ENCYCLOPEDIA OF RELIGION

SECOND EDITION

ENCYCLOPEDIA OF RELIGION

SECOND EDITION

8

KAʿBAH
•
MARX, KARL

LINDSAY JONES
EDITOR IN CHIEF

MACMILLAN REFERENCE USA
An imprint of Thomson Gale, a part of The Thomson Corporation

THOMSON
GALE

Detroit • New York • San Francisco • San Diego • New Haven, Conn. • Waterville, Maine • London • Munich

THOMSON
GALE

Encyclopedia of Religion, Second Edition

Lindsay Jones, Editor in Chief

For more information, contact
Macmillan Reference USA
An imprint of Thomson Gale
27500 Drake Rd.
Farmington, Hills, MI 48331-3535
Or you can visit our Internet site at
http://www.gale.com

LIBRARY OF CONGRESS CATALOGING-IN-PUBLICATION DATA

Encyclopedia of religion / Lindsay Jones, editor in chief.— 2nd ed.
p. cm.
Includes bibliographical references and index.
ISBN 0-02-865733-0 (SET HARDCOVER : ALK. PAPER) —
ISBN 0-02-865734-9 (V. 1) — ISBN 0-02-865735-7 (v. 2) —
ISBN 0-02-865736-5 (v. 3) — ISBN 0-02-865737-3 (v. 4) —
ISBN 0-02-865738-1 (v. 5) — ISBN 0-02-865739-X (v. 6) —
ISBN 0-02-865740-3 (v. 7) — ISBN 0-02-865741-1 (v. 8) —
ISBN 0-02-865742-X (v. 9) — ISBN 0-02-865743-8 (v. 10)
— ISBN 0-02-865980-5 (v. 11) — ISBN 0-02-865981-3 (v.
12) — ISBN 0-02-865982-1 (v. 13) — ISBN 0-02-865983-X
(v. 14) — ISBN 0-02-865984-8 (v. 15)
1. RELIGION—ENCYCLOPEDIAS. I. JONES, LINDSAY,
1954-

BL31.E46 2005
200'.3—dc22
2004017052

This title is also available as an e-book.
ISBN 0-02-865997-X
Contact your Thomson Gale representative for ordering information.

Printed in the United States of America
10 9 8 7 6 5 4 3 2 1

EDITORS AND CONSULTANTS

Harvard Forum on Religion and Ecology
Ecology and Religion

JOSEPH HARRIS
Francis Lee Higginson Professor of English Literature and Professor of Folklore, Harvard University
Germanic Religions

URSULA KING
Professor Emerita, Senior Research Fellow and Associate Member of the Institute for Advanced Studies, University of Bristol, England, and Professorial Research Associate, Centre for Gender and Religions Research, School of Oriental and African Studies, University of London
Gender and Religion

DAVID MORGAN
Duesenberg Professor of Christianity and the Arts, and Professor of Humanities and Art History, Valparaiso University
Color Inserts and Essays

JOSEPH F. NAGY
Professor, Department of English, University of California, Los Angeles
Celtic Religion

MATTHEW OJO
Obafemi Awolowo University
African Religions

JUHA PENTIKÄINEN
Professor of Comparative Religion, The University of Helsinki, Member of Academia Scientiarum Fennica, Finland
Arctic Religions and Uralic Religions

TED PETERS
Professor of Systematic Theology, Pacific Lutheran Theological Seminary and the Center for Theology and the Natural Sciences at the Graduate Theological Union, Berkeley, California
Science and Religion

FRANK E. REYNOLDS
Professor of the History of Religions and Buddhist Studies in the Divinity School and the Department of South Asian Languages and Civilizations, Emeritus, University of Chicago
History of Religions

GONZALO RUBIO
Assistant Professor, Department of Classics and Ancient Mediterranean Studies and Department of History and Religious Studies, Pennsylvania State University
Ancient Near Eastern Religions

SUSAN SERED
Director of Research, Religion, Health and Healing Initiative, Center for the Study of World Religions, Harvard University, and Senior Research Associate, Center for Women's Health and Human Rights, Suffolk University
Healing, Medicine, and Religion

LAWRENCE E. SULLIVAN
Professor, Department of Theology, University of Notre Dame
History of Religions

WINNIFRED FALLERS SULLIVAN
Dean of Students and Senior Lecturer in the Anthropology and Sociology of Religion, University of Chicago
Law and Religion

TOD SWANSON
Associate Professor of Religious Studies, and Director, Center for Latin American Studies, Arizona State University
South American Religions

MARY EVELYN TUCKER
Professor of Religion, Bucknell University, Founder and Coordinator, Harvard Forum on Religion and Ecology, Research Fellow, Harvard Yenching Institute, Research Associate, Harvard Reischauer Institute of Japanese Studies
Ecology and Religion

HUGH URBAN
Associate Professor, Department of Comparative Studies, Ohio State University
Politics and Religion

CATHERINE WESSINGER
Professor of the History of Religions and Women's Studies, Loyola University New Orleans
New Religious Movements

ROBERT A. YELLE
Mellon Postdoctoral Fellow, University of Toronto
Law and Religion

ERIC ZIOLKOWSKI
Charles A. Dana Professor of Religious Studies, Lafayette College
Literature and Religion

ABBREVIATIONS AND SYMBOLS USED IN THIS WORK

abbr. abbreviated; abbreviation
abr. abridged; abridgment
AD *anno Domini,* in the year of the (our) Lord
Afrik. Afrikaans
AH *anno Hegirae,* in the year of the Hijrah
Akk. Akkadian
Ala. Alabama
Alb. Albanian
Am. *Amos*
AM *ante meridiem,* before noon
amend. amended; amendment
annot. annotated; annotation
Ap. *Apocalypse*
Apn. *Apocryphon*
app. appendix
Arab. Arabic
ʿArakh. *ʿArakhin*
Aram. Aramaic
Ariz. Arizona
Ark. Arkansas
Arm. Armenian
art. article (pl., arts.)
AS Anglo-Saxon
Asm. Mos. *Assumption of Moses*
Assyr. Assyrian
A.S.S.R. Autonomous Soviet Socialist Republic
Av. Avestan
ʿA.Z. *ʿAvodah zarah*
b. born
Bab. Babylonian
Ban. Bantu
1 Bar. *1 Baruch*
2 Bar. *2 Baruch*
3 Bar. *3 Baruch*
4 Bar. *4 Baruch*
B.B. *Bavaʾ batraʾ*
BBC British Broadcasting Corporation
BC before Christ
BCE before the common era
B.D. Bachelor of Divinity
Beits. *Beitsah*
Bekh. *Bekhorot*
Beng. Bengali
Ber. *Berakhot*
Berb. Berber
Bik. *Bikkurim*
bk. book (pl., bks.)
B.M. *Bavaʾ metsiʿaʾ*
BP before the present
B.Q. *Bavaʾ qammaʾ*
Brāh. *Brāhmaṇa*
Bret. Breton
B.T. Babylonian Talmud
Bulg. Bulgarian
Burm. Burmese
c. *circa,* about, approximately
Calif. California
Can. Canaanite
Catal. Catalan
CE of the common era
Celt. Celtic
cf. *confer,* compare
Chald. Chaldean
chap. chapter (pl., chaps.)
Chin. Chinese
C.H.M. Community of the Holy Myrrhbearers
1 Chr. *1 Chronicles*
2 Chr. *2 Chronicles*
Ch. Slav. Church Slavic
cm centimeters
col. column (pl., cols.)
Col. *Colossians*
Colo. Colorado
comp. compiler (pl., comps.)
Conn. Connecticut
cont. continued
Copt. Coptic
1 Cor. *1 Corinthians*
2 Cor. *2 Corinthians*
corr. corrected
C.S.P. Congregatio Sancti Pauli, Congregation of Saint Paul (Paulists)
d. died
D Deuteronomic (source of the Pentateuch)
Dan. Danish
D.B. Divinitatis Baccalaureus, Bachelor of Divinity
D.C. District of Columbia
D.D. Divinitatis Doctor, Doctor of Divinity
Del. Delaware
Dem. *Demaʾi*
dim. diminutive
diss. dissertation
Dn. *Daniel*
D.Phil. Doctor of Philosophy
Dt. *Deuteronomy*
Du. Dutch
E Elohist (source of the Pentateuch)
Eccl. *Ecclesiastes*
ed. editor (pl., eds.); edition; edited by

ʿEduy. *ʿEduyyot*
e.g. *exempli gratia,* for example
Egyp. Egyptian
1 En. *1 Enoch*
2 En. *2 Enoch*
3 En. *3 Enoch*
Eng. English
enl. enlarged
Eph. *Ephesians*
ʿEruv. *ʿEruvin*
1 Esd. *1 Esdras*
2 Esd. *2 Esdras*
3 Esd. *3 Esdras*
4 Esd. *4 Esdras*
esp. especially
Est. Estonian
Est. *Esther*
et al. *et alii,* and others
etc. *et cetera,* and so forth
Eth. Ethiopic
EV English version
Ex. *Exodus*
exp. expanded
Ez. *Ezekiel*
Ezr. *Ezra*
2 Ezr. *2 Ezra*
4 Ezr. *4 Ezra*
f. feminine; and following (pl., ff.)
fasc. fascicle (pl., fascs.)
fig. figure (pl., figs.)
Finn. Finnish
fl. *floruit,* flourished
Fla. Florida
Fr. French
frag. fragment
ft. feet
Ga. Georgia
Gal. *Galatians*
Gaul. Gaulish
Ger. German
Giṭ. *Giṭṭin*
Gn. *Genesis*
Gr. Greek
Ḥag. *Ḥagigah*
Ḥal. *Ḥallah*
Hau. Hausa
Hb. *Habakkuk*
Heb. Hebrew
Heb. *Hebrews*
Hg. *Haggai*
Hitt. Hittite
Hor. *Horayot*
Hos. *Hosea*
Ḥul. *Ḥullin*
Hung. Hungarian
ibid. *ibidem,* in the same place (as the one immediately preceding)
Icel. Icelandic
i.e. *id est,* that is
IE Indo-European
Ill. Illinois
Ind. Indiana
intro. introduction
Ir. Gael. Irish Gaelic
Iran. Iranian
Is. *Isaiah*
Ital. Italian
J Yahvist (source of the Pentateuch)
Jas. *James*
Jav. Javanese
Jb. *Job*
Jdt. *Judith*
Jer. *Jeremiah*
Jgs. *Judges*
Jl. *Joel*
Jn. *John*
1 Jn. *1 John*
2 Jn. *2 John*
3 Jn. *3 John*
Jon. *Jonah*
Jos. *Joshua*
Jpn. Japanese
JPS Jewish Publication Society translation (1985) of the Hebrew Bible
J.T. Jerusalem Talmud
Jub. *Jubilees*
Kans. Kansas
Kel. *Kelim*
Ker. *Keritot*
Ket. *Ketubbot*
1 Kgs. *1 Kings*
2 Kgs. *2 Kings*
Khois. Khoisan
Kil. *Kilʾayim*
km kilometers
Kor. Korean
Ky. Kentucky
l. line (pl., ll.)
La. Louisiana
Lam. *Lamentations*
Lat. Latin
Latv. Latvian
L. en Th. Licencié en Théologie, Licentiate in Theology
L. ès L. Licencié ès Lettres, Licentiate in Literature
Let. Jer. *Letter of Jeremiah*
lit. literally
Lith. Lithuanian
Lk. *Luke*
LL Late Latin
LL.D. Legum Doctor, Doctor of Laws
Lv. *Leviticus*
m meters
m. masculine
M.A. Master of Arts
Ma ʿas. *Maʿaserot*
Ma ʿas. Sh. *Maʿ aser sheni*
Mak. *Makkot*
Makh. *Makhshirin*
Mal. *Malachi*
Mar. Marathi
Mass. Massachusetts
1 Mc. *1 Maccabees*
2 Mc. *2 Maccabees*
3 Mc. *3 Maccabees*
4 Mc. *4 Maccabees*
Md. Maryland
M.D. Medicinae Doctor, Doctor of Medicine
ME Middle English
Meg. *Megillah*
Me ʿil. *Meʿilah*
Men. *Menaḥot*
MHG Middle High German
mi. miles
Mi. *Micah*
Mich. Michigan
Mid. *Middot*
Minn. Minnesota
Miq. *Miqvaʾot*
MIran. Middle Iranian
Miss. Mississippi
Mk. *Mark*
Mo. Missouri
Moʿed Q. *Moʿed qaṭan*
Mont. Montana
MPers. Middle Persian
MS. *manuscriptum,* manuscript (pl., MSS)
Mt. *Matthew*
MT Masoretic text
n. note
Na. *Nahum*
Nah. Nahuatl
Naz. *Nazir*
N.B. *nota bene,* take careful note
N.C. North Carolina
n.d. no date
N.Dak. North Dakota
NEB New English Bible
Nebr. Nebraska

Ned. *Nedarim*
Neg. *Nega'im*
Neh. *Nehemiah*
Nev. Nevada
N.H. New Hampshire
Nid. *Niddah*
N.J. New Jersey
Nm. *Numbers*
N.Mex. New Mexico
no. number (pl., nos.)
Nor. Norwegian
n.p. no place
n.s. new series
N.Y. New York
Ob. *Obadiah*
O.Cist. Ordo Cisterciencium, Order of Cîteaux (Cistercians)
OCS Old Church Slavonic
OE Old English
O.F.M. Ordo Fratrum Minorum, Order of Friars Minor (Franciscans)
OFr. Old French
Ohal. *Ohalot*
OHG Old High German
OIr. Old Irish
OIran. Old Iranian
Okla. Oklahoma
ON Old Norse
O.P. Ordo Praedicatorum, Order of Preachers (Dominicans)
OPers. Old Persian
op. cit. *opere citato,* in the work cited
OPrus. Old Prussian
Oreg. Oregon
'Orl. *'Orlah*
O.S.B. Ordo Sancti Benedicti, Order of Saint Benedict (Benedictines)
p. page (pl., pp.)
P Priestly (source of the Pentateuch)
Pa. Pennsylvania
Pahl. Pahlavi
Par. *Parah*
para. paragraph (pl., paras.)
Pers. Persian
Pes. *Pesahim*
Ph.D. Philosophiae Doctor, Doctor of Philosophy
Phil. *Philippians*
Phlm. *Philemon*
Phoen. Phoenician
pl. plural; plate (pl., pls.)
PM *post meridiem,* after noon
Pol. Polish
pop. population
Port. Portuguese
Prv. *Proverbs*
Ps. *Psalms*
Ps. 151 *Psalm 151*
Ps. Sol. *Psalms of Solomon*
pt. part (pl., pts.)
1Pt. *1 Peter*
2 Pt. *2 Peter*
Pth. Parthian
Q hypothetical source of the synoptic Gospels
Qid. *Qiddushin*
Qin. *Qinnim*
r. reigned; ruled
Rab. *Rabbah*
rev. revised
R. ha-Sh. *Ro'sh ha-shanah*
R.I. Rhode Island
Rom. Romanian
Rom. *Romans*
R.S.C.J. Societas Sacratissimi Cordis Jesu, Religious of the Sacred Heart
RSV Revised Standard Version of the Bible
Ru. *Ruth*
Rus. Russian
Rv. *Revelation*
Rv. Ezr. *Revelation of Ezra*
San. *Sanhedrin*
S.C. South Carolina
Scot. Gael. Scottish Gaelic
S.Dak. South Dakota
sec. section (pl., secs.)
Sem. Semitic
ser. series
sg. singular
Sg. *Song of Songs*
Sg. of 3 *Prayer of Azariah and the Song of the Three Young Men*
Shab. *Shabbat*
Shav. *Shavu'ot*
Sheq. *Sheqalim*
Sib. Or. *Sibylline Oracles*
Sind. Sindhi
Sinh. Sinhala
Sir. *Ben Sira*
S.J. Societas Jesu, Society of Jesus (Jesuits)
Skt. Sanskrit
1 Sm. *1 Samuel*
2 Sm. *2 Samuel*
Sogd. Sogdian
Soṭ. *Soṭah*
sp. species (pl., spp.)
Span. Spanish
sq. square
S.S.R. Soviet Socialist Republic
st. stanza (pl., ss.)
S.T.M. Sacrae Theologiae Magister, Master of Sacred Theology
Suk. *Sukkah*
Sum. Sumerian
supp. supplement; supplementary
Sus. *Susanna*
s.v. *sub verbo,* under the word (pl., s.v.v.)
Swed. Swedish
Syr. Syriac
Syr. Men. *Syriac Menander*
Ta'an. *Ta'anit*
Tam. Tamil
Tam. *Tamid*
Tb. *Tobit*
T.D. *Taishō shinshū daizōkyō,* edited by Takakusu Junjirō et al. (Tokyo,1922–1934)
Tem. *Temurah*
Tenn. Tennessee
Ter. Terumot
Ṭev. Y. *Ṭevul yom*
Tex. Texas
Th.D. Theologicae Doctor, Doctor of Theology
1 Thes. *1 Thessalonians*
2 Thes. *2 Thessalonians*
Thrac. Thracian
Ti. *Titus*
Tib. Tibetan
1 Tm. *1 Timothy*
2 Tm. *2 Timothy*
T. of 12 *Testaments of the Twelve Patriarchs*
Ṭoh. *ṭohorot*
Tong. Tongan
trans. translator, translators; translated by; translation
Turk. Turkish
Ukr. Ukrainian
Upan. *Upaniṣad*
U.S. United States
U.S.S.R. Union of Soviet Socialist Republics
Uqts. *Uqtsin*
v. verse (pl., vv.)
Va. Virginia
var. variant; variation
Viet. Vietnamese

viz. *videlicet,* namely
vol. volume (pl., vols.)
Vt. Vermont
Wash. Washington
Wel. Welsh
Wis. Wisconsin
Wis. *Wisdom of Solomon*
W.Va. West Virginia
Wyo. Wyoming
Yad. *Yadayim*
Yev. *Yevamot*
Yi. Yiddish
Yor. Yoruba
Zav. *Zavim*
Zec. *Zechariah*
Zep. *Zephaniah*
Zev. *Zevaḥim*

* hypothetical
? uncertain; possibly; perhaps
° degrees
+ plus
– minus
= equals; is equivalent to
× by; multiplied by
→ yields

K

KA'BAH. The Ka'bah (cube), located in Mecca, is the shrine at the center of the Muslim world. Referred to as the "House of God," (*bayt Allāh*), it is the central point (*qiblah*) on earth toward which all Muslims face when performing daily prayers (*salāt*). Making pilgrimage (*ḥājj*) to the Ka'bah at least once in a Muslim's life if able, is one of the major religious obligations in Islam. It is also referred to in the Qur'ān (5:95, 97), where it is called *al-bayt* (his house), and also *masjid al-ḥaram* (the sacred mosque).

The present Ka'bah is a cubelike building made of local Meccan granite and Yemeni mortar. It is 50 feet high, 40 feet on its longest side and about 33 feet on its shorter walls. It is hollow, with a door on the long side about 7 feet above the ground, necessitating rolling stairs to enter. The corners are situated roughly on the points of the compass, with the eastern corner containing the Black Stone (*al-ḥajar al-aswad*) that has been the major feature of the structure since pre-Islamic times. Inside the Ka'bah, there are gold and silver lamps hanging from a ceiling supported by wooden pillars. The Ka'bah is covered by a black cloth brocaded in gold and silver, called the *Kiswah* (curtain), containing the words of the declaration of faith (*shahādah*) and quotations from the Qur'ān. This covering is renewed each year, with the old cloth cut into pieces as relics for the pilgrims.

The history of the Ka'bah demonstrates that the Black Stone is the primary focal point of Muslim veneration, but is not an object of worship, since only the aniconic Allāh is worshiped. While there is only slight mention outside of Muslim accounts of the history of the Ka'bah, the story told is that it was destroyed and rebuilt several times in Muḥammad's lifetime and afterward by war, fire, and flood. In one incident, the Black Stone, which is really a dark reddish brown, was cracked into three pieces and several fragments, and is now encased in a heavy silver bezel. During Muḥammad's farewell pilgrimage, he kissed the Stone during his circumambulation (*ṭawāf*), which action has become customary for pilgrims since. The circumambulation, which is counter clockwise, is made as close to the Ka'bah as possible on a pavement of granite called the *maṭāf.*

The pre-Islamic records of the Ka'bah indicate that it was an ancient shrine and place of sacrifice. The geographer Ptolemy refers to Mecca as *Macoraba,* a term that is likely

---

Clockwise from top left corner. Kṛṣṇa playing the flute. Kanchipuram, India. *[©Lindsay Hebberd/Corbis]*; Relief of a winged, lion-headed goddess from Meroe, Sudan. Sudan Archaeological Museum, Khartoum. *[©Werner Forman/Art Resource, N.Y.]*; Stone victory stele of Naram-Sin, c. twenty-third century BCE. *[©Gianni Dagli Orti/Corbis]*; A time-exposure photograph of devout Muslims performing ṭawāf, the circumambulation of the Ka'bah in Mecca, during the ḥājj. *[Photo by Keystone Features/Getty Images]*; The Khmer horse-headed god Vajimukha, sixth-century, Cambodia. Musée des Arts Asiatiques-Guimet, Paris. *[©Scala/Art Resource, N.Y.]* .

cognate with South Arabian *mikrab* (temple), and Northwest Semitic *qurbān* (sacrifice). Arabic records indicate that the Kaʿbah was a place of pagan sacrifice until the arrival of Islam. Qurʾanic verses and Muslim legends assign an importance to the Kaʿbah similar to the position of the Jerusalem Temple for Judaism. Many Western scholars have pointed to similarities among stories about the two shrines. It is said to be at the center of the earth and the location at which Adam first performed worship of God. It is thought to be directly beneath a heavenly counterpart that some hold to be the "real" Kaʿbah. Under heavenly guidance, it is said to have been first constructed by Abraham (Ibrāhīm) and his son Ishmael (Ishmāʾīl) when the *Sakīnah* circled the spot and instructed them to build. The Black Stone is believed to have been brought from heaven by the angel Gabriel (Jibrīl), giving rise to modern, secular speculation that the stone is a meteorite. The nearby well of Zamzam was the source of water for Ishmael and Hagar when they were cast into the desert. Abraham was the first to institute the pilgrimage (*ḥājj*), and it is held to be the location of the graves of Abraham, Ishmael, Hagar and a number of prophets. In the process of rebuilding the Kaʿbah in Muḥammad's early life, a pry bar was placed under the foundation stone to move it, and the whole earth is said to have shook, indicating that it was the foundation of the world. In this reconstruction, Muḥammad acted to resolve a conflict over who would have the honor of restoring the Black Stone by placing it in his cloak and having a representative of each Meccan clan lift the stone into place.

With Muḥammad's conquest of Mecca in 8/629, the accretions and numerous pagan idols that had become associated with the Kaʿbah were purged, and Islamic worship established. It is believed that there were over 360 different idols that had been moved into the Kaʿbah. According to tradition, Muḥammad left an image of Maryam, the mother of Jesus, intact inside of the cleansed Kaʿbah, put there by the Coptic craftsman who helped the Meccans rebuild the shrine. This image was destroyed in the civil wars during the Umayyad period. The sacred precinct around the Kaʿbah thus became the place that Muslims perform the *ḥājj* and the lesser pilgrimage (*umrah*), including the annual ritual sacrifice.

In 64/683, during the attempt of ʿAbd Allāh b. al-Zubayr to gain the caliphate, the Kaʿbah was nearly destroyed in the siege, and a subsequent fire cracked the Black Stone into three pieces. When the siege was lifted, the Black Stone was repaired with a silver bezel, and the Kaʿbah was rebuilt and enlarged. In 74/693, the Umayyad conquered Mecca, killed al-Zubayr, and undid many of the alterations, returning the Kaʿbah to a simpler form, which it still retains. In 317/929, the Qaramatians (Qarāmitah) carried off the Black Stone, which was restored after twenty years. While the Kaʿbah itself has retained the general size and form it had in Muḥammad's lifetime, much work has been done to improve the surrounding areas to accommodate the *ḥājj* visitors. Since 1376/1956, the stones that paved the *matāf* were relayed, an electric lighting system replaced the oil lamps, water taps have been provided and the walkway between Safā and Marwah used for the *Saʿy* has been covered by a tall ceiling. In keeping with Nahhabi doctrines, the improvements in the Kaʿbah have resulted in the elimination of saint-shrines and other historical and religious spaces.

Nearly all branches of Islam near the Kaʿbah regard the Kaʿbah as a central part of Islamic religious practice. In addition to facing th Kaʿbah during *salāt,* Muslims also bury the dead facing towards it. In the Islamic mystical tradition, its importance has been reinterpreted and linked with a heavenly Kaʿbah that is, according to some, directly above the earthly shrine. Above all, the experience of visiting the Kaʿbah is not veneration of the building or the Black Stone, but an aid to contemplation of God.

SEE ALSO Ḥaram and Hawtah; Pilgrimage, article on Muslim Pilgrimage.

BIBLIOGRAPHY

Descriptions of the Kaʿbah are readily found in pilgrim accounts of the *ḥājj,* some of which are available on the Internet. A comprehensive study of the pilgrimage with an extensive bibliography is F. E. Peters, *The Hajj* (Princeton, 1994). Also recommended is his *Jerusalem and Mecca: The Typology of the Holy City in the Near East* (New York, 1987). Beverly White Spicer's *The Kaʿbah* (Lanham, Md., 2003), examines the intersection of the Kaʿbah and human psycho-physiology. For a concise summary of the rites associated with the Kaʿbah, see Noah Ha Mim Keller, ed. and trans., *The Reliance of the Traveler; A Classic Manual of Islamic Sacred Law by Ahmad ibn Naqib al-Misri* (Dubai, 1991). For literary accounts of the *ḥājj* and descriptions of the Kaʿbah, see Michael Wolfe's *One Thousand Roads to Mecca: Ten Centuries of Travelers Writing about the Muslim Pilgrimage* (New York, 1997). See also Gerald Hawting's "Ka'ba," in *Encyclopedia of the Qurʾān,* Vol. III (Leiden, 2003). For a recent film, see *Hajj, The Pilgrimage: A Videorecording* (Princeton, 2003). The presentation in art is reflected in Ann Parker's *Hajj Paintings: Folk Art of the Great Pilgrimage* (Washington, D.C., 1995).

GORDON D. NEWBY (2005)

KABALLAH SEE QABBALAH

KABERRY, PHYLLIS M.

Phyllis Mary Kaberry (1910–1977), the first anthropologist to study religion and culture from the vantage point of Aboriginal women in Australia, showed that the benefits and responsibilities of the *Ngarrangkarni*—spelled by Kaberry as *Narungani* and translated by her to mean "The Time Long Past"—were equally relevant to women as they were to men. *Ngarrangkarni,* or "The Dreaming," as it is known in the Kimberley, northern Australia, embraces a profound body of Aboriginal religion and law. Often described as a creative epoch that lives on in the present via myth, ritual, art, and oral traditions, the powers of the Dreaming ancestors formed the human and physical world, while also revealing a way of life for humankind to follow. Arguing against peers such as Bronislaw Malinowski (1913), Géza Róheim (1933), and especially W. Lloyd Warner (1937) that Aboriginal religion was an all-male domain, and critical of Émile Durkheim's (1915) sociological thesis that religious beliefs and behaviors could be organized into distinct secular and nonsecular spheres, Kaberry made her findings explicit in *Aboriginal Woman, Sacred and Profane,* first published in 1939.

A graduate of Sydney University and the London School of Economics, Kaberry worked among Bunuba, Gooniyandi, Jaru, Kija, Malgnin, Nyikina, and Walmajarri groups between 1934 and 1936. According to Kaberry, the Time Long Past encompassed various totemic beliefs (such as conception, birth, and clan totems) and complementary symmetrical social divisions or moieties, which provided connections between people and all other life forms. She interpreted conception totems and the animation of spirit children, ultimately born as human beings, as central to the culturally complex and integrated nature of Aboriginal religion and law (Kaberry, 1936, 1937, 1937a, 1939).

Mythological narratives (given expression through performance, song cycles, trading, and artworks) were also described by Kaberry as a medium through which the cosmology occupied a practical socializing role. She wrote, for example, about the mythic rainbow snake, or *kalpurtu,* as the maker of rivers and rain, about social classifications known as subsections, and about marriage laws. Rainmaking also fell into the category of "increase ceremonies," where rituals ordained by ancestral beings were enacted to ensure the stability and replenishment of food and other resources.

In keeping with a holistic approach to Aboriginal religion, Kaberry discussed death as well as birth. She recorded how death and grieving were incorporated into the "sacred and profane" lives of men and women (Kaberry, 1935, 1939). Death in old age was often accepted, but when a child or young adult died, relatives sought reason in the supernatural, such as that a taboo had been broken, an avoidance relationship ignored, or that unauthorized contact with sacred objects had occurred. Kaberry claimed that spirits had the power to influence the living in positive or negative ways. If the deceased was old or very young, for instance, the corpse was buried in the ground. When this was not the case and the cause of death was unclear, the body was placed on a platform in a tree, covered with soft bark, and then left for as long as it took for the flesh to disintegrate. The purpose of this kind of burial was to allow the deceased's juices to fall on stones placed beneath the corpse so that the cause or murderer could be divined. While this took place, the husband or wife and in-laws would smear themselves with mud. Other kin, such as the mother, father, sisters, sons, and daughters, would be painted by grieving family members with ochre. Wives shaved their hair and the belongings of the deceased were distributed to distant kin or burnt. Mourning taboos restricted the consumption of meat, leaving vegetable foods or small fish, grubs, and so on to be eaten. Such taboos could be removed only when the required period for mourning was over.

Kaberry paid some attention to religious rites associated with the initiation of young men, but as a female observer of and participant in a society where both joint and gender-specific activities occurred, her account of men's rituals was understandably limited. She described, however, the role of women during the initiation of male kin (such as men related to them as sons or brothers) and about women-only ceremonies, including *yoelyu.*

There are several features that define Kaberry's contribution to the study of religious beliefs and practices. Firstly, she analyzed the *Narungani* as a rich body of religion, law, and lore central to the reproduction of Aboriginal society and human/land/water relationships. Secondly, in contrast to Durkheim, she argued that cosmological and temporal beliefs, ideas, and actions merged into and were dependent upon each other. Kaberry rejected entirely the notion that Aboriginal religion could be demarcated into disparate religious and secular domains. Thirdly, Kaberry challenged Malinowski, Róheim, and Warner who, when writing about Australian Aboriginal religion, portrayed women as "profane." It is the latter for which Kaberry is most well known, an assessment that has perhaps restricted a full appreciation of her contribution to the study of Australian Aboriginal religion.

BIBLIOGRAPHY

Durkheim, Émile. *The Elementary Forms of the Religious Life.* London, 1915.

Kaberry, Phyllis M. "Death and Deferred Mourning Ceremonies in the Forest River Tribes." *Oceania* 6, no. 1 (1935): 33–47.

Kaberry, Phyllis M. "Spirit Children and Spirit Centres of the North Kimberley Divisions." *Oceania* 6, no. 4 (1936): 392–400.

Kaberry, Phyllis M. "Subsections in the East and South Kimberley Tribes of North-west Australia." *Oceania* 7, no. 1 (1937): 436–458.

Kaberry, Phyllis M. "Totemism in East and South Kimberley." *Oceania* 8, no. 1 (1937a): 265–288.

Kaberry, Phyllis M. *Aboriginal Woman, Sacred and Profane.* London, 1939.

Malinowski, Bronislaw. *The Family among the Australian Aborigines: A Sociological Study.* London, 1913.

Róheim, Géza. "Women and Their Life in Central Australia." *Royal Anthropological Institute Journal* 63 (1933): 259–265.

Warner, W. Lloyd. *A Black Civilization: A Social Study of an Australian Tribe.* New York, 1937.

SANDY TOUSSAINT **(2005)**

KABĪR (fifteenth century CE) was one of the most famous saints and mystics in the Indian tradition. Kabīr is unique in that he is revered by Hindus and Muslims alike, yet his personality and his biography remain shrouded in mystery. The only certain fact about him is that he was born a Julāhā, a low-caste Muslim weaver, in or near the city of Banaras toward the middle of the fifteenth century CE, at a time when North India was under the rule of the Lodi dynasty. The Julāhās were probably recent converts to Islam, and it is not certain that Kabīr himself was circumcised. He refers to the Muslims as "Turks."

The legendary biography of Kabīr includes his alleged persecution by the Muslim ruler Sikander Lodi and his initiation (presumably in the Rāmāite faith) by a rather mysterious Hindu saint known as Rāmānand. The most famous story about Kabīr, however, concerns the saint's death and burial-cremation at Magahar, a small town of ill repute in northeastern Uttar Pradesh, near Gorakhpur. As Kabīr was about to die, two armed parties of his followers allegedly converged on Magahar, ready to fight in order to secure possession of the saint's body. Kabīr retired into a small tent to die, and immediately after his death his body disappeared. Nothing was found but a heap of flowers, which was divided between the two parties: The Muslims buried their share of the flowers on the spot and erected a cenotaph over it; the Hindus cremated their share and later built a *samādhi* (memorial tomb) over it, although most sectarian devotees of Kabīr believe the flowers were cremated at the important Kabīr Chaurā Maṭh in Banaras itself. In later times, Kabīr's fame continued to grow among Hindus. In an attempt to "Hinduize" the saint, devotees told of his having been born miraculously of a brahman virgin widow; she committed the child to the Ganges, but he was saved and reared by Julāhās.

There is no fully authoritative version of the *Kabīrvāṇīs,* the "words of Kabīr." The poet was probably illiterate, and it is certain that he himself never committed anything to writing. His utterances took the form of the popular couplets known as *dohās*, or the equally popular form of short songs (*padas*) set to a refrain. His language was a nondescript form of Old Hindi, which may have served as a sort of lingua franca for the wandering holy men of his time. So great was his eloquence, however, that his "words" spread like fire over a large area of Hindustan, at least from Bihar in the east to the Panjab and Rajasthan in the west. Immensely popular, the *Kabīrvāṇīs* were largely imitated and interpolated even before they could be written down. The oldest dated written record is found in the *Guru Granth* of the Sikhs, compiled by Guru Arjun in the Panjab around 1604. In the *Granth,* Kabīr's utterances are recorded as the words of the foremost among the *bhagats* (devotees or saints) who were the predecessors of Guru Nānak, the founder of the Sikh Panth ("path" or "way"). Two more undated recensions of Kabīr's "words" are known: one in Rajasthan, preserved in the *Pāñcavāṇīs* compiled by the Dādūpanthīs of Rajasthan (c. 1600) and known as *Kabīr Granthāvalī,* and the other, known as the *Bījak,* popularized, if not compiled, in Bihar by putative disciples of Kabīr who called themselves Kabīrpanthīs, although Kabīr himself never founded a sect. The *Bījak* represents the eastern recension of Kabīr's words. A fair idea of Kabīr's teachings, however, can be inferred only from a comparison of the three main recensions.

Some Muslims in the past tended to view Kabīr as a Ṣūfī, because many of his "words" are somewhat similar to those of the most liberal and unorthodox Indian Ṣūfīs. Modern Hindus and Muslims tend to see him as the champion of Hindu-Muslim unity, although Kabīr himself expressed outright rejection of the "two religions" and bitterly castigated their official representatives: pandits and *pāṇḍes* on the one side, *mullas* and *kāzis* on the other. For Kabīr, there could be no revealed religion at all—no Veda, no Qurʾān. All scriptural authority he emphatically denied, and he warned people against searching for truth in "holy books": "Reading, reading, the whole world died—and no one ever became learned!"

There is a tendency in modern times, especially among Hindu scholars with Vaiṣṇava leanings, to view Kabīr as a "liberal" Vaiṣṇava, one opposed—as indeed he was—to caste distinctions as well as to "idol worship," but a Vaiṣṇava all the same, because he made use of several Vaiṣṇava names to speak of God. Actually, Kabīr's notion of God seems to go beyond the notion of a personal god, despite the fact that he may call on Rām or Khudā. If he often mentions Hari, Rām, or the "name of Rām," the context most often suggests that these are just names for the all-pervading Reality—a reality beyond words, "beyond the beyond," that is frequently identified with *śūnya* ("the void") or the ineffable state that he calls *sahaj.* In the same way, though Kabīr often speaks of the *satguru* (the "perfect guru") it is clear that he is not alluding to Rāmānand, his putative guru, nor to any human guru. For Kabīr, the *satguru* is the One who speaks within the soul itself. Although he often borrows the language of Tantric yoga and its paradoxical style to suggest the "ineffable word," Kabīr held all yogic exercises to be absurd contortions and the yogis' pretention to immortality as utter nonsense.

Kabīr's view of the world is a tragic one. Life is but a fleeting moment between two deaths in the world of transmigration. Family ties are insignificant and rest on self-interest. Woman is "a pit of hell." Death encompasses all: Living beings are compared to "the parched grain of Death, some in his mouth, the rest in his lap." There is no hope, no escape for man but in his own innermost heart. Man must search within himself, get rid of pride and egoism, dive within for the "diamond" that is hidden within his own soul. Then only may the mysterious, ineffable stage be achieved within the body itself—a mystery that Kabīr suggests in terms of fusion:

> When I was, Hari was not.
> Now Hari is and I am no more.

For one who has found the hidden "diamond," for one who has passed "the unreachable pass," eternity is achieved. Mortal life seems to linger, though in truth nothing remains but a fragile appearance. In Kabīr's own words:

The yogin who was there has disappeared:
Ashes alone keep the posture.

In its rugged, terse, fulgurant brilliance, Kabīr's style is unique. His striking metaphors and powerful rhythms capture the heart of the listener. His scathing attacks on brahmans and the "holy men" of his time have never been forgotten by the downtrodden people of India. Probably no greater voice had been heard on Indian soil since the time of the Buddha, whom Kabīr resembles in more ways than one. His pessimistic view of worldly life, his contempt for holy books and human gurus, his insistent call to inwardness have not been forgotten. His own brand of mysticism may appear godless if one takes "God" as a divine personality. In one sense, Kabīr is not only an iconoclast, he may even be called irreligious—and yet he appears as a master of the "interior religion."

SEE ALSO Adi Granth; Hindi Religious Traditions; Poetry, article on Indian Religious Poetry.

BIBLIOGRAPHY

For the *Kabīr Granthāvalī,* see the editions prepared by Shyam Sundar Das (Banaras, 1928); by Mata Prasad Gupta (Allahabad, 1969), which includes a modern Hindi paraphrase; and by Parasnath Tiwari (Allahabad, 1965), which is a critical edition. The *Kabīr Bījak* has been edited a number of times. The standard edition is by S. Shastri and M. Prasad (Barabanki, 1950), and has been partially translated into English by Linda Hess and Shukdev Singh as *The Bijak of Kabīr* (San Francisco, 1983). Kabīr's words in the *Guru Granth* have been collected and edited by S. K. Varma in *Sant Kabīr* (Allahabad, 1947); this edition includes a paraphrase in modern Hindi.

For a translation of Kabīr's *dohās* in the Western recensions, see my *Kabīr* (Oxford, 1974) and my *Kabīr-vāni; The Words of Kabīr in the Western Tradition* (Pondicherry, 1983). See also my "Kabīr and the Interior Religion," *History of Religions* 3 (1964).

New Sources

Mehta, Rohit. J. *Krishnamurti and Sant Kabir: A Study in Depth.* Delhi, 1990.

A Touch of Grace: Songs of Kabir. Translated by Linda Hess and Shukdev Singh. Boston, 1994.

CHARLOTTE VAUDEVILLE (1987)
Revised Bibliography

KAGAN, YISRAʾEL MEʾIR

KAGAN, YISRAʾEL MEʾIR (c. 1838–1933), also known as Ḥafets Ḥayyim, was a rabbi, ethical writer, and Talmudist. Born in Zhetel, Poland, Yisraʾel Meʾir Kagan (or ha-Kohen) revealed his scholarly abilities at an early age, and his father decided to devote his life to developing the talents of his son. He took the ten-year-old Yisraʾel to Vilna; there the boy studied Talmud and came under the influence of the Musar movement, which sought the revitalization of the ethical life within the framework of traditional Judaism. After his marriage at the age of seventeen (which was normal for his circle), he moved to Radun, the hometown of his wife. At first he devoted himself to study while being supported by his wife, who ran a grocery store. For a short time afterward he served as the town rabbi, but he left the position when he found himself unsuited for it.

At the age of twenty-six, Kagan took a position as a Talmud teacher in Minsk, and in 1869 he returned to Radun and opened a *yeshivah* there. A few years later he published his first book, *Ḥafets ḥayyim* (Seeker of life), the title of which is the epithet by which he became best known. It is an impressive work on the seriousness of the sins of gossip and talebearing as violations of Jewish law. His concern with morality attracted many students to him and gave him a position of leadership in the developing Jewish Orthodoxy of eastern Europe.

His messianic beliefs led Kagan to set up a program in his *yeshivah* in which students descended from the priestly clan studied intensively the laws of the Temple so that they would be prepared upon its rebuilding. He also published a compilation of laws and texts dealing with the Temple service. At the end of the century he began to publish a commentary on the parts of the *Shulḥan ʿarukh* (a standard code of Jewish law) that deal with rituals, ceremonies, and holidays. This commentary, known as the *Mishnah berurah* (Clear teaching), incorporated the views of the later legal decisors and became the authoritative commentary.

After spending the years of World War I in Russia, Kagan returned in 1921 to newly independent Poland, where he reestablished his *yeshivah.* In his later years he was active in Agudat Yisraʾel (the world Orthodox organization), and during the interwar period he was probably the most influential rabbi in Poland. His influence was due not so much to his intellect as to his absolute honesty, his modesty, and his energy.

SEE ALSO Musar Movement.

BIBLIOGRAPHY

The first full-scale biography, which still has value and charm, though it is clearly hagiographical, is Moses M. Yoshor's *Saint and Sage* (New York, 1937). A more recent treatment, with an academic apparatus, though still somewhat hagiographical, is Lester S. Eckman's *Revered by All* (New York, 1974). At least one of Kagan's works has been translated into English: see Leonard Oschry's translation *Ahavath Chesed: The Love of Kindness as Required by G-D,* 2d rev. ed. (New York, 1976).

New Sources

Fishbane, Simcha. *The Method and Meaning of the Mishnah Berurah.* Hoboken, N.J., 1991.

SHAUL STAMPFER (1987)
Revised Bibliography

KAGAWA TOYOHIKO

KAGAWA TOYOHIKO (1888–1960) was a Japanese Christian novelist, social worker, statesman, and evangelist.

He alerted a whole generation of Japanese to the need for a practical expression of Christian ethics and symbolized to non-Japanese the power of faith in action.

Both of Kagawa's parents died before the boy entered school. As a middle-school student he was befriended by American missionaries who converted him to Christianity and treated him like a son. Extremely gifted mentally but weak physically, he spent four months in the hospital and then nine months alone in a hut recuperating shortly after he had entered a theological seminary. His close encounter with death became the basis of his later novel *Shisen o koete* (translated as both *Across the Death Line* and *Before the Dawn*). For the rest of his life, glaucoma and tuberculosis threatened his many activities.

Back in the seminary, Kagawa concurrently started social work in the Kobe slums. After ordination into the Japanese Presbyterian church and marriage, he traveled to the United States to study at Princeton University and Princeton Theological Seminary. This experience abroad began a pattern that developed into frequent lecture trips to many parts of the world. To the West he brought a message of hope based on his experience; in Japan he threw himself into social reform. He supported his slum work by royalties from his writing. He also organized both urban workers and farmers to improve their livelihoods.

In the late 1920s Kagawa moved to Tokyo, which became his headquarters. There he helped found consumer cooperatives and led pacifist movements. On a 1941 trip to the United States, he vigorously opposed militarism. Back in Japan, police incarcerated him several times; his foreign friends made him suspect. Then, when World War II ended, he was made a member of the cabinet formed to proffer Japan's surrender. In the liberal postwar climate after 1945, Kagawa helped form the Socialist party and worked to return Japan to the world community under the United Nations. In 1955 he was nominated for the Nobel Peace Prize. Until his death, he served as the pastor of a Tokyo congregation.

Kagawa's thought reflected the accomplishments born of his great energy. Quick to analyze a problem, he would form an organization to remedy it, assign it to trusted associates, and move on, giving his friends the sense that he considered the problem solved. Those who questioned problems more deeply found his expression of faith facile. Nevertheless, they could not disagree with his postmillenarian conviction that work in service of the Social Gospel would help realize his aims. His writings all reflected this combination of faith and the need for hard work. The novel *Mugi no hitotsubo* (A grain of wheat) showed how an individual could change the moral climate of a whole village through his dedication to reform. Kagawa's nonfiction works included analyses of economics that showed how cooperation serves the interests of the community better than competition.

Kagawa's tireless writing and other activities drew attention to the very practical aspects of the Christian gospel. He used royalties from the sixteen printings of *Shisen o koete* to help start the Japanese labor movement. He led and assisted groups that worked to alleviate various social wrongs and thereby gained the respect of many individuals who otherwise had little interest in Christianity. He had the highest profile among Japanese Christian leaders. In contrast to most of them, Kagawa also showed respect to foreign missionaries, a number of whom translated his writings for publication in their homelands and arranged speaking tours for him. With more than a dozen titles in English, he remains one of the most translated Japanese writers. During the thirties his message of faithful economic improvement brought hope to North American communities whose self-confidence had been severely eroded by the Great Depression. His name, along with those of other world figures such as Mahatma Gandhi and Jiang Gaishek, became a household word as an example of the fruits of Christian mission.

Events near the end of World War II tarnished Kagawa's saintly image. He broadcast over the Japanese national radio network, invoking Lincoln's second inaugural address (1865) as he urged American troops to lay down their arms. Other Japanese, themselves concerned with war responsibility, felt that this cooperation with the government, however well intentioned, had compromised Kagawa's pacifism. Yet only four decades later his countrymen began to reassess his true worth. More than any other Japanese Christian of his generation, Kagawa tried to implement the Christian gospel in everyday life and formed a bond with Christians throughout the world.

BIBLIOGRAPHY

The works of Kagawa Toyohiko are collected in *Kagawa Toyohiko zenshu,* 24 vols. (Tokyo, 1962–1964), which forms the basis for all further studies. *Kagawa Toyohiko den* (Tokyo, 1959), by Haruichi Yokoyama, is considered the standard biography. Charley May Simon's *A Seed Shall Serve: The Story of Toyohiko Kagawa, Spiritual Leader of Modern Japan* (New York, 1958) presents a summary Western view of the man and his work. George Bikle, Jr.'s *The New Jerusalem: Aspects of Utopianism in the Thought of Kagawa Toyohiko* (Tucson, 1976) deals with Kagawa's ideas. Yuzo Ota's "Kagawa Toyohiko: A Pacifist?" in *Pacifism in Japan: The Christian and Socialist Tradition,* edited by Nobuya Bamba and me (Kyoto, 1978), discusses the quite differing attitudes in Japan and abroad toward Kagawa's work.

JOHN F. HOWES (1987)

KAIBARA EKKEN (1630–1714) was a Japanese Neo-Confucian scholar. Ekken was born in Fukuoka on the island of Kyushu in southern Japan. Although he was the son of a samurai family, he had early contacts with townspeople and farmers of the province. This no doubt influenced his later decision to write in simplified Japanese in order to make Confucian teachings available to a wide audience. His father taught him medicine and nutrition, awakening a lifelong interest in matters of health that would culminate in the composition of his well-known book *Yōjōkun* (Precepts for Health Care), completed in 1713. It was his older brother Sonzai, however, who urged Ekken to abandon his early interest in Buddhism and to immerse himself in the Confucian classics. Under Sonzai's tutelage, Ekken became well versed in the classics and in the Neo-Confucian writings of Zhu Xi. During a seven-year stay in Kyoto under the patronage of the lord of the Kuroda domain, he came into contact with the leading Confucian scholars of his time, including Nakamura Tekisai, Kinoshita Jun'an, the botanist Mukai Gensho, and the agronomist Miyazaki Yasusada. These contacts continued throughout his life by virtue of Ekken's numerous trips to Kyoto and Edo. Ekken's tasks as a Confucian scholar included lecturing to the lord of the Kuroda domain and tutoring his heir. In addition, he was commissioned to produce lineage of the Kuroda family that required some sixteen years of research and writing. He also recorded the topography of Chikuzen Province, in a work that is still considered a model of its kind. Ekken's other major research project, entitled *Yamato honzō,* consisted of a classification and description of the various types of plants in Japan. It has been praised by Japanese and Western scholars alike as a seminal work in the history of botany in Japan.

Ekken's enduring interest, however, was the popularization of Confucian ethics and methods of self-cultivation for a wide audience. Accordingly, he wrote a number of *kunmono,* instructional treatises for various groups such as the samurai, the lord, the family, women, and children. His work *Onna Daigaku* (Learning for Women) is especially well known. In addition, he wrote on methods of study, on literature, on writing, on precepts for daily life, and on the five Confucian virtues. Although a devoted follower of Zhu Xi, toward the end of his life he wrote *Taigiroku,* a work that records his "great doubts" about Zhu's dualism of Principle (*li*) and material force (*qi*). Ekken's ideas were influenced by the thought of the Ming scholar Luo Qinshun (1416–1547), who had articulated a monistic theory of *qi.* Ekken felt that the dynamic quality of Confucianism had been lost by certain Song and Ming thinkers, and he hoped through the monist theory of *qi* to reformulate a naturalism and vitalism that he, like Luo, viewed as essential to Confucian thought. Consequently, Ekken was concerned to articulate the vital impulse of the material force that suffused all reality. His thought can thus be described as a naturalist religiosity rooted in profound reverence and gratitude toward Heaven as the source of life and earth as the sustainer of life. He felt that by recognizing one's debt to these "great parents," human beings activated a cosmic filiality toward all living things. This idea of filiality implied that one should preserve nature, not destroy it. The highest form of filiality was humaneness (*jin*), through which humans formed an identity with all things. Ekken, then, was a reformed Zhu Xi scholar whose broad interests, voluminous writings, and naturalist religiosity mark a high point in Japanese Neo-Confucian thought.

See Also Confucianism in Japan.

Bibliography

Kaibara Ekken's works are collected in *Ekken zenshu,* 8 vols. (Tokyo, 1910–1911) and *Kaibara Ekken, Muro Kyūsō,* "Nihon shiso taikei," vol. 34, edited by Araki Kengo and Inoue Tadashi (Tokyo, 1970). Works on Ekken include Inoue Tadashi's *Kaibara Ekken* (Tokyo, 1963); *Kaibara Ekken,* Nihon no meicho, vol. 14, edited by Matsuda Michio (Tokyo, 1969).

Mary Evelyn Tucker (1987)

KALĀBĀDHĪ, AL-

KALĀBĀDHĪ, AL- (d. AH 380/5, 990/5 CE), more fully Abū Bakr Muḥammad ibn Isḥāq ibn Ibrāhīm al-Kalābādhī; was the author of a famous treatise on early Sufism. As his name indicates, he was a native of the Kalābādh district of Bukhara. Details of his biography are lacking, but he is stated to have been a pupil of the Ṣūfī Abū al-Ḥusayn al-Fārisī and a Ḥanafī jurist with pro-Māturīdī views who studied jurisprudence (*fiqh*) under Muḥammad ibn Faḍl.

Of the works attributed to al-Kalābādhī, two are extant. The *Maʿānī al-akhbār,* also known as *Baḥr al-fawāʾid* and by other titles, was compiled in 985 and remains as yet unpublished. It consists of a brief ethical commentary, Ṣūfī in coloring, on 222 selected traditions of the Prophet and includes parallel passages cited in al-Kalābādhī's principal work, the *Kitāb al-taʿarruf li-madhhab ahl al-taṣawwuf.* This masterpiece has been edited several times, most reliably by A. J. Arberry (Cairo, 1933), who also translated it into English with a detailed introduction as *The Doctrine of the Sufis.*

The work is a principal source for the development of early Sufism (second/eighth to fourth/tenth centuries). It is divided into seventy-five chapters that fall into two parts. Beginning with a sketchy introductory survey of important early Ṣūfīs, the first part sets out the tenets of Islam as accepted by the Ṣūfīs; these can be traced back to the articles of faith elaborated in the creed known as *Al-fiqh al-akbar II* (The Greater Understanding II), which, it seems, al-Kalābādhī quotes directly. The second part discusses the ascetic endeavors, spiritual experiences, technical terms, and miraculous phenomena of the Ṣūfīs, based on their sayings and verses.

Throughout the work it is al-Kalābādhī's stated purpose to stave off the decay of Sufism and to prove that Sufism lies within the boundaries of Islamic orthodoxy. As a primary source for the history of early Sufism, al-Kalābādhī's *Taʿarruf* may rank with the works of al-Sarrāj (d. 988), Abū Ṭālib al-Makkī (d. 996), and al-Sulamī (d. 1021).

The *Taʿarruf* reflects the Ṣūfī tradition that became current in Transoxiana during Samanid times. It soon achieved the status of an authoritative treatise on Sufism, and commentaries were written on it. The most important of these is the Persian *Nūr al-murīdin wa-fa-zīhat al-muddaʿīn,* also known as *Sharḥ-i Taʿarruf* (Commentary on the *Taʿarruf*), of Abū Ibrāhīm Ismāʿīl ibn Muḥammad ibn ʿAbd Allāh al-Mustamlī (d. 1042), a Ṣūfī of Bukhara. The work is the oldest surviving Ṣūfī treatise in Persian prose and is extant in several manuscripts, one of them copied in 1081. The value of this voluminous source for the development of Sufism in Transoxiana lies in its copious comments on each Ṣūfī statement quoted in the *Taʿarruf*, and in the fact that it was compiled with apparently no motive other than the instruction of Ṣūfī disciples. From the point of view of the Persian language, the work gives testimony to dialectal forms of tenth-century Persian, with an extraordinarily frequent occurrence of Arabic words.

The commentary on the *Taʿarruf* ascribed to ʿAbd Allāh ibn Muḥammad al-Anṣārī (d. 1089) appears to be lost, while the *Ḥusn Al-taʿarruf*, an Arabic commentary on the work written by the Shāfiʿī judge ʿAlāʾ al-Dīn ʿAlī ibn Ismāʿīl al-Qūnawī (d. 1327 or 1329), is extant in manuscript. There is also an anonymous Arabic commentary that is erroneously ascribed to Yaḥyā Suhrawardī (d. 1191), who nonetheless summed up the importance of the *Taʿarruf* in the watchword: "But for the *Taʿarruf* we should not have known of Sufism."

BIBLIOGRAPHY

Anawati, Georges C., and Louis Gardet. *Mystique musulmane.* 3d ed. Paris, 1976.

Arberry, A. J. *The Doctrine of the Sufis.* Cambridge, 1935.

Lazard, Gilbert. *La langue des plus anciens monuments de la prose persane.* Paris, 1963. See pages 67–71.

Nwyia, Paul. "Al-Kalābādhī." In *The Encyclopaedia of Islam,* new ed., vol. 4. Leiden, 1978.

GERHARD BÖWERING (1987)

KĀLACAKRA

KĀLACAKRA ("Wheel of Time"; Tib., *dus kyi 'khor lo;* Mong., *čay-un kürdü*) is the Sanskrit name for the principal male deity and personification of the *Kālacakra Tantra,* an Indian Buddhist esoteric treatise belonging to the class of unexcelled yoga-tantras (*anuttarayoga-tantra*). In this Tantric tradition, the deity Kālacakra represents spiritual knowledge (*vidyā*) and the state of immutable bliss, which is attainable only through the yogic practices that are specific to the Kālacakra tradition. Kālacakra is a single, unified reality, which is given different names in the Kālacakra tradition: Ādibuddha (Primordial Buddha), *sahajakāya* (innate body), *jñānakāya* (gnosis body), *viśuddhakāya* (pure body), *vajrayoga* (indestructible union), and the like. This nondual reality has two main aspects: the phenomenal world of multiplicity (*saṃsāra*) and the unitary ultimate reality (*nirvāṇa*).

The Kālacakra tradition is the latest Buddhist tantric system to appear in India. While retaining its distinctive Buddhist tradition, the Kālacakra tradition integrates a variety of non-Buddhist Indian elements. The most prominent of these are Śākhya and Jainism. Likewise, a number of non-Buddhist Indian deities encountered in Hindu tantric systems have a place in the Kālacakra pantheon. Although the *Kālacakra Tantra* shares some general characteristics with other Unexcelled Yoga Tantras in terms of tantric yogic practice, it differs from others in its goal of the attainment of the empty form (śūnyatā-bimba) that is devoid of matter, and in the path to that goal, namely, the *Kālacakra Tantra's* six-phased yoga.

Another unique feature of the Kālacakra tradition is its close affiliation with the mythical land of Śambhala and its kings, not only in terms of its history but also in its future role in Buddhism. It prophesizes an apocalyptic battle between Raudra Cakri, the King of Śambhala, and the malevolent King of the barbarians, whom Raudra Cakri will defeat. The calculations pertaining to the time of the battle are contained in Kālacakra's elaborate astrological system.

Regarding the individual, the term *kālacakra* signifies the circulation of vital energies (*prāṇa*) within the circular passages in the body; in terms of the cosmos, it designates the passing of days, months, and years in the cycle of time. Regarding the ultimate reality, the term *kālacakra* refers to the nonduality of the two facets of enlightened awareness-emptiness (*śūnyatā*) and compassion (*karuṇā*), or wisdom (*prajñā*) and method (*upāya*). It further denotes the unity of the Buddha's mind, or the supreme, indestructible knowledge, and his body, or a phenomenal world, which is the object of that knowledge. Kālacakra's consort is Viśvamātā (Tib., Sna tshogs yum; Mong., Visiyamada), who is the personified perfection of wisdom.

HISTORY OF THE KĀLACAKRA TRADITION. The early history of the Kālacakra tradition in India is abstruse, since the earliest holders of the tradition remain shrouded by pseudonyms. The most prominent early masters of the Kālacakra tradition in India were Piṇḍo, Dīpaṃkaraśrījñāna (also known as Atīśa), Nāro, Śrībhadrabodhi, Somanātha, Anupamarakṣita, Abhayākāragupta, Raviśrījñāna, Śakyaśrībhadra, and Vibhūticandra. An important reference for establishing the period of the propagation of the Kālacakra tradition in India is found in the *Kālacakra Tantra* (chap. 1, v. 27) and in the *Vimalaprabhā* (Stainless light) commentary. These two sources mention the end of the sexagenary cycle that comes 403 years after the Hijirī era of 623 CE as the earliest period in which the *Kālacakra Tantra* was promulgated in India. Thus, the year 1026 CE, which was the last year of the reign of King Mahīpāla of Bengal, a great supporter of Buddhism in India, is established as the year of the *Kālacakra Tantra's* composition.

According to the legendary accounts of the Kālacakra tradition, the existing version of the *Kālacakra Tantra* is said to be an abridged version of a larger original Tantra called the *Paramādibuddha Tantra* (Tantra of the primordial Buddha), which reportedly consisted of twelve thousand verses. According to the *Vimalaprabhā* (chap. 1), the extant version of the *Kālacakra Tantra* was taught by Buddha Śākyamuni to Sucandra, the king of Śambhala, and an emanation of Bodhisattva Vajrapāṇi in the Dhāṇyakaṭaka stupa, situated in the vicinity of the present-day village of Amarāvatī in Andhra Pradesh. Having returned to Śambhala, King Sucandra wrote it down and disseminated it throughout his kingdom.

Sucandra's six successors continued to maintain the Kālacakra tradition, and the eighth king of Śambhala, Mañjuśrī Yaśas, composed the abridged version, known as the *Laghukālacakratantrarāja* (Sovereign abridged *Kālacakra Tantra*). Existent Sanskrit variants of the abridged version are written in the *śradgharā* meter (four lines of twenty-one syllables each) and contain between 1,030 and 1,037 verses. The tradition holds that Mañjuśrī Yaśas's successor Puṇḍarīka, an emanation of the Bodhisattva Avalokiteśvara, composed the *Vimalaprabhā,* an extensive 12,000-line commentary on the *Kālacakra Tantra.*

Tibetan sources on the history of the *Kālacakra Tantra* differ in their accounts of the *Kālacakra Tantra's* history in India. According to the Tibetan Rwa tradition, Indian Buddhist master Cilupā of Orissa, after studying the *Kālacakra Tantra* in Ratnagiri in the second half of the tenth century, set out on a journey to Śambhala to receive further teachings on the text. Having returned to India in 966 CE, Cilupā taught the *Kālacakra Tantra* to his three disciples and wrote a commentary on it. His most important disciple, Piṇḍo Ācārya, later taught the *Tantra* to Kālacakrapāda the Senior, from Bengal, who in turn passed on the tradition to his disciples, among whom the most important is Kālacakrapāda the Junior. To facilitate the propagation of the Kālacakra tradition in all of the regions of India, Kālacakrapāda the Junior built a Kālacakra temple at Nālandā in the present-day state of Bihar, where he taught the *Kālacakra Tantra* and wherefrom the Kālacakra tradition widely spread. A disciple of Kālacakrapāda the Junior by the name of Mañjukīrti passed on the tradition to the Newari *paṇḍita* Samantaśribhadra, who in the later part of the eleventh century assisted the Tibetan translator Rwa lo tsa ba rdo rje grags pa (Ra lotsawa dorje drak pa) in translating the *Kālacakra Tantra* and *Vimalaprabhā* into Tibetan. This translation marked the beginning of the Kālacakra Rwa lineage in Tibet, which became influential in the Sa skya (Śākya) school of Tibetan Buddhism.

According to the Tibetan 'Bro tradition, the *Kālacakra Tantra* was brought to India during the reign of Kalkī Śrīpāla in Śambhala. He gave a transmission to Kālacakrapāda the Senior, from whom the Kālacakra tradition was successively transmitted through Kālacakrapāda the Junior to the Kāśmiri *paṇḍita* Somānātha. In the early eleventh century, Somānātha assisted Tibetan translator 'Bro shes rab grags (Dro sherap drak) in translating the Kālacakra literature into Tibetan. This initiated the Kālacakra 'Bro lineage in Tibet, which was passed on to Bsgom pa dkon mchog gsum (Gompa Könchok sum) of the Bka' gdams (Kadam) pa school, subsequently to the eighth Karma pa, Mi bskyod rdo rje (Mikyo Dorje, 1507–1554), and then to Dol bu pa shes rab rgyal mtshan (Dölbupa sherap gyaltsan; 1292–1361) of the Jonang school. It was later transmitted by Tārānātha (1575–1643), through whom it reached the Zhang pa Bka' brgyud (Zhangpa Kagyu) school.

An important figure in bringing together the Rwa and 'Bro lineages was Bu ston rin chen grub (Butön rinchendrub, 1290–1364). His disciple transmitted both traditions to Rje Tsong kha pa (1357–1419), the founder of the Dge lugs (Geluk) pa school, who in turn transmitted it to his disciple Mkhas grub Dge legs dpal bzang (1385–1438).

A later tradition called Tsami was established by Tsa mi sangs rgyas grags pa (Tsami sangye drakpa) and Siddha Orgyen pa, who passed it on to the third Karma pa Rang byung rdo rje (Rangjung Dorje, 1284–1339). Gyi jo zla ba'i 'od zer (Gyijo dawei özer), who was the first to translate Kālacakra texts into Tibetan under the guidance of Indian *paṇḍita* Śrībhadrabodhi in 1026 CE, established the earliest Kālacakra lineage in Tibet. His lineage was passed on to 'Brom lo tsa ba padma 'od zer (Drom lotsawa padma özer), and it reached the Jonang pa school through Jonang Kun spang thugs brtson 'grus (Jonang Künpang tuk tsöndrü) (1243–1313), the founder of Jonang monastery.

Among the Tibetan scholars who produced an extensive amount of commentarial literature on the *Kālacakra Tantra,* Rgyal tshab dar ma rin chen (Gyaltsap darma rinchen; 1364–1432), Stag tshang lo tsa ba (Taktsang lot sawa), and 'Ju Mi pham rgya mtsho (Ju mipan gyatso; 1846–1912) are also worthy of mention.

CONTENT OF THE *KĀLACAKRA TANTRA*. The *Kālacakra Tantra* is divided into five chapters, which are categorized by the Tibetan tradition into three main divisions—the Outer, Inner, and Alternative Kālacakra.

1. The Inner Kālacakra (chap. 1: "The Cosmos") deals with cosmology, astrology, chronology, and eschatology. It describes in detail the nature of time and the elementary particles of the cosmos, along with the origination, configuration, measurements, and dissolution of the cosmos and its constituents. It interprets the cosmos as a four-tiered *maṇḍala* and as the cosmic body of the Buddha.

2. The Outer Kālacakra (chap. 2: "The Individual") deals with human embryology and subtle psychophysiology, astro-medicine, medical botany, yogic and ritual therapies, and alchemy. It discusses the formation, functions, and disintegration of the human body, speech, and mind. It interprets the individual as a microcosmic representation of the cosmic *maṇḍala,* as a cycle of time, and as an abode of the four bodies of the Buddha (*sahajakāya, dharmakāya, saṃbhogakāya,* and *nirmāṇakāya*).

3. The Alternative Kālacakra (chaps. 3–5: "Initiation," "Sādhana," and "Gnosis") deals with the practice of Kālacakra, which is generally divided into three main stages—initiation (*abhiṣeka*), the stage of generation (*utpattikrama*), and the stage of completion (*saṃpannakrama*).

Kālacakra initiation involves the initiate's entrance into the Kālacakra *maṇḍala,* purification and empowerment by the deities in the *maṇḍala,* a series of meditations and recitations of *mantras,* and the taking of Tantric vows and pledges. The stage of initiation consists of eleven successive initiations. The first seven initiations are the water, crown, crown pendant, *vajra* and bell, conduct, name, and permission initiations; the four higher initiations are the vase, secret, wisdom, and gnosis. The successive initiations are analogous to the individual's progression on the Buddhist path from a layperson to a buddha.

The stage of generation involves the practice of conceptual meditation in which one mentally creates the Kālacakra *maṇḍala* with its various deities and imagines oneself as the Kālacakra deity standing in the center of the *maṇḍala,* holding the *vajra* and bell, and embracing Viśvamātā. The *maṇḍala* represents a sublimated cosmos and a mother's body insofar as the mental creation of the *maṇḍala* and its deities is analogous to the individual's conception, development in the mother's womb, and birth. The deities in the *maṇḍala* represent the purified aspects of the Buddha's four bodies, or the sublimated aspects of the individual's gnosis, mind, speech, and body. The *maṇḍala* embodies the Kālacakra *mantra: oṃ haṃ kṣa ma la ca ra ya svāhā.* The stage of generation also involves certain sexual yogic practices with either an actual consort or an imagined consort. The goal of this stage of practice is the accumulation of merit and further purification through the transformation of the individual's conception of the world.

The stage of completion involves meditation on the form of emptiness (*śūnyatā-bimba*) by means of the practice of the six-phased *yoga* (*ṣaḍ-aṅgayoga*). This six-phased yoga of Kālacakra consists of the following phases: retraction (*pratyāhāra*), meditative stabilization (*dhyāna*), breath control *(prāṇāyāma),* retention (*dhāraṇā*), recollection (*anusmṛti*), and *samādhi.* The *samādhi* phase is characterized by the generation of 21,600 moments of the immutable bliss, which, coursing through the six bodily chakras, eliminate the material aspects of the four drops in the individual's body and facilitate their manifestation as the four bodies of the Buddha. Thus, 21,600 moments of bliss transform the material and perishable nature of the individual's body and mind into the empty form and the gnosis of imperishable bliss, called *Kālacakra.*

ICONOGRAPHY OF KĀLACAKRA. In Buddhist iconography, Kālacakra is depicted as standing on a lotus, which is on the disks of the sun, moon, and Rāhu, with the right knee advanced and the left leg retracted (the *ālīḍha* posture), crushing Kāmadeva and Rudra with his two feet. He has a dark blue body, symbolizing day and night; three throats, each of which represent four zodiac signs; four faces, each of which represent three zodiac signs; twelve shoulders, representing the twelve months of the year; twenty-four arms holding various weapons; and 360 joints of the hands, symbolizing 360 days of the year. He is embraced by a yellow, twelve-eyed Viśvamātā, standing with the left foot advanced and the right leg retracted (the *pratyālīḍha* posture).

Since the 1980s, the Kālacakra tantric system has been gaining popularity in Europe and the United States, in part because the Dalai Lama has offered initiations each year in Western countries in the belief that the time of Śambhala is approaching and in order to generate a karmic connection for Buddhist practitioners to Śambhala.

BIBLIOGRAPHY

Broido, Michael M. "Killing, Lying, Stealing, and Adultery: A Problem of Interpretation in the Tantras." In *Buddhist Hermeneutics,* edited by Donald S. Lopez Jr., pp. 71–118. Honolulu, 1988. Addresses a hermeneutical problem in Buddhist Tantric literature by concentrating on specific passages from the Kālacakra literature and on the variety of interpretations given to them in different sources.

Gen Lamrimpa. *Transcending Time: An Explanation of the Kālacakra Six-Session Guru Yoga.* Translated by B. Alan Wallace. Boston, 1999. Discusses in detail the three areas of the Kālacakra practice—preliminary practices, six-session *guru* yoga, and the stage of completion—as they are interpreted by the Tibetan Dge lugs pa tradition.

Geshe Lhundup Sopa, Roger Jackson, and John Newman, eds. *The Wheel of Time: The Kalachakra in Context.* Madison, Wis., 1985. Contains five articles by different authors giving a brief summary of the broader context of the *Kālacakra Tantra* and its history and practice.

Gyatso, Tenzin (Dalai Lama XIV), and Jeffrey Hopkins. *Kalachakra Tantra: Rite and Initiation.* London, 1989. This volume consists of the three main parts: (1) a general introduction to the Kālacakra rite of initiation and its preliminary practices; (2) an English translation of Kay drup ge lek bel sang bo's text, *Kālacakra Initiation Rite: Stage of Generation,* with the Dalai Lama's commentary; and (3) a translation of the Dalai Lama's composition on the three versions of the six-session yoga.

Harrington, Laura, ed. *Kalachakra.* 2d ed. Rome, 1999. A pictorial guide with explanatory notes to the Kālacakra *maṇḍala* and its deities.

Newman, John. "The Outer Wheel of Time: Vajrayāna Buddhist Cosmology in the *Kālacakra Tantra.*" Ph.D. diss., University of Wisconsin, Madison, 1987. This dissertation concentrates primarily on the analysis of the first chapter of the *Kālackra Tantra.* It contains a translation of several cosmological and eschatological passages of the *Kālacakra Tantra* and the *Vimalaprabhā;* in footnotes, it gives useful interpretations from several Tibetan commentaries on those passages.

Newman, John. "The *Paramādibuddha* (*The Kālacakra-mūla-tantra*) and Its Relation to the Early Kālacakra Literature." *Indo-Iranian Journal* 30 (1987): 93–102.

Newman, John. "Buddhist Siddhānta in the *Kālacakra Tantra.*" *Wiener Zeitschrift für die Kunde Südasiens* 36 (1992): 227–234. Analyzes philosophical statements found in the second chapter of the *Kālacakra Tantra* from historical and philological perspectives.

Newman, John. "Eschatology in the Wheel of Time Tantra." In *Buddhism in Practice,* edited by Donald S. Lopez Jr., Princeton, 1995. Includes brief introductory notes and a translation of a short, eschatological passage from the first chapter of the *Kālacakrata Tantra.*

Steams, Cyrus. *The Buddha from Dolpo: A Study of the Life and Thought of the Tibetan Master Dolpopa Sherab Gyaltsen.* Albany, N.Y., 1999. Offers an insight into the Tibetan *zhan stong* view based on teachings in the *Kālacakra Tantra* and unique teachings of Dolpopa, a great Kālacakra master from the Tibetan Jonang tradition.

Wallace, Vesna A. "The Buddhist Tantric Medicine in the *Kālacakratantra.*" *Pacific Journal of the Institute of Buddhist Studies,* n.s. 10–11 (1995): 155–174. Discusses the concept of science in the *Kālacakra Tantra,* the *Kālacakra Tantra's* medical theories and practices, and their soteriological significance.

Wallace, Vesna A. *The Inner Kālacakratantra: A Buddhist Tantric View of the Individual.* New York, 2001. Analyses the Kālacakra tradition's various interpretations of the individual and the individual's place in the universe. It discusses the individual in terms of the Kālacakra deity's cosmic, social, gnostic, and transformative bodies.

VESNA A. WALLACE (2005)

KALĀM. In common usage *kalām* signifies speech, language, sentence, proposition, words, but in the field of Muslim religious thought it has two particular meanings: the word of God (*kalām Allāh*) and the science of *kalām* (*ʿilm al-kalām*), which may be understood as dogmatic theology or more precisely the defensive apologetics of Islam. Apart from a few preliminary remarks on *kalām* as the word of God, the present article is devoted to *kalām* in the latter sense.

ETYMOLOGY AND DEFINITIONS. *Kalām Allāh* is mentioned several times in the Qurʾān (for example, *sūrahs* 2:75, 9:6, 48:15). God spoke to the Prophets (2:253). He "spoke clearly to Moses" (4:164, 7:143, and elsewhere). However, one finds neither *kalām* nor *mutakallim* (speaking) in the list of the most beautiful names of God (*asmāʾ Allāh al-ḥusnā*). Rather, it was the theologians who, on the basis of Qurʾanic evidence, ascribed the attribute of *kalām* to God and designated the Qurʾān as *kalām Allāh.* From this development arose the very controversial problem of the relationship of the Qurʾān to the Word as a divine attribute. Here it may be mentioned in passing that during the European Middle Ages, Thomas Aquinas described the *mutakallimūn* (whose occasionalism and negation of causality he refuted) as "loquentes in lege maurorum" ("those who speak on behalf of Islam").

As for the science of *kalām,* this term came to mean Muslim dogmatic theology. In his effort to determine the origin of the usage, Harry A. Wolfson suggests that the word *kalām* was used to translate into Arabic the different meanings of the Greek term *logos* as "word," "reason," "argument." It was also used to signify the act of expounding or discussing a specific science, and the *mutakallimūn* became those who deal with this science, for example *al-kalām al-ṭabīʿī, peri phuseos logoi.* The "physicians" (*phusikoi, phusiologoi*) are sometimes called *al-mutakallimūn fī al-ṭabīʿīyat,* those who deal with questions of physics. The Greek term *theologoi* is translated by *aṣḥāb al-kalām al-ilāhī* or *al-mutakallimūn fī ilāhīyāt* (i.e., those who deal with the divine). Gradually, the term came to signify the specific, perfectly defined science that is the object of the present study.

In his renowned *Muqaddimah,* Ibn Khaldūn gives the following definition of *ʿilm al-kalām:* "The science of *kalām* is a science that involves arguing with logical proofs in defense of the articles of faith and refuting innovators who deviate in their dogmas from the early Muslims and Muslim orthodoxy. The real core (*sirr*) of the articles of faith is the oneness of God" (Cairo, n.d., p. 321; trans. Rosenthal, New York, 1958, vol. 3, p. 34).

This role of defensive apologia and of apologetics attributed to the science of *kalām* has remained standard in Islam. The modernist *shaykh* Muḥammad ʿAbduh wrote that the purpose of *kalām* was the "fixing of religious beliefs for the aim of working to conserve and consolidate religion" (*Riṣālat al-tawḥīd,* p. 5; trans., p. 5).

Al-Ījī (d. 1356), commented on at length and intelligently by al-Jurājnī (d. 1413), initially defines the function of *kalām* as seeking "to guarantee the proof (of the existence) of the Creator and of his unicity" (*Mawāqif,* vol. 1, p. 26). Later in the same work he explains that "*kalām* is the science that bears the responsibility of solidly establishing religious beliefs by giving proofs and dispelling doubts" (pp. 34–35). He goes on to state explicitly the purpose, the usefulness, the degree of excellence, the questions treated, and the explanation of the chosen term.

Finally, to cite a nineteenth-century popular manual, al-Bājūrī's gloss on the *Jawharat al-tawḥīd, kalām* or *tawḥīd* is defined as "the science that enables one to establish clearly religious beliefs, based on definite proofs of these beliefs" (*Ḥāshiyah ʿalā Jawharat al-tawḥīd,* p. 8). For al-Bājūrī this definition is the first of the ten "foundations" that converge to form each branch of knowledge. The second element is the subject: God, the envoys and the prophets, the contingent being insofar as he serves to give existence to his Maker, and the *samʿīyāt,* or traditionally accepted truths. The third element is its utility: the knowledge of God supported by decisive proofs and the acquiring of "eternal happiness." The fourth is the degree of excellence, and the fifth, the relationship of this science to the other disciplines. The people of *kalām* consider their science to be the most noble of all because of its subject and see it as the basis of all other fields of knowledge. The sixth element specifies the founders of the science: for orthodox *kalām,* al-Ashʿarī (d. 935) and al-Māturīdī (d. 956), who "coordinated the writings related to this science and refuted the specious ambiguities introduced by the Muʿtazilah." The seventh element is the name: *tawḥīd* or *kalām.* The eighth is the means used, namely rational and traditional arguments. The ninth is its legal category, because the study of *kalām* is considered obligatory by its adherents. Finally, the tenth includes the questions treated, which deal with what is necessary and impossible to attribute to God and to the prophets.

ORIGINS AND SOURCES OF THE SCIENCE OF KALĀM. Among the influences that can be detected in the science of *kalām,* direct sources include the Qur'ān, *ḥadīth,* consensus of the community, and reason, while indirect sources can be traced to the pre-Islamic religions of the Byzantine and Sasanid empires and Greek philosophy as well as political dissensions of the early Islamic period.

The Qur'ān. This is the primary element on which the science of *kalām* is built. Islam is first of all the religion of the Book: It is a surrender to a God who, in the eyes of the believers, reveals himself in the book *par excellence,* the Qur'ān, his uncreated word. The Qur'ān is neither a history of the people of God nor a life of Muḥammad; it is rather a "discourse" that God holds with humanity in the first person.

The Qur'ān presents itself in effect as an absolute beginning of revelation. The earlier revelations (Jewish and Christian) have not been preserved in the authentic versions and thus cannot serve a "given." Consequently Muslim theology finds itself before an all-encompassing document, transmitted by a single man and corresponding to a very limited period of time. There is no progressive revelation, no *preparatio coranica* according to a divine plan, no development comparable to that of the Old Testament in relation to the New, or that within the New Testament itself. All the dogma is explicitly given in the Qur'anic text.

This Qur'anic core, the starting point of the science of *kalām,* is not systematic. It is essentially a collection of "revelations" stretched out over approximately twenty years, in which the Prophet informs his followers of the orders of God according to the circumstances, some of which are political.

A person knowledgeable in *kalām* finds four elements in the Qur'ān. First there is a theodicy: the existence of God, his unity, his eternal self, his omnipotence, the source of life and death, his fixity, his omniscience, and his mercy. God is endowed with speech and with will. He is the Creator. Second comes an anthropology: God created humankind from dust. He breathed his spirit into humanity (*wa-nafakha fīhi min rūḥihi*). The human intelligence is superior to that of the angels. Adam disobeyed God, but his sin is not passed down to his descendants; thus, there is no original sin in Islam. The human being is the vicegerent of God (*khalīfat Allāh*) on earth, the ruler of the created world, which must be submitted to God's will. Third there is an eschatology: the judgment of the individual, heaven, hell, and the Last Judgment; God is the master of death. Finally there is morality: personal, familial, social; the rights of God.

Although the Qur'ān presents itself as a divine revelation, it nonetheless communicates no mysteries that are truly supernatural. There is the global mystery of the divine being (*al-ghayb*), which is transcendent and entirely inaccessible in itself to human intelligence, but no mystery of the Trinity nor of the incarnation, nor of the redemption, and therefore no mystery of the church or of the sacraments. Quite the contrary, the very idea of the incarnation is vigorously rejected. Thus the theologians, those knowledgeable in *kalām,* have only to organize the elements of a natural theodicy in their attempt at synthesis. If one disregards the pejorative connotation that the word *rationalism* has acquired in Western Christian milieus since the eighteenth century, one can say that Muslim theology is basically rationalist: In practice it denies the possibility of access to an order of supernatural mysteries. For its clearest representatives who are not necessarily always the most religious, Muslim theology is essentially a superior metaphysical system to which are added, in an incidental manner, a few positive notions relating to matters of cult, which are revealed by God in the Qur'ān.

Finally, the Qur'ān was revealed in Arabic. For Muslim theologians this fact indicates an essential link between the religious notion and the nature of God. The Arabic Qur'ān is the very word of God himself. Consequently the Arabic language is seen as itself revealed, or at least as the one that best expresses the word of God. This explains the primary role played by language in the elaboration of Muslim theology and the importance of the schools of grammar in the interpretation of the sacred texts.

Ḥadīth. This term refers to the corpus of words and actions of the Prophet, the "perfect model" whose least word assumes normative value. In dogmatic and moral authority, the canonical collections of these *ḥadīth* are second only to the Qur'ān, at least according to traditional Muslim thinkers.

The consensus of the community *(Ijmāʿ).* This consensus of the community as represented by its doctors is an internal factor of regulation. According to Henri Lammens, it is a kind of instinct of the people, who when faced with certain innovations react according to the spirit of Islam. The Prophet had said, "My community will never agree on an error," and from this his disciples concluded that the community is infallible as far as its beliefs and religious practices are concerned.

The idea of *ijmāʿ,* although quite complex in theory, showed itself to be effective in practice to maintain a traditional line of orientation through the stirrings caused by new conditions. Because Islam has neither an official ministry nor an advisory body, the *ijmāʿ* exercises more or less tacitly the role of regulator within the Muslim community. Qualified reformers aroused by God could legitimately undertake to reestablish the Muslim community in the purity of its original line or could propose solutions to the demands of the modern world in conformity with the religious law.

Reason. For a certain number of narrow traditionists, especially in the early period, the only acceptable attitude from the religious point of view was an exclusive loyalty to the Qur'ān and the *ḥadīth* with no rational elaboration. Nevertheless, for traditional theology reason became an essential factor in the problem of faith. It is necessary for every adult, who should not be satisfied with a blind acceptance of tradition (*taqlīd*) but must be able to demonstrate rationally the existence of God and the truth of the Muslim religion. The theologians themselves use reason to establish the authenticity of their historical notions, to criticize evidence, to defend dogmas, and to refute objections. This tendency went so far that in certain treatises on theology the major part is devoted to *ʿaqlīyāt,* those truths that reason can reach on its own, with the Qurʾān serving as a confirmation. A certain number of positive notions, the *samʿīyāt,* are known only by revelation; these are concerned with eschatology, prophetology, the caliphate, and similar matters. The degree to which reason is used also varies with the schools: Some restrict its use to logic as instrument; others apply an untiring dialectical zeal to the smallest theological problems.

Christianity. The influence of Christianity was felt either in an informal way, notably through the Bible itself or through contacts that Muslims had with Christians living in Muslim lands, or formally via discussions with Christian theologians, especially in Damascus and Baghdad. Among these theologians were the Nestorians concentrated in Hira, the Jacobites (monophysites), and finally the Melkites, including John of Damascus and his disciple Abū Qurrah, as well as several dissident sects that were more or less Christian. As they attempted to defend the dogma of Islam in discussions with these groups, Muslim theologians were led to address certain problematic issues such as free will and predestination, the divine attributes, and the uncreated Qurʾān. (In the Qurʾān Jesus is considered to be the word of God.)

Greek philosophy. In the eyes of Muslim thinkers, Greek philosophy was perceived as a single body of knowledge within which Plato and Aristotle, far from being in opposition, played complementary roles in relation to each other. Apocryphal Neoplatonic writings such as *De causis* and the *Pseudo-Theology of Aristotle* served to reinforce this conviction. These Greek teachings, known directly or via the commentators, exercised an influence in two directions. Certain Muslim thinkers adopted an orientation that was straightforwardly rational in the eighteenth-century French sense of the term. They denied all revelation, maintaining only a vague notion of a distant philosophical God. This was especially true of Abū Bakr al-Rāzī, the Rhazes of the Latins.

Other thinkers, loyal to their faith, took on the task of defending the principal dogmas of their religion with this instrument newly placed between their hands—Greek thought. These were the Muʿtazilah, the first theologians of Islam. They soon split into two main groups. The dissidents among them, such as al-Ashʿarī, wished to retain only the minimum of philosophy indispensable for theological elaboration and stressed more the properly religious core of the Qurʾān. The other group, the *falāsifah,* including hellenizing philosophers such as al-Kindī, al-Fārābī, Ibn Sīnā, Ibn Rushd, and others, were more philosophers than Muslims; for them religious ideas were only a superstructure or a pretext for philosophizing. The *ijmaʿ* came to favor the first trend, and the ideas of the Ashʿarīyah became the shared philosophy of Islam, while the second tendency was met with great reticence, and its doctrine was hardly tolerated.

Manichaeism and Mazdakism. The invasion of Iran brought the Muslims in contact with a very rich and complex cultural climate, where the Armenian and Syrian Christians in particular were already engaged in controversies with the Mazdaeans and the Magians. The ardent monotheism of Islam, which for fear of taking anything away from God's omnipotence made God the creator of evil as well as good, offered a new battlefield for Mazdaean apologists, as is demonstrated by the *Shkand gumānīk vichār,* a ninth-century Mazdaean apologetic treatise. The theologians responded by elaborating treatises against the dualists.

As for the Manichaeans, their survival in the tenth-century East, attested by Ibn al-Nadīm's *Fihrist,* leads one to believe that with the fall of their Mazdaean persecutors and the period of calm that followed the Muslim conquest, their doctrine was able to find a new lease on life.

Political dissensions. The political struggles among Muslims mark the starting point for the elaboration of theological problems. Given that traditional Islam is inseparably *dīn wa-dawlah,* "religion and state," it is normal that everything concerning the polity, the transmission of power, legitimacy, and the struggle for public authority should express itself in religious terms and provoke violent conflicts among the partisans of opposing opinions. It was in this way that the problems of the nature of faith, of its relationship to works, of the possibility for faith to increase or decrease, of the status of the unrepentant sinner who is nevertheless a believer, of the caliphate, and like questions developed among the Muslims.

THE PRINCIPAL SCHOOLS AND MAJOR THEMES. Here this article shall pursue a mainly chronological order that will permit the author to trace the emergence and development of the problem.

The early creeds. The earliest surviving documents that give an official expression of doctrine are the first creeds, some of which have been studied by A. J. Wensinck in *The Muslim Creed.* From what has been observed concerning the fragmentary nature of the Qurʾān, it is not surprising to find no systematic résumé of doctrine there. What Muḥammad affirms above all are the divine transcendence and unity, the declaration in fiery terms of the horrors of the judgment, and the prophetic character of his message.

But a few decades after Muḥammad's death, the expansion of the new religion and the political and social questions that arose led the heads of the community to express the essential traits of Islam and to condense them into a formula that was easy to recite and easy to remember. Some of these formulas are found in the *ḥadīth* collections. For example, Muḥammad is asked, "What is Islam?" and he answers, "It is to associate nothing with God, to perform the ritual prayer, to give the prescribed alms, and to fast during Ramaḍān." When he is asked, "And what is faith?" he answers, "It is to believe in God, his angels, his book, his meeting [with believers in Paradise], and his Prophet, to believe in the resurrection and the final destiny."

The development of Islam, the struggle with the tribes in revolt, and the conquests slowly necessitated a distinction between *islām* ("submission") and *īmān* ("faith"). It is possible to be Muslim in different ways, and external posture is not necessarily a sign of inner faith. It was at this point that the "five pillars of Islam" were defined. These are usually expressed in the following terms: "Islam is built on five pillars: faith, ritual prayer (*ṣalāt*), the tithe (*zakāt*), the fast of Ramaḍān, and the pilgrimage." Thus Islam presents itself in its entirety as faith and acts. The holy war is not yet mentioned.

However, conversion to Islam prompted the development of a simple formula expressing in a few words the essential message of the new religion: the *shahādah* ("witnessing") served this function. By reciting it, the new converts entered the Muslim community; it was their profession of faith: "There is no god but God, and Muḥammad is the messenger of God."

A profession of faith reduced to its simplest expression, the *shahādah* would be sufficient as long as internal discussions did not pit the disciples of the same master against one another. But once dissension arose, there was inevitably an orthodox party that sought to set down its position in precise terms and heaped anathema on those who did not accept it in its entirety. It was in this context that the first creeds would appear.

The Fiqh al-akbar. One of the principal creeds to come down to the present is the *Fiqh al-akbar.* Although it is tempting to see it as nothing more than the simple development of the formula of the profession of faith, such is not the case. The *shahādah* is a formula of adherence to the Muslim community; the creed is the profession of faith of the community itself, which wishes to state its position in relation to the dissenting sects. This particular profession mentions neither the unity of God nor the mission of Muḥammad, because neither is called into question. It states the following articles:

(1) We consider no one (of those who profess Islam) to be an unbeliever on account of his faith, nor do we deny his faith.

(2) We command the good and forbid the evil.

(3) What reaches you could not have missed you, and what misses you could not have reached you.

(4) We do not disavow any of the companions of the Apostle of God, nor do we adhere to any one of them in particular.

(5) We leave to God the question of ʿUthmān and ʿAlī. He alone knows the secret and hidden matters.

(6) Knowledge in matters of religion is better than knowledge in matters of the law.

(7) The difference of opinions in the community is a blessing of God.

(8) Whoever believes what should be believed but says, "I do not know if Moses and Jesus are prophets or not," is an unbeliever.

(9) Whoever affirms that he does not know if God is in heaven or in hell is an unbeliever.

(10) Whoever says he does not know the punishment in the tomb belongs to the sect of the Jahmīyah, which is condemned to perdition.

The Waṣīyah. It is with the *Waṣīyah* (Testament) of Abū Ḥanīfah (d. 767) that the major problems begin to emerge; it is true that these are not yet classified in homogenous groups, but one feels that the work of conflicting has started. The twenty-seven articles of this creed can be separated into the following themes.

1. The problem of faith. The text affirms that faith resides in witnessing with the tongue, believing with the mind, and knowing with the heart. It does not increase or decrease (art. 2). The believer and unbeliever really are such (art. 3). Muslim sinners do not cease to be Muslim (art. 4). Works are distinct from faith (art. 5). Finally, faith allows people to be classified in three categories: believers with pure intentions, unbelievers who recognize their lack of belief, and hypocrites (art. 14).

2. Predestination. This problem is treated throughout the *Waṣīyah.* First of all it is affirmed against the dualists and the Qadarīyah that God alone controls good and evil (art. 6), that mortal acts are created by God (art. 11) because human beings have no natural power (art. 12), and that God creates the faculty at the same time as the act (art. 15). Finally it is God who orders the (celestial) pen to write (art. 17); that is to say, he determines all things.

The theme of human actions is very closely associated with that of predestination, because these actions are totally dependent on divine will. The relationship between these two forms the crucial problem of speculative moral philosophy. Along with predestination, the distinction of three kinds of actions is affirmed: These are the obligatory, the optional, and the reprehensible. About ten affirmations follow to detail the eschatological beliefs: the punishment of the tomb (art. 18), questioning in the tomb (art. 19), heaven and hell (art. 20 and 27), the scale (art. 21), the reading of the book (art. 22), the resurrection (art. 23), God's meeting with the inhabitants of Paradise (art. 24), the intercession of the Prophet (art. 25), and God's sitting on the throne (art. 8). In addition there are affirmations concerning the uncreated or created nature of the Qurʾān (art. 9), the order of precedence of the first caliphs (art. 10), the precedence of ʿĀʾishah (art. 26), and the validity of ablutions performed on shoes (art. 16).

Fiqh al-akbar II. The *Fiqh al-akbar* II leads one onto much more defined ground, for debate had obliged the religious leaders to clarify beliefs, to reject anything that could threaten the transcendence of God, and to specify the role of the prophets and the value of their message.

From the very first affirmation, the global content of the faith reveals itself: God, the angels, his envoys, the resurrection, the decree concerning good and evil, the calculation of sins, the scale, heaven and hell. The entire theological base to date is thus set out: Theology already possesses all the material it will have to systematize. The different articles of the creed, about forty in all, take up each point in turn and develop them slightly without, however, following the order proposed at the start.

Muʿtazilī problematic and theses. The Muʿtazilah, "the first thinkers of Islam," gave the science of *kalām* a systematic form. The great Muʿtazilah lived either in Basra (Abū al-Hudhayl al-ʿAllāf, d. 849; al-Naẓẓām, d. 846; al-Jāḥiẓ, d. 872) or in Baghdad (Bishr ibn al-Muʿtamir, d. 825; Abū Mūsā al-Mirdar, d. 841; Thumāmah ibn al-Ashras, d. 828).

Although they did not teach the same doctrine on all matters, they nonetheless shared a common spirit. Historians and heresiographers have not been wrong in summarizing the characteristics of their doctrine in five affirmations called *al-uṣūl al-khamsah:* the unity of God *(al-tawḥīd),* his justice *(al-ʿadl),* the promise and the threat *(al-waʿd wa-al-waʿīd),* the "neutral" position in relation to the sinner (*al-manzilah bayn al-manzilatayn*), and finally the "commanding of good and forbidding of evil" (*al-amr bi-al-maʿrūf wa-al-nahy ʿan al-munkar*).

First thesis: tawḥīd. Concerned with avoiding the slightest anthropomorphism in the question of divine attributes, the Muʿtazilah applied in all its vigor the *via remotionis,* God's transcendence (*tanzīh*). The anthropomorphic verses should be "interpreted" symbolically, and in some cases even rejected. Similarly, contradictory *ḥadīths* were set aside. Against the "people of *ḥadīth*" and the ʿAlids, the Muʿtazilah could affirm their agnosticism on the matter of the nature of God. Without going as far as the Jahmīyah, who completely denied the attributes of God, they affirmed that all these attributes are identical with God's essence and that they have no real existence. Against the Dahrīyah (materialists) they affirmed a personal creator God. If God is completely spiritual, he cannot be seen by the senses, from which came their rejection of the "vision of God" in the future life, the *ruʾyah* of the traditionists. The absolute transcendence of God in relation to the world led them to distinguish rigorously between the preeternal and the *muḥdath* (that which has begun to be) and made them reject energetically any notion of *ḥulūl* (the infusion of the divine into the created).

The Muʿtazilah accepted a "contingent" or "created" divine knowledge of free intentions and of possibilities in general. They studied the object and the limits of divine power, analyzed human control over their actions, and affirmed that they created such actions by "generation" (*tawallin*).

With the same concern to eliminate any suspicion of associationism, they affirmed the created character of the Qurʾān, the word of God. In the history of the Muʿtazilah, this position attracted the most attention because of its political repercussions. The Qurʾān, they held, is a "genus" of words, created by God. It is called the "word of God" because, in contrast to human words, the Qurʾān was created directly.

Second thesis: the justice of God. In conjunction with *tawḥīd,* this belief served to describe the Muʿtazilah, or rather, they proudly described themselves as the "people of justice and unity." By analyzing the notion of human justice and extending it to God, they drew two conclusions.

1. As an intelligent and wise being, God must necessarily act according to a purpose, with a view to a determined plan. There is a chosen, objective order in the universe, and thus intermediary purposes, themselves related to an ultimate purpose. Consequently there are an objective good and evil prior to the determination brought by religious law. God is obliged always to do the best, *al-aṣlaḥ;* he can wish only the good.

2. God does not want evil. He does not order it because his wish (*irādah*) and his commandment (*amr*) are identical. Evil is created by humans, as is good for that matter, because people create all their actions, good or evil. They have in effect received from God a "power" (*qudrah*), that allows them to act freely. For this reason they will inevitably receive a reward for their good actions and a punishment for their evil ones.

Third thesis: the promise and the threat. This concerns the fate of the believer (*muʾmin*), the sinner (*fāsiq*), and the unbeliever (*kāfir*) in the hereafter. The term "the names and the statutes" (*al-asmāʾ wa-al-aḥkām*) is also used, referring to the juridical statutes that determine the fate of each group. The basic problem is that of faith and disbelief. For the Muʿtazilah, to have faith is not merely to assent in the heart and to make the verbal profession (*shahādah*) but also to avoid the "major sins" (*kabāʾir*). The unbelievers and the unrepentant Muslim sinners are condemned to hell.

Fourth thesis: the "intermediate position" between faith and disbelief. This is a corollary to the Muʿtazilī concept of divine justice and faith and is easily assimilated to the preceding thesis. The position of the Muslim sinner (*fāsiq*) is intermediate between that of the believer and that of the unbeliever. Although condemned in the hereafter to eternal damnation (albeit one less rigorous than that of the *kāfir*), the sinner remains nonetheless a member of the Muslim community while on earth.

Fifth thesis: "commanding the good." In contrast to those who saw internal criticism as sufficient, the Muʿtazilah favored direct action. Order must be reestablished "by the sword." If there is a hope of defeating adversaries one must overthrow the guilty leaders, even kill them if necessary, and force them, on pain of death, to accept the true doctrine.

This is not the place to discuss the history of the Muʿtazilah, their temporary triumph and final defeat. History books recount different stages of the *miḥnah* (inquisition), which represents the final struggle of the upholders of rational doctrines against the narrowly traditionalist thinkers. The rationalists were defeated and the "people of *ḥadīth*" triumphed decisively. The fact remains nevertheless that the Muʿtazilah represent a turning point in the history of Muslim thought and they left a definitive mark, even if by reaction, on the problematic of *kalām.*

It was one of the deserters from the Muʿtazilah, Abū al-Ḥasan al-Ashʿarī, who succeeded in finding the conciliatory *via media* between their rationalism and the literalism of the traditionists. A longtime disciple of al-Jubbāʾī, the head of the Muʿtazilah of Basra, he broke publicly with his teacher and turned violently against his former companions. At first he attempted to win over the literalists by expressing his admiration for Ibn Ḥanbal, as can be seen at the start of his *Ibānah,* or "elucidation" of the principles of religion.

However, his real theological work would consist of attempting to reconcile the different schools. By his conversion he intended to rediscover the meaning of traditional doctrine, to "return" to the Qurʾān and to the teaching of the first Muslims. In the field of exegesis he energetically rejected the overly drastic *tanzīh* of the Muʿtazilah as this led to *taʿṭīl,* a complete dissection of the notion of God. He wished to maintain a literal interpretation of the text and in this respect appeared to present himself as a faithful disciple of Ibn Ḥanbal. This was a literalism peculiar to al-Ashʿarī, however, because the later Ashʿarīyah would distance themselves considerably from the rigid literalism of their founder and thus would provoke the anger of Ibn Ḥazm and the Ḥanābilah themselves (Laoust, *Ibn Taymiyya,* pp. 81–82). Likewise on the question of the "vision of God" and of the anthropomorphic terms and the attributes (*Ibānah,* p. 47), he presented positions to which Ibn Ḥanbal would have ascribed without hesitation.

Such was the al-Ashʿarī of the direct sources. But for al-Juwaynī (d. 1085), who became al-Ghazālī's master, al-Ashʿarī was not a theologian following the opinions of Ibn Ḥanbal but rather a conciliator of two extreme positions. In his *Tabyīn* (pp. 149ff.) Ibn ʿAsākir demonstrates how his master, when dealing with the principal questions, followed a middle course between the exaggerations of the Muʿtazilah and those of the *ḥashwīyah* who, it is true, were recruited among the extremist Ḥanābilah. Table 1 summarizes the principal Ashʿarī positions in comparison with those of the extremists. All later *kalām* would see al-Ashʿarī as its founder.

Al-Māturīdī was a follower and contemporary of al-Ashʿarī. His disagreements with al-Ashʿarī stemmed above all from the fact that they followed different legal rites. Al-Ashʿarī was probably a disciple of al-Shāfiʿī. Al-Māturīdī was by contrast a clear disciple of Abū Ḥanīfah, a Persian like himself. He favored liberal, rational solutions, staying as close as possible to the Muʿtazilah while remaining within the limits of orthodoxy. An example of this approach is seen in his attitude toward the problem of liberty and *kasb.* Al-Māturīdī's solution attempted to respect the intervention of the human being, to whom he attributes the "qualification" of acts. Similarly al-Māturīdī affirms that the believer can say, "I am a believer in truth," whereas al-Ashʿarī required the restriction, "if God wishes it." (This is the problem of the *istithnāʾ*.) For the Māturīdīyah it was inconceivable that God would punish those who had obeyed him, while the Ashʿarīyah accepted the possibility, at least in theory. For the Māturīdīyah, often called "shameful Muʿtazilah," reason, even without the religious law, would have taught that there is an obligation to know God; for the Ashʿarīyah, this awareness comes exclusively from revelation. The different points of divergence, which number about fifty, remain secondary and in no way prevent the Ashʿarīyah and Māturīdīyah from being considered without distinction as "people of tradition and *ḥadīth,*" the former in the western part of the empire (Syria, Iraq, Egypt), and the latter in the eastern part.

The Ashʿarīyah spread into Persia under the Seljuks, then into Syria and Egypt under the Ayyubids and the Mamluk sultans, and finally into the Maghreb under the Almohad dynasty led by Ibn Tūmart (d. 1130?). This triumph was characterized by ongoing development of the doctrine, with the names of the *qāḍī* al-Bāqillānī, al-Juwaynī (Imām al-Ḥaramayn), and finally al-Ghazālī serving to demarcate the principal stages.

From the via antiqua to the via moderna. In his famous *Muqaddimah,* Ibn Khaldūn (d. 1406) presents the time of al-Ghazālī (d. 1111) as a watershed in the evolution of *kalām.* The *via antiqua,* characterized by a dialectic inspired primarily by the logic of the doctors of the law, gave way to the *via nova,* which relied on the Aristotelian syllogism. This break should not be overemphasized, however: At least from the point of view of the subjects discussed, influences must have been felt earlier via the Muʿtazilah, some of whom had read Aristotle. This tendency can already be seen in the writings of al-Bāqillānī (d. 1013), himself an untiring opponent of the Muʿtazilah, and even more strongly in those of his disciple al-Juwaynī. The latter was indeed an ancient in his dialectic, but an ancient who foretold the victory of the new method, which would triumph through his disciple al-Ghazālī and come even closer to the *falāsifah* with later theologians.

This article shall now trace this evolution in the *Tamhīd* of al-Bāqillānī, the *Irshād* of al-Juwaynī, and the *Iqtiṣād* of al-Ghazālī. It shall finish with the treatises in which the new tendency takes full shape.

The Tamhīd of al-Bāqillānī. In his *Tamhīd,* al-Bāqillānī, who has not yet broken away from his apologetic preoccupations, mixes his presentation of beliefs with long

Extreme by Default	Al-ash'arī	Extreme by Excess
The attributes		
Denied *(ta'ṭīl, ibṭāl)* by the Mu'tazilah, Jabarīyah, Rāfiḍah.	They are real, but not like human attributes.	They are like human attributes *(ḥashwīyah).*
Human acts		
People have a power *(qudrah).* They are susceptible to acts *kasb* (Qadarīyah, Mu'tazilah).	No power. God creates the of human beings, who are endowed with *kasb* (attribution, juridical charge).	Neither power nor *kasb* (Jabarīyah).
The vision of God		
Denied by the Mu'tazilah, Jahmīyah, and Nājjarīyah.	God will be seen (by the eyes) but without *ḥulūl,* without terms, without modes, as he sees us.	God will be seen like things of the senses *(ḥashwīyah).*
Omnipresence of God		
God is everywhere without *ḥulūl* or direction (Mu'tazilah).	God existed before there was place. He created the throne and the seat. He has no need of place. The creation of place has in no way changed his nature.	God is "infused" *(ḥulūl)* in the throne. He is seated on the throne which is his place *(ḥashwīyah).*
Ta´wil (interpretation)		
Hand = power and grace; face of God = his existence; descent of God = descent of certain verses, or of his angels; sitting on the throne = domination (Mu'tazilah).	The hand and face are real attributes like hearing and sight . . . = attribute . . . = attribute. . . .	The hand is a real limb, the face is a face with human form. The descent is real, as is sitting on the throne *(ḥashwīyah).*
The Qur´ān		
It is the created word of God (Mu'tazilah).	The [eternal] Qur'ān is the uncreated word of God, eternal, unchangeable. The individual letters, the ink with which it is written are created.	All is uncreated *(ḥashwīyah).*
Faith		
It is created (Mu'tazilah, Jahmīyah, Najjārīyah).	Faith is of two kinds: that of God, uncreated; that of the believers, created.	Faith is absolutely uncreated *(ḥashwīyah).*
The eternal punishment		
The Muslim who commits a grave sin is eternally damned (Khārijīs, Mu'tazilah).	The Muslim sinner is given up to divine goodwill. God can accept that person immediately into Paradise or mete out punishment in a temporary Hell.	The fate of the Muslim sinner will be debated only on the Day of Judgment (Murji'ah).
Intercession		
The Prophet does not have the power of intercession (Mu'tazilah).	Intercession of the Prophet on behalf of believing sinners with the permission of God.	Muhammad and 'Ali can intercede without God's order or permission, even for unbelievers (Rāfiḍah).
The caliphate		
Mu'āwīyah, Ṭalḥah, Zubayr, and `Ā´ishah are guilty. Their testimony is not accepted (Mu'tazilah). They are not guilty (Umayyads).	Every *mujtahid* achieves a result. There is general agreement on this principle.	All these people are unbelievers (Rāfiḍah).

SOURCE: Gardet and Anawati (1948), pp.58-59

TABLE 1. The conciliating position of al-Ashʿarī, according to the Qāḍī Abū al-Maʿali ibn ʿAbd al-Malik (al-Juwaynī) as reported by Ibn ʿAsakir, Tabyīn (pp. 149ff.)

discussions against non-Muslim sects and dissident Muslims themselves. The following is the schema of his presentation:

Preliminary. Science; nature; foundations.

I. *De Deo Uno.* (1) Existence of God: (a) division of known objects; (b) accidents; (c) created nature of the word and proof of the existence of God. (2) His attributes: he is one, living, knowing, hearing, seeing, speaking, willing; he has no appetite. (3) Divine action: neither motive *(gharaḍ)* nor cause *(ʿillah);* he acts freely.

II. *Apologetic Section.* Refutation of the astrologers, dualists, Magians, Christians, Brahmans (Hindus), Jews, and corporalists (*mujassimah,* i.e., those who maintain a literal interpretation of the anthropomorphic verses of the Qurʾān).

III. *The Caliphate.* (1) Principles of methodology and nature of the caliphate. (2) Qualities required of the caliph. (3) The first four caliphs. (4) Validity of their caliphate. (See also Gardet and Anawati, 1948, pp. 154–156.)

The Irshād of al-Juwaynī. Al-Ghazālī's master, also called Imām al-Ḥaramayn ("imam of the two holy places"), presents the principles of his classification more than once in his *Irshād.* At some points he divides his treatise between what exists necessarily in God and what is possible, that is to say, between what God can and cannot accomplish. At others he distinguishes between matters accessible to reason and those attainable only through the traditional path. Although it is not easy to find one's way through the *Irshād,* its plan can be drawn up in the following manner:

Introduction. The character of reason; the nature of science.

I. *The Existence of God.* (1) Contingency of the world (its beginning in time). (2) Proofs of the existence of God (*a novitate mundi*).

II. *What Necessarily Exists in God.* (1) Attributes of the essence: the unity of God. (2) Attributes of qualification: (a) knowledge of the attributes; (b) knowledge of the attributes themselves (the word; the divine names; other attributes).

III. *What God Can and Cannot Accomplish.* (1) Visibility of God: the creation of human acts. (2) The promise and the threat. (3) Prophetology. (4) The "traditional" questions (*samʿīyāt*): (a) sundry aspects: terms assigned to things, subsistence for maintaining life, censure of human actions; (b) eschatology; (c) names and the juridical qualifications; (d) the caliphate.

The Iqtiṣād of al-Ghazālī. The author of the *Iḥyāʾ* discussed *ex professo* and with precision the science of *kalām* in a compendium entitled *Al-iqtiṣād fī al-iʿtiqād* (The just mean in belief). He intended to remain loyal to Ashʿarī orthodoxy, simplifying to the extreme the dialectical debates and eliminating the philosophical investigations that his master al-Juwaynī had integrated into his treatises.

Al-Ghazālī devotes four chapters to a general introduction on *kalām.* The first underlines the importance of this science: It allows the reader to know God, his tributes, and the work of his messengers. However, he takes pains to state in the second chapter that this concerns only a certain number of people, because, with relation to the truths of faith and the doubts that can arise, one must distinguish different categories of people who are not equally able to devote themselves to this science. *Kalām* is safely used only to resolve certain doubts of the believers and to try to convince intelligent unbelievers. Finally, the fourth chapter analyzes the sources.

Next al-Ghazālī divides all the questions considered into four large sections, each precisely articulated. Because God is the object of *kalām,* one must first study him in his essence; this is the aim of the first section. The second section deals with the attributes; the third, with the action of God and his personal acts; and the fourth, with his envoys. The following is a general outline of the whole work:

Preliminaries. The nature of *kalām;* its importance; its methodology.

I. *The Divine Essence.* (1) God exists. (2) He is eternal. (3) He is permanent. (4) He is insubstantial. (5) He is incorporeal. (6) He is nonaccidental. (7) He is undefined. (8) He is not localized. (9) He is visible and knowable. (10) He is one.

II. *The Attributes of God.* (1) The attributes in themselves: life, knowledge, power, will, hearing, sight, speech. (2) The "status" of the attributes: (a) they are not the essence; (b) they are in the essence; (c) they are eternal; (d) the divine names.

III. *The Acts of God* (what God can or cannot do). (1) God can choose (is free) to impose no obligation on his creatures. (2) Or he can choose to impose on them what they cannot do. (3) God does nothing in vain. (4) He can make innocent animals suffer. (5) He can fail to reward one who obeys him. (6) The obligation of knowing God comes from revelation alone. (7) The sending of prophets is possible.

IV. *The Envoys of God.* (1) Muḥammad. (2) Eschatology (and faith). (3) The caliphate. (4) The sects.

Evolution of the via moderna. Elsewhere (Gardet and Anawati, 1948) this author has shown the evolution of the *via moderna* with the progressive introduction of philosophy through an examination of *kalām* treatises such as the *Nihāyat al-aqdām* of al-Shahrastānī (d. 1153), the *Muḥaṣṣal* of Fakhr al-Dīn al-Rāzī (d. 1209), and the *Ṭawālīʿ al-anwār* of al-Bayḍāwī (d. 1286). Here shall be given the end result of this evolution as it is crystallized in the *Mawāqif* of al-Ījī with the commentary of al-Jurājnī. With this work is reached the high point of the science of *kalām* in Sunnī Islam. Ījī/Jurājnī, with the glosses of other commentators, represent the largest (four volumes of more than five hundred pages each) and most systematic work of orthodox Muslim speculative thought. The work supplied material for years of specialization in the great Muslim universities, and one is obliged to recognize, especially by comparison with previous works, that its fame is well deserved. Even if the truly traditional parts, and the theology strictly speaking, are treated soberly, the philosophical part with its long critical introduction receives ample development. Consisting of six treatises and an appendix, the work is divided and subdivided with care:

I. *Preliminaries.* (1) The presuppositions of *kalām* and all knowledge. (2) Science (or knowledge) *in genere.* (3) The division of knowledge (the first two operations of the spirit). (4) The existence of sciences or necessary knowledges. (5) Reasoning. (6) The different forms of reasoning.

II. *General Principles.* (1) Being and nonbeing. (2) Essence. (3) The necessary and the possible. (4) The one and the many. (5) Cause and effect.

III. *The Accidents.* (1) *In genere.* (2) Quantity. (3) Quality.

(4) The relations (*nisab*): local relations, space, movement. (5) Relationship (*iḍāfah*).

IV. *Substance.* (1) The body. (2) Accidents of bodies. (3) The separate soul. (4) The intellect.

V. *"Rational" Theology* (*Ilāhīyāt*). (1) The divine essence. (2) The transcendence of God (the *via remotionis*). (3) His unity. (4) The positive attributes. (5) "Possible" attributes: visibility, knowability. (6) The acts of God (problem of human acts). (7) The divine names.

VI. *The Traditional Questions* (*Samʿīyāt*). (1) Prophethood. (2) Eschatology. (3) Statutes and names. (4) The caliphate.

Appendix. The sects.

Rigid Ashʿarīyah. The so-called way of the "modernists" was in effect the most original line of thought in the fully evolved Ashʿarī *kalām.* One can note among the most characteristic representatives al-Shahrastānī, Fakhr al-Dīn al-Rāzī, and al-Isfahānī (d. 1348). Al-Rāzī, although he called himself an Ashʿarī, did not hesitate to adopt Māturīdī theses, or even Muʿtazilī influences.

Other modernists, possibly less daring, nonetheless did not hesitate to borrow in their turn from *falsafa* various ideas on logic, nature philosophy, or metaphysics. This was the most orthodox of the tendencies that issued from the thought of al-Ījī, including al-Jurājnī, who called himself an Ashʿarī. Very close to him in methodology was his adversary al-Taftāzānī (d. 1389), who attempted to oppose the conclusions of *falsafa* while still placing himself on the same plane as philosophy.

The glosses, commentaries, and discussions multiplied, often with a great richness of argumentation and certain original views. But this did not serve the elaboration of *kalām* as a theological science: The clearest result of such studies was to throw the teaching of *kalām* by reaction into the constraints of "rigid conservatism."

Kalām would soon ossify under the Ashʿarī writ, and, losing the freshness of its early years, it would become frozen in the stereotyped forms of "manuals" endlessly commented and recommented. If one compares the nineteenth-century *Jawharat al-tawḥīd* of al-Bājūrī with the *Muḥaṣṣal* of al-Rāzī, one finds the same major divisions, the same responses, the same "intemporality." The manuals of that age are often a compendium of all the past, but framed and codified by the most rigid solutions of the school.

An enumeration of these manuals and their authors would be lengthy indeed; suffice it to mention the two writers who are situated at the beginning and the end of this long period, and who had and still have an important place in official teaching. One is al-Sanūsī, from the fifteenth century, famous for his *kalām* treatises set out according to the three cycles of teaching (*Umm al-barāhin*) called *Al-ṣughrā* (The small), or the *Sanūsīyah,* then *Al-wusṭā* (The median) and *Al-kubrā* (The great). The other is Ibrāhīm al-Bājūrī, (d. 1860), rector of al-Azhar, who wrote commentaries on his predecessors, al-Sanūsī himself, al-Laqānī, and his own master, al-Faḍālī. The differences are minimal between al-Sanūsī and al-Bājūrī. One of those who would attempt to arouse theology from its sleep, Shaykh Muḥammad ʿAbduh (d. 1905), would write of this period, "Whoever studies the works of this era will find only discussions on words, studies on methodology. And he will find these in only a small number of works chosen by weakness and consecrated by impotence."

Reformist period. It was precisely Muḥammad ʿAbduh, the disciple of the reformer Jamāl al-Dīn al-Afghānī (d. 1897), who would try to renew the problematic of *kalām* within the scope of the general renaissance of the Middle East. His originality in this field was his religious rationalism. He believed deeply in Islam, but he wanted a thoroughly interpreted religion that could respond intellectually to the demands of criticism, socially to the desire of the humble to live a decent life, and politically to the ardent passion among the people for liberty.

Against the traditional Ashʿarī ideas that crushed the believer under the weight of a fatalist predestination, he would state the existence of human liberty as the basis of all action and responsibility. He did not want to concern himself with what he considered metaphysical subtleties and turned instead to a somewhat agnostic pragmatism. It was practice that interested him above all. Thus divine law, reason, conscience, and common sense affirm human responsibility and therefore human freedom. It was useless to go over the old discussions again on the bases and nature of this freedom. It was enough to recognize that it did not contradict God's omnipotence, because, as he said, "God is the cause to the extent that people act, and people are the cause to the extent that God acts." This is far from the Ashʿarī *kasb* ("acquisition") that denies any real power to human beings.

He added to this clear attitude toward human freedom an affirmation of natural law, which once again suggests the influence of the Muʿtazilah. Like the latter he recognized that there are things objectively good or evil, naturally beautiful or ugly, and concludes that a "natural law" is possible. Religious law does not differ essentially from natural morality. "The law came simply to show what exists (*al-wāqiʿ*). It is not the law that makes it good" (*Risālah,* p. 80, trans., p. 56).

In his discussion of prophecy, he shows similarly rationalist tendencies. While keeping the orthodox position, he stresses the psychological and social aspects of prophecy (ibid., p. 127/86).

In discussing *kalām* he insists above all on the political factor in the formation and differentiation of the schools. He recognizes that foreign elements integrated into the community prompted the first dogmatic discussions (ibid., intro., p. 55). The rational character of the science of *kalām* is affirmed forcefully: It is reason that is called upon to examine the proofs of the beliefs and rules of conduct imposed by religion in order to show that they truly come from God (ibid., p. 129/88). In response to Hanotaux he does not hesitate to write, "In the case of a conflict between reason and tradition, it is reason that must decide. This is a position that would only be opposed by a few people, from among those whose views cannot be taken into consideration" (Gardet and Anawati, 1948, p. 86, n. 3).

In his *Riṣālat al-tawḥīd,* Shaykh ʿAbduh spends little time on the metaphysical introductions so common in traditional manuals. After stating the usual definitions of the impossible, the contingent, and the necessary, he establishes the classic proof of the existence of God and his attributes. To be necessary, endowed with life, knowledge, and will, to be all-powerful, free, one—these are all attributes that reason can discover on its own. He is very circumspect on the question of the relationship of the attributes with the essence of God: He advises [the believer] to have the wisdom to "stop at the limit that our reason can reach" (*Risālah,* p. 52/37).

The "new theology" of the Egyptian grand *muftī* also shows itself in his attitude toward the origins of faith: He contests the authority of the juridical schools resting on the consensus of the community (*ijmāʿ*) and rejects servile traditional imitation (*taqlīd*). Only the Qurʾān and authentic *sunnah* should serve as the base of *ijtihād,* this effort of personal elaboration of religious positions by qualified theologians. The same concern for adaptation is shown in his commentary on the Qurʾān, which he wished to be pragmatic and oriented essentially toward "moral direction" (*hidāyah*); it was to be in accord with modern civilization and encourage activity, energy, and personal labor. The anthropomorphic passages should be interpreted by using reason (*taʾwīl ʿaqlī*) in the manner of Ibn Rushd. God's transcendence (*tanzīh*) must be ensured at all costs.

Muḥammad ʿAbduh was able to inspire the best of his disciples with a spirit of openmindedness and renewal. Especially worthy of mention is Shaykh Muṣṭafā ʿAbd al-Rāzīq, who was appointed rector of al-Azhar in 1945.

Parallel to this reformist movement in Egypt and the Near East a no less sustained effort for renewal, *sui generis,* occurred in British India. This was particularly due to the work of Sayyid Aḥmad Khān (d. 1898), whose *Tabyīn al-kalām* (Commentary on the Holy Bible) dates from 1862 to 1865; Syed Ameer Ali (d. 1928), author of *The Spirit of Islam* (London, 1922), and Muḥammad Iqbāl, whose *Six Lectures on the Reconstruction of Religious Thought in Islam* was published in 1934.

TWO FINAL REMARKS. A complete presentation of *kalām* in Islam should also take into consideration Shīʿī *kalām,* in particular the disciples and successors of Mullā Ṣadrā (d. 1640) in the nineteenth and twentieth centuries. These include among others Ḥājī Mullā Hādī Sabziwārī, Ashtiyānī, Ṭabāṭbāʾī, Rāfiʿī Qazwīnī, and Muḥammad Amūlī (see Seyyed Hossein Nasr's articles on the school of Isfahan and Mullā Ṣadrā in M. M. Sharif's *A History of Muslim Philosophy,* vol. 2, Wiesbaden, 1966).

Among contemporary Muslim writers a certain number outside the traditional framework of theology have tried to speak of God and Muslim doctrines in a way adapted to the modern world, including Kāmil Ḥusayn, Sayyid Quṭb, Tawfīq al-Ḥakīm, ʿAbbās Maḥmūd al-ʿAqqād, and Muṣṭafā Maḥmūd. The historian of *kalām* should not overlook their contributions.

SEE ALSO Ashʿarīyah; Creeds, article on Islamic Creeds; Imān and Islām; Muʿtazilah; Qurʾān.

BIBLIOGRAPHY

General Works

The best works on *kalām* for the general reader are Harry A. Wolfson's overview, *The Philosophy of the Kalam* (Cambridge, Mass., 1976); D. B. Macdonald's article "Kalām" in the first edition of *The Encyclopaedia of Islam* (Leiden, 1934); and Louis Gardet's "ʿIlm al-Kalām" and "Kalām" in the new edition of *The Encyclopaedia of Islam* (Leiden, 1960-). Louis Gardet's and my *Introduction à la théologie musulmane* (1948; 2d ed., Paris, 1970) and W. Montgomery Watt's *Islamic Philosophy and Theology,* 2d rev. ed. (Edinburgh, 1984), are useful surveys. J. Windrow Sweetman's *Islam and Christian Theology,* 2 vols. (London, 1942–1947), and A. S. Tritton's *Muslim Theology* (1947; reprint, Westport, Conn., 1981) should also be consulted.

Sources in Translation

The works of al-Ashʿarī have been translated by several scholars. *Al-ibānah ʿan uṣūl al-diyānah* has been translated and edited by Walter C. Klein as *The Elucidation of Islam's Foundation* (New Haven, Conn., 1940); *The Theology of al-Ashʿarī,* edited and translated by Richard J. McCarthy (Beirut, 1953), contains translations of two creeds by al-Ashʿarī; and D. B. Macdonald's *Development of Muslim Theology, Jurisprudence and Constitutional Theory* (1903; reprint, New York, 1965) contains translations of creeds by al-Ashʿarī as well as al-Ghazālī, Abū Ḥafṣ al-Nasafī, and al-Faḍālī. Ibn Qudāmah's *Taḥrim al-naẓar fī kutub ahl al-kalām* has been edited and translated by George Makdisi as *Censure of Speculative Theology* (London, 1962). Al-Shahrastānī's *Kitāb nihāyat iqdām fī ʿilm al-kalām* has been edited and translated by Alfred Guillaume as *The Summa Philosophiae of al-Shahrastānī* (Oxford, 1934). Al-Taftāzānī's *Sharḥ al-ʿaqāʾid al-nasafīyah* has been edited and translated by E. E. Elder as *A Commentary on the Creed of Islam* (New York, 1950).

Critical Studies

An excellent study is A. J. Wensinck's *The Muslim Creed: Its Genesis and Historical Development* (1932; reprint, New York, 1965), which contains translations of three Ḥanafī creeds. Michel Allard's *Le problème des attributs divins dans la doctrine d'al-Ašʿarī et de ses premiers grands disciples* (Beirut, 1965) is a detailed study of the works and teachings of al-Bāqillānī, al-Baghdādī, al-Bayhaqī, and al-Juwaynī. Also useful are Max Horten's *Die philosophischen Systeme der spekulativen Theologen im Islam* (Bonn, 1912) and my article, with R. Caspar and M. El-Khodeiri, "Une somme inédite de théologie moʿtazilite: le *Moghni* du qāḍī ʿAbd al-Jabbār," in *Mélanges de l'Institut Dominicain d'Études Orientales* 4 (1957): 281–316.

For modern developments in India and Pakistan, see Aziz Ahmad's *Islamic Modernism in India and Pakistan 1857–1964* (London, 1967); Syed Ameer Ali's *The Spirit of Islam,* rev. ed. (London, 1922); A. A. Fyzee's *A Modern Approach to Islam* (Bombay, 1963); Wilfred Cantwell Smith's *Modern Islām in India,* rev. ed. (London, 1972); and Christian Troll's *Sayyid Ahmad Khan: A Reinterpretation of Muslim Theology* (New Delhi, 1978).

GEORGES C. ANAWATI (1987)
Translated from French by Richard J. Scott

KALEVALA See LÖNNROT, ELIAS

KĀLĪ See GODDESS WORSHIP, *ARTICLE ON* THE HINDU GODDESS

KALISCHER, TSEVI HIRSCH (1795–1874),

rabbi, messianic theorist, and activist. Kalischer spent his entire life in the Posen district of Prussia. He received an intensive education in Talmudic literature and independently studied Jewish philosophy. With his wife's financial support, he pursued a life of community service and scholarship. His works include commentaries on Jewish law, exegeses of the Bible and Passover Haggadah, and philosophical studies reconciling religion and reason. In his messianic writings he argued that Judaism encouraged efforts to accelerate the arrival of the messianic age. Historically, this opinion was accepted by only a few religious authorities; the dominant rabbinic tradition regarded messianic activism as a rebellion against God.

Starting with the rationalist assumption that God steers the course of history toward the messianic age without abrogating natural laws, Kalischer asserted that human participation in the redemptive process was essential. He contended that biblical prophecies, when interpreted through the ideology of messianic activism, indicated that the messianic age would arrive in gradual stages. A nonmiraculous stage, in which the Holy Land would be repopulated and made agriculturally productive by Jews, would be followed by a miraculous stage consisting of the other features described in biblical prophecies. The miraculous stage would be ushered in when the Jews reestablished their intimate connection with God by offering sacrifices on the rebuilt altar in Jerusalem.

In 1836, encouraged by European interest in the Jews' return to Zion and the Orthodox rabbinate's insistence on retaining in the liturgy prayers for the restoration of sacrificial worship, Kalischer wrote to Meyer Anschel Rothschild and several influential rabbis about acquiring the Temple Mount and studying the possibility of restoring sacrificial worship. Most Jewish leaders withheld their support when they realized that to Kalischer the sacrifice renewal was not academic and was actually part of a messianic plan. By 1860 he realized that focusing only on the agricultural development of Palestine would receive wider support; he still believed that the sacrifice renewal and other messianic events would flow naturally from that. This tactical change has led some historians to the mistake of describing Kalischer as a Zionist rather than a messianist.

Kalischer's writings and activities eventually helped legitimize messianic activism, and religious Jews who regard the State of Israel as a step toward the messianic age have adopted his formulation of this ideology.

BIBLIOGRAPHY

The only comprehensive examination of Kalischer's messianic ideology is my *Seeking Zion: Modernity and Messianic Activism in the Writings of Tsevi Hirsch Kalischer* (Oxford; Portland, Ore., 2003). A complete bibliography of Kalischer's writings and secondary literature is included. A critical edition of Kalischer's major work, *Derishat Tsiyyon* (Lyck, 1862), and most of his messianic writings are collected in *Ha-ketavim ha-tsiyyonim shel ha-Rav Tsevi Hirsch Kalischer,* edited and with an introduction by Israel Klausner (Jerusalem, 1947).

JODY ELIZABETH MYERS (1987 AND 2005)

KAMALAŚĪLA (c. 740–795)

was an Indian Buddhist scholar and monk, who was famed for his role in the legendary Bsam yas debate in Tibet and for his prolific writings on Buddhist philosophy and practice. A disciple of Śāntarakṣita (c. 725–790), he is known for his strong commitment to inferential reasoning, his integration of diverse schools of Indian Buddhism, and his teachings on Buddhist meditation and practice. His many works, preserved mostly in Tibetan, include independent philosophical tracts, commentaries on Mahāyāna Buddhist *sūtras*, and an encyclopedic commentary on Śāntarakṣita's *Tattvasaṁgraha* ("Collection of Realities"). Although little is known of his life in India, later Tibetan sources indicate that Kamalaśīla was a preceptor at the renowned Nālandā monastic university in present-day Bihar.

THE DEBATE AT BSAM YAS. Historical records show that Kamalaśīla did not accompany Śāntarakṣita to Tibet but was summoned there some time after his teacher's death. According to legend, near the end of his life Śāntarakṣita and his followers at the court of the Tibetan king Khri srong lde btsan (c. 740–798) came into conflict with the followers of Hva-shang Mahāyāna, a Chinese Buddhist monk also resident at the court. At the heart of the dispute was the question of whether awakening (*bodhi*), the ultimate goal of these Buddhist practitioners, must be obtained gradually, as Śāntarakṣita maintained, or whether it could occur suddenly, as held by the Chinese camp. Apparently Śāntarakṣita foresaw on his deathbed (c. 788) that the followers of Hva-shang Mahāyāna would gain ground in Tibet, and he therefore asked the king to invite Kamalaśīla from India to challenge the Chinese monk to a debate. Kamalaśīla arrived, and the debate (or debates—the duration and precise nature of the event is unclear) was held in the presence of the king. According to Tibetan records, Kamalaśīla vanquished his opponent, and the king decreed that henceforth only Indian Buddhist practices and texts would be adopted in Tibet. Perhaps not surprisingly, Chinese sources claim Hva-shang Mahāyāna the victor. Despite the lingering uncertainties about the debate, however, it is certainly the case that the vast majority of the many Buddhist texts translated into Tibetan over the following centuries was translated from Sanskrit and not from Chinese.

Kamalaśīla is said to have died in Tibet, murdered by assassins who killed him by "squeezing" his kidneys. Because the dates of both the debate and the death remain somewhat murky, precisely how much time Kamalaśīla spent in Tibet is unclear. However, he did stay long enough to compose four of his most influential works: three texts all bearing the title *Bhāvanākrama* ("Stages of Meditation") and his magnum opus on Madhyamaka thought, the *Madhyamakāloka* ("Illumination of the Middle Way").

THE STAGES OF MEDITATION. According to traditional Tibetan accounts, Kamalaśīla wrote the three *Bhāvanākramas* after the Bsam yas debate at the request of King Khri srong lde btsan to clarify the stages of the gradualist (*rim gyis pa*) path to awakening and to refute the doctrines of the suddenist (*cig car ba*) approach. The emphasis in these works is on the proper way to cultivate one's mind to become a fully awakened buddha. Kamalaśīla articulates numerous steps, beginning with the generation of compassion and the altruistic aspiration to attain awakening for the sake of others. With compassion and altruism firmly in place, the practitioner next cultivates two distinct mental achievements: calm abiding and special insight. Calm abiding refers to the ability to easily rest the mind on a single object without distraction. Special insight is the wisdom that realizes that all things are devoid of any fixed identity or essence. Kamalaśīla's message in these texts is that neither calm abiding nor special insight alone will do; rather, the two must be united by taking the object of special insight, or "essencelessness" as the focus of single-pointed meditation (calm abiding).

One important consequence of Kamalaśīla's presentation is that it preserves a strong role for rational analysis and conceptual thought on the Buddhist path. That is, whereas calm abiding is generally understood to be a mental state that is free from concepts, special insight is brought about through the measured application of conceptual analysis. Although Kamalaśīla agrees that the ultimate state of transcendent wisdom attained in awakening is entirely free from conceptual thought, he nonetheless stresses that without conceptual analysis one cannot eliminate the negative mental states and primordial ignorance that are the roots of all the suffering in *saṃsāra* (the beginningless and involuntary chain of birth, death, and rebirth fueled by negative acts and ignorance). Kamalaśīla likens special insight to a fire produced by rubbing together the wooden sticks of conceptual analysis, which in the end consumes the very concepts that produced it. When calm abiding and special insight are united in meditation, the practitioner comes to have a nonconceptual experience of the essencelessness that had previously been determined through conceptual reasoning to be the ultimate reality of all things.

Kamalaśīla's presentation of the gradual path to awakening in the three *Bhāvanākramas* has been very influential among Tibetans, who frequently see the texts as having been written especially for them. To this day, Tibetan lamas often advise students to implement Kamalaśīla's instructions on the generation of compassion and the integration of meditative concentration with the wisdom that realizes emptiness.

THE ILLUMINATION OF THE MIDDLE WAY. The fourth text that Kamalaśīla wrote in Tibet is the *Madhyamakāloka*. This is an ambitious treatise on the Madhyamaka or "Middle Way," school of Indian Buddhist thought that seeks to demonstrate conclusively the negative thesis that things are devoid of fixed identity or essence (*svabhāva*) by employing the tools of the Buddhist logical and epistemological traditions. In this, the text builds on Śāntarakṣita's *Madhyamakālaṃkāra* (on which Kamalaśīla had already written a subcommentary), and indeed, Tibetan sources maintain that Kamalaśīla undertook the work due to his concern that his teacher's thought might be misunderstood or inappropriately criticized in Tibet. The *Madhyamakāloka* addresses a variety of objections to the Madhyamaka teachings and to the arguments that are intended to demonstrate their truth. Tibetans have frequently turned to this work as a resource for working through some of the difficult logical issues that arise when attempting to demonstrate essencelessness. This work is also probably the first Madhyamaka treatise to present a catalogue of five logical reasons that demonstrate that things are essenceless.

Later Tibetans classify Kamalaśīla, along with Śāntarakṣita, as a member of the Yogācāra-Svātantrika-Madhyamaka school. In brief, this means that Kamalaśīla is understood, first, as accepting the basic Yogācāra position that objects of knowledge do not exist outside the mind and, second, as endorsing the use of autonomous (*svatantra*) inferences, that is, inferences that operate independently of the positions held by the two parties in a debate. For many later Tibetans, such inferences are improper in the context of Madhyamaka, because they would require things to have essences to function. Instead, it is preferable for a Mādhyamika, a follower of the Madhyamaka, to use inferences that operate on the basis of positions accepted by the opponent alone, as is held to be the case in the so-called Prāsaṅgika-Madhyamaka school. Although the terms *Svātantrika* (Autonomist) and *Prāsaṅgika* (Consequentialist) were not used as doxographical categories in India, their Tibetan equivalents became axiomatic in discussions of Madhyamaka in Tibet. Although many Tibetans have expressed qualms about the so-called Svātantrika elements of

Kamalaśīla's approach to Madhyamaka, he is still widely admired among Tibetans for his role in defending the gradualist path at the Bsam yas debate, his presentation of Buddhist meditation and practice, and the depth and subtlety of his philosophical thought.

See Also Buddhism, article on Buddhism in Tibet; Śāntirakṣita; Tibetan Religions, overview article.

Bibliography

Demiéville, Paul. *Le concile de Lhasa. Une controverse sur le quiétism entre bouddhistes de l'Inde et de la Chine au VIIe siècle de l'ère chrétienne.* Paris, 1952. Historical study of the Chinese and Tibetan records concerning the Bsam yas debate.

Dreyfus, Georges B. F., and Sara L. McClintock, eds. *The Svātantrika-Prāsaṅgika Distinction: What Difference Does a Difference Make?* Boston, 2003. Collection of articles on the Svātantrika-Prāsaṅgika distinction, with several contributions touching on the Madhyamaka philosophy of Śāntarakṣita and Kamalaśīla.

Gyatso, Tenzin (the XIVth Dalai Lama). *Stages of Meditation.* Translated by Ven. Geshe Lobsang Jordhen, Ven. Losang Choephel Ganchenpa, and Jeremy Russell. Ithaca, N.Y., 2001. An excellent introduction to Kamalaśīla's teachings on Buddhist practice; includes a translation and Tibetan edition of the second *Bhāvanākrama* accompanied by a clear commentary by the Dalai Lama.

Houston, Garry W. *Sources for a History of the bSam yas Debate.* Monumenta Tibetica Historica. Sankt Augustin, Germany, 1980. Selections in Tibetan and English from a variety of Tibetan sources on the Bsam yas debate.

Jha, Ganganatha, trans. *The Tattvasaṅgraha of Shāntarakṣita with the Commentary of Kamalashīla.* 2 vols. Baroda, India, 1937; reprint, Delhi, 1986. The only complete translation of the encyclopedic *Tattvasaṃgraha* and its commentary; although valuable for gaining a sense of the work's overall structure and arguments, the work should be used with caution as the translation is, at points, deeply misleading.

Keira, Ryusei. *Mādhyamika and Epistemology: A Study of Kamalaśīla's Method for Proving the Voidness of All Dharmas.* Vienna, 2004. The first in-depth study in English of the *Madhyamakāloka*, Kamalaśīla's most important philosophical treatise; includes a translation and edition of sections of the work's second chapter.

López, Donald S., Jr. *A Study of Svātantrika.* Ithaca, N.Y., 1987. Exploration of the category of Svātantrika-Madhyamaka based principally on Tibetan (especially Dge lugs pa) sources.

Seyfort Ruegg, David. *Buddha-nature, Mind and the Problem of Gradualism in a Comparative Perspective: On the Transmission and Reception of Buddhism in India and Tibet.* London, 1992. An important study of the philosophical concerns underlying the Bsam yas debate.

Tucci, Giuseppe. *Minor Buddhist Texts, Parts 1 & 2.* Rome, 1956; reprint, Delhi, 1986. Includes a Sanskrit edition, Tibetan edition and English translation of the first *Bhāvanākrama*, as well as an extended discussion of the debate at Bsam yas.

Tucci, Giuseppe. *Minor Buddhist Texts, Part 3.* Rome, 1971. Includes Sanskrit and Tibetan texts and English translation of the third *Bhāvanākrama.*

Sara L. McClintock (2005)

KAMI

KAMI. From a historical and religious viewpoint, what is meant by the Japanese word *kami* cannot be exhausted by the term itself, for it is also often expressed in other terms, such as *tama* (spirits), as well as by names for natural things beginning with such prefixes as *mi* (sacred), *hi* (spiritual, sacred forces) and *itsu* (sacred power). These can refer to concrete landscapes of place, sky, mountain, hill, river, sea, or forest, or sometimes to the nameless and extraordinary. In some expressions, the whole universe is permeated by the sacred *kami* nature, thus constituting a monistic universe. The characteristics of *kami* in the early phases of Japanese history share many common elements among the primary religious traditions of various communities in the world.

Characteristics of *Kami*. There are several important characteristics of *kami* in the early Japanese expressions. First of all, the *kami* in the archaic level of religious experience, manifests its totality, and it is ambivalent. The term *kami* refers to all beings—good and evil—that are awesome and worthy of reverence. The *kami* who is in charge of fertility of a territory or the well-being of its society usually reigns over the territory and can harm or destroy it when disregarded. And the *kami* must be well respected; otherwise, it punishes people. There are numerous cases in which *kami* reveals awesome and dreadful natures, and yet the same awesome *kami* often shows gentle and loving natures at the same time. Those *kami* who are in charge of epidemics have the power to spread illness, and also to heal. In that sense, *kami* is regarded as a terrible being who has superhuman powers to reign over territory, a being in charge of fertility and well-being. One of the most famous examples appears in the *Kojiki* (chapter 92) that the emperor Chuai had to die because he disregarded the will of *kami* revealed through an oracle. There are many cases of the *kami* that curses *(tatari-gami)*, who harms people when disrespected, but bestows blessings when the *kami* is well respected.

The invisible and concealed *Kami*. Secondly, the *kami* is basically concealed and invisible. The most original seven *kami* "at the time of the beginning of heaven and earth" in Japanese myth, are all "not visible," or "they hid their bodies" in the myth (the *Kojiki*, pp. 47–48.) There are many evidences of the invisible nature of *kami*. As basically concealed and invisible, *kami* responds to prayer by descending to earth and dwelling in tangible objects such as sacred space, tree or rock, or human beings. The prayers are addressed to *kami* through ritual, and then, following the ritual, *kami* returns to the invisible world. The above story of the emperor Chuai involved the trance of the empress Okinaga-tarashi-hime through whom the invisible *kami*-spirit delivered the message. Not only in the classical texts, but also in the whole history of Japanese religions, the visible world of religious phenomena is intensely affirmed because it is connected to and sustained by the invisible world of *kami*-spirits through the "seamlessness of the border-space" by various channels of mediation between the two worlds, the visible and the invisible, the world of *kami* and that of the human. This seamlessness of the border-space as well as the frequent passage of the *kami*-spirit through it ensured the monistic spiritual universe of early Japanese people. (Kitagawa, 1987, pp. 44–45) The sacred fall of Nachi, as it is seen, is described and worshipped as the sacred body of *kami*, as is the sacred mountain of Miwayama. They are among the specific examples of the manifestations of *kami*, which remains, however, basically hidden.

Following the introduction of Buddhism into the Japanese archipelago (c. 550 CE), indigenous religions, now influenced by Buddhist expressions, began building shrines and producing fewer *kami* images. Prior to Buddhism, people prayed only at specific *iwakura* (sacred rocks) or *go-shinboku* (sacred trees), or other special places where *kami* visited in response to requests for their presence.

Itinerancy of the *kami*. A third characteristic of *kami* in early Japanese expressions is that it visits, drifts about, but does not stay in one place forever; it visits sacred places, possessing the medium to deliver oracles in response to requests. This mobility of *kami* makes possible the periodic visits by the sacred visitors in various local communities; it also means that *kami* can have various places to visit or vehicles to possess. *Kami* moves and drifts horizontally and vertically, freely. It is important to remember Joseph Kitagawa's remarks about the *kami* spirit moving through the seamless border-space between the human and the divine world, or between the world of the living and that of the dead, as evidence of this mobility.

***Kami* of different natures.** A fourth characteristic of *kami* in this early Japanese world is that it seems that many *kami* of different natures coexist. This multiplicity has been often mistakenly interpreted as a "polytheistic" nature of Japanese religious tradition by Japanese scholars in modern times. However, these concepts—polytheism, monotheism, and pantheism—come from the Western philosopher Baruch Spinoza (1632–1677). In other words, they are concepts that were imposed upon Japanese religious phenomena from Western culture, and do not do justice for interpreting such phenomena in Japanese history.

The existence of numerous *kami* does not necessarily mean "polytheism." In various religious traditions of the world there is clear evidence of the dialectic between one god and many gods within the same tradition. Japanese history traces the emergence of "monolatory" religions (religions of one-god worship) in the serious crisis situations of society in the late Heian (794–1185 CE) and Kamakura (1185–1333 CE) periods, as well as in the late Tokugawa (1600–1868) to early Meiji (1868–1912) eras. Yet when the crisis situations were over and an ordinary life returned, people reverted to the world of numerous *kami*.

Early Japanese history also shows the manifestations of numerous *kami* the people prayed to. It is possible, therefore, to say that one of the important characteristics of early Japanese history is the coexistence of various *kami*. In the oldest Japanese chronicles of the *Kojiki* (The records of ancient matters), the names of more than three hundred *kami* are mentioned. In the *Engishiki* (Procedures of the Engi era), the prayers are addressed to various *kami*, not only to the *kami* of the High Heaven but also to the *kami* of the earth, such as a land, an oven, the *kami* of road, or the *kami* of the palace gate. In other words, each *kami* was assigned to the specific role within the world of meaning in the religious life of the early Japanese people.

The *kami* of locative type and of Utopian type. A fifth characteristic of the Japanese *kami* also manifests the aspects of the tutelary *kami* of local tribes, concrete places, matters, and affairs, which possess them and are in charge of them. People pray to the *kami* of the road, to the *kami* of mountain, or the *kami* of the river, with offerings, asking for protection and permission to get through or cross over. The *kami* of the wind, of the fire, or of the oven responds to the prayers of the respective person who is concerned with the place. But if he or she ignores the *kami*, the *kami* becomes a terrible *kami* that harms him or her. As is the case with the religious world of primary culture, the *kami* of the place dominates the place, territory, border, pass, or doorway, and often they are called by the name of the place, as the *kami* of the doorway, the *kami* of the pass, or the *kami* of a particular village. In other words, the *kami* manifest awesome, terrible natures as well as gentle, loving, fascinating natures. In the contradistinction with this type of *kami*, there are utopian types of *kami* that drew and attracted people to the far-away, sacred centers. In the famous millenarian movement of the *tokoyo-gami* (*kami* of the eternal paradise), people gave up their properties and ran dancing and singing to Mt. Fuji, where the *kami* promised to descend with the paradise of longevity and wealth. The movement was quickly suppressed by the government in 644 CE, the third year of the emperor Kogyoku right before the establishment of the Ritsu-ryo state. Also, various types of pilgrimages were developed throughout Japanese history, in which people left the place of their daily life temporarily for the blessings of the *kami* in far-away centers.

***Kami* in prehistoric cultures.** From a historical and cultural viewpoint, the tradition of the prehistoric Jomon period (about 10,000 BCE to fourth century CE) embraced the evidences of the *kami* closely entwined with the hunting-and-gathering culture, that is, the tradition of the slash-and-burn agriculture as well as that of fishing. The representative *kami* of this tradition were the earth-goddess-type *kami* of mountain and of sea. In the Yayoi culture (fourth century BCE to seventh century CE) the paddy-rice cultivation in the low land areas became the important source of production. Whereas in the slash-and-burn agricuture, people had to move to change the field of cultivation every three to twenty years for the fertile soils, in the paddy-rice cultivation, people had to stay in one place to enrich the soil through generations. In the paddy-rice agriculture tradition, the *kami* of the land (field), water (rain), sun and moon, as well as the spirit-*kami* of rice *(ina-dama)* among others, all with specific and articulate functions, were organically integrated and synthesized into a world of the *kami* of rice-spirit to constitute a pantheon of various *kami.* The resulting pantheon was the basis of the myth of the ancient state.

THE *KAMI* IN THE MYTH OF THE STATE. Various *kami* in the *Kojiki* point to the new historical stages into which Japanese people entered socially and religiously. In other words, new orientations of the human had entered into Japanese history. These were "new" in the sense that they were no longer simply primary; rather, they were the elements of civilization as the state entered into the story and nature of *kami.*

Motoori Norinaga (1730–1801), the founder of the Shinto theology of the Tokugawa period, treated the *Kojiki* as the sacred text of the Shinto and came up with the interpretation of *Kami* as "any entity with unusually powerful spiritual function that imparts a feeling of awe." His delineation of *kami* is profound and broad. However, it could be misleading if the *Kojiki* is treated as the only channel to the sacred in Japanese religious tradition.

As is often pointed out, the *Kojiki* is already colored by the ideology of the ancient Ritsuryō state. When Motoori interpreted the historical events by going back to the *Kojiki,* the interpretation itself was influenced by the state ideology of ancient Japan. The *Kojiki* is the text that interprets the origin of the state in the genealogy of various *kami*; therefore all *kami* in this text are situated in the story for the legitimatization of the state. Here, *kami* tend to have a more impersonal nature, and all *kami* are organized in the mythic structure of the state as the originator and ancestors of the state, as well as of the people and their descendants. The *kami* of the High Heaven and earthly *kami* are organized into the ideology of the unity of the state. The divinity that once was the tutelary *kami* of some specific local clan or village community is thus separated from the community and developed into the tutelary *kami* of the whole state-land—the ancestor *kami* of the nation. But evidence in folklore and in Japanese texts indicates that people have experienced *kami* not spoken about in the *Kojiki* and the *Engishiki.* Such a variety of *kami* is observed in the later development of Japanese history.

BUDDHISM AND *KAMI.* When Buddhism was introduced into Japan, the Buddha was treated as a foreign *kami.* Soon, however, Buddhism and Shinto began interacting, and with the establishment of the ancient state, Buddhist schools, the Shinto pantheon, Confucian ideology, and Yin-Yang Daoist specialists were all organized into and monopolized by the government system of the Ritsuryō state during the Nara (710–784 CE) and most of the Heian period. When persons belonging to these religions were controlled by the government, various folk-religious movements emerged spontaneously to fulfill the needs of the populace outside of the religio-political hierarchy of the government.

Various crises during the Nara and Heian period, including the gradual erosion of the state system of Ritsuryō and repeated famines and epidemics in the central Japan, led to a new expression of *kami* known as the *goryo-shin* (the Sacred Spirit-*Kami*). The *kami* of the *goryo* were originally the *onryo* (the vengeful spirits of the dead) whose lives went unfulfilled because of their tragic deaths, often through political strife. Still, they were turned into graceful *kami* in response to the veneration of people.

These *onryo* and *kami* of *goryo* became popular among the ordinary people, which in itself symbolized the agony of the unfulfilled living and dead. But these *kami* were also accepted as those who would harm people who did not pay due respects to the *kami.* All sectors of Buddhism responded with various counter-magic against *onryo,* from which new Buddhist movements emerged.

The emergence of these new Buddhist sects, called "Japanese Buddhism," was preceded by the violent movement of *onryo* and *goryo.* Also, through the Heian and Kamakura period, syncretic relationships were developed between Japanese *kami* and foreign *kami* (Buddha), in which various Japanese *kami* were interpreted first as an incarnation of Buddha (*honji suijaku*), then later reversed—it was *kami* that had gone to India to become Buddha.

The influences of Buddhism remained overwhelmingly strong in the Kamakura period. During the Tokugawa period, however, neo-Confucian ideologues began interpreting the indigenous tradition of Shinto as separate from Buddhism. This tendency was most clearly seen in the development of National Learning represented by Motoori's study of the *Kojiki,* in which he attempted to wipe away all foreign influences in the study and interpretation of the *Kojiki.* Furthermore, Motoori's interpretation of the *Kojiki* as the sacred text, as well as his way of understanding *kami,* was succeeded—and developed more nationalistically—by A. Hirata and later theologians. In this scholarhip, *kami* and the Buddha were not only separated from each other theoretically, but also practically. This concept of *kami,* and this tradition of interpretation, is therefore also a new development.

SYNCRETIC RELIGIONS. One of the problems of *kami* in folk and popular religions is that Buddhists practially lost their religious freedom during the Tokugawa period. This was undertaken by the *jidan seido,* the Tokugawa neo-Confucian regime's control of the Buddhist temples as the official temples to which all people had to register to be certified as a nonmember of malicious religions, including Chrisianity. Shinto shrines were also controlled as one of the official religions under the the regime. People's religious needs were thus met by the emergence of numerous phenomena of fragmented—but very rich—elements of the syncretic integration of folk religion, such as pilgrimage movements and folk religious practices of various magico-religious activities (e.g., divinations, amulets, incantations, and many kinds of prayer in urban and rural areas).

From the lower strata of society, then, three (popular) founded religions—the Kurozumi, the Konko, and Tenri—emerged spontaneously through the religious experiences of each of their founders. Each of these religions, while critically reassessing their contemporary civilization and the structure of society including Buddhism and Shinto, created universalistic and egalitarian teachings in which all the influences of Buddhism, Shinto, Confucianism, and Taoism were organically blended together but integrated through their religious experience on the basis of strong undercurrents of folk religion. They had all-inclusive *kami* in the center of their teaching, and they responded to the religious needs of the alienated. These three religions thus became the historical prototypes of new religions in modern Japan.

Another point is that through the contact with the Western powers, Japanese people achieved the Meiji restoration—the establishment of the new unity of the state by restoring the sacred emperor, the living-*kami*, as the descendant of the sun goddess Amaterasu. This allowed them to achieve a modernization and westernization of Japan—the powerful modern state. The living *kami*, as the focal point of national identity and indigenous culture, thus came to be exposed to the secular history of the modern international struggles. This is indeed a new, paradoxical context for Japanese *kami*. In addition, through the missionary activities of Christian groups the notion of the Japanese *kami* came to be influenced by the notion of the god of transcendence, for Christian missionaries applied the Japanese word *kami* to explain their god, Yahweh, or the absolute.

SEE ALSO Japanese Religions, article on The Study of Myths; New Religious Movements, article on New Religious Movements in Japan; Shintō; Study of Religion, article on The Academic Study of Religion in Japan; Transculturation and Religion, article on Religion in the Formation of Modern Japan.

BIBLIOGRAPHY

Bock, Felicia G., trans. *The Engi-shiki* (The procedures of the Engi era). Tokyo, 1972.

Hardekar, Helen. *Shinto and the State, 1868-1988.* Princeton, N.J., 1991.

Kitagawa, Joseph M. *Religion in Japanese History.* New York, 1966.

Kitagawa, Joseph M. *On Understanding Japanese Religion.* Princeton, N.J., 1987.

Nippon Gakujutsu Shinkokai, trans. *The Mannyō-shū* (Collection of leaves). Princeton, N.J., 1981.

Philippi, Donald L, trans. *The Kojiki* (Records of ancient matters). Tokyo, 1969.

Shigeyoshi Murakami. *Japanese Religion in the Modern Century.* Translated by H. Byron Earhart. Tokyo, 1980.

Susumu Ono. *Kami* (in Japanese). Tokyo, 1997.

Tetsuo Yamaori. *Kami to Hotoke* (*Kami* and buddhas). Tokyo, 1983.

MICHIO ARAKI (2005)

KAMO NO MABUCHI (1697–1769), Japanese scholar of classical studies in the Tokugawa period (1600–1868); he wrote classical poetry under the pen names Shōjyō, Moryō, Iyō, and Agatai.

Mabuchi was born on March 4, 1697, into the Okabe family, descendants of the overseers of Kamo Shrine in Kyoto, at Iba, Ōmi province (modern Shizuoka Prefecture). Mabuchi's father was a Shintō priest and part-time farmer who encouraged his son to write poetry. At the age of ten (eleven by Japanese count) Mabuchi, who received initial instruction from the poet Kada Masako and then from her renowned husband, Sugiura Kuniakira, began taking active part in poetry tournaments.

At the age of twenty-five, Mabuchi made the acquaintance of Kada Azumamaro (1668–1736), scholar of classical studies and headmaster of the school of National Learning (Kokugaku) in Kyoto. Through his association with Watanabe Myōan, a scholar of Ogyū Sorai's school of Ancient Rhetoric (Kobunjigaku), Mabuchi met the Confucian Dazai Shundai, who introduced him to the study of classics in the manner developed by Sorai. Later, as he turned away from Chinese influences to embrace things Japanese, Mabuchi repudiated the scholarship of the members of the Sorai school as the work of eccentrics.

In 1734, after enrolling in Kada Azumamaro's school, Mabuchi began work on the eighth-century collection of poetry known as the *Man'yōshū*. Following Kada's death in 1736, Mabuchi moved to the capital at Edo (modern Tokyo), but returned frequently to Iba, for he believed it was possible to see the reality of human existence in the naiveté of the rural people. Thus he developed his concept of society based on an agricultural economic model combined with the Daoist principle of natural life. At the same time, he composed poetry and participated in poetry competitions. In 1742, he joined the service of Lord Tayasu, a member of the Tokugawa family, as a teacher of classical studies.

Opposing the tradition that saw the right of succession in schools of scholarship passed down through families, Mabuchi considered himself the successor to the Kada school. The number of his followers increased to almost 350, and three subschools emerged. In 1763, when Mabuchi was returning from a trip to the Yamato area (modern Nara), he met Motoori Norinaga (1730–1801), his future successor and a leading figure in the National Learning school.

It was Mabuchi's aim to understand the terminology and ideology of ancient (pre-Nara) times. He advocated adherence to Shintō doctrine and a return to the "natural" concepts of the ancient period as a means of discovering the supreme and correct *kokoro* ("soul, spirit") of the Japanese people. Influences from China and Confucian ideology were, in his interpretation, unnatural. In opposition to the principles set down by Confucians and Buddhists, Mabuchi stressed the philosophy of nonaction, or naturalness, by which it would be possible to unite one's *kokoro* with the spirit of the universe. He maintained that "artificial" knowledge, such as that propounded by Confucians and Buddhists, would only harm the spirit of the people. Therefore, since Japan's ancient period was based on what was pure and natural, it was essential that there be a return to the things of the past. In adoration of such an ideal concept, he attempted to revive the spirit of the classical times not only through the doctrines he propounded, but also in his style of clothing and the furnishings of his home. He studied ancient poetry and literature as a means of practicing the principles of old, thereby setting a high value on the myths of Japan's ancestral gods, the emperor, and the elements of nature.

Mabuchi pointed to the virtuous character of a bright, naive, and pure *kokoro*, a soul that was brave, honest, and gentle. This type of spirit would only manifest itself in a subject who was courageous and loyal to the emperor. Yet he did not regard the Tokugawa regime as suppressive of the interests of the emperor but rather praised its founding ruler, Tokugawa Ieyasu (1542–1616), for establishing a government with Shintō as its base.

See Also Kokugaku.

Bibliography

One may find useful the details concerning the poetry of Kamo no Mabuchi in the book by Tamura Yoshinobu entitled *Kamo no Mabuchi wakashū no kenkyū* (Tokyo, 1966). The following biographical accounts are recommended for their detail: Koyama Tadashi's *Kamo no Mabuchi den* (Tokyo, 1938), and Terada Yasumasa's *Kamo no Mabuchi shōgai to gyōseki* (Hamamatsu, 1979). Descriptions of Mabuchi's religious philosophy can be found in Ōishi Arata's *Kamo Mabuchi* (Tokyo, 1942) and in Araki Yoshio's *Kamo no Mabuchi no hito to shisō* (Tokyo, 1943). On the scholarship of Mabuchi, see Inoue Minoru's *Kamo no Mabuchi no gakumon* (Tokyo, 1943). For Inoue's evaluation of the accomplishments of Mabuchi and his successors, see his *Kamo no Mabuchi no gyōseki to monryū* (Tokyo, 1966). The part that the interest in agriculture played in forming his philosophy is taken up by Saegusa Yasutaka in *Kamo no Mabuchi, jimbutsu sōsho* (Tokyo, 1962).

New Sources

Nosco, Peter. *Remembering Paradise: Nativism and Nostalgia in Eighteenth-Century Japan.* Cambridge, U.K., 1990.

Okumura Kōsaku. *Kamo no Mabuchi: den to uta.* Tokyo, 1996.

Saigusa Yasutaka. *Kamo no Mabuchi.* Tokyo, 1987.

Haga Noboru (1987)
Translated from Japanese by Irene M. Kunii
Revised Bibliography

KANG YUWEI (1858–1927), political reformer and Confucian thinker of modern China. Kang Yuwei first attained national prominence as leader of the political reform movement that ended in the defeat of the Hundred Days Reform of 1898. Although primarily political, the movement also had a spiritual and moral dimension. Kang called not only for the "protection of the nation" but also for the "preservation of the faith," by which he meant the spiritual revitalization of Confucianism and the promotion of its teachings as the state religion. This position was partly a response to the cultural and political crises that China was undergoing at the time. By revitalizing Confucianism, Kang hoped to strengthen China's self-esteem and national solidarity. But his call for the "preservation of the faith" must not be seen solely in this practical light; it was also the culmination of a moral and spiritual quest that had started in his early youth.

Kang Yuwei was born to a family of scholars and officials in Nanhai County, Guangdong Province. His father died while Kang was still a child, and thereafter his grandfather, a devoted Neo-Confucian scholar, personally took charge of the boy's education. Shortly before the age of twenty, Kang entered a period of spiritual restlessness, triggered by the sudden death of his grandfather and by the beginning of his subsequent apprenticeship under an inspiring Confucian teacher. He rebelled against his conventional Confucian education and temporarily withdrew from society altogether. Plunging into a frantic intellectual search, he fell under the influence of various non-Confucian persuasions, especially Mahāyāna Buddhism, philosophical Daoism, and "Western learning."

Kang's intellectual quest finally culminated in the formation of a moral and historical worldview that he expressed in a series of writings published in the decade from the early 1890s to the early 1900s. Based on a bold and comprehensive reinterpretation of Confucianism that centered on the pivotal Confucian ideal of *ren* (human-heartedness), this view also reflected, in its redefinition of *ren*, ang's interest in non-Confucian thought. *Ren* provided Kang with a worldview that saw the essential and ultimate state of the cosmos as a selfless all-encompassing whole. Kang also retained the Confucian belief central to *ren* that the intrinsic goal of human existence is the moral perfection of individual and society. But his definition of moral perfection bears the profound influence of non-Confucian thought, for his vision of the ideal society, the "great unity" (*datong*), was that of a universal moral community where egalitarianism, libertarianism, and hedonism would prevail. Since his conception of hedonism resulted from the impact of the materialistic doctrines of Western industrial society, his ideal society offered the radical combination of moral perfection, technological development, and material abundance.

The radical tendencies in Kang's conception of *ren* were tempered by his teleological notion of histroy heavily influenced by the modern Western thought. In his view, the full realization of the ideal can be attained only through the gradual course of historical developement. Borrowing a scheme from an ancient commentary on the Confucian classic *Chun qiu*, Kang took the view that human history evolves through three stages, from "the age of chaos," which lay in the past, through an intermediate age of "emerging peace," to the final stage of "universal peace," or "great unity," to be realized in the future. Kang insisted that it was for this latter age alone that his radical reevaluation of *ren* was appropriate. He believed that, meanwhile, in the era preceding the "age of great unity," many of the conventional values of Confucianism remained relevant. These were the tenets of the moral-historical worldview that lay at the core of his efforts to have Confucianism accepted as a state religion.

Kang's reform movement culminated in 1898, when, under his guidance, the Guangxu emperor attempted to put into practice a wide-ranging program of political reform. The intervention of the dowager empress Cixi, who moved to imprison the emperor and nullify the imperial edicts little more than three months after they were issued, brought Kang's reforms to an abortive end. Together with his student Liang Qichao, Kang fled China and began an exile that lasted until 1913. During this period he continued his reformist efforts abroad and traveled extensively, deepening his understanding of the social and political forces that were shaping the modern world.

Upon his return to China, Kang resumed his efforts to implement the promotion of Confucianism as a state religion. Convinced that the revolution of 1911, in which the traditional monarchy had been replaced by a republican form of government, had only served to impede the historical evolution of the ideal society, he joined the warlord Zhang Xun in an ill-fated attempt to restore Manchu rule in 1917. In the writings of his later years, Kang remained faithful to the interpretation of Confucianism that he had formulated in the 1890s, but, because the intellectual climate of China had changed, his views never regained their former influence.

BIBLIOGRAPHY

Hsiao Kung-chuan. *A Modern China and a New World: K'ang Yu-wei, Reformer and Utopian, 1858–1927.* Seattle, 1975.

Lo Jung-pang, ed. and trans. *K'ang Yu-wei: A Biography and a Symposium.* Tucson, 1967.

Thompson, Laurence G., trans. *Ta T'ung Shu: The One-World Philosophy of K'ang Yu-wei.* London, 1958.

Fang Delin. *Ruxue di Weiji yu Shanbian: Kang Youwei Yu Jindai Ruxue.* Taipei, 1992.

Zang Shijun. *Kang Youwei datong Sixiang Yenjiu.* Guangdong, 1997.

HAO CHANG (1987 AND 2005)

KANNON SEE AVALAOKITEŚVARA

KANT, IMMANUEL (1724–1804), German philosopher. Kant was born in Königsberg, a provincial town in East Prussia. He grew up in a religious family of relatively low social status. His father was a saddler, and both his parents were dedicated members of the Pietist movement, which stressed the interior devotion of the heart in opposition to the prevailing Lutheran practice of external observances. The spirit of Pietism pervaded not only Kant's family but also the Collegium Fridericianum, a local school, where he received his early education from 1732 to 1740.

In 1740 Kant entered the University of Königsberg, where he studied science and philosophy for six years. After graduation, he earned his living as a private tutor for a number of East Prussian families. During this period he kept up his studies and earned his master's degree at the university in 1755, which allowed him to teach as a privatdocent, a private lecturer accepted as a member of the faculty without compensation from the university. He occupied this financially precarious and academically undistinguished position for fifteen years. In 1770 he was appointed professor of logic and metaphysics.

While holding this position, Kant produced a stream of masterpieces. His best-known works are his three critiques: the *Critique of Pure Reason* (1781), the *Critique of Practical Reason* (1788), and the *Critique of Judgment* (1790). These three volumes expound Kant's critical idealism, or critical philosophy, which has also been known as Kantianism. Kantianism was the first phase of German Idealism, which gained fuller development in the writings of Johann Fichte (1762–1814), Friedrich Schelling (1775–1854), and G. W. F. Hegel (1770–1831). Kant's religious ideas not only constitute essential features of his critical philosophy but also play a pivotal role in the transition from his critical idealism to the absolute idealism of his intellectual successors.

KANTIANISM AS A WORLDVIEW. Kantianism was an attempt to reconcile British empiricism and continental rationalism. British empiricism had been developed by a succession of British and Scottish philosophers, namely, Thomas Hobbes (1588–1679), John Locke (1632–1704), George Berkeley (1685–1753), and David Hume (1711–1776). Continental rationalism had been advocated by René Descartes (1596–1650), Gottfried Leibniz (1646–1716), and Christian Wolff (1679–1754). During his formative years, Kant learned his philosophy from Leibnizians and Wolffians, but he later came to appreciate the importance of empiricism, especially Hume's theory of ideas.

The central point of the dispute between rationalists and empiricists was the theory of ideas. Since all our ideas are derived from sensation, the empiricists maintained, the objects of sensation are the only proper objects of knowledge. In opposition to this view, the rationalists argued that some of our ideas are not derived from sensation but are innate to reason. They further claimed that these innate ideas give us a knowledge of supersensible reality such as God. The idea of a supersensible reality, although espoused by some early empiricists, became unpopular with the later empiricists, because they considered it incompatible with empiricism. This later tendency of empiricism amounted to recognizing sensible reality, or the physical world, as the only reality. Thus the dispute that had begun with the epistemological issue concerning the origin of ideas came to have the ontological implication of admitting or not admitting any reality beyond the domain of sensation.

Kant's *Critique of Pure Reason* is a critical assessment of these two contending views. He holds that there are two kinds of ideas: those derived from sense and those innate to reason. The latter are the a priori elements of cognition; the former are its a posteriori elements. These two are equally indispensable for human knowledge. Kant is emphatic on the mutual dependence of sensibility and understanding: "Percepts without concepts are blind; concepts without percepts are empty." Although the domain of knowledge is limited to the domain of sensation, as the empiricists claimed, Kant argues, knowledge of sense objects requires the use of a priori concepts such as the concept of cause and effect. He derives twelve a priori concepts from twelve forms of judgment and calls them the categories of understanding. He uses the categories to construct a priori principles of understanding, which function as the framework for organizing the objects of sensation.

This epistemological compromise between rationalism and empiricism has the following ontological consequence: Kant maintains that the objects of sensation are not reality itself (things-in-themselves) but its appearance. He bases this claim largely on his argument that space and time are not objective entities but subjective forms of intuition, that is, the manner in which human beings are given objects of sensation. Since all objects of sensation are given through space and time, Kant holds, they cannot be objective realities. They are only appearances to us. Kant calls these appearances "phenomena" and the things-in-themselves "noumena."

Unlike phenomena, noumena are not located in space and time; nor are they given as objects of sensation. They are the supersensible realities. That the domain of knowledge is limited to the world of phenomena means that we can never know the true reality but only its appearances. That we can have no knowledge of noumena, however, does not mean that we have no ideas about them. Kant maintains that we have a priori ideas about the supersensible reality. But to have these ideas is not to know the world of noumena, because there is no way of proving their truth or falsity.

In Kant's view, knowledge is inseparable from the power of demonstrating the truth or falsity of an idea, and that power is inexorably limited to the domain of sensibility. For this reason, knowledge is limited to the world of phenomena. The rationalists have assumed that the truths of a priori ideas can be demonstrated by rational arguments alone, that is, without appealing to sensibility. But rationalist arguments divorced from the constraint of sensibility can produce only sophistical illusions and confusions, according to Kant. He gives the name "transcendental dialectic" to the pseudoscience constituted by those sophistical arguments, because they are dialectical arguments transcending the domain of sensibility.

Kant recognizes three branches of transcendental dialectic: transcendental psychology, transcendental cosmology, and transcendental theology. These three are supposed to prove the immortality of the soul, the freedom of the will, and the existence of God. In the *Critique of Pure Reason,* Kant provides a systematic examination of their arguments and exposes their common error, namely, the error of employing a priori concepts beyond the domain of sensibility.

The immortality of the soul, the freedom of will, and the existence of God are three of the central dogmas in many religions. That none of them can be proved, however, should not be mistaken to mean that they can be disproved. Kant is emphatic on this point. A transcendental assertion can neither be proved nor be disproved, because sensibility is essential not only for proofs but also for disproofs. Hence the three religious dogmas can still be regarded as possible truths of the supersensible reality. As such, they can be accepted in faith.

Kant demarcates matters of faith from matters of fact. The latter are the objects of knowledge; the former are the objects of belief. The objects of knowledge are situated in the world of phenomena; the objects of faith belong to the world of noumena. The objects of faith transcend the domain of sensibility, while the objects of knowledge are immanent in it. Although theoretical reason cannot settle the question of accepting or rejecting the objects of faith, Kant says, practical reason has a way of ruling over their admissibility.

KANTIANISM AS A MORAL VIEW. Practical reason is the rational faculty concerned with human conduct, and a critical examination of this faculty is given in his second critique, the *Critique of Practical Reason.* Kant recognizes two mainsprings for human conduct: the will and the inclination. The inclination is the working of our desires and feelings, which are subject to the causal laws of the phenomenal world. The will is the rational faculty for moral actions. Unless the freedom of this faculty is presupposed, Kant says, it makes no sense to talk of the moral worth of human conduct. Since freedom is impossible in the phenomenal world of causal necessity, it can be accepted only as an entity belonging to the noumenal world. Kant calls the noumenal world the domain of freedom and the phenomenal world the domain of necessity. Thus he installs the noumenal world as the practical ground for morality and the freedom of the will as the first postulate (presupposition) of practical reason.

Besides the postulate of freedom, Kant says, two other postulates are demanded by morality: the existence of God and the immortality of the soul. The immortality of the soul is required for moral perfection. Our inclination has the natural propensity to go against the moral dictates of pure reason, and our moral perfection can be achieved by transforming this natural propensity into the willing obedience to the moral law. Since this moral transformation of the soul is infinitely time-consuming, it can be accomplished only if the soul continues to live after the death of its body. For this reason, Kant says, the postulate of the immortality of the soul is dictated by the practical ideal of moral perfection.

In Kant's ethics, the ideal of moral perfection is inseparably connected with another practical ideal, the notion of the complete good (*summum bonum*). Kant defines it as the harmony of moral perfection and happiness (natural good).

He regards moral perfection as the absolutely necessary condition for rendering human beings worthy of happiness. In this world, however, happiness can be denied to a person morally worthy of it, while it can be given to a person morally unworthy of it. The dispensation of happiness in proportion to each person's moral worth is their harmony, that is, the ideal of the complete good. This ideal can, Kant maintains, be fulfilled only by God in the other world. This is the third and the final postulate of practical reason.

Kant's third postulate has sometimes been known as the moral proof for the existence of God, and as such it has been the object of many disputes and misunderstandings. But to call it a proof is highly misleading; a "proof" for the existence of God generally means the demonstration or assurance of his existence. In Kantianism, as we have already seen, demonstration or assurance can be given only for the objects of the phenomenal world. Therefore the reasons Kant gives for the existence of God cannot constitute a proof. It is only a postulate. Whereas a proof can give certainty or assurance, a postulate can give only possibility, a supersensible ground for hope.

Kant's notion of rational postulates is inseparable from his ideal of practical rationality. To regard the harmony of moral and natural goods as an ideal of practical reason means that the world in which this ideal is fulfilled is a rational one and, conversely, that the world in which it is not fulfilled is an irrational one. It is impossible to find out whether our world is ultimately rational or irrational in this regard. As rational beings, however, we can, for practical purposes, opt and hope for the possibility that our world is ultimately rational. If this possibility is to be true, Kant argues, there must be a God who assures the harmony of moral and natural goods for every moral being. This is all that is meant by this and other postulates of practical reason.

KANT'S CONCEPTION OF GOD AND THE RELIGIOUS. In Kant's philosophy, God does not stand as a power that has its own laws and commands different from the moral law and its dictates. What God demands from ethical subjects is none other than what is dictated by moral reason. To do the will of God is to perform the duties of the moral imperative. There is no way to please God other than to be morally perfect. To be religious is to be moral; to be moral is to be religious. As far as human behavior is concerned, morality and religion are functionally identical, and their functional identity is expressed in Kant's statement that religion and God are internal to morality.

Kant's internalism, as he admits, goes against the traditional view that assumes an external relation between morality and religion. In general, the traditional religions portray God as a powerful being, whose will is independent of our will, whose commands can override even our moral dictates, and whose favor can be sought by special rituals and devotions. In short, the traditional religions stand on the existence of powers and values external to the powers and values of morality. Kant rejects such externalism because it is incompatible with the autonomy of practical reason.

In Kant's view, externalism is the anthropomorphic misconception of God and his relation to us, that is, the error of understanding God as someone like a powerful human being who demands our service and devotion. This misconception lies behind the religions of what Kant calls "*cultus externus.*" These religions impose on their devotees a set of obligations or observances that consists of prayers, rituals, services, and various prohibitions. Furthermore, the gods of these religions are assumed to be pleased or displeased by the performance or nonperformance of these religious duties. Most of these religions have specially ordained experts called priests, ministers, or shamans, who have the power of officiating and facilitating the performance of religious duties.

Cultus externus, Kant insists, makes no sense to anyone who correctly understands the nature of God as the most perfect being, that is, omniscient, omnipotent, and, above all, morally perfect. It makes no sense to render any service to such a being, because he is in need of nothing and can derive no benefit from our services. Even the praise of his perfection cannot add anything to his perfection any more than flattery can to his honor. God does not need our prayers to find out what we need. Nor can he be moved by our supplication, because his mind is governed only by moral dictates. The *cultus externus* can fulfill none of the religious functions that it has been assumed to fulfill.

Kant uses the label "natural religion" to designate his view of religion, because it can be fully comprehended by the natural power of human reason, that is, without the aid of supernatural revelation. Kant's idea of natural religion may appear to reduce religion to morality. But he insists that natural religion retains all the essential features of traditional religions. In his view, those features are the moral attributes and functions of the supreme being, as the holy lawgiver, the benevolent ruler, and the just judge. Any other attributes of God such as omniscience, omnipotence, and omnipresence are only supplementary to his moral attributes; they are the requisite conditions for discharging his moral functions.

Kant argues that Christianity is the only moral religion, while the others are servile religions. The central function of servile religions is to curry favor from the supernatural powers; they place human beings in a servile relation to those powers. This servile relation has, Kant holds, been transformed into a moral one by Jesus of Nazareth. Jesus transformed the "old" law of Moses, the rules for external observance, into the "new" law, the rules for internal disposition. Kant finds Jesus' moral interpretation of religious life most conspicuously in his Sermon on the Mount, and he reads its concluding remark—"Therefore be perfect, as your heavenly father is!"—as an exhortation for moral perfection.

In *Religion within the Limits of Reason Alone* (1793), Kant offers his moral interpretation of Christian dogmas. The dogma of original sin concerns our innate propensity to do evil, which is to flout the maxims of duty and to succumb to the maxims of inclination. Kant regards it as a superstition to believe that this propensity was generated by Adam's fall from grace and then passed on to his posterity. On the contrary, Kant holds that the innate propensity to go against the moral law is in the very nature of man. No doubt, original human nature is said to be good. This original goodness, however, is not incompatible with the innate propensity to do evil. The original goodness of man means the freedom to obey the moral law by disciplining and mastering inclinations. Hence, original goodness and the innate propensity to evil are two essential features of every human being.

Kant interprets the incarnation of God in Christ not as a miracle of the supernatural order but as the manifestation of a moral ideal. As moral agents, he says, all of us have the ideal of a morally perfect human being. Such an ideal, if ever realized in this world, can be called an incarnate God, because the ideal in question belongs to pure practical reason, whose dictates are one with the dictates of God. Kant calls the ideal of moral perfection the archetype of moral life. But this archetype, he insists, cannot be identified with Jesus Christ himself. For he is only an instance or example, while the archetype belongs to all of us as agents of practical reason.

The relation of archetype and example, Kant says, is misrepresented in the traditional dogma of the incarnation, which exalts Jesus as a member of the Holy Trinity. He regards the dogma of the Trinity as theoretically incomprehensible and practically unserviceable. If the Son of God is so exalted as to stand above all human temptations and struggles, he is too remote from our existence to serve as a useful model. The value of the Son of God as our practical model lies in his essential identity with all human beings, and every human being who strives to achieve moral perfection can be called a son of God, a man well-pleasing to God.

Kant interprets the kingdom of God as an ethical commonwealth, a community of moral agents each of whom treats the other as an end-in-itself by obeying the moral law. He distinguishes the ethical commonwealth from the political commonwealth by virtue of the former's freedom from coercion. Whereas the power of coercion is indispensable for the maintenance of a political commonwealth, the freedom of the will is sufficient for the administration of an ethical commonwealth. The constitution of such a harmonious community, Kant says, becomes possible only through the moral rebirth of its members, which involves the radical transformation of their hearts from the propensity to follow inclination into the willing obedience to the moral law, that is, through conversion. The same moral transformation is required for the admission to the ethical commonwealth.

Kant shows special caution in handling the claims of supernatural revelation. He rejects the claim that revelation has the authority of discovering and authenticating the supernatural truths inaccessible to human intelligence. He also rejects the view that revelation is totally gratuitous with respect to the discovery of religious truths. Although the truths of natural religion can be discovered by natural reason, revelation makes easier their discovery and propagation. Since he recognizes only the practical value of expedition, he rejects the traditional distinction between natural and revealed religion. As in Christianity, he says, a natural religion can be a revealed one.

Since natural religion belongs to the pure practical reason, Kant asserts the unity of all religions. There is only one true religion, he says, although there can be many different faiths. He distinguishes the particular ecclesiastical faiths from pure religious faith. Whereas pure faith consists of the ideals of practical reason, the particular faiths are the manifestations of those ideals through the historically instituted churches. Since the formation and development of those institutions have been influenced by historical contingencies, Kant holds, the ecclesiastical faiths are bound to show their differences. Nevertheless, he is confident that they can still display the unity of pure religious faith insofar as they are faithful to their original ideals.

KANT'S CRITICS AND HIS INFLUENCE. Kant's idea of natural religion provoked the charge among his contemporaries that he was a Deist. Deism was the view, prevalent among the scientific-minded intellectuals of the eighteenth century, that God does not intervene in the running of the universe because it has been placed under the working of immutable laws since its creation. Kant categorically denied the charge of being a Deist and attributed it to the misrepresentation of his position.

The misrepresentation in question was largely due to Kant's skeptical attitude toward miracles, God's interventions par excellence in the running of the world. Because miracles contravene the laws of nature, they cannot be reconciled with the use of reason. Both in theoretical and practical functions, human reason appears crippled in the presence of miracles. Furthermore, he says, miracles are not essential for the functions of true religion, because these functions can stand securely on moral beliefs alone. In fact, any demand for miracles as the authentication of religious beliefs betrays the lack of firm faith in the authority of moral commands, which are engraved upon the heart of man through reason. Because of this, Kant says, Christ rebuked the miracle-seekers: "Unless you see signs and wonders, you will not believe" (*Jn.* 4:48). In spite of these reservations about miracles, Kant categorically refused to impugn their possibility or reality.

Another charge against Kant was that he compromised his doctrine of moral autonomy by retaining the traditional doctrine of grace. Grace, for Kant, means God's help; it presupposes man's weakness, dependence, and heteronomy. The Pietists under whose influence Kant had grown up stressed the indispensability of grace and tended to take a passive attitude toward life. Kant rejects this passive attitude and praises the positive value of active efforts in moral life. Nevertheless, he admits the possibility that even our best efforts may fail to secure moral perfection. In that event, he says, we can hope that God will, in his wisdom and goodness, make up for our shortcomings.

His critics have pointed out that man is not a truly autonomous moral agent if even his best moral efforts are not enough to secure his moral perfection. They have further argued that Kant's notion of moral autonomy is also incompatible with his notion of the complete good. In their view, the intimate connection between worthiness and happiness makes morality too dependent on the idea of happiness, which is admittedly outside the control of a moral agent. Kant had guarded himself against this charge by stressing that the connection in question was a matter of belief rather than knowledge. Even if it is only a belief, his critics have maintained, it compromises the notion of moral autonomy as long as it is acted upon in the practical world.

Perhaps the most serious charge against Kant was addressed to his demarcation between phenomena and noumena. At the time he was concluding his second critique, the *Critique of Practical Reason,* he was not terribly disturbed by this criticism. So he confidently singled out the starry heavens above and the moral law within as two objects of awe and admiration, respectively representing the world of phenomena and the world of noumena. This observation was intended to mark the end not only of the second critique but of his entire critical enterprise. For he believed that his two critiques had fulfilled his ambition of critically assessing the two worlds of phenomena and noumena.

Shortly thereafter, however, Kant became preoccupied with the question of transition and mediation between the two worlds. Although moral precepts belong to the noumenal world, they can be realized in the phenomenal world. Kant found it difficult to explain the transition from the world of precepts to the world of practice, because one was supposed to be governed by necessity and the other by freedom.

In order to resolve this problem of transition, Kant wrote his third critique, the *Critique of Judgment,* and introduced reflective judgment as the faculty of mediation between the two worlds. But his theory of mediation was far from convincing, and most of his intellectual heirs resolved his problem by collapsing his two worlds into one. This post-Kantian development in German idealism made it impossible to retain Kant's postulates of immortality and the other world, because there was only one world left.

The fusion of Kant's two worlds into one was the climax of the progressive secularization that had begun in the Renaissance. Kant played a pivotal role in this development. His demarcation between phenomena and noumena was a modification and retention of the medieval demarcation between the natural and the supernatural orders. Unlike the medieval demarcation, however, Kant's did not completely coincide with the demarcation between this world and the other world. Kant made the transcendent noumenal world functionally immanent for moral life, thereby initiating the descent of the transcendent reality to the immanent level. The post-Kantians completed this process of descent and converted Kant's theism into pantheism. Kant's transcendent God became their immanent force in history.

The resulting pantheism also resolved the tension in Kant's notion of human autonomy. Although he claimed autonomy and independence for moral life, he acknowledged heteronomy and dependence for happiness. He stressed this admixture of dependence and independence in his notion of the complete good and the postulate for the existence of God. But this admixture was unacceptable to his successors, because they insisted on the total autonomy of human reason. The totally autonomous human reason became indistinguishable from the immanent God, and the two-in-one came to be called the "Absolute Spirit" by Hegel. With Kant, religion and morality became functionally identical; with Hegel, God and man were given their ontological identity.

See Also Deism; Empiricism; Free Will and Predestination; Pietism; Proofs for the Existence of God.

Bibliography

Kant's Works in English Translation

Critique of Judgement. Translated by J. C. Meredith. 1928; reprint, London, 1973.

Critique of Practical Reason. Translated by Lewis White Beck. Chicago, 1949. Kant's preliminary view of this subject is given in his *Foundations of the Metaphysics of Morals,* translated by Lewis White Beck (Chicago, 1949).

Critique of Pure Reason. Translated by Norman Kemp Smith. New York, 1929. An abridged version is available in Kant's *Prolegomena to Any Future Metaphysics,* edited by Lewis White Beck (Indianapolis, 1950).

Lectures on Ethics. Translated by Louis Infield. London, 1979. These lectures are not from Kant's own writings but from his students' notes.

Religion within the Boundaries of Mere Reason. Translated and edited by Allen Wood and George Di Gionvanni (Cambridge, 1998).

Works on Kant's View of Morality and Religion

Beck, Lewis White. *A Commentary on Kant's Critique of Practical Reason.* Chicago, 1960.

Cassirer, Ernst. *Kant's Life and Thought.* Translated by James Haden. New Haven, 1981. This is perhaps the most comprehensive introduction available in English to Kant's life and philosophy. A shorter general introduction to his philosophy can be found in Stephan Körner's *Kant* (1955; reprint, New Haven, 1982) and in Ralph C. S. Walker's *Kant* (Boston, 1978).

Collins, James D. *The Emergence of Philosophy of Religion.* New Haven, 1967. This volume provides a good account not only of Kant's conception of religion but also of what comes before and after Kant's conception, especially Hume's and Hegel's ideas on the issue.

England, F. E. *Kant's Conception of God.* New York, 1929.

Green, Ronald Michael. *Religious Reason: The Rational and Moral Basis of Religion.* New York, 1978.

Paton, Herbert J. *The Categorical Imperative: A Study in Kant's Moral Philosophy.* Chicago, 1948.

Silber, John R. "Kant's Conception of the Highest Good as Immanent and Transcendent." *Philosophical Review* 68 (1959): 469–492.

Silber, John R. "The Moral Good and the Natural Good in Kant's Ethics." *Review of Metaphysics* 36 (December 1982): 397–437.

Webb, Clement C. *Kant's Philosophy of Religion.* Oxford, 1926.

Wood, Allen W. *Kant's Moral Religion.* Ithaca, N. Y., 1970.

T. K. SEUNG (1987 AND 2005)

KAPLAN, MORDECAI (1881–1983), American rabbi, author, and religious leader, was the creator of the theory of Reconstructionist Judaism and the founder of the Reconstructionist movement. The son of Rabbi Israel Kaplan, a Talmudic scholar, Mordecai Menahem Kaplan was born in Svenciony, Lithuania, on June 11, 1881. The family left eastern Europe in 1888 and reached the United States in June 1889. Kaplan was instructed in traditional Jewish subjects by private tutors while attending public schools in New York City. He received degrees from the City College of New York (1900) and Columbia University (1902) and rabbinic ordination from the Jewish Theological Seminary of America (1902). In 1909, following a tenure as minister and rabbi of Kehillath Jeshurun, an Orthodox congregation in New York City, Kaplan returned to the Jewish Theological Seminary, where he served for more than fifty years, first as principal (later dean) of the Teachers Institute until 1945, then as professor of homiletics and philosophies of religion until his formal retirement in 1963.

Beyond his roles as a leader within the Conservative rabbinate and the Zionist movement, and as an important contributor within the field of Jewish education, Kaplan's major achievement remains his formulation of Reconstructionism. He presented Reconstructionism to the public through a series of lectures and publications, chiefly *Judaism as a Civilization* (1934). Kaplan developed his theories in response to his own loss of faith in the traditional concept of revelation (known as *Torah mi-Sinai,* "the Law from Sinai"), one result of his studies with the iconoclastic Bible scholar Arnold Ehrlich. Attempting to rebuild a personal cosmology, Kaplan drew from Western philosophers and social scientists as well as Jewish sources, using the sociological findings of Émile Durkheim (1858–1917), the pragmatic philosophy of John Dewey (1859–1952) and William James (1842–1910), and the theological insights of Matthew Arnold (1822–1888) in combination with the Spiritual Zionism of Aḥad ha-ʿAm (Asher Ginzberg, 1856–1927).

Kaplan considered Durkheim "the most significant influence" on his conception of religion (Libowitz, 1983). Durkheim maintained that religions did not arise as individual phenomena that spread to a group but out of a societal matrix, representing collective representations of collective realities. Religion was a vital phenomenon shared by members of a group, who came together for more than religion. For Kaplan this theory refuted the Reform (and general Western) definition of Judaism as a religion and Jewry as the members of a church, membership in which was the only link between Jews in different lands. The Durkheimian understanding meant that any solution to Judaism's problems required a program that transcended religion. Kaplan began to study the earliest known forms of Judaism, noting the onset of innovations through the centuries, some of which were accepted and absorbed into the mainstream of Jewish society whereas others died away or separated from Judaism.

The search for a general philosophic guideline directing his experiments and proposals for Judaism led Kaplan to pragmatism, as expounded by James and Dewey. He accepted James's understanding of pragmatism as an approach combining the best of both empiricist and rationalist philosophy, without being limited by abstraction or fixed principles. This included rejection of the notion of absolute truth(s), while seeking understanding through concreteness, facts, and action. He disagreed with James's focus upon the individual, however, believing that religion is primarily "a group consciousness" (Libowitz, 1983), and he sought to combine James's method of evaluation with Durkheim's group-centered understanding of religious development.

Dewey provided Kaplan a guide in this endeavor. Dewey argued that society developed as humans sought practical solutions to specific problems. Knowledge grew from experience, in matters of ethics and morality just as in science. Intelligence would direct improvements upon experience. This intelligence was never finite but in constant evolution. Kaplan applied Dewey's theories to religion, replacing traditional claims to truth with a collective search for truth based upon the actual experiences of the Jewish people. This led him to understand Judaism "functionally" rather than as "pure" philosophy or theology. This synthesis of resources made Kaplan unique among twentieth-century Jewish thinkers as a redactor who sought to combine modern science with an affirmation of Judaism.

At the heart of Kaplan's thought is his definition of Judaism as an "evolving religious civilization." Opposing those who sought the maintenance of Jewish life solely through preservation of the religion, he argued that a Jewish civilization—including within it a land, language and literature, mores, laws and folkways, arts, and a social structure—transcended religion. Kaplan also presented a radical change in the God idea. Preferring to use the term *divinity,* he rejected notions of an anthropomorphic and personal God active in human history, favoring instead a functional understanding of God as the creative source within the universe, the power that engenders a salvation to which the Jewish people have long been particularly responsive. These conceptual shifts infuriated Orthodox Jewry, creating a division exacerbated further by Kaplan's efforts to transfer the center of concern and authority from divinely revealed text to the Jewish people itself, as well as by his justification of the transcendence of Jewish law *(halakhah)* and custom *(minhag)* when those sources no longer met the needs of the Jewish people. Kaplan differed from his Conservative colleagues in his use of extratraditional resources; his approach remained distinct from that of Reform Judaism through his efforts to retain traditional forms while providing new content.

Kaplan also sought to modernize Jewish organizational structure. Realizing the superior strength of the Diaspora cultures, he argued that emancipated Jews lived within two civilizations and that, on most occasions, the general (Gentile) culture exerted the primary hold upon the individual. In an effort to counterbalance the impetus toward total assimilation, Kaplan called for maximal development of opportunities for the individual to function within a Jewish environment. The locus of those activities was to be the synagogue, which Kaplan sought to transform from a simple prayer room to a modern institution, the focus for worship, study, and recreation. Attracting supporters for these theories, Kaplan supervised the creation of the first such community and synagogue center, the Jewish Center on Manhattan's West Side, in 1918. The commitment of the lay leadership to Orthodox Jewish practice, as well as Kaplan's own temper, soon led to difficulties, however, resulting in his resignation from the center in 1922. Kaplan next established the Society for the Advancement of Judaism, which served thereafter as the living laboratory for his experiments with Jewish worship, such as the inclusion of women within the minyan (prayer quorum) and the creation of bat mitzvah as a young woman's rite of passage equivalent to the bar mitzvah.

When editing the *Sabbath Prayer Book* (1945), Kaplan retained the traditional service structure but replaced statements regarding resurrection of the dead with declarations that God remembered the living. In a similar manner, prayers for restoration of the Temple and the coming of the Messiah were removed in favor of recollections of the faith of those who had worshiped in the Temple and prayers for a messianic age, to be achieved through human efforts. Perhaps most controversial, because it was most readily apparent, was Kaplan's replacement of the phrase "who has chosen us from all the nations" in the benediction prior to reading from the Torah with "who has brought us near in His service." Copies of the prayer book were burned at a rally of Orthodox Jews in New York City in 1945, and a ban *(issur)* was pronounced against Kaplan.

Kaplan's followers included the Conservative rabbis Eugene Kohn (1887–1977), Ira Eisenstein (1906–2001), and Milton Steinberg (1903–1950), as well as laypeople throughout the country. Kaplan resisted their desire to establish Reconstructionism as a fourth movement within American Judaism, and Reconstructionism thus remained identified as the "left wing" of Conservative Judaism until the 1960s. Only upon his retirement from the Jewish Theological Seminary did Kaplan devote himself to the establishment of a distinct Reconstructionist movement; by then many of his concepts and practices had diffused and become accepted within Reform and Conservative Judaism. As a result, although the influence of Kaplan's ideas has been broad, the Reconstructionist movement has remained small.

SEE ALSO Reconstructionist Judaism.

BIBLIOGRAPHY

Works by Kaplan not mentioned above include *The Future of the American Jew* (New York, 1948; reprint, New York, 1967), which examines the needs of Jews and Judaism following the creation of the State of Israel. For an examination of religion and the concept of God as it functions within the Jewish civilization, there is *The Meaning of God in Modern Jewish Religion* (New York, 1937; reprint, New York, 1994). *The Greater Judaism in the Making* (New York, 1960; reprint, New York, 1967) studies the modern evolution of Judaism, and *The Religion of Ethical Nationhood* (New York, 1970) is an advocacy of the idea of ethical nationhood as the only means of avoiding world disaster. Studies of the life and works of Kaplan include Richard Libowitz, *Mordecai M. Kaplan and the Development of Reconstructionism* (New York, 1983), an intellectual biography drawing upon Kaplan's personal papers. Other biographical studies include Emanuel S. Goldsmith, Mel Scult, and Robert M. Seltzer, eds., *The American Judaism of Mordecai M. Kaplan* (New York, 1990); and Scult, *Judaism Faces the Twentieth Century: A Biography of Mordecai M. Kaplan* (Detroit, Mich., 1993). Analyses of Kaplan's thought and his place in the Reconstructionist movement include Gilbert S. Rosenthal, *Four Paths to One God* (New York, 1973); Ira Eisenstein, *Reconstructing Judaism: An Autobiography* (New York, 1986), by Kaplan's son-in-law and successor as leader of the Reconstructionist movement; S. Daniel Breslauer, *Mordecai Kaplan's Thought in a Postmodern Age* (Atlanta, 1994); and Jack J. Cohen, *Guides for an Age of Confusion: Studies in the Thinking of Avraham Y. Kook and Mordecai M. Kaplan* (New York, 1999), by a leading voice in Reconstructionism for more than half a century. William James, *The Varieties of Religious Experience* (New York, 1961) was a valuable source for Kaplan's understanding of religion and its role in society.

RICHARD L. LIBOWITZ (1987 AND 2005)

KARAITES.

KARAITES. The Karaites (Heb., *Qara'im*; Arab., *Qarā'īyūn*) are a Jewish sect that recognizes the Hebrew Bible as the sole source of divinely inspired legislation, and denies the authority of the postbiblical Jewish tradition (the Oral Law) as recorded in the Talmud and in later rabbinic literature. The term, which apparently first occurs in the writings of Benjamin al-Nahāwandī (ninth century CE), is variously interpreted as "scripturalists, champions of scripture" (from the Hebrew *qara'*, "to read," particularly "to read scripture") and as "callers," that is to say, those who call for a return to the original biblical religion (from the alternate meaning of *qara'*, "to call, to summon"). Apart from the Samaritans, the Karaites are the oldest surviving Jewish sect and have produced an extensive scholarly literature, much of which has been preserved.

The Rise of Karaite Judaism ("Karaism"). Sectarian dissent in Judaism goes back to the Second Temple period, when it was represented by the Pharisees, the Sadducees, and the Essenes (with whom the Qumran community is likely to be identified). The growth and eventual codification of the postbiblical rabbinic tradition in turn gave rise to further dissent. The Karaites are one of several groups that have claimed the Hebrew Bible to be the one and only repository of God's word, which may not be modified by any subsequent, traditional law.

According to one early Rabbanite account, the Karaite movement originated circa 750 CE with an aristocratic, Babylonian scholar named ʿAnan ben David, who should have succeeded to the Exilarchate (secular leadership) of the Iraqi Jewish community. Because of his excessive wildness and irreverence, however, he was rejected in favor of his younger brother Hananiah. Consequently, ʿAnan declared himself head of a dissident group; these Ananites formed the nucleus of what later became the Karaite sect.This simplistic account suffers from a number of historical and psychological difficulties. Already in the late seventh and early eighth centuries, the anti-traditional leaders, Abū ʿĪsā and Yūdghān, had been active in the vicinity of Iraq. In the ninth and early tenth centuries, other leaders such as Ismāʿīl and Mīshawayh in ʿUkbarā (Iraq), Benjamin al-Nahāwandī in Iran, Mūsā al-Zaʿfarānī in Iraq and then Armenia, and Malik al-Ramlī in Palestine, presided over their own sectarian followings. All of these separate dissident groups developed their own heterogeneous teachings, although they seem to have vaguely regarded themselves as members of the larger community of anti-rabbinic sectarians.

Theological disagreement seems to have been only one of several causes of this new flowering of schisms; others were political, social, and economic. The large autonomous Jewish community in Iraq was administered by a bureaucracy serving the exilarch and the presidents (called the *geʾonim*) of the academies, who codified, interpreted, and developed the rabbinic tradition and acted as supreme courts of appeal. This bureaucracy was maintained by internal taxation that added to the heavy taxes already paid by non-Muslims to the Muslim state. The poorer classes of the Jewish community—and they formed the great majority—thus had ample reason for dissatisfaction with their lot. At the same time, the extension and consolidation of the Muslim empire in the seventh and eighth centuries enabled such discontented elements in the Iraqi community to emigrate to the sparsely settled and less regulated mountainous provinces of the east and north, where they observed the conquered Persian population, united under the banner of Shiism, seething with resentment and resistance against their Arab masters. Finally, the speed and ease with which the Arabs conquered the Byzantine and Persian dominions must have aroused anew Jewish hopes for the end of exile, the restoration of Zion, and the ingathering of the exiles in the Holy Land under their own government. But this hope was quickly shattered: the new Muslim masters, like their Christian and Zoroastrian predecessors, had not the slightest interest in Jewish national aspirations and dreams. All these factors probably contributed to discontent with the status quo, particularly among the disadvantaged elements of the Iraqi Jewish community.

By the beginning of the tenth century, the schism had expanded from its Iranian-Iraqi birthplace into Syria-Palestine. The leading figure was Daniel al-Qūmisī (originally from northern Iran), who preached a spiritual return to biblical Judaism and a physical return to the Holy City. By returning to Jerusalem, studying scripture, leading an ascetic existence, and mourning for the destroyed Temple, these "Mourners for Zion" sought to hasten the divine salvation and the messianic era which they believed to be imminent. The Mourners would become the spiritual and intellectual core of the Karaite movement during the tenth and eleventh centuries, subsuming other sectarian groups such as the Ananites. Zealous Karaite missionaries traveled far and wide to the Jewish settlements in the Near East, preaching to both Karaite and Rabbanite audiences. During the second quarter of the tenth century, however, they encountered stiff opposition. Saʿadyah ben Joseph al-Fayyūmī (882–942), the polymath *gaon* of the Sura academy in Baghdad, published several polemical works against Karaite teachings, condemning their proponents as outright heretics. Saʿadyah's prestige and forceful scholarly argumentation effected a decisive break between the two camps that has never healed. It also seems to have kept the Karaite mission from ever making serious inroads among Rabbanite populations in the Near East.

Bitter though it was in its earlier stages, the Karaite-Rabbanite controversy stimulated Jewish literary creativity in the East during the tenth and eleventh centuries. Influenced by Islamic and Christian models, Rabbanites and Karaites had begun to experiment with new genres in the fields of theology, philosophy, biblical exegesis, and Hebrew philology. But undoubtedly, the inter-denominational feuding motivated members of both camps to produce scholarship of the highest standard. A Karaite academy flourished in Jerusalem during this period, giving advanced training to students from sectarian settlements as far-flung as Muslim Spain and Byzantium.

Much closer to home, the Karaite community of Egypt grew in wealth and importance, which derived in no small part from the success of several members of the Tustarī family, prominent members of the Fatimid court. Since Syria was under Fatimid control for much of this period as well, Karaite prestige increased throughout the area and on the whole, relations with Rabbanites improved dramatically. Marriage documents and formularies from the eleventh century attest to Karaite-Rabbanite intermarriages, in which bride and groom agreed to recognize each other's respective religious practices. Such alliances—which took place within the highest strata of Jewish society—indicate a general interest in maintaining communal unity and harmony.

During the eleventh and twelfth centuries, the Karaite population began to shift geographically. The Turcoman invasion of Syria (1071–1074) and then the Christian victory in the First Crusade (1099) all but ended Jewish settlement—Rabbanite and Karaite alike—in Palestine. While the Cairo community remained intact—surviving *in situ* until the late twentieth century—it seems to have declined in prestige during the twelfth century. Meanwhile, the Karaites of Byzantium, who had imbibed the teachings of the Jerusalem school, emerged as a distinctive, independent community which created a substantial scholarly literature over the course of seven centuries (see below). Constantinople remained the leading Karaite center until the seventeenth century when it went into a steep decline. In Islamic Spain, on the other hand, the presence of Karaites elicited sharp reactions from leading twelfth-century Rabbanite scholars including Judah Halevi, Abraham Ibn ʿEzraʾ, and Avraham Ibn Daud. Likely because of their isolation from fellow-sectarians and this unrelenting Rabbanite opposition, the Andalusian Karaites seem to have vanished by the end of the twelfth century. New communities were emerging, however, in Eastern Europe. The Rabbanite traveler Petahyah of Regensburg (1180), mentions a scripturalist group he encountered in the Crimea who appear to have been Karaites; there is clear-cut evidence of a community there by the late thirteenth century. Settlements in Poland and the Ukraine may date to the thirteenth century; they were certainly established by the early fifteenth century, when the Lithuanian community in Troki (Trakai, near Vilnius) emerged as the European center of the sect.

There are large gaps in the Karaite historical record between the twelfth and early nineteenth centuries. For thirteenth- and fourteenth-century Byzantium, for example, the sole witnesses are Aaron ben Joseph the Physician and Aaron ben Elijah of Nicomedia, whose writings contain few contemporary references. Bio-bibliographic works, by David Ibn al-Hiti (fifteenth century), Mordecai ben Nisan (1699), Simḥah Isaac Lutski (1757), and others, provide the skeleton for a history of scholarship and are invaluable guides to Karaite self-perceptions and historical consciousness, but yield scant information about social, religious, and cultural developments. Travel accounts—by Karaites, Rabbanites, and non-Jews—correspondence, and topical treatises, on the other hand, give glimpses of communal life and concerns at specific moments. Thus, a dispute with Rabbanites in Cairo (1465) or an internal controversy in Constantinople over Sabbath lights (late fifteenth–early sixteenth centuries) are relatively well documented, while basic data concerning both communities in subsequent decades are lacking. All the same, certain generalizations seem warranted. Not infrequently, Karaite and Rabbanite communities existed in close proximity. Usually, the Christian and Muslim authorities did not differentiate between the two groups, regarding them both as Jews. Since Karaite populations almost invariably seem to have been smaller, they tended to remain on correct, if somewhat distant terms with their Rabbanite brethren. In one striking exception to this pattern, several Karaite scholars in mid-fifteenth-century Constantinople—including Elijah Bashyatchi, Caleb Afendopolo, and Judah Gibbor—studied with an eminent Rabbanite teacher, Mordecai Comtino. Typically, teacher and disciples treated each other with respect, while attacking each other's legal views vigorously.

In general, conversions from one group to the other seem to have been relatively rare. The anti-Karaite polemic of some Rabbanite authors is merely theoretical, and is not grounded in any actual fear of defection to the Karaite cause. Moses Maimonides (Mosheh ben Maimon, 1135/8–1204), the most outstanding Jewish scholar of the medieval period, summed up the Rabbanite attitude by advising reserved but helpful behavior toward Karaites as fellow Jews, albeit wayward ones, so long as they desisted from hostile attacks on Rabbanite dogma and practice.

In the seventeenth century, the Karaite communities in the Crimea, Lithuania, and Poland assumed the leading role. By the end of the eighteenth century, these communities had all come under Russian rule. In the nineteenth century, several energetic leaders succeeded in obtaining from the tsarist government full citizenship rights for Karaites; this set them even further apart from the Rabbanite majority in Russia, which continued to bear the full weight of the oppressive and discriminatory anti-Jewish laws.

World War I affected the Russian Karaites only where they found themselves directly in the way of military operations. During World War II, the Karaites in the occupied territories of Poland and western Russia were generally not molested by the German authorities, on the ground—generously supported by Rabbanite representatives consulted by the Germans—that they were ethnically not Jewish but rather were descended from the ancient Turkic nation of the Khazars, converts to Judaism who once ruled southern Russia. These Karaites were therefore not subject to wholesale extermination, as were their Rabbanite brethren. The nineteenth-century campaign to achieve independent, official recognition and the generally negative attitude in Russia after the 1917 revolution toward religion in general and Judaism in particular, led Karaites in the U.S.S.R. to distance themselves entirely from Jewish history, religion, and culture. In the Middle East after 1945, the Arab-Israeli conflict had a serious effect on the Karaite communities in the neighboring Arab states. Owing to emigration, the ancient community of Hīt, in Iraq, ceased to exist, and the equally ancient community in Cairo was vastly reduced when most of its members moved to Israel, Europe, and the Americas. At present, there are perhaps twenty-five thousand Karaites in the world (in Israel, Eastern and Western Europe, and the United States), though no truly reliable statistics exist.

KARAITE LITERATURE. Fragments of ʿAnan's code of law have survived in the original Aramaic. Both in language and in style, the work bears strong affinities to classical rabbinic texts. Benjamin al-Nahāwandī and Daniel al-Qūmisī also wrote codes, and al-Qūmisī composed the earliest surviving

Jewish Bible commentaries; these works were all written in Hebrew. Between the tenth and fifteenth centuries, Karaite scholars in Muslim lands produced an extensive religious literature in Arabic. In Asia Minor, the Crimea, and Poland-Lithuania, the Karaite language of scholarship between the eleventh and twentieth centuries was Hebrew. Beginning in the fifteenth century, the Karaites of Eastern Europe and the Crimea also wrote in their vernacular Turkic dialects.

The first major scholar of the golden age of Karaite literature was Yaʿqūb al-Qirqisānī (second quarter of the tenth century), whose magnum opus is a two-part Arabic commentary on the Pentateuch. The first part, titled *Kitāb al-anwār wa'l-marāqib* (Book of light-houses and watchtowers), comments on the legal parts of the Pentateuch and forms not only a detailed code of Karaite law but also a veritable encyclopedia of early Karaite lore. The second part, *Kitāb al-riyāḍ wa'l-ḥadā'iq* (Book of gardens and parks), deals with the nonlegal portions of the Pentateuch. Al-Qirqisānī also wrote an extensive commentary on *Genesis* that seems to have dealt in detail with various philosophical problems, such as the nature of God and of matter, creation *ex nihilo,* and good and evil. Of all his works, only *Kitāb al-anwār* has been published in full. In the tenth and eleventh centuries, Karaite scholars connected with the academy in Jerusalem produced a number of important works, mostly in Arabic, in the areas of exegesis, philology, theology, law, apologetics, and polemics. Among the most important authors were Salmon ben Yeruḥīm (a polemicist and exegete), Japheth ben Eli (the first Jew to compose commentaries on the entire Bible), Sahl ben Maṣliaḥ (an exegete, legal scholar, and polemicist), David al-Fāsī (a lexicographer), Joseph ben Noah (president of the Jerusalem academy), Abu'l-Faraj Hārūn (Hebrew: Aaron ben Jeshua; a grammarian and exegete), Yūsuf al-Baṣīr (Hebrew: Joseph ha-Ro'eh; an eminent theologian), and Abu'l-Furqān ibn Asad (Hebrew: Jeshua ben Judah; an exegete and legal authority).

With the growth of the Greek-speaking community in Asia Minor, it became necessary to translate the Karaite Arabic classics into Hebrew, the literary language of Byzantine Jewry. Translators such as Tobiah ben Moses and Jacob ben Simeon produced Hebrew versions which are notable for their awkward syntax, strange technical vocabulary, and Greek glosses. In the twelfth century, a more natural Hebrew style appears in an extensive encyclopedia of Karaite scholarship begun in 1148 by Judah Hadassi and titled *Eshkol ha-kofer* (Cluster of henna), and in Jacob ben Reuben's terse Bible commentary. By the late thirteenth century, the Karaites of Byzantium were writing a fluent Andalusian Rabbanite Hebrew. Drawing upon Maimonides and Abraham Ibn ʿEzra', Aaron ben Joseph wrote a philosophical commentary on the Pentateuch; he is best known, however, as the redactor of the official Karaite liturgy. Subsequently, Aaron ben Elijah (d. 1369), composed an invaluable trilogy: *ʿEṣ ḥayyim* (The tree of life), a Karaite *Guide of the Perplexed; Gan ʿEden* (The Garden of Eden), a code of law; and *Keter torah* (The crown of the Torah), a commentary on the Pentateuch. Elijah Bashyatchi (d. 1490) and his brother-in-law Caleb Afendopolo (d. after 1522) compiled another code, *Adderet Eliyyahu* (The mantle of Elijah), which became the most esteemed legal manual among modern Karaites. A versatile scholar, Afendopolo indexed older books (such as *Eshkol ha-kofer* and *ʿEṣ ḥayyim*), wrote scientific works, and composed Hebrew belles-lettres. A contemporary, Judah Gibbor, composed an important Pentateuch commentary in verse, which was the subject of later Karaite supercommentaries. Other authors of note include Moses Bashyatchi (d. 1572?), who incorporated Arabic citations of al-Qirqisānī into his own treatises, Moses Messorodi, who composed an important collection of sermons, and Elijah Yerushalmi (d. c. 1700), who sought to bring traditional Karaite learning from Constantinople to the Crimea.

Egypt produced a few important Karaite authors. Born in Alexandria, Moses Darʿī (thirteenth century?) was the group's preeminent Hebrew poet, writing an impressive body of secular verse in the style of the great Andalusiams. In the fifteenth century, Samuel al-Maghribī wrote the last known Arabic code of Karaite law and a popular set of homilies on the Pentateuch, while David Ibn al-Hītī composed a brief but important chronicle of Arabic scholars from ʿAnan down to his own time. Moses ben Samuel produced a corpus of Hebrew poetry, including an epic account of his tribulations in the service of the emir of Damascus, who in 1354 forced him to become a Muslim and to join a pilgrimage to Mecca. He finally escaped to Egypt, where he seems to have returned to his ancestral faith.

As the Ottoman Empire progressively declined, the center of Karaite literary activity again shifted northward, to the Crimea, Lithuania, and Poland. The Karaite community of Troki counted as one of its most illustrious sons Isaac ben Abraham Troki (d. 1594, or perhaps 1586), the author of a critical tract against Christianity titled *Ḥizzuq emunah* (Fortification of the faith), which was later admired by Voltaire. In the seventeenth and eighteenth centuries, a group of Protestant theologians (Rittangel, Peringer, Puffendorf, Warner, Trigland) drew parallels between the Karaite secession from the Rabbanite synagogue and the Protestant secession from the Church of Rome. They encouraged the composition of several works by Polish Karaite informants, including Mordecai ben Nisan of Kukizów (near Lviv, in Polish Galicia) and Solomon ben Aaron of Troki (d. 1745), which set forth their view of Karaite history, dogma, and ritual. Simḥah Isaac ben Moses of Lutsk (d. 1766) composed the first substantial Karaite literary history.

In the nineteenth century, the outstanding Karaite man of letters was Abraham Firkovitch (1786–1874), who during his travels in the Crimea, the Caucasus, Syria, Palestine, and Egypt amassed a large collection of Karaite manuscripts, one of the richest in the world, now in the Russian National Library in St. Petersburg. He was also a prolific writer, although the authenticity of many historical data he cited from colophons and from tombstones has been rejected. An older contemporary of his, Mordecai Sultansky (d. 1862), wrote several works, among them a history of Karaite Judaism, *Zekher ṣaddiqim* (Memorial of the righteous), valuable mainly as an exposition of the modern official version, authorized by the leading circles of the Russian-Polish-Lithuanian community.

During the twentieth century, several members of the Egyptian community were active authors: Mourad Farag (1867–1956), a jurist and poet; Tobiah Babovitch (1879–1956), the last Karaite Chief Hakham (Rabbi) in Cairo; Mourad El-Kodsi (1919–), a communal historian; and Yoseph El-Gamil (1943–), a historian and editor of texts.

The invention of printing with movable type was eagerly seized upon by Rabbanite Jews to produce an enormous library of religious and secular literature from the 1470s down to the present day. On the Karaite side the picture is quite different. No Karaite incunabula were printed, and only four Karaite books—the first, an edition of the Karaite liturgy, published by the Christian bookmaker Daniel Bomberg in Venice in 1528–1529—appeared in the sixteenth century, all set in type and run off the press by Rabbanite compositors and pressmen. Only one Karaite book came out in the seventeenth century, printed in 1643 at the Amsterdam press of Menasseh ben Israel, a Rabbanite scholar and publisher known also for his negotiations with Lord Protector Oliver Cromwell on the readmission of Jews into England. The earliest Karaite presses were those of the brothers Afeda and Shabbetai Yeraqa in Istanbul (1733) and in Chufut-Kale, in the Crimea (1734–1741); there was also another press in Chufut-Kale (1804–1806). They were short-lived and succeeded in publishing only a few books. The first more or less successful Karaite press was established in 1833 in Eupatoria (or Gözlöw), in the Crimea, and published several important old texts.

One can only guess at the reason for the typographical backwardness of the modern Karaites. One factor was very likely their historical dislike of innovative change. Their limited number and the comparative paucity of prospective purchasers and interested readers among them probably also made printing unprofitable unless supported from time to time by a wealthy patron from their own midst. In recent years, however, the Karaites in Israel have issued a large number of texts; some are photomechanical reproductions of nineteenth-century prints, but many more have been newly set and published by Yoseph El-Gamil.

Dogma and Practice. Karaite Judaism is epistemologically grounded in scripture and reason. During its formative period, it borrowed its theology wholesale from the teachings of the Muslim Mutazilites of Basra. The Karaite Yūsuf al-Baṣīr (d. c. 1040) and his Rabbanite contemporary Samuel ben Hophni Gaon thus shared common views on many doctrinal points. While Rabbanite scholars distanced themselves from Mutazilite theories, successively embracing Neoplatonism and then Aristotelianism, the Karaites held fast to their old theology until the thirteenth and fourteenth centuries. In his *ʿEṣ ḥayyim,* Aaron ben Elijah actually attempts to synthesize the *kalām* teachings of Yūsuf al-Baṣīr with Maimonidean Aristotelianism. Although the experiment cannot be said to have succeeded in full, it remained influential within the Byzantine Karaite camp.

In his code of law, *Adderet Eliyahu,* Elijah Bashyatchi formulated the Karaite creed in ten articles, corresponding to the Ten Commandments: (1) that the physical universe was created; (2) that it was created by God, who is eternal; (3) that the Creator has no form and is unique; (4) that He sent Moses, His prophet; (5) that He sent the Torah, which is perfect, with Moses; (6) that the believer must know Hebrew, the language of the Torah; (7) that God inspired all other true prophets who came after Moses; (8) that God will resurrect the Dead on the Day of Judgment; (9) that God rewards and punishes all human beings according to their deserts; (10) that God has not abandoned the people in exile, and that though they suffer, they must anticipate the coming of the Messiah who will effect the divine salvation. No Rabbanite could find any of this objectionable.

Where the two groups have always differed, however, is in their attitude toward the postbiblical (Talmudic and rabbinic) tradition: for Rabbanites, the Oral Law is of Mosaic origin and mediates the understanding of Scripture; for Karaites it is at best a body of non-authoritative knowledge, and at worst a malignant, man-made fabrication. But even the rejection of the rabbinic tradition has turned out to be not quite absolute, for with the passage of time, changing conditions have forced the formation of a native Karaite tradition in order to cope with new situations and problems that were not anticipated by Moses the lawgiver. Hence the development of the three pillars of Karaite legislation: (1) the scriptural text (Heb., *katuv;* Arab., *naṣṣ*); (2) analogy (Heb., *heqesh;* Arab., *qiyās*) based on scripture; and, in cases where the first two pillars are of no help, (3) the consensus of scholarly opinion (Hebrew *qibbuṣ* or *ʿedah,* "community," the latter term possibly influenced by the Arabic *ʿādah,* "customary practice, common law"; Arabic *ijmāʿ,* "agreement"; later termed in Hebrew *sevel ha-yerushah,* "burden of inheritance").

Consequently, the Karaites and Rabbanites finally part ways in their religious practices, and here the differences are substantial and fundamental. For the Jewish calendar, which governs the fixing of the dates of holy days, the Karaites rejected the rabbinic mathematical reckoning and depended solely on the observation of the phases of the moon; only comparatively recently was limited reckoning admitted. In dietary law, the scriptural interdict against seething a kid's flesh in its mother's milk was not broadened (as it was in rabbinic law) to cover all meat and dairy foods. In the law of consanguinity, the Karaites originally followed the so-called catenary (chain) theory (Heb., *rikkuv;* Arab., *tarkīb*), which permitted piling analogy upon analogy to deduce further forbidden marriages from those explicitly listed in scripture.

The social consequences of this practice finally became so threatening to the physical survival of the Karaite community that Jeshua ben Judah succeeded in modifying it, although the Karaites still employ a much more extensive definition of consanguinity than the Rabbanites do. This remains, however, the only instance of a major reform in Karaite law. The scriptural prohibition of kindling fire on the Sabbath day is interpreted literally to mean the total absence of all fire, even if kindled before the onset of the Sabbath and left to continue burning, as permitted by rabbinic law. The modest relaxation of this rule in the Byzantine, Crimean, and Eastern European communities, where the absence of light and heat throughout the cold and sunless winters inflicted real hardship, aroused strong opposition. Other differences relate to ritual cleanness—particularly rigorous for Karaite women—inheritance (the Karaite husband has no claim upon his deceased wife's estate), and various dietary laws. Polygyny is not officially prohibited—as it was by a medieval European rabbinical enactment recently extended to eastern Jewries as well—but it seems to have been quite uncommon even in Muslim countries, probably for social and economic reasons; in Western countries it was, of course, outlawed and was recognized as such by Jewish law. The Karaite liturgy, originally limited to selected biblical psalms and prose passages, was eventually developed into a large corpus of both prose and verse—some written by Rabbanite poets—quite distinct from the Rabbanite one.

The connection between the Karaites and Sadducees, suggested by some early Rabbanite polemicists, or between the Karaites and the Qumran sect, as advanced by some modern scholars, remains hypothetical. Similarities in some observances may be nothing more than earmarks of the age-old continuous chain of dissent in Judaism. (The outstanding example, the rule that Shavuʿot must always fall on a Sunday, seems to be one of the oldest points in Jewish dissent.) Verbal parallels between certain early Karaite writings and the Dead Sea Scrolls are more suggestive. The chief stumbling block here is the hiatus of some five hundred years between the Sadducees and the Qumran community on the one hand, and the earliest known Karaites on the other. The most that can safely be said at present is that the primitive Karaites may possibly have had access to some Sadducee or Qumranite literary documents. Whether they have been influenced by them, and if so, to what extent, cannot yet be determined.

Bibliography

The modern critical study of Karaite Judaism dates back about a century and a half. Until recently, very few scholars devoted their full attention to the subject, despite the existence of a large and extremely important Karaite literature which remains in manuscript, awaiting publication and analysis. Certain aspects of Karaite history—for example, the role of social and economic factors—have only now begun to attract interest. Many of the older works retain their basic value, but require updating. Fortunately, the situation seems to be changing. During the past two decades, there has been growing interest in Judeo-Arabic literature generally, and Karaite writings in particular. Since 1989, moreover, the great collections of Karaite manuscripts in St. Petersburg at the Russian National Library (RNL) and the Institute of Oriental Studies have become accessible. The RNL manuscripts, which had been assembled by Abraham Firkovitch during the nineteenth century, are now being catalogued for the first time. They will serve as the basis for a comprehensive rewriting of early Karaite history and literature. At the same time, Karaite texts in Hebrew from Byzantium, the Crimea, and Eastern Europe are now being studied critically and analyzed in their proper contexts. Despite their historically small numbers, the Karaites, their forms of belief and practice, and their place in Jewish history, are now beginning to receive the attention they deserve.

Ankori, Zvi. *Karaites in Byzantium: The Formative Years, 970–1100.* New York, 1959.

Astren, Fred. *Karaite Past and Jewish History.* Columbia, S.C., 2004.

Baron, Salo W. *A Social and Religious History of the Jews.* 2d ed. 18 vols. New York and Philadelphia, 1952–1983, 5: 209–285.

Ben-Shammai, Haggai. "The Karaite Controversy: Scripture and Tradition in Early Karaism." In *Religionsgespräche im Mittelalter,* edited by Bernard Lewis and Friedrich Niewöhner, pp. 11–26. Wiesbaden, Germany, 1992.

Birnbaum, Phillip, ed. *Karaite Studies.* New York, 1971.

El-Kodsi, Mourad. *The Karaite Jews of Egypt, 1882–1986.* Lyons, N.Y., 1987.

Frank, Daniel. "The Study of Medieval Karaism, 1989–1999." In *Hebrew Scholarship and the Medieval World,* edited by Nicholas De Lange, pp. 3–22. New York, 2001.

Frank, Daniel. *Search Scripture Well: Karaite Exegetes and the Origins of the Jewish Bible Commentary in the Islamic East.* Leiden, 2004.

Gil, Moshe. *A History of Palestine, 634–1099.* Cambridge, U.K., 1992. See pages 777–820.

Goldberg, P. Selvin. *Karaite Liturgy and Its Relation to Synagogue Worship.* Manchester, U.K., 1957.

Lasker, Daniel J. "Karaism in Twelfth-Century Spain." *Journal of Jewish Thought and Philosophy* 1 (1992): 179–195.

Mann, Jacob. *Texts and Studies in Jewish History and Literature,* vol. 2: *Karaitica.* Philadelphia, 1935; reprint, New York, 1972.

Miller, Philip E. *Karaite Separatism in Nineteenth-Century Russia: Joseph Solomon Lutski's Epistle of Israel's Deliverance.* Cincinnati, 1993.

Nemoy, Leon. *Karaite Anthology.* New Haven, Conn., 1952.

Olszowy-Schlanger, Judith. *Karaite Marriage Documents from the Cairo Geniza: Legal Tradition and Community Life in Mediaeval Egypt and Palestine.* Leiden, 1998.

Polliack, Meira. *The Karaite Tradition of Arabic Bible Translation: A Linguistic and Exegetical Study of Karaite Translations of the Pentateuch from the Tenth to the Eleventh Centuries.* Leiden, 1997.

Polliack, Meira, ed. *Karaite Judaism: A Guide to Its History and Literary Sources.* Leiden, 2003.

Poznanski, Samuel. "The Karaite Literary Opponents of Saadiah Gaon." Originally published in the *Jewish Quarterly Review*, old series vols. 18–20 (1906–1908), reprinted, London, 1908; reprinted again in *Karaite Studies*, edited by Phillip Birnbaum (see above).

Rustow, Marina. "Rabbanite-Karaite Relations in Fatimid Egypt and Syria: A Study Based on Documents from the Cairo Geniza." Ph.D. diss, Columbia University, New York, 2004.

Vajda, Georges. *Al-Kitāb al-Muhtawī de Yūsuf al-Basīr.* Edited by David R. Blumenthal. Leiden, 1985.

Wieder, Naphtali. *The Judean Scrolls and Karaism.* London, 1962.

LEON NEMOY (1987)
DANIEL FRANK (2005)

KARBALA, a city located sixty-five miles southwest of Baghdad, constitutes the pivot of devotion for more than a hundred million Shīʿī Muslims. Although the estimated population of this palm-grove-laden city is approximately 500,000, during seasons of pilgrimage it draws more than a million devotees. The city owes its significance to the battle that was waged on its soil in 680 CE between Ḥus b. ʿAli, the younger grandson of the prophet Muḥammad, and Yazid b. Muʾawiya, the ruling head of the Ummayad dynasty at the time. During the battle, Ḥusayn and a small group of followers and family members were killed by the forces of Yazid after refusing to acknowledge the latter as a legitimate authority. Ḥusayn, for his devotees, has remained the most significant martyr of Islam, *Sayyid al-shuhada*, and Karbala, the site of this martyrdom, *Mashhad al-Ḥusyan.* For the Shīʿī Muslims, Ḥusayn is also one of the legitimate spiritual leaders (*imāms*) of the community, who protected Islam from decay. Notwithstanding his significance in Shīʿī piety, Ḥusayn and his Karbala battle have also had a strong appeal in various Sunnī, Ṣūfī, and non-Muslim contexts.

Although the etymology of Karbala is most likely rooted in Aramaic and Assyrian, in the Shīʿī devotional lore it is invoked as a combination of two Arabic words, *karb* (anguish) and *balā* (calamity). In all likelihood Karbala rose in the devotional hierarchy of Ḥusayn's followers right after his martyrdom in 680 CE. That the Prophet had loved his grandson and bestowed upon him various honorific titles was never doubted in the Muslim world. After the battle of Karbala, Ḥusayn's family members and friends journeyed to the site of his martyrdom and burial, commencing the cherished tradition of *ziyārah* (pilgrimage to a sacred site) to Karbala. The high season of pilgrimage has remained around the day that marks Ḥusayn's martyrdom (*ʿāshura*, tenth day of the first Islamic month, Muḥarram) and the fortieth-day commemoration of this martyrdom (*arbaʿen*, forty days after *ʿāshura*).

Pilgrims to Ḥusayn's grave also make the rounds of graves of other companions of Ḥusayn, especially his half-brother ʿAbbās. Prescribed prayers and lamentation accompany the pilgrims as many wish that they had fought alongside Ḥusayn. The soil and clay from Karbala acquires a remedial touch and is fashioned into tablets upon which Shīʿah prostrate during their prayers. Not only do Shīʿah wish to make a pilgrimage to Karbala in their lifetime, many also aspire to be buried in Karbala. Corpses of devotees from all over Asia and Africa have been sent to Karbala in order to atone for a sinful life and secure for the deceased an enduring stamp of redemption. Some Shīʿah have devotionally conceded that a pilgrimage to Karbala is more meritorious than the pilgrimage to Mecca (*ḥājj*). Karbala along with its sister city Najaf (where Ḥusayn's father and the first Shīʿī *imām*, ʿAlī ibn Abī Ṭālib, is buried), and the two Iranian cities of Qom and Mashhad, also house important centers of Shīʿī learning (*madrasahs* or *hawzas*). Students from Iraq, Iran, Lebanon, Syria, India and Pakistan make up most of the student body at these institutions.

In the course of a millennium and three centuries, Karbala changed hands many times. As a center of Shīʿī piety, it was often seen by Sunnī political authorities as a threat to their rule. The ʿAbbāsid caliph, al-Mutawakkil, for example, had Ḥusyan's shrine destroyed in 850 CE. Severe restrictions were placed on the pilgrims who desired to visit Karbala. The Shīʿī Buyid rulers who wrested power from the ʿAbbāsids restored the architectural as well as the devotional aura to Karbala. Subsequent generations of Shīʿī Muslims, from Iran to India, festooned the shrines of Karbala with golden and silver sarcophaguses, expensive chandeliers and carpets, and exquisite tile work and ornamentation. The endowments for the maintenance of the Karbala shrines came not only from the Shīʿī rulers of Iran and India but also from the Sunnī Ottoman leaders who ruled over this region from the sixteenth to the twentieth centuries. Many times during these four centuries, the Ottoman rulers and their Shīʿī Safavid rivals from Iran sought to control Karbala in order to consolidate their respective political clout in the region. Karbala during this time remained a testimony to the riches of its patrons. In 1801, the Wahhābī forces, comprised of anti-Shīʿah and anti-shrine culture Sunnī Muslims, wreaked havoc on various pilgrimage sites and killed scores of inhabitants of this city. But as in the past, Ḥusyan's devotees from around the world once again garnered resources to restore the regal aura to the shrines. In 1919, after the defeat of the Ottomans, Iraq came under the British mandate. At the 1921 Cairo Conference, the British named Prince Faisal, a Mecca-based Sunnī descendant of the Prophet, as Iraq's ruler. In 1932 the nation-state of Iraq was born amidst much dismay and contested geographical borders. These borders, mostly drawn at the discretion of the British, have continued to remain the cause of several political conflicts in the Arab world. Various ethnic groups living in the newly created nation state of Iraq, including the Kurds and the Shīʿah (who are a majority) felt disenfranchised at various levels. Such a feeling was compounded by the policies of various leaders, most notably Ṣaddām Ḥusayn. Ruling from 1979 to 2003 as Iraq's president, Ṣaddām Ḥusayn, dealt brutally with any challenge to his authority. To assure that the Shīʿī majority of the country was in check, Ḥusayn imposed severe restrictions on the cultural practices of the city of Karbala. Prominent Shīʿī opponents of the Iraqi government were killed, put under surveillance, or driven into exile as Ṣaddām Ḥusayn and his Baath Party created a climate of intimidation. Life in Karbala only got worse after the beginning of the eight-year Iraq-Iran war in 1980. This war, in which Iraq was supported in part by the United States, drained Iran and Iraq of valuable resources and especially devastated the city of Karbala, which was economically dependent to a great degree on the Iranian pilgrims. Ṣaddām Ḥusayn imposed his presence on Karbala by lacing the walls of the Shīʿī shrines with his own pictures and forbidding large commemorative assemblies. These assemblies resurfaced after Ṣaddām Ḥusayn was defeated by the United States and its allies in 2003. Over a million Shīʿah marked the day of Ḥusyan's martyrdom in 2004 by walking in the pathos-laden processions at Karbala. The Shīʿī sense of relief after the fall of Ṣaddām Ḥusayn, however, quickly gave way to dismay as the U.S. armed forces battled anti-American elements in Karbala, causing many deaths. Not withstanding a long history of conflict, Karbala is likely to retain its importance as a center of pilgrimage and scholarship.

Karbala, apart from standing as a bustling pilgrimage city, also holds status as a metaphor for a righteous struggle. Although physically contained in Iraq, its spiritual, aesthetic and political ramifications transcend geographical confines and narrow religious allegiances. It has inspired traditions of theater (the *taʿziyah* of Iran), paintings and modern political movements of Lebanon, Iran, Central Asia and South Asia. It has spoken to a wide range of reformist and revolutionary yearnings from a variety of traditions, including those of the Ayatollah Khomeini, Muhammad Iqbal and Mohandas Gandhi. To those drawn to Karbala as a metaphor and trope, it seems to provide testimony to the sentiment that numerical strength does not necessarily insure a spiritual and moral victory. In spite of suffering at the hands of Yazīd's massive force, Ḥusayn and his small band of companions secured enduring legacies through the rich idioms of Karbala.

SEE ALSO Shiism.

BIBLIOGRAPHY

Al-Serat: Papers from the Imam Ḥusayn Conference, London, July 1984. London, 1986.

Ayoub, Mahmoud. *Redemptive Suffering in Islam, a Study of the Devotional Aspects of ʿAshuraʾ in Twelver Shiʿism.* Religion and Society Series, No.10. The Hague, 1978.

Chelkowski, Peter J. ed. *Taʿziyeh: Ritual and Drama in Iran.* New York, 1979.

Cole, J. R. I. *Roots of North Indian Shiism in Iran and Iraq: Religion and State in Awadh, 1722–1859.* Delhi, 1989.

Fischer, Michael M. J. *Iran, from Religious Dispute to Revolution.* Cambridge, Mass., 1980.

Halawi, Majed. *A Lebanon Defied: Musa al-Sadr and the Shīʿah Community.* Boulder, Colo., 1992.

Korom, Frank. *Hosay Trinidad: Muharram Performances in an Indo-Caribbean Diaspora.* Philadelphia, 2003.

Mottahedeh, Roy. *The Mantle of the Prophet: Religion and Politics in Iran.* New York, 1985.

Nakash, Yitzhak. *The Shiʿis of Iraq.* Princeton, N.J., 1994.

Tripp, Charles. *A History of Iraq.* Cambridge, U.K., 2000.

SYED AKBAR HYDER (2005)

KARDECISM is the name given the system of spiritist doctrines and practices codified by the French spiritist Allan Kardec. Kardec's religio-philosophical principles and therapeutic techniques have been especially influential in the development of spiritism among the urban middle classes in Brazil from the mid-nineteenth century until the present.

KARDEC'S LIFE AND WORK. Allan Kardec was born Hyppolyte Léon Denizard Rivail on October 3, 1804, in Lyons, France. The son of Justice Jean-Baptiste Antoine Rivail and Jeanne Duhamel, Rivail received a thorough education. Descended on his father's side from a family of magistrates, and on his mother's side from a family of theologians, writers, and mathematicians, Rivail was sent as a boy to Switzerland, to study under the famous pedagogue Henri Pestalozzi. He distinguished himself with his intelligence and precocity: At fourteen, Rivail had a command of several languages and was conversant in Greek and Latin.

Having received training as a teacher, he returned to Paris, and earned a bachelor's degree in sciences and letters. According to some of his biographers, Rivail concluded the course in medicine at twenty-four years of age. During his studies, he taught French, mathematics, and sciences. Having failed at his attempt to create a teaching institution after Pestalozzi's model, he survived by doing translations and teaching courses at schools and institutes. Notwithstanding his medical studies, the eight books written from 1824 to 1849 deal with mathematics, grammar, and the physical sciences in general, in which his pedagogical concerns prevail. He joined several professional, pedagogical, and scientific associations.

In short, Rivail was a typical European scholar of his time, with a classical training in letters, positivist beliefs, an interest in the theoretical and applied development of science, and a professional specialization in teaching. But Rivail was not an orthodox positivist. Imbued with a great curiosity about phenomena unheeded and even shunned by official science, he belonged to the French Society of Magnetists. Hypnotism, sleepwalking, clairvoyance, and similar phenomena strongly attracted him. He studied them as physical phenomena resulting from unknown causes, an approach resulting from his being a follower of the theory of animal magnetism, called Mesmerism, expounded by Franz Anton Mesmer (1734–1815).

Magnetism brought Rivail in contact with spiritism. He was by then fifty-one years old and had consolidated his scientific background. In the years 1854 and 1855, the so-called turning table and talking table invaded Europe from the United States and created an intense curiosity. Several people would sit around a table, hand in hand, in a state of mental concentration; after a certain lapse of time, the table would begin to rotate, to produce noises, and even to answer, in code, questions proposed by the participants. This practice became quite a fad, especially in the more elegant circles. Rivail was introduced by magnetist friends to such sessions, which were already accepted by their promoters as demonstrations of spiritual phenomena. He was initially skeptical about their authenticity but was soon to revise his opinion. Under his supervision, the sessions were no longer dedicated to frivolous consultations and guessing games but became serious study sessions.

Rivail considered such phenomena both relevant and natural, though invisible, and believed one should adopt a "positivist and not an idealist" attitude toward them. If the conditions in which such phenomena manifested themselves hindered the use of common scientific instrumentation, he believed that one should at least employ the scientific method of "observation, comparison, and evaluation."

Inspired by his own experiences, stimulated by illustrious spiritists who supplied him with fifty notebooks containing messages from the souls of deceased persons, and guided by the spirits that conferred on him the role of codifier of spiritism, Rivail became Allan Kardec; he adopted this pen name under the inspiration of one of his guiding spirits, who revealed that it had been his name in a former incarnation, in which he had been a druid in ancient Gaul. In 1857 he published his fundamental work, *Le livre des esprits,* which contained 501 questions answered by the spirits themselves. By the time of its twenty-second and definitive edition, the number of questions had grown to 1,019.

Thereafter followed his other works: *Qu'est-ce-que le spiritisme?* (1859); *Le livre des médiums* (1861); *Refutation aux critiques au spiritisme* (1862); *L'évangile selon le spiritisme* (1864); *Le ciel et l'enfer, ou La justice divine selon le spiritisme* (1865); and *La genèse, les miracles et les predictions* (1868). The literature further includes his *Œuvres posthumes,* published in 1890, and an incalculable number of articles published over a period of eleven years in the *Spiritist Journal,* issued by the Parisian Society for Spiritist Studies that had been founded by Kardec in 1858 and of which he was the chairman to his death in 1869.

Kardecism, as codified by Kardec, defines the spiritist doctrine in this way: There are souls, or spirits, of deceased persons that are capable of communication with the living through mediumistic phenomena. They belong to an invisible but natural world; there is no discussion of magic, miracles, and the supernatural in Kardecism. This invisible and nonmaterial world is, as part of the natural world, susceptible to experimentation, but, unlike the natural world, it is eternal and preexistent and is identified with goodness, purity, and wisdom. There is a spiritual hierarchy ranging from that most closely identified with the material plane (and hence with evil, impurity, and ignorance) up to that of spiritual fullness.

God is the primary cause that generates the material and the spiritual; the spirits are engendered by him, and although they receive a mission and submit to the law of constant progress, they are endowed with free will. Spirits continually progress toward perfection, and they fulfill their missions through successive reincarnations, not only on earth (considered a planet of atonement) but also on other worlds. The law of cause and effect explains human happiness or misfortune as consequences of good or evil practiced in previous incarnations. Christian charity is the supreme virtue (Christ is considered the most elevated spirit that has ever incarnated) that makes spiritual evolution possible; it is closely followed in importance by the virtue of wisdom. As the locus of the activity of the developing but morally free spirits and as the product of evolution, the social world, even with its injustices and inequalities, is seen as ultimately just, and the search for perfection is ruled by individualistic ethics.

It is a rather curious fact that Kardec remained practically unknown for a long time outside French spiritist circles. Approximately sixty years after his death, Arthur Conan Doyle, as chairman of the London Spiritist League and honorary chairman of the International Spiritist Federation, only devoted a few scanty pages to Kardec in one of the twenty-five chapters of his comprehensive *History of Spiritualism* (1926). There seem to be two related reasons for this obscurity: British spiritism did not accept the idea of reincarnation, and, except in France, Kardec's claim to be the true codifier of spiritism by virtue of a mission entrusted to him by the spirits was not readily accepted. Although this role currently tends to be universally accepted by spiritists, the name of Kardec (or Rivail) is not mentioned in the main European encyclopedias, and he remains known only within spiritist circles.

Kardecism in Brazil. Originally introduced in Brazil in the middle of the nineteenth century in the form of "talking tables," spiritism mainly attracted teachers, lawyers, physicians, and other intellectuals. One of the reasons for its appeal was the pseudoscientific character of Kardecism. Kardecist groups were soon organized, first in Bahia (1865), and later in Rio de Janeiro (1873, where the Brazilian Spiritist Federation was created in the following year), São Paulo (1883), and gradually throughout the entire country. Kardecism was already attracting large sectors of the urban middle class.

Although Kardec did not consider spiritism a religion (but rather a philosophy of science with religious implications), Kardecism in Brazil was soon to take on a religious character, centering on the idea of charity, which led to therapeutical practices such as the "pass." Kardecism followed the same pattern of evolution as positivism, which had already become a religion in Brazil, with an organized church and cult.

The 1940 and 1950 censuses in Brazil showed an intense expansion of spiritism: Though its adherents did not exceed 2 percent of the population in 1950, it was growing at a much more rapid pace than any other religion, including Catholicism, the unofficial but dominant creed (then adhered to by about 90 percent of Brazil's people). For this reason, the Catholic Church initiated an antispiritist campaign during the fifties.

A distinguishing feature of Brazilian spiritism is the fact that it is an almost exclusively urban phenomenon. In these regions, however, Kardecism is not the only spiritist current that manifests itself. Another trend is that of Umbanda spiritism, a syncretic product of Afro-Brazilian religions under the influence of Kardecism. While Kardecism proper tends to be a religion of those of the urban middle classes who have been city-dwellers for several generations, drawing people who have a certain level of secular education and who are disposed to accept its pseudoscientific discourse, Umbanda remains a religion of the unschooled lower classes of more recent urbanization. Unlike Kardecism, Umbanda is still linked to a magical conception of the universe.

Currently, Kardecism and Umbanda encompass significant population groups in Brazil. The censuses, however, do not register their extension, because both Kardecists and Umbandists often also declare themselves to be Catholics, especially for social purposes such as christenings, marriages, funerals, and statements given in official forms. In spite of the evident importance of spiritism in Brazil—an importance that is easily verified by other indicators (e.g., the medium Chico Xavier's book sales are exceeded only by those of the novelist Jorge Amado)—the census still reports the number of spiritists as approximately 2 percent.

Despite census data to the contrary, it seems fairly certain that Umbandists outnumber Kardecists in Brazil. Though until the forties Kardecism was predominant, in the sixties the situation was utterly reversed in favor of Umbanda. It should be noted, however, that the fifties mark the stage of the greatest penetration of Umbanda by Kardecism. Up to that time, Umbanda subsisted as a semiclandestine cult under severe and tyrannical police control. From 1953, many Kardecists, disenchanted with the prevailing intellectualism of their spiritist centers, turned to Umbanda. Under their leadership, federations were organized that grouped Umbanda adherents into units called "yards" and "tents," and these disenchanted Kardecists took over, in a less repressive and more persuasive fashion, the control that formerly had been exercised by the police. The price Umbanda had to pay for this protection was its adjustment to a rationalization and moralization of the cult—processes that were based on Kardecist models. One may therefore conclude that although Umbanda has grown much more rapidly than Kardecism over the last few decades, the influence of Kardecism in the context of Brazilian spiritism continues to remain strong.

See Also Afro-Brazilian Religions.

Bibliography

Sociological, anthropological, and historical studies on Kardecism are scarce. With respect to the historical aspects, one will search in vain for a single work by any specialist in the field; the only texts available are biographies of Kardec written by spiritist intellectuals. Among these the best are José Herculano Pires's *O espírito e o tempo: Introdução histórica ao espiritismo* (São Paulo, 1964), a scholarly and interesting work, and the voluminous book by Zeus Wantuil and Francisco Thiesen, *Allan Kardec, pesquisa bibliográfica e ensaios de interpretação,* 3 vols. (Rio de Janeiro, 1979–1980), which offers a comprehensive analysis and represents the official view of Brazilian Kardecism on the life and work of its inspirer.

Among sociological and anthropological studies, the following are worth mentioning: Cândido Procópio Ferreira de Camargo's *Kardecismo e Umbanda: Una interpretação sociológica* (São Paulo, 1961); Roger Bastide's article "Le spiritisme au Brésil," *Archives de sociologie des religions* 12 (1967): 3–16; and Maria Viveiros de Castro Cavalcanti's work, *O mundo invisiuel: Cosmologia, sistema ritual e noçao de tempo no espiritismo* (Rio de Janeiro, 1968). The first two are solid sociological analyses of Kardecism in Brazil, with Umbanda as a counterpoint; studies solely dedicated to Kardecism, such as Cavalcanti's interesting and lucid book on Kardecist cosmogony, are few and far between.

Finally, one can mention the doctoral dissertation of J. Parke Renshaw, "Sociological Analysis of Spiritism in Brazil" (University of Florida, 1969), which contains historical data and analyses, and Donald Warren, Jr.'s articles "The Portuguese Roots of Brazilian Spiritism," *Luso-Brazilian Review* 5 (December 1968): 3–33, and "Spiritism in Brazil" in *Journal of Inter-American Studies* 10 (1968): 393–405.

New Sources

Hess, David. *Spirits and Scientists: Ideology, Spiritism, and Brazilian Culture.* University Park, Pa., 1991.

Hess, David. *Samba in the Night.* New York, 1994.

Santos, José Luiz dos. *Espiritismo: Uma Religiã Brasileira.* São Paulo, 1997.

Wulfhorst, Ingo. Discernindo os Espíritos: O Desafio do Espiritismo Eda Religiosidade Afro-brasileira. São Leopoldo, Brazil, 1989.

Lisias Noguera Negrão (1987)
Revised Bibliography

KARELIAN RELIGION.

The term *Karelia* (Finnish, *Karjala*) has had different meanings throughout history. Historically, it was the borderland between Finland and Russia where most Karelians (Finnish, *karjalaiset*) lived. At present, it typically refers to specific areas in contemporary Russia and Finland.

Recent Russian-Finnish research—around Lake Ladoga and on the Karelian Isthmus, on the Elk and Guri Islands, in Bes Nos and other places on the shores of Lake Onega, around Uiku River, and in territories near the Kola Peninsula—has uncovered abundant archaeological evidence dating back to around 8000 BCE that indicates migrations by several indigenous peoples with an ethnic makeup different from today. Elk, snake, bear, swan, goose, and sturgeon motifs found on objects from graves and petroglyphs dating back to 5500 BCE provide hints of sacred histories, animal ceremonialism, and mythological pairings of man and animals.

The experience of living in a spatial and temporal borderland, and of being compelled to cross back and forth over various borders as the countries, cultures, and peoples around them change, has deeply affected Karelians. It has shaped their lifestyle, their worldview, and their religious history.

The Karelian language belongs to the Baltic Finnish group, and is closest to Finnish, with its "Karelian dialects" being spoken in the two eastern Finnish provinces of South Karelia (Etelä-Karjala) and North Karelia (Pohjois-Karjala). People living in the Autonomous Republic of Karelia in Russia speak five Baltic Finnish languages: Veps, Lude, and three forms of Karelian—Livvi or Onega, South, and Viena (Dvina) or White Sea Karelian. The Izhor *(inkeroiset)* population (consisting of around 1,000 people living in Ingria on the south coast of the Gulf of Finland) speaks a Karelian-related language.

Tver, Novgorod, and Pihkova Karelians are descendants of Orthodox refugees who escaped from Karelian and Ingrian territories around Lake Ladoga to remote settlements throughout Russia after the signing of the Stolbova Treaty of 1617, which allowed Sweden to annex the province of Ingria. This exodus left space for Lutheran settlers entering from Savo *(savakot)* and Karelia *(äyrämöiset)*. Lutheran identity became one of the main features of Ingrians, who endured Siberian exile after World War II, then relocated to Karelia, Estonia, and the district of St. Petersburg, and since 1990 to Finland, where around 25,000 Ingrians have entered as returnees. Today, their total population numbers around 100,000.

Throughout the course of the nineteenth and twentieth centuries, violent religiously based transfers, Russian colonization, and Soviet deportation policies kept the Karelian portion of the population small wherever Karelians lived. Karelian speakers in the Autonomous Republic of Karelia number less than 60,000, under 10 percent of the total population. A group of around 30,000 Tver Karelians are the strongest Karelian ethnic group in Russia, both demographically and culturally.

Karelian history has been shaped by both political and religious struggles between Eastern and Western power blocs within Northern Europe. Along with other territories occupied by indigenous peoples, such as Livonia, Vatja (Votes), Ingria, Estonia, Bjarmia, Scridfinnia, and so on, Karelia was divided between East and West—for the first time by the Pähkinänsaari Treaty of 1323, which split it between Sweden and Novgorod (Russia). Religiously, Karelia was a battleground between Western (Roman Catholic) and Eastern (Byzantine Greek Orthodox) churches. Wars won by the kingdom of Sweden brought the Lutheran faith to Karelia, and the religious border between East and West was accordingly moved eastward. As Finland remained Lutheran, Karelians with different faiths moved across the Russian-Finnish border repeatedly until 1809, when Finland was annexed by Czarist Russia.

The October 1917 Revolution both led to Finland's independence and brought new divisions into Karelian history. Some Karelian-speaking territories became part of Finland in the north (villages in Kuusamo, Suomussalmi, Kuhmo, Ilomantsi) and south (Border and Ladoga Karelia). Within the Karelian-speaking territory not ceded to Finland, there was disagreement about whether Karelians should attempt to form an independent nation, should integrate themselves into the Soviet system, or should seek integration with Finland. After the pro-Soviet side won out, pro-independence Karelians staged the Karelian Rebellion of 1921–1922; when this was crushed around 33,500 refugees fled to Finland. The largest wave of refugees in Finnish history crossed the newly established Soviet-Finnish border, culminating in February 1922 with thousands of refugees who came from White Sea (Dvina) Karelia to northern Finland. Accounts of this exodus, consisting of the oral and written narratives of refugees and eyewitnesses (detailed in Pentikäinen, 1978, and Hyry, 1994), show that interaction between the inhabitants of northern Finland and White Sea Karelia continued in spite of the border. Refugees crossed back and forth over the border publicly and then secretly, using the routes they already knew and engaging in traditional cultural practices, such as singing poems, together with people from the other side. Soon, however, the border was totally closed, and Dvina Karelians living on both sides became divided from one another.

The narratives of the refugees indicate the strong influence of the Dvina Karelian tradition. The refugees who told and sang their history to Finnish scholars (Samuli Paulaharju, Martti Haavio, Pertti Virtaranta, Juha Pentikäinen, Katja Hyry, etc.) expressed themselves in the language of oral narrative and epical poetry, using Karelian genres such as the rune and the lament and calling on legends of the saints and folk tales. In the descriptions of the eyewitnesses to their flight, however, the refugees are considered as a kind of crowd or mass. They are seen either as part of "Us"—that is, as relatives of the Finns—or as the "Other": a poor, helpless people who need our (Finns') help. The attitude of these eyewitnesses—shared by some Finnish scholars at the time—was somewhat Social Darwinist: Dvina Karelians are thought of as a vanishing people whose traditions should be recorded for posterity's sake, but whose language should be replaced by Finnish as soon as possible. The problem of Karelian-language instruction remained unsolved today, due to this attitude, and because of the fact that for a number of Karelian languages no textbooks have been written and no writing systems have been devised.

Karelian literature is largely comprised of long narratives written by peasant authors, such as Antti Timonen. Exceptional length is also characteristic of Karelian oral expression, such as the epic cycles of White Sea Karelian male singers, which served as the basis for Elias Lönnrot's celebrated *Kalevala* (1835; rev. 1849). The folklore repertoire of refugees such as Marina Takalo (studied by Juha Pentikäinen, 1971, 1978) included all the basic genres of Karelian oral narrative and poetry. With their conservative Old Believer mentality and deep roots in folk culture, refugees favored those narratives and poems with the highest testimonial value concerning their orally transmitted folk and religious beliefs.

Self-identification as Old Believers, together with strong female leadership and emphasis on oral memory, has continued to characterize Russian- and Karelian-based Eastern Orthodox Christianity in Finland, in spite of official ties to the Byzantine Orthodox Church in Istanbul. The first contacts between Baltic Finnish people and Russian Old Believers took place as early as 800 CE in Novgorod in the heart of Finnish-speaking Russia. Vocabulary related to various aspects of Christianity (*risti,* cross; *kirkko,* church; *pappi,* priest: *raamattu,* the Bible) was taken into Finnish from Russian via these encounters. It was through Karelia that Finland absorbed the first traces of Christianity in its Russian Pre-Orthodox form, before the 1651 schism that led to the division of Russian Eastern Christianity into the mainstream Russian Orthodox Church and the conservative Old Faith *(staraya verh).* Karelia, with its location far from the centers of the Czarist empire, became the favored locale for Old Believer monasteries and a place to which Old Believers could escape. The majority of Karelians throughout Russia were Old Believers, to such an extent that the terms Karelian and Old Believer became synonymous.

The *Kalevala,* Finland's national epic, has its own importance for Karelians, as a sacred history rather than as a recording of oral mythology. Lönnrot, the author of the *Kalevala* and also a collector of runes, became the mythographer of the Finns. His research led him to identify the ancient basis of Finnish religion in the worship of Ukko, the Finnish deity of thunder.

Michael (Mikael) Agricola, the Lutheran reformer of Finland, was the first to recognize the cultural divide between East and West. The preface to his translation of the Psalter includes two lists of gods, one set worshiped by Tavastians in the west, the other by Karelians in the east. Uno Harva's *Suomalaisten muinaisusko* (The ancient religion of the Finns, 1948), and Martti Haavio's *Karjalan jumalat* (Karelian gods; 1959) both owe a debt to this early document on the most important border inside Finland—that between East and West. Finnish religion has Western (Finnish), Karelian, and Northern nuances.

SEE ALSO Finnish Religions; Finno-Ugric Religions.

BIBLIOGRAPHY

Alho, Olli, et al., eds. *Finland: A Cultural Encyclopedia.* Finnish Literature Society editions no. 684. Helsinki, 1987.

Haavio, Martti. *Karjalan jumalat.* Porvoo, Finland, 1959.

Harva, Uno. *Suomalaisten muinaisusko.* Porvoo, Finland, 1948.

Hyry, Katja. *Rajakansan historia ja historian kokijat: Vienankarjalaisten vaiheet 1900–luvulla.* M.A. thesis, Helsinki University, 1994.

Järvinen, Irma-Riitta. "Communication between the Living and the Dead through Rituals and Dreams in Aunus Karelia." In *Folklore and the Encounters of Traditions: Proceedings of the Finnish-Hungarian Symposium, 18–20 March 1996, Jyväskylä, Finland.* Edited by P. Suojanen and R. Raittila. Jyväskylä, Finland, 1996.

Kaukonen, Väinö. *Elias Lönnrotin Kalevalan toinen painos.* Suomalaisen Kirjallisuuden Seuran toimituksia no. 247. Helsinki, 1956.

Kuusinen, Otto-Ville. "Kalevala ja sen luojat." In *Kalevala: Karjalais-suomalainen kansaneepos.* Edited by G. Stronk. Petroskoi, Russia, 1956.

Pentikäinen, Juha. *Marina Takalon uskonto: Uskontoantropologinen tutkimus.* Suomalaisen kirjallisuuden Seuran toimituksia no. 299. Helsinki, 1971.

Pentikäinen, Juha. *Oral Repertoire and World View: An Anthropological Study of Marina Takalo's Life History.* Folklore Fellows' Communications no. 219. Helsinki, 1978.

Pentikäinen, Juha. *Kalevala Mythology.* Translated and edited by Ritva Poom. Folklore Studies in Translation series. Bloomington, Ind., and Indianapolis, 1989.

Pentikäinen, Juha, ed. *"Silent as Waters We Live": Old Believers in Russia and Abroad: Cultural Encounter with the Finno-Ugrians.* Studia fennica Folkloristica no. 6. Helsinki, 1999.

Ravdonikas, F. V. *Lunarnye znaki v naskal'nyh izobrazeniah Onetskogo ozera.* Novosibirsk, Russia, 1978.

Stoljar, A. D. *Dreivneishi plast petroglifov Onetskogo ozera.* Peterburgski archeologicheski vestnik no. 9. Saint Petersburg, 1995.

Stoljar, A. D. "Oleneostrovski mogilnik i yego progrebeniye n 100 kak agenty mezolitischeskogo etnokulturogeneza Severa." In *Drevnosti Severo-Zapadnoi Rossii,* edited by V. M. Massova, E. N. Nosova, and E. A. Râbinina. Saint Petersburg, 1995.

Timonen, Antti. *Me karjalaiset.* Petroskoi, Russia, 1971. A novel.

Virtaranta, Pertti. *Vienan kansa muistelee.* Porvoo, Finland, 1958.

JUHA PENTIKÄINEN (2005)

KAREN RELIGION

SEE SOUTHEAST ASIAN RELIGIONS, *ARTICLE ON* MAINLAND CULTURES

KARMAN

This entry consists of the following articles:

KARMAN: HINDU AND JAIN CONCEPTS

As diverse as the culture of India may be, one common assumption undergirds virtually all major systems of South Asian religious thought and practice: a person's behavior leads irrevocably to an appropriate reward or punishment commensurate with that behavior. This, briefly stated, is the law of *karman.*

The importance of the idea of *karman* is not limited to the religions of the subcontinent. It is likely that no other notion from the sacred traditions of India has had more influence on the worldviews assumed by non-Indian cultures than that of *karman,* for in it lie the foundations of a wealth of astute ethical, psychological, metaphysical, and sacerdotal doctrines. Translations of the word (Pali, *kamma*; Tib., *las*; Chin., *yeh* or *yin-kuo*; Jpn., *gō* or *inga*) have for centuries been a key part of the religious lexica of the various canonical languages of Asia. Furthermore, the word *karma* (the nominative form of the Sanskrit *karman*) has in the last few generations also entered the vocabulary of European languages, appearing first in technical Indological works and more recently in popular or colloquial use as well.

The term is based on the Sanskrit verbal root *kṛ,* meaning "act, do, bring about," the idea being that one makes something by doing something; one creates by acting. It may be of interest to note that some linguists see the Indo-European root of the word *karman* (namely, **kwer,* "act") in the English word *ceremony,* which can mean either a combination of sacred acts performed according to prescribed norms or a system of proper behavior that keeps the world running smoothly. The same meanings hold, in part, for *karman.* Originally referring to properly performed ritual activity, the notion was ethicized to include the larger meaning of any correct activity in general. Granting this view, the religious, social, and medical philosophers of India, particularly those intrigued by the doctrines of rebirth and of the origins of suffering (but also of the related problems of the source of personality and the justification of social status), expanded the meaning of the term. Under this new understanding, *karman* came to denote the impersonal and transethical system under which one's current situation in the world is regarded as the fruit of seeds planted by one's behavior and dispositions in the past, and the view that in all of one's present actions lie similar seeds that will have continuing and determinative effect on one's life as they bear fruit in the future.

The language here ("fruit," Skt., *phala*; "seed," *bīja*; etc.) is remarkably consistent throughout the long history of Indian religions. Some scholars have seen in it evidence of an agricultural ecology and value system that knows that a well-planted field yields good crops; that the land will give birth repeatedly if healthy seeds find in it a place to take hold and grow; that the apparent death of a plant in the fall is merely the process by which that plant assures its own renewal in the spring; and that life, therefore, is a periodic cycle of death and then rebirth determined by the healthy or unhealthy conditions of former births.

Possibly originating, therefore, in the agrarian experience of aboriginal India, the notion of an impersonal law of cause and effect subsequently pervaded the (often decidedly un-agricultural) ideology of Vedic ritualism, Yoga, the Vedanta, Ayurvedic medicine, and sectarian theism, and it stands as a central theme in the lessons recorded in the scriptures of Jainism and Buddhism. This is not to say that all of these traditions share the same teachings regarding the nature of action, the desirability of the result, and the effective mechanism that links the two. On the contrary, views vary widely in this regard. This means that there is no single South Asian notion of *karman.*

EARLY RITUAL NOTIONS. The poets who composed the sacred hymns of the Vedic Mantrasaṃhitās in the twelfth century BCE sang praises to the gods in reverential, supplicatory, and sometimes cajoling tones. Deities were powerful beings who held control over the lives of the people on earth but who nevertheless could be propitiated and pleased with sacrificial gifts and who enjoyed staged battles, chariot racing, gambling, and riddles. The Vedic Brāhmaṇas (900 BCE and the following few centuries) present images of elaborate priestly actions performed in order to offer these gifts and entertainment to the gods, to the advantage—wealth, prestige, immortality, and so on—of the person who paid for the expert services of the priests and their assistants. This sacerdotal performance was known as *karman,* the "action" of the ritual undertaken to gain a particular end. The rites were often quite expensive and the rewards not always immediately realized, so the patrons were reassured that their support of the ceremony would benefit them sometime in the future.

Arguments in defense of this notion that the reward for one's present ritual action is reaped in the future laid part of the foundation for later doctrines of rebirth and transmigration. This development can be seen in the use of synonyms or near-synonyms for the word *karman.* For instance, the term *iṣṭāpūrta* ("the fulfillment of that which is desired") refers to a kind of package, as it were, that holds all of one's deeds and that precedes a person to the world to come, where it establishes a place for him (see *Ṛgveda* 10.14.8). The Brāhmaṇas also describe the rewards as events that will happen in the future and describe the sacrifice as *apūrva-karman,* "action the results of which have not yet been seen."

Evidence suggests that in the early Brahmanic period the gods were generally free to accept or reject the gifts and therefore were not bound to respond in kind. Over time, though, the Pūrva Mīmāṃsā philosophers came to view the ritual in magical terms: if the priest performed the prescribed actions correctly, he controlled the gods, who were forced by the devices of the ritual to respond in the way the priest desired. Conversely, the priest's improper performance of the ceremony led to the certain ruin of him or his patron. *Karman* for these thinkers therefore did not involve divine will; it was part of an impersonal metaphysical system of cause and effect in which action brought an automatic manipulated response. The Brahmanic notion of *karman* thus centers on the view that a person is born into a world he has made for himself (see *Kauṣītakī Brāhmaṇa* 26.3, for example). This meant that every action in the ritual was important and that every action brought a result of one kind or another, and did so irrevocably.

RENUNCIANT NOTIONS. The renunciant tradition provided two principal contexts for the elaboration of the notion of *karman.* The Upaniṣads speculate, among other topics, on human action and its consequences in this and in subsequent lives; the Yoga literature provides a more systematic and pragmatic approach to liberation from the consequences of action.

Karman in Upanisadic thought. The composers of the major Upaniṣads (eighth to fifth century BCE) generally saw two paths open to the deceased at the time of death. The lower path, one on which the person eventually returns to earth in a subsequent birth, is described as the "way of the fathers" (*pitṛyāna*) and is traveled by those who perform the rituals in hopes of material gain. The higher path, the way of the gods (*devayāna*), is one that does not lead to rebirth on earth and is taken by those who have renounced worldly ends and practice austerities in the forest. *Bṛhadāraṇyaka Upaniṣad* 4.4.4 describes the process with the doctrine that, as a goldsmith forms a new and more beautiful form out of a rough nugget, the soul leaves the body at death and fashions for itself a new and fairer body. Human happiness is said to be a fraction of the bliss known by a celestial man-spirit (*manuṣya-gandharva*), which in turn is meager compared to that of a *karma-deva,* a human who has become a god by his actions (see *Taittirīya Upaniṣad* 2.8 and *Bṛhadāraṇyaka Upaniṣad* 4.3.33).

Seeking to understand the Brahmanic notion of the ritual in anthropological rather than sacerdotal terms, the Upaniṣadic sages taught that all physical and mental activity was an internal reflection of cosmic processes. Accordingly, they held that *every* action, not only those performed in the public ritual, leads to an end. One's behavior in the past has determined one's situation in the present, and the totality of one's actions in the present construct the conditions of one's future. Thus, the *Bṛhadāraṇyaka Upaniṣad's* assertion that "truly, one becomes good through good action, bad by bad" (3.2.13) represents the encompassing Upaniṣadic scope of *karman.* From this notion arises the idea that one's worldly situation and personality are determined by one's desire: that is, one's desire affects one's will; one's will leads one to act in certain ways; and, finally, one's actions bring proportionate and appropriate results.

For the most part the composers of the major Upaniṣads disdained actions performed for the resulting enjoyment of worldly pleasures, for such material pursuit necessarily leads from one birth to another in an endless cycle characterized by dissatisfaction and, thus, to unhappiness. "The tortuous passage from one birth to another [*sāmparāya*] does not shine out to who is childish, careless and deluded by the glimmer of wealth," the Lord of the Dead tells Naciketas. "Thinking 'this is the world, there is no other,' he falls again and again under my power" (*Kaṭha Upaniṣad* 2.6).

The only way to break this turning wheel of life and death (*saṃsāra*) was to free oneself of the structures and processes of *karman.* The composers of the Upaniṣads understood this liberation to take place through the practice of *yoga* or through the intervention of a personal supreme deity who lived beyond the karmic realm.

Karman in classical Yoga. The practioners and philosophers of classical Yoga agreed with the Upaniṣadic idea that one's circumstances are determined by one's actions. Like some of those sages they, too, understood *karman* to involve what might be called a substance that leads the soul from one body to another as it moves from birth to birth. Patañjali's *Yoga Sūtra* (the pertinent passages of which were composed in the second century BCE) analyzes the ways in which such transfer takes place. Any act (*karman*) performed as a result of desire creates what is known as *karmāśaya,* the "accumulation for receptacle of *karman*" that is either beneficial or harmful depending on the quality of the act itself. *Karmāśaya* can be understood as a kind of seed that will mature either in one's present life or, if not fully ripened, in another lifetime (*adṛṣṭajanman*). That seed includes one's personal dispositions (*saṃskārā*), including those themes or memories imprinted at the unconscious levels of one's mind (*vāsanā*) and that serve as the source of the five habitual personal "afflictions" (*kleśa*) of ignorance, ego, hatred, and the will to live (see *Yoga Sūtra* 2.3). The *kleśas* tend to reinforce the ignorant notion that activity directed to some end is desirable, and in so doing are the main reason that people stay trapped in the wheel of life and death. If a person dies before all of his accumulated *karmāśaya* is gone, that karmic residue joins with his unfulfilled thoughts, desires, and feelings in search of a new body whose nature is receptive to his pertinent dispositions, which it then enters (*āpūra,* literally, "making full") and through which the unripened seeds can come to fruit. A person with a passion for food thus may be reborn as a hog. One eventually gets what one wants, even though it may take more than one lifetime to do so. That's the problem. For in order to get what one wants one needs a body, and in order to have a body one needs to be born. Birth leads to death, death leads to birth. Unless the cycle is broken it never stops.

Without values directed towards the attainment of worldly goals a person will cease to behave according to one's desire, and without that desire no karmic residue, no unmatured seeds, can accumulate. Classical Yoga, as represented by Patañjali, presents the *yogin* with a set of practices by which that person can be free of the karmic process. In these exercises the meditator reduces the power of the *kleśas* by performing actions that are opposed to their fulfillment. Traditionally this meant the practice of ascetic renunciation of physical pleasures. Thorough renunciation makes it impossible for new *kleśas* to arise, and through more and more subtle meditations the *kleśas* that remain from the past are diluted so much that they no longer produce any *karmāśayas.* At this point the person (*puruṣa*) within the *yogin* no longer needs a body because it no longer has any unripened *karmāśaya,* and at the death of the present body the person no longer migrates to another life. The *puruṣa* is liberated from the entrapping demands of habitual afflictions and experiences *kaivalya,* "autonomy."

Ontological or Materialistic Notions. The terms *bīja* (seed), *karmāśaya* (karmic residue), *vāsanā* (pychological traces) and others suggest a general South Asian notion that some "thing" is created and left behind by one's actions. At times the Upaniṣads describe *karman* almost as a substance that not only influences one's subsequent births but can also be passed from one person to another, especially from father to son. The *Kauṣītakī Brāhmaṇa Upaniṣad*, for example, tells a dying father to transfer his *karman* to his son, saying "let me place my deeds in you" (2.15). The son is then able to perform atoning actions such that the father is free of the consequences of his own improper behavior (see *Bṛhadāraṇyaka Upaniṣad* 1.5.17).

Ritual practices in which one either supplements or attenuates the *karman* acquired by one's ancestors take place in various Vedic *śrauta* and Hindu *pūjā* ceremonies that have been practiced from the time of the Brāhmaṇas and Dharmaśāstras. They appear, for example, in the postclassical *sāpiṇḍīkaraṇa* and *bali* rites in which balls of rice and other foods that are said to contain an ancestor's *karman* are ceremonially offered to the deceased.

Indian medical texts of the Ayurveda traditions agree that *karman* is a material entity of sorts that can be passed from one generation to the next. The *Caraka Saṃhitā* (first century CE), for example, maintains that *karman* resides in substance (*dravya*) and is one of the causes of physical health and disease. Accordingly, *karman* is seen as an important factor in medical etiologies and in techniques of fertility in which a father and mother perform certain actions so that the embryo (*garbha*, sometimes called the "seed") can acquire the most desirable or auspicious karmic elements and thus be born a strong person with admirable character.

By far the most assertive thinkers concerning the material nature of *karman*, however, are the Jains, who since the sixth century BCE have followed the teachings and traditions surrounding the founder of Jainism, Mahāvīra Vardhamāna. Central to Jain doctrine in general is the notion that the living entity (*jīva*, "life") within a person is by nature blissful and intelligent. Traditional teachings sometimes describe the *jīva* as a pure, colorless, and transparent energy and maintain that all of the infinite creatures in the universe—including animals, plants, and rocks as well as human beings—possess such an ethereal crystalline life within them. But, also according to Jain thought, the spatial world occupied by the *jīvas* is permeated with a kind of subtle dust or stained liquid that has existed since time immemorial and that "sticks," as it were, to each *jīva*, soiling and infecting its original nature with a color (*leśya*), the hue and intensity of which corresponds to the amount of desire, hatred, and love with which that being performs any given action. This glutinous blurry stuff is *karman*. Virtuous and selfless action attracts to the *jīva* the lighter and less cloudy colors, which hardly obscure the *jīva*'s nature at all, compared to the dark and muddy colors brought together by acts engendered in self-concern. The amount and color of the *karman* that adheres to any given *jīva* determines the conditions and circumstances of its subsequent rebirth. Competitive, violent, self-infatuated people carry the heavy weight of *karman* and will sink downwards through their many lifetimes as demons or as animals who live by eating others; gentle, caring, and compassionate beings gradually cleanse their *jīva* of its encumbering *karman* and rise through rebirth towards enlightenment.

Even unintentional violence, however, burdens the *jīva* with the stain of *karman*. Thus, Jain tradition demands absolute *ahiṃsā*, a complete unwillingness to kill or injure any and all living beings. Jains, therefore, are absolute vegetarians, some of whom in their attempts to sustain themselves with food in which no living creature has met a violent death refuse even to pick the living fruit from a tree, waiting instead until it falls of its own (ripened) accord.

A *jīva* finds release from the bonds of rebirth only when it stops accumulating new *karman* and removes that *karman* already there. This is described as a long and arduous task, one that takes many lifetimes to complete. Although the necessary discipline can be practiced by lay members of the community, traditionally only renunciate Jains can undergo the physical austerities and rigorous mental concentration that are needed to remove the *karman* from their *jīvas*. One who through many ascetic lifetimes has completely removed the cloud of *karman* from his *jīva* is known as a *siddha* (one who has "succeeded") or a *kevalin*, an omniscient and enlightened being. The paradigmatic ascetic here is Mahāvīra Vardhamāna, who, according to Digambara tradition, wandered naked and homeless as he practiced nonviolence, truthfulness, honesty, renunciation of possessions, and sexual abstinence.

A Theistic Notion: Karman in the *Bhagavadgītā*. Some thinkers in ancient India found practical problems in the renunciate attitude towards *karman*. For example, if all actions, including good actions, bring consequences, don't all actions, including good actions, lead inevitably to rebirth? Does this mean that one must renounce all actions, even good ones? Isn't renunciation itself an act, and therefore constitutive of karmic residue; isn't the desire for liberation still a desire? Doesn't the final end of renunciation of all action result in willful death, since one must actively eat and breathe in order to live; yet isn't suicide itself considered an evil and thus entrapping action?

The author or authors of the *Bhagavadgītā* (c. first century BCE) seem to have been aware of these problems. Generally supportive of the value of disciplined meditation (see *Bhagavadgītā* 6.10–6.13), those philosophers nevertheless saw the impossibility of complete inaction, for "even the maintenance of your physical body requires activity" (3.8).

Noting that one cannot remain inactive, and aligning themselves with the social philosophy presented in the Dharmaśāstras and related Hindu orthodox literatures on law outlining specific responsibilities incumbent on people in various occupations and stages of life, the authors of the

Bhagavadgītā present the idea that one should perform those actions that are obligatory (*niyata*) to one's position in society (*svadharma*), and the better one performs those actions the purer their result (*Bhagavadgītā* 18.23, 2.31). Personal preference should have nothing to do with one's duties. In fact, to perform someone else's responsibilities well is worse than performing one's own badly (3.35, 18.45–48).

The *Bhagavadgītā* justifies its teaching with a theological argument: social responsibilities arise from divine law (*Bhagavadgītā* 3.15a). Therefore, priests should perform rituals, soldiers should fight battles, and merchants should conduct the affairs of business (18.41–44) not because they want to but because it is ordained by God to do so. If done properly, such action cannot be considered evil and therefore does not lead to rebirth.

But if action itself does not lead to rebirth, then what does? The authors of the *Bhagavadgītā* supported the general South Asian notion that karmic action arises from desire; from this idea they developed the doctrine that it is the desire for certain results, and not the action itself, that gives rise to the mechanism of karmic processes. For these sages, freedom from the bonds of *karman* comes not when one ceases acting but when one acts without desire, when one renounces the attachment one has for the fruits of one's actions (*Bhagavadgītā* 4.19–23).

According to the *Bhagavadgītā* and similar devotional texts, this renunciation of desire for specific ends can be obtained only through *bhakti-yoga*, the loving surrender to God's will. Ritual actions properly performed are meritorious, and ascetic meditation leads to release. But these two modes of action either require wealth or are difficult to perfect. Purportedly quoting Kṛṣṇa (that is, God) himself, the *Bhagavadgītā* offers a theological response to these difficulties: "Those who dedicate all of their actions [*karman*] to Me, intent on Me, with unwavering discipline, meditating on Me; those who revere Me—for those I am the Savior from the sea of the cycle of deaths" (12.6–12.7b); those who see their actions as God's actions and the results as God's will "are also liberated from the traps of *karman*" (*mucyanti te'pi karmabhiḥ*, 3.31d).

See Also Bhagavadgītā; Bhakti; Dharma, article on Hindu Dharma; Jainism; Mahāvīra; Upaniṣads; Yoga.

Bibliography

Bhattacharyya, Haridas. "The Doctrine of Karma." *Visva-Bharati Quarterly* 3 (1925–1926): 257–258.

Bhattacharyya, Haridas. "The Brahmanical Concept of Karma." In *A. R. Wadia; Essays in Philosophy Presented in His Honor*, edited by Sarvepalli Radhakrishnan et al., pp. 29–49. Madras, 1954.

Bhattacharyya, Kalidas. "The Status of the Individual in Indian Metaphysics." In *The Status of the Individual East and West*, edited by Charles A. Moore, pp. 29–49. Honolulu, 1968.

Dilger, D. *Der indischer Seelungswanderungsglaube*. Basel, 1910.

Falke, Robert. *Die Seelenwanderung*. Berlin, 1913.

Farquhar, J. N. "Karma: Its Value as a Doctrine of Life." *Hibbert Journal* 20 (1921–1922): 20–34.

Glasenapp, Helmuth von. *The Doctrine of Karman in Jain Philosophy*. Translated by G. Barry Gifford. Bombay, 1942.

Hall, Rodney. *The Law of Karma*. Canberra, 1968.

Henseler, Éric de. *L'âme et le dogme de la transmigration dans les livres sacrés de l'Inde ancienne*. Paris, 1928.

Kalghatgi, T. G. *Karma and Rebirth*. Ahmadabad, 1972.

Keyes, Charles F., and E. Valentine Daniel, eds. *Karma: An Anthropological Inquiry*. Berkeley, 1983.

O'Flaherty, Wendy Doniger, ed. *Karma and Rebirth in Classical Indian Traditions*. Berkeley, 1980.

Silburn, Lilian. *Instant et cause: Le discontinu dans la pensée philosophique de l'Inde*. Paris, 1955.

Steiner, Rudolf. *Die Offenbarungen des Karma: Ein Zyklus von elf Vorträgen*. Dornach, 1956.

William K. Mahony (1987)

KARMAN: BUDDHIST CONCEPTS

The Indian religious worldview emerging about the time of the Buddha centered on three interrelated notions: rebirth, *karman*, and liberation. These concepts informed the cosmology, eschatology, and soteriology of the developing traditions, which taught that sentient beings have been reborn repeatedly in diverse forms of life, in places ranging from various hells to the highest heavens, over vast tracks of time. This process of rebirth is guided and even generated by the force of a person's actions (*karman*), which possess the power of inevitably working their consequences. Thus, deeds in the present will unfailingly bear their fruit in this or a future life, and present conditions, pleasurable or disagreeable, including one's form of existence, length of life, social station, and personal appearance, are the effects of deeds performed in the past. The span of one's existence through cycles of birth and death (*saṃsāra*) stretches back endlessly into the past and will continue without limit into the future, unless liberation is attained. The understanding of the mechanism of karmic bondage and the nature of emancipation evolved variously within the different traditions, and—although notions of *karman* are also found in pre-Buddhist Upaniṣads and in Jain thought—the precise relationships among the traditions remains uncertain.

Karman in Early Buddhist Thought. The concept of *karman* as causal action and its consequence is often said to be the cornerstone of Buddhist philosophy and its basis for explaining human existence and the physical world. It is, however, less a clearly articulated doctrine than an elemental insight, in terms of which Buddhists have apprehended the temporal, existential dimension of human life rooted in the realization of non-self. Perhaps the most distinctive aspect of Buddhist thought within the Indian context, non-self is expressed in the early tradition as the rejection of the bifurcation of experience into subject and object (five aggregates), and further as release from painful, repetitive existence through the eradication of delusional egocentric craving (dependent arising).

Although *karman* in Indian thought originally presupposed an enduring entity as both agent of action and recipient of rebirth, it also appears in legendary accounts of the Buddha's enlightenment. The early tradition teaches that he attained three insights during the three watches of the night following his awakening: he saw his own previous lives and how each conditioned subsequent ones; he saw that beings everywhere also underwent repeated rebirths, receiving the results of acts performed in past lives; and he perceived the desires and attachments that bound one to further painful rebirth and the method by which to eradicate them. The critical role of *karman* in constituting samsaric existence was expressed by the notion of *dependent arising,* the core motif of which was formulated as: "When this arises, that arises; when this is not, that is not" (*Majjhima-nikāya* I, 262–263).

The concept of dependent arising was developed into a twelve-link chain: conditioned by ignorance, mental formations arise; conditioned by formations, consciousness arises; and so forth, leading finally to old age and death. These links are seen as elements within phases of past karmic acts (ignorance, formations) leading to present conditions (consciousness, mind-objects, six senses, sensory contact, feeling) and present actions (craving, grasping, becoming) leading to future consequences (birth, old age and death). The reverse chain leads from eradication of ignorance to the cessation of the successive links and liberation from *karman*-formed existence. Thus, the earliest strata of Buddhist texts state: "One who sees dependent arising rightly sees *karman* and its matured fruit" (*Suttanipāta*), and further, "One who sees dependent arising sees dhamma [*dharma*]" (*Majjhima-nikāya* I, 190–191).

THE ETHICIZATION OF *KARMAN* IN THERAVĀDA THOUGHT. In early Buddhist tradition, *karman* is understood not only as an aspect of the Buddha's awakening, but also as broadly ethical in implication, in contrast to the Brahmanic tradition, in which the notion of *karman* concerned the efficacy of sacrificial rites. In Vedic tradition, it is the enactment of sacrifice itself and its ritual correctness, rather than moral quality, that are determinative of the result. *Karman* in early Buddhist thought also differs from the contemporaneous Jain tradition, in which it is conceived as material accretion or residue, so that, for example, any act destructive of sentient life will bear fruit, even though it may have been unintended. Buddhist tradition asserts intention (*cetanā*) or the originating impulse as the critical element of any karmic act. The Buddha states: "Monks, I say that intention is acting; by intention, one performs an action of body, speech, or mind" (*Aguttara-nikāya* III, 415). It is the intention functioning as the motive force giving rise to deeds that determines their quality and thus their karmic effect. Hence, harm inflicted inadvertently does not necessarily bespeak an evil act entailing unwholesome retribution, and even meritorious acts may in fact be injurious. The monk Nāgasena explains that since the offering of a meal to Śākyamuni by Cunda was done with good intentions, even though the Buddha fell ill and died upon eating it, Cunda was not at fault (*Milindapañha*).

This emphasis on intention as determinate of the quality of acts was developed by early Buddhists through various classifications. All human activity is classified in terms of three modes of action: bodily, vocal, and mental. Thoughts of theft or murder bear karmic effects, even though not physically enacted. In addition, a twofold classification of acts centering on intention was expounded: the act of intending and acts performed having been intended. The former category consists of mental acts, while the latter consists of bodily and verbal acts that arise as manifestations of volition (*Abhidharmakośa*).

THE MORAL QUALITY OF ACTS. *Karman* is classified by moral quality as good or wholesome (*kuśala*), unwholesome (*akuśala*), and indeterminate (*avyākṛta*). Unwholesome or "unskillful" acts result in unhappy rebirth (in the realms of hell, animals, or spirits), and a list of "ten evil acts" is organized in terms of bodily, vocal, and mental deeds: taking life, taking what is not given, sexual misconduct; false speech, slander, harsh speech, frivolous talk; greed, malice, and false views. Good or "skillful" acts, given in a corresponding list of ten admonitions, result in propitious rebirth (as a human or *deva*). Indeterminate acts do not produce a karmic result. Here again one sees the centrality of intention in early Buddhist thought, for present conditions, which are the results of past actions, are themselves indeterminate. In this way, Buddhists sought to avoid any determinism of the moral quality of present acts by direct causation from the past.

Further, the early tradition asserts the strictness of the causal working of *karman.* One's *karman* is one's own; whether good or bad, it is like "a treasure not shared with others, which no thief can steal" (*Khuddakapātha,* p.7). Thus, the consequences of one's actions will return upon oneself alone. Karmic effect is open to various forms of conditioning, and the results of a particular act may vary depending on when it is performed (the time of death is particularly potent), the combination with other acts, the quality of habitual conduct that forms its context, or the attitude taken toward the act before or even after it has been performed. For example, the degree of deliberation preceding an act, and the presence of regret or of repentance and expiation after, may influence the karmic effect of both good and evil acts, either intensifying or meliorating the result. Nevertheless, however conditioned, *karman* unfailingly brings about consequences. It may ripen quickly in the present life or bear its fruit only in some future life, but its effect will not be lost and its potency not exhausted or nullified until it works itself out.

Karman in early Buddhist tradition thus suggests a moral eschatology in which one's future depends on the moral qualities of the thoughts underlying one's acts in the present. The ethical import is to shun evil acts and strive to do good: "Watchful of speech, well restrained in mind, / One would not do what is unwholesome by body too; / These three modes of action one would purify; / Let one fulfill the path made known by the sages" (*Dhammapada,* verse 281). This vision, however, is complicated by two intertwined issues: the soteriological aim of liberation from karmic functioning itself, rather than skillful application of it, and the rejection of enduring, substantial existents, including a "self" that can inherit the consequences of its own past acts.

MERIT AND LIBERATION. While *karman* expresses the moral logic at work within the cosmos of living beings, liberation in the Buddhist path ultimately involves transcendence of existence as continual rebirth, which is karmically generated and characterized as delusionally driven and painful. Because the notion of *karman* continued to underpin ideas of merit (*puṇya*) accumulation originating in the Vedic context of sacrificial rite, two general goals were upheld by early Buddhist practitioners, reflecting distinct attitudes toward *karman.*

On the one hand, acts may be distinguished as sources of merit or demerit, the former leading toward happy future conditions and the latter toward painful states. In the early tradition, meritorious action is enumerated as giving (*dāna*), moral conduct (*śīla*), and meditative practice (*bhāvanā*), but *dāna* as almsgiving is given particular attention as a source of merit for laity. Further, the degree of merit accrued in an act of giving is said to turn on the worthiness of the recipient, who is a "field of merit" in which the gift as seed is brought to fruition. Any act of charity may bear fruit, but the greatest rewards lie in the supreme field of merit, the community of monks (*saṃgha*) led by the Buddha. The practical significance of this metaphor for the symbiotic relationship between monks and laity is evident, but it has also been suggested that the importance placed on the recipient stems from the original sacrificial context of the act of almsgiving as a form of worship.

On the other hand, the goal of the Buddhist path is not higher states of existence or ascension through the five "courses," including human and *deva,* of the realm of desire into the loftier realms of form and formlessness. Rather, one seeks to sever the bonds to samsaric existence altogether. This is *nirvāṇa,* which, in terms of *karman,* is "extinction" of afflicting passions giving rise to acts of karmic retribution and cessation of the resultant pain of continual rebirth. Since any thoughts of attachment within the realms of rebirth, even to meritorious acts or blissful states of life, are themselves *karman* that will bind one to further samsaric existence, liberation is attained only when one produces no *karman* and one's *karman* from the past has been exhausted. Acts performed with detachment and equanimity (*upekṣā*) bear no further results, whether good or bad. Hence, it is by purification of the mind through right conduct, meditation, and religious insight, so that one's acts are free of greed, malice, and delusional thinking, that *nirvāṇa* is attained.

Some studies of the present Theravāda tradition have distinguished these two patterns of religious acts as kammatic and nibbanic, the former emphasizing giving and right conduct and directed toward achieving higher states within samsaric existence, while the latter focuses on meditative practice leading to liberation from *saṃsāra.* The former turns on the karmic effects of merit-making, while the latter seeks the eradication of *karman* through perfect disinterestedness.

The working of *karman,* however, also serves to conjoin these two patterns. Since the path to liberation traverses many lifetimes, present merit may be understood to lead to conditions favorable to purifying practice and eventual attainment of *nirvāṇa.* In addition, through transference of merit, one may generously turn the effects of a meritorious act to benefit another. That persons must each bear the results of their own deeds is a fundamental postulate of the notion of *karman* emphasized in the early tradition. At the same time, however, examples are recorded of a person ascribing a good deed, such as a gift of food to monks, to other beings, including famished spirits and *devas,* so that they might receive the merit. Such a notion of compassionate transference later developed into a hallmark of Mahāyāna tradition.

THE ANALYTIC STANCE OF THE SCHOLASTIC TRADITIONS. Scholastic traditions developed in the monastic communities in the centuries following the Buddha's death, resulting in a literature of doctrinal systematization and categorization known as *abhidharma* (further teaching). Adopting an objectifying stance of exhaustive analytical reflection, the *abhidharma* broke down all existents and phenomena into constituent, elemental factors (*dharmas*) categorized as consciousness, mental attitudes, material elements, elements neither mental nor material such as causal relation, and the uncreated. These psychological and physical *dharmas* (numbering seventy-five in the Sarvāstivāda school and eighty-two in the Theravāda *abhidharma*) were said to arise in composites in the present instant, then immediately pass away. Thus, although normally experienced as continuous and integral, mental functioning is merely a rapid series of discrete instants of consciousness, each arising as a psychophysical combination of numerous *dharmas,* and objects grasped as enduring and real are no more than momentary aggregates of *dharmas* informed by conceptual construction. What is actually and irreducibly existent are only the elemental factors coming together and passing away.

In the *abhidharma* schools, the notion of *karman* functioned as a fundamental causal principle underlying the linear, temporal flow of all things, but a number of contentious issues relating to it were debated. For example, although the Theravāda tradition emphasized intention as determinant of the moral quality of even physical acts, Sarvāstivādins asserted that bodily and vocal acts, being material, manifest but are distinct from intention as a mental act. Further, major issues arose regarding karmic causation. How can actions occurring in the present moment and then passing away bring about consequences in the future? The Sarvāstivādins argued that *dharmas* themselves, as elemental factors, exist in the future and past as well as in the present, although the modes of existence differ. *Dharmas* existing in the future move, through causes, into the present and arise in fusion with countless other *dharmas* as actions or composite things before slipping into the past. Since the *dharmas* continue to exist even though they have vanished from the present, they hold the energy to cause their results to appear upon maturation. How can there be continuity between the agent of an act and the receiver of its fruit? If there is only flux, there can be no reception of karmic results, but if there is continuity, an enduring entity seems implied. The early tradition teaches that the person who commits the act and the person who receives the fruit are neither wholly identical nor wholly different. In order to explain the continuity of the series of psychophysical moments that is the subject of karmic working, Sarvāstivādins argued that there exists a *dharma* of "possession" (*prāpti*), which functions with all karmic acts, so that each act or thought, though immediately passing away, creates the "possession" of that act in the continuum of instants we experience as a person. This possession itself is momentary, but continually reproduces a similar possession in the succeeding instant, even though the original act lies in the past. Through such continual regeneration, the act is "possessed" until the actualization of the result.

Such views were rejected as contrary to the Buddha's teaching of impermanence by other schools, notably the Sautrāntikas, who insisted that each act exists only in the present instant and perishes immediately. To explain causation, they taught that with each karmic act a "perfuming" occurs which, though not a *dharma* or existent factor itself, leaves a residual impression in the succeeding series of mental instants, causing it to undergo a process of subtle evolution eventually leading to the act's result. Good and bad deeds performed are thus said to leave "seeds" or traces of disposition that will come to fruition.

THE MAHĀYĀNA VIEW OF *KARMAN*. The Prajñāpāramitā sūtras (c. first century CE) and early Mahāyāna thinkers rejected the realism of scholastic traditions that presupposed the enduring own-being (*svabhāva*) of all *dharmas* and fixed the transcendent, uncreated *dharma* of *nirvāṇa* as the ultimate religious goal. Instead, they sought to articulate the soteriological realization of non-self in terms of a thoroughgoing nondiscriminative wisdom in which the dissolution of the subject-object dichotomy and the nature of all things as dependently arising were expressed as emptiness or voidness (*śūnyatā*).

Nāgārjuna (c. 150–250 CE), in *Mūlama-dhyamaka-kārikā*, sought to demonstrate the logical incoherence of the substantialist assumptions governing ordinary human experience of—and speech about—the world, including causation. He argued, for example, that notions of agent and act are mutually dependent, so that any conceptual reification will render the whole—action itself—untenable. Further, if *karman* persists until its result arises, it is permanent and unchanging; if it expires, it cannot function as cause. In either case, it cannot produce a result. *Karman* must be neither continuous nor discontinuous; this eradication of objectifying conceptual bifurcation pervades the world of non-self or emptiness. To go beyond emptiness-contemplation as the elimination of discriminative discourse only and to explore the active functioning of wisdom, the Yogācāra thought of Asaṅga (c. 320–390 CE) and Vasubandhu (c. fourth century CE) adapted, from a Mahāyāna perspective, such *abhidharma* conceptions as the subconscious mind (*bhavaṅga*), from which conscious processes arise and into which they subside and the karmic seeds (*bīja*) of mental activity. Time is a succession of discontinuous instants, with mind and all things mutually giving rise to each other and perishing moment by moment. This instantaneous "other-dependent" co-arising of mind and world is not different from emptiness, wisdom, or true reality.

By asserting "form is itself emptiness, emptiness is form," Mahāyāna thought departed from earlier tendencies toward mutually exclusive, substantialist-leaning conceptions of samsaric and nirvanic realms, or the *karma*-created and uncreated, and thus from the ethical focus developed in Theravāda tradition and the atomistic analyses of karmic causation in the scholastic tradition.

KARMIC EXISTENCE AND TRANSCENDENT WISDOM. The implications regarding *karman* of the notion of nonduality in Mahāyāna thought may be considered from the perspectives of both the being of wisdom (a *bodhisattva*) and the person of karmic existence (a foolish, unenlightened being). For the *bodhisattva*, the strictness of karmic working emphasized in the early tradition is broken in several ways by the wisdom in which such dichotomies as form and emptiness, *saṃsāra* and *nirvāṇa*, and blind passions and enlightenment are simultaneously established and dissolved. Although the early tradition asserts that *karman* is personal, the *bodhisattva's* transcendence of the dichotomy of self and other leads to the practice of merit transference, by which one vows to ferry all beings to the other shore of *nirvāṇa* before crossing over oneself, giving the merit of one's practice to others. Self does not exist merely as self, but upon the foundation of both self and other arising in mutual dependence, that is, in emptiness. This thinking is developed in Yogācāra writings in the concept of "shared *karman*," in which *karman* is at once individual and conjoint.

Further, although the notion of *karman* asserts a correlation between the moral quality of past deeds and the circumstances of rebirth, the *bodhisattva* may choose to be reborn in realms of suffering to save beings there. Above all, the *bodhisattva* relinquishes the earlier view that liberation lies in departing from *saṃsāra* and entering *nirvāṇa*, abandoning all attachments, even to *nirvāṇa*.

While attainment of nondiscriminative wisdom is a prominent feature in most East Asian Buddhist traditions, including Huayan, Tiantai, and Chan, realization of nonduality from a stance within karmic bondage has also been developed, most clearly by Shinran (1173–1263), founder of the Japanese Shin Buddhist tradition (Jōdo Shinshū) of the Pure Land school. In Shinran's thought, persons come to know the depths of their karmic bondage, reaching back into the unknowable past, through receiving the wisdom of Amida Buddha as the genuine entrusting of themselves (*shinjin*) to the Buddha's vow to bring them to enlightenment though his own fulfillment of practices. They awaken to their inability to free themselves from blind passions through religious practices or meritorious acts, which are inevitably tainted by self-attachment, and at the same time they realize that their birth in the Pure Land and attainment of enlightenment are fully settled, for they have attained the Buddha's mind as *shinjin.* Thus in *Tannishō,* Shinran states, "Hell is decidedly my home," and also speaks of "the attainment of buddhahood by the person who is evil" (*akunin jōbutsu*), expressing the nonduality of karmic existence and Buddha's wisdom found throughout Mahāyāna tradition.

The notion of *karman* has been considered an integral element of Buddhist awakening to human existence. At the same time, however, the significance of moral action—in relation to religious practice in the Theravāda tradition and to nondichotomous wisdom in Mahāyāna traditions—has been a recurring issue throughout Buddhist history, and recent concerns to formulate a Buddhist social ethics have drawn renewed attention to issues of *karman.*

SEE ALSO Buddhist Philosophy; Dharma, article on Buddhist Dharma and Dharmas; Sarvāstivāda; Sautrāntika.

BIBLIOGRAPHY

Carter, John Ross, and Mahinda Palihawadana, trans. *The Dhammapada.* Oxford, 1987.

Egge, James R. *Religious Giving and the Invention of Karma in Theravāda Buddhism.* Richmond, UK, 2002. Considers the harmonization of the ethicized and soteriological strains of *karman* in Theravāda texts.

Heine, Steven. *Shifting Shape, Shaping Text: Philosophy and Folklore in the Fox Kōan.* Honolulu, 1999. Highlights the tensions between the ethical and the nondiscriminative treatments of *karman* in Chan/Zen tradition.

Hirota, Dennis, trans. *Tannishō: A Primer.* Kyoto, 1982. A parallel translation with original text. Also in Dennis Hirota et al., trans., *The Collected Works of Shinran,* Kyoto, 1997.

Keyes, Charles F., and E. Valentine Daniel, eds. *Karma: An Anthropological Inquiry.* Berkeley, 1983. Includes articles on modern Tibet and Southeast Asia.

Kumoi Shōzen, ed. *Gō shisō kenkyū.* Kyoto, 1979. Includes articles on a wide range of Buddhist traditions and a bibliography of research in Japanese and European languages.

Lamotte, Étienne. *Karmasiddhi Prakaraṇa: The Treatise on Action by Vasubandhu.* Translated by Leo M. Pruden. Fremont, Calif., 1987. Introduction includes a summary of views on *karman* in various abhidharmic schools.

Lusthaus, Dan. *Buddhist Phenomenology: A Philosophical Investigation of Yogācāra Buddhism and the Ch'eng Wei-shih lun.* London, 2002. Considers Buddhist conceptions of *karman* on the way to arguing a phenomenological understanding of Yogācāra.

McDermott, James Paul. *Development in the Early Buddhist Concept of Kamma/Karma.* New Delhi, 1984. Lucid survey of the issues in the literature of the early tradition through Vasubandhu's *Abhidharmakośa.*

Neufeldt, Ronald W., ed. *Karma and Rebirth: Post Classical Developments.* Albany, N.Y., 1986. Includes articles on Buddhist traditions in China, Tibet, and Japan.

Obeyeskere, Gananath. *Imagining Karma: Ethical Transformation in Amerindian, Buddhist, and Greek Rebirth.* Berkeley and Los Angeles, 2002. Surveys the notion of rebirth in diverse cultures and delineates a theory of its evolution in Indian traditions through ethicization based on *karman* to a notion of salvation as transcendent *nirvāṇa.*

O'Flaherty, Wendy Doniger, ed. *Karma and Rebirth in Classical Indian Traditions.* Berkeley, 1980. Includes several articles on Buddhist tradition and an extensive bibliography.

Ueda Yoshifumi. "Freedom and Necessity in Shinran's Concept of Karma." Translated by Dennis Hirota. *Eastern Buddhist* 19, no. 1 (1986): 76–100. An adaptation and translation of *Bukkyō ni okeru gō no shisō.* Kyoto, 1957. See also Ueda Yoshifumi and Dennis Hirota, *Shinran: An Introduction to His Thought.* Kyoto, 1989.

Warren, Henry Clarke. *Buddhism in Translations* (1896). Cambridge, Mass., 1953. Convenient collection of important passages in Theravāda tradition in a section on "Karma and Rebirth."

DENNIS HIROTA (2005)

KARMA PAS are among the most prominent lines of reincarnated Tibetan Buddhist masters, or *tulkus.* They are also often referred to as the Shanak pas, or "Black Hat" masters, after the black crown passed down from each incarnation to the next that has come to symbolize the lineage. The first Karma pa, Dus gsum mkhyen pa (Dusum Khyenpa, 1110–1193), was an important leader in twelfth-century Central and Eastern Tibet. As of 2004 the seventeenth Karma pa resided in the Tibetan diaspora community in Dharamsala, India. Throughout the centuries, the successive Karma pas have played a large role in the religious, cultural, and political life of Tibet.

The Karma Kamtshang school, of which the Karma pas are the leaders, is but part of a larger school of Tibetan Buddhism known as the Bka' Brgyud (Kagyu) school or "Oral Tradition" school. The Bka' Brgyud school is one of the principle traditions of Tibetan Buddhism, with a history that extends from the twelfth century to the present day. The names and dates of the successive Karma pas, as well as their allied lineage, the Shamar pas, are listed at the end of this entry.

Although the first two Karma pas were posthumously recognized as "Karma pas" only in the late thirteenth century at the time of the third Karma pa, Rang byung rdo rje (Rangjung Dorje, 1284–1339), they are nevertheless important figures in the tradition. The first Karma pa was born in the village of Treshö, situated in the eastern Tibetan region of Kham. At the age of thirty he became a student of Sgam po pa (Gampopa, 1079–1153), well-known disciple of Mi la ras pa (Milarepa, 1028/40–1111/23), wellspring of many strands of Bka' Brgyud tradition. Dus gsum mkhyen pa founded two monasteries. Karma Gon (or Karma Densa), founded in 1147 in Kham, gave the Karma pas their name ("those of Karma Gon"), though it did not play a central role in the tradition. Tsurphu, founded in 1189 in the Tolung Valley of Central Tibet, some fifty miles west of Lhasa, was to become the true seat of the lineage, a status that it has enjoyed up to the present day. The second Karma pa, Karma Pakshi (1204–1283), was a monk at Tsurphu when he traveled to Mongolia in 1154, a journey that marked the entry of the Karma pas into Central and East Asian politics. While he is remembered by tradition principally as a great magician who beguiled the Mongol leaders, he was also the author of a massive philosophical compendium known as the *Limitless Ocean Cycle*, in which he integrated doctrines from both the Bka' Brgyud and the Rnying ma (Nyingma) traditions of Tibetan Buddhism.

The third Karma pa, Rang byung rdo rje, was born in southwest Tibet in 1284. According to early stories of his life, at the age of five he received a blessing in the form of a white light striking his head from the famous statue of the *bodhisattva* of compassion, Avalokiteśvara, in Kyirong on the southwest border of Tibet. This miraculous event led his parents to bring him before Master Orgyanpa Rinchenpal (1230–1309), who identified him as his deceased teacher, Karma pakshi. At the age of seven, Rang byung rdo rje took vows as a novice monk at Dusum Khyenpa's monastery of Tsurphu. At age twenty he took full monastic vows, again at Tsurphu. As an adult, while not studying at Tsurphu or maintaining solitary yogic practice in nearby hermitages, the third Karma pa traveled throughout Central and Eastern Tibet giving religious instruction, founding and renovating religious institutions, and acting as a political mediator in times of regional conflict. In 1331 the third Karma pa received an order from a Mongol leader of the Chinese Yuan dynasty (1206–1368) to join him at his capitol. Rang byung rdo rje grudgingly acquiesced to this long journey, and in 1332 arrived at the court. Rang byung rdo rje returned a second time to China in 1338, dying at the capitol a year later. His close relationship with the Yuan emperors gained Tsurphu Monastery tax-exempt status under Mongol sovereignty and ensured subsequent Karma pas favorable ties with later Chinese imperial leadership.

Rang byung rdo rje was a prolific writer on all aspects of Buddhist culture, authoring over a hundred works on Buddhist ritual practice, esoteric philosophy, medicine, astrology, and ethics. He is often credited with combining the contemplative precepts of the "great seal," or *mahāmudrā*, with the Great Perfection system of esoteric practice developed in the Rnying ma school. A verse from the *Great Seal Prayer* makes this identification clear: "Free from subjective activity, this is the Great Seal. Free from extremes, this is the Great Middle Way. This is also called the all-encompassing Great Perfection. May we attain certainty that the awareness of one is the realization of all." This inclusive approach to soteriological doctrine has earned Rang byung rdo rje a place in the canon of the nonsectarian movement of nineteenth-century Tibetan religious history. Indeed, Jamgön Kongtrul (1813–1899), the movement's most important proponent, wrote commentaries on all three of Rang 'byung rdo rje's most famous works. These three works are often considered by tradition as a trilogy on Buddhist theories of ontology, consciousness, and soteriology. The first of these is the *Treatise on Buddha Nature*. In this brief work of only 225 verse lines, the third Karma pa synthesizes ontological notions from exoteric and esoteric Buddhist scriptures, thereby presenting a comprehensive vision of buddha nature—the innate potential for enlightenment in all living beings—as seen in both its latent state and its fully revealed state. The *Treatise* is in many ways an elaboration on two famous quotes from Buddhist canonical literature, with which he begins his work—albeit without citing his sources.

The first is from the *Mahāyāna Abhidharma Sūtra*, a work oft quoted yet unknown in its entirety in Tibet. The popularity of this verse is no doubt due to its bold assertion that buddha nature exists—and is in fact the very reason enlightenment is possible at all: "The beginningless essence is the support of all phenomena. Because it exists, so do all beings, as well as the attainment of liberation from suffering." The second quote is from the *Hevajra Tantra*: "Sentient beings are simply buddhas, save for being obscured by adventitious impurity. If just this [impurity] is removed, there is buddhahood." The rest of the work describes the nature of these impurities, which hide from human beings their true nature, as well as the nature of the fully awakened buddha that results from spiritual practice. Rang byung rdo rje leaves his presentation of the practices for removing these impurities to the third work in his trilogy. The second, *Differentiating Consciousness and Wisdom*, draws heavily on Yogācāra sources to detail the difference between ordinary human perception and the enlightened perception of buddhas, as well as the mechanism by which the former transforms into the latter through contemplative practice.

Finally, the third work of the trilogy, the *Profound Inner Meaning*, outlines the means by which one attains buddhahood according to esoteric Buddhist tradition, particularly the literary cycles of the *Hevajra Tantra* and the *Kālacakra Tantra*. This is perhaps Rang byung rdo rje's most important work, and it has formed the basis of esoteric praxis to the present day. Taking the notion of buddha nature as his starting point, he systematically presents the ontological foundations of human existence, the psycho-physical development of the human body and its physiology as seen from an esoteric Buddhist perspective, the nature of human ignorance and suffering, and finally the nature of enlightenment, as well as the esoteric practices leading to it.

Though neither the fourth or the fifth Karma pas were as prolific as Rang byung rdo rje or as influential in doctrinal matters, both had relations with the imperial court of Ming China (1368–1644), thus contributing substantially to both the prestige and the wealth of the lineage. Later Karma pas would each be remembered for particular aspects of their careers. The seventh authored the authoritative work on logic and epistemology (*pramāṇa*) in the Karma pa scholastic tradition, and the ninth systematized the contemplative teachings of the great seal traditions in several influential works. The sixteenth Karma pa fled Tibet in 1959 under fear of Chinese rule, and in 1962 he founded Rumtek Monastery in Sikkim, an institution that was to become of seat of the Karma Bka' Brgyud in exile. He was also responsible for introducing the Karma Bka' Brgyud Buddhist tradition to an increasingly interested North American and European populace of Buddhist converts, first visiting the United States in 1974. He died in Chicago in 1981. Political battles surrounded the recognition of the seventeenth Karma pa, with opposing camps continuing to support their Karma pa as the authentic member of the lineage. O rgyan 'phrin las rdo rje (Orgyan Trinlay Dorje, b. 1985) has received the seal of authority by the fourteenth Dalai Lama, and after spending his youth at Tsurphu Monastery in Tibet, moved to the Dalai Lama's center in Dharamsala, India.

It is impossible to speak of the Karma pas without mentioning their Bka' Brgyud brethren, the Shamar pa incarnation lineage, which currently numbers twelve. Rang byung rdo rje himself recognized the first Shamar pa, despite the fact that Grags pa sengge (Drakpa Senge, 1283–1349) was his senior by one year. In subsequent centuries the Karma pa and Shamar pa incarnations would share religious authority in Central Tibet, the senior of the two assuming control of the Karma Kamtshang School. The fourth Shamar pa was intimately involved in the sectarian and political rivalries of the late fifteenth and early sixteenth centuries, most notably between the Karma Kamtshang and the Dge lugs (Geluk) schools. While the Karma pa lineage has continued uninterrupted to the present day, the Shamar pa lineage was disbanded by the central Tibetan government in 1792 due to the ninth Shamar pa's complicity in the Nepalese invasion of Tibet, to be reinstated a century later.

According to the *Blue Annals* of the famed Tibetan historian 'Gos Lo tsa ba Gzon nu dpal (Go Lotsawa, 1392–1481), the Karma pas and the Shamar pas were, respectively, the first and second incarnation lineages in Tibet. The situation proves to be more complicated than this, however, and 'Gos Lo tsa ba likely links the origins of reincarnated religious masters in Tibet to the Karma pas and Shamar pas because of his close relations with the Karma Bka' Brgyud pa leaders of fifteenth-century Tibet. Nevertheless, his assertion does emphasize the foundational role of these two lineages in making the phenomenon of incarnation an integral part of Tibetan religion and politics. For it is likely upon these two that the most powerful incarnation lineage to develop in Tibet was modeled, the succession of the Dalai Lamas, who would decisively wrest political and cultural hegemony from the Karma pas and Shamar pas in the seventeenth century, forever changing the face of rule by rebirth in Tibet.

The Karma pa Lineage

1. Dus gsum mkhyen pa (Dusum Khyenpa): 1110–1193
2. Karma pakshi (Karma Pakshi): 1204–1283
3. Rang byung rdo rje (Rangjung Dorje): 1284–1339
4. Rol pa'i rdo rje (Rolpay Dorje): 1340–1383
6. Mthong ba don ldan (Tongwa Dondan): 1416–1453
7. Chos grags rgya mtsho (Chodrak Gyatso): 1450/1454–1506
8. Mi bskyod rdo rje (Mikyo Dorje): 1507–1554
9. Dbang phyug rdo rje (Wangchuk Dorje): 1556–1603
10. Chos dbyings rdo rje (Choying Dorje): 1604–1674
11. Ye shes rdo rje (Yeshe Dorje): 1675–1702
12. Byang chub rdo rje (Jangchup Dorje): 1703–1732
13. Bdud 'dul rdo rje (Dudul Dorje): 1733/1734–1797/1798
14. Theg mchog rdo rje (Tekchok Dorje): 1799–1869
15. Mkha' khyab rdo rje (Khakyap Dorje): 1870/1871–1921/1922
16. Rang byung rig pa'i rdo rje (Rangjung Rikpay Dorje): 1924–1981

17 (1). O rgyan 'phrin las rdo rje (Orgyan Trinlay Dorje): 1985–

17 (2). 'Phrin las mtha' yas rdo rje (Trinlay Taye Dorje): 1983–

The Shamar pa Lineage

1. Grags pa sengge (Drakpa Senge): 1283–1349
2. Mkha' spyod dbang po (Kacho Wangpo): 1350–1405
3. Chos dpal ye shes (Chopal Yeshe): 1406–1452. Chos grags ye shes (Chodrak Yeshe): 1453–1524
5. Dkon mchog yan lag (Konchok Yenlak): 1525–15836. Chos kyi dbang phyug (Chokyi Wangchuk): 1584–1630. Yeshe Nyingpo ye shes snying po: 1631–1694
8. Dpal chen chos kyi don grub (Palchen Chokyi Dondrup): 1695–1732
9. Dkon mchog dge ba'i 'byung gnas (Konchok Geway Jungnay): 1733–1740
10. Chos grub rgya mtsho (Chodrup Gyatso): 1741/1742–1792
11. 'Jam dbyangs rin po che (Jamyang Rinpoche): 1892–1946

12. Mi pham chos kyi blo gros (Mipam Chokyi Lodro): 1952–

BIBLIOGRAPHY

Richardson, Hugh. "The Karma-pa Sect: A Historical Note." In *High Peaks, Pure Earth: Collected Writings on Tibetan History and Culture*, pp. 337–378. London, 1998.

Roerich, George, trans. and ed. *The Blue Annals.* Calcutta, 1949–1953; reprint, New Delhi, 1976.

KURTIS R. SCHAEFFER (2005)

KARO, YOSEF (1488–1575), Talmudic scholar, codifier of rabbinic law, and qabbalist. Yosef Karo (or Caro) grew up and lived in the century following the expulsion of the Jews from the Iberian Peninsula (first from Spain in 1492 by the Catholic rulers Ferdinand and Isabella, then from Portugal in 1497). It was a period of turmoil, major demographic shifts, messianic longings, and mystical revival. Karo was the scion of a family of illustrious scholars. Whether he was born in Toledo or whether his family had already left Spain for Turkey (either directly or via Portugal) before the expulsion is uncertain. His father and first teacher, Efrayim, died when Yosef was still very young, and his place was taken by Yosef's uncle, Yitsḥaq Karo, to whom he frequently and respectfully refers in his writings as "my uncle and master."

We do not know exactly at which schools Yosef Karo studied, but most of the first half of his life was spent in the Balkan provinces of the Ottoman empire (Salonika, but mainly Adrianople and Nikopol). The influx of Iberian Jewish (Sefardic) refugees had turned Ottoman Turkey into one of the most important centers of sixteenth-century Jewry, and Jewish communities and academies of learning were flourishing. In Salonika Karo also met Yosef Taytazak, one of the leading Talmudic scholars and qabbalistic charismatics of his generation, as well as the young ex-Marrano enthusiast and visionary Shelomoh Molkho. The latter's death at the stake in 1532, after his ill-fated mission to the pope, left a deep impression on Karo and no doubt inspired his unfulfilled desire to die a martyr's death. (In fact he died in Safad at the ripe age of eighty-seven.)

In addition to the academies of rabbinic learning, circles of qabbalistic and mystical pietists also flourished in the various Jewish centers of the Ottoman empire, especially in the Balkans, and Karo and his friend and disciple Shelomoh Alkabets were among their most prominent figures. These circles undoubtedly were the seedbed of the great mystical, and subsequently messianic, revival that took place in Safad in Galilee and from there swept over world Jewry. Because of the deaths of his wives, Karo married at least three times and had several children, of whom three survived him.

The dates of Karo's biography and literary activity have to be pieced together from incidental references in his writings. By 1522 he was settled in Nikopol and already enjoyed a reputation as one of the foremost rabbinic scholars. In that year he began work on his monumental commentary on the code of the great Talmudist Ya'aqov ben Asher (1270–1343). He finished this work, the *Beit Yosef,* twenty years later in Safad. Whereas the classic and most complete code, that of Moses Maimonides (Mosheh ben Maimon, 1135/8–1204), simply and clearly set forth the law without argument or discussion, Ya'aqov ben Asher's *Arba'ah ṭurim* (Four Rows, i.e., four main parts) also reviewed the opinions of earlier authorities. Such review may have been the reason why Karo chose this code as the basis of his commentary, which is, in fact, a complete digest of the whole relevant halakhic literature. Ya'aqov ben Asher's code, however, unlike that of Maimonides, omits all subjects not applicable in exile and after the destruction of the Temple (e.g., laws concerning the Temple, its priesthood, ritual, and sacrificial cult; legislation concerning kingship, the Sanhedrin, the Jubilee year, and so on). On the basis of his *Beit Yosef,* Karo subsequently produced the *Shulḥan 'arukh* (Set Table, or Short Book, as he himself called it). This précis and synopsis soon established itself as the standard code of Jewish law and practice, especially after Mosheh Isserles of Cracow (d. 1572) had added glosses incorporating the sometimes divergent customs of Ashkenazic Jewry. Since then Karo's code has served as the revered or, alternatively, reviled symbol of orthodox rabbinic Judaism. Karo also wrote a commentary, *Kesef mishneh,* on the code of Maimonides, supplementing the earlier commentary *Maggid mishneh* by the fourteenth-century Spanish scholar Vidal of Tolosa.

Many *responsa* of Karo are also extant. Although of less historical influence than the aforementioned works, they throw much light on the social history of the period, in addition to illustrating Karo's standing as a leading Talmudic authority.

In Safad an attempt was also made—probably inspired by the messianic temper of the age—by one of the foremost Talmudic authorities, Ya'aqov Berab, to renew full rabbinical ordination, which had lapsed in the first centuries of the common era. Karo was one of the four scholars ordained by Berab, but the initiative proved abortive, mainly because of the opposition of the scholars in Jerusalem.

It was probably mystical and messianic ideology that prompted many qabbalists and devout scholars to move from the Diaspora to the Holy Land. Around 1536 Karo, too, realized his long-standing intention and settled in Safad in upper Galilee, which soon became a center of intense mystical and devotional life. The leading qabbalists of the time had converged there, among them Mosheh Cordovero (who belonged to Karo's intimate circle) and Isaac Luria. Karo, like most rabbis of his generation, was also a qabbalistic scholar but, in addition, led a somewhat unusual (though by no means unique) charismatic life. According to various reports, Karo was visited every night by a heavenly mentor who, in the form of what psychology would describe as "automatic speech," revealed to him qabbalistic mysteries, exhortations to ascetic practice, and other matters related to his personal life and to his Talmudic studies. Afterward Karo wrote down the communications received from his celestial *maggid* ("speaker"), who identified himself (or perhaps herself) as the heavenly archetype of the Mishnah. Among Karo's writings there is, therefore, a "mystical diary," printed later in edited form under the title *Maggid mesharim.* Unconvincing attempts have been made to deny the authenticity of the diary, probably because scholarly rationalism, especially in the nineteenth century, could not come to terms with the idea that the great Talmudist, legal scholar, and codifier Yosef Karo was also an ascetic qabbalist and mystical enthusiast, subject to paranormal experiences. While as a qabbalist Karo was less outstanding than many of his Safad contemporaries, the existence of the *Maggid mesharim,* in the shadow, as it were, of the *Beit Yosef* and the *Shulḥan ʿarukh,* is indicative of the complexities of rabbinic Judaism and of the role that Qabbalah played in it, especially in the sixteenth century.

BIBLIOGRAPHY

Twersky, Isadore. "The *Shulḥan ʿAruk*: Enduring Code of Jewish Law." In *The Jewish Expression,* edited by Judah Goldin, pp. 322–343. New York, 1970.

Werblowsky, R. J. Zwi. "Caro, Joseph ben Ephraim." In *Encyclopaedia Judaica.* Jerusalem, 1971.

Werblowsky, R. J. Zwi. *Joseph Karo: Lawyer and Mystic.* 2d ed. Philadelphia, 1980.

R. J. ZWI WERBLOWSKY (1987)

KARUṆĀ, normally translated as "compassion," is a term central to the entire Buddhist tradition. When linked with *prajñā* ("wisdom") it constitutes one of the two pillars of Buddhism. *Karuṇā* is frequently described as the love for all beings, as exemplified by a mother's love for a child. However, *karuṇā* is quite unlike conventional "love" (Skt., *priya, kāma, tṛṣṇā*), which is rooted in dichotomous thinking (*vijñāna, vikalpa*) and centered on self-concern. Love in this latter sense is egoistic, possessive, clouded by ignorance (*avidyā*), and easily subject to its opposite passion, hate.

In contrast, *karuṇā* is manifested in the non-dichotomous mode of *prajñā* that has broken through the self-other discrimination. Thus freed of self-centeredness, *karuṇā* is concerned only with the welfare of the other. The root meaning of *karuṇā* is said to be the anguished cry of deep sorrow that elicits compassion. Love in the conventional sense and compassion in its Buddhist sense may be loosely equated to *eros* and *agapē,* respectively.

The life of Śākyamuni Buddha, especially his missionary work of forty-five years, is a manifestation par excellence of compassion. The cruciality of compassionate deeds for the attainment of supreme enlightenment is evident in the *jātakas,* a collection of fables recounting the previous lives of the Buddha. The evolution of Buddhism in Asia and its spread throughout the world are, from a Buddhist point of view, none other than the unfolding of *karuṇā* in history.

In Buddhist doctrine, *karuṇā* is most commonly found as the second of the Four Immeasurable Attitudes (*catvāri apramāṇāni*) that are to be cultivated in meditative practice: *maitrī* ("friendliness"), *karuṇā* ("compassion"), *muditā* ("sympathetic joy"), and *upekṣā* ("equanimity"). Friendliness is said to give pleasure and happiness to others, compassion uproots pain and suffering, and sympathetic joy refers to one's joy for the happiness of others. Finally, equanimity frees one from attachment to these attitudes so that one may go forth to practice them in the service of all those in need.

The Mahāyāna scriptures, in spite of their diversity and differences, reveal the multifaceted dimensions of *karuṇā.* Central to all Mahāyāna texts is the *bodhisattva* vow, which puts the deliverance of all beings from *saṃsāra* (i.e., the cycle of births and deaths) before one's own deliverance. To put it in a more personal way, the vow states, "As long as there is one unhappy person in the world, my happiness is incomplete." The vow acknowledges the absolute equality of self and other (*parātmasamatā*) and the interchangeability of self and other (*parātmaparivartana*), such that one willingly takes on the suffering of others.

Philosophically, the justification of compassion is rooted in the notion of *śūnyatā* ("emptiness"), which sweeps away all divisions and discriminations—self and other, good and bad, like and dislike, and so forth—that are created by the arbitrary conceptions of the subjective mind. This clearing away of all forms of discursive thinking, originating from the fictive self, is none other than the working of *prajñā,* which is inseparable from *karuṇā.* Wisdom and compassion are said to be like two wheels of a cart or two wings of a bird.

Another important dimension of compassion that figures in Mahāyāna Buddhism is *mahākaruṇā* ("great compassion"). The adjective "great" connotes the transcendent nature of the compassion that is an essential quality of Buddhahood. All Buddhas—whether Śākyamuni, Vairocana, Bhaiṣajyaguru, Amitābha, Akṣobhya, and others—manifest great compassion. Amitābha (Jpn., Amida) Buddha, for example, reveals great compassion in his "primal vow" (Jpn., *hongan*), which states that his attainment of supreme Buddhahood was contingent upon the guarantee of the selfsame enlightenment for all beings who have faith in him. The practitioner of the Mahāyāna path, then, becomes a recipient of great compassion. In fact, it is said that the *bodhisattva* progresses on the path to enlightenment by virtue not of his own powers but of the powers of great compassion.

Historically, however, *karuṇā* is also manifested in such practical expressions as acts of generosity or charity (*dāna*). Among the *puṇyakṣetra* ("merit-fields", i.e., sources for creating religious merit) available to the devotee are compassion, wherein those in need, helpless beasts, and even insects are the objects of care and concern; gratitude, where parents, all sentient beings, rulers, and the Three Treasures (Buddha, Dharma, Sangha) are revered; the poor, where the destitute are fed, clothed, and housed; and animals, which are to be released from human enslavement. In premodern times, *karuṇā* was also understood and appreciated in much more concrete forms: planting fruit orchards and trees, digging bathing ponds, dispensing medicine, building bridges, digging wells along highways, making public toilets, establishing clinics and orphanages, teaching sericulture, farming methods and irrigation, building dikes and canals, and countless other welfare activities.

See Also Prajñā.

Bibliography

There is no single monograph on *karuṇā* in any Western language. Because it permeates Buddhist literature, it is best to go to the original sources. A good sampling may be found in Edwin A. Burtt's *The Teachings of the Compassionate Buddha* (New York, 1955). For the relationship between *śūnyatā* and compassion, see *The Holy Teaching of Vimalakirti,* translated by Robert A. F. Thurman (University Park, Pa., 1976); for the working of wisdom, compassion, and *upāya* (liberative technique), see *The Threefold Lotus Sutra,* translated by Bunnō Katō and others (New York, 1975); and for the Primal Vow of compassion, see "The Larger Sukhāvatī-vyūha," in *Buddhist Mahāyāna Texts,* edited by E. B. Cowell, in "Sacred Books of the East," vol. 49 (1894; reprint, New York, 1969).

New Sources

Clayton, Barbra. "Ahimsa, Karuna and Maitri: Implications for Environmental Buddhism." *Ecumenism* 134 (1999): 27–31.

Jenkins, S. L. "The Circle of Compassion: An Interpretive Study of Karuna in Indian Buddhist Literature." Ph.D. diss., Harvard University, 1999.

Viévard, L. *Vacuité (Sunyata) et Compassion (Karuna) dans le Bouddhisme Madhyamaka.* Paris, 2002.

Taitetsu Unno (1987)
Revised Bibliography

KASHMIR ŚAIVISM See Śaivism

KASHRUT, from the Hebrew word *kasher* (Eng., kosher), meaning "acceptable" (see *Est.* 8:15), denotes anything permitted by Jewish law for use. More specifically, it connotes the Jewish dietary laws. Kashrut pertains directly to (1) permitted and forbidden animals, (2) forbidden parts of otherwise permitted animals, (3) the method of slaughtering and preparing permitted animals, (4) forbidden food mixtures, and (5) proportions of food mixtures prohibited ab initio but permitted *ex post facto.* The rules of *kashrut* are derived from biblical statute, rabbinic interpretation, rabbinic legislation, and custom, as outlined below.

Biblical Law. According to the Bible, animals permitted for Jewish consumption must have fully cloven hooves and chew the cud (*Lv.* 11:3). Forbidden fowl are listed (*Lv.* 11:13–19, *Dt.* 14:11–18), as are forbidden insects (*Lv.* 11: 21–22, *Dt.* 14:20), but no characteristics are presented for determining their forbidden status. Fish must have fins and scales (*Lv.* 11:9, *Dt.* 14:9). Both Jews and gentiles are forbidden to eat flesh torn from a living animal (*Gn.* 9:3). Jews are not to consume the blood of permitted animals or the fat that covers their inner organs (*Lv.* 3:17, 7:23), that is, tallow or suet. Both this blood and this fat were to be offered on the altar of the Temple in the case of animals fit for sacrifice (e.g., *Lv.* 1:11–12). In the case of an animal permitted for ordinary consumption but not for sacrifice, the blood is to be poured on the ground and covered (*Lv.* 17:13, *Dt.* 12:16). The same is the case with the blood of fowl slaughtered for ordinary use. Animals that died of internal causes or that were killed by other animals are not to be consumed (*Ex.* 22:30). Also, the sciatic nerve of slaughtered animals is not to be eaten (*Gn.* 32:32). Finally, a kid is not to be cooked in the milk of its own mother (*Ex.* 23:29, 34:26; *Dt.* 14:21).

Rabbinic Interpretation. The rabbinic sources present a number of important and wide-reaching interpretations of these biblical laws which are seen as being themselves "oral Mosaic traditions" *(halakhah le-Mosheh mi-Sinai).* Thus, the rabbis determined that all birds of prey are forbidden for Jewish consumption (*Ḥul.* 5.6). The requirement that fish have fins and scales was qualified to include any fish that had scales at any point in its development even if they subsequently fell off (B.T., *Ḥul.* 66a–b). Milk from nonkosher animals was forbidden because it was judged as having the status of its source (*Bekh.* 1.2). An important exception to this rule is the honey of bees, which the rabbis determined does not have anything from the bee's body in it (see B.T., *Bekh.* 7b). The Babylonian Talmud presents criteria for distinguishing between permitted and forbidden fat (B.T., *Ḥul.* 49b). The blood drained from permitted animals and fowl after slaughter is covered with soil or ashes (*Ḥul.* 6.7).

Sheḥiṭah. The method of slaughtering permitted animals and fowl, known as *sheḥiṭah,* is not explicated in scripture but is seen as the prime example of a law commanded orally by Moses, to whom it was divinely revealed (B.T., *Ḥul.* 28a). The throat of the animal or bird must be slit with a perfectly smooth blade by a highly trained and supervised slaughterer (*shoḥeṭ*), who recites a blessing before cutting across the gullet and windpipe, severing the jugular. Detailed regulations govern the process; internal irregularities found in the lungs and other organs render even properly slaughtered animals unfit for consumption by Jews (*ṭerefah, Hul.* 3.1ff.). Various procedures are presented for draining the blood from the slaughtered animal, such as opening the arteries and veins, soaking and salting the meat, and broiling the meat over a flame. The laws that required Jews to eat meat slaughtered by a trained *shoḥeṭ* often determined where Jews could and could not live, and the presence of a kosher butcher has, in modern Jewish history, often symbolized the existence of an observant Jewish community.

Milk and meat. In the area of mixing milk and meat, rabbinic interpretation considerably expanded the biblical prohibition of simply not "cooking a kid in its mother's milk." The rabbis extended this law from animals fit to be offered on the altar (i.e., the lamb) to all animals and fowl in order to avoid any possible confusion (B.T., *Ḥul.* 104a). The Talmud interprets the threefold mention of this prohibition in the Pentateuch as entailing three distinct prohibitions: (1) eating, (2) cooking, and (3) deriving any monetary benefit from such a mixture of meat and milk. These prohibitions were elaborated by requirements for the use of separate dishes and utensils for meat foods and milk foods.

RABBINICAL LEGISLATION. In addition to the interpretations presented as ultimately Mosaic, the rabbis legislated additional rules in connection with those seen as biblical or traditional. All insects were forbidden because it was assumed that there was no longer to be found the necessary expertise to distinguish between those permitted and those forbidden. (*Ṭaz* [David ben Shemu'el ha-Levi] on *Shulḥan ʿarukh, Yoreh deʿah* 85.1). Because of concern that gentiles might mix milk from nonkosher sources in the milk they sell to Jews, and that cheese from gentiles might contain nonkosher rennet, the precaution arose that milk and cheese must be prepared under Jewish supervision (*ʿA.Z.* 2.6). When this was not a likely possibility, however, this precaution was relaxed (*Responsa Tashbatz,* 4.1.32). The rabbis ruled that whereas one may follow a milk meal with a meat meal (except when hard cheese was eaten), after washing the hands and rinsing the mouth, one must wait a period of time before consuming a milk meal after a meat meal.

Because at times meat foods and milk foods are accidentally mixed, the rabbis developed a number of rules to determine whether or not the mixture could be used ex post facto. Generally, if the ratio is 60 to 1 or more, then the smaller substance is considered absorbed (*baṭel*) in the larger substance (B.T., *Ḥul.* 97b), provided the smaller substance neither changes the flavor of the larger substance, or gives the larger substance its actual form, and provided the smaller substance is not still found intact.

In order to discourage social contact between Jews and gentiles which might lead to intermarriage and assimilation (B.T., *ʿA.Z.* 36b; J.T., *Shab.* 3c), and because non-Jewish wine might have been produced for idolatrous purposes, the rabbis forbade Jews to drink wine or wine products made by non-Jews (B.T., *ʿA.Z.* 29b). However, because certain non-Jews were no longer considered idolators, and for other reasons, a number of authorities relaxed some (but not all) of these prohibitions. (See, for example, Maimonides' *Mishneh Torah,* Forbidden Foods 11.7; Mosheh Isserles's *Responsa,* no. 124.)

CUSTOM. Custom determines a number of *kashrut* regulations, often being divergent in different communities. If certain fowl is not customarily eaten in a particular community, then this custom has the force of law there for no other reason. Although the hindquarters of permitted mammals may be eaten after the sciatic nerve has been totally removed, because of the great amount of energy and time required by this procedure, and because of the greater availability of meat in modern times, it has become the custom in Western Europe and America (but not in Israel) for the hindquarters of slaughtered animals to be sold to non-Jews as a regular practice rather than their being eaten by Jews.

Because of the rabbinic requirement for the internal examination of slaughtered animals (*bediqah*) to determine whether or not any abnormalities were present before slaughtering, elaborate methods of certification have evolved to guard against error or fraud. Often there are today competing rabbinical groups giving approval to different sources of kosher meat inasmuch as demands for reliability vary. Also, advances in food technology have led to the requirement that most processed foods be rabbinically certified (*hekhsher*) as not containing any forbidden substances.

Because of the custom in many Hungarian communities not to consume meat with certain irregularities nevertheless permitted by rabbinical legislation, the practice of certifying meat as *glaṭ kosher* (Yi., "smooth," without blemish) arose. In America, since the immigration of many Hungarian Orthodox Jews after World War II, *glaṭ kosher* has become a connotation of a stricter and more reliable level of *kashrut.*

Custom varies as to how long one is to wait after consuming meat before consuming milk. Moses Maimonides (1135/8–1204), followed by most other authorities, required a six-hour interval (*Mishneh Torah,* Forbidden Foods 9.28). Other authorities require a much shorter interval (B.T., *Ḥul.* 105a; Tos., s.v. *le-seʿudata*). Customarily, eastern European Jews and Sephardic Jews and their descendants follow Maimonides; German Jews and their descendants wait three hours; and some Dutch Jews of Sephardic origin wait as little as slightly over one hour.

Orthodox and Conservative Judaism generally follow the same standards of *kashrut,* based on biblical, rabbinic, and customary rules. Conservative Judaism, however, tends to follow more lenient options within the law itself, such as not requiring cheeses manufactured in the United States to be certified kosher. Reform Judaism, because it does not regard *halakhah* in toto as authoritative, does not, therefore, regard *kashrut* as binding. Some Reform Jews as an individual option do follow *kashrut* completely, and others follow at least those rules that are biblically explicit.

THEOLOGICAL INTERPRETATION. Although scholars have long recognized similarities between the biblical laws and other ancient Near Eastern customs, the laws of *kashrut* are traditionally considered to be *ḥuqqim,* that is, laws about which "Satan and the gentiles raise objections" (B.T., *Yoma'* 67b), namely laws without apparent reasons. Nevertheless, Jewish theologians have attempted to penetrate their deeper meaning to discover hidden reasons for them.

Because of the frequent biblical mention of holiness (*qedushah*) in connection with these laws (e.g., *Lv.* 11:44–45), a number of the rabbis emphasized that their very unintelligibility is a test of one's full acceptance of the authority of God's law (e.g., *Gn. Rab.* 44.1). However, even here the general reason of holiness is taken to mean separation of Jews from gentiles (*Lv.* 20:26). The importance of this general motif is seen in texts from the Maccabean period (c. 150 BCE), when the forced assimilation of Jews usually began with making them eat forbidden foods (*Dn.* 1:8, *2 Mc.* 7:1ff., *4 Mc.* 5:1ff.). In rabbinic law one is required to die as a martyr rather than violate *kashrut,* when the violation is clearly symbolic of general apostasy (B.T., *San.* 74a).

Some of the earliest and latest rationales for *kashrut* have emphasized the moral intent of having Jews refrain from foods that are either taken from cruel animals (*Letter of Aristeas,* 142–147) or, also, symbolize bad moral traits (S. R. Hirsch, *Horeb,* trans. M. Hados, New York, 1951). Interestingly, early Christian criticism of Judaism argued that Jewish preoccupation with these laws actually leads to the neglect of morality (*Mk.* 7:14–23).

Maimonides saw the reasons for these laws as being based on both considerations of safe and healthy diet and the avoidance of some ancient idolatrous practices (*Guide of the Perplexed,* ed. Shlomo Pines, Chicago, 1963, 3.48; cf. *Ḥinukh,* no. 92). This emphasis on physiological reasons is followed by other Jewish scholars, such as Shemu'el ben Me'ir in the twelfth century (e.g., on *Lv.* 11:30 re B.T., *Shab.* 86b) and Moses Nahmanides in the thirteenth century (e.g., on *Lv.* 11:9 in his *Commentary on the Torah*). Others, however, reject this whole approach as unduly secular (e.g., Avraham ben David of Posquières on *Sifra: Qedoshim,* ed. I. H. Weiss, 93d; *Zohar* 3:221a–b). The qabbalists, based on their view that every mundane act is a microcosm of the macrocosm of divine emanations (*sefirot*), worked out elaborate symbolic explanations of how the laws of *kashrut* reflect the cosmic economy and of their spiritual effect on human life. Among these mystics were, in the fourteenth century, Menahem Recanati, author of *Ṭa'amei ha-mitsvot* and, in the fifteenth century, Yitsḥaq Arama, author of *'Aqedat Yitsḥaq.* In these classic qabbalistic treatments of *kashrut,* forbidden foods were seen as imparting the cosmic impurity of the demonic forces that work against the godhead.

SEE ALSO Food; Passover.

BIBLIOGRAPHY

The literature on kashrut is enormous, in both English and Hebrew. The following English works are particularly useful: J. J. Berman's *Shehitah: A Study in the Cultural and Social Life of the Jewish People* (New York, 1941); Samuel H. Dresner and Seymour Siegel's *The Jewish Dietary Laws,* 2d rev. ed. (New York, 1966); Isidor Grunfeld's work by the same name, especially volume 1, *Dietary Laws with Particular Reference to Meat and Meat Products* (New York, 1972); Isaac Klein's *A Guide to Jewish Religious Practice* (New York, 1979); and my *Law and Theology in Judaism,* vol. 2 (New York, 1976). Two very different approaches to understanding the relationship between dietary and other purity laws can be found in Jacob Neusner's *The Idea of Purity in Ancient Judaism* (Leiden, 1973) and Mary Douglas's *Purity and Danger* (London, 1966), and in Douglas's "Critique and Commentary" on Neusner in his volume, pp. 137–142.

DAVID NOVAK (1987 AND 2005)

KĀŚI SEE BANARAS

KATHENOTHEISM SEE HENOTHEISM

KAUFMANN, YEḤEZKEL (1889–1963), was an Israeli Bible scholar and philosopher of Jewish history. Born in the Ukraine, Kaufmann was educated in Bible, Talmud, and Jewish history and received a doctorate in philosophy from the University of Bern in 1918. From 1914 to 1928 he lived in Germany, writing on Jewish nationalism. Immigrating to Israel (then Palestine) in 1928, he published a four-volume historical-sociological interpretation of Jewish history, *Golah ve-nekhar* (Exile and alienage; 1928–1932). His eight-volume *Toldot ha-emunah ha-Yisre'elit* (A history of the religion of Israel; 1937–1956) is the most comprehensive study of biblical religion by a modern Jewish scholar. From 1949 until 1957 he was professor of Bible at the Hebrew University of Jerusalem.

Kaufmann's major writings, historical and ideological, are distinguished by philosophical sophistication, methodological reflectiveness, and detailed textual analysis. In *Toldot,* a comprehensive, detailed analysis of the Bible and biblical religion, he argues (1) that the idea of one God ruling over nature was the unique creation of the nation of Israel, (2) that monotheism arose during the early stages of the nation's history, and (3) that, far from being influenced by genuine paganism, Israel was virtually ignorant of it. This work, which criticized prevalent ideas of modern biblical scholarship regarding the dating of the Torah texts, Israelite monotheism, and the impact of paganism on Israelite religion, had a decisive influence on an entire generation of Jewish Bible scholars.

In *Golah ve-nekhar,* Kaufmann employs historical-sociological arguments to demonstrate (1) that Israel's commitment to the monotheistic idea was the decisive factor ensuring the nation's survival in exile and (2) that in the modern era of secularization and nationalism, only a Jewish homeland could ensure the people Israel's survival. Like his biblical studies, this work is distinguished from other works on Jewish history both by its scope and by its mode of argumentation.

BIBLIOGRAPHY

Works by Kaufmann

Kaufmann's major works remain untranslated. An abridged translation of *Toldot ha-emunah ha-Yisre'elit,* containing Kaufmann's major arguments, is *The Religion of Israel from Its Be-*

ginnings to the Babylonian Exile, translated and abridged by Moshe Greenberg (Chicago, 1960). An English essay, "The Biblical Age," in *Great Ages and Ideas of the Jewish People,* edited by Leo W. Schwarz (New York, 1956), covers the development of Israelite religion to the end of the Second Temple. A preliminary presentation of his Hebrew studies of *Joshua* and *Judges* is *The Biblical Account of the Conquest of Palestine,* translated by M. Dagut (Jerusalem, 1953).

Works about Kaufmann

A critical discussion of Kaufmann's basic arguments regarding biblical Israel is Moshe Greenberg's "Kaufmann on the Bible: An Appreciation," *Judaism* 13 (Winter 1964): 77–89. For Kaufmann's interpretation of Jewish history, see my own "Religion, Ethnicity and Jewish History: The Contribution of Yehezkel Kaufmann," *Journal of the American Academy of Religion* 42 (September 1974): 516–531. Kaufmann's historical-sociological method is discussed critically in my "Historical Sociology and Ideology: A Prolegomenon to Yehezkel Kaufmann's *Golah v'Nekhar,*" in *Essays in Modern Jewish History: A Tribute to Ben Halpern,* edited by Frances Malino and Phyllis Cohen Albert (East Brunswick, N.J., 1982), pp. 173–195.

New Sources

Luz, Ehud. "Jewish Nationalism in the Thought of Yehezkel Kaufmann." *Binah* 2 (1989): 177–190.

LAURENCE J. SILBERSTEIN (1987)
Revised Bibliography

KAZAKH RELIGION SEE INNER ASIAN RELIGIONS

KEIZAN (1264–1325), more fully Keizan Jōkin, was the founding abbot of the Sōjiji Zen monastery. Since the late nineteenth century, he has officially been designated, along with Dōgen (1200–1253), as one of the two founding patriarchs of the Japanese Sōtō Zen school.

Born in 1264 (not 1268 as previously assumed), Keizan entered Eiheiji, the Zen monastery founded by Dōgen in Echizen province, in 1276. Keizan studied Zen directly under four of Dōgen's leading disciples: Ejō (1198–1280), Jakuen (1207–1299), Gien (d. 1313), and Gikai (1219–1309). In 1298 Keizan succeeded Gikai as second abbot of Daijōji monastery in Kaga province. Eventually Keizan entrusted Daijōji to his disciple, Meihō Sotetsu (1277–1350), and began constructing a new monastery in Noto province named Tōkoku-san Yōkōji, which he envisioned as the future headquarters of the Sōtō Zen lineage in Japan. With Yōkōji as his base, Keizan founded six more monasteries nearby, including Hōōji, the first Sōtō nunnery, and Sōjiji, which he entrusted to his disciple Gasan Jōseki (1276–1366).

Keizan worked hard to establish a firm religious and institutional basis for the nascent Sōtō Zen school. Toward these ends, he authored a history of the Sōtō Zen lineage (the *Denkōroku*), founded a memorial hall at Yōkōji to enshrine relics of five generations of Sōtō Zen patriarchs, wrote beginner's guides to Zen training, and compiled detailed instructions for every aspect of Zen monastic life. His most influential contribution was his detailed instructions on how the abbotship of his monasteries should be rotated among several lines of succession so as to ensure united support and avoid schisms. This method of rotating abbotship became widely adopted among subsequent Sōtō monasteries. It was implemented most successfully not at Yōkōji, but at Sōjiji, which eventually grew to have more affiliated branch temples than any other Sōtō institution. By the beginning of the twenty-first century, Sōjiji, relocated in 1910 to Yokohama (next to Tokyo), had become one of the two headquarter temples (along with Eiheiji) of the Sōtō Zen school. In 1909 the Meiji emperor (Mutsuhito, 1852–1912) awarded Keizan with the posthumous name Jōsai Daishi.

Keizan's life and its significance have been the subject of much unsubstantiated speculation. Many modern Japanese interpretations of Keizan reflect an artificial structural antagonism between him and Dōgen, with the latter's teachings being portrayed as more pure, more elitest, and more monastic in orientation, in contrast to which Keizan's teachings are seen as more eclectic, more common, and more accessible to laypeople. This narrative of Keizan as the purported popularizer of Dōgen's so-called strict Zen rests not on the historical evidence but on simplistic apologetics that attempt to justify Sōjiji's modern preeminence over and above Dōgen's Eiheiji. Keizan, as much as Dōgen, focused his life's efforts on providing strict monastic training for monks and nuns. Likewise, Dōgen, as much as Keizan, worked to build an institutional foundation for Japanese Zen. Keizan was long departed before subsequent generations of monks at Sōjiji and its affiliates began effecting the rapid growth and transformation of Sōtō Zen into an institution consisting primarily of local temples that service the religious needs of laypeople who themselves do not practice Zen.

It is also true, however, that Keizan was a man of his times. In addition to Zen history, Zen training, and Zen monasticism, his writings reveal many religious themes common to other fourteenth-century Japanese religious writings. Keizan openly described, for example, his reliance on inspired dreams as a source of religious authority, his use of astrology, his devotion to his mother and grandmother, his invocation of the local gods who protect Buddhism, and his devout faith in the bodhisattva Avalokiteśvara (Japanese, Kannon). These kinds of trans-sectarian religious values exerted, no doubt, a greater influence on the lives of ordinary people than did Keizan's difficult Zen practices or abstruse Zen doctrines. For this reason, Keizan's surviving writings constitute prime sources for the study of medieval Japanese religiosity and the ways that it interacted with sectarian doctrinal traditions (such as Zen) and their institutions.

Keizan's numerous writings were not collected, edited, or published during his lifetime. Extant manuscript versions, as well as published editions, are marred by numerous textual defects, copyist errors, and arbitrary editorial deletions, additions, and rearrangements. Scholars have not begun to resolve all the difficulties these texts present. Nonetheless, Keizan's authorship of the major works traditionally attributed to him is no longer considered doubtful. These major words include the following: *Denkōroku* (History of the transmission of the light); *Zazen yōjinki* (How to practice sitting Zen); *Tōkoku gyōji jijo* (Procedures at Tōkoku monastery), also known as *Keizan shingi* (Keizan's monastic regulations); and *Tōkokuki* (Chronicle of Tōkoku monastery).

See Also Dōgen; Zen.

Bibliography

Azuma Ryūshin. *Keizan Zenji no kenkyū* (A study of Zen teacher Keizan). Tokyo, 1974.

Bodiford, William M. *Sōtō Zen in Medieval Japan.* Honolulu, 1994.

Bodiford, William M. "Keizan's Dream History." In *Religions of Japan in Practice,* edited by George J. Tanabe Jr., pp. 501–522. Princeton, 1999.

Faure, Bernard. *Visions of Power: Imagining Medieval Japanese Buddhism.* Translated by Phyllis Brooks. Princeton, 1996.

Hirose Ryōkō. "Eiheiji no suiun to fukkō undō" (The decline and revival of Eiheiji monastery). In *Eiheijishi* (The history of Eiheiji monastery), edited by Sakurai Shūyū, vol. 1, pp. 379–541. Fukui Pref., 1982.

Keizan Zenji Hōsan Kankōkai, eds. *Keizan Zenji kenkyū* (Researches on Zen teacher Keizan). Tokyo, 1974.

Sahashi Hōryū. *Ningen Keizan* (Keizan as a human being). Tokyo, 1979.

"Taiso Keizan Zenji roppyaku gojūkai daionki hōsan." (Special issue dedicated to the 650th anniversary of the Great Patriarch Keizan.) *Shūgaku kenkyū* 16 (1974).

Takeuchi Kōdō. "Keizan Zenji ryaku nenpyō (seju rokujūni sai)" (Brief chronology of Zen teacher Keizan's sixty-two-year lifetime). *Sōtōshū kenkyūin kenkyūsei kenkyū kiyō* 18 (1986): 151–164.

William M. Bodiford (2005)

KEMPE, MARGERY

KEMPE, MARGERY (c. 1373–c.1440), English pilgrim, autobiographer, and professional holy woman. Kempe was the daughter of a prosperous merchant of King's Lynn, England. Although happily married, she tended to have hysterical fits during which God spoke to her. At about the age of forty, having had fourteen children, she persuaded her husband that God wished them to take a vow of chastity. By this time the Deity was conversing agreeably with her nearly every day. Her meditations tended to concentrate on the Passion and to bring on wild lamentations, uncontrollable floods of tears, and rollings on the ground. These were widely acceptable signs of grace in the Middle Ages, but there were always some who declared her a fraud. Such charges were dangerous, as they several times led to her arrest as a heretic and a narrow escape from burning. For about twenty-five years, Kempe was a perpetual pilgrim, visiting not only every shrine in England but also the Holy Land, Rome, Santiago de Compostela in Spain, and various northern German centers, gradually establishing a reputation as a prophetess and seer among the less learned.

Kempe's importance for history lies in her autobiography, the first in English, a book intended for the edification of nuns. Although full of moralizing and sermons, it has a saving shrewdness and interest in the world. In the course of her travels, Kempe had numerous alarming encounters and met a host of people, from the archbishops of Canterbury and York, the holy Julian of Norwich, and innumerable friars to a wide range of fellow pilgrims and lesser government officials. It was her wish to write a mystical treatise, such as the famous *Cloud of Unknowing,* but what she did, in her autobiography, was to lay the fifteenth-century world before the reader in all its violence and piety; its blend of the spiritual and the venal, ignorance and learning, feudalism, democracy, and petty officialdom; its magnificence and utter filth. Here is the authentic background to Chaucer's *Canterbury Tales.* No other medieval document enables one so clearly to realize what it was actually like for a humble pilgrim to live and to travel in fifteenth-century Europe.

Bibliography

The Book of Margery Kempe, edited by Hope E. Allen and Sanford B. Meech (London, 1940), is the text dictated by Kempe to a priest about 1438, in the original spelling and fully annotated. The narrative is confused in many places, and the reader will be greatly assisted by the only modern study, *Memoirs of a Medieval Woman: The Life and Times of Margery Kempe,* by Louise Collis (New York, 1964), also published under the title *The Apprentice Saint* (London, 1964). This biography places Kempe's adventures in their proper historical perspective, relating them to the wider political, social, and religious issues of the day.

Louise Collis (1987)

KENYON, KATHLEEN

KENYON, KATHLEEN. Kathleen Mary Kenyon (1906–1978) was born in London on January 5, 1906. She graduated from Somerville College, Oxford, in 1929, and in 1934 she cofounded, with Mortimer Wheeler and Tessa Wheeler, the University of London's Institute of Archaeology. Kenyon served as the institute's first secretary, then as interim director during World War II. She was a lecturer in Palestinian archaeology (1949–1962); was appointed honorary director of the British School of Archaeology in Jerusalem in 1951; and excavated Jericho between 1952 and 1958 and Jerusalem from 1962 to 1967. She served as principal of Saint Hugh's College from 1962 to 1973 and upon her retirement in 1973 received the title Dame of the Order of the British Empire, 1973. After her death on August 24, 1978, in Wrexham, Wales, the British School of Archaeology in Jerusalem was renamed the Kenyon Institute in her honor (2003).

Kenyon is a significant figure in the history of Near Eastern archaeology. She created the Wheeler-Kenyon excavation method, contributed to establishing a dating system for Iron II occupation levels, established the Neolithic origins of biblical Jericho, and uncovered the occupational history of Samaria. She was a teacher as well as a practitioner of archaeology. In addition to lecturing at the University of London's Institute of Archaeology, she also conducted field schools at her excavations in Jericho and Jerusalem. There she trained the next generation of archaeologists from England, the United States, and Europe who in turn handed on her legacy to their students.

Kenyon began her distinguished archaeological career in 1929 as a photographer of Gertrude Canton-Thomson's excavation of the ruins of Zimbabwe in Rhodesia. When she returned to England, Kenyon worked with Mortimer Wheeler and Tessa Wheeler at Verulamium (Saint Albans), directing the excavation of the Roman theater during the summer field seasons from 1930 to 1935. Wheeler was considered the founder of modern British archaeology, and Kenyon learned his box-grid excavation system. The Wheeler system divided a site into five-meter squares with one-meter balks (walls) between them in order to uncover and excavate horizontally the layered remains of human occupation according to their natural contours. Layers (strata) differed in color, consistency, and contents—information generally previously unrecorded on excavations whose major goal was recovering a site's architecture. Diagnostic ceramics (for example, jar handles, rims, and bases) helped to date the strata from which they were recovered.

Kenyon's first foray into Near Eastern archaeology was her collaboration with John Crowfoot and Grace Crowfoot at Samaria (1931–1933). Kenyon used Wheeler's method to excavate trenches across the top of the mound and down its northern and southern slopes, uncovering evidence of human occupation from the Roman period to Iron II. Her findings provided important ceramic dating material for Palestinian Iron II stratigraphy and for the study of *terra sigilata* ware. Colleagues considered Kenyon's fieldwork at Samaria a high point in Palestinian archaeology.

Kenyon directed her career-defining excavation of Tel es-Sultan, ancient Jericho, from 1952 to 1958. Building on her work in Samaria, she created the Wheeler-Kenyon method, which is still a popular technique among Near Eastern archaeologists. By this method, she dug a deep, stepped trench down to bedrock on one side of the site in order to trace its history of human occupation. To follow a surface or a building's foundations, for example, she excavated horizontally in a series of five-meter squares, leaving balks intact.

Jericho was one of the first sites excavated in Palestine. The British engineer Charles Warren surveyed the site in 1868. Two German archaeologists, Carl Watzinger and Ernest Sellin, conducted the first scientific excavations (1907–1909, 1911). They uncovered remains of a massive city wall and palace—validation, they claimed, of the Old Testament story of Jericho's destruction (*Jos.* 6). However, after analyzing stamped jar handles and Egyptian scarabs associated with the wall, Watzinger concluded that the wall had been destroyed during the Middle Bronze period, much earlier than the Israelite conquest. The excavations of the British archaeologist John Garstang (1930–1936) revealed remains of a network of walls whose collapse, he argued, resulted from military destruction rather than disrepair or erosion. He dated the walls to about 1400 BCE and, dismissing Watzinger's conclusions, announced that the archaeological evidence confirmed the Israelite destruction of Jericho.

Kenyon's Jericho project uncovered evidence of Natufian culture just above bedrock and, in the next strata, a mud-brick tower dated to the Neolithic period (c. 8000 BCE), making Jericho the earliest-known walled city. Her excavation of tombs in the same strata city provided evidence for Neolithic funeral rites: clay-covered skulls decorated with paint and shells. She found that the mud-brick city walls had been repaired and rebuilt some seventeen times, probably because of earthquake damage. The building of the most recent wall Kenyon dated to around 2300 BCE; it was destroyed in about 1550 BCE. Only a small, unfortified settlement existed on the site when the Israelites entered Canaan (c. 1400 BCE). Her interpretation prevails, despite subsequent criticism (see Wood, 1990).

Kenyon's final excavation (1962–1967) focused on the City of David, just south of the Temple Mount, the oldest inhabited part of Jerusalem. The most important architectural features she uncovered were stepped-stone structures whose function and dating remain ambiguous. The 1967 Six-Day War terminated Kenyon's excavation. She died before she could publish final field reports on her work in Jerusalem.

See Also Archaeology and Religion.

Bibliography

Kenyon, Kathleen. *Digging up Jericho.* London, 1957.

Kenyon, Kathleen. *Excavations at Jericho.* 2 vols. London, 1960, 1965.

Kenyon, Kathleen. *Amorites and Canaanites.* London, 1966.

Kenyon, Kathleen. *Royal Cities of the Old Testament.* London, 1971.

Kenyon, Kathleen. *Digging up Jerusalem.* London, 1974.

Kenyon, Kathleen. *The Bible and Recent Archaeology.* London, 1978; rev. ed., 1987.

Wood, Bryant G. "Did the Israelites Conquer Jericho?" *Biblical Archaeology Review* 16 (March–April 1990): 44–58.

Kathleen S. Nash (2005)

KEPLER, JOHANNES (1571–1630), was the discoverer of the laws of planetary motion named after him. He was born at Württemberg, Germany. Owing to his family's poverty, the young Kepler had to leave school to work in the fields, but his physique was too frail for such labor. In 1584, therefore, he decided to train for the priesthood. His brilliant academic record earned him acceptance at the University of Tübingen, where he was introduced to the ideas of Copernicus. In 1594 he was appointed to the professorship of astronomy at Graz. There, in addition to preparing astrological almanacs, he devoted himself to studying the solar system. His publication of *Mysterium cosmographicum* (1595) attracted the attention of the great Danish astronomer Tycho Brahe, who invited him to Prague and whom he succeeded as imperial astronomer to the emperor Rudolf II, in 1601. Kepler published some optical discoveries in 1604 and, in 1609, found that the orbit of Mars was elliptical in shape. In the latter year he also explained the cause of tides. In his *Dioptrice* (1611), Kepler developed the principle of the astronomical (or inverting) telescope. Deeply anguished by the untimely death of his favorite child and, soon after, that of his wife, Kepler sought release by plunging into his studies of the heavenly bodies. By 1619 he had discovered the last of his three famous laws, which he published in *De harmonice mundi.* It should be remarked that "Kepler's laws of motion" were scattered amid many other conjectures and planetary relationships postulated by Kepler and that he himself did not attach particularly great importance to them (as opposed to other relationships that did not prove so fruitful for later science).

Kepler's work is permeated with his conviction that the book of nature is written in mathematical symbols and that reality can be grasped only through mathematics. "Just as the eye was made to see colors, and the ear to hear sounds," he said, "so the human mind was made to understand, not whatever you please, but quantity." Kepler seems never to have shown any opposition to or disrespect for theology, although he regarded the realms of the theologians and the natural philosophers as quite different. He insisted that the Bible, when it refers to natural objects and events, should not be taken literally.

Kepler took his religion, in which he displayed an unyielding individualism, seriously. He was expelled from his home and from his position at Graz for refusing to embrace Roman Catholicism, and he was excluded from communion in the Lutheran church in Linz both for his refusal to give a written statement of conformity with the Lutheran doctrine and also on suspicion of being a secret Calvinist. He wanted to find a genuine harmony among these three factions: "It hurts my heart that the three factions have miserably torn the truth to pieces between them, that I must collect the bits wherever I can find them, and put them together again."

In his astronomical work—discovering laws and harmonies of the solar system and the music of the spheres, to which he assigned specific musical notes—Kepler regarded himself as priest of God in the temple of nature. Having insisted in his *Astronomia nova* (1609) that the biblical references to nature are not natural philosophy, he goes on to say:

> And I urge my reader also not to be forgetful of the divine goodness imparted to men, when the Psalmist invites him particularly to contemplate this, when having returned from the temple, he has again entered the school of astronomy. Let him join with me in praising and celebrating the wisdom and greatness of the Creator which I disclose to him from the deeper explanations of the form of the universe, from the enquiry into its causes, from the detection of errors of appearance. Thus not only let him recognize the well-being of living things throughout nature, in the firmness and stability of the world so that he reveres God's handiwork, but also let him recognize the wisdom of the Creator in its motion which is as mysterious as it is worthy of all admiration.

BIBLIOGRAPHY

The definitive biography of Kepler is Max Casper's *Johannes Kepler* (Stuttgart, 1950), which has been translated and edited by C. Doris Hellman as *Kepler* (New York, 1959). A popular and very readable account is Arthur Koestler's *The Watershed: A Biography of Johannes Kepler* (New York, 1960). Books 4 and 5 of Kepler's *The Epitome of Copernican Astronomy* and book 5 of his *Harmonies of the World* can be found in the series "The Great Books of the Western World," vol. 16 (Chicago, 1952).

New Sources

Ferguson, Kitty. *Nobleman and His Housedog: Tycho Brahe and Johannes Kepler: The Strange Partnership that Revolutionised Science.* London, 2002.

Field, J. V. *Kepler's Geometrical Cosmology.* Chicago, 1988.

Gingerich, Owen. *Eye of Heaven: Ptolemy, Copernicus, Kepler.* New York, 1993.

RAVI RAVINDRA (1987)
Revised Bibliography

KERÉNYI, KÁROLY (1897–1973), was a Hungarian-born scholar of classical philology, the history of religions, and mythology. He was born in the southeastern corner of the Austro-Hungarian Empire in the town of Temesvár (now Timisoara, Romania). Growing up in a Roman Catholic family of small landowners, Kerényi learned Latin and was drawn to the study of languages. Classical philology was his major subject at the University of Budapest; his doctoral dissertation (1919) was entitled "Plato and Longinus: Investigations in Classical Literary and Aesthetic History." He spent several years as a secondary-school teacher, traveled in Greece and Italy, and undertook postdoctoral studies at the universities of Greifswald, Heidelberg, and Berlin, under Hermann Diels, Ulrich von Wilamowitz-Moellendorff, Eduard Norden, Eduard Meyer, and Franz Boll. To Boll he dedicated his first book, *Die griechisch-orientalische Romanliteratur in religionsgeschichtlicher Beleuchtung* (1927), the scholarly reception of which led to Kerényi's appointment as *privatdo-*

cent in the history of religions at the University of Budapest. He became professor of classical philology and ancient history at Pécs in 1934 and at Szeged in 1941, while retaining his docentship at Budapest.

During a visit to Greece in 1929, Kerényi met Walter F. Otto (1874–1958), whose approach to the history of religions influenced him profoundly. He resolved to combine the "historical" and the "theological" methods and to go beyond the limits of academic philology. His first works in this new direction were the essay collection *Apollon* (1937) and *Die antike Religion* (1940).

Two significant influences from outside his field came to bear on Kerényi in the 1930s. In 1934 he began a correspondence with Thomas Mann (1875–1955) that, except for a wartime hiatus, lasted until Mann's death. In the late 1930s Kerényi came into contact with C. G. Jung (1875–1961), and their first joint publication on mythology appeared in 1941. Jung encouraged Kerényi's move to Switzerland in 1943 as a cultural attaché charged with maintaining contact with the Western democracies, in spite of Nazi domination of Hungary; the following year, when the Germans occupied his homeland, Kerényi could not return to Hungary and chose permanent exile in 1947. Fifteen years later he and his family became Swiss citizens. They lived near or in Ascona, in the Italian-speaking canton of Ticino, where Kerényi led the life of an independent humanist, though he taught occasionally in Basel, Bonn, and Zurich. He was a cofounder in 1948 of the C. G. Jung Institute in Zurich, where he also lectured.

In the course of his work with Jung, Kerényi conceived a plan to study the Greek gods with the aim of developing a view of the Greek pantheon that modern people could encompass; to this end he took the findings of psychology into consideration, while maintaining that he followed a path separate from that of Jungian psychology. As Kerényi saw it, every view of mythology is a view of human culture. Thus, every "theology" is at the same time an "anthropology." Kerényi's method was to test the "authenticity" of mythological tradition by examining stylistic traits. The essence of his work, Kerényi thought, consisted in establishing a science of ancient religion and mythology based not merely on a detailed knowledge of the literature and archaeology but also on a reciprocal sympathy between the interpreter and his material; this would broaden the field of learning already opened by traditional historical methods. *Mythologie der Griechen* (1951) and *Die Heroen der Griechen* (1958) are his most comprehensive achievements in this regard.

In exile, Kerényi's reputation as a mythologist prospered among scholars, and he also became known as a popular interpreter of myths. His honors included membership in the Norwegian Royal Academy of Sciences, an honorary doctorate from the University of Uppsala, the Humboldt Society gold medal, and the Pirckheimer Ring of Nuremberg. In addition, he was a Bollingen Foundation fellow from 1947 until his death in 1973. Between 1941 and 1963 he lectured frequently at the annual Eranos conferences in Ascona.

THE SCIENCE OF MYTHOLOGY. Kerényi's approach to Greek religion in his first book on Hellenistic romance literature was consistent with the standard historical method. In the 1930s he followed Otto's interpretation of the Greek godheads as "forms of being" (*Seinsgestalten*), that is, ideal figures corresponding to particular spheres of reality in the common experience of the world, whose essential aspects are represented by means of symbolic features. The exposure to these "forms" has a strong emotional impact, but the impact is not merely a psychic phenomenon, because it has an objective reference. Kerényi, like Otto, made use of the anthropologist Leo Frobenius's *Ergriffenheit*—the idea of "being-grasped" by prominent phenomena of the external world—which promotes myth-making activity in human cultures. Kerényi claimed that scientific inquiry into religions does not face the mind's "illusions" but rather its "realities" ("*Realitäten der Seele*," in *Apollon*, 1937, p. 27). Mythology, in other words, is grounded in actual human life, not insane or childish imagery, as positivism had envisaged it. At the same time, however, such fundamental "humanism" cannot be understood, as historicism understands it, by explaining religion as if it were only the output of a given cultural and social setting. The human "reality" reflected in myths and symbols is something deeper than a simple matter of facts. It is a complex interaction between a human being's consciousness and the riddles of the existence by which he or she is "grasped" and stimulated to reflect and to interpret. Kerényi's perspective is thus equally distant from metaphysical theology and from atheistic anthropology—though it is "theological" (in a Greek sense), because the representations of the gods are taken seriously, and also "anthropological" insofar as the human being is the ultimate concern of religious discourse. For this reason it has been defined as a peculiar form of religious phenomenology or hermeneutics (Magris, 1975).

The basic difference with respect to Otto lies in the fact that Kerényi shares only partially his mentor's neoclassical patterns of thought. Kerényi does not consider the Greek mythological figures as exclusively luminous and positive forms of being contemplated by the Hellenic "spirit." He aims to analyze the divine forms to underline their negative aspects or "dark side" (*Schattenseite*). For example, Apollo appears on one hand as linked to beauty and light; but on the other hand he is a gloomy death-bringing god, whose symbol is the wolf. The objective experience of the polarity of life and death, of world and afterworld, is part of the complexity of human reality: this is what can actually "grasp" the mind and be given a mythological form.

While working out this research project, Kerényi found Jung to be a natural partner; their collaboration lasted for a couple of decades after their joint programmatic work, *The Science of Mythology* (1941). The founder of analytical psychology had been keenly interested in mythology since his break with Sigmund Freud's psychoanalytical movement.

Jung assumed that along with the individual unconscious, which owed its existence to personal experience, a second psychic system existed—the collective unconscious—inherited by all individuals and consisting of primordial forms, the so-called archetypes, whose main manifestations within human history were mythological constructs. According to this view, which Kerényi accepted in principle, a comparison among different cultures was suitable because essentially the same archetypes appear everywhere as a common heritage of humankind. In *The Science of Mythology*, for example, the Greek myth of Persephone parallels the religious tradition of a remote Indonesian tribe (discovered by Adolf Jensen, a pupil of Frobenius), although any historical link between the two cultures is highly hypothetical.

Another issue Jung and Kerényi shared was the analogy between the internal structure of myths and dreams, so that, as Kerényi put it, the myth can be defined as a "collective dream," and the dream as an "individual myth." The mythologist is allowed to apply the method of free association that Jung had been using with his patients, thus uncovering in apparently minor details a decisive connection between different mythological figures or events, in which an analogous archetypal theme is expressed (e.g., the femaleness portrayed in different ancient goddesses). But the most important thing Kerényi derived from Jung was undoubtedly the idea of the essential ambivalence of human nature. The Jungian distinction not simply between consciousness and unconscious, but also between the soul and the "shadow," and between *animus* and *anima* (the male and female aspect of each individual soul), should have stimulated Kerényi's view of the mythological thought as expressing the human ambivalence through the polarity of light side and dark side, and through the deep meaning of gender symbolism. Moreover, Kerényi applies, in a way, to the understanding of mythology the method of the analytical therapy, according to which the formation of the "self" takes place when one is able to establish a constructive interaction with one's hidden "double." In a similar way, the protagonist of a mythological narrative also has to cope with and overcome the manifold figures of death. This is the archetypal meaning of the different situations Kerényi investigated with profound sensitivity: the fight against a dragon; travel in unknown lands; the descent to the underworld; initiation; and the heroic contest. Psychology enhances the study of myths by adding a keener insight into the basic questions all humans generally face (*allgemeinmenschlich*). The mythologist thus performs a "humanistic inquiry on the soul" (*humanistische Seelenforschung*).

Nevertheless, Kerényi carefully avoided appearing as a psychologist or a Jungian historian of religions like Eric Neumann. Kerényi adopted a softer version of the archetype theory. He proposed that this term should be employed (in keeping with ancient Greek) only as an adjective, not as a noun. There exist no "archetypes" as everlasting psychical structures in human minds, but rather "archetypal" images, meanings, and situations that are deeply rooted in the universal human experience. Moreover, these archetypal images and meanings are given historical consistency only in one specific cultural setting, or more than one, provided that their being interconnected is supported by anthropological evidence. The science of mythology deals with "culture-typical" phenomena (*kulturtypisch*), but it achieves its goal as a "humanistic" discipline by trying to grasp their "archetypal" relevance (*archetypisch*) at a deeper level than the historical one.

Kerényi carried out this kind of "excavation" (the method of archaeology offering in his view the nearest resemblance to the mythologist's work) in the fifteen books and several brilliant papers he wrote from 1942 to 1962, the most creative period of his scientific career. The Greek religion emerged in the Mycenaean and archaic age on the background of the pre-Greek Mediterranean substrate, mainly evidenced in the Minoan culture of ancient Crete. Its general frame seems to have been a dialectic of life and death, as well as a sort of circularity between the natural world and the underworld. This dialectic was symbolically exhibited in such ritual performances as the labyrinth dance (*Labyrinth-Studien*, 1942; *Werke* 1) or portrayed in key mythological figures that underwent a complicated "culture-typical" evolution. Initially, the female godhead prevails, whereas the male godhead plays a subordinate function as begetter (Poseidon-type) or divine child (Dionysos-type). The archetypal mother-begetter scheme evolved eventually to the husband-wife couple (*Zeus und Hera*, 1972). The idea of the origin of life also appears in a masculine version in the Cabyrian couple (father-son) around whom the mysteries of Samothrace were centered (*Mysterien der Kabiren*, 1944).

The idea of life as being essentially exposed to death but nevertheless triumphant over death and suffering is another basic archetypal idea expressed in different ways by the figures of Hermes and Dionysos (*Hermes*, 1943; *Dionysos*, 1976). The feminine version of the same idea is embodied in the mother-daughter couple (Demeter and Persephone) of the Eleusinian mysteries. In this case, the rape of the maiden by Hades (for Kerényi a form of chthonic Dionysos) emphasizes the dark side of the gender relationship, but the male's violence also implements the female's transition from virginity to motherhood, whereby a divine child (a form of younger Dionysos) is given birth miraculously within the realm of the dead. It is noteworthy that many issues were interlaced in an apparently simple tale: the complexity of the female nature; the process of the mother-daughter, father-son duplication; the switching from negative to positive; and the knowledge, transmitted by the mystery cult, that even the sinister sphere of death allows life to endure and the deceased to join it again (*Mysterien von Eleusis*, 1962).

The science of mythology does not aim to build a systematic theory. Its work consists in analyzing definite blocks of mythical and ritual tradition; its requirements are cleverness and extensive acquaintance with philology, archaeology, and even the "indirect tradition" offered by the very sites and landscapes to which mythological tales were linked. Moreover, as Kerényi pointed out in his only methodological essay (*Umgang mit Göttlichem*, 1955; *Werke*, 5.1), the historian of religions, as well as the historian of art, cannot operate as a pure scholar, since dealing (*Umgang*) with the divine requires a certain sense or taste for its object. The historian of religions must appreciate in the mythological figures the attempt made by the human mind to elaborate in symbolic form its experience of something transcending it. Even if mythological figures did not "exist" anywhere, they ought not to be dismissed as a bare human invention, for the divine represents the deeper levels of being that humans actually experience every day (though they are unable to master them). The foremost mythogenic situations are birth, begetting, and death (the "high moments of life," *Höhepunkte des Lebens*); in Kerényi's formula, "the myth is myth of man."

In his last years, the debate on the "demythologization" question raised by Rudolf Bultmann (1884–1976) offered Kerényi the opportunity to clarify his own assumptions. Religion ought not be "demythologized" in order to be authentic, because it is grounded neither on doctrines nor fables, but on events (*Geschehen*) in which the divine dimension of reality is perceived while crossing the dimension of ordinary life. Only the myth is appropriate for expressing the deeper level of the experience. Thus the Greek word for "god" (*theos*) originally had an adjectival rather than a substantive meaning—it stood for a property of the experienced event and was not a definition of an abstract object (see *Werke* 7).

See Also Brelich, Angelo; Jung, C. G.; Otto, Walter F.

Bibliography

Works

Kerényi (Károly, Karl, Charles, or Carlo, according to the language in which his work appeared) produced 295 separate original works, chiefly in German, but also in Hungarian and Italian. With different versions and translations, the total number of his publications is more than five hundred; some 470 appeared during his lifetime and some forty were issued posthumously. Kerényi's first book is *Die griechisch-orientalische Romanliteratur in religionsgeschichtlicher Beleuchtung* (Tübingen, Germany, 1927, second edition Darmstadt, Germany, 1962). The collected works, including monographs on philology, mythology, and literature, as well as diaries and travel journals, have been published in eight volumes (twelve were originally projected) as *Werke in Einzelausgaben*, published by Langen-Müller (Munich and Vienna), and originally under the editorship of Kerényi's wife, Magda Lukács. For a complete bibliography, excluding articles published in periodicals, updated to 1975 by Lukács, see the Langen-Müller edition of *Dionysos* (1976), pp. 447–474.

The Langen-Müller program was suspended after publishing eight volumes, each one containing several essays under a general title:

1. *Humanistische Seelenforschung* (1966)
2. *Auf Spuren des Mythos* (1967)
3. *Tage- und Wanderbücher* (1969)
4. *Apollon und Niobe* (1980)

5.1. *Wege und Weggenossen I* (1985)

5.2. *Wege und Weggenossen II* (1988)

7. *Antike Religion* (1971)
8. *Dionysos: Urbild des unzerstörbaren Lebens* (1976)

Klett-Cotta (Stuttgart, Germany) later republished vol. 8 (1994), vol. 7 (1995), and vol. 1 (1996), adding *Mythologie der Griechen* (1997), *Töchter der Sonne* (1997), and *Urbilder der griechischen Religion* (1998, containing *Hermes, Asklepios, Mysterien von Eleusis* and *Promethus*). See also the correspondence with Thomas Mann, *Gespräch in Briefen* (Zurich, 1960) and with Hermann Hesse, *Briefwechsel aus der Nähe* (Munich and Vienna, 1984). Also of biographical interest is the correspondence with Furio Jesi, *Demone e mito: Carteggio 1964–1968*, edited by Magda Kerényi and Andrea Cavalletti (Macerata, Italy, 1999). Kerényi's writings in Italian have also been published under the title *Scritti italiani (1955–1971)*, edited by Giampiero Moretti (Naples, Italy, 1993). After the fall of the Communist regime in Hungary, Kerényi's early writings in Hungarian, along with some Hungarian translations of his German works, were published.

Many of Kerényi's major works have been translated into English:

Apollon: The Wind, the Spirit, and the God (1937). Translated by Jon Solomon. Dallas, Tex., 1983.

The Religion of the Greeks and Romans (1940). Translated by Christopher Holme. New York, 1962.

Essays on a Science of Mythology (1941). Coauthored with C. G. Jung. Translated by Richard Francis C. Hull. Princeton, N.J., 1969; reprinted as *The Science of Mythology;* London and New York, 2001.

Hermes, the Guide of the Souls (1942). Translated by Murray Stein. Zurich, 1976.

Goddesses of Sun and Moon (1944). Translated by Murray Stein. London, 1979; reprint, Dallas, Tex., 1991.

Prometheus: Archetypal Image of Human Existence (1946). Translated by Ralph Manheim. Princeton, N.J., 1997.

The Gods of the Greeks (1951). Translated by Norman Cameron. New York, 1951; reprint, London, 1974.

Athene: Virgin and Mother in Greek Religion (1952). Translated by Murray Stein. New York, 1978.

Asklepios: Archetypal Image of the Physician's Existence (1954). Translated by Ralph Manheim. New York, 1959; reprint, 1997.

The Trickster: A Study in American Indian Mythology (1954). Coauthored with Paul Radin and C. G. Jung. Translated by Richard Francis C. Hull. Reprint, New York, 1990.

The Heroes of the Greeks (1958). Translated by Herbert Jennings Rose. London, 1974; reprint, Princeton, N.J., 1997.

Eleusis: Archetypal Image of Mother and Daughter (1962). Translated by Ralph Manheim. New York, 1967; reprint, Princeton, N.J., 1991.

Zeus and Hera: Archetypal Image of Father, Husband, and Wife (1972). Translated by Christopher Holme. Princeton, N.J., 1975.

Mythology and Humanism: The Correspondence of Thomas Mann and Karl Kerényi. Translated by Alexander Gelley. Ithaca, N.Y., 1975.

Dionysos: Archetypal Image of the Indestructible Life. Translated by Ralph Manheim. Princeton, N.J., 1976; reprint, 1996.

Literature

Earlier evaluations include Charles Picard, "Un bilan moderne de la religion antique," *Diogène* 25 (1959): 125–141; Hervé Rousseau, "La présentification du divin: L'oeuvre de Karl Kerényi," *Critique* 15 (1959): 433–454; Geo Widengren, "Karl Kerényi siebzig Jahre," *Numen* 14 (1967): 164–165; *Karl Kerényi: Der Humanismus des integralen Menschen* (Mannheim, 1971); Furio Jesi, *Letteratura e mito* (Turin, Italy, 1968), see pp. 35–44; and Hellmut Sichtermann, "Karl Kerényi," *Arcadia: Zeitschrift für vergleichende Literaturwissenschaft* 11 (1976): 150–177.

The only encompassing monograph as of 2004 is Aldo Magris, *Carlo Kerényi e la ricerca fenomenologica della religione* (Milan, 1975). Several further studies are available in Italian, including Furio Jesi, *Materiali mitologici* (Turin, Italy, 1979), pp. 3–80, where Magris's work is strongly criticized. A survey on Kerényi's theory of language is presented by Serena Cattaruzza Derossi, "Il problema linguistico in K. Kerényi," in *Miscellanea* 4 (Udine, Italy, 1984): 81–119.

Several papers illustrate Kerényi's relationships with leading Italian scholars of the history and philosophy of religion. These include Dino Pieraccioni, "Mario Untersteiner e Carlo Kerényi: Due spiriti europei in un epistolario," *Nuova antologia* 2162 (1987): 293–328; Nicola Cusumano, "Károly Kerényi in Italia," *Il Veltro* 37 (1993): 161–170; Riccardo Dottori, "Karl Kerényi ai Convegni internazionali di Enrico Castelli (1955–1971)," *Mythos* 7 (1995): 33–57; Paola Pisi, "Dioniso da Nietzsche a Kerényi," *Studi e materiali di storia delle religioni* 69, no. 27 (2003): 129–218; and Natale Spineto, "Károly Kerényi e gli studi storico-religiosi in Italia," *Studi e materiali di storia delle religioni* 27, no. 2 (2003): 385–410. See also Giampiero Cavaglià, "Karl Kerényi e Hugo von Hofmannsthal: Il viaggio ermetico," *Rivista di estetica* 24 (1984): 18–31; and Volker Losemann, "Die Krise der 'alten Welt' und die Gegenwart: Franz Altheim und Karl Kerényi im Dialog," in Peter Kneissl and Volker Losemann, eds. *Imperium Romanum: Studien zur Geschichte und Rezeption* (Stuttgart, 1998).

Miscellaneous books dedicated to Kerényi include, *Kerényi Károly és a humanizmus* (Zurich, 1977); Edgar C. Polomé, ed., *Essays in Memory of Károly Kerényi* (Washington, D.C., 1984); Luciano Arcella, ed., *Károly Kerényi: Incontro con il divino* (Rome, 1999); and János György Szilágyi, ed., *Mitológia és humanitás* (Budapest, 1999).

William McGuire (1987)
Aldo Magris (2005)

KEROULARIOS, MICHAEL See CERULARIOS, MICHAEL

KESHAB CHANDRA SEN See SEN, KESHAB CHANDRA

KEYS.

Doors held shut with bars, and bars and bolts, were common long before locks and keys became prevalent. Some of the oldest myths reflect this. In Babylonian mythology, for example, Marduk makes gates to the heavens and secures them with bolts. Many later divinities in the ancient world were both guardians of closed doors and bearers of keys.

The possession of keys usually signified power over regions guarded by the locks that the keys could open or close. The regions in question were often the underworld or places of the afterlife—for example, the realm of Hades, the Abyss in the *Book of Revelation,* and the Mandaean "dark worlds" that had locks and keys different from all others. The keeper of keys was charged not only with guarding the passage as human beings went from this world to the next but also with keeping the dead where they belonged. A Babylonian funerary chant entreats the gatekeeper of the underworld to keep close watch over the dead, lest they return.

The locked realm can also be this earth, the seas, or even the cosmos itself. In Greek mythology Cybele holds the key to Earth, shutting her up in winter and opening her again in the spring. Similarly, Janus opens the door of the sky and releases the dawn. In Mesopotamian myth, Ninib guards the lock of heaven and earth and opens the deep, while Ea unlocks fountains. The Egyptian Serapis has keys to the earth and sea. In Breton folklore menhirs are the keys to the sea and also the keys to hell; if they were turned in their locks and the locks should open, the sea would rush in.

Because in the ancient world many divinities were key bearers, their priestesses bore keys signifying that the divine powers belonged to them as well, or that they were guardians of the sanctuaries of the gods. Priestesses were represented carrying on their shoulders large rectangular keys. A key pictured on a gravestone indicated the burial place of a priestess.

There is a morphological relationship between the key and the *nem ankh* sign, where the anserated cross of the Egyptian gods is carried by its top as if it were a key, especially in ceremonies for the dead. Here the cross, playing the role of the key, opens the gates of death onto immortality.

Keys also symbolize a task to be performed and the means of performing it. In the Hebrew scriptures the accession to kingly power occurred through "laying the key of the House of David upon [his] shoulders" (*Is.* 22:22). For ancient Jewish and some non-Jewish royalty, the passing on of keys was a natural symbol for the transfer of the monarch's task and the power to accomplish it.

The key symbolizes initiation into the mysteries of the cult. In Mithraic rites the lion-headed figure who is central to the ceremony holds in his hands two keys. It is possible that they function in the same way as the two "keys of the kingdom" held by Saint Peter in Christianity: One represents excommunication whereby the door is locked against the unworthy soul, while the other represents absolution whereby the door is opened and the initiate achieves salvation.

BIBLIOGRAPHY

Information about the symbolism of keys can be found in various primary sources. J. A. MacCulloch's "Locks and Keys," in the *Encyclopaedia of Religion and Ethics,* edited by James Hastings, vol. 8 (Edinburgh, 1915), contains material covering the development of locks, locks and bolts, and keys as mechanical contrivances as well as symbols. Franz Cumont in *The Mysteries of Mithra,* 2d ed., translated by Thomas J. McCormack (New York, 1910), and Robert C. Zaehner in *Zurvan: A Zoroastrian Dilemma* (Oxford, 1955) both discuss at length the initiation rites of Mithraism and speculate about the keys of the lion-headed god.

New Sources

Lurker, Manfred. "Schlüssel." In *Wörterbuch der Symbolik.* Stuttgart, Germany, 1983, p. 603.

Ortner, S. B. "On Key Symbols." *The American Anthropologist* 75 (1973).

ELAINE MAGALIS (1987)
Revised Bibliography

KHAN, SAYYID AHMAD SEE AHMAD KHAN, SAYYID

KHĀNAGĀH

KHĀNAGĀH is a Persian word for the lodge or hospice where Ṣūfī masters (*mashā'ikh*) reside, teaching disciples (who sometimes are also residents), conversing with visitors, welcoming travelers, and feeding the poor. The word is functionally interchangeable with equivalent technical terms of Ṣūfī vocabulary, such as *ribāṭ, tekke, takīyah, zāwiyah, dā'irah,* and *dargāh,* though each has a distinct, region-specific connotation.

Mystics must live in the world. Literature by or about mystics frequently emphasizes the importance of escaping not only involvement in the world but, by extension, concern with all material needs and desires. *Khānagāh,* together with its lexical equivalents, inverts that emphasis, riveting attention to the physical spaces that Ṣūfīs inhabit, interacting with others and relying on instruments from the very world that they seek to escape.

Usage of the word *khānagāh* dates back to the tenth century, although its actual origin remains obscure. The modern attempt to relate it to *khān,* the widely used term for commercial way stations, has been dismissed by those who argue that the Ṣūfī concept of a hospice bears no relation to the mercantile institution of *khān.* But the distinction seems specious because both *khān* and *khānagāh* were clearly places for Muslim wayfarers, whether they sought rest on a trade route or guidance on a spiritual path.

The *khānagāh* itself is embedded in a pre-Muslim, pre-Ṣūfī history from which it was never fully disentangled. It derives from Manichaean antecedents as well as pre-Ṣūfī ascetic communities (the Karrāmiyah of Khorasan in eastern Iran). One of the earliest Ṣūfī masters to establish a *khānagāh,* Shaykh Abū Sa'īd ibn Abī al-Khayr (d. 1049), also laid down rules that were to apply to its inmates: He is extolled in a posthumous family biography for the firm but moderate spiritual discipline he imparted to the residents of his *khānagāh.* Later Ṣūfī masters were less collegial and more autocratic, but they, like Abū Sa'īd, utilized a *khānagāh* or similar facility for engaging in a variety of communal relations.

It was also in the late eleventh century, beginning with the Seljuk rulers of Egypt and Syria and continuing under their successors, that the establishment of *khānagāhs* and their equivalents became widespread. The most renowned hospices were clustered in places that were also the commercial and political capitals of major Muslim dynasties—Cairo, Baghdad, Mosul, Lahore, and Delhi. Their persistence is suggested by the fact that *ribāṭs* founded in Baghdad in the eleventh and twelfth centuries were replicated, at least in their broad outlines, by *zāwiyahs* built in North Africa during the nineteenth century.

Although one would expect to find accounts detailing *khānagāh* architectural design and physical layout, few exist from the medieval period. One of the most graphic relates to the foremost saint of pre-Mughal North Indian Sufism, Shaykh Niẓām al-Dīn Awliyā' of Delhi (d. 1325). His *khānagāh* was a huge building, consisting of a main hall (*jamā'at khānah*), courtyard, veranda, gate room, and kitchen. It accommodated several senior disciples in lower rooms, but its crowning structure was also the least imposing: an isolated, small room on the roof where the shaykh passed his late evening and early afternoon hours in prayer, meditation, and (rarely) sleep. The plan seems to have been repeated, with adaptations to local taste, in many regions of Central and South Asia.

The appeal of the *khānagāhs* as the most visible expression of institutional Sufism was multiple. To the outer circle of disciples, including Muslims and non-Muslims of mixed social background who came to visit at irregular intervals, it housed at once a saintly presence deemed to be magical and a public kitchen dispensing free food. Closer to the shaykh were disciples who pursued mystical studies and began meditative exercises at his behest; they would frequent the *khānagāh* on a regular basis and occasionally take up residence there. The most intimate circle of disciples were the permanent residents designated as successors (*khalīfahs*) to the shaykh: Not only did he entrust them with his deepest insights, but he also allowed them to initiate others into the tradition of his order (*ṭarīqah;* pl., *turuq*).

Despite the continuous and widespread association of the *khānagāh* with Ṣūfī orders and their masters, the nonmystical dimension of *khānagāhs* was never fully excised. Throughout the medieval and early modern periods, there is ample evidence of non-Ṣūfī hospices and also nonmystical

Muslims in charge of Ṣūfī hospices. The reason is evident: The source of support for every *khānagāh* was lay; it derived from the income, earned or not, of those who dwelled outside its walls. Even in those not-so-rare instances of rural hospices where inmates engaged in agricultural pursuits, their continued existence depended on contributions from the wider lay circle of the shaykh's followers and admirers. Not all sources of income were acceptable to all Ṣūfīs, however. For the Chishtī and Naqshbandī masters, it was normative (despite major exceptions) that they reject all governmental assistance, while for the Suhrawardi and Qādirī communities, any benefactor from the wealthy mercantile and ruling classes was usually welcome to make occasional offerings or even to set up permanent charitable endowments (*awqāf;* sg., *waqf*) supporting the *khānagāh* and its operations. Those saints who attempted to refuse governmental offers of assistance were often overruled and compelled to yield: Such was the power of the medieval state that few Ṣūfī masters or their successors could resist a headstrong ruler who wished to use the spiritual power of a *khānagāh* and its saintly denizens to undergird his own legitimacy.

That the *khānagāh* continued for centuries to be the mainstay of institutional Sufism has never been questioned, but its vitality has. Some chart a decline in the major orders from the time that the *khānagāh* ceased to house a fraternal group of like-minded Ṣūfīs and became instead a tomb complex. This institution may have retained the name of *khānagāh,* but in fact it perpetuated the memory of a dead shaykh through greedy relatives who ignored his legacy yet lived off his spiritual capital by accepting all forms of public and private subsidy. Indeed, as early as the fourteenth century, the *khānagāh* was commonly linked to a tomb, as well as to an adjacent mosque and *madrasah.* Most Muslims, however, accepted this extension of the public profile of Ṣūfī agencies, because they acknowledged the *mashā'ikh* as exemplars of the prophetic standard (*sunnah*) and boons for their own local communities.

Nonetheless, and no matter how one evaluates the *khānagāh* and institutional Sufism, the theory of diachronic decline and charismatic sclerosis is weakened, if not refuted, by the emergence of North African reformist orders, especially the Sanūsīyah, during the nineteenth century. Even that most extreme of puritanical groups, the Wahhābīyah, tacitly acknowledged the benefits that accrued to all Muslims from the extension of Sanūsī influence. The instrument for that extension was a network of hospices (*zāwiyahs*), deliberately located in areas that would maximize support for the Sanūsī armed resistance to Italian colonial administration.

Nor was the Sanūsī movement the death rattle of institutional Sufism or the last dramatic staging of fraternal lodges. Their continued influence in modern Egypt and Algeria has been well chronicled, and for many Muslims the physical abode of saints, by whatever name it is denoted, continues to embody the cosmic quality attributed to it by the thirteenth-century Kubrawī saint Najm al-Dīn al-Rāzī: "The world is in truth like a hospice where God is the shaykh and the Prophet, upon whom be peace, is the steward or servant" (Hamid Algar, trans., *The Path of God's Bondsmen from Origin to Return,* New York, 1982, p. 485).

SEE ALSO Madrasah.

BIBLIOGRAPHY

There is no single book to consult on the *khānagāh* or its equivalent terms. For an appreciation of its origin and medieval development, the best starting points are the two articles by Jacqueline Chabbi, "*Khānḳah,*" in *The Encyclopaedia of Islam,* new ed. (Leiden, 1960–), and "La fonction du ribāṭ à Bagdad du cinquième siècle au début du septième siècle," *Revue des études islamiques* 42 (1974): 101–121. On the contribution of Abū Sa'īd, there is the incomparable study by Fritz Meier, *Abū Sa'īd-i Abū L-Ḥayr* (Leiden, 1976), especially pages 296–336. The South Asian evidence is set forth in a number of articles and monographs, the best being K. A. Niẓāmi's "Some Aspects of Khānqah Life in Medieval India," *Studia Islamica* 8 (1957): 51–69; Fritz Lehmann's "Muslim Monasteries in Mughal India," unpublished paper delivered to the Canadian Historical Association, Kingston, June 8, 1973; and Richard Maxwell Eaton's *Sufis of Bijapur, 1300–1700: Social Roles of Sufis in Medieval India* (Princeton, N.J., 1978), especially pages 165–242.

To understand the Sanūsīyah in their North African setting, one can do no better than consult the comprehensive analysis of Bradford G. Martin, *Muslim Brotherhoods in Nineteenth Century Africa* (Cambridge, U.K., 1976), chap. 4. Also indicative of the persistent role of the *zāwiyahs* in another vital context are two monographs on Egyptian Sufism: F. de Jong's *Turuq and Turuq-Linked Institutions in Nineteenth Century Egypt* (Leiden, 1978) and Michael Gilsenan's *Saint and Sufi in Modern Egypt* (Oxford, 1973). J. Spencer Trimingham's *The Sufi Orders in Islam* (New York, 1971), despite its seeming comprehensiveness, is unfortunately limited by pseudo-typological explanations and an Arab puritan bias.

BRUCE B. LAWRENCE (1987)

KHANTY AND MANSI RELIGION. Together with Hungarian, the Mansi (Vogul) and Khanty (Ostiak) languages form the Ugric branch of the Finno-Ugric (and, ultimately, the Uralic) language family. During the first millennium BCE, the proto-Ob-Ugrians withdrew along the Ob River northward from the forested steppe region of southwest Siberia, simultaneously assimilating the autochthonous population and losing their own Iron Age culture and equiculture. The Ob-Ugrians (Khanty and Mansi) thus became secondarily primitivized, emerging as a fishing, hunting, and reindeer-breeding sub-Arctic people. Between the twelfth and sixteenth centuries the Ob-Ugrians split into quasi-tribal or clan-based "chiefdoms," a system that disintegrated as a consequence of sixteenth-century Russian colonization. The Eastern Orthodox church began conversion of the Ob-Ugrians in the eighteenth century, but the character of this conversion was formal and thus did not essentially influence the original religion.

The Mansi number 7,700, the Khanty, 21,000; of these, respectively 49 and 68 percent speak their ancestral language. The ethnographic macrogroups correspond to dialect groupings. Yet, while the culture and language of the various macrogroups is divergent enough to justify their classification as distinct peoples, the Mansi and Khanty *within* the same microgroup differ from one another only in language and in their consciousness of identity. The ethnographic subgroups (i.e., dialects) subdivide according to fluvial regions. The religion of the Mansi and Khanty is identical: Within one and the same macrogroup the same supernatural beings are revered regardless of which people's territory they are affiliated with. Mansi and Khanty folklore, too, is uniform on a nearly word for word basis. A few general nature deities are known to all groups; key figures of mythology are associated with the northwest region, although these same figures may appear in the religion of the other groups under different names. The Northern macrogroup, for instance, is familiar both with a high-ranking spirit from the Eastern Mansi and with another high-ranking spirit from the Western Mansi. On the other hand, Eastern Khanty spirits are completely unknown to them. From the perspective of both system and cult, the religion of the Vasjugan Khanty is the most complex. Ob-Ugric culture as a whole is of a marginal West Siberian type, distinct in quite a few traits. Its study is complicated by the factor of secondary primitivization.

The following is a description of the best documented macrogroup, the Northern. Characteristic of this society are a dual moiety system (*moś* and *por:* the former relatively positive, the latter relatively negative in connotation) and the loose agglomeration of patriarchal consanguineous groups that trace their origins to spirit ancestors conceptualized as simultaneously anthropo- and zoomorphic. This description, however, must unavoidably portray a more archaic form of social organization than is actually the case today. When technical terms are referred to, they derive from either the Sosva Mansi (Man.) or the Kazim Khanty (Kh.).

Anthropomorphy is dominant in Ob-Ugrian religion today, but a latent zoomorphic character can be demonstrated for many categories of supernatural beings. The cult of spirits that arise from the shadow souls of the dead is a productive element in many forms, supporting (1) the ancestor cult in general; (2) the cult of hegemonic personalities, of which the earlier (chiefdom period) variant is a hero cult, and the later variant is the cult of shamans and other worthies; and (3) the cult of those who have died extraordinary deaths. It is a peculiarity of the northern groups that they have incorporated both the major mythological personalities and various individuals of the unindividuated classes into a system of guardian spirits tied to concrete places and societal units. This category, which may be termed "warlord guardian spirits," became primary in both the religious system and cultic life.

Roughly speaking, the following categories may be distinguished according to the degree of the cult:

(1) The true individual cult beings. These have their own prescriptions and prohibitions and their own regular festivals and sacrifices; in folklore they have their own summoning songs and prayers. The terms *pupigh* (Man.) and *iungx* (Kh.) refer to their most general class (which may be represented in idol form as well).

(2) The higher-level belief beings. Relations with these beings are well regulated, and their benevolence may be won with the practice of hospitality or, in unusual cases, by means of more serious sacrifice. A lower level of belief being is also acknowledged. It is connected only with prohibitive and preventative practices. The lesser forms of word *magic* (incantation, short prayer) are addressed to the belief beings, who are portrayed in plays at the bear festival. Certain belief beings have no cult whatsoever. Folklore beings play no role in either belief or cult.

CONCEPTIONS OF THE UNIVERSE. Ob-Ugric cosmology was originally vertical and tripartite: upper (sky), middle (earth), and lower (underworld). A conception of these worlds as seven-layered is known, but not concretely elaborated. In the lower sphere of the sky dwell the Wind Old Men, named after the cardinal points. In the various upper layers of the sky revolves Sun Woman, with her team of horses, or Moon Old Man with his arctoid dog sled. Later, this worldview became contaminated with a horizontal system: Upper-Ob (southern), Middle-Ob, and Lower-Ob (northern). Accordingly, the productive region is located in the South, which sends migratory birds and which is the home of the world tree and the fountain-of-youth lake. Conversely, at the mouth of the Ob, on the Arctic Ocean, lies the dark land of the dead. At present, syncretistic twofold conceptualizations predominate.

The earth, brought up as a chunk by two bird representatives of the netherworld (a little and a big loon), is spread out over the primeval sea; it is disk-shaped: A fish or a fantastic animal holds it up. In the present-day version, the son of the mythic ancestral pair (identified either with the Pelim god or with World-Overseeing Man, both warlord guardian spirits) plays a salient part. With the collaboration of the chief god's counterpart, the folklore figure Kul, he created humankind; he then decimated his progeny with a fiery flood and scattered them over the world. Before the present-day Mansi and Khanty, the myth alleges, there were many other periods: In folklore the most richly depicted are the period of the moiety ancestors and the heroic time of the origin of the warlord guardian spirits.

General mythological personalities. In the vertical system, the upper sphere is embodied by the positive-functioning chief god, Upper Sky Father (Man., Num Torem Aś; Kh., Nŭm Turem Aśi). Symbolized by the vault of heaven, he has the form of an old man and is active in climatic changes connected with the change of seasons, passive in regard to humans. He may be approached only through the intervention of high-ranking spirits, having scarcely any cult. His wife is (Lower) Earth Mother (Man., [Joli-]Mā

Angkw). His counterpart is the lord of the netherworld. Admixture with the horizontal worldview and the localization of cults to particular places produced syncretistic personality trinities. Above Sky Father there appeared two ancestors (Man., Kośar Tōrem and Kores Tōrem, both folklore figures), or there appeared alongside him two other personifications (the Khanty folklore figures Nŭm Sĭwes and Nŭm Kŭres). His wife was reinterpreted as belonging to the same category, with the name Sky Mother (folklore figure). Elsewhere she was identified with the warlord guardian spirit goddess Kalteś. This same female fertility principle is repeated in the trinity South Woman, Kalteś, Gold Woman. Concrete incarnations of the lord of the netherworld include the warlord guardian spirits Sickness Lord and Lower-Earth Old Man, and "Devil," the fictive master of the harmful spirits called *kul.*

Warlord guardian spirits. These are nature deities tied to societal units of a higher level (moieties, perhaps at one time tribes). Their antiquity is evidenced by the fact that their *attributa* often preserve features of the equiculture of the steppe rim. Their most representative group is now indigenous to the Middle-Ob territory of the Mansi and Khanty, the once-famous region of the Koda principality. The members of this group, listed here with corresponding zoomorphy, associated moiety, and cult center, are as follows:

(1) Kalteś, popularly, Mother (Man., Śān; Kh., Ăngki; female wild goose, swan, hare; *moś* moiety; village of Kaltisjan). Originally a sky goddess, Kalteś is the only equestrian female warlord guardian spirit. It is she who decides the number, sex, and longevity of children; she also aids in childbirth. Her persona is interpreted variously as wife, sister, or daughter of the sky god. Among her properties there is a negative one: infidelity or stubbornness.

(2) World-Overseeing Man (Man., Mir Susne Xum; Kh., Mĭr Šawijti Xu; wild goose, crane; *moś* moiety; village of Belogorje). His other names include Golden Lord, Horseman, and Upriver Man. He is the youngest son of the sky god, the central figure of Ob-Ugric religion, and functions as a mythic hero in the creation of the world order. Married to the daughters of persons symbolizing nature, he excels in providing humans with their needs. His sphere of activity ranges through all three worlds. His is the highest position of honor among his brothers: the overseeing of the world and of humans. He accomplishes this by circling the world on his winged horse. In early formulations he is a solar god; later formulations preserve traces of the shamanistic mediator: He is the chief communicator with Sky God.

(3) Holy City Old Man (Man., Jalp-ūs Ōjka; Kh., Jem Woš Ĭki), also known as Clawed Old Man (Man., Konsing Ōjka; Kh., Kŭnšeng Ĭki; bear, mouse; *por* moiety; village of Vežakar). In the region of his cult center he is held to be a son of the sky god. Functionally, he is the counterpart of World-Overseeing Man: In the shape of a mouse he goes under the earth and regains the shadow souls of sick people from underworld spirits who have stolen them. He is a totem ancestor of the *por* moiety.

(4) Sickness Lord (Man., Xuĺ Ōter; Kh., Xĭń Wurt; big loon, village of Sumutnyol) and Lower-Earth Old Man (Kh., Ĭł Mŭw Ĭki; little loon; Sumutnyol) are two incarnations of the lord of the netherworld. The former steals souls; the latter either rules over them or eats them. In their empire they have a family and teeming army of servants consisting of illness spirits. They are also the source of unpleasant insects and vermin. Some versions interpret the lord of the netherworld as the son of the sky god; in any case, he functions as the subordinate of the sky god in the vertical system and the subordinate of Kalteś in the horizontal system. Under the name Downriver Man he also constitutes a complement to World-Overseeing Man.

Models of the middle world. Beliefs concerning the middle world reveal a general but not extensive symbolization of natural elements. The most significant is Fire Mother, but Earth Mother and Water Mother enjoy lesser cults.

The land-water opposition. Such an opposition is clearly represented by the forest and aquatic variants of the positive-functioning *łungx*-type spirits; these oversee the natural resources of a particular territory. In eastern and southern areas they are important cult beings; in the north, they have been overshadowed by local warlord guardian spirits and the cult of the *mis* people. Closely connected with their cult is that of the more individualized *łungx*-type spirits associated with particular natural objects (high places, boulders, trees, whirlpools). Their negative counterparts are the forest and aquatic *kul,* beings that represent the netherworld.

The forest sphere. In the animal world-model there is no notion of lord over the individual animal types. In addition to the totemistic animal cult, the greatest veneration surrounds the larger aquatic birds (symbols of fertility), the elk (because of its celestial references), and the bear. Around the bear, merged with the totem ancestor of the *por* moiety, developed a highly characteristic feature of Ob-Ugrian culture: a bear cult that is one of the most elaborate in the world.

The bear cult. The fusion of conceptualizations from various periods has conferred upon the bear the character of universal mediator. His origins tie him to the upper world; his dwelling place and connections with human society tie him to the middle world; his mouse-shaped soul ties him to the netherworld. Child of the sky god, he acquired knowledge of the middle world despite paternal prohibition and conceived a desire to descend there. His father permitted the descent but prescribed the most harmless manner of acquiring food. (At the same time he makes the bear the judge of societal norms, the guardian of the bear oath.) But the bear violates the prohibitions, thus becoming fair game for humans.

The slain bear is a divine guest who, after the ritual consumption of his flesh, transfers into the heavens the sacrifices dedicated to him and the cultic folklore performed for his benefit, thereby ensuring his own rebirth and that of the natural order. A separate taboo language exists in connection with the bear and the bear hunt, and the activities therein are highly ritualistic.

What follows is a description of the bear festival in its most characteristic (northern) variant. After purifying ceremonies, the bear (i.e., the bear hide, placed on a stand) is regaled for three to seven nights (depending on the bear's age and sex) with performances of a hospitable, educational, and amusing nature. Only men may participate as performers. The diurnal repertoire begins with a didactic section in which the offense of murder (of the bear) is brushed aside and epic songs are sung about the origin of the bear, the first bagging of a bear by a mythical personage, the bear's function as judge, and the death of the particular bear present at the ceremony. Thereafter follows a section punctuated by danced interludes, intended as entertainment for the bear, although its function for humans is didactic. Players in birchbark masks perform brief plays with song and pantomime. The plays are only a few minutes in duration, but they may number in the hundreds. These reflect the key motifs of nature and society and supranormal and everyday categories and their interdependence. Their aesthetic quality ranges from the comic to the sublime. Separate genres are represented by songs and games that depict the proliferation, way of life, and capture of various animal species, and by songs and games performed by a mythical being or clown figure who draws the spectators into the action.

In the most sacred section of the festival the warlord guardian spirits are summoned. Portrayed by costumed performers, they perform a dance that ensures the well-being of the community. When the bear meat is consumed, it is consumed under the illusion that birds are feasting. After this, the bear is instructed on the manner of returning to the heavens. Meanwhile, the bear's skull and the festival paraphernalia are taken to a special place where cult objects are stored.

The mirroring of social structure in the forest sphere. Two types of anthropomorphic forest beings pursue daily activities similar to those of the human community and may even intermarry with humans. The *mis* people are outstanding hunters; their benevolence provides humans with a good hunt. The *mis* take as their mates those people who disappear in the forest without a trace. The *mengk* people are supposed to be simple-minded malevolent giants. Northern Mansi associate the *mis* people with the *moś* moiety and the *mengk* people with the *por* moiety. The origins of certain warlord guardian spirits is derived—with the mediation of the cult of the dead—from these beings.

The aquatic sphere. While the dominant being of the forest is the bear, the lord of the waters, Water King (Man., Wit Xōn; Kh., Jĭngk Xon, Jĭngk Wurt) is similar to a high-ranking warlord guardian spirit. Water King is not tied to a societal unit, but each group thinks it knows of his dwelling place, which in each case is the stream from which fish migrate (e.g., northern groups place it in the mouth of the Ob, southern groups in the mouth of the Irtysh). Water King has a family and is the superior of water sprites and other beings. The chief function of Water King is the direction of the migration of fish; warlord guardian spirits that dwell at the outlets of tributaries supply a redistribution network.

The forest-settlement opposition. The sylvan pantheon is much richer than its aquatic counterpart. This is explained, in part, by the fact that the forest participates in the opposition of forest and settlement. The proper place of *łungx*-type spirits is indicated by the location of their sacred place; certain lower-ranked beings (e.g., the Eastern Khanty ghostlike *potčak*) are subdivided into explicitly forest or village variants. Other figures may lack pertinent counterparts but may nevertheless be construed in terms of this opposition. Examples include the birchbark-rucksack woman, identified with the (folkloristic) figure of the anthropophagous *por* woman, the elf called Village-Square Being, Trash-Heap Woman, Bathhouse Woman, Sinew-String-Making Woman, and others.

The Human Sphere. The warlord guardian spirit that is tied to a concrete place is not only the sole form representing the community but also the central category of all of cultic life. The primary functions of the warlord guardian spirit are to ward off harmful (especially disease-causing) spirits, to provide succor in situations of peril, and to ensure good fortune in hunting and fishing. The warlord guardian spirit appears in two forms: as a human, generally in the form of a luxuriantly ornamented woman or a warrior in sword and armor, or as an animal, in the form of a specific species of wild beast, which is then taboo for the pertinent social unit. These may be portrayed by wooden images in the form of a human (or, more rarely, an animal), sometimes with the addition of metal disks, or made entirely of metal. The appurtenances of the image are a sacred spot outside the settlement and the items stored there: the idol and/or its *attributa,* a small chamber built on stilts for preserving offerings, a sacrificial table, poles or trees called *tir,* and a sacred tree. The warlord guardian spirit addresses his kindred group as his "little ones" or "children"; as a projection of the actual relations within the group, he enjoys spirit kinship both ascendant and descendant, agnate and cognate. Characteristic features of the cult are a special idol guardian or shaman and prescriptions concerning both cyclical communal ceremonies and sacrificial animals and objects.

Although tied to a concrete place, a warlord guardian spirit may appear anywhere and at anyone's summons. Its connection with the individual is manifested by the fact that it selects a protegé. Every human has a warlord guardian spirit "master of his head." Higher-ranked spirits can select anyone as protegé; lower-ranked spirits are restricted to members of their own community. Ob-Ugrians oriented themselves with one another in terms of the relations obtaining among their warlord guardian spirits; they identified the spirits according to the village held to be the center of a given cult.

Hierarchy of warlord guardian spirits. The community associated with a spirit can be of various levels in the social hierarchy—upper (moiety, base clan), middle (roughly, units corresponding to a clan and its branches), or lower (smaller, local groups). The rank of a spirit is determined by this hierarchy and by the "power" and functions attributed to it, which are generally in direct proportion to the antiquity of the spirit and the complexity of its typological profile. Roughly speaking, the Ob-Ugrians distinguish three hierarchical categories of spirits. Spirits belonging to the high (and upper middle) rank are qualified as "powerful" (Man., *ńangra;* Kh., *tarem*). Among these, the children of the sky god are set apart as a separate group. To this rank belong, besides mythological personae in general, Old Man of the Middle Sosva, the Lozva Water Spirit, the Tegi Village Old Man, and the Kazim Lady. The middle category, which is the chief locus of the hero cult, is subdivided in terms of the opposition between indigenous and immigrant groups. The spirits of immigrant groups are called "land-acquiring" spirits. Among the lower-ranked spirits, those of local character are sometimes distinguished by the terms "master of the village" or "master of the region." The superior of the spirits is the chief deity.

The warlord guardian spirits, like the social groupings associated with their cults, do not form a clearly structured system. The interpretation of their rank and kinship varies from one fluvial region to another. Genealogical, local, or functional subsystems, however, can develop in particular regions. The basis of the genealogical order resides in the fact that migrating groups either bring a copy of their original spirit with them or declare the indigenous spirit of their new home to be their original spirit's offspring. The range of the cults of higher-ranked spirits roughly corresponds to dialect areas. Their descendants may appear with names differing from those of their parents, and may even appear in animal form. The children of middle-ranked spirits are often—at least with regard to name and form—exact copies of one another. For example, spirits named Winged Old Man or Old Man with the Knife, in eagle and firefly form, respectively, crop up in villages at far remove from one another. In local subsystems, the high-ranked spirits are the superiors of all other spirits in their cult sphere.

The development of these spirits was determined along two lines: diverse nature cults and multiple intertwinings of cults of the dead. Both lines of development contain zoomorphic and anthropomorphic elements that are reflected in the diploid form of the spirits. The animal symbology of natural forces is zoomorphic. The oldest layers of this symbology (e.g., the cult of aquatic birds) date to at least the Finno-Ugric period. The other zoomorphic component is totemistic in character; its earlier layer may be Ugric, while its more recent layer is arctoid and may bear the influence of the religion of assimilated autochthonous Siberian populations. The oldest demonstrable layer of the anthropomorphic component is a group of nature deities that preserves traces of southern equiculture. Similarly anthropomorphic are the ancestor cult and hero cult, which are the source of the dominant mark of warlord guardian spirits. To the cult of warlord guardian spirits was juxtaposed the cult of those persons whose decease is in some way extraordinary. A further component is the cult of proprietary spirits of natural places and objects.

Family guardian spirits. Termed "house spirits" (Man., *kol puping;* Kh., *xot łungx*), these anthropomorphic spirits are difficult to differentiate from the lower-ranked warlord guardian spirits. They are variously conceived as descendants of a warlord guardian spirit or its spirit assistant, as the spirit of a deceased relative, or as the proprietary spirit of an object that is interesting in some way (e.g., an archaeological find made of metal). Its votaries approach them through dream or the instructions of a person with cult functions. Such spirits serve to protect and to ensure success in hunting and fishing. Successful execution of this latter office may occasion a widening of its circle of devotees; in case of failure, on the other hand, its idol representations suffer mistreatment or even complete destruction as punishment. The idol, its *attributa,* and ceremonies associated with the family guardian spirit are miniature duplicates of those of the warlord guardian spirits; its folklore, however, is on the wane. Individual protective spirits have similar typological profiles.

Mediator spirits. Documentation for the individual shaman spirit assistant—known as a "living spirit" (Man., *liling puping;* Kh., *łileng łungx*) or, when functioning purely as an acquirer of information, a "talking spirit" (Man., *potertan puping*)—is extremely poor. Typologically, such a being is similar to family and individual spirits and probably serves merely as a messenger in the interactions of shaman and warlord guardian spirits.

Conceptions of the soul. Conceptions of the soul are syncretistic and not always clear even to the Ob-Ugrians. Originally, they were twofold: breath spirits (Man., *lili;* Kh., *łił*) and shadow spirits (Man., Kh., *is*).

The breath spirit—roughly, a symbol of the individual personality—has the form of a small bird; its seat is the hair or crown of the head. Characters in heroic epics could send birds that lived on the crown of their heads or caps to fetch information; they also practiced scalping, by which they were able to take possession of any enemy's soul. The soul called *is* may have been regarded as a posthumous variation of the breath spirit (in men, it consists of five parts, in women, three; it is reborn in consanguineous progeny).

The shadow souls—symbols of emotional and vegetative functionings—have the form of humans or birds. One subtype may leave the body during sleep or in case of fear or fainting; it may also fall prey to illness spirits. After death it remains for a certain time in the vicinity of the house, then departs, northward, for the land of the dead. The other subtype has a more material character; its properties are roughly those of shadows. After death it lives a quasimundane life in the cemetery until the body fades away. The free soul is a type of sleep soul living in the form of a grouse; its destruction results in sleeplessness, then death. Under unfavorable circumstances shadow souls turn into ghosts.

Conceptions of the hereafter. The hereafter is a mirrorlike inversion of the real world, lacking, however, the celestial bodies. The soul lives the same life, in the same form, as its owner did on earth, but backwards. Once returned to the time of birth it reappears in the real world as an insect or spider. Differentiation is minimal, but separation and punishment of the souls of suicides is known. Atonement for moral offenses seems to be the result of nonindigenous influence.

The soul of a dead person can have three material representations. It was obligatory to make for the reincarnating soul a doll of wood, cloth, or hair (Man., *iterma;* Kh., *šungŏt;* literally, "suffering one"; *upet akań,* "hair baby"). Long ago, this figure was so identified with the deceased that widows fed it regularly and slept with it. Among certain groups, the doll was passed from generation to generation; among others it was eventually placed in the grave or burned. A special wooden figure was carved for the souls of outstanding individuals. Through time, the worship of such a figure made it possible for these souls to achieve the status of family guardian spirits. Finally, for those whose remains were inaccessible, in some regions a figure was made and kept in a separate storing place after a symbolic burial ceremony.

Mediators. The Ob-Ugrians belong to the marginal zone of Siberian shamanism. The figure of the shaman is relatively unimportant, the shaman's significance being somewhat overshadowed by mediators who function without deep ecstatic trance. Overall, the study of Ob-Ugrian shamanism is hampered by extraordinarily imprecise documentation.

If as a hypothesis one limits true shamanism to the practice of drum-accompanied deep ecstatic trance, one is left with two types of people who fall outside this strict delimitation. The first group, the "one-sided interaction type," includes those who transmit from the human sphere to the spirits, but who cannot perceive the spirits' reactions. To this class belong the idol guardian in the role of master of ceremony, the "praying man," and epic singers, whose activity is not of a healing nature. The second group, the "two-sided interaction type," consists of those capable of obtaining information from the spirits, and who—to a certain degree—can set them into motion. They can perform these feats in sleep, however, or in a light trance. The only categories known among the Eastern Khanty are those who mediate through singing accompanied by string instruments, dreams, or the summoning of the spirits of forest animals. To the north, a possible equivalent is the Mansi *potertan pupgheng xum* ("talking spirit-man"), who summons his prophetic spirits by means of a stringed instrument.

Terminologically, the Ob-Ugrians make little distinction between the activity of shamans and that of persons who mediate by means of iron objects (ax, knife) and light trance: The noun "magic" (Man., *pēnigh;* Kh., *śărt*) and its verbal derivate "perform magic" (Man., *pēnghungkwe;* Kh., *śărtti*) can refer, in both languages, to the activity of either practitioner. The Mansi consider the "magic(-performing) person" who operates without the use of a drum (Man., *pēnghen xum*) to belong to a lower degree of the shaman category; they do, however, distinguish terminologically between this degree and the full-fledged drum shaman.

Destructive magic, which moves the spirits to negative ends, is used by the "spell-casting one" (Man., *sepan;* Kh., *sepan[eng] xu;* the latter term is also used to refer to the shaman) and by the Mansi "destructive person" (*surkeng xum*) or "spell-knowing person" (*mutrang xum*). These persons are capable of spoiling luck in hunting; they can also cause sickness and death. While terminologically distinct, they stand in an unclear relation to the shaman.

Shaman. Shamanism among the Ob-Ugrians is apparently a rather developed variant of a Paleo-Asiatic type that lacked the shamanistic journey. Exceptionally, and owing to foreign influence, there exists among the Eastern Khanty a more elaborated system of journeying and assistant spirits. No special folklore is associated with the shaman. Similarly, the figure of the female shaman who prophesizes by means of a gyratory dance appears conspicuously late, in a more recent type of heroic song. There is no specific evidence of the influence of neighboring peoples on Ob-Ugrian shamanism; although in peripheral regions certain features have been adopted from every possible donor, none of the various influences can be called dominant.

The shaman can provide any cultic service. His chief task is the defense of one's shadow soul against disease spirits. The shaman also fills an extremely important role as acquirer and interpreter of information (given that at least a dozen different supernatural causes may give rise to unfavorable events). His functions also include prophesy, the finding of lost objects, inquiry after the souls of the dead, and the steering of a sacrificial animal's soul to the spirits. The number of functional elements that may be demanded of the shaman varies from region to region. The shaman's participation in rites of passage, the bear festival, and lesser sacrificial ceremonies is not typical. There is no evidence of the shaman possessing the role of conductor of souls. The shaman acquires the greatest significance in situations of peril that affect the community.

There are no explicit categories of shamans among the Ob-Ugrians. The shaman's strength depends on the nature and number of his spirit assistants, or on the warlord guardian spirits, which are susceptible to influence. Stronger and weaker shamans are distinguished, but without special terminology. There are no reliable data for a distinction between "black" and "white" shamans. In fact, the activity of the shaman is ambiguous, because he may, to redeem the sick person's soul, offer up the soul of another; at times of rivalry he endangers the life of himself and his family.

The shaman, like all other mediative persons, is in principle at everyone's disposal. His activity, whether unreciprocated or remunerated with minor gifts and/or hospitality, is insufficient for independent subsistance. The shaman can increase his income only as the preserver of high-ranked warlord guardian spirits. Both men and women can be shamans, but in general the former have higher status.

There are no reliable data for special shamanic attire or accoutrements; the cap and the headband, however, are documented as headgear. The primary type of drum is oval, with a frame both decorative and resonating; its Y-shaped handle is sometimes embellished with representations of a spirit's face. The skin is unadorned; the position of the pendants (made of metal) varies. The drum may be replaced by a stringed instrument. Fly agaric is the usual narcotic.

Selection and recruitment of apprentice shamans is passive; it is generally attributed to the will of the chief deity, or World-Overseeing Man. Sensitivity, deviant behavior, and musical proclivities are required; somatic marks, illness, and inheritance are also documented but not universal. The candidate rehearses his repertoire as an assistant without benefit of initiation, only gradually assuming his role.

The shamanic séance takes place in a darkened house, where the shaman communicates—with drum-accompanied song, then with gyratory dance—with the warlord guardian spirits appropriate to the occasion. Metal objects (such as arrows) set out for the purpose announce by their rattling that the spirits have arrived (through the roof). When contact is established, the shaman is overcome by a warm breeze. Thereafter a protracted, dramatized debate takes place on the following subjects: (1) determining the cause of the problem; (2) summoning the spirit responsible or contacting it through an assistant spirit; (3) probing the cause of the problem and the nature of the sacrifice needed for its termination; and (4) ensuring the benevolence of the spirits. The role of the shaman is limited to setting events in motion; the actions themselves (i.e., journey, recovery of the sick person's soul) are carried out by the spirits, who, should they resist, can torment the shaman severely. The shaman ends his state of trance and announces the result; he may also take part in the offering of a sacrificial animal.

OTHER FEATURES OF THE CULTIC LIFE. Characteristic of the entire region are the restrictions on religious practice for women considered impure. If invested with any kind of special significance or cultic character, an object, living creature (especially the horse), place, or ceremony carried a list of prohibitions for such women. They were not allowed to visit the sacred locales of warlord guardian spirits. At the bear festival they could participate only in the interlude dances. Customs connected with birth and death were in the hands of the old women. Women sometimes had a separate sacred place near the village and a separate cult rendered to Kalteś. Among males, those who had assumed the care of the family idols after their parents' death were most fully esteemed.

In the cult of warlord guardian spirits there were presumably differences of ceremony according to moiety (especially with regard to the bear cult) and according to consanguineous group. Accordingly, at joint ceremonies the proprietors of the cult being played active roles, while newcomers or guests played relatively passive roles.

Periodic communal holidays were important in the maintenance of social relations. The most inclusive and involved such holiday was the festival organized by the *por* moiety in the village of Vežakar. Held every seven years, it lasted three months and followed the pattern of the bear festival. Several hundred participants were attracted to this event from northern regions. Periodic visits to warlord guardian spirits were sometimes prescribed, during the course of which the devotees made joint sacrifices. Regularly intermarrying groups invited one another to the larger festivals, which could be linked with cultic competitions, prophetic practice, the singing of epics (for the entertainment of the spirits), plays, and amusements. Generally prescribed pilgrimages to high-ranking warlord guardian spirits brought about more extensive relations, as did various alms-collecting tours undertaken in the interest of maintaining the cults of such spirits.

Sacrificial ceremonies. There are two kinds of sacrifices. (1) In bloodless sacrifice (Man., *pūri;* Kh., *por*) the spirits absorb the vapors (or "strength") of the food and alcoholic beverages that have been set out for them; later, the humans present eat it. (2) In blood sacrifice (Man., Kh., *jir*) the spirits receive a portion of the animal's soul-bearing body parts (the blood, certain organs, the head, the entire skin) and thus take possession of the animal's shadow soul. The most precious sacrificial animal is the horse, which was sacrificed to high-ranking mythological personalities (especially World-Overseeing Man) throughout the entire region irrespective of the presence or absence of an equestrian culture. In addition, reindeer (in the north) and horned cattle and roosters (in the south) were usual sacrificial animals. Spirits of the upper sphere were said to favor light-colored animals; those of the nether sphere favor dark-colored animals. In a typical northern sacrifice, the animal is either strangled or dealt a blow to the head with the back of an ax; simultaneously, the spirit is summoned by shouts. The animal is then stabbed in the heart with a knife and its blood is let. The blood and entrails are consumed raw on the spot; there are separate prescriptions concerning the cooking and distribution of the flesh. In addition to animals, fur, cloth, and coins may serve as objects of sacrifice. Among metals, silver has the highest value.

Periodic sacrifices may be classified into two types, annual and macroperiodic (every three or seven years). Required communal sacrifices are tied to the economy of the seasons; so, for example, in spring (fishing season) and autumn (hunting season) sacrifices carried out to ensure a good catch and bountiful quarry were frequent at the beginning of the season, while thanksgiving sacrifices were generally at the end of the season. For animal sacrifices autumn was the most propitious season. During important communal sacrifices the shaman would take part, and men in a light ecstatic trance would perform sword dances in commemoration of the ancient heroic deeds of certain warlord guardian spirits.

It should also be mentioned that the idol-like representation of spirits among the Ob-Ugrians is not fetishistic in character and is thus not absolutely obligatory. It is of importance only as an exterior representation or as a dwelling-place for the spirit; if necessary, the image can be replaced with a new representation.

Nonindigenous influences. The most archaic (but far from the oldest) exterior influence may be found in the cultural elements derived from assimilated sub-Arctic populations. These elements are evident in magic related to production, in certain elements of totemism, and in the bear cult. If one accepts the hypothesis that the *por* moiety is connected with this unknown sub-Arctic people, the number of such elements grows larger. Iranian-speaking and Turkic speaking peoples influenced the proto-Ob-Ugrians in several phases from the Finno-Ugric period (fourth millennium BCE) through the Ugric period (until circa 500 BCE). These peoples played an important role in the development of equiculture among the Ob-Ugrians. Traces of steppe culture are preserved in the dominant role of the horse as a sacrificial animal and divine *attributa,* in the representation of mythological persons from the upper sphere dressed in open, wide-sleeved garb, and in the symbology of images found on hitching posts. Contact with Turkic peoples also brought, most recently, elements of Islam (from the Siberian Tatars), as can be seen in the book of destiny that occurs as an *attributum* and in elements of relatively differentiated conceptions of the netherworld. A surprisingly large number of religious terms were borrowed from or through the Komi (Zyrians), especially in connection with conceptions of the soul and the goddess of fertility. Such Komi influence may have been enhanced when the Komi fled into Siberia to escape conversion to Christianity by Stephen of Perm (fourteenth century).

The first intention of Eastern Orthodox efforts at conversion (which began in the eighteenth century) was the annihilation of the most important idols. This external threat had two consequences: heightened solicitude for cultic objects and a disassociation of spirits from their representations. Within a century, a network of church-centered villages had developed, displacing, wherever possible, the cult centers of ranking warlord guardian spirits. At times, the clergy exploited the possibilities of identifying the personalities of the two religions; formulas of correspondence thus quickly gained ground; the sky god was equated with God the Father, Kalteś with the Virgin Mary, World-Overseeing Man with Jesus, Pelim with Saint Nicholas. Ob-Ugrians understood the new religion entirely in terms of their own categories. Thus, a church was the idol chamber of the Russian god, the icon was the idol itself (before which even animals were sacrificed), the cross worn about the neck was an amulet for warding off harmful forest beings, and so on. The Christian worldview brought little change other than a gradual increase in the significance of the sky god. Qualitative change arose in step with Russification, especially for southern groups. At present, in consequence of the spread of civilization and atheism, Ob-Ugrian young people are ill-informed about religious matters, and their attitude toward their religious heritage is inconstant.

SEE ALSO Bears; Finno-Ugric Religions; Num-Tūrem; Shamanism.

BIBLIOGRAPHY

Folklore Collections

Avdeev, I. I. *Pesni naroda mansi.* Omsk, 1936.

Chernetsov, V. N. *Vogul'skie skazki.* Leningrad, 1935.

Kálmán, B. *Manysi (vogul) népköltési gyüjtemény.* Budapest, 1952.

Kannisto, Artturi. *Wogulische Volksdichtung.* 4 vols. Helsinki, 1951–1963.

Kulemzin, V. M., and N. V. Lukina. *Legendy i skazki khantov.* Tomsk, 1973.

Munkácsi, B. *Vogul népköltési gyüjtemény.* 4 vols. Budapest, 1892–1921.

Pápay, J. *Osztják népköltési gyüjtemény.* Budapest and Leipzig, 1905.

Patkanov, S. *Die Irtyschostjaken und ihre Volkspoesie.* 2d ed. Saint Petersburg, 1900.

Reguly, A., and J. Pápay. *Osztják hofsénekek.* Budapest, 1944.

Reguly, A., and J. Pápay. *Osztják (changi) hősénekek.* Budapest, 1951.

Steinitz, W. *Ostjakische Volksdichtung und Erzählungen,* vol. 1. Budapest, 1975.

Steinitz, W. *Beiträge zur Sprachwissenschaft und Ethnologie.* 4th ed. Budapest, 1980.

Vértes, E. *K. F. Karjalainens südostjakische Textsammlungen,* vol. 1. Helsinki, 1975.

Secondary Sources

Chernetsov, V. N. "Fratrial'noe ustroistvo obsko-ugorskogo obshchestva." *Sovetskaia etnografiia* 2 (1939): 20–42.

Chernetsov, V. N. "K istorii rodovogo stroia u obskikh ugrov." *Sovetskaia etnografiia* 6–7 (1947): 159–183.

Chernetsov, V. N. "Concepts of the Soul among the Ob-Ugrians." In *Studies in Siberian Shamanism,* edited by Henry N. Michael. Toronto, 1963.

Gondatti, N. L. *Sledy iazychestva u inorodtsev Zapadnoi Sibiri.* Moscow, 1888.

Hoppál, Mihály. "Folk Beliefs and Shamanism among the Uralic Peoples." In *Ancient Cultures of the Uralic Peoples,* edited by Péter Hajdú, pp. 215–242. Budapest, 1976.

Karjalainen, K. F. *Die Religion der Jugra-Völker.* 3 vols. Helsinki, 1921–1927.

Kulemzin, V. M. "Shamanstvo vas''iugansko-vakhovskikh khantov." In *Iz istorii shamanstva,* pp. 3–155. Tomsk, 1976.

Kulemzin, V. M. *Chelovek i priroda v verovaniiakh khantov.* Tomsk, 1984.

Sokolova, Z. P. *Sotsial'naia organizatsiia khantov i mansov v XVIII–XIX vekakh.* Moscow, 1983.

Toporov, V. N. "On the Typological Similarity of Mythological Structures among the Ket and Neighbouring Peoples." *Semiotica* 10 (1974): 19–42.

Tschernejtzow, V. N. "Bärenfest bei den Ob-Ugrien." *Acta Ethnographica* (Budapest) 23 (1975): 285–319.

Bibliographies

Nikol'skii, N. P. "Obzor literatury po etnografii, istorii, fol'kloru i iazyku khantov i mansov." *Sovetskaia etnografiia* 2 (1939): 182–207.

Novitskii, G. "Kratkoe opisanie o narode ostiatskom" (1715). Reissued in Hungarian in "Studia Uralo-Altaica," no. 3. Szeged, 1973.

New Sources

Balzer, Marjorie Mandelstam. *The Tenacity of Ethnicity: A Siberian Saga in Global Perspective.* Princeton, N.J., 1999.

EVA SCHMIDT (1987)
Translated from Hungarian by Daniel Abondolo
Revised Bibliography

KHĀRIJĪS are the "third party" in Islam, who anathematize both the majority Sunnīs and the Shīʿī partisans of ʿAlī. Although few in number today, the Khārijīs played a role of great importance in the history of Muslim theology and political theory.

Their origins lie in the agreement between the fourth caliph, ʿAlī, and his challenger, Muʿāwiyah, kinsman and avenger of the murdered third caliph, ʿUthmān, to submit their quarrel to arbitration, following the Battle of Ṣiffīn (AH 37/657 CE). A group of ʿAlī's followers, at first mostly from the Arab tribe of Tamīm, held that ʿAlī had, by agreeing to treat with rebels, committed a great sin and could no longer be considered a Muslim. They made an exodus (*khurūj*) from his camp and collected at Ḥarūrāʾ near ʿAlī's capital of Kufa in Iraq: Hence Khārijīs ("those who went out") are sometimes referred to as Ḥarūrīyah. From the beginning they insisted on the equality of all Muslims regardless of race or tribe, "even if he be a black slave," and they found an important following among the non-Arab converts.

Despite all efforts, ʿAlī was unable to conciliate them. In the end he was forced by their raids and provocations to attack their headquarters on the Nahrawān canal (July 17, 658). This attack became more of a massacre than a battle, and it aroused sympathy for the Khārijīs. Within three years ʿAlī was murdered at the door of his mosque in Kufa by Ibn Muljam al-Murādī, a Khārijī seeking revenge for the slain of Nahrawān.

The intellectual center of Khārijī doctrine for the next century was the great Iraqi port of Basra, but then moved to North Africa. There Khārijī doctrine struck a responsive chord among the Berber tribes, and North Africa became the Scotland of these Muslim Puritans. Khārijī revolts making effective use of guerrilla tactics helped to weaken Muʿāwiyah's Umayyad dynasty before it was overthrown by the Abbasid revolution in 750. Their revolts continued under the early Abbasids, and the appellation *khārijī* came to mean "rebel."

Being from the first people who could not compromise, the Khārijīs quickly separated into sects: Muslim heresiographers list more than twenty. Each sect usually elected an imam, a "commander of the faithful," and regarded itself as the only true Islamic community. Basic to Khārijī doctrine are the tenets that a Muslim who commits a major sin has apostatized, and the shedding of his blood is lawful; that any pious Muslim is eligible to become an imam; and that if he sins or fails to be just, he may be deposed. Non-Khārijī Muslims were regarded as either polytheists or infidels. Jews or Christians who accepted Khārijī rule were, however, scrupulously protected. Khārijīs who sought death in *jihād* (religious war) against other Muslims were considered *shurāt,* or "vendors" (of this world for paradise).

The principal sects were the Azāriqah, the Ṣufrīyah, and the Ibāḍīyah. The Azāriqah probably took their name from Nāfiʿ ibn al-Azraq, son of a former Greek slave and blacksmith. They excluded from Islam all those who were content to coexist peacefully with non-Khārijī Muslims or who believed in *taqīyah,* dissimulation of their true beliefs, and all who would not make the *hijrah,* or emigration, to join them. They practiced *istiʿrāḍ,* or "review" of the beliefs of their opponents, putting to death those who failed to pass their catechism, often including women and children, and held that infants of "polytheists" went to hell with their parents. They maintained that even a prophet was not immune from sin, and hence from final infidelity; that menstruating women should still pray and fast; that a thief's "hand" should be cut off at the shoulder; and that it was not lawful to stone adulterers, because this punishment is not prescribed in the Qurʾān. They broke with the other Khārijīs of Basra in 684 and left the city to conduct a terrible civil war in the southern provinces of Iraq and Iran. This was led by Zubayr ibn Māhūz until 688, then by Qaṭaī ibn Fujāʾah until their final defeat in 699. Qaṭaī was one of a series of gifted Arab Khārijī poets.

The Ṣufrīyah are said to have originated among the followers of ʿAbd Allāh ibn Ṣaffār al-Tamīmī. They believed that peaceful coexistence with other Muslims was legally permissible; unlike the Azāriqah they did not practice *istiʿrāḍ,* and unlike the Ibāḍīyah they held that non-Khārijī Muslims were polytheists rather than merely infidels. They emerged as an active sect in 695 and found an enthusiastic following among the Arab tribes of the upper Euphrates Valley. Under a series of fierce leaders they made their own bid for supreme power in the troubled events at the close of the Umayyad caliphate. From 745 to 751 they fought in Iraq, then Fārs, then Kishm Island, and finally in Oman, where their imam was slain by an Ibāḍī imam. The sect's activities then moved chiefly to North Africa, where it had found Berber adherents after 735. Berber Ṣufrīyah captured the important caravan city of Sijilmāsah in southern Morocco in 770 under an imam named Abū Qurrah. Like many other Khārijīs they were active traders. They maintained an imamate for about a century but at last seem to have been converted to the Ibāḍīyah and to Sunnism.

The Ibāḍīyah are the only surviving division of the Khārijīs, and because they have preserved their writings, they are also the best known. Numbering probably fewer than a million, they are found in the oases of the Mzab and Wargla in Algeria, on the island of Jerba off Tunisia, in Jabal Nafūsah and Zuwāghah in Libyan Tripolitania, in Zanzibar, and in Oman, where the ruling family is Ibāḍī. The merchants of the Mzab, Jerba, and Oman present a good example of closed religious trading communities similar to the Jews, the Parsis, or the Ismāʿīlī Muslims. Practicing Ibāḍīyah do not tolerate tobacco, music, games, luxury, or celibacy, and must eschew anger. Concubinage can be practiced only with the consent of wives, and marriages with other Muslims are heavily frowned upon. They disapprove of Ṣūfīsm, although they have a cult of the saintly dead. Sinners in the community are ostracized until they have performed public admission of guilt and penance.

The sect was first mentioned about 680, in Basra. It took its name from ʿAbd Allāh Ibn Ibāḍ, who broke with the Azāriqah in 684 and continued to live in Basra, where he presided over a secret council called the Jamāʿat al-Muslimīn (Collectivity of the Muslims). His work was continued under Jābir ibn Zayd, an eminent scholar and traditionist. The earliest *mutakallimūn,* or theologians, of Islam were Ibāḍīyah who debated with the circle of Ḥasan of Basra. Jābir was from the Omani tribe of Azd and did much to organize the sect. It had close contacts with the Basran Muʿtazilah and, like them, held that the Qurʾān was created, that humans have power over their own acts, and that there will be no beatific vision. The Ibāḍīyah have also been called the Wāṣilīyah, after Wāṣil ibn ʿAṭāʾ, an early Muʿtazilī.

After Jābir, the Basra collectivity was headed by Abū ʿUbaydah Muslim al-Tamīmī. He retained the Basra headquarters as a teaching and training center and prepared teams of teachers (*ḥamalat al-ʿilm*) to go and spread the doctrine in remote Muslim provinces. When the time was ripe, these teams were to set up imams: Like the Zaydī Shīʿīah and many Muʿtazilah, the Ibāḍīyah hold that there can be more than one imam if communities of widely separated believers need them. At other times, when circumstances dictate, Ibāḍī communities may legally dispense with the imamate, to be ruled by councils of learned elders.

Ibāḍī imamates rose and fell in Yemen, Oman, and Tripolitania in the eighth century. Omani traders carried the doctrine to East Africa in the ninth century. The greatest Ibāḍī imamate was that of Tāhart, founded in central Algeria around 760, which became hereditary in a family of Persian origin, the Rustamīs. During the latter part of the eighth century and the first half of the ninth century, the imams of Tāhart were recognized by Berber tribes from Morocco to Tripolitania, as well as by the Ibāḍīyah of Basra, Iran, and Oman. Their traders were early missionaries of Islam in sub-Saharan Africa. In the latter half of the ninth century, this state was weakened by a series of religious schisms and by external enemies, and many of its Berber supporters converted to Sunnism. The remains of the state were destroyed in 909 by the rise of the Fatimid caliphate, based in Kairouan. The last imam fled to Sadrātah in the oasis of Wargla. The descendants of the fugitives of Tāhart live today in the oases of the Mzab, deep in the Sahara.

Twelve subsects of the North African Ibāḍīyah are mentioned by historians of the sect. Three of these, the Nukkārīyah, the Nafāthīyah, and the Khalafīyah, have survived to modern times in small numbers, chiefly in Tripolitania.

See Also Caliphate; Imamate; Muʿtazilah; Ummah.

Bibliography

The best sources on the Khārijīs are, of course, in Arabic, with others in French, German, and Italian. Most of these will be found listed after three excellent articles in *The Encyclopaedia of Islam,* new ed. (Leiden 1960–): G. Levi Della Vida's "Kh̲āridj̲ites," Tadeusz Lewicki's "Ibāḍīyya," and R. Rubinacci's "Azāriḳa." Two classic Sunnī heresiographies have been translated into English, however, and are valuable reading, though written from a distinctly hostile stance. These are ʿAbd al-Qāhir al-Baghdādī's *Moslem Schisms and Sects* (*Al-Farḳ Bain al-Firaḳ*), translated by Kate Chambers Seelye (New York, 1919–1935), pp. 74–115, and A. K. Kazi and J. G. Flynn's "Shahrastānī: Kitāb al-Milal wa'l Niḥal (The Khārijites and the Murjiʾites)," *Abr-Nahrain* 10 (1970/71): 49–75. A valuable article by a leading scholar of the Ibāḍīyah is Tadeusz Lewicki's "The Ibádites in Arabia and Africa," parts 1 and 2, *Cahiers d'histoire mondiale* 13 (1971): 51–130. An older but still useful introduction is William Thomson's "Khārijitism and the Khārijites," in *The Macdonald Presentation Volume: A Tribute to Duncan Black Macdonald* (1933; reprint, Freeport, N. Y., 1968).

John Alden Williams (1987)

KHILĀFAH See CALIPHATE

KHMER RELIGION.

KHMER RELIGION. The majority of Khmer, the dominant ethnic population of Cambodia, identify themselves as practitioners of Theravāda Buddhism. As in other contemporary Southeast Asian cultures with strong Theravadin identities, the Buddhism practiced in Cambodia is characterized by two trends. Although the Theravadin history of Cambodia is understood by most Khmer to extend back to ancient times, the self-conscious construction of Cambodia as a Theravadin nation is largely a modern development. Khmer Buddhism is (and has long reflected) a complex interweaving of local and translocal religious ideas, movements, rituals, practices, and persons. This history includes, first, the blurring of clear distinctions between Theravāda, Mahāyāna, and Tantric historical development in Cambodia, and second, the incorporation of Buddhist values into local spirit cults and healing practices. As Buddhist scholars have only recently begun to recognize, the older normative presentation of a monolithic "Theravāda" tradition dominating Southeast Asia is largely a scholarly fiction.

Buddhism in Cambodia during the past two millennia has been marked by numerous transformations as it was blended, in different forms, with local and Hindu-influenced cults; as diplomats, missionaries, monks, and traders imported new interpretations, monastic lineages, and practices; and as Buddhism rose and fell from official patronage. There are striking continuities in Khmer religious history as well: the political potency of religion in various Khmer kingdoms, states, and regimes; the intertwining in all periods of Buddhist, Brahmanic, and spirit cults and practices; and, at least since the widespread popularization of Theravāda Buddhism after the fourteenth century, the important role of Buddhist ideas and values in the moral vocabulary and ritual practices of Khmer people.

Based on Pali scriptures, many Khmer Buddhists have understood their national religion to originate in the Aśokan missions of the third century BCE. Archeological evidence, however, suggests a somewhat later introduction of Buddhism, possibly as early as the second century CE, when Khmer-speaking peoples were congregated in small chiefdoms referred to in Chinese records as *Funan.* Buddhism was likely introduced into the Khmer regions by Indian merchants, explorers, and traveling monks, but the extent to which this movement should be regarded as a full-scale "implantation" has been debated. The theory of the importation and spread of Buddhism and other Indian ideas and cultural forms into Southeast Asia has been termed *Indianization* by scholars. In the nineteenth and early twentieth centuries, a historical account of the "origin" of Southeast Asian cultural forms through the mode of a dominant Indian civilization was widely accepted by colonial scholars of Cambodia, presumably because of its resonance with dominant colonial views of race and civilizational development. By the 1930s, the work of the French Indologist Paul Mus (soon joined by other historians) began to call into question the extent to which the Khmer and other Southeast Asian cultures were shaped by Indian influence, arguing instead that Indian forms had been easily absorbed in Southeast Asia because they complemented existing indigenous ideas and practices, and that the cultural influences moved both ways, not just one way.

More recently, a consensus has emerged among many historians that Indians probably never established a political and economic process akin to modern-era colonization by Europeans in Southeast Asia; nor is there thought to have been a large movement of Indian settlers to Southeast Asia. Rather, aspects of the language, arts, literature, and philosophical, religious, and political thought of Indians were assimilated and reinterpreted by Khmer and other Southeast Asian peoples during the first centuries CE, possibly through a combination of trade, diplomatic, and religious contacts both with India and Indians directly and also through trade and court relations with Southeast Asian neighbors. Among the most important borrowings from India for the Khmer was the introduction of Sanskrit writing and literature. Archeological evidence from the pre-Angkorian (seventh to ninth centuries) and Angkorian (ninth to fourteenth centuries) periods shows that the Khmer utilized both Sanskrit and Khmer for inscriptions: they used Sanskrit for expressive literary purposes, such as extolling the virtues of the gods, and Khmer for more documentary purposes, such as listing donations of slaves to temples. Sanskritist Sheldon Pollock has suggested that the attraction of Sanskrit as a cosmopolitan language was aesthetic; it provided a powerful medium for imagining the world in a larger, more complex, and translocal way. By the middle- or post-Angkorian period (fifteenth to nineteenth centuries), the use of Sanskrit for literary purposes had been replaced by the vernacular, which had developed its own cosmopolitan idiom. For the Khmer, this process of the thorough transformation of the Indian literary imagination is evident in the celebrated Khmer rendering of the *Rāmāyaṇa,* known in Khmer as the *Rāmakerti* (pronounced "Ream-ker"), the *Glory of Rām.* The Khmer adaptation of the Indian epic transforms the hero, Rām, into a *bodhisattva,* reflecting Khmer ethical and aesthetic concern with the biography of the Buddha. The *Rāmakerti* appears as a frequent theme in Khmer art in temple murals and paintings and in bas reliefs on the galleries of Angkorian temples. It has also been reenacted in elaborate traditional dance forms, composed as narrative poetry, and retold in many oral versions, including shadow puppet plays known as *spaek dhaṃ* and *lkhon khol* performances used ritually as spirit offerings.

From the second century onward, historical evidence suggests that Buddhist and Brahmanic practices coexisted and became intertwined with local animist traditions and spirit beliefs in the Khmer regions. Chinese records indicate that Khmer court rituals during the Funan period included the worship of Śiva-liṅgam, suggesting devotion to Śiva, as well as evidence of local spirit cults. The transregional movements of Buddhist missionaries and pilgrims may well have introduced Buddhism into Southeast Asian courts. Chinese histories reveal that Chinese monks en route to India by sea visited sites in Southeast Asia, and likewise that a Buddhist monk from Funan named Nāgasena traveled to China in the sixth century. At Oc-Eo, a port city of the Funan era, archeologists have discovered Buddha images associated with the Mahāyāna tradition.

Epigraphic records of religious life began to appear in the seventh century, during the period referred to as *pre-Angkor,* when the Khmer regions were apparently dominated by a group of chiefdoms or kingdoms referred to in Chinese sources as *Chen-la.* These inscriptions, primarily composed in Khmer and Sanskrit, suggest that the pre-Angkorian rulers were for the most part devotees of Śiva or Viṣṇu. Contemporary historians warn against over-interpreting this evidence to suppose that an Indian-like "Hinduism" was in existence. Rather, drawing on persuasive linguistic evidence, Michael Vickery has pointed to the practice among pre-Angkor Khmer of attributing Indian names to their own indigenous deities.

These inscriptions also suggest the simultaneous practice or at least the presence of diverse religions, including Buddhism, which was tolerated and to different degrees supported by most pre-Angkorian rulers. Buddhism was apparently practiced alongside or synthesized into the activities of indigenous cults with some Indian features. These sources also reveal that pre-Angkorian Buddhist influences were drawn from India, China, Sri Lanka, and other parts of Southeast Asia, such as Dvaravati and Champa, with more than one form of Buddhism in evidence. Numerous Avalokiteśvara figures, as well as a reference to the name *Lokeśvara* in an inscription from 791 (found in present-day Siemreap), indicate Mahayanist influence. Yet some early Pali inscriptions from the pre-Angkor period have also been found along with Sri Lankan and Dvaravati style Buddha images showing Theravadin presence.

The end of the pre-Angkor period was a period of political and economic expansion and centralization in the Khmer region. As kings enlarged their territories, the Khmer political linking of king and deity began to emerge, a concept referred to in Sanskrit inscriptions as *devarāja,* which may have grown out of older indigenous traditions linking rulers and local deities of the earth. This association developed more fully during the Angkor period, starting with the kingship of Jayavarman II (802–854). While the ideological details of the *devarāja* cults remain unclear—whether or to what extent kings understood themselves as embodied deities or as supplicants to or patrons of particular deities remains contested—scholars have surmised that the considerable political and economic influence wielded by Angkorian kings was inseparable from their close ties to cycles of agricultural production and fertility, their roles as moral exemplars and protectors and patrons of religious life. These dimensions of kingship were manifested in the building projects undertaken by the Angkorian kings, in reservoirs, images, and mountain temples such as Angkor Vatt, the fabulous religious monument constructed by Sūryavarman II (1113–c.1150) and dedicated to Viṣṇu.

Most of the early Angkorian kings were Saivites or devotees of Harihara, a Khmer deity incorporating aspects of both Śiva and Viṣṇu. But Mahāyāna Buddhism was also in evidence and became increasingly connected with royal patronage and political power during the Angkorian period. Yasovarman, regarded as the founder of Angkor (889–900), dedicated hermitages to Śiva, Viṣṇu, and the Buddha; Rājendravarman II (c. 944–968), Jayavarman V (c. 968–1001), Sūryavarman I (1001–1050), and Jayavarman VI (1080–1107) all patronized Buddhism in addition to other religious cults. Mahāyāna Buddhism came to the forefront, however, toward the end of Angkorian predominance, during the reign of Jayavarman VII (1181–c.1218). Historian David Chandler has suggested that Jayavarman VII may have developed an interest in Mahāyāna Buddhism during a stay in Champa, where Mahāyāna Buddhism was flourishing. Influenced by Buddhist ideas, Jayavarman VII followed a period of bloody warfare in his reign by constructing public works, such as rest houses, hospitals, and reservoirs, as well as the temples Ta Prohm and Preah Kan to honor his parents in combination with the goddess of wisdom, Prajñāpāramitā, and the Bodhisattva Lokeśvara (symbolizing compassion). He also erected the Bayon temple in the center of his capital containing the central image of the Buddha, with four-faced images of Lokeśvara on its towers and exteriors, an image that has been widely associated in modern times with Cambodian identity and with a widespread romantic fascination with Angkor. This image has sometimes been interpreted as a likeness of Jayavarman VII as well, possibly representing a further reinterpretation of the earlier *devarāja* concept, now connecting king and *bodhisattva.*

During the eleventh to thirteenth centuries, as inhabitants of the Southeast Asian maritime regions were adopting Islam, people in mainland areas, including Cambodia, were turning to Theravāda Buddhism. Although there is a generally acknowledged acceptance among scholars of the "ascendancy" of Theravāda Buddhist ideologies and practices during this period, it is not exactly clear why or how. Victor Lieberman explains the popularization of Theravāda Buddhism after about 1400 in connection to expanding trade and prosperity moving from coastal to inland regions. He suggests that Theravāda Buddhism became associated with this movement and that it perhaps provided a larger, more cosmopolitan and universal vision of the world for its new adherents. Given the syncretic nature of Khmer religion in general, it is likely that Theravadin ideas and practices continued to intermingle with other Buddhist forms. As the dominant political and economic influence of Angkor waned and the kingdoms of Pagan and Sukothai (in present-day Burma and Thailand) replaced it as regional powers, trade, diplomatic, and other cultural contact with these Theravadin kingdoms spread Theravadin ideas to Khmer-speaking people. A Khmer prince, possibly a son of Jayavarman VII, is supposed to have been among a group of Southeast Asian monks who traveled to Sri Lanka to study Buddhism at the end of the twelfth century and ordained in the Mahaviharin order, a lineage that was carried back and established in Pagan. During the next two centuries, Theravāda Buddhism became assimilated into all levels of Khmer society and synthesized with older Brahmanic and spirit practices, such as agricultural and life-cycle rites, worship of *qnak tā* (local spirits), spirit mediumship, alchemy, and healing practices.

During the post-Angkorian or "middle period," the population and agricultural centers of the Khmer region gradually shifted southward. While Khmer religion retained its syncretic character, Theravadin forms and idioms dominated. Cultural historian Ashley Thompson sees this movement reflected in the appearance of wooden Theravadin *vihāras* built adjacent to Angkorian Brahmanic stone temples, and in the shift in iconography from images of deities such as Śiva, Viṣṇu, and Harihara to images of the Buddha. Pali replaced Sanskrit as the language of inscriptions and literature along with Khmer, and much of the classical Khmer literature was composed during this time. Along with the development of Buddhist interpretations of the *Rāmakerti,* Khmer art and literature began to assume Theravadin ideas of the relationship between Buddhist virtue and kingship, and merit-making and *karma;* they also developed an emphasis on the cosmic biography of the *bodhisattva* perfecting virtues in his different rebirths on the path to buddhahood, and a cosmology and ethical orientation reflecting notions of rebirth and moral development in the three-tiered world of the Trai Bhūm. A sixteenth-century inscription translated by Thompson, for example, refers to the merit produced by a royal couple, the king's subsequent rebirth in Tuṣita Heaven, and his resolve to become an *arahant* at the time of the Buddha Maitreya.

While Khmer scholars tend to situate the end of the middle period and the beginning of the modern period in the mid-nineteenth century with the advent of French colonial rule in 1863, a significant shift in the fate of modern Khmer Buddhism began to occur toward the end of the eighteenth century. From this point until the early nineteenth century, Cambodia was involved in almost continual warfare with its Siamese and Vietnamese neighbors, followed by unrest and violence later in the nineteenth century, as a result of internal revolts, Buddhist millenarian rebellions, piracy, and banditry. The Buddhist material culture that had developed during the middle period was damaged or destroyed as a result of this warfare and social chaos. A nineteenth-century Khmer official wrote in his memoir that in the late 1840s, once a relative peace was restored for the first time in more than a century, the countryside of Cambodia was "shattered," poverty and starvation were apparent everywhere, and Buddhist temples were destroyed or broken apart. Orphaned and poor, he recalled, "I knew only suffering and misery and my heart was broken. I wanted to ordain in the discipleship of the Lord Buddha. . . . But in Vatt Sotakorok there were no *Dhamma-attha-sāstra-pali* [Buddhist scriptures] and in the *vatt* [temple] where I was ordained as a *bhikkhu,* there remained only ignorant and backward monks."

The destruction of Buddhist texts, temples, educational facilities, and generations of scholar-monks over a sustained period of time, as well as the weakening of the Cambodian monarchy, the influence of Thai Buddhist reforms, and the colonial religious policies imposed by the French, all contributed to a shift in the religious landscape of Cambodia during and after the reign of King Ang Duong (r. 1848–1860). In his path-breaking work on Khmer Buddhism, which has also held wider repercussions for challenging a rigid historiography of a dominant Pali Theravadin tradition in the region, François Bizot has argued that Khmer Buddhism prior to the period of renovation initiated by Ang Duong was characterized by strong Tantric influences, which were largely eradicated during the nineteenth and early twentieth centuries. Bizot's current translations seek to preserve remnants of these traditions, marginalized and preserved in the esoteric teachings, texts, and meditation practices of small numbers of adherents.

Beginning in 1848, when Ang Duong was installed on the Khmer throne under Siamese patronage, he initiated a Buddhist purification movement that lasted for nearly a century, and which formed the basis for the creation of modern Khmer Buddhism during the early decades of the twentieth century. Ang Duong, who composed a number of well-known literary works himself, gathered Buddhist-trained literati in his court, and turned his attention toward revitalizing Buddhist education and rebuilding Buddhist material culture. The strong court ties with Siam, affinities between Khmer and Thai Buddhism, as well as the vibrancy of Buddhist literary culture in Bangkok during much of the nineteenth century, led the Khmer to turn to Bangkok for Buddhist texts and education. Modern Khmer Buddhism, as it developed, was thus also strongly influenced by the Thai Buddhist reforms introduced in the nineteenth century by King Mongkut and his sons, King Chulalongkorn and (in the Khmer transliteration) Supreme Patriarch Vajirañāṇavarorasa.

This Siamese influence is evident in the biographies of the two leading Khmer monks of the nineteenth century, who both received their ordinations in Bangkok. Samtec Braḥ Sangharāj Dīeṅ (1823–1913), the *saṃgha* chief who oversaw most of the Buddhist renovation in Cambodia, was captured as a prisoner of war by the Siamese army as a young boy and taken to Bangkok as a slave, where he became connected to the entourage of the exiled Ang Duong. Dīeṅ was ordained as a novice at the age of eleven, and by the time he was ordained as a monk in 1844, he had already won the notice of Rama III for his brilliance. By the age of twenty-five, his reputation as a scholar and monk-scribe was well established in monastic circles in Bangkok, and his works included a translation of the *Trai Bhūm* from Thai, as well as the *pātimokkha,* a section of the Vinaya or monastic code regularly recited by monks. Dīeṅ returned to Cambodia at the request of Ang Duong to head up the restoration of Buddhism in the kingdom, and following a Thai model of administrative centralization, he began to conduct the first of several reorganizations of the *saṃgha* that occurred between the 1850s and 1880. Appointed to the rank of supreme patriarch in 1857, Dīeṅ also instituted monastic Pali exams, beginning in 1858. He retained his close connections with the Khmer throne during Norodom's reign (r. 1864–1904), and was venerated by the general populace until his death in 1913.

The other highly regarded Khmer monk of the nineteenth century was Samtec Braḥ Sugandhādhipatī Pān (c.1824–1894), the monk credited with the importation of the Dhammayutnikāy (Mongut's reformist sect) to Cambodia. Born in Battambang, Pān was ordained as a novice in 1836 at Vatt Bodhivāl in Battambang; in 1837 he went to Bangkok to study Pali, his biography states, because of "the deplorable state of Buddhist education in his [natal] pagoda." He was ordained in the Mahānikāy sect as a *bhikkhu* at the age of twenty-one, but in 1848, he was exposed to an influential teacher of the Dhammayut sect; one biography states that he also studied Pali under the direction of Mongkut, who was still in the monkhood at this time. Pān reordained as a Dhammayut *bhikkhu* in 1849, with Mongkut presiding at the ceremony.

The date of Pān's return to Cambodia and the founding of the Dhammayut sect in Cambodia has been attributed to the reigns of both Ang Duong and Norodom, either in 1854 or 1864. While the exact date is uncertain, it is clear that in symbolic and political terms, the erudite monk Pān—and with him, the establishment of the Dhammayut sect—emanated from the highest court circles in Bangkok. Pān was accompanied on his return to Cambodia by a number of Siamese monks, who presented the kingdom with a collection of eighty Siamese texts, presumably the *tipiṭaka,* which had been "lost" in Cambodia during the years of warfare. Under Norodom, Pān constructed the seat of the Dhammayut order in Vatt Bodum Vaddey in Phnom Penh. He was apparently literate in Pali, Sanskrit, Thai, Lao, Burmese, and Mon, and could also read ancient Khmer inscriptions. Dhammayut sources suggest that he was an important compiler of Vinaya commentaries, monastic training manuals, and manuals on merit-making rituals.

While these two widely-respected and well-educated monastic leaders were able to foster the renovation of Buddhism envisioned by Ang Duong from the 1850s onward, monks and novices seriously interested in advanced Pali studies were still better served in Bangkok, usually after receiving a basic primary and novitiate education in Cambodia. Monastic biographical sources suggest that prior to about 1910, young boys studying in Khmer temples learned Khmer literacy, writing, arithmetic, vernacular religious literature such as *cpap'* (didactic poetry), *jātaka, lpaeṇ* (narrative poetry), and sometimes *kpuan* (manuals) or *tamrā* (technical treatises) on astrology, medicine, or ritual procedures. Monks and novices who traveled to Bangkok for study or text collection purposes, such as Ukñā Suttantaprījā Ind (1859–1924), Braḥ Mahāvimaladhamm Thoṅ (1862–1927), and Braḥ Mās-Kaṅ (1872–1960), encountered new methods of Pali grammar instruction, translation, and textual analysis that went beyond the older pedagogical traditions employed in most Khmer monasteries of the day of rote memorization, often without clear understanding of the Pali verses being chanted.

Although the Dhammayutnikāy imported from Siam and patronized by the royal family never took wide hold outside of urban areas, the wider imprint of Thai reformism influenced young Khmer monks in the more traditional Mahānikāy order in Cambodia. These young monks, led in particular by Chuon Nath (1883–1969) and Huot Tath (1891–1975), pushed for a series of innovations in the Khmer *saṃgha* beginning in the early twentieth century: they advocated the use of print for sacred texts (supplanting the traditional inscription of palm-leaf manuscripts mandated by *saṃgha* officials for Buddhist texts into the 1920s in Cambodia); a higher degree of competence in Pali and Sanskrit studies among monks; a vision of orthodoxy based on understanding of Vinaya texts for both *bhikkhu* and laypersons; and modernization in pedagogical methods for Buddhist studies. As the modernist and reformist ideas of Nath and That developed, the two monks came to champion the understanding and practice of a rationalistic, scripturalist, demythologized Buddhism, similar in many respects to the reformed Buddhism of Mongkut.

Chuon Nath, often considered to be the greatest Khmer monk of the twentieth century, was born in Kompong Speu and ordained as a *bhikkhu* at Vatt Bodhi Priks in Kandal in 1904; he was educated as a novice first at Vatt Bodhi Priks and later at Vatt Uṇṇālom. After his ordination as a *bhikkhu* he returned to Vatt Uṇṇālom, where he continued his Pali studies under the direction of Braḥ Mahāvimaladhamm Thoṅ, who was in turn a student of Braḥ Samtec Sangharāj Dieṅ. Nath's younger colleague and long-time collaborator, Huot Tath, was also born in Kompong Speu, and was ordained in 1912 at Vatt Uṇṇālom. Both men generated controversy and were held in scorn by some of their older colleagues within the Mahānikāy during their early years as reformers, but they rose to prominent monastic ranks during the late 1920s and 1930s, serving as professors at the Sālā Pali and as key members of the Commission for the Production of the *tipiṭaka.* Nath was appointed as *saṃgha* head in 1963; Tath followed as *sangharāj* in 1969, after Nath's death, holding this title until his execution by the Khmer Rouge in 1975.

The reforms envisioned by the faction of Nath and Tath were not uniformly accepted within the Khmer *saṃgha.* Early attempts by Nath to introduce print met with resistance from established *saṃgha* officials and led to increasing factionalism between modernists and traditionalists within the Mahānikāy that continued into the 1970s. The reformist efforts led by modernist monks did however coincide with both the pedagogical ideologies and political interests of French colonial administrators who backed Nath and Tath in an effort to reinvigorate Buddhist education within the protectorate. The French administration took on the role of *saṃgha* patron in part to foster European models of scientific education but also, fearing Siamese and Vietnamese influence, to stem the flow of Khmer Buddhist literati to Bangkok, as well as the movement of monks within French Indochina. The modernist agenda also helped to counter the influence of millenarian Buddhism in the provinces, which threatened French rule. In French Cambodia, as well as in southern Vietnam, peasant insurrections linked anticolonialism with predictions of a Buddhist *dhammik* ("righteous ruler") who would usher in the epoch of the Buddha Maitreya.

The Buddhist reform movement advocated by Nath, Tath, and their fellow professors and scholars at the Sālā Pali—known initially as Dharm-thmī ("modern *dhamma*") and later as Dhammakāy or simply *smāy* ("modern") Buddhism—shaped the contours of official scholarly Buddhism in Cambodia as these reformers taught in advanced Buddhist educational institutions and *dhamma*-Vinaya schools, and prepared textual compilations. But this textually-oriented Buddhism was never the only or even the dominant expression of religious life in modern Cambodia, and even while a figure such as Chuon Nath was widely respected as a great scholar, he was also venerated by the Cambodian populace as the possessor of extraordinary powers of *iddhi,* such as the ability to understand the speech of birds.

In urban as well as rural areas, Khmer religious life during most of the twentieth century was deeply ritualistic, involving the daily or seasonal worship of deities of the earth, water, rice fields, and cardinal directions, as well as local tutelary spirits and ancestors, along with the care and manipulation of the relationships between humans and these powerful spirit beings. (Some of these generalizations remain current, but since so many aspects of Khmer life were altered after 1975, it is more accurate to confine these descriptions to the pre-1975 religious context documented by ethnographers such as Eveline Porée-Maspero and May Ebihara). Spirit houses in fields and outside of houses were often attended daily, while shrines within the house were maintained for ancestor spirits, known as *mebā,* whose dissatisfaction or disapproval could potentially cause illness in family members. While Buddhist monks were invited to offer prayers and blessings or sprinkle sacred water at weddings, funerals, housewarmings, and other life-cycle events, other religious practitioners besides monks often presided at these kinds of events. These included *āchāry,* lay teachers at the *vatt* who assisted with life-cycle rituals, protective amulets, and so on; *grū Khmaer,* traditional healers who could diagnose and cure many illnesses, including those connected with the spirit world; *rūp arakkh,* spirit mediums who could communicate with the spirits of the dead, *arakkh;* and *chmap,* midwives who assisted with the rites and practices necessary to assure safety for mothers and infants during the highly vulnerable passage of childbirth.

The ethical ideas underlying these religious practices reflect several central themes. First and perhaps most important, is a belief in the efficacy of the law of *karma* (*kamm* in Khmer). Summarized by the contemporary Khmer monk Venerable Maha Ghosananda, this law states: "*Karma* means action. . . . I am the owner of my *karma.* And the heir of my *karma.* I am related to my *karma,* and abide supported by my *karma.* Whatever *karma* I shall do, whether good or evil, of that I will be the heir. What we do we will reap, what we sow we will reap." Given this understanding, moral behavior and especially the attainment of high levels of moral purification—most often by monks and other religious virtuosos—were highly valued. But even for lay people, religious participation was marked by the frequent ritual invocation of the five Buddhist precepts (*sīl praṃ* in Khmer: to abstain from taking life, stealing, false speech, improper sexual relationships, and the use of intoxicants), as well as by ceremonies of homage and taking refuge in the "triple gem" (the Buddha, *dhamma,* and *saṃgha*), and by merit-making through offering gifts of food and robes to monks, through the copying or dedication of Buddhist texts, and for those with enough means, through sponsoring religious building projects. Gratitude to parents or teachers, to whom one could dedicate merit, and veneration toward monks, the king, and the nation were increasingly intertwined with ideologies of merit-making during the twentieth century. A Khmer proverb translated by Bounthay Phath conveys the understanding of impermanence and *dukkha* that inscribed the religious ethos of her childhood in Phnom Penh during the 1950s and 1960s: "Wherever one goes, suffering will go along just as the shadow follows the body."

While modernist *saṃgha* officials and scholarly Buddhists in the 1920s and 1930s sometimes decried the religion practiced by the majority of Khmer as "non-Buddhist," for the most part, the spirit practices, Brahmanist court rituals, ancestor propitiation, and healing cults amply documented by ethnographers coexisted with reformist forms of Theravāda Buddhism. This complementarity between "popular" and textual interpretations of Buddhism was visible even in 1930 when the Buddhist Institute was established under the directorship of French curator Susanne Karpelès, a French Indologist who promoted Nath's and Tath's reform Buddhism; Karpelès and her staff happily orchestrated colorful processions and merit-making festivals in the countryside as they collected copies of Buddhist manuscripts for the Buddhist Institute and Royal Library. The major project of the institute was to produce a critical Khmer-Pali printed edition of the Tipiṭaka, culled by a commission of Buddhist scholars from palm-leaf manuscripts donated by the Khmer populace, and finally completed in 1968. After 1930, the Buddhist Institute continued to lead the development of modern Buddhism in Cambodia, and historian Penny Edwards has argued for its role as a site for imagining Khmer nationalism. Monks were among the most prominent dissidents against the French colonial regime, and the institute also helped give rise to the development of the Communist Party in Cambodia; Mean (Son Ngoc Minh) and Sok (Tou Samouth), later leaders of Khmer communism, were both recruited by Susanne Karpelès for Buddhist education.

In spite of this early connection between Buddhism and the Communist Party, after the Khmer Rouge took power in April 1975, they quickly sought to eradicate Buddhism in Democratic Kampuchea. Ian Harris estimates that 63 percent of monks died or were executed during the Democratic Kampuchea years; many others were forced to disrobe, Buddhist monasteries were destroyed or used for other purposes, Buddhist text collections were discarded, and Buddhist practices were forbidden. Nearly two million people died as a result of Khmer Rouge policies enacted between 1975 and 1979.

Since the Vietnamese invasion of 1979 that brought an end to the murderous Democratic Kampuchea regime, Buddhism has slowly reemerged in Cambodia, in some ways resembling Buddhism before 1975 and in other ways altered. The People's Republic of Kampuchea allowed the reorganization of the Khmer *saṃgha* under the Venerable Tep Vong, but imposed severe restrictions on Buddhist participation and expression. These were gradually lifted by the People's Republic of Kampuchea and the subsequent (1989) State of Cambodia government. Since 1989, many temples (*vatt*) have been rebuilt, often from contributions by overseas Khmer, and Buddhist life has been widely reconstituted.

Research by anthropologists John Marston and Judy Ledgerwood, among the first to begin to document the new religious context, suggests that older strains of Khmer Buddhist thought, such as tensions between "modernists" (*smāy*) and "traditionalists" (*purāṇ*), as well as millenarian movements (connected in some cases with the nineteenth-century versions), have reemerged in this new period. Ledgerwood's work has also begun to document the ways in which contemporary political leaders such as Hun Sen are returning to the pre-revolutionary model of political rulers as patrons of the *saṃgha* in order to establish authority and legitimacy. On the other hand, the loss of so many monks, intellectuals, and texts and a whole generation of young lay people raised without any religious education during the Democratic Kampuchea period is seen by some contemporary Buddhist leaders as a major obstacle to the rebuilding process and an irreparable break with the past. The traumatic experience of the Democratic Kampuchea period and its aftermath has in some cases ushered in new kinds of cynicism and questioning of basic Buddhist truths, such as the efficacy of the law of *karma;* in contemporary Phnom Penh, the classic karmic formula, "If you do good, you will receive good in return; if you do evil, you will receive evil," is sometimes sardonically rephrased to reflect a widespread perception of governmental corruption: "If you do good, you will receive good; if you do evil, you will receive a car." Other contemporary Khmer now identify even more strongly with Buddhism; many seek to remember the dead through merit-making ceremonies or to ease traumatic memories through meditation practice. Lay meditation movements have begun to flourish in Phnom Penh, a trend already decades old in other Theravadin countries such as Burma and Thailand.

As diasporic Khmer establish new Buddhist centers around the world in cities such as Lowell, Massachusetts, and Long Beach, California, and as Japanese and Western Buddhists and aid workers visit Cambodia, new global Buddhist ideas are reaching contemporary Khmer Buddhists, including "engaged Buddhism," models for Buddhist-led care for AIDS patients, and human rights education and conflict mediation techniques taught through the medium of Buddhist concepts. The internationally known Khmer monk, Mahā Ghosananda, a student of Gandhian ideas, began leading peace marches across Cambodia in 1989 known as *dhammayātrā* (*dhamma* pilgrimages), which crossed war zones and called attention to injustices in contemporary society. Nadezhda Bektimirova reports that after the 1997 coup, seven hundred monks marched for peace in Phnom Penh, carrying the slogan "May peace come to the home of every Cambodian."

See Also Buddhism, article on Buddhism in Southeast Asia; Hinduism in Southeast Asia; Samgha, article on Samgha and Society in South and Southeast Asia; Southeast Asian Religions, article on Mainland Cultures.

Bibliography

The classic, indispensable synthetic work on Khmer history is David Chandler's *A History of Cambodia,* rev. 3d ed. (Boulder, Colo., 2000). *The Khmers,* by Ian Mabbett and David Chandler (Oxford, 1995), emphasizes early Khmer history. The essays by Keith Taylor, Ian Mabbbett, J. G. De Casparis, Barbara Watson Andaya, and Anthony Reid in *The Cambridge History of Southeast Asia,* vol. 1: *From Early Times to c. 1800,* edited by Nicholas Tarling (Cambridge, UK, 1992), along with Victor Lieberman's *Strange Parallels: Southeast Asia in Global Context, c. 800–1830* (Cambridge, 2003), can provide a picture of the history and development of the Khmer in a larger regional perspective. Chandler, a student of Paul Mus and strongly influenced by his theories about indigenous culture, reflects the turn toward producing "autonomous" histories of Southeast Asia. Together with Ian Mabbett, he translated and edited Mus's *India Seen from the East: Indian and Indigenous Cults in Champa* (Cheltenham, Australia, 1975). While Indianization theories have been challenged, George Coedès's *The Indianized States of Southeast Asia,* translated by Sue Brown Cowing, remains an important comprehensive regional treatment of Southeast Asia. Louis Finot's *Le Bouddhisme, son origine, son evolution* (Phnom Penh, 1956), which shares the Indianization bias, was written in the early 1920s in part to convey this notion to Khmer Buddhist monks. It deals primarily with Indian Buddhist history rather than Khmer Buddhism, and was influential for both Chuon Nath and Huot Tath, who studied Buddhist history and epigraphy with Finot in Hanoi in the early 1920s.

Bizot's most important work, in which he lays out his theory of Tantric influence in Cambodia, is *Le Figuier à cinq branches* (Paris, 1981); he continues to translate and publish vernacular works in this vein. Relatively few synthetic works are available on Khmer Buddhist history in European languages. Ian Harris' new *Cambodian Buddhism: History and Practice* (Honolulu, 2004), drawing primarily on European sources, provides a much-needed overview of Khmer Buddhist history. This work can be supplemented with Charles F. Keyes, "Communist Revolution and the Buddhist Past in Cambodia," in *Asian Visions of Authority: Religion and the Modern*

States of East and Southeast Asia, edited by Charles F. Keyes, Laurel Kendall, and Helen Hardacre (Honolulu, 1994), and the topical essays on historical and contemporary religion included in *History, Buddhism, and New Religious Movements in Cambodia,* edited by John Marston and Elizabeth Guthrie (Honoloulu, 2004). In Khmer, Huot Tath has a history of Khmer Buddhism called *Braḥbuddh-sāsanā nau Prates Kambhujā Sankhep* (An abbreviated account of Buddhism in Kampuchea; Phnom Penh, 1961).

Michael Vickery's brilliant and meticulous reading of Khmer epigraphy and other historical sources in *Society, Economics, and Politics in Pre-Angkor Cambodia: The 7th–8th Centuries* (Tokyo, 1998) treats the pre-Angkor period, while Ian Mabbett's *Patterns of Kingship and Authority in Traditional Asia* (London, 1985) and Stanley Tambiah's *World Conqueror and World Renouncer* (Cambridge, U.K., 1976) examine historical relationships between kingship and religion in Cambodia and elsewhere in the Theravadin world. Helpful works on Angkor (and after) include the collected essays in *Sculpture of Angkor and Ancient Cambodia: Millennium of Glory,* edited by Helen Ibbitson Jessup and Thierry Zephir (Washington, D.C., 1997); Charles Higham's *The Civilization of Angkor* (Berkeley, 2001); and Eleanor Mannikka's *Angkor Wat: Time, Space, and Kingship* (Honolulu, 1996). Michael Vickery's Yale University dissertation, "Cambodia After Angkor: The Chronicular Evidence for the Fourteenth to Sixteenth Centuries" (1977), and Ashley Thompson's "Introductory Remarks Between the Lines: Writing Histories of Middle Cambodia," in *Other Pasts: Women, Gender and History in Early Modern Southeast Asia,* edited by Barbara Watson Andaya (Manoa, Hawai'i, 2000), both deal with post-Angkorian epigraphy. Reid's edited volume *Southeast Asia in the Early Modern Era: Trade, Power, and Belief* (Ithaca, N.Y., 1993), and Khin Sok's *Le Cambodge entre le Siam et le Viêtnam (de 1775 à 1860)* (Paris, 1991), take different approaches, one broadly cultural and regional, one closely focused on Khmer social stratification and political history, but both help one to understand Khmer society in the late middle/early modern period. David Chandler's "Going Through the Motions: Ritual Aspects of the Reign of King Duang of Cambodia, 1848–1860" in *Facing the Cambodian Past,* by David Chandler (Chiangmai, Thailand, 1996), discusses royal patronage of Buddhism on the eve of colonialism.

There are a number of helpful works in reference to Khmer literature, which is largely religious in nature. Saveros Pou's work is extensive, but of special note in reference to religion is her study, *Études sur le Rāmakerti (XVI–XVII siècles)* (Paris, 1977), and her translation and analysis of the *cpap', Guirlande de Cpāp'* (Paris, 1988). François Bizot's *Rāmaker ou l'amour symbolique de Rām et Setā* (Paris, 1989) is a study and translation of a Khmer version of the text used as a manual for the practice of Tantric meditation in which the Buddhist adept follows the journey of *Rām* as a form of spiritual instruction. A contemporary oral version of the *Rāmakerti* used for ritual purposes has been collected and edited by Pic Bunnin as *Rāmakerti bol daoy Tā Say* (*Rāmakerti* as recited by Grandfather Say [Phnom Penh, 2000]).Khing Hoc Dy has written a comprehensive survey of Khmer literature and authors, *Contribution à l'histoire de la littérature khmère: Littérature de l'epoque "classique" (XVème–XIXème siècles)* (Paris, 1990), and *Ecrivains et expressions littéraires du Cambodge au XXème siècle* (Paris, 1993), as has Judith Jacob in her highly useful *The Traditional Literature of Cambodia: A Preliminary Guide* (Oxford, 1996). In Khmer, the most-cited work on literature is by Lī Dhām Teṅ, *Aksarsāstr Khmaer* (Khmer literature [Phnom Penh, 1961]).

The classic work on colonial Buddhism is still Adhémard Leclère's *Le bouddhisme au Cambodge* (Paris, 1899); this work is particularly useful for its records of Leclère's conversations with Khmer monks of the period. His numerous translations of Buddhist vernacular works from the period are also available. Alain Forest's *Le Cambodge et la colonisation française: Histoire d'une colonisation sans heurts (1897–1920)* (Paris, 1990) touches on many aspects of Buddhist organization during the French Protectorate period, and *The French Presence in Cochinchina and Cambodia: Rule and Response (1859–1905)* by Milton E. Osborne is especially helpful for understanding millenarianism (Ithaca, N.Y., 1969). Essays by Penny Edwards and Anne Hansen in *History, Buddhism, and New Religious Movements in Cambodia* (cited above) treat the role of religion in "imagining" Khmer identity during the colonial period. The most helpful published source in Khmer on the early twentieth century is Huot Tath's memoir *Kalyāmitta rabas' khñu* (My *Kalyāmitta* [Phnom Penh, 1993]). Bunchan Mul's essay "The Umbrella War of 1942" in *Peasants and Politics in Kampuchea, 1942–1981,* edited by Ben Kiernan and Chantou Boua (London, 1982) considers later involvement of monks in anticolonialism, and the introductory chapters of Ben Kiernan's *How Pol Pot Came to Power* (London, 1985), offer a tightly condensed overview of Buddhist developments during the colonial period. Many Khmer reformist writings from 1914 and later are still available; they were often reprinted decades later (without revision) by the Buddhist Institute. These are largely Buddhist ethical works by monk-scholars such as Uṃ-Sūr and Lvī-Em, as well as Nath and Tath. Tauch Chhuong's oral historical work, *Battambang during the Time of the Lord Governor,* which contains chapters on religious life in Thai-ruled Battambang, was translated by Hin Sithan, Carol Mortland, and Judy Ledgerwood (Phnom Penh, 1994).

In addition to the ethnographic works on Khmer ritual life discussed above, Eveline Porée-Maspero's *Étude sur les rites agraires des Cambodgiens* (Paris, 1962–1969), and May Ebihara's Columbia University Ph.D. dissertation, "Svay: A Khmer Village in Cambodia" (1968) and "Interrelations between Buddhism and Social Systems in Cambodian Peasant Culture" in *Anthropological Studies in Theravada Buddhism,* edited by Manning Nash et al., (New Haven, Conn., 1966); Ang Choulean's *Les êtres surnaturels dans la religion populaire khmère* (Paris, 1986); and Alain Forest's *Le culte des genies protecteurs au Cambodge: Analyse et traduction d'un corpus de texts sur les neak ta* (Paris, 1992), give a thorough treatment of spirit cults and practices. Work on Buddhism in the Democratic Kampuchea period is still emerging, but published works include Yang Sam, *Khmer Buddhism and Politics 1954–1984* (Newington, Conn., 1987), and Boua Chanthou, "Genocide of a Religious Group: Pol Pot and Cambodia's Buddhist Monks" in *State Organized Terror: The Case of Violent Internal Repression* (Boulder, Colo., 1991). Many works are available on diasporic Khmer religion, including several essays collected in *Cambodia Culture Since 1975: Homeland and Exile,* edited by May Ebihara et al. (Ithaca, N.Y., 1994) and Nancy Smith-Hefner's *Khmer-American: Identity and Moral Education in a Diasporic Community* (Berkeley, 1999). Some of the work cited above is from unpublished sources; ethnographic research on Khmer religion by Judy Ledgerwood and John Marston (referred to above) is not yet available. An overview on contemporary religion appears in Nadezhda Bektimirova's "The Religious Situation in Cambodia in the 1990s" in *Religion, State, & Society* 30, no. 1 (2002): 63–72.

ANNE HANSEN (2005)

KHOI AND SAN RELIGION. The Khoi and San are the aboriginal peoples of southern Africa. The appellations formerly applied to them (*Hottentot* and *Bushmen*, respectively) have gone out of use because of their derogatory connotations. Properly, the terms *Khoi* and *San* refer to groups of related languages characterized by click consonants and to speakers of these languages, but they are frequently applied in a cultural sense to distinguish between pastoralists (Khoi) and foragers (San). In historical time (essentially, within the past 250 years in this region), these people were found widely distributed below the Cunene, Okavango, and Zambezi river systems, that is, in the modern states of Namibia, Botswana, Zimbabwe, and South Africa. Smaller numbers were, and are, to be found in southern Angola and Zambia. The once large population of San in South Africa has been completely eliminated; perhaps 20 percent of contemporary Khoi still live in that country. Accurate censuses of these people are available only for Botswana, where today about half the estimated forty thousand San live. The fifty thousand Khoi (except as noted above) are concentrated in Namibia.

Archaeological and historical evidence document the coexistence in these areas of herding and foraging economies for at least the past fifteen centuries. Bantu-speaking as well as Khoi and San agropastoralists have been in the region along with foragers during this entire span of time. The first ethnographies were compiled by German ethnologists in the last decade of the nineteenth century; a few accounts by missionaries, travelers, and traders are available for the preceding one hundred years.

All of these herders and foragers were seasonally migratory, circulating within group-controlled land tenures in response to seasonal distributions of pastures and plant and animal foods. The basic residential group was an extended family often with close collateral extensions; it seldom exceeded fifty persons in size. Two or more of these units, or segments thereof, came together for social, economic, and ritual reasons at specified times, and contact among adjacent groups was maintained by frequent visiting. Descent among the San is bilateral. Patrilineal clans are attributed to the Khoi. Neither social system contains hierarchical strata at present, although there is evidence for them in the past.

On the surface, Khoisan cosmological concepts are not uniformly coherent. The apparent ad hoc and sometimes ambivalent quality of explanations about natural phenomena has led anthropologists to treat these concepts in a descriptive, folkloristic manner. Yet there is an underlying order of shared symbolic categories that represents an inclusive process of cultural management. In its broad outlines, this system is common to all Khoisan groups, even though there is variation in content and emphasis from one group to another.

The key to understanding Khoisan cosmology lies in its creation myths. In the beginning of time all species were conflated. Body parts were distributed in a haphazard, capricious manner by the creator and were intermixed among the different animals. These beings moved through mythical time, eating and mating with each other and being reincarnated in different forms. In the process, each species assumed the identity suggested by its name and thereafter lived in the surroundings and ate the food appropriate to it. As order was achieved, the creator played an ever smaller active role in events; now he lives in the sky, relatively remote from earthly affairs. Generally positive values are attributed to him. Another being has the role of administrator; he is responsible for and is the cause of everything that occurs on earth. He is said to be stupid because he continues to make mistakes. One of the principal mistakes is that people continue to die when, in the logic of creation, they should not be mortal. He also capriciously sends or withholds rain, interferes in the conception and birth of children, and dictates success or failure in food production.

There is, accordingly, a dual conception of death. The death of animals is properly a part of their being; they are food. Human death is rationalized as the caprice of the administrator and justified on the grounds that he eats the dead, whose spirits then remain with him. These spirits have an incorporating interest in death because "their hearts cry for their living kin," and they wish to perpetuate the social order from which they came. The dead are thus agents of the administrator and a danger to the living, especially during dark nights away from camp.

This duality is pervasive in Khoisan cosmological thought. Aside from the obvious oppositions between life and death, earth and sky, that are found among so many peoples, a deeper configuration of a dialectical nature is present. Comparative data is scarce; however, a good deal is known about the Žu/hõasi San (!Kung) of Namibia and Botswana; these people are by far the most numerous living San. This, plus the fact that they share some specific details with Nama Khoi, is suggestive ground for using the data obtained from them for a paradigm case. The Žu/hõasi creator, !xo, and the administrator, //angwa, may be seen—and are sometimes described by informants—as a contrasting pair.

In other words, !xo is a completed proper being, as is a Žu/õa person. (The name *Žu/hõasi* means "completed people": *žu* means "person," */hõa* "finished" or "complete," and *si* is a plural suffix.) //angwa is incomplete, chaotic, "without sense." !xo's attributes are desirable, //angwa's despicable.

!XO	//ANGWA
Creative	Destructive
Passive	Active
Cool	Hot
Clean	Dirty
Hairless	Hirsute
Bees/Honey	Flies/Feces
Cattle/Sheep	Horses/Goats
The color blue	The color red
Cultural order	Natural order

The one gives life, the other takes it away. Some Žu/hõasi think of them as alternative aspects of the same person. That this division, and by implication the cosmological system of which it is a part, may have considerable time depth is suggested by the attribution of cattle and sheep to the cultural order of!xo, while horses and goats are assigned to the unfinished domain of //angwa. Archaeological evidence places both cattle and sheep firmly within the first millennium CE in southern Africa; horses are much more recent. Linguistically, cattle and sheep are derived from a single native stem in most Khoisan languages; horses and goats, on the other hand, are called by a term borrowed from Setswana or—in the case of horses—by extensions of the local word for zebra.

Among the Nama, the creator (rendered Tsui //goab by Schapera) has functions identical to those of !xo and, like his Žu/hõasi counterpart, had an earthly trickster manifestation during the time of creation. It was this trickster (≠gaun!a among Žu/hõasi; Heitsi Eibib among the Nama) who carried out the actual acts of creation. Khoi, in the past, had annual rain ceremonies in which several groups joined. Pregnant cattle and sheep were slaughtered on these occasions and their flesh consumed; their milk, blood, and the water in which they were boiled were used to douse the fire on which they had been cooked. Prayers for rain were offered to Tsui //goab as this was done. The Nama counterpart of //angwa is //gaunab, derived from *//gau,* "to destroy." Their administrative roles are parallel. Earlier writers claim that southern Khoi and southern San worshiped the moon, but as Schapera notes, these reports are inadequate and unsystematic; it is, therefore, difficult to give full credit to such claims. Contemporary San use the moon as a quite specific and accurate timepiece. When referring to the time of occurrence of an event, they will point to a position of the moon in the sky or state that the moon's return to a position will coincide with some event. Women mark their menstrual cycles and the durations of their pregnancies in like manner, but they do so strictly for calendric purposes. It is possible Europeans interpreted these actions as "moon worship."

Although the mythological past is not thought to be active in the present natural world, many of its elements are very much involved in the control of this world. The administrator eats not only humans but also flies, which he attracts by smearing honey around his mouth. This reversal of propriety and the fact that he is covered with long hair (Khoisan have little body hair) is taken as further proof of the confused incompleteness that situates him in residual mythological time. Shamans enter this time while in trance to confront the administrator.

Žu/hõasi shamans go in disembodied flight to the sky and wrestle with //angwa in an attempt to force him to correct some error—an illness, a social disfunction, or an uncertainty about events. In entering this state, shamans take on some of its attributes; they sprout body hair or feathers, become partly or wholly animal, and fly. To be able to participate in this realm they must partake of it. They eat the bile of a lion, the musk gland of a skunklike weasel, the fat from an eland and a porcupine, and the roots of the three plants that grow in the supernatural world. Bitterness (of bile and gland) and fat are the dual sources of strength, as are the roots of extrasensory vision. These elements—eaten once during the course of learning to be a shaman—empower ordinary men to challenge the strength of the supernatural and, by overcoming it, to restore order to the social and natural universe.

The ritual context in which these activities take place involves the entire kin-based community. Only a few people who are directly affected may participate in minor cases, but, small or large, the form of both divinatory and curing rituals is the same. Both involve trance as the essential visionary condition in which the shaman is enabled to exercise his or her power. Women and girls sit in close physical contact, forming a circle facing a fire; they sing and clap songs that are associated with specific natural elements, usually animals but also plants or their products. Men and boys dance closely around the circle, chanting a counterpoint to the songs. Certain dancers are identified with particular animals and their songs; they are more likely to enter trance during performances of these songs. As a dancer feels the trance state approaching, he or she intensifies his or her movements and vocalizations, uttering piercing cries and calling for help, which is signified by heightening the intensity of the music. It is said that in the mythological past, the actual animal being danced (an eland, for example) was attracted to the performance, but now only its spirit attends.

During divinatory trances, Žu/hõasi shamans shout descriptions of their encounter with //angwa in which the cause of the social or physical illness under investigation is revealed. This cause is almost invariably some transgression on the part of either the patient or a close kinsman, usually involving the violation of rights to property (especially the products of land) or personal rights (infractions of obligations, sometimes extending to ancestors). But this direct cause is always expressed indirectly as having disrupted the cosmological order through some mediating agency; for example, the offender may have eaten (or only have killed) a forbidden animal. During the curing trance, the shaman rubs the patient and everyone else present with his hands and arms, thereby transferring healing energy through the mediating agent—sweat.

Thus the myths and their reenactment constitute the conceptual dimensions of Khoisan reality. They integrate subjective experience with the larger structural context through a repertoire of causal principles that, though not expressly verbalized in ordinary discourse, are based on an underlying symbolic order. Trance rituals mediate between these realms. Although couched in causal metaphors, responsibility is normally allocated to living individuals (through their having transgressed the cosmological order) and almost always involves a consensus solution to current social disruptions. The act of divination translates the cosmological constructs in terms of the specific instance at hand. The random, amoral, impersonal forces of nature—which have an order of their own, personified by the administrator and his domain—are temporarily neutralized by this dialectic between culture and society. In the process, although the internal logic remains intact, both are transformed.

There is abundant evidence that these contemporary systems of thought are derived through transformations of more ancient systems. Many rock paintings throughout southern Africa depict persons in postures identical to those assumed during trance today. Therianthropic and theriomorphic figures comparable with those of current creation myths abound among these paintings. The basic structure of these myths and many specific referents (rain bulls whose blood brings rain; water snakes that have hair, horns, limbs, and ears; beings that partake of the mythic past in the present) are shared by many Khoisan and southern Bantu-speaking peoples, suggesting a long history of associated cosmological construction. There is also evidence for comparatively recent change from more active totemic association with natural elements, especially animals, prominent today in trance. The colonial era and its aftermath disrupted the political and economic lives of Khoisan as well as Bantu-speaking peoples; in this process, it is possible but not yet certain that destructive, uncontrollable elements of the cosmological system became emphasized over the constructive forces of creation, and that today the administrator (//angwa of Žu/hõasi) has disproportionate power when compared historically with the role that the creator (!xo) has played.

BIBLIOGRAPHY

Biesele, Megan. "Sapience and Scarce Resources." *Social Science Information* 17 (1978): 921–947.

Lee, Richard B. *The !Kung San: Men, Women, and Work in a Foraging Society.* New York, 1979. The first comprehensive view of the San. Although it falls prey to many traditional faults of evolutionary theory in anthropology, it is much more systematic than its predecessors.

Lewis-Williams, David. *Believing and Seeing: Symbolic Meanings in Southern San Rock Paintings.* London, 1981. Excellent integration of prehistoric and historical rock art with contemporary and archival stories. Points the way toward further fruitful research.

Marshall, Lorna. "!Kung Bushman Religious Beliefs." *Africa* 32 (1962): 221–252. Narrative and descriptive account containing useful information but no comprehensive analysis.

Schapera, Isaac. *The Khoisan Peoples of South Africa.* London, 1930. Based on accounts of missionaries and travelers. Valuable information but outdated synthesis.

Silberbauer, George B. *Hunter and Habitat in the Central Kalahari Desert.* Cambridge, Mass., 1981. Primarily an ecological, evolutionary study, but also includes information on the religious system of the G/wi San.

Wilmsen, Edwin N. "Of Paintings and Painters, in Terms of Žu/hõasi Interpretations." In *Contemporary Studies on Khoisan in Honour of Oswin Köhler on the Occasion of His Seventy-fifth Birthday,* edited by Rainer Vossen and Klaus Keuthmann. Hamburg, 1986. An economic and political analysis of prehistoric and contemporary San paintings.

New Sources

Deacon, Janette and Thomas A. Dowson, eds. *Voices from the Past: /Xam Bushmen and the Bleek and Lloyd Collection.* Johannesburg, 1996.

Gall, Sandy, *The Bushmen of Southern Africa: Slaughter of the Innocent.* London, 2001.

Kent, Susan, ed. *Cultural Diversity among Twentieth-Century Foragers: An African Perspective.* Cambridge, U.K. and New York, 1996.

Sanders, A. J. G. M., ed. *Speaking for the Bushmen: A Collection of Papers Read at the 13th International Congress of Anthropological and Ethnological Sciences.* Gaborone, South Africa, 1995.

Smith, Andrew B. *The Bushmen of Southern Africa: A Foraging Society in Transition.* Athens, Ohio, 2000.

Steyn, Hendrik Pieter. *Vanished Lifestyles: The Early Cape Khoi and San.* Pretoria, South Africa, 1990.

Suzman, James. *"Things from the Bush": A Contemporary History of the Omaheke Bushmen.* Basel, Switzerland, 1999.

Wannenburgh, Alf. *The Bushmen.* Cape Town, South Africa, 1999.

EDWIN N. WILMSEN (1987)
Revised Bibliography

KHOMIAKOV, ALEKSEI (1804–1860), was a Russian Orthodox lay theologian. Khomiakov was influential in determining the character of the Russian intelligentsia in the 1840s and 1850s; the emergence of one of its principal schools of thought, Slavophilism, is closely linked with his name. He was a member of the landed gentry and a participant in the salons of Moscow. His skills as a dialectician and debater were respected even by those (such as Herzen) who shared few of his views. Khomiakov's skills as a writer were less evident in his own milieu as the result of censorship or at least the anticipation of censorship. Virtually all his writings on religion were published abroad and in French. Most of these were published posthumously in their country of origin; few were available in Russian before 1879.

Khomiakov graduated from the University of Moscow as a mathematician but never received any formal instruction in theology. In view of the limitations under which Russian academic theology labored at this time, this was probably an advantage. It allowed him to probe church life for the essentials of the Orthodox faith and to delineate them in a remarkably succinct and forceful fashion. Most notable among his theological compositions was the essay *The Church Is One* (c. 1850).

In this essay Khomiakov adumbrated his celebrated teaching on *sobornost'*, the cornerstone of his theology. The term—a Russian neologism—defies translation, and Khomiakov invariably preferred to transliterate rather than translate it. He himself objected to the French translation, *conciliarité*. In modern times no one word has been found as an acceptable, equally comprehensive, alternative.

Khomiakov derived *sobornost'* from the ninth-century (and subsequently standard) Church Slavonic translation of the Nicene Creed, where the term *catholic* (*katholikos*) had been rendered as *sobornaia*. For him, the word denoted more than mere universality. It spoke rather of a church in which free and complete unanimity prevailed. Such freedom could admit of no constraint. Papal authoritarianism was indicative of a profound malaise in Western Christendom, and Khomiakov campaigned vigorously against it. Indeed, for Khomiakov, any kind of authoritarianism contradicted the very nature of the church. His intuition on this subject was to receive confirmation in 1848 when the Eastern patriarchs and bishops replied to the papal encyclical of that year. Their reply was enthusiastically echoed by Khomiakov (1850) in his correspondence with William Palmer: "The unvarying constancy and the unerring truth of the Christian dogma does not depend upon any Hierarchical Order: it is guarded by the totality, by the whole *people* of the church, which is the Body of Christ" (Birbeck, 1895, p. 94). By the same token, the individualism of the Protestant world was to be rejected. In 1851 he declared that it is in the Orthodox church that "a unity is to be found more authoritative than the despotism of the Vatican, *for it is based on the strength of mutual love*. There [also] a liberty is to be found more free than the license of Protestantism, for it is *regulated by the humility of mutual love*" (Birbeck, 1895, p. 102).

In the teaching of the Slavophiles, as of Khomiakov himself, a social expression of such mutuality was to be found in the Russian peasant commune, the *obshchina*. That the principles of *obshchinnost'* ("communality") and of *sobornost'* were interrelated, if not interdependent, was emphasized by Khomiakov's use of the one term *obshchina* ("commune") to designate both the ecclesiastical community (*koinonia*) and the peasant commune proper. But with the increasing disrepute and ultimate disappearance of the latter, this strand of Khomiakov's thought was itself to be obscured in later years. By contrast, his teaching on *sobornost'* was to capture the imagination of Russian religious thinkers throughout succeeding decades and to play its part also in the ecumenical debates of the century to come.

BIBLIOGRAPHY

Birbeck, William J., ed. *Russia and the English Church during the Last Fifty Years: Containing a Correspondence between Mr. William Palmer Fellow of Magdalen College, Oxford and M. Khomiakoff, in the Years 1844–1854* (1895). Reprint, Farnborough, 1969. Includes also the invaluable *The Church Is One.*

Bol'shakov, Sergius. *The Doctrine of the Unity of the Church in the Works of Khomyakov and Moehler.* London, 1946. Originally a doctoral dissertation which juxtaposes Khomiakov's thought with that of his Roman Catholic contemporary J. A. Möhler. The latter's *Die Einheit in der Kirche* (1825) provides important parallels for Khomiakov's work, even if it cannot be considered as its source.

Christoff, Peter K. *An Introduction to Nineteenth-Century Russian Slavophilism: A Study in Ideas*, vol. 1, *A. S. Xomjakov.* The Hague, 1961. A wide-ranging study of Khomiakov's work as a whole; the only such study in English to date.

SERGEI HACKEL (1987)

KHUSRAW, AMĪR

KHUSRAW, AMĪR (AH 651?–725?/1254?–1325? CE), was a distinguished Indo-Persian poet, musician, and panegyrist. His father, Sayf al-Dīn Shamsī, was most probably a slave-officer in the court of the Delhi sultan Iltutmish (r. 1211–1236). Orphaned at an early age, Khusraw was brought up in the household of his maternal grandfather, ʿImād al-Mulk, another high-ranking nobleman and a former Hindu Rajput who must have converted to Islam following the establishment of Turkish rule in India in the early thirteenth century.

Almost every aspect of Khusraw's life and work has been mythologized to the point where it is difficult to separate the true historical personage from his current popular image. He is today hailed as a great patriot and is counted among the foremost Ṣūfīs of India. Credited with the composition of many lyrics used for *qawwālīs*, a genre of Ṣūfī devotional music, as well as numerous works in Hindi, he is also renowned as a creator of ragas and inventor of musical instruments, including the sitar. Popularly referred to as Ḥaẓrat Amīr Khusraw, he is accorded an honorific title raising him to the stature of a saint. His *ʿurs* (lit., "wedding," the anniversary of a saint's death) is celebrated with tremendous enthusiasm and devotion. He is also known as Turk Allah ("God's Turk") and Tutī-yi Hind ("the parrot of India").

Khusraw displayed his precocious poetic talents at an early age. Seeking his livelihood in the only way open to poets of his time, in the service of rich patrons, he finally found a position at the royal court and had no scruples about flattering a series of royal masters, one of whom had acquired the throne after murdering his former benefactors. Khusraw was first employed by Sultan Kayqubād (1287–1290), at whose request he wrote a long poem, *Qirān al-saʿdayn* (The conjunction of the two auspicious stars). He continued in the service of the next ruler, Jalāl al-Dīn Khiljī (1290–1296), whose achievements he lauded in his *Miftāḥ al-futūḥ* (The key to victories). The reign of ʿAlāʾ al-Dīn Khiljī (1296–1316) saw Khusraw at his most prolific, with *Khazāʾin al-futūḥ* (The treasury of victories) and *ʿĀshiqah* (the love story of Khiḍr Khān and Dewal Rani). He also paid eloquent poetic tributes to the next ruler, Mubārak Shāh Khiljī (1316–1320), who was by all accounts vain and debauched, in *Nuh sipihr* (The nine skies). When the Tughlaqs replaced the Khiljīs, Khusraw continued in the service of Ghiyāth al-Dīn Tughlaq (1320–1325), the history of whose reign he encapsulated in the *Tughlaq-nāmah.*

Khusraw was the first poet in India to compose war and court epics in Persian. As a prose writer he was remarkably eloquent; as a poet he was the master of all forms of verse: *rubāʿīs* ("quatrains"), *qaṣīdahs* ("odes"), and *ghazals* ("lyrics"). A superb lyricist, Khusraw confidently mixed Persian and Hindi metaphors with striking results.

But it was his association with Shaykh Niẓām al-Dīn Awliyāʾ (d. 1325), a saint of the Chishtī order, that is responsible for Khusraw's present stature. The Chishtīyah, a Ṣūfī order that flourished only in India, were at the height of their popularity during the spiritual reign of Shaykh Niẓām al-Dīn. As liberal interpreters of Islam, they provided an effective counterpoint to the orthodox version of Islam as propounded by the court-associated *ʿulamāʾ*. The liberalism of this order was reflected not only in their attitude toward non-Muslims but also in their patronage of cultural activities. As firm believers in the power of music and dance to induce mystical ecstasy, for which they were constantly attacked by the orthodox, they naturally attracted poets and musicians to their hospices (*khānagāhs*). In fact, almost all literary activity among the Muslims of this period was influenced by the ideology of the Chishtīyah. Among notable contemporaries of Khusraw also associated with the Chishtī *khānagāh* were Amīr Ḥasan Sijzī, the great poet and mystic, and Ẓiyā al-Dīn Baranī, the courtier and historian.

Khusraw came into contact with Shaykh Niẓām al-Dīn in 1272, and though he was never initiated into the mystic order, his wit and poetical and musical talents endeared him to the saint. Remarks attributed to the shaykh indicate the special fondness that he had for Khusraw.

The atmosphere of Shaykh Niẓām al-Dīn's *khānagāh* was particularly conducive to Khusraw's sensibilities. As a crucible where a composite culture was evolving from the interaction between Islamic and Indic elements, it suited the genius of Khusraw, who was by birth the product of a similar fusion. As a poet he thrived on mystic themes and imagery; as a gifted musician he moved the audiences at sessions of devotional music (*samāʿ*) to ecstasy, and with his special ear for languages he contributed greatly to the evolution of a lingua franca that made communication possible among the various groups. In brief, Khusraw came to represent almost every aspect of the Ṣūfī tradition in India.

Khusraw also embodies the contradictions arising from his situation. As a courtier dependent on the political survival of the Muslim rulers, he vocalizes an intense and often crude hatred for the Hindus, identifying in them the main threat to his class. But as a poet inspired by the ideology of the Chishtīyah, he displays a touching sensitivity and respect for the religion and culture of India. For this reason Khusraw represents a fine example of the evolving synthesis between the Islamic and the indigenous cultures of the Indian subcontinent.

BIBLIOGRAPHY

Although there are many studies on Amīr Khusraw, most of them unfortunately lack critical analysis of the man or his writings. The most adequate work on Khusraw in English continues to be Mohammad Wahid Mirza's *The Life and Works of Amir Khusrau* (1935; reprint, Lahore, 1962). See *Amir Khusrau: Memorial Volume* (New Delhi, 1975) for a collection of some erudite articles by experts on various facets of his personality. Mohammad Habib's *Hazrat Amir Khusraw of Delhi* (Bombay, 1927), also included in *Politics and Society during the Early Medieval Period: Collected Works of Professor Mohammad Habib,* edited by K. A. Nizami (New Delhi, 1974), is a historical analysis of Khusraw by a leading scholar of medieval Indian history. For a list of Khusraw's works, see C. A. Storey's *Persian Literature: A Bio-Bibliographical Survey,* vol. 2, part 3 (London, 1939).

SALEEM KIDWAI (1987)

KHVARENAH is the Avestan term for "splendor" (OPers, *farnah;* MPers, Pahl., *khwarr;* NPers, *khurrah* or *farr*), designating one of the most characteristic notions of ancient Iranian religion. It is often associated with the aureole of royalty and of royal fortune, thanks to its identification in the Hellenistic period with Greek *tuchē* and Aramaic *gad,* "fortune" (*gdh* is also the ideogram with which *khwarr* is written in Pahlavi), but its meanings go beyond the sphere of royalty, and its influence transcends the confines of the Iranian world. Aspects of the concept of *khvarenah* are found in Manichaeism and Buddhism and are interwoven with similar concepts characteristic of other cultures, as in the Turkish notion of *qut* and the Armenian *pʿaṙkʿ*. In the Avesta and in Zoroastrian tradition in general, *khvarenah* is also personified as a *yazata* or a being "worthy of worship."

Fundamental to the concept of *khvarenah* are its connections with light and fire, attested in the root from which it is derived, *khvar* ("to burn, to glow"), which is probably—despite the opposing opinion of H. W. Bailey, author of an important essay on the question (1943, pp. 1–77)—connected with the same root as *hvar,* "sun" (Duchesne-Guillemin, 1963, pp. 19–31). This explains why *khvarenah* is sometimes translated in Greek as *doxa* ("glory") and in Arabic-Persian as *nūr* ("light").

The *khvarenah* is a luminous and radiant force, a fiery and solar fluid that is found, mythologically, in water, in *haoma,* and, according to Zoroastrian anthropogony, in semen. It is an attribute characteristic of Mithra, of royalty, of divine and heroic figures in the national and religious tradition, of Yima, the first king, of Zarathushtra, and of the three Saoshyants, who perform their tasks (Pahl., *khwēshkārīh*) on earth thanks to the *khwarr* that they possess. It has the power to illuminate the mind and to open the eye of the soul to spiritual vision, enabling those who possess it to penetrate the mysteries of the otherworld.

Recently the winged disk in Achaemenid reliefs has been interpreted as the *khvarenah* (Shahbazi, 1980, pp. 119–147). Deified Khvarenah (Pharro) is depicted on coins from the Kushan empire as a standing man with flames rising from his back.

BIBLIOGRAPHY

Bachhofer, Ludwig. "Pancika und Harītī, *Pharo* und *Ardochro.*" *Ostasiaatische Zeitschrift,* n. s. 23 (1937): 6–15.

Bailey, H. W. *Zoroastrian Problems in the Ninth-Century Books* (1943). Oxford, 1971.

Bombaci, Alessio. "Qutlug Bolsun!" *Ural-Altaische Jahrbücher* 36 (1965): 284–291 and 38 (1966): 13–44.

Boyce, Mary. *A History of Zoroastrianism,* vol. 2. Leiden, 1982.

Bussagli, Mario. "Cusanica et Serica." *Rivista degli studi orientali* 37 (1962): 79–103.

Corbin, Henry. *Terre céleste et corps de résurrection.* Paris, 1961.

Cumont, Franz. *Textes et monuments figurés relatifs aux mystères de Mithra.* 2 vols. Brussels, 1896–1899.

Duchesne-Guillemin, Jacques. "Le 'X̌arenah.'" *Annali dell'Istituto Universitario Orientale di Napoli,* Sezione Linguistica, 5 (1963): 19–31.

Eliade, Mircea. "Spirit, Light, and Seed." *History of Religions* 11 (1971): 1–30.

Gnoli, Gherardo. "Un particolare aspetto del simbolismo della luce nel Mazdeismo e nel Manicheismo." *Annali dell'Istituto Universitario Orientale di Napoli,* n.s. 12 (1962): 95–128.

Gnoli, Gherardo. "Über das iranische *hu̯arnah-*: lautliche, morphologische und etymologische Probleme. Zum Stand der Forschung." *Altorientalische Forschungen* 23 (1996): 171–180.

Gnoli, Gherardo. "Nuove note sullo *hu̯arnah-*." In *Oriente e Occidente. Convegno in memoria di Mario Bussagli,* edited by Chiara Silvi Antonini, Bianca Maria Alfieri and Arcangela Santoro, pp. 104–108. Rome, 2002.

Hertel, Johannes, ed. and trans. *Die awestischen Herrschafts- und Siegesfeuer.* Leipzig, 1931.

Itō, Gikyō. "Gathica." *Orient* 11 (1975): 1–10.

Jacobs, Bruno. "Das Chvarnah—Zum stand der Forschung." *Mitteilungen der Deutschen Orient-Gesellschaft zu Berlin* 119 (1987): 215–248.

Litvinskii, B. A. "Das K'ang-chü-Sarmatische Farnan." *Central Asiatic Journal* 16 (1972): 241–289.

Lubotsky, Alexander. "Avestan *x*ᵛ*arənah-*: The Etymology and Concept." In *Sprache und Kultur der Indogermanen,* pp. 479–488. Innsbruck, 1998.

Shahbazi, A. S. "An Achaemenid Symbol." *Archaeologische Mitteilungen aus Iran,* n.s. 13 (1980): 119–147.

GHERARDO GNOLI (1987)

Translated from Italian by Roger DeGaris

KIERKEGAARD, SØREN

KIERKEGAARD, SØREN (1813–1855), was the most outstanding writer in the history of Danish letters and one of the leading religious philosophers of the nineteenth century. Kierkegaard's novel interpretation of the structure and dynamics of individual selfhood formed the basis of his radical critique of European cultural Protestantism and its philosophical counterpart, Hegelianism. His innovative ideas have remained extremely influential.

LIFE. Søren Aabye Kierkegaard was a person of unusual complexity whose outward life was relatively uneventful. Having received a substantial inheritance, he never needed to secure a regular professional position. He devoted most of his short life to the production of an immense body of philosophical and religious literature. The formative events in Kierkegaard's life centered around two individuals: his father, Michael Pedersen Kierkegaard, and his one-time fiancée, Regine Olsen; and two public conflicts: the *Corsair* affair, and his celebrated attack upon the Danish church.

Michael Pedersen Kierkegaard was a successful Copenhagen businessman who retired at an early age to pursue his theological interests. The elder Kierkegaard was a sober, brooding man who was possessed by a profound sense of personal guilt. In an effort to come to terms with his malaise, he became deeply involved in the Protestant Pietism that was then sweeping Denmark. Michael subjected his favorite son, Søren, to a rigorous and austere religious upbringing. The psychological and intellectual complexity of the father-son relation left a lasting impression on Kierkegaard and indirectly informed much of his theological reflection.

The other personal relationship that was decisive for Kierkegaard was his brief engagement to Regine Olsen. Shortly after proposing marriage to Regine, Kierkegaard precipitated a break with her. The apparent reason for this unexpected reversal was twofold. In the first place, Kierkegaard discovered an unbridgeable gap between his own introspective, tormented personality and the seemingly innocent, inexperienced Regine. Second, Kierkegaard became convinced that his religious vocation precluded marriage and family life. Many of Kierkegaard's most important works focus on issues raised by his perplexing relation to Regine.

The two major public events in Kierkegaard's life involved him in bitter controversy. Late in 1845, Kierkegaard published a criticism of the *Corsair,* a sophisticated Danish scandal sheet, in which he exposed the association of several leading intellectuals with this notorious journal. The embarrassed authors and editors responded by unleashing an abusive personal attack on Kierkegaard in which he was held up to public ridicule. This episode marked a turning point in his life. After 1846, Kierkegaard's writings became more overtly Christian. The full implications of this shift emerged clearly in Kierkegaard's attack on the Danish church. Kierkegaard believed that God had chosen him to expose the scandal of a society that espoused Christian principles but in which citizens lived like "pagans." In a series of articles titled *The Moment,* Kierkegaard argued that the Christianity preached in the established church of Denmark was actually the opposite of the religion practiced by Jesus. His penetrating criticisms of church and society created a public furor. In the midst of this controversy, Kierkegaard died (November 11, 1855).

WORKS. Few authors have written as wide a variety of works as Kierkegaard. Most of his writings can be grouped in four major categories.

(1) Pseudonymous works. Between 1841 and 1850, Kierkegaard wrote a series of works under different pseudonyms. These are his best-known books: *Either-Or* (1843), *Repetition* (1843), *Fear and Trembling* (1843), *Philosophical Fragments* (1844), *The Concept of Anxiety* (1844), *Stages on Life's Way* (1845), *Concluding Unscientific Postscript* (1846), *Crisis in a Life of an Actress and Other Essays on Drama* (1848), *The Sickness unto Death* (1849), and *Training in Christianity* (1850). Not until the last pages of *Concluding Unscientific Postscript* did Kierkegaard publicly claim responsibility for his pseudonymous writings.

(2) Edifying discourses. It was Kierkegaard's custom to accompany each of the pseudonymous texts with one or more religious works published under his own name. He frequently complained that while his pseudonymous writings received considerable attention, his religious works were virtually ignored. Two kinds of works make up the edifying discourses: ethical discourses and Christian discourses. While the ethical discourses consistently exclude Christian categories, the Christian discourses explore religious life from the perspective of Christian faith. The former are more common before 1845 and the latter more numerous after that date. The most important Christian discourses are: *Works of Love* (1847), *Christian Discourses* (1848), *The Lilies of the Field and the Birds of the Air* (1849), *For Self-Examination* (1851), and *Judge for Yourself* (1851–1852).

(3) Polemical tracts. Since he understood himself as a necessary "corrective" to "the present age," Kierkegaard remained an irrepressible polemicist. As was the custom in Denmark at that time, he presented his views on current intellectual and social matters in the public press and in pamphlets that were directed to a general audience. Kierkegaard's most important polemical writings appeared in a newspaper, *The Fatherland,* and his own publication, *The Moment.* These articles provide a glimpse of Kierkegaard's immediate impact on Danish society.

(4) Journals and papers. Throughout his life, Kierkegaard kept a detailed journal, which he knew would be published after his death. The journal, which runs to twenty volumes, contains a wealth of information about Kierkegaard's personality, writings, and his views of other philosophers and theologians.

Two important books do not fall within this general grouping. *The Concept of Irony, with Constant Reference to Socrates* (1841) was Kierkegaard's dissertation for the master of arts degree. This work presents an early version of his critique of Hegel and leading nineteenth-century Romantics. In addition, the analysis of Socrates developed in this book forms the basis of Kierkegaard's understanding of his own role as an author. This becomes obvious in the final text that deserves mention: *The Point of View for My Work as an Author* (written in 1848 and published posthumously in 1859). In this short book, Kierkegaard insists that in spite of appearances to the contrary, his diverse writings form a coherent whole that is constantly guided by a religious purpose.

THOUGHT. Kierkegaard's sense of religious mission informs all of his writings. The overriding goal of his work is nothing less than "the reintroduction of Christianity into Christendom." Since Kierkegaard believes that authentic human existence is decisively revealed in Christianity, he is convinced that the struggle to lead a Christian life involves the attempt to realize true selfhood. Kierkegaard's writings represent a sustained effort to provide the occasion for individuals to make the difficult movement of faith. The most important part of Kierkegaard's carefully conceived strategy is his intricate pseudonymous authorship. The pseudonymous writings can best be understood by considering three interrelated assumptions that they all share: the notion of indirect communication, the understanding of the structure of selfhood, and the theory of the stages of existence.

Kierkegaard's method of communicating indirectly through pseudonyms reflects his effort to address problems peculiar to nineteenth-century Denmark and expresses his general conception of the nature of religious truth. He repeatedly insists that most of his fellow Danes were simply deluding themselves when they claimed to be Christians. The established Lutheran church had so domesticated Christian faith that the spiritual tensions that characterized original Christianity had all but disappeared. In this situation, Kierkegaard views his task as inversely Socratic. Rather than engaging in a rational dialogue that is supposed to uncover the truth implicitly possessed by all human beings, Kierkegaard tries to bring individuals to the brink of decision by offering them the opportunity to discover the errors of their ways. Each pseudonym represents a different point of view that reflects a distinct form of life. Kierkegaard presents these works as mirrors in which people can see themselves reflected. The self-knowledge that results from this encounter with the text creates the possibility of decisions that redefine the self.

Kierkegaard's method of communication is also a function of his conviction that religious truth is subjectivity. In contrast to Hegel's speculative approach to Christianity, Kierkegaard maintains that religious truth cannot be conceptually grasped but must be existentially appropriated through the free activity of the individual agent. In matters of faith, there can be neither knowledge nor certainty. Human existence in general and religious belief in particular always involve absolute risk. Kierkegaard's aim is to serve as a "midwife" who can attend but not effect the birth of the authentic self.

This understanding of indirect communication presupposes a specific interpretation of the structure of human selfhood. In *The Sickness unto Death,* Kierkegaard ironically employs Hegelian language to formulate an account of selfhood that overturns Hegel's understanding of subjectivity. The self, Kierkegaard argues, is a structure of self-relation that is created and sustained by the wholly other God. Each human being is called upon to relate possibilities and actualities through the exercise of his or her free will. This view of the self forms the basis of Kierkegaard's penetrating psychological analyses. In *The Concept of Anxiety,* Kierkegaard defines anxiety in terms of the subject's recognition of the possibilities opened by its own freedom. Despair is the subject's failure or refusal to be itself. Anxiety and despair combine to disclose the self's responsibility for itself.

The analysis of the structure of selfhood forms the foundation of the theory of the stages of existence. Although each person is irreducibly individual, Kierkegaard maintains that it is possible to discern recurrent patterns amid the variety of human lives. He identifies three basic stages of existence: aesthetic, ethical, and religious. Each stage represents a distinct form of life that is governed by different assumptions and expectations. Taken together, the stages provide an outline of the entire pseudonymous authorship. While Kierkegaard examines aesthetic existence in the first part of both *Either-Or* and *Stages on Life's Way,* the second section of each of these works is devoted to a consideration of ethical experience. The analysis of the religious stage is more complex. In *Fear and Trembling, Philosophical Fragments,* and *Concluding Unscientific Postscript,* Kierkegaard approaches questions and dilemmas posed by religion from the perspective of nonbelief. *The Sickness unto Death* and *Training in Christianity,* by contrast, are written from an avowedly Christian point of view. Finally, the third part of *Stages on Life's Way* is a tortuous account of the inner struggle of an individual who is caught between belief and unbelief.

These three stages of existence are not randomly selected and arbitrarily presented. Rather, the stages are carefully ordered in such a way that as one advances from the aesthetic through the ethical to the religious, there is a movement toward authentic selfhood. Generally conceived, this progression charts the subject's advance from undifferentiated identification with its environment, through increasing differentiation from otherness, to complete individuation, in which the self becomes a concrete individual, eternally responsible for itself. The aesthetic stage of existence is characterized by the absence of genuine decision. The lack of free resolution results from either unreflective immersion in sensuous inclination and social life or the dispassionate absorption in abstract reflection. From the ethical point of view, the self has an obligation to become itself through free activity. Deliberate decision marks an essential moment in the process of individuation and forms a crucial stage in the journey to selfhood. The ethicist, however, is insufficiently sensitive to the self's radical dependence on God. The ethical actor eventually realizes that he actually divinizes the social order by regarding moral obligation as divine commandment. The "infinite qualitative difference" between the divine and the human creates the possibility of a conflict between obligation to other people and obedience to God. Kierkegaard labels this collision a "teleological suspension of the ethical." This clash between religious and moral responsibility effectively overturns ethical life.

The religious stage of existence represents the full realization of authentic selfhood. Kierkegaard's analysis of the self culminates in the paradoxical coincidence of opposites created and sustained by the faithful individual's absolute decision. Faith is the free activity of self-relation in which the self becomes itself by simultaneously differentiating and synthesizing the opposites that make up its being. In this critical moment of decision, a person who is fully conscious of his responsibility for his life constitutes his unique individuality by decisively distinguishing himself from other selves and defining his eternal identity in the face of the wholly other God. The qualitative difference between God and self renders impossible any immanent relation between the divine and the human. Left to himself, the sinful individual cannot establish the absolute relation to the absolute upon which genuine selfhood depends. The possibility of the proper relation between God and self is opened by the incarnate Christ. The God-man is an absolute paradox that can never be rationally comprehended. This absolute paradox poses an irreconcilable either-or: *either* believe, *or* be offended. Faith is a radical venture, an unmediated leap in which the self transforms itself. By faithfully responding to the absolutely paradoxical divine presence, the self internalizes the truth of the God-man. In this moment of decision, truth becomes subjective and the subject becomes truthful. Such truthful subjectivity is the goal toward which Kierkegaard's complex authorship relentlessly leads the reader.

INFLUENCE. Largely ignored in his own day, Kierkegaard's writings emerged during the early decades of the twentieth century to become a dominant force in theology, philosophy, psychology, and literature. Kierkegaard's theological impact is evident in Protestant neo-orthodoxy. Karl Barth and Rudolf Bultmann developed many of the themes that Kierkegaard had identified. In the thought of Martin Buber, Kierkegaard's influence extends into the domain of Jewish theology.

Kierkegaard's work also forms the foundation of one of the most important twentieth-century schools of philosophy: existentialism. Kierkegaard set the terms of debate for major Continental philosophers such as Martin Heidegger, Karl Jaspers, and Jean-Paul Sartre. By underscoring the importance of the problems of individual selfhood, authenticity, transcendence, absurdity, temporality, death, desire, guilt, despair, anxiety, and hope, Kierkegaard's texts provided rich resources for an entire generation of philosophers.

Less often recognized is Kierkegaard's role in modern psychology. His groundbreaking analyses of the psychic states of the individual self have been expanded and extended by psychologists such as Ludwig Binswanger and R. D. Laing. The psychological theories that have arisen from the work of Kierkegaard tend to complement and correct currents in traditional Freudian analysis.

Finally, it is important to stress Kierkegaard's influence on twentieth-century literature. The hand of Kierkegaard can be seen in the works of creative authors as different as Albert Camus, Franz Kafka, John Updike, and Walker Percy.

This summary can only suggest the extraordinary importance of Kierkegaard's work. The insights of this lonely Dane pervade contemporary thought and shape the way many people now understand their lives.

See Also Existentialism.

Bibliography

Primary Sources

The standard Danish editions of Kierkegaard's writings are *Søren Kierkegaards Papirer,* 11 vols., edited by P. A. Heiberg et al. (Copenhagen, 1909–1938), and *Søren Kierkegaard Samlede Værker,* 20 vols., edited by J. L. Heiberg et al. (Copenhagen, 1962–1964). The best English translations of these works are *Søren Kierkegaard's Journals and Papers,* 7 vols., edited and translated by Howard V. Hong and Edna H. Hong with Gregory Malantschuk (Bloomington, Ind., 1967–1978), and *Kierkegaard's Writings,* edited by Howard V. Hong (Princeton, 1977–).

Secondary Sources

There is an enormous body of secondary literature on Kierkegaard. Emanuel Hirsch's *Kierkegaard-Studien,* 2 vols. (Gütersloh, 1933), remains the most comprehensive intellectual biography of Kierkegaard. Gregor Malantschuk's *Kierkegaard's Thought* (Princeton, N.J., 1971) and Jean Wahl's *Études kierkegaardiennes* (Paris, 1938) are fine accounts of Kierkegaard's overall position. James D. Collins's *The Mind of Kierkegaard* (Chicago, 1953) provides a good introduction to Kierkegaard's thought. For a helpful examination of the importance of Kierkegaard's pseudonymous method, see Louis Mackey's *Kierkegaard: A Kind of Poet* (Philadelphia, 1971). Stephen Crites's *In the Twilight of Christendom: Hegel vs. Kierkegaard on Faith and History* (Chambersburg, Pa., 1972) and my own *Journeys to Selfhood: Hegel and Kierkegaard* (Berkeley, Calif., 1980) analyze the complex relationship between Kierkegaard and Hegel.

Mark C. Taylor (1987)

KIMBANGU, SIMON (1889–1951), African religious prophet and founder of the Church of Jesus Christ on Earth through the Prophet Simon Kimbangu. Kimbangu was born on September 24, 1889, in the village of N'Kamba, located in the Ngombe district of what is now the Democratic Republic of the Congo. In Kikongo, the word *kimbangu* means "one who reveals the hidden truth." Many legends surround Kimbangu's youth and early religious activities. Some accounts claim that both his mother and father were traditional Kongo healers and that his visionary activities were related to theirs. Only since the mid-1970s has much of the original missionary and government documentation on Kimbangu's early activities become available to scholars.

Kimbangu attended a Baptist Missionary Society school at Wathen, near his home village. He became a Christian as a young man and was baptized on July 4, 1915, along with his wife, Marie-Mwilu, in the Baptist mission at Ngombe-Luete. He was trained as a catechist and religious instructor by the Baptist Missionary Society but failed his examination to become a pastor. During the typhoid epidemic of 1918 and 1919, in which many residents of his area died, Kimbangu is reputed to have received a calling to heal the sick. He is alleged to have heard a voice that said, "I am Christ. My servants are unfaithful. I have chosen you to bear witness before your brethren and convert them. Tend my flock" (Martin, 1975, p. 44). Frightened, Kimbangu was unable to respond and fled to the capital city of Kinshasa (then Léopoldville), where he worked briefly as a migrant laborer at an oil refinery.

Upon returning to his village, Kimbangu again received the calling to heal. On April 6, 1921, he performed his first public act of faith healing. He is reported to have laid hands on a critically ill woman and healed her. This act marked the beginning of Kimbangu's healing revival and six months of intensive religious activity. N'Kamba, the seat of Kimbangu's healing ministry, became known as the "New Jerusalem," and over five thousand local converts are reported to have flocked to him.

As the healing movement spread in popularity, colonial officials and merchants began to perceive it as a revolutionary threat. Missionaries were skeptical of Kimbangu's new teachings, and merchants complained that he incited followers to abandon their work and neglect the payment of taxes. With a small cadre of leaders to assist him, Kimbangu continued to preach and perform inspired acts of healing. On June 6, 1921, Léon Morel, a Belgian official, attempted to arrest Kimbangu and four of his most loyal assistants. Kimbangu eluded colonial officials until, prompted by a divine vision, he voluntarily surrendered on September 12.

On October 3, 1921, Kimbangu was sentenced to death by 120 strokes of the lash for sedition and hostility toward the colonial authorities. His court-martial was characterized by arbitrary proceedings and legal irregularities. In November, the death sentence was commuted to life imprisonment by King Albert, who was reportedly influenced by the pleas of Belgian missionaries to exercise some leniency. Kimbangu was transported to Lubumbashi (then Elisabethville) in Shaba province, where he was imprisoned until his death on October 12, 1951, in the "hospital for Congolese." There is some debate concerning whether Kimbangu, whose teachings resembled those of fundamentalist Protestantism, converted to Catholicism on his deathbed. This possibility has been vehemently denied by his family and followers.

Kimbangu's arrest augmented the aura of mystery surrounding him as a prophetic figure and increased the popular appeal of his charismatic movement. Between 1924 and 1930, Belgian colonial authorities continued overt attempts to suppress the movement. Kimbangu's principal followers were imprisoned at Lowa, and others were confined over the years in thirty detention centers spread throughout the country. The Kimbanguist church estimates that there were 37,000 exiles, of whom 34,000 died in prison between 1921 and 1956. Recent scholarship, however, has established that this figure resulted from a typographical error in a newspaper article; the official exile and imprisonment figure was closer to 2,148. Although Kimbanguist detainees were isolated and kept under martial surveillance, the policy of detention eventually led to the spread of the Kimbanguist movement in various regions of the Belgian Congo.

The movement gained strength, forming itself into a group that became known as the Church of Jesus Christ on Earth through the Prophet Simon Kimbangu. Followers were called *ngunza* ("prophets" or "preachers"). Kimbanguist offshoots, such as Salutism and Mpadism, and other manifestations of Kimbangu's influence appeared throughout the region among populations with whom Kimbangu never had direct contact.

Between 1955 and 1957, Kimbangu's movement experienced a renewal and continued to spread throughout the Belgian Congo. After the prophet's death, his youngest son, Kuntima (Joseph) Diangienda, assumed leadership of the church in accordance with Kimbangu's wishes. He formalized its doctrine, sacraments, and egalitarian organizational structure. In 1969, the Kimbanguist church was admitted to the World Council of Churches, and in 1971, it was proclaimed as one of the four officially recognized ecclesiastical bodies in the newly formed nation of Zaire. By the end of the 1980s there were nearly four million Kimbanguists in Zaire.

Simon Kimbangu's direct and indirect influence on African prophetic movements has been far-reaching. The Kimbanguist church is one of the most extensively documented African religious groups. It is possible to view the history and transformation of the Kimbanguist church as a prototype for many contemporary African religious groups that have made the transition from grass-roots movements to established churches.

BIBLIOGRAPHY

Andersson, Effraim. *Messianic Popular Movements in the Lower Congo.* Uppsala, 1958. A historical account of Kimbanguism and other prophetic movements in the Lower Kongo; analyzes the history of religious protest in the area and describes Kimbanguism as a messianic movement in the context of offshoot and related groups arising between the 1930s and the 1950s.

Asch, Susan. *L'église du prophète Kimbangu: De ses origines à son rôle actual au Zaïre.* Paris, 1983. A comprehensive study of the growth and development of the Kimbanguist church. Contains a historical and sociological analysis of the transition of the group from a popular movement to a church, spanning the years 1921-1981. Includes discussions of the group's origin, changing organizational structure, distribution throughout the region, and relations with the colonial and postindependence governments.

Chomé, Jules. *La passion de Simon Kimbangu.* Brussels, 1959. An account of the life and trial of Kimbangu by a Belgian lawyer who studied the legal documents in detail. Parallels Kimbangu's arrest and sentencing to the Passion of Jesus and outlines the legal irregularities of Kimbangu's trial.

MacGaffey, Wyatt. *Modern Kongo Prophets: Religion in a Plural Society.* Bloomington, Ind., 1983. An analysis of prophetism among the Kongo, including a detailed discussion of Kimbanguism and related offshoot movements in the context of local cultural history and traditions.

Martin, Marie-Louise. *Kirche ohne Weisse.* Basel, 1971. Translated by D. M. Moore as *Kimbangu: An African Prophet and His Church* (Oxford, 1975). A history of the Kimbanguist movement in central Africa from 1918 to 1960, with discussions of responses to colonial authority, doctrine and ritual of the movement, and political attitudes of the followers. Contains a comprehensive bibliography on the Kimbanguist movement up to 1970.

Sinda, Martial. *Le messianisme congolais et ses incidences politiques: Kimbanguisme, matsouaisme, autres mouvements.* Paris, 1972. This book presents a comparative analysis of Kongo messianic movements as forms of religious protest. The author raises many interesting questions concerning leadership in prophetic groups and the history and motivations of African prophets and religious leaders in the context of the colonial government.

BENNETTA JULES-ROSETTE (1987)

KIMḤI, DAVID (c. 1160–c. 1235), known by the acronym RaDaK (Rabbi David Kimḥi), was a biblical exegete. David was the son of Yosef Kimḥi and the brother of Mosheh Kimḥi, exiles from Almohad Spain to Narbonne, where David was born. Both Yosef and Mosheh, David's principal teacher, were grammarians and exegetes of note, heavily influenced by contemporary Hispano-Jewish rationalism. David was the best-known graduate of the school of exegetes that the elder Kimḥis founded in Narbonne, a city whose tradition of biblical studies had been established by the eleventh-century Mosheh the Preacher.

Kimḥi was the author of a masoretic guide, the *'Et sofer* (Scribe's pen); the *Sefer ha-shorashim* (Book of roots), a dictionary of biblical Hebrew; and the *Mikhol* (Compendium), the most authoritative Hebrew grammar of the Middle Ages. However, he is chiefly known for his biblical commentaries, which include expositions on *Genesis,* the Former and Latter Prophets, *Psalms, Proverbs,* and *Chronicles.* He also wrote two allegorical commentaries, employing Maimonidean philosophical concepts, on the Hexaemeron (chapters 1 and 2 of *Genesis*) and the chariot vision of Ezekiel.

Kimḥi's commentaries evince great interest in masoretic questions, and he traveled considerable distances to consult reliable manuscripts such as the *Sefer Yerushalmi* in Saragossa and the *Sefer Hilleli* in Toledo. His avowed aim was to follow the twelfth-century Andalusian grammarian Avraham ibn ʿEzraʾ and his own father and brother in establishing a *peshaṭ* ("plain sense") based on philological and contextual analysis. His extensive knowledge of rabbinic Hebrew, Aramaic, and Provençal, as well as his acquaintance with Arabic, contributed to his explication of the text. Concern for internal syntax within verses and for the general sequence of the biblical narrative became the hallmark of his commentaries. Yet despite Kimḥi's emphasis on *peshaṭ,* he cited abundant *midrashim,* or rabbinic interpretations—some because he felt them useful in explicating the plain sense, some as a foil against which he could highlight the *peshaṭ,* and some to add interest and liveliness to his text. His rationalism frequently comes to the fore in brief digressions on the nature of providence, prophecy, epistemology, and the rationales for observance of the commandments. He generally explained miracles naturalistically. Although the influence of Saʿadyah Gaon, Avraham ibn ʿEzraʾ, and Yehudah ha-Levi can clearly be felt, the dominant tone of his work was set by Maimonides.

Kimḥi demonstrated his loyalty to Maimonides when, in his seventies, he journeyed across Languedoc and Spain to defend Maimonides' *Guide of the Perplexed* when that work came under attack by traditionalist Jews during the so-called Maimonidean controversy. He engaged in external polemics as well, and a number of anti-Christological and anti-Christian remarks can be found in his writings. Many of these were censored and survive only in manuscript. Kimḥi's depiction of exile and redemption in terms of darkness and light—a theme he developed at length—was prompted by his sensitivity to the tribulations of Israel brought about by internal division and external oppression.

Because of its accessibility, Kimḥi's work left an indelible mark on that of the Hebraists and humanists of the Renaissance and Reformation, and its influence on the King James Version of the Bible is unmistakable.

Bibliography

An intellectual biography and analysis of Kimḥi's exegesis is my *David Kimhi: The Man and the Commentaries* (Cambridge, Mass., 1975), which contains a complete bibliography up to the date of publication. His philological work is analyzed in *David Kimchi's Hebrew Grammar (Mikhlol)*, translated and edited by William Chomsky (Philadelphia, 1952). Specific themes are treated in the following articles by me: "R. David Kimhi as Polemicist," *Hebrew Union College Annual* 38 (1967): 213–235; "David Kimhi and the Rationalist Tradition," *Hebrew Union College Annual* 39 (1968): 177–218; and "David Kimhi and the Rationalist Tradition: 2, Literary Sources," in *Studies in Jewish Bibliography, History, and Literature in Honor of I. Edward Kiev,* edited by Charles Berlin (New York, 1971), pp. 453–478. Much detailed data in tabular form can be found in Ezra Zion Melamed's *Mefarshei ha-miqraʾ: Darkheihem ve-shitoṭeihem,* vol. 2 (Jerusalem, 1975), pp. 716–932.

New Sources

Bartelmus, Rüdiger. "'Prima la Lingua, Poi le Parole': David Kimchi und die Frage der hebräischen Tempora: sprachwissenschaftliche und exegetische Überlegungen zu IISam 14,5b und 15,34a." *Theologische Zeitschrift* 53 (1997): 7–16.

Grunhaus, Naomi. "The Dependence of Rabbi David Kimhi (Radak) on Rashi in His Quotation of Midrashic Traditions." *Jewish Quarterly Review* 93 (2003): 415–430.

Katz, Ben Zion. "Kimchi and Tanhum ben Joseph Hayerushalmi on Chronicles." *Jewish Bible Quarterly* 26 (1998): 45–51.

Frank Talmage (1987)
Revised Bibliography

KING, MARTIN LUTHER, JR. (1929–1968), was a Baptist minister and civil rights leader. The son and grandson of Baptist preachers, Martin Luther King, Jr., was born into a middle-class black family in Atlanta, Georgia. As an adolescent, King grew concerned about racial and economic inequality in American society. Sociology classes at Morehouse College taught him to view racism and poverty as related aspects of social evil, and reading Henry David Thoreau's essay "Civil Disobedience" (1849) convinced him that resistance to an unjust system was a moral duty. At Morehouse, King decided to become a minister, and after graduation he enrolled at Crozier Theological Seminary to study divinity. There he acquired from Walter Rauschenbusch's *Christianity and the Social Crisis* (1907) the conviction that the Christian churches have an obligation to work for social justice. In Mohandas Gandhi's practice of nonviolent resistance he discovered a tactic for transforming Christian love from a merely personal to a social ethic.

King's interest in theology, philosophy, and social ethics led him to enter the graduate program at Boston University School of Theology, where he earned a Ph.D. degree and developed his own philosophical position based upon the tenet that "only personality—finite and infinite—is ultimately real." In Boston, he met and courted Coretta Scott, and in 1953 they were wed. A year later, King accepted a call to be pastor of Dexter Avenue Baptist Church in Montgomery, Alabama. Chosen by E. D. Nixon, president of the Montgomery National Association for the Advancement of Colored People, to lead a boycott of the city's segregated buses, he gained national recognition when the boycott resulted in a Supreme Court decision that declared laws requiring segregated seating on buses unconstitutional.

Following the Montgomery bus boycott, King founded the Southern Christian Leadership Conference (SCLC) to coordinate scattered civil rights activities and local organizations. Operating primarily through the black churches, the SCLC mounted successive attacks against segregation in the early 1960s. Public demonstrations, especially in the South, dramatized for the nation the violence of white segregationists in contrast to the nonviolence of black demonstrators. Although immediate gains at the local level were often minimal, King's strategy drew national attention to the racial problem, awakened moral concern in many, pressured the federal government to act, and helped gain passage of legislation protecting the rights of blacks to vote and desegregating public accommodations. As the most eloquent speaker of the movement, King moved thousands to commit themselves to civil rights as both a moral and a political issue. For his nonviolent activism, he received the Nobel Peace Prize in 1964.

Against the arguments of militants, King maintained that nonviolence was the only practical and moral means for African Americans to achieve equality. Violence would bring only more violence; nonviolence might convert the racist's conscience. Linking the cause of African Americans to the struggle for independence of colonized peoples worldwide, King opposed the Vietnam War and condemned international violence.

While organizing a "poor people's campaign" to persuade Congress to take action on poverty, King accepted an invitation to participate in marches for striking sanitation workers in Memphis, Tennessee. There, on April 4, 1968, he was assassinated. Considered a modern prophet by many, King ranks with Gandhi as a major ethical leader of the twentieth century.

BIBLIOGRAPHY

Works by King

The best introduction to King's own version of his goals and values is *Stride toward Freedom: The Montgomery Story* (New York, 1958), which contains a chapter explaining his intellectual development in the midst of an eyewitness description of the bus boycott. *Strength to Love* (New York, 1963) is a collection of sermons. *Why We Can't Wait* (New York, 1964) includes "Letter from Birmingham Jail," one of King's most cogent justifications of his philosophy of nonviolent direct action. *Where Do We Go from Here: Chaos or Community?* (New York, 1967) outlines his detailed program for social justice in the United States.

Works about King

Of the many biographical sketches, the best critical treatment is David L. Lewis's *King: A Biography,* 2d ed. (Urbana, Ill., 1978). Stephen B. Oates's biography, *Let the Trumpet Sound: The Life of Martin Luther King, Jr.* (New York, 1982), is factually more complete but lacks interpretive analysis. *Martin Luther King, Jr.: A Profile,* edited by C. Eric Lincoln (New York, 1970), is a collection of insightful evaluations of King and his role in the civil rights movement. John Ansbro's *Martin Luther King, Jr.: The Making of a Mind* (Maryknoll, N.Y., 1982) is a valuable explication of King's thought.

ALBERT J. RABOTEAU (1987)

KINGDOM OF GOD.

Among the central concepts of the great religions, that of the kingdom of God may be the most hopeful, for while it recognizes the reality of death and injustice, it affirms that a just and living transcendent reality is entering history and transforming it. This article discusses the concept of the kingdom of God in postbiblical Judaism, the New Testament, and the history of the Christian church, together with its antecedents in the ancient Near East, Israel, and Greece.

DIVINE KINGSHIP IN THE ANCIENT NEAR EAST, ISRAEL, AND GREECE. Although the notion of divine kingship is defined in human political terms, it is not a mere projection of human kingship onto a divine realm. Rather, the successive phrases in which this notion occurs show that divine kingship was understood as transcending and rejecting human kingship.

"King of the gods." This phrase implies sovereignty over the created order. In a pantheon, one god can emerge as supreme (1) through political shifts, as does, for example, Enlil, the tutelary god of Sumerian Nippur, who becomes "lord, god, king . . . the judge . . . of the universe" (J. B. Pritchard, ed., *Ancient Near Eastern Texts relating to the Old Testament,* 3d ed. with supp., Princeton, 1969, p. 575); (2) through syncretism in favor of a solar deity such as Shamash (Pritchard, p. 387) or the Egyptian deity Amun-Re, who is the chief, lord, and father of the gods as well as creator of life (Pritchard, pp. 365–366); or (3) through the acclamation of one god as king by the others for his victory over the powers of chaos. This final form of acquiring sovereignty springs from a widespread mythical pattern illustrated in the texts of four ancient societies.

Babylon. The creation epic *Enuma elish,* recited at the spring New Year festival, describes the victory of Marduk over the sea monster Tiamat, from whose body Marduk creates heaven and earth. Even before the contest the other gods proclaim, "We have granted you kingship [*sharruta*] over the universe entire" (4.14), and "Marduk is king!" (4.28). After the battle, the gods ratify these proclamations and give Marduk the chief of his fifty Sumerian titles, "king of the gods of heaven and the underworld" (5.112).

Ugarit (modern Ras Shamra, Syria). Although the god El is routinely addressed as king in this literature (Pritchard, pp. 133 and 140), Baal is elevated to kingship after his victory over Yam, "Prince Sea." The craftsman-god tells Baal, "Now you will cut off your adversary, you will take your eternal kingship [*mlk 'lmk*], your everlasting dominion" (Pritchard, p. 131); and goddesses tell El, "Baal is our king [*mlkn*], our judge, and there is none above him" (Pritchard, pp. 133 and 138).

Greece. In the Homeric poems, Zeus is called the "father of gods and men" and is once called the "highest and best of the gods" (*Odyssey* 19.303). In Hesiod's *Theogony* (700 BCE?), Zeus leads the Olympian gods in battle against the Titans, who include Chaos (v. 700) and the dragon Typhoeus. Hesiod recounts that after the battle, "the blessed gods, at the urging of Earth [Gaia], requested far-seeing Zeus to reign and rule over them" (i. e., as *basileus* and *anax,* vv. 881–885). It is from this victory over the Titans that Zeus acquires the title "king of the gods" (v. 886). Similarly, in Pindar's *Sev-*

enth Olympian Ode (464 BCE), Zeus is called "great king of the gods" (v. 34).

Israel. In the face of Israel's ostensible monotheism, a group of other gods, called *benei Elim* (lit., "sons of gods"), is also acknowledged. These gods, however, are not like the one God (who in this context always has the name whose consonants are YHVH, conventionally transcribed "Yahveh," *Ps.* 89:5–8); they must ascribe glory to him (*Ps.* 29:1), for it was Yahveh who crushed the sea-monster of chaos, Rahab (*Ps.* 89:10), or Leviathan (*Ps.* 74:13–14). And in *Psalms* 95:3, Yahveh is given the same title that Pindar gives Zeus, "a great king above all gods."

"Yahveh is king." This phrase implies sovereignty over the people of Israel. In the historical books of Israel, the kingship of Yahveh is cited solely to refute the claims of human kings (*1 Sm.* 8:7, 12:2; cf. *Jgs.* 8:23). The concept is most fully developed in the *Book of Psalms,* the dating of which is problematic; however, Isaiah's vision of Yahveh as king (*Is.* 6:5) shows that this was a living belief in 742 BCE. In a compact group of Psalms, Yahveh is called "king" (*melekh*) or is made the subject of the corresponding verb *malakh* (*Ps.* 93:1, 96:10, 97:1, 99:1). These Psalms display a unique cluster of motifs associated with Yahveh's kingship: (1) his theophany in lightning or earthquake over Lebanon (*Ps.* 29) and elsewhere (*Ps.* 97, 99); (2) his supremacy over other gods who bow down to him or are reduced to "idols" (*Ps.* 29, 95–97, 47:2 in some texts); (3) his entrance into his holy place (*Ps.* 24) or ascent to his throne (*Ps.* 47; cf. *Ps.* 93, 97); (4) his act of creation (*Ps.* 24, 95, 96), portrayed as a conquest of great waters (*Ps.* 29, 33), where the personified elements sing a new song (*Ps.* 96, 98) and the floods, now beneficent, "clap their hands" (*Ps.* 98:8); (5) his sovereignty over other nations or over all the earth (*Ps.* 47, 96, 98); and (6) his future coming to judge the earth (*Ps.* 96, 98) as he has previously come to Israel (*Ps.* 99:4).

Sigmund Mowinckel, in his *Psalmenstudien* (2 vols., Oslo, 1921–1924), searching for a liturgical occasion for these psalms in the Temple, boldly hypothesized a festival of Yahveh's enthronement, a *Thronbesteigungsfest,* which he assigned to the autumn feast of Tabernacles (Sukkot) on the basis of *1 Kings* 8:2 (cf. *Zec.* 14:16). This theory, much developed by Scandinavian and British scholars, assumed that the king dramatically enacted the role of Yahveh in conquering chaos and the nations, in the god's enthronement, and, perhaps, even in a mock death, resurrection, and sacred marriage. But Roland de Vaux, in his *Ancient Israel* (vol. 2, New York, 1965, pp. 502–506), finds no evidence for such a festival. And while the theme of Yahveh's entrance to the holy place or ascent to his throne suggests a Temple liturgy, *Psalms* 132:8 suggests that the god was represented in this liturgy by the ark rather than by the king.

As the contrast between these affirmations of divine kingship and Israel's state of exile (587/6–538 BCE) became too great, the concept is split up between present and future. In the present, God's kingship is individualized and he becomes "my king" (*Ps.* 5:3ff.); in an indefinite future, Yahveh as king will regather dispersed Israel (*Ez.* 20:33) and reign in Jerusalem (*Is.* 24:23, *Mi.* 4:7; cf. *Is.* 52:7–10).

"Kingship from heaven." This Babylonian phrase introduces various concepts of the divine sovereignty in the state. Hammurabi in the prologue to his laws (c. 1700 BCE) tells how Anu established for Marduk an "enduring sovereignty" over the world. At first, the Babylonian myth *Etana* states, "the people had not set up a king"; but later "kingship descended from heaven" (Pritchard, p. 114). Although the concept of kingship as bestowed from the divine realm served to legitimate the state in Mesopotamia, in Zoroastrianism it provided an alternative to the state. One of the aspects of Ahura Mazdā is Khshathra, who combines the ideas of divine and human "kingship." In *Yasna* 44.7, kingship is presented as his creation along with Ārmaiti ("piety"); *Yasna* 33.10 speaks of "kingship and justice [*asha*]" in parallel just as *Matthew* 6:33 does in the New Testament. But the prophetic Zoroastrian sense of kingship is co-opted for political ends by Darius, who begins his Behistun inscription (520 BCE), "I am Darius, the Great King, King of Kings . . . Ahura Mazdā bestowed the kingship upon me" (cited in Roland G. Kent's *Old Persian: Grammar, Texts, Lexicon,* 2d ed., New Haven, 1953, p. 119).

There are hints of such a semi-autonomous kingship in Stoicism, as in Epictetus's notion of the "kingship" (*basileia*) of the philosopher (Arrian, *Epictetus* 3.22.76). But the principal inheritor in the West of the concept of a quasi-independent divine kingship was later biblical Judaism. *Psalms* 22.28 affirms that "kingship *[melukhah]* belongs to Yahveh." The editor who wrote *1 Chronicles* 28:5 replaced the kingship (*mamlekhet*) of David and Solomon, which he found in his source, *1 Kings* 9:5, by substituting the divine *malkhut.* Echoing an Ugaritic theme, *Psalms* 145:11–13 proclaims, "thy kingship is a kingship of all the ages." This theme is developed in *Daniel:* "The God of heaven will set up an everlasting kingdom" (*Dn.* 2:44; cf. *Dn.* 4:3), which is to be handed over to one who is "like a son of man" (*Dn.* 7:14ff.) or to "the people of the saints of the Most High" (*Dn.* 7:27).

Among the Covenanters of Qumran it was believed that the "covenant of the kingship" (*berit malkhut*) over God's people was given to David and his descendants for ever (Edmund Lohse, *Die Texte aus Qumran,* Munich, 1964, p. 247). The Old Testament Pseudepigrapha sometimes ascribe the kingship to a Messiah (which may, however, be a Christian interpolation); for example, the Syriac *Apocalypse of Baruch* affirms that the "anointed one" will sit "in eternal peace on the throne of his kingship" (73:1).

"King of kings." This phrase indicates first human, then divine, sovereignty over earthly kingships. It was first applied to human rulers annexing vassal kingships. It was standard among Old Persian royal inscriptions (cf. *Ezra* 7:12), and it is ascribed to the Babylonian king Nebuchadrezzar by *Ezekiel* 26:7 and *Daniel* 2:37 (but not by cuneiform sources). The Romans knew it as a Parthian title. Plutarch writes that Pompey refused the title to the Parthian king (*Pompey* 38.2) and that Antony called his sons by Cleopatra "kings of kings" (*Antony* 54.4).

In Stoicism and the Judeo-Christian tradition, this title is transferred to the God who rules over all human kingship. Cleanthes, in his *Hymn to Zeus* (270 BCE), names the abstract god of Stoicism "Zeus" and calls him "highest king"; a later Stoic gave him the Persian title "great king of kings" (Dio Chrysostom 2.75). Yahveh is called "God of gods and Lord of lords" in *Deuteronomy* 10:17—conceivably a late enough text to be under Babylonian-Persian influence. Once in Greek Judaism God appears as "king of kings" (*2 Maccabees* 13:4). Rabbi ʿAqavyaʾ (c. 60 CE) expanded the title to underline God's claim over the highest of earthly monarchies, teaching that humans are to give account "before the King of the kings of kings" (Mishna *Avot* 3.1). These usages are combined in *Revelation* 19:16 and 17:14 where the victorious Christ is proclaimed "King of kings and Lord of lords." The title became the rallying point for simple Christians to reject the divine status of the Roman emperor; thus the African martyr Speratus (180 CE) before a Roman proconsul confessed "my Lord, the Emperor of kings and of all peoples" (*dominum meum, imperatorem regum et omnium gentium;* text in Herbert Musurillo, *The Acts of the Christian Martyrs,* Oxford, 1972, no. 6).

"Kingship of heaven." In the rabbinic tradition this phrase expresses an understanding of the universal sovereignty of God, future and/or eternal. The rabbis saw *Exodus* 15:18 ("Yahveh will reign for ever and ever") as the recognition that established God's kingship on earth (*Exodus Rabbah* 23.1). As the sovereignty assigned to the God of Israel grew, his name was replaced by the term *heaven.* The obligation to recite the Shemaʿ twice daily is called "taking on the yoke of the kingship of heaven [*ʿol malkhut shamayim*]" (Mishna *Berakhoth* 2.2); Rabbi ʿAqivaʾ ben Yosef did so during his execution under Hadrian (135 CE, Babylonian Talmud *Bera-khot* 61b). Eventually the recognition of the divine sovereignty by Jews alone seemed to the rabbis insufficient: Thus the great universalistic prayer *ʿAlenu* of Roʾsh ha-Shanah has the petition that all the inhabitants of the world "should accept the yoke of thy kingdom; and do thou reign over them speedily and forever; for the kingship is thine, and forever wilt thou reign in glory."

One set of rabbinic texts partially identifies the divine kingship with Israel's political autonomy. Rabbi Ayyvu (c. 320 CE) said: "Formerly the kingship was vested in Israel, but when they sinned it was taken from them and given to the other nations. . . . But tomorrow when Israel repents, God will take it from the idolaters, and the kingship shall be to the Lord" (*Esther Rabbah*). The fortunes of Israel are seen by the rabbis as coloring universal history: Thus the Midrash on Psalm 99 states, "As long as the children of Israel are in exile, the kingship of heaven is not at peace and the nations of the earth dwell unperturbed."

Another set of texts portrays the coming sovereignty of God as wholly universal. In the *Mekhiltaʾ de-Rabbi Yishmaʿeʾl* (Jacob Z. Lauterbach, trans., 3 vols., Philadelphia, 1933, vol. 2, p. 159) one reads: "At the time when idolatry shall be uprooted . . . and the Place [*Maqom,* 'God'] shall be recognized throughout the world as the One, then will his kingship be established for the age of the ages of ages." The Aramaic Targums, which regularly translate "The Lord will reign" as "The kingship [*malkhut*] will be revealed" (e.g., *Is.* 24:23; *Ex.* 15:18), twice attribute the kingship to the Messiah: The Targum on *Micah* 4:7–8 states that "to you, O Messiah of Israel, hidden because of the sins of the congregation of Zion, the kingship is to come," and the Targum on *Isaiah* 53:10 affirms that God's people, after being purified from sin, "shall look upon the kingship of their Messiah."

THE KINGDOM OF GOD IN THE WORDS OF JESUS. "The kingdom [*basileia*] of God" is the sole general phrase expressing the object of Jesus' proclamation. (In *Matthew* it mostly appears as "kingdom of heaven," probably as an artificial restoration of the rabbinic usage.) His affirmations about this kingdom are the unifying thread on which all his other sayings are strung.

Jesus' contemporaries shared with the rabbinic tradition at least a political coloration of the concept: Thus *Acts* 1:6 represents disciples asking the risen Jesus, "Will you at this time restore the kingdom to Israel?" But the gospel narratives that presuppose Jesus' most characteristic ideas already in the minds of others, such as John the Baptist (*Mt.* 3:2), Joseph of Arimathea (*Mk.* 15:43), the Pharisees (*Lk.* 17:20), or the disciples (*Mt.* 18:1, *Lk.* 14:15), are unsupported by the rabbinic texts and are probably the work of the evangelists.

In the sayings of Jesus, the "kingdom of God" replaces the state of affairs that he calls "this generation"; for they are given exactly parallel introductions. Over against the obdurate "men of this generation" (*Lk.* 7:31–34), the kingdom of God grows from its tiny hidden beginnings like a man's mustard seed or a woman's leaven (*Lk.* 13:18–21). Into the present "faithless" and "adulterous" generation (*Mk.* 9:19, *Mt.* 12:29) there has broken a new historical reality. Four types of sayings each illustrate one dimension of Jesus' vision: (1) the kingdom as subject of verbs of coming; (2) the kingdom as object of verbs of entering; (3) the kingdom as object of search or struggle; (4) "in the kingdom of God" in the context of a banquet. (But the extended parables of *Matthew* are mostly omitted here, because their introduction "The kingdom of heaven is like . . ." seems editorial rather than organic.)

"The Kingdom of God is at hand." Here is implied a preliminary but decisive victory over injustice and death. In the first group of sayings, the kingdom of God is presented as a quasi-autonomous reality whose arrival is being announced. In *Mark* 1:15 the expression "The kingdom of God is at hand" is placed, perhaps editorially, as a motto or summary over Jesus' entire work.

The Lord's Prayer. This prayer contains the petitions "Hallowed be thy name, thy kingdom come" (*Lk.* 11:2, *Mt.* 6:9). They echo the Qaddish, the oldest Aramaic part of the synagogue liturgy: "Magnified and sanctified be his great name in the world which he created according to his will. And may he establish his kingdom [*yamlikh malkhuteh*] during your life and during your days and during the life of the house of Israel, even speedily and at a near time." The Qaddish plainly includes a covert petition for the political independence of Israel. And both texts by implication are asking for an end to those crimes against persons that are described in the Hebrew Bible as a "profanation" of God's name: debt-slavery and prostitution (*Amos* 2:6–8), enslavement (*Jer.* 34:14–16), and murder (*Lev.* 18:21).

Victory over dark powers. In *Luke* 11:20 Jesus proclaims, "But if I by the finger of God cast out demons, then the kingdom of God has come upon you." What is asked for in the Lord's Prayer is here announced as already operative. Jesus instructed his missionaries to "heal those who are sick and say to them, 'The kingdom of God has drawn near you'" (*Lk.* 10:9). Proofs that the kingdom has broken into history are the healing of sickness, often of psychosomatic types of sickness, and victory over the destructive social forces called "demons," such as Legion, so named as a sign of military oppression (*Mk.* 5:9), and Mammon (*Lk.* 16:13). God's "finger" is the creative force by which the heavens were made (*Ps.* 8:3), oppressors overthrown (*Ex.* 8:19), and the Law given (*Ex.* 31:18). No less a power, Jesus implies, could do what has already been done through him; hence God's sovereignty has already broken into history.

"To enter the kingdom of God." A second group of sayings defines the condition for entering the kingdom: becoming like the poor. Jesus expresses the condition negatively: "It is easier for a camel to go through the eye of a needle than for a rich man to enter the kingdom of God" (*Mk.* 10:25). He also expresses it positively: "Allow the children to come to me and do not forbid them, for of such is the kingdom of God" (*Mk.* 10:14–15; cf. *Mt.* 18:13–14, *Jn.* 3:3–5). With far-reaching irony he says, "The tax collectors and harlots enter the kingdom of God before you" (*Mt.* 21:31). The kingdom of God is further reserved for the handicapped (*Mk.* 9:47), the persecuted (*Mt.* 5:10), and those in tribulation (*Acts* 14:22). The rabbinic background for these sayings is the concept of "the coming age" (*ha-ʿolam ha-ba'*): "Master, teach us the paths of life so that through them we may win the life of the coming age" (B.T., *Ber.* 28b).

The link among these groups is a deep structure of Jesus' thought underlying Luke's "Sermon on the Plain." The beatitude "Blessed are you poor, for yours is the kingdom of God" (*Lk.* 6:20) shows that possession of the kingdom is the coming reward for the poor, hungry, and mourning. The saying "Love your enemies . . . and your reward will be great" (*Lk.* 6:35) shows that the characteristic of this ideal poor is love of enemies, that is, nonretaliation to evil. Hence Gerd Theissen (*Sociology of Early Palestinian Christianity*, John Bowden, trans., Philadelphia, 1978, p. 99) concludes: "The best description of the functional outline of the Jesus movement for overcoming social tensions is an interpretation of it as a contribution towards containing and overcoming aggression." Later, Jesus' criterion is reformulated with increasing degrees of legalism: To enter the kingdom of God one must keep two great commandments (*Mk.* 12:34); show persistence (*Lk.* 9:62); do the will of God (*Mt.* 7:21); serve the Christ hidden in the poor (*Mt.* 25:34); have a higher righteousness (*Mt.* 5:20); and avoid certain listed sins (*1 Cor.* 6:9–10, *Gal.* 5:21).

The kingdom of God as object of search or struggle. A third group of sayings defines the kingdom of God as the highest object of desire. Although certain forces "lock up the kingdom of heaven" (*Mt.* 23:13), the reader is told "seek first God's kingdom and all these shall be added to you" (*Lk.* 21:31; cf. *Mt.* 6:33). The kingdom is symbolized by the "treasure hidden in a field" and the "pearl of great price" (*Mt.* 13:44–46). But the nature of the "mystery of the kingdom of God" is left unexplained at *Mark* 4:11; and Paul only vaguely suggests with the expression "fellow workers for the kingdom of God" (*Col.* 4:11) the modern idea that the kingdom can be promoted by human energy.

"In the kingdom of God." This phrase in a fourth group of sayings is always used in connection with a banquet at the end of time. When Jesus affirms, "I shall no more drink of the fruit of the vine until that day when I drink it new in the kingdom of God" (*Mk.* 14:25), he implies that the kingdom can only come in through his suffering. The greatest and least in the kingdom are paradoxically reversed (*Mt.* 5:19, 18:4; *Lk.* 7:28 and *Mt.* 11:11) as in the parable of the banquet (*Mt.* 22:2–14, *Lk.* 14:16–24). The final event will be inaugurated by the apostles: To them Jesus says, "I bequeath you as my Father bequeathed me a kingdom, that you may eat and drink at my table in my kingdom and sit on thrones judging the twelve tribes of Israel" (*Lk.* 22:29–30; cf. *Mt.* 19:28).

At the inauguration of the banquet, Jesus says, there will be a final division of humanity "when you see Abraham . . . and all the prophets in the kingdom of God, but you yourselves cast out; and they shall come from the east and the west . . . and recline in the kingdom of God" (*Lk.* 13:28–29; cf. *Mt.* 8:11–12). Two themes are combined in this text: the pilgrimage of all peoples to Jerusalem (*Is.* 49:12, etc.) towards the "house of prayer for all peoples" (*Is.* 56:7); and the banquet described in *Isaiah* 25:6–9, which ends with the archaic Ugaritic motif of Yahveh swallowing up death forever.

The Kingdom of God in Christian Tradition. Luke in his gospel and in the *Acts* when writing narrative regularly speaks of "preaching the good news of the kingdom of God." Paul inherits the phrase "kingdom of God" in fixed phrases from the gospel tradition; the structural parallel that plays the same role as the kingdom in his thought is the "righteousness [*dikaiosune*] of God." The remaining letters of the

New Testament, where, as Rudolf Bultmann says, Jesus "the Proclaimer becomes the one proclaimed" by the church, mostly speak of the kingdom of Christ. In the writings of the Greek church fathers the notion of the kingdom of God loses any sociopolitical connotation and is seen as the state of immortality or the beatific vision as entered through baptism. But in his commentary on *Matthew* 14:7 (244 CE), Origen coins a word that contains much of the original sense: As Christ is "wisdom itself, righteousness itself and truth itself," so is he also "the kingdom itself" (*autobasileia*).

The development of the concept of the kingdom of God occurred primarily in the church of the West. In the thought of the Latin theologians and the official Reformation, it served to legitimate the state through Augustine's doctrine of two cities and Luther's of two kingdoms. The Enlightenment, while discovering the primacy of the kingdom of God in Jesus' thought, tried to accommodate it to rational categories. It was the radical Reformation that most fully recovered Jesus' original understanding, and that transmitted the most vital form of the concept to contemporary Christian believers today.

Two cities, two kingdoms. These concepts served to accommodate the church to the state. In his *City of God* (413–426 CE), Augustine developed his grandiose contrast between the *civitas Dei,* with a biblical basis in *Psalms* 87:3 and 46:5, and the *civitas terrena,* the "earthly city," with no biblical antecedent. This work laid a basis for relations between church and state that was not decisively challenged until the resistance to Hitler by the German Confessing church.

Augustine's concept of the earthly city is especially ambiguous. Sometimes (e.g., *Sermons* 214.11) he identifies the city of God with the historical church and attributes to the earthly city aspects of the state; here he has a predecessor in the rabbinic parallelism of the "kingdom [*malkhut*] of the earth" and the "kingdom of the firmament" (B.T. *Ber.* 58a), and in one interpretation of Jesus' saying about the "things of Caesar" and "things of God" (*Mk.* 12:17). Elsewhere for Augustine the city of God is the society of the redeemed, and the earthly city is the society of the devil; here the good and evil principles of the Manichaeism that Augustine previously embraced resurface.

While Augustine's language about church and kingdom fluctuates, his underlying thought is consistent. His predecessor Cyprian saw both distinction and continuity between present church and future kingdom: "One who abandons the church which is to reign [*regnatura est*] cannot enter the kingdom [*regnum*]" (*On the Unity of the Church* 14). So Augustine distinguishes the temporary "inn" of the church from the permanent "home" of the kingdom (*Sermons* 131.6). Hence there are two ages of the church, now with a mixture of wheat and tares, in the future transformed into a kingdom without evil. Correspondingly Augustine distinguishes two periods of the kingdom: a present "kingdom of militancy" (*regnum militiae*), and a future "peaceable kingdom," a *pacatissimum regnum* (*City of God* 20.9). When he goes on then to say that "the church even now is the kingdom of Christ and the kingdom of heaven" he does not imply it is that already perfected.

Two kingdoms in Luther. In the High Middle Ages, Hugh of Saint-Victor (1096–1141) crystallized Augustine's two cities unambiguously into the "spiritual power" of the church and the "secular power" of the state, with the church in theory superior and in practice subservient. Martin Luther restored the New Testament term "kingdom of God" (*Reich Gottes*) but placed over against it a "kingdom of the world" (*Reich der Welt*). God's kingdom is one of grace and mercy; the world's kingdom, one of wrath and severity (Martin Luther, *Works,* ed. Jaroslav Pelikan, Saint Louis, 1955–1976, 46.69, 30.76). In Luther's *On Temporal Authority* (1523) the children of Adam are divided between the two kingdoms (*Works,* 45.88). The sayings "Render to Caesar what is Caesar's" (*Mk.* 12:17) and "The powers that be are ordained of God" (*Rom.* 13:1) carry great weight for Luther (*Works* 45.99)—in part because of his dependence on the German princes for protection against Rome. Only when a political leader gives false religious commands does Luther permit the stance expressed in *Acts* 5:29, "We must obey God rather than men" (*Works* 45.111).

In a sermon of 1544, Luther boldly defined the two kingdoms as distinct operations of the one God:

> The worldly government [*das weltlich Regiment*] also may be called God's kingdom. For he wills that it should remain and that we should enter it; but it is only the kingdom with his left hand [*nur des reych mit der lincken hand*]. But his right-hand kingdom [*rechtes reych*], where he himself rules, and is called neither . . . Kaiser nor king . . . but rather is himself, is that where the Gospel is preached to the poor. (*D. Martin Luthers Werke,* Weimar, 1883–, 52.26; cf. 36.385)

Luther calls these two operations of God his "alien" and "proper" work (*opus alienum, proprium;* cf. *Is.* 28:21 Vulgate). In an early sermon of 1516 he maintains, "since God could justify only those who are not just, he is forced before his proper work of justification to carry out an alien work in order to make sinners" (*Works* 51:19; cf. 33.140).

Sometimes Luther opposed to God's kingdom not the kingdom of the world but Satan's kingdom (*Works* 33.227). Unlike Augustine he closely integrates the devil's work with the work of God. On *Hebrews* 2:14, Luther comments: "God pierced the adversary with that one's weapon . . . and so completes his proper work with an alien work" (*Works* 29.135). While he protests that "God does not wish us like the Manichaeans to imagine two gods, one the source of good, the other of evil" (*On Psalms* 90:16, *Works* 13.135), Luther comes close to postulating a duality within God, with the devil as God's dark side. Thus he holds that on occasion "God wears the mask [*larva*] of the devil" (*On Galatians* 5:11, *Works* 27.43).

Only one kingdom. The doctrine of "only one kingdom" was the affirmation of the German Confessing church.

Luther's scheme of two kingdoms was pushed to an extreme in the 1930s by German theologians such as Paul Althaus and Emanuel Hirsch, who favored National Socialism. In their *Zwei-Reiche-Lehre* ("doctrine of the two kingdoms") the state is autonomous over against the church. Opposition to this doctrine led to a rethinking of Luther's position. For example, Dietrich Bonhoeffer in his *Ethics* (trans. N. H. Smith, London, 1955, p. 62) condemns any thinking about God and the world "in terms of two spheres," especially when "in the pseudo-Lutheran scheme the autonomy of the orders of the world is proclaimed in opposition to the law of Christ."

During World War II, Karl Barth wrote that the "illusory paganism of the German people" had been confirmed rather than restrained by the "heritage of the greatest Christian of Germany, by Martin Luther's error on the relation between . . . the temporal and spiritual order" (*A Letter to Great Britain from Switzerland,* London, 1941, p. 36). On the one hand Barth uses Luther's language when he states that "nothingness" (i.e., evil) is "on the left hand of God as the object of his *opus alienum*" (*Church Dogmatics,* trans. G. T. Thomson et al., 5 vols. in 14, Edinburgh, 1936–1977, vol. 3, part 3, p. 361). But, contrary to Luther, he emphasizes the uniqueness of God's kingdom, insisting on the radical "antithesis of the kingdom of God to all human kingdoms" and also to the "sphere of Satan" (*Church Dogmatics* 4.2.177, 2.2.688). "There is no collateral rule [*Nebenregierung*] side by side with [God's] and no counter-rule opposed to it. He alone can rule, and ought to rule, and wills to rule; and he alone does so" (*Church Dogmatics* 3.3.157).

Barth's views were accepted in principle by the newly formed German Confessing church at the Synod of Barmen (May 31, 1934) in opposition to the Nazi state church. The fifth thesis of Barmen, drafted by Barth and going beyond previous Lutheran or Reformed confessions, says that "the State has by divine appointment the task of providing for justice and peace. . . . The Church acknowledges the benefit of this appointment. . . . It calls to mind the Kingdom of God . . . and thereby the responsibility both of rulers and of the ruled." The document contains nothing about the nature of the state, much less its alleged status as a parallel kingdom; it refers only to the state's assigned task (Cochrane, 1962, pp. 192, 241).

The legacy of the Enlightenment. Here the concept of the coming of the kingdom of God is accommodated to rational categories. Hermann Samuel Reimarus (1694–1768), in a posthumously published manuscript, was the first modern scholar to recognize that the coming of the kingdom of God was Jesus' central theme (*Reimarus: Fragments,* ed. C. H. Talbert, Philadelphia, 1970, pp. 136–138). Reimarus presumes that Jesus' contemporaries expected no other savior "than a worldly deliverer of Israel, who was to release them from bondage and build up a glorious worldly kingdom for them." When to announce his kingdom (*Mt.* 10:7) Jesus "chose for his messengers men who were themselves under the common impression," Reimarus concludes, he could have had "no other object than to rouse the Jews . . . who had so long been groaning under the Roman yoke." Thus he sees Jesus as simply a political revolutionary or Zealot.

From an opposite, but no less rationalistic, perspective, Immanuel Kant argued for a universal philosophic interpretation of the kingdom of God. He took the title of the third book of his *Religion within the Limits of Reason Alone* (1793) from the language of Jesus: "The victory of the good over the evil principle, and the founding of a kingdom of God on earth." He ends the work by citing the phrase from *Luke* 17:22 ("the kingdom of God is in your midst") in the translation "the kingdom of God is within you," thus giving the saying the "spiritual" interpretation that remains popular: "Here a kingdom of God is represented not according to a particular covenant (i.e., not messianic) but moral (knowable through unassisted reason)."

Most nineteenth-century German New Testament scholars interpreted the Gospels according to Kant's presuppositions. This accommodation, however, collapsed with the publication in 1892 of the first edition of Johannes Weiss's *Jesus' Proclamation of the Kingdom of God* (trans. R. H. Hiers, Philadelphia, 1971, p. 130). Weiss concluded that "although Jesus initially hoped to live to see the establishment of the kingdom of God, he gradually became certain" that he must die first, but that after his death he would "return upon the clouds of heaven at the establishment of the kingdom of God, . . . within the lifetime of the generation which rejected him." He frankly recognized that this historical reconstruction contradicted the "modern Protestant worldview" that he shared with his contemporaries, because he could not take the "eschatological attitude" that the world was passing away. Likewise, Albert Schweitzer conceived of Jesus as an eschatological visionary awaiting an imminent end of the world. In his *The Mystery of the Kingdom of God* (1901; trans. W. L. Lowrie, New York, 1950, p. 55), Schweitzer explained the radical demands of the sermon on the mount as an *Interimsethik,* too rigorous for normal life, in the brief period before the full establishment of the kingdom.

A number of twentieth-century scholars defined Jesus' idea of the kingdom of God as basically completed in his own work. Charles Harold Dodd in his *The Parables of the Kingdom* (London, 1935) rejects Schweitzer's "thoroughgoing eschatology" and argues that Jesus regarded the kingdom of God as having already come. He interprets "the ministry of Jesus as 'realized eschatology,' that is, as the impact upon this world of the 'powers of the world to come'" (p. 151). Rudolf Bultmann in his *Jesus and the Word* (1926; trans. L. P. Smith et al., New York, 1934, pp. 52, 131), anticipating his later program of "demythologization," interprets the absolute certainty of the coming of the kingdom as a "crisis of decision" in which every hour is the last hour. He defines the kingdom as "an eschatological deliverance which ends everything earthly" by confronting the human being with a decision in crisis as in Kierkegaard's "Either/Or."

Schweitzer laid much weight on the saying in *Mark* 9:1, "There are some standing here who will not taste death before they see the kingdom of God coming with power." If this verse is both historically attributed to Jesus and understood literally, Jesus will seem to have been in error. There have been many efforts to account for the apparent error. In his *On Being a Christian* (New York, 1978, p. 220), Hans Küng argues that Jesus' "apocalyptic horizon," the expectation of an immediate end of the world, is "not so much an error as a time-conditioned . . . worldview which Jesus shared with his contemporaries." Erich Grässer, in his *Das Problem der Parusieverzögerung in den synoptischen Evangelien* (Berlin, 1960), sees the entire development of the early church as a response to the "delay of the *parousia* [i.e., 'expected coming']," citing especially *2 Peter* 3:4: "Where is the promise of his coming?" John G. Gager in his *Kingdom and Community: The Social World of Early Christianity* (Englewood Cliffs, N.J., 1975, p. 39) explains the whole original Christian mission by analogy to a contemporary millenarian sect that, after its prediction of an immediate end is disconfirmed, "may undertake zealous missionary activity as a response to its sense of cognitive dissonance." Other scholars, such as Werner G. Kümmel and Norman Perrin, have characterized the supposed error as springing from the adoption of a literalistic antithesis of present/future.

A kingdom of righteousness and peace. This kingdom was the heritage of the radical Reformation. Both the centrality and the original meaning of Jesus' concept of the kingdom of God were grasped by the radical reformers, less through their scholarship than through the conformity of their lives to Jesus' pattern. Menno Simons (c. 1496–1561), rejecting the violence of the Peasants' Revolt of 1525 under Thomas Münzer but speaking from the same social situation, based his stand of nonretaliation on the sermon on the mount. He wrote, "Christ has not taken his kingdom with the sword, although he entered it with much suffering" (*The Complete Writings of Menno Simons,* trans. L. Verduin et al., Scottsdale, 1956, p. 49). And again, "We acknowledge . . . no other sword . . . in the kingdom or church of Christ than the sharp sword of the Spirit" (p. 300). While leaving "the civil sword to those to whom it is committed," Menno's only kingdoms are those of "the Prince of Peace and the prince of strife" (p. 554). Similarly, in his *Journal,* George Fox, recording his famous testimony of November 21, 1660 before Charles II, characterizes the kingdom of God as wholly pacific: "The Spirit of Christ, which leads us into all truth, will never move us to fight and war against any man with outward weapons, neither for the kingdom of Christ nor for the kingdoms of this world."

The visual arts. The church early developed pictorial versions of the human scenes of the Gospels. But an adequate symbol of the kingdom of God first appears in the nineteenth century in the many versions of *The Peaceable Kingdom* painted by the American Quaker primitive Edward Hicks (1780–1849). These paintings illustrate *Isaiah* 11:6–8: Against a Delaware River landscape the wolf and lamb, leopard and kid lie down together, the cow and bear feed side by side, and the lion eats straw with the ox; one child leads them, another plays on the serpent's den. In a background vignette William Penn signs his peace treaty with the Indians.

The popular piety of Hymnody. Even for Luther, when he turned hymn-writer, the only opposite to God's kingdom can be Satan's: In *Ein feste Burg* (1529) God's opposite is the "Prince of this world" (*John* 12:31), and the sole kingdom is the one we inherit, *Das Reich muss uns doch bleiben.* The masters of English hymnody, who always attribute the kingdom of Jesus, suffuse it with the social witness Evangelical revival. Thus Isaac Watts in his paraphrase (1719) of the messianic Psalm 72: "Jesus shall reign where'er the sun . . . his kingdom stretch from shore to shore." Charles Wesley's Christmas hymn (1739) once began "Glory to the King of kings!"; congregations still sing, "Hail, the Sun of Righteousness! / Hail, the heav'n-born Prince of Peace!" Their focus on the person of Jesus is especially plain in their transformation of the "kingship Psalms": Watt's Christmas hymn (1719) "Joy to the world! the Lord is come; / Let earth receive her King" adapts Psalm 98; Charles Wesley's ascension hymn "Hail the day that sees him rise . . . Take the King of Glory in!" reworks Psalm 24.

Puritanism and the Social Gospel. English Puritans commonly speak of God as king. In his *A Holy Commonwealth* (1659), Richard Baxter affirms that "the world is a kingdom whereof God is the King . . . an absolute Monarchy . . . All men are subjects of God's kingdom" (Richard Niebuhr, 1937, p. 52). It is a false boast when in John Milton's *Paradise Lost* Satan claims "Divided Empire with Heaven's King I hold" (4.111). In America, where the symbolism of monarchy was less apt, the emphasis merely shifts to the kingdom of God. Jonathan Edwards in his *History of Redemption* regards the kingdom of heaven upon earth as a prosperous age of the church before the apostasy and last judgement. The Puritan inheritance was secularized in Walter Rauschenbusch's notion of the Social Gospel, in which the realization of the kingdom is identified with historical progress. In a manuscript of about 1891, posthumously published as *The Righteousness of the Kingdom* (Nashville, 1968), Rauschenbusch holds that the "program of the Christian revolution," namely, the kingdom of God on earth, "includes a twofold aim: the regeneration of every individual to divine sonship and eternal life, and the victory of the spirit of Christ over the spirit of this world in . . . all the institutions formed by human society" (p. 110).

The theology of the future. After the reaction to nineteenth-century liberal theology in Bultmann's existentialism and Barth's neo-orthodoxy, the 1960s saw new theologies that were oriented toward the future. For example, Wolfhart Pannenberg in his *Theology and the Kingdom of God* (Philadelphia, 1969) writes: "If the Kingdom of God and the mode of his existence (power and being) belong together, then the message of the coming kingdom implies that god in his very being is the future of the world" (p. 61). And Jürgen Moltmann in his *Theology of Hope* (trans. J. W. Weitch, London, 1967) holds that "the kingdom is present here as promise and hope for the future horizon of all things" (p. 223).

Councils, Catholic and Protestant. Paul had defined the kingdom of God as "righteousness and peace and joy in the Holy Spirit" (*Rom.* 14:17). Those identifications are taken up in the documents of the Second Vatican Council (1963–1965): "To the extent that [earthly progress] can contribute to the better ordering of human society, it is of vital concern to the kingdom of God" (*Gaudium et Spes* 39, cf. *Lumen Gentium* 5). Similarly, the Sixth Assembly of the World Council of Churches (Vancouver, 1983) affirms "the identification of the churches with the poor in their witness to God's kingdom"; and in its statement rejecting nuclear weapons says that "as we witness to our genuine desire for peace with specific actions, the Spirit of God can use our feeble efforts for bringing the kingdoms of this world closer to the kingdom of God."

The theology of liberation. A unity of piety with political struggle marks a new life in the Latin American church. A key spokesman is the Peruvian Gustavo Gutiérrez, who writes: "The process of liberation will not have conquered the very roots of oppression . . . without the coming of the kingdom of God, which is above all a gift. . . . The historical, political liberating event *is* the growth of the kingdom . . . but it is not *the* coming of the kingdom" (*A Theology of Liberation: History, Politics and Salvation,* trans. Caridad Inda and J. Eagleson, Maryknoll, N.Y., 1973, p. 177). This theology is adapted to North American experience by James H. Cone, who in his *A Black Theology of Liberation* (Philadelphia, 1970, p. 220) writes: "The appearance of Jesus as the Black Christ also means that the Black Revolution is God's kingdom becoming a reality in America. . . . The kingdom of God is what happens to a person when his being is confronted with the reality of God's liberation."

The movement for justice and peace. Dom Helder Câmara of Recife has often said that the current world faces twin threats: the actual "M-bomb" of misery and the potential holocaust of the A-bomb. In that situation, the most critical in history, many readers of the New Testament are finding that its apocalyptic images of the end of the world, far from being alien to their mentality, are merely literal. To many Christian believers in the movement for justice and peace the kingdom of God has become the primary name for what is at work in them. James W. Douglass, in his *Resistance and Contemplation: The Way of Liberation* (Garden City, 1972, p. 107), writes: "The way of revolution is the kingdom because the revolution is the people coming together in a new humanity, ignited by a divine symbol given through the man of truth—Jesus in the Temple and on the cross, Gandhi by the sea [on the salt march], the Berrigans at Catonsville [destroying draft files]." In the slums of São Paulo a French priest, Dominique Barbé, drawing on an indigenous Brazilian tradition of nonviolent resistance, writes (*La grâce et le pouvoir,* Paris, 1982, p. 206): "If I have been snatched out of the empire of darkness to enter into the kingdom, that is, into that part of reality where death has been eliminated, the only means of combat left me is the Cross and not the revolver." After Martin Luther King Jr., the disciple of Rauschenbusch and Gandhi, delivered his speech "I have a dream" at the Lincoln Memorial on August 28, 1963 (*A Testament of Hope,* ed. J. M. Washington, San Francisco, 1986, p. 217), Coretta King commented: "At that moment it seemed as if the Kingdom of God appeared." She added, "But it only lasted for a moment." Contemporary belief in the kingdom of God requires it to be reappropriated freshly by human beings at each historical turning point.

SEE ALSO Christian Social Movements; Kingship; Political Theology; Theocracy.

BIBLIOGRAPHY

No comprehensive study of the topic exists. For a well-documented source of texts from the ancient Near East and an extensive bibliography, see Thorkild Jacobsen's *The Treasures of Darkness: A History of Mesopotamian Religion* (New Haven, Conn.,1976). The Ugaritic data with relation to Hebrew are clearly presented by Werner H. Schmidt in *Königtum Gottes in Ugarit und Israel: Zur Herkunft der Königsprädikation Jahwes,* 2d ed. (Berlin, 1966). The most reliable surveys for the biblical material as a whole are Rudolf Schnackenburg's *God's Rule and Kingdom* (New York, 1963) and "Basileus" and related entries in the *Theological Dictionary of the New Testament* (Grand Rapids, Mich., 1964). For excellent surveys of Old Testament scholarship on Yahveh's kingship, see Joseph Coppens's contribution to the entry "Règne (ou Royaume) de Dieu," in the *Supplément au Dictionnaire de la Bible,* vol. 10 (Paris, 1981), and the article "Melek" by Helmer Ringgren et al. in the *Theologisches Wörterbuch zum Alten Testament,* vol. 4 (Stuttgart, 1984). Martin Buber's *Kingship of God,* translated from the third German edition (New York, 1967), is more theological than exegetical in its handling of the topic. John Gray restates the "enthronement-festival theory" uncritically but offers a thorough bibliography in *The Biblical Doctrine of the Reign of God* (Edinburgh, 1979).

The rabbinic sources were first analyzed by Gustaf H. Dalman in *The Words of Jesus Considered in the Light of Post-Biblical Jewish Writings and the Aramaic Language,* rev. Eng. ed. (Edinburgh, 1909); see especially pages 91–102 in volume 1 on the "kingship of heaven." Thousands of rabbinic texts in German translation are included in Hermann L. Strack and Paul Billerbeck's *Kommentar zum neuen Testament aus Talmud und Midrasch,* 6 vols. in 7 (Munich, 1922–1961); see especially the collection on "kingdom of God" in volume 1, pages 172–180. The use of the term *kingdom* in the Targum is analyzed by Bruce D. Chilton in "Regnum Dei Deus Est," *Scottish Journal of Theology* 31 (1978): 261–276.

For an introduction to the teachings of Jesus, see Hans Küng's *On Being a Christian* (Garden City, N.Y., 1976) and Günther Bornkamm's *Jesus of Nazareth* (New York, 1960). The "form-criticism" (*Formgeschichte*) of the gospel materials, important for assessing the historicity of the different sayings on the kingdom, was begun and almost ended with Rudolf Bultmann's *The History of the Synoptic Tradition,* 2d ed. (New York, 1968). On the Aramaic background of the sayings, consult Joachim Jeremias's *New Testament Theology: The Proclamation of Jesus* (New York, 1971). The case for making Jesus a political revolutionary has been restated by S. G. F. Brandon in *Jesus and the Zealots* (Manchester, 1967).

For a bibliography of the research on Jesus' sayings on the kingdom, together with scrupulous exegesis of key ones, see Jacques Schlosser's *Le règne de Dieu dans les dits de Jésus,* 2 vols. (Paris, 1980). Two articles on the subject of Jesus' sayings are especially useful: Hans Windisch's "Die Sprüche vom Eingehen in das Reich Gottes," *Zeitschrift für die neutestamentliche Wissenschaft* 27 (1928): 163–192, and Heinz Kruse's "The Return of the Prodigal: Fortunes of a Parable on Its Way to the Far East," *Orientalia* 47 (1978): 163–214.

Ernst Staehelin offers a very large annotated compilation of texts from the Christian church in *Die Verkündigung des Reiches Gottes in der Kirche Jesu Christi,* 7 vols. (Basel, 1951–1965). The early church fathers' treatment of the concept is indexed in "Basileia," in *A Patristic Greek Lexicon,* edited by G. W. H. Lampe (Oxford, 1961). A reliable guide to Augustine's thought is Étienne Gilson's *The Christian Philosophy of Saint Augustine* (New York, 1960), especially pp. 180–183. For a brief introduction to the thorny controversy surrounding Luther's doctrine, consult Heinrich Bornkamm's *Luther's Doctrine of the Two Kingdoms in the Context of His Theology* (Philadelphia, 1966). Arthur C. Cochrane narrates the struggle within the German church in *The Church's Confession under Hitler* (Philadelphia, 1962).

Read in sequence, three works provide the history of scholarly research into the meaning of the kingdom in Jesus' sayings: Christian Walther's *Typen des Reich-Gottes-Verständnisses: Studien zur Eschatologie und Ethik im 19. Jarhundert* (Munich, 1961) offers the perspective of nineteenth-century thinkers; Albert Schweitzer's *The Quest of the Historical Jesus: A Critical Study of Its Progress from Reimarus to Wrede,* 2d ed. (London, 1911), moves from Reimarus to Schweitzer himself; and Gösta Lundström's *The Kingdom of God in the Teaching of Jesus: A History of Interpretation from the Last Decades of the Nineteenth Century to the Present Day* (Edinburgh, 1963) moves forward to the 1960s. The most extensive contemporary work is the lifetime opus of Norman Perrin: *The Kingdom of God in the Teaching of Jesus* (Philadelphia, 1963), *Rediscovering the Teaching of Jesus* (New York, 1967), and *Jesus and the Language of the Kingdom: Symbol and Metaphor in New Testament Interpretation* (Philadelphia, 1976). Werner B. Kümmel's *Promise and Fulfillment: The Eschatological Message of Jesus* (Naperville, Ill., 1957) is also useful.

Numerous texts otherwise barely accessible are cited in H. Richard Niebuhr's *The Kingdom of God in America* (Chicago, 1937); his schematism is to be taken with reserve.

New Sources

Blumenfeld, Bruno. *The Political Paul: Justice, Democracy, and Kingship in a Hellenistic Framework.* London, 2001.

Chilton, Bruce. *Pure Kingdom: Jesus' Vision of God.* Grand Rapids, Mich., 1996.

Fuellenbach, John. *Church: Community for the Kingdom.* Maryknoll, N.Y., 2002.

Humphries, Michael L. *Christian Origins and the Language of the Kingdom of God.* Carbondale, Ill., 1999.

Kainz, Howard P. *Democracy and the "Kingdom of God."* Milwaukee, Wis., 1995.

Liebenberg, Jacobus. *The Language of the Kingdom and Jesus.* New York, 2000.

Malina, Bruce J. *The Social Gospel of Jesus.* Minneapolis, 2001.

O'Donovan, Oliver. *The Desire of the Nations: Rediscovering the Roots of Political Theology.* Cambridge,1996.

Phillips, Paul T. *A Kingdom on Earth: Anglo-American Social Christianity, 1880–1940.* University Park, Pa., 1996.

Viviano, Benedict T. *The Kingdom of God in History.* Wilmington, Del., 1988.

JOHN PAIRMAN BROWN (1987)
Revised Bibliography

KINGSHIP

This entry consists of the following articles:

AN OVERVIEW
KINGSHIP IN THE ANCIENT MEDITERRANEAN WORLD
KINGSHIP IN SUB-SAHARAN AFRICA
KINGSHIP IN MESOAMERICA AND SOUTH AMERICA
KINGSHIP IN EAST ASIA

KINGSHIP: AN OVERVIEW

The term *kingship* refers to a relatively complex and hierarchical structure of society in which a central figure—a king or, in certain cases, a queen—undertakes a unifying role that acts as a value reference for the various groups that constitute the society. Depending on whether or not this function involves a direct exercise of political power on the part of the person who is discharging it, the king may be considered a monarch, and the kingship may be identified as a *monarchy,* a word that technically may mean only a particular form of government and nothing else. That the two terms do not correspond is well expressed by the saying that, in many cases, the king "reigns but does not govern." It is also possible to govern in an absolute fashion, as a monarch, by holding military office or administering justice without being legitimately entitled to do so. In such cases the one who governs does so by relying almost entirely upon force, making the role of engendering social cohesion difficult, which is the first duty of a king.

On this basis, then, one can understand that the interest in the subject shown by anthropologists and religious historians stems from the fact that the word *kingship* refers not only, and not so much, to a form of government but also to a supposed quality belonging to the person who embodies the king that sanctions his legitimacy—if not to govern, then at least to reign. This quality has been given various names, even in the Western tradition, such as *majesty* or *dignity*—and the word *kingship* itself has been used. It consists of precisely those attributes that mark out the king as exceptional, that make him, in the eyes of his subjects, a sacred person, a moral authority, a common reference point because of his universal value, with consequent displays of devotion and respect toward his person and his family, ancestors included. The analysis of this sacred role has had important consequences for the broad understanding of power in general. If it is indeed true that any form of power is still considered sacred—inasmuch as it represents a kind of transcendency, expressing a cultural method that humankind has at its disposal by which it can escape from the condition of contingency—it is also true that, in acquiring such an awareness, which finds its most extreme expression in the idea that political science is a chapter in the comparative historical study of religion (Debray, 1981; Heusch, 1987), thinking regarding the particular forms of power that constitute kingship, typified by association with a detailed set of rituals and a rich mythology, has played no small part.

DEFINING KINGSHIP. Examples of kingship may be drawn from all four corners of the world, from ancient China to Mexico, from the Egypt of the pharaohs to Mesopotamia, from the kingdoms of equatorial Africa to those of Polynesia. Although far apart in space and time, these societies often show surprising similarities even when they differ markedly in other respects, such as their size. Indeed, it has been noted that the traits that largely identify kingship (insofar as not being exclusively a form of government) are also present in forms of tribal organization, and their ultimate roots come directly from Neolithic social structures. This seems to suggest the importance attributed to the cult of ancestors—or even the well-known motif symbolically identifying the figure of the king with the father figure, understood not so much as a parent but rather as one who provides nourishment and, more generally, as a principle of authority.

The African continent provides numerous examples of this model of kingship (e.g., Mair, 1977; Vansina, 1966), where the main function of the king is not so much to govern as to engage directly with the forces of nature to ensure fertility and prosperity for the community. He has powers, such as the ability to ensure rain, and he must demonstrate their supposed effectiveness or, in certain cases, must pay with his life for his ineffectiveness. These are some of the traits that make up what is sacral in the broadest sense and in many cases differ only in detail. Generally, the idea is that the king guarantees the order of the universe via his privileged contact with the restless world of nature, inhabited by many invisible forces. This enhanced closeness is clear from his being permitted to transgress the laws of the land, which indicates that he does not belong to the social group that is obliged to follow rules by which he is not bound. Among these transgressions, one of the most significant is the practice of incest that often accompanied enthronement—a kind of hierogamy, according to Luc de Heusch (1987), that reveals to the greatest degree the alienation of the king from the obligation to obey the rules that bind the community.

Nevertheless, the emphasis upon the alienation and separateness of the king from the general populace means not only an exemption from the obligation to obey normal rules but also the observation of rules that on this occasion apply only to him. For the most part this involves submitting to a whole series of taboos, which serve to conceal the clearly human traits of the sovereign. Thus, in many traditional societies—the Jukun in Nigeria, for example—he cannot be seen while doing everyday things such as drinking, eating, sleeping, or directly touching the ground. Various figures—wives, sisters, dignitaries, and servants who always gravitate around the court—ensure strict adherence to this protocol. They share in the sacred nature of the king to varying degrees and are particularly involved at those moments most loaded with symbolism, such as during the actual investiture ceremony, when the new king is dressed in his robes, changes his name, and receives his royal insignia; or at the time of the funeral rites, which may also involve killing his relatives or particularly close servants, such as someone who is regarded as his double.

DEATH OF A KING. The death of a king is a highly significant event. It is the most dramatic event for the community, exposing the fiction that the sovereign is different from mere mortals. It is an event best kept secret for as long as possible and surrounded with the utmost discretion, from a practical point of view, to ensure the future plans for the succession and because of the worry such news can provoke among the general populace, who regard as an apocalyptic event the termination of the cosmic and social order the king ensured. Hence, the concern in many societies is to keep the interregnum to a minimum, because it is a period of chaos, real or imagined. To appoint a successor in advance or to appoint a figure to function as regent (in many cases the queen mother) is one measure adopted to deal with this situation.

This attitude toward the dangers of interregnum is not the exclusive concern of societies that are little more than tribal, but is a danger every kind of kingship must face. It shows one of the most symbolically specific characteristics of the institution itself. The solutions adopted may be different, but the guiding spirit that lies behind them remains the same. A glance at historical events in Europe tells the story more eloquently than numerous ethnographic examples, because it also serves as a better antidote to any attempt to diminish the importance of that mystical aspect that is a constant mark of kingship all over the world and at every level of social complexity.

To deny the interregnum is to deny the mortality of the king. This fiction was maintained in Renaissance Europe by the French and British monarchies by creating an effigy of the dead king, which was waited upon as if it were the living king himself (Giesey, 1960). This ritual practice was the starting point for the doctrinal elaboration (the subject of a masterly 1957 study by Ernst H. Kantorowicz) according to which the king possessed two bodies: one natural and one political. Only the first one was mortal, whereas the second was regarded as a *corporation sole*, constituted of a single person considered eternal. The insignia, which symbolized the eternal nature of the royal institution, was the crown.

The analogies are more significant than the differences, evidence of a political symbolism, a reality encompassing both tribal and centralized states. For these reasons, too, as with the distinctions between kingship and monarchy, some modern scholars of kingship consider it necessary to move to a less-marked identification between the kingship and the state (Simonse, 1992), and this has widened the field of study, especially from an ethnological perspective. Ideas such as the segmentary state (Southall, 1956) or the clan state (Adler, 1982) now rank alongside the more classical division between societies based upon ancestral lineage and those based upon the state, considered a throwback to nineteenth-century thinking (Tardits, 1980). It has thus become easier to agree with the argument of Roland Mousnier (1989), stating that groups deal with a kingship every time a leader is deemed to be in a privileged relationship with surrounding forces that, on the basis of accepted categorization, are considered supernatural.

"Ritual" and "politics" can be found together also in simpler societies than those traditionally defined as kingships or monarchies. To assume this seems to be the only way to agree with those authors, for example Valerio Valeri (1980), who warn that, as far as kingship is concerned, to try to establish an evolutionistic relationship between the categories above mentioned is misleading.

To return to the theory of the ritual origin of kingship formulated by James G. Frazer (1890) and restated by Arthur M. Hocart (1927) and the Myth and Ritual school (Ackerman, 1991), it should be clear that this will never mean the ritual origin of politics itself, an activity that, at least in the generally accepted sense of the guidelines about decisions taken with regard to matters of common concern, presumably has existed in all human societies. As far as the theory of the ritual origin of the kingship is concerned, its fortunes stem at least in part from the fact that it flourished in a period when it was firmly believed that politics was an activity that took place exclusively in those societies considered states.

A further implication of the distinction between kingship and monarchy may be the fact that the sacred nature of the king may be more clearly specified when one defines categories such as *legitimacy* and *sovereignty*. Thus, Mousnier, in his attempt to clarify the distinction between a king and a monarch, uses various figures to illustrate the differences between the two. In seventh- and sixth-century BCE Greece, for example, the term *tyrant* had not yet acquired any pejorative connotation but indicated simply an illegitimate king, one not meant to take the throne. The tyrant was thus a usurper who, albeit for the common good, illegitimately assumed power in particular circumstances.

Origin of Kingship. Vladimir Volkoff (1987) states that whereas a monarchy might be abruptly established, this is not so with kingship, which may only exist as a shared institution with a real or mythical past presenting a stable and reassuring figure, an intersection between the microcosmos and the macrocosmos. Volkoff thus restates in an elegant fashion that *legitimacy* best describes the fundamental difference between a king and a pure and simple monarch.

How then is the legitimacy of a monarch established? In other words, what is it that makes a *rex*—a term with a much older meaning, as the studies of Émile Benveniste (1969) suggest—more concerned with the figure of the priest than of the sovereign? Of the two main theories on the origin of kingship, the first holds that it originates from within the social group, while the other holds that it has external origins, such as the result of military conquest. The majority of available historical and ethnographic data supports the second hypothesis.

In the theory of the ritual origin of the kingship, which proposes the internal origin of the institution, the problem of legitimacy is in a sense already solved. To repeat the above distinction, it could be said to be a matter of demonstrating the transition from king to monarch, from an individual symbol—the moral and religious reference point of a broad range of groups who remain autonomous in terms of political, judicial, and administrative decisions—to an individual with the power to command all of these groups, which are reduced to unimportant objects and accept his authority.

For the opposing theory, which supports the external origin of the kingship, the problem is to analyze the transition from monarch to king, the shift from a character originating as a result of force to one accepted by the group because of a recognition of his exceptional nature, which makes him appear sacred and gives him legitimacy in the eyes of the entire community. The historical dynamics are naturally different. When the king and the monarch are not the same person, the legitimization of power almost always occurs in the form of a dyarchy. Analysis of a specific example clarifies how all this develops and the different institutional arrangements that may occur.

Two qualifications become appropriate. The first is that the force with which a stranger imposes himself upon a populace is still perceived, on the part of those subdued, in cultural terms as the expression of a superior power—of which he is the embodiment, or with which he has privileged relations. In this sense, the warring conqueror already has a sacred dimension, for he is already seen as the expression of a power with which he enjoys a privileged relationship. The second qualification is closely linked to the broad definition of kingship that has been adopted. On this basis the majority of ethnographic and historical examples put forward by scholars to illustrate the appearance of kingship deal with simply the appearance of a new kind of kingship, that is, a different institutional arrangement of the relationship between the mystical and political elements of power. Finally, it should be added that it is not always clear, when talking of kingship established via conquest, if the society from which the conquerors come is already familiar with a reasonably stable, regal organizational structure of some sort, or if a particular kind of leadership has been drawn up to carry out the conquest.

However that may be, to recall some classical examples, the documentary evidence related to both ancient Egypt and Mesopotamia refers to the existence of an earlier form of kingship. In the first case, the theriomorphic symbolism associated with the kingship (e.g., falcon, scorpion) is too varied not to allude to previous models of regal organizational structure predating the glory of the pharaonic age. As for Mesopotamia, the royal Sumerian genealogy recalls ancient nomad kings, leaders who "live in tents," suggesting a model of kingship, perhaps rather uncertain, that preceded the complex organization of the city-state centered on the temple.

The origins of the kingship of the Congolese, a Bantu people of West Africa, provide a good example of a frequent model for the construction of legitimacy by a foreign king. Lukeni, a fourteenth-century warrior not in command in his own circle of influence, emigrated with some of his followers and subdued the Ambundu, who were organized in small chiefdoms. He married the daughter of a powerful local priest, the *mani cabunga*, the guardian of supernatural powers, and he ordered his men to marry local women and take on their tribal name. In this way he began a process of territorial expansion, whereas the priest, as well as retaining his traditional ritual functions, was to play an important part in the enthronement ceremony of future kings and thus legitimize their governance.

Japan provides a different model. Here the mikado, or emperor, was considered a descendant of the sun goddess Amaterasu and was surrounded by an ostentatious ritual. He was regarded as endowed with miraculous powers and was perceived as an intermediary between the people and the divine cosmos. He did not engage in governmental functions, which was the role of the shogun who held military power.

Western Christianity offers yet another model based upon the fact that monotheism puts forward a transcendent god in contrast to the equality of all humanity. In this instance the king cannot be considered divine in origin, as in Japan, or be confused with a god, as with the Egyptian pharaoh. The religious realm remained firmly in the hands of a complex ecclesiastical apparatus that was involved in coronations from the eighth century until the time of Charles X in 1825 in France at Rheims, during which period the king was religiously anointed. The entire history of Europe consists of continuous attempts by the church and the state to assert their own superiority. The result was not so much a differentiation of roles, as in the preceding examples, but rather, as Kantorowicz has explained, an attempt to imitate each other, which is particularly evident in certain rituals of clothing and which culminated, as far as the king was concerned, in the claim that the sovereignty was divine in origin.

Alongside this institutional scenario, which in historical terms was interrupted by the French Revolution, there is a persistent popular image of the king. Marc Bloch (1924), in his now classic study, described the magical powers attributed to the medieval king, such as the ability to cure scrofula, and Yves-Marie Bercé (1990) investigated the equally fascinating topic of the king who is not dead but in hiding and will return to his people. These works provide evidence of the important mythological background that surrounds kingship even in Europe, which experienced the formation of the modern state, and evidence of the profitable use of the results of more than a century of anthropological research on this subject.

The Divine King and the Ritual Regicide. The history of this research can be traced back to the publication of *The Golden Bough* by James G. Frazer in 1890. This work deals with the theme of kingship, in particular its magic and sacred aspects, expanded upon in subsequent editions. It was the first important theoretical comparative formulation. It expresses the idea that the attribution to certain individuals of presumed magical powers that enabled them to interact with the forces of nature and positively influence it was decisive in them assuming the roles of chiefs and kings in the first human societies. One of the consequences of their privileged contact with the forces of nature would have been concern for their physical condition, the fear that their degeneration would drag down the whole universe with it. To prevent this catastrophic hypothesis from becoming reality, it was thought necessary to anticipate the natural death of the king and kill him first, which would allow his soul to be transferred to a stronger successor, and his physical well-being would thus be harmoniously linked via the sympathetic principle of magic to that of the whole universe.

In the first edition of *The Golden Bough,* the killing of the king does not appear as a relevant feature when the author speaks of the "divine King," a person distinct from the "magical King," the most meaningful example of which is provided by the Japanese mikado. It does appear in the third edition (1911–1915), when Frazer inserts a reference in the fourth volume of the work (1911), which eventually reached twelve volumes, to the Shilluk of the Sudan, among whom, according to a letter sent him by Charles G. Seligman on December 13, 1910, regicide was practiced until a few years previous. The subject of ritual regicide acquired a central place in the discussion of sacred or, as Frazer put it, "divine" kingship. Perhaps because the paroxysm seemed to embody it best, or perhaps because he was deliberately referring to the most archaic period of the institution of the kingship, Frazer thought it the expression of a still savage sense of the sacred that shed light upon the nature of the kingship in his subsequent histories. Scholars were naturally reluctant to ignore the importance of these references in the picture of an evolutionistic interpretation of the kingship.

This evolutionary outlook still retains its appeal when kingship and, particularly, ritual regicide are discussed. In the late twentieth century, William G. Randles (1968) gathered the various references to this subject in subsequent anthropological literature into a structured plan that identifies four possible stages in the evolution of the kingship. At the first level, the society actually determines in advance the length of the king's reign, thus indicating the maximum control over his fate. At the second level, regicide takes place at the first signs of the sovereign growing old. At the third, the sovereign is obliged to prove that he is worthy of the throne by undergoing trials in which he risks his own life. Only at the fourth stage does the king gain control of his own fate and acquire the right to die a natural death.

This representation is useful in that it attempts to incorporate a wide range of ethnographic evidence within an apparently logical sequence where certain events, regarded as horrifying to modern sensibilities, are not denied as such but are instinctively moved back to the distant past. This, however, encourages an inflexible interpretation, which is still unacceptable.

The diffusionist viewpoint is similar and can be considered a less rigid form of evolutionism, with more regard for the definite historico-geographical links of cultural factors. The most important works of this school, such as the monograph by Charles K. Meek (1931) on the Jukun of Nigeria, in which he adduces symbolic parallels with ancient Egypt, remain essentially faithful to Frazer's view. The first attempted classification of this representation was by Seligman (1934), who in his Frazer Lecture of 1933 summarized the essential features of the so-called divine king. For him a king was divine if:

1. He was able to exercise influence, voluntary or otherwise, over the forces of nature;
2. He was regarded as the dynamic center of the universe;
3. His daily actions were meticulously controlled and constantly checked;
4. He had to be put to death when his powers declined so that his weakness did not drag down the whole kingdom with it.

The final point is the most interesting one because it became the criterion by which to identify the figure of the divine king and distinguish him from the sacred king. In practice, divine kings were those who were not able to die natural deaths but had to be ritually killed. The fact that this characteristic has remained difficult to demonstrate from empirical evidence, and in many kingdoms is not hinted at even in mythological traditions, has led the majority of scholars to prefer the expression sacred (or sacral) kingship. This may be seen from the title "The Sacral Kingship" given to the Eighth International Congress of the History of Religions, on the subject of kingship, held in Rome in 1955. Its proceedings were published in 1959.

In the meantime, the diffusionist trend has been giving way to a functionalist interpretation that provided the first real alternative to Frazer's model. What had previously been analyzed in terms of cast of mind and superstitions was now seen in institutional terms. These were viewed by Frazer as the result, or at least the reflection, of certain beliefs. The similarities between societies that were far apart from each other in terms of space and time were, for Frazer, an indication that the societies were at more or less the same stage of intellectual development. For the functionalists the reverse was the case. Beliefs were no longer the central issue; it was the need for structured social integration that was important and that provided the key to interpreting the ideology and symbolic practices, including those in which such societies were similar. The analysis was therefore mainly synchronic in nature, so origins are discussed only in a figurative sense. The "origins" of a cultural phenomenon are only found within the society in which it is exhibited. They are the place it occupies and the function it performs taken as a whole. The rich symbolism associated with the kingship is thus essentially seen in terms of the need for group social cohesion.

One of the most important monographs with this approach was published by Hilda Kuper (1947) and concerned the Swazi, who celebrate the *ncwala* ritual. This provided the starting point for Max Gluckman to provide details of the category in "Rituals of Rebellion" (1963). The category allowed the various phenomena of puppet kings, scapegoat kings, or kings humiliated or mocked in literature to be interpreted as dramatic representations of the conflict that would end with the reaffirmation of the unchangeable nature of the existing order, the renewal and re-endorsement of the kingship. The evidence may be ethnographic as well as historic, as in the case of the New Year ceremony (*akitu*) of the ancient Babylonians, the Roman Saturnalia, or various rituals that accompanied Carnivals in European history. Once again it raises, albeit only indirectly, the matter of the interregnum. It raises fear of the specter of anarchy in order to forestall it.

With regard to the question of regicide, the clearest expression of the functionalist view is the reinterpretation of the case of the Shilluk in the work of Edward E. Evans-Pritchard (1963/1948). For this people, the author contests the previous picture of a centralized society and holds that the king reigns but does not govern. The Shilluk lands are subdivided into autonomous areas, with regard to which the king acts as the focus of social cohesion. He is regarded as the descendant of Nyikank, the hero and founder of the entire people. This identification makes him the center of moral values, leading to the creation of a system that links together religion, cosmology, and politics. Furthermore, sacrality, according to Evans-Pritchard, was not an attribute of the king himself but of the office of kingship. The legitimacy of an individual king's reign could thus be revoked if it was felt that he did not satisfactorily embody the kingship. The belief that the king should be killed in particular circumstances was cleverly exploited by those who had ambitions of power and were excluded from it. The regicides were therefore nothing more than political murders disguised as ritual killings.

The concern to dispense with Frazer meant that this interpretation held sway for some time, although it was in fact somewhat contradictory. To begin with, it talked of a king who reigns but does not govern, though at the same time it considered the regicide as motivated by ambitions of power.

A further unconvincing point concerns the clear distinction between the person and the office, with the resulting transfer of the sacrality issue to the latter. Michael W. Young (1966) drew attention to this in an essay that began by reconsidering the case of the Jukun. In his view the position taken by Evans-Pritchard considered the body of the sovereign as a mere vessel. The fact that a social and cosmic bond may conceivably be identified with a physical body must have repercussions (in terms of the sacrality) for the individual whose body is thus identified. Referring to the distinction made by Kantorowicz concerning medieval and Renaissance English kings, Young makes the point that, for the Jukun, the body of the king is different from those of the common populace in that it is linked to *juwe*, a quality that can be compared to what English jurists saw as the *dignitas* of the political body of the king, which was immortal, as opposed to his physical body. The regicides were thus ritual acts with political consequences, rather than the opposite.

The strength of the arguments against the Evans-Pritchard position could not be clearer. They were reinforced by so-called neo-Frazerians, the most representative of whom is Heusch, who began his own study of sacred kingship in 1958, concentrating in particular on the symbolism of royal incest and more generally advancing a comparative analysis with the Bantu kings on the figure of the sacred king as a transgressor of rules. The same subject was dealt with by other authors, such as Laura Makarius (1974) or Alfred Adler (1982) with respect to the Mundang of Chad and Jean-Claude Muller (1980) regarding the Rukuba of Nigeria. The last two authors regarded the kingship as an essentially symbolic structure, thus restoring the theoretical plausibility of ritual regicide.

Nevertheless, despite an inclination to consider ritual regicide as widely practiced, the neo-Frazerians, by paying scant attention to historical dynamics, are unable to get past the idea that it should be placed at the beginning of institutional history. They thus ignore important occurrences of ritual killing that are much more recent and do not tally with an implicitly evolutionist outlook.

A theoretically important suggestion to overcome the limitations of this outlook could be to adopt the idea of the *sacré sauvage* put forward by Roger Bastide (1975). Bastide uses this idea to highlight the fact that, in contexts that are particularly dramatic in terms of cultural impact, the sacred manifests itself not in a tame, domesticated manner but in all its explosive violence, giving rise to unexpected events that most people would be inclined to relegate to the remote past. Colonial impact has certainly been one of those situations that have produced a kind of historical reversal.

The most profitable application of these suggestions has been a reinterpretation of Congolese kingship in the work of Kajsa Ekholm Friedman (1985). This author demonstrates that, contrary to the frequent representation of the kingship as the transition from a "purely symbolic" king to a plenipotential king, in the case of the Congo the situation is precisely the opposite. Whereas initially the king's sovereignty and effective power are clearly displayed, in more recent times, as a result of the disintegration produced by colonial impact, events have led to the scapegoat procedure, the coronation of marginal individuals who are given the title of king and humiliated in every possible way. Thus, what one would prefer to think of as a remnant of a previous age is more effectively interpreted if related to current events.

Allowing for the plausibility of ritual regicide does not necessarily imply adherence to an evolutionist view of kingship. This important lesson, which is based upon an open attitude to actual historical investigation, was illustrated by the comparative analysis of Nilotic societies by Simon Simonse in *Kings of Disaster* (1992). This important study not only includes instances of regicide as the result of a failure to make the rains fall—including in the late twentieth century (in 1984 in the case of the queen of the Sudanese Bari), it also stresses that regicide per se is not necessarily the definite outcome but only one possible result, albeit the most dramatic, among a series of alternatives that remain open to the society until the last moment.

Similar historical observations are made by Claude Tardits (1980, 1990) and Dario Sabbatucci (1978). Tardits rejects the concept of the divine king and is reluctant, as far as Africa is concerned, to use even the notion of the sacred king, remarking how, in this case, one may speak of sacrality and transcendence only by referring to the cult of ancestors and is still, it may be added, a form of eschatology. Sabbatucci is even more skeptical. He starts by correctly urging caution about whether the populations studied by ethnologists may really shed retrospective light upon previous millennia, as based upon a conjectural model of history. He then turns to an extreme theory, according to which eschatology was an entirely Egyptian creation, produced by the historical experience of kingship. Life in the next world, previously the exclusive privilege of the pharaoh, became available to the people.

This process, in so far as it is real, should not be regarded as something absolute, as a one-way journey. Power may not be redistributed unless it has previously been assumed. If societies are indebted to kingship for the creation of more sophisticated models of transcendence, this is not the case when it comes to the longing for transcendence per se. The immortality gift historically offered by kingship was appreciated because people could recognize the fulfillment of a previous shared aspiration in it.

Kingship and Transcendence. The idea that kingship represents a particularly attractive model of transcendence, as one of the principal gauntlets thrown down by humans in the face of death, may be recognized in the fact that poets and writers have long been interested in this custom. Authors such as Homer, William Shakespeare, Luigi Pirandello, Eugène Ionesco, Italo Calvino, VladimirVolkoff, Elias Canetti, and many others have produced memorable writing on the subject of kingship. They have enlightened readers in many ways, and even as far as regicide is concerned, one may begin to understand that the most incisive writing may be contained in literary works (Vaughan, 1980). The sacrality of the king may only be understood when one sees the kingship of humanity, and in this regard poets have great vision. Thus, in the analysis of kingship, more so than in other fields, Aristotle's theory that poetry expresses a more philosophical and universal form of knowledge than history may be productively cited (Riccardo, 1997).

However, bringing this kind of thinking to bear concerning kingship involves the danger of becoming involved in the actual political defense of kingship. In other words, if the figure of the king is perceived as extremely close to, if not directly linked to, human nature itself, a little like God in the philosophy of Saint Augustine, empirical consideration of his absence from the political and institutional stage may be transformed into a kind of disquiet, rather like that presumably felt by those traditional societies at the physical decline of their sovereign. In this case, analysis of kingship and what it may have symbolized for peoples who experienced it is cloaked in a thinly disguised nostalgia for a bygone age. Kingship is seen as a panacea for the ills of the modern world, whereas modernity itself is considered in its turn to be a kind of interregnum, a void to be filled in the near future. One moves from kingship as poetry to kingship as therapy.

Such ideas are common in certain general studies on kingship. Thus Jean Hani (1984) is interested in the subject of kingship as a way to denounce modern Western secular thinking and the idea that sovereignty resides in the people. He highlights the unifying role of kingship, that individuals thus become part of a mystical Body, whereas secular political regimes operate in the opposite way, fragmenting society with subsequent conflict between its different parts, which are completely divided. It is clear that the historical advance of pluralism is denigrated here, perceived as irremediable chaos, a kind of interregnum, as opposed to those systems in which the sacrality of power would be able to ensure harmony between the whole and the parts.

The thinking on royal, or rather imperial, symbolism of Claudio Bonvecchio (1997) is mostly similar in tone. His analysis starts from a statement of the degeneration of the current liberal idea of popular sovereignty, where the king (*rex*) is replaced by the law *(lex),* a barren standard that will never be able to replace the symbolic richness, particularly as expressed imperially, because this is the best embodiment of the original model of sovereignty. Even more so than Hani, he emphasizes the "prescriptive emptiness of character" of sovereignty in the secular age, which is like "a pathology which denies any meaning to man, alienating man from himself, from society, from nature, from the cosmos" (Bonvecchio, 1997, p. 36). To rediscover the original idea of sovereignty would therefore mean to master the real self, and thus be not so much a political battle as an existential one. Can one consider this battle politically neutral? Maybe so, but only on condition of avoiding the temptation to try to buttress it with the firm support of an institution to justify and promote it. A true poet does not need it.

See Also Charlemagne; Constantine; Myth and Ritual School; Theodosius.

Bibliography

Ackerman, Robert. *J. G. Frazer: His Life and Work.* Cambridge, U.K., 1987.

Ackerman, Robert. *The Myth and Ritual School.* New York, 1991.

Adler, Alfred. *La mort est le masque du roi.* Paris, 1982.

Balandier, Georges. *Sociologie actuelle de l'Afrique noire.* Paris, 1955.

Bastide, Roger. *Le sacré sauvage et autres essais.* Paris, 1975.

Benveniste, Émile. *Le vocabulaire des institutions indo-européennes.* Paris, 1969.

Bercé, Yves-Marie. *Le roi caché: Sauveurs et imposteurs; Mythes politiques populaires dans l'Europe moderne.* Paris, 1990.

Bertelli, Sergio. *Il corpo del re: Sacralità del potere nell'Europa medievale e moderna.* Florence, 1990.

Bloch, Marc. *Les rois thaumaturges: Étude sur le caractère surnaturel attribué à la puissance royale particulièrement en France et en Angleterre.* Strasbourg, France, 1924.

Bonvecchio, Claudio. *Imago imperii imago mundi: Sovranità simbolica e figura imperiale.* Padua, Italy, 1997.

Canetti, Elias. *Masse und Macht.* Hamburg, Germany, 1960.

Cerulli, Ernesta. *Ma il re divino viaggiava da solo? Problemi e contraddizioni di un "complesso culturale" di diffusione quasi universale.* Genoa, Italy, 1979.

Debray, Régis. *Critique de la raison politique.* Paris, 1981.

Ekholm Friedman, Kajsa. "Sad Stories of the Death of Kings." *Ethnos* 50 (1985): 248–272.

Evans-Pritchard, Edward E. "The Divine Kingship of the Shilluk of the Nilotic Sudan." 1948. Reprinted in *Essays in Social Anthropology,* pp. 66–86. New York, 1963.

Feeley-Harnik, Gillian. "Issues in Divine Kingship." *Annual Review of Anthropology* 14 (1985): 273–313.

Frazer, James G. *The Golden Bough.* London, 1890.

Frazer, James G. *The Golden Bough.* 3d ed., 12 vols. London, 1911–1915. See vol. 4, *The Dying God.*

Giesey, Ralph E. *The Royal Funeral Ceremony in Renaissance France.* Geneva, 1960.

Gluckman, Max. "Rituals of Rebellion in South-East Africa." In *Order and Rebellion in Tribal Africa,* pp. 110–136. London, 1963.

Hani, Jean. *La royauté sacrée: Du pharaon au roi très chrétien.* Paris, 1984.

Heusch, Luc de. *Ecrits sur la royauté sacreé.* Brussels, 1987.

Hocart, Arthur M. *Kingship.* London, 1927.

International Congress for the History of Religions. *The Sacral Kingship.* Leiden, Netherlands, 1959.

Kantorowicz, Ernst H. *The King's Two Bodies: A Study in Mediaeval Political Theology.* Princeton, N.J., 1957.

Kuper, Hilda. *An African Aristocracy.* London, 1947.

Mair, Lucy. *African Kingdoms.* Oxford, U.K., 1977.

Makarius, Laura Levi. *Le sacré et la violation des interdits.* Paris, 1974.

Meek, Charles K. *A Sudanese Kingdom.* London, 1931.

Meillassoux, Claude. *Anthropologie de l'esclavage.* Paris, 1986.

Mousnier, Roland. *Monarchies et royautés: De la préhistoire à nos jours.* Paris, 1989.

Muller, Jean-Claude. *Le roi bouc émissaire.* Quebec, 1980.

Randles, William G. L. *L'ancien royaume du Congo des origines à la fin du XIXe siècle.* Paris, 1968.

Riccardo, Gaetano. *L'immortalità provvisoria: Antropologia del regicidio rituale in Africa.* Turin, Italy, 1997.

Sabbatucci, Dario. *Il mito, il rito, e la storia.* Rome, 1978.

Seligmam, Charles G. *Egypt and Negro Africa: A Study in Divine Kingship.* London, 1934.

Simonse, Simon. *Kings of Disaster.* Leiden, Netherlands, 1992.

Southall, Aidan W. *Alur Society.* Cambridge, U.K., 1956.

Tardits, Claude. *Le royaume bamoum.* Paris, 1980.

Tardits, Claude. "A propos du pouvoir sacré en Afrique: Que disent les testes." *Systèmes de pensée en Afrique noire* 10 (1990): 34–48.

Valeri, Valerio. "Regalità." In *Enciclopedia Einaudi*, vol. 11, pp. 742–770. Turin, Italy, 1980.

Valeri, Valerio. *Kingship and Sacrifice: Ritual and Society in Ancient Hawaii.* Chicago, 1985.

Vansina, Jan. "A Comparation of African Kingdoms." *Africa* 32, no. 4 (1962): 324–335.

Vansina, Jan. *Kingdoms of the Savanna.* Madison, Wis., 1966.

Vaughan, James H. "A Reconsideration of Divine Kingship." In *Explorations in African Systems of Thought*, edited by Ivan Karp and Charles S. Bird, pp. 120–142. Bloomington, Ind., 1980.

Volkoff, Vladimir. *Du roi.* Paris, 1987.

Young, Michael W. "The Divine Kingship of the Jukun: A Re-Evaluation of Some Theories." *Africa* 36 (1966): 135–152.

GAETANO RICCARDO (2005)
Translated from Italian by Paul Ellis

KINGSHIP: KINGSHIP IN THE ANCIENT MEDITERRANEAN WORLD

It is important to underline that the concept of "oriental despotism" deriving from the Bible is an ethnocentric concept that must be left aside. The general features of the Near Eastern kingships show a steady and strict bond with the cosmic order, just as the gods wanted it to be and to be maintained. The sovereign, therefore—far from giving way to his whims—constantly had to conform his behavior to superior heavenly principles.

A second point has to be highlighted: our knowledge of the forms of kingship in the ancient civilizations of the Mediterranean depends almost exclusively on written sources; if these are lacking, our research is forcefully limited. The oldest epigraphs appear around 3100 BCE in the town of Uruk, in lower Mesopotamia, when the phenomenon of the birth of the first cities was culminating. Unfortunately, these give no insight into the kind of government ruling the society at that time. After a short period, writing also appeared in Egypt (c. 3000 BCE). It is a common opinion that Mesopotamian influence played a major role in the birth of writing in Egypt, which is probably true, but the hieroglyphic system has distinct and different features from the Mesopotamian cuneiform. In Mesopotamia a certain number of archives and libraries throw light on its institutions, but there is a grave lack of continuity and homogeneous information. Even more sporadic are the written sources from the Syro-Palestinian area where, before the first millennium BCE, we find only the great archive of Ebla (twenty-fourth century BCE), Mari (from the same period to the eighteenth century BCE), and Ugarit and Emar (Late Bronze Age). Anatolia, as well, has provided scattered bits of information; one has the documents of the Assyrian traders of the beginning of the second millennium and, afterwards, the archives and library of Hattushash-Bogazköy up to about 1200 BCE. Recent discoveries have added minor archives, although these, too, contain material restricted to the same time span. The first millennium is not very well documented by the Hittite hieroglyphic inscriptions (from the Hittite period to the eighth century BCE) nor by the epigraphs written in the local languages and writings. Ancient Iran is almost completely undocumented (with the remarkable exception of the *Avesta*, written—*terminus ante quem*—before the fifth century BCE), in spite of the epigraphic heritage of the so-called proto-Elamic and Elamic, which are both very limited. It is unnecessary here to list all classical sources in Greek and Latin; one must mention however that for various reasons, both the Linear B for Greece and the heritage of the Etruscan and Italic epigraphs provide insufficient information. As can be seen, extremely widespread areas and long periods are completely obscure or inadequately documented by the sources. This situation greatly limits our present possibilities of knowledge.

MESOPOTAMIA. According to the present state of knowledge, the most ancient form of kingship is connected to the birth of an urban society in the Low Mesopotamia toward the end of the fourth millennium BCE. A rich stock of technical experience from the Chalcolithic era, certain favorable ecological and climatic changes, and an increase in population contributed to the birth of the first city, Uruk (perhaps an analogous yet independent process started in High Mesopotamia). This process was connoted by the creation of a bureaucratic apparatus and by the hierarchical partition of depersonalized work. However, it is not possible to obtain any direct information about the form of government of this society. Notwithstanding the privileged condition afforded by the great amount of written documents discovered, it is yet not possible—due to the characteristics of the texts themselves—to adequately answer any questions on fundamental topics related to Mesopotamian kingship.

The whole Mesopotamian civilization constantly strove to conform human society to the model offered by the divine world. In the pantheon, below the remote heaven god An was Enlil (Lord Wind), who, as the only one who could touch the unreachable sky of his father, An, played a very forceful role on earth. Enlil was the king of all gods, and they would travel to his see, his temple in Nippur, to draw from him his superior divine power. Under his rule, the demiurge god, Enki, ascribed specific tasks to every single divinity, each of whom had his see in a particular city. Enlil (named "the trader" for his mediating function) constituted the paradigm of kingship: from their various sees and tasks the gods were unified under his authority and, through him, could reach—albeit in an indirect way—the summit of the sky. In the same way, the king, being the vertex of society, acted as the point of contact between the latter and the world of the gods. Wolfgang Heimpel presented a theory (1992), based on consistent clues, about the passage from a form of a kingship, which was temporally limited and elective (by means of oracles, related to the royal title *en*), to a dynastic form, legitimized by royal birth (related to the royal title *lugal*). Sumerian literature explicitly states that kingship, besides being of divine origin because it descends from the heaven of the gods, makes possible civilization, the acme of which resided in worship (the relationship with the gods) and justice (the preservation of the order the gods wanted). Humanity, being the consignee of such an important gift, must certainly play a central role in the universe.

Various anthropogonic myths tell how humans were created from the gods in order to relieve the inferior divinities from the trouble of running the cosmos. The human task, therefore, is a task of divine level, and it was with this aim that man had been brought into being by mixing clay with the flesh and blood of a killed god. The sovereign is, therefore, he who leads society towards the realization of the divine design, which is made known to him by means of divinatory practices: according to one tradition, the primeval sovereigns were the keepers of the divinatory science (Lambert, 1967). In relation to the gods, the king is thus the vertex of humanity. The reign is therefore thought of as an ordered area (cosmos), departing from a "center"—the point where the horizontal surface of the world of men meets the vertical axis elevating to the heaven of the gods; it is this connection that defends the reign (i.e., cosmos) against the unruliness of chaos. The breaking of this axis causes the collapse of the kingdom's defenses, thereby allowing the devastating forces of chaos to rush in. As is unequivocally clear, this "center" is represented on a social level by the temple (the see of the city-god) and by the king. In this context the king is seen as the steward of the god housed in the temple. It is the god who is the veritable owner of the kingdom. Thus, the building of his temple is the culminating point of the king's activity, and the king demonstrates in this way that he has achieved the god Enki/Ea's knowledge (Matthiae, 1994) after having first established justice, enlarged the cosmos or contained chaos (all errands exalting his solar character).

Although these ideas have remained the same for more than three thousand years, it is understandable that their forms in history changed with the times. The spatial representation of the king as the center of his kingdom shifted onto a time level when large kingdoms of nomadic origin took form in Mesopotamia (the comparison with the biblical patriarchs is immediate [Hallo, 1970]). Their legitimation stemmed from the long list of their nomadic ancestry, whereas in the Sumerian world it was the town, as the see of the god and thus the point of contact between the divine and human spheres, which legitimized the king's position. The dynastic tallies listing the nomadic ancestors corresponded to the "Sumerian King List," a long text arranged as a sequence of cities. This catalog, which begins with the words "When kingship descended from heaven," lists—city by city—the kings who ruled them. It begins with the mythical kings who lived before the Flood and reigned for thousands of years each; then the list continues on until historical times. According to the organization of the list, only one city at time was dominant in Mesopotamia (which is surely historically incorrect). The end of a certain city's dominion is marked by the entry of the sum of the years of reign of its single kings and with the sentence "its (of that city) kingship was carried to . . . (name of another city)." As Claus Wilcke (1989) demonstrated, the series of the dominant cities follows a predetermined order, which is regularly repeated—a further element indicating a function unconnected with the recording of historical events. In fact, this list was probably composed during the dynasties of Ur III (2112–2004 BCE) and Isin (2017–1794 BCE), and its compilation aimed at legitimizing those dynasties.

The contact between the king and the divine took on peculiar forms, such as the Holy Wedding (*hieros gamos*) when the king, playing the god Dumuzi, married the goddess Inanna in order to attract divine benevolence down onto his reign. Another form was the divination of the king. Both forms are found in the second half of the third millennium until the second half of the second: they overlapped but were not directly connected and were extinguished during the Old Babylonian period (twentieth–sixteenth century BCE). The king was legitimized politically by his birth, but from a religious point of view, it was necessary that he have a divine rebirth (probably through a royal initiation) from which he appeared to have been generated by particular divinities (Sjöberg, 1972). It must be stressed, however, that even those sovereigns who were divinized while yet living and whose images were worshipped after their deaths were never considered to be living divinities, such as the Egyptian pharaohs, and their conduct was constantly and exclusively guided by the oracles.

In Assyria in the earliest period, before Shamshi-Adad I's reign (1812-1780 BCE), the king appeared as the executor of the citizen's assembly; he did not have the title *king,* which belonged to the city-god Ashur, but rather that of his *vicar,* a title also connected to sacerdotal functions. It was only when Assyria began an expansionistic policy that this frame was changed and became definitive—after discontinuous events, under King Tukulti-Ninurta I (second half of the thirteenth century BCE), until the end of the empire (612–610 BCE). The earliest phase of this transformation, due to Shamshi-Adad I, saw the introduction of the idea of legitimation by means of the list of ancestors, as happened in Babylonia (king Ammi-saduqa: 1646–1626 BCE). A further form of legitimating—not excluding the preceding ones—is given by the divinity's choice by means of divination. This may have been the condition that allowed Asarhaddon (680–669 BCE) to ascend the throne (Asarhaddon was the youngest son of king Sennacherib and was chosen by his father to succeed to the throne on grounds of many oracular responses; as a matter of fact it was his mother who managed to have his son chosen instead of his elder brothers, sons of other wives and concubines of the king), or that endorsed the result of a conjure, taken as an ordeal, as in the case of Nabonedo (555–539 BCE) (Nabonedo was a usurper who took power illegally, delcaring himself the legitimate successor because astrological and oneiromantic *omina* decreed he had to be the heir of the previous kings). In other very numerous occurrences the gods' choice blended royal descent with gods' will, for the dynasty itself was but a manifestation of the latter.

EGYPT. The peculiar feature of the Egyptian king, the pharaoh, consisted in his being the image of the supreme sun god of the Egyptians, Re-Atum, who wanted him as his successor in the world of the living so that he could maintain worship and justice between humans (as did his Mesopotamian counterpart). However, the Egyptians had a more complex idea of their sovereign's function than the Mesopotamians had: they saw in him one who would fulfil the concept of *maat,* thereby annihilating *isfet* at the same time. The word *maat* conveys the idea of an all-pervading cosmic order: it is the principle according to which the universe had been created. The world lost touch with this principle, and therefore no longer corresponded to its original state of order. The opposite of *maat, isfet* (defect) conveys the sense of disorder that comes into being wherever and whenever the relationship with the creator principle is lost: illness, crime, misery, war, lies—everything, in short, that makes history—are all episodes of *isfet.* The pharaoh, helped by the two cosmic forces *sia* (knowledge) and *hu* (word), can restore the primeval "wealth" that conforms to *maat.* He is, consequently, one of the three poles of a triad formed with the god and the *maat.* When he identifies himself with the latter, he becomes "one body with the god," and his will cannot but be good. From a cosmological point of view, after the divine world had been set apart from the human world, only the god of the air, Shu, the prototype of kingship, could make possible a form of communication between the worlds, while at the same time keeping the heaven of the creator Sun-god and the other gods at a distance. (It must be noted that the Sumerian king of the gods, Enlil—whose name means "Lord Wind"—played an analogous role of separation and connection.) Indeed, kingship finds its raison d'être in this detachment, for it is the king who must guarantee the continuity of the relationship with the now-distant gods. Jan Assmann (1990) points out the analogy with the Christian church, whose very existence was made necessary by the distance between man and Christ's coming. It thus becomes clear why Egypt did not leave any codices or collections of laws: every single pharaoh was the only one to determine justice, because it was he who made the realization of *maat* possible. As the opponent of *isfet,* the pharaoh was also the defender of the poor.

The pharaoh was at the center of other binary systems, even if on completely different levels. Every king, at the moment he assumed his power, thereby also renewed the unification between High and Low Egypt (the diversity of which is expressed even in their names, Shema and Mehu, which respectively referred to the gods Horus and Seth). The opposition of the two gods, which is the basis of the Egyptian kingship, is not merely geographic, but also corresponds to the opposition between order and chaos, right and violence. Horus must prevail over the wild Seth by taming him into a form of unity in a continuously repeated dynamic process. For this reason, the pharaoh wore the crowns of both High and Low Egypt; as king of High Egypt he was named *njswt,* and as king of Low Egypt, *bjt.* At the sides of his throne the images of the gods Horus and Seth held the hieroglyph meaning "to unify."

The pharaoh was thought to be destined to join the sun god after his death, when "his divine body coalesces with its sire." In each kingly succession, indeed, there was a reenactment of the mythical struggle between the god Osiris (son of Geb, the earth god, and Nut, the sky goddess)—the first king and Nile god, god of cereals, and lord of the dead—and his brother and murderer, Seth, followed by the revenge taken on Seth by Osiris's son and successor, the young god Horus. Even until much later times, the destructiveness of Seth was a fundamental power in the creation of the universe, because only by its working alongside order was the birth of the cosmos possible. In the end, as the direct heir of Osiris, and therefore of Geb, Shu, and Ra, Horus himself assurged to the undivided power. So, in Egyptian religious thought, Horus was the living pharaoh, and Osiris was his dead predecessor.

Kings, "souls," and ancestors. The superiority of the monarchs was expressed not only by their connection or identification with deities: the king was also superior to his subjects because his *ka* (vital force, a spiritual twin that lives on after the death of the physical body) was different from that of commoners. The pharaoh's *ka* was shown on monuments in the shape of the monarch's identical twin; as the king's protector in death, it announced the arrival of the dead monarch to the gods in heaven, and it was identified (Frankfort, 1948) with the placenta enwrapping the newborn king.

One of the standards that accompanied the king during festivals and processions probably represented the royal placenta, and may have been the image of the king's *ka.*

Other standards accompanying the king represented his ancestral spirits (in Egyptian, *ba*), whose functions were to give life to the pharaoh, thus protecting the land, and, after his death, to prepare his ascent to the heavens. The standards thus played an important part in kingly rituals. The fact that they were classified in two subgroups, the souls of Pe and the souls of Nekhen, may point to an early artificial combination of two series of kingly ancestors, from southern and northern Egypt, respectively. Pe was an ancient town of the Delta, and Nekhen was one of the South. In a certain way both towns represent the two original distinct political units of the period before the unification.

Kingly rituals. The main rituals of the Egyptian state were kingly rituals sanctioning the various aspects of the royal succession, a delicate mechanism that ensured the continuity of the social order. The death of the old king was followed by a period during which the new pharaoh assumed power, visited sanctuaries throughout Egypt, and issued his protocols, while his father's body and funerary temple were prepared for the burial rites. During this period, the *kas* rested.

On the day of the royal funerary ritual, a series of litanies, spells, and incantations were probably recited, insisting on the identification of the dead pharaoh with Osiris (and of the pharoah's son with Horus), and on the dead monarch's glorious survival in heaven, where he was embraced by the god Atum or received by the souls of Pe and Nekhen. The king was buried as an embalmed mummy in his funerary abode, and was symbolically located in the regions where his life continued (the netherworld, the west, and the north near the circumpolar stars). While the dead king ruled as Osiris among the dead, his son ruled on earth, in perfect continuity.

The day after the celebration of the dead king's heavenly survival, the coronation of the new pharaoh took place. It was usually made to coincide with the New Year's Day or with some other important beginning in nature's cycle. The ritual involved cultic practices in the dual shrines of the royal ancestral spirits of Pe and Nekhen, and it culminated in the placing of the two crowns of Upper and Lower Egypt on the pharaoh's head. A further important kingly ritual was the *Sed* festival, which took place once or several times during a pharaoh's reign. This renewal of the kingly power was held on the anniversary of the pharoah's coronation. It included a procession; the offering of gifts to the gods; pledges of loyalty by the king; visits to shrines; the dedication of a field to the gods by the pharaoh, who twice ran across it in the four directions of the compass, first as king of Upper, then Lower Egypt; and the shooting of arrows by the king in these four directions, symbolically winning him control of the whole universe.

SYRIA AND PALESTINE, INCLUDING ISRAEL. In spite of the great efforts of specialized scholars (including Giovanni Pettinato and Pelio Fronzaroli), it is still impossible to outline a reliable picture of kingship in Ebla (about 70 kilometers south of Aleppo; mid-third millennium BCE). Through the nomenclature it is evident that the Eblaite queen had a particular role, but the mechanism of the institution is far from clear. In Mari (medium Euphrates; early second millennium BCE), the two concepts of the holiness of the king and of the king's role in assuring justice became intermingled and formed one inseparable idea. (This passed—through the mediation of the Bible—into the Christian concept of kingship.) The king was anointed (a habit alien to Mesopotamia, yet documented in Ebla, where it was not restricted to sovereigns alone), and by means of this rite, his state was changed and he consequently acquired major authority. The practice of anointing was directly related to the main function of the king, namely that of "king of justice," "the good shepherd" who protects the weak. This idea of justice, therefore, went beyond the boundaries of the law and centered on the king's personal subjective beliefs, which determined the king's interference and were completely unrelated to the kind of justice that the judges were expected to apply. According to the law, the weak might be in the wrong, but the sovereign would protect them. Another peculiar feature that is also found in the Bible was the use of the donkey as the proper mount for the legitimate king. In contrast to the horse, which was used in war and thus conveyed an idea of violence, the donkey became the symbol of the triumphant peace, which the king was seen to have realized through his submission to the gods (Lafont, 1998, pp. 161–166).

In the Ugaritic texts (late second millennium BCE), however, we find an important trait of kingship ideology in Bronze Age Syria: the cult of the dead kings, which apparently began at the time of the Amorite dynasties. In Ugarit the royal ancestors, the most ancient of which were probably mythical, called *rapium* ("healers, saviors"; compare with the biblical *refa'im*), were worshipped with offerings and periodic rites.

In the first millennium BCE, traces of both the Phoenician and Aramean kingship ideology are attested to by alphabetic inscriptions. The godlike qualities of monarchs were sometimes indicated, but the main aspects of kingship were the ruler's upholding of justice and peace and his role as a servant of the gods. They repaid him by giving peace and abundance to his kingdom. One Aramaic inscription, however, seems to present the king as enjoying a special existence ("drinking" with the storm god) after his death.

The Israelite monarchy in the Bible was not devoid of such "sacral" traits, and specific ritual aspects such as royal anointing and royal burial rites are described in the biblical texts with some precision. Yet, the Bible presents the kings as mere servants of the heavenly king and sole true god, Yahweh, and it denies them any superhuman powers or destiny. Moreover, kingship is presented as a foreign institution adopted by the Israelites, and most Israelite kings are depicted as unfaithful to the national deity, whereas the prophets of Yahweh play an important role in condemning monarchs on behalf of their god, and sometimes in anointing new and more pious kings to replace them. In the exilic and postexilic texts, many aspects of the Near Eastern kingship ideology (but not the divine nature of monarchs) seem to have converged in the eschatological expectations of the Israelites, who had no kings of their own, but awaited the return of a descendant of the Davidic dynasty. In this sense, the roots of Jewish and Christian messianism must be sought in the kingship ideology of the ancient Near East.

HITTITE KINGSHIP. By far the most important form of writing used in Anatolia was the cuneiform script imported from Mesopotamia (naturally, also ideograms and standard forms of handwriting were used). Thus, even if one knows that the Hittite word for king is *hashshu-* (this term, though infrequent, is written in the cuneiform Hittite texts), one does not know for certain whether the Sumerian and Akkadian terms (respectively *lugal* and *sharru,* both used as ideograms, even if written in cuneiform) for the title of sovereign corresponded exactly to the local usage. This problem was already evident at the time of the paleo-Assyrian colonies (beginning of the second millennium BCE). In texts, the Hittite sovereigns used the ideogram *LUGAL* ("king" in Sumerian) not only for themselves but also for the sovereigns for neighboring states. In Late Bronze Age politics the title *LUGAL.GAL* (Sumerian for "great king") was used to refer to the sovereigns of Egypt and Babylonia as well as to the Hittite king himself, to distinguish them from sovereigns of politically less important states. In this period the Hittite king was referred to with the epithet "my sun" (*shamshi* in Akkadian script), which was perhaps of Egyptian derivation or an elaboration of Mesopotamian elements. The characteristic title, however, was *tabarna,* derived from the name of the first great Hittite king, Labarna (a process analogous to Latin "Cæsar," *t* and *l* refer to intermediate sounds); the feminine form, *tawananna,* referred to the king mother, to whom special cultural functions were given. The significance given to divine support was a characteristic of the Hittite monarchy, which was taken to extremes by Hattushili III (1275–1260 BCE) to legitimate his coup d'état. Numerous have been found that bear oracles for the interpretation of divine will and thus provide clues to the reasons that determined unfavorable political events. After the king's death a complex ritual based on the cremation of his body took place, and food was ritually offered to the dead monarch. When the texts refer to a king's death, they speak of his "becoming a god." These elements cannot, however, be taken to indicate the divinization of the sovereign during his lifetime, although this did happen—to an extent—later, from the middle of the thirteenth century BCE onwards, in the major celebration of monarchy from Hattushili III until the fall of the empire.

IRAN. From the nomadic life in a semidesertic land, the tribes of the Persians and the Medes became—in a relatively short period of time—the conquerors of great kingdoms, the capitals of which were fully developed cities. This rather sudden change bore important consequences. In order to control their new acquisitions, the Achaemenid kings incorporated the royal ideology of the defeated people into their own one. In the extension of their wide empire, therefore, the Achaemenids everywhere impersonated the legitimate successors of the former dynasties, but it was the conquest of Babylon (539 BCE) that determined this political choice. The basic concepts of the Achaemenid kingship are traced back to the ideology of the Assyrian-Babylonian monarchy rather than to the Indo-European political institutions, as Gnoli demonstrated. This borrowing however, was tempered by the peculiar feature of the Zoroastrian thought that patently differentiated it from the other religious worlds of the ancient Near East—the dualistic opposition between Ohrmazd-Ahuramazda and Ahreman. This opposition mirrored a deeper cosmological level than the idea of contrast between chaos and order in Mesopotamian thought. The expected conclusive victory of Ohrmazd, with the final annihilation of Ahreman, is a unique component in all the Ancient Near East. The forms of kingship, from that of the Achaemenids to that of the Sasanians, are all determined by this fundamental idea of rigid dualism, which Pettazzoni (1920) drew nearer to monotheistic than to polytheistic religions—this is not a paradox. It was then inconceivable that a sovereign appears as a god. The Greeks, for their convenience, translated with the same term, *theos,* both the Iranian words *bay* and *yazad,* but only the former (which also means "[divine] distributor") actually referred to the king; the latter term was limited to the divinities only. *Bay* was a king's title because of his role in the first line against the forces of evil, not because of his divinization. The king, indeed, played a key role in creation, in which the battle between Ohrmazd and Ahreman is fought. For this reason an initiatory rite, perhaps based on the mystical union with the deceased ancestors, became necessary in the enthroning process during the Achaemenid period, and some buildings in Pasargade and Naqsh-i Rustam may have been mainly destined for that function. In the Sasanian period, on the other hand, the king assumed those astral traits, which made him a "cosmocrator." Indeed, like the stars, the king was endowed with *xwarrah* (roughly translated as "brightness, glory," also to vital energy), and because his "form" is an image of the gods, this makes his *xwarrah* similar to theirs as well. In any case, alive or dead, the Iranian king never became a god, even if while living he assumed some distinctive traits which were to make him different from all other men, and notwithstanding the fact that he was a living image of the gods (although he never identified himself with them). He was allowed to enjoy "rightness" in the netherworld for his right behavior while living, as could any other person who had done the same.

GREECE AND HELLENISM. Four very different forms of kingship succeeded in ancient Greece: the Mycenaean, the Homeric, the archaic and the classical, and the Hellenistic. Little is known about kingship in Crete in Minoan times (c. 2500–c. 1500 BCE), and in Greece and Crete in Mycenaean times (c. 1600–c. 1100 BCE), because the relevant texts have either not yet been translated (the Minoan Linear A inscriptions) or are concerned mainly with problems of administration (the Mycenaean Linear B texts, in a language that is an ancestor of ancient Greek). Archaeology and the study of the Egyptian texts (where the Cretans were named *Keftiu*) provide evidence of the regular relationship—which was not limited to trade—that flourished from the third millennium BCE between the Aegean civilizations and Egypt and Syria (city of Biblos).

Minoan and Mycenaean kingship. These relations had an incisive influence on the Aegean world as well as on the institution of the Mycenaean kingship, about which limited information exists. As for the Minoan kingship, it could be of some interest that the sovereigns were embalmed with the oil of Syrian firs. The lack of royal tombs in Crete before the Santorini eruption (c. 1530 BCE) and the uncertain destination of the "palaces" (perhaps only cultic places) demonstrate against a possible divine or divinely inspired kingship (on which, see Marinatos, 1995), which was introduced only later, after that disaster (Driessen, 2003).

The Mycenaean kingship covered both political and religious spheres. The king *(wanax)* was an overlord who ruled over the local kings (whose title was the archaic form of *basiléus*). His kingdom never reached an extent comparable to that of the Near Eastern empires, even if it was formed on their model. Besides civil functions, the administrative records in Linear B show that the king had at least partial control of the cultic organization. It is unclear whether this twofold role is related to the Indo-European heritage (see Dumézil, 1977). The term *wanax* disappeared with the fall of the Mycenaean civilization. When indeed this state system collapsed around 1100 BCE, many other aspects of that cultural tradition, including writing, were lost.

Homeric kingship. Kingship, as it was represented in the Homeric world, seems to have kept few traits of continuity with what is known of the Mycenaean civilization. It has to be stressed that since the depiction of the social and political institutions is always coherent in both the Homeric poems (the *Iliad* and the *Odyssey*), it is evident that in the age of their composition, the eighth century BCE, these institutions still existed. The poet described them in a slightly more archaic way as they actually were (Carlier, 1996, p. 294). The king is named *basileus*—an approximate translation of the Greek term, which must be understood as "king of a community," not of a state; the word is also employed to indicate the chief of an aristocratic *oikos* ("household, manor"). The royal power seemed to have been related to the power of a clan, and the king himself rather resembled a *pater familias.* The mechanisms of the succession are obscure, but a conflict between the aristocracy and the royal family, willing to affirm the dynastic principle, is evident. The king therefore appears to have been a *primus inter pares*; a vague hint of the *wanax* is kept in Agamemnon's attribute "*anax andron.*" Carlier compares *wanax* to Imperial Latin *dominus,* "lord" (1996, p. 268).

Kingship is an expression of strength. M. I. Finley (1956) mentions the term *iphi* ("with strength") in theorizing why Odysseus's father, Laertes, was not the king in the twenty-year absence of his son because, being an aged person, he was not strong enough to assure his rule, and his family, in which the young Telemachus was the only man, could not guarantee it. It is also not clear why marriage to Penelope would have legitimated the new king, chosen among her suitors (in the same way, the usurper Aegistus, in Argos, married Agamemnon's wife). Power is personal, and supported by the family. Central to this system was the *oikos,* an almost self-sufficient productive unit where relatives assembled, *hetairoi* ("comrades") rallied to war campaigns, and different classes of servants and helpers set to everyday tasks. The king summoned an assembly of the citizens, but it was merely a consultative organ, and decision making was held firmly in the king's own hands. The social pattern of the organization of power may be defined thus: the assembly listens, the elders propose, the king disposes. In particular circumstances such as warfare and journeys, the king might celebrate sacrifices to the gods, as had the Mycenaean *wanax.* The king was always at the head of his army, which he personally led in war, and the aristocracy would lend him their men as warriors (all the heroes of the Homeric poems are aristocrats, if not kings). In conclusion, it may be safely stated that the Homeric king enjoyed *geras* ("privilege" and "honor," which is also expressed by *time*) that made him owner of the *temenos,* a plot of particularly fertile land (also, shrines of the gods); as a leader, he had to show both *metis* ("prudence") and valor. In every circumstance, he had to demonstrate that he deserved his *time.*

Kingship in the *poleis* and Spartan diarchy. After many centuries, a profound social transformation led to the birth of a new organization, the typically Greek *polis,* or city-state. Although kingdoms survived in the periphery of the new Greek world, the *polis* was a structure that had no place for monarchies of the type discussed above, although some kingly functions were inherited by magistrates, and there is even evidence of restricted forms of kingship (e.g., the Spartan diarchy). The diarchy was more a concurrent lifetime leadership of two *strategoi* ("strategists," a sort of magistrates) than a true form of kingship, notwithstanding its hereditary characteristic. It was this feature that qualified the two kings of Sparta with respect to their magical and religious functions, based on the reference of the divine couple of twins, the Dioscuri (Carlier, 1984, pp. 296–301). The system was very stable, and it lasted for about five centuries.

The same religious concerns are to be found in the Athenian monarchy. Both the king (*basileus*) and, when monarchy disappeared, the magistrate (also called *basileus*) were active characters in the rites of the city cults, which included the hierogamic ceremony symbolizing the union of the city (represented by the queen) with the god Dionysos.

The monarchical tendencies of some rulers *(tu-rannoi)* of cities in the seventh to fourth centuries BCE were exceptional and short-lived, though they arose again and again, especially in the colonial worlds of Sicily and Asia Minor. It was only when the polis system declined and the peripheral Macedonian dynasty gained control over Greece and later conquered the Iranian Empire that the Greek-speaking world had to come to terms with the power of the Macedonian kings *(basileis),* while most cities maintained, at least formally, their traditional regimes.

After the death of Alexander the Great of Macedonia (323 BCE), his empire was divided among his successors. The Near East of the Hellenistic age became a series of monarchies headed by kings of Macedonian descent. These kingdoms were ruled, and profoundly influenced culturally, by an elite of Greek soldiers and administrators. Hellenistic kingship ideology, like Hellenistic culture in general, was a combination of Greek (Macedonian) and traditional Near Eastern traits. Kings were believed to be descendants of divine ancestors (through Alexander), godlike—in some cases, divine—in life, and surviving as gods after their death. The court etiquette and the rituals of kingship, so far as can be ascertained, were derived mainly from the Iranian, Egyptian, and other Near Eastern traditions.

ETRUSCANS. In modern times some progress in the research on the mechanism on the Etruscan kingship was achieved by integrating the scarce data from the written Etruscan sources (because of their celebrative character, most of the funerary epigraphs are of little relevance in this kind of inquiry) with the comparison of the data related to the earliest Roman history and of the archaeological documentation. Apart from the Greek metropolises of the south (*Magna Gaecia*) of a clearly foreign tradition, the development of urban civilization in Italy can be ascribed to the Etruscans. Etruscan urbanization grew through subsequent phases, each of which produced its relative form of government. In the first phase villages merged, under the stimulus of their aristocracies, into a single unit of superior order, thus beginning the growth of metropolises (from the ninth to the sixth centuries BCE). The city was ruled by a king (*lucumo*) whose institutional features are unfortunately obscure. A lictor preceding him, his gold crown, his ivory throne, his sceptre surmounted by an eagle, and his purple toga and mantle were all signs of his rank. The ceremony of the triumph, in which the king personified a deity, together with the *ludi* and other insignias of regal power, was probably introduced in Rome by the Etruscan dynasty of the Tarquini.

The assembly of the twelve *lucumones* of the Etruscan dodecapolis was held near the *Fanum Voltumnae* (the temple of the protector god, or genius, of Etruria—*deus Etruriae princeps*), most probably located near present-day Orvieto. There a magistrate was elected whose functions were superior to the particularism of the single *polis* and who was, therefore, preceded by twelve lictors as a sign of his position. The subsequent progression of the mercantile middle class led to seigniories similar to Greek "tyrannies." Toward the end of the sixth century and during all of the fifth century BCE, republican oligarchies took control; besides an *ordo principum* (probably analogous to the Roman senate), one or more likely more *zilath / zilach* (*praetor*) were ruling. The dodecapolis league was active in the republican period as well, and elected the *zilath mechl rasnal* (i.e., the *praetor Etruriae).*

ROME. The mythology regarding the foundation of Rome gives expression to different phases of the beginnings of the city and of its primitive kingship. Romulus, who founded the city of Rome on the Palatine hill and whose name the city therefore bears, was a foreign king—an Alban from a region about 40 kilometers to the south. The phrase *populus Romanus Quiritesque* (the Roman people and the Quirites) thus indicates the superimposition of Rome on the inhabitants of the proto-urban settlements of the other nearby hills, specifically the Quirites, who had the system of the curiae (the curia was a division of the three original Romulean tribes, Ramnes, Tites and Luceres, and was the basic element of the assembly, *comitia curiata*), which Romulus's reign centralized into a unique political formation. On the one hand, the murder and dismemberment of Romulus by the senators, each of whom carried home limbs of his body, represents the transformation of Romulus into Quirinus, the god of the Quirites, but on the other hand, it also expresses the return of the power to the *curiae,* who will choose the new king. This system was in use up until the reign of Tarquinius Priscus (Carandini, 2002, pp. 197–207). With this latest king the Etruscan influence became very incisive, and it continued to be decisive until the fall of the monarchy. The forms of cult changed dramatically; amongst other innovations, the *triumphus,* originally a theophany in which the god Jupiter appears to guarantee an incipient welfare, was introduced. Though often changed in its constitutive traits, celebration of the *triumphus* was to last in the Roman tradition (Versnel, 1970).

From the sixth century BCE, Rome was a republic headed by an aristocracy of *senatores* and governed by elected magistrates. Indeed, the antimonarchic ideology of ancient Rome was such that when—after the Roman conquest of most of the Mediterranean world—the crisis of the republican state led to the rise of a new form of monarchy, the rulers did not take on the traditional title of Indo-European origin, *rex* (king), but were called *imperator,* a word denoting the triumphing war leader of republican times. The Roman Empire lasted from the first century BCE to the late fifth century CE, and the ideology of rulership changed profoundly during its history. Its original traits included the cult of the emperor's *genius* (personality, double) and the deification of the dead emperor through a complex ritual involving cremation and the flight of his spirit to the heavens in the form of an eagle flying from the funeral pyre. But these soon gave way—first in the eastern provinces and then in the entire imperial territory—to other forms of ruler worship, such as the identification of the emperor with mythical figures or gods, which were often directly imported by monarchs from the local cultures of their provincial homelands.

The emperor Constantine's conversion to Christianity in the late fourth century was the starting point of a further profound transformation in the imperial ideology. Obviously, the new Christian rulers could not be considered divine, yet many aspects of the system of beliefs, rituals, and etiquette typical of the imperial monarchy were adapted to the new religious context. According to the *Triakontaeterikos,* a treatise on imperial power by the Christian writer Eusebius of Caesarea (fourth century), the whole cosmos is a monarchic state *(basileia, monarchia)* ruled by the Christian God, and it is the emperor's task to imitate the divine monarch. The final result of the process of ideological transformation that began with Constantine was the ideology of the Christian ruler. This was the basis of Byzantine kingship ideology, and it later joined with other (mainly Celtic and Germanic) traditions to form medieval theories of kingship.

SEE ALSO Dumuzi; Twins; Utu.

BIBLIOGRAPHY

The bibliography on this subject is huge, and it is not always easy to select from it without omitting important contributions. On the sacral kingship of the ancient Near East, one should see the following.

General Studies

Gadd, Cyrill J. *Ideas of Divine Rule in the Ancient Near East.* Oxford, 1948.

Frankfort, Henri. *Kingship and the Gods: A Study of Ancient Near Eastern Religion as the Integration of Society and Nature.* 1948; reprint, Chicago, 1978.

Mesopotamia

Finkelstein, Jacob J. "The Antidiluvian Kings: A University of California Tablet." *Journal of Cuneiform Studies* 17 (1963): 39–51.

Hallo, William W. "Antediluvian Cities." *Journal of Cuneiform Studies* 23 (1970): 57–67.

Heimpel, Wolfgang. "Herrentum und Königtum im vor- und frühgeschichtlichen Alten Orient." *Zeitschrift für Assyriologie* 82 (1992): 4–21.

Labat, René. *Le caractère religieux de la royauté assyro-babylonienne.* Paris, 1939.

Lambert, W. G. "Enmeduranki and Related Matters." *Journal of Cuneiform Studies* 21 (1967): 126–138.

Lambert, Wilfred G. "The Seed of Kingship." In *Le palais et la royauté, Comtes rendues de la Réncontre d'Assyriologie Internationale 19 (1971),* pp. 427–440. Paris, 1974.

Matthiae, P. *Il sovrano e l'opera.* Rome and Bari, Italy, 1994.

Michalowski, Piotr. "History as Charter—Some Observations on the Sumerian King List." *Journal of the American Oriental Society* 103 (1983): 237–224.

Seux, J.-M. "Königtum." In *Reallexicon der Assyriologie,* vol. 6, edited by Otto Dietrich Edzard, pp. 140–173. Berlin and New York, 1983.

Sjöberg, Ake. "Die göttliche Abstammung der sumerisch-babylonischen Herrscher." *Orientalia Suecana* 21 (1972): 87–112.

Wilcke, Claus. "Genealogical and Geographical Thought in the Sumerian King List." In *DUMU E2-DUB-BA: Studies in Honor of Å Sjöberg,* edited by E. Leichty, et al., pp. 557–569. Philadelphia, 1989.

Egypt

Assmann, Jan. *Maat: Gerechtigkeit und Unsterblickeit im alten Ägypten.* Munich, 1990.

Assmann, Jan. *Herrschaft und Heil. Politische Theologie in Altägypten, Israel, und Europa.* Munich and Vienna, 2000.

Frankfort, Henri. *Ancient Egyptian Religion.* New York, 1948.

Syria-Palestine

Coppens, Joseph. *Le messianisme royal.* Paris, 1968.

De Fraine, Jean. *L'aspect religieux de la royauté israélite.* Rome, 1954.

Fronzaroli, Pelio. *Archivi reali di Ebla. Testi –X I. Testi rituali della regalità (Archivio L. 2769).* Rome, 1993.

Lafont, S. "Le roi, le juge, et l'étranger à Mari et dans la Bible." *Revue d'Assyriologie et d'Archéologie Orientale* 92 (1998): 161–181.

Pettinato, Giovanni. *Il rituale per la successione al trono ad Ebla.* Rome, 1992.

Widengren, Geo. *Sakrales Königtum im Alten Testament und im Judentum.* Stuttgart, Germany, 1955.

Iran

Gnoli, Gherardo. "Politica religiosa e concezione della regalità sotto gli Achemenidi." In *Gururajamañjarika. Studi in onore di G. Tucci,* pp. 23–88. Naples, Italy, 1974.

Gnoli, Gherardo. "L'Iran tardoantico e la regalità sassanide." *Mediterraneo Antico. Economie società culture* 1, no. 1 (1998): 115–139.

Panaino, Antonio. "The Bagan of the Fratrakas: Gods or 'Divine' Kings?" In *Religiuos Themes and Texts of Pre-Islamic Iran and Cantral Asia. Studies in Honour of Prof. G. Gnoli on the Occasion of His 65th Birthday on 6th December 2002,* edited by C. G. Cereti, M. Maggi, and E. Provasi, pp. 265–288. Wiesbaden, Germany, 2003.

Panaino, Antonio. "Astral Characters of Kingship in the Sasanian and Byzantine Worlds." In *Atti del Convegno internazionale "La Persia e Bisanzio,"* edited by Antonio Carile et al., pp. 555–594. Rome, 2004.

Hittite

Giorgieri, M., and C. Mora. *Aspetti della regalità ittita nel XIII secolo a. C.* Como, Italy, 1996.

Pettazzoni, Raffaele. *La religione di Zarathustra nella storia religiosa dell'Iran.* Bologna, Italy, 1920.

Szabó, G. "Herrscher -§ 7.1." In *Reallexicon der Assyriologie IV,* edited by Dietrich Otto Edzard, pp. 342–345. Berlin and New York, 1975.

Van den Hout, Theo P. J. *Tudhalija Kosmokrator. Gedachten over ikonografie en ideologie van een hettitische koning.* Amsterdam, 1993.

Greece

Carlier, Pierre. *La royauté en Grèce avant Alexandre.* Strasbourg, France, 1984.

Carlier, Pierre. "La regalità: beni d'uso e beni di prestigio." In *I Greci,* vol. 2, edited by S. Settis, pp. 255–294. Torino, Italy, 1996.

Driessen, Jan. "The Court Compounds of Minoan Crete: Royal Palaces or Ceremonial Centers?" *Athena Review* 3, no.3 (2003): 57–61.

Dumézil, George. *Les dieux souverains des Indo-Européens.* Paris, 1977.

Finley, M. I. *The World of Odysseus.* London, 1956.

Marinatos, Nanno. "Divine Kingship in Minoan Crete." In *The Role of the Ruler in the Prehistoric Aegean,* Aegaeum 11, edited by P. Rehak, pp. 37–48. Liège, Belgium, 1995.

Schubart, Wilhelm. *Die religiöse Haltung des frühen Hellenismus.* Leipzig, Germany, 1937.

West, Martin L. *The East Face of Helicon.* Oxford, 1997.

Etruscans

Cristofani, Mauro. "Società e istituzioni nell'Italia preromana." In *Popoli e civiltà dell'Italia antica,* vol. 7, edited by Massimo Pallottino, pp. 51–112. Rome, 1978.

Staccioli, Romolo. *Gli Etruschi, un popolo tra mito e realtà.* Rome, 1980.

Torelli, Mario. *Storia degli Etruschi.* Rome and Bari, Italy, 1985.

Rome

Bickermann, Elias. J., et al., eds. *Le culte des souverains dans l'Empire romain.* Entretiens sur l'antiquité classique, vol. 19. Geneva, Switzerland, 1973.

Carandini, Andres. *Archeologia del mito.* Torino, Italy, 2002.

Cornell, T. J. *The Beginnings of Rome.* London and New York, 1995.

Versnel, H. S. *Triumphus—An Inquiry into the Origin, Development, and Meaning of the Roman Triumph.* Leiden, Netherlands, 1970.

CRISTIANO GROTTANELLI (1987)
PIETRO MANDER (2005)

KINGSHIP: KINGSHIP IN SUB-SAHARAN AFRICA

Kingship is always ritualized to some extent. Since the beginning of the twentieth century scholars have sought unsuccessfully to define a particular type of cultic complex in Africa as "divine kingship." Many now prefer the looser term "sacred kingship." Two opposed arguments dominate this and other anthropological discussions of ritual. One, derived from the work of the English anthropologist James G. Frazer (1854–1941), dwells on a purportedly distinct set of ideas in which the personal, physical health of the king is responsible for the generosity of nature and the well-being of his people. The other, derived from the great French sociologist Émile Durkheim (1858–1917), treats such ideas as expressions of sociopolitical realities rather than as primary factors. The sociological view predominated in the 1940s, but in the 1960s anthropologists renewed their interest in Frazer's thesis.

Although many of Frazer's data were drawn from Africa, he thought of divine kingship as characteristic of a particular phase of cultural evolution, not of a particular continent, and he also drew upon European and Middle Eastern ethnography, to which his model may have been more appropriate. Frazer supposed that primitive societies preoccupied with agricultural problems put their faith in a king whose vitality magically ensured the abundance of the harvest and whose death at the hands of a stronger challenger corresponded efficaciously to the seedtime planting of the next crop. Early ethnographic reports concerning the Shilluk people of the Sudan seemed to provide a contemporary example of such ritual regicide.

Dwelling on the association between the king's health and natural fertility, Frazer explained the kingship but not the kingdom. In the first modern treatment of the subject, in 1948, E. E. Evans-Pritchard, relying on better ethnography and a wholly different theory, asserted that the spiritual role of the king expressed the political contradiction between the corporate unity of the Shilluk people and the lack of any central authority capable of subordinating factional interests. In the absence of real control, the king's identity with the moral values of the nation could only be expressed in spiritual terms. Evans-Pritchard found no hard evidence of ritual regicide and suggested that the tradition merely reflected the fact that many kings came to a violent end at the hands of princely challengers.

Meyer Fortes modified this sociological thesis, arguing that all offices were social realities distinct from the individuals who held them. The function of ritual was to make such offices visible and to effect the induction of the individual into his office; as it is said in some parts of Africa, in rituals of investiture the kingship "seizes" the king. Rituals were not simply passive or even imaginary reflexes of the social order but instruments that maintained it and convinced the participants of the reality of royal powers; after the ritual process, the king himself felt changed in his person and took credit for ensuing events (a fall of rain, mysterious deaths) that seemed to confirm the efficacy of the ritual. In this respect, however, kingship did not differ from other social roles such as that of a diviner or an adept in a healing cult.

Another kind of sociological explanation, the reverse of the first, was advanced by Max Gluckman with respect to the Swazi people (Swaziland). Gluckman suggested that the great Ncwala ceremonies provided the people with an annual opportunity to express their resentment of the king's rule and thus stabilized the political system. This "rituals of rebellion" thesis, though widely cited, seems to be based on a misreading of the hymns sung at the Ncwala; on this, more below.

Explanations of rituals in terms of their political functions fail to account for the elaborate content of the rituals, which often involve hundreds of titleholders, experts, courtiers, and lineage heads in rich textures of song, dance, eulogy, costume, taboo, and medication extending over many days and weeks of the year. Rereading the Swazi ethnography, T. O. Beidelman argued that the purpose of the Ncwala was to set the king apart so that he might take on the supernatural powers necessary to his office. He showed how such details as the black color of a sacrificial ox, the king's nudity during the ritual, and the emptiness of his right hand while he danced are consistent with Swazi cosmology and symbolic usage. The color of the ox refers to the powerful but disorderly forces of sexuality that the king must incorporate and master; the king's nudity expresses his liminal status as the "bull of his nation," mediating between the supernatural and the living.

Other writers pointed out that many kings, such as the *ọba* of Benin (Nigeria) or the *mwami* of Bunyoro (Uganda), were powerful rulers whose spiritual powers seemed to express their real authority rather than compensate for the lack of it. In other instances, the rituals of kingship and respect for the king's supernatural powers remained constant despite pronounced, long-term changes in his real political importance. The same ritual complex might or might not be associated with a hierarchical organization of important functions, so that among the Kongo people, legends and rituals alone fail to make it clear whether the chief to whom they refer is a ruler of thousands or of dozens. Among the Nyakyusa (Tanzania) the divine king remained essentially a priest, whereas among the neighboring Ngonde, who share the same culture and traditions of origin, the king acquired real powers through his control of the trade in ivory and other goods. In Bunyoro, princes fought to succeed to the throne, whereas among the Rukuba (Nigeria) and Nyakyusa the chosen successor must be captured by the officiating priests lest he abscond.

These and other commentaries tended to place Frazer's thesis in doubt. The components of what Frazer thought was a single complex are now seen to vary independently of each other. Also, it has proved impossible to verify any tradition of regicide, although both the tradition and, apparently, the practice of not allowing kings to die a natural death are also associated with some ritual figures who are not kings. Other observances once thought to be specific to divine kings, such as prescribed incest and taboos against seeing the king eat or drink, are present in some instances but not in others. Chiefs among the Dime (Ethiopia) are regarded as having a spiritual power called *balth'u* that seems to meet Frazerian expectations since, if the power is "good," it is believed to make the crops grow and livestock multiply, whereas if the harvest is poor the people say, "We must get rid of him; the thoughts he has for the country don't work." A Dime chief is not required to be in good health, however, and eventually dies a natural death.

Africans themselves often speak of the powers vested in kings as independent entities with organic properties. The spiritual power known as *bwami* among the Lega, for example, is thought to grow and forever renew itself, like a banana tree; this *bwami* may be vested in a king *(mwami)* (as among the eastern Lega) or in a graded association (as among the western Lega). From this point of view the purpose of ritual is to favor the growth of kingship as a public resource. Whether or not the king rules as well as reigns, his person is one of the instruments of the process necessary to maintain the kingship. Relics of dead kings are often part of the regalia of their successors or are used to make medicines conferring royal powers. The jawbone of a *kabaka* of Buganda (Uganda) was enshrined after his death; in Yorubaland, an *ọba* of Ọyọ (Nigeria) consumed the powdered heart of his predecessor. More generally, the body of a living king is itself a sacred object, modified and manipulated for ritual purposes; among these manipulations, the observances that set him apart from ordinary people often bear more onerously upon him than upon anyone else.

This African perspective is consistent with the sociological one of Fortes, and it is here, perhaps, that we may discover the secret of regicide. Kingship, itself a perpetual office, stands for the corporate unity and perpetuity of the kingdom. Time is therefore intrinsic to the idea of kingship. Time, in turn, has two components: transience and constant renewal. The continuity of the body politic, and of human life within it, may be symbolized by the agricultural cycle or other natural phenomena, by communal rites of passage and succession, or by similar rites in which the king's own life, death, and replacement are made to embody the life process of the community. In such instances, agricultural cycles, initiation cycles, and the succession of kings are not merely metaphors for the continuity and vitality of the social order but substantial constituents of it.

It is not surprising, therefore, among widely separated peoples, including the Lovedu (South Africa), the Nyakyusa, the Rukuba, and the Mundang (Chad), that the death of a ruler or of a surrogate is supposed to coincide with a phase in the cycle of initiations whereby the succession of generations is regulated, although in all these examples the real timing of the events is obscure. The Rukuba king is required to ingest, at his installation, material from the bodies both of his deceased predecessor and of an infant, specially killed for the purpose, whose status is such that he might have been chosen to be king had he lived; these and other Rukuba rituals, which clearly express the theme of renewal and continuity, are believed to cause a long and therefore successful reign. The king himself is not burdened with many taboos; he may be deposed if his "blood" is not strong enough to keep misfortunes from afflicting his people, but he is not himself killed.

During the 1970s anthropologists expressed increasing interest in the subjective perspective in kingship cults, in the content of ritual and its capacity to shape the cognitive experience of participants. The reductionist view that ritual merely expresses political realities seemed inconsistent with the quasi-organic character attributed to kingly powers and with the intense secrecy that in many cases surrounds complex and central cultic performances.

This revival of Frazer's intellectualism did not extend, however, to his evolutionary assumptions about primitive thought, and it emphasized the particularity of symbols whose meanings should be sought in their local context. For example, the skull of a dead Temne chief (Sierra Leone) is kept in a shrine at which daily sacrifices are performed for communal well-being, but that of a Mundang king serves only as a magical device to force his successor to commit the expected suicide. The hair and nails of a deceased *mwami* of Bunyoro are cut after his death, to be buried with him, whereas those of a *lwembe* of the Nyakyusa must be taken before he has drawn his last breath, "so that Lwembe might not go away with the food to the land of the shades, that the fertility of the soil might always remain above," and they are used in a powerful fertility medicine. There can be no universal dictionary of symbols, and even in one context a ritual element usually has several kinds and levels of significance, some better defined than others.

In her review of the subject, "Keeping the King Divine," Audrey I. Richards (1969) recommended that in future more attention should be paid to kingship in its relation to other elements of the society in which we find it; for example, other forms of ancestor worship, other kinds of control over nature, other political authorities. Or as an ethnographer of eastern Zaire put it, "chiefship is simply a variant of Bashu ideas about healers, sorcerers, and women." The cultural pattern of the Shilluk (shared by the Anuak, Dinka, and other Nilotic peoples) is very different from that of the Azande (southern Sudan), in which the cultic attributes of kingship are minimal, and from those of the Temne, Rukuba, or Dime, all of which are in turn strongly dissimilar.

In a pattern that is widespread in central, southern, and parts of West Africa, violent powers associated with chiefs and the activities of men in hunting and war were supposedly derived from ancestors. Ancestral cults were paired and contrasted with those of local or nature spirits, from whom powers were procured that were beneficial to the fertility of nature, the activities of women, and the well-being of local communities. During the eighteenth and nineteenth centuries, such local cults were merged with the institution of kingship during the process of state formation; the Swazi, Luba and Bushong, and Benin kingdoms provide examples.

In this pattern, the symbolization of violence is often intentionally shocking. A Luba chief, after being anointed with the blood of a man killed for that purpose, put his foot on the victim's skull and drank his blood mixed with beer. Such acts showed that the king possessed superhumanly destructive powers, similar to witchcraft, with which he would be able to defend his people against the attacks of witches and criminals. The Ncwala confers similiar powers on the Swazi king; the hymns sung are a national expression not of rebellion but of sympathy for him in his lonely struggle against such enemies. As the Swazi themselves say, the Ncwala is intended to strengthen the kingship and "make stand the nation." In some kingdoms, designated groups engage in looting, rape, and other disorderly behavior to show that the power that should contain violence is temporarily in abeyance. Often, however, the ritual representation of the chief's violent powers was greatly disproportionate to the amount of real force he commanded; he had authority as the embodiment of the social order but little power.

In contrast, local cults devoted to community well-being emphasized growth and fertility, employing as ritual symbols the color black (associated with rain clouds) and farming implements such as hoes rather than the color red and various weapons associated with war. In other configurations, as among the Nyakyusa, life-giving and death-dealing powers are not segregated in this way. In yet others, such as the Mundang, whose king was as much bandit as sovereign, looting at home and abroad, there was no cult of violence.

Although kings are "made" by the rituals that enthrone them, their powers are maintained by daily observances. The unfortunate leader of the Dime, known as *zimu,* though he had real political and military responsibilities, was so restricted in his diet and personal contacts as to be virtually an outcast. Besides installation and funerary rites and daily observances, kingship cults include bodies of myth and the ritual organization of space. The plans of royal palaces and grave shrines, even the distribution of shrines in the country, organize rituals in space in conformity with cosmological models. The bodies of some kings, as among the Mundang, are casually thrown away, but for the Nyakyusa the graves of the original kings are among the most fearfully sacred of all shrines. The dynastic shrines of the Ganda are replicas of the royal court, with their own elaborate rituals and personnel centered on a queen sister.

Royal myths commonly refer to the founding of the state and its subsequent history, which the rituals of investiture and periodic festivals may reenact. Until the 1970s, scholars tended to take such myths literally, especially those that attributed the origin of a kingdom to immigrants. Paradoxically, the intellectualist reappraisal of ritual was accompanied by a new view of myths as narrative expressions of real, contemporary sociopolitical relations. The "stranger" status of the king expresses his difference from ordinary people or the separation of dynastic, chiefly functions from local, priestly ones, just as prescribed incest or murder marks the king's removal from his ordinary status and his accession to a new one.

Colonial rule abolished or profoundly modified all kingships and their rituals, appropriating many of their powers and banning some practices deemed essential by the people to create true kings. Central mysteries of surviving cults were and are known only to the participating experts. Consequently, we have few descriptions of the working of kingship in practice, and only one extensive set of ritual prescriptions, for the kingdom of Rwanda. Even much better information, however, would not render unambiguous the functions of kingship, which have always been responsive to changing circumstances, or reveal beyond doubt the relationship between ritual prescription and actual event. Kings as well as anthropologists debate whether regicide is a necessary practice or symbolic truth; in the mid-nineteenth century an *ọba* of Ọyọ refused to submit to regicide, and in 1969 the king of the Jukun (Nigeria) was reported in the press to be sleeping with a loaded revolver under his pillow. Part of the power and mystery of kingship is its refusal to be bound by rules and its centrality to the political process.

See Also Bemba Religion; Southern African Religions, article on Southern Bantu Religions; Swazi Religion.

Bibliography

James G. Frazer's ideas on divine kingship can be found in the various editions of *The Golden Bough;* his one-volume abridgment (New York, 1922) has been frequently reprinted. The modern revival of Frazer begins with Michael W. Young's article "The Divine Kingship of the Jukun: A Re-evaluation of Some Theories," *Africa* 36 (1966): 135–152, and includes Luc de Heusch's *Sacrifice in Africa* (Bloomington, Ind., 1985). Recent neo-Frazerian accounts of divine kingship include Alfred Adler's *La mort est le masque du roi: La royauté sacrée des Moundang du Tchad* (Paris, 1982), Jean-Claude Muller's *Le roi bouc-émissaire: Pouvoir et rituel chez les Rukuba du Nigéria* (Quebec, 1980), and Dave M. Todd's "Aspects of Chiefship in Dimam, South-West Ethiopia," *Cahiers d'études africaines* 18 (1978): 311–332. De Heusch has returned to Frazer's thesis in his "The Symbolic Mechanisms of Sacred Kingship: Rediscovering Frazer," *Journal of the Royal Anthropological Institute* 3, 2 (1887): 213–232, which includes references to recent studies, and has applied his version of the concept in L.de Heusch, *Le Roi de Kongo et les monstres sacrés* (Paris, 2000).

E. E. Evans-Pritchard established the sociological approach in opposition to Frazer in his *The Divine Kingship of the Shilluk of the Nilotic Sudan* (Cambridge, U.K., 1948). Relevant essays by Meyer Fortes include "Of Installation Ceremonies," *Proceedings of the Royal Anthropological Institute for 1967* (London, 1968). Max Gluckman's "rituals of rebellion" thesis is to be found in his *Order and Rebellion in Tribal Africa* (London, 1963). Audrey I. Richard's review, "Keeping the King Divine," is in *Proceedings of the Royal Anthropological Institute for 1968* (London, 1969).

Classic ethnographic accounts of kingship cults include John Roscoe's *The Bakitara or Banyoro* (Cambridge, U.K., 1923), in which he gives, for Bunyoro, the best account of a king's daily observances. Hilda Kuper's *An African Aristocracy: Rank among the Swazi* (London, 1947) sets a vivid description of the Ncwala in an analysis of the political system; T. O. Beidelman interprets the symbolism in "Swazi Royal Ritual," *Africa* 36 (1966): 373–405. Monica Wilson's richly detailed *Communal Rituals of the Nyakyusa* (London, 1957) includes trancripts of interviews with senior participants in kingship and other cults. Ray E. Bradbury's illustrated article "Divine Kingship in Benin," *Nigeria* 62 (1959): 186–207, is a useful companion to the film *Benin Kingship Rituals,* made by Bradbury and Francis Speed. The only extensive published set of esoteric ritual prescriptions is *La royauté sacrée de l'ancien Rwanda* (Tervuren, Belgium, 1964), edited by Marcel d'Hertefelt and André Coupez. Ritual features of Luba kingship, with special reference to art works and attitudes concerning them, are presented in M. N. Roberts and A. N. Roberts, *Memory: Luba Art and the Making of History* (New York, 1996).

Among recent historical accounts of the development of divine kingships are, on the Bashu, Randall Packard's *Chiefship and Cosmology* (Bloomington, Ind., 1981), which explains the relationship between chiefly power and control of natural forces; on the Luba, Thomas Q. Reefe's *The Rainbow and the Kings* (Berkeley, 1981); and, on the Kuba, Jan Vansina's *The Children of Woot* (Madison, Wis., 1978).

Wyatt MacGaffey (1987 and 2005)

KINGSHIP: KINGSHIP IN MESOAMERICA AND SOUTH AMERICA

Of essential importance for the study of kingship in Mesoamerica and South America is the profound connection between supernatural authority and political power residing in an elite class of sacred kings who directed the interaction of the natural environment, the human population, technology, and developments in social structure from sacred precincts and ceremonial cities. In the Aztec, Maya, and Inca patterns of sacred kingship are found distinct versions of this connection.

Aztec Sacred Kingship. The supreme authority in Aztec Mexico was the *tlatoani* (chief speaker), who resided in the imperial capital of Tenochtitlan. This pattern of rulership grew out of earlier forms of sacred and social authority in which each political-territorial unit (*altepetl* in Nahuatl) was governed by a titled lord, or *tecuhtli,* living within a noble estate or elite social and geographical domain. This local ruler was understood to be the living image of the *altepetl's* patron deity and communicated directly with him. As one scholar notes:

> The *tlatoani* headed a large, multifaceted bureaucracy composed of other lords and lesser nobles, and his palace (*tecpan, tecalli*) was the principal government administration building. . . . The king, like other high-ranking lords, was the titular head of a patrimonial demesne (complex of holdings, privileges, and obligations) that consisted of the provision of agricultural, public works, manufacturing and military services by commoners, tribute payment, the allegiance of lesser (including nontitled) nobility, and various other sumptuary privileges. (Gillespie, 2001)

During the later stages of Aztec history, the *tlatoani* governed with the assistance of the Council of Four, which included the second in command, who occupied an office called the Cihuacoatl (snake woman). The occupant of the Cihuacoatl office was always male. The elite status of the Council of Four is indicated by the fact that the members were chosen from the royal family and included the king's brothers, sons, and nephews. Under normal circumstances this group chose the successor to a dead king from one of its members. A primary qualification for the Aztec king was military leadership, and a truly great king was a victorious general who conquered many towns, which led to the organization of tributary payments to the royal and capital storehouses. In broad terms, the Aztec *tlatoani* was responsible for agricultural fertility, order and success in warfare, the maintenance of the ceremonial order, the stability of bureaucratic systems, and above all the orderly parallelism between society and the cosmos. The dominant symbol of sacred rulership in Mesoamerica was the throne that took the form of a woven mat or a seat with a high back in which the ruler was also carried in public settings. In Aztec society the word for throne was *petlatl, icpalli,* or the "reed mat"—the seat that also became a metaphor for the ruler.

By the beginning of the sixteenth century, the Aztec *tlatoani* Motecuhzoma Xocoyotzin (Moctezuma II, r. 1503–1520) was surrounded by an elaborate court dedicated to carrying out the expressions of authority and pomp of the monarch. According to Hernán Cortés's second letter to the king of Spain, Motecuhzoma changed clothes four times a day, never putting on garments that had been worn more than once. The formation of this privileged position came about as the result of two decisive transformations in the social and symbolic structures of Aztec life—the acquisition in 1370 of the sacred lineage of kingship associated with the Toltec kingdom, and the consolidation of authority and power in the office of the king and a warrior nobility known as the *pipiltin* during the war against the city-state of Atzcapotzalco in 1428.

When the Aztec precursors, the Chichimec (from *chich,* meaning "dog," and *mecatl,* meaning "rope" or "lineage"), migrated into the Valley of Mexico in the thirteenth century, they encountered an urbanized world of warring city-states. The basic settlement pattern in the valley was the *tlatocayotl,* a city-state that consisted of a small capital city surrounded by dependent communities that worked the agricultural lands, paid tribute, and performed services for the elite classes in the capital according to various ritual calendars and cosmological patterns. Within this world of political rivalries, the most valued legitimate authority resided in communities tracing their royal lineage to the great Toltec kingdom of Tollan (tenth through twelfth centuries CE), which was remembered as the greatest city in history, noted for agricultural abundance, technological excellence, and cosmological order.

As the Aztec slowly but systematically integrated themselves into the more complex social world of *tlatocayotls,* they sought a means to acquire access to the Toltec lineage. According to a number of sources, they turned to the city-state of Culhuacan, which held the most direct lineal access to the authority represented by the Toltec, and asked to be given a half-Aztec, half-Culhuacan lord by the name of Acamapichtli as their first *tlatoani,* or royal leader. The successful transfer of legitimate kingship to the Aztec resulted in an internal adjustment of Aztec society. The first several *tlatoanis* were forced to negotiate their authority with the traditional social unit of Aztec life, the *calpulli.* The *calpulli* was most likely a type of conical clan in which members were interrelated by family ties but hierarchically stratified according to lines of descent from a sacred ancestor. This sharing of authority took an abrupt turn at the collapse of the Tepanec kingdom between 1426 and 1428 and the formation of a new political order known as the Triple Alliance. During the last half of the fourteenth century the Mexica (Aztec) were military vassals of the powerful Tepanec kingdom centered in the capital of Azcapotzalco.

During their tutelage to the Tepanec, the Aztec became the most powerful military unit in the region and adapted their political and economic structure to the more urbanized systems of the valley. When the king of Azcapotzalco died in 1426, the Tepanec kingdom was ripped apart by a war of succession. The Aztec *tlatoani* Itzcoatl, with his nephews Motecuhzoma Ilhuicamina and Tlacaellel, formed a political alliance with two other city-states and successfully took over the lands, tribute, and allegiances that formerly belonged to the Tepanec. In the process these three leaders restructured the Aztec government by concentrating power and authority in the *tlatoani,* the Council of Four, and to a lesser extent in the noble warrior class known as the *pipiltin.* The *calpulli* were incorporated into less powerful levels of decision making. This restructuring marked the beginning of the rise of Aztec kingship on a road to the status of god-king.

Subsequent Aztec kings—such as Motecuhzoma Ilhuicamina (Moctezuma I)—issued decrees defining the different classes of nobles, traders, warriors, and commoners according to their privileges, manner of dress, ownership, and education. Beginning around 1440 the cosmological traditions undergirding Aztec society were reinterpreted to legitimate the rise of sacred kingship and the concentration of authority in the elites. As a sign of this cosmic and political authority, each king following Itzcoatl took the responsibility of enlarging the Great Temple of the capital and acquiring large numbers of enemy warriors to be sacrificed to the imperial gods Tlaloc and Huitzilopochtli.

Interestingly, the symbolic sources for the legitimation of Aztec kingship come from two lines of descent. On the one hand, Aztec kings drew their legitimacy from the Toltec priest-king Topiltzin Quetzalcoatl, while on the other hand they drew their power from the "all-powerful, the invisible, the untouchable" Tezcatlipoca, whom one chronicler called "the first among all the gods" and who was strongly related to the patron Aztec god Huitzilopochtli. This combination demonstrates both the strength and, surprisingly, the vulnerability of Aztec kings. The most intimate inspiration for Aztec kings came from the twisting maneuvers of the principal god, Tezcatlipoca. While Quetzalcoatl was an ancient underpinning of Aztec kingship, Tezcatlipoca's influence on the legitimacy, power, and conduct of Aztec rulers was immediate and pervasive. Guilhem Olivier summarizes the major feast of Tezcatlipoca:

> The king personally decorated "his beloved god," a young man impersonating Tezcatlipoca, who was destined to be sacrificed. The king sacrificed himself symbolically through the man who was the image (*ixiptla*) of his tutelary divinity. Likewise, during the royal enthronement rites, the future sovereign wore pieces of fabric that covered the sacred bundles (*tlaquimilolli)* of

> Huitzilopochtli and of Tezcatlipoca, ritually reproducing the death and rebirth of the two major Aztec divinities. (Olivier, 2001)

Perhaps the most vivid example of Tezcatlipoca's influence appears in the prayers recited at the installation of a ruler and upon his death. When a new king was installed in Tenochtitlan, Tezcatlipoca was invoked as the creator, animator, guide, and potential killer of the king. The ceremony, according to book 6 of Fray Bernardino de Sahagún's *Historia general de las cosas de la Nueva España* (compiled 1569–1582; also known as the Florentine Codex), begins at the moment when "the sun . . . hath come to appear." The particular phrasing of the description of the sunrise in the prayer reported by Sahagún is related to the story of the creation of the Sun in the official cosmogonies of the Aztec elites. The king's installation and Tezcatlipoca's presence are seen as cosmogonic acts that result in the dawning of a new day. As the ritual proceeds, Tezcatlipoca is called the "creator . . . and knower of men" who "causes the king's action, his character," even the odors of his body. This intimacy is best stated when Tezcatlipoca is asked to inspire the king: "Animate him . . . for this is thy flute, thy replacement, thy image." This intimacy is carried to a surprising turn when, later in the narrative, the prayer asks Tezcatlipoca to kill the king if he performs badly. This resonates with the tradition about Tollan, in which the king Quetzalcoatl broke his vows of chastity and was sent away by the sorcerer Tezcatlipoca. The omnipotence of Tezcatlipoca is also evidenced in the repeated statement that the new king, like all the other previous rulers, was merely borrowing the "reed mat" (symbolic of kingship) and "thy [i.e., Tezcatlipoca's] realm" during his kingship. The invocation to Tezcatlipoca ends when the god is asked to send the king "to be on the offensive" in the "center of the desert, to the field of battle." Kings in Aztec society were expected above all to be successful in warfare.

As this historical narrative demonstrates, the Aztec sense of legitimacy was derived, in part, from their acquired connection to the ancient kingdom of Tollan, where Quetzalcoatl ruled a world of abundance, artistic creativity, and cosmic balance, only to be undone by his counterpart Tezcatlipoca. This connection and conflict apparently influenced Aztec kingship and provided to some degree an ironic destiny for the last Aztec *tlatoani*, Motecuhzoma Xocoyotzin (Moctezuma II). In fact, the vulnerability of Aztec kingship is reflected in a series of episodes involving Motecuhzoma Xocoyotzin and Hernán Cortés, the leader of the conquering Spanish expedition (1519–1521). According to the account of the conquest of Tenochtitlan told in book 12 ("The Conquest") of Sahagún's work, when word reached the magisterial city of Tenochtitlan that "strangers in the east" were making their way toward the high plateau, "Moctezuma thought that this was Topiltzin Quetzalcoatl who had come to the land. . . . It was in their hearts that he would come . . . to land . . . to find his mat . . . his seat. . . . Moctezuma sent five emissaries to give him gifts."

This passage demonstrates how, at least in the eyes of some of his descendants and Spanish chroniclers, an Aztec king used an ancient mythological tradition of kingly abdication in a new situation for the purpose of interpreting a threatening development. According to this tradition, the kingdom of Tollan (centuries before the Aztec arrived in the central plateau of Mexico) was ruled by the brilliant priest-king Topiltzin Quetzalcoatl, but it collapsed when a sorcerer (Tezcatlipoca) from the outside tricked him into violating his kingly vows and abdicating his throne. Topiltzin Quetzalcoatl left his kingdom for the eastern horizon, where, according to different traditions, he either sacrificed himself and became the morning star or sailed away on a raft of serpents promising to return one day and reclaim his throne. In the crisis of 1519, according to some interpreters, the last Aztec king applied to a series of reconnaissance reports the archaic mythologem of Quetzalcoatl's flight and promised return to regain his throne. Moctezuma sent jeweled costumes of Aztec deities, including the array of Quetzalcoatl, to Cortés, and he instructed his messengers to tell Cortés that the king acknowledged the presence of the god for whom he had been waiting to return and sit in the place of authority. As the Spaniards advanced, Moctezuma fell into an emotional crisis ("He was terror struck . . . his heart was anguished"), and he made two gestures of abdication. First, he moved out of his kingly residence into a palace of lesser authority, and second, he sought escape in a magical cave where he believed he could pass into the supernatural world. When Cortés arrived at the capital, a series of encounters took place in which Moctezuma instructed his nobles to transfer their power to the returning king. In this situation, a form of "imperial irony" appears in the tradition of Aztec kingship. On the one hand, the Aztec drew their legitimacy from the tradition that depicted Tollan as a city-state characterized by agricultural stability, artistic achievement, and religious genius. But in drawing their legitimacy as Toltec descendants, they were also heirs to a tradition of kingly abdication and dramatic political changes. Like Topiltzin Quetzalcoatl, who gave his kingdom to Tezcatlipoca, Moctezuma opened the royal door for Cortés to enter.

It must be noted that this interpretation, found in both the sixteenth-century chronicles and a group of modern studies, is in constant dispute by some scholars who believe these episodes were largely fabricated during the early decades of Spanish colonial domination in central Mexico. In this view, the application of Quetzalcoatl's return to the arrival of Cortés was part of a vigorous sixteenth-century prose project designed to justify the holy and just war propaganda of the Europeans and to celebrate the genius of their triumphs.

In the case of the last great civilization of Mesoamerica, sacred kingship was an urban institution acquired by the Aztec, who utilized borrowed and indigenous religious symbols to legitimate their imperial expansion and social character.

MAYA SACRED KINGS. In the last several decades, our overall view of the long, complex history of Maya society, culture, and rulership has undergone something of a revolution. Where once were imagined peaceful kingdoms ruled by astronomer priests who had mastered the human tendencies of aggression and warlike domination, it is now known that Maya peoples, despite their superb artistic, mathematical, and architectural capacities, struggled violently among their various city-states, kingdoms, and extended families. Stunning breakthroughs in deciphering Maya forms of writing have led to a complex understanding of how Maya societies were organized around stunning ceremonial centers in which resided, supreme among an ever pulsating elite community, the *ajaw* or *k'uhl aja*-lord (ruler or holy lord or supreme ruler). As one Maya scholar writes, "Perhaps the most famous Mesoamerican scenes of accession appear on the so-called niche stelae of Piedras Negras; they represent the new king on a scaffold throne, surrounded by cosmological symbols of heaven. Like the Mexica emperors, the new Maya ruler is shown at the central point of the cosmic order" (Stuart, 2001).

Scholarship has shown that in many ways the Maya replicated the basic pattern of ruler-deity relations, control of natural and cultural resources, dominance through military aggression, and administration of tributary payments outlined above in the central Mexican world. But the Maya world also had many distinctive royal practices and variations of sacred authority during the many centuries of urban development. In exquisitely constructed civic ceremonial centers such as Tikal, Copán, Quirigua, Caracol, Calakmul, and many others, rulers and their elite families occupied and controlled high-status compounds from which they ruled a large populace by directing ritual performances in imposing stone temple precincts, spacious plazas, and even ballcourts. Kkings and their families reenacted cosmological narratives, sometimes of bellicose and warlike character in these ballcourts. Royal authority, as William Fash (2001) has shown, was powerfully reinforced through public displays of portrait sculptures, dynastic genealogies, and accounts of military victories against neighboring city-states. In Maya centers throughout a long, complex history, rulers skillfully used public architecture to not only map the course of the time and the heavens but also to persuade the populace of their individual dynastic interests and interpretations.

Certainly by what is called the "Late Classic" period, the holy lords of many Maya centers passed on their authority from father to son, unless a younger brother was deemed more fit for the accession to the throne. Among the Maya, as archaeological and ethnohistorical evidence clearly shows, women sometimes governed as regents and played crucial roles in interdynastic marriage alliances. The record also shows that Maya rulers lived in an unstable social world. As one scholar writes:

> Despite the sumptuous royal tombs, impressive building programs, and texts extolling military exploits, marriage alliances, and visits by honored foreign leaders, royal authority was clearly subject to challenge. Titles for subsidiary lords proliferated in the Late Classic, suggesting growing recognition of sub-royal entitlements. A "council house" (*popul na*) is material evidence that Copan's rulers shared formal governance with high-ranking nobles by the late eighth century CE. (Ashmore, 2001)

What seems particularly outstanding through the Maya world, especially in places like Copan and Tikal, is a profound respect given to the founders of kingdoms and their real or imagined well-being. Ancestor worship as social and symbolic sites where each new generation discerned the will of the gods seems profoundly intertwined with the rise, florescence, and waning of Maya society.

INCA SACRED KINGSHIP. When Spanish soldiers led by Francisco Pizarro arrived on the Pacific coast of South America in 1527, they encountered the Inca empire, called Tahuantinsuyu (land of the four quarters). At its height, the empire extended from the northern border of present-day Ecuador south for more than 4,300 kilometers to the Maule River in Chile. This kingdom contained more than twelve million people organized into a tightly knit series of local, regional, and imperial administrative units, with authority centered in the capital city of Cuzco. When subsequent researchers attempted to reconstruct the history of the Inca empire, they found two impressive facts. First, the Inca achieved a meteoric rise from a modest village settlement in the valley of Cuzco to an imperial power in less than one hundred years. Second, the Inca recorded their own historic developments in terms of the lives and achievements of their kings and the care of dead kings by the royal mummy cult.

The term *Inca*, according to the social context to which it refers, can have one of three meanings. As Michael A. Malpass writes,

> It can refer to a people, an empire, or even a single person—the Inca king. The term as it is used by experts refers only to the small ethnic group that originally lived in the area around Cuzco. All others were not originally Incas; we may refer to them as Inca subjects, but not as Incas. To be an Inca was to have certain privileges not allowed to others; to wear a particular kind of headband and to wear earplugs that were so large that they stretched out the earlobe. This caused the Incas to be given the Spanish nickname *orejonjes*, or "big ears." Not to be an Inca was to be subject to the orders of the reigning Inca king, who claimed ownership of your land and rights to your labor. Thus the differences between the Inca and the Inca subject were great (Malpass, 1996, p. 37).

The origin myth of the Incas explains the sacredness of the royal Inca lineage. Eight ancestors of the Inca kings, four women and four men, emerged from a cave near the town of Pacariqtambo. One of them, Maco Capac, became the first Inca ruler, and from him all subsequent kings descended. After other people emerged from nearby caves, the royal ancestors gathered them together and sought a place to settle. They drove out the original inhabitants of the town of Cuzco and there established a capital city. From this myth, it is gathered that Inca kingship was intimately related to:

1. The powers of the earth, for example, caves.
2. A cosmology of wholeness symbolized by the number eight, with four males and four females constituting a balance of gender.
3. The site of Cuzco, which served as the axis of the Inca world.
4. A direct line to Manco Capac.

At its most basic social level, the world of these kings and their royal mummies was organized by *ayllus*, which appear to have been composed of well-ordered endogamous kinship groups that traced their descent to a common ancestor. *Ayllu* members emphasized self-sufficiency by rigorously practicing certain traditions such as assisting one another in the construction of homes and public buildings, the farming of lands together, and the care of specific deities within local ceremonial centers. In fact, certain common plots of land were used to produce goods for sacrifices at the shrine of ancestral deities.

These *ayllus* were organized into larger units such as villages and chiefdoms that were involved in intense raiding and small-scale warfare among themselves. The social setting of *ayllus* and competing chiefdoms helped to produce the emergence of *sinchis*, or war leaders, who possessed the additional capacity to organize groups of men into firm alliances. These leaders were chosen from the prominent adult male members of the *ayllus*, and if one was particularly successful in warfare and conquest of new lands, he utilized his acquisitions to achieve more permanent positions of leadership.

It appears that the earliest Inca kings were particularly prominent *sinchis* who achieved a semblance of permanent and legitimate authority by manifesting an intimacy with the Inca sun god Inti. The actual reconstruction of the process of the rise of sacred kingship in the Inca culture is difficult to discern. However, the standard Inca histories hold that all Inca kings descended from this great solar god. Different primary sources include a standard list of thirteen Inca kings dating back to mythical times, but serious historical reconstructions reveal that the expansion of Inca power beyond the chiefdom level and the consolidation of authority in kings took place with the career of the ninth Inca king, Pachacuti.

The sacred histories of the Inca tell of a crucial turning point in the creation of their empire. In 1438 the fledgling Inca village of Cuzco was attacked by the aggressive army of the Chanca. A threatening siege of the settlement resulted in the flight of the Inca king Viracocha and his designated successor, his son Urcon, from the capital. Another son, Cusi Yupanqui, commanded the defense of Cuzco. Just before the expected final attack, the commander had a vision of a terrifying deity that identified itself as the Inca sky god; the sky god called Cusi Yupanqui "my son," and he told Cusi Yupanqui that if he followed the true religion he would become the Sapay (great) Inca and conquer many nations. Driven by this powerful vision and supported by increased political alliances, the Inca leader drove the invaders away, which resulted, after factional intrigues against his father and brother, in his ascension to the throne. The new king then embarked on an intense series of conquests resulting in the expansion of Inca lands and the laying of the foundation for the Inca empire. He became known as Pachacuti, which means "cataclysm" or "he who remakes the world." This remarkable episode, which is recorded in a number of sources, combines two major patterns of Inca religion: the sacred legitimacy of Inca kinship and the responsibility of the king to acquire new territories through conquest and warfare.

While it is difficult to present a satisfactory outline of Inca religion, recent studies have identified three major components, each relating to the power and authority of Inca kings: the omnipotence and omniscience of the creator sky god Viracocha, the cult of ancestor worship and mummies, and the pervasive pattern of the veneration of *huacas*.

Inca kings derived their sanctification from what Arthur Andrew Demarest (1984) calls the "upper pantheon" of Inca religion. According to Demarest's useful formulation, the single Inca creator sky god manifested himself in at least three subcomplexes organized around Viracocha (the universal creator), Inti (the sun god), and Illapa (the thunder and weather god). Ritual cycles and ceremonial events associated with political, astronomical, and economic schedules revealed the many aspects and versions of this upper pantheon. At the center of the sacred schedule of activities stood the Sapay Inca, who was venerated as the manifestation of Viracocha, as the descendant of Inti, and, upon his death, as the power of Illapa.

Cult of ancestor worship. The second aspect of Inca religion related to kingship is the fascinating cult of ancestor worship and mummies. A pan-Andean tradition of ancestor worship, in which the bodies of dead family members were venerated as sacred objects and ceremonially cared for by the living, permeated Inca existence. Central to this tradition was the practice of oracular communication with the dead. The ancestral remains, in the form of a mummy or simply a collection of bones, were called *mallquis*. Specific questions concerning all aspects of life were put to the *mallquis*, and specific answers resulted. Specialists known as the *mallquipvillac* (they who speak with the *mallquis*) were influential in Inca life. The ancestral spirits also manifested themselves in hierophanies of stones and plants, and, most powerfully, in the sparks of fires. Specialists called the "consultors of the dead" communicated with the ancestors through fire.

The quintessential expression of this pattern of ancestor worship was the royal mummy cult of Cuzco. As already noted, the king was considered a descendant of the sky god Inti or Viracocha. At the death of a Sapay Inca, the authority to govern, wage war, and collect taxes passed on to one of his sons, ideally a son born of a union with the king's sister. However, all possessions of the dead king, including his palaces, agricultural lands, and servants, remained the property of the mummy. These possessions were to be administered by his *panaqa*, a corporate social unit made up of all the descendants in the male line. While the *panaqa* lived off a small portion of these lands, the group's primary purpose was to function as the dead king's court and to maintain his mummy in private and public ceremonial events, relaying his wishes through oracular specialists and carrying out his will. The public display of these mummies was a major element in Inca ceremonial life. Processions of kingly mummies, arranged according to their seniority, traveled through the fields at rainmaking ceremonies and paraded through the streets of the capital to the ceremonial center of Cuzco, where they observed and participated in state rituals. They also visited one another to communicate through oracular specialists and participated in the dances, revelries, and ceremonies in their honor. All kings, alive and dead, were considered the living spirit of Inti.

What is vital to understand is the degree of influence the cult of mummies had on the conduct and destiny of the living king. For instance, when the Spanish captured the Inca ruler Atahuallpa and condemned him to death, he was given a choice of remaining a pagan and being burned at the stake or converting to Christianity and being garroted. Atahuallpa chose conversion and garroting, not because he believed in Christianity but so that his body would not be destroyed. After receiving a Christian burial, some surviving Incas secretly disinterred his body, mummified it, and then hid the mummy, continuing to treat it in the traditional manner. More impressive perhaps is the political and military pressure placed on the living king by his mummified father. Powerful in privilege but much poorer in lands and riches, the new Inca was spurred on to carry out expansive conquests in order to acquire his own territorial lands and riches so he could live in the expected manner. This forced him to carry out his kingly responsibilities of establishing short- and long-distance trading routes, building agricultural projects to sustain himself and his growing kingdom, building temples to the sky god Viracocha throughout the new regions of the empire, and establishing the local and imperial administration units into which the kingdom was organized.

At the more popular level, Inca religion was organized by the veneration of *huacas*. *Huacas* were the endless hierophanies in stones, plants, or other objects that animated the entire Inca landscape. The countless *huacas* were objects of offerings, sacrifices, and oracular events. Even major family relationships expressed in the concept of *villca* (ancestor, descendant) were examples of *huacas*. Ancestors were *huacas*, and in this way the Inca mummies were the most sacred of *huacas*.

The last great civilization of South America, the Inca developed their concept of sacred kingship by combining their practice of ancestor worship with the historical process of imperial expansion and warfare. As in Mesoamerica, sanctified legitimacy was derived from connection with ancient and contemporary hierophanies, deities, and their human representatives.

See Also Aztec Religion; Inca Religion; Maya Religion; Quetzalcoatl; Tezcatlipoca.

Bibliography

Adams, Robert M. *The Evolution of Urban Society: Early Mesopotamia and Prehistoric Mexico.* Chicago, 1966. This concise study of urban development in Mesopotamia describes the step-by-step process of the rise of intense social stratification. It includes insightful passages on the persistence of the sacred in periods of secular growth.

Ashmore, Wendy. "Maya Lowlands." In *Oxford Encyclopedia of Mesoamerican Cultures,* edited by Davíd Carrasco, vol. 1, pp. 242–243. New York, 2001.

Brundage, Burr C. *Empire of the Inca.* Norman, Okla., 1963. Though dated in some respects, Brundage's study provides a useful description of the religious forces contributing to the integration of the Inca empire.

Carrasco, Davíd. *Quetzalcoatl and the Irony of Empire: Myths and Prophecies in the Aztec Tradition.* Niwot, Colo., 2001. This work discusses the ironic dimensions of Aztec kingship and the roots of sacred kingship in five Mesoamerican capitals. This revised version has a new chapter on the controversy surrounding the "return of Quetzalcoatl" tradition and the conquest of Mexico.

Carrasco, Pedro. "Los linajes nobles del Mexico antiguo." In *Estratificación social en la Mesoamérica prehispánica,* edited by Pedro Carrasco, Johanna Broda, et al., pp. 19–36. Mexico City, 1976.

Cobo, Bernabé. *History of the Inca Empire: An Account of the Indians' Customs and Their Origin, Together with a Treatise on Inca Legends, History, and Social Institutions.* Austin, Tex., 1979. One of the valuable post-Conquest primary sources for the study of various aspects of Inca history and religion.

Demarest, Arthur Andrew, and Geoffrey W. Conrad. *Religion and Empire: The Dynamics of Aztec and Inca Expansionism.* Cambridge, U.K., 1984. This study makes a significant contribution to the comparative study of social dynamics, religion, and imperialism in the two regions of New World primary urban generation.

Fash, William. *Scribes, Warriors and Kings: The City of Cópan and the Ancient Maya.* London, 2001. This beautifully illustrated book illuminates the ways that rulers, warriors, and Maya scribes interacted to consolidate the Maya worldview and conceptions of authority.

Gillespie, Susan D. "Rulers and Dynasties." In *Oxford Encyclopedia of Mesoamerican Cultures,* edited by Davíd Carrasco, vol. 3, pp. 96–98. New York, 2001. This is the best overview of up-to-date scholarship on the varieties and powers of sacred rulership in Aztec and Maya societies.

Katz, Friedrich. *The Ancient American Civilizations.* Chicago, 1972. The standard starting point for a comparative analysis of the material and social character of Aztec and Inca kingship.

Malpass, Michael A. *Daily Life in the Inca Empire.* Westport, Conn., 1996. A very useful summary of scholarship on the religion, politics, and daily life in the Inca world.

Nicholson, H. B. *Topiltzin Quetzalcoatl: The Once and Future Lord of the Toltecs.* Niwot, Colo., 1999.

Olivier, Guilhem. *Mockeries and Metamorphoses of an Aztec God: Tezcatlipoca, "Lord of the Smoking Mirror."* Niwot, Colo., 2004. This is the finest and most detailed analysis of the evidence about Tezcatlipoca's significance in Mesoamerican society and the relationship to kingship.

Reed, Kay. *Time and Sacrifice in the Aztec Cosmos.* Bloomington, Ind., 1998.

Schele, Linda, and David Freidel. *A Forest of Kings: The Untold Story of the Ancient Maya.* New York, 1990. A detailed study of the lives of individual rulers in lowland Maya cultures.

Stuart, David. "Ruler Accession Rituals." In *Oxford Encyclopedia of Mesoamerican Cultures,* edited by Davíd Carrasco, vol. 3, pp. 95–96. New York, 2001.

Wheatley, Paul. *The Pivot of the Four Quarters: A Preliminary Enquiry into the Origins and Character of the Ancient Chinese City.* Chicago, 1971. Wheatley places Inca and Aztec social and symbolic structures within a broad comparative analysis of the rise of primary urban generation.

Zuidema, R. Tom. "The Lion in the City: Royal Symbols of Transition in Cuzco." *Journal of Latin American Lore* 9 (Summer 1983): 39–100. One of the many important articles by Zuidema explaining the myths and rituals associated with kingship and authority in Inca religion.

DAVÍD CARRASCO (1987 AND 2005)

KINGSHIP: KINGSHIP IN EAST ASIA

The central focus of East Asian civilization until the beginning of the twentieth century remained the king. He was the center of the universe, whether it was in China, Korea, or Japan, and he was supremely responsible for the well-being and prosperity of the society over which he reigned. The king's political authority was ultimately based on the religious claim that he possessed the mandate of Heaven, whether temporarily or perpetually. Moreover, the heavenly origin of the king was acknowledged almost invariably in East Asia. His status was generally defined as (1) the earthly representative of heaven or heavenly will, (2) the descendant of a god, or (3) the god incarnate.

The earliest institution of kingship to emerge in East Asia developed on the mainland of China with the establishment of the Shang kingdom (c. 1500–1050 BCE). The Shang state centered around the king (*wang*) for, according to oracle-bone inscriptions, he was the "unique man" who could appeal to his ancestors for blessings or, if necessary, dissipate ancestral curses that affected the state. It was believed that determining and influencing the will of the ancestral spirits were possible through divination, prayer, and sacrifice. The king's ancestors interceded, in turn, with Di or Shangdi, the supreme being in heaven, who stood at the apex of the spiritual hierarchy of the Shang.

The question of whether or not the Shang people defined the status of their king as Shangdi's "descendant" has not yet been settled. The Shang dynasty was founded by members of the Zi clan, who were descendants of the clan's founder, Xie. According to the *Shi jing,* Xie was born miraculously; his mother became pregnant after swallowing an egg dropped by a dark bird in flight. This mythic story might be taken to suggest that the Shang people believed in a blood link between Shangdi and the king. It may be noted, however, that no oracle-bone inscription has thus far pointed to the genealogical relationship. According to David N. Keightley, the doctrine of the "mandate of Heaven" (*tianming*), usually considered a creation of the Zhou dynasty (1150–256 BCE), has deep roots in the theology of the Shang. Di, the supreme god of the Shang, is most impersonal in character; that is, it was not generally thought that he could be "bribed" by the sacrifices offered by the members of the royal family. It was precisely this impersonality that made it possible for Di to harm the dynasty by sponsoring the attack of the Zhou, the dynasty that followed the Shang.

The state religion of the Zhou times centered on sacrifice to Tian (Heaven) and the gods of the soil (*she*). A vast ceremonial was elaborated in which the Zhou king played the leading role and on which the well-being of his state was deemed to depend. Two kinds of sacrifices were offered to Tian, the supreme god of the Zhou: in the ancestral temple and in the open fields. The sacrifice in the open fields, called the "suburban sacrifice," was the religious act *par excellence* of a reigning king; a burnt offering of an unblemished calf was offered to Tian at the winter solstice, on the round hillock in the southern suburbs of the royal city.

The *Shi jing* narrates the origin of the Zhou people: a woman named Yuan stepped on the big toe of Shangdi's footprint and then gave birth to Hou Ji (Prince Millet), the god of agriculture, who was considered the primordial ancestor of the Zhou. This notion of divine descent probably helped to establish the Zhou's claim to the royal throne, and it may also have contributed to the Zhou conception of the king as "son of Heaven" (*tianzi*).

The Son of Heaven was one who received the mandate of Heaven. This mandate signified that imperial authority could not become a permanent possession of the ruler, that Heaven had the complete freedom to confer or withdraw its charisma or "gift of grace" from the ruler on earth. Whether or not the king was given the divine mandate was generally determined by his acceptance by the "people" (the ruling class and their clients, i.e., the literati and landowners). If the people recognized his rulership, it was an indication that the heavenly mandate remained with him, but if they deposed him or killed him, it was a clear sign that he had lost Heaven's moral support. Under these circumstances, the Zhou conception of the Son of Heaven tended to lose in the course of time whatever genealogical implications it may have had in its beginnings.

The classical Chinese conception of sovereignty took shape in the Qin and Han periods (221 BCE–220 CE). While the sovereign adopted the title, connoting supreme power, of *huangdi* (emperor), he was never considered divine, at least while he was alive, nor was he regarded as an incarnation of a divine being. Rather, he was a "unique man" representing Heaven's will on earth and serving as the link between Heaven and earth. The Chinese notion of the Son of Heaven in its classical form had nothing to do with the genealogical conception of kingship, such as in ancient Egypt or Japan, that the king was the descendant of a certain god or the god incarnate; the emperor was simply the earthly representative of Heaven or heavenly will. The essential function of the Chinese emperor, as formulated in the Han period, was to maintain the harmonious cosmic order by means of ceremonials. "The Sage-Kings did not institute the ceremonies of the suburban sacrifices casually," states the *Han shu* (chap. 25). "The sacrifice to Heaven is to be held at the southern suburb. Its purpose is to conform to the yang principle. The sacrifice to earth is to be held at the northern suburb. Its purpose is to symbolize the yin principle." In short, the emperor maintained the cosmic balance by assisting Heaven and earth in the regulation and harmonization of the yin and yang principles.

In the centuries that followed the fall of the Han empire, China was often threatened and invaded by the nomadic peoples of Central and Northeast Asia. Here, too, the king (*khagan, khan*) was considered a sacred person, deriving his sacredness and authority from Tengri (Heaven); he was heavenly in origin, received the mandate from Heaven, and was a supremely important spokesman of heavenly will, serving as Heaven's representative on earth.

Significantly, the sacred nature of the king in Central Asia was often conceived after the archaic model of the shaman. Among the Tujue, who dominated the Mongolian steppes from 552 to 744, a series of strange rituals was performed when a new king acceded to the throne (*Zhou shu*, bk. 50): the high-ranking officials turned a felt carpet, on which the king was seated, nine times in the direction of the sun's movement, and after each turn they prostrated themselves, making obeisance to him. Then they throttled him with a piece of silken cloth to the point of strangulation and asked him how many years he was to rule. In an almost unconscious state, the king uttered his answer.

This ceremony is somewhat reminiscent of the shaman's rite of initiation in Central Asia in which the felt carpet played a role. Seated on a felt carpet, the shaman was carried nine times around nine birches in the direction of the sun's movement and made nine turns on each of them while climbing. Nine turns symbolize the shaman's ascent to nine heavens. According to the belief of the Tujue, the king in his accession makes a symbolic ascent to the highest heaven through the nine cosmic zones, starting his journey from the felt carpet on which he is seated; then, after reaching the top of heaven, he descends onto earth. In this sense, the king was heavenly in origin. It seems also certain that the number of reigning years he uttered in an unconscious state was accepted as an announcement from Tengri, the supreme being in heaven.

The use of the felt carpet was not confined to the T'ujue. It was also used among the Tuoba, the Turkic or Mongolian people also known as the Xianbei, who established the Northern Wei dynasty (493–534) in China. When the enthronement ceremony for Tuoba Xiu was celebrated in 528, seven dignitaries held up a carpet of black felt on which the new emperor, facing west, made obeisance to heaven (*Bei shi*, bk. 5). In the Khitan state of Liao (907–1125), the enthronement ceremony had as its essential scenario the elevation of the new emperor on a felt carpet (*Liao shi*, bk. 49). Chinggis Khan, the founder of the great Mongol empire, was also lifted in his accession on a carpet of black felt supported by seven chiefs.

In ancient Korea, several states competed with each other for political supremacy until 676, when they became united by the kingdom of Silla. The beginnings of these nations are inseparably interwoven with myths narrating the miraculous birth of the founders, which point almost invariably to the heavenly origin of sovereignty.

The myths can be classified into two major types, one of which may be illustrated by the myth of Puyŏ: Tongmyŏng, the founder of Puyŏ, was born of a woman who became pregnant by a mystical light descending from heaven. A similar story is also told of Zhu Mong, who founded Koguryŏ. This type of foundation myth is associated, outside of Korea, with Taiwudi (r. 424–452), the third emperor of the Northern Wei dynasty; with A-pao-chi, who founded the Khitan state of Liao; and with Chinggis Khan. There is no doubt that this mythic theme was widespread among nomadic peoples such as the Manchus and the Mongolians.

The other type of myth is characterized by the story of how the founder of a nation or a dynasty descended from Heaven onto mountaintops, forests, and trees. According to the myth of ancient Chosŏn, Hwang-wung, a son of the celestial supreme being Hwang-in, descended from Heaven onto Mount Tehbaek to establish a nation. The supreme god in Heaven approved of Hwang-wung's heavenly descent and granted him three items of the sacred regalia. He descended, accompanied by the gods of the wind, rain, and clouds as well as three thousand people. Similar stories of heavenly descent are known of Pak Hyŏkkŏse and Kim Archi of Silla. Also noteworthy is the myth of Karak, a small state variously known as Kaya or Mimana: Suro, the founder of Karak, descends from Heaven onto the summit of Mount Kuji at the command of the heavenly god; a purple rope is seen coming down from Heaven, and at the end of the rope there is a box containing six golden eggs covered by a piece of crimson cloth. Suro is born of one of the eggs.

Significantly, the heavenly origin of sovereignty is also recognized by the pre-Buddhist tradition of ancient Tibet:

Gñya'-khri Btsam-po, the first mythical king, descended from Heaven onto the sacred mountain of Yar-lha-śam-po in Yarlung, by means of a rope or a ladder. He agreed to descend on the condition that he be granted ten heavenly magical objects. According to Giuseppe Tucci, the Tibetan royal ideology owes much to the religious tradition of the pastoral Turco-Mongolians.

Japanese kingship emerged at the end of the fourth century CE. The ruler called himself the "king [*ō* in Japanese; *wang* in Chinese] of Wa" or "king of the land of Wa" when he addressed the court in China. These designations simply followed what had become customary between the Chinese suzerains and the Japanese local princes since the middle of the first century CE. However, these titles were never used within Japan; the sovereign was called *ō-kimi* (*dawang* in Chinese; "great king") by local nobles. It is not until the beginning of the seventh century that the Japanese sovereign began to employ such titles as *tenshi* ("son of Heaven") and *tennō* ("emperor") to refer to himself, both of which have been in use until modern times.

In 600 Empress Suiko sent an envoy to the Sui dynasty, the first Japanese mission to China since 502. The *Sui shu* reports of that mission: "The king of Wa, whose family name was Ame and personal name Tarishihiko, and who bore the title of Ō-kimi, sent an envoy to visit the court." Meaning "noble son of Heaven," *Ametarishihiko* (or *Ametarashihiko*) was roughly equivalent to the Chinese *tianzi*, although its implications could be different. "Son of Heaven" in the Japanese conception of sovereignty referred invariably to the ruler who claimed his direct genealogical descent from the sun goddess Amaterasu as well as his vertical descent from the heavenly world. The Japanese mission to China was followed by another one in 607: "The Son of Heaven in the land where the sun rises addresses a letter to the Son of Heaven in the land where the sun sets" (*Sui shu*). According to the *Nihongi* (compiled in 720), in 608 Suiko forwarded a letter to China with the greeting: "The Emperor of the East respectfully addresses the Emperor of the West."

The classical Japanese conception of sovereignty took shape in the second half of the seventh century. It was an era when, under the influence of the Chinese legal system, a highly centralized bureaucratic state was created. Significantly, the creation of this political structure was accompanied by the completion of the sacred-kingship ideology that had been developing in the previous centuries; not only was the state conceived as a liturgical community with its paradigm in heaven, but also the sovereign who ruled the state was explicitly called the *akitsumikami*, manifest *kami* (god), that is, the god who manifests himself in the phenomenal world.

The essential part of the sacred-kingship ideology was the belief in the emperor's heavenly origin, and this belief was clearly expressed in the myths of Ninigi, as narrated in the *Kojiki* (compiled in 712) and the *Nihongi*. Genealogically, Ninigi is connected with both the god Takaki (Takamimusubi) and the sun goddess Amaterasu through the marriage of Takaki's daughter to Amaterasu's son, to whom Ninigi is born. He is born in the heavenly world and, at the command of either Takaki or Amaterasu or both, descends onto the summit of Mount Takachiho. When Ninigi is about to descend, accompanied by the five clan heads, Amaterasu gives him rice grains harvested in her celestial rice fields, after which he comes down in the form of a newborn baby covered by a piece of cloth called *matoko o fusuma*. Especially noteworthy is the fact that Ninigi is granted the sacred regalia as well as the mandate of Heaven guaranteeing his eternal sovereignty on earth. Ninigi's heavenly descent was reenacted by the emperor at the annual harvest festival in the fall as well as on the occasion of his enthronement festival.

SEE ALSO Amaterasu Ōmikami; Chinese Religion, article on Mythic Themes; Japanese Religions, articles on Religious Documents, The Study of Myths; Shangdi; Tengri; Tian; Tibetan Religions, overview article.

BIBLIOGRAPHY

There is no single book dealing with the problem of sacred kingship in East Asia as a whole. On kingship in ancient China, there is a classic study in Marcel Granet's *La religion des Chinois* (Paris, 1922), translated with an introduction by Maurice Freedman as *The Religion of the Chinese People* (New York, 1975), pp. 57–96. Valuable information is also presented in D. Howard Smith's "Divine Kingship in Ancient China," *Numen* 4 (1957): 171–203. David N. Keightley has made an excellent analysis of the kingship ideology of Shang China in "The Religious Commitment: Shang Theology and the Genesis of Chinese Political Culture," *History of Religions* 17 (February–May 1978): 211–225. More recently, kingship in ancient China has been brilliantly discussed in Guangzhi Zhang's *Art, Myth, and Ritual: The Path to Political Authority in Ancient China* (Cambridge, Mass., 1983).

The conception of kingship among the nomadic peoples in Central Asia has been skillfully analyzed in Jean-Paul Roux's "L'origine céleste de la souveraineté dans les inscriptions paléo-turques de Mongolie et de Sibérie," in *La regalità sacral The Sacral Kingship* (Leiden, 1959), pp. 231–241. I have examined the symbolism of the felt carpet with special reference to both shamanism and kingship in my article "Notes on Sacred Kingship in Central Asia," *Numen* 23 (November 1976): 179–190.

On the ancient Tibetan conception of kingship, see Giuseppe Tucci's study "The Sacred Characters of the Kings of Ancient Tibet," *East and West* 6 (October 1955): 197–205.

The Tibetan conception of kingship has been compared with that of ancient Korea and Japan in my "Symbolism of 'Descent' in Tibetan Sacred Kingship and Some East Asian Parallels," *Numen* 20 (April 1973): 60–78.

The formation of kingship and its ideology in ancient Japan is discussed in my "Sacred Kingship in Early Japan: A Historical Introduction," *History of Religions* 15 (May 1976): 319–342. See also my article "Conceptions of State and Kingship in Early Japan," *Zeitschrift für Religions- und Geistesgeschichte* 28 (1976): 97–112.

New Sources

Butler, Lee. *Emperor and Aristocracy in Japan, 1467–1680: Resilience and Renewal.* Cambridge, U.K., 2002.

Ching, Julia. *Mysticism and Kingship in China: The Heart of Chinese Wisdom.* Berkeley, 1997.

Fujitani, Takashi. *Splendid Monarchy: Power and Pageantry in Modern Japan.* Berkeley, 1996.

Piggot, Joan. *The Emergence of Japanese Kingship.* Stanford, Calif., 1997.

Wakabayashi, Bob Tadashi. *Japanese Loyalism Reconstrued: Yamagata Daini's Ryushi Shinron of 1759.* Honolulu, 1995.

MANABU WAIDA (1987)
Revised Bibliography

KINJIKITILE (d. 1905) was a religious leader in southeastern Tanganyika (now Tanzania) who provided inspiration for the anticolonial struggles known as the Maji Maji Wars. In 1904, Kinjikitile became famous as a medium in a place called Ngarambe in Matumbi country, where the oppressions of the German colonial system were severe. He was possessed by Hongo, a deity subordinate to the supreme being, Bokero, whose primary ritual center was at Kibesa on the Rufiji River. At Ngarambe, Kinjikitile blended the spiritual authority of Bokero and Hongo with more local elements of ancestor veneration at a shrine center where he received offerings from pilgrims seeking intercession with the spiritual world and relief from the adversities they faced, both natural and political. In the later part of 1904 and early 1905, Kinjikitile advised the pilgrims to prepare themselves to resist the Germans and dispensed a medicine that he promised would turn the enemy's bullets into water when combat commenced. The rebellion broke out in late July 1905 without the order coming from Kinjikitile, but the ideological preparation provided by his message and the system of emissaries that spread the word and the medicine have been viewed as critical in the struggles called the Maji Maji Wars.

The Maji Maji Wars continued from July 1905 to August 1907, extending over more than 100,000 square miles and causing terrible loss of life, estimated officially at 75,000 by the Germans and at over 250,000 by modern scholars. Out of this struggle, Kinjikitile emerged as a figure of epic proportions; he is said to be a religious innovator who devised a spiritual appeal that transcended particularism and allowed the people to unite against German rule.

By 1904, resentment of colonial rule and the desire to overthrow it had become widespread in southeastern Tanganyika. The times were especially troubled in Matumbi country, which experienced a succession of adversities that went beyond the capacity of political agents to handle. In 1903 there was a severe drought, and from 1903 to 1905 the Germans increasingly insisted that the people of Matumbi engage in communal cotton growing, promising payment for the crop once it had been marketed and the administration's overhead covered. Much to the anger of the people, the payments did not materialize.

Of Kinjikitile the person very little is known. The most certain event in his biography was his death by hanging on August 4, 1905, when, together with an assistant, he became the first opposition leader to be summarily executed by the German military forces. He had lived in Ngarambe for some four years prior to this time and had emerged as an influential person; the recipient of many gifts, he had become an object of jealousy on the part of local political leaders.

Kinjikitile was a synthesizer of many religious elements. There had long been a territorial shrine to Bokero on the Rufiji to which the people had recourse in times of drought. The drought of 1903 had activated this shrine and extended its range of influence as pilgrims came from greater and greater distances. Kinjikitile's teachings drew upon this longstanding religious institution, joining the territorial authority of Bokero with local beliefs in divine possession. His use of *maji* as a new war medicine, which helped to convince people to join the rebellion, combined Bokero's preeminent association with water with traditional beliefs concerning the efficacy of sacred medicines in protecting hunters. At Ngarambe, he also built a huge *kijumba-nungu* ("house of God") for the ancestors; drawing on a resurrectionist theme, he announced that the ancestors were all at Ngarambe, ready to help their descendants defeat the Germans and restore the earthly realm. Furthermore, Kinjikitile's teachings contained elements of witch cleansing, whereby the evil within society was to be eliminated and the community morally purified. By drawing upon these traditional beliefs and using them to create an innovative ideology, Kinjikitile provided a regional and polyethnic basis for the spread of his message of resistance.

Maji Maji warriors knew that their weapons were inferior to those of the colonial forces, but the German presence was not so strong as to overawe them. They hoped for a political restoration, not of indigenous rulers, but of the Sultan of Zanzibar, whose regime became idealized because of the relatively benign form of commercial hegemony with which it was associated. Hence there was room for the Germans to investigate the possibility that Islamic propaganda or belief had played a role in the mobilization of resistance. Their conclusions were negative. Indeed, although Kinjikitile wore the traditional garb of Muslims, a long white robe called the *kanzu,* his message and idiom were decidedly drawn from traditional sources. Whether he really forged a universalistic traditional religion, as the Tanzanian historian G. C. K. Gwassa has claimed, demands closer scrutiny. Certainly his career obliges students of religion to pay well-merited attention to the structures and functions of territorial cults, ancestor veneration, and concepts of personal spiritual power and charisma. The context of the Maji Maji Wars must also be carefully weighed to refine notions of thresholds of moral outrage, recourse to religious leaders, and willingness to subscribe to a common ideology of resistance.

BIBLIOGRAPHY

Gwassa, G. C. K. "The German Intervention and African Resistance in Tanzania." In *A History of Tanzania,* edited by Isaria N. Kimambo and A. J. Temu, pp. 85–122. Nairobi, 1969.

Gwassa, G. C. K. "Kinjikitile and the Ideology of Maji Maji." In *The Historical Study of African Religion,* edited by T. O. Ranger and Isaria N. Kimambo, pp. 202–217. Berkeley, Calif., 1972.

Iliffe, John. *A Modern History of Tanganyika.* Cambridge, 1979.

MARCIA WRIGHT (1987)

KINSHIP is both a social phenomenon found in all human societies and one of the most central and contested concepts in anthropology. It is a pervasive symbolic practice of creating socially differentiated categories of people and the relationships among them, especially those relationships that concern the reproduction of people and that constitute human "being." A significant aspect of kinship relationships is that they apply not only to contemporaries, but transcend the living to include predecessors and ancestors as well as descendants and future generations.

Who is a relative and how relations of kinship are defined varies from culture to culture. But the ideas and principles underpinning these different kinships systems are often closely associated with religious ideas, addressing existential questions for all human beings, such as: What makes people humans? How do people come into the world? What constitutes a person? What happens to persons when they die? Wherein consists the continuity of social relationships that transcends generations?

THE CONCEPT. Early anthropologists noticed that the various peoples they studied differed greatly in the ways they named and categorized kin, defined appropriate behavior among kinspeople, reckoned descent, regulated marriage, and organized succession among the generations. Kinship and its diversity became the central issue in anthropology for much of the twentieth century, mainly for two reasons. First, both an explanation for the diverse systems of kinship and, in the face of such diversity, a universal definition needed to be found. This taxing issue led to most of the central debates in anthropology until quite recently. Arguments over what the term *kinship* designates, and what its analytical validity is, resulted in a robust reconfiguration of kinship studies since the 1970s. Second, many of the societies anthropologists studied were societies without state organization, and one of the leading questions was how social order and political structure were defined and maintained in such societies.

Kinship was considered to play the key role in providing a basic structure for the organization of the social life of stateless and, as they came to be called, as a type, "primitive" societies. Their social structure, Meyer Fortes stated in *The Web of Kinship among the Tallensi,* was "kinship writ large" and "kinship . . . is one of the irreducible principles on which their organized social life depends" (1949, p. 340). At the time, this was a progressive approach, emphasizing the rationality, functionality, and essentially human creativity of such societies. But it became untenable, both because it is too reductionist and because of the inherent evolutionist dichotomy between "primitive" and "civilized"—the former designating a more natural state of social life and the latter higher cultural development and social institutions—which suggested a great, substantive divide among all forms of human society. Rather than substantive, the differences and contrasts of sociality between societies came to be seen as relative. Although research in "civilized" societies revealed many structural similarities with "primitive" societies, reducing the social structure of more egalitarian societies to the principles of kinship disregards influential factors such as the division of labor, gender, or inequality. The link between kinship and social structure is critical in some societies, but it cannot be made at the expense of disregarding the dynamics of religious or political or economic factors.

At the same time, the ethnographic evidence across cultures does not uphold the typologies of social order proposed on the ground of a supposed correlation between kinship constructs such as descent, kinship terminology, or marriage patterns and aspects of social organization such as gender relations, social roles, the allocations of rights and obligations, or the distribution of power. In this regard, studies that combined the analysis of kinship and gender since the 1970s contributed critically to dismantling formal models that linked kinship institutions to social organization. The way kinship is conceptualized and structured in a society does not predict the totality of social life.

KINSHIP AND THE NATURAL. For much of the twentieth century, anthropologists defined kinship as genealogical relatedness, that is, as relationships based on consanguinity (the idea that related people share blood or biogenetic substance) and affinity (relationships forged as a result of marriage). This meant that the diverse ways in which people in different cultures define who is a relative and organize their systems of kinship relationships were explained by falling back on the notion that this diversity nevertheless must have a referent in the natural facts of life, the natural processes of human sexual reproduction. A critical distinction, between social kinship and biological kinship, was introduced. Biological relations were considered given in nature, and therefore kinship could be singled out as the primary structure ordering social relations in simple societies. The social relations of kinship were regarded as cultural constructs and representations that more or less recognized and interpreted biological ties and the given facts of life.

In the 1960s and 1970s a debate erupted concerning what kinship is all about and engendering a rethinking of the concept. It resulted in the analytical separation of physical kinship from biological kinship. The cultural notions of physical procreation and consubstantiality—how people considered themselves to be related through shared physical substance, whether it was blood, or semen, or food—should be seen as separate from true biological facts and as cultural interpretations of genealogical ties (see Holy, 1996 for a useful discussion). A major turning point in the still ongoing reconfiguration of kinship was *A Critique of the Study of Kinship* (1984) by David Schneider, who targeted the analytical distinction between biological and social kinship, which he identified as stemming from a European and American cultural bias, from Western folk models of kinship which are embedded in what he called the "general characteristic of European culture toward what might be called 'biologistic' ways of constituting and conceiving human character, human nature, and human behavior" (1984, p. 175). Reflecting a general shift in anthropology from function to meaning, Schneider's pioneering work on kinship in American culture analyzed "the distinctive features which define the person as a relative" (1968, p. 19), examining American kinship as a symbolic system in which biological relatedness and sexual relations play a fundamental role as symbols for social relationships. In many non-European traditions, kinship relationships are not necessarily conceptualized as an elaboration of natural processes or as the tracing of genealogical connections (and where biological ideas have gained purchase in the course of the global spread of Western culture, they are often being reworked and innovatively amalgamated with existing cultural ideas). Cultural concepts of procreation may involve critical religious elements unrelated to biological processes.

The people of the Micronesian island of Yap, for example, single out human existence as categorically different from the existence of animals such as their domestic pigs. In Yap culture, human procreation and descent involve not only bodily processes but also a spiritual component, the reincarnation of ancestral souls. Descent only exists in humans. It charts the reincarnation of ancestral souls and is distinct from reckoning parentage for the breeding of pigs. Anthropologists have always insisted that descent is a concept of social organization, referring to relatedness based on common ancestry, which may include people not related biologically and only those genealogical relationships that are socially recognized. In the Yap definition, however, descent and the relationship to ancestry is part of the process of conception.

Since Schneider's critique, anthropologists approach kinship cross-culturally, with an increased reflective sensitivity to preconceived ideas about what kinship is. As Ladislav Holy points out in *Anthropological Perspectives on Kinship* (1996), "the most significant development in the study of kinship has been the growing awareness of the cultural specificity of what were previously taken to be the natural facts on which all kinship systems were presumed to be built" (p. 165). The resulting challenges made kinship again one of the most innovative areas of study, connecting research across diverse disciplinary, analytical, theoretical, and ethnographic sites. Recent studies of local and specific conceptualizations of kinship foreground the questions of what kinship means and who is a relative and why, and they seek to answer them empirically rather than take them as given by definition.

DEFINITION. If the defining moment of kinship is not referenced to biology, what kind of definition can be put forth that enables cross-cultural comparison but avoids the pitfalls of previous definitions? Current working definitions of the concept—and there is no single agreed-upon definition—tend to go back to first principles. They focus on those relationships that in any given cultural context are considered constitutive of personhood and social human being, of how people come into being, achieve personhood, and attain a socially recognized afterlife. There may be exceptions, but in most human societies these constitutive relationships are marked as distinct among all social relations. They often articulate fundamental ideas about relationality itself, about how social relationships can be forged, maintained, and properly dismantled. They also tend to articulate a temporal component so that such constitutive relationships provide a person with a past, with relationships to predecessors, such as ancestry, descent, and collective history.

Raymond C. Kelly offered a comprehensive and cross-culturally useful definition of kinship in *Constructing Inequalities* (1993). Significantly, he connects kinship to the concepts of the *body* and the *person*:

> Kinship relations are social relations predicated upon cultural conceptions that specify the processes by which an individual comes into being and develops into a complete (i.e., mature) social person. These processes encompass the acquisition and transformation of both spiritual and corporeal components of being. Sexual reproduction and the formulation of paternal and maternal contributions are an important component of, but are not coextensive with, the relevant processes. This is due to the ethnographic fact that a full complement of spiritual components is never derived exclusively from the parents. Moreover, the sexually transmitted ingredients of corporeal substance are frequently transmitted in other ways as well. (p. 521)

These further processes of manipulating and modifying substances and spiritual components involved in attaining full personhood and in forging kin relations should not be disregarded because of a biologically based definition of kinship. As Kelly points out, "there is no analytic utility in artificially restricting the category of kin relations to relations predicated on some but not all the constitutive processes of personhood because these processes are culturally formulated as components of an integrated system" (1993, p. 522).

By dissociating the concept of kinship from biology and integrating it with the process of how persons come into being, the investigative focus shifted to ways in which kinship is embedded in the social life of people and to its connections to aspects of culture such as religion.

KINSHIP, PERSON, AND BODY. The approach to kinship and social organization through the concepts of the person and the body was most powerfully developed by Marilyn Strathern in *The Gender of the Gift* (1988), a comparison of social life across the diverse cultures of Melanesia. She generalized the Melanesian person as "a microcosm of relations" and the body as "a register, a site of . . . interaction . . . composed of the specific historical action of others" (pp. 131–132), and both concepts are keys to understanding social organization and social units such as descent, group formation, exchange, and marriage arrangements. The approach echoes well beyond that region, inspiring studies triangulating kinship, the person, and the body elsewhere, including the West. Examining kinship in conjunction with personhood also sheds new light on the structuring of rituals, particularly life-cycle rituals such as initiation, marriage, and mortuary rituals in which the body often takes center stage. As Kelly's definition suggests, life-cycle rituals modify and complement the composition of the body and the constitution of the person, which began with procreation. Death rituals often involve the dismantling of the network of relationships centered on the deceased and the final repayment of contributions towards the deceased person by others. This history of relationships, contributions, and obligations is literally embodied in the deceased person, and, with the body gone, the person and the obligations need to be discharged by the surviving kin of the deceased. Kinship and life-cycle rituals are analyzed here in a combined approach, and such rituals, which often articulate and realize religious ideas, are part of the process of attaining personhood.

Some recent kinship studies reveal the importance of feeding and nurture to the process of kinship. Janet Carsten showed that while the people of Langkawi (Malaysia) regard blood as a substance with which a child is born and which differentiates kin, blood as a kinship substance is modified and transformed by breast-milk which the child ingests, and later by the food the child eats; through the daily food that was cooked on the hearth of the house and that members of a household share, they have a substance in common which has qualities similar to blood. The body of a Langkawi person undergoes a social process that reflects the relationships of commensality, the sharing of food, and cohabitation that the person maintains. One consequence of this processual conceptualization of kinship is that birth siblings and adopted siblings are not socially differentiated if they were nursed by the same woman and fed from the same hearth, because the substance that makes them related to others is considered to be the same.

The cultural understanding of procreation and personhood among Trobriand Islanders (Papua New Guinea) incorporates significant religious and relational concepts that structure social organization. Trobriand procreation not only involves bodily substance and the reincarnation of spirits, but also the creation of form. The Trobriand model of human reproduction preoccupied many observers and was debated as an instance of virgin birth, or denial of physiological paternity and sexual intercourse as a condition for procreation. This is based on a fundamental misconception of Trobriand traditional belief that conception takes place when an ancestral soul enters the womb of a woman who belongs to the same landholding descent group with which the ancestor is associated. Souls thus retain the descent and kin classification they had as living beings, and they are reincarnated into the same kin group. Sexual intercourse is critical to this process because it provides the soul with a material human form, the body, which is made from blood, a kinship substance provided by the mother, and which is shaped by the father's activities during sexual intercourse with the mother. Both the maternal and paternal contributions are vital to this process. The mother's contribution consists of providing blood (essence) and spirit, and the father's of forming the child's body, which takes an appearance that resembles the father, and of enabling the child's growth and eventual separation from the maternal body. A Trobriand father will contribute to feed and shape his child's bodily form and appearance by affectionately taking care of the child, in what is expressed by Trobrianders as paternal nurture and which remains a vital factor in the course of a person's life. The different maternal and paternal contributions to the making of a child are symbolized in the relationships between the child and wider sets of maternal and paternal kin. They also shape the relationships between different descent groups who maintain relations of paternal nurture with each other, expressed in various exchange events. These collective relationships acknowledge their mutual interdependence from each other for the regeneration of the descent group. Like an ancestral soul, they depend on paternal nurture to be able to exist in a material, bodily form.

Recent scholarship on kinship and new reproductive biotechnology, international adoption, and gay and lesbian families shows that a more flexible concept of kinship, emphasizing relationality and process, may be at work significantly in European and North American practices. At the same time, these new contexts for kinship raise new questions about how relatives, especially parents, are defined, challenging traditional Euro-American notions that human reproduction is a natural process through which the ties of kinship emerge unproblematically. The new reproductive technologies manipulate what were deemed to be natural processes so that biological relatedness no longer figures as a given ground for kin relations. Marilyn Strathern succinctly states the problem as "what is interfered with is the very idea of a natural fact" (1992, p. 41); nature assisted by technology becomes part of culture. Shared substance, rather than biology, may also be a powerful connection for members in families created through adoption. These innovative ways of making kinship suggest that, in the European tradition, the ground for relationality as it is experienced by people is no longer, or may never have been, simply biology and nature after all.

Ancestors and Descent. Ancestors are important in most kinship systems. Shared ancestry can be the basis for the classification of kin into social categories, particularly descent categories. Ancestors are, by definition, remembered kin, but not all kin are remembered as ancestors, and which kin become ancestors varies. Among some Amerindian peoples only personally known kin become ancestors, whereas in many African and Asian cultures ancestors and their relationships are remembered for many generations. In yet other cultures ancestors may be remembered as names rather than as deceased kin, but as names associated with land and people who, by bestowing the names to children, forge descent as a relationship between ancestral name, land, and kinspeople. Among the Dobu Islanders of Papua New Guinea, the physical remains of ancestors are the focus of descent. Dobuans return their dead kin to their village of origin and bury them in the center of the village. The burial mound thus symbolizes lineal descent unadulterated by affinal relations. Among Australian Aboriginals it is often the memory of the ancestors' journeys in the country, and their activities and experiences at places in the landscape, that is the content of descent and connects people to ancestors, the landscape, and their past.

Ancestors may be the focal point for the definition of kin categories and groups, in the case of lineages and clans for example, which comprise persons related through descent exclusively through either the male (patrilineal) or the female (matrilineal) line. In societies with a strongly developed patrilineal descent structure, such as the Lugbara of Uganda, different categories of patrilineal male and female ancestors are distinguished depending on their descent status and whether they contributed significantly to the polity of the descent group during their lifetime. In these societies, genealogies record effective ancestors.

In community-based religions the offices of ritual experts and access to esoteric knowledge may be organized by kinship statuses and succession through descent. Only people categorized as descendants of a particular ancestor may be permitted to have certain knowledge or the right to perform rituals. Such experts often employ this knowledge and perform rituals on behalf of the whole community or society. In many Australian Aboriginal, lowland South American, and Native American cultures of the Southwest, the kinship system involves a form of dual organization in which people are classified into moieties (halves into which the total society divides), which are part of a dual cosmology. Moiety organization is related to kinship and descent, but it is often relatively flexible and may involve multiple differentiations, which enables cooperation between the moieties. Depending on the specific system, a person may belong to one or several cross-cutting moieties. Moiety affiliation may be strictly through descent, or it may change according to the specifics of marriage exchanges or of residence. Some moieties are not linked to kinship, but are ritual moieties. Among Yolngu, an Australian Aboriginal people of Arnhem Land, there are named matrilineal and patrilineal moieties as well as ceremonial nonlineal moieties. Moieties own certain cults and rituals which they perform for the whole community, which in turn supports these services by organizing the performances.

Extending the Morality of Kinship. Many communities extend the use of kinship terms—the specific names for the different kinship relationships and those used to address kin—to refer to non-kin. This is a metaphorical or classificatory use of kinship which is significant, because it extends the morality of kinship to other people and sometimes to other beings. In Christianity, God is addressed as Father, and Jesus is addressed as the Son of God. Similarly, members of Christian faith communities and monasteries use kinship terms to express relationships within their communities. In doing so they express their separation from their families of origin and their commitment to the social relations of the community. It has also been suggested that the sharing in the Holy Spirit serves as a basis of essence for the social relationships of kinship in Spirit. From an anthropological point of view, one understands such uses in different Christian communities across the world as reflecting cultural diversity and diverse views of God as Father—depending on the way in which the role of father is culturally conceived, for example.

In some societies, kinship and ancestry is extended to animals and other beings who live together with people in the same environment. The Nayaka, a people living in the Nilgiri Hills of Tamil Nadu (South India), regard the forest in which they live as a parent. Nurit Bird-David (1999) reports that Nayaka refer to features in the forest such as hills or rocks in the same terms they use to refer to the spirits of those who were their immediate predecessors (their recently deceased ancestors)—as "big father" or "big mother"—and they refer to themselves as children. In relation to their forest they see themselves as children of the forest, and they maintain relationships of sharing. The morality of kinship, specifically the sharing morality and intimacy of the parent-child relationship, extends to the environment. As Tim Ingold notes, "the environment shares its bounty with humans just as humans share with one another, thereby integrating both human and non-human components of the world into one, all embracing 'cosmic economy of sharing'" (Ingold, 2000, p. 44).

Such use of kin terms is part of a wider phenomenon by which people attribute personhood to the beings with whom they share an environment (e.g., animals, trees, rocks, places), whether or not they address them by kin terms. Attributing personhood means that one regards other beings as capable of maintaining social relationships among themselves and with other beings. It indicates what Bird-David calls a "we-ness which absorbs differences" (1999, p. 78), and subsumes kinship, or what Roy Wagner (1977) identified among Papuan cultures as the very ground of being rather than merely of humanity, namely the innate capacity for social relationship both with those similar and with those differentiated, which renders all beings of an environment akin.

See Also Ancestors, article on Ancestor Worship; Community; Family; Genealogy; Marriage; Totemism.

BIBLIOGRAPHY

Bird-David, Nurit. "Animism Revisited: Personhood, Environment, and Relational Epistemology." *Current Anthropology* 40, suppl. (February 1999): 67–79, 86–91.

Bloch, Maurice. "Zafimaniry Birth and Kinship Theory." *Social Anthropology* 1 (1993): 119–32. This concise article outlines the processual nature of kinship and marriage among Zafimaniry (Madagascar), where a couple emerges through the children they raise and the increasing solidity of the house they build over their lifetime; the house turns into a family shrine upon their death.

Bloch, Maurice, and Jonathan Parry, eds. *Death and the Regeneration of Life.* Cambridge, U.K., 1982. Various excellent articles dealing with death, kinship, descent, and funeral rituals.

Carsten, Janet. *The Heat of the Hearth: The Process of Kinship in a Malay Fishing Community.* Oxford, U.K., 1997. A readable and evocative ethnographic account of kinship on the island of Langkawi, Malaysia, and a grounded theoretical discussion of the nature of kinship, especially the concept of substance.

Carsten, Janet, ed. *Cultures of Relatedness: New Approaches to the Study of Kinship.* Cambridge, U.K., 2000. A collection of articles providing detailed ethnographic accounts of various cultural idioms of relatedness in an attempt to rethink kinship theory.

Collier, Jane Fishburne, and Sylvia Junko Yanagisako, eds. *Gender and Kinship: Essays toward a Unified Analysis.* Stanford, Calif., 1987. A milestone in kinship studies, dismantling the idea of kinship as a separate domain of social life and putting forth the cultural construction of difference as the central issue in understanding both kinship and gender.

Desjarlais, Robert. *Sensory Biographies: Lives and Deaths Among Nepal's Yolmo Buddhists.* Berkeley, Calif., 2003. Insightful and beautifully written biographical accounts of several persons portraying the many ways kinship and religion shape a life and are closely interwoven in a person's experience of life.

Fortes, Meyer. *The Web of Kinship Among the Tallensi.* London, 1949. A classic ethnographic monograph of kinship in the structural-functionalist mode of a culture where kinship is closely linked to ancestral authority.

Franklin, Sara, and Susan McKinnon, eds. *Relative Values: Reconfiguring Kinship Studies.* Durham, N.C., 2001. A major recent contribution towards repositioning kinship studies, particularly in response to empirical and theoretical challenges posed by international adoption, reproductive technology, and genetic projects in a globalized world.

Holy, Ladislav. *Anthropological Perspectives on Kinship.* London, 1996. A sensitive and well-argued introductory text on the concept of kinship and its history, and still the best available today.

Ingold, Tim. *The Perception of the Environment: Essays on Livelihood, Dwelling, and Skill.* London, 2000. An innovative, highly synoptic approach to understanding human culture through relationality, environment, personhood, and interaction.

Kelly, Raymond C. *Constructing Inequality: The Fabrication of a Hierarchy of Virtue among the Etoro.* Ann Arbor, Mich., 1993.

Kuper, Adam. *The Invention of Primitive Society: Transformations of an Illusion.* London and New York, 1988. A comprehensive and influential critique of the notion of the primitive, kinship-based society representing the origins of human society, discussing different theoretical traditions such as totemism, lineage theory, and alliance theory.

Middleton, John. *Lugbara Religion.* London, 1960; new edition, Oxford, 1999. A classic account of kinship and ancestor worship in Africa.

Mosko, Mark. "On 'Virgin Birth,' Comparability, and Anthropological Method." *Current Anthropology* 39, no. 5 (1998): 685–687. A short but concise discussion of Trobriand Islanders' cultural theory of conception, including relevant references.

Morphy, Howard. *Ancestral Connections: Art and the Yolngu System of Knowledge.* Chicago, 1991. A readable ethnography on the complex relations of ceremony, art, land, ancestry, and kinship among an Aboriginal Australian people.

Ortiz, Alfonso. *The Tewa World: Space, Time, Being, and Becoming in a Pueblo Society.* Chicago, 1969. An encompassing ethnographic account of a system of dual classification, of the dynamic of its inherent division and unity, tracing its application in all aspects of culture.

Schneider, David M. *American Kinship: A Cultural Account.* Englewood Cliffs, N.J., 1968.

Schneider, David M. *A Critique of the Study of Kinship.* Ann Arbor, Mich., 1984.

Schweitzer, Peter, ed. *Dividends of Kinship: Meanings and Uses of Social Relatedness.* London and New York, 2000. These articles examine kinship as a practice and explore how kinship is embedded in social life through the way people in various cultures make kinship concepts work to address specific opportunities and pursue social strategies.

Strathern, Marilyn. *The Gender of the Gift.* Berkeley, Calif., 1988. One of the most theoretically innovative and influential comparative works by a leading anthropologist, a synthesis addressing kinship, personhood, gender, and sociality in Melanesia.

Strathern, Marilyn. *After Nature: English Kinship in the Late Twentieth Century.* Cambridge, U.K., 1992. An account of English kinship in the context of knowledge production, assisted human reproduction, and consumer society, tracing the wider implications of producing natural ties through reproductive technology for the way human knowledge is conceptualized.

Wagner, Roy. "Are There Social Groups in the New Guinea Highlands?" In *Frontiers of Anthropology,* edited by Murray J. Leaf. New York, 1974. A seminal essay showing how the exchange of food substances connects with kinship substance in a New Guinea society and how kin groups are elicited temporarily through the use of named differentiations and constitute themselves in the process of such successive exchange events, rather than in a given kinship structure.

Wagner, Roy. "Scientific and Indigenous Papuan Conceptions of the Innate." In *Subsistence and Survival: Rural Ecology in the Pacific,* edited by Timothy P. Bayliss-Smith and Richard G. Feachem, pp. 385–410. London and New York, 1977.

Weiner, Annette. *Women of Value, Men of Renown: New Perspectives on Trobriand Exchange.* Austin, Tex., 1976.

CLAUDIA GROSS (2005)

KIREEVSKII, IVAN

KIREEVSKII, IVAN (1806–1856), was a Russian publicist and Slavophile. In his early years Kireevskii's literary criticism gained him the patronage of Vasilii Zhukovskii (1783–1852) and the approval of Aleksandr Pushkin (1799–1837). He founded and was briefly the editor of a promising journal, *Evropeets*, closed by the authorities in 1832. This event drove Kireevskii into semiretirement, from which he was to emerge only occasionally and with reluctance. Only in the last decade of his life was he to find a cause that helped to justify his withdrawal from society: collaboration with the monastic elders of the hermitage at Optino. This in its turn provided him with a theological diagnosis for what in 1853 he called "the disorder of my inner forces."

In his early years Kireevskii was a proponent of Westernization. But by the late 1830s he insisted on the role of Russia as a lodestar for a western Europe in decline. Without any marked chauvinism or aggressiveness (in this he differed from several of his contemporaries and successors), he had become one of the founding fathers of the Slavophile movement.

For Kireevskii this undertaking had involved a conversion or at least a return to the Orthodox church. At the prompting of his wife, Natal'ia Arbeneva, Kireevskii had turned his attention from Friedrich Schelling (1775–1854) to the church fathers. His first guide in Orthodox church life was his wife's confessor, Filaret (d. 1842), a monk of the Novo-Spasskii monastery in Moscow. But in his search for guidance Kireevskii also visited the Optino community, which was in the forefront of a Russian hesychast revival. Here he found two profound and subtle guides—the elder Leonid (1768–1841) and his successor Makarii (1788–1860). Kireevskii's acceptance of their guidance presaged the reconciliation of the Westernized gentry and (subsequently) intelligentsia with the church; and it anticipated what is so often termed the Russian "religious renaissance" of the early twentieth century.

At Optino Kireevskii committed himself to an ambitious, unprecedented program—the editing, translation, and publication of Greek patristic texts. The program attracted the patronage of Metropolitan Filaret of Moscow and proved to be a landmark in the history of Russian publishing. Among the authors made available were Isaac the Syrian (d. 700?), Maximos the Confessor (c. 580–662), John Climacus (c. 570–649), Symeon the New Theologian (949–1022), and, representative of Russian mystics, Nil Sorskii (1433–1508). The first volume issued (1847) was, appropriately enough, called *The Life and Writings of the Moldavian Starets Paisii Velichkovskii* (1722–1794). Paisii's influence had stimulated the resurgence of hesychast spirituality at the Optino community.

With all his concern for the traditional spiritual disciplines, Kireevskii had no intention of discarding reason. Nor did he see Orthodox tradition as something finite. He spoke of patristic teaching as "an embryo for the philosophy of the future." That future philosophy must not be the task of an isolated individual. Kireevskii's "integrality" of the soul was to be attained solely by "the common endeavor of all who believe and think." The concept of *sobornost'*, first formulated by Kireevskii's friend Aleksei Khomiakov (1804–1860), was equally congenial to Kireevskii himself. Each was eager to promote that sense of Orthodox community and organic fellowship to which *sobornost'* refers.

Several of Kireevskii's insights were to prove seminal for Russian thinkers of succeeding decades. He died an early death of cholera and was buried at Optino, his spiritual home. Despite the neglect of Kireevskii's reputation and depredations of Optino during the Soviet period, his tombstone has recently been recovered and restored.

BIBLIOGRAPHY

Kireevskii's complete works were edited by M. O. Gershenzon as *Polnoe sobranie sochinenii I. V. Kireevskago* in two volumes (1911; reprint, Farnborough, 1970). To these should be added the German translation of Kireevskii's diaries for 1852–1854 (the original remains unpublished): "Das Tagebuch Ivan Vasil'evic Kirejevskijs, 1852–1854," translated by Eberhard Müller, *Jahrbücher für Geschichte Osteuropas* 14 (1966): 167–194. Two monographs may be mentioned: Abbott Gleason's *European and Muscovite: Ivan Kireevsky and the Origins of Slavophilism* (Cambridge, Mass., 1972) and Peter K. Christoff's *An Introduction to Nineteenth-Century Russian Slavophilism: A Study in Ideas*, vol. 2, *I. V. Kireevskij* (The Hague, 1972).

SERGEI HACKEL (1987)

KISSING

KISSING SEE POSTURES AND GESTURES; SALUTATIONS; TOUCHING

KITAGAWA, JOSEPH M.

KITAGAWA, JOSEPH M. (1915–1992) was a historian of religions, humanist, Asianist, priest, theologian, educator, and administrator. The career of Joseph Mitsuo Kitagawa, who served as an editor of the first edition of *The Encyclopedia of Religion* (1987), spanned a number of continents, traditions, disciplines, and roles.

EARLY YEARS. Born to Japanese Christian parents in Osaka, his father an Episcopal priest, from his youth Kitagawa lived within the minority Christian tradition in Japan, but was attuned to the variety and depth of Asian thought and belief. Reflecting on his life, Kitagawa wrote that:

> I have always been awed, fascinated and inspired by the lives of two men, Confucius and the Apostle Paul. . . .[P]ersons like myself, born and raised in the Far East, lived in the shadow of the towering figure of Confucius. We were inspired by his view of common human nature, his insistence on the educability of all men and women, and his vision of ethical universalism based on the cultivation of human goodness. His vocation was the training of scholars (*Ju*), who would influence the administrative policies of the nation. Although

> he himself failed miserably during his lifetime to persuade the rulers to adopt his policies, Confucius left a high standard for his disciples to follow. . . .An educated person had a vocation to master the saving knowledge of the sacred past, to transmit it to the present generation, and to interpret contemporary experience in the light of accumulated wisdom. . . .As a child of a parsonage, I have been exposed from my earliest days to the name of another important figure, namely the Apostle Paul. . . .I have come to appreciate over the years the very human qualities of the Apostle Paul. Also his piercing insight into human nature and its predicament resonates in many of us. . .Paul. . .is a man of unusual talents coupled with human weaknesses, completely dedicated to his vocation of spreading the gospel. . . .For this vocation he joyfully endured afflictions, hardships, calamities, beatings, imprisonments, and hunger. Significantly, it was his spiritual maturity which brought him to a profound understanding of the meaning of love as the mystery of God. . . .The lives of these two persons. . .remain constant reminders to me that our worth must be measured not primarily by our accomplishments, not even by scholarly accomplishments, but by the quality of vocation we find in life. (Kitagawa, 1979, pp. 18–20)

Kitagawa's own experiences and studies led him to a life-long commitment of mediating between and among contrasting viewpoints. He graduated from Rikkyo University, affiliated with the Episcopal Church, and like his brother followed their father in becoming an Episcopal priest. Coming to the United States to continue his theological studies just before World War II, he was caught in the internment of Japanese and Japanese-Americans for the duration of the war. He commented later that, while ministering to the religious needs of fellow internees, these relocation camps were his real introduction to American society. He embraced America's democratic ideals, and yet noted, with sadness, "America's failure to fulfill her creed of democratic equality" (Kitagawa, 1992, p. 128), not only in his own internment experiences, but domestically on racial issues and internationally on refugee matters. Not until after the war, in October 1945, could he resume his studies, first taking a bachelor of divinity degree at Seabury-Western Theological Seminary in Evanston, Illinois, in 1947. During this time he also organized an Episcopal mission to Chicago's Japanese population; this endeavor eventually became the Asian ministry of the diocese. He studied for his doctorate under Joachim Wach at the Divinity School of the University of Chicago, completing his dissertation on "Kobo-daishi and Shingon Buddhism" in 1951.

ACADEMIC CAREER. Kitagawa joined the faculty of his alma mater in 1951 and served in a number of capacities, first assisting his mentor Joachim Wach in cultivating the postwar interest in the study of religion. Their efforts to combine the earlier American tradition of comparative religion with the European notion of *Religionswissenschaft* were cut short by Wach's premature death in 1955. Kitagawa was instrumental in securing the appointment of Mircea Eliade at the University of Chicago; together with Charles H. Long, and later other scholars, they established the "history of religions" approach, as epitomized in the journal they founded, *History of Religions: An International Journal for Comparative Studies* (1961–). While promoting the study of religion on the graduate level, Kitagawa helped educate a large group of historians of religion, and trained a number of doctoral students in the area of Japanese religion, who helped develop the field of "Japanese religion" within North America. He was an indefatigable advocate of comparative religion as a component of undergraduate education, and of the role of trained historians of religions to teach such courses; he foresaw the role of state institutions as playing a prominent function in the teaching about religion, once undertaken only in private institutions. Kitagawa's students, both those in his special area of Japanese religion, and in other fields of the history of religions, found academic positions throughout the world, especially in the United States and Japan. He is remembered by his colleagues and students as impeccable in dress and manners, a consummate diplomat, and an able and tireless administrator.

Kitagawa interrupted his own academic work to serve for two terms from 1970 to 1980 as dean of the Divinity School. As dean he looked back to the vision of William Rainey Harper (the academic founder of the University of Chicago, a scholar of biblical and Middle Eastern studies who also insisted on the scientific study of religion), finding in him a role model for mediating both between academic and professional roles and among various fields. Following Harper's lead, Kitagawa promoted a threefold graduate and professional mission for the Divinity School: balancing theological inquiry, the humanistic (or scientific) study of religion, and the development of professional religious leadership. Kitagawa's work as dean has been summed up by his close colleague, Martin Marty: "Kitagawa regularly remarked on the ways the Harper model could be used to criticize excesses in today's world. Thus he was not impressed by neo-positivist, 'more secular than thou' scholars of religion who pretended that believing communities did not exist, or disdained them. He was equally unimpressed by professional ministerial or theological schools which underestimated the need for critical scholarly inquiry" (Marty, 1985, p. 13).

Kitagawa was furthering these goals when he was instrumental in establishing the Institute for the Advanced Study of Religion (now the Martin Marty Center) at the University of Chicago. In the United States he was a founding member and mainstay of the American Society for the Study of Religion, and he was prominent in his support of the International Association for the History of Religions. Kitagawa's service to the field was international, sitting on the board of directors for both the International Institute for the Study of Religion (Tokyo) and the Fund for Theological Education; he was editorial advisor to the *Encyclopaedia Britannica* and on the board of editors for *Numen.* He lectured widely throughout the world, and delivered a number of major lectures, including the Joachim Wach Memorial Lecture at the

University of Marburg, the Charles Wesley Brashares Lectures on the History of Religions at Northwestern University, the Charles Strong Memorial Lecture in Comparative Religions at Australian universities, the Rockwell Lecture Series at Rice University, and Lectures on the History of Religions (sponsored by the American Council of Learned Societies). For his scholarship he received a number of honorary degrees.

SCHOLARLY CONTRIBUTION. Several autobiographical statements can serve to characterize Kitagawa's work. "Having a father who was a Confucian-turned-Christian minister and growing up in the Yamato area, the oldest district of Japan, with the children of Buddhist and Shinto clerics as my playmates, made me realize the importance of religion early in life" (Kitagawa, 1987, p. ix). In contrast to some Japanese scholars who began with the study of religion and ended up in the pursuit of theology, Kitagawa notes: "I found that my own academic pilgrimage moved in the opposite direction: from theology to the philosophy of religion to *Religionswissenschaft* (known as the history of religions, or *Shūkyō-gaku*)" (1987, p. ix). Grounded in his own experience as a Japanese Christian, Kitagawa reached out to Asians to broaden their perspective of Christianity, at the same time chiding Westerners for their Eurocentric conception of Christianity. Having received his earliest academic training in Japan, and then undergoing a harsh introduction to American democracy through internment, he completed his graduate work in an American setting under the European influence of Wach, and later refined his understanding of religion in collaboration with his colleague Eliade; he parlayed Wach's notion of *Verstehen* (understanding) and *Religionswissenschaft* into the more recent category of history of religions. Like Eliade, Kitagawa deplored the fact that we do not have a more precise term than *religion*, but insisted that "the point of departure of *Religionswissenschaft* is the historically given religions" (Eliade and Kitagawa, 1959, p. 21). He acknowledged in a critique of the history of religions approach that "there are no purely religious phenomena," but agreed with Eliade that "the meaning of a religious phenomenon can be understood only if it is studied as something religious," viewing it religio-scientifically or religio-historically (Eliade and Kitagawa, 1959, p. 21).

SEE ALSO Japanese Religions, overview article.

BIBLIOGRAPHY

From early in his career Kitagawa wrote on a wide range of issues for a general audience in various publications, voicing his concerns about social and political issues, such as the wartime internment of Japanese-Americans and the treatment of refugees, and speaking to theological issues (especially the situation of Asian churches and the character of missionary activity). The best source for such materials is in the *Festschrift* edited by Frank E. Reynolds and Theodore M. Ludwig, *Transitions and Transformations in the History of Religions: Essays in Honor of Joseph M. Kitagawa* (Leiden, 1980); the bibliography, pp. 3–9, includes a comprehensive listing of both books and articles to 1980. Reynolds and Ludwig have also provided (pp. 11–21) an overview of Kitagawa's methodology. Some of his publications undertook the editing of posthumous works of his mentor, Joachim Wach: *The Comparative Study of Religions* (New York, 1958); *Understanding and Believing: Essays* (New York, 1968); and *Essays in the History of Religions* (New York, 1988). He also authored *Gibt es ein Verstehen fremder Religionen?: Mit einer Biographie Joachim Wachs und einer vollst(ndigen Bibliographie seiner Werke* (Leiden, 1963). Kitagawa was generous in editing the work of others, such as (with Alan L. Miller) Ichiro Hori, *Folk Religion in Japan: Continuity and Change* (Chicago, 1968); he co-edited (with Charles H. Long) *Myths and Symbols: Studies in Honor of Mircea Eliade* (Chicago, 1969); he also co-edited a number of volumes in Japanese, and some of his articles and books were translated into Japanese.

Kitagawa's own contribution to the field is found in articles such as "The History of Religions in America," in *The History of Religions: Essays in Methodology*, ed. Mircea Eliade and Joseph M. Kitagawa (Chicago, 1959), reprinted in *The History of Religions: Understanding Human Experience* (Atlanta, 1987), a collection of his key articles on the history of religions and *Religionswissenschaft*. Kitagawa is best known for his work in Japanese religion. His doctoral dissertation, "Kobo-daishi and Shingon Buddhism" (Chicago, 1951), although not published, has been used widely (in photoduplicated copies in university libraries). His major work is *Religion in Japanese History* (New York, 1966), an overview still utilized as a textbook; his key articles are collected in *On Understanding Japanese Religion* (Princeton, N.J., 1987). While continuing his scholarly work, he remained in touch with his concern for social issues, editing *The American Refugee Policy: Ethical and Religious Reflections* (Minneapolis, 1984). At the end of his career Kitagawa turned to broader themes: the theological work *The Christian Tradition: Beyond its European Captivity* (Philadelphia, 1992), and the synthetic works *The Quest for Human Unity: A Religious History* (Minneapolis, 1990) and *Spiritual Liberation and Human Freedom in Contemporary Asia* (New York, 1990). He wrote a brief autobiographical account, "Vocation and Maturity" (pp. 18–20), in *Criterion: A Publication of the University of Chicago Divinity School* 18, no. 2 (1979). Appreciations of Kitagawa's contributions as a scholar, educator, and administrator are included in *Criterion* 24, no. 3 (1985), which includes Robert Wood Lynn, "The Harper Legacy: An Appreciation of Joseph M. Kitagawa"(pp. 4–8); Martin E. Marty, "Joseph M. Kitagawa, the Harper Tradition, and this Divinity School" (pp. 9–13); and D. Gale Johnson, "Comments on Joseph Kitagawa's Day" (pp. 14–16). A memorial tribute in *Criterion* 32, no. 1 (1993) is Nancy Auer Falk and H. Byron Earhart, "Perfect in Dress and Address: Remembering Joseph Mitsuo Kitagawa, 1915–1992" (pp. 10–16).

H. BYRON EARHART (2005)

KLIMKEIT, HANS-JOACHIM. Hans-Joachim Klimkeit (1939–1999) was born in Ranchi, Bihar, in India, the son of a German Lutheran missionary. Klimkeit spent his youth in different parts of the subcontinent, and from early on he became acquainted with such languages as English, Hindi, Urdu, Bhojpuri, and Tamil. In 1955 Klimkeit moved to Germany, where he passed his school-leaving examination in 1958. Afterwards he took up studies of Protestant theology, first at a small ecclesiastical academy, then, from 1959 onwards, at the university of Tübingen. There, besides theology, he also studied mathematics and, more importantly, philosophy with the hermeneutician Otto Friedrich Bollnow and Indology with Helmuth von Glasenapp, who both would have a lasting impact on him. In 1961 Klimkeit went to study at Bonn under the phenomenologist Gustav Mensching, whose successor he became in 1972.

Klimkeit took his Ph.D. with a thesis on Ludwig Feuerbach's ideas about miracles from the point of view of the phenomenology of religion (*Das Wunderverständnis Ludwig Feuerbachs in religionsphänomenologischer Sicht,* 1964). Afterwards he spent one year at the Center for the Study of World Religions at Harvard University, where Wilfred Cantwell Smith encouraged him to add a historic-philological approach to the sort of phenomenology represented by Mensching. Klimkeit then began studying Sanskrit, and after he returned to Bonn he wrote his *Habilitation* on antireligious movements in Southern India (*Anti-religiöse Bewegungen im modernen Südindien: Eine religionssoziologische Untersuchung zur Säkularisierungsfrage,* 1971). The work was intended as a contribution to the issue of secularization from the point of view of the sociology of religion. His interest in recent developments in Indian religious history would culminate in *Der politische Hinduismus: Indische Denker zwischen religiöser Reform und politischem Erwachen* (1981), which was published before "political Hinduism" had become a standard agenda. Klimkeit's knowledge of Sanskrit left fruitful traces in his book on the Buddha (1990), in which he emphasized the importance of the Northern Buddhist Sanskrit texts, as against the later Pali books.

During the 1970s, by learning several other languages (Uighur, Middle Iranian, Sogdian, Tibetan, and Mongolian) Klimkeit laid the groundwork for his later studies on Manichaeism (e.g., Klimkeit, 1982, 1989, 1993) and the Silk Road (e.g., Klimkeit 1986, 1988). These were mainly published during the 1980s, the peak period of his scholarly output, while the 1990s were increasingly overshadowed by the illness that ended in his tragic death in 1999.

Both in his teaching and his research, Klimkeit worked on a remarkable number of different religions, most importantly Hinduism, Buddhism, (Nestorian) Christianity (e.g., Gillman and Klimkeit, 1999), Zoroastrianism, and in particular Manichaeism (Klimkeit was instrumental in the revival of Manichaean studies). Apart from writing and coauthoring monographs and papers on single religions, Klimkeit devoted several important studies to different forms of encounter and interaction between religions and cultures, in particular (but not exclusively) on the Silk Road. Apart from his work with textual sources (culminating in his collection of Manichaean texts and a series devoted to the Hami manuscript of the Maitrisimit, undertaken with Geng Shimin, Jens Peter Laut, and Helmut Eimer), Klimkeit was much concerned with questions of religious iconography.

While he added a sense of history and a rich variety of source materials to the abstract phenomenologist sketches of his teacher and predecessor Mensching, Klimkeit would always remain heavily influenced by the phenomenology of religion and hermeneutics as represented by Bollnow and Joachim Wach (see Klimkeit, 1972). In his later work, Klimkeit advocated the idea of a "problem-centered" (and humanist) phenomenology of religion (see Klimkeit, 1986, 1999), and he intended a comparative study of the "answers" that different religions give (or have given) to a number of fundamental problems of humankind, such as good and evil, human autonomy, and divine heteronomy (see Gantke, who continued this approach in his own work).

As a teacher and supervisor, Klimkeit had a remarkably open and kind attitude. Rather than founding a school in the strict sense, he actively encouraged his students to pursue their own paths, even if they were leading into territories beyond Klimkeit's frame of mind. During his time there, the tiny Religionswissenschaftliches Seminar at Bonn University experienced an unprecedented increase in enrollment. Klimkeit was the editor of several books and series (most importantly the series Studies in Oriental Religions), and he served as coeditor of the *Zeitschrift für Religions- und Geistesgeschichte,* the series Nag Hammadi and Manichaean Studies, and the *Theologische Realenzyklopädie.* In addition, Klimkeit served on the boards of several academic societies. Even before the fall of the Iron Curtain, he had established important and lasting contacts with colleagues in many countries ranging from the former German Democratic Republic to China, which would greatly facilitate the progress of research on the Silk Road and Manichaeaism.

BIBLIOGRAPHY

For a complete bibliography of Klimkeit's writings (360 items) and a survey of the courses and classes taught by him in Bonn, as well as the thirty Ph.D. theses and four *Habilitation* supervised by him, plus obituaries, see Ulrich Vollmer, "Hans-Joachim Klimkeit—Werk, Wirken, Würdigung" in *Religionsbegegnung und Kulturaustausch in Asien: Studien zum Gedenken an Hans-Joachim Klimkeit,* edited by Wolfgang Gantke, Karl Hoheisel, and Wassilios Klein, pp. 11–48 (Wiesbaden, Germany, 2002). For Wolfgang Gantke's personal recollections plus an evaluation of Klimkeit's approach to the phenomenology of religion, see his essay in this volume, "Mut zur Offenheit: Erinnerung an Hans-Joachim Klimkeit und einige seiner zentralen Überlegungen zur religionswissenschaftlichen Methodendiskussion," pp. 72–80.

See also:

Gillman, Ian, and Hans-Joachim Klimkeit. *Christians in Asia Before 1500.* Richmond, UK, 1999. Klimkeit contributed the chapters on Christians in Central Asia and Christians in China.

Klimkeit, Hans-Joachim. "Das Prinzip des Verstehens bei Joachim Wach." *Numen* 19 (1972): 216–228. A comprehensive reconstruction of Wach's hermeneutic system.

Klimkeit, Hans-Joachim. *Der politische Hinduismus: Indische Denker zwischen religiöser Reform und politischem Erwachen.* Wiesbaden, Germany, 1981. A survey of major thinkers of political Hinduism and an investigation of some of its "archetypal," basic structures with their respective religious roots.

Klimkeit, Hans-Joachim. *Manichaean Art and Calligraphy.* Leiden, 1982. The first ever general study of Manichaean iconography.

Klimkeit, Hans-Joachim. *Die Begegnung von Christentum, Gnosis und Buddhismus an der Seidenstrasse.* Opladen, Germany, 1986.

Klimkeit, Hans-Joachim. *Die Seidenstrasse: Handelsweg und Kulturbrücke zwischen Morgen- und Abendland.* Köln, Germany, 1988; 2d ed. 1990. A richly illustrated cultural history and panorama of the Silk Road (mostly focusing on pre-Islamic times) comprising history of research, geography, cultural centers, people, and religions.

Klimkeit, Hans-Joachim. "Der leidendende Gerechte in der Religionsgeschichte: Ein Beitrag zur problemorientierten 'Religionsphänomenologie.'" In *Religionswissenschaft: Eine Einführung,* edited by Hartmut Zinser, pp. 164–184. Berlin, 1988. A global comparison of the motif of the suffering righteous meant as an example of his "problem-centered" phenomenology of religion.

Klimkeit, Hans-Joachim. *Hymnen und Gebete der Religion des Lichts: Iranische und türkische liturgische Texte der Manichäer Zentralasiens.* Opladen, 1989. A collection of Manichaean (ritual) texts in several Iranian languages and Old Turkish with extensive introductions. A revised and augmented English translation was published under the misleading title *Gnosis on the Silk Road: Gnostic Texts from Central Asia.* San Francisco, 1993.

Klimkeit, Hans-Joachim. *Der Buddha: Leben und Lehre.* Stuttgart, 1990. A study of the figure of the Buddha intended for a broader audience and illustrative of Klimkeit's approach in that he seeks to combine historic-philological methods and hermeneutic principles of understanding.

Klimkeit, Hans-Joachim. "Religionswissenschaft." In *Theologische Realenzyklopädie,* edited by Gerhard Müller, Vol. 29, pp. 61–67. Berlin and New York, 1998. Expresses Klimkeit's ideas about the history of religions.

Klimkeit, Hans-Joachim, Shimin Geng, Helmut Eimer, and Jens Peter Laut. *Das Zusammentreffen mit Maitreya: Die ersten fünf Kapitel der Hami-Version der Maitrisimit.* 2 vols. Wiesbaden, Germany, 1988.

MICHAEL STAUSBERG (2005)

KLONG CHEN RAB 'BYAMS PA (LONGCHENPA).

KLONG CHEN RAB 'BYAMS PA (LONGCHENPA). Longchenpa (1308–1363) is perhaps the most important philosophical author in the history of the Rnying ma (Nyingma) school of Tibetan Buddhism and one of the great figures in fourteenth-century Tibet, a time of larger-than-life authors and systematizations of sectarian traditions. His renown stems from his huge literary corpus, and three distinctive facets of it. Firstly, he is renowned as the systematizer of the Nyingma tradition of the Great Perfection (*Rdzogs chen* [Dzogchen]), which he expounded in a series of brilliant texts that balanced architectonic structure, aphoristic poetry, and philosophical nuance and precision. While his writings span the earliest phases of Great Perfection literature, he above all else focused on the eleventh- and twelfth-century Seminal Heart (*Snying thig* [Nyingthink]) revelations and their highly distinctive reinterpretation of the Great Perfection. Longchenpa articulated a deeply systematic approach to Seminal Heart to create one of the most powerful statements of philosophical Vajrayāna. His writings systematize doctrines and contemplative practices into a structured and integrated whole, while simultaneously definitively defining key terminology with innovative nuance. In large part due to the influence of his corpus, the Seminal Heart came to be the dominant tradition of the Great Perfection right into the present.

Secondly, Longchenpa was one of the few premodern Nyingma authors to incorporate broad learning in exoteric Buddhist literature directly into his writings. He is famed for his integration of the insights, terminology, and practice of the Great Perfection into the broader framework of an encyclopedic overview of the entire Buddhist tradition. While many other Nyingma authors appear to have had solid training in the exoteric literature, relatively few wrote at any great length on the subject, preferring to work in esoteric veins and narrative materials. Longchenpa is thus often discussed within the Nyingma tradition in connection with two other such prominent authors, Rongzom Chökyi Zangpo (eleventh century) and Mipham (1846–1912). These three stand out within the tradition for their great learning in exoteric Buddhist scholasticism, and the expression of that learning in extensive writings.

Thirdly, the Nyingma tradition until the fourteenth century was dominated by the practice of revelations, whereby important new bodies of literature were produced as "treasures" (*gter ma,* terma) attributed to the distant past of Tibet's imperial greatness (seventh to ninth centuries) rather than to the authorial hand of the present. Longchenpa's writings at times utilized the rhetoric of revelation, but in general were clearly presented as his own personal compositions. While certainly such personal compositions had appeared elsewhere in Nyingma circles from the eleventh to thirteenth centuries, the emergence of such a huge corpus of major religious writings attributed to a contemporary figure was a watershed in the history of the Nyingma tradition.

Longchenpa's life can be roughly divided into his first twenty years of youth and earlier studies, his twenties during which he received his seminal intellectual and yogic training, his thirties when he emerged as a major teacher and author, his forties marked by political turmoil and exile even as his literary output continued unabated, and finally his return to Tibet and final years in his fifties. His studies, social experiences, and literary writings were all deeply interwoven into the fabric of his life, with common motifs and images running through both.

Past Lives and Prophecies. Tibetan accounts of the life of a saint begin at starting points that are highly Tibetan and Buddhist in character: past lives and prenatal prophecies concerning birth and life. Longchenpa did not arrive on the historical scene as a recognized member of an established reincarnational line with a clear pedigree and institutional power, though certainly his gestation and birth are framed with prophecies said to indicate his unusual spiritual accomplishments. His most interesting and relevant reincarnational associations, however, are with an obscure visionary from the late twelfth and thirteenth centuries, Tsultrim Dorjé (1291–1317), with intimate associations to the Seminal Heart. Through Tsultrim Dorjé, also known as Pad ma las 'brel rtsal (Pema Ledreltsel), he came to be further identified as the direct rebirth of the Tibetan princess Lhacam, daughter of Khri srong lde'u btsan (Trisong Detsen, 742–797), and a direct disciple of Padmasambhava. He was also identified eventually as a divine emanation of Mañjuśrī, the *bodhisattva* of wisdom. Such emanatory identity is common place for great scholars, given Mañjuśrī's traditional function as the patron *bodhisattva* of intellectual and monastic pursuits.

The Early Years: Samye, Sangphu, and Nomadic Yogis. Longchen Rabjampa was born on the tenth day of the second month of the earth-monkey year of the fifth sixty-year cycle (Saturday, March 2, 1308). He appears to have been a member of an aristocratic family with strong spiritual associations on both sides of his family, including a paternal ancestor dating back to the imperial period and Padmasambhava's original circle of disciples, namely Rgyal ba mchog dbyangs (Gyelwa Chokyang). It is possible that Longchenpa's sense of himself as possessing a certain social and spiritual heritage with corresponding entitlements may explain the tensions and self-perception in his adult life discussed below.

Longchenpa's early education consisted of studying various rites, ceremonies, and "sciences" (*rig gnas*) such as medicine and astrology with his father. As a teenager, he memorized lengthy texts, and expanded his interest into the study of Tantric texts from both the ancient (*rnying ma*) and modern (*gsar ma*) traditions. At the age of twelve, Longchenpa journeyed to Bsam yas (Samyé), Tibet's first monastery, where he took up the study of monastic discipline. Longchenpa's association with Samyé dates back to his paternal ancestor, Gyelwa Chokyang, who was one the original monks ordained there in the eighth century. His own studies there accompanied by his intellectual brilliance led him to be known later as "the polymath from Samyé," which could also be interpreted as "the recipient of Samyé's many scriptural transmissions."

Among the most significant events in Longchenpa's education as a young adult was his entry into the Sang phu ne'u thog (Sangphu Neutok) monastic college. Sangphu, founded by the translator Ngogs legs pa'i shes rab (Ngok Lekpé Sherap, c. eleventh century), was the preeminent institution for the study of logic and epistemology in Tibet. It was the most important institutional support for the rise of scholastic learning during the twelfth and thirteenth centuries, and remained a dominant academic seat during Longchenpa's lifetime. His educational focus thus shifted during this time from ritual and meditation to syllogism and philosophy in the form of works by Asaṅga (c. 315–390), Dignāga (c. 480–540), Dharmakīrti (seventh century), and others. By all accounts he excelled in his studies, and it was this seven-year stay at Sangphu that gave him the superb mastery of traditional Buddhist thought that came to be a hallmark of his literary output.

However, Longchenpa's decisive educational experience was the period he spent living and practicing with his principal teacher Kumārāja (Kumārādza, Gzhon nu rgyal po, 1266–1343) during his late twenties. Besides receiving his most important Great Perfection teachings from Kumārāja, Longchenpa was also much influenced by the peripatetic way of life of his followers. The biographical materials mention that Kumārāja and his small band of disciples wandered from place to place, living like virtual nomads, exposed to the elements, living and sleeping in crude sack garments. Such a yogic lifestyle stands in clear contrast to the institutional life of so many Tibetan scholars based in large monasteries, presiding over systematic institutional processes, and often bound up with or even directly wielding political power. This quasi-nomadic lifestyle is also consonant with tropes and metaphors commonly found in Great Perfection literature valorizing space, the absence of boundaries, natural freedom, simplicity, and spontaneity. Hence, this training with his teacher Kumārāja may be understood as a period during which these literary images became associated with vivid sociological experiences connected to specific behaviors and lifestyles for Longchenpa.

Teaching and Composition. After approximately two years living and practicing with his principal *guru* Kumārāja, Longchenpa is said to have been designated as his successor, after which he embarked on a period of intensive teaching and meditation. Thus, during his thirties, Longchenpa emerged as a teacher in his own right and began to pen some of his greatest works. Although Longchenpa's fame as a practitioner and teacher were increasing significantly during this time, he never founded or became affiliated in any significant way with a large religious institution. On the contrary, he apparently preferred the relatively remote hermitage setting of his home monastery called *Gang ri thod dkar* (White-Skull Mountain). It was here that he composed many of his greatest works.

Longchenpa's corpus consists of compilations typically referred to in terms of the number of texts belonging to each compilation. The most famous is undoubtedly *The Seven Treasures* (*Mdzod bdun*), which integrates standard scholasticism with philosophical poetry to offer a systematic survey of Buddhist thought and practice from its earliest phases up to and including the distinctive synthesis of the Seminal Heart. These seven texts as a set are famous among his fellow Nyingmas, as well as other sects, for their philosophical acumen, their systematization of the Great Perfection, and their ability to integrate distinctive Nyingma esoteric traditions with pan-sectarian Buddhist scholastic traditions. *The Wish-Fulfilling Treasury (Yid bzhin mdzod)* and *The Treasury of Philosophical Systems (Grub mtha' mdzod)* focus on the basic Buddhist scholastic systems with modest influence from the Great Perfection. In contrast, *TheTreasury of Words and Meanings (Tshig don mdzod)* and *TheTreasury of the Supreme Vehicle (Theg mchog mdzod)* offer a scholastic treatment of the Seminal Heart in its own right. Finally, *The Treasury of Reality's Expanse (Chos dbyings mdzod)* and *The Treasury of Abiding Reality (Gnas lugs mdzod)* constitute masterpieces of philosophical poetry focused on the Seminal Heart, while *TheTreasury of Esoteric Precepts (Man ngag mdzod)* is a lesser work devoted to lists of precepts.

Longchenpa authored at least six other major compilations, each a trilogy devoted to Nyingma esoteric traditions. *The Trilogy of Resting-at-Ease* (*Ngal gso skor gsum*) and *The Trilogy of Natural Freedom* (*Rang grol skor gsum*) are both lovely root poems around which a variety of other commentarial texts have been associated, all of which center around earlier traditions of the Great Perfection known as "mind series" (*Sems sde*). In contrast, *The Trilogy of Qintessences* (*Yang ti gsum*) constitute three individual compilations of scores of individual works covering the rituals, yogas, history, philosophy, and other areas of the Seminal Heart tradition. These constitute his ritual and yogic masterpieces of the Seminal Heart, in addition to detailed discussions of many other aspects of the tradition. These were integrated with two similar compilations deriving from the older revelations associated with the Indian saint Vimalamitra, and the more recent revelations associated with the Indian saint Padmasambhva to form *The Seminal Heart in Four Parts* (though in fact it has five parts). Thus this famous anthology compiles the two main strands of exegetical literature of the tradition along with Longchenpa's extension and integration. Finally, *The Trilogy of Dispelling Darkness* (*Mun sel skor gsum*) was his masterly commentary on *The Nucleus of Mystery Tantra* (*Gsang ba snying po*; Skt., *Guhyagarbha*), the chief Tantra of the Nyingma tradition and the center of the Mahāyoga corpus. This trilogy was famed not only for its detailed study of the Tantra, but also for its innovative Great Perfection-based reinterpretation of many of its particulars. Longchenpa wrote widely on many other topics, including exoteric Buddhist scholasticism. However, it appears that the vast majority of these compositions have been lost to the ravages of time and the relative lack of concern for exoteric writings by the Nyingma tradition in premodern times.

Social and Political Conflict. Longchenpa had a lifelong tendency to remain somewhat in the margins of religious institutions and political powers, and yet he was also explicitly critical of social, political, and religious trends and events in Tibet. We have already seen such tendencies in his nomadic years with his teacher Kumārāja, and his proclivity for the isolated retreat center of White-Skull Mountain. The tendency to social criticism and feeling in conflict with the prevailing social norms was equally evident from his early years. For example, toward the end of his stay at Sangphu, we can see Longchenpa's impatience with what he perceived to be the frivolous behavior of ostensibly religious figures. He came into conflict with a group of scholars from Kham (*Khams*), who appeared to him to be sectarian and of poor moral character. The literary result of his disgust with these scholars was a thirty-line alphabetically arranged poem entitled "The Thirty Letters of the Alphabet" (*Ka kha sum cu*). This bitter but witty work is a savage attack on the dubious conduct of the persons in question, likening them to demons and accusing them of such actions as killing, boozing, and whoring.

The mid-fourteenth century in Tibet was a time of political and social upheaval, yet also a time of consolidation of literary canons and sectarian identity. The sa skya (Sakya) hegemony, together with its Yuan dynasty patrons, was reaching a state of collapse. Religious and regional factions were in open and often violent conflict. Central Tibet in particular was a contested area, with sites like Samyé coming under the control of belligerent factions allied with specific clans and religious sects. Families, politics, and religion were inextricably interwoven throughout the time. Among the prominent competing factions active in Central Tibet at that time were the Sakyapas, the *'Bri gung pa* (Drigungpas), and the Phag mo gru pa (Phakmodrupas), whose leader was Ta'i situ byang chub rgyal mtshan (Tai Situ Jangchub Gyaltsen, 1303–1364). It is roughly during this period that we come upon further literary evidence of Longchenpa's profound antipathy toward these factions and his dissatisfaction with political and religious developments in Central Tibet as he entered a period of political turmoil and even exile during his forties.

Longchenpa's attempts to process his feelings of discontent at the situation in Central Tibet are well documented in a series of didactic narrative poems in which the characters are animals. The plots of several of these narratives revolve around the protagonist—invariably an exalted spiritual personality—being set upon by irreligious forces and being compelled to depart for regions more conducive to religious practice. These stories all take the appearance of a subtle social critique, and convey the impression of being thinly veiled autobiography. Probably the best example is *The Swan's Questions and Answers* (*Ngang pa'i dris lan sprin gyi snying po*). In this work, Longchenpa's perception of himself as an unjustly ostracized pariah is clearly evident, and the references to his specific situation are more explicit than in other examples. The story chronicles a noble swan's flight from the formerly sacred precincts of Samyé to more hospitable environs. The swan in the story is in reality an emanation of the Bodhisattva Avalokiteśvara, and is clearly patterned on Longchenpa himself.

From here we must turn briefly to the critical issue of Longchenpa's relationship with Tai Situ Jangchup Gyaltsen, who was the leading political figure in Tibet during the latter years of Longchenpa's life. Not only was he a key figure behind many of the trends in Tibet that Longchenpa found so problematic, but in fact the two came into direct conflict in the 1350s. Jangchup Gyaltsen and the clan he led, the Phakmodrupas, were in constant conflict with various other competing groups throughout most of the early fourteenth century. Among the more prominent of the competing groups were the religious factions of the Sakyapas and the Drigungpas. Longchenpa, while no fan of the increasing military presence in Central Tibet, became implicated in a bitter feud between the leader of the Drigungpas and the leader of the Phakmodrupas, that is, Jangchup Gyaltsen. Jangchup Gyaltsen reportedly came to view Longchenpa as a significant enemy, to the extent that he tried to have him assassinated. This conflict, together with all his other frustrations and disappointments, eventually led Longchenpa to flee to Bhutan in approximately 1353.

Final Years in Bhutan and Tibet. Longchenpa was reportedly very active during his time in Bhutan, establishing and renovating many monasteries and retreat facilities. He taught widely, and is credited with reviving the fortunes of the Nyingma and Great Perfection traditions in that region. He composed several important texts there, very likely including *The Treasury of Abiding Reality.* His home base was the famous Thar pa gling (Tharpa Ling) monastery, still standing today in Bumthang. He also fathered at least one son with a nun during his stay in Bhutan, indicating that his monastic vows either lapsed at some point or that he viewed his realization as enabling the integration of monastic vows and sexual activity. During this period of exile, Longchenpa received numerous visitors from Tibet who encouraged him to return to Central Tibet. Eventually, a reconciliation between Longchenpa and Jangchub Gyaltsen was negotiated by Sangs rgyas dpal (Sangyepel), such that Jangchub Gyaltsen invited Longchenpa to return to Tibet, made offerings to him, and received Tantric initiations and other teachings from him. In fact, there is a tradition that Longchenpa's most famous epithet (*klong chen rab 'byams pa,* "infinite open space") was given to him by Jangchup Gyaltsen himself, although the veracity of this story is uncertain. Although we have no definite dates for Longchenpa's sojourn in Bhutan, it may have lasted from roughly 1353 to 1360.

In 1363, when he was fifty-six years old, Longchenpa took ill, and began to prepare for his eventual passing by composing his final testaments (*zhal chems*). Finally, late in that same year, Longchenpa had a series of visions and gave his final advice to his disciples. His hagiographies describe his death in terms typical for a saint, specifying that he entered a state of deep meditation, and manifested many miraculous signs such as rainbows, earthquakes, and showers of flowers in his final hours and for twenty-five days following his death.

Influence: Books, Future Lives, and Visions. Religious influence in Tibet can be measured on many registers, but a useful fourfold measure is to consider the institutional, literary, intellectual, incarnational, and visionary impact a figure has after his death. Measured by institutional standards, Longchenpa had minimal impact on his own school, much less on Tibetan Buddhism as a whole. He offered no new institutional models, his disciples were not particularly vigorous in founding new monasteries and temples, and his institutional legacy was limited to modest sites such as the retreat center White-Skull Mountain and the temple in Bumthang. It appears that a family lineage did persist over the centuries in Bhutan from his offspring there.

Longchenpa's most significant contribution is undoubtedly in the intellectual and literary domains, where he is a towering figure historically both within the Nyingma tradition, and outside it in other traditions. Curiously, however, he did not spawn a cottage industry in exegetical literature directly commenting on his work, quite in contrast to many of the other great Tibetan philosophical authors. The reason for this lacuna is twofold. Firstly, Longchenpa's impressive range of scholarly expertise and philosophical nuance in the exoteric traditions remained unusual in Nyingma traditions until the last few centuries. Secondly, ongoing revelation remained a dominant influence in subsequence centuries among Nyingma lineages, and its historical focus on the imperial past discouraged the development of exegesis of post-imperial Tibetan authors. Despite this absence of direct commentarial literature, Longchenpa's influence was pervasive, even if mediated through vision and the explicit citation often thus sublimated. His impact on Great Perfection traditions can already be seen in the revelations of Rig 'dzin rgod ldem (Rinzin Godem, 1337–1409), or in the later revelations of 'Jigs med gling pa (Jikmé Lingpa, 1729/30–1798). In addition, his masterly synthesis of esoteric Nyingma traditions with mainstream Buddhist scholasticism was the inspiration for the Mipham's later extensive corpus of exoteric writings, which undergirds much of the Eastern Tibetan ecumenical movement *(ris med),* and forms the most important basis for the modern monastic curriculum of Nyingma institutions. Over time he thus achieved renown within and without the Nyingma tradition as its greatest intellectual.

Longchenpa never spawned a clear incarnational institution of his own rebirths, not surprising given his contentious relationship with institutions. Incarnational lines known as "tulku" (*sprul sku),* literally "emanated bodies," of course refer to the phenomenon in Tibet of religious personages being identified after death in young children believed to be their rebirths, and to whom the previous life's title, position, and property were transmitted. This institution of cross-life inheritance was naturally bound up with monastic institutions, which had the institutional resources, memory, and record keeping to maintain such incarnational lines. Longchenpa's failure to found his own large monastic institution almost guaranteed the lack of such an incarnational heritage. There were of course various figures identified as, or claiming to be, his incarnation, right into the present—the most famous being the Bhutanese Pad ma gling pa (Pema Lingpa,

1450–1521)—but none of these crystallized into a high-profile and continuous series of incarnations in the way of, say, the Karma pa or Dalai Lama incarnational lines. In contrast, Longchenpa has had a highly successful visionary career since his death, and his presence in visions and dreams has become a pervasive feature among Nyingma scholars and yogis. The most important of these is undoubtedly the famous visions experienced by Jikmé Lingpa, which were crucial to his revelation of the Great Sphere (*"longchen"*) of the Seminal Heart in the eighteenth century. This cycle came to be the dominant Great Perfection ritual cycle right into the present, and while perhaps subliminal, the use of the term *longchen* in its title is obviously deeply resonant of Longchenpa's own centrality in the tradition overall.

BIBLIOGRAPHY

Aris, Michael. *Bhutan: The Early History of a Himalayan Kingdom.* Warminster, U.K., 1979. A study of the early history of Bhutan, including issues relevant to Longchenpa's exile there.

Aris, Michael. *Hidden Treasures and Secret Lives: A Study of Pemalingpa (1450–1521) and the Sixth Dalai Lama (1683–1706).* Delhi, 1988. A study of the life of Pemalingpa, including an account of his identification with Longchenpa.

Dudjom Jigdrel Yeshe Dorje (Dudjom Rinpoche). *The Nyingma School of Tibetan Buddhism: Its Fundamentals and History.* Translated and edited by Gyurme Dorje and Matthew Kapstein. Boston, 1991. An encyclopedic work covering the history and religious traditions of the Nyingma school, with a substantial biography of Longchenpa.

Germano, David F. "Architecture and Absence in the Secret Tantric History of rDzogs Chen." *The Journal of the International Association of Buddhist Studies* 17 no. 2 (1994): 203–335. This surveys the various forms of the Great Perfection with a concern for Longchenpa's systematization of them.

Germano, David, and Janet B. Gyatso. "Longchenpa and the Possession of the Dakinis." In *Tantra in Practice,* edited by David Gordon White, pp. 239–265. Princeton, N.J., 2000. A look at events of possession and prophecy marking the emergence of Longchenpa in his early thirties as a prominent teacher within yogic circles.

Guenther, Herbert. *Matrix of Mystery: Scientific and Humanistic Aspects of rDzogs-chen Thought.* London and Boulder, Colo., 1984. A highly interpretative study of Longchenpa's writings on *The Nucleus of Mystery Tantra.*

Gyatso, Janet. *Apparitions of the Self: The Secret Autobiographies of a Tibetan Visionary.* Princeton, N.J., 1998. A study of Jigme Lingpa's visionary experiences of Longchenpa.

Kapstein, Matthew. *The Tibetan Assimilation of Buddhism: Conversion, Contestation, and Memory.* New York, 2000. A survey of how Tibetans assimilated Buddhism, including a chapter on the integration of the Great Perfection and exorcistic esotericism within the school by Longchenpa and others.

Kuijp, Leonard W. J. van der. "On the Life and Political Career of Ta'i-Si-tu Byang-chub rgyal-mtshan (1302–c. 1364)." In *Tibetan History and Language: Studies Dedicated to Uray Géza on his Seventieth Birthday,* edited by Ernst Steinkellner, pp. 277–328. Vienna, 1991. A survey of the life of Tai Situ Jangchub Gyaltsen and his political activities.

Longchenpa. *Kindly Bent to Ease Us.* 3 vols. Translated by Herbert Guenther. Berkeley, 1976. A translation and interpretative study of the root verses from Longchenpa's *The Trilogy of Resting-at-Ease.*

Longchenpa. *Looking Deeper: A Swan's Questions and Answers.* Translated by Herbert Guenther. Porthill, Idaho, 1983. A translation and interpretative study of Longchenpa's semi-autobiographical didactic narrative *The Swan's Questions and Answers.*

Longchenpa. *The Precious Treasury of the Way of Abiding.* Translated by Richard Barron. Junction City, Calif., 1998. A translation of Longchenpa's *The Treasury of Abiding Reality* and its auto-commentary.

Longchenpa. *A Treasure Trove of Scriptural Transmission.* Translated by Richard Barron. Junction City, Calif., 2001. A translation of Longchenpa's *The Treasury of Reality's Expanse* and its auto-commentary.

Roerich, George, trans. *The Blue Annals.* Delhi, 1976.

Tulku Thondup. *Buddha Mind: An Anthology of Longchen Rabjam's Writings on Dzogpa Chenpo.* Ithaca, N.Y., 1989. An anthology of different selections of writings by Longchenpa ranging from the more exoteric to the more esoteric.

Tulku Thondup. *Masters of Meditation and Miracles: The Longchen Nyingthig Lineage of Tibetan Buddhism.* Boston, 1996. Biographies of saints involved in the lineage of *The Great Sphere of the Seminal Heart,* including detailed accounts of the lives of Longchenpa and Jikmé Lingpa.

DAVID GERMANO (2005)
GREGORY A. HILLIS (2005)

KNEES. The knees have long been closely associated with religious attitudes of penitence, prayer, surrender, and humility. In the Near East since ancient times kneeling has sometimes been connected with prostration; Islam developed full prostration as the climax of a cycle of postures that includes a combined sitting and kneeling position. In ancient Israel, people considered the knees to be associated with the generation of new life and with adoption; thus Bilhah, Rachel's maidservant, bore a child on Jacob's knees (*Gn.* 30:3), for a baby born on a man's knees in biblical times and places was considered legally to be his child. There may be a reflection or survival here of a prehistoric notion of an intimate relationship between the knees and the reproductive process (Onians, 1951, pp. 174–180).

In ancient Rome, adoration at sacred temples included falling to the knees as well as kneeling during supplication and prayer. Romans also knelt when presenting pleas before earthly authorities. In ancient Greece, only women and children knelt before deities. The early Christians practiced kneeling, according to accounts given in the New Testament, and the posture appears to have been inherited directly from earlier Jewish practice. In the Hebrew scriptures, Solomon, Ezra, and Daniel are reported to have knelt at prayer (*1 Kgs.* 8:54, *Ezr.* 9:5, *Dn.* 6:10). It is likely that the ancient Israelites adopted kneeling as a religious posture from other

Near Eastern peoples. Buddhists also kneel, when paying respects at sacred sites, for example.

Kneeling is not the only prayer posture mentioned in the Bible. Standing in prayer is recorded as well (*1 Sm.* 1:26, *Mk.* 11:25, *Lk.* 22:41). In fact, only once in the Gospels is Christ reported to have knelt, namely, on the Mount of Olives before his arrest (*Lk.* 22:41). But the *Acts of the Apostles* depicts both Peter and Paul kneeling in prayer (9:40, 20:36, 21:5), and Paul's great kenotic Christological passage in the *Letter to the Ephesians* ends with this declaration: "In honor of the name of Jesus all beings in heaven, and on earth, and in the world below will fall on their knees, and all will openly proclaim that Jesus Christ is Lord, to the glory of God the Father" (2:10–11). The penitential aspect of kneeling was noted in the fourth century by Ambrose: "The knee is made flexible by which the offence of the Lord is mitigated, wrath appeased, grace called forth" (*Hexaemeron* 6.9.74.287).

The early Christians appear to have practiced both standing and kneeling at prayer. Later the Roman Catholic church appears to have encouraged standing for prayer, especially in Sunday congregational worship, but recommended kneeling for penitential and private prayer. Protestantism has emphasized kneeling as the prayer posture above all others, whereas Catholicism has regulated the postures of worship and prayer fairly rigorously, for example prescribing standing on Sundays and festival days and in praise and thanksgiving at all times. During Low Mass, the worshipers kneel except during the reading of the gospel.

Popular Christianity employs a kneeling posture for both supererogatory prayer and adoration. These practices sometimes extend to rather arduous ascending of stairs of shrines on the knees while uttering pious formulas at each step, as at Saint Joseph's Oratory in Montreal, where many supplicants have been healed of crippling afflictions. Cured persons have long left their crutches at this shrine, displayed in the sanctuary like sacred relics. Within the precincts of the Shrine of the Virgin of Guadalupe in Mexico City many pilgrims can be seen approaching the sacred places on their knees. Similar practices can be observed at other Christian holy places in both the Old World and the New.

Kneeling has been practiced not only in the presence of God but also in the presence of royalty in many cultures. The early Roman rulers required the northern Europeans, the Egyptians, and Asian peoples to bend the knee in submission, whereas earlier still Alexander the Great required it of all, declaring himself to be divine. When making supplication, ancient Greeks and Romans are reported to have knelt while kissing the hand of the superior person, at the same time touching his left knee with the left hand. Modern British subjects curtsy and bend the knee when in the presence of their sovereign.

Extreme flexing of the knees was once entailed in the binding of corpses for burial in a fetal position, as has been reported in ethnographical accounts and in reports on prehistoric burials. The reasons are unclear, as it is not certain whether the bent knees were especially significant in themselves. Certainly the corpse's submissive incapacity can at least be conjectured from this position, whether in order to prevent the spirit of the deceased from wandering about and haunting the living or to prepare the deceased for initiation into the secrets of the afterlife, which might possibly have included a ritual symbolism of returning to the fetal position.

BIBLIOGRAPHY

A. E. Crawley's article entitled "Kneeling," in the *Encyclopaedia of Religion and Ethics*, edited by James Hastings, vol. 7 (Edinburgh, 1914), is a useful source for Near Eastern, biblical, and Christian kneeling practices; the evolutionary perspective from which the topic is addressed must be rejected, however. For a convenient reference work, consult Betty J. Bäuml and Franz H. Bäuml's *A Dictionary of Gestures* (Metuchen, N.J., 1975); here are found numerous documented reports about knee symbolism and kneeling in the ancient Near East and Mediterranean world as well as in later European history and literature. For stimulating insights and observations on the knees and other parts of the body, see Richard B. Onians's *The Origins of European Thought about the Body, the Mind, the Soul, the World, Time, and Fate* (Cambridge, U.K., 1951).

FREDERICK MATHEWSON DENNY (1987)

KNOTS. The sacred value attributed to knots throughout human history, and amid the most diverse cultures, has interested historians of religions since the nineteenth century. As products of the activity of tying or binding, knots have usually been studied in the context of the more general phenomenon of sacred bonds. It is not surprising, therefore, that research into the religious value of knots has followed the same general pattern that one finds in the study of binding. In particular, the problems have been formulated in similar terms, similar methods have been employed, and consequently the results obtained have also tended to coincide.

Thus the leading students of the religious significance of binding and bonds have also led the way in the study of knots. Scholars such as James G. Frazer, Isidor Scheftelowitz, Walter J. Dilling, Georges Dumézil, and Mircea Eliade have made important contributions in both areas. In general, these scholars have expended considerable effort on the collection of data that are then subjected to comparative-historical study. Closer examination shows, however, that several quite different methods have been employed. Some scholars have been content with a simple exposition of individual instances of knots in particular cultures (Frazer, Dilling). Others have defined their study in terms of a definite cultural area (Dumézil). Finally, there has been an attempt at a phenomenological analysis of knots aimed at the identification of an archetype of the bond (Eliade). The results obtained by these methods, from Frazer to Eliade, have generally been formulated in exclusively symbolic terms, for the most part in the context of magical beliefs and practices. What has not been adequately studied up to now is the symbolic value that knots may have in the context of everyday life and the wholly secular and functional importance of binding and knots in that context.

Beginning with the work of Frazer at the beginning of the present century, scholars have repeatedly affirmed that the sacred action of tying or untying a knot serves to establish or remove some restraint and that it has either a positive or a negative effect, depending upon the specific circumstances under which it is done and the motives of the person doing it. Countless examples of such symbolic action have been furnished, drawn from both primitive cultures and higher civilizations. Every imaginable type of bond has been analyzed, bonds both concrete (such as are made from string or rope, or again, rings and chains) and abstract. Instances have been provided of knots tied in both public and private rituals as well as in nonritual contexts. Knots are found to be tied by superhuman beings as well as by ordinary mortals, and in the latter case by those who are religiously inspired as well as by those who are not. In all of this description, however, the deeper motives behind such widespread forms of activity have not been sought.

It has long been known that the activity of binding in its various forms has the essential goal of permitting human beings to extend their control over reality. The most striking example consists of the knotted ropes used in many preliterate societies as a means of organizing and storing information. Knots tied into ropes, often of different colors, are used to represent numbers, objects, persons, situations, actions, and so forth. Such knotted ropes are useful in resolving specific problems of a practical nature, because they extend the human ability to count, inventory, register, list, and in general to organize and communicate information. The problems solved in this way are not exclusively secular problems, however. They can often have a decidedly religious aspect. The practical function of such knots, and in fact, of all types of bond, even those of a purely symbolic nature, does not preclude their having a sacred function as well. Indeed, these two functions may exist in a relation of strict complementarity.

In the specific context of the ritual confession of sins, Raffaele Pettazzoni has shown how certain knots combine a symbolic value with the quite concrete purpose of restraining or fixating the sin, so that the guilt associated with it may be more effectively confronted and neutralized. Thus, for example, in preparation for their ritual journey in search of the sacred *hikuri* (a cactus used in a festival), the Huichol of Mexico require that each person making the trip indicate the number of his lovers by tying the appropriate number of knots in a rope, which is then destroyed by fire. A similar operation is performed by the women who remain at home. The Zapotec symbolically knot up the sins of the year by tying blades of grass together two by two, soaking them in the blood of the penitent, and then offering them to a superhuman being. In ancient Babylonia, one finds the idea of sin as a knot that has to be undone by various divinities, such as Nergal, "lord of the untying." In Vedic India, it is the god Varuna who captures the guilty with his knotted lasso. In the Shinto purification ritual, a piece of paper (*katashiro*) is cut out by the penitent, bound in bundles of wicker, and thrown into the flames.

The calculation of sacred and profane time can also be managed through the use of knots tied into a rope at set intervals. A mere glance at such a rope is enough to allow a person to comprehend a situation and act appropriately. Martin P. Nilsson has shown how various primal cultures use such ropes for measuring the duration of menstrual impurity (for example, the Nauru of the Gilbert Islands), the period during which justice should be administered (the Gogo of Tanzania), the period during which intertribal dances should be prepared (the Miwok of California), or the days to be dedicated to the celebration of a great festival (the Melanesians of the Solomon Islands).

In all these cases, knots are used to control a reality that is itself abstract, fluctuating, evanescent. Guilt, time, or fate itself, by being concretized in a knot, comes under the control of the person who ties it and who thereby resolves a given situation. But it is not only determinate problems that can be resolved through the use of knots and the control they give. The complexities of an entire empire can be made manageable thanks to the use of knotted ropes. This was the case in pre-Columbian Peru, where the use of knotted ropes called *quipu* as instruments for keeping records was essential for the orderly functioning of the Inca Empire. The use of the *quipu* made it possible for the *quipu-camayoc* (keeper of the *quipu*) to manage the enormous mass of data collected by local officials and thereby keep tabs on the complex economic and military situation of the empire.

Moreover, in every period, in the most diverse types of civilization, technology strives not only to gain control over the world but also to enhance human creativity by providing humankind with new tools with which to confront life's difficulties. The fabrication of such implements, however, involves the binding, weaving, and knotting together of the most diverse materials. It is precisely the enormous importance of the technology of binding that stands behind the transposition of all its means and forms from the mundane to the sacred. Forms of transposition that are particularly widespread include the attribution of extraordinary value and power to knots in magical rites; the creation of the type of the "god who binds," armed with ropes, lassos, and nets; and above all, the development of the majestic conception of a universe created by means of the art of weaving.

In this regard, Eliade's concept of the woven cosmos requires further development. Eliade's study of the symbolism of knots went beyond the study of knots per se to investigate those cases in which the universal order is believed to be produced by various types of tying and weaving, in much the same way as one would produce a rope, a chain, or a net.

Among the Babylonians, for example, the *markasu* (rope) was both the cosmic principle that unites all things and the divine power or law that provides the framework for the universe. Similarly, the Vedic *prāṅa* (breath) was believed to have woven human life (*Atharvaveda* 10.2.13), while *vayu* (air) bound all beings to each other like a thread (*Bṛhadāraṇyaka Upaniṣad* 3.7.2). In China, the Dao, which was the ultimate principle of the universe, was described as the chain of all creation. Now it is precisely comparisons from the history of religions that teach that a motif of this type, far from being the distillate of an extremely sophisticated philosophical thought, is in fact an image of great antiquity, sinking its roots beneath the higher civilizations into the traditional patrimony of primitive peoples.

Indeed, the conception of creation as a whole—both the cosmic order and humanity's place within it—as the product of some type of binding activity, whether of knotting, tying, twining, or weaving, is quite widespread. One finds, for instance, in the origin myths of several primal cultures the conception of the creator as a spider who weaves the universe just as a normal spider weaves its web. Similarly, specific forms of ropes or bonds are sometimes assigned cosmic functions. The rainbow, for example, can be interpreted as the belt with which the supreme being fastens his robe, as among the western Galla. Among the Witóto of Colombia, the "thread of a dream" binds together a creation that is believed to emerge out of nothingness. The Maidu of south-central California believe that a superhuman being once descended beneath the waters to procure the soil needed for creation by means of a rope woven of feathers. The Nootka of Vancouver Island and the Polynesians of Hoa Island relate that the light of the sun, having taken on the form of a basket, is lowered down to the earth by means of a rope. In a similar vein, the cosmogonic myths of various peoples of California tell of how, in a primordial epoch, the sea was put into a wicker container (the Salina), the world was sewn together like a small, tarred reed basket (the Yuki), or the entire universe took shape through the patient work of weaving as though it were a knotted mat (the Wintu).

In this cosmos, structured and woven like fabric, the creator taught human beings to tie fibers to make ropes and lassos. In this way the wild and unruly clouds were captured and humans began to exert a degree of control over the climate (the Wintu). Similarly, bindings were used to control the sun at the time of origin of the universe, when it was either too hot or too cold, and therefore threatened humans, animals, and plants. The sun, caught in a trap like a lynx (the Chipewyan), half-tied like a slipknot (the Montagnais-Naskapi, the Alonquian Cree, the Ciamba of Nigeria), and captured in snares of various types (the Pende of the Kongo and the natives of the Gazelle Peninsula, Oceania, and Melanesia, as well as others), was forced to diminish or strengthen its rays, change its course, and settle into what must henceforth be its proper path. Neither could the moon avoid being caught with a rope and receiving thereby the spots that would forever mark it (the Naskapi). As for the stars, they are so high because one day the vine woven between earth and sky was cut in two (the Boróro of the Mato Grosso).

In this universe, variously knotted, tied, and woven, the differentiation of animals and humans likewise was the result of binding. When the rope that had permitted access to the celestial sphere was broken, the animals tumbled hopelessly to earth (the Boróro). And once on earth, their existence was determined by the activity of binding. The armadillo, for example, set about weaving the "shirt" that would belong to it, and it is because it hurried too much and tied stitches of unequal size, now small and thick, now large and broad, that it looks the way it does today (the Aymara of Bolivia). The trout, for its part, while still in the hands of its creator felt drawn to its own fate so that it lamented and despaired, crying out for a net in which it could make its first appearance on earth (the Athapascan-speaking Kato).

As for human beings, bonds characterize their very existence in the details of their own body and in the countless components of the human condition. The Pomo of north-central California relate that Marunda created the first humans by weaving and knotting together his own hair, while among the Melanesians of the island of Mota this usage is associated with an archetypal woman named Ro Vilgale ("deceptive bond") who is created from twigs, branches, and leaves woven and knotted together, much like the masks of a Melanesian secret society in historical times. Alternatively, primordial man may descend to earth by means of a skein let down from the sky (the Toba Batak of Indonesia) or a rope (the Carisi of Brazil, the natives of Belau [Palau]). The breaking of this rope, sometimes due to the clumsiness of the person who wove it, brings about human mortality (the Keres of New Mexico, the natives of Belau), and the resulting fall causes the articulation of the human body into joints or knots (the Carisi). In order to cover human nakedness, the superhuman beings who preside over weaving gave these first humans cotton and taught them to spin and to weave (the Caduveo of South America, the Ifugao of the Philippines). To provide them with various necessities, they also taught them the art of weaving wicker (the Pomo).

At a certain point, however, humans themselves became capable of using bonds to improve their own economic condition by capturing superhuman beings and forcing them to yield to their demands. A myth from Namoluk Island (Micronesia) tells how certain spirits, captured with a net, taught the cultivation of taro to those who until then had lived exclusively on fish. Stories are also told among numerous cultures of humanity's rescue from various cataclysms by means of specific products of binding: the net of the spider (the Pomo), a basket (the Wiyot of Algonquin language), and so on.

From this brief survey, it should be clear that knots and other types of bonds need to be studied not only in historical perspective but also in relation to the technology of the culture in question. Behind the motif of knots is found the exaltation of *homo faber,* who redeems himself from the infinite miseries and multitudinous limitations of his existential condition precisely by means of his ability to bind things together. It is he who catches spirits in nets, weaves the rope that permits him to live on earth, sets snares and traps in order to capture the stars and fix them in their course, weaves the basket in which he saves himself from the flood—in short, spins and weaves the mortal condition. In his full appreciation of manual ability as a creative force, in his elevation of this creativity to the cosmogonic level, and in his sublimation of his own work by means of implements and tools capable of controlling reality, humankind proves itself capable of binding and loosening the entangling and knotty problems that fill his existence: He shows himself to be the uncontested artificer of his own fate.

SEE ALSO Binding; Labyrinth; Webs and Nets.

BIBLIOGRAPHY

Three works discuss the theme of knots and the binding action central to it: James G. Frazer's *The Golden Bough,* 3d ed., rev. and enl., vol. 3, *Taboo and the Perils of the Soul* (London, 1911); Isidor Scheftelowitz's *Das Schlingen- und Netzmotiv im Glauben und Brauch der Völker* (Giessen, 1912); and Walter J. Dilling's "Knots," in the *Encyclopaedia of Religion and Ethics,* edited by James Hastings, vol. 7 (Edinburgh, 1914). More detailed approaches are taken by Georges Dumézil in *Ouranos-Varuna* (Paris, 1934) and *Mitra-Varuna* (Paris, 1940) and by Mircea Eliade in *Images and Symbols: Studies in Religious Symbolism* (New York, 1961).

Concerning the use of knotted ropes, the Peruvian *quipu* and art of weaving are the subject of P. Matthey's "Gli esordi della scienze" and Enrica Cerulli's "Industrie e techniche," both in *Ethnologica,* vol. 2, *Le opere dell'uomo,* edited by Vinigi L. Grottanelli (Milan, 1965). Martin P. Nilsson discusses the measurement of time with the aid of knotted ropes in *Primitive Time-Reckoning* (Lund, 1920), pp. 320ff. On the use of ropes in the confession of sins, see Raffaela Pettazzoni's *La confessione dei peccati,* vol. 1 (1929; reprint, Bologna, 1968), and on the use of knots in divination, see William A. Lessa's "Divining by Knots in the Carolines," *Journal of Polynesian Society* 68 (June 1959): 188–204. For a discussion of the metaphor of the universe as something woven, see Pettazzoni's well-documented study *Miti e leggende,* 4 vols. (Turin, 1948–1963).

New Sources

Dupré, Louis. *Symbols of the Sacred.* Grand Rapids, Mich., 2000. A study on the nature of religious symbols.

Faraone, Christopher A. *Talismans and Trojan Horses. Guardian Statues in Ancient greek Myth and Ritual.* New York and Oxford, 1992. Knots and knotted chords as prophylactic devices in ancient magic.

Humphrey, Caroline. *Shamans and Elders. Experience, Knowledge, and Power among the Daur Mongols.* Oxford, 1996. Knots in shamanic performances.

Lurker. "Knoten." In *Wörterbuch der Symbolik.* Stuttgart, Germany, 1983, p. 50. Bibliography.

McKenna, Megan. *Praying the Rosary.* New York, 2004. A theological and historical guide to symbols related to rosaries in Catholicism and various religious traditions using knots in praying.

Meuli, Karl. "Die gefesselten Götter." In *Gesammelte Schriften,* vol. 2, Basel and Stuttgart, 1975, pp. 1035–1081. A classic study on binding symbolism throughout ancient Mediterranean traditions.

GIULIA PICCALUGA (1987)
Translated from Italian by Roger DeGaris
Revised Bibliography

KNOWLEDGE AND IGNORANCE.

A cognitive element is essential to most religions and probably to all, but exactly what constitutes religious knowledge is problematic. Strong belief, for example, may be subjectively indistinguishable from knowledge. In a 1984 BBC interview, Billy Graham asserted that he *knows* there is to be a second coming of Christ. At a lecture, the Hindu scholar Swami Bon declared that "transmigration is not a dogma, it is a fact." This article will examine the various and conflicting conceptions of religious knowledge that have emerged in the major traditions through history.

PRIMAL PEOPLES. "It appears," Dominique Zahan has written, "that every religion, however primitive, contains a cognitive element" ("Religions de l'Afrique noire," *Histoire des religions* 3, 1976, p. 609). In primal religions, according to Åke Hultkranz, religious knowledge rests on a fundamental division of experience: "A basic dichotomy between two levels of existence, one orderly or 'natural'—the world of daily experience—the other extraordinary or 'supernatural'—the world of belief—conditions man's religious cognition" (Hultkranz, 1983, pp. 231, 239). The world of belief is in turn divided into that of the sorcerer and that of the magician. "They are opposed to one another on the plane of knowledge and wisdom, as a tortuous, obscure knowledge full of contradictions and uncertainties, over against a clear knowledge, imbued with evidence and conforming to the logic of a thought at the service of the community" (ibid., p. 632).

More simply, though, the world of belief may be identified with the invisible. As the Kiowa Indian N. Scott Momaday has said, "We see the world as it appears to us, in one dimension of reality. But we also see it with the eye of the mind" (ibid., p. 248). A slightly different note is struck by an Eskimo woman: "You always want the supernatural things to make sense, but we do not bother about that. We are content not to understand" (ibid., p. 247).

INDIA. In India a cognitive element is conspicuous in the whole tradition that sprang or claimed to spring from the Veda. The *Ṛgveda* already comprised some speculative hymns, and the Brāhmaṇas were essentially an interpretation of ritual by means of myth. Finally, in the Upaniṣads, ritual itself gives way to speculation: Salvation is achieved through recognizing one's identity with the essence of the universe, the *brahman.*

In classical Brahmanism, philosophy is a mere rationalization of the Vedic revelation (Biardeau, 1964). Contrary to what happened in both Christianity and Islam owing to the clash of two different traditions, in Brahmanism no distinction was made between philosophy and theology. But in Hinduism there was always "a deep-seated tension between the ascetic ideal as personified in the holiness of the *śramaṇa* and the ideal or ritual propriety for the ordinary believer" (Bendix, 1960, p. 192). One of three or four approaches to this tension was *jñānayoga* ("the way of knowledge"), which held that even a good action, because it is connected with ignorance (*avidyā*), can only produce the fruit of all attachment to things and beings, namely, reincarnation. In the Nyāya ("logic") school, there is finally only one mode of knowledge, that of perception, but in certain circumstances contact with the external senses is not required: Contact between *ātman* ("soul") and *manas* ("inner sense") is sufficient. Natural and revealed knowledge are on the same plane: "The gods, the men and the animals make use of the [revealed] means of right knowledge, and there is no other" (*Nyāyabhāṣya* 1.1.17).

Concepts of nondualism and *brahman* have long had precise meanings in India. Both refer to a mystical doctrine of salvation through knowledge: As the Veda is endowed with the ontological fecundity of the *brahman,* so the latter is, in turn, the spring of all knowledge. In the Sāṃkhya school the most fatal attitude is nescience, or nondiscrimination between *puruṣa* (spectator spirit) and *prakṛti* (creative energy): This failure to discriminate is *avidyā* ("ignorance"), which keeps one in the bonds of the cycle of transmigration. But if language speaks only of things in themselves, it cannot express becoming, or change, Bhaṛtrhari objects, and he finds a way out of this difficulty not by suppressing permanence, as did the Buddhists, but by allowing thought to transcend perception without relinquishing being. He eventually does away with the authority of perception and relies only on interior revelation, which is essentially religious and nonrational. Bhaṛtrhari does not mention *avidyā* or *māyā* ("illusion"), which will be the pivots of Vedantic thought. Vedāntism—the further development of Brahmanism—cannot be understood without reference to Buddhism.

BUDDHISM. The teachings of the Buddha presupposed a high level of schooling among his disciples: There were systematic, dispassionate discussions in which appeal was made to the intellect, in contrast to the popular similes, ironical retorts, and emotional preaching of Jesus or the visionary messages of Muḥammad (Bendix, 1960, p. 192). Buddhism is based on an illumination (*bodhi*) experienced by Śākyamuni. Its object was expressed in the form of a chain of causes and effects (Skt., *pratītya-samutpāda;* Pali, *paṭicca-samuppāda*). The list given in the *Mahānidāna Sutta* comprises only nine links, ending in (or starting from) *viññāṇa* ("consciousness"), without ignorance being mentioned. Not so in the *Mahāvagga,* which counts twelve terms, starting from *avijjā* ("ignorance"), in the chain of psychic formations, a notion parallel to that in Brahmanism where, unlike the Buddhist understanding, pure being shrouds itself, out of ignorance, in psychic formations. Essentially the Buddhist message is this: Living is suffering, suffering stems from desire, and desire from *avidyā.* In order to be delivered one should vanquish ignorance and obtain wisdom, mystical lucidity (Pali, *paññā;* Sanskrit, *prajñā*), also called *āryaprajñā* ("noble knowledge"), which produces extinction, *nirvāṇa.* But, contrary to what is taught in Brahmanism, this knowledge implies the negation of all permanence, of all substance, of *ātman* as well as of *brahman,* the two terms whose equation was the foundation of the Brahmanic doctrine. This is the view of Hīnayāna Buddhism.

Mahāyāna Buddhism refines this negative position. The perfection of wisdom, *prajñāpāramitā,* does not give omniscience by providing a foundation of knowledge: The very lack of such a foundation constitutes omniscience, which is the revelation of emptiness. Still, there are two degrees of this revelation. According to the Vijñānavādins, pure thought is an absolute to which all things are reduced, while the Mādhyamikas go one step further: For them the doctrine of emptiness is itself emptiness (Bugault, 1968, p. 48). The effort toward knowledge results in nonknowledge, nescience.

According to Asanga, *prajñā* is only obtained subsequent to *dhyāna* ("appeased, introverted concentration"; in Chinese *chan,* in Japanese *zen*) and is a sort of *noēsis* without *noēta* (ibid., p. 41). *Prajñā* and *dhyāna* are like the two sides of a coin. *Dhyāna* concentrates; *prajñā* liberates. Supreme knowledge, *bodhi,* is only the realization that there is nothing to comprehend. This kind of knowledge would seem to be tantamount to sheer ignorance, but it is not, for then "the deaf, the blind and the simpletons would be saints" (*Majjhima Nikāya* 3.498). It must be remembered that Buddhism arose amid ascetics who practiced control of the senses, of breath, even of blood circulation—and of thought. In Chinese Buddhism, the direct approach of Huineng (seventh to eighth century) to sudden awakening rejected all distinctions between enlightenment and ignorance.

VEDĀNTA. The ruin of Brahmanic ontology under the assault of Hinayana Buddhism had resulted in Hinayana positivism, which led to the Mahāyāna doctrine of absolute emptiness. This in turn brought about in Brahmanism Vedantism, a return to ontology on the basis of *avidyā* ("nescience"), as formulated by its first major exponent, Śaṅkara, in the eleventh century. The idea of the ego is produced by nescience; so are, in their literal sense, the Vedic texts. Nescience is the cause of all error, of suffering and of evil. *Brahman* is the only true object of knowledge, to which the soul goes back by exercising nescience. Substituting the word *nirvāṇa* for the word *brahman* would result in a perfect formula of Buddhist orthodoxy. But Rāmānuja (twelfth century), the second important exponent of Vedantism, went one step further. He admits, not unlike Śaṅkara, that subject, object, and the act of knowledge are only arbitrary distinctions created by *avidyā,* that the chain of acts is only a trick of nescience, and that salvation consists in the cessation of nescience through knowledge of *brahman,* which is accessible in the Veda. But this is transcendent knowledge, an intuitive revelation only made possible in a mystical union with *brahman,* which is also conceived as the universal lord. "He who possessing knowledge untiringly strives and is devoted to me only, to him I am infinitely dear and he is dear to me" (*Bhagavadgītā,* 7.17).

Rāmānuja also restored to the individual soul its reality and substantiality. Whereas in the Upaniṣads and the teachings of Śaṅkara the divinity was conceived as sheer consciousness, in medieval Hinduism, whether Vaiṣṇava or Śaiva, it becomes a force in action, a sovereign energy. And knowledge must be fulfilled in *bhakti,* that is, unrelenting love of God. Rāmānuja refutes the notion of *avidyā* Śaṅkara had inherited from the Buddhists. To assume that the *brahman* necessarily develops into illusory nescience and plurality is to admit that the *brahman* itself is illusory, that ultimate reality is error and lie. This is, he says, to fall into the error of Mādhyamika Buddhism, which is contradicted by the teachings of the Upaniṣads, the *Bhagavadgītā,* and the *Viṣṇu Purāṇa* (Grousset, 1931, p. 391).

DAOISM. Chinese thought, on the whole, aims at culture, not at pure knowledge. In Daoism, humankind falls by acquiring knowledge. Whereas for the Confucians humans learn to use and to improve on nature, for the Daoists this is a profanation of nature: "Banish wisdom, discard knowledge, and the people will be benefited a hundredfold, for it was only when the great Dao declined, when intelligence and knowledge appeared, that the great Artifice began. . . . In the days of old those who practiced Dao with success did not, by means of it, enlighten the people, but on the contrary sought to make them ignorant. The more knowledge people have, the harder they are to rule. Those who seek to rule by giving knowledge are like bandits preying on the land. Those who rule without giving knowledge bring a stock of good fortune to the land" (*Dao de jing*). Daoism is the declared enemy of civilization. Civilization based on knowledge is to be replaced by another kind of knowledge, the intuitive knowledge of Dao, through which humanity becomes the Dao.

THE GREEKS. The notion of Logos in Heraclitus implies that the universe can be known. He was the first philosopher to pose the epistemological problem. Still, for him "questions of cognition are inseparable from questions of action and intention, of life and death. The blindness he denounces is that of men who do not know what they are doing" (Kahn, 1979, p. 100).

The Pythagoreans were divided into acousmatics and mathematicians, the former following the tradition of *fides ex auditu,* the latter following reason and *veritas ex intellectu,* thus already exemplifying, as Léon Brunschwicg noted, the contrast between theosophy and philosophy. With the emergence of philosophy a conflict was bound to arise between reason and religion, between *logos* and *muthos.* It tended to be resolved, for instance by Theagenes of Rhegium (fourth century BCE), through the allegorical interpretation of myths.

In the sixth century BCE Xenophanes ridiculed the anthropomorphism of the myths and emphasized God's spirituality and omniscience. A century later Socrates (according to Xenophon) rejected the study of the world machine, wrought and ruled by the gods, and instead recommended studying human affairs. He equated virtue with knowledge and vice with ignorance (Xenophon, *Memorabilia* 3.9, 4. a; Plato, *Protagoras, Meno,* etc.).

According to Plato, faith, mystical enthusiasm, is but a stage in the pathway to knowledge; the knowledge of God is the soul's marriage with her ideal. Above the Logos, or Reason, is the Nous, or Intellect, the faculty of perceiving the divine, the instrument of contemplation. But the supreme idea, the Good, was raised by Plato beyond both being and knowledge, as the principle of their unity.

Aristotle replaced Plato's *anamnēsis* by abstraction. Humankind is like a mortal god, for it possesses a divine reality, the intellect, capable of knowing God. God, the Unmoved Mover, is *noēsis noēseōs.* This still reflects the primacy of the intellect and implies superiority of contemplation over any other way of life.

The Cynics reacted against the almost unlimited confidence in education as a means to form and transform man that had prevailed in Athens since the time of the Sophists. Virtue, said Antisthenes, lies in action and has no need of many discourses or of science. But the saying attributed to him by Diogenes Laertius (6.103) that "if one were wise, one would not learn to read, lest one should be corrupted by other people," is probably an exaggeration of his position.

For the Stoics the human intellect is not only akin to God, it is part of the divine substance itself. They appealed to Heraclitus, but their Logos was not, like his, simply a principle of explanation. It probably owed much to the notion of the commanding word, *davar,* which in Hebrew expressed the divine will.

In the Platonic tradition, according to Philo Judaeus, the human intellect is the source of, on the one hand, perception, memory, and reaction to impulses; on the other hand, as *apospasma theion* ("divine fragment"), it makes possible suprarational intuition.

THE HEBREWS. To the Hebrews, knowing was less a logical, discursive process than a direct psychological experience, less the expression of objective truths than a personal engagement. (The Hebrew for "to know," *yada'*, signifies sexual intercourse.) Knowledge of the law was the basis of the moral life. In the *Book of Genesis,* however, a negative appraisal of knowledge was reflected in the story of the Fall: Evil and death entered the world through humanity's "knowledge of good and evil." The myth resembles the Daoist one in which the loss of happiness results from the acquisition of knowledge.

In Israel, however, this conception remained isolated and, perhaps, misunderstood, over against the more widespread feeling that knowledge is from God, who "teaches man knowledge" (*Ps.* 94:10) and, in the Qumran texts, is even called "God of knowledge," and "source of knowledge." Such a notion also prevails in Jewish apocalyptic literature (Gruenwald, 1973, p. 63). Finally, skepticism is not absent from the Bible; *Ecclesiastes* expresses skepticism but compensates for it by adherence to authority.

Early Christianity. The role of knowledge in the Christian faith has varied considerably. Its importance was already recognized by Paul the apostle, who considered it the supreme virtue: ". . . after I heard of your faith . . . and love . . . [I prayed] that . . . God . . . may give unto you the spirit of wisdom and revelation in the knowledge of him" (*Eph.* 1:15–18; cf. *Col.* 2:2), which agrees with the educational ideal of a Jewish doctor of the law and with the mystical aspiration of apocalyptic; however, the ultimate object of knowledge, the love of Christ, "passeth knowledge" (*Eph.* 3:19), and Paul conformed to the specific Christian ideal when, addressing the Corinthians, he put charity above everything: "and though I have the gift of prophecy, and understand all mysteries, and all knowledge; and though I have all faith, so that I could move mountains, and have no love, I am nothing" (*1 Cor.* 13:2); "knowledge puffeth up, love edifieth" (*1 Cor.* 8:1).

Only John attempts a synthesis of love and knowledge: "for love is of God, and every one that loveth is born of God, and knoweth God" (*1 Jn.* 4:7). And in the prologue of the Fourth Gospel he identifies Jesus himself with the Logos. Contact with paganism, however, had already brought about in Paul a completely different reaction: "But we preach Christ crucified, unto the Jews a stumbling block, and unto the Greeks foolishness" (*1 Cor.* 1:23). A conflict between natural wisdom and revealed truth thus developed in Christianity and later, parallel to it, in Islam. On the other hand, Justin Martyr, the first Christian apologist, headed a long series of authors for whom the Christian revelation was the culmination of a more ample one that would include the thought of the pagan philosophers, also Christian in its own way because it came from the Word (Logos), and Christ was the Word incarnate.

Gnōsis. In the second century, when Plutarch, with his Platonic use of myth, bore witness to philosophy's overture toward mysticism and to the challenge of the primacy of the Logos, people were seeking to attain through revelation a kind of knowledge allowing union with God. There ensued a heated dialogue between faith (*pistis*) and intellectual knowledge (*gnōsis*), the latter already suspect to Paul (*1 Tim.* 6:20: *pseudonumos gnōsis*). Thus arose two conceptions of the knowledge accessible to the Christian: The one (*gnōsis*) is to replace faith; the other submits to faith in order to fathom its mystery. Gnosticism "traces back the origin of the world to an act of ignorance, the removal of which through knowledge is the aim of the Gnostic doctrine of redemption" (Rudolph, 1983, p. 71). The element earth has been produced by horror, water by fear, air by pain; within those three elements there is fire, a vehicle of death and destruction, as within the three passions is hidden ignorance (Irenaeus, *Against Heresies* 1.5.4).

Jewish apocalyptic contributed to gnosticism by its new idea of knowledge as a religious ideal (Gruenwald, 1973, p. 104), but the gnostics, according to Celsus, called the god of the Jews the "accursed god" because he created the visible world and withheld knowledge from humans (Rudolph, 1983, p. 73). According to various gnostic texts the "tree of knowledge" imparts to Adam his appropriate godlike status over against the lower creator god, who prohibited the enjoyment of this tree out of envy. The serpent functions at the behest of the highest god for Adam's instruction, and thus has a positive task (ibid., p. 94). According to Irenaeus, however, mundane knowledge is to be rejected (*Against Heresies* 2.32.2). And according to Hippolytus, God will extend the great ignorance to all the world, so that each creature will remain in its natural condition and no one will desire anything against nature.

Direct information about gnosticism is available thanks to the discovery in Upper Egypt of the Nag Hammadi Coptic manuscripts. *Gnōsis* is a hidden, esoteric knowledge. One of the tractates bears the significant title *The Interpretation of Knowledge.* The *Gospel of Truth* states that "ignorance of the Father brought about anguish and terror. And the anguish grew solid like a fog so that no one was able to see. For this reason error became powerful; it fashioned its own matter" (Robinson, 1977, p. 38). In the *Gospel of Thomas:* "The Pharisees and the scribes have taken the keys of knowledge and hidden them. They themselves have not entered" (ibid., p. 122). In the *Authoritative Teaching:* "Even the Pagans give charity, and they know that God exists . . . but they have not heard the word" (ibid., p. 282). The God of this world is evil and ignorant, according to *The Second Treatise of the Great Seth.* In contrast, the Logos "received the vision of all things, those which preexist and those which are now and those which will be" (ibid., p. 77). Further: "The invisible Spirit is a psychic and intellectual power, a knowledgeable one and a foreknower" (ibid., p. 383). The function or faculty by means of which *gnōsis* is brought about is personified: It is Epinoia, a transformation of Pronoia, or Providence (*Apocryphon of John*). The world, on the contrary, was created through the union of Ialdabaoth, the demiurge, with Aponoia, the negative counterpart of Ennoia and a symbol of his intellectual blindness.

Knowledge liberates: "The mind of those who have known him shall not perish" (ibid., p. 52); The "thought of Norea" is the knowledge necessary for salvation. The *Testimony of Truth* contrasts knowledge with empty hopes for martyrdom and a fleshly resurrection. The tractate *Marsanes* speaks of the rewards of knowledge. But knowledge is not sufficient: According to the *Apocryphon of John,* Christ is sent down to save humanity by reminding people of their heavenly origin. Only those who possess this knowledge and have lived ascetic lives can return to the realm of light. In fact, says the *Testimony of Truth,* "No one knows the God of truth except the man who will forsake all of the things of the world."

In sum, "Gnosis is not a 'theology of salvation by nature,' as the heresiologists caricature it; it is rather thoroughly conscious of the provisional situation of the redeemed up to the realization of redemption after death." (Rudolph, 1983, p. 117). Similarly, in Mandaean religion (Manda d-Hiia, literally "knowledge of life"), a gnostic sect that survives to the present day in Iraq, knowledge alone does not redeem: The cultic rites, primarily baptism and the "masses for the dead," are necessary for salvation.

But God, according to the gnostics, is the incomprehensible, inconceivable one, who is superior to every thought, "who is over the world," "the one who is ineffable," "the unknowable" (Robinson, 1977, pp. 209, 213, 411).

GREEK FATHERS. In the third century Clement of Alexandria, "with his conscious use of the concept *gnōsis* for the Christian knowledge of truth, attempts to overcome the breach between faith and knowledge in the Church and not to remain stuck in a mere denial of the claims of the 'false' gnosis" (Rudolph, 1983, p. 16). "Should one say," he writes in *Stromateis* 2.4, "that knowledge is founded on demonstration by a process of reasoning, let him hear that the first principles are incapable of demonstration. . . . Hence, it is thought that the first cause of the universe can be apprehended by faith alone." But Clement's God is as unknowable as that of Plato or Philo Judaeus, who placed him above being. This is also the position of Plotinus, a contemporary of Clement.

In the fourth century at Antioch John Chrysostom wrote on God's incomprehensibility. According to Gregory of Nazianzus God's existence can be inferred from the order of the world, but we cannot know what he is. The motto of Theodoret of Cyrrhus (fourth to fifth century) was "first believe, then understand."

The Desert Fathers, in their simplicity, sometimes resented the intrusion of more sophisticated views from Alexandria or, later, from Cappodocia. In contrast to the newly converted intellectuals who were bringing to Christianity the aristocratic tradition of the pagan teachers, monachism reaffirmed, as the Franciscans were to do in the thirteenth century, the primacy of the unsophisticated, one of the essential teachings of the Gospels. *Libido sciendi* and excessive pretension to wisdom were regarded as temptations of the devil just as were sensuality or ambition. (Brunschwicg, [1927] 1953, p. 107).

In the sixth century a gnostic tendency expressed already in the *Gospel of Philip* was developed by Dionysius the Areopagite, who applied to God all the names the scriptures give him (affirmative theology), but only in order to afterward deny them (negative or apophatic theology). God is beyond affirmation or negation; he is a superbeing (superlative theology). The world is a theophany, the only means of knowing its author. Universal illumination is an immense circulation of love. Knowledge is above every affirmation or negation. This is the mystical ignorance, the supreme degree of knowledge. The other kinds of knowledge are defective, this one is superabundant.

To Maximos the Confessor (seventh century), man in his progress toward God through knowledge only ascends back, in a movement opposite to his fall, toward the eternal idea of himself that, as his cause, has never ceased to exist in God.

LATIN FATHERS. Among the Latin church fathers in the second and third centuries Tertullian (like Tatian among the Greeks) radically opposed philosophy. He wrote that the desire for knowledge leads to faith. This is perhaps rather simple, but not quite the same as the motto often attributed to him: "Credo quia absurdem."

The Platonic tradition survived and in the fourth and fifth centuries produced the philosophy of Augustine of Hippo, who after hoping to proceed through Manichaeism from reason to faith, always maintained the necessity of the preparatory role of reason but held that reason had also another role to play, subsequent to faith. Thus: "Intellige ut credas, crede ut intelligas." All one's knowledge stems from one's sensations, which, however, do not teach one the truths. This is done by something in one that is purely intelligible, necessary, motionless, eternal: a divine illumination. To know oneself (as Socrates recommended) is to recognize an image of God, therefore to know God.

ISLAM. Muḥammad's message presents itself as knowledge, so much so that the times preceding his coming are called the Jāhilīyah ("state of ignorance"). The same idea is found in *Acts of the Apostles* 17:30: "And the times of this ignorance God winked at; but now commandeth all men everywhere to repent." Islam initiated the times of illumination and right knowledge. But when the Muslims encountered the Greek philosophical heritage through Syriac texts, the problem of the relationship between philosophy and the Qur'anic tradition was bound to arise. Some Muslims quoted the Prophet in support of their contention that speculation was one of the duties of the believers; others, on the contrary, maintained that faith should be obedience, not knowledge.

As related in the Jewish philosopher Maimonides' *Guide for the Perplexed,* "when the Muḥammadans began to translate the writings of the Greek philosophers from the Syriac into the Arabic, they likewise translated the criticisms of those philosophers by such Christians as John Philoponus, the commentator of Aristotle" (Gilson, 1937, p. 39). Al-Kindī (ninth century) seems to have found in Philoponus the germ of his notion of a harmony between Greek philosophy and Muslim faith. He suffered under the repression of all philosophical activity ordered by the Abbasid caliph al-Mutawakkil.

According to Abū Bakr al-Rāzī, a tenth-century physician, only philosophy, especially that of the Greek sages, could lead to happiness. For him, there was no possible reconciliation between philosophy and religion.

"Where the revealed truth is, by hypothesis, absolute truth," writes Étienne Gilson, "the only way to save philosophy is to show that its teaching is substantially the same as that of revealed religion" (1937, p. 37). This was the purpose of al-Ashaʿrī (Baghdad, tenth century), who inaugurated Muslim scholasticism (*kalām*) in the Sunnī tradition, but whose doctrine "is a remarkable instance of what happens to philosophy when it is handled by theologians, according to theological methods, for a theological end" (ibid., p. 39). His contemporary al-Fārābī was a typical representative of the main current in Muslim philosophy: Everything is known through a cosmic agent, the Active Intellect, whose final aim is to enable everyone to know God. Al-Fārābī's tendency culminated in the teachings of the Iranian Ibn Sīnā (Avicenna). AbūḤāmid al-Ghazālī (Iran, eleventh century) turned Aristotle's own weapons against the Aristotelianism of al-Fārābī and Ibn Sīnā in order to establish religion—accessible only through mystical knowledge—on the ruins of philosophy.

Faith could, in principle, be based either on authority *(taqlīd)* or on knowledge *(ʿilm)* or on the intuition of the mystic *(aʿyān)*. Islamic mysticism seems to have originated in some form of gnosticism, and in the tenth century Neoplatonism was adapted. Twelver Shiism distinguishes, in its epistemology, two parallel series. On the side of external vision are eye, sight, perception, and sun; on the side of internal vision, heart, intelligence *(ʿaql)*, knowledge (*ʿilm*), and active intelligence *(ʿaql faʿʿāl)*. This, so far, is the philosophical approach. The prophetic approach considers as its source the Holy Spirit, Gabriel, the angel of revelation, who is distinct from the Active Intellect. But the two modes of perception ultimately converge. This is due, according to the Twelver Shīʿī theoretician Mullā Ṣadrā Shirāzī (seventeenth century), to the existence and activity, halfway between pure sense perception and pure intellection, of a third faculty of knowledge: creative imagination. (Aside from his Aristotelian theory of passive imagination, Ibn Sīnā held another, "Oriental" one, of active imagination, which was to be developed in Suhrawardī's "philosophy of light").

But to return to al-Ghazālī's destruction of philosophy: "There was bound," writes Gilson, "to appear a philosopher who, on the contrary, endeavored to found philosophy on the ruins of religion" (ibid., p. 35). Such was the Andalusian philosopher Ibn Rushd (Averroës, twelfth century). He distinguished between knowledge accessible to the lower classes and interpretations reserved for the philosophical elite. Philosophy was supreme in attaining absolute science and truth; next came theology, the domain of dialectical interpretation and verisimilitude; at the lowest level, religion and faith were adequate for those who needed them. His adversaries accused him of professing the doctrine of double truth. This, according to Gilson, is inaccurate and unfair. Ibn Rushd maintained only that reason's conclusions are necessary *and* that he adhered to faith's opposite teaching. His Latin followers supported his view that philosophy, when given the liberty to follow its own methods, reaches necessary conclusions that are contradictory to the teachings of religion.

THE SCHOOLMEN. Scholasticism was largely an answer to the challenge of Ibn Rushd (Averroës); it might also be seen, however, as little more than an obstinate endeavor to solve one problem, the problem of universals. The answer was far from unanimous.

Peter Abelard (eleventh to twelfth centuries) always insisted on the continuity between ancient wisdom, based on the natural usage of reason, and Christian wisdom, which, far from destroying the previous, fulfills it. But he soon reached the conclusion that he had no universal ideas. God alone has. Scientific and philosophical skepticism is compensated for by a theological appeal to the grace of God. Anselm of Canterbury (eleventh century) had written, "For I do not seek to understand that I may believe, but I believe in order to understand. For this also I believe, that unless I believed, I should not understand." Hence his motto: "Fides quaerens intellectum."

Hugh of Saint-Victor (twelfth century) wrote that from the beginning God wished to be neither entirely manifest to human consciousness nor entirely hidden. "If He were entirely hidden, faith would indeed not be added unto knowledge, and lack of faith would be excused on the ground of ignorance. . . . It was necessary that He should conceal Himself, lest He be entirely manifest, so that there might be something which through being known would nourish the heart of man, and again something which through being hidden would stimulate it" (*De sacramentis* 1.3.2). Further: "Faith is a form of mental certitude about absent realities that is greater than opinion and less than knowledge" (ibid., 1.10.2).

The position of the Franciscan Bonaventure (thirteenth century), like that of Abelard, was destructive of natural knowledge. This was a difficulty another Franciscan, John Duns Scotus, endeavored to deal with, but his own doctrine was "the death warrant of early Franciscan epistemology" (Gilson, 1937, p. 59).

The Dominican Albertus Magnus and his disciple Thomas Aquinas (who was almost exactly contemporaneous with Bonaventure) vindicated Aristotle's "abstraction" as a way of knowing God against the "divine illumination" of Augustine, Anselm, and Bonaventure, as well as against the Active Intellect of Ibn Rushd. But in an irenic mood Thomas observed that because God is the ultimate cause, his illumination is implied in abstraction also. Faith differs from knowledge in being determined in part by the choice of the believer, and from opinion in being held without misgiving:

> Faith implies intellectual assent to that which is believed, but there are two ways in which the intellect gives its assent. In the first way, it is moved . . . by the object iself. . . as are conclusions which are known scientifically. In the second way, the intellect gives its assent not because it is convinced by the object itself, but by voluntarily preferring the one alternative to the other. (*Summa theologiae* 2.2.1.4)

Commenting on *James* 2:19 ("Even the demons believe—and shudder"), Thomas further writes:

> The demons are, in a way, compelled to believe by the evidence of signs and so their will deserves no praise for their belief as they are compelled to believe by their natural intellectual acumen. (ibid., 2.2.5.2)

Moreover, while philosophy only teaches about God what is known *per creaturas* (Paul, *Rom.* 1:19), theology also teaches, thanks to revelation, "quod notum est sibi soli" ("what only He himself knows"; ibid., 1.6). Thomas's position has been characterized as intellectualist, fideistic, and voluntarist by John Hick (1966), who attempts to refute it.

William of Ockham (fourteenth century), yet another Franciscan, discusses various philosophical problems as if any theological dogma, held by faith alone, could become the source of philosophical and purely rational conclusions. Intuitive knowledge is self-evident. Not so abstractive knowledge. William denies the existence of ideas representing the genera and the species, and this even in God (thus outstripping Abelard). The universal mystery is but a concrete expression of the supreme mystery of God, a position that anticipates Hume's skepticism.

According to Gregory Palamas (fourteenth century), who lived in Constantinople and was thus outside Latin Scholasticism, knowledge acquired through profane education is not only different from but contrary to veritable, spiritual knowledge (*Triads in Defense of the Holy Hesychasts* 1.1.10).

After the breakdown of medieval philosophy, there seemed to be two ways of saving the Christian faith: either to resort, with Petrarch, Erasmus, and others, to the gospel, the fathers of the church, and the pagan moralists, which might lead to the skepticism of Montaigne (who, nevertheless, practiced Catholicism, to the extent of making a pilgrimage to Our Lady of Loretta), or to resort to mysticism. A mystical tide swept over Europe during the fourteenth and fifteenth centuries. Johannes (Meister) Eckhart's God is not simply beyond the reach of human knowledge, but in a truly Neoplatonic manner escapes all knowledge, including his very own: Even if it be true that God eternally expresses himself in an act of self-knowledge, his infinite essence is unfathomable even to himself, for he could not know himself without turning this infinite essence into a definite object of knowledge. "It is only when man reaches that silent wilderness where there is neither Father, nor Son, nor Holy Ghost, that his mystical flight comes to an end, for there lies the source of all that is: beyond God, in the fullness of Godhead" (Gavalda, 1973, p. 111).

Copernicus had put an end to geocentrism, but an accommodation between a newer cosmology and an older theology was nevertheless to prevail for a long time to come: Kepler and others saw the Holy Trinity reflected in the solar system, with the sun as God the Father.

PROTESTANTISM. In reaction to accomodating tendencies within monachism and Scholasticism, Luther loathed philosophy and ancient culture: Reason was "the devil's highest whore"; hence his polemic against Erasmus. Calvin thought that humanity cannot know God in itself, but only as the Lord revealing himself to humans. A Calvinist (as noted by Max Weber), because of his particular view of the relationship between the creator and the creature and of his own "election," would live and work in a certain way: "Puritanism's ethic of trade, which applied to believers and nonbelievers alike, was related to both religious doctrine and pastoral practice. Intense religious education, together with the threat of social ostracism, provided powerful incentives and sanctions" (Reinhard Bendix, *Max Weber: An Intellectual Portrait,* Garden City, N. Y., 1960, p. 91).

To combat Protestantism, the Roman Catholic church took an obscurantist stance, forbidding the reading of the Bible in translation, while it also attempted to reinforce its doctrines by the institution of catechism. Ignorance could be considered culpable, and a person could, "like a diseased limb . . . [be] cut off and separated by his ignorance and sin" (Miguel de Cervantes, *Don Quixote,* chap. 40). But ignorance could also be an excuse if it be, in terms of Catholic theology, "invincible," that is, if the agent is wholly unaware of his obligations or of the implications of a specific act (see G. H. Joyce, "Invincible Ignorance," in *Encyclopaedia of Religion and Ethics,* edited by James Hastings, vol. 7, Edinburgh, 1914).

For Pascal, there is an order of the spirit above that of the flesh; but above the order of the spirit there is that of love: "Le coeur a des raisons que la raison ne connaït pas" ("The heart has its reasons, which reason does not know"). And: "It was not then right that [Christ] should appear in a manner manifestly divine, and completely capable of convincing all men [through reason] . . . and thus [He was] willing to appear openly to those who seek Him with all their heart" (*Pensées* 430).

CARTESIANISM. Descartes's doctrine was "a direct answer to Montaigne's scepticism" and "a recklessly conducted experiment to see what becomes of human knowledge when moulded into conformity with the pattern of mathematical evidence: He had the merit of realizing that two sciences—geometry and algebra—hitherto considered as distinct were but one: Why not go at once to the limit and say that all sciences are one? Such was Descartes's final illumination" (Gilson, 1937, pp. 127, 133). After confessing in the *Discourse on Method* that one could not talk of things sacred without assistance from heaven, he showed in the *Meditations* "the way to attain knowledge of God with more ease and certainty than that of things of this world" (ibid., p. 137).

Leibniz, Spinoza, and Malebranche were Cartesians: From God proceeded the unknown force that linked mind to matter and matter to mind. According to Spinoza, the mysticism of literal faith belongs to a kind of inferior knowledge that dissolves in the light of intelligence. Above imagination there is reason, but above reason, intellectual intuition, which leads to the unique and absolute truth, God.

Malebranche, although holding that everything in God is known, still believed in the existence of a concrete and actually subsisting world of matter. Not so Berkeley. Finally, Hume said that if one has no adequate idea of "power" or "efficacy," no notion of causality that one can apply to matter, where could be obtained one that would be applied to God?

For Jakob Boehme, knowledge was a way of salvation. Under the influence of Boehme and Paracelsus, Christian esotericism tried more and more to unite faith and knowledge. But in eighteenth-century Europe, particularly in France, Germany, and England, the pursuit of happiness tended to prevail over concern for salvation; besides, unhappiness was regarded as due to a lack of knowledge or to erroneous judgment, and it was consequently believed that the progress of reason would bring happiness. For Leibniz, evil results from ignorance. Locke entitled a book *The Reasonableness of Christianity* (1695).

None of the German *Aufklärer* was inclined toward atheism; each tried to fit God into a rational scheme of things. For Samuel Reimarus, whose work was published by G. E. Lessing, religion did not proceed from a letter, Bible, or Qurʾān, dictated by some God; God was the presence, in one's soul, of universal, eternal reason.

It was thought that one should stop bothering about what cannot be known and that morality could be free of any transcendent element and based on nothing more than the self-knowledge of conscience. If all that seemed superstitious in the beliefs of the Roman church and reformed religion were purged, only the unknown supreme being would remain. Pierre Bayle paved the way for Holbach, Voltaire, Shaftesbury, Locke, Montesquieu, Rousseau, and, eventually, Kant.

While the Encyclopedists were trying to apply the methods of the sciences to the improvement of the practical arts and of social institutions, Rousseau's opposition exploded like a bomb: His philosophy was to dominate the period before the French Revolution and the years that followed its failure. God had created man not only innocent but ignorant, wishing thereby to "preserve him from knowledge just as a mother would wrench a dangerous weapon from the hands of her child" (*Discours sur les sciences et les arts,* quoted in Zaehner, 1970, p. 330). "Reason too often deceives us," says the Vicaire Savoyard, but "conscience never deceives" (*Émile,* quoted in Brunschwicg, 1927, p. 271). Conscience is the soul's divine instinct. Such was the religion of instinct, already advocated by Swiss pietists. Bolingbroke had written that one cannot know what God is, only that there is a God—which was, more or less, Hume's position.

KANT. What was Hume, after all, asks Gilson (1937, p. 223), but a sad Montaigne? Hume's voice was soon to be heard by Immanuel Kant. So long as one's mind applies itself to the mere mental presentation of possible objects, it does not form concepts of things, but mere ideas; these do not constitute scientific knowledge, but that illusory speculation that people call metaphysics. If reason does not lead to God, if, given Hume's skepticism, reason is destructive of the very principles of philosophical knowledge and morality, Rousseau's passionate appeal to feeling and to moral conscience, against the natural blindness of reason, is to Kant the revelation of a wholly independent and self-contained order of morality. But to posit God as required by the fact of morality is not the same as to know that God exists.

Maine de Biran, when young, surmised that the origin of belief lay in the sense of smell, but in his old age he wrote that Augustine, when meditating on his relation to God, found or proved that there might be a subtler, more refined organization above the coarse one of human sense (Brunschwicg, 1927, p. 618).

Hegel was in very much the same situation as Nicholas of Cusa in the fifteenth century. There had to be contradiction everywhere in the universe for the contradictions of philosophy to give a true picture of reality: This was another form of learned ignorance. But finally Hegelianism, by confining reason to the sphere of pure science, enslaved philosophy to the blind tyranny of the will (Gilson, 1937, p. 252).

COMTE. At a primary level of each social group there is, according to Comte, a definite state of intellectual knowledge; at a secondary level, determined by the first, is a specific form of government; finally, a third element flows from the first two: a specific form of civilization. "We have only to reverse this doctrine to get Marxism," remarks Gilson (1937, p. 257). In his synthesis of positivism with the Hegelian tradition, Marx made possible a sociology of knowledge (actually founded by Karl Mannheim), a science that tries to explain ideas (including religion) as the outcome of social conditions.

By driving metaphysics out of its final position, Comte had ensured the uniformity of human knowledge. But science had failed to provide mankind with a systematic view of the world. By making love the ultimate foundation of positivism Comte was repeating in his own way Kant's famous step of decreeing the primacy of practical reason. Condemnation of metaphysics in the name of science invariably culminates in the capitulation of science to some irrational element (Gilson, 1937, p. 298).

Eighteenth-century rationalism believed it could eliminate the religious tradition simply by determining its human conditions through historical and psychological observation. The nineteenth century, on the contrary, established a psychology and a sociology of religion that, far from eliminating their object, posited its objective reality through the very principles of their method. This reality is attained by intuition (Léon Brunschwicg, *Les étapes de la philosophie mathématique,* Paris, 1912, p. 432).

THE PROTESTANT PERSPECTIVE. The problem of religious knowledge has been dealt with extensively from the Protestant point of view by Douglas Clyde Macintosh (1940). He distinguishes not only between realism and idealism but between dualism and monism: "The object consciously experienced and the object existing independently of experience are, according to dualism, two wholly different existences, and, according to monism, existentially one, at least in part and sufficiently for some knowledge of the independently existing reality to be humanly possible" (Macintosh, 1940, p. vii). After excluding from the sphere of knowledge mysticism, ecstasy, the love-dialogue with God, and whatever is redolent of monasticism as "extreme monistic realism," Macintosh proceeds to an examination of "monistic idealism in religion."

MONISM. Under the rubric "Religious Psychologism" Macintosh deals with the views of Hegel and others. Hegel's definition of religion is "the Divine Spirit's knowledge of itself through the mediation of a finite spirit." For Feuerbach religion is man's earliest, indirect form of self-knowledge. For Édouard Le Roy dogmas are concerned primarily with conduct rather than with pure reflective knowledge. Barukh Spinoza wrote in his *Tractatus Theologico-Politicus* that faith does not demand that dogmas shall be true, but that they shall be pious—such as will stir up the heart to obey. For Durkheim, science refuses to grant religion its right to dogmatize upon the nature of things. For Freud, insofar as religion conflicts with science or would offer a substitute for scientific investigation of the cause and cure of human ills, it is open to criticism. Macintosh would strongly maintain that any tenable religious worldview must do full justice to science, including whatever scientific knowledge there may be in the field of religion, but such a worldview has the right to supplement scientific knowledge through a reasonable formulation of religious faith based upon the tested value of spiritual life.

Under "Philosophical Antecedents of Humanism" Macintosh deals with John Dewey, whose functionalism implies a behaviorist theory of thinking and knowing, which crowds out of the definition of knowing all elements of mental contemplation and rules out as "nonempirical" not only the idea of a transcendent God but even that of a persisting metaphysical ego as the individual subject of experience.

Under "Theological Antecedents of Humanism" Macintosh cites the work of George Burman Foster, whose early thought inclined to a dualistic theory of religious knowledge according to which the independently real but theoretically unknowable religious object was made the subject matter of judgments of religious faith and feeling, an attitude obviously inspired by Kant's. But Foster came to feel that he must give up the dualistic supernaturalism of all doctrines of a purely transcendent God.

Under "Humanism, Ecclesiastical and Other" Macintosh cites, among others, William Brown, who wrote that the world's savior, God, is knowledge, that the Gods of all the supernaturalistic interpretations of religion are so many creations of the dominant master class, and that "my God, Nature, is a triune divinity—matter, form, and motion—an impersonal, unconscious, non-moral being." Brown was expelled from the Episcopal church for espousing these ideas.

Under "Logical Idealism" Macintosh ranks Georg Simmel, Wilhelm Windelband, George Santayana, Benedetto Croce, and Giovanni Gentile. While the religious man, wrote Simmel, must be assured that God is, even if he may be in doubt as to what God is, the typical modern man knows very well what God is, but is unable to say that God is. Similarly, to Dean Inge the important question is not whether God exists but what is meant when speaking of God—the value of values, the supreme value. One could add Léon Brunschwicg, for whom God is the formal ideal of knowledge (as well as the intentional value of actions). Such a philosophy of religion is common to Platonism and Christianity.

In Croce's fusion of logical with psychological idealism, to the extent that religion as cognition intuits what is beautiful or thinks what is true, it is nothing beyond aesthetics or logic: To the extent that it intuits as beautiful what is not, or thinks to be true what is not true, it is not valid, theoretically considered. Gentile's attitude, even more than Croce's, is absolute idealism without the Absolute.

Under "Critical Monistic Realism" Macintosh endorses a form of religious knowledge that includes adequate and adequately critical (i.e., logical) certitude of the validity of ideals and values considered as divine (i.e., as worthy of universal human devotion). He cites as predecessors Friedrich von Hügel, Henri Bergson, and a few others. Von Hügel was convinced that people have real experience and knowledge of objects and that in religion in its higher reaches there is real contact with superhuman reality. For Bergson, the true metaphysical method is an immediate intuition or vision of reality, and in religious mysticism there is such a thing. According to Macintosh, "Bergson carried the needed reaction against intellectualism and rationalism to an equally objectionable irrationalism and anti-conceptualism." (Macintosh, 1940, p. 181).

"Empirical Theology" is the title under which Macintosh presents his own program. Whereas scholastics, he writes, defined theology as the science of God, a deductive science proceeding from assured premises, some theologians have occasionally claimed to proceed by the inductive method. Macintosh meets such objections as that of Georg Wobbermin, who as a confirmed Kantian dualist cannot but feel that all such terms as "empirical theology" involve a contradiction in terms. Macintosh finally formulates thirteen laws of empirical theology. But he never gives an example of what he means by "a truly reasonable belief."

DUALISM. According to dualism, the divine reality is never experienced immediately, never perceived directly. How then can there by any knowledge? There is reason to question the conclusiveness of the so-called proofs of God's existence, the ontological, cosmological, anthropological, theological arguments. These proofs will be replaced by argument from moral values (as in Kant) or religious values.

But this has in fact led to agnosticism (a term coined in 1870 by Thomas Huxley), notably with Charles Darwin, who wrote that "the whole subject is beyond the scope of man's intellect," and with Herbert Spencer, the prophet of agnostic religion. For the agnostic, only the inductive method and the positive results of the empirical sciences can serve as an adequate check upon the too easy dogmatizing of theology and the speculative vagaries of metaphysics.

Friedrich Schleiermacher, "the father of modern theology," oscillated between pantheism and dualistic epistemological agnosticism. Theology, he thought, can only be a description of subjective states of mind. Albrecht Ritschl was, along with Schleiermacher, the most influential Protestant theologian of the late nineteenth century; he reacted vigorously against intellectualism in favor of the autonomy of religious consciousness. He found Schleiermacher guilty of the old error of making the doctrine of God a natural, as distinct from a revealed, theology, but in both cases, "religious knowledge" is distinguished from science, philosophy, and theoretical knowledge generally. "But," Macintosh asks (1940, p. 247), "how can be justified the use of the term religious knowledge as applied to the God and Father of our Lord Jesus Christ?" It should be recognized that the intuition in question is not perceptual but imaginal, that so-called religious knowledge is not knowledge in the scientific sense of empirically verified judgments and so on.

Adolf von Harnack agreed with Ritschl that Christianity is essentially ethico-religious and experiential rather than metaphysically speculative and intellectualistic. Ritschlians have much to say about revelation, but the concept is left vague from the epistemological point of view.

Wilhelm Herrmann was quite as suspicious of the influence of mysticism as of the encroachments of metaphysics. For Julius Kaftan, Kant is the philosopher of Protestantism, as Aristotle is the philosopher of Catholicism. The object of religious knowledge is not religion, but God; theology can never be a science of the objects of faith, however, only a science of faith itself. Religious knowledge, as opposed to knowledge in the theoretical sense, presupposes an authentic revelation of God.

Wobbermin agreed with Ritschl in excluding from theology all the mixed articles in which the faith-knowledge of God was combined with and modified by the now discredited "natural" knowledge of God. "But," Macintosh concludes (ibid., p. 278), "no consideration of the value of a belief can establish it as knowledge in the absence of any possibility of 'first-hand experience.'"

Under "Critical Rationalism" Macintosh lists the Religionsgeschichtliche Schule, which gave promise of liberating modern theology from its perpetual oscillation between helpless agnosticism and the sheer dogmatism of exclusive supernaturalism. The comparative historical study of religions shows that the uniqueness of Christianity consists not in the manner of its proof, as resting upon a supernatural revelation, but in its content: An inclusive supernaturalism would acknowledge revelation and miracle in all religions. (How is religious knowledge possible? A "fourth critique," after Kant, should investigate the *a priori* conditions of religious experience.)

Rudolf Otto assumed that besides *Glaube,* which apprehends the rationally necessary idea of an ultimate reality, there is also *Ahnung,* a non-rational foundation for religion in human nature, the instinctive sense of a mysterious reality (*das Heilige*), transcendent and wholly other.

Under "Religious Pragmatism" Macintosh ranks, of course, William James, but also his less well-known precursor A. J. Earl Balfour, who wrote that one assents to a creed merely because of a subjective need for it, and who predicted the advent of a critical science of religion whereby what valid religious knowledge there may be will be given the universal form of an empirical science.

Under "Reactionary Irrationalism" Macintosh analyzes Søren Kierkegaard, Miguel de Unamuno, and the theologians of crisis. This tendency began as a response to the monistic idealism of Hegel. Kierkegaard rebelled against Hegel's equation of actuality and the rational Idea. For Kierkegaard, Christian faith is always contrary to reason: "The absurd is the proper object of faith, and the only thing that lets itself be believed."

Similarly, for Unamuno, reason and faith are enemies, and reason is the enemy of life. His despair of finding any theoretical defense of the Roman Catholic system of dogma led him to underestimate the arguments vindicating a Christlike God and the immortality of the soul.

KARL BARTH. The theology of crisis in Germany was a consequence of World War I. But Karl Barth was also heir to Kant, Schleiermacher, Troeltsch, Herrmann, Otto, Kierkegaard, and Feuerbach. He condemned modern liberalism for its emphasis upon divine immanence, for "except in His Word, God is never for us in the world." As Kierkegaard insisted, following *Ecclesiastes,* "God is in Heaven, and thou upon Earth." The image of God, Barth argued, has been wholly destroyed in man by sin. The Bible is to be read in the old way, namely, not to find what people thought about God, but to find what God says to people. "This is," writes Macintosh, "pretty much the old externally authoritarian, irrationalistic theology of the Evangelical Calvinism of two or three hundred years ago."

Barth, hearkening back to Luther as well as to Calvin, emphasizes the distinction between faith, which he embraces, and religion, which he almost identifies with Roman Catholicism and abhors. In an essay on Barth's theology, Brand Blanshard offers this critique ("Critical Reflections on Karl Barth," in *Faith and the Philosophers,* ed. John Hick, Ithaca, N.Y., 1957):

> Faith, according to Barth, is itself the highest knowledge; but this knowledge differs completely from anything else which man calls knowledge, not only in its

> content, but in its modes of origin and form as well. (p. 159) That revelation is to be considered a kind of knowledge is detected by his entitling one of his books *Knowledge of God.* But he holds, with Ayer and Carnap, that the attempt by rational thought to go beyond nature to the supernatural is inevitably defeated, though of course he draws a different conclusion from the defeat. He concludes that since we cannot reach a knowledge of God through radical means, we must do so through non-natural means; the positivists conclude from the same premises that the attempt itself is meaningless. (p. 170) In the face of all the projectionists who, like Freud and Feuerbach, would make religious "knowledge" an imaginative fulfilling of need, of all the pragmatists who, like Dewey, would make it merely a means to human betterment, of all the rationalists who, like Hegel, would make it philosophy half grown-up, of all the psychologists who, with Schleiermacher and Ritschl, would make it essentially a matter of feeling, Barth proclaimed a full-fledged return to the theology of the Reformation, in which God is set over against the world as "wholly other," known indeed to faith, but unknowable, unapproachable and unimaginable by any natural faculties. (p. 160)

BULTMANN AND JASPERS. Aside from Barth's (or Luther's) distinction between religion and faith, Rudolf Bultmann discerns within faith a core of message (*kerygma*) that is to be extracted from the letter of the Bible through *"Entmythologisierung."* The Bible failed to eliminate philosophy, which tends to make the *kerygma* a reality subject to reason's grasp. Knowledge of God does not refer to his essence, but to his will. God is neither in nature nor in history and cannot be attained there. The biblical authors are not completely innocent of the sin of natural humankind; they sometimes understood God's word through a naive kind of rationalism, mythological rationalism, which is as sinful as scientific rationalism. Serious, cultivated believers reject that popular mythology. They can accept science and technology because they affirm that science and faith belong to two wholly different orders. But although they discard magic, spiritism, and all forms of pagan miracles, they nevertheless accept Christian mythology, except in its most objectionable instances. Contrary to Barth's contention, faith should not utilize any philosophy. All philosophies are human projections of God, of man, and of the world and are as such incompatible with faith. It was the mistake of the *philosophia perennis* to limit itself to the domain of knowledge and objectivity. The destruction of metaphysics that was attempted by Heidegger helped Bultmann to reject all *Selbstsicherung.*

Karl Jaspers's philosophy appears to be "the last word of irrationalism," the last stage in the great movement of reaction against *Aufklärung.* Remembering Kant's motto: "I must suppress knowledge in order to make room for faith," Jaspers finally yields to the prestige of the ineffable. However, he expresses his philosophical irritation about the theologians' claim that the Christian faith is something absolute. Christians should give up the idea that Jesus was the one incarnation of transcendence; they should accept the fact that dogmas are symbols, ciphers, lacking all objective value, and they should renounce their claim to the monopoly of truth.

Jaspers's position is extreme, and exceptional in Germany. The general difference in philosophy between Germany and France is clearly formulated by Raymond Aron:

> German philosophers, especially in the last century, often belonged to a milieu of civil servants, chiefly clerical. Even when turned miscreants, they retain a sense of religion as a supreme form of spiritual aspiration; tending to a non-dogmatic religiosity, they distinguish between science, objectively true, and religion, humanly valuable although not liable to demonstration or refutation. This godless religiosity implies acknowledging the role of feeling, irreducible to that of reason. In France, the direct rivalry of religion and philosophy prompts both of them to thorough and contradictory claims. Profane philosophy (at least in its most characteristic exponents) is anti-Christian, even anti-religious. It is rationalistic and scientistic. (Aron, 1983, p. 135)

THE ROMAN CATHOLIC PERSPECTIVE. The Roman Catholic point of view, in its most conservative aspect, was put forward by Étienne Gilson in many admirable books, especially in *Réalisme thomiste et critique de la connaissance* (1939). Religion justifies philosophy, which in turn illuminates religion through intelligence. Gilson writes on Bergson in *La philosophie et la théologie* (Paris, 1960):

> Bergson had a clear idea of two types of knowledge, that of intelligence, of which the purest expression is science, and that of intuition, akin to instinct, which becomes explicitly conscious in metaphysics. If questioned about faith, he could not for one instant imagine that it was, properly speaking, knowledge. The word "faith" suggested to him primarily the notion of obedience. To accept a number of doctrinal positions as true although accessible neither to intelligence nor to intuition, out of sheer submission to an external authority, was all this philosopher would resign himself to. (p. 177)

Gilson sums up his own attitude as follows:

> There is on the one hand scientific progress, on the other hand Christian faith, incarnated in the Church and defined by tradition. To speak summarily but not inexactly, there arises from the contact between the two a third kind of knowledge, distinct from both but akin to both, whose data are provided by science but whose main object is to achieve as complete a comprehension as possible of the Christian revelation received by faith. (p. 233)

But Roman Catholics are far from unanimous. They never were. They disagreed in the Middle Ages, as has been seen, as to whether one knows truth in the light of one's own intelligence, or in a divine light added to that of the intellect. The present time has witnessed the painful controversies surrounding Maurice Blondel's obstinate attempt at deducing the supernatural from the natural and Teilhard de Chardin's fusion—or confusion—of cosmology with Christology, of evolution with revelation. Both incurred anathema. Ever since the Counter-Reformation the church has been trying to combat Protestantism, or to catch up with it, not only (as seen above) by instituting catechism, but also by encouraging biblical studies. It has also tried to counter Kant's influence by reviving Thomism; by condemning, in the ninteenth century, all forms of fideism; and by condemning modernism in the early twentieth century, only to yield to liberal tendencies at the Second Vatican Council.

Roman Catholicism, in its existentialist variety, is represented by Henry Duméry, who also owes much to Blondel—and to Spinoza and Plotinus. He distinguishes, in his *Philosophie de la religion* (Paris, 1957), different noetic levels; he speaks of "a specified intelligible plane, halfway between God and empirical consciousness"—perhaps what he calls "le troisième genre de connaissance"—and treats faith as "un object spécifique, irréductible à tout autre." He speaks of "mentalité projective," "intentionalité vécue," "visée de transcendance." Although recognizing that the philosophy of religion should apply to all known religions, he bases his own attempt exclusively on Christianity. One example may be quoted from his *Phénoménologie de la religion* (Paris, 1958): "It would be erroneous to objectify the typical existence of the Virgin Mary onto a profane—nay, profaning—plane of registry office" (p. 57). Duméry, a Roman Catholic priest, has been granted permission to relinquish priesthood.

In the Anglican church the situation is different, as suggested by the appointment as bishop of Durham in 1984 of David Jenkins, who had declared that teachings concerning the virgin birth and the resurrection might be more symbolic than literal, and that a person could be a good Christian even while doubting the divinity of Christ.

EPISTEMOLOGY. In England, modern epistemology is represented by, among others, Bertrand Russell and A. J. Ayer. In *Mysticism and Logic* (London, 1918) Russell defines the mystical impulse in philosophers such as Heraclitus, Plato, Spinoza, and Hegel as the "belief in the possibility of a way of knowledge which may be called revelation or insight or intuition, as contrasted with sense, reason and analysis, which are regarded as blind guides leading to the morass of illusion" (p. 16). But he calmly remarks that what is knowledge is science, and what is not science is not knowledge. In *The Problem of Knowledge* (1956) Ayer simply ignores religion altogether, as does Rudolf Carnap in his work. Both Ayer and Carnap belong to the logical positivist movement, based on the analysis of language, which started in Vienna with Ludwig Wittgenstein, who later migrated to England and was in close contact with Russell. But Wittgenstein's attitude toward religion was far less simple than that of those he influenced. Admittedly, he thought that religious creeds, in contradistinction to scientific concepts, are not more or less probable hypotheses: Never have propositions pertaining to religion expressed positive possibilities. Their whole significance stems from their place in human existence; science and religion are entirely separate; between them there can be no conflict or relation whatsoever. But he writes in his *Tractatus Logico-Philosophicus* (6.54): "He who understands me finally recognizes my propositions as senseless, when he has climbed out through them, on them, over them," a position uncannily reminiscent of Mahāyāna Buddhism. Finally, Wittgenstein writes: "Whereof one cannot speak, thereof one must be silent" (ibid., 7.0). However, *Notebooks 1914–1916* affirms that "to believe in God means understanding the question of life, means seeing that life makes sense" (11 June 1916), which amounts to what has been called Wittgensteinian fideism.

A brave attempt at overcoming positivism was made by Michael Polanyi, another scientist and philosopher, who migrated from central Europe (in his case, Hungary) to England. In his great book *Personal Knowledge* (London, 1958), he refutes the Laplacean ideal of objective knowledge and calls for a return to Augustine in order to restore the balance of cognitive human powers and to recognize belief once more as the source of all knowledge. He tries to define a form of knowledge neither purely objective nor purely subjective, namely, personal knowledge: "Into every act of knowing there enters a tacit and passionate contribution of the person knowing what is being known, and . . . this coefficient is no mere imperfection but a necessary component of all knowledge" (p. 312). Unfortunately, in the vast field of religion he only takes into account Christianity. Even more narrowly, he subscribes to the following statement by Paul Tillich: "Knowledge of revelation, although it is mediated primarily through historical events, does not imply factual assertion, and it is therefore not exposed to critical analysis by historical research. Its truth is to be judged by criteria which lie within the dimension of revelatory knowledge" (*Systematic Theology,* London, 1953, vol. 1, p. 144). The phrase "revelatory knowledge" begs the whole question of the nature of religious knowledge.

Yet another scientist and philosopher, Alfred North Whitehead, who migrated to the United States from England, dealt with the problem of religious knowledge, especially in his book *Religion in the Making* (1928) and again in his great *Process and Reality* (1929), in which one reads: "Religion is the translation of general ideas into particular thoughts, emotions, and purposes; it is directed to the end of stretching individual interest beyond its delf-defeating particularity. Philosophy finds religion, and modifies it" (*Process and Reality,* New York, 1978, p. 15). On Christianity, his position is summed up as follows:

> The notion of God as the "unmoved mover" is derived from Aristotle, at least as far as Western thought is concerned. The notion of God as "eminently real" is a favourite doctrine of Christian theology. The combination of the two into the doctrine of an aboriginal, eminently real, transcendent creator, at whose fiat the world came into being, and whose imposed will it obeys, is the fallacy which has infused tragedy into the histories of Christianity and of Mahometanism. (ibid., p. 342)

Whitehead's own ideas, albeit somewhat obscure, have produced process theology.

Research has recently been started to try to locate, in the brain, a specific area of the mythical function (Eugene G. d'Aquili and Charles D. Laughlin, Jr., "The Neurobiology of Myth and Ritual," in *The Spectrum of Ritual,* ed. Eugene d'Aquili et al., 1979); and the symbolic approach has brought forth a new discipline: theolinguistics (J. P. Van Noppen, *Theolinguistics,* Brussels, 1981).

In the fervent, adventurous notebooks of a modern gnostic, Simone Weil, published posthumously under the title *La connaissance surnaturelle* (Paris, 1950), one reads: "Intelligence remains absolutely faithful to itself in recognizing the existence, in the soul, of a faculty superior to itself and leading thought above itself. This faculty is supernatural love" (p. 80). And: "Since evil is the root of mystery, suffering is the root of knowledge" (p. 43).

Two recent writers, Terence Penelhum and John Hick, have developed the idea of faith as a form of knowledge. "There is," writes the latter, "in cognition of every kind an unresolved mystery" (Hick, 1966, p. 118). "But," writes Basil Mitchell, "there is an important sense of 'know' in which even the 'great religious figures' cannot be said to know that there is a God (let alone the Christian doctrines) so long as it remains a genuine possibility that some non-theistic interpretation of their experience might turn out to be true" (Mitchell, 1973, p. 112). However, as Nicholas Lash writes: "The possibility of theological discourse constituting a mode of rational knowledge could only be excluded if religious faith could be shown to be in no sense experimental knowledge of its object" (Lash, in Peacocke, 1981, p. 304).

SEE ALSO Epistemology; Esotericism; Faith; Neuroscience and Religion, article on Neuroepistemology; Philosophy, article on Philosophy and Religion; Truth.

BIBLIOGRAPHY

Aron, Raymond. *Mémoires: Cinquante ans de réflexion politique.* Paris, 1983.

Bendix, Reinhard. *Max Weber: An Intellectual Portrait.* Garden City, N. Y., 1960.

Biardeau, Madeleine. *Théorie de la connaissance et philosophie de la parole dans la brahmanisme classique.* Paris, 1964.

Brunschwicg, Léon. *Le progrès de la conscience dans la philosophie occidentale* (1927). 2d ed. Paris, 1953.

Bugault, Guy. *La notion de 'prajña' ou de sapience selon les perspectives du 'Mahāyāna.'* Paris, 1968.

Gavalda, Berthe. *Les grands textes de la pensée chrétienne.* Paris, 1973.

Gilson, Étienne. *The Unity of Philosophical Experience.* New York, 1937.

Gilson, Étienne. *La philosophie et la théologie.* Paris, 1960. Translated by Cécile Gilson as *The Philosopher and Theology* (New York, 1962).

Grousset, René. *Les philosophies indiennes.* 2 vols. Paris, 1931.

Gruenwald, Ithamar. "Knowledge and Vision." *Israel Oriental Studies* 3 (1973): 63ff.

Hick, John. *Faith and Knowledge.* 2d ed. Ithaca, N.Y., 1966.

Hultkrantz, Åke. "The Concept of the Supernatural in Primal Religion." *History of Religions* 22 (February 1983): 231–253.

Kahn, Charles H. *The Art and Thought of Heraclitus.* Cambridge, 1979.

Macintosh, Douglas C. *The Problem of Religious Knowledge.* London, 1940.

Mitchell, Basil. *The Justification of Religious Belief.* New York, 1973.

Peacocke, A. R., ed. *The Sciences and Theology in the Twentieth Century.* London, 1981.

Robinson, James M., ed. *The Nag Hammadi Library in English.* San Francisco, 1977.

Rudolph, Kurt. *Gnosis.* Translated by Robert M. Wilson. San Francisco, 1983.

Swinburne, Richard. *Faith and Reason.* Oxford, 1981.

Zaehner, R. C. *Concordant Discord.* Oxford, 1970.

New Sources

Alston, William. *Perceiving God: The Epistemology of Religious Experience.* Ithaca, N.Y., 1991.

Dubuisson, Daniel. *The Western Construction of Religion: Myths, Knowledge, and Ideology.* Translated by William Sayers. Baltimore, Md., 2003.

Frisina, Warren. *The Unity of Knowledge and Action: Toward a Nonrepresentational Theory of Knowledge.* Albany, N.Y., 2002.

Hayes, Brain. *The Concept of the Knowledge of God.* Basingstoke, U.K., 1988.

Marurana, Humberto. *The Tree of Knowledge.* 1987; reprint Boston, 1992.

Petitot, Jean, Francisco Varela, Bernard Pachoud, and Jean-Michel Roy, eds. *Naturalizing Phenomenology: Issues in Contemporary Phenomenology and Cognitive Science.* Writing Science series. Stanford, Calif., 2000.

Turner, James. *Language, Religion, Knowledge: Past and Present.* Notre Dame, Ind., 2003.

Varela, Francisco, Evan Thompson, and Eleanor Rosch. *The Embodied Mind: Cognitive Science and Human Experience.* Cambridge, Mass., 1992.

Varela, Francisco, and Jonathan Spear, eds. *The View from Within: First-person Approaches to the Study of Consciousness.* Charlottesville, Va., 1999.

Zimmerman, Michael. "Controlling Ignorance: A Bitter Truth." *Journal of Social Philosophy* 33 (fall 2002): 483–491.

JACQUES DUCHESNE-GUILLEMIN (1987)
Revised Bibliography

KNOX, JOHN (c. 1514–1572), was a Protestant reformer of Scotland. Born in Haddington, Knox likely studied at Saint Andrews under the nominalist theologian John Major. He was ordained to the priesthood at the age of twenty-five, held the post of apostolical notary, and served as a tutor to the children of gentlemen in East Lothian.

Knox was a rugged political fighter, but he was also, as his biographer Jasper Ridley writes, a person of "profound and sincere religious sensitivity." The source of this sensitivity was the Bible, which he apparently studied with devotion early in life. When dying, he asked his wife to "go read where I cast my first anchor" in the seventeenth chapter of *John.*

Knox, converted to Protestantism by the preaching of Thomas Gwilliam in Lothian, was confirmed in the Protestant movement by his association with George Wishart. After the burning of Wishart, Protestants took the castle at Saint Andrews and the life of Cardinal Beaton, Scotland's Catholic leader. Knox, under threat of persecution, moved from place to place, eventually taking refuge in the castle with his students. Protestant leaders urged him to "take up the public office and charge of preaching," a role that would identify him with Gwilliam, John Rough, and Wishart. He was reluctant to accept the vocation, as he emphasized in his *History,* but having done so, he filled it with remarkable skill and became a leading spokesman of the Protestant cause.

The castle fell to the French fleet in 1547, and Knox became a galley slave until his release was arranged by the English. For five years (1549–1554) he was active in the Puritan wing of the English Reformation movement. With the accession of Mary, Knox left England and was named the minister of the church of the English exiles in Frankfurt. The exiles soon divided over the use of *The Book of Common Prayer,* whether to revise it or to substitute a new liturgy. As a result of the controversy, Knox left Frankfurt for Geneva, where he became pastor of the English congregation. Knox's stay there was significant for the consolidation of his own theology, as he was impressed by Calvin's achievement in establishing the Reformed church in Geneva.

Knox visited Scotland briefly in the autumn of 1555 to encourage the Protestant leadership. When the religious and political struggle came to a crisis in 1559, Knox left Geneva to assume a leading role in the Protestant cause. His powerful preaching, political wisdom, and determination contributed significantly to the Scottish Parliament's action in 1560 abolishing the papal jurisdiction and approving a confession of faith as a basis for belief in Scotland.

In addition to his public leadership, Knox had a role in three major documents of the Scottish Reformation of 1560. The Confession of Faith was written in four days by John Knox and five others. It conveys the intensity of the moment and the personal quality of the confession of believers who were putting their lives at risk for their faith. It has been described as "the warm utterance of a people's heart." It states the Protestant faith in plain language and is more pictorial and historical than abstract in style.

The *First Book of Discipline* was written by Knox in collaboration with four others. It is notable not only for its reform of the church but also for its vision of universal compulsory education up to the university level and for its provisions for relief of the poor. The book was never adopted by Parliament because its members did not want the wealth of the church expended on Knox's "devout imaginings."

Knox's third contribution to the official documents of the church was *The Book of Common Order,* which Knox and his collaborators had written in Frankfurt and used in Geneva. It now became the worship book of the Church of Scotland.

Knox disavowed speculative theology, but his writings, filling six volumes, were as powerful as his preaching. "The First Blast of the Trumpet against the Monstrous Regiment of Women" (1558), although dealing with the situation in Scotland, caused him difficulty with Elizabeth I of England when he needed her support. Knox's *History of the Reformation of Religion within the Realm of Scotland* is a history of the man and the cause and a justification of both. Other notable writings include "Letter of Wholesome Counsel" and "Treatise on Predestination."

Knox was a remarkable human being. Scholars have debated whether or not he was a man of courage, perhaps because of his own misgivings. He took precautions, but he did "march toward the sound of guns." Scholars have accused him of demagoguery, but a supporter declared that he was able in one hour to do more for his contemporaries than five hundred trumpets continually blustering in their ears. He believed that he had been called by God, that through his life God's purposes were being fulfilled, and that the Reformation was God's cause and must triumph.

Knox's biographer, Jasper Ridley, points to the Church of Scotland as Knox's greatest achievement. Catholicism would probably have been overthrown without Knox, but it is due to Knox that the Church of Scotland was Calvinist rather than Anglican, and that after his death it became Presbyterian rather than Episcopal. Knox also contributed significantly to the struggle for human freedom. His emphasis on the responsibility not only of lower magistrates but of individuals to resist evil rulers, and the dramatic way he expressed this idea in his own life, especially in his encounters with Queen Mary, and in his sermons and writings cannot be overestimated. His Presbyterian and Puritan followers made these ideas part of the tradition of public and political life in the English-speaking world.

BIBLIOGRAPHY

Cheyne, Alec. Review of *The Scottish Reformation* by Gordon Donaldson. *Scottish Journal of Theology* 16 (March 1963): 78–88.

McEwen, James S. *The Faith of John Knox.* London, 1961.

Percy, Eustace. *John Knox.* London, 1937.

Ridley, Jasper. *John Knox.* New York, 1968.

Shaw, Duncan, ed. *John Knox: A Quartercentenary Reappraisal.* Edinburgh, 1975.

JOHN H. LEITH (1987)

KŌBEN (1173–1232), also known as Myoe Shonin, was an important figure in the Kamakura-period revival of Nara Buddhism. This revival consisted of criticism of the exclusivist doctrines of the Pure Land and Nichiren sects and a renewed interest in, and devotion to, the historic Buddha, Śākyamuni. As a prominent Kegon (Chin., Huayan) mentor, Kōben attempted to introduce Tantric elements into Kegon practice, as evidenced by his compilation of Kegon-Tantric (*gommitsu*) rituals and consecrations. He also worked for the revival of traditional Kegon learning, emphasizing the study of Fazang's works rather than those of Chengguan, whose doctrines were transmitted within the Shingon tradition, and the cultivation of Kegon visualization meditations.

Kōben was born in the village of Yoshiwara, on the Ishigaki estate, in Aritakoori in the province of Kii (present-day Wakayama prefecture). In the fall of 1181, following the death of his parents, the boy was sent to the Jingoji monastic complex, located on Mount Takao north of Kyoto, where he began his studies under the master Mongaku. Kōben subsequently studied Tantric doctrines (*mikkyō*) and Fazang's *Wuzhiao zhang.* At the age of fifteen (sixteen by Asian reckoning), Kōben became a novice and received the full monastic precepts (the *gusokukai*) at the Kaiden'in monastery of the Tōdaiji, in Nara. Following his ordination in Nara, Kōben began his study of the *Kusharon* (Vasubandhu's *Abhidharmakośabhāṣya,* a major Hīnayāna Abhidharma text). At the age of eighteen Kōben received the transmission of the dual *maṇḍalas* of the *jūhachidō* tradition from the *ācārya* Kōnen. Following this transmission, which centered around an eighteen-part Tantric *sādhana* to be undertaken by new initiates, Kōben began the cultivation of the *butsugen* ritual, a ritual centered on a visualization of the eyes of the Buddha, and his biography records that he experienced many miracles due to this practice.

In 1193, Kōben received an imperial order commanding him to work for the restoration of the Kegon tradition; thereafter, he took up residence as abbot in the Shōson'in of the Tōdaiji in Nara. Seeing the conflicts that racked the Buddhist world at this time, Kōben decided to retire from all worldly and ecclesiastical concerns. In 1195, Kōben left the Jingoji monasteries, and building himself a rude hut in the Kii mountains he retired, spending his time in the cultivation of *sādhana* rituals and in meditative visualizations. During this time he read the bulk of the commentaries and subcommentaries to the *Kegongyō* (Skt., *Avataṃsaka Sūtra*). This task, it is recorded, was also rewarded with many miracles and visions.

Later, returning to Mount Takao, Kōben began the teaching of the Kegon doctrines, lecturing on the *Kegon tangenki* (Chin., *Huayan tanxuan ji*), a major Huayan commentary composed by Fazang. It was here that Kōben initiated a series of lectures and debates on Kegon doctrine. In 1198 a number of disturbances between monastic factions on Mount Takao broke out, and Kōben, taking with him the chief image (*honzon*) of the monastery and its sacred texts, once more retired to his hermitage in the province of Kii. Here he constructed another hut with the aid of a local military leader and, as previously, he devoted himself to meditation, the recitation of scriptures, and writing.

In the eleventh month of 1206, the retired emperor Go-Toba presented Kōben with the Togano-o monastic complex in the hope that it would long be a center for the revival of the Kegon tradition. The monastic complex was given the new name of Kōzanji, and Kōben soon set to work repairing the buildings and reviving the tradition. Kōben was asked many times to administer the precepts to both the retired emperor Go-Toba and the Lady Kenreimon'in, his two most important patrons. After the death of her husband, Emperor Takakura, and her son, the infant emperor Antoku, Lady Kenreimon'in became a nun.

Kōben's fame came to the attention of the shogun in Kamakura, Hōjō Yasutoki, and on numerous occasions he would visit Kōben at his mountain monastery and receive his teachings. Subsequently, Yasutoki left the householder's life to become a monk under the guidance of Kōben.

After Kōben fell ill and died, at the age of fifty-nine, his many disciples continued their master's work toward the revival of the Kegon tradition. Modern scholars have attributed some forty-two works to Kōben. Included among them are essays on Kegon practice and doctrine, numerous ritual texts, literary works, and Japanese poems (*waka*), which are preserved in both the *Shinzoku kokinshū* and the *Shin shūishū*.

SEE ALSO Fazang; Huayan; Shingonshū.

BIBLIOGRAPHY

For a chronology of the life of Kōben and a complete list of his works see the article "Kōben," in *Bukkyō daijiten,* edited by Mochizuki Shinkō (Tokyo, 1933–1936), vol. 2, pp. 1083c–1084c. For a general overview of Kegon doctrine and its Japanese development, see Sakamoto Yukio's *Kegon kyōgaku no kenkyū* (Tokyo, 1976), Ishii Kyōdō's "Gommitsu no shisō Kōben," *Taishō Daigaku gakuhō* 3(1928):48–72, traces Kōben's attempt to establish purely Kegon Tantric rituals, thereby making the Kegon tradition of his day fully Tantric. On the orthodoxy of Kōben in the Kegon tradition, see Kamata Shigeo's "Nihon Kegon ni okeru seito to itan," *Shisō* (November 1973). A popular work on Kōben is Tanaka Hisao's *Myōe* (Tokyo, 1961). Like many other Buddhist monks of his day, Kōben kept a record of his dreams, *Yume no ki.* For a study of this work, see Yamada Shōzen's "Myoe no yume to *Yume no ki,*" in *Kanazawa Bunko kenkyū* (Tokyo, 1970). An English-language summary of Kōben's criticisms of Hōnen's doctrines is Bando Shojun's "Myoe's Criticism of Hōnen's Doctrine," *Eastern Buddhist,* n.s. 7 (May 1974): 37–54.

LEO M. PRUDEN (1987)

KOHANIM SEE LEVITES

KOHELETH See ECCLESIASTES

KOHLER, KAUFMANN

KOHLER, KAUFMANN (1843–1926), Reform rabbi, scholar, and theologian. Born in Fürth, Bavaria, into a pious Orthodox family of rabbinical ancestry, Kohler entered the *Gymnasium* in Frankfurt in 1862 and continued his earlier rabbinic training with Samson Raphael Hirsch, leader of German Neo-Orthodoxy, whose crucial religious impact on him Kohler frequently acknowledged. Gradually, however, with exposure to modern science and the critical studies of philology, the Bible, history, and comparative religion at the universities of Munich, Berlin, and Erlanger (where he received his Ph.D. in 1867), his faith in Orthodox Judaism was shattered.

Attracted to the religious orientation of Abraham Geiger, leader of German Reform Judaism, Kohler embraced Reform as an outlet for both his profound religious faith and his scholarly proclivities. When a rabbinical appointment in Germany was not forthcoming, he moved to the United States in 1869 and served congregations in Detroit and Chicago until, in 1879, he succeeded his father-in-law, David Einhorn, in one of the most prestigious Reform temples in the country, Beth El in New York City.

During the next decade, through his books and articles, Kohler became recognized as a preeminent advocate of classical Reform Judaism. Undaunted by controversy, he defended Reform against critics such as Felix Adler and Alexander Kohut; in the wake of his celebrated polemic with the latter, Kohler convened the Pittsburgh Rabbinical Conference in November 1885 and steered its eight-point statement of principles to reflect his own views; these corresponded to and articulated most Reformers' religious self-understanding for the next two generations. From 1903 to 1921, Kohler served as president of the Reform seminary at Hebrew Union College in Cincinnati.

Kohler's scholarship included works in theology, Semitics, Hellenistic studies, comparative religion, and intertestamental literature. These were consistently marked by the application of modern scientific analysis to Jewish literary sources, an approach reflecting the nineteenth-century *Wissenschaft des Judentums.* He assumed that this historicist reassessment of Judaism and its texts uncovered the essence of Judaism, which he identified with the central beliefs of Reform Judaism. His scholarship therefore was often an adjunct to his religious beliefs.

Recognized as a giant in his day, Kohler now has scant influence. His scholarship is generally dated, and his rationalist, anti-Zionist Reform orientation has long since been set aside by the mainstream of Reform Judaism. Nevertheless, he typified one of its most significant stages and expressed its major ideals in a bygone era.

Bibliography

Kohler's most notable work, well reviewed in its day, is *Jewish Theology Systematically and Historically Considered* (1918; a revised edition of the 1910 German version); the current edition (New York, 1968) includes a fine introductory essay by Joseph L. Blau that combines biographical data with a critical assessment of Kohler's text. His other scholarly writings can be found in *Hebrew Union College and Other Addresses* (Cincinnati, 1910), *Heaven and Hell in Comparative Religion* (New York, 1923), and two posthumously published books, *The Origins of the Synagogue and the Church* (1929; New York, 1973) and *Studies, Addresses, and Personal Papers* (New York, 1931). The best retrospective on Kohler, written by an admirer and colleague, is H. G. Enelow's "Kaufmann Kohler," *American Jewish Year Book* 28 (1926–1927): 235–260.

Benny Kraut (1987)

KO HUNG See GE HONG

KOKUGAKU

KOKUGAKU. The Japanese intellectual movement known as Kokugaku (Native Learning) includes the Shintō revival that began in the middle of the Edo period (1603–1867). Inspired by the spirit of nationalism, Kokugaku thinkers deplored the lack of scholarship on Japanese history and literature and attacked the wholesale adoption of such foreign influences as Confucianism and Buddhism. According to Kokugaku thinkers, Japanese history can be divided into three periods: antiquity, during which Japan's indigenous, original spirit emerged and was manifest in its purest form; the Middle Ages, when this spirit became "contaminated" and was suppressed by the introduction of Chinese culture, in particular Confucianism and Buddhism; and the modern age, when Japan's ancient, original spirit was revived and rediscovered. Although the Kokugaku movement encompassed various fields of study, among them literature and philology, this discussion is limited to its concern with religion.

In the Genroku period (1688–1704), which marks the rise of the Kokugaku movement, the Buddhist priest Keichū (1640–1701) proposed that the poetic conventions popular during the Middle Ages in Japan be abolished so as to allow free composition of the Japanese *waka* poems. Keichū applied philological analysis to the *Man'yōshū,* but said only that Shintō differed from both Confucianism and Buddhism and that the *kami* were beyond the understanding of people. Kada Azumamaro (1669–1736), a Shintō priest at Inari Shrine in Kyoto, opposed the synthesis of Confucianism and Shintō in which Confucian terms and concepts—for example, the principles of yin and yang and the Five Elements (*wu xing*)—were used to interpret Shintō. Although he also advocated the founding of a college for "Native Learning" to combat the influence of Confucianism, he did not engage in the study of ancient Shintō himself.

The men considered the most representative thinkers of the movement—Kamo no Mabuchi (1697–1769) and Motoori Norinaga (1730–1801) among the second generation of

Kokugaku scholars and Hirata Atsutane (1776–1843) among the third generation—were also the most prominent of the advocates of Native Learning to focus their attention on religious issues. Kamo no Mabuchi founded the school of Kogaku (Ancient Learning) Shintō, which sought a reawakening of and a return to ancient Shintō. That is, he called for a revival of Shintō as expressed and practiced prior to the introduction of Buddhism and Confucianism. His main ideas are presented in his *Kokuikō* (On the spirit of the nation).

Motoori Norinaga further clarified and developed Ancient Learning Shintō. He established the *Kojiki,* the earliest recorded Japanese history, as the scriptural authority for the movement and wrote a commentary on it, the *Kojikiden.* Others of his works include *Naobi no mitama* (Straightening *kami*) and *Tamaboko hyakushu* (One hundred poems on the way). Hirata Atsutane argued even further the religiosity of Ancient Learning Shintō and asserted that Shintō was superior to other religions. His works include *Tama no mihashira* (The pillar of the soul), *Tamadasuki* (The jeweled sash), and *Honkyō gaihen* (Supplement to my theory of Shintō).

Whereas they called for an end to the influence of all foreign ideas and for a revival of Shintō in its original form, in reality these three men found certain foreign ideas conducive to the advancement of Kokugaku ideology. Both Mabuchi and Norinaga turned to the philosophy of Laozi and Zhuangzi, with Mabuchi borrowing from the former and Norinaga from the latter. Atsutane, however, made use of the teachings of Christianity, a religion that had been proscribed during the Tokugawa era (1600–1868). Their purpose in doing so was to eradicate the influence of Confucianism and Buddhism and to clarify the identity of Shintō and establish its supremacy. For example, believing that the teachings of the Buddhists and Confucians were "unnatural," that is, products of mere human artifice, Mabuchi used Laozi's notion of *ziran wu-wei* (Japanese, *shizen mui,* "spontaneity and nonactivity") to reject their interpretations of Shintō. He argued that Shintō, or the way of life of the ancient Japanese, was completely in accord with the nature of heaven and earth and thus did not give rise to the artificial systems found in China.

Accepting Mabuchi's basic thesis, Norinaga applied the knowledge gained through his research of the Japanese classics to criticize even more fervently than Mabuchi the precepts and doctrines of neo-Confucianism. Norinaga borrowed Zhuangzi's philosophy of nature (the philosophically exclusive principle of causality whereby there is no cause for an occurrence other than from the self) to reject the synthesis of neo-Confucianism and Shintō that had been popular in the previous century. As a physician, Norinaga refused to accept the complex neo-Confucian methodology that used the metaphysical theories of yin and yang and the Five Elements to determine the causes of diseases and their cures. He devoted himself to the task of reviving the ancient practices of medicine *(koihō)* that limited medicine to the sphere of empiricism. Accordingly, he asserted that all existence and phenomena arise from the self through divine will and that both the cause and the reason for the occurrence of things cannot be fathomed by people—daring to inquire into such causes showed disrespect for the *kami.* Thus Norinaga sought absolute obedience to the *kami.* He maintained that since the activities of the *kami* recorded in the *Kojiki* had actually been witnessed by the people of that early era, they should be accepted as fact and should be studied with the same empiricist method as that used for *koiho.* According to the Mito scholar Aizawa Yasushi (1781–1863), Norinaga's concept of the creator and sovereign *kami* was influenced by Christianity. Norinaga did read Christian doctrine, but one can also see in his work an adaptation of the neo-Confucian concept of tai chi (Japanese, *taikyoku,* meaning "ultimate principle" or "great ultimate").

Following the Shintō theories of Norinaga, Atsutane continued to develop Kokugaku Shintō, giving it a theological foundation. Although he showed it to no one, Atsutane's most important work is *Honkyō gaihen,* which he subtitled *Honkyō jibensaku* (Flagellation of my theory of Shintō). All of his theologically important works were written after this. Muraoka Tsunetsugu (1884–1946) has verified that this work is composed of adaptations or selected translations of books on Christian doctrine that had been written by missionaries in Chinese during the Ming dynasty (1268–1644). Atsutane was impressed by such missionaries as Matteo Ricci (1552–1610), whose works presented arguments in support of Christianity, particularly in the face of Confucian opposition. Atsutane adapted these arguments to elevate Shintō over both Confucianism and Buddhism. He reasoned that the three *kam*—Ame no Minakanushi, Takamimusubi, and Kamimusubi—were a "Trinity," which he identified as Musubi no Okami (great creator *kami).* He also advanced the notion that the human soul receives final judgment by Okuninushi no Mikoto in the netherworld and that one's eternal happiness or hardship was based on one's deeds during life.

Atsutane held that ancestor worship was central to Shintō practice. Unlike Chinese ancestor worship, which was limited to consanguineous relationships, Shintō ancestor worship especially revered the creator and sovereign *kami* as the ancestral *kami* of the entire nation, the head of which was the imperial family. Atsutane institutionalized the religious observances celebrating the ancestral *kami,* the writing of prayers, and the promotion of Shintō practices.

The legacy of Atsutane's ideas lay in their political implications. In asserting that the imperial system, in which the emperor *(tennō)* was supreme ruler over all the people, was the original form of the Japanese polity, he held that system as the purest and most natural structure of government. In his view the (Tokugawa) shogunate was a later accretion that was not in accordance with Shintō and was thus disrespectful of the divine origins of the imperial family. Atsutane's criticisms provided a religious foundation for the nineteenth-century political movement that resulted in the Meiji Restoration of 1868.

Kokugaku was largely responsible for the construction of collective identity and "Japaneseness" that occurred during the second half of the Tokugawa period. Later, during the Meiji period (1868–1912), ideas rooted in the Kokugaku tradition similarly contributed to those ideological constructions that supported the emergent nation-state. These ideas included the proposition that Japanese monarchs had traditionally constituted the heart of the polity—and the polity construed as extended family—as well as the articulation of a privileged place and destiny for Japan and Japanese people within Asia the world beyond. These same ideas of course also contributed substantially to Japan's international excesses, particularly during the first half of the twentieth century.

Subsequent to Japan's defeat in the Pacific War, expressions of the traditional essentialism became virtually taboo for several decades, and in their place there arose what were generally deemed to be less-offensive expressions of a Japanese national character, said to include:

an emphasis on harmony and industriousness;

a tradition of group decision making and subordinating one's own interests to those of the group;

a distinctive affinity for nature and seasonal change;

and an unusually refined aesthetic sense juxtaposed against a distinguished martial tradition.

These were inevitably represented as being both natural (and hence inescapable) and of great antiquity. It is likewise clear that these virtues also served the interests of national reconstruction and economic development.

By the 1980s, many of the earlier Kokugaku expressions of distinctiveness and superiority were once again recast under the rubric of Nihonjinron, or "theories of Japaneseness." They acquired a genuinely popular character in this guise.

SEE ALSO Hirata Atsutane; Kamo no Mabuchi; Motoori Norinaga.

BIBLIOGRAPHY

Selected writings of *Kokugaku* thinkers are in Ryūsaku Tsunoda, William Theodore de Bary, and Donald Keene, eds., *Sources of Japanese Tradition*, vol. 2 (New York, 1958). Three quite different studies of *Kokugaku* are Susan L. Burns, *Before the Nation: Kokugaku and the Imagining of Community in Early Modern Japan* (Durham, N.C., 2003); Harry D. Harootunian, *Things Seen and Unseen: Discourse and Ideology in Tokugawa Nativism* (Chicago, 1988); and Peter Nosco, *Remembering Paradise: Nativism and Nostalgia in Eighteenth-Century Japan* (Cambridge, Mass., 1990). See also Muraoka Tsunetsugu's *Studies in Shinto Thought* (Tokyo, 1964) and Masao Maruyama's *Studies in the Intellectual History of Tokugawa Japan* (Tokyo, 1974).

ISHIDA ICHIRŌ (1987)
PETER NOSCO (2005)

KOMI RELIGION.

The Komi peoples (the Zyryans and Permians) comprise a group of Finno-Ugric peoples who from time immemorial have lived in northeastern Europe. The Zyryans were Christianized at the end of the fourteenth century, the Permians in the second half of the fifteenth century. The study of the traditional Komi culture started only in the second half of the nineteenth century. Klavdij Alekseevich Popov (1874), Alexandr Vasilevich Krasov (1896), and Kallistrat Faloleevich Zhakov (1901) made attempts to reconstruct the ancient religion of the Komi-Zyryans; Nikolai Abramovich Rogov (1858, 1860), Nikolai Dobrotvorsky (1883), Ivan Nikolaevich Smirnov (1891), and Vladimir Mikhailovich Yanovich (1903) made attempts to reconstruct the Komi-Permian nature religion, separate manifestations of being in ancient cults (fire, water, and trees), animistic ideas on spirit masters, dual conception of cosmogenesis, and ideas on the dual function of a soul (soul-shadow and soul-breath). The profound study of separate aspects of the religious world outlook started at the beginning of the twentieth century. Vasilij Petrovich Nalimov, the Komi-Zyryan ethnographer, worked productively in this direction. He analyzed in detail the ideas of the Komi on the creation of the world, the role of demiurgians-antipodes in the cosmogenesis and in further world organization, the dual ideas on the essence of a soul, the attitude toward the dead, the cult of ancestors, and gender interdictions in both the hunting (men) and the household (women) spheres of activity (Nalimov, 1903, 1907, 1908). Uno Holmberg, the Finnish ethnographer, studied the Komi water cult and ideas on water spirits (Holmberg, 1913).

Pitirim Alexandrovich Sorokin, a prominent American sociologist, published a number of articles on the Komi beliefs on the soul, the cult of ancestors, and trees (Sorokin, 1910, 1911, 1917). In the 1920s Alexei Semenovich Sidorov described the religious world outlook of the Komi peoples and the cults of fur-bearing animals and trees. In "Sorcery, Witchcraft, and Spoiling in the Komis" (1928) he considered their ideas on witchcraft and magic based on interesting and original material he collected (Sidorov, 1924, 1926, 1928). In 1937 Sidorov was arrested for nationalism; he was set free in 1940. After that he did not devote himself to the Komi ethnography.

Ethnographic studies in the Komi land renewed in the beginning of the 1950s, and the first large scientific work reconstructing the ancient Komi religion was published in 1975. Ljubov Stepanovna Gribova, a Komi ethnographer, in her monograph *Permian Animal Style: The Problems of Semantics* (1975), suggested a totemic conception of the semantics of ancient cult casting of the Komi ancestors, which caused a number of serious remarks from other ethnographers. Gribova collected interesting and valuable material on the mythology and pagan beliefs of the Komi.

Analyses of the Komi calendar and ceremonial rites have shown that they represented syncretism of the Christian, pre-Christian Komi, and Russian traditions (Konakov, 1993).

The reconstruction of the ideas of the Komi on the surrounding world, space, and time has shown that, according to ancient beliefs, the world of people is in constant and close interaction with the world of spirits. Especially clear were the interrelations of Komi hunters with the forest spirits, whereas fishermen associated with the water spirits (Konakov, 1996).

Irina Vasiljevna Ilyina, in her monograph *Folk Komi Medicine* (1998), considered rational as well as irrational ways of healing, depending on the traditional beliefs regarding the causes for the disease. Komi beliefs on the next world and its interaction with the earthly world were generalized by Pavel Fedorovich Limerov in *Mythology of the Next World* (1998). *Komi Mythology*, a volume of the *Encyclopaedia of Uralic Mythologies*, edited by Anna-Leena Siikala, Vladimir Napolskikh, and Mihály Hoppál, appeared in Russian in 1999 and in English in 2003. This volume recorded for the first time the data on different aspects of the ancient religious world outlooks of the Zyryans and Permians surviving in the rites, cults, folklore, and fine arts.

In the Komi cosmogony two gods-demiurgians—Yon and Omol' to the Zyryans, En and Kul' to the Permians—participated in the creation of the world. The world before its creation was represented as a boundless water element, and the god-creators were represented in their ornithomorphous images: En as a swan or a duck, Omol' (Kul') as a loon. A loon took the earth from the bottom of the deep water. The earth grew spontaneously, first to the size of a small island, gradually to its present size. In another version, two brother ducklings, who were hatched by a mother duck or loon, took eggs dropped into the water by the mother duck from the bottom of the "sea-ocean." The body of the mother duck turned into the earth when the En duckling broke the eggs taken from the bottom of the water against it. The earth was covered with forest and grass, and its relief was created without the help of the demiugrians. En created stones, which grew and stretched toward the sky until En stopped their growth. Mountains appeared, and rivers filled the paths made by mammoths.

After the earth was formed, En created the sun and Omol' (Kul') created the moon. Initially the luminaries were placed close together in the center of the sky. They were pulled apart without the participation of the demiurgians and began their daily routes in the sky. According to the Komi-Zyryan version, this event took place when the Sun (sister) and the Moon (brother) played hide-and-seek and lost sight of each other. The Komi-Permians thought this took place because a powerful magician wanted to separate a loving couple whom he had placed on the luminaries. The creation was finished when En made the sky. En, victorious over Omol' (Kul') in the struggle for the cosmic height, went to live in the sky, intending not to interfere in the affairs of the earth. Omol' (Kul') went to live under the ground—in one version voluntarily, in another version placed there by En. Thus ended the creation of the structure of the cosmos.

En, the supreme deity, made the first person out of ground or clay. The Komi-Zyryans believed En made a man and vivified him with no aid from Omol', who tried to profane En's creation. Omol' was partly successful. According to the Permians, Kul' took part in the creation of a man. En made a body, and Kul' added some small details. But En vivified the man. According to the Komi, two demiurgians took part in the creation of animals. The Komi-Zyryans thought En and Omol' rivaled over that activity: En created a squirrel for man to hunt, then Omol' created a marten to eat squirrels, and then En created a dog to help man hunt the marten. En created a cock, a hen, a black grouse, a ptarmigan, a hazel grouse, and a duck. In response, Omol' created beasts and birds of prey. The bear had a special status among the animals. It was thought to be En's son who had come down from the sky to live on the earth. According to the Komi-Permians, En and Kul' created all the animals together and at the same time. First they made them of parti-color clay, then En vivified the animals. Under the influence of Christianity the images of demiurgians among the Komi in many respects began to resemble the images of God and Satan, especially among women, who thought En acted as the creator and Omol' (Kul') hampered him.

Few early literary sources on the ancient Komi religion have survived. According to *The Life of Saint Stefan, the Bishop of Perm* (1897) by Epiphany the Wise, Komi ancestors had many deities, whose anthropomorphous wooden images stood in the cult sanctuaries. Periodically, sacrifices of valuable furs were made, with Pam, the supreme priest, leading. In response, good luck in hunting and fishing was granted. There were also domestic deities whose images were kept in the dwellings. Of the deities of the highest rank, only one is known. In 1501 Simon, a bishop, sent a message to the Komi-Permians appealing to them not to pray to the idol Voipel and not to sacrifice. In the Permian folklore, Voipel is a kind deity who protects people from various misfortunes and enemies. In the pre-Christian sanctuary, Voipel's image took the central place. The name of this deity is not fixed in the folklore of the Komi-Zyryans. Evidently the images of ancient Komi deities merged with the images of the Christian saints. Discoveries of the early twentieth century indicate the custom of collective sacrifices on the days of the saints, especially on Ilya Day.

According to Komi animistic ideas, there existed an irreal world of various spirits that in many respects determined the life and well-being of people. In the traditional Komi world outlook, the water masters and especially the forest masters dominated in the hierarchy of the lower-ranking deities. En divided the riches of the forests and waters between people and the spirits. People could obtain their share of riches only with the agreement of the forest and water masters. A hierarchy was implied among the forest masters: there was senior forest spirit and spirit masters of separate kinds of animals, such as squirrels and hares. Vorsa was a common name for a forest spirit among the Komi-Zyryans, whereas the Permians used the name Voris'. The ideas of the image of the forest spirit were diverse: it could be invisible or appear as a whirlwind, an ordinary man, or a man with some peculiar features. A bear was though to be the forest spirit's living embodiment. The forest spirit was the guarantor of hunting morals to be observed by the hunters, and the spirit thus deprived the infringers of good luck. The Komi made offerings to the forest spirit before the beginning of the hunting season, and they left their first catch for him. The two Komi peoples had different attitudes toward a forest spirit in a nonhunting village environment. Among the Komi-Zyryans, especially the women, the spirit's image was often understood as identical to that of the evil spirit. The Permians' attitude to Voris' was most respectful, however, giving him wider functions than simply power over the forest. They asked him to give health and well-being to the people and the cattle, and he was addressed in epidemic and epizootic cases.

Vasa was the most widely used name for a water spirit master among the Komi-Zyryans, whereas the Permians preferred the name Vais'. They pictured this spirit as a man, as a man with a fish tail, or more often as a man with a large pike. The water spirit master monitored the observance of the hunting morals, and an infringer was deprived of good luck. Sacrifices, such as bread, butter, and eggs, were made to water spirits before the beginning of the fish catch. The loss of people and cattle in waters was understood as the harmful activity of the water spirits.

Other deities of lower rank inhabited the environment where people lived. In the period of rye flowering, a female spirit in the field protected the crops. This spirit deprived people of good harvests as punishment for whistling, for linen rinsing, and for touching the flowering crops. This spirit did not receive sacrifices. Spirit masters of dwellings and household constructions lived in the peasant farmsteads. The spirit master living in a barn protected it and crops from fire. People left food for this spirit. The bathhouse spirit master (Pyvsyansa) was though to be terrible, and one had to ask permission before entering the bathhouse. After the third steam, people did not wash in the bath, as it was thought the infringer might be tortured to death. This spirit was offered water and baked onion before people washed. The spirit master of the house and the cattle shed was considered primary among the spirit masters of the farmstead, and the Komi had many names for it. This spirit assured the well-being of people and cattle. It lived behind a stove or in a cellar under the floor, and people left food at the door to the cellar as a treat.

Clear traces of animism cults are also preserved. The Komi believed animals, birds, and fish understood human speech. According to the rules of the cult of fur animals, it was forbidden to say disapproving words to any catch. The hunters used various allegories (euphemisms) so as not to frighten off a beast. If the catch was valuable, they made a festive meal. The first fish caught was thrown back into the water. They believed that a killed animal would reincarnate in some other species if its remains were collected and buried in some secluded place. It was forbidden to bring a live catch to a hunting hut or home. In particular, hunting bear or elk was strictly regulated, for these animals possessed calendar significance: the bear was a symbol of the spring and summer, whereas the female elk was a symbol of autumn and winter.

According to folklore data, large birch trees stood in the main sanctuaries where the important pre-Christian festivities took place. The sites of many Komi villages have huge birch, pine, or spruce trees nearby, where it is said the population used to gather for some calendar festivities. In the beginning of the twentieth century the sacred groves still could be found near some villages. People held special attitudes toward some trees. They thought willow, alder, rowan, and juniper trees could frighten away evil spirits. Birch and fir trees were related to females, and pine and spruce were related to males. Birch is a symbol of the upper world, pine of the middle world, and spruce of the lower world. Thus, hunters making lodging for the night under a tree asked its permission. They thought trees not only understood human speech but also communicated with one another.

Traces, though not strong, of a fire cult are also preserved. Fire, especially "live" fire obtained from friction, had cleansing power. Before meals the hunters performed the rite of feeding the fire by throwing bread crumbs into it. It was forbidden to spit or urinate into fire or to trample the fire down with one's feet. Fire could only be quenched with water. It was believed that En created the fire.

The water cult required a sacrifice to water. Every spring the Komi made presents to rivers and springs as soon as the ice was broken up. To avoid diseases they threw a present into the water after drinking it. Newly married couples went to the river to wash their hands and faces on the third day after their weddings, they then threw presents, such as bread, cheese, money, and yarn, into the water. When crossing the river for the first time after the ice had broken up, people threw some bread into the water, asking it to protect them in their run. Some springs were considered health-giving. Those who came to use its waters threw bread or silver coins into it as a present. The invocated (charmed) water was also believed to be health-giving and was used for healing diseases caused by spoiling and the evil eye.

The ancestor cult was closely related to ideas of soul and death. The Komi thought people had two souls. Ort (soul shadow), a person's invisible double, accompanied him or her from birth to death. It became visible only before a person's death, appearing before the person or his or her relatives, thus informing them of the imminent death. But Ort could also inform of death while remaining invisible by making sounds: firewood hewing predicted a man's death, while the noise of a spinning wheel predicted a woman's death. After a person's death, Ort stayed on the earth for forty days, visiting all the places the dead person used to go when alive. The spirit then left for the other world. Komi villagers, especially women, retained ideas on Ort even in the early twenty-first century. Lov (soul breath) was located inside a person's body. After the person's death Lov stayed inside the house near the body until the fortieth day, the day of the funeral repast. Then it also left for the other world.

The idea of the world of the dead was dual. On the one hand there were the Christian ideas of paradise and hell. On the other hand there existed a belief that the habitation place of the souls of the dead, not localized concretely, was close to the world of people, which explained the close interrelation between the world of the dead and the world of their living relatives. These ancient pre-Christian ideas found reflection in the traces of the ancestor cult that survived into the early twentieth century. Before performing any important work (sowing, reaping), the Komi addressed their "parents." It was believed that the dead constantly took care of their living relatives. In turn, the living, to ensure this aid, had to periodically make the funeral repast, to remember the dead with a kind word, and to invite them to wash when going to a bathhouse. The dead who were offended by insufficient attention punished their living relatives with bad luck in household affairs or by making them fall ill. The souls of the dead forgotten by their relatives and descendants left for some other world that did not interact with the world of the living. Few ancient Komi beliefs and cults survive, only some superstitions.

See Also Finno-Ugric Religions.

Bibliography

Dobrotvorsky, N. "The Permians: Everyday and Ethnographic Sketch." *Bulletin of Europe* 11, book 3 (1883): 228–264; book 4 (1883): 544–580.

Epiphany the Wise. *Life of Saint Stefan, the Bishop of Perm.* St. Petersburg, 1897.

Gribova, Liubov S. *The Permian Animal Style: Problems of Semantics.* Moscow, 1975.

Holmberg, Uno. "Die Wassergottenheiter der finnischugrischen Volker." *Suomalais-ugnischen seran toimitska* 32 (1913).

Ilyina, Irina Vasiljevna. *Folk Komi Medicine.* Syktyvkar, Russia, 1995.

Konakov, Nikolaĭ D. *From Christmas Tide to Christmas Eve: Komi Traditional Calendar Rites.* Syktyvkar, Russia, 1993.

Konakov, Nikolaĭ D. *Traditional World Outlook of the Komis: Surrounding World, Space, and Time.* Syktyvkar, Russia, 1996.

Krasov, Aleksandr V. *The Zyryans and Saint Stefan of Perm.* St. Petersburg, Russia, 1896.

Limerov, Pavel Fedorovich. *Mythology of the Next World.* Syktyvkar, Russia, 1998.

Nalimov, V. P. "Some Traits from the Pagan World Outlook of the Zyryans." *Ethnographic Review* 2 (1903): 38–59.

Nalimov, V. P. "The Next World in the Beliefs of the Zyryans." *Ethnographic Review* 1–2 (1907): 88–101.

Nalimov, V. P. "Zur Frage nach der ursprunglichen Bezichungen der Gesclehter bei den Syrjanen." *Journal de la Societe/Finno-ougriene* 25 (1908): 1–31.

Popov, K. A. "The Zyryans and the Zyryan Land." *Transactions of the Society of Natural Science, Anthropology, and Ethnography Lovers* 13, book 3, no. 2 (1874): 24–182.

Rogov, N. A. "Materials for Describing the Permians' Everyday Life." *Journal of the Ministry of Internal Affairs* 4 (1858): 45–126.

Sidorov, Aleksi S. "Traces of Totemic Ideas in the World Outlook of the Zyryans." *Komi Mu* 1–2 (1924): 47–50.

Sidorov, Aleksi S. "Survivals of the Cult of Fur Animals in the Komi Hunters." *Komi Mu* 5 (1926): 29–33.

Sidorov, Aleksi S. *Sorcery, Witchcraft, and Spoiling in the People of Komi.* Leningrad, 1928.

Siikala, Anna-Leena, Vladimir Napolskikh, and Mihály Hoppál, eds. *Encyclopaedia of Uralic Mythologies,* vol.1, *The Komi Mythology.* Moscow and Syktyvkar, Russia, 1999; English translation by Sergeĭ Belykh, Budapest, 2003.

Smirnov, I. N. "The Permians." *Transactions of the Kazan Society of Archaeology, History, and Ethnography* 9, no. 2 (1891): 184.

Sorokin, Pitirim A. "Survivals of Animism in the Zyryans." *Transactions of Arkhangelsk Society on the Study of the Russian North* 20 (1910): 24–52.

Sorokin, Pitirim A. "The Present Zyryans." *Transactions of Arkhangelsk Society on the Study of the Russian North* 18 (1911): 525–536; 22 (1911): 811–820; 23 (1911): 876–885; 24 (1911): 941–949.

Sorokin, Pitirim A. "To the Problem of Primitive Beliefs of the Zyryans." *Transactions of Vologda Society on the Study of the Northern Land* IV (1917): 38–49.

Yanovich, V. M. "The Permians: Ethnographic Sketch." *Living Antique* 1 (1903): 1–223; 2 (1903): 52–171.

Zhakov, Kallistrat F. "Pagan World Outlook of the Zyryans." *Scientific Review* 3 (1901): 68–84.

Nikolai Konakov (2005)

KONGO RELIGION.

KONGO RELIGION. The Kikongo-speaking peoples of the Niger-Congo linguistic group represent a rich and diverse cultural heritage associated with the ancient kingdom of Kongo. By the late twentieth century, they were three to four million strong and lived in rural and urban areas of the western part of the Democratic Republic of the Congo, the Republic of Congo, Angola (and Cabinda), from 4° to 7° south latitude to 11° to 14° east longitude, as well as in several New World settings. Since the fourteenth century they have gained their livelihood primarily from the cultivation of various food crops (oil palm, yams, plantains, manioc, and so forth), and from hunting, fishing, and livestock tending. Smithing (of weapons, tools, jewelry, and ritual articles), weaving, tanning, sculpting, and carpentry, as well as trading in the famous Kongo markets, have been important commercial skills.

Increasingly from the late fifteenth century on, Kongo peoples were profoundly affected by contacts with European merchants, missionaries, and travelers, especially in connection with the great coastal trade, which included (from the eighteenth to late nineteenth centuries) massive slave traffic. Hardly had the slave trade ended in the 1860s when the Kongo region became the launching ground for colonial exploration and the establishment of the Congo Free State and the Belgian Congo. One indicator of the social dislocation and upheaval suffered by Kongo peoples is their gradual decline in population. From the fifteenth century to the early twentieth century it was reduced by half, despite a high birthrate. Only in 1930 did this population trend change to one of growth.

Life in Kongo society is characterized by a sense of unity of all aspects, articulated through numerous complementary oppositions. An individual is born, and remains, a juridical member of his mother's lineage and clan, yet the tie to the father and the father's kin is also strong and provides a source of spiritual identity. An individual's property relations lie inherently with the matrilineal estate, yet throughout life a child may enjoy rights to use the father's property. The collective children of a matrilineage's men constitute a continuing source of political consolidation of such a lineage. Alliances between lineages, often in reciprocal father-to-child marriages, reinforce existing bonds and create the basis of the social fabric.

Kongo religious beliefs and practices derive from these pervasive social realities. There are a number of basic Kongo religious concepts that have persisted amid the profound vicissitudes of Kongo history. Among them is the belief in a supreme being, known as Nzambi Kalunga or Nzambi Mpungu Tulendo, who is thought to be omnipotent. Although Nzambi Kalunga is the creator and the ultimate source of power, lesser spirits and ancestors mediate between humanity and the supreme being. Evil, disorder, and injustice are believed to be the result of such base human motives as greed, envy, or maliciousness. As constant sources of life and well-being, both the land and the matrilineal ancestors buried in it form the basis of the preoccupation in Kongo thought with fertility and the continuity of the community. Patrifilial relations and other alliances formed in the public sphere bring forth in Kongo religion a concern with the nature of power, its sources, applications, and the consequences of beneficent and malevolent uses of it.

KONGO RELIGIOUS HISTORY. The range of diverse cults, movements, and beliefs in the religion of the Kikongo-speaking peoples may best be presented in terms of a historical sketch. By 1500, the period when historical records were first kept, Kongo agrarian communities had been drawn into numerous kingdoms and large chiefdoms established centuries earlier; on the coast there were the Loango, Kakongo, and Ngoyo kingdoms; inland on the north bank of the Congo River, there was Vungu and numerous other chiefdoms; on the south bank, Nsundi and Kongo. In all these polities, shrines and insignia of authority represented the complementarity of power: the autochthonous spirits of the land and the awesome, detached, acumen of conquering, alliance building, and conflict judging.

The Portuguese explorer Diogo Cão contacted the king at Mbanza Kongo, the capital, in the late fifteenth century, and later the Portuguese king and merchants entered into diplomatic, mercantile, and missionary relations with Kongo, unleashing significant forces of change. In a succession struggle between the traditional prince Mpanzu and Christian prince Afonso in 1510, the victory of the latter brought about the official endorsement of Catholicism, schools, and the Europeanization of Kongo culture. A more centralized model of government prevailed, with Portuguese backing. At the same time, but against the king's wishes, the slave trade began to have serious repercussions in the kingdom. After Afonso's death in the mid-fifteenth century the kingdom began to disintegrate and, although usually supported by Portuguese militia and Catholic missionaries, it became increasingly subject to extended succession feuds between contending houses and lineages. During the centuries of the coastal trade, especially the slave era (eighteenth to late nineteenth century), all of the region's historical kingdoms gradually lost their control over tax levying, trade, and orderly administration. A variety of cults and renewal movements made their appearances.

Crisis cults and movements in Kongo history must be seen against the background of more long-term, focused, therapeutic rituals and life-cycle rituals, with which they share the underlying symbolic logic that will be described later. To a degree the crisis cults of Kongo history arise from the ground of routine rituals. Thus, initiation rites of Kimpasi (widespread south of the river) and Kinkhimba (north of the river), mentioned as early as the seventeenth century, are known to have had a periodicity of occurrence that intensified with droughts, political chaos, and rising perception of witchcraft activity. Both types of initiation were promoted by chiefs and sought to instruct youth and to legitimate political regimes.

As chiefdoms and kingdoms suffered loss of legitimacy in the trade or because of the decline of central states, new insignia and charms of power spread to enhance authority. As infertility and population decline became acute, especially in areas subjected to venereal disease and other epidemics, fertility and birthing medicine cults emerged, such as Pfemba, organized by midwives in the western north bank region. As the coastal trade increased in intensity and caravans moved from the coast to inland markets and trading points, challenging local polities and demanding provisions, medicine cult networks arose to buttress regional market and alliance structures and to protect those who were involved in the trade from the envy of their subordinates; Lemba, the great medicine of markets and government, is an important instance of this. Nkita, an ancient medicine of lineage structure, emerged wherever segmentary lineage fragments were beset by misfortune and sought to restore authority and ties to ancestors.

Kongo cultic history may be seen as a veritable tradition of renewal, either at the local lineage level, the national level, or in terms of a specific focus. Often the appeal is for restoration of public morality and order; individualized charms are commanded to be destroyed, the ancestors' tombs are restored, cemeteries purified, and group authority is renewed. Although often the originators of new cultic forms are unknown, some exceptional founding individuals are remembered and may be identified.

An especially severe and prolonged succession crisis in the Kongo kingdom in the eighteenth century brought to the fore a Kongo Joan of Arc, the prophetess Kimpa Vita, or Dona Béatrice, to reconcile the contending factions and restore authority to the capital. Her syncretic doctrine of national salvation combined royalist ideals of restoration of the capital with the call for fertility and the appeal to Christian love, subsumed under the banner of Saint Anthony, for whom the prophetess's followers were named Antonines. Kimpa Vita's work was cut short when she was charged with heresy by the Capuchin missionary Bernardo da Gallo, who supported one of the other political factions; after her execution the Antonine movement continued for several decades. Renewal movements became increasingly common, and better documented, during the Free State era (1875–1908) as colonial labor recruitment, epidemic diseases, population decline, and renewed missionary efforts to defame traditional beliefs subjected the Kongo peoples to a loss of values and the disintegration of leaders' authority. By 1920 Kongo chiefs were generally ineffective; their judicial techniques were bypassed by the colonial authorities or banned. Especially important in the context of Kongo religious leaders is the twentieth-century Kongo prophet Simon Kimbangu, whose widely influential teachings eventually gave rise to the largest independent church in Africa.

Mission Christianity, implanted during the Free State and subsequent colonial era by British, Swedish, and American Protestant groups and by Belgian, French, and Portuguese Catholics has given rise to many congregations and conferences, as well as to schools, hospitals, seminaries, and other specialized institutions. Furthermore, it has brought about the far-reaching Christianization of the Kongo populace. However, paradoxically, most Kongo Christians still subscribe to the fundamental tenets of the Kongo religion and worldview.

KONGO BELIEFS AND PRACTICES TODAY. In the twentieth century large numbers of Kongo people migrated to the urban centers of Brazzaville, Kinshasa, Matadi, Pointe Noire, Luanda, and lesser towns, yet reverence for lineage ancestors and offerings made to them continue to be integrally tied to the maintenance of lineage land estates and to the guardianship of the matrilineal kin unit. Many of the eighteenth- and nineteenth-century initiatory and curing rites have been abandoned, yet many dimensions of life continue to be sacralized. For example, religious beliefs continue to revolve around providing assurance for women's reproductive capacity and male fertility; guaranteeing the legitimacy of authority roles at lineage and clan levels; presiding over rites of passage—naming, puberty, marriage, bride price payment, death; restoring ancestral ties where lineages have been segmented or where, in urban settings, lineage fragments seek to return to their roots.

Dealing with misfortune remains an important issue in Kongo religion, although the list of common occurrences has grown from hunting and gardening activities and related accidents (e.g., being gored by a wild boar, falling from a palm tree) to include accidents and misfortunes of industrial society (e.g., automobile crashes and factory accidents). The old desires for influence, love, justice, and success have remained current, along with the need to explain failures in these areas. Misfortunes, and the desire for good fortune, are dealt with in the perspectives of historical Kongo divining, mediumship, protective magic, and healing. The axioms of this worldview, apparently quite persistent over centuries, explain the fate of humans in terms of the priority of the invisible spirit world over the visible material world or the tendency of the former to regularly break in upon the latter. Normal events in the order of things and relationships created by Nzambi require no particular piety or devotion to continue. By contrast, abnormal or unusual events are considered to be caused by humans who, willfully or inadvertently, affect others' destinies (mostly for the worse) by spiritual or direct means. The Kongo word often translated as witchcraft or sorcery is *kindoki,* from *loka* (to use charged words toward others). The power of words in interpersonal discourse is greatly respected. Human ties, frequently polluted and muddled with ill will, malicious intentions, and envy, or the threat of becoming so, must regularly be renewed with gift exchanges, purification rites, and harmonious discourse.

When ordinary people cannot cope with their misfortunes and conflicts, they turn to the *nganga* (specialized priests and doctors). The *nganga* are diviners, religious specialists skilled in manipulating spirits, humans, and symbols; agents of power who inaugurate offices of authority; and healers who deal with sicknesses of mind and body. They use esoteric codes relating the visible realm of plants and substances and apply them to the invisible realm of emotions, society, and the beyond. These mediatory roles of the *nganga* (as well as those of chiefs, prophets, and other powerful people) require legitimation from the white otherworld (*mpemba*), the realm of ancestors and spirits. As a natural cosmology *mpemba* is most often associated with water, the realm of nature, and with ancestor spirits. Land, the abode of mundane human powers, is associated with black, the realm of defective, partial, and evil forces. The sky is a third realm, not associated with any color; it is the abode of other spiritual forces. Redness, often used to describe the ambiguous or transitional areas of life, may be tied to power, or to the sun and other astral bodies, and it expresses the cycles and rhythms of natural and human life. This cosmology of natural realms and color qualities may be associated with the more explicit human ideology of matrilineal and patrilateral kinship, in a ritual grammar that amplifies the complementary dependencies of mother and child, father and child, siblings and spouses. At the most abstract level, the white may be contrasted to the world and used as a metaphor of renewal, postulating the ever-ready tendency of *mpemba* to pervade the human world, to replace, renew, and purify it.

Kongo religion is more complex and profound than any single doctrine or congregation represented within it. It is a set of perspectives about life, of symbolic traditions and roles that have formed over centuries of human experience at the mouth of the Congo River. This experience includes the adversities of the slave trade, massive depopulation, epidemics, colonialism, and droughts, as well as the challenges of Christianization and independence. Kongo religion is at the heart of one of the great historic, yet living, human civilizations.

See Also Kimbangu, Simon.

Bibliography

The English reader may begin a study of Kongo religion with John M. Janzen and Wyatt MacGaffey's *An Anthology of Kongo Religion: Primary Texts from Lower Zaire,* "Publications in Anthropology, University of Kansas," no. 5 (Lawrence, Kans., 1974), an introduction to several facets of the subject as seen in fifty-two translated texts. Wyatt MacGaffey's *Religion and Society in Central Africa: The BaKongo of Lower Zaire* (Chicago, 1986), is a major synthesis of all aspects of historical and current Kongo religion. Kongo religion as reflected in mortuary art is depicted in Robert Farris Thompson's *The Four Moments of the Sun: Kongo Art in Two Worlds* (Washington, D.C., 1981). The double entendre of Thompson's title, refering to the dichotomies of visible-invisible and Africa-New World in Kongo belief and ceremonial space, is derived from one of the clearest renderings of Kongo cosmology, A. Fukiau kia Bunseki-Lumanisa's *N'kongo ye Nza / Cosmogonie Kongo* (Kinshasa, Congo, 1969).

Classics in Kongo culture, including religion, are Jan van Wing's *Études baKongo* (Brussels, 1959), especially part 2 on religion and magic, and Karl Edward Laman's *The Kongo,* 4 vols., "Studia Ethnographica Upsaliensia," nos. 4, 8, 12, and 16 (Uppsala, 1953–1968). Specialized studies include, on Kongo messianism, Effraim Andersson's *Messianic Popular Movements in the Lower Congo* (Uppsala, 1958); on witchcraft and consecrated medicines, Tulu kia Mpansu Buakasa's *L'impensé du discours: "Kinodoki" et "nkisi" en pays kongo du Zaïre* (Kinshasa, Congo, 1973); on Christian missions in Kongo, Effraim Andersson's *Churches at the Grass Roots: A Study in Congo-Brazzaville* (London, 1968); and on historic healing cults, John M. Janzen's *Lemba, 1650–1930: A Drum of Affliction in Africa and the New World* (New York, 1981).

New Sources

Bockie, Simon. *Death and the Invisible Powers: The World of Kongo Belief.* Bloomington, Ind., 1993.

Friedman, Kajsa Ekholm. *Catastrophe and Creation: The Transformation of an African Culture.* Philadelphia, 1991.

John M. Janzen (1987)
Revised Bibliography

KONG SPRUL BLO GROS MTHA' YAS (KONGTRUL LODRO TAYE) (1813–1899).

Kong sprul was the founder of an extraordinary movement emphasizing the internal harmony of the various spiritual traditions of Tibet. The essential outlook of the nonsectarian or Rime approach in Tibetan Buddhism is respect for all approaches to realization. But followers of this approach believe equally in the necessity of personal practice, initiations, deity yoga, and guru devotion derived from one of the other traditions.

Kong sprul, his friend the Sa skya (Sakya) master 'Jam dbyang Mkhyen brtse'i dbang po (Jamyang Kyentse Wangpo, 1820–1892), and the visionary revealer of concealed teachings Chogyur Lingpa (1829–1870) together changed the spiritual landscape in eastern Tibet and eventually brought forth a renaissance of Tibetan culture, education, and spiritual practice. Their friends included teachers from all the competing religious traditions of the Tibetan lands. They met often to exchange teachings and profoundly influenced each other.

Buddhism and other written religious traditions came into Tibet from India, China, and central Asia over centuries, beginning in the seventh century. During the Royal Dynastic period (seventh to ninth centuries) Buddhism and Bon struggled for supremacy, each of their claims supported by different factions at court. Buddhist monastic practices were gradually standardized, and methods and terminology for translation into Tibetan were decreed. But Tibet was then and remains largely local, and the local weather makers and ritual specialists provided religious needs for the vast majority of the population. These followed a bewildering variety of practice forms, some of which had little to do with the Buddhism and Bon of the court circles.

With the collapse of the central dynasty and the breakup of a national political authority, family-based religious businesses became the rule. Members of these families began to travel in quest of special teachings, which were passed to family members and favored students within protected transmissions. There were great rivalries for patronage from local princes and nomadic headmen.

The roots of eclecticism and tolerance are sunk as deep into the soil of the Tibetan tradition as those of sectarianism and bigotry. Early masters of the Tibetan systems of practice sought teachings and methods of spiritual transformation from a variety of sources. There was a continuing and vital sustenance between the religious philosophy of the greater tradition and the practice of village wizards.

Kong sprul was born in Rong rgyab (Rongyab), a remote area in Kham. His father was a lay village priest of the Bon tradition. Kong sprul was a remarkable student and mastered in a short time the writing and all of the books available in his area. Kham was filled with turbulence and war during these years. Eventually the young Kong sprul's skills as a scholar and secretary came to the attention of a Rnying ma (Nyingma) monastery in Kham.

These were times of tremendous sectarian conflict between followers of Bon and the Buddhist traditions as well as within the Buddhist traditions in all of eastern Tibet. The young Kong sprul moved to Dpal spungs (Palpung), where he became a valued scribe and scholar. In order to prevent him from being taken by the Sde dge (Derge) authorities into the service of the court, he was recognized as an incarnation of a former monk at Palpung from Kong po (Kongpo) far to the west. This meant that he could not be inducted by the prince, and he became and remained a monk of Palpung.

During his long career at Palpung, Kong sprul penned over ninety volumes. The first of his five great treasuries is *Kagyu ngak dzo* (Treasury of Tantric empowerments of the Mar pa Bka' brgyud [Kagyu] school). The second is *Damngag dzo* (Treasury of practice instructions). The third and longest of the five, *Rinchen ter dzo,* is an anthology of all of the hidden teachings that had appeared in Tibet. The fourth is the Treasury of Extensive Teachings, *Gyachen ka dzo,* which comprises Kong sprul's own writings. The fifth, the three-volume *Sheja dzo* (Treasury of the knowable), is the shortest and is an encyclopedic work. The essence of the Rime movement is expressed in *Damngag dzo,* which enshrines the empowerments and instructions that had been transmitted by all of the Buddhist lineages that had come into Tibet.

The emphasis is shifted from colors of hats and sect names to a broad system of eight lineages of practice. Each of the eight lineages were passed on by masters who taught special insights into methods of spiritual transformation. Four of these persist in Tibet in the early twenty-first century as the four Buddhist orders. The other four at the time of Kong sprul had almost died out as active functioning sects; they survived only as transmissions of word and a few empowerments. Kong sprul and Mkhyen brtse gathered together these rare word transmissions from all over Tibet. Kong sprul included them in his eightfold architecture, and the teaching transmissions were spread throughout the land and became revived and revitalized.

Of course no mortal can attempt to practice all of the eight systems in one lifetime. The followers of the Rime movement emphasize that what is important is the development of an attitude of respect for all systems and philosophical outlooks while maintaining a firm commitment to a personal practice. Many great masters of the Indo-Tibetan tradition taught the moral dangers of denigrating proponents of any practice, even the adherents of the Hindu and Jain traditions. What is important is the commitments to one's own spiritual master and to the practice that the teacher has enjoined.

The Eight Systems. The first of the systems is the Early Translation school or the Rnying ma. These teachings consist of the practice of the three yogas: *mahāyoga, anuyoga,* and *atiyoga.* The master who systematized these teachings and their philosophy was Klong chen Rab 'byams pa (Longchen Rabjampa) ((1308–1364), although the teachings first began to be translated into Tibetan in the eighth century. The highest fundamental outlook of this tradition is Rdzogs chen (Dzogchen) or the Great Perfection. In the eighteenth century 'Jigs med gling pa (Jigme Lingpa, 1729/1730–1798) produced the cycle of revelations known as the *Longchen Nyingtig* after receiving profound visions of Longchen Rabjampa. The Early Translation school has maintained its strength because of ongoing revelation.

The second of the systems, the Bka' gdams (Kadam) pa, flourishes strongly in the early twenty-first century in its offshoot, the Dge lugs (Geluk) pa, founded by Je Tsong kha pa (1357–1419). This school became the paramount sect of Tibet under the Dalai Lama. The basic teachings of the Bka' gdams pa and Dge lugs pa are mental training (*lojong*), the graduated path, and careful observance of monastic discipline. The Bka' gdams pa approach has profoundly influenced all of the other systems of Tibet.

The third system is centered around the teachings of the Path and Its Fruition (Lamdre) derived from the *Vajra Verses.* The empowerments of the Lamdre system are derived from the *Hevajra Tantra.* These teachings became widely spread through the efforts of Sa chen Kun dga' snying po (Sachen Kunga Nyingpo, 1092–1158), the first of the five great patriarchs of the Sa skya school. The teachings remain strong in the early twenty-first century among the followers of the Sa skya tradition.

The Mar pa Bka' brgyud school begins in Tibet with the great translator Mar pa Chos kyi blo gros (Marpa Chokyi Lotro, 1002/1012–1097). The Mar pa Bka' brgyud school subsequently split into a multitude of kindred traditions following the *mahāmudrā* outlook, realized through the practice of the *Six Yogas of Nāropa.* The empowerments for the Mar pa Bka' brgyud are the Chakrasamvara and Vajravarahi.

All of the above four traditions survive as separate sects or schools to the early twenty-first century. The other four were absorbed into the four major schools and did not enjoy a separate sectarian presence after the seventeenth century.

The Shang pa Bka' brgyud school has experienced a great revival because of the teachings of Kong sprul and Khenpo Kalu (1905–1989). The teachings passed from Niguma, the female counterpart of Nāropa (1016–1100), and another *ḍākinī,* Sukhasiddhi, to Khyung po Rnal 'byor (Khyungpo Naljor) (978/990–1127). The primary sources are a set of *Vajra Verses,* the outlook of *mahāmudrā,* and the practice of the Six Doctrines of Niguma. The teachings were amplified by the long-lived builder of bridges, Thang stong rgyal po (Thangtong Gyalpo) (1361–1485), and Jo nang Rje btsun Tā rā nā tha (Jonang Jetsun Tārānātha) (1575–1634). These precepts are widely practiced in the Bka' brgyud in the early twenty-first century.

The sixth system is the Zhi byed (Zhije) school with its auxiliary system known as Gcod (Cho).The Zhi byed, or Quelling of Suffering, came to Tibet with the eleventh-century Pha Dam pa sangs rgyas (Pha Dampa Sangye,

d. 1105/1117). The Gcod, or Severance, teachings come from a great female disciple of Pha Dam pa, Ma gcig lab sgron (Machig Labdron, c. 1055–1149). These practices have spread through almost all of the other traditions of Tibet.

Vajra Yoga, the seventh system, exists in two flavors, the Zhwa lu (Zhalu) and the Jonang, both of which at one time had separate identities. The focus is upon the *Kālacakra* (Wheel of time) *Tantra* and the methods enshrined in the Six Branches of Union. The Jonang school survives as a sect in 'Dzam thang (Dzamthang) and a number of affiliated monasteries in Sichuan Province. The Zhwa lu sect has largely merged with the Dge lugs tradition.

The final and last of the eight systems is no longer extant except as empowerments and textual transmissions among the Bka' brgyud. These were received by O rgyan pa (Orgyenpa) from enlightened women in Swat in the borderlands where India, Pakistan, and central Asia meet.

The followers of the Rime movement began to question the banning of books of sects regarded as heretical. Many of these had been banned beginning as early as the fifteenth century. Zhwa lu Ri sbug Blo gsal bstan skyong (Shalu Ribug Losal Tenkyong) (b. 1804) was ultimately successful in persuading the Tashilhunpo authorities to permit the opening of the Dga' ldan Phun tshogs gling (Ganden Phuntso Ling) and Byang Ngam ring (Jang Ngamring) printeries in Gtsang (Tsang). The writings of Jo nang masters, including Dol po pa Shes rab rgyal mtshan (Dolpopa Sherab Gyaltsen) (1292–1361) and Jo nang Rje btsun Ta rā na thā (Jonang Jetsun Tarānathā) (1575–1634), were again permitted to be printed and distributed. The blocks for many of the banned works of great Sa skya masters, such as (Go rams pa) Gorampa (1429–1489), and Karma Bka' brgyud thinkers like the eighth Karma pa Mi bskyod rdo rje (Mikyo Dorje, 1507–1554) were recarved onto blocks at the great Rime centers of Sde dge Dgon chen (Derge Gonchen) and Palpung.

Under the influence of Mkhyen brtse and Kong sprul a resurgence of interest in histories took place. Many new religious histories were written and distributed throughout Tibet. Important figures in this movement included Zhwa lu Ri sbug, Dga' ldan The bo Ye shes bstan pa rgya mtsho (Ganden Thewo Yeshe Tenpa Gyatso) (b. nineteenth century), Brag dgon Zhabs drung (Dragon Shabdrung) (1801–1866), and Mkhyen brtse himself. This new historiography was infected with the ideals of the Rime.

RELIGIOUS EDUCATION. Religious education was another area in which the teachers of the Rime tradition had a great impact. Mkhyen brtse and his teaching school at Rdzong gsar (Dzongsar) served as a model for new forms of religious education. The Rdzong gsar syllabus, created by Mkhan po Gzhan dga' (Khenpo Zhenga) or Gzhan phan chos kyi snang ba (Zhenpen Chokyi Nangwa) (1871–1927), focused on a return to the Indian *śastra* tradition and the memorization of thirteen basic verse texts (gzhung chen [*zhungchen*]). Zhenga wrote annotated commentaries to each of these. The annotations simply attempted to explain the grammatical meaning of the great Indian authors and eschewed sectarian polemic and debate. Their purpose was simply to lead the student into the understanding of the difficult phraseology of the Indic originals. While the great Dge lugs monasteries of Tibet and their affiliates continued to use the time-honored syllabi (*yigcha*) presented for debate, the students at Rdzong gsar and affiliates focused on mastering the basic texts. Even here there were attempts to rewrite the *yigcha* of the great Dge lugs monastic colleges.

Finally, teachers who had been inspired by the ideals in the air began to write more simply and produce works intended to improve the spiritual lives of ordinary laypeople, villagers, and nomads. Dpal sprul (Patrul Rinpoche) (1808–1887) and nomad teachers like Rig 'dzin Gar dbang (Rigdzin Garwang) (1858–1930) began to pen simple literature intended for common people, which included exhortations to give up hunting and adultery and to practice the ideals of the simple Buddhist life. There are few Tibetan Buddhist teachers living in the early twenty-first century who have not been influenced by the ideals of the Rime movement.

BIBLIOGRAPHY

Barron, Richard (Chökyi Nyima), trans. and ed. *The Autobiography of Jamgön Kongtrul: A Gem of Many Colors.* Ithaca, N.Y., 2003.

Smith, E. Gene. *Among Tibetan Texts: History and Literature of the Himalayan Plateau.* Boston, 2001.

E. GENE SMITH (2005)

KONKŌKYŌ is a modern Japanese religion founded in 1859. In 1984 it boasted some 469,153 members. The founder of Konkōkyō, known by the honorary title Konkō Daijin (1814–1883), was born Kandori Genshichi to a peasant family in Ōtani village, Bitchū province (present-day Okayama prefecture). Adopted at the age of twelve, he became head of the Kawate (later renamed Akazawa) family at twenty-three and took the name Akazawa Bunji. Under his direction, his family began to cultivate cotton in addition to the traditional rice crop, thereby raising their living standard above the norm of the local cultivating class. However, while Akazawa's diligence and initiative brought material benefit, he also experienced profound grief. Four of his children died of sickness, and in 1855 he himself became very ill.

As a young man, Akazawa was deeply religious and participated in the multifaceted religious life of rural Japan. While his village was principally affiliated with the Tendai school of Buddhism, it was also deeply influenced by the cult of sacred mountains, Shugendō. Shugendō ascetics (*yamabushi*) were prominent in village religion as healers, an activity from which they derived significant income. In addition, priests of local Shintō shrines sponsored pilgrimages to the Ise Grand Shrines. Akazawa assisted traveling Ise priests (*oshi*) in distributing Ise talismans and almanacs in the village. He also joined village confraternities (*kō*) in pilgrimage to a circuit of eighty-eight temples on Shikoku island. He scrupulously observed horoscopic and geomantic prescriptions in planning any significant activity, such as travel or construction.

TEACHING AND SCRIPTURE. Akazawa's illness of 1855 was diagnosed as resulting from an offense against Konjin, who, according to local folk notions, was a malevolent deity ruling the northeast. It was believed that to offend Konjin was to precipitate his wrath in the form of possession or sickness. Akazawa's cure, thought to have been realized through earnest prayers to Konjin, marked the beginning of a complete reorientation of his life, culminating in a new understanding of humanity's relation to the deity Konjin and in the founding of Konkōkyō. Akazawa began to serve Konjin in 1858 and devoted increasing amounts of time to religion. Followers came to seek his advice and to have him mediate (*toritsugu*) Konjin's will to them. He received instructions (*shirase*) from the deity about agriculture, construction, sickness, and a host of other matters. From Konjin, Akazawa received a series of honorary titles marking his spiritual progress, and the deity revealed a corresponding set of titles of his own. Through Akazawa's spiritual development and earnest prayer the deity gradually manifested its true nature and desire for humanity's salvation.

While Akazawa originally conceived of Konjin as an evil being, he realized that the deity did not willfully cause suffering, and that the being he originally knew as Konjin was in fact the one, true God of the universe (Tenchi Kane no Kami), the source of all being. Akazawa's final title, Ikigami Konkō Daijin, reflects the concept that humanity and deity are originally united and indivisible.

In 1859 Akazawa, now called Konkō Daijin, gave up agriculture to devote himself fully to the service of Tenchi Kane no Kami (Great Living Deity Konkō); Konkōkyō dates its founding from that event. Two years later, Konkō Daijin began to record his consultations with followers, most of whom came from Okayama and Hiroshima. As the number of believers increased, the group encountered suppression and persecution from domain officials and *yamabushi.* Many followers believed they were healed by Konkō Daijin's mediation (*toritsugi*), but as such healings detracted from the *yamabushi*'s prayer healings, and hence from their income, Konkō Daijin incurred considerable enmity from these powerful religious practitioners. In order to continue *toritsugi* and avert further persecution, Konkō Daijin took a license from the Shirakawa house of Shintō. Although this gave the organization limited recognition as a variety of Shintō, Tenchi Kane no Kami was not an authorized Shintō deity, nor did *toritsugi* bear any relation to the usual practices of the Shintō priesthood.

Konkōkyō's central doctrine is rooted in the concept of reciprocity between humanity and God. Both are said to be fulfilled through humanity's self-cultivation. The task of the religious life is to awaken to God's eternal love and to realize that everyone is endowed with life and sustained by Tenchi Kane no Kami and that all things in the universe derive from him. Because all people are believed to be the children of God, human equality is a fundamental tenet. Faith and spiritual strength, rather than healing rites or medication, are the keys to physical health. Konkō Daijin denied fatalistic ideas of horoscopy and geomancy and derided food taboos and pollution notions regarding women. The record of Konkō Daijin's *shirase* and *toritsugi*, as well as accounts of the lives and conversions of early followers, are collected in Konkōkyō's scripture, *Konkōkyō Kyōten.*

RELATION TO SHINTŌ. Konkōkyō's relation to Shintō is a complex and much debated issue among the ministry. Konkō Daijin's certification by the Shirakawa was acquired more in order to protect the group than as an expression of its faith. Between 1870 and 1884, during the Meiji government's campaign to promote Shintō (called the *taikyō senpu undō*), Konkō Daijin's son Hagio became a *kyōdōshoku* ("national evangelist") and his main disciple, Satō Norio, became a vigorous activist for the movement. It was Satō who was most influential in aligning the group's doctrine with State Shintō. In spite of the direct and repeated protests of Konkō Daijin, who denied that Konkōkyō was a variety of Shintō and refused to meet with local Shintō officials, Satō and other early leaders sought, and eventually gained, recognition for Konkōkyō as one of the thirteen sects of Shintō. The group accepted this designation, no doubt partially owing to their fear of suppression.

Since the early 1980s, however, the group has rejected Shintō rites and vestments, and many ministers repent the part Konkōkyō played in prewar Shintō. They see Shintō as having contributed to militarism and nationalism, traits they wholeheartedly reject. Yet a change of such magnitude, requiring a rejection of much of the group's history, is difficult for many to accept, even when carried out in the name of a return to the true spirit of the founder's teaching. At present, the group is in the midst of a true religious revolution, and the outcome seems sure to bring in a new order.

SEE ALSO New Religious Movements, article on New Religious Movements in Japan; Shugendō.

BIBLIOGRAPHY

Articles of high scholarly merit often appear in *Konkōkyōgaku* (Konkō-machi), a journal published by Konkōkyō. In addition to this basic source, the following works may be profitably consulted.

Holtom, D. C. "Konkō Kyō—A Modern Japanese Monotheism." *Journal of Religion* 13 (July 1933): 279–300. General description and discussion of the group in terms of monotheism.

Konkō Churches of America. *Konkō Daijin: A Biography.* San Francisco, 1981. A shortened translation of the official biography of the founder.

Konkōkyō kyōten. Konkō-machi, 1983. A revised version of the sacred scriptures of the group plus much valuable information on the founder's life and those of early disciples.

The Sacred Scriptures of Konkōkyō. Konkō-machi, 1973. An abridged version of sacred texts.

Schneider, Delwin B. *Konkōkyō, a Japanese Religion: A Study in the Continuities of Native Faiths.* Tokyō, 1962. The only book-length study in a Western language, the book concentrates on the theology of the group.

HELEN HARDACRE (1987)

KOOK, AVRAHAM YITSḤAQ. Rabbi Avraham Yitsḥaq Kook (1865–1935) was the first Ashkenazi chief rabbi of the Land of Israel in the modern era, a religious thinker and *halakhic* authority, and one of the prominent leaders of the New (Jewish) Settlement at the beginning of the twentieth century. Rabbi Kook was born in Grieva, Latvia. His father was of Lithuanian Jewish descent, and his mother came from a Lubavitcher Hasidic family. Kook was the spiritual and *halakhic* authority who laid the foundations for a religious Zionism that did not settle for the political pragmatism of the Mizraḥi (the religious Zionist movement) or that of Theodor Herzl, the founder of the Zionist movement. Kook sought to view Zionism as a process of redemption, of repentance, and of an overall Jewish renaissance. He was a man of complexity whose persona unified opposing spiritual worlds: the Lithuanian Torah scholarship with the Hasidic spiritual experience, a commitment to *halakha* and Jewish tradition with a modern worldview and Western culture and philosophy, a tendency toward spirituality and mysticism with full involvement in the practical matters of rabbinic and public leadership.

At a very early age, Kook was appointed rabbi of Zaumel and later of Boisk. In 1904 he made a pilgrimage to the Land of Israel and was appointed chief rabbi of Jaffa and the surrounding towns. World War I broke out while he was attending a conference of the Agudath Israel movement in Germany, and he was forced to spend the war years (1914–1918) in Switzerland and England. When he was finally able to return, he moved to Jerusalem to serve as chief rabbi and was elected the first Ashkenazi chief rabbi of the Land of Israel when the chief rabbinate was established in 1921. Rabbi Kook became an outstanding rabbinic leader, one who played an active role in many controversies but won the respect of diverse groups, from the devoutly observant members of the Old Settlement to the atheist pioneers of the New Settlement and the leaders of the second emigration.

Rabbi Kook's extensive writings traverse a wide range of literary styles and forms. He wrote contemplative compositions, *halakhic* books, ideological articles and essays, commentary to the Talmud, poetry, and many letters. His language and style reflect the complex nature of his spiritual world. The unique synthesis found in his writings between mystical concepts and qabbalistic ideas, on the one hand, and philosophical thought and his bold and novel interpretation of the meaning of Judaism, on the other, as well as the personal and original nature of his thought required the creation of a new mystical language.

Rabbi Kook's thought is based on a mystical intuition and on a radically monistic perception. He viewed reality as an absolute unity whose source is the divine infinity and is expressed in all dimensions of existence: in the cosmic, natural, and physical dimension, in the historical-political, and in the cultural dimension. Kook viewed all reality as a revelation or manifestation of the divine, leading to his tolerant and pluralistic outlook, which sees all cultures, each worldview, and every ideology as partial expressions of the divine truth. Despite Kook's basic assumption that no single philosophical or qabbalistic theory can contain the multiple dimensions of existence and that therefore each theory is partial and relative, he nonetheless usually formulated his ideas within a Neoplatonist mystical framework, using concepts borrowed sometimes from the Qabbalah and sometimes from idealistic European philosophy of the nineteenth century. He saw the Qabbalah not simply as an ancient tradition but also as a discipline of free thought and creativity, which springs from the depths of a person's spirit and deciphers the secrets of the Torah.

Kook's contemplative writings were, for the most part, not written in a systematic fashion; his writing was automatic and spontaneous, and in general he did not later edit and arrange these writings in book form. His student and friend, Rabbi David Cohen (HaNazir), who edited a large portion of his works, arranged them in the book *Lights of Holiness,* according to the major topics of philosophical inquiry: epistemology, ontology, and anthropology (including ethics and morality). His nationalistic thought is mostly found in several essays collected in the book *Lights,* which was edited by his son, Rabbi Tsvi Yehudah Kook.

REPENTANCE. Several of Rabbi Kook's main and most fundamental ideas were formed in an original fashion. In Kook's thought, repentance is not merely a psychological process that takes place in the consciousness of the individual but instead a cosmic process taking place in all dimensions of existence, which has sought to return to its source from the moment of creation. This cosmic process is apparent in the movement found in nature, history, and culture toward higher, superior levels of existence. Thus all progress made in the history of the Jewish people and the entire world, in the natural sciences, medicine, and technology, are understood as manifestations of the process of redemption. In this context, sin is also understood as a metaphysical concept that signifies the failure to reach the original goal of creation and a deviation from creation's proper state of wholeness. The redemption of the world is therefore a metaphysical necessity.

FREEDOM. The idea of freedom and the striving for freedom were characteristic of the spirit of the nineteenth century in Europe. However, the idea of freedom in Rabbi Kook's writings is not limited to the realm of political thought; it exists also as a metaphysical principle, as a trait and a basic drive of humans, and as a lofty religious ideal. The concept of freedom is understood foremost as a cosmic dialectical process of self-realization.

HOLINESS. The idea of holiness, according to Rabbi Kook, expresses the immanence of the divine in the world and is described as a current flowing forth invisibly from the source of existence and spreading throughout all dimensions of existence: in space, in time, and in humanity. From this perspective, there is no essential difference between the sanctity of the Land of Israel and that of other places. The difference is only that in the Land of Israel the hidden holiness bursts forth and is revealed like a wellspring. The same is true in terms of time, since the holiness that flows forth in secret each day reveals itself on the Sabbath day, and so it is in the other dimensions of existence. One of the distinguishing characteristics of humanity is the ability to recognize holiness and to have religious aspirations. The capacity for religiosity is common to all people, and in the people of Israel this capacity is also realized in their collective spiritual creation.

Kook's approach to the Zionist movement was based both on his "historiosophical" religious and metaphysical worldview and on his personal experiences of direct contact with the pioneers of the second emigration. In his eyes, Zionism was an opportunity for an overall Jewish renaissance, and he yearned to witness a far-reaching renewal not only of the Hebrew language and the Jewish settlement in Israel but also of Jewish literature, Torah scholarship, and the creative arts as well as an expansion of the meaning of the Torah itself. All of these changes, he believed, would bring about the establishment of the state of Israel in the Land of Israel, an ideal state that would actualize in all dimensions of its existence the noble ideals of Judaism and thus reveal the kingship of God in the world. He valued the Zionist movement as a practical-political instrument whose function was to realize this vision. He also admired and loved the pioneers, in whom he saw unadulterated idealism and innate moral values. However, he also voiced harsh criticism of both wings of the Zionist movement, the religious and the secular, for their narrow understanding of their role. Rabbi Kook was actively involved in the Zionist public life, and the British Mandate related to him as one of the representatives of the Zionist leadership.

Rabbi Kook's impact on the development of ideological-political and spiritual-religious trends was greater after his death than during his lifetime. He was very highly respected and revered by most sectors of Jewish society, despite the fact that his opinions were controversial. At the same time, he did not have many students and did not succeed in creating a mass movement. The yeshiva he established in Jerusalem and led for many years, Merkaz HaRav, did not, after his death, make an impact on wider circles. However, Rabbi Kook's ideas permeated religious Zionist society, and after the Six Day War in 1967, during which territories under Arab rule were captured, all the dreams, the ideas, and the great prophecy of the redemption of the people of Israel returning to their biblical homeland surfaced and came to life in the real world. Youth movements, many religious educational institutions, yeshivas, and high schools educated their students in light of his teachings. Students of the yeshivas and movements influenced by his thought established new settlements in Judea and Samaria; those groups even established a political-ideological movement, Gush Emunim, in the aftermath of the Yom Kippur War in 1973. Of course these movements and trends express only one particular dimension of Rabbi Kook's thought and his multifaceted writings.

Thus Gush Emunim's claim to be the true continuation of Rabbi Kook's legacy put it at the center of a controversy that was both political and ideological in nature. Supporters of this claim emphasize the movement's devotion to the idea of settling in the entire Land of Israel as an integral part of the complete redemption of the people of Israel. Opponents emphasize the fact that this settlement comes against the will of the Arab residents, sometimes takes away their lands, and prevents a peace treaty between Israel and the Palestinians. Seemingly Rabbi Kook's thought is the source of both perspectives.

Unquestionably the love of the Land of Israel, settlement as part of the process of redemption, and the establishment of the state of Israel were essential elements in Rabbi Kook's vision. At the same time, sensitivity toward the dignity and will of the Arabs was also part of his approach (as evidenced by his testimony before the British governor of Jerusalem after Arab rioters attacked Jews at prayer at the Western Wall).

Any attempt to estimate what Rabbi Kook's political position about the Israeli-Palestinian conflict of the late-twentieth century and early-twenty-first century would have been is nothing more than speculation. His perspective and worldview were wide and complex to such an extent that many can find support in them for their contradictory positions; this does not mean that their views should be seen as necessary conclusions or realizations of his thought.

Kook's successors established communities and residential neighborhoods with the characteristics of closed, separate societies. At the same time, in particular over the last two decades of the twentieth century, some of these groups have displayed a trend of openness toward and involvement in all the realms of activity and production of the general society: in academia, in the economy, in the army, in culture, and in the arts. Furthermore the spiritual-mystical trends developing in the climate of the New Age and postmodernism in Israel also have roots in the mystical thought of Rabbi Kook, and its magnetism grows, especially among the religious youth.

BIBLIOGRAPHY

Goldman, Eliezer. "Rav Kook's Relation to European Thought." In *The World of Rav Kook's Thought,* edited by Benjamin Ish

Shalom and Shalom Rosenberg, translated from the Hebrew by Yovel Orot, pp. 115–122. New York, 1991.

Ish-Shalom, Benjamin. *Rav Avraham Itzhak HaCohen Kook: Between Rationalism and Mysticism.* New York, 1993.

Ish-Shalom, Benjamin. "Tolerance and Its Theoretical Basis in the Teaching of Rav Kook." In *Abraham Isaac Kook and Jewish Spirituality,* edited by L. Kaplan and D. Shatz, pp. 178–204. New York, 1995.

Ross, Tamar. "Rav Kook's Concept of the Divine" (in Hebrew; two-part series). *Daat* No. 8 (Winter 1982): 109–128, No. 9 (Summer 1982): 39–70.

Schwartz, Dov. *Challenge and Crisis in Rav Kook's Circle* (in Hebrew). Tel Aviv, 2001.

BENJAMIN ISH-SHALOM (2005)

KORAN SEE QUR'ĀN

KORE SEE DEMETER AND PERSEPHONE; ELEUSINIAN MYSTERIES

KOREAN RELIGION.

KOREAN RELIGION. The earliest religious practice of the peoples of the Korean peninsula is a form of Siberian shamanism, or *musok* in Korean. Neolithic archaeological excavations on the peninsula have produced pottery with geometric designs identical to those found in regions of Siberia, Manchuria, and Mongolia, suggesting that Koreans of the Neolithic period (beginning around 4000 BCE) can be traced back to the same ethnic stock. The label *shamanism* as the native religion of Korea has encountered some definitional problems, however. Mircea Eliade supplied the essential definition of *shamanism* as the technique of ecstasy, or the separation of the soul from the body to journey to heaven or to the underworld. Modern Korean shamans do not undergo such flights of the soul. Instead, they become possessed by spirits, who "descend" into the shaman and speak through her. Ethnographic data contravenes the definitional problem, however, by attesting to the inherent diversity of shamanic practice even within central Asia itself. In central and eastern Siberia, for example, the possession séance predominates, as in contemporary Korea, whereas the soul flight is more typical to the western and northern regions.

Although *musok* is the most native and persistent form of religious practice in Korea, surviving into the contemporary era, its position in Korean society experienced a sharp reversal between the ancient era and the advent of Chinese cultural influence upon the Korean peninsula. In the earliest period, shamans (*mudang,* from the Mongolian/Tungus *utagan*) were males closely aligned to ruling powers, and shamanism was integral to the establishment of sacred kingship. During the unified Silla, Koryŏ, and Chosŏn dynasties, *musok* was regarded by ruling elites as a form of superstition and was similarly disparaged by Christian missionaries and Japanese colonists in the early twentieth century. Today, *mudangs* are primarily women from reduced economic and social circumstances. They are held in low esteem by the general population, but their services are nevertheless sought out by people of all classes who struggle with inexplicable illness or misfortune.

Shamanism's persistence as a Korean religious practice can be attributed to the basic nature of its ritual objectives—the bringing of good fortune and the warding off of ill via the manipulation of spirits—and its tremendous adaptability to cultural change, particularly to the introduction of other religious systems. Its pantheon of gods, its mythology, and its rituals have been augmented throughout the centuries by the rise of more organized religious traditions passed on by China: Buddhism, Confucianism, and to a lesser extent, Daoism. One might reverse this picture, however, to also observe that the success of these foreign traditions—particularly Buddhism—was a function of their ability to accommodate the primary practice of shamanism. The success of Christianity in Korea beginning in the late nineteenth century can be described in the same manner.

SHAMANISM AND STATE FORMATION. The history of the Korean peninsula can be traced back to about 4000 BCE, with the Neolithic peoples. They lived by hunting, fishing, and gathering and began the shift to agriculture in the third millennium BCE. The basic social unit consisted of the clan, or consanguineous social groupings that occupied distinct territorial regions, and they differentiated among themselves through totemic practices. As the population increased, tribes were created through the merger of clans, primarily through marriage.

The metallurgic technology of the Bronze Age spread down through the Korean peninsula between the first millennium and 600 BCE and was brought by the Tungus, a separate racial stock originating in central and southeastern Siberia. The merger of the two peoples led to an increase in political stratification, as the superior weapons of the Tungus led to the domination of the Neolithic inhabitants. Bronze implements, such as the mandolin-shaped dagger and the knobbed mirror, were emblems of this new authority. The construction of dolmen tombs in this era also testifies to the ability of new leaders to command vast labor sources.

During this era, distinct states evolved from tribal leagues and established themselves throughout the peninsula and present-day eastern and southern Manchuria. They include the Puyŏ, in the region of the Sungari River (present day Manchuria); the Koguryŏ, just to the south, in the region of the Yalu River; the Okchŏ and Tong-ye, in the central peninsular region between the Taedong and Han Rivers; and the three Han tribes—Mahan, Pyŏnhan, and Chinhan—south of the Han River in the southern tip of the peninsula. The strongest and most evolved "state," however, was that of ancient Chosŏn, in the northwestern region of the peninsula closest to China. The chieftan of this tribal confederation adopted the title of *wang,* or king, emulating the northern Chinese state of Yan during the decline of the Zhou dynasty. The dates of ancient Chosŏn largely parallel the Warring States period of China (403–221 BCE).

During this era in which political organization became more complex, shamanism manifested itself as an intimate aspect of state formation. Shamans were males who possessed political as well as ritual power. With the development of hereditary rulership, the exercise of power maintained its religious dimension by expanding the animistic belief system of shamanism into ancestor worship and a belief in divine kingship.

Shamanistic belief fundamentally entails the idea that all natural objects—mountains, rivers, trees, the sun, as well as human beings—are animated by a soul, or spirit. These spirits are divided between those that bring good fortune and those that bring ill. Human ancestors can be benign or troublesome, depending on whether or not they have been properly dispatched into the spirit world. In all cases, spirits are forces that can be propitiated and controlled through the technology of ritual. In the southern regions, "heavenly princes" *(ch'ŏn'gun)* engaged in ceremonial dance and chanting to do their work. Chinese historical sources also attest to ancient Korean tribal festivals uniformly associated with points in the agricultural calendar such as the sowing and harvest seasons. These celebrations entailed sacrifices to heaven on mountaintops or sacred groves. The use of drums and bells at these festivals is characteristic of Siberian shamanic practice. The drum, in particular, was an important instrument in creating the ecstatic trance that enabled Siberian shamans to journey to heaven. Besides mountaintops, sacred groves marked off by a bell and drum signified the presence of spirits and functioned as ritual sites.

The belief in heaven, and a ruler of heaven (*hananim* or *hanŭnim*), was the by-product of nature worship, particularly that of the sun, and was the basis for narratives about divine kings who descended from the upper realm. A legend from the state of Koguryŏ, for example, attests that its founder, Chumong, was conceived by the rays of the sun and finally born of an egg. Each foundation myth of the ancient states establishes the principle of sacred kingship by tracing the ruling clan to a progenitor who is of heavenly origin. One of the most complex, and certainly the most historically significant, of these foundation myths is the story of Tan'gun, who is the progenitor of the state of ancient Chosŏn. Through an analysis of this myth, one can discern the relationship between shamanism and kingship in the early period of Korean history, as well as the evolution of this relationship into the political phenomenon of national identity in more recent eras.

The myth of Tan'gun. It is recorded that in ancient times, the king of heaven (Hwanin) had a son who wished to descend into the world of men. The king descended onto the three great mountains, and finally chose Mount T'aebaek (presently in North Korea) as the site of his son's domain. With three thousand spirits, the son descended onto Mount T'aebaek via the path of a sandalwood tree, under which a sacred altar was established. The realm was called the Sacred City, and the son was known as the Sacred King *(ch'ŏnwang).* With the ministers of wind, rain, and cloud, the king ruled the people.

At that time a tiger and a bear petitioned the king to be made human. The king gave them mugwort and garlic as their food and instructed them to live in a cave for one hundred days. The tiger failed to follow these instructions, but the bear succeeded, and it was rewarded by being transformed into a woman. The king married the Bear Woman, and she gave birth to a son named Tan'gun. Tan'gun established the nation of Chosŏn and ruled for fifteen hundred years, until King Hu of Zhou (China) enfeoffed the nation to Kija. Tan'gun departed for some time but then returned to Chosŏn and became the Mountain God.

The myth of Tan'gun is a synthesis of political and shamanic narratives. The story explains the divine origins of the founder of ancient Chosŏn. In addition, the story moves beyond mythic time into historical time, which is signified by reference to the Chinese state of Zhou. The historical aspect of the narrative accounts for the ultimate displacement of the Tan'gun dynastic line. The mythical portion of the narrative is replete with shamanistic symbolism. *Tan'gun* appears to be cognate to the Mongolian *tengri* and other central Asian terms for *heaven.* The descent of the heavenly king Hwanin, his son, and the three thousand spirits into the human world evokes the primary aspect of shamanic practice, which is the descent of spirits. Mount T'aebaek, the sandalwood tree, and the sacred altar signify cosmic axes through which spirits descend and attest to the shamanic practice of sacrifices on mountaintops and sacred groves. The three ministers of wind, rain, and cloud are nature spirits that shamans propitiate for the purpose of bringing good fortune, particularly by making rain.

The tiger and the bear, particularly the latter, function as totem spirits in Siberia. The marriage of the king with the Bear Woman indicates the alliance of the solar clan with the bear clan in the creation of the dynastic line. The connection between political power and shamanic power is clearly denoted by the successful transformation of the bear into a woman: the conversion suggests the shaman's initiation, which is enacted as a rite of death and rebirth signified by the eating of special foods and submersion into the womb of a cave.

Besides the ingredients of the Tan'gun myth itself, the preservation and use of the myth has maintained the connection between shamanism and the state. The Tan'gun myth was recorded in the thirteenth century by the Buddhist monk Iryon (1206–1289), who compiled the miscellany of legends and folklore known as the *Samguk yusa.* This unofficial compilation is one of the earliest sources available on Korean history and culture. Part of its title, *samguk,* refers to the Three Kingdoms period, when the states of Koguryŏ, Paekche, and Silla emerged in the fourth century as the most powerful states on the peninsula. The era endured until the late seventh century, when victorious Silla emerged as the first unified Korean state. The *Samguk yusa,* however, does not confine itself to the period of the Three Kingdoms. It begins with the founding myths of the earliest states, such as ancient Chosŏn, and proceeds through the united Silla up until its fall to the Koryŏ dynasty in 935.

A centrally important fact about the *Samguk yusa* is that Iryon compiled it during the Mongol rule of Korea, which commenced with the invasions of 1231 and 1254 and which solidified with the formal proclamation of the Mongol Yuan dynasty in 1271. The political and cultural humiliations that Koreans endured under Yuan rule yielded a literary bounty of prose tales, anecdotes, and poetry that aimed to preserve and enhance a sense of native identity. Not only do these sources appear in *Samguk yusa,* but the compilation of the *Samguk yusa* itself was the result of this cultural preservationist impulse. The myth of Tan'gun, in particular, emerged into broad social consciousness and functioned as the foundation myth of all of Korea. This conceit solidified most completely during yet another period of foreign rule—the Japanese colonial era of the twentieth century (1910–1945). After independence, the new Republic of Korea adopted a calendar based on the purported year of Tan'gun's ascension to rule, in 2333 BCE. This calendrical system remained official until 1961, when it was abolished by the military regime of Park Chung Hee.

The survival of Tan'gun mythology into the modern period can also be credited to actual *musok* practices. From the beginnings of the Chosŏn dynasty (1392–1910), Tan'gun shamanism was expressed most directly in the reascension of Tan'gun as a shamanic spirit. The precedent for this is given in the original myth, where it is recounted that after Kija took over the rule of ancient Chosŏn, Tan'gun became the Mountain God. In actual practice, however, Tan'gun became the most prominent member of a "holy trinity" *(samsŏng)* that includes his father, the Sacred King, and his grandfather, the Heavenly King. Tan'gun is to this day an important member of the shamanic pantheon and is pictured as an old man of a decidedly Daoist flavor, mounted on a tiger. In October sacrifices are offered to Tan'gun on mountaintops, the most significant one being Mount Mani on Kanghwa Island. Interestingly, the "holy trinity" is augmented by five historical kings and fifteen culture heroes in the Mani shrine. All of these individuals, dating from the earliest period of Korean history up to the twentieth century, are recognized as culture heroes. The shamans who deify them and petition them for national security and prosperity carry on one of the oldest functions of shamanism—that of protecting the state.

SHAMANISM IN TRANSITION. The period of the Three Kingdoms, briefly mentioned above, was characterized by inner struggles for political domination and union of the peninsula, particularly by Koguryŏ in the north, Paekche in the south, and Silla in the southeast. In 475, the forces of Koguryŏ sacked the Paekche capital, forcing the latter kingdom into an alliance with Silla, its eastern neighbor. Silla in turn seized most of Paekche's territory in the Han River Valley, as well as tribal territories along the Naktong River. By the seventh century, Silla was ready to challenge Koguryŏ. The Chinese unification under Tang rule (618–907) provided Silla the needed ally to thwart its northern rival, which posed a threat to China's own northeastern boundary. By the end of the 660s, both Paekche and Koguryŏ collapsed under combined Tang-Silla attack. Silla then drove off the Tang forces from the Korean peninsula, finally establishing its northern border at present-day P'yŏngyang.

The pivotal role of China in the dynastic union of Korea under Silla rule was only one result of the opening of the Korean peninsula to relations with the Chinese. From the fourth century on, Korea states were increasingly drawn into the Chinese cultural sphere, primarily through the adoption of the Chinese written language, Chinese Confucian texts, and with that, Chinese statecraft. Buddhism was introduced during this period as well, and regular pilgrimages by Korean monks to China, as well as to India, elevated Korea into a new epoch of transregionalism. In the sixth century, Korean monks from Paekche carried Buddhist texts to Japan, the most famous being Hyeja, who served as tutor to the crown prince Shōtoku Taishi (574?–622?). Paekche monks served as the primary transmitters of Chinese Buddhism and Chinese culture to Japan. Along with Buddhist scriptures and Buddhist art, Korean artisans were sent to aid in the construction of Buddhist temples. In return, Japanese monks traveled to Paekche for study.

THE IMPACT OF BUDDHISM. Buddhism was formally recognized by Koguryŏ in 372; by Paekche in 384; and Silla in 529. These dates parallel the timing of each respective kingdom's establishment of formal contacts with China. In this respect, not only was Buddhism a cultural import but, more importantly, it functioned as a vehicle of political relations. The *Samguk yusa* relates that the Chinese missionary monk Sundo arrived in Koguryŏ during the reign of King Sosurim (r. 371–384), bearing scriptures and religious images. Sundo was sent by King Fujian of the Former Qin (351–394), who had defeated the Former Yan—an enemy of Koguryŏ. Hence, Sundo was an envoy-missionary who came to cement political relations between the two states. The ambassadorial nature of the visit is indicated by the fact that King Sosurim made the extravagant gesture of meeting Sundo at the city gate.

The political import of Buddhism in Koguryŏ is augmented by the fact that Chinese Buddhism had already set the precedent for close relations between kings and Buddhist clergy, in the belief that the magical powers of Buddhism were capable of protecting the state. State interest and royal patronage explain the rapid establishment of Buddhist temples and the intense evangelization of the population. The large numbers of Korean monks who traveled to China for study and to Japan as missionaries during this early period was yet another facet of state patronage.

The transmission of Buddhism into Paekche came at the hands of the Serindian monk Mŭlŭnanda, who arrived via the Chinese state of Eastern Jin (317–420). It is similarly related that the Paekche king greeted the monk at the city gate. In Paekche, too, Buddhism was established initially as a royal cult. The arrival of the first Buddhist monks in Silla (from Koguryŏ), on the other hand, was met with suspicion and persecution on the part of the ruling elites—perhaps in part because of their origins from a rival state. When a monk cured King Nulchi's (r. 417–458) daughter of an illness, however, the royalty was converted. This story suggests that the success of Buddhism in Korea hinged on its ability to replicate key functions of shamanism. The curing of illness is the central element here, and the establishment of Buddhism as a state religion replicates the close ties between kingship and shamanism in the pre-Buddhist period.

Throughout the unified Silla (668–935) and Koryŏ (918–1392) dynasties, Buddhism maintained its status as a state religion, and in this capacity it displaced the function and prestige of the *mudang*. As a direct result, the *mudang*'s social and political standing became decidedly ambiguous. The dynastic records of Koryŏ describe the presence of *mudangs* (who appear to have been primarily female) in the palace and the fact that some court ladies and officials deferred to them. On the other hand, the records also detail the persecution of *mudangs* by other officials and royal proclamations against "licentious" *musok* festivals within the city walls. The levying of taxes on *mudang* also suggests that the court sought to discourage people from taking up the shamanic calling. The records paint a picture in which most individuals still adhered to the traditional cosmology of spirits and believed in the efficacy of the *mudang*, but in which the rise of an official and elite ideology led to the repression of *musok* as superstitious and morally corruptive.

On the other hand, it is interesting to note that in overtaking the role of state protector, Buddhism took on the very same ritual tasks so central to *musok*. The P'algwanhoe, a ceremony first performed in 572, was a state-sponsored Buddhist festival that ostensibly encouraged lay people to adhere to the eight ascetic precepts (*p'algwan*) of the monk. The most significant aspect of the ceremony, however, was the prayers for the state, which consisted of spirit propitiation as well as supplication of the Buddha. The Heavenly spirit, mountain spirits, river spirits, and Dragon Spirit were regularly recognized in the annual festivals of the Koryŏ era. The other significant aspect of these festivals was their gaiety, being an occasion for singing, dancing, and feasting. Following *musok* custom, entertainment was considered integral to the task of pleasing the spirits and sending them on their way.

It might very well be claimed that the P'algwanhoe is simply a case of native shamanic practice in Buddhist garb, but the more significant point is that the garb of official choice had direct, negative consequences for the continuing practice of *musok*. From its close association with kingship, still symbolically visible in the royal regalia of Silla kings, *musok* became the province of peasants who augmented their profession with fortune-telling and sorcery. To be sure, Buddhism stretched its ideology in order to accommodate the native Korean spirit world, and *musok* in turn incorporated Buddhas and *bodhisattvas* into its pantheon. Beyond this, however, Buddhism ultimately trumped *musok* because of its political support and because of the plasticity and sophistication of the Buddhist belief system.

These latter qualities are particularly visible in Buddhism's dissemination into the larger populace. The practice of mortuary rites provides the best illustration. The aforementioned P'algwanhoe, from its early sixth-century origins, functioned as a feast for the dead, particularly for the spirits of men fallen in battle. From the early Koryŏ period, the festival of Manghon-il (Day of the Dead) was celebrated on the fifteenth day of the seventh lunar month, and it had the same function of propitiating the spirits of the dead. This festival, however, was quite explicitly enveloped in a Buddhist scriptural and ritual web, and it demonstrates the deftness with which the pervasive concern with ancestral spirits was integrated into the Buddhist worldview.

Manghon-il derives from the Chinese "ghost festival," which emerged during the Tang dynasty. The festival got its charter myth from a popular tale about Mulien, a disciple of the Buddha, who journeys to the lowest of Buddhist hells in order to rescue his mother. The tale fuses the Buddhist cosmology of rebirth and the Chinese value of filial piety, testifying to the manner in which the ghost festival allayed the charge that Buddhist monasticism was antifamily. The festival celebrated the emergence of the monastic community from its rainy season meditative retreat. By making donations of food, clothing, and other necessities to the monastic community at this time (which also coincided with the harvest season), the laity reaped the benefit of the heightened ascetic and religious power of the monks, which translated into significant karmic merit. This merit in turn was dedicated to the lay ancestors for the purpose of ensuring their favorable rebirth.

The Chinese ghost festival was a significant community celebration that operated with the financial assistance and ritual participation of the emperor. The Chinese Buddhist canon acquired two sūtras (*Yulanpen* and *Offering Bowls to Repay Kindness*) that narrate how the historical Buddha himself founded the ghost festival and that emphasize the key role of monks as intermediaries between ancestors and descendents. The festival and the texts demonstrate how Buddhism was able to mythically and ritually co-opt the native Chinese worship of ancestors. Transmitted to Korea, which also received the tale of Mulien, the Buddhist belief in rebirth finessed the more fundamental fear of malicious spirits and the need to properly dispatch them from the world of the living. The P'algwanhoe reflects the idea that those who die violently or unexpectedly come back as disgruntled spirits who harass the living through illness and misfortune. Aside from the annual festivals, Buddhist monks were steadily employed to offer sūtra readings at private funerals—a practice that continues into the present day. The ability of Buddhism to usurp the function of spirit propitiation was a key element in the spread of Buddhism among the masses.

The mortuary rituals of *musok* may have remained competitive with Buddhist ones, but its cosmological beliefs were simple in contrast to the great metaphysical and doctrinal systems of Buddhism. During the united Silla, the rise of Buddhist doctrinal schools and renowned monks such as Wŏnhyo (617–686) and Ŭisang (625–702) established a learned religious tradition that was kept vibrant by frequent travel within an international community that included not only China and Japan but also India and Central Asia. Particularly in its missionary travels to Japan, Korean monks acted the role of conduits of culture from the West. The full emergence of Korea into the international scene bred an elite culture and learned community that grew increasingly unkind in its view of the native tradition of *musok*.

The Chosŏn Era (1392–1910). When the military general Yi Sŏnggye (1335–1408) betrayed his Koryŏ king to establish the Chosŏn dynasty (as King Taejo, r. 1392–1398), he chose Confucianism as the new state ideology. Buddhism curried the favor of kings throughout the previous Koryŏ period, but by the end of this era, the cultural and religious vitality of Buddhism had dissipated from privilege and came to pose an enormous financial burden on the state. Taejo looked, as in previous eras, to China for a model of state, but this time to Confucianism, paralleling China's own ideological shift. Integral to the new state was a system of learned Confucian scholars who functioned as ministers and advisors to the king. Hence the official learning of the land became Confucian, although Buddhist learning and piety was never fully abandoned by the aristocracy (and royalty). Buddhist monasteries, however, were banished beyond the capitol to remote mountains, and monks were reduced to the status of pariahs. In a sense, monks joined the ranks of *mudang*, and the intermingling of Buddhism and shamanism at the popular level allowed Confucians to dismiss both as "superstition."

Official ideology, however, tends to paint a picture far simpler than the richness and ironies of actual life. Chosŏn kings and queens lived by the Confucian institutions that maintained the state—such as the Confucian education system that supplied the court with its scholar-officials. These same kings and queens, however, routinely turned to Buddhism in their private lives, particularly when vicissitudes in the exercise of power brought home the Buddhist message that all worldly gains are ultimately empty. Taejo himself bestowed the title of "Royal Preceptor" (*wangsa*) on the Buddhist monk Muhak (1327–1405), who functioned as his confidante and spiritual advisor. King Sejong (r. 1418–1450), considered to be the most illustrious of Chosŏn kings, vigorously suppressed Buddhism but turned to it at the end of his life, going so far as to build a temple within the palace precincts. King Sejo (r. 1455–1468), who ruthlessly assumed the throne by murdering his nephew, the boy-king Tanjong, also turned to Buddhism in the course of his reign.

Chosŏn dynastic history is replete with royalty who not only embraced Buddhist piety but who also shaved their heads and put on Buddhist robes in the final chapter of their checkered lives. These tendencies were shared by the ministers and officials, who were also vulnerable to swings in political fortune. The evidence of this appears in literary works that gave voice to personal feelings. The longing for nature and retirement from political life was a persistent Buddhist-Daoist theme in literati poetry, for example. Kim Sisŭp (1435–1493), Hŏ Kyun (1569–1618), and Kim Manjung (1637–1692) are some of the better known literati whose lives and works of fiction testify to Buddhism's continuing centrality to the way Koreans understood the world. Buddhism's cultural presence straddled the social hierarchy, reaching down to the peasants. Pure Land Buddhism and the cult of Amida (Sanskrit: Amitābha) promised rebirth in the Western Paradise to all, and the compassion of Bodhisattva Kwanŭm (Sanskrit, Avalokiteśvara) promised intercession in a variety of life's difficulties.

If the fortunes of Buddhism officially waned during the Chosŏn, the fate of *musok* was consistently dire, with its rites routinely referred to as *ŭmsa*, or "obscene." Like Buddhism, however, these ritual technologies maintained a secure place on all levels of Korean society, and the tradition of *musok* formed the most basic substratum of folk religion. The *musok* rite, known as *Kut* (Tungus, *kutu*), means "happiness" and "good fortune," and it was performed for private individuals and families, as well as for the community. The basic categories of *Kut*, which continue to the present day, were mortuary rites for ancestors, healing rites, and good-luck rites that invoked heavenly and natural spirits, as well as village tutelary gods. Significantly, *mudang* maintained their presence even in the Chosŏn palaces, where special buildings were prepared for them. The *mudang* who had access to these residences were known as *kongmu*, or "national shamans."

From the Confucian perspective, the most offensive aspect of *Kut* was perhaps its liminoid qualities, in which uninhibited dancing and singing induced frenzied trance in the *mudang* and the abandonment of decorum by everyone else present. This is the reason behind the designation *ŭmsa*, or obscene rites. The strict rules of relation between parents and children, mothers-in-law and daughters in-law, and village hierarchies were temporarily suspended for cathartic celebrations in which spirits and humans enjoyed themselves and entertained each other into a renewed harmony. Unlike Confucian ancestral rites, in which social order and familial obligations are sanctified, *musok* rites were dramatic, improvisational affairs in which personal feelings and grievances are aired by humans and spirits alike.

The significant difference between the Confucian concept of ancestors and the human spirits propitiated by *Kut* bears elaboration here. The basic purpose of Confucian ancestor worship is to define and revere the family line, which is traced through the male side. The continuity of the clan is maintained through marriage and the birth of legitimate male offspring. Firstborn sons carry out the ancestral rites, which pay homage to agnatic ancestors who have bequeathed property to the descendents. This selective definition of ancestors not only excludes collateral family members, such as second-born sons, daughters, secondary wives, and concubines, but also eliminates anyone who has died a violent or unnatural death. *Musok*, on the other hand, is attentive to these very ancestors who have reason to be restless and troublesome to the living. In addition to those who die before their time, there are others whose lives are "incomplete," such as females who never marry and mothers who fail to bear legitimate heirs. In addition, there are those who are disgruntled simply because they are ignored by their descendents. It is these "polluted" ancestors to which *musok* attends, not with the formality and decorum of Confucian rites but with complete abandon to interpersonal drama.

The inherent drama of the *Kut*, with its tradition of music, song, and dance, is not limited to family affairs. Shaman songs (*muga*), particularly in the southern region of Korea, took on the form of epic recitations that recount creation myths and the stories of heavenly gods. The function of the recitation was to summon the spirits to the *Kut*. From a purely cultural perspective, *muga* has become the repository of folk literature that exhibits popular Buddhist and Confucian worldviews as well as shamanic beliefs. In the "Ballad of the Abandoned Princess" (*Pari kongju muga*), for example, a filial daughter travels to the underworld in order to fetch medicine for her parents, in a tale quite reminiscent of the story of Mulien. The saga is populated by *bodhisattvas*, as well as the Buddha himself, and the plot is driven by the law of karmic retribution. The princess's parents fall ill due to their sin of abandoning their daughter, but the princess's Confucian piety drives her to save her parents, nonetheless. She is rewarded with deification, and her sons become the Ten Kings of the underworld. This *muga* is recited during mortuary *Kut*s to assist the dead safely through the underworld.

A cultural legacy of *muga* is a form of oral performance and storytelling called *p'ansori* that formed in the early eighteenth century. *P'ansori* is secular entertainment that arose among the lower classes but that grew popular across all levels of society. Its limited repertoire of stories derives in part from *muga*. The tale of Simchŏng, in which a filial daughter saves her blind father by sacrificing herself to the Dragon King, survives both as a *p'ansori* tale and *muga* recitation. The most popular of *p'ansori* tales—that of Chunhyang—also expresses the prototypical elements of the oppressed or socially disadvantaged female who preserves her familial devotion (in this case, to her husband) despite severe trial, and who is rewarded in the end. The prominence of female protagonists certainly reflects the preponderance of female *mudangs*, who are also lowborn and socially disadvantaged. The plight of such women in these tales, however, came to represent all of those who suffer from social inequity, including, at times, the entire peoples of Korea under foreign domination.

P'ansori performances are given by a single storyteller, the *kwangdae*, who narrates and acts out the characters. Much like the *mudang*, who summons a pantheon of spirits for the assembled participants, the *kwangdae* enlivens the tale's dramatis personae for an audience. A good performing voice is a requisite for both *mudang* and *kwangdae*, both of whom are accompanied by the all-important drum. The *kwangdae*'s only prop is a fan, which can stand for any object, and it is a standard implement (among many others) of shamanic *Kut*. The most compelling aspect of *p'ansori* performance is the *kwangdae*'s ability to improvise upon a standard oral text and to customize it in interaction with the audience. The livelihood of the *mudang*, too, rests upon her ability to negotiate the *Kut* and bring her clients and spirits into a communication that is satisfying and therapeutic.

THE MODERN PERIOD. Korea's modern era begins in the late nineteenth century, when Japan, followed by the United States, the United Kingdom, and Germany, broke down the barriers of the "hermit kingdom" by insisting upon trade treaties. This enforced internationalization showed up the internal weaknesses of Korean society, particularly of its rulers, and the outcome was loss of self-rule to the Japanese between 1910 and 1945. Even after liberation from colonial rule, Korea's dependency on foreign powers led to the north-south division of the country under Soviet and U.S. patronage, respectively. On June 25, 1950, the communist north launched an attack on South Korea, creating the civil conflict that concluded three years later with the north-south division firmly reinforced.

The transmission of Christianity. The opening of Korea to the West also meant the advent of Christianity. Jesuit missions in China in the seventeenth century led to a modest infiltration of Catholicism into Korea. Although missionary attempts to gain entry into Korea largely failed, Jesuit tracts on Christian doctrine found their way in. In the eighteenth century, these pamphlets drew the interest of politically disenfranchised aristocrats. Members of the *namin* ("southern") faction, in particular, formed themselves into a church after Yi Sŭnghun (1756–1801) received baptism from a priest in Beijing and returned to Korea to evangelize. Throughout the nineteenth century, however, the Korean court suppressed Catholicism, in part due to fear of the *namin*, in part because of the importation of the rites controversy from China. The major reason, however, was the association of Catholicism with the aggression of Western powers against Korea. During this period, Catholicism lost its foothold within the aristocracy and shifted largely to petty bureaucrats and peasants, whose persecution made them particularly receptive to a theology of suffering as represented by the Passion of Christ. The Catholic population numbered around fifteen thousand in 1857 but was cut nearly in half by the Great Persecutions from 1866 to 1871, in which eight thousand Catholics were executed.

The story is quite different for the Protestant evangelization of Korea, which began even while Catholics were suffering martyrdom. The seminal event was the arrival in Manchuria of the Scottish Presbyterian missionary John Ross (1842–1915) in 1874. From there Ross succeeded in publishing a Korean translation of the New Testament, as well as a dictionary and grammar of the Korean language. Hence, even before the arrival of official missionaries to Korea, a Protestant Korean community existed in Manchuria, and the circulation of the Bible and native evangelization had begun in Korea itself. Before the end of the century, an array of Presbyterian, Methodist, and Anglican missionaries from Europe and America established themselves. When the American Presbyterian Dr. Horace Allen saved the life of Prince Min in the wake of a palace coup in 1884, Western medicine and Protestant missions received sanction from the Korean king and queen. Dr. Allen's petition to establish a Western medical institution—the Kwanghye-wŏn—was readily granted and opened the following year.

The social and altruistic outreach of Protestant missions was a significant factor in their missionary success. In addition to hospitals, Protestants established the first modern schools in Korea, creating the foundation for the contemporary educational infrastructure, in which forty universities and nearly three hundred schools are of Christian provenance. By the first decade of the twentieth century, seminaries were opened to train native clergy, and the first generation of Korean ministers was ordained prior to the Japanese annexation in 1910, when the Protestant population had already reached 1 percent of the country. Protestant Christianity was the welcome harbinger of progress and new learning, and the Korean court and aristocracy looked increasingly to the West for aid and even personal protection.

The phenomenal success of Protestantism made Christianity respectable overall, and by the turn of the century, the fortunes of Catholicism had also improved. By 1880 the persecution of Catholics had tapered off significantly, and by 1900 there were ten native Korean priests. After surviving the suppressions of the Japanese colonial government and the persecutions by the communist north, Korean Christianity in the Republic of Korea entered a period of uninhibited growth in the 1960s. The gap in Protestant and Catholic success maintained itself, however. According to the 1995 national census, self-identifying Catholics numbered almost three million, whereas Protestant adherents reached nine million, representing 20 percent of the population.

The extraordinary growth of Protestantism in the twentieth century can be attributed initially to the goodwill generated by its philanthropic and social activism. But with the parity of the Catholic Church in these respects since the Second Vatican Council (1962–1965), other factors appear to be at play. Protestantism was from the beginning comparatively more open to native Korean culture, hence encouraging deeper implantation. It translated the Bible into the Korean *han'gul* script, whereas Catholicism favored Chinese translations. It chose the native Korean *musok* term *hanŭnim* for God, whereas Catholicism favored the Sino-Korean *ch'ŏnju*, which imports a set of Chinese meanings. The explosion of evangelical Protestantism since the 1960s is notable for its emphasis on faith healing, with its obvious parallel to *musok* practice.

Like Buddhism, Christianity swept into Korea with a wholly new and sophisticated complex of beliefs, rituals, and institutions. The dramatic ascendance of a new religion in Korea seems to rely upon a combination of such innate complexity, which inspires conversion and adherence, on the one hand, and an ability to adopt or equal key paradigmatic functions of Korean religiosity, on the other. The history and evolution of the syncretic religion known as Ch'ŏndogyo ("Heavenly Way Teaching") offers an interesting counterexample. Ch'ŏndogyo initially began as the Tonghak ("Eastern Learning") movement led by Ch'oe Che'u (1824–1864), who was executed for being a Catholic. Tonghak was actually a mixture of Christian, Buddhist, and Daoist elements with a strong nationalist overlay. Its primarily characteristics, however, are a belief in a supreme heavenly ruler and the practice of healing. In spite of these central religious elements, the numbers of followers have dramatically declined in the course of the twentieth century. This suggests that Ch'ŏndogyo is fated to be an epoch-specific movement that could not long survive the death of its charismatic founder nor compete against the doctrinal and infrastructural sophistication of Christianity.

The survival of *musok*. The advent of Christianity in Korea, as with the arrival of Buddhism in an earlier age, has not spelled the demise of native shamanism. To be sure, the modern age produced new adversaries of *musok*—Christians, Japanese colonialists, and communists alike vilified the persisting tradition as an ancient superstition in need of eradication. On the other hand, foreign aggression toward Korea, as well as the north-south national division, spurred both scholarly and popular interest in *musok* as the survival of a united folk (*minjung*) culture. As a result, in the twentieth century Korean and Western scholars devoted serious attention to *musok* and *mudangs*, providing detailed ethnographic accounts of contemporary practice.

A notable feature thereof is the existence of two distinct kinds of Korean shamans, the charismatic *kangsinmu*, who predominates in the northern and central parts of Korea (but who can be found throughout the peninsula), and the hereditary *sesŭmmu*, who are found in the southern Chŏlla and Kyŏngsang provinces. These latter *mudang* are also known as *tan'gol mudang*, named for the regional districts (*tan'gols*) over which they preside, and they can be distinguished from the *simbang* of Cheju Island (located off the southern coast of Korea), which forms a distinct shamanic region. Both *tan'gol* and *simbang mudangs* are *sesŭmmu* who inherit the authority to preside at shamanic rituals, but quite distinctively, they do not experience the descent of spirits into their bodies. Their primary role is to entertain the gods with songs and dances, but they do not interact directly with the spirits.

True to the dynamic of institutional charisma, the hereditary shamans inherit their spiritual authority and maintain it through their ritual expertise. Shamanism in this instance is a family profession, and the personal history of the shaman is not at issue, nor is her ability to be possessed by the gods. Personal contact with the gods, and their inherent power, are in fact of secondary importance relative to the power of the ritual itself. As an institutionalized form of *musok*, hereditary shamanism functions as a cultural performance that is as artistic as it is religious. The evolution of *p'ansori* from the mythic recitations of *sesŭmmu* demonstrates how *musok* has expanded into a broader cultural tradition.

Kangsinmu, on the other hand, keeps alive the tradition of spirit possession that is at the center of shamanic practice. Rather than inheriting their role, these *mudangs* typically exhibit symptoms of "spiritual sickness" that can last for years until they are initiated as *mudangs* through an exorcism *Kut.* The illness is believed to be caused by spirit possession, and the subject's descent into physical and mental illness can only be cured by a shamanic ritual in which she identifies the god inhabiting her body. From there on, the subject apprentices herself to a senior *mudang* in a spiritual mother/daughter relationship until she becomes a fully initiated shaman. If the subject gives up this function as a *mudang* for a prolonged period of time, the spiritual illness returns.

The overwhelming majority of *kangsinmu* are female. The female-to-male ratio of *mudangs* is estimated to be between 80 to 20 and 70 to 30. The term *mudang* is now reserved for female shamans, generally, and male shamans are known as *paksu.* Although the ritual authority of *sesŭmmu* is passed down through the male line, women also play the dominant role (except on Cheju Island), marrying into shaman families and apprenticing with the mother-in-law, who passes on her ritual expertise. The son/husband learns how to sing and play instruments for the purpose of assisting in the mother's/wife's rites.

The gender disparity has led observers to note that *musok* is a religious and cultural realm that empowers women, particularly of the lower class. The informal, improvisational, and intuitive qualities of shamanic rituals (particularly of the *kangsin* variety) also suggest a female domain in contrast to the formal and male-centered rituals of Confucianism, Buddhism, and Christianity.

Kut is most often sponsored by a family or village in the event of misfortune—typically diseases but also natural disasters, accidents, and deaths. Before a full-scale *Kut,* which can last up to three days, is determined to be necessary, the *mudang* will perform divination to determine the cause of the misfortune and the necessary extent of the remedy. Most often, possession by troublesome spirits who have been neglected or ill-treated are the culprits. These ancestral spirits or gods are placated by prayer and ritual offerings and then driven out, often through a sacrificial scapegoat such as an animal or a doll.

A full scale *Kut* is performed in the event of grave and prolonged disease, assuming the adequate financial resources of the sponsoring family. Its central element consists of the descent of the spirit into the *mudang.* The identity of the spirit is determined through divination, and the possessed *mudang* proceeds to talk, cajole, complain, cry, dance and otherwise interact with the assembled participants. The spirit's presence through the *mudang's* body allows family members to address departed relatives, often on matters of unresolved grief or misfortune—the deceased's suicide or untimely death, for example. The outpouring of tears, resentments, and feelings address not only past history and suffering but ongoing conflicts between living family members and/or neighbors.

Musok still has its image problems, particularly among the educated adherents of Confucianism, Buddhism, and Christianity. The press toward modernization in South Korea since the 1960s, moreover, condemned shamanism as irrational and regressive. It is interesting to note, however, that at the end of the twentieth century, barely half of the population self-identified with the three aforementioned "great traditions." Although *musok* was not classified as a religion with which to self-identify, its persistence is evident in its rehabilitation as native *minjung* culture. Since the 1980s South Korea's emergence as a global economic power has expressed itself through the state's rapid westernization, on the one hand, and through the self-conscious formation of a unique national identity, on the other. Hence, while private *Kuts* have been banned for being too noisy in urban areas such as Seoul, public performances routinely sponsored by cultural centers and universities have taken their place. Accordingly, even Koreans who do not partake of *Kut* in a religious vein nevertheless affirm it as an important cultural performance.

For their part, *mudangs* quite consciously embrace the role of preservers of Korean culture and identity. The alliance between *musok* and Korean nationalism took on an explicit political dimension with the formation in 1971 of the Korean Spirit Worshippers' Association for the Victory over Communism. The anticommunist sentiments of *mudangs* can be traced back to their persecution under the North Korean regime. This experience has spawned fear for their fate in the event of a North Korean takeover of the South. The response has been to enhance the traditional role of the *mudang* as a protector of the state. The modern *musok* pantheon includes not only Tan'gun as the progenitor of the Korean peoples but also military heroes who have defended Korea's sovereignty in the past. *Kuts* often include a portion known as the "state *Kut*" in which the *mudang* prays for the welfare of the Republic of Korea and its president.

In the meantime, *musok*'s presence finds inroads even into the newest of the great traditions—Protestant Christianity—in the form of *minjung* theology. Like liberation theologies around the world, *minjung* theology speaks directly to the suffering of the ethnic and national community, caused by centuries of political and social misrule, both foreign and domestic. In underscoring the people, or *minjung,* as the primary theological entity, this indigenized Christianity parlays biblical narratives of emancipation and salvation into the story of the Korean people. In defining the people, *minjung* theology looks in particular to cultural performances such as *musok,* as well as to other folk traditions, as its locus.

CONCLUSION. The history of religions in Korea is characterized by both innovation and conservatism. As a small peninsular state subject to the presence and influence of much mightier nations, Korea has embraced a steady flow of religious innovation in the forms of Buddhism, Confucianism, and Christianity. These new traditions have been adopted with a sense of ownership that at times sees itself as the most faithful bearer of the originally foreign religion. In this respect, one can note the relative absence of xenophobic rhetoric against these adoptive traditions, in contrast to the history of, say, Buddhism in China and Japan.

It is this same faithfulness that has preserved and perpetuated the native shamanistic religion of *musok* throughout the periods of religious innovation. Although it has been vilified since the establishment of Buddhism, *mudangs* have provided a fundamental technology for dealing with the basic predicaments of illness and misfortune—predicaments that visit the privileged and the educated as well as the poor. While lacking in doctrinal and metaphysical sophistication, *musok* conveys a therapeutic, interpersonal, performative, and communal value that accounts for its longevity and pervasiveness.

BIBLIOGRAPHY

The most general introduction to Korean religions is offered by James Huntley Grayson's *Korea—A Religious History,* 2d ed. (New York, 2002). Its attention to Korean shamanism is relatively brief compared to other religions, but it nevertheless offers a comprehensive survey of Korean religious history. Grayson's *Early Buddhism and Christianity in Korea* (Leiden, Netherlands, 1985) considers more closely the factors that led to the implantation of these religions in Korea, and his *Myths and Legends from Korea* (London, 2001) deals with native Korean materials, such as the Tan'gun myth.

English-language scholarship on Korean shamanism by Korean scholars has proliferated in the past few decades. Monographs worthy of mention begin with Kim Tae-kon's *Korean Shamanism—Muism* (Seoul, 1998), which focuses on contemporary rituals, beliefs, and social organization. Hyun-key Kim Hogarth's *Korean Shamanism and Cultural Nationalism* (Seoul, 1999) consists of the same general introductory materials but includes a useful discussion of the Tan'gun myth in relation to Korean national identity (chapter 6). Hogarth's *Syncretism of Buddhism and Shamanism in Korea* (Seoul, 2002) consists primarily of separate discussions of the history of these two traditions but offers useful considerations of contemporary syncretic practices. Her full translation of three popular *muga,* or shamanic epic songs, is of particular value, but the analysis is limited to literary and structural interpretation. A study of the historical evolution of the oral storytelling tradition of *p'ansori* from the synthesis of Buddhist narrative elements and shamanic performance has yet to be written. Both the Hogarth titles and the Kim title are published in the Korean Studies Series of Jimoondang Publishing Company of Seoul. These monographs consist to a large degree of the personal reportage of the authors, who are cultural insiders and who are aligned with the contemporary native view that *musok* embodies an enduring cultural tradition.

Ethnographic studies of *mudangs,* particularly in terms of their experience as women, have been the norm of scholarship based in the West. Standard titles include Youngsook Kim Harvey's *Six Korean Women: The Socialization of Shamans* (St. Paul, Minn., 1979), which analyzes the life histories of *kangsinmu;* and Laurel Kendall's *Shamans, Housewives, and Other Restless Spirits* (Honolulu, 1985), which frames *mudang* rites and beliefs in relation to the social realities of Korean women. Kendall followed up this work with *The Life and Times of a Korean Shaman: Of Tales and the Telling of Tales* (Honolulu, 1988). Roger L. Janelli and Dawnhee Yim Janelli detail the structures of Korean family, kinship, and class in relation to ancestor rites in *Ancestor Worship and Korean Society* (Stanford, Calif., 1982).

A number of articles deal with the rise of folklorism in South Korea since the 1960s and the way *musok,* and peasant culture generally, have become the idealized foci of an anti-foreign *minjung* ideology. Kim Kwang-ok's "Rituals of Resistance: The Manipulation of Shamanism in Contemporary Korea," in *Asian Visions of Authority,* edited by Charles F. Keyes, Laurel Kendall, and Helen Hardacre (Honolulu, 1994), looks at how *Kut* rituals have been adapted by university students into dramas of political protest against the state in the 1970s and 1980s; and Chungmoo Choi's "Hegemony and Shamanism: The State, the Elite, and Shamans in Contemporary Korea," in *Religion and Society in Contemporary Korea,* edited by Lewis R. Lancaster and Richard K. Payne (Berkeley, Calif., 1997) traces the emergence of a culture industry in which media, scholarship, and political conflict drive the rise of superstar shamans who function as culture specialists and performers.

Two articles on Christianity in the previously mentioned volume, *Religion and Society in Contemporary Korea,* are worthy of mention. Kwang-ok Kim's "Ritual Forms and Religious Experiences: Protestant Christians in Contemporary Korean Political Context" links the explosion of evangelical Protestantism in the 1970s and 1980s with its political conservatism and its alliance with the government, and looks also at its indigenous, including shamanistic, elements. Donald Clark's "History and Religion in Modern Korea: The Case of Protestant Christianity" looks particularly at the development and beliefs of *minjung* theology and the question of its relation to shamanism. A native voice that clearly affirms the relationship can be found in theologian David Kwang-sun Suh's *Theology, Ideology, and Culture* (Hong Kong, 1983), in which he invokes the hybrid category of the "Christian *mudang*."

FRANCISCA CHO (2005)

KORESH, DAVID. On Sunday morning, February 28, 1993, David Koresh (1959–1993), the messianic leader of the small band of approximately 130 followers known as the Branch Davidians, dramatically captured headline attention throughout the United States. The Bureau of Alcohol, Tobacco, and Firearms (ATF) had staged an armed raid on Mount Carmel, the Branch Davidians' communal residence outside Waco, Texas. The rambling wood-frame building was home to forty-one men, forty-six women, and forty-three children under age eighteen, all fiercely loyal to their leader.

The ATF arrived at the property in an eighty-vehicle convoy including two cattle car trailers loaded with seventy-six heavily armed agents, while three helicopters circled overhead. A fierce gun-battle followed, lasting for several hours and leaving four ATF agents killed and twenty wounded. Koresh and four of his followers were also wounded and six others were fatally shot. Who shot first remains in dispute.

The ATF had a warrant authorizing it to search for improperly registered firearms. Koresh, claiming that the stockpile of weapons the Branch Davidians collected were all legally acquired and were for self-defense in case the government did try to interfere with its activities, said that he had nothing to hide and that when the agents charged the building with guns blazing he and his followers had acted in self-defense. The ATF maintained that its attempt to serve the warrant was met with a hail of bullets. Koresh and his followers refused to exit the building and surrender.

With federal agents dead the Federal Bureau of Investigation (FBI) was immediately called in and took over what became a fifty-one-day stand-off that attracted worldwide media attention. Although Koresh agreed to send out a selected group of thirty-five, mostly elderly folk and children, eighty-three Branch Davidians remained through the entire period. (Six Branch Davidians were off the property at the time of the raid.)

The stand-off ended on April 19, 1993, when the FBI attempted to force Koresh and his followers to surrender by an assault with tanks equipped to disassemble the building while inserting a military-grade tear-gas inside. After several hours, and not a single surrender, a fire mysteriously broke out and the entire place quickly went up in flames. How the fire began, and who might have been responsible, remains unresolved. At the end of the day, Koresh and seventy-three of his followers were dead, including twenty-one children. Only nine followers managed to escape the fire.

KORESH'S EARLY YEARS. Before this tragic confrontation with U.S. federal authorities David Koresh was virtually unknown outside his tiny band of followers, the bulk of whom were living with him in Texas.

He was born Vernon Howell on August 17, 1959, in Houston, Texas, to Bonnie Clark, a fifteen-year-old unwed mother. (It was not until he was thirty-one years old, in August 1990, that he legally changed his name to David Koresh based on his own messianic claims.) Howell's grandmother, Earline Clark, assisted in his upbringing during his early years. His mother married Roy Haldeman in 1964.

Howell grew up in various east Texas towns and eventually dropped out of high school in the tenth grade. He worked as a carpenter and took various other odd jobs. As early as junior high school, he showed an avid interest in three things: playing the electric guitar, working on old cars, and studying the Bible. He had an uncanny ability to memorize, and as a teenager could quote hundreds of chapters of the Bible with word-for-word exactitude.

KORESH'S SPIRITUAL DEVELOPMENT. When Howell was twenty years old he was baptized into his mother's Seventh-day Adventist Church in Tyler, Texas. He avidly accepted the basic doctrines of the Adventist denomination, including its belief that the nineteenth-century founder of the movement, Ellen G. White (1827–1915), was a divinely inspired prophetess of the last days.

Although Howell amazed all who heard him with his knowledge of the Bible, he was a vocal and controversial figure and began to develop certain apocalyptic views considered heretical by his church, causing his membership to be revoked. He was convinced that the "living voice of prophecy" had surely not ceased when Sister White died in 1915. He maintained that the Seventh-day Adventist Church had become complacent, lethargic, and worldly, having lost the original apocalyptic fervor generated in 1844 by the preaching of William Miller (1782–1849).

KORESH AND THE BRANCH DAVIDIANS. In 1981 Howell visited, and subsequently joined, the Branch Davidian community headquartered on the Mount Carmel property ten miles outside Waco, Texas. At the time, the group was led by Lois Roden, a former Seventh-day Adventist in her late sixties, who claimed to represent a continuation of the prophetic inspiration that had once resided with White. The origins of the group trace back to 1934 when Seventh-day Adventist Victor Houteff (1885–1955), a Bulgarian immigrant to the United States, broke with the parent body to form his own movement that he called the Davidian Seventh-day Adventists. He was convinced of his own prophetic gifts and saw as his divinely appointed mission the gathering of a final remnant group of God's faithful (144,000 taken from *Revelation* 7) before the imminent second coming of Christ. Lois and her husband, Ben Roden, had assumed leadership of the group in the early 1960s and the name Branch Davidian took hold. The Branch Davidians emphasized four main beliefs in contrast to the parent body:

1. A living succession of contemporary prophets following White.
2. The calling together of a remnant group of God's faithful and obedient followers.

3. The imminent return of Christ and his literal worldwide reign in Jerusalem.

4. The observance of the biblical Jewish festivals such as Passover, Pentecost, and the Feast of Tabernacles.

Howell's fervor, dedication, and particularly his vast knowledge of the Bible served him well. It became obvious to all that he was becoming Lois Roden's anointed successor, despite the opposition of her son, George. The two traveled to Israel together in 1983, and rumors of a sexual relationship, and even a nonlegal "wedding," were rampant. (Ben Roden died in 1978, three years before Howell's arrival.) In 1984 George Roden and Howell got into a gunfight when Roden claimed he could raise a deceased member of the group from the dead and Howell was trying to take a photograph of the corpse to show to the sherriff's department. By this time Howell was claiming to have received the Seventh Angel's Message mentioned in *Revelation* 10:7, thus joining the ranks of seven inspired end-time prophets that included, as Koresh counted them, Miller, White, Houteff, his wife Florence, and Ben and Lois Roden.

THE COMING OF A SECOND CHRIST. In 1984 Howell legally married Rachel Jones, the fourteen-year-old daughter of longtime Branch Davidian Perry Jones and Mary Jones. By this time he had become the dominant influence in the group and several of the leading members had accepted his claim to be the herald of the final prophetic message before Christ's return. In 1985 Howell and now-pregnant Rachel visited Israel where he, like Jesus of old, hoped to confound the rabbis in Jerusalem with his prophetic message.

It was there he had his greatest and most defining religious experience. He claimed that he was taken up to heaven, that he was shown and taught all the prophetic mysteries of the Bible, and that he was given the ability to open the book "sealed with seven seals" mentioned in *Revelation* 6. Implicit in this claim was the idea that Howell had become a kind of second Christ or Messiah figure, in that he, as the chosen "Lamb," was the only one in Heaven or on Earth empowered to open the Seven Seals. He subsequently took the name Koresh, the Hebrew name for the Persian king Cyrus, who is actually called a "messiah" in *Isaiah* 45:1. Just as the ancient Cyrus conquered the Babylonian empire, Koresh saw himself as a kind of spiritual counterpart who would vanquish the forces of the "Babylonian" governments of the world. The first name David signified his spiritual link with the messianic line of King David of ancient Israel.

David Koresh never claimed to be Jesus Christ, though he did claim that as a kind of second or final messiah, he had received the same level of inspiration that Jesus had received at his own baptism. He referred to this as the "Christ-spirit." He pointed to messianic texts such as *Psalm* 40 and 45 that he was convinced predicted the coming of a final "sinful" messiah who would appear at the end of the age. Not only would this figure have the normal weaknesses and "sins" of any ordinary human being, but he would marry multiple wives and sire children who were destined to rule with him in Jerusalem as King of the Earth. While Jesus would maintain his heavenly rule at the right hand of God, Koresh interpreted the second coming of Christ as the coming of a *second* Christ. Like Jesus, he, too, would be slain by his enemies, but would be resurrected thereafter to establish the Kingdom of God on Earth. Those faithful Branch Davidians who remained with him to the end would have places of honor in the new world government.

KORESH'S FINAL YEARS. In 1989 Koresh dissolved all marriages among the Branch Davidian members and instituted a policy of celibacy for the group. He promised each person that he or she would find his or her true soul mate when the Kingdom of God arrived. He took several of the women, some underage, and others previously married, as his own wives and fathered twelve of the children who died in the fire. Koresh claimed these special children were the firstborn of the new millennial generation, uncontaminated by the corruptions of society. (Although Koresh and his followers had been previously investigated for allegations of child abuse the Texas authorities had found no substance to the charges.)

Koresh prided himself as a Texan and a legal gun owner exercising his constitutional rights. The group was adamant that the stockpile of weapons they collected were all legally acquired and were for self-defense in case the government did try to interfere with their activities. Koresh had prepared his followers for a final confrontation with the forces of Babylon, as he called them. However, he expected that to happen in 1995, and in Jerusalem, not in Texas. The irony in the whole Waco tragedy is that the FBI unwittingly delivered to Koresh and the Branch Davidians a kind of preemptive apocalypse—but in a place and at a time that they never anticipated.

SEE ALSO New Religious Movements, articles on New Religious Movements and Millennialism, New Religious Movements and Violence, and Scriptures of New Religious Movements; White, Ellen Gould.

BIBLIOGRAPHY

Lewis, James R., ed. *From the Ashes: Making Sense of Waco.* Lanham, Md., 1994. An edited collection of essays dealing with various aspects of the Waco events.

Moore, Carol. *The Davidian Massacre: Disturbing Questions about Waco Which Must Be Answered.* Franklin, Tenn., 1995. A sharply polemical indictment of the Federal mishandling of all aspects of the Waco situation.

Reavis, Dick J. *The Ashes of Waco: An Investigation.* New York, 1995. A balanced account, but mostly critical of the government, by a seasoned reporter who spent months investigating after the tragedy.

Tabor, James D., and Eugene V. Gallagher. *Why Waco?: Cults and the Battle for Religious Freedom in America.* Berkeley, Calif., 1995. A full account that not only covers Waco and the theology of Koresh and his followers but also explores the more general issue of when and how groups get the label of "cult" in our society

Thibodeau, David, and Leon Whiteson. *A Place Called Waco: A Survivor's Story*. New York, 1999. One of the only full accounts from a member of the group who lived through the siege and survived the fire.

Wessinger, Catherine. *How the Millennium Comes Violently: From Jonestown to Heaven's Gate*. New York, 2000. Contains a chapter on "Waco" that offers a wider interpretation related to millennial visions and the issue of violence.

Wright, Stuart A., ed. *Armageddon in Waco: Critical Perspectives on the Branch Davidian Conflict*. Chicago, 1995. An excellent collection of academic essays dealing with all aspects of Waco and the matter of "cults" in our society.

JAMES D. TABOR (2005)

KOSMAS AITOLOS

KOSMAS AITOLOS (1714–1779), also known as Father Kosmas, was a Christian saint, priest, monk, popular preacher, and educator. Kosmas was born in Aitolia, Greece, and received his elementary education in his home province. After spending some time as a teacher, he entered the theological academy on Mount Athos then headed by Eugerios Voulgares, one of the eminent Greek educators of the eighteenth century. Shortly afterward, Kosmas became a member of the monastery of Philotheou (one of the twenty monasteries of Mount Athos), where he later was ordained a priest.

Within a year, Kosmas felt called to leave the monastery and become an itinerant preacher. With the permission of the patriarch of Constantinople, Serapheim II (r. 1761–1763), Kosmas began his preaching ministry, which lasted until his death by hanging in 1779 at the hands of the Ottoman authorities, who accused him of, among other things, being a Russian spy.

What alarmed the Ottoman authorities was the great popularity enjoyed by Kosmas. His honesty and direct manner of preaching in the language of the people, his reputation for sanctity, his frequent visits to remote villages and hamlets, and his total disregard for material possessions caused hundreds, sometimes thousands, of men and women to follow him while he traveled from village to village.

Kosmas preached a gospel of love and concern for the fair and just treatment of women and children. In addition, he laid great stress on education, founding ten secondary schools and over two hundred elementary schools. Often he secured both teachers and funds for these schools. He believed that an educated laity would be able to rise to a higher standard of moral and ethical living and thus be better prepared to resist the temptation, due to discrimination as well as social and economic pressures, to convert to Islam. Kosmas can truly be credited with effecting enormous changes in education and in the moral behavior of the people of western Greece and southern Albania.

Honored as a saint in his lifetime, Kosmas remains one of the most popular saints of the Greek Orthodox church. He has been given the sobriquet "teacher of the nation."

BIBLIOGRAPHY

A complete bibliography on Kosmas would include more than two thousand items. The best work on him and his times is Markos A. Gkiokas's *Ho Kosmas Aitolos kai hē epochē tou* (Athens, 1972). The most complete account of his teachings in English is my own book *Father Kosmas, the Apostle of the Poor* (Brookline, Mass., 1977).

NOMIKOS MICHAEL VAPORIS (1987)

KOTLER, AHARON

KOTLER, AHARON (1892–1962), was a rabbi and prominent educator in eastern Europe and the United States. A child prodigy, Kotler was sent as a youth to study in the famous *musar-yeshivah* of Slobodka (near modern-day Kaunas, Lithuania), which emphasized Talmudic studies as well as ethics and self-improvement. After his marriage to the daughter of Isser Zalman Meltzer, the head of the *yeshivah* in Slutsk, White Russia, Kotler moved to Slutsk and began to teach in the *yeshivah*. In the wake of World War I he moved the *yeshivah* from the Soviet-controlled area to Kletzk in Poland. There he became one of the best-known figures in Polish rabbinical circles. He was the youngest member of the Council of Scholars and Sages of Agudat Yisra'el.

In 1935 Kotler visited the United States, where he discussed the need for an American *yeshivah* that would be designed not for the training of rabbis and religious professionals but for the study of Torah for its own sake. The discussions came to naught and he returned to Poland.

Following the German occupation of Poland, Kotler immigrated in 1941 to the United States, where he was to have his most lasting influence. He was driven by the concern that with the destruction of the *yeshivot* in eastern Europe, new centers of Torah study would have to be established in America. Despite widespread doubt that the atmosphere of intense Torah study that had prevailed in eastern Europe could be re-created in the United States, Kotler persevered and in 1943 established the Beit Midrash Gevohah in Lakewood, New Jersey. The school was designed for students of post-high-school age, and its curriculum was made up solely of religious studies with no admixture of secular studies. The school grew rapidly and by the 1980s had more than eight hundred students. Active in the Jewish day-school movement as well, Kotler also helped to intensify Jewish education on the primary level. One result of his influence was a decrease of cooperation between Orthodox and non-Orthodox Jewish groups, for he was strongly opposed to the participation of Orthodox bodies in associations that included Reform or Conservative rabbis.

BIBLIOGRAPHY

There is no full-scale biography of Aharon Kotler. An interesting and highly complimentary study of the Beit Midrash Gevohah, which deals, of course, with Kotler, is Sidney Ruben Lewitter's "A School for Scholars" (Ph. D. diss., Rutgers University, 1981). Much relevant material can also be found in William B. Helmreich's *The World of the Yeshiva* (New York, 1982).

New Sources

Finkelman, Yoel. "Haredi Isolation in Changing Environments: A Case Study in Yeshiva Immigration." *Modern Judaism* 22 (2002): 61–82.

SHAUL STAMPFER (1987)
Revised Bibliography

KOU QIANZHI (373–448), Celestial Master *(tianshi)* at the Northern (Tuoba) Wei court between the years 425 and 448, an office that marked a unique era of Daoist ascendancy in Chinese political history. A member of a traditionally Daoist gentry family of Fengyi (Shaanxi), Kou at an early age developed an intense interest in such occult sciences as astrology, alchemy, and knowledge of transcendental herbs. At about the age of thirty (c. 403) he went into reclusion on the western sacred peak of Mount Hua (Shaanxi) with his master the Daoist adept Chenggong Xing (d. 412?), a student of the Buddhist monk and mathematician Shi Tanying (d. before 418), who had been a colleague of the great Central Asian translator Kumarajiva while the latter was in Chang'an (modern Xi'an) between 402 and 413. After a brief sojourn on Mount Hua the two traveled to the central sacred peak, Mount Song (in Henan). Chenggong died after seven years, and Kou continued his cultivation of Daoist arts alone on the mountain. In 415 he was rewarded with a visitation from the deified Laozi (Taishang Laojun), who delivered to him a document labeled *Yunzhong yinsong xinke zhi jie* (Articles of a new code to be chanted to Yün-chung musical notation), which corresponds to the *Laojun yinsong jiejing* of the present Daoist canon (Harvard-Yenching Index No. 784). At the same time the god revealed to him certain secret breathing and calisthenic techniques, and soon he began to attract disciples. Eight years later, in 423, when he was fifty, he was visited again by a divine being, this one a Li Puwen, who identified himself as Laozi's great-great grandson (*xuansun*). Li Puwen presented Kou with a second document, *Lutu zhenjing* (The true scripture of talismanic designs). It has not survived, but was probably similar to other collections of talismanic designs (fantastic characters) that can be found in the canon.

The *Yunzhong yinsong* appears to have been influenced indirectly by translations of the Buddhist Vinaya that had recently appeared in China. It set forth rules for the selection and ceremonial roles of religious officers and the conduct of ceremonies, confessionals, and charitable feasts (*chuhui*), and laid down principles for moral behavior among the "chosen people" (*zhongmin*), that is, among the adherents of the Celestial Masters Sect (Tianshi Dao). The code seems to have been directed specifically at reforming certain practices that had emerged since the founding of the sect by Zhang Daoling in the late second century and that were now felt to pose a threat to civic order in the Northern Wei state. These included the apocalyptic expectation of messianic deliverers (who often turned out to be fomenters of rebellion), the hereditary transmission of religious offices within particular families, and the extragovernmental levies of grain or silk (*zumi*) to support them, which tended to create subgovernmental enclaves within the state. The code was also directed against the sexual ritual known as the "union of vital forces" (*heqi*), which was seen as a threat to public morals. It is for these reasons that when in 424 Kou Qianzhi arrived in the Northern Wei capital of Pingcheng (in Shanxi), he was eagerly welcomed by such diverse constituencies as the non-Chinese Tuoba rulers and the Confucian-oriented minister Cui Hao (381–450). It was Cui Hao who sponsored Kou's induction into the Northern Wei administrative hierarchy as Celestial Master in 425.

In his alliance with Kou Qianzhi, Cui Hao had his own agenda. He was the scion of an old Chinese gentry family that looked forward to the restoration of a unified Han rule over the fragmented non-Chinese kingdoms of the north and the weakened Chinese exilic regimes of the south. Cui utilized Kou's essentially conservative *Yunzhong yinsong* as a spiritual base from which he could promote his own goals. He saw to it that the *Yunzhong yinsong* was promulgated to every corner of the Tuoba Empire, which at its peak included nearly all of China north of the Yangtze River and by 439 appeared ready to incorporate the south as well. He also took advantage of the confidence placed in him by Emperor Taiwu (r. 424–452) to institute some reforms of his own. These culminated in the devastating purge of the Buddhist clergy and the proscription of the Buddhist religion and confiscation of its monasteries between the years 444 and 446. Kou Qianzhi has been accused of instigating the attacks in an attempt to eliminate a rival faith, but this is unlikely, although his acquiescence is probable. His own master, Chenggong Xing, had studied with Buddhist teachers and had inculcated in his disciple a high regard for the foreign faith. Kou seems to have acquiesced in Cui Hao's purges primarily because they were also aimed at local heterodox cults (*yinsi*). It was these pockets of popular religion where blood sacrifices and other unacceptable forms of worship were still practiced which Kou, as head of an established Daoist orthodoxy, could not tolerate.

Kou Qianzhi's term as Celestial Master is sometimes compared to a theocracy because of the unique establishment of religion in the Northern Wei state, in which the Celestial Master as *pontifex maximus* mediated between the celestial divinities and the earthly ruler. The climax of Kou's career was the inauguration of the reign period "Perfect Ruler of Grand Peace" (Taiping Zhenjun), which lasted from 440 to 451. The title was unmistakably Daoist, recalling the ideal of universal peace proclaimed by the Yellow Turban leader Zhang Jue in 184. His movement, known as the Way of Grand Peace (Taiping Dao), was presumably based in turn on teachings found in the *Scripture of Grand Peace* (*Taiping jing*). In a magnificent public ceremony conducted on a newly constructed Daoist platform (*tan*) south of the capital, on New Year's Day of the year 442 Kou Qianzhi, splendidly arrayed in Daoist robes, personally presented to Emperor

Taiwu certain sacred talismans (*fulu*) in recognition of the emperor's sage virtue as "Perfect Ruler." The ceremony instituted a tradition of Daoist investiture that was continued by the Tuoba states well into the next century. The "theocracy," however, ended with Kou's death in 448. Four years later Taiwu was murdered by a palace eunuch. His successor, Wencheng (r. 452–465), was an ardent Buddhist and in an orgy of penitential restitution reestablished Buddhism as the state religion. Under him began the construction of the monumental cave-temples of Yungang that have come down to the present day.

SEE ALSO Daoism, overview article, article on the Daoist Religious Community.

BIBLIOGRAPHY

The primary source for Kou Qianzhi is the "Monograph on Buddhism and Daoism" (*Shi Lao zhi*) in fascicle 114 of the *Wei shu* (Beijing, 1974), pp. 3048–3055. The Daoist portion has been translated by James R. Ware in "The *Wei Shu* and the *Sui Shu* on Taoism," *Journal of the American Oriental Society* 53 (1933): 215–250. The most complete study of this text is found in Tsukamoto Zenryū's *Gisho Shakurōshi no kenkyū* (Kyoto, 1961), pp. 313–356. An annotated text of the "Articles of a New Code" attributed to Kou Qianzhi may be found in Yang Liansheng's "*Laojun yinsong jiejing jiaoshi*," *Bulletin of the Institute of History and Philology, Academia Sinica* 28 (1956): 17–53. Two secondary studies are my own "K'ou Ch'en-chih and the Taoist Theocracy at the Northern Wei Court, 425–451," in *Facets of Taoism*, edited by Holmes Welch and Anna Seidel (New Haven, 1979), and Anna Seidel's "The Image of the Perfect Ruler in Early Taoist Messianism: Lao-tzu and Li Hung," *History of Religions* 9 (1969–1970): 216–247.

RICHARD B. MATHER (1987)

KRAEMER, HENDRIK (1888–1965), was a Dutch historian of religions. Kraemer spent his professional career mainly in three significantly different settings: working with the Dutch Bible Society in Indonesia (1921–1935), serving as professor of the history and phenomenology of religions at the University of Leiden (1937–1947), and functioning as the first director of the Ecumenical Institute Chateau de Bossy in Switzerland (1948–1955). His guest lectureships included, among many others, a stay at Union Theological Seminary in New York (1956–1957), and the Olaus Petri Lectures at the University of Uppsala (February 1955).

Beginning with the Second International Missionary Conference held in Tambaram, India (December 1938), Kraemer played a major role in the ecumenical theological discussions on the relations between Christian faith and other religions. His works *The Christian Message in a Non-Christian World* (1938), *Religion and the Christian Faith* (1956), and *World Cultures and World Religions: The Coming Dialogue* (1960) explore this theme.

Among the less well known titles that are important for an assessment of Kraemer's work as a historian of religions and of how he viewed religio-historical data "in the light of Christ, the 'kritikos' of all things," four publications deserve special attention. The earliest of these is the article "Geloof en Mystiek" (Faith and Mysticism), which appeared in the missionary journal *Zendingstijdschrift "De Opwekker"* 79 (Bandeong, Netherlands Indies, 1934). Next is Kraemer's inaugural address in Leiden, *De Wortelen van het Syncretisme* (The Roots of Syncretism; 1937). Third is the study "Vormen van Godsdienstcrisis" (Forms of Crisis of Religion), originally published in *Mededelingen der Koninklijke Nederlandse Akademie van Wetenschappen, Afdeling Letterkunde,* n.s. 22 (1959): 103–134, and later reissued as a booklet (Nijkerk, n.d.); it is based on four lectures given in 1959 on the place of the history of religions in the faculty of theology. Finally, of particular interest are Kraemer's remarks on W. Brede Kristensen (who was his predecessor at Leiden) in the introduction to Kristensen's *The Meaning of Religion,* edited by John B. Carman (1960).

Without ever abandoning his earlier thesis of a discontinuity between the biblical revelation and all forms of religion—most radically expressed in his 1938 study for the Tambaram conference—Kraemer tried later, in his own words, "to improve upon" that view of "the non-Christian religions [as] . . . great human achievements" by paying careful attention to "the religious consciousness as the place of dialectic encounter with God" (*Religion and the Christian Faith,* p. 8). He affirmed religiosity as a fundamental aspect of human structure and as manifesting the permanence, amid various forms of religious crisis, of the *sensus divinitatis* and *semen religionis* "whatever the content of the 'divinitas' and whatever the quality of the 'semen'" ("Vormen van Godsdienstcrisis," p. 134). As the notion of "communication," including communications between people of different traditions, became a key concern for Kraemer in the later years, he stressed the need for participants in an interfaith dialogue to "be open to new insights through the instrumentality of contact with one another," and he called for "a real openness to truth wherever it may be found" (*World Cultures and World Religions,* pp. 356–365).

From 1938 onward the debate on Kraemer has focused on his theological views, and relatively little attention has been given to the question of the extent to which his theological perspectives and the categories derived from them influenced his description and analysis of world religions.

BIBLIOGRAPHY

Kraemer's extensive studies of Islam include his doctoral dissertation, *Een Javaansche Primbon uit de estiende eeuw* (Leiden, 1921); "Eenige grepen uit de moderne Apologie van de Islam," *Tijdschrift voor Indische Tall-, Land- en Volkenkunde* 75 (1935): 1–35, 165–217; and *Een nieuw geluid op het gebied der Koranexegese* (Amsterdam, 1962). Kraemer discussed Christian-Muslim relations in "L'Islam, une religion, un mode de vie: L'Islam, une culture; Points de confrontation entre l'Islam et le Christianisme," *Revue de l'évangélisation* 41 (1959): 2–38; "Die grundsätzlichen Schwierigkeiten in der

Begegnung von Christentum und Islam," in *Neue Begegnung von Kirche und Islam,* edited by Walter Holsten (Stuttgart, 1960), pp. 15–27; and "Islamic Culture and Missionary Adequacy," *Muslim World* 50 (1960): 244–251.

For a bibliography of Kraemer's works, see Carl F. Hallencreutz's *Kraemer towards Tambaram* (Lund, 1965), pp. 309–317. A comprehensive list of biographies and works of appreciation can be found in Jacques Waardenburg's *Classical Approaches to the Study of Religion,* vol. 2, *Bibliography* (The Hague, 1974), pp. 133–135.

New Sources

Perry, T. S. "The Significance of Hendrik Kraemer for Evangelical Theology of Religions." *Didaskalia* 9, no 2 (1998): 37–59.

Perry, T. S. *Radical Difference: A Defence of Hendrik Kraemer's Theology of Religions.* Waterloo, Ont., 2001.

WILLEM A. BIJLEFELD (1987)
Revised Bibliography

KRAMRISCH, STELLA (1896–1993), was an art historian and educator who specialized in the arts and cultures of South Asia. Born in 1896 in Moravia (then Austrian crown land, later a part of Czechoslovakia), Kramrisch worked steadily through a long century of intellectual ferment. She died in Philadelphia in 1993. Trained in part as a dancer, she brought firm visual skills to her analysis of India's artistic legacies and strong European standards to her insights into India's intellectual and ritual worlds. Many myths mask her personal history; her work was always the legacy she wished observed. She introduced European art-historical methods to many of her students in India, and her take on indigenous understandings of India's art to many students in the West. Her early labors were based on fieldwork and work with pundits on texts, and her interests ranged widely—from temple architecture and iconography to folk and textile arts—with a powerful commitment to all of the material cultures of South Asia.

Kramrisch was trained in Vienna and London—and by long living in India—with older mentors such as Joseph Strzygowski and Rudolf Steiner and, as prewar peers, such scholarly companions as Ananda Coomaraswamy, Alain Daniélou, Louis Renou, and Heinrich Zimmer. She traveled first to India in 1921, presenting herself at Rabindranath Tagore's Vishva-Bharati University at Shantiniketan, where she lectured until she was appointed at the University of Calcutta the next year.

Kramrisch moved from Calcutta to Philadelphia in 1950, invited by the Sanskritist W. Norman Brown to teach in the newly formed Department of South Asia Regional Studies at the University of Pennsylvania. She served as curator of Indian art at the Philadelphia Museum of Art from 1954 to 1979 and as emeritus curator until her death. Following her retirement from the University of Pennsylvania in 1969, she continued to train graduate students at the Institute of Fine Arts in New York for another two decades. She was throughout her work intellectually curious, alive to contemporary art but unfazed by intellectual fashions. One of her late essays was written for an exhibition of the artist Francesco Clemente.

One of Kramrisch's first experiences in India was to visit the great cave-temple dedicated to Śiva on the island of Elephanta in Bombay's harbor. Her long meditation on that deity led to an authoritative essay, "The Image of Mahdevā in the Cave-Temple on Elephanta Island," published in the Archaeological Survey of India's *Ancient India* in 1946; to her exemplary catalog and exhibition for the Philadelphia Museum of Art, *Manifestations of Shiva* (1981); and to her definitive personal study, *The Presence of Śiva,* in 1981. Kramrisch's final reformulation, "The Great Cave Temple of Śiva in Elephanta: Levels of Meaning and Their Form," appeared in 1984 in the proceedings of an international symposium held at the University of Pennsylvania in association with her Śiva exhibition.

Kramrisch's lifetime meditations on Śiva and the processes and stages of his manifestation were personal, rich, and fruitful. She saw his quintessential form at Elephanta finally as that of the eternal Śiva (Śad'ivā) and drew parallels between his three stages of emergence and the concept of a "triple body" for the Buddha. Her long exposure to India's myths and texts forms a rich mosaic in her later scholarship, impressionistic and literary in its presentation but deeply layered and felt (her students nicknamed *The Presence of Śiva* the "Stella Pur ṇā").

Kramrisch's early art-historical work in India moved her gradually from an ideological position brought from Europe to one recognizing India's praxis. She responded deeply to first-century BCE Buddhist sculptures from Bharhut and to the aesthetic merits of art in the Gupta period (c. fifth century CE). She matched texts to techniques to study Ajanta's Buddhist painting, explored medieval Kerala in South India, and finally focused her prodigious efforts on the Indian temple. Combining close knowledge of monuments with a study of available texts, Kramrisch attempted to restore knowledge of indigenous meanings to the Indian temple and its forms. Articles appeared over many years in *Ūpam* and the *Journal of the Indian Society of Oriental Art,* both of which she edited in Calcutta; then finally, written in sight of the Himalayas, her essential two-volume study *The Hindu Temple* was published by Calcutta University in 1946. Both essential and essentializing, Kramrisch's volumes returned the temple's architecture from a century of archaeological caretakers to its meaning as a manifest form of divinity. What they do not do is approach issues of daily and changing ritual. The history of Hindu architecture became instead "an exchange of forms within a community of symbols" (Kramrisch, 1946, p. 220). Without Kramrisch's emphasis on the temple's symbolic scaffolding, however, religious and architectural studies in South Asia might never have met.

Following publication of *The Hindu Temple* and throughout her many years in Philadelphia, Kramrisch combined curatorial entrepreneurship of a high order—organizing groundbreaking exhibitions, including The Art of Nepal (1964) and Unknown India: Ritual Art in Tribe and Village (1968) as well as The Manifestations of Śiva (1981)—with continuing text-based scholarship that increasingly sought for the origins of symbolism in Vedic literature. The essays "Linga," "Eka-Vratya," and "The Indian Great Goddess" were in part preparation for her major study *The Presence of Śiva* (1981), but in part they also document Kramrisch's retreat from her early encounters with praxis in India at a time when a new generation of scholarship had begun to delineate "temple Hinduism" through much different means. The fabric of her perceptions, however, continued to inform her deep engagement with the objects of India under her care, her sensuous and impassioned response to which remains a great part of her lasting legacy. That she was able to restore a religious dimension to an art and architecture largely subsumed by orientalist agendas, and to do so in the name of indigenous knowledge, had roots in early-twentieth-century thinking but flowered in India, fed by her living experiences as well as her scholarship. Her methodologies were as layered, personal, and reimagined, as are religious and aesthetic experiences themselves.

BIBLIOGRAPHY

Kramrisch, Stella. *Indian Sculpture.* Calcutta, 1933. This is an incomparable attempt to bring a European-trained vision to recreate indigenous categories for India's sculpture. Where Kramrisch is led by her eyes, not by European theories, her observations still can seem revelatory.

Kramrisch, Stella. *The Hindu Temple.* Calcutta, 1946. This is Kramrisch's definitive achievement. Initially planned as an introduction to an album of photographs by Raymond Burnier, these volumes have become a monument of twentieth-century scholarship.

Kramrisch, Stella. *The Art of Nepal.* New York, 1964. By means of this Asia Society exhibition, Kramrisch first introduced New York to the important art of this previously closed Himalayan kingdom.

Kramrisch, Stella. *Unknown India: Ritual Art in Tribe and Village.* Philadelphia, 1968. Kramrisch used her major exhibitions in the United States to break new ground, here introducing the art world (and in part India too) to "subaltern" artistic traditions she valued as much as India's courtly cultures.

Kramrisch, Stella. "The Indian Great Goddess." *History of Religions* 14 (1975): 235–265. This essay, a major example of Kramrisch's later scholarship, combines an understanding of the importance of India's essentialized "great" goddess and of her myriad and multiple sources.

Kramrisch, Stella. *Manifestations of Shiva.* Philadelphia, 1981. Kramrisch worked on this major exhibition for more than a decade to summarize her involvement with and knowledge of the great god Śiva.

Kramrisch, Stella. *The Presence of Śiva.* Princeton, N.J., 1981. It is difficult to say whether this volume, in which Kramrisch reprocesses all her knowledge of Śiva's myth, is a supplement to the exhibition above or the other way around.

Meister, Michael W. "Display as Structure and Revelation: On Seeing the Shiva Exhibition." *Studies in Visual Communication* 7, no. 4 (1981): 84–89. This review is a tentative exploration of Kramrisch's intuitive understandings of art and display.

Meister, Michael W., ed. *Discourses on Śiva.* Philadelphia, 1984. These are proceedings of an international symposium on religious imagery held in conjunction with Kramrisch's Manifestations of Shiva exhibition in Philadelphia.

Miller, Barbara Stoller, ed. *Exploring India's Sacred Art.* Philadelphia, 1983. This well-edited selection of a lifetime of Kramrisch's widely disbursed essays has a biographical introduction by Miller and a bibliography of Kramrisch's writings by Joseph M. Dye III.

Percy, Ann, and Raymond Foye, with essays by Stella Kramrisch and Ettore Sottsass. *Francesco Clemente: Three Worlds.* Philadelphia, 1990. Kramrisch throughout her life engaged with living artists. Clemente's interactions with Kramrisch and India are particularly fascinating.

MICHAEL W. MEISTER (2005)

KRATOPHANY SEE POWER

KRISHNA SEE KṚṢṆA

KRISHNAMURTI, JIDDU (1895–1986), an Indian spiritual leader, attained fame through his presentation of a unique version of Indian philosophy and mysticism in a charismatic, even mesmerizing style of lecturing that attracted large audiences around the world. Although Krishnamurti taught a philosophy that seemed to border on atheism, it is clear in his authorized biography that throughout his life he was subject to a profound spiritual purgation. This purgation came to be called "the Process" and suggested to those who witnessed it that his "higher self" departed from his body and entered into what appeared to be a transcendent state of consciousness. This state was accompanied at times by severe pain in his head and back. The suffering accompanying this experience occurred only under certain circumstances and did not impede his teaching work. In fact, it was understood to contribute to the exalted state in which Krishnamurti knew the oneness with all life and the unconditioned freedom that he tried—through his continual lecturing and the books, tape recordings, and videotapes published by his organization—to convey to thousands of persons under his influence.

Krishnamurti was born in Madanapalle, a small town in what is now the state of Andhra Pradesh, north of Chennai (Madras). He was of *brahman* caste. His mother, Sanjeevama, died when Krishnamurti was ten years old. His father, Narianiah, cared for Krishnamurti and his brothers until he retired from government service and was granted permission to move to the estate of the Theosophical Society, located at Adyar, just outside Chennai. This move occurred in January 1909, when Annie Besant was the international president of the Theosophical Society. Her close collaborator was Charles W. Leadbeater, whose clairvoyant powers, he claimed, enabled him to recognize Krishnamurti's potential for spiritual greatness when he observed the boy's aura as he was playing on the beach at the seaside edge of the Theosophical Society estate.

Leadbeater and Besant taught that the Lord Maitreya, the World Teacher, would become incarnate in this age in a manner similar to the way Śri Kṛṣṇa (the Hindu deity) and Jesus had appeared in the world in earlier eras. They taught that the Lord Maitreya was a master residing in the Himalayas in a place described by Leadbeater in a metaphorical and symbolic manner. The Lord Maitreya occupied the office of the Christ or the *bodhisattva* in the occult hierarchy of masters. Leadbeater and Besant expected that a portion of the consciousness of the Lord Maitreya would occupy an appropriate vehicle to present a teaching that would raise humanity's awareness of unity and lead to a "new civilization." Krishnamurti was a likely candidate to become the vehicle for such a manifestation, but it remained for him to be trained and tested before he could actually take on such a role.

Krishnamurti and his brother Nityananda, usually called Nitya, were understood to have been "put on probation" (i.e., rigorously tested and prepared for spiritual leadership) by a master in the occult hierarchy named Kuthumi on August 1, 1909, when Krishnamurti was fourteen years old. From that time onward Krishnamurti was nurtured and financially supported by a circle of upper-class English and American men and women and was under the scrutiny of the larger group of Theosophists who saw him at public gatherings.

Krishnamurti and Nitya left India in 1911 for their first visit to England. After their return to India, Krishnamurti's father allowed Krishnamurti and Nitya to be taken back to England for education by Besant, signing a document to that effect in 1912. By the end of 1912 Narianiah had filed suit against Besant to regain custody, charging that Leadbeater and Krishnamurti were involved in a sexual relationship. In 1914, after a judgment against her in the Indian courts, Besant won an appeal to the Privy Council in London. Both she and Leadbeater were exonerated from the charges brought by Narianiah. Krishnamurti and Nitya remained in England during this period and were prepared by a tutor for university studies. However, Krishnamurti was not able to pass the entrance examinations and never obtained a university degree, although he studied for many years privately and learned English, French, and some Sanskrit.

From about 1920 on, Krishnamurti's extraordinary gifts as a public lecturer and his independent viewpoint on the spiritual quest became evident. He spoke more and more frequently at gatherings of the Theosophical Society in India, the Netherlands, and North America. At some of these meetings he referred to himself in a way that implied he was speaking as the World Teacher. (Krishnamurti's brother, Nityananda, died of tuberculosis in Ojai, California, on November 13, 1925; Krishnamurti's struggle with the ensuing sorrow was formative of his judgment about the "bondages of the mind.") However, the articulation of his own special teachings alienated him from the inner circle of the leadership of the Theosophical Society, including Besant, Leadbeater, George Arundale, and C. Jinarajadasa, each of whom claimed to have received communications from the masters consisting of instructions for the Theosophical Society that were contrary to Krishnamurti's increasingly independent course. In 1926 Krishnamurti dissolved the Order of the Star, built up by Annie Besant, an organization of about thirty thousand members expecting the World Teacher. Besant's death in 1933 ended Krishnamurti's ties to the Theosophical Society. Krishnamurti was repudiated for some time by leading officials of the Theosophical Society. However, Jinarajadasa's successors to the presidency of the Theosophical Society, Nilakanta Sri Ram and Radha Burnier, sought cordial relations with Krishnamurti.

There was no apparent single turning point in the development of Krishnamurti away from and beyond the confines of the role created for him in the Theosophical Society by his early mentors Leadbeater and Besant. It is undoubtedly true that Leadbeater had a dominating and charismatic personality in his own right. Krishnamurti was the center of an extensive circle of young people who faithfully followed Leadbeater in the work of the Co-Masonic Order and the Liberal Catholic Church and other subsidiary organizations, including the Order of the Star, that provided—and mostly continue to provide—a total way of life for members of the Theosophical Society. Krishnamurti had been appointed a further pivotal figure in the formation of one of these groups, the Bharata Samaj, which offers a reformed Hindu ritual, based on Vedic mantras and traditional ceremonies, for Hindu members and others in the Theosophical Society. Under Leadbeater's direction, Krishnamurti had performed the first public rite of the Bharata Samaj, in effect as its first priest. (Priesthood of women is also allowed in the Bharata Samaj.) One can suppose that Krishnamurti's own internal spiritual dynamic had finally profoundly rejected the complex system of organizations and rituals increasingly promoted by Besant, Leadbeater, and other leaders of the Theosophical Society, as they believed, under the guidance of the masters. There is no other apparent explanation than a matter of temperament on Krishnamurti's part to reject these developments.

Ever afterward, Krishnamurti continued to express the emergence of his spirituality from a type of experience beyond all physical and particularly mental forms. It was the offering of that ultimate abstraction from all the inherited limitations of the million-year-old human brain (that he liked to refer to in evolutionary terms) that was the cause he promoted tirelessly until his death in his ninetieth year. To his most committed followers, it was this radical insight that drew them to try to grasp his teachings. To others in the Theosophical Society and elsewhere, his teaching was incomprehensible. In his later years Krishnamurti sometimes made comparisons between what the Buddha had taught and what he taught, and he also accepted such comparisons. But that seemed to be as far as he would go in defining his status. Pupul Jayakar records the context of these extensive discussions and dialogues in *Krishnamurti: A Biography* (1986).

Krishnamurti's work as an independent teacher eventually combined two approaches. First, he traveled around the world on a schedule of lectures. In India he spoke often in Chennai and Bombay, and occasionally in Delhi and Banaras. He lectured at Saanen in Switzerland, Brockwood Park in England, and New York City and Ojai, California, in the United States. Second, he founded several schools in the United States, Canada, Europe, and India, where students through high school age are instructed in ways to reduce aggression and to aid in acquiring Krishnamurti's universal insight. In his later life he participated in various dialogues with groups or individuals from the scientific community on the possible connection between his teachings and contemporary theories of, for example, physics. One of the last books he published, *The Ending of Time* (1985), was cowritten with David Bohm, a professor of theoretical physics at Birkbeck College, University of London.

Scattered throughout the Krishnamurti writings and in the various transcripts of discussions and dialogues are reports of the unusual psychic experiences of Krishnamurti when he was in touch with the source, beyond language or thought or the vacillations of the emotions, that convinced him of the correctness of what he taught. The following passage from Jayakar's biography was given in a dialogue in January 1980 in Bombay and speaks of the certitude Krishnamurti had that he was in touch with that which is beyond all limitations. The reader must judge whether Krishnamurti has succeeded in this and other similar statements in portraying the underlying reality or "emptiness" upon which he tried to construct the language to propose his doctrine of an absolute freedom for himself and humanity as a whole. It is on such a judgment that claims made about Krishnamurti as a World Teacher should be based.

> Recently, when I was in Rishi Valley [the location of his school in southern India], a peculiar thing happened. For several nights, one actually touched the source of the energy of all things. It was an extraordinary feeling, not from the mind or brain, but from the source itself. And that has been going on, in Madras and here. It is as though one was totally isolated—if one can so use that word without a sense of withdrawal. There was a sense of nothing existing except "that." That source or feeling was a state in which the mind, the brain, was no longer in operation—only that source was in operation. . . . So I am extremely careful to see that that thing remains pure. The word pure means clear, unspotted, not corrupted. It is like pure water, distilled water, a mountain stream which has never been touched by human mind or hand. (Jayakar, 1986, pp. 392–393)

From 1968 to 1986 Krishnamurti was involved in an increasingly bitter dispute with D. Rajagopal, Rosalind Rajagopal (D. Rajagopal's divorced wife), and other officials and workers in the company called Krishnamurti Writings, Inc., and in other organizations controlled by D. Rajagopal. Rajagopal had been an associate of Krishnamurti's from the early days of their connection with the Theosophical Society. As the World Teacher—however it was understood—Krishnamurti for many years did not take an active role in the management of the groups that gathered monetary contributions and gifts of properties and undertook to publish his many books. Rajagopal was in charge of most of these enterprises to the extent that he even allocated pocket money to Krishnamurti for expenses while traveling.

When the disputes finally erupted openly, from Krishnamurti's point of view, Rajagopal appeared to have mismanaged the work for his personal gain. Krishnamurti instituted legal proceedings in California, England, and India to recover money, property, and even publication rights to his own books. Rajagopal countersued, and approximately four major legal proceedings with various settlements developed. Krishnamurti severed all ties with Rajagopal's organizations. In their place he established the Krishnamurti Foundation, which in the early twenty-first century is his designated organization to disseminate his teachings.

It is important to note and even study the issues that were raised in the conflict between Krishnamurti and Rajagopal, because they are representative of the difficulties faced by the successors of a spiritual teacher who try to preserve both the integrity of the teaching and some kind of organization that will guarantee the survival of the teacher's charisma for future generations. Various strategies are in operation, but the most viable seems to be the appointment of someone, or of a group of individuals, who can embody and transmit the charisma. The twelve apostles of Jesus Christ are exemplary of this formula. Krishnamurti did not choose that route of succession and transmission. He seemed to believe that under a kind of corporate banner of his own devising—the Krishnamurti Foundation—his work can continue. The theoretical basis for the analysis of these issues in one of the Hindu systems is in Charles S. J. White's article "Structure and the History of Religions: Some Bhakti Examples" (1978).

See Also Besant, Annie; Theosophical Society.

Bibliography

Mary Lutyens's biographies, *Krishnamurti: The Years of Awakening* (New York, 1975) and *Krishnamurti: The Years of Fulfilment* (New York, 1983), were, according to Lutyens, read by Krishnamurti prior to their publication, and their factual contents and interpretations were approved by him. Emily Lutyens, *Candles in the Sun* (London, 1957) (Mary Lutyens's mother) recounts her relationship with Krishnamurti during the time she and others took charge of his welfare in adolescence and early manhood. The bond between them was one of the closest in Krishnamurti's life.

Krishnamurti's own *Krishnamurti's Notebook* (New York, 1976) contains firsthand descriptions of "the Process." Alcyone [J. Krishnamurti], *At the Feet of the Master* (Wheaton, Ill., 2001), has run to more than forty editions since it was first published in 1910. It recounts teachings from the Master Kuthumi that Krishnamurti received during astral projection while asleep and under the guidance of Leadbeater. For an analysis of the esoteric side of Krishnamurti's life experience, as against the often-repeated claims that Krishnamurti completely rejected occultism and religion in general, see Aryel Sanat [Miguel de Sanabria], *The Inner Life of Krishnamurti: Private Passion and Perennial Wisdom* (Wheaton, Ill., 1999).

Radha Rajagopal Sloss, *Lives in the Shadow with J. Krishnamurti* (Reading, Mass., 1991), by D. Rajagopal's daughter, recounts her long association with Krishnamurti but also criticizes Krishnamurti and justifies her parents' actions. To refute Sloss, the Krishnamurti Foundation published *Statement by the Krishnamurti Foundation of America about the Radha Sloss Book "Lives in the Shadow with J. Krishnamurti"* (1995); Mary Lutyens, *Krishnamurti and the Rajagopals* (1996); and Erna Lilliefelt, *History of the KFA: Report on the Formation of Krishnamurti Foundation of America and the Lawsuits Which Took Place between 1968 and 1986 to Recover Assets for Krishnamurti's Work* (1995), which contains much legal documentation. Catherine Lowman Wessinger, *Annie Besant and Progressive Messianism,* Studies in Women and Religion, vol. 26 (Lewiston, N.Y., 1988), discusses the role of Krishnamurti as the World Teacher promoted by Annie Besant. Pupul Jayakar discusses her personal relationship with Krishnamurti and records his ideas extensively and historically in *Krishnamurti: A Biography* (San Francisco, 1986). As with much else written about Krishnamurti, this work contains little analytical apparatus to help the reader understand its subject. Charles S. J. White, "Structure and the History of Religions: Some Bhakti Examples," *History of Religions* 18, no. 1 (1978): 77–94, discusses the issues surrounding a spiritual leader's succession and the transmission of his or her ideas.

CHARLES S. J. WHITE (1987 AND 2005)

KRISTENSEN, W. BREDE (1867–1953), was a Norwegian historian of religions. From 1901 to 1937, he was professor of the history and phenomenology of religion at the University of Leiden. Virtually unknown outside of Scandinavia and the Netherlands during his lifetime, he was the teacher of many of the next generation of Dutch historians of religions and has exerted some influence on methodological discussion through the posthumous publication in English translation of his class lectures at Leiden on the phenomenology of religion (*The Meaning of Religion,* 1960).

Kristensen was the son of a Lutheran minister, born in Kristiansand, Norway, on June 21, 1867. He went to the University of Kristiania (present-day Oslo) to study theology. After a year, however, he switched to the study of languages, which he later continued in Leiden and Paris. In addition to Latin, Greek, and Hebrew, he studied ancient Egyptian, Assyrian, Sanskrit, and Avestan. He did his dissertation research in the British Museum in London on Egyptian ideas of the afterlife and then returned to Kristiania to study and lecture on the ancient Zoroastrian text, the Avesta. In 1901 he was appointed to the chair of his teacher C. P. Tiele (1830–1902) at the University of Leiden, where he remained professor until his retirement in 1937; he lived in Leiden until his death in 1953. After World War II he returned briefly to Norway to give a course of introductory lectures on history of religions (posthumously published both in Norwegian as *Religionshistorisk studium,* 1954, and in a Dutch translation by Mevrouw Kristensen). Much of Kristensen's scholarly work consisted of papers dealing in some detail with various specific aspects of religious life in the ancient Near East. Many of the papers were presented at the annual meetings of the Dutch Royal Society. They were collected and published in two volumes in Dutch, *Verzamelde bydragen tot kennis der antieke godsdiensten* (Collected Contributions to the Knowledge of the Ancient Religions; 1947) and *Symbool en werkelykheid* (Symbol and Reality; 1954).

Kristensen rejected the prevailing evolutionist theory of his teacher and predecessor C. P. Tiele and tried to base his understanding of a given religion on its believers' own estimate of it; he found such estimates expressed in written documents, in languages he himself had learned to read. He believed that the religions of the ancient (preclassic) Mediterranean and Near East each had a distinctive nature but that all shared important underlying features basic enough to make comparison among them extremely fruitful. The aim of such comparison is not to define certain general ideas, such as the meaning of sacrifice, but to illuminate the meaning of some particular practice. In this respect the systematic work of the phenomenologist always remains in the service of the more particular investigation of the historian. For Kristensen, however, there was in practice very little difference, because he was interested neither in a philosophical theory of historical development in religion nor in tracing stages in the development of a particular religion. For him historical change becomes significant at the point that a particular religious apprehension comes to an end. The historian's task is thus not to focus on historical change but to find a bridge to understanding a vanished world of religious reality on the other side of the decisive change to the rationalistic consciousness of the modern world. Kristensen's work is full of polemics against this rationalism, not because he was antimodern, but because he felt that such rationalism led to the misunderstanding of ancient religions.

Kristensen did not regard informative comparison as a scientific method that would guarantee correct results. He sought to gain a certain inkling or intuition of what is important in the religion under examination, which requires in negative terms, that one not mix one's praise or blame with what the believer relates, and, in positive terms, that one seek a sympathetic and loving understanding of the alien faith. This understanding can be no better than approximate, because the alien religious language cannot be fully learned and because the other religion does not become a power in one's own life, but the effort is worthwhile, because across the barrier of languages and epochs and civilizations the truth perceived by believers in the alien religion can be glimpsed Those who make this effort can grow, Kristensen maintained, not only intellectually but religiously.

BIBLIOGRAPHY

An extensive bibliography of Kristensen's works can be found in Jacques Waardenburg's *Classical Approaches to the Study of Religion,* vol. 2, *Bibliography* (The Hague, 1974).

New Sources

Of Kristensen's many works, two have been translated into English: *The Meaning of Religion: Lectures in the Phenomenology of Religion,* 2d ed. (The Hague, 1960) and *Life out of Death. Studies in the Religions of Egypt and Ancient Greece* (Louvain, Belgium, 1992). For an application of the latter book's methodology see Giovanni Casadio, "Osiride in Grecia e Dioniso in Egitto," in *Plutarco e la religione,* edited by Italo Gallo (Naples, 1996), pp. 201–227. The definitive publication on all aspects of Kristensen's intellectual enterprise and his legacy to the discipline of religious studies is *Man, Meaning, and Mystery: 100 Years of History of Religions in Norway. The Heritage of W. Brede Kristensen,* edited by Sigurd Hjelde (Leiden, 2000). Prominent specialists examine the European and Scandinavian background (Hans Georg Kippenberg and Einar Thomassen among the others), Kristensen's contribution to the study of Ancient Religions (Anders Hultgård, Jan N. Bremmer, Jens E. Braarvig) and the foundation of religious phenomenology (John B. Carman, Willem Hofstee, Igvild Sælid Gilhus). A masterful essay by Jacques Waardenburg on "Progress in Research on Meaning in Religions" concludes the volume (a full, detailed bibliography of publications by and on Kristensen is included).

JOHN B. CARMAN (1987)
Revised Bibliography

KROCHMAL, NAḤMAN (1785–1840), was a Jewish philosopher and historian. A major figure in the Haskalah (Jewish Enlightenment movement), Krochmal is noted for his contributions to Jewish historiography and his program for a metaphysical understanding of Judaism using German idealist philosophy.

Born in the city of Brody in Galicia, Krochmal lived most of his life in the town of Żołkiew near Lvov. To supplement his traditional Talmudic education, he learned Latin, Syriac, Arabic, French, and German, giving him access to a broad range of medieval and modern philosophical literature. Despite an unsuccessful career as a merchant, Krochmal rejected the offer of a rabbinical post in Berlin and supported himself as a bookkeeper. His last years were spent in the Galician cities of Brody and Ternopol.

In the nineteenth century the large Jewish population of the Polish districts of the Hapsburg empire was an integral branch of the east European Jewish milieu both in its economic and social patterns and its traditional Jewish piety. Galicia was a center of Hasidism, as well as of rabbinic learning and leadership of Hasidism's opponents. Krochmal himself was a religiously observant Jew who was highly critical of the "delusions" and "folly" of the Ḥasidim, with whom he and his circle from time to time came into bitter conflict. Krochmal was one of the preeminent figures of the Galician phase of the Haskalah, then in its heyday and consisting of writers who advocated such reforms of Jewish life as the modernization of Jewish education and livelihood, a greater knowledge of natural sciences and European languages, and the introduction into Hebrew literature of the genres and ideas of modern European literature. A major aim of Krochmal's scholarship was to further the rapprochement between the modern rational, critical, and historical spirit and the Talmudic-rabbinic worldview.

Krochmal was a brilliant conversationalist but published little in his lifetime. After his death his papers were sent, according to his instructions, to the eminent German Jewish scholar Leopold Zunz, who edited and published them in 1851 as *Moreh nevukhei ha-zeman* (A guide for the perplexed of the time), a title deliberately reminiscent of Moses Maimonides' *Guide for the Perplexed.*

Krochmal's book is an incompletely developed but suggestive work that covers the following topics: the connection between philosophy and religion, the philosophical significance of the Israelite conception of God, the cycles of Jewish history in relation to the cyclical history of nations, aspects of postbiblical Jewish literature (including a pioneering treatment of the evolution of the *halakhah* and *aggadah*), the logic of Hegel, and the philosophy of Avraham ibn ʿEzraʾ.

Like Hegel, Krochmal conceived of the dynamic totality of reality as an absolute Spirit whose nature is pure cognition, which for Krochmal was the philosophical meaning of the God of Judaism. Like Hegel, Krochmal believed that religion conveys through the faculty of imagination that which philosophy conveys through reason, so that it is the task of philosophers to make explicit what remains implicit in religious imagery. The extent of Krochmal's indebtedness to Vico, Herder, Schelling, and Hegel has been a matter of scholarly controversy: Apart from his rendition of Hegel's logic and use of the terminology of post-Kantian idealism, Krochmal does not hold to a temporal unfolding of the absolute. Equally, if not more important to Krochmal's metaphysics were Maimonides, Abraham ibn ʿEzraʾ, and Qabbalah.

Krochmal grounded the truth of Judaism in a general concept of religion and cultural nationalism. The intelligibility of reality and the lawfulness of nature derive from a system of spiritual powers that, in turn, is generated by an unconditioned absolute Spirit. All positive religions intuit some aspect of this supersensuous reality. Moreover, a particular national spirit expresses the unity and individuality of the nation during its history. All nations are finite organic entities, passing through a cycle of growth, maturity, and death. Only the people of Israel have avoided eventual extinction, because their singular, infinite God is the dynamic principle of absolute Spirit that generated all the particular spiritual powers. The people of Israel were the "eternal people" inasmuch as they worshiped and were sustained by the force that accounted for the entire cosmic process and that renewed the spiritual strength of Jewish culture after periods of stagnation and decline. The God of Judaism did not change as the Jewish people passed three times through the cycle of national historical existence. The first cycle of national growth, maturity, and decay extended from the time of the biblical patriarchs to the destruction of Judaea in 587/6 BCE. The second cycle began with the return from the Babylonian exile and ended with the failure of the Bar Kokhba Revolt in the second century CE. The third commenced with the codification of the Mishnah, culminated in the philosophical and mystical flowering of medieval Judaism, and declined in the late Middle Ages. Krochmal does not explicitly develop the notion of a fourth cycle of Jewish history, but he probably envisioned such a rebirth as beginning in the seventeenth century or with the rise of the Haskalah. As the Jewish people passed through these cycles, the Jewish idea of God attained greater articulation and the meaning of the people's existence became transparent to reason.

Because Krochmal proposed a metaphysics that took Jewish history with the utmost seriousness, he can be seen as a pioneer both in Jewish religious thought and in modern theories of Jewish nationhood.

BIBLIOGRAPHY

The standard edition of Krochmal's works is *Kitvei RaNaK* (Writings of Rabbi Naḥman Krochmal), edited by Simon Rawidowicz (Berlin, 1924; reprint, Waltham, Mass., 1961). On Krochmal's place in Jewish thought, see Julius Guttmann's *Philosophies of Judaism,* translated by David W. Silverman (New York, 1964), pp. 321–344; Nathan Rotenstreich's *Jewish Philosophy in Modern Times* (New York, 1968), pp. 136–148; and Rotenstreich's *Tradition and Reality: The Impact of History on Modern Jewish Thought* (New York, 1972), pp. 37–48. Two articles of value are Ismar Schorsch's "The Philosophy of History of Nachman Krochmal," *Judaism* 10 (Summer 1961): 237–245, and Jacob Taubes's "Nachman Krochmal and Modern Historicism," *Judaism* 12 (Spring 1963): 150–164.

New Sources

Amir, Yehoyada. "The Perplexity of Our Time: Rabbi Nachman Krochmal and Modern Jewish Existence." *Modern Judaism* 23 (2003): 264–301.

Cooper, Eli Louis. *Am Segullah: A Treasured People.* New York, 1983.

Harris, Jay Michael. *Nachman Krochmal: Guiding the Perplexed of the Modern Age.* New York, 1991.

ROBERT M. SELTZER (1987)
Revised Bibliography

KṚṢṆA

KṚṢṆA, whose name means "black" or "dark," is customarily said to stand alongside Rāma in the Hindu pantheon as one of the two preeminent *avatāras* of the great god Viṣṇu. Although present-day Hindus do not dispute such divine genealogy, they and most of their ancestors who have lived in the last millennium have found Kṛṣṇa more important to their faith than Viṣṇu. In Vaiṣṇava circles one often hears it emphasized, in a quote from the *Bhāgavata Purāṇa,* that "Kṛṣṇa is God himself" ("Kṛṣṇas tu bhagavān svayam"; 1.3.27), not merely a portion or manifestation of the divine fullness. In the devotion of contemporary Hindus, he more than any other figure symbolizes divine love (*prema*), divine beauty (*rūpa*), and a quality of purposeless, playful, yet fascinating action (*līlā*) that bears a peculiarly divine stamp. In recent centuries Kṛṣṇa has been adored principally as a mischievous child in the cowherd settlement (Vṛndāvana) where he chose to launch his earthly career and as a matchless lover of the women and girls who dwell there. In earlier times, however, heroic and didactic aspects of Kṛṣṇa's personality have played a more forceful role in his veneration.

ORIGINS AND HISTORY. Many scholars feel that Kṛṣṇa and Viṣṇu were originally two independent deities. On this view, Kṛṣṇa is to be understood as more closely associated with a warrior milieu than Viṣṇu, since most early information about him comes from epic texts. Viṣṇu, by contrast, appears in the Vedas, so knowledge about him would have been transmitted by *brahmans.* It is unclear at what point in time the two cults merged, if they were ever truly separate. Certainly this happened by the time of the *Viṣṇu Purāṇa* (c. fifth century CE), which declares Kṛṣṇa to be an *avatāra* of Viṣṇu; yet there are a number of indications that the interidentification was much older than that. A pillar at Ghoṣuṇḍi has often been interpreted as implying that Kṛṣṇa was worshiped alongside Nārāyaṇa, who in turn is closely related to Viṣṇu, in the first century BCE; and in a series of icons from the Kushan period (first and second centuries CE) Kṛṣṇa bears a series of weapons associated with Viṣṇu: the club, the disk, and sometimes the conch.

The Kṛṣṇa to whom reference is made in each of these cases is usually designated Vāsudeva. This patronymic title is one he inherits as head of the Vṛṣṇi lineage of Mathura. Vāsudeva Kṛṣṇa liberates the throne of Mathura from his evil kinsman Kaṃsa; he struggles with the Magadhan king Jarāsaṃdha for continued control of the Mathura region and apparently loses; he travels to the western city of Dvārakā on the shores of the Arabian Sea, there to establish a flourishing dynastic realm; and he serves as counselor to his cousins the Pāṇḍavas in their monumental battle with the Kauravas.

Early reports of these actions are found in various sections of the *Mahābhārata,* and reference is made to certain of them in Patañjali's *Mahābhāṣya* (c. second century BCE) and the Buddhist *Ghaṭa Jātaka.* None of them, however, is depicted in sculpture before the Gupta period. Instead one finds sets of icons that imply no narrative context. One group of sculptures from the Kushan period depicts

Vāsudeva Kṛṣṇa in conjunction with his brother Saṃkarṣana/Balaramā and adds a third figure, a sister Ekānaṃśā, whose role in the epic texts is minimal and not altogether clear. Another set enshrines a different grouping, wherein Vāsudeva is accompanied by his brother and two of his progeny. This set corresponds to a theological rubric in force in the Pāñcarātra and perhaps the Bhāgavata sects, according to which Vāsudeva is said to be the first in a series of four divine manifestations (*vyuhas*) of Nārāyaṇa in the human realm.

In addition to the many icons of Vāsudeva Kṛṣṇa that survive from pre-Gupta times, one finds a handful of narrative reliefs, and these depict quite another aspect of Kṛṣṇa. This is Kṛṣṇa Gopāla, the cowherd, and he seems as distinct from Vāsudeva Kṛṣṇa in the texts as he does in sculpture. The texts report that although Kṛṣṇa was born into the Vṛṣṇi lineage in Mathura, he was adopted by the simple Ābhīra herdspeople of the surrounding Braj countryside for the duration of his childhood and youth. Only as a fully developed young man did he return to Mathura to slay Kaṃsa. The involvements of Vāsudeva Kṛṣṇa and Kṛṣṇa Gopāla are sufficiently distinct that it has been suggested the two figures were initially separate. On this hypothesis, Kṛṣṇa Gopāla would originally have been worshiped by the Ābhīra clan, a nomadic group that extended its domain of activity from the Punjab and Indus regions to the Deccan and Gangetic plains by the third century CE. As the clan expanded its terrain, it moved into the Braj region and would have encountered the Vṛṣṇis, whose mythology of Vāsudeva Kṛṣṇa was then integrated with the Ābhīra cult of Kṛṣṇa Gopāla.

THE SUPREMACY OF KṚṢṆA. The *Viṣṇu* and *Bhāgavata Purāṇas* (c. fifth and ninth centuries CE) clearly understood Kṛṣṇa in both his pastoral and royal roles to be an *avatāra* of Viṣṇu. In the *Bhāgavata,* however, which is the more important of the two, Kṛṣṇa occupies so much attention that the text is preeminently his. The same thing is true in the *Bhagavadgītā* (c. second century BCE), a portion of the *Mahābhārata* that vies with the *Bhāgavata Purāṇa* for the honor of being the most influential Vaiṣṇava text in the early twenty-first century. There, too, it is Kṛṣṇa who occupies center stage, not Viṣṇu. Indeed, Kṛṣṇa asserts that it is he who has issued forth in several *avatāras*, he who comprehends the many forms by means of which the divine makes itself manifest.

In the *Gītā* one has a glimpse of how Vāsudeva Kṛṣṇa could be interpreted as the supreme divinity. He enters the *Gītā* not as a combatant but as an adviser to his Pāṇḍava cousin Arjuna, who must fight. He himself is not implicated in the battle but is willing to serve as a resource. In the battle of life, similarly, one can act dispassionately by placing trust in the One who is too great to have any narrow interest in earthly conflict. Kṛṣṇa's oblique relation to the Pāṇḍavas' battle becomes a metaphor for his transcendence of the world altogether, and it enables Arjuna to transcend himself.

In the considerably later *Bhāgavata Purāṇa* one has a comparable vision of Kṛṣṇa's supremacy, but this time the supremacy of Kṛṣṇa Gopāla is more at issue than that of Vāsudeva Kṛṣṇa. Here the playful cowherd dances with all the milkmaids (*gopīs*) of Braj at once, multiplying himself so that each woman feels he is dancing with her alone. This amorous dance *(rāsa-līlā)* is an image of divinity and humanity wholly identified in one another, an absorption made possible by intense devotion *(bhakti).* Like Arjuna's encounter with Kṛṣṇa, this meeting, too, relativizes the importance of worldly involvements. In the *rāsa-līlā* the idyllic quality that always separated the pastoral life of Kṛṣṇa Gopāla from the royal world of Vāsudeva Kṛṣṇa attains its apotheosis.

The most important icon of Kṛṣṇa as the divine lover becomes prevalent in Orissa and Karnataka in the twelfth and thirteenth centuries and later spreads throughout the subcontinent. In this image Kṛṣṇa is shown with his neck tilted, waist bent, and ankles crossed as he plays his irresistible flute to summon the *gopīs*—symbolically, human souls—from their mundane preoccupations.

Two icons that enjoy a great prominence from Gupta times onward suggest still another way in which the supremacy of Kṛṣṇa Gopāla was experienced. One of these represents Kṛṣṇa lifting Mount Govardhana to protect the inhabitants of Braj from the angry, rainy torrents unleashed by Indra when at Kṛṣṇa's advice they turn their veneration away from that distant Vedic god and toward the symbolic center of the nourishing realm in which they live, Mount Govardhana itself. A second popular image shows Kṛṣṇa taming the evil snake Kāliya, whose presence had poisoned the Yamuna River upon whose waters all of Braj—humans and cattle alike—depend. In both moments Kṛṣṇa wrests order from chaos; in both he guarantees safe and habitable space; and in both he displaces and incorporates the powers earlier attributed to other figures in the pantheon. When he lifts the mountain he overcomes the sky gods captained by Indra, and when he tames the snake he subdues the nether spirits symbolized by snake deities (*nāgas*). The preeminence of these images of Kṛṣṇa as cosmic victor is only gradually displaced by that of Kṛṣṇa as cosmic lover in the course of time.

TWO FORMS OF LOVE. Kṛṣṇa is principally accessible to the love of his devotees in two forms—as a child and as a youth—and the affections elicited by each are distinct, though related. In systematic treatises such as the *Bhaktirasāmṛtasindhu* of the sixteenth-century theologian Rupa Gosvami, these two are described by separate terms. The first is "calf love" (*vātsalya*), the emotion felt by parents and especially mothers for their children, and the second is "sweet love" (*mādhurya*), the emotion that draws lovers together. Kṛṣṇa serves as the ideal focus for both sets of feelings. As a child Kṛṣṇa is impish and irrepressible, and modern Hindus adore him as such, displaying his most lovable moments on the calendars and posters that provide India with a great proportion of its visual diet. As a youth he is charming and unabashed; and in Rajput miniature painting as well as a strand of love poetry broad enough to include the Sanskrit *Gītagovinda* of Jayadeva and the Hindi *Rasikapriyā* of Keśavdās, he serves as the "ideal hero" or "leading man" (*nāyaka*) known to secular erotic literature.

In both these roles there is an element of contrariness that sets Kṛṣṇa apart from others. His mischievous deeds in childhood contribute greatly to his fascination and are epitomized in his penchant for stealing the *gopīs*' freshly churned butter. Kṛṣṇa's naughtiness and outsized appetite further stimulate the *gopīs*' desire to have him as their own, yet he can never be possessed. As the young lover he remains unattainable. Though he makes himself present to all the *gopīs* in his *rāsa* dance, he does so on his own terms, never allowing himself to be brought within the confines of a domestic contract. The love he symbolizes exceeds the bounds set by any relationship that can be conceived in terms of *dharma.*

Child or adolescent, Kṛṣṇa is always a thief, for he is a thief of the heart. Hence even Rādhā, the maiden whom tradition recognizes as his special favorite, frequently and powerfully senses his absence. Much of the poetry that has been dedicated to Kṛṣṇa is in the nature of lamentation (*viraha*). The women who speak in such poems give voice to the unquenched yearnings of the human heart, as in the following composition attributed to the sixteenth-century Hindi poet Surdas:

> Gopāl has stolen my heart, my friend.
> He stole through my eyes and invaded my breast
> simply by looking—who knows how he did it?
>
> Mother, father, husband, brothers, others
> crowded the courtyard, filled my world,
> As society and scripture guarded my door—
> but nothing was enough to keep my heart safe.
>
> Duty, sobriety, family honor:
> using these three keys I'd locked it away
> Behind eyelid gates and inside hard breasts.
> Nothing could prevail against efforts such as these.
>
> Intellect, power of discretion, wit:
> an immoveable treasure, never once dislodged.
>
> And then, says Sūr, he'd stolen it—
> with a thought and a laugh and a look—
> and my body was scorched with remorse.

In this mode it is the elusiveness of Kṛṣṇa that gives evidence of his divine supremacy. Intimately accessible as he seems, whether as child or lover, he can never quite be grasped.

CULT AND RITUAL. Kṛṣṇa is worshiped in homes and temples throughout India and has become the devotional focus of the Hare Krishna movement (International Society for Krishna Consciousness [ISKCON]) beyond Indian shores. Rituals vary from place to place and caste to caste, but some of the most impressive are those associated with the Gauḍīya and Puṣṭimārgīya Sampradāyas, which trace their lineage back to the fifteenth- and sixteenth-century divines Caitanya and Vallabha. In temples and homes belonging to these communities, Kṛṣṇa is worshiped in a series of eight daily *darśans* (ritual "viewings") in which the god allows himself to be seen and worshiped in image form by his devotees. His clothing, jewelry, and flower decorations may be altered many times in the course of a day, and different forms of devotional song are sung as the god's daily cowherding routine is symbolically observed. Vestments, food offerings, and musical accompaniment vary seasonally as well, with the festivals of Holī and Kṛṣṇajanmāṣṭami occupying positions of special importance.

In the Braj country surrounding Mathura, which attracts pilgrims from all over India in festival seasons, these ceremonial observances are amplified by dramas in which Kṛṣṇa makes himself available in an especially vivid manner to his devotees through child actors. These *brahman* boys native to Braj are thought to become actual forms (*svarūpas)* of Kṛṣṇa and his companions as they present events in Kṛṣṇa's childhood life. A dancing of the *rāsa-līlā* is the starting point for every performance, hence the genre as a whole is called *rāsa-līlā.* In Sanskrit aesthetic theory, drama is thought to comprehend all the arts, and owing to his essentially aesthetic nature Kṛṣṇa is more frequently depicted in Indian art, dance, and music than any other god. Drama is a particularly appropriate mode in which to experience him, however, because Kṛṣṇa's antics so clearly embody the Hindu conviction that life itself is the product of divine play (*līlā*). To surrender to play, to plays, and to the sense that all life is play, is to experience the world as it actually is.

SEE ALSO Avatāra; Bhagavadgītā; Holī; Kṛṣṇaism; Līlā; Rādhā; Rāma; Vaiṣṇavism; Viṣṇu; Vṛndāvana.

BIBLIOGRAPHY

Two works serve as basic references for the study of Kṛṣṇa. On the textual side there is the encyclopedic work of Walter Ruben, *Krishna: Konkordanz und Kommentar der Motive seines Heldenlebens* (Istanbul, 1944), and on the art historical side the somewhat more personal study of P. Banerjee, *The Life of Krishṇa in Indian Art* (New Delhi, 1978). A third major work, which calls for a wholesale reexamination of Bhāgavata religion and Kṛṣṇa's place in it from the sixth century BCE through the tenth century CE is Dennis Hudson's *The Body of God* (New York, forthcoming). A recent issue of the *Journal of Vaishnava Studies*—volume 11:1 (2002)—explores his ideas.

A broad study of materials relating to Vāsudeva Kṛṣṇa is provided in Suvira Jaiswal's *The Origin and Development of Vaiṣṇavism* (Delhi, 1967), critical portions of which are deepened by recent investigations on the part of Doris Srinivasan, including her "Early Kṛishṇa Icons: The Case at Mathurā," in *Kaladarsana,* edited by Joanna G. Williams (New Delhi, 1981). Several recent studies make it possible to enter imaginatively into the religious world of Braj, which is so thoroughly animated by Kṛṣṇa. My *At Play with Krishna* (Princeton, N.J., 1981) focuses on the *rāsa-līlās* of Vṛndāvana; Margaret Case's *Seeing Krishna* (New York, 2000) describes the ambience that sponsors and surrounds them; and David Haberman traces a pilgrims' circumference for all of Braj in *Journey through the Twelve Forests* (New York, 1994). Shrivatsa

Goswami articulates an insider's view of Vṛndāvana in *Celebrating Krishna* (Vṛndāvana, 2001) and Robyn Beeche matches it with a set of peerless photographs. The scholarly background for all this is set forth in Alan Entwistle's *Braj, Centre of Krishna Pilgrimage* (Groningen, 1987). Readers who suspect this focus on Braj of being overly centrist, even hegemonic will appreciate the essays collected by Guy Beck in *Alternative Krishnas* (Albany, N.Y., forthcoming).

Two large thematic studies relating to Kṛṣṇa Gopāla are Friedhelm E. Hardy's *Viraha Bhakti* (Oxford, 1983), which emphasizes South Indian materials and focuses on Kṛṣṇa as a lover; and my work *Krishna, the Butter Thief* (Princeton, N.J., 1983), which emphasizes North Indian material and concentrates on the child Kṛṣṇa; the appendixes provide a digest of information relating to the iconography of Kṛṣṇa Gopāla.

JOHN STRATTON HAWLEY (1987 AND 2005)

KṚṢṆAISM. The god Kṛṣṇa has been one of the most popular figures of Hinduism and of Indian culture generally. Episodes from his life story have found innumerable expressions in literature and art. Against this larger cultural background one witnesses a more specifically devotional and theological preoccupation with Kṛṣṇa that can be reduced to basically two different trends. On the one hand, there is the development of religious systems in which Kṛṣṇa is defined as an earthly *avatāra* (incarnation) of the god Viṣṇu. Here Viṣṇu plays the central role and one must thus speak of Vaiṣṇava (alternately, Vaiṣṇavite or Viṣṇuite) systems; these can be grouped together under the rubric "Vaiṣṇavism" ("Viṣṇuism"). But the global assumption that Kṛṣṇa is an *avatāra* of Viṣṇu is derived from an inadequate interpretation of the facts. This assumption has its origin in the Indian conceptualization of the religious situation and later came to be accepted uncritically by scholars. The concept "Vaiṣṇavism" has tended to subsume all Kṛṣṇaite phenomena and has thus proved to be far too wide. "Kṛṣṇaism" (along with parallel terms such as "Rāmaism," "Rādhāism," "Sītāism," etc.) is a useful heuristic tool, as long as it is understood to denote not a single system but a whole range of systems.

The strictest definition of a system according to traditional Indian understanding is that of a *sampradāya*, a religious movement that proves its orthodoxy and orthopraxy through detailed exegesis of the Vedanta scriptures. In this sense, one finds only three such Kṛṣṇaite systems (those of Nimbārka, Caitanya, and Vallabha). On the other hand, there are many further instances in which Kṛṣṇa appears de facto as the central religious figure. Whether textual, theological, ritual, or devotional, such contexts can be described as types of Kṛṣṇaism, even when not dealing with a *sampradāya*. Finally, there are many examples of partial Kṛṣṇaism, whereby a religious system is Kṛṣṇaite on one level and, say, Vaiṣṇava on another.

EARLY KṚṢṆAISM. The first Kṛṣṇaite system known is the theology of the *Bhagavadgītā*. When read as a self-contained work, and not automatically in the light of the Vaiṣṇava theology that pervades the *Mahābhārata* into which it was inserted, its Kṛṣṇaite character is unmistakable. There is no suggestion here that in the person of the physical Kṛṣṇa a different being, that is, an eternal, unmanifest Viṣṇu, is contained. Thus when it is said (in 4.7): "Whenever *dharma* is suffering a decline, I emit myself [into the physical world]," or (in 4.8): "In different ages I originate [in physical form]," there is not the slightest hint in the text that this "I" is different from that used in the previous verse (4.6): "I am without birth, of immutable self. . . ." Similarly, in the grand vision that Arjuna, by means of his "divine eye," has of Kṛṣṇa in his cosmic form, no change in person is suggested. Even more important are verses like 14.27 or 18.54, in which Kṛṣṇa's relationship to *brahman* is indicated: Here *brahman* somehow is dependent on, and subsumed in, Kṛṣṇa. On the basis of these theological premises, the *Gītā* advocates a complex spiritual path leading ultimately to human salvation. Attention to the demands of society is combined with the need for inner spiritual growth; but both must be carried out in total "loyalty" (the primary meaning of *bhakti*) to Kṛṣṇa. At the end appears "love" (called "highest *bhakti*") coupled with a sharing in Kṛṣṇa's "working" in the universe.

The remaining portions of the epic, of which the *Bhagavadgītā* is but a minute part, are on the whole Vaiṣṇava. Eventually, by about the fourth or fifth century CE, the concept of the *avatāra* was introduced to clarify the relationship between Kṛṣṇa and Viṣṇu. This had very far-reaching consequences for the interpretation of Kṛṣṇaite material, including the *Gītā* itself. Thus the earliest source on the childhood and youth of Kṛṣṇa, the *Harivaṃśa* (third cent. CE?), an appendix to the *Mahābhārata*, presented the myths within a Vaiṣṇava framework, just as did the *Viṣṇu Purāṇa* (fifth cent. CE?), which contains a very much enlarged account of Kṛṣṇa's early life. By no means, however, did the *avatāra* concept acquire spontaneous, universal validity.

DEVELOPMENTS IN THE SOUTH. When turning to southern India, the region where Tamil was spoken (modern Tamil Nadu, Kerala, and southernmost Andhra Pradesh), one finds the figure of Māyōṉ documented from the beginning of the common era. Although he is assumed by some to have been an autonomous Dravidian god, no evidence for this theory can be found. Instead, a closer analysis of the sources shows that they are dealing here with here is Kṛṣṇa, or better, a god-figure of predominantly Kṛṣṇaite features who also incorporates elements of Viṣṇu. (Thus, strictly speaking one ought to use "Māyōṉism" rather than "Kṛṣṇaism" here.) The name itself, and synonyms like Māl and Māyavaṉ, denote a person of black complexion—a precise translation into Tamil of the Sanskrit Kṛṣṇa. Different milieus deal with the situation differently. In the context of temple worship, the emphasis is on Viṣṇu-Nārāyaṇy. But in the area of folk religion, and, of central importance in later developments, among the (secular) literati, Māyōṉ appears as Kṛṣṇa, particularly the young Kṛṣṇa living among the cowherds, dallying with the girls and playing his tricks on the women. One also hears about his favorite, the milkmaid Pinnai, for whom he subdued seven vicious bulls. To the extent that one can infer from the literary allusions something about the religious situation during the first half of the first millennium CE, the songs, dances, and rituals celebrating those events appear decidedly Kṛṣṇaite.

With the Āḻvārs (sixth to ninth centuries), considerable changes in the conceptualization of Kṛṣṇa take place. Overall, a more pronounced Vaiṣṇava orientation emerges in their works. Yet even they do not introduce the conceptual distinction of Kṛṣṇa and Viṣṇu by means of the notion of *avatāra*, and the names by which they address their god fuse the Kṛṣṇaite with the Vaiṣṇava. The central range of myths that they develop in their poems and the eroticism that pervades their devotion have remained fundamentally Kṛṣṇaite. The emphasis is here on "love-in-separation."

This situation changes only with the emergence of Rāmānuja's Śrī Vaiṣṇavism (from the eleventh century, with antecedents in the tenth). Although institutionally links with the Āḻvārs are maintained, the formation of a definite Vaiṣṇava theology, which in turn has close historical links with the Vaiṣṇava temple tradition of the Pāñcarātras (and Vaikhānasas), encouraged a very different form of *bhakti*. Even so, Kṛṣṇa remains here the central *avatāra*, only eventually to be overtaken by Rāma.

Śrī Vaiṣṇavism was not the only heir to the devotional Kṛṣṇaism of the Āḻvārs. Two Sanskrit works have to be mentioned in this connection. One is the *Kṛṣṇa-karṇāmṛta* by one Vilvamaṅgala (also called "Līlāśuka," or "Playful Parrot"), of unknown date and possibly from Kerala. By 1200 the work is known in Bengal, and at a later stage was a favorite text of Caitanya. From ever-new angles, the erotic attraction of the youthful Kṛṣṇa is explored in this poem. Yet the importance of this work dwindles compared with the second text, the *Bhāgavata Purāṇa*. Written in the Tamil country around the ninth or early tenth century by an unknown poet, in Vedic-sounding and highly poetic language, this text is far more than a traditional *purāṇa*. It attempts to fuse a great variety of contemporary religious and cultural strands, and it does so in a decidedly Kṛṣṇaite manner. While for its "plot" it uses as its model the *Viṣṇu Purāṇa* (where Kṛṣṇa is an *avatāra* of Viṣṇu), in two important respects, devotional-literary and metaphysical, Kṛṣṇa is presented as the central deity. Book 10 and part of Book 11 comprise the structural center of the work: They have become the most famous source on the life of Kṛṣṇa among the cowherds of Vraja. Translating or paraphrasing here poems of the Āḻvārs (PeriyĀḻvār on Kṛṣṇa's childhood, Āṇṭāḷ, Nammāḻvār, and Parkālaṉ on his amours and on "love-in-separation"), Kṛṣṇaite *bhakti* finds here powerful expression. This devotional emphasis is complemented by a Kṛṣṇaite metaphysical framework. Thus in 1.3.28 one reads: "Kṛṣṇa is Bhagavān himself." Or in 10.33.36: "He who moves in the heart of all corporeal beings, here took on a body through playfulness." Kṛṣṇa is *brahman*, and—to make matters more complicated in this *purāṇa*—the ultimately sole real. Thus, an illusionist *advaita* teaching (in which Kṛṣṇa's love-play with the milkmaids can be compared to a child's playing with his own image seen in a mirror—10.33.17) is expounded in its metaphysical frame. Historically, this particular combination of *advaita* (metaphysical nondualism), sensuous *bhakti*, and the identification of Kṛṣṇa with *brahman* proved enormously influential. Most subsequent developments of Kṛṣṇaism in northern India are unthinkable without the *Bhāgavata Purāṇa*.

EARLY DEVELOPMENTS IN THE NORTH. Current knowledge of the situation in northern India during the first millennium CE is far more limited and patchy. No instances of Kṛṣṇaism can be cited, and yet a number of factors were essential in the formation of later types of Kṛṣṇaite religions. Numerous references in the various literatures of the period make it clear that Kṛṣṇa enjoyed enormous popularity. In predominantly secular works his amours with the milkmaids were explored and given a definite place in the imaginary landscape of classical Indian lovers. Moreover, already from the very beginning of the common era one encounters Rādhikā (later usually Rādhā) as his favorite beloved among the milkmaids. She is clearly different from the Tamil Piṉṉai, whom Sanskrit works present as Nīlā or Satyā. (Not that there is much of a story here, apart from the conventional amatory situations envisaged in the poetics of love.) But what was important was the inevitable association in the popular mind of Kṛṣṇa with Rādhikā. The religious works (the *Harivaṃśa*, Purāṇas, etc.) knew nothing about Rādhā, and broke the anonymity of the crowd of Kṛṣṇa's beloved ones only after his departure from Vraja, when he abducted and married the princess Rukmiṇī.

This whole popular interest in Rādhā and Kṛṣṇa reaches its culmination in Jayadeva's *Gītāgovinda* (written in Bengal c. 1185 CE), a kind of libretto for a dance-drama about the lovers' quarrels due to Rādhā's jealousy, and about their eventual reconciliation and their passionate lovemaking. While the *Bhāgavata Purāṇa*, which became known during this period in the north, provided the metaphysical and devotional frame, the *Gītagovinda* acted as the focusing mechanism for mythical episodes in Kṛṣṇa's complex earthly life.

A further contributory factor, *rasa* speculation, must be mentioned. Here one is dealing with academic aesthetics, which in India tended to focus on drama and poetry. By the ninth century CE a conceptual framework had evolved for the analysis of art and aesthetic experience that centered around the notion of *rasa* (literally, "flavor"). A good poem is supposed to contain one of eight possible emotions (love being by far the favorite among the poets) that, by means of poetic-linguistic devices, can be transferred to the reader (listener), to appear in the reader now in a transformed state as the reader's aesthetic relish, as *rasa*. Given that most of the sources on Kṛṣṇa's life were in poetry, that over the centuries an increasing concentration on his amours had taken place, and that in the devotee's emotions vis-à-vis Kṛṣṇa "aesthetic relish" could be found, it was perhaps natural for this to be developed systematically as *bhakti-rasa.* Particularly in the school of Caitanya, the scholastic exploration of *bhakti-rasa* (along with the production of Sanskrit poetry based on it) reached its climax.

Regional Trends in the North. Kṛṣṇaism makes its first documented appearance in the north with the beginning of the second millennium CE in a ritual context. This is the temple-culture of Paṇḍharpur in southern Maharashtra. The god in the temple is variously called Viṭṭhala or Viṭhobā. Although etymologies from *Viṣṇu* have been suggested, the personage described here, from at least a certain stage in the development onward, is clearly Kṛṣṇa. His consort is Rakhumāī, the Marathi form of Rukmiṇī. Particularly through the popularizing activities of Marathi poets such as Jñāneśvar, Nāmdev, and Tukārām, and many other (often pseudonymous) poets and texts, a markedly individual religious system of great popularity evolved in Maharashtra and also in Karṇāṭaka. Heaven and eternity, with Viṭhobā and Rakhumāī as king and queen, take visible form in Paṇḍharpur. Instead of the amorous episodes in Kṛṣṇa's earthly life (which do appear in numerous poems associated with this religious tradition), the emphasis is on secondary myths about the saints connected with Paṇḍharpur.

Maharashtra produced (from the thirteenth century onward) yet another type of Kṛṣṇaism, the very austere and idiosyncratic movement of the Mānbhāv (Mahānubhāva). Here five Kṛṣṇas are listed: Kṛṣṇa himself (husband of Rukmiṇī, etc.), who is closely connected with Parameśvara, the Absolute in the system; Dattātreya (a god-figure of Maharashtrian Hinduism); and three historical persons (Cakrādhār, the founder of the movement, and two predecessors) who are identified with Kṛṣṇa.

As a further example of regional forms of Kṛṣṇaism centered around temples, mention may be made of Jagannātha in Puri, Orissa, the building of whose temple was started around 1100 CE. Accompanied by Baladeva and Subhadrā, he is evidently envisaged in a Kṛṣṇaite context. This connection was strengthened in the sixteenth century through the *bhakti* culture developed in the temple by Rāmānanda Rāya and Caitanya.

The first Kṛṣṇaite *sampradāya* was developed by Nimbārka. Unfortunately, very little reliable information is available on him and thus it is difficult to place him accurately in the history of Kṛṣṇaism. A date before the sixteenth century would emphasize his originality in terms of Kṛṣṇaite theology, but make his alleged residing in Bṛndāvan (a locality near Mathurā, thought to correspond to the mythical Vṛndāvana) very doubtful. Here for the first time in the Vedanta school-tradition is found *brahman* identified with Kṛṣṇa (and not, as earlier on in Rāmānuja and also in Madhva, with Viṣṇu). Moreover, Kṛṣṇa is here envisaged in the company of Rādhā.

A further contributing factor to the increasing popularity of Kṛṣṇa throughout northern India was the appearance of vernacular poets who, in different languages and in varying approaches, dealt with Kṛṣṇa's amours and childhood pranks. While the Bengali poet Caṇḍīdās (1400 CE?) sang about his own tragic love in the imagery of Rādhā's separation, the Maithilī poet Vidyāpati (c. 1350 to 1450) fused the erotic culture of a royal court with the amours of Kṛṣṇa and the milkmaids.

But what about the locality on earth where myth places these amours, that is, Vṛndāvana? The Śrī Vaiṣṇavas had certainly listed it among their 108 primary places of pilgrimage (and in a prominent position) from the tenth century onward. But to what extent anybody from Tamil Nadu traveled all the way up to Mathurā during the period up to the sixteenth century is unknown.

Bṛndāvan. Toward the close of the fifteenth century, the longing to live in the actual place where Kṛṣṇa spent his childhood takes on concrete and documented form. At this point there a number of Kṛṣṇaite devotees, originating from various parts of India, settling in Bṛndāvan along with their disciples. Many temples are constructed on sites that had been (usually miraculously) "rediscovered" as the localities mentioned in Puranic episodes. These developments may well be connected with the transfer of the Mughal capital from Delhi to Agra (in 1506) and the construction of a major road between these two cities that passed through Mathurā. Certainly the tolerant reigns of Akbar (1556–1605) and Jahāngīr (1605–1627) were decisive factors as well.

While the claim that Nimbārka (at an earlier date) had lived in Bṛndāvan is of doubtful validity, both the Caitanyites and Vallabhites refer to an otherwise nebulous Mādhavendra Purī (late fifteenth century) as the original "rediscoverer" of the site of the mythical Vṛndāvana. He in turn appears to have inspired Caitanya to visit the place around 1516 and to settle his disciples there from 1516 onward. Vallabha (c. 1480–1533) and Haridās (c. 1500–1595) arrived somewhat later. During the sixteenth century a whole cluster of Kṛṣṇaite religious movements had their center in the locality of Bṛndāvan. These included Nimbārka's followers and Hit Harivaṃś (c. 1500–1552), who was native to the region. While as religious systems they preserved their separate identities, the common milieu nevertheless produced great similarity of theology and devotion. Although Vallabha himself, and then the branch of his movement that eventually arose in Gujarat, ignored Rādhā and concentrated on the child Kṛṣṇa and his various pranks, through Vallabha's son Viṭṭhaladeva (c. 1518–1586) Rādhā gained prominence theologically, and through the vernacular poetry of Sūrdās (from c. 1480 to between 1560 and 1580), whom the Vallabhites consider as one of their poets, attention is focused upon Rādhā's and Kṛṣṇa's lovemaking. The poetry of Haridās and Hit Harivaṃś is very similar to this. In contrast, the Caitanyites emphasized the *viraha* ("separation") of Kṛṣṇa and Rādhā.

This milieu shares generally the following features. The Absolute, namely, *brahman*, is Kṛṣṇa together with Rādhā (whom the Vallabhites, in this aspect, call Svāminī-jī). Their relationship may be formulated as that of *śaktimān* ("powerful") and *śakti* ("power"), which—according to the *advaita* stance employed—is one of "nonduality." The older, Upaniṣadic definition of *brahman* as *saccidānanda* ("being, consciousness, bliss") is transformed through emphasis on the "bliss" aspect (in which the other two become subsumed); Rādhā is Kṛṣṇa's *hlādinī-śakti*, the "bliss-causing power." Their lovemaking (and separation), which scriptures locate in the mythical Vṛndāvana, is on the one hand envisaged as denotative of the nature of *brahman* (ultimate unity of Kṛṣṇa and his *śakti*, differentiation within an *advaita* sense, etc.). On the other hand, it is perceived as taking place, more literally, in eternity, in a heaven usually called Goloka far above the world (and even above Viṣṇu's heaven, Vaikuṇṭha). Yet the earthly Bṛndāvan remains central, for here the eternal love mysteries and the events that took place in the mythical Vṛndāvana fuse invisibly. Thus, by living here and meditating through song and poetry on Kṛṣṇa and Rādhā—by cultivating *bhaktirasa*—the devotee has direct access to the divine mysteries.

A large corpus of scriptures (devotional poetry along with learned treatises) evolved from all this. Even anonymous works such as the *Brahmavaivarta Purāṇa* and the *Garga Saṃhitā*, or later sections of the *Padma Purāṇa*, show an affinity, if no direct connection, with this Bṛndāvan milieu.

Further Diffusion. The centripetal forces that Bṛndāvan exerted on the north soon were balanced by a centrifugal diffusion of the type of Kṛṣṇaism developed here. Thus Vallabha's son Viṭṭhala moved to Gujarāt in about 1570, where the *sampradāya* acquired a large following. Kṛṣṇa's temple in Dvārakā served as ritual center and the *maharajas*—descendants of Vallabha and *gurus* of the community—as Kṛṣṇa's personal embodiments. A personal, devotional Kṛṣṇaism is expressed by the Rajput princess Mīrā Bāī (c. 1500–1565). In her famous poetry she sang about her love for Kṛṣṇa who is fused with her *gurū*. A contemporary of hers was the Gujarāti poet Narsī Mehtā (c. 1500–1580), who wrote about Kṛṣṇa's and Rādhā's Vṛndāvana amours. In the east, the Caitanyites continued to flourish in Bengal and influenced Bengali poetry on Kṛṣṇa. Śaṇkardev (died c. 1570) and others introduced versions of Kṛṣṇaism into Assam. During the eighteenth century Calcutta witnessed the rise of the Sakhībhāvakas, whose members wore female dress in order to identify themselves even externally with the female companions of Rādhā. In modern times, the Hare Krishna movement exemplifies the continuation of devotional Kṛṣṇaism.

In Kerala ritual Kṛṣṇaism flourishes in connection with the temple of Guruvāyūr, which attracts nowadays large numbers of pilgrims from all over India. Popular texts such as the *Kṛṣṇavilāsa* (by Sukumāra, possibly thirteenth or fourteenth century) and the *Nārāyaṇīyam* (by Mēlpathūr Nārāyaṇa, 1560–1646)—both based on the *Bhāgavata Purāṇa*—provide a literary backing for it.

The term *Kṛṣṇaism*, then, can be used to summarize a large group of independent systems of beliefs and devotion that developed over more than two thousand years, through the interaction of many different cultural contexts. Given the composite nature of the Kṛṣṇa-figure itself (as prankish child, lover, king, fighter of demons, teacher of the *Bhagavadgītā*, etc.), the selective emphasis in these systems on such individual aspects is worth noting. No grand theological synthesis was attempted. Instead, one notices centralizing trends (on an abstract level, in the *Bhāgavata Purāṇa*, and in concrete form, in the influence of the Vṛndāvana milieu) that in turn produced localized expressions. As an overall trend, a concentration on Kṛṣṇa the lover can be recognized, and it is only in the twentieth century that people such as Gandhi or Bal Gangadhar Tilak began to explore the role of Kṛṣṇa's teaching in relation to the demands of modern politics and society. The move "beyond Kṛṣṇa" in the direction of a "Rādhāism" (as found, for example, in the later teaching of the Rādhāvallabhīs or with the Sakhībhāvakas) was, on the other hand, tentative and of limited appeal.

See Also Āḻvārs; Bhagavadgītā; Bhakti; Caitanya; Hindi Religious Traditions; Indian Religions, article on Rural Traditions; Jayadeva; Kṛṣṇa; Marathi Religions; Mīrā Bāī; Nimbārka; Rādhā; Śrī Vaiṣṇavas; Sūrdās; Tamil Religions; Vaikhānasas; Vaiṣṇavism, article on Pāñcarātras; Vallabha; Viṣṇu; Vṛndāvana.

Bibliography

No single book has thus far surveyed the whole range of Kṛṣṇaism. William G. Archer's charming *The Loves of Krishna in Indian Painting and Poetry* (New York, 1957) can serve as a first introduction to the subject. Four more recent works explore different aspects of the Kṛṣṇa figure, but mainly of the earlier period. My *Viraha-Bhakti: The Early History of Kṛṣṇa Devotion in South India* (New Delhi, 1983), deals primarily with early North Indian material as received and developed in the South (particularly by the Āḻvārs and in the *Bhāgavata Purāṇa*). The Kṛṣṇa of the classical Purāṇas is envisaged in Benjamin Preciado-Solís's *The Kṛṣṇa Cycle in the Purāṇas: Themes and Motifs in a Heroic Saga* (New Delhi, 1984) in the context of heroic poetry and Indian art history, and in Noel Sheth's *The Divinity of Krishna* (New Delhi, 1984) from a theological point of view. In his *Krishna, the Butter Thief* (Princeton, N.J., 1983), John Stratton Hawley concentrates on the prankish child as treated in later Hindi poetry, but he includes earlier textual and art-historical material on the theme. Two collections of individual articles contain much relevant information: *Krishna: Myths, Rites, and Attitudes*, edited by Milton Singer (Honolulu, 1966), and *Bhakti in Current Research, 1979–1982*, edited by Monika Thiel-Horstmann (Berlin, 1983). Surendranath Dasgupta's *A History of Indian Philosophy*, vols. 3 and 4 (Cambridge, U.K., 1949–1955), may be consulted on the more technical side of the philosophical and theological discussion.

New Sources

Vaisnavi: Women and the Worship of Krishna. Edited by Steven J. Rosen. Delhi, 1996.

Varma, Pavan K. *Krishna, the Playful Divine.* New Delhi, 1993.

FRIEDHELM E. HARDY (1987)
Revised Bibliography

KṢITIGARBHA, called Dizang in China and Jizō in Japan, is, after Avalokiteśvara, the most important *bodhisattva* of Buddhist East Asia. Kṣitigarbha is also well known in Tibet. His name is usually interpreted to mean "receptacle (womb, storehouse) of the earth"; as such, he may be a Buddhist transformation of the Vedic earth goddess Pṛthivi.

Information about the cult of Kṣitigarbha in the esoteric and exoteric Buddhist traditions comes from a number of sūtras. Principal among these are two texts:

(1) *Dasheng daji dizang shilun jing* (Mahāyāna Mahāsaṃnipata sūtra on Kṣitigarbha and the ten wheels; T.D. no. 411). This *sūtra* was translated into Chinese by Xuanzang (596?–664) in the year 651, but there may have been an earlier translation of the same Sanskrit original made about 400. This scripture is the only exoteric sūtra concerning Kṣitigarbha whose pre-Chinese origin is undoubted.

(2) *Dizang pusa benyuan jing* (Sūra of the original vow of the Bodhisattva Kṣitigarbha; T.D. no. 412). This sūtra is said to be translated from Sanskrit by Śikṣānanda (652–710), but in fact this attribution is impossible to substantiate. Many contemporary scholars believe that the sūtra was written in China as late as the tenth or eleventh century.

HISTORY IN INDIA. An independent cult of Kṣitigarbha apparently never developed in India. The seventh-century Chinese pilgrims to India do not mention Kṣitigarbha. *Maṇḍalas* in the cave-temples of Ellora do include Kṣitigarbha, but there are no separate images of him. Textual references to Kṣitigarbha are found as far back as the first or second century CE, as well as quotations from an *Ārya Kṣitigarbha Sūtra* in a text from the seventh or eighth century. In Central Asia, Kṣitigarbha was more important: Separate images have been found in caves at Dunhuang in what is now Gansu province.

According to the *Dasheng daji,* Kṣitigarbha's special characteristic is that Śākyamuni Buddha has entrusted him with the task of rescuing sentient beings during the buddhaless interval between Śakyamuni's *parinirvāṇa* and the enlightenment of the next Buddha, Maitreya. For countless aeons, the scripture maintains, he has worked to lead sentient beings toward buddhahood in worlds bereft of buddhas. Kṣitigarbha is said to respond to those who call upon his name and rely on him singlemindedly, meeting their immediate needs, eliminating their suffering, and setting them firmly on the path to *nirvāṇa.* He softens the hearts of those mired in evil and brings them repentance. Similarly, those in hells obtain release through his intercession.

HISTORY IN CHINA. Knowledge of Kṣitigarbha (Dizang) was probably introduced to China around 400, but there is no evidence that Dizang became an object of widespread devotion there until much later. An important stimulus for the popularity of faith in Dizang's vows seems to have come from the Sanjie Jiao, or Sect of the Three Stages, a group that believed that various of the teachings of the Buddha were designed to be beneficial in each of three historical ages. Xinxing (540–594), the founder of the sect, promoted the worship of Dizang as appropriate to the present, the third and most evil of the three ages. Judging from the number and dates of images in the Buddhist caves at Longmen, worship of Dizang became popular among the aristocracy, in tandem with that of the Buddha Amitabha, from 650 to 700.

The *Dizang pusa* and other texts very possibly written in China made central the notion of Kṣitigarbha's special intention to rescue those in the hells. Filial piety is another theme that emerges in these texts. Of four stories in the *Dizang pusa* that relate the origin of Kṣitigarbha's vow to rescue all beings from suffering, two tell of his previous births as women who are moved to take such a vow after they have learned that their own mothers are suffering in the Avici hells. In certain "counterfeit" sūtras (i.e., sūtras whose provenance is clearly Chinese) showing obvious Daoist influence, Kṣitigarbha was linked to the "ten kings" who were the judges of the Chinese "dark regions," and prayed to specifically in order to lengthen life and ward off disaster. In these sūtras, Dizang both judges and saves beings.

Reliance on Dizang's vow remains part of Buddhist practice in Chinese cultural areas today. In the seventh lunar month the *Dizang pusa* is widely recited and special offerings made in gratitude for his rescuing of ancestors reborn in the various hells.

HISTORY IN TIBET. Kṣitigarbha is known in Tibet as Sahi snying po. There is a Tibetan translation of the *Dasheng daji* but not of the *Dizang pusa.* Kṣitigarbha is most frequently honored as one of the grouping of "eight great *bodhisattvas*" whose *maṇḍalas* are important in the Esoteric (i.e., Vajrayāna) tradition.

HISTORY IN JAPAN. The first unquestioned evidence of the enshrining of an image of Jizō in Japan and the conducting of an offering service in his temple dates from the year 850. From the ninth century onward, ceremonies of offerings called Jizōkō were widely observed to avert illness and to rescue beings from the hells. Jizō also became honored throughout the country as a protector of children as well as a provider of various blessings sought by the common people. Jizō's festival (Jizōbon), on the twenty-fourth day of the seventh month, usually centers on prayers for the safety of children.

In Japan, many carved stone images of Jizō can still be found at roadsides or in the wild. (Some scholars say that these images gradually replaced an indigenous tradition of erecting stone phallic symbols by the roadside.) In this form, Jizō is the subject of many children's songs and folk songs from ancient times. Today, as in the past, when people mourn victims of war or traffic accidents, or pray for children or for the *mizunoko* (the souls of children who died before birth, usually by miscarriage and abortion), they still often dedicate a small Jizō image at a temple.

ICONOGRAPHY. Although Kṣitigarbha appears in the princely garb of a *bodhisattva* in the Esoteric tradition and in all traditions in China, in Japan he usually appears with the shaved head and monk's robes of a *śravāka,* or Hīnayāna monk, a devotee of the first of the "three vehicles" that, in Mahāyāna thought, comprehend the three soteriological paths recognized by the tradition. He usually carries a pearl and a staff. In the Japanese Shingon (Vajrayāna) tradition he appears in both the Taizōkai (Womb Realm Maṇḍala) and the Kongōkai (Diamond Realm Maṇḍala). Another highly developed tradition in Japan is the depiction of "six Jizōs," each with different attributes according to the path of rebirth in which he appears.

SEE ALSO Buddhas and Bodhisattvas, article on Celestial Buddhas and Bodhisattvas; Xinxing.

BIBLIOGRAPHY

In English, M. W. de Visser's *The Bodhisattva Dizang (Jizō) in China and Japan* (Berlin, 1914), although somewhat dated, remains the best reference. The *Dizang pusa* has been translated into English by Heng Jing and the Buddhist Text Translation Society as *Sutra of the Past Vows of Earth Store Boddhisattva: The Collected Lectures of Tripitaka Master Xuan Hua* (San Francisco, 1974).

The literature in Japanese is extensive. Among the best works are Manabe Kōsai's *Jizō bosatsu no kenkyū,* 2d ed. (Kyoto, 1969), which includes a history of texts; Hayami Tasuku's *Jizō shinkō* (Tokyo, 1975), a well-researched, popular book with a good bibliography; and *Jizō shinkō,* edited by Sakurai Tokutarō (Tokyo, 1983), which includes essays on all aspects of the topic by a number of scholars.

New Sources

Gabain, Annemarie von. "Ksitigarbha-Kult in Zentralasien. Buchillustrationen aus den Turfan-Funden." In *Indologen-Tagung: Verhandlungen der Indologischen Arbeitstagung im Museum für Indische Kunst Berlin, 7. – 9. Oktober 1971, Wiesbaden 1973,* pp. 47–71, edited by Herbert Härtel and Volker Moeller. Wiesbaden, 1973.

Kamstra, J. H. "Jizo on the Verge of Life and Death: The Bodhisattva-god of Japan's Buddhism of the Dead." In *Funerary Symbols and Religion: Essays Dedicated to Professor M. S. H. G. Heerma van Voss on the Occasion of His Retirement from the Chair of the History of Ancient Religions at the University of Amsterdam,* edited by J. H. Kamstra, H. Milde, and K. Wagtendonk, pp. 73–88. Kampen, 1988.

LaFleur, William R. *Liquid Life: Abortion and Buddhism in Japan.* Princeton, 1992.

Miyazaki, Fumiko, and Duncan Ryuken Williams. "The Intersection of the Local and the Translocal at a Sacred Site: The Case of Osorezan in Tokugawa Japan." *Japanese Journal of Religious Studies* 28, nos. 3–4 (2001): 399–440.

Wang-Toutain, Françoise. *Le bodhisattva Kṣitigarbha en Chine du Ve au XIIIe siècle.* Paris, 1998.

MIRIAM LEVERING (1987)
Revised Bibliography

KUAN-YIN SEE AVALAOKITEŚVARA

KUBRĀ, NAJM AL-DĪN.

Al-Kubrā, Shaykh Abū al-Jannāb Najm al-Dīn Aḥmad ibn ʿUmar, Khīwaqī, known as Najm al-Dīn Kubrā, was a Ṣūfī master (AHsixth–seventh centuries/twelfth–thirteenth centuries CE) and founder of the Kubrawīyah Order. Najm al-Dīn was born circa AH540/1145 CE at Khiva in Khwārizm (Khorezm, Uzbekistan), then a flourishing region of Central Asia. As a student his talent for theological disputation earned him the epithet al-Kubrā, an abbreviated form of the Qurʾanic phrase *al-ḳiāmmat al-kubrā,* "the greatest calamity" (84:34)

Kubrā's travels in search of religious learning—chiefly *ḥadīth* (prophetic tradition) and *kalām* (theology)—took him to Egypt, where he spent several years, and also to Iran and Asia Minor. Najm al-Dīn received initiation into Sufism in Egypt from Rūzbihān al-Wazzān, a sheikh of the Suhrawardīyah Order. Najm al-Dīn continued to study theology in Iran until he had a decisive encounter in Tabriz with Bābā Faraj, after which he devoted himself wholly to the mystical path, first under Ismāʿīl al-Qaṣrī (d. 589/1193) in western Iran and then under ʿAmmār ibn Yāsir al-Bidlīsī (d. 582/1186). Finally ʿAmmār sent him back to Rūzbihān to complete his training. Probably between 581/1185 and 586/1190, Kubrā returned to Khwārizm with authorization as a Ṣūfī master in his own right.

The remainder of Najm al-Dīn's life was devoted to the Ṣūfī path, the training of disciples, and the composition of treatises. He founded the Kubrawīyah *ṭarīqah* (order), whose offshoots spread far and wide. Its genealogical line of successive sheikhs is traced back to the Prophet through Rūzbihān al-Wazzān and Abū al-Najīb al-Suhrawardī (Gramlich, 1965). Owing to the stature of his disciples, Kubrā acquired a second nickname, Walī-Tarāsh ("Fashioner of Saints"). He died a martyr's death in battle when the Mongol army attacked Urganj, present-day Kunya-Urgench in Turkmenistan.

Najm al-Dīn Kubrā's principal writings are mostly in Arabic. *Ṣifāt al-ādāb,* in Persian (Meier, 1999), expounds the basics of the Ṣūfī path, including rules of discipline. Kubrā's rules are also set out in *al-Uṣūl al-ʿasharah,* which inspired several commentaries, and in Persian in both *Risālat al-hāʾim al-khāʾif min lawmat al-lāʾim* (Letter to the ecstatic one fearful of blamers' blame) and the more wide-ranging exposition *Ādāb al-sulūk il aẓrat Mālik al-Mulk wa Mālik al-Mulk* (Rules of traveling to the presence of the Master of the Kingdom and King of Kings). To summarize, they prescribe constant observance of ritual purity, fasting, silence, seclusion, and invocation of God. Disciples must keep their hearts focused on the sheikh, abandoning their own will and referring all questions to him; discard all thought impulses, the various types of which, good and bad, must nevertheless be rigorously distinguished; and surrender entirely to the Divine Will.

Sleep must be minimized and moderation observed in breaking the fast.

Najm al-Dīn probably wrote only a small part of *Baṣr al-Ṣaqā'iq* (The ocean of divine realities), also known as *'Ayn al-Ṣayāt* (The source of life), the profound and highly original Qur'ān commentary (*tafsīr)* begun by him and completed in turn by two other Kubrawīs, Rāzī and Simnānī. Several brief tracts and some mystical quatrains (*rubā 'iyyāt*) in Persian are also attributed to Kubrā.

Kubrā's best-known work, *Fawā'iḥ al-jalāl wa fawātiḥ al-jamāl*, contains instructions on Ṣūfī discipline; reminiscences of incidents in the author's outward and inner lives; and interpretive descriptions of mystical states, encounters, visions, and revelations. Prolonged retreat for intensive invocation and fasting, often for forty days, was central to Kubrawī methodology as a means of opening the heart to experiential knowledge of God. The *Fawā'iḥ* describes with exceptional openness experiences of a highly personal nature in both the everyday and the suprasensory realms. Its primary themes include that everything in the created universe can be found within the human microcosm; that humans have innate knowledge of spiritual realities, but to actualize it they must "un-forget" (cf. Neoplatonic anamnesis); that because like can only be known by like, inward purity and outward purity are prerequisites for gaining *ma'rifah;* the *latā'if*, subtle centers of perception; and the significance of visions of lights seen during invocation in relation to spiritual states and the *latā'if*. The *Fawā'iḥ* also contains unusual hermeneutical interpretations (*ta'wīlāt*) of Qur'anic verses and of other texts and sayings.

Mainly because of the Mongol invasion, Kubrā's followers dispersed widely. His successors, direct and later, varied greatly in background and outlook. Several made significant contributions to Kubrawī doctrine and methodology. Majd al-Dīn Baghdādī (d. 616/1219) composed some short treatises before his untimely death. Sa'd al-Dīn Ḥammū'ī (d. 650/1252) and the Shī'ī 'Azīz al-Dīn Nasafī (d. before 1300) wielded much influence in Iran. Both were prolific authors. While Ḥammū'ī tends to be abstruse, Nasafī, like Rāzī, is distinguished by his clarity of exposition. Kamāl al-Dīn (also known as Bābā Kamāl) Jandī, later Sighnaqī (d. 672/1273), played a major part in transmitting the order in Khwārizm and surrounding regions, especially among the Turkic population. In the Bukhara region Sayf al-Dīn Bākharzī (d. 658/1260) was revered as Shaykh-i 'Ālam (the Sheikh of the World). Both Razī al-Dīn 'Alī Lālā Samarqandī (d. 642/1244) and Baghdādī's disciple Najm al-Dīn Dāyah Rāzī (d. 654/1256) brought Kubrawī teachings to Asia Minor. Coauthor of *Baṣr al-ṣaqā'iq*, Rāzī also wrote one of the finest Persian treatises on Islamic mysticism, ethics, and eschatology, *Mirsad al-'ibad* (The path of God's servants). The work traveled far, and one extant manuscript has annotations in a Chinese dialect. Another Iranian Kubrawī sheikh, 'Alā' al-Dawlah Simnānī (d. 736/1336), produced several treatises, lyric poetry, and also much of *Baṣr al-ṣaqā'iq*. His *Risālah-'i Nūrīyah* adds to Kubrā's and Rāzī's earlier interpretations of visions of light.

Some Kubrawī masters acquired influence in the outside world. Berke, khan of the Mongol Golden Horde, converted to Islam at Sayf al-Dīn Bākharzī's *kh ānaqāh.* Ḥammū'ī's son and successor officiated when Ghāzān Khan, Mongol ruler of Iran, embraced Islam in 694/1295. Simnānī also moved in court circles. As for literati, notable Persian poets who were disciples or associates of Kubrawī sheikhs include Humām Tabrīzī, Muḥammad Shīrīn Maghribī, and Sayyid Qāsim al-Anwār.

The Kubrawīyah prospered for some generations in parts of central Asia and Iran. A few offshoots of the order have survived into the twenty-first century. By 699/1300 it reached India, where it became known as the Firdawsīyah and produced a didactic classic in the *Maktūb-i adī* (Hundred letters of Sharaf al-Dīn Manerī [d. 772/1371]). The missionary activity of Sayyid 'Alī Hamadānī (d. 786/1385), a Persian Kubrawī, played a great part in the spread of Islam in Kashmir, where the Hamadānīyah branch is still active. Far to the west the Ottoman sultan Sulaymān II the Magnificent (r. 926–974/1520–1566) was initiated into Sayyid 'Al'ī's litanies *(awrād)*. Even in the nineteenth century some Turkish sheikhs of other orders claimed a Kubrawī affiliation as well, though the order seems never to have become established on Ottoman soil. In Iran the Nūrbakhshīyah branch endured into the tenth/sixteenth century. The rival Barzishābādī faction, also descended from Hamadānī, eventually evolved into the Shī'ī Dhahabīyah Order, which still has two active branches, and during the fourteenth/twentieth century it produced many writings.

The Kubrawīyah's later history in Central Asia has been brilliantly investigated by Devin De Weese (1988, 1994). The ninth/fifteenth century saw the rise of the Naqshbandī Order, which largely supplanted all its rivals there by the end of the eleventh/seventeenth century. Ḥusayn Khwārazm (d. 958/1551) temporarily revived Kubrawī fortunes in Samarkand and elsewhere; in India his deputy Ya'qūb Ṣarfī initiated the famous Naqshbandī Mujaddid Sheikh Aḥmad Sirhindī. In Java (van Bruinessen, 1994) several Ṣūfī orders included Najm al-Dīn Kubrā's name in their genealogy (*silsila*), and Kubrawī teachings conceivably had some actual influence, for example, on the interpretation of visions. Heavily mythologized, Kubrā also features in Javanese quasi-Islamic folklore under the name of Jumadil Kubra, who has several *maqāms* (centers of pilgrimage). Some Kubrawī groups possibly existed in modern times in Chinese-ruled Central Asia, though hard evidence is lacking. Najm al-Dīn Kubrā's shrine remains among the most revered in Central Asia.

BIBLIOGRAPHY

Corbin, Henry. *The Man of Light in Iranian Sufism.* Translated from French by Nancy Pearson. Boulder, Colo., and London, 1978.

De Weese, Devin. "The Eclipse of the Kubravīyah in Central Asia." *Iranian Studies* 21, nos. 1–2 (1988): 45–83.

De Weese, Devin. "Bābā Kamāl Jandī and the Kubravī Tradition among the Turks of Central Asia." *Der Islam* 71, no. 1 (1994): 58–94.

Elias, Jamal J. "A Kubrawī Treatise on Mystical Visions: The *Risāla-yi Nuuriyya* of ʿAlāʾ ad-Dawla as-Simnānī." *Muslim World* 83, no. 1 (1993): 68–80.

Elias, Jamal J. "The Sufi Lords of Bahrabad: Saʿd al-Din and Sadr al-Din Hamuwayi." *Iranian Studies* 27, nos. 1–4 (1994): 53–75.

Elias, Jamal J. *The Throne Carrier of God: The Life and Thought of ʿAlāʾad-Dawla as-Simnānī.* Albany, N.Y., 1995.

Gramlich, Richard. *Die schiitischen Derwischorden Persiens.* Vol. 1, *Die Affiliationen.* Wiesbaden, Germany, 1965.

Maneri, Sharafuddin. *The Hundred Letters.* Translated by Paul Jackson. New York, 1980.

Meier, Fritz. "A Book of Etiquette for Sufis." In *Essays on Islamic Piety and Mysticism,* translated by John O'Kane, edited by Bernd Radtke, pp. 49–92. Leiden, Netherlands, 1999. A paraphrase with commentary of Kubrā's *Ṣifāt al-ādāb.*

Molé, Marijan. "Les Kubrawiya entre sunnisme et shiisme aux huitième et neuvième siècles de l'Hégire." *Revue des etudes islamiques* 29 (1961): 61–142.

Najm al-Dīn al-Kubrā. *Die Fawāʾiḥ al-jamāl wa fawātiḥ al-jalāl.* Edited with introductory study by Fritz Meier. Wiesbaden, Germany, 1957. A French translation is *Les éclosions de la beauté et les parfums de la majesté,* translated by P. Ballanfat. Paris, 2001.

Najm al-Dīn al-Kubrā. "Traités mineurs de Najm al-Dīn Kubrā." Edited by M. Molé. *Annales islamologiques* 4 (1963): 1–78.

Najm al-Dīn Rāzī. *The Path of God's Bondsmen from Origin to Return.* Translated by Hamid Algar. Delmar, N.Y., 1982.

Ridgeon, Lloyd V. J. *ʿAzīz Nasafī.* Richmond, Va., 1998.

Van Bruinessen, Martin. "Najmuddin al-Kubra, Jumadil Kubra, and Jamaluddin al-Akbar: Traces of Kubrawiyya Influence in Early Indonesian Islam." *BKI* (*Bijdragen tot de Taal- Land- en Volkerkunde*) 150, no. 2 (1994): 305–328.

Waley, Muhammadisa I. "Najm al-Dīn Kubrā and the Central Asian School of Sufism (the Kubrawiyyah)." In *Islamic Spirituality: Manifestations,* edited by Seyyed Hossein Nasr, pp. 80–104. World Spirituality vol. 20. New York, 1991.

MUHAMMADISA WALEY (2005)

KUIJI (632–682), religious name of the first patriarch of the Faxiang school of Chinese Buddhism, also known by the titles Dasheng Ji and Ci'en Dashi. Kuiji was the foremost disciple of the great pilgrim-monk Xuanzang, under whose tutelage he came to play an instrumental role in the second major transmission of Indian Yogācāra Buddhist thought into China.

Born into a family of famous generals, the Yuzhi, Kuiji received a classical Confucian education in preparation for the life of a court official, but decided while still in his teens to enter the Buddhist monastic order instead. In 645 Xuanzang returned from his extended study of Buddhism in India and was commissioned by Taizong, the second Tang emperor, to oversee the translation of the numerous Buddhist texts he had brought back to China. Upon his ordination several years later, Kuiji was assigned by imperial order to Xuanzang's translation team and soon became one of his most capable students. As Xuanzang's main assistant for much of the project, Kuiji appears to have been the actual editor of the influential *Cheng weishi lun,* a synopsis of early Indian scholarship on Yogācāra Buddhism.

After the death of Xuanzang (664), Kuiji turned from translation to exegesis, writing extensive commentaries on most of the works translated by the imperial project, a corpus reflecting his interest in a wide range of Buddhist issues both philosophical and practical. He was especially concerned with the doctrine of *vijñaptimātratā,* which holds that the world as we know it is the result of a psychologically conditioned process of cognitive construction. Kuiji also devoted considerable literary effort to working out scholastic problems associated with the stages of progression along the path to liberation. In addition, he wrote important works on Buddhist logic and, consistent with his Yogācāra affiliation, his personal religious practice emphasized devotion to the *bodhisattva* Maitreya.

In spite of its early prominence, the Faxiang school soon experienced a rapid decline, beginning with a shift in imperial patronage that was already apparent in Kuiji's lifetime. The conservative, highly technical, and very scholastic version of Indian Yogācāra thought represented by the school proved antithetical to the prevailing fashion of Tang Buddhism, which had begun to develop independently of the continuing Indian tradition. To bridge this gap Kuiji sought to interpret unfamiliar Indian Yogācāra ideas in terms of contemporary Chinese Buddhist vocabulary (see especially his *Weishi zhang,* or *Essay on Vijñaptimātratā*). His views became the subject of increasing polemic, however, and the school was soon eclipsed by the more indigenous Huayan and Tiantai doctrines. Particularly unacceptable to Kuiji's contemporaries was the Yogācāra affirmation of three distinct (and unequal) religious careers and its corollary that some beings, the *icchantikas,* were inherently incapable of any religious development and were thus forever barred from liberation.

Despite the eclipse of the Faxiang school, Kuiji's commentaries and essays continued to be widely read throughout East Asia. His students introduced Faxiang thought to Japan, where, as Hosso Buddhism, it became the basis for one of the historically most influential of the Nara schools. While the full range of Kuiji's contribution has not yet been fully assessed by modern scholarship, his greatest achievement may be seen in his effort to catalog and preserve details of the scholastic period of Indian Yogācāra thought, especially since he recorded material from texts that now no longer survive in the original Sanskrit.

SEE ALSO Xuanzang; Yogācāra.

BIBLIOGRAPHY

Besides his extensive commentaries, Kuiji wrote a number of essays, many of which were collected in his doctrinal compendium, the *Dasheng fayuan yilin zhang* (T. D. no. 1861). For a translation and study of the most important of these, his *Essay on Vijñaptimātratā* (*Weishi zhang*), see my study "The Vijñaptimātratā Buddhism of the Chinese Monk K'uei-chi" (Ph. D. diss., University of British Columbia, 1980). On Kuiji's relation to the Indian Yogācāra tradition, see my article "The *Trisvabhāva* Doctrine in India and China: A Study of Three Exegetical Models," *Bukkyō bunka kenkyūjo kiyō* 21 (1982): 97–119. In his *Buddhist Formal Logic* (London, 1969), Richard S. Y. Chi has written an excellent study of early Indian Buddhist Nyāya in China based primarily on Kuiji's commentaries to the *Nyāyapraveśa.* The rather limited traditional sources for Kuiji's biography have been thoroughly analyzed and summarized by Stanley Weinstein in "A Biographical Study of Tz'ŭ-ên," *Monumenta Nipponica* 15 (April–July 1959): 119–149.

New Sources

Shih, Heng-ching, trans. *A Comprehensive Commentary on the Heart Sutra (Prajñāpāramitā-Hṛdaya-Sūtra). Translated from the Chinese of K'uei-chi in Collaboration with Dan Lusthaus.* Berkeley, 2001.

Sponberg, Alan. "Meditation in Fa-hsiang Buddhism." In *Traditions of Meditation in Chinese Buddhism,* edited by Peter N. Gregory, pp. 15–43. Honolulu, 1986.

Williams, Paul. *Mahāyāna Buddhism: The Doctrinal Foundations.* London, 1989. See Chapter 4.

ALAN SPONBERG (1987)
Revised Bibliography

KULTGESCHICHTLICHE SCHULE SEE MYTH AND RITUAL SCHOOL

KULTURKREISELEHRE.

Kulturkreiselehre (doctrine of culture "circles"), also called the cultural-historical method, refers to a model developed at the beginning of the twentieth century by German-speaking ethnologists to provide ethnology with a cultural-historical perspective. The intention of these scholars was to change the study of preliterate peoples into a historical science, freeing it from the naturalistic approaches that, influenced by positivism, had been dominant since the beginning of the nineteenth century and that still form a theoretical model of reference.

In anthropological works in English and the main Romance languages, the German word *Kreis* is often translated as "circle" or "cycle," but this translation is inaccurate because the use of *Kulturkreis* as a concept is intended to indicate the context—the complex of conditions in which a particular culture is developed and spread and, at the same time, the entire extent of its important characteristics. These aspects are not an integral part of the concept of a "circle," whereas the term *cycle* is concerned exclusively with the chronological aspect. For this reason it would be more appropriate to use the expression *culture ambit-complex,* which is, like the common expression *culture area,* a concept particular to modern historical and idiographic thought developed in the United States through criticism of the generalized ideas of history devised by writers such as Franz Boas (1940). This article, however, retains the traditional term to avoid confusing the reader.

By setting up culture "circles," that is, various areas governed by the same or a dominant culture (in the view of the cultural-historical school) ethnology ceased to be either the unsystematic collecting of artifacts or the binding of disparate artifacts under the concept of evolutionism or unilinear development. Cultural historians also maintain that their method allows them to identify the differences between preliterate peoples, to characterize cultural phases, and to provide a concrete demonstration of the historical relationships between cultural phenomena, avoiding inadequately argued references to the a priori psychological unity of the human race.

From what has been stated above, it can be concluded, as Marvin Harris (1968) stresses, that from a cultural-historical perspective the culture circles are also strata or phases of a universal chronological plan (based upon the assumption that cultures should be placed in an evolutionary sequence according to the level of civilization attained). For many, this was what evolutionists had already done—construct a completely hypothetical history. The notion of the "cultural stratum" has a long history developed by authors such as Gian Battista Vico (1668–1744) and Johann Jakob Bachofen (1815–1887), who identified three *Kulturstufen.* This notion, which seems to precede the organicism of some cultural historians, is based upon the belief that every cultural form is a living thing that comes into being, develops, and disappears (Casadio, 1994).

The precursors of the cultural-historical method were the Russian naturalist Nikolaj Yakovlevič Danilevsky (1822–1865) and the German geographer Friedrich Ratzel (1844–1904). In his *Anthropogeographie* (1882–1891) and *Völkerkunde* (1885–1888), Ratzel attempted to resolve the conflict between convergence theory (egregiously represented in Adolf Bastian's notion of *Elementargedanken*) and diffusionism, in favor of the latter. Ratzel applied, for the first time, the zoological migration theory to explain the expansion, migration, and layering of cultures. He used the "form criterion"—based upon the identification of material objects that have been made in the same form, not determined by their function or the physical properties of the material employed—to confirm contacts, often across great distances, between cultures. Ratzel's pupil Leo Frobenius, however, is considered the founder of the cultural circle theory. According to Paul Leser (1964), however, Ratzel devised the concept of *Kulturkreis,* even if Frobenius was the first to use the expression in the modern sense. With the aid of the "quantitative criterion" (the more numerous the similarities between two cultural elements, the more likely there will be a historical-genetic relationship between them), Frobenius proposed a "West African culture area" in his *Der Ursprung der afrikanischen Kulturen* (1898). From this concept, however, he later developed the notion of "culture morphology," in which culture was conceived as a living organism whose development was determined by a soul (*paideuma*). Adopting an irrational position, Frobenius held that the inner meaning of culture can only be understood by intuition.

Frobenius's work was joined by the scholarship of Bernhard Ankermann, in "Kulturkreise und Kuhurschichten in Afrika," and Fritz Graebner, in "Kulturkreise und Kulturschichten in Ozeanien," which appeared in *Zeitschrift für Ethnologie* 37 (1905). With his *Die Methode der Ethnologie* (1911), Graebner created the methodological basis for ethnology and introduced methods of historical inquiry, especially the methods developed in Ernst Bernheim's *Lehrbuch der historischen Methode* (5th ed., 1908). Another important methodological contribution to the cultural-historical school is found in the work of the Jesuit historian and theologian Henri Pinard de la Boullaye (1929–1931), who added new criteria to be used for a more precise historical analysis of cultural phenomena. A majority of the young ethnologists of the period gathered under the banner of the cultural-historical method, even if they did not always make use of *Kulturkreis*, which was replaced by other similar concepts.

WILHELM SCHMIDT'S CONTRIBUTION. The Viennese linguist and ethnologist Father Wilhelm Schmidt (1868–1954) developed the concept of the culture circle into an extended system by unifying it and incorporating new elements. In his *Handbuch der Methode der kulturhistorischen Ethnologie* (1937), Schmidt wrote that a culture complex can be called *Kulturkreis* if it embraces all the essential categories of human culture, such as material culture, economy, and religion. Through the continuing scholarship of Wilhelm Koppers, Martin Gusinde, and Paul Schebesta, the concept of the cultural circle acquired acceptance in the history of religion and periodically dominated discussion in the area of the ethnology of religion. In his twelve-volume work *Der Ursprung der Gottesidee* (1912–1955), Schmidt used the *Kulturkreiselehre* to support the theory of primordial monotheism (*Urmonotheismus*).

In 1906 the periodical *Anthropos* became the mouthpiece of Schmidt's Viennese school. To quantitative and form criteria, Schmidt added the criteria of continuity and relatedness as a means of determining relatively uniform cultural complexes. He emphasized the temporal factor and the succession of cultural strata in time, and thus introduced the question of the origin and development of the culture areas. The Viennese ethnologist employed the cultural stratum idea (*Kulturschicht*), which, like *Kulturkreis*, was an organic complex produced by an almost biological determinism, but he did not recall his predecessor Bachofen (Casadio, 1994). According to some scholars, among the followers of the historical-cultural school there is variation between the atomistic concept of culture, in which diverse cultural characteristics coexist, and the organic conception, which instead opens the way to the functionalism moderated by the historical approach of Richard Thurnwald and Wilhelm Mühlmann.

According to Schmidt, cultural elements can be compared only if they are related to each other or occur within the same cultural complex. In determining the origin of the cultural complex, a double rule applies: a cultural element can be explained only within its own cultural complex, and in this explanation the oldest cultural forms are of primary significance. The *Kulturkreise* proposed by Schmidt are:

1. *Primitive cultures,* characterized by preliterate hunters and gatherers:

1.1 Central primitive culture; exogamous and monogamous marriages.

1.2 Southern primitive culture; exogamous marriages and sex totems.

2. *Primary cultures,* characterized by preliterate agriculturalists:

2.1 Exogamous marriages, patrilineal kinship; totemism, higher-stages hunting; "city" culture.

2.2 Exogamous marriages, matrilineal kinship; horticulturist; "village" culture.

2.3 Patrilineal kinship, undivided families; pastoral nomads who become ruling races.

3. *Secondary cultures,* characterized by picture writing:

3.1 Free patrilineal cultures (e.g., Polynesia, the Sudan, western India, western Asia, southern Europe).

3.2 Free matrilineal cultures (e.g., southern China, eastern India, Melanesia; the northeast of South America).

4. *Tertiary cultures,* characterized by alphabet use (the oldest civilizations of Asia, Europe, and the Americas).

Schmidt presumes a succession that is distinguished from the older evolutionism schema but that assumes, in effect, a reverse evolution, or a "devolution." This reversal becomes particularly obvious in Schmidt's religious historical schema. In primitive cultures the belief in a Supreme Being dominates; this belief is interpreted as primordial monotheism. In the next stage, primary cultures, the belief in spirits (animism), magic, and totemism (animal worship) emerges. These beliefs increasingly stifle monotheism and eventually result in the polytheism of the higher cultures, but the earlier monotheistic stage is finally revived by the biblical religions.

Nineteenth-century British evolutionists were lined up against a similar concept of religious history, defined as "degenerationism," supported, for example, by the Anglican archbishop of Dublin Richard Whately. In particular, Edward B. Tylor (1871) produced a timely critique of degenerationism to demonstrate the validity of his progressive concept of history inspired by the thinking of the followers of the Enlightenment.

Without a doubt, Schmidt sought through the use of the *Kulturkreiselehre* a historical proof of the existence of God. It is small wonder, then, that this school has fallen into disrepute among ethnologists, because it appears to serve the aims of Catholic theology more than those of unbiased research. The members of the Viennese school, especially Josef Haekel and Walter Hirschberg, have increasingly distanced themselves from Schmidt's ideas.

METHODOLOGICAL DEBATE. The establishment and research of cultural historians gave rise to an interesting debate, in which anthropologists and religious historians pointed out what, in their opinion, were the strong and weak points of this ethnological point of view, which had spread in German- and Italian-speaking circles (with the occasional French exception, such as Georges Montandon). This convergence of Italian- and German-speaking scholars is particularly owed to the fact that both groups were Catholics. In addition, some of them were priests and played an important part in the political life of the Catholic Church.

Italian diffusionists include Renato Biasutti, Renato Boccassino, Padre Luigi Vannicelli, Vinigi L. Grottanelli, and Guglielmo Guariglia, who as well as devising important criticisms of the theories of the Viennese school were also followers of it. Subsequently, Italian ethnology and cultural anthropology were influenced by other sources, such as British functionalism, American anthropology, and French structuralism.

The above debate has concerned both the purely methodological aspects of *Kulturkreiselehre* and the application of its principles to specific cultural contexts. The article "Some Reflections on the Method and Theory of the *Kulturkreiselehre*" (1936) by the U.S. anthropologist Clyde Kluckhohn is an important piece of writing in this debate. Kluckhohn proposes to identify the assumptions (influenced by scholastic philosophy) and objectives of the historical-cultural method, avoiding misunderstandings due to the unspoken premises and emotional involvement of every scholar. He considers the form criterion to be subjective, in that its application implies a choice on the part of the scholar. He also identifies a contradiction in the historical-cultural point of view. On the one hand, it claims that ethnology is historically authentic; on the other hand, it treats cultural facts as facts of nature, extrapolating them atomistically from their context. In his opinion, its extensive use of naturalistic metaphors means that it is dominated by biological thinking and is particularly concerned with identifying genetic-causal links between phenomena. For this reason it seems to ignore the fact that, to understand the history of cultural phenomena, one ought to identify the close relationships between them. On this point the criticism of Kluckhohn agrees with that of the Italian ethnologist Ernesto de Martino (1941), who considers unacceptable the mechanistic and naturalistic concept of history typical of the historical-cultural school, like evolutionism and French sociology. This concept seems to be based upon the lack of interest in psychology shown by cultural historians and pointed out by some scholars.

The link with biology, not unknown in fields such as social anthropology, is also identified by Boas and Robert H. Lowie. Boas, for example, states that *Kulturkreiselehre* bases the stability of cultural complexes upon the biological principal of the permanence of the characteristics of a particular entity (Boas, 1911, p. 807). Although Kluckhohn and Lowie recognize that the cultural historians refer to the basic tenets of the Catholic *Weltanschauung,* they still do not maintain that these, more than others, invalidate the results of their research. After all, they seem to be supporters of methodological pluralism, convinced that cultural anthropology benefits from the use of different methods.

Another important moment in the development of the theory of cultural environment was the publication of Robert Heine-Geldern's "One Hundred Years of Ethnological Theory in German Speaking Countries" (1964). Heine-Geldern reconstructs the history of ethnology in German-speaking countries, setting out elements of continuity between the various scholars. In his opinion, the work of Ratzel is of great importance, as he brought to an end the stagnation that had characterized German thinking, which had been dominated by the doctrine of *Elementargedanken* in the period 1860–1890 (Heine-Geldern, 1964, pp. 411–412). He notes that the historical-cultural school has a candid and dogmatic belief in the temporal stability of cultural complexes, denying the dynamic nature of culture (Heine-Geldern, 1964, p. 413). Such a claim, however, is denied by Paul Leser (1964, p. 417). For Leser, Graebner was convinced that two cultural elements, if not functionally linked, tend to separate in time.

The criticism of evolutionism and the naturalistic approach produced diffusionism in Europe and particularism in the United States. Both incorrectly identified evolutionism with the denial of the processes of diffusion and the exclusive acceptance of independent invention. The two trends thus had these two aspects in common, but they parted company over psychological interpretation and several specific ethnographical problems. In the United States the particularists, who made extensive use of diffusion to explain the similarities between different social groups, developed the idea of "cultural area." As Harris (1968) writes, this concept, used for the first time by Otis T. Mason in 1895, allowed the Amerindian scholars, such as Clark Wissler and Alfred L. Kroeber, to describe and classify the societies of North and South America.

Thus the discussion surrounding the culture circles has continued outside the Vienna School. Hermann Baumann and Wilfred D. Hambly have presented different models for Africa, and Clark Wissler, Edward Sapir, Melville J. Herskovits, and A. L. Kroeber have done the same for the Americas. There is no longer the problem of identifying the oldest culture in which the prehistorical "primitive stage" has survived, as found in Oswald Menghin's *Weltgeschichte der Steinzeit* (1931).

Many anthropologists have gone beyond the contradiction between independent invention and diffusion, because they are convinced that the presence of a cultural institution in a particular context is the result of so-called structural causality. From this point of view, the various aspects of sociocultural life are explained and interpreted by reference to the complex interaction of structural and environmental conditions. It is therefore held that similar structures have produced similar institutions in different contexts, or that a cultural trait has been received or adopted as useful to the social organization by the process of transculturation.

SEE ALSO Evolution, article on Evolutionism; Frobenius, Leo; Graebner, Fritz; Schmidt, Wilhelm.

BIBLIOGRAPHY

Baumann, Hermann, Richard Thurnwald, and Diedrich Westermann. *Völkerkunde von Afrika.* Essen, Germany, 1940.

Boas, Franz. "Review of Graebner's Methode der Ethnologie." *Science* 34, no. 884 (1911): 804–810.

Boas, Franz. "The Limitations of the Comparative Method of Anthropology." In *Race, Language, and Culture.* New York, 1940.

Brandewie, Ernest. *Wilhelm Schmidt and the Origin of the Idea of God.* Lanham, Md., 1983.

Casadio, Giovanni. "Bachofen, o della rimozione." In *Agathē elpis: Studi storico-religiosi in onore di Ugo Bianchi,* edited by Giulia Sfameni Gasparro, pp. 63–78. Rome, 1994.

De Martino, Ernesto. *Naturalismo e storicismo nell'Etnologia.* Bari, Italy, 1941.

Fiedermutz-Laun, Annemarie. *Der kulturhistorische Gedanke bei Adolf Bastian.* Wiesbaden, Germany, 1970.

Grottanelli, Vinigi L. "Ethnology and/or Cultural Anthropology in Italy: Traditions and Developments." *Current Anthropology* 18, no. 4 (1977): 593–614.

Haekel Josef, Anna Hohenwart-Gerlachstein, and Alexander Slawik, eds. *Die Wiener Schule der Völkerkunde.* Vienna, 1956.

Harris, Marvin. *The Rise of Anthropological Theory: A History of Theories of Culture.* New York, 1968.

Heine-Geldern, Robert. "One Hundred Years of Ethnological Theory in German Speaking Countries: Some Milestones." *Current Anthropology* 5, no. 5 (1964): 407–418.

Kluckhohn, Clyde. "Some Reflections on the Method and Theory of the *Kulturkreiselehre.*" *American Antropologist* 38, no. 2 (1936): 157–196.

Kroeber, A. L. *Cultural and Natural Areas of Native North America.* Berkeley, Calif., 1939.

Langness, Lewis L. *The Study of Culture.* San Francisco, 1974.

Leser, Paul. "Zur Geschichte des Wortes Kulturkreis." *Anthropos* 58 (1963): 1–36.

Leser, Paul. "Comment to 'One Hundred Years of Ethnological Theory in German Speaking Countries: Some Milestones.'" *Current Anthropology* 5, no. 5 (1964): 407–418.

Lowie, Robert H. *The History of Ethnological Theory.* New York, 1937.

Mühlmann, Wilhelm E. *Geschichte der Anthropologie.* 3d ed. Wiesbaden, Germany, 1984.

Pinard de la Boullaye, Henri. *L'étude comparée des religions.* 4th ed. 3 vols. Paris, 1929–1931.

Poirier, Jean. "Histoire de la pensée ethnologique: L'ethnologie italienne." In *Ethnologie générale,* edited by Jean Poirier. Encyclopédie de la Pléiade. Paris, 1968.

Schmidt, Wilhelm, and Wilhelm Koppers. *Völker und Kulturen,* vol. 1, *Gesellschaft und Wirtschaft der Völker.* Regensburg, Germany, 1924.

Tylor, Edward Burnett. *Primitive Culture: Researches into the Development of Mythology, Philosophy, Religion, Art, and Custom.* London, 1871.

KURT RUDOLPH (1987)
ALESSANDRA CIATTINI (2005)
Translated from Italian by Paul Ellis

KUMĀRAJĪVA (343–413; alternative dates: 350–409) was renowned as the founder of the Sanlun ("three treatise," i. e., Mādhyamika) school in China and as an adept translator into Chinese of many important and influential Mahāyāna Buddhist texts.

Kumārajīva was born of noble lineage in the Central Asian city of Kuchā. His father was an emigrant Indian brahman and his mother a Kuchean princess. During the fourth century Kuchā was a major city along the northern trade route of the Silk Road connecting China with India and the West. There is ample testimony from the travelogues of Faxian and Xuanzang that cities along this route were strongholds of Hīnayāna Buddhism, especially the Sarvāstivāda sect, which had been introduced from its center in Kashmir. The works of this sect were thus the first he was to study.

Kumārajīva became a novice monk at the early age of seven. His mother, who wanted to become a nun, also abandoned lay life at this time. He spent the next two years studying the Āgamas and Abhidharma texts. When he was nine he went with his mother to North India (to Chipin, in Kashmir), where for three years he studied the *Dirghāgama,* the *Madhyamāgama* and the *Kṣudraka* under the master Bandhudatta. At twelve he again set out with his mother for Kuchā. On the way they stopped for more than a year in Kashgar, where he studied the *Jñānaprasthāna Śāstra,* a Sarvāstivādin Abhidharma treatise, as well as the Vedas and the five sciences (grammar, logic, metaphysics, medicine, and the arts and crafts). While in Kashgar he met the Mahāyānist Sūryasoma, who converted him to the Mahāyāna. In Kashgar, Kumārajīva also met the Dharmagupta master Buddhayaśas. After returning to Kuchā, Kumārajīva received full ordination in the royal palace at age twenty. He studied the Vinaya of the Sarvāstivāda school with the North Indian master Vimalākṣa. More significantly, however, he spent the next twenty years concentrating on Mahāyāna *sūtras* and *Śāstras.* His biography reports that he studied the three *Śāstras* of Nāgārjuna and Āryadeva that were later to become the central texts of the Sanlun tradition, all of which he may have obtained in Kashgar. A Chinese account of 379 mentions Kumārajīva as an accomplished monk, and it is from this period that his fame reaches China.

KUMĀRAJĪVA'S TRANSLATIONS. The *Chu sanzang ji ji* (early sixth century) attributes thirty-five works in 294 fascicles to Kumārajīva. The central corpus of these works is well attested by contemporary prefaces, and dates of translation are known for twenty-three titles. The core of works translated by Kumārajīva shows that his main interest was in the Śūnyavādin *sūtras*, particularly those of the Prajñāpāramitā class, and the Mādhyamika treatises. His interests were catholic, however, and he also translated pietist, Vinaya, and *dhyāna sūtras*, as well as the *Satyasiddhi Śāstra*, a Bahuśrutīya treatise by Harivarman.

Chief among the translated Śūnyavādin works were the *Pañcaviṃśati* (T.D. no. 223), the *Aṣṭasāhasrikā* (T.D. no. 227), the *Vimalakīrtinirdeśa* (T.D. no. 475), the *Vajracchedikā* (T.D. no. 235), and the *Prajñāpāramitāhṛdaya* (T.D. no. 250). He also translated the three Mādhyamika treatises that form the basis for the Sanlun school in China and Japan: the *Mūlamadhyamaka Śāstra*, a treatise consisting of verses by Nāgārjuna and commentary by Piṅgala (T.D. no. 1564; Chin., *Zhong lun*); the *Śata Śāstra* of Āryadeva (T.D. no. 1569; Chin., *Bo lun*); and the *Dvādaśanikāya Śāstra* of Nāgārjuna (T.D. no. 1568; Chin., *Shier men lun*). Three other important Mādhyamika treatises that he translated are the *Daśabhūmivibhāṣā Śāstra* attributed to Nāgārjuna (T.D. no. 1521), the *Faputixisnjing lun* attributed to Vasubandhu (T.D. no. 1659), and the *Mahāprajñāpāramitā Śāstra* attributed to Nāgārjuna (T.D. no. 1509; Chin., *Da zhidu lun*). Four treatises on meditation are attributed to Kumārajīva; chief among them is the *Zuochan sanmei jing* (T.D. no. 614), also called the *Bodhisattvadhyāna*. The major Vinaya works that he translated are the Sarvāstivāda *Prātimokṣa Sūtra* and, according to tradition, the *Pusajieben (Bodhisattva-pratimokṣa)*. His pietist translations include the *Saddharmapuṇḍarīka* (T.D. no. 262), the *Smaller Sukhāvativyūha* (T.D. no. 366), and two Maitreya texts (T.D. nos. 454 and 456). He also translated the *Daśabhūmika* (T.D. no. 286) in collaboration with his friend from Kashgar Buddhayaśas. All of these texts became central to the Chinese Buddhist community.

Kumārajīva, his chief assistants, and the translation bureau devised new transcriptions of names and Buddhist technical terms and utilized interpolated glosses when specific words could not be translated adequately. Although his translations betray careless editing, they are famous for their florid and elegant style. They may not preserve the original words of a Sanskrit *sūtra*, but they clearly express the intended meaning.

The most important evidence for Kumārajīva's religious thought is contained in the commentary on the *Vimalakīrtinirdeśa* (T.D. no. 1775) and the collection of correspondence (T.D. no. 1856) between Huiyuan and Kumārajīva. From these works it is clear that Kumārajīva was an unqualified adherent of the Mādhyamika tradition. His critique of causation is the same as that of Nāgārjuna.

There is no evidence that Kumārajīva intended to found a lineage. Nevertheless, his influence in China, Korea, and Japan was pervasive. Although the *Saddharmapuṇḍarīka Sūtra*, the *Smaller Sukhāvativyūha Sūtra*, and the *Vimalakīrtinirdeśa a Sūtra* had been translated earlier by Dharmarakṣa, Kumārajīva's more accurate translations further stimulated the growth and popularity of Mahāyāna Buddhism in the Far East: The *Saddharmapuṇḍarīka Sūtra* became the basic text of the Tiantai school and, later, of the Nichiren sect in Japan; the *Smaller Sukhāvativyūha* became one of the three major texts of the Pure Land Tradition; the *Vajracchedikā* continues to be esteemed as a basic text of the Chan school; the *Da chidu lun* was very influential in the Zhenyan or Shingon (i. e., Vajrayāna) school in China and Japan; while the *Vimalakirtinirdesa* popularized the ideal of the *bodhisattva*. Other of his translations also helped shape the history of medieval Chinese Buddhism. The *Satyasiddhi Śāstra*, which had many commentaries written on it, became the most widely studied and influential work in the South during the Southern Qi (479–502) and Ling dynasties (502–557), and the Sarvāstivāda Vinaya became one of the two Vinaya systems prevalent in China and Japan. The old line transmission of the Sanlun school persisted until the time of Jizang (549–623) of the Sui dynasty (581–618). In summary, Kumārajīva's activities ushered in the second period of Chinese translations (fifth and sixth centuries), characterized by greater accuracy and widespread influence in the Chinese Buddhist community.

SEE ALSO Buddhism, Schools of, article on Chinese Buddhism; Buddhist Books and Texts; Huiyuan; Mādhyamika; Nāgārjuna; Sengzhao.

BIBLIOGRAPHY

The standard traditional account of the life of Kumārajīva can be found in Huijiao's *Gaoseng zhuan* (T.D. nos. 50. 330–333). For a German translation of the biography, see Johannes Nobel's "Kumārajīva," *Sitzungsberichte der preussischen Akademie der Wissenschaften* 26 (1927): 206–233. Erik Zürcher's *The Buddhist Conquest of China*, 2 vols. (1959; reprint, Leiden, Netherlands, 1979), treats the development of Buddhism in China through the end of the fourth century and thus provides an invaluable introduction to the religious and intellectual climate Kumārajīva encountered upon reaching Chang'an. For a general survey of Kumārajīva's career see Kenneth Chen's *Buddhism in China: A Historical Survey* (Princeton, N.J., 1964). Other critical discussions include the following:

Kimura Eiichi, ed. *Eon kenkyu*. 2 vols. Kyoto, 1960–1962. Contains a translation of Kumārajīva's correspondence with Huiyuan.

Koseki, Aaron K. "'Later Mādhyamika' in China: Some Current Perspectives on the History of Chinese *Prajñāpāramitā* Thought." *Journal of the International Association of Buddhist Studies* 5 (1982): 53–62.

Liebenthal, Walter. "Chinese Buddhism during the Fourth and Fifth Centuries." *Monumenta Nipponica* 11 (April 1955): 44–83.

Liebenthal, Walter, ed. and trans. *The Book of Zhao.* Beijng, 1948.

Robinson, Richard H. *Early Mādhyamika in India and China.* New Delhi, 1976.

Sakaino Koyo. *Shina bukkyo seishi* (1935). Tokyo, 1972. See pages 341–417.

Tang Yongtong. *Han Wei liangjin Nanbeichao fojiao shi.* Shanghai, 1938.

Tsukamoto Zenryu. "The Dates of Kumārajīva and Sengzhao Reexamined." *Jinbum kagaku kenkyusho* (Silver Jubilee Volume, 1954): 568–584.

Tsukamoto Zenryu, ed. *Joron kenkyu.* Kyoto, 1955.

DALE TODARO (1987)

KUMAZAWA BANZAN (1619–1691), Japanese Confucian thinker of the Wang Yangming school. Born in Kyoto, the son of a *rōnin,* or masterless samurai, Banzan probably suffered deprivation during his early years. In 1634, however, he was employed as a page to Ikeda Mitsumasa (1609–1682), daimyo of Okayama, who was later acknowledged to be one of the enlightened rulers of his age. Banzan left the service of Mitsumasa in 1638. In 1641 and 1642 he studied under Nakae Tōju (1608–1648), the founder of the Wang Yangming school of neo-Confucianism (Ōyōmeigaku) in Japan, an experience that permanently molded Banzan's attitude to the Confucian tradition.

Reentering Mitsumasa's service in 1645, Banzan appears to have been employed mainly as a Confucian adviser and teacher. He rose dramatically in the service of the domain, attaining the rank of *bangashira* (divisional commander) in 1650. Undoubtedly, his participation in domain adminstration further influenced his intellectual development, particularly his sense of the limited practicability of certain aspects of Confucianism to the Japanese social and intellectual condition. Banzan's resignation from Mitsumasa's service in 1657 probably resulted from a combination of internal domain rivalries and external pressure from the Tokugawa government to suppress *shingaku,* or "the learning of the heart," as Banzan's style of Confucianism was then known.

Banzan next lived for a number of years in Kyoto, where he associated with and taught court nobles and pursued a life of high culture. In 1667, however, his activities appear to have aroused the suspicion of the authorities and, subsequently, he was forced to leave the city. Thereafter, he lived under official surveillance in the castle towns of Akashi and Yada until finally he was placed under house arrest in Koga.

Banzan's extensive written works date mainly from the period of his retirement from service in Okayama. Among them are miscellanies relating to Confucianism in Japan and to contemporary affairs, including financial and economic matters; commentaries on the Confucian classics; an important treatise on contemporary political economy titled *Daigaku wakumon* (Questions on the *Great Learning*); a series of dialogues in which speakers from different social groups discuss a wide range of issues; and a remarkable commentary on the *Tale of Genji.*

Banzan belonged to that generation of early Tokugawa-period thinkers who first explored seriously the practical relevance to their own society of Chinese neo-Confucianism as established during the Song (960–1279) and Ming (1368–1644) dynasties. He accepted in broad outline the metaphysical assumptions of that tradition, including the concept of a dualistically structured world of *li* (Jpn., *ri,* "principle") and *ch'i* (Jpn., *ki,* "ether"). He was also a proponent of the neo-Confucian doctrine of the mind, asserting that it is man's duty to regenerate himself through self-cultivation. Like most of his Confucian contemporaries, he was anti-Buddhist and anti-Christian. Banzan's thought is further characterized by an eclecticism that is evident in his attempts to combine the intellectual traditions of Wang Yangming (1472–1529) and Zhu Xi (1130–1200). Banzan adhered to the former's emphasis on introspection as a technique for self-cultivation and on the subjective conscience in determining action. Following the thought of Zhu Xi, Banzan upheld the idea of *ri* as a rationally accessible and objective principle underlying the natural and social worlds. His pragmatism can be seen in his resolutely antidoctrinaire stance and his willingness to accommodate to Japanese conditions many conventional Chinese Confucian institutions such as earth burial of the dead, the prohibitions on nonagnatic adoption and agnatic marriage, and the rituals of mourning. This pragmatism was underpinned by sophisticated theories of history and geography that related national temperament to physical and historical environment.

Banzan's Confucianism, therefore, was not profoundly innovative or original. Rather, it bears the stamp of a vigorous and practical attempt to adapt the Chinese neo-Confucian heritage to the complex realities of early Tokugawa Japan. Banzan himself had no major disciples, but his thought influenced the ideas of Ogyū Sorai (1666–1728) and several Confucian thinkers of the late Tokugawa period, including Yokoi Shōnan (1809–1869).

SEE ALSO Confucianism in Japan.

BIBLIOGRAPHY

Gotō Yōichi and Tomoeda Ryūtarō, eds. *Kumazawa Banzan.* Nihon shisō taikei, vol. 30. Tokyo, 1971.

Taniguchi Sumio et al., eds. *Zōtei Banzan zenshū.* 7 vols. Tokyo, 1980.

I. J. MCMULLEN (1987)

KUMBHA MELĀ. The Kumbha Melā is a Hindu pilgrimage fair that occurs four times every twelve years, once in each of four locations in North India: at Haridvār, where the Ganges River enters the plains from the Himalayas; at Prayāg, near Allahabad, at the confluence of the Ganges, Yamunā, and "invisible" Sarasvatī rivers; at Ujjain, in Madhya Pradesh, on the banks of the Kṣiprā River; and at Nāsik, in Maharashtra, on the Godavari River. Each twelve-year cycle includes the Mahā ("great") Kumbha Melā at Prayāg, which is the largest pilgrimage gathering in the world. These *melās* ("fairs"), also known as Kumbha Yoga or Kumbha Parva, occur during the conjunctions (Skt., *yoga, parva*) of celestial beings who performed important acts in the myth that forms the basis of the observance. In one version of the story, the gods and the antigods had concluded a temporary alliance in order to churn *amṛta* (the nectar of immortality, ambrosia) from the milky ocean. Among the "fourteen gems" they churned from the ocean was a pot (*kumbha*) of *amṛta.* One of the gods, Jayanta, took the pot and ran, chased by the antigods. For twelve divine days and nights (the equivalent of twelve human years) they fought over the *amṛta.* The Moon protected it from "flowing forth," the Sun kept the pot from breaking, Jupiter preserved it from the demons, and Saturn protected it from fear of Jayanta. During the battle, drops of *amṛta* fell at eight places in the inaccessible worlds of the gods and four places (Haridvār, Prayāg, Ujjain, and Nāsik) on the earth.

The Kumbha Melā is celebrated at the four earthly points where the nectar fell, during the conjunctions of planets (*graha*) with astrological houses (*rāśī*) that are characters in the story—for example, at Haridvār when Jupiter (Guru) is in Aquarius (Kumbha) and the Sun (Sūrya) is in Aries (Meṣa). It is popularly thought that a ritual bath (characteristic in all Hindu pilgrimages) at the Kumbha Melā confers extraordinary merit, not only by cleansing the pilgrim of "sin" (*pāpa*), but also by immersing him in waters infused with *amṛta.* Major baths are done at different times in each of the four Kumbha Melās, chiefly on new-moon and full-moon days.

The historical origin of the Kumbha Melā is an open and indeed almost uninvestigated question. The authenticity of its purported mention in the *Atharvaveda* has been challenged, although certain *khila* verses of unknown date in the *Ṛgveda* demonstrate familiarity with some of the sites and relevant astrological conjunctions. The Chinese Buddhist pilgrim Xuanzang visited Prayāg in the seventh century, but there is no evidence that he witnessed a Kumbha Melā.

Traditions regarding the determination of the time of the Kumbha Melā are not unanimous. This is partly due to the absence of a single, authoritative scripture sanctioning the *melā.* It is mentioned only in late texts, notably the *Skanda Purāṇa,* which has several notoriously inconsistent recensions. Thus there are occasional disagreements between those who say that the Kumbha Melā should be held every twelve years and those who claim that, in exceptional instances, the precise astrological conjunction may occur in the eleventh year. Matters are complicated by the fact that Haridvār and Prayāg have traditions of *ardha* ("half") Kumbha Melās, which occur six years after the Kumbha Melās. Nevertheless, there is at present a rough consensus of learned opinion regarding the appropriate times of its occurrence.

Kumbha Melās are popularly understood to be not only pilgrimage fairs at which sins can be cleansed and merit gained but also religious assemblies at which doctrine is debated and standardized and Hindu unity affirmed. This is perhaps an apt characterization of present-day Kumbha Melās, but historical evidence indicates that in centuries past they were the scenes of bloody battles, chiefly between the militant sections of rival orders of Hindu monks. The main object of contention in these battles, which occurred as recently as 1807, was the right to bathe in the most auspicious place at the most powerful instant. The conflicts were so fierce that indigenous and British courts finally had to establish and enforce specific bathing orders at the various sites of the Kumbha Melā. The *sāīs*, processions of monks to the bathing place, are still focal events in the Kumbha Melās.

With the advent of modern transport and communications, contemporary Kumbha Melās are sometimes attended by several million people in a single day. The government of India provides safety, order, sanitation, and preventive inoculations for this multitude, which besides innumerable devout Hindus includes merchants, representatives of religious organizations, casual tourists, groups of monks, and others. Many of those who attend the Kumbha Melā hope to gain some specific "fruit," such as a job, a son, success in studies, and so on. The special power of the Kumbha Melā is often said to be due in part to the presence of large numbers of Hindu monks, and many pilgrims seek the *darśan* (Skt., *darśana*; "auspicious mutual sight") of these holy men. Others listen to religious discourses, participate in devotional singing, engage *brahman* priests for personal rituals, organize mass feedings of monks or the poor, or merely enjoy the spectacle. Amid this diversity of activities, the ritual bath at the conjunction of time and place is the central event of the Kumbha Melā.

SEE ALSO Pilgrimage, article on Hindu Pilgrimage.

BIBLIOGRAPHY

An excellent description of a recent Kumbha Melā is given in Ved Mehta's *Portrait of India* (New York, 1970), pp. 77–111. A more scholarly analysis of the Kumbha Melā, based on Sanskrit sources, is Giorgio Bonazzoli's "Prayāga and Its Kumbha Melā," *Purāṇa* 19 (January 1977): 81–179. This article also discusses the scriptural glorifications (*mahātmyas*) of Prayāg at length and contains useful information regarding the history of the Kumbha Melā. A good example of a learned Hindu's ideas concerning the Kumbha Melā is Veṇirāmaśarma Gauḍ's *Kumbhaparva Mahātmya* (Varanasi, n.d.) in Hindi. The best general introduction to Hindu pilgrimage is still Agehananda Bharati's "Pilgrimage Sites and Indian Civilization," in *Chapters in Indian Civilization,* edited by Joseph W. Elder, vol. 1, rev. ed. (Dubuque, 1970), pp. 84–126. The author discusses Hindu pilgrimage in general, the Kumbha Melā in particular, and also catalogs numerous pilgrimage places in India. For the significance of *parva,* see John M. Stanley's excellent article "Special Time, Special Power: The Fluidity of Power in a Popular Hindu Festival," *Journal of Asian Studies* 37 (November 1977): 27–43. This essay contains a clear exposition of Hindu astrological and astronomical ideas relating to *melās*.

New Sources

Rai, Subas. *Kumbha Mela: History and Religion, Astronomy and Cosmobiology.* Varanasi, 1993.

Tully, Mark. *No Full Stops in India.* New Delhi; New York, 1991.

WILLIAM S. SAX (1987)
Revised Bibliography

KUNAPIPI SEE GADJERI

KUṆḌALINĪ.

The Sanskrit term *kuṇḍalinī* is used in Hindu yogic and Tantric literature to refer to the divine female energy (*śakti*) that lies dormant within every human body. Derived from *kuṇḍala,* a word meaning "coil," *kuṇḍalinī* is imagined in the form of a coiled serpent who sleeps at the base of the spine in the lowest energy center of the body, called the *mūlādhāra cakra.* Through specialized techniques of meditation, physical postures, and breath control, *kuṇḍalinī* can be aroused and raised through the body to unite with the divine male principle (personified as Lord Śiva) that resides at the top of the head. Although *kuṇḍalinī* is used primarily in Hindu yogic traditions, Buddhist Vajrayāna texts describe an analogous kind of fiery internal energy that is usually called *caṇḍālī,* the "outcaste woman" or, in Tibetan, *gtum mo,* the "inner heat."

The figure of *kuṇḍalinī* does not appear in the early Indian yoga literature, such as Patañjali's *Yoga Sūtra,* but only emerges in the later Tantric and Haṭha Yoga texts from roughly the eighth century onwards. The earliest reference to a coiled internal energy appears to be in the *Tantrasadbhāva Tantra* (eighth century), which describes the serpent goddess Kuṇḍalī—"she who is ring-shaped"—imagined as a snake lying in deep sleep. The first mention of *kuṇḍalinī* as it is understood today seems to be in such Tantric texts as the Jayadrathayāmala (eleventh century) and Rudrayāmala Tantra (thirteenth to fourteenth century). The latter describes Kuṇḍalinī as the "master" and "mother of yoga," who is "like poison" when dormant in the lower body and "like nectar" when uncoiled and raised to the top of the skull. Finally, in the later Haṭha Yoga literature, Kuṇḍalinī is portrayed as a serpent coiled three and a half times around an internal *liṅgam* (phallus), with her hood or mouth covering its top.

However, this image of Kuṇḍalinī as a coiled, slumbering serpent may well have much older roots in Indian mythology, iconography, and architecture. It appears in the mythology of the Purāṇas, a body of texts composed from roughly 300 CE to 1000 CE. In the Purāṇas, the great serpent Śeṣa, or Ananta, floats on the cosmic ocean, serving as Lord Viṣṇu's couch; Indian temples are symbolically supported by a serpent that coils around their foundations, and images of Buddha, Viṣṇu, and Jain saints are often represented seated upon a coiled serpent, whose hood provides a protective umbrella over their heads.

In most human beings, this coiled energy lies dormant, representing the sleep of ignorance in which most beings are lost in the world of *saṃsāra* (rebirth). The aim of yogic practice is to awaken this coiled energy and direct her upward through the body, using a variety of methods, such as yogic postures, locks and bonds (*bandhas,* postures in which organs or parts of the body are contracted), repetition of *mantras* (*japa*), regulation of breath (*Prāṇayāma*), and intense meditation (*dhyāna, bhāvanā*).

Once aroused and uncoiled, Kuṇḍalinī becomes a fiery energy which is then made to rise through the central channel (*nāḍī*) of the body, the *suṣumṇā nāḍī.* As she ascends, she successively pierces a series of vital energy centers (*cakras*), awakening the various powers associated with each one, until she reaches the top of the head. Here, Kuṇḍalinī—as the divine female energy or *śakti*—is united with the divine male principle, Lord Śiva, who dwells in a thousand-petalled lotus in the highest center of energy. The result of this internal union is an intense ecstatic bliss, a kind of internal orgasm, which is no less than the union of the individual self (*ātman*) with the absolute reality (*brahman*). The yogi who achieves this inner union is said to achieve the most supreme worldly and otherworldly benefits, including supernatural powers (*siddhis*) in this life, as well as the ultimate goal of spiritual liberation (*mokṣa*). In some Tantric traditions, *kuṇḍalini* may also be awakened using techniques of ritual sexual intercourse (*maithuna*). Here, the union of male and female partners in orgasm serves as the physical embodiment of the wedding of the divine male and female principles in ecstatic union within the individual self.

The awakening of Kuṇḍalinī is not, however, without certain dangers. Indeed, Kuṇḍalinī is also described as a tigress who can drain a man of his vital energy and semen. If not properly controlled, she can cause all manner of physical and psychological disturbances. One of the more striking cases is the account of a modern Indian author, Gopi Krishna, who accidentally awakened the serpent power, which then proceeded to rise not through the central *suṣumṇā* channel but through one of the side *nāḍīs.* After a period of intense physical distress and near insanity, Krishna sought the advice of a guru who helped him return Kuṇḍalinī to her seat in the *mūlādhāra cakra* and then raise to raise her through the proper, central *nāḍī.*

Today, the practice of Kuṇḍalinī yoga is found widely throughout South Asia in many non-Tantric and even non-Hindu traditions, including some forms of Sufism and Sikhism. Since the 1964 publication of Arthur Avalon's *The Serpent Power,* moreover, Kuṇḍalinī has also made her way to the West, and has now been popularized in various forms of occult, New Age, and alternative spirituality throughout Europe and the United States.

SEE ALSO Cakras; Jīvanmukti.

BIBLIOGRAPHY

For good historical discussions of Kuṇḍalinī and her symbolism, see David Gordon White, *The Kiss of the Yoginī: "Tantric Sex" and Its South Asian Contexts* (Chicago, 2003) and *The Alchemical Body: Siddha Traditions in Medieval India* (Chicago, 1996). A good discussion of *kuṇḍalinī,* mainly in the Kashmir Śaivite tradition, is Lilian Silburn, *Kuṇḍalinī: Energy of the Depths* (Abany, N.Y., 1988). The earliest and most famous work on *kuṇḍalinī* in English was Arthur Avalon's translation, *The Serpent Power, Being the Ṣat-cakra-nirūpaṇa and Pādukā-pañcaka* (Madras, 1964). Other important sources include *The Haṭhayogapradīpikā* of Swāmi Svātmārāma with the commentary *Jyotsnāof Brahmānanda,* translated by Srinivasa Iyangar (Madras, 1972) and the *Yoga Upanishads,* edited by A. Mahadeva Sastri (Adyar, 1968). A fascinating modern account of *kuṇḍalinī* by an Indian practitioner is Gopi Krishna, *Living with Kundalini: The Autobiography of Gopi Krishna* (Boston, 1993).

HUGH B. URBAN (2005)

K'UNG-TZU SEE CONFUCIUS

KUO HSIANG SEE GUO XIANG

KUROZUMIKYŌ is a popular charismatic religion founded in Japan in the early nineteenth century (the late Edo period) by Kurozumi Munetada (1780–1850). Kurozumi began to spread his teachings in 1814, and in the 1840s a formal religious body called Kurozumikyō was established. After the Meiji restoration the group was persecuted for a time, but in 1872 it received formal recognition from the government.

Its teachings include a belief in Amaterasu Ōmikami, the sun goddess and supreme deity of the universe. Another major tenet is that since all people are emanations of the *kami* (deities), they may themselves become *kami* through certain spiritual practices. Further, it is taught that when a person becomes one with the *kami* (*ikitōshi*) that person will achieve life without end. All are exhorted to "live cheerfully" and to obey the *kami.* At the time of its founding, the religion included a strong element of magic, including rituals for curing illnesses. Later, it came to stress the virtues of popular morality: frugality, diligence, filial piety, and harmony. The purpose of spiritual practices was to cultivate these virtues. The teachings of Kurozumikyō are characterized by a combination of popular morality and syncretic Shintō; believers seek immediate benefits in this world for the sake of popular salvation.

These beliefs, implying as they do that happiness may be garnered not by changing the realities of life but by changing one's spiritual attitude, tended to perpetuate a passive acceptance of the harsh realities of life. This is significant, given that most of the movement's followers were common people of subordinate status within the feudal order. On the other hand, they were also taught that all people have a kind of spiritual potentiality whereby life and death, poverty and wealth may be affected by pious practices. Furthermore, the idea of the spiritual independence and equality of all people was a part of Kurozumikyō's teachings. In this sense, the religion might be seen as the first step in the spiritual modernization of the late Edo period.

Kurozumi Munetada's proselytization was confined to the Okayama area, but thanks to the vigorous activities of his major disciples, the religion later extended from the Shikoku and Chugoku districts as far as the central Kyoto area. Akagi Tadaharu (1816–1867) in particular spread the teachings in Kyoto, and even converted aristocrats like Kujō Naotada, the imperial regent. Tadaharu, deeply influenced by the movement to restore direct imperial rule, envisioned a utopia in which all would be equal under the emperor. But his activities were so extreme that he was expelled from the religious organization.

In the 1880s Kurozumikyō grew dramatically and at one point boasted a membership of six or seven hundred thousand. In 1885, Munetada Shrine was established as its headquarters at Ōmoto in Okayama City. But as government control of religion tightened, the popular salvation aspect of Kurozumikyō gradually waned and the nationalistic component came to the fore.

After World War II, Kurozumikyō became chiefly a provincial religion based in western Japan. By the late 1970s its membership stood at around four hundred thousand. In 1974 a large *kami* hall (Shintōzan) was built in Okayama, and the organization's headquarters was moved there. The present and sixth-generation head is Kurozumi Muneharu. Three large religious festivals are held each year: the founder's festival on the first Saturday in April, a purification festival on July 30, and the winter solstice festival. *Kuni no hikari* and *Keisei zasshi,* two magazines published by the group before the war, were followed by a third, *Nisshin,* published after the war.

SEE ALSO New Religious Movements, article on New Religious Movements in Japan.

BIBLIOGRAPHY

Hirota Masaki. *Bunmei-kaika to minshu-ishiki.* Tokyo, 1980.

Murakami Shigeyoshi. *Kindai minshu shukyoshi no kenkyu.* Kyoto, 1963.

Murakami Shigeyoshi and Yasamaru Yoshio. *Minshu shukyo no shiso.* Tokyo, 1971.

New Sources

Hardacre, Helen. *Kurozumikyō and the New Religions of Japan.* Princeton, 1986.

Kurozumi, Tadaaki, and Willis Stoesz. *Kurozumi Munetada: Founder of Kurozumikyō.* Lanham, Md., 1994.

Stoesz, Willis. *Kurozumi Shinto: An American Dialogue.* Chambersburg, Pa., 1989.

HIROTA MASAKI (1987)
Translated from Japanese by Suzanne Gay
Revised Bibliography

KURUKṢETRA, "the field of the Kurus," is today an important Hindu pilgrimage site (*tīrtha*) in Haryana state, about eighty-five miles north-northeast of Delhi. Its history can be traced from the period of the Brāhmaṇas to modern times; in 1014 CE its earliest shrines were destroyed by the invading Mahmud of Ghazni. The site forms part of the plain on which the two pivotal battles of Panipat were fought, marking the rise of the Mughals in 1526 and the defeat of the Marathas in 1761. Since at least the sixteenth century pilgrims have come to Sannihita Lake at Kurukṣetra at times of eclipses. According to contemporary *māhātmyas* ("glorifications" of the place that serve as pilgrims' manuals), a mendicant named Rāmācandra Swāmi came there several centuries after the early shrines had been destroyed and relocated the sites according to information he received in dreams. In all there are said to be 360 *tīrthas* within Kurukṣetra. Current lists include many sites associated by local tradition with the brave deeds and deaths of the heroes in the great war of the Bhāratas, which is said to have been fought at Kurukṣetra at the beginning of the present age. Other than these epic-related *tīrthas*, the pilgrim manuals of today mention much the same sites as are described in the *Mahābhārata* epic and the Purāṇas.

One of Kurukṣetra's traditional names, Samantapañcaka, indicates that the field is supposed to be "five *[yojanas]* on each side," or roughly a 160-mile circuit. The boundaries given in the *Mahābhārata* are little altered in Puranic sources and can be harmonized with this description. Kurukṣetra is thus bordered on the north and south by the rivers Sarasvatī and Dṛṣadvatī. Especially sacred, Sarasvatī is said to have gone underground at the Vināsana *tīrtha* within Kurukṣetra to avoid coming into contact with low castes. The epic mentions four *yakṣa* gatekeepers (*dvārapālas*) on the boundaries at the intermediate cardinal points. According to a nineteenth-century account (Cunningham, 1880), these *yakṣas* sang and danced during the great war of the Bhāratas and drank the blood of the slain.

The first texts to expound upon the sacredness of Kurukṣetra are the Brāhmaṇas, and it is likely Kurukṣetra was a heartland for Brahmanic learning in the period of both the Brāhmaṇas and early Upaniṣads. Thus *Śatapatha Brāhmaṇa* 14.1.1.2 describes it as "the gods' place of divine worship," and several passages speak of the gods' sacrificial performances there. It is also the territory of the Kurus and Pañcālas, or Kuru-Pañcālas, famed for their Brāhmaṇas. These are the central peoples of the *Mahābhārata,* and several epic characters are already mentioned in Brāhmaṇa and Upaniṣadic texts.

It is through the *Mahābhārata,* however, that Kurukṣetra attains its renown. One passage ranks Kurukṣetra as the foremost *tīrtha* in the three worlds. Twice it is said that the dust of Kurukṣetra, blown by the wind, leads even those of bad *karman* to heaven. It is further described as the altar or northern altar (*vedī, uttara-vedī*) of Brahmā or Prajāpati, and thus the preeminent place of sacrifice. Numerous sacrificial acts are said to have occurred there prior to the great war of the Bhāratas, including the destruction of the *kṣatriya* caste twenty-one times over by Rāma Jāmadagnya (later the *avatāra* Paraśurāma), which left in its wake five lakes of blood. But most significant is the legend told in the epic of the origins of Kurukṣetra. The field is named after King Kuru, ancestor of the epic heroes. Kuru had plowed the field for many years, seeking from Indra the boon that those who die there should go straight to heaven. The gods counseled Indra not to grant the boon, because it would mean that human beings could attain heaven without sacrificing to them, thus endangering the gods' existence. So Indra offered a compromise. Two types of beings could directly attain heaven there: yogins who practice *tapas* (asceticism), and *kṣatriyas* who were slain in battle. Thus the traditional Brahmanic sacrifices are dispensed with, but doubly transformed. *Kṣatriyas* will attain heaven by the epic's "sacrifice of battle," and yogins and pilgrims will do so by acts of *tapas,* which the epic repeatedly exalts above the traditional rites performed there. Indra's compromise is further sanctioned by Viṣṇu, Śiva, and Brahmā (the *trimūrti*), thus indicating the subordination of these transformed sacrificial acts to the higher ideals associated with *bhakti.* All this is thus in accord with the *Bhagavadgītā,* which begins with the proclamation that Kurukṣetra is a *dharmakṣetra* ("field of *dharma*"). There, Kṛṣṇa instructs Arjuna to perform the sacrifice of battle on Kurukṣetra as a *karmayogin,* and thus perform acts disciplined by yoga that are offered as if in sacrifice to God. Biardeau (1976) suggests that the name Kurukṣetra has come in the epic to mean the "field of acts," *kuru* being the imperative of the verb *to do.* It is thus analogous to the Puranic concept of the earth as the "world of acts" (*karmabhūmi*). The act of plowing, here undertaken by King Kuru, is further a common Indian metaphor for sowing the seeds of *karman.*

SEE ALSO Mahābhārata.

BIBLIOGRAPHY

The main *Mahābhārata* passages are translated in *The Mahābhārata,* vol. 2, edited and translated by J. A. B. van Buitenen (Chicago, 1975), pp. 378–386, and in *The Mahābhārata of Krishna-Dwaipayana Vyasa,* vol. 7, 2d ed., translated by P. C. Roy and K. M. Ganguli (Calcutta, 1970), pp. 158–159. For still the best on-site description, see Alexander Cunningham's *Report of a Tour in the Punjab in 1878–*

79, vol. 14 (1880; reprint, Varanasi, 1970), pp. 86–106. On textual references, see Sasanka Sekhar Parui's *Kurukṣetra in the Vamana Purāṇa* (Calcutta, 1976). On symbolic overtones, see Madeleine Biardeau's "Études de mythologie hindoue, Chap. II, Bhakti et avatāra," *Bulletin de l'École Française d'Extrême Orient* 63 (1976): 111–263, esp. pp. 259–262.

ALF HILTEBEITEL (1987)

KUSHITE RELIGION.

Kush was the name given in ancient times to the area of northeast Africa lying just to the south of Egypt. It is the Aethiopia of Herodotus and other classical writers, and it corresponds in a general way to the Nubia of today. Its peoples were and are African in race and language, but since very early times their culture has been strongly influenced by that of their northern neighbors.

The northern part of Kush was under direct Egyptian control during the New Kingdom (c. 1580–1000 BCE). Egyptians did not settle in the country in large numbers, but they oversaw the building of temples, towns, and fortresses and the inauguration of the typical pharaonic system of administration and of worship. When the colonial overlords departed, around 1000 BCE, they had laid the basis for an Egyptianized successor-state that was to emerge a little later as the empire of Kush. The Kushite rulers assumed all the titles and trappings of the pharaohs, and for a brief period (751–656 BCE) were even accepted as rulers in Egypt itself. Kushite authority in Egypt was ended by an Assyrian invasion, but the empire later expanded southward at least as far as the confluence of the Blue and White Niles, and possibly much farther.

The original capital of Kush was at Napata, near the Fourth Cataract of the Nile, where a great temple of Amun had been erected during the Egyptian colonial regime. Later, as the empire expanded southward, the capital was moved to Meroe, near the mouth of the Atbara River. The earlier and later phases of Kushite civilization are often designated as Napatan and Meroitic, after the respective capitals. The empire of Kush was finally overrun and destroyed by barbarian invaders in the fourth century CE, but some of its traditions persisted until the coming of Christianity two centuries later.

Detailed information about the religion of Kush is scanty. The accounts of classical writers are unreliable, and the indigenous language of Kush (called Meroitic) is largely undeciphered. Most of our information is based on the interpretation of reliefs carved on temple and tomb walls and on votive objects.

In the beginning, the religion of Kush appears to have differed little from that of pharaonic Egypt. The principal state deity was Amun, whose cult was celebrated at the great state temples of Napata and Meroe, and at many other places. Other Egyptian deities who are depicted in Kushite temple reliefs include the moon god Khonsu, the ibis-headed Thoth, and the goddesses Isis, Hathor, and Mut. The ram-headed Khum, god of cataracts, was especially venerated in the cataract region of northern Kush. Horus, who in Egypt symbolized the pharaonic authority, was another deity especially popular in the north.

In Kush as in Egypt, mortuary ritual was associated with the Osirian family of deities: Osiris, his sister-wife Isis, and Nephthys, the sister of Isis. The jackal-headed Anubis also played an important part in mortuary ritual. In later centuries the cult of Isis became especially highly developed, and was no longer primarily a mortuary cult. Isis became the chief tutelary of the most northerly district of Kush (later known as Lower Nubia), but there were also Isis temples at Meroe and elsewhere in the south.

In the Meroitic period (c. 350 BCE–350 CE) the Kushite pantheon came to include a number of deities who were apparently not of Egyptian origin. The most important of them was Apedemak, a lion-headed male god who was a special tutelary of the ruling family. He was a god of victory and also of agricultural fertility. There were temples of Apedemak at Meroe and at several other towns in the southern part of Kush, but his cult seems to have been little developed in the more northerly districts, which were far from the seats of royal authority. Two other possibly indigenous deities were Arensnuphis and Sebiumeker, who are sometimes depicted as guardians standing on either side of temple doors. There was, in addition, an enigmatic goddess with distinctly negroid features, whose name has not been recovered.

Cult animals were evidently important in Kushite religion, as they were in Egypt. Cattle are often depicted in temple procession scenes, and at the southern city of Musawwarat there was apparently a special cult of the elephant.

Kushite religious architecture shows very strongly the influence of Egypt, though with some distinctive local touches. Temples are of several types, but they fall into two broad categories. The largest temples, comprising from three to five rooms, are purely Egyptian in type, with pylon gate, forecourt, hypostyle hall, pronaos, and one or more sanctuaries. All of the temples dedicated to Amun are of this type. A much smaller type of temple comprises only a pylon gate and one or two adjoining chambers, with or without interior colonnading. Most if not all of the temples of Apedemak are of this type.

We know almost nothing about the details of ritual, but we can deduce from temple and tomb scenes that offerings of food and drink played an important role. Processions of priests and animals were probably also common. Pilgrimage was an important act of personal piety, to judge from the number of votive graffiti on temple walls and floors as well as on cliff faces. Funerary texts from northern Kush suggest that there were several ranks of priesthood attached to the temples, although the precise meaning of these texts is very far from clear.

As in Egypt, the afterlife was a major focus of concern. The Kushite rulers and their families were buried under steep-sided stone pyramids, each of which had attached to it a mortuary chapel like a miniature temple. Underground there were two or three chambers adorned with painted scenes of the afterlife. The royal dead were often laid out on a bed (a uniquely Kushite practice), accompanied by lavish offerings that sometimes included animal and human sacrifices. More ordinary folk were interred in an undecorated underground chamber, which might be surmounted by a brick platform or a miniature pyramid. These too usually had an adjoining chapel or at least an offering niche. A unique feature of mortuary ritual in the northern part of Kush was the making of *ba* statuettes, in the form of a bird with human head. These were placed outside the tomb superstructure, and symbolized that part of the soul (the *ba*) that remained on earth after death, while another manifestation of the soul (the *ka*) journeyed to the afterworld.

BIBLIOGRAPHY

There is no single, detailed work on the religion of Kush, as is to be expected in view of the scanty available evidence. Brief, popular summaries can be found in Peter L. Shinnie's *Meroe: A Civilization of the Sudan* (New York, 1967), pp. 141–152, and in my book *Nubia: Corridor to Africa* (Princeton, 1977), pp. 325–328, 336–338, 374–378. More technical discussions include those of Jean Leclant, "La religion Méroïtique," in *Histoire des religions,* edited by Henri-Charles Puech (Paris, 1970), vol. 1, pp. 141–153, and Nicholas B. Millet, "Meroitic Religion," in *Meroitische Forschungen 1980* (*Meroitica* 7), edited by Fritz Hintze (Berlin, 1984), pp. 111–121. L. V. Žabkar's *Apedemak, Lion God of Meroe* (Warminster, 1975) discusses at length one particular aspect of Kushite religion.

New Sources

Török, Laszlo. *The Image of the Ordered World in Ancient Nubian Art: The Construction of the Kushite Minad, 800 B.C. – 300 A.D.* Leiden, Netherlands, 2002.

Welsby, Derek A., ed. *Recent Research in Kushite History and Archaeology: Proceedings of the 8th International Conference for Meroitic Studies.* London, 1999.

Wildung, Dietrich, ed. *Sudan: Ancient Kingdoms of the Nile.* New York, 1997.

WILLIAM Y. ADAMS (1987)
Revised Bibliography

KŪYA (903–972), also called Kōya, a charismatic Japanese monk who devoted himself to popularizing the Nembutsu (Chin., Nianfo), the oral invocation of Amida Buddha. Kūya's origins are unknown, but some sources claim that he may have been a grandson of Emperor Ninmyō (810–850) or a son of Emperor Daigo (885–930). In his youth, as an itinerant lay priest (*ubasoku*), Kūya traveled in rural areas, directing and assisting in the repair of roads and bridges, improving wells and dikes, and supervising burials. In these activities he closely resembled Gyōgi (or Gyōki, 668–749), a revered monk of the Nara period.

In 924, Kūya formally entered the priesthood at the Kokubunji in Owari Province (modern Aichi Prefecture). He later spent periods of devotion and study at Mineaidera in Harima Province (modern Hyōgo Prefecture), at Yushima on the island of Shikoku, and perhaps in the far northern provinces as well. But beginning in about 938, his public demonstrations of the Nembutsu in the markets of Heiankyō, the capital city (modern Kyoto), began to attract a large following among the common people. He soon became known as *ichi no hijiri* ("the holy man of the markets") and *Amida hijiri* ("the holy man of Amida").

In 948 he received full ordination at Enryakuji, the headquarters of the Tendai school, and took the priestly name Kōshō. When an epidemic swept Heiankyō in 951, Kūya undertook several projects designed to ease the sufferings of the people, including the carving of images of the eleven-headed Kannon and other benevolent deities, the copying of the *Daihannyakyō* (*Mahāprajñāpāramitā Sūtra*) in gold letters, and the founding of a temple, originally named Saikōji, and now called Rokuharamitsuji. The temple, near Higashiyama in Kyoto, remains closely associated with Kūya, and it was also the site of his death, at age sixty-nine, in 972.

Kūya's Nembutsu, a chant accompanied by dancing to the beat of a small cymbal or drum, was probably an adaptation of shamanic practices. He also praised Amida and the Nembutsu in simple verses that were posted in the marketplace. Before Kūya, the Nembutsu was used as a magical charm, at funerals, and in the intense meditations of Tendai monks. Kūya was the first to prescribe it as a simple expression of faith to be used by the uneducated and the poor, and he is even said to have taught it to prostitutes and criminals. He thus contributed to the Heian-period developments that carried Buddhism beyond the confines of court and monastery and prefigured the founders of the Pure Land (Jōdo) schools that emerged in the Kamakura period (twelfth and thirteenth centuries), advocating exclusive devotion to the Nembutsu and appealing to persons from all social strata.

Like Gyōgi and the Kamakura innovators, Kūya functioned on the periphery of the ecclesiastical establishment while maintaining ties with influential, aristocratic patrons, and he was thus free to convey his teachings to a diverse audience. There are many legends about his deeds, and the wooden image of him enshrined at Rokuharamitsuji (done in the Kamakura period) emphasizes his *hijiri* character: he is clad as an ascetic and carries his cymbal and a staff topped with antlers; he leans forward as if to begin his dance, and from his mouth issue six tiny images of Amida Buddha, representing the six characters of the written Nembutsu.

SEE ALSO Gyōgi; Nianfo.

BIBLIOGRAPHY

The most reliable account of Kūya's life and career is a memorial biography, *Kūya rui,* written in 972 (the year of his death) by Minamoto Tamenori. The biography in Yoshishige Yasutane's *Nihon ōjō gokuraku ki* (c. 986) and most other traditional versions are closely based on Tamenori's. These and other variants are reproduced in and were the basis for the first comprehensive modern study in Japanese, Hori Ichirō's *Kūya* (Tokyo, 1963), no. 106 of "Jimbutsu sōsho." For a more recent study, see Ishii Yoshinaga, *Kūya shōnin no kenkyū: sono gyōgō to shisō* (Kyoto, 2002).

In Hori's English works, Kūya is discussed as one of several similar Heian period figures; see "On the Concept of *Hijiri* (Holy-Man)," *Numen* 5 (April 1958): 128–160 and (September 1958): 199–232; and *Folk Religion in Japan,* edited by Joseph M. Kitagawa and Alan L. Miller (Chicago, 1968), pp. 107ff. See also Yuishin Itō, "Kūya," in Yūsen Kashiwahara and Kōyū Sonoda, eds., *Shapers of Japanese Buddhism* (Tokyo,1994), pp. 52–62.

EDWARD KAMENS (1987 AND 2005)

L

LABOR See WORK

LABYRINTH. The word *labyrinth* refers to a large variety of drawings and patterns, some intricate, some less so, ranging from prehistoric rock engravings to modern art, as well as to highly complex symbolic and mythological structures around which an immense richness of meaning has accumulated during the course of many centuries and civilizations. The word is used to describe:

(1) a difficult path, or passage, or tunnel, often underground, through which it is extremely hazardous to find one's way without guidance

(2) a seemingly unending building of innumerable rooms and galleries intended to confound intruders and lead them astray

(3) metaphorically, any kind of complexity from which it is almost impossible to extricate oneself.

In this last and more general use, and under the pressure of the growing complexities of the contemporary world, the very old symbol of the labyrinth has come back with renewed vitality to haunt the subconscious of modern humankind and reenter the vocabulary of art and literature. What makes the labyrinth, in its wealth of analogical associations, so relevant today is the fact that it is an emblem of the existential dilemmas of modern urbanites, who find themselves trapped in a prisonlike world and condemned to wander aimlessly therein. However, the labyrinth catches the imagination not just because it reminds one that one is lost in its bowels and about to be devoured by the Minotaur but also because it suggests that somewhere in the dark pit there must be an almost forgotten center from which, after the ultimate trial confronting terror and death, one may find the way out to freedom. These hints of fear and hope are, in fact, echoes of very ancient myths, among which stands the famous story of Theseus and the Minotaur.

The Myth of the Minoan Labyrinth. In concise terms the myth of the Minoan labyrinth tells of Minos, who became king of Crete when Poseidon, god of the sea, sent him

---

Clockwise from top left corner. A labyrinth on the floor of Chartres Cathedral in France. *[©Foto Marburg/Art Resource, N.Y.]*; The Stele of Hammurabi. Lion capital of Aśoka at Sarnath, India. *[The Art Archive]*; Marble Sappho by James Pradier (1792–1852). Musée d'Orsay, Paris. *[©Giraudon/Art Resource, N.Y.]*; Japanese Buddhist wood carving depicting a spirit holding a lotus. *[©Foto Marburg/Art Resource, N.Y.]*.

a bull from the sea in answer to his prayers. But Minos failed to sacrifice the animal, as ordered by Poseidon, and so became sterile. Pasiphaë, daughter of the Sun and wife of Minos, conceived a passion for the bull; she placed herself inside an artificial cow, built for the purpose by Daedalus, and made love with the animal. The Minotaur, a monster half man and half bull, was born of this union. King Minos, appalled by this event, ordered Daedalus to build a labyrinth from which no one could escape and had the Minotaur hidden within it.

The town of Athens, which had been recently conquered by Crete, was ordered to send every eight years seven youths and seven maidens to be devoured by the Minotaur. The time came when the Athenian hero Theseus decided to put an end to this dreadful tribute and offered himself as one of the seven young men to be sacrificed. He entered the labyrinth and killed the monster, finding his way out again with the help of a ball of string he had spun out behind him, a gift to him from Ariadne, the enamored daughter of Minos.

After this triumph, however, things began to go wrong. First, on his way back to Athens, on the island of Naxos, the proud hero abandoned Ariadne while she was asleep and decided to marry her sister Phaedra—a decision that later proved disastrous. Then he forgot to substitute the black sails of his ship for white ones, as he had promised his father, King Aegeus, he would do if he had slain the Minotaur; the old Athenian king, on seeing the black sails in the distance, believed that Theseus was dead and so jumped off a cliff to his death. Meanwhile, the furious Minos punished Daedalus by incarcerating him and his son Icarus in the maze. Although Daedalus was the architect of the labyrinth, he could not find his way out. Therefore he decided to escape by the only possible route: upward. With feathers and wax he manufactured two pairs of wings; he warned his son not to ascend too high, and the two flew away. Icarus, however, intoxicated by the wonders of flight, forgot his father's advice and soared too near the sun; the wax of his wings melted, and he plunged into the sea and disappeared. The more cautious Daedalus landed safely in Sicily.

Many aspects of this story require careful study before one can fully grasp its meaning. Four of its more relevant themes are these:

(1) There is the suggestion that the labyrinth is related to an unresolved conflict that carries a costly toll of guilt and fear—the annual sacrifice of the seven boys and girls—that can only be settled through the intervention of a "hero."

(2) It is also suggested that the way out of this conflict depends on mnemonics and feats of memory—Ariadne's thread—and on the ability to "fly," that is, to achieve a higher level of consciousness.

(3) The myth points to the ultimate failure of the hero. It is important that Theseus, apparently the hero, meets a dismal end when later he descends to hell, helped this time not by a loving woman but by a bandit named Peritoos, in an attempt to abduct Persephone, the wife of Hades; the project fails. Peritoos is dismembered by the three-headed dog Kerberos, and Theseus, lost in the labyrinth of Hades, is turned into a stone. This implies that the killing of the Minotaur is less heroic than it seems, for it involves the brutal suppression of a problem instead of the attempt at a harmonious solution.

(4) Finally, the story of Theseus in the labyrinth can be seen as symbolizing the dangers of initiation according to a well-known pattern of *descensus ad inferos*, symbolic death and return to life.

THE LABYRINTH AS SYMBOL. This article shall now briefly review some of the more significant connotations of the idea of the labyrinth itself. It should be kept in mind that all symbols and myths can be interpreted on many different levels and ask for a continuing effort of hermeneutics.

Descent into the unconscious. Entering the labyrinth stands for what a psychoanalyst would describe as a descent into the subconscious layers of the psyche, with its obscurities and terrors, its traumas, complexes, and unresolved emotional conflicts.

Regressus ad uterus. Entry into the labyrinth recalls as well a retreat into the bosom of Mother Earth, conceived also as *yoni*, grave, and magic oven, and related to the "V. I. T. R. I. O. L." injunction of alchemy attributed to Basilius Valentinus—"Visitabis Interiora Terrae Rectificando Invenies Occultum Lapidem" ("Visit the interior of the earth and by rectifying thou wilt find the secret stone"). This connotation is particularly strong in cave and underground labyrinths. In fact, many megalithic stone engravings seem to associate labyrinthine patterns simultaneously with the cult of the dead and symbols of fecundity, as for instance in the drawings in Val Camonica, Italy. In many cases prehistoric drawings show what seem to be the female genitalia; sometimes they show concentric circles with a straight or serpentine line running to the center, suggesting spermatozoa reaching the ovum. This is the kind of drawing Moritz Hoerner and Oswald Menghin called *Ringwallbilder* and considered the simplest and most common of labyrinthine patterns found in Europe. Explicit sexual symbolism can be found also in the Etruscan vase of Tragliatella (Museum of the Capitolium, Rome) and in connection with Knossos-type labyrinths.

Nekuia or the descent into Hades. In close association with the symbolism of a *regressus ad uterus* is that of a *nekuia*, or descent into Hades, to the underworld abode of the dead where an invisible fire transforms all bodies that enter it. Inner fire destroys and melts, but as the *athanor* (the symbolic furnace of physical or moral transmutation) of the alchemist, it also purifies, regenerates, transmutes, and produces "gold."

Meeting the monster. Visiting the underworld entails meeting its guardians: Kerberos, old women and magicians, monsters and demons. Horned figures identical with the Minotaur can be found in many prehistoric drawings, as in Val Camonica, Italy, and the Cueva de los Letreros, Spain, as well as in ancient Egypt; they bring to mind the traditional images of the devil in Christian and other traditions.

The Minotaur's horns can be related to the idea of a crown, not only through etymology but also through symbolic associations. In Delos was an altar, named Keraton, made of the horns of bulls and goats and linked to the cult of Apollo Karneios, protector of horned animals. Another interesting link can be established between horns and the *labrus*, or the double ax. William H. Matthews (1922) reports that the German archaeologist Heinrich Schliemann, during his researches at Mycenae, unearthed from one of the graves an ox head of gold plate with a double ax between the upright horns. The double ax was the sign of the Zeus worshiped at Labraunda, and it occurs frequently in the Minoan palace of Knossos discovered by Arthur Evans; it was obviously an object of great importance and was linked with the cult of the bull. There was even a tomb shaped like a double ax that contained a big ax and some smaller ones. Evans, in the light of these and other discoveries, concluded that the palace of Knossos was the labyrinth, or "house of the Labrys," although some scholars dispute this. Confirming the initiatory symbolism of the labyrinth, some authors think that the ax signifies the "power of light" and is the equivalent to sword, hammer, and cross (Juan-Eduardo Cirlot); it corresponds to the Indian *vajra* and to Jupiter's lightning, symbols of the celestial illumination at the center, and as such it may reveal the symbolic reversal of polarities implied by Gemini (Luc Benois); in any case, the ax and the labyrinth respond to each other as representations of the supreme center and of a supreme principle (Mario Pasotti).

Temenos, or the enclosed space. Burying the dead and sowing seeds consecrates the ground. This creates a privileged place, a place of sacred mystery, of a *conjunctio oppositorum*, where life and death, light and darkness, male and female principles transform and melt into each other. Such a place is a *campo santo* and has to be protected from profane intrusion and invisible threat. In this connection the labyrinth acquires new symbolic functions, becoming a prophylactic device, a defensive wall, a trap for hostile invaders, while remaining at the same time, for those who know it, the secret path to the initiation chambers in which the "second birth" takes place. Both in magical terms and in actual fact, it comes to represent the protective ramparts of the most precious spiritual treasures of the clan. And then it becomes also the defense of the house of the living, the rampart of the town and the town itself. In southern India the Tamil women draw labyrinthine patterns on the threshold of their houses in the month of Margali, or Mṛgaśira, corresponding to the period of the winter solstice, during which the sun is "dead"; some of these patterns, called *kolams*, are named *brahmamudi* ("Brahma knot") and form a continuous line with no beginning and no end.

Daedalus. Labyrinthine defense develops with the rise of agrarian empires. The need to protect crops creates the need to build secure storage places; the silo foretells the stronghold. Soon the labyrinth becomes the emblem of the treasure house, of the king's palace (as in Knossos), of the defensive walls of the town, of the *urbs*. It is not surprising, thus, to find out that the name *Daedalus*, the inventor and mythic architect of the Minotaur's labyrinth, means "to build well"; Daedalus's ascendency is also significant, for his ancestors are Hephaistos, god of underground fire and an architect himself; Gaia, the earth, mother of all things; and Erecteion, their son, a half god whose nature is partly that of human, serpent, and wind.

According to Homer the ramparts of Troy were built by Apollo and Neptune disguised as humans; metaphorically, form-giving intelligence and solar reason combine with the energy-giving depths of the collective psyche to create the urban labyrinth symbol. In Indian myth the god of heavens, Varuṇa, whose power is symbolized by a knotlike emblem, commands the divine architect Visvakarman to build a castle of one hundred rooms where the sun woman Sutya shall be kept.

It is interesting, from this point of view, to recall some of the popular names of labyrinths current in Europe, like the Scandinavian "Ruins of Jerusalem," "City of Nineveh," "Walls of Jericho," and "Babylon," as well as the frequent names meaning "the castle of Troy," like *Trojin, Trojeburg, Troburg, Treiborg, Truberslot*, and so forth. This suggests that popular imagination sees the labyrinth as the symbol of a legendary town doomed to destruction. In contrast, the labyrinths that can still be seen on the floor of European churches and cathedrals, where penitents used to walk on their knees as the equivalent of a pilgrimage to the holy places were called, among other names, La Lieue de Jerusalem ("the Jerusalem mile"). In them is found a clear symbol of the archetypal town, taken now as the promised celestial bride, the Heavenly Jerusalem glorified by the apostle John, as opposed to the doomed City of Destruction of the biblical apocalypse.

Ascent to the sacred mountain. If the labyrinth, as has been seen, denotes the underworld in its catharsis, in its descent "to the left" (the "sinister" direction), it also implies the meaning of an *anarsis*, or ascent to life and light in its turnings "to the right." These opposed movements are both comprised in the wholeness of the symbol. The link between them is evident in the wholeness of the symbol. The link between them is evident in the rapid passage from the maze's bottom, or from the pit of hell, into the mountain's ascent, or the liberating flight. In the legend of Minos, Daedalus escapes the prison by using artificial wings. In his *Commedia* Dante reaches the depths of hell only to find that he is at the bottom of the mountain of purgatory, which he subsequently climbs with his guide Vergil. Similarly, at the entrance of the cave leading to the Maya kingdom of the dead stands the stairway pyramid, symbolizing ascent to the heavens, and, according to Codex Borgia, after the terrifying journey to the abyss, the soul turns right into the realm of regenerating water and purifying fire, to be born again.

In the archetypal town the center represents this place of rebirth and ascent and is occupied by an empty space, which marks the vertical axis that links the different planes of the cosmos, or by a temple, which symbolizes the sacred mountain. The temple or the mountain's axis is again the central passage along which the underworld communicates with the world of humans and the world of the gods. Such is the symbolism of the Temple of Solomon, built on Mount Moriah; of the sacred Mount Tabor; of the Samaritans' Mount Gerizim; of the Batu-Ribn, the cosmic rock of the Semang of Malacca, on which once stood a tree rising to heaven; of the subterranean temples of the Pueblo Indians of North America, in which a hole in the ground and a ladder to the ceiling link the netherworld to the worlds above; of the Kaʿbah in Mecca, the sacred stone that fell from the sky, leaving a hole corresponding to the North Star that is known as the Door of Heaven; and so forth. The center of the labyrinth, the *axis mundi*, the vertical alignment of the centers of the abyss, of the earth and of the heavens, the temple, the sacred mountain, and the infinite number of variations on these themes—all are parts of the same symbolic constellation.

Dance, playground, garden, and game. As shall be seen below, there is a profound link between the labyrinth and dance. Legend says that Daedalus built in the agora of Knossos the first place for sacred dances. After the victory of Theseus over the Minotaur, the feat was reenacted on the island of Delos in a nightly dance dedicated to the goddess of love that was known by the name of *geranos*, a word coming from the Greek for "cranes," probably because these birds fly in a straight line.

Things sacred do not disappear with time, even when they are seemingly abandoned in favor of other traditions, beliefs, and cultures; they often survive in folklore, in popular and peasant festivals and traditions, in children's games, in plays and playgrounds. Labyrinthine games were extremely popular in England; witness the many surviving "turf-mazes," sometimes called "Troy towns" or "Caerdroia," which follow the pattern of the labyrinths seen on coins from Knossos. The art of trimming hedges of evergreens is very old; it made possible the creation of the hedge mazes in gardens that became popular in the seventeenth century, especially in Holland, France, and England. And the type of game in which a path must be followed to a center, like *jeu de l'oie*, snakes and ladders, and so many others everywhere is an example of how the symbol of the labyrinth has survived in children's games and puzzles.

TYPES OF LABYRINTH. Such a wealth of connotations and interlinked meanings combine in the single symbolic structure of the labyrinth. This article can give only a pale idea of its riches. They show its antiquity and the accumulation of many layers of magical, religious, intuitive, rational, and metaphysical significance. Over the centuries the idea of the labyrinth has evolved and acquired new meanings that have influenced its design. The discussion that follows will attempt to categorize these different labyrinthine patterns.

The serpentine linear labyrinth. A type of proto-labyrinthine pattern of wandering or undulating lines, sometimes going in one direction and then turning back in the opposite one, is frequent in prehistoric rock engravings; in some cases it appears in combination with spiral labyrinths. Serpentine lines evoke a voyage "to the left and to the right" and connote a fate decided by various opposing influences, visible and invisible—the path of the nomad or the hunter, the passage of humanity through space and time.

Ringwallbilder. A type of drawing known to scholarship as a *Ringwallbilder* consists basically of concentric circles penetrated by a straight or serpentine line. The central point corresponds to origin, to the *fiat*, to the manifestation of divine energy. In its dimensionless recesses is concealed the mysterious inmost womb of all creation and all creatures. Thus new life and fertility depend on the hidden center—of being, of the earth, of the mother. *Ringwallbilder* relate to a cosmogonic vision, to the mystery of life-generating processes, to fertility and sexual symbolism.

The spiral labyrinth. Basically the spiral labyrinth is made of a spiral line turning around a center; it implies a double movement, inward and outward, sometimes drawn into a double spiral. Many types of design are possible; the well-known representation of yin and yang and the Grecian motifs can be considered variations of the spiral. Because a spiral leaves no alternative paths, some authors prefer to call it a pseudolabyrinth. Spiral labyrinths are very frequent. Their first appearance is probably linked to the human revolutionary passage from neolithic nomadism to the settled agrarian life, a passage that forced a reappraisal of fertility, cosmic cycles, and earthly and motherly deities. Agriculture implies a fixed life and the creation of privileged loci, as well as the belief in the "resurrection" of seeds by invisible forces hidden in the earth, which is conceived as an inner fire capable of "digesting" whatever goes underground. It is not surprising, then, to find an ancient relation between the spiral and intestines, as in several drawings of the so-called Röntgen-style, frequent among Arctic populations, or in certain Japanese ceramics of the Jomon period. Károly Kerényi studied what he considered the first kind of labyrinth—the spiral—in the most ancient examples available: several clay plaquettes found during excavations in Babylon that show drawings of intestines. According to some scholars, the inscription on this drawing is *êkal tirâni* ("palace of viscera"); these plaquettes were probably used for divination. The bowels, through internal heat, or "fire," were supposed to create a form of energy that is analogous to the inner fire of the earth as shown in the slow "digestion" of seeds, ores, and crystals and in the sudden eruption of volcanoes.

The spiral labyrinth is simultaneously the intestine, digestion, and energy, as can be seen in some ancient documents—in the *Epic of Gilgamesh*, for example, the face of the horned monster Huwawa is made of viscera—as well as in much more recent ones—like the Romanesque paintings in which the abdomen of the figure of Christ in majesty displays the arms of a spiral and the frescoes that depict the triumph of Death in the Campo Santo of Pisa, in which a sinner's exposed bowels form a spiral. To eat and to be eaten are correlative moments in the cosmic balance; digestion in *viscera terrae* corresponds to death and dissolution, to the interchange of energies, to transmutation, and to promised resurrection. Jurgis Baltrusaitis says that until Carolingian times sepulchers often contained spiral-shaped snail shells, to symbolize a tomb from which humankind will rise again. Similarly, in Kansu, China, funerary urns of the Ma Chang period have been found decorated with cowrie patterns, also known as death patterns, spiral motifs that symbolize the promise of an afterlife. The earth, like an abdomen, ingests the seed, the dead, the sun, or the virgin before it allows the revival of plants, of souls, or of spring and fruits.

Several known myths of distinct areas and epochs follow an identical pattern of a virgin's sacrifice and burial that is necessary to ensure future crops. In one such myth, collected by Adolf E. Jensen from among the Maros of the island of Ceram in Indonesia, the virgin Hainuwele is put to death after a dance that lasts nine nights, during which men and women move along a big spiral centered upon a hole in the ground; the virgin is gradually pushed into that hole and, after the sacrifice, is buried in it; Malua Satene, probably a death divinity, infuriated by the murder of Hainuwele, forces every person to pass through a door decorated with a spiral of nine circumvolutions; those incapable of passing the portico are transformed into animals or spirits.

A definite link connects the spiral labyrinth with ritual dance. In Kerényi's opinion, all research into the labyrinth should take dance as its starting point. Peasants in many places still dance around a tree or pole (the maypole in Anglo-Saxon areas), often using bands or threads to create a spiral, as in the *geranos* dance performed in Delos in honor of Ariadne. The German *Bandltanze* are often performed inside a labyrinth made of stones aligned on the ground; such stone labyrinths are known in Germany as *Steintanz* and in Scandinavia as *jungfrudans* ("dance of the maidens"). There is also a possible link between the paramilitary ritual games of the Ludus Troiae in ancient Rome, corresponding to an equestrians' dance, and what became the tournaments of horsemen in the Middle Ages, as well as to the *ludus draconis* ("dragon's play") of France, Germany, and England, a feast related to the cult of Saint George and the return of the spring. In fact, a vast number of sacred dances of great antiquity were associated with funeral, fertility, and shamanistic rites and were performed around a center that symbolized the *axis mundi,* the entrance to hell, or "Jacob's ladder" to the heavens; in the *geranos* dance of Delos the women held a string or band and moved along a spiral, first to the left, into death, and then to the right, to rebirth. Many types of such dances could be mentioned, like the shamanistic ones of Central Asia, the first element of which is spinning around a center. According to the *Kojiki,* a collection of narratives and myths written in Japan at the beginning of the seventh century, the marriage of the male and female aspects of divinity was preceded by a dance around the "august celestial pilaster."

Spiral labyrinths connote symbolically also the serpent, as Indian tradition represents it implicitly in the first *cakra,* able to rise up the spine or *axis mundi.* The serpent motif, so charged with energy and meaning in Tantric as well as in Christian and many other cultures, is an ancient symbol connected with the earth that appeared on ceramics at the rise of agrarian civilization and spread to vast regions of Mesopotamia, India, and Mesoamerica. It is relevant to remember that in Vergil's *Aeneid,* after the description of the equestrian dances that closed the funerary feats in honor of Anchises, it was told that a serpent crept out of the tomb and twisted its body in seven knots.

The cross labyrinth. The cross labyrinth combines the spiral motif with the partition of space in four directions. The transition from spiral to cross labyrinth results perhaps from the psychic situation created by the rise of agrarian and subsequent urban cultures. The city becomes the privileged and protected area where wealth, knowledge, and power, both material and spiritual, are concentrated. The center of the city, as center of the labyrinth, is turned into a crossroads from which distances are measured and time calculated. Four is the basic number of directions: sunrise, sunset, north, and south. A cross is the sign of their spreading from the central heart. The square, which evolves from the cross, then becomes the emblem of the rational *urbs* and the dwelling place of the new urbanite. The settlement of towns requires a mental revolution: people must make accurate forecasts and long-range plans; draw up laws and regulations, which implies a police force (the words *police* and *policy* both come from *polis,* "town"); and, last but not least, develop a "town memory" in the form of registers and archives, an act that requires the invention of writing. This change in thinking finds its visual expression in the orderly vertical and horizontal arms of the cross, which when repeated create geometric patterns based on squares. This type of geometric arrangement appeared in Mesopotamia and then, more suddenly, in Egypt in predynastic times, around the end of the fourth millennium; as René Huyghe points out, it served as a link in the passage from nomadism to settled life. The knife of Jebel el Arak, found near Dendera, a village on the Nile, is probably the first Egyptian example; the figures appear in parallel rows, not randomly, as in prehistoric art. This labyrinthine pattern eventually evolves into the classical model seen in the Knossos coins: a cross with its arms bent and turning around the center in curvilineal or, more often, straight movements at right angles. Examples of this type occur most frequently, from antiquity to modern times.

A walled, strong, and organized city may reveal itself as a prison to its inhabitants, just as the labyrinth, after some authors, may have been used in a remote past to trap wild animals. Lost is the freedom of movement and direct contact with the spirits of nature. The mythical Minotaur is, thus, also the symbol of the repressed part of human nature, prerational and vital, which the new city hero wants to subdue; the artifices of Daedalus and the needs of the emerging state hide the "monster" in the underground, and Theseus, with the help of artful memory tricks, decides to suppress it. But this is a fatal mistake on the part of the hero, for the Minotaur is also the hidden source of his own energy and power; killing the monster brings tragic forgetfulness, loss of purpose, decay, and disaster. In fact, the Minotaur cannot die. He takes his revenge in the same labyrinth, which is turned now into hell, for the Minotaur is also the promise of the sun's rebirth (as the constellation Taurus brings back spring's vitality), and through the sun's rays Icarus is punished for his arrogance in trying to evade complexity and enjoy a new, marvelous freedom in the belief that he has to thank his own inflated ego alone.

The cross inside the spiral suggests a divine sacrifice necessary to redeem those who became lost in the "city of perdition"; Christ, like Theseus, descends to hell, but instead of killing the monster, he redeems the condemned. As an *iter mysticum* to salvation, the cross labyrinth was extensively used in Christian ethics and symbolical art, in illuminated manuscripts, on the floor of cathedrals, in painting, and in heraldic and esoteric emblems, especially after the twelfth century. In literature the connotations of this type of labyrinth have inspired poems, stories, and Hermetic and symbolic writings, from the cycle of the Holy Grail legends to the seventeenth-century writings of John Bunyan and Johannes Amos Comenius.

The cross is an immensely rich symbol. It reconciles opposed directions and divided drives at its center, where the revolutions of the labyrinthine universe find their fixed axis, just as in one of the coins from Knossos one sees the arms of a squared spiral turn around the polestar or the fixed sun.

The thread and the knot. The red thread of Ariadne is a symbol of memory, as mentioned before; it symbolizes as well the sun's rays and the way to liberation. But the thread also binds when it turns and twists itself into knots, both as the cords tie the prisoner and as words compromise or the vow commits an honest person. The knots of Varuṇa are the symbol of the god's power to tie and untie, of the magic forces of sovereignty concentrated in the king or chief—justice, administration, public security, political decision, in fact, all the "powers," as Georges Dumézil established when he studied the Ouranos-Varuṇa symbolism. The knot contributes to the labyrinth as a tying device, a symbol of centralized urban power and "amazing" artifice, and as such is linked to Daedalus, the artist and the inventor. But the knot also symbolizes initiation and, through its intricate detours, the journey of the soul to salvation.

The native peoples of the Malekula Islands in Vanuatu believe in a "journey of the dead," as John Layard (1937) has observed; according to one of the oldest variants of their myth, the soul must pass the "waters of death" and then, at the entrance of the cave leading to the kingdom of the souls, be confronted with the "female devouring ghost." This ghost has previously drawn with her finger on the sand of the floor of the cave, a geometric "knotty" pattern of considerable complexity: It is made of one uninterrupted line, named "the way" or "the path." Half of the drawing has been erased by the ghost, however, and the soul must remake the missing half correctly before being admitted into the cave. The female devouring ghost will eat those who are unable to complete the drawing. In preparation for this journey the Malekula islanders practice the ritual drawing of difficult patterns on the sand.

One is reminded here of the cave of the sibyl of Cumae, in the sixth book of Vergil's *Aeneid*, and of the labyrinth drawn at its entrance. One-line, complex patterns evoke as well the famous *Concatenation* drawn by Leonardo da Vinci, Albrecht Dürer's *Sechs Knoten*, and the arabesques of Muslim art (in architecture, in frontispieces to the Qurʾān, in tile and carpet motifs). One is also are reminded of many well-known Celtic labyrinthine designs sculpted on crosses and stones, such as the Carndonagm Cross at Donegal, in Ireland, and the Jelling Stone in Denmark.

The thread symbolizes guidance through a difficult path or through initiatory rites, the loving or charitable gift of secret knowledge, and the promise of freedom. In India the monks of Viṣṇu receive a sacred thread, and neophytes learn to perform symbolic exercises with it. Metaphysically, the thread is that with which God made all things, his divine logos; with it the sun, like a spider, unites the worlds. The *Satapatha Brahmana* calls it the "wind" thread, and the *Brhadaranyaka Upaniṣad* comments that the knowledge of this thread and of *brahman* is the supreme knowledge of being in all its manifestations. Knowing that there is only one thread in spite of the infinite variety of its knots, as Ananda Coomaraswamy ponders, brings one safely to the end of the path, to the center, and to the cosmic architect, himself the way and the door.

The celestial city and the *maṇḍala*. Finding the way through a labyrinth, conceived as a mental, spiritual, and metaphysical enigma, corresponds to the successful conclusion of an *iter mysticum*. It can be expressed visually by transformation of the labyrinth drawing into what in Indo-Tibetan terms is known as *maṇḍala*. The *maṇḍala* (the more schematic linear variations are called *vantras*) basically consists of a circle enclosing a square divided into four triangles; in the center of each triangle, as well as in the center of the whole drawing, are circles that contain the images of deities. This pattern can take an infinite number of variations, some of which are similar to the classical pattern of the labyrinth: Many *maṇḍalas* show bastions, ramparts, towers, and gardens. All are conducive to yogic meditation; they are meant to protect the meditator from distraction caused by unconscious impulses and lead him or her to a *descensus ad inferos* where the meditator meets his or her "ghosts," and, recognizing their true nature, conquers them. Step by step the meditator is led out of the ocean of *saṃsāra*—the overpowering illusion of the complexity of appearances—to gain a new realization of being.

The *maṇḍala* is therefore a chart of the cosmos, including the *axis mundi,* the cosmic mountain of Sumeru, the palace of the *cakravartin* ("universal monarch"), and, according to the Tantric text, the *Sādhanamāla* ("city of liberation"). The city of liberation evokes the celestial Jerusalem that descends from the heavens at the end of time; like a *maṇḍala,* the celestial city expresses the final unification of opposites and the emergence of the transcendental ego—the "secret self" or *ātman* of the Vedānta, the Self in Jung's terminology. The rose windows in medieval churches and cathedrals of the West, considered one of the greatest achievements of European art, are *maṇḍalas,* symbolizing the process leading to the ultimate metamorphosis of humankind. Their colored light, circular shape, and geometric crystalization suggest the attained final radiance of the "adamantine body."

SEE ALSO Center of the World; Crossroads; Descent into the Underworld; Knots; Maṇḍalas.

BIBLIOGRAPHY

Borgeaud, Philippe. "The Open Entrance to the Closed Palace of the King: The Greek Labyrinth in Context." *History of Religions* 14 (1974): 1–27.

Coomaraswamy, Ananda K. "The Iconography of Dürer's 'Knots' and Leonardo's 'Concatenation.'" *Art Quarterly* 7 (1944): 109–128. A brilliant essay on the symbolism of knots.

Cowen, Painton. *Rose Windows.* San Francisco, 1979. A valuable recent book on the history and, especially, the symbolism of the *maṇḍala*-type rose windows of Western churches.

Deacon, A. Bernard. "Geometrical Drawings from Malekula and Other Islands of the New Hebrides." *Journal of the Royal Anthropological Institute* 64 (1934): 129–175.

Deacon, A. Bernard. *Malekula: A Vanishing People of the New Hebrides.* London, 1934. See pages 552–579.

Deedes, C. N. *The Labyrinth: Further Studies in the Relation between Myth and Ritual in the Ancient World.* Edited by Samuel Henry Hooke. New York, 1935. An authoritative study on the subject, with emphasis on Egyptian seals and the use of labyrinths as a protection in Mesopotamian tombs.

Eliade, Mircea. *Images and Symbols: Studies in Religious Symbolism.* New York, 1961. See especially chapter 4.

Freitas, Lima de. *O labirinto.* Lisbon, 1975. A richly illustrated general essay on the symbolic meaning of the labyrinth.

Hocke, Gustav René. *Die Welt als Labyrinthe: Manier und Manie in der europäischen Kunst.* Hamburg, 1957. A scholarly conspectus of the labyrinthine complex through the evolution of Western art.

Kerényi, Károly. *Labyrinth-Studien.* Amsterdam, 1941. A brilliant essay on the spiral labyrinth.

Knight, W. F. Jackson. *Cumaean Gates: A Reference of the Sixth Aeneid to the Initiation Pattern.* Oxford, 1936.

Layard, John. "Labyrinth Ritual in South India: Threshold and Tattoo Designs." *Folk-Lore* 48 (1937): 115–182.

Layard, John. "The Malekulan Journey of the Dead" (1937). In *Papers from the Eranos Yearbooks,* edited by Joseph Campbell, vol. 4, pp. 115–150. New York, 1960.

Matthews, William H. *Mazes and Labyrinths: Their History and Development* (1922). Reprint, New York, 1970. A classic general conspectus of the subject written with great care and scholarship.

Mumford, Lewis. *The City in History.* London, 1973. A masterly study of the evolution of towns. The first eight chapters are especially relevant to the understanding of the labyrinth.

Purce, Jill. *La spirale mystique.* Paris, 1974. A readable essay on the sacred meaning of the spiral.

Santarcangeli, Paolo. *Le livre des labyrinthes: Historie d'un mythe et d'un symbole.* Paris, 1974. A general overview of the development of the labyrinth through history, including a good bibliography.

Tucci, Giuseppe. *The Theory and Practice of the Maṇḍala, with Special Reference to the Modern Psychology of the Subconscious.* London, 1969. An enlightening study by one of the world's leading authorities in the field.

New Sources

Artress, Lauren. *Walking a Sacred Path: Rediscovering the Labyrinth as a Sacred Tool.* New York, 1995.

Attali, Jacques. *Labyrinth in Culture and Society: Pathways to Wisdom.* Berkeley, 1999.

Bord, Janet. *Mazes and Labyrinths of the World.* London, 1976.

Castleden, Rodney. *The Knossos Labyrinth: A New View of the 'Palace of Minos' at Knossos.* New York and London, 1990.

Doob, Penelope Reed. *The Idea of the Labyrinth from Classical Antiquity through the Middle Ages.* Ithaca, N.Y., 1990.

Granger, Penny. "Religious Symbolism in Mazes." *Caerdroia* 29 (1998): 11–13.

Michell, John. *The Dimensions of Paradise: The Proportions and Symbolic Numbers of Ancient Cosmology.* London, 1988.

Pennick, Nigel. *Sacred Geometry: Symbolism and Purpose in Religious Structures.* Freshfields, U.K., 1994.

Saward, Jeff. *Magical Paths: Labyrinths and Mazes in the 21st Century.* London, 2002.

Saward, Jeff, and Kimberly Saward. "Is That a Fact?" *Caerdroia* 33 (2003): 14–28.

LIMA DE FREITAS (1987)
Revised Bibliography

LADY OF THE ANIMALS.

The term *Lady of the Animals* is a scholarly convention used to describe anthropomorphic images of Godesses with companion animals. The image of the Lady of the Animals is well known to readers of the classics: Aphrodite riding a goose or in a chariot drawn by doves, Athena with her owl, and Artemis with her deer. But the image goes back much further than the classical age of Greece (fifth and fourth centuries BCE), even much further back than the times of Homer (before 700 BCE) and Hesiod (c. 700 BCE). Female images with zoomorphic body parts (wings, beaks, snakelike bodies, bear heads, and the like) are common in the Neolithic era in Old Europe (6500–3500 BCE) and elsewhere. Their origins can probably be traced to the Upper Paleolithic (30,000–10,000 BCE). The Lady of the Animals is found in almost all cultures.

Because prehistory has left no written records, interpretation of the meaning of the earliest images called Lady of the Animals cannot be certain. She was known to her earliest worshipers as "Mother of All the Living" (a phrase used to refer to Eve in *Genesis* 3:20), as "Creatress," "Goddess," "Ancestress," "Clan Mother," "Priestess," by a place or personal name, or, simply, as "Mother," "Ma," or "Nana." Whatever she was called, the Lady of the Animals is an image of the awesome creative powers of women and nature. The term *Mother of All the Living* may in fact be more accurately descriptive of the wide range of creative powers depicted in images commonly called "Lady of the Animals."

A very early sculpture of a Lady of the Animals was found in Çatalhüyük, a Neolithic site in central Anatolia (central Turkey), dating from 6500 to 5650 BCE. Made of baked clay, she sits on a birth chair or throne. She is full-breasted and big of belly, and she seems to be giving birth, for a head (not clearly human) emerges from between her legs. Her hands rest on the heads of two large cats, probably leopards, that stand at her sides. From Sumer (c. 2000 BCE), a Lady of the Animals appears in a terra-cotta relief, naked and winged, with two owls at her sides and her webbed feet resting on the backs of two monkeys. From Minoan Crete comes a small statue unearthed in the treasury of the new palace of Knossos (c. 1700–1450 BCE); staring as if in trance, she holds in her outstretched arms two striped snakes; her breasts are exposed, and a small snake emerges from her bodice.

In Ephesus, an enormous image of a Lady of the Animals dominated the great temple of Artemis or Diana (rebuilt 334 BCE and known as one of the seven wonders of the ancient world). Her many egg-shaped breasts symbolized her nurturing power, while the signs of the zodiac forming her necklace expressed her cosmic power. Her arms were extended in a gesture of blessing, and her lower body, shaped like the trunk of the tree of life, was covered with the heads of wild, domestic, and mythical animals. At her feet were beehives; at her sides, two deer. The city crowned her head.

In Asia Minor the Lady of the Animals is known as Kubaba or Cybele and is flanked by lions. In Egypt she is Isis the falcon or Isis with falcon wings and a uraeus (snake) emerging from her forehead; she is also Hathor the cow goddess or Hathor with the cow horns. In Canaan she is Ashtoret or Astarte holding snakes and flowers in her hands. In India she is Tārā or Parvati astride a lion or Durgā riding a lion into battle and slaying demons with the weapons in her ten arms. In Japan she is Amaterasu, the sun goddess, with her roosters that crow at dawn and her messengers the crows. In China she is Kwan Yin standing on a dragon that symbolizes good fortune. To the Inuit (Eskimo) she is Sedna, goddess of the sea and sea animals, especially seals, walruses, and whales. To the Hopi she is Kokyanguruti, or Spider Woman, the creatress and guardian of Mother Earth, who presides over emergence and return. To the Algonquin she is Nokomis, the Grandmother, who feeds plants, animals, and humans from her breasts. In Mexico she is Chicomecoatl, Heart of the Earth, with seven serpent messengers. In Africa she is Osun with peacocks and Mami Wata with snakes. In Christianity her memory remains in the images of Eve with the snake and Mary with the dove. She lingers, too, in such folk images as Mother Goose, the Easter bunny, and the stork who brings babies.

Composed between 800 and 400 BCE, the *Homeric Hymns,* some of which may reflect earlier religious conceptions, provide two powerful written images of the Lady of the Animals that can help us interpret earlier drawn and sculpted images. In the "Hymn to Earth" she is "well-founded Earth, mother of all, eldest of all beings. She feeds all creatures that are in the world, all that go upon the goodly land, and all that are in the paths of the seas, and all that fly." In the "Hymn to the Mother of the Gods" she is "well-pleased with the sound of rattles and timbrels, with the voice of flutes and the outcry of wolves and bright-eyed lions, with echoing hills and wooded coombes."

In these songs the Lady of the Animals is cosmic power, mother of all. The animals of the earth, sea, and air are hers, and the wildest and most fearsome animals—wolves and lions, as well as human beings—praise her with sounds. The Lady of the Animals is also earth, the firm foundation undergirding all life. The hills and valleys echo to her. In these images she would not be called a "lady of the plants," which suggests that the conceptions reflected in these hymns may have originated in preagricultural times. Jane Harrison (1903) has suggested that the "lady of the wild things" becomes "lady of the plants" only after human beings become agriculturalists.

THE PALEOLITHIC AGE. Marija Gimbutas, Gertrude R. Levy, and E. O. James are among those who concur with Harrison in tracing the Goddess symbolism of the Neolithic and later periods to the Upper Paleolithic, or Old Stone Age (c. 30,000–10,000 BCE). Therefore, we must ask whether the image of the Lady of the Animals also goes back to the Paleolithic era.

Many small figures of so-called pregnant Venuses have been dated to the Upper Paleolithic. Abundantly fleshed with prominent breasts, bellies, and pubic triangles, they were often painted with red ocher, which seems to have symbolized the blood of birth, the blood of life. These images have been variously interpreted.

These images may be understood in relation to the cave art of the Paleolithic era. Paleolithic peoples decorated the labyrinthine paths and inner recesses of caves with abstract line patterns and with drawings and paintings of animals, such as bison and deer. Small human figures, both male and female, were sometimes painted in the vicinity of the much larger animals. The drawings and paintings of these animals, and the rituals practiced in the inner reaches of the caves, have often been understood as hunting magic, done to ensure the capture of prey. But Gertrude R. Levy argues that the purposes of these rituals cannot have been simple "magic compulsion" but must have involved a desire for a "participation in the splendor of the beasts" (Levy, 1963, p. 20). If, as was surely the case later, Paleolithic peoples also understood the caves and their inner recesses to be the womb of Mother Earth, then is it not possible to recognize the aniconic image of the Lady of the Animals in the womb-cave onto which the animals were painted? And can we not also see the Lady of the Animals in the well-known Paleolithic carving found in Laussel of an unclothed full-bodied woman holding a bison horn? Must we not, then, interpret prehistoric rituals in the labyrinthine recesses of caves as a desire to participate in the transformative power of the creatress, the mother of all, the Lady of the Animals?

OLD EUROPE. Anthropomorphic images of the Lady of the Animals appear in abundance in the Neolithic, or early agricultural period, which began about 9000 BCE in the Near East. Marija Gimbutas coined the term *Old Europe* to refer to distinctive Neolithic and Chalcolithic (or Copper Age) civilizations of Central and Southern Europe that included the lands surrounding the Aegean and Adriatic Seas and their islands and extended as far north as Czechoslovakia, southern Poland, and the western Ukraine. There is reason to believe that Neolithic-Chalcolithic cultures developed along similar lines in other parts of the world, including, for example, Africa, China, the Indus Valley, and the Americas.

In Old Europe (c. 6500–3500 BCE), Gimbutas found a pre–Bronze Age culture that was "matrifocal and probably matrilinear, agricultural and sedentary, egalitarian and peaceful" (Gimbutas, 1982, p. 9). This culture was presided over by a goddess conceived as the source and giver of all. Although originally this goddess did not appear with animals, she herself had animal characteristics. One of her earliest forms was as the snake and bird goddess, who was associated with water and represented as a snake, water bird, duck, goose, crane, diving bird, or owl or as a woman with a bird head or birdlike posture. She was the creator goddess, the giver of life.

The goddess of Old Europe was also connected with the agricultural cycles of life, death, and regeneration. Here she appeared as, or was associated with, bees, butterflies, deer, bears, hares, toads, turtles, hedgehogs, and dogs. The domesticated dog, bull, male goat, and pig became her companions. To the Old Europeans she was not a power transcendent of the earth but rather the power that creates, sustains, and manifests itself in the variety of life-forms within the earth and its cycles. Nor did the goddess represent "fertility" in a narrow sense of human, animal, and plant reproduction; rather she was the giver of life, beauty, and creativity. Instead of celebrating humanity's uniqueness and separation from nature, Old Europeans honored humanity's participation in, and connection to, nature's cycles of birth, death, and renewal. A combination of human and animal forms expressed her power more fully than the human figure alone. Many animals, such as the caterpillar-chrysalis-butterfly, the bird that flies in the air and walks on the earth, and the snake that crawls above and below the earth, have powers that humans lack.

In Old Europe, the creator goddess who appeared with animal characteristics was the primary image of the divine. According to Gimbutas, the "male element, man and animal, represented spontaneous and life-stimulating—but not life-generating—powers" (Gimbutas, 1982, p. 9). Gimbutas stated that women were symbolically preeminent in the culture and religion of Old Europe. Although women were honored, the culture itself was not "matriarchal," as women did not dominate men but shared power with them. It is generally thought that women invented agriculture, which led to the Neolithic "revolution." As the gatherers of plant foods in Paleolithic societies, women would have been the ones most likely to notice the connection between the dropping of a seed and the springing up of a new plant. Women are also the likely inventors of pottery and weaving in the Neolithic era, for pottery was used primarily for women's work of food preparation and food storage, and weaving clothing and other items for use in the home is women's work in almost all traditional cultures. Each of these inventions of the Neolithic era is a mystery of transformation—seed into plant into harvest, earth and fire into pot, wool and flax into clothing and blankets. If these mysteries were understood to have been given to women by the goddess and handed down from mother to daughter, this would have provided a material and economic basis for the preeminence of the female forms in religious symbolism.

ÇATALHÜYÜK. The culture of Çatalhüyük, excavated by James Mellaart, seems similar to that found by Gimbutas in Old Europe. Like Gimbutas, Mellaart found a culture where women and goddesses were prominent, a culture that he believed to have been matrilineal and matrilocal and peaceful and in which the goddess was the most powerful religious image. In Çatalhüyük the Lady of the Animals was preeminent. Wall paintings in the shrines frequently depict a goddess, with outstretched arms and legs, giving birth, sometimes to bulls' or rams' heads. Other shrines depict rows of bull heads with rows of breasts; in one shrine, rows of breasts incorporate the lower jaws of boars or the skulls of foxes, weasels, or vultures. Besides the small figure, mentioned earlier, of the seated goddess, hands on her leopard companions, giving birth, Mellaart also found a sculpture of a woman in leopard-skin robes standing in front of a leopard. One shrine simply depicts two leopards standing face-to-face.

Wall paintings of bulls were also frequent at the site. Mellaart believes that the religion of Çatalhüyük was centered on life, death, and rebirth. The bones of women, children, and some men were found buried under platforms in the living quarters and in the shrines, apparently after having been picked clean by vultures. According to Mellaart, vultures were also associated with the goddess, thus indicating that she was both giver and taker of life.

As Mellaart states in *Earliest Civilizations of the Near East* (1965), the land-based matrifocal, sedentary, and peaceful agricultural societies of the Near East were invaded by culturally inferior northern peoples starting in the fifth and fourth millennia BCE. These invaders and others who followed set the stage for the rise of the patriarchal and warlike Sumerian state about 3500 BCE. According to Gimbutas, the patriarchal, nomadic, and warlike proto-Indo-Europeans infiltrated the matrifocal agricultural societies of Old Europe between 4500 and 2500 BCE. As a result, in both the Near East and Old Europe, the creator goddess was deposed, slain, or made wife, daughter, or mother to the male divinities of the warriors. The Lady of the Animals did not disappear (religious symbols linger long after the end of the cultural situation that gave rise to them), but her power was diminished.

MINOAN CRETE. In the islands, which were more difficult to invade, the goddess-centered cultures survived and developed into Bronze Age civilizations. In Crete the Lady of the Animals remained supreme until the Minoan civilization fell to the Mycenaeans about 1450 BCE. In the old and new palace periods of Minoan Crete (c. 2000–1450 BCE), a highly developed pre-Greek civilization based on agriculture, artisanship, and trade emerged. From existing archaeological evidence (Linear A, the written language of the Minoans, has not been translated), it appears that women and priestesses played the prominent roles in religious rituals. There is no evidence that women were subordinate in society. Indeed, there is no clear evidence that the "palaces" were royal residences. The celebrated throne of "King Minos," found by excavator Arthur Evans, is now thought by several scholars (including Nano Marinatos, Jacquetta Hawkes, Stylianous Alexiou, Helga Reusch, and Ruby Rohrlich) to have been occupied by a priestess or a queen, while others suggest that it dates from the time of Mycenean occupation of Knossos.

In Minoan Crete the goddess was worshiped at natural sites, such as caves or mountaintops, and in small shrines in the palaces and homes. She had attributes of both a mountain mother and a Lady of the Animals. In Crete the Lady of the Animals is commonly found in the company of snakes, doves, and trees, particularly the olive tree, which may have first been cultivated in Crete. In a seal ring found in the Dictean cave, the goddess appears with bird or snake head between two winged griffins, the same animals that flank the throne of "Minos."

Other pervasive symbols in Crete include the stylized horns of consecration, which evoke not only the cow or bull but also the crescent moon, the upraised arms of Minoan goddesses and priestesses, and the double ax, which may originally derive from doubling the sacred female triangle, the place where life emerges. Heiresses and heirs to Neolithic religion, the Minoans continued to understand the divine as the power manifesting itself in the cycles of nature. Thus, Cretan pottery and frescoes abound in rhythmical forms; images of waves, spirals, frolicking dolphins, undulating snakes, and graceful bull leapers are everywhere. The Minoans captured life in motion. Exuberant movement must have represented to them the dance of life, the dance of the Mother of All the Living, the Lady of the Animals.

GREECE. Eventually all the Neolithic and (isolated) Bronze Age cultures in which the creator goddess was supreme fell to patriarchal and warlike invaders. By the time of decipherable written records, we begin to see evidence that societies are ruled by warrior kings; goddesses are no longer supreme and women are subordinated by law to their husbands. On mainland Greece, Apollo took over the holy site of Delphi, sacred first to Mother Earth and her prophetess, after slaying the python, the sacred snake that guarded the sanctuary. This act can be compared to Marduk's slaying of the female sea snake (or dragon) Tiamat, to the association of the formerly sacred snake with sin and evil in *Genesis* 2–3, to St. George's slaying the dragon-snake, and to St. Patrick's driving the snakes out of Ireland.

According to the Olympian mythology found in Homer, Hesiod, and the Greek tragedies, Zeus, the Indo-European sky God, is named father and ruler of all the gods and goddesses. Hera, an indigenous goddess whose sanctuary at Olympia was older than that of Zeus, becomes his never fully subdued wife. Athena is born from the head of Zeus, but her mountain temples (for example, the Parthenon) and her companions, the owl and snake, indicate her connection to the mother of the living, the Lady of the Animals. Aphrodite retains her connection to the dove and the goose. Artemis is the goddess of the untamed lands, mountain forests, and wild animals such as bears and deer. Although she is named a virgin goddess, she aids both human and animal mothers in giving birth. Of all the Olympian goddesses, Artemis retains the strongest connection to the Mother of All the Living, the Lady of the Animals.

What happened to the goddesses in ancient Greece happened elsewhere. They were slain, tamed, made defenders of patriarchy and war, or relegated to places outside the city. Yet the attempt to banish the image of the Mother of All the Living, the Lady of the Animals, was never completely successful. Like an underground spring, she burst forth in images of Mary and the female saints throughout Christian history. In the twentieth and twenty-first centuries she has reemerged in the work of feminist artists and in a widespread Goddess movement.

SEE ALSO Animals; Goddess Worship, overview article; Lord of the Animals; Megalithic Religion; Prehistoric Religions.

BIBLIOGRAPHY

The reconstruction of Old European religion and culture by Marija Gimbutas can be found in *The Language of the Goddess* (San Francisco, 1989) and *The Civilization of the Goddess* (San Francisco, 1991); a summary of her conclusions can be found in "Women and Culture in Goddess-Oriented Old Europe," in *The Politics of Women's Spirituality*, edited by Charlene Spretnak (Garden City, N.Y., 1982), pp. 22–31. Gimbutas's work has incited scholarly controversy, some of which may reflect a backlash against feminist uses of her work; see *From the Realm of the Ancestors*, edited by Joan Marler (Manchester, Conn., 1997); *Ancient Goddesses*, edited by Lucy Goodison and Christine Morris (Madison, Wis., 1998); and *Varia on the Indo-European Past (Journal of Indo-European Studies* Monograph 19), edited by Miriam Robbins Dexter and Edgar C. Polome (Washington, D.C., 1997). The works of James Mellaart, particularly *Çatal Hüyük: A Neolithic Town in Anatolia* (New York, 1967) and *Earliest Civilizations of the Near East* (London, 1965), are essential for understanding Goddess symbolism in Neolithic civilization. For a brief overview of reconsiderations of Mellaart's work, see Michael Balter, "The First Cities: Why Settle Down? The Mystery of Communities," *Science*, November 20, 1998, pp. 1442–1443; visit the website of the new excavation, "Çatalhöyük" at http://catal.arch.cam.ac.uk/catal/catal.html. Gertrude R. Levy's *Religious Conceptions of the Stone Age* (New York, 1963), originally titled *The Gate of Horn* (London, 1948), remains a valuable resource on prehistoric religion, especially on the question of cave symbolism. Jane E. Harrison's *Prolegomena to the Study of Greek Religion* (1903; reprint, Atlantic Highlands, N.J., 1981) has never been superseded as a comprehensive reference on Greek religion with particular emphasis on the prepatriarchal origins of goddesses. Jacquetta Hawkes presents a dramatic contrast between patriarchal and prepatriarchal Bronze Age societies in *Dawn of the Gods* (New York, 1968). Nano Marinatos presents an original scholarly reconstruction in *Minoan Religion* (Columbia, S.C., 1993). For a general overview of Goddess symbolism in many cultures, E. O. James's *The Cult of the Mother Goddess* (New York, 1959) remains extremely useful. Erich Neumann's *The Great Mother*, 2d ed., translated by Ralph Manheim (New York, 1963), contains a wealth of information mired in androcentric Jungian theory. Buffie Johnson's *Lady of the Beasts* (San Francisco, 1998) is also written from a Jungian and therefore ahistorical perspective. Anthropological research on Goddess symbolism and ritual in numerous cultures, most of them contemporary, can be found in *Mother Worship*, edited by James J. Preston (Chapel Hill, N.C., 1982). *The Book of the Goddess: Past and Present*, edited by Carl Olson (New York, 1983), presents research, some of it feminist, on historical and contemporary Goddess religions. *Women and Goddess Traditions in Antiquity and Today*, edited by Karen King (Minneapolis, 1997), addresses the role of women in Goddess religions. The emergence of Goddess symbolism in contemporary women's art and spirituality is discussed in Elionor Gadon, *Once and Future Goddess* (San Francisco, 1989).

CAROL P. CHRIST (1987 AND 2005)

LAESTADIUS, LARS LEVI

LAESTADIUS, LARS LEVI (1800–1861), Sami minister, writer, ecologist, mythologist, and ethnographer who became the founder of Laestadian Lutheran revivalist movement. Laestadius was born January 10, 1800, in the Swedish Lappland village town of Jäkkvik to a Sami mother and a Swedish father. After Laestadius's alcoholic father lost his job, the family went to live with Lars's half-brother, Carl Erik, a Lutheran pastor in Kvikkjokk. Carl Erik was an also amateur botanist and encouraged his younger brother's interest in the subject.

When Lars was 16, he entered the Härnösand Gymnasium. Three years later his avid interest in botany led him to take part in a botanical excursion to Helgoland, Norway; when his report of the journey was published, the Swedish Academy of Science and Letters was so impressed that it promised to underwrite his future excursions. In 1820 Laestadius enrolled at the University of Uppsala, where he studied botany and theology—excelling in both.

He was ordained in1825, and became the vicar of Karesuando a year later. During his years as a minister, Laestadius continued his botanical studies, joining the scientific society of Uppsala publishing articles on the flora of Samiland, and serving as botanist during the years 1838 to 1840 on a French botanical expedition to the region.

In 1844, after nineteen years in the ministry, Laestadius underwent a significant "conversion" from inside the Lutheran Church from its "highly churchly" mainstream to the pietist movement of the "Readers." He became a revivalist minister, campaigning for temperance, organizing of education for the Sami people, and serving as a newspaper editor. His dynamic evangelism won him many followers, and eventually prompted a following that spread throughout the region. This religious movement, now known as Laestadianism, began among the Sami Readers in Karesuando and spread to the Finns at Pajala in the Tornio river valley. Sami and Finnish immigrants brought Laestadianism to America, particularly northern states like Michigan, Minnesota, and Oregon. Laestadius's role as founder of the biggest religious movement in northern Scandinavia eventually overshadowed his scholarly career, which expanded into several disciplines:

1. As an ecologist and botanist he was the successor to Carolus Linnaeus; he took part in Prof. Wahlenberg's botanical expeditions from Skåne to Lapland. His unique herbarium, containing 6,700 plants, was sold to the French Academy after his death.

2. As a theologian and religious philosopher Laestadius used his considerable knowledge of Enlightenment psychology, philosophy, and theology to preach forceful and dynamic sermons against alcohol and other social eveils. He published many of these, including his pastoral thesis *Crapula mundi* (Hangover of the world, Hernoesandie, 1843), the three-volume book *Dårhushjonet* (The madhouse inmate, written before 1851), as well as sermons in Finnish, Swedish, and Sami. Many of these writings expressed his protest against the spiritually dead doctrinalism taught by traditional church leaders.

3. Laestadius was a philologist of some stature; in addition to his mother's Southern Sami tongue, he spoke Pite

Sami and Finnish. He learned the latter two to be able to preach in those languages. He transcribed Pite and Luleå Sami using his own "Lodge Lappish" Sami-based orthography.

4. Laestadius was an ethnographer, mythographer, and a mythologist of the Sami people. He collected information about the ancient Sami, and compiled folk beliefs and legends into a system he called a mythology; and as mythographer used this mythology to write a history for the Sami. His achievement as mythologist and ethnographer, *Fragmenter i lappska mythologien* (Fragments in Lapp mythology), was finally translated into English in 2002. This manuscript, written between1840 and 1845, was not even published fully in Swedish until 1997.

Laestadius did field work in the heart of Sami territory as rector of Karesuando and inspector of Sami parishes in Sweden. In these capacities, he visited every lodge in Swedish Lapland, as he stated in the *Fragmenter* preface. Both this work and *Crapula mundi* were written during his religious conversion.

As a religious man he lived wholeheartedly inside the "interior household of the Sami," as he called their world view—or more properly their religion. His 1845 letter to another Lapp mythologist, Jacob Fellman (1795–1875), rector of Utsjoki, offers evidence of the change already begun within him: "I can no longer undertake any further actions with regard to this worthy manuscript, because my attention has become directed elsewhere and been overwhelmed by matters belonging to the sphere of religion, which seem to me to be considerably more important than mythology."

Laestadius's writings in Latin, Swedish, Finnish and Sami are extensive. His Sami-language works, *Hålaitattem Ristagase ja Satte almatja kaskan* (1839), a talk between a Christian and an ordinary man, and *Tåluts Suptsahah, Jubmela pirra ja Almatji pirra* (1844), an ancient tale about God and man, make him one of the first Sami writers. *Fragmenter i lappska mythologien* was originally produced for J. P. Gaimard, leader of Laestadius's 1838 royal French arctic expedition to Scandinavia, the Faroes, Iceland, and Spitzbergen. Both Gaimard and historian Xavier Marmier recognized Laestadius' knowledge of Lappish history and lore. Mythology and history are intermingled in *Fragmenter;* the borderline between the two was extremely vague.

Part I of *Fragmenter*, "Gudalära" (Doctrine on divinity), was written in 1840; the next three chapters, including one called "Comments to Fellman" were completed five years later. The other parts are *offer-lära* (sacrifice), *spådomslära* (prophesy), Lapp *nåjdtro* (shamanism), and *valda stycken af Lapparnes Sagohäfde* (selection of Lappish folk tales).

Laestadius's *Fragmenter* details his vast knowledge of the Sami people, languages, and religion. His careful criticism and field observations make him one of the founders of the Northern Ethnography school.

SEE ALSO Finno-Ugric Religions; Sami Religion.

BIBLIOGRAPHY

Franzén, Olle. *Naturalhistorikern Lars Levi Laestadius.* Tornedalica 15. Luleå, 1973.

Jonsel, Bengt, et al., eds. *Lars Levi Læstadius: botaniker-lingvist-etnograf-teolog.* Oslo, 2000.

Laestadius, Lars Levi. *Dårhushjonet.* In Suomen Kirkkohistoriallisen Seuran toimituksia L:1, 2, 3. Vasa (1949), Åbo (1964).

Laestadius, Lars Levi. *Fragmenter i lappska mythologien.* In Svenska landsmål och svenskt folkliv, B 61. Uppsala, 1959.

Laestadius, Lars Levi. *Hulluinhuonelainen.* Helsinki, 1968.

Laestadius, Lars Levi. *Katkelmia lappalaisten mythologiasta.* Tallinn, 1994.

Laestadius, Lars Levi. *Fragments in Lappish Mythology.* Edited by Juha Pentikäinen, translated by Börje Vähämäki. Beaverton, 2002.

Larsson, Berngt. *Lars Levi Laestadius—Hans liv och verk & den laestadianska väckelsen.* Skellefteå, 1999.

Norderval, Øivind og Nesset, Sigmund, ed. *Vekkelse og vitenskap. Lars Levi Læstadius 200 år.* Tromsø, 2000.

Pentikäinen, Juha. "Lars Levi Laestadius Revisited: A Lesser-Known Side of the Story." In *Exploring Ostrobothnia*, edited by Börje Vähämäki (Special Issue of *Journal of Finnish Studies* Vol. 2). Toronto, 1998.

JUHA PENTIKÄINEN (2005)

LĀHORĪ, MUḤAMMAD ʿALĪ (1874–1951),

scholar of Islam and founder of the Lāhorī branch of the Aḥmadīyyah movement. Born in Murar (Kapurthala), India, Lāhorī completed advanced degrees in English (1896) and law (1899) in Lahore. His life and works are closely intertwined with the Aḥmadīyyah (also known as Qādiyānī) movement, a minor sect of Islam founded in 1889 by Ghulām Aḥmad (c. 1839–1908), at whose suggestion Lāhorī undertook his two major works, a translation of the Qurʾān and *The Religion of Islam.* In 1902, Lāhorī was appointed co-editor of the Aḥmadīyyah periodical, *Review of Religions*, through which he propagated the movement's news and views to the non-Muslim world. This appointment marked the beginning of Lāhorī's prolific career. He translated Ghulām Aḥmad's writings into English, defended his views in the face of the Sunnī majority's growing opposition, and wrote on various aspects of Islam.

In 1914, with the death of Ghulām Aḥmad's successor, Nūr al-Dīn—a prominent scholar of Qurʾān considered the mastermind of the Aḥmadīyyah movement by its opponents—the community split over doctrinal issues such as Ghulām Aḥmad's claim of prophethood. Lāhorī headed the splinter group, the Aḥmadīyyah Anjuman-i Ishaʿat-Islam, Lahore, known as the Lāhorī group, which regarded Ghulām Aḥmad a reformer *(mujaddid)*, not the prophet. This group was more liberal and closer to the mainstream of Sunnī Islam, but also more aggressive in its outreach and more vocal in explaining its doctrinal differences with the parent group. Muḥammad ʿAlī was the main force behind the literary and missionary activities of this group (directed to the converts to Islam not to the group itself), including the opening of new centers in Western Europe and North America.

Lāhorī wrote profusely in Urdu and English. Equipped with Western research methodology and linguistic tools, he explained and defended various precepts of Islam to counterbalance criticism of Christian missionaries and to help develop a sense of pride among Western-educated Muslims in their heritage. He was the first Muslim to publish an English translation, with explanatory notes, of the entire text of the Qurʾān (1917), followed by *Muḥammad the Prophet* (1924), and a sequel, *Early Caliphate* (1932). He also addressed issues of the time. Responding to the crisis of the Ottoman caliphate, for example, he wrote a short monograph entitled *The Khilafāt in Islam* (1920). His major work, *The Religion of Islam* (784+ pages), was written in response to a book of the same title published in 1906 by F. A. Klein. The abridged and third edition of this work was published with two additional chapters, "Muslim State" and "Ethics of Islam" (1971).

The tenor of Lāhorī's writings reflects the mood of the times—polemical, apologetic, and missionary—*Islam and the Present War* (n.d.); *Muḥammad and Christ* (1921); *The New World Order* (1944); *Islam the Religion of Humanity; The Living Thoughts of the Prophet Muḥammad* (1947), to name only a few. Lāhorī clearly ranks with the intellectuals of the period, such as Sayyid Aḥmad Khān (d. 1898), Syed Ameer ʿAlī (d. 1928), Alṭāf Ḥusayn Ḥālī (d. 1914), Chirāgh ʿAlī (d. 1895), and Shiblī Nuʿmānī (d. 1914). Among his followers he is considered the most prominent scholar of the century and, according to Mumtāz Aḥmad Farūqī, the "savior of the Aḥmadīyyah movement." Through the efforts of various centers established in Western Europe, North America and Indonesia, Lāhorī's works have received wide recognition. It is claimed that a copy of his translation of the Qurʾān, presented to Elijah Muhammad, had far-reaching effects on the Black Muslim movement in North America. In the Indo-Pakistan subcontinent, however, the controversial character of the movement and ensuing polemic debates, and his split from the parent movement have adversely affected the popularity of his works among the non- Aḥmadīyyah Muslims as well as his among fellow Aḥmadīyyahs belonging to the parent Qādiyānī group.

BIBLIOGRAPHY

For Muḥammad ʿAlī Lāhorī's life and works, see Mumtāz Aḥmad Farūqī and Muḥammad Aḥmad, *Mujāhid-i Kabīr* (Lahore, 1962) in Urdu, translated in an abridged version as *Muhammad Ali: The Great Missionary of Islam* (Lahore, 1966). Muḥammad ʿAlī Lāhorī, *The Ahmadiyyah Movement*, translated by Muḥammad Ṭufail with a biographical section and bibliography (Lahore, 1973).

For the split of the movement, see Muḥammad Ali Lāhorī, *True Facts about the Split* (Lahore, 1966). Yohanan Friedmann, *Prophecy Continuous: Aspects of Aḥmadī Religious Thought and its Medieval Background* (Berkeley and Los Angeles, 1989), pp. 147–162.

For the issue of prophethood and renewal (*nubuwwat va tajdīd*), see Muḥammad Ali Lāhorī, *The Call for Islam* (Lahore, 1926, 2d ed.), pp. 7–34. For a scholarly discussion, see Friedmann, *Prophecy Continuous*, pp. 105–146.

For an insider appraisal of the movement, see Muḥammad Ali Lāhorī, *True Conception of Ahmadiyyat* (Lahore, n.d.), translated by S. M.Ṭufail from *Taḥrik-i Aḥmadiyyat* (in Urdu). Muḥammad ʿAlī Lāhorī, *Mirza Ghulām Aḥmad of Qadian: His Life and Mission* (Lahore, 1951). For a judicious historical survey of the movement and references to the primary and secondary sources, see Yohanan Friedmann, cited above, pp. 1–46. For critical views on the movement, see Muḥammad Iqbal, *Islam and Ahmadism* (Meerut, n.d.). Abu'l-Hasan ʿAlī Nadwī, *Qādiyānīyat*, in Urdu, translated by Zafar Ishaq Ansari as *Qadianism: A Critical Study* (Lucknow, 1967), and Ehsan Elahi Zaheer, *Qadiyaniat, An Analytical Survey* (Lahore, 1972).

SAJIDA S. ALVI (1987 AND 2005)

LAIMA is one of the few goddesses of the Baltic peoples who can be said to personify a number of elemental concepts. She incorporates a wide variety of both individual and societal functions, of which two are particularly noteworthy: architect of destiny and agent of fertility. In connection with the former, the etymological link should be noted between the name *Laima* and the common noun *laime*, which in its general sense means "happiness." Notwithstanding the apparent restrictions of this definition, Laima embraces a wide range of functions. As goddess of destiny, Laima holds supreme power to determine an individual's life. Her decisions in this context are not rationally motivated; they are radical and unchangeable.

In Baltic religion, Laima's role became prominent at life's critical moments. The first and most significant of these was birth. Here Laima acted as determiner of the individual life of both mother and child. Her concern for the woman in childbirth began before the onset of labor. Traditionally, the place appointed for childbirth was the sauna, and in preparation for the event the woman was ritually cleansed, as was the route to the sauna, so that Laima could make her way unimpeded to aid the woman. As childbirth was frequently a life-threatening event, the woman would offer prayers to Laima before giving birth, asking her assistance in ensuring that both mother and infant would survive the birth. The prayer was accompanied by offerings to Laima (generally in the form of dyed threads and woven braids of wool or flax). On a religious level, the most significant moment occurred after successful childbirth: it took the form of a thanksgiving meal, held in the sauna and consisting of flat cakes, honey, and ale. Only married women were allowed to participate, with the place of honor reserved for Laima.

A similarly fateful moment was marriage, and Laima traditionally was held responsible for a happy as well as an unhappy married life. It is understandable, therefore, that an unmarried girl turned directly to the goddess with prayers that she be provided with a good and suitable husband so that her life might be happy. As determiner of the future, Laima alone was responsible if the girl was later unhappy because her husband was a drunkard or because he had died an untimely death, leaving her a young widow with sole responsibility for young children. In such cases, the conflict between the unfortunate woman and Laima could grow into an open feud. Folklore material shows that in these circumstances a woman might demand that Laima carry a heavy load of stones as punishment or even threaten to "drown" the goddess.

Laima also determined a person's death. Two forms of dialogue took place around the time of death. The first involved the dying person, who attempted to persuade Laima that it was not yet time to die because important work still had to be accomplished, of which the care of children was the most compelling. This form of appeal was generally unsuccessful. In the other type of dialogue, the dying person was represented by Dievs, the Baltic god of the heavens. An argument took place between Dievs and Laima over the issue of the person's death and whether it should occur at that particular moment. Clearly, Laima was one of the most rigid and extreme of the goddesses of destiny, and the extent of her radicalism was demonstrated by her inability to alter her own decisions. If the individual's future was determined at any one moment, it then remained unaltered, whatever the circumstances. If a man was destined to suffer all his life, then Laima could do no more than weep with him. A possible explanation for the evolution of this fatalist conception in Baltic religion is what many have seen as the centuries-long enslavement of these peoples by the German colonialist Christian church.

In addition to her role as determiner of the future, Laima's obligations included the encouragement of fecundity and of well-being in general. This is comprehensible in light of the structure of Baltic religion, which is that of an agrarian community. The basis of existence and well-being was determined by the fertility of the fields and animals. As Laima's name indicates, her primary raison d'être was happiness. Consequently she alone could make the farmer happy, and by dint of this she takes her place alongside the other fertility gods of Baltic religion. In this context she is further differentiated. Depending on which animals she was considered to aid, Laima was given an attributive qualification: thus she became Laima of Zirgu ("horses"), Laima of Govu ("cows"), Laima of Aitu ("sheep"). In the oldest agricultural tradition, the horse was held to be of particular worth; hence Laima was linked most closely with horse rearing. Yet she also aided crop cultivation by participating in hoeing and by circling the farmer's fields to protect them from evil spirits.

The iconography of Laima is very clearly delineated in the sources. She is represented as a beautiful young blonde woman dressed in clothes such as those worn by the wives of wealthy farmers on festive occasions. On her head is a splendid garland and on her shoulders a colorful shawl held together with one or more silver brooches. Only on rare occasions does she disguise herself as a poor old woman.

The interpretation of the essential qualities of Laima is nevertheless complicated by certain unresolved questions, one of which concerns the source of her frequent description as *Laimas māte* ("mother fortune"). On the one hand, it could be argued that the idea of "mother," one of the fundamental notions of religion, is clearly linked with Laima. Yet on the other hand, it is also true that for centuries the Baltic peoples were subject to the influence of Christianity, particularly the Marian cult. Hence it could be held that Laima's description as "mother" is a later development based on this influence.

Another problem concerns Laima's creative role. In the sources she is occasionally described as *laidēja* ("mainspring"), from the verb *laist* ("to let," in the dynamic sense of "to cause to happen"; its synonym is *radīt,* "to create"). The epithet *laideja* and the name *Laima* are etymologically derived from the same root *(lei),* and this common derivation suggests that the act of creation is one of Laima's basic functions. Precise statements to this effect are sparse, however.

BIBLIOGRAPHY

Biezais, Haralds. *Die Hauptgöttinnen der alten Letten.* Uppsala, 1955. An exhaustive critical monograph, including a bibliography.

Velius, Norbertas. *Mitines lietuvių sakmių butybes.* Vilnius, 1977. Analyzes the texts of Lithuanian legends and discusses relevant problems. An English summary is included on pages 294–302.

New Sources

Kokare, Elza. *Latviešu galvenie mitoloģiskie tēli folkloras atveidē.* Riga, 1999. Major Latvian mythological figures as depicted in folklore.

Kursīte, Janīna. *Latviešu folklora mītu spogulī.* Rīga, 1996. Latvian folklore as reflected by myth.

Kursīte, Janīna. *Mītiskais folklorā, literatūrā, mākslāy (The mythical in folklore, literature, art).* Riga, 1999.

Latviešu tautas dzīveszīņa 2, ed. by Anta Rudzīte. Riga, 1990.

Mitoloģijas enciklopēdija II. Riga, 1994. Encyclopedia of mythology.

HARALDS BIEZAIS (1987)
Revised Bibliography

LAITY

LAITY is a term that has emerged in the Western religious and theological traditions to refer to those members of a religious community who, as a group, do not have the responsibilities of fulfilling the priestly functions appropriate to the offices of the clergy or ordained ministers.

ETYMOLOGY AND ORIGINS OF CONCEPT. The adjective *lay* is derived from the Greek word *laikos* (Lat., *laicus*) meaning "of or from the people." In early Christianity the term came to connote "the chosen people of God," a meaning derived from the Greek *laos* ("people of unknown origin"). In the New Testament a distinction is made between the Jewish "people" (*laos*) and their priests and officials (as in, for example, *Acts* 5:26, *Matthew* 26:23, *Hebrews* 7:5, 7:27).

Before the end of the first century CE the term *laos* took on a more ecclesiastical connotation. The term *laikos* is used by Clement of Alexandria (c. 200 CE) to distinguish a layman from a deacon and a presbyter. In the *Apostolic Canons,* laity (*laikoi*) are distinguished from clergy. The early Christian distinction between laity and clergy was informed by a political differentiation of Greek origin, that is, that between the *klēros* (from which *clergy* is derived) and "the people" (*laos*), the two groups that comprised the administration of the polis. As the Christian community continued to develop ecclesiastically, the *klēros,* the leaders or those with an "office," became the ones through whom the means of grace were extended to the believers, "the people" (*laos*). By the time of the Council of Nicaea (325) the organization and structure of the church was understood basically in terms of the clerical order, with authority vested in the bishops and the councils as distinguished from the laity.

While the notion of laity, derived as it is from Western sources, is not relevant to the study of all religious communities, it is a helpful heuristic category for the study of those traditions in which a fundamental distinction is drawn between two styles of the religious life, two modes of pursuing spiritual fulfillment. One mode, for the majority of persons within a given tradition, involves the religious quest in conjunction with full participation in the ordinary life of society. In this mode one will assume the responsibilities of some role as a member of a functioning society while at the same time pursuing the goals of the religious life. A second mode is characterized by a different way of life, involving total absorption in the religious quest, generally in association with a renunciation or turning away from full participation in the ordinary life of society. The following discussion will explore such a distinction in these two basic styles of the religious life as they are manifest in selected religious traditions: Christianity (Roman Catholic, Eastern Orthodox, Protestant), Theravāda Buddhism, and Jainism. I shall then proceed to suggest the possibilities and limits of the category "laity" with respect to some other traditions: Hinduism, the religions of Japan, and Islam.

CHRISTIANITY. The Roman Catholic tradition makes a clear differentiation between "laity" and "religious." The religious are those who take orders, and they comprise two groups, priests and monastics. The ecclesiastical use of the term *order,* which had been a designation prevalent in Roman civil life, included reference in the time of Tertullian (c. 155–220 CE) to both clergy and laity. By the sixth century CE, however, *order* was used to specify appointment by a bishop to a given office, with both authorization and responsibility to carry out the duties thereof. The distinction between the clergy and the laity is held to be divinely established. The priesthood, set apart by the sacrament of "holy orders" or ordination, is commissioned to fulfill the threefold function of the priestly office: teaching, directing and administering, and sanctifying. Thus, the priest as a member of the episcopate fulfills the divinely established mission of the church as teaching authority and sacramental agent, making available to the laity the means of God's grace through the sacraments. The laity, in turn, receive the teaching and the grace of God by participation in the worship and liturgy of the church and share the responsibility of fulfilling the church's mission in the world, the sphere of their activity. Through their participation in the affairs of the world, the truth and values of the church are to permeate society.

The distinction between laity and clergy in the Roman Catholic tradition is correlative with a distinction between church and world. The church is conceived as a *societas perfecta* but *inequalis,* with the *status clericalis* and the *laicalis,* each group having its respective rights and responsibilities. The clergy, with the right and responsibility of administering the sacraments, is ordained to a sacred vocation. The laity, who are to receive the sacraments and teaching and to obey the teaching, are to pursue their work in the world, the profane realm. Ecclesiastically, the church, the realm of the sacred, is given priority over the profane. Implied in this distinction is a valorization of the office of the clergy. The monastics, who renounce ordinary participation in the world (i.e., the profane) by taking the vows of celibacy, poverty, and obedience, are committed to the pursuit of spiritual perfection and fulfillment.

In the Eastern Orthodox church a similar distinction is made between clergy and laity, with ecclesiastical authority and the responsibility for administering the sacraments residing in the clergy. The designated roles of clergy and laity are manifest during the weekly ritual drama of the Divine Liturgy, in which the most sacred area of the sanctuary behind the iconostasis is entered by the priest as mediator between God and the people but is not accessible to laypersons. In at least two regards, however, the demarcation between laity and clergy was qualified. First, the formulation of the interpretation and explanation of the truth affirmed to have been revealed by Jesus Christ and contained in the Bible is accomplished through the ecumenical councils. This truth comprises the "holy tradition," as distinguished from the church tradition that developed through the centuries of church life. The authority of the councils rests on the understanding that they represent the consensus of the faithful and the conscience of the entire church, viewed as a sacramental unity of love inclusive of the laity as well as the clergy. Second, although since the seventh century CE only the celibate clergy and monks have been eligible for the episcopate, ordination through the holy orders of the priesthood may be conferred on married men, thus qualifying the distinction between clergy and laity.

A significantly different approach to the status and role of laity was evident in the Protestant Reformation that began in the sixteenth century. Martin Luther (1483–1546), in his *To the Christian Nobility,* rejected the hierarchical structure of the Roman Catholic church as well as the distinction between clergy and laity. The principle of the universal priesthood of all believers, viewed as an essential teaching of the word of God, provided a basis for insistence on the preeminence of the laity in Protestant churches. The vocation of ministry, viewed as necessary for the life and practice of the church, was the delegated responsibility of persons from the community of believers who were commissioned by the congregation to teach, to preach, to lead in worship, and to administer Holy Communion and baptism.

Although the administering of Holy Communion and baptism were held to be the right of every baptized Christian, those who were commissioned to minister became the officiants for ritual occasions. John Calvin (1509–1564) stressed the importance for all members of the church, who collectively were the laity, to so live that the reality of their state of election by God would be evident in their work in the world, which was to be pursued diligently. While the theological principle of the universal priesthood of all believers has been central to Protestantism, in practice the ordained ministry is accorded a priority in keeping with the importance of its teaching, preaching, and liturgical responsibilities, for which special training and education were needed.

The changes associated with the Protestant Reformation in social and political as well as religious life required the exercise of power and authority on the part of political officials, providing opportunity for them, as laity, to exercise influence in church affairs. Also, it was necessary for practical reasons for those set apart (i.e., the ministers) to assume responsibility for church administration. It should be noted that in the churches of the more radical "left-wing" Reformation and in free and dissenting churches (Anabaptists, Baptists, Congregationalists, Methodists, Universalists, and Unitarians), even greater prominence was given to the laity.

BUDDHISM. The relationship between the *bhikkhus* (monks) and the *upāsakas*/*upāsikās* (laymen/laywomen) in the Theravāda Buddhism of the countries of Southeast Asia (e.g., Thailand, Laos, Myanmar, and Sri Lanka) is characterized by a full measure of reciprocity. Just as the members of the *bhikkhu sangha* provide exemplary models for the laity, teach the Dhamma, and fulfill priestly functions by presiding at festival and ritual occasions, so the laity provide for the material support of the monastic community. Indeed, reliance of the *bhikkhu sangha* on the laity for daily provisions of food, for the erecting and maintenance of the buildings within the monastic compound, for the supplying of basic necessities (especially through lay offerings during the Uposatha rituals) provides cherished opportunities for merit making on the part of the laity.

The support of the laity, so rendered, invites the *bhikkhus* to sustain and extend their compassionate service to society. In this way the life of the *sangha* (the all-encompassing Buddhist community) is sustained through the reciprocity of *bhikkhus* and laity. The laity, by assuming responsibility for maintaining a stable civil and political order as well as by filling the basic needs of the monastics, provide the *bhikkus* with the opportunity to seek spiritual perfection (liberation, *mokkha, nibbāba*) by being free from the struggle to provide the necessities of samsaric existence. The laity, by their merit making, make progress toward fulfillment themselves by assuring a favorable rebirth. It should be noted that there are two orders of laity in Theravāda Buddhism, those who have never taken the full monastic orders and former *bhikkus*, who are extended higher status than laypersons of the first category. (It is customary in certain Southeast Asian societies for young men to be ordained for a brief period prior to assuming the economic and social responsibilities of adulthood.) Such former *bhikkus* preside at certain ritual occasions that do not require an active *bhikku* as officiant.

JAINISM. In Jainism a definitive distinction is made between the laity and monastics, the vows of the latter requiring the practice of a rigorous asceticism in a disciplined effort over numerous existences to free the *jīva* (soul) from contaminating *karman.* Because this asceticism involves the practice of *ahiṃsā* (noninjury to any living thing), the support of the laity in providing the necessities of life for Jain monks and nuns is indispensable. The principles of Jainism necessitate the avoidance of professions or vocations that involve the violation of *ahiṃsā,* and the nurturing of the qualities of honesty and industry is commended. As a consequence, Jain laypersons have generally pursued business and professional occupations, at which they have been very successful. Among the vows taken by the laity are those commending the sharing of wealth and the providing of support for monks and nuns. Although they are a comparatively small religious community (between two and three million adherents) that has never spread beyond India, the Jains have maintained their tradition over a millennium and a half, largely because of the vital interdependent relationship of the monastics and the laity.

OTHER TRADITIONS. As has been noted earlier, the category "laity" has limitations with respect to its capacity to illuminate the structures and dynamics of certain religious traditions. It has little to contribute, for example, to a discussion of Judaism in the common era. To be sure, there did develop among the ancient Israelites a priestly group (as members of the tribe of Levi came to be regarded, and later, at the time of the Babylonian exile, the Jerusalem priests, or Zadokites) distinct from those who were not involved in performing priestly functions, hence laity. After the destruction of the Temple by the Romans (70 CE), the continuity of a priestly order became moot, and the tradition of a rabbinate developed. The rabbinic tradition in Judaism is a learned tradition. Rabbis may be viewed as scholars of the Jewish texts and traditions—a learned laity—whose authority as teachers rests in their competence as scholars of the tradition.

With respect to Confucian China also, the notion of laity has limited applicability. Although religious Daoism and the schools of Mahāyāna Buddhism (especially Pure Land, Tiantai and Zhenyan) observed distinctions between priests and laity, the Confucian tradition looked upon the secular as sacred, and authority was vested in the sage and the educated Confucian gentry. However, it may be useful to explore briefly the relevance of the notion of laity with reference to Hinduism in traditional India, the religio-social context of Japan, and the tradition of Islam.

Hindu traditions. The most highly structured and hierarchical social organization in which there is a definitive distinction between those who have responsibility for specific and formal religious functions and other members of society who do not (hence, "laity") is the caste system of traditional India, a system that is inseparably interwoven with classical Hinduism. The four basic divisions of society had their roots in the Vedic era (1500–800 BCE) and assumed definitive form by the sixth century BCE. The *Mānava Dharmaśāstra* (Laws of Manu; 200 BCE–200 CE) is a codification of the normative behavior and duties of castes that has informed traditional Hindu society. The *varṇas* are hereditary; one's birth in a particular caste is determined by a repository of karmic consequences from previous lives in accordance with the law of *karman* (often referred to as the law of moral retribution). Each caste has its duty (*dharma*); it is one's social as well as religious responsibility to fulfill the *dharma* of one's caste. Caste may thus be viewed as class undergirded by religious sanction and metaphysical principle.

The inequality of the castes is evident in the definition of rights and responsibilities of each as well as in the restrictions concerning the relationships between persons of different castes. The *brāhmaṇas*, for example, whose duty it is to study the sacred texts (the Vedas), to teach, to perform sacrifices and other rituals, and to see that the stipulations concerning caste are honored, are at the top of the religio-social hierarchy. They are thought to be superior by virtue of their karmic repository and spiritual accomplishment.

The other groups of the social structure comprise what may be termed the laity. The *kṣatriyas*, next in descending hierarchical order, are the ruling, bureaucratic, and warrior caste. The third caste, the *vaiśyas*, is composed of artisans, merchants, traders, and farmers (although farming has been largely turned over to the *śūdras*). These three castes comprise the "twice-born" groups, that is, those who may study the Vedas as they pass through the four *āśramas*, or stages of spiritual progression: student, householder, forest dweller (one in retreat), and *saṃnyāsa* (holy person). Persons in each of these top three castes may pursue an occupation of a lower caste, should circumstances require it. The fourth caste, the *śūdras*, are to do the manual labor of society and to serve the needs of the castes above them.

There is considerable distance—social, economic, and religious—between the *vaisyas* and the *śūdras*. For example, the *śūdras* are prohibited from participating in Vedic ceremonies, traditionally are not to marry persons of a higher caste, may not engage in the duties of other castes, are denied, along with outcastes and women, entry into the *āśramas*, and so forth. Below the *śūdras* are those outside the caste system altogether, whose work includes the undesirable occupations of leather worker, hunter, latrine cleaner, handler of corpses, etc. Each of these social groupings is divided into subcastes or subgroups, each with its own duties and responsibilities. Although this religio-social structure appears to be rigidly entrenched, it must be remembered that it served traditional India well over many centuries, providing for stability, order, and the sure accomplishment of the many and diverse tasks essential to the effective functioning of society. In no society have differentiated groups of laity been addressed by more specifically assigned duties and responsibilities. While changes in the caste system are occurring in contemporary urban India, largely in the direction of increased fluidity, its major characteristics persist in Indian villages, which comprises about 75 percent of the subcontinent.

Japanese religions. The sociological expression of religious community in the distinctive religio-social context that is Japan invites an exploration of the possible relevance of the notion of laity in interpreting Japanese religious traditions. Although a diversity of religions has emerged in Japanese culture, there is among Japanese people a permeating and encompassing sense of sacred community that is coextensive with national identity. Rooted in the indigenous traditions of Shintō, a sense of the continuity between the people, the land, the ancestors, the nation, and *kami* (sacred and mysterious power) provides a cosmic orientation that sustains and informs the Japanese whatever the particularities of religious affiliation. To be Japanese is "to participate in the task of unfolding the underlying meaning of the national community which is their sacred trust" (Kitagawa, 1968, p. 309). There are, of course, priestly officials who are distinguished from lay members of the major religions, including Sectarian and Shrine Shintō, Pure Land (Jōdo and Shin), Shingon, Tendai, and Nichiren Buddhism, and Christianity. But the vitality of these particular religions is dependent upon the participation and support of the laity associated with each.

In addition to the sense of identity and meaning that is derived from participation in these particular religious communities, there is an encompassing sense of what it means to be Japanese. This feeling is grounded in a historic apprehension of Japan as "a communal manifestation of the sacred" (Kitagawa, 1968, p. 309). In this latter sense, all of the people of Japan can be viewed as participants in the corporate manifestation of sacrality. One question addressing contemporary Japan is whether this corporate sense with a cosmic dimension can be maintained alongside the continuing development of Japan as a modern nation-state within which there is a plurality of particular religions. A phenomenon of considerable interest has been the emergence of new religious movements (*shinkō shūkyō*) in Japan during the nineteenth and twentieth centuries, and especially after World War II. These new religions have been, in the main, lay movements. It is not incidental that they have developed during a time of rapid cultural and political change. The new religious movements, whether of Shintō (Tenrikyō, Konkōkyō, Tenshō Kōtai Jingukyō), Buddhist (Sōka Gakkai or Nichiren Shōshū, Reiyūkai, Risshō Kōseikai) or Christian origin, have frequently been inspired by a shamanistic manifestation of *kami* in a charismatic leader (who usually becomes a primary source of authority); they also provide a strong sense of corporate solidarity, emphasize the active participation of laity, and assure the realization of lay values (e.g., health and prosperity).

Islam. Because there is no clergy as such in Islam, there is technically no laity either. The sources of authority in Islam—Qurʾān, *sunnah,* analogical reasoning (*qiyās*), and consensus (*ijmāʿ*)—are the foundation of all Muslim teaching, and there is the need for commentary and interpretation of these authoritative sources as well as of the *sharīʿah* (divine law). For Sunni Islam (the normative religion of about 85 percent of Muslims, dominant in the Muslim world outside of Iran and southern Iraq) there are the imams (preachers and teachers of the Muslim law) and the jurists (specialists in *fiqh,* or jurisprudence, and the study of the *sharīʿah*). They have a special responsibility to the *ummah* (the community of Muslims) but no special privileges before God.

For Shīʿī Islam (dominant in Iran and southern Iraq, with minorities in Yemen, India, Pakistan, and Lebanon) there is held to be a line of divinely ordained and authoritative successors (imams) of Muḥammad through his cousin and son-in-law, ʿAlī, as teachers of the faithful. Although there are variations among the Shīʿīs with respect to the specific figures accepted as legitimate in the line of succession, there is a general expectation that the authentic imam, now hidden, will return as the Mahdi to establish justice. Meanwhile, authority is vested in leaders of the various Shīʿī groups, who are thought, in the interim, to act on behalf of the hidden imam. All Muslims, in submission and commitment to God, are to be obedient to the revelation contained in the Qurʾān and are to follow "the straight path." All are equal before God, with no distinctions in this regard among those within the *ummah.* Thus, to speak of "laity" and "clergy" within the community of Islam is to introduce categories that are more likely to distort than to illuminate the religio-social dynamics of this tradition.

SEE ALSO Merit, article on Buddhist Concepts; Saṃgha.

BIBLIOGRAPHY

Chatterjee, Satischandra. *The Fundamentals of Hinduism.* 2d ed. Calcutta, 1970. A basic discussion of the cardinal aspects of traditional Hinduism.

Fingarette, Herbert. *Confucius: The Secular as Sacred.* New York, 1972. A discerning interpretation of the formative influence of Confucius and Confucianism on traditional China.

Ghurye, G. S. *Caste and Class in India.* 2d ed. Bombay, 1950. A definitive presentation of the history and features of the caste system in India.

Glasenapp, Helmuth von. *Der Jainismus, eine indische Erlösungsreligion.* Berlin, 1925. A classic and unsurpassed treatment of the thought and practice of Jainism that is worthy of careful attention even though it does not profit from the findings of the most recent scholarship.

Hodgson, Marshall G. S. *The Venture of Islam.* 3 vols. Chicago, 1974. A comprehensive and accomplished treatment of Islam as a religion and of Islamic culture and history.

Kitagawa, Joseph M. *Religion in Japanese History.* New York, 1966. One of the most complete and authoritative accounts of the religions of Japan portraying their historical developments.

Kitagawa, Joseph M. *Religions of the East.* Enl. ed. Philadelphia, 1968. An interpretation of the major religions of Asia focusing on the theme of religious community.

Kraemer, Hendrik. *A Theology of the Laity.* Philadelphia, 1958. A Protestant interpretation of the role and status of the laity within the Christian tradition.

Latourette, K. S. *A History of Christianity.* New York, 1953. A competent and informative account; a work of careful scholarship and artful, judicious interpretation.

Lester, Robert C. *Theravada Buddhism in Southeast Asia.* Ann Arbor, Mich., 1973. This study, informed by field experience, depicts the modern situation and dominant features of Theravada Buddhism in the countries in which it is strongest.

Maclean, A. J. "Laity, Laymen." In *Encyclopaedia of Religion and Ethics,* edited by James Hastings, vol. 7. Edinburgh, 1914. Although dated, this article presents in a concise and lucid manner the origins and derivations of the concept "laity" in early Christianity.

Rahman, Fazlur. *Islam.* 2d ed. Chicago, 1979.

Rahner, Karl. *Theology for Renewal: Bishops, Priests, Laity.* New York, 1964. A provocative theological statement about the responsibilities of and opportunities afforded the various offices and constituent groups of the Roman Catholic church in the contemporary era.

Seltzer, Robert M. *Jewish People, Jewish Thought: The Jewish Experience in History.* New York, 1980. An account of Jewish intellectual history by a foremost scholar of the basic texts and seminal figures of the tradition.

Zimmer, Heinrich. *Philosophies of India.* Edited by Joseph Campbell. Princeton, 1951. Zimmer's study remains one of the most illuminating treatments of the classical thought systems of India.

New Sources

Ahir, D. C. *The Status of the Laity in Buddhism.* Delhi, 1996.

Astell, A. W. *Lay Sanctity, Medieval and Modern: A Search for Models.* Notre Dame, Ind., 2000.

Boisvert, L. *Laïcs Associés à un Institut Religieux.* Saint-Laurent, Québec, 2001.

Carré, O. *L'islam laïque, ou, Le retour à la Grande Tradition.* Paris, 1993.

Harris, Elizabeth J. "Internal and External Authority among Lay Buddhist Women in Contemporary Sri Lanka." *Scottish Journal of Religious Studies* 18, no. 1 (1997): 51–75.

Lancaster, L. R., R. K. Payne, and K. M. Andrews. *Religion and Society in Contemporary Korea.* Berkeley, 1997.

Sauvage, M. *Vie religieuse laïque et vocation de frère: recueil d'articles.* Rome, 2001.

Schopen, G. *Bones, Stones, and Buddhist Monks: Collected Papers on the Archaeology, Epigraphy, and Texts of Monastic Buddhism in India.* Honolulu, 1997.

F. Stanley Lusby (1987)
Revised Bibliography

LAKES. Water, essential to life on earth, has occupied a preeminent place in religious thought and imagery, together with the land and sky. In many cultures it is considered to be procreative, a source of forms and of creative energy. The life-giving property of water has been projected in its almost universal perception as *fons et origo,* "spring and origin," the element that preceeds solid form and is the support of all earthly creation. In this context, from remote times to the present, among peoples who have perceived the world in terms of sacred and profane phenomena, springs, ponds, and lakes have figured importantly in the realm of water symbolism. In many regions of the world where lakes are major geographic features, they often have been the setting of cosmogonic myths and have been invested with many meanings, historical associations, and ritual functions.

The importance of sacred lakes in cultural context will be discussed by examining the ritualistic and mythic significance of two American lakes, Titicaca and Texcoco, associated with the Andean and Mexican civilizations respectively. The areas around both these lakes have been heavily populated in ancient, colonial, and modern times. Accounts of the ancient ceremonial pageantry, mythology, and human-made or natural sacred places in and around these lakes have been reported since the sixteenth-century Spanish conquest. Their meanings and functions in the evolution of native American civilizations continue to form an expanding field of inquiry in archaeology, art history, and ethnology, as well as in the history of religions.

Lake Titicaca. Lake Titicaca lies between southern Peru and northwestern Bolivia, where the Peruvian intermontane valleys and rugged cordilleras give way, at the 12,500-foot level, to the spacious Altiplano. This lake is impressive in its size and is the highest navigable body of water in the world. It sustained the agricultural and economic life of the surrounding areas. As the mainstay of complex societies, the religious meaning of the lake was most dramatically defined in the case of the civilizations of the Tiahuanaco (c. 100 to 1000 CE) and the Inca (c. 1400 to 1532 CE). Near Lake Titicaca, the principal archaeological ruins are those of Tiahuanaco, located in Bolivia a few miles inland from the southern shore. This was an important political and religious center whose influence spread over large section of Bolivia and southern Peru. The Titicaca basin came again within the orbit of an imperial state during the fifteenth century, when the Inca nation extended political control from the capital of Cuzco, some 200 miles to the north. At this time the Inca nation affirmed a spiritual and historical connection with the earlier Tiahuanaco state, and the Inca ruler Tupac Yupanqui visited the islands of Titicaca and Koati on the lake and commissioned shrines there. Inca interest in the lake was expressed in religious art and architecture, the location of major shrines, and the incorporation of ancient myths concerning the lake into their own mythology. By these means the lake's ancient significance continued to remain part of an imperial sacred geography.

In Andean religion the border between the notion of deities and the phenomena of nature was entirely open, with emphasis placed on direct communication with the elements of nature. The worship of *huacas* and major nature deities was a basic theme of Andean religion. A *huaca* was an object or phenomenon that was perceived to have unusual presence or power beyond the range of everyday life, where the sacred may have been manifested or where the memory of some past momentous event resided. It could be the locus of an oracle, a cave, or a curiously indented boulder where a people were thought to have emerged from the earth during the time of creation. This belief system was closely tied to the formation of sacred geographies and formed part of a cosmological religion with an array of gods associated with natural epiphanies.

The island of Titicaca, about seven miles long, serves as a good example of how a lake figured in Andean sacred geography. Adolph Bandelier's explorations and interpretive report of 1910 remain fundamental to an understanding of the island and its ruins. Toward the northern end of the island there is a construction, and it was across this isthmus that a precinct wall was built to separate sacred from proface space. Early Spanish accounts record that three gates were arranged in succession here and that confessions were required of all who sought to pass through. The religious and ritual focus of the site lay beyond the gates. The sacred feature was comprised of a great rock about 25 feet high and 190 feet long, with a broad plaza or assembly ground built in front. This was the chief *huaca* of the island, named in Aymara *titi* ("wild cat") *kaka* ("rock"), the latter word a substitution for *kala* ("stone"). The shrine rock was thus the source for the name of the lake itself. Also included within this sacred precinct were burial cysts with offerings and paraphernalia, storehouses, and residences for cult priests, officers, and aides. In this context it is important to mention the Pilco-Kayma building on Titicaca Island, which corresponds to another structure called Inyak-Uyu on Koati Island nearby. The design and siting of these two buildings reveal an important aspect of Andean religion. Both buildings stand near the eastern shores of their respective islands, and the principal apartments in each ruin, with the most elaborate entrances and prominent niches, open toward the majestic snow-capped peaks of Sorata and its neighbors across the lake on the Bolivian (eastern) side. These grand mountains even today continue to be worshiped by the people in their vicinity. Considered in relation to Lake Titacaca and the island of Titicaca with its huge rock *huaca,* the mountains complete the *imago mundi* of Altiplano peoples.

The Inca people paid homage to Titicaca Rock as the dominant and central feature associated with the lake. This is illustrated by Spanish written accounts of an annual pilgrimage made to the island across the straits from a shrine on nearby Copacabana Peninsula. In that festival, which centered around solar events, two principal idols were brought in reed boats from Copacabana: a statue of the sun father, Inti, and one of the moon mother, Mama Quilla. These two effigies were regarded as husband and wife, and they were transported with other idols dedicated to thunder and other natural forces. The sun was represented in the form of an Inca of gold embellished with much brilliant jewelry; the moon was represented as a queen of silver; and thunder was a man of silver, also very brilliant. Once landed, they were placed in splendid litters decorated with flowers, plumage, and plates of gold and silver, and they were carried to the sacred enclosure. The idols were set up in a plaza, almost certainly in front of the sacred rock. After having placed the idols, the attendant Inca priests and nobles prostrated themselves, first worshiping the effigy of the sun, then that of the moon, afterward that of the thunder, and then the others. The prostrations were concluded by blowing kisses to the images and to the *huaca* itself. Dances, banquets, and amusements were then held to close the festival.

Even today, Titicaca Island is known as the "island of the sun," while Koati is the "island of the moon." Yet it is clear that, although the cult of these celestial bodies was maintained upon the islands by the Inca, they remained subordinate to the primary cult of Titicaca Rock itself.

What then, was the meaning of the sacred rock, the dominant icon of the island? What was its relationship to the surrounding waters of the lake? The answers lie in mythology. Bandelier's compilation of myths recorded by the sixteenth-century Spanish chronicler Cieza de León include a text in which the Indians tell of an event that occurred before the Incas ruled in these lands. Long ago, they went without seeing the sun for a long time and suffered greatly, so they prayed to their gods, begging them for light. The sun then rose in great splendor from the island of Titicaca, within the great lake of the Collao (the ancient name of province), so that all were delighted. Then from the south there came a white man of large size who showed great authority and inspired veneration. This powerful man made heights out of level plains and flat plains out of great heights, and created springs in live rock. Recognizing in him such power, they called him Maker of All Created Things, Beginning Thereof, and Father of the Sun. They also said that he gave humans and animals their existence and that they derived from him great benefits. This being, called Ticciviracocha, was regarded as the supreme creator. Another myth, recorded by Juan de Betanzos before Ceiza, also connects two successive "creations" of the world by "Con Tici Viracocha" to Lake Titicaca (Bandelier, 1910, pp. 298–299). In yet another version, the sun and moon were said to have risen from Titicaca itself. In this mythological context, "wild cat rock" must be seen as a cosmogonic place of origin.

Rising from the windswept sheet of reflecting water, the island hills and promontories are removed from the sphere of ordinary life. On the ridges, marine fossil strata underscore the theme of aquatic emergence at this unusual site. The placement of the *huaca* and the relationship of buildings to the distant mountains are joined with ritual and mythic imagery in a powerful metaphor of humanity and land. The sense of place, of being "at the center," is also linked to notions of history, for the ancient myths and the architectural features of the Pilco-Kayma building (designed in an archaic style) reminded the Inca of Tiahuanaco and established a succession to that old imperial tradition. In this respect, the Inca shrine incorporated a sense of the past and signaled territorial possession. Woven into these levels of meaning was a still more fundamental theme. Most of all, the setting was designed to bring to mind the time and place of the beginnings. The sacred lake was the primordial natural icon, a reminder of *illud tempus.* Passive in the mythic imagery, the lake formed the fluid cosmogonic field from which all forms came forth in darkness. Upholding the island birthplace of the sun and moon, Lake Titicaca, as the home of Viracocha, who gave form to mountains, plains, and people, was the element from which the world itself was made.

LAKE TEXCOCO AND THE VALLEY OF MEXICO. Rimmed by mountains and snowcapped volcanoes, the Valley of Mexico is a spacious basin that formerly contained a system of shallow interconnected lakes. The central lake, known as Texcoco, was saline from evaporation, but the southern lakes of Chalco-Xochimilco were fed by abundant aquafers that issued from the base of the steep Ajusco Mountains. To the north, lakes Zumpango-Xaltocán depended more on seasonal rain, but there is evidence that in ancient times the surrounding hills and open fields were watered by abundant springs and streams. In a collective sense, the entire set of lakes may be referred to as Lake Texcoco.

By the first century CE, the city of Teotihuacan began to dominate the lesser settlements in the Texcoco lakeshore region. A powerful manufacturing, trading, and religious center of some one hundred thousand people, Teotihuacan became the center of a trade network that ramified to the most distant parts of Mesoamerica. With the violent eclipse of this metropolis in the seventh century, power was transferred to other capitals throughout the neighboring highlands. The old ascendancy of the Valley of Mexico was not restored until the fifteenth century with the rise of the Méxica-Aztec capital of Tenochtitlán and its allied neighbor, the city of Texcoco. Built on an island and reclaimed marshes near the western shore of Lake Texcoco, Tenochtitlán became the most feared and powerful city, the seat of the most powerful empire in Mesoamerican history.

An agricultural economy, supplemented by fishing and the gathering of natural products, remained fundamental to urban life throughout the long history of the valley, and the problem of maintaining fruitful relationships between humans and nature formed an underpinning of religious life. To express this relationship in symbolic form, monumental works of art and architecture were built as stage sets and memorials for seasonal rites as well as the important ceremonies of government and war. The ruined pyramids of Teotihuacan were the largest in Mesoamerica, and long after the city was destroyed they were visited in pilgrimage by the rulers of the later México-Aztec state. In the middle of the México-Aztec capital, Tenochtitlán, a new pyramid and attendant temples were built in a great quadrangular enclosure, with gates at the cardinal directions. The main pyramid, representing a symbolic mountain with dual shrines to the rain god, Tlaloc, and the México national ancestor hero, Huitzilopochtli, established the vertical *axis mundi* of the cosmological design. A similar but smaller ritual center was constructed in the allied city of Texcoco.

In addition to such urban monuments, other shrines and temples were scattered throughout the valley on mountaintops, in caves, by springs and rivers, and in the waters of the lake itself. These places were the shrines of nature deities whose cults were also represented in the temples of the city. These cults, in addition to those of conquered nations, were woven into the religious fabric of the city in an effort to form an embracing state religion. The many divinities were impersonated by ritual performers on festival occasions. The costumes often visually corresponded to the cult names themselves: For example, Chalchiuhtlicue, a female deity of water on the ground, that is, a lake, river, or spring, would appear with a green-painted skirt or a skirt sewn with pieces of jade. *Chalchiuhtlicue* means "jade skirt" in the Nahuatl language. Thus the costume was an ideogram, and the impersonator became a living, moving metaphor naming the element of nature that she represented.

An illustration of this custom is recorded by the sixteenth-century chronicler Alvarado Tezozomoc, who describes a ceremony that took place to inaugurate an aqueduct built from mainland springs to the island of Tenochtitlán. The emperor Ahuizotl instructed two high priests to be attired as Chalchiuhtlicue and go welcome the incoming water. As the water arrived, they sacrificed quail and burnt copal incense. After drinking, the chief priest spoke directly to the water: "Be very welcome, my lady, I come to receive you because you shall be coming to your home, to the middle of the reeds of Mexico-Tenochtitlan" (Alvarado Tezozomoc, 1975). The passage shows how a deity impersonator would also address the natural element whose symbolic form he represented. In this way of thought, the elements themselves were seen to have life-force and were considered inherently sacred. Lake Texcoco was spoken of as Tonanhueyatl, "our mother great water," a provider of moisture to agricultural fields who was teeming with edible algae, aquatic plants of various kinds, mosquito eggs (also edible), shrimp, a diversity of fish, as well as frogs, ducks, and other aquatic birds. As a sustainer of life, the lake was looked upon as the mother of Tenochtitlán.

Pilgrimages were made by the Aztec and their neighbors to sources of water at springs, streams, and lakes, as well as in hidden caves and ravines on cloudy mountaintops. At such places it was common practice to offer green stones and jewelry as well as sacrifices. A preoccupation with fertility was paramount among the reasons why water was so widely venerated. Nowhere was this more apparent than in an elaborate annual pilgrimage made by the ruler of Tenochtitlán and three allied rulers to shrines on the summit of Mount Tlaloc and in the middle of Lake Texcoco. The relationship between these two water shrines shows that no part of the natural setting could be considered in isolation, and that the imagery of sacred geography, based upon the ecological structure of the land, established fundamental integrating bonds between society and nature.

The bonds between humans and nature are evident with the sequence of rituals, beginning at Mount Tlaloc. The archaeological ruins of the Tlaloc temple are located below the summit of this mountain, close by a grassy vale where springs are still located. Here the ruins of a square courtyard enclosed by masonry are entered via a long narrow walkway that had a controlling function in ritual procedure. Within, there was a flat-roofed chamber housing the main Tlaloc effigy, around which were clustered a group of lesser idols. These were intended to represent the other mountains and cliffs surrounding Mount Tlaloc. Thus the arrangement was a microcosm of the land itself, the symbol of a geographical setting where rain and springs were seen to originate.

This shrine was visited in late April, at the height of the dry season, by the ruler of Tenochtitlán and the allied rulers of Texcoco, Tlacopán, and Xochimilco (the number four was a ritual requirement). The pilgrimage was the duty and privilege of royalty alone. The ceremonies opened with the sacrifice of a male child, followed by a hierarchical procession in which the kings approached the idol in order of rank (Tenochtitlán first). One by one, they proceeded to dress the idols with splendid headdresses, breechcloths, various mantles, jewelry, and so on, according to the status of each monarch.

The next phase again involved a procession in order of rank, as the rulers approached with food for a sumptuous repast. After the food was put before the images, a priest entered to sprinkle everything with blood from the sacrificed child. The blood offering at Mount Tlaloc had a contractual function. As chief ritualists of their respective nations, the rulers set in motion a vital principle that unified the rain and mountains with their people, circulating life and energy throughout the social and ecological orders. Correspondingly, the structure of political alliances was reinforced through sacramental rites.

While these events were taking place, another rite was unfolding in the main religious precinct of Tenochtitlán. A large tree was brought in and erected in the courtyard of the dominating pyramid, on the side of the Tlaloc shrine. This tree, called Tota ("father"), was surrounded by four smaller trees in a symbolic forest designed according to the center and the cardinal directions. A girl attired as Chalchiuhtlicue to represent the great lake and other springs and creeks was brought to sit within the forest. A long chant with drums was then begun around the seated figure, until news was finally received that the rulers had completed the Mount Tlaloc offerings and were now at the Texcocan lake-shore, ready to embark in their canoes. At this time, the Chalchiuhtlicue impersonator was placed in a canoe at Tenochtitlán, and the Tota tree was also taken up and bound upon a raft. Accompanied by music and chanting, a vast fleet of canoes filled with men, women, and children embarked with the symbolic figures to a sacred place within the lake called Pantitlan. This was the site of a great spring, an aquifer that welled up from the lake bottom with remarkable turbulence. At this site the two processions met and, as the rulers and population watched, the Tota tree was unbound and set up in the muddy lake bottom by the spring. The Chalchiuhtlicue child was then sacrificed and her blood was offered to the waters, along with as much jewelry as had been given on Mount Tlaloc. The theme of water as *fons et origo* was strikingly expressed, incorporating the renewal of vegetation and of life itself at the height of the dry season. The ceremonies were then concluded and everyone departed, leaving the Tota to stand along with others of previous years. Diego Durán (1971) remarks that the peasantry went on to the preparation of the fields, continuing to make offerings at local springs and rivulets.

The imagery of this long and remarkable sequence of ceremonies was directly based on the ecological structure of the highland basin. The relationship of mountains to rain, mountains to springs, and springs to the great lake was symbolically acknowledged in covenants and pleas for water, crops, and vegetation. This communal ceremony, in which the major rulers and lords of the valley participated, affirmed a topographic metaphor: *atl tepetl* (lit., "water-mountain"), which means "city" or "community." In the Nahuatl language, the habitat of humanity was defined in terms of landscape elements that made life possible. The structure of the ceremony and the metaphor it brought to mind represent a powerful integrating principle that was known and recognized by everyone. Rooted in what was seen and experienced in the land itself, the imagery of the Tlaloc-Chalchiuhtlicue rites represented a sense of order in the highland way of life and symbolically legitimized the governments with which it was identified.

CONCLUSION. In the Andes and Mexico, sacred lakes formed part of religious systems that grew out of landscapes. The patterns become evident upon considering the ethnohistoric texts, archaeological monuments, and new ethnological reports of religious practices in the context of topography. At the time of the Inca and Méxica-Aztec empires, lakes were seen as sources of life where the generative, procreative qualities of water were especially concentrated. The properties of lakes were acknowledged in myths and metaphors, as in Andean cosmogonic stories and the *atl tepetl* theme of highland Mexico; in the powerful imagery of ritual; and in the design and disposition of monuments in the city and the country. These symbolic forms of representation celebrated the dynamic relationship of lakes and other features of the natural and human-fashioned environment.

These concerns were fundamentally bound with fertility and agriculture, but the imagery of lakes was also creatively employed by ruling elites in building imperial domains. Myths, rites, and monuments affirmed territorial claims, consolidated alliances, and validated the larger interests and policies of state organizations. Rooted in cosmogony and the seasonal cycle, the symbolism of lakes was inseparably interwoven with the imagery of history. In New World Indian religions, the order of the cosmos and the structure of the state were inseparably bound.

SEE ALSO Caves; Mountains; Water.

BIBLIOGRAPHY

Alvarado Tezozomoc, Fernando de. *Crónica mexicana.* Mexico City, 1975.

Bandelier, Adolph F. *The Islands of Titicaca and Koati.* New York, 1910.

Barlow, Robert Hayward. *The Extent of the Empire of the Culhna Mexica.* Berkeley, 1949.

Bastien, Joseph W. *Mountain of the Condor: Metaphor and Ritual in an Andean Ayllu.* Saint Paul, 1978.

Bennett, W. C. *Excavations at Tihuanaco.* New York, 1934.

Betanzos, Juan de. *Suma y narración de los Incas.* Edited by Márcos Jiménez de la Espada. Madrid, 1880.

Carrión, Rebecca C. "El culto al agua en el antiguo Perú." *Revista del Museo Nacional de Antropología y Arqueología* (Lima) 11 (1955).

Cieza de León, Pedro de. *Segunda parte de la crónica del Perú, que trata del senorió de los Incas Yupanquis y de sus grandes hechos y gobernación,* vol. 5. Edited by Márcos Jiménez de la Espada. Madrid, 1880.

Cobo, Bernabé. *Historia del Nuevo Mundo.* 4 vols. Edited by Marcos Jiménez de la Espada. Seville, 1890–1895.

Demarest, Arthur Andrew. *Viracocha: The Nature and Antiquity of the Andean High God.* Cambridge, Mass., 1981.

Díaz del Castillo, Bernal. *The Discovery and Conquest of Mexico.* Translated by A. P. Mandslay. Edited by Eudora Garrett. Mexico City, 1953.

Durán, Diego. *Book of the Gods and Rites and the Ancient Calendar.* Translated and edited by Fernando Horcasitas and Doris Heyden. Norman, Okla., 1971.

Eliade, Mircea. *Patterns in Comparative Religion.* New York, 1958.

Kolata, Alan L. "The South Andes." In *Ancient South Americans,* edited by Jesse D. Jennings, pp. 241–285. San Francisco, 1983.

Million, René, ed. *Urbanization at Teotihuacán, Mexico,* vol. 1, *The Teotihuacán Map.* Austin, 1973.

Posnansky, Arthur. *Tiahuanacu, the Cradle of American Man.* 4 vols. Translated by James F. Shearer. New York, 1945–1958.

Reinhardt, Johan. *The Nazca Lines: A New Perspective on Their Origin and Meaning.* Lima, 1985.

Rowe, John Howland. "Inca Culture at the Time of the Spanish Conquest." In *Handbook of South American Indians,* vol. 2, pp. 183–330. Washington, D. C., 1946.

Sahagún, Bernardino de. *Historia general de las cosas de la Neuva Espana* (compiled 1569–1582; first published 1820). Translated by Arthur J. O. Anderson and Charles E. Dibble as *Florentine Codex: General History of the Things of New Spain.* 13 vols. in 12. Santa Fe, N. Mex., 1950–1982. See especially book 1, *The Gods;* book 2, *The Ceremonies;* and book 12, *The Conquest.*

Soldi, Ana Maria. "El agua en el pensamiento andino." *Boletín de Lima* (1980).

Sullivan, Thelma D. "Tlaloc: A New Etymological Interpretation of the God's Name, and What It Reveals of His Essence and Nature." In *Proceedings of the Fortieth International Congress of Americanists,* vol. 2, pp. 213–219. Rome, 1974.

Townsend, Richard F. "Pyramid and Sacred Mountain." In *Ethnoastronomy and Archaeoastronomy in the American Tropics,* edited by Anthony F. Aveni and Gary Urton, pp. 37–62. New York, 1982.

Townsend, Richard F. "Deciphering the Nazca World." *Museum Studies* 11 (1985): 116–139.

New Sources

Demarest, Arthur A. *Ideology and Pre-Columbian Civilizations.* Santa Fe, 1992.

Los Misteros del Lago Sagrado (Mysteries of the sacred lake). Marco A. Ninamango Jurado, editor. Lima, 1998.

Palao Berastain, Juan. *La Religión del Titikaka: Revelaciones del Yatiri.* Puno, Peru, 2001.

Salles-Reese, Veronica. *From Viracocha to the Virgin of Copacabana: Representation of the Sacred Lakes at Lake Titicaca.* Austin, Tex., 1997.

Smith, Michael E. *The Aztecs: The Peoples of America.* Cambridge, Mass., 1998.

Stuart, Gene S. *The Mighty Aztecs.* Washington, D.C., 1981.

Townsend, Richard F. *The Aztecs.* New York, 1992.

RICHARD F. TOWNSEND (1987)
Revised Bibliography

LAKOTA RELIGIOUS TRADITIONS. *Lakota,* meaning "friends or allies," are Plains Indian peoples. They represent the largest of three divisions within the political body known as the Titonwan, along with the Dakota and Nakota. The Lakota are also known as the Western Sioux, although the latter is a pejorative name meaning "snakes in the grass," applied to them by Algonquian-speaking neighbors to the east. *Lakota* also designates the language spoken by the seven bands of the Oceti Sakowin (seven council fires): Oglala, Sicangu, Mnicoujou, Itazipco, Oohenumpa, Sihasapa, and Hunkpapa. In the past, the Lakota occupied areas of what are now Montana, Wyoming, North and South Dakota, and Nebraska. As of the 2000 census, over 108,000 U.S. residents identify as Lakota, many living on or near reservations in South Dakota, North Dakota, and Minnesota.

Often represented in media and film as the typical Indians of the Plains, the Lakota have historically been a nomadic people who organize their lives and ceremonies around the movement of the sun and stars. They acquired the horse around 1700 and became a dominating force within the Missouri River Basin by virtue of their skills as mounted equestrians. In 1851, Lakota bands, along with other Plains tribes, signed a treaty with the federal government at Fort Laramie, Wyoming, creating an aboriginal territory that encompassed parts of Nebraska, Wyoming, North Dakota, and South Dakota. In 1868, they signed another treaty that established the entire western portion of modern-day South Dakota as a reservation for their "undisturbed and exclusive use."

Included in Lakota-held lands was He Sapa, the Black Hills. After the discovery of gold by Custer's forces in 1875, He Sapa was taken illegally for white settlement, something still contested and in litigation today, although in the early 1980s the U.S. Supreme Court established once and for all that the Lakota hold exclusive title to the Black Hills. He Sapa, sometimes known as Paha Sapa, is land considered sacred by the Lakota and other Plains tribes. It is known as *wamaka ognaka y cante* (the heart of everything that is).

During the westward movement by gold seekers and immigrants, the Lakota actively participated in the defense of their lands under such leaders and strategists as Red Cloud, Crazy Horse, Sitting Bull, Gall, American Horse, and Rain in the Face. The Lakota were notably present at the victory of Greasy Grass (the Little Bighorn) and the subsequent defeat of George Armstrong Custer and the Seventh Calvary on June 25, 1876.

By 1888, intense suffering, starvation, and death on the reservations prompted people to participate in the Ghost Dance movement in an effort to restore lost relatives and the traditional way of life. Allegedly for their participation in the movement, over three hundred disarmed Lakota men, women, and children of Chief Big Foot's band of Mnicoujou were massacred by the Seventh Calvary, Custer's reconstituted force, on December 29, 1890, at Wounded Knee, South Dakota. In 1986, Birgil Kills Straight and several other descendents of the Bigfoot Band survivors led the first Big Foot Memorial Horseback Ride, which led up to a spiritual ceremony called *istamniyanpi wasigla* "to wipe the tears" of the people for this sorrowful event. In December of 1990 the fifth and final ride took place, marking the hundred-year anniversary of the massacre.

RELIGIOUS SYSTEM. The notion of a religious system is more applicable to Western ideology and Christian missionaries' efforts to understand a spiritual philosophy different from their own than it is to the beliefs of the Lakota. For the Lakota, religion is not compartmentalized into a separate category. More appropriately, Lakota traditions can be characterized as a system of spirituality that is fully integrated into a rhythm of life that includes all aspects and patterns of the universe. At the center of this rhythm is Wakan Tanka or Tunkashila, sometimes translated as Grandfather and often as Great Spirit or Great Mystery, but better left untranslated. Cannupa Wakan (the sacred pipe) and the subsequent smoke carries messages from humans to *Wakan Tanka.* The system is based on respect and emphasizes that the virtues or values of bravery, fortitude, wisdom, and generosity be followed and perpetuated.

James R. Walker, a physician at Pine Ridge, South Dakota, between 1896 and 1914, was one of the most influential non-Indian revisers of Lakota spirituality. Ella Deloria expressed her skepticism in the 1930s about his work, and, more recently, his interpretations have been considered specious by William K. Powers. It has been hypothesized that George Sword, an Oglala Lakota, gave Walker an explanation of the Lakota system in Christian theological terms to make it understandable to him, and Walker misinterpreted and further changed some of Sword's descriptions based on his own Christian notions and ideology.

Some of Walker's work accurately reflects Lakota belief and information from Sword. His work describes a number of Lakota spirits who inhabited the earth prior to humans. Takuskanskan (that which moves-moves); Wi (Sun), who is married to Hanwi (Moon), with whom he has one daughter, Wohpe (Falling Star); Old Man and Old Woman, whose daughter *Ite* (Double Face) is married to Tate (Wind), with whom she has four sons, Tate Topa (the Four Winds). An important spirit is *Iktomi* the trickster. Iktomi conspires with Old Man and Old Woman to increase their daughter's status by arranging an affair between the Sun and Ite. The discovery of the affair by the Sun's wife leads to punishments by Takuskanskan, who gives the Moon her own domain, and in the process separates her from the Sun. Old Man, Old Woman, and Ite are sent to earth, but Ite is separated from Tate, who, along with the Four Winds and a fifth wind establishes space as the universe known today. The daughter of the Sun and the Moon, Wohpe, falls to earth and later resides with South Wind.

The emergence. Alone on the newly formed earth, Ite prevails upon Iktomi to find her people, Pte Oyate (the Buffalo People or Nation). In the form of a wolf, Iktomi travels beneath the earth and discovers a village of humans. Iktomi tells them about the wonders of the earth and convinces one man, *Tokahe* (the first), to accompany him to the surface. Tokahe does so and upon reaching the surface through the emergence place, located in Wind Cave in the Black Hills of South Dakota, marvels at the green grass and blue sky. Iktomi and Ite introduce Tokahe to buffalo and show him tipis, clothing, and hunting utensils. Tokahe returns to the village and appeals to six other men, and their families to travel with him to the earth's surface. When they arrive, they discover that Iktomi has deceived them. The weather has turned bad, and they find themselves starving. Unable to return to their home, but armed with a new knowledge about the world, they survive with the help of their relative the buffalo. The skull of this animal is a significant symbol that represents Lakol Wicoh'an (the traditional way of life).

The Seven Sacred Rites. According to contemporary Lakota oral historical accounts and discussions with elders, the following is a description of the Seven Sacred Rites of the Lakota and of how these rites came to the people. Many years ago, during a period of starvation, there appeared to the Lakota a beautiful woman who was met by two hunters. One hunter lusts for her, and is covered by a mist and reduced to bone. The other hunter, who possesses a good and pure heart, is instructed to return to camp and tell the chief and people that she, Ptehincalaskawin (White Buffalo Calf Woman), will appear to them the next day for she has something of importance to tell them. He obeys, and a great council tipi is constructed. Ptehincalaskawin presents to the people a bundle containing the sacred pipe and tells them that in time of need they should smoke and pray with the pipe for help. The smoke from the pipe will carry their prayers upward.

She then instructs them in the great Wicoh'an Wakan Sakowin (Seven Sacred Rites), the basis of Lakota spirituality, which have been recorded by Joseph Brown in the words of Nicholas Black Elk in *The Sacred Pipe: Black Elk's Account of the Seven Sacred Rites of the Oglala Sioux.* Ptehincalaskawin pledges to watch over the people and to return someday. Upon leaving, she walked a short way off and lay down in the grass. When she stood again she had turned into a white buffalo calf, and walked over the hill, out of sight. The Sacred Buffalo Calf Pipe remains among the people today.

First rite. The first of the Seven Sacred Rites (though they are not chronological) is Inikagapi or Inipi (to renew life). A sweat lodge is held in a dome-shaped structure made of saplings and covered with hide or tarps that symbolizes the shape of the universe and/or the womb of a pregnant woman. Heated stones are placed in a central hole in the lodge and water is poured over them by an *itancan* (leader) to create steam. The purpose of the ceremony is to pray for health and well-being, spiritually and physically. The lodge "utilizes all the Powers of the universe: earth, and the things which grow from the earth, water, fire, and air" (p. 31).

Second rite. The second rite is Hanbleceyapi (crying for a vision). The vision quest is undertaken by an individual with the help and guidance of a holy man. A person elects to go on a vision quest to pray, communicate with the spirits, and attempt to gain knowledge, strength, and understanding. The person pledges to stay on an isolated hill for one to four days with a blanket and a pipe, but without food or water. Upon returning, the vision may be discussed with the *wicasa wakan* (holy man). Often the meaning of the vision is not readily apparent and the individual may be told to wait for knowledge and understanding.

Third rite. The third rite is Wanagi Wicagluha (keeping of the spirit). Spirit keeping is a rite performed by a mourner for one year to grieve for a lost loved one. When a person dies the spirit can linger around the family and community. According to Black Elk, "this rite purifies the souls of our dead, and our love for one another is increased" (p. 10). A special place is set up for the spirit, who is fed every day. Members of the family and community can come and visit, eat, and sit with the spirit and family. After one year the spirit is ceremonially released and the mourning period is formally ended. It is usual among the Lakota for the mourning family to refrain from attending or participating in secular activities, gatherings, or events during this formal grieving period.

Fourth rite. The fourth rite is Wiwanyang Wacipi (sun dance). The Sun Dance is often considered the most important rite, and it is held during the summer when the moon is full. In times past a number of Plains bands of the Lakota would gather at a prearranged location for the annual meeting of the Oceti Sakowin; this was the occasion prior to Greasy Grass. It was during this annual gathering that the Sun Dance ceremony was held. During the ceremony, dancers pledge to make offerings of their flesh so that "much strength would be given to the nation" (p. 99) and to fulfill personal vows. The choice to participate is solely that of each individual. It is usually the result of receiving a sacred dream or is undertaken to seek assistance in healing a sick loved one. The sacred tree that is placed at the center of the dance area symbolizes Wakan Tanka, the center of the universe.

Fifth rite. The fifth rite is Hunkapi (making relatives). It establishes a "relationship on earth, which is a reflection of that real relationship" with Wakan Tanka (p. 101). It was usually performed to unite a younger person with a family, and it can be a way of solidifying relationships with other individuals as well as Wakan Tanka. This ceremony represents the formal adoption of people as relatives.

Sixth rite. The sixth rite is Isnati Awicalowanpi (puberty ceremony). The ceremony takes place after a girl's first menses, and prayers are said to ensure the girl will grow up to have all the virtues of a Lakota woman and understand the meaning of her new role, and to formally announce her eligibility as a potential wife and mother.

Seventh rite. The seventh rite is Tapa Wankayeyapi (throwing the ball), a game "which represents the course of a man's life" (p. 127). A young girl stands at the center and throws a ball upward and to the four corners as people vie to catch it. The person to catch the ball is considered more fortunate than the others, for the ball is symbolically equated with knowledge.

Essential beliefs. For the Lakota, the nature of the universe is a whole, and above, below, and around are all part of that whole. Life is seen as a series of recurrent travels, and each person has a purpose to fulfill, one that will support and benefit the community.

People live through four generations: childhood, adolescence, maturity, and old age. When a person dies, one of his four souls travels southward, along the Wanagi Tacanku (spirit path, identified with the Milky Way), where it meets with an old woman who examines its earthly virtues, directing the soul either to the spirit world, where there is an unending supply of buffalo and where people rejoin their kin, or back to earth where they are reborn and given another chance to live in harmony. Because of this the birth of children is a joyful event since they are closest to the spirit world and considered sacred. Twins are particularly auspicious and considered intellectually mature at birth. Many rites help develop the proper behavior of children through observation and listening.

The sacred is the domain of the *wicasa wakan* (holy men), who conduct all spiritual ceremonies. The most important symbol is the sacred pipe, whose smoke represents prayers offered to Wakan Tanka. In addition to its general interpretation as something like "great spirit," this single name refers to important beings and powers, half of which existed prior to the creation of the earth, and half as a result of it. Wakan Tanka, in the sacred language of the medicine men, underscores the belief that all sacred things come in fours. The root *wakan* (sacred) is a dynamic concept indicating the potentiality of anything to transform from the secular to sacred. Iktomi the trickster named all things, taught culture to humans, and remains on the earth to continually deceive them. The trickster is smart and works to fool humans for his own benefit. His is the power to deceive. Iktomi stories frequently are told with humor and serve as lessons for young children as well as adults since Iktomi often plays the fool. But he is capable of bringing real danger and destruction, as well.

Contemporary religion. All of the Seven Sacred Rites are still performed, with the exception of Tapa Wankayeyapi. In addition, a vital religious practice known as Yuwipi became popular in the twentieth century. It encompasses a number of cultural concepts related to traditional life and problems confronting contemporary Lakota peoples. This rite is performed in a darkened room under the supervision of a Yuwipi man or *wicasa wakan*. The object is to cure a person and at the same time to pray for the general welfare of all Indian people and for long life for the kinship group. Some Yuwipi men possess an exceptional ability that allows them to locate lost items or people.

BIBLIOGRAPHY

Brown, Joseph Epes, ed. *The Sacred Pipe: Black Elk's Account of the Seven Sacred Rites of the Oglala Sioux.* Norman, Okla., 1953. An interview during the winter of 1947 with the Lakota medicine man Nicholas Black Elk on the Seven Sacred Rites, inspired by earlier interviews by John G. Neihardt.

Deloria, Ella C., ed. *Dakota Texts.* New York, 1932. The best bilingual compilation of Lakota mythological texts by an author who was both Lakota and an anthropologist.

Densmore, Frances. *Teton Sioux Music.* Washington, D.C., 1918. Contains a number of interviews with Hunkpapa medicine men, transcriptions and translations of sacred songs, and vivid ethnographic accounts of most of the sacred ceremonies.

Garrett, James J. "The Cheyenne River Tribal College *Tatanka* (*Bison-bison*) Management Program." Masters of Science Thesis, Humboldt State University, Acata, Calif., 2001.

Neihardt, John G. *Black Elk Speaks* (1932). Lincoln, Neb., 1979. Although only a few chapters relate to Lakota traditions, this interview between Nicholas Black Elk and John Neihardt is a popular reference for American Indian spirituality. The problem lies in the reader's inability to distinguish between what is Neihardt's and what is Black Elk's. Brown's interview with Black Elk is much more authentically Lakota.

Powers, William K. *Yuwipi: Vision and Experience in Oglala Ritual.* Lincoln, Neb., 1982. A translation of a Yuwipi ceremony indicating the relationship between Yuwipi, sweat lodge, and vision quest. Includes a chapter on the history of Yuwipi at Pine Ridge.

Rice, Julian. *Before the Great Spirit: The Many Faces of Sioux Spirituality.* Albuquerque, N.M., 1998. A publication on Sioux spirituality with chapters that examine a variety of aspects, including tricksters, symbols, the Thunders, and James Walker in light of Ella Deloria's writings.

Valandra, Edward Charles. "Lakota Buffalo Theology: Implications for Buffalo Reintroduction into the Great Plains." Masters Thesis, University of Colorado, Boulder, Colo., 1993.

Walker, James R. *The Sun Dance and Other Ceremonies of the Oglala Division of the Teton Dakota.* New York, 1917. An early publication on the cosmology and rituals of the Oglala. Some of the myths should be read judiciously as they are obvious romantic reconstructions of Lakota myth from a classical Greco-Roman perspective.

Walker, James R. *Lakota Belief and Ritual.* Edited by Raymond J. DeMallie and Elaine Jahner. Lincoln, Neb., 1980. Previously unpublished papers of J. R. Walker, mainly interviews with Oglala men, some of whom were medicine men.

White Hat, Albert, Sr. *Reading and Writing the Lakota Language.* Edited by Jael Kampfe. Salt Lake City, 1999. Well-written and adapted language text that presents the interplay between culture and language through stories as well as the importance of language in reflecting the characteristics of the people.

Wissler, Clark. *Societies and Ceremonial Associations in the Oglala Division of Teton Dakota.* New York, 1912. One of a number of monographs by the former curator of the American Museum of Natural History on Lakota religion. This monograph addresses the nature and function of dream cults and the modern Yuwipi.

Young Bear, Severt, and R. D. Theisz. *Standing in the Light: A Lakota Way of Seeing.* Lincoln, Neb., 1994. Documents the founder and for many years lead singer of the Porcupine Singers, Severt Young Bear. His narrative presents Lakota culture, the importance of names, and rich detail on the significance of music in Lakota life.

William K. Powers (1987)
James Garrett (2005)
Kathleen J. Martin (2005)

LAKSMĪ See GODDESS WORSHIP, *ARTICLE ON* THE HINDU GODDESS

LAMAISM See TIBETAN RELIGIONS

LAMOTTE, ÉTIENNE

LAMOTTE, ÉTIENNE (1903–1983), Belgian specialist in Indian Buddhist doctrine and history. A Roman Catholic priest, Lamotte was a professor at the Catholic University of Louvain. His two most significant achievements in the field of Buddhist studies were his *Histoire du bouddhisme indien des origines à l'ère Śaka* (1958), the most elaborate work thus far on the history of early Buddhism, and his *Le traité de la grande vertu de sagesse* (1944–1980), an annotated translation of a large portion of the *Ta chih tu lun* (Skt., **Mahāprajñāpāramitopadeśa*), which is an encyclopedic treatise on Mahāyāna Buddhism attributed to Nāgārjuna and translated into Chinese by Kumārajīva.

His ten years of collaborative work with Louis de La Vallée Poussin (1869–1938) were more decisive in the formation of Lamotte's thought than were his short periods of study in Rome (1926–1927) and Paris (1931–1932). If the monumental writings of these two masters of the French-language school of Buddhist philology are compared, one realizes a great complementarity in their achievements. La Vallée Poussin's glittering genius is swift and full of illuminating and often paradoxical insights into every part of his field of study. Lamotte's genius is reflected in the remarkable organization of the exegetical work that formed his voluminous books. Each element of his books—chapter, paragraph, footnote (often constituting a comprehensive monograph)—contributes to the brightness of the synthesis of a broad range of information by diffusing its own particular light.

Lamotte's exegetical work centered on doctrinally important texts, mostly of the *śāstra* (treatise) type preserved primarily in Tibetan or Chinese. At first attracted to the Yogācāra (Idealist) school, he produced a study (1935) on the *Saṃdhinirmocana Sūtra* and a commentary (1938–1939) on Asaṅga's *Mahāyānasaṃgraha* titled *La somme du grande véhicule d'Asaṅga* (*Mahāyānasaṃgraha*). His interest shifted to Vasubandhu's *Karmasiddhiprakaraṇa* and to the seventeenth chapter of Candrakīrti's *Prasannapadā*, a commentary to the *Madhyamakakārikā*s by Nāgārjuna. This last work initiated his choice of Mādhyamika texts for the remainder of his career. In addition to the already mentioned *Traité* (*Mahāprajñāpāramitopadeśa*), he translated two related Mahāyāna sūtras: the *Vimalakīrtinirdeśa* (1962; translated into English as *The Teaching of Vimalakīrti*, 1976) and the *Śūraṃgamasamādhi* (1965).

Lamotte's *Histoire du bouddhisme indien des origines à l'ère Śaka* is an epoch-making synthesis based on multilingual documents (including Greek and Chinese) and incorporating the latest developments in Indian epigraphy, archaeology, and linguistics. The first volume traces the development of Buddhism up to the emergence of the Maitreya cult. The second volume was never finished. Some parts of this projected second volume, however, have been published separately, including "Mañjuśrī," *T'oung pao* 48 (1960): 1–96, and "Vajrāpaṇi," in *Mélanges Demiéville*, vol. 1 (1966), pp. 156–168.

Bibliography

Biographical and bibliographical information on Lamotte is available in the *Notice* published by the Imprimerie Orientaliste

(Louvain, 1972). This work has been supplemented by D. Donnet's "L'œuvre de Mgr É. Lamotte," in *Indianisme et bouddhisme: Mélanges offerts à Mgr Étienne Lamotte* (Louvain, 1980), pp. vii–xvi.

Lamotte, É. *Śūraṃgamasamādhisūtra. The Concentration of Heroic Progress.* Translated by Sara Boin-Webb. Surrey, U.K., 1998.

HUBERT DURT (1987 AND 2005)

LANDVÆTTIR in Old Norse means literally "land wights," the guardian spirits of an area. The *Landnámabók* (the Icelandic "book of settlements," extant in thirteenth-century redactions but based on still older traditions) tells of a tenth-century settler who struck a deal with one of the *landvættir* and thereafter became a wealthy man. The same text cites an ancient law warning that the dragon-head ornament on a ship's prow should be removed before land is sighted, so as to avoid frightening off the *landvættir.* The early-thirteenth-century *Egils saga* tells that Egill once erected a pole with a horse's head and uttered a magic formula intended to arouse the *landvættir* to drive off the land's king. The *Óláfs saga helga* (Saga of Olaf the Saint, in Snorri Sturluson's *Heimskringla*), reports that Harald II once sent a man of magic powers on an out-of-body journey to Iceland; there the man saw that the mountains and mounds were full of *landvættir,* both large and small.

The emphasis on *landvættir* in Icelandic sources, particularly the *Landnámabók,* may have to do with Iceland's status as a newly discovered and settled land where, according to folk tradition, the supernatural "owners" of nature had previously ruled unhindered by humans. The *Landnámabók* tells also about a man killed by the *landvættir.* Insofar as Iceland was unknown and hence mysterious, its supernatural beings were threatening; but as people settled the land and made it theirs, these beings became increasingly friendly and potentially helpful. The distinction may be viewed in the modern Scandinavian descendants of the *landvættir: nisser* and *tomtar* live on and about farms and are helpful if treated with respect, whereas trolls and similar creatures live in uninhabited forests and mountains and are always dangerous.

Icelandic folklore tells of a "hallowing" of the island Drangey by the thirteenth-century bishop Guđmundr the Good, in which he drives off the *landvætttir,* here understood as evil spirits and trolls; he leaves a small portion of the island for them to inhabit. The *landvætttir* seem therefore to belong more to pre-Christian than to Christian Iceland. The term is not common in more recent folklore; when encountered, it seems to be a collective for supernatural nature beings.

Even so, belief in the *landvætttir* may have persisted even after the conversion to Christianity. This is indicated by a prohibition of such belief in medieval Norwegian law. Although one cannot truly speak of "worship" of the *landvættir,* ritual activity to ensure their cooperation and protection (such as leaving out food for them in uninhabited areas) persisted as part of this belief.

SEE ALSO Sagas.

BIBLIOGRAPHY

There is no comprehensive treatment of the *landvættir,* although the literature on similar beings in recent Scandinavian lore is extensive. The fullest treatment is in the chapter "Landvættir," in Ólafur Briem's *Heiđinn siđur á Íslandi* (Reykjavík, 1945), pp. 71–90.

JOHN LINDOW (1987 AND 2005)

LANG, ANDREW (1844–1912), was a Scottish anthropologist and folklorist. Born in Selkirk, Scotland, Lang received his education at Saint Andrews, Glasgow, and Oxford universities. For seven years he was a fellow of Merton College, where he was regarded as a brilliant and promising classicist. After his marriage, he left Oxford, embarked upon a career as a literary journalist, and became widely known for his editions of fairy tales, his contributions to folklore and anthropology of religion, and his literary essays and reviews. Although Lang's range of interests and learning was considerable, his scholarly work was devoted to topical intellectual issues, and he made no major contribution to the development of knowledge. He was an astute critic of the theories of others rather than an original thinker. He was among the founders of the British Folklore Society and near the end of his life was president of the Society for Psychical Research.

As a professional man of letters, Lang wrote prodigiously. He was the author of 120 books (including pamphlets) and was involved in more than 150 others either as editor or as contributor, and his periodical articles number in the thousands. At a time when the growing British and American intelligentsia were intensely interested in issues of science and scholarship, Lang's penetrating intellect and skillful writing made him a leading figure, especially in the newly developing fields of anthropology, folklore, and history of religions.

Lang is credited with demolishing the great Max Müller's philological approach to the study of myth and his popular theory that all myth was the result of a "disease of language." In *Modern Mythology* (1897) Lang used his extensive knowledge of comparative mythology to show that the themes in Indo-European mythology that Müller explained in terms of Indo-European philology, many of them concerning solar phenomena, were also present in myths from other parts of the world and could be accounted for by the more universal tendency to personify nature. Although Lang did not himself offer a new theory of myth, he regarded mythology as the key to the "actual condition of the human intellect" (*Myth, Ritual, and Religion,* 1887, vol. 1, p. 29), and he thought that myth had to be understood according to its own form of rationality. In this respect, Lang anticipated major developments in the contemporary study of myth in anthropology and history of religions.

In *Magic and Religion* (1901) Lang wrote a detailed criticism of the illustrious James G. Frazer's theory of magic and religion. He exposed the flaws in Frazer's evolutionary theory that magic preceded religion and that religion arose from the perceived failures of magic. Lang also took Frazer to task for explaining the divinity of Christ in terms of ritual king-killing and myths of dying-rising gods, and he produced a devastating criticism of Frazer's theory of ritual regicide and his comparative method in *The Golden Bough,* questions on which later scholarly opinion agreed.

Although Lang was a proponent of E. B. Tylor's evolutionary theory of animism, he rejected Tylor's view that the idea of God arose as a late development from the animistic notions of souls, ghosts, and spirits. He pointed out in *Myth, Ritual, and Religion* that the concept of a creator god who is moral, fatherly, omnipotent, and omniscient is found among the most culturally primitive peoples of the world. Hence, on the evolutionists' own grounds, the idea of God, having been found among the culturally simplest peoples, could not have arisen from ideas of ghosts and souls as a later development. Lang's criticism on this point was among the first of many that eventually led to the downfall of evolutionism in anthropology. Lang's own view was that the idea of the soul-ghost and the idea of God had totally different sources and that the idea of God may have preceded animism, though he recognized that the issue of priority could never be historically settled. Lang thought, however, that the idea of God may have been prior and that it may have been corrupted and degraded by later animistic ideas and pushed out of its originally central position. Although Lang's emphasis upon the presence of "high gods" among culturally primitive peoples was largely ignored in England, it was taken up by other scholars and made the subject of major investigation in anthropology (Wilhelm Schmidt, E. E. Evans-Pritchard) and history of religions (Nathan Söderblom, Raffaele Pettazzoni, Mircea Eliade).

In later life, Lang developed an interest in psychic phenomena—ghosts, telepathy, crystal gazing, fire walking, apparitions, spiritualism—and he wrote two books on the subject. Although he treated ghost stories as a form of folklore, he thought that the psychological experience that gave rise to them might have some foundation in reality and that it might have been the original source of religious belief. In this matter, however, Lang stood alone and somewhat in disgrace among his folklore colleagues. What Lang seems to have been groping for was a way of documenting and exploring the experience of what Rudolf Otto was later to call "the numinous," which Otto and subsequent phenomenologists of religion held to be both the ancient source and the continuing foundation of religious belief.

See Also Supreme Beings.

Bibliography

Noteworthy among Lang's many contributions to the study of religion and mythology are *Custom and Myth* (1885), 2d rev. ed. (1893; Oosterhout, 1970); *Myth, Ritual, and Religion,* 2 vols. (1887), rev. ed. (1899; New York, 1968); *Modern Mythology* (1897; New York, 1968); and *Magic and Religion* (1901; New York, 1969). His two works on parapsychological phenomena are *Cock Lane and Common-Sense* (1894; New York, 1970) and *The Book of Dreams and Ghosts* (1897), rev. ed. (1899; New York, 1970). A useful source for information regarding Lang's life and his enormous literary output is Roger L. Green's *Andrew Lang: A Critical Biography with a Short-Title Bibliography of the Works of Andrew Lang* (Leicester, 1946).

New Sources

Turner, Bryan S., ed. *The Early Sociology of Religion,* vol. 4: *The Making of Religion by Andrew Lang.* London, 1997.

Benjamin C. Ray (1987)
Revised Bibliography

LANGER, SUSANNE.

Susanne Katherina Knauth Langer (1895–1985) was a German-American philosopher. She was born the second of five children in an affluent banking family. Educated at the Veltin School in Manhattan, Langer primarily spoke German as a child. Nurtured in a culturally rich environment, she developed an interest in aesthetic forms that would mark her philosophy. Educated at Radcliffe College, she tutored there (1927–1942) and held positions at the University of Delaware (1943), the Dalton School (1944–1945), New York University (1945–1946), Columbia University (1945–1950), Northwestern University (1951), Ohio State University (1951), the University of Washington (1952–1953), the New School (1950), the University of Michigan (1954), and Wesleyan University (1954). Her first permanent appointment was at Connecticut College for Women (1954–1962) in New London. In her later years (1962–1985), she lived alone in a farmhouse in Olde Lyme, Connecticut, and her research was funded by the Edward J. Kauffmann Foundation. By this time in her life, she had been honored with many degrees, the Radcliffe Founders Award, and election to the American Academy of Arts and Sciences. She died at the age of eighty-nine, only three years after her final book appeared.

Although Langer was a philosopher, her later insights on symbols, myth, and aesthetic experience made her influential throughout all of the humanities. Langer's early writing demonstrates her interest in symbols and their relationship to human potential. Influenced by Alfred North Whitehead's earlier work on symbols, Langer's *Practice of Philosophy* (1930) considers the nature of revolutionary thinking, anticipating paradigm theories of science. *An Introduction to Symbolic Logic* (1937) argues that logic is a concept central to philosophy, not mere tautology, but part of meaning.

Langer's mature work begins with *Philosophy in a New Key: A Study in the Symbolism of Reason, Rite, and Art* (1942). Here she names the symbolic as the defining mark of humanity and develops a theory that originates symbolic action in feeling rather than logic. In doing so, she frees the binaries of mind and body, reason and impulse, autonomy and law. According to *Philosophy in a New Key*, from the flux of bodily sensation (the sense data), human minds constantly abstract the forms that affect them. Symbols are far more than communicative devices or descriptions of the empirical world; the brain endlessly makes them, as evidenced by dreams, religious experience, art, ritual, and even science. For Langer, symbols worked as both an end and an instrument, a human characteristic and compulsion. All of one's conceptions are only held through symbols. While the biological and social origin of the symbolic is inflected differently in myth, religion, art, or science, the human drive to symbolize characterizes every form, and they are equally human acts of meaning-making.

An account of human emotion, *Feeling and Form: A Theory of Art* (1953) extends the symbolic into forms that are less linguistic, and it offers a fuller account of expression and reception. Langer extends the earlier example of music to develop an aesthetic theory that includes the place of time, virtual space, magic, poesis, and traumatic forms. She argues that art is a symbolic form that through its dynamic structure expresses the forms of experience that language is unfit to convey. Language—limited by its discursive, sequential form—cannot express the emotional content as well as can presentational forms, such as music and painting. The creation of aesthetic forms, however, is not an emotional experience; it is an intellectual one of understanding and objectifying emotions.

Langer's philosophy is often connected to that of the German philosopher Ernst Cassirer. Although they were friends—she translated Cassirer's *Language and Myth* (1946)—too frequently their philosophical systems are collapsed and fruitful distinctions lost to the detriment of each. Unlike Cassirer, who values science over art, and reason and numbers over feeling and language, Langer offers a nonhierarchical model of symbolic forms, one based in biological evolution (*Mind*, 1967–1982), and she avoids a communicative model of language, instead conceiving language as forming and expressing concepts. Furthermore, Langer developed a full aesthetic theory and, through it, a more complex sense of symbolic reception and production.

Langer's own influence has been significant if underrecognized. Although women philosophers faced resistance in the mid-twentieth century, Langer's books were widely read. Her work remains vital to theology, rhetoric, and aesthetic philosophy, and references to her writings continue to appear in anthropology, psychology, education, and communications.

BIBLIOGRAPHY

Langer's books include a collection of German children's stories, *The Cruise of the Little Dipper and Other Fairy Tales* (Greenwich, Conn., 1923); as well as *The Practice of Philosophy* (New York, 1930); *An Introduction to Symbolic Logic* (Boston, 1937); *Philosophy in a New Key: A Study in the Symbolism of Reason, Rite, and Art* (Cambridge, Mass., 1942); *Feeling and Form: A Theory of Art Developed from Philosophy in a New Key* (New York, 1953); *Problems of Art: Ten Philosophical Lectures* (New York, 1957); *Philosophical Sketches* (Baltimore, Md., 1962); and *Mind: An Essay on Human Feeling*, 3 vols. (Baltimore, Md., 1967–1982). Langer's papers are housed at the Houghton Library at Harvard University; a large collection of her annotated books are archived at Connecticut College. For the most complete bibliography, see Rolf Lachmann, "Der Philosophische Weg Susanne K. Langer (1895–1985)," *Studia Culturologica* 2 (1993): 65–114. Donald Dryden's biography in *Dictionary of Literary Biography*, vol. 270: *American Philosophers before 1950*, edited by Philip B. Dematteis and Leemon B. McHenry (Farmington Hills, Mich., 2003), pp. 189–199, offers a full picture of her intellectual life. A centennial retrospective symposium on Langer appears in *Transactions of the Charles S. Peirce Society* 33 (1997): 131–200.

ARABELLA LYON (2005)

LANGUAGE

This entry consists of the following articles:

SACRED LANGUAGE
BUDDHIST VIEWS OF LANGUAGE

LANGUAGE: SACRED LANGUAGE

Language, as a fundamental form of human expression, is a central element in every religious tradition and can be examined from a variety of perspectives. This article will not be concerned with the theological issue of how to assess the truth of religious statements; that is, rather than dealing with language's function of making propositions about a sacred reality, the focus will be on the kinds of sacral functions to which language has been put, such as consecration and prayer, and on the ways in which language itself has been regarded as a manifestation of the sacred.

The enormous advances made in the disciplines of linguistics and the philosophy of language over the last few decades have provided the scholar of religion with the means for more precise characterization of sacred language and its functions. Traditional terms used to describe the forms of sacred language—such as *prayer*, *praise*, and *magic spell*—though they stand for important thematic concerns, are too broad and imprecise by themselves to express adequately the rich variety of religious functions performed by language and the complexities involved in accomplishing those ends. The key to the modern understanding of language is to see it as an integrated system of components that are concerned with form and purpose, as well as with meaning. Spoken language manifests itself in the speech act, a type of purposeful human activity that can be analyzed in terms of its intended effect within a social context. A speech act involves (1) a language in which to embody a message, (2) a speaker to send the message, (3) a hearer to receive it, (4) a medium by which it is transmitted, and (5) a context to which it makes reference. Sacred language can be examined in terms of how it gives distinctive treatment, in turn, to each of these elements of a speech act situation. Then we will see how these components are combined to achieve the various goals of sacred speech acts.

Language as a Manifestation of the Sacred. Perhaps the most interesting examples of the intersection of religion and language are those cases in which language has been viewed not just as a means for referring to or communicating with the sacred realm but as an actual manifestation of a sacred power. Some of the most sophisticated understandings of language as a sacred power entail the belief that it was a fundamental force in the creation of the cosmos. Such ideas are widespread.

Language and creation. The Karadjeri of Australia, for example, say that it was only from the moment that the first two humans gave names to all the plants and animals, on the first day of creation, that those things really began to exist. The texts of ancient Sumer provide the first example of the commonly found Near Eastern doctrine of the creative power of the divine word. The major deities of the Sumerian pantheon first plan creation by thinking, then utter the command and pronounce the name, and the object comes into being. Well-known is the biblical version of this same theme, in which God brings order out of chaos by simply speaking ("Let there be light," *Gn.* 1:3) and by naming ("God called the light Day, and the darkness he called Night," *Gn.* 1:5). Adam's giving of names to the plants and animals in the second chapter of *Genesis*, like the Australian example above, confirms mere physical existence with linguistic existence.

The religions of India, extending back into the earliest recorded forms of Hinduism in the Vedic period (c. 1000 BCE), contain the most developed speculations about the cosmic role of language. Several of the Vedic texts record the story of a primordial contest between speech and mind to see which is the most fundamental and essential force. While mind always wins, there is still the acknowledgement that speech is a basic cosmic force. One Vedic god, Prajāpati, who in the Brāhmaṇas (c. 800 BCE) figures most prominently as the god of creation, speaks the primal syllables *bhūr, bhuvaḥ, svar* to create the earth, atmosphere, and heaven. He is said to give order to the world through name and form (*nāmarūpa*), which are elsewhere called his manifest aspects. These two terms are key elements in much of later Hindu philosophy, standing for the two basic dimensions of reality. The single most important term from this earliest stratum of Indian thought on language is *vāc.* Meaning "speech," it has been personified as an independent deity, the goddess who is Prajāpati's wife and who is, in some places, given the role of the true active agent in creating or, more accurately, becoming the universe.

Among the Western religious traditions, a comparable idea has been expressed in the doctrine of the *logos.* It was developed in the ancient world through a combination of Platonic, Aristotelian, and Stoic ideas. *Logos* was viewed as the rational principle that pervaded and gave order to nature. It was a demiurge that mediated between the created cosmos and the transcendent god, in whose mind existed the eternal forms. This idea was taken over by Hellenistic Judaism (in the writings of Philo Judaeus, 30 BCE–50 CE), where *logos* was identified with the biblical "Word of God"; from there it came to influence Christianity, which around 150 CE began to refer to Jesus as the *Logos.* The Christian view of the *Logos* seems to stress its quality as language, word, and message, rather than as mere thought; and besides the world-ordering function, there is the idea that the *Logos* is a principle of salvation as well, delivering the message that shows the way to return to the condition of original cosmic purity. Such a conception of the double movement of creative language is found within the Indian Tantric system also.

The widely influential Tantric philosophy (which began to reach its classical articulation around 1000 CE) developed earlier strands of Indian speculation on language into a full-blown cosmogonic and soteriological system. The supreme deity of Hindu Tantrism, Śiva, is pure consciousness and thus silent. But in his first manifest form he unites with his consort, Vāc ("speech"), who is also termed Śiva's *śakti* ("power"), the female agency through which the process of creation will proceed. Creation begins with a subtle vibration that develops into the "mothers of the letters" of the Sanskrit alphabet, then into the words of speech, and finally into the referents of those words, namely, the concrete objects of the world. Certain monosyllabic vocables, called *bīja mantras* (*mantras* are syllables, words, or whole sentences that serve as both liturgical utterances and meditational devices), are regarded as the primordial forms of this linguistic evolution and, therefore, as sonic manifestations of basic cosmic powers: literally "seeds" of the fundamental constituents of the universe. For example, *yāṃ* is equivalent to wind, *rāṃ* to fire. Importantly, the Tantric adept who masters the use of *mantras* is felt to know how to control the process of cosmic evolution, and to be able to reverse that process to take himself back to the condition of primordial unity and silence that constitutes the goal of Tantric practice.

A very similar conception of cosmic evolution as identical with linguistic evolution was developed in Qabbalah, the medieval tradition of Jewish mysticism. The main idea here was that God himself was totally transcendent, but flowing forth from him were a series of ten emanations of light (*sefirot*) that were his manifest and knowable aspects. However, parallel to the emanation doctrine existed the conception of creation as the unfolding of the divine language. Instead of realms of light, there issued forth a succession of divine names and letters, namely, the twenty-two consonants of the Hebrew alphabet. As in Indian Tantrism, such a belief led to a tradition of powerful word-magic; the initiate into the practices of Qabbalah was supposedly capable of repeating acts of cosmic creation through proper combination of the Hebrew letters.

Language as a sacred substance. A hallmark of the modern understanding of language is the realization that meaning rests on a conventional relationship between the signified and the signifier. The latter (e.g., a word) is comprised of both form (e.g., phonological and grammatical rules of proper formation) and substance (e.g., its sounds, if a spoken word). The meaning of a word, however, is not inherent in either its form or substance. In premodern attitudes toward language, such distinctions were not usually made. In particular, to regard some linguistic manifestation as sacred did not imply that it was exclusively, or even primarily, the meaning that was taken to be holy. More often it was the exact form or even the veritable substance in which it was expressed that was felt to be the locus of the sacrality. This is seen most clearly in the reluctance or refusal to allow translation of certain religious expressions into equivalent statements. Religious traditions have often held the position that synonymy does not preserve sacrality. After a brief look at some examples of language substance that are regarded as sacred, we will turn to some of the important ways in which language form has taken precedence over meaning in various religions.

The Dogon of Africa believe that the speech used by the priest during ritual action contains a life force, or *nyama*, that is conveyed by his breath and becomes mixed with the life force of the invoked gods and the sacrificial offerings that are to be redistributed for the benefit of all the people. The *nyama* is given to the priest by a snake deity who appears at night and licks his body, thereby conveying the moisture of the word—the same creative power used by God at the beginning of the world to fertilize the cosmic egg. The Chamula, a Maya community of Mexico, have a similar notion of the useful power inherent in the substance of sacred speech used in ritual, believing that this more formal and redundant language contains a "heat" that is consumed by the gods along with the other offered substances.

Sacred languages. It is well known that many religions have developed the idea that an entire language, usually other than the vernacular, is sacred. Such languages are then often reserved for liturgical or for other functions conveying sacred power, such as healing or magic. A sacred language usually begins as a vernacular through which a revelation is believed to have been received. This can lead to the belief that that language is particularly suited for revelation—that it is superior to other languages and thus inherently sacred. For example, Sanskrit, the language of the Vedas, the earliest sacred scriptures of Hinduism, means literally "perfected," or "refined" (*saṃskṛta*). In Islam, the Arabic wording of the Qurʾān is regarded as essential to its holiness; as is said in many passages of the book itself, "we have sent it down as an Arabic Qurʾān." This has sometimes led to the inference that translations of the Qurʾān are not themselves sacred scriptures, but more like mere commentaries. Such belief in the sacrality of what originally was a vernacular seem to be special cases of the widespread idea that one's people and culture are the best, superior to others by virtue of a special closeness to the gods. For example, the Chamula of Mexico say that the sun deity gave them the best of all the languages of mankind; thus they call it "true language."

Furthermore, the Chamula distinguish three different forms of their own language, the most important of which is "ancient words," those which were given to their ancestors during the first stages of world creation. These are the formal phrases used in ritual. This example well illustrates a general principle. Many traditional peoples, as well as high cultures, recite sacred doctrines and rituals in an archaic form of speech that is only barely comprehensible to contemporary speakers. But the language is regarded as sacred, not primarily because it is different from the vernacular, but because it contains the doctrines of revered figures from the past, such as gods, prophets, or ancestors. The desire to express the unchanging, eternal validity of some scripture or liturgy by not allowing any change over time in its language will necessarily result in the language becoming largely unintelligible to those without special training. Such is the case for many of the prayers (*norito*) that are spoken by the priests in Shintō shrines, having been preserved in their original classical Japanese of the tenth century CE. The further passage of time can yield a fully distinct, now "sacred," language, as the offspring vernaculars develop into independent forms. Such was the case for Sanskrit in relation to its vernacular offshoots, the Prakrits, as well as for Latin in relation to the Romance languages.

The most prominent place a sacred language will be found, aside from in the scriptures, is in the cult. Here the preservation of archaic forms of language is part of the general conservatism of liturgical practice. The inclusion in the Latin Mass of such ancient and foreign-sounding elements as the Hebrew and Aramaic formulas "Halleluja," "Amen," and "Maranatha" and the Greek prayer "Kyrie eleison" added an element of mystery and sense of connectedness to a religiously significant past, which even the Latin phraseology would eventually come to represent.

Whenever language has become mere form to the common person, having lost the ability to convey any message beyond its symbolic representation of a particular manifestation of sacrality, there will be a reaction by those who see a need for a scripture or liturgy that can once again speak and teach. Many religious movements have begun on this note, railing against frozen formalism and demanding—and usually producing—vernacular expressions of their religious feelings. Buddhism began in this manner, as did many *bhakti* movements in medieval India. The latter stressed vernacular compositions—devotional poetry—that often became the foundation for the flowering of literature in the regional language. In the West, Luther's insistence on hearing, understanding, and responding to the divine word led to the Protestant use of vernaculars and to the elevation of liturgical practices, such as the sermon, that stressed not just presentation of the scriptural forms but interpretation of the scriptural message.

Sets of sacred words. While not every religion develops the idea of an entire language as sacred, many—perhaps most—do regard some special subset of speech as an embodiment of the sacred. The mere uttering or hearing of words from this set, which usually takes the form of a collection of sacred scriptures, will be believed efficacious, whether or not the meaning is understood. This emphasis on formulaic, as opposed to spontaneous, language brings with it a stress on techniques of preservation and precise recitation of the given texts, rather than on methods for inspiration and creation of new expressions. The sacred words of scripture are a divine gift to man, which relieve him of the burden of inventing his own, merely human, response to the sacred.

Within the set of sacred scriptures, a single passage may stand out as the holiest of all, and therefore the most efficacious. Hinduism recognizes the mystic syllable *oṃ* as the essence of all the Vedas, and the hymn known as the Gāyatrī (*Ṛgveda* 3.62.10), has achieved a place of preeminence among all *mantras.* The smallest unit of sacred language is the single word, and there have been many candidates for the one that should be regarded as the holiest. However, the most widely recognized sacred word is the name of a god. This stems from a common association of the name of someone with that person's soul. Utterance of the name was felt to give power over the being. So the name of God in various religions has alternately been taboo—to be avoided because likely to incite the awesome power of the deity—and a focal point of prayer, meditation, or magic. The Igbo of Africa try to avoid using the names of gods they consider particularly capricious, employing instead such circumlocutions as "The One Whose Name Is Not Spoken." On the other hand, for the Ṣūfīs, the mystics of Islam, the intense repetition of the divine name over and over again in the practice of *dhikr* is regarded as one of the most effective means of achieving the highest state of pure, undivided consciousness of God.

The Speaker. Just as form may take precedence over content, so too the messenger may be a more important determinant of the sacrality of language than the message. Certainly the characteristics possessed by the speaker have often been regarded as significant factors contributing to, or detracting from, the sacral impact of the words uttered. The greatest impact comes when the speaker is regarded, in effect, as being a god. Very dramatic are those cases where a god is believed to talk directly and immediately through a person in the present. Here we have what has been called prophetic or charismatic speech, which stands in contrast to liturgical speech by representing a fresh and instantaneous infusion of sacrality. It may take such forms as speaking in tongues (glossolalia), or acting as a medium, oracle, or prophet.

For human speakers, in any case, their status will affect the sacrality attributed to their words; particular status may even be a necessary precondition for the use of sacred words. Priests, for example, may have exclusive rights to the use of liturgical utterances. In India, only the three upper classes were allowed to perform rites with Vedic *mantras.* Certainly high status will enhance the effectiveness of one's speech. Thus the Dinka of Africa believe that their priests' words are more effective in invoking, praying, and cursing because they have within themselves the power of the deity Flesh, who manifests himself in their trembling while they speak.

At some point in their history, most religions have struggled with the problem of keeping their tradition of rites and prayers from becoming an empty formalism. One approach has been to insist that a certain quality of heart or mind accompany the recitation of the sacred formulas. This usually involves a greater attention to the meaning of the language and requires a different attitude on the part of the speaker than does mere exactness in the repetition of the forms. In Vedic India, where precise articulation of the *mantras* became an essential ingredient of an effective ritual, there also developed the idea that the priest who had esoteric knowledge of the symbolic import of the ritual, and who silently rehearsed that knowledge during the performance, had the most effective ritual of all. In Indian Tantrism, the *mantra* became a meditational device that had to be uttered with the proper consciousness to be effective. The goal was to have the worshiper's consciousness blend with the thought-power represented by the *mantra.* A final example is the Jewish concept of *kavvanah.* In Talmudic writings, this was a state of mental concentration appropriate for prayer. But in the system of the Qabbalah, this became, during the recitation of a prayer, a form of single-minded meditation on the cosmic power to which the prayer was addressed. This gave one power over that cosmic element or allowed one's soul to ascend to that cosmic realm.

The Hearer. There may be a great difference in perspective on the issue of the sacrality of language between the speaker and the hearer or audience. The characterization of a sacred language as unintelligible and valued only for its form, discussed above, would apply, then, only to the untutored audience, and not to the priestly speaker who had been taught that language. Often, however, even a priest will be ignorant of the meaning of the words he uses, as is the case today, for example, among many of the Hindu *brahmans* who use Sanskrit recitations in their rituals, or the Buddhist monks who chant the Pali scriptures.

In many applications of sacred language, the intended hearer is a god. However, unlike the addressee in ordinary conversational situations, the addressed gods seldom speak back. The pattern of use most typical for sacred language—as in ritual or prayer—is not dialogue, with responsive exchanges between a speaker and hearer who alternate roles, but monologue. Or, in a ritual, there may be multiple speakers, but seldom are they responding to or addressing one another; rather they are prompted by cues of form to utter what the text calls for next, in a pattern that could be called orchestrated.

The Medium. The spoken word uses the medium of sound for its transmission. This gives it qualities that make it quite distinct from the written word, conveyed through the medium of print. This article focuses on sacred language as spoken, leaving to others the discussion of sacred forms of written language.

Many scholars in the past few decades have come to understand and emphasize the numerous differences between oral cultures and literate cultures. One key difference is that preliterate peoples regard the speaking of an utterance as an act that manifests power; the word is viewed as an active force that is immediately involved in shaping the world. In contrast, the written word comes to stand for lifeless abstraction from the world.

The medium of sound has a number of flexible qualities that can be manipulated to express nuances of power and sacrality in ways that go beyond the meaning of the words. These range from variation in tone and speed to the use of sound patterns such as rhythm and rhyme. The simplest of these vocal but nonverbal (or paralinguistic) features is variation in loudness. In the high cult of Vedic India, for example, three major variations were used for the *mantras:* (1) aloud, for the priest who recited the hymns of praise; (2) muttered, for the priest who performed most of the physical handiwork; and (3) silent, for the priest who sat and watched for errors in the performance. The loud recitations of praise were further divided into high, medium, and low tones, with the louder portions also spoken at a faster pace. The instructions for the traditional (Tridentine) Mass of Catholicism also called for three different tones, from aloud to inaudible.

While heightened sacrality, as in a liturgical climax, is sometimes marked by the loudest dynamic, often it is just the opposite. Silent speech or pure silence have often been regarded as the highest forms of religious expression. Thus, many times in the history of the Mass, the Canon—the climactic hallowing and offering of the sacraments—has been recited inaudibly, or so softly that only those immediately around the celebrant can hear. In Indian Tantra an explicit doctrine developed according to which "prayer without sound is recommended as the most excellent of all." Among the Zuni of North America, a person's most prized prayers are said only "with the heart."

Other modifications of sound may be used to set off some speech as particularly sacred. For example, the Zuni have another category of nonordinary language, used primarily in ritual, that they say is "raised right up." In this form they give strong stress and high pitch to ordinarily weak and low syllables. The most refined way of giving form to the sounds of language is to craft them into poetry or song. Adherents of many religions have felt that these forms possessed more magical power than prose or are more fitting modes of expression for the very solemn. For example, the traditional distinction between low and high Mass is based primarily on the use in the latter of a sung or chanted liturgy. In the Vedic high cult, the more lavish and important rituals were marked by the addition of a sung portion taken from the *Sāmaveda.*

The Context. Full understanding of any speech act requires knowledge of the context in which it occurs. Language regarded as sacred quite often has for its context a ritual setting. In that case, the intended effects of the speech acts are largely confined to the domain of the ritual. Some rituals do, of course, intend their effects to carry over into the nonritual environment as, for example, when the priest says "I now pronounce you man and wife." Sacred language may also find expression in settings other than ritual, in the case of spontaneous prayers or the occasional use of magic spells, for example.

The relationship between ritual language and its context is much different from that between ordinary language and its context. Since ritual language is, for the most part, the repetition of a fixed text, it precedes and, in effect, creates its context rather than reflecting and representing in speech a context regarded as prior and already defined. Therefore, much ritual language is directed toward defining the characteristics of the participants and the nature of the ritual situation. The rich symbolism of both object and action that marks off ritual behavior from ordinary behavior will add yet another distinctive trait to ritual language. Its message is often paralleled in the symbolic systems of those other media—the visual and tactile properties of the physical objects, the kinesthetic sensibilities of gesture and movement—which then serve to reinforce, enhance, or even complete the verbal meaning. For example, as the Dinka priest recites an invocation over the animal victim during a sacrifice, he accompanies each phrase with a thrust of his sacred spear to ensure that his words "hit the mark" and weaken the beast for the final physical act of killing. During the reciting of the Institution in the Mass, the priest breaks bread and offers the cup of wine to reenact the Last Supper and, thus, give parallel reinforcement to the words that make reference to the same event.

Language in Sacred Function. The several speech act components just surveyed, from language itself to the context in which it is spoken, combine to achieve the final product of the sacred utterance. There has been a wide variety of terms used to describe the possible intended effects (or, in linguistic terminology, illocutionary forces) of words used in the service of religious ends. However, it seems possible to reduce this multiplicity to two basic categories of purpose: (1) transforming some object or state of affairs and (2) worshiping spiritual beings. These categories correspond, in some measure, to the traditional views of sacred language as either magic spell, the self-effective word of power, or prayer, the petitionary communication with a god. That phrasing, however, overstates the dichotomy. It is all too customary to regard the formulas in one's own religion as prayers and those of another's as spells.

There is, in fact, an important trait held in common by both transforming and worshiping forms of language when they are employed in the context of ritual. As remarked earlier, most ritual language comes from a preexisting text and is repeated verbatim during the performance. It conveys little or no information to any of the ritual participants, since nothing new is being said. Therefore, it might be best to characterize the overall purpose of ritual language as creating and allowing participation in a valorized situation, rather than communicating information.

Language and transformation. It has already been noted above that there is a significant difference between sacred language uttered within the context of a ritual and that spoken outside of such a setting. A ritual is a self-contained and idealized situation in which the participants and objects momentarily take on changed identities in order to play out sacred roles. The words of the liturgy are the chief instruments by which these transformations take place.

The human participants. First of all, the human observants need to express their pious qualifications for undertaking the ritual. First-person indicative utterances are most frequently used to accomplish this task. In Christianity, for example, the proper identity of a repentant sinner and believer in the correct doctrine becomes manifest through the recitation of the Confession, "I confess to almighty God . . . that I have sinned," and the Creed, "I believe in one God . . ."

Some ritual traditions involve transforming the human into a divine being, in many cases by using language that states an identity between parts of their bodies. This is a common theme in Navajo healing rites. One prayer, for example, describes the deeds of two Holy People at the time of creation, and then continues: "With their feet I shall walk about; . . . with their torso I shall walk about." The priest in a Vedic ritual must also establish his partial identity with the gods, using such *mantras* as, "I pick you [grass bundle] up with the arms of Indra."

The ritual objects. The transmundane character of the ritual objects is, in a parallel fashion, often conferred or made explicit by indicative phrases. Most of the implements at a Vedic sacrifice are addressed by the priest with second-person utterances, such as this one to a wooden sword: "You are the right arm of Indra." The words spoken over the sacraments of the Christian Eucharist ("This is my body") also typify utterances of this category, whose function could appropriately be labeled consecration.

The ritual goals. Once the ritual setting has been transformed into an assemblage of divine or cosmic personages and forces, the transforming language of the liturgy will be directed to the task of prompting those powers to bring about some desired end. At the simplest level, there are the wishes that the ritual will produce a positive result. These may be first-person optatives (the optative is the grammatical mood for expressing a wish) of a condition one desires for oneself, as in this *mantra* said by the patron of a Vedic sacrifice: "By the sacrifice to the gods for Agni may I be food-eating." The patron will utter a wish in the same form after each offering is poured onto the fire. A similar connection between ritual activity and desired end is expressed in the Catholic Mass by a third-person optative: "May the body of our Lord Jesus Christ preserve my soul for everlasting life." This is said by the priest when he takes communion himself. But when he offers the sacrament to others he turns the wish into a blessing: "May the body of our Lord Jesus Christ preserve your soul for everlasting life." When one utters a wish that some negative condition may come about for another, it is a curse.

One may also direct the ritual objects to bring about a goal, as when the Vedic priest calls on the firmly fixed baking tile: "You are firm. Make the earth firm. Make life firm. Make the offspring firm." Or, finally, past-tense indicative utterances may be used simply to declare that the wished-for state of affairs has indeed come about. Navajo blessing prayers regularly conclude on such a note of verbal accomplishment.

There are some transformations that are supposed to carry over into, or take place in, nonritual settings. The marriage pronouncement is one such instance. These verbally accomplished acts that bring about a change in status were closely studied first by the philosopher J. L. Austin, who called them "performative utterances." Following his lead, some scholars have interpreted the magic spell as a simple case of a performative act that is felt to bring about a change in condition through the proper application of wholly conventional rules—just as turning two single people into a married couple requires only the recitation of the correct set of words under stipulated circumstances. Others, however, have pointed out that there is a difference between the conventional, socially recognized condition of being married and the brute, physical facts of illness or even death, which magic spells have regularly been employed to bring about. Thus when the priest at a Vedic sacrifice thrusts a wooden sword into the ground and says "O gods, he who hates me . . . his head I cut off with Indra's thunderbolt," words are being used to connect a ritual or magical action with a desired end that is more than just a conventional reality.

Language and worship. The most prominent sacred task to which language is put is the worship of the gods. The transformation of the ritual setting is usually an activity preparatory to the climactic offering of praise. The service of the gods demands a complex verbal etiquette. Interaction with the gods cannot be a matter of simple manipulation; instead, every act must be cushioned with words of explanation and concern. Furthermore, the intangible nature of the gods demands a linguistic means to make their presence take on a more concrete reality.

Most religious traditions have decided that worship of the gods must follow a particular form. The topics of the liturgy have a proper order. In Judaism there is the principle enunciated by the rabbis: "A man should always utter the praises of God before he offers his petitions." The opening lines of the official worship service dedicated to the Chinese earth god display a typical pattern: "She [the earth god] defends the nation and shelters the people. . . . Now during the mid-spring, we respectfully offer animals and sweet wine in this ordinary sacrifice. Deign to accept them." Indicative statements of the god's praiseworthy activity are followed by a first-person announcement of the act and objects of offering. Last comes the request to the god to accept the sacrifice. Most of the fundamental themes of worship will be found within the structure: invocation, praise, offering, and petition.

Invocation. Logically the first topic of any service of worship, securing the gods' presence at the rite—usually with second-person imperatives requesting them to come—will form an elaborate early portion of many liturgies. Hindu Tantric ritual, for example, uses an invocation to bring about the presence of the god in the concrete image that is the focus of worship: "O Lord who protects the world, graciously be present in this lingam [phallic image of Śiva] until the end of worship."

Praise. Essentially to *praise* means to pronounce publicly and thereby acknowledge recognition of a god's praiseworthy characteristics. If these involve deeds accomplished in the past that were of benefit, one expresses thanksgiving. There is always the hope, and probably expectation, that mentioning such deeds of benevolence will prompt the deity to act again on the celebrant's behalf. Certainly uttering praise is intended to make the god favorably disposed, or even to fill the god with renewed energy.

The simplest way to give linguistic expression to praise is to say "I praise," as in the Christian Gloria: "We praise thee, we bless thee, we adore thee, we glorify thee. . . ." Also typical are optative phrases, hoping that praise will become the universal response to the god. There is, for example, the Lesser Doxology: "Glory be to the Father, the Son, and the Holy Ghost." That is a common form for Hindu *mantras* of praise as well. The most basic verbal expression of piety for followers of Śiva is the "root *mantra*" (*mūlamantra*), "Namo Śivāya," meaning "[Let there be] reverence to Śiva." This Sanskrit form was carried by Buddhism all the way to Japan, where the favorite way of showing devotion in the Pure Land sects became the constant repetition of "Namu Amida Butsu," meaning "[Let there be] reverence to Amida Buddha."

A further development of the theme of praise comes through indicative statements of a god's praiseworthy characteristics, either present-tense declarations of constant attributes or past-tense statements of a god's great deeds. Both help to give a vivid sense of the god's actual presence, especially when made in the intimate form of second-person direct address. The Jewish *berakhot* ("blessings") combine the two methods of praise just presented. They usually have the form "Blessed are You O Lord, who has done [or does] such-and-such." The phrase "Blessed are You O Lord" ("Barukh attah Adonai") is equivalent to the optative expression "Let there be reverence (or glory) to you."

Offering. The high point of many worship services is the act of offering some gift to the invoked and praised gods. Words are necessary accompaniments to the physical act to define it as an act of offering, motivated by the appropriate intention on the part of the worshiper. There must also be statements expressing the proper concern for the god's feelings. Again, the simplest way to establish an act as one of offering is to say "I offer." This is usually accompanied by an enumeration and description of the objects offered. Almost always there will be a request that the god accept the offerings. In the Mass one finds "Holy Father . . . accept this unblemished sacrificial offering." Hindu worship includes such phrasing as "What has been given with complete devotion, . . . do accept these out of compassion for me."

Petition. The logically final act of worship, petition is in many cases the motive force behind the entire service. There are religious traditions, however, that downplay this goal. The worship service (*pūjā*) of Hindu Tantra, for example, is intended primarily as a spiritual discipline to be valued in its own right, rather than for any boon that might be obtained by prayer to the worshiped deity. The liturgy of Islam also has little in the way of petition. However, in the standard weekday service of rabbinic Judaism, the central element, the Amidah, contains a set of twelve supplications, the *tefillot,* accompanied by praise. And in the traditional Mass, the most prominent single type of utterance is a second-person imperative addressed to God the Father—for example, "Deliver us from every evil" or "Grant us this day our daily bread." The term *prayer,* though often used in the widest sense to refer to almost any form of language used in dealing with the gods, might best be restricted to this function of petition.

See Also Alphabets; Calligraphy; Glossolalia; Incantation; Logos; Magic; Mantra; Names and Naming; Oracles; Prayer.

Bibliography

General Works

Still the only major general and cross-cultural treatment of forms of sacred language is Friedrich Heiler's *Prayer: A Study in the History of Psychology and Religion* (London, 1932). Its usefulness is limited, however, because it gives primary emphasis to the psychology of spontaneous prayers and downplays the worth of liturgical compositions. Overviews of the traditional ways of characterizing religious conceptions and uses of language, with examples drawn from around the world, can be found in Heiler's *Erscheinungsformen und Wesen der Religion* (Stuttgart, 1961), chap. 7, "Das Heilige Wort"; and in a number of chapters in Gerardus van der Leeuw's *Religion in Essence and Manifestation,* 2d ed., 2 vols. (Gloucester, 1967).

Theoretical Studies

In order to appreciate the newer studies of sacred language that employ the insight of modern linguistics, it would be useful to consult the seminal work on speech acts by J. L. Austin, *How to Do Things with Words,* 2d ed. (Cambridge, Mass.,

1975), or the sophisticated development of his ideas in John Searle's *Speech Acts: An Essay in the Philosophy of Language* (London, 1969). One of the first and most successful attempts to clarify the category of prayer, using contemporary linguistic tools, is Antti Alhonsaari's *Prayer: An Analysis of Theological Terminology* (Helsinki, 1973). Some of the most insightful applications of speech act theory to religious language have come from anthropologists. Of particular significance is the work being done by Stanley J. Tambiah, particularly his article "The Magical Power of Words," *Man*, n. s. 3 (June 1968): 175–208, and chapter 12, "Liberation through Hearing," in *Buddhism and the Spirit Cults in North-East Thailand* (Cambridge, 1970). The former gives some important new discussion to the concept of the magic spell, and the latter proposes useful ways for understanding sacred languages and sacred scriptures. The relevance of much linguistic theory to the understanding of ritual language is summarized in Wade T. Wheelock's "The Problem of Ritual Language: From Information to Situation," *Journal of the American Academy of Religion* 50 (March 1982): 49–71. Groundbreaking work in examining the factors that make sacred language distinctive in its actual context of use, in both tribal societies and high cultures, has been done in the several fine studies in *Language in Religious Practice*, edited by William Samarin (Rowley, Mass., 1976).

Studies of Specific Traditions

Sam D. Gill's *Sacred Words: A Study of Navajo Religion and Prayer* (Westport, Conn., 1981) represents both an important theoretical study on methods for the thematic analysis of liturgical texts and a fine introduction to Navajo religious practices. The fascinating and complex theory of sacred language of the Dogon of West Africa is presented in Marcel Griaule's *Conversations with Ogotemmêli* (London, 1965). Pedro Laín Entralgo's *The Therapy of the Word in Classical Antiquity*, edited and translated by L. J. Rather and John M. Sharp (New Haven, 1970), gives a comprehensive discussion of the views on the power of charms and prayers in ancient Greece and Rome. The language theory of the Jewish mystical tradition is best presented in Gershom G. Scholem's *On the Kabbalah and Its Symbolism* (New York, 1965). The best discussion of the difficult philosophy of language of Indian Tantrism, as well as a useful overview of other Indian speculations on language, is André Padoux's *Recherches sur la symbolique et l'énergie de la parole dans certaines textes tantriques* (Paris, 1963).

WADE T. WHEELOCK (1987)

LANGUAGE: BUDDHIST VIEWS OF LANGUAGE

Any tradition that seeks mystical silence becomes intensely involved with the question of the role of language in religion. Silence presupposes speech; concern with the former reflects a concern with the latter. Even a brief survey of Buddhism would reveal a number of important strands within its tradition that depend heavily, or focus primarily, on some concept of sacred language.

DOCTRINAL BACKGROUND. Pre-Mahāyāna Buddhist literature tends to subsume all forms of discourse into the category of discursive thought. At this early stage there is already a tendency to identify language with "discursive or conceptual thought," and to identify the latter with erroneous knowledge. The Nikāyas and Āgamas suggest—certainly not as strongly as in Mahāyāna—the ineffable character of the Buddhist religious goal. The Buddha is beyond the "paths of speech" (*Suttanipāta* 1076), he cannot be conceived in visual or auditory images (*Theragāthā* 469).

Buddhist scholastics, on the other hand, downplay the nonconceptual. For them, liberating wisdom (*prajñā*) has discursive, as well as nondiscursive, dimensions. Still, their view of Buddhism unquestionably pictures the religion as a critique of conventional perceptions and descriptions of reality. The *dharma* theory of the Abhidharma can be interpreted as an attempt to establish a technical language of liberation—a set of concepts that will replace the misconceptions inherent in the ways of speaking about the world. These reflections find expression in the Abhidharmic concept of *prajñapti,* as developed in particular in the Sautrāntika school. *Prajñapti,* or "conventional designation," is the term used to explain the role and function of conventional language in contrast to the language of truth (*paramārtha*), which describes accurately the nature of reality as seen by the enlightened.

Prajñapti is also the key link between Abhidharmic thought and the philosophy of the Mādhyamika school. In the latter school human experience of reality is seen as being of two kinds: conventional views and the perception of ultimate reality. Language is an important aspect of the former, and as such it is perceived as a tool for the construction of a mock reality. Yet language also serves to express, or point at, the nonlinguistic sphere, that is, at the nature of things.

The Sautrāntika logicians also sought to attack what they perceived as reification of language in the philosophy of their Hindu rivals. The extremes to which these Buddhist philosophers went in trying to show the deceptive nature of language are particularly obvious in their theory of *apoha*—language as "exclusion." According to this theory, words do not correspond or refer to objects, for their meaning is the exclusion of whatever is not the object of reference. The word *cow,* for instance, means only "the absence of non-cow." Among Buddhist philosophers after the eighth century (e.g., Śāntirakṣita, Kamalaśīla, Ratnakīrti) several refinements and qualifications of this view became the standard theories of meaning. Application of these theories to the religious sphere, however, does not seem to have occurred to their formulators.

Nevertheless, it is difficult to imagine that doctrines of meaning and negation could remain unconnected to Buddhism as a religious practice—that is, as a type of apophatic mysticism. In the Sūtra literature the connection is established explicitly. For instance, the *Laṅkāvatāra Sūtra* sees the world of speech as the world of delusion, which is identical with the world of the disturbed and illusory mind. Accordingly, the Buddha is said to have abided in "the silence of the sage." He never spoke a word. The *Vimalakīrtinirdeśa*

Sūtra likewise, while asserting that everything is language, claims that only silence can express ultimate reality.

It is impossible, however, to remain in the realm of pure silence yet claim to practice a religion in a religious community. The Buddhist must therefore find a doctrinal bridge that will reach out beyond the sphere of mystical silence. Two doctrines are selected for this purpose by the scriptural and scholastic traditions: the doctrines of conventional truth (*saṃvṛti*) and "skillful means" (*upāya*). These are in part a theoretical recognition of the fact that Buddhism as a living religion is seldom a practice of literal silence. The silence of the Buddha is manifested in his speech; his words take the form that is understood by his listeners. Language is therefore not necessarily false. It is not misleading under all circumstances, because it can be used "skillfully" as a "means" (*upāya*). This is the ultimate statement on language made in texts such as the *Laṅkāvatāra Sūtra* and the *Tathāgataguhya Sūtra.*

RELIGIOUS PRACTICE. Concern with the sacred word and acceptance of language as a practical tool play a much more significant role in Buddhist religious life than does the philosophical understanding of Buddhist silence, although they are never understood as contradicting the apophatic doctrine.

The importance of language and "the word" in the general history of religions in India is well attested (e.g., the Hindu *kirtan,* the pan-Indian *mantra,* and the school of Mīmāṃsā). What is characteristic of Buddhism is its concern with a critique of language. This concern is often found mixed, paradoxically, with a strong sense of the importance of the invariant word, the holy manifested in utterance, silence embodied in words. There are, however, many instances in which the sacred word is just that—its immutable character endowing it with power to protect and redeem.

Typology of the word. One can speak of a typology of the sacred word in Buddhism as ranging from the canon of scriptures, through the book, the sacred phrase, the (single) sacred word, the sacred syllable, and the sacred sound or letter. The following are a few major examples of the use of sacred words in Buddhism.

The vow. Perhaps the most important of these beliefs are the Mahāyāna doctrines of the *bodhisattva*'s solemn utterance of a vow (*praṇidhāna*), to follow the path of buddhahood, and the ritual formulation of the vow and the precepts (*saṃvara-grahaṇa*). The vow is a kind of "act of truth," in which the will of an extraordinarily virtuous human being cooperates with the power of truth inherent in any statement of fact.

The book. Even in the sober Theravāda there is a strong sense of the authority of scriptural pronouncement as the ipsissima verba of Gautama the Buddha. As such, the sacred text is sacred regardless of the devotee's capacity to understand the conceptual content of the text. Concrete manifestations in ritual of this Buddhist reverence for the sacred word—including the literal text and the material book—are also well attested in Mahāyāna traditions. For example, the "perfection of wisdom" (*prajñāpāramitā*) stands not only for the "highest experience" of absolute nonduality, but also represents the expression of this experience in words. The words themselves, and even the material "book" in which the words are preserved, embody the *prajñāpāramitā,* they are the *prajñāpāramitā.* Thus, scripture, as the "embodiment" of the Buddha as Dharma, becomes a living relic of the Buddha, so that every place where the text is made known becomes a sacred location, a reliquary, as it were (*Vajracchedikā* 12.15c; *Aṣṭasāhasrikā Prajñāpāramitā* 3.57). The preservation of the sacred word, therefore, is tantamount to the preservation of the Buddha's own being.

The ritual recitation of the scriptures as a source of merit is a common practice throughout Buddhist Asia. This practice can extend from the actual study and expounding of the Sūtra as doctrinal discourse to the cult of the collection of scriptures (cult of the Tripiṭaka), from the study of extensive collections of texts to the symbolic repetition of the text by copying it, or merely by turning a revolving bookcase containing the whole canon of scriptures or a praying wheel with copies of a short incantation. The enshrinement of texts—a common practice in Tibetan Buddhism—is not qualitatively different from the acceptance of a single fragment of text as an embodiment of the *Dharma.*

Incantation. The concept of words as summary or embodiment of the sacred has its most extreme manifestation in the symbolization of the *Dharma* in short segments of speech that are either fragments of natural expressions (the title of sūtras, the *Prajñāpāramitā in a Single Syllable*), or strings of phonemes with little or no signification in the natural language (*mantra, dhāraṇī*). These texts are also regarded as a condensation of the sacred power of the enlightened, and can be protective formulas as well as instruments of meditation. The latter function is reserved primarily, although not exclusively, for the *mantra.*

The use of sacred texts or fragments of sacred speech (e.g., *paritta* and *dhāraṇī*) as incantations to guard off evil or eliminate negative influences or as propitiatory formulas plays an important role in both popular and "great tradition" Buddhist practice. A mysterious Dhāraṇī Piṭaka seems to have formed part of the canon of the Dharmaguptaka Buddhists in Andhra (in Southeast India), and may have been the repository of many of these formulas, otherwise attested in inscriptions, in anthologies (e.g., Śāntideva's *Śikṣāsamuccaya*), and as part of sūtras (e.g., the *dhāraṇī* sections of the *Saddharmapuṇḍarīka,* chap. 21, and *Laṅkāvatāra,* chap. 9). In the same way that the book comes to stand for the source of Buddhahood, the *dhāraṇī,* as epitome of the wisdom and power of the Dharma, can be conceived as a protective deity. The word becomes personified power in the mythology of figures, for example, the "Five Protective Deities" (*pañcarakṣā*).

Sectarian manifestations. The importance of these religious phenomena becomes even more obvious when one considers their central role in the development of some of the most successful sectarian traditions of Buddhist Asia. In all of the examples given below, a practice connected with the sacred word has become the characteristic doctrinal or practical axis of a distinct school.

Pure Land. Pure Land Buddhism, as a generalized religious ideal in India, epitomizes Buddhist doctrines of grace and the sacred word. The *bodhisattva* or the Buddha is the source of grace, the savior who can be reached by merely calling his name. The classical examples of this tradition are the chapters on the *bodhisattva* Avalokiteśvara in the *Gaṇḍavyūha Sūtra* and the *Saddharmapuṇḍarīka Sūtra.*

The practice of the recitation of the name of Buddha Amitābha, on the other hand, is usually not separated from the traditions of faith and meditation, as found, for instance in the *Sukhāvatīvyūha.* The mythology behind the practice reveals that it can be conceived as something more than faith in the magical power of words. Amitābha, in a former existence as the *bodhisattva* Dharmākara, pronounced a solemn vow, the power of which is such that it can produce the effect (the goals sought by the vow) by the sheer power of the truth of the words uttered. This vow and its effects are embodied, and can be evoked or reached by another sacred word—the name of Amitābha. The power is not in the name as such, but in the intention of the Buddha's former vows.

Nevertheless, a belief that the repetition of the names of Buddhas is intrinsically meritorious is amply attested. In China, the incantation of the name of Amitābha Buddha became an independent religious form. The most extreme example of the mechanical application of this practice is the custom of keeping accurate accounts of how many times one repeats the name of Amitābha. Whether one is attempting to visualize the Buddha or not is irrelevant; the merit accrues regardless of the state of mind or degree of spiritual advancement of the believer.

In the Pure Land traditions of Japan the repetition of the name of Amitābha (Jpn., Amida) is divorced from the doctrine of merit altogether. The invocation itself becomes the primary practice, the only access to Amida's saving grace. The simplicity of this practice (known as the Nembutsu) is such that many believers would even deny that it is a ritual of invocation. Rather, it is conceived as the simple enunciation of the formula "Namu Amida Butsu" (the Japanese pronunciation of the Chinese phrase "Namo O [or A]mituofo," itself an attempt to reproduce the Sanskrit sentence: "Namo 'mitābhāya buddhāyā"). This short phrase is considered equivalent to the "true name" of the Buddha—that is to say, the essence of the Buddha as Buddha.

Nichirenshū. Related to this faith in the power of the name is the Buddhist trust in the power of particular sūtras. The most successful development of this belief is the Japanese sect founded by Nichiren (1222–1282). For him, the title *(daimoku)* of the *Lotus Sūtra* recited in the formula "Namu *Myōhō-renge-kyō*" becomes the powerful source of all spiritual and material well-being. Nichiren himself is said to have inscribed the phrase on a scroll. This inscription is considered the primary object of veneration in the sect. It is conceived—following Japanese esoteric tradition—as a *maṇḍala.*

Tantra. Perhaps the most obvious manifestation of concern with the sacred character of language within Buddhism is in the phenomena encompassed by the broad term Buddhist Tantra or Tantric Buddhism. In the Tantric tradition the sacred word is at the same time the embodiment of multiple dimensions of the holy. Tantric texts such as the *Guhyasamāja Tantra* develop homologies linking the Buddha's silence (the ineffable), his mind (the experience of meditation), his speech (the expression of his experience), and his power (apotropaic formulas).

The sacred formula (*mantra*) or syllable (*bīja*) serves both as a powerful tool of incantation and a vehicle for visualization. A sacred and esoteric language or code (*saṃdhā-bhāṣā, saṃdhyā-bhāṣā*) is developed to convey the meaning of ritual symbolism as the embodiment of religious experience. The latter use of sacred language is perhaps an interpretive device that tends to reduce the sacred word to the experience of meditation. The reduction takes place by means of homologies similar to the ones at the heart of the mystical tradition of the Brāhmaṇas and the early Upaniṣads. Thus, the *mantra* conveys meaning primarily as a code—a multivalued icon embodying a system of sacred identities.

Therefore, one can rightly speak of "the word as icon" in the Tantric tradition. In Tibet, for instance, the sacred word acquires a life of its own. The sacred *mantra* of the *bodhisattva* Avalokiteśvara, "Oṃ maṇi padme huṃ," is inscribed on building walls, on rooftops, and on stones in the road. It is inserted in praying wheels, where the mere mechanical turning of the inscribed syllables is supposed to invoke the presence of the *bodhisattva,* and allow the devotee to gain access to his grace or visualize his image.

The Japanese Kūkai (774–835), the founder of the esoteric tradition of Japanese Tantra, regarded all language as sacred, although he also adopted the philosophical critique of language. He regarded *mantras* as the primary form of the sacred (the "true word," *shingon*), but at the same time he considered that all words, even syllables and letters, stood ultimately for the silent meditation of Vairocana Buddha. Words, but above all Sanskrit sounds, were the embodiment of the highest reality.

Zen. Chan or Zen Buddhism also represents an important manifestation of both a concern with language and a predilection for the development of specialized sacred languages. The Zen tradition is avowedly the Buddhism of Vimalakirti's silence—a claim that is explicitly reinforced by the practice of silent meditation. However, the excesses of blank mental concentration have been criticized in the sect since its inception in the eighth century, and an important segment of the tradition also practices meditation on "words"—*kanna-zen.* The use of the *kōan* (Chin., *gongan*) or *mondō* as sacred text (even in ritual contexts) is well attested; the *kōan* collections became the sacred canon of the sect. Nevertheless, even as the tradition concedes the immutable character of the sacred utterance it emphasizes the critical function of the *kōan* as expression of the dialectic nature of the enlightenment experience. For the *kōan* is also regarded as the embodiment of the enlightenment experience of the great masters of the past and a test case for the aspirant to that experience—hence its name, "public (*kung*) case or precedent (*an*)."

The general category of "sacred language," however, does not exhaust or explain the specific meanings of the sacred word in Pure Land, Tantra, and Zen. Each one has a particular context. They represent only polarities in a wide range of possibilities within the Buddhist tradition. The three types of sacred word—*nembutsu, kōan,* and *mantra*—share a common element insofar as they represent forms of nonnatural linguistic expression, but the analogy ends there. On the one hand, the *mantra* and the *dhāraṇī* express or embody the enlightenment experience as the manifestation in sound of a nonlinguistic sphere. They usually convey sacred meaning with only a token or minimal regard for linguistic sense. The title of a sūtra or the name of a Buddha, on the other hand, are clearly exact names that correspond to well-formed names in the natural language. The Nembutsu may embody Amida's enlightenment and true nature, but only by way of the actual name found in the myth of Dharmākara. Last, the *kōan* also claims to contain the actual linguistic form of a sacred, yet natural utterance "attested" in the quasi-historical context of hagiography; unlike the title of a sūtra, however, it alludes explicitly to the mythic context, and unlike the calling on the name of a Buddha, it claims to preserve a segment of meaningful, albeit paradoxical discourse.

INTERPRETIVE FRAMEWORKS. Among the religious traditions, explicit discussion of the nature of language occurs mainly within the Tantra, which in Tibetan and late Indian Buddhism constitutes the practical branch of the eclectic philosophical schools. In conformity with its philosophical roots Tantrism falls back on two Mādhyamika principles that are no doubt the most important hermeneutic devices in Buddhist philosophy—the concept of "two truths" and the concept of "explicit" and "implicit" meanings (*nīta-* and *neya-artha*). As convention, language has a certain validity, but its claim to represent something more than convention or to depict reality are spurious. The experience of reality as such, or of things as they are "before language," is the experience of the highest goal, the ultimate meaning, or the most real object (*paramārtha*). Although this experience lies beyond all linguistic procedures or operations, beyond all conceptualization, it is accessible only through some form of linguistic index. Thus, linguistic convention, while merely conventional and relative, is necessary for liberation as well as for everyday practical activities.

Furthermore, the rejection of linguistic convention and conceptual thought is seldom unconditional or unqualified. In some Buddhist traditions the conventional world is not to be rejected because it is convention. The linguistic realm is deceptive and false only when it claims to be something more than a conventional construct. Therefore, certain forms of linguistic convention—everyday use of language and special sacred language tools or substitute linguistic conventions—are acceptable. This is especially clear in late Mādhyamika thought, where the realm of the conventional is further divided to distinguish a "true" conventional from a "false" conventional usage. For instance, the Indian philosopher Kamalaśīla (fl. eighth century) regards the logic of everyday transactions as true in a certain manner of speaking. It is in fact the only logic possible, and discourse about the absolute only serves to clear away metaphysical language games. Thus, even the ultimate reality of emptiness is subject to a critique that corrects its apparent isolation from the world. Conventional and religious discourse alike may be illusions, but so is talk about the silence of emptiness. This is the theoretical context in which religious practices such as Tantra see themselves as a means to a practical and effective resolution of the tension between absolute and relative, silence and speech, liberating knowledge (*prajñā*) and skillful application of liberating means (*upāya*).

SEE ALSO Amitābha; Buddhism, Schools of, article on Tantric Ritual Schools of Buddhism; Buddhist Books and Texts, article on Exegesis and Hermeneutics; Chan; Jingtu; Jōdo Shinshū; Jōdoshū; Kamalaśīla; Mantra; Mīmāṃsā; Nianfo; Nichirenshū; Oṃ; Prajñā; Śāntarakṣita; Sautrāntika; Shingonshū; Tantrism, overview article; Upāya; Zen.

BIBLIOGRAPHY

Bharati, Agehananda. *The Tantric Tradition.* London, 1965. A study of Indian Tantrism in general, and Hindu Tantra in particular.

Bhattacharyya, Benoytosh. *An Introduction to Buddhist Esotericism* (1932). Reprint, Varanasi, 1964. A work of uneven quality, but still indispensable. The reprint edition contains a new preface by the author, but chapter 7, "The Mantras," is unfortunately too short.

Blacker, Carmen. "Methods of Yoga in Japanese Buddhism." In *Comparative Religion: The Charles Strong Trust Lectures,* 1961–1970, edited by John Bowman, pp. 82–98. Leiden, 1972. An accessible, yet scholarly comparison of the practice of the *kōan* method of Rinzai Zen, and the *mantras* of Shingon Buddhism.

Dasgupta, Shashibhusan. *An Introduction to Tantric Buddhism* (1958). Reprint, Berkeley, Calif., 1974. The reprint edition of this work contains a foreword by H. V. Guenther, in which he points to some of the book's shortcomings. Like Bhattacharyya, this work is still one of the standard surveys, in spite of its problems.

Hakeda, Yoshito S., trans. *Kūkai: Major Works.* New York, 1972. A study of Kūkai, and a translation of some of his works. Includes his most important work on the meaning of language and the sacred word, the *Shōji jissō gi.*

Hamlin, Edward. "Discourse in the *Laṅkāvatāra-Sutra.*" *Journal of Indian Philosophy* 11 (September 1983): 267–313. An original interpretation of the sūtra's view of language as *upāya.*

Hopkins, Jeffrey, ed. and trans. "The Great Exposition of the Secret Mantra." Hopkins's translation of Tsoṅ-kha-pa's classical treatise on the Tantric path, *Sṅags rim chen po,* was published in two volumes under two different titles: *Tantra in Tibet: The Great Exposition of the Secret Mantra,* Wisdom of Tibet Series, no. 3 (London, 1977), and *The Yoga of Tibet: The Great Exposition of the Secret Mantra, 2 and 3,* Wisdom of Tibet Series, no. 4 (London, 1981).

Huntington, C. W., Jr. "A 'Nonreferential' View of Language and Conceptual Thought in the Work of Tsoṅ-Kha-pa." *Philosophy East and West* 33 (October 1983): 325–340. Highlights the elements of "linguistic philosophy" found in Tsoṅ-kha-pa's interpretation of Indian Mādhyamika. With Williams (1980), this paper adds to the strength of the linguistic interpretation of Mādhyamika.

Ñāṇananda, Bhikkhu. *Concept and Reality in Early Buddhist Thought.* Kandy, 1971. An imaginative interpretation of the Buddhist critique of conceptual thought in the Pali tradition.

Padoux, André. *Recherches sur la symbolique et l'énergie de la parole dans certains textes tantriques.* Paris, 1963. A general discussion of sacred language in Hindu Tantra. Many of the author's interpretations could apply to Buddhist Tantra.

Saunders, E. Dale. "Some Tantric Techniques." In *Studies in Esoteric Buddhism and Tantrism,* pp. 167–177. Koyasan, 1965. Surveys various Tantric ritual and meditation styles, including the use of *mantras* in meditation.

Schopen, Gregory. "The Phrase *'sa pṛthivīpradeśaś caityabhūto bhavet'* in the *Vajracchedikā:* Notes on the Cult of the Book in Mahāyāna." *Indo-Iranian Journal* 17 (November–December 1975): 147–181. This essay lays the groundwork for Schopen's views on the cult of the book in Mahāyāna.

Sen, Sukumar. "On Dharani and Pratisara." *In Studies in Esoteric Buddhism and Tantrism,* pp. 67–72. Koyasan, 1965. A study of *pratisarā* as emblematic of the so-called "deified" utterances.

Shama, Dhirendra. *The Differentiation Theory of Meaning in Indian Logic.* The Hague, 1969. An edition and translation of Ratnakīrti's (fl. 1070) *Apohasiddhi.*

Snellgrove, David L., ed. and trans. *The Hevajra Tantra: A Critical Study.* 2 vols. London, 1959. An edition and translation of an important Tantric text of the Indo-Tibetan tradition.

Tambiah, Stanley J. "The Magical Power of Words." *Man* 3 (June 1968): 175–208. The role of nonhuman language forms in the "little tradition" of Theravāda.

Ueda, Yoshifumi, ed. *Notes on Once-Calling and Many-Calling: A Translation of Shinran's Ichinen-tanen mon'i.* Kyoto, 1980. An annotated translation of one of Shinran's most lucid expositions on the meaning of Nembutsu practice.

Waddell, L. Austine. "'Dharani,' or Indian Buddhist Protective Spells." *Indian Antiquary* 43 (1914): 37–42, 49–54. This essay contains translations of Tibetan *dhāraṇīs.* See also the same author's "The Dhāraṇī Cult in Buddhism, Its Origin, Deified Literature and Images," *Ostasiatische Zeitschrift* 1 (1912): 155–195, which is dated, but remains the most complete attempt to establish a history of Buddhist *dhāraṇī.* Includes a discussion of the personified protective formulas (*pañcarakṣā*).

Waldschmidt, Ernst. "Das Paritta: Eine magische Zeremonie der buddhistischen Priester auf Ceylon." *Baessler-Archiv* 17 (1934): 139–150. Reprinted in *Von Ceylon bis Turfan: Schriften zur Geschichte, Literatur, Religion und Kunst des indischen Kulturraumes von Ernst Waldschmidt* (Göttingen, 1967), pp. 465–478. Analysis of the use of *parittā* in Sri Lanka, and its sources in the Pali tradition.

Wayman, Alex. "Concerning saṃdhā-bhāṣā/saṃdhi-bhāṣā/saṃdhya bhāṣā." In *Mélanges d'indianisme à la mémoire de Louis Renou,* pp. 789–796. Paris, 1968. Summarizes earlier research on the subject and proposes Wayman's theory of "twilight language." This thesis is developed further in "Twilight Language and a Tantric Song," chapter 11 of Wayman's *The Buddhist Tantras: Light on Indo-Tibetan Esotericism* (New York, 1973). Other aspects of the problem of language in Buddhism have been explored by Wayman in "The Hindu-Buddhist Rite of Truth: An Interpretation," in *Studies in Indian Linguistics,* edited by Bhadriraju Krishnamurti (Poona, 1968), pp. 365–369. In this essay the author considers the connections between the "act of truth" and other "pan-Indian" notions of the "true word." Wayman studies early instances of the tension between the ideals of silence and truth in Indian religious thought in "Two Traditions of India—Truth and Silence," *Philosophy East and West* 24 (October 1974): 389–403. He has also written extensively on the *Guhyasamāja* and the symbolism of the *mantra* in *Yoga of the Guhyasamājatantra: The Arcane Lore of Forty Verses: A Buddhist Tantra Commentary* (Delhi, 1977).

Williams, Paul M. "Some Aspects of Language and Construction in the Madhyamaka." *Journal of Indian Philosophy* 8 (March 1980): 1–45. Summarizes, with new data and insight, the linguistic aspects of Mādhyamika dialectic.

New Sources

Abe, R. *The Weaving of Mantra: Kukai and the Construction of Esoteric Buddhist Discourse.* New York, 1999.

Cabezón, José Ignacio. *Buddhism and Language: A Study of Indo-Tibetan Scholasticism.* Albany, N.Y., 1994.

Hayes, R. P. *Dignaga on the Interpretation of Signs.* Boston, 1988.

Kalupahana, D. J. *The Buddha's Philosophy of Language.* Ratmalana, Sri Lanka, 1999.

Lang, Karen C. "Poetic License in the Buddhist Sanskrit Verses of the Upalipariprccha." *Indo-Iranian Journal* 44, no. 3 (2001): 231–240.

McPhail, M. L. *Zen in the Art of Rhetoric: An Inquiry into Coherence.* Albany, N.Y., 1996.

Salomon, Richard. "'Gandhari Hybrid Sanskrit': New Sources for the Study of the Sanskitization of Buddhist Literature." *Indo-Iranian Journal* 44, no. 3 (2001): 241–252.

Smits, Gregory. "Unspeakable Things: Sai On's Ambivalent Critique of Language and Buddhism." *Japanese Journal of Religious Studies* 24 (1997): 163–178.

Tilakaratne, A., and University of Kelaniya. Postgraduate Institute of Pali & Buddhist Studies. *Nirvana and Ineffability: A Study of the Buddhist Theory of Reality and Language.* Sri Lanka, 1993.

LUIS O. GÓMEZ (1987)
Revised Bibliography

LAO RELIGION. The Lao people inhabit both banks of the Middle Mekong, from Louang Phrabang in the north to Khong Island in the south. Properly speaking, they represent only half of the population in the country that bears their name; the number of Lao in neighboring Thailand is five times as great. A variety of influences have contributed to the religious contours of the Lao. Tai-speaking peoples from south of the Chinese empire introduced into the autochthonous Austroasiatic culture of the region a variety of myths and rites exhibiting Chinese influence. In the ensuing process of assimilation elements of both cultures were preserved. The dominant cultural vector, however, stems ultimately from the Indian subcontinent. When asked his or her religion, a Lao invariably will answer that he is a Buddhist, more specifically, a follower of the Theravāda ("doctrine of the elders") school. The center and symbol of the rural collectivity, indeed, of all action that is communal in Lao society, remains the *vat* (Pali, *vatthu*; Skt., *vāstu*) or Buddhist monastery. Within its precincts matters both sacred and secular—religious instruction, public meetings, community rituals, the election of a village chief—are conducted. Conversion to Buddhism remains the principal means of assimilation of minorities into the sphere of Lao culture.

Coextensive with Buddhism, and functionally integrated with it, is the so-called phī cult, or cult of local spirits. While belief in local spirits predates the introduction of Buddhism, it is important to recognize that it is impossible to extrapolate from contemporary practice the contours of Lao religion prior to the introduction of Buddhism. Nor is it consistent with the society's own understanding of its religious system to see the phī cult as formally or functionally distinct from Buddhism. Centuries of syncretization have forged an internally consistent religious ideology that has rationalized the mutual interdependence of both systems. The separate consideration of the two in the discussion that follows is merely a heuristic device, designed to illuminate the prevailing religious concerns of each.

THE PHĪ CULT. The term *phī* is common to all Tai-speaking populations (one finds the term *fī* among certain non-Buddhist Tai in northern Vietnam) and typically designates an ensemble of various entities such as souls, ancestors, evil spirits, and celestial deities. The cult probably originated in pre-Buddhist Tai society, enriched by contact with Austroasiatics, the previous inhabitants of the region. The influence of the *phī* cult is seen in the concern to maintain the integrality of the person, as it is held that the departure of one (or several) souls provokes sickness and death. Here, it is the therapeutic aspect that dominates, Buddhism having appropriated the funerary rites. The performance of *sū khwan* ("calling back the souls") is mandated at times of risk: illness, before a voyage or examination, or at the passage to another stage of life. This "call" is accompanied by invocations and the recitation of votive formulas and is concluded by the tying of ligatures of cotton threads to the wrist, thus connecting the souls to the body.

The Lao have recourse equally to specialist healers (*mọ̄*) and occasionally to female mediums (*nāng thiam*). The most powerful among the former is the *mọ̄ thēvadā*, or "master of divinities," a shaman who invokes the aid of his auxiliary spirits, the *phī thēvadā*. The *mọ̄ thēvadā* have a double competence, as shamans and as mediums, as demonstrated by the "sacrifice to the talisman protectors" (*liang khọ̄ng haksā*). In this ceremony, master and disciples stage a séance of successive possessions by diverse deities, among them a class of spirits known as *khā*, said to include both Austroasiatic authochthones and Vessantara, the Buddha in his last rebirth prior to that in which he achieved enlightenment as Gautama. Richard Pottier (1973) has exposed this same double competence among the *nāng thiam* of the Louang Phrabang region, who undergo possession in public rites but act as shamans in the course of healing consultations. However, the *nāng thiam* function principally on the level of the collectivity, where they intervene in ceremonies honoring the guardian deity of the territory (*phī muang*) or of the individual village (*phī bān*).

The cult of the tutelary deity of the village is headed by a master of ritual known as a *caw cam*, a position that is gained through village elections. It is the role of the *caw cam* to announce to the *phī* all events affecting the life of the collectivity, notably events in which the *phī* is directly implicated. He addresses to the spirits the personal requests of the villagers; when these requests are granted it is his duty to officiate at the *kẹ̄ba*, or sacrifice of thanksgiving. His principal task, however, is to organize and execute the annual sacrifice to the tutelary deity, the *liang phī bān*, or "nourishing of the village spirit," in which all households participate.

BUDDHIST INFLUENCES. Buddhism and the *phī* cult are not simply juxtaposed in Lao popular religion; over the course of several centuries they have become syncretized. Those who compiled the royal annals have presented the introduction of Buddhism at the time of the Lao kingdom's foundation as a victory over the *phī* cult that had predominated. They recall the vigorous campaign carried against the *phī* by King Pothisarath, who passed an edict in 1527 prohibiting them and ordering the destruction of all sanctuaries consecrated to the *phī*. His successors showed more understanding toward the *phī*, and Buddhism had to accommodate itself to the persistence of the cult's hold on the population. Some concepts and practices were "civilized" by assuming an outwardly Hindu form—it is likely that this phenomenon predates the arrival of Hīnayāna Buddhism.

This syncretism shows up constantly in daily life and in grand public celebrations. For example, one utilizes Buddhist formulas for magical purposes and seeks without hesitation the knowledge of a monk before drawing a number in the lottery. It would never enter anyone's mind to reproach the *caw cam phī bān* for indulging in acts contrary to *tham* (Pali, *dhamma*; Skt., *dharma*), because one generally elects to this position a man known for his devotion to the Perfect One; in fact, before going to officiate at this altar of the tutelary deity, this ritual master first prays at the pagoda. We see within the very compound of the *vat* the presence of a replica in miniature of the altar of the tutelary deity: this altar, the *hǭ phī khun vat*, is dedicated to the spirit benefactor of the monastery, the monk who was its founder. The tutelary deity, in the majority of cases, is also the founder of the village, and it happens frequently that the master of the *phī bān* ritual is the same as that of the *phī khun vat*.

One of the great village feasts is the Bun Bang Fai ("rocket festival"). There is no need to overemphasize the sexual symbolism of the giant rockets that are shot against the sky just before the coming of the monsoon with its fecundating rains; moreover, the carnivalesque processions with their ribald songs and provocative exhibition of enormous wooden phalluses for the benefit of young maidens points more explicitly to the nature of the festival. That the Buddhist clergy sanctions and effectively participates in this festival is evidenced by the fact that the rockets are placed within the compound of the pagoda under the supervisions of the monks. It is also in the monastic compound that the dancing *nāng thiam* enter into trances and where rockets of invited neighboring pagodas are collected for the rites. In numerous villages the festival of Bun Bang Fai is connected with the feast of the tutelary deity. Fertility, bawdiness, the drinking of alcoholic beverages, entering into trances, gambling (with betting on the rockets)—all of these are against Buddhist law. However, in the eyes of the Lao farmer, the festival of the rockets commemorates the Visākhā Pūjā—the triple anniversary of the birth, the enlightenment, and the death of the Buddha.

The Buddhist notion that has most profoundly permeated Lao popular religion seems to be that of *bun* (Pali, *puñña*), "merit." One must acquire merit to enrich one's *kam* (Pali, *kamma*; Skt., *karman*), which permits the attainment of spiritual liberation in the cycles of transmigration. The Lao thinks very little of *niphān* (Pali, *nibbāna*; Skt., *nirvāṇa*), but remains concerned with a mundane counterpart of merit: prestige, wealth, power. It should be noted that the Lao layman preoccupies himself even less with the inverse notion, that of *bāp* (Pali, Skt., *pāpa*), "error." He is particularly concerned with the acquisition of merits, best obtained through gift giving. Moreover, the gift most laden with merit is that which has as its beneficiary the *pha sang* (Pali, *sangha*; Skt., *saṃgha*), the community of monks. Thus, one who has chosen monastic asceticism by his sacrifice enriches not only his own *kam* but offers to others the possibility of acquiring merit, even if only through the food alms that he must collect each day. To this daily source of *bun* must be added the massive enrichment procured through offerings of paraphernalia for the ordination of a monk or for the celebration of Buddhist feasts. Moreover, it should not be forgotten that at least once in his life every man must wear the saffron robe, a trial that constitutes a sort of initiation and preparation to adult life.

Another outwardly Buddhist component of Lao society that also serves non-Buddhist functions is the *vat*, or monastery. The monastery rises and grows with the collective it represents. After having cleared a section of the forest and forming a sufficiently autonomous hamlet, a group of farmers may decide to establish a hermitage (*vat pā*, "forest pagoda") for a monk. This small wooden house on stilts becomes the first *kutdī* (Skt., *kutī*; monks' quarters) and grows with the hamlet itself. Consequently, this growth brings an increase in voluntary manpower and thus the construction of a more sophisticated building, the *sālā*, a public hall. Once this grand square hall on short stilts has been completed, the collective is able to invite a greater number of monks and laity to the village's religious ceremonies. The *sālā* does not function solely as a religious center, however. It serves also as a forum for meetings where the local inhabitants convene to debate on matters concerning the entire collective, such as the election of village chief, common works to undertake, and feasts to celebrate. It also serves as a warehouse for materials needed for the realization of these projects, a shelter for hawkers and travelers, and as classroom for any occidental-type schools built in the rural area. When a village attains a degree of development and reputation such that it has at its disposal the means to pay hired labor (thanks to collections made during feasts or gifts offered by individuals), it undertakes the construction of a sanctuary (*sīm*; Pali, Skt., *sīmā*). We see, therefore, that the monastery is the center not only of the religious life of the rural collective but also, by virtue of its multifunctional role, of all activity that is communal in character.

The two currents of Buddhist and indigenous folk religious belief intermingle to form Lao religion, but their respective proportions vary with the epochs and regions. As the reigning power reinforces itself and develops the teaching of Buddhism, the *phī* cult's influence tends to diminish. Despite this, Lao farmers do not completely abandon this recourse to nature's forces, which guarantee them the resources necessary for the maintenance and renewal of life. Even when they concern the whole village, the *phī* ceremonies take place beyond the sight of strangers. On the other hand, the monastery bears witness to the adherence of its members to a universalistic religion. The individual finds therein refuge for the most important phases of his spiritual life. But the *vat* is not there to serve the spiritual activities of Buddhism only; it caters also to all aspects of collective life. By its openness, it bears testimony to a social space comprising the totality of peasant system of relations: state officials on inspection tours hold meetings there, monks whom it shelters come from a hierarchy paralleling that of state administrative divisions, and festivals held in the monastery take all forms, sacred or profane, of Lao culture.

SEE ALSO Buddhism, article on Buddhism in Southeast Asia; Merit, article on Buddhist Concepts; Southeast Asian Religions, article on Mainland Cultures; Theravāda; Worship and Devotional Life, article on Buddhist Devotional Life in Southeast Asia.

BIBLIOGRAPHY

First and foremost, a portion of the many but dispersed publications of Charles Archaimbault has been compiled in one volume, *Structure religieuses lao: Rites et mythes* (Vientiane, 1973). Archaimbault's article "Les ceremonies en l'honneur des phi fà (phi celestes) et des phi t'ai (phi précieux) à Basăk," appears in *Asie du Sud-Est et monde insulindien* 6 (1975): 85–114. Richard Pottier's "Notes sur les chamanes et médiums de quelques groupes thaï," *Asie du Sud-Est et monde insulindien* 4 (1973): 99–103, is supplemented by his very important dissertation, "Le système de santé lao et ses possibilités de développement" (Ph.D. diss., University of Paris, 1979). Another indispensable work on Lao religion is Marcel Zago's *Rites et cérémonies en milieu bouddhiste lao* (Rome, 1972). For more details, I refer the reader to my own essay, "Notes sur le bouddhisme populaire en milieu rural lao," which appeared in consecutive issues of *Archives de sociologie des religions* 13 (1968): 81–110, 111–150. A small section of this essay has been translated into English under the title "*Phībān* Cults in Rural Laos," in *Change and Persistence in Thai Society: Essays in Honor of Lauriston Sharp*, edited by G. William Skinner and A. Thomas Kirsch (Ithaca, N.Y., 1975), pp. 252–277.

Concerning the Thai-Lao of Phaak Isaan, see Stanley J. Tambiah's *Buddhism and the Spirit Cults in North-East Thailand* (Cambridge, 1970). A useful general bibliographical reference is Frank E. Reynolds's "Tradition and Change in Theravāda Buddhism: A Bibliographical Essay Focused on the Modern Period," in *Contributions to Asian Studies*, edited by Bardwell L. Smith, vol. 4 (Leiden, 1973), pp. 94–104.

New Sources

Archaimboult, Charles. *Le Sacrifice du Buffle, a S'ieng Khwang (Laos).* Paris, 1991.

Condominas, Georges. *Le Bouddhisme au Village: Notes Ethnographiques dans la Société Rurale Lao, Plaine de Ventiane.* Vientiane, 1998.

Donnelly, Nancy D. *Changing Lives of Refugee Hmong Women.* Seattle, 1994.

Evans, Grant. *Lao Peasants under Socialism.* New Haven, Conn., 1990.

Evans, Grant, and Kevin Rowley. *Red Brotherhood at War: Vietnam, Cambodia, and Laos.* London, 1990.

Wilson, Constance M. "The Holy Man in the History of Thailand and Laos." *Journal of Southeast Asian Studies* 28 (September 1997): 345–365.

Zasloff, Joseph, and Leonard Unger, eds. *Laos: Beyond the Revolution.* New York, 1991.

GEORGES CONDOMINAS (1987)
Translated from French by Maria Pilar Luna-Magannon
Revised Bibliography

LAO-TZU SEE LAOZI

LAOZI,

a quasi-historical figure who came to be revered as a supreme godhead in Chinese Daoist and popular religious traditions. His divinity is understood to be both transcendent and immanent. The *Dao de jing*, also known simply as the *Laozi*, is traditionally attributed to him. By mid-Han times (206 BCE–220 CE), this text and the *Zhuangzi* (c. fourth to third century BCE) were regarded as the cornerstones of early Daoist thought.

LAO DAN, THE TEACHER OF CONFUCIUS. There is no textual evidence that the *Dao de jing* itself existed prior to about 250 BCE, although various sayings in the text were in circulation somewhat earlier. It is thought that those who valued this literary heritage as an alternative to the teachings associated with Confucius began to attribute it only retrospectively to a Laozi. The source of inspiration for this hypothetical spokesman was a presumably historical figure known only as Lao Dan, "Old Dan." According to the *Li ji* (Book of rites; c. 100 BCE), Lao Dan's reputation as an expert on mourning rituals was well established. On four occasions, Confucius is reported to have responded to inquiries about ritual procedure by quoting Lao Dan. It was knowledge he had apparently gained firsthand, for Confucius recalls how he had once assisted Lao Dan in a burial service. Lao Dan, on the other hand, is quoted as addressing Confucius by his given name, Qiu, a liberty only those with considerable seniority would have taken. It is no mere coincidence that those at odds with the Confucian tradition should have found a spokesman in someone said to be a mentor of Confucius, for Lao Dan is in fact the only teacher of Confucius about whom there is any documentation.

Unlike the *Li ji*, texts outside the Confucian legacy drew on an oral tradition that emphasized the humiliation rather than the enlightenment of Confucius before his teachers. Chief among his detractors was none other than Lao Dan. The *Zhuangzi*, which is the earliest text to speak of Lao Dan and Laozi as one, appears to have taken the lead in presenting this version of the education of Confucius. There is one allusion to Confucius as a pupil of Lao Dan in the *neipian* ("inner chapters") of this text. The passage is particularly significant, for the inner chapters are the only portion ascribable to a Zhuangzi (c. 320 BCE), and the characterizations given here for both Lao Dan and Confucius differ substantially from those recorded in the *Li ji*. Lao Dan is no longer presented as a specialist in ritual protocol, nor is Confucius regarded as an exemplar of his teachings. Rather, Lao Dan here counsels a way of life that Confucius is thought too dull to master.

This difference between Confucius and Lao Dan is expanded upon in the *waipian* ("outer chapters") of the *Zhuangzi*, the product of heterogeneous authorship. Seven episodes supposedly document instances when Confucius sought advice from Lao Dan on various principles of the

Dao. In one of the passages, Lao Dan is identified for the first time as an archivist in retirement from the court of Zhou (c. 1046–221 BCE). On each encounter, Confucius is invariably made to look the fool, slow to grasp the subtleties of the Dao. Internal evidence suggests that some of these accounts were perhaps not composed until after the beginning of the Han dynasty. It may have been only a few decades earlier that this reputed superior of Confucius became associated with the *Dao de jing*. Although the text is never mentioned by title in the *Zhuangzi*, the outer chapters do draw occasionally on its sayings and twice ascribe them to Lao Dan. Both the *Han Feizi* (third century BCE) and *Huainanzi* (c. 130 BCE) are more specific, and attribute citations from a *Laozi* text to Lao Dan. By the first century BCE, the legend that Laozi was the author of the *Dao de jing* had entered the annals of Chinese history as accepted fact.

LI ER AND THE JOURNEY WEST. Sima Qian (145–86 BCE) is the first known to have attempted a biography of Laozi. His *Shi ji* (Records of the historian, c. 90 BCE) gives Laozi's full name as Li Er or Li Dan. The Li clan is identified as native to Hu district, modern Luyi near the eastern border of Henan province. In specifying the surname Li, Sima appears to have had no authority other than an imperial tutor named Li who traced his ancestry to Laozi. Only two episodes are recorded from the life of Laozi. One appears to have drawn on the legacy of both the *Li ji* and *Zhuangzi*. Confucius is said to have sought out Laozi explicitly for instruction on ritual *(li)*, a venture that left him befuddled as well as in awe of the archivist. The second episode centers on Laozi's disappearance. It is said that after living in the domains under Zhou rule for a considerable time, Laozi took his leave when he perceived the imminent downfall of the regime. Heading west, he left the central plains of China, but at the Hangu Pass he was detained by a gatekeeper named Yin Xi and asked to compose a text on the concepts of *dao* and *de*.

The text Laozi completed was reported to have contained altogether five thousand words filling two folios. That Sima Qian incorporates this legend on the origins of the *Dao de jing* into Laozi's biography suggests that the text was fairly well established by his time. The earliest extant versions of a *De jing* and a *Dao jing* were in fact found among silk manuscripts unearthed in 1973 at a Han tomb known as Mawangdui, located outside modern Changsha in Hunan province. One of the manuscripts appears to have been made sometime prior to 195 BCE and the other sometime between 180 and 168 BCE, both predating Sima's *Shi ji* by a century or so.

Apocryphal though the attribution to Laozi may be, the *Dao de jing* became a fundamental text not only for students of pre-Han thought but also for those who came to venerate Laozi as a divine being. Sima himself says no more about the history of the text or its following. He appears instead to have been genuinely puzzled as to the true identity of Laozi and what writings he may have left behind. His main conclusion seems to be that Laozi was a recluse who, according to popular traditions, may have had a life span of 160 to over 200 years. Such supernatural longevity Laozi presumably attained by an ascetic cultivation of the Dao. So although Sima does not ascribe a divine status to Laozi, he does retain in his account the suggestion of otherworldly characteristics. This motif and that of the journey west, with its apocalyptic implications of the fall of the Zhou, came to be two of the predominant features in the lore that developed around Laozi.

LAOZI AND YIN XI, MASTER AND DISCIPLE. Among the earliest texts to expand upon Sima's account is the *Liexian zhuan* (Lives of the immortals), ascribed to Liu Xiang (77–6 BCE). This work, the current redaction of which dates to no earlier than the second century CE, includes separate entries for Laozi and the gatekeeper Yin Xi. As the exemplary disciple of Laozi, Yin was also eventually revered as a Daoist patriarch. The *Liexian zhuan* makes special note of how master and disciple were each aware of the other's uniqueness. Not only did Yin Xi reportedly recognize Laozi as a *zhenren* ("true man"), but Laozi is also said to have seen in Yin the rare qualities that made him deserving of instruction.

The master-disciple relationship between them served as a model for generations. According to the hagiographic lore, Yin begged to accompany Laozi on his westward trek. This he could not do, he was told, until he had cultivated the Dao as his master had. Thus it seems that the supernatural qualities that had permitted Laozi to undertake his vast travels abroad were regarded as equally within the reach of his disciple. After an appropriate period of concentrated study, Yin had but to await his master's summons at the Qingyang marketplace in what came to be known as the Sichuan city of Chengdu. The Qingyang Gong (Palace of the Blue Lamb), newly restored in Chengdu, stands today in testimony to this ideal discipleship.

THE DIVINIZATION OF LAOZI. An equally important shrine in the history of the veneration of Laozi lies far to the northeast of Chengdu, at Luyi, his putative birthplace. It is at this site, the Taiqing Gong (Palace of Grand Clarity), that Emperor Huan (r. 147–167) of the Latter Han dynasty is known to have authorized sacrifices to Laozi in the years 165–166. Commemorating the imperial offerings is the *Inscription on Laozi* (*Laozi ming*), composed by a contemporary local magistrate named Bian Shao. While Bian honors Laozi as a native son of his district, he goes far beyond Sima's *Shi ji* to convey for the first time something about popular beliefs regarding his apotheosis. He describes Laozi as coeval with primordial chaos, from which he emerged prior to the evolution of the universe itself. After a series of cosmic metamorphoses, Laozi is said to have finally achieved an incarnate form and thus to have begun his descent as savior to the mortal realm. He then became, according to Bian, counselor to successive generations of the great sage-kings of China. It is clear from Bian's inscription that by the late Han, Laozi was viewed as a cosmic force capable of multiple reincarnations in the role of preceptor to the ruling elite. The messianic purpose of his descent became the single most important theme in Laozi's divinization, one that subsequently served all classes of Chinese society, from emperor to revolutionary.

Laozi as Buddha. At the time that Emperor Huan ordered sacrifices at Luyi, he also presided over an elaborate ritual at court held in honor of both Laozi and the Buddha. An academician named Xiang Kai was moved to comment on this service in a memorial that he submitted to the throne in 166. Xiang alludes in his address to a belief that Laozi transformed himself into the Buddha after having ventured west of his homeland. Thus did the legend of Laozi's disappearance at Hangu Pass lead to the claim that the Buddha was none other than Laozi, and that his journey was a mission to convert all mortals to the "way of the Dao." This is what came to be known as the *huahu* ("conversion of barbarians") theory. Initially, the proposal that Laozi was the Buddha seems to have reflected no more than an amalgamation of Daoist and Buddhist traditions in their formative stages. But as the Buddhist heritage became better articulated and more firmly established on Chinese soil, this notion served as a point of dispute.

By the early fourth century, debates between a prominent Buddhist monk named Bo Yuan (d. 304) and the polemicist Wang Fou appear to have inspired the first full treatise on Laozi as the Buddha. Following his defeat in these debates, Wang is said to have composed the *Laozi huahu jing* (Scripture on Laozi's conversion of the barbarians). Not surprisingly, those who sought to assert the preeminence of Laozi took every opportunity to enlarge upon the legacy of the *huahu* myth. Such efforts did not go unchallenged. Twice during the Tang dynasty *huahu* literature was proscribed by imperial command. The decrees were clearly issued at times when defenders of the Buddha's uniqueness held the upper hand at court. Their influence was felt even more strongly during the Mongol regime, when formal debates on the subject were conducted before the throne. The success of the Buddhist monks over the Daoist priests led, in 1281, to the burning of all Daoist texts deemed forgeries. Officially, only the *Dao de jing* itself was to be spared.

Laozi as a Messiah. The vision of Laozi as a messiah, moving freely between the celestial and mundane realms, inspired a large body of sacred literature. Just as the motives of the authors of these texts varied, so too did their conceptions of what was meant by a deified Laozi. One of the earliest and most enigmatic sources to take up the soteriological theme is the *Laozi bianhua jing* (Scripture on the transformations of Laozi). This text was among the manuscripts recovered by Sir Aurel Stein in 1907 at Dunhuang in Gansu province. Although fragmentary, the work can be identified as the tract of a popular sect in the Chengdu region, dating to the end of the second century CE.

The *Laozi bianhua jing* reflects some of the same beliefs articulated in the contemporary *Inscription* of Bian Shao. Laozi is seen as coeval with primordial chaos, circulating in advance of the creation of the universe. He is portrayed as the ultimate manifestation of spontaneity (*ziran*), the source of the Dao itself, and as the "sovereign lord" (*dijun*) of the spirit realm. Such is his transubstantiality that Laozi, according to this text, not only nourishes his own vital principle within the cosmos, but also emerges at various times as an imperial counselor. His series of corporeal transformations is enumerated from legendary times down to the year 155. The final passage appears to be a sermon of Laozi himself, addressed to the faithful masses awaiting his reappearance. He promises them relief from all their tribulations and at the same time vows to overthrow the Han. Precisely what politico-religious sect produced this text is not known, but it was unmistakably intended to set the scene for the reincarnation of Laozi in a charismatic figure who harbored dynastic aspirations. This messianic vision of Laozi's imminent physical transformation continued to inspire generations of rebel leaders, most notably those who also bore the surname Li.

In the Name of Laozi. The documents available on the early Celestial Master tradition (Tianshi Dao), which originated in the same area of Sichuan province as the sect associated with the *Bianhua jing*, suggest a distinctly different view of Laozi. To the founder, Zhang Daoling (c. 142), and his successors, Laozi was known as Lord Lao the Most High (Taishang Laojun). Although Lord Lao was thought capable of manifesting himself at times of political unrest, the Celestial Masters apparently never entertained the possibility of his reincarnation. Rather than assume a worldly identity, Lord Lao was seen as a transmitter of sacred talismans and registers and, eventually, newly revealed scriptures. He thereby designated the Celestial Masters as his personal envoys and gave them alone responsibility for restoring order on earth.

As agents of their Lord Lao, the Celestial Masters themselves often assumed the role of imperial preceptor that Laozi was traditionally thought to have fulfilled for the sage-kings. Thus Zhang Lu (c. 190–220) and Kou Qianzhi (d. 448), for example, served the monarchs of the Wei and Northern Wei regimes, respectively. Crucial to their success as counselors to the throne was the emperor's perception of his own divine rank. It was advantageous, in other words, to identify the head of state as a deity incarnate, just as Kou proclaimed the emperor Taiwu (r. 424–452) to be the Taiping Zhenjun ("true lord of grand peace"). As the influence of the Celestial Masters declined, the Tang imperial lineage, surnamed Li, laid claim to being the direct descendants of Laozi. In support of this assertion, there seems to have been a renewed interest during the Tang in witnessing the epiphanies of Lord Lao.

Laozi as a Focus of History. The histories of the faith that survive in the Daoist canon (*Daozang*) are remarkably uniform in that they are organized as chronicles of Laozi's unending transmigrations. An early example of this annalistic approach is found in the *Lidai chongdao ji* (A record of historical reverence for the Dao), compiled by the preeminent ritual specialist Du Guangting (850–933) in 884. The Tang portion of this chronicle is devoted primarily to a record of Laozi's providential manifestations, from the founding of the dynasty to the suppression of the Huang Chao rebellion (c. 878–884).

Later historians also sought to link the vitality of their age to the beneficence of Laozi. Jia Shanxiang (c. 1086), for example, paid special tribute to the favors Lord Lao granted during the early part of the Song dynasty. He wrote his lengthy treatise, the *Youlong zhuan* (Like unto a dragon), while stationed at the Palace of Grand Clarity in Luyi, the site to which Laozi reputedly made many return visits following his "historical" birth there. While Jia writes extensively about the mythical manifestations of Laozi, it is to his incarnation as Li Er that he devotes an unprecedented amount of detail, much of it parallel to the legends surrounding the Buddha. Just as Śākyamuni was, according to some traditions, born of his mother's right armpit, so was Laozi said to have emerged from his mother's left armpit. Laozi was also conceived to be equally precocious for, according to legend, he, too, took his first steps immediately after birth. The latter episode is among those given further elaboration in the *Hunyuan sheng ji* (A chronicle of the sage from the primordiality of chaos), compiled a century later. The compiler of this work, Xie Shouhao (1134–1212), extends the chronology of Laozi's manifestations down to the end of the Northern Song dynasty (960–1126) and offers a thoughtful commentary on many controversial points such as the *huahu* theory.

Of note in the writings of both Jia and Xie is the wide range of revealed literature associated with the successive rebirths of Laozi. Chronicles of this type also typically record the honorary titles bestowed upon Lord Lao by imperial decree, thus calling attention to the periods when state patronage was at its height. The title of Xie's work is in fact based on the epithet granted Laozi in 1014.

Laozi Embodied. The feature of the hagiographic lore that came to serve as a primary focus of Daoist meditative practice is the process by which Laozi came to his earthly incarnation. An early account of his "historical" nativity appears in the late second-century *Laozi bianhua jing*. There it is said that by a metamorphosis of his spirit (*shen*), Laozi assumed the form of his mother and then within her womb, after a long gestation, he achieved carnal form. This concept of Laozi as his own mother is ultimately derived from the *Dao de jing*, where the Dao that bears a name is said to be the mother of all things. It is understood, in other words, that Laozi is the body of the Dao itself. The transformations he undergoes prior to his incarnation are thought to be analogous to the evolutionary stages of the universe. Laozi arises from primordial chaos as the Dao incarnate to become the mother of all things, the source of creation. The reenactment of this process of Laozi's birth is precisely what lies at the heart of the early manuals on meditative practices associated with "nourishing the vital principle" (*yangxing*). Just as Laozi, the embodiment of the Dao, is himself perceived to be a microcosm of the universe, so too does the Daoist adept view his own body as a vast kingdom. Within this internal landscape, the adept strives to transform his vital forces into the image of a newborn babe, a homunculus modeled after Laozi.

In the legacy of *neidan*, physiological alchemy, this creation has come to be referred to as the enchymoma, or inner macrobiogen. The generation of an enchymoma is achieved by a variety of psycho-physiological means, including respiratory exercises, visualization procedures, and controlled sexual practices. It is as if the adept strives to replicate within his body the elixir of immortality that alchemical reaction vessels were designed to produce. Consequently, to attain physiological rejuvenation through the enchymoma is to attain longevity and to become impervious to any external threats from demonic sources. Some manuals spell out even higher goals, including liberation from the bonds of mundane existence and promotion to the ranks of heavenly transcendents.

Such techniques of regeneration are also commonly applied by a Daoist priest in the liturgies, such as the Jiao ceremony, held on behalf of the living and dead he serves. By re-creating the "sovereign lord" embryo within, the priest promotes not only his own transcendent status but that of his entire parish as well. Thus does the embodiment of the cosmogonic image of Laozi lead to the salvation of all.

Patterns of Devotion. The importance of the *Dao de jing* in various scriptural guides to the Daoist way of life cannot be overemphasized. In a preface to his analysis of the work, the thirty-ninth Celestial Master Zhang Sicheng (d. 1343) laments the fact that many who regarded themselves as disciples of Lord Lao had no understanding of his teachings. Many such commentaries to the *Dao de jing* were compiled upon imperial command, following the model of the emperor's personal exegesis. The opaque language of the text easily lent itself to countless reinterpretations and metaphorical applications.

As early as the Han dynasty, the *Dao de jing* was apparently recited not only for magico-religious purposes, but also as a guide to deportment. Additionally, a number of separate tracts appeared, offering advice to the adept on how to conduct one's life in accordance with the principles of the *Dao de jing*, namely, limited activity (*wuwei*), pure quiescence (*qingjing*), and noncontention (*buzheng*). According to hagiographic lore, it was not unusual for exemplars of these principles to find themselves bearing witness to an epiphany of Laozi, an experience that in turn frequently presaged their own spiritual transcendence. From at least the thirteenth century, Laozi was ritually evoked as the primary patriarch of the Quanzhen lineage on the putative date of his birth, the fifteenth day of the second lunar month. It was also customary, according to the Quanzhen tradition established by Wang Zhe (1112–1170), to call upon Lord Lao to preside over ritual commemorations of immortals sacred to the lineage. These ceremonies no doubt drew large crowds of clergy and laity alike.

To the individual lay believer, Laozi appears to have offered a wide range of solace. The texts of stone inscriptions preserved from the sixth to the thirteenth century attest to the various demands devotees put on their compassionate messiah. Two inscriptions dating to the Northern Qi (550–577), which mark the crafting of an image of Laozi, express the hope that the deceased will be granted ascent to the heavenly realm. By the Tang dynasty, many images and shrines to Laozi had been created as talismans to ensure the welfare of the emperor, reflecting thereby the close relation between church and state.

Large quantities of newly revealed scriptures written in the name of Taishang Laojun took equal account of both this-worldly and otherworldly concerns. These texts, especially popular during the Tang and Song, purport to be the Lord Lao's personal instructions on everything from the art of prolonging life to the quelling of all the malevolent forces thought to threaten humankind. As was the case with the *Dao de jing*, it was believed that the full efficacy of the new scriptures could only be realized after repeated recitation. To Laozi were also attributed very specific behavioral codes, designed to reinforce traditional Chinese values as well as to promote the goals of a utopian, socialist society. Laozi, in other words, was a source of inspiration for many special interests from all levels of society. During waves of spiritual innovation, many shrines to Lord Lao arose throughout the countryside, while others were restored or enlarged. Worshipers at these shrines were often rewarded by visions of their Lord, appearing in response to individual pleas for divine intervention. According to one inscription dated 1215, Lord Lao was expressly evoked by Daoist priests in an elaborate ritual to exorcise a victim of possessing spirits.

IMAGES OF LAOZI. In his *Baopuzi*, a compilation of southern Chinese religious beliefs and practices, Ge Hong (283–343) offers one of the earliest descriptions of Laozi's appearance. According to a passage in the *neipian* ("inner chapters"), one was to envision Lord Lao as a figure nine *chi* (about seven feet) tall, invested with cloudlike garments of five colors, a multitiered cap, and a sharp sword. Among the distinctive facial features he is reputed to have are a prominent nose, extended eyebrows, and long ears, a physiognomy typically signifying longevity. Ge Hong concludes that the ability to call forth this vision of Lord Lao gave one assurance of divine omniscience, as well as everlasting life.

Later resources propose a far more elaborate scheme of visualization. For example, nearly an entire chapter of a seventh-century anthology, the *Sandong zhunang* (A satchel of pearls from the three caverns) of Wang Xuanhe (fl. 682), is devoted to citations on the salient features of supramundane beings. Among the more notable passages is one from the *Huahu jing* that asserts that Laozi is endowed with seventy-two distinguishing attributes, an obvious parallel to the Buddha's thirty-two *lakṣaṇa*. The specification of these divine features varies according to the meditation guide quoted. One manual speaks of meditating on the nine transformations of Laozi, the last and most imposing of which bears all seventy-two attributes. In this ultimate vision, the cosmogonic body of Laozi is said to emerge as a radiant simulacrum of the heavens above and earth below.

A variation on this visualization technique is found in an anonymous account of the Lord Lao of the early eleventh century, the *Hunyuan huangdi sheng ji* (A chronicle of the sage and majestic sovereign from the primordiality of chaos). Two meditative techniques prescribed in this text invite comparison with the changing conceptualizations of the Buddha's *dharmakāya*. The initial procedure is based on a recall of each of the seventy-two attributes of Laozi's "ritual body," or *fashen*, which is the standard translation of the term *dharmakāya*. The focus of the second type of meditation is on the "true body" or *zhenshen* of Laozi, as he is perceived suspended in the cosmos, utterly tranquil, beyond all transmigrations. The *Hunyuan huangdi sheng ji* also discusses the settings in which the ever-radiant Lord Lao may be envisioned, for example, seated Buddha-fashion on a lotus throne or in command of a jade chariot harnessed to divine dragons. The vividness of these descriptions suggests that they may very well have served as guides to those who crafted images of Laozi or painted temple murals.

Later hagiographic accounts supplement the teachings on visualization with reports on the miraculous impressions of Lord Lao upon both natural and manmade landmarks. Although these visions commonly proved to be equally ephemeral, their memory was often reportedly preserved in works of art. Details on early icons are otherwise scarce, for even in the epigraphic records little more is specified than the choice of material to be worked, such as stone, jade, or clay. A Tang dynasty rendition of Laozi in stone, now housed in the Shanxi Provincial Museum of Taiyuan, is one of the few such images to survive. The right hand of this seated figure, dating to 719, holds a short-handled fan in the shape of a palm leaf. This type of fan became the defining feature of the Lord Lao as he is most commonly depicted in a grouping of the Celestial Worthies of the Three Clarities (Sanqing Tianzun). A remarkable representation of this trinity in wood is once more on view in the upper story of the rear pavilion at the Baiyun Guan (White Cloud Abbey) in Beijing, a Quanzhen shrine that is now home to the Chinese Daoist Association.

SEE ALSO Confucius; Daoism; Ge Hong; Jiao; Kou Qianzhi; Millenarianism, article on Chinese Millenarian Movements; Wang Zhe; Zhang Daoling; Zhang Lu.

BIBLIOGRAPHY

Tao Te Ching, rev. ed., translated by D. C. Lau (Hong Kong, 1982), includes a translation of the Wang Bi text of the *Laozi*, together with a rendition based on the Mawangdui manuscripts. Of special interest in this work are Lau's introductions on Laozi and the Mawangdui texts, and two appendixes on "The Problem of Authorship" and "The Nature of the Work." *Chuang-tzu; The Seven Inner Chapters and Other Writings from the Book Chuang-tzu*, translated by A. C. Graham (London, 1981), includes a thoughtful analysis of the passages that bear on Laozi's encounters with Confucius. Annotated translations of Liu Xiang's biographies of Laozi and Yin Xi are found in *Le Liesien tchouan: Biographies légendaires des Immortels taoïstes de l'antiquité*, edited and translated by Max Kaltenmark (Beijing, 1953). Anna K. Seidel's *La divini-*

sation de Lao tseu, dans le taoïsme des Han (Paris, 1969) is an invaluable monograph based on a critical reading of the *Laozi ming* and the *Laozi bianhua jing*. For a comprehensive study of the *huahu* issue from the second to the sixth century, Erik Zürcher's *The Buddhist Conquest of China*, 2 vols. (1959; Leiden, 1972), remains unsurpassed. Outstanding documentation of the techniques for prolonging life with which Laozi became associated is available in Henri Maspero's *Le taoïsme et les religions chinoises* (Paris, 1971), translated by Frank A. Kierman, Jr., as *Taoism and Chinese Religion* (Amherst, Mass., 1981). Norman J. Girardot's *Myth and Meaning in Early Taoism* (Berkeley, 1983) examines the mythology of Laozi's transformations as it pertains to early cosmogonic theory. His analysis is based in large part on Seidel's work, taken together with Kristofer Schipper's "The Taoist Body," *History of Religions* 17 (1978): 355–386. Schipper offers a more detailed interpretation of Laozi's "cosmogonic body" in *Le corps taoïste* (Paris, 1982). Extensive documentation of the *neidan* tradition is found in Joseph Needham and Lu Gwei-Djen's *Science and Civilisation in China*, vol. 5, pt. 5 (Cambridge, 1983). For a survey of pertinent hagiographies, historical chronologies, and exegeses on the *Dao de jing*, see my *A Survey of Taoist Literature, Tenth to Seventeenth Centuries* (Berkeley, 1987).

JUDITH MAGEE BOLTZ (1987)

LAPP RELIGION SEE ARCTIC RELIGIONS; FINNO-UGRIC RELIGIONS; SAMI RELIGION

LARES.

LARES. The ancient Roman name for the deified souls of the dead was *lases* (*Inscriptiones Latinae liberae rei publicae* 4), a term for which the only possible comparison is *Lasa*, the Etruscan name for a nymph. An old theory according to which the *lares* (singular, *lar*) were originally guardians of fields, roads, and other areas (Wissowa, 1912, pp. 166–174) is not convincing. A fragment of the *Proceedings of the Arval Brotherhood* (*Inscriptiones Latinae selectae* 9522) and a fourth- to third-century BCE dedication to the *lar Aeneas* indicate that the "mother of the *lares*" was a chthonic deity and that common ancestors were believed to be *lares*. Therefore the theory (Samter, 1901) that the *lares* were deified souls of ancestors is preferable.

The argument concerning whether *lares* originated outside the house (Wissowa) or inside (Samter) is probably a false problem, because the spirits of dead protected Romans everywhere. The ancient tradition is unanimous in maintaining that *lares* were deified souls (e.g. Festus 273; *Glossaria Latina* 2, 104); some authors suggest *lares* were the gods' *manes*, that is, the deified dead (Varro by Arnobius 3,41; Servius, *On Aeneis* 3,302); or they identify *lares* with the Greek *daimones* (Cicero, *Timaeus* 38; *Glossaria Latina* 2,121.17; 265.62); or with heroes (Dionyso of Halikarnassos 4,2,3–4; 14,3; Plutarch, *On the Fortune of Romans* 10; *Glossaria Latina* 2,121; 3, 290). Servius (*On Aeneis* 6,152) maintains that the *lares* cult can be traced back to an ancient custom of domestic burials. In fact, an Iron Age custom of burials in oak trunks is known, as are the cults of the *lares Querquetulani* (Varro, *De lingua Latina* 5,49) and the *virae Querquetulanae* (Festus 314), which were male and female spirits living in oak trees and oak bushes.

The Dionysian religion clearly exerted an influence upon the *lares* cult because both Dionysos and the *lares* were meant to connect and harmonize the world of life and the world of death. The *lares* were deified souls, and Greek deification was celebrated by a Dionysian triumphal parade from earth to Olympus, whereby the *lares* were conceived as drinking wine, wearing crowns, and sometimes accompanying satyrs.

Few myths related to the *lares* are known. King Servius Tullius was allegedly the son of the *lar* living in the hearth of royal palace, and because of that he founded the *lares* cult in the town and villages, which included the festivals of Compitalia and Paganalia (Dionyso of Halikarnassos 4,14; Pliny, *Historia naturalis* 36, 204). According to Ovid (*Fasti* 2, 583–616) the *lares praestites*, protectors of Rome, were sons of the nymph Lara, who was raped by Mercurius.

The public cult of the *lares* was democratic in character and was seen as an alternative to the ancestor cult of noble families. The standard image of the *lares*, dancing and pouring wine, had no personalized features, whereas the ancestor masks of the aristocracy were believed to represent the precise personality of the deceased. The only *lares* with identifiable personalities were associated with Aeneas (Guarducci, 1956–1958) and Hercules (Floriani Squarciapino, 1952), who were common heroes to all Romans. In addition, the sow and the thirty piglets of Lavinium, which appeared to Aeneas as a forecast of the thirty Latin towns, were believed to be *lares Grundiles* (Schilling, 1976). In the first century BCE a popular politician, Marius Gratidianus, merited a cult organized by the city's quarters. This cult was similar to that of the *lares* (Cicero, *On the Duties* 3, 80; Seneca, *Ira* 3, 12, 1; Pliny, *Historia naturalis* 33, 132; 34, 27). The cult of the emperor's genius was first organized by Augustus in 7 BCE together with the *lares* cult in every city quarter (Cassius Dio 55,8.1; Suetonius, *Augustus* 30–31; Ovid, *Fasti* 5,145 ff.; Niebling, 1956).

In the towns of central Italy the most important festival for the *lares publici* was the Compitalia, which was called Paganalia in the villages. The features of this festival survived late into the Christianized empire and constituted the core of paganism. The Compitalia occurred at the beginning of January near crossroads, where small altars or chapels stood. Every family hung wool dolls at the crossroad, and slaves hung balls (Festus, 273, Lindsay). People also offered cakes, garlic, and poppyheads, and a sow was sacrificed to the Mater Larum (*Inscriptiones Latinae selectae* 3615; Propertius 4,1,23). The festival's presidents were four *magistri vici*, authorities of the quarter or village, who often were also heads of craft guilds (Asconius, *On Cicero's Pisonianam* 7, Clark) and freedmen. The wall paintings of the Italic quarter at Delos show scenes of these plebeian meetings. The *magistri* can be seen wearing *toga praetexta* and accompanied by lictors and flute-players. The paintings also depict scenes of boxing matches and other games. Simple theatrical plays were presented during this festival (Nonius, 288, Lindsay; Propopertius 2,22,1; Suetonius, *Augustus* 43; Euantius, *On the Comedy* 5,2; *Grammatici Latini* 1, 488). Everyone, even the slaves, was permitted to drink a large amount of wine (Cato, *On Agriculture* 57; Persius 4, 25–26). The *lares* were conceived as young men who danced, drank wine, and participated in the games. The Compitalia and Paganalia had the features of the great winter festivals (Lanternari, 1976), which took place during the seasonal pause in work, when the souls of the dead came back among the community and were entertained with banquets, dances, and other rituals, and the normal hierarchical structure of the society was suspended.

The public *lares* were also protectors of roads (*lares viales:* e.g., Plautus, *The Merchant* 865; *Corpus inscriptionum Latinarum* VI, 2103; VIII, 9755; XII, 4320), of enterprises of the Roman fleet (*lares permarini,* whose temple was dedicated in 179 BCE: Livius 40, 52, 4; Macrobius 2, 10, 10), and of the army (*lares militares*: Martianus Capella 1, 46, 48; *Corpus inscriptionum Latinarum* III 3460; 3463; *Acta fratrum Arvalium* 86 Henzen). Two *lares praestites,* wearing dogs' coats over their heads and accompanied by dogs, were the protectors of Rome; their festival was celebrated on May 1 (Ovid, *Fasti* 5, 129–146; Plutarch, *Roman questions* 51 and the Republican denarius of L. Caesius).

In private cult the *lares* were the ancestors of families (cf. *lares Volusiani*: *Corpus inscriptionum Latinarum* 6, 10266–102667; *lares hostilii*: Festus, 90, Lindsay) and every Roman house had a *lararium,* a chapel where offerings were brought to the statues or paintings of the *lares* and the genius in form of a snake. The hearth was the most ancient seat of the *lar domesticus* or *lar familiaris* (e.g. Plautus, *Aulularia* 1–8; Ovid, *Fasti* 6, 306; Petronius 60). The *lares* were endowed with fecund might and were supposed to have made certain mythical girls pregnant, such as the slave who gave birth to Servius Tullius. In fact, the cult of the *lares domestici* was often entrusted to home slaves. The most important moments in the life of each Roman were marked by cultic acts in honor of the *lares*: birth, death, disease, and the liberation of slaves, as well as a young person's attainment of the legal age of adulthood, the rituals of which inherited features of initiatory rituals in which the *lares* played a major role. During the festival of Liber Pater, the Liberalia of March 17, fathers presented sons who had reached legal age as new citizens; the young man dedicated to the *lares* his *bulla* (hanging personal amulet) and was clothed with a toga (e.g., Persius 5, 31). A similar ritual for daughters corresponded to marriage, before which the bride dedicated her toys, a hair net, and the bandage that had been wrapped around her upper body to conceal her bosom. (Scholia to Horace, *Satyres* 1, 5, 65; Nonius, 863, Lindsay.) When the bride first went to her new husband's house, she dedicated coins to the *lar* of the hearth and to the *lares* of the crossroad (Nonius, 852, Lindsay), showing that she had arrived under the protection of these divine souls.

The souls of Roman ancestors had a "mother," the Mater Larum, who was a female divinity, or queen of dead, comparable to Ceres and the Greek Hekate. Her names Larunda, Lara, Larentia, and Acca (= mother) Larentia derive from the word *lar,* and the names Mania and Genita Mana derive from *manes*; she was also called Tacita and Muta; that is, "silent goddess." Acca Larentia, a famous personage in the myths of Roman origins, played a role as the mother of Roman ancestors. At first she was a girl with whom Hercules once flirted (e.g., Plutarch, *Romulus* 5; *Roman Questions* 35); later she was the wet-nurse of Romulus (e.g., Livy 1, 4, 7; Plutarch, *Romulus* 4). In addition, the first eleven Arvales, Romulus's brothers, were her sons (Gellius 7, 7, 8; Pliny, *Historia naturalis* 18, 6). During the Compitalia families displayed hideous images of the face of Mania in order to gain protection against bad ghosts; people also offered garlic and poppyheads, which stood for human heads. This ritual was introduced by Junius Brutus when he founded the Republic, and by means of the ritual sought to appease Mania, who had been offended by Tarquinius Superbus (Macrobius 1, 7, 34–35).

Mater Larum was honored during other festivals of the dead—she was seen as Tacita at the Feralia of February 21, and as Larenta/Larunda at the Larentalia of December 23. On that day the pontiffs and the *flamen Quirinalis* brought offerings to the burial site of Acca Larentia (Varro, *De lingua Latina* 6, 23; Gellius 7, 7, 7), the *sacellum Larundae* on the Roman Forum (Tacitus, *Annales* 12, 24; Varro, *De lingua Latina* 5, 74), where Romulus's nurse was buried and Hercules' beloved disappeared. In the archaic age this area was covered by the Velabrum marshes and was believed to be a gateway to the netherworld. On May 13 the Arval Brothers sacrificed two sheep to the Mater Larum (*Acta fratrum Arvalium* 145 Henzen) and during another ritual they prepared pots of cornmeal mush as her dinner (*Inscriptiones Latinae selectae* 9522). Similar pots were employed at the Greek Anthesteria, a Dionysiac festival celebrating the return of souls from the netherworld.

SEE ALSO Ancestors; Arval Brothers; Penates; Roman Religion, article on The Early Period.

BIBLIOGRAPHY

Aronen, Jaakko. "Iuturna, Carmenta e Mater Larum: Un rapporto arcaico tra mito, calendario e topografia." *Opusc. Inst. Rom. Finlandiae* 4 (1989): 65–88.

Bezerra de Meneses, Ulpiano, and Haiganuch Sarian. "Nouvelles peintures liturgiques de Délos." In *Études déliennes,* pp. 77–109. Paris, 1973.

Bulard, Marcel. *La religion domestique dans la colonie italienne de Délos, d'après les peintures murales et les autels historiés.* Paris, 1926.

Carandini, Andrea. *La nascita di Roma: Dèi, lari, eroi, e uomini all'alba di una civiltà.* Turin, Italy, 1997.

De Marchi, Attilio. *Il culto privato di Roma antica.* 2 vols. Milan, Italy, 1896–1903.

Flambard, Jean-Marc. "Clodius, les collèges, la plèbe et les esclaves: Recherches sur la politique populaire au milieu du Ier siècle." *Mélanges de l'École Française de Rome (Antiquité) (MEFRA)* 89 (1977): 115–153.

Floriani Squarciapino, Maria. "L'ara dei lari di Ostia." *Archeologia classica* 4 (1952): 204–208.

Fröhlich, Thomas. *Lararien- und Fassadenbilder in den Vesuvstädten.* Mainz, Germany, 1991.

Guarducci, Margherita. "Cippo Latino arcaico con dedica ad Enea." *Bullettino commissione archeologica comunale Roma* 19 (1956–1958): 3–13.

Hano, Michel. "A l'origine du culte impérial: Les autels des lares Augusti." In *Aufstieg und Niedergang der römischen Welt (ANRW)* II, 16, no. 3 (1986): 2333–2381.

Lanternari, Vittorio. *La grande festa: Vita rituale e sistemi di produzione nelle società tradizionali.* Bari, Italy, 1976.

Mastrocinque, Attilio. *Lucio Giunio Bruto.* Trento, Italy, 1988.

Niebling, Georg. "Laribus Augustis magistri primi." *Historia* 5 (1956): 303–331.

Piccaluga, Giulia. "Penates e lares." *Studi e Materiali di Storia delle Religioni (SMSR)* 32 (1961): 81–98.

Radke, Georg. "Die Dei Penates und Vesta in Rom." *Aufstieg und Niedergang der römischen Welt (ANRW)* II, 17, no. 1 (1981): 343–373.

Samter, Ernst. *Familienfeste der Griechen und Römer.* Berlin, 1901.

Scheid, John. *Romulus et ses frères: Le collège des Frères Arvales, modèle du culte public dans la Rome des empereurs.* Rome, 1990. See pages 578–598.

Schilling, Robert. "Les lares Grundiles." In *L'Italie préromaine et la Rome républicaine: Mélanges offerts à Jacques Heurgon,* pp. 947–960. Paris, 1976.

Settis, Salvatore. "Severo Alessandro e i suoi lari." *Athaeneum* 50 (1972): 237–251.

Tabeling, Ernst. *Mater Larum: Zum Wesen der Larenreligion.* Frankfurt, Germany, 1932.

Wissowa, Georg. *Religion und Kultus der Römer.* 2d ed. Munich, 1912.

ATTILIO MASTROCINQUE (2005)

LAS CASAS, BARTOLOMÉ DE

LAS CASAS, BARTOLOMÉ DE (1474–1566), was a Christian missionary. Las Casas was born in Seville, Spain. In 1502 he went to the island of Hispaniola (present-day Dominican Republic and Haiti), where he participated in the conquest of the Indians. As a reward he received lands and Indians under the *encomienda* system, a kind of indentured servanthood. He exercised the lay office of catechist, worked to evangelize the Indians, and was ordained a priest about 1512. His commitment to evangelization did not keep him from participating in the bloody conquest of Cuba, for which he received additional lands and Indians. However, in 1514, at forty years of age, he was converted to concern for the plight of the Indians while reading *Ecclesiasticus* (*Ben Sira*) 34:22. Four months later he preached his famous sermon in the Church of the Holy Spirit, denouncing the grave injustices being committed, and turned his Indians over to the governor of Cuba. Until his death at ninety-two, he was the tireless "Defender of the Indians," a title conferred on him in Madrid in 1516.

Las Casas returned to Spain four times, in attempts to save the Indians from the cruelties of the Spanish conquest and to find new methods to convert them to Christianity. In his efforts he became a court reformer in Spain (1515); the leader of the unsuccessful colony of peace in Curmaná, Venezuela (1520), which attempted to establish agricultural communities of Spanish and Indian workers; a Dominican monk and prior in Santo Domingo (1523); the unrelenting foe of the unjust wars of suppression in Nicaragua (1535); a defender of the Indians against ecclesiastics in Mexico (1532); a promoter and participant in the project to colonize and Christianize the natives of Guatemala by peaceable means (1537); a successful attorney for the Indians before Charles V, urging the adoption of the New Laws (1542), which, for example, negated the rights of the *encomienda* over Indian children; and the rejected bishop of Chiapas (1545). When he returned to Spain for the last time in 1547, it was as a legal adviser and theologian in defense of Indian rights.

In his prophetic crusade, alternately encouraged and denounced by creoles and clerics, Las Casas doggedly and dogmatically followed what he conceived to be his life's purpose. With a missionary conviction that his truth could not be negotiated, he proclaimed, "All peoples of the earth are men." He categorically denied the claims of Juan Ginés de Sepúlveda that "the Indians are inferior to the Spanish as are children to adults, women to men, and . . . almost as monkeys to humans." Rather, he lauded the cultural and artistic achievements of Indian cultures, which he considered equal to that of ancient Egypt. In some respects, he declared in his *Apologetic History,* Indians are superior to Spaniards.

Las Casas wrote in reaction to what he viewed as horrible inhumanities committed with hypocritical religious justification. Must people be converted by slavery and the sword? In his *Only Method of Attracting All People to the True Faith* (1537), he argued for means that persuade by exhortation and gentle attractions of the will. With furious verbal assaults and chilling realism, he recounted the relations of the Indians with their European conquerors in his *History of the Indies,* on which he worked from 1527 to 1566. Equally brutal in exposing the grave crimes against the Indian race, his *Very Brief Account of the Destruction of the Indies* (1542) and eight more tracts for public dissemination (1552) raised storms of protest against Las Casas. But the prophet was unbending: His *Advice and Regulations for Confessors* (1545) advocated denial of the sacraments of the church to all who had Indians and did not "pay a just wage." In later years British royalists, New England colonists, French rationalists, and Latin American nationalists freely used his condemnation of the Spanish atrocities as propaganda for their own causes.

Crusader, traitor, prophet, paranoiac, servant of God, anarchist, visionary, pre-Marxist, egalitarian—these are but a few of the epithets hurled at his memory. The issues Las Casas raised are dangerously modern.

BIBLIOGRAPHY

An admirable collection of the principal writings of Las Casas is *Orbras escogidas,* 5 vols., edited by Juan Pérez de Tudela (Madrid, 1957–1958). The missionary's view that the gospel requires a peaceful evangelization of the Indians without the use of arms is contained in his *Del único modo de atraer a todos los pueblos a la verdadera religión,* edited by Augustín Millares (Mexico City, 1942). Two of his principal works are available in English: *Devastation of the Indies: A Brief Account,* translated from Spanish by Herman Briffault (New York, 1974), and *In Defense of the Indians,* edited and translated from Latin by Stafford Poole with Lewis Hanke, V. Friede, and Benjamin Keen (De Kalb, Ill., 1974). The first work defends the thesis that the cause of the destruction of an "infinite number of souls" by Christians is solely the latter's thirst for gold and "to become fat with riches in a few brief days." The second work denounces the imperialistic exploitation of the Indians inspired by the conquistadors' greed and ambition; as such, it may be considered a tract for all times against economic and social exploitation.

A useful bibliography is Lewis Hanke and Manuel Giménez Fernández's *Bartolomé de las Casas, 1474–1566: Bibliografía crítica y cuerpo de materiales para el estudio de su vida* (Santiago de Chile, 1954). Though dated, this work gives a valuable accounting of studies on historical background and additional bibliographical sources. Manuel Giménez Fernández's *Bartolomé de las Casas,* 2 vols. (Seville, 1953–1960), is an excellent, though unfinished, biography of the first part of his life.

SIDNEY H. ROOY (1987)

LATTER-DAY SAINTS SEE MORMONISM

LATVIAN RELIGION SEE BALTIC RELIGION

LA VALLÉE POUSSIN, LOUIS DE (1869–1938),

was a Belgian Indologist and specialist in Buddhist philosophy. Educated in Liège, Louvain, Paris, and Leiden, La Vallée Poussin became professor at the University of Ghent. He entered his field of research at a time when Buddhist studies were dominated by the study of the Pali canon and Sanskrit narrative literature with an emphasis either on psychological and ethical aspects or on mythology and social concerns. (A more doctrinal approach did exist, mostly in the French and Russian traditions.) La Vallée Poussin dedicated all the strength of his philological genius to this field and thus contributed to a reorientation of Buddhist studies toward the languages of northern Buddhism (Sanskrit and Tibetan) and toward Buddhist philosophy considered in its historical perspective. He produced two main types of studies: scholarly editions, and translations with exegeses. These correspond roughly to the two periods of his activity, that before and that after World War I.

During the first period, there was a need for accurately edited texts. It remains La Vallée Poussin's major contribution to Buddhist studies that he compiled several text editions, some published in Belgium, others in the classical series "Bibliotheca Indica," Calcutta, and others in the series "Bibliotheca Buddhica," Saint Petersburg. He began with some of the then-neglected Tantric texts, *Pañcakrama* (1896) and *Adikarmapradīpa* (1898), and continued with important Mādhyamika writings, among them Nāgārjuna's *Mādhyamikasūtras* (1903–1913) and Prajnākaramati's *Panjikā* commentary on the *Bodhicaryāvatāra* of Śāntideva (1901–1905). Other texts he edited included some fragments then newly discovered by Aurel Stein.

Besides this editorial oeuvre, La Vallée Poussin produced numerous translations, exegetical studies, and text analyses. He also wrote several essays (including some that were to appear in Christian publications) that show his preoccupation with and perpetual reassessment of what he called Buddhist dogmatics.

After World War I, La Vallée Poussin, who had in the meantime mastered the languages of the Chinese Buddhist translations, undertook the enormous enterprise of translating and critically annotating two *summae* of Buddhist scholastics: Vasubandhu's *Abhidharmakośa,* the masterwork of the northern Hīnayāna *abhidharma* school, and Xuanzang's *Vijnaptimātratāsiddhi,* the best compendium of the tenets of the Yogācāra, or Idealist, current of the Mahāyāna. For his *Abhidharmakośa* (1923–1931), La Vallée Poussin had to master the huge Kashmirian *Mahāvibhāṣā,* which even today has not been translated into a Western language. With his *Vijñaptimātratāsiddhi: La Siddhi de Xuanzang* (1928–1929) he took the lead in the study of Idealist Buddhism, a field in which Sylvain Lévi had laid the foundation and which Paul Demiéville and La Vallée Poussin's pupil Étienne Lamotte were to continue.

These exegetical exercises did not keep La Vallée Poussin from pursuing other areas of Buddhist thought. Paradoxically, La Vallée Poussin was both fascinated and reticent regarding the Mādhyamika; he was attracted by the critical stance of Mādhyamika thought, but this attraction was resisted by his strong personal convictions. His attitude is reflected in numerous publications on the meaning of *nirvāṇa* (annihilation or bliss?) and in his polemics with Theodore Stcherbatsky on the interpretation of *sūnyatā* (emptiness or relativity?). La Vallée Poussin submitted the ancient history of India to his Nagarjunian criticism in three volumes: *Indo-Européens et Indo-Iraniens* (1924), *L'Inde aux temps des Mauryas* (1930), and *Dynasties et histoire de l'Inde* (1935).

BIBLIOGRAPHY

Besides the writings mentioned in this article, the thirty-six articles La Vallée Poussin contributed to the *Encyclopaedia of Religion and Ethics,* edited by James Hastings (Edinburgh, 1908–1926), yield much information on the results of the studies of his first period. A good overview of his second period can be gained from his "Notes bouddhiques" in the *Bulletin de la classe des lettres* of the Académie Royale de Belgique (Brussels, 1921–1929) and from his numerous contributions to the first five volumes (Brussels, 1932–1937) of the publication series he founded in 1931, the "Mélanges chinois et bouddhiques."

Works on La Vallée Poussin include Marcelle Lalou's article "Rétrospective: L'œuvre de Louis de la Vallée Poussin," in *Bibliographie bouddhique,* fasc. annexe 23 bis (Paris, 1955), pp. 1–37; and Étienne Lamotte's article "Notice sur Louis de la Vallée Poussin," *Annuaire de l'Académie Royale des Sciences, des Lettres et des Beaux-arts* 131 (1965): 145–168.

New Sources

Wedemeyer, Christian K. "Tropes, Typologies, and Turnarounds: A Brief Genealogy of the Historiography of Tantric Buddhism." *History of Religions* 40, no. 3 (2001): 223–259.

HUBERT DURT (1987)
Revised Bibliography

LAW, WILLIAM (1686–1761), was an English devotional writer. Born at King's Cliffe, Northamptonshire, William Law came from a family "of high respectability and of good means." He entered Emmanuel College, Cambridge, in 1705 to prepare for the Anglican ministry; he achieved the B.A. in 1708 and the M.A. in 1712, the same year in which he received a fellowship and ordination. He read widely from the classics, the church fathers, and the early mystics and devotional writers, and he studied science and philosophy as well. Law's refusal to take oaths of allegiance and abjuration upon the accession of George I deprived him of his fellowship and his right to serve as minister in the Church of England. He remained loyal to the state church, however, throughout his life. After an extended period as tutor to Edward Gibbon, father of the historian, Law took up permanent residence at his birthplace, King's Cliffe, where he served as spiritual adviser to many, engaged in acts of charity to the deprived of the community, and wrote the nine volumes that make up his major works.

Law's early writings include *Remarks upon the Fable of the Bees* (1723), a refutation of Bernard Mandeville's work; *The Unlawfulness of Stage Entertainment* (1726); *The Case of Reason or Natural Religion* (1731); and two better-known works, *Treatise upon Christian Perfection* (1726) and *A Serious Call to a Devout and Holy Life* (1729). These latter contribute significantly to a tradition of devotional prose literature that includes such writers as Augustine, Richard Baxter, Jeremy Taylor, John Donne, and Lancelot Andrewes. Law's devotional writing has as its controlling purpose the aiding of persons in their quest of the "godly life," and it reveals several distinguishing themes: preoccupation with the scriptures and Christ as the bases and models for perfection; self-denial as a necessary antidote to vainglory and passion; prayer and meditation; and ways and means for implementing Christian doctrine in practical affairs.

Among Law's later work were responses to various religious writers: *The Grounds and Reason for Christian Regeneration* (1739), *An Appeal to All Who Doubt the Truths of the Gospel* (1740), *An Answer to Dr. Trapp's Discourse* (1740), and *A Refutation of Dr. Warburton's Projected Defense of Christianity* (1757). More influential, however, were the mystical writings *The Spirit of Prayer* (1749), *The Spirit of Love* (1752), and *The Way to Divine Knowledge* (1752). These three works reveal the influence of Jakob Boehme, who professed visionary encounters with God. Many Christian critics have objected to the oversubjectivism and implicit universalism in Law's later writings, branding them as "mystical," a term often held as opprobrious by traditional religious thinkers. However, if one considers an intuitive approach to reality, awareness of unity in diversity, and a passion for a spiritual reality that underlies and unifies all things to be typical of mysticism, one realizes that this desire for union with God lies at the root of all religious devotion. In this light, Law's "mystical" works reflect his earlier theological beliefs and have a close kinship with his *Christian Perfection* and *A Serious Call.*

Many readers have paid tribute to Law's simple, clear, and vivid prose style, and scholars have pointed to his pronounced religious influence on such minds as Samuel Johnson, John Wesley, John Henry Newman, Charles Williams, and C. S. Lewis. His intellectual power, incisiveness, and piety wielded a marked influence both within and without organized church ranks. Law's major achievement lay in his significant contribution to the English tradition of devotional prose literature.

BIBLIOGRAPHY

Primary Source

Law, William. *The Works of the Reverend William Law, M.A.* (1762). Reprint, 9 vols. in 3, London, 1892–1893.

Secondary Sources

Baker, Eric. *A Herald of the Evangelical Revival.* London, 1948. Examines basic views of Law and Jakob Boehme and shows how Law kindled in Wesley a passion for an unimpaired "ethical ideal."

Hopkinson, Arthur. *About William Law: A Running Commentary on His Works.* London, 1948. Recognizes works with different subjects: religious controversy, morality, mysticism, and theology. Sketchy but informative.

Overton, John H. *William Law: Nonjuror and Mystic.* London, 1881. Still the best single source for Law's life and thought.

Rudolph, Erwin P. *William Law.* Boston, 1980. Examines the range of Law's thought and contribution to devotional prose literature.

Walker, Arthur K. *William Law: His Life and Thought.* London, 1973. Examines Law's intellectual biography, focusing on the people whom Law knew and the writings with which he was familiar. Sometimes digressive and biased but generally useful.

Erwin P. Rudolph (1987)

LAW AND RELIGION

This entry consists of the following articles:

LAW AND RELIGION: AN OVERVIEW

"Law" and "religion" denote vast, imperial realms that are, for the most part, each understood to be clearly bounded and independent. On closer inspection, these terms prove to be curiously amorphous and resistant to precise definition. Each is also, in present common usage, peculiarly the product of modernity. Linking the two terms, as in "law and religion," compounds these ambiguities. The ancient roots of these two terms, the definitional difficulties associated with employing them cross-culturally, and, above all, the problematic understanding of "modernity" they encode are only some of the challenges that complicate an analysis of their interconnection. The purpose of the present article is to begin this work of definition in a manner that introduces and synthesizes some of the key themes in the articles on law presented both in this section and elsewhere in the *Encyclopedia,* and to specify a range of historical and structural connections between law and religion that illuminate the possible meanings of each of these terms, and of their intersection. (In an article of this size and scope it is, of course, impossible to treat comprehensively the manifold religious and legal traditions of human history and their intersections. This section will focus primarily, although not exclusively, on the Anglo-American common-law tradition, reflecting the legal training of its authors. Other parallel and related stories centering on other legal traditions are presented in the articles that follow).

Introduction. There is a widespread tendency in modern, secular society to view law and religion as unrelated except insofar as they may, from time to time, come into conflict. According to a commonplace of post-Enlightenment thought, the "secularization thesis," societies as they modernize move progressively away from religious norms toward a complete regime of secular law that permits only such religion as does not inhibit its administration. From the standpoint of secular law, religion is regarded as largely irrelevant, or even as a source of sectarian partisanship, in contrast with the presumed universalism of law. The sole positive role allowed to religion is the subordinate one of reinforcing norms otherwise determined and enforced by the state. The evolutionary hypothesis that religion, as an irrational vestige of pre-modern or "primitive" culture, will gradually disappear, views the continuation and especially the resurgence of religion as a problem and challenge for secular law. For many inside and outside the academy, this view is the only one that continues to have relevance (and, with few exceptions, it is also the only one incorporated in the law school curriculum in the United States and most other modern, secular states). Consequently, it is crucial to note at the outset that this manner of conceiving the relation between law and religion is quite parochial and, in some respects, fundamentally flawed. Historically, there have been close connections, extending in some cases to an identity, between law and religion in many societies. Moreover, structural and historical connections between law and religion continue into modernity. These connections demonstrate that the concept of law as inherently secular is highly anachronistic and ought to be regarded with greater suspicion and criticism. (In other words, "law" as a category ought to be regarded by scholars of religion as problematic to the same extent as the category "religion.")

The contemporary separation between law and religion has been taken for granted both by those who endorse and by those who deplore this separation. Both the British legal historian Henry Maine (1822–1888) and the French sociologist Émile Durkheim (1857–1917), among others, argued for the convergence of law and religion in ancient or "primitive" society. (Arthur S. Diamond's [1897–1978] argument against Maine that law has always been to a greater or lesser extent autonomous from religion is a minority view.) Neither Maine nor Durkheim took a strong normative position as to the desirability of this separation. However, Maine's advocacy of gradualism in the evolution of law and Durkheim's association of primitive law with the strong social functioning of "collective representations"—the comparative weakness of which in modern society presented a problem for social cohesion—may suggest the potentially negative effects of this separation. More recently, the American law professor Harold Berman has consistently called into question the desirability of the present extreme separation of law from religion. This perspective—which we may call "religionist" in order to distinguish it from the "secularist" position to which it is opposed—shares with the latter the conviction that law today is, indeed, separate from religion. Both positions tend not to address definitional difficulties. The differences of opinion are largely as to when, how, and why this separation came about; as well as, of course, its desirability.

Although the roots of the secular legal autonomy of the modern state lie deep in medieval Europe, a decisive point of separation between law and religion within the Anglophone common-law tradition occurred in nineteenth-century legal theory. The English jurist Matthew Hale

(1609–1676) declared that Christianity is a part of the common law. William Blackstone (1723–1780), author of the influential *Commentaries on the Laws of England,* identified divine law and natural law among the sources of the common law. Against such views, the founding figures of legal positivism, which continues to be the reigning political theory of law, argued that law is necessarily separate from religion and morality. The English Utilitarian philosopher and legal reformer Jeremy Bentham (1748–1832) argued that law ought to be embodied in a written code enacted by the legislature, to the exclusion of other sources, including religious ones. His follower John Austin (1790–1859) rejected Blackstone's argument that human laws that conflict with divine laws are not valid. Through their intellectual descendants, such as the Oxford legal philosopher Herbert Hart (1907–1992), Bentham's and Austin's views have largely won this debate within modern jurisprudence.

Recently, legal positivism has been the subject of sustained critique from several quarters. (Here we will focus on the problematic aspects of legal positivism from the point of view of religious studies. Other critiques of legal positivism have focused on expanding our understanding of law from other critical perspectives, including those of gender and post-colonial theory, and have focused on legal positivism's tendency to fixate on law as rules rather than as cases. These other critiques are, of course, also related to the problematic separation of law and religion.) Positivism's insistence on the separation of law from both religion and history has increasingly been seen to encourage the neglect and ignorance of these domains and of their importance for law. When one approaches law historically, however, it becomes apparent not only that law was not always so separate from religion, but also, and more surprisingly, that the modern separation of law from religion was in part the result of particular religious developments that either originated in or accelerated during the Protestant Reformation. Although these developments are further described below, some brief indications may be given here. The English critical legal historian Peter Goodrich argues that the common-law tradition in the sixteenth and seventeenth centuries established itself through an "antirrhetic," a polemic against images that borrowed from religious iconoclasm. Law borrowed its foundational narrative from religion and located its authority in an increasingly written canon of reified tradition. From a longer-term perspective, French socio-legal theorist Marcel Gauchet has argued for the compatibility of secularism with certain tendencies in Judaism and Christianity. Increasingly, it appears that law is, for us moderns, "our religion" not merely in the sense of having inherited part of religion's role as an arbiter of values and guide to conduct, but also in the sense of being historically or genealogically related to older modes of religiosity. Following such demonstrations, it becomes increasingly difficult to maintain the secularization thesis, or the idea of a clean separation between law and religion, in its usual, overly simplified form. Yet if the secularization thesis, which is a founding narrative not only of modern law but of modernity itself, is no longer quite so believable, then there is greater reason to inquire into the relations between law and religion, and especially their historical connections, both as a means of better understanding the present, and as a potential guide to the future.

The present article initiates this inquiry, and makes a plea for further conversation between scholars of religion and scholars of law. In modern times, the separation between law and religion is paralleled by a separation between the two academic disciplines of legal studies and religious studies. These two fields, reflecting the strengths of secular legal positivism and religious antinomianism, have led mostly independent lives. On the one hand, despite the best efforts of legal anthropologists, scholars of law remain almost exclusively focused on Western, secular legal materials. In contrast, comparative religious historians have exhibited little interest in either law or the West. However, there is precedent for a deeper engagement between these two groups. Maine coined the term "comparative jurisprudence" on the model of comparative philology and comparative mythology, the predecessor of the history of religions. Citing this forgotten precedent, the present article attempts to initiate a conversation between legal studies and religious studies.

RELIGION AND SECULAR LAW: STRUCTURAL DIFFERENCES AND SIMILARITIES. The historical convergences of law and religion are perhaps most obvious in what is sometimes called "religious law," a term used to refer to those parts of many religious traditions that prescribe and regulate norms of conduct, as encoded, for example, in such sources as the Ten Commandments (*Exodus* 20), the *sharīʿah* and the Hindu *Laws of Manu,* and which include many aspects of conduct that are now within the purview of secular law. It was these traditional legal forms that inspired Maine's and Durkheim's theses regarding the "primitive" or traditional lack of separation between law and religion. Some legal theorists today contend that the category "religious law" makes sense only in such an evolutionary scheme defined by secularization. They argue that all legal regimes, whether religious or secular, are more usefully characterized by referring to the styles of reasoning and decision-making they employ. From this perspective, the argument goes, *qadi*-administered law, for example, might be better understood by seeing its resemblance to English common law than by classifying it with other "religious" laws, some of which may exhibit radically different legal characteristics. Although acknowledging such views, the present section explores the value of the term "religious law" for distinguishing key features of many legal systems prior to modernity.

In many pre-modern legal traditions, the connection between law and religion is underscored by the absence of a separate or secular term for "law." For example, in Hinduism the term *dharma* means not only "law" but also "religion" and "proper conduct," among other things. Torah and sharīʿa can refer both to operating community legal regimes and to the overall religious path or discipline of an individual or community. In this latter sense, law may be understood metaphorically as extending to the realm of conscience. Of course, even in many so-called traditional societies, whether ancient or modern, there are legal norms, processes, and institutions—particularly those associated with royal administration, taxation, and trade—that are relatively autonomous from religion, as narrowly construed, although generally not to the same extent as in the modern West.

In general, religious, or pre-modern, law exhibits certain differences from those forms of law that have become normative in modernity. If we follow the legal positivists and define law as a norm of general or even universal application promulgated by the state and enforced by its sanction (although some positivists place less emphasis on the role of sanctions in constituting law), then it is clear that many religious laws deviate from this standard in one or more respects. In some cases, they may lack universality. The Ten Commandments apply to an entire population and therefore are nearly universal. However, the Vinaya, the monastic code of the Buddhists, regulates the conduct of religious professionals only. Often, as in the *Laws of Manu,* provisions of general and group-specific (gender- or caste-based) application are announced within the same text.

Many religious laws also lack the element of an effective, state-enforced sanction. The Ten Commandments themselves prescribed no sanction for their violation; this was done for most of its provisions elsewhere in the Pentateuch. The presence of alternative or even contradictory norms can also vitiate the certainty of the sanction. Consider, for example, the provisions on vegetarianism in the *Laws of Manu.* There is a blanket provision on eating any meat. However, if one does eat meat, then only certain meats should be consumed under certain circumstances by certain persons. Finally, if one violates these provisions, penances or expiations are prescribed to restore purity. For modern theorists, this kind of flexibility in enforcement has counted against the status of religious law as "real" law. Conversely, the law of retribution ("an eye for an eye") in the Hebrew Bible (e.g., *Exodus* 21:23–24) has been interpreted, probably erroneously, as mandating an inflexible punishment. An even more noteworthy aspect of many religious laws is that they prescribe a sanction to be visited upon the offender in the afterlife or next life through the agency of the deity or the cosmos itself. In *Manu,* for example, many actions are punished or rewarded through the operation of *karma.* This is what Bentham termed the "religious sanction." Such punishments were either cumulative with or in place of punishments to be imposed by the state. From the standpoint of positive law, religious sanctions lack the certainty sufficient to create valid, binding legal norms.

Religious laws also differ from secular ones with respect to their sources of authority, processes of dispute resolution, and mechanisms of enforcement. The source of authority of religious law is often said to be the deity or the first ancestors. One of the hallmarks of law in modern democratic societies is that the authority to create law resides exclusively in a popularly elected legislature, subject in many cases to a more fundamental constitution also held to embody the popular will, which may in turn be constrained by universal secular norms. Some religious law has in the past used trials by ordeal as a method of dispute resolution. In Hinduism and Medieval Christianity, for example, ordeals placed the outcome of the trial at least nominally in the hands of the deity. In modern trials, the outcome rests in the hands of human decision makers, whether judge or jury. Without the imperative of the modern state, religious law may in many cases operate most effectively at a local level—taking as its function the return of parties to social competency rather than acting as an instrument of state legitimacy, authority, and power.

So far the main consideration of this section has been to highlight some of the principal differences of religious law from modern, secular law. There are also numerous parallels and convergences between secular law and religion more generally, not limited to the most "law-like" aspects of religious traditions. Some of these convergences are evident in the special importance to each of ethical concepts; of rituals, including especially formulaic utterances; of narratives; of canons, especially of the written variety; and of hermeneutics or modes of interpretation. Other parallels could certainly be discussed, but these are among the most important.

Religion and law have both given attention to how humans ought to live their lives. Modern western legal concepts of crime and punishment, for example, closely resemble their predecessors, the Western religious concepts of sin, expiation, and purity. In religious law, sin is regarded as a violation of the cosmic order. Punishments or expiations may be designed to restore order and purity for the individual or the community. In its origin, then, crime often was not distinguished from sin. Even today, a number of the practices and articulated purposes of punishment—including retribution, the ghost of which has proved difficult to exorcise from the law—echo earlier, non-utilitarian religious ideas. Law and religion have therefore shared the dubious distinction of administering violence. In addition to the threatened religious sanction of punishment in the afterlife, religious law also frequently prescribed punishments in this world, together with voluntary expiations, ascetic practices, and sacrifices.

Both law and religion depend heavily on ritual operations, as evident in the structured, dramatic procedures of courtroom and temple, with their organization of public spaces, choreography of events, and use of specialized costumes. Both law and religion rely on verbal techniques, including formulaic utterances. Pre-modern law was often exacting in its demand for conformity to prescribed procedure and has been accused of an excessive formalism whereby, for example, a small mistake in the pronunciation of a petition could lead to its dismissal. Many oaths, vows, and declarations of legal effect were, like spells, poetic in form. In early English and German law, as represented respectively in the eleventh-century Anglo-Saxon charms and the thirteenth-century *Sachsenspiegel* and catalogued by the German folklorist Jacob Grimm (1785–1863) in his essay *On Poetry in Law* (*Von der Poesie im Recht,* 1816), rhythmic parallelisms such as "unbidden and unbought" and "for goods or gold" were common. These are the ancestors of the formula "to have and to hold" in the marriage ceremony as still prescribed in the Anglican *Book of Common Prayer.* Poetic devices not only made such formulas more memorable, a function of special importance in an oral culture, but also reinforced their persuasive, "binding" function. Rhetorical devices were also used frequently in early law to reinforce the connection between crime and punishment.

Today the ritual formulas of law are seldom poetic. The transition in early modern Europe from an oral culture to one based on literacy and the medium of print certainly played an important role in the disappearance of such formulas. With the greater availability of writing, poetic forms were no longer needed as mnemonic devices. Both religion and law were deeply influenced by the new medium, as evidenced by their increasing emphasis on written canons, as further described below. There was also a religious component to these developments. Protestant biblical literalism contributed to a polemic against verbal images. For example, Thomas Cranmer's (1489–1556) introduction to the *Book of Common Prayer* (1549) justified the removal of "vain repetitions" and other superstitious formulas from the liturgy. Among the regional variants excluded from the new, more prosaic marriage ceremony were the phrase "for fairer for fouler" and the bride's promise "to be bonour and buxom at bed and at board" (i.e. gentle and obedient). Although the phrase "to have and to hold"—a key declaration of legal ownership—was retained, the net effect was to strip away much of the poetry of the law. Positivists have continued a polemic against poetry. Bentham in his original attack on Blackstone charged that early law often depended on poetic "harmony" for its persuasiveness, and that modern law continued this dependence in more hidden form. More recently, the English philosopher John Langshaw Austin (1911–1960), Hart's colleague at Oxford, used the declaration "I do" (the actual declaration is "I will") in the marriage ceremony as his first example of a "performative utterance," meaning a statement that accomplishes something (such as a legally binding marriage) through the act of utterance itself (*How to Do Things with Words,* 1962). By ignoring the history of this declaration, including its earlier, more poetic forms, Austin produced a theory of legal and ritual language that continued the repression of poetry, albeit through neglect rather than overt animosity.

In addition to employing poetry and other verbal formulas, law and religion both also depend on narrative. In religion and religious law, myths are used to found a moral cosmos. For example, the *Laws of Manu* begins with an account of the cosmogony. Although modern law eschews the explicit use of myth, it remains dependent on foundational narratives, as Robert Cover emphasized, and there is even, in Peter Fitzpatrick's term, a particular "mythology of law." In addition to such grand narratives, narratives of a simpler sort—in the form of stories that make sense of people's actions—constitute an important part of the everyday business of law. The examination of witnesses, lawyers' arguments during trial, and judicial opinions all use narrative techniques to construct compelling fact scenarios and resolve disputes over the interpretation of the law. As legal anthropologists and sociologists have shown, ordinary people also tell stories to make sense of the law and their relationship to it. Law, like a story, is directed toward a definite conclusion and is peopled by actors who are engaged in a clash of interests that are often intensely personal, of dramatic public importance, and engaged with fundamental social values. Like literary interpretations, the answers law affords to such dilemmas may remain provisional and uncertain. These characteristics shared by law and literature are also shared by many religious texts, and especially by myths, the interpretation of which assumes a similar hermeneutic irreducibility, if not undecidability.

A related parallel that points to the "closed" rather than "open" nature of both law and religion is the frequent dependence of each on a canon, which now usually means a corpus of texts. Canon, in Jonathan Z. Smith's definition (*Imagining Religion,* p. 43), represents a delimitation to a set (for example, of texts), which is then subjected to ingenious and varied interpretation. Canon therefore combines the opposed gestures of restriction and expansion: the first is aimed at control and the second at completeness. Although this is obviously a distinctive feature of many religious traditions and especially of collections of scripture, it is also a point of contact between law and religion. Under the sign of canon, the work of both law and religion becomes one of interpretation or hermeneutics. Within this work, different degrees of flexibility may be pursued, as described by Paul's phrase "the letter killeth, but the spirit giveth life" (*2 Corinthians* 3:6). Paul appears to dismiss the adherence to black-letter law as a narrow formalism and to embrace flexibility in interpretation. The distinction in religious law between "letter" and "spirit" can be seen to correspond to the distinction in modern law between "formal" and "substantive" justice or between "law" and "equity." Although the tendency away from formalism is often regarded as one of the hallmarks of modern as opposed to pre-modern law and religion, some more restrictive modern forms of canon belie such a simple dichotomy. The form of canon most common in modern law is the "code": the reduction of the law to a set of written statutes that is comprehensive and unequivocal. Not only the canon itself but the interpretation thereof has been restricted in accordance with the image of law as a perfect, and perfectly unambiguous, language. As described below, codification bears historical connections to Protestant biblical literalism. However, the influence of religion on legal interpretation has operated in different ways. In *Vichy Law and the Holocaust in France* (1996), Richard Weisberg argues that lawyers in Nazi-occupied France used a certain flexibility in interpretation, a form of casuistry inspired in part by religious and other cultural factors, to justify anti-Semitic laws. Other scholars of law and literature emphasize the inflexibility of modern law and its hostility to multivocal interpretation. For example, Goodrich ("Europe in America: Grammatology, Legal Studies, and the Politics of Transmission," *Columbia Law Review,* 2001) identifies this rigidity as a source of resistance to Jacques Derrida's philosophy of deconstruction, which he associates with Talmudic interpretation.

The modern bias toward canon or the location of culture in texts has long distorted scholarly interpretations of both law and religion. Many religious laws are embodied in a textual corpus of rules and therefore resemble modern law, which is now promulgated primarily in written statutes and judicial opinions. This bias has facilitated the over-emphasis on such texts to the detriment of customs, not only in scholarship but also in the colonial administration of laws in such countries as India. The valorization of texts, although not new, has increased in recent centuries. Its apex in England can be traced to Bentham's codification proposal and attack on Blackstone's celebration of the largely customary common-law tradition. The first edition of this *Encyclopedia* included a number of articles on the laws of the world religions, namely those traditions that, in addition to having many adherents, have coalesced historically around collections of scripture. The laws of oral, indigenous, tribal, or "primitive" traditions were largely ignored. This bias has affected our understanding even of the law of literate societies. Anthropologists and historians have worked against this textual bias and recovered the importance of customary and unwritten traditions of both religion and law. Some further historical dimensions of the emphasis on a written canon are described below.

Another bias that has distorted our understanding of religious law is the modern tendency to reduce religion to belief, to the exclusion of practice. Rules that prescribe, often minutely, both everyday and ritual conduct have constituted historically a central part of many religious traditions. Increasingly since the Reformation, religion or its "essence" has come to be defined as belief, meaning the voluntary and affective assent to a particular doctrine. Religious conduct has often been defined as non-essential to religion or even, in the case of ritual conduct, as "superstitious." Not coincidentally, it is precisely these particularistic religious practices, such as those involving diet, dress, and marriage, that have tended to come into conflict with secular law, with its universalizing tendencies. Freedom of religion now means primarily freedom of conscience, and the expression of one's religious convictions becomes more problematic when it extends beyond verbal modes of expression. These developments have also operated as a barrier to our historical understanding of the practical or legal dimensions of religious traditions—what we are here calling "religious law."

Religious Genealogies of Secular Law. In modernity, as previously noted, law and religion are generally regarded as separate. This view has already been challenged by examinations of both pre-modern religious law and the continuing structural parallels between law and religion. There are also important genetic or, to invoke the increasingly popular Nietzschean term, genealogical connections between law and religion. In contradiction of the secularization thesis, not only did much of modern law originate in religion, but it remains, in an important sense, "religious" in character. Even the process by which law separated from religion is, as previously indicated, related to religious developments, especially and most proximately those arising in the Protestant Reformation. Although there are, of course, many competing narratives of the process by which modern law came to be as it is, the following narrative is offered as a partial corrective to the standard trope of secularization.

The emergence of regional legal regimes in Europe and elsewhere and the development of international law have stimulated a renewed interest in the sources of Western law. The history of law in the West is the history of the complex interactions among the tribal laws of Europe, Roman law, and the institutions of the Roman church. With the decline of its Western empire, Roman law fell into disuse. Law in Europe was a highly diffuse collection of local customs and institutions, which depended on local religious ideologies and symbols. The rediscovery of Roman law in the form of Justinian's *Institutes* in the early twelfth century and its subsequent elaboration and influence on both the canon law of the papacy and on emerging national legal regimes, fundamentally altered the relationship of law and religion in Europe. This Roman-derived law served as the prototype for the autonomous secular and universalistic law of the modern period. The separation of law and religion already occurred in one form in the theological elaboration of the idea of two domains of law, one spiritual and the other secular. Harold Berman has described this as a "revolution" of the highest importance in the development of modern law, though not the last.

Other scholars have focused attention on the period during and after the Reformation as a key phase in the development of modern law, including its separation from religion. Goodrich's account of the parallels in English Protestant and common-law foundationalism, each of which opposed a reified, and increasingly written, canonical tradition to the "idolatry" of images, has already been mentioned. These developments, although heavily influenced by the rise of literacy and printing, also represented a religious dynamic. A later phase of this development occurred with Bentham's proposal for codification of the still largely unwritten common-law tradition. This proposal drew on the opposition of a now exclusively written canon to the "idolatry" of custom. Earlier English codes, from Alfred's in the ninth century to the one promulgated in the Massachusetts Bay Colony in the 1640s, had drawn on scripture for their substantive law. Bentham's code had a more subtle, indirect relation to religion that emerged most clearly in his criticism of "fictions," linguistic pathologies that he generally argued should be expunged both from the law and from language. One of his key complaints was the habit of reifying language or taking words for things. He argued that only words that referred to really existing things should be permitted. As the common law, being nowhere written down, could not be pointed to, the phrase "common law" was, he said, a fiction used by lawyers to dupe their opponents. The sole remedy was codification. Although arguably an atheist, Bentham in his jurisprudence drew upon religious sources. One indirect source was English linguistic empiricism, which, beginning with Francis Bacon's (1561–1626) critique of "idols of the marketplace," had applied Protestant literalism to language. Another source was scripture, which, in his papers on codification (*Works,* vol. 10, p. 483), Bentham directly invoked in condemning the invocation of the "common law" as a form of personification and idolatry.

Given Bentham's profound influence on both legal reform and the philosophy of legal positivism, it has seemed especially appropriate to detail these connections between his jurisprudence and certain strains of Protestantism. The positivists' contention of the separation between law and religion is belied by a closer examination of the work of one of their founding figures. Regarded as a "vanishing point" at which religion effectively transformed into modern, secular law, Bentham is a crucial figure for a genealogical analysis of law. His example suggests that secularization was, in at least some of its dimensions, influenced by a specifically religious dynamic. The relationship between religion and legal rationalization thus outlined parallels the relationship the German sociologist Max Weber (1864–1920), himself a trained lawyer, identified between religion and capitalist economic rationalization. Bentham's example further suggests a reevaluation of the separation between legal and religious studies. The founder of the history of religions, Friedrich Max Müller (1823–1920), drew on many of the same linguistic and religious ideas as Bentham for his concept of myth as a "disease of language," a form of radical metaphor where a word is reified and, ultimately, deified. The founding narratives of both legal and religious studies owe more to the history of particular religious developments than either discipline cares to acknowledge.

Religion and Human Rights. The phrase "religion and law" today is not infrequently also understood to denote an expanding arena of modern life purportedly governed by guarantees of religious freedom under national constitutions, transnational conventions, and other international legal instruments. The rather limited legal accommodation made for religion in the West under the Enlightenment guarantees of religious freedom is proving inadequate in the face of demands to accommodate an ever widening spectrum of religious practices from both traditional religious communities and new religious movements, some of which refuse to accept the implications of the secularization thesis for law. The strong desire by many to acknowledge (or to be seen to acknowledge) the powerful demands of religion on individuals and communities is handicapped by the underlying claims to universalism of modern, secular law.

Various legal and political arrangements have been made to handle demands for legal accommodation of religious practices. The complex and sometimes explosive mix of religious and ethnic diversity, the global dynamism of diaspora religious communities, and the vestiges of legal structures reflecting prior religio-political histories have inspired different legal strategies. A simple, and perhaps deceptively clean, solution has been the United States Supreme Court's interpretation of the First Amendment to that country's Constitution. The First Amendment religion clauses have increasingly been interpreted in such a way as to efface the legal significance of religion. The state may not discriminate against religious persons and practices, but neither is it required to provide legal exemptions or accommodations for them. Furthermore, the state may fund and contract with religious institutions for the provision of government services, but only on the same terms as it extends to secular organizations. Religion as a legal category has less and less relevance. In cases in the United States and in other jurisdictions where legal instruments are interpreted to privilege religiously motivated persons or institutions, persistent questions have arisen concerning the boundaries of such exemptions, particularly in light of the usual accompanying provision that the state may regulate religious conduct to protect the health and safety of its citizens, a provision that has allowed states a wide latitude in suppressing, or even criminalizing, religious ways of life. This is especially ironic, given that recent revisionist scholarship on religious human rights has emphasized the influence of religious ideas, including those of the fascinating but historically rather remote Puritan Roger Williams (c.1603–1683), on the historical development of the First Amendment.

Other secular constitutional democracies are often less dominated by an ideology of equality than the United States and have for historical reasons been more likely to privilege some religious communities in their dealings with the state and to carve out exemptions for religiously motivated persons. An example is India, a country with a very different history, level of development, and experience of colonialism, where the continuing existence of separate domains of private law for different religious traditions and recent political developments favoring communalism, have inspired a fierce debate over the meaning of secularism and its permissible cultural variations.

Questions have recently arisen about whether human rights language is so indebted to the history and culture of the West that it may be inadequate to protect individuals and communities from or in non-Western cultures and societies. The human rights paradigm is understood, according to this critique, to privilege a "Protestant" view of religion as private, individual, voluntary, and constituted by belief rather than practice. What is clear is that many of the foundations of international human rights law were laid by scholars such as Hugo Grotius (1583–1645) on a religious basis and in response to the wars of religion in seventeenth-century Europe. After several centuries, and with the extension of this historically contingent (and evolving) paradigm to other cultures, the religious roots of the modern doctrine of freedom of religion may be more exposed and shakier than they have been for some time.

Two often-stated goals of U.S. foreign policy today are first, international enforcement of guarantees of religious freedom, and second, global extension of the rule of law. A particular understanding of religion and law is regarded as the *sine qua non* for the spread of democracy. Religion freely chosen by the individual and secular law impartially and democratically administered by a state dedicated to due process and human rights are proclaimed together as the "natural" and necessary characteristics of a society that respects human dignity. The anthropologist Richard Shweder calls this American stance "imperial liberalism." Alternative models for negotiating the competing demands of religion and modern, secular law are being developed in various forums, including the agencies of the United Nations.

CONCLUSION. This article has sketched some of the contours of the religious dimensions of law and the legal dimensions of religion as an invitation to scholars of religion to avoid reproducing the modern Western positivist self-understanding of law as autonomous, state-produced and state-enforced, and secular. The standard narrative of secularization has damaged our understanding of both law and religion by rendering each incomprehensible to the other. On the contrary, the numerous historical connections, the continuing structural parallels, and above all the genealogical relationships between law and religion suggest new pathways for exploring the reciprocal relevance of these two fundamental categories and the relevance of both for the comprehension of modernity. For those studying contemporary religio-political structures, in particular—although the same could be said of many earlier societies—conditions of religious and legal pluralism vastly complicate the matter. The comprehensive explanatory and disciplinary pretensions of both law and religion are moderated by the presence and constant interaction of multiple systems.

The remaining articles in this section provide an approach to the interactions of law and religion across a number of axes. First in order are several articles that examine law and religion within or respecting particular cultural traditions, which are for the most part bounded geographically and/or historically ("Law and New Religious Movements," "Law and Religion in Medieval Europe," "Law and Religion in The Ancient Mediterranean World," "Law and Religion in Hinduism," "Law and Religion in Buddhism," "Law and Religion in Chinese Religions," "Law and Religion in Indigenous Cultures"). After these come several articles that consider the interaction of law and relation in relation to a third category or from a particular methodological perspective ("Law, Religion, and Critical Theory," "Law, Religion, and Human Rights," "Law, Religion, and Literature," "Law, Religion, and Morality," "Law, Religion, and Punishment"). The reader is referred also to articles elsewhere in the *Encyclopedia* that are relevant to the topic of law and religion.

SEE ALSO Afterlife; Atonement; Canon; Codes and Codification; Covenant; Islamic Law; Israelite Law; Ordeal; Purification; Revenge and Retribution; Secularization; Sin and Guilt; Vows and Oaths.

BIBLIOGRAPHY

Berman, Harold. *Law and Revolution: The Formation of the Western Legal Tradition.* Cambridge, Mass., 1983.

Berman, Harold. *Law and Revolution II: The Impact of the Protestant Reformations on the Western Legal Tradition.* Cambridge, Mass., 2003.

Casanova, José. *Public Religions in the Modern World.* Chicago, 1994.

Comaroff, John L., and Simon Roberts. *Rules and Processes: The Cultural Logic of Dispute in an African Context.* Chicago, 1981.

Cover, Robert. "Foreword: *Nomos* and Narrative." *Harvard Law Review* 97 (1983): 4–68.

Fitzpatrick, Peter. *The Mythology of Modern Law.* New York, 1992.

French, Rebecca. *The Golden Yoke: The Legal Cosmology of Buddhist Tibet.* Ithaca, N.Y., 1995.

Gauchet, Marcel. *Le désenchantement du monde: une histoire politique de la religion.* Paris, 1985.

Geertz, Clifford. "Local Knowledge: Fact and Law in Comparative Perspective." In *Local Knowledge: Further Essays in Interpretive Anthropology.* New York, 1983.

Goodrich, Peter. *Oedipus Lex: Psychoanalysis, History, Law.* Berkeley, Calif., 1995.

Hamburger, Philip. *Separation of Church and State.* Cambridge, Mass., 2002.

Howe, Mark deWolfe. *The Garden and the Wilderness: Religion and Government in American Constitutional History.* Chicago, 1965.

Huxley, Andrew, ed. *Religion, Law and Tradition: Comparative Studies in Religious Law.* London, 2002.

Jacobsohn, Gary. *The Wheel of Law: India's Secularism in Comparative Constitutional Context.* Princeton, N.J., 2003.

Kahn, Paul. *The Cultural Study of Law: Reconstructing Legal Scholarship.* Chicago, 1999.

Levack, Brian. *The Witch-Hunt in Early Modern Europe.* New York, 1995.

Levinson, Sanford. *Constitutional Faith.* Princeton, N.J., 1988.

Llewellyn, Karl N, and E. Adamson Hoebel. *The Cheyenne Way.* Norman, Okla., 1941.

McConnell, Michael. "The Origins and Historical Understanding of Free Exercise of Religion." *Harvard Law Review* 103 (1990): 1409–1517.

Moore, Sally Falk. *Social Facts & Fabrications: "Customary" Law on Kilimanjaro, 1880–1980.* Cambridge, U.K., 1986.

Murphy, Tim. *The Oldest Social Science: Configurations of Law and Modernity.* Oxford, 1997.

Pocock, J. G. A. *Barbarism and Religion.* Cambridge, U.K., 2000.

Rawls, John. *The Law of Peoples.* Cambridge, Mass., 1999.

Roberts, Simon. *Order and Dispute: An Introduction to Legal Anthropology.* New York, 1979.

Rosen, Lawrence. *The Anthropology of Justice: Law as Culture in Islamic Society.* New York, 1989.

Rouland, Norbert. *Anthropologie juridique.* Paris, 1988.

Smith, Jonathan Z. *Imagining Religion: From Babylon to Jonestown.* Chicago, 1982.

Sousa Santos, Boaventura de. *Toward a New Common Sense: Law, Science and Politics in the Paradigmatic Transition.* New York, 1995.

Tierney, Brian. *Religion, Law and the Growth of Constitutional Thought, 1150–1650.* Cambridge, U.K., 1982.

van der Vyver, Johann D., and John Witte, Jr., eds. *Religious Human Rights in Global Perspective: Legal Perspectives.* The Hague, 1996.

Williams, Robert A., Jr. *The American Indian in Western Legal Thought: The Discourses of Conquest.* Oxford, 1990.

WINNIFRED FALLERS SULLIVAN (2005)
ROBERT A. YELLE (2005)

LAW AND RELIGION: LAW AND RELIGION IN THE ANCIENT MEDITERRANEAN WORLD

Most scholars of the ancient world assume that Roman law did not fundamentally affect ancient religions. In 1905, Theodor Mommsen argued that in antiquity the only civil requirement religions had to meet was loyalty toward the rulers. In case of default the believers were forced to comply. Likewise, church historians tend to ignore any impact Roman law may have had on ancient Christianity. The jurist Harold J. Berman (1983) corroborates this view. In ancient Roman society law remained secular, he argues. Though the modern Western legal tradition derived crucial elements from it—a sharp distinction between legal and other social institutions, for example, religion, politics, and morality; an administration of law by a class of specialists; and a legal training of these professionals and the existence of a legal science—a closer relation between law and religion did not arise before the Middle Ages, when the Roman law was adopted by the Christian nation.

When Berman agues that the ancient Roman law was pervasively secular, he has the Near Eastern law codes in mind, which were promulgated by rulers on behalf of the gods or revealed by prophets in the name of God as the biblical book of the covenant (*Genesis* 20:22–23:19) or *Deuteronomy* (12–26). But is a hierarchical relation between religion and law the only one possible or even obvious? Tim Murphy (1997) proposes to consider also a horizontal one. He conceives of religion and law as two autonomous "systems," separate, but not unrelated. Law can be studied as a cultural system that turns religion into a legal subject, and religion as a cultural system that turns law into a religious issue (Geertz, 1983, p. 184). Using this approach, Winnifred Fallers Sullivan (1994) studied the notions of religion in U.S. Supreme Court rulings on First Amendment cases. Her study confirms that the disestablishment clause did not terminate a link between legislature and religion, but instead evoked among jurists legal discourses about defining religion. Likewise, Roman law despite its secular origin turned ancient religious practices into legal subjects and established legal discourses on religious issues.

FROM THE TWELVE TABLES TO THE LATE ROMAN LAW CODES: PRINCIPLES OF THE GROWTH OF THE ROMAN LEGAL TRADITION. "The most celebrated system of jurisprudence known to the world begins, as it ends, with a code" (Maine, 1905/1861, p. 1). The Twelve Tables were drawn up by a special commission in 451–4500 BCE and published on tablets in the Forum. Their demolition in 390 BCE did not undermine their authority, as Elizabeth A. Meyer (2004) shows. Until the end of the Roman Empire they were cited as a fountainhead of all public and private law (Livy 3, 34, 6). For that reason the code is known only through quotations—in an adjusted, but still archaic language—by Roman authorities: Cicero (106–43 BCE), Gaius (third quarter of the second century CE), Seneca the Younger (4 BCE–65 CE), Pliny (23–79 CE), and others, but also by Christian Church fathers such as Augustine of Hippo (354–430), as Michael H. Crawford's reconstruction of the Twelve Tables shows (1996, pp. 555–721).

Law making in Rome was not restricted to only one institution. There were the *leges,* resolved by the people in a meeting and regarded as eternally valid, as the Twelve Tables. Other institutions legislated different kinds of law: the Senate's *senatus consultum;* Roman officials' *edictum;* and the emperor's *constitutio principis,* which could take the form of an *edictum* (an enactment of a general character), *decretum* (a judicial decision), *rescriptum,* in the form of a letter (*epistola*), or an endorsement appended to a petition (*subscriptio*) (Bretone, 1998, pp. 153–157). Finally, there were the legally binding opinions of the jurists (*responsa prudentium*) when all agreed on a certain issue (Gaius, Inst. 1, 7).

Before the Twelve Tables were promulgated, the legal field was divided between human law (*ius*) and divine law (*fas*). Afterward, the main division became between public and private law (*ius publicum* and *ius privatum*) as Alan Watson shows (1992, pp. 21–29). Religious matters belonged to the realm of public law. Since public law was based on the principle of a common benefit (*utilitas*), it could not be annulled by private decisions or agreements. It also restricted private religious practices.

The Roman legal system, particularly during the empire, revolved around an institutionalized practice of questions and answers as Fergus Millar shows (1992, pp. 240–252). An official, a citizen, or a community confronted with an unusual legal case could send a petition (*libellus*) to the emperor. When the case was deemed important enough, the emperor, assisted by his council, responded. The wording of the answer was entrusted to jurists. In their function as imperial advisors (*iurisconsulti*) they introduced their professional knowledge into the process of law making. Likewise, on the local level jurists were indispensable. Since Roman officials had also the task of settling disputes, often without being legal specialists themselves, jurists had to find the laws applicable to the disputed cases (Bretone, 1998, pp. 138–169).

The efficacy of the laws differed profoundly from that of modern societies, at least in their ideal form. In pagan antiquity law abiding was not a value in itself. Roman citizens invoked laws when it was in their self-interest (Harries, 1999, p. 81). When people obtained a ruling from the emperor, they had to convince local officials to enforce it. Ramsay MacMullen observes that "[a] law reflects somebody's pressing need at a certain time. It does not show what was . . . common practice in the empire" (1984, p. 95). This practice was responsible for the many repetitions, tensions, and contradictions in the Roman legal tradition. Pagan Roman emperors made attempts to reduce the incoherence by determining officially the legal authorities that could be cited in court and by commissioning collections of laws. In the end only the Christian rulers succeeded. This was not by chance, however. In the pagan culture every city and nation lived according to its own laws, which differed from each other, whereas Christian theologians believed in one true law for all of humanity.

After Theodosius II (401–450) had decreed that all "constitutions" of Christian emperors should be collected, the *Codex Theodosianus* (*CTh;* Honoré, 1986; Harries and Wood, 1993) was promulgated in 438 CE. In 529–534 Emperor Justinian I (483–565) commissioned the *Codex Justinianus,* the *Digests,* and the *Institutions.* The committee in the *Digests* collected the legal tradition of the pagan Roman jurists and included in the *Codex* not only the laws of former Christian emperors, but also of their pagan predecessors. Justinian thought of his own empire as a restoration of ancient Rome. After the entire legal oeuvre was rediscovered in the twelfth century, it was called *Corpus Iuris Civilis* and became a fountain for the modern Western legal tradition.

LEGAL DISCOURSES ON PRIVATE RITUALS. The Twelve Tables prohibited casting bad spells (*carmina*), harming somebody else by incantations, bewitching fruits, and enticing the harvest of a neighbor (8:1, 8:4, Crawford, 1996). Not all ritual practices called magic were prohibited, but merely those that violated the property and the reputation of a fellow citizen (Graf, 1997, pp. 41–43). In an ongoing civil discourse on this provision, the focus gradually shifted to spells and rituals (Kippenberg, 1997). The *Lex Cornelia,* proclaimed in 82/81 BCE, prohibited the possession of particular substances. "Who for the purpose of killing a man" has prepared, sold, bought, or administered a wicked drug (*venenum malum*), shall be tried on a criminal charge (Crawford, 1996, pp. 752–753). Because the notion of *venenum* covered natural as well as supernatural devices, Roman lawyers included spells and rituals. Because of a lack of a theory of natural causation, poison and "unsanctioned religious activity" were brought under the same rubric (Phillips, 1991). In political trials where the defendant was accused of treason (*maeistas*), the charge of sorcery (*veneficia*) was often added. The *Pauli Sententiae,* compiled around 300, prohibited the art of magic and the possession of magical books as such and prescribed severe punishment. It even applied to secret nocturnal rites (Paulus, *Sententiae* 25, 17–18). Practicing magic had become a crime in itself, whether it caused damage or not. Even recognized rituals could be suspected of being "magic," provided their performance was unauthorized and of malicious intent.

After the Catholic Church was established within the Roman legal tradition (Gaudemet, 1947), the Christian emperors continued prohibiting magic. For example, an edict of Constantius II (317–361) stated, "Superstition (*superstitio*) shall cease; the madness of sacrifices (*sacrificiorum insania*) shall be abolished" (*CTh* 16, 10, 2; 341 CE). Yet, the content of this ruling was open to different understandings. Pagan officials understood it as a license of prosecuting magic, and Christian officials, of suppressing paganism (Salzman, 1987). While the Christian rulers and their jurists preserved the existing legal notions, they reversed their reference. This applied in particular to the category *superstitio.* When Christianity spread in the Roman Empire, pagan authors from the early second century CE—Pliny (ep. X 96f), Tacitus (c. 56–c. 120; ann. XV 44, 2–5), and Suetonius (c. 69–after 122; Nero 16, 2)—decried it as a new *superstitio.* By adding *nova et malefica* to *superstitio,* Suetonius even suspected it of magical practices. In pagan times *superstitio* was defined by its opposite, *religio,* and could refer either to foreign origin or to unlawful practices. Since the reference of the pair shifted according to its user (Sachot, 1991), Christians were able to claim to be the *religio,* while denouncing paganism as *superstitio* (Grodzynski, 1974).

Another striking example of the continuity from Roman law to Christianity and a reversal of the categories at the same time is Augustine. In *De civitate Dei* (8, 19) he dealt with the *artes magicae* and pointed out that the Romans, not the Christians, had started prosecuting them. Pagan public opinion (*lux publica*) was strongly against magical arts, as the Christians were. Augustine was so enamored of the Roman law that he transmitted quotations of the Twelve Tables, which have become highly valuable for the modern reconstruction.

LEGAL DISCOURSES ON PRIVATE ASSOCIATIONS. The other provision of the Twelve Tables that was elaborated in the legal tradition and that affected religion concerned unauthorized meetings of citizens (*coetus*) (8:14–15; Crawford, 1996). Since early times, citizens of Rome were remarkably free to establish private associations, as the lawyer Gaius reported in the second century CE about the Twelve Tables.

"A statute (*lex*) gives the members of an association (*sodales*) the power to enter into any agreement (*pactio*) they like, so long as they do not contravene the public statute." Gaius added that this statute appeared to have been adopted from the law of Solon (*Digests* 47, 22, 4 "De collegiis et corporibus").

The creation of a great variety of professional and religious associations in ancient Roman society was because of that freedom. But that freedom also generated conflicts. When the Dionysian rituals, the Bacchanalia, spread clandestinely in Italy, Roman officials in 186 BCE severely punished its adherents and abolished the status of a *collegium.* The rituals for the benefit of Dionysos/Bacchus were permitted, though only under restricted conditions (Baumann, 1990). After that, the Romans never forgot that unauthorized nocturnal meetings were unlawful (Livy XXIX).

This was only the beginning of restrictive politics toward associations. In the first century BCE, when associations participated in the civil strife at the end of the Republic, Julius Caesar dissolved them all, "besides those that were long ago established" (Suetonius 42, 4). An ancient descent was required from all authorized associations. While Jews answered that requirement and were at least in principle allowed to establish associations under that law (Rajak, 1984), Christian associations did not. "How [were] the Christians . . . able to exist un-interfered with . . . in the face of the imperial policy in regard to associations?" a scholar asked long ago (Hardy, 1971/1874, p. 168). The solution probably lies in the different kinds of legal status of associations. While some *collegia* were officially acknowledged by a *senatus consultum,* an imperial letter, or a civic decree, and while others were prohibited and abolished as illicit, there existed in-between associations without an official recognition, but tolerated by state officials and city councils because of their useful social function as societies of humble people (*collegia tenuiorum*). As such, Christian associations before the fourth century were probably tolerated as belonging to this third category (Kippenberg, 2002).

The legal restrictions had repercussions on the diffusion of religions. When Christians spread in the Greek cities, they expressed their beliefs and rituals in Hellenistic forms and conceptions. That the truth divine was hidden from the profane marketplace was evident to Greeks. Christian Gnostics shared this view and decried the material world as filled with lies and deceit. Accordingly, they kept their faith secret and rejected martyrdom. When Christians established their associations within the range of Roman law, the Latin church fathers Irenaeus (c. 120 to 140–c. 200 to 203) and Tertullian (c. 155/160–after 220) defended Christian associations and practices as public phenomena, in agreement with Roman law. They also engaged in a struggle against Christian Gnostics, who denied the public status of their faith. The category of *hairesis* arose during that struggle (Kippenberg, 1991, pp. 369–402).

LATE ROMAN LAW CODES TURNING RELIGIOUS DIVERSITY IN A LEGAL HIERARCHY. While Christian emperors and the Catholic Church were hostile to religious paganism, their attitude toward the Roman legal tradition was different. The official recognition of Christianity occurred in terms of the Roman legal tradition. The Catholic Church had been recognized by Constantine in 313 as a *religio* equal to all the other religious associations; Theodosius acknowledged it as the only true *religio* of the entire Empire in 380.

The associations of private Christian believers became a legal body with laws, property rights, and an official hierarchy of its own, and their worship was protected by the ruler. The emperor and Catholic Church adopted legal notions such as *religio, superstitio, maleficium, magia, corpus* (*collegium*), and *hairesis* to define the recognized place of the Catholic Church in the public realm of the Roman Empire, as various documents show (Coleman-Norton, 1966).

The *Codex Theodosianus* (*CTh;* Mommsen and Meyer, 1904; Pharr, 1952) arranged the imperial constitutions in a way that still reflects the point of departure from the Twelve Tables. The prohibition of harmful private rituals and of unauthorized associations informs the arrangement of the laws. In book 12, which is dedicated to public crimes, title 16 collected imperial constitutions concerning "Magicians, astrologers and all other like Criminals." Christians adopted and intensified the practice of prosecuting them, as Augustine had already demanded. Book 16 collected rulings regarding religious associations. The notion *religio* was reserved for the Catholic Church alone. Heretics, Jews, and pagans belonged to the category of *superstitio* and were virtual threats to the common well-being of the empire. Jews were allowed to keep their old privileges, but were prohibited from building new synagogues. Heretics were forbidden, but not all were prosecuted alike. "Not all should be punished with the same severity" (*CTh* 16:5, 65 [2]). The sanctions for the various groups ranged from being tolerated to merciless prosecution (Manicheans). Apostates had to forfeit their right to make a will. And pagan sacrifices, both public and private, were strictly forbidden. The entire composition is imbued with the idea that the Catholic Church alone may represent the true *religio* in public and that *res publica* is sustained more by religion, than by official duties and labor (*CTh* 16:2, 16). By means of Roman legal notions, the *Codex Theodosianus* turned the religious diversity of the late Roman Empire into a hierarchical order (Salzman, 1993).

The *Codex Iustinianus* (*CI;* Krüger, 1929; Scott, 1932), composed about a hundred years later, moved chapter 16 of the *Codex Theodosianus* on religious associations to the very beginning. A comparison reveals that the legal distinctions between various heretics in chapter 16, title 9 of the *Codex Theodosianus* disappeared. Membership in all non-Catholic Christian groups became a public crime (*CI* 1:5, 4); the perpetrators were punished like the Manicheans and forfeit their civic rights. In book 9, which addressed public crimes like the *Codex Theodosianus,* the *Codex Iustinianus* adopted the constitutions of the *Codex Theodosianus* on "Magicians, astrologers and all other like Criminals" (*CI* 9:18). It added two constitutions of earlier pagan emperors: Antoninus Pius

(r. 138–161 C.E.) and Diocletian (r. 284–305; *CI* 9, 18, 1, 2). The continuation of the Roman criminalization of magic was in agreement with Justinian's aspiration: to restore ancient Rome.

But it would be rash to infer from these prohibitions that religious diversity disappeared. The consequence of this takeover of the Roman legal tradition was the introduction of a new kind of legal reasoning into the rising Christian social order. While the Christian monotheistic creed knew merely the biblical distinction between idolatry and the true worship of the One God, the Roman legal terms applied other criteria: whether a cult was ancient or not and foreign or not; whether rituals were performed in public and therefore salutary or unauthorized in secret and therefore pernicious; and whether associations were lawful or unlawful. By adopting the pagan legal distinctions, the Catholic Church established a worldview, in which paganism, Judaism, magic, and heresy continued to exist, though theologically and legally devalued. MacMullen points out that the triumph of the Catholic Church "did not and could not conclude in any sort of total eclipse or displacement of the past" (1997, p. 159). The hierarchy was in line with the early and persistent Christian faith: that Christ had subdued the pagan demonic forces. That belief allowed the continuous existence of the non-Christian powers in an inferior status (Flint, 1999).

SEE ALSO Codes and Codification.

BIBLIOGRAPHY

Baumann, R. A. "The Suppression of the Bacchanals: Five Questions." *Historia* 49 (1990): 334–348.

Berman, Harold J. *Law and Revolution: The Formation of the Western Legal Tradition.* Cambridge, Mass., 1983.

Bretone, Mario. *Geschichte des Römischen Rechts: Von den Anfängen bis zu Justinian.* Munich, 1992.

Codex Justinianus: Codex Iustinianus, vol. 2. Edited by Paul Krüger. *Corpus Iuris Civilis.* Berlin, 1929.

Codex Theodosianus: Theodosiani libri XVI cum Constitutionibus Sirmondianis et Leges novellae ad Theodosianum pertinentes. Edited by Theodor Mommsen and Paulus M. Meyer. Berlin, 1904.

Codex Theodosianus. Translated by Clyde Pharr. Princeton, N.J., 1952.

Coleman-Norton, Paul R. *Roman State and Christian Church: A Collection of Legal Documents to A.D. 535.* 3 vols. London, 1966.

Crawford, Michael H. *Roman Statutes,* vol. 2. London, 1996.

The Digest of Justinian. Latin text edited by Theodor Mommsen with the aid of Paul Krueger; English translation edited by Alan Watson. Philadelphia, Pa., 1985.

Flint, Valerie. "The Demonisation of Magic and Sorcery in Late Antiquity: Christian Redefinitions of Pagan Religions." In *Witchcraft and Magic in Europe,* edited by Valerie Flint, Richard Gordon, Georg Luck, and Daniel Ogden, vol. 2. London, 1999.

Gaius. *Institutes.* Edited with translation by W.M. Gordon and O. F. Robinson. Ithaca, N.Y. 1988.

Gaudemet, J. "La législation religieuse de Constantin." In *Revue de l'histoire de l'Église de France* 33 (1947): 25–61.

Geertz, Clifford. "Local Knowledge: Fact and Law in Comparative Perspective." In *Local Knowledge: Further Essays in Interpretive Anthropology,* pp. 167–234. New York, 1983.

Graf, Fritz. *Magic in the Ancient World.* Translated by Franklin Philip. Cambridge, Mass., 1997.

Grodzynski, Denise. "'Superstitio." *Revue des Études Anciennes* 76 (1974): 36–60.

Hardy, E. G. *Christianity and the Roman Government: A Study in Imperial Administration* (1874). New York, 1971.

Harries, Jill. *Law and Empire in Late Antiquity.* Cambridge, U.K., 1999.

Harries, Jill, and Ian Wood, eds. *The Theodosian Code.* Ithaca, N.Y., 1993.

Honoré, Antony M. "The Making of the Theodosian Code." *Zeitschrift der Savigny Stiftung* 103 (1986): 133–222.

Kippenberg, Hans G. *Die vorderasiatischen Erlösungsreligionen in ihrem Zusammenhang mit der antiken Stadtherrschaft: Heidelberger Max Weber-Vorlesungen 1988.* Frankfurt, 1991.

Kippenberg, Hans G. "Magic in Roman Civil Discourse: Why Rituals Could Be Illegal." In *Envisioning Magic: A Princeton Seminar and Symposium,* edited by Peter Schäfer and Hans G. Kippenberg, pp. 137–163. Leiden, Netherlands, 1997.

Kippenberg, Hans G. "Christliche Gemeinden im Römischen Reich: Collegium licitum oder illicitum." In *Hairesis: Festschrift für Karl Hoheisel zum 65. Geburtstag,* edited by Manfred Hutter, Wassilios Klein, and Ulrich Vollmer, pp. 172–183. Münster, 2002.

Livy. *History of Rome.* 14 vols. Cambridge, Mass., 1919–1959.

MacMullen, Ramsay. *Christianizing the Roman Empire (A.D. 100–400).* New Haven, Conn., 1984.

MacMullen, Ramsay. *Christianity and Paganism in the Fourth to Eighth Centuries.* New Haven, Conn., 1997.

Maine, Henry Sumner. *Ancient Law: Its Connection with Early History of Society and Its Relation to Modern Ideas* (1861). London, 1905.

Meyer, Elizabeth A. *Legitimacy and Law in the Roman World: Tabulae in Roman Belief and Practice.* Cambridge, U.K., 2004.

Millar, Fergus. *The Emperor in the Roman World (31 BC–AD 337).* Ithaca, N.Y., 1992.

Mommsen, Theodor. "Religionsfrevel nach römischem Recht." *Gesammelte Schriften* (Berlin) 3 (1905): 389–422.

Mommsen, Theodor, and Paulus M. Meyer. *Theodosiani libri XVI cvm Constitvtionibvs Sirmondianis et Leges novellae ad Theodosianvm pertinentes.* Berlin, 1904.

Murphy, Tim. *The Oldest Social Science? Configurations of Law and Modernity.* Oxford, 1997.

Pharr, Clyde. *The Theodosian Code and Novels, and the Sirmondian Constitutions: A Translation with Commentary, Glossary, and Bibliography.* Princeton, N.J., 1952.

Phillips, C. R., III. "'Nullum Crimen sine Lege': Socioreligious Sanctions on Magic." In *Magika Hiera: Ancient Greek Magic and Religion,* edited by Chris A. Faraone and D. Obbink, pp. 260–276. New York, 1991.

Rajak, Tessa. "Was There a Roman Charter for the Jews." *Journal of Roman Studies* 74 (1984): 107–123.

Sachot, Maurice. "'Religio/Superstitio': Historique d'une subversion et d'un retournement." *Revue de l'histoire des religions* 208 (1991): 355–394.

Salzman, Michele R. "Superstitio in the Codex Theodosianus and the Persecution of Pagans." *Vigiliae Christianae* 41 (1987): 172–188.

Salzman, Michele R. "The Evidence for the Conversion of the Roman Empire to Christianity in Book 16 of the 'Theodosian Code.'" *Historia* 42 (1993): 362–378.

Scott, Samuel P. *The Civil Law.* 17 vols. Cincinnati, 1932.

Sullivan, Winnifred Fallers. *Paying the Words Extra: Religious Discourse in the Supreme Court of the United States.* Cambridge, Mass., 1994.

Watson, Alan. *The State, Law, and Religion: Pagan Rome.* Athens, Ga., 1992.

Zeddies, Nicole. *Religio et sacrilegium: Studien zur Inkriminierung von Magie, Häresie und Heidentum (4.–7. Jahrhundert).* Frankfurt, 2003.

HANS KIPPENBERG (2005)

LAW AND RELIGION: LAW AND RELIGION IN MEDIEVAL EUROPE

The distinctive relationship between law and religion is one of the main features of the Western political tradition. The origins can be traced, in part, to a set of principles incorporated in the corpus of the Roman law and its later medieval developments. The legal status of religion and religious institutions in Roman public law was defined by a set of principles and rules regulating the use of sacred buildings and the status of priests and magistrates. By the time of the compilations of all the Roman laws under the emperor Justinian in sixth-century Byzantium, Christianity had given a new meaning to law and religious relations. Legal rules and religious norms developed in a symbiotic environment. Outside the Byzantine Empire, however, the Western part of Christendom was no longer ruled by Roman law. Rome had ceased to be the capital of an empire. The memory of its past imperial glory rested now on the claims of Peter's successors at the head of the Catholic Church. The people newly established inside the frontiers of the former empire followed their own law and customs. The revival of the concept of empire during the Carolingian Renaissance had little consequence for the existing systems of customary law. With the many obstacles faced by the church in the early Middle Ages, interest in Roman law declined.

In the eleventh century, the vast intellectual movement of the Gregorian Reform restored the church's discipline and its authority. The Gregorian Reform also generated a renewed interest for the texts of the church's legal tradition But in their search for the texts suitable to their purpose, the reformers, with perhaps the exception of Ivo of Chartres (c. 1040–1115), rarely bothered to harmonize the contradictions found in the texts then collected in their compilations. They chose instead simply to suppress the texts which did not support their own conclusions. While the reformers did provide the intellectual impulse for the reinterpretation of the spiritual foundations of the ecclesiastical institutions, sacramental law as understood by the reformers did not aim at the construction of a unified juridical order. They focused on the defense of the spiritual and pastoral nature of the church's mission and the function of its clergy. The legal revolution came later, once the long forgotten compilations of Justinian were rediscovered in the West.

The rediscovery of Justinian's compilations in northern Italy and the resulting exegesis of Roman legal texts brought about dramatic changes. Within a few decades, the renewal of jurisprudence gave rise to a novel legal culture (c. 1130). As the teaching of the first generations of jurists spread outside the limited circle of the schools, the new legal reason attracted a larger audience. By the turn of the twelfth century, princes and prelates, teachers and students, judges and lawyers, merchants and clergymen were readily using the new law. But to these men, law was more than a technical tool. An image of a prestigious past, it was also described as the *ratio scripta* and a mode of thinking encompassing the whole field of human affairs, both secular and sacred. The new law transformed feudal society and shaped forever the legal tradition of Western Europe. Viewed as the legacy of the former empire, the new law was clearly distinguished from religion at a time when the conflict between the popes and the heirs of the Holy Roman Empire divided medieval Europe. Yet the practices and belief of a deeply religious medieval society could not but influence the definition and the perception of the legal norms in both the private and the public spheres. In turn, legal reasoning would also contribute to shaping religious doctrine. This combination would be achieved by the new canonical jurisprudence within a few decades.

Around 1140, an Italian monk named Gratian produced his *Concord of Discordant Canons,* otherwise known as the *Decretum* or *Decreta,* establishing the science of canon law. In its first version, this compilation of church law attempted to reconcile various legal sources from the Holy Scriptures to conciliar canons, the writings of the church's fathers, as well as papal decretals. Gratian also added a treaty on penance and one on sacraments as if in his eyes these two sacramental elements could not be dissociated from an ecclesiastical model founded on the law. But Gratian's project became more than a mere collection of contradictory texts. Bringing together works and authorities excerpted from a pluralistic, complex religious tradition, Gratian rewrote the vibrant history of the Catholic Church through the recalling of an uninterrupted chain of authorities and sometimes dissonant voices. The suppression of discordances and the harmonization of the textual material paved the way toward a unified church leading a united Christian world.

Anders Winroth has recently shown with great care how little Roman law Gratian initially knew or considered to be worthy of the canonists' attention. But the general conception of a harmonious legal system as the foundation of a unified society clearly reminds one of Justinian's effort to find in the confirmation of an age-old Roman legal tradition the intellectual and cultural strength to revive a declining empire.

The renewal of jurisprudence was part of an intellectual movement that had already affected the other fields of learning among which theological inquiry enjoyed primacy of place. At the crossroads of theology and law, it provided a model for the development of a new science of canon law which aimed at blending harmoniously the sacramental tradition with more practical Roman legal principles. In doing so, as Walter Ullmann has pointed out, religious doctrine has transformed into legally sanctioned rules of conduct that governed the acts and the beliefs of each member of the Christian community. Law acquired an essential function in the life of the church. It contributed to a new definition of its purpose and transformed its institutions for the coming centuries. From the start, Gratian's message was clear and confident. "Mankind is governed in two ways by natural law and by mores." For the twelfth-century canonist, long before Thomas Aquinas and the revival of Aristotelian philosophy, natural law was the expression of God's will. The world was ruled by divine law and human law.

Writing in the 1160s, the canonist Stephan of Tournai (1135–1203) had bemoaned the difficulty of bringing together theologians and jurists at the same intellectual banquet. Begging his reader to be patient, Stephan proceeded to serve "the promised feast to the diners":

> In the same city here are two peoples under the same king, and with the two peoples two ways of life, and with two ways of life two dominions, and with two dominions a double order of jurisdiction emerges. The city is the Church; the king of the city is Christ; the two people are the two orders in the Church, of clerics and lay people. The two ways of life are the spiritual and the physical; the two dominions are the institutional Church and secular government; the double order of jurisdiction is divine and human law. Render to each its own and all will be in accord.

What made the history of the medieval church different from other religions was precisely the clear distinction between the two jurisdictions. To the medieval person, divine and human laws were the indispensable foundations of the Christian society. The authority of both laws transcended the separation of the society into two distinct spiritual and temporal partitions. By the turn of the following century, this doctrine was undermined by the renewed interest in Roman law. The misgivings of the first decretists such as Rufinus (d. 1192) were no longer heard and the "sirens of Roman law" were tempting the *decretorum nauta.* With few exceptions, the success of Roman law as the *ratio scripta* and the primary source of legal science did not, in fact, prompt the demise of canon law. On the contrary, the canonists' interest in Roman law gave it a new status. Hence canonical jurisprudence transformed the original character of Roman law while diluting its imperial essence mostly in response to the political claims made by Frederic Barbarossa and his successors. As heir to the past Roman emperors, Frederic maintained that his authority as lord of the world *(dominus mundi)* could not be challenged by any one. Praised as the living law *(lex animata)* by the Bolognese envoys to the Diet at Roncaglia (1158) after the defeat of the rebellious Italian cities, Frederic shared with his Roman predecessors the unique knowledge of the law and placed under his protection law students and teachers. The authority of Roman law was closely associated with the imperial power. The teaching of the new Roman Jurisprudence was the constant reminder of the emperor's legislative authority. Outside Northern Italy, the success of Roman law in the Parisian schools diverted the students from theological studies and might also have offended the French king who did not consider himself as the emperor's subject. One of the canonists' achievements consisted in dissociating Roman law from its imperial background. In 1219, Honorius III's famous interdiction of the teaching of Roman law in Paris did not deter the canonist's attention to the secular law.

This legal development came at a time when the teachings of the Catholic Church were contested by various popular movements that challenged the authority of its institutions and the legitimacy of its clergy. Heresies gained popular support while the spiritual enthusiasm once energized by the call for the defense of the Holy Land was losing its momentum. In 1204, the sack of Constantinople ended the Fourth Crusade well before it reached the Holy Land. At the same time, the claims of the emboldened secular powers, imperial as well as royal, reached new proportions. The continuous conflict between the Holy Roman Empire and the papacy fostered the opposition between the secular and the spiritual spheres of political power. It led progressively to a reinforcement of church hierarchy around the growing authority of the popes who adapted the Roman model of imperial power to the conduct of the papal office. The resulting tensions shifted the issue of religious belief and the practice of one's faith from the spiritual to the secular sphere of the public order.

In 1215, when Pope Innocent III convened the Fourth Lateran Council, these political tensions had become acute. The preachings of the medieval Catharists treated the ecclesiastical hierarchy and the church's institutions with contempt while more esoteric prophecies announced the coming of a new age of the Spirit. Beginning with the strong reaffirmation of the true Catholic faith and belief in the Holy Trinity, the assembly of church dignitaries outlined the steering principles for the governance of the universal church and the government of Christian society. Although there is reason to believe that Innocent III himself was not an accomplished jurist, the church prelates who gathered under his leadership attempted to rethink the dual mission of the medieval church comprised of pastoral duty to the faithful and the government of Christian society. The council had three goals: to strengthen the Catholic faith, to fight heresy, and to restore Catholic life. The result was a two-pronged attempt to discipline individual behavior and to restore order in the Christian society. Considered as the most important council of medieval Christendom, Lateran IV marks a turning point in the shaping of a juridical model that blended religious norms and legal rules. The canons of the councils outlined a new order in which private belief and public interest merged into one all encompassing definition of Catholic life. A century after the final outcome of the Gregorian reform, the restatement of the Catholic faith was backed by a legal apparatus in which religious norms had acquired a new significance. Faith and Christian doctrine were thus rethought in order to fit within the new paradigms. Once more, the canonists turned to the Roman law.

In the fourth century, Emperor Theodosius's edict establishing the Catholic faith as the religion of the empire ordered all the people subjected to his imperium to embrace the religion of Peter and belief in the Holy Trinity. This famous edict was later inserted at the beginning of Justinian's codex in the opening title on the Holy Trinity and the Catholic faith. It is not surprising therefore that it found pride of place in the teachings of the medieval legal scholars. For the jurists who painstakingly interpreted Roman law, Theodosius's edict was the perfect illustration of the imperial power. Faith was defined both as belief in the Holy Trinity and as obedience to the emperor's order. The subject who dared reject this religion was guilty of a double offense in the eyes of God and in the eyes of the emperor. Punishment was handed down swiftly by divine will and imperial justice. Religion was the law, as later pointed out by Accursius, one of the most famous medieval jurists; it was the expression of the emperor's pleasure. Reading the early glosses and comments to this famous text, the canonists did not fail to notice the striking parallel between the imperial edict and the first canon of the council. By the time of Lateran IV (1215), however, the pope had replaced the emperor as defender of the faith and ecclesiastical justice combined the legitimacy of the spiritual jurisdiction with the authority of legal procedure. The earlier distinction between sin and crime, which had long defined the economy of salvation, was also reinterpreted.

The changes envisioned by Innocent III (d. 1216) rested firmly upon the view that the unity of the church both as a mystical body and a hierarchical institution was the expression of a universal order. For the canon lawyers pastoral function and jurisdictional power coincided in the divine order of salvation. Within a few years, however, the delicate balance between the care of the soul and the reason of state faced an increasing challenge. The initial quest for harmony was gradually replaced with a different quest for unity that rested on a faith sanctioned by canon law.

By the time of the promulgation of the Decretals by Pope Gregory IV in 1234, the development of jurisprudence in both canon and civil law had brought into question many legal doctrines. The first half of the thirteenth century marked a period of renewed legal dynamism in which the identity and authority of canon law was defined by a new generation of jurists and ecclesiastics who readily adopted a more emancipated attitude toward Roman law. This intellectual movement was also shaped by the intense political debate that contributed to the redefinition of the papal power. The first compilations of Decretals fostered an interest for the new law and confirmed the pope's function as guardian of church doctrine and source of its law. The analysis and exegesis of legal texts reached a new dimension while theological inquiries extended the predicament of salvation to the broader conception of the medieval political order and the common good of human society. A new generation of canonists known as the decretalists gave more importance to the harmonious relationship between law and theology. Henry of Suza, known as Hostiensis, later cardinal-bishop of Ostia, taught in his lectures that "Theology was the science of the angels, while Roman law was the science of the animals and Canon law the science of the human beings." The three conditions of the living creatures corresponded with the trilogy of theological, Roman, and canonical knowledge as well as the three conditions of the soul—*synderesis*, sense, and reason—that corresponded to the three forms of life.

By the end of the thirteenth century, however, Hostiensis's beliefs were challenged by the practical needs of a rising administration and the strengthening of the papal government. Faced with political challenges and theological disputes, the church increasingly relied upon the legal doctrines developed in the previous century to maintain and expand its authority. In doing so, the rigid interpretation of the legal rules widened the gap between the pastoral and sacramental commitments and the governmental institutions.

During the last centuries of the Middle Ages, the conflict between civil and ecclesiastical jurisdiction was often reduced to what Stephan Kuttner described in his book *Reflections on Gospel and Law in the History of the Church* as the "petty reality of legalism" (Kuttner, 1976, 199–209). For a time, the spirit of the first canonists continued through a conception of canon law and ecclesiastical justice which was grounded in the biblical precedents and the sacred canons. But the growing bureaucratic and administrative process of the church's institutions transformed the canonical norms into a set of technical rules and regulations increasingly detached from the daunting goals of an economy of salvation. Canon law seemed no longer able nor interested to foster the spiritual and the temporal dimensions of human life. This failure expressed the decline of the intellectual movement which had shaped the distinctive features of ecclesiastical law. This decline explains to some extent the inability of the church's institutions to respond to the expectations of Christian society until the Reformation.

BIBLIOGRAPHY

Benson, Robert L., and Giles Constable with Carol D. Lanham, eds. *Renaissance and Renewal in the Twelfth Century.* Cambridge, Mass., 1982.

Berman, Harold Joseph. *Law and Revolution: The Formation of the Western Legal Tradition.* Cambridge, Mass., 1983.

Brentano, Robert. *Two Churches; England and Italy in the Thirteenth Century.* Princeton, N.J., 1968.

Brundage, James A. *Medieval Canon Law.* 3d ed. London and New York, 1997.

Evans, G. R. *Law and Theology in the Middle Ages.* London and New York, 2002.

Helmholz, Richard H. *The Spirit of Classical Canon Law.* Athens, Ga., and London, 1996.

Kantorowicz, Ernst H. *The King's Two Bodies; A Study in Mediaeval Political Theology.* Princeton, N.J., 1957; 6th ed., 1981.

Kuttner, Stephan. *Harmony from Dissonance; An Interpretation of Medieval Canon Law.* Latrobe, Pa., 1960.

Kuttner, Stephan. *Studies in the History of Medieval Canon Law.* Aldershot, U.K., and Brookfield, Vt., 1990.

Kuttner, Stephan. *The History of Ideas and Doctrines of Canon Law in the Middle Ages.* Aldershot, U.K., and Brookfield, Vt., 1992.

Post, Gaines. *Studies in Medieval Legal Thought.* Princeton, N.J., 1964.

Tierney, Brian. *Church Law and Constitutional Thought in the Middle Ages.* London, 1979.

Tierney, Brian. *Religion, Law, and the Growth of Constitutional Thought, 1150–1650.* Cambridge, U.K., and New York, 1982.

Tierney, Brian. *Rights, Laws, and Infallibility in Medieval Thought.* Aldershot, U.K., and Brookfield, Vt., 1997.

Ullmann, Walter. *The Church and the Law in the Earlier Middle Ages: Selected Essays.* London, 1975.

Ullmann, Walter. *The Papacy and Political Ideas in the Middle Ages.* London, 1976.

Vodola, Elisabeth. *Excommunication in the Middle Ages.* Berkeley, Calif., 1986.

Winroth, Anders. *The Making of Gratian's Decretum.* Cambridge, U.K., and New York, 2000.

LAURENT MAYALI (2005)

LAW AND RELIGION: LAW AND RELIGION IN INDIGENOUS CULTURES

Taken individually, the four principal terms that make up the title of this entry—law, religion, indigenous, and culture—are extraordinarily broad and problematic. The conjunction of the terms does little to narrow the field of analysis, prompting questions often asked by scholars of law, religion, and indigenous cultures: Whose law? What is religion? Indigenous by what standards? Culture in what sense? Moreover, scholars must make sense of the discrepancies and overlap between academic categories and the real world while being alert to various ways indigenous peoples represent themselves in diverse contexts, which are occasionally achieved in ways that appear paradoxical. Some scholars have observed that in the course of legal struggles indigenous peoples embody postmodern notions of culture—at times with inventiveness and play—while claiming quite the opposite: they represent themselves as timeless, autochthonous, and cohesive. That they do so is an indication of the domain in which they must act: an international legal arena configured by conflicting impulses and histories that has not yet evinced principled and consistent ways of addressing native claims. Such is the predicament of native peoples who seek to maintain their identities and legal autonomy in the face and by way of the institutions of politically ascendant nation-states.

In order to do justice to the complex field defined by the engagement of indigenous cultures, religion, and law, several related points must be emphasized: the concerns of law and religion are quite ultimate; the stakes of both are amplified in their intersection; and, finally, in the post-colonial world this urgency pertains directly to self-determination and human rights—how these are imagined (as individual or collective), articulated, and, on occasion, resisted or denied. Before addressing these themes and the tensions they imply, several perspectives from within the field will be considered.

APPROACHES. The vast possibilities for the study of law and religion in indigenous cultures are a source of both promise and potential confusion. To begin to address some of the issues raised above, scholars in the field have historically limited their frames of analysis in three general ways. One approach is to address jurisprudence within indigenous cultures, which is best represented by early work in the field of legal anthropology. A classic of this genre is *The Cheyenne Way: Conflict and Case Law in Primitive Jurisprudence* by K. N. Llewellyn and E. Adamson Hoebel. In the African context, the work of Max Gluckman did much to consolidate the field, particularly as he grappled with questions of social stability in the face of crisis. A wonderful account of the sorts of issues addressed by this approach to religion, culture, and law is found in Elenore Smith Bowen's anthropological novel *Return to Laughter.* By the mid-twentieth century legal anthropology was becoming increasingly comparative, a trend best represented by the classic text edited by Laura Nader, *Law in Culture and Society.* Religion, and particularly ritual, has long been a concern of legal anthropologists in this tradition, but it often is relegated to the status of a secondary concern.

A somewhat different approach to the study of law and religion in indigenous cultures has addressed native religious traditions more fully by way of focusing on the post-contact influences of European colonial practices and policies around the globe, particularly in North America. This area of study has been developed most extensively by legal experts like Robert A. Williams, Jr., whose *The American Indian in Western Legal Thought: The Discourses of Conquest* links pre-colonial religious and legal functions to colonial practices, and native authors such as Vine Deloria, Jr. (*For This Land: Writings on Religion in America*), Gerald Vizenor, Walter Echo-Hawk, and Lilikala Kame'eleihiwa. Religious studies scholars have been influential here as well, with notable contributions being made by, among others, Robert Michaelsen, Christopher Vecsey, whose *Handbook of American Indian Religious Freedom* addresses issues ranging from land access to repatriation, and Huston Smith, who collaborated with Hochunk religious leader Reuben Snake to write *One Nation Under God: The Triumph of the Native American Church.*

A third trajectory of scholarship in the field builds upon the insights of the former two traditions in order to emphasize resilient and novel qualities of indigenous agency. The central insight of this scholarship shows the radically contingent quality of religious and legal claims, and its emphasis is on the decolonization of native identities. This approach explores the ways indigenous people are able to participate in rights discourse in ways that raise complex questions about the meanings of, for example, citizenship, tradition, and entitlement. This is an interdisciplinary movement that offers significant contributions from critical legal theory, political theory, history, and anthropology. Such work includes, for example, studies of cultural movements in Latin America (as analyzed in an engaging volume edited by Kay Warren and Jean Jackson, *Indigenous Movements, Self-Representation, and the State in Latin America*), Australia (see, e.g., Elizabeth Povinelli, *The Cunning of Recognition: Indigenous Alterities and the Making of Australian Multiculturalism*), and Africa (as explored by John and Jean Comaroff in their magisterial *Of Revelation and Revolution: The Dialectics of Modernity of a South African Frontier*).

Creative scholarship in the study of law and religion in indigenous cultures from all of the perspectives described above follows a model described by Susan Staiger Gooding in her article, "At the Boundaries of Religious Identity: Native American Religions and American Legal Culture." She argues that the scholar's job is "to take account of legal discourse as an historical force, without taking it as our framework for understanding" (Gooding, p. 159). Substituting religion in place of law, Gooding's model is equally descriptive of the quest and tension at the heart of the study of religion. Achieving this dual goal—the critical assessment of religion and law—requires a willingness on the part of the scholar to de-privilege both discourses: to view them as human, historical, interested, and necessarily ideological. In this way, it is analytically productive to view religion and law as discourses of authenticity. However, following Warren and Jackson, scholars of religion and law should not take their focus to be the question of what constitutes authenticity; rather, attention should be centered on the construction of authenticity, which entails attending both to its production and consumption. The study of indigenous traditions and law is, then, fundamentally devoted to analyzing the strategies people(s) pursue in the process of identity articulation in the course of legal struggles.

Scholars have made considerable headway in understanding the relationships of law and religion by conceptualizing them as modes of speech and, more specifically, as modes of rhetoric (i.e., forms of speech as persuasion). Furthermore, critical scholars have discerned that religion and law are modes of rhetoric that, on occasion, share common venues and audiences, construct themselves in starkly similar ways (e.g., as authoritative, defining of the social body, normative, and eternal), and which sometimes run parallel or even function in complementary ways but run at cross purposes at other times (see Goodrich 1990; Fitzpatrick 1992). Religion and law do not exist as abstractions, but only as articulations of historical orators. As such, each mode of rhetoric is open to reformulation by persuasive speakers so that a range of tendencies and possibilities for the uses of each develops over time. To cite a basic example, Christianity can be viewed in a number of lights vis-à-vis native traditions in the Americas: it was a primary source of Western law; it was invoked to provide colonial legal rationale against native ceremonies; and it has become, at times, a source of native religious and legal resurgence. The first two of these historical observations accords with common sense, the last does not. The task of the scholar of religion and law in indigenous contexts is to make sense of the relationships of law and religion even, perhaps especially, when they appear to be counterintuitive.

INDIGENOUS AS CULTURE, CATEGORY, AND CLAIM. Perhaps the most counterintuitive aspect of the field is the category indigenous. Indigenous legal action in the contemporary political moment is likewise counterintuitive and rife with apparent and real paradoxes, the analysis of which will keep scholars of law and religion busy for years to come. The salient features of indigeniety on the world stage include its relative youth and its global reach. Further complicating the picture, the category indigenous signals (1) a term of self-designation; (2) an analytic concept; and (3) a legal construction. Much of the power of the category is vested in the interplay of these meanings—in respects, indigenous is a self-referential metaphor that accrues meaning to itself precisely because of the gaps and overlaps between its assumed meanings. This is especially so in legal contexts. Consider Ronald Niezen's account of indigenous identity espoused in his wide-ranging and provocative book, *The Origins of Indigenism: Human Rights and the Politics of Identity*:

> Indigenous identity, sometimes used to designate the distinctiveness of indigenous societies in the constitutional and moral orders of nation-states, carries significant authority and some degree of power, especially when legally articulated. It is largely an outcome of unintentional cultural and political collaboration. The concept "indigenous peoples," developed principally within Western traditions of scholarship and legal reform, has nurtured the revival of "traditional" identities. It has transcended its symbolic use by acquiring legal authority. It is the focus of widening struggles by increasing numbers of "peoples" for recognition, legitimacy, and validation. It has been taken control of by its living subjects—reverse-engineered, rearticulated, and put to use as a tool of liberation. (Niezen, 2003, p. 221)

It is crucial to any understanding of indigenous identities and discourse that scholars appreciate their oppositional component. As Niezen writes,

> When we look for things that indigenous people have in common, for what brings them together and reinforces their common identity, we find patterns that emerge from the logic of conquest and colonialism. These patterns apply equally to peoples otherwise very different in terms of history, geography, method of subsistence, social structure, and political organization. They are similarities based largely on the relationships between indigenous peoples and states. (Niezen, 2003, p. 87)

The relationship of indigenous claims to the states against which they are articulated points to profound imbalances in resources for identity articulation. When material bases of identity are so compromised, symbolic sources of identity are amplified by way of compensation and response. Claims that emerge in such contexts tend toward religious formulations insofar as their referents are transcendent (even while being grounded in the natural world). For example: we emerged from the earth here; the spirits conveyed knowledge to us here; we are descendants of the timeless ones who must care for this land. This is not to say that such claims are invented, for the people who make them are often members of groups with long traditions of connection to and veneration of the land and nature itself—nature is, in many native traditions, always supernatural. The point to be made here concerns the way such sentiments are given oppositional articulation as a form of cultural criticism that calls upon state powers to relieve crises they are perceived to have caused. In making such claims in legal contexts, native representatives attempt to bridge a chasm between their acutely local concerns and the predilections of audiences trained in the Western tradition of law and saturated by exotic images of "the Other." The category indigenous provides a framework for this bridge. It appears manifestly historical and rooted while simultaneously enabling the articulation of transcendent claims by appealing to tendentious habits of imagination that view native peoples as timeless stewards of nature.

Numerous nation-states are increasingly attentive to native claims and the U.N. now has a regular forum for addressing native concerns, which suggests that an international indigenous discourse is functioning to link local grievances to global responsiveness. However, this bridge is not without potential pitfalls. One regular impasse faced by legal audiences of indigenous claims is akin to that provoked by religious claims in the context of the United States with reference to the First Amendment: auditors are caught in the position of wanting to protect religious claims and actions without thereby establishing any particular religion as receiving special treatment under the law. Or, in the terms most often used to describe this scenario with regard to indigenous claims, legal audiences are faced with tension that emerges in the disjuncture between supporting human rights (based on liberal individualism) without endorsing collective rights. This tension points to other paradoxes.

Perhaps the foundational paradox upon which others rest in this context is that between relativism and universalism. This is not a merely abstract or philosophical issue. The problem here takes on embodied dimensions: namely, those who announce indigenous claims do so from relative positions of political weakness versus the assumed universal security of those who judge. This embodied aspect of the paradox is also historical, as speakers are the discovered, listeners the discoverers, and so forth. As indicated above, this tension is most evident and taut when conceptions of identity are at stake. Indigenous advocates espouse collective claims; human rights universalism is anchored in the identity of the individual. Not only are these positions mutually exclusive at some levels, they are also mutually suspicious: indigenous claimants worry that treaty rights and other collective entitlements will be ignored; universalists worry that individual rights might be subordinated to and even extinguished by zealous pursuit of collective aspirations. However, it is not the space between these positions that renders this dichotomy worthy of sustained investigation; it is the bridge-building capacity of indigenous discourse that deserves analysis, for occasionally indigenous representatives are able to reach across this historical, geo-political, and conceptual gulf.

A Hawaiian Example. If the linkage of human rights and self-determination is the quintessential goal of indigenous movements, then contemporary Hawai'i offers much to ponder. Sovereignty disputes have long been visible in Hawai'i. Students of Hawaiian culture are aware that battles over rule of the islands predated European contact. However, contests over native autonomy—what some have called inherent jurisdiction—have flared over the last 200 years, with notable inflammations at the time of missionization, the overthrow of the Hawaiian nation, the military conquest by the United States, and at the time of the Hawaiian Renaissance (1970s) to the present. Sovereignty disputes have been especially acute in recent years, as the alignment of local, state, federal, and international legal bodies has been destabilized in ways suggestive to native advocates that the time is ripe for political action. Numerous sovereignty groups have emerged in this context, most of which articulate a familiar set of concerns: environmental degradation, educational disadvantages, generalized cultural decay, religious desecration, and land access. As generally univocal as the many sovereignty groups are in stating their concerns, their suggestions for redress are less monolithic. Their primary point of divergence is with regard to differing visions of ideal relations to the state and federal governments. All share an emphasis on self-determination, but just what this means in practice can be remarkably divergent. To illustrate this point, two groups that represent positions at either end of a spectrum will be considered.

The first is a group led by veteran activist Dr. Kekuni Blaisdell. The position of his group is that of maximal sovereignty: Dr. Blaisdell and his group agitate vocally for complete decolonization of Hawai'i. Their argument has several prongs. First, they situate themselves as the unambiguous heirs of the land. Preserving the land, they argue, is a religious and moral duty. Second, they argue against U.S. jurisdiction, claiming that Hawai'i was a self-governing nation that was subjected to illegal overthrow by the United States. Third, as a remedy to this situation, the group represents itself as the legitimate political arm of the Hawaiian Nation. As such, it seeks audiences with other nation-states through international forums such as the UN. To graphically announce and enact its position, the group held a tribunal in 1993, during which an international panel of legal experts and indigenous representatives assessed claims against the United States (Ball, 2000, pp. 93–96). The United States was found guilty of all charges, which ranged from illegal occupation of the land to environmental abuse.

The second group is Hui Mālama I Nā Kūpuna O Hawai'i Nei (Hui Mālama). Focused primarily on repatriation and reburials issues (Johnson, 2003), Hui Mālama is no less vocal than Dr. Blaisdell's group. However, Hui Mālama's self-understanding vis-à-vis the state and federal governments is based implicitly on the model of federally recognized Indian tribes (as stipulated in the Native American Graves Protection and Repatriation Act). Hui Mālama operates within federal guidelines and often by way of federal grants to pursue the repatriation and protection of ancestral cultural objects and human remains. Doing so, they represent their cause as one fundamentally concerned with Hawaiian identity. This assertion took on greater relevance from 2000 forward, as a piece of federal legislation (The Native Hawaiian Recognition Act) was under consideration by the Senate in 2005. The pending legislation is designed to grant native Hawaiians "tribal" status within the state and federal governments. The intent of the legislation is to stabilize and define the status of native Hawaiians with regard to governmental policies and programs in a way that establishes "limited sovereignty" for native Hawaiians, particularly with reference to issues of education, land use, and cultural heritage. Politically and legally, the function of the bill is to recast the terms by which special entitlements for native Hawaiians may be constitutionally defended by shifting the basis of entitlements from the criterion of race to the criterion of tribal status. This is in response to the Supreme Court's 2000 decision in *Rice v. Cayentano,* which held that voting for trustees of the state Office of Hawaiian Affairs could not be limited by race. Hui Mālama is in support of this legislation and sees it as a "realistic" redressive mechanism. Dr. Blaisdell's group, by contrast, considers the bill anathema to sovereignty and a form of continued colonization.

The two indigenous Hawaiian movements briefly considered here both make religious claims for their positions, engage the media, attend and address national and international meetings, and have legal experts in their ranks. What these groups share above all else, beyond a contested Hawaiian identity, is a struggle with the web of modern statism. Dr. Kekuni Blaisdell's group has constructed itself as a nation that pushes on the border of statist aspirations, precisely as a means to gain an audience with influential states and as legitimated stance from which to engage in the politics of embarrassment and radical decolonization. Hui Mālama, from the other side, constructs itself as a self-determining entity within the boundaries of a nation-state. In ways that are sometimes countervailing and sometimes convergent, both groups use indigenous discourse to express and advance their positions in navigating a path toward substantial preservation of human rights based in—not held against—their collective identities. However differently pursued, their common quest is simultaneously ancient and futuristic. Moreover, their actions point to the fact that things scholars often take for granted—native identities and the borders of nation-states, for example—are constantly being (re)defined in the here and now.

SEE ALSO African Religions, overview article; Oceanic Religions, overview article.

BIBLIOGRAPHY

Ball, Milner. *Called by Stories: Biblical Sagas and Their Challenge for Law.* Durham, N.C., and London, 2000.

Bowen, Elenore Smith. *Return to Laughter: An Anthropological Novel.* New York, 1954.

Comaroff, John, and Jean Comaroff. *Of Revelation and Revolution: The Dialectics of Modernity on a South African Frontier.* Chicago, 1997.

Deloria, Vine, Jr. *For This Land: Writings on Religion in America.* New York and London, 1999.

Fitzpatrick, Peter. *The Mythology of Modern Law.* London, 1992.

Gooding, Susan Staiger. "At the Boundaries of Religious Identity: Native American Religions and American Legal Culture." *Numen* 43 (1996): 157–183.

Goodrich, Peter. *Languages of Law: From Logics of Memory to Nomadic Masks.* London, 1990.

Johnson, Greg. "Ancestors Before Us: Manifestations of Tradition in a Hawaiian Dispute." *Journal of the American Academy of Religion 71/2* (2003): 327–346.

Llewellyn, K. N., and E. Adamson Hoebel. *The Cheyenne Way: Conflict and Case Law in a Primitive Jurisprudence.* Norman, Okla., 1941.

Nader, Laura, ed. *Law in Culture and Society.* (1969.) Berkeley, Calif., 1997.

Niezen, Ronald. *The Origins of Indigenism: Human Rights and the Politics of Identity.* Berkeley, Calif., 2003.

Povinelli, Elizabeth. *The Cunning of Recognition: Indigenous Alterities and the Making of Australian Multiculturalism.* Durham, N.C., 2002.

Smith, Huston, and Reuben Snake. *One Nation Under God: The Triumph of the Native American Church.* Santa Fe, 1996.

Vecsey, Christopher, ed. *Handbook of American Indian Religious Freedom.* New York, 1991.

Warren, Kay, and Jean Jackson, eds. *Indigenous Movements, Self-Representation, and the State in Latin America.* Austin, Tex., 2002.

Williams, Robert A. *The American Indian in Western Legal Thought: The Discourses of Conquest.* New York, 1990.

GREG JOHNSON (2005)

LAW AND RELIGION: LAW AND RELIGION IN HINDUISM

The distinction between law and religion is one that does not exist in classical Hindu thought. Instead, both law and religion are parts of the single concept known as *dharma.* This fact is the key to understanding the legal system of classical India and its eventual acceptance and adaptation in Southeast Asia. *Dharma,* the basis for the legal system, is a system of natural laws in which specific rules are derived from an ideal, moral, and eternal order of the universe. The fact that the laws are based on this eternal order is their source of validation and authority. In classical Hindu society, the rights and responsibilities of an individual were determined by status. In general, the role and place of women were of marginal concern in the legal texts. The texts were composed by men, and they deal with matters of concern to all. In addition to gender, the determiners of one's status are caste (*varṇa* or *jāti*), stage of life (*āśrama*), age, and so forth. Every caste, age group within that caste, and stage of life has certain generic responsibilities that must be fulfilled (*varṇāśramadharma*). The king was charged with the responsibility of seeing to it that the populace adhered to its *dharma,* but this charge of the king's was itself a part of his *dharma,* so it is difficult to distinguish between the political, legal, and religious aspects of the South Asian legal tradition.

SOURCES OF *DHARMA*. The pervasive idea of *dharma* influences all aspects of a Hindu's life. It is a natural and moral order, and its disturbance has grave consequences for individuals and society. In theory, at least, every act of every Hindu's life should be done in accordance with this natural and moral order, so a righteous person would wish to perform every act in accordance with *dharma.* There are four sources of *dharma* enumerated in the legal literature (see, for example, *Manu* 2.12 and 1.108): the Veda (*śruti,* sometimes translated as "revelation"), *smṛti,* custom (i.e., *sadācāra;* literally, "the practice of the good"), and whatever seems correct to one's conscience (*ātmatuṣṭi*). The Veda is the ultimate source; all of the statements concerning *dharma* are theoretically traceable to the Veda. Both *smṛti* and custom are, according to the commentators, dependent on the Veda, in that the practices described in *smṛti* and followed in the customs of various groups and localities can all be traced, at least theoretically, to the Veda. The last source of *dharma*—whatever seems correct to one's conscience—is the most vague and least discussed, but it seems to have been included to cover those circumstances where no specific rule exists. In this last case it is presumed that the individual in question is one who has been instructed in *dharma* and is familiar with the sacred tradition. In all four of these cases, the connection with the Veda is the validation of their teachings on *dharma.*

The enormous corpus of Sanskrit literature called *smṛti* ("what has been remembered") attempted to teach the rules for conducting a righteous life. The ways in which this literature taught *dharma,* that is, taught righteousness as reflected in the conduct of one's life, varied considerably. One subcategory of *smṛti,* the Purāṇas, is made up of narrative texts that relate mythological stories focused on the incarnations of various gods. The great epics of India, the *Mahābhārata* and the *Rāmāyaṇa,* constitute another branch of *smṛti* literature and contain large amounts of didactic teaching. These two genres are designed to convey *dharma* by the examples of the characters in their stories.

A much more technically and strictly "legal" literature that constitutes a subcategory of *smṛti is* the *Dharmaśāstra,* or literally, the "science of *dharma.*" These *Dharmaśāstra* texts are all presumed by Hindus to teach the eternal and immutable *dharma* contained in the Vedas. The presumption of these texts was that the reader was familiar with the ritual texts and was a practitioner of the Vedic ritual. It was the purpose of the literature on *dharma* to unify the Hindu's world. This was done by enabling the members of society to harmonize their existence with the universal order. The range of topics in this literature is extensive, and includes: rules on the conduct of daily life including diet, cleanliness, times for sleeping and waking, the selection of mates, criminal laws, rules governing social interaction, relations between castes, sexual norms, laws of commerce, and rules relating to agricultural activity. In addition there is detailed treatment of the rules of procedure and of evidence. The latter includes witnesses, documents, and a sophisticated treatment of the use of ordeals to settle disputes.

Precisely because this literature dealt with *dharma,* its rules and regulations were held to be inviolable: the fact that *dharma* is itself the order of the universe validates rules pertaining to it. In an ideal sense the literature on *dharma* served to define who and what a righteous believer in the Veda was. The *Dharmaśāstra* literature comprises four types: (1) the earliest, aphoristic texts, the *Dharmasūtras,* each of which are attributed pseudonymously to a famous sage of antiquity; (2) later metrical texts, also pseudonymous, often referred to by the term "metrical *smṛtis*" and (somewhat confusingly) when in opposition to the *Dharmasūtras* by the term *dharmaśāstra;* (3) commentaries (*bhāṣyas*) on both of the preceding; and (4) legal "digests" called *nibandhas.*

The earlier texts, the *Dharmasūtras,* were taught as part of the literature of a particular Vedic school (*caraṇa*), whereas the later texts, the metrical *smṛtis,* were not connected with any particular school. This fact indicates that the study of *dharma* had become much broader and more specialized than it was at the time of the *Dharmasūtras.* The *dharma* literature is often very difficult to date (for the earlier texts, especially, only tentative relative chronologies may be established), but the extant texts probably range in date from the fourth century BCE to the late eighteenth century CE. It is in this body of literature that we find the most explicit descriptions of the legal system of classical India. The most authoritative of these explicitly legal writings is the earliest metrical *smṛti*, the *Mānava Dharmaśāstra* or *Manusmṛti* (c. 100 BCE–100 CE, hereinafter "*Manu*"), which is attributed to the semidivine mythical figure Manu Svayambhu.

PRINCIPLES OF RIGHTEOUSNESS. Both the *Dharmasūtras* and the metrical *smṛtis* claim to be the teachings of great sages who have made *dharma* known to humankind. The rules contained in these texts are specific statements of the principles of righteousness (*dharma*) and world order (*ṛta*) that are taught in the Veda. While the Veda is the theoretical source for all of the law contained in the *smṛti* literature, very little of what is contained in Vedic literature could itself be called "law." The exact way in which specific laws are derived from the largely ritual, sacerdotal literature of the Vedas is never made clear; therefore, the connection between the Vedas and *smṛti* is not obvious except for their shared theoretical concern for *dharma.* The test of the orthodoxy of any *smṛti* or interpretation *of smṛti* was its acceptance in practice by the educated and righteous men of the community. This is most probably the real connection between the Vedas and the *dharma* literature—the *dharma* literature records the practice of those steeped in the teachings of the Veda.

Acceptance of a rule did not always mean that its purpose was clearly understood by the educated and righteous men of the community. Indeed, the very obscurity of the reason for some rules is an important interpretative device. Since *dharma* is not "visible" or apparent to ordinary human beings, and since the *smṛti* literature teaches *dharma*, whenever there is "no visible purpose" (*adṛṣṭārtha*) for a rule, then that rule is of greater importance than a rule for which there is an obvious purpose (*dṛṣṭārtha*). Rules with an obvious purpose relate to the realm of the practical (*artha*) or that of the pleasant (*kāma*) and are therefore of less consequence to the metaphysical well-being of a person than rules that relate to *dharma.* For example, the metrical *smṛti* of the sage Yājñavalkya (at 1.352) states that the king should strive to make friends because friends are worth more than material possessions. This is a rule with an obvious purpose—the welfare of the king. The same text (at 2.1) later states that the king must administer his judicial court impartially and according to *Dharmaśāstra.* The purpose of this rule is not apparent (*adṛṣṭārtha*), except that to fulfill this rule is to engage in righteous behavior (*dharma*); thus, it is a rule which is more compelling than the earlier one advising the king to make friends. The sum of these rules, then, is that the king is not allowed to use his position as administrator of justice to cultivate friends. Indeed, when he is in court, he must be equally impartial to both friends and enemies (*Yājñavalkasmṛti 2.2*). This principle of the superiority of rules relating to *dharma* is stated explicitly in several places in the *smṛti* literature (see, for example, *Yājñavalkyasmṛti* 2.1).

***DHARMA* AND "LAW."** It is important to make a distinction between the rules contained in the *smṛti* literature and what we might call "the law of the land." In general, we have such limited evidence for daily practice that we cannot say with much certainty what the actual law was in a given place in the subcontinent at a given moment in history. What we can say is that the *Dharmaśāstras* and the *Dharmasūtras* record the foundation on which the legal system was based. The level of technical sophistication of the *Dharmaśāstra* was considerable, and it seems unavoidable that the adjective law found in the texts was born of a long process of actual practice that resulted in the elaborate legal procedure described there. (The quintessential text on legal procedure is the *Nāradasmṛti.*) *Dharmaśāstra* represents real legal principles. Even though the record of these legal principles is refracted through the lenses of the priestly class who recorded and interpreted it, *Dharmaśāstra* is of great value in reconstructing the history of Indian society because these texts tell us how—if not where and when—people actually lived.

The commentators and digest writers (and to some extent the texts themselves) tell us that local custom was of overriding authority. This means that the *Dharmaśāstras* and the *Dharmasūtras* were not uniformly statements of substantive law as actually applied; rather, they may be viewed as theoretical guidelines that conveyed in specific statements the ways that members of society might adhere to *dharma.* The actual implementation of these guidelines was fragmentary and localized. Local custom played a significant part in these variations. The *Dharmasūtras* and the *Dharmaśāstras* explicitly provide for variations in local custom and also indicate that these local customs are valid sources for knowledge of *dharma.* There was no concern for precedent, and although the decisions of courts were recorded, the records, as far as we known, were then usually given to the litigants themselves, who were responsible for the maintenance of the documents of their respective trials.

The fragmentary nature of the administration of the Hindu legal system was in part a function of the fact that there was no centralized legal hierarchy that had the capacity to uniformly enforce "the law." The king had appellate jurisdiction, and there were very few matters that he could prosecute on his own initiative without first having had a case brought to him by a plaintiff. The purpose of the entire legal system was not so much to deliver justice as it was to ensure that the entire populace adhered to the duties and obligations of *dharma.* The administration of law courts and the enforcement of "law" was not a purely political matter (although it had a political dimension); it was a religious concern. The fact that there is no central ecclesiastical authority in the Hindu tradition also contributed to the fragmentariness of the development of this legal tradition. This fragmentary and localized administration was also a result of the idea that every individual has a unique *dharma* and therefore a unique set of responsibilities. Accordingly the circumstances of every case would be unique, there would be no reason to record for reference the previous deliberations of a court.

ENFORCEMENT OF THE LAW. The validation of the "laws" in this system was to be found in the religious belief that the world is organized according to the natural and moral order of *dharma.* The enforcement of the laws was primarily the responsibility of the king, who was viewed as semidivine (see *Manu* 7.4–5), and this semidivine nature legitimized his temporal power. Within this natural and moral universal order, any polity without a king was one that suffered calamities; thus, the monarchy was essential to the well-being of the people. The reason that a polity without a king suffered calamities is that the primary task of the king was to protect his subjects. The most important part of his protection was seeing to it that *dharma* was adhered to by all of his subjects. Therefore, the king was the punisher of violators of *dharma* and the ultimate guarantor that *dharma* was adhered to in his kingdom. The *Mahābhārata,* for example, states in several places that the king's *dharma* is the culmination and sum of all other *dharmas.* His court was the court of final jurisdiction. There was no appeal from a judgment of the king's court. The king himself was the judge, but he was also urged to appoint a number of experts in *Dharmaśāstra* (preferably *brāhmaṇas*) to serve as judges in his court. One of these could be appointed the chief judge, and this judge would preside in the king's absence. Even though he has the assistance of these experts, and even though he could appoint them to serve in his absence, the king was still ultimately responsible for the adherence to *dharma*; if there were wrong judgments handed down by his court, the judges were liable to punishment, but so was the king.

Though the king was seen as semidivine—he is even addressed as *deva* (god) in Sanskrit drama—there was no real idea of the "divine right of kings." To be sure, the monarch was endowed with extraordinary powers, but the literature contains references to kings who were dethroned for their failure to adhere to their own *dharma* or who had failed to see to it that others did so. The *smṛti* literature recognized this as a legitimate response of the people to an unrighteous king. A related genre of Sanskrit technical literature, the *arthaśāstra,* is intended as a handbook for governance. Whereas the focus of the *arthaśāstra* literature is matters of concern specifically to the king (as opposed to other members of society): his training, conduct of war, foreign policy, intelligence, policing, and administrative organization, there is a detailed treatment of the administration of justice. The *arthśāstra* passages parallel similar treatments of judicial procedure in the *Dharmaśāstra* literature.

The concept of punishment was closely tied to the concept of penance. Any violation of *dharma* means that the violator incurred sin. To expunge this sin it was necessary to undergo some penance. The punishment meted out for a crime was thus viewed as purifying (*Manu* 8.318). It was also possible to mitigate the corporal or financial punishment of a crime by undergoing a specific penance (*Manu* 9.240). Neither punishment nor penance is described as a deterrent or as a way of compensating for injury or tort, but they are ways of compensating for the violation of the natural and moral order of *dharma.*

The *Dharmaśāstras* and the *Dharmasūtras* are the most succinct statements of *dharma,* but, as in all legal systems, the power to interpret the law is the power to make the law. In classical India this power was in the hands of the king and his judges, but we have very little record of their rulings. There has been controversy among scholars over the question of whether or not the king had the power to "legislate." The texts tell us that any ruling of the king had to be obeyed, but at the same time there are indications that existing custom had such a superior claim to validity that the king was bound not to interfere with it (so long as it was not depraved) but to enforce it.

Commentators on the *smṛtis* and digest writers were also interpreters of the law, and we have a huge corpus of literature recording their views. The function of interpretation served to keep the legal texts attuned to the changing needs of society. It was the task of the commentators and the digest writers to relate the general principles found in the texts to the current society in which the commentator was writing. Interpretation of *Dharmaśāstras* and *Dharmasūtras* was regulated by two factors. First, an interpreter had to use the codified hermeneutical techniques of the Mīmāṃsā school of philosophy. These techniques were originally developed for interpretation of Vedic texts to determine the exact procedures for the ritual. Since the *smṛti* literature is seen as a sort of continuation of the Vedic tradition, it is appropriate that the same techniques of interpretation be applied to it. The second factor controlling the interpretation of *smṛti* was the acceptance/implementation or rejection/ignoring by the community of any interpretation. Thus, the validation of any interpretation was found in its implementation.

CONTENTS OF THE *DHARMAŚĀSTRAS* AND THE *DHARMASŪTRAS.* The contents of the *Dharmaśāstras* and the *Dharmasūtras* may be divided into three broad categories: rules for "good conduct" (*ācāra*), those for legal procedure (*vyavahāra*), and those for penance (*prāyaścitta*). It was the design of these texts to prescribe rules that would guide each member of society so that he might live his life as fully in accordance with *dharma* as possible. This meant that as society changed, the prescriptions for righteousness contained in the texts needed to be adapted to those changes. This adaptation was done by the commentators on the *Dharmasūtras* and the *Dharmaśāstras* and by the digest writers. Because it was their responsibility to adapt the teachings of the *Dharmasūtras* and the *Dharmaśāstras,* their role as arbiters of *dharma* (righteousness) became central in the development of classical Hindu law.

The range of human activity regulated by the provisions of these texts is remarkable. Large categories such as marriage, ritual purity, inheritance, criminal law, and a basic commercial law are covered, but so are the minutiae of daily life: what and what not to eat, how to brush one's teeth, when and where to move one's bowels, how to detect suitable marriage partners, and more. The sophistication of the rules of legal procedure indicate a long-standing juridical tradition whose evolution can be vaguely traced through the increasingly sophisticated treatment of topics such as the administration of ordeals. The earliest texts know only two ordeals: fire and water. Later texts know as many as nine ordeals.

Every individual has a *dharma* that is a constellation of duties and responsibilities that are unique to him, because each individual has different capacities for righteousness. An individual's capacity for righteousness is determined by his birth, and his birth is determined by his *karma.* Thus every individual cannot be expected to meet the same standard. In broad terms, a *brāhmaṇa* and a *śūdra* (the highest and lowest *varṇas,* respectively) are therefore qualitatively different members of society. The social, religious, and legal expectations and requirements of a *brāhmaṇa* and a *śūdra* were different in accordance with their qualitative differences. For example, the killing of a *brāhmaṇa* was a very serious crime requiring harsh penances lasting twelve years (*Manu* 11.73–82), while the killing of a *śūdra* was a minor offense requiring a penance that lasts only six months; this penance was the same one prescribed for the killing of lizards (*Manu* 11.131, 11.141). Thus, to kill a *brāhmaṇa* was to do greater violence to the universal order than to kill a *śūdra* because of their qualitative differences in ritual status. The same reasoning is employed in the standards of behavior applied to members of society. A *brāhmaṇa* must take great care to perform penance for offenses, whether committed knowingly or unknowingly (*Manu* 11.45–46), but many of the things for which a *brāhmaṇa* would be outcasted are not even offenses for a *śūdra* (*Manu* 10.126).

THE COLONIAL PERIOD. It was this aspect of the Indian legal tradition that most alienated the British when in 1772 they decided that they should assume the responsibility for the enforcement of laws in the territories controlled by them. They mistrusted the traditional *paṇḍitas* because they appeared to discriminate between litigants on the basis of "religious" matters such as caste. Only after they had instituted sweeping changes in personal laws (such as those dealing with inheritance, marriage, adoption, etc.) did the British come to understand that the concept of *dharma* was different from the concepts of justice and equity found in the common-law tradition. In their defense it must be said that the traditional lack of concern for precedent, the fragmentary nature of the legal system, and the reliance on largely uncodified custom made the task of British administrators of Hindu law extremely difficult. It was the intention of the British to remove these uncertainties by providing a codified "Hindu Law." The British commissioned such a code, the *Vivādārṇavasetu,* and for a time the English translation of this code (*A Code of Gentoo Laws,* first published in 1776) served as the basis for the British courts' adjudication of Hindu personal law. Eventually, by the mid-nineteenth century, British scholarship had learned enough about the *Dharmaśāstra* to point out the errors that had been committed by the British-Indian judiciary, but by that time the corpus of judicial precedent was so large that it had an inertia of its own, and it was not possible to retrace all the steps that had been taken in the name of justice and equity. This corpus of judicial precedent continued to grow and was inherited by the judiciary of independent India so that the Hindu personal law of modern India is only nominally based upon *smṛti.* Having created it judicially, the British and their heirs in independent India were left with the task of legislatively reforming this new "Hindu Law." An attempt to systematically codify Hindu Law in newly independent India was unsuccessful, and the result is a piecemeal attempt to bring consistency or, sometimes, rationality to the law. Thus one finds the Hindu Marriage Act of 1955, the Hindu Adoptions and Maintenance Act of 1956, the Hindu Succession Act of 1956. The courts of modern India continue the process.

SOUTHEAST ASIAN DEVELOPMENTS. Since the Indian "legal" tradition is so integral a part of the religious and philosophical ideas of the Hindu tradition, it was inevitable that it would be exported to Southeast Asia when that region became "Indianized" (a process lasting for centuries, but beginning in the early centuries of the common era). The Indianization of Southeast Asia involved the adoption of Indian culture and religion (Hinduism and Buddhism), including the use of the Sanskrit language, the mythology of the Purāṇas and the epics, the concept of kingship, and the reliance on the *Dharmaśāstra* as a statement of the generalized standard of conduct.

As a result of the adoption of these Indian religious and philosophical ideas by the Southeast Asian countries, the idea of *dharma* came to be central in the legal systems of this region as well. Burma, Thailand, Cambodia, Java, and Champa all adopted the Hindu ideal of law based on a natural and moral order of the universe. As an integral part of this idea of *dharma* the Hindu concept of kingship was also adopted in these regions of Southeast Asia. Though these were originally Hindu ideas, they were integrated into Buddhist kingdoms by the convention of explaining in the introductions to legal texts that a sage by the name of Manu was inspired by the Buddha to discover the eternal laws and to make them available to the world. In some texts of the Southeast Asian tradition, the organization of the Indian *Mānava Dharmaśāstra* is followed fairly closely, but in other texts it is not adhered to at all. There is generally less concern with the technical aspects of law in the Southeast Asian tradition, and unlike the Indian *Dharmaśāstra* the texts do not recognize and incorporate custom as a source of law. This fact probably contributed to the role assumed by these texts, which function much more as exemplary statements of general standards of conduct than as statements of actual law.

Each of the cultures of Southeast Asia adopted the Indian legal tradition in slightly different ways. There are significant variations in the formal aspects of each legal system, and generally it may be said that the further the geographical distance from India, the greater the formal differences. In every case, however, the religio-philosophical basis of the Indian legal system was accepted: namely, that *dharma is* the natural, moral order of the universe and that it is this concept that defines and validates the law.

SEE ALSO Dharma, article on Hindu Dharma; Ṛta; Śāstra Literature; Sūtra Literature.

BIBLIOGRAPHY

Coedès, George. *The Indianized States of Southeast Asia.* Translated by Susan Brown Cowing and edited by Walter F. Vella. Canberra, Australia, 1968. On the career of Indian law in Southeast Asia.

Derrett, J. D. M. *Religion, Law and the State in India.* New York, 1968. Discusses the influence of *dharma* literature on modern Hindu law.

Direck Jayanama. *The Evolution of Thai Laws.* Bonn, West Germany, 1964. Discusses how *Manusm ti* and other texts contributed to the formation of the Thai legal tradition.

Gharpure, Jangannatha Raghunatha. "*Yājñavalkya smṛti,* or the *Institutes of Yājñavalkya,* Together with the Commentary Called the *Mītākṣara* by Sri Vijñāneśvara, Book the Second: And English Translation." In *Collections of Hindu Law Texts,* vol. 2., Bombay, 1914.

Hooker, M. B. *A Concise Legal History of South-East Asia.* Oxford, 1978.

Jolly, Julius. *Hindu Law and Custom.* Translated by Batakrishna Ghosh. 1928; reprinted, Varanasi, India, 1975.

Kane, P. V. *History of Dharmaśāstra.* 2d ed., 5 vols. Poona, India, 1968–1975. The most encyclopedic treatment of the topic.

Kangle, R. P. *The Kauṭilīya Arthaśāstra.* Part 2, Translation. Bombay, 1972.

Lariviere, Richard W. *The Divyatattva of Raghunandana Bhaṭṭācārya: Ordeals in Classical Hindu Law.* New Delhi, 1981. The most comprehensive treatment of the subject of ordeal in Hindu law.

Lariviere, Richard W. "*Dharmaśāstra,* 'Rea' Law and 'Apocryphal *Smṛtis.*'" In *Law, State, and Administration in Classical India,* edited by Bernhard Kölver, pp. 97–109. Munich, 1997. A discussion of the status of *dharma* literature as "law."

Lariviere, Richard W. *The Nāradasmṛti: Critical Edition and Translation,* 2d ed. Delhi, 2003. The most thoroughly juridical of all of the classical Indian texts.

Lingat, Robert. *The Classical Law of India.* Translated by J. D. M. Derrett. Berkeley, Calif., 1973. A superb, concise overview of the entire topic of classical Hindu law.

Menski, Werner F., *Hindu Law: Beyond Tradition and Modernity.* New Delhi, 2003. An attempt to discuss the topic of Hindu law in terms of post-modern analysis.

Olivelle, Patrick. *Dharmasūtras: The Law Codes of Āpastamba, Gautama, Baudhāyana, and Vasiṣṭha.* Delhi, 2003. The best translations of these very early texts.

Olivelle, Patrick. *The Law Code of Manu.* Oxford, 2004. A landmark translation of the most important of all of the traditional legal texts.

Rocher, Ludo. "Hindu Law and Religion: Where to Draw the Line." In *Malik Ram Felicitation Volume,* edited by S. A. J. Zaidi, pp. 167–194. New Delhi, 1972. A contribution to the discussion of the status of law in the ancient Indian tradition.

Sarkar, Upendra Chandra. *Epochs in Hindu Legal History.* Hoshiarpur, India, 1958.

Sen Gupta, Nares Chandra. *Evolution of Ancient Indian Law.* London, 1953. Important contributions by Indian scholars to the ongoing problem of periodization of the history of the Hindu legal tradition.

RICHARD W. LARIVIERE (2005)

LAW AND RELIGION: LAW AND RELIGION IN BUDDHISM

The study of secular law in Buddhist culture and society is a relatively new and intriguing area of research. This entry will first describe the Buddha's view of society and his legal decision making. Then it will review monastic offenses, punishments, and procedures, followed by a discussion of the first Buddhist king, Aśoka, and the growth and spread of Buddhism. In the final sections, three patterns for transmission of Buddhism will be described, one with a legal system, one without, and one in an area of legal pluralism. Then four other types of religious influence on a legal system will be discussed, foundational concepts; rituals; legal subject matters; and stories, art, and literature. The conclusion will present the current state of the field.

LAW AT THE TIME OF THE BUDDHA. Distinctions in modern academic discourse among politics, religion, law, and morality would have been incomprehensible in the intellectual culture of Brahmanic India of the fifth century BCE. When Siddhārtha Gautama first sat under the pipal tree, law and justice were connected to the idea of *dharma,* the proper and natural development of the social and universal orders through morality and religious teaching. Given these interconnections, there is still little doubt that Siddhārtha Gautama was concerned with legal matters as we now define them. He was born heir apparent to the throne of the regional kingdom of Śākya in a time when princes were trained extensively in the Sanskrit *smṛti* legal literature, especially the *Dharmaśāstras* and the *Dharmasūtras.* He was taught the ritual and legal roles of a king who stood as the ultimate authority for maintaining the peaceful relations of his subjects. His turn away from his family obligations, from the opportunity to be king, and more specifically, from the administration of legal power was a personal renunciation but not an indicator of either a lack of interest in or a rejection of the importance of rules of conduct and social order.

BUDDHA'S VIEW OF SOCIETY. The enlightened Buddha conceived of society as having two parts—a monastic *saṅgha* seeking enlightenment through his teachings and a supportive patron laity that donated to the *saṅgha* to make merit. He began immediately to teach, collect disciples, and form the new monks into a social order by expounding the rules and requirements of the group. These rules were later collected and written down as the Vinaya Piṭaka. As a central Buddhist teaching and one third of the *Tripiṭaka,* the Vinaya provides us with the clearest information about the Buddha's prescriptions as to the required behavior for ordained monastic practitioners.

DECISION MAKING BY THE BUDDHA. The *Suttavibhaṅga* section of the Vinaya is a series of encounters between the

Buddha and a monk defendant. In a standardized narrative sequence, a monk accuser approaches the Buddha and presents the infraction; then, the Buddha asks questions of the perpetrator to determine his state of mind and knowledge of the event. Finally, he makes a casuistic determination about the propriety of the act, often berating the defendant repeatedly, and announces the punishment that should follow as well as possible mitigating factors. Through a case-by-case process of institutional definition, the Buddha built a legal outline of the proper behaviors, speech, clothing, and rituals of the *saṅgha.*

MONASTIC OFFENSES, PUNISHMENTS, AND PROCEDURES. The *Prātimokṣa,* or precepts, is a list of offenses in the Vinaya numbering from 218 to 263 for males and more for females. They range from the most serious—a violation of celibacy, theft, and intentional murder—to the least significant, concerning attire and walking style. To inculcate the rules of the social order, all Buddhist *saṅghas* chant the *Prātimokṣa* twice a month. Each of these offences is matched with a category of punishment, from permanent dismissal, called "defeat," to a combination of formal hearing in front of the *saṅgha,* probation, forfeiture, expiation, and acknowledgment. Suspension and formal reprimand were also possible.

The *Prātimokṣa* also contains a list of the procedures for resolving legal disputes within the monastery itself. It outlines types of verdicts that are possible, the definition of innocence, seven ways to settle a case, the definition of a majority verdict, insanity pleas, and levels of culpability. The *Khandhaka* section of the Vinaya provides the working structure of the monastery, the rules by which the community is organized. It regulates the wearing and sewing of robes, types of food, drink, medicine, and times of eating and sleeping. Each monastery could also develop its own separate constitution. The Buddha determined that after his death, legal decisions were to be made by a quorum of monks reaching a consensus, each monk having an equal vote. The resultant decisions of the *saṅgha,* called announcements of action, could concern any aspect of monastic life, including ordination, debate, ceremonies, and discipline. The rules of the Vinaya are similar in content and form throughout the Buddhist monastic world.

THE ROLE OF MONASTERIES IN THE COMMUNITY. Until more recent times with the advent of state-supported schools and bureaucratic offices, Buddhist monasteries were often the local repositories for documents, artistic training, and medicine, as well as centers for education in writing and reading. In some societies but not all, Buddhist monks are tightly embedded in their communities as the ritual specialists. They provide ceremonies for the laity for house openings, new businesses, births, dangerous periods, exorcisms, illness, and death, all functions currently legally regulated by modern states through certification, licensing, business contracts, and social work. In pre-1960 Tibet monks were also often the literate legal specialists, maintaining legal records, drafting documents, presenting and arguing cases, and fashioning legal settlements for both monastic and lay parties.

THE LAITY. The lay patrons of the *saṅgha,* who ranged in status from the lowest outcaste to local kings such as King Bimbisāra of Māgadha and King Prasenajit of Kośala were expected to adopt their own set of vows. As patrons, they were charged by the Buddha with providing the necessities of food, clothing, and shelter in the form of *vihāra,* resting lodges and *ārāma,* residences for the monks. These patrons also requested teachings from the Buddha on religious, political, and legal matters. To King Prasenajit, inclined to the pleasures of wealth, the Buddha lectured about subduing sense pleasures, living righteously, and the inevitability of impermanence. In legal matters, the Buddha advised him to not elevate himself above others, to exercise judicious reason, and to always observe the traditional rules of royal conduct. In the last days of the Buddha's life, King Ajātaśatru, the son of King Bimbisāra, sent his minister to inquire whether an attack against an enemy would be successful. The Buddha responded with a discourse on the seven conditions necessary for a just and prosperous state.

THE MODEL OF A BUDDHIST KING. The *Sutta Piṭaka* section of the Buddhist canon contains discourses of the Buddha on kingship that praise the election of leaders who then rule through compassion, morality, and social justice. The first exemplar of a Buddhist king, King Aśoka (third century BCE) of the Māgadhan Empire, came to power a hundred years after the Buddha's death. While uniting much of the South Asian continent, Aśoka experienced a particularly bloody victory and converted to Buddhism. He placed stellae as a confirmation of his faith at every outpost of his realm that described the importance of the Buddhist principles of noninjury, truthfulness, gentleness and generosity. King Aśoka made the welfare of his subjects the primary objective of his government and sent out officials to build way stations for travelers, dig wells, provide medicine, and care for orphans, the sick, and the elderly. Abolishing torture and the death penalty, he sought equal legal treatment of criminal infractions throughout the empire. His reign remains the best example of a government committed to putting Buddhist principles into practice.

GROWTH AND DIFFUSION OF BUDDHISM. From the huge monasteries of classical India, the teachings of the Buddha moved out with great rapidity for over fifteen hundred years until the destruction of Nālandā University in 1198 and then the influx of Muslims three hundred years later. As early as 250 BCE, Aśoka's own son, the monk Mahinda, took the Buddhist *dharma* in the form of the Pali Theravādan canon to Sri Lanka. With translation of these texts into the local Sinhala dialect, an ideology that fused race, religion, and region, was adopted and continued by successive Buddhist states. Today, Buddhism remains the major religion of the island.

Historical transmission of Buddhism with law. Sri Lanka is an example, along with states such as Tibet, Burma, and Thailand, of areas that received Buddhist teachings from another country at the same time that they unified and developed advanced legal and administrative procedures. This is the first type of historical transmission of law that occurs in a Buddhist context. From this acculturation process evolved jurisprudential cultures, legal processes, rituals, and law codes that were heavily inspired by Buddhism. Recalling the reign of King Aśoka, the idea of the compassionate *chakravartin*, or wheel-turning king, often became the model for the ruler in these states.

The first king to unify Burma was King Anawrata of Bamar, who created a Buddhist capital at Pagan in 1057 CE. This Pali Buddhist king worked with monks to create the *dhammasat* and *rajasat* secular law codes based on Buddhist treatises, Hindu law, and the Sinhalese version of the Vinaya. In the following centuries, these law codes spread across what are now Burma, Thailand, Cambodia, and Laos, adapting to the local areas, languages, and spirit cults. In succeeding dynasties, especially under the Konbaung Empire (1752–1885), Burmese Buddhism moved down into the village level, with local monasteries taking over the functions of educating the youth, providing a standardized Buddhist ethical code, and unifying the country culturally and legally.

Transmission of Buddhism to a developed state. A second type of Buddhist transmission occurred when the religion entered a state that already had an advanced literate tradition, including a legal and political administrative apparatus. China is perhaps the best example of this second type. Traveling along the Silk Route, merchants brought Buddhism into several Central Asian kingdoms, but when it reached the area of what is now known as China around 50 CE, it encountered resistance in the form of an in-place legal system already strongly based in Daoism and Confucianism, with its ties to family and a prescribed set of harmonious social relations.

While Buddhism had a strong influence on Chinese ethics, art, architecture, and literature, some scholars have argued that it did not have a strong legal impact on the various Chinese Buddhist states from the Han (206 BCE–220 CE) through the Tang (618–907) into the Song (960–1279) dynasties, or even in the brief revival of Buddhism under the Mongolian Yuan dynasty (1215–1368). Instead, they describe a legal administration controlled largely by Confucian-trained officials, with Buddhist monasteries vying for local political power and popular support. While this is an enormous simplification of a very long period of complex history, it is a thesis that is worth investigating as Buddhist legal research continues. In the Tang period, for example, a time of flourishing Buddhism, the great Law Code (*Ku T'ang-lu shu-yi*) was concerned in its four main divisions—the code, the statutes, the regulations, and the ordinances—with the prevention, apprehension, and punishment of crime and with commercial law from a Confucian point of view. Scholars also report the use of the legal system to persecute and harass Buddhist monasteries at various points in Chinese history.

The record of the outer-lying kingdoms is mixed. The Tanguts of the Xixia dynasty (1038–1223), located in the current Chinese provinces of Gansu and Ningxia, produced law codes strongly influenced by Buddhism. However, the Vietnamese law codes derived from Chinese states such as the Lê code is described by its translators as having a Confucian core. The situation in Korea and Japan is similarly problematic. King Sosurim of the north state of Koguryŏ officially introduced Buddhism into what is now called Korea in 372 BCE and at the same time established a school for Confucian learning. The legal codes and centralized administrative system that he promulgated during his reign are arguably not heavily influenced by Buddhism. Similarly, although Prince Shōtoku promoted Buddhism as the state religion of Japan at the end of the sixth century CE, scholars have argued that the Confucian tradition has always accompanied and superceded Buddhism's effect on the Japanese legal system and law codes. As more research is done on the relationship between law and Buddhism in these cultures, new information and perspectives will emerge.

Buddhism in legal pluralism. A third category of the relationship between Buddhism and law is legal pluralism. Many modern states such as Sri Lanka, Vietnam, Laos, and Mongolia have layers of colonialism, fragmentation, ethnic struggles, and global influence that have resulted in particularized legal pluralisms. Sri Lanka, an original Buddhist legal state, has overlays of Kandyan law, Catholic Portuguese influence (c.1505–1658), Calvinist Dutch law in certain regions (c. 1658–1796), and a period of English colonial rule from 1795 until independence in 1948. With ethnic struggles between Buddhists, Hindus, and Muslims, the recognition of the fishing laws of the Mukkuvar people and the Tesavalami legal code of the Tamil people of the Jatna region, legal pluralism defines modern Sri Lanka. This complex interplay of legal forces has resonance in modern-day Vietnam as well, with several forms of Theravādan Buddhism overlaid by Chinese Mahāyāna Buddhism and Confucian legal codes from an invasion in the fifteenth century. Spanish Catholicism in the sixteenth century was followed by French colonists, the rise of the Viet Minh, and occupation by the United States in the 1950s and 1960s.

A TYPOLOGY OF NONSTATE BUDDHIST INFLUENCES ON A LEGAL SYSTEM. Interactions between Buddhism and law also occur when (1) basic Buddhist principles and reasoning processes, (2) Buddhist practices, rituals, and procedures, and (3) Buddhist ideas about legal subject matters such as murder, theft, inheritance, and land tenure are employed by the population when using the legal system. Finally, (4) Buddhist ideas can be captured in literature such as the *jātaka* tales of the former lives of the Buddha, in puppet plays, art, or numerous other aspects of culture and then influence the way in which a legal system operates.

Foundational concepts. First, legal systems are strongly influenced by the foundational ideas that their participants employ, such as the concepts of causation, intention, cosmology, conflict, notions of the community, *karma*, compassion, identity and subjectivity, status, jurisdiction, sanctuary, shame, apology, and evil. For example, in Buddhism the Christian theological problem of evil does not exist. Instead, an illegal, evil, or immoral act committed by a human being is the result of either received *karma* from a previous life or an intentional choice made during this lifetime. Illegal acts are an inevitable part of the human state of *saṃsāra* that is defined by *duḥkha*, suffering due to human hatred, greed, and delusion. These three elements of suffering are the root cause of all antisocial acts by individuals. Given that individuals who do not follow the *dharma* are ignorant of the perpetual cycle of *saṃsāra*, open conflict in the form of lawsuits and altercations are to be expected. Even legal categories such as lying and theft exist only as a result of human greed and pride. Thus, legal controversies in most Buddhist societies indicate a lack of knowledge and understanding of the *dharma*.

Karma is another Buddhist concept that can influence legal proceedings. The reason for an illegal occurrence in this lifetime could be found in one of several previous lives or in this life; the punishment of an illegal act in this life could occur in this life or in a future life. Studies of the use of *karma* as a rationale for not pursuing an injury case in a modern Thai city have demonstrated this. One scholar has found that individuals who do not sue commonly state that their current injury is the karmic result of their own previous, perhaps unintended, negative acts. Strikingly, injury suits are decreasing in this city and karmic rationales are being used more frequently with the increase in globalism.

Legal practices and rituals. In pre-1960 Tibet, monastic ritual debate techniques were one of the foundations of legal argumentation. Specialists in monastic legal decision making were often appointed to represent a monastery in a secular civil suit. Also, ritual ceremonies of catharsis and apology often follow lawsuits in Tibet, Japan, and Burma. This is a rich area for further investigation.

Legal subject matters. Third, ideas about the nature of theft and the factors that should be considered in assessing a case of theft in the Tibetan law codes were closely tied both to the customary rules of the plateau and to the discussion of theft in the Vinaya. Criminal cases were assessed by the four factors of Nāgārjuna, a great Indian Buddhist scholar of the second century, who looked to the object of the action, the motivation of the actor, the action itself, and the completion of the act. These four factors were written into the Law Codes of the Dalai Lamas. By several reports, these ideas of how to factor a case of theft were employed by the Tibetan population in their legal decision making even after the Chinese takeover in 1960; here, litigants are applying Buddhist factoring concepts in a new non-Buddhist, colonial court.

Narratives and art. Fourth, the story of the personal enlightenment of the Buddha was cited in Tibetan courts for the importance of fashioning punishments that would uniquely fit a defendant and improve his *karma*. As the Buddha taught that each individual was an impermanent collection of ever changing physical and mental states, conditioning the person's mind to a tranquil life and the *dharma* was often seen as the best form of punishment. Also, legal oaths were taken in front of artistic renderings of the Dalai Lama or the Buddha.

CONCLUSION. The study of secular law in Buddhist culture and society is a relatively new area that requires a multidisciplinary approach including comparative law, Buddhist studies, anthropology, history, religious studies, sociology, and sociolegal studies. There is little doubt that Buddhism has strongly influenced and been strongly influenced by legal culture in vast parts of Asia. The role of communism, for example, in extinguishing Buddhist practices has not even been touched in this review. Other categories that need to be more fully investigated are Buddhist law and women, violence and Buddhism, uprisings based on Buddhism, monastic martial arts training, messianic movements, and animist spirit traditions. While a few in-depth projects have been completed, it is an open and exciting field ready for detailed research, both historical and current, and more textual translations, comparisons, and theorizing.

SEE ALSO Buddhist Books and Texts, article on Canon and Canonization—Vinaya.

BIBLIOGRAPHY

Bodiford, William. *Soto Zen in Medieval Japan.* Honolulu, 1993.

Brook, Timothy. "Patronage and the County Magistrate: Dangyang County Hubei." In *Praying for Power: Buddhism and the Formation of Gentry Society in Late-Ming China.* Cambridge, Mass., 1993.

Ch'en, Paul Heng-chao. *Chinese Legal Tradition under the Mongols: The Code of 1291 as Reconstructed.* Princeton, N.J., 1979.

Dunnell, Ruth W. *The Great State of White and High: Buddhism and State Formation in the Eleventh Century Xia.* Honolulu, 1996.

Dutt, S. *Buddhist Monks and Monasteries of India.* London, 1962.

Engel, David. *Code and Custom in a Thai Provincial Court: The Interaction of Formal and Informal Systems of Justice.* Monographs for the Association of Asian Studies. Tucson, Ariz., 1978.

French, Rebecca R. "The Cosmology of Law in Buddhist Tibet." *Journal of the International Association of Buddhist Studies* 18, no. 1 (1994): 4.

French, Rebecca R. *The Golden Yoke: The Legal Cosmology of Buddhist Tibet.* Ithaca, N.Y., 1995.

Gombrich, Richard. "Buddhist Karma and Social Control." *Comparative Studies in Society and History* 17, no. 2 (1975): 212–220.

Gunawardena, R. A. L. H. "The People of the Lion: Sinhala Consciousness in History and Historiography." In *Ethnicity and Social Change in Sri Lanka,* ed. Colombo: Social Scientists Association, pp. 55–107. Dehiwala, Sri Lanka, 1985.

Hinuber, Oskar von. "Buddhist Law According to the Theravada Vinaya: A Survey of Theory and Practice." *Journal of the International Association of Buddhist Studies* 18, no. 1 (1995): 7–45

Horner, Isaline B., trans. *The Book of Discipline*. London, 1938–1966.

Horner, Isaline B. *Women under Primitive Buddhism*. London, 1930. Reprinted Delhi, 1975.

Huxley, Andrew. "The Reception of Buddhist Law in Southeast Asia, 200 BCE–1860 CE." *La réception des systèmes juridiques: implantation et destin*, ed. Michel Douchet and Jacques Vanderlinden, pp. 139-237. Brussels, Belgium, 1994.

Johnson, Wallace. *The T'ang Code*. Princeton, N.J., 1979.

Ketelaar, James. *Of Heretics and Martyrs in Meiji Japan: Buddhism and Its Persecutions*. Princeton, N.J., 1990.

Lingat, Robert. *The Classical Law of India*. Translated by J. Duncan Derrett. Berkeley, Calif., 1973.

McKnight, Brian, and James T. C. Liu. *The Enlightened Judgments: Ch'ing-Ming Chi, the Sung Dynasty Collection*. Albany, N.Y., 1999.

Nikam, N. A., and Richard McKeon, trans. *The Edicts of Asoka*. Chicago, 1959.

Nguyen, Ngoc Huy. *The Lê Code: Law in Traditional Vietnam*. Athens, Ohio, 1987.

Prebish, Charles S. *Buddhist Monastic Discipline: The Sanskrit Prātimokṣa Sūtras*. University Park, Pa., and London, 1975.

Reynolds, Frank E. "Dhamma in Dispute: The Interactions of Religion and Law in Thailand." *Law and Society Review* 28 (1994): 433.

Rhys-Davids, T. W., and C. A. F. Rhys-Davids, trans. *The Dialogues of the Buddha (Dīgha Nikāya)*. 3 vols. London, 1899–1921.

Schopen, Gregory. *Bones, Stones and Buddhist Monks: Collected Papers on the Archaeology, Epigraphy and Texts of Monastic Buddhism in India*. Honolulu, 1997.

REBECCA R. FRENCH (2005)

LAW AND RELIGION: LAW AND RELIGION IN CHINESE RELIGIONS

Over the past three thousand years, religion and law in China have been contemporaneous forms of social control. Many of the multiple forms of dynamics between the two have centuries-old roots.

INTRODUCTION. Any thorough discussion of law and religion in China that attempted to cover a three thousand year time span would require multiple volumes. Even then, source limitations engender further obstacles to comprehensiveness. For instance, for one period there may be complete legal codes, whereas for another only ritualistic records of legal events might remain. Some evidence comes from government sources, others are products of popular religion. Cultural spheres may also affect practice and belief. Nonetheless, certain recurrent and often overlapping patterns are detectable in the relationships between law and religion in China. For instance, there is the relationship between law and the spirit realm, where religious authority often enhances legal authority, or, may serve as a deterrent to illegal behavior. Then there is law as regulator of religious bodies, often as protection for the state against the potential challenge of religious authority and popular superstition. There is also the situation wherein law helps to enforce the implementation of religious practices and ritual protocol. Conversely, religion may relate to law inasmuch as it may help to further politico-legal aims. Other associations between law and religion, in a more broad sense, would be law as an embodiment of custom; ritual prescriptions and proscriptions as para-legal behavior; and law modeled on and implemented in harmony with the cosmos.

"Religion" in China encompasses what in the Judeo-Christian tradition might be considered secular behavior. While Buddhism, Daoism, Christianity, Islam, Judaism, Manichaeism, and Zoroastrianism are all woven to varying degrees into the fabric of Chinese history, the most pervasive features of Chinese culture continue to be its patriarchal social order and its *li*, which can be defined as "ritual, rites, decorum." *Li* encompasses a range of behavior, including the correct performance of religious ritual; religious and secular ceremonial behavior and institutions that enable a harmonious, usually Confucian society; and socially correct deportment, especially the observance of obligations between superior and inferior. Many manifestations of *li* have some religious and certainly spiritual dimensions to them. The patriarchal order (itself supported by ritual texts and behavior) was at the core of ancestor worship, which, at times, was intimately connected to notions of legal authority, punishment, and criminality.

Li worked sometimes in concert with and sometimes separately from law to form the framework for social control. As a check on improper behavior (which is often but not always simultaneously illegal behavior), *li* served as an ever-present, sometimes quasi-legal, sometimes para-legal force. And even though a fundamental tenet of Confucian ideology presumed a dichotomy between *li* and law (*fa*), still, *li* broadly defined sometimes provided validation for legal proceedings. At other times, *li* was itself protected by the law.

At the same time that the referent to "religion" in this entry necessarily changes according to the materials available for study, so does that of "law." Law was often inseparable from the ruling political authority, which thus also served as the legislative authority, law enforcer, and/or lawgiver. In this entry, reference is made to a wide range of legal behavior, documents, and legislation.

CATEGORIES OF RELATIONSHIPS BETWEEN LAW AND RELIGION. The following proposed categories of relationship are explored here as a means to present in a manageable way an overwhelming amount of information about a highly intricate web of relationships between law and religion.

Law and the spirit realm. In the early historical period in China, the division between religion on the one hand, and politics and law on the other was blurred. The first potentially legal information dates to approximately 1200 BCE and comes to us from the oracle-bone inscriptions of the late Shang state (c. 1200–1050 BCE). These were divinations to the king's deceased ancestors conducted by the king and his diviners, the contents and sometimes the results of which were later inscribed on turtle plastrons or cattle scapulae. It was thought that the ancestors not only could communicate with the God on High, but also that they were among the significant otherwordly powers that could influence earthly happenings and guide the king in his decision-making. These politico-religious writings are the only extant documents of significant length from the Shang period, but they were certainly not the only ones to have existed. Legal documents probably would have been part of an estimated vast administrative corpus, and these likely would have served as the primary documents recording legal activity and rules. Thus, while a mere handful of the approximately 200,000 known oracle-bone inscriptions seek advice from the spirit world on implementing punishments or on conducting legal matters—and such an interpretation of those inscriptions is not definitive—they cannot necessarily be considered representative of all the legal activity occurring during the late Shang. At the same time, we cannot ignore the implications of this sacred form of ancestral communication on the validation of politico-legal behavior.

The Shang were overthrown by the Zhou around 1150 BCE, an event recorded in many historical texts, some of which are closely contemporary to the actual conquest. Much of the language in these documents couches the Shang downfall and subsequent Zhou conquest in legalistic terms. The fall of the Shang was viewed as a result of moral decline and criminality on the part of the last Shang king, while the conquest by the Zhou was the punishment for such behavior. In order to legitimate control over the subjugated Shang people, the Zhou utilized a rhetorical device, "the Mandate of Heaven" (*tian ming*). It was not that the Zhou invaded and overthrew the Shang, but rather Heaven (*tian*), acting much like judge and jury, decreed that the privilege to rule be stripped from the Shang and transferred to the Zhou. Although the Shang did not share with the Zhou the belief in Heaven as the most potent deity, the Zhou's reliance on this rhetorical religious device must have bolstered their claim to power.

Dating to the Western Zhou dynasty (1050–770 BCE) are a couple dozen ritual bronze vessels inscribed with legalistic contents: appointments to positions entailing legal duties, records of court cases, land transfers, contractual agreements, and private sales transactions. Again, these inscriptions not only comprise a miniscule fraction of all inscribed ritual vessels, they also would not have been the primary vehicle for recording legal matters. Bronze inscriptions tended to be records of noteworthy events that were transmitted to deceased ancestors of the vessel owner through their ritual cooking and feasting using the vessel on which the inscription was cast. Of interest here is the use of religious rhetoric in legal contexts. While Western Zhou legal proceedings were conducted with a high degree of rationality and secularity, the inclusion of religious rhetoric in legal activities may have enabled the legal process and legal decisions to invoke age-old religious authority to lend validity to earthly proceedings and humanly determined verdicts. The ritually enacted transmission of legal decisions to the ancestors also would have authorized the proceedings and their outcomes.

Oaths containing self-imprecations are found in both legal and religious contexts. Those sworn by losing litigants paralleled the syntactical structure of later pledge and loyalty texts from the early fifth century BCE state of Jin, which were spirit-sanctioned contracts between individuals of a common lineage. These covenant texts, inscribed on jade and stone tablets and later buried in pits containing animal sacrifices, were appeals to the ancestral spirits of Jin's deceased rulers to help the covenantor serve the covenant lord and protect the Jin state. They called down punishment from the ancestral spirit world upon the covenantor and his lineage should he breach the stipulations he swore to uphold, thus functioning as a means of spirit-sanctioned deterrence and para-legal enforcement.

Connections between the spirit world and earthly affairs are evidenced in some excavated sources dating to the Warring States period (from the mid-fifth century to 221 BCE). In an inscription on a jade tablet from the state of Qin, the owner, in order to petition the spirit of Hua Mountain to cure his disease, first stipulates that he is "without guilt." Almanacs from throughout the Eastern Zhou period also testify to the belief that events could be determined by unearthly powers through divination. Many of the entries in these texts indicate that a robber may be caught on a particular day, or that a crime will occur. Some even provide partial names of robbers, and/or descriptions of their personalities and physical features.

Chinese folk religion which developed from at least the Han period (206 BCE–220 CE), and especially folk Buddhism of the sixth through ninth centuries CE, gradually incorporated supernatural laws and elaborate spirit worlds that were expected to be morally superior to the earthly realm. They contained references to multiple hells for earthly offenses. These were populated by lawyers and judges, and trials were conducted therein. Certain hells existed to mete out additional punishment on criminals who had already been executed on earth for their crimes. The deep-rooted nature of such popular beliefs necessarily bolstered earthly propensities to obey the law.

The interplay between the two spheres of law and religion was most marked with the notion that the head of state was often simultaneously the supreme religious authority. A person's ancestors were powerful in their own family's lives, but those of a ruling lineage could affect the entire state. This is especially evident when the two authorities came together in the person of the one true king or emperor—titled "The Son of Heaven" (*tian zi*)—who, theoretically if not in practice, usually also stood at the apex of the legal bureaucracy.

Moral rectitude, and correct performance of state-level secular and religious rituals were among the factors validating the emperor's right to rule as well as the decisions (legal and otherwise) that he made. Such was the case, for example, of the *feng* and *shan* sacrifices dedicated to Heaven and Earth, or the fasting rituals of absolution performed by the Qing (1644–1911) emperors at the Temple of Heaven.

Law as regulator of religious authority and enforcer of ritual. China's ruling powers periodically have had to grapple with how to protect themselves from the omnipresent threat of insurgence from religious groups, primarily unofficial ones, as well as how to keep in check the authority of formal and widely practiced religions. The earliest extant, complete legal code which was generated by a central government dates to the Tang dynasty (618–907). The Tang Code evinces what was a lasting practice of close supervision by and even interference from the central government in religious affairs. The 737 revision of the imperial code stipulated legal provisions governing religious activity, a practice that continues to this day under the constitution. The banning of heterodox (i.e., not government-approved) practices, such as witchcraft, fortune-telling, prophecies, treating disease by exorcism, and supplications for offspring was common, especially when such practices had political implications. Examples can be found in Articles 161, 162, and 165 of the Great Qing Code, and in the 1999 Decision of the Standing Committee of the National People's Congress. Article 36 of the 1982 constitution has similar implications.

Since the Six Dynasties period, the clergy also were subject to varying forms of bureaucratic control. They enjoyed certain privileges, such as exemption from land tax on their monasteries and temples, and reprieves from corvée labor (state-mandated) and military conscription. Thus, religious clergy and institutions came to be considered by many to be societal parasites. Buddhism presented a further problem. Upon ordination, its monks and nuns were required to sever all ties and obligations with their families, society, and the state, and instead to operate under Buddhism's own hierarchy and system of property ownership. Such autonomy was antagonistic to a culture based in large part upon a complex formula of social and familial relationships and obligations. Legislation specifically aimed at the clergy is found in the Tang, Song (960–1279), Ming (1368–1644), and Qing codes. For example, the Tang and Song codes incorporate statutes governing property ownership by religious clergy, as well as the relations between the clergy and the state. Similarly, Article 176 of the Great Qing Code stipulates that Buddhist and Daoist clergy must observe proper Confucian ritual observances for their parents and sacrifices to their ancestors. This can be seen as a means to keep religious orders under the control of the greater political order, and of protecting the patriarchal Confucian social order.

Weakening of religious authority is seen in other ways, too. According to the reconstructed Yuan Code of 1291, special jurisdiction was granted to Buddhist and Daoist clergy. Minor offenses by a clergy member fell within the jurisdiction of the temple, while serious offenses (such as sexual assault, homicide, robbery) were to be tried in a court of law. During the Song (960–1279), the government repeatedly tried to prohibit Manichaeism, whose adherents were often rebelling against the state. By separating its leaders from their followers, and by regulating their gatherings, the state succeeded in slowly diffusing Manichaeism's threat to the central government. (This practice has been employed repeatedly throughout China's history, more recently with the exile of Tibetan Buddhism's spiritual leader, the Dalai Lama.) State intervention in religion is also evident in the conferring of living buddhas. During the Ming dynasty, the state assumed legal jurisdiction over the identification of the reincarnation of living buddhas and the approval of their enthronement. This was done in accordance with established religious rituals and historical conventions of Tibetan Buddhism. This practice was followed by the Qing, and is still upheld today under the jurisdiction of the State Council's Bureau of Religious Affairs.

The regulation by law of religious acts also had another dimension. At times throughout China's history it would seem that the social force behind ritual observances was not always sufficient. In the Tang and later codes, articles were included which enforced certain ritual activities. The Ming and Qing codes include entire sections concerning the Board of Rites (*li bu*). The Tang Code also contains articles which essayed to enforce officials to properly conduct their duties regarding the imperial sacrifices; to ensure the practice of the purification ritual according to the ritual schedule; to protect sacrificial objects and structures; to punish non-observance of rules of proper ceremony (*li*) and demeanor (*yi*); to enforce proper mourning for parents and husbands, proper care for ill or critically disabled parents, and proper burial etiquette; and to uphold ritually correct village wine-drinking activities. All of these behaviors are among those that were generally dictated by *li*.

The Tang, Song, and Qing codes also invoked ritual texts of previous periods to support laws regulating extra-religious activities. For instance, Song legal conservatives appealed to Warring States ritual texts as support for reduction of penalties. The Great Qing Code also incorporated many stipulations from earlier ritual texts, especially the *Zhou li* (Rituals of Zhou), as well as some general ritual observances. Certain legal organs protected the presumed chastity of women of a particular social standing by requiring a male relative to appear in court in her stead. And while the state did not sanction the long-standing custom of vendetta, the Tang and Song codes, following the example of preceding dynasties, did grant some leniency for sons or grandsons who attempted to avenge the murder of their elders. Under the Song, even more lenient treatment than that prescribed by law was sometimes granted.

Religion and law in Communist China. The relationship between religion and law in Communist China (1949 to the present) is a complex one, and incorporates historical antecedents like those discussed above. With the exception of the Cultural Revolution (1966–1976), when all religious activity was banned, religious freedom is protected under the Chinese Constitution as well as under the criminal, civil, electoral, military, and compulsory education laws. The central government instated departments of religious affairs to ensure that this freedom is honored. Additionally, Article 36 of the constitution grants equal rights and protection from discrimination to citizens practicing "normal religion," that is, those five religions recognized by the state (Buddhism, Daoism, Catholicism, Christianity/Protestantism, and Islam). Parties, including state officials, who harm the religious feelings or freedom of an individual or group are to be dealt with according to the law, although this is not always carried out.

Government-recognized religious organizations receive financial assistance from central and local governments for repairs to churches, mosques, temples, and monasteries, as well as tax exemptions for land and buildings used for religious purposes. The Chinese government also offers services for Chinese Muslims who wish to make the pilgrimage to Mecca, and financial support for the printing of religious scriptures.

On the surface it appears that legal institutions protect religious freedom. However, this protection is not without qualification. Religious freedom is subordinate to China's political aims. For example, one of the tenets underpinning Communist Party rule is the building of "spiritual civilization," specifically, "socialist spiritual civilization," a role that the state itself strives to monopolize rather than leave to independent religious organizations. The ultimate goal of the party is to make religion obsolete in China. However, current trends in various localities, wherein the prestige of and interest in joining the Communist Party is waning as that of religion is on the rise, suggest that the people prefer religious organizations in the role of spiritual leaders. China's constitution is written in such a way as to permit the state broad control over religious freedom as a means of ensuring the state's "supremacy," and of stemming the tide of any movements that are potentially harmful to the state. It stipulates that no individual may use religious beliefs or activities to undermine the government. This includes disrupting public order, interfering with the state educational system, or harming another citizen. Local and central governments also grant or deny permission for the restoration and opening of places of worship. Most importantly, only religions that are formally recognized by the state may exist, and these must be law-abiding and patriotic by supporting the Communist leadership and socialist system. Furthermore, their leadership structures must be identifiable, possibly so that they may be more easily controlled by the state. Government suspicion of religions or cultic movements has ample historical precedent. The Five Pecks of Rice Rebellion of 184, and the Yellow Turban Rebellion of 190, are among the earlier examples in a long line of religiously inspired uprisings that sought to challenge State authority. The government's repeated suppression and regulation of Muslim religious activities in Xinjiang are considered by the state to be legal because they are linked to separatist activities. Similar concerns influence government control of Buddhism in Tibet. The recent crackdown on Falun Gong practitioners may, perhaps, also be viewed in this light.

Religion's subordination to China's political agenda is seen in other ways as well. For example, the Vatican is considered first and foremost to be a political entity, and religious interaction with it will only be permitted once it supports China's "one-country policy" by severing relations with Taiwan. China's religious bodies must also be self-governing and independent of foreign control, although it does permit interaction between Chinese and foreign religious bodies when the latter recognizes the former as their equals. Where Catholicism is concerned, this effectively prevents relations between the Vatican and the Chinese Catholic Church, as the state's policy requires that its bishops be consecrated by the Chinese church. Furthermore, each of the five recognized religions is monitored by a "patriotic association" (which, among other things, approves religious leaders for applicant congregations), and they, in turn, are responsible to the state's Bureau of Religious Affairs. All religious activity and fixed places of worship which are not registered with the appropriate patriotic association are considered illegal. Additionally, Communist Party members are prohibited from practicing even state-recognized religions.

CONCLUSION. The preceding discussion and sample evidence serve as a springboard for further investigation into the complex relationship between law and religion from the late second millennium BCE. At times symbiotic, at times antagonistic, law and religion have been two indispensable elements of social control in China. While the specific dynamics of their relationship have varied according to historical and social circumstances, many have endured for centuries, if not millennia.

SEE ALSO Buddhism; Buddhism, Schools of, article on Chinese Buddhism; Chinese Religion; Confucianism; Dalai Lama; Falun Gong; Tian.

BIBLIOGRAPHY

Balazs, Etienne. *Le traité juridique du "Souei-Chou."* Leiden, 1954.

Ch'en, Paul Hen-chao. *Chinese Legal Tradition under the Mongols: The Code of 1291 as Reconstructed.* Princeton, N.J., 1979.

Ch'ü, T'ing-tsu. *Law and Society in Traditional China.* Paris, 1961.

Eberhard, Wolfram. *Guilt and Sin in Traditional China.* Berkeley, Calif., 1967.

Huang, Philip C. C. *Code, Custom, and Legal Practice: The Qing and the Republic Compared.* Stanford, Calif., 2001.

Johnson, Wallace, trans. *The T'ang Code.* 2 vols. Princeton, N.J., 1979.

Jones, William C., trans. *The Great Qing Code: A New Translation.* With introduction by William C. Jones. Oxford, 1994.

MacCormack, Geoffrey. *The Spirit of Traditional Chinese Law.* Athens, Ga., 1996.

McKnight, Brian E. *Law and Order in Sung China.* Cambridge, U.K., 1992.

Skosey, Laura A. "The Legal System and Legal Tradition of the Western Zhou, c. 1045–771 BCE." Ph.D. diss., University of Chicago, 1996.

Wechsler, Howard. *Offerings of Jade and Silk: Ritual Symbol in the Legitimation of the T'ang Dynasty.* New Haven, Conn., 1985.

Weld, Susan. "The Covenant Texts from Houma and Wenxian." In *New Sources of Early Chinese History: An Introduction to the Reading of Inscriptions and Manuscripts,* edited by Edward L. Shaughnessy, pp. 125–160. Berkeley, Calif., 1997.

Yang, C. K. *Religion in Chinese Society.* Berkeley, Calif., 1961.

LAURA A. SKOSEY (2005)

LAW AND RELIGION: LAW, RELIGION, AND LITERATURE

The critique of "the textual bias" in studies of culture is important, and we ignore the implications at our peril: interpretation never exists independently of social context or setting, especially the institutional. Yet it is inevitably and decisively the case that language and its conventions play a dominant and decisive role in the complexly variegated realms of law and religion, and perhaps most acutely at their myriad intersections. Scholars of religion and scholars of law have each acted explicitly on this recognition, generating the fields of "religion and literature" and "law and literature." This shared "turn to the literary" reflects some common questions and interests. First, and most generally, there is the common recognition that to grasp securely the cultural standing of religion or of law mandates sustained attention to specific forms of expression; and that, in turn, that the relationship is dialogical, so that literature is understood to influence religion and law even as law and religion are understood to influence literature. It also reflects, secondly, a recognition that questions of linguistic construction and deconstruction, of determinate and indeterminate linguistic meaning and the degree to which social context addresses such concerns, is a central question. And, finally, in each instance but with differing degrees of emphasis and controversy, each includes on the part of some an attempt to correct or augment a deficiency in scholarship. The debate about the "turn to the literary" in law and literature is discussed below and is nascent by comparison to the discussions in religion and literature. Readers should consult relevant entries for its history in religion and literature.

That both legal systems and religions arbitrarily deploy language has as its crucial corollary the fact that in doing so they generate and employ literary conventions of both usage and form. The shared concept of "canonical" writings, whether sacred scripture or constitution and statute, extending in turn to commentary and judicial opinion, indexes the deep family resemblances between religion and law. It is the source as well of their common fascination with questions of hermeneutics. Elucidation of the canon is a great religious and a great legal expertise, hallowed alike in courtroom argument and Sabbath sermon, legal brief and scriptural commentary. Canons of sacred scripture include law in both literal and figurative modes: literally, as exemplified in the Jewish Torah by the Decalogue and the related prescriptions in *Leviticus, Numbers,* and *Deuteronomy,* and figurally in the Christian formulation penned by St. Paul in his *Epistle to the Romans*—itself an exegesis of Torah—regarding the spirit and the letter. Legal opinions and briefs deploy a range of narrative techniques to plot the "facts of the case" and thus shape the appropriate purview of juridical deliberation, and the writing of judicial opinions is, among other things, a rhetorical art of interpretation, whether in explication or dissent. The point is not to elide distinctive legal and religious traditions, but to underscore the less frequently noted, yet crucial and foundational, literary and interpretive connections between law and religion.

If law and religion both take innate recourse to literary expression, it is equally the case that works of imaginative literature frequently and vigorously engage religion or the law, or both. It is striking that scholars of law and literature whose work engages in sustained literary interpretation have lavished more attention on the novel. While there are important studies of law and poetry, and especially of law and drama (most notably Sophocles and Shakespeare), the modern novel's susceptibility to plurality in both linguistic expression and social setting, its sheer plasticity, afford it a particular fascination for the innately adversarial processes of argument and evidentiary discussion that characterize most modern legal systems. Standard citations tend to focus on twentieth-century works, and range from Franz Kafka's *The Trial* (1914) and Albert Camus's *The Stranger* (1940) to Truman Capote's self-proclaimed journalistic work of historical fiction, *In Cold Blood* (1965) and William Gaddis's *A Frolic of His Own* (1994). But the range, even limiting the purview to the novel, is extraordinarily wide and diverse. Henry Fielding (1707–1754), both a distinguished jurist and one of the first great English novelists, deployed in the creation of his self-proclaimed "new Species of Writing" the literary forms of sermon and legal brief in the service of cultivating his hallowed virtue of "readerly sagacity." *The History of Tom Jones, A Foundling* (1749), Fielding's greatest novel, displays its author's familiarity with classical legal argument in its sophisticated use of ongoing commentary, intercalary tales, and retrospective viewpoint. The novel constructs a scenario in which the maxim (averred by both the theology and the law of the day) "that Virtue is the certain Road to happiness, and Vice to misery" is brought into severe question but ultimately affirmed.

Also noteworthy for the interactions of law, religion and literature is the corresponding emergence, also as early as Fielding's own time, of the figure of the literary critic who renders learned judgment on literary works toward the formation of an authoritative canon of "the classics." What is perhaps the first major controversy of *belles letters* had to do with the concept of poetic justice, and its appropriate use in drama. Two English "men of letters," Joseph Addison and John Dennis, debated hotly the question of whether the drama ought to reflect the justice of this world or the next, of death or the Final Judgment. Instigated by the production and popularity of Nahum Tate's revised version of William Shakespeare's *King Lear*—in which Tate excised hundreds of lines from the original, and rewrote the ending to transform tragedy into comedy in the name of poetic justice—the Addison/Dennis debate was such that some seventy years later Samuel Johnson was constrained to take up the case in his authoritative *Preface to Shakespeare* (1765). Citing the popularity of Tate's version and his own aversion to the terrors of the original, Johnson effectively "found for" Tate's revision. While Johnson's judgment lacked the binding authority of a judicial ruling, Tate's *King Lear* rather than Shakespeare's was performed on the English stage for the next one hundred and fifty years.

As these brief and necessarily selective examples underscore, the engagement of law and religion in the realm of imaginative literature and literary criticism is manifest. Scholarship, however, has not kept pace with history in this regard. While scholars of religion and of law have in recent decades explored in systematic and parallel ways the relationship of their respective fields to literature and hermeneutics, their common efforts have not intersected. Before sketching these developments and discussing a particularly important and illustrative dispute in the domain of "law and literature," a brief *caveat* may be in order. The point of stressing these parallels is to underscore the prospect of comparative analysis rather than direct analogy. The Jewish tradition of *halakhah,* rabbinic exegesis addressing the proper understanding of (sometimes obscure) scriptural tenet to (sometimes challenged or compromised) religious practice, has no direct analogue in the Christian tradition. Yet both *halakhah* and Martin Luther's commentary on the *Book of Genesis* reflect an ongoing recourse in the Jewish and Christian traditions to interpret their scriptures in ways that inform the theological and moral livelihoods of their respective communities. Comparison that is principled—that does not fall into reduction or assimilation—affords clarity both about fundamental human cultural practices and their distinctive manifestations in individual communities. An excellent example of this concerns ongoing debates in American jurisprudence concerning the relationship of the Constitution to the rendering of legal opinion. When a Supreme Court Justice argues that his job is to elucidate the intent of the Founding Fathers, and only that, he is in fact engaging a set of hermeneutical issues that have a history dating to ancient Greece, and a relevance to a broad range of humanistic work in both religion and literature. Longstanding debates about the inspiration and interpretation of the sacred scriptures of Judaism and Christianity revolve around precisely the question the Justice invokes in his declaration. The European hermeneutical tradition is also represented, especially in the work of Juergen Habermas, Hans-Georg Gadamer, and Paul Ricoeur, and in important traditions in twentieth-century literary studies ranging from the American New Critical tradition of John Crowe Ransom, William Wimsatt, and Cleanth Brooks, to the deconstructionist theories of Jacques Derrida. A more vigorous comparative scholarship integrating law, religion, and literature can only enhance thought about canonical inspiration, its relation to exegesis and its obligations, and the interplay of the authorities of scripture, tradition, and experience in elucidating authoritative sources for contemporary life. The obverse also holds: Charles Dickens' *Bleak House* is deprived of its moral scope when it is not understood to be as fully engaged with social questions about the status of law in Victorian England as is any halakhic text with conceptions of Jewish duty in modern civil society. Correspondingly, halakhic discourse is deprived of its imaginative scope and figural discretion if we do not attend to its literary conventions and hermeneutical presuppositions. Only in such comparative contexts is it possible fully to recognize and appreciate the complex interplay of received tradition and contemporary practice that characterizes legal, religious, and literary practice.

The Turn to Literature in Study of the Law. If scholars have not pursued these conjunctions, recent decades have set the stage for the possibility of doing so through the turn, both in scholarship on the law and in scholarship on religion, to the study of literature and the complementary study of interpretive theory. The last two decades of the twentieth century witnessed an efflorescence of the "law and literature" field: courses exploring the interface now study legal curricular across North America, and the publications have kept pace. The field of religion and literature has a somewhat earlier pedigree, dating at least to the late 1940s and arguably to the earliest decades of the twentieth century. Its integration into the broader study of religion—witnessed by the widespread prevalence of the category of narrative in the study of religion, and the recourse to the hermeneutical tradition across nearly all dimensions of the study of religion—has been more systematic. Such has been the success of religion and literature so conceived that its integration across historical, theological, and human scientific study is manifest.

Such integration is less clear in the case of study of the law and literature. Central to the field is a debate about the use and abuse of the literary turn in the study of law. Two of the most important figures in this debate are James Boyd White and Richard Posner: each offers a formulation of the field, and each has engaged the other's work critically. White, whose *The Legal Imagination* (1973) served to crystallize interest in the field, argues that two predominant conceptions tend to delineate studies of law and literature: the "findings" conception, in which the law uses literature to establish truths about the inhumanity of law; and the "technologies" conception, in which the *au courant* terminologies of critical theory are deployed to perpetuate longstanding debates about legal interpretation. Dissatisfied with both conceptions, White argues for a third, better option: that law is best understood as a compositional art in which the mind uses language to make meaning and establish community. Because the law has this role, it follows that it is essential for lawyers to establish a voice, one that is both professionally excellent and individually authentic. White argues that, examined carefully, this recognition is not unique to the law: lawyers are in this regard one professional group contributing to the broader cultural matrix of professionals, including poets, politicians, priests, and indeed all citizens, who aspire to the same. White's conception thus seeks to move beyond the correlative formulation of law *and* literature to the descriptive formulation of law *as* literature: to the understanding that literature is not a recourse to expand reference or elucidate theory in the law, but is rather its essence. Law is neither more nor less than a cultural form of literary expression.

At stake for White in this claim is the public culture of a social order. Worried that law may simply take over and transform a culture into one that operates by adversarial argumentation, White advocates for the recognition—against the mechanistic tendencies that he sees to run very deep in our culture—that fundamental to our lives as human beings is the use of language to make meaning. Framed in this way, law is understood to be one of the fundamental processes by which society argues about its values. Promoting a kind of "negative capability," the Romantic poet John Keats' phrase for the ideal receptive state for poetic reception, White advocates a sensibility in which this recognition eases adversarial opposition and its ensuing isolation: we can admire opinions with which we disagree and condemn aspects of opinions with which we are in concord. This capacity will both underscore the commonality of the endeavor, and lead us to the essential recognition that the world is, in the end, a matter of conversation and discourse.

In contrast, Richard Posner regards the law precisely as a set of rules for social control, and he is dubious that literary criticism or works of literature can or do present a formalizable theory or method that can inform the law. Posner allows that lawyers and literary critics are both close readers, but they read very different materials, and therein lies all the difference. *Hamlet* and the United States Constitution both present puzzles, but the natures of the puzzles differ and there are few telling commonalities. There are, to be sure, craft values from reading literature, and perhaps literary criticism, that help judges to think and write better than they would otherwise. But the bottom line, in Posner's judgment, is that law and literature represent different realms of literary discourse that require different valuations.

Posner thus articulates distinctive approaches to law and to literature, and must formulate as well a rationale for their conjunction that is more willed than innate. He advocates respectively for a pragmatic approach to the law, and a formalist approach to literature. Following his claim that the problems of literary and legal texts are different, Posner argues that these approaches most fully honor the nature of their object: law adjudicates disputes and establishes the social arrangements that ameliorate them; literature delights us with its beauty and wit. One body of texts exerts social control, while the other is an art. Posner is in turn skeptical about establishing even a willed conjunction. He finds White's "law as literature" conjunction to be based on a view of literature as edification that is both vague and didactic—terms which together describe the antithesis, in Posner's view, of great art and thus do not persuade him. There is for Posner the further problem of social utility: what new insights does the study of literature bring to specific fields of the law? Here Posner contrasts literary theory unfavorably with economic theory, asserting that applications of economics permeate many standard fields of legal study and even create new ones. While Posner avers that law and literature should be understood to be complementary rather than competitive, it is clear that their conjunction is more social than dialectical.

As it stands this debate is intractable because of the stilted relationship in each case between meaning and power. For White, meaning is central and must trump pure power, while for Posner power in an important sense simply is meaning. The late Robert Cover, in a suggestive and necessarily incompletely developed but seminal article, anticipates precisely this dilemma. Postulating that every community has a *nomos*, or regulative code—it is telling that Cover reintroduces religion into the conversation by drawing a parallel between the Greek term and the Hebrew Torah—Cover argues that it is internally tensive in its parts: "For every constitution there is an epic," he writes, and "for each Decalogue a scripture" (Minow, Ryan, and Sarat, p. 96). Society constructs a nomos not solely of law, then, but of law and literature, to encompass power and meaning, and thus acknowledge the degree to which uncontrolled meaning destabilizes power, and uncontrolled power destabilizes meaning. The central point, Cover argues, is to recognize this conjunction for the fundamental tension that it is, and to expect the discretion of judges, and by implication artists, to be informed by it.

Cover's untimely death, and a style of writing that defies apodictic summary, leaves his readers without the full development of the idea of nomos, and its implications for the relationship between power and meaning, that one might wish. But the analogy of *nomos* to Torah that informs his work has its complementary development in both the Jewish and Christian traditions. Thus Jon D. Levenson shapes his treatment of theodicy in Judaism around the juxtaposition in the Scriptures of the Covenant between God and Israel. In that Covenant, fealty to the law assures divine guidance and protection. Yet the Jewish canon also includes the story of Job, in which a man utterly faithful to the Covenant nonetheless experiences tragedy and the utter absence of God. In strictly logical terms, the juxtaposition bespeaks a contradiction. Levenson has no wish to understate that fact or its impact. Yet, like Cover, he argues that the canonical incorporation of the covenant promise and the story of Job into one common scripture acknowledges that power and meaning do not fully accord in human experience. Religions of the book construct canons precisely to afford themselves both law and story, both power and meaning, and the crucial capacity to acknowledge their sometimes uneasy juxtaposition and even conflict in human experience. Religion adds to the study of law and literature a crucial umbrella of coherence, that enables full engagement and obviates the otherwise destructive impasses effected by the Posner/White debate. Through its processes of canon formation, and the intertextual reference the canon enables, religions of the book afford the fullest possible informing relationship and ongoing conversation—between the legal regulation of power, and the literary expression of vagaries of personal identity and experience.

CONCLUSION. Legal theorist and philosopher Ronald Dworkin proposes a view of legal reasoning as analogous to a chain novel, in which a judge inherits a history of opinion to which she or he must add the latest chapter. Dworkin seeks to capture with this formulation what he regards as the exquisite equipoise necessary for a responsible judiciary: it is constrained both by what has been written, and by the demand of a new chapter. Dworkin's formulation would not pass muster with either White or Posner: for White, it would fall into the technologies conception of theorizing, while for Posner the founding statutes of the U.S. Constitution are not analogous to the opening chapter of a novel. The above survey would appear to suggest, however, that White may underestimate the need for a requisite theoretical architecture to support his claim that law is one of a set of cultural expressions under the aegis of literature; and, correspondingly, that Posner may underestimate the degree to which a Shakespeare or a Tolstoy can accomplish a great deal in an opening scene or chapter. Dworkin's formulation appropriates and makes usefully concrete Hans-Georg Gadamer's conception of "the history of effects": the idea that, when we encounter a work of the imagination, we encounter not only it but its recensions and valorizations through time. Such a formulation honors the power of imagination in the human adventure with ideas, and underscores how central the imaginative capacity is not only to literature, but to religion and the law.

BIBLIOGRAPHY

Dworkin, Ronald. *Law's Empire.* Cambridge, Mass., 1986.

Fish, Stanley. *The Trouble with Principle.* Cambridge, Mass. 1999.

Law and Literature (formerly *Cardozo Studies in Law and Literature*), New York, 1989–. The longest running, and arguably the best, journal devoted to the field.

Minow, Martha, Michael Ryan, and Austin Sarat, eds. *Narrative, Violence, and the Law: The Essays of Robert Cover.* Ann Arbor, Mich., 1992.

Nussbaum, Martha C. *Poetic Justice: The Literary Imagination and Public Life.* Boston, 1995.

Posner, Richard A. *Law and Literature.* 2d ed., rev. and enl. Cambridge, Mass., 1998. The most useful and most complete extant survey, and a lively if at times tendentious treatment of major themes.

Rose, Gillian. *Mourning Becomes the Law: Philosophy and Representation.* New York, 1996. An exercise in the philosophy of law, deeply informed by continental thought.

White, James Boyd. *Justice as Translation: An Essay in Cultural and Legal Criticism.* Chicago, 1990. The best summary statement from White of his view of the field.

RICHARD A. ROSENGARTEN (2005)

LAW AND RELIGION: LAW, RELIGION, AND CRITICAL THEORY

In the course of a case concerned with contempt of court, an English judge not long ago remarked: "if any secular relation is analogous to that between priest and penitent, it is that between lawyer and client" (*X Ltd* v. *Morgan Grampian*). The judge in question, officially entitled Master of the Rolls, or in a vernacular idiom, Lord of the legal writings, appears to have meant that there is no higher duty than that owed to the law. The relationship between lawyer and client is a fiduciary one, it is based upon faith, and it relays the truths contained in the texts or scripture of law.

This judicial aside can help to remind us that for all of its seemingly secular aura, the contemporary legal tradition still harbors theological roots and practices, a hermeneutics that developed first as a dogmatics or unraveling of canonical, text-based truths. The great scriptural moments of law, from the eighteenth-century BCE Code of Hammurabi to the U.S. Constitution, from the civilian codes to the books of common law, still place law apart or purport to remove it from the mundane political domain, and so perpetuate a religious function. In that the interpenetration of law and religion is structural rather than always immediately apparent, its reconstruction is best illustrated historically as well as conceptually.

UNDER GOD AND LAW. The modern Western legal tradition has its roots in a dual law whose source is first divine and only latterly spoken through the mouth of the mundane sovereign or judge. The Judeo-Christian tradition of law depended heavily upon the image of a divine legislator whose orders governed both nature and society. From the very beginnings of the tradition, the source of law was the dictate, commandment, or tables of an invisible God whose decrees were enigmatic and in need of protection and interpretation by authorized human intermediaries, oracles, and, later, lawyers.

The Renaissance inherited a theistic—specifically, monotheistic—conception of law through the *Corpus Iuris Civilis,* or great code of Roman law that the Eastern Emperor Justinian I (482–565) had ordered compiled in early-sixth-century Byzantium (Berman, 1983). The text had been lost for several centuries before its rediscovery in Bologna toward the end of the twelfth century, and it became both the source of law and the rule of its method (Legendre, 1964). Although no more than a collection of fragments, maxims, and opinions of long-deceased Roman lawyers, the *Corpus Iuris* represented to the later age the irrefragable truth of law. It was preserved and studied as a sacred text. This means, in essence, that what mattered was the status of the text and the rites of access to it rather than the vagaries of its content. In the description of one humanist lawyer, early jurists would travel to Italy to study the original text of the law, which was "guarded like a sacred relic, only being very rarely shown accompanied by candles and torches, thus did the ancient mystagogues show their law to the faithful" (Hotman, 1567, p. 120). The source of such a view is not hard to discern. The *Corpus* indeed begins by announcing that God is its author—*Deo Auctore*—but also early on indicates that the study of law is the study of all things, both divine and human. So too, within the early common-law tradition, it was God and law that governed, and those who represented the law were expressly the delegates of *maiestatis,* or divine authority. In a characteristic phrase from a guide to the study of law authored by an English lawyer writing at the very end of the sixteenth century, "law and religion do lie together" (Fulbecke, 1599, p. 103). They are between the same persons and about the same things.

The rules of legal method, both in Europe and in the anglophone common-law world, are derived from the inherited Roman exemplars. Although God was from the early modern period onward decreasingly the explicit source of law, the Western tradition remained bound to a series of religiously inspired dogmatic axioms. First and paradoxically, the source of law remained a mystery, or *arcanum,* that exceeded the bounds of temporal human knowledge. Law was founded upon something other than law. The text was simply a visible manifestation of an invisible cause; the law was in the end the expression of a law of law and thus only the *iuris peritus,* or legally wise, could excavate and interpret the proper meaning of rules that by this definition were necessarily too old to be uncovered by historians or too technical to be understood by the untrained. In good Christian fashion, lawyers believed that the text was simply a mnemonic or sign of a higher order of truth, and hence it was a primary rule of method that it was not the letter of the law, but according to the Roman jurists, it was rather its interlinear force and power, the intention that spoke through it, that had to be observed. For the English legal sage Sir Edward Coke, it was equally "*non verba sed veritas est amanda*—not the words, but the truth that is to be loved" (Maclean, 1992, p. 33).

Second, although the source of law existed prior to and exceeded any specific written representation, the immediate secular presence of law was to be found in a text or series of texts that were the bearers of the esoteric but visible rule of law. Law was a system of texts, and it was in and through the scripture of law that the sanctity or separateness of law was maintained. A chief marker of such distance from the mundane lay in the language of law, which was explicitly that of written reason, or *ratio scripta,* namely Latin rather than the vernacular, because God and law were best protected from both the blandishments of popular use and the depredations of the local tongue (Goodrich, 2003).

Third, the textual basis of law imposed hermeneutics, or the science of textual interpretation, as the proper method of legal study. Encoded in a foreign tongue and surrounded by rites of solemnization and authority, only the chosen few—the sovereign and its various delegates—could properly pierce the veil of the text, and embody and interpret the laws. The historical trajectory of law from the divine ruler to the human subject meant that legal hermeneutics was not simply bound to the doctrine delivered through texts, but also was under the duty of discovering the singular and primary truth that underpinned any given legal text. Monotheism in short dictated that just as there was only one God, so too there could only be one meaning of law, and that was the meaning that accorded best with the hermeneutic labor or divination of what the deity—or latterly the emperor, the founding fathers, or sovereign—intended (Legendre, 1988).

The Normative Function of Law. Dogmatics, the patient exegesis or exposition of the meaning of an incorrigible text, is common to religion and law. To the extent that theologian and jurist are alike concerned with expounding not the letter but the spirit, not the words but the truth of the text, the technical role of interpretation is secondary to its normative function. The text must produce not simply a meaning but an object of reverence: an image, concept, or term that the subject can love. The text must bind the social, and to do so it must get under the skin of its subjects and attach them to law. Within the Western tradition such veneration of the law was both explicit in the *Decretals*—the primary source of ecclesiastical law, which directly ordained a love of texts in the injunction *venerandae romanae leges* (the laws of the Romans must be venerated)—and more structurally in instituting the image of authority: a pontiff, sovereign, or other social father figure who acted as the living emblem of a divine law.

The term *dogmatics* derives from the Greek *dokein* and means "to think," but it also has a secondary meaning of "reverie," or the recounting of dreams and visions. The alternate connotations capture the dual function of the textual art of law. According to the Roman tradition it was the function of law *vitam instituere,* or "to institute life," and this function can be interpreted plausibly to include two principal projects. The first was broadly aesthetic and amounted to enacting the social or instituting a theater of justice and truth (Gearey, 2001). The second was more strictly ethical—instituting a subject who would take up his or her role in the hierarchy of textually assigned places and thus live faithfully, according to the dictates of the social father, and within the law.

"The theater of justice and truth" is an expression that derives from the early modern era, and it captures well the essentially symbolic function of law that more contemporary law formulates less elegantly in the maxim that "justice must not only be done, but must be seen to be done." To have its effects, law has to be staged. It has to establish a scene of law, and this means not simply an image of authority or authorship of law, but a series of ceremonies or rites of solemnization through which the sanctity of law can be promulgated or made socially present. This depends first upon a spatial metaphor—the separation of the legal from the social within an elaborate architecture of courts and codes of procedure that include control of both how the law is represented and what can be said about it (Haldar, 1999). The architecture of law signals a hierarchy and power that is apparent not only in the often dramatic scale of the courthouse (its columns, domes, and rotunda) but also in the courtroom itself, with its familiar bar that marks the separation of law (the bench) from the social, and across which the law will sound. The bar is what Franz Kafka (1883–1924) framed as the gate or door before which the peasant protagonist of his parable "Before the Law" waited uselessly, or at least under a misapprehension for the entirety of what remained of his life (Kafka, 1976).

The law requires both a physical demarcation of its distance from the mundane, as well as a professional caste of lawyers, the fiduciaries who will mediate and disseminate the protocols that institute and maintain that distance. The role of the lawyer is that of guardian of the secrets of texts, because it is the texts of law that establish the hierarchical places and legitimate roles of the social. In classical law, the text is not simply something to read, it is the space people inhabit. Hence the life and death significance of hermeneutics, the legal art of manipulating the arcane elements of legal texts, the foreign languages, the enigmas, archaisms, and other protocols through which the law gains its legitimacy and its force. It is indeed the unique feature of the Western legal tradition that it is fundamentally enigmatic. The ritual character of legality is not directly a feature of celebration or education, but rather it separates and distances so as to establish hierarchy and inculcate reverence for a theistically derived truth and law. Whereas non-Western traditions, such as that in China, have frequently relied upon governance through the simplicity of laws, the Western tradition has used the complexity of legal language and the intricacy of texts as one further symbol of the divine provenance of law (Soupiot, 2002).

Critical Theories. The beginning of all critique lies in the critique of religion. This Marxist axiom probably stands in need of revision. The beginning of all critique now probably lies in the critique of law, although as elaborated above, this means critique of a law that is both divine and human in its origins. In a recent study of the "mediocracy," the contemporary French intellectual leftist Dominique Lecourt offers the view that it is precisely the failure to challenge an unthinking adherence to the sanctity of law that undermines critical theory: "Today," he opines, "there is no more emphatic discourse than that extolling the virtues of the 'state of law'. . . . When we hear encomia to a form of state that respects duly established judicial rules and procedures, another little tune insinuates that the state is 'law' in the sense that wine is 'Bordeaux'. . . . Has the structure via which the normativity of juridical and political institutions operates in the West really changed? Has the absolute reference point constituted by God remained vacant?" (Lecourt, 2001, p. 129).

Viewed in historical perspective, the separation of church and state was a displacement of the religious function from the former to the latter, involving a juridification of the rites of solemnization rather than their erasure. In good Roman fashion, modern people go to court for the truth, to the market for credit or belief, but only privately attend the confessional, mass, synagogue, or Sunday service (Saunders, 1997). Reason appears to be free of the church but remains staunchly Christian, indelibly Western, and resolutely singular. In the manner of the earlier juristic tradition of *universalia,* or imperial and global statements of legal truth, it should also be pointed out that reason attaches to institutions that are hierarchically ordered, organized according to systems of authorized texts, and generally dogmatic in their methods. The legal function, in other words, takes over the public space of religion or the founding image of the social, yet renders itself more or less impervious to the political critique of religion by adopting an increasingly secular and economical, or efficient, appearance in its more visible social forms of presence, whether on *Court TV* or in the various grandstand trials that more or less continuously perturb the media.

In a contemporary critical idiom, the key question that remains to be fully addressed is that of what the residual religious function of law entails. From an anthropological perspective it is evident that the rites, rituals, arcane languages, and architectural and artistic insignia of law all convey significant social and political messages, and not least the attributes of authority and attachment. In these terms, law both provides a sense of community and models the modes of belonging, of citizenship, and of social role. These begin with the family and end with the sovereign and the reason of state. Their logic, if not always their religious roots, has been the object of a variety of critiques based loosely in gender studies, social theory, and critical race studies.

In many senses the most obvious and potentially the most far-reaching of critiques of the religious function of law lies in the critique of the paternal role of the law, and specifically of the father figure in whose name the lawyer speaks. The tradition is explicitly and expressly patristic, and the law speaks in the name of a singular father. This has had a variety of detractors based in feminist theory and in gender and transgender studies. At its most basic, the tradition models a singular law and an equally monolithic reason. A logic of identity and a privileging of the same thus take precedence over difference and diversity. As Luce Irigaray, one of the most legally oriented of feminist critics, has put it, this means that there is in doctrinal terms only one sex and only one form of legal personality or citizenship. Using the fact that there are two sexes—three if one counts the relationship between the sexes as a further distinct form of sexuality—she argues for explicit legal definition, protection, and rights for a feminine legal personality (Irigaray, 1992). She continues to advocate a doctrinal accounting of the feminine and so interestingly proposes a diversification of both the texts and methods of law. Doctrinal difference here requires attention to the body as well as to the more familiar abstractions of law, and favors the reason of emotion, the aesthetic and poetic, as supplements to the rigid morality of law.

Parallel to the argument for difference predicated upon gender is the broadly sociological critique of the caste and class, or priesthood, of lawyers (Kairys, 1990). Here the social class and political place of the legal profession is subjected to a substantive critique of the instrumental function of legality. Law protects private wealth rather than public good. It favors the rich, or corporate interest, over the poor. The profession itself both represents and belongs to a ruling elite. The political economy of lawyering inexorably supports the hierarchical and singular logic of established power, or the *status quo ante*, leading critical legal scholars—a brief but expressive conference of radical legal academics—to the position that law is indistinguishable from politics, and that legal reason is simply theology by other means (Schlag, 2000).

Writing within a Christian tradition is inevitably a Trinitarian enterprise, and so there is ineluctably a third position to depict. Critique of the gender bias and class interests of law, of the residual paternal function and priestly status of lawyers, was in cultural terms an internal critique. Feminism and gay and lesbian studies had their roots in white, middle-class, and frequently legal circles. The critical legal studies movement was overwhelmingly masculine and rooted in a white, middle-class academy. Concerned primarily with projecting their own anger at their exclusion from power onto the juridical structure, they ironically adopted a legalistic stance in critique of law, and paradoxically offered a series of universal solutions to the problem of the extant universalism. Critique here tended to represent most directly the interests of the critics themselves, and at best simply spoke for—rather than empowering or giving voice to—the majority of those excluded by the sexism or elitism of the juristic tradition. Amongst the various flaws in such a position was the absence of any sustained attention to racial difference or to non-Western cultures.

The final branch of critique thus has been critical race theory. It has introduced the history and the plural forms of diverse non-Western cultures into the analysis of law. Histories of slavery have been introduced into the analysis of the law of property, and fiction, dance, and jazz have been culled for their expressions of alternative norms and laws (Williams, 1988). Although authored primarily from within the Western legal tradition, critical race theory provides at least one impetus for perceiving the limits of Western law. Viewed as the expression of a social form, the limit of the Western legal tradition is coincident with the limits of the religious culture and history that it represents. That the Christian tradition was both imperialistic and universalizing gains expression contemporarily in the expansionist tendencies of law and economics. The fact that the discipline of law is not any longer expressly religious in its self-presentation should not obscure the fact that lawyers currently undertake the fiduciary role and bear the status insignia that in previous eras belonged to the priest and enjoyed the protection of the church.

See Also Canon; Codes and Codification; Justinian I; Literature, article on Critical Theory and Religious Studies.

Bibliography

Berman, Harold. *Law and Revolution: The Formation of the Western Legal Tradition.* Cambridge, Mass., 1983.

Debray, Régis. *A Critique of Political Reason.* London, 1983.

Fulbecke, William. *Direction or Preparative to the Study of Law.* London, 1599; reprint, Clark, N.J., 2003.

Gearey, Adam. *Law and Aesthetics.* London, 2001.

Goodrich, Peter. *Oedipus Lex: Psychoanalysis, History, Law.* Berkeley, Calif., 1995.

Goodrich, Peter. "Distrust Quotations in Latin." *Critical Inquiry* 29 (2003): 193–215.

Haldar, Piyel. "The Function of the Ornament in Quintilian, Alberti, and Court Architecture." In *Law and the Image: The Authority of Art and the Aesthetics of Law,* edited by Costas Douzinas and Lynda Nead. Chicago, 1999.

Hotman, François, *Anti-Tribonian.* Paris, 1567.

Irigaray, Luce. *I Love to You: Sketch for a Felicity in History.* New York, 1992.

Kafka, Franz. *The Trial.* London, 1935; reprint, 1976.

Kairys, David, ed. *The Politics of Law: A Progressive Critique.* New York, 1990.

Lecourt, Dominique. *The Mediocracy: French Philosophy since the Mid-1970s.* London, 2001.

Legendre, Pierre. *La Pénétration du droit romain dans le droit canonique classique.* Paris, 1964.

Legendre, Pierre. *Le Désir politique de Dieu: Étude sur les montages d'Etat et du Droit.* Paris, 1988.

Maclean, Ian. *Interpretation and Meaning in the Renaissance: The Case of Law.* Cambridge, U.K., 1992.

Saunders, David. *Anti-Lawyers: Religion and the Critics of Law and State.* London, 1997.

Schlag, Pierre. *The Enchantment of Reason.* Durham, N.C., 2000.

Soupiot, Alain. "Ontologies of Law." *New Left Review* 13 (2002): 107–121.

Williams, Patricia. *The Alchemy of Race and Rights.* Cambridge, Mass., 1988.

Case Reference

X Ltd v. Morgan Grampian (1991) 1 AC 1.

Peter Goodrich (2005)

LAW AND RELIGION: LAW, RELIGION, AND HUMAN RIGHTS

The roots of human rights reach back into history as long as human beings have struggled for liberty and justice, yet the modern international human rights movement only took shape, through the agency of the United Nations, in the wake of World War II. Despite the voluminous output of literature on human rights, scholarly analysis of the promotion and protection of the freedom of religion and belief, and the ambivalent relationship of human rights concepts to religious traditions, only started to become apparent in the 1980s—subsequent to the development of specific international human rights instruments. The manifold reasons for this orphan status include secularist perceptions of religion as privatized, irrelevant or dangerous, sensitivity of religion questions, relativist concerns, and difficulty of achieving consensus and definition across many different traditions. Yet the rise of religion to prominence on the world stage has added new impetus to analyzing and engaging religious ideas and institutions from a human rights perspective, and vice versa.

CONTOURS AND CHALLENGES. Several specialized texts on the ambivalent relationship between religion and human rights emerged in the 1990s. Arguably the most influential publication was the two-volume *Religious Human Rights* (Witte and Vyver 1996; van der Vyver and Witte 1996). It represented the first attempt to bring together different religious traditions and scholarly disciplines to examine, from an international perspective, the various permutations of the relationship between religion and human rights. By the end of the 1990s it also became possible to consult reports on how freedom of religion is understood, protected or denied around the world.

International developments in the last few years with regard to freedom of religion and belief have forced the hand of scholars to pay more attention to what is possibly the most controversial of rights.

1. There is a growing awareness of the role of religion in social and ethnic conflict (e.g. the Balkans, Nigeria, Indonesia, etc.), and in international terrorism.
2. The former communist countries of Europe and Eurasia have embraced, at least in theory, democracy and human rights, occasioning significant religious pluralization and conflict.
3. The United States took steps to make religious freedom a central aspect of its foreign policy in the form of the International Religious Freedom Act of 1998. As a result of this law there is now an Ambassador-at-Large for International Religious Freedom, an office in the State Department, an Advisory Commission, and annual report on the state of religious freedom worldwide; in addition, the President is required to act to oppose all violations of religious freedom and employ the tools of U.S. foreign policy to promote religious freedom, as well as to activate sanctions against countries that are major violators of this freedom.
4. A number of European countries have in the last few years imposed or proposed restrictions on newer religious formations ("sects" and "cults"), as well as on immigrant religious communities, such as Islam. These new developments have served to shift the focus onto actual violations of religious freedom by individual states, as well as bringing it closer to "home." It is predominantly minority religions who continue to suffer the worst forms of human rights abuses on a global scale.

DETERMINING ORIGINS AND DEFINING TERMS. More than fifty years after the drafting and adoption of the historic Universal Declaration of Human Rights in 1948, with its purpose of establishing a "common standard of achievement for all peoples and all nations," human rights parlance has now achieved the status of a global *lingua franca*. Yet the origins and trajectory of the human rights movement are contested by both its proponents and opponents, notably over its religious or secular foundations. Paul Gordon Lauren refers more constructively to the evolution of the human rights vision as the many "tributaries" of the "ever expanding and evolving river of human rights" (Lauren, p. 9). There are also valuable accounts of the semantic, political, and theological wranglings that shaped the emergent human rights discourse.

David Little rejects any pretensions to a single methodological approach to the complex and uncertain interrelationship of religion and human rights. His analytical framework is predicated on the two fundamental interests of religious people: being able to affirm, express, and manifest their convictions, and being able to avoid unfair discrimination or bias on account of religion. Little defines a "human right" as:

1. A moral right advanced as a legal right.
2. Protecting something of indispensable human importance.
3. Ascribed naturally.
4. "Non-derogable" (if primary), or subject to limitations under prescribed conditions.
5. Universally claimable by all people against all others, or by certain generic categories of people such as "women" or "children"(Little, 1996).

The lack of theoretical and conceptual clarity of rights language troubles a number of scholars. Preferring to eschew the confusing array of philosophical theories proposed to account for human nature and human rights, Jack Donnelly describes human rights as "the social and political guarantees necessary to protect individuals from the standard threats to human dignity posed by the modern state and the modern markets" (Donnelly, pp. 20–22). Defining religion is even more of a challenge. The complexity and variability of definitions of religion from a legal perspective are cogently presented by Jeremy Gunn (Gunn, 2003).

Legal Protection and Interpretation. Four major modern instruments are concerned with the protection of freedom of religion and belief, although we should not overlook the significant norms regarding freedom of religion established by both the Treaty of Westphalia (1648) and the Minorities Regimes of the post-World War I system. The first is the 1948 Universal Declaration of Human Rights with its most crucial provision, Article 18: "Everyone has the right to freedom of thought, conscience and religion; this right includes the freedom to change his [*sic*] religion or belief, and freedom, either alone or in community with others and in public or private, to manifest his religion or belief in teaching, practice, worship and observance." The first clause guarantees the right to freedom of thought (and the inclusion of theistic, non-theistic, and atheistic belief is a feature of these international documents), and the second enumerates the specific rights therein. Kevin Boyle and Juliet Sheen write that this article constitutes a paradigm of the widespread debates over the nature of human rights in general, because it "raises the issue of the universality and indivisibility of rights, of the primacy of international law over national law and religious codes, of individual, minority and collective rights and of the relationship between rights, duties and community."

In 1959 followed Arcot Krishnaswami's much-cited *Study of Discrimination in the Matter of Religious Rights and Practices.* Krishnaswami was appointed by the Subcommission on Prevention of Discrimination and Protection of Minorities to study rights pertaining to religion and belief, and to draw up a program of action to eradicate religious discrimination. He concluded that the collective aspect of the freedom to manifest religion or belief was especially important, as it was prone to state intervention and regulation. He noted the particular vulnerability of minorities in this regard. The International Covenant on Civil and Political Rights (ICCPR) and the International Covenant on Economic, Social and Cultural Rights (ICESCR) were adopted in 1966 and ratified in 1976. The ICCPR is the only global human rights treaty with articles on religion and belief that contains measures of implementation.

In 1981 (after years of intensive lobbying and complicated negotiations) came the landmark Declaration on the Elimination of All Forms of Intolerance and Discrimination Based on Religion or Belief. It served to elaborate what the 1966 Covenant adumbrated. To placate non-religious believers "whatever" was inserted before the word "belief" in Article 1(1), and explicit references to "changing one's religion" were deleted from the text at the behest of Muslim delegations, although this had already been partly degraded in the ICCPR.

A number of legal scholars have helped illuminate the theory and practice of the freedom of thought, conscience, religion and belief in international law. Many consider that it is preferable to strengthen existing norms and mechanisms rather than move toward a more legally binding convention. Boyle and Sheen acknowledge the considerable agreement that has been reached on the content of these freedoms in international law, notwithstanding the remaining disputes, chiefly over the interpretation of the requirements of these international standards. They see the more serious reality as the "open repudiation in practice" (Boyle and Sheen, pp. 4–5) of norms accepted by the majority of states in the United Nations in binding international agreements. These allegations of violations, generally pertaining to restrictions on practice and association, are forwarded to states, which must then respond. They are also documented biannually in the reports by the Special Rapporteur of the Sub-Commission on Freedom of Religion and Belief of the United Nations Commission on Human Rights. These reports are integral to the normative interpretation and development of the international norms pertaining to religion, as are the views of the Human Rights Committee of the ICCPR. However, the U.S. State Department is more effective in documenting abuses.

Many scholars point to the nature of the relationship—practical and not just legal—between religion and the state ("church-state" is proving less and less applicable as a descriptor in the face of religious pluralization) as being formative in accounting for the substantive differences in the achievement of religious freedom around the world. There is a growing body of literature on Europe in matters of freedom of religion and belief—which is to be expected given its historical significance—and a surge of cases raising difficult questions under Article 9 of the European Convention on Human Rights (ECHR). The Organization for Security and Co-Operation in Europe (OSCE) has been described as a "trendsetter" for the way it has raised the profile of religious freedom on the international agenda of participating states and focused critical international attention on their respective practices, although its far-reaching norms are politically, rather than legally, binding.

Compatibility/Incompatibility Arguments. A large portion of the scholarship on the relationship between religion and human rights addresses the issue of their compatibility or incompatibility. For Louis Henkin (1998) religious ideologies differ from the human rights ideology principally in terms of sources and bases of authority. Religious traditions are more totalizing, and oriented (notably smaller, minority religions) toward the rights of their own adherents, or religious rights more generally. While acknowledging the shared concept of human dignity, he highlights recurring differences in contemporary interests and concerns, namely the areas of freedom of religion and religious choice, equality and nondiscrimination, gender distinctions, and capital punishment.

Those who advocate the compatibility approach tend to opt for a strong foundationalist orientation, believing human rights to be the modern political outcome of ancient religious beliefs and practices. In addition to the numerous works on Christianity and human rights, some focus on other traditions such as Buddhism, Judaism, Hinduism, or traditional African religions. There exist also several comparative works, often driven by an ecumenical, Golden Rule approach. Some studies explore differing points of emphasis, such as the interdependence of rights and duties, the concept of personhood, and the dynamic between individual and collectivity in religious communities. The case of Islam is viewed as particularly challenging in terms of whether Islamic law and theology support the modern notion of human rights.

CULTURE MATTERS. Culture both complicates and enriches the whole question of human rights theory and implementation. The truth-claims and traditions of religious and ethnic groups feed into, and even exacerbate, the unending debates about universalism and relativism, or cultural domination and subordination. Frequently these are centered on concerns for the rights of peoples or populations identified as indigenous who have suffered both under colonialism and postcolonialism. In the case of Latin America, for example, some scholars have argued that religion provided the foundation for the defense of the rights of indigenous peoples in Latin America, as well as legitimating the atrocities against them. The protection now available to ethnic minorities in the form of Articles 18 and 27 of the ICCPR to maintain their language, culture, and religion is predicated on the control of sacred sites, skeletal remains, burial artifacts, and other items of religious and cultural significance.

Others would consider that it is the challenge that these indigenous peoples, along with other ethnic minorities, are mounting to the individualistically oriented human rights paradigm that is more preoccupying. There is a rich body of literature emerging on "group rights," some of it framed within current discourse on multiculturalism and cultural self-determination, in which religious identity often features prominently. The particular problems of religious rights come about as they constitute classic "civil" or "individual" rights and yet are fundamental to the protection of the rights of minority, indigenous, and other groups. The dichotomy of group versus individual rights is also a major issue as far as how countries and societies view the right to freedom of religion or belief, and one which adversely affects minorities.

Proponents of "Asian values" or "Islamic values" argue that the communitarianism, authoritarianism, and emphasis on economic development in their societies are antithetical to Western liberal conceptions of human rights. Such advocates have been challenged for using cultural reservations as a "smokescreen" for human rights violations, and for promoting a static and polarized image of the human rights movement. Some question the univocality of terms such as *universal* or *freedom*.

Human rights scholar and advocate Abdullahi An-Na῾im has been one of the most prominent proponents of the need for human rights to seek cultural legitimacy through internal and cross-cultural dialogue and to support more inclusive and equitable processes of change. He realistically sees how individual rights and collective rights complement, but also contradict each other—which is to be expected, as all rights are instruments of negotiation and mediation of competing claims. Similarly, he stresses the contingency of universalist projects to date, while calling for more global participation in the construction of the human rights ideal. This is reiterated by such critical theorists as Boaventura De Sousa Santos, with his concern to transform the conceptualization and practice of human rights from a globalized localism into a cosmopolitan project. This reconfiguring of the relationship between culture and rights is considered as arguably the most important development in recent rights theory and practice. Yet sensitivity to believers' positions, while not conceding to relativist arguments, continues to represent one of the most pressing challenges for the field of human rights.

PROSELYTIZATION. Some consider that the right to engage in missionary activity is perhaps the most controversial aspect of religious freedom. This is closely linked to the disputed right of changing and exiting one's religion. The new "war for souls," precipitated by the globalizing forces of democracy and capitalism, became the focus of an international project conducted by Emory Law School's Law and Religion Program.

Perhaps the most problematic issue to emerge from the research was the clash between the right of an individual or group to promote, teach or propagate his or her religion or belief, and the right of an individual or group to resist such disruptive incursions. Disseminating one's religion is protected by both individual and group rights. Asymmetrical power relations are generally inherent in the proselytization exercise, although this type of interreligious encounter can arguably stimulate cultural exchange and self-critique. With the growth of religious revivalism and militancy within our global network society, the human rights community is gradually waking up to the potent influence of the media in promoting both tolerance and intolerance.

WOMEN'S RIGHTS. A strong focus of the scholarship on the no less controversial case of women within the overall picture of religion and human rights has been on the religious traditions themselves. This is hardly surprising given the denial of their rights that many women experience both as citizens and as members of religious communities, and the fact that religious norms frequently underpin social practices of exclusion and domination. Women's rights to equality under state and international human rights law frequently clash with the rights of religious collectivities to self-determination. Religion is also a source of liberation or repression for women from a variety of textual, historical, legal, cultural and social perspectives.

The freedom of choice is important for women within religious systems, but not at the expense of their basic human capabilities. Conflicts frequently arise between religious and customary laws and international human rights norms over the equality and freedom of women in matters of land allocation, inheritance, marriage, and divorce. External freedoms, or the public manifestations of religion, are areas where women's rights to freedom of religion and belief are often compromised, as in dress codes and female genital mutilation.

Conclusion: Lingua Franca, Lingua Sacra? Now more than ever the convergences and divergences of human rights culture(s) and religious culture(s) in our globalizing world calls for new interpretations. Scholars of religion need to examine the ways in which both mainstream and minority religious organizations resist and accommodate the increasingly powerful discourse of international human rights as part of the strategies of these groups for recognition in the public sphere. The naturalization of human rights norms can lead to the objectification and standardization of religion. It also serves to blur conventional distinctions between public and private. Similarly, it points to the capacity of religious communities to generate much-needed political will for the implementation of human rights standards. Likewise, an appropriate focus on the cultural translation of human rights in diverse settings would illuminate the ambivalence surrounding their reception and implementation. Attention to the new strategies being developed by many states to regulate freedom of religion and belief would enhance understanding of patterns of discrimination more generally. In other words, the critical and comparative study of religion can help raise questions about the troubling question of human rights *qua* religion, in other words, the (occasional) intolerance of the human rights movement toward its detractors, and its functioning at times as a new world religion. For that reason, it has been argued that because religious thinking has contributed to the conceptual and practical development of human rights, and legal regulation draws increasingly on human rights norms, it should resist being coopted.

In sum, the particular skills that religion scholars bring to the table in terms of what Ninian Smart called "worldview analysis." The critical interpretation of sacred symbol, sound, text, space, ritual, object, community, as well as cultural difference and identity, are highly germane in the analysis of human rights discourse and practice. Moreover, the location of religious studies scholarship at the intersection of the humanities and social sciences, together with its focus on religious belief and practice as embedded historical and contemporary realities, can serve to complement, if not healthily challenge, the domination of human rights questions by legal, political, and philosophical theorists.

See Also Human Rights and Religion.

Bibliography

Good overview articles on the nature and history of the human rights idea can be found under "human rights" at http://www.britannica.com. For a range of texts on religion and human rights, see the invaluable http://www1.umn.edu/humanrts/links/religion.html, as well as http://www.religlaw.org/interdocs/rhrbdtoc.htm. For reports on freedom of religion and belief, see the annual reports by the U.S. State Department (http://www.state.gov) and the U.S. Commission on International Religious Freedom (http://www.uscirf.gov), and the biannual reports of the U.N. Special Rapporteur on freedom of religion and belief (http://www.unhchr.ch/html/menu2/7/b/mrei.htm). See also the news service on religious intolerance and discrimination from Human Rights without Frontiers (http://www.hrwf.net).

An-Na'im, Abdullahi A., ed. *Human Rights in Cross-Cultural Perspectives: Quest for Consensus.* Philadelphia, Penn., 1992.

An-Na'im, Abdullahi A., ed. *Proselytization and Communal Self-Determination in Africa.* Maryknoll, N.Y., 1999.

Barry, Brian. *Culture and Equality: An Egalitarian Critique of Multiculturalism.* Cambridge, Mass., 2001.

Bloom, Irene, J. Paul Martin, and Wayne L. Proudfoot, eds. *Religious Diversity and Human Rights.* New York, 1996.

Boyle, Kevin, and Juliet Sheen, eds. *Freedom of Religion and Belief: A World Report.* London, 1997.

Cowan, Jane K., Marie-Benedicte Dembour, and Richard A. Wilson, eds. *Culture and Rights: Anthropological Perspectives.* New York, 2001.

Danchin, Peter, and Elizabeth Cole, eds. *Protecting the Human Rights of Religious Minorities in Eastern Europe.* New York, 2002.

Evans, Caroline. *Freedom of Religion under the European Convention on Human Rights.* New York, 2001.

Evans, Malcolm D. *Religious Liberty and International Law in Europe.* New York, 1997.

Gunn, T. Jeremy. "The Complexity of Religion and the Definition of 'Religion' in International Law." *Harvard Human Rights Journal* 16 (Spring, 2003): 189–215.

Hackett, Rosalind I. J., Mark Silk, and Dennis Hoover, eds. *Religious Persecution as a U.S. Policy Issue.* Hartford, Conn., 2000.

Hackett, Rosalind I. J., and Winnifred Fallers Sullivan. "A Curvature of Social Space." *Culture and Religion* 16, no. 1 (2005).

Hastrup, Kirsten, and George Ulrich, eds. *Discrimination and Toleration: New Perspectives, International Studies in Human Rights.* The Hague, Netherlands, 2001.

Henkin, Louis. "Religion, Religions, and Human Rights." *Journal of Religious Ethics* 26, no. 2 (1998): 229–239.

Howland, Courtney W., ed. *Religious Fundamentalisms and the Human Rights of Women.* New York, 1999.

Lauren, Paul Gordon. *The Evolution of International Human Rights: Visions Seen.* Philadelphia, 1998.

Lerner, Natan. *Religion, Beliefs, and International Human Rights.* Maryknoll, N.Y., 2000.

Little, David. "Studying 'Religious Human Rights': Methodological Foundations." In *Religious Human Rights in Global Perspective: Legal Perspectives,* edited by J. D. v. d. Vyver and J. Witte, pp. 45–78. The Hague, Netherlands, 1996.

Mayer, Ann Elizabeth. *Islam and Human Rights: Tradition and Politics.* 3d. ed. Boulder, Colo., 1998.

Ministry of Foreign Affairs, ed. *Seminar on Freedom of Religion or Belief in the OSCE Region: Challenges to Law and Practice.* The Hague, 2001.

Nussbaum, Martha C. *Women and Human Development: The Capabilities Approach.* New York, 2000.

Richardson, James T., ed. *Regulating Religion: Case Studies from Around the Globe.* Dordrecht, Netherlands, 2004.

Santos, Boaventura Sousa de. *Toward a New Legal Common Sense: Law, Globalization, and Emancipation.* Evanston, Ill., 2003.

Sharma, Arvind. *Hinduism and Human Rights: A Conceptual Approach (Law in India).* New York, 2004.

Stahnke, Tad. "Proselytism and the Freedom to Change Religion in International Human Rights Law." International Religious Liberty Association. Available from http://www.irla.org/documents/articles/stahnke-proselytism.html.

Stahnke, Tad, and J. Paul Martin, eds. *Religion and Human Rights: Basic Documents.* New York, 1998.

Steiner, Henry J., and Philip Alston. *International Human Rights in Context, Law, Politics, Morals.* 2d ed. New York, 2000.

Tahzib-Lie, Bahia. "Applying a Gender Perspective in the Area of the Right to Freedom of Religion or Belief." *Brigham Young University Law Review* 3 (2000): 967–988.

Van der Vyver, Johan D., and John Witte, eds. *Religious Human Rights in Global Perspective: Legal Perspectives.* The Hague, 1996.

Witte, John. "A Dickensian Era of Religious Rights: An Update on Religious Human Rights in Global Perspective." *William and Mary Law Review* 42 (2001): 707–799.

Witte, John, and Johan D. van der Vyver, eds. *Religious Human Rights in Global Perspective: Religious Perspectives.* The Hague, Netherlands, 1996.

ROSALIND I. J. HACKETT (2005)

LAW AND RELIGION: LAW, RELIGION, AND MORALITY

The relation between law, morality, and religion in the West has grown progressively more complex and fragmented over the last five hundred years. Historically, two paths emerged in Western thought regarding the relation of transcendent justice and positive law secured in the secular political order. The natural-law tradition followed Platonic philosophy by locating human cognition of true justice in a rational awareness of the divinely sanctioned order of the universe. The other tradition arose from conceptions of obedience to divine command. Such movements were more skeptical of human apprehension, reserving knowledge about justice to that received by revelation of the Divine Will. The Hebraic tradition, typified by the Ten Commandments, was structured around the community's faithful response to the laws of the God who created and sustained them. The Christian apostle Paul claimed that only through fideistic awareness of God's activity can true justice be revealed, and that only absolute reliance on faith alone as the means of grace could deliver one from evil. For Augustine, the world of things below is for security only—to restrain evil—and the true focus of the believer's attention was the heavenly kingdom, known through faith alone. Human knowledge could not achieve any awareness of true justice.

There are many approaches to the study of the changing connections of these spheres of human life. Some theorists focus on philosophical accounts of the validity of legal, moral, and religious claims and concepts. Others emphasize the many structural similarities between law, morality, and religion, since each sphere claims authority and obedience over the lives of adherents, each reproduces itself through a tradition of concepts and rituals, and each claims universality and a comprehensive character. Still others hope to articulate a religious or moral worldview which unites each of the spheres in some comprehensive fashion, often subordinating legal goals and processes to religious or moral claims. Whichever method is adopted, the fact remains that the social structure of law continues to develop as an increasingly isolated sphere. Law in the West has grown more unified as an instrumental mode of social formation, purged of the supposedly extraneous elements of religious and moral culture. At the same time, religion and morality, to their adherents, continue to be comprehensive in their claims about the proximate and ultimate goods for human life. But as a mode of culture, religion has exploded into countless, disconnected ways of life. One major problem for the relation between modern law, religion, and morality is whether these social spheres relate to each other any longer, and if so, how they relate.

Modern democratic legal systems usually accommodate some form of religious plurality and refrain from establishing or privileging any particular religious entity or practice through legal sanction. But these legal systems are often unable to account fully for the idea that religion is not just a distinct set of religious rituals, a defined community, and a discrete body of doctrines. Religion is also a worldview, a set of ideas and beliefs of conscience about the nature of the world, that for many people shape all of their moral, economic, social, and personal affairs and choices. Religion and morality have become increasingly private and individual affairs, formed by interaction between the human subject, his or her culture, and his or her conscience.

Until the late Middle Ages, a predominant idea in the West was that the cosmos and all of nature contain intrinsic rational principles which human beings can apprehend in order to understand how to form their political, moral, and legal affairs. This "natural law" was an eternal order invested by the Creator in all reality. While it could be apprehended independently from religious revelation, natural law was thought to be consistent with deeper cosmological truths. The Protestant tradition broke from this structure and adopted an Augustinian anthropology in which humans live in two realms simultaneously, the empirical reality of time and space and the transcendental sphere of the numinous experienced by faith alone. The claims of religion about the transcendent Divine cannot be verified or denied by empirical or rational investigations, and the location of religious experience is the individual's conscience. Under the conditions of modernity, fueled by these Protestant ideas, it has become increasingly the case that claims can only enter legal discourse if they are universalizable and empirically testable. Law deals with discovery of facts and adjudication of testable claims—what the law "is" has an empirically verifiable character. Therefore, modern law as it has developed does not directly relate to claims of religious revelation, private intuition, or other sources of "ought-claims."

Western law has often, especially in recent centuries, focused on the concept of sanction, that element of the law's origin in a legitimate process of legislation which gives any law its authority as a command that must be obeyed. With the decline of natural law as a persuasive model, the human process by which law is created took on greater importance. If law can no longer be discovered in the nature of things, for modern people its authority comes from the legitimacy of the institutional procedures of the legal system, accorded by its subjects who have authorized it to have power on their behalf. Positive law—that law which is posited or willed through the legislative process—has nearly become the exclusive focus of obedience and legitimacy. Positive law so conceived bears only historical relations to moral and religious culture, and any direct links are historically contingent once adopted into legal code. In modernity, the human ruler or community sanctions human law, using criteria of efficiency and utility to achieve social, economic, and political goals desired for any number of practical reasons. Conceptions of political goals and legal rights are increasingly identified with individual preferences and prevention of harm, rather than transcendental or religious goods.

The problem for law and politics under these new conditions is a crisis of legitimacy: how, under conditions of such radical social upheaval, can political will-formation and legal obedience be achieved and successfully reproduced? From the new American society, where writers worry about increasing individualism and decreasing religious checks on such unbridled drives, to the old Europe, where the church has lost most of its grip over the hearts and minds of the citizenry, many have seen a profound crisis develop in how society can remain cohesive and functional under law when, from a moral and/or religious standpoint, there exist a vast plurality of uncoordinated societies.

Law, Morality, and Religion in Classic Modern Theory. Niccolò Machiavelli (1469–1527), in *The Prince* (1517), dismissed the concept of the common good as the primary telos of the sovereign's legislative activity, replacing it with the hallmark of political realism, the *raison d'état.* Machiavelli's prince only needed to concern himself with the balance and preservation of power while exercising statecraft. Thomas Hobbes (1588–1679), in his *Leviathan* (1651), carried this vision forward by claiming that the goal of self-preservation was the primary function of individuals who organized themselves into a legal state to achieve greater and lasting security. The right of nature, according to Hobbes, is the simple liberty each human has to use his or her own power, as desired, for the preservation of his or her life and to do anything which, according to his or her own judgment and reason, he or she conceives to be the most appropriate means to reach that goal. Hobbes's break with the medieval worldview can be seen here since the greatest good for each individual is his or her own natural preservation, not flourishing as defined by a transcendental moral or religious good.

Hobbes argued that since the natural condition of humankind was a war of each against all, self-interested agents must recognize by reason that their surest possibility of achieving self-preservation can only come through transfer of their natural liberty to a common and ultimate authority who can adjudicate disputes, provide an established law, and create conditions of security for each individual. In Hobbes's view, humans are not naturally social as Aristotle had held; rather they enter society by convention, for the promotion of their own interest. The social contract is the mechanism whereby individuals mutually and equally lay down their rights to every other citizen, forming a society which transfers their collective, natural liberty over to the coercive power of the sovereign. Thus the will of the sovereign alone, authorized by the contract between citizens, creates the force of law. The legislating sovereign is not bound by nor aims toward transcendental moral or religious goods, nor does the civil law aim for anything other than external compliance. The sovereign must, however, institute order in the earthly kingdom. And, as Hobbes knew well, skirmishes over religious doctrines had caused many of the bloodiest conflicts in human history. To alleviate these conditions, he argued that the political sovereign must judge doctrinal disputes and shape a coherent and unified set of religious beliefs and practices for the political community, lest their squabbles cause civil unrest.

John Locke's (1632–1704) *Second Treatise on Government* (1690) shaped a legal philosophy to support the English Revolution of 1688 and espoused perhaps the most influential theory of modern liberal democracy. He argued, against Hobbes, that the sovereign was bound by a criteria of transcendental justice known by natural reason. Locke demonstrated the creation of civil society in a manner similar to Hobbes, basing its legitimacy in the state's role of protecting property rights and serving as a fair, common arbitrator of disputes. However, Locke decreed that God appointed the government to restrain the partiality and violence of humans and to remedy the inconveniences of the state of nature. According to Locke, each individual recognizes by natural reason the fundamental law of nature: each human, being equal and independent, should not harm any other in his or her life, liberty, health, or property. Under the social contract, the sovereign must legislate toward the common good of the collective members. The only legitimate end of state action is the peace, safety, and public welfare of the people. If the legislator acts against the ends of security and preservation of the people, Locke contended that the people, using natural law as their guide, have the right to rebel and to establish the government anew, since an unjust or arbitrary sovereign would be in a state of war against them.

Civil authority is here limited to the preservation of material property and earthly security, not to the creation of a pietistic or moralistic state. Locke thereby rules out the ecclesiastical authority from having anything to do with the governance of common affairs. Further, he contends that, being free and equal, each individual should have freedom of conscience over his or her own thoughts and affairs. In his *Letter Concerning Toleration,* Locke argues, also against Hobbes, that the care of souls, the management of estates or health, the choice of religious rituals, and private judgments about doctrine or political matters all belong to the individual, and toleration must therefore be accorded by the sovereign and fellow citizens for various patterns of life.

Locke does merge religious claims and law together, however. All human actions ought to be conformable to the law of nature, which he equivocates with both natural reason and the will of God. The fundamental law of nature is a declaration of the basic good of the preservation of life, written into the very fabric of human life. No human law can be good or valid that cuts against this law. However, the criteria by which a law is judged remain exclusively rational. This is not a contradiction, since Locke assumes that the proper operation of natural reason—the gift of God—would yield a result that correlates with the intention of the Divine. Locke also articulated two instances where the sovereign could interfere with an individual's personal beliefs. Locke argued that those who claim allegiance to a foreign prince should not be tolerated (such as Catholic allegiance to the papacy), since they would hold higher allegiance to someone other than the political sovereign of the territory. Thus moral conscience can be intruded upon when obedience to the authority of the legislator is compromised. Secondly, Locke argued that atheists must not be tolerated. Locke holds that if belief in God is taken away, then the ability to hold promises, covenants, and oaths—the bonds of society itself—is made impossible. But a more subtle and profound point is at stake, one that shows the extent of the relation of law and religious claims in Locke. Natural reason teaches that all humans, being equal, are not to be harmed in the pursuit of life, liberty, health, or property. Locke does not argue that reason teaches that humans are equal. Rather, this conclusion derives from a religious claim that humans are the created property of God, sent to earth about God's business, and thus there can exist no subordination between humans that authorizes another's destruction or use. Humans are equal since they are created equal. At the very heart of Locke's arguments for the establishment of civil law is a fundamental religious claim about the human being.

In the German tradition, Immanuel Kant (1724–1804) argued that the civil law is created by rational, autonomous agents, who aim to institute a self-imposed structure to protect and guide their lives. Kant argued that the civil law achieves moral ends for all persons, yet the state must extract legal claims and institutions from particular religious and moral claims. For Kant, the civil condition institutes justice, which he defined as the universal moral end of making possible each individual's self-determination in a way that is consistent with the freedom of every other individual. The civil law is posited by the common sovereign who acts in a manner consistent with universal reason, promulgating law that all rational subjects could have agreed to for themselves. The only direct goal of the civil state is the achievement of this coexistence of external free actions. The civil law does not have as its goal the moral betterment of the social agents nor religious community-building, but simply to provide the conditions upon which free agents could pursue these or other ends. Kant held that religion can provide important motivation for pursuing a moral life under the civil law, but this meant that religion must be elevated to its rational meaning, and its subjective and impassioned elements must be tamed by reason.

LAW, RELIGION, AND MORALITY IN MODERN JURISPRUDENCE. William Blackstone (1723–1780) strongly espoused natural-law theory in his *Commentaries on the Laws of England* (1765–1769). Human positive law must be subsumed under the natural order, and "no human laws are of any validity, if contrary to this." Alexis de Tocqueville (1805–1859), in the first volume of his *Democracy in America* (1835), described how such a practical fusion of religion, law, and morality was present throughout the early American colonies. The penal laws of early America were above all concerned with reproducing moral order in society. Thus, laws often addressed the domain of conscience and were pietistic in scope—such as forbidding unmarried persons from keeping company, prohibiting kissing, laziness, or drunkenness; insistence on attending religious services; or disallowing blasphemy—besides more obvious crimes such as rape and incest. Tocqueville was most fascinated by the fact that these laws often were not arbitrarily imposed but freely adopted by the citizenry who wanted laws reflecting their religious mores.

But Blackstone's contemporary, David Hume (1711–1776), articulated skepticism about natural law that has held lasting influence over jurisprudence; his analyses of human nature and philosophy rendered all ideas of justice dependent upon invention, social custom, and habit. Jeremy Bentham (1748–1832) defined political society in a way that followed directly from Hume. Political society is formed when a number of subjects are in the habit of paying obedience to a person, or an assemblage of persons, the sovereign. The command of the sovereign is law. In *A Comment on the Commentaries,* he directly refuted Blackstone's notion of natural law as a criterion by which positive law is to be judged. For Bentham, although a duly legislated law might be bad according to moral or religious criteria, it is still law. He argued that law should be based on the calculative capacity of the human mind to apprehend how the outcome of actions will maximize pleasure, and thereby chart a course of action that will end in relative happiness. Bentham, like John Stuart Mill (1806–1873), believed that legislation should aim to maximize social utility rather than institute transcendent moral principles in society. Legal codes evolve as particular societies develop. The law of any particular polity is not transcendent and static, but dynamic and fluid, incorporating social customs, practices, and moral preferences into the civil law. Further, the only legitimate constraint over individual behavior is to prevent that action which inflicts harm upon others (the "harm principle").

It was John Austin (1790–1859), a disciple of Bentham, who explicitly distinguished positive laws from other cultural elements in his *Province of Jurisprudence Determined* (1832). Such "extraneous materials" include the divine law, natural law, and particular moral claims. Austin does hold that there are moral criteria that may be applied to the law, tests that can determine if a positive law is what it ought to be. But positive laws are sufficient in their own power, not being fashioned on the law of God but posited by utility. Austin famously declared, contrary to Blackstone, what has become known as the "separability thesis," which holds that "the existence of law is one thing; its merit or demerit another." What law is by social agreement, and what it ought to be according to moral or religious ideals, are distinct and not necessarily related.

Law, Morality, and Religion in Later Theory. According to Max Weber (1864–1920), modern Western societies developed on the basis of "functional differentiation" between social spheres. This process of social division has changed the basis of societal solidarity and disrupted social integration by rationalizing and minimizing the impact of traditional forms of cultural cohesion, a process often termed "secularization." Where the medieval worldview had created a homogenous social structure, modern life is marked by a vast plurality of social modes of existence and underlying worldviews, which splinter individuals into increasingly diverse modes of life. With traditional forms of religious and moral community no longer capable of producing social cohesion, complex forms of bureaucratic structures have emerged with a monopoly of power to regulate activity, social functions, and interaction. Social power has become increasingly centralized in the state bureaucracy, resulting in the monopolization of power into the state. The state, as the legitimate political authority through law, has colonized other aspects of society, increasing its domination through steering mechanisms of policy and planning. For Weber, the existence of a society's rules and laws is not dependent on their satisfaction of moral purposes or goals; rather the laws are legitimate solely by reference to their origin in the procedures of the social system. Since laws are made to regulate social reality, an analysis of the law is primarily a description of how effective law is at meeting its goals. Such goals are arbitrary from the standpoint of the descriptive analysis of law, as well as from the standpoint of jurisprudence; the question is not what law ought to accomplish but whether law achieves the desired goals of utility. This idea is basic to the "Legal Realism" and "Law and Economics" movements.

H. L. A. Hart (1907–1992) argued that a legal proposition which ran counter to a moral proposition was still a valid law. Yet, for Hart, there was nothing to prevent societies from holding that a rule is a valid law and that it should be overturned, modified, or resisted. The processes by which law exists allowed the conversion and transformation of the law, and these processes were driven by ideals that came from a variety of sources—moral, legal, economic, and utilitarian. While there is often a coincidence between legal and moral rules, a law is valid as a rule of law on the simple condition that it is enacted according to and consistent with the procedures given in the society. The mere fact that the rule might conflict with a moral criterion is insufficient to invalidate the rule as a law.

But where the utilitarians argued that the validity of law was sufficient in the capacity of the state to coerce those subject to it, Hart argued that the laws resonate more deeply in citizens than is accounted for by the concepts and motives of mere obedience or the avoidance of coercion. As he articulated in "Positivism and the Separation of Law and Morals" (1958), the proper distinction between law and morality should be between "what is" (the law) and what from many different points of view "could be" or "ought to be."

Hart's concern in *Law, Liberty, and Morality* (1963) was to investigate the legal status of a class of actions that are considered immoral by communal standards but result in no harm to others. This work was written in response to Lord Patrick Devlin's attack on the Wolfenden Report of 1957, which had argued that because no public harm issued from homosexual relations between private, consenting adults, it ought to not be illegal in England any longer. Hart agreed with the report that without an external harm committed, the law's legitimate scope could not enforce some conception of communal moral standards against the private affairs of consenting adults. Yet he did allow that the harm principle was too narrow: the state could have a compelling interest to intervene in protecting a citizen from him or herself or when the citizen's actions contend with standards of public decency. Fundamentally, however, Hart argued that moral facts and values change, that the proposition that any deviation from a society's shared morality threatens its continued existence is unsustainable when faced with the simple fact of the continuous evolution of social norms.

The natural law tradition has continued to garner interest despite the realism and positivism that characterizes modern law. Hart's primary interlocutor and critic, Lon Fuller, in *The Morality of Law* (1969), argued for a vision of the moral characteristics of any valid legal system, the so-called internal morality of law. By looking at certain formal characteristics or procedures that Fuller maintained must be obtained in any legal system, he contended that these characteristics—such as comprehensibility and promulgation—display a moral purpose and structure inherent to the law. In order to garner widespread compliance, the laws need these characteristics to render them tasteful to the citizenry. Further, any legal structure must ensure respect for human dignity and treat humans as subjects of their own actions, all moral goals. Since the purposiveness of law is directed to societal balance, Fuller contends this goal is inherently moral.

For John Finnis, a contemporary theorist working in the tradition of Thomas Aquinas (1225–1274) and Blackstone, the natural-law tradition still has validity as a theory of the obligatory force of positive law. In a nonsectarian fashion, Finnis set out to describe those "basic forms of human good" that organize the goals of positive law, goods to which all humans naturally subscribe. Civil laws aim to solve coordination problems in the common pursuit of these basic, natural goods. For Finnis, a law which is unjust according to moral criteria may still have the force of law, but the law in question has not fully achieved the character of law.

Jürgen Habermas (1929–), a neo-Kantian, recognizes the splintering of social groups described by Weber and the destructive effects this can have on social cohesion and formation of political will, but refuses to return to religious-based or natural-law conceptions. As a remedy to social disintegration, he argues for a conception of legal procedure that allows a society to protect the rights of subjects and to achieve common interests while maintaining the diversity of basic social structures. This is the only way out of the modern deconstruction of traditional norms of social conduct without turning social organization entirely over to the objectivizing strategic calculations of social scientists and legal theorists. Habermas aims to reconstruct the contemporary system of law around the notion of popular sovereignty in such a way that legal subjects organize for themselves the political power they possess and structure their social interactions so as to achieve certain strategic interests in a social order that is otherwise diverse, plural, and incommensurable.

Legal structures can thus be the result of both the rational reflection and the willful intention of humans who create social order through processes of interaction, using all of the capacities that human beings can creatively bring to bear on the task. While this rational intentionality can be utilitarian and calculative, many modern theorists have shown how the law is also infused with moral intentions based in rational reflection, natural desires, subjective goals, and religious belief. Indeed, it could be argued that legal systems are not simply institutions that are obeyed through threat of coercion, but depend for their smooth operation and flourishing on persons who, ennobled by their religious and moral sentiments, actively cooperate and participate in social order through law. Since legal structures safeguard individuals and communities from harmful and destructive forces, regulate interaction so that freedom is maximized, and create conditions of stability and order which allow humans to flourish, the law achieves goals important for many persons of moral and religious goodwill. Thus, the pursuit of earthly justice is sufficiently described by non-moral criteria, which, for some, can be at the same time a religious and moral task. Yet in the modern state, participation as a legislator or citizen is largely a task driven by legal criteria and goals.

Bibliography

Augustine. *City of God* (413–426). Translated by George E. McCracken. Cambridge, Mass., 1957.

Austin, John. *The Province of Jurisprudence Determined* (1832). Edited by Wilfrid E. Rumble. Cambridge, U.K., and New York, 1995.

Bentham, Jeremy. *A Fragment on Government* (1776). Edited by J. H. Burns and H. L. A. Hart. London, 1968.

Bentham, Jeremy. *An Introduction to the Principles of Morals and Legislation* (1789). Edited by J. H. Burns and H. L. A. Hart. London, 1970.

Bentham, Jeremy. *Comment on the Commentaries* (edited by Charles Warren Evertt, 1928). Edited by J. H. Burns and H. L. A. Hart. London, 1968.

Berman, Harold. *Faith and Order: The Reconciliation of Law and Religion.* Atlanta, 1993.

Blackstone, William. *Commentaries on the Laws of England* (1765–1769). 4 vols. Chicago, 1979.

Dworkin, Ronald. *Taking Rights Seriously.* Cambridge, Mass., 1978.

Feldman, Stephen M., ed. *Law and Religion: A Critical Anthology.* New York, 2000.

Finnis, John. *Natural Law and Natural Rights.* Oxford, and New York, 1980.

Fuller, Lon. *The Morality of Law.* New Haven, Conn., 1969.

George, Robert P., ed., *Natural Law Theory: Contemporary Essays.* Oxford, and New York, 1992.

Greenawalt, Kent. *Conflicts of Law and Morality.* New York, 1989.

Habermas, Jürgen. *Legitimation Crisis.* Translated by Thomas McCarthy. Boston, 1975.

Habermas, Jürgen. *Between Facts and Norms: Contributions to a Discourse Theory of Law and Democracy.* Translated by William Rehg. Cambridge, Mass., 1996.

Hart, H. L. A. *Law, Liberty, and Morality.* Stanford, Calif., 1963.

Hart, H. L. A. "Positivism and the Separation of Law and Morals." In *Essays in Jurisprudence and Philosophy.* Oxford, and New York, 1983.

Hart, H. L. A. *The Concept of Law.* 2d ed. Oxford, and New York, 1994.

Hobbes, Thomas. *Leviathan* (1651). Edited by Richard Tuck. Cambridge, U.K., and New York, 1996.

Hume, David. *An Enquiry Concerning Human Understanding* (1748). Edited by Eric Steinberg. Indianapolis, 1977.

Kant, Immanuel. *The Metaphysics of Morals* (1875). Translated by Mary Gregor. Cambridge, U.K., and New York, 1991.

Locke, John. *Two Treatises of Government* (1690). Edited by Peter Laslett. Cambridge, U.K., 1960.

Machiavelli, Niccolò. *The Prince* (1517). Translated by Harvey Mansfield. Chicago, 1998.

Mill, John Stuart. *On Liberty* (1859). In *The Basic Writings of John Stuart Mill.* New York, 2002.

Patterson, Dennis, ed. *A Companion to Philosophy of Law and Legal Theory.* Cambridge, Mass., 1996.

Pound, Roscoe. *An Introduction to the Philosophy of Law.* New Haven, Conn., 1954.

Rawls, John. *A Theory of Justice.* Cambridge, Mass., 1971.

Rawls, John. *Political Liberalism.* New York, 1993.

Raz, Joseph. *The Authority of Law: Essays in Law and Morality.* Oxford, and New York, 1979.

Raz, Joseph. *Ethics in the Public Domain: Essays in the Morality of Law and Politics.* Oxford, and New York, 1994.

Tocqueville, Alexis de. *Democracy in America* (1835, 1840). Translated by Harvey C. Mansfield and Delba Winthrop. Chicago, 2000.

Weber, Max. *The Protestant Ethic and the Spirit of Capitalism* (1905). Translated by Talcott Parsons. London, 1992.

Weber, Max. "Politics as a Vocation." In *From Max Weber: Essays in Sociology.* Translated by H. H. Gerth and C. Wright Mills, pp. 77–128. New York, 1946.

Witte, John Jr., and Frank Alexander, eds. *The Weightier Matters of the Law: Essays on Law and Religion.* Atlanta, 1988.

MICHAEL KESSLER (2005)

LAW AND RELIGION: LAW, RELIGION, AND PUNISHMENT

Punishment represents a crucial intersection between law and religion. As many scholars have noted, in its origins law was closely connected with and often indistinguishable from religion, and much of this early law was penal. The areas of private law and contract developed more gradually, although the relationships and transactions that these areas of law formalized were always present in society. This primacy of penal law is hardly surprising, if we consider that the first obligation of the law, even before the advent of a concept of the state, was to preserve the security and well-being of individuals. Prior to modernity, law was often reinforced by an explicitly religious cosmology. Violations of the law were interpreted as transgressions against the cosmic order, and were punished accordingly. As the French sociologist Émile Durkheim (1858–1917) argued, offenses against our "collective representations" were treated with special severity in early society.

Modern, secular law no longer invokes an explicitly religious cosmology. The term *law* is now applied almost exclusively to positive law, meaning discrete rules promulgated by the state or its agents, and enforced by their sanctions. The state now has a monopoly on punishment. Compliance with religious rules or norms, which are often called "morals" to distinguish them from positive law, is voluntary rather than coercive. The process by which religion lost its ability to enforce its provisions, and by which, at the same time, a secular legal order developed that no longer required the explicit sanction of religion, is one of the key transformations in the history of law. The present article focuses primarily on describing this transformation in Western law and conceptions of punishment, although examples from other cultures are occasionally provided.

PUNISHMENT AND ASCETICISM IN RELIGIOUS LAW. In the vast majority of premodern traditions, religion played an important role in reinforcing a moral order. Ancient punishment was often a ritual of purification that, once completed, discharged fully the guilt of the offense. Although this may run counter to the modern understanding of punishment as designed to prevent further harm, it did contribute to the maximization of certainty within the legal system. Punishments enforced by authorities in this world were supplemented, and occasionally replaced, by threatened punishments in the afterlife or next life, which the English Utilitarian legal reformer Jeremy Bentham (1748–1832), the foremost philosopher of punishment in the common law tradition, referred to as "religious sanctions." Christian representations of Hell are paralleled by Hindu and Buddhist depictions of the suffering caused in hells or other realms, or in subsequent reincarnations in this world, through the consequences of one's actions (*karma*) in this life. The social function of such devices is to enhance obedience to the law by augmenting the severity and/or certainty of punishment, especially in the absence of other effective mechanisms of legal enforcement. As Bentham argued, when such threats are no longer taken seriously, they are mere fictions that do not serve the purposes of law.

One of the difficult questions, from a modern perspective, is how far to extend the definition of "punishment" to religious law. If this term is restricted to the type of punishment associated with positive law, namely a sanction enforced by authorities in this world for violation of a command, then it excludes many types of religious law. Some religious laws prescribe no specific punishment for their violation. An example is the Ten Commandments (*Ex.* 20), which express commands ("Thou shalt [not]") without specifying sanctions. (However, sanctions for many of its commands were specified elsewhere in the Pentateuch.) Threatened retributions in the afterlife or next life lack, from a modern perspective, the certainty of state-enforced sanctions. Many expiations and penances prescribed by religion are self-imposed, rather than being imposed by the state. Ascetic practices are prospective and prophylactic rather than retributive: they seek to bring about a condition of religious purity, rather than to compensate for some offense already committed. Trials by ordeal and judicial torture, on the other hand, are regarded as processes of truth-finding, rather than substantive punishments for crimes for which guilt has already been determined. Despite these differences, there are also profound similarities among these religious phenomena. They are all types of violence, often employing the same techniques, and they serve moral or spiritual ends, or what we may in a broader sense call "justice."

The German philosopher Friedrich Nietzsche (1844–1900), in *On the Genealogy of Morals* (1887), emphasized the continuities among punishments, religious ideas of retribution, and asceticism. He argued that all of these phenomena were manifestations of a fundamental "will to power." In asceticism, the human organism turned this will against both the world and its own nature. The ultimate expression of this cruelty was the idea of God as both sacrifice and executioner.

The greater physical cruelty of pre-modern punishments was a means of impressing moral obligations upon the memory.

Among the aspects of religious law most alien to modern law is its association of moral purity or innocence with physical or ritual purity, as evidenced by restrictions on diet, dress, and sexual behavior, which we may broadly term "rules of asceticism." *Leviticus* and the *Laws of Manu* provide numerous examples within the Jewish and Hindu traditions, respectively. More severe forms of asceticism included the self-infliction of bodily pain. Although similar restrictions, and voluntary practices such as vegetarianism, tattooing, and body-piercing, are prevalent in modernity, they are, with few exceptions, no longer part of positive law. Rules of asceticism often appear to conflate law with punishment. In other words, the command that constitutes the law in many cases also itself entails physical suffering or deprivation. Although any law is in some sense a restriction, modern, positive law clearly separates a command from a sanction attendant upon its violation.

In his *Introduction to the Principles of Morals and Legislation* (1781), Bentham argued that the sole rational basis for law was utility, meaning the principle of the greatest good for the greatest number. He understood "good" and "pleasure" as synonyms. Pain of any sort, including punishment, was an evil that could be justified only in the interest of avoiding greater pain. Consequently, he opposed the principle of utility to that of "asceticism" associated with religion. From his view, asceticism maximized pain for its own sake. He also argued that deriving the idea of moral purity from that of physical purity was a pernicious fiction. (In her analysis of the dietary provisions of *Leviticus*, the anthropologist Mary Douglas presented a more sympathetic analysis of the contribution of such ascetic regulations in contributing to a symbolic moral order.) From the religious perspective, the purpose of asceticism, as a kind of prophylactic punishment, is often precisely the avoidance of greater pain in the future, such as an eternity in Hell. Therefore, even from the perspective of a utilitarian calculus, asceticism can be rational. What explains Bentham's rejection of asceticism is not its application of pain, but rather his disbelief in such future punishments, and in the ability of asceticism to prevent them.

Suffering is, of course, universal, even when we do not impose it on others as punishment, or on ourselves as asceticism. The problem of accounting for suffering or evil is perennial, and it shows the close connection of punishment with theodicy, or the vindication of God's justice. People look for meaning even, and perhaps especially, where there is none apparent. This explains the tendency to interpret suffering as a punishment for wrongs previously committed. The Hindu and Buddhist doctrine of *karma* is often invoked not only to threaten future punishment, but also to explain present suffering as the result of actions in a past life. Among biblical texts, the *Book of Job* grapples most explicitly with this problem of suffering, but ultimately preserves the inscrutability of God's interventions. More common among religious groups is the tendency to view prosperity as a sign of Providence, and misery as a sign of God's wrath. One response to these "divine punishments" is the attempt to ward them off by means of sacrifices and self-imposed punishments. An example is the Massachusetts Bay Colony during the seventeenth century, which progressively added rules against frivolous and irreligious conduct such as gambling, idling, and sabbath-breaking. These were in part extensions of religious law, and in part responses to the hardships and depredations of colonial life viewed as retribution for moral backsliding. Such legal developments culminated, infamously, in the Salem witch trials at the end of the century, which Mary Beth Norton (*In the Devil's Snare*, 2002) interprets as an internal response to attacks from forces outside, including native Americans. Speaking more generally and from a sociobiological perspective, Walter Burkert explains sacrifice, scapegoating, and atonement as measures for alleviating anxiety (*Creation of the Sacred*, 1996). Although such attitudes and practices may appear to be quite distant from modern legal punishment, they remain deeply entrenched in human psychology.

Similar ideas served within the Christian tradition to structure a grand narrative of history, both communal and individual. Adam's sin of disobeying God was inherited by all humans as "original sin." Christ redeemed this sin through the Passion, which combined the ideas of sacrifice and punishment. However, individuals still needed to give their voluntary assent and belief to this salvation, or they would be subjected to the terrors of Hell. While threatening future punishment, this system emphasized moral and spiritual reform, in marked contrast with the modern emphasis on the deterrence and isolation of offenders. The Christian system of punishment may have reached its fullest development with the proliferation of penitential manuals in the Middle Ages. These manuals elaborated different rules for different social groups, extending to the populace at large a system of discipline that had previously been confined to the monastery. The anthropologist Talal Asad argues that the goal of penance was to produce disciplined social bodies; the quest for individual spiritual perfection was pursued within communities and manifested in social relations. He emphasizes the connection of such penitential practices with the rise of the inquisitorial system, which used judicial torture as its basic method of truth-finding.

RETRIBUTION: FROM RELIGION TO MODERN LAW. Another feature of pre-modern religious law that presents problems of interpretation from a modern perspective is its emphasis on retribution or retaliation. The so-called "law of talion" (*lex talionis*) provided a strict equivalence between the punishment imposed on the criminal and the original injury imposed on his or her victim. Perhaps the most famous example is the formula that occurs in several places in the Hebrew Bible: "a life for a life, an eye for an eye, a tooth for a tooth" (*Exodus* 21:23–24; *Deuteronomy* 19:21; cf. *Leviticus* 24:20). Variations of talion are also found in many other, especially pre-modern cultures.

Modern theorists frequently have characterized retribution as "barbaric" or "primitive." Durkheim emphasized the connection of retribution with primitive forms of social organization. For him, retribution represented a kind of blind passion striking out against any potential target. The English legal historians Frederick Pollock (1845–1937) and Frederic William Maitland (1850–1906) condemned the adoption in medieval England of the law of talion as a throwback to Judaism. Part of the modern attitude toward retribution can be traced to the secular Enlightenment, as exemplified by the Italian philosopher Cesare Beccaria's (1738–1794) influential treatise *Of Crimes and Punishments* (1764), which argued against the use of torture and other cruel and unnecessary punishments. Another part of the modern attitude toward retribution, however, echoes Christian sources. Jesus said: "You have heard it said, 'An eye for an eye and a tooth for a tooth.' But I say to you, . . . if any one strikes you on the right cheek, turn to him the other also. . . ." (*Mt* 5:38–39). Of course, no actual legal system can operate without the use of sanctions. Christian antinomianism is more an ideal than a reality.

A primary reason for the modern ambivalence toward retribution is a transformation in the understanding of the purpose served by punishment. Modern legal theory generally recognizes several legitimate reasons for punishment: deterrence of prospective crimes; the separation of offenders from society ("isolation"), especially through incarceration; and the reform and rehabilitation of offenders. Each of these serves the basic goal of preventing further or future harm. Retribution, except to the extent that it coordinates with one of these other purposes, does not prevent future harm. For this reason, it has a somewhat disreputable status in modern law. However, the continuing use of capital punishment and the introduction of a concept of victim's rights in the United States show that the concept of retribution still has some popular appeal.

For Bentham, as noted above, punishment was a further evil that could be justified only by its deterrent effects. On these grounds, punishment for the sake of retribution alone was no more justified than asceticism. Threats of retribution at the hand of the deity might be justified as deterrents. However, if actually imposed, an eternal punishment in the afterlife for offenses already committed would be grotesquely disproportional and devoid of deterrent justification. Despite his rejection of retribution for its own sake, Bentham embraced retribution as a device for enhancing the deterrent effect of punishments. Following an older English philosophical tradition that regarded mental operations as the result of the association of ideas, he argued that the function of the law was to create an ideal association between crime and punishment, so that when the criminal thought of committing a crime, the idea of the punishment would immediately come to mind and deter the commission of the offense. Some of the means of reinforcing the mental association between crime and punishment were to increase the speed and certainty of punishment. Another means was to employ punishments that were "characteristic" of the offense, namely that bore some analogy to it. For example, arsonists might be burned, and forgers might have their hands pierced with iron pens. Bentham explicitly approved talion, or strict equivalence of injury, among the means of making punishments characteristic. Such punishments were not only more memorable, but more popular among the public. Bentham's concept of punishment as a form of rhetoric, combined with his principle of minimizing (real) suffering, led him to endorse the use of illusory punishments, such as hangings in effigy, if these could serve the same deterrent effect as real punishments.

Bentham's modern philosophy of punishment as a form of communication or rhetoric suggests a new interpretation of retribution in pre-modern law. In many cases, retribution may have been used to reinforce the association between crime and punishment. The primary devices used to promote this association were metaphor (similarity) and metonymy (contiguity), although, as described below, sometimes rhyme or other verbal associations were also used. Talion itself prescribed one form of similarity, namely equivalence of injury. Other punishments based on similarity are found, for example, in *Manu* 11:104, according to which a student who sleeps with his teacher's wife is supposed to embrace a red-hot iron statue of a woman. An example of a punishment based on contiguity is *Manu* 8:334, which prescribes that whatever limb a thief uses to commit a crime should be cut off. Retribution, far from being primitive, was in many cases a carefully orchestrated ritual practice designed to deliver the "message" of a connection between crime and punishment. As James G. Frazer (1854–1941) pointed out in his classic *The Golden Bough*, magical rituals also often depend on relations of similarity and contiguity. To harm an opponent, a magician may stick a pin into a voodoo doll resembling the intended victim, or burn an article of their hair or clothing. These relations of similarity and contiguity are interpreted as both causes and signals of the goal the ritual seeks to bring about. Although punishment looks backward to an offense already committed, it depends on similar associations.

The communication function of punishment may be clearest in those cases where the association with the crime is verbal and rhythmic. *Manu* 5:55 prescribes vegetarianism with a pun: "The being whose flesh (*maṃsa*) I eat in this world, that creature (*sa*) will eat me (*mam*) in the next world." Probably the most elaborate "poetic punishment" occurs in Dante's *Divine Comedy*, which used the new verse form of rhymed tercets to make everything in the poem reflect the Holy Trinity: even the three-headed Satan, who appears at the end of the *Inferno* as the upside-down, mirror-image of the Holy Trinity revealed at the end of the *Paradise*. Another example, discussed by Bernard Jackson, is *Leviticus* 24:13–23, which encompasses the talionic formula ("an eye for an eye") at its center in an elaborate chiasmus or quasi-palindrome, where the first sentence parallels the last, the second the second-to-last, and continuing along in that vein. The entire passage imitates, on a larger scale, the reciprocity of the talionic formula. The passage narrates God's command to punish a blasphemer, and the community's obedience to this command. It therefore depicts a successful act of communication, in which God's message has been heard. Palindromes, or inversions of word order, are used in many languages to promote communication, for example in greetings and questions. Talion may have used similar devices to reinforce the "message" of punishment.

RELIGION IN MODERN PUNISHMENT. The concept of retribution, if not its more elaborate symbolic formulations, has been difficult to exorcise from modern law. In other respects, however, modern punishment appears quite different from its pre-modern ancestors. One of these differences is its greater emphasis on incarceration. Michel Foucault's (1926–1984) classic *Discipline and Punish* identified several stages in the development of punishment, beginning with the "symbolic tortures" of the ancien régime in pre-Enlightenment France. In a fashion closer to the older practices of penance and torture, these punishments operated directly upon the body of the offender, producing visible signs of the law's power. Such punishments gave way to the "analogical penalties" of the Enlightenment reformers, in which the goal was instead to construct a sign-relation or association between the ideas of crime and punishment, so as to deter the prospective criminal. Torture was now viewed as an evil connected with the cruelest and most superstitious aspects of religion. As we have seen, Bentham belongs mainly to this stage of punishment.

Foucault, however, took another aspect of Bentham's system of punishment, the circular prison called the Panopticon, as the prime illustration of the modern stage of punishment based on incarceration, regimentation, and constant surveillance. The Panopticon consisted of a ring of prison cells surrounding a guard tower at the center. The cells were lighted from behind and their occupants were visible to the guards, who were shuttered and invisible from the standpoint of the prisoners. As no one knew when she was under surveillance, the structure itself was supposed to promote good behavior. As Foucault convincingly demonstrated, the Panopticon was a paradigmatic, if extreme, example of certain modern institutions, such as the factory and the school, which also promote surveillance and self-policing.

Although Foucault did not address the religious dimensions of Bentham's philosophy of punishment and of modern practices of incarceration, several considerations suggest the continuity of such ideas and practices with older religious models. The first is that the modern prison bears numerous structural and functional parallels to cenobitic monasticism, which gave us the original meaning of the terms *cell* and *penitent(iary)*. Asad has drawn on Foucault's work to illuminate aspects of this older tradition. In each case regimentation, including confinement, served the goal of producing a subjection that was internal as well as external. Bentham often grappled with the question of how to replace the religious sanction, or threat of punishment from the deity, given the decline in religious belief. One response was the "Pannomion," a comprehensive legal code that supplied the lack of clear and effective sanctions. The Panopticon, as the architectural counterpart of this code, similarly replaced the policing function of an omniscient deity, and reintroduced the fear of retribution from an invisible guardian. Bentham may even have had such religious parallels in mind: the Panopticon incorporated, within its inner circles, space for a chapel; its inmates were supposed to be occupied in religious devotion; and, perhaps most revealingly, Bentham acknowledged the religious connotations of the "apparent omnipresence" he attributed to its guards (Bentham, vol. 4, p. 45).

Furthermore, religion, including especially evangelical movements for social reform, played an important role in the rise and development of the modern penitentiary system. Specifically, the ideas of reform and rehabilitation owed much to evolving Christian models. The influence of such ideas continues, especially in the form of voluntary programs of religious instruction offered in prisons. As previously noted, the modern law of punishment minimizes—in actual practice if not in rhetoric— the goals of reform and rehabilitation, and maximizes deterrence and, increasingly, the isolation of offenders through incarceration. Religious programs in prisons, although extra-legal, fill for some prisoners the important function of rehabilitation, especially through the well-known phenomenon of "jail-house conversions." In this way, older religious models of punishment as spiritual reform make a significant contribution to prisoners' constructions of narratives of redemption. Famous examples are *The Autobiography of Malcolm X* (1965) and the film *Dead Man Walking* (1995).

In the sentencing of offenders in the modern United States, there are further intersections between law and religion. Religious arguments play an important role on both sides of the debate over capital punishment. A less sensational but more widespread aspect of modern punishment is the statutory prescription of mandatory, fixed sentences for particular offenses, to the exclusion of judicial discretion. Critics of mandatory sentences usually point to the unduly harsh punishments that may result when individual circumstances are not taken into account. On the other hand, allowing judicial discretion can lead to the inequitable result that different punishments are awarded to different defendants for the same offense. This debate echoes the Christian dichotomy between strict justice and mercy, and potentially places the latter in opposition to modern egalitarianism, which also has religious roots.

CONCLUSION. The separation of religion from positive law poses a potential problem for law, in that it represents the decline of the belief in a moral cosmos, and the loss of an earlier consensus regarding the purposes of punishment. Modern law has provided its own replacements for the religious sanction, but the difficulties of promoting deterrence, the absence of effective mechanisms of reform, and, above all, the reliance on mass incarceration illustrate the nature of the challenge. Tim Murphy (*The Oldest Social Science?*, 1997) argues that the older system of religious law constituted a "penetrative scheme" in which outer practices shaped the interior being, or "juridical soul." By contrast, the modern, social scientific view of punishment emphasizes the constraint of external conduct, and may weaken the hold of law on the subject. Bentham struggled to preserve a penetrative scheme of punishment by borrowing elements from religion: the principle of retribution, ritual displays including illusionism, the fiction of an omnipresent prison guard. Apart from the proliferation of techniques of surveillance, these recommendations have, by and large, not been followed in modern punishment. In response to the arguments by some communitarian theorists in favor of the use of symbolic "shaming" punishments, Martha Nussbaum argues against the appropriateness, and indeed the humanity, of such practices and the emotions they produce (*Hiding from Humanity: Disgust, Shame, and the Law*, 2004). As the debate over how to constitute a system of punishment that is both moral and effective continues, questions of religion are never far from view.

See Also Afterlife; Atonement; Ordeal; Purification; Revenge and Retribution; Sin and Guilt.

Bibliography

Alighieri, Dante. *The Divine Comedy*. Translated by John Sinclair. New York, 1939.

Asad, Talal. *Genealogies of Religion: Discipline and Reasons of Power in Christianity and Islam*. Baltimore, 1993.

Bartlett, Robert. *Trial by Fire and Water: The Medieval Judicial Ordeal*. Oxford, 1986.

Beauchamp, Philip [Jeremy Bentham and George Grote]. *Analysis of the Influence of Natural Religion on the Temporal Happiness of Mankind*. London, 1822; reprint, Amherst, N.Y., 2003.

Beccaria, Cesare. *Of Crimes and Punishments*. Translated by Jane Grigson. Oxford, 1964.

Bentham, Jeremy. *Works*. Edited by John Bowring. 11 vols. Edinburgh, 1843.

Doniger, Wendy, and Brian K. Smith, trans. *The Laws of Manu*. London, 1991.

Douglas, Mary. *Purity and Danger: An Analysis of the Concepts of Pollution and Taboo*. London, 1984.

Durham, W. Cole, Jr. "Religion and the Criminal Law: Types and Contexts of Interaction." In *The Weightier Matters of the Law: Essays on Law and Religion*, edited by John Witte, Jr. and Frank S. Alexander, pp. 193–227. Atlanta, 1988.

Durkheim, Émile. *The Division of Labor in Society*. Translated by George Simpson. Glencoe, Ill., 1947.

Foucault, Michel. *Discipline and Punish: The Birth of the Prison*. Translated by Alan Sheridan. New York, 1995.

French, Rebecca. *The Golden Yoke: The Legal Cosmology of Buddhist Tibet*. Ithaca, N.Y.,1995.

Jackson, Bernard. *Studies in the Semiotics of Biblical Law*. Sheffield, U.K., 2000.

Lea, Henry C. *Superstition and Force*. 2d rev. ed. Philadelphia, 1870.

Malinowski, Bronislaw. *Crime and Custom in Savage Society*. London, 1926.

Megivern, James J. *The Death Penalty: An Historical and Theological Survey*. New York, 1997.

Merback, Mitchell. *The Thief, the Cross, and the Wheel: Pain and the Spectacle of Punishment in Medieval and Renaissance Europe*. Chicago, 1999.

Nietzsche, Friedrich. *On the Genealogy of Morals*. In *Basic Writings of Nietzsche*, translated by Walter Kaufmann, pp. 439–599. New York, 1968.

Smith, Peter Scharff. "A Religious Technology of the Self: Rationality and Religion in the Rise of the Modern Penitentiary." *Punishment and Society* 6 (2004): 195–220.

Yelle, Robert A. "Rhetorics of Law and Ritual: A Semiotic Comparison of the Law of Talion and Sympathetic Magic." *Journal of the American Academy of Religion* 69 (2001): 627–647.

Robert A. Yelle (2005)

LAW AND RELIGION: LAW AND NEW RELIGIOUS MOVEMENTS

New religious movements (NRMs), sometimes referred to pejoratively as "cults" or "sects," have tested the boundaries of social control in many societies in the West since they developed several decades ago, first in the United States, and then in other countries. Indigenous NRMs, have also developed in non-Western countries such as China, where the Falun Gong emerged some years ago, much to the consternation of the Chinese government. Legal solutions have often been sought to the perceived need to exert social control over NRMs. This need for control is often promoted in Western countries by participants in what sociologists refer to as the "anticult movement" (ACM), made up of disaffected former members, parents of participants, leaders of a few traditional religious groups, political leaders, and even, on occasion, journalists. In both Western and non-Western countries, political, legal, and judicial officials at every level have occasionally combined in efforts, often supported by the media, to exert control over NRMs. Thus the law, in some societies, has become a major instrument of social control over NRMs, encouraging the courts to affirm community norms and values as well as political ideology to the disadvantage of NRMs and other minority faiths.

Legal actions against NRMs in various societies have used preexisting laws, creative extensions of existing laws and legal procedures, and even new legislation. The application of law to NRMs in different countries and regions of the world has varied considerably. These major applications of law as an instrument of social control over NRMs will be examined, as will efforts by NRMs to make use of the law to challenge their detractors.

Conservatorships and NRMs. When NRMs first came to the attention of the general public and policymakers in the United States, they were not viewed as a social problem. That changed quickly when it became clear that many NRMs in the U.S. and other Western societies were high-demand religions—that is, religions requiring extensive commitment and lifestyle changes in the lives of their members. Young, relatively affluent members of society were dropping out of school, becoming missionaries, or fund-raising on the streets of the United States and elsewhere. Parents of some recruits in the United States sought help from government officials, but that was not easily obtained, given that the First Amendment of the United States Constitution guarantees religious freedom, and because most participants in NRMs were of legal age. This impasse led some parents to self-help solutions, such as kidnapping and "deprogramming," sometimes combined with legal efforts to exert control. In countries without First Amendment protections and with a more paternalistic approach toward citizens, direct state intervention often replaced such self-help methods.

The first use of the legal system against NRMs in the United States was to seek temporary guardianships or conservatorships. This gave parents legal control over their children and the assistance of law enforcement in the effort to secure physical custody over, and even to deprogram, the young convert. Conservatorship laws are pervasive in the United States, but their main focus is to allow adult children to assume responsibility for elderly parents who can no longer fend for themselves. Use of conservatorship laws against participants in NRMs began in the mid-1970s, and it was successful for several years, with the courts conveniently forgetting that the subjects of the laws were not elderly people, but young people who had joined a religious group of which their parents did not approve. The courts being asked by a parent to grant a conservatorship sometimes made a problematic assumption that young people who had chosen to participate in a newer religious group were, by so doing, demonstrating a lack of mental competence akin to that sometimes seen in elderly people suffering from dementia.

Such uses of the law were dealt a severe blow in the United States in 1976. In *Katz v. Superior Court,* the California Supreme Court overruled a lower-court decision allowing parents of several adult members of the Unification Church to apprehend the members by court order for purposes of deprogramming them. This case occurred in California, but it became persuasive precedent in other parts of the country, and the use of conservatorship laws for purposes of deprogramming waned. Efforts were made in a number of American states to change conservatorship laws to apply to young adults joining NRMs, but none of these efforts was ultimately successful, although some came close.

Brainwashing Claims in Legal Actions. Claims that participants in NRMs had been brainwashed surfaced early in the United States as a part of efforts to exert social control over NRMs. Such claims were initially considered almost prima facie evidence that a conservatorship was needed. While such claims ultimately failed in legal contests over conservatorship, they were found to be quite useful for a time in civil actions against unpopular religious groups by former members and their parents. While there is no sanctioned legal action that can be based on a claim of brainwashing, these claims were used to underpin a number of other traditional civil legal actions, such as fraud, deception, and intentional infliction of emotional distress.

For a number of years, judges and juries in the United States often accepted such claims and sometimes awarded large monetary damages. Eventually, legal claims based on brainwashing were disallowed, this time by decisions in federal courts. The major decision was *Fishman v. United States* (1990, N.D. California), a criminal case involving a former member of the Church of Scientology who was charged with mail fraud. He claimed an insanity defense and said he was brainwashed by Scientology into committing criminal acts. His defense was not allowed, on the grounds that brainwashing was not a concept generally accepted within relevant scientific disciplines. A federal civil case had also disallowed a claim of brainwashing two years earlier in a case involving a suit by a former practitioner of Transcendental Meditation (*Kropinski v. World Plan Executive Council,* D.C. Circuit, 1988). After these decisions, brainwashing-based actions became less prevalent in the United States.

Legal theories based on brainwashing were more successful as a defense in the United States when used, not by former NRM members, but by those who had kidnapped them for purposes of deprogramming and had then been sued for false imprisonment or even charged with criminal kidnapping. Deprogrammers would use a "necessity" or "choice of evils" defense, claiming that, because the NRM or "cult" member had been brainwashed and was under mind control, the deprogrammer had committed the lesser of two evils. Such defenses, which were usually allowed, permitted the defendant to introduce evidence concerning the beliefs and lifestyle of the NRM in question, something that was usually not permitted under the First Amendment of the United States Constitution. However, such cases have become increasingly rare, as incidents of deprogramming and, indeed, sentiments against NRMs have declined in recent years.

At the same time, legal claims based on brainwashing have been gaining credence outside the United States in a number of countries where NRMs are viewed by some as a major social problem. Such theories have become an important cultural export from the United States, where they first came to prominence during the decades-long battle against communism, but then were transformed for application against NRMs. Countries where the concept of brainwashing has achieved some legal currency include some in western Europe, in Catholic regions such as South America, and in countries that were affiliated with the former Soviet Union. Early in the twenty-first century, claims of brainwashing continued to justify hundreds of deprogrammings in Japan, especially of members of the Unification Church, sometimes by Protestant ministers. The term *brainwashing* has even surfaced in China, as part of efforts by the state to exert control over the spread of Falun Gong.

In some other countries claims of brainwashing have been used to undergird new legislation designed to make it harder for NRMs to secure new converts. In France, for example, new legislation was passed in 1990 making "mental manipulation" a crime. In Russia, a 1997 revision of a liberal new law concerning religions attempted to prevent NRMs from coming into the country. Often, as in Russia, such new laws have the backing of traditional churches.

Legal Concerns Deriving from the Presence of Children in NRMs. Another major arena of legal action against NRMs involved children. As the NRMs in Western countries matured, families were often formed, and children were born into the groups—a development that had significant "domesticating" effects on the NRMs. The presence of children also eventually led to two major, and sometimes related, types of legal problems. First, custody battles erupted when one member of a couple in the group decided to divorce the partner or leave the group with their children. A second problem arose when the state entered the picture to varying degrees, exerting control over how the children were cared for and schooled. Indeed, the state was often obligated to intervene if certain types of accusations were made, and sometimes graphic accusations of child abuse, including sexual abuse, were made in the heat of a custody battle.

Custody of children is always a major issue when couples divorce. The issue becomes even more salient when one member of a couple is of a different faith, particularly a member of a "high demand" religion that has strict expectations about how to rear children. Courts in most modern societies are supposed to make custody decisions based on the criterion of "best interest of the child," which is a very flexible guideline allowing much discretion on the part of the judge or other authorities of the state. Often custody decisions are made that favor the party who is not a member of an NRM or other controversial religious group. The court may exercise its judgment in a manner that illustrates the normative function of courts of making decisions that reflect the basic values of a society. The view of what is, and is not, an acceptable religion is often used to justify custody decisions by the courts.

When custody battles become rancorous, claims of various kinds of child abuse may surface, and these may be communicated via the media or directly to state authorities who may choose, or be obligated, to act on them. In many modern Western societies since the 1980s, a plethora of laws designed to protect children have been enacted. These laws have had the overall effect of increasingly redefining children as the property of the state, as opposed to being the property of their parents. These new laws have made it easier to attack NRMs for not treating children as the society expects. Four major areas of law come into play concerning some NRMs: schooling, corporal punishment, health care, and the possible sexual abuse of children.

Home schooling is legal in some Western countries if carried out with reasonable supervision of the state authorities to ensure that the child is being given at least a minimal education level. However, in some societies, such as France and Germany, home schooling is not legal to the degree it is in the United States and elsewhere. The very attempt to school children at home may be viewed by state authorities and the general public as a form of child abuse.

Some religious groups also practice corporal punishment with children, such as spanking them for misbehavior. Spanking can be, and has been, quickly translated by the media into "beating" the children, which is thought to be child abuse by most citizens and policymakers. Such claims have arisen in custody disputes involving NRMs in a number of countries. Some episodes of extreme physical punishment have occurred in a few religious groups, and those have been seized by the media, leaving an impression that all or most unconventional religious groups beat their children and, therefore, commit child abuse.

Health-care needs of NRM children are also of concern for authorities of the state. These concerns have been made more prominent in recent decades by controversies over the refusal of blood transfusions by Jehovah's Witnesses and the rejection of standard health care in favor of "spiritual healing" by Christian Scientists. The experience of these groups, and their treatment by the media and the courts, have established important precedents for the way that health concerns relating to children in NRMs are dealt with. A common stereotype regarding NRMs is that they do not use traditional medical care, but rely only on prayer or similar methods when children become ill. Although this stereotype is generally false, its prevalence has supported state intervention into the health and well-being of NRM children.

The most significant accusation that can be and has been raised against some NRMs is that of child sex abuse. Such accusations, which have become more prevalent in child-custody disputes involving ordinary members of society, change the entire dynamic of a divorce action. When they are made in a situation involving a controversial NRM, as they have been by some in the anticult movement or in child-custody disputes, then the impact is even greater and can lead to immediate state intervention in the NRM in a number of countries around the world. Large numbers of children of NRM members have been seized in raids by state authorities in Argentina, Australia, France, and the United States, and there have been interventions involving smaller numbers of children in other countries. In all of these instances, the children have eventually been returned to their parents and the charges dropped. In Australia, damages were even eventually paid to one group that had seen nearly 150 of its children seized in predawn raids to rescue them from what the media called a "sex cult."

Other Legal Issues Raised with NRMs. There are many other legal issues concerning NRMs that have been raised around the world. Communal NRMs have sometimes run afoul of zoning regulations that limit the number of unmarried adults who can live in a residence. Solicitation laws have been enforced in various countries in an attempt to stop NRMs from raising money. The Unification Church has won many such battles in the United States, but in other countries the legal precedents are not so helpful for NRMs. Even in the United States, the Hare Krishnas (members of the International Society for Krishna Consciousness) have found limits placed on their solicitation of funds in airports and other public settings. Laws requiring contribution to social security and health schemes have been applied to communal NRMs in some countries, as have minimum wage statutes, thereby undercutting some of the benefits of communal living. Immigration laws have been used to limit the ingress of members of some NRMs to various countries, including the United States and the former Soviet Union.

One of the most complicated legal situations involving an NRM may be that of the Bhagwan Shree Rajneesh group that settled in Antelope, Oregon, in the 1980s. The Rajneesh group bought up the entire town and controlled all that occurred there. Only members or invited guests could be present in the town. This had many ramifications, as the group ran the local schools and police force and was serving as the local government for the town. The state of Oregon, working closely with federal government agencies and the courts, managed to exert control over the situation after numerous legal battles. Oregon successfully claimed that to assist the town in any way, including sending state revenues to fund operation of the schools and law enforcement, would violate the Establishment Clause of the United States and Oregon constitutions. The Rajneesh group ceased operations in Oregon, although not without a violent backlash. For instance, some leaders of the group devised a plan to poison members of the general public by placing salmonella bacteria in salad bars in several restaurants in Oregon, causing several hundred people to become ill.

Use of Law by NRMs. NRMs have sometimes been able to use the legal system in their defense, especially in countries such as the United States, which has Constitutional protection for religious freedom. Many other Western countries have statutory or constitutional provisions that allow NRMs to take legal action against those who criticize them. This includes tax officials who might have exercised their judgment so as to preclude an NRM from claiming tax exemptions available to other religious organizations. The Church of Scientology has had some success in legal battles with tax officials and other governmental agencies in a number of countries, and thus has succeeded in securing for the organization some legal privileges otherwise unobtainable. A number of NRMs and other minority religions are attempting to use the European Court of Human Rights (ECHR) to deter the exercise of legal social control over them by the over forty-member Council of Europe, which includes a growing number of countries of the former Soviet Union. Early in the twenty-first century, the record of these legal efforts was decidedly mixed, as the ECHR preferred a posture of deferring to member countries in matters having to do with religion.

Some NRMs have launched major legal attacks on their detractors in the United States and other countries, and they have also attempted to make use of the ECHR when not dealt with in a manner that seems fair to leaders of the NRM. Scientology is perhaps best known for using legal action as a way to deter detractors and promote its organization. Other NRMs have also developed legal prowess, even if only out of the necessity of defending the organization or its leaders and members in court actions. This allocation of group resources toward legal defense occurred first in claims of brainwashing for damages by former members in civil actions. But, particularly with the advent of efforts by various governments to assume authority over children of group members, some groups, such as The Family (formerly known as the Children of God), have invested heavily in developing an adequate legal defense.

Some NRMs have also launched libel and defamation actions against their detractors, a tactic that is only occasionally successful, but which also serves as a deterrent. In Hungary the Hare Krishnas (ISKCON) won a major victory against a prominent religious leader who had published a brochure defaming the group. In Russia, however, a major defamation action failed against a prominent representative of the Russian Orthodox Church who was publishing extreme accusations against a number of NRMs and other minority faiths. This case was actually used by the Russian Orthodox Church and political authorities in the successful effort to gain approval for restrictive legislation that would limit the activities of NRMs in Russia.

Of course, there are limitations on NRM use of the courts. In societies such as China, where the courts are controlled to a considerable extent by the government, it is difficult for NRM members to defend themselves in court, much less to mount legal offenses such as has been done by some groups in Western societies.

Conclusions. In many societies, particularly those dominated by one particular traditional religious organization or by a political ideology such as communism, the exercise of legal rights by NRMs has been decidedly difficult. Indeed, NRMs usually lose in legal actions whatever the societal context, as the courts exercise their normative function and make decisions in line with the basic values of a given society. It is surprising when NRMs win in court as they have sometimes done in Western countries, and it demands explanation. NRMs have sometimes successfully defended themselves against legal attacks, and some have been able to launch their own legal battles that have occasionally had a positive outcome for the organization. In such cases, the religious group has gained some legitimacy, and perhaps at least the right to be left alone.

See Also Anticult Movements; Brainwashing (Debate); Christian Science; Cults and Sects; Deprogramming; Falun Gong; Family, The; International Society for Krishna Consciousness; Jehovah's Witnesses; New Religious Movements, article on New Religious Movements and Children; Rajneesh; Scientology; Unification Church.

Bibliography

Anthony, Dick. "Pseudoscience and Minority Religions: An Evaluation of the Brainwashing Theories of Jean-Marie Abgrall." *Social Justice Research* 12 (1999): 421–456.

Anthony, Dick. "Religious Movements and Brainwashing Litigation: Evaluating Key Testimony." In *In Gods We Trust,* 2d ed., edited by T. Robbins and Dick Anthony, pp. 295–344. New Brunswick, N.J., 1991.

Bromley, David. "Conservatorships and Deprogramming: Legal and Political Perspectives." In *The Brainwashing/Deprogramming Controversy,* edited by D. Bromley and J. T. Richardson, pp. 267–293. New York, 1983.

Edelman, Brian, and James T. Richardson. "Falon Gong and the Law: Development of Legal Social Control in China." *Nova Religio* 6 (2003): 312–331.

Flinn, Frank. "Criminalizing Conversion: The Legislative Assault on New Religions." In *Crime, Values, and Religion,* edited by J. M. Day and W. S. Laufer, pp.153–192. Norwood, N.J., 1987.

Ginsburg, Gerald, and James T. Richardson. "'Brainwashing' Evidence in Light of *Daubert.*" In *Law and Science,* edited by H. Reece. pp. 265–288. Oxford, UK, 1998.

LeMoult, John, "Deprogramming Members of Religious Sects." In *The Brainwashing/Deprogramming Controversy,* edited by D. Bromely and J. T. Richardson, pp. 234–257. New York, 1983.

Palmer, Susan, and Charlotte Hardman, eds. *Children in New Religions.* New Brunswick, N.J., 1999.

Richardson, James T., ed. *Regulating Religion: Case Studies from Around the Globe.* New York, 2004. This volume has thirty-three chapters describing efforts to regulate and control minority religions in North and South America, western, eastern, and central Europe, including a number of former Soviet Union countries, as well as in Australia and the Far East.

Richardson, James T. "State and Federal Cooperation in Regulating New Religions: Oregon versus the Bhagwan Rajneesh." In *Regulating Religion,* edited by J. T. Richardson, pp. 477–490. New York, 2004.

Richardson, James T. "Law, Social Control, and Minority Religions." In *Chercheurs de Dieux dans l'espace Public—Frontier Religions in Public Space,* edited by Pauline Cote, pp.139–198. Ottawa, Canada, 2001.

Richardson, James T. "Social Control of New Religions: From 'Brainwashing' Claims to Child Sex Abuse Accusations." In *Children in New Religions,* edited by S. Palmer and C. Hardman, pp. 172–186. New Brunswick, N.J., 1999.

Richardson, James T. "'Brainwashing' Claims and Minority Religions Outside the United States: Cultural Diffusion of a Questionable Legal Concept in the Legal Arena." *Brigham Young University Law Review* 1996 (1996): 873–904.

Richardson, James T. "Minority Religions ('Cults') and the Law: Comparisons of the United States, Europe, and Australia." *University of Queensland Law Journal* 18 (1995): 183–207.

Richardson, James T., and Massimo Introvigne. "'Brainwashing' Theories in European Parliamentary and Administrative Reports on Cults and Sects." *Journal for the Scientific Study of Religion* 40 (2001): 143–168.

Shterin, Marat and J. T. Richardson. "Effects of the Western Anti-Cult Movement on Development of Laws Concerning Religion in Post-Communist Russia." *Journal of Church and State* 42 (2000): 247–272.

James T. Richardson (2005)

LAWRENCE, PETER (1921–1987), a pioneer in the study of Melanesian religions and a native of Lancashire, England, came to Australia as a child and was educated at Geelong Grammar School. As an undergraduate he studied classics at Cambridge University and after serving in naval intelligence during World War II returned to Cambridge to study anthropology under Meyer Fortes. In 1949 and 1950 he undertook field research for his doctoral dissertation among the Garia of the Madang district of what was then the Territory of New Guinea. For the rest of his life he returned regularly to the Madang area and concerned himself with Australia's preparation of New Guineans for self-government and independence.

Lawrence and his wife, Fanny, made Australia their home as he took appointments in Australian institutes of higher learning and continued his research in New Guinea. He served at the Australian National University (1948–1957), the Australian School of Pacific Administration (1957–1960), the University of Western Australia (1960–1963), the University of Queensland (1966–1970), and the University of Sydney (1963–1965 and 1970–1986). Lawrence visited North America frequently and was a visiting professor at Queens University (1969), the University of Pittsburgh (1970), and Victoria University (1975). He participated in the meetings of the Association for Social Anthropology in Oceania, a scholarly society founded in North America with a focus on the study of the cultures of the Pacific, and was elected an honorary fellow of the association. He was also active in the Australian Anthropological Society and served the journal *Oceania* as associate editor (1977–1979) and editor (1979–1985). Papers on Melanesian religion given at a symposium in his honor in 1986 at LaTrobe University in Melbourne were published posthumously as a special issue of *Oceania* (volume 59, number 1).

Lawrence's theoretical interest was in the intellectual life of indigenous peoples; he saw himself continuing the intellectualist approach to magic and religion promoted by Sir E. B. Tylor. In their introduction to *Gods, Ghosts, and Men in Melanesia,* Lawrence and coeditor Mervyn Meggitt followed Robin Horton in defining religion as "the putative extension of men's social relationships into the non-empirical realm of the cosmos" (p. 8); in Melanesia, they pointed out, gods, ghosts, ancestors, demons, and totems are closely associated with the settlements of human beings. Lawrence's *Road Belong Cargo* became a classic in the study of cargo cults and in the study of Melanesian religion. In it he traced a complex of beliefs and ritual activities in the southern Madang area from 1871 to 1950. He presented this cargo movement as a process of changing myths and rites. In the various phases of the movement the cultists appealed to traditional myths, embraced European myths, and combined myths from both sources in attempts to discover the secret of the Europeans' cargo. The term "cargo cult" seems to have first been used in 1945 (Lindstrom, p. 15) and is not original with Lawrence although he employed it. In the post-colonial Pacific the appropriateness of the term has been questioned. Lamont Lindstrom, for example, suggests that "cargo cults" probably reveal less about Melanesians than about the ideas and the motivations of the colonial officials and missionaries who reported on them. That is, the construction of "cargo cults" may point to a deficiency in Western understandings of other peoples. Elfriede Hermann, who worked in the Southern Madang area in the 1990s, and is more familiar than most with the ideas and practices of the people in the region as well as with Lawrence's work, wondered whether is was advisable to use the term at all.

Lawrence also wrote on social structure, politics, and law. The Territory of New Guinea was a United Nations trusteeship administered by Australia that in 1975 merged with the Australian Territory of Papua to become the independent state of Papua New Guinea. Lawrence believed that because he was conducting research in the region he had a responsibility to educate colonial officials and missionaries so that they could carry out their tasks with greater cultural awareness. During his time with the Australian School of Pacific Administration (ASOPA) he developed an anthropology curriculum for the teachers and public servants training for work in Australia's overseas territories. Later he was influential in the transformation of ASOPA into the International Training Institute, under the auspices of the Australian Department of Foreign Affairs, to provide education for administrators from Third World countries.

Lawrence enjoyed the engagement with patrol officers and teachers at ASOPA. He was similarly gracious and helpful to missionaries, many of whom studied with him at the University of Sydney. Raised Anglican, Lawrence professed to be an atheist, although, as he once wryly remarked, "an atheist with doubts." Lawrence's sense of humor, and his frustration with British structural-functionalism, found an outlet in a satirical poem, *Don Juan in Melanesia*. Peter Lawrence retired from the University of Sydney at the end of 1986. He died of a stroke on December 12, 1987. At the time of his death he was working on a book on the nature of religion.

SEE ALSO Cargo Cults.

BIBLIOGRAPHY

Hermann, Elfriede. "The Yali Movement in Retrospect: Rewriting History, Redefining 'Cargo Cult.'" *Oceania* 63, no. 1 (1992): 55–71.

Jebens, Holger. "How the White Man Thinks. Peter Lawrence: *Road Belong Cargo*." *Paideuma* 47 (2001): 203–221.

Jebens, Holger, ed. *Cargo, Cult, and Culture Critique*. Honolulu, 2004.

Lawrence, Peter. *Road Belong Cargo: A Study of the Cargo Movement in the Southern Madang District, New Guinea*. Manchester, U.K., 1964.

Lawrence, Peter, and Mervyn J. Meggitt, eds. *Gods, Ghosts, and Men in Melanesia*. Melbourne, 1965.

Lawrence, Peter. "Daughter of Time." Inaugural lecture as foundation professor and head of the Department of Anthropology and Sociology. St. Lucia, Queensland, 1967.

Lawrence, Peter. *Don Juan in Melanesia*. Saint Lucia, Australia, 1967.

Lawrence, Peter. *The Garia: An Ethnography of a Traditional Cosmic System in Papua New Guinea*. Manchester, U.K., 1984.

Lindstrom, Lamont. *Cargo Cult: Strange Stories of Desire from Melanesia and Beyond*. Honolulu, 1993.

MARY N. MACDONALD (2005)

LEACH, EDMUND

LEACH, EDMUND (1910–1989), a prominent British social anthropologist, is known for his critical adaptation of Claude Lévi-Strauss's structuralist principles in the interpretation of myths and social institutions.

LIFE. Edmund Ronald Leach was born into a large, upper-middle-class family of entrepreneurs in Sidmouth, Devon, England. He studied mathematics and engineering at Cambridge University, graduating in 1932. The next year he obtained a commercial position with a trading firm with offices in China. The administrative duties it entailed soon grew onerous, but the country itself fascinated him, and he seized opportunities to travel and to study the language and culture. Before returning home in 1936, he visited Botel Tobago, a small island off Formosa, where he encountered a "primitive" people, the Yami, on whom he made extensive notes.

Back in England, he met Bronislaw Malinowski (1884–1942) and began attending his seminar at the London School of Economics. Here he decided upon anthropology as a career and embraced Malinowski's distinctive type of functionalism. Leach's most important and extensive fieldwork took place during World War II, under exceptional circumstances. He arrived at the intended study site in northeast Burma in August 1939, just before the outbreak of conflict in Europe. Burma was then a British colony, and Leach enlisted in the Burma Rifles. However, before being called to active duty nine months later, he was able to engage in preliminary fieldwork among the Kachin, a remote mountain people, and write up a draft of his notes. (This draft subsequently was lost, rewritten, then lost again.) After the Japanese invaded and overran Burma in 1940 to 1941, Leach continued his military activities clandestinely behind the lines, rendering invaluable service by recruiting and leading Kachin troops because of his fluency in their language. Both before and after the liberation of the colony, Leach's duties took him to many tribal communities. On the basis of this extraordinary, though nonsystematic research, plus intensive study of documents upon his return to England, he wrote his doctoral thesis at the London School of Economics in 1947 under D. Raymond Firth and A. R. Radcliffe-Brown.

Following a short government research mission to Sarawak, Leach was appointed lecturer in primitive technology at the London School of Economics in 1948. Soon he took a leave of absence to work on the book *Political Systems of Highland Burma* (1954), which became a classic in social anthropology. In 1953, Meyer Fortes, formerly of the London School of Economics and by now head of the anthropology department at Cambridge University, invited Leach to join his faculty. Thereafter, this university would be Leach's base of operations. From July to November 1954 he engaged in concentrated fieldwork in a peasant village in Ceylon, on the basis of which he wrote *Pul Eliya* (1961a). In 1960 he was elected fellow of King's College, and in 1966 he became its provost. From 1971 until 1975 he served as president of the Royal Anthropological Institute. He was named to the British Academy in 1972, and was knighted in 1975.

Sir Edmund retired from the Department of Anthropology in 1978 and the next year from the provostship, but he continued to be active while health permitted: writing, attending meetings, and lecturing at universities in England, the United States, and elsewhere. His last public lecture was given in the United States in April 1986. After a long struggle with cancer, he succumbed to a brain tumor on January 6, 1989.

Theory and Method. The social anthropology in vogue in England and the United States when Leach was a student and began his career was functionalism. While this term covers a variety of individual approaches, functionalism in general may be defined as the attempt, using empirical data obtained from fieldwork, to determine how a society "functions" as a system. Furthermore, the elements that comprise a social system, such as marriage rules, economics, and religion, must be studied not as isolated entities, but in their total social context, as parts of a working whole. Malinowski exemplified this methodology.

Contrasted with this approach is that typified by James Frazer (1854–1941), who in his monumental *The Golden Bough* (1911–1915), a compendium of data about folklore, magic, and primitive religion, sought to discover fundamental truths about human psychology through comparison of apparently similar data, selected unscientifically from all times and places. Leach's fieldwork in northeast Burma focused on kinship structures, and his first published article on the Kachin (1945, in 1961b) was dominated by Malinowski's functionalism. However, when he read Claude Lévi-Strauss's *Les structures élémentaires de la parenté* (1949), he was strongly drawn to the French anthropologist's "structuralism." Thereafter, without renouncing all functionalist principles, he employed a method that owed much to Lévi-Strauss, but was not, he insisted, a "Lévi-Straussian methodology" (1983a, p. 2).

In a sense, structuralism can be classified as a continuation of Frazerian anthropology in that it seeks to establish facts true of "the human mind." Although Lévi-Strauss traveled extensively for some months in 1938 among "primitive" tribes in Brazil, his fieldwork is deemed shallow by functionalist standards, and his writings are not truly dependent upon it. Rather, his method derives from the structural linguistics of Ferdinand de Saussure (1857–1913) and Roman Jakobson (1896–1982). Significantly, Lévi-Strauss and Jakobson were colleagues in 1945 at the New School for Social Research in New York. (Similarly, Leach was Jakobson's colleague at Stanford from 1952 to 1953.) Just as Jakobson taught that in all languages, humans code and decode sounds into meaningful speech by combining them into bundles of binary oppositions, so Lévi-Strauss taught that the myths, rituals, eating customs, and all other aspects of a society express contrasting pairs (left/right, male/female, and so on), between which mediating elements intervene. This is the logic by which the human mind functions, he insisted, and his writings analyze these oppositions and mediations. Once a structure is identified in one society or text, comparisons can be made with others. In his later work, especially, he came under criticism from Leach for departing from empirical data in his search for universals applicable to all humanity (Leach, 1970, p. 104). Leach criticized him too for distinguishing between "cold" (primitive, ahistorical) and "hot" (historically conscious) societies (1983a, p. 21–22).

Leach has said of his own magnum opus (1954) that it is a kind of "dialogue between the empiricism of Malinowski and the rationalism of Lévi-Strauss" (1982, p. 44). The latter's *Les structures élémentaires* had contained much about the Kachin, based on data obtained wholly from documentary sources. Although Leach made early use of Lévi-Strauss's structuralism in his 1954 book, he signaled ethnological errors in Lévi-Strauss's statements on marriage relations among these people. The criticism led to a protracted polemics, eventually ending in a rupture between the scholars when Lévi-Strauss refused, in the revised version of his book (1967, 1969), to acknowledge Leach correct. Nevertheless, there were numerous friendly exchanges between them from 1962 to 1966, when Leach was writing structural analyses of myths, and in 1970 Leach penned a lucid, concise, and mostly positive study of Lévi-Strauss that became a standard introduction to his thought.

To the end of his career, Leach continued to adhere to a basic principle of functionalism, namely, that "the real subject matter of social anthropology is the actual social behavior of human beings" (1970, p. 105), while also employing methods of structural analysis derived from Jakobson and Lévi-Strauss.

MYTH AND RELIGION. In private life, Leach was a Humanist (Leach, 1972), and his beliefs carried over into his scholarly work. Once when a fellow anthropologist called him a "vulgar positivist" (Clifford Geertz, in Banton, 1966, p. 35), he retorted, "This intended insult I take as a compliment," adding, "positivists, whether vulgar or otherwise, usually show signs of knowing what they are talking about, whereas theologians, even when disguised as Professors of Anthropology, do not" (Leach, 1969b, p. 86). When he wrote about the Kachin *nats* (spirits), he dismissed them as "nothing more" (1954, p. 182) than ways of describing relationships among persons and groups in the society. Religion, as such, did not interest him at this time.

Having been won over, largely, to the structuralist or symbolist view of myth by 1959 (Leach, 1961b), in the 1960s and 1980s Leach wrote several structuralist interpretations of biblical narratives and Christian doctrine (1969b, 1983a), fields his Parisian counterpart eschewed. The most complex of these is "The Legitimacy of Solomon" (1966), a tour de force of the Jewish scriptures, which disregards biblical criticism, theology, and historical concerns, and instead treats the text as "myth," taking it as a whole. Leach identifies recurring binary patterns concerning incest, murder/sacrifice, endogamy/exogamy, descent, and inheritance, and shows how the writers (consciously or unconsciously) found mediating agencies to resolve the "unresolvable" dilemmas in the narratives. For this article, Leach won the commendation of two prominent Jewish scholars, Jacob Neusner and Abraham Malamat (Tambiah, 2002, pp. 303–305). In another article, "Virgin Birth" (1966) he shows how Christians can believe that Jesus was both supernaturally conceived (by the Holy Spirit through the Virgin Mary) and the human messiah, descended from David through Joseph. In this case, both Jesus and Mary are mediators between earth and heaven. Then Leach uses this illustration to contradict the claim of certain anthropologists that some primitive tribes are ignorant of the connection between copulation and conception.

Only once did Leach write expressly about the history of religions: in a 1966 review of Mircea Eliade's 1965 book *Mephistopheles and the Androgyne.* Since a major theme of this book is the *coincidentia oppositorum,* it was an appropriate volume for him to review, but in doing so, he also discussed nine other works by Eliade. He charged the author with being a "Frazerian," a "Jesuit," and a Jungian, with inflating his outdated bibliographies, with believing in a prelogical archaic mentality, and with speaking like "an enlightened prophet." He commends Eliade for stressing notions of polarity (sacred/profane, heaven/earth) and the necessity for connecting links between them, such as the yogin and the shaman, but he says that the true implications of these ideas have escaped him. Leach believed that "because Eliade has recognized that religious symbols occur not singly but as binary pairs, he is really committed to an analysis of *structure.*"

The value of structuralist analyses of religious texts, for Leach, was not that they reveal truth or meaning, but that they afford the basis for looking at familiar materials in a new way. "Mediation between opposites is precisely what religious thinking is all about," he once said (Leach, 1983a, p. 16).

Leach also reviewed numerous books on religion by fellow anthropologists and wrote structuralist studies of religious art and architecture (1971b, 1978, 1983b, 1985). Although a few American religion scholars utilize Lévi-Straussian structuralist principles (e.g., Penner, 1989; Doniger, 1998), Leach is seldom cited. Leach is much better known and referenced by anthropologists, especially in the United Kingdom.

SEE ALSO Structuralism.

BIBLIOGRAPHY

Cambridge Anthropology. Special Issue: Sir Edmund Leach 13, no. 3 (1989–90).

Doniger, Wendy. *The Implied Spider: Politics and Theology in Myth.* New York, 1998. A great many references to Lévi-Strauss, but Leach is cited only three times.

Eliade, Mircea. *Mephistopheles and the Androgyne: Studies in Religious Myth and Symbol.* Translated by J. M. Cohen. New York, 1965.

Frazer, James G. *The Golden Bough.* 3d ed., rev. and enl., 12 volumes. London, 1911–1915.

Geertz, Clifford. "Religion as a Cultural System." In *Anthropological Approaches to the Study of Religion,* edited by Michael Banton, pp. 1–46. London and New York, 1966.

Leach, Edmund R. *Political Systems of Highland Burma: A Study of Kachin Social Structure.* London, 1954.

Leach, Edmund R. *Pul Eliya, a Village in Ceylon: A Study in Land Tenure and Kinship.* Cambridge, U.K., 1961a.

Leach, Edmund R. *Rethinking Anthropology.* London, 1961b. Besides "Jinghpaw Kinship Terminology: An Experiment in Ethnographic Algebra" (1945): 28–53 and the groundbreaking essay, "Rethinking Anthropology" (1959): 1–27, the volume contains two short essays of interest to religion scholars on symbolic representations of time: "Chronus and Chronos": 124-132; and "Time and False Noses": 132-136.

Leach, Edmund R. "Sermons by a Man on a Ladder." Review of *Mephistopheles and the Androgyne,* by Mircea Eliade. *New York Review of Books* (October 20, 1966): 28–31.

Leach, Edmund R. "High School." Review of *The Teachings of Don Juan: A Yaqui Way of Knowledge,* by Carlos Castaneda. *New York Times Review of Books* (June 5, 1969a). A caustic critique of "the fashionable mysticism of hippydom."

Leach, Edmund R. *Genesis as Myth and Other Essays.* London, 1969b. Contains "Genesis as Myth" (1962), "The Legitimacy of Solomon: Some Structural Aspects of Old Testament History" (1966), and "Virgin Birth" (1966).

Leach, Edmund R. "'Kachin' and 'Haka Chin': A Rejoinder to Lévi-Strauss." *Man* (n.s.) 4, no. 2 (1969c): 277–285.

Leach, Edmund R. *Claude Lévi-Strauss.* London and New York, 1970.

Leach, Edmund R. "Mythical Inequalities." Review of *The Death and Rebirth of the Seneca* by Anthony F. C. Wallace; *Natural*

Symbols: Explorations in Cosmology by Mary Douglas; and *Myth: Its Meaning and Functions in Ancient and Other Cultures* by G. S. Kirk. *New York Review of Books* (January 28, 1971a).

Leach, Edmund R. "The Politics of Karma." Review of *Buddhism and Society* by Melford Spiro, *Religion and Change in Contemporary Asia*, edited by Robert F. Spencer, and *Islam Observed* by Clifford Geertz. *New York Times Review of Books* (November 18, 1971b).

Leach, Edmund R. "A Personal View." *Humanist News* (January–February, 1972).

Leach, Edmund R. "Michelangelo's Genesis: Structural Comments on the Paintings of the Sistine Chapel Ceiling." *Times Literary Supplement* (March 18, 1978).

Leach, Edmund R. *Social Anthropology*. Glasgow, 1982.

Leach, Edmund R. "Anthropological Approaches to the Study of the Bible during the Twentieth Century" (1980): 7–32; "Against Genres: Are Parables Lights Set in Candlesticks or Put under a Bushel?" (1982): 89–112; "Why Did Moses Have a Sister?" (1980): 33–66; and "Melchisedeh and the Emperor: Icons of Subversion in Orthodoxy" (1983) 67–88. In *Structuralist Interpretations of Biblical Myth*, edited by Edmund R. Leach and D. Alan Aycock. Cambridge, UK, and New York, 1983a. This book also includes an important methodological introduction: pp. 1–6.

Leach, Edmund R. "The Gatekeepers of Heaven: Anthropological Aspects of Grandiose Architecture." *Journal of Anthropological Research* 39, no. 3 (1983b): 243–264.

Leach, Edmund R. "Michelangelo's Genesis: A Structuralist Interpretation of the Central Panels of the Sistine Chapel." *Semiotica* 56, nos. 1–2 (December 1985): 1–30.

Leach, Edmund R. "Noah's Second Son." *Anthropology Today* 4, no. 4 (1988): 2–5. Opposing racial discrimination.

Lévi-Strauss, Claude. *Les structures élémentaires de la parenté*. Paris, 1949. 2d rev. ed. Paris and the Hague, 1967. Translated as *The Elementary Structures of Kinship* by James Harle Bell, John Richard von Sturmer, and Rodney Needham. Boston and London, 1969.

Malamat, Abraham. "Comments on E. Leach: 'The Legitimacy of Solomon—Some Structural Aspects of Old Testament History.'" *Archives Européennes de sociologie* 8 (1967): 165–167.

Neusner, Jacob. "The Talmud as Anthropology." Annual Samuel Friedland Lecture, the Jewish Theological Seminary of America (1979). See Tambiah (2002): 301–303.

Penner, Hans. *Impasse and Resolution: A Critique of the Study of Religion*. New York, 1989.

Tambiah, Stanley J. *Edmund Leach: An Anthropological Life*. Cambridge, UK, 2002. Thorough, sympathetic treatment of Leach's life and work, by a former pupil. Indispensable resource.

MAC LINSCOTT RICKETTS (2005)

LEADERSHIP. The concept of religious leadership, although indispensable to general discourse, has been of limited value to the social scientific study of religion, which has advanced little beyond the pioneering studies of Max Weber and Joachim Wach. While a great deal is known about individual religious leaders and have accumulated a reservoir of case studies of such leaders, far less is known about the phenomenon of leadership. Indeed, what is lacking at present is a generally accepted concept of religious leadership. Scholars working in different religious traditions use diverse modes of theorizing and analysis and do so in pursuit of differing and often unrelated questions. Important but largely unrecognized work in the psychology of leadership in small groups, social exchange models of interaction processes developed by sociologists, and shifts in focus from power to leadership in political science thinking all provide new bases for generalizations about religious leadership across differing cultures and times.

Religious leadership may be defined as the process by which leaders induce followers to act for certain transcendental goals that embody the values, motivations, and aspirations of both leaders and followers. Such leadership involves the exercise of power in religious collectivities, but its domain is more limited than that of power. Unrestricted power over others is exercised to realize the goals of the power-wielder whether or not these goals are shared by the followers. The essence of leadership lies in the manner in which leaders perceive and act on their own and their followers' values and needs (Burns, 1978).

WEBER'S TYPOLOGY OF RELIGIOUS LEADERSHIP. The groundwork for a comparative study of religious leadership was laid by the German sociologist Max Weber in his *Wirtschaft und Gesellschaft* (1925), the first strictly empirical comparison of the social structure and normative order of societies in world-historical depth. He contributed the outlines of a typology of religious leaders as well as a major statement on forms of domination and the bases of legitimization of authority underlying different types of leadership. In spite of his stress on the independent significance of religious values and ethics, he acknowledged the importance of the social vehicles through which the impact of religion is effected. His analysis of religious groups, as one instance of a variety of nearly universal types of human groups found at differing phases of historical development, highlights the crucial importance of religious leadership as a vehicle of religiosity and religious change.

Weber isolates the features peculiar to three major types of leaders—magicians, prophets, and priests—through a comparison with each other as well as with the subsidiary leadership roles of lawgivers, teachers of ethics, and mystagogues. The emergence of priests as distinct from practitioners of magic centers on several points of differentiation: (1) priests influence the gods by means of worship, whereas magicians coerce demons by magical means; (2) priests are "functionaries of a regularly organized and permanent enterprise concerned with influencing the gods," whereas magicians engage in "individual and occasional efforts"; (3) priests are actively associated with some type of social organization by which they are employed, in contrast to magicians who are typically self-employed; and (4) the priest exerts influence by virtue of his professional expertise in fixed doctrine and his vocational qualifications, whereas magicians exert their influence by virtue of personal gifts and charisma made manifest in miracles. The nature of the learning of these leadership roles differs; priests undergo rational training and discipline and magicians are prepared through an "awakening" using nonrational means and proceeding in part as a training in purely empirical lore.

Weber recognized that in reality the contrasts just noted are fluid and by no means unequivocally determinable so that empirically the two contrasted types often flow into one another. The crucial feature of the priesthood is centered on "the specialization of a particular group of persons in the continuous operation of a cultic enterprise permanently associated with particular norms, places, and times and related to specific social groups."

Building on Adolf von Harnack's typology, Weber isolates the sociologically distinctive traits of the prophet as a "purely individual bearer of charisma who by virtue of his mission proclaims a religious doctrine or divine commandment." For Weber, it is this personal call that is the decisive element distinguishing prophet from priest. It is the latter who claims authority by virtue of his service in a sacred tradition, whereas the prophet's claim is based on personal revelation and charisma. It is no accident that almost no prophets have emerged from the priestly class. The priest typically dispenses salvation by virtue of his office even in instances in which personal charisma may be involved. It is the hierarchical office that confers legitimate authority upon the priest as a member of an organized collectivity.

A second and closely linked point is Weber's focus on the prophet as an agent of change who takes personal responsibility for breaking with the established normative order, declaring this break to be morally legitimate. The leadership role of the priest by contrast is exercised typically in the service of an established order.

Unlike the magician, the prophet claims definitive revelations, the core of his mission being doctrine or commandment, not magic. Again, Weber acknowledged that this distinction was fluid; magicians are frequently knowledgeable experts in divination and prophets often practice divination as well as magical healing and counseling like the *nevi'im* mentioned in the Old Testament. What distinguishes the prophet from both the magician and the priest in this regard is an economic factor, namely, that prophecy is unremunerated. Weber further differentiates prophets from the religious leadership roles of lawgivers, epitomized in the Greek *aisumnētai*, teachers of ethics, and mystagogues. While the transition historically from prophet to each of these types is not clearly defined, Weber separated out from the category of prophet these other types, treating them as analytically distinguishable leadership roles for "sundry purveyors of salvation." Of these, only the mystagogue—Weber's neologism for the religious counterpart of the demagogue—shared with the prophet a leadership role that demands a break with the established order. But whereas the prophet legitimates that break in ethical and moral terms, the bases of legitimation for the mystagogue are primarily magical.

Central to Weber's delineation of the role of prophet was his differentiation of two subtypes. One was the *ethical* prophet, who preaches as one who has received a commission from God and who demands obedience as an ethical duty. He is represented most clearly by Muhammad and Zarathushtra (Zoroaster). The Buddha by contrast typified the *exemplary* prophet, who by his personal example demonstrates to others the way to religious salvation.

A discussion of Weber's typology of religious leaders is distorted unless it includes reference to his discussion of the laity whom prophets and priests sought to influence. For a prophecy is successful only if the prophet succeeds in winning permanent helpers. These include the *amaga*, or members of the inner circle of devotees of Zoroastrianism; the disciples of the Hebrew Bible and of the New Testament; and the intimate companions of Hinduism and Islam. The distinctive characteristic in all these cases is that these are personal devotees of the prophet who, in contrast to those of the priest, are not organized into guilds or office hierarchies. In addition to these most active co-workers, there is a widening circle of followers who support the prophet and expect to obtain their salvation through his mission. These followers may engage in intermittent action or associate themselves continuously in a congregation. The latter community does not arise in connection with every type of prophecy; generally it is the result of routinization, that is, of a process securing the permanence of the prophet's preaching and the congregation's role as distributor and recipient of grace.

Weber reserves the term *congregation* for situations in which the laity has been organized permanently in such a manner that it becomes an active participant. Thus a mere administrative unit that delimits the jurisdiction of priests is a parish but not yet a congregational community. From this point of view, one finds that in medieval Christianity in the West and Islam in Near East the parish was essentially a passive ecclesiastical tax unit with the laity generally lacking the character of a congregation. By contrast, it is the distinctive characteristic of sects that they are based on a restricted association of individual local congregations. In such circumstances the relationship between priesthood and laity becomes of crucial significance for the practical consequences of religion and for the exercise of religious leadership.

Weber here argues that every type of priesthood is to some extent in a similar position: To maintain its own power it must meet the needs of the laity to a very considerable degree. Because as a rule both the ethical and the exemplary prophet are themselves laymen, the prophet's power position depends in both cases also on that of his lay followers. To what extent the prophet would succeed as a leader depended on the outcome of a struggle for power. All prophets made use of the prestige of their prophetic charisma and the support it gained them among the laity. The sacredness of the radically new revelation was continuously opposed to that of tradition. Depending on the success of the propaganda by each side, the priesthood might compromise with the new prophecy, outbid its doctrine, eliminate it, or be subjugated itself. Religious leadership, in short, is exercised typically in competition or conflict with others in which the different leaders contend for the support of their potential followers.

In Weber's ensuing discussion of the major social classes and their affinities for religion, he provides a comparative frame of reference for assessing the influence of class factors in conditioning the outcome of specific religious leaders' claims for support by the laity. This includes a discussion of intellectuals and of the conditions under which priests and monks become intellectual elaborators of religion, as was true, for example, in India, Egypt, and Babylonia. In the religions of the ancient city-states, however, notably among the Phoenicians, Greeks, and Romans, the development of all metaphysical and ethical thought became the province of nonpriests. Weber further emphasized the predominance of high-status intellectuals as religious innovators and leaders.

The Bases of Legitimation of Authority. Weber's typology of religious leadership is intricately linked to his sociological analysis of forms of domination, with its threefold typology of the bases of legitimation of authority to which such leaders made claim. [*See* Authority.] Domination was defined by Weber as "the probability that certain specific commands (or all commands) will be obeyed by a given group of persons." Domination ("authority") for Weber could be based on diverse motives of compliance "all the way from simple habituation to the most purely rational calculation of advantage." But he makes clear that every form of domination implies at least a minimum of voluntary compliance and thus represents obedience based on self-interested calculation.

For Weber, the key to leadership had to be found in the kind of legitimacy claimed by the leader, the type of obedience demanded, the kind of administrative support developed to guarantee its success, and the modes by which such authority is exercised. All of these would differ fundamentally depending upon which of three types of legitimization was most prevalent. The validity of claims to legitimacy, according to Weber, were based on (1) rational grounds, resting on a belief in the legality of enacted rules and the right of those elevated to authority under such rules to issue commands, that is, legal authority; (2) grounds resting on an established belief in the sanctity of traditions and the legitimacy of those exercising authority under them, that is, traditional authority; and (3) charismatic grounds "resting on devotion to the exceptional sanctity, heroism, or exemplary character of an individual person and of the normative patterns or order revealed or ordained by him, i.e., charismatic authority."

The concept of charisma, "gift of grace," was taken from the vocabulary of early Christianity and drew heavily on writings of the church and legal historian Rudolf Sohm, in particular his *Kirchenrecht* (1892). The term *charisma* as elaborated by Weber refers to "a certain quality of an individual personality by virtue of which he is considered extraordinary and treated as endowed with supernatural, superhuman, or at least specifically exceptional powers or qualities. These . . . are regarded as of divine origin or as exemplary and on the basis of them the individual concerned is treated as a 'leader.'" What is crucial is how the individual is regarded by those subject to charismatic authority, that is, by the leader's followers or disciples. Such recognition is freely given and guaranteed by "what is held to be proof, originally always a miracle, and consists in devotion to the corresponding revelation, hero worship, or absolute trust in the leader."

Weber notes that where charisma is genuine, the basis lies not in such proof per se but rather in the conception that it is the duty of those subject to charismatic authority to recognize its genuineness and to act accordingly. Psychologically, such recognition is a matter of complete personal devotion to the possessor of the quality, arising out of enthusiasm or alternately out of despair or of hope. The charismatic leader's legitimacy to act is thus not derived from the follower's consent or from custom or law, but from a transcendental realm.

The right of the leader to rule is determined by the follower's recognition of the godlike qualities either imputed to him by the follower or bestowed on him through ascension to a charismatic office. The success of the charismatic leader in developing a community of disciples or followers gives rise to the charismatic community. But if that community is to take on a degree of permanence—a matter of considerable interest to the disciples and followers if their own positions are to be put on a stable, everyday basis—it becomes necessary for the character of the original charismatic authority to be altered radically.

The problem of leadership transfer from the charismatically endowed leader to his successor is thus inherently unstable. How this problem is met, if it is met at all, is amenable to a range of solutions. These include the search for a new leader, using as criteria qualities that will fit him for the position of authority, as has historically been so with the search for a new Dalai Lama; revelation manifested in the use of lots or divine judgment or other techniques of selection; designation on the part of the original charismatic leader of his own successor (a very common form); designation of a successor by the charismatically qualified administrative staff together with his recognition by the community; and transmission of charisma by heredity or by ritual means. In the last case, charisma becomes disassociated from a particular individual, is objectified, and becomes a transferable entity that may be transformed into a charisma of office. A critical example is the transmission of priestly charisma by anointing, consecration, or the laying on of hands.

The Weberian typology of religious leadership was subsequently enlarged by Joachim Wach in his *Einführung in die*

Religionssoziologie (1931). Wach attempts to classify the variety of types of religious authority "according to the principle of personal and official charisma," although he recognizes that a given type can include a combination of both elements. Even though the critical issue of leadership as deriving from different forms of charismatic authority is never explicitly addressed by Wach, his typology has generally been presumed to constitute both a delineation of types of religious leaders and an analysis of the underlying types of legitimation of their rule. In addition to the categories of priest, prophet, and magician already developed by Weber to which Wach's delineation provides little that is analytically new, Wach adds the following types: founder, reformer, seer, diviner, saint, and *religiosus.* As with Weber, Wach's analysis is directed not only to an examination of the charismatic basis of their claims to authority, but also to an elaboration of the variety of religious roles played by such leaders. Even as a classificatory tool, however, Wach's typology needs to be substantially enlarged if it is to encompass the diversity of religious leadership known to contemporary scholars. Still more crucial is the fact that with Wach, the emphasis shifted from typology as a tool of analysis and explanation to a tool of description and classification. It is to these analytic and explanatory concerns to which this article must now return.

CURRENT THEORIES IN THE SOCIAL SCIENCES. Research in the fields of psychology, political science, and sociology may be drawn on to suggest a number of new directions for the study of religious leadership.

Origins of religious leadership. One key to understanding leadership lies in recent findings and concepts in psychology, psychiatry, and psychohistory. Despite its cultural limitations, psychobiography can be an important tool in analyzing the formative influences on religious leadership, as Erik H. Erikson's studies of Luther and Gandhi have documented. Viewing some of the influences in the early years of great religious leaders, one may come to better understand the powerful influences of family, peer group, class, and adolescent experience. Such studies, however, will always be inadequate, because they deal with only one segment and tend to slight the effects of religious learning, political and institutional contexts, and the role of followers in shaping the behavior of leaders.

Social sources of leadership. Typologies of leadership by virtue of their abstraction tend to disassociate leadership from its social-situational context. Leadership occurs, as Weber's discussion of hierocracy, theocracy, and caesaropapism documents, in an immensely complex social network of structured and patterned relationships. The psychology of small-group research documents, moreover, how leadership adheres not in an individual but in a role that is imbedded within some specified social system. Variations in the social context within which religious leadership is deemed to be critical represent an important historical variable. Thus, studies of religious organizations that have focused on their leadership in modern industrial societies in the period since World War II rarely if ever address the kinds of issues dealt with by Weber. The study of religious leadership in these contexts typically involves an analysis of personnel recruitment, socialization, professionalization, training for the ministerial or priestly role, and delineation of the various role segments of administrator, preacher, counselor, teacher, and pastor. A recent review of the literature by the American sociologist Edgar W. Mills (1985) decried the absence of a concern with leadership in most contemporary studies of the ministry. These themes reflect, as Roland Robertson (1970) has noted, organizational constraints upon the exercise of leadership in societies in which religion has become increasingly differentiated and compartmentalized.

Personal traits. Religious leadership like other forms of leadership cannot be reduced to some specific set of abilities or personal attributes. Even the prophet is not born with "the gift of grace"; he must claim it. Natural endowment, intellectual or emotional predisposition, and training are only accessory, and they vary considerably.

A mixing of variables. Typologies of leadership, including those of religious leadership, have too often drawn on a variety of analytical and theoretical considerations without adequately differentiating the specific variables according to which a given religious leader is classified within one type rather than another. Indeed the very delineation of these types and their nomenclature suggest a mixing of variables. Thus a delineation of religious leaders as founders, reformers, revolutionaries, and conservationists focuses on the role of such leadership in challenging, revitalizing, or maintaining the existing social and religious order. By contrast, a typological distinction between expressive and instrumental types of leaders emphasizes differences in the ways in which leadership is exercised and followers exhorted, as was also true of Weber's original distinction between exemplary and ethical forms of prophetic leadership. Other typologies have focused on segmental roles or functions assumed by specific religious leaders, such as miracle workers, exorcists, moral teachers, mediators, ritual specialists, administrators, and scribes, as well as intellectual leaders and educators.

REVISED ASSUMPTIONS. Underlying the Weberian approach to religious leadership, and subscribed to equally by Wach, are a number of assumptions that recent research has either seriously questioned or forced to abandon altogether. Classic sociological treatments of religious leadership have leaned heavily on conceptions applying to elites, to authoritarian systems and to rigid caste- and class-based societies. The literature on religious leaders (and on leadership in general) has generally been committed to images of strong-willed leaders and mindless masses. Weber emphasized the authoritarian character of such leadership, especially charismatic leadership, by focusing on the exclusive prerogative of leaders to command and the unquestioning obligation of subordinates to obey. As a result there has been an unfortunate emphasis on the "great man" theory of leadership.

The role of gender—to the extent to which it enters into these studies of religious leadership at all—has simply reinforced the sterotyped image of religious leaders as male. The conditions under which women claim and successfully exercise such leadership has only recently become a topic of serious scholarly investigation. The focus on the great men who exercised religious leadership has moreover ignored the vital network of secondary, tertiary, and even "lower" leadership in most societies and most religious communities.

Weber's delineation of charismatic leadership has been a source of considerable confusion. This confusion has arisen because he integrated two distinct analytic components, the one social-structural and the other psychological, into his discussion of charismatic legitimations of authority. Each of them highlights different aspects of leaders and of their relationships to their followers. Yet, in focusing on the personal and affective dimensions of the relationship between charismatic leaders and their followers, Weber himself tilted the balance toward an emphasis on personality. The dominant thrust of his analysis was toward linking charisma with certain structural strains that are likely to be pronounced during periods of accelerated social change. But his analysis of the social conditions that give rise to charismatic leadership remained sketchy. These ambiguities in Weber's own discussion of charismatic leadership are reflected and magnified in the recent literature dealing with charisma, which has often used historical materials in an undiscriminating way to refer to almost all nonbureaucratic forms of leadership.

Although Weber never adopted the traditional image of leadership as unilateral—one was either leader or follower—his analysis of the relationship between the two, seen in the light of more recent research findings from the social sciences, tends to underplay the degree to which followers condition, shape, and mold both their leaders and the religious movements of which they form a part.

Similarly, Wach's discussion of the groups "corresponding to religious authority" is entitled "the audience" and includes references to the ephemeral audience of the migrating preacher or prophet, the crowd attending a religious celebration, and the permanent circle accompanying the founder and prophet. Such labeling of the group of followers as an audience betrays the passivity with which they are presumed to function and relate to their leader. While past studies of religious leaders generally portrayed their followers as a passive audience or mere aggregation minus the leader, more recent psychological and sociological research drawing on interaction theory and social exchange theory has demonstrated conclusively that the concepts of leading and following are reciprocal. Thus, religious leaders are by no means exclusively and always engaged in acts of leading. Leaders and followers do at times exchange roles, with the most active followers and disciples initiating acts of leadership. The expectations of followers and the acceptance accorded the leader may be as influential in shaping the character and consequences of that leadership as the resources of the leader himself. A more systematic attention to followers is likely to lead to the development of typologies not only of followers but of various models of leader-follower relationships.

The topic of religious leadership needs to draw on the empirical findings, concepts, and theoretical insights of recent research by social scientists working for the most part outside the realm of religious studies. The rapid proliferation of case studies of individual religious leaders, both past and present, has yet to be systematically integrated into a conceptual framework capable of subsuming the complex character of religious leadership. Greater integration is necessary if one is to move beyond description and classification to a level of analysis that will incorporate the determinants, processes, character, and consequences of such leadership.

See Also Charisma; Intellectuals; Priesthood; Prophecy; Shamanism.

Bibliography

Bendix, Reinhard. "Reflections on Charismatic Leadership." In *State and Society: A Reader in Comparative Political Sociology*, edited by Reinhard Bendix, pp. 616–629. Boston, 1968.

Bierstedt, Robert. "The Problem of Authority." In *Freedom and Control in Modern Society*, edited by Morroe Berger, Theodore Abel, and Charles H. Page, pp. 67–81. New York, 1954.

Burns, James MacGregor. *Leadership*. New York, 1978.

Erikson, Erik H. *Young Man Luther: A Study in Psychoanalysis and History*. New York, 1958.

Erikson, Erik H. *Gandhi's Truth: On the Origins of Militant Nonviolence*. New York, 1969.

Gibb, Cecil A. "Leadership: Psychological Aspects." In *International Encyclopedia of the Social Sciences*, edited by David L. Sills, vol. 9, pp. 91–101. New York, 1968.

Mills, Edgar W. "The Sacred in Ministry Studies." In *The Sacred in a Secular Age*, edited by Phillip E. Hammond. Berkeley, Calif., 1985.

Robertson, Roland. *The Sociological Interpretation of Religion*. New York, 1970.

Sohm, Rudolf. *Kirchenrecht*. Leipzig, 1892.

Tannenbaum, Arnold S. "Leadership: Sociological Aspects." In *International Encyclopedia of the Social Sciences*, edited by David L. Sills, vol. 9, pp. 101–107. New York, 1968.

Wach, Joachim. *Einführung in die Religionssoziologie* (1931). Translated by the author as *Sociology of Religion*. Chicago, 1944.

Weber, Max. *Wirtschaft und Gesellschaft: Grundriss der verstehenden Soziologie* (1922). 2 vols. Translated by Ephraim Fischoff et al. as *Economy and Society*, edited by Guenther Roth and Claus Wittich. Berkeley, Calif., 1978.

Willner, Ann Ruth. *The Spellbinders: Charismatic Political Leadership*. New Haven, Conn., 1984.

New Sources

Aberach, David. *Charisma in Politics, Religion and the Media: Private Trauma, Public Ideas*. Basingstoke, U.K., 1996.

Afsaruddin, Asma. *Excellence and Preference: Medieval Islamic Discourses on Leadership.* Boston, Mass., 2002.

Clarke, Andrew. *Serve the Community of the Church: Christians as Leaders and Ministers.* Grand Rapids, Mich., 2000.

Elazar, Daniel, ed. *Authority, Power and Leadership in the Jewish Polity.* Lanham, Md., 1991.

Fuller, Timothy, ed. *Leading and Leadership.* The Ethics of Everyday Life series. Notre Dame, Ind., 2000.

Harris, James. *The Courage to Lead: Leadership in the African American Urban Church.* Lanham, Md., 2002.

Hutch, Richard. *Religious Leadership: Personality, History, and Sacred Authority.* New York, 1991.

GILLIAN LINDT (1987)
Revised Bibliography

LEAH SEE RACHEL AND LEAH

LEAVEN.

LEAVEN. The Hebrews and other peoples of the Middle East were taught to use leaven by the Egyptians, who may have discovered its use as early as 2600 BCE. Although leavened bread took on importance as a religious symbol during the Azyme Controversy that finally divided Eastern and Western Christianity in 1054, the use of unleavened bread has had far greater significance in religious ritual. As a consequence, the ritualistic use of unleavened bread and the symbolic meaning of leaven merit special attention.

The best-known use of unleavened bread is described in the twelfth chapter of *Exodus,* where Ḥag ha-Matsot, the Feast of Unleavened Bread, and Passover are interfused in a historical commemoration of Israel's deliverance from Egypt. Other texts in the Hebrew scriptures indicate that the two feasts had different origins (*Dt.* 16:1–8, *Lv.* 23:5–6). Whereas Passover was a pastoral festival, the Feast of Unleavened Bread was agricultural. Because natural dough, a harvest gift of Yahveh, was considered holy, the addition of yeast would profane it. In addition, fermentation may have been viewed as a form of corruption.

Unleavened bread was prescribed for the night of Passover also to remind the Hebrews of the great haste with which they ate during their anxious flight from Egypt. During the Feast of Unleavened Bread, which began on the day following Passover and lasted seven days, the Israelites were directed to destroy all leavened bread that remained in their homes and eat only the "bread of misery."

When the Israelites celebrated Shavuʿot, the Feast of Weeks (or Pentecost), at the end of the wheat harvest, they offered leavened bread as first fruits because it had become their common bread in Canaan. Although they associated leavened bread with the giving of the Law of Moses, the ritual for communion sacrifices stipulated that unleavened cakes mixed with oil and unleavened wafers smeared with oil be used. Leavened bread, however, was also to be given to the priest for the sacrificial meal (*Lv.* 7:11–15).

The Israelites seem to have been ambivalent about adding leaven to dough. Although its use conflicted with their eating habits as nomads, once they settled in Egypt and Canaan they routinely consumed leavened bread.

In the New Testament, leaven has at least three symbolic meanings: It is a sign of the Old Covenant that must yield to the New Covenant; it is symbolic of corrupting influences; and it typifies small beginnings that have enormous potential for growth. Paul instructed the Corinthians to rid themselves of the old yeast of evil and wickedness and to become instead the unleavened bread of sincerity and truth (*1 Cor.* 5:8). In this way, they would be united with the risen Christ in an unending Passover. Paul thus turned the cultic practice of the Israelites into an ethical injunction. The suggestion that leaven corrupts is also found in the admonition of Jesus to be on guard against the yeast of the Pharisees, that is, their hypocrisy (*Lk.* 12:1). Like many other symbols, yeast had a positive as well as a negative aspect. The parable comparing the kingdom of heaven to a yeast that spreads through three measures of flour (*Mt.* 13:33) refers to the fact that something as small and unpretentious as yeast can have astonishing potential.

Plutarch recounts that in Greco-Roman culture, the priest of Jupiter was forbidden to touch unleavened bread because it was unclean and corrupt. For Philo Judaeus, unleavened bread was a symbol of humility and leavened bread a symbol of pride.

The bread used for the Eucharist was leavened in the Eastern church and unleavened in the Western rite. These geographical variations caused no difficulty until the Middle Ages, when the discrepancy gradually became a point of contention. It reached a climax in 1054 in the Azyme Controversy preceding the Great Schism that divided the Eastern and Western churches. Mohlan Smith, tracing the controversy in his book *And Taking Bread,* suggests that Eastern and Western liturgical traditions involving different types of eucharistic bread are based on an apparent disagreement in the scriptures about the date of the last supper. The synoptic gospels seem to indicate that the last supper took place on the first day of the Feast of Unleavened Bread. A reading of *John,* on the other hand, suggests that Jesus was crucified on the day of preparation. If this interpretation of *John* is accepted, the last supper would not have been a Passover meal, and leavened bread would have been used. The Eastern church's liturgical use of leavened bread also has theological overtones: It accentuates the break between the Old and New Covenants. Western rituals, on the other hand, emphasize the continuity of Hebrew and Christian traditions.

SEE ALSO Bread; Passover.

BIBLIOGRAPHY

Smith, Mohlan H. *And Taking Bread: Cerularius and the Azyme Controversy of 1054.* Paris, 1978. An excellent study of the correspondence concerning the use of leaven in the eucharistic bread that was one of the issues in the schism between the Eastern and Western churches in 1054.

Wambacq, Benjamin N. "Les Massôt." *Biblica* 61 (1980): 31–54. A scholarly work that questions whether the Feast of Unleavened Bread was an agricultural feast.

JAMES E. LATHAM (1987)

LEE, ANN (1736–1784), English visionary and founder of the American Shakers. Growing up in a poor, working-class family in Manchester, England, Ann Lee was attracted in 1758 to the Shakers, a religious group that engaged in ecstatic dancing and other charismatic activities. Married in 1762, Lee had four children, all of whom died in infancy or early childhood. She interpreted these losses and the pain that she experienced in childbirth as a judgment on her concupiscence. In 1770 a vision convinced her that lust was the original sin in the Garden of Eden and the root of all human evil and misery. Only by giving up sexual intercourse entirely, following the heavenly pattern in which "they neither marry nor are given in marriage," could humankind be reconciled to God.

The Shakers and the celibate message that Ann Lee introduced among them experienced little success in England, where the group was sporadically persecuted but generally ignored. In 1774 Lee and eight of her followers emigrated to America and two years later settled at Niskeyuna (now Watervliet), New York, near Albany. Between 1781 and 1783, during the troubled aftermath of the American Revolution, Lee and the Shakers undertook a major proselytizing effort in New York and New England in the course of which they attracted support primarily from Free Will Baptists. Ensuing persecution, including brutal beatings and harassment, weakened Ann Lee and her brother William, contributing to their premature deaths in 1784.

Although Ann Lee's involvement with the Shakers in America lasted only a decade, her influence at that time was profound and has continued to be so during the groups's subsequent two-hundred-year history. Intelligent, dynamic, and loving, she was revered by her followers. They came to believe that in "Mother Ann," as they affectionately called her, God's spirit had been incarnated in female form just as they believed that in Jesus, God's spirit had been incarnated in male form. Whether Lee herself ever claimed such quasi divinity—except in ecstatic utterances subject to symbolic interpretation—is questionable. Yet the conviction that Ann Lee was the second embodiment of Christ's spirit and the inaugurator of the millennium is central to the Shaker faith.

SEE ALSO Shakers.

BIBLIOGRAPHY

Scholarly treatments of Ann Lee are found in Clarke Garrett's *Spirit Possession and Popular Religion: From the Camisards to the Shakers* (Baltimore, 1987), and Edward Deming Andrews's *The People Called Shakers*, new enl. ed. (New York, 1963). Anna White and Leila S. Taylor's *Shakerism: Its Meaning and Message* (Columbus, Ohio, 1904) provides a perceptive Shaker assessment of the life and spirit of Ann Lee. The most valuable primary source on Ann Lee's life and beliefs is the rare *Testimonies of the Life, Character, Revelations, and Doctrines of Our Ever Blessed Mother Ann Lee and the Elders with Her*, edited by Rufus Bishop and Seth Y. Wells (Hancock, Mass., 1816).

LAWRENCE FOSTER (1987 AND 2005)

LEENHARDT, MAURICE (1878–1954), was a French Protestant missionary and ethnographer. In the French ethnographic tradition of the era before World War II, Leenhardt stands out as a fieldworker of uncommon depth. From 1902 until 1926 he was a liberal evangelist in New Caledonia. His active defense of the Melanesians against colonial abuses and his stress on vernacular education and on the growth of autonomous local churches anticipated what would later be called liberation theology. His extremely subtle work in linguistics and Bible translation led him to ethnography. He had a relativist's understanding of cultural process and invention that brought him to challenge the notion of religious conversion as a discrete event. Leenhardt envisaged a longer, locally rooted historical development leading to a fresh articulation of Christianity, an experience of personal authenticity that would transcend, not abolish, Melanesian totemism and myth.

Upon leaving his mission field in 1926, after a successful, albeit embattled and unorthodox, career, Leenhardt turned his attention more directly to ethnographic description and ethnological theory. With the help of Lucien Lévy-Bruhl and Marcel Mauss he obtained a professorship at the École Pratique des Hautes Études and a post at the Musée de l'Homme. He published four works of detailed New Caledonian cultural description: *Notes d'ethnologie néo-calédonienne* (1930), *Documents néo-calédoniens* (1932), *Vocabulaire et grammaire de la langue houailou* (1935), and *Langues et dialectes de l'Austro-Mélanésie* (1946). He also wrote a synthetic ethnography, *Gens de la grande terre* (1937; rev. ed., 1952), and what is perhaps his best-known work, *Do Kamo: La personne et le mythe dans le monde mélanésien* (1947; translated into English as *Do Kamo: Person and Myth in the Melanesian World,* 1979). These works are characterized by rigorous attention to issues of linguistic and conceptual translation, by an emphasis on cultural expressivity and change over structure and system, and by an analytic focus on the person.

Leenhardt's chief ethnological contribution is his experiential concept of myth. In this view, myth should be freed from the status of a story or even of a legitimating social charter. Myth is not expressive of a "past." Rather, myth is a particular kind of engagement with a world of concrete presences, relations, and emotional participations. It is a "mode of knowledge" accessible to all human experience. There is nothing mystical, vague, or fluid about this way of knowing; it does not preclude logical, empirical activities, as Lévy-

Bruhl tended to assume. Myth is fixed and articulated by a "socio-mythic landscape." For Leenhardt, place has a density inaccessible to any map; it is a superimposition of cultural, social, ecological, and cosmological realities. (The valleys of New Caledonia provided his most potent examples.) Orienting, indeed constituting, the person, this complex spatial locus is not grasped in the mode of narrative closure by a centered, perceiving subject. Rather, the person "lives" a discontinuous series of socio-mythic "times"—less as a distinct character than as a loose bundle of relationships. This *mythe vécu* ("lived myth") calls into question a Western view of the self as coterminous with a discrete body, a view that values identity at the expense of plenitude.

BIBLIOGRAPHY

For a full account of Leenhardt's life and writings, see my work *Person and Myth: Maurice Leenhardt in the Melanesian World* (Berkeley, 1982). Useful collections assessing his career appear in the *Journal de la société des océanistes* 10 (December 1954) and 34 (March–June 1978) and in *Le monde non chrétien* 33 (January–March 1955). On his work in the light of liberation theology, see Jean Massé's "Maurice Leenhardt: Une pédagogie libératrice," *Revue d'histoire et de philosophie religieuse* 1 (1980): 67–80, and Pierre Teisserenc's "Maurice Leenhardt en Nouvelle Calédonie: Sciences sociales, politique coloniale, stratégies missionnaires," *Recherches de science religieuse* 65 (July–December 1977): 389–442.

New Sources

Centenaire, Maurice Leenhardt, 1878–1954: Pasteur et Ethnologue. Nouméa, 1994.

Clifford, James T., and Raymond Henri Geneviève. *Maurice Leenhardt, Personne et Mythe en Nouvelle-Calédonie.* Paris, 1987.

JAMES CLIFFORD (1987)
Revised Bibliography

LEESER, ISAAC (1806–1868), was an American rabbi, writer, and leader of Jewish traditionalism.

Born in Neunkirchen, Westphalia (Prussia), Leeser was orphaned at an early age. He received his secular education at a *Gymnasium* in Münster, and his religious tutelage from Benjamin Cohen and Abraham Sutro. At the age of eighteen he joined his uncle Zalman Rehiné in Richmond, Virginia, where he began to prepare for a business career and assisted the local religious functionary, Isaac B. Seixas. An article he published in defense of Judaism brought him to public attention and resulted in an invitation to occupy the pulpit of Philadelphia's congregation Mikveh Israel in 1829. During the next forty years he was the most prolific American Jewish writer and the most creative communal architect.

Leeser's *Instruction in the Mosaic Law* (1830) was followed by *The Jews and Mosaic Law* (1834), "a defence of the Revelation of the Pentateuch"; *Discourses, Argumentative and Devotional* (1837), "delivered at the Synagogue Mikveh Israel"; and *The Form of Prayers according to the Custom of the Spanish and Portuguese Jews,* 6 vols. (1837–1838), edited and translated by Leeser, as was *The Book of Daily Prayers . . . according to the Custom of the German and Polish Jews* (1848). An edition of the Pentateuch in 1845 was followed by a translation of the entire Hebrew Bible into English in 1853, the first to be done by a Jew. In 1867 his collected sermons and essays, *Discourses on the Jewish Religion,* were published in ten volumes. His chief literary monument is *The Occident and American Jewish Advocate,* which he edited for twenty-five years (1843–1868).

Leeser inspired the establishment of the first Jewish Sunday school in America (1837), helped establish the Hebrew Education Society of Philadelphia (1848), and founded and headed the first rabbinical seminary in the New World, Maimonides College (1867). "His far seeing vision," Mayer Sulzberger wrote in 1868, "years and years ago projected a Hebrew College, a Jewish Hospital, a Foster home, a Union of Charities, a Board of Delegates of American Israelites, an Educational Society, an American Publication Society."

Religiously, Leeser was a staunch traditionalist who resisted and battled the rising Reform movement. His Orthodoxy, however, kept him neither from fully partaking of world culture nor from introducing the English sermon. Both Conservative and modern Orthodox Jews claim him and acknowledge his influence.

BIBLIOGRAPHY

Davis, Moshe. *The Emergence of Conservative Judaism.* Philadelphia, 1963. See pages 347–349.

Korn, Bertram W. "Isaac Leeser: Centennial Reflections." *American Jewish Archives* 19 (November 1967): 127–141.

Morais, Henry Samuel. *Eminent Israelites of the Nineteenth Century.* Philadelphia, 1880. See pages 195–201.

Seller, Maxine S. "Isaac Leeser's Views on the Restoration of a Jewish Palestine." *American Jewish Historical Quarterly* 58 (1968): 118–135.

Whiteman, Maxwell. "Isaac Leeser and the Jews of Philadelphia." *Publications of the American Jewish Historical Society* 48 (1959): 207–244.

New Sources

Sussman, Lance Jonathan. *Isaac Leeser and the Making of American Judaism.* Detroit, Mich., 1995.

ABRAHAM J. KARP (1987)
Revised Bibliography

LEEUW, GERARDUS VAN DER (1890–1950), was a Dutch historian of religions, theologian, and phenomenologist.

LIFE. Born and raised in the Hague, van der Leeuw studied theology at the University of Leiden (1908–1913), with history of religions as his main field and W. Brede Kristensen as his principal teacher. The faculty also included P. D. Chantepie de la Saussaye, who himself had taught history of religions at the University of Amsterdam and who influenced the young man. Van der Leeuw specialized in ancient Egyptian religion and studied for a year in Germany (1913–1914), first in Berlin under Adolf Erman and Kurt Sethe, and then in Göttingen under Wilhelm Bousset. He obtained his doctorate in 1916 from Leiden. After having been a minister in the Dutch Reformed church for two years, van der Leeuw was called to Groningen in 1918 to occupy the chair of history of religion and history of the doctrine of God, with responsibility for the "theological encyclopedia" in the faculty of theology. He also taught Egyptian language and literature in the literary faculty. "History of the doctrine of God" was later dropped from his chair's title and after World War II phenomenology of religion was added to van der Leeuw's official assignment; after 1940 he also taught liturgics.

Van der Leeuw was active in the Dutch Reformed church where, like Chantepie de la Saussaye, he adhered to the so-called ethical theology, which stressed the value of religion as a reality of the heart and as an existential datum. Later he was particularly active in the liturgical movement in his church and in attempts to reform it. From 1945 to 1946 he was minister of education, arts, and sciences. In 1950 van der Leeuw became the first president of the newly founded International Association for the History of Religions; this put the seal on his international reputation. He died shortly afterward in Utrecht.

PRINCIPAL WORKS. Van der Leeuw's books that are relevant to the study of religion fall into a number of categories. Most of his scholarly work was in the field of comparative studies and phenomenology, for which he wrote an introductory work, *Inleiding tot de godsdienst-geschiedenis* (1924), later completely revised as *Inleiding tot de phaenomenologie van den godsdienst* (1948), and the famous handbook titled *Phänomenologie der Religion* (1933), subsequently translated into English as *Religion in Essence and Manifestation* (1938). Further, he produced articles and books on subjects as varied as sacrifice, mysticism, representations of Paradise, children in worship, the image of God, and the God-human relationship as well as articles on myth and mythology and on immortality.

In other categories, van der Leeuw's works are almost as numerous. His major historical studies concern ancient Egyptian religion, although he also wrote on ancient Greek religion and produced studies of ancient calling-songs and lamentations and on the meeting of early Christianity and paganism. Also important are his books on liturgics, on religious art, and on music and religion—including books treating the works of Bach and the history of church hymns—and his several theological works, which often derive their insights from the history and phenomenology of religion. Another category of van der Leeuw's works comprises his writings on his phenomenological method and on issues of philosophical and theological anthropology. He also wrote extensively on Christian topics and on various literary and cultural subjects. The total number of his publications amounts to about 650.

MAJOR CONTRIBUTIONS. Van der Leeuw's most original contribution may be his phenomenological approach to the study both of religious data and of the phenomenon of religion itself. Guided by a particular vision of religion as a whole, he looked for structure and meaning in the multitude of religious data. With this approach van der Leeuw rejected certain parochial theological schemes of interpretation, evaluation, and judgment that were current in his time. He thus cleared the terrain for new kinds of inquiries into the various meanings pertaining to religious data and into the potential religious meaning of basic natural and human phenomena. Van der Leeuw's phenomenology was characterized by its psychological orientation and its status as a theological discipline.

In his approach, van der Leeuw leans heavily on psychology and in particular on structural psychology in Dilthey's sense, as he states himself in 1928. He was then even prepared to speak of the "psychology" instead of the "phenomenology" of religion. His concept of psychology, however, is not that of present-day empirical psychology; he sees it instead as a way of approaching a subject through one's own experience. Understanding rather than explanation should be the aim of the study of religion, he believes, echoing a similar aim formulated in psychology in the 1920s by such scholars as Karl Jaspers, Eduard Spranger, and Ludwig Binswanger. In this psychological understanding-through-experience, the "subjectivity" of the researcher is an indispensable datum. In order to understand a religious phenomenon as a human expression, the researcher should allow it to affect him in its wholeness, and van der Leeuw contends that this should be done methodically, in the field of religion as well as in such other humanistic fields as history and psychology. This particular way of understanding implies that the researcher interpolates the religious phenomenon into his own life and "experiences" it, while bracketing (*epochē*) both its factual and ultimate reality. Van der Leeuw describes this procedure in the "Epilegomena" of his handbook and adds that such a psychological understanding should be followed by empirical research to control and correct what has been understood. It is precisely the subjective nature of the experience of understanding, as propounded by van der Leeuw, that has given rise to scholarly objections, because this approach may lead to abuse in hermeneutical investigations. The discussion of the value for hermeneutics of van der Leeuw's psychologically oriented phenomenology is still continuing.

Phenomenology of religion had a theological foundation for van der Leeuw. The "sacramental" experience of reality on the one hand and the tension between subject and object of religious experience on the other, which are at the basis of his phenomenology of religion, find their theological basis, according to him, in the doctrine of the Incarnation. As a discipline, phenomenology of religion had for van der Leeuw a theological status; he did, in fact, also speak of it as "phenomenological theology." Basically, it was a theological discipline concerned with the meaning of religious data in the experience of the believers, and van der Leeuw wanted to see this phenomenological theology as an intermediary stage between "historical" theology, concerned with literary and historical facticity, on one hand and "systematic" theology, concerned with ultimate truth and reality, on the other. Because it leaves open the status of the phenomenon with regard to ultimate values, phenomenological theology limits itself to the problem of "meaning" and "significance." In practice, however, a theological phenomenologist will interpret the meaning of religious phenomena finally in the light of the "true" religious meaning known in faith, and van der Leeuw's *Religion in Essence and Manifestation* bears witness in fact to its author's faith as a Christian. This book describes religious phenomena in five parts. The first three parts represent the classical structure given by Chantepie de la Saussaye: the object of religion, the subject of religion, and object and subject in their reciprocal operation. Part 4 deals with "the world" and part 5 with "forms" (religions and founders). Religion, for van der Leeuw, is humankind's encounter with "power," and it implies being "overpowered," for he understood "power" as a philosophical category with theological overtones. Philosophically, in van der Leeuw's view, religion is one of the consequences of the fact that humans do not accept life as given to them: They seek power in life, something that is superior, and they try to find meaning in life and to arrange this into a significant whole. For van der Leeuw, consequently, religion is intimately linked to culture as humanity's creative effort.

APPRAISAL OF OEUVRE. Theological schools have not been prepared to accept van der Leeuw's theological vision, and its most elaborate expression, his *Sacramentstheologie* (1949), has had little resonance. Nor have scholars of religion, whatever their orientation and persuasion, been prepared to accept van der Leeuw's subordination of the phenomenological enterprise to theology. Further objections have been raised against van der Leeuw's relative neglect of the historical and social realities in which religious phenomena are embedded, and against his notion of "understanding."

Apart from the information it offers and the insights contained in it, one of the definite contributions of van der Leeuw's erudite oeuvre is the attention it draws to the problem of the scholar's role in research in the humanities in general and in religious studies in particular. In his phenomenological work there is an evident tension between the researcher's "participation" and his "distance" with regard to the subject matter; these stances he even considered as representative of two basic anthropological structures, the "primitive" and the "modern" mentality. In many respects van der Leeuw anticipated problems that were to be explored by postwar existential and hermeneutical philosophy in Germany and France. His own presuppositions were largely determined by Dutch theological thought of the beginning of the twentieth century, and this allowed him to be receptive to the ideas of Dilthey, Husserl, Spranger, Lucien Lévy-Bruhl, and others. In his search for the right view of human phenomena he protested against any idealistic interpretation of humanity.

Throughout van der Leeuw's oeuvre is a broad mosaic of statements that bear witness to his sensitivity, realism, and open mind. Even now, his insights into his materials sometimes must be recognized as brilliant, and that is why his work, mostly in Dutch, still counts: Suddenly, connections are revealed in an original, striking, and somehow convincing way.

BIBLIOGRAPHY

The following books by van der Leeuw are available in English: *Religion in Essence and Manifestation: A Study in Phenomenology* (1938), rev. ed. (1963; reprint, Gloucester, Mass., 1967); and *Sacred and Profane Beauty: The Holy in Art* (London, 1963; reprint 2005), a translation of the third edition, completely revised by E. L. Smelik, of *Wegen en grenzen: Studie over de verhouding van religie en kunst* (Amsterdam, 1955).

A bibliography of van der Leeuw's publications up to 1950 was compiled by Wiebe Vos, "Dr. G. van der Leeuw: Bibliografie zijner geschriften," in *Pro Regno, Pro Sanctuario,* edited by Willem Jan Kooiman and Jean Marie van Veen (Nijkerk, Netherlands, 1950), pp. 553–638. For lists of works about van der Leeuw and of van der Leeuw's main publications in religious studies, see my *Classical Approaches to the Study of Religion,* vol. 2, *Bibliography* (The Hague, 1974), pp. 149–156. Further bibliographical information can be found in my article "Gerardus van der Leeuw," in *Biografisch lexicon voor de geschiedenis van het Nederlandse Protestantisme,* vol. 1, edited by D. Nauta and others (Kampen, Netherlands, 1978), pp. 114–120, and in my *Reflections on the Study of Religion* (The Hague, 1978), which volume also contains my essay "Gerardus van der Leeuw as a Theologian and Phenomenologist," pp. 186–253. See also Jan Hermelink's *Verstehen und Bezeugen: Der theologische Ertrag der 'Phänomenologie der Religion' des G. van der Leeuw* (Munich, 1960). For an autobiographical statement by van der Leeuw, see his "Confession scientifique," *Numen* 1 (1954): 8–15.

New Sources

Hubbeling, Hubertus Gezinus. *Divine Presence in Ordinary Life: Gerardus van der Leeuw's Twofold Method in His Thinking on Art and Religion.* Amsterdam, 1986.

James, Alfred. *Interpreting Religion: The Phenomenological Approaches of Pierre Daniel Cantepie de la Saussaye, W. Brede Kristensen, and Gerardus van der Leeuw.* Washington, D.C., 1995.

Molendijk, Arie L. "At the Cross-Roads: Early Dutch Science of Religion in International Perspective." In *Man, Meaning and Mystery: 100 Years of History of Religions in Norway,* edited by Sigurd Hjelde, pp. 19–56. Leiden, 2000.

Plantinga, Richard J. "An Ambivalent Relationship to the Holy: Gerardus van der Leeuw on Religion." In *Religion in History: The Word, the Idea, the Reality,* edited by Michel Despland and Gérard Vallée, pp. 93–100. Waterloo, Ontario, 1992.

Religionswissenschaft und Kulturkritik: Beiträge zur Konferenz (The History of Religions and Critique of Culture in the Days of Ge-

rardus van der Leeuw). Hans Kippenburg and Brigitte Luchesi, editors. Marburg, 1991.

Jacques Waardenburg (1987)
Revised Bibliography

LEFT AND RIGHT. Symbolic differentiations of left and right are virtually universal cultural classifications among humankind. Research interest in the asymmetrical functioning of the left and right hemispheres of the brain and in the dominance of right-sided dexterity arose about a century ago. From a growing body of clinical evidence a variety of theories have evolved about the presumed physiological and neurological causes of right versus left preferences and performances in human behavior. Less well studied is the significance of right and left in the matrix of textual and contextual symbols that comprise a given culture. In 1909, French sociologist Robert Hertz established the first genuine social-science approach in his article "The Preeminence of the Right Hand: A Study of Religious Polarity" by making the following observation: "To the right hand go honors, flattering designations, prerogatives: It acts, orders, and *takes.* The left hand, on the contrary, is despised and reduced to the role of a humble auxiliary: By itself it can do nothing; it helps, it supports, it *holds*" (Hertz, in Needham, 1973, p. 3). Since Hertz's pioneering study, social scientists have explored the religious polarity of left and right in both literate and nonliterate societies, although the bulk of research has been on nonreligious aspects. As E. E. Evans-Pritchard has observed, much work on the cultural significance of left and right symbolism remains to be done.

The views advanced by Hertz on left and right have been affirmed by Émile Durkheim, Marcel Mauss, E. E. Evans-Pritchard, and Rodney Needham, among others, and may be summarized as follows. First, a preference for the right hand or foot to perform the noble tasks of life, in religious rituals as well as ordinary social intercourse, is widely observable among world cultures, both civilized and primitive. Conversely, the left hand and foot are regularly assigned secondary, converse, and even debasing tasks. From these widely observed sets of asymmetrical behavior it is often concluded that it is characteristic of human beings to regard the right side as exalted and auspicious and the left, by contrast, as despised and inauspicious.

A second characteristic of much of the ethnographic literature on left and right is the general tendency to see their opposition as part of a generic capacity in humans to classify the world around them and to derive the meanings of things in relation to their opposites. Thus, the binary oppositions of right and left, male and female, positive and negative, cooked and raw, up and down, noble and ignoble, and sacred and profane, indicate some of the fundamental modes human groups use to organize the world and to determine how to act within it. The structural properties of these schemata become more complex and interesting when, for example, sacrality, right-sidedness, and maleness are associated in some contexts. Is asymmetrical binary opposition a fundamental feature of the mind and of social symbolization and thus a key to unlock the cultural codes of left- versus right-sidedness in those religions where it appears?

Associated with the question of asymmetrical binary oppositions, of which left and right differentiation is presumed to be a species, are other issues that still divide scholars. One is the cultural versus the physiological (or neurological) question of origins. Are humans primarily and by preference right-handed because the corresponding left hemisphere of the brain predominates, or do the left hemisphere and right hand function as they do in most cases because of cultural conditioning? Another issue concerns the differences among societies regarding left-and-right symbolism and the increasing amount of evidence that in some cases the left is considered to be more auspicious than the right.

It is not the primary task of religious studies to attempt to answer these questions, however important they may be in establishing or confuting theories propounded by neurologists, psychologists, and ethnographers. The historian of religions works with a variety of textual and contextual materials, such as sacred texts and rituals, religious worldviews, and symbols. In this regard the interest of religious studies in left and right symbolism lies more in the interface of textual and cognitive valuations of left versus right with contextual and behavioral patterns.

The evidence for left and right symbolism in Islam was examined by Joseph Chelhod in a 1964 essay titled "A Contribution to the Problem of the Right, Based upon the Arabic Evidence" (Chelhod, in Needham, 1973). As Chelhod and other Near Eastern specialists have shown, the differential roles of the left and right hands were already entrenched in ritual practices among Arabs at the sacred shrine in Mecca prior to the seventh century CE and shared some common characteristics with ancient Near Eastern practices. Much of the scholarship on pre-Islamic Arabian culture has adduced the probability that a solar cult gave directional orientation to ritual activities at the Kaʿbah in Mecca, where one would face toward the east in ritual activities. Correspondingly, the Arabic word for "right" is *yamīn* (root, *ymn*), whose cognates include terms that mean "south," the prosperous land of the Yemen, and "felicity" (*yumn*); the word for "left," on the contrary, is *shimāl,* whose cognates and synonyms include terms for "bad luck," "north," and Syria, a land associated with ill omen.

The Qurʾān assigns auspiciousness to the right side, including a person's right hand and foot and the symbolic circumstance of being situated on the right side of God. Corresponding inauspiciousness and servility are assigned to the left. As in other civilizations, so in the early Islamic culture of Arabia certain ambiguities clouded a clear-cut association between right and left with good and evil, respectively. For example, Chelhod points out that the Qurʾanic term *yasār* means both "left" and "prosperity." Does this constitute evidence of the inversion of values that W. Robertson Smith and others saw in the sacred as distinct from secular realms? Whether or not this is so, the solution to the problems raised by linguistic evidence lies in a study of the semantic fields of terms for "right" and "left" that would determine in what contexts such terms are used, especially in cases where single lexical items seem on the surface not to conform to general cultural pairings of right with good and auspiciousness and left with bad and inauspiciousness.

Early Islamic textual and more recent ethnographic evidence further attest to such practices as setting out for the mosque or on the pilgrimage to Mecca on the right foot but setting out on the return trip from these places on the left foot; eating and drinking with the right hand but touching the genitals for toilet activities with the left hand; seating one's honored guest to one's right, and so forth. Today, non-Arab Muslims of Africa and Asia generally adhere to the normative Islamic patterns for behavior involving the right and the left side. Thus, for example, in Indonesia it is considered offensive to pass food to another with the left hand. The fact is, however, that in both Africa and Asia forms of left-and-right cultural symbolism preceded the historical arrival of Islam, and hence the role of Islam was probably that of linking local meanings and myths about left-and-right symbolism with the more universal meanings of the great tradition.

The application of Hertz's thesis on the religious polarity of left and right in China was discussed by the French sociologist Marcel Granet in 1933 (trans. in Needham, 1973). The Chinese textual and ethnographic evidence differs from that of the Western monotheistic religions insofar as the Chinese regard the left side as a place of honor even though right-handedness is encouraged by social convention. Granet found that preference for the left or right varies in traditional Chinese culture, depending upon the context. For example, children are taught to eat with the right hand, but males greet others by bowing, presenting the left hand and covering the right, while females reverse the pattern, concealing the left hand and exposing the right. Male/female differentiation of right-and-left symbolic acts corresponds to the yin/yang metaphysical polarity. Left, yang, and male are associated symbols in opposition to right, yin, and female. The opposition is not diametric, however, but circumstantial, conforming to strict social codes and rites that determine etiquette throughout society. Thus, at the levels of the universe (cosmos), society as a whole (etiquette), and the human body (physiology), left and right are differentiated, though both are valued in their symbolic association with yin and yang, sky and earth, male and female as opposing but complementary forces in the universe. The Chinese case differs from most others, because neither side of the interactive polarity is consistently valued over the other; preference is determined by context.

Tribal societies exhibit left-and-right symbolic differentiation at the levels of cosmic myth, social interaction, and physiological performance. In Africa, for example, there is greater similarity to the patterns described in Islamic culture. South of the Sahara, ethnic groups tend to associate the right side with male sexuality, moral good, good fortune, and auspicious directions and orientations, while the left side is associated with female sexuality, evil, misfortune, and inauspicious or bad places. H. A. Wieschhoff provided several examples of these patterns, noting that in Cameroon and parts of northeast Africa some ethnic groups regard the left hand as symbolic of good fortune and the right of misfortune (Wieschhoff, in Needham, 1973).

Although the Chinese evidence fits less well with Hertz's widely accepted "exalted right / debased left" theory, Granet's approach to right-and-left symbolism in Chinese culture illumines more appropriately the religious significance of right-and-left differentiation. Continuing research on the different roles of the right and left hemispheres of the brain in neurology and cognitive psychology may eventually reveal the extent to which right- or left-handedness is physiologically determined. The religious character of such symbolism lies, however, in the combined cultural media of cosmology, ritual performance, and social interaction. The study of right-and-left religious symbolism must take all of the textual and contextual fields into account in order to appreciate the full dynamics of the symbolism for each group studied.

BIBLIOGRAPHY

The articles referred to above can be found in *Right and Left: Essays on Dual Symbolic Classification,* edited by Rodney Needham (Chicago, 1973). Still valuable is Ira S. Wile's *Handedness: Right and Left* (Boston, 1934). Bibliographic references to right and left symbolism and physiological differentiation are generally classified under the heading "right and left," while "left and right" normally designates political subject matters.

New Sources

Crandall, David P. "Female over Male or Left over Right: Solving a Classificatory Puzzle among the Ovahimba." *Africa* 66, no. 3 (1996): 327–348.

Dalton, C. W. *The Right Brain and Religion: A Discussion of Religion in the Context of the Right- and Left-Brain Theory.* Lakeside, Calif., 1990.

Lytton, Ursula. "Aspects of Dual Symbolic Classification: Right and Left in a Japanese Kyu-Dojo." *Asian Folklore Studies* 48, no. 2 (1989): 277–291.

RICHARD C. MARTIN (1987)
Revised Bibliography

LEGALISM. Legalism refers to theories of statecraft that emerged in China after the weakening of the Zhou confederation in 403 BCE. Legalist thinkers never formed a school of thought that matched the Confucian establishment. It was later Han dynasty (206 BCE–220 CE) syncretists who labeled certain early thinkers *fajia* for their commitment to clear, public laws (*fa*) backed by predictable, harsh punishments as the foundation of government. The most famous early practioners of Legalism associated themselves with the state of

Qin, which eventually conquered its rival kingdoms and established the first Chinese empire in 221 BCE. But Legalist ideas filter through many other texts from the Warring States period (403–221 BCE) and inform later political theories that developed to accommodate the centralized, imperial state.

THE ROLE LAW IN GOVERNMENT. Shang Yang (fl. 359–338 BCE) presented a strong case for replacing local customs with a unified state-sponsored legal system. As a young man he is said to have studied criminal law, which suggests that by the fourth century in China a conception of law that was backed by punitive measures already existed. He lived in a world in the midst of massive social upheaval, as kings grew ever more powerful, "new men" free from ascriptive ties served as court advisers, and taxpaying peasants replaced aristocrats in warfare. The proper role of law in this new world was a matter of much discussion, and Shang Yang's views are identified in a book, *Shangjunshu* (*The Book of Lord Shang*), that most likely represents the collective wisdom of a group of like-minded realists. According to the text, Shang Yang's service at the court of Duke Xiao of Qin in 359 BCE involved him in court debates with a ruler wary of tampering with the laws and courtiers committed to maintaining the status quo. Shang Yang addressed their concerns about the dangers of replacing laws based on kinship, custom, and historical precedent with more universal standards. He declared the past so varied and complex that it could not serve as a reliable guide for contemporary governments: "If the Emperors and Kings [of old] did not copy one another, what standards should we follow?" But Shang Yang himself wasn't above manipulating contested historical precedent to legitimate his claim that law has a time-honored place in government. He noted, for example, that some of the most effective rulers in the golden age did in fact use laws and punishments with good results.

Shang Yang and later Legalists concerned themselves with the character of laws, which in their view must be clearly written, universally disseminated, and backed by consistent, appropriate punishments in order to operate as effective deterrents. Legalist writers displayed an absolute commitment to guard the welfare of the state rather than serve the will of the ruler or accede to the demands of the populace. Shang Yang advocated measures designed to strengthen state control over the common people and the noble class alike. He proposed to organize commoners into taxpaying groups whose members would suffer if any member failed to pay taxes or committed a crime, failed to ensure that households supply the manpower to support the armies, or failed to outlaw private vendettas and to mete out rewards for meritorious service rather than family status. In his scheme, there was no room for human caprice. Shang Yang echoed Aristotle when he argued that good rulers are so rare that only laws could check their mistakes and protect their position: "An enlightened ruler is cautious in the face of the laws and regulations."

Early Legalist and Confucian writers disagreed about the place of law and institutions in an ideal society, but the lines between adherents of the major schools of thought often blurred. For example, it was the greatest Confucian scholar of his day, Xunzi (310–220 BCE), who trained two of the most influential Legalist reformers of the late classical era, Han Fei and Li Si.

LAW AND PUNISHMENT. Xunzi based his legal theory on a realistic assessment of the costs and benefits of the state and its institutions. More pragmatic than earlier Confucians, he believed that humans by nature compete for resources and must be restrained by a strong state and strict laws. But he recognized as well that laws are only as effective as the men who administer them. His student, Han Fei, moved one step further and placed his faith squarely on mechanistic laws that would restrain the bureaucrats and punish the deviant. Living in a time when it had become clear that only a strong centralized state could put an end to warfare that had become constant and costly, Han Fei proposed measures that bolstered the state and its institutions rather than the welfare of local communities. He advocated clearly defined and appropriate rewards and harsh punishments to control all human behavior—including the acts of rulers and bureaucrats. Codified law, in his scheme, would mitigate the arbitrary, whimsical decisions that brought so much chaos to the world. "Law is confused if private standards are used," and "When laws are established, punishments will be consistent." Han Fei's concern that laws be clear and public and punishments consistent and predictable resonated with other Warring States writers, especially when the death penalty was involved. The eclectic text *Guanzi*, for example, bluntly declares, "When the people know the death penalty is inevitable, they will fear it."

Predictable laws and legitimate punishments worked best if they were based on immutable standards that could withstand human manipulation, and for some third-century thinkers, a universal natural principle, the *dao*, rather than the old books and ways of the past, seemed to best serve that purpose. Han Fei discussed the *dao* as a workable standard for law, but other texts more clearly link human standards with the law of nature. For example, the *Jingfa*, a text unknown to the world of scholarship until tomb excavations in 1974, clearly links law with nature. According to this newly discovered work, "The *dao* gives birth to law, and law marks what is crooked from what is straight." A demand for clear laws and predictable punishments emerges as a major theme as well in other familiar texts transmitted in the late Warring States and early Han dynasty. The *Guanzi*, for example, declares: "Therefore it is said that statutes, regulations and measures must be modeled on *dao*. Commands and ordinances must be clear and open, rewards and punishments trusted and definite. These are the constant standards for bringing justice to the people." By the time the empire coalesced during the Han dynasty, legal reformers regularly urged the emperors to clarify the laws and maintain consistency in punishments.

LAW AND EMPIRE. Arguments for clear, consistent, universal laws make sense in light of the move toward empire that these late third-century thinkers witnessed. Universal rule would require standards that transcended local customs and particular histories. It is not surprising that one of the most comprehensive blueprints for linking all human activities with cosmic patterns was produced in the state of Qin, which unified China in 221 BCE. The *Lushi Chuqiu*, compiled around 239 by a group of scholars retained by Lu Buwei, a merchant and high-level official in the state of Qin, set forth an intricate scheme for managing political and religious duties according to the patterns of the natural world. The text incorporates Legalist notions of the importance of consistent laws and punishments, firmly rejects the standards of the past as being too unreliable for present circumstances, and creates an almanac for scheduling punishments in a manner that would not upset the cosmic balance. Archaeological excavations in China after 1975 have yielded legal materials that allow scholars today to check the literary and historical record with a new perspective. The Qin materials unearthed at Shuihudi, for example, demonstrate that the low-level official in charge of local legal matters who took his administrative guidelines to his grave was bound by strict procedures himself and in turn enforced draconian measures on his charges.

The first emperor of China boasted in 221 that his creation would last ten thousand generations, but the task of imposing legal and religious uniformity in the new territories under its control proved so onerous that the dynasty collapsed after less than two decades. The succeeding Han dynasty legitimated the use of force to destroy Qin by promising to simplify and mitigate Qin's harsh laws. But contrary to early Han claims to reject the harsh laws of Qin, the Han code recently unearthed at Jiangjiashan shows that to the contrary, the laws of Qin remained as the foundation for the new dynasty's legal system. Indeed, law codes, case manuals, and literary materials from medieval and late imperial China reveal that Legalist conceptions of law as a means of exercising control and centralized power lived on in China, despite the attempts of orthodox Confucian scholars and bureaucrats to associate themselves with more benign forms of control through education and sound leadership.

Modern views of the early Legalists are mixed. Some thinkers blame them for creating a draconian legal system that undergirded despotism, while others see them as prescient realists who did not shirk from evaluating traditions with a utilitarian eye. After the Chinese empire suffered internal and external attacks in the mid-nineteenth century, some thinkers rejected Confucian conservatism and turned to the early Legalists for inspiration as they attempted to reform the imperial apparatus. During the Maoist period, when Confucianism represented all that was feudal and decadent, the Legalist thinkers were touted as realistic men of action. In the post-Maoist reform era in China, debates about the efficacy of law have become urgent as China enters a global economic and legal order. Some contemporary Chinese political thinkers point to Legalist thought as an early expression of the rule of law that subordinates rulers to the law, while others see them as the creators of a system of rule by law that places the rulers above the laws.

SEE ALSO Han Fei Zi; Law and Religion, article on Law and Religion in Chinese Religions.

BIBLIOGRAPHY

The most accessible recent account of Legalism in the context of early Chinese culture and intellectual currents is by Benjamin Schwartz, *The World of Thought in Ancient China* (Cambridge, Mass., 1985). Li Yuning offers an interesting survey of perspectives about Shang Yang in relation to Maoist politics in China in *Shang Yang's Reforms and State Control in China* (White Plains, N.Y., 1977). Randall Peerenboom discusses Legalist theories in China with a historical introduction and contemporary evaluation in *China's Long March Toward Rule of Law* (Cambridge, U.K., 2002). A selection of translations of original materials related to law in early China can be found in *Sources of Chinese Tradition.* Vol. 1: *From Earliest Times to 1600.* Compiled by Wm. Theodore De Bary and Irene Bloom (New York, 1999).

KAREN TURNER (2005)

LEGITIMATION is a process in which new situations in society are sought, or current ones sustained, through reference to widely shared values and/or qualities. Law and order, tradition, justice, patriotism, class affiliation, and ethnic identity are common legitimating values; charismatic leadership, the status quo experience of success, and the sting of oppression are common legitimating qualities. Legitimation is a feature of all formal governance but must not be construed exclusively as such. Nongovernmental groups also seek to preserve or alter social arrangements, and their success similarly depends upon their capacity to link goals with common values and qualities, somtimes for and sometimes against the interests of governments. By "social action" we mean efforts by nongovernmental groups to promote or resist social change. It is not our task here to discuss legitimation of and by governments in general or social action promoted by secular, nongovernmental groups, although in both cases religious and parareligious values and qualities are sometimes used as legitimating references. The scope of this article is social action undertaken by religious communities and legitimated by reference to values and qualities preferred within their own traditions. Religiously legitimated social action can refer to actions undertaken by religious hierarchies, denominational agencies, local congregations, groups within congregations, or church members who act through voluntary associations outside their religious institutions.

The fact that social action is promoted by religious groups and is religiously legitimated does not insure its positive worth. Religious social action, as we understand it, injects into a situation new sensitivity to issues and attempts to undercut spurious legitimations of power. Spurious legitimations often have appeared in the interests of nationalism, and the church often has become a legitimating authority for imperial power.

The examination of legitimation is largely a study of ambiguity, of value orientations amenable to a variety of meanings or interpretations. The reasons for this include the variety of situations in which ostensibly the same sanctions are appealed to, the variety of interests that come into play in a single situation, the mixture of good and evil, the conflict among values, and the difficulty of providing a rational, unambiguous formulation of the legitimation claimed.

SOCIAL ACTION. The unique context of social action is the modern community in which diverse groups coexist under the rubrics of freedom of association, freedom of assembly, and freedom of speech. Within pluralistic society, government is generally viewed as the one association that holds a monopoly on legitimated coercion. Modern pluralism implies that associations may hold conflicting values. In an open society, where change and conflict are common, dissent is entitled to a hearing and to constitutional protection. In fact, one role of associations (James Madison called them factions) is to guard the state against demonic usurpation of authority by any group; they do so by means of an ongoing dialogue among rival conceptions of what is legitimate. The growth of voluntary associations in modern society has enhanced the importance of public opinion as a factor in social reality. Social action, therefore, is concerned to affect public opinion.

The means for social change are viewed differently by different parties. Some prefer subjective means aimed at modifying larger social realities through the power of transformed persons and the spread of influence from person to person and from persons to social structures. This approach depends upon good character rather than organized planning and action by groups. A second approach, philanthropy, offers assistance to persons and groups whose efforts show signs of positive outcome for the larger society. This approach, important as it sometimes is, aims more at remedying the consequences of social (structural) dysfunction than at criticism and change of social structures. Finally, some believe that meaningful social change must occur at the level of socioeconomic and political structures. It is this approach that we call social action.

Social action is concerned with what H. Richard Niebuhr (1954) calls the macro, meso, and micro levels or dimensions of human experience. It is concerned primarily with the macro and meso levels although changes in these levels affect and are affected by the micro level. Ernst Troeltsch (1968), through his distinction between subjective and objective values, deals with these same conceptions in a somewhat different way. For Troeltsch, subjective values spring from an individual's direct relation to God, one's direct relation to other persons, and one's internal dialogue in the striving for integrity. Here truthfulness, openness, benevolence, and loyalty are characteristic values. Objective values, on the other hand, are the social-ethical claims that inform or guide action in the realm of "history"—the structured sphere of group life with its particular roles and rules. Objective values attach to the structures of society, the family (especially in its relation to other spheres), the state, the community, property and production, education, science, art, and "organized" religion.

Moral life, then, comprises both subjective and objective values, and they are of course interrelated. Social action must relate to all these levels. Martin Luther King, Jr., Mohandas Gandhi, and current theologians of liberation all agree that there is a clear and direct link between personal spirituality and a person's social praxis.

Values sometimes are widely held and are central for an entire society, while others are held only by a few and are marginal for the society. Marginality, however, is not irrelevance. Radical transforming insights frequently originate at the margins of society, calling into question central values while also expressing a desire for community based on alternative values. This was true of ancient prophecy and is true as well of many modern movements. Most Western monasticism, for example, may be understood as socially marginal, subjective withdrawal from the social community. But, as many have observed, monasticism has often reentered the community at large in objective, world-affirming ways: service, reform, intellectual leadership, and contemplative inspiration. This two-sidedness has existed in the Gandhian ashrams, in the black churches that supported the civil rights movement, in contemporary Latin American base communities, and in many communitarian experiments of the past two centuries. There is a dynamic interaction of values back and forth, between the margins of society and the center.

THE DECLINE OF AUTHORITY. Legitimation is aligned with authority and is dependent on it. Many would agree, however, with Hannah Arendt's disconsolate view that "authority has vanished from the world." The modern world has an authority crisis, therefore a legitimation crisis (see Arendt, 1958; Habermas, 1975). Since Plato, it has been understood that power rests on authority outside the present situation: nature, God, eternal ideas, custom, or some historical event of great importance. These outside authorities have been referred to by some as elements of "numinous" legitimation (see Sternberger, 1968). In past times of effective authority such as the Roman Empire and the Christian Roman Empire, those authoritative elements have been persuasive, legitimating whole societies. In modern times, they are undercut and we are left in a myopic state of individualistic want-orientation with far-reaching implications for all realms of life from the most public to the most private, including political organization and religion (see Tribe, 1976; Arendt, 1958). The value that most frequently replaces traditional legitimating values is the state. In modern Western states, the problem of authority is complicated by the fact that individualism carries within itself seeds of dissonance; capitalistic individualism and democratic individualism contradict one another in theory and practice (Troeltsch, 1968). The goal of the latter is freedom, whereas that of the former is want-satisfaction. The latter leads toward a broadening recognition of personhood and rights with attendant pluralism and a stress on community; the former leads toward bureaucratization of production and suppression of opportunities for democratic expression of individuality.

The impact of social change is greater in the modern epoch than in former ones. The rapid rate of change in recent generations is unique in history and destabilizes enduring values. Legitimation is more difficult in the context of unprecedented change.

Likewise, the impact of modern pluralism and responses to it have raised other problems for legitimation. In Roman Catholicism, for example, Vatican II has been a watershed, opening the way for a more pluralistic emphasis in the church. At the same time, the Roman church is experiencing strong internal conflict on some key issues such as human sexuality, the roles of women, and the place of popular religious movements within the church. The Vatican is faced with a dilemma about whether to impose traditional monolithic authority upon its increasingly pluralistic and worldwide constituency; the issues of liberation theology and popular religion in Latin America are current cases in point. Protestant evangelicals are experiencing analogous difficulties. They no longer can claim unity of political goals. A progressive wing attacks the conservative political values and programs of right-wing evangelicals.

Nationalism and Civil Religion. When the "constitution of the everyday world" is examined in terms of its "preferred and preeminent modes of being," there are "structures of faith and reason" that express the actual religious commitments of cultures, their orientations toward what is deemed by them to be sacred, "with or without the benefit of a transcendent referent or supervening unity" (George Pickering). Seen in this light, nationalism has become a dominant form of religion in the modern world, preempting a void left by the deterioration of traditional religious values. What appear to be conflicting legitimations often are evidences of rival nationalisms. Nationalism, devotion to nation as an ultimate reality or to one nation to the exclusion of others, must not be confused with civil religion, values transcending a nation by which that nation is both legitimated and judged (see Mead, 1975; Bellah, 1967). Indeed, nationalism and civil religion may often conflict. Nationalism, without any means for self-transcending criticism, is inclined toward the demonic. Its primary interest is unquestioning loyalty. Civil religion, on the other hand, tests present reality by reference to transcending values that represent the ideals and values of a nation.

Carl Schmitt (1932) saw that nationalism is fueled by the fear of an enemy. Hitlerism was promoted as a means for saving Germany from Bolshevism. The lengthening conflict between the Soviet Union and the United States in this century may be understood, at least in part, by the same dynamic. But nationalism is ambiguous. Gandhi appealed to national interests, or "home rule," both as a way of overcoming the unwieldiness of deep-seated village sovereignty and as a way of uniting India against British rule. And Martin Luther King, Jr., effectively appealed to the national interest by forcing issues into federal jurisdiction in order to overcome the segregationism that dominated Southern state and local courts. In the sections that follow, the thread of nationalism as a major legitimating value runs through virtually every situation examined.

Praxis. In 1851, Stephen Crowell, a trustee of Princeton Theological Seminary, in his volume *New Themes for the Protestant Clergy* (Philadelphia, p. 15), asserted, "The whole socialist movement is one of the greatest events of this age. . . . The works of socialists have exposed this hideous skeleton of selfishness—they have pursued it with unfaltering hatred; and this constitutes our main obligation to them" (cited in Stackhouse, 1985). This exposure, he argued, calls for a new application of Christian principles to the economic order. The book was published three years after the *Communist Manifesto* and three years after the appearance of the Christian Socialists sponsored in England by Frederick Denison Maurice and Charles Kingsley "to socialize Christianity and Christianize socialism."

Earlier in the nineteenth century, Roman Catholic writers had mounted a similar attack. Social action in the following period of well over a century concerned itself not only with a critique of the legitimacy of the industrial system but also with experiments in alternative social groupings. These experiments presupposed new conceptions of legitimacy.

Growth of the idea of social salvation. The search for alternative societies may be traced to the writings of Plato, Thomas More, and Tommaso Campanella, and also to the heretical sects of the Middle Ages and the withdrawing as well as the aggressive sects of the Reformation. Most influential of all have been the monastic communities from which the concept of sainthood emerged. In these efforts, one can see the deliberate formation of nonoppressed, marginal groups in contrast to the oppressed margins in which the labor movements were born as well as the U. S. civil rights movement and grass-roots liberation movements in the Third World.

Of special character and significance were the social actions associated with communitarian movements in the United States and Europe. The fantastic schemes of Samuel Taylor Coleridge and Robert Southey are familiar. In the United States these experiments, religious and secular, appeared from New Hampshire to Oregon, from the Rappites and the Owenites to the Shakers and Brook Farm. In the nineteenth century, there were over a hundred known communities of more than one hundred thousand men, women, and children. Writing to Carlyle in 1840, Emerson said, "We are all a little wild here with numberless projects of social reform. Not a reading man but has a draft of a new community in his waistcoat pocket."

Egalitarianism was a major nerve of these movements. Their conceptions of legitimacy issued in the demand for equality of sex, nationality, and color, the abolition of private property, the abolition of slavery, the humane treatment of domestic animals, and the practice of nonresistance.

Experiments have continued into the present century, for example, the interracial community Koinonia Farm in Americus, Georgia, and the mainly Roman Catholic Focolare ("fireplace") movement. The latter, an international group with four thousand members, emphasizes face-to-face "family" groups stressing unity toward the end of transforming structures of domination through praxis rather than doctrine, and uses mass media for wider communication. Especially significant too are the *kibbutsim* in Israel, the oldest extant communal experiments among marginal, alternative societies.

In England, the philosophy of individualism may be traced to left-wing Puritanism, with its attack on chartered monopoly and its promotion of the dispersion of power in church and state. Legitimation was found in the alleged congregational polity of primitive Christianity. Here was the birth of the bourgeois revolt against feudalism. Later, the work of Adam Smith gave birth to belief in automatic harmony issuing from a free market. This hope for automatic harmony constituted an eschatological form of legitimation. This eschatology was fueled by the belief in progress, a restatement of the doctrine of providence. Marxism in dialectical fashion, centering attention on economic analysis and on the hope for a classless society, also adopted an optimistic eschatology.

Automatic harmony failed to appear. Smith had not anticipated the advent of large corporations and the coalitions among them, nor had he foreseen greater success in production than in the capacity to expand markets, maintain employment levels, and encourage consumption. This economic system left in its wake a residue of faceless poverty that over a long period has remained undiminished in proportion to the middle class. Legitimation became more difficult to maintain as prebourgeois social solidarity eroded. In this century, as New Deal politics shifted from the older individualism, Roscoe Pound would speak of a return to features of feudalism. The legal system, however, stood in opposition, concerned about order more than justice.

In an environment of individualistic pietism and privatization, the idea of "social salvation" appeared in the United States and Europe. From the ecumenical movement and the World Council of Churches arose the idea of "a responsible society." The secular articulation of these new religiously conceived ideas helped to legitimate the welfare state.

Meanwhile, the deprivations of Third World peoples were coming into sharper focus and it rapidly became evident that bureaucratization of business and the welfare state was inimical to training for democratic citizenship. For example, the percentage of eligible voters in the United States who participate in presidential elections has diminished by nearly half in this century. As these conflicts became more obvious, the crisis of legitimations became more acute. In this period of attacks upon prevailing legitimations, increasing appeals were made to the teachings of Jesus as a final authority, for example, by Walter Rauschenbusch in the earlier years of this century and later by John Bennett, Walter Muelder, Reinhold Niebuhr, and others (see Stackhouse, 1985).

The movement Christians for Socialism in Europe, North America, and Latin America is more pluralistic in goals and methods. Here there is recognition of the church as an economic and political power sometimes inimical to a socialist reorganization of society. Marxist tools of analysis have been employed, but the major thrust is against inequality among classes, regions, and production sectors. The emergence of new "base communities," especially but not only in Latin America, has provided grass-roots support with a new religious awareness in the face of institutional concentrations of power, ecclesiastical or economic.

This trend has continued, for example in papal encyclicals since the end of the nineteenth century and, in the period since Vatican II, in the official statements issued by councils of bishops in Latin America and the United States. These Protestant and Catholic views in part have rearticulated a century-old religious socialism with its numinous legitimation of freedom in community.

Gandhi's appeal to religion. Mohandas Gandhi was born to a political father and a religious mother. The Gandhis were *vaiśya* Hindus, though both mother and father, according to Gandhi's reflections, were tolerant and actively interested in persons and ideas outside their own religious tradition. Gandhi's mature religious views, consequently, were grounded in Hindu wisdom but also mingled with non-Hindu, especially Christian wisdom. With this beginning, it is not surprising that, for Gandhi, God is greater than any concept of God, Hindu or Christian. Gandhi interchangeably used terms like truth, life, light, and love to describe God. In his view, one draws close to God by struggling against evil in the world, even at the risk of death. He saw no distinction between religion and politics. Whereas many saw him as a religious figure involved in politics, he saw himself as a political individual trying to be religious.

The motivating vision for Gandhi was *Rāma rājya*, an ideal state of harmony in which the "welfare of all" (*sarvodaya*) would characterize the systemic interconnections of society. There would be "rights alike of prince and pauper," "sovereignty of the people based on pure moral authority," and "self-rule." Human relations in *Rāma rājya*, therefore, will manifest the principle of "noninjury" (*ahiṁsā*). *Ahiṁsā* is more than refraining from hurting by active aggression; it is subtle harmony of all living things; it is love in action. Because truth is beyond human grasp, one is bound to respect the truth claims of others. One may not inflict injury (*hiṁsā*) upon others in the name of one's own truth. Truth is larger than any person's or group's comprehension of it; it is always beyond, judging every human truth. One must "hold on to truth" (*satyāgraha*) in the latter sense, that is, one must be committed to the truth one knows with humility, knowing that one's commitment is ultimately to the greater, unseen truth (see Chatterjee, 1983).

In the Gandhian movement, we find the three legitimating forces discussed by German sociologist Max Weber: tradition, charisma, and law. Gandhi himself was charismatic; Hindu values were traditional; and Gandhi, an attorney by training, believed in law even when he took exception to it through civil disobedience.

Gandhi met many forms of resistance to his work, even from some who shared his general desires for transformation. His differences with Rabindranath Tagore are well known; both were religious, but Tagore seriously disliked many of Gandhi's methods. Gandhi's conflict with B. R. Ambedkar over how to deal with the issue of untouchability was even more serious. Ambedkar, born an untouchable himself, saw Gandhi's approach as bourgeois, therefore ineffective and even harmful in perpetuating the very oppressions in question. The final irony is that Gandhi's assassin belonged to a Hindu group whose members resented Gandhi's openness to Muslims.

Transformations in recent Buddhism. In Japan since World War II, numerous new religions (voluntary associations) have enjoyed phenomenal growth. From among these we select the lay Buddhist movements Sōka Gakkai and Risshō Kōseikai for a brief account. Both these new religions trace their heritage to the Buddhist "Nichiren sect" stemming from the thirteenth century.

Literally translated, the name *Sōka Gakkai* means "the value-creating society." The movement, characterized by family membership, has claimed to have sixteen million on its rolls. Its mushroom growth sprang from the ashes of the second world war. These value preferences, it is claimed, can be traced to Nichiren who seven centuries ago brought Buddhism to the common people and who traced authority to the *Lotus Sutra* of the fourth century.

The characteristic ideas of this *sūtra* are that every living being possesses the Buddha in embryo and should, through meditation and discipline, achieve the enlightenment of Buddhahood and also assist others on the *bodhisattva* path. All are heirs of the Buddha who engage in *bodhisattva* practice that leads to happiness in this world and the next.

The basic faith issues from worship of the mandala and the repetition of prescribed words of prayer enabling one to get rid of delusion, to achieve merit toward happiness in this world and the next, to enter the state of Buddhahood, and also to contribute to world peace. Happiness consists in material satisfaction (promised to everyone) such as economic prosperity, freedom from bad personal habits and adversity, sound health, peace of mind, and a bubbling over with joy—a markedly utilitarian, cash-value religion. The search for Buddhahood in Sōka Gakkai is the sign of the one and only true religion; other religions are to be uprooted. Conversion of nonmembers requires "a stern strategy" of pummeling ("breaking and subduing") the unbeliever, which is the highest form of compassion. There is confidence that inner reform (subjective virtue) will move outward to infuse politics, economics, art, and all spheres of life with new value.

Sōka Gakkai has been politically active, at one time establishing a political party and gaining several representatives in the national legislature. Its successful international missionary efforts have generated mass peace rallies. In a volume sponsored by the rapidly growing Youth Division, *Peace Is Our Duty* (1977), many individual statements recount vividly the brutalities of war and the callousness of former military training. It is not quite clear what the work for peace is apart from rallies; economic questions relating to world peace are not taken into account.

The fundamental motivation (or legitimation) of this "value-creating" movement resides in Buddhahood, though legitimation has been scarcely a pressing matter; the possession of truth suffices. The authoritarian, nationalist ethos and concern for individual happiness are readily evident. But still more evident is the transformation from early Buddhism's escape from history to a dynamic, utilitarian this-worldliness, yet with no social action in the strict sense.

Risshō Kōseikai, possessing six million members, also traces its heritage to Nichiren and earlier Mahāyāna Buddhism. Oriented to the *Lotus Sūtra*, members of Risshō Kōseikai interpret the way of the *bodhisattva* as the path of those who, in compassion, strive to achieve salvation for themselves and others "who shed tears of sorrow." All people have the potentiality of attaining Buddhahood; conflict prevails in the world because people have forgotten this potentiality. One aims to be loyal to one's own country, but through religious faith one hopes to be united with other peoples in a spirit transcending national boundaries.

This movement was founded in 1934 by Niwano Nikkyō, who was thoroughly familiar with the *Lotus Sūtra*, and by a prophetess, Naganuma Myōkō, who from time to time received revelations regarding immediate situations. They tirelessly visited the sick, claimed miraculous healings, and offered pastoral counseling; these elicited personal transformation and public testimonials. In all situations, they emphasized the reading of the *sūtra*; later Niwano published numerous articles of commentary on it. As Risshō Kōseikai has grown in size, close interpersonal relations of the early days have been retained in the form of the *hōza*, small groups in which personal, family, neighborhood, and business problems are discussed with the assistance of leaders who are appointed and trained by the hierarchy.

The general ethos is authoritarian, reflecting the charismatic and administrative leadership of Niwano.

Institutionalized dissent is unknown. Various social activities are encouraged, including community projects and also vigorous assistance to the "boat people" in Southeast Asia. These philanthropic concerns, however, have not led to political-social action, though there is some educational interest in such matters; young members going abroad are studying international affairs and social sciences (and other world religions). Risshō Kōseikai, like Sōka Gakkai, has aroused widespread interest in world peace, stimulated of course by the memory of the American destruction of Hiroshima and Nagasaki.

Niwano has vigorously promoted an international thrust, for example, becoming active in the International Association for Religious Freedom and in the World Conference on Religion and Peace. He has served as president of both these organizations with their global constituencies, searching in world religions for common bonds conducive to peace. It should be noted, in addition, that concern for world peace is widely prevalent in Japanese society and not only in these new religions.

Legitimation is provided in general by the *Lotus Sūtra* and to some extent by modern conceptions of tolerance and interfaith cooperation. One does not, however, discern any tendency to alter the authoritarian, hierarchical structure of Risshō Kōseikai itself. The question of legitimation, though not fully formulated in Risshō Kōseikai, is becoming more important, as is evident in Niwano's personal growth, which is centered in traditional Buddhism but reaches out to Western and Eastern non-Buddhist concepts, including the New Testament and the writings of Gandhi.

It can be seen, from this brief discussion, that social action within the group is still largely undeveloped. To be sure, some new Buddhist groups are interested in philanthropic effort. However, in Risshō Kōseikai as well as in Sōka Gakkai, political participation is not explicitly promoted. We can see how objective values are beginning to engage attention in the Nichiren groups but more in practical, microcosmic, and mesocosmic (e.g., neighborhood) ways than in systematic macrocosmic ways—that is, apart from the peace movements. Yet, in all this a return to this-worldliness is markedly evident.

In recent decades a turn toward this-worldliness is increasingly apparent in Theravāda Buddhism, too, especially in Burma, though not without tensions that render the outlook ambiguous. This turn is taking place at both the macrocosmic and the microcosmic levels. Indeed, the evaluation of the world has become so positive that escape from it in complete detachment is not a primary or immediate goal.

This change of outlook has appeared strikingly in the sphere of objective, institutional values. Winston L. King, in his writings, has delineated these changes of recent decades. In his article "Samsara Re-Valued" (1964), he succinctly defines *saṃsāra,* the round of births and deaths, as a synonym for "all that is evil," as compounded in the impermanence, suffering, and insubstantiality of the world, as well as in the "no-souledness of individuatedness of space-time existence," a malady from which one escapes through complete detachment. Yet today practical changes are being sought, for example, emancipation from "economic strangulation." The inspiration for this stance is found in the career of the Buddha himself, who realized during the course of ascetic practices that privation did not conduce to spiritual liberation, or, in other words, that dharma can be better practiced on a full stomach. This emancipation will bring freedom from want, economic well-being for the entire people, an end to exploitation of man by man. In short, what is required is a Buddhist national socialism—adumbrated by U Nu, the first premier of independent Burma in 1948 (though his effort was aborted, to be resumed by the revolutionary government). Other changes are also demanded, for example, a new role for the meditating lay person, who should have equality with the monks. Meditation is useful for both this world and *nirvāṇa,* maintaining detachment for both worlds. A new meaning for *karman* makes room for change of the self and for self-reliance. The *bodhisattva* ideal from Mahāyāna Buddhism is reinterpreted to give sanction for public service in the community, to be sure not without a strong element of nationalism. Detachment can accompany activity in the world toward achieving *nirvāṇa* peace in daily life. For the understanding and enhancement of daily existence, the study of the sciences is encouraged, something traditionally found in the teachings of Buddha.

In these ways, *saṃsāra* is being revalued. Legitimation for this way of life is claimed by appeal to the intentions of the true Lord Buddha for the sake of otherworldliness within this world. Since thousands of lives lie ahead of us, there need be no hurry about striving for the achievement of *nirvāṇa.* King (1964) describes this paradox as having one's cake and eating it, too. With an absolutely straight face, the defender can say that these developments provide a new hope for transformation in this world in preparation for the next, while at the same time maintaining the rule of *dharma* against false consciousness and greed. In all this, one can detect influences from the West and from Marxism.

The civil rights movement in the United States. The civil rights movement of the 1950s and 1960s in the United States is significant for our present purposes because the movement claimed legitimations that were largely, though not entirely, religious in a traditional sense. The movement was a religiously legitimated mass social-action movement. Black church networks provided the talent, energy, and institutional connections that were determinative for the wisdom, strength, and durative power of the movement.

Martin Luther King, Jr., added a charismatic presence to the movement and became its focal personality and symbolic leader. As one whose father, grandfather, and great-grandfather had been Baptist ministers, whose father and grandfather had been civil rights leaders in Atlanta, and as one who had himself earned a doctorate in systematic theology, King was well prepared in many respects to lead a social-action movement legitimated by religious values and based in churches. Within the black church tradition, King knew the symbolism, the characteristic networking, and the style of male-oriented, charismatic leadership. He also knew the ins and outs of the liberal Protestant social theology that echoed in many Northern churches and seminaries. He could preach extemporaneously from his thorough familiarity with the ideas of Walter Rauschenbusch, Paul Tillich, Reinhold Niebuhr, Henry Nelson Wieman, and the Boston University personalist theologians, as well as the rich theological heritage of the black church.

From his church tradition and theological education, King emphasized community ("beloved community," he called it), faith in a personal God who struggles in history side by side with those who suffer and work for justice, an eschatological vision of liberation, and a doctrine of human personality rooted in God as personal. With these he interpreted the significance of being free and fully human on the one hand, and the destruction of human personality by racism on the other. The means of social transformation and liberation had to be in accord with the goal of the beloved community. For King only nonviolence, rooted in Christian love and influenced by the example of Gandhi's nonviolent *satyāgraha* campaigns in South Africa and India, could produce change and create "beloved community." For King, these values were grounded in a willingness to suffer and a belief that unmerited suffering can be redemptive. These legitimating values were the heart of the movement.

In spite of religious values at the center of the movement, many in the churches did not follow King's lead. In his famous 1963 "Letter from Birmingham Jail" King lamented the failure of churches, especially white church leaders, to support the movement. Even before 1966, there was tension within the movement when King and his supporters were challenged by a group of younger black leaders who wished to move ahead faster and with greater militancy. In 1966, this challenge within the movement became public and serious when the cry of "black power," supported by Stokely Carmichael and Floyd McKissick, struck a resonant note among civil rights workers and created a legitimation crisis in the movement, a crisis that was not resolved at the time of King's murder and is not yet resolved in liberation struggles around the world. The struggle against apartheid in South Africa and the revolutionary struggle against poverty in Latin America are current examples of the same crisis over which values will legitimate and guide social transformation.

The civil rights movement also precipitated an old tension in American life between the legitimating ideals of the Constitution and federal courts on the one hand, and persistent attempts of regions to resist federal domination on the other. On both sides of the conflict, people felt they were in a moral struggle. One of King's most repeated aphorisms was "The moral arc of the universe is long but it bends ultimately toward justice." On the other hand, some supporters of Jim Crow also believed their struggle was a moral one. It was part of King's genius to understand their feelings and the history from which such feelings come into being. This moral element, despite its ambiguity, helps to explain the depth of feeling, commitment, and sacrifice that characterized the movement on all sides but especially among the inner ranks of the nonviolent workers.

We find again Weber's three kinds of legitimation—tradition, charisma, and law. The black church and liberal theology were traditional elements; the black minister model of leadership was charismatic, and King was its consummate manifestation; and civil rights work in the South before 1955, especially the work of the National Association for the Advancement of Colored People (NAACP), focused very often on legal redress and on respect for the courts and bringing pressure to bear on them. Most interpretation of this movement overemphasizes the role of charisma, mistakenly following Weber's thesis that charisma is the chief legitimating force that produces social change. Such a view distorts the role of King even as it intends to elevate his importance, and it also undervalues the importance of indigenous leadership in southern black church communities (see Morris, 1984).

Theologies of liberation. Since 1960, theologies of liberation have emerged from theologians identified with the experiences of oppressed groups, groups that have been pushed to the margins of society by economic and political systems. From this new perspective, earlier traditional theologies too often have been unwitting expressions of privileged interests that serve to further the oppression of groups such as women, the chronically poor, and black people. This section will concentrate primarily on Latin American theologies of liberation. Feminist theologies, black theologies, and liberation theologies from Africa and Asia also offer much to this conversation as they challenge traditional legitimating values.

One thing is common to Latin American theologies of liberation—the view that theology is never ideologically neutral, that no theology is Christian if it is aligned ideologically with privileged groups and against the welfare of already oppressed groups. Theology, these theologians believe, must serve as an element of liberation rather than oppression.

In most liberation theologies, scripture is placed side by side with the suffering of the poor. The God of scripture is one who liberates, who is on the side of the poor against their oppressors. In the faces of the poor one meets God in history; the liberation of the poor in history is the work of God. Liberation praxis is the way of meeting and serving God in history; it is the way of discipleship.

In light of the strong emphasis on scripture as a primary legitimating authority for many liberation theologians, it is important to note that some feminist theologians believe that scripture is so thoroughly accommodated to past cultures of oppression which produced it, that it cannot legitimate liberation; legitimations for liberation, especially the liberation of women, must be sought elsewhere. It is at this point that certain feminist theologians suggest such alternative sources as goddess traditions to legitimate theology and social praxis. Among black theologians also, there is debate about the role of scripture as a legitimating source. In the black churches of the United States, there is no doubt that scripture has been central; some, however, believe it would be better to draw more of African culture as a central source of liberating praxis. But in Latin American theologies of liberation, scripture is fundamental.

There are areas of ambiguity in these theologies. For instance, if God favors the oppressed, how is the concept of the church as God's people to be reconciled with the historical reality of the church in which there are both oppressed and oppressors? This has been a central question for liberation leaders such as Oscar Romero, Helder Camara, and Camilo Torres. If social transformation is legitimated by appeal to God's preference for the poor and oppressed, does that introduce partisan divisions into the body of the church? On the other hand, appeal is made to an image of the church as a harmonious whole, as one body in Christ, undisturbed by historical injustices. History has shown, however, how the church denies and rationalizes the bitter conditions of the poor and oppressed in order, with a clear conscience, to sustain the ideal of wholeness as a credible legitimating ideal. One can see these ambiguities in current discussions surrounding the Vatican instruction on liberation theology and the Vatican's silencing of the Brazilian theologian Leonardo Boff.

In the Ecumenical Association of Third World Theologians (EATWOT), which includes among its members many of the Latin American theologians of liberation, there has been disagreement about the order of importance of legitimating principles. Oppression, and therefore liberation, are viewed by some as matters of class, by others as matters of race, and by still others as matters of culture. These differences, serious as they are, should not divert attention from the wide agreement among these theologians about liberation as the essence of the gospel: liberation from sin, of course, but also liberation in history from the oppressions of history.

The social form of theology of liberation in Latin America is the base community movement. Concerns are largely practical—work, food, health care, freedom from political oppression and terror, and empowerment for political participation. Liberation thought stresses the primacy of social transformation at the macro level, but is also keenly aware of the interconnectedness of the personal with the sociohistorical, the micro with the macro level. Objective virtue is valued above subjective virtue, although the connections between them are clearly seen and appreciated (see Gutiérrez, 1984). Marginality is a key feature of the liberation movements. The poor are the central subjects of this historical process and theology. The phrase "the irruption of the poor" points to that process by which the poor in the margins of society are speaking, organizing, and acting for themselves in a new way.

The Weberian elements are visible in the liberation movement in Latin America. Scripture and the church, the two great elements of Catholic authority, continue to be affirmed even when reinterpreted; they are traditional elements. There are charismatic leaders, heroes, and martyrs in the movement—Helder Camara, Camilo Torres, Gustavo Gutiérrez, Rutillo Grande, and Oscar Romero among others; but there is no one person who marks this movement as King marked the civil rights movement in the United States or Gandhi marked the work in India. This is a more diffuse, more people-oriented movement in which democratic organization and participation transcend the role of charisma. The result is a different kind of people empowerment. The element of law can be seen in the ongoing role of church authority; it can be seen also in the desire to transform society, if possible, by lawful means.

Concluding remarks. In the so-called secular, modern world of the past century and a half, the role of religious legitimation has been highly ambiguous. Progressive secularization has driven religion to the margins of contemporary culture. Some have lamented this while others have welcomed "a world come of age." This article has noted several major movements of social transformation whose primary legitimating values are religious.

The social-reform movements represent a focus on world affirmation or social salvation. In the case of Gandhian applications of Hindu values and new Buddhist socialism, world affirmation is a reversal of traditional world negation or contempt for the world. In the case of Latin American liberation movements, world affirmation is the reclaiming of a prophetic tradition that until recently was recessive in the Latin American church. In the civil rights movement, prophetic world affirmation was a continuation of the black church's traditional emphasis on historical liberation. However, scholars of black religions maintain that, from the United States Civil War until the civil rights movement, the prophetic edge of black church theology, so common in the antebellum period, was in recession. In spite of these recent examples of religiously legitimated social action, the barriers to such change remain substantial. Bureaucratization of military, governmental, and economic powers increases the difficulty of effective social action. The global extent of these problems is only now becoming fully apparent. In addition, religious groups generally are divided about social action.

What characterizes the present situation is a movement, by no means universal, toward world affirmation in the religious legitimation of social action. This is not a recent turn, parallel with the birth of the so-called postmodern era, but rather a slowly spreading phenomenon with roots in the nineteenth century. It represents an extension of the modern emphasis on the world, with a peculiar twist that world affirmation in these movements is religious, not secular (see Cox, 1984). This change is occurring in Eastern and Western religious traditions. Even pietistic religious groups have taken an interest in social transformation. Cases in point are the recent emergence in the United States of the "moral majority" as well as socially minded evangelical theology (see Mott, 1982). Especially interesting is the recent legitimation of "democratic capitalism" with religious sanctions and, at the same time and by the same writers, a sharp criticism of recent statements on the economy issued by the Catholic bishops of the United States.

The growth of prophetic, world-affirming religiousness is one manifestation, a notable one, of the search for moral meaning in a modern world (see Tipton, 1982). It is not the only one, however; modernism is pluralistic and the search for moral meaning is drawn in many directions, especially by the lure of nationalism. It would seem, however, judging from the vitality of world-affirming religious movements during the past 150 years, that religious legitimation of social action is destined to play a continuing role in the struggles for social transformation in both East and West. It is worth noting, in this connection, the Catholic church's historic transition toward world affirmation in the events of Vatican II (see *Gaudium et Spes*, documents of the Consejo Episcopal Latino-americano conferences at Medellín, 1968, and Puebla, 1979, and the declarations of the Conference of United States Bishops on Nuclear Weapons and the American Economy.) Secularization has contributed to that expansion by helping to clarify the conflict of rival legitimations inherent in it. The future of social action legitimated by traditional religious values, when pitted against powerful rival religions or rival structures of faith and reason such as nationalism, remains to be seen.

See Also Authority; Religious Communities, article on Religion, Community, and Society; Utopia.

Bibliography

Arendt, Hannah. "What Was Authority?" In *Authority*, edited by Carl J. Friedrich, pp. 81–112. Cambridge, Mass., 1958.

Bellah, Robert N. "Civil Religion in America." *Daedalus* 96 (Winter 1967): 1–21.

Bellah, Robert N., and Phillip E. Hammond. *Varieties of Civil Religion.* San Francisco, 1980.

Berger, Peter L. *The Sacred Canopy: Elements of a Sociological Theory of Religion.* Garden City, N.Y., 1967. This is an especially useful book for consideration of the complex issues of legitimation.

Berger, Peter L., and Thomas Luckmann. *The Social Construction of Reality: A Treatise on the Sociology of Knowledge.* Garden City, N.Y., 1966.

Boulding, Kenneth. *The Organizational Revolution.* New York, 1953.

Chatterjee, Margaret. *Gandhi's Religious Thought.* South Bend, Ind., 1983.

Cox, Harvey. *Religion in the Secular City: Toward a Post-Modern Theology.* New York, 1984.

Gerth, Hans H., and C. Wright Mills, eds. and trans. *From Max Weber.* Oxford, 1958. See especially chapters 4 and 11.

Gutiérrez, Gustavo. *A Theology of Liberation.* Maryknoll, N.Y., 1973.

Gutiérrez, Gustavo. *We Drink from Our Own Wells.* Translated by Matthew J. O'Connel. Maryknoll, N.Y., 1984.

Habermas, Jürgen. *Legitimation Crisis.* Translated by Thomas McCarthy. Boston, 1975.

Hartshorne, Charles. "Toward a Buddhisto-Christian Religion." In *Buddhism and American Thinkers*, edited by Kenneth K. Inada and Nolan P. Jacobson, pp. 1–130. Albany, N.Y., 1984.

King, Winston L. "Samsara Re-Valued." In *Midwest Conference on Asian Affairs.* Carbondale, Ill., 1964.

Mead, Sidney E. *The Nation with the Soul of a Church.* New York, 1975.

Mead, Sidney E. *The Old Religion in the Brave New World.* Berkeley, 1977.

Morris, Aldon. *The Origins of the Civil Rights Movement.* New York, 1984.

Mott, Stephen C. *Biblical Ethics and Social Change.* New York, 1982.

Niebuhr, H. Richard. "The Idea of Covenant and American Democracy." *Church History* 23 (June 1954): 126–135.

Niebuhr, Reinhold. *Moral Man and Immoral Society.* New York, 1932.

Niebuhr, Reinhold. *An Interpretation of Christian Ethics.* New York, 1935.

Niebuhr, Reinhold. *The Nature and Destiny of Man.* 2 vols. New York, 1941, 1943.

Parsons, Talcott. "Authority, Legitimation, and Political Action." In *Authority*, edited by Carl J. Friedrich, pp. 197–221. Cambridge, Mass., 1958.

Pickering, George. "Reflections on the Task of Social Ethics." *Journal of the Interdenominational Theological Center* (in press).

Schmitt, Carl. *The Concept of the Political* (1932). Translated and edited by George Schwab. New Brunswick, N.J., 1976.

Stackhouse, Max L. "Jesus and Economics: A Century of Christian Reflection on the Economic Order." In *The Bible in American Law, Politics, and Political Rhetoric*, edited by James T. Johnson. Chico, Calif., 1985.

Sternberger, Dolf. "Legitimacy." In *International Encyclopedia of the Social Sciences*, edited by David L. Sills, vol. 9, pp. 244–248. New York, 1968. Contains an interesting discussion of the history of the concept of legitimation.

Tillich, Paul. "Kairos." In his *The Protestant Era.* Chicago, 1948.

Tillich, Paul. *Love, Power, and Justice.* New York, 1954.

Tipton, Steven M. Getting *Saved from the Sixties: Moral Meaning in Conversion and Cultural Change.* Berkeley, 1982.

Tribe, Laurence H. "Ways Not to Think about Plastic Trees." In *When Values Conflict*, edited by Laurence H. Tribe et al. Cambridge, 1976.

Troeltsch, Ernst. "Fundamental Problems of Ethics." In *The Shaping of Modern Christian Thought*, edited by Warren F. Groff and Donald E. Miller. Cleveland, 1968.

James Luther Adams (1987)
Thomas Mikelson (1987)

LEHMANN, EDVARD (1862–1930), was a Danish historian of religions. Born in Copenhagen, Edvard Johannes

Lehmann began studying theology at the university there in 1880. Frants Buhl, in Old Testament, and Karl Kroman, in philosophy, exercised the greatest influence on the young scholar. In 1886 he obtained his theological degree, and until 1892 he earned his living as a schoolteacher while continuing his theological and philosophical studies.

In 1890 he received the gold medal of the University of Copenhagen for his treatise *Den religiøse Følelses Natur og psychologiske Oprindelse og dens etiske Betydning* (The nature and psychological origin of the religious feeling and its ethical importance). He had already conceived an interest in the history of religions and felt the need to acquire knowledge of Near Eastern languages. The gold medal provided a scholarship that enabled him to study in Germany, Holland, England, and France.

In Holland, Lehmann became closely acquainted with scholars in the comparative study of religion and the history of religions, including C. P. Tiele and P. D. Chantepie de la Saussaye. Lehmann was invited by Chantepie to write on Greek, Indian, and Persian religion in the second edition of Chantepie's *Lehrbuch der Religionsgeschichte,* which appeared in 1897. (Lehmann later became the coeditor, with Alfred Bertholet, of the fourth edition of the *Lehrbuch,* 1925.) The immediate result of Lehmann's studies abroad was his doctoral thesis of 1896, "Om Foroldet mellem Religion og Kultur i Avesta" (On the relationship between religion and culture in the Avesta). In this work, Lehmann addressed the problem of the animosity toward culture that he found characteristic of religion in general. According to Lehmann himself, however, this little work is to be considered only a preliminary study to his magnum opus, *Zarathustra: En Bog om Persernes ganmle Tro* (Zarathustra: A book on the ancient faith of the Persians), 2 vols. (1899–1902).

The first volume of this work made such an impression on the academic authorities that Lehmann in 1900 was made docent at the University of Copenhagen. In 1904 he published *Mystik i Hedenskab og Kristendom,* which was translated into a number of languages, including English, and in 1907 *Buddha: Hans lære og dens gærning* (Buddha: His teaching and work), dedicated to Nathan Söderblom. Both works, though widely read and of no small influence, reveal a weak point in Lehmann's scholarship: his profound attachment to the ideals of Protestantism and his conviction of its superiority, which he thought was confirmed by the study of other religions.

In 1910 Lehmann was invited by the theological faculty of the University of Berlin to take the post of *professor ordinarius* of the history and the philosophy of religion, but only three years later he left Berlin to accept to a similar invitation from the University of Lund in Sweden. He held the latter chair until his retirement in 1927; from then on he lived in Copenhagen until his death in 1930.

With the passage of time, Lehmann's interest in strictly religio-historical studies gradually receded into the background. In 1914 he published (with Johannes Pedersen) the treatise "Der Beweis für die Auferstehung im Koran" (The proof of the resurrection in the Qurʾān) in *Der Islam,* vol. 5, pp. 54–61; but his *Stället och vägen: Ett religionshistorisk perspektiv* (1917), on the static and dynamic elements in the history of religions, marks a turning point in his activity. He now felt his most important role to be that of a folk-educator who was to rouse interest in general cultural (including religio-historical) matters and problems; to this end he wrote a number of books on cultural themes and current social issues.

BIBLIOGRAPHY

Only one of Lehmann's books is available in English: *Mysticism in Heathendom and Christendom* (London, 1910) is the English version of *Mystik i Hedenskab og Kristendom* (Copenhagen, 1904). Lehmann's contributions to a number of encyclopedias and other collective works are important in that they call attention to his inspired style, breadth of view, and strong endeavors to promote the study of world religions. These include "Die Religion der primitiven Völker," in *Die Kultur der Gegenwart,* part 1, section 3 (Leipzig, 1906), pp. 8–29; several articles on Iranian religion and one on Christmas customs in the *Encyclopaedia of Religion and Ethics,* edited by James Hastings, vol. 3 (Edinburgh, 1910); "Erscheinungswelt der Religion," in *Die Religion in Geschichte und Gegenwart* (Tübingen, 1910); and articles in *Textbuch zur Religionsgeschichte* (Leipzig, 1912). Lehmann also edited and was a contributor to *Illustreret Religionshistorie* (Copenhagen, 1924).

A bibliography of Lehmann's works can be found in *Festskrift udgivet af Københavns Universitet i anledning af universitetets aarsfest, November 1930* (Copenhagen, 1930), pp. 148ff. A biography, written by Arild Hvidtfeldt and Johannes Pedersen, appears in *Dansk biografisk leksikon,* vol. 8 (Copenhagen, 1981), pp. 657–659.

JES P. ASMUSSEN (1987)

LEIBNIZ, GOTTFRIED WILHELM

LEIBNIZ, GOTTFRIED WILHELM (1646–1716), was a German polymath. Leibniz was born in Leipzig on July 1, 1646. Trained in the law, he earned his living as a councillor, diplomat, librarian, and historian, primarily at the court of Hanover. Leibniz made important intellectual contributions in linguistics, geology, historiography, mathematics, physics, and philosophy. Although he did not view himself primarily as a theologian, he devoted considerable time and energy to church reunion projects, engaging in extended efforts to provide a basis for reunion among Catholics and Protestants, and, that project having failed, attempting to provide a basis for reunion between Lutherans and Calvinists.

Leibniz completed the arts program at Leipzig University in 1663 with a philosophical dissertation titled *Metaphysical Disputation on the Principle of Individuation.* He then entered a program at the university leading to the doctorate of law. By virtue of a quota system, he was not awarded the doctorate in 1666, although his final dissertation was written. Offended, Leibniz enrolled in the law program at the University of Altdorf in October 1666 and almost immediately submitted his completed dissertation, *Disputation concerning Perplexing Cases in the Law,* which was accepted. He was awarded the doctorate in 1667.

After declining a teaching position offered at Altdorf, Leibniz was employed first by Baron Johann Christian von Boineburg, and, then, by Boineburg's sometime employer, Johann Philipp von Schönborn, elector of Mainz. While in the employ of the elector he initially worked on a project aimed at a codification of German civil law, and later as an officer in the court of appeal. During his time in Mainz Leibniz produced work in physics, the law, and philosophy, especially philosophy of religion. It was in this period that he formulated the idea of writing a definitive apology for Christianity, under the title *The Catholic Demonstrations.* While at Mainz he outlined the entire project and filled in some of the details. The aims of the project included proofs of the propositions of natural theology, proofs of the possibility of Christian dogmas not included in natural theology, and the adumbration of a philosophical system that would provide a basis for reunion among the Christian churches.

In the winter of 1671–1672 Leibniz drew up a plan for the French conquest of Egypt, which appealed to his German superiors because, if carried out, it would have provided Louis XIV with a task they assumed to be incompatible with his attacking Germany. Leibniz was sent to Paris to present his plan to Louis. He was never granted an audience with the French king, but during his protracted stay there (spring 1672 to December 1676) he met and conversed with some of the leading intellectuals of Europe, including Antoine Arnauld, Nicolas Malebranche, and Christiaan Huygens. Huygens became Leibniz's mentor in mathematics. When Leibniz arrived in Paris his mathematical knowledge was out of date and superficial; by the time he left he had developed the basic theory of calculus, which he first published in 1684. Later in his life a storm of controversy was to arise over whether he or Isaac Newton deserved credit for laying the foundations of calculus. Modern scholarship seems to have reached the verdict that Leibniz and Newton both developed the idea of calculus independently. Newton was the first to develop calculus, Leibniz was the first to publish it. A time of intensive effort in mathematics, Leibniz's Paris period was also a period of serious work in philosophy and, in particular, philosophy of religion. During the Paris years he wrote *The Faith of a Philosopher,* apparently for Arnauld, a work that considers many of the same problems treated in his only philosophical monograph published in his lifetime, *The Theodicy.*

Leibniz left Paris in October 1676 to accept a position as councillor and librarian to Duke Johann Friedrich in Hanover. During the trip from Paris to Hanover Leibniz had a four-day visit with Spinoza, which generated Leibniz's particular contribution to the ontological argument for the existence of God. He believed that the ontological argument, as formulated by Descartes, for example, established the conditional proposition that if the existence of God is possible, then the existence of God is necessary. Leibniz set out to prove the antecedent, that is, that the existence of God is possible. The main idea of the proof is that God may be characterized as a being having all and only perfections; perfections are positive simple qualities, and, hence, collections of them must be consistent.

During his years of service to Johann Friedrich, a convert to Catholicism, and his early years of service to Ernst August, a Lutheran, Leibniz was deeply involved in reunion projects, first with the apostolic vicar Nicholas Steno, who read and commented on Leibniz's *The Faith of a Philosopher,* and then with Cristobal de Rojas y Spinola, the representative of the emperor Leopold I, who, with papal approval, engaged in extensive negotiations in Hanover in an effort to find compromise positions acceptable to both Catholics and Protestants. Although not an official party to the negotiations, Leibniz produced various documents intended to further their progress, including *A System of Theology,* a document that has generated considerable debate about Leibniz's attitude toward Catholicism. What is clear is that the work considers some of the problems relating to church reunion from the Catholic standpoint. What is less clear is the extent to which Leibniz accepted its contents.

Much of Leibniz's intellectual effort went into his extensive correspondence. The most famous of his irenic correspondences was with Jacques-Bénigne Bossuet, bishop of Meaux and leading French prelate, a correspondence that began in earnest in 1691 and continued with some interruptions until 1702. Leibniz aimed at compromise, Bossuet at capitulation. Neither succeeded.

Leibniz himself dated his philosophical maturity from 1686 and the writing of *The Discourse on Metaphysics.* Leibniz's original work in dynamics, begun prior to *The Discourse on Metaphysics* and reaching its culmination in the *Specimen Dynamicum* of 1695, and his original work in logic, begun in 1679 and reaching a high point in the *General Inquiries concerning the Analysis of Concepts and Truth* of 1686, partially motivate the metaphysics of *The Discourse on Metaphysics.* But so do the theological aims of *The Catholic Demonstrations,* previously mentioned. Thus it is plausible to see *The Discourse on Metaphysics* as attempting to provide a philosophical framework adequate to permit a satisfactory account of the relation of human freedom to divine causality. Indeed, the major project of *The Discourse on Metaphysics* is an attempt to provide a theory of individual created substances that will permit a distinction between those actions properly attributed to creatures and those properly attributed to God, yet a distinction so drawn that it is consistent with God's universal conservative causation.

Much of Leibniz's philosophical work in the mature period may be seen as a contribution to the aims of *The Catholic Demonstrations.* Thus, in *The Theodicy* (1710), Leibniz set out to show, contrary to the claims of Pierre Bayle, that the tenets of Christianity are not contrary to the dictates of reason; in particular, that the Christian view that God is omnipotent, omniscient, omnibenevolent, and the creator of the world is consistent with the fact that there is evil in the world. He believed that his views about the structure of possible worlds, composed of independent possible substances, from which God chose at creation in accordance with the principle of sufficient reason, provided a suitable framework for resolving the problem of evil, as well as the problem of the relation of human freedom to divine grace. The basic idea of Leibniz's solution to the problem of evil is this: God's choice among possible worlds, like every choice of every agent, is subject to the principle of sufficient reason. God's reason in connection with creation is based on the principle of perfection; hence, God chooses the best possible world. There is evil in the world and there are possible worlds containing no evil. Still, this is the best possible world, so the evil it contains must be necessary for good things without which the overall perfection of the world would be diminished.

Leibniz's major metaphysical thesis, articulated in his mature period, is that there is nothing in the world except simple substances (monads) and, in them, nothing except perceptions and appetites. He believed that monads, although capable of spontaneous action, could not causally interact, but that they were so programmed by their creator that they appeared to interact in accordance with the principle of preestablished harmony. An extensive correspondence with Bartholomew des Bosses, a Jesuit professor of theology in Hildesheim, dating from 1706 until Leibniz's death, considers, among other things, whether Leibniz's major metaphysical thesis is consistent with the Catholic dogma of transubstantiation and the Christian understanding of the incarnation.

Leibniz traveled extensively in connection with his historical research and on various diplomatic missions, particularly to Berlin and Vienna. During the same period he made efforts to bring about the establishment of scientific academies, particularly at Berlin, Dresden, Vienna, and Saint Petersburg. Of these proposals, only the plan for an academy at Berlin came to fruition in his lifetime. In 1700 the Brandenburg Society of Sciences was founded in Berlin, with Leibniz its president for life.

The later period of Leibniz's life produced important philosophical work in addition to *The Theodicy,* for example, *The Monadology* (1714); *The New Essays on Human Understanding* (1703–1704), a commentary in dialogue form on John Locke's philosophy; and the correspondence with Samuel Clarke, a disciple of Isaac Newton, on the nature of space and time.

BIBLIOGRAPHY

Works by Leibniz

Much of the material Leibniz wrote on philosophical and theological topics was not published in his lifetime, in part, because it was not intended for publication. Some remains unpublished. The work of producing a definitive edition has been undertaken jointly by various German academic groups. The "academy edition," as it is usually called, is being produced under the title *Gottfried Wilhelm Leibniz: Sämtliche Schriften und Briefe.* Until that grand project reaches fruition it will be necessary to rely on partial editions, among which the most useful is Charles James Gerhardt's *Die philosophischen Schriften von G. W. Leibniz,* 7 vols. (Berlin, 1875–1890). The most complete edition available in English is Leroy E. Loemker's *Philosophical Papers and Letters,* 2d ed. (Dordrecht, 1969).

Works about Leibniz

The Leibniz manuscript material available in Hanover is cataloged in two volumes by Eduard Bodemann: *Der Briefwechsel des Gottfried Wilhelm Leibniz* (1895; reprint, Hildesheim, 1966) and *Die Leibniz: Handschriften* (1889; reprint, Hildesheim, 1966). Two major works of Leibniz bibliography are Émile Ravier's *Bibliographie des œuvres de Leibniz* (1937; reprint, Hildesheim, 1966) and Albert Heinekamp and Kurt Müller's *Leibniz Bibliographie: Verzeichnis Der Literatur über Leibniz bis 1980* (Frankfurt, 1983).

A scholarly exploration of some aspects of Leibniz's theological thinking is Gaston Grua's *Jurisprudence universelle et théodicée selon Leibniz* (Paris, 1953). On the specific topic of Leibniz's reunion efforts, see Paul Eisenkopf's *Leibniz und die Einigung der Christenheit: Überlegungen zur Reunion der evangelischen und katholischen Kirche* (Munich, 1975). Two penetrating studies of his philosophy in English are Bertrand Russell's *A Critical Exposition of the Philosophy of Leibniz,* new ed. (London, 1937), and G. H. R. Parkinson's *Logic and Reality in Leibniz's Metaphysics* (Oxford, 1965). An excellent introduction to Leibniz's philosophy is Nicholas Rescher's *Leibniz: An Introduction to His Philosophy* (Totowa, N.J., 1979). The scholarly journal *Studia Leibnitiana* (Wiesbaden, 1969–) is devoted to the study of Leibniz.

R. C. SLEIGH, JR. (1987)

LEMMINKÄINEN is one of the heroes of the Finnish national epic, the *Kalevala.* Elias Lönnrot, who published his redaction of the *Kalevala* in 1835, composed those sections concerning the adventures of Lemminkäinen by combining elements from the stories of five other heroes, a process already begun by the traditional rune singers on whose songs his work was largely based. Lemminkäinen thus came to play such diverse roles as Don Juan, belligerent adventurer, skier, sailor, and witch.

The only poem incorporated into the *Kalevala* having Lemminkäinen as its original hero describes his journey as an uninvited guest to a place variously named Luotola ("homestead of the archipelago"), Pohjola ("homestead of the north"), or Päivölä ("homestead of the sun"). There he overcomes various supernatural obstacles: the fiery grave, the rapids, the fence coiled with snakes (or one giant serpent), and the fettered beasts that guard the yard. His host there serves him a flagon of beer with snakes hidden beneath the foam, which he nevertheless drinks. After this he kills his host in a battle of magical skills.

The description of Lemminkäinen's journey has features in common with medieval vision poetry and the visionary journeys described by arctic shamans. It also finds close parallels in the oral traditions of the Saami (Lapps) and others, which include poems about battles of magic between shamans of different communities.

A few of the three hundred variants of the Lemminkäinen poem contain a sequel that has attracted the attention of many scholars of mythology and religion. In one of its episodes a herdsman shoots (or, in some versions, stabs) Lemminkäinen with the only weapon against which he has taken no magical precautions and throws him into the black river of Tuonela (the realm of death). As Lemminkäinen dies, his mother notices that a brush has begun oozing blood, fulfilling Lemminkäinen's prophesy of his own death. Taking this as a sign that her son is in danger, she sets out in search of him. She rakes parts of his body out of the river, but, according to most versions, does not succeed in restoring him to life.

Scholars have noted the similarity of this story to the ancient Egyptian myth of Osiris, as well as to the religious legends concerning the death of Christ and Balder. The poem contains clear influences from the Russian bylina *Vavilo i skomorokhi,* a poem through which it is believed motifs from the Osiris myth were conveyed from Byzantium to northern Europe.

A Christian poet-singer has reshaped the poem, adding to it, among other things, a passage describing Lemminkäinen's power to cure the blind and the crippled. At the end of the poem, Lemminkäinen delivers a homily on the horrors that await the wrongdoer in the world beyond.

See Also Finnish Religions; Ilmarinen; Tuonela; Väinämöinen.

Bibliography

Krohn, Kaarle. "Lemminkäinens Tod 'Christi' Balders Tod." *Finnisch-ugrische Forschungen* 5 (1905–1906): 83–138. Includes a German translation of the last portion of the poem.

Kuusi, Matti, Keith Bosley, and Michael Branch, eds. and trans. *Finnish Folk Poetry: Epic; An Anthology in Finnish and English.* Helsinki, 1977. Pages 205–223 and 538–540 contain three extensive variants with translations and comments in English.

Matti Kuusi (1987)

LENSHINA, ALICE (c. 1919–1978), was the founder of the African prophetic movement referred to as the Lumpa church. A barely literate peasant woman, Alice Lenshina Mulenga, from Kasomo village, Chinasali district, in the northern province of Northern Rhodesia, started the movement among the Bemba, a matrilineal Bantu-speaking people of Northern Rhodesia (now Zambia). In 1953, Lenshina claimed to have had a spiritual experience in which she died, went to heaven, and met a Christian spirit, described variously as Jesus, God, or an angel, who told her to return to earth to carry out God's works. She told her story to the minister of the nearby Church of Scotland mission at Lubwa (founded by David Kaunda, the father of Kenneth Kaunda, the president of Zambia) and was baptized into the church, taking the name Alice. In 1954, she began holding her own services and baptizing her followers. Her meetings drew large crowds, and by 1955 her following was more or less distinctive from the Church of Scotland mission. One characteristic feature of Lenshina's movement was the singing of hymns, many of which were closer in form to traditional Bemba music than were the hymns of the Church of Scotland. Moreover, Lenshina's followers believed that she could provide protection against witchcraft, the existence of which the Church of Scotland denied.

By 1956 the Lenshina movement, with a membership of more than 50,000, could be considered a church of its own. As the movement grew it drew members from different ethnic and religious backgrounds—matrilineal and patrilineal peoples, urban workers and rural subsistence farmers—and from a range of social statuses, although its appeal was strongest among the poorer, less educated sections of Northern Rhodesian society. The movement spread along the line of the railroad into the towns of the Copper Belt, one of the main urban, industrial regions of central Africa. It also spread to the remote rural areas of the northern and eastern provinces, and poor peasants would walk hundreds of miles to contribute their labor and money to construct the monumental cathedral at Kasomo, Lenshina's religious headquarters. Lenshina's followers became known as *Lumpa* (a Bemba term meaning "excelling," "the most important").

In its early years, from the mid-1950s to the early 1960s, the Lumpa church, with its anti-European stance, was viewed as a political ally of the independence movement in Northern Rhodesia, and Lumpa meetings incorporated nationalist propaganda. Afterward, however, the church became increasingly nonpolitical and otherworldly in its outlook, and conflicts developed with the United National Independence Party, a political party founded under the leadership of Kenneth Kaunda and the main political contender to establish Zambian independence from colonial rule. In 1957 the Lumpa church, in its constitution, had stated that it was not opposed to the laws of the country; its solution to the problem of colonialism, African political nationalism, and rapid economic change was withdrawal. By 1963 church members refused to obey the laws of the colonial state or to join political parties. They believed that the end of the world was at hand, and they withdrew from the secular world and built their own separate communities in anticipation of the end. These communities were believed to be sacred domains, immune from the evils of the external world, which was thought to be under the control of Satan and his evil influence and agents.

By 1964, at a time when Northern Rhodesia's independence was imminent, both the colonial administration and the African independence movement attempted to control the Lumpa church. This led to fighting between church members and the recently elected Northern Rhodesia government, and between July and October 1964 more than 700 people were killed. The Lumpa, armed with indigenous weapons such as spears, axes, and muzzle loaders, confronted soldiers with automatic weapons. As the Lumpa attacked they shouted, "Jericho!" in the belief that the walls of evil would tumble down and that they would triumph in battle. As they were shot they shouted, "Hallelujah!" in the belief that they would be transported directly to heaven, only to return to rule the world. The Lumpa were defeated, the church was banned, and Lenshina herself was imprisoned. Some of her followers fled to Zaire, where the Lumpa church continued to exist.

In its beliefs and practices, the Lumpa church combined both African and European elements. Movements of this type were and are characteristic of southern and central Africa. At the core of such movements is a prophet who is believed to have had a Christian experience. As is typical of such movements, Lenshina's prophecy was ethical in that it imposed a strict, puritanical moral code upon her followers. She forbade adultery, polygamy, divorce, dancing, and drinking. Lenshina herself was the ultimate source of authority, and some Lumpa hymns even represented Lenshina as the savior. Baptism, the most important rite of the church, could only be performed by Lenshina herself, using water that she claimed to have received from God himself. Baptism was believed to wash away sins and ensure salvation.

In Lumpa theology, God was viewed as the creator of all things. Satan was thought to have been created by God as a good spirit who turned against God. Witchcraft, thought to stem from Satan, could be safeguarded against by church membership. Unlike the European mission churches, the Lumpa church did not deny the existence of witchcraft; instead it gave its members a means of combating it. Lenshina was believed to be the personification of good and to provide protection against evil. For the Lumpa, evil came to be the world outside their church, including the colonial administration, and the United National Independence Party represented evil.

The movement gradually acquired a structure, with Lenshina, her disciples, and spiritual and secular advisers at the center. Deacons supervised congregations, and within congregations preachers and judges ministered to the needs of local members and adjudicated their disputes. The church was itself a complete community, meeting its own spiritual, social, judicial, and economic requirements. In the historical context of the struggle for Zambian independence, a movement that demanded the complete allegiance of its members was bound to come into conflict with secular authorities. The Lenshina cult was not an atypical African religious expression; what brought it into prominence and led to its destruction was its unfortunate timing and conflict with the movement for Zambia's independence.

BIBLIOGRAPHY

Binsbergen, Wim van. "Religious Innovation and Political Conflict in Zambia: The Lumpa Rising." In his *Religious Change in Zambia.* Boston, 1981.

Bond, George Clement. "A Prophecy That Failed: The Lumpa Church of Uyombe, Zambia." In *African Christianity,* edited by George Clement Bond, Walton Johnson, and Sheila S. Walker, pp. 137–160. New York, 1979.

Calmettes, J.-L. "The Lumpa Sect, Rural Reconstruction, and Conflict." M.Sc. (Econ.) thesis, University of Wales, 1978.

Roberts, Andrew D. "The Lumpa Church of Alice Lenshina." In *Protest and Power in Black Africa,* edited by Robert I. Rotberg and Ali A. Mazrui. Oxford, 1970.

Rotberg, Robert I. "The Lenshina Movement of Northern Rhodesia." *Rhodes-Livingston Journal* 29 (June 1961): 63–78.

Taylor, John Vernon, and Dorothea A. Lehmann. *Christians of the Copperbelt.* London, 1961.

GEORGE CLEMENT BOND (1987)

LEO I (d. 461), pope of the Roman Catholic Church (440-461), called "the Great." Nothing is known for certain about Leo's early life, although according to the *Liber pontificalis,* he was born in Tuscany probably at the turn of the fourth to the fifth century. Leo is one of the most important Roman pontiffs and one of the architects of papal authority. He served as a deacon of the Roman church under both Pope Celestine I (422–432) and Pope Sixtus III (430–440), and in that position exercised great influence. He took an active role in the theological controversies with the Nestorians and the Pelagians and was also involved with institutional matters. While Leo was on a mission to Gaul in early 440, Sixtus died, and the legate returned to Rome to find himself elected pope. He was consecrated as bishop of Rome on September 29, 440.

The energy that Leo had devoted to religious questions before he became pope carried into his pontificate. In the first decade of his papacy, Pelagians, Manichaeans, and Priscillianists were at different times condemned in his writings and even in public debate. Of Leo's undoubtedly extensive homiletical and epistolary production, only 96 sermons and 123 indisputably authentic letters survive. Yet even this legacy is unusually large for a pope in antiquity and permits insight not only into Leo's papal activities, but also into his ideas and beliefs.

Leo considered himself to be, as bishop of Rome, the successor of Peter in a transhistorical sense. When Leo spoke it was the apostle who spoke. Just as all bishops are responsible for the care of their own flocks, so, in Leo's conception, the successor of Peter in the Roman church is charged with the care of all churches, for it was to Peter that Christ gave the keys of binding and loosing in heaven and on earth (*Mt.* 16:16-19). Just as it was for Peter's faith alone that Christ prayed when all the apostles were threatened (*Lk.* 22:32), so firmness to the apostolic tradition of the Roman church will strengthen all bishops. With a strikingly deep sense of the traditions both of his office and of Roman law, and with a conviction about the presence of apostolic authority in his words and actions, Leo stands out among other fourth- and fifth-century architects of papal claims, such as Celestine I and Damasus I (366–384). With deft use of such a dossier, it is small wonder that notions such as the contrast between *plenitudo potestatis* ("fullness of power") and *pars solicitudinis* ("part of the responsibility")—terms that emerge from a letter of Leo's to Anastasius, his vicar in Illyricum—over time became central in the tradition of describing the powers of Rome vis-à-vis other churches.

Leo was not, however, merely a theoretician of papal claims. He was deeply committed to effective action, whether in a pastoral role at Rome or in the larger sphere of empire-wide ecclesiastical politics. He promoted the claims of Roman authority in various ways, whether negotiating in the West with barbarian invaders, or dealing with issues in regions as far removed as Egypt and Gaul. In the former instance, although he acknowledged Dioscorus as successor of Cyril on the patriarchal throne of Alexandria, Leo urged uniformity between the two churches in certain liturgical practices. Tradition stated that the evangelist Mark had founded the Alexandrian church, and Mark was a disciple of Peter, who had "received the apostolic principate [*apostolicum principatum*] from the Lord, and the Roman church preserves his teachings" (*Regesta pontificum Romanorum,* JK406). Leo reasoned that teacher and disciple ought not to represent disparate traditions.

The pope asserted papal authority in Gaul in the face of staunch opposition. The archbishop of Arles had been granted a primacy over the Gallican church by Pope Zosimus I (417–418). The vigorous exercise of that privilege and the objection of local churchmen gave Leo an opportunity to have recourse to the prerogatives of the Roman church. The pope restored to Besançon a bishop who had been deposed by Bishop Hilary of Arles and was able to gain support from Emperor Valentinian III against Hilary. When the latter challenged Leo's authority, the pontiff had him confined in 445 to his diocese by an imperial decree in which the primacy of the bishop of Rome was acknowledged.

The most famous instance in which Leo's claims were manifest involved the renewed Christological dispute in the East in the 440s. When the troubles over Eutyches began at Constantinople, Leo felt that they should have been referred to Rome at once. In 449 the pope sent to Bishop Flavian of Constantinople his famous *Tome* in the custody of legates destined for the synod held at Ephesus, a synod that Leo later condemned as a *latrocinium* (a band of robbers, or an act of banditry), rather than a *concilium.* The problem with Ephesus as Leo saw it was that the gathering was controlled by Dioscorus of Alexandria and concluded by condemning Flavian and rehabilitating Eutyches and his Alexandrian Monophysite Christology.

The events of 449 were reversed through the concerted efforts of Leo, in association with powerful allies in Constantinople, both in the imperial household and in the church. The Roman pontiff's legates and *Tome* had been ignored in Ephesus. When a new synod was convened at Chalcedon in 451 by the recently elevated emperor Marcian, the opponents of the Alexandrians were firmly in charge. Leo's *Tome* was received, to quote Henry Chadwick, "with courteous approval" (*The Early Church,* 1967, p. 203), and it became the basis of the Chalcedonian definition of faith (not a new creed, in deference to the tradition that no faith different from that of the Council of Nicaea, 325, should be proclaimed). The definition set forth a Christology of two natures, divine and human, in Christ, within one person, and represented a triumph for Western views and Roman authority within the complex Eastern world. Chalcedon also, in its twenty-eighth canon, which was enacted without the approval of the Roman legates, elevated the see of Constantinople to a rank in ecclesiastical dignity equal to that of Rome. The pope was furious, refused to accept this decree into the Latin canonical tradition, and even delayed affirming the council's theological decisions.

With Leo, Roman ecclesiastical authority became both a concept and a force to be taken seriously in the Christian world. Scholars debate the extent of his contributions to the sacramentary that bears his name, although Leo may have composed some of the material. There can be no question, however, of Leo's contribution to the development of the papacy as a religious and political force. Together with Damasus I, Gelasius I, and Gregory I, he stands out as one of the most important Roman pontiffs of antiquity, and throughout papal history only Leo and Gregory have been remembered with the sobriquet "the Great."

BIBLIOGRAPHY

Readers should begin with the sections on Leo by Karl Baus and others in *The Imperial Church from Constantine to the Early Middle Ages,* "History of the Church," no. 2 (New York, 1980), pp. 264–269, with a bibliography. The best guide to Leo's letters is still *Regesta pontificum Romanorum,* vol. 1, 2d ed., edited by Phillip Jaffé (Leipzig, 1885). The letters are usually cited by number preceded by J(affé) K(altenbrunner); an English translation of Leo's letters and sermons by Charles Lett Feltoe is in "A Select Library of Nicene and Post-Nicene Fathers," 2d series, vol. 12 (New York, 1895). Useful still is the informative article by G. N. Bonwetsch in *The New Schaff-Herzog Encyclopedia of Religious Knowledge,* 13 vols., edited by Samuel M. Jackson (Grand Rapids, Mich., 1953). See also Henry Chadwick's *The Early Church* (Harmondsworth, 1967) and *The Church in Ancient Society* (Oxford, 2001).

ROBERT SOMERVILLE (1987 AND 2005)

LEO XIII (Vincenzo Giacocchino Pecci, 1810–1903), pope of the Roman Catholic church (1878–1903). The sixth child of noble parents, Giacocchino Pecci was born in Carpineto in the Papal States on March 2, 1810. Educated at the Jesuit college in Viterbo (1818–1824), the Roman College (1825–1832), and the Roman Academy of Noble Ecclesiastics (1832–1837), he was made a domestic prelate in 1837 and began a career as a papal civil servant.

Following his ordination as a priest in late 1837, he held the post of papal delegate (provincial governor) successively at Benevento (1838–1841), Spoleto (briefly in 1841), and Perugia (1841–1843). As a result of his success as an administrator, in 1843, Pope Gregory XVI made him papal nuncio to Belgium and promoted him to the rank of bishop. At the request of King Leopold I, he was recalled to Rome and named to the vacant see of Perugia in 1846.

During his long Perugian tenure (1846–1878), he developed and displayed the complex attitude toward modernity (combining a principled resistance to the currents of the age with a pragmatic accommodation to the same for the church's welfare) that was later to mark his pontificate. Thus, on the one hand, he identified with Pius IX's program calling for the definition of papal infallibility and the convening of an ecumenical council to solidify the church's teaching authority. He also reflected Pius's views in condemning both the Sardinian annexation of Perugia (1860) and the anticlerical legislation that followed it. On the other hand, he revamped the seminary curriculum of his diocese to include the study of modern developments, founded the Academy of Saint Thomas to help the church meet the philosophical challenges of the age, praised the advances of modern science, technology, and scholarship in a series of pastoral letters (1874–1877), and sought accommodation with the Sardinian regime.

Pecci's complex stance toward modernity produced mixed reactions. Giacomo Antonelli, the cardinal secretary of state, distrusted him, while some bishops hailed his perspicacity. Although he did not sympathize with him entirely, Pius IX recognized Pecci's abilities. Consequently, in 1853 he made him a cardinal, and in 1877 he appointed him the camerlengo, the cardinal to whom fell the responsibilities of governing the church and organizing the electing conclave during a papal interregnum.

Following Pius's death in 1878, Pecci was elected pope. At the time of his election, the church's prospects were not very promising. Leo's sympathy with Pius's attitudes toward modernity led him to continue or at least to echo some of the latter's sentiments and policies, most notably concerning compensation for the loss of church lands (the Roman Question), the centralization of church authority, and a distaste for modern political developments (which in 1878 he voiced in the encyclical *Inscrutabili*). But his contribution to modern Catholicism lay in his discerning that Pius's strident hostility to modernity had not won for the church the influence that both men desired.

With a pragmatism that his detractors interpreted as rank opportunism, Leo realized that the church had to come to terms with the intellectual, political, and socioeconomic conditions of the times. Although his statesmanship succeeded both in ending German repression of the Catholic church *(Kulturkampf)* and in establishing correct relations with Britain and cordial ties with the United States, it was Leo's revitalization of the church's philosophical tradition that allowed Catholicism effectively to come to terms with the two major currents of the age: democracy and industrial life.

In 1879, Leo issued *Aeterni patris* and called for a Catholic return to the study of Thomism. As time went on, it became clear that in his plan for a revival of Thomas, Leo revered him above all as a methodological mentor who pointed the way to a reconciliation of church and world. As Thomas had used the intellectual advances and categories of his day to reconcile faith and reason, enhancing the teaching prestige of the church by giving it a philosophy that was solid, plausible, and useful, so also Leo wished to enhance the prestige of the modern church by advancing a philosophical system that was solid because it was based on natural-law principles and both plausible and useful because these same principles could be translated into modern terms. Once this translation had been made, Leo believed that the church would be able to understand the modern world, converse with the natural-law adherents of the Enlightenment, and offer plausible and lasting solutions to the problems of contemporary society.

In Leo's hands, Neo-Thomism proved a remarkably supple and useful instrument for confronting the political and socioeconomic conditions of the age. Spurred on by crises in the French church, Leo used his new philosophical method to rehabilitate democracy for the church. In a series of encyclicals running from *Diuturnum illud* (1881) to *Au milieu des sollicitudes* (1892), he used natural-law thought to distinguish between the forms and functions of states. Although he never personally reconciled himself with the idea of popular sovereignty or the revolutionary aspects of modern democracies, he was able to accept democratic republics as long as they fulfilled the functions assigned them by natural law and did not interfere in the religious sphere.

Leo likewise used his Neo-Thomist method to frame a universal Catholic response to the problems of worker unrest, unionization, and socialism. Building on the work of ecclesiastics such as Henry Manning (d. 1892) and Wilhelm von Ketteler (d. 1877), in 1891 Leo issued *Rerum novarum.* In this encyclical, he used natural-law social thought to condemn both liberalism and socialism and to champion the rights of workers both to earn a living wage and to organize in unions. In addition, he used the natural-law understanding of the positive function of the state (i.e., the promotion of the common good) to sanction state intervention for the alleviation of worker distress. Although Leo's encyclical came relatively late in the history of European industrial growth, and although it was frequently construed as a purely antisocialist document, it earned for him the sobriquet Pope of the Workingman, and its sympathy for the rights of labor was generally credited with stopping or at least slowing the exodus of industrial workers from the church.

Although he met with defeats (most notably his failure to interest European governments in his plans for the return of the papacy's temporal power) and although he never gained for the church that degree of power for which he yearned, Leo XIII did, through his diplomacy, his revitalization of Catholic scholarship, his social concern, and his sincere desire to touch the world, leave the church more secure, more respected, and more able to deal with the modern world than it had been at the time of his accession to the papal throne in 1878.

BIBLIOGRAPHY

Camp, Richard L. *The Papal Ideology of Social Reform: A Study in Historical Development, 1878–1967.* Leiden, 1969. Deals with the growth of sophistication in papal social documents from Leo XIII to Paul VI. Helpful for seeing Leo's long-term influence on the church.

Gargan, Edward T., ed. *Leo XIII and the Modern World.* New York, 1961. A collection of essays marking the sesquicentennial of Leo's birth. Joseph N. Moody's contribution on Leonine social thought and James Collins's article on Leo's philosophical program are especially helpful.

Jedin, Hubert, and John Dolan, eds. *The Church in the Industrial Age,* vol. 9 of *The History of the Church.* New York, 1981. This work benefits from the contributions of Oskar Kohler, which place Leo in his historical context.

Moody, Joseph N., et al., eds. *Church and Society: Catholic Social and Political Thought and Movements, 1789–1950.* New York, 1953. Has the virtue of gathering together extended essays and primary sources that, among other things, shed light on the development of Catholic social thought.

Murray, John Courtney. "Leo XIII on Church and State: The General Structure of the Controversy," "Leo XIII: Separation of Church and State," "Leo XIII: Two Concepts of Government," *Theological Studies* 14 (1953): 1–30, 145–214, 551–567; and "Leo XIII: Government and the Order of Culture," *Theological Studies* 15 (1954):1–33. A series of four important articles that offer a progressive and historically sophisticated interpretation of the political thought of Leo XIII.

Soderini, Eduardo. *The Pontificate of Leo XIII.* 2 vols. London, 1934–1935. Written with the aid of the Vatican Archives. Only two of the original volumes have been translated into English.

Wallace, Lillian P. *Leo XIII and the Rise of Socialism.* Durham, N.C., 1966. Argues that the rise of socialism forced the church to come to terms with the problems of industrialization, and that the church's entrance into the field of economics blunted the advance of socialism.

JOSEPH M. MCSHANE (1987)

LEONTIUS OF BYZANTIUM

LEONTIUS OF BYZANTIUM (c. 500–c. 543), Orthodox Christian monk and theologian, was the author of a brief corpus in the Christological controversies of the Greek East just before the Second Council of Constantinople (553). The manuscript tradition calls Leontius only "monk" and "eremite," but modern scholarship identifies him as Leontius of Byzantium, an Origenist monk of Palestine, who appears in the *Life of Sabas* by the sixth-century hagiographer Cyril of Scythopolis. This Leontius, born probably in Constantinople, entered the monastery called the New Laura near Tekoa in Palestine around 520 with his spiritual master Nonnus, a disciple of the Origenist monk Evagrios of Pontus (345–399). Coming to Constantinople in 531, he became the nucleus of an Origenist party led by his friend Theodore Askidas (d. 558), which defended the Council of Chalcedon against the Monophysites. Back in Palestine in 537, Leontius returned to Constantinople around 540 to defend the Origenists against charges of heresy. In 543 the emperor Justinian condemned Origenism. Leontius's polemic against Theodore of Mopsuestia (c. 350–428) probably initiated the campaign that led to Justinian's publication of the "Three Chapters" edict (a collection of condemned texts attributed to three representatives of the school of Antioch: Theodore of Mopsuestia, Theodoret of Cyrrhus, and Ibas of Edessa), which persuaded the Second Council of Constantinople (553) to condemn the school as teaching the heresy of Nestorius (that in Jesus exist two distinct "sons" or persons, the one divine, the other human).

Three of Leontius's works survive, all defending and interpreting the Christological formula of Chalcedon. The first work collects three different treatises but is usually called by the name of the first: *Against the Nestorians and Eutychians.* This treatise, the best known of Leontius's works, defends the formula of Chalcedon both against those who "divide" or "separate" (and not simply "distinguish") Christ's divine and human natures (that is, the Nestorians) and against those who collapse the two natures into "one incarnate nature of God the Word" (the formula of the Orthodox father Cyril of Alexandria adopted by the Monophysites). Leontius represents Chalcedon as a middle way between heresies, defending it by means of a common metaphor: Just as soul and body, although different by nature, are united to form a single human being, so also the Son of God (bearing the divine nature) is united with human nature to form Jesus Christ.

The second treatise, *Dialogue against the Aphthartodocetists,* attacks the Monophysite Julian of Halicarnassus (d. after 518), who had taught that the body of Jesus had become incorruptible not at his resurrection (the Orthodox view) but at the very moment of the Son's entering it. The third treatise, *Critique and Triumph over the Nestorians,* argues that Theodore of Mopsuestia was the spiritual father of the heretic Nestorius. Leontius's other works include *Resolution of the Arguments Opposed by Severus, Thirty Propositions against Severus,* and *Against the Frauds of the Apollinarists,* the last work attested to be genuine (on the strength of only a single manuscript).

The Origenism ascribed to Leontius of Byzantium by Cyril of Scythopolis derived not from Origen (c. 185–c. 254) himself but from Evagrios of Pontus, who taught that Jesus was not, strictly speaking, the Son of God, but rather an eternally spiritual intellect (nous) who had, without losing his primordial unity with the Son, transformed himself into a soul capable of uniting its flesh to the Son. Modern scholarly interpretations divide over the question whether the Christology of Leontius reflects this Origenism. The best-known of Leontius's teachings is the formula "one person in two natures," in which the term *nature* is understood as an "enhypostasized nature." The traditional scholarly view maintains that for Leontius only the human nature of Jesus is enhypostasized; it exists only in the hypostasis or person of the Son of God. Leontius is therefore a "strict Chalcedonian" who rejected the extremes of both Alexandria and Antioch. Others interpret Leontius as an Origenist: Both natures of Christ are enhypostasized in a third entity, the "intellect" Jesus.

Although known to Maximos the Confessor (c. 580–662) and John of Damascus (c. 679–c. 749), Leontius's works exercised almost no influence in the later Byzantine tradition and were unknown in the Latin West until Heinrich Canisius published a Latin translation by Francisco Torres in 1603.

BIBLIOGRAPHY

Daley, Brian. "The Origenism of Leontius of Byzantium." *Journal of Theological Studies* 27 (October 1976): 333–369.

Evans, David B. *Leontius of Byzantium: An Origenist Christology.* Washington, D.C., 1970.

Evans, David B. "Leontius of Byzantium and Dionysius the Areopagite." *Byzantine Studies* 7 (1980): 1–34.

Gray, Patrick T. R. *The Defense of Chalcedon in the East, 451–553.* Leiden, 1979.

Guillaumont, Antoine. *Les "Kephalaia gnostica" d'Evagre le Pontique et l'histoire de l'Origénisme chez les Grecs et chez les Syriens.* Paris, 1962.

Loofs, Friedrich. *Leontius von Byzanz und die gleichnamigen Schriftsteller der griechischen Kirche.* Leipzig, 1887.

Richard, Marcel. "Léonce de Byzance était-il origéniste?" *Revue des études byzantines* 5 (1947): 31–66.

DAVID B. EVANS (1987)

LESBIANISM.

LESBIANISM. The field of lesbian studies has burgeoned in the last two decades. In response to the social and political changes of the 1960s, as well as to the 1963 U.S. Supreme Court decision concerning the legality of teaching about religion in public institutions of higher education, lesbian studies has emerged as a dynamic arena that engages questions of lesbian identities and religious experience, comparative religions, and religious studies at its broadest. Rooted historically in the medical discourses that defined homosexuality in the late nineteenth century, studies of lesbianism, or the homosexuality of women, have self-consciously grappled with definitions of the term and methodological implications, as well as more straightforward documentations of cases of "lesbianism" around the world and throughout history.

One of the most significant debates to shape the field is the relationship scholars have sought to articulate between the fields of lesbian studies and gay and, more recently, queer studies. In response to questions articulated by Mary Daly and others in the 1970s, scholars have asked whether lesbian studies share any part of their analysis with studies that do not seek to critique the larger framework of patriarchy. Studies of gay male sexuality and some queer theorists do not consistently engage critiques of patriarchy, and thus they have been called into question by scholars in lesbian studies. The central question in this conversation focuses on the nature of experiences of lesbians as women, and thus it embraces an analysis of the oppression of women across cultures and throughout history. In distinction to studies that focus primarily on lesbians, recognizing a necessary breadth of the term in relation to specific periods and places under examination, queer studies and queer theories seek to be more inclusive than lesbian or gay theories. The term *queer* includes bisexual and transgendered people; fundamentally, "queer" embraces anyone who falls outside of traditional heterosexual orientations.

Contemporary scholarship in lesbian studies and religious studies draws in part on two studies that stand at the foundation of studies of gay male experiences: Michael Foucault's *History of Sexuality* (1976) and John Boswell's *Christianity, Social Tolerance, and Homosexuality* (1980). Also in 1980, Adrienne Rich published her classic essay "Compulsory Heterosexuality and Lesbian Existence," arguing for a "lesbian continuum" that embraced women who were sexually attracted to other women as well as nonsexual friendships between women-identified women. Following Boswell's monumental survey and engaging Rich's methodological questions, Judith Brown's study of the life of Benedetta Carlini was published in 1986 as *Immodest Acts: The Life of a Lesbian Nun in Renaissance Italy.* Critically drawing upon Foucault, Janice Raymond published *A Passion for Friends* in 1986 and called for women to document the genealogies of gyn/affection, or female friendship. These works were situated in the explosion of scholarship in lesbian studies outside the study of religion that emerged in the first half of the 1980s. Other works of this period that have been foundational for lesbian and religious studies include Audre Lorde's "Uses of the Erotic: The Erotic as Power," which appeared in her book *Sister Outsider* (1984), and, of course, the works of Mary Daly. A good overview of the early decades of scholarship in the field may be found in the introduction of Bernadette Brooten's *Love between Women* (1996).

At the core of this generation of scholarship in lesbian studies and religion were questions of, first, biological essentialism or social construction, and second, the use of categories such as "homosexuality," "gay," or "lesbian" across vastly different cultural and historical periods. These issues have not abated in recent years. In stark contrast to popular assumptions about gay identity found in the press around the end of the twentieth century about how gay people are "born that way," scholarship that emerged in the 1980s staunchly argued for the social construction of lesbianism in clear historical and cultural contexts. Scholars such as Rich, Daly, and Raymond have since been classified by others as "cultural feminists" and have thus been labeled as biological essentialists. However, Tania Lienert (1996) demonstrates that these reinterpretations were rooted in different strategies for social change. Questions of essentialism have also been taken up by queer and postmodern theorists and have become inextricable from discussions of identity. Scholars who locate themselves within queer studies have sought to unravel different threads of this issue, examining assumptions about sexual identities, constructions of gender, and the significance of power with the tools of poststructural and postmodern approaches. Amanda Swarr and Richa Nagar (2003), for example, provide insightful critiques of the category of "lesbian" in relation to issues of class, cultural location, and heterosexism in India and South Africa, raising questions about the centrality of a woman's choice to identify as a lesbian. Though not explicitly focused on lesbians, one of the most useful anthologies that deliberately positions itself at the intersections of religious studies and lesbian/gay/queer studies and that engages the question of identity is the anthology *Que(e)rying Religion* (1997), edited by add Gary David Comstock and Susan E. Henking.

Arguments about what to call women who are attracted—sexually or not—to other women marked the early studies in the 1980s and continue to characterize scholarship today. For example, Marilyn Brown (1986) rejected Rich's notion of a "lesbian continuum" as ahistorical, but she still retained the category of "lesbian" as useful for studying the life of Renaissance nuns. This assertion, though, did not enter the field uncontested: Mary D'Angelo (1990) used Rich's notion of a lesbian continuum to explore women who appear partnered with other women in the New Testament. The relationship between scholarship on gay men and lesbians was also at stake in these terminology battles. John Boswell (1980) argued for the use of the term *gay* in contrast to *homosexual* on the grounds that *gay* had a richer history in the experiences of same-sex attractions than *homosexuality* and that it was broad enough to encompass the experiences of women. Despite Boswell's claims for his inclusive approach to the study of gay studies, he has been soundly critiqued for his lack of attention to gender and the experiences of women. In part as a response to both of Boswell's studies, Brooten chose the term "homoeroticism" to denote erotic attraction for members of the same sex, distinguishing between female and male homoeroticism when appropriate. She found this term to be broader than the term homosexual, and more useful than terms used by male authors in the early centuries of Christianity to describe homoerotically oriented women.

It is essential to note that some of the most striking contributions of lesbian studies have been to liberal theologies of different religious traditions, most notably Christianity and Judaism. The writings of such authors as Mary Daly and Carter Heyward have transformed feminist theologies in the United States. Similarly, recent books by Rebecca Alpert not only document the experiences of lesbian rabbis but offer new ways of looking at traditional Jewish theologies from lesbian-feminist points of view. Such theologians as Renita Weems, Kelly Douglas, and Renee Hill have taken up questions of homophobia within Womanist theologies. Each of these studies seeks to incorporate the experiences of lesbians/bisexual/gay/transgendered individuals into the traditionally proscribed territory of Christian theology, transforming Christianity in the process. Any search on the internet shows that Muslim lesbians are beginning to speak out in ways similar to Christian and Jewish lesbians; however, we have yet to see the beginnings of a Muslim lesbian theology emerge within the academic sphere. There is a plethora of resources from the point of view of lesbians within Hinduism and South Asian traditions—South Asian sources rarely make distinctions on the basis of religion. One of the earliest collections was edited by Rakesh Ratti, *A Lotus of Another Color* (1993), and one essay of note is a piece on the 1987 marriage of two policewomen in Bhopal, India.

There is hardly any tradition around the world that does not have first-person reflections from lesbian members of that culture available on the Internet. Will Roscoe has been particularly active in seeking out the voices of lesbian/bisexual/gay/transgendered individuals in different cultures. Roscoe (1988) has edited a volume on Native American two-spirit traditions and, with Stephen Murray (1997), he has also published volumes on homosexuality in Muslim cultures and in African traditions. In each of these collections, the authors provide material on lesbians, often critiquing the traditional category of lesbian. In almost all of these non-Anglo cultures, a critique of colonialism goes hand-in-hand with the need to identify the indigenous concepts of gender and sexuality that may or may not intersect with the familiar Western concepts. One of the most provocative findings to come out of many of the studies of lesbianism in indigenous traditions has been the challenge to the fixed system of two genders, as in the study of traditional women healers in South Africa conducted by Ruth Morgan and Graeme Reid (2003). Finally, since its inception in the 1970s, the study of same-sex relationships between women has suffered from "lesbian invisibility," a widely recognized phenomenon in the field that stems from both sexism and heterosexism. Religion, too, suffers a similar neglect: while there are increasing numbers of articles on lesbianism in specific cultures, religion is not often pursued as a line of analysis. Nonetheless, there is a growing body of research available to scholars of lesbianism and religion that may draw on the wealth of first-person narratives available online.

One of the advantages of studying lesbianism and male homosexuality in religious traditions is that there is usually a detailed enumeration of the type of same-sex identities or behaviors that are forbidden by a given religion. Setting aside indigenous religions, such as those in Africa and the Americas, every major religion prohibits homosexuality at the most explicit level. The Hebrew Bible is actually an exception, insofar as it makes no reference to same-sex sexual relationships between women. Hindu, Jain, Buddhist (from India to Japan), and Muslim sacred texts proscribe sexual practices between women—but to widely varying degrees. Islamic jurisprudence rarely identifies sexual acts between women but does prohibit all homosexual activity insofar as it falls outside of the bounds of marriage. There are very few references to sexual activity between women contained in the juridical texts, but there are a few more in Arabic, Turkish, and Persian literature; Everett Rowson (1991) discusses the references found in Arabic literature, and Paul Sprachman (1997) focuses on Persian sources. Ironically, lesbianism in Turkish harems was one of the classic stereotypes about Islam at the height of colonialism, as Marilyn Brown (1987) has eloquently demonstrated. There are few studies of same-sex relationships between women within Islam; the references are scattered throughout studies of male homosexuality. In the South Asian arena, however, Ruth Vanita has recently emerged with a few excellent studies on same-sex relationships between women in Hinduism that draw on both local and Sanskrit myths, rituals, and linguistic analyses (in Vanita and Kidwai, 2000).

The normative standard in all Indian traditions is heterosexual intercourse. Almost all violations of the usual strictures incur a higher penalty than male-male sex, and the price for sexual acts between women falls even lower on the scale. Thus, in the Hindu *śastra* tradition, the *Arthaśastra* declares that women who have sex with each other are required to pay a lower fine than men who have sex with each other. In the *Manusmriti*, a woman who has sex with a virgin pays a much higher fine than two women who are no longer virgins are required to pay. The *Kāmasūtra* details a variety of sexual acts between women, and like other sources of the period, describes a type of "third gender" described as biologically male. Leonard Zwilling (1992) has written on the detailed taxonomies of sexual "identities" described within Indian texts, but he has not paid as close attention to terms for "women" as he has for "men." Within the Indian sphere, but from a different angle, Buddhist Vinaya texts go into detail on the kinds of sexual activity prohibited to monks and nuns; unlike the Hindu tradition, one's intent weighs more heavily than the actual act itself. Thus, the punishment for monks who willfully violate the prohibitions on sexual intercourse (*maithuna*) with women is to be expelled from the *sangha* (order). However, the penalty for two nuns who engage in "patting each other" (i.e., mutual manual stimulation) falls into the category of minor offenses. Because the Buddhist Vinaya texts were carried along with Buddhism as it moved into China, Japan, and throughout Southeast Asia, the same descriptions of proscribed behaviors for nuns appear throughout Asian Buddhist traditions, though with some variations in how the terms are understood in the commentaries.

Sources for understanding same-sex relationships between women are relatively scarce in East Asia. There is one passage in the *Dream of the Red Chamber* (also known as *The Story of the Stone*) that describes the attractions that a young actress has for other actresses with whom she worked. Hinsch also devoted an appendix to lesbianism in *Passion of the Cut Sleeve* (1990), but there are relatively few studies of lesbianism in Chinese literature. Some have argued that the strong affiliations between women at certain moments in Chinese history should be considered as same-sex affections, as in the case of Chinese marriage resisters. It may be that the relationships between women such as these should be considered in the same light as female friendships in the nineteenth century, in which the relationships are enduring, passionate, and stable but contain no references to sexual activity between the partners (Smith-Rosenberg, 1985; Raymond, 1986). Paul Schalow's article on Kukai and male love in *Buddhism, Sexuality, and Gender* (1992) is a fascinating study. There is a growing literature on the lives of gay men and lesbians in contemporary China—known collectively as *tongzhi*—and Japan—where the term for lesbian is *rezubian*, or *rezu* for short. One good guide to the literature by geographical area is the *Reader's Guide to Lesbian and Gay Studies,* edited by Timothy F. Murphy (2000).

See Also Gender and Religion, overview article; Gynocentrism; Homosexuality; Human Body, article on Human Bodies, Religion, and Gender; Nuns, overview article; Patriarchy and Matriarchy.

BIBLIOGRAPHY

Alpert, Rebecca. *Like Bread on the Seder Plate: Jewish Lesbians and the Transformation of Tradition.* New York, 1997.

Boswell, John. *Christianity, Social Tolerance, and Homosexuality: Gay People in Western Europe from the Beginning of the Christian Era to the Fourteenth Century.* Chicago, 1980.

Brooten, Bernadette J. *Love between Women: Early Christian Responses to Female Homoeroticism.* Chicago, 1996.

Brown, Judith C. *Immodest Acts: The Life of a Lesbian Nun in Renaissance Italy.* New York, 1986.

Brown, Marilyn R. "The Harem Dehistoricized: Ingres' *Turkish Bath.*" *Arts Magazine* 61 (Summer 1987): 58–68.

Cabezòn, José Ignacio, ed. *Buddhism, Sexuality, and Gender.* Albany, N.Y., 1992.

Cao Xuequin, and Gao E., trans. *Story of the Stone,* vol. 3, pp. 375, 551–553. New York, 1973–1987.

Chalmers, Sharon. *Emerging Lesbian Voices from Japan.* London, 2002.

Chao, Antonia. "Global Metaphors and Local Strategies in the Construction of Taiwan's Lesbian Identities." *Culture, Health and Sexuality* 2, no. 4 (2000): 377–390.

Comstock, Gary David, and Susan E. Henking, eds. *Que(e)rying Religion: A Critical Anthology.* New York, 1997.

Daly, Mary. *Gyn/Ecology: The Metaethics of Radical Feminism.* Boston, 1978.

D'Angelo, Mary Rose. "Women Partners in the New Testament." *Journal of Feminist Studies in Religion* 6, no. 1 (1990): 65–86.

Foucault, Michel. *The History of Sexuality*, vol. 1. Translated by Robert Hurley. French orig. 1976; New York, 1978.

Heyward, Carter. *Touching Our Strength: The Erotic as Power and Love of God.* San Francisco, 1989.

Hinsch, Brett. *Passion of the Cut Sleeve: The Male Homosexual Tradition in China.* Berkeley, Calif., 1990.

Leyland, Winston, ed. *Queer Dharma: Voices of Gay Buddhists.* San Francisco, 1998.

Lienert, Tania. "On Who Is Calling Radical Feminists 'Cultural Feminists' and Other Historical Sleights of Hand." In *Radically Speaking: Feminism Reclaimed,* edited by Diane Bell and Renate Klein, pp. 155–168. North Melbourne, Australia, 1996.

Lorde, Audre. *Sister Outsider: Essays and Speeches.* Trumansburg, N.Y., 1984.

Morgan, Ruth, and Graeme Reid. "'I've Got Two Men and One Woman': Ancestors, Sexuality and Identity among Same-Sex Identified Women Traditional Healers in South Africa." *Culture, Health and Sexuality* 5, no. 5 (2003): 375–391.

Murphy, Timothy F., ed. *Reader's Guide to Lesbian and Gay Studies.* Chicago, 2000.

Murray, Stephen O., and Will Roscoe, eds. *Islamic Homosexualities: Culture, History, and Literature.* New York, 1997.

Murray, Stephen O., and Will Roscoe, eds. *Boy-Wives and Female Husbands: Studies in African Homosexualities.* New York, 1998.

Ratti, Rakesh, ed. *A Lotus of Another Color: An Unfolding of the South Asian Gay and Lesbian Experience.* Boston, 1993.

Raymond, Janice. *Passion for Friends: Toward a Philosophy of Female Affection.* Boston, 1986.

Rich, Adrienne. "Compulsory Heterosexuality and Lesbian Existence." *Signs: Journal of Women in Culture and Society* 5 (1980): 631–660.

Roscoe, Will, ed. *Living the Spirit: A Gay American Indian Anthology.* New York, 1988.

Rowson, Everett K. "The Categorization of Gender and Sexual Irregularity in Medieval Arabic Vice Lists." In *Body Guards: The Cultural Politics of Gender Ambiguity,* edited by Julia Epstein and Kristina Straub, pp. 50–79. New York, 1991.

Smith-Rosenberg, Carole. "The Female World of Love and Ritual: Relations between Women in Nineteenth Century America." In *Disorderly Conduct: Visions of Gender in Victorian America,* pp. 53–76. New York, 1985.

Sprachman, Paul. "*Le beau garon sans merci*: The Homoerotic Tale in Arabic and Persian." In *Homoeroticism in Classical Arabic Literature,* edited by J. W. Wright and Everett K. Rowson, pp. 192–109. New York, 1997.

Swarr, Amanda Lock, and Richa Nagar. "Dismantling Assumptions: Interrogating 'Lesbian' Struggles for Identity and Survival in India and South Africa." *Signs: Journal of Women in Culture and Society* 29, no. 2 (2003): 491–516.

Te Awekotuku, Ngahuia. "Maori—Lesbian—Feminist Radical." In *Radically Speaking: Feminism Reclaimed,* edited Diane Bell and Renate Klein, pp. 55–61. North Melbourne, Australia, 1996.

Thomas, Wesley, and Sue-Ellen Jacobs. "'. . . And We Are Still Here': From Berdache to Two-Spirit People." *American Indian Culture and Research Journal* 23, no. 2 (1999): 91–107.

Vanita, Ruth, and Saleem Kidwai. *Same Sex Love in India: Readings from Literature and History.* New York, 2000.

Zwilling, Leonard. 1992. "Homosexuality as Seen in Indian Buddhist Texts." In *Buddhism, Sexuality, and Gender,* edited by José Ignacio Cabezòn. Albany, N.Y., 1992

CAROL S. ANDERSON (2005)

LESSING, G. E. (1729–1781), was a German dramatist, historian, and essayist. Born in Kamenz, the son of a Lutheran pastor, Gotthold Ephraim Lessing went to university in Leipzig in 1746 to study theology, which his interest in drama soon caused him to abandon. He moved to Berlin in 1748 and there became acquainted with noted Enlightenment figures. Between 1755 and 1760 Lessing spent time in Leipzig and Berlin as a journalist. In 1760 he took up residence in Breslau, where he wrote his famous drama *Minna von Barnhelm* (1767–1777) and his treatise comparing literary and visual arts criticism, *Laokoon* (1766). In 1766 Lessing became resident critic for a new theater in Hamburg and composed the *Hamburg Dramaturgy* (1767). The theater soon failed, and Lessing finally became librarian at the library of the duke of Brunswick in Wolfenbüttel. Here he pursued intently his heretofore intermittent theological and historical studies. His publication of anonymous fragments from a manuscript by Samuel Reimarus (1694–1768), attacking Christianity, provoked heated opposition from orthodox Lutherans, and Lessing eventually became embroiled in polemics with the Hamburg pastor Johann Melchior Goeze (1717–1786). Upon being placed under censorship by the duke in 1778, Lessing answered with his famous play *Nathan the Wise* (1779), which pleads for religious toleration. He died in Braunschweig in 1781. Lessing's theological tracts include *Vindication of Hieronymous Caradanus* (1754); *Leibniz on Eternal Punishments* (1773); *Berengarius Turonesis* (1770); "Editor's Counterpropositions," prefacing Reimarus's fragments (1777); *New Hypotheses Concerning the Evangelists Seen as Merely Human Historians* (1778); *Axiomata* (1778); and *The Education of Mankind* (1780).

Lessing's theological reflections have produced divergent interpretations. He is variously seen as an Enlightenment rationalist, basing knowledge upon mathematical models, or as an irrationalist influenced by British empiricism. There are sound textual grounds for both positions, but both presuppose a consistent and relatively complete theory on Lessing's part. Lessing is most effectively interpreted not as a consistent theorist, however, but as one caught up in the cognitive crisis of precritical philosophy between 1750 and 1781. Rationalistic and empiricist paradigms are evident as organizational principles in his handling of religious data.

Religion, specifically revealed religion, became an acute problem for Lessing because its medium is history. "Accidental truths of history can never become the proof of necessary truths of reason," he wrote in *On the Proof of the Spirit and the Power* (1777). Reason, he argued, posits a mathematical mode for all reality. The inner truth of being evinces the formal features of necessity, universality, and intelligibility; truth about God must accord with the formal structure of reason. Historical truth is, on the other hand, always concerned with what, empirically, has occurred. But empirical events are structurally accidental, that is, their contradiction is always possible; this generates the accidental essence of the historical. To base metaphysical and moral truth about God and human relation to God on accident would accordingly constitute *metabasis eis allo genos* (passage into another conceptual realm). Lessing does not flatly deny, for instance, the historical truth of Christ's resurrection. Letting it be accepted as historically possible, he nevertheless balks at drawing a conclusion of salvational importance from such an "accidental" event. History would thereby become a "spider's thread," too weak for the weight of eternity.

Because Lessing freed himself from orthodox dependence upon the literal word of the Bible, he was able to entertain various theses concerning the purely historical origins of the books of the New Testament. He can thus be considered an early exponent of higher criticism.

Through Lessing's reflections there runs an empiricist, if not irrationalist, counterthesis: Humankind as it really is—in history and as historical being—is not a rationalist, grounding moral activity on rational insight into the nature of God. From his youthful poetic fragment "Religion" to his late "collectanea to a book," *The Education of Mankind*, Lessing complained of the benightedness of human consciousness. Indeed, he sometimes viewed reason as a destructive force that has removed humanity from a primitive innocence. At any rate, humankind, left to its own powers, would wander about for "many millions of years" in error, without reaching moral and religious perfection. De facto, humanity has fallen from a primordial state (be it in fact or only in allegory) and is cognitively limited. De facto, humans do not possess a rational consciousness; they are limited to "unclear" ideas. In short, human consciousness is sensate-empirical. Along with humanity's benighted cognition goes its essentially emotional psychology. Images, not abstract ideas, move humans to action.

Lessing clearly separated himself from Lutheran orthodoxy, but he expressed his appreciation for it: Historical Christianity at least addresses humans as they de facto are. Neological and rationalist theologies, on the other hand, assume humans to be rational; this, history proves false. Lessing thus repeatedly opposed theological "liberals" such as J. A. Eberhard (1739–1809).

Lessing reconciled rationalism and Christianity by distinguishing between Christianity as history and Christianity's contemporary meaning; he then brought the two together through the notion of the progressivity of history. Humankind, clearly incapable of reaching moral perfection, is in need of a directional impulse from beyond. Lessing accordingly accepts hypothetically the basic Christian position that God has entered history. But for Lessing, God enters history as an educator who uses prerational means (e.g., miracles) to stimulate human evolution toward rational self-sufficiency. The Old and New Testaments are thus stages leading to a new eternal covenant, not unlike that envisioned by some rationalists, in which humankind will reach perfection.

In the modern period, revealed religion is valid independent of any historical proofs because it has the function to stimulate humankind's progressively improving capacity for rational self-reflection. The effects (still evident) of a maturing Christianity, not its historical miracles, become the criterion of the inner truth of Christianity. True religion improves humankind.

Lessing's theology does not constitute a worked-out philosophy; rather, it evinces a laborious and painful encounter with revolutionary tendencies of the modern world. His progressive view of history constitutes an early link in the great theodicies of historical evolution developed in the eighteenth and nineteenth centuries, particularly by Hegel.

Lessing's influence on posterity has been ambiguous. He founded no school and had no followers, yet his theological efforts encompass and epitomize the theological currents of the eighteenth century, currents that influenced subsequent developments critically. In addition, he was a master stylist and rhetorician. Lessing's writings are masterfully, even dramatically, constructed. Here is the source of his lasting influence. He has historical importance because of the content of his theologizing and enduring appeal because of the creative form of his writing.

BIBLIOGRAPHY

An agreed-upon interpretation of Lessing's theology is lacking, and great divergencies among scholars are evident. In the twentieth century some found Lessing to be a secular rationalist. In this connection, see Martin Bollacher's *Lessing: Vernunft und Geschichte; Untersuchungen zum Problem religiöser Aufklärung in den Spätschriften* (Tübingen, 1978) and Martin Haug's *Entwicklung und Offenbarung bei Lessing* (Gütersloh, 1928). Bollacher's study is a particularly good presentation of this view. Since the 1930s some scholars have found Lessing to be a theist, even Christian to a degree—at any rate, at least receptive to the idea of revelation. For two very important works concerning this thesis, see Arno Schilson's *Geschichte im Horizont der Vorsehung: G. E. Lessings Beitrag zu einer Theologie der Geschichte* (Mainz, 1974) and Helmut Thielicke's *Offenbarung, Vernunft und Existenz: Studien zur Religionsphilosophie Lessings,* 3d ed. (Göttingen, 1957). My study *G. E. Lessing's Theology: A Reinterpretation* (The Hague, 1977) is an attempt to integrate the two traditions by viewing Lessing not as a systematic thinker but as one who evinced contradictions and hovered between secularism and Christianity. For two introductions in English to Lessing's theology, see Henry Allison's *Lessing and the Enlightenment* (Ann Arbor, Mich., 1966) and Henry Chadwick's "Introduction," in *Lessing's Theological Writings* (Stanford, Calif., 1957), pp. 9–49.

L. P. WESSELL, JR. (1987)

LEUBA, JAMES H. (1868–1946), was an American psychologist and one of the leading figures of the early phase of the American psychology of religion movement (1880–1930). Born in Switzerland, Leuba came to the United States as a young man and studied at Clark University under G. Stanley Hall. In 1895 he graduated from Clark and became a fellow there, and in 1896 he published the first academic study of the psychology of conversion. In 1889 he had begun teaching at Bryn Mawr College, where he spent all his active academic life. His numerous publications on the psychology of religion gave him a position of prominence in the field through the 1930s.

Leuba was responsible for the classic study on religious beliefs among scientists and psychologists. He found that the more eminent the scientist, the less likely he was to profess religious beliefs. The same finding held for psychologists. The results accorded with Leuba's own sympathies, for he was a critic of religion, a skeptic reporting on other skeptics. In his book *The Psychology of Religious Mysticism* (1926) he emphasized the importance of sexual impulses in motivating religious rituals and of the sexual symbolism of religious ecstasy. Leuba's work has been described as empiricist, reductionist, and antireligious. There is no doubt that in his time he was the least inclined among the leading psychologists to show any respect for conventional religion.

As Leuba himself reported, his early experiences in Switzerland led him to his critical views regarding religion and religious people. Raised in a Calvinist home, he began to have doubts, but then came under the influence of the Salvation Army and had a conversion experience. After he began his scientific studies he became an atheist. He remained, throughout the rest of his life, a critic of religion, much in the same vein as Freud, and a critic of religious hypocrites. He accused Hall and others of keeping up the appearance of religiosity for the sake of their social standing, or as a way of maintaining the authority of religious institutions in order to keep the "ignorant masses" under control. The current standing of Leuba's contribution can be gauged by the fact that of the six books he published during his lifetime, four are still in print, and one of them (*The Psychology of Religious Mysticism*) was reissued as recently as 1972. His brilliant ideas regarding the origins of religion and magic presaged those of Freud and Malinowski, and should keep Leuba numbered among the true greats of the study of religion.

BIBLIOGRAPHY

Argyle, Michael, and Benjamin Beit-Hallahmi. *The Social Psychology of Religion.* Boston, 1975.

Beit-Hallahmi, Benjamin. "Psychology of Religion, 1880–1930: The Rise and Fall of a Psychological Movement." *Journal of the History of the Behavioral Sciences* 10 (1974): 84–90.

Leuba, James H. *A Psychological Study of Religion.* New York, 1912.

Leuba, James H. *The Belief in God and Immortality.* Chicago, 1921.

Leuba, James H. *The Psychology of Religious Mysticism* (1926). Boston, 1972.

New Sources

Hay, David. "Psychologists Interpreting Conversion: Two American Forerunners of the Hermeneutics of Suspicion." *History of the Human Sciences* 12, no. 1 (1999): 55–73.

Leuba, James H. "Sources of Humanism in Human Nature." *Humanist* 61, no. 2 (2001): 12–15.

Wulff, David M. "James Henry Leuba: A Reassessment of a Swiss-American Pioneer." In *Aspects in Contexts*, edited by Jacob A. Belzen, pp. 25–44. Amsterdam; Atlanta, 2000.

BENJAMIN BEIT-HALLAHMI (1987)
Revised Bibliography

LÉVI, SYLVAIN (1863–1935), French Sanskritist, Orientalist, and cultural historian. "Sylvain was—always and from the very first—my second uncle," Marcel Mauss declared, recalling his fateful introduction to Sylvain Lévi in 1895; "I owe to Sylvain the new directions of my career." Many other scholars, European and Asian, owed Sylvain Lévi similar debts, and twentieth-century studies of South and East Asia's cultural and religious legacy owe numerous insights and new directions to Lévi's scholarship and personal example.

Just as Marcel Mauss was indebted to Sylvain Lévi for crucial advice, so Lévi owed a similar debt to Ernest Renan, who urged that he sit in Abel Henri Joseph Bergaigne's Sanskrit course at the École des Hautes Études in 1882. Born in Paris, March 28, 1863, Lévi was nineteen when he took Renan's advice, and his career was set after the first hour with Bergaigne. Three years later, in 1885, he was appointed to the second Sanskrit post at the École, and the following year he also took up a lectureship in the newly established section on sciences religieuses. In 1889, the year after Bergaigne's death, he became head of Sanskrit instruction at the École. He resigned that post to become professor of Sanskrit language and literature at the Collège de France in 1894, a position he held until his death, October 30, 1935.

Initially fascinated by the possible impact of Greek culture on ancient India, Lévi remained captivated by the nature and extent of cross-cultural influences in Asia. The extensive domain of his own scholarship on primary sources ranged from the first systematic study of Sanskrit drama to Buddhist studies, in which he was, in effect, the successor of Eugène Burnouf. In pursuit of these latter studies, he learned Chinese, Tibetan, and Japanese, and also mastered the Tocharian dialects of Central Asia. Broad and imaginative in his scholarly vision and speculation, Lévi remained a versatile specialist who insisted that the discovery of a single text, the confirmation of a single historical fact, the decipherment of a single stanza, was more significant than any theoretical construct.

Having become a close friend of two young Japanese while still a student, Lévi always sought to strengthen living cross-cultural associations and to recover dimensions of cultural heritage for the benefit of all. These humanistic concerns were evident not only in his scholarship but in his numerous activities as an unofficial cultural ambassador. Instrumental in establishing the École Française d'Extrême Orient, the Institut de Civilisation Indienne, and the Musée Guimet, Lévi founded the Maison Franco-Japonaise and was its first director. His close friendship with the ruling family of Nepal resulted in his classic three-volume work, *Le Népal.* As a friend and adviser of such Indians as Rabindranath Tagore and as a teacher of students, such as Takakusu Junjirō, who came to him from Japan, India, and other Asian countries, Lévi internationalized Asian religious studies and was perhaps Europe's first "postcolonial" Orientalist.

An important element in Lévi's background as a scholar was his abiding interest in Judaism of the Diaspora. The son of Alsatian Jewish immigrants, he worked tirelessly on behalf of world Jewry, becoming the president of the Alliance Israélite Universelle. In the last years of his life, efforts on behalf of Jewish refugees from Germany consumed much of his energy. Clearly, he saw parallels between the adventure of Buddhism in Asia and the impact of Jewish life and thought in Europe. The one historical verity reinforced the other; together the two helped shape and direct a career that changed European Orientalism and inaugurated an epoch in scholarship and in the human interaction between Europe and Asia. Lévi was, as one of his admirers put it, more than an Orientalist: he was a humanist.

BIBLIOGRAPHY

Lévi's writings remain untranslated from the French. A fairly complete bibliography concludes Victor Goloubew's tribute, "Sylvain Lévi et l'Indochine," *Bulletin de l'École Française d'Extrême Orient* 35 (1935): 551–574. The volume *Mémorial Sylvain Lévi*, edited by Louis Renou (Paris, 1937), contains forty-two articles by Lévi that eloquently illustrate the nature and range of his interests and scholarship. Renou's preface to this collection, "Sylvain Lévi et son œuvre scientifique" (first published in the *Journal asiatique*), is an informative and affectionate evaluation of the scholar and the man. Ivan Strenski continues his useful exploration of Levi's influence on Émile Durkheim and his school in *Durkheim and the Jews of France* (Chicago, 1997).

The essays (including an address in English) published as *L'Inde et le monde* (Paris, 1925) may be the most accessible introduction to Lévi's thought. Of his longer works, three are indisputable classics: *Le théâtre indien*, 2 vols. in 1 (Paris, 1890), *La doctrine du sacrifice dans les Brāhmaṇas* (Paris, 1898), and *Le Népal: Étude historique d'un royaume hindou*, 3 vols. (Paris, 1905–1908). Among his numerous editions, translations, and studies, two that remain especially important are *Asanga: Mahayana-sutralamkara; Exposé de la doctrine du Grand Véhicule selon le système Yogacara*, 2 vols. (Paris, 1907–1911), and *Un système de philosophie bouddhique: Matériaux pour l'étude du système Vijñaptimātra* (Paris, 1932).

G. R. WELBON (1987 AND 2005)

LEVI BEN GERSHOM SEE GERSONIDES

LEVITES.

[*This entry discusses the role of the* leviyyim *("Levites") and* kohanim *("priests") in Israelite religion and in Judaism.*]

The origin of the Levites remains obscure despite considerable scholarly attention. Without contemporary documentation of the sort available on the larger societies of the ancient Near East, scholars must rely largely on the Hebrew Bible and later Jewish sources for information, making it difficult to trace the early development of this priestly group. What is known is that religious life in antiquity, from an institutional point of view, always required special places of worship with priests who were trained to perform cultic rites, make oracular inquiry, record temple business, and instruct worshipers on religious matters. Like the scribe, the priest had a set of skills unknown to most other members of society, and the need for skilled personnel generated a system of "schools" attached to temples and other cult centers to recruit, support, and educate priests. In ancient societies three factors interact: training and skill, family and clan, and place of residence. The family provided an ideal setting for teaching priestly skills and retaining exclusive control over them. In Israel, as elsewhere, families and clans tended to concentrate in certain locales, where their members lived in proximity to each other. Clans were not strictly ancestral, contrary to the impression made by certain biblical texts, and it was not uncommon to admit an outsider to learn the skills practiced by the clan, and eventually to grant clan membership as well.

Some biblical traditions regard the Levites as one of the original twelve tribes, whose members were collectively consecrated to cult service; other less systematic but perhaps more authentic biblical evidence regards them as a professional group, whose members came from various tribes and clans. Initially, priestly groups may have formed along professional lines, subsequently developing into clans and even larger units. Biblical writers probably began to regard the Levites as a tribe only after the interaction of training, locale, and family affiliation had progressed to a considerable degree. Biblical historiography has shown a strong tendency toward fitting social groups into neat, genealogical categories, which may account for the traditional identity of the Levites as a tribe.

Of the professional titles and terms used in Hebrew sources to designate priests of different types, the most common is *kohen* (pl. *kohanim*), cognates of which are found in the Ugaritic, Aramaic, Phoenician, and Arabic languages. The term *komer* ("priest"), with cognates in Akkadian, the el-Amarna dialect, and again Aramaic, is used in Hebrew scriptures only for pagan priests, and then rarely (*2 Kgs.* 23:5, *Hos.* 10:5, *Zep.* 1:4).

There is no feminine form for *kohen* because there was no role for women in the official Yahvistic cult of Israel. And yet there is a term for priestess, *qedeshah,* which literally means a (female) "consecrated person." (The masculine equivalent, *qadesh,* also occurs.) Based upon biblical evidence, these terms would be considered solely derogatory (e.g., *Dt.* 23:18, *Hos.* 4:14). However, in Ugaritic, *qadishuma* is an administrative term for priests and in Akkadian, *qadishtu* designates a priestess class widely known in the Old Babylonian period. Thus, biblical usage of *qedeshah* and *qadesh* as terms of derision to designate improper or pagan priests is more a matter of attitude than of nomenclature. The terms *kohen, komer,* and *qadesh/qedeshah* are professional titles.

A bigger problem arises in defining the term *levi* (Levite). A number of etymologies have been posed along professional lines, ranging from the notion of "carrying, bearing," to camping "around" the sanctuary. Poor documentation aside, what these etymologies are actually positing is more logical than linguistic, reflecting known cultic functions, such as carrying cultic artifacts, guarding temples, and so on. If the term derives from a single verbal root, it is not presently established and any definition must be according to context and usage.

Early History in Biblical Tradition. The earliest biblical reference to a *levi* is probably to be found in *Judges* 17–18. Micah, a man who lived somewhere in the Ephraimite hills before there was a monarchy in Israel, built a temple and installed in it several cult objects. He appointed one of his sons as priest. About that time, "a young man from Bethlehem, from the clan of Judah, who was a *levi"* (*Jgs.* 17:7), arrived at Micah's residence while en route to seek his fortune in northern Israel. After conversing with him, Micah invited him to live in his household and serve as priest in his temple; more precisely, to be a father (*av*) and priest (*kohen*). Micah offered him ten shekels of silver a year, clothing, and room and board. The *levi* accepted, and Micah was assured that God would grant him good fortune now that he had a *levi* of his own.

Chapter 18 opens with the tribe of Dan, then living in the southern plain, seeking territory elsewhere because of pressure from the Philistines. The Danites sent spies to northern Israel, where they stopped at Micah's home, and the *levi* assured them that God was with them. They later found suitable land in upper Galilee, and when the entire tribe began its migration northward, they once again stopped at Micah's home. The spies informed the others that valuable cult objects were to be found in the local temple, and they persuaded the young *levi* to abandon Micah and serve as priest for their tribe. The Danites stole Micah's cult objects, including a statue, an *efod* (a vestment with pockets, containing lots used in oracular divination), and *terafim* (statuettes that probably served as family gods). Then they proceeded to Laish, took it without an attack, and renamed it Dan, and thus the cult of Dan was established.

The story has all the earmarks of authenticity precisely because it does not conform to traditional notions about Yahvistic religion. The *levi* was of the clan of Judah and from Bethlehem. But it was his profession, as distinct from clan affiliation, that was valued all over the country, affording him a certain degree of mobility. He was appointed *av* and *kohen,* the former a term sometimes used to designate a "teacher" or "master," quite apart from its use in a familial sense.

From this story it could be concluded that a *levi* was a mobile professional who might have come from any tribe or clan, employed by a family or at a temple or other cult site, supported by them and serving at their pleasure. In contrast to other members of clans, who normally tended agricultural lands, a *levi* could move about. This portrait, probably more accurate for the early period of Israelite settlement than for the later, sheds light on the question of origins, and corrects the traditional and less historical picture found in biblical priestly literature.

Hebrew scriptures tell little about the status of Micah himself except that he owned a temple, which indicates that he was a local leader. Leading residents of towns built temples, appointing members of their own families as priests. Some biblical historians claim that in the early Israelite period the head of the clan or household was the priest, an image that seems to fit the patriarchs of Israel, who built altars and endowed cults.

An early story about the training of a priest is preserved in *1 Samuel* 1–3. Samuel, a cult prophet, officiated at sacrifices but also spoke with the authority of a prophet who communicated God's word to the people. Before his birth, he was dedicated to temple service by his mother, pledged as a *nazir* ("Nazirite") to serve all his life in the temple at Shiloh. This form of cultic devotion, which parents might perform for a variety of reasons, was one of the ways of recruiting priests. With Samuel the motive given was the gratitude of his onetime barren mother, but in reality economic deprivation often prompted parents to seek security for their sons in the priesthood. *1 Samuel* 2:36 intimates as much in predicting that the sinful priests of the House of Eli would beg to be accepted in a priestly group just to have bread to eat.

It was Eli, the chief priest of Shiloh, to whom young Samuel was brought by his mother. Samuel's prophetic role is anticipated by a divine theophany whose message Eli does not fail to comprehend. Samuel is taught the priestly arts by Eli, whose own sons were greedy and improper in the conduct of the sacrificial cult. Here is seen an instance in which an outsider rose to prominence at a major temple, while the

APPROPRIATION AND IDENTITY

Whatever else they are, images are always deposits of previous forms of image-making, traces of visual thought inherited from the past. This fact makes any given image a particular configuration of preservative or backward-looking impulses and present or even forward-looking ones. In the case of religious imagery, this means that images are something like cultural fossils that are especially useful to religious belief because of their ability to appropriate old motifs for new uses. It is possible, therefore, to plot the changes and cultural developments of religious thought and practice in the material record of art and architecture. Images (as well as song, dance, verse, and music) are not merely incidental to religion, but often the very medium in which belief takes shape.

Images live long lives. Their features and motifs travel far, are copied and often modified by successive generations of artisans, and are used as patterns for new ideas and put to purposes for which they were not originally intended. In some cases, there is no question of intentional appropriation of a visual motif. Haitian Vodou makes explicit use of Catholic iconography and the cult of saints in its imagery and visual practices. Vodou societies possess flags, such as the one illustrated here **(a)**, to represent their group and the gods or goddesses whom they worship. The flag of Sen Jak or Ogou is clearly taken from imagery of Saint Jacques or Saint James, the mounted soldier well known for his pilgrimage church, Santiago de Compostella, in Spain. Ogou is the principal male deity in Vodou, the master of iron and lord of battle who is invoked dur-

(a) A Haitian Vodou flag *(drapo sevis)*, sewn by Silva Joseph for the male deity Ogou (Sen Jak). *[UCLA Fowler Museum of Cultural History; photograph by Don Cole]*

ing times of crisis and conflict. Among the many Haitians who practice both Vodou and Catholicism, the duality of the image is important. As a consequence of French colonialism, the dual nature of the image signifies both the authority of the dominant religion and the strategy of resistance adopted by Haitians. In other instances, original meanings are readily lost or detached from images and new significance discerned within them. The frontispiece of a medieval Muslim manuscript (not pictured) offered protection from snakebite and did so by combining originally Babylonian iconography (the symbol of the moon in the center) with the visual organization of a Buddhist *maṇḍala*. It has been said of this image that popular belief understood an eclipse to occur when a celestial monster swallowed the sun or moon. It is known that the manuscript was written during an eclipse, which may have been thought to enhance the power of the image and the text's prescriptions to protect against snakebite. Registered in the image, therefore, are pre-Muslim beliefs and an archive of non-Muslim visual motifs that may or may not be associated with the image's meaning.

In yet a third scenario, images (in this case, architectural styles and decorative iconography) offer the select appropriation of many traditions and their deliberate integration into a new religious ideal, as in the case of the Bahāʾī religion. This religion teaches that a single, universal deity has been revealed by important messengers, including Moses, Buddha, Jesus, and Muḥammad, and that a single, universal religion is being progressively revealed. Unity of belief and diversity of believers goes to the heart of the faith and is visually conveyed by the architectural design of Bahāʾī temples around the world **(b)**, each of which integrates elements from many faiths.

(b) The Bahāʾī House of Worship in Wilmette, Illinois. *[©Richard Hamilton Smith/Corbis]*

As Buddhism developed in northern India and elsewhere, the life of Siddārtha Gautama was understood in terms borrowed from Hinduism, the parent religion of Buddhism. The Buddha himself maintained major features of Hindu thought and practice in his new way, so it is not surprising that elements used to define and affirm the distinctiveness of Buddhism clearly derive from Hinduism, such as the serpent Mucalinda, who arose to protect Siddārtha from the rain as he meditated **(c)**. The small company of Hindu ascetics with whom he had practiced for several years saw in the act of the serpent something that might have reminded them of Viṣṇu **(d)**, who was often shown recumbent on a bed of a multiheaded serpent, which provided shade for the resting deity. Emerging from Buddhist and Hindu traditions, Jainism borrowed the motif for portraying the Jina named Parshvanatha, one of the religion's enlightened few

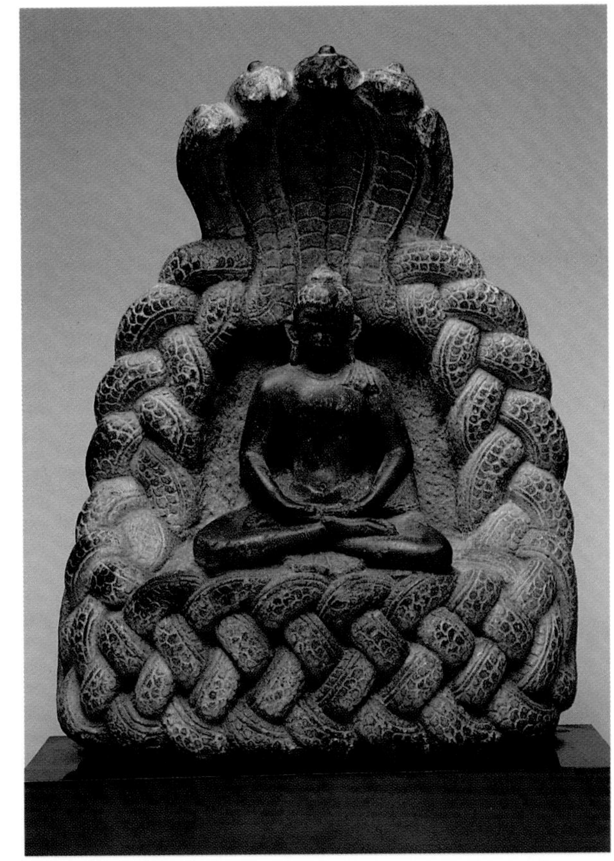

(c) Right. Buddha sheltered by the serpent Mucalinda during meditation, eleventh to twelfth century, Nepal, Kathmandu. *[The James W. and Marilynn Alsdorf Collection, 193.1997; photograph by Michael Tropea; reproduction, The Art Institute of Chicago]* **(d) Bottom.** Viṣṇu and Lakṣmī resting on the multiheaded serpent Garuḍa, Kangra school, c. 1870. *[©Victoria & Albert Museum, London/Art Resource, N.Y.]*

(the equivalent of a *bodhisattva*) who lead the way out of rebirth **(e)**.

Buddhism is an especially resourceful religious tradition, adapting itself to locale and cultural milieu to great effect. As with the saints in many other religions, such as Catholicism and Vodou, the *bodhisattvas* often assume the greatest variety of accommodation. Avalokiteśvara, the *bodhisattva* of compassion, who enjoyed enormous popularity among Mahāyāna Buddhists in India and the Himalayan regions (often receiving even greater attention than the Buddha himself), was portrayed with many heads and arms to signify the watchfulness and abundance of his compassion **(f)**. When Buddhism took root in China, however, Avalokiteśvara morphed into a female equiva-

(e) TOP. Ninth-century bronze of the Jain teacher Parshvanatha flanked by attendants, beneath the canopy of a multiheaded serpent, Maitraka region, India. *[©Angelo Hornak/Corbis]* **(f)** RIGHT. Eleven-headed Avalokiteśvara, 1800, bronze and silver gilt, polychromed and inlaid with semiprecious stones, Eastern Tibet. *[The Walters Art Museum, promised gift of John & Berthe Ford]*

lent known as Guanyin, the *bodhisattva* of mercy **(g)**, a pre-Buddhist figure who had been dedicated to assisting mothers in the birth and care of children. As often happens in the history of Buddhism, this transformation was effected by imperial influence: Avalokiteśvara became female when the portrait of an empress was inserted into his depictions in the decorations of her tomb. A Japanese counterpart, Kannon, accompanied the rise of Buddhism in Japan and served as the meeting point of Christianity and Japanese Buddhism when Jesuit missionaries portrayed the Madonna and Child for Japanese converts to Roman Catholicism in the sixteenth century.

It will always be a matter of debate among specialists (as well as among believers, perhaps) what such borrowings and transformations mean. Is the Egyptian motif of Isis suckling Horus on her lap **(h)** the source of early

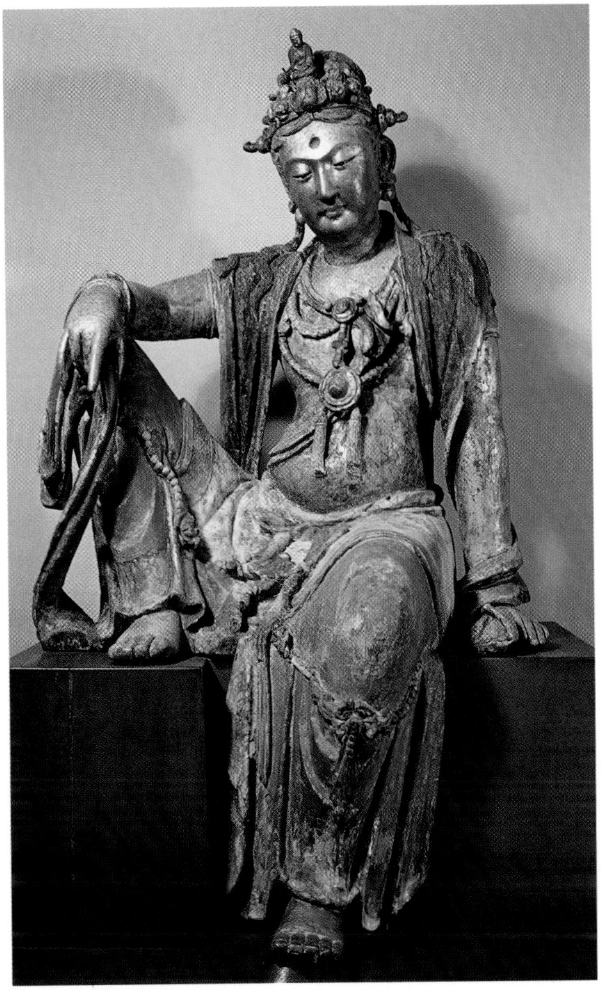

(g) ABOVE. Guanyin, the Chinese *bodhisattva* of mercy, Yuan dynasty, c. 1279–1369, polychromed wood. *[©Burstein Collection/Corbis]* **(h)** LEFT. Bronze sculpture of the ancient Egyptian goddess Isis suckling the infant Horus. *[©Réunion des Musées Nationaux/Art Resource, N.Y.]*

(i) A Roman catacomb image depicting the Magi with Mary and the infant Jesus, from the Catacomb of Priscilla in Rome, c. 200 CE. *[©Scala/Art Resource, N.Y.]*

Christianity's portrayal of the Virgin and Child? If so, does any of the meaning of the Egyptian motif remain in its Christian appropriation? By the same token, the three figures approaching the seated Madonna in a Roman catacomb painting **(i)** are the magi mentioned in the Gospel of Luke, wise men from the East, possibly Zoroastrian priests from Persia (modern Iran), who practiced a monotheistic faith that maintained understandings of soul, conflict of good and evil, afterlife, and eschaton that were shared by Christianity. As an early competitor of Christianity, Zoroastrianism may have deliberately been portrayed in the subordinating motif of the wise men's visit to the newborn Christ. If so, the representation of the three figures, whose form recalls the repetitive silhouettes of Persian relief sculpture, may have been keyed to the visual and theological sensibilities of Zoroastrian converts to Christianity in third-century Rome. Sometimes images may be intended to retain their older associations as a way of subordinating them to their new religious contents.

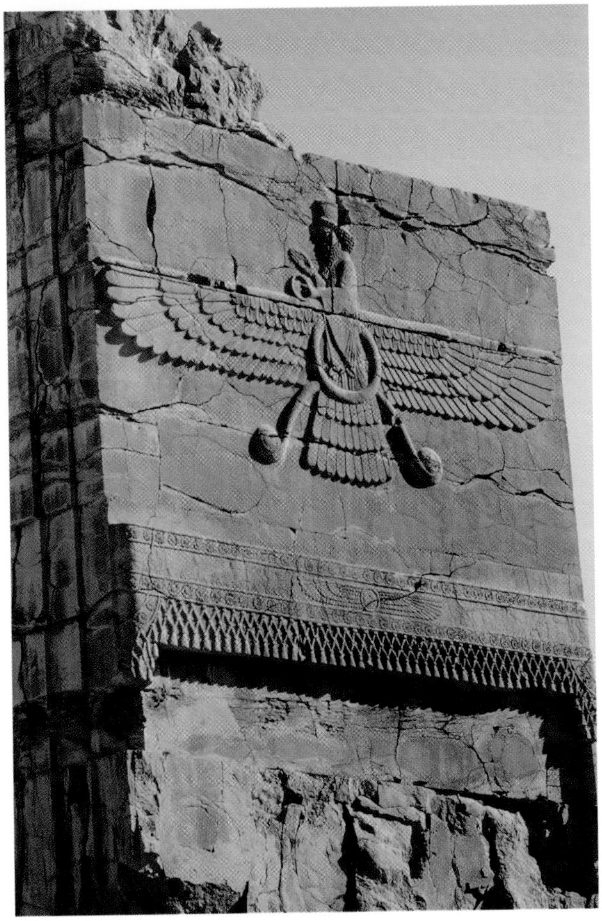

But the survival of visual features does not always mean a continuity of meaning or specific intention. Winged figures, for instance, are a familiar aspect of many different religions and might be historically traced in a long descent from antiquity to the present. In ancient Nimrud winged creatures were depicted on the palace walls of Assyrian kings as divine protectors **(j)**. Winged figures were reported in the Hebrew Bible when writers described angels or messengers of God and apocalyptic figures such as those in the *Book of Ezekiel.* Zoroastrianism portrays the human soul with a winged figure **(k)**, and angels perform important roles in both Islam and Christianity. Gabriel appears to Mary to announce the birth of the messiah and, according to the Qurʾān, to many prophets from Adam to Muḥammad. And it was Gabriel who brought to Muḥammad the revelations that

(j) Above. Limestone relief of Ashurnasirpal II offering protection to the Assyrian kings, 875 BCE, Nimrud, Assyria. *[©The Trustees of the British Museum]* **(k) Right.** Iranian relief of Ahura Mazdā, the chief Zoroastrian deity, c. sixth century BCE, Persepolis, Iran. *[©Charles & Josette Lenars/Corbis]*

(I) Pietro da Cortona, *The Guardian Angel*, seventeenth century. *[©Araldo de Luca/Corbis]*

are recorded in the Qurʾān. Another function of winged angels occupies popular Christian piety in the modern age: the benevolent guardian angels who accompany their charges in daily life in order to protect them from mishap or evil **(I)**.

BIBLIOGRAPHY

Davis, Richard H. *Lives of Indian Images*. Princeton, 1997.

Hillenbrand, Robert. *Islamic Art and Architecture*. London, 1999.

Ning, Qiang. *Art, Religion, and Politics in Medieval China: The Dunhuang Cave of the Zhai Family*. Honolulu, 2004.

Pal, Pratapaditya. *The Peaceful Liberators: Jain Art from India*. Los Angeles and New York, 1994.

Polk, Patrick Arthur. *Haitian Vodou Flags*. Jackson, Miss., 1997.

Shafer, Byron E., ed. *Religion in Ancient Egypt: Gods, Myths, and Personal Practice*. Ithaca, N.Y., 1991.

Weidner, Marsha, ed. *Latter Days of the Law: Images of Chinese Buddhism, 850–1850*. Lawrence, Kans., and Honolulu, 1994.

DAVID MORGAN (2005)

family that had controlled the priesthood lost power. The hereditary succession did not always work and one adopted into the priesthood might assume leadership if he had superior gifts. In *1 Chronicles* 6:13, the name of Samuel is inserted in a Levitical genealogy. At that late period, it would have been inconceivable that a legitimate priest and leader of the people such as Samuel would not have been the descendant of a Levitical clan.

The story of the Canaanite king of Salem, Melchizedek, characterized as "a priest of El, the most high," adds yet another dimension to the status of priests in early Israel. In *Genesis* 14 (by all accounts an early biblical text), Melchizedek greets the patriarch Abram (later Abraham) after a victorious battle fought against foreign kings. He blesses Abram in the name of his own god, El ʿElyon. Here the king of a Canaanite city-state serves as a priest, showing the priestly office to be a corollary of civil status.

Little else is known about priests, generally, in the premonarchic period. Quite coincidentally, *Judges* 19:1 reports that the man whose concubine was raped and murdered in Gibeah of Benjamin was a *levi* living in the Ephraimite hills. That he had originally taken a concubine from Bethlehem suggests that he, like Micah's *levi,* may also have been from Bethlehem.

Curiously, the term *levi* most often appears in north Israelite literature. Indeed, it may be a north Israelite term for "priest," which would explain its general absence from Judahite sources and its occurrence in *Deuteronomy,* a book essentially northern in origin.

Monarchic period. The biblical narratives about Saul, the first king of Israel, reveal two aspects of the role of priests during the early monarchy. Saul employed an elderly professional priest, a descendant of Eli, from Shiloh (it having since been destroyed by the Philistines), who made oracular inquiry for Saul and the Israelite forces using the *efod* (*1 Sm.* 14). There is also the recurring theme of Saul's own involvement in priestly functions. At one point, Saul officiated at a sacrifice when, after seven days of waiting, Samuel failed to arrive (*1 Sm.* 13). Although Samuel was enraged over what Saul had done, it was probably in accordance with contemporary custom: Kings often assumed sacral roles.

David also employed professional priests, appointing and dismissing them at will. The first priest he encountered was Ahimelech, priest of Nob—the town of priests (*1 Sm.* 21). Ahimelech sided with David against Saul, offering him and his band comfort and aid. Saul eventually murdered the priests of Nob, but one escaped, Abiathar, Ahimelech's son (*1 Sm.* 22:20f.), who joined David's forces and regularly undertook oracular inquiry for David (*1 Sm.* 23:10f., 30:7f.). Later, David had two priests with him, Ahimelech and Zadok, whose origins are not revealed (*2 Sm.* 8:17, 15:24). These two lines of priests continued to serve David throughout his career until a priest of the Abiathar line sided with David's son, Adonijah, in an attempt to claim the succession and this line of priests was rejected (*1 Kgs.* 1:7, 1:19). Solomon banished the priest to his hometown, and henceforth only the line of Zadok served the Judahite royal house (*1 Kgs.* 2:35). The list preserved in *1 Kings* 4:25, which still mentions Abiathar, is apparently a later source, showing how literary tradition often ignores historical sequence.

In priestly families, as in many royal lines, sons were named after their grandfathers, a method known as "papponymy," so that names like Zadok reappear in subsequent generations (*Ez.* 40:46).

The narratives of David and Solomon reveal how certain priestly families were appointed under the monarchy and were expected to be loyal to their royal sponsors. At one point David used the priest Zadok to spy for him and to report on Absalom's activities (*2 Sm.* 15:26f.).

Considerable information is found in the Bible about priestly families during the period of the Judahite and northern Israelite monarchies, but there is hardly any mention of Levites. *1 Kings* 12:31 states that Jeroboam I did a wicked thing by appointing non-Levitical priests to officiate at his heterodox temples, but this statement occurs in a later insertion into the text. For the most part, *Samuel* and *Kings* know nothing about a tribe of Levi.

The reference to Nob as a town of priests introduces the factor of locale. The law of *Leviticus* 25:32–34 provides tax exemptions for Levitical towns, justifying such exemptions by the fact that the Levites had no territory of their own. The same justification underlies the provisions in *Numbers* 35:1–8. Both are late texts.

The lists of *Joshua* 21 and *2 Chronicles* 6 present a different problem because they specifically name forty-eight Levitical towns, most of which have been located. Benjamin Mazar argues that these lists ultimately reflect the situation under the united monarchy of the tenth century BCE. According to Mazar, these towns were first established by David and Solomon as part of a system of royal outposts, especially in newly conquered territories.

Aside from the fact that these lists show signs of lateness, there is some difficulty in ascertaining whether the sites listed were actually settled by Israelites in the tenth century BCE. Recent archaeological surveys in Israel show a different pattern of early settlement. Then too Mazar must rest his case on the traditions of *Chronicles,* to the effect that Levites specifically were involved with David and Solomon. Given the generally biased character of *Chronicles,* these traditions may not reflect an earlier reality. In any event, the concentration of Levites in certain locales is logical in the earlier periods of biblical history, as is the existence of certain towns of asylum, often located where priests lived (*Nm.* 35:9f.).

Deuteronomy, essentially derived from the northern Israelite kingdom of the eighth century BCE, refers to all priests as Levites. Its classic designation is "the Levitical priests, the entire tribe [Heb., *shevet*] of Levi" (*Dt.* 18:1). Clearly, in the north Levites were regarded as having a tribal identity: All legitimate priests were Levites, and all Levites were priests.

From what *Deuteronomy* says about Levites elsewhere one notes that the tribe of Levi was not like other tribes. Levites lived throughout the land (*Dt.* 14:26f.) and had no territory of their own, relying on cultic service for support (*Dt.* 18:6f.). The concern in *Deuteronomy* with the Levitical priests stems from its doctrine, expressed in chapters 12 and 16, that sacrifice is proper only at one central temple in a town to be selected by God. The habitation patterns of the Levites had corresponded to the decentralized pattern of worship at local and regional centers. Tithes and votaries remitted at these centers henceforth were to be collected only at a central temple. Once *Deuteronomy* legislated against the customary, decentralized pattern, provision had to be made for those Levitical priests who had served throughout the land. They therefore were granted the right to be maintained at the central Temple in Jerusalem, and assigned to cultic duties there.

The "Tribe of Levi." Current scholarship is only able to explain the traditions concerning a tribal origin for the Levites in broad, sociological terms. The biblical record of twelve tribes, into which that set of traditions fits, is questionable historically. The number twelve is maintained quite artificially in various tribal lists that sometimes include a tribe named Levi, sometimes not.

Apart from the genealogical recasting of the early Israelites, so characteristic of Priestly literature, the tradition of a tribe named Levi occurs in two poetic passages. In *Genesis* 49, Levi, the eponym of one of Jacob's sons, is the head of a tribe like all the others. Nothing is said about any cultic function associated with Levi, but there is the telling threat to disperse Levi throughout the Land of Israel, suggesting what came to be the real situation of the Levites.

In *Deuteronomy* 33, the Levites are a tribe, but a tribe of priests. This same chapter, verses 8 through 11, contains an oblique reference to the incident of the golden calf, recounted first in *Exodus* 32:26–29, and again in *Deuteronomy* 9:16f. Of all the Israelites, the Levites alone rallied to Moses' side. For their loyalty to God they were rewarded by being granted the Israelite priesthood. The cult of Yahveh was threatened when the golden calf, an allusion to the calves installed by Jeroboam I at Dan and Bethel, became the object of worship (*1 Kgs.* 12:29f.). The Levites are not characterized as a tribe, but rather as a group bound by the commitment to a proper Yahvistic cult that superseded their various tribal affiliations.

The reference to a tribe of Levi in *Genesis* 49 is less readily explained. Some historians have suggested that *Genesis* 49 is a very ancient passage that proves the early existence of a tribe called Levi. This is doubtful, because the incident of Shechem, recounted in *Genesis* 35, may be a late story of priestly origin.

Priests and Levites. The distinction between priest and Levite, basic to certain Priestly traditions, may have first emerged during the Babylonian exile. In *Ezekiel* 44:9f., the prophet, in his vision of a restored Temple in Jerusalem, favored the priestly line of Zadok exclusively. The Levites who had turned away from Yahveh (when, is not clear) were no longer to officiate at the cult, but were demoted (as it were) to supporting tasks in maintaining the Temple. In effect, the Levites were to take over tasks formerly performed by foreign workmen (or, perhaps, foreign Temple slaves), whose presence in the Temple was condemned by Ezekiel.

This is the first indication outside of the Priestly texts of the Torah of a differentiation between Levitical priests and ordinary Levites, laying the groundwork for the postexilic system wherein priests were considered superior to Levites. Most biblical historians have explained this distinction as a consequence of Josiah's edict (c. 622). Josiah had closed down the local *bamot* ("high places") and summoned the priests serving them to Jerusalem (*2 Kgs.* 23). The reconstruction that Ezekiel's heterodox Levites were, in fact, these priests is logical but still only conjecture.

Classes of priests, with differentiated functions, were characteristic of Near Eastern temples, and undoubtedly applied to the Temple in Jerusalem at one time or another. Conceivably, the poem of *Genesis* 49 served to explain the demotion of the Levites, which is attributed to some outrageous act.

Postexilic references to priests and Levites appear in *Ezra, Nehemiah,* and *Chronicles,* a pattern continuing through and even subsequent to the destruction of the Second Temple in Jerusalem in 70 CE. In *Kings,* as in *Jeremiah* with its strong historical orientation, priests are in charge of the First Temple, before the exile. Recent archaeological discoveries have added to information on the succession of high priests from the eve of the exile through to the Hellenistic and Roman periods. By correlating postexilic writings with the works of Josephus Flavius and apocryphal books such as *1 Esdras,* Frank Moore Cross (1975) uses the Aramaic Samaria papyri of the fourth century BCE to propose an uninterrupted succession of high priests. From Jehozadak, who served on the eve of the Babylonian exile, Cross moves forward to Simeon I, born in 320. Based on the custom of "papponymy," Cross traces the priestly names.

High-born priestly families, such as those recorded in the lists of returning exiles in *Ezra* 2 and *Nehemiah* 7, owned estates outside of Jerusalem and probably derived their income from sources other than mere priestly emoluments. It can be logically assumed that of all the Jewish exiles in Babylonia, priestly families may have been particularly motivated to return to the Holy Land. By contrast, the Levites seem a deprived group in the early postexilic period. Ezekiel's differentiation between Zadokite priests and Levites may, in the last analysis, reflect the different economic standing of priestly families.

Thus far the history and formation of priestly groups in Israel have been discussed, but scripture highlights Priestly traditions on the origin and character of the priesthood that cannot be regarded historically, certainly not in detail. It would be fruitful to attempt a synthesis of history and tradition, both subjects for the historian but each requiring different methods in studying the past.

The Priestly traditions trace the origin of the priesthood, as well as the origin of the Yahvistic cult, to the time of Moses, prior to the settlement of Canaan. When the reader first encounters Aaron in the earliest traditions of *Exodus* (in the source known as JE, which combines Judean and north Israelite texts), he is Moses' brother certainly, but serves as a spokesman and emissary, and not as a priest. In *Exodus* 2:1f., Moses is affiliated with a Levitical family, and 4:14 refers to Aaron as "your brother, the *levi,*" but these references are the work of the Priestly editors. The identification of Moses and Aaron as Levites was part of the overall Priestly historiography, linking the cult and the priesthood to the Sinai theophanies.

The consecration and investiture of Aaron and his sons as priests are themes woven into the Tabernacle texts of *Exodus* 24:12–31:18 and 35–40, and into *Numbers,* especially 1–10:28, and 26, as well as in the descriptions of the investiture of Aaron and his sons in *Leviticus* 8–10. G. B. Gray (1971) regarded Moses as a priest, primarily on the basis of Psalm 99:6. It is preferable, however, to interpret the Priestly traditions of the Torah as a mirror image of reality: Moses, like other leaders and like the Judahite and northern Israelite kings, is portrayed as a priest maker, not a priest. He oversees the transfer of priestly authority to Eleazar, Aaron's son, before Aaron's death (*Nm.* 20:22f.); Moses never actually performs cultic functions, apart from the investiture of the first priests. As for Psalm 99, it is actually a late, postexilic composition and it endorses the Aaronic priesthood.

Aaron the priest, as opposed to Aaron the person, is nowhere mentioned in *Deuteronomy.* A Priestly addendum in *Deuteronomy* 32:50 speaks of his death, and *Deuteronomy* 9:20f. merely retells the episode of the golden calf. Even in that episode, with its cultic context, Aaron functions as leader of the people. The Aaronic priesthood is never referred to in the historical books of the Bible—*Judges, Samuel, Kings*—except in a few interpolated passages (such as *Jgs.* 20:28).

It is in *Chronicles,* however, that Aaronic genealogies are presented in detail, much in the spirit of the Priestly writings of the Torah (*1 Chr.* 5–6, 23–24, etc.). In this fourth-century BCE recasting of early Israelite history, Aaronic priests are projected into the preexilic period of the Judahite monarchy, as though to compensate for their absence in *Samuel* and *Kings.* Julius Wellhausen (1957) was logical in concluding that the Priestly Torah traditions originated in the period of *Chronicles,* but it would be more precise to place them somewhat earlier in the postexilic period, the fifth century BCE.

Ezra, Nehemiah, and *Chronicles* present a dual situation: on the one hand, the Aaronic tradition, and on the other, evidence of a more historical character on the history of the priesthood. In *1 Chronicles* 5:27–41 Aaron and his sons launch the priestly line, but then the narrative returns to historical reality, listing known priestly families. In *1 Chronicles* 6:1–27 the names are entirely different, and generally match those in *Numbers.* Thus even within *Chronicles* a distinction must be drawn between history and tradition. The same is true in *Ezra* and *Nehemiah.*

This and other information confirms the unreliability of the Aaronic genealogy, while at the same time confirming the postexilic books as the repository of historical information, as well as tradition.

Yehoshuʿa Ben Sira, a sage very much in the priestly tradition, writing in the late third or early second century BCE, endorses the Aaronic line (*Ben Sira* 50). Ellis Rivkin (1976) conjectures that beginning in the time of Ezra, around the mid-fifth century, a group of priests claimed descent from Aaron, and it was this group who promulgated the tradition of the Aaronic priesthood continued by Ben Sira.

The Torah also preserves Priestly traditions on the consecration of the Levites. In *Numbers* 8–10 the description of Levitical devotion parallels that of priestly investiture in *Leviticus* 8–10. The tasks of the Levites are set forth in *Numbers* 3–4 according to clans.

In the Priestly tradition, priests and Levites shared a common descent. All priests were of the tribe of Levi, but not all Levites were priests. *Nehemiah* 10 has the population registered in a stratified way: priests, Levites, and the people at large.

ORGANIZATION. The internal organization of the Israelite priesthood probably changed little over the centuries, from the inception of the monarchies to the destruction of the Second Temple. A priest was usually in charge of a temple/cult center, and he was referred to simply as *ha-kohen* ("the priest") or as the priest of a particular locality or temple. The chief priest of Jerusalem in the near-exilic period was called *kohen ha-roʾsh* ("the head priest," *Jer.* 19:1), and the second in charge *kohen ha-mishneh* ("the deputy head"). The title *ha-kohen ha-gadol* ("the high priest") that occurs in several passages in *Kings* (*2 Kgs.* 22:10, 23:3f.) is probably a later designation based on the characterization of the head priest in the Holiness Code (*Lv.* 21:10) as *ha-kohen ha-gadol me-ehav* ("the priest who is higher than his kinsmen"). From the fifth-century BCE Jewish mercenary community at Elephantine comes the Aramaic counterpart, *khnʾ rbʾ* ("the high priest"), and it is entirely possible that the Hebrew *ha-kohen ha-gadol* is a translation from the Aramaic. The Torah includes the epithet *ha-kohen ha-mashiah,* "the anointed priest" (*Lv.* 4, 6), reflecting a Priestly tradition that has only Aaron receiving unctions, not his sons (*Lv.* 8:12). The rabbinic tradition has the additional title *ha-segan,* or *segan ha-kohanim* ("the director of the priests"); the term *segan* is a cognate of the Akkadian *shaknu* ("govern"). This terminology reflects the widely attested practice of applying political and administrative nomenclature to cultic offices (*Yomaʾ* 3.9, 4.1; *Tam.* 7.3). In

2 Kings 19:2 is found the designation *ziqnei ha-kohanim* ("the elders of the priests"), perhaps the "curia" of the priesthood. In rabbinic literature, apprentice priests were called *pirhei ke-hunah* ("the budding flowers of the priesthood," *Yoma'* 1.7, *Tam.* 1.1). Certain postexilic sources refer to *sarei ha-kohanim* ("the leaders of the priests," *Ezr.* 8:24) who had a role in governing the people.

The Mishnah (*Tam.* 3.1) mentions *ha-memunneh* ("the appointed priest"), who served either as an "officer of the day," or was in charge of a specific bureau or set of rites. In short, the priesthood of the Temples of Jerusalem was organized along royal, administrative lines.

From early times priests likely were assigned to Temple duty for one-week periods. Nehemiah is said to have instituted these *mishmarot* (*Neh.* 13:20; cf. *1 Chr.* 7:6) and indications are that this was the arrangement in the Jerusalem Temple during the monarchy. In *2 Kings* 11:5f., groups of priests are designated as *ba'ei ha-shabbat* ("going on duty on that Sabbath") and *yots'ei ha-shabbat* ("going off duty on that Sabbath"), suggesting weekly tours of duty for the priests.

SUPPORT SYSTEMS. While on duty, priests lived in the Temple complex, apart from their families; this arrangement helped ensure a state of purity.

Priests were supported by levies and donations, and enjoyed the privilege of partaking of sacred meals; their families also benefitted from Temple support. There is evidence, however, that as time went on, prominent priestly families amassed independent wealth and owned large estates.

FUNCTIONS. The skills required for the priestly functions (see below) were learned from masters and based on written "instructions" (or manuals) called *torot* (sg. *torah*). The term *torah,* which has enjoyed wide applications in the Jewish tradition, derives from the priestly context: It is the priest who knows the *torah,* as is indicated in many biblical characterizations of the priesthood (*Jer.* 18:18, *Ez.* 7:26, *Hg.* 2:11). In the Priestly laws of the Pentateuch captions such as *zo't ha-torah* ("this is the instruction," *Nm.* 19:2) and *zo't torat* ("this is the instruction for," *Lv.* 6:2) introduce guides for purification and sacrifices.

The Mishnah describes how priests were guided or directed step by step in the celebration of cultic rites. In ancient Egypt, officiating priests were actually followed around by a "lector priest" who held before him a tablet with precise instructions that he read aloud to the officiant. Failure to carry out the specific instructions could render the rite ineffective, disqualify the priest, and in severe cases defile the sanctuary.

In addition to their roles as skilled professionals, priests were consecrated persons. The Torah preserves detailed descriptions of the procedures followed in consecration (*Lv.* 8–10, *Ex.* 28–29), including prophylactic rites (involving the use of blood and oil), ablutions, and investiture—all accompanied by purification or expiatory sacrifices. Once consecrated, the priest officiated for the first time and partook of expiatory sacrifice.

The priestly vestments are described in *Exodus* 28 and are referred to in *Leviticus* 8 and 16. The high priest (Aaron was the first) wore distinctive garb; linen was used extensively, as was dyed cloth, and both were embroidered with gold. The high priest wore an *efod* decorated with twelve gemstones symbolizing the tribes of Israel, a breastpiece on which were sewn the binary oracles Urim and Tummim (two small stones), a headdress, diadem, robes, and pantaloons. These vestments were worn only while officiating, or when present in a sacred precinct.

Ezekiel's vision of the restored Temple (44:15f.) includes more information on priestly vestments as well as grooming: Wool was to be avoided, and priests were to crop their hair but refrain from shaving their head. They probably officiated barefoot.

The priesthood was bound by a rigid law of purity. First were fitness requirements for officiating priests, who had to be free of blemishes, as were the sacrifices. Priests at all times were to avoid impurity, and as necessary would undergo purification in order to be readmitted to the Temple and allowed to officiate once again. The most severe impurity was contact with dead human bodies. According to their law, priests were forbidden to attend burials, which removed the cult of the dead from the priesthood's functions. An ordinary priest was permitted to attend the burial of his most immediate, consanguineous relatives, but even that was denied the high priest. Purity involved marriage law as well. A priest was forbidden to marry a divorced woman, because adultery was originally the basis of divorce; similarly unfit (at least in later law) was a woman who had committed harlotry, or whose fathers had been pronounced unfit for the priesthood. An improper wife would disqualify a priest's son from cultic service. A priest could only marry an Israelite, and the high priest only a virgin.

All of these regulations originate in the Priestly laws of the Pentateuch and were expanded and variously applied by the rabbinic authorities of a later age. How early they applied is not certain, but they were in force during the early postexilic period. In late Second Temple times, priestly families kept marriage records and were presumed to adhere to a stricter code. *Ezra* 2 and *Nehemiah* 7 mention priests who had been declared impure, and removed from the priesthood on that account, an obvious reference to violations of the priestly marriage code.

Sacrificial and cultic functions. The primary responsibility of the priest was to officiate at sacrificial worship; quite possibly, others than priests may have officiated at certain periods in biblical history. As stated earlier, the priestly laws of the Pentateuch include the *torot* ("instructions") for this function, spelled out in detail. Apart from actually officiating, priests were undoubtedly responsible for sacrificial *matériel*—mixing spices and incense, preparing flour for grain offerings, and preparing proper oils for various purposes, including lighting of the *menorah* ("candelabra") and the like. According to the later pattern, Levites attended to certain of the preparations, but actual slaughtering of sacrificial animals was a priestly function.

The function of the priest as officiant was indispensable to the efficacy of the sacrificial cult, and priests were required to partake of sacrifices in sacred meals. Certain sacrifices were not valid if the priest failed to partake of them. The priests invoked God's blessing of the people on certain occasions; *Numbers* 6:24–26 preserves the text of the benediction. "May the Lord bless you and watch over you. May He cause the light of His countenance to shine over you, and may He be gracious to you. May the Lord lift His face toward you and grant you peace." The benediction was usually pronounced at the end of the sacrifice, when the priest emerged from the Temple and its inner courtyard to face the people. This blessing is one of the rare instances of recitation in the priestly laws of the Torah, which otherwise fails to preserve the many formulas employed by priests in the Israelite cult.

In addition to sacrificial *matériel,* priests were clearly responsible for maintaining the purity of the Temple and of all cultic utensils, vestments, and such. The Torah's priestly laws assign some of these "maintenance" tasks (*mishmeret*) to the Levites, but they usually required priestly supervision.

Oracular functions. Again, some of the earliest biblical references to priests are in connection with oracular activity. Micah and the Danites were served in this way by a young Levite, and the priests who accompanied Saul and David into battle provided similar service. Very likely the laws of *Deuteronomy* 20 are to be understood against the background of oracular inquiry. Before battle the Israelites were addressed by the priest, undoubtedly the high priest, who assured them that God would stand at the side of his people and grant them victory. The priest then stipulated certain deferrals and exemptions from military service, an act reminiscent of the ancient custom of "clearance" (in Akkadian, *tebibtu*), known from the archives of Mari, a Syrian capital of the eighteenth century BCE. Soldiers had to be "cleared" by checking to see if their obligations on the "home front" had been met. Presumably, the priest was asked whether the contemplated military venture had God's support. While priests provided such services most of the time, in some instances prophets advised kings in this way, as in *1 Kings* 22, a reflection of the overlapping of priestly and prophetic functions.

Most forms of divination were expressly forbidden in official Israelite religion, but surprisingly the casting of lots was not. The best known form of this practice was using the Urim and Tummim. Comparative evidence suggests that the Urim and Tummim consisted of two somewhat flat stones similar to the *puru* ("lots") known in Mesopotamia. The Tummim, a term derived from *tamam* ("perfect, without blemish"; hence, "innocent, right"), probably indicated an affirmative response, or a response establishing innocence. It is therefore assumed that Urim was negative, establishing guilt, although its precise meaning remains unclear. Casting lots was intended to yield a response: Either the stones were similar to dice, each with affirmative and negative markings, or one was affirmative, the other negative.

The Urim and Tummim were kept by the priest in a pouch sewn into an embroidered cloth breastpiece. They are mentioned also in connection with the *efod,* a finely embroidered garment. In the depiction of the vestments of the high priest (*Ex.* 28, *Lv.* 8), the two stones were carried in a separate breastpiece, called *hoshen,* fastened to the *efod,* but it is quite obvious that they were an important part of the *efod,* the essential oracular vestment. The depiction of carved gemstones, symbolizing the tribes of Israel, further indicates the vestments' oracular function. The term *hoshen ha-mishpat* ("breastpiece of judgment," *Ex.* 28:15, *Lv.* 8:8) reflects the use of the Urim and Tummim in determining guilt and innocence, a process also indicated by the phrase *mishpat ha-urim* ("the judgment of the Urim," *Nm.* 27:21).

The casting of lots (*goral*) by priests was not always directly associated with the Urim and Tummim, at least not explicitly. In the Yom Kippur ritual (*Lv.* 16), the high priest cast lots to determine which of two goats was to be designated the scapegoat and which the sin offering. Priestly traditions, found primarily in *Numbers* and *Joshua,* portray the division of the Promised Land among the tribes by casting lots (*Nm.* 26, 33–36; *Jos.* 17–21). Priests again conducted the proceedings.

Oracular inquiry is generally viewed as characteristic of the earlier period of Israelite history, fading out as time went on, an opinion not borne out, however, in the priestly writings that give prominence to oracular, priestly functions. *Ezra* (2:63) and *Nehemiah* (7:65) each include a curious statement about the disqualification of certain priestly families among the returning Judahite exiles that, unable to produce genealogical records, were denied the right to partake of sacrificial meals, "until a priest with Urim and Tummim should appear."

It would be erroneous to minimize the lasting importance of oracular inquiry in early religion, a function shared by priests and prophets. The term *darash* (to inquire) often connotes oracular inquiry in biblical Hebrew, perhaps more often than is generally realized. Other than the casting of lots, very little is known about the mechanics of oracular inquiry in Israelite Jewish religion.

Therapeutic functions. *Leviticus* 13–15 prescribes a quasi-medical role for priests in the treatment of skin ailments that were considered contagious, and that in similar form appeared as blight on leather, cloth, and plaster-covered buildings and stones. Such a role was assigned to priests in other parts of the ancient Near East; Mesopotamian magical texts, for instance, speak of the activities of the *ashipu* ("magical practitioner") who combined magical and sacrificial activity with medical methods to heal the afflicted, often "purifying" them through exorcism. In *Leviticus* the priest orders quarantine, examines patients, shaves the hair of the afflicted, and diagnoses skin ailments on the basis of a set of given symptoms, observing the course of the disease. Along with these procedures, he conducts expiatory rites, involving the utilization of sacrificial blood in magic, as well as making sanctuary offerings. It is the priest who declares one either "impure" or "pure."

Such functions were akin to the instructional and juridical roles of the priest: All involved interpreting the contents of the priestly *torot* ("instructions"). As with oracular inquiry, these functions were probably shared by prophets and other "men of God."

Instructional and juridical functions. The cult role of the priest cast him in a sacred, somewhat detached light, for he officiated within sacred precincts from which the people at large were excluded. In contrast, the instructional and juridical functions of the priesthood, like the less known therapeutic ones just discussed, brought the priesthood into contact with the people. The same applies to its administrative role discussed later.

The instructional and juridical roles were, of course, closely interrelated. *Ezekiel* 44:23–24 gives a fairly comprehensive definition of these priestly functions:

> They [the Zadokite priests] shall declare to My people what is sacred and what is profane, and inform them what is pure and what is impure. In lawsuits, too, it is they who shall act as judges: they shall decide therein in accordance with My rules. They shall preserve My teachings and My laws regarding all My fixed occasions, and they shall maintain the sanctity of My Sabbaths.

Deuteronomy 17:8f. relates that a court was to be located in the central temple of the land where priests and magistrates could hear cases referred to them by local and regional courts. The high court of the Jews, the Sanhedrin, convened in the Temple complex and was composed largely of priests. The early Pharisees, members of a lay movement, eventually gained predominance in the courts, but not until after the destruction of Jerusalem's Second Temple.

The epitome of the instructional role of the priest is preserved in *2 Kings* 17:24f. Foreigners settling in northern Israel (Samaria) following its annexation by the Assyrians in 722 suffered misfortunes, and they attributed their sad state to not knowing how to worship "the god of the land" properly. Sargon, the Assyrian king, sent back an Israelite priest who established residence in Bethel. "He went about instructing the people how they should worship Yahveh" (*2 Kgs.* 17:28). The verb *horah* is most often used to convey the instructional role of the priests, who answered the questions brought to them by the people and their leaders.

The early exilic prophecy of Haggai (*Hg.* 2:11–13) contains an actual inquiry that, although it was rhetorical and symbolic in the prophetic context, is worded precisely; it is dated to 520:

> Inquire of the priests *torah* ["instruction"] as follows: If a person should carry sacrificial flesh in a fold of his garment, and if this fold should touch bread, stew, wine or oil, or any other foodstuffs, would it [that foodstuff] become sacrificial? The priests responded by saying, "No!" Haggai continued: Should a person impure by reason of contact with a dead human body touch any of these materials, would it [that foodstuff] be rendered impure? The priests responded by saying, "It would become impure!"

An entire body of ancient Near Eastern literature of priestly texts has to do with the interpretation of dreams, often a function of the priest. Indeed, the instructional and juridical roles of the priesthood would be clearer if similar Israelite texts had survived.

Administrative and political functions. In addition to conducting the cult of worship, priests were responsible for the overall administration of the Temple and its affairs.

Temple business. The Temples of Jerusalem were hubs of activity: Worshipers often purchased sacrifices in the Temple bureaus; they remitted votary pledges (the so-called vows); they paid their dues (tithes to the Levites, and in later times priestly levies, the firstlings of the herd and flocks). In *2 Kings,* chapters 12 and 22, one learns that Temple business was administered by the priests often in collaboration with agents of the king. In the postexilic recasting of these earlier accounts, such as in *2 Chronicles* 24, priests and Levites are sent out to collect dues from the people, as well as voluntary contributions for the Temple.

Maintenance. Cult vessels had to be replaced and purified from time to time, as did the Temple. The Temple complex had to be kept in good repair, and priestly vestments fashioned. Temple maintenance meant not only repair but purification, and the priesthood was in charge of these activities.

In the postexilic period when Jerusalem and Judah were under foreign domination, the high priest and heads of other important priestly families often served as heads of the Jewish community, especially in conducting its relations with the imperial authorities. This political arrangement is referred to as "hierocracy," government by priests. Something of this atmosphere colors the *Letter of Aristeas,* which reports on delegations to the high priest of Jerusalem, and the writings of Josephus of the first century CE.

Throughout most of the period of the Second Temple the power of the priesthood was more than it had been in the preexilic period. In the wake of the Hasmonean Revolt (167–164 CE) the priests assumed both political and spiritual power, a situation that lasted for about a century and correlated well with the imperial policy of various foreign rulers throughout their empires.

The political function of the priesthood is more specific during the postexilic period, although it is likely that, as in most societies, leading priests had exercised power and influence under Judahite and northern Israelite kings as well. Whereas such earlier historic books as *Samuel* and *Kings* are primarily concerned with the monarchy, and therefore say little about priestly power, it is the later *Chronicles* that create the myth of deep cooperation between the two establishments—the royal and the sacerdotal—especially during the reign of the "upright" Judahite kings.

In the postexilic period, Levites had specific functions distinct from priests. In *Numbers* 1–4, Levites are assigned the task of guarding the sanctuary, in addition to "bearing" its appurtenances, and other duties. They are encamped around it, barring entry to all unfit to approach the sacred precincts. This role coincides with the postexilic *Ezra, Nehemiah,* and *Chronicles* concerning Levitical "gatekeepers" (*Neh.* 7:1, *1 Chr.* 9:18). In the later literature Levites are also the Temple singers and musicians, a role further suggested by some of the captions in *Psalms,* attributing them to Levitical authors, members of musical guilds, and affiliates of the Levitical clans, such as "the sons of Korah."

Postexilic traditions also speak of Levites as "teachers, interpreters" (*Ezr.* 8:16, *Neh.* 8:7, *2 Chr.* 35:3), thereby endorsing the ancient instructional role of priestly and Levitical groups as teachers. Levitical names have turned up at Arad, in the Negev, during the late preexilic period, thus affirming that such families were assigned to royal outposts where there were also temples.

Worship was never the end-all of religious life in biblical and later Jewish traditions, and prophets continually criticized the common belief that God was more desirous of praise than of obedience to his laws. The prophet Samuel put the matter as follows (*1 Sm.* 15:22): "Does the Lord delight in burnt offerings and sacrifices, as much as in obedience to the Lord's command?" And yet, it was through the institution of religion, as conducted by sanctified and trained priests, that the people of Israel were able to secure the presence of God, in sacred places and in celebration. No institution was more volatile, more subject to abuse and exploitation than the priesthood (except, perhaps, the monarchy and political leadership), and none was more indispensable to the expression of Israel's unique religion. Whereas the Hebrew scriptures and later Jewish literature never spared priests from criticism and rebuke and faithfully recorded their misdeeds from Aaron to Menelaus, the same tradition held forth the idea of the devout and learned priest:

> True teaching was in his mouth,
> Nothing perverse was on his lips.
> He served Me with complete loyalty,
> And held the many back from iniquity.
> For the lips of a priest preserve knowledge,
> And men seek instruction from his mouth.
> For he is a messenger of the Lord of Hosts!
> (*Mal.* 2:6–7)

See Also Aaron; Biblical Temple; Dreams; Israelite Religion; Oracles; Priesthood, article on Jewish Priesthood; Prophecy, article on Biblical Prophecy; Purification; Tithes; Torah.

Bibliography

The higher critical point of view regarding the development of Israelite religion and its priestly institutions, according to which these are relatively late phenomena in biblical history, is best presented in Julius Wellhausen's *Prolegomena to the History of Ancient Israel,* translated by J. Sutherland Black (1885; reprint, New York, 1957). In contrast, Yeḥezkel Kaufmann's *The Religion of Israel,* translated and abridged by Moshe Greenberg (Chicago, 1960), offers a learned argument against the higher position, insisting on the greater antiquity of priestly institutions.

The best, and virtually the only, overall history of the Israelite priesthood is Aelred Cody's *A History of Old TestamentPriesthood* (Rome, 1969). G. B. Gray's *Sacrifice in the Old Testament* (1925), reissued with a prolegomena by myself (New York, 1971), devotes a section to the priesthood (pp. 179–270), analyzing its character primarily on the basis of the biblical textual evidence, and that of postbiblical ancient sources.

Several recent encyclopedia articles summarize and assess scholarly research. They include: Menahem Haran's "Priests and Priesthood," in *Encyclopaedia Judaica* (Jerusalem, 1971); my own "Priests," and Ellis Rivkin's "Aaron, Aaronides," in *Interpreter's Dictionary of the Bible: Supplementary Volume* (Nashville, 1976).

New light is shed on the history of the high priesthood by Frank Moore Cross in his "A Reconstruction of the Judean Restoration," *Journal of Biblical Literature* 94 (1975): 4–18, drawing on the evidence of the Samaria Papyri of the fourth century BCE. The religious and political roles of the postexilic priesthood, in particular, are discussed with considerable insight in Morton Smith's *Palestinian Parties and Politics That Shaped the Old Testament* (New York, 1971). The less explored functions and status of the Levites, as distinct from priests, are investigated, on the basis of biblical terminology, in Jacob Milgrom's *Studies in Levitical Terminology,* 2 vols. (Los Angeles and Berkeley, Calif., 1970–1974). All of the above references provide extensive bibliographical information.

The reader will also want to consult ancient sources outside the Bible referred to in this article. The best available English translation of the Mishnah is Herbert Danby's *Mishnah* (Oxford, 1933). The writings of the ancient historian Josephus Flavius, translated by Henry St. J. Thackeray and Ralph Marcus, are available in volumes 1–5 and 7 of the "Loeb Classical Library" (Cambridge, Mass., 1950–1961). *The Apocrypha and Pseudepigrapha of the Old Testament,* 2 vols., edited by R. H. Charles (Oxford, 1913), includes such works as *Ben Sira. Aristeas to Philocrates, or the Letter of Aristeas* has been edited and translated by Moses Hadas (New York, 1951).

The discoveries at Arad, a Negev site principally excavated by the late Yohanan Aharoni, have been carefully summarized in the article by Ze'ev Herzog and others, "The Israelite Fortress at Arad," *Bulletin of the American Schools of Oriental Re search* 254 (Spring 1984): 1–34. The inscriptions, originally published with a Hebrew commentary by Aharoni, have been translated by Judith Ben-Or and edited and revised by Anson F. Rainey as *Arad Inscriptions* (Jerusalem, 1981). These inscriptions and the information received from the excavations shed light on the functioning of Levitical priests at such royal outposts as Arad in the late preexilic period.

New Sources

Abegg, Martin G., Jr. "1QSb and the Elusive High Priest." *Emanuel* (2003): 3–16.

Broyde, Michael J. "A Mathematical Analysis of the Division of the Tribes and the Role of the Levites on Grizim and Aval in Deuteronomy 27." *Tradition* 27 (1992): 48–57.

Dahmen, Ulrich. *Leviten und Priester im Deuteronomium: literarkritische und redaktionsgeschichtliche Studien.* Bonner biblische Beiträge, no. 110. Bodenheim, 1996.

Dequeker, Luc. "*1 Chronicles* 24 and the Royal Priesthood of the Hasmoneans." *Oudtestamentische Studiën* 24 (1986): 94–106.

Haran, Menahem. *Temples and Temple-service in Ancient Israel: An Inquiry into Biblical Cult Phenomena and the Historical Setting of the Priestly School.* Winona Lake, Ind., 1985.

Leithart, Peter J. "Attendants of Yahweh's House: Priesthood in the Old Testament." *JSOT* 85 (1999): 3–24.

Millar, William R. *Priesthood in Ancient Israel.* Understanding Biblical Themes. St. Louis, Mo., 2001.

Nurmela, Risto. *The Levites: Their Emergence as a Second-class Priesthood.* South Florida Studies in the History of Judaism, no. 193. Atlanta, 1998.

O'Brien, Julia M. *Priest and Levite in Malachi.* Dissertation Series Society of Biblical Literature, no. 121. Atlanta, 1990.

Schaper, Joachim. *Priester und Leviten im achämenidischen Juda: Studien zur Kult- und Sozialgeschichte Israels in persischer Zeit.* Forschuzum Alten Testament, no. 31. Tübingen, 2000.

BARUCH A. LEVINE (1987)
Revised Bibliography

LEVI YITSḤAQ OF BERDICHEV

LEVI YITSḤAQ OF BERDICHEV (c. 1740–1810), was a Hasidic master and is one of the best-beloved figures of the east European Jewish folk tradition. Born into a distinguished rabbinical family, Levi Yitsḥaq joined the circle of disciples around Dov Ber of Mezhirich (Międzyrzecz, Poland) in 1766. He served as rabbi of Richwal, Żelechów, and Pinsk before being appointed to the important Ukrainian rabbinate of Berdichev in 1785. As both statutory rabbi and Hasidic *rebe* of that city for twenty-five years, he made Berdichev a center of Hasidic influence and played an important role as a leader of Russian Jewry. While in his earlier rabbinical positions he had been hounded by the *mitnaggedim* (the "opponents" of Hasidism; he was apparently deposed in both Żelechów and Pinsk), his strong position in Berdichev allowed him to serve as convener of rabbinical conferences, author of important communal legislation, and defender of Hasidism from attack. He also worked to ameliorate the oppression of the Jews by their newly acquired Russian masters, but to little avail. Better known are his reputed attempts to "storm the gates" of heaven, demanding of God, sometimes in harsh terms, that he better the lot of his beloved Israel. It is this image of Levi Yitsḥaq as defender of Israel and advocate of individual Jews before the heavenly tribunal that is especially prevalent in the later folk literature. The relationship between the Levi Yitsḥaq of these tales and the actual historical figure has yet to be tested.

Widely revered among the Ḥasidim even in his own day, Levi Yitsḥaq worked to stem the growing discord within the Hasidic movement at the turn of the nineteenth century. He served as intermediary in the disputes between his friend, Shneʾur Zalman of Lyady, and Barukh of Medzhibozh, as well as in Barukh's dispute with his own nephew, the young Naḥman of Bratslav.

The homilies of Levi Yitsḥaq, *Qedushat Levi,* were issued in two parts; the extended treatises on the meaning of Hanukkah and Purim were published during his lifetime (Slavuta, Ukraine, 1798), while the better-known treatment of the weekly Torah portions were edited after his death and appeared in Berdichev in 1811. This work was largely a popularization of Dov Ber's teachings but in a readable and homiletically creative setting.

Levi Yitsḥaq was a sounding board for all the major ideas of Dov Ber's circle, and all are well represented in *Qedushat Levi.* The call for ecstatic self-negation in *devequt* (communion with God) is adumbrated but is coupled with warnings about its potentially antinomian implications. Levi Yitsḥaq was well aware of the more radical implications of Hasidic teaching and sought to warn against them. Thus he places in the mouth of the snake in Eden the notion that because all things are created by God there can be no category of the forbidden; he saw the authority of the *mitsvot* (commandments) potentially challenged by the notion, so loudly and uncompromisingly proclaimed in the early Hasidic movement, that all is holy. He agreed with the elevation of the *tsaddiq* (holy man) to a place of primacy in Hasidic Judaism and speaks of the cosmic power such a figure has in the ongoing development of Torah. The sense of communal responsibility he felt as rabbi is frequently reflected in his homilies, in which there is also to be seen a touch of regret about the fate of his own intense spiritual life, as he was forced to devote his energies to communal matters.

BIBLIOGRAPHY

The biography by Samuel H. Dresner, *Levi Yitzhaq of Berditchev: Portrait of a Hasidic Master* (New York, 1974) retells the traditional tales but also contains notes of scholarly interest. Michael J. Luckens's "Rabbi Levi Yitzhak of Berdichev" (Ph.D. diss., Temple University, 1974) surveys both the life and thought of Levi Yitsḥaq.

New Sources

Blumenthal, David R. *God at the Center: Meditations on Jewish Spirituality.* San Francisco, 1988.

Klepfisz, Heszel. "Rabi Levi Itzjak Berdichever, maestro Jasidico del judaismo polaco." *MEAH* 29 (1980): 163–184.

Waintrater, Meïr. "Lévi-Yitzhak ou le sens migratoire." *Genre Humain* 19 (1989): 137–145.

ARTHUR GREEN (1987)
Revised Bibliography

LÉVY-BRUHL, LUCIEN (1857–1939), French philosopher and sociologist. Lévy-Bruhl devoted most of his attention to the analysis of the human mind in primitive societies. He studied mental functions and mystical experience, symbols and myths, and notions of the soul and of the supernatural.

Lucien Lévy-Bruhl was born in Paris. A student at the École Normale Supérieure, he passed his *agrégation* in philosophy in 1870. He then taught successively at three *lycées*. In 1884 he was awarded the *docteur ès-lettres* with a thesis on the idea of responsibility. At the École des Sciences Politiques, he gave a remarkable course of lectures on the history of ideas in Germany since Leibniz. As senior lecturer (1895) and then professor (1907) at the Sorbonne, he taught the history of modern philosophy and developed his ideas about primitive peoples. He became the editor of the *Revue philosophique* in 1916, was elected to the Académie des Sciences Morales et Politiques in 1917, and, with Paul Rivet and Marcel Mauss, founded the Institute d'Ethnologie.

Without ever openly disagreeing with Émile Durkheim, Lévy-Bruhl diverged from the leader of the French sociological school—a divergence that was made apparent when his book *La morale et la science des mœurs* (1904) criticized Durkheim's theory of *métamorales* and what he took to be Durkheim's confusion of moral philosophy with the sociology of moral life. In *Les fonctions mentales dans les sociétés inférieures* (1910), Lévy-Bruhl examined what he took to be fundamentally different kinds of mental activity. This work sought to establish the existence of a "primitive" mentality, an attitude of mind characterized by mystic participations and exclusions and by alogical liaisons not subject to the principle of contradiction.

In *La mentalité primitive* (1922), he emphasized the difference between the "primitive mind" and the "civilized mind." These terms describe the distinctive tone or quality of the "collective representations" of two basic types of society. A society finds representation in the concepts and beliefs of its members; the members share a mental attitude and hence a manner of experiencing the world.

According to Lévy-Bruhl, the "primitive" mentality and the "civilized" mentality each embodies its own irreducible logic: respectively, the magico-religious and the critical. Differing conceptions of causality and representations of time and space define these contrasting modes of thought. The magico-religious, or "prelogical" mentality, judges no event (e.g., accident, sickness, death) to be natural and fortuitous but instead attributes it to the direct action of supernatural powers belonging to an invisible extraspatial and extratemporal world. Dreams, omens, divinatory practices, and ordeals are given great importance as signs of a primary mystic causality, the only truly efficient cause. Without the critical mentality's concern for the causal interconnections of phenomena, the "primitive" mind is indifferent to secondary causation. Immediate and intuitive, the "primitive" concept of causation does not employ the inductive method of the scientific West.

In *L'âme primitive* (1927) Lévy-Bruhl argues that the "primitive" personality appears stronger than the "civilized" personality, because the ego and the cosmos are integrated there through a network of mystic relations. In his later works, Lévy-Bruhl develops the notion of the "law of participation," according to which various aspects of reality comprise a single mystical unity based on resemblance, contrast, or contiguity and thereby enable a being to be simultaneously himself and something other. This "law of participation" is a way of living, of acting, and of being acted upon. Lévy-Bruhl attempts to show that symbols are the vehicles of participation; he claims that extrarational reality does not permit itself to be systematized into a conceptual framework.

Lévy-Bruhl's theories were controversial in their day and met criticism from a variety of perspectives. Most contemporary anthropologists have rejected the notion of a specifically primitive mentality. In his posthumous *Carnets* (1949), Lévy-Bruhl himself considerably tempers the difference between prelogical and logical mentalities, showing that they coexist to various degrees in all kinds of societies and that participatory thought is never entirely eclipsed by pure rationality.

BIBLIOGRAPHY

Several works by Lévy-Bruhl have been translated. These works include *Les fonctions mentales dans les sociétés inférieures* (Paris, 1910), translated as *How Natives Think* (London, 1926); *La mentalité primitive* (Paris, 1922), translated as *Primitive Mentality* (New York, 1923); *L'âme primitive* (Paris, 1927), translated as *The "Soul" of the Primitive* (New York, 1928); and *Le surnaturel et la nature dans la mentalité primitive* (Paris, 1932), translated as *Primitives and the Supernatural* (New York, 1935). Two additional works, though not translated, deserve to be mentioned: *La mythologie primitive* (Paris, 1935) and *L'experience mystique et les symboles chez les primitifs* (Paris, 1938).

For a brief assessment of the context and application of Lévy-Bruhl's theories, see the chapter entitled "Lévy-Bruhl" in E. E. Evans-Pritchard's *Theories of Primitive Religion* (Oxford, 1965). The repercussions of Lévy-Bruhl's notion of mystic participation are examined in Jonathan Z. Smith's article, "I Am a Parrot (Red)," *History of Religions* 11 (May 1972): 391–413. For discussions of his life and work, see Jean Cazeneuve's *Lucien Lévy-Bruhl* (Paris, 1963), translated under the same title (New York, 1972); and Georges Davy's *Sociologues d'hier et d'aujourd'hui,* 2d ed. (Paris, 1950).

Claude Rivière (1987)
Translated from French by G. P. Silverman-Proust

LEWIS, C. S. (1898–1963), was an Anglican scholar, novelist, and theologian. Clive Staples Lewis was born in Belfast on November 29, 1898. As a boy he read omnivorously and wrote remarkably imaginative stories about a world he called Boxen. He was educated at Malvern College, and then privately. Soon after discovering Celtic and Norse mythology, in 1913, he became convinced that Christianity was one of the inferior mythologies of the world and that God, if he existed, was a cosmic sadist. After one term at University College, Oxford, in 1917, he went to France with the Somerset Light Infantry, and on April 15, 1918, he was wounded in the Battle of Arras. Upon his return to Oxford in 1919 he took first-class degrees in classics, philosophy, and English. Between 1925 and 1954 he was the fellow of English language and literature at Magdalen College, Oxford, and he won acclaim as a medievalist for *The Allegory of Love* (1936).

Lewis's efforts to keep God at bay gave way slowly as he began to find his own arguments philosophically untenable. His friend and colleague J. R. R. Tolkien (1892–1973) did much to unsettle his atheism when he convinced Lewis that the Christian myth differed from all others in that it ended in the Word made flesh. After his conversion in 1931, Lewis published the partly autobiographical *The Pilgrim's Regress* (1933), whose main theme is that everyone's experiences of inconsolable longing (which he was later to call "joy") are longings for and pointers to God. Another theme of the book—afterward developed in his *Miracles* (1947)—is that, while all mythologies contain hints of divine truth, Jewish mythology was chosen by God and culminates in myth becoming fact. A clearer account of Lewis's almost purely philosophical conversion is his autobiography, *Surprised by Joy* (1955).

Lewis was happiest with a few male friends, and especially at the weekly meetings of the "Inklings," a group that included his brother Warren (1895–1973), Tolkien, Merton College English scholar Hugo Dyson (1896–1975), the novelist Charles Williams (1886–1945), the philosopher Owen Barfield (1898–1997), and a few others. The influence of these men on Lewis was important, as they read and criticized one another's writings.

Lewis relished "rational opposition," and in debate his inexorable logic was unanswerable. His *Abolition of Man* (1943) is considered one of the most carefully reasoned defenses of natural law ever formulated. Able to adapt to any audience, Lewis became well known in Britain from his talks over the BBC from 1941 to 1944, which were expanded into the book *Mere Christianity* (1952). One of his most popular works, *The Screwtape Letters* (1942), was rapturously received in America. These and many other books established him as a brilliant and lucid defender of orthodox, supernatural Christianity, and through them he won a wide hearing for Christianity. A great many people have been introduced to Christian ideas through Lewis's three science fiction novels, of which the first is *Out of the Silent Planet* (1938), and his seven fairy tales of the mythical land of Narnia, beginning with *The Lion, the Witch and the Wardrobe* (1950). A brilliant popularizer of the faith and an apologist acceptable to an exceptionally wide spectrum of Christians, Lewis, through his books, sheds light from unexpected angles on the faults and foibles of men and women. Lewis was made professor of medieval and Renaissance literature at Cambridge University in 1955. In 1956 he married Joy Davidman Gresham, who died in 1960. Lewis died at Oxford on November 22, 1963.

BIBLIOGRAPHY

For a complete list of C. S. Lewis's writings, see my "Bibliography of the Writings of C. S. Lewis," in *C. S. Lewis at the Breakfast Table, and Other Reminiscences,* edited by James T. Como (New York, 1979), pp. 250–276. *Miracles: A Preliminary Study,* rev. ed. (New York, 1960), is Lewis's most solid work of theology, and *Mere Christianity* (London, 1952) is his most popular. For information about Lewis, see his *Surprised by Joy: The Shape of My Early Life* (London, 1955) and *C. S. Lewis: A Biography,* by Roger Lancelyn Green and myself (London, 1974).

WALTER HOOPER (1987)

LI. The homophones *li* and *li*, two distinct Chinese graphs, are seminal concepts in Chinese moral philosophy and metaphysics. Although they are both pronounced the same in the modern Beijing dialect, they differed in ancient pronunciation and were originally unrelated: one *li*, meaning "principle," terminated in the consonant sound *g*, according to Karlgren's reconstruction, while the other, meaning "rites," ended in the consonant sound *r*. While the meaning and usage of these terms converge to some extent, they will be discussed separately in this article.

LI AS PRINCIPLE. The root graph for this *li* combines the elements "field divided into sections for planting" with "earth," and means "village." To this is added the element "jade," in consequence of a derived meaning—thought by later philosophers to be the original sense—"cut and polish jade" so as to make its inner pattern of veins visible. The original meaning as found in the *Shi jing* (Classic of odes), however, apparently was to mark out divisions in a field for planting, and so to organize it for agricultural work. Thus *li* has the senses "put in order," "govern," and the resulting (good) "order" in society, as well as "inner structure." In antiquity these senses already converge in the sense "natural order or structure."

In the *Mengzi* the word occurs in a moral sense in the term *li yi*, "order and right," which Mengzi says is what "all human hearts have in common" and what naturally "pleases" our moral sensibility (6A.7). By the early Han dynasty, the term had gone through a semantic evolution: from just "patterns observable here and now" to patterns in temporal extention; hence a pattern developing through history; hence potential or ideal as well as what is actual; hence not only patterns observed in particulars but also general patterns in types or classes; and hence also one overarching pattern through time, branching out from a simple beginning to the complexity of observables in the present; thus both one and many, both explanatory and normative. The *Huainanzi* (c.

130 BCE) says, "As for the *dao*, when unity is established the myriad creatures are produced. For this reason, the *li* of unity permeates the entire world, and the expansion of unity reaches the bounds of Heaven and earth." This sense is further developed by Wang Bi (226–249), who speaks of *zhi li* ("ultimate *li*"), and Kuo Xiang (d. 312). However, one already finds the expression *tian li* ("heavenly" or "natural" *li*) in *Zhuangzi* and in the *Li ji*. *Li* thus approaches the sense of a single first "principle," intelligible but distinct from sensible phenomena, linked with *dao* and Heaven. It was not yet, perhaps, an object of religious awe.

The word acquired this religious sense when Buddhists, realizing its importance, appropriated it to refer to the primary object (and state) of saving contemplation. The *Sūtra in Forty-two Sections* (c. 100 CE) says that the saint who has cut ties to the world "attains to the deep *li* of Buddhahood," gaining enlightenment and *nirvana*. Zhi Dun (314–366) uses the word interchangeably with the Daoist *wu* ("nothing" or "nonbeing") and the Buddhist *kong* (Skt., *śūnyatā*; "emptiness"), the ultimately real character ("divine *li*") of things. Still later, proponents of Huayan Buddhism such as Dushun (557–640), retreating from the negativistic Mādhyamika terminology of *kong* and *se* ("phenomena"), offered a dualism of *li* ("principle"?) and *shi* (things and events), in which *li* are both one and many, "pervading" and "pervaded by" *shi*, so that the one-and-many *li* of everything is instanced, for example, in each mote of dust.

The word next is repossessed by the Confucians of the Song and following dynasties; *li* is now both one and many, it becomes the object of religious veneration insofar as it is identified with their first principle, under various names and aspects—*tai ji* ("supreme ultimate"), *dao* ("way"), *tian* ("heaven"), and *xing* ("human nature"). In the dualism of Zheng Yi (1033–1108), *li*, "principle(s)," sometimes redescribed as *dao*, is "above form" (*xing er shang*), while *qi*, "embodiments," are "within form" (*xing er xia*). Different attempts were made to overcome this dualism by such thinkers as Lu Xiangshan, Wang Yangming, and Dai Zhen; some of them (Lu, Wang, but also even Zheng Yi himself) identified *li* with *xin* ("mind"). *Li* is (are) both normative (*dangran*) and explanatory-descriptive (*so-i-jan*). As described by Zheng Yi and Zhu Xi, after long study (*gewu*, "investigating things") the Confucian sage attains a sudden unitary vision of all *li*. The concept is often illustrated by reference to natural objects; however, the Confucians usually have in mind the "principles" of social institutions and relationships.

LI AS RITES. The graphic root of this *li* represents a type of ritual vessel (called a *li*), to which is added the graph for "altar stand," an element commonly marking graphs for religious objects or activities. The basic sense was "religious rite." By the time of the earliest moral-philosophical writings the term had already taken on an expanded meaning: not merely a rite in a religious ceremony, but formal, patterned behavior of any kind, from court ceremonial—and hence, the functions and duties of officials—to the ordinary forms of everyday polite behavior. In early Confucian writings great attention was paid to *li* in all senses; Confucius frequently complained about eminent people's use of ceremonials to which they were not by rank entitled. Some schools of his followers specialized in the study and practice of *li*. Of particular importance were observances for the dead, such as the three-year period of mourning for parents (*Mengzi* 3A.1–3).

As the meaning evolved during the first millennium BCE two concurrent tendencies developed. First, there was a progressive secularization of certain originally religious concepts, not only "rite" but also Heaven (*tian*). This latter term originally denoted an anthropomorphic deity, but by the third century BCE it had become for many simply the physical heaven and the order of nature. The other tendency was a persisting sacralization of the concept of ordinary civilized behavior (Fingarette, 1972). Both of these developments came to fruition in the subtle moral philosophy of Xunzi, in whose writings the ubiquitous term *li yi* ("rites-and-right") means in effect "morality," much like *renyi* in Mencian thought. Xunzi was cognitively and explicitly atheist, yet attitudinally deeply religious, devoting a major chapter to the utility, beauty, and cosmic appropriateness of *li*. Earlier, Mengzi had taken *li*, in the sense of a disposition to propriety, as one of man's four natural virtues.

The different sorts and aspects of *li* were explained and cataloged in a group of the Confucian classics that probably date from Han times (with older material): the *Zhou li*, on the organization of the early Zhou state and functions of its officers; the *Yi li*, on ceremonies in everyday life; and the *Li ji*, which contains miscellaneous treatises on ritual and related moral-philosophical matters, and which was probably the cumulative product of Han court specialists on ritual.

Li has continued to have a double importance in Confucian moral thought. On the one hand, its observance is evidence of the moral health of society or of the individual. On the other hand, observing the rites is thought to develop moral character and the moral health of society (see Ouyang Xiu's *Ben lun*). The *li*, therefore, are thought of as the patterns of behavior of a good society, a good government, or a good life.

In this sense the concept overlaps with the *li* meaning "pattern" or "principle." The convergence of *li* and *li* was noticed by Xunzi: "Music [i.e., the standard modes and traditional pieces] is harmonies that are unchangeable; rites [*li*] are patterns [*li*] that are unalterable" (*Xunzi*, chap. 20). That is, the rites are forms of social behavior that are valid throughout history. Much later, Wang Yangming offers a very different idea. In his *Chuanxii lu* (Instructions for practical living) Wang argues that "*li* [rites] means *li* [principle]," because "restraining oneself with *li* [rites]" means that "this mind" must become completely identified with the "principle of nature," the *li* of Heaven (3.9).

SEE ALSO Confucianism; Ren and Yi; Tian.

BIBLIOGRAPHY

Chan, Wing-tsit. "The Evolution of the Neo-Confucian Concept of *Li* as Principle." *Tsing-hua Journal of Chinese Studies*, n.s. 4 (February 1964): 123–148.

Demiéville, Paul. "La pénétration du bouddhisme dans la tradition philosophique chinois." *Cahiers d'histoire mondiale* 3 (1956): 19–38.

Fingarette, Herbert. *Confucius: The Secular as Sacred.* New York, 1972.

Gimello, Robert M. "Apophatic and Kataphatic Discourse in Mahayana: A Chinese View." *Philosophy East and West* 26 (April 1976): 117–136.

Graham, A. C. *Two Chinese Philosophers: Ch'êng Ming-tao and Ch'êng Yi-ch'uan.* London, 1958.

Moran, Patrick Edwin. "Explorations of Chinese Metaphysical Concepts: The History of Some Key Terms from the Beginnings to Chu Hsi (1130–1200)." Ph. D. diss., University of Pennsylvania, 1983.

Waley, Arthur, trans. and ed. *The Analects of Confucius.* London, 1938.

DAVID S. NIVISON (1987)

LIANG WUDI (464–549), or Emperor Wu of the Liang dynasty, also known as Xiao Yan; first emperor of the Liang dynasty (502–557), man of letters, and patron of Buddhism. Although from a Daoist family and versed, like all educated gentlemen of his time, in the Confucian principles of morality and statecraft, Xiao Yan came to be fascinated by Buddhism through exposure as a young man to the teachings of Buddhist monks at the court of Prince Jingling, Xiao Ziliang, of the Southern Qi dynasty (479–502). Xiao Yan later overthrew the Qi and declared himself emperor of the Liang dynasty, but he maintained his interest in Buddhism and became a full convert after three years on the throne.

Endeavoring to fashion state policy according to Buddhist ideals, Emperor Wu softened the traditionally harsh penal code by minimizing the application of torture, capital punishment, and other excesses of government. He also forswore meat and alcohol and built numerous temples, including the Tongtai Si, where he often sponsored a kind of Buddhist symposium, known as an "open assembly" (*wuzhe dahui*), so called because it was open to men and women, clergy and laity, regardless of class. The emperor, who sometimes delivered lectures on Buddhist doctrine at these assemblies, four times used the occasion to announce that he was surrendering himself to voluntary servitude to the Tongtai temple. He of course expected his imperial officials to ransom him, and so they did, each time for prodigious sums. Each ransoming was followed by a full reenactment of the imperial enthronement ceremony. Emperor Wu's behavior, which had precedents in the history of Indian Buddhism and may have been suggested by the newly translated *Aśokāvadāna* (Legend of King Aśoka), was intended to raise money for the propagation of the Buddhist religion. The emperor also established "inexhaustible treasuries" (*wujin zang*), institutions that provided safe-deposit vaults and repositories for donations made to the religion. These funds were often used in financial transactions the profits of which reverted to the church.

Emperor Wu was overthrown by the rebel Hou Jing in 548. Some anti-Buddhist critics attributed his fall to the slackening effect of Buddhist principles on governmental control. Such a view unjustifiably ignores the political complexities of the period. Nor are his deeds to be comprehended merely in terms of whether or not they conform to Buddhist principles. Although versed in Buddhist doctrine beyond the level of the ordinary layman, Emperor Wu also devoted an important part of his energies to his literary work, much of which is still preserved and admired. This artistic bent, as much as his religious proclivities, must be taken into account in any effort to assess his fitness to rule.

BIBLIOGRAPHY

Annals of the reign of Emperor Wu can be found in fascicles 1 to 3 of the *Liang shu* and in fascicles 6 and 7 of the *Nan shih.* His writings are collected in Yan Kejun's *Quan shanggu sandai Qin Han sanguo liuchao wen* (1930, available on microfilm at the University of Chicago library). See also Mori Mikisaburo's *Ryo no Butei* (Kyoto, 1956).

MIYAKAWA HISAYUKI (1987)

LIANG WU-TI SEE LIANG WUDI

LIBATION is one of the oldest and perhaps least understood religious rituals, the sacrificial pouring out of liquid. Its primary importance seems to lie in the act of pouring, because the liquids that are poured out (wine, milk, honey, water, oil, and in some cases even blood) and the places where this is done (on the ground, into chasms, upon the altar, over the sacrificial victim, into a sacrificial bowl) vary and change. Libation can be traced back as far as the Bronze Age by means of libation pitchers and bowls discovered in excavations or depicted in stone reliefs and vase paintings or on gems, seals, and rings. The ritual is found in almost every culture and geographical area, but the kinds of libations and their performance, place in the cult, relations to other rituals, sacrificial materials, and possible meanings and functions differ from one religion to another and even within the same religion.

In spite of a wealth of evidence, many of the basic problems have remained unsolved. The information about Greek religion is extraordinarily complicated, but the situation may have been just as confusing in other religions where data have not been as fully preserved. Further, in this regard there is a remarkable degree of similarity between religions that otherwise have little connection, as for instance the sacrificial rites of Classical Greece and the Priestly tradition of the Old Testament.

Name and Terminology. The word *libation* is derived from the Latin *libatio* ("sacrificial offering of drink"). The word is connected with the Greek noun *loibē* ("libation") and the verb *leibō* ("to pour out a libation"), used since Homer. More common than these poetic terms, however, are the synonyms *spendō, spondē* (Hittite, *shipand-;* Latin, *spondeo;* German, *spenden;* English, *spend*) and *cheō, choē.* The word-field points to an Indo-European religious ritual with the wider range of social and legal functions.

Meaning. The meaning of the libation offering can vary as much as the way it was performed. It is not known for certain what the original meaning of the ritual was, if, in fact, there was only one original meaning. Perhaps the original meaning or meanings are still found among the many seemingly secondary applications and developments. The ritual itself, being rather simple and of no great interest, may have attracted what appeared to be deeper interpretations and connections with other rituals. In these matters history may provide some clues.

The most ancient sources treat libations as separate gift offerings, and this is probably what they originally were. In Babylonian and Assyrian religion, it was primarily the king's office to offer libations to the gods. Libations were part of the meals presented to the gods on altar tables, around which the divinities gathered eagerly. In purifications and magic, however, the purpose of libations was different. The ancient Egyptian sources provide a similar picture, so that the common performances of the ritual may not have changed much over the centuries down to the Greco-Egyptian period, when libations are found in all their variety in the Greek Magical Papyri. These sources show libations of wine, honey, milk, water, and oil as standard features of most religious rites, either separately or in connection with other ceremonies. Originally they seem to have been separate from animal sacrifices, with which they were often later connected. If at the beginning libations were gift offerings, they were most likely understood as gifts to the deity in return for benefits received. By the seemingly wasteful giving up of some vital resources, libations constituted fundamental acts of recognition and gratitude as well as hope for future benefits. Thus they were part of the communication with the divine sphere of life through the exchange of gifts. This may also explain why the gods themselves are often shown offering libations.

Greek Religion. Libations were common as early as the Minoan-Mycenaean period (c. 2000 BCE). Gems often depict sacrificial scenes with libation pitchers and offering tables laden with bread and fruit. While these pictures generally separate such gift offerings from animal sacrifices, there is at least one noted exception: the Hagia Triada sarcophagus from the late Minoan period (c. 1500 BCE; Long, 1974). Here one scene shows a procession of women and men carrying buckets of liquid; the first person, a priestess, is pouring her bucket into a krater (mixing bowl). This scene probably depicts the mixing of wine and water as preparation for the libation. In another scene altars are shown in a tree sanctuary. A priestess officiates before one of these altars, on which stand a libation pitcher and a basket of bread and fruit. Behind this altar, however, appears a table bearing a newly slaughtered bull, his blood flowing from his throat into a vessel on the floor. The data provided by these pictures suggest that later Greek sacrifice dates back to this Archaic period, when the originally separate gift offerings had already become associated with animal sacrifice.

It is difficult to understand the relationship between libations and the special blood sacrifices performed in funerary rites for heroes (see Pindar, *Olympian Odes* 1.90, with the technical expression *haimakouria,* "a fill of blood"; Homer, *Iliad* 23.34; Plutarch, *Aristides* 21). Whether these blood rites are to be regarded as different from libations, or in some instances as adaptations to libations, is far from clear.

While the gift offerings continued in Classical Greek religion, libations also made their way into a variety of other rituals and became a part of them. Animal sacrifice had libations as part of its preliminary sacrifice (as in Aristophanes' *The Peace* 431–435) and used libation as well in its conclusion, when wine was poured into the fire that consumed the remains of the victim. Wine drinking at symposiums involved libations by all participants, together with invocations and prayers. Concern for protection and a safe return is evident in libations made just prior to sea voyages (Thucydides, 6.32.1–2; Pindar, *Pythian Odes* 4.193–200) and battle (*Iliad* 16.220–252). Libations in connection with legal agreements had a different meaning, signifying the entering into obligation. The more magically oriented libations for the dead, of which there are literary accounts, were again different, but their specific role and function, despite ancient attempts at explanation, remain somewhat ambiguous (e.g., the epithet *gapotos,* "to be drunk up by Earth," in Aeschylus, *The Libation Bearers* 97, 164, and *The Persians* 621). A reflection of popular beliefs is found in Lucian's remark (*On Funerals* 9) that the souls of the dead receive nourishment from libation. Libations of oil, another very old custom, develop more in a magical direction: Anointing stones and funerary stelae was customary in much of the ancient world.

Whatever the original purpose of water libations may have been, they were later understood mostly in terms of purification. This is true especially of the ablution of hands (*chernips*) at the beginning of the offering ceremonies. Yet water libations were also performed at tombs by putting the water on them or pouring it into them. Mythology may have provided secondary explanations: They are bathwater (*loutra*) from the underworld (Sophocles, *Electra* 84.434) or a fresh drink for the thirsty dead (cf. *Luke* 16:24). The origins of water-carrying festivals (*hudrophoria*), which existed since ancient times, were different still, the purpose perhaps originally being purification. Yet another water ritual found its way into the mysteries of Eleusis, when at their conclusion two jugs were filled and then overturned, one toward the east and the other toward the west. This probably happened while the initiates shouted "Hue kue," telling the heavens, "Rain!" and the earth, "Conceive!"

Israelite Religion. Israelite libations, as known from the Hebrew scriptures and the Mishnah (*Suk.* 4.9), were remarkably similar in appearance to ancient Greek rituals. Similar too are some of the ambiguities, such as the role of blood in relation to libations (see McCarthy, 1973; Kedar-Kopfstein, 1978). The formation of the composite sacrifice in the Priestly texts can be compared to the formation of the Greek sacrifice. No attempt is made in the Hebrew scriptures to explain the purpose of the libations. If reasons are given, they apply as caricatures of foreign religions and express sarcasm (*Is.* 1:11; *Ps.* 50:13). Together with other parts of the sacrificial cult, libation was taken over from the Canaanites. The root of the term designating libation (*nsk*) also occurs in Ugaritic and Phoenician-Punic. Direct takeover of a foreign ritual including libations is reported in connection with King Ahaz's imitation of the royal cult of Damascus (*2 Kgs.* 16:10–18) and in Artaxerxes' decree to Ezra (*Ezr.* 7:17). The sharp polemics by the prophets also reflect the non-Israelite origin of libations (*Jer.* 7:18, 19:13, 32:29; *Ez.* 20:28; *Dt.* 32:38; *Ps.* 16:4). Texts dealing with libations mention them either alone (*Gn.* 28:18, 35:14; *Jer.* 7:18, 19:13, 32:29, 44:17–19, 44:25; *Ez.* 20:28; *Ps.* 16:4) or in connection with the *minhah,* the gift offering of cereals (*Jl.* 1:9, 1:13, 2:14; *Is.* 57:6). The Priestly legislation shows the combination of *minhah* ("gift offering") and *nesekh* ("libation") with the burnt offering (*'olah*) (*Lv.* 23:13, 23:18, 23:37; *Nm.* 6:15, 6:17, 15:10, 28:7–31, 29:39), as do the morning and evening offerings in *Exodus* 29:40–41. References to libation utensils confirm what is known from excavations (*Ex.* 25:29, 30:9; *Nm.* 4:7; *1 Chr.* 29:21; *2 Chr.* 29:35). Anointing of stones with oil was perhaps traditional at Bethel (*Gn.* 28:18, 35:14); water libations are also mentioned (*1 Sm.* 7:1; *2 Sm.* 23:16; *1 Chr.* 11:18). The notion of wine symbolizing blood is late (*Sir.* 50:15).

Special Developments. Some religions and cultures have developed special forms of libation offerings, several of which should be mentioned. The Iranian cult of *haoma* goes back to great antiquity. This drink of immortality was encountered by Zarathushtra (Zoroaster, c. 600 BCE), who attacked it. Its later revival suggests that he reformed the ritual and thus continued it. The *haoma* cult corresponds to the Vedic cult of *soma. Soma* is at once a deity and the plant from which the juice comes that, when pressed and then mixed with water and milk, makes the *soma* drink. This drink is offered to the gods, but it is also consumed by the people during feasts and conveys immortality (*Ṛgveda* 8:48).

Ancient Chinese religion developed the festival of Shidian ("pouring a drink offering"). The cult seems to have its origin in ancestral worship and is connected with the veneration of Confucius and his pupil Yen Hui. It consisted of a sacrifice and a banquet. During the Ming dynasty (1368–1644), the Shidian ritual was greatly expanded along with the Confucius cult.

The sacrifice of the legendary first emperor, Jimmu, in Shintō religion is also interesting because of its antiquity. The offering includes the essential means for life, food, and drink and is followed by a feast. Ceremonial beer-drinking rituals were conducted by the Vikings of Scandinavia. The *drykkeoffer* was a sumptuous beer party with three ceremonial cups of mead offered to Óðinn (Odin), Þórr (Thor), and Freyja. The three offerings have a curious parallel in Greek sacrifice, but beer-drinking rituals are found elsewhere as well, as for instance in Southeast Asia.

For different reasons, several major religions have discontinued libations altogether. Buddhist religion is opposed to external sacrifices in principle. Jewish religion was compelled to abandon its sacrificial ritual, and with it libations, because of the destruction of the Jerusalem Temple in 70 CE. Christianity has no room for libations in its cult. It uses water in baptism; sees in wine the blood of Christ, the sacramental drink of the Eucharist (substituted in some instances by milk or honey), which is offered not to but by the deity, and certainly must not be spilled; and uses oil for sacramental anointing. Islam has no sacrifices in the proper sense of the term. The pre-Islamic libations of milk, predominant among the Arabs, were discontinued, but in some quarters those offerings persist.

Bibliography

No scholarly investigation exists that takes adequate account of the libations in the various religions, nor do most encyclopedias include a separate article on this important ritual. The following bibliography lists items that summarize the evidence of specific religions, provide surveys, or contain bibliographies.

Asmussen, Jes P., and Jørgen Laessøe, eds. *Handbuch der Religionsgeschichte.* 2 vols. Göttingen, 1971–1975. Sections on the various religions give attention to libations; see the index, s.v. *Opfer* (*Trink-, Libations-*).

Bonnet, Hans, ed. *Reallexikon der ägyptischen Religionsge-schichte.* 2d ed. Berlin, 1952. See pages 424–426, s.v. *Libation.* Surveys the evidence in Egyptian religion; includes a useful bibliography.

Borghouts, J. F. "Libation." In *Lexikon der Ägyptologie,* vol. 3. Wiesbaden, 1980. Presents evidence for Egyptian religion on the basis of current research.

Burkert, Walter. *Homo Necans: The Anthropology of Ancient Greek Sacrificial Ritual and Myth.* Berkeley, Calif., 1983. Basic study of Greek sacrificial rituals and their prehistory.

Burkert, Walter. *Greek Religion.* Cambridge, Mass., 1985. Best account of the current state of research on Greek religion, with sections on libation. Contains a wealth of bibliographical, textual, and archaeological references.

Gill, David. "*Trapezomata:* A Neglected Aspect of Greek Sacrifice." *Harvard Theological Review* 67 (1974): 117–137. Discusses Greek gift offerings set up for the gods on tables.

Graf, Fritz. "Milch, Honig und Wein: Zum Verständnis der Libation im griechischen Ritual." In *Perennitas: Studi in onore di Angelo Brelich,* pp. 209–221. Rome, 1981. Important study of the complexities of the Greek ritual, especially with regard to the substances of milk, honey, and wine. Bibliographic references.

Hanell, Krister. "Trankopfer, Spenden, Libationen." In *Real-Encyclopädie der klassischen Altertumswissenschaft,* 2d series, vol. 6. Stuttgart, 1937. Collection of the evidence of libations in Greek religion.

Herrmann, Wolfram. "Götterspeise und Göttertrank in Ugarit und Israel." *Zeitschrift für die alttestamentliche Wissenschaft* 72 (1960): 205–216. Compares the evidence from Ugarit and the Old Testament.

Kedar-Kopfstein, Benjamin. *"dam"* (Blood). In the *Theological Dictionary of the Old Testament,* vol. 3. Grand Rapids, Mich., 1978. Deals with the evidence and literature on blood sacrifice in the ancient Near East and the Old Testament.

Latte, Kurt. *Römische Religionsgeschichte.* Munich, 1960. Summary of the evidence in Roman religion.

Long, Charlotte R. *The Ayia Triadha Sarcophagus: A Study of Late Minoan and Mycenaean Funerary Practices and Beliefs.* Göteborg, 1974. Investigation of the sacrificial scenes on the sarcophagus from Hagia Triada (Crete), with good photographic material.

McCarthy, Dennis J. "The Symbolism of Blood and Sacrifice." *Journal of Biblical Literature* 88 (1969): 166–176.

McCarthy, Dennis J. "Further Notes on the Symbolism of Blood and Sacrifice." *Journal of Biblical Literature* 92 (1973): 205–210. Discusses the evidence and possible meaning of blood sacrifice in the ancient Near East and Israel and in Greek religion.

Meuli, Karl. "Griechische Opferbräuche." In *Phyllobolia für Peter von der Mühll zum 60. Geburtstag,* edited by Olof Gigon and Karl Meuli, pp. 185–288. Basel, 1946. Reprinted in Meuli's *Gesammelte Schriften,* vol. 2, edited by Thomas Gelzer (Basel, 1975). A seminal study.

Michel, Otto. *"Spendomai, spendō."* In the *Theological Dictionary of the New Testament,* vol. 7. Grand Rapids, Mich., 1971. Surveys the evidence in the Old Testament, Judaism, and Christianity. Contains a rich bibliography, for which also see the supplement in *Theologisches Wörterbuch zum Neuen Testament,* vol. 10, pt. 2 (Stuttgart, 1979).

Mitropoulou, Elpis. *Libation Scenes with Oinochoe in Votive Reliefs.* Athens, 1975. Collects evidence from the perspective of art history.

Nilsson, Martin P. *The Minoan-Mycenaean Religion and Its Survival in Greek Religion* (1950). 2d rev. ed. New York, 1971. Especially important for the pictorial material.

Nilsson, Martin P. *Geschichte der griechischen Religion.* 3d ed. 2 vols. Munich, 1967–1974. A monumental work, especially important for bibliographical references.

Rendtorff, Rolf. *Studien zur Geschichte des Opfers im alten Israel.* Neukirchen-Vluyn, West Germany, 1967. The only modern critical study of the Old Testament traditions concerning libations. Contains a comprehensive bibliography.

Smith, W. Robertson. *Lectures on the Religion of the Semites: The Fundamental Institutions* (1889). 3d ed. New York, 1969. This nineteenth-century classic is still indispensable.

Stengel, Paul. *Opferbräuche der Griechen.* Leipzig, 1910. Basic study of the Greek sacrificial terminology and practices.

Stengel, Paul. *Die griechischen Kultusaltertümer.* 3d ed., rev. Munich, 1920. Standard work concerning Greek cultic practices. See pages 103–105 on libations.

Wachsmuth, Dietrich. "Trankopfer." In *Der Kleine Pauly,* vol. 5, edited by Konrat Ziegler. Munich, 1975. Update of the articles by Krister Hanell and Ludwig Ziehen with additional references.

Wendel, Adolf. *Das Opfer in der israelitischen Religion.* Leipzig, 1927. A basic study that is still of value.

Ziehen, Ludwig. *"Nephalia."* In *Real-Encyclopädie der klassischen Altertumswissenschaft,* vol. 16. Stuttgart, 1935. Surveys wineless libations in Greek religion.

New Sources

Schechner, Richard, and Willa Appel, ed. *By Means of Performance: Intercultural Studies of Theatre and Ritual.* New York, 1990.

HANS DIETER BETZ (1987)
Revised Bibliography

LIBERAL JUDAISM SEE REFORM JUDAISM

LIBERATION, as a goal to be attained or as a designation of a process or activity contributing to this goal, has a central place in many religious traditions, but this should not belie the fact that quite different terms are used in these traditions to convey the protean variability of the meanings typically associated with this concept. These differences of meaning may reflect a wide range of religious conviction and practice, even as these meanings happen to overlap. Thus, in English alone, *redemption, salvation, purification, absolution, freedom, illumination, enlightenment, forgiveness, expiation, deliverance,* and *rescue* form a cluster of terms with close affinities to *liberation.* These affinities notwithstanding, significant differences may exist in the import conveyed by these expressions. Thus, and this is just one example, *deliverance,* as in the Christian prayer "Deliver us from our travails, O Lord," clearly presupposes the indispensable agency of the author of this sought-for deliverance, while, by contrast, *illumination* does not necessarily carry with it the presumption of the activity of any kind of external agent or power. The differences between these terms are also indicated by their contrasts: to be purified is to be removed from a state of uncleanliness, whereas to be illuminated is to be extricated from a condition of ignorance. Of course, one may be said to be ignorant because one is unclean, or vice versa, but ignorance is banished by one's gaining in wisdom, while uncleanliness is removed by one's extrication from a state of defilement or corruption. Someone may be cleansed without necessarily being any wiser about it, or anything else, as when an infant undergoes a cleansing ritual, but it is impossible to become significantly wiser without being aware in some way that one has undergone a more or less decisive cognitive or spiritual transformation. Different patterns of belief and practice may therefore surround a particular term—*expiation,* for instance, presupposes a gesture of atonement on the part of the one whose putative transgressions are being expiated (a substitute may also undertake this act of expiation on behalf of the one who is being redeemed by the expiation in question), and so expiation qua act is never fortuitous or gratuitous, while, by contrast, *rescue* can be, and indeed in many religious traditions is thought to be, entirely gratuitous and undeserved, the outcome of an act of grace (to use a theological formulation). To gain an appreciation of the significance and complexity of these assorted patterns of belief and practice, the individual undertaking a scientific study of "religion" has to be aware of the complex conditions that give these expressions their particularities of meaning. This is not likely to be easy.

For one thing, an expression like *liberation* (and its several cognate terms) is always an abstraction, and by virtue of being an abstraction it is unavoidably detached, albeit in ways that are not insurmountably problematic, from the full range of the ritual, doctrinal, and textual particularities that go into the constitution of liberation's putative goals or processes. Thus the Buddhist *mārga* (path to liberation) is treated in such exegetical texts as the *Bhāvanākrama* (Stages of practice), *Bodhisattvabhūmi* (Stages on the *bodhisattva* path), and *Mo-ho-chih-kuan* (Great calming of contemplation). These works are commonly depicted by scholars of Buddhism as descriptions of contemplative states achieved by individuals who happen to be skilled practitioners of the meditative arts. This is in fact a misrepresentation, since the authors of these texts derive their influence not from their achievement of some kind of inner enlightenment attested to in the texts in question, but rather from their disciplined observance of Buddhist scripture (Sharf, 1995). The "path to liberation" delineated in these sacred texts therefore is found not so much in the undergoing of a process of spiritual illumination, but in the discipline of mastering sacred scriptures (though illumination is not an accidental by-product of this scriptural mastery). Texts, even scriptural texts, are not always free of inconsistencies and ambiguities, and any characterization of liberation has to take these into account, more often than not by relating the texts in question to the complex of practices associated with them. This in turn poses important and sometimes difficult questions of description and interpretation.

How do we know that a particular term adequately expresses what goes on in a particular religious practice, or that it is providing an appropriate version of the meanings that inhere in a scriptural text? For instance, can we be certain that the English term *liberation* is an appropriate rendition of the Hindu notion of *moksha,* or that the English *destiny* properly translates the Homeric *moira,* and so forth? The history of religions provides examples of how, despite purporting to be free of theological presuppositions, a religion's renditions of the practical elements and doctrinal principles of other religions can nonetheless be tacitly influenced by theological or quasi-theological normativities. An important case in point is provided by the work of the great scholar of comparative religion Mircea Eliade (1907–1986), who sought in his work to eschew reliance of any kind on theological premises, but whose delineation of the sacred is nonetheless thought by such critics as Jonathan Z. Smith to involve just such a theological dependence. Eliade believed that there is an essential sacred in the world, to which religions sought to give expression, and that the task of the student of religion was to analyze both this *expressivity* and the structure of the essential sacred conveyed through its myriad modulations. Smith and others have criticized Eliade's key proposition that there is an irreducible "religious" way of being in the world possessing an essential structure. For Smith this proposition can only be regarded as residually theological, and he prefers instead to view *sacred* as a term used in the construction and discovery of worlds of meaning. For someone like Smith, therefore, it is not obvious that there are readily available bridging concepts, invoking sacred "essences," which enable us to establish commonalities and affinities between the rituals and doctrines constitutive of the various religious traditions.

The above animadversions notwithstanding, the person interested in propounding a concept of liberation may find useful the general theory of the concept of salvation formulated by the sociologist Max Weber (1864–1920). A general theory of this kind, which will of course need to be mindful of the differences that exist among peoples, their communities, and their religious traditions, can link otherwise disparate phenomena into a general narrative that will be a useful complement to the more piecemeal ethnographies or phenomenologies of religious practice and conviction. (It is fairly clear, however, that a satisfactory account of the concept of liberation requires both this general theory and the more finely grained ethnographies and phenomenologies.) *Liberation,* like parallel concepts such as *creation, human flourishing, providence,* or *cosmic harmony,* has in some sense to function as a narrative that aspires to be a "story of everything." Weber's sociology of religion provides a pioneering overarching narrative of liberation, motivated by just this ambition to be a "story of everything" about "stories of everything" (or *metanarrative,* in other words).

Weber wanted to formulate a general theory for understanding the many different conceptions of religious salvation, and he employs the notion of an *ideal-type* to identify and describe aspects of the different religious traditions that for him embodied certain transhistorical and transcultural soteriological principles. The *ideal-type* is thus an analytical construct *(Gedankenbilder)* that enables its user to pinpoint and synthesize certain features of the phenomenal or historical world, and to form these events and observable processes into an abstraction that is then returned to the historical and empirical world to furnish interpretations of it. Weber harnesses the tool of the ideal-type to a comparative mythology of salvation to formulate a number of interlinked typologies that furnish some important theses about *salvation* in the different religions.

The resultant Weberian theory of salvation, his metanarrative, hinges on a number of distinctions that have become standard in the sociology of religion. It exploits important distinctions between religions that understand salvation in terms requiring or positing the necessary agency of supernatural beings (such as the so-called Abrahamic religions), and those that do not (such as early Buddhism); between ways to salvation based on the satisfaction of "ethical demands" and others based on "pure faith"; between a salvation premised on a "world-renouncing asceticism" *(weltablehnende Askese)* and one resulting from "this-worldly asceticism" *(innerweltliche Askese);* between "contemplative" and "active" religious methods; and so on. These divisions are then further complicated, as when Weber distinguishes between schemas that involve a "salvation from. . ." and those that embody a "salvation [attained] for. . ."—examples of the former being "liberation from the machinery of Satan" or "liberation from the wheels of *kharma* causality," and examples of the latter being "salvation [attained] for the eternal rest that is *nirvana* " or "salvation [attained] for the bliss that is heaven."

As was the case with Mircea Eliade, critics soon made the point that these Weberian formulations are not as innocently "ideal-typical" as Weber himself took them to be. Thus, his important demarcation between "pure faith" and "ethical demands" (or "works") is palpably influenced by a post-Reformation version of Christianity. This being so, the application of these schemas to the soteriological systems of non-Christian religions will probably traduce or distort the latter—Weber, for instance, saw no problems with the distinctions he made between "the divine," "the human," and "the world," and in this respect he resembles Eliade. For all these weaknesses, Weber's sociology of salvation is the first notable attempt to systematize the affirmations made by the various religious traditions about the means by which salvation is attained, the states associated with its attainment, and the powers and figures deemed to be responsible for this attainment. He was a pioneer when it came to systematizing, at the level of a wide generality, the various dispositions toward "the world" that underlie the different religions. This is an essential undertaking for any theorist of liberation. Especially important here is Weber's assertion that the fundamental motivation behind the various conceptions of liberation is the pressing need to find a solution to the "problem" of the world, since the desire of the seeker of liberation pivots on the quest for a resolution of the predicaments posed by a basic recalcitrance of the world. Liberation is thus glossed as liberation *from* some unsatisfactory state of the world, and this principle becomes an axiom for the theory or higher-order narrative of salvation.

Liberation, therefore, is inextricably bound-up with the lineaments of a certain structure of desire—namely, the desire to surmount, bypass, or mitigate a fundamentally unsatisfactory state of being, whether it happens to be individual or collective or both. Liberation can then be glossed as a concept intrinsically linked to that desire (and this includes the desire for the ending of *all* desire). For this reason, liberation as a concept has to be understood by delineating the structures and functions of this elemental desire, its nomenclatures, its conditions, its consequences, its practical ramifications for those who are followers and believers. The constitution of the world as a place where meaning and value are to be discovered and interpreted can only be approached theoretically through an analysis of this primordial desire. As a result of this axiomatic principle, an ethics of liberation has to depend on the human powers that subtend this desire (though it is of course possible for the devout to locate the source of this desire in some supernatural figure or power); and reflection on liberation will, in turn, rest on an ontology that elucidates the various conceptual amplifications of this primal desire. It will take this ethics to be the outcome of a disciplined reflection focused on this prior and enabling knowledge of desire. This ontology of human constitutive power will specify what it is that the configurations of desire that happen to go by the name of the "human" can accomplish, what their repulsions and attractions are capable of, and this will include those impulses that gesture towards what is seemingly beyond the compass of all that is currently taken to constitute "the human." The great philosophical projects—and here Aristotle's *Metaphysics,* Barukh Spinoza's *Ethics,* G. W. F. Hegel's *Phenomenology,* Alfred North Whitehead's *Process and Reality,* Martin Heidegger's *Being and Time,* and Gilles Deleuze and Félix Guattari's *A Thousand Plateaus* come to mind as exemplary instances—undertake this ontological task that is a necessary first step in developing the ethics of liberation.

The problematic of the relation between transcendence and the doctrines of *immanence*—which picture consciousness either as existing solely within the self or as being part of a universal whole—is thus central to reflection on the project of liberation, a project that may or may not go by the name of "religion" or be associated with religion's appurtenances. For religions in their very nature provide for their adherents the figuration of an ontology of the kind mentioned above. Religious traditions with a soteriological dimension, it is easy to see, purport not only to provide a path towards liberation, but also seek to account for the origin or ground of this very desire to find such a path. Soteriologies are thus mechanisms for producing truth or "true ways" for those who adhere to them. Axiomatic for these mechanisms is the notion that to be liberated is to have found the true way, whether this finding is attributed to an external agent or is depicted as the individual achievement of the religious person. Can a religion really do without a basis in some kind of transcendence, can it be wholly and unreservedly immanent, and can an uncompromising immanence form the core of a project of liberation? These are the crucial questions for an ethics of liberation. Necessary here is a distinction between the transcendent (that which transcends all subjects and objects) and the transcendental field (which is a nontranscendent that accounts for the possibility of immanence itself). Liberation's ontological script could be one that occupies a transcendental field without making any appeal to a transcendent being or power. This would be the perspective of a Spinoza, Heidegger, or Deleuze. We cannot be sure that such an ontological script would be compatible with the religions of the Abrahamic traditions for instance, since these seem irreducibly to be wedded to an ontology of the transcendent. But the possibility of these religions being able to incorporate an ontology of unqualified immanence is one that cannot be ruled-out *tout court.* Or it may be that we cannot, after all, obviate the transcendent, despite what Spinoza, Heidegger, Deleuze, and others have argued for, in which case the ontological preeminence of the religious transcendent is guaranteed. If this were the case, then it and only it can be the foundation of liberation.

BIBLIOGRAPHY

It is virtually impossible in a brief bibliography to do full justice to the range of fields that have to be covered in an adequate treatment of the concept of liberation: the history of religions, comparative religion, hermeneutics, the history of ideas, cultural anthropology, philosophy, theology and other doctrinal studies, psychology, sociology, and political theory. The following have been useful in producing this entry, which of course represents a primarily philosophical and hermeneutical approach to the concept of liberation that needs to be complemented by studies in other intellectual fields.

Numerous works convey the hermeneutical difficulties in matching later or contemporary interpretations to earlier practices and doctrines. Robert Sharf's "Buddhist Modernism and the Rhetoric of Meditative Experience," *Numen* 42 (1995): 228–283, has been used here, but a dozen other works can easily be cited. For an understanding of religion that accords broadly with this hermeneutical approach, see Jonathan Z. Smith's *To Take Place: Toward Theory in Ritual* (Chicago, 1987). Max Weber's general theory of salvation is to be found in *Gesammelte Aufsätze zur Religionssoziologie* (Tübingen, Germany, 1922), translated by Ephraim Fischoff as *The Sociology of Religion* (Boston, 1963). A fuller version of the position developed here is to be found in Kenneth Surin's "Liberation," in *Critical Terms for Religious Studies,* edited by Mark C. Taylor, pp. 173–185 (Chicago, 1998).

KENNETH SURIN (2005)

LIBERATION THEOLOGY. Liberation theology is defined as critical reflection on the historical praxis of liberation in a concrete situation of oppression and discrimination. It is not a reflection on the theme of liberation but "a new manner" of doing theology. The perspective of the poor and the commitment of Christians to the transformation of the world are the privileged places of the theological task. This theology should be considered as a theological and pastoral movement and not as theoretical expositions by important personages.

The stages of development of liberation theology are: preparation (1962–1968), formulation (1968–1975), systemization (1976–1989), and diversification of specific perspectives (since 1990).

THE STAGE OF PREPARATION (1962–1968). The first reflections in the direction of liberation theology have their origins in the 1960s. This was a period characterized by a structural crisis (economic, political, and ideological) of the systems of domination, the proliferation of popular liberation movements, and the appearance of military dictatorships. Critical reflections from the Christian faith emerged as an answer to the challenges that were presented not only by the liberation movements but above all by Christians who became involved in those movements.

Although elements were taken from new German political theology (Johann Metz, Jürgen Moltmann, Dorothee Solle), the theological themes coming from the European academy were considered insufficient to accompany the faith of Christians in a time of an "awakening of consciousness" of belonging to a dependent and oppressed continent that needed to free itself. This "awakening of consciousness" appeared in different parts of Latin America and from different rationales. Among those, Frantz Fannon wrote against colonialism in *The Wretched of the Earth.* Paulo Freire of Brazil spoke out in *Education as the Practice of Freedom* (1967) and *Pedagogy of the Oppressed* (1970). Many writers expressed themselves through literature, for example, Gabriel García Márquez with his novel *One Hundred Years of Solitude* (1967). Philosophy spoke of the social movements on the continent; economics produced the theory of dependence in confrontation with the theory of development (André Gunder, Theotónio Dos Santos, Celso Furtado, and others). In fact, the history of this continent was read from Eduardo Galeano's *The Open Veins of Latin America* (1973). The awakening of Christians to the challenges of the liberation movements and their active participation in those movements led theologians to elaborate a theology that took seriously the reality of poverty and exploitation and to take up the clamor of the poor. The climate of the church in the Catholic world was opportune. The Second Vatican Council (1962–1965) had begun a great opening with its concern and reflections on Christianity confronted by the modern world, and the Medellín Conference of Latin American Bishops contextualized its significance for the "oppressed and believing" Latin American continent. Within the Protestant tradition there were also groups (ISAL; Iglesia y Sociedad en América Latina, or Church and Society in Latin America) and theologians (Rubén Alves, Richard Shaull, and José Migues Bonino) who bore witness on the basis of Christian faith in the face of a reality that needed liberation.

THE FORMULATION (1968–1975). Gustavo Gutiérrez, a Catholic Peruvian theologian, is the principal figure in the formulation of liberation theology. His classic book *A Theology of Liberation* (1972) appears as an amplified and deepened version of previous expositions. Among other important persons who contributed to the debate of this reformulation were, among Catholics, Hugo Assmann, Leonardo Boff, Juan Luis Segundo, Enrique Dussel, and later Clodovis Boff; among Protestants, Rubén Alves, José Migues Bonino, and Julio de Santa Ana.

In this stage, theology is defined as a critical reflection on historical practice in the light of faith. The poor, as in "exploited classes, marginalized races, depreciated cultures" (Gutiérrez), is the privileged place of the theological task. It becomes clear that liberation theology is more than a theology with a single theme, or one of fixed contents. It is a manner of doing theology. Interested in the relation of theory and practice, the major contribution of liberation theology is precisely its method, considered as "an epistemological rupture" with traditional theology in which ideas are applied to practice. Its newness, thanks to the method, is in the application of the social sciences as instruments that help it analyze the reality out of which the theological reflection comes. Theology, insists Gutiérrez, is a second act. It is the rationality or intelligence of faith that emerges from the praxis of transformation and the encounter with God in history: praxis and contemplation are the first act.

The Systemization (1975–1989). This is a productive period in writings as well as in the growing eruption of Christian base communities. Theologians during this period took great care to spell out the method and to re-create Christology and ecclesiology.

As for the method in the process of the theological task, there are three mediations. The socioanalytic mediation analyzes the reality where theology is done. Here the social sciences are used as tools to reflect theologically on the analyzed reality. The hermeneutical mediation interprets the Bible and tradition to reflect theologically on the analyzed reality. The praxiological or pastoral practice seeks to make visible the commitment to justice in favor of the poor. This method is common in the Christian base communities; it is expressed in a simple way with the terms: "see, judge, and act." Later the term "celebrate" was added in the sense that within the communities, in the process of a contextual rereading of the Bible, God's solidarity is celebrated as read in the Scriptures and in life.

The utilization of some Marxist elements as instruments for the analysis of reality generated controversy with the Vatican and certain Protestant sectors. The Sacred Congregation for Doctrine and Faith published *Instruction on Various Points of Liberation Theology* (1984), questioning this aspect because of the risk of ideologizing faith. If indeed liberation theology has adopted some elements of Marxism for class analysis and social change, it has rejected its atheism.

The Christology of liberation theology is characterized by the insistence on following Jesus (Jon Sobrino), who preached not himself but the reign of God. The following of Jesus underlines the practical character of the demands of a liberating Jesus Christ, whose "passion is also the passion of the world," in the words of Leonardo Boff (1987), which suffers injustices. In the Christology of liberation, historic liberations also form a part of the eschatological promise of salvation in Christ, although it is not identified with salvation in Christ. Because of certain critiques, theologians are careful to make clear that the reign of God is not limited to human history. From the beginning Gutiérrez affirmed that the reign of God "is realized in liberating historical acts, but denounces their limitations and ambiguities. It announces complete fulfillment and moves toward total communion." Because of the "radicality of the salvific gift, nothing escapes it, nothing is outside the action of Christ and the gift of the Spirit" (1973, p. 240).

The ecclesiology of liberation has as its point of reference the experience of a new way of being a church in the Christian base communities. It is a church that understands itself and emerges from the poor. For that reason it has been called the church of the poor or church that is born from the people. This ecclesiology is critical of a form of church that gives privilege to power concentrated in hierarchy instead of privileging charisma. According to Brazilian theologian Leonardo Boff (1981), charisma is the spiritual force that maintains the life of institutions and is more fundamental for the church than institutional element. Neither the hierarchy nor the institution constitutes what is fundamental in charisma, though they are not excluded (p. 254). This theme caused certain difficulties with the official Catholic Church. In 1984 Boff was called on by Cardinal Ratzinger, head of the Catholic Church's Congregation for the Doctrine of the Faith, to clarify some aspects of his book, published in English as *Church: Charism and Power* in 1985. Boff was silenced; the punishment was suspended a year later.

The term *iglesia popular* (church of the poor) was refuted in the document of the Episcopal Conference held in Puebla (1979) because of the danger of seeing it as a parallel church to the official church. In the 1980s a shift began within theology: reflection based on the deepening of the dialectical relation between faith-politics and life-economy. According to Enrique Dussel, it is not the Christian demand to opt for the poor and to commit oneself in the process of liberation, but rather "the hunger of the majorities is the imperative to modify unjust systems of production. It is the relationship bread-production and from there the centrality of the Eucharist as bread of life through justice" (1995, p. 152). *La idolatría del mercado* by Hugo Assmann (1989) and Franz Hinkelammert; Hinkelammert's *A idolatria do mercado* (1989); and the Costa Rican Ecumenical Department of Research's *La Lucha de los dioses* (1979) are reflections from the economy that mark Latin American theological thought. Within the movement of the theology of liberation there are different emphases; some give more importance to political action, others to church ministries, and others to liberating spirituality.

The Diversification of Specific Perspectives (from 1989). New contributions followed in the 1990s. Among those that stand out are reflections on the significance of evangelization in light of the five-hundred-year commemoration of the Spanish and Portuguese conquest; human beings as subjects (agents); law and grace; and more contributions to Christology. But what was new at this time were two facts: the participation of new subjects in the theological reflection and the biblical movement.

Women, blacks, and indigenous peoples have always participated in the movement of liberation theology. Since the 1980s women and black theologians have declared themselves as specific subjects in writings and at congresses. Nevertheless, since the 1990s, the recomposition of the world and the strengthening of the struggles for the emancipation of women, indigenous peoples, and blacks have multiplied and given much more strength to these particular perspectives of liberation theology. New challenges appeared. Liberation theology had included the aspirations of these sectors in its preferential option for the poor. In fact, Gustavo Gutiérrez frequently made clear that the word *poor* was a broad term that included the races and ethnic groups depreciated by racism and women who are doubly exploited for being poor and being women. But that was not sufficient for these groups. On becoming agents of theological production and assuming the method of liberation theology, they prefer to speak of the "option for those excluded" because it is a more ample category than the "option for the poor." These groups are introducing new themes that challenge the discourse of liberation theology: racism, the spirituality of the non-Christian African and indigenous ancestors, and a nonpatriarchal ecclesiology and epistemology. These perspectives seek to transcend the limited use of economics and sociology in analytic mediation and introduce new tools that take into account sexism, racism, and culture. Liberation theology has also in this decade confronted problems that had not been dealt with deeply, such as ecology, culture, and interreligious dialogue. These themes are now being taken up from the liberation perspective by some theologians. Nevertheless, because of the Latin American context and the presence of men and women theologians in church institutions, theological reflection from the perspective of those discriminated against because of their sexual orientation and reflections on reproductive rights, especially for women, are still pending. Recently there have appeared timid initiatives produced by the new generation.

The most developed current of the new theologies is feminist theology. An analysis of the origins and development of this theology appears in Pilar Aquino's book, *Clamor por la vida. Teologia latinoamericana desde la perspectiva de la mujer* (1992; in English, *Our Cry for Life: Feminist Theology from Latin America,* 1993). One of the pioneers and representative theologians is the Brazilian nun Ivone Gebara. In recent years three currents can be distinguished: feminist theology of liberation, ecofeminist theology, and black feminist theology of liberation.

Another innovating fact in liberation theology is the Bible movement that extends over the whole continent. In communities, workshops, and courses the Bible is being reread from the perspective of the excluded—the poor, blacks, indigenous peoples, and women. This reading, which employs a liberating hermeneutic, is called a popular (communitarian or pastoral) reading of the Bible. Among its founders are Carlos Mesters and Milton Schwantes. *The Journal of Latin American Biblical Interpretation* (RIBLA), founded in 1989, constitutes a permanent contribution to biblical hermeneutics of liberation. This movement is distinguished by a solid group of women biblical scholars.

In this time of theological formulation there were two convergences with other theologies of liberation that were born simultaneously: German political theology and black theology within the United States. History registers dialogue and tensions between these theologies: in Geneva in 1973 with European theology and in Detroit in 1975 with black theology and feminist theology. The convergence with European political theology is in the analysis of the relation of faith-world, but they differ in their theological discourse given the great difference of the interlocutors. While European political theology reflects faith from an atheist, secularized, adult world, liberation theology is challenged to reflect from the nonperson and the scandal of poverty. The convergence with black theology is the search for liberation in a context of oppression, but black theology permanently critiques the theology of liberation for not taking seriously the problem of racism in Latin American society.

Apparently the theology of liberation that was launched originally as a theology with a universal vocation became a theology of the Third World after the foundation of the Association of Third World Theologians in Dar es Salaam in 1976. During these last years it has been conceived more as a contextual theology of Latin America. Liberation theology and Latin American theology have become synonymous.

BLACK LIBERATION THEOLOGY. Black liberation theology was born among African American clergy and theologians in the United States out of the experience of humiliation and suffering of blacks in the historical and contemporary system of racism. Its task is to analyze that condition of oppression in the light of the revelation of Jesus Christ with the goal of creating a praxis of liberation from white domination and a new understanding of black dignity among black people (James Cone). The praxis of liberation in a racist system and the affirmation of blackness are the privileged place of their theological task. To affirm God's solidarity with the oppressed, black theology refers to God and Christ as black.

The black slaves brought from Africa to the United States appropriated the Bible and read it in a liberation key, in spite of the fact that their white masters used the Bible as a tool of oppression. The book of *Exodus* was a source of inspiration for their own liberation. Before the beginnings of the formulation of black theology, a black community had already been founded by independent black churches, both Baptist and Methodist, in the eighteenth and nineteenth centuries. This explains why the clergy had permanent participation in the declarations, their position in the face of racism, and their place in the movements of black liberation. Also antecedent to black theology was the development of liberation thought among activists against slavery (Nat Turner, 1800–1831); against racial segregation (Marcus Garvey, 1887–1940), considered by many of his people "the apostle of black theology"; in the struggle for human rights (Martin Luther King Jr., 1929–1968); and in the Black Power movement (the Muslim Malcolm X, 1930–1965).

Black liberation theology was born within the heat of political and racial tumults of the 1960s and 1970s. It searched for a Christian answer to the black political movement. The first work of black theology as a formal discipline came out in 1969 with the title *Black Theology and Black Power,* written by the most important figure in the formulation of black theology, James Cone. A year later, Cone published his well-known work *Black Theology of Liberation,* in which he presents the contents of that theology. The fundamental question behind this work is, "What does the gospel of Jesus Christ have to do with the struggle of blacks for freedom in a society that denies African Americans as human beings?"

There are two important theological affirmations that distinguish black liberation theology: (1) The knowledge of God that reveals God's self as liberator. The God of Exodus, the prophets, and Jesus can only be known in the liberation struggles of the oppressed. (2) The blackness of God and of Christ as a theological symbol that looks to articulate the concrete presence of Jesus Christ in the history, culture, and experience of African Americans. Blacks are oppressed in the United States; therefore, God is on the side of the oppressed blacks and takes on the condition of the black. God is black, Christ is black; the blackness of God and Christ means that God and Christ have made the condition of the oppressed their own condition. For Cone, there is a distinction of colors. To say there is no difference means that God makes no differences between justice and injustice, between reason and irrationality, between good and evil. God is in solidarity with the blacks. As for Christology, Cone refers to Jesus as the *Oppressed par excellence* and the *Liberator par excellence.* The black Christ is the norm, the hermeneutical principle that integrates black theology, that is to say, the black experience, black history and black culture. This black experience, history, and culture are illuminated by the biblical testimony, but above all by the norm, that is, the black Christ. For Cone, sin is all that denies the liberating dimension of God revealed in Jesus Christ. Salvation, therefore, is not reduced to a future without transforming the situation of this world. The liberation of African Americans involves empowerment and the right of self-definition and self-affirmation, in addition to the transformation of social, political, economic, and religious oppression.

The debate between black theologians has been fruitful. The historians Gayraud Wilmore (1972) and Cecil Cone (1975) propose religious experience as the point of departure for black theology and not the political struggle or black power. Deotis Roberts (1974) represents a more moderate line by proposing the need for a liberating reconciliation in black-white relations. Cornel West (1979) underlines the importance of the dialogue with Marxism.

The new generation is working from three perspectives: womanist theology (Jacquelyn Grant, Katie Cannon, Delores Williams, Emilie Towns), who do theology from the experience of black women within a racist and patriarchal system; biblical hermeneutics, which questions Eurocentric scholarship and begins to discover the African presence within the Bible as well as the racial problems that the Bible itself presents. Another important perspective appears in the 1991 collective work directed by Cain H. Felder, *Stony the Road We Trod: African American Biblical Interpretation,* and the religion of the black slaves (Dwight Hopkins, George Cumming) that gathers the religious experience of the black slaves through stories, meditations, sermons, petitions and songs.

Of these three perspectives, the most developed is womanist theology. Since the 1980s black women have protested their invisibility in black theology and in white feminist theology. They feel that these theologies do not take into account the experiences of black women, who have to endure both racism and sexism in a context of poverty. The term "womanist" is from Alice Walker's work *In Search of Our Mother's Garden* (1982). It comes from the black folk expression "You acting womanish," meaning outrageous, audacious, courageous, and willful. Womanist theology takes into account the daily situation of survival as well as the structures that affect the lives of women.

***MINJUNG* THEOLOGY.** *Minjung* theology is a Korean liberation theology. It emerged in the 1970s as a Christian response to the struggle of the *minjung,* meaning "the people." This term comes from the combination of two Chinese characters. *Min* signifies people and *jung* means mass. *Minjung* theology is the theology of people who are oppressed politically and economically. It is a political hermeneutic of the gospel and a political approach to the experiences of the Korean people. For this theology Jesus was a *minjung,* was in solidarity with the *minjung,* and his life was an example of liberation. Among its most important contributions is the use of the term *han* (accumulated anger, just indignation), introduced by Suh Nam Dong. The term is taken from a poem "The Story of Sound" (1972) by the poet Kim Nam Ha. The poem expresses the pain of a poor prisoner. This is better understood in the following words of the poet Kim: "This little peninsula is filled with the clamor of aggrieved ghosts. It is filled with the mourning noise of the *han* of those who died from foreign invasions, wars, tyranny, rebellion, malignant disease and starvation. I want my poems to be the womb or bearer of these sounds, to be the transmitter of the *han* and to communicate a sharp awareness of our historical tragedy" (*Minjung Theology,* p. 26). For *minjung* theologians the term *han* refers to the sentiments of interiorized injustice of the oppressed; one of the tasks of *minjung* theology is to help people to recognize these feelings. The most important figures of this theology besides Suh Nam Dong are David Kwang Sun Suh, Ahn Byung Mu, Kim Yong Bock, and HyunYoung Hak. Within this current has emerged the feminist Korean Chung Hyun Kyung.

After the founding of Ecumenical Association of Third World Theologians, in which theologians from Latin America, Africa, and Asia and blacks from the United States began their dialogue, theologies of liberation multiplied. These theologies were not imports of the Latin American or black theologies but critical theological reflections that arose from their own particular contexts. What unites the theologies of liberation is the objective of the theological task: "liberation." All the theologies of liberation are ecumenical.

In Africa there are four strong currents: South African black theology, inspired by black theology from the United States and the struggle against racism; African (Christian) inculturation theology, which has culture as its point of reference; African liberation theology, which underlines socioeconomic and political analysis along with religious and ecclesial analysis; and African women's theology, with it theological focus against androcentrism and patriarchalism present in church structures and in African traditions.

In Asia, along with *minjung* theology, the Filipino theology of struggle and other contextual theologies of liberation stand out. The theology of struggle of the Philippines is seen in its struggle of resistance. Asian theologies of liberation differ from the rest of the liberation theologies because of their predominant context of religious plurality. Christians are a minority among large non-Christian religions. In order for a theology of liberation to have an impact in this context, Christians are challenged to dialogue with the other religions and to reconsider valuable elements of Hinduism, Buddhism, or Shamanism that promote liberation and an enrichment of Christian theology. Among other theologies coming out of Asia are Indian *dalit* theology, which struggles against the caste system, and Burakumin liberation theology, which focuses on persons marginalized by ritual impurity systems. In Asia, as in the theologies of Africa, Latin America, and minorities in the United States, women theologians have a strong voice. Their publications appear in the well-known theological journal *In God's Image* founded by Asian women theologians.

Among the minorities of the United States new theologies have emerged: Latino theology reflects their racial mixture, culture, and popular religion. It does theology in the symbolic framework of "being" on the border. Within this theology women's voices have created the *mujerista* theology. Native American theology does theology out of their experience without forgetting their presence in America before the arrival of Christians and Christian American colonialism. This theology rescues ancestral spiritual values. Asian-American theologies present the particularities of the Japanese-, Chinese-, and Korean-American experiences.

These theologies of liberation recognize that a good number of Christians in their own countries do not share their point of view because of, above all, the political commitment inherent in liberation. Nevertheless, new contextual theologies of liberation continue to proliferate as this new way of doing theology, in which subjects take their concrete reality as the point of departure to speak of God, has spread throughout the world.

SEE ALSO Feminist Theology; Political Theology.

BIBLIOGRAPHY

Boff, Clodovis. *Teología de lo político. Sus mediaciones.* Salamanca, 1980. English version, *Theology and Praxis: Epistemological Foundations.* New York, 1987.

Boff, Leonardo. *Iglesia, carisma y poder.* Santander, 1981.

Boff, Leonardo. *Passion of the Christ, Passion of the World: The Facts, Their Interpretation, and Their Meaning, Yesterday and Today.* Translated by Robert Barr. Maryknoll, N.Y., 1987.

Boff, Leonardo, and Clodovis Boff. *Introducing Liberation Theology.* New York, 1987.

Commission on Theological Concerns of the Christian Conference of Asia, ed. *Minjung Theology: People as the Subjects of History.* London and New York, 1983.

Cone, James. *Black Theology and Black Power.* New York, 1969.

Cone, James. *A Black Theology of Liberation.* New York, 1970.

Dussel, Enrique. *Teología de la liberación. Un panorama de su desarrollo.* México D.F., 1995.

Ellacuría, Ignacio, and Jon Sobrino. *Mysterium Liberationis: Conceptos fundamentales de la teología de la Liberación.* San Salvador, 1990. English version, *Mysterium Liberationis: Fundamental Concepts of Liberation Theology.* New York, 1993.

Fabella, Virginia and R. S. Sugirtharaja, eds. *Dictionary of Third World Theologies.* New York, 2000.

Gutiérrez, Gustavo. *Teología de la liberación. Perspectivas.* Salamanca, 1972. English version, *A Liberation Theology.* New York, 1973.

Hopkins, Dwight. *Introducing Black Theology of Liberation.* New York, 1999.

Loysius, Pieris. *An Asian Theology of Liberation.* New York, 1988.

Martey, Emmanuel. *African Theology: Inculturation and Liberation.* New York, 1993.

Musala, Itumeleng J., and Tlhagalr Buti. *The Unquestionable Right to Be Free: Black Theology from South Africa.* New York, 1986.

Roberts, James Deotis. *A Black Political Theology.* Philadelphia, 1974.

West, Cornel. *Black Theology and Marxist Thought.* Boston, 1979.

Wilmore, Gayraud, and James Cone. *Black Theology, a Documentary History, 1966–1979.* New York, 1979.

ELSA TAMEZ (2005)

LIELE, GEORGE (1752–1825) was the first black Baptist in Georgia and perhaps the founder of the first black church in North America. He was also the first black missionary from the United States to Jamaica, West Indies, and the founder of the first black congregation there.

George Liele was born a slave in Virginia and manumitted by his owner just prior to the War of Independence.

Liele's owner, Henry Sharp, was a Baptist deacon. Liele was converted to Christianity by Matthew Moore, a white minister, while on a trip with Sharp to Burke County, Georgia. Liele quickly expressed a desire to preach and was encouraged by Sharp to do so. After Liele was licensed, around 1773, he began preaching to the local black population at Silver Bluff, South Carolina. David George (1742–1810) was one of Liele's early converts and became an exhorter at the Silver Bluff congregation. The Silver Bluff congregation may have been the first black congregation to be organized in North America. The date of its founding has been variously given between 1773 and 1775. The date on the church's cornerstone is 1750, which identifies its founding as earlier than that of the black Baptist church organized on the William Byrd plantation in Mecklenburg, Virginia in 1758.

After Sharp died in battle in 1778, his relatives tried to re-enslave Liele but were prevented from doing so by the British troops who had occupied Savannah, Georgia, where Liele was then residing. He continued to preach in Savannah to a congregation of slave as well as free black Baptists. In 1782 Liele baptized one of his gifted converts, Andrew Bryan (1737–1812). This was the same year he departed Savannah with the British for Jamaica. In 1788 Bryan was officially ordained and the church was certified. The church was reorganized as the First Baptist Church of Savannah in 1800.

When Liele accompanied the British troops when they left Savannah in 1782 and relocated to Jamaica, it was as an indentured servant to Colonel Kirkland. In 1783 Kirkland transferred Liele's indenture to the governor of Jamaica, General Campbell. By 1784 Liele had worked off his indenture, and he thus had nothing to encumber the exercise of his preaching gifts except the objections of some Anglican clergymen. His congregation in Kingston soon boasted 350 members, mostly former slaves. The construction of their first sanctuary was completed in 1793. Liele was incarcerated in 1801 on the charge of preaching sedition, but he was released for lack of evidence. He was jailed a second time because the payments on the church building had fallen into arrears. Liele's ministry continued in spite of these hardships, and in spite of the fact that a law was passed on the island in 1805 that made preaching to slaves illegal. Liele referred to his members as "Ethiopian Baptist" and the importance of such a term and what "Ethiopianism" later signified for the Garvey and Rastafarian movements in the twentieth century has led some scholars to view him as their intellectual father.

SEE ALSO African American Religions, overview article and article on History of Study; Baptist Churches.

BIBLIOGRAPHY

Davis, John W. "George Liele and Andrew Bryan, Pioneer Negro Baptist Preachers." *Journal of Negro History* 2 (1918): 119–127.

Gayle, Clement. *George Liele: Pioneer Missionary to Jamaica.* Kingston, Jamaica, 1982.

Holmes, Edward A. "George Liele: Negro Slavery's Prophet of Deliverance." *Foundations* 9 (1966): 333–345.

Pinn, Ann H., and Anthony B. Pinn. *Black Church History.* Minneapolis, 2002.

JAMES ANTHONY NOEL (2005)

LIFE. Across the centuries and the continents, human beings have revealed, through myths, rituals, religious and cultural institutions, social histories, and various other modes of symbolic expression, a central and overriding preoccupation with the creation and prolongation of life. Most of the human cultures known to us today have one or more terms to designate life, being, existence, or other cognate concepts, which have occupied a core position in the intellectual life of each tradition. The Chinese language, for instance, which does not possess an exact equivalent of the term *life,* does contain a number of other words to describe the seat of life or basis of the life process (such as *yu,* "being," and its counterpart, *wu,* "nonbeing"). So, too, Hebrew has *nefesh/ruah,* Greek *psyche/pneuma,* Latin *spiritus,* Sanskrit *ātman / jīva / prāṇa / puruṣa,* Arabic *ʿumrʿishah,* and Nuer *yiegh.*

The identity of the human faculty or function that is regarded as an undeniable indication of the presence of life in an animated organism varies from one culture to another. By and large, however, the seal of life has been identified with the tangible signs of the presence of breath, with consciousness or mental functioning, and with physical movement or—in the modern scientific fields of physiology and neurology—pulsebeat and measurable brain-wave activity.

In many cultures, it is perhaps breath, more than any other single human function, that has been designated as the most dependable sign of life. This designation is confirmed by the fact that in many languages, both ancient and modern, the words for "life" and "breath" are one and the same. A particularly intriguing illustration of this phenomenon appears in one of the most ancient Hindu texts, the *Bṛhadaranyaka* Upaniṣad (composed around the sixth century BCE), where a debate as to which of the human faculties is indispensable to the maintenance of life is resolved in favor of breath (*prāṇa*).

Many religious traditions have attributed the existence of the world and its entire population of living inhabitants to the creative act of a god or gods at the beginning of time. According to various cosmologies, from both oral and written traditions, the divine creator fashioned the universe as we know it either out of nothing or from some type of preexistent *materia prima* (such as water, earth, fire, mind, or substances like tears or semen, emitted by the creator). Such traditions believe that the cosmos is therefore suffused with and supported by the sacred energies of the creator deity, and human life is linked physically and spiritually with the life of the cosmos as a whole. That is, the human realm is established within and directed by a cosmic, celestial, or divine dimension of reality, of either a personal or a transpersonal nature. As a consequence, human existence is believed to possess, both a human and a divine, a temporal and an atemporal dimension, with the latter being both logically and metaphysically prior to the former.

In addition, many religions and philosophies make a qualitative distinction between two contrasting and mutually exclusive modes or styles of life. The two categories of existence have been characterized variously as profane and sacred, impure and pure, fallen and redeemed, ignorant and enlightened, bound and liberated, alienated and authentic. In cultures having experienced colonization by Western countries, such a dichotomy can also take on the more politicized valence of indigenous/Western imperialist styles of life; or pre-colonial and postcolonial ways of being.

The first category pertains to life in a state of separation from or in opposition to the will of a god or gods in theistic systems or in opposition to the natural law or the principle of ultimate reality within non-theistic systems (such as *dharma* in Hinduism and Buddhism, *moira* or *logos* in ancient Greece, and *dao* in China and Japan). Life in this state is depicted as a realm of sin and ignorance, suffering and misery, and death (linked, in certain cases, with rebirth).

Achievement of the second, more salutary state of existence (conceived as one of wholeness, physical and spiritual integration, redemption, or liberation), is realized by living in compliance with the cosmic law or the will of God. For many cultures, human existence is viewed as real and meaningful only insofar as it is experienced as organically rooted in a divine realm of existence. This divine realm is conceived to be a celestial abode of God or the gods or the shadowy domain of the cultural ancestors. It is the function of the network of myths and symbols, cultic rituals, and cultural customs to preserve and strengthen the connection between the human and divine realms and, thereby, to guarantee to human beings the sense of reality and value that makes life not only bearable but fulfilling.

Clearly it is impossible to cover all the beliefs about life held by all the peoples of the world. The present article will merely select one or two salient examples from a few geographical or religious traditions, in hope that readers will be inspired to find out more on their own. Due to space limitations, moreover, coverage of the religious traditions themselves will focus only on their formative and classical periods.

AUSTRALIA. The indigenous inhabitants of Arnhem Land in Australia believe that the world existed from the beginning; only human beings were lacking. Human life originated with the peregrinations of a primal ancestor and his two sisters. They wandered about the landscape, paused from time to time, engaged in sexual intercourse, and thereby produced human offspring and various totemic emblems known as Dreamings (that is, the world as it now is). The peoples who inhabit this territory trace the origin of all entities that constitute the world in which they live back to a "Dreaming period." It was during this timeless, mythical epoch that the life-world as we know it was established. To explore a further example: in Murngin society of Northeastern Australia, the sacred well, or water hole, contains the essence of all life. The soul (warro) returns to this water hole to be renewed by contact with the ancestors—both those long dead, who are most pure, and those recently dead, who are still in contact with the living. Animals sacred to the Murngin are also part of this life-giving cycle of returning to the water to be purified and renewed.

NATIVE AMERICANS. Like the vast array of the Australian indigenous peoples, the equally vast array of Native American practices is united by a deep respect for the natural world. The power of life inheres in the powers of nature. Natural objects are imbued with sacred meaning, and in their ceremonial use they become supernaturally as well as naturally powerful. Native American groups tend not to make any distinction between ritual and theology, and therefore a successful life is something to be ritually enacted as well as imagined in a more abstract way. Many of these ceremonies include the insurance of a successful hunt, as well as contemporary hopes for life on the reservation. The Lakota, for instance, understand life to be comprised of seven rituals: The Sweat Lodge, The Vision Quest, Ghost Keeping, The Sun Dance, Making Relatives, Puberty Ceremony, and Throwing the Ball. One new ceremony, the Yuwipi, specifically incorporates the post-colonial life of the Lakota. The Apache believe that life endures through successful negotiation with the larger power that informs the universe, as well as with one's individual power, attained during visionary experiences—sometimes alone and sometimes with the mediation of a holy person. The number four is central to the performance of these rituals and considered a basis for wholeness and healing in life. So, too, the Navaho's understanding of a prosperous life involves harmonious relations with the Holy People. Their rituals, especially the complex practice of chanting called the Blessingway, remember the creation of their own life on earth: their Emergence from the Underworld, as well as their travails and challenges after the Emergence.

INDONESIA. According to the people of West Ceram in the Sulawesi Islands, human beings emerged from bananas that grew at the base of a sacred mountain. Living beings of all sorts, together with various foodstuffs and diverse sources of wealth, resulted from the sacrifice (literally, the "murder") of a coconut maiden, Hainuwele, and the implantation of the several parts of her body in the surrounding landscape. By this means, her bodily parts became sources of sustenance for all living creatures. But this primal murder was also the occasion for the advent of death. Hence, death is understood to be a necessary precondition for the creation and maintenance of life.

This kind of complementarity is also reflected in the beliefs other traditional Indonesian peoples, where sacred geography involves the upstream and downstream flow of rivers and other bodies of water, an upper world and a netherworld, inside and outside, and other opposites. For the Sumbanese, the major deity is a dual entity of Amawolo/Amarawi; for the Toraja, the marriage of heaven and earth gives rise to the universe. Such an idea of the life-giving balance between opposites has even influenced the religious traditions of peoples who later came and settled in Indonesia, such as Hinduism, Buddhism, Christianity, and Islam, and is shown in current cultural forms such as the *wayang*, or shadow theater.

AFRICA (SOUTH OF THE SAHARA). In the words of Richard Nyombi, for African peoples, "religion is literally life and life is religion." Doctrine and creed as such are less central to various African traditions than the force of sacred place and the power of sacred objects, especially as they are used in dance and art forms, as well as in festivals, ceremonies, and rituals. Each individual comes into being through social rites of passage, and gains, through these rites, the capacity to become an ancestor after his or her death. Each ritual preserves the web of relationships that give life and protects against those forces that would destroy it. J. S. Mbiti calls this African view of the world a "relational metaphysics": "I am because we are and because we are therefore I am" (Mbiti, 1990).

For example, according to the Nuer, a tribe of cattle keepers in the southern Egyptian Sudan, life is bestowed upon the universe and all its inhabitants by the cosmic spirit (Kwoth), invoked variously as "spirit of the sky," "grandfather of the universe," or "spirit who created the ancestors." This omnipresent spirit of the sky is credited with creating the world and its offspring and determining the course of its operations. From his lofty perch, he rewards and punishes human actions and upholds the moral order of the universe, by which all life is governed.

In addition, for the Nuer there are smaller and more localized spirits (*kuth*) of the sky, atmosphere, and earth, through whose mediating powers the life energies of Kwoth are transmitted to animals and human beings. Specifically, this transmission of power is effectuated by the killing and partaking of the flesh and blood of the ox, the totemic ancestor of the Nuer. Even as birth necessitates a temporary separation from the primordial spirit, death is the return of the individual soul to the great spirit and its near-complete isolation from the realm of the living. The deceased are transmuted into ghosts at the moment of death but retain the capacity to return to the living in dreams, visions, and various types of misfortune.

Kwoth is only one example of such an idea of a Supreme Being, and kuth only one example of the mediating deities who maintain life. The Supreme Being is known by several names in other African traditions (and there are arguments to this day as to whether there is one African tradition or many): To the Ibo, the Supreme being is Chukwu; to the Akan in Ghana he is Nyame, to the Yoruba he is Ọlọ́run, and in Central Africa he is Jok, to name a few. In most African traditions, he is a life-preserver who is a parent figure to the other gods, and charges them with maintaining cosmic processes; to the earth he is a husband standing behind her creative forces.

JUDAISM. In the Book of *Genesis*, the world is created by divine fiat. In accordance with most of the Hebrew tradition, biblical thought identifies the basis of human life as the blood (*Lv.* 17:14).

The writers of the various books in the Hebrew scriptures are in general agreement that the relative length of life is determined by human virtues and vices, as exemplified by the travails of the first man and woman, Adam and Eve, in the Garden of Eden. God is the lord of life and death by virtue of his sovereign rulership over the book of life.

In biblical thought, therefore, life reveals its presence through breath (*ruah*) and blood. Hence, God is the prototypical living being whose life is eternal, whereas the existence of all created beings and entities is fragile and perishable, "like the grass of the field" (*Ps.* 103:15, *Is.* 40:6). God's life is manifested through action and creativity. He is the creator and therefore the lord of life (*Jb.* 43:14f.). Hence, to live in rebellion against his will is equivalent to experiencing death in the midst of life (*Jb.* 3:11–26, *Jon.* 4:9). Such an existence will be filled, inwardly, with misfortune and misery, however favorable the external circumstances may be.

The realization that death is the fate of all living beings brings into question the ultimate value of life and its various aspects (*Eccl.* 1:1–11), but in the final analysis the judgment is rendered that those who live in submission to God's will can expect to enjoy a long and happy life and, in the end, be gathered to the fathers (*Gn.* 15:15, *Jb.* 42:17). All persons, therefore, face a choice between the way of life and the way of death (*Prv.* 5:6, 14:12).

In the biblical period, the life of Israel was believed to be maintained and revitalized through sacrifice. The community of Israel as a whole appropriates the divine power resident within the sacrificial oblation and shares in the sanctity created by the sacrifice. Likewise, by offering the sacrifice to God, the sacrificer also strengthens both God's nature and, through his revitalization, that of the world and its inhabitants. The covenant between God and Israel is expressed and strengthened though a system of sacrifice.

In rabbinic Judaism as it developed after the destruction of the Second Temple in 70 CE, prayer and study of the Torah replaced sacrifice as the form of service to God. Rabbinic Judaism, whose central tenets are expressed in the Mishnah and the Talmud, posits the parallel existence of the written Torah and the Oral Torah. (The Oral Torah was written down between the third and sixth centuries CE). These two written documents, as interpreted by the Sages, are the sources of *halakhah* (the "way" or "path"), often called Jewish law. Life should be lived by following this path, according to the prescriptions of *halakhah*, a term that includes religious rituals as well as rules that govern the conduct of everyday life.

CHRISTIANITY. The New Testament concept of life rests upon the distinction between mere existence, or natural life (*bios*, as the ancient Greeks used the term), and true or authentic life in Christ. In the first instance, human life is finite, fragile, and mortal. As in the Hebrew Bible, to be alive is to possess the capacity to perform one's intended function and act efficaciously (*Acts* 7:38) and to do so in a state of health (*Mk.* 5:23). While animal life is sustained by nourishment, human life is dependent upon the continued presence of the soul (*psyche*), or life breath (*pneuma*), which is a gift of God. Since God is the only being who possesses life inherently (*Jn.* 5:26) and, hence, alone lives eternally, it follows that all living creatures derive their existence from him. In recognition of the fact that life is a divine dispensation, the believer does not live for himself, nor primarily for his fellow creatures, but for his creator and redeemer (*Rv.* 14:7f., *Gal.* 2:19). He who lives for his own selfish pleasure will come, in the end, to sin and death (*2 Cor.* 5).

While the life of redemption is available in the present as a consequence of the establishment of the new regime of faith through Christ's resurrection as the second Adam (*1 Cor.* 15:20–22), its complete realization must await the end of time, when Christ is to deliver the kingdom of God and, thereby, put "all enemies under his feet." Since life in its truest and most efficacious form lies in the future, beyond the grave, then all present conduct is but a preparation for that eventuality. But, in the final analysis, this indestructible form of life is the result of divine grace (*Jn.* 3:16, *Rom.* 8:1–11), extended to those who repent past sins and accept the promise of salvation (*Lk.* 13:3, *Acts* 2:38, *Rom.* 2:4). The doctrine of the immortality of the soul is entirely foreign to the New Testament.

Building upon certain key concepts in the Hebrew Bible, the New Testament writers declare that authentic life is based not upon God's nature in general, but rather upon God's expression of his love and compassion for the sufferings of humanity and his readiness to forgive and redeem all those who seek his forgiveness through the life, death, and resurrection of his only son, Jesus, the Christ (*Jn.* 3:16, *1 Pt.* 1:18–19). According to Paul, the consummate realization of the benefits of the "life in Christ" will occur only after the Day of Resurrection. Hence, true life can be appropriated in the present time only in the form of hope (*Rom.* 5:1–11, *1 Cor.* 15). Whereas the letter of the law kills (i.e., destroys the freedom of life in the spirit), the spirit gives life (*2 Cor.* 3:6). Where the spirit is present there is life, eternal and indestructible (*2 Cor.* 3:17f.). This life is embodied in and offered through the preached word (*kerygma*), the "power of God for salvation to all those who have faith" (*Rom.* 1:16).

According to Augustine, the wide panorama of living beings is distinguished by the divine creator according to a hierarchical order of existence. At the lowest level are the merely nutritive life forms such as plants, devoid of sensibility or consciousness. Then come sentient forms of life, devoid of mind or soul, such as cattle, birds, and fishes. Third, there is the human being, the crown of God's created order by virtue of his possession of mind and will. Ultimately, transcendent to humans, whose life is conditioned by the vicissitudes of change and death, there is the eternal, unchanging, absolute existent, God, "who is wisdom itself."

Augustine, like other Christian writers who followed him, understood God to be living in a highly exceptional, and indeed, absolute sense. He possesses the capacity to give life to the multitude of creatures that inhabit the world. He is the boundless and inexhaustible reservoir of power from which all other living beings derive their existence. He is, in short, the alpha and omega, the source and final resting place for all living beings.

ISLAM. In the Qur'ān, God (Allāh) creates humans from a "blood clot." (*Sūrah* 96.2: "Read: 'In the name of the Lord who creates humanity from a clot.'") God controls and supervises all of life, and is frequently envisioned in a magisterial and yet caring and compassionate capacity. God determines the span and quality of human life in accordance with the behavior of each individual. Humans are also judged at two moments: first, at their own time of death, and second, "at the hour"—the day of judgment for all humanity.

The rules and standards by which the lives of Muslims will be judged are expressed in the *sharī'ah* ("path") or system of Islamic law. The sources of *sharī'ah* are the Qur'ān and the *ḥadīth*—the tradition of the actions and utterances of the prophet Muḥammad (d. 632 CE), both as told by the Prophet himself and as included in narratives and regulations about him recorded after his death.

A life well-lived is best judged by the capacity to which men and women might engage in the service and worship of God. As expressed in the rules of *sharī'ah*, such service and worship are often organized as the Five Pillars of Islam. They are: the profession of the faith (*shahādah*); prayer five times a day (*ṣalāt*); fasting during the month of Ramaḍān (*ṣawm*); charity to the needy (*zakāt*); and pilgrimage to Mecca (*ḥājj*). Later Muslim tradition saw this ideal life as being contained in the early history of Islam. For example, the Life of Muḥammad by the Muslim philosopher Ibn Ishaq describes much of the setting for the establishment of these regular practices in Muḥammad's own example; thus, Muḥammad's life becomes the model life *par excellence.*

Many Muslim thinkers have argued that following this Five-Pillar structure is the most life-giving practice, infusing the world with a sense of God. The rich Ṣūfī mystical tradition frequently emphasized the recollection of the Name of God as a particularly enlivening custom, in which God's merciful light could be shown on the faces of those engaged in prayer. All of the nature of creaturely existence can be known only when one fully surrenders to God—thus the Arabic word *slm*, or surrender, from which we derive the words "Muslim" and "Islam," also implies knowledge of the nature of life itself.

The more orthodox Sunnī and Shī'ah traditions also taught that ritual prayer and ritual acts in general give one a deeper sense of this life and of the life to come. The great twelfth-century lawyer and theologian al-Ghazālī writes that, during the ritual preparation for prayer, each person should say, "Oh God, I am purposing to read Your Book and to have Your name many times on my lips; through the steadfast word make me steadfast in this life and the world to come." (*The Beginning of Guidance*, 8).

The value of human life is emphasized in the Qur'anic dictum that "If anyone slew a person it would be as if he slew the whole of humankind, and if anyone saved a life it would be as if he saved the life of all of humankind." (Śūra 5.32) In addition, the Qur'ān often mentions the physical resurrection of the dead at the end of time. "Does man think that we cannot assemble his bones? Nay we are able to put together, in perfect order, the very tips of his fingers." (Śūra 75.1–2) Thus, the creation of life and resurrection are imaginatively linked.

HINDUISM. The Vedas (c. 1500–900 BCE), the earliest strata of Hindu texts, attribute the creation of the life-world to a variety of divine agents or cosmogonic entities, with no apparent compulsion toward consistency among the many theories of creation. The cosmos was believed to have originated from the primordial sacrifice of a cosmic superman (*puruṣa*) and the distribution of the parts of his body throughout the universe to form the sun, moon, stars, sky, earth, and so forth (*Ṛgveda* 10.90). Alternatively, the universe arose from the mysterious breathing, windlessly, of "That One" (*tad ekam*) within the realm where "there was neither existence nor nonexistence" (*Ṛgveda* 10.129), or it resulted from the fragmentation of a primordial "Golden Germ" (*hiranyagarbha*) floating upon the cosmic ocean (*Ṛgveda* 10.121). At least one sage expressed skepticism that the origins of the world can be known even to the highest deity (*Ṛgveda* 10.129.7).

The Brahmanas (c. 800 BCE), liturgical manuals employed by Brahmanic priests, attribute the creation of the universe and its multitudinous inhabitants to a god addressed as Prajāpati ("lord of creatures"). The later traditions recorded in the Hindu epics and Purāṇas explain the creation of the universe as the work of other deities, each regarded as supreme among a pantheon of other gods. Chief among these are Viṣṇu, Śiva, and Devī (the Goddess), each worshiped under many different names and in many different forms. The actual task of making the world, however, is still often assigned to the god Prajāpati, usually under his later name, Brahmā, now regarded as a minor god under the direction of one of the supreme gods.

In the Upaniṣads, the basis of Vedānta, the focus shifts from cosmology to spiritual psychology, from accounts of the origin and operations of the universe to the birth, death, and rebirth of the human soul (*ātman*). It is also here that the Hindu doctrines of *karma* and rebirth burst into full flower. From the Vedāntic perspective, creaturely existence (including that of the gods) is the direct result of action (*karma*) performed in past lives in a state of metaphysical ignorance (*avidya*). This ignorance, which pervades the existence of all creatures and is the cause of transmigration (*saṃsāra*), results from the confusion of the finite and evanescent self (*ātman*) with the absolute, unchanging self of the universe (also called *ātman*, but also *brahman*). This phenomenal self or human personality is composed of five sheaths or layers of faculties, which account for a person's conscious existence and which, if identified egoistically as the ultimate basis of reality, serve as the causal basis of rebirth (*saṃsāra*). The cyclical recurrence of rebirth can be terminated, and permanent liberation achieved, only after the person has come to a transformative knowledge (*prajñā*) of the quintessential identity of the human self (*ātman*) and the self of the universe (*ātman /brahman*).

The *Bhagavadgītā* attempts a synthesis of Vedic and Upaniṣadic conceptions of the world and creaturely existence. The *Gītā* embraces the view that the life of the cosmos and all its inhabitants is the result of the formative activities of God, who appears here in the form of Kṛṣṇa. Kṛṣṇa is both the womb of the universe and its final resting place (*Bhagavadgītā* 7.6). He is the primal spirit (*puruṣa*), the source of all beings (10.8), the seed of all creatures (7.10, 10.39), and the universal father who plants the seeds from which all living entities arise. The world, in turn, is God's body (11.7). All beings abide in him (9.6). Hence, all states of existence arise from God alone (10.5). Abiding within the hearts of all beings and by means of his celestial power of creation (*māyā*), he causes them to revolve (*saṃsāra*) around the circuit of rebirth as though they were mounted on a machine (18.61).

When the life process is viewed *sub specie aeternitatis*, God projects creatures into being, time after time, by means of his material nature (*prakṛti*) through the instrumentality of his magical power (*māyā*). He implants spirit (*puruṣa*) within the physical organism as the basis for the experience of pleasure and pain. The human being, in turn, appropriates the material nature of God by identifying with the three strands (*gunas*) of creaturely existence (passion, lethargy, and mental clarity), rather than with the *ātman*, which is the spiritual essence of the divine nature.

Human beings, then, are bound to the factors of material nature. Their emotional and appetitive attachment to these factors provokes them to perform egoistical actions (*karma*), which bind them to self-deluding ignorance and, thereby, to the round of death and rebirth. They are bound by their own past actions and also, paradoxically, by the will of God, who controls the ultimate course of events throughout the universe.

Once the embodied soul transcends the three strands that arise from physical existence, it is freed from bondage to death and rebirth and, in the end, it achieves immortality in God. Those persons who renounce the fruits of their actions and submit themselves completely to the divine will pass beyond the sphere of sorrow and death and arrive at the final termination of the cyclical life process to enjoy eternal bliss (*ānanda*) in perfect union with the godhead. This tradition, in which union with God through passionate commitment is the aim of life, is frequently referred to as *bhakti*, or devotion.

Buddhism. The Buddha himself declared that the search for answers to all metaphysical questions concerning life (Was the universe created by God or is it eternal? Is the source of birth and death traceable to a divine agent? Does the human soul survive the death of the body?) is detrimental to the human quest for lasting peace and contentment. The sole *raison d'être* of the whole of his life and teachings was the identification of the human cause of human misery and the means to its permanent eradication. In one sense, therefore, it could be said that the Buddha was one of the first proponents of a philosophy of life.

The Buddha declared that creaturely existence is characterized by three distinguishing marks or factors: impermanence (*anitya*, Pali *anicca*), suffering or unsatisfactoriness (*duḥkha* / *dukkha*), and no-selfhood (*an ātman* / *anattā*). With this teaching, the Buddha undercut, by a single stroke, the Hindu Vedāntic conviction that the life-world (*nama-rūpa*), with its myriad of arising and perishing creatures, is established upon a single, universal, eternal, and unchanging reality (*ātman-brahman*).

While the Buddha embraced the twin Hindu beliefs in *dharma/dhamma* (the universal law that governs the operations of the entire life-world) and *karma* (the principle that all past actions condition all current life situations), he radically redefined both concepts by rejecting the notion of an eternally enduring and unchanging soul or self. In place of the Vedāntic notion of soul, or *ātman*, he declared that the human personality is constituted of five aggregates (*skandhas*) or clusters of physical and psychological factors that form the core of human consciousness and behavior. The five groups of factors are:

1. The body (*rūpa*), or physical context of sentient existence.
2. The feelings (*vedana*), or physical and psychological sensibilities.
3. The perceptual group (*samjña*), from which arise the perceptions of physical objects.
4. The mental factors (*saṃskārās*), or tendencies of mind and will in combination.
5. The consciousness proper (*vijñāna*), the property of awareness in the fullest personal sense of the term and the factor that binds together the other elements to form a unified personality.

It is these five collections of psychosomatic factors, therefore, that constitute the functional apparatus of all human beings, the operations of which account for the birth, existence, death, and rebirth of each person. Nor are these factors to be thought of as real and permanent entities. They are physical and mental components of life that condition the multitude of situations under which a person exists within each moment of consciousness. Ultimately, viewed against the backdrop of the one, unchanging reality (called *nirvāṇa*, "cessation," or *śūnyatā*, "emptiness"), the aggregates or components of life are discovered to be an ever-fluctuating (hence, unreal) succession of psychosomatic events.

But the Buddha's teaching concerning the nature of creaturely existence becomes fully comprehensible only when interpreted within the context of the doctrine of causality or the universal law of karma. The Buddhist view of causation, succinctly stated, is as follows: "When this is present, that comes to be; from the arising of this, that arises; when this is absent, that does not come to be; on the cessation of this, that ceases" (*Samyutta Nikāya* 2.28).

The law of causation, which governs the coming to be and passing away of all forms of life, is depicted through the image of the wheel of life and death (*saṃsāra - maṇḍala*). The wheel is composed of two causally interlocking aspects or links in a chain of causes and effects. Each of the pairs of links in the chain is dependent, causally, upon the one or ones preceding it, and each, in turn, is a precondition for the link or links that follow it. In this way, the two aspects of existence form a closed circle.

Again, properly understood, the doctrine of causation (or dependent co-origination) is to be viewed not as a set of abstract metaphysical principles but as the theoretical basis of a therapeutic system by means of which the infirmities of sentient existence can be diagnosed and an antidote administered. By demonstrating that the miseries of existence (death followed by rebirth) arise out of a series of finite conditions governed by a state of ignorance (*avidya*), the teaching of causation defines the various points at which the succession of causally related symptoms can be broken and a cure achieved. Such a view of conquering ignorance proved to be compatible with other indigenous views of life where Buddhism traveled, such as the idea of *kami*, or life force in Japan, or the Bon practice of life-giving visualization in Tibet.

According to the teachings of Buddhism, therefore, the ultimate objective of human existence is to become conscious of and transcend all thoughtless desires, obliterate the causes of ignorance, suffering, and rebirth, and thereby to terminate the ever-recurrent cycle of death and rebirth in the bliss of *nirvāṇa*.

Conclusions. Human beings realize the aims of their existence through the medium of self-consciousness. Their possession of the faculty of self-consciousness enables them to exercise the capacity to transcend the sheer flux and flow of sensual experience and to reflect upon the nature of their existence, its origins, and the direction they wish it to take. Hence, they can imagine other ideal states of existence that are preferable to the one in which they find themselves at any given moment. They can, then, exercise their will in choosing among preferred states in hope of bringing those states closer to realization. For many people, mere physical survival is not an adequate legitimation of human life. They find human existence acceptable only when it can be experienced within the framework of a meaningful and purposeful order.

For many religious people, a meaningful life is predicated upon the confidence that the world and all the creatures who inhabit it are the handiwork of divine creative forces or beings, who also, in some cases, are believed to provide a cosmic milieu that is hospitable to the growth of plant, animal, and human species. Such people look to a transhuman order of being for the revelation of the basic structure of the universe and of the moral and spiritual laws that govern its various operations. For them, even the performance of such commonplace activities as eating and dying, working and sleeping, marriage and reproduction is patterned after celestial or transtemporal models. Other traditions have taught that life and death are inextricably interconnected aspects of a single reality and that all beings exist under the inexorable law of mortality. Most religious and cultural institutions that compose the fabric of the social life of a people (from temple or church to family and educational system, from fertility and puberty rites to funeral and ancestral ceremonies) have been established in response to the recognition that finitude and death are inescapable realities. Such religious communities sanction these and all other institutions in the belief that the *élan vital* that undergirds and nourishes all living beings can be augmented and either the event of death can be postponed or the remaining period of life can be enriched by means of these performative rites.

In addition, many religious traditions embrace social history, or their own version of such history, as a crucial element that gives meaning to life. For example, during the Passover Seder, Jews recite the life of the Israelites wandering in the desert as if they, too, were present. Historical reality becomes meaningful religious reality. Many Native American groups now tell their mythical histories in such a way that they end with recent social history, especially the ways in which colonial practices have stolen powers of life inherent in the earth and the world of nature.

Colonial and postcolonial realities, too, play a role in contemporary religious traditions' views of what is and is not life-giving. For some, the work of Christian missionaries has created a permanent shift in worldview in postcolonial times; previously colonized peoples must choose which god is more life-giving than another. The African thinker Bolagi Idowu writes of African converts "with two Gods in their hands," who are therefore "peoples of ambivalent spiritual lives." Ideas of life and human flourishing look very different in countries that have been colonized, where dominant/colonial and indigenous traditions have been engaged in ultimate struggles and negotiations for power, detente, or even simple coexistence. Christian traditions of resurrection may take on aspects of indigenous ideas about life-giving ancestors; so, too, indigenous practices may take on healing and life-giving powers of Christian saints. The practice of Santeria, in both America and the Caribbean, is one example of such a merging of traditions in the wake of the colonial and postcolonial effects of the slave trade. "Life" in these religious contexts must also be viewed politically and historically.

Many religious traditions also distinguish between an imperfect and ultimately unsatisfactory state in which human existence is set, and a more satisfying, long-lasting, and fulfilling state beyond the grave (variously referred to as Heaven, Paradise, the Pure Land, the Land of the Blessed, the state of enlightenment, or *nirvāṇa*), toward which human life, in response to its loftiest aspirations, is striving. Among the world's religions, certain traditions within Judaism, Christianity, Islam, Hinduism, and Mahāyāna Buddhism teach that access to this loftier, purer, and more enduring postmortem existence comes in the form of a gift, or an act of grace on the part of God, or some other celestial bearer of salvation.

How can we define life in the religious context? The very act of posing the question produces an initial sense of bafflement and perplexity. Augustine's statement that he knows the meaning of the term *love* until asked to define it could be echoed in this context. Yet the vast array of semantic values that have been attributed to the word for "life" in the various languages of humankind might lead us to conclude that a precise, distinct, and universally acceptable concept need not accompany the use of the term. Instead, merely asking the question brings in its wake a sense that life is a realm of endlessly self-perpetuating novelties, in which the solution to any given problem gives rise to a plethora of other questions. These questions force us to seek further for additional answers or, at least, to search out more intellectually refined, morally elevating, and spiritually salutary ways of pursuing the quest.

SEE ALSO Afterlife; Archetypes; Breath and Breathing; Nirvāṇa; Sacrifice; Soul, article on Christian Concepts; Subaltern Studies.

BIBLIOGRAPHY

Creation

Eliade, Mircea. *Birth and Rebirth.* New York, 1958.

Gleiser, Marcello. *The Dancing Universe: From Creation Myths to the Big Bang.* New York, 1997.

Harvey, Graham. *Indigenous Religions: A Companion.* New York, 2000.

Leeming, David Adams. *A Dictionary of Creation Myths.* New York, 1995.

Lincoln, Bruce. *Myth, Cosmos and Society: Indo-European Themes of Creation and Destruction.* Cambridge, Mass., 1986.

Long, Charles H. *Alpha: The Myths of Creation* (1963). Reprint, Chico, Calif., 1983.

Olupona, Jacob K. *Beyond Primitivism: Indigenous Religious Traditions and Modernity.* New York, 2004.

Sproul, Barbara C. *Primal Myths: Creating the World.* San Francisco, 1979.

Von Ditfurth, Hoimar. *The Origins of Life: Evolution as Creation.* San Francisco, 1982.

Native Americas
Hultkrantz, Ake. *Native Religions of North America.* San Francisco, 1987.

Jones, David M., and Brian L. Molyneaux. *The Mythology of the Americas: An Illustrated Encyclopedia of Gods, Spirits, and Sacred Places in North America, MesoAmerica, and South America.* New York, 2001.

Sullivan, Lawrence E. ed., *Native Religions and Cultures of North America: Anthpology of the Sacred.* New York, 2000.

Versluis, Arthur. *Native American Traditions.* Shaftesbury, U.K., 1994.

Australia and Indonesia
Charlesworth, Max. *Religious Business: Essays on Australian Aboriginal Spirituality.* Cambridge, U.K., 1998.

Geertz, Hildred. *The Life of a Balinese Temple: Artistry, Imagination, and History in a Peasant Village.* Honolulu, 2004.

Kipp, Rita Smith. *Indonesian Religions in Transition.* Tuscon, Ariz., 1987.

Pattel-Gray, Anne. *Aboriginal Spirituality: Past Present and Future.* Blackburn-Victoria, Australia, 1996.

Africa
Blakely, T.D., Walter E. A. van Beek, and Denis L. Thomson, eds. *Religion in Africa: Experience and Expression.* London, 1994.

Evans-Pritchard, E. E. *Nuer Religion.* Oxford, 1956.

Gyekye K. *African Cultural Values: An Introduction.* Accra, Ghana, 1996.

Mbiti, John S. *African Religions and Philosophy,* 2d ed. Oxford, 1990.

Olupona, J.K., ed. *African Traditional Religion in Contemporary Society.* New York, 1990.

Islam
Martin, Richard, Editor. *Encyclopedia of Islam and the Muslim World.* New York, 2004.

Rahman, Fazlur. *Islam.* Chicago, 1979.

Ruthven, Malise. *Islam in the World.* New York, 2000.

Judaism
DeLange, Nicholas. *An Introduction to Judaism.* Cambridge, U.K., 2000.

Epstein, Isadore. *Judaism: A Historical Presentation.* London, 1966.

Neusner, Jacob, ed. *The Blackwell Companion to Judaism.* London, 2000.

Christianity
Nystrom, Bradley Paul, and David Paul Nystrom. *The History of Christianity: An Introduction.* Boston, 2004.

Tillich, Paul. *A History of Christian Thought.* New York, 1968.

Weaver, Mary Jo, with David Bernhard Brakke and Jason Bivins. *Introduction to Christianity.* Belmont, Calif, 1998.

Hinduism
Flood, Gavin, ed. *The Blackwell Companion to Hinduism.* Malden, Mass., 2003.

King, Richard. *Indian Philosophy: An Introduction to Hindu and Buddhist Thought.* Washington, D.C., 1999.

O'Flaherty, Wendy Doniger, with Daniel Gold, David Haberman, and David Shulman, eds. and trans. *Textual Sources for the Study of Hinduism.* Chicago, 1990.

Buddhism
Harvey, Peter. *An Introduction to Buddhism: Teachings, History, and Practices.* Cambridge, U.K., 1990.

Kalupahana, David J. *A History of Buddhist Philosophy: Continuities and Discontinuities.* Honolulu, 1992.

Lamotte, Etienne. *History of Indian Buddhism: From the Origins to the Saka Era.* Translated from the French by Sara Webb-Boin, under the supervision of Jean Dantinne. Louvain-la-Neuve, France, 1988.

J. Bruce Long (1987)
Laurie Louise Patton (2005)

LIGHT AND DARKNESS are basic natural phenomena as well as symbolic or metaphorical meanings that are often equated with the pairs of Being and Non-Being, primordial chaos and world order. According to the most ancient conceptions from the early civilizations of the Middle East, light and darkness are experienced in rhythmical alternation and hence as being contingent on each other. Darkness is the mysterious, impenetrable ground and source of light; and light becomes associated with creation. It grants and is therefore a symbol for the primal conditions of life: warmth, sensuality, and intellectual and spiritual enlightenment. In the course of the history of ideas, however, another concept was developed, in which darkness is an outcome of failure within the creational process.

If light and darkness are interpreted as alternate stages relieving one another, they are viewed as complementary rather than oppositional. Stipulating one another's occurrence, both are necessary phases of the life cycle that is altogether perceived as a harmonious totality. While the passage from light to darkness is performed without further problems, the reemergence of light out of darkness is precarious. Therefore, the vanishing of light into darkness has always caused anxieties and given rise to special rites and precautions. However, even with such implications, this conceptualization of light and darkness needs to be distinguished from the other, later one, in which the predominance of light no longer means its ever-new salvation through but its final salvation from darkness. Ideas about the possibility of a total, eternal victory over and abolition of darkness come along with a worldview that has detected a fundamental corruption of and within creation. Its flaws result from the mixture of light and darkness, which happened accidentally and against the original plan. Such a concept—it may be called binary or dualistic as opposed to the original complementary concept—does not interpret light and darkness in a mutual conditionality and, accordingly, in their relativity, but as only self-identical, irreconcilable entities rather than states.

This considerable change in conceptualizing light and darkness as well as other comparable polarities (male-female, right-left, heaven-earth, day-night, sacred-profane, exogamous-endogamous, truth-falsehood, and so on) is observable from about the sixth century BCE and may be explained by the emergence of transcendental, logical thought, which characterizes the "Axial Age," according to Karl Jaspers and adherents of his cultural theory (Benjamin Schwartz, Shmuel Eisenstadt, and others).

While complementary notions of light and darkness, which can be studied, for example, in ancient Egyptian religion, always stick to imageries resulting from close observation of natural processes, the dualistic concept is largely independent from the appearances of light and darkness in the cosmos, as will be shown in the discussion of Iranian, Gnostic, and Manichaean ideas below.

HISTORY OF RELIGIONS. Many cosmologies begin their accounts of the creation with the emergence of light (or the sun or an equivalent light principle) out of a primeval darkness, and conversely many mythologies describe the end of the world as a twilight or darkness of the gods, that is, the disappearance of light in a final darkness that engulfs all. There is an obvious connection between light and the sun as the source of light, though not all gods of light are always and necessarily solar deities. Nevertheless, perhaps because of the conspicuous presence of sun, moon, and stars, these celestial bodies often appear as manifestations of the gods. There seems to be a correlation between light and the "ouranic" gods of the heavens, on the one hand, and between darkness and the "chthonic" gods of the earth and the underworld, on the other. Originally, there appears to have been no ethical valuation of the opposition between light and darkness, but since the sun above is also all-seeing, he (that is, the god connected with the sun) becomes guardian of the law, of the faithful keeping of treaties, of justice, and ultimately also of the ethically good.

Generally speaking, light serves as a symbol of life, happiness, prosperity, and, in a wider sense, of perfect being. As a symbol of life, light can also serve as a symbol of immortality. Darkness, on the other hand, is associated with chaos, death, and the underworld. However, even if this polarity appears to the modern mind as an opposition with one positive and one negative side, it must not be forgotten that in nonlogical, complementary thinking the two are not exclusive to each other. At a cosmic as well as at a social and individual level, darkness guarantees the continual existence of light by its regular renewal.

When light is personified and worshiped, it tends to become associated either with the sun or with hearth fire, or both. Solar worship was central to ancient Egyptian religion. Thus, the ancient Egyptian god Amun became identified, in due course, with the sun god Ra as Amun-Ra (whose predecessor may have been Ra-Atum). As the sun god, Amun-Ra was threatened every day to be swallowed by Apophis, the serpent monster of darkness (the night). Amenhotep IV (Akhenaton; fourteenth century BCE) even attempted—unsuccessfully—to impose a quasi-monotheistic sun cult on Egypt. After the reinstallation of Egyptian polytheism in the Ramessid era, theologians developed a new, monistic concept, according to which sun and Sun-God were only expressions of the visible side of reality, whereas the source of existence was the secret divinity shrouded in darkness. Later, the same idea became prominent in Hermeticism, the various mysticisms of the Western world (including Islam), and in Esotericism. Sun worship and symbolism also figured in Mesopotamian religion and established themselves—probably because of Asian influences—in later Roman religion, with the great Roman festival of Sol Invictus ("invincible sun") subsequently becoming the date of the Christian celebration of the Nativity.

The complementarity of light and darkness was most radically formulated and transferred into ritual life in the ancient religions of Mesoamerica. According to Mayan and Aztec belief, the continuation of the sun, light, and world order could even for a limited time only be guaranteed by sacrifice of godheads and humans. Ages of creational order, which were cyclically replaced by periods of chaos and darkness, were initiated through an archetypal act of self-sacrifice. After its sacrificial death, a mythical figure appeared in the east as the sun and established itself as the ruler of the world. In order to persist, it needed the sacrificial blood of humans. Finally, however, the sun would not be able to resist the attacks of enemy gods and the whole cosmos would perish in an apocalyptic cataclysm.

In ancient Iranian religion, the empirical, natural polarity of light and darkness is of surprisingly little importance. Attributes of light are ascribed to Ahura Mazdā, the Lord Wisdom and highest god of the sky; to Asha, the implicit order of the world; and to paradise and afterlife. Yet, the *devas,* evil spirits and enemies to Ahura Mazdā, are also of shining quality. In Zoroastrian literature it is explicitly stated that Ahura Mazdā figures as creator of both light and darkness. Thus, despite the blatantly dualistic structure of Iranian religion, a light-and-darkness dichotomy was not obtrusive in it. This might be explained by the high degree of abstraction characterizing the Zoroastrian faith in the morally good. Compared to Egyptian and even to Greek thought, Zoroastrianism made little use of natural imagery in its concept of Being as it is represented by Ahura Mazdā and of Non-Being, which is the domain of the latter's enemy, Angra Mainyu.

Light is an attribute of many divinities. As regards the religious history of the West, the eastern Mediterranean area (Egypt, Syria, Mesopotamia) seems to have been the cradle of many gods of light who gained considerable importance in the Hellenistic period and played a major role in the mystery cults of the period, although here too it is difficult to distinguish clearly between light and solar deities. Most mystery rites performed their function of mediating salvation by having the sun/light deity bring the "initiate" (*mustēs*) "from darkness unto light." Divine manifestations are usually described as epiphanies of light. In the Magical Papyri, the gods frequently are endowed with light attributes, and in the collection of writings known as the *Hermetic Corpus*, spirit and light are practically identical. In fact, as man rises to greater spiritual heights "he is turned into light" (*Corpus Hermeticum* 13). Similar motifs are frequently mentioned in the Indian Upaniṣads. Here too, Absolute Being (*brahman*) as well the mind through which spiritual knowledge is acquired, is identified as light. Accordingly, the central experience of the inner self as identical with *brahman* is depicted as a light experience.

Light symbolism in Western religions (including Islam) was decisively influenced by Greek philosophy, which gave to light a simultaneously intellectual and ethical connotation. Here again it is difficult to distinguish sharply between light and sun symbolism or to evaluate the precise extent of the influence of Syrian and Egyptian sun cults. Greek philosophy seems to have shifted the meaning of light as a primal symbol of life to one of consciousness. For Minoan religion it is still obvious that a sun cult was connected to tombs and the belief in an afterlife. For Greek philosophers, however, the sun as the "light of the world" represents mainly cosmic reason. Light also represents Wisdom since it is through her that things are apparent. A particular feature, which then had a great impact on the Western history of ideas, was the connection of the light and darkness theme with a presumed opposition between the physical and the spiritual.

Some of the pre-Socratic philosophers took the light and darkness dichotomy as a starting point for their metaphysical speculations. While Anaximander (c. 610–550 BCE) stated that becoming and decaying of all things were connected and Heraclitus (c. 500 BCE) still viewed change as the only reliable norm of the world, Parmenides of Elea (sixth–fifth century BCE) attempted to trace one stable principle behind or within the phenomenal oppositions like the one of light and darkness. The method of pursuing this aim was, however, not a mental reunification of empirical antagonisms but, on the contrary, the confirmation of their heterogeneity and their separateness. Therefore, the ultimate reality of Being, an opposite of which, according to Parmenides, does not exist, was to be sought beyond the visible world. As a mediating and encompassing principle between light and night, Parmenides set up *anankē* (fate), who could still be represented mythically by the goddess Aphrodite.

Pre-Socratic philosophy (for example, Parmenides, Pythagoras) already associated light and darkness with the light and heavy elements, respectively, and hence ultimately with spirit (soul) and matter (body). According to Plato (*Republic* 506d), the idea of the Good (which illuminates the soul) in the supersensual world corresponds with Helios (the sun) as the light of the physical world. The opposition of light and darkness is thus not so much an ethical one as a distinction of degrees of purity between the higher world of ideas and its copy, the lower world. According to some thinkers, it was the fire of the heavenly bodies that begot human souls. The ascent from a low, material, "dark" existence to a higher, spiritual, and divine level of being is expressed in terms of illumination (*photismos*)—a concept that came to play an increasingly important role in mysticism. The main connecting link between philosophy and mysticism in the Hellenistic world, especially regarding the terminology and symbolism of light, was Neoplatonism. The Neoplatonic system supposes a downward movement of light in the course of the creation process. This concept entails that the lower hemisphere, which is Earth, is heavier and darker than the upper one; matter is thus considered light in a degraded condition. Accordingly, the relationship between light and darkness is here not construed as one of necessarily alternating states and or as one of binary oppositions completely exclusive of each other; light and darkness are rather construed as different grades of the same substance.

Light symbolism spilled over from the mystery cults and the philosophical traditions to influence magic, Hermeticism, and Gnosticism. Some expressions of Hermeticism have inherited the Greek dichotomy of light and darkness, even though the Hermetic tradition is genuinely rooted in the ancient Egyptian worldview, which is free of any depreciation of the material cosmos. The devaluation of matter had a more important impact on Gnosticism. Gnostic dualism equates the opposition of light and darkness with that of spirit and matter, and hence tends to develop a hostile attitude to "this world," which is the creation of an inferior or even evil power. Salvation consists in leaving behind this lower world of darkness and rejoining the principle of light. Often, salvation is brought about by the supernal light principle (or a part of it) descending from above in order to redeem the particles of light (for example, souls) from the realm of darkness into which they have fallen and in which they are imprisoned. The idea of an inferior nature of the material, which had made its first appearance in Orphism and probably from here entered the Platonic tradition, was intensified by the mythic imagery of a fall that had not been foreseen in the original plan of the creation. This dramatization of the subsequent downward movement of the light rays or particles, which became impure only because of the distance from their source, led to an approximation of the Greek conceptualization of the light-darkness polarity to the Iranian type of glaring dualism in Gnosticism. Thus, the monism of the light, which was philosophically perceived as one substance of different qualities, could very easily turn into a dualism of two irreconcilable substances in Gnostic mythology. (It must be stressed here that this kind of light-darkness dualism is not genuinely Iranian. It resulted from a fusion of Greek speculations about light and darkness and the Zoroastrian overall dualism as the structure of the cosmos.) Gnostic texts present a wide range of interpretations of the light and darkness theme. Some of the myths are heavily dualistic, while other Gnostic treatises in a more philosophical style stress the homogeneity of light and darkness.

In Mandaeism and Manichaeism, a fundamentally dualistic structure in conceptualizing the world was prevalent, but this does not mean that light and darkness were consequently subsumed under it. According to Mandaean myths, the sun, the moon, and the seven planets are evil beings, yet the splendid appearance of the King of Light is compared to the sun. In Manichaeism, too, light symbolism was strongly emphasized, but there were also lights of the cosmos that belonged to the reign of darkness. While the sun and the moon were very important light beings and played a considerable part in the salvational processes, the stars were considered evil. This shows that the opposition between good and evil in Mandaean and Manichaean religion was expressed by the light-darkness dichotomy, but good as light and evil as darkness could be attributed to different phenomena. Particularly in Manichaeism, light and darkness became abstract qualities rather than appearances in the natural world. Similarly, there is no indication that the "King of the Darkness," who attacked the "Hemisphere of Light" and thereby initiated the Manichaean cosmogonic drama, represents the material world or any particular realm of the universe; rather, he seems to be opposed to any imaginable mode of existence. The "Father of Greatness," on the contrary, is the lord of the world as it is known and experienced by human beings, even though it is infiltrated with particles of darkness in a metaphorical sense. This observation confirms that the Manichaean kind of symbolism does not generally correlate to the appearances of light and darkness in the cosmos. Paradoxically, Manichaeism turned the strictest kind of dualism and light-darkness dichotomy ever developed in the history of religions into a positive attitude toward nature and the cosmos. It is notable in this context that the same elements, namely fire, water, and wind, occur under the reign of light as well as under the one of darkness, while only air under darkness is corrupted as smoke.

Of all the gnostic-type religions, Manichaeism emphasizes the light symbolism most. Since Manichaeism also penetrated Central Asia and even farther east, as far as China, it is not impossible that certain forms of Buddhist light symbolism were influenced by it. This must be particularly taken into consideration with certain light- and sun-related representations of the Buddha: the cosmic Buddha (Mahāvairocana) in Vajrayana Buddhism, who is equated to the sun, and Amida (or Amitābha), the Buddha of Eternal Light in Pure Land Buddhism.

Certain aspects of Manichaeism have analogies in Christianity, but the exact nature of these analogies and of the relationship between Christianity and gnosticism in general are still a matter of scholarly controversy. Surprising analogies with the gnostic systems can also be found in the medieval Jewish Qabbalah, especially in the form that it assumed in the sixteenth century.

The Hebrew Bible begins with an account of the creation of light, followed by the creation of the sun and the celestial bodies, but it has no original light or solar mythology. In due course, however, light became a symbol of divine presence and salvation: "The Lord is my light and my salvation" (Ps. 27:1); "In thy light we shall see light" (Ps. 36:10); "Let us walk in the light of the Lord" (Isa. 2:5); sun and moon will no longer be the sources of light, for "the lord shall be unto thee an everlasting light" (Isa. 60:19). The association of light and sun is preserved in many other biblical passages, especially Malachi 4:20: "The sun of righteousness shall arise."

Early Christianity inherited both the biblical and the contemporaneous Hellenistic (philosophical as well as religious) light symbolism. Christ was the *sol iustitiae* (see Mal. 4:20), and hence there was nothing incongruous about celebrating the Nativity on the date of the pagan Roman festival of the "invincible sun." According to the Gospel of John (8:12), Jesus said of himself, "I am the light of the world," and his followers would possess the "light of life." Easter is therefore celebrated with fire and light rituals. In the Roman Catholic rite, the paschal candle is carried into a pitch-dark church with the thrice-repeated exclamation "Lumen Christi." In fact, the equation of God with the Absolute and the pure light essence finds expression also in the creed where the Son (Christ) is defined as "God of God, Light of Light, very God of very God." The Logos is also described as light in the prologue to the Gospel of John. Paul's experience on the road to Damascus was a typical light experience.

The Jewish Qumran community had already divided Israel into "children of light" (to be ultimately saved) and "children of darkness" (doomed to eternal damnation)—a distinction that was subsequently taken over by Christianity. The Prince of Evil and Darkness, Satan, was originally an angel of light, and hence one of his names is Lucifer (Gr., *Phosphoros*), literally "bearer of light." The imagery is derived from Isaiah 14:12, where the king of Babylon, who in his overweening pride fell from glory to destruction, is called the morning star who fell from heaven. But the same term (*phōsphoros,* "morning star") is also applied to Christ in the Second Letter of Peter. The expectation of the advent of Christ was like "a light that shineth in a dark place until . . . the daystar arose" (2 Pet. 1:19).

Practically all religions give symbolic expression—in mythology, worship, and iconography—of their valuation of light as a symbol of blessing. Even when light and darkness are not diametrically opposed as two hostile principles but are conceived as complementary cosmic modes and creative agents (the Chinese yin and yang), there is a marked preference for light. Thus, yang is light, heaven, active, constructive, masculine, while yin is the opposite. Chinese religious history, too, has its goddesses of light as well as its sects and religious movements (including secret societies) in which light symbols play a role. There even was a women's sect—officially classified as a "heterodox sect"—called the Light of the Red Lamp, which gained some notoriety through its connections with the Boxer Rebellion around 1900.

The significance of light is also illustrated by the ritual use of lamps or candles in temples, on altars, in or near tombs, near holy images, or in processions, and by the lighting of fires on special occasions. Christmas has become a festival of light; so is the Jewish Ḥanukkah, the Hindu Dīvālī, and many other rituals, festivals, and customs in both the ancient (compare, for example, the ancient Greek torch race known as Lampadedromia or Lampadephoria) and the modern world.

Light symbolism is also conspicuous in religious iconography: saints or divine figures have a halo surrounding their head or their whole body or a flame above their head. This is particularly conspicuous in Buddhist iconography, especially in its Mahāyāna forms (for example, in many *maṇḍalas*). Amida is easily identifiable by the halo of "infinite" rays emanating from his head. Similarly, the Buddha Mahāvairocana (in Japan, Dainichi-nyorai), the "Great Illuminator," who radiates the most intense light, appears in many Tibetan *maṇḍalas* as the radiant center. For many Buddhist sects, such as the Japanese Shingon, he is the supreme reality. In Japanese Buddhist-Shintō syncretism, he was also identified with Amaterasu, the sun goddess (and chief goddess) of the Shintō pantheon. The holy city of Banaras in north India is also called Kāśī, "city of light." From the seven-armed candelabrum in the Temple in Jerusalem to the secularized ritual of a permanently burning flame at the Tomb of the Unknown Soldier, the symbolism of light has shown a power and persistence unparalleled by most other symbols.

The Qur'ān, too, has its famous "light verses." In due course, a prophetic and ultimately metaphysical doctrine of light developed. With the assimilation of Neoplatonic philosophy into Islam after the ninth century, light began to be identified with the divine light principle (that is, the intellect, according to some philosophical thinkers) emanating into this world, a process corresponding to the elevation of the human soul to the divine light. The ultimate goal of the mystic is to behold the pure light and beauty of God. Light speculations can be found among orthodox Muslim theologians, mystics, and gnostics (including those that were suspected of gnosticizing heresies).

MYSTICISM AND ESOTERICISM. Enough has now been said to indicate the special role of ideas and experiences of light (illumination, *photismos*) in mystical systems. It seems that mysticism almost automatically resorts to a terminology of light. Greek Orthodox mystical theology emphasizes the doctrine of the divine, "uncreated light" through which the mystic achieves union with God. The New Testament account of the transfiguration of Christ (Luke 9) supplied the basis for this mystical theology, and hence Mount Tabor is one of its central symbols. This doctrine, rejected as heretical by the Roman Catholic Church, exhibits some interesting analogies with the qabbalistic doctrine of the *sefirot.* Sufism, especially its Persian branch in the fourteenth century CE, unfolded an original way of speculation about mystical significances of light and darkness in their relation to the Sufic doctrine of the oneness of existence (*wahdat al-wujúd*).

While mysticism of light and illumination (cf. the technical term *via illuminativa*) is a commonplace that hardly calls for a detailed account—Buddhist meditation systems also lead through innumerable light spheres and worlds—there is one noteworthy and highly paradoxical exception. That is the doctrine of mystical darkness, variants of which can be found in many religious traditions. A comparable concept becomes already apparent as the concealment of god in the Ramessid theology during the New Kingdom of ancient Egypt (thirteenth century BCE). The idea can be interpreted as a mystical translation of the mythical night. It can also be equated to qabbalistic Ayin (Nothingness), and Indian, Chinese, and Japanese concepts of Shunyata (Emptiness). The Christian doctrine of mystical darkness appears first in the New Testament as *Kenosis. Kenosis* is mentioned in Philippians 2:6 and presumably goes back to a pre-Pauline source. It designates Christ's negation of divine power in order to take up the sufferings of humans and the whole world in his own person. The concept of mystical darkness was then taken up and elaborated in the writings of Dionysius the Areopagite (probably c. 500 CE), a pseudonymous writer whose mysticism combined Neoplatonic and Christian elements. His influence, mediated to the medieval West by John Scotus Eriugena (c. 810–after 877 CE), was strongly felt in the later Middle Ages. Philo Judaeus (c. 20 BCE–after 42 CE) had already declared that the divine splendor was so radiant as to be blinding. For Dionysius, God is so utterly unknowable, and his essence so utterly beyond our reach, that all our knowledge of him is perforce "negative." The experience that he expounds in his *Mystical Theology* is essentially an "unknowing." It is beyond human thought. It is not light but, from the point of view of human understanding, utter darkness. (This doctrine reappears in the famous fourteenth-century English mystical treatise *The Cloud of Unknowing.*) The sixteenth-century Spanish mystic John of the Cross similarly describes the path of the soul to total union with God as the ascent through two "dark nights": that of the senses (that is, loss of all discursive thought, feeling, and images) and that of the spirit. In other words, mysticism is not the enjoyment of charismatic graces, illuminations, or supernaturally infused higher knowledge. Using an Old Testament image, it is not the Pillar of Fire that went before the camp of the Children of Israel at night, but rather the Cloud of Darkness. In this tradition, we do not, however, deal with an option of darkness as opposed to light in the ordinary sense but rather with a dialectically paradoxical response to the traditional and commonplace "mysticism of light," which is here represented as totally inadequate to describe the nature of the mystical union with the utterly unknowable absolute divine transcendence. Even more thoroughly, the Persian Sufī Muhammad Gīlanī Lāhījī (died c. 1506 CE) explained the experience of divine oneness by use of a paradoxical merging of light and darkness in terms like "Black Light" (*nur-e siyāh*) or "Bright Night" (*shab-e rowshan*).

SEE ALSO Dualism; Manichaeism, overview article; Moon; Mystical Union; Nimbus; Sol Invictus; Stars; Sun; Via Negativa.

BIBLIOGRAPHY

Apart from the entries "Light and Darkness" by J. A. MacCulloch et al. in the *Encyclopaedia of Religion and Ethics,* edited by James Hastings, vol. 8 (Edinburgh, 1915), Gustav Mensching's, "Die Lichtsymbolik in der Religionsgeschichte," in *Studium Generale* 10 (1957): 422–432, and "Licht und Finsternis" by K.-W. Tröger, Bernd Janowski, and Kurt Erlemann in *Die Religion in Geschichte und Gegenwart,* 4th ed., vol. 5 (Tübingen, 2002), there are only specialized works that deal with the topic, and mostly only with light symbolism, in a certain religious tradition or even only in a certain text. Volume 18 (1965) of the German journal *Studium Generale* provides a number of separate articles on light and darkness in ancient Egyptian religion, ancient Iranian traditions, Greek poetry, and alchemy.

Further single treatments are listed below:

Aalen, Sverre. *Die Begriffe Licht und Finsterniss im Alten Testament im Spätjudentum and im Rabbinismus.* Oslo, 1951.

Bultmann, Rudolf. "Zur Geschichte der Lichtsymbolik im Altertum." *Philologus* 97 (1948): 1–36.

Cumont, Franz. *Lux perpetua* (1949). New York, 1985.

Filoramo, Giovanni. *Luce e gnosi.* Rome, 1980.

Fröbe-Kapteyn, Olga. *Alte Sonnenkulte und die Lichtsymbolik in der Gnosis und im frühen Christentum.* Zurich, 1943.

Goodenough, Erwin R. *By Light, Light: The Mystic Gospel of Hellenistic Judaism.* New Haven, 1935.

Izutsu, Toshihiko. "The Paradox of Light and Darkness in the Garden Mysteries of Shabastarī." In *Creation and the Timeless Order of Things. Essays in Islamic Mystical Philosophy,* pp. 38–65. Ashland, Ore., 1994.

Turner, Denys. *The Darkness of God. Negativity in Christian Mysticism.* Cambridge, 1995.

Wetter, G. P. *Phos.* Uppsala, 1915.

Woschitz, Karl Matthäus, Manfred Hutter, and Karl Prenner. *Das Manichäische Urdrama des Lichtes. Studien zu koptischen, mitteliranischen und arabischen Texten.* Wien, 1989.

R. J. ZWI WERBLOWSKY (1987)
JULIA IWERSEN (2005)

LĪLĀ is a Sanskrit noun meaning "sport" or "play." It has been the central term in the Hindu elaboration of the idea that God in his creating and governing of the world is moved not by need or necessity but by a free and joyous creativity that is integral to his own nature. He acts in a state of rapt absorption comparable to that of an artist possessed by his creative vision or to that of a child caught up in the delight of a game played for its own sake. The latter comparison is the basis for speaking of God's acts as *līlā,* or sport. Although the translation is the best available, the English word *sport* is a rough rendering that suggests a frivolity not necessarily implied by the word *līlā.* In the Hindu thought world in which this term arose, the description of God's acts as sport was intended to negate any notion that they are motivated, like the acts of human beings, by acquisitive desire (*kāma*) or are necessitated by the retributive impetus of the actor's previous deeds (*karman*) or by the requirements of duty. Because God forever possesses all, he has no wants and no desires. His ever-desireless acts entail no retribution. He is not the instrument of duty but duty's creator. The spontaneity and autonomy of his actions are absolute.

The word *līlā,* used in this theological sense, began to appear in Hindu religious literature in about the third or fourth century CE. Partial sources of the concept are found in earlier writings that mention, even in the Vedic age, the frolicsome nature of the gods and the ease and freedom of their acts. The attribution of joyous freedom to the one supreme being made its appearance in the Upaniṣads in reports of experiences of unity with the Divine that were expansive states of blissful release from care. It was not in the monistic systems, however, but in the great Hindu monotheisms that the notion of divine sportiveness became a major concept. Even the worshipers of Śiva—a violent and dangerous deity not easily credited with playfulness—explained the universe as formed in the gyrations of a cosmic dance in which, as Naṭāraja, or Lord of Dancers, Śiva ecstatically creates and sustains and destroys. The elaboration of the idea of *līlā* into a studied doctrine has been primarily the work of the Vaiṣṇava tradition; in particular, the cult of Kṛṣṇa as Gopāla, the young cowherd, carried the teaching of *līlā* to its most advanced development. This later Kṛṣṇaism was shaped decisively by the idea of *līlā* in almost every aspect of its religious system—in its theology, its mythology, its mysticism, and its conception of salvation.

THE THEOLOGY OF LĪLĀ. The first appearance of *līlā* as a theological term is apparently a use of the word in the *Vedānta Sūtra* of Bādarāyaṇa (third century CE?). In 2.1.33 of that work the author defends belief in a personal Creator against an objection that the God of monotheistic belief who is all and has all cannot be credited with creation, because persons create only in order to come into possession of something that they do not already have. The author replies that, even in the ordinary world, some people carry out creative acts not for the satisfaction of any wants, but merely sportively, for the sheer joy of the activity itself. Faith in a personal Creator is thus reasonable and possible.

The theological literature on *līlā* consists primarily of the commentarial writings on this passage that have been written by the founders and other recognized scholars of the various Vaiṣṇava sects. In the twelfth century, for example, Rāmānuja illustrates the meaning of *līlā* by the example of a great monarch who, though he has no unsatisfied desire, sports enthusiastically on the playing field just for the amusement of the game. The Caitanyaite commentator Baladeva compares the Creator's activity to that of a healthy man just awakened in the morning from deep sleep, who breaks into a dance simply to express his own exuberance.

Because all schools of Vedānta accept the *Vedānta Sūtra,* in some fashion they must accept also its teaching on divine sportiveness. The adherents of the illusionist school of Advaita Vedānta have been obliged, of course, to understand the sports of God to have only such reality as belongs to the personal God himself. For them, the absolute being is not in truth a person, nor in reality has any world been created, nor have any sports been performed. The teaching of *līlā* is provisional only, expressing how unenlightened persons must understand the course of the apparent world so long as they remain under the influence of the deluding cosmic ignorance (*māyā*) that creates the appearance of a world that is false. Over against this illusionist cosmology those who fully embraced the *līlā* teaching were able to maintain that the creative process is real and that the creation is not an obscuration but a manifestation of the nature of God. Indeed, some Hindus have been able to use the *līlā* doctrine to support appreciation of the world in a spirit of religious wonder and to sustain a joy in living. But the general world-weariness of medieval India did not encourage such positive applications. It was more common to use the idea of divine sportiveness to domesticate the tragedies of life by reflecting that wealth and poverty, health and sickness, and even death itself are apportioned to creatures by God in his mysterious play. The reasons for such fateful interventions are beyond human comprehension, but devotees who understand their fortunes to be the sport of God will know that it is not blind fate that controls their lot, and hence they will accept their condition as providential.

Some tension exists between the conception of God's sportiveness and the older picture presented in the *Bhagavadgītā* (3.21–25, 4.5–14) of God as acting in order to assist devotees, to maintain righteousness, and to preserve the integrity of the world. Thinkers of the school of Caitanya (1486–1533) have gone so far as to insist that God acts solely for his own sport and without thought of benefiting his creatures; creatures are in fact benefited by God's sportive acts, but only because those acts are the pleasure of a supreme being whose nature includes compassion. In other Vaiṣṇava circles it has been more common to see no difference between the two explanations of the divine motivation: God's sportive acts and his supportive acts are one because both are done without calculation of any selfish gain that might be made through them. Both are therefore desireless (*niṣkāma*) in terms of the ethical ideal of the *Bhagavadgītā,* and between God's *līlā* and his grace there is no inconsistency.

Līlā Mythology. Although such Vaiṣṇava reasonings could reconcile the old and new views of the divine motivation to each other at the level of theological doctrine, a lavish new mythology was arising in the same period that could not be reconciled so easily with the narratives of earlier forms of Kṛṣṇa worship. The theological development of the *līlā* idea was overshadowed in mass and influence by a profuse literature that expressed the new conception of the deity in myth. A diversion of attention away from the earnest Kṛṣṇa of the *Bhagavadgītā* is evident in the *Harivaṃśa Purāṇa,* composed about 300 CE. Chapters 47 to 77 of that work relate for the first time a famous set of tales about how Kṛṣṇa as a child disobeyed his parents, played tricks on his elders, spread lighthearted havoc in his cowherd village, disposed of demons with jocular nonchalance, and flirted with the cowherdesses with a daring naughtiness. About a century later these whimsical stories were retold in the fifth book of the *Viṣṇu Purāṇa,* where Kṛṣṇa's antics are called *līlās* and the whole of his earthly career is described as his *manuṣyalīlā,* or human sport (5.7.38). About the ninth century CE these pranks were fully elaborated in the tenth book of the *Bhāgavata Purāṇa,* a text that remains the foremost scripture of the family of Vaiṣṇava sects that worship Kṛṣṇa in the form of Gopāla. The stories contained in the *Bhāgavata Purāṇa* have been retold endlessly in dependent literature in the regional languages of India. The major poets of Hindi, of whom Sūrdās was the greatest, have created in the Braj dialect an especially honored literature on the sport of the child Kṛṣṇa. The attractiveness of these myths has made the worship of Gopāla Kṛṣṇa one of the most prominent forms of Hinduism throughout the past thousand years.

In the Gopāla cult's portrayal of Kṛṣṇa's childhood behavior, the flouting of Hindu moral codes was a prominent element already in the *Viṣṇu Purāṇa,* and the antinomian tendency increased steadily thereafter. The stories of the god's infancy have remained relatively innocent in spirit, but the tales of his childhood and youth soon focused particularly upon his lying, stealing, violation of sexual taboos, and other mischievous tricks. His nocturnal flirtations in the *rāsa* dance with the *gopīs*, or cowherdesses, and in particular with a *gopī* named Rādhā, became more and more explicitly sexual. In recent centuries a major stream of Bengal Vaiṣṇavism has insisted that Kṛṣṇa's amours must be construed as adulterous. At the same time the story of Kṛṣṇa's dance with the *gopīs* has become ever more important, a central and revelatory mystery of the faith. The lesson that Kṛṣṇa worshipers have drawn from this myth has been purely devotional, however: The ideal devotee must surrender the self to God with a passion as total as that of the straying Hindu wife who, love-mad, sacrifices reputation and home and security in her ruinous devotion to a paramour.

Līlā in Meditation. The myths of Kṛṣṇa's *līlās* provide the mental material for most of the religious observances of the Gopāla cults. The purpose of their characteristic practices is to preoccupy the consciousness with visionary perception of the *līlās* of Kṛṣṇa. Simple conditioning begins with participation in assemblies where the stories are presented in dance, drama, the singing of narrative poetry, or the chanting of sacred texts. Brahman actors called *rāsdhārīs* enact the sports of Kṛṣṇa in a Hindi drama called the *rāsa-līlā.* Professional declaimers called *kathakas*, *purāṇikas*, or *kathāvācakas* read out the scriptural tales and explain them publicly. Devotees move toward a more inward absorption in the *līlās* by quiet and reflective reading of mythological books. Aspiration to yet deeper Kṛṣṇa consciousness leads some further into elaborate meditational practices analogous to yoga, carried out under the spiritual direction of a sectarian teacher. Because yogic instruction has traditionally been confidential, and particularly because meditation in this tradition focuses upon matter that is shockingly erotic by usual Hindu standards, the pattern of these disciplines has remained secret to an exceptional degree. A little can be learned from manuscript works of early scholastic writers of the Bengal school, however.

One plan of meditation requires the devotee to follow in imagination the erotic interplay between Rādhā and Kṛṣṇa through all the eight periods of the traditional Hindu day, from their arising in the morning to their retiring at night. Another requires long focus of the inner imagination upon one or another mythical meeting of the divine lovers in the bowers, the meditator assuming the role of one of the female attendants (*sakhīs*) whose names are mentioned in late Vaiṣṇava legends. The hope of the meditator is to perceive his chosen *līlā* no longer merely in his imagination but in its ongoing celestial reality. By meditating on the manifested (*prakaṭa*) *līlās* that are known to all because Kṛṣṇa performed them in the light of history when he descended to earth as an *avatāra,* it is possible to develop a spiritual eye and to attain vision (*darśana*) of the same sports as they are being played eternally in Kṛṣṇa's transcendent paradise in unmanifested (*aprakaṭa*) form. It helps one's meditation to take up residence in the holy region of Mathurā because that earthly city stands directly beneath the celestial city of that name where Kṛṣṇa sports unceasingly, and is its shadow and a point of special contact between the two. Such contemplations focus upon divine acts that have the form of human sexual activities, and success in meditation involves the deliberate arousal and sublimation and use of the meditator's own erotic sensibility. However, the divine love sports that meditators sometimes see are not understood to be acts of lust (*kāma*), but acts of spiritual love (*prīti*). It is believed that they will remain forever invisible to those who cannot rise above longings that are carnal.

The religious experience that is idealized by this tradition is exemplified in Narsī Mehtā, a Kṛṣṇa devotee of sixteenth-century Gujarat. His career as a major poet sprang from a vision in which he found himself in a celestial region at night, an attendant holding a blazing torch in his hand and privileged to see the heavenly sports of Rādhā, Kṛṣṇa, and the *gopīs*. So fascinated did he become as he witnessed their eternal dance that his torch burned down through his hand, he said, without his having taken any notice. In visions such as this, intense devotion to Kṛṣṇa is produced and devotees receive assurance of divine assistance and of final liberation.

LĪLĀ IN SALVATION. The idea of Kṛṣṇa's eternal sport dominates the Gopāla worshipers' understanding of the nature of ultimate blessedness also. They do not expect a merging with the deity but participation forevermore in his celestial sports. It is a state of liberation that can be achieved by attaining on earth a state of total mental absorption in the *līlās*. The schools of Vallabha and of Caitanya hold that such raptness of attention is not a mere means of liberation but is the state of liberation itself, and say that those who truly attain this ecstatic state do not care whether they shall be taken into transcendency on death or shall be reborn forever into the world. The usual anticipation, however, is mythological in its imagery. According to the *Brahmavaivarta Purāṇa* (4.4.78ff.), the sainted visionary will rise not merely to Vaikuṇṭha, the paradise of Viṣṇu, but to its highest level, Goloka, the paradise of Kṛṣṇa. There the liberated become cowherdesses belonging to the sportive entourage of Kṛṣṇa. As delighted observers and helpers, they attend forever upon the love sports of Rādhā and Kṛṣṇa, expressing through their joyful service their love for Kṛṣṇa as the center of all existence.

Hindu critics of the notion of *līlā* have felt that it trivializes God's motives and obscures his active benevolence as savior. Rāmānuja avoids the use of the word when not obliged to explain it in his role as a commentator on a sacred text, and never mentions the mythology of the *Bhāgavata Purāṇa,* which was already widely known in his day. The Śaiva theologian Umāpati in section 19 of his *Śivap Pirakācam* declares that all five classes of divine activities recognized in the system of Śaiva Siddhānta must be understood to spring from God's gracious concern for the deliverance of souls, and that it is not permissible to say that Śiva's acts of creation, preservation, destruction, and so forth, are his sports. Nor have the chief spokesmen of modern Hinduism been attracted generally by the conception of *līlā* or by its myths. Swami Dayananda in his *Satyārthaprakāśa* denounces the sportive Kṛṣṇa and his supposed acts as immoral human fabrications. Moved by their social and civic concerns and influenced by the ethical stress in Christian theology, most modern Hindu leaders have preferred the morally earnest Kṛṣṇa of the *Bhagavadgītā* to the pleasure-seeking Gopāla. Yet a few have responded to the world-affirming implications of *līlā* as a cosmological idea and have used it in interpreting the natural and human realms. In his book *The Life Divine,* Aurobindo teaches that the Lord as a free artist creates real worlds and real beings, and sports with souls and in souls in order to lead his creatures to ever-higher levels of consciousness. Rabindranath Tagore uses the language of traditional *līlā* teaching in testifying to his intuitions that a joyful, ever-creative God is continually revealing himself in the play of natural forces and in the interactions of human beings (see his *Gitanjali,* poems 56, 59, 63, 80, and 95).

Appraisals of the *līlā* doctrine have usually recognized its contribution to theology in providing a solution to an important question in cosmology and in supporting a positive appreciation of the world and of life. On the other hand, the *līlā* idea has been condemned widely as a negative development in Hindu ethics. The judgment assumes that thinking about God arises necessarily out of moral concern and must be applied immediately to the governing of the moral life. The *līlā* literature is entirely separate, however, from the *dharma* literature that is the repository of moral guidance for Hindus. The worshipers of the young Kṛṣṇa have never understood the sports of the god to be models for their own actions. Indeed, the *Bhāgavata Purāṇa* itself in 10.33.32f. admonishes ordinary mortals never to behave as Kṛṣṇa does, not even in their minds. The Kṛṣṇa cults have been orthodox in their submission to the social patterns prescribed in the Dharmaśāstras and the folk codes. Their sportiveness has manifested itself in cultic matters that are marginal to social ethics: in the exuberance of their religious assemblies, in the easy emotionality of their pathway of salvation through devotion, in the madcap behavior that they tolerate in their saints, and in the spirit of abandon that pervades their fairs and pilgrimages and a few saturnalian festivals such as the licentious Holī. The great problem with which this religion deals is not a chaotic world's struggle for order, but the struggle for emotional freedom in a world already firmly and tryingly regulated. There is a clear correlation between the religion of sportiveness and the closed world of caste, as confirmed by the contemporaneity of their historical origins.

Fascination with Kṛṣṇa's *līlās* became strong in the fourth century CE, when the writing of mature Dharmaśāstras had become a full tide and the rules of caste were being systematically enforced for the first time by brahmanical dynasties after centuries of foreign rule. Thereafter Hindus found little meaning in the *Bhagavadgītā*'s call to save an anarchic world from disintegration; instead, they sought release from bondage, and found it in new tales about Kṛṣṇa as an irresponsible and irrepressible child. Seeking in the supernatural what was most desperately lacking in their lives, what they now cherished most in Kṛṣṇa was the spirit of sport. For many centuries, imaginative participation in the frolics of a boy-god helped them to endure the restrictions of the life of caste.

SEE ALSO Drama, article on Indian Dance and Dance Drama; Kṛṣṇa; Kṛṣṇaism; Rādhā; Vaiṣṇavism, article on Bhāgavatas.

BIBLIOGRAPHY

Banerjea, Akshay Kumar. "The Philosophy of Divine Leela." *Prabuddha Bharata* 49 (1944): 275–281, 311–316.

Banerjea, Akshay Kumar. "The Conception of the Sportive Absolute." *Prabuddha Bharata* 56 (1951): 170–173, 216–218, 258–261, 290–296. Banerjea's articles provide the beginner with a useful philosophical introduction to the concept of *līlā*.

Bäumer, Bettina. "Schöpfung als Spiel: Der Begriff Līlā im Hinduismus, seine philosophische und theologische Deutung." Ph.D. diss., Ludwig-Maximilians-Universität, Munich, 1969. This work is the sole monograph on the theological conception of *līlā*. In her conclusion, the author provides a comparison with Christian cosmogonies.

Coomaraswamy, Ananda K. "Līlā." *Journal of the American Oriental Society* 61 (1941): 98–101. An inconclusive etymological study of the word *līlā* and the associated verbal root *krīḍ-* or *krīḷ-*, "play."

Kinsley, David R. *The Divine Player: A Study of Kṛṣṇalīlā*. Delhi, 1979. A loose survey of the concept of *līlā* and of some of the Hindu narratives in which it finds expression. Includes notes on related extra-Indian materials.

New Sources

The Gods at Play: Lila in South Asia. Edited by Williams S. Sax. New York, 1995.

NORVIN HEIN (1987)
Revised Bibliography

LILITH

LILITH. In postbiblical Judaism, Lilith is a female demon who seduces men and kills unsuspecting children. Lilith (Hebrew, Lilit) became identified as Adam's first wife, created from dust to be her husband's equal. As the name of a demon, Lilit is etymologically related to the Sumerian *lil* ("wind") and not, as some once supposed, to the Hebrew *laylah* ("night"). Yet like the Sumerian wind demon and her later Babylonian counterpart, *lilitu,* a succuba who seduces men in their sleep, Lilith is active at night, seizing men and forcing them to copulate with her. In ancient Babylonian religion, the *lilitu* has a male counterpart, the *ardat lili,* who seduced women in their sleep. Both were once human, identified as women and men who died young and who after death sought the husbands and wives they had never enjoyed in life. The figure of the Babylonian demon Lamashtu, known as a child slayer, eventually converged with that of the *lilitu* demon to form the image of Lilith.

In the Hebrew Scriptures, there is only one clear reference to Lilith. *Isaiah* 34:14, describing the devastation of Edom, maintains that Lilith shall be at rest in the desert, among wild animals, screech owls, and satyrs. This reference to Lilith as demon is more fully developed in postbiblical Jewish literature, where Lilith is one of the *lilin,* a class of demons that includes both females and males. In the Babylonian Talmud Lilith is portrayed as having a woman's face, long hair ('Eruv. 100b), and wings (Nid. 24b). Her identity as demon is underscored in Bava' Batra' 73a, referring to the demon Hormiz or Ormuzd as Lilith's son, and in Shabbat 151b, where men are warned against sleeping alone lest they be seized by Lilith.

Pesahim 112b, warning men not to go out alone on Wednesday and Sabbath evenings because of the presence of "Agrat, the daughter of Mahalat," has been taken by some commentators as a further reference to Lilith. However, as Gershom Scholem maintains in his essay on Lilith in the *Encyclopaedia Judaica* (1971), the identification of Lilith with Agrat, although both are night demons, seems to have no real foundation. In a midrashic commentary on the Bible (Nm. Rab. 16.25), Lilith is portrayed as a child killer, slaying her own children when no others are available to her.

The liliths, as a class of demons, appear many times on the Aramaic incantation bowls from Babylonia (Montgomery). These are earthenware bowls (400–800 CE) inscribed with incantations to expel demons from the house or exorcise them from the body of the clients named on the bowls. The drawing of a fettered lilith with wings and wild, spiky hair often appears in the center of the bowl. The liliths appear in lists of evil spirits that refer to both the "male and female liliths," and one text denounces the liliths "who appear to human beings, to men in the likeness of women and to women in the likeness of men."

It is in the *Alphabet of Ben Sira,* an often misogynist satirical Hebrew work from between the seventh and tenth centuries CE, that Lilith appears as a fully rounded individual character for the first time. Here, we find earlier descriptions of her as night demon and child killer combined with a number of rabbinic midrashim. According to the *Alphabet of Ben Sira,* when God created Adam, he realized that it was not good for man to be alone, so he created a woman out of the earth, just as he had created Adam, and he called this woman Lilith. Immediately, Lilith and Adam began to quarrel. Insisting that they were equals, Lilith refused to lie beneath Adam, while he argued that it was proper for him, as a man, to lie on top. Uttering God's ineffable name, Lilith flew away. In response to Adam's complaints, God sent three angels—Sanvi, Sansanvi, and Semangelaf—to bring Lilith back, telling them that if she refused, one hundred of her demon children would die each day. The angels found Lilith at the Red Sea and implored her to return. She refused to do so. When informed of her impending punishment, she vowed to inflict harm on male infants up until the eighth day after birth, presumably until their circumcision, and on females up until the twelfth day. Lilith made one additional vow: if she saw an amulet bearing the name of the three angels, she would not harm the infant in any way.

Illustrations of such amulets can be found in the *Sefer Razi'el,* first printed in 1701 but largely based on the writings of El'azar of Worms, a mystic of the late twelfth and early thirteenth centuries. Describing certain mysteries supposedly revealed to Adam by the angel Razi'el, this work includes an incantation against Lilith that identifies her as *Havvah ri'shonah* (the "first Eve"), the one who seeks to harm newly born infants and women in childbirth. The iconography of the angels in *Sefer Razi'el* and the wording of the incantation against Lilith are still found in contemporary amulets printed to this day in Israel. In other medieval mystical works, Lilith becomes a figure of cosmic evil. In the thirteenth-century qabbalistic work by Rabbi Yitshaq ha-Cohen, *Treatise on the Left Emanation,* she appears for the first time as the female consort of the demon Sama'el, the chief of all the demons. This work speaks of two Liliths: Lilith the Elder, the wife of Sama'el, and Lilith the Younger, the wife of Asmodeus (Ashmed'ai), another demon king.

According to the late thirteen-century qabbalistic work the Zohar, Lilith and Sama'el emanated together from one of the divine powers, the *sefirah* of Gevurah (Strength). On the side of evil (the "other side") they correspond to the holy divine male and female. "Just as on the side of holiness so on 'the other side' there are male and female, included one with the other" (Tishby, 1989, II: 461). In the Zohar, Lilith's demonic sexuality comes to the fore. She is the seductive harlot who leads men astray, but when they turn to her, she transforms into the angel of death (Sama'el) and kills them. Lilith attempts to seduce men and use their seed to create bodies for her demonic children. The Zohar even recommends a special ritual to be performed before sexual intercourse between husband and wife in order to prevent Lilith from stealing the man's semen.

Other suggestions found in the Zohar are further developed in later qabbalistic texts. These include the view that Lilith, along with the demon Na'amah or Agrat, was one of two harlots who stood in judgment before Solomon and that the Queen of Sheba was actually Lilith, a claim first made in the Targum to *Job* 1:15. Belief in Lilith as child killer persisted in traditional European and Middle Eastern Jewish communities at least through the early twentieth century. According to Scholem (1971), protective amulets would be placed either above the bed of a woman about to give birth or on all four walls of the room in which she lay. As mentioned before, it is still possible to purchase amulets against Lilith to protect the mother and her newborn child.

The image of Lilith as it developed from antiquity through the early twentieth century represents an antitype of desired human sexuality and family life, a wild and unkempt woman whom Jewish society could not control. This image was demonic because Lilith represented everything that traditional Jews, both women and men, feared could go wrong in the arena of sexuality and childbearing: extramarital attractions and sexual intercourse, and the premature death of children.

Lilith's freedom from traditional constraints on Jewish women's lives has served, since the mid-1970s, as a model of female strength and independence for American Jewish women. A Jewish feminist magazine named *Lilith* has been published since 1976, and a number of Jewish feminist theologians, reexamining the accounts of creation in *Genesis* 1:27 *ff.,* have worked to create midrashim of their own. In one such midrash, Judith Plaskow (in Koltun, 1976) restores Lilith's independence and belief in her equality with Adam, as portrayed in the *Alphabet of Ben Sira,* and replaces the myth of Lilith's supercession by Eve with an optimistic vision of the two first rejecting, then returning to, the garden of Eden to rebuild it together. Since the mid-1970s interest in Lilith has only grown among Jewish feminists, neopagans, musicians (the Lilith Fair), poets, and other writers. *Whose Lilith?* (1998) collects many articles and poems on Lilith, with a focus on her importance for Jewish women. These reclamations of Lilith can be seen as a part of a more general awakening of interest in female images and symbols within Jewish tradition.

SEE ALSO Folk Religion, article on Folk Judaism; Women's Studies in Religion.

BIBLIOGRAPHY

A good, brief account of Lilith in the Hebrew Bible and cognate ancient Near East literature can be found in M. Hutter, "Lilith," in *Dictionary of Deities and Demons in the Bible,* edited by Karel van der Toorn, Bob Becking, and Pieter W. van der

Horst (Leiden, 1995). Lilith in the Aramaic incantation bowls is evidenced in James Montgomery, *Aramaic Incantation Texts from Nippur* (Philadelphia, 1913); Joseph Naveh and Shaul Shaked, *Amulets and Magic Bowls: Aramaic Incantations of Late Antiquity,* 2d ed. (Jerusalem, 1987); and Joseph Naveh and Shaul Shaked, *Magic Spells and Formulae* (Jerusalem, 1993). Lilith's role in the incantation bowls and rabbinic texts is discussed in Rebecca Lesses, "Exe(o)rcising Power: Women as Sorceresses, Exorcists, and Demonesses in Babylonian Jewish Society in Late Antiquity," *Journal of the American Academy of Religion* 69 (2001): 343–375. The story of Lilith in the *Alphabet of Ben Sira* can be found in Eli Yassif, *Tales of Ben Sira in the Middle Ages* (Jerusalem, 1984). There is a good English translation in David Stern and Mark J. Mirsky, eds., *Rabbinic Fantasies* (Philadelphia, 1990). Gershom Scholem published the *Treatise on the Left Emanation* in "The Kabbalah of R. Jacob and R. Isaac, the sons of R. Jacob ha-Kohen" (Hebrew; *Madda'ei ha-Yahadut* 2 [1927]: 244–264), and discusses the development of Lilith extensively in his 1971 article in the *Encyclopedia Judaica. The Wisdom of the Zohar* by Isaiah Tishby, translated by David Goldstein (Oxford, 1989) publishes translations of many of the Zoharic passages dealing with Lilith and Sama'el. Joshua Trachtenberg's *Jewish Magic and Superstition* (1939; reprint, New York, 1982) discusses the appearance of Lilith in medieval incantations. *Voices within the Ark,* edited by Howard Schwartz and Anthony Rudolph (New York, 1980), is an example of the resurgence of interest in Lilith, under various guises, in Jewish poetry and fiction. Judith Plaskow's midrash about Lilith and Eve is found in her essay "The Jewish Feminist: Conflict in Identities," in *The Jewish Woman,* edited by Elizabeth Koltun (New York, 1976). Enid Dame, Lilly Rivlin, and Henny Wenkart edited *Which Lilith? Feminist Writers Re-create the World's First Woman* (Northvale, N.J., 1998).

REBECCA M. LESSES (2005)

LIMINALITY. *Liminality,* "being on a threshold," is the condition that prevails during the inner phase of rites of passage, those rituals performed in many societies to transfer a person from one stage of life to another. Liminality is the experience of being betwixt and between. In his book *The Rites of Passage* (1909), the folklorist Arnold van Gennep first isolated and named the rites of passage that accompany changes of place, state, social position, religious calling, and age in a culture. His study mainly focused on the life crisis rituals of birth, puberty, marriage, and death. Van Gennep found that as a general rule there were three stages in the rites: separation, margin or limen, and reaggregation. The first phase detaches the ritual subjects from their old places in society; in the second, the liminal phase, the subjects pass into a cultural and spiritual realm that has few of the attributes of either the past or coming state; the last phase installs them, inwardly transformed and outwardly changed, in a new place in society. Van Gennep used the word *limen*—the Latin for "threshold"—for the middle stage, because his researches showed much door symbolism in the rites, the participants often entering the new ritual life over a threshold or entryway.

During the forty years following the publication of van Gennep's book the special stage of mid-transition was rarely examined by researchers, except in Henri Junod's exemplary study of the circumcision rituals of the Thonga of Mozambique (1912–1913). From 1951 to 1954, during anthropological studies of ritual, Victor Turner and Edith Turner participated in the rites of passage of the Lunda-Ndembu of Zambia. In 1964 Victor Turner, using his understanding of the betwixt-and-between milieu of the boys in the Ndembu circumcision lodge and of the girls in their initiation seclusion, wrote a general article, "Betwixt and Between: The Liminal Period in Rites of Passage," newly establishing the word *liminality* as the description of the midphase of the rites and employing for his examples the liminal phases from the rites of a number of different societies. His further work (Victor Turner 1969, 1974, 1982, 1986) opened up a broad view of liminality worldwide, existing in hitherto unrecognized forms; subsequently the concept was recognized in anthropology, theology, performance studies, literature, psychiatry, psychology, and education.

The liminal phase is ambiguous because it is a threshold between more or less stable phases of the social process. It has frequently been likened to death; to being in the womb; to invisibility, darkness, bisexuality, and the wilderness. The initiates are stripped of their status, removed from a social structure maintained and sanctioned by power and—ultimately—force, and leveled to a homogeneous social state through ordeal. However, in seclusion their secular powerlessness is compensated for by a sacred power, in this place that is not normal to life at all, a "no-place," at a time taken right out of normal life, a "no-time"—a realm of pure possibility that resists classification. The sacred power is the power of the weak, derived from the resurgence of nature when structural power is removed and from the experience of spiritual beings and things, inseparable from the power of nature. Much of what has been bound up by social structure is liberated, notably the sense of comradeship—*communitas*—even communion, the oneness between person and person, whereas sooner or later the subjects begin to experience more fully the wisdom traditions of their society in a visionary, unified way—traditions that are able to achieve great conjunctive power. Turner demonstrated in anthropology that this liminal period is an essential component of human experience, one that has been obscured by an erroneous equation of the "social" with the "social-structural." Liminality, then, in its manifestation is not identifiable as a social construction of reality.

THE PREINDUSTRIAL RITES OF LIMINALITY. The actual rites may vary greatly, but it is instructive to learn the main patterns recurring in the liminal phase of the numerous well-documented puberty rites of preindustrial peoples (for example, Bateson, 1958; Farrer, 1991; Junod, 1912–1913; Richards, 1956; Turner, 1967; and Walens, 1981). The general term *liminality* refers not only to the middle phase of the rite of passage but also to the period from the beginning of the separation phase through the marginal or seclusion period and until the person is back in normal life. The whole is a period of liminality.

In the first phase, separation, the novices are physically separated from the other members of the community and take the entryway into the seclusion area. In the liminal phase the elders may strip off the novices' clothing, leaving them just as simple human beings. The helpers then wash them in order to purify them from evil influences and dress them in special clothing. Then the initiates pass through an ordeal to test their spiritual or physical stamina. They may only eat certain foods and have no name, just "novice." In this period the novices are the babies of the culture, belonging to the future, or they become as animals in the wilderness, or they may be spiritually invisible or spiritually in trance and "dead." Indeed the main theme of most initiations is the death and rebirth of the novices, dying to their old life in order to move to a new life. At this time the novices and those in the lodge enjoy the spirit of *communitas,* a sense of fellowship.

The initiates live for some time in their seclusion lodge, a nonordinary place in nonordinary time. In the heart of the liminal period occur some of the greatest rites of the culture. Music and song draw the spirits near, giving an immediate sense of the unity of people and spirits. Certain objects and images help to bring the spirit to the place, or the elders make special objects that are the spirit itself. These are rites of revelation that the novices actually experience. The initiates may share in the sacred objects and become deeply aware of spirit presence. The spirits, through the elders, give the novices new names or mark their bodies in some way, making them full members of the community.

Masked figures may appear. They are the spirits of ancient times or beings half-human and half-animal; they can appear with both fearsome and comic aspects. These figures constitute "symbolic types," sometimes humorously in the form of clowns or dirty old men or women. Finally, the novices share in a communion feast, which unifies the participants in a group and with the spirit beings from beyond the mortal sphere.

At the end, during the reaggregation phase, the initiates go through rites of rebirth and return to the community as initiated members. Celebration marks the end of the ritual. Such is the power of these rituals that the physical and inner aspects working together can bring about changes of the person's consciousness and identity.

Thus the biological change of a person, whether at the exact moment of bodily change or not, becomes the occasion for a plunge into the fount of all change, which is a mystery—especially to the subject. This is very different from an ordinary change, such as changing one's supermarket when moving to a new area. The sacred objects of initiation, often having to do with ancestral beings and their present power, radiate this power and show the neophyte what all have discovered—that they too, the neophytes, belong with such an array of beings and will eventually become ancestors themselves.

It is this sense that also explains the important class of liminality that has to do with the coming of a vocation—a spiritual call—bringing the gift of healing and other gifts and arts of humanity. The same pattern holds, except that in the life pattern of the one who is called, the initiative commonly comes from a spiritual source and is not prompted by natural bodily changes. (For an example of liminal trance and the inception of the shamanic healing gift, see Friedson, 1996.)

Liminality in the Contemporary World. Liminality is even further extended in the developed and modern world. Here it refers to broad areas of life within the mainstream, on its margins, and below it. In the mainstream, the rites of passage of contemporary religions still exist. However, as most religions only claim optional memberships, the rites are not universal. Their life-crisis rites may be circumcisions, christenings, shaving as a Hindu or Buddhist, bar mitzvahs, marriages, funerals, and so forth. The time of child education is liminal in the sense of being betwixt and between infancy and adulthood, but schools have so structured education that only the playground scene and street corners after school have the character of true liminality (McLaren, 1985).

Examples of those in marginal liminality are pilgrims, monks and nuns, critics of the structure, members of the counterculture, revolutionaries, writers, poets, philosophers, and novelists—a group that shades into the world of theater, film, television, music, sports, and at the folk level, clowning, charivari, celebration, and carnival. In the twenty-first century one may include vegetarians, alternative healers, and members of a great number of new religions; even the new world of the internet has a strongly liminal character. Victor Turner identified most of the marginal genres as those practiced in leisure time in industrial societies and not within the necessary structures of earning one's living. The term he used for them was *liminoid genres,* that is, genres broken off, as it were, from the former curious features of the inner rites of passage and migrating to the margins of society, the center of which is now ruled by business, industry, and law; the marginal genres then developed independently (Turner, 1982, pp. 32–55). However, in the twenty-first century the term *liminoid* is rarely employed. The anthropologist Gananath Obeyesekere opposes the use of the term: "The restriction of the liminal to special localized arenas in complex societies makes for too artificial a distinction between preliterate and industrial cultures" (Obeyesekere, 1986, p. 821). The problem of terminology is not yet solved.

The freedom from set social structures enjoyed by marginal genres has liberated them to develop and ramify still further: they are more liminal than the rites of passage genres. They are above all creative; they are plural and tend to be fragmentary, experimental, idiosyncratic, quirky, subversive, and utopian. They are produced by identifiable individuals, sometimes using what is akin to the shamanistic gift and thus extending the faculties of the human being. Those in the genre tend to follow a calling; they may suffer from their marginality and are hard to categorize. They are often practitioners and performers, but even their more passive followers, such as the readers of their books, spectators of performances, students, or church congregations, also belong to a varying extent in the liminal, liberated, non-workaday category.

As for the liminality of the lowly, it is seen in subjugated native peoples in the early twenty-first century. They have no chance of a level playing field while the whole of modern technology is stacked against them. People of color and strangers of different race are in this category as well as the poor, outcasts, and anyone physically or mentally impaired. The most telling group is women, who are physically smaller than men and even now often are subjugated by law and custom to the other sex because structural power tends to be on the men's side. The battle of the feminists still rages. Nevertheless, a rich culture of inclusiveness has grown around those low in the structure, and they often have been assigned the symbolic function of representing humanity without status qualifications or characteristics (Turner, 1974, p. 234). This sense is that of the powers of the weak. The Universal Declaration of Human Rights showed the same ethic in 2004, and the idea of democracy is founded on the value of the simple human being seen as undifferentiated, beyond social structures and human-made distinctions.

In the last decades of the twentieth century another class of the liminal has risen to the fore out of the class of the lowly, that of bad liminality or permanent *negative liminality.* This is the state of people who fall through the cracks—the suicides and the hopeless. The group is represented by those who suffer nervous breakdowns or depression; the subjects of violence; those with post-traumatic stress disorder; those suffering from cancer, HIV, psychiatric disorders, alcoholism, and self-abuse; those who are alienated, such as the Dostoevskian figure of Raskolnikov; the socially invisible; the "disappeareds," immigrants, those with no identity or qualifications, homeless, and without health insurance, and thus often with physical impairments and therefore unemployable, constituting an unrecognized "lower caste," even in U.S. society. Then there are those in conditions of misfortune, or devastating wars, or disasters such as the nineteenth-century Irish famine. Finally, people of very great age exist, enduring circumscribed lives in assisted-living facilities, perhaps on permanent dialysis, or in hospice, facing a lonely death.

The spectacle of their suffering continually hangs before one's eyes and one does not know what to do about the problem. Some of those who have helped the sufferers have been beatified, such as Mother Theresa of Calcutta. The liminality of the negative group seems to be in other hands. Phenomena that have the power to tip the scale on these states may be the visit of a divine spirit bringing healing and salvific gifts, such as at Knock in Ireland; the coming of a prophet, such as Moses leading the Hebrews to the promised land; the spontaneous *communitas* that arises in disasters, for instance, the Dunkirk spirit; the stimulation of the mainstream that produces activists and revolutionaries, such as Mahatma Gandhi and Nelson Mandela; movements, such as Methodism in its day and liberation theology; and for the individual, conversion, as in the case of Thomas Merton, or the experience of Alcoholics Anonymous, or the near-death experience. In conclusion, liminality is the "time out" from the everyday that has become available for humans to reflect, reevaluate, comment, critique, challange, and possibly change routines and structures. They are still free to "drop out, turn on, and tune in." Liminality is pure possibility, creativity, a venue or means for personal, social, and cultural change, growth, and healing.

SEE ALSO Gennep, Arnold van; Rites of Passage; Turner, Victor.

BIBLIOGRAPHY

Daly, Robert. "Liminality and Fiction in Cooper, Hawthorne, Cather, and Fitzgerald." In *Victor Turner and the Construction of Cultural Criticism,* edited by Kathleen Ashley, pp. 70–85. Bloomington, Ind., 1990. Liminality in U.S. society as seen through the eyes of novelists.

Friedson, Steven. *Dancing Prophets: Musical Experiences in African Healing.* Chicago, 1996. The liminal spirit world of Tumbuka healers, with a detailed discussion of ritual music.

Holmes, Urban T. "Liminality and Liturgy." *Worship* 47, no. 5 (1973): 386–397. An Episcopal scholar and pastoral leader claims liminality for Christianity.

MacAloon, John, ed. *Rite, Drama, Festival, Spectacle.* Philadelphia, 1984. The liminality of charivari, clowns, diviners, demon exorcism, carnival, and the Olympic Games.

McLaren, Peter. "Classroom Symbols and the Ritual Dimensions of Schooling." *Anthropologica,* n.s., 27, nos. 1–2 (1985): 161–189. Liminality among school students.

Nichols, J. Randall. "Worship as Anti-Structure: The Contribution of Victor Turner." *Theology Today* 41, no. 4 (1985): 401–409. A Presbyterian theologian examines worship in the light of liminality.

Obeyesekere, Gananath. "Stages of the Social Drama" (review of *On the Edge of the Bush* by Victor Turner). *Times Literary Supplement* (July 25, 1986): 821. Contains a critique of the *liminoid.*

Prosise, Theodore O. "Prejudiced, Historical Witness, and Responsible: Collective Memory and Liminality in the Beit Hashoah Museum of Tolerance." *Communication Quarterly* 51, no. 1 (Summer 2003): 351 (16). The Holocaust museum at Los Angeles planned as a liminal experience.

Turnbull, Colin. "Liminality: A Synthesis of Subjective and Objective Experience." In *By Means of Performance: Intercultural Studies of Theatre and Ritual,* edited by Richard Schechner and Willa Appel, pp. 50–81. Cambridge, U.K., 1990. Liminality as the sacred itself among the Mbuti hunters of Congo.

Turner, Victor. "Betwixt and Between: The Liminal Period in Rites of Passage." In *The Proceedings of the American Ethno-*

logical Society for 1964, pp. 4–20. Seattle, 1964. Also published in *The Forest of Symbols,* by Victor Turner, pp. 93–111. Ithaca, N.Y., 1967. Turner's original statement on liminality.

Turner, Victor. *The Ritual Process: Structure and Anti-Structure.* Ithaca, N.Y., 1969. A full-scale exposition of liminality, its place in society, and its variations. Examples are taken from African peoples; from the Hindu Caitanya movement, Bauls, and Holī festival; from the Buddha, Gandhi, and Tolstoy; from Saint Francis and the Benedictine order; from Melanesian millenarianism; and from hippies and gang life.

Turner, Victor. "Passages, Margins, and Poverty: Religious Symbols of Communitas." In *Dramas, Fields, and Metaphors: Symbolic Action in Human Society,* by Victor Turner, pp. 231–271. Ithaca, N.Y., 1974. An essay on genres of liminality, including rock music.

Turner, Victor. "Liminal to Liminoid, in Play, Flow, and Ritual." In *From Ritual to Theatre: The Human Seriousness of Play,* by Victor Turner, pp. 20–60. New York, 1982. An explanation of the liminal and its continuation in the liminoid genres.

Turner, Victor. "Rokujo's Jealousy: Liminality and the Performative Genres." In *The Anthropology of Performance,* by Victor Turner, pp. 99–122. New York, 1986. The liminality of Japanese Noh theater and Lady Murasaki's *Genji.*

Van Gennep, Arnold. *The Rites of Passage* (1909). Chicago, 1960. The discovery of rites of passage.

Ethnographies illustrating the liminal phase of puberty initiations among indigenous peoples

Bateson, Gregory. *Naven: The Culture of the Iatmul People of New Guinea as Revealed through a Study of the "Naven" Ceremonial.* Stanford, Calif., 1958. Boys' and girls' initiation.

Farrer. Claire. *Living Life's Circle: Mescalero Apache Cosmovision.* Albuquerque, N.M., 1991. Girls' initiation.

Junod, Henri A. *The Life of a South African Tribe* (1912–1913), vol. 1: *Social Life,* pp. 71–99. New York, 1962. The circumcision rites of the Thonga of Mozambique.

Richards, Audrey I. *Chisungu.* London, 1956. Girls' initiation among the Bemba of Zambia.

Turner, Victor. "Mukanda: The Rite of Circumcision." In *The Forest of Symbols,* by Victor Turner, pp. 151–279. Ithaca, N.Y., 1967. Boys' initiation among the Ndembu of Zambia.

Walens, Stanley. *Feasting with Cannibals: An Essay on Kwakiutl Cosmology.* Princeton, N.J., 1981. Young men's initiation among the Kwakiutl of the northwest coast of Canada.

EDITH TURNER (2005)

LIN-CHI SEE LINJI

LINGAM SEE ICONOGRAPHY, *ARTICLE ON* HINDU ICONOGRAPHY; PHALLUS AND VAGINA; ŚIVA

LIṄGĀYATS SEE ŚAIVISM, *ARTICLE ON* VĪRAŚAIVAS

LINGUISTIC ANALYSIS SEE ANALYTIC PHILOSOPHY

LINGUISTIC THEORY SEE MÜLLER, F. MAX

LINJI (d. 867 CE), known also by his initiatory name Yixuan; Chinese Buddhist monk of the Chan school. Linji (Jpn., Rinzai) is considered the eponymous "ancestor" (founder) of the Linji sect, one of five major Chan schools. In Japan, Linji's Chan was transmitted though the Rinzai lineage, one of the principal Zen schools there.

Like most Chan monks, Linji studied the canonical teachings of Buddhism while still in his youth and eventually progressed from doctrinal to practical studies. An early source of Chan history, the *Zu tang ji,* suggests that he took particular interest in the doctrines of the Weishi (Skt., Vijñāptimātratā, or Representation Only) school. Some of the emphases in his own teaching, his concern to expose the mental nature of the actualities underlying Buddhist doctrines and the artificiality of their formulations, are reminiscent of Weishi Buddhism. In Linji's teaching, the notion of nonattachment as a means of freedom is extended to include intellectual and spiritual matters as well as emotional and material concerns. In common with many Chan teachers, he pointed out that striving for higher attainments may be no more than a disguised form of greed, a kind of agitation that in fact inhibits realization of enlightenment. Linji recommended nonseeking, in the sense of noncontrivance, contending that the spiritual noble is the one who is free from obsessions, not the theoretician or the devotee of transic exercises. In Linji's terms, the task of Chan is to be free, to be immune to psychological coercion by practices or ideas, people or circumstances; the fundamental experience he called for is what he referred to as "the true human being without status," the original, "ordinary" human being, of which all states, mundane or spiritual, are merely, in Linji's terms, "clothing." To this end he repeatedly called attention to what he called the formless light of the mind, the giver of names and definitions, which itself cannot be defined or grasped but only experienced through itself.

Linji's recorded sayings include descriptions of the teacher-student interaction, an important part of Chan activity, which outline the perceptive capacity needed in a genuine teacher, various didactic strategies, and typical barriers to understanding. This aspect of Linji's work provides valuable material for understanding processes of Chan Buddhist teaching as relational or situational rather than dogmatic.

In his own teaching, Linji was famed for his shout, which he described as a technique that might be used in a number of ways, such as to interrupt a train of thought, dislodge fixed attention, test a student by observing the reaction, draw a student into an interchange, or express the nonconceptuality of being in itself. Such was the impact of this method that it was extensively imitated, to the point that certain of Linji's heirs expressly denounced such mimetic behavior as void of true understanding. Nonetheless, "Linji's shout" became a stock expression in Chan lore, and continued to be employed ever after.

Linji's sayings contain elaborations of themes and structures used by his predecessors; several of these became standard items of later Chan teaching material. Among the most famous of Linji's formulations is his "four views," in which he sums up basic processes of Chan in terms of (1) effacing the environment while leaving the person, (2) effacing the person while leaving the environment, (3) effacing both person and environment, and (4) effacing neither person nor environment. Like other Chan devices, these views allude to actual experiences to be undergone by the practitioner in accordance with need.

Although most of Linji's twenty-odd spiritual successors are obscure and his lineage did not flourish until more than half a century after his death, he became one of the outstanding figures of tradition. The record of his sayings, *Linji lu* (T.D. no. 1958), is one of the great classics of Chan Buddhism. Excerpts from this collection appear in numerous Chan books of later times, used as illustrative stories or points for meditation. Less-well-known materials of a somewhat different tradition also appear in the tenth-century *Zu tang ji* and *Zong jing lu.*

See Also Chan.

Bibliography

Linji's recorded sayings, the *Linji lu,* have been edited by Takahashi Shinkichi as the *Rinzairoku* (Tokyo, 1970). Paul Demiéville's translation of Linji's sayings, *Entretiens de Lintsi* (Paris, 1972), is informed by the translator's own superb Sinological and Buddhological skills and contains much valuable commentarial material. Readers of English will want to consult Ruth Fuller Sasaki's *The Recorded Sayings of Ch'an Master Lin-chi Hui-chao of Chen Prefecture* (Kyoto, 1975).

Thomas Cleary (1987)

LIONS. Largest of the cat family and feared by most wild animals, the lion is almost universally known as the "king of beasts." Its physical appearance, size, strength, dignified movements, and fierceness in killing other animals have, since early times, left a deep imprint on the human psyche. Associations with the concept of royalty (i.e., power, majesty, control of others) have elevated the status of the lion as symbol; such figures as Richard the Lion-Hearted; various Catholic popes who have taken the name of Leo; the Buddha, who was known as the "Lion of the Śākya Race"; and Christ, called the "Lion of Judah," have all been identified with this animal through their imputed possession of certain heroic qualities. Sekhmet, Gilgamesh, Herakles, Samson, David, Daniel, Aeneas, and Aphrodite all share some of the "lionlike" qualities of ferocity, strength, valor, dignity, and nobility.

In astrology, such connotations of royalty were taken a step further: The lion was equated with the solar principle, which is often identified as the illumination of consciousness. The constellation of Leo was assigned the sun as its ruler, and the zodiacal sign of Leo appearing during the hottest time of the year (July–August). This relationship between the sun and Leo is central to an understanding of the major role played by the solar principle in this complex symbolism.

In early Western mythology, sun/lion attributes were identified as powerful cosmic forces, eventually replacing the moon/bull themes that had dominated earlier myths. In Sumer and Crete, the lion was associated with the blazing sun, which slays the moon and parches vegetation. In Egyptian art and mythology, representations of lions were frequently stationed at the end of tunnels and placed at palace doors and tombs to protect against evil spirits. Sekhmet appears as a lion-headed woman holding a sun disk. She was known as a war goddess and became associated with the Temple of Mut during the reign of Amunhotep II (1450–1425 BCE). In his study *The Great Mother* (New York, 1963), Erich Neumann sees Sekhmet as a symbol of fire—the devouring, negative aspect of the solar eye that burns and judges.

In the Hebrew scriptures (Old Testament), the lion appears as a symbol of strength and power and an object of fear intended as a catalyst in humanity's relationship to God. The allusion in *Judges* 14:18—"What is stronger than a lion?"—and the story in *Daniel* 6 of the prophet who was sent into the lion's den as a test of his faith in God exemplify the awe-inspired associations of the lion with God's power to judge humankind.

In Christian iconography Mark the evangelist is depicted as a winged lion, perhaps because the first chapter of the *Gospel of Mark* refers to "the voice of one crying in the wilderness" (*Mk.* 1:3), a voice that reputedly resembled a lion's roar. The lion is also symbolic of Christ's royal dignity. The *Book of Revelation* contains a reference to the lion as symbolic of Christ, particularly his ability to conquer evil and overcome darkness: "Weep not, the Lion of Judah, the Root of David, has conquered" (*Rv.* 5:5). The lion also came to symbolize resurrection. According to popular legend, lion cubs, when born in litters of three, were stillborn; they were brought back to life by their father, who after mourning for three days, revived them with his breath. Similarly, Jesus, three days after his death, was resurrected by God the Father.

Royal and superhuman qualities are also reflected in the portrayal of the Hindu Great Mother goddess, Śakti, who rides upon a lion. In one of Viṣṇu's many incarnations, he manifests himself in the form of Narasimha, the "man-lion," to defeat the demon Hiraṇyakaśipu. Numerous references in the *Bhagavadgītā* demonstrate the importance of the lion as a symbol. In battle scenes, Bharata, chief of warriors, is compared to Indra and described as an "invincible lion of a man."

Well-known representations of the lion in Indian Buddhist art include the Aśoka pillar, capped by a four-faced lion, and the Sarnāth pillar, crowned by a lion upholding a great wheel or disk indicative of the solar principle. In Tantric Buddhist art, the bodhisattvas Avalokiteśvara and Mañjusrī are seated on lions, and the fierce goddess Siṃhamukha is depicted as having the head of a lioness. The stylized posture called the Buddha Entering *Nirvāṇa* is also known as the Lion Posture and forms part of the ritual for disciples being initiated into certain ceremonies.

In addition to its function as a representation of the solar principle, the lion symbol has also been variously used to depict contemplation and the solitary life. These qualities are best illustrated in the lives of certain Christian saints, especially Euphemia, Ignatius, Jerome, Paul the Hermit, and Mary of Egypt.

Rebirth motifs have also focused on the lion. In the Mithraic cult, the lion-headed god Aion (Deus Leontocephalus) is associated with time and the shedding of light so that rebirth may ensue. C. G. Jung regarded the lion, as discussed in alchemical literature, as a "synonym for mercurius . . . or a stage in transformation." "The fiery lion," he concludes, "is intended to express passionate emotionality that precedes recognition of unconscious contents."

According to Heinrich Zimmer, the insatiable qualities of the lion as devourer are demonstrated in Śiva's creation of a lion-headed monster. The *Book of Job* (4:10) also notes the destructive, fear-inspiring characteristics of the lion in epitomizing its roar as the "voice of the fierce."

BIBLIOGRAPHY

Bleek, W. H. I., and L. C. Lloyd, eds. *Specimens of Bushman Folklore* (1911). Reprint, Cape Town, 1968.

Goodenough, Erwin R. "The Lion and Other Felines." In his *Jewish Symbols in the Greco-Roman Period,* vol. 7, *Pagan Symbols in Judaism,* pp. 29–86. New York, 1958.

Gray, Louis H., et al., eds. *The Mythology of All Races.* 13 vols. Boston, 1916–1932. Consult the index, s.v. *Lions.*

Gubernatis, Angelo de. "The Lion, the Tiger, the Leopard, the Panther, and the Chameleon." In his *Zoological Mythology, or The Legends of Animals,* vol. 2, pp. 153–161. London, 1872.

Thompson, Stith. *Motif-Index of Folk Literature.* 2d ed., rev. & enl. 6 vols. Bloomington, Ind., 1955–1958. Consult the index, s.v. *Lions.*

New Sources

Stith, D. Matthew. "Whose Lion Is It, Anyway: The Identity of the Lion in *Amos* 3-12." *Koinonia* 11 (Spring 1999): 103–118.

KATHRYN HUTTON (1987)
Revised Bibliography

LI SHAO-CHÜN SEE LI SHAOJUN

LI SHAOJUN

LI SHAOJUN (second century BCE), magician and alchemist at the court of the Chinese emperor Han Wudi (140–87 BCE). According to a contemporary history, the *Shi ji,* Li, like many earlier magicians, first gained prominence in the northeastern coastal area of China, present-day Shandong. There he won a reputation among the nobility for his magical remedies and especially for warding off old age. Though he never explicitly claimed to be more than seventy himself, he let it be known that he had witnessed events decades or even centuries earlier than would have been possible for a septuagenarian. In 133 BCE Li attracted the attention of the emperor himself. He recommended that Wudi should worship the God of the Stove (Zaojun) as a preliminary to transforming cinnabar into gold; this gold was then to be used to make eating utensils that would confer on the food served from them longevity-producing powers. Eating these foods was in turn a precondition for sighting the immortal beings of the magic isle of Penglai, off the Shandong coast. Only then would Wudi's performance of the imperial *feng* and *shan* sacrifices on the sacred Mount Tai win immortality for himself as well. Li claimed that he had already visited Penglai and there had met the immortal Master Anqi.

Although Li's career at court was cut short by his death before the emperor had succeeded in encountering immortals himself, Wudi continued to send out expeditions in search of Master Anqi, on the assumption that Li had in fact not died but had himself been transformed into an immortal. A legend (attested in the fourth century CE) claims that before Li's death, the emperor dreamed that an emissary riding on a dragon flew down and announced that Li had been summoned by the god Taiyi. Some time after Li's death, Wudi had his coffin opened and found in it only his gown and hat. According to another account, Li came to court only in order to acquire for his own use the ingredients for an elixir of immortality too expensive for an impoverished private citizen. The emperor's well-attested concern with the supernatural inspired further legends during the period of disunion that followed the fall of the Han in 220 CE. These elaborated on Li's career in yet greater detail. In some he is confused with the necromancer Shaoweng, a later thaumaturge at Wudi's court.

To modern scholars Li remains a significant figure as the first recorded alchemist in Chinese history, the first devotee of the pursuit of immortality who was said to have feigned death, and the first of many known to have worshiped the God of the Stove. The *Shi ji* account also states that Li practiced the avoidance of cereal foods, a discipline that would figure prominently in later ages as a means of achieving longevity or even immortality. Later hagiography is probably correct, however, in depicting him as but one among many magicians of his day with similar preoccupations.

SEE ALSO Alchemy, article on Chinese Alchemy.

BIBLIOGRAPHY

The *Shi ji* account of Li Shaojun's activities is translated in volume 2 of Burton Watson's *Records of the Grand Historian of China* (New York, 1963), pp. 38–39. For a translation of some early legends, see James R. Ware's *Alchemy, Medicine, and Religion in the China of A.D. 320: The Nei P'ien of Ko Hung* (Cambridge, Mass., 1967), p. 47. A modern assessment of Li Shaojun is Holmes Welch's *Taoism: The Parting of the Way,* rev. ed. (Boston, 1965), pp. 99–102.

New Sources

Strickmann, Michel. *Chinese Magical Medicine.* Edited by Bernard Faure. Stanford, Calif., 2002.

T. H. BARRETT (1987)
Revised Bibliography

LITERATURE

This entry consists of the following articles:

LITERATURE: LITERATURE AND RELIGION

The most apparent and apposite justification for including literary materials in the study of religion is the historical one. What is most obvious, however, is often overlooked. In virtually every high-cultural system, be it the Indic, the Islamic, the Sino-Japanese, or the Judeo-Christian, the literary tradition has, though in vastly different forms and guises, developed in intimate—indeed, often intertwining—relation to religious thought, practice, institution, and symbolism. Without paying due heed to Greek myth and thought, to Hebrew saga and wisdom, and to Christian symbolism and piety, the twenty-five-hundred-year "drama of European literature," as German scholar Erich Auerbach calls it, simply cannot be understood. Conversely, our knowledge of these three religious traditions, of their self-expression and cultural impact, would be grossly truncated without specific consideration of their literary legacy in both canonical and extracanonical writings. In a similar way, Daoist rituals, Buddhist dogmas, and Confucian ethics joined, in imperial China, to shape and sustain the classic forms of Chinese lyric poetry, drama, and prose fiction. The itinerant Buddhist priest and his exorcistic exploits in medieval Japan have provided numerous plots for Nō drama, while subtle debates on the buddhahood of trees and plants (*somoku jobutsu*) underlie many of the exquisite *waka* of Saigyo, the twelfth-century poet. In Hinduism, Judaism, Christianity, and several major divisions of Buddhism, sacred and secular hermeneutics have developed, at various periods, in a parallel or mutually influential manner. To ignore this interrelatedness of holy and profane texts and the interdependence of their interpretive sciences is to distort large segments of the world's literary and religious history.

THE TESTIMONY OF LITERATURE. Scholars have frequently suggested that certain genres of literature, notably poetry and drama, may have arisen directly from religious rituals. While such a view may not be applicable to all forms of literature, the Romanian-born American religious scholar Mircea Eliade determined that the origin of some types of epic is traceable to the practice of shamanism. One of the most important and conspicuous features of literature's relation to religion is thus that of affirmation, in the sense that literature—both oral and written—functions to preserve and transmit religious ideas and actions. Witness the detailed description of Sibylline prophecy in the Roman poet Virgil's *Aeneid* (6.77–102) or haruspicy (foretelling the future) in the Roman dramatist Seneca's *Oedipus* (303ff.). Sometimes in a particular culture, as in the case of ancient India, literature may be the principal record of a religious tradition.

German scholar Albin Lesky noted in *A History of Greek Literature* (1966) that the "relation between gods and men is central in the world of Homer" to an even greater extent, Lesky's observation would describe a vast amount of ancient Near Eastern and Indian literature. Dubbed "une initiation manquée" by Eliade in *Histoire des croyances et des idées religieuses* (1976), the *Epic of Gilgamesh,* in its Sumerian and Old Babylonian versions, is a classic example of religious materials commingling with entertainment and adventure, the accepted hallmark of secular literature. Although its action is concerned with the ostensibly human quest for knowledge and escape from mortality, and though there is no firm evidence that the poem was ever recited as part of religious ritual (as was *Enuma elish,* the Babylonian poem of creation), *Gilgamesh* itself nonetheless provides its readers with a full and intricate view of Mesopotamian cosmology and theogony. As the story of Gilgamesh and Enkidu unfolds through its several extant episodes—the siege of a city, a forest journey, the routing of a fickle goddess, the lamented death of a tutelary companion—the epic simultaneously describes the character and activity of a host of deities. The vast pantheon and the important role these deities play in the poem reveal important conceptions of the divine in this ancient civilization. Moreover, the story of the Deluge and vivid accounts of the underworld have, understandably, elicited illuminating comparison with Hebraic notions of creation and eschatology.

To students of the Indian tradition, it is entirely appropriate, indeed even commonplace, to assert that religion provides both form and substance for virtually all of its classical literary culture. So indivisible are the two phenomena that in *The Literatures of India: An Introduction* Edward Dimock and his colleagues write that "until relatively modern times in India—meaning by India the Indo-Pakistan subcontinent—it is sometimes difficult to distinguish literature from religious documentation. This is not because there has been an imposition of a system of religious values on the society; it is rather because religion in India is so interwoven with every facet of life, including many forms of literature, that it becomes indistinguishable" (1974). The truth of such a sweeping declaration is to be found first and foremost in the exalted doctrine of the spoken word in Indian antiquity, in every sense a potent equal to the Hebraic *davar* or the Johannine *logos.* This view holds that literary speech, not that of home or court but a way of speaking that is deliberately cultivated, is virtually identical with divinity, "the Goddess herself, the first utterance of Prajapati, Lord of Creation, and herself coterminous with creation" (Dimock). Literary speech is the language enshrined in the Vedas, four collections of hymns with origins dating to the second millennium BCE. Although these hymns are themselves magnificent and majestic ruminations on humankind's place in the cosmos and our relation to our fellow creatures, and on the great questions of life and death, it is the language itself that was supremely revered long before the texts were transcribed. It is as if the serene sublimity of the text, called *sruti* ("revelation" or "that which one has sacramentally heard"), demands of its earthly celebrants a method of transmission that would defy the corrosive power of time. To the long line of priests entrusted with this awesome responsibility, this concept means the obsessive concern for letter- and accent-perfect recitation of these sacred hymns and sacrificial incantations. This profound respect for the word not unexpectedly gave rise also to a science of linguistic analysis, in which detailed etymological investigation complements the exhaustive, minute dissections of words and their linguistic components. The Sanskrit grammar of Pāṇini (fl. around 400 BCE), comparable in effect to the minister Li Si's codification of the Chinese radical system (c. 213 BCE) and Xushen's compilation of the first great dictionary, *Shuowen Jiezi* (c. 121), exemplified this science and standardized Sanskrit as a national literary language.

That language, of course, is also the mother tongue of many of India's major literary monuments. As the texts of the Vedas have led to the development of philosophical speculations later embodied in the Aranyakas and the Upaniṣads, so the literature in Sanskrit, as defined according to Pāṇini's grammar, encompasses the two monumental epics, the *Mahābhārata* (compiled between 500 BCE and 400 CE) and the *Rāmāyaṇa,* authored by the poet Valmiki in the first century. The length of the former is unique in world literature; it is a one-hundred-thousand-line poem about the protracted conflict between two rival brothers, Dhrtarastra and Pandu, and their descendents, the Kauravas and the Pandavas. Sometimes called "the fifth Veda," it is also a massive compendium of mythologies, folk tales, discourses, and dogmas (the *Bhagavadgītā* is an insertion in the sixth book of the poem) that epitomizes what scholar Northrop Frye has termed "the encyclopedic form."

Unlike its companion, the *Rāmāyaṇa* is a shorter work with a more unified perspective, a romantic tale in which the hero, Rāma, assisted by a host of magical monkeys led by Hanuman, their simian leader, routs the god Ravana, abductor of Rāma's wife. Similar to the compendious nature of the two epics are the Purāṇas, a repository of "stories and tales and sayings that document the thoughts, the religious attitudes, and the perceptions of self and world of the Indian peoples" (Dimock). The first century CE, which saw the *Rāmāyaṇa*'s composition, also witnessed the birth of the *kavya* style of writing, the poetic expressions of which include both the longer narrative form (the *mahakavya*) and the short lyric (the *subhasita*).

Sanskrit is just one of the major linguistic and literary currents in the history of India. Other significant tributaries which must be mentioned include the Dravidian literatures, of which the four primary languages are Tamil, Telugu, Kannada, and Malayalam, each having its own forms and conventions and its own epic, lyric, and narrative works. There are also rich and varied specimens of Hindi and Bengali religious lyric, and for students of Buddhism, Pali and Prakrit literatures constitute the indispensable vehicle for both canonical and extracanonical writings. Though the scholar of Indian religions, like all scholars of religions, must also study art and architecture, rites and institutions, icons and cults, social structures and cultural patterns, the length and breadth of that nation's literary history offers a magnificent panoply of virtually all the salient themes of religion: cosmology and eschatology, theogony and theomachy, *dharma* and *karma,* sin and redemption, pollution and purification, fertility and immortality, initiation and apotheosis, austerity and piety, and the thousand faces of the divine. In *From Myth to Fiction: The Saga of Hadingus* (1973), the French scholar Georges Dumézil demonstrates in his studies the inextricable link between the gods and heroes in an epic like the *Mahābhārata.* The five Pandava heroes, as well as countless others, are bonded to the mythic by divine parentage. These heroes replicate on earth the tripartite function of their parents: sovereignty, force, and fecundity. Moreover, whole mythological scenarios have been "transposed," according to Dumézil, onto the human level to undergird the characters and their actions in the epic. The eschatological conflict at the end of the world becomes the great battle of the *Mahābhārata* and numerous other Indo-European epics. The ancient opposition between the Sun and the Storm God in the Vedas is transplanted in the famous duel between Karna (son of the Sun) and Arjuna (son of Indra). To understand this aspect of the epic characters and their exploits is therefore to recognize "an entire archaic mythology," displaced but nonetheless intact. For this reason also, Dumézil can claim that what we know of the formation of such epics is equivalent "to the same thing in many societies, the formation of 'the history of origins'" (*Du mythe aux roman,* 1970).

India is not the only culture wherein a developed body of literary texts serves as a fundamental datum for the scholar of religion. In a well-known passage, the Greek historian Herodotos has observed that "Homer and Hesiod are the poets who composed our theogonies and described the gods for us, giving them all their appropriate titles, offices, and powers" (*Histories* 2.15). This claim is not in dispute, though the picture drawn by these two poets must be supplemented by the Homeric *Hymns* and the works of Stesichorus, Pindar, and the tragedians.

Theogony, a work attributed to Hesiod and composed soon after 700 BCE, contains meticulous descriptions of the underworld. This feature indicates the Greeks' deep interest in the condition and physical locale of the departed; moreover, the thematic resonance of the subject would, through Book Eleven of the Odyssey, spread beyond Hellenic culture to touch such subsequent Western poets as Vergil and Dante. As befits its name, however, *Theogony* is centrally concerned with the processes of divine emergence, differentiation, and hierarchy. Since it purports to trace the successive stages by which Zeus (a sky and storm god of unambiguously Indo-European origin) attained his unchallenged supremacy, the poem devotes greater attention to those immediately related to this deity and his dynastic struggles (Kronos, Hekate, Prometheus, and a motley crew of monsters and giants) than to other prominent members of the Olympian circle of Twelve Gods. While the earlier portion of the work focuses on cosmogonic development in which Ouranos and Gaia, sky and earth, were first enveloped and then separated by Chaos, the latter part chronicles among other events the series of Zeus's marriages—to Metis, Themis, Eurynome, Mnemosyne, and Hera. The significance of these multiple unions and erotic adventures is discernibly both religious (hierogamy) and political. Eliade notes, "By taking to himself the local, pre-Hellenic goddesses, worshiped since time immemorial, Zeus replaces them and, in so doing, begins the process of symbiosis and unification which gives to Greek religion its specific character" (*Histoire,* vol. 1, 1976). This portrait of Zeus's growth and triumph has its literary counterpart in the depiction of the central heroes of the *Iliad* and *Odyssey,* who are also transformed from local cultic figures to the Panhellenic heroes of immortal songs.

The Homeric poems offer possibly the earliest and certainly the fullest account of the gods after they have achieved their permanent stations and functions. Throughout the two epics, the presence is felt not only of Zeus but also of martial and tutelary deities like Athena, Hera, Apollo, and Poseidon and of gods with particular functions like Hermes and Hephaestus. The critical roles such deities assume, as well as their unpredictable behavior, confer on the relation between gods and men its characteristic antinomies: distance and nearness, kindness and cruelty, justice and self-will.

Of the heroes of Greece, Herodotos has said that they "have no place in the religion of Egypt," implying that the worship of noteworthy dead men and women, real or imaginary, is peculiar to Hellenic culture. In fact, however, because these sorts of individuals do populate other Indo-European literatures, their presence in Homer sheds an odd, distinguishing light on these poems as both literary masterpieces and religious documents. The fact that they are local cultic figures celebrated by a Panhellenic epic tradition means that the central heroes "cannot have an overtly religious dimension in the narrative," according to Gregory Nagy in *The Best of the Acheans* (1979). On the other hand, it is not the near-divinity of the Greek heroes—their cultic background, their fully or semidivine parentage, or their elicitation of subsequent speculation on how virtuous humans can become gods—that makes them impressive. It is, rather, says author Paolo Vivante in *The Homeric Imagination* (1970), the "disconcerting ambiguity" of their humanity—"to be born of gods, and yet to be human"—that sets apart figures like Achilles and Prometheus (in Greek dramatist Aeschylus's trilogy) and endows them with problematic magnitude.

The Homeric poems are famous for their portrayals of the deities in the image of human virtues and vices, of precipitous actions and petulant emotions. These anthropomorphic features, however, cannot obscure the one profound feeling pervading all classical Greek literatures: that between gods and men a great gulf exists. Whereas the blessed Olympians are immortal, humans are miserable, short-lived creatures who may, in the words of Apollo, "glow like leaves with life as they eat the fruits of the earth and then waste away into nothing" (*Iliad* 21.463).

Only against this background of life's brevity and human insignificance can the strivings of heroic virtue be seen in their greatest intensity and special poignancy. Only in the light of the constant injunction against excess and aspiration to divinity, that one should not forget one's mortality, can the heroic epithet "godlike" attain its fullest ironic impact. In Homer and in the tragedians, the gods are free to uphold or to dispose, to confirm or to deceive, to enable or to destroy. They may even be tied to particular individuals (Apollo and Hector, Athena and Odysseus) by means of an affinity that is both natural and ideal; yet at no point in this divine-human encounter are the gods to be trusted. "The gods have made us suffer," declares Penelope to her husband Odysseus at their long-awaited reunion, "for they are jealous to think that we two, always together, should enjoy our youth and arrive at the threshold of old age" (*Odyssey* 23.210-212). The pathos of this utterance notwithstanding, the mood of this epic is not one of bitter regret for what fulfillment life might have brought had the divine powers been more benign. The *Odyssey* is, rather, a celebration of the exercise of human intelligence, resourcefulness, courage, and loyalty in the presence of overwhelming odds, as is the *Iliad* also, specifically when depicting Hector's farewell and departure for battle, or Priam's solitary confrontation of Achilles. In *After Babel* (1975), George Steiner writes, "The totality of Homer, the capacity of the Iliad and Odyssey to serve as repertoire for most of the principal postures of Western consciousness—we are petulant as Achilles and old as Nestor, our homecomings are those of Odysseus."

To speak of the gods' jealousy and self-will is to confront the character of their morality, already a problem disturbingly felt in the Homeric poems but reserved for the keenest scrutiny by the tragic dramatists. The fundamental issue is whether human suffering is an affair of crime and punishment, as when Paris in his sin brought down divine wrath (*nemesis*) upon his city (*Iliad* 13.623), or whether suffering is the result of capricious interference by the gods (often referred to as *atē*).

Tragedy's enduring bequest to Western civilization, and its first paradox, is the arresting but troubling spectacle of the failure of an extraordinary individual. Men and women like Ajax, Philoctetes, Oedipus, Antigone, and Medea, because of their exalted station in life and nobility of character, should in all likelihood enjoy success. Tragedy, however, disabuses us of that expectation by showing us that, as the classicist James Redfield puts it in *Nature and Culture in the "Iliad"* (1975), "virtue is insufficient to happiness." Its second paradox stems from the realization that such a spectacle can be intensely pleasing. Aristotle's *Poetics,* attempting to explain both these phenomena, concentrates on the ideal properties of tragedy's internal structure and its designed effect on the audience. Many modern interpreters believe that catharsis, whatever its precise meaning, represents the key to the Aristotelian understanding of tragic pleasure. The aesthetic appeal of tragedy lies in its capacity to neutralize or purge the tragic emotions of pity and fear aroused by the incidents in the plot, much as the mimetic medium itself delights the audience by working to remove the repugnance caused by certain natural objects (*Poetics* 1448b). The realization of tragedy's aesthetic power, however, hinges on the proper resolution of the first paradox. Hence Aristotle highlights the concept of *hamartia:* an good but not perfect person fails, not out of his or her own vice or crime, but through error or ignorance.

Such a formulation clearly reflects the philosopher's perception of the necessarily unequal balance between culpability and consequence. The protagonist must not be wholly innocent or wholly wicked, for his suffering should neither revolt nor exhilarate. Only undeserved suffering or the kind that is disproportionate to one's offense can arouse the requisite tragic emotion of pity (cf. Aristotle, *Rhetoric* 1386b). The audience's cognitive and emotive response thus depends on its accurate assessment of the hero's situation, which in turn depends on how a drama unravels the causes of faulty knowledge or ignorance of circumstance that can initiate a disastrous sequence of action. Although Aristotle's explanation stresses human motivation and action, the literary texts themselves are more ambiguous, for they frequently point to the complementary image of divine interference as the ultimate cause of evil in human existence.

Whereas *atē* in Homeric religion invariably implies the awful delusion instigated by capricious deities, writers such as Hesiod, Solon, Theognis, and Pindar tend to see it also as a form of punishment for human arrogance and violence. Both strands of emphasis converge in the theology of the dramatists. In Aeschylus's *The Persians,* for example, Xerxes is both victimized by a demon, which exacerbates his actions, and guilty of hubris, for which he is further afflicted by delusion. In the *Oresteia,* Zeus is extolled as all-seeing, all-powerful, the cause of all, and the bearer of justice. Against such a high view of the godhead, nonetheless, there is at the same time the discordant and jarring emphasis, notably in *Prometheus Bound,* on Zeus as a cruel and truculent despot, one who is hardhearted (160) and is not open to reason or entreaty (184–185). The string of testimonies on divine malevolence extends even further in the plays of Sophocles and Euripides. Perhaps the extreme expression of the god who blinds and dooms is to be found in the latter's *Heracles* when Lyssa, at Hera's command, appears in palpable form to madden the pious hero, who kills his wife and children, mistaking them for the sons of Eurystheus.

Even in the dramas which make no use of such sensational devices as the *deus ex machina,* in *Hamartia: Tragic Error in the "Poetics" of Aristotle and in Greek Tragedy* (1969), Jan Bremmer notes that there is a constant depiction of "an arbitrary and malicious interference of the gods with human action, causing infatuation in man and resulting in disaster." In the language of the dramatists, *atē* has consequently been interpreted by contemporary scholars as the counterbalance to Aristotle's concept of *hamartia.* Though it neither exculpates the guilty nor exempts the person from accountability, *atē* helps the reader think the unthinkable. The momentous error leading to disaster cannot be "explained" fully by human irrationality, excess of passion, or finitude of knowledge alone. "When adverse circumstance seems to give evidence of a hidden pattern hostile to man," as Redfield notes, the dramatists invariably invoke the deed of the god who strikes for producing the ironic perversion of purposive action (including Oedipus's desperate moves to save his city and Phaedra's tactics under the influence of Aphrodite). This aspect of tragedy is what shocks Plato, for its explicit formulation, as the French philosopher Paul Ricoeur succinctly points out in *Symbolism of Evil* (1967), "would mean self-destruction for the religious consciousness." Therefore, the notion of evil's divine origin cannot be suggested or made explicit in reflective wisdom, cultic worship, or the reasoned discourse of formal theology. It can come into thought only through the concrete, albeit circuitous, medium of art. The figure of the wicked god is not, however, an isolated cultural aberration of ancient Greece; the historian of religion Wendy Doniger O'Flaherty notes in *The Origins of Evil in Hindu Mythology* (1976) that the Indian tradition also embodies many paths of theodicy and antitheodicy. The literary data that enshrine tragic theology, scandalous though its implications may be, will therefore always be pertinent to the study of certain types of religious phenomena—from primitive sacrifices to the modern anomaly of a Jonestown massacre.

If Greek religion has had lasting impact on major genres of classical literature, the effect of the Christian religion on Western literary tradition is even more pronounced and far-reaching. In the incisive observation by author E. R. Curtius in *European Literature and the Latin Middle Ages* (1953), "It was through Christianity that the book received its highest consecration. Christianity was a religion of the Holy Book.

Christ is the only god whom antique art represents with a book-scroll. Not only at its first appearance but also throughout its entire early period, Christianity kept producing new sacred writings—documents of the faith such as gospels, letters of apostles, apocalypses; acts of martyrs; lives of saints; liturgical books." There is, however, one crucial difference between Classical Greek literature and Christian writing. Whereas the former is largely reflective of a religious ethos peculiar to one culture, the latter is by no means the unique product of one solitary community. Even the language and form of Christian canonical writings bear the imprint of antecedent religious milieus, notably the Jewish and the Greco-Roman. In his zeal to defend Christian particularism, the second-century apologist Tertullian once posed the famous question "What has Athens to do with Jerusalem?" In this rhetorical question, however, he failed to remember that Jerusalem as a sacred city and a symbol of faith was not solely a Christian notion. Throughout its long history, Christianity and its environing culture have always developed in a dialectical fashion of discreteness and syncretism, invention and adaptation, disjunction and harmony.

Such a process is apparent at the outset of Christian literary history, in the twenty-seven documents that make up the New Testament. Virtually all four major literary types found in the canon—gospel, acts, letters, and apocalypse—possess the paradoxical features of distinctiveness and newness in utterance on the one hand and affinity and alliance with local literary cultures on the other. In its formal totality, the gospel may be regarded as a novel genre created by the early Christian community, since its synthetic amalgamation of narrative, biography, history, dialogue, and sermonic materials defies easy classification. When analyzed in the light of historical and form criticism, however, many of the gospel's smaller, constitutive units are demonstrably comparable to other verbal forms and expressions found in the religious and philosophical movements of the Hellenistic world. There are, for example, elements of the biographical apothegm, which chronicles the life of a sage climaxing in pregnant sayings or dramatic dialogues; and there are tales of the miracle worker or healing hero common to Mediterranean religions of that era. The permanent legacy of Jesus as master teacher may well have been his highly individualized use of the parable, but the form itself was long known in rabbinic instruction. The content of Jesus' teachings on many occasions again may show striking originality or deviation from tradition, but the language in which his teachings and actions are cast (e.g., the marked series of anaphoras that introduce the Beatitudes, and the deliberately crafted introduction to *Luke* and *Acts*) can also significantly reveal the author or redactor's familiarity with classical rhetoric and literary form.

This phenomenon of originality joined with conventionality also characterizes the named, anonymous, or pseudonymous epistolary writings of the New Testament. Students of the apostle Paul's letters are understandably prone to stress their distinctive features: the Christian transformation of the opening and address; the special use of the diatribe; the vivid autobiographical accounts; the intimate, personal tone of his concerns; and the powerful texture woven out of both *kerygma* (the proclamation of Christ as crucified and risen Lord) and *parenesis* (exhortations and advice to churches). To balance such an emphasis, it must be pointed out that these apostolic documents are not isolated instances of letter writing. Letters in the ancient world were used, among other purposes, as a medium for the exposition of ideas, and such writings as those of Epicurus on philosophy, Archimedes and Eratosthenes on science, and Dionysius of Halicarnassus on literary criticism still provide an illuminating context for the study of Christian epistolary achievement. Increasingly, contemporary New Testament scholarship has come to recognize that Paul's education may well have included exposure to the rhetoric of Roman law courts, the practices of itinerant Greek philosophers, and the conventions of Greek letter-writers. For example, Hans Deiter Betz has analyzed the letter to the churches in Galatia in terms of the classical apology (whose form includes the exordium, narration, proposition, proof, and conclusion), and Wayne A. Meeks sees the famous chapter on love in Paul's first letter to the Corinthians (*1 Cor.* 13) as a possible imitation of a Greek encomium on virtue.

In the subsequent centuries of the Christian era in the West, the tension between "pagan learning" and an emergent Christian literary culture continues to be evident. Anticipating by more than a millennium some of the sentiments of Milton's Christ in *Paradise Regained,* the *Didascalia apostolorum* (Teachings of the Apostles, 12) solemnly instructs the faithful:

> But avoid all books of the heathen. . . . If thou wouldst read historical narratives, thou hast the Book of Kings; but if philosophers and wise men, thou hast the Prophets, wherein thou shalt find wisdom and understanding more than that of the wise men and philosophers. And if thou wish for songs, thou hast the Psalms of David; but if thou wouldst read of the beginning of the world, thou hast the Genesis of the great Moses; and if laws and commandments, thou hast the glorious Law of the Lord God. All strange writings therefore which are contrary to these wholly eschew.

The persistence of Greco-Roman *paideia* (education and acculturation) in the schools and the gradual increase of educated converts, however, rendered it inevitable that a narrow parochialism had to modify itself. In his *On Christian Doctrine,* Augustine of Hippo (354–430) epitomizes the alternate attitude in a rhetorical question: "While the faculty of eloquence, which is of great value in urging either evil or justice, is in itself indifferent, why should it not be obtained for the uses of the good in the service of truth?" Once Christians had settled on this prosaic but potent justification for art, realizing that beauty could be enlisted for the cause of faith, incentives for adapting alien cultural forms and creating original productions multiplied. Echoing Augustine's sentiments, the seventeenth-century poet George Herbert asked of his God:

> Doth poetry Wear Venus' livery, only serve her turn?
> Why are not sonnets made of thee, and lays Upon thy altar burn?

In view of such zealous concern, it is not surprising that Catholic meditative techniques and Protestant biblical poetics would combine to produce in the late English Renaissance an abundance of the finest Christian devotional lyrics.

Although the bulk of patristic prose literature remains in the categories of dogmatic treatises, apologetics, exegetical and hermeneutical writings, homiletics, and pastoral disquisitions, Christian writers of the early centuries have also contributed to noteworthy and lasting changes in literary language. While the likes of Minucius Felix (d. about 250) and Cyprian (d. 258) faithfully and skillfully emulated classical models, Tertullian forged a new style through translation, word-borrowing (Greek to Latin), and the introduction of new Latin diction based on vernacular usage. By means of extensive translations (of both sacred scriptures and other Christian writers), letters, lives of saints, travelogues, and the continuation of Eusebius's chronicle, Jerome (c. 342–420) also mediated between classical antiquity and Christian letters.

Within this context of continuity and change, Augustine of Hippo justifiably occupies a place of pivotal importance. Not only did he set forth a profound and mature theological vision that across the centuries has exerted abiding influence on both Catholic and Protestant thought in the West, but his mercurial mind and voluminous speculations also directly funded such divergent developments as medieval literature, science, and aesthetics. More than any other figure in early Christian history, Augustine exemplifies the near-perfect fusion of pagan wisdom and Christian invention, of thought and style, of ideology and language.

As the astute analysis of German scholar Erich Auerbach has shown, the sermons of Augustine are masterful transformations of the Ciceronian model of oratory. To the ornate abundance of rhetorical figures and tropes at his disposal, the bishop of Hippo brought new depths of passion, piety, and inwardness. Of the three styles (magna, modica, and parva) that defined the ancient gradations of writing, the last and the lowliest is now endowed with unprecedented dignity and employed with new flexibility, precisely because *sermo humilis* is structured to mirror the threefold *humilitas* of the Incarnation, the culture of the Christian community, and the relative linguistic simplicity of scripture.

Just as Augustine's *Confessions* exists for all posterity as the undisputed prototype of both spiritual and secular autobiographies, and his *City of God* as an unrivaled exemplum of Christian philosophy of history and historiography, so his *On Christian Doctrine* remains a milestone in the history of interpretation theory and homiletics. The Augustinian understanding of rhetoric, hermeneutics, poetry, and allegory pervades medieval formulations of literary theory, notable in the works of Isidore of Seville (c. 560–636), Vergil of Toulouse (fl. seventh century), Bede (c. 673–735), Alcuin (c. 730–804), Rabanus Maurus (c. 780–856), John Scottus Eriugena (fl. 847–877), and Thomas Aquinas (c. 1225–1274). The grand themes of his theology—creation, the human image as analogy to the divine, the fall, the incarnation, election, redemption, history, providence, temporality, and eternity—and his particular mapping of the *ordo salutis* find reverberations and echoes, not only in such specifically Christian poets as Spenser and Milton, but also in some of the Romantics and moderns.

Unlike writing in prose, poetry had a discernibly slower development within Christianity. Although three of the largest works in the Hebrew canon are essentially poetical—*Job, Psalms,* and *Proverbs*—and long passages of poetry stud the historical and prophetic books, what passes for verse in the New Testament amounts to no more than bits and fragments. Christians had to wait for over a thousand years before they produced devotional and liturgical verse of comparable intensity and complexity to "the songs of David." The author of *Colossians,* in a well-known passage (*Col.* 3:16), bids his readers to sing "psalms, hymns, and spiritual songs," and hymn singing was apparently a common act of worship among the early Christians (cf. *1 Cor.* 14:26, *Eph.* 5:19, *Mk.* 14:26, *Acts* 16:25). But the texts of such hymns or songs are all but unknown. Even the so-called *Magnificat,* preserved in the first chapter of *Luke,* displays greater indebtedness to Hebraic sentiment and diction than to Christian feeling. Beyond the canonical corpus, examples of early Christian versification in classical languages may be found in such diverse contexts as the pseudo-Sibylline Oracles (additions by Judaic Christians in the late first to third centuries); an anonymous poem at the end of *Paidagogos* by Clement of Alexandria (early third century); the partly allegorical *Symposium of the Ten Virgins* by Methodius (fourth century); the *Peristephanon, Cathemerinon,* and *Psychomachia* by the Spaniard Prudentius (late fourth century); the *Carmen Paschale* by Sedulius (mid-fifth century); and in such verse paraphrases of the Bible as Juvencus's *Historia evangelica* (fourth century) and Marius Victor's *Alethia* (fifth century). With the possible exception of those by Prudentius, these works are now read more for their historical than for their literary merit. The ensuing Carolingian age produced verse (both accentual and quantitative) on a variety of subjects, which would eventually fill four massive volumes (in *Monumenta Germaniae Historica*), but no poet ranking with the immortals. As for vernacular literature, such poems as the *Chanson de Roland, Beowulf,* and the *Víga-Glúmssaga* continue to fuel scholarly debate about the extent to which Christian conceptions of virtue and piety colored pagan notions of heroism and fate.

In contrast to the relative simplicity of their predecessors' accomplishments, the poetic genius of Dante, Spenser, and Milton seems all the more remarkable, for the Christian tradition would be immeasurably impoverished if it did not possess their writings. These eminent theological poets, however, are so well known and their works have been the subject of so much sustained commentary that additional analysis may be superfluous. Yet, their permanent greatness in the annals of Western religious poetry surely rests on their creation of original, large-scale works of art that are at the same time monuments in the history of religions. Neither ponderous paraphrases of scripture or doctrinal treatises nor the unassimilated union of poetic forms and religious substance, the texts of the *Commedia, The Faerie Queene,* and *Paradise Lost* represent the fullest, most systematic exploration and embodiment of the poets' faith. Each in its respective manner is, as Dante said of his own masterpiece, "a sacred song / To which both Heaven and Earth have set their hand" (*Paradiso* 25.2–3). Their luminous, mellifluous sacredness is measured not only by the way they faithfully reflect or document tradition, but also by the creativity and acuity wherewith they challenge and revise tradition. According to Curtius, for example, Dante claims for his poem "the cognitional function Scholasticism denied to poetry in general," and Auerbach, in *Dante: Poet of the Secular World* (1961), holds that Dante reverses Thomas Aquinas's *Summa Theologia* by disclosing "divine truth as human destiny, as the element of Being in the consciousness of erring man." Milton's attempted theodicy significantly alters patristic and reformed dogmas (Christology, election, creation, and sin) to stress a dynamic conception of the image of God and the import of free will and human love in the drama of fall and redemption. Their distinctive elucidation of scripture and embroidery of tradition render these articulate canticles part of Christian exegesis and theology, for they participate as much as any work of "the doctors of faith" in seeking to comprehend and interpret the original mystery of faith, of revelation itself.

THE STUDY OF LITERATURE. The foregoing survey of religious and literary history has sought to demonstrate how individual texts, figures, genres, movements, and periods may provide crucial data for the student of religion. The survey has been deliberately focused on more traditional materials, since its principal thesis is manifestly more restricted in the modern era, given the undeniable shifts in historical development and cultural climate. However, inasmuch as the study of religion frequently, if not exclusively, involves the study of verbal texts, the discipline is even more indissolubly bound with the study of literature. Both disciplines entail the deepest and most wide-ranging engagement with the analysis of language, and this engagement implicates all the concerns of the human sciences.

Prior to any textual interpretation there must be an acceptable text. This truism forcefully reminds us that textual criticism, the science developed since the Renaissance for the establishment of the so-called proper text, already locates the unavoidable convergence of classical scholarship, biblical criticism, and the techniques of literary analysis. Most religious communities are not as fortunate as the Church of Jesus Christ of Latter-day Saints, which has in its possession both partial and complete versions (the latter in the church's reorganized branch) of the *Book of Mormon*'s original manuscript. For Jews, Christians, and Buddhists, however, the original documents of revelation exist only in a scholarly construct called the "ur-text" and, if even that seems an impossible ideal, in a family or group of the best texts, critically ascertained and adjudged to approximate the original form. Of necessity, therefore, the study of sacred texts at its most fundamental level already employs procedures and methods that transcend the provenance of any particular religious tradition or community. The author of *2 Timothy* may claim that "all scripture is inspired by God" (*2 Tim.* 3:16), but all scripture is not thereby protected from wayward readings by errant mortals or the corruptions of temporal transmission. As Jerome McGann puts it in *A Critique of Modern Textual Criticism* (1983), "To repair the wrecks of history" requires the use of "a historical method," and any religion of the book or books must rely on this most venerable of humanistic disciplines (that is, textual criticism, which for McGann depends on the historical method) for its continuance and propagation.

Were textual criticism merely an affair of the mechanical activities of editing, collation, and application of the canons of textual criticism, the consequence of its pursuit might not appear to be immediately relevant. But scholars have long recognized that in many instances, textual criticism does bear powerfully on textual interpretation. On the one hand, the modes of critical reasoning used to determine variant readings are identical with or similar to those engaged in the determination of verbal meaning, in exegesis, and in translation. On the other hand, the difference of a single word or of an entire edition can drastically alter the text's meaning. Whether Christians, as a result of their "justification by faith," are told that they in fact *have* peace with God or that they *are to have* peace with God depends on the selection of either the indicative *(echomen)* or the hortatory subjunctive *(echōmen)* found in the different manuscript traditions of *Romans* 5:1. Even modern literature is not free of the accidents of textual indeterminacy. "Soiled fish of the sea," a phrase lodged in the Constable Standard Edition of Herman Melville's works, led the great American critic F. O. Matthiessen to speak unwittingly in *American Renaissance: Art and Expression in the Age of Emerson and Whitman* (1944) of "the *discordia concors,* the unexpected linking of the medium of cleanliness with filth, [which] could only have sprung from an imagination that had apprehended the terrors of the deep," only to have his eloquence vitiated by the cruel discovery of a typesetter's oversight, when "coiled," not "soiled," proved to be in both the English and American first editions of the 1849 novel *White Jacket.* The publication in 1984 of James Joyce's *Ulysses: A Critical and Synoptic Edition,* edited by Hans Walter Gabler, with five thousand corrections and additions heretofore unavailable, has led critics to reexamine and revise many previous interpretations of this modern classic.

Because textual criticism wishes to retrieve a text as free as possible of historical corruptions, its goal is often taken as the starting point for textual interpretation. Paradoxically, however, such criticism can also set one kind of limit for interpretation. The authoritative text in such a discussion means that which is closest to the author's final intentions, whether those intentions are perceived to be identified with a manuscript or one of the first printed editions. Although such considerations are germane to many modern texts, they become unsuitable for editing (and thus for interpreting) many medieval and older texts. In *A Critique of Modern Textual Criticism* (1983), Jerome G. McGann notes:

> In their earliest "completed" forms these texts remain more or less wholly under the author's control, yet as a class they are texts for which the editorial concept of intention has no meaning. These texts show, in other words, that the concept of authorial intention only comes into force for criticism when (paradoxically) the artist's work begins to engage with social structures and functions. The fully authoritative text is therefore always one which has been socially produced; as a result, the critical standard for what constitutes authoritativeness cannot rest with the author and his intentions alone.

In the example from *Romans* 5 cited above, even the recovery of the original manuscript may not be decisive enough to decipher authorial intention, since the fact that the Greek words are homonyms could easily have dictated the particular spelling of the amanuensis known to have been used by the apostle. Short of questioning Paul himself, the reader is left with two perhaps equally plausible readings, but with definitely different meanings. A scholar can recover, independently and without difficulty, the meaning of these two Greek words, but no amount of attention to what the literary theorist E. D. Hirsch in *Validity in Interpretation* (1967) calls the "shared experiences, usage traits, and meaning expectations" can determine exactly what Paul wished to convey by this particular sequence of linguistic signs. Inability to discern final intention in this instance is also synonymous with inability to discern original intention, but the indeterminancy of textual meaning is not caused so much by the historicity of modern understanding as it is by the historicity of the text.

In his effort to elevate the discourse of contemporary literary criticism, author Geoffrey Hartman, in *Beyond Formalism* (1970), wants to make it "participate once more in a living concert of voices, and to raise exegesis to its former state by confronting art with experience as searchingly as if art were scripture." This noble proposal unfortunately does not make clear how searchingly scriptural exegesis has been confronted with experience. More importantly, it overlooks the fact that scriptural exegesis itself throughout its history, much as any other kind of exegesis, has always had to struggle with the question of how a verbal text is to be read, how its language—from a single word to an entire book—is to be understood. If biblical critics of late, according to the scholar Frank Kermode in *The Genesis of Secrecy* (1979), "have been looking over the fence and noting the methods and achievements of the secular arm," this tendency is not radically different from the Alexandrian school's appropriation of Philonic allegory to interpret Christian scriptures or the Protestant reformers' use of humanistic philology to advance their own grammatical-historical mode of exegesis. Wary of misreadings through willful or unintended anachronism, some contemporary biblical scholars are justifiably skeptical of the current movement to read the Bible as literature, and to expound upon sacred writ by means of secular norms and literary classifications.

Although comparing Hebrew narrative with Homeric epic or analyzing a parable of Jesus' in terms of plot and character can yield limited results, the reverent affirmation that scripture must be read as revelation or the word of God does not itself explain how language is used in divine literature. The confusion here arises from the too-ready identification of literature with fiction, itself a common but nonetheless a particular view of the nature of literature. The rejection of this view, on the other hand, in no way absolves the biblical reader from wrestling with the linguistic phenomenon that is coextensive with the text. Does the Torah or the New Testament or the *Lotus Sūtra* use language as human beings do, and if not, what other contexts are there for their readers to consider and consult? What sort of literary competence or what system of conventions ought to be operative in reading sacred texts?

The history of Christian biblical exegesis is filled with examples of how interpretation changes along with different reading assumptions and conventions. A particular view of language has led patristic writers to understand in a certain way the terms *image* and *likeness* (Heb., *tselem, demut;* Gr., *eikona, homoiosin;* Lat., *imaginem, similitudinem*), used in the first creation narrative of *Genesis*. Irenaeus, in the second century, thought the former signified the *anima rationalis* (rational soul) in human nature, whereas the latter referred to the *donum superadditum supernaturale* (an additional divine gift of perfection) which will be lost in the fall. Later interpreters, notably the Protestant reformers, challenged this developed Catholic doctrine of the *imago dei* on the ground that it missed the Hebraic convention of linguistic parallelism (pairs of words or phrases with closely related meanings), though the reformed interpretation itself is by no means free of dogmatic presupposition. Similarly, the precise meaning of the Eucharistic formula, "This is my body . . . this is my blood," has eluded interpreters and divided Christendom for centuries because the issue of whether it is a literal or a figurative statement is as much linguistic as it is theological.

These examples of biblical exegesis reinforce one basic insight of the German Protestant theologian and philosopher Friedrich Schleiermacher (1768–1834), namely that special or sacred hermeneutics "can be understood only in terms of general hermeneutics" (MS 2, in *Hermeneutics: The Handwritten Manuscripts,* ed. H. Kimmerle, 1977). For this very reason, every significant turn or development in literary theory and the culture of criticism should, in principle, be of interest to scholars of religion. Because verbal texts are more often than not the objects of their inquiry, author Robert Alter believes they must know "the manifold varieties of minutely discriminating attention to the artful use of language, to the shifting play of ideas, conventions, tone, sound, imagery, syntax, narrative viewpoint, compositional units, and much else" (*The Art of Biblical Narrative,* 1981). That last amorphous category, in the light of the American and European critical discourse since the mid-twentieth century, would certainly include such large and controversial subjects as phenomenology, philosophical hermeneutics, psychoanalysis, feminist criticism, genre theory, reception theory, communication and information theory, linguistics, structuralism, and deconstruction. Although space does not permit extensive treatment of any single facet of this new "armed vision," a brief review of the problem of where to locate textual meaning may be instructive.

In the heyday of New Criticism, distinguished by its apologetic zeal to honor literature's intrinsic worth and mode of being, meaning was virtually identical with the text. In contrast to scientific denotative language, literary language was held to be reflexive and self-referential; hence the perimeters of a single text constituted its most proper context. Meaning was generated by the text's essential form or verbal structure, which Cleanth Brooks, in his 1947 book *The Well Wrought Urn,* said resembled "that of architecture or painting: it is a pattern of resolved stresses." Because the poem represented the most felicitous union of ontology and praxis— "it is both the assertion and the realization of the assertion"—its meaning was thus paradoxically comprehensible but supposedly could not be paraphrased. Similarly, the act of interpretation was itself something of a paradox. On the one hand, the aim of interpretation was to ascertain "the way in which the poem is built . . . the form it has taken as it grew in the poet's mind." Since interpretation was thought to be determined by no factor other than that single object of the text, even the consideration of its origin or effect (the celebrated "intentional" and "affective fallacies") was deemed extraneous and irrelevant. Because the text was taken as the privileged vehicle of meaning, its integrity could be preserved only if the interpreter were purged as much as possible of his or her own assumptions, prejudices, beliefs, and values. Despite such noble effort, the New Critics confessed, the interpreter's act carries the pathos of a quixotic quest, for the adequacy of criticism will always be surpassed by the adequacy of the poem.

In various ways, the history of literary theory since the mid-twentieth century may be regarded as a steady and increasingly stringent attack on such New Critical doctrines of the text and the interpreter. The Heideggerian notion of *Vorverstädnis* (fore-understanding), mediated by the writings of the German biblical and philosophical scholars Rudolf Bultmann and Hans Gadamer, demonstrated the impossibility of unprejudiced, objective interpretation, because no act of knowing can be undertaken without a "pre-knowing" that is necessarily bound by the person's history and culture. In fact, both texts and the historical "horizon" of the interpreter, when scrutinized by such hermeneuticians of suspicion as Marxists, neo-Marxists, and Freudians are inevitably obscured by ideology, false consciousness, or the subversive language of repression. In place of the "closed readings," in which purity and objectivity are ensured by an innocent and submissive critical consciousness, the languages of both text and critic seem more likely to wear the masks of deceit and desire, as well as those of domination and violence. Instead of the text being the bearer of meaning as intended by the author, textual meaning is regarded as a product either of readers or communities of readers or of the dialectical interplay of the text and the reading process. Meaning may be actualized by uncovering the deep structures—the equivalences and oppositions—buried within a poem's semantic, syntactic, and phonological levels, by the delineation of the vision and world projected "in front of" the text, or by the perception of generic codes that at once familiarize and defamiliarize.

The most radical treatment of the problem of text and meaning is certainly that fashioned by French philosopher Jacques Derrida and his followers. The traditional view of language in Western civilization has been essentially a mimetic one: that is, language can faithfully and fruitfully mirror the interchange between mind, nature, and even God. Deconstruction, however, undertakes the most trenchant and skeptical questioning of the symmetrical unity between words and meaning. According to Terry Eagleton in the 1983 book *Literary Theory: An Introduction,* "For the signified 'boat' is really the product of a complex interaction of signifiers, which has no obvious end-point. Meaning is the spin-off of a potentially endless play of signifiers, rather than a concept tied firmly to the tail of a particular signifier. . . . I do not grasp the sense of the sentence just by mechanically piling one word on the other: for the words to compose some relatively coherent meaning at all, each one of them must, so to speak, contain the trace of the ones which have gone before, and hold itself open to the trace of those which are coming after." (For this reason, meaning in the Derridean view must be qualified by the characteristics of *différance* [in the sense of both difference and deferral], absence [in the sense that signs are forever inadequate to "make present" one's inward experiences or phenomenal objects], and decentering [in the sense of rejecting the "transcendental signified" and reconceptualizing any notion of the fixed origin or metaphysical *Urgrund* as merely the product of desire.]) To speak of the stability and determinancy of textual meaning is therefore meaningless, just as it is futile to refer to a poem's language as its proper context. The context of a poem, rather, is the entire field of the history of its language, or, in commentator Jonathan Culler's apt dictum, "Meaning is context bound, but context is boundless" (*On Deconstruction: Theory and Criticism after Structuralism,* 1982). Meaning is thus finally coincidental with the Nietzschean concept of free play, both labyrinthine and limitless; and interpretation, far from being an affair of passive mimesis, is another form of mediation and displacement, of substituting one set of signifiers for another.

The merit of deconstruction for literary study remains hotly debated. To the study of religion, a discipline committed to investigating the infinite varieties and morphologies of "the irreducibly sacred," a program so replete with logocentrism, the challenge posed by the uncanny, Cassandra-like utterances of Derrida seems all too apparent.

Deconstruction and Religion. By the end of the twentieth century, the term *deconstruction* had become commonplace in popular culture and across the humanities and social sciences. Its effects on inquiry into religion have proven to be as paradoxical as Derrida himself, who has written of religion appreciatively as well as critically. To grasp this perhaps surprising development requires noticing how Deconstruction differs from other critical practices.

In many ways, it resembles what Ricoeur calls the "hermeneutics of suspicion." Derrida exposes arbitrary, seemingly innocent dualities in texts and traditions (e.g., where "depths" are assumed to be truer than "surfaces," and "originals" more authentic than "copies"). He intersects with feminist, psychoanalytic, Nietzschean, and Marxist-related critiques of gendered interests, racism, collective neuroses, and unacknowledged power. Some of the earliest deployments of Deconstruction sought to dismantle the "logocentric" assumptions it detects in both classical and modern reasoning.

Deconstruction follows a distinctive trajectory, however. First, it must indicate its own norms cautiously, ironically, or "under erasure," since principles of justice or compassion would also be part of the disconcerting play of signifiers. Secondly, deconstructive readings—almost as if they were guests, hosts, or parasites—insinuate themselves into the language at hand. The reader, after all, has no place to be other than amid the play of differences in the texts and traditions being read. This strategy of textual interplay can make reading Derrida's writings quite challenging. When he writes of religion, he locates himself in proximity not only to theory about religion but also adjacent to scriptures and practices. And appropriately so, for he is a francophone Jew born in Algeria, who remains both apart from yet in contact with Judaism; his work has affinities with midrashic commentary. So one should be cautious in assuming that deconstructive criticism is only suspicious, since its attentions to linguistic and rhetorical details often elucidate textual meaning.

Derrida himself has encouraged one of the positive appropriations of Deconstruction in religious thought, acknowledging its resonance with apophatic, or negative, ways of knowing God. Clearly, his numerous near-synonyms for *différance* (*écriture,* trace, dissemination, supplement) do not name some unnamable, ultimate referent of negative theology. Since *différance* is but a neutral possibility, which both enables and destabilizes language and knowing, it is neither the hidden God nor the death of God. Yet some have observed that when *différance* is described as "wholly other" (*tout autre)* than being and knowing, its convergences with theological ideas of transcendence are hard to ignore. Dutch Philosopher Hent de Vries considers Deconstruction and negative theology to have become "silent companions in an attempt to establish new discursive forms and practices of philosophical and cultural analysis, of ethical deliberation and political engagement" (*Philosophy and the Return to Religion,* 1999).

Other religious responses to Deconstruction have attended less to its emphasis on *différance* than to its critiques of modernity. If one comes to doubt the self-sufficiency of Enlightenment beliefs about the autonomy of reason, then modern reductions of religion to social categories can begin to seem insecure. Deconstructive-like interpretation has cleared openings for reappraisals of religious practice and thought, such as Daniel Boyarin's *Intertextuality and the Reading of Midrash* (1990) and Jean-Luc Marion's *God Without Being* (1991). Some who have otherwise appreciated its critiques of modernity, however, have strenuously dissented from what they regard as the nihilism of Deconstruction, viewed less as a critical practice than an ideology that regards writing as another instance of Nietzsche's will-to-power. Similarly, Deconstruction has been valued for unmasking the political and religious rationalizations so often evident in histories of oppression, and for listening carefully to the silences in testimony about such events—as when survivors of the Shoah (Holocaust) challenge consoling ways of coming to terms with evil. Nevertheless, its approach to texts that bear witness to great harm or injustice has prompted the worry that postmodern critique can be rather ahistorical; it may risk reducing the limits of mimesis in suffering to a general theory of linguistic limits, instead of considering how history may rupture reflective language in particular ways.

Derrida addresses these issues of particularity and universality in his works on religion. He learned much from Emmanuel Levinas, one of his earliest interlocutors. Their decades-long exchange concerned how far one may universalize the encounter with the "face of the other," which creates, for Levinas, the ethical imperative that precedes all philosophical issues. If this encounter reduces to a universal "otherness," then particular others may be eclipsed. Because Deconstruction does not understand the other reductively, however—it claims only to probe the intertextual milieus in which others are met—then arguably it is an approach that respects particularity.

Rhetorical innocence may be a quixotic dream, yet religion is most intriguing, believes Derrida, when it desires "the impossible." It is more compelling in its practices of prayer, mourning, giving, confession, circumcision, hospitality, and testimony than when conceptualizing the divine. In his essay "Faith and Knowledge" (in *Acts of Religion,* 2002), Derrida likens religion, as least in the West, to an ellipse, whose foci are the idioms of faith (belief, trust, obligation) and of the holy (the sacred, "the unscathed," purity). This unstable structure figures in ancient and modern histories of "enlightenment" and can now be seen globally in perplexing, even contradictory alliances. Derrida observes how religious personalities and institutions frequently attempt to use the machinery of telecommunication and cyberspace to preserve identity and resist the ways that the machine alienates persons from one another. Yet there also remains, anterior to the shifting terms of religion, the metaphor of the "desert." While Derrida alludes to Sinai and to eremites and mystics, by the desert he means the all but impossible "place" of *différance,* where the other is met. His late ruminations invite us to contemplate the inherited and contingent uncertainties of signs, as they play host to protean transformations of meanings and identities in literature and religion.

SEE ALSO Aesthetics, article on Philosophical Aesthetics; Augustine of Hippo; Bhagavadgītā; Biblical Exegesis; Biblical Literature, article on New Testament; Brāhmaṇas and Āraṇyakas; Buddhist Books and Texts; Cosmogony; Dante Alighieri; Deconstruction; Drama, articles on Ancient Near Eastern Ritual Drama; Enuma Elish; Epics; Evil; Gilgamesh; Hermeneutics; Heroes; Language; Law and Religion, article on Law, Religion, and Literature; Mahābhārata; Myth, overview article; Poetry, articles on Christian Poetry, Indian Religious Poetry; Quests; Rāmāyaṇa; Scripture; Shamanism, overview article; Upaniṣads; Vedas.

BIBLIOGRAPHY

Auerbach, Erich. *Mimesis: The Representation of Reality in Western Literature.* Princeton, N.J., 1953.

Auerbach, Erich. *Literary Language and Its Public in Late Latin Antiquity and in the Middle Ages.* New York, 1965.

Betz, Hans Dieter. *Galatians.* Philadelphia, 1979.

Booth, Wayne C. *A Rhetoric of Irony.* Chicago, 1974.

Bultmann, Rudolf. *Jesus Christ and Mythology.* New York, 1958.

Critchley, Simon. *The Ethics of Deconstruction.* Oxford, 1992.

Derrida, Jacques. *Of Grammatology.* Baltimore, 1976.

Derrida, Jacques. *Dessemination.* Chicago, 1981.

Derrida, Jacques. *On the Name.* Stanford, Calif., 1995.

Derrida, Jacques. *Adieu to Emmanuel Levinas.* Stanford, Calif., 1999.

Derrida, Jacques. *Acts of Religion.* New York, 2002.

Dumézil, Georges. *Mythe et épopée.* 5 vols. Paris, 1968–1973.

Eliade, Mircea. *Shamanism: Archaic Techniques of Ecstasy.* New York, 1964.

Fairchild, Hoxie N. *Religious Trends in English Poetry.* 6 vols. New York, 1939–1968.

Farnell, L. R. *Greek Hero Cults and Ideas of Immortality.* Oxford, 1921.

Fish, Stanley. *Surprised by Sin: The Reader* in "Paradise Lost." Berkeley, Calif., 1971.

Frye, Northrop. *The Great Code: The Bible and Literature.* New York, 1982.

Gadamer, Hans-Georg. *Truth and Method.* New York, 1975.

Girard, René. *Deceit, Desire, and the Novel.* Baltimore, 1965.

Girard, René. *Violence and the Sacred.* Baltimore, 1977.

Girard, René. *The Scapegoat.* London, 1986.

Gunn, Giles B. *The Interpretation of Otherness: Literature, Religion, and the American Imagination.* Oxford, 1979.

Handelman, Susan A. *The Slayers of Moses: The Emergence of Rabbinic Interpretation in Modern Literary Theory.* Albany, N.Y., 1982.

Jacobsen, Thorkild. *The Treasures of Darkness: A History of Mesopotamian Religion.* New Haven, Conn., 1976.

Kennedy, George A. *Classical Rhetoric and Its Christian and Secular Tradition from Ancient to Modern Times.* Chapel Hill, N.C., 1980.

LaFleur, William R. *The Karma of Words: Buddhism and the Literary Arts in Medieval Japan.* Berkeley, Calif., 1983.

Lesky, Albin. *A History of Greek Literature.* Translated by James Willis and Cornelius de Heer. New York, 1966.

Lewalski, Barbara Kiefer. *Protestant Poetics and the Seventeenth-Century Religious Lyric.* Princeton, N.J., 1979.

Lieb, Michael. *Poetics of the Holy: A Reading of "Paradise Lost."* Chapel Hill, N.C., 1981.

Lord, Albert Bates. *The Singer of Tales.* Cambridge, Mass., 1960.

Meeks, Wayne A. *The Writings of St. Paul.* New York, 1972.

Milbank, John. *The Word Made Strange: Theology, Language, Culture.* Oxford, 1997.

Miner, Earl, ed. *Literary Uses of Typology from the Late Middle Ages to the Present.* Princeton, N.J., 1977.

O'Flaherty, Wendy Doniger, ed. *The Critical Study of Sacred Texts.* Berkeley, Calif., 1979.

Poland, Lynn M. *Literary Criticism and Biblical Hermeneutics: A Critique of Formalist Approaches.* Chico, Calif., 1985.

Ramsaran, John A. *English and Hindi Religious Poetry.* Leiden, 1973.

Redmond, James, ed. *Drama and Religion.* Cambridge, U.K., 1983.

Ricoeur, Paul. *Interpretation Theory: Discourse and the Surplus of Meaning.* Fort Worth, Tex., 1976.

Ricoeur, Paul. *Time and Narrative.* 3 vols. Chicago, 1984–1988.

Rohde, Erwin. *Psyche: The Cult of Souls and Belief in Immortality among the Greeks.* London, 1925.

Scott, Nathan A., Jr. *The Poetics of Belief.* Chapel Hill, N.C., 1985.

Shaffer, E. S. *"Kubla Khan" and the Fall of Jerusalem: The Mythological School in Biblical Criticism and Secular Literature, 1770-1880.* Cambridge, U.K., 1975.

Smith, Jonathan Z. *Imagining Religion: From Babylon to Jonestown.* Chicago, 1982.

Sternberg, Meir. *The Poetics of Biblical Narrative.* Bloomington, Ind., 1984.

Strier, Richard. *Love Known: Theology and Experience in George Herbert's Poetry.* Chicago, 1983.

Tigay, Jeffrey H. *The Evolution of the Gilgamesh Epic.* Philadelphia, 1982.

Wilder, Amos N. *Early Christian Rhetoric: The Language of the Gospel.* Cambridge, Mass., 1972.

ANTHONY C. YU (1987)
LARRY D. BOUCHARD (2005)

LITERATURE: RELIGIOUS DIMENSIONS OF MODERN WESTERN LITERATURE [FIRST EDITION]

In the West, the major literature of the modern period forms a canon reaching from Stendhal to Faulkner, from Leopardi to Stevens, from Gogol to Malraux, from Rimbaud to Rilke and Yeats and Montale; and this is a canon that, in its predominant tone and emphasis, is secular. Indeed, the modern writer, in his characteristic manifestations, is commonly regarded (in the phrase from Wallace Stevens's *Esthétique du Mal)* as a "shaken realist" who, in a time left darkened by the recession of traditional codes and patterns of belief, has had to steer his own course without compass or guiding star. The Christian mythos has, of course, steadily retained its power to offer certain figures a controlling vision of the world; and, in this connection, one will think of such poets and novelists and dramatists of the present century as Georges Bernanos, Paul Claudel, François Mauriac, Gertrud von le Fort, T. S. Eliot, David Jones, W. H. Auden, R. S. Thomas, Graham Greene, and Flannery O'Connor. But these and numerous others who might also be spoken of are writers who, for all the immense distinction of an Eliot or an Auden, form nevertheless a minority tradition that does not carry (in Matthew Arnold's phrase) "the tone of the centre."

This is by no means, however, to say that the literature of the modern period is without significant religious interest. For even when it has thrown away, as Stevens would say, all the lights and definitions of the past and when it will no longer use "the rotted names" for what it vaguely and agnostically descries of *theos* "in the dark," it may, by the very radicality of its unbelief, awaken sensibilities of a contrary order, so that by way of a kind of *coincidentia oppositorum* it becomes an instrument of religious recovery. One classic case in point is Paul Claudel's testimony (in his preface to the *Œuvres de Rimbaud*, Paris, 1924) about how his early admiration for the poet of *Une saison en enfer* came to be a decisive *praeparatio* in his own life for a deeper entrance into the Christian faith. And similar testimonies have been made by others about the poetry of Baudelaire and the fiction of Kafka and the theater of Beckett.

The analysis of the interrelations in the modern period between religious and literary forms finds its greatest challenge, however, in the kind of subterranean life that religious modalities often have in literature that announces itself as radically secular. Remarking this paradox often provokes, to be sure, a certain vexation among those literary scholars and critics who like a tidier state of affairs. So when, for example, a Christian interpreter of culture detects in this body of poetry or in that body of drama phases of Christian thought and feeling that have, as it were, gone underground and taken on strange new accents and guises, he may be irritatedly told that it is appropriate for literary criticism to make reference to the Christian firmament of value only when it is dealing with a literature that explicitly relies on a particular tradition of Christian orthodoxy, on its symbolism and conceptual structures and cultic forms and all its protocol. But (as Amos Wilder reminds us, in his book *Modern Poetry and the Christian Tradition*) it ought to be regarded as one of the great lessons of the Incarnation that a faith grounded in a divine act of self-*emptying* (kenosis) will itself always be an affair of diaspora—dying in order to live, wedding itself to changing forms and sensibilities "in a daring surrender of life, and [thus introducing] creative energies and perspectives which then make their appearance in secular form," and in ways undistinguished by any evangelical stamp.

The chief paradigm here is, of course, that of the Romantics, that "visionary company" of such people as Blake and Wordsworth and Chateaubriand and Hölderlin and Schiller. For these and numerous other strategists of the Romantic insurgency, though they were seeking a way out of the wilderness that had been created by Enlightenment iconoclasm, had yet lived through the Enlightenment, which meant that, eager as they were to retrieve the religious *possibility*, they could not simply reinstate without revision the traditional dogmatic system of Christian belief. Just as Romantic philosophers like Schelling and Hegel were adapting biblical themes and categories to the new requirements of speculative metaphysics, so, too, their literary counterparts were approaching their religious inheritance as in Wallace Stevens's phrase, a "poem of the mind in the act of finding / What will suffice" (*Of Modern Poetry*, in *The Collected Poems*). But, now that "the theatre was changed," if the poem of the mind were "to learn the speech of the place" and "to face the men of the time," it had "to construct a new stage." So, inevitably, it underwent the sort of profound hermeneutic transformation that had to be administered, if the received heritage of faith were to be so reconstituted as to be intellectually and emotionally appropriable in an altered climate. And very often (as M. H. Abrams has shown in his book *Natural Supernaturalism*) the result proved to be one or another kind of project for naturalizing the supernatural and for humanizing the divine.

Yet in Blake's *The Four Zoas* as in Hölderlin's *Hyperion*, in Wordsworth's *Prelude* as in Novalis's *Hymnen an die Nacht*, the pressure of biblical forms and categories is manifest: the central realities are alienation and reunion, death and rebirth, hell and heaven, paradise lost and paradise regained. And we can discern the formative influence of the archetypes of the old Christian story of man as an exiled pilgrim who, having lost an original state of felicity through a tragic fall, must undertake a difficult *Bildungsweg*, a circuitous journey in search of a new Jerusalem.

Now, it is this Romantic pattern—of the religious heritage being submitted to a process of revision and secularization but of the themes and issues of that heritage retaining a powerful underground life—that, improbable as it may at first seem, is frequently to be encountered in the literature of the modern period. It may well be, therefore, that in this connection we ought not to use the term *secularization*.

True, the idea of the world as the creation of a *deus faber*, of some sort of immaterial Person behind the myriad phenomena of experience who periodically perforates or breaks into the realm of nature and history to set things aright, is, indeed, an idea in which the modern writer does not characteristically take any great interest, and his tendency has been to endorse something like the famous word that the French astronomer Laplace offered Napoleon, when he said, "I have no need of that hypothesis." Which is not, however, to say that the literary imagination has not regularly sought to assure itself that the world is something more than the inert blankness of what Coleridge called "fixities and definites": on the contrary, again and again it searches for evidence that things are charged (in Stevens's phrase) with "a kind of total grandeur at the end," for evidence that, inconceivable though the idea of Grace "overhead" may be, the world does itself tabernacle grace and glory. Transcendence, in other words, is to be found in and through the secular, or, to borrow the terms of the French philosopher Jean Wahl, the route to be taken toward felicity and plenitude is not "transascendence" but "transdescendence"—or, in the familiar formulation of Dietrich Bonhoeffer's *Letters and Papers from Prison*, the "Beyond" is to be found "in the midst of our life." It is such an axiom as this that comes close to forming the basis of the period style in large ranges of twentieth-century literature, and it may be descried to be a guiding principle for writers as various as William Butler Yeats and Wallace Stevens, D. H. Lawrence and William Carlos Williams, Jorge Guillén and René Char, Marianne Moore and Charles Olson, Elizabeth Bishop and Gary Snyder, Jules Supervielle and Czeslaw Milosz.

The poetry of Stevens, for example, provides a great case of this relocation of transcendence into the dimension of immanence. Taking it for granted, as he does, that "the author of man's canons is man, / Not some outer patron" (*Conversation with Three Women of New England*, in *Opus Posthumous*), he is, to be sure, a "shaken realist" who finds it impossible to avoid the conclusion that something *else* "must take the place / Of empty heaven and its hymns" (*The Man with the Blue Guitar*, in *The Collected Poems*). So, as he says, "We seek / Nothing beyond reality" (*An Ordinary Evening in New Haven*, in *The Collected Poems*), since the "essential integrity" of things must be found within "The actual landscape with its actual horns / Of baker and butcher blowing." But this actual landscape is by no means for Stevens merely a huge *res extensa*, silent and dead and immeasurable. On the contrary, the "Is-ness" of everything that exists is invested with a most extraordinary radiance and presence: in the poem *Metaphor as Degeneration* he says, "It is being." This it is that lights up the things and creatures of earth—"mere Being," which is, as he says in *The Sail of Ulysses*, that

> Life lighter than this present splendor,
> Brighter, perfected and distant away,
> Not to be reached but to be known,
> Not an attainment of the will
> But something illogically received. . . .
> (*Opus Posthumous*, p. 101; used by permission)

So we need not, therefore, cast about for some *scala sacra* leading up beyond the phenomenal world into the timelessness of eternity, since that which is steadfast and reliable, which is gracious and deserving of our trust, is already at hand in "the vulgate of experience," in the uncreated Rock of reality—"mere Being"—which offers us "the imagination's new beginning." And most especially in the great poems of his last years—in *Chocorua to Its Neighbor*, *Credences of Summer*, *Notes toward a Supreme Fiction*, *A Primitive like an Orb*, *An Ordinary Evening in New Haven*, *To an Old Philosopher in Rome*, *The Rock*—all his "edgings and inchings" appear to be calculated at the end to speak of "the final goodness" of things, of a holiness indwelling every nook and cranny of the world, which invites "a fresh spiritual," one untouched by any sort of supernaturalist figuralism. It is a poetry of immanence. But, for all Stevens's impatience with traditional metaphysical theism, it can hardly be declared to be a poetry that fails to line itself up behind any significantly religious outlook, and its accent and emphasis require us to pay deference to what he himself on one occasion wanted to insist upon when, in a Christmas letter of 1951 to the critic Sister M. Bernetta Quinn, he said, "I am not an atheist although I do not believe today in the same God in whom I believed when I was a boy."

Yet, however much modern literary sensibility may be distinguished by the determination of such a writer as Stevens to find the possibility of transcendence in and through the secular, many of the old paradigms and archetypes of the Judeo-Christian story continue to endure with a remarkable persistence. More than three hundred years after the first publication of Milton's *Paradise Lost* the myth of the Fall, for example, has lost none of its power to captivate and focalize the literary imagination. In part, this is no doubt consequent upon the disclosures that have come from modern psychology of the furies of unreason that rage deep within the human interior. And in the twentieth century the gas ovens and concentration camps that have been devised for the obliteration of millions of people and the nightmares of nuclear warfare have surely provided the most compelling incentive for subsuming the human condition at large under this ancient apologue. But, for whatever reason, it has been used almost endlessly as a framing structure for narrative, and not only by writers sustained by some mode of religious orthodoxy but by, say, the Conrad of *Heart of Darkness*, the Hesse of *Demian*, the Camus of *La chute*.

Indeed, the English novelist William Golding is so obsessed by what is broken and deformed in the human situation that in book after book—in *Lord of the Flies*, in *Free Fall*, in *The Spire*—he uses in one way or another imagery of "fallenness." In, for example, his novel of 1954, *Lord of the Flies*, he builds his narrative around a group of English schoolboys who survive a plane crash on a tropical island. But this remote fastness turns out not at all to be any sort of Isle of the

Blessed: its shoreline is "torn everywhere by the upheavals of fallen trees," the heat is felt as "a threatening weight," and the forests roar and flail, the thorny underbrush is a reminder of how nearly the adjacent jungle presses in, and the fruits of the place induce diarrhea. Such is the uncongenial precinct amid which the little company of refugee schoolboys must undertake to organize a makeshift confederation for their common welfare. But, almost immediately, their life together is so perverted by the will to power that it collapses into a savage kind of depravity. They invent absurd taboos and barbaric blood-rituals. And their cruel aggrandizements against one another erupt at last into murder. Golding was for many years a teacher in Bishop Wordsworth's School, Salisbury; so, as an ex-schoolmaster, he has the requisite experience of boys for making the whole tale fully plausible. But his novel does not want to say "You see? This is what *boys* are like, once they escape the civilizing disciplines of family and church and school." On the contrary, it intends to say "Here is the naked reality of elemental human nature itself." Nowhere, to be sure, is any explicit reference made to the story about the garden of Eden in *Genesis*, but Golding's very refusal to submit the Fall to anything resembling logical or historical analysis is an indication that he, like the numerous other modern writers who work with this theme, takes for granted the lesson laid down by the English theologian John Seldon Whale (in his book *Christian Doctrine*), when he says: "Eden is on no map, and Adam's fall fits no historical calendar. Moses is not nearer to the Fall than we are, because he lived three thousand years before our time. The Fall refers not to some datable aboriginal calamity in the historic past of humanity, but to a dimension of human experience which is always present. . . . Everyman is his own 'Adam,' and all men are solidarily 'Adam.'"

Or, again, like the myth of the Fall, the Christic image is frequently invoked in the literature of recent decades. What is here being referred to is not, however, the kind of fictionalized biography of Jesus that occasionally provides the focus for historical novels in the mode of Robert Graves's *King Jesus* and Nikos Kazantzakis's *The Last Temptation of Christ.* Nor is reference being made to the various literary presentations—as in Gerhart Hauptmann's *Hanneles Himmelfahrt* or Upton Sinclair's *They Call Me Carpenter*—of Christ in modern garb, of the figure whom Theodore Ziolkowski (in his book *Fictional Transfigurations of Jesus*) speaks of as the *Jesus redivivus.* Nor, again, to insert still another negative, is reference being made to the phenomenon that Ziolkowski denominates as "Christomania," the condition that is being explored (as in Nathanael West's *Miss Lonelyhearts* or Kazantzakis's *The Greek Passion*) when the novelist takes as his subject a personage who, often under the pressure of a pathological psychology, commits himself to the exactions of an *imitatio Christi.* What is rather in view are the various examples in modern literature of sanctity and of redemptive suffering that are rooted in the archetype of Christ, in the same manner that other dramatic patterns are grounded in the archetypes of Prometheus and Orpheus and Parzival and Faust.

When poets and novelists and dramatists begin, out of whatever framework of personal belief, to explore what is involved in life releasing itself as an offering to other life, surely it is inevitable that this *leitourgia* should be apprehended, even if unconsciously, within the terms of the Passion story, since this is the most familiar and the most pervasive narrative in Western culture of what Dietrich Bonhoeffer (in his book *Ethics*) called "deputyship." When we act *for* others—as, said Bonhoeffer, when a "father acts for the children, working for them, caring for them, interceding, fighting and suffering for them" and thus undertaking to be "their deputy"—something is being given up: what is one's own is being handed over to another, for the sake of the human communion. And, at least on one level, it is of such sacrificial service that Christ stands in our culture as the primary archetype. So, when "deputyship" forms a part of the experiential reality with which the literary imagination seeks to deal, it ought not to be regarded as surprising that the figure of Christ should often be found hovering in the background.

One will not, of course, be surprised to find the Christic image being invoked by a Roman Catholic novelist like François Mauriac (in the character of Xavier Dartigelongue in *L'agneau*) or Graham Greene (in "the whiskey priest" of *The Power and the Glory*). But it is also to be encountered over and again in the fiction of many writers who, if not representing some mode of secular humanism, stand in at least a very ambiguous relation to Christian doctrine.

In American literature one will think, for example, in this connection of John Steinbeck's *The Grapes of Wrath.* Its moving account of the flight to California of a family of tenant farmers from an Oklahoma ruined by the dust storms of the 1930s established it as the dominant social novel of its period on the American scene, and it remains a minor classic. On their long and difficult journey the Joads are accompanied by Jim Casy, an ex-preacher who has lost his faith and who, in his lighthearted womanizing, does not conform in any conventional way to a saintly norm. But, in his steadfast loyalty to the Joads throughout all their hazardous journeying to the Promised Land (not unlike the journeying of the ancient Israelites) and in his sympathy for all those who are in need of succor and encouragement, he proves his role in the design of the novel to be that of showing that, indeed, the Good Place is not so much a particular region or tract of land as it is that space among human beings that is made radiant by reverence for the sacrality of the neighbor. And, not unnaturally, his fidelity to the insulted and the injured leads to his death at the hands of strikebreakers in California who are sent to hunt him down for the part he has played in leading a strike. Tom Joad, who kills the man who struck Casy, becomes a fugitive, and, when Ma Joad reaches him in his place of hiding, he says:

> Lookie, Ma. I been all day an' all night hidin' alone. Guess who I been thinkin' about? Casy! He talked a lot.

> Used ta bother me. But now I been thinkin' what he said, an' I can remember—all of it. Says one time he went out in the wilderness to find his own soul, an' he foun' he didn' have no soul that was his'n. Says he foun' he jus' got a little piece of a great big soul. Says a wilderness ain't no good, 'cause his little piece of a soul wasn't no good 'less it was with the rest, an' was whole. Funny how I remember. Didn' think I was even listenin'. But I know now a fella ain't no good alone.

So it seems that this Christlike man in death has at least one disciple, for Tom Joad appears to have mastered Casy's great lesson, that "two are better than one."

Nor will it be forgotten how regularly the Passion of Jesus guided William Faulkner's imagination. Though the principal action of *The Sound and the Fury* occurs in the year 1928, the chronology of the novel is, clearly, that of Passion Week. At the center of *Light in August* is not only Joanna Burden but also Joe Christmas, who is marked by the invisible "cross" of the Negro blood that flows in his veins and who, after a lifetime of being badgered and abused, is finally slaughtered on a Friday, at the same age of Christ at the time of his crucifixion. And he, too, achieves a kind of apotheosis, for, after being castrated by a white racial maniac while he is dying of gunshot wounds, "from out the slashed garments about his hips and loins the pent black blood . . . seemed to rush out of his pale body like the rush of sparks from a rising rocket; upon that black blast the man seemed to rise soaring into their memories forever and ever." Or, again, Ike McCaslin in *The Bear* and Nancy—"Negro, dopefiend, whore"—in *Requiem for a Nun* want in various ways to say, as Nancy puts it, "Trust in Him." And the book of 1954, *A Fable*, presents the culminating instance of Faulkner's dependence upon the imagery of the Passion, for his central protagonist here is an obscure pacifist corporal who, by the manner of his death in the attempt to bring to an end the carnage in the French theater of World War I, appears unmistakably to be an analogue of Christ.

Steinbeck and Faulkner are, of course, but two of many other writers who might be cited in this context, for, from the time of Melville's *Billy Budd* on to the present, the American literary imagination has been repeatedly drawn to the archetype of Christ. Nor does modern European literature represent any great difference in this respect. The fiction of the Italian novelist Ignazio Silone, for example—*Bread and Wine, The Seed beneath the Snow, The Secret of Luca*—recurrently presents a dramatic economy that is knit together by its parallels to the gospel of the New Testament, and Silone's play *And He Hid Himself,* which is essentially a dramatization of *Bread and Wine*, makes explicit how much Pietro Spina, the protagonist of the novel and of *The Seed beneath the Snow*, is intended to be a figure of Christ.

Or, again, odd as it may at first seem in the work of a writer apparently so distant from any sort of Christian position, the great climactic moment of André Malraux's last novel, *Les noyers de l'Altenburg*, is nothing if it is not a rehearsal of the Passion of Christ. The action occurs on June 12, 1915 on the Eastern Front, where the narrator's father Vincent Berger (a native of Alsace, then a part of Germany), as an officer of the German intelligence service, is observing a bombardment being launched by German troops against the Russians. A newly developed poisonous gas is to be used, and, once it is released and begins to float down the adjacent valley toward the Russian trenches, the German troops wait and wait, and continue to wait, but they can discern through their binoculars no trace of any activity in the neighborhood of the enemy's advance positions. So, after a long interval, they decide to move forward; but no fire comes from the Russian artillery. And, finally, Berger and the other staff officers begin to wonder why it is that, long after plunging into the Russian trenches, the foot soldiers in their advance guard do not reappear. At last they are seen, but instead of continuing their advance, they return in a great swarm, and the officers, as they peer through their binoculars, are baffled by what they seem to be carrying, which, at a distance of a mile or so, appear to be only white spots. As it turns out, the Germans, in making their way back to their own lines, are carrying the bodies of gassed Russian infantrymen. "No," says one, "man wasn't born to rot!" Berger, as he contemplates the scene, slowly realizes that this mutiny is not merely an expression of pity, that it attests to "something a good deal deeper, an impulse in which anguish and fraternity were inseparably mingled." And, as he passes a German infantryman struggling to carry on his shoulders a dying Russian out of "the sordid world of the liquefied forest," he notices that the two together in silhouette form an outline like that of the Descent from the Cross.

So the old images and myths and archetypes of the Christian story persist in the secular literature of the modern period, although often in altered form. But not only do these protoplastic forms continue to have a significant subterranean life; so, too, do certain habits of spiritual perception. The works, for example, of D. H. Lawrence—the Lawrence of *Women in Love* and *The Plumed Serpent* and *Lady Chatterley's Lover*—are a case in point. T. S. Eliot laid it down (in *After Strange Gods*) that Lawrence was "an almost perfect example of the heretic," that his vision was "spiritually sick," and that it could appeal only "to the sick and debile and confused." And no doubt Lawrence's quest of "mindlessness" and the "dark gods" and his commitment to "savage pilgrimage" will still prompt many to blurt out some such impatient dismissal as Eliot ejaculated. But such a response will only reflect, as it did in Eliot, a failure of intelligence, for Lawrence's whole emphasis on "phallic consciousness," as it was combined with his polemic against "mental consciousness," was intended to rescue human carnality from the kind of "scientific" reductionism that, in the manner of a Marie Stopes, would make it merely an affair of calculation and mechanism (as it is for "the young man carbuncular" of Eliot's *Waste Land).* In Lawrence's short story *Glad Ghosts*, Lord Lathkill is speaking to Colonel Hale about the latter's wife, now deceased, and he says: "You may have been awfully good to her. But her poor woman's body, were you ever good to that? . . . That's the point. If you understand the marriage service: with my body I thee worship. That's the point. No getting away from it." And in his richest work—in *The Rainbow*, in *Women in Love*, in *St. Mawr*, in many of his finest poems—it is precisely his purpose to advance such a sacramental view of the sexual act as may indeed be far more authentically Christian than the frequent tendency of the theological tradition, in both its Catholic and Protestant phases, to pronounce *concupiscentia* as valid only insofar as, within the bond of marriage, it is instrumental toward procreation.

Or, in another direction, we may turn to a writer as different from Lawrence in style of vision as Ernest Hemingway, and, immediately, the common tendency will be to think of him as having been a votary of *nada*, as one who was prepared to say (in the language of his famous story *A Clean, Well-Lighted Place*), "Our nada who art in nada, nada be thy name thy kingdom nada thy will be nada in nada as it is in nada. Give us this nada our daily nada and nada us our nada as we nada our nadas and nada us not into nada but deliver us from nada; pues nada. Hail nothing full of nothing, nothing is with thee." And many of Hemingway's readers may be inclined to posit—not, indeed, without some reason—that it is this "nothing full of nothing" that defines the basic metaphysical situation forming the background of his fiction. But, then, one may remember the glorious interlude of those five days that Jake Barnes and Bill Gorton in *The Sun Also Rises* spend together fishing in waters up in the Pyrenees, where the air is crisp and clean and where they exchange, as it were, a smile of complicity with the golden Basque uplands, with the clear trout streams and the dense beech woods and the untraveled sandy roads and the rising sun—and one will remember that the novel's epigraph from *Ecclesiastes* speaks of how "the earth abideth forever." Or one will remember Santiago in *The Old Man and the Sea* and his reverential amazement at how beautiful and wondrous are the creatures of the sea and the sky. Though he beseeches the Holy Mother after he has hooked his great marlin to "pray for the death of this fish," he thinks to himself, "Never have I seen a greater, or more beautiful, or a calmer or more noble thing than you, brother." And he is "glad we do not have to kill the stars." Or, again, in a similar vein, one will think of the Nick Adams stories in Hemingway's first major book, *In Our Time*, and of how Nick is touched by the healing power of the good earth as he fishes deep in the back country of the north woods of Michigan, sometimes tenderly unhooking the barb from the mouth of a trout he has caught and dropping it back into the water. And, throughout the novels and the short stories, there is so much else in this mode that it is difficult finally not to conclude that this writer often sounds one of the most primitive meanings of the Christian doctrine of Creation, that the world at hand is touched by a transcendent glory, that indeed (as it is said by the canticles of the Morning Office) the mountains and the hills, the nights and the days, the dews and the frosts, the sun and the moon, and all the things of earth "uttereth speech" and "sheweth knowledge" and are exalted forever.

Now it is into this general order of discrimination that we shall be taken when we begin to reckon with, say, Joyce's *Portrait of the Artist as a Young Man*, with many of Pound's *Cantos*, with Kafka's *Das Schloss*, with Brecht's *Der gute Mensch von Sezuan*, with Beckett's *En attendant Godot*, with William Carlos Williams's *Paterson*, and with a vast number of other focal modern texts. Which is not at all to say that, for all its secularity, the characteristic literature of the modern period reveals itself to be somehow controlled by an *anima naturaliter Christiana*. What requires rather to be acknowledged is that the great symbolic forms of Christendom never (as Mircea Eliade says of symbols generally, in *Images and Symbols*) simply disappear from the reality of the psyche: "the aspect of them may change, but their function [often] remains the same; one has only to look behind their latest masks." And it is the uncovering of what is hidden and disguised that constitutes the difficult effort to be undertaken when literature in the age of Joyce and Kafka and Sartre begins to be viewed from the standpoint of its relation to our religious inheritance.

BIBLIOGRAPHY

Abrams, M. H. *Natural Supernaturalism: Tradition and Revolution in Romantic Literature.* New York, 1971.

Brooks, Cleanth. *The Hidden God.* New Haven, 1963.

Killinger, John. *The Fragile Presence: Transcendence in Modern Literature.* Philadelphia, 1973.

Moseley, Edwin M. *Pseudonyms of Christ in the Modern Novel: Motifs and Methods.* Pittsburgh, 1962.

Otten, Terry. *After Innocence: Visions of the Fall in Modern Literature.* Pittsburgh, 1982.

Scott, Nathan A., Jr. *Negative Capability: Studies in the New Literature and the Religious Situation.* New Haven, 1969.

Scott, Nathan A., Jr. *The Wild Prayer of Longing: Poetry and the Sacred.* New Haven, 1971.

Turnell, Martin. *Modern Literature and Christian Faith.* London, 1961.

Webb, Eugene. *The Dark Dove: The Sacred and Secular in Modern Literature.* Seattle, 1975.

Wilder, Amos N. *Modern Poetry and the Christian Tradition: A Study in the Relation of Christianity to Culture.* New York, 1952.

Ziolkowski, Theodore. *Fictional Transfigurations of Jesus.* Princeton, 1972.

NATHAN A. SCOTT, JR. (1987)

LITERATURE: RELIGIOUS DIMENSIONS OF MODERN WESTERN LITERATURE [FURTHER CONSIDERATIONS]

The most important development in Western literature since the 1960s is the rise of a movement that is generally known as postmodernism. Postmodern literature is characterized by a rejection of the Enlightenment's belief in a rational and authoritative narrative viewpoint in favor of an emphasis on the virtual, the fragmentary, and the subversive. Nathan A. Scott, Jr. concludes his essay "Tillich's Legacy and the New Scene in Literature" (1985) by recognizing that postmodern writing has firmly rejected "the old myth of 'depth'" (p. 147) upon which Tillich's theology of culture relied. He turns to Warner Berthoff, who suggests, with a nod to Robert Musil's novel in which "no serious attempt [will] be made to. . . enter into competition with reality" (147), that postmodern writing is "a literature without qualities" (p. 152). Postmodern literature, Scott notes, "hardly gives off even the slightest intimation of the sacred" (p. 152); it seems "utterly dry and vacant and unpromising" (p. 153). Yet the writers in contention—Donald Barthelme, John Barth, Raymond Federman and Thomas Pynchon—are, he admits, highly gifted, and it would be best for us to do as Tillich would have done—to wait and see before we make judgments about them, while at the same time remembering that great literature seeks to cope with the human situation and gives "a shape and a significance" to our lives (p. 153).

If we survey the "new scene" in the early twenty-first century, however, we will find ourselves obliged to extend Scott's vocabulary and to include other writers. Where Scott took Paul Tillich (1886–1965) as his theological reference point when associating religion and literature, we would be more likely in the early 2000s to cite Hans Urs von Balthasar (1905–1988), whose influence has increased significantly since his death. In the seven volumes of *The Glory of the Lord* (1961–1969; English translation, 1982–1989), the Swiss theologian provides a theological aesthetics rooted in the Hebrew Bible, the New Testament and the Church Fathers, and nourished by theologians as recent as Karl Barth (1886–1968). Von Balthasar attempts nothing less than a rereading of the entire Christian tradition in terms of the third transcendental—beauty—which he believes to have been bypassed in recent centuries by modernity's absorption in being and truth, the first two transcendentals. Revelation has an irreducible aesthetic dimension, *Gestalt*, or form, and aesthetics has an equally resistant theological component. Especially in the third volume of his series, von Balthasar writes illuminatingly on a range of authors from Dante Alighieri (1265–1321) to the French poet Charles Péguy (1873–1914). Yet his sympathies stop well short of postmodern writers. Von Balthasar's admirers are impressed by his diagnosis of modernity as misrepresenting being by discussing it as a concept rather than reality, and as relentlessly representing time in spatial terms. Yet they can put this critique to work only on modern aesthetics, thereby allowing the possibility of a postmodern theological aesthetics but without having any positive guidance from von Balthasar.

CHARACTERISTICS OF POSTMODERN LITERATURE. Scott was entirely correct to say that postmodern literature rejects depth as a hermeneutical value. A play of surfaces with nothing beneath them has been one of the signature motifs in literature since the early 1980s. It would be a hasty induction, however, to say that postmodern writing has no sense of the sacred. Postmodern emphasis on the fragmentary has led in unforeseen ways to a new way of thinking about religion. Attention to fragments of narrative and personality characterized both Romantics of the Jena tradition, such as Novalis (1772–1801) and Friedrich von Schlegel (1772–1829), and such high modernists as T. S. Eliot (1888–1965) and Ezra Pound (1885–1972). For all these writers, the fragment is a part of an absent whole. The fragmentary, on the other hand, attempts to pass beyond wholes and unities and to establish what Maurice Blanchot (1907–2003) calls a "relation without relation" or an "infinite relation" (Blanchot, *The Infinite Conversation*, 1993, pp. 73, 296). The fragmentary cannot be folded into any unity, past or future, and certainly not into any of the "grand narratives" that Jean-François Lyotard (1925–1998) took as characteristics of modernity (Lyotard, 1984, xxiii). Rather, it would be mobile and plural, forever unsettled and unsettling. For Blanchot, this new mode of relation bespeaks a rigorous atheism: it takes us beyond the One on which all notions of God rely. For theologian David Tracy, however, the fragmentary is precisely our way of grasping God. The Eliot of *The Waste Land* (1922), he argues, was a modernist, using fragments to shore him up against ruins of Western civilization, while the poet of *Four Quartets* (1943) now seems strangely postmodern in his use of fragmentary passages to suggest the intersections of time and eternity.

Looking back on Scott's essay, one can only be surprised to see how thoroughly the sense of "heteronomy" has changed in twenty years. For Tillich, a heteronomous culture (from the Greek word *hetero*, "other") is one in submission to a law that is alien to the creativity of the individual. His examples include the Catholic Church of the Middle Ages as well as the communist and fascist movements of the twentieth century. Opposed to heteronomy is an autonomous culture characterized by a spirit of "self-sufficient finitude" (Scott, 1985, p. 138). And at variance with both autonomy and heteronomy is what Tillich calls "theonomy," a state in which cultural creations embody a spiritual content.

One of the main theses of postmodern thought, however, has been that the other exceeds and is prior to the self, and that only if one affirms this asymmetric relation can one escape from the threat of totalitarianism. At times, this heteronomy is inhuman, as in what Blanchot calls the Outside (an impotent collection of images that constantly presses on people without yielding any meaning or having any point) or in what Jacques Derrida (1930–2004) dubs *la différance*, or difference, which he defines as the condition of possibility for meaning that perpetually differs from itself, ensuring no final convergence of text and meaning. At other times heteronomy is the very image of the human: Emmanuel Lévinas (1906–1995) argues that ethics is possible only if the other person is regarded as speaking from a position of height. And at yet other times otherness is in effect one of the divine names, as it is for Jean-Luc Marion (b. 1946) who seeks a "God without being," a deity who reveals himself as Love.

The writers that Scott named in 1985 have all been absorbed into mainstream North American literary culture. They are not, however, the authors most talked about under the sign of the postmodern. Where Scott cited Wallace Stevens (1879–1955), a postmodern critic would quote John Ashbery, while also noting that Stevens has survived the transition from modern to postmodern canons far more easily than have most of his contemporaries. The spirituality of Stevens, especially the lyrics of his final phase, has become more evident since the 1980s, when the poet's lack of a dogmatic confession of belief in the Judeo-Christian God poses fewer problems for readers of a religious disposition. "Final Soliloquy of the Interior Paramour" has a prayerful quality, not in the affirmation of a transcendent deity but in its strong Romantic sense that the divine is one with the human imagination. A spiritual longing also emerges from time to time in Ashbery. "Self-Portrait in a Convex Mirror," a long poem that has come to exemplify postmodern questioning of both depth and the truthfulness of representation, begins with a traditional image of the soul as "a captive, treated humanely, kept / In suspension." Yet the poem captures postmodern pathos in its modulation to the realization that "the soul is not a soul, / Has no secret, is small, and it fits / Its hollow perfectly" (Ashbery, 1975, pp. 68–69). The secret, as postmodernists like to say, is that there is no secret: all "depths" are already on the surface.

God in Postmodern Literature. The word "God" appears often in recent writing, although it is not always evident what it means. For Edmund Jabès (1912–1991), God is sometimes a figure of endless contestation—"God is a questioning of God" (Jabès, 1976–1984, vol. 1, p. 138)—and sometimes a metaphor for emptiness. *The Book of Questions* (1963–1973), elaborated over seven volumes, is a fragmentary work that is neither fiction nor poetry, neither drama nor essay. As Jacques Derrida would say, it participates in all these genres without belonging to any of them. The book was translated into English over the period from 1976 to 1984, and its importance requires us to distinguish between books written since the mid-1980s and books that have become prominent in that same period. Much seminal postmodern writing falls into the latter category. The first volume of Jabès's work introduces a story that is never quite completed of two lovers, Sarah and Yukel. Sarah is deported to a concentration camp and returns to Yukel after she has gone insane. Questioned about the stories he tells, Yukel answers, "I brought you my words. I talked to you about the difficulty of being Jewish, which is the same as the difficulty of writing. For Judaism and writing are but the same waiting, the same hope, the same wearing out" (Jabès, 1976–1984, vol. 1, p. 122). The work multiplies itself in gnomic remarks by imaginary rabbis and voices that come from nowhere. One voice interrupts another, yet the overall impression is of an endless sifting of a small group of themes: the book, the desert, exile, God, the Jewish people, and writing.

One of Jabès's most appreciative and exacting readers has been Blanchot, whose own narratives have been translated into English only in recent years—several of them by no less a writer than Lydia Davis—and have marked the literary sensibility of the past two decades. Blanchot does not believe in revelation, but he maintains that literature is necessarily tied to the sacred. He wonders, now that the gods have departed, what will become of literature. The last vestige we have of the sacred is what he calls the Outside, an empty depth of images, and all his narratives brood on its eerie approach. It returns eternally without ever quite arriving and divides the "I" of anyone who is attuned to it, especially writers. *Death Sentence*, which appeared in France in 1948, was published in English in 1978, yet has become better known only with its reissue in 1998 and its inclusion in *The Station Hill Blanchot Reader* (1999). Its story of the resuscitation of a woman, J., by the narrator is a powerful rewriting, in terms of the myth of Orpheus, of the story of Jesus' revival of Jairus's daughter in *Mark* 5: 21–43. More recently, *The Instant of My Death*, published in France in 1994, relates the story—apparently autobiographical—of a young man almost executed by the Germans in 1944. Faced with imminent death, the young man "experienced then a feeling of extraordinary lightness, a sort of beatitude (nothing happy, however)—sovereign elation?" (Blanchot, 2000, p. 5). The protagonist has what Georges Bataille (1897–1962) calls a "limit-experience," a moment of ecstasy akin to mystical rapture, though one in which God does not appear.

Much translated in the last two decades, the poetry of Paul Celan (1920–1970) has been a touchstone for many poets. A lyric such as "Psalm," with its play on God as "No one," offers a model of how God can be simultaneously named and erased, and how a poet can express a longing for God without being committed to his existence. An affinity with Celan is apparent in the poems of the English poet Geoffrey Hill (b. 1932) in *Tenebrae* (1978) and *Canaan* (1996). The earlier volume in particular offers an anguished yet ambivalent relation to the Christian God, drawing heavily on Spanish lyricism. More relaxed in tone than Hill, the American Charles Wright (b. 1935) expresses a religious longing throughout his writing life but is perpetually frustrated by a God who seems incredible to him. In a recent poem, "Cicada Blue" (1998), he says, "We've tried to press God in our hearts the way we'd press a leaf in a book" (Wright, 2000, p. 157). The mystics attract him, as do Eastern sages, and he finds he must content himself with registering "ripples of otherworldliness" rather than worshiping God (Wright, 2000, p. 81).

A nature mysticism that is leagued with science can be found in another American, Archie Randolph Ammons (1926–2001). In "Hymn," the search for God is on earth and in space, and the deity is acknowledged to be "on the inside of everything and on the outside" (Ammons, 1972, p. 39). Later, in 1997, he speaks "as a nonreligious person" to God and hopes that, in the absence of a revelation that can be experienced, we "can work / this stuff out the best we can" and "walk with / you as long a line of trees" (Ammons, 1997, pp. 4–5). Charles Simic (b. 1938), also American, has had a tangential relation with mysticism, though his sense of the eternal in the world also has dark moments. "To the One Upstairs" (1999) addresses God as "Boss of all bosses of the universe / Mr. know-it-all, wheeler-dealer, wire-puller" and at the end contemplates this new set of divine names that "I keep inventing, / As I scribble this note to you in the dark" (Simic, 1999, p. 63). Angry as it is, the poem remains a prayer.

There are few female poets who are both postmodern and religious, in any strong sense of either word. One of these is the Canadian poet Anne Carson (b. 1950). In her sequence called "The Truth about God" (1995), she tells us right at the beginning, "My religion makes no sense / and does not help me / therefore I pursue it" (Carson, 1995, p. 39). In some ways her lines could stand as an epigraph to postmodern religion, but with two important provisos. The dominant religious mode of postmodern times is fundamentalism. This mode must be distinguished from postmodern reflections on religion, which take two main forms: a reduction of revelation to ethics ("religion without religion"), and an affirmation that God is Love and is therefore beyond being. The former helps people make their way through life, although sometimes at the cost of discounting natural reason, while the latter makes sense although at the risk of helping only those who can enter into sophisticated theological speculation.

SEE ALSO Poetry, article on Poetry and Religion.

BIBLIOGRAPHY

Ammons, A. R. *Collected Poems, 1951–1971.* New York, 1972.

Ammons, A. R. *Glare.* New York, 1997.

Ashbery, John. *Self-Portrait in a Convex Mirror.* New York, 1975.

Balthasar, Hans Urs von. *The Glory of the Lord.* Edited by John Riches and translated by Erasmo Leiva-Merikakis et al. 7 vols. San Francisco, 1982–1989. Volume 1 presents the argument for a theological aesthetics, while volume 5 contains the critique of modernity.

Blanchot, Maurice. *The Infinite Conversation.* Translated by Susan Hanson. Minneapolis, 1993.

Blanchot, Maurice. *The Station Hill Blanchot Reader.* Edited by George Quasha and translated by Lydia Davis et al. Barrytown, N.Y., 1999. The volume is a collection of Blanchot's major fiction and some important essays.

Blanchot, Maurice. *The Instant of My Death.* Bound with Jacques Derrida, *Demeure: Fiction and Testimony.* Both translated by Elizabeth Rottenberg. Stanford, Calif., 2000. Blanchot's testament of atheistic mysticism.

Carson, Anne. *Glass, Irony and God.* Introduction by Guy Davenport. New York, 1995.

Celan, Paul. *Poems.* Translated by Michael Hamburger. New York, 1984.

Hart, Kevin. *The Dark Gaze: Maurice Blanchot and the Sacred.* Chicago, 2004. Study of Blanchot and religion.

Hill, Geoffrey. *Collected Poems.* Harmondsworth, U.K., 1985.

Hill, Geoffrey. *Canaan.* London, 1996.

Jabès, Edmond. *The Book of Questions.* Translated by Rosemary Waldrop. 7 vols. Middletown, Conn., 1976–1984.

Lyotard, Jean-François. *The Postmodern Condition: A Report on Knowledge.* Translated by Geoff Bennington and Brian Massumi. Minneapolis, Minn., 1984. Early and influential account of postmodernism.

Scott, Nathan A., Jr. "Tillich's Legacy and the New Scene in Literature." In *The Thought of Paul Tillich,* edited by James Luther Adams et al., pp. 137–155. San Francisco, 1985. Important early survey of postmodern writing with reference to Tillich's theology of culture.

Simic, Charles. *Jackstraws.* New York, 1999.

Tracy, David. "Fragments: The Spiritual Situation of Our Times." In *God, the Gift, and Postmodernism,* edited by John D. Caputo and Michael J. Scanlon, pp. 170–184. Bloomington, Ind., 1999. Includes a response by Jacques Derrida.

Wright, Charles. *Negative Blue: Selected Later Poems.* New York, 2000.

KEVIN HART (2005)

LITERATURE: CRITICAL THEORY AND RELIGIOUS STUDIES

Interpretation and understanding of literature has been closely linked with the development of religious thought in nearly all cultures. Literary theory and theology are rarely separated, especially in contemporary, postmodern critical theory. The term hermeneutics, or the theory of interpretation, contains a reference to Hermes, the messenger of the gods according to Greek mythology. He helped humans to understand the decisions of the Olympians. Hermeneutics seeks not only to clarify the relationship between the text and the minds of those seeking to understand it, but also to bridge the gap between the earthly and the divine. In its origins, it is a profoundly theological task, closely associated with evolving from an oral to a written scriptural tradition and of translating texts from one language and culture to another. Transmitting sacred texts using the fallible sign systems of human language requires careful and methodical thought as a preservative against the taboos often associated with the translations of such texts. George Steiner, in his foreword to the 1973 book *Translating Religious Texts,* noted that in one tradition, the translation of the Hebrew Bible into the Greek Septuagint (probably begun in the third century BCE) was the result of angelic guidance. On the other hand, another tradition preserved in the *Megillath Taanith* (first century CE) records that three days of darkness enveloped the earth as mourning for expressing the Law in profane Greek.

HINDUISM AND BUDDHISM. In the Vedic period of Hinduism (c.1500–500 BCE), scholars memorized the learning (the word *Veda* means "knowledge") and handed it down orally; eventually, the ancient rulers and sages joined forces with the

Brahmin, who provided religious legitimization of their power, to begin composing written texts. The *Brahmanas* and the Upaniṣads discuss the meaning and purpose of Vedic ritual practices, the latter frequently indicating that nothing of value can be achieved by them in this changing world. By the fifth century, the Brahmins had developed a sophisticated system of phonetics and grammar (notably Panini's grammar of Sanskrit) which enabled the development of thinking in a wide range of literature, from mathematics texts of Hindu theology, and to poetry, most notably the *Mahābhārata,* within which is to be found the *Bhagavadgītā.* This poem gave rise to a vast tradition of commentary in Sanskrit and other Indian languages.

As Buddhism entered China, traveling through Central Asia, the process of assimilation occurred in three phases: first, the period of translation; next, the interpretation phase, called Ko-yi Buddhism, and finally, the philosophical systematization of the T'ien-t'ai and Hua yen schools. In the second century CE, Buddhist monks in Central Asia who were competent in Sanskrit and Chinese (as well as other languages) translated the texts. Consequently translation also resulted in interpretation, as Mahāyāna Buddhism shifted from interest in the historical Buddha to more philosophical concerns. Early translations gave rise to a new sort of hermeneutics, or phase of interpretation, called Ko-yi Buddhism. Based upon an analogical method (*ko-yi* means "extending the idea"), this approach explores the similarities between the Daoist "nothing" and the Buddhist "emptiness." Finally, by the sixth century CE, Kiyoshi Tsuchiya notes in *Major World Religions* that Chinese Buddhists of the T'ien-t'ai and Hua-yen schools had reinterpreted all the major doctrines into a synthetic whole, describing enlightenment in a sophisticated and speculative philosophical language, in contrast to the simple theology of Pure Land Buddhism.

THE RELIGIONS OF THE BOOK. In Sura 29.45 of the Qur'ān, it is urged: "Do not dispute with the People of the Book: say, we believe in what has been sent down to us and what has been sent down to you; our God and your God is one." The People of the Book are adherents of the three monotheistic religions: Judaism, Christianity, and Islam. These believers share a sense of the revealed nature of their sacred texts, but each faith adopts a very different understanding of textuality as well as its own distinct hermeneutical approach.

In a sense, the Qur'ān is not actually a text; rather, it is the recitation (qur'ān) of revelations by God, the *umm al-kitāb* (the "Mother of the Book"). In other words, it is fundamentally oral, and therefore it provokes a very different hermeneutics than, for example, the written tradition of the Christian Bible. Translation is literally impossible (rather than forbidden), while reading is not understood as an appropriation of the text but rather as a participation in it. As Gerald Bruns noted, in the 1992 book *Hermeneutics Ancient and Modern,* "To understand the Qur'ān is to disappear into it."

One of the greatest hermeneutical scholars of the Qur'ān was Abū Hāmid Muhammad al-Ghazāli (twelfth century CE). Al-Ghazāli's hermeneutics stress the primacy of seeing God for oneself within a mystical experience rather than relying on the authority of exegesis. He sets scriptural interpretation firmly at the level of individual experience; on this foundation, al-Ghazāli establishes rules for recitation, including posture instruction and reading speed. Recitation thus performed will lead the reader to a direct experience of God. Al-Ghazāli states that no darkness resides within the text itself, but only in the human mind; he describes the four veils that obscure understanding, such as adhering to dogma rather than witnessing mystical visions. But the purpose of recitation, he believes, is not exegesis or interpretation; instead, it is to experience the speech of God. In these hermeneutics, understanding of the text is not mediated by tradition; rather, understanding of the tradition is mediated by experience of the text.

Vast differences exist between such hermeneutics and the hermeneutics of Torah; the rabbinic tradition is rooted in utterly different understandings of its sacred texts. The Qur'ān exists only as recitation, while Torah exists only in, or as, its letters. As Susan Handelman explains in her 1982 book *The Slayers of Moses,* "Every crownlet of every letter is filled with significance, and even the forms of letters are hints to profound meanings." Jewish scholars have always understood the Torah, not as divinely inspired human words, but as the very words of God; not as a physical book, but as the blueprint and essence of creation. Thus, Erich Auerbach can say of the stories of *Genesis* that "doctrine and promise are incarnate in them and inseparable from them" (*Mimesis,* 1945), and their purpose is not to yield any clear meaning, but rather to leave traces and to provoke and demand many and different voices of interpretation. Against this background stands the genre of biblical exegesis known as *midrash,* which began with oral transmission in the rabbinic schools, and flourished at the time of the Tannaitic and Amoraic Sages (70–220 CE, and 220–400 CE). In his 1987 book *What is Midrash?,* Jacob Neusner defines midrash as "biblical exegesis by ancient Judaic authorities." He divides it into three approaches: first, Midrash as paraphrase, in which the commentator participates in the composition of the text; second, Midrash as prophecy; and third, Midrash as parable or allegory. Above all, midrash is to be seen as a process, rather than as an interpretative exercise seeking definite meaning. The midrashic was one of four overlapping schools of Jewish hermeneutics; the other three were the Literalist, which was applied particularly to deuteronomistic legislation, the Pesher, which was characteristic of the Qumran community and claimed particular knowledge of divine mysteries, and the Allegorical, which understood the text symbolically and pointed beyond itself to a deeper reality (Jeanrond, *Theological Hermeneutics,* 1991).

Before discussing early Christian hermeneutics, to the reader should briefly review classical literary theory; in particular, Plato, Aristotle, and the tradition of rhetoric, originating in ancient Greece and transmitted into Christian literature largely through the writings of Cicero (106–43 BCE). These traditions mingled with Jewish hermeneutics to form a body of hermeneutics that continues to serve as the foundation for literary critical theory in Western thought. As observed by Raman Selden in *The Theory of Criticism* (1988), Plato regarded the artist or poet as an imitator of imitations, twice removed from the "essential nature of a thing": the poet imitates a physical object which is merely a faint copy of the Idea (or Form) of the thing itself. In Plato's *Republic,* "imitation" (*mimesis*) is regarded negatively and seen as a decline from the purity of the original. Aristotle, on the other hand, in the *Poetics,* regards *mimesis* as a basic and instinctive human faculty; he sees literature not as an imitation of the illusion of reality, but as an imitation of what is essential to reality itself. Aristotle both develops and diverges from Plato, indicating that art and poetry do not simply appeal to the more inferior human faculties but to the natural human instinct to imitate.

These fundamental differences in classical literary understanding underlie the divergences between the two schools of Christian interpretation of the Bible, based at Alexandria and Antioch in the third and fourth centuries CE, respectively. Between them, they represent the most developed forms of early Christian hermeneutics. Both schools were deeply influenced by traditions of Jewish interpretation theory and practice. The first great scholar of the Platonic Alexandrian school, Clement of Alexandria (c. 150–215), received a broad education from both Jewish and Greek teachers. He established an allegorical reading of Scripture, understood as a language of symbols; this interpretation was taken up and systematized by Origen (c. 185–c. 254 CE). For Origen, because scripture contains the ultimate mystery, the texts can never be literal and are thus to be read allegorically. At the school of Antioch, however, following the local Jewish traditions of interpretation with an Aristotelian bent, scholars read scripture literally. They believed it described historical events and had no hidden meanings; its stories were therefore clear and available to all. One of its principal scholars, Theodore of Mopsuestia (c. 350–428), dismissed the Alexandrian interpreters as "stupid people."

The greatest of the early Christian scholars in the field of hermeneutics is undoubtedly St. Augustine of Hippo (354–430). Before his conversion to Christianity, Augustine was a teacher of classical rhetoric, deeply influenced by Cicero, and well read in classical philosophy. His influential work *De Doctrina Christiana* (On Christian Doctrine) is essentially a systematic hermeneutics, balancing both allegorical and literal readings of scripture, advocating a careful linguistic analysis of the texts, and developing a theory of signs (semiotics) which anticipates modern scholarship. Arguing that words are only signs, Augustine regarded the Bible as human texts that refer to God. He also insisted upon a proper attitude or perspective when reading Scripture, namely that of love, an insight that can only be derived from reading the Bible itself. He thus established the principle of the "hermeneutic circle," which was only fully acknowledged centuries later by scholar Friedrich Schleiermacher (1768–1834). Augustine's sophisticated theory of reading scripture remained largely unchallenged through the Middle Ages, and continues to provide the basis of much contemporary hermeneutical theory and practice.

Medieval and scholastic hermeneutics continued to insist that scripture offers not merely one way of reading; for example, Nicholas of Lyra (c. 1270–1349) described four ways—the literal, the allegorical, the moral, and the anagogical. Even so, biblical hermeneutics tended to take second place to the "science" of the theology of the Church. Change came about with the rise of the Christian Humanism of Renaissance thinkers like Desiderius Erasmus (c. 1466–1536) and the Protestant hermeneutics of Martin Luther and John Calvin. For Luther, the principle of *sola scriptura* ("scripture alone"), accompanied by the development of vernacular translations of the Bible, established a clear division between sacred and profane literature that would eventually separate the processes of studying the Bible from developments in the understanding of all other literature and literary theory. Thus, although scholar Terry Eagleton ascribes the growth of professional English studies in the later nineteenth century to one major cause, "the failure of religion" (Eagleton, *Literary Theory: An Introduction,* 1983), its roots also lie deep in Protestant hermeneutics. In the seventeenth century, the poet Andrew Marvell feared that John Milton's incursion into biblical space in *Paradise Lost* might result in the ruin of sacred truths ("On Mr. Milton's Paradise Lost"), and in the next century, Dr. Johnson remarked that Milton was preserved only "by religious reverence from licentiousness of fiction" (*The Lives of the Poets,* 1779–1781).

The eighteenth century in Germany and England saw the development of a technical science of hermeneutics that profoundly affected the way in which the Bible was read—changing to a hermeneutics of suspicion rather than a hermeneutics of faith. German theologian Schleiermacher established a critical balance between faith and reason, setting the pattern for contemporary biblical hermeneutics. Similar to St. Augustine, Schleiermacher insisted that scriptural reading be divided into two parts: *psychological interpretation,* which is concerned with the interplay between the text and the reader, and *grammatical interpretation,* which requires the careful examination of the linguistic and grammatical structures of the text. Later in the nineteenth century, German theologian David Friedrich Strauss (1808–1874), in his great 1835 work *Das Leben Jesu* (The Life of Jesus), read the gospels critically, seeking to undercut the Christian religion and its assumptions using a radical hermeneutics which anticipated a Christianity suited to the modern age, separate and distinct from its historical origins and scriptural traditions.

Biblical hermeneutics in the early part of the twentieth century was dominated by two figures, Swiss theologian Karl

Barth (1886–1986) and German theologian Rudolf Bultmann (1884–1976). Early in his career, Barth wrote: "The Historical-critical Method of Biblical investigation has its rightful place: It is concerned with the preparation of the intelligence–and this can never be superfluous. But, were I driven to choose between it and the venerable doctrine of Inspiration, I should without hesitation adopt the latter, which has a broader, deeper and more important justification" (preface to the first edition of *The Epistle to the Romans,* 1918). Barth admits his debt to such writers as Søren Kierkegaard (1813–1855) and Fyodor Dostoevsky (1821–1881) in his interpretation of the New Testament. Bultmann, on the other hand, bases his biblical hermeneutics firmly within the context of existentialist philosophy and the thought of the German philosopher Martin Heidegger (1889–1976), concentrating not upon a reconstruction of the beginning of the text's life (historical criticism of the Bible tends to focus on the origins of the text as the place of interpretation), but upon the present "existential" moment of encounter between the text and the reader. In the early twenty-first century, attention has turned to more recent developments in critical theory, hermeneutic, and religious studies; one of the major contributors has been French thinker Paul Ricoeur (1913–) whose long and multi-disciplinary career has been largely devoted to exploring the relationship between religious thought and literary reflection. In *The Symbolism of Evil* (1960), Ricoeur explores the notion of "evil" as always requiring a process of interpretation, a hermeneutics, for its very identification. In his more recent *Thinking Biblically* (1998), written in collaboration with the biblical scholar André LaCoque, he comments on specific passages from the Hebrew Bible, highlighting their metaphorical structure and indicating how they have acted as catalysts for philosophical reflection. For example, in his discussion of *Psalm* 22, Ricoeur explores how the structure and "poetic composition" of the psalm become the condition of its "reactualization" in prayer and religious reflection.

FROM MODERNITY TO POSTMODERNITY. In his article on literature and religion in the first edition of this encyclopedia, scholar Anthony Yu outlines the increasing importance of literary critical theory to biblical criticism and religious thought, giving particular emphasis to the effects of New Critical thinking and suggesting that "the history of literary theory over the past thirty years may be regarded a steady and increasingly stringent attack on . . . New Critical doctrines of the text and the interpreter." At the same time, however, many of the underlying doctrines of New Criticism have remained influential and tenacious in literary theory, even while the privilege given to the text as the vehicle of meaning has been eroded. In Yu's brief discussion, which concludes with comments on deconstruction and the earlier works of the French thinker Jacques Derrida and his "Cassandra-like" utterances against logocentrism and the "irreducibly sacred," he pays little attention to the globalization and politicization of critical theory, the merging of religious traditions in common critical discourses, the interaction between liberation ethics and theologies and literary and cultural theory, and the theological shift—often with a deeply mystical quality—represented in varieties of post-foundational thinking that owe much to poetic theory and practice. Such topics must be explored more fully.

Many of the most important figures working in contemporary and postmodern literary theory write from a Jewish background: Harold Bloom, Jacques Derrida, Geoffrey Hartman, Robert Alter, Emanuel Levinas, among others. Susan Handelman (*The Slayers of Moses* [1982], *Fragments of Redemption* [1991]) has examined the theological bases of current interpretation theory, suggesting a shift from the predominantly abstract and philosophical preoccupations of Hellenic thought to a more text-based approach reminiscent of rabbinic thought and practice. In *Kabbalah and Criticism* (1975), Harold Bloom addresses the "mysticism" of Jewish Kabbalah, differentiating it from Christian or Eastern mysticism as an interpretative tradition that sought knowledge in the Book and was centered in the Bible. If today literary criticism has become a kind of substitute theology, it is because arguably its concern for text and textuality is rooted in the theology of the Book, and Derrida, who often reminds others of his background in rabbinic traditions by autograph signatures ("Reb Derissa"—the laughing Rabbi) or graphic devices in his texts reminiscent of Talmudic commentary, promotes the matter of endless writing as if to set the Jewish against the more definitive Greco-Christian tradition (Christopher Norris, *Derrida,* 1987). The loss of certainty, which is often perceived as the deepest characteristic of postmodernity, is located by Derrida in "the absence of the Jewish God (who himself writes, when necessary). . . . As the absence and haunting of the divine sign, it regulates all modern criticism and aesthetics" (Derrida, *Writing and Difference,* 1978). From such beginnings was fashioned the "a/theology" of Mark C. Taylor's *Erring: A Postmodern A/theology* (1984), with its sense of the unending play of signification in the mazes of "erring Scripture," though Taylor's work begins by relocating Derrida's sense of the absent God in the "death of God," an "event" within the Christian tradition, as reported in the parable of the madman in German philosopher Friedrich Nietzsche's *The Gay Science* (1882).

Thus, close affinities exist between the hermeneutical practices of midrash and much of postmodern literary theory—the open-ended nature of the text, the emphasis on writing, the sense of the struggle with the text, and the participation in endless debate rather than the search to establish meaning. The claims of "literary approaches" to the Bible, however, as opposed to the scholarly approaches of the historical critical method—source, form and redaction criticism—began much earlier, and can be traced back at least to the work of scholar Austin Farrer in the 1950s, and the later debates over his work between Helen Gardner and Frank Kermode. It was Kermode, in his key text *The Genesis of Secrecy* (1979), writing as a "secular" critic, who reintroduced the narratives of Scriptures, and in particular the *Gos-*

pel of Mark, to the arena of literary debate alongside texts from fiction and poetry. Within Kermode's project are two strands, studying the Bible *as* literature (an activity denounced by poet T. S. Eliot as early as 1935, but taken up in the 1960s by literary scholars like T. R. Henn), and studying the Bible *within* the canons of literature. The pursuit of the first of these approaches resulted in the volume, which Kermode edited with Robert Alter, entitled *The Literary Guide to the Bible* (1987); this work sought to avoid the duplication of "traditional historical scholarship" and to celebrate the Bible as literature of major significance. Alter and Kermode specifically rejected the "cultural or metaphysical ruminations" of political or postmodern readings of the text—their literary approach remains profoundly based in New Critical assumptions. Such literary preoccupations, however, can never be as innocent as Kermode and Alter might seem to imply, and the redefinition of the task of interpretation in hermeneutics and contemporary literary theory has shifted biblical studies away from its traditional emphasis on historical origins and authorial intention towards greater attention to the reader and "reader-response." At the same time, the claims of deconstruction have challenged notions of the coherence and unity of the text; they also question the repressions inherent in such notions (Francis Watson, ed.; *The Open Text,* 1993). These two shifts have spawned various forms of liberation criticism that seek to expose the coherencies of power perceived both within the texts of the Bible and in the traditions of reading and interpreting them. Two major forms of such criticism exist: first, within various kinds of feminist critique; and second, within the growing field of post-colonial criticism of the Bible.

For example, feminist scholar Mieke Bal claims to establish a "countercoherence" in the *Book of Judges* which exposes the patriarchal narrative of salvation history as effecting an extreme, gender-bound violence against women, both within the social institutions of the book and its politics of history. Reading the stories of unnamed young women, such as that of the Levite's concubine in chapter 19, she develops an interdisciplinary hermeneutics, drawing upon narratology, anthropology, and other disciplines within the human sciences, to challenge what she calls the arbitrary and biased limits of biblical scholarship. A similar interdisciplinarity characterizes the newer project of postcolonial criticism of the Bible (R. S. Sugirtharajah, *Postcolonial Criticism and Biblical Interpretation,* 2002). This approach seeks a hermeneutics that exposes the imperialist oppression effected by biblical interpretation, accompanying colonial rule as the twin pillars of imperial control in the nineteenth-century empires of Great Britain, France, and Portugal. In his 1947 book *The British Empire in the Light of Prophecy,* Bernard Bateson identifies that imperial powers perceived their colonial acquisitions as fulfilling the prophecy of *Genesis* 28:14: "Thou shalt spread abroad to the west, and to the east, and to the north, and to the south."

Contemporary critical theory has affected theology and the interpretation of the Bible in four areas: representation, history, ethics, and aesthetics (Graham Ward, *Theology and Contemporary Critical Theory,* 1996).The work of Derrida and others on issues of text and textuality radically deconstruct traditional assumptions about subjectivity and text as representation, with massive implications for religious thought. Thus, scholar Luce Irigaray has stated: "We need to reinterpret everything concerning the relations between the subject and discourse, the subject and the world, the subject and the cosmic, the microcosmic and the macrocosmic. Everything, beginning with the way in which the subject has been written" (*An Ethics of Sexual Difference,* 1993). Moreover, the history, especially in the reading of the Bible, has been deconstructed by critics such as Michel Foucault, resisting and breaking up those continuities which, he suggests, silence the articulation and voice of the imprisoned and oppressed. Far from advocating, as some would suggest, a kind of nihilistic textual free play, postmodern criticism opens up radical ethical perspectives and "an unconditional categorical imperative or moment of affirmation" (Critchley, *The Ethics of Deconstruction,* 1992) that are deeply rooted in ancient and neglected forms of theological thinking. Finally, a renewed interest in aesthetics relates closely to questions of representation and the importance of the poet and the artist in primary religious reflection and experience.

Although Jewish and Christian perspectives have been predominant in all such contemporary critical theory, a great deal of such activity has been characterized by a non-adherence to any particular religious tradition or confession. Indeed, much of modern literary theory is atheistic, first heavily dependent upon Enlightenment thought and later upon Marxist, psychoanalytic, and other skeptical forms of analysis. In *The Death of the Author* (1968), Roland Barthes describes the post-structuralist emphasis on textuality as "an anti-theological activity." At the same time, with increasing critical globalization, broad discussions within literary theory have also begun to embrace the texts and theologies of Eastern religions and Islam. But scholars continue to vigorously defend Christian literary theory, even after recognizing the modern objections to it, arguing that an act of faith is present in all systems of thought (Luke Ferretter, *Towards a Christian Literary Theory,* 2003). Within the interdisciplinary study of literature and religion in North America and the United Kingdom over the past fifty years, bold advances in literary theory and textual analysis have either provoked defenses of theology and biblical critics—within the terms of a Christian anthropology which still recognize the possibilities for the Christian critic and post-structuralist and postmodern thought—or else have driven new forms of theological thinking (though often within ancient ancestors) that are radical yet continue to claim Christian roots. Kevin Mills, for example, in his 1995 book *Justifying Language,* reads the Pauline letters through the lens of contemporary hermeneutics, which he claims can be thereby a Christian hermeneutics of faith, hope, and charity.

In the decade after biblical criticism finally produced the widely read *Postmodern Bible* (1995), written by "the Bible and Culture Collective," and its companion volume *The Postmodern Bible Reader* (2001), which has entered the arena of cultural studies, others have begun to acknowledge the passing of postmodernism. Yet before the majority of theologians have even begun to take seriously the possibility of a "postmodern theology," some have started to ponder what a post-postmodern theology might be like. In his book *After Theory* (2003), Terry Eagleton argues for the end of the age of "high theory" in literary and cultural studies. He claims that the new narrative of global capitalism exposes those questions that cultural theory has largely overlooked—the ancient issues of love, evil, death, morality, and religion. When a literary theorist like Eagleton, who was nurtured on Cambridge Marxism in the 1960s, concludes his latest book with a chapter entitled "Death, Evil and Non-being," those whose acknowledged business is religious studies need to take note.

Hermeneutics was nurtured on the reading of sacred texts, while the histories of religious thought and hermeneutics are bound together in all the great religious traditions. In Western thinking, the radical beliefs of the "death of God" theologians (Thomas J. J. Altizer, William Hamilton, and others) emerged from a profound interaction with poetry and literature; they asked radical questions about the identity of Christianity. In the 1966 book *Radical Theology and the Death of God,* Altizer asked, "Must Christianity be identified with its given or orthodox dogmatic form?" What had begun to appear was a form of non-foundational theology, in the work of the British theologian Don Cupitt, for example, based on the radical critique of the western metaphysics of presence by Heidegger and Derrida, and sharing much in common with the ancient theologies of mysticism and the *via negativa.* Scholar Mark C. Taylor has been defined as the first American "post-ecclesiastical theologian . . . free of the scars or perhaps even the memory of Church theology" (Altizer). It remains to be seen if, in the aftermath of a critical revolution which much religious thought has yet to acknowledge, religious studies can survive as more than a form of historical enquiry, or whether the reading and interpretation of sacred texts will continue as other than merely a branch of wider literary studies outside the closed communities of traditional faith. Critical theory has offered a challenge to hermeneutics and religious thought that will not be denied if reading and thinking are to remain universal activities based on defensible universal principles. According to Cupitt, scholars must learn how to re-read Scripture in a radically different way: "The remedy is to learn to read the text horizontally, from sign to sign, and then we will see that the sideways resonance of the metaphoric is directly ethical. . . . And if we thus relearn reading, then perhaps the text will not seem quite so intellectually obsolete as we feared it was" (*The Long-Legged Fly,* 1987).

BIBLIOGRAPHY

Alter, Robert. *The Art of Biblical Narrative.* London, 1981.

Bible and Culture Collective, The. *The Postmodern Bible.* New Haven, Conn., 1995.

Bloom, Harold. *Kabbalah and Criticism.* New York, 1975.

Bloom, Harold. *Ruins the Sacred Truths: Poetry and Belief from the Bible to the Present Day,* Cambridge, Mass. 1987.

Bruns, Gerald L. *Hermeneutics Ancient and Modern.* New Haven, Conn., 1992.

Budick, Sanford and Wolfgang Iser, eds. *Languages of the Unsayable: The Play of Negativity in Literature and Literary Theory.* New York, 1989.

Detweiler, Robert and David Jasper, eds. *Religion and Literature: A Reader.* Louisville, Ky., 2000.

Exum, J. Cheryl and Stephen D. Moore, eds. *Biblical Studies/Cultural Studies.* Sheffield, U.K., 1998.

Ferretter, Luke. *Towards a Christian Literary Theory.* London, 2003.

Fiddes, Paul S. *Freedom and Limit: A Dialogue between Literature and Christian Doctrine.* London, 1991.

Handelman, Susan A. *The Slayers of Moses: The Emergence of Rabbinic Interpretation in Modern Literary Theory.* New York, 1982.

Hartman, Geoffrey H. and Simon Budick, eds. *Midrash and Literature.* New Haven, Conn., 1986.

Jasper, David and Stephen Prickett, eds. *The Bible and Literature: A Reader.* Oxford, U.K., 1999.

Jeanrond, Werner G. *Theological Hermeneutics: Development and Significance.* London, 1991.

Kermode, Frank. *The Genesis of Secrecy: On the Interpretation of Narrative.* Cambridge, Mass., 1979.

Kermode, Frank and Robert Alter, eds. *The Literary Guide to the Bible.* London, 1987.

Selden, Raman. *The Theory of Criticism from Plato to the Present: A Reader.* London, 1988.

Steiner, George. *After Babel: Aspects of Language and Translation.* 2d ed. Oxford, U.K., 1992.

Sugirtherajah, R. S. *Postcolonial Criticism and Biblical Interpretation.* Oxford, 2002.

Taylor, Mark C. *Erring: A Postmodern A/theology.* Chicago, 1984.

Ward, Graham. *Theology and Contemporary Critical Theory.* London, 1996.

DAVID JASPER (2005)

LITHUANIAN RELIGION SEE BALTIC RELIGION

LITURGICAL DANCE SEE DANCE, *ARTICLE ON* THEATRICAL AND LITURGICAL DANCE

LITURGY. The English term *liturgy,* like its parallels in other languages, is primarily Christian. It denotes acts and scripts of worship in Christian experience. By now, however, the word is widely used for similarly ritualized phenomena in other religions too. By extension, it may even be applied to ritual that occurs outside of religion (strictly speaking) altogether. It is derived from the Greek *leitourgia,* meaning work "performed for the public good," in this case sacrificial acts that served the gods on whom civic welfare ultimately depended. The Septuagint used the term as the Greek equivalent to the Hebrew Bible's *avodah,* "the sacrificial service," and Christianity retained it for the priestly work of Jesus (*Heb.* 8:6) and the ministry of Paul (*Rom.* 15:16). In Judaism, *avodah* is still found in some prayer-book titles, prayer being seen as the replacement for sacrifice.

The Greek-speaking church, in the East, used liturgy to denote the eucharist. In the West, churches adopted other nomenclature: *mass* or the *sacrament* for eucharist; and *divine, daily,* or *ecclesiastical office* to mean non-eucharistic daily prayer. By the 1830s, however, as part of a hunt for liturgical origins, liturgy was revived to designate corporate church prayer in general. The Oxford movement, for example, proclaimed liturgy central to the Church of England; and Roman Catholics developed a Liturgical movement variously traced to the Benedictine revival in France of Prosper Gueranger (1805–1875), the pastoral work in Belgium of Lambert Beauduin (1873–1960), and others. Other primary figures were theologian Odo Casel (1886–1948); Virgil Michael (1890–1938), who brought the Liturgical Movement to the United States and founded its primary organ of liturgical research in 1926 (*Orate Fratres,* renamed *Worship* in 1951); and scholars Anton Baumstark (1872–1948) and Gregory Dix (1901–1952), whose *Comparative Liturgy* and *The Shape of the Liturgy* (respectively) became classics. These developments culminated in Vatican II (1962–1965) within Roman Catholicism, and similar movements for liturgical renewal in other churches.

Liturgy frames issues around which matters of identity have been fought—for instance, the Calvinist preference (dating from the Reformation) for purely biblical prayer; the institutionalization of Taoist ritual under K'ou Ch'ien-chih (365–448); and Islamic processions to mourn the killing of the prophet's grandson. Cultural rifts among modern Christians have revolved around other issues, primarily:

- the language of prayer (its register, inclusivity, and doctrinal precision);
- the musical canon (inherited hymns alone or contemporary jazz);
- inculturation (altering the liturgy to reflect the culture of the people assembled);
- ordination of women; and
- the status of gays and lesbians.

Contemporary liturgical change in Judaism reflects these same cultural rifts, but centers also on the relative importance of prayer in Hebrew rather than the vernacular.

FROM TEXT TO RITUAL. As a modern scholarly discipline, liturgy has focused on the origins and evolution of ritual texts. It emerged in nineteenth-century evolutionary theory, which Romanticism applied to literary traditions, seeing them as plants that are seeded and then grow through time, sometimes attracting weeds that sully the garden's purity. Religions were thus assumed to have an authentic liturgical canon, the history of which can be traced through scientific attention to manuscript recension. Some liturgists have dedicated themselves simply to unearthing liturgical manuscripts and preparing scientific versions of them. Others have applied this scholarship to implicit religious concerns, citing discoveries of ancient or alternative liturgies to support the status quo or to challenge it, reviving some traditions and jettisoning others.

The most significant recent development in the study of liturgy is its identification as ritual, not just literature. Like drama, liturgies may exist in printed modes, but the written text of *Hamlet,* for example, is not the actual play—the performance is. Unlike letters, stories, and chronicles, liturgy is a text (usually composite), written or oral, intended for ritual performance. It can even be the performance itself: its words, gestures, melodies, clothing, spaces, props, and roles. *Worship* (from the old English *weorthscipe,* implying "worth–ship"), is the term most employed to characterize the faithful playing out of such a liturgy.

Liturgy, then, is a kind of ritual, presumably a religious ritual. But differentiating it as distinctively religious is as difficult as defining religion itself, and definitions derived from Christian practice may not do justice elsewhere. It is common, for instance, to limit liturgy to public corporate celebrations, but Buddhism, Hinduism, and Judaism feature significant domestic ritual that should be included in the category. Then too, the blurring of the division between religious and secular results in modern liturgies that reflect both influences: civil marriages with religious components, for example, or national and civic liturgies with at least once–religious connotations, like American Thanksgiving services, or even the national anthem of the Third Reich—originally a Haydn hymn. In 2003, an American prison population claiming expressly not to be a religion won the legal right to celebrate its own liturgy anyway.

Liturgies can be variously catalogued—like liturgies of protest, such as a gay-pride parade, and liturgies of anguish, such as ceremonies attendant on the 9/11 disaster. Since the 1960s, increasing inventiveness has provided variations on established liturgical practice, such as a feminist eucharist with a female "Christa" on a cross; but new traditions have sprung up too, such as the displaying of an ever-growing AIDS quilt. Some would even include as liturgy such rituals as opening a major sporting event.

Liturgies can be considered internally and externally. Internally, liturgies are open to whatever specific critique a particular religion applies to itself: theology for Christians; *halakhah* for Jews; *shariah* for Muslims; or *dharma* for Hindus and Buddhists. External considerations apply objective measures, like the literary model through which the study of liturgy first arose. Defining liturgy as ritual performance has spawned other methods of investigation, like studies of artistic communication, or even studies of how technology influences liturgical expression: invention of coffee brought about all-night ritual to Jewish mysticism; moveable type universalized prayer texts, erasing local variation; and nineteenth-century rail transportation permitted suburban cemeteries that prompted liturgies for funeral homes.

The terms liturgy and ritual are somewhat difficult to disentangle, especially because ritual has its own religious usage in, for example, Methodism. Narrowly conceived, liturgy is the ritual side of religion. But more broadly, liturgy becomes a subsection of the larger discipline of ritual studies (Grimes, 1982), so that insight into ritual informs the understanding of liturgy as well.

The turn to ritual studies came primarily in the post-industrial west where liturgical renewal was responding to modern sensitivities such as gender egalitarianism; internal anachronisms like the marginalization of worshipers from full liturgical participation in Roman Catholicism; and an inherited protest against ritual in many Protestant churches and Reform Judaism. Nearly every discipline in the human sciences has subsequently provided insight, but anthropology and linguistic philosophy have proved most helpful.

ANTHROPOLOGY. The contemporary application of cultural anthropology to liturgy has had to contend with four challenges from prior research. A psychological attack is associated with Sigmund Freud (1856–1939), for whom ritual is merely obsessive–compulsive neurosis: both are marked, paradigmatically, by strictly controlled touching and eating. Freud's tracing of ritual's origins to an elemental act of incest has been widely dismissed, but liturgy does, in fact, often resemble obsessive behavior, and is still popularly attacked as religiously undesirable, or at least subservient to doctrine and morals (Freud, 1913).

A sophisticated neo-Marxist approach (Bloch, 1989) emphasizes liturgy's verbal form: song, chanting, and repetitive but invariable wording. Communications theory measures cognitively meaningful messages according to the extent that a listener can predict what the speaker will say. Liturgy such as hymns, chants, or intoning praise, provides almost total predictability, so has little or no cognitive content to debate and is therefore charged with underwriting the ineluctable "rightness" of traditional authority among people who would be better off resisting oppression.

The sociological attack is more subtle in that its founder, Emile Durkheim, actually lauded religious ritual for the powerful way it underwrites the legitimacy of social morality. But Durkheim anticipated the replacement of religious liturgies by nationalistic secular alternatives that would accomplish the same thing (Durkheim, 1912).

A fourth challenge came from early armchair anthropologists like Edward Tylor (1832–1917) and James Frazer (1854–1941), who forced primitive liturgies of which they had read or heard into a straightjacket of social evolutionism.

These approaches suffer from reductionism: isolating some specific aspect of ritual (and therefore liturgy) and then identifying it as a sorry, and even immoral, remnant of early human history. Liturgy does follow fixed sequences of behavior, but it need not be a compulsive disorder. Liturgical language features linguistic redundancy, but this is not necessarily a ploy by authorities. And even though liturgy claims to access the sacred, the sacred is not solely a socially useful phantasm that supports the social order. Liturgists may agree with some characterizations made by Freud, Marx, Durkheim, and their followers, but liturgists draw different conclusions than they did.

Philologists studying origins and history of liturgical texts claim scientific absoluteness: the prayer is either rightly or wrongly dated to a certain era and author; there can be only one right answer. Ritualists are more like drama critics watching a liturgy and interpreting its messages. Their claims are what philosopher Susanne Langer (1895–1985) called presentational, not scientific: rather than true or false, they are judged by how compelling they appear, and there is more than one right answer. As cultural ethnographers, liturgists posit interpretations in keeping with a particular religion's internal explanations, but also according to the way liturgies seem externally to function. Other liturgists still study just the liturgical scripts, keeping in mind, however, that they are scripts for performances, not literary works alone. Yet others are musicologists or ethnomusicologists, concerned predominantly with the history or cultural performance of liturgical music.

Cognitively speaking, it is possible to see liturgies as expressions of metaphysical reality for their participants. In that regard, it is convenient to think in terms of three variables: (1) theology (the nature of God or some other higher power, organizing force, principle or reality, like the Upanisad Brahman); (2) religious anthropology (the nature of human beings—born to original sin; reincarnations according to the principle of Karma; or the absolute servants of God, as in Islam); and (3) cosmology (the nature of the universe–neutral as to human action, as in Epicureanism, or perfectible by human action, as in Jewish Kabbalah). Participants take their existential stand at the convergence of these three metaphysical variables, which liturgies expound through word and action. Liturgies posit sacred places; shape time with sacred fasts and festivals; define ideal lives by imposing life-cycle moments (first communion, marriage, ordination); conceptualize human nature (given free will, prone to sin); posit human projects (the Buddhist eight-fold path, the pillars of Islam); and cement relationships with the universe (through sacred soil, perhaps) and with each other (born into a caste, predestined as chosen elect). Along the way liturgies shape sacred history, not just what has been, but what can still be expected to pass, and, therefore, the hopes participants may rightly hold. Liturgies express the rules by which human destiny unfolds: the logic of daily experience. They rehearse formative or revelatory moments of original visionaries by including them in sacred narratives that may be read, chanted, sung, or acted out so as to map their categories on the world and instruct religious adherents on how to find their way within it. More immediately, liturgies organize relations of power, gender difference, and social classby rooting them in assumed metaphysical reality.

Typical of anthropological influence has been rite-of-passage theory, going back to Arnold van Gennep (1908): liturgies separate participants from an old status, transition them betwixt and between, and incorporate them into a new status. Victor Turner (1969) emphasized the potential of transitional (liminal) moments, when neither the old nor the new limit creative vision. Other theorists widely cited are Clifford Geertz, who saw liturgies as symbolic demonstrations of a people's ethos and world view (Geertz, 1973) and "the kind of lives [their] societies support" (Geertz, 1983); and Mary Douglas, who emphasized the body as a symbolizing entity and linked forms of ritualism to specific social structures (Douglas, 1970). Using Turner's emphasis on the potential of liminal moments to produce social and psychological transformation, liturgy's advocates have argued that liturgy is morally empowering (Driver, 1991).

Contemporary theory is multidisciplinary, bringing together such studies as mythology from Lévi-Strauss in 1963 and Eliade in 1954; performance practice from Turner in 1982; and even ritual's biogenetic basis from Newberg, D'Aquilli, and Rause in 2001. Most theorists assume overall that liturgies posit systems of meaning—a view that goes back to pioneers like Max Weber (1864–1920)—especially in "limit" moments, Clifford Geertz describes as intellectual bafflement, inexplicable suffering, and ethical paradox (Geertz, 1973).

LINGUISTIC PHILOSOPHY. By the end of the nineteenth century, western philosophy seemed mired in two equally undesirable alternatives: British empiricism, according to which the world is available only through the senses; and René Descartes's (1596–1630) claim that only introspection determines certainty. The latter solution could not guarantee that sensations from within represent the universe without; but the empiricists fared no better, because in the end, what one sees (as it were) is not at all what one gets. Neither school could guarantee a genuine world beyond one's own invention. Immanuel Kant's (1724–1804) attempt to admit the role of a constructing mind, while yet saving external reality, was whittled away by Georg Wilhelm Friedrich Hegel (1770–1831), for whom reality was pure spirit.

These philosophical wars over the nature of reality had consequences for liturgical traditions that posit experience of God, hope, *atman,* salvation, *samsara, jihad,* and other presumably real entities, which ought to fit dominant theory of what can be reliably known. The question became whether what liturgy posits is not just chimerical, and if so, how one can know it.

A variety of responses have therefore arisen to justify liturgical claims. Hermeneuticist Paul Ricoeur, for instance, admitted the right to suspect naive theological assumptions. But he thought a new and sophisticated naivete would penetrate the world of symbols and see truths that ordinary sense–data miss. By far the most impactful modern philosophical trend has been what philosopher Gustav Bergmann (1906–1987) labeled "the linguistic turn." It began with scientifically influenced philosophers who denied all reality to statements that are neither empirical nor logically deducible from empirical bases. Propositions in liturgy (like those of aesthetics, ethics, and religion generally) are, therefore, neither true nor false, but simply meaningless. If liturgy is not saying anything meaningful, what is its point?

Ludwig Wittgenstein (1889–1951) provided the philosophical possibility of meaningful liturgical statements. His *Tractatus Logico-Philosophicus* (1921) concluded that even though empirical reality was all that could be spoken about, anything that really mattered existed beyond speech and would have to be shown. Wittgenstein's later *Philosophical Investigations* (1953) described language as a series of games, only one of which is the description of empirical reality. Other games include naming, ordering, or offering to do something; these do not describe reality, but are not on that account meaningless.

With Wittgenstein, emphasis switched from determining what liturgical language describes to asking what it does. If liturgy does not describe empirical reality, perhaps it shows it, the way art, for instance, demonstrates truths that elude simple declarative sentences. Or, following contemporary pragmatists, perhaps liturgy manufactures truths as much as it discovers them (Rorty, 1999; Putnam, 1994; Goodman, 1978). Here liturgy meets philosophy and the human sciences, which also see ritual as accomplishing something, such as life-cycle passages. A particularly influential approach derives from J. L. Austin (1911–1960), who called some speech-acts "performative" in that the very act of uttering them performs certain tasks: Saying, "I bet you fifty dollars," establishes a wager; similarly, saying, "I declare you husband and wife" accomplishes what it says in the very saying of it—as long as apt circumstances accompany the remark (husband and wife cannot be a dog and a cat, for example). In both the wager and the wedding, a speech act provides words that are measurable not as true or false, but as "felicitous or infelicitous"—it works (because done properly) or it does not (Austin, 1962).

With Austin, and then with John Searle, liturgy emerged as a ritualized creative act bringing into being institutional facts like marriage, a new year, pardon from sin, and other states constituted by a religion's internal category scheme. Liturgy is universal to human society because it defines into being the categories of social life, religious or otherwise, without which there would be no social life at all (Searle, 1969, 1995).

THE FUTURE OF LINGUISTIC STUDY. Contemporary trends in liturgical study still include historical reconstruction. They also encompass whatever internal studies a religion finds meaningful, as well as insights from the human sciences and philosophy, and the role of the arts in what is increasingly perceived as a performative discipline. Still in their relative infancy, for example, are studies of the way space and music transform script into performance. In addition, studies of Christian and Jewish liturgy have much to learn from the expansion of purview beyond western experience to include the vast panorama of liturgical expression worldwide.

BIBLIOGRAPHY

From a Christian perspective, the history of the Eucharist is most fully covered in Joseph A. Jungmann, *The Mass of the Roman Rite,* 2 vols. (Westminster, Md., 1986). For an excellent survey overall, see Theodor Klauser, *A Short History of the Western Liturgy* (1965: Eng. Ed. Oxford, 1979). Protestant liturgy is surveyed in James F. White, *Protestant Worship* (Louisville, Ky., 1989). Reuven Hammer's, *Entering Jewish Prayer* (New York, 1994) and *Entering the High Holy Days* (Philadelphia, 1998) provide a modern and accessible survey of traditional Jewish liturgy. *My People's Prayerbook* (Woodstock, Vt., 1997–2004, Lawrence A. Hoffman, ed.) provides traditional Jewish liturgy in detail, alongside modern commentaries. During its brief existence, *Liturgy Digest* (Nathan Mitchell, ed., 1994–1997) devoted exceptionally fine treatment to a variety of liturgical topics, along with bibliographic details. *Worship,* the North American journal of record for Christian liturgy, has been available since 1926. In 1987, the newly launched *Journal of Ritual Studies* began publishing significant articles on ritual aspects of liturgy. Paul Bradshaw, ed., *The New Westminster Dictionary of Liturgy and Worship* (Louisville, Ky., 2002), includes specific prayers and liturgical items; and Edward Foley, ed., *Worship Music: A Concise Dictionary* (Collegeville, Minn., 2000) briefly defines musical entries. Paul Bradshaw, Lawrence A. Hoffman, and Janet Walton, eds., provide a six-volume series, *Two Liturgical Traditions* (Notre Dame, 1991–1999), tracing parallels and differences in Jewish and Christian liturgy.

A sampling of other recent books of significance includes the following:

Austin, J. L. *How to Do Things with Words.* Oxford, 1962.

Bell, Catherine M. *Ritual Theory, Ritual Practice.* New York, 1992.

Bloch, Maurice. *Ritual, History and Power.* London, 1989.

Driver, Thomas, *The Magic of Ritual* [*Liberating Rites*]. New York, 1991.

Douglas, Mary. *Natural Symbols.* London, 1970.

Durkheim, Emile. *The Elementary Forms of Religious Life* (1912). English ed., New York, 1995.

Eliade, Mircea. *The Myth of the Eternal Return.* Princeton, N.J., 1954.

Freud, Sigmund, *Totem and Taboo* (1913). English ed., London, 1950.

Geertz, Clifford. *The Interpretation of Cultures.* New York, 1973.

Gill, Sam D. *Native American Religious Action.* Columbia, S.C., 1987.

Goodman, Nelson. *Ways of Worldmaking.* Indianapolis, 1978.

Grimes, Ronald L. *Beginnings in Ritual Study,* Washington, D.C., 1982

Grimes, Ronald L. *Ritual Criticism.* Columbia, S.C., 1990.

Hoffman, Lawrence A. *Beyond the Text.* Bloomington, Ind., 1987.

Hoffman, Lawrence A. *The Way into Jewish Prayer.* Woodstock, Vt., 2000.

Langer, Ruth. *To Worship God Properly.* Cincinnati, Ohio, 1998.

Levi–Strauss, Claude. *Structural Anthropology.* New York, 1963.

Newberg, Andrew, Eugene D'Aquili, and Vince Rause. *Why God Won't Go Away.* New York, 2001.

Putnam, Hilary. *Pragmatism.* Cambridge, Mass., 1995.

Rappaport, Roy. *Ecology, Meaning and Religion.* Berkeley, Calif., 1979.

Rorty, Richard. *Philosophy and Social Hope.* New York, 1999.

Schechner, Richard and Willa Appel, eds. *By Means of Performance: Intercultural Studies of Theatre and Ritual.* New York, 1990.

Schulz, Hans-Joachim. *The Byzantine Liturgy* (1980). English ed., New York, 1986.

Turner, Victor W. *The Ritual Process.* Chicago, 1969.

Turner, Victor W. *From Ritual to Theatre.* New York, 1982.

Searle, John R. *Speech Acts.* London, 1969.

Searle, John R. *The Construction of Social Reality.* New York. 1995.

Van Gennep, Arnold. *Rites of Passage* (1908). English ed., Chicago, 1960.

Wittgenstein, Ludwig. *Philosophical Investigations.* New York, 1958.

Wittgenstein, Ludwig. *Lectures and Conversations on Aesthetics, Psychology and Religious Belief.* Berkeley, Calif., n.d.

LAWRENCE A. HOFFMAN (2005)

LIU AN (c. 180–122 BCE), second king of Huainan, also known as Huainanzi; Chinese philosopher, poet, and essayist. Liu An was the grandson of Liu Pang (d. 194 BCE), founder of the Han dynasty. Shortly after the birth of An's father, Liu Chang (b. 199 BCE), the woman who bore him committed suicide when denied formal recognition by the emperor. The seventh of eight sons of the emperor by different women, Liu Chang was twice passed over in the imperial succession, which left him bitter and resentful. In 172 BCE Liu Chang, then king of the vassal state of Huainan, was banished to a remote corner of the empire for insulting his half brother, the emperor Wen. He died en route, leaving Liu An and his two younger brothers. In 164 BCE Liu Chang's fief of Huainan was divided among his three sons, with the eldest, Liu An, receiving the title of King of Huainan. He also inherited his father's disdain for the imperial line; twice he plotted rebellion.

CENTER OF CULTURE AND LEARNING AT HUAINAN. The biographies of Liu An all speak of him as a youth who eschewed martial pursuits in favor of literature, music, and philosophy. He quickly developed his literary talent and at the age of twenty-two is said to have written, upon imperial command, a brilliant essay on the famous Chu poem the *Li Sao* in the few hours between dawn and breakfast. In 154 BCE, Liu An almost took part in the unsuccessful rebellion of Liu Pi but changed his mind at the last moment. Some time later he decided to establish his court as a center of learning. He opened his court in Shouchun to philosophers, poets, and masters of esoteric techniques *(fangshi).* History speaks of a major center developing there, a focal point for the last flourishing of the ancient culture of Chu, a region renowned for its mysticism and shamanism. In the great tradition of King Xuan of Qi (c. 310 BCE), the founder of the Jixia Academy at which the *Guanzi* was probably written, and Lü Buwei (c. 240 BCE), sponsor of the *Lüshi chunqiu,* Liu An was patron to many of the finest religious and philosophical minds of his time. However, unlike these earlier patrons, An took an active part in philosophical discussions and the writing of essays and poems. He also collected an extensive library that contained all the major pre-Han philosophical texts, including his favorite, the *Zhuangzi.*

The center of culture and learning founded by Liu An was distinctly oriented toward Daoism and rivaled the largely Confucian center at the imperial court in Chang'an. It lasted for almost three decades and toward its end became a target of powerful officials in the imperial court. In 122 BCE Liu An was convicted of plotting rebellion, and imperial representatives were sent to Huainan to punish him. Before they arrived, Liu An took his own life. Despite the conviction, the challenge presented by the rival Daoist-based intellectual center in Huainan was undoubtedly a more powerful motivation for the successful prosecution of Liu An than his hopeless plans for rebellion. Whatever the reason, Liu An and his family perished, and the vibrant center he established came to a tragic and untimely end.

WRITING THE *HUAINANZI*. Today all that remains of this last flourishing of Chu culture is one book, the *Huainanzi,* and an extensive list of others that attest to the vibrancy of the Huainan court. Among the writings produced are a number in which Liu An was directly involved. Two essays on the *Zhuangzi* and a collection of eighty-two poems, all now lost, are credited to him. Also listed under his name are three treatises identified simply as the "Inner Book," which discussed the Dao; the "Outer Book," which discussed miscellaneous doctrines; and the "Middle Book," which dealt with esoteric alchemical techniques. Of the three, only the "Inner Book," which Liu An presented to Emperor Wu in 139 BCE, has survived intact. This is the work that has come down to us under the name of *Huainanzi.* It stands as his major contribution to Chinese thought.

Of the reportedly several thousand philosophers and adepts at the court of Liu An, eight are named with him in the authorship of the *Huainanzi.* Liu An probably established the scope and format of the work, wrote some of the essays, and then edited the essays and wrote the final summary and overview. The resulting text consists of twenty-one essays on topics ranging from cosmology, astronomy, and geography to self-cultivation, human relations, and government. It was clearly intended to be a compendium of knowledge about the nature of the universe and the human role within it. Its extensive use of pre-Han philosophical and religious sources indicates not the mere repetition of earlier ideas, as some have maintained, but rather a bold and innovative attempt at their synthesis and an application to contemporary concerns.

The topics considered and the viewpoints represented in the essays of the *Huainanzi* occur in the context of a consistent cosmology that is best described as a blend of the Daoism of the *Laozi* and *Zhuangzi* and the Naturalist philosophy of *yin* and *yang* and the Five Phases *(wuxing)* of energy *(qi),* first systematized by Zou Yan (c. 340–270 BCE). Some scholars identify this synthesis as the syncretic Daoist philosophy associated with the long-lost intellectual lineage that historical sources call "The Way of the Yellow Emperor and Lao Tzu" *(Huang-Lao zhi Dao).* This synthesis remains faithful to the earlier Daoist cosmology of an organismic universe of totally interrelated phenomena, which spontaneously tend toward harmony and are interfused by the unifying and creative power of the Dao. However, the *Huainanzi* provides a more detailed explanation of the actual mechanisms of this universe in terms of *yin* and *yang* and the Five Phases. Because human beings are an integral part of this universe and are thus subject to its laws, all human activity, from politics to warfare to spiritual self-realization, must take these universal forces into account. The *Huainanzi* balances both cosmological and social-political perspectives in its thorough emphasis on the universal context of human nature and human activity. In so doing, it has made a significant contribution to the evolution of the unique Chinese worldview.

THE *HUAINANZI* AND INNER CULTIVATION. As might be expected in light of the number of religious adepts at the court of Liu An, the *Huainanzi* has left its mark in the area of spiritual self-cultivation as well. A number of passages stress the importance and provide examples of meditative techniques of "nourishing one's inherent nature" *(yangxing)* and "nourishing the spirit" *(yangshen),* such as controlled breathing and calming the mind. An important contribution of the *Huainanzi* lies in its elaboration of how these techniques function in terms of Five-Phases philosophy. This elaboration places the *Huainanzi* firmly within the meditative tradition of "inner cultivation" that reaches back to the fourth century BCE "Inward Training" *(Neiye)* text in the *Guanzi* and ahead to the physiological alchemy that was later developed and expanded in the Daoist religion. There were undoubtedly adepts who followed these practices at the court of Liu An, perhaps the *fangshi,* and it was the spiritual descendants of such people who were involved in the early organization of the Daoist church some three centuries later. It is no surprise that the *Huainanzi* was later included in the comprehensive collection of Daoist canonical works, the *Daozang.* Another contributing factor must be the legend that Liu An did not die, but attained immortality after consuming an elixir given him by the *fangshi.*

While most of the works written by Liu An and his associates have regrettably been lost, their contribution to the development of Chinese religion and philosophy has survived in the form of the *Huainanzi.*

See Also Daoism, article on Daoist Literature; Fangshi; Yinyang Wuxing.

Bibliography

The most complete Western source on the life of Liu An is Benjamin E. Wallacker's "Liu An, Second King of Huai-nan," *Journal of the American Oriental Society* 92 (January–March 1972): 36–49. The *Shiji* biographies of Liu An and his father have been translated in Burton Watson's *Records of the Grand Historian of China,* vol. 2 (New York, 1963), pp. 359–381. In *The Huainanzi and Liu An's Claim to Moral Authority* (Albany, N.Y., 2001), Griet Vankeerberghen has written an insightful study of the philosophy of the *Huainanzi* in the historical context of the events of 123–22 BCE that led to Liu An's suicide and the destruction of his intellectual center. The most thorough textual study of the *Huainanzi* is *The Textual History of the Huai-nan Tzu* (Ann Arbor, Mich., 1993) by Harold D. Roth. A summary of this history can be found in Charles LeBlanc's article in *Early Chinese Texts: A Bibliographical Guide* (Berkeley, Calif., 1993), edited by Michael Loewe. There is one complete French translation of the *Huainanzi* made by a team of eight scholars under the direction of Charles LeBlanc and Rémi Mathieu: *Philosophes taoïstes, tome 2: Huainan zi* (Paris, 2003). There are also a number of partial translations; Evan Morgan's *Tao, the Great Luminant: Essays from Huai-nan tzu* (1935; reprint, New York, 1969) is a translation of eight of the twenty-one essays in the text but suffers from poor scholarly methodology and antiquated renderings of key terms. Nonetheless, it is superior to the idiosyncratic mishmash of unidentified *Huainanzi* fragments, from a variety of chapters, assembled and translated by Thomas Cleary in *The Book of Leadership and Strategy: Lessons of the Chinese Masters* (Boston and London, 1990). Three scholars, Claude Larre, Isabelle Robinet, and Elisabeth Rochat de la Vallée, provide a lucid French translation of chapters 1, 7, 11, 13, and 18 in *Les Grand Traités du Huainan zi* (Paris, 1993). Eva Kraft's "Zum Huai-nan-tzu: Einführung, Übersetzung (Kapitel 1 und 2) und Interpretation," *Monumenta Serica* 16 (1957): 191–286; 17 (1958): 128–207, uses the questionable method of basing her translation on parallel passages in the *Wenzi.* John S. Major's *Heaven and Earth in Early Han Thought* (Albany, N.Y., 1993) translates the three most challenging essays in the text, 3–5, which deal with astronomy, geography, and calendrics, and renders them intelligible to a modern reader through meticulous explanatory notes. There are also a number of studies of individual essays that contain translations: chapter 1: D.C. Lau and Roger T. Ames, *Yuan Dao: Tracing Dao to its Source* (Albany, N.Y., 1998); chapter 6: Charles LeBlanc, *Philosophical Synthesis in Early Han Thought. The Idea of Resonance (Kan-Ying)* (Hong Kong, 1986); chapter 7: Claude Larre, *Le Traité VII du Houai nan tseu. Les esprit légers et subtils animateurs de l'essence* (Taipei, 1982); chapter 9: Roger T. Ames, *The Art of Rulership: A Study in Ancient Chinese Political Thought* (Honolulu, 1983; reprint Albany, N.Y., 1994); chapter 11: Benjamin E. Wallacker, *The Huai-nan Tzu, Book Eleven: Behavior, Culture, and the Cosmos,* "American Oriental Series," vol. 48 (New Haven, Conn., 1962). There are translations of short passages from the *Huainanzi* in *A Sourcebook in Chinese Philosophy,* translated and compiled by Wing-tsit Chan (Princeton, N.J., 1963); in Fung Yu-lan's *The Period of the Philosophers,* vol. 1 of *A History of Chinese Philosophy,* 2d ed., translated by Derk Bodde (Princeton, N.J., 1952); in *Chinese Philosophy in Classical Times,* edited and translated by E. R. Hughes (New York, 1942); and by Harold D. Roth in the second edition of *Sources of Chinese Tradition,* vol. 1, edited by W.T. DeBary and Irene Bloom (New York, 1999).

Harold D. Roth (1987 and 2005)

LIU DEREN (1122–1180), Daoist master of the Jin period and founder of the Zhenda sect of Daoism. His Daoist clerical name was Wuyouzi. In 1126, the year the Northern Song dynasty fell, Liu moved from Luoling Prefecture in Shandong Province to the Taiping district of Yanshan Prefecture in Hebei Province, where he studied Confucianism as a youth. It is alleged that early one morning in the eleventh month of 1142, a white-haired old man riding a cart pulled by a blue calf gave Liu the fundamental principles of the *Dao de jing,* along with a writing brush. The old man declared, "If you can fully understand the essentials of the *Dao de jing,* your own religious education will be complete and you will be able to enlighten others." Liu followed the old man's advice, deepened his knowledge of Daoism, and attracted an ever greater number of disciples.

In teaching his followers, Liu stressed nine points, including loyalty, filial piety, sincerity, purity, humility, sufficient knowledge, acceptance, and the prohibition of cruelty, lewdness, slander, stealing, gambling, consuming the five pungent substances, drinking intoxicants, and taking life. Zhenda Daoism represents a syncretization of China's three teachings: Confucianism, Buddhism, and Daoism. But while the influence of Confucianism was pronounced, Daoist magical practices and the use of talismans, incantations, and elixirs of immortality (*jindan,* "gold and cinnabar") found little room in his teaching. The Zhenda sect promoted a rational philosophy centered on practical morality in accordance with the demands of the time.

Liu's teachings were quickly embraced by the people of northern China, who at the time were plagued by social instability. The sect's rapid rise in influence brought Liu's name to the attention of Emperor Shizong of the Jin dynasty. The emperor summoned Liu to the capital and in 1161 established Liu in residence at the Tianzhang temple, which thereby became the head temple of Zhenda Daoism. In 1167 the emperor bestowed on Liu the title Dongyue Zhenren ("perfected one of the eastern peak"). Liu thus developed important ties with the court, thereby paving the way for the expansion of Zhenda Taoism. He died in 1180.

See Also Daoism, overview article, and article on The Daoist Religious Community.

Bibliography

Chen Yuan. *Nan Song chu Hebei xin daojiao kao.* Beijing, 1958.

Kubo Noritada. *Chugoku no shukyo kaikaku.* Tokyo, 1967.

Kubo Noritada. *Dokyoshi.* Tokyo, 1977.

Kubo Noritada (1987)
Translated from Japanese by James C. Dobbins

LIU TE-JEN See LIU DEREN

LLULL, RAMÓN See LULL, RAMÓN

LOCKE, JOHN

LOCKE, JOHN (1632–1704), English Christian writer on religious toleration, epistemology, political theory, theology, education, and economics. Locke was admitted to Westminster School, London, upon the recommendation of a Puritan family friend and proceeded as a King's Scholar to Christ Church, Oxford, where in 1658 he was chosen as a senior student (fellow) to teach moral philosophy. He studied chemistry and medicine, the practice of which contributed to his friendship with Anthony Ashley Cooper, earl of Shaftesbury and leader of the Whig Party. This political association led to Locke's self-imposed exile in Holland and the loss of his Oxford studentship in 1684. With the "Glorious Revolution" of 1689, he returned to England, where he devoted the remainder of his life largely to writing.

Locke's earliest extant writings of substance (not published until the twentieth century) set the course, though not the content, of his later, most influential works. After the restoration of Charles II to the throne in 1660, Locke conformed to the Church of England and wrote two essays defending the right of the civil magistrate to determine and enforce *adiaphora,* indifferent matters of religious worship. He believed that such authoritarianism was the only means to religious and political peace after the conflicts of the interregnum. In 1661 he reiterated this position in an essay on infallibility, which subject perhaps initiated his interest in the relationship between issues of knowledge and religious policy. By 1667, after his association with Shaftesbury, Locke changed his position and defended religious toleration in *An Essay concerning Toleration,* which foreshadowed the liberal views of his *Epistola de tolerantia* (1689), his classic defense of religious liberty. There he argued that religious opinions, even in "matters indifferent," could not and ought not be imposed upon subjects since a government magistrate had no more certain or infallible knowledge than anyone else.

From his consideration of religious toleration, Locke turned his attention to two fundamental attendant issues: the nature of government and the nature of knowledge. His *Two Treatises of Government* (1689) sets forth both a biblical interpretation attacking the basis of traditional patriarchal political theory and a model of human society in which every person has a direct relation to God under natural law. In accord with his views on toleration, Locke's theory of government does not require a uniformity of religion but is instead based on the right and need of individuals to preserve their lives, liberty, and property under natural law, even to the point of revolution.

His *Essay concerning Human Understanding* (1690) addresses issues of epistemology with an eye toward their religious and political implications. He attacks the theory of "innate principles," charging that its proponents (Hobbesians, Enthusiasts, and Roman Catholics) used it to impose their opinions on others as infallible so that they might govern by demanding unquestioning faith in their judgments. He seeks to show how little proper knowledge, that is, certainty, is available and asserts that religion rests primarily upon faith, not on knowledge. By "faith" Locke meant an assent to revelation; such an assent is essentially a judgment of probability, however great an assurance or confidence it carries. Thus, his epistemology supports his claim, with regard to toleration, that the leaders of society have no basis for imposing religion on subjects. However, he firmly believed that each individual could determine what was essential to his or her own salvation and moral life.

In *The Reasonableness of Christianity* (1695), Locke sets forth his own understanding of true religion, which he describes as a simple, intelligible Christianity derived from scripture alone. Drawing on an old tradition, he argues that the fundamental articles of Christian faith had been clearly designated by Jesus and the apostles, and that they are evident to anyone who reads the Bible. Focusing on the Gospels and the *Acts of the Apostles,* he attempts to reconstruct the life and teachings of Jesus and the apostles so as to show that they required for salvation belief only that Jesus was the Messiah, which presupposes belief in the existence of God and carries with it certain "concomitant articles" (such as Jesus' miracles, resurrection, and ascension) that proved him to be the Messiah. He admits that other scriptural doctrines must be believed as one comes to know them and emphasizes that moral obedience must accompany faith. Locke seems to have hoped that such a vision of Christianity, founded on a simple article of faith and clear morality set forth plainly in scripture, could provide a basis for social and political unity in which secondary matters of difference would be tolerated.

Locke's method in *Reasonableness* was also influential in the history of biblical criticism. His attempt to reconstruct the earliest teachings of Christianity led him to write a virtual "life of Jesus," including attention to what would later be called the "messianic secret." He emphasized what he thought were the more historical portions of the New Testament over the more doctrinal letters. His later *Paraphrases and Notes on the Pauline Epistles,* published posthumously

(1705–1707), also contributed to the perspective and style of subsequent biblical interpretation.

Locke's views on religion have been labeled as Hobbesian, Socinian or Unitarian, and deistic. The thesis of *Reasonableness* is nearly identical to that of Hobbes, and modern Marxist interpreters have revived the charges of Hobbesian inclination made by a few of Locke's contemporaries. However, non-Marxist historians have countered with alternative interpretations of Locke's meaning and broad intentions. Locke's ownership of numerous Socinian books, his several Unitarian friends, and manuscript records of antitrinitarian sentiments have often been cited as evidence of his secret sympathies. Yet such claims depend largely on silence and association, and recent analyses of manuscript sources have revealed that nearly all of Locke's "Unitarian" manuscript writings were not his own opinions but notes taken from his readings. His epistemology became a standard foundation of eighteenth-century Deism, but *Reasonableness* may well have been directed in part against the Deists and was used as a source of anti-Deist polemics. Locke strongly denied that his religious opinions were either the same as or influenced by Hobbes, the Socinians, or the Deists. If he is to be classed with any group or party, he might best be labeled as an independent thinker of the English Latitudinarian tradition.

BIBLIOGRAPHY

Maurice Cranston's *John Locke: A Biography* (London, 1957) is more comprehensive in its biographical detail than compelling in its interpretations of Locke's thought. Peter Laslett's edition of *Two Treatises of Government,* 2d ed. (Cambridge, 1964), provides the best critical text, as well as a revolutionary interpretation that has been widely accepted. The best work on the religious influence of Locke's epistemology is John W. Yolton's *John Locke and the Way of Ideas* (Oxford, 1956).

New Sources

Anstey, Peter R., ed. *The Philosophy of John Locke: New Perspectives.* New York, 2003.

Jolley, Nicholas. *Locke: His Philosophical Thought.* New York, 1999.

Marshall, John. *John Locke: Resistance, Religion, and Responsibility.* New York, 1994.

Simmons, A. John. *The Lockean Theory of Rights.* Princeton, N.J., 1992.

Wollerstorff, Nicholas. *John Locke and the Ethics of Belief.* New York, 1996.

JOHN C. HIGGINS-BIDDLE (1987 AND 2005)
Revised Bibliography

LOGIC. In the words of Petrus Hispanus, logic is both "ars artium et scientia scientiarum, ad omnium aliarum scientiarum methodorum principia viam habens." Roughly, we may take this to say, in modern terms, that logic concerns itself with the methods of correct statement and inference in all areas of inquiry whatsoever. Traditionally logic has divided into the study of deduction and of induction. The former has had an enormous development in the last hundred years or so, whereas the latter is still lagging behind, awaiting its coming of age.

Deductive logic does not dictate the principles or statements with which a given line of reasoning or inference starts; it takes over after these have been initially decided upon. Such principles or statements are decided upon, in turn, by direct insight, by revelation, by direct experience, by induction from instances, and so on. Deductive logic steps in only in the secondary capacity of directing the course of inferences once the so-called "premises" have been accepted or determined. The principles and rules of correct inference are stated in complete generality and hence are applicable to all kinds of subject matter. They are stated within a limited logical vocabulary—primarily that providing for the notions "not," "and," "or," "for all," "for some," and so on—to which the statements of any discipline must be brought into conformity by the use of suitable nonlogical constants providing for the given subject matter. Logic is thus indeed a kind of straitjacket that enforces correct statement and inference, just as moral norms enforce correct behavior and aesthetic norms enforce the beautiful or the artistically acceptable. In logic, however, there is less variation in the norms than in moral or aesthetic matters. Although many varieties of "deviant" logics have been invented, all of these turn out to be mere applications of the one standard logic. This is essentially the logic of Aristotle, brought up to date with the important contributions of DeMorgan, Boole, Peirce, Frege, Schröder, Whitehead and Russell, and Lesniewski.

Principles of logic have played a central role in theology throughout the long history of both, and each has influenced the other in significant ways. To be noted especially is the development, between roughly 1200 and 1500, of the Scholastic logic that aimed at providing the wherewithal for proofs of God's existence, especially those of Anselm, Thomas Aquinas, and Duns Scotus. In recent years, so-called process theology, stemming from the work of Whitehead, owes its origins to Whitehead's early work in logic, and much of the current discussion of the language of theology, especially in England, has been decisively influenced by the contemporary concern with the logic of natural language. In the East, especially in India, logic began to flourish in the first century CE within the confines of the methodology of theological and moral discussion and had a vigorous development that has persisted to the present day.

Logic, especially in its modern form, is a helpful adjunct to theology and should not be viewed with the fear that it will reduce the subject to a long list of sterile formulas. On the contrary, it should be viewed as an instrument that can help theology regain the high cognitive regality it once had as the queen of the sciences.

Bibliography

Bochenski, Joseph M. *The Logic of Religion.* New York, 1965.

Carnes, John. *Axiomatics and Dogmatics.* Oxford, 1982.

Martin, R. M. *Primordiality, Science and Value.* Albany, N.Y., 1980.

New Sources

Allen, James. *Inference from Signs: Ancient Debates about the Nature of Evidence.* New York, 2001.

Bowell, Tracy, and Gary Demp. *Critical Thinking: A Concise Guide.* London, 2001.

Falmagne, Rachel Joffe, and Marjorie Hass. *Representing Reason: Feminist Theory and Formal Logic.* Lanham, Md., 2002.

R. M. Martin (1987)
Revised Bibliography

LOGICAL POSITIVISM. Narrowly defined, logical positivism was an organized, science-oriented movement centered in Vienna during the 1920s and 1930s, a movement severely critical of metaphysics, theology, and traditional philosophy. Also known as logical empiricism, logical positivism may be more broadly defined as a doctrine born of classical empiricism and nineteenth-century positivism and sharpened by an empirical interpretation of the early logical writings of Ludwig Wittgenstein (1889–1951).

In either case, the distant origins of logical positivism lie in the long history of philosophical empiricism, the tradition holding that all knowledge must be derived from human experience alone. More particularly, the empiricism of John Locke (1632–1704), George Berkeley (1685–1753), and David Hume (1711–1776), with their cumulatively ever more radical elimination of nonempirical sources of knowledge, served as inspiration for the scientific views of the influential Vienna physicist and theorist of science, Ernst Mach (1836–1916). In addition, the positivist movement of the nineteenth century, founded by Auguste Comte (1798–1857), with its intense admiration for natural science, its anticlerical and antimetaphysical commitments, and its self-conscious programs for social and religious reform, lay behind not only Mach but also the small group of mathematical, natural, and social scientists who gathered in Vienna as early as 1907 to discuss Mach's views. In 1922 this group was successful in bringing Moritz Schlick (1882–1936), who was scientifically trained under the great German physicist Max Planck (1858–1947) but also keenly interested in philosophical issues, to the chair once held by Mach at the University of Vienna. Schlick quickly drew around him a circle of like-minded thinkers, mainly from the sciences, some of whom formed in 1928 the Verein Ernst Mach (the Ernst Mach Society). What soon became known as logical positivism was formulated by this group. The Vienna Circle, as they came to be known, issued a "manifesto" in 1929, organized international meetings, and in 1930 took over a journal, renamed *Erkenntnis,* for the advancement of its increasingly sharp position.

The distinctively "logical" character of the radically empiricist Vienna Circle was derived from the careful study (a line-by-line examination from 1924 to 1926) of Wittgenstein's *Tractatus Logico-Philosophicus,* which had been completed by 1918 and first published in 1921 (in German under the title *Logisch-philosophische Abhandlung*), just prior to the formation of the Vienna Circle. Wittgenstein was never a member of the Circle and was not sympathetic either to its party spirit or to the "grandiloquence" of its pronouncements, but from 1927 to 1929 he engaged in conversations with Schlick and other members of the Circle. Wittgenstein's logical doctrine formed the Circle's sharpest weapon against metaphysics and theology: the characterization of them not merely as false or outmoded, as Comte and the classical positivists had claimed, but as strictly "nonsense."

It was from Wittgenstein that the Vienna Circle drew its insistence that all meaningful statements are either analytic (and logically certain merely because they are tautologies) or synthetic (and "truth-functionally" analyzable into basic propositions corresponding to ultimately simple facts). The Circle gave its own characteristic interpretation of what qualified as these "atomic facts": sense-experiences. With this interpretation came support for two of the Circle's three primary positions: (1) the doctrine of the unity of science, Mach's key project, on the ground that all the sciences can be reduced equally to variously complex ("molecular") reports on experience; and (2) the doctrine of the valuelessness of metaphysics, on the ground that metaphysical utterances, by attempting to go "beyond" experience, fail to point to simple sense-experiences and thus are devoid of cognitive content.

Both doctrines were incorporated in and defensible by the third, the single most characteristic doctrine enunciated by the logical positivists: the verification principle of meaning, fashioned in light of Wittgenstein's analysis of the logic of language. The principle itself, "the meaning of a proposition is the method of its verification," though not appearing in the *Tractatus Logico-Philosophicus,* was attributed to a remark by Wittgenstein and was first published in the initial volume of *Erkenntnis* (1930–1931). In all its many later versions, the verification principle was taken to mean that for any nonanalytic (i.e., any would-be informative) statement, the factual meaning of the statement is equivalent to the set of observations (or sense-experiences, or "observation-statements") that would be sufficient to confirm the assertion's truth. Thus a thoroughgoing empiricist interpretation was given to Wittgenstein's more general dictum, and the authority of a powerful theory of meaning was placed behind the old disavowal of metaphysical or theological claims.

Those purported claims, it was said, must (if nontautological) be equivalent to the sensory experiences that might be obtained by an observer ideally positioned to verify the claim. Such confirming experiences, in the end, are alone what the utterances can mean. But if there are (and could be) no such specifiable experiences, as in the case of utterances allegedly "about" nonsensory entities like "God" or the "Absolute," then literally nothing is conveyed by the language, no real claims are made, and no "entity" can be conceived, much less believed in. So ran the fresh, essentially polemical argument of the logical positivists.

This polemic was generally ignored in the German-speaking philosophical world, doubtless because the Vienna Circle was not perceived (and to a large extent did not perceive itself) as engaging in philosophy so much as in a critique, enunciated mainly by professional scientists on behalf of a scientific method and worldview, of philosophy itself. Some English-speaking philosophers, however, long nurtured in the empiricist tradition that had inspired Mach and the Vienna Circle, were quick to notice the logical positivists. Alfred Jules Ayer (1910–1989) and Gilbert Ryle (1900–1976), of Oxford, and John Wisdom (1904–1993) and Susan Stebbing (1885–1943), of Cambridge, were early interpreters of the movement. Ayer, visiting Vienna in 1933, attended the meetings of the Circle, and in 1936 his book *Language, Truth and Logic*, containing a logical positivist critique of theology and ethics, exploded onto the English-speaking scene.

This radical challenge to the logical intelligibility of central theological utterances—those ostensibly about God, the soul, life after death, and the like—provoked a reaction that, though muted by the outbreak of World War II, intensified again in the early 1950s after a renewed challenge was issued by Antony Flew (b. 1923). Flew drew upon a variation of the verification principle for his question: what empirical observations would be incompatible with (would "falsify") theological assertions? If the answer is none, then are not the assertions in fact empty of definite, thinkable content? Theologians in the Catholic tradition (Roman or Anglican) tended to answer in terms of traditional doctrines of analogy. Members of the reformed tradition replied in fideistic terms. Neither group offered direct responses to the logical positivist attack. On the other hand, a third group, mainly liberal Protestants (including some Anglicans), attempted to vindicate the cognitive meaningfulness of theological discourse by satisfying the conditions set by the verification principle, specifying experiences that would be relevant to the verification or falsification of the claims in question. John Hick (b. 1922) proposed that claims about God could be verified, but only by postmortem experiences. Basil Mitchell (b. 1917) suggested that ordinary historical events or personal experiences are relevant to the verification of these claims, though not conclusively (as in many complex or ambiguous situations in life). He further suggested that faith-commitments are shown to be cognitively significant precisely because of the anguish sometimes felt in maintaining them against the evidence. R. M. Hare (1919–2002) and John Wisdom agreed that ordinary cognitive content is missing from theological claims but that these utterances might still have importance otherwise, offering comprehensive interpretations of particular experiences.

This variety of replies, to which many others could be added, underscores the distance that the postwar discussion had come from the rigorous either/or position of the Vienna Circle. But the sharp sword of the verification principle had already been blunted on issues at the very center of logical positivist concern: issues involving the adequate analysis of scientific assertions themselves. Try as they might, the members and allies of the Vienna Circle were not able to make good their program to include with the same criteria all scientifically essential statements but to exclude all metaphysical and theological ones. It soon became clear that the laws of science, being entirely universal in form, are not conclusively verifiable, since finite numbers of observations cannot in principle verify a universal assertion. ("Some" examples, however many they may be, cannot verify claims about "all.") Furthermore, the proffered suggestion that scientific laws are not, after all, assertions, as they seem to be, but disguised "rules" or other logical entities was too paradoxical for most science supporters. Again, the apparently definite meaning of even straightforward, particular factual assertions of science and daily life was found to melt away under verificational analysis into an infinite series of possible observations. Reversing the problem to the criterion of "falsification" did not help, since although a universal proposition can be falsified (in principle) by a single negative observation, no particular assertion can be so falsified; furthermore, universal laws of science are not, either in logic or in historical fact, at once falsified by negative observations. At most a whole network of theories is shown to need revision by a negative observational result (since it is not immediately clear which of the premises ought to be discarded and which retained). Moreover, as argued by such historians of science as Thomas S. Kuhn (1922–1996), science does not actually develop in any such logically neat way.

Other applications, not directly fashioned by the Vienna Circle, of verificationism to science—for instance, the attempt of the Harvard physicist P. W. Bridgman (1882–1961) to reduce all concepts in science to descriptions of specific procedures ("operationalism")—resulted in the unsatisfactory conclusion that entirely different concepts (for example, of "length" or "time") would be fashioned by the various sciences, depending on their subject matter and characteristic methods. Far from supporting the unity of science, which was a central motive in the founding of the logical positivist movement, operationalism tended to make it logically impossible for astronomy, which measures distance by various sorts of procedures, to share a common concept of distance with geology, biology, or microphysics, which rely upon others. Indeed, even within the same science—or within the same laboratory on different occasions—scientifically essential conceptual generality was seen to be forfeited by the particularistic reductionism of operationalism.

Equally alarming to many more realistically minded scientists and friends of science was the problem of retaining a (non-"metaphysical") concept of the common world studied by science if the meanings of all factual propositions are to be literally equated with those experiences that could verify them. Since experiences are personal and private, the traditional problem of "other minds" (i.e., of how I can escape solipsism if other centers of consciousness are not directly observable by me) was added to the problem of escaping from absolute idealism (i.e., the alarmingly traditional metaphysical view that nothing exists except mentality), even if the egocentric predicament somehow could be avoided.

Finally, the logical status of the verification principle itself could not withstand verificationist analysis. The principle is not just another empirical hypothesis: that is, it certainly does not offer a foothold for confirmation (or falsification) by sense-experiences. Is it then an empty tautology? Most logical positivists took the latter position, holding that the principle was an "important" tautology that had many good reasons for being "recommended" to the intellectual community. This tack, however, allowed others, like Hare and Wisdom, to speak of equally "important" nonverifiable utterances and to make more complex counterrecommendations about the meaning of "meaning."

The disintegration of the organized Vienna Circle can be dated from the murder by a deranged student of Schlick in 1936. Viewed with hostility by the Nazis, the Vienna Circle was formally disbanded in 1938, and in the same year *Erkenntnis* was moved out of Hitler's direct sphere of control, to Holland, where it lasted only another two years. The end of the broader movement is harder to trace, and in some fashion it remains influential as an overtone in the more radically empirical voices of our time. Still, the gradual abandonment by Wittgenstein of his own either/or position on meaning in the *Tractatus Logico-Philosophicus*, in favor of a much more pluralistic approach to the functions of human language, pulled the logical rug out from under logical positivism. Its significance for religion and theology continues to lie in the fact that theologians now have been forced to acknowledge the extent to which their claims cannot be treated as simple empirical hypotheses, open to "crucial experiments," as in the contest between Elijah and the priests of Baal (*1 Kgs.* 18:17–40). Indeed, it may be thought that theology has emerged the better for its cold bath in verificationism, if only because theologians are now required to be aware of the subtlety of their speech and of the many functions it may have both in their technical discourses and in the living religious speech of the faithful.

SEE ALSO Analytic Philosophy; Comte, Auguste; Empiricism; Hume, David; Locke, John; Positivism; Science and Religion; Wittgenstein, Ludwig.

BIBLIOGRAPHY

No single book is more important for the understanding of logical positivism than Ludwig Wittgenstein's difficult but fascinating *Tractatus Logico-Philosophicus* (London, 1922). As a general guide to Wittgenstein's thought and to the *Tractatus* in particular, one might turn to part 1 of George Pitcher's helpful *The Philosophy of Wittgenstein* (Englewood Cliffs, N.J., 1964). The thought of the founder of the Vienna Circle is reflected in Moritz Schlick's posthumously published *Gesammelte Aufsätze 1926–36* (1938; reprint, Hildesheim, 1962). Other representative writings of the Vienna Circle can be found in Rudolf Carnap's *The Logical Structure of the World* (London, 1967) and in *Foundations of the Unity of Science*, vol. 2 of *International Encyclopedia of Unified Science*, edited by Otto Neurath, Rudolf Carnap, and Charles Morris (1938–1962; reprint, Chicago, 1955–1970). The explosive introduction of logical positivism to the English-speaking world was through Alfred Jules Ayer's *Language, Truth and Logic* (London, 1936). After World War II, the key book in focusing the theological aspect of the controversy was *New Essays in Philosophical Theology*, edited by Antony Flew and Alasdair MacIntyre (London, 1955). One of the important sustained efforts to meet the challenge by offering theological verification of a sort, though not in this life, was John Hick's *Faith and Knowledge*, 2d ed. (Ithaca, N.Y., 1966). A detailed analysis of the arguments leading to the verificationist challenge to religious belief, of various attempted replies, and of the transformation of the issues resulting from this debate can be found in the first chapters of my *Language, Logic, and God* (New York, 1961). The best recent survey of the whole phenomenon of logical positivism, readable and authoritative, is Oswald Hanfling's *Logical Positivism* (New York, 1981).

New Sources

Coffa, Alberto. *The Semantic Tradition from Kant to Carnap: To the Vienna Station.* 1991; reprint New York, 2003.

Fitch, G. W. "On Theoretical Identifications." *Philosophical Perspectives* 11 (October 2001): 379–393.

Friedman, Michael. *Reconsidering Logical Positivism.* New York, 1999.

Jones, Todd. "The Virtues of Nonreduction, Even When Reduction Is a Virtue." *Philosophical Forum* 34 (Summer 2003): 121–141.

Sarkar, Sahotra. *Decline and Obsolescence of Logical Empiricism: Carnap vs. Quine and the Critics.* Science and Philosophy in the Twentieth Century: Basic Works of Logical Empiricism. New York, 1996.

Schaffer, Jonathan. "Is There a Fundamental Level?" *Nous* 37 (September 2003): 498–518.

FREDERICK FERRÉ (1987)
Revised Bibliography

LOGOS

LOGOS. The noun *logos* is as old as the Greek language itself. It has acquired, over the course of time, a large number of different meanings, which only with difficulty can be drawn into a simple unity. "Reason" is the translation that causes perhaps the least trouble, but "reason" itself is of course far from unambiguous. Perhaps it will help to carve up the vast semantic field covered by the word *logos* if the three principal meanings are distinguished, even though this entails considerable simplification. First there is an objective meaning: the rational ground or basis (Ger., *Grund*) for something. This is often of a numerical or logical nature and functions as a principle of explanation. Second, there is a subjective meaning: the power or faculty of reasoning (Ger., *Vernunft*) or thought. Third, there is what shall be called an expressive meaning: thought or reason as expressed in speech or in writing (the "speech" may be either vocalized or purely cerebral).

STOIC VIEWS OF LOGOS. No one of these three meanings is limited specifically to the study of religious thought and experience. One specific use of the word did, however, come to have pride of place in some of the philosophical schools of the ancient world, and especially among the Stoics. In these circles *logos* came to mean the rational order of the universe, an immanent natural law, a life-giving force hidden within things, a power working from above on the sensible world. This use of the word has obvious affinities with the first of the meanings listed above. Clearly we have to do here with the idea of rational ground or basis. There is, however, the obvious difference that we are dealing not with the rational ground of some one particular entity as distinct from some other, but with the cosmos as a whole. It is this extension in the scope of the word, an extension reaching out to embrace the confines of the universe, that gives to this particular use of *logos* a religious dimension. Hence the willingness of the Stoics to call this *logos* "God." Deeply embedded in the matter of the universe, God does not demand our worship, does not cry out for temples built by human hands. He does nonetheless call forth a theology, and he does stir in us a sense of piety; but theology and piety are centered on the cosmos.

The point to appreciate is that, for the Stoics, *logos* is associated with all the functions that are normally attributed to the divine. Logos is destiny and providence. Chrysippus, one of the founders of Stoicism, tells us for example that "it is in conformity with the Logos that what has happened, has happened, that what is happening, is happening, that what will happen, will happen" (*Stoicorum veterum fragmenta* 2.913). The Logos impregnates the world, from within, with its order and rhythm. The Stoic emperor Marcus Aurelius (5.32.2) tells us that wisdom consists in coming to know "the Logos that extends through the whole of matter, and governs the universe for all eternity according to certain fixed periods." For all that, the Logos is not limited to controlling nature. "If there is any common bond between gods and men, it is because both alike share in the Logos, which Logos is the natural law" (*Stoicorum veterum fragmenta* 2.528).

Such were the theses upheld by the oldest of the Stoics, in the third century before the common era. Were these Stoics taking over an earlier set of ideas that had been worked out even before their time by Heraclitus of Ephesus toward the end of the sixth century? Heraclitus believed in the existence of a Logos common to all humans, shared by all, over and beyond their private thoughts, a Logos by which all things happen as they do, a Logos clothed with many of the attributes of divinity. There were, besides, many readers in the ancient world who thought that Heraclitus's Logos was close to the Logos of the Stoics and could therefore be taken as the first mapping out of the Stoic conception. On the other hand, one must remember how laconic are the very few quotations from Heraclitus on the nature of his Logos that have come down to us, and how very different are the meanings that can attach to the word. There can therefore be no certainty that the Logos of Heraclitus was really the principle guiding and underlying the universe that the Stoics were going to call by the same name.

It is certain, nevertheless, that of all the theological thinkers of pagan antiquity who made use of the idea of a Logos, the Stoics took the idea furthest and had the greatest influence. Although the great philosophers of the classical period made much use of the word *logos*, they did not attach to it a meaning capable of sustaining the same religious development. Nor can such development be traced in any of the later spiritual movements rooted in the tradition of Greek thought. Contrary to what one might have expected, the Neoplatonists gave only a very limited place to the Logos within the framework of their religious ideas. The Logos does not belong to the hierarchy of hypostases set up by Plotinus. In the *Enneads* there are only two short treatises, both called *On Providence* (3.2.3 [47, 48]), in which Plotinus plays with the idea, perhaps under the influence of Gnostic beliefs. Where Jewish and Christian speculative thinkers are to be found giving the word *logos* the full depth of its religious value, they, no less than their pagan counterparts, draw upon ways of thinking that are recognizably Stoic in origin.

Should we then look upon the Stoic philosophers as the fountainhead of the entire subsequent development of a theology of the Logos? Not quite: Stoic influence would hardly have been capable, without reinforcement, of stimulating such a profound development. But as it happened, the Stoic conception was joined by a new way of thinking that probably originated in the Near East and that encouraged people to see as independent and separate personifications what had hitherto been understood as different psychological aspects of a single divine being. What had been simply modes of the divine essence now came to be thought of as substances in their own right, each of which had issued from the divine by a process neatly epitomized in the title of a thesis presented by Helmer Ringgren: *Word and Wisdom: Studies in the Hypostatization of Divine Qualities and Functions in the Ancient Near East* (Lund, 1947). This same shift in thought is brought out by the Christian Tertullian in a treatise against the Gnostics (*Against the Valentinians* 4.2), in which he writes of the difference between Valentinus and his disciple Ptolemy. In the thought of Ptolemy, "the Aeons, each distinguished by its own name and by its own number, became personalized substances, characterized independently of God, whereas Valentinus had included them in the divine whole itself, and had taken them as thoughts, feelings and emotions of the divine." Earlier, Irenaeus (*Against Heresies* 1.12.1) had written in a similar vein of the same Ptolemy's belief that there had issued forth from the Father Aeons that had earlier been thought of as mere "dispositions" (*diatheseis*) of the Father.

The Logos should be seen as the chief of these dispositions. As the name itself testifies, it originally designated the divine reason before becoming a reality in its own right, distinct from God, and soon to be personified by taking on the characteristics of the Son of God. A parallel transformation into a hypostasis distinct from God was undergone by another divine faculty, Wisdom (Sophia). Both developments took place in the first two centuries of the common era, in the Hellenized Jewish circles of Alexandria, and reached their fullest expression in the works of Philo Judaeus (first century CE). The conceptual effort required by these transformations bears all the marks of Stoicism, but the change has been made on the basis of underlying doctrinal shifts. The personalized Logos, distinct from God insofar as accounted the Son of God, is far removed from the supreme principle immersed in matter that the Stoics called by the same name. A difference in terminology brings out just how far the idea has traveled: the "god Logos" of Stoicism has given way, more often than not, to the "Logos of God," or "divine Logos" (e.g., Philo, *On the Maker of the World* 5.20). This change takes on its full meaning when the Christian Origen contrasts his own belief with that of his adversary Celsus, who on this point can be taken for all intents and purposes as a Stoic. Origen writes as follows (*Against Celsus* 5.24): "The Logos of all things, according to Celsus, is God himself, whereas we believe that the Logos is the Son of God. In our philosophy it is he of whom we say: 'In the beginning was the Logos, and the Logos was with God, and the Logos was God' (*Jn.* 1:1)."

LOGOS AND WISDOM. The theology of Wisdom is inseparable from the theology of the Logos. The theology of Wisdom stems from the Old Testament, where in *Proverbs* (8:22–23) Wisdom speaks: "The Lord created me at the beginning of his work, the first of his acts of old. Ages ago I was set up, at the first, before the beginning of the earth," and so on. Wisdom is plainly presented here as the first of God's creatures and as God's collaborator in the creation of all that was yet to be created. How Wisdom is to be thought of in conjunction with Logos may be gleaned from a Hellenistic Jewish text, the *Wisdom of Solomon* (9:1–9): "God of my fathers and Lord of thy mercy, thou who hast made all things in thy Logos, and who by this Wisdom has called forth man . . . grant me the Wisdom seated by thy throne."

Jews and Christians have devoted much commentary to these two passages. Philo sees the Wisdom of *Proverbs* as the mother of the universe. In accordance with an obviously Stoic train of thought (*Stoicorum veterum fragmenta* 2.1074), she is held to have received from God the seeds (*spermata*) of creation (*On Drunkenness* 8.30–31; *On the Cherubim* 14.49). Elsewhere (*Allegorical Interpretation* 1.19.64; *On Flight and Finding* 20.109; *On Dreams* 2.37.245), she is identified in his eyes with the Logos, and either can be taken as typified by the manna from heaven in *Exodus* 16. These apparent inconsistencies in Philo's thought have a great deal to do with his allegorical exegesis. They also show how ideas of Wisdom and Logos became intertwined in the Judeo-Greek world of Alexandria. Things worked out differently, however, in the purely Jewish tradition, the tradition we speak of as Palestinian. The rabbinical commentators took Wisdom in *Proverbs* 8:22 to mean the preexistent Torah, conceived by them as being the plan according to which God had created the world.

The Christians of the second century exercised their minds on the same pages of the Bible and came up with conclusions that were not dissimilar. This, for example, is how Justin Martyr interprets the text from *Proverbs*, just before quoting liberally from it: "As a principle prior to all his creatures, God has called forth from himself a Power that is like a Logos [*dunamin logikēn*]". He goes on to say that in different contexts, scripture calls this power Son, Wisdom, God, and Logos (*Dialogue with Trypho* 61.1, 129.3–4). But there is a difference, and one with important ramifications, in the way in which Philo and Justin quote from the same verse of *Proverbs*. Philo reads the text in a Greek translation that has Wisdom say: "The Lord, to whom I belong [*ektēsato*], has made me the principle of his ways." But Justin, in common with other Christian writers of his day, follows another Greek translation, the so-called Septuagint, which rightly or wrongly gives the verse as: "The Lord has created me [*ektise*]." One can hardly mistake the significance of the idea of creation that has thus been introduced into the passage.

Justin's aim, an aim that will be shared by the whole of ancient Christianity, is to read this verse from *Proverbs* in the light of the prologue to the gospel according to John, and so to see in Wisdom a prophetical foretelling of the Logos or the preexistent Son of God. But such an aim is not supported by the fact that Wisdom is said to be "created," which obviously could not be applied to the Son of God. This explains why Justin, as we just saw, abandons the idea of creation and adopts instead the idea of generation, an idea altogether more suited to describe the arrival of the Christian Word. Nonetheless, the idea that Wisdom had been "created" was a constant irritant, impeding any attempt at a syncretistic explanation of Wisdom as the Word. It is not until the fourth century that Eusebius of Caesarea (*Ecclesiastical Theology* 3.2.14ff.) resurrects and insists upon the reading *ektēsato* that had been given by Philo of Alexandria, while Jerome, when he comes to translate the same word in his Latin version of the Hebrew scriptures, chooses the meaning of *possessio* and excludes the idea of *creatio* (see his *Letter* 140.6).

Shortly after Justin, the Christian Theophilus of Antioch takes up the association of the Logos and Wisdom and sometimes seems even to identify the two (*To Autolycus* 2.10, 2.22). In other passages, however, he distinguishes them (1.7, 2.8), while once (2.15) he uses a very striking formula to tell us of a triad made up of God, his Logos, and his Wisdom. It is tempting to see at this point a preliminary version of the doctrine of the Trinity, with Wisdom occupying the place of the Holy Ghost. The different ways that Theophilus has of expressing himself on the subject show, however, that the doctrine has not as yet really taken on definite shape in his mind. Not until Irenaeus, who never wavers in his identification of Wisdom with the Holy Ghost, does the idea of the Trinity become a consistent and self-conscious doctrine.

SEMINAL LOGOS. We can see here how, from the very beginning, the Christian theology of the Logos, or of the Word, was deeply rooted in the particular way in which theologians read and understood *Proverbs* and the *Wisdom of Solomon* in the cultural circles of Hellenistic Judaism. No less important was the influence that Stoicism exerted on these Jewish speculations, though its importance was of another kind. Stoicism provided the theoretical framework that made it possible for images and ideas drawn from scripture to take on definite doctrinal shape.

Take, for example, the Stoic idea of *logos spermatikōs*, seminal or spermatic *logos*. This was an idea that the Stoics had worked out to explain how every being contains within itself a principle of development suitable to itself—an idea that they applied to the individual beings within the cosmos as well as to the cosmos itself in its entirety. When applied to individual beings, the formula is used in the plural. We are told, for example, that God, "in looking to the birth of the world, holds within himself all the seminal *logoi*, according to which each thing is produced, as required by necessity" (*Stoicorum veterum fragmenta* 2.1027). We have already seen how Philo makes use of this way of thinking when he writes of Wisdom receiving from God the seeds of creation.

Justin is no less indebted to the same mode of thought, although the turn of ideas in his case is very different. Justin wonders how pagan philosophers and poets have been able to utter certain truths, despite their having had no access to the truths of revelation. He decides that it is "because of the seed of the Logos that has been implanted in the whole human race," with the difference that the pagans respond to only "a part of the seminal Logos," whereas the Christians' rule of faith is founded on "the knowledge and the contemplation of the whole Logos, that is, of Christ" (*Second Apology* 8.1, 8.3). The same Stoic concept underlies the thought of the Gnostic Ptolemy at about the same time (as reported by Irenaeus in *Against Heresies* 1.8.5): Ptolemy claimed that the Father, in the Son, had called forth all things seminally (*spermatikōs*).

INNER LOGOS AND SPOKEN LOGOS. Stoic psychology emphasized the lack of coincidence between the reasoning power, which rests within, and language, which gives outward expression to the powers of reason. Since the same word *logos* was used to designate both the power of reasoning and reason as expressed in speech, the difference came to be stated as a difference between two *logoi*. One might no less properly express this as a distinction between two types or states of language. A language within, or an inner language (*logos endiathetos*), is then distinguished from a language that we have in common with talking birds, a language expressed in speech (*logos prophorikos*). We should refrain, however, from giving too much importance to the significance that the Stoics themselves attached to this distinction, for the accounts of it are few and far between. Thus we find in Heraclitus, a commentator on Homer (first century CE?), the claim that if Hermes, god of the *logos*, is given double honors, "this is because language is double. The philosophers call one an 'inner' language and the other a 'spoken' language. The 'spoken' language is the messenger of the thoughts that pass within us, whereas the 'inner' language stays enclosed within the fastness of our heart" (*Homeric Problems* 72.14–16).

From small beginnings, this Stoic way of thinking came to cut deep into the Christian theology of the Logos. No one threw himself with greater abandon into the description of the idea and its transposition into a Christian context than Theophilus of Antioch, at the end of the second century. In his treatise *To Autolycus* (2.2), he gives brilliant proof of the idea outlined earlier, according to which the Jewish and Christian Logos resulted from exteriorizing and personifying what had originally been God's own internal faculty of reflection. At first God is alone, and the Logos is quite simply God's weighing up of things within himself; then, when he wishes to create, God brings forth the Logos to be his instrument and his messenger. By cleverly cutting off the opening of the prologue of John's gospel, Theophilus is able to drum up a scriptural warrant for this Stoic representation of the two *logoi*. The evident weakness in the process lies in introducing into the condition of the Logos a kind of historical development that is ill-suited to the nature of the divine. Because Theophilus has taken over the movement *ad extra* by which the Stoics passed from the *logos endiathetos* to the *logos prophorikos*, the Word of God has to pass through two different and successive states, and it seems clear that his begetting, for all that it is the essential mark of his relation to the Father, belongs only to the second state.

The danger inherent in this view of the Trinity did not escape the eagle eye of Origen, who very neatly seizes upon it in a passage (*De principiis* 1.2.2) written around 230. By means of a subtle philosophical argument, proceeding by dilemma, he establishes that from all eternity God is, and always has been, the Father of his only Son.

Theophilus of Antioch probably best typifies the tendency that we have found in him. Yet he is by no means the only writer able to manipulate such ideas. In the second century and at the beginning of the third, almost all Christian theologians write of the Logos in a way that implies development: starting from a lack of distinction within the innermost being of God, they make the Logos "proceed" from out of God and take upon himself the work of creation. To be sure, only some of these authors deliberately and explicitly draw upon the Stoic model of the two *logoi* and cast their ideas in the technical terms of the theory; but they all have the same model in mind. One may quote Justin (*Dialogue* 61.2) and his disciple Tatian (*Speech to the Greeks* 5), and in the Latin-speaking world Tertullian (*Against Praxeas* 5–7) and finally Hippolytus of Rome (*Against Noëtus* 10; *Refutation* 10.33.1–15). Hippolytus virtually repeats the analyses given by Theophilus, although there are some differences of nuance: for example, Hippolytus splits in two the outward state of the Logos and sees therein a separate stage for the Word incarnate. Yet two noteworthy exceptions should be mentioned: Clement of Alexandria (*Stromateis* 5.1.6.3) and even more so Irenaeus (*Against Heresies* 2.13.8, 2.28.5). His struggle against the Gnostics (who in practice shared the views of Theophilus and others) gave Irenaeus an additional reason for forcefully rejecting any assimilation of the generation of the Word with happenings related to the human Logos.

Irenaeus's negative approach won the day. The analogy with Stoic theory of the two *logoi* is heard of no more for a while, then reappears during the fourth century in the theology of the Word expounded by Marcellus of Ancyra and Photinus. Both these writers were condemned and anathematized by synods in 345 and 351. The declaration of faith in 345 ran as follows: "But as for us, we know that Christ is not merely a Logos of God uttered outwardly or resting within [*prophorikos ē endiathetos*]. He is the Logos God, living and subsisting of himself, Son of God, Christ" (*Macrostich Formula* of the third synod of Antioch, pt. 6, in August Hahn, *Bibliothek der Symbole und Glaubensregeln der alten Kirche*, 3d ed., Breslau, 1897, para. 159, p. 194). This conciliar statement had in any case been anticipated by Eusebius of Caesarea (*De ecclesiastica theologia* 1.17; 2.11; 14; 15), and was shortly to receive the approval of Cyril of Jerusalem (*Catechesis* 11.10) and Athanasius (*Speech against the Arians* 2.35). Marcellus of Ancyra and Photinus, then, were fighting rearguard battle. In the dogmatic formula approved in 325 by the ecumenical council of Nicaea (the Nicene Creed), the word *logos*, which Eusebius had suggested, had already disappeared in favor of "Son of God" (Hahn, 1897, pp. 160–161). This substitution obviously brought on the demise of the old Stoic ways of thinking that had been indissolubly linked to the term *logos*. Not until the fifth century, and then only in the Latin-speaking world, does one find, in the great trinitarian synthesis of Augustine, a new way in which the two states of human language (*verbum quod intus lucet, verbum quod foris sonat*) can again be employed to mark out similarities with the divine Word; yet even then the comparison has to be handled with the greatest circumspection. Augustine differs from the theologians of the second century in holding that the spoken human word finds for its analogue not the begotten Logos seen against the background of its participation in creation, but the Word made flesh (*De trinitate* 15.10.19–11.20).

FUNCTIONS OF THE LOGOS. Philo of Alexandria, as well as the early Christians, confers upon the Logos a number of different functions. The chief of these can be described by three words: *creation, revelation, mediation.*

The idea of speech as creative is hardly likely to have arisen in Greece, where men thought instead in terms of an antithesis between the two nouns *logos* and *ergon:* the antithesis of talking and doing, of words and acts, of the lips and the heart. Quite other is the world of the Old Testament, where sentences abound such as those in Psalm 33:9: "For he spoke, and it was done; he commanded, and it stood fast." (See also *Ps.* 148:5, 42:15 et al.) Philo was especially struck by the fact that this temporal coincidence between the divine command and its effect was nowhere to be found in the culture of the Greeks: "At the moment that he speaks, God creates, and there is no gap in time between the two; alternatively one might say, if one wished to improve upon the truth of this opinion, that his Word was act [*logos ergon*]" (*On the Sacrifices of Abel and Cain* 18.65).

This moment in Christian doctrine led naturally to giving the Logos (which is also the divine Word) a part in the creation of the cosmos. Its role was that of an instrument (*organon*), and Philo takes care to distinguish between the instrument and God himself, who is cause, or *aition* (*On the Cherubim* 35.127). This is the same instrumental causality, a subordinate form of causality, that early Christians normally attributed to the Logos. The idea was nearly always expressed by the preposition *dia* with the genitive, and one should translate it (or at least understand it as meaning) "by means of," starting from *John* 1:3: "All things were made by the Logos."

Philo does, however, take the instrumental role of the Logos in a fairly wide sense and makes room for what the Greek philosophical tradition called the "exemplary cause" (which was distinguished thereby from the idea of instrument; see Basil of Caesarea, *On the Holy Ghost* 3.5). An extract from the *Allegorical Interpretation* (3.31.96) makes clear how the Logos is at one and the same time instrument (*organon*) and model (*archetupos, paradeigma*). And Philo's analyses help us in turn to understand some later texts. Toward the year 177 Athenagoras, no different in this from other Christian writers of the time, writes that "God, by means of the Logos that comes from him, has called the universe into being, has set it in order, and keeps it beneath his governance" (*Legatio* 10). But a little later he adds, and indeed repeats, that "the Son of God is the Logos of the Father in idea and in act [*en ideai kai energeiai*]." These final words would be shrouded in mystery, did we not recall the dual role that Philo assigned to the Logos in creation since, for Philo, the Logos is at one and the same time the ideal model and the agent of creation. At this point, therefore, the influence of Greek philosophy makes itself felt again in the thought of Philo and no less in that of Athenagoras. Thus a pagan contemporary of Athenagoras, the Platonist Albinus, will write of a principle that he calls the first Intellect: "its activity [*energeia*] is itself idea [*idea*]" (*Didascalicos* 10).

In the loose and widespread Platonism with which Jewish and Christian ideas of the time were saturated, the impossibility of an adequate knowledge of God was stressed. In such an intellectual climate the Logos inevitably took on a second function, whereby it became a means of revealing the

Father to us. This idea becomes so commonplace that I shall only allude to it. There is, however, one very early noncanonical Christian writer who gives the idea a novel twist. Ignatius of Antioch (d. 107) writes as follows (*Letter to the Magnesians* 8.2): "There is only one God, who makes himself known to us through Jesus Christ his Son, who is his Logos who comes forth from his silence [*logos apo sigēs proelthōn*]." Sigē (Silence) is a figure well known to us from the theogonies current in Simonian and Valentinian Gnosticism, where one of the first Aeons—that is, one of the earliest emanations—is called by this name. Are we to conclude that Ignatius has drawn his inspiration on this point from the Gnostic theory of divine emanations, as Marcellus of Ancyra later did (according to Eusebius, *Ecclesiastical Theology* 2.9.4)? The possibility cannot be ruled out. But it is more likely that Ignatius made use of this gripping expression to describe how, when the Logos comes forward to reveal the Father, he breaks the silence that God had kept for ages past.

Entrusted from on high with the creation of the cosmos and the revelation of the Father, the Logos is in some ways closer to humanity than is the Father. The Logos stands on the borderline (*methorios stas*), so to speak, between the Father and the human race, and so can play the part of a mediator. To God he offers the prayers and worship of mortal men, while to mortal men he gives the assurance of a divine help that will never fail them. That, at least, is how Philo shapes his ideas, sometimes applying these trains of thought deliberately and explicitly to the Logos (*On Dreams* 2.28.188–189; *On the Special Laws* 1.23.116). But the role of mediator finds its fullest scope only in Christianity, where the incarnate Logos draws together and makes of itself a center for human and divine nature and is thereby in the ideal position to facilitate the communication of one nature with the other. There are some famous passages in Augustine that one could quote as answering exactly to this point (*Confessions* 7.18.24; *City of God* 9.15–17). No less apposite, but less hackneyed, is the following quotation from Clement of Alexandria, where a flavor of baroque archaism results from his quoting Heraclitus: "Heraclitus was quite right to say: 'The gods are men, and men are gods. For the Logos is one and the same.' Light shines through this mystery: God is in man, and man is God, and the Mediator [*mesitēs*] fulfills the will of the Father; for the Mediator is the Logos, which is the same for man and for God, at one and the same time Son of God and savior of men, God's servant and our Teacher" (*Teacher* 1.2.1).

The Christian Logos. With the rise of Christianity, old words and ideas became charged with a new meaning, and new wine was poured into old skins, with all the risks attendant upon such an enterprise, as we have already seen in our study of the Stoic theory of the two *logoi.* Some Christian authors take up with confidence and determination the earlier pagan prehistory of this idea and see therein a providential pattern mirroring sacred history itself: "Those who lived with the Logos are Christians, even if in their day they passed for atheists: among the Greeks, such are Socrates, Heraclitus, and their like; among the barbarians, Abraham, Ananias, Azarias, Misaël, Elijah, and many others." Such is the claim of Justin Martyr (*First Apology* 46.3), who revels in ferreting out from Greek philosophy and religion ideas that are compatible with the Christian Logos. He draws attention to Mercury, who was called the angelic word of God (22.2), and most of all to the world soul that Plato (*Timaeus* 36B) says is embedded in the universe in the shape of a cross or the Greek letter chi, a symbol for the cross of Christ (60.5–7).

This movement toward harmonizing pagan Greek and Christian beliefs, a movement that reflects a grandiose conception of the theology of history, did not keep early Christianity from becoming clearly aware of what, in its conception of the Logos, was most peculiarly its own. Thus the prologue to the *Gospel of John* shows a writer deeply aware of the historical background from which he has sprung (which included the Wisdom of Hellenistic Judaism and the Torah of Palestinian Judaism). But the prologue is also without peer in revealing the overriding importance given to the perfect coincidence between the preexisting Logos and the Jesus of history. Even so, in *John,* the personality of this Logos is taken as the known, and not spelled out, a point to which the early theologians will direct their efforts. Such, for example, is Justin's preoccupation when he writes against those (possibly Jews taking their lead from Philo) who believe that individuality of the Logos is no more distinct from that of the Father than light is distinct from the sun. In his *Dialogue with Trypho* (128.4, 129.3–4), Justin argues instead in favor of a distinction that is not merely nominal but a distinction of number. As proof, he takes his stand on the bringing forth of the Logos: for "what is brought forth is numerically distinct from him who brings forth; anyone must allow us that."

To be perfectly accurate, Justin does not write of the Logos as "numerically distinct," but as "other [*heteros*] in virtue of number." In writing thus, Justin hit upon a word full of pitfalls, a word that could suggest the existence of two gods as well as a debasement of the Logos in relation to the Father. It could even suggest both ideas at once, as seen in another sentence from the same *Dialogue,* a sentence truly staggering in its lack of theological foresight: "There is, as has been said, another [*heteros*] god and lord below the Creator of the universe . . . the Creator of the universe has no other [*allos*] god above him" (56.4). Perhaps Justin's pen has run away with him, forcing his ideas in a direction that he did not really intend. Others, whose thinking was really no different from his, will take much greater care in how they express themselves (e.g., Hippolytus, *Against Noëtus* 11). Origen himself will downgrade the Logos in calling it "second [*deuteros*] god" (*Against Celsus* 5.39, 6.61, etc.) or again in writing "god" (*theos*) without the article, whereas he calls the Father *ho theos,* "the God" (*Commentary of Saint John* 2.2.13–18).

The analyses quoted above may seem oddly archaic in the light of later theology, but they lose a good deal of this quality if we take account of two points. In the first place, the expressions employed by Justin and Origen can already be found in Philo, whose use of them naturally occasions much less surprise. Thus Philo had used the presence or absence of the article to distinguish the "true" God from the Logos god (*On Dreams* 1.39.229–230), and had marked out the Logos as being "the second god" (*Questions and Answers on Genesis* 2.62). Before Justin and Hippolytus, Philo sees in the Logos "another god" (ibid.). The second point to bear in mind is that the Platonist philosophers of the day also contribute to the movement toward giving the Logos only a diminished form of divinity. They refer regularly to a first principle or a first god, obviously implying the existence of a god of second rank. One such Platonist writer, Numenius (later than Philo but known to Origen), uses the term *second god* for the demiurge (fragments 11, 15, 16, 19). It is hard to avoid the conclusion that the Christian theologians of the second and third centuries, even theologians of the caliber of Origen, were simply prisoners of the *Zeitgeist* when they came to see the Logos as a god of second rank. They were as yet unequipped with the conceptual apparatus that their successors were going to need so as to share, without loss of identity, the divine nature between Persons Three.

SEE ALSO Archetypes; Hypostasis; Jesus; Kalām; Sophia; Torah.

BIBLIOGRAPHY

Aeby, Gervais. *Les missions divines de saint Justin à Origène.* Fribourg, Switzerland, 1958.

Daniélou, Jean. *Gospel Message and Hellenistic Culture,* vol. 2 of *A History of Early Christian Doctrine before the Council of Nicea.* Translated by John A. Baker. London, 1973.

Harl, Marguerite. *Origène et la fonction révélatrice du verbe incarné.* Paris, 1958.

Hatch, Edwin. *The Influence of Greek Ideas on Christianity* (1888). Reprint, New York, 1957.

Holte, Ragnar. "Logos Spermatikos: Christianity and Ancient Philosophy according to St. Justin's Apologies." *Studia Theologica* 12 (1958): 109–168.

Kretschmar, Georg. *Studien zur frühchristlichen Trinitätstheologie.* Tübingen, 1956.

Kurtz, Ewald. *Interpretation zu den Logos-Fragmenten Heraklits.* Spudasmata, vol. 17. Hildesheim, 1971.

Lebreton, Jules. *Histoire du dogme de la Trinité des origines au Concile de Nicée,* vol. 1, *Les origines,* and vol. 2, *De Saint Clément à Saint Irénée.* 6th ed. Paris, 1927–1928. This is an essential work for the study of the Logos doctrine in early Christianity.

Lebreton, Jules. "La théologie de la Trinité chez Clément d'Alexandrie." *Recherches de science religieuse* 34 (1947): 55–76, 142–179.

Orbe, Antonio. *En los albores de la exegesis iohannea.* Analecta Gregoriana, vol. 65. Rome, 1955.

Orbe, Antonio. *Hacia la primera teología de la procesión del Verbo.* 2 vols. Analecta Gregoriana, vols. 99–100. Rome, 1958. The two works by Orbe are important for the study of the notion of *logos* in Gnostic traditions.

Prestige, G. L. *God in Patristic Thought.* London, 1952.

Rendel, Harris J. "Athena, Sophia and the Logos." *Bulletin of the John Rylands Library* 7 (July 1922): 56–72.

Ringgren, Helmer. *Word and Wisdom: Studies in the Hypostatization of Divine Qualities and Functions in the Ancient Near East.* Lund, 1947.

Wolfson, Harry A. "The Trinity, the Logos, and the Platonic Ideas." In his *The Philosophy of the Church Fathers,* vol. 1. Cambridge, Mass., 1964.

New Sources

Bonetskaia, N. K. "The Struggle for Logos in Russian in the Twentieth Century." *Russian Studies in Philosophy* 40 (Spring 2002): 6–40.

Desjardins, Rosemary. *The Rational Enterprise: Logos in Plato's Theaetetus.* Albany, 1990.

Lee, Bernard H. *Jesus and the Metaphors of God: The Christs of the New Testament.* New York, 1993.

Montiglio, Silvia. *Silence in the Land of Logos.* Princeton, N.J., 2000.

Rauser, Randal. "Logos and Logoi Ensarkos: Christology and a Problem of Perception." *International Journal of Systematic Theology* 5 (July 2003): 133–147.

Roochik, David. *The Tragedy of Reason: Toward a Platonic Conception of Logos.* New York, 1990.

Swearingen, C. Jan. *Rhetoric and Irony: Western Literary and Western Lies.* New York, 1991.

Wilcox, Joel. *The Origins of Epistemology in Early Greek Thought.* Lewiston, N.Y., 1994.

JEAN PÉPIN (1987)
Translated from French by Denis O'Brien
Revised Bibliography

LOISY, ALFRED (1857–1940), French scholar who held a dual role in the religious history of France: as a Roman Catholic biblical critic who employed the methods pioneered by German Protestant scholars and as the center of the conflict in Catholicism that would come to be known as the modernist controversy.

Alfred Firman Loisy was born in Ambrières (Marne) on February 28, 1857, and died on June 1, 1940, in Paris. While Loisy was a student in a rural seminary, he undertook the study of Hebrew as an antidote to the mediocrity of his theological education. His familiarity with the language gave him a taste for reading biblical texts for their original sense, a taste that developed into a lifelong preference for historical as opposed to theological approaches to biblical questions. In 1878 he was assigned to the fledgling Institut Catholique de Paris to complete his seminary education. There he attracted the attention of the church historian Louis Duchesne, who encouraged Loisy's interest in modern methods of historical research. There, too, he attended classes of Ernest Renan at the Collège de France; Renan embodied the conviction that it was not possible to be both a historian and a

Catholic. Loisy's youthful ambition was to prove Renan wrong, to demonstrate in his own life and work that, as he put it, "the great march of history did not pass by Renan's door."

Nevertheless, Loisy's journals for these years indicate that he was deeply distressed by what seemed to be the unwillingness of the church to understand or explain its past in any but the most doctinaire theological categories. However troubled his private thoughts may have been, Loisy exhibited in his studies the clarity of mind, attention to detail, and remarkable discipline that would characterize all his later work. As a result, he was appointed instructor (1882) and then professor of New Testament (1890) at the Institut Catholique. In that position, Loisy began to expose his students to the requirements of a historical study of Christian origins. However, church authorities were wary of scientific studies that would alter or overturn traditional doctrines, and it was inevitable in this environment that a controversy would arise. Loisy soon found himself embroiled in an argument over the nature of biblical inspiration that led first to his demotion and finally to his dismissal.

Loisy's next appointment, to the chaplaincy of a convent school outside Paris, was probably intended to keep him out of higher education. However, unable to do technical research, Loisy began to think about the problem of modern religion in its wider bearings. He developed an entire program for teaching the Catholic faith in a way that would be consistent with the discoveries of modern historical research. When, in 1902, Adolf von Harnack's popular book on the essence of Christianity, *Das Wesen des Christentums* (English title, *What Is Christianity?*), appeared in French translation, Loisy saw an opportunity to demonstrate that Catholics could have the better of an argument with Protestant historians simply on historical grounds; one could show, for example, that Harnack's conclusions were wrong, not because they violated doctrine but because they rested on inadequate research and hasty conclusions. Loisy's book *L'évangile et l'église*, published that same year, created a sensation. However, what proved significant about the book was not so much the success of Loisy's argument with Harnack as his acknowledgment that history allowed for considerably fewer claims about Jesus' divinity and foreknowledge than Catholic theology had traditionally made. When Loisy confirmed this position in a companion volume (*Autour d'un petit livre*) the next year, the issue crystallized into a conflict between historians who would alter doctrine to suit their vision of history and theologians who would refuse historical fact to preserve doctrine. Loisy spent the next several months defending his position while trying to avoid condemnation by the church on whose behalf he understood himself to be speaking. By the end of 1903, he realized that the project to which he had given so much of his life was failing. When, in March 1904, Pius X's accusation that Loisy was not sincere in his wish to remain in the church was conveyed to him, "something inside came apart."

Loisy was excommunicated in 1907. Earlier that year, the encyclical *Pascendi dominici gregis* was issued by Pius X, describing and condemning "modernist" errors; prominent among them were the principles of biblical research drawn from Loisy's work.

During this controversy, Loisy had begun to teach courses at the Collège de France and to return to the kind of technical research he said he preferred. After his excommunication, he was appointed to the chair of history of religions, where he remained until his retirement in 1931. Loisy continued to publish a remarkable number of books until just before his death at the age of eighty-three. Besides his technical work on aspects of Christian origins, he continued his interest in the nature of religion and its place in the modern world. He understood these latter works as a kind of series that began with *L'évangile et l'église* in 1902 and concluded in 1937 with *La crise morale du temps présent et l'éducation humaine.*

Bibliography

For analysis of Loisy's thought and influence, see Maude D. Petre's *Alfred Loisy: His Religious Significance* (Cambridge, U.K., 1944) and John Ratte's *Three Modernists: Alfred Loisy, George Tyrrell, William L. Sullivan,* New York, 1967.

Several of Loisy's works have been translated into English. *The Gospel and the Church* (1903), Christopher Home's translation of *L'évangile et l'église,* has been reissued (Philadelphia, 1976) with a good introduction by Bernard Scott, and Loisy's autobiography, *Choses passées* (1913), translated by Richard W. Boynton with Loisy's approval and issued as *My Duel with the Vatican* (1924), is still available in a reprint edition (New York, 1968). Loisy's later three-volume *Mémoires pour servir à l'histoire religieuse de notre temps* (Paris, 1930–1931) has not been translated. His last major work on Christian origins, *La naissance du Christianisme* (1933), was translated by L. P. Jacks as *The Birth of the Christian Religion* (London, 1948) but is currently out of print.

New Sources

Heaney, John J. "Metaphor and Modernist: The Polarization of Alfred Loisy and His Neo-Thomist Critics." *Theological Studies* 49D (1988): 781.

Hill, Harvey. "French Politics and Alfred Loisy's Modernism." *Church History* 67, no. 3S (1998): 521–536.

Hill, Harvey. *The Politics of Modernism: Alfred Loisy and the Scientific Study of Religion.* Washington, D.C., 2002

Jodock, Darrell. "Introduction II: The Modernists and the Anti-Modernists." In *Catholicism Contending with Modernity,* pp. 20–27. Cambridge, U.K.; New York, 2000.

Kieran, Patricia Mary Brigid. "New Light on Alfred Loisy: An Exploration of His Religious Science in Essais d'Histoire et de Philosophie Religieuses (1898–1899)." Ph.D. diss., University of London, 1995.

RICHARD J. RESCH (1987)
Revised Bibliography

LOKI is an enigmatic figure in Scandinavian mythology. There is no evidence for the worship of Loki, nor any evidence of his being known elsewhere in the Germanic world. He turns up only rarely in skaldic poetry and not at all in the *Gesta Danorum* of Saxo Grammaticus. Even in Eddic poetry he turns up less frequently than Óðinn or Þórr. And yet he is something like the lynchpin of the mythology proper in its vernacular Icelandic form.

According to Snorri Sturluson's *Gylfaginning*, part of his *Edda* (c. 1220–1230), Loki is the son of the giant Fárbauti. With the giantess Angrboða, Loki is the father of three monsters who threaten the gods: the wolf Fenrir, the serpent Jǫrmungandr, and the woman Hel. Óðinn, with his foresight, saw the threat and had the monsters brought to him. The wolf was bound; the serpent was cast into the sea, where he lies coiled around the earth and hence is known as the Midgard serpent; and Hel was cast down into the underworld, where she rules over the realm of the dead. These monsters remain checked until Ragnarǫk, the end of the world.

Despite his giant heritage and these threatening offspring, Loki lives among the gods in the time before Ragnarǫk. At the end of his catalogue of the Æsir (gods) in *Gylfaginning*, Snorri Sturluson wrote that Loki "is also enumerated among the Æsir." This puzzling expression may in fact hold the key to understanding Loki. He is numbered among the gods, but is not apparently one of them. Much of his activity during the period up to Ragnarǫk supports the gods in their struggle against the forces of chaos, but some of his actions are ambiguous. One good example involves another monstrous offspring, Óðinn's eight-legged horse Sleipnir, best of horses. Loki bore Sleipnir after seducing, in the form of a mare, the workhorse that a giant was using to construct the wall around Valhǫll. The giant was to have done the work without help, but when he requested the use of his horse the gods consented, with Loki's specific approval. The horse did more work than the giant, and it began to appear that the giant would fulfill the contract, for which he was to receive the goddess Freyja, the sun, and the moon. When the horse ran off to mate with Loki in the form of a mare, the giant was unable to finish the wall on time and had to forfeit his life. Giving up Freyja and the celestial bodies to the giants would have meant the end of the gods' order, so here Loki caused a problem for the gods, solved it, and protected them, and he also produced a valuable treasure for Óðinn.

In another case, Loki was once captured by the giant Þjazi and agreed to deliver Iðunn and her golden apples, which kept the gods young. Loki did so, but then the gods forced him to retrieve her. This he did in the form of a falcon. The myth, which is found in skaldic poetry as well as in Snorri's *Edda*, highlights Loki's ambivalence. He begins the myth traveling together with Óðinn and Hœnir. His agreement to deliver Iðunn nearly leads to the demise of the gods; his retrieval of Iðunn restores order and reinforces the mythological rule that females move only from giants to gods, never in the opposite direction, and in the end of the story the gods kill Þjazi, thus reinforcing their hierarchical supremacy over the giants.

The story goes on in Snorri's version. Þjazi's daughter Skaði demands compensation for the death of her father. The gods agree to allow her to choose a husband from among them, and she chooses Njǫrðr. But they must also make her laugh, and it is Loki who meets this challenge. He ties one end of a rope around his testicles and the other around the beard of a she-goat, and as both howl, Loki falls on Skaði's knee; then she laughs. Here Loki sacrifices his honor, and perhaps more, to right the original wrong of his giving Iðunn and her apples into the hands of the giants. He also helps procure for the gods a wife from among the giantesses.

Snorri has several stories of this kind. Captured and starved in bird form by the giant Geirrǫðr, Loki agrees to deliver Þórr to the giant without his hammer or belt of strength. Loki accompanies Þórr on the arduous journey, which ends with Þórr killing the giant's daughters and the giant himself. We have the same myth in a late tenth-century skaldic poem, *Þórsdrápa of Eilífr Goðrúnarson*; in it the motivation for the journey is not provided, and Þjálfi, not Loki, accompanies Þórr.

Perhaps the most important of these stories of Loki's ambivalent position, all retained in Snorri, begins when he cuts the hair from the head of Sif, the wife of Þórr. How he does so is unknown, but it is not impossible that he was cuckolding Þórr at the time (as Margaret Clunies Ross suggests). To avert Þórr's rage, Loki agrees to acquire gold hair from the dwarfs. He returns with six great treasures, which are divided in Dumézilian triads: the spear Gungnir for Óðinn, the gold hair for Þórr's wife, and the ship Skíðblaðnir for Freyr; and the ring Draupnir for Óðinn, Þórr's hammer, and the golden-bristled boar Gullinborsti for Freyr. The second set was made by Brokkr, with whom Loki had bet his head that the dwarf could not make better items than those in the first set. Turning himself into a fly, Loki bit the smith mercilessly, but the only effect was that the hammer ended with a short handle. Even so, the gods declared it the greatest treasure, but when Loki declared that he had wagered his head, not his neck, the dwarf sewed Loki's lips shut.

In each of these cases Loki acts to right an initial misbehavior, and the outcome is favorable to the gods. Every case involves shape-changing, and bearing a foal and having his lips sewn shut represent significant losses of honor for Loki.

Bodily injury, dishonor, shape-changing, and especially the shortsighted or impulsive behavior that leads to significant cultural acquisition make Loki look much like the common narrative and mythological type of the *trickster.* Georges Dumézil (1948) contrasts this impulsive intelligence with that of Hœnir, who cannot speak without counsel, but the better comparison would be with the deep-thinking Óðinn. Both Óðinn and Loki are shape-changers and both are sexually ambiguous.

While Loki clearly plays the trickster and shows impulsive behavior in many myths, he by no means does so in every case. In the Eddic poem *Þrymskviða,* for example, he helps Þórr to retrieve his hammer from the giant who has stolen it. Although both he and Þórr must dress as women (Þórr as Freyja, whom the giant has demanded in exchange for the hammer), there is no indication that Loki had anything to do with the loss of the hammer, and Loki's wise responses to the giant's questions make possible the ultimate retrieval of the hammer. Similarly, in *Gylfaginning* Loki is one of Þórr's party when the god visits the giant Útgarðaloki and helps him wholeheartedly in the contests that follow. In neither case is there indication of any ambivalence in or about Loki.

Just as there are stories in which Loki unequivocally works on the side of the gods, so are there stories or indications of stories in which he opposes them unequivocally. Stanza 37 of the Eddic poem *Hymiskviða* charges Loki with having lamed Þórr's goat. The skald Úlfr Uggason, describing the carvings in a chieftain's hall in western Iceland circa 985, left us one stanza about a battle between Loki and the god Heimdallr. It is obscure, but Snorri tells us that the gods fought in the form of seals, and that they were fighting over the Brísingamen, the precious necklace of Freyja. Since some kennings (metaphors) call Loki the thief of this object, and since Freyja has it in the mythological present, it is possible that the battle between Heimdallr and Loki took place in the mythic past and that Heimdallr won the battle and got the necklace back. In the poetic language Heimdallr is known as Loki's adversary.

We may conjecture that the battle with Heimdallr and the siring of the three monsters with the giantess Angrboða both occurred in the mythic past. We have Loki's own voice testifying to his joining the gods during the mythic past as well:

> Do you not remember, Óðinn, when we two in days of yore Blended our blood together? You said you never would taste beer, Unless it were served to both of us. (*Lokasenna* 9)

According to medieval Icelandic literature, an oath of blood brotherhood meant that the sworn brothers would avenge each other as though they were actual brothers; that is, each would be obliged to revenge the other, and an injury done to one could be regarded as an injury done to both. On the obverse side, sworn brothers agreed never to harm each other. We have no information on this oath taken in days of yore between Óðinn and Loki, but Óðinn and the gods would appear to be the beneficiaries, as Loki was the father of monsters and adversary of Heimdallr, and the oath would have neutralized his natural enmity toward Óðinn and the family of gods.

Lokasenna (Loki's quarrel) puts the oath to the test and indicates its failure. Loki has been excluded from the feast which is the scene of the poem because, according to the prose header, he killed the host's servants. His appeal to Óðinn matches the context—the gods are drinking—but it is ominous, because beer is a weapon Óðinn uses against the giants; Óðinn obtained the mythic mead of poetry and is a master of wisdom. The rest of the poem is a series of poetic dialogues, usually Óðinn's arena, in which Loki humiliates the gods by telling home truths, including his own role in the death of Óðinn's son Baldr. In the end only the threat of Þórr's hammer silences him.

The prose colophon tells of the punishment of Loki. The gods bind him with the guts of his son with the goddess Sigyn, and another of these sons turns into a wolf. The gods hang a pot of dripping poison over his face. Sigyn catches it in a bowl, but when she goes to empty the bowl the poison torments Loki and his writhings cause earthquakes. According to Snorri, the gods visited this punishment on Loki for his role in the death of Baldr. In Snorri's version of the story, Loki learns that only mistletoe will kill Baldr; guides the arm of the blind Hóðr when he throws the mistletoe at Baldr; and then, disguised as the old hag Þǫkk, refuses to join all creation in weeping for Baldr, to meet the condition that Hel has set for his release. Snorri's presentation of Loki, then, shows that Loki is ultimately a giant and that he shares the enmity of the giants toward the gods. The fictive kinship implied by an oath of blood-brotherhood or by Loki's being "enumerated among the Æsir" is less strong than the blood kinship of Loki's patrilines. Son of a giant, he arranges the death of Óðinn's son at the hands of another son. Any vengeance Óðinn takes must be hollow: he can sire an avenger to kill his own son, Hóðr, or he can have one of Loki's sons kill another (as Snorri has it) and bind Loki, but the damage is done. The first death of a god, as Baldr's is, must lead to Ragnarók, the end of the world.

When Ragnarók arrives, all bonds break. Human kin kill each other and kinship is spoiled. Loki steers a ship full of giants to the last battle, and he and his monstrous offspring are free to face the gods. The wolf kills Óðinn (and is avenged by another son of Óðinn). Þórr and the Midgard serpent kill each other, as do Loki and Heimdallr according to Snorri. In the new world that springs up after the battle, Baldr and Hǫðr return, their enmity annulled. Loki and the other giants are no more.

See Also Eddas; Jötnar; Óðinn; Snorri Sturluson.

Bibliography

The scholarship on this enigmatic figure is vast. Older scholarship pointed to Loki's byname, Loptr, which appears to be related to the noun *lopt* (air) to buttress various notions familiar to nature mythology. Jan de Vries, *The Problem of Loki* (Helsinki, 1933), offers the connection with the trickster figure. Georges Dumézil's notion of Loki's impulsive intelligence is to be found in his *Loki* (Paris, 1948). In his *Gods of the Ancient Northmen* (Berkeley, 1973), Dumézil adduces supposed Ossetic parallels to Loki's role in the death of Baldr. Folke Ström's *Loki: Ein mythologisches Problem* (Göteborg, Sweden, 1956) argues on the basis of the patent similarities between the two figures that Loki was an hypostasis of Óðinn. Anna Birgitta Rooth, *Loki in Scandinavian Mythology* (Lund, Sweden, 1961), applies a very strict version of folklore mythology that regarded everything found elsewhere as not original to

Loki; stripping away these supposed layers, she is left with an original notion of Loki as a spider, a notion that finds no support in the texts. Jens Peter Schødt, "Om Loke endnu en gang," *Arkiv för nordisk filologi* 96 (1981): 49–86, offers an insightful exploration of Loki as mediator. Anatoly Liberman, "Snorri and Saxo on Útgarðaloki, with Notes on Loki Laufeyjarson's Character, Career, and Name," in *Saxo Grammaticus: Tra storiografica e letteratura*, edited by Carlo Santini (Rome, 1992), pp. 91–158, speculates on the etymology of the name and on the relationship between Loki and Útgarðaloki. John Lindow, *Murder and Vengeance among the Gods: Baldr in Scandinavian Mythology* (Helsinki, 1997), discusses the fictive kinship between Óðinn and Loki and the narrative implications of myth told in a society that used blood feud to resolve disputes.

JOHN LINDOW (2005)

LOMBARD, PETER SEE PETER LOMBARD

LONERGAN, BERNARD

LONERGAN, BERNARD (1904–1984), Roman Catholic philosopher-theologian and methodologist. Bernard Joseph Francis Lonergan was born on December 17, 1904, at Buckingham, Quebec, not far from Ottawa. Of Irish-English stock, he was the eldest of three sons. His early education took place in the local schools and at Loyola College in Montreal. In 1922 he joined the Jesuits and followed their regular course of study: Greek and Latin classics at Guelph, Ontario, philosophy at Heythrop College in England (with an external bachelor of arts degree from the University of London in 1930), and theology at the Gregorian University in Rome, where he was ordained priest in 1936 and completed his doctoral work in 1940. He taught theology for twenty-five years, thirteen in the Jesuit seminaries at Montreal and Toronto and twelve at the Gregorian University. In 1965 major surgery for lung cancer forced his partial retirement, but he continued writing, first for a decade as research professor at Regis College in Toronto (with a year's leave as Stillman professor at Harvard University, 1971–1972) and then as visiting distinguished professor at Boston College from 1975 to 1983. On taking full retirement in 1983 he returned to his native Canada, where he died at the Jesuit Infirmary in Pickering, Ontario, on November 26, 1984.

Lonergan's first major works were studies of Thomas Aquinas generously laced with references at Aristotle: *Grace and Freedom* (his doctoral dissertation) and *Verbum: Word and Idea in Aquinas.* The latter was a revolutionary study in Thomist cognitional theory and a springboard to the independent *Insight: A Study of Human Understanding* (published in 1957, but completed in 1953), a monumental work that went far beyond Thomas into twentieth-century science, psychology, and social and political theory. Lonergan's second major work, *Method in Theology* (1972), incorporated hermeneutics and history and added personal notions of dialectic and foundations to provide not a theology but an integral framework in which creative theology could be done.

Meanwhile Lonergan was producing theological instruction of considerable importance (though it needs redoing in the light of his own method) for his Latin-language courses, writing articles and reviews, and giving occasional lectures. Toward the end of his life he went back to an early interest in economics and the dialectic of history and had almost completed a work that may turn out to be as revolutionary in those two fields as *Insight* had been in philosophy and *Method* had been in theology.

Although his early focus on questions proper to Roman Catholic theology left religion in general in the margin, Lonergan's relentless drive toward a comprehensive view of things, and his special methodological interest in foundations of thought and conduct, led him eventually to reflection on religion too. His views on this topic are set forth succinctly in chapter four of *Method,* but that account can be enlarged from other writings and set in the context of his general concerns.

Lonergan comes to the question from the two questions of philosophy and theology. First, a thoroughgoing philosophy will raise the question of God's existence and nature. The question is the key step, and Lonergan raises it in his own characteristic way: through inquiry into the possibility of fruitful inquiry, through reflecting on the nature of reflection, and through deliberating on the worthwhileness of deliberation. With the question raised and answered affirmatively, thought may take different routes to arrive at complementary aspects of religion. One route starts with the problem of evil, to work out the anticipated general lines of the solution that a wise, good, and powerful God may be expected to provide: in effect religion as pertaining to the objective order of the universe; this was the approach of chapter twenty of *Insight.* The second is the route of religious experience taken in chapter four of *Method* (though the problem of evil still provides an introduction to the question, p. 288); personal fulfillment is achieved in self-transcendence, love is the crown of self-transcendence, and love of God is the primary religious experience: in effect, religion as a differentiation of human consciousness.

The theological approach starts from the Roman Catholic doctrine that God wills the salvation of the whole human race and so offers everyone the divine transforming grace needed for salvation. On this basis Lonergan proceeds to the love of God flooding everyone's hearts through the Holy Spirit given to all and links this as inner word to the outer word of tradition deriving from the Son. Thus he arrives at a concretely identifiable charismatic and institutional religion to which philosophical inquiry had pointed in a general way.

There remains the question of dialogue, in particular between Christianity and the world religions. Lonergan's starting point is not the institutional church as evangelizing the nations (outer word, Son of God, Christianity), but religious experience (inner word, Holy Spirit, a community enjoying God's love). He does not impose his theological a priori on students of religion but leaves it to them to decide whether his model of religious experience is verified in the data, though he finds support in their writings (*Method,* pp. 108–109). Again, the gift from God that he affirms is fundamentally a reality—experienced, but not thematized. It must be thematized and given expression in a process that has its difficulties for the Christian as well as for others (*Method,* p. 290). Further, each religion will have its own categories of expression, so there is then the problem of a common language and communication. He recognizes that his own language (God's love flooding our hearts) is Christian (*Method,* p. 240), but he hopes that the core reality as reality will be a base for cross-cultural discussion (*Method,* pp. 11, 284). That is, the orientation to the otherworldly, the conversion to the transcendent, the being seized by the mystery of love and awe, the fateful call to a dreaded holiness—whatever the language, and all these phrases are culturally conditioned—all this as a reality would bring people together in discussion. But then the first and fundamental need is for self-appropriation (the great thrust of *Insight*), and the further, more specific need is for studies of religious interiority (*Method,* p. 290).

BIBLIOGRAPHY

In addition to the works mentioned above, Lonergan's views on religion can be found in various chapters of *Collection* (New York, 1967), *A Second Collection* (Philadelphia, 1974), *A Third Collection* (New York, 1985), and in *Philosophy of God, and Theology* (Philadelphia, 1973). Since 1988 reference must be made to the *Collected Works of Bernard Lonergan,* University of Toronto Press. Twenty-some volumes are projected, of which numbers 1–7, 10, 15, 18, and 21 have been issued as of late 2003.

The difficulty of drawing up a bibliography of secondary literature stems from the fundamental nature of Lonergan's ideas, which involve study of basic generalities before specific application can be made, and allow ramification into many seemingly disparate areas. But two dissertations can be mentioned: Vernon J. Gregson, Jr.'s "Bernard Lonergan and the Dialogue of Religions: A Foundational Study of Religion as Spirituality" (Ph.D. diss., Marquette University, 1978), somewhat rewritten and published as *Lonergan, Spirituality, and the Meeting of Religions* (Lanham, N.Y., 1985), and Emil J. Piscitelli's "Language and Method in the Philosophy of Religion: A Critical Study in the Development of the Philosophy of Bernard Lonergan" (Ph.D. diss., Georgetown University, 1977). A more recent publication is *Symposium: Lonergan's Philosophy and the Religious Phenomenon,* published as a special issue of *Method: Journal of Lonegan Studies* (Fall 1994). The foundational aspect of Lonergan's work, especially in relation to Jungian psychology, is studied in two works of Robert Doran: *Psychic Conversion and Theological Foundations: Toward a Reorientation of the Human Sciences* (Chico, Calif., 1981) and *Subject and Psyche; Ricoeur, Jung, and the Search for Foundations* (Washington, D.C., 1977). Considerable interest is emerging in the relation of Lonergan's work to mystical theology; see, for example, Harvey D. Egan's *What Are They Saying about Mysticism?* (New York, 1982) and William Johnston's *The Inner Eye of Love: Mysticism and Religion* (San Francisco, 1978). The elation of Lonergan's trinitarian theology to world religions is studied in my own *Son of God, Holy Spirit, and World Religions: Bernard Lonergan's Contribution to the Wider Ecumenism* (Toronto, 1984). A new and important field of application is that of popular religions (Philippines, Africa), but the literature is scattered; for this material and for Lonergan's unpublished works, the Lonergan Research Institute, Toronto, can be consulted.

FREDERICK E. CROWE (1987 AND 2005)

LÖNNROT, ELIAS (1802–1884), Finnish folklorist and philologist, the compiler of the *Kalevala,* the Finnish national epic. Lönnrot was born in the parish of Sammatti, province of Uusimaa, Finland, as a son of a tailor. In a childhood full of poverty, his schooling was difficult and often interrupted. In 1822 he became a student at the University of Turku, where he supported himself as a private tutor. He received his M.A. degree at Turku in 1827 with his thesis "On Väinämöinen, a Divinity of the Ancient Finns." After the university was destroyed in the fire of Turku, Lönnrot undertook a folklore collecting trip across Finland as far as Finnish Karelia. Part of the material he collected was published under the title *Kantele* (The harp, 1829–1831).

In 1828, Lönnrot resumed his studies, this time in medicine at Helsinki University. There he came into close contact with a number of young literati who were filled with the national spirit. In 1831, the Finnish Literature Society was founded to further the development of Finnish culture and to collect and study folklore. Lönnrot became its first secretary. This society financed Lönnrot's numerous folklore collection trips. After defending his thesis, "The Magical Medicine of the Finns," he received the M.D. degree in 1832 and was assigned as the district physician in Kajaani, northern Finland.

Lönnrot then got the idea of combining the folk songs of Finland into bigger units. Thus came about the cycles of songs about the major Finnish heroes that constitute the first stage of the Finnish epic. A journey during which he met the greatest folk singers of Karelia yielded a rich harvest that was incorporated into the first version of the *Kalevala,* the so-called *Old Kalevala* (1835–1836), which consisted of thirty-six songs comprising 12,078 lines. From extensive additional folk song material, recorded partly by Lönnrot himself but mostly by others in eastern Karelia and eastern Finland, Lönnrot prepared a greatly expanded and changed version of the *Kalevala.* Published in 1849, it has 22,795 lines and is divided into fifty songs. It is this so-called *New Kalevala* that is considered the Finnish epic.

In the 1830s, Lönnrot published a few popular books on food substitutes and health care and edited some journals.

He compiled a large collection of lyrical songs and ballads, titled *Kanteletar* (The spirit of the harp; 1840–1841), which was followed by books of proverbs (1842) and riddles (1844). In 1844 he was granted a leave for five years for the preparation of a comprehensive Finnish-Swedish dictionary.

After defending his inaugural thesis on the Vepse language, Lönnrot was named professor of the Finnish language and literature at Helsinki University in 1853. In this capacity, he had greater significance as a practical linguist than a theoretical scholar. He retired in 1862 and settled down in his native parish of Sammatti, to continue his work. He revised Finnish hymns, completed the Finnish-Swedish dictionary (1866–1880), and published a collection of Finnish charms (1880). His last years were spent in conducting religious services in his community, treating people without charge, and participating actively in numerous charitable enterprises.

The *Kalevala* is not only Lönnrot's greatest accomplishment; it is the most important work in Finnish literature. It is, in its entirety, Lönnrot's compilation, based on the best and most complete variants of about thirty folk songs. Lönnrot made certain changes and modifications in them, adding verses from other variants and even from other songs, increasing the parallelism, and creating linking verses. He had a tendency to reduce the Christian and legendary features while strengthening the heathen and the historical-realistic elements. The songs are, however, not copies of reality, but instead they convey a fictional picture of the ancient Finns' way of life. While the *Kalevala* itself cannot be used as material for folklore study, its heroes and problems have strongly stimulated research into Finnish folklore and mythology.

The *Kalevala* has been called a shamanistic epic, since its great deeds are accomplished by magical means—by the power of words and incantations. All the heroes of the Kaleva group—Väinämöinen, Ilmarinen, and Lemminkäinen—are mythic and/or shamanistic figures and, as a group, are opposed to the people of the North, headed by the witch Louhi. The plot, created by Lönnrot, centers on fights over the possession of a fertility-promoting object, the Sampo, and competition for the Maiden of the North.

The *Kalevala*, according to Martti Haavio, was not only "the symbol of Finnish nationalism, but it was actually its crown symbol." The *Kalevala* gave faith and confidence to the people living under Russian rule. It influenced the development of the Finnish language, literature, and arts, and it played a substantial role in the adoption of Finnish as the language of the country.

BIBLIOGRAPHY

Anttila, Aarne. *Elias Lönnrot: Elämä ja toiminta.* 2 vols. Helsinki, 1931–1935. A detailed and very broad survey of Lönnrot's life and work, presented against the background of his time. An excellent work.

Anttila, Aarne. *Elias Lönnrot.* 2d ed. Helsinki, 1962. An abbreviated version of the preceding work.

Fromm, Hans. "Elias Lönnrot als Schöpfer des finnischen Epos Kalevala." In *Volksepen der uralischen und altaischen Völker*, edited by Wolfgang Veenker, pp. 1–12. Wiesbaden, 1968. A survey of Lönnrot's work on the compilation of *Kalevala.*

Haavio, Martti. "Elias Lönnrot." In *Leading Folklorists of the North*, edited by Dag Strömbäck, pp. 1–10. Oslo, 1971. A splendid essay about Lönnrot.

Honko, Lauri."The *Kalevala* and Myths." *Nordisk Institut for Folkedigtning Newsletter* (Turku, Finland) 12 (1984): 1–11. Discusses the interpretations of the *Kalevala* and the authenticity of the epic.

Magoun, Francis P., Jr. "Materials for the Study of the *Kalevala.*" In *The Kalevala, or Poems of the Kaleva District*, compiled by Elias Lönnrot; prose translation with foreword and appendixes by Francis Magoun, Jr., pp. 341–361. Cambridge, Mass., 1963. A concise biography of Lönnrot and discussion of his work on the *Kalevala.*

New Sources

Wargelin Brown, K. Marianne. "Kalevala as Western Culture in Finland and America." In *Finnish Americana* 7 (1986): 5–12.

FELIX J. OINAS (1987)
Revised Bibliography

LORD OF THE ANIMALS. The concept of a special type of deity or spirit that reigns over the animal kingdom is common among many Old and New World peoples. The universality of this conception suggests that formerly some form of cultural contact existed that bridged the continents. As a fundamental element in the life of the human as hunter, a lord of the animals is a familiar figure among hunting cultures, but he also occurs, in modified forms, in many agrarian and pastoral societies. In the latter instance the concept is often associated with a spiritual herdsman of wild game, a spirit analogue to human domesticators of animals. But the idea of an animal lord or spirit can be traced even further back than the development of herding—indeed, as concrete evidence shows, into the Old Stone Age.

The lord of the animals often appears as a lord of the forest, mountain, or sea—natural areas that may possibly have been inhabited by individual spiritual sovereigns that eventually blended together to form a lord of animals. For many cultures, the forest (or tree), the mountain, and the cave are the preferred residence of the animal lord, though for hunters of sea mammals and fish, the sea floor and the deep sea are conceived as his abode. Occasionally the lord is associated with the sun, the moon, a star, or a constellation.

The lord of the animals is often a helper of mankind. He guides the animals to the hunter or helps him discover the trail of his prey. In addition, he often provides a magical weapon or a mystical spell that assures success in finding game. Such assistance, however, often assumes that certain conditions are fulfilled or specific regulations observed: the lord of the animals punishes the malicious, those who wantonly kill more game than is needed and those who are disrespectful of the dead game, especially in handling the bones, which must be meticulously saved, for from the bones, the same type of animal will be re-created (with or without the intervention of the lord of the animals). It is most often assumed that the soul of the dead animal returns to its spiritual master, from whom it will receive another body. Frequently, the lord of the animals is held to be the creator of the game and is therefore often named "Father" or "Mother." At the very least, he gives the animals their names or other distinguishing features. In cases of misbehavior on the part of the hunter, the animal lord either retains the game (which is often believed to reside with him) or strikes the guilty hunter down with sickness, or punishes him by withdrawing his luck in the hunt. To win his favor, the lord of the animals must be called upon before the hunt with a plea to release some of the game, and afterwards must be given thanks. Frequently a small offering is also made before the expedition, some tobacco for example, while after the hunt a portion of the game might be left behind as an offering.

Precise physical descriptions of the lord of the animals vary considerably from culture to culture. He may appear in anthropomorphic as well as zoomorphic form, as a mixture of these or as some other fabulous creature, or as a giant or dwarf. In the majority of instances the lord of the animals is masculine, but we often find a feminine conceptualization and in some instances a bisexual character. When envisioned in zoomorphic form, the lord of the animals often combines various parts or markings of different types of animals, thereby emphasizing and enhancing his authority over all game.

In addition to belief in a lord of all animals, a corresponding or supplementary belief may exist in an individual master or lord of each separate kind of animal. Such a being is classified ethnologically as a "species spirit." This spirit, when envisioned theriomorphically, may also represent another animal type besides its own—a relationship that is often alleged to exist naturally. Many scholars maintain that the belief in species spirits is a more recent manifestation of older, more general conceptions of the lord of the animals.

When the lord of the animals is associated with an individual representative of a specific kind of animal, a different situation develops. Such instances occur among hunting groups when a defined game animal plays a predominant role in tribal subsistence patterns. Frequently, the lord of the animals must be propitiated when a member of that particular species is killed. This expression of the idea of an animal lord can be accepted as a more ancient form, especially when it appears concurrently with the conceptualization of this deity as a prototypical or exaggerated version of that animal species. In such cases the spirit is often envisioned as an exceptionally large, and therefore supernatural, member of the species in question. Sometimes he is conceived in human form riding the animal with which he is particularly associated. In general, scholars hold the theriomorphic version of the lord of the animals to be older, in cultural-historical terms, than the anthropomorphic form. In this respect, frequent observation of ceremonies performed for the ritual handling of slain large game (bear, lion, elephant, etc.), and even prehistoric testimony about such ceremonies, have proved to be of great importance. The reverence shown to large game is closely associated with the original form of the lord of the animals and deserves further study.

A distinctive characteristic of the animal lord is the fact that, despite his role as protector of wild game, he makes certain concessions when considering the needs of the hunter. To the extent that this is true, the animal lord functions as a god of the hunt, which in some cases is the predominant role. This aspect has caused many researchers to seek his origin outside a purely zoological sphere. The question remains open, however, whether or not this hunting-god aspect is connected with the anthropomorphic aspect of the lord of the animals. An ethno-religious order can be arranged as follows. In many cases, particularly among hunting peoples, past as well as present, the lord of the animals is clearly a real god, distinctively named and sovereign over his realm. In other cases, however, he is merely a game spirit, who is named solely by his association with a particular animal species. Such a game spirit is sometimes outwitted because of his awkwardness and may be characterized by unpredictability, arbitrariness, and tomfoolery (i.e., he is a trickster); in many conceptions he has the ability to transform himself into many forms and thereby confuse the hunter. In still other cases, the lord of the animals may have shrunk to a mere mythological or legendary figure disengaged from the immediate life of the society.

The distinctions between these different categories are, of course, not rigid. The relationship between the lord of the animals and other supernatural beings varies also. He may be incorporated within the character of a tribal father or of the supreme being that creates life and provides subsistence. Many ethnologists of the Vienna school, following Wilhelm Schmidt, viewed the lord of the animals as an offshoot of the supreme being. This theory contradicts an understanding of the lord of the animals as an older, independent god who served as a fundamental element in the construction of the idea of a supreme being. In the opinion of the notable historian of religions, Raffaele Pettazzoni, the supreme being himself was the lord of the animals.

The primary areas of diffusion for the concept and veneration of a lord of the animals include northern Eurasia, ancient Europe, and Africa, as well as the regions occupied by the indigenous inhabitants of the Americas, from the extreme north to the southernmost tip. Such beliefs are also found elsewhere, but only occasionally.

It is in ancient Greece that one encounters the most familiar animal deity, Artemis, whose double role as goddess of the hunt and mistress of the animals was never fully understood. In Homer's *Iliad* and other sources from antiquity, she is described in an obviously preexisting formula as *potnia thērōn*, or "mistress of the wild animals." Although she cares for the animals as a mother does her children, she also hunts them with bow and arrow. The deer is her devoted companion, consistently appearing beside her in works of art, and she is sometimes referred to as the "deer huntress" in the Homeric Hymns. She is also mistress over the entire wild animal kingdom, which includes not only land animals but the birds in the sky and fish in the waters.

Artemis herself is depicted as wild and uncanny and is sometimes pictured with a Gorgon's head. The rituals by which she was venerated also took on an archaic character. Reverence was displayed by the hunter's hanging the skin of the animal, including the antlers, on a tree or special pole. Besides the deer, Artemis had other favorite animals, including the lion and, especially, the bear, which has led some researchers to the opinion that, although this was not understood by the Greeks, she originally appeared as a female bear. In keeping with this interpretation, Artemis has been associated with the lord of the animals in the Northern Hemisphere, where bear rituals were an essential religious element. Even among the ancient Greeks, Artemis was the central figure at the bear feast, and her tradition can be traced to a Cretan or Minoan goddess of animals. Diana was her counterpart among the Roman goddesses. During the period in which the Romans occupied Gaul, the goddess who was interpreted as the indigenous parallel to Diana was known as Artio (from the Celtic *artos,* "bear"; *arta* "female bear"). This information comes down to us in the form of a bronze votive offering with a Latin inscription found in Muri (near Bern, Switzerland), an area occupied by the Helvetii. It depicts a sitting female who is being approached by a bear that has come out of a tree. The veneration displayed in Gaulish ceremonials to the slain bear as a lord of the animals closely resemble the rites dedicated to this animal over an extensive area. According to A. Irving Hallowell (1926), bear ceremonials are widespread among peoples of northern Eurasia, from the Finns, Saami (Lapps), and Mansi (Voguls) in the west, eastward through Siberia to the Yakuts and the Tunguz, further east to the Paleosiberian Nivkhi (Giliaks), the Chuckchi and the Ainu, and across the Bering Sea to the northern regions of North America. Although it cannot be generalized, the most suggestive interpretation of the intent of such ceremonies is that of the Japanese ethnologist Kyosuke Kindaichi concerning the bear feast of the Ainu. Kindaichi suggests that the bear itself is god. All animals are deities that live in human form in another world. When these deities occasionally come to this world, they appear in the form of animals. The bear is the highest of these gods. Any animal that is not captured, killed, and eaten by the Ainu has the unfortunate fate of wandering aimlessly throughout the world. The killing of an animal is therefore a sacred act, since the god himself has come into their midst. And with his coming he brings presents to mankind: his meat and fur. This divine animal, however, is satisfied, since it will now be able to return to its eternal home ("The Concepts behind the Ainu Bear Festival," *Southwest Journal of Anthropology* 5, 1949).

To ascertain the antiquity of such bear cults, we must return to Europe. Caves in Switzerland, southern Germany, France, Silesia, Hungary, and Yugoslavia, dating from the middle to early Stone Age, have revealed small manmade stone chambers containing the skulls, teeth, and long bones of bears, arranged in orderly fashion. In addition to these bear burial sites, however, particularly important evidence of a bear cult dating from the early Paleolithic period has been obtained from a cave near Montespan in Haute-Garonne, France. In a vault at the end of a tunnel, a clump of molded clay was found that obviously represented a bear. Although headless, the animal figure was distinguishable by its legs and high, rounded withers. In the flat surface at the top of the figure, a hole was bored, apparently to support a forward-projecting pole. Instead of a clay head, which was sought in vain, a bear skull was discovered between the front legs. This led to the conclusion that the figure was a base constructed to support the head and skin of the animal on ceremonial occasions.

This conclusion found substantial support in a similar animal figure reported among the Mande in the western Sudan. A slain lion or leopard, either of which is equivalent to the bear in Europe, was skinned with the head attached. This skin was then laid over a headless clay figure of the animal. Such a figure was placed within a circular hedge of thornbushes especially constructed for ceremonial purposes. The existence of a Eur-African hunting culture has become an accepted doctrine among many ethnologists, most notably Hermann Baumann (1938). This example, along with many others, fits quite appropriately into a scheme of unifying factors that suggest connections between the two continents.

The conceptual figure of a lord of the animals, appearing among less advanced hunting cultures like the San and the Pygmies in Africa, remains to this day a functional belief; one example should suffice. The creator god Khmwum is the supreme being among the Pygmies of Gabon. He lives in heaven and appears to humans as a rainbow in the eastern sky when he sees that they need his help. A singer raises his bow in the direction of this heavenly "bow" and intones: "Most powerful bow of the hunters that follows a herd of clouds that are like startled elephants, rainbow, give him [Khmwum] our thanks" (R. P. Trilles, *Les pygmées de la forêt équatorial,* Paris, 1931, p. 78). In this way the supreme deity is identified with the lord of the animals. Khmwum also manifests himself to humans in dreams, appearing as a huge elephant who reports the location of an abundance of game. This gigantic elephant is called Gor, and he towers over the tallest tree in the forest. Blue in color, he supports the sky on his shoulders, and since he is immortal, no one can kill him. Gor is the chief of all elephants; he is responsible for giving them life and preserves them from the threat of extinction. He directs the elephants to those paths that the hunters take care to follow. A slain bull elephant is decorated with a bright blue liana, and the chief of the Pygmies dances on the carcass and sings to "father elephant." This song is a solemn incantation in which the chief expresses the conviction that the elephant should not be outraged at being killed but pleased that he is going to the land of the spirits; he also says that the spear that erroneously took the elephant's life was misguided. Such excuses are made to the hunted animal out of fear of revenge and a guilty conscience at having killed the animal; this is a widespread phenomenon, typical of a hunting mentality.

In northern Eurasia we encounter the concept of a lord of the animals who either is anthropomorphic or has affinities with predominant animals other than the bear. Although such a concept occurs among numerous peoples in Eurasia, specific examples need not be mentioned here.

In the New World there exists, among the central and eastern Inuit (Eskimo), an extraordinary deity named Sedna, who is known as the goddess of the sea animals. She is an old woman who lives on the ocean floor and sends sea animals to the world above as long as humans do not aggravate her. If she does become angry, however, the shaman must venture on a dangerous journey to visit her below. Such an undertaking is made to pacify her so that she will release the animals once again. To accomplish this, the shaman must comb Sedna's hair, which has become soiled by humans—particularly women—whose violation of taboos causes her anger. Through combing, the shaman cleanses her hair of dirt and parasites, an act that Sedna herself cannot perform, since she has no fingers. According to the mythology, Sedna lost her fingers as a young girl because of an undesirable suitor, the storm bird. He appeared as a human and followed Sedna and her father, who fled in a kayak across the water. In his fear Sedna's father threw her into the water, but she held on tightly to the side of the boat. Her father then cut off all her fingers, and as they fell into the water they turned into seals and walruses. Sedna in turn sank to the ocean floor, where she took up her abode and became the mother of sea animals. The souls of these sea animals reside with her for a short period after their deaths; then, when the time has come, she restores them to life once again.

Among the Inuit of western Alaska, a male moon spirit replaces Sedna as lord of the animals. When the shaman is called upon to represent the moon spirit, he wears a mask encircled by miniature figures of reindeer, seals, and salmon, which symbolically depict authority over the animals when the spirit is implored.

The lord of the animals plays an important role among many North American Indians, as for example the Algonquin tribes of the eastern woodlands. According to the Delaware, Misinghalikun ("living solid face"), the "boss" or master of the deer, who himself rides a deer, is the mentor of those placed under his protection. His position was obtained directly from the creator. When a hunter is leaving for the hunt, Misinghalikun will appear to him in person, wearing a bearskin with a large oval mask that is painted red on the right side and black on the left, a form that reflects his name. This masked figure accompanies the hunters a short distance into the woods, during which time a spokesman drops six pinches of tobacco in each of two fires while begging Misinghalikun to seek out deer and help the hunters.

Numerous examples of the conceptual form of the lord of the animals in North America could be mentioned. Josef Haekel (1959) collected all available material source concerning the lord of the animals among the ancient, culturally advanced peoples of Mesoamerica and their descendants. Although the concept arose prior to the full development of these cultures, it becomes apparent that the lord of the animals also possessed qualities of an agrarian deity of the earth and master over cultivated plants. Even among the descendants of the advanced Andean cultures—the Quechua, Aymara, and others—this combined conceptual variation is known to occur. These characteristics are displayed in Pachamama, the Quechua earth mother who is at the same time the maternal progenitor of plants and of humans and animals. She is viewed as the actual owner of all llamas and alpacas, which she lends to humankind; if they are mishandled by humans, she repossesses them. A part of the ritual slaying of the llama involves the interment of the bones of that animal in a burial ground near the area in which the sacrifice took place. Such an act expresses trust that the earth mother will create a new animal from the bones of the old one—a notion typical of hunters.

Sometimes, however, Pachamama also functions as the mistress of the wild animals; thus, creatures like the guanaco, vicuña, and deer are referred to as "animals of the earth." This is reflected in practices like the offering (by burial) of a sacrifice to Pachamama before the start of a vicuña hunt.

Ideas and rites such as these, which either evolve in a hunting culture and are then superimposed on a pastoral one, or vice versa, are also found in the Old World; they have been observed, for instance, among the people of the Hindu Kush, particularly when the animals are conceived as being related. Like the Peruvians, the people of the Hindu Kush associate the wild and domesticated animals—in this instance, goats.

European chroniclers of the sixteenth and seventeenth centuries in the tropical lowlands of the Amazon continually encountered mention of a lord of the animals and a wild game spirit known as Korupira or Kaapora, a familiar figure among the Tupi-Guaraní tribes and comparable to a deity of other agricultural Indians. Among the mixed population of Brazil, belief in Korupira has likewise remained alive. Korupira's characteristic traits were collected and recorded in 1920 by Theodor Koch-Grünberg, a renowned researcher of the Indians of the Amazon whose primary source materials included the sixteenth- and seventeenth-century chronicles.

Among the hunting and planting tribes of eastern Brazil, the Sun is often viewed as the protector of hunted game. The Ge-speaking Indians of this region turn to this male deity with a plea for the maintenance and increased abundance of the various animal species. An appearance of Father Sun to a hunter ensures a successful expedition. Similarly, the hunting and gathering tribes of Tierra del Fuego conceive of a masculine sun (Kran or Lem), who is the "owner" of the animals; he is called upon by the Selk'nam (Ona) and Yaghan peoples to help them acquire subsistence. Watauineiwa of the Yaghan, who is viewed by many researchers as the supreme deity of these people, is in actuality the creator and owner of all animals. He entrusts his animals to humans for food and other essential uses, but only to the extent to which they are needed for survival. He watches out for his animals and assures that they are not killed wantonly, lest the meat be wasted. All these traits can be identified most precisely in describing a lord of the animals, and have also been used by Pettazzoni in describing a supreme being.

SEE ALSO Animals; Artemis; Bears; Bones; Lady of the Animals; Sedna; Supreme Beings; Tricksters.

BIBLIOGRAPHY

Baumann, Hermann. "Afrikanische Wild- und Buschgeister." *Zeitschrift für Ethnologie* 70 (1938): 208–239. A basic work on the lord of the animals and related deities in Africa.

Dirr, Adolf. "Der kaukasische Wild und Jagdgott." *Anthropos* 20 (1925): 139–147. A specific study, incorporating what was then groundbreaking research, of belief in the lord of the animals in the Caucasus.

Friedrich, Adolf. "Die Forschungen über das frühzeitliche Jägertum." *Paideuma* 2 (1941): 20–43. An exceptionally good overview of the topic, including the lord of the animals in Siberia among ancient hunting cultures.

Haekel, Josef. "Der Herr der Tiere im Glauben der Indianer Mesoamerikas." *Mitteilungen aus dem Museum für Völkerkunde in Hamburg* 25 (1959): 60–69. A study of the relevant concepts of the pre-Columbian peoples of Mesoamerica. Haekel also writes extensively on the basic phenomena of the lord of the animals.

Hallowell, A. Irving. "Bear Ceremonialism in the Northern Hemisphere." *American Anthropologist* 28 (1926): 1–175. The doctoral thesis of this well-known American anthropologist presents a comprehensive investigation of bear ceremonials and is of great importance for the concept of the lord of the animals.

Hultkrantz, Åke, ed. *The Supernatural Owners of Nature.* Stockholm Studies in Comparative Religions, vol. 1. Stockholm, 1961. An article presented at a symposium for Northern studies, about the religious conceptualization of "master spirits" of places and animal types.

Paulson, Ivar. *Schutzgeister und Gottheiten des Wildes (der Jagdtiere und Fische) in Nordeurasien.* Stockholm Studies in Comparative Religions, vol. 2. Stockholm, 1961. A standard work concerned with the lord of the animals and the species spirits of the animals of northern Asia.

Schmidt, Leopold. "Der Herr der Tiere in einigen Sagenlandschaften Europas und Eurasiens." *Anthropos* 47 (1952): 509–538. A study that traces the motif of the restoration of life to slain animals from their bones, in Eurasia.

Zerries, Otto. *Wild und Buschgeister in Südamerika.* Studien zur Kulturkunde, vol. 11. Wiesbaden, 1954. The only work that deals exclusively with the lord of the animals and related manifestations in South America.

OTTO ZERRIES (1987)
Translated from German by John Maressa

LORD'S PRAYER.

LORD'S PRAYER. When his disciples asked Jesus to teach them to pray, *Luke* 11:2–4 records the Master's reply in words similar to the teaching in the Sermon on the Mount at *Matthew* 6:9–13. In a slightly simplified tabulation, the two versions of the text may be compared as follows, with the Matthean surplus and variations in brackets and two particularly difficult expressions in parentheses:

> [Our] Father [who art in heaven], Hallowed be thy name, Thy kingdom come, [Thy will be done, On earth as it is in heaven]. Give us [this day] our (daily) bread, And forgive us our sins [*Mt.:* debts], For [*Mt.:* As] we [have] forgive[n] our debtor[s], And lead us not into (temptation) [But deliver us from evil].

USE IN CHRISTIAN WORSHIP. The church has taken the Lord's Prayer as indicating both the spirit of Christian prayer and a formula to be employed in worship. The Matthean form is at almost all points the more usual in the liturgy. Liturgical use is the probable source of the concluding doxology, "For thine is the kingdom, the power, and the glory for ever," which is found—though not yet with the addition of the word *kingdom*—in a text that is as early as the first- or second-century church manual the *Didache* (8.2). The Lord's Prayer has been used, formally and informally, in daily worship as well as in the eucharistic liturgy. In the latter case, its place has usually been between the great prayer of thanksgiving and the communion, whither it was doubtlessly attracted by the bread to be consumed.

CLASSICAL COMMENTARIES. The early Fathers taught the prayer's meaning to their catechumens, and it has remained a favorite subject of exposition by spiritual writers. Tertullian and, in his wake, Cyprian both wrote pastoral tracts entitled *On (the Lord's) Prayer.* Origen dealt with it in his theological treatise *On Prayer* (chaps. 18–30). Cyril of Jerusalem expounded it to the newly baptized in his *Mystagogical Catechesis* 5.11–18, while Augustine of Hippo preached sermons 56–59 on it to the *competentes* (candidates for baptism) and also treated it as part of his commentary *The Sermon on the Mount* (2.4.15–2.11.39) and elsewhere. John Chrysostom devoted to the Lord's Prayer his *Nineteenth Homily on the Gospel of Matthew.* Gregory of Nyssa discoursed on it in his five *Sermons on the Lord's Prayer.* Conferences on it are ascribed to Thomas Aquinas. Luther explained the prayer in his *Large and Small Catechisms* and in other writings, such as *A Simple Way to Pray,* written in 1535 for his barber. Calvin presented it in the first edition of his *Institutes of the Christian Religion* (1536; cf. 3.20.34–49 in the final edition of 1559) and commented on it in his *Harmony of the Gospels* (1555). Teresa of Ávila used the Lord's Prayer to instruct her religious communities in *The Way of Perfection* (chaps. 27–

42). John Wesley devoted to the prayer one of his Standard Sermons (numbered variously 21 or 26) and versified it in the hymn "Father of All, Whose Powerful Voice." Karl Barth treated it in his 1947–1949 seminar notes entitled *Prayer* and developed the address and the first two petitions in the unfinished part 4.4 of his *Church Dogmatics.* Simone Weil's thoughts on the subject are contained in her *Waiting on God.*

A CONTEMPORARY EXEGESIS. The best contemporary exegesis of the Lord's Prayer is that of Raymond E. Brown, who interprets it as an eschatological prayer. Jesus announced the coming of the kingdom of God. His followers prayed for the definite establishment of God's eternal rule and intimated their own desire to be part of it. They requested a place at the messianic banquet and asked for forgiveness in the divine judgment as well as for deliverance from the mighty struggle with Satan that still stood between the community and the final realization of its prayer. As hopes for the imminent advent of the final kingdom faded, interpreters adapted the prayer to continuing life in the present age with the assurance that God's kingdom had at least begun its entry into the world through the life, death, and resurrection of Jesus.

RECURRENT THEMES OF ANALYSIS. The Lord's Prayer opens with a bold filial salutation. To address almighty God as "Abba, Father" (*Rom.* 8:14, *Gal.* 4:6) is to share by grace a privilege that Jesus enjoyed by nature (*Mk.* 14:36, cf. *Mt.* 11:25–27). Liturgically, believers do in fact proclaim that they "make bold to say" (*audemus dicere*) this prayer. The heavenly Father is near. Moreover, to address the Father as "*our* Father" is to acknowledge that the Christian faith is a communal matter with brothers and sisters who are, at least potentially, as numerous as the human race. After this opening address six petitions follow, which typically attract the kind of comments next summarized.

1. Hallowed be thy name. God is by definition holy, and strictly speaking, only God can hallow the divine name: he does so in history by vindicating his holiness (*Ez.* 36:22–27, *Jn.* 12:28). But humans join in by not despising the Lord's name (*Ex.* 20:7 and, identically, *Dt.* 5:11), by praising the name of the Lord (*1 Chr.* 29:13 and often in *Psalms*), by calling on the name of the Lord for salvation (*Jl.* 2:32, *Acts* 2:21, *Rom.* 10:13), and by living in accord with the name put upon them in baptism (Augustine, sermon 59; cf. *1 Cor.* 6:11).

2. Thy kingdom come. Instead of "Thy kingdom come" a minor variant reads "May thy Holy Spirit come upon us and purify us." Here outcrops the common view that God's rule may at least begin in the present in human lives. Yet the primary agency in establishing the kingdom remains God's.

3. Thy will be done. In the garden of Gethsemane, Jesus accepted the Father's will (*Mk.* 14:36, *Mt.* 26:39, 26:42; cf. *Jn.* 6:38, *Heb.* 10:7–10). Thereby God's eternal will for salvation was implemented (*Eph.* 1:5, 1:9, 1:11). Humans benefit through faithful and obebient participation. The scope of God's plan is no less than heaven and earth.

4. Give us this day our daily bread. The adjective qualifying bread (Gr., *epiousios*) is otherwise practically unknown. Suggested possibilities for its meaning include: food "suited to our spiritual nature" (Origen); the bread "we need" for our "everyday" lives (Syriac and Old Latin traditions—cf. *Mt.* 6:34); an "excellent" bread surpassing all substances (the Vulgate's *supersubstantialis*). The original eschatological tone of the prayer favors the reading "tomorrow's bread," as in some Egyptian versions and in Jerome's report on the "Gospel of the Hebrews" wherein he employs the Latin word *crastinus* ("for tomorrow"); it is an urgent prayer for the feast of the age to come. Whatever their interpretation of *epiousios*, commentators regularly emphasize the graciousness of the divine provision and the human obligation to share the blessings of God, and most of them make a link with the eucharistic Communion.

5. Forgive us our sins. The parable of the unforgiving servant in *Matthew* 18:23–35 suggests that the final execution of God's will to forgive sinners depends on the sinner's readiness to forgive others (cf. *Mt.* 6:14f., *Lk.* 6:37). While humans cannot compel God's gracious forgiveness, they can be prevented from receiving it by their own unforgiving spirit.

6. Lead us not into temptation. Commentators have stressed the indirect character of God's testing of humans (*Jas.* 1:12–14) and insisted that God "will not let you be tempted beyond your strength" (*1 Cor.* 10:13). Some modern liturgical translations have restored the strictly eschatological character of the petition: "Save us from the time of trial" (cf. *Rv.* 3:10). In the present, the devil still "prowls around like a roaring lion, seeking whom he may devour" (*1 Pt.* 5:8; cf. *Eph.* 6:11–13, *1 Jn.* 5:19), but his defeat has already been assured by Christ, and the deliverance of believers is certain (*2 Thes.* 3:3, *Jn.* 17:15).

BIBLIOGRAPHY

Studies on the Jewish background to the Lord's Prayer can be found in Jean Carmignac's *Recherches sur le "Notre Père"* (Paris, 1969) and in *The Lord's Prayer and Jewish Liturgy*, edited by Jakob J. Petuchkowski and Michael Brocke (New York, 1978). Raymond E. Brown's "The *Pater Noster* as an Eschatological Prayer" is contained in his *New Testament Essays*, 3d ed. (New York, 1982), while other contemporary exegesis includes Ernst Lohmeyer's *The Lord's Prayer* (New York, 1965), Joachim Jeremias's *The Prayers of Jesus* (London, 1967), and Heinz Schürmann's *Das Gebet des Herrn*, 4th ed. (Leipzig, 1981). The tightly packed lectures of Thomas Aquinas are accessible in a translation by Lawrence Shapcote under the title *The Three Greatest Prayers: Commentaries on the Our Father, the Hail Mary and the Apostles' Creed by St. Thomas Aquinas* (London, 1956). Modern devotional works include William Barclay's *The Plain Man Looks at the Lord's Prayer* (London, 1964), Gerhard Ebeling's *On Prayer: Nine Sermons* (Philadelphia, 1966), Romano Guardini's *The Lord's Prayer* (New York, 1958), Alexander Schmemann's *Our Father* (Crestwood, N.Y., 2002), and

Kenneth Stevenson's *The Lord's Prayer: A Text in Tradition* (London, 2004).

GEOFFREY WAINWRIGHT (1987 AND 2005)

LOTUS. A poem from a twelfth-century anthology of Sanskrit court poetry, in which the poet visualizes the whole world in the form of a spreading lotus, suggests how comprehensive and intricate a symbol the lotus can be. In it, the lotus encompasses the worlds of gods and humans:

> Its seed is the god Brahmā, its nectar are the oceans and its pericarp Mount Meru, its bulb the king of serpents and the space within its leaf-bud is the spreading sky; its petals are the continents, its bees the clouds, its pollen are the stars of heaven: I pray that he, the lotus of whose navel forms thus our universe, may grant you his defense. (Ingalls, 1965, p. 107)

It is especially in Indian art, literature, and religion that the lotus has been a frequent and central symbol. Indeed, lotus symbolism has accompanied Indian cultural influence wherever it has spread, especially in Southeast Asia and East Asia, where it is part of the symbolic language of Buddhism. But the lotus also appears as a symbol in East Asia without any obvious Indian connection, and in ancient Egypt.

The lotuses considered in this article are aquatic plants belonging to the *Nymphaeaceae* (water lily) and *Nelumbonaceae* families. They grow from rhizomes in the mud, and their leaves and blossoms float on the water or rise above its surface. Because the lotus grows out of water, early Indian tradition identified it with the waters (cf. *Śatapatha Brāhmaṇa* 7.4.1.8), with the creative and life-giving potential of the waters, and even with creation itself. So, for example, the *Taittirīya Brāhmaṇa* (1.1.3.5–6), relates that at the beginning of time the creator, Prajāpati, existed alone amid the primordial waters. As he was wondering how to create, he saw a lotus leaf, the sole other existing object. Diving down, he found the mud from which it was growing and brought some to the surface. He then spread the mud on the lotus leaf, and this, supported by the lotus leaf, became the surface of the earth. The later Indian tradition envisioned the world as having the shape of a lotus blossom (cf. *Matsya Purāṇa* 41.86). In either case, the lotus, rising out of the mud and the waters, is a mediating symbol, bridging the amorphous waters and the created earth.

In classical Indian mythology, the lotus as the bridge of creation is preserved in another expression, which forms the basis for the poem quoted above. At the beginning of a new world cycle, the god Viṣṇu lies on a serpent amid the primordial waters. From his navel grows a lotus, which blossoms to reveal Brahmā, the agent of creation. Here, the growth and unfolding of the lotus is both the vehicle for the generation of Brahmā and the image of the emergence of creation from the mind and body of Viṣṇu.

The association of the lotus with the concept of creation appears also in ancient Egypt. According to one tradition from Hermopolis, the highest deity appeared, self-begotten, on a lotus. In the temple at Edgu, built during the Greco-Roman period, an inscription equates the First Primeval One, who "caused the Earth to be when he came into existence," with the Great Lotus. Egyptian mythology connects the lotus especially with the creation of the sun.

The lotus opens not only as the world but also within each person. In both Hindu and Buddhist symbolism, a lotus encloses the center of one's being, which is located in the heart. The lotus is thus not only a bridge between precreation and creation but also a symbol linking the macrocosm and the human microcosm. "For this heart lotus," says the *Maitri Upaniṣad*, "is the same as space. The four regions and the four intermediate regions constitute its leaves. The vital breath and the sun move downward toward its base" (6.2). This symbolism of an inner lotus corresponding to the outer world is elaborated in Tantric yoga. Forms of this yoga identify five or seven lotiform centers in the body; these centers correspond to bodily locations and functions, to particular deities, and to aspects of the macrocosm. Likewise, in the Indo-Tibetan *maṇḍalas*, the opening of the lotus symbolizes the manifestation of divine powers, the world, the mind, and insight. In a typical *maṇḍala*, a principal deity occupies the center. Arranged around this center are four or eight other deities, who are visualized as emerging from it, like petals spreading out from the center of a lotus. Indeed, the fields on which their images or symbols appear are occasionally depicted as lotus petals. The lotus symbolism is also carried to the outer part of the *maṇḍala* which includes at least one circle of lotus petals. These confirm the lotus form of the whole *maṇḍala* and represent, among other possible meanings, the extension of divine power from the center.

Because the opening and closing of the lotus follows the rising and setting of the sun, the lotus is also a solar symbol. According to Indian iconographic texts, Sūrya, the Sun, should stand on red lotuses placed in his chariot or on a single lotus, and he may carry a lotus in his hand. Such solar symbolism was developed especially in ancient Egypt. According to one tradition, the newborn sun, identified with the child Horus, arose from the lotus. Corresponding to this conception, Horus was often depicted in the Greco-Roman period as a sun-child on a lotus blossom. In another tradition, the lotus, deified as the god Nefertem, gave life to the sungod Re and, by means of his fragrance, continues to give vitality to Re every day. Therefore, Re is, according to the *Book of Going Forth by Day* 15, the "golden youth, who came forth from the lotus." Elsewhere Nefertem also identified with Re and hence with the sun.

In addition to the Sun, various other Hindu deities have special connections to the lotus. The Moon is symbolized by the night-blooming white lotus. The lotus is also one of the characteristic signs of Viṣṇu. Of all the Indian deities, however, the one most closely associated with the lotus is Śrī, or Lakṣmī, the goddess of prosperity, good fortune, and wealth. The *Śrīsūkta*, which became her principal hymn of praise, surrounds her with lotuses and merges the image of the goddess and the lotus. There, she is called "moist"; she is garlanded and surrounded by lotuses; she is lotus-colored, is perceptible by her scent, and stands within the lotus. Her son is Slime (Kardama), who is asked to dwell with the poet and to make Śrī dwell with him. The widespread image of Gaja-Lakṣmī, the elephant Lakṣmī, also portrays the goddess's close connection with the lotus. Standing on a lotus, she holds two lotuses (or a woodapple and a lotus) and is sprayed with water by two elephants. This image of Lakṣmī is interpreted in the Puranic accounts of her origins. According to the *Viṣṇu Purāṇa* (1.9.100ff.), for example, Śrī emerged from the Ocean of Milk seated on a blossoming lotus and bearing a lotus in her hand. The Ocean himself appeared in human form and presented her with a garland of never-wilting lotuses, and Indra, king of the gods, praised her, saying, "I bow down before Śrī, the mother of all, who resides on the lotus, who has eyes of blossoming lotuses, and who reclines on the heart of Viṣṇu." In all these representations, the lotus blends with the waters and the goddess herself to symbolize fertility, prosperity, and bounty.

The lotus also underscores the beauty of the goddess, for it is a strikingly lovely flower that has become a conventional sign of beauty. According to Indian texts on erotica, the ideal woman is the Padminī, the woman of lotus scent. The hands, feet, and face of a beautiful woman are like lotus blossoms. Her eyes, especially the pupils of her eyes, are like lotuses. The lotus also possessed even more specifically erotic connotations. Iconographically, Kāma, the personification of sexual desire, is ornamented by the conch shell and the lotus, both symbols of the vulva. Lotuses were used in aphrodisiacs, in concoctions to ensure potency and fertility, and in scents to attract a lover. The "lotus position" is not only a yogic posture but a sexual one as well. Such simultaneous religious and erotic connotations were exploited particularly by the Tantric traditions of Buddhism and Hinduism to show the interpenetration of the two realms.

In China, too, the lotus was an erotic symbol. In the following song by Song Huangfu, the lotus helps create an erotic atmosphere:

> Water lilies and fragrant lotus across the vast stretch of water, A young girl exuberant and playful, picks lotus until late; Evening comes, the splashing water dampens her in the boat, Making her remove her red skirt and wrap up the ducks. The boat glides, the lake shines, overflowing with autumn. With desire she watches a young boy letting his boat drift, Impetuously across the water she throws lotus seeds, As the news spreads and people hear of it, she is bashful for half a day. (Wagner, 1984, p. 146)

The lotus exemplifies the beauty and passion of the young girl. The lotus seeds she throws are love tokens.

The lotus also represents birth as well as beauty and sensuality. In the folk traditions of India and China, the lotus has the power to make a person potent or fertile: both folk traditions have legends of virgin births that occurred after young women bathed in lotus ponds or ate lotus blossoms. A dramatic Indian image of a lotus-headed goddess in a birthing position has been identified by Stella Kramrisch (1983) as the divine Mother, who has given birth to all creatures. In ancient Egypt, too, the lotus was a symbol of birth or, more especially, of rebirth. The god Osiris was reborn from a lotus after he was killed. Such rebirth is the hope of humans as well, and for this reason the lotus appears as a decoration on Egyptian tombs and mummy cases. Because it was a symbol of regeneration, the lotus was a funerary flower also among the Greeks, Romans, and early Christians. One reason for this symbolism may be that the seedpods, open flowers, and buds of a lotus are all visible at the same time. The flower thus contains past, present, and future life.

But if the lotus is a symbol of sensual beauty, it can also be a symbol of transcendence or purity. It grows from the mud, but shows nothing of its origins. Nor are its leaves or petals affected by water, which beads and falls away. Untouched and breaking the surface of the water, the lotus is a natural symbol for rising above the world. It is, in this sense, applied especially to the Buddha in a well-known passage from the Pali texts *Saṃyutta Nikāya* (vol. 3, p. 140) and *Anguttara Nikāya* (vol. 2, pp. 38f.): "Likewise, monks, the blue lotus, the pink lotus, or the white lotus, born in the water and grown in the water, rises beyond the water and remains unsoiled by the water. Thus, monks, the *tathāgata*, born in the world, grown up in the world, after having conquered the world, remains unsoiled by the world." This metaphor is usually taken to mean that the Buddha, after his enlightenment, lives within the world but is not affected by it or by the passions that normally govern human life. Within the Buddhist tradition, however, different sects have interpreted the passage in various ways. The "supernaturalist" sects, as Étienne Lamotte calls them (e.g., the Mahāsāṃghikas and the Vibhajyavādins), interpret it to mean that the Buddha's birth is purely apparent. Because his existence is a fiction, his body spiritual, and his human acts and qualities actually foreign to his true nature, the purity of the Buddha is absolute. The lotus as a symbol of purity also occurs in Hinduism. Two passages from the Upaniṣads (*Chāndogya* 4.14.3 and *Maitri* 3.2) reverse the Buddhist metaphor. In them the self is compared to a drop of water on a lotus leaf; it does not cling to the leaf, even while it remains upon it. In China, too, the white lotus is a symbol of purity.

The lotus is associated not only with Gautama Buddha but with other figures in the Buddhist pantheon, especially Prajñāpāramitā, Avalokiteśvara (Chin., Kuan-yin), and Amitābha. In connection with Prajñāpāramitā (Perfection of Wisdom), the lotus signifies purity, transcendence, and beauty. Avalokiteśvara and Amitābha belong to a Buddha "family" whose characteristic mark is the lotus. Here, the lotus functions both as an auspicious sign and as a reminder that these beings act compassionately while remaining unattached.

Like other central symbols of religious traditions, therefore, the lotus has many possible meanings within a cultural sphere; for that reason, it may not have a determinate meaning in a specific context. For example, the lotus is encountered frequently in art as a pedestal or throne for Buddhist and Hindu deities. Those viewing such an image might understand many of the associations outlined above: it could suggest purity, transcendence, the unfolding of a vision of divinity, beauty, the power to create, the centrality of the deity in the world, or the auspiciousness of the image. Moreover, the lotus is a surprisingly complex symbol, which is able to express the contradictory realities of divine and human life. It is both an erotic symbol and a symbol of purity. It signifies the creation of the world as well as the transcendence of it. The same lotus is the world and is within each person. It is the unformed waters and the visible world. And it is much else besides, for having established itself as a central symbol, the lotus gives rise to further interpretation. Blofeld (1978, p. 151), for example, gives a list of the principal emblems of Kuan-yin and their meanings taken from the Chinese edition of the *Heart of the Dhāranī of Great Compassion Sutra.* In this sūtra, four lotuses of four different colors serve as the emblems of Kuan-yin: the white lotus signifies the attainment of merit, the blue lotus signifies rebirth in a Pure Land, the purple lotus signifies that one will behold bodhisattvas, and the red lotus signifies that one will attain rebirth in a heaven of the gods. Here, the meanings of the lotus pass beyond ideas directly suggested by its colors and parts.

SEE ALSO Maṇḍalas.

BIBLIOGRAPHY

References in this article to the Nidāyas are to the text edited by the Pali Text Society.

Anthes, Rudolf. "Mythology in Ancient Egypt." In *Mythologies of the Ancient World,* edited by Samuel Noah Kramer, pp. 15–92. Garden City, N. Y., 1961. A useful introduction and overview of Egyptian mythology and symbolism.

Blofeld, John. *Bodhisattva of Compassion: The Mystical Tradition of Kuan Yin.* Boulder, 1978. A study of the Chinese transformation of the bodhisattva most closely associated with the lotus.

Bosch, F. D. K. *The Golden Germ: An Introduction to Indian Symbolism.* The Hague, 1960. This work studies the cosmic lotus and the world tree; according to Bosch, Indian and Southeast Asian artists envisioned the genesis and structure of the macrocosm and the human microcosm through these symbols.

Coomaraswamy, Ananda K. *Elements of Buddhist Iconography* (1935). New Delhi, 1972. Part 1 presents the symbolism of the tree of life, the earth-lotus, and the word-wheel; part 2 treats the development of the lotus-throne in Buddhist art.

Ingalls, Daniel H. H., trans. *An Anthology of Sanskrit Court Poetry: Vidyākara's "Subhāṣitaratnakośa."* Cambridge, Mass., 1965. These poems show the mature development of Indian poetry and literary symbolism.

Ions, Veronica. *Egyptian Mythology.* Rev. ed. New York, 1983. This is a splendidly illustrated, easily accessible introduction to Egyptian symbolism.

Kramrisch, Stella. "An Image of Aditi-Uttānapad." In *Exploring India's Sacred Art,* edited by Barbara Stoler Miller, pp. 148–158. Philadelphia, 1983. This article is a study of an image of a goddess who has a lotus blossom in place of her head and who appears to be giving birth.

Lauf, Detlef Ingo. *Tibetan Sacred Art: The Heritage of Tantra.* Berkeley, 1976. This introduction to Tibetan art mentions the lotus frequently, although in passing.

Siegel, Lee. *Sacred and Profane Dimensions of Love in Indian Traditions as Exemplified in the Gītagovinda of Jayadeva.* Oxford, 1978. On pages 195 and following, Siegel offers a short but helpful discussion of the lotus as an erotic and religious symbol.

Wagner, Marsha L. *The Lotus Boat: The Origins of Chinese Tz'u Poetry in T'ang Popular Culture.* New York, 1984. According to Wagner, *tz'u* poetry originated in the popular songs sung by courtesans and other musical entertainers. The lotus appears as a symbol of love and erotic desire.

Zimmer, Heinrich. *Myths and Symbols in Indian Art and Civilization.* Edited by Joseph Campbell. New York, 1946. See pages 90–102 for Zimmer's study of the development of lotus symbolism in connection with goddess figures of Hinduism and Buddhism.

JOEL P. BRERETON (1987)

LÖW, YEHUDAH BEN BETSAL'EL OF PRAGUE (1520?–1609), known by the acronym MaHaRaL (Morenu ha-Rav Leib, "our teacher Rabbi Löw"). Löw was a Jewish teacher, preacher, and mystic, a social and religious reformer, and a community leader in Poland, Bohemia, and Moravia.

In the course of his long, eventful, and often controversial life, Löw served as chief rabbi of Moravia, of Poznán in Poland, and of Prague. Celebrated as a wonder-worker in both Jewish and Czech legend, Löw was deeply immersed in rabbinic and qabbalistic tradition. His enormous literary output articulates a comprehensive although unsystematic mystical theology. His popularization of recondite qabbalistic notions establish him as a forerunner of Hasidism.

In Löw's epistemology, Jewish tradition, particularly Jewish mystical tradition, is both the essential source of and the only promising gateway to truth. Philosophical speculation can merely offer what tradition has already established. Löw sharply attacked the Jewish philosophical enterprise for its dependence on rational analysis and empirical observation, which he deemed epistemologically subordinate to tradition in the quest for truth. Moreover, Löw considered philosophy faulty, predicated on assumptions considered anathema by tradition (e.g., the eternity of the world), and therefore potentially heretical in its conclusions. For Löw, the higher truth of tradition measures the truth of philosophy; philosophy cannot evaluate tradition.

In his discussion of the nature of the Torah, Löw used a theory of complementary and contradictory opposites.

Complementary opposites fulfill and complete one another. For example, male and female are incomplete when apart and are individually complete only when they are both together. Contradictory opposites conflict with one another and cannot coexist unresolved. The conflict may, however, be resolved through a synthesis of the two opposing factors. God and the world are such contradictory opposites. The Torah represents a synthesis of the spiritual God and the material world and therefore effectively mediates between God and the world.

Utilizing a notion of "natural place," Löw argued that until the Jews are restored to the Land of Israel—their natural place and origin—the world remains in disorder. This physical, geographic restoration will occur only in the messianic era after disturbances in the natural order have been rectified through a penultimate process of restoration. The goal of this process, according to Löw, is to restore the Jewish people to its proper and essential nature, thus fulfilling the necessary conditions for the act of divine grace that will initiate the messianic era. Löw maintained that proper study and observance of the Torah, which he felt were lacking in his time, are necessary for the Jewish people to realize its essential nature. Therefore, this restoration process entails a reformation of Jewish life. These theological assumptions served as the premise for Löw's program of social and religious reform. Most noteworthy in this regard are his plans for the reformation of rabbinic leadership and Jewish education.

Löw considered the poor rabbinic leadership and faulty education during his time as conditions vitally requiring rectification. For Löw, the rabbi is to his community what the heart is to the body. A rabbi was ideally a "saint-scholar" serving on the authority of his scholarship and piety, rather than a "political" figure, appointed and sustained through the influence of secular government authority and accountable to a board of Jewish laymen. Löw's educational reforms included the intensified study of the Bible (neglected in his day) and the restoration of study of the Mishnah as the basis for subsequent studies in rabbinics, as opposed to the dominant emphasis upon *pilpul* (hairsplitting dialectical reasoning). He advocated curricular reforms that correlated content studied and methods utilized to the intellectual and psychological development of the student and he favored a complete rejection of "secular" studies in the curriculum—a reaction to the Italian Jewish trend in response to the influence of the Renaissance, of including such studies in Jewish education. Löw called for reliance upon the entire scope of Jewish legal tradition rather than only upon legal codes in the process of decision making in matters of Jewish law and rejected contemporary trends that permitted socioeconomic factors to intrude upon the processes of legal adjudication.

Löw is popularly identified with the Jewish legend of the *golem*, an artificial man created by magical means. Those versions of the legend that connect Löw with the *golem*, maintain that Löw created the *golem* to defend the Jews of Prague during pogroms related to a "blood libel" (a claim that Jews used the blood of Christian children in religious rites). The *golem* legend seems to have influenced Mary Shelley in the composition of *Frankenstein*, Goethe in the writing of the *Sorcerer's Apprentice*, and Karel Čapek in his drama *R.U.R*, in which the term *robot* was first coined. The *golem* legend has been developed in contemporary literature in the works of Halper Leivick, Max Brod, Gustav Meyrink, and Jorge Luis Borges, among others.

BIBLIOGRAPHY

Most of Yehudah Löw's works are contained in *Kol sifrei Maharal mi-Prag*, 12 vols. (New York, 1969), and *Gur Aryeh*, 5 vols. (Benei Beraq, 1972). Comprehensive works on Yehudah Löw's life and works are Ben Zion Bokser's *From the World of the Kabbalah: The Philosophy of Rabbi Judah Loew of Prague* (New York, 1954) and both my *Mystical Theology and Social Dissent: The Life and Works of Judah Loew of Prague* (London, 1982) and my *The Golem Legend: Origins and Implications* (Lanham, Md., 1985).

New Sources

Jacobson, Yoram. "The Image of God as the Source of Man's Evil, according to the Maharal of Prague." *Binah* 3 (1994): 135–158.

Neher, André. *Mishnato shel ha-Maharal mi-Prag*. Jerusalem, 2003. (Translation of the French edition, *Le puits de l'exil: tradition et modernité: la pensée du Maharal de Prague [1512–1609]*, 1991.)

Winkler, Gershon. *The Golem of Prague: A New Adaption of the Documented Stories of the Golem of Prague*. Illustrated by Yochanan Jones. New York, 1997.

BYRON L. SHERWIN (1987)
Revised Bibliography

LOWIE, ROBERT H. (1883–1957), American anthropologist. Lowie was born in Vienna and emigrated to New York in 1893. After graduation from City College with honors in classics and an interlude of public-school teaching and additional training in science, he enrolled at Columbia for graduate study in anthropology under Franz Boas. His student cohort included Edward Sapir, Alexander Goldenweiser, Frank Speck, and Paul Radin, all of whom were to exert continuing influence on Lowie's ideas and approach to anthropology. Clark Wissler served as Lowie's principal fieldwork mentor and directed his formative research among the Shoshoni and various Plains tribes. He obtained his doctorate in 1908 with a comparative dissertation, "The Test-Theme in North America Mythology."

While employed by the American Museum of Natural History (1907–1917), Lowie conducted extensive fieldwork among the tribes of the Great Basin, the Southwest, and the Plains, eventually focusing on the Crow Indians of Montana. From this rich and varied data base he produced an impressive corpus of detailed ethnographic writings.

After holding a visiting professorship in 1917–1918, Lowie received a permanent appointment at the University of California, where he remained for the rest of his academic career. At Berkeley he proved a beloved teacher and an able administrator, and he broadened his theoretical horizons and range of ethnological expertise. In the 1930s he developed an interest from afar in the Ge-speaking Indians of eastern Brazil, an interest that was expressed through his promotion and translation of the valuable researches of Curt Nimuendajú. Near the end of his career Lowie studied complex societies and published two books on postfascist Germany.

Lowie's reputation rests primarily on his substantive contributions to ethnography and to theoretical issues in kinship and social organization, but he maintained an abiding interest in problems of religion. Although a freethinker, he came to view religion sympathetically as a vital and perduring force in human culture and society. His approach to religion was essentially psychological. Influenced by the work of the German critical empiricist Ernst Mach (1838–1916), Lowie felt it possible to reach objective analyses of such subjective phenomena as magical thinking, symbolic associations of meaning, and individual religious experience.

Lowie's *Primitive Religion* (1924; rev. ed., 1948) is a loosely integrated composite treatment of the subject. In his autobiography (1959), he comments that the book "met with a cold reception and I doubt whether it has exerted any influence." Nevertheless, *Primitive Religion* repays careful study as an exemplary document of the Boasian approach to religion. After a cautious consideration of the problem of defining religion, Lowie plunges directly into particularistic ethnographic data by offering synthetic sketches of four tribal religions from different regions of the world. Next he offers philosophically informed critiques of major anthropological theories of religion, taking direct aim at E. B. Tylor, James G. Frazer, and Émile Durkheim. The final section of the book comprises an uneven yet suggestive treatment of such diverse topics as individual variability in religious matters, religious movements, the role of women in religion, and relations of religion to art and economics.

Lowie's main legacy to the study of religion consists in his own rich corpus of field materials and his critical assessments of the theories of others. His significance lies in the questions he posed rather than in any synthesis he achieved.

Bibliography

Details of Lowie's life and work are readily available in his entertaining autobiography, *Robert H. Lowie, Ethnologist: A Personal Record* (Berkeley, 1959). This volume contains his vita, outlining his professional career and listing the many honors he received, as well as a nearly complete bibliography of his many publications. A representative collection of Lowie's articles, including some of his more technical essays on myth, ceremonialism, and comparative religious ethnology, can be found in *Lowie's Selected Papers in Anthropology*, edited by Cora DuBois (Berkeley, 1960); DuBois's introductory essay lends valuable perspectives on his work, and the volume contains a fascinatingly detailed syllabus for a graduate seminar that Lowie led on his own work. The biographical picture, along with an acute modern appraisal of his theories, is sensitively filled out in Robert F. Murphy's *Robert H. Lowie* (New York, 1972), which also reprints some of Lowie's articles, including a posthumously published essay titled "Religion in Human Life." Lowie's major statement on religion, *Primitive Religion*, rev. ed. (New York, 1948), is summarized above. The flavor of Lowie's ethnographic description of religion can be sampled in his classic monograph, *The Crow Indians* (1935; reprint, New York, 1956), and in the chapter on religion in his popular survey *Indians of the Plains* (New York, 1954), reissued, with an introduction by Raymond J. De Mallie, in 1982.

Raymond D. Fogelson (1987)

LOYOLA, IGNATIUS See IGNATIUS LOYOLA

LUBA RELIGION.

LUBA RELIGION. The woodlands south of the African equatorial forest have been the homeland of different Luba tribes and subtribes since the first half of the first millennium, according to the latest archaeological evidence. The area stretches roughly from 5° to 10° south latitude and from 22° to 29° east longitude. Most of the peoples living in this region of central Africa share certain cultural traits and a more or less common language. In terms of political organization, however, there are fundamental differences. Four main groups can be distinguished according to political structure. The political centerpiece of the entire region is the ancient Luba empire, situated west of the Kongo River between the Lomami and Lualuba rivers. Political structure in the area of the Luba empire is based on the sacred authority of a paramount chief, an individual who is crucial to the survival of the people and success of the land. Several minor kingdoms derived their structure from the central empire; sometimes these kingdoms were vassals to the larger Luba state. The second group in terms of political structure is best represented by the matrilineal Hemba-speaking groups east of the Lualuba. The Luba Hemba, the most important of the Hemba-speaking groups, were part of the central Luba empire (at least temporarily) and pretended to derive their political institutions from the central royal court. The third group is composed of the western Luba groups that lack overriding political authority: the Luba Kasai, the Bene Luluwa, and the Bakwa Luntu. In contrast to the central and eastern groups, the western Luba peoples constitute a strict segmentary society. The fourth group, known as the Luba Songye, lives in big, well-organized villages on the southern fringe of the forest, north of the central empire. Although the Songye and the central Luba have clearly influenced each other, when the Songye reached the peak of their power as allies of the Swahili ivory and slave traders coming inland from Zanzibar in the nineteenth century, they liked to entertain a sense of superiority toward the other Luba groups. All of the Luba peoples believe in a more or less common origin, more for the sake of prestige than on historical grounds.

Luba Concepts of Body and Soul. The Luba concept of the human being provides an excellent vantage point for understanding their religious worldview. Basically the Luba believe that each human being (*muntu*) has a single essence. However, this essence has many manifestations. For instance, empirical reality is the manifestation of a deeper level of being that is tied to the Luba concept of spirit (*vidye*). The essential part of each human being is the life shadow (*umvwe wa bumi*), the soul (that is, the seat of thinking and feeling). The distinction between physical and spiritual reality, or body (*umbidi*) and soul (*muja*), is also fundamental to the Luba vision of reality as such. According to circumstances and context, a person's inner spiritual reality, which shows through external appearances and constitutes the human being, can be symbolized in various ways: shadow, life breath, blood, voice, and so on. The two elements (body and soul for the sake of simplicity) are interdependent. Whoever destroys the body also destroys the soul—that is, weakens the whole person until finally the soul departs. Anyone who destroys the soul—for example, by casting a spell—at the same time attacks the physical person of the victim. However, there is no special link between body and soul. A slight particle of bodily matter can be sufficient to support and transfer the soul without endangering the life force of the person concerned. If an individual seeks to kill his neighbor and is successful in forcing his neighbor's soul to leave its bodily abode, the neighbor's life is endangered. However, if the same individual performs the same ritual with the intention of protecting his neighbor's life against attacks by evildoers, then the neighbor will feel safe and his life will flourish. The outcome depends upon the intention of the ritual performer. The Luba conception of a human being as a dual entity, coupled with changing modes of interpreting how the body relates to the soul, leads to a wide variety of symbolizations. Hence one hears of hiding a soul in the bush for protection or tying up a soul in the bush to destroy a person or transferring the soul of an enemy into the body of an animal so that this person starts acting like an animal. The soul of a person who dies in a modern city can be buried in ancestral ground by transferring some hair, nail clippings, or some other particle from the dead body to the village.

Unity of Spiritual and Physical Worlds. Anything belonging to the body or having been in contact with it can be used as a reduced and sufficient support for the soul. But conversely, any form of intimate contact with the body impregnates an object, piece of clothing, tool, or utensil with that person's spiritual reality. Getting hold of any such element gives a person power over the owner of the object. Destroying such an object with the intention of harming its owner represents a direct attack against the owner's life. Property, land, crops, dust sticking to a person's body, anything associated with the physical reality of a person is stamped with the owner's personal being. The dirt on a road retains something vital of the people walking over it. A gift is always more than a simple transfer of material objects. This view of reality has a wide range of applications. Principally, it gives rise to sexual taboos and the avoidance of physical contact in certain situations; it also leads to the belief that a blessing can be bestowed by touching a person or that the power of the soul can be depleted by coming into contact with ill-intentioned people.

The unity between humans and their environment manifests itself in a much more complicated way in the patterns of dependence within the human community. The relationship between father and son or mother and daughter seems to be a universal model to express the essence of most relationships (whether the society is matrilineal or patrilineal, the same parent model is used—that of initiator and initiate). Among the Luba, the chief is seen as the father of his subjects. The parents are spirits in relation to their children while the husband is the wife's spirit as well. The social fabric is rooted in this unified spiritual interdependence. Vital ties between members of the community not only support the essential institution of the social group, that is, the lineage: they are the real substance of group dynamism, group restraint, and group cohesion.

Worlds of the Living and the Dead. The Luba believe that when people die they go to the invisible world of the dead. This world of the shades, located under the earth, is structured according to the world of the living. There the dead live as they did on earth: in family groups, in villages, with forests and gardens and so on. From the world of the dead, the ancestors watch over their children, contacting the living through dreams, in divination sessions, and by making all sorts of strange and unusual things happen. The dead come back to the world of the living, giving their names to newborn children. The Luba Songye are unique in that they believe in the transmigration of the soul. This soul "seems normally to return three times to earth in a human body and the fourth time in the body of an animal before it goes to Efile Mukulu to remain indefinitely" (Merriam, p. 298).

The dead constantly interact with the living. Their attitude toward their descendants is ambiguous. The living must remember the dead and honor them through the performance of rituals because the survival of the dead depends on the devotion of their relatives. If their descendants neglect to show filial piety, the dead will withhold their favor and show their anger by causing crop failures, disease, bad dreams, and evil omens. Of course, the duty to remember bears most directly upon recently deceased lineage members (deceased parents or grandparents). Those people who have died in the more distant past are referred to as a collectivity under the vague title *ancestors*; among this group, only the most important people and former political leaders are directly named.

Beyond the world of human involvement, the Luba have an almost innate idea of the world as a unified whole; transcending the various Luba representations of human institutions is the idea of a creator god. There is only one creator god and he made this one world, man and woman, and nature and all it contains, including the curative qualities of herbs and roots. The creator owns all the world—all the countries, as the Luba say. The human species is one and so the human mind is one; it transcends empirical reality. From whatever angle the Luba look at their world, they always end up, from perception to perception, at the concept of a universal. When the Luba declare, time and again, that *vidye udiko* (spirit does exist), they mean exactly that: spirit transcends and founds all other reality and, above all, the reality of the ancestors. God is not a sublimation of the idea of the ancestors; on the contrary, the ancestors can exist only because there was first the concept of a creator god. In the old stereotyped prayers God is always the father of all and everything, the one "who carved the fingers in our hands" (or a similar praise-name is used).

Creator God. Human life can only be conceived of as a part of a universal concept of an absolute. The Luba call this absolute Vidye, Mvidie, Efile Mukulu, Maweja, or Mulopo. Usually they use these names in combination with one or more of the praise names that are so abundant in Luba prayers and invocations. Although God is ever present in the back of their minds as the great creator spirit, the Luba do not have shrines where prayers or sacrifices can be offered to God. God is in no place—God is everywhere. Wherever there is power, there is spirit; be it a mighty tree or a thundering waterfall, the Luba will say here is spirit. From consulting the dead in divination to the ancient poison ordeal, from chasing the rain to stopping the sun from setting, there is one vision at work. Mythic language gives this visible world its true dimension.

It is not as if there was a fundamental opposition between ancestors, lineage founders, and political institutions on the one hand and the creator god on the other. Worship of the ancestors or lesser spirits does not mean that the creator god is consigned to oblivion. Indeed, the ancestors, whatever their status and function, are linked to the supreme being; they are sons of the spirit. Their lives continue to be the existential feeding ground of the living generations. They are heroes, mediators between God and their descendants. At the beginning God worked through agents known as culture heroes who received responsibility for certain domains. These towering figures are the focus of myths and legends. The distinction between culture heroes and ancestors is not always very clear. The Songye developed a well-defined trickster figure in Kafilefile, God's opponent from the beginning. Elsewhere the trickster figure took on less dramatic features.

Medicine, Witchcraft, Sorcery. The Luba believe in a general spiritual force that pervades all nature. Here again, the Songye take an outspoken leading position: "Efile Mukulu is considered to exist in everything, and to be everything, and thus everything is a part of Efile Mukulu" (Merriam, p. 297). This concept might not be as clearly phrased by other groups, but the idea that a shadow or soul operates in everything is present in all Luba thought. This hidden force is created by God himself in the works of God's own hands. It is as if God left something of his own being in all created things, just as humans communicate something of themselves to the things they create and manipulate. To know the name and the inner life force of things, so as to be able to use them safely for the good of humanity, is to know medicine or witchcraft, that is, power based on knowledge and creative skills. For the central Luba, God is Shamanwa (the father of skills). Sorcery—using the forces hidden in things with an evil intention to kill people or destroy things—is bad. Just as people mold their world by the power of their words and through the skills of their hands, so too they try to master the invisible life force behind all material appearances. They try to get on top of this invisible reality, the hidden forces, to mold them into visible material forms. They give them names and animal or human figures to bring them within the reach of the human imagination, vision, and language. They carve them into stone or wooden statues and so doing, give them individuality, so that they may be talked to, aroused, praised, or even cursed. The world of medicine, amulets, and other ritual objects is the link between spiritual realities and the empirical world.

Ritual Life. Ritual activities such as prayers, invocations, and offerings can be performed by individuals or by officials. Officials derive their ability to officiate from their function and position in the group (e.g., head of the household, leading elder of a lineage, head of a village) or from a special initiation as a diviner and traditional healer. The prophetic type of performer takes over from the official one at particular occasions for a variety of reasons: divination, healing, the cleansing of defiled persons or villages, and so on. These ritual actions take place when the dead interfere with the living by claiming attention or demanding to be consulted; rituals can also be required because the ancestors want to be honored through prayer and sacrifice.

The main characteristic of the duly initiated traditional healer is spirit possession accompanied by prophetic utterances. Diviners and traditional healers constitute a kind of informal guild, one initiating the other, but this guild should not be confused with the secret societies that formerly were abundant in Lubaland. Spirit possession usually occurs at shrines. The shrines themselves consist of tiny huts containing different kinds of receptacles in which simple objects, symbolizing the presence of the spirit during rituals, are placed. Sometimes the shrine is a tree planted to honor an ancestor. Ritual objects, usually receptacles of medicine, can also be placed at the entrance of a village (e.g., hunting spirits) or can be hidden together with special medicine under the roof of the main hut. A man's principal wife will then be entrusted with the keeping of the sacred objects. At certain times standardized rituals take place: first-fruit rituals, fertility rituals at the full moon, rites of passage, burial, and so on. Luba traditional religion forms a well-balanced whole in which the living and the dead can find peace and rest from the anxieties of human existence and through which the Luba find themselves inserted into the universal world of religious quest and spiritual concern.

BIBLIOGRAPHY

Burton, W. F. P. "Luba Religion and Magic in Custom and Belief." *Annales du Musée Royal de l'Afrique Centrale, Sciences Humaines*, vol. 8, no. 35. Tervuren, Belgium, 1961. Written by a member of the Congo Garanganze Mission after many years of living and traveling among the central Luba.

Colle, R. P. *Les Baluba.* 2 vols. Collection de Monographies Ethnographiques, vol. 10. Brussels, Belgium, 1913. Also written by a missionary. Still one of the basic sources, especially for the Luba Hemba.

Göhring, Heinz. *BaLuba: Studien zur Selbstzuordnung und Herrschaftsstruktur der baLuba. Studia Ethnologica*, vol. 1. Meisenheim am Glan, Germany, 1970. A wonderful synthesis; a scholarly work offering with an extensive bibliography; the indispensable introduction to any further research.

Merriam, Alan P. "Death and the Religious Philosophy of the Basongye." *Antioch Review* 21 (Fall 1961): 293–304. Excellent.

Mukenge, Leonard. "Croyances religieuses et structures sociofamiliales en société luba: 'Buena Muntu,' 'Bakishi,' 'Milambu.'" *Cahiers économiques et sociaux* 5 (March 1967): 6–94. The thèse de license of a Luba student at the Lovanium University (now Unaza). Outstanding.

Reefe, Thomas Q. *The Rainbow and the Kings: A History of the Luba Empire to 1891.* Berkeley, Calif., 1981. Essential to any further study of Luba culture. Outstanding.

Theuws, J. A. (Th.). "De Luba-mens." *Annales du Musée Royal de l'Afrique Centrale, Sciences Humaines*, vol. 8, no. 38. Tervuren, Belgium, 1962. Göhring called this work by a missionary an "intuitive synthesis." The information is based on prolonged field research in central Lubaland.

van Caeneghem, P. R. *La notion de Dieu chez les BaLuba du Kasai. Memoires de l'Académie Royale des Sciences Coloniales, Classe des Sciences Morales et Politques*, vol. 9, fasc. 2. Brussels, Belgium, 1956. The best work of a missionary priest who lived for years among the Luba Kasai.

van Overbergh, Cyrille. *Sociologie descriptive: Les Basonge.* Collection de Monographies Ethnographiques, no. 3. Brussels, Belgium, 1908. Based on early reports of travelers and civil service members. Still worthwhile.

Verhulpen, Edmond. *Baluba et Balubaïsés du Katanga.* Anvers, Belgium, 1936. A detailed study of Luba groups by a former civil service member. As a first orientation, the administrative information is still useful.

New Sources

Kalulambi Pongo, Martin. *Etre Luba au XXè Siècle: Identité Chrétienne et Ethnicité au Congo-Kinshasa.* Paris, 1997.

Mudimbe, V. Y. *Parables and Fables: Exegesis, Textuality, and Politics in Central Africa.* Madison, Wis., 1991.

Petit, Pierre. "Hunters, Mediums and Chiefs: Variations on the Theme of the Luba Ritual Object" in Mireille Holsbeke, ed. *The Object as Mediator: On the Transcendental Meaning of Art in Traditional Cultures.* Antwerp, Belgium, 1996.

J. A. THEUWS (1987)
Revised Bibliography

LUBAVITCH SEE HASIDISM, *ARTICLE ON* HABAD HASIDISM

LUCK SEE CHANCE

LUDI SAECULARES, the centennial games of ancient Rome, were rites celebrated in fulfillment of a vow pronounced at the beginning of the previous *saeculum.* Because a *saeculum,* in the wider sense of the term, was a period of time longer than the longest human life, no one could attend the games twice. It seems that initially the games went on for three nights; in any case, from the time of Augustus onward they lasted three days and three nights and were held, in principle, every 100 or 110 years, depending on the computation. The functioning and arrangement of this festival changed in the course of time, but its purpose remained the same: to purify the *res publica* at the beginning of a new era, by putting a hopeful end to a given period of time.

We do not know how far back the centennial games go. The ancients, followed by some modern scholars, sometimes claimed an early date: the fifth century BCE; it is certain at any rate that centennial games were celebrated in 249 BCE at the urging of the Sibylline Books; these games included nocturnal sacrifices in honor of Dis Pater (god of the underworld) and Proserpina, to which were added chariot races. It may be, however, that in one or another manner these games replaced a cult of the Valerian gens, which clearly was of greater antiquity but was celebrated on the same site as the centennial games: in the Campus Martius (Field of Mars), near the Tiber River, level with the modern Ponte Vittorio Emmanuele, in that part of the Field of Mars known as the Tarentum (though the connection with the Tarentum is doubtful).

At the beginning of the reign of Augustus, in 17 BCE, centennial games were celebrated with great pomp in order to mark the end of a period of destruction and bloodshed and the beginning of a golden age. It was in the form the games acquired at this time that they were subsequently celebrated in 88 and 204 CE. (A parallel series of festivities was held on April 21 of the years 248, 147, and 47 BCE to commemorate the centenaries of the foundation of Rome; the rites were simpler but also went by the name of centennial games.) The new liturgy comprised a complex series of nocturnal and diurnal rites. The nocturnal rites, which opened each day's festival after midnight and were regarded as a prolongation of the games of antiquity, marked the close of the preceding century with a sacrifice to the Fates (June 1), the Ilithyiae, goddesses of childbirth (June 2), and Mother Earth (June 3). The daytime sacrifices were offered to Jupiter Optimus Maximus (June 1, on the Capitoline), Juno Regina (June 2, on the Capitoline), and Apollo and Diana (June 3, on the Palatine). During the three nights, after the sacrifices, *sellisternia* or religious banquets were celebrated on the Capitoline in honor of Juno and Diana; 110 matrons of senatorial and knightly rank took part, and then plays were presented on the Campus near the Tiber. During the daytime these plays were continued from June 1 to 3 after the sacrifices to Apollo and Diana; other plays were added, known as Latin plays, and there were more banquets in honor of Juno and Diana. The climax of the entire festival came on the third day after the sacrifice to Apollo and Diana: 27 boys and 27 girls of senatorial rank, whose fathers and mothers were still living, recited a *Carmen saeculare* on the Palatine and the Capitoline (the centennial ode for 17 BCE was composed by Horace). After the celebration of the banquets and other rites, the plays ended, and chariot races, held in a temporary arena, brought the liturgy proper to an end.

Along with the festivals of the Arval Brothers, the centennial games of the emperors Augustus and Septimius Severus (193–211) are the Roman religious liturgies best known to us, thanks to the discovery of extensive records in epigraphic form.

BIBLIOGRAPHY

Brind'amour, P. "L'origine des jeux séculaires." In *Aufstieg und Niedergang der römischen Welt*, vol. 2.16.2, pp. 1334–1417. Berlin and New York, 1978.

Gagé, Jean. *Recherches sur les jeux séculaires.* Paris, 1934.

Pighi, Giovanni Battista. *De ludis saecularibus populi Romani Quiritium libri sex.* 2d ed. Amsterdam, 1965.

New Sources

Altheim, Franz. "Poetry and Cult: The Secular Hymn of Horace." In *A History of Roman Religion*, translated by H. Mattingly, pp. 394–407. London, 1938.

Gagé, Jean. *La reforme apollinienne des jeux et le chant séculaire d'Horace; l'achèvement suprème du 'ritus graecus' à Rome des origines à Auguste.* Paris, 1956. See pages 629–637.

Guittard, Charles. "Les prières dans la célébration des jeux séculaires augustéens." In *Dieux, fêtes, sacré dans la Grèce et la Rome antiques*, edited by André Motte and Charles M. Ternes, pp. 205–215. Turnhout, 2003.

Pavis d'Escurac, Henriette. "Siècle et Jeux Séculaires." *Ktèma* 18 (1993): 79–89.

Poe, Joe Park. "The Secular Games, the Aventine, and the Pomerium." *Classical Antiquity* 3 (1984): 57–81.

Schnegg-Köhler, Bärbel. *Die augusteischen Säkularspiele.* Munich and Leipzig, 2002 (a monographic issue of *Archiv für Religionsgeschichte*, 4).

JOHN SCHEID (1987)
Translated from French by Matthew J. O'Connell
Revised Bibliography

LUGBARA RELIGION. The Lugbara are a Sudanic-speaking people of northwestern Uganda and the northeastern portion of the Democratic Republic of the Congo, culturally related to the Azande and Mangbetu to the northwest. They are largely peasant farmers who grow grains and keep some cattle and other livestock. Their land is about 4,000 feet above sea level, well watered and fertile, with a population density of over two hundred people to the square mile in the central areas. The Lugbara have a politically uncentralized society in which traditional authority is held by the elders of small patrilineal lineages. Such lineages are the bases of local settlements and are linked into a segmentary lineage system of the classic kind. Above the elders, ritual and political authority is exercised by rainmakers, one to each clan, and occasionally by prophets. Since colonial rule was established by the Belgians in 1900 and the British in 1914, there have been administrative chiefs and headmen, but these stand very much outside the religious system. Catholic Verona Fathers and the Protestant African Inland Mission have been active since World War I and have had considerable success in education and conversion; there are relatively few Muslims. In the 1950s, when the main anthropological research was carried out, the mass of the people adhered to the traditional religion. Since then this situation may have changed, due mainly to the political upheavals and population movements under presidents Amin and Obote: the traditional lineage system has been severely weakened, and the cults associated with it have lost their importance.

MYTH. The Lugbara have a corpus of myth that tells of the creation of the world and the formation of their society. One myth tells that at the beginning humans dwelt and conversed with the Deity in the sky, coming daily down a rope or tower to farm; a woman who was hoeing cut it down, and since then people have lived on earth, ignorant of divine will and subject to change and death. Another myth states that the Deity (Adroa—the diminutive form of the word *adro*, connotating his distance from humankind, not lack of power) created a man and a woman far to the north. The woman was created pregnant and gave birth to animals and to a son and a daughter. This sibling pair gave birth to another, and several such generations followed. Each is credited with the invention of processes of transformation of natural products into domestic ones: smithing, potmaking, hunting, and so on. Finally there were born two sons, the culture heroes who formed society as it ideally is today. Each of the two culture heroes hunted with his sons, killing and eating a son each day; this filial cannibalism led to their expulsion, and each hero (accompanied by a sister's son and a bull) was compelled to cross the Nile and to go to the mountains in the middle of the country. There the two heroes hunted and killed buffalo but lacked fire to cook the meat. Each hero then descended to the plains and found there a leper woman with fire. After cooking and eating the meat, each hero cured one of the leper women (thus making her physically complete) and impregnated her. The armed brothers of the leper women forced the heroes to marry the women and provide cattle bridewealth. Each hero eventually did the same with some thirty women, whose sons were the founders of the present sixty or so clans. The heroes then retired to their mountains and died.

The myth explains the existence of social groups and settlements, of marriage and the legitimacy of offspring, and of feuds (the traditional basis for the maintenance of social order). The preheroic period is timeless, asocial, amoral, and marked by lack of order and authority; the postheroic period, structured by the passing of time, is both social and moral, with order maintained by genealogically sanctioned authority. The periods are bridged by the heroic mediators. The same pattern may be seen in spatial terms, with related lineages in a settlement's neighborhood, then a belt of people feared as magicians, and beyond them an amoral wilderness of strange, incestuous, and cannibalistic people. The myths explain the form of society, its relationship with the Deity, and the distinction that runs through Lugbara cosmology between the inside of home and settlement and the outside of the bushland, where spirits and other manifestations of the extrahuman power of the Deity dwell. Lugbara ritual is concerned essentially with the maintenance of the boundary between these two moral spheres.

Sacrifice to the Dead and Spirits. Sacrifice is not made to the Deity. The central cult is that of the dead, who are considered senior members of their lineages and who bridge the main cosmological boundary. The Lugbara concept of the person is important here. Men are considered persons of the home and women things of the bushland, having the potentially dangerous power of procreation that links them with the Deity. A person is composed of physical elements such as body and blood and the mystical ones of soul, spirit, and influence. Only men have souls (*orindi*), the seat of lineage authority, although those women born first of a set of siblings may have souls when they grow old; both men and women have spirit (*adro*), the seat of idiosyncratic and antisocial behavior; and both have *tali*, the seat of influence gained over others. At death the soul goes to the deity in the sky and may later be redomesticated by a diviner as a ghost (*ori*) as well as an ancestor (*a'bi*). Only the heads of lineage segments who leave sons are usually made into ghosts; others join a collectivity of ancestors. The spirit goes to the bushland, where it dwells with the immanent and evil aspect of the Deity (*Adro*); the *tali* merges with a collectivity of *tali*.

Death is marked by elaborate mortuary rites, which are the only important rites of transition. The corpse is buried and dances are held at which men of lineages related to the deceased dance competitively and aggressively to demonstrate their relative seniority within the total lineage structure. When death occurs, it is said that disorder has entered the community, and clan incest is permitted as a sign of this disorder; after a certain period has elapsed, order is reestablished by more dances and the distribution of food and arrows.

Ghosts are given individual shrines (in the shape of miniature huts) where they may be offered sacrifices; other patrilineal ancestors have collective shrines; and there are shrines for matrilateral ancestors. The ghost shrines for the recently dead are located in the compound, but after a few generations they are moved outside, a sign that their incumbents have merged spiritually with the Deity. The forms, distribution, and details of oblation with regard to these many shrines cannot be given here.

Sacrifice at the ghost shrines is part of the process by which lineage authority is exercised by the elders. Hence, it lies at the heart of the maintenance of social order within the community. Sacrifice follows on the invocation of the ghosts. It is believed that an elder whose authority is flouted by a dependent sits near the shrines in his compound and ponders the offense; the ghosts hear him and decide to send sickness to the offender to show him the error of his behavior; the offender then falls sick; the elder consults oracles that state which ghost is responsible and what oblation is demanded. In actuality a person falls sick and the process only then begins. If the patient recovers, then a sacrifice is made (if he or she dies, then the Deity is responsible and nothing can be done). The animal (ox, sheep, goat, or fowl) is consecrated and slaughtered. Part of the meat and blood is placed in the shrines; part is cooked and eaten later by the congregation. Some of the cooked meat is divided and taken home by the members of the congregation, who are members of lineages that share the same ghosts. The elder and others concerned discuss the case until a consensus has been reached that the original offense or dispute has been settled and atoned; they bless the patient with their breath and spittle, and the assembled kin, seated by generation and so representing the unity of normally competitive lineages, consume the cooked meat and beer. The stated purpose of this rite is to purify the home, to remove conflict and ensure unity and continuity. Sacrifice is also made, usually on behalf of junior kin, to the collectivity of lineage ancestors and to matrilateral ancestors.

Offerings are also made to many kinds of spirits (*adro*), invisible powers that are of a different order of existence than that of humans. Such spirits are beyond the understanding or control of normal people. Spirits are held to be innumerable. At one time or another, some are attached to prophets; others represent expressions of divine power (lightning, winds). All have as a central attribute the ability to possess a living person and to make the victim tremble or shake, a condition curable only by a diviner. Initial communication with a spirit is by its possession of a living person; almost all cases are of women, in particular those in an ambiguous moral situation (such as that of a persistently barren wife). The possessed woman consults a diviner to discover the identity of the offended spirit, then places a small shrine for it where she periodically makes offerings of grain and milk. There are no spirit cults as such; offerings are only made by individuals.

Divination. The need for the living to know the identity of the dead and the spirits with whom they come into contact requires divination. There are several kinds of oracles and diviners. Oracles, operated by men in the public space of the open air, consist essentially of material artifacts that select names put to them by those consulting them. Diviners are postmenopausal or barren women, who divine under possession in the darkness of their huts with only the client present. They confirm the identity of a spirit or of a witch or sorcerer (which oracles cannot do) and also redomesticate the soul when it has gone outside of the social realm to live with the Deity in the sky. Their power is thought to come directly from the Deity and is feared as being spiritual and dangerous.

EVIL. Evil is represented as the work of harmful human beings assumed to be witches and sorcerers. Using the classic distinction made for the Azande by Evans-Pritchard, witches are believed to harm others by an innate mystical power; among the Lugbara they are older men who bewitch their own kin because of envy or anger. Sorcerers use material objects or medicines, and among the Lugbara they are women and young men who lack the authority that witches have to pervert power for their own ends; because of this lack, sorcerers must turn to material means (including both poisons and nonpoisonous objects). Sorcerers are especially held to be women who are jealous of their co-wives. Both witches and sorcerers are believed to cause sudden and painful sicknesses, and their identities may be discovered by diviners who can also cure the affliction, usually by sucking its essence from the victim's body. Whereas witchcraft is traditional and, although evil, not particularly morally reprehensible (since the witch merely has the innate power and may not always be able to control it), sorcery is seen as a modern phenomenon and an abomination because it is deliberate and malign in its purpose.

RAINMAKERS AND PROPHETS. Each subclan has one rainmaker, the senior man of the senior descent line. He is believed to be able to control the rainfall by manipulating rain stones kept in a pot buried in his rain grove. In the past he was expected to end interlineage feuds by cursing the antagonists with impotence if they crossed a line drawn by him between their territories. He tells his community the times for planting and harvesting. And he is thought to be able to end epidemics and famines by beseeching the Deity. In brief, he is able to regulate the rain that links sky and earth, to control the fertility of human beings and of crops, to mark territorial and moral space, and to establish the orderly passage of time. He is held to be a repository of some of the secret truth and knowledge of cosmic categories held by the Deity. A rainmaker is symbolically buried at his initiation by other rainmakers, and later, at his actual death, he is buried silently at night in a manner opposite to that of ordinary people.

Prophets have appeared among the Lugbara on rare occasions, as emissaries of the Deity with a message to reform society in the face of disasters. The most famous was Rembe, a man of the neighboring Kakwa people. In the 1890s the Lugbara approached Rembe requesting that he give them a sacred water. This water was intended to remove the epidemics that were killing both humans and cattle, as well as the Arabs and Europeans who were entering the region at the same time. In 1916 Rembe entered Lugbaraland, called by elders for his help in removing further epidemics and Europeans. He established a cult known as Dede (grandmother, as it protected people) or Yakan (from the root *ya*, to make tremble). Adherents drank water from a sacred pool in which dwelt the power of the Deity; this would drive away the Europeans and bring back ancestors and dead cattle. Members of the cult attempted to establish a new egalitarian community and no longer recognized differences of descent, age, or sex. After the threat of revolt Rembe was deported by the British colonial authorities and hanged in the Sudan. Today he is still remembered and given mythopoeic attributes of sacredness and inversion, and it is said that he can never die and will one day return.

BIBLIOGRAPHY

Middleton, John. *Lugbara Religion: Religion and Authority among an East African People.* New ed., Oxford, England, 1999.

JOHN MIDDLETON (1987)
Revised Bibliography

LUGH. The pagan Irish deity Lugh (Shining One)—the model of kingly leadership and master of all arts and crafts—corresponds to the Gaulish god Lugus as well as to the Welsh Llew Llaw Gyffes. Lugus—who had widely scattered sites dedicated to him, from Loudun and Laon in France, and Leiden in Netherlands (from Lugu-dunum, or fort of Lugus) to Carlisle in Britain—is taken to be the Gaulish Mercury whom Julius Caesar identifies as the god most worshipped by the Gauls, a patron of prosperity and inventor of all the arts. Both Lugh and Lugus were honored on or near August 1, the beginning of the harvest quarter. Celebration of Lughnasa, the August festival honoring Lugh in Ireland, may have commemorated his symbolic ritual marriage to the land of Ireland. It included fairs and assemblies; hilltop gatherings; the first meal from the new crops; games and trials of strength; and horse racing. Traditions about Lugh may have survived in legends of the many Irish saints with the names Lugh or Lughaidh, as well as in legends about Saint Patrick, and early sites associated with his cult may have become associated with these Christian saints.

In the detailed picture of the Irish gods and their society found in *The Second Battle of Mag Tuired*, a text that includes language from as early as the ninth century, Lugh appears among the gods (called the Tuatha Dé Danann) as the unique practitioner of all the arts (*samildánach*, meaning skilled in many arts together). When Lugh arrives, the Tuatha Dé are anticipating an attack by the supernatural Fomhoire, who are trying to restore the reign of Bres, whose greed and incompetence forced him to leave Ireland. Bres is the son of the Fomhorian king Elatha and of Ériu (Ireland), a woman of the Tuatha Dé. When his misdeeds drive him from his kingship of the Tuatha Dé, Bres flees to his father's people, the Fomhoire, to gather an army. In response, the Tuatha Dé invite Lugh to lead their defense. Lugh is also half-Fomhorian, but on his mother's side: Eithne, daughter of Balar was given in marriage to Cian, son of the divine physician Dian Cécht, to form an alliance between the two peoples.

Asking what contribution each god will make to the battle, Lugh coordinates the work of the tribe's professionals and artisans—from weapon makers to physicians, druids, and witches—making the tribe stronger through collaborative effort. A master strategist, Lugh sends Eochaidh Ollathair, called the Daghdha (the Good God), to the Fomhorian camp to arrange a truce until Samhain (November 1), the beginning of winter and the start of the Celtic new year, so that the timing of the conflict will be favorable to the Tuatha Dé. Once the battle begins, Lugh's skill at arms tips the balance in favor of the Tuatha Dé. He defeats his Fomhorian grandfather Balar in single combat and deprives the Fomhoire of their greatest weapon, the magical power of Balar's baleful eye. Lugh assumes the responsibilities of a king after Bres's successor Nuadhu is slain, and he arranges the peace treaty between the two peoples. Lugh's bargain for the life of the Fomhorian poet Loch wards off Fomhorian aggression forever, and Lugh's decision to spare the captured Bres brings the Tuatha Dé knowledge of the most favorable days in the agricultural cycle: when to plant, when to sow, when to reap. By his judicious decisions, Lugh establishes a lasting peace and gives the Tuatha Dé access to Bres's power over agricultural prosperity.

In the later, related tale *Oidheadh Chloinne Tuireann,* Lugh appears as his father's avenger, exacting from the kinsmen who murdered Cian a wergild that includes having to win magical weapons that will be used against the Fomhoire. The guilty cousins are killed completing the final task of the wergild, but Lugh himself commits no act of violence and thus avoids perpetuating a cycle of kinslaying. In the epic tale *Táin Bó Cuailnge* (The cattle raid of Cooley), a tale known from manuscripts that include language from as early as the eighth century, Lugh appears as the father of Cú Chulainn, the preeminent Ulster hero whose single combats determine victory for his province against forces drawn from the rest of Ireland. In *Baile in Scáil,* a ninth-century text associated with the political claims of Irish kings, Lugh foretells and legitimizes an extended succession of Uí Néill rulers.

Lugh is said to be the originator of assemblies and to the inventor of an Irish game of strategy resembling chess (*fidhchell*), as well as ball-playing and horseracing. He is also said to have founded an assembly held on Lughnasa at Tailtiu in honor of his foster mother. Lugh's marriages link him symbolically to the land of Ireland, and his queens include Buí, a goddess of Munster, and Nás, eponym of a site in Leinster. He dies at Uisnech when he drowns fleeing grandsons of the Daghdha, who seek to avenge their father, slain by Lugh through jealousy over one of his queens.

See Also Celtic Religion, overview article.

Bibliography

Gray, Elizabeth A., ed. *Cath Maige Tuired: The Second Battle of Mag Tuired.* Naas, Ireland, 1982. Provides text and translation; contains extensive indices of references to the Tuatha Dé Danann and Fomhoire in early and later medieval Irish literature.

Gray, Elizabeth A. "Lug and Cú Chulainn: King and Warrior, God and Man." *Studia Celtica* 24/25 (1989–1990): 38–52. Explores key facets of the mythological dossier of Lugh and his heroic offspring.

Mac Cana, Proinsias. *Celtic Mythology.* New York, 1970. Succinct, authoritative, and comprehensive survey, extensively illustrated with photographs of significant items of Celtic material culture; includes chapters on the Tuatha Dé Danann and on the Irish heroic tradition.

MacNeill, Máire. *The Festival of Lughnasa: A Study of the Survival of the Celtic Festival of the Beginning of the Harvest.* 2 vols. Dublin, 1982. Provides an extensive discussion of both learned and popular literary sources related to Lugh and details folk customs associated with the celebration of Lughnasa.

Rees, Alwyn, and Brinley Rees. *Celtic Heritage: Ancient Tradition in Ireland and Wales.* London, 1961. Far-reaching and ahead of its time; explores the range of Celtic mythic tradition in the Indo-European context, including reference to the work of Georges Dumézil, with exhaustive notes that provide access to both specialist studies and more general works.

Elizabeth A. Gray (2005)

LU HSIANG-SHAN *See* LU XIANGSHAN

LU HSIU-CHING *See* LU XIUJING

LUKE THE EVANGELIST, according to Christian tradition the author of both the third canonical gospel and *Acts of the Apostles.* The *Gospel of Luke* and *Acts* are linked by similarities of style and theology, by their dedications to a certain Theophilus, and by reference to a first book, almost certainly the *Gospel of Luke,* in *Acts* 1:1. Unlike the other evangelists, Luke indicates that he was not an eyewitness to the events of Jesus' ministry that he describes (*Lk.* 1:1–3).

Luke is mentioned three times in the New Testament in letters ascribed to Paul (*Col.* 4:14, *2 Tm.* 4:11, *Phlm.* 24). Although a Lucius (a variant of the same name) appears in *Acts* 13:1 and *Romans* 16:21, there is no explicit link between this figure and Luke. In *Colossians* 4:14, Luke, who is with Paul, is called "the beloved physician." In the same context colleagues only are to be identified as Jewish; apparently Luke was a Gentile. Only the reference to Luke in *Philemon* can be certainly ascribed to Paul, inasmuch as *2 Timothy* is probably, and *Colossians* quite possibly, pseudonymous. In any event, each reference supports a traditional association of Luke with Paul. That association may also be attested to by the so-called "we-passages" of *Acts.* In four separate instances (*Acts* 16:10–17, 20:5–15, 21:1–18, 27:1–28:16) the narration of Paul's travels unaccountably switches from third person to first person plural, creating the impression that the narrator accompanied Paul. Although other explanations are possible, the traditional one, that Luke had joined Paul's party at those points, is a reasonable one. Since Luke is otherwise not a prominent figure in early Christianity, the attribution of two major New Testament books to him becomes understandable if it is, indeed, historically grounded. (A Timothy or Titus would otherwise have been a more obvious choice for such an attribution.) That Luke's understanding and presentation of Pauline theology is in some respects inadequate scarcely disproves a personal relationship between them in *Acts. Acts* was written a couple of decades after Paul's death.

Irenaeus (c. 180) names Luke as the third evangelist and a companion of Paul and describes Luke as having recorded the gospel as preached by Paul (*Against Heresies* 3.1.1). The Muratorian canon (probably late second century) gives a rather full description of Luke that agrees with Irenaeus and with the slim biblical evidence. Eusebius (c. 325) reports that Luke was "by race an Antiochian," a physician, and a companion of Paul (*Church History* 3.4.6).

Luke's vocabulary was once thought to reflect his medical training, but comparative studies have shown that his medical terminology does not surpass what might be expected of a Hellenistic author. According to an ancient, anti-Marcionite prologue to the gospel, Luke remained unmarried and lived to a ripe old age. While this is entirely possible, there is no way to confirm such a report. The same goes for the tradition that he was from Antioch, or that his remains, with those of the apostle Andrew, were interred in the Church of the Holy Apostles in Constantinople in 357. Luke's feast is celebrated on October 18. The evangelist's symbol, the ox, can be traced back to the late second century; it has been thought to mirror the importance of the Jerusalem temple and its sacrifices in Luke's presentation of Christ.

BIBLIOGRAPHY

Aside from the New Testament the most important primary source is Eusebius's *Church History*, which brings together earlier testimony of Christian writers on the origin and authorship of the Gospels. The most convenient edition is the two-volume "Loeb Classical Library" text and translation of Kirsopp Lake, J. E. L. Oulton, and Hugh J. Lawlor (Cambridge, Mass., 1926).

Werner G. Kümmel's *Introduction to the New Testament,* rev. ed. (Nashville, 1975), pp. 147–150, 174–185, finds the difficulties of Lucan authorship insurmountable. On the other hand, *The Gospel According to Luke, I-IX,* translated and edited by Joseph A. Fitzmyer, volume 28 of the Anchor Bible (New York, 1981), pp. 35–53, makes a guarded defense of the Luke tradition, in part because Fitzmyer does not regard the objections to it as entirely cogent. Raymond E. Brown, in his *Introduction to the New Testament* (New York, 1997), p. 327, finds the traditional ascription to Luke "not impossible."

D. MOODY SMITH (1987 AND 2005)

LULL, RAMÓN (c. 1232–1316), Catalan philosopher, poet, and missionary. Lull was born in Majorca shortly after the Arab occupation of the island had ended. He certainly was acquainted with spoken Arabic, but must have known classical Arabic as well. In his youth he was interested in chivalry and courtly occupations, but the visions of Christ that he experienced around 1265 transformed him into an ardent missionary whose aim was to create an understanding between Christianity, Judaism, and Islam and to resolve their differences. To this end he composed a great number of books in his native Catalan and is said to have traveled to various Islamic countries. Among Lull's works, his *Libre del contemplacio en Deu* (originally written at least partly in Arabic; see *Obres,* vol. 8, p. 645) is a seven-volume encyclopedia in which he sets forth his idea that by contemplation the truth of the Christian religion would be revealed to everyone.

In a vision in 1272 Lull saw the whole universe reflecting the divine attributes, a vision reminiscent of Islamic traditions. There has been much scholarly debate on the extent to which Lull was conversant with Arabic sources. His great novel, *Blanquerna,* best expresses his attitude to and understanding of Islam. Here, as in other early works, he expresses his concern for those who are lost despite many good aspects of their faith and life; he praises the Muslims' faith in the unity of God, which he views as the basis on which the three "Abrahamic" religions could understand one another; he acknowledges the importance of the Ṣūfī practice of *dhikr* ("recollection of God") and describes it as a useful step on the way to God; finally, he expresses the opinion that Muslims are closer to Christians than are other nonbelievers because Muslims accept the virgin birth of Mary. The novel *Blanquerna* closes with the "Book of the Lover and the Beloved," a collection of 365 aphorisms, many of which can be found verbatim in Arabic Ṣūfī sources and may come partly from al-Ghazālī, whose works Lull apparently knew well (he is even said to have translated one of his books) and who may have strengthened Lull's aversion to "philosophy," that is, to Averroism. Again, some of the symbols, his images, letter mysticism, and the use of prose rhyme are reminiscent of Arabic Ṣūfī works, especially of some of Ibn al-ʿArabī's writings.

On the other hand, Lull was very critical of the Muslims in other regards and repeated the traditional medieval accusations against them, such as the sensual image of Paradise, polygamy, and so forth. His attitude hardened over the years, and in the place of his earlier irenic attitude an increasingly militant missionary zeal fills his later works. He requested the church to emphasize the study of Arabic so that disputations with Muslims could be carried out more successfully and he succeeded in persuading James II of Aragon to establish a school of oriental languages in Miramar on Majorca. Later, in 1312, the Council of Vienne decided to found chairs for Arabic in several universities to train missionaries. In 1316, on one of his trips to North Africa, Lull was imprisoned and probably stoned to death. Many years later, in 1376, some of his teachings were condemned by Gregory XI.

Lull was a complex figure, and he himself complained of not being properly understood; this attitude is typically expressed in his *Disputatio clerici et Raymundi phantastici,* in which he portrays himself as the eccentric idealist. Lull's philosophy is based on the mystery of the Trinity: the three powers of the soul reflect the trinitarian principles. He tried to achieve a reduction of all knowledge to first principles so as to establish perfect unity as the underlying structure of the universe. Among his numerous books, the *Ars magna;* the *Arbor scientiae* (The Tree of Knowledge), with its mysterious diagrams; and the *Liber de ascensu et descensu intellectus* (Book of Intellectual Ascent and Decline) best reflect his philosophical ideas and his way of using the various branches of medieval science, from mathematics to alchemy. Some of his ideas were later taken over and elaborated by Nicholas of Cusa.

In each of his writings Lull strove to show that faith and intellect must work together to prove that Christianity is the true religion. His ardent striving to lead to the true faith those who knew it only fragmentarily, and to whom he himself was indebted to a certain degree, is summed up in an aphorism from the "Book of the Lover and the Beloved," which translates an old Ṣūfī saying: "The ways in which the lover seeks his Beloved are long and dangerous; they are populated by meditation, sighs, and tears, and illuminated by love."

Bibliography

Lull's works have been printed from the sixteenth century onward; the latest edition is *Obres: Edició original,* 20 vols. (Palma de Mallorca, 1906–1936). The best biography is still E. Allison Peers's *Ramon Lull: A Biography* (London, 1929). Peers has also translated *Blanquerna: A Thirteenth Century Romance* (London, 1925), and its last chapter, published separately, *The Book of the Lover and the Beloved* (New York, 1923). Jean Henri Probst's *La mystique de Ramon Lull et l'arte de contemplació* (Münster, 1914) and Otto Keicher's *Raymundus Lullus und seine Stellung zur arabischen Philosophie* (Münster, 1909) are both critical of the extent of Lull's knowledge of classical Arabic. A good selection from Lull's works is *Selected Works of Ramon Llull,* edited and translated by Anthony Bonner (Princeton, 1985), which is well-balanced and readable.

Annemarie Schimmel (1987)

LUPERCALIA.

LUPERCALIA. The Lupercalia, inscribed in the calendar on February 15, belongs by virtue of its suffix to the category of Roman feasts that have names ending in *-alia,* such as the Feralia on February 21. The word is a derivative of *Lupercus* and is semantically related to *Lupercal.* The Luperci were the officiants and were divided into the Luperci Quinctiales (or Quintiliani; Paulus-Festus, ed. Lindsay, 1913, p. 78 L.) and the Luperci Fabiani; the former bound themselves to Romulus, the latter to Remus (Ovid, *Fasti* 2.375–378). For a long time the word was thought to have come from *lupus* ("wolf") and *arceo* ("to keep off") and so to mean "protectors against wolves" (Servius, *Ad Aeneidem* 8.343; Wissowa, 1912, p. 209). But *Luperci* is more a derivative of *lupus* with the ending *-ercus* (analogous to the formation of *noverca,* "mother-in-law") and so means "wolf-men." The Luperci, appearing naked (Servius, *Ad Aeneidem* 8.663), or rather "nude except for a simple loincloth" (Plutarch, *Romulus* 21.7, *Quaestiones Romanae* 68), brought to mind a precivilized state and constituted a "truly savage brotherhood" (*fera quaedam sodalitas;* Cicero, *Pro Caelio* 26).

When the Luperci ran around the Palatine in the midst of a crowd of people, the act had a purifying purpose that Varro (*De lingua Latina* 6.34) sums up thus: "[in February] the people are purified [*februatur*], insofar as the old fortress on the Palatine was circled by nude Luperci for purposes of lustration [*lustratur*]." This ceremony began with a sacrifice in the grotto of Lupercal, located at the southwest corner of the Palatine (Plutarch, *Romulus* 21.5); the offering was a she-goat (Ovid, *Fasti* 2.361; see also Plutarch, *Romulus* 21.6) or a he-goat (Servius, *Ad Aeneidem* 8.343). During their run, they would carry lashes, called *februa,* made from hides of she-goats or of he-goats (Paulus-Festus, op. cit., p. 76 L.). With these lashes they would strike the spectators, especially women, "in order to ensure their fertility" (Servius, *Ad Aeneidem* 8.343). Ovid (*Fasti* 2.441) proposes a strange etiology for this rite: it would be the application (discovered by an "Etruscan augur") of an order from Juno, "Let a sacred he-goat . . . penetrate Italian mothers" ("Italidas matres . . . sacer hircusi-nito").

Other unusual or unexplained elements enter into the ceremonial. According to Plutarch (*Romulus* 21.8; *Quaestiones Romanae* 68, 111), who seems to be our only source, the Luperci also sacrificed dogs. Stranger still, he tells how "two young people from noble families are led forth: some touch their foreheads with bloody knives while others wipe them with wool soaked in milk. Once they are wiped, they start to laugh" (*Romulus* 21.6–7). Another problem is far from being clarified: what divinity was patron of this feast? Vergil (*Aeneid* 8.344) does not hesitate to designate Pan of Arcadia. Ovid (*Fasti* 2.423–424) interprets *Lupercus* as transposition of the "Arcadian" *Lycaeus:* the cult was supposedly established by the hero Evander on behalf of Pan-Faunus. This late syncretism leaves open the patronage question, for the Latin equivalent of Pan in the third century BCE was not Faunus but Silvanus (Plautus, *Aulularia* 674, 766).

Bibliography

Dumézil, Georges. *La religion romaine archaïque.* 2d ed. Paris, 1974. See pages 352–356. This work has been translated from the first edition by Philip Krapp as *Archaic Roman Religion,* 2 vols. (Chicago, 1970).

Latte, Kurt. *Römische Religionsgeschichte.* Munich, 1960. See pages 84–87 and especially note 4 on page 84.

Michels, Agnes Kirsopp. "The Topography and Interpretation of the Lupercalia." *Transactions of the American Philological Association* 84 (1953): 35–59.

Wissowa, Georg. *Religion und Kultus der Römer.* 2d ed. Munich, 1912. See pages 209–212.

New Sources

Bannon, Cynthia J. *Brothers of Romulus.* Fraternal Pietas in Roman Law, Literature and Society. Princeton, 1997.

Bianchi, Ugo. "Luperci." In *Dizionario Epigrafico di Antichità Romane* 4.3 (1980): 2204–2212.

Capdeville, Gérard. "Jeux athlétiques et rituels de fondation." In *Spectacles sportifs et scéniques dans le monde étrusco-italique. Actes de la table ronde organisée par l'Équipe de recherches étrusco-italiques de l'UMR 126 (CNRS, Paris) et l'École française de Rome. Rome, 3–4 mai 1991*, pp. 141–187. Rome, 1993.

Holleman, A.W.J. *Pope Gelasius I and the Lupercalia.* Amsterdam, 1974

Holleman, A.W.J. "Lupus, Lupercalia, lupa." *Latomus* 44 (1985): 609–614.

Marchetti, Patrick. "Autour de Romulus et des 'Lupercalia.' Une explication préliminaire." *Les Etudes Classiques* 70 (2002): 77–92.

Piccaluga, Giulia. "L'aspetto agonistico dei Lupercalia." *Studi e Materiali di Storia delle Religioni* 33 (1962): 51–62.

Pötscher, Walter. "Die Lupercalia-Eine Strukturanalyse." *Grazer Beiträge* 11 (1984): 221–249.

Ulf, Christopher. *Das römische Lupercalienfest. Ein Modellfall für Methodenprobleme in der Altertumswissenschaft.* Darmstadt, 1982.

Wiseman, Timothy Peter. "The God of the Lupercal." *Journal of Roman Studies* 85 (1995): 1–22.

ROBERT SCHILLING (1987)
Translated from French by Paul C. Duggan
Revised Bibliography

LURIA, ISAAC

LURIA, ISAAC (1534–1572), known also by the acronym ARiY (ha-Elohi Rabbi Yitsḥaq, "the godly Rabbi Isaac"); Jewish mystic. Isaac Luria was the preeminent qabbalist of Safad, a small town in the Galilee where a remarkable renaissance of Jewish mystical life took place in the sixteenth century. Not only did Luria's original mythological system and innovative ritual practices achieve great popularity in Safad itself; they also exerted profound influence upon virtually all subsequent Jewish mystical creativity. By the middle of the seventeenth century, Lurianic theology and ritual practices had permeated much of the Jewish world. It has been observed that Lurianism was the last premodern theological system to enjoy such widespread acceptance within Judaism.

Luria was born in Jerusalem, where his father had settled after migrating from Germany or Poland. Following his father's death his mother took him to Egypt, where he lived in the home of his uncle, a wealthy tax gatherer. In Egypt, Luria studied with two prominent rabbis, David ibn Abi Zimra and Betsal'el Ashkenazi, and collaborated with the latter on legal works. During this period Luria apparently immersed himself in the study of the *Zohar* and other qabbalistic texts. In late 1569 or early 1570, Luria traveled to Safad and began studying with Mosheh Cordovero, the principal master of esoteric studies in this community. Luria quickly attracted a circle of students to himself that included Ḥayyim Vital, his chief disciple, as well as Yosef ibn Ṭabūl and Mosheh Yonah.

It appears that Luria possessed the traits of a genuinely inspired and charismatic individual. He became known in Safad as an extraordinarily saintly person who had been privileged to experience personal revelations of qabbalistic knowledge from the Holy Spirit, the prophet Elijah, and departed rabbis. He was regarded as having knowledge of such esoteric arts as metoposcopy and physiognomy and the ability to understand the language of animals. He was able to diagnose the spiritual condition of his disciples and others and provided them with specific acts of atonement for restoring their souls to a state of purity.

To his formal disciples, who numbered about thirty-five, Luria imparted esoteric wisdom, vouchsafing to each one mystical knowledge pertinent to his particular soul, such as its ancestry and the transmigrations through which it had gone. He also gave his disciples detailed instructions on the meditative techniques by which they could raise their souls up to the divine realm, commune with the souls of departed rabbis, and achieve revelatory experiences of their own.

Luria developed an intricate mystical mythology that served to explain, on a cosmic level, the meaning of the exile of the Jewish people, which was felt especially strongly after their expulsion from Spain in 1492. The three elements of this myth correspond to three dramatic events within the life of God. In an attempt to explicate how the world could come into being if God originally filled all space, Luria taught that God had withdrawn into himself, so to speak, thereby creating an "empty space." This divine act of self-withdrawal, known in Hebrew as *tsimtsum,* made possible the existence of something other than God. The second part of the cosmic process, called the "breaking of the vessels" *(shevirat ha-kelim),* concerns the emanation or reemergence of divinity back into the primordial space produced by *tsimtsum.* During this process of emanation, some of the "vessels" containing the light of God were shattered. While most of the light succeeded in reascending to its divine source, the remainder fell and became attached to the now-broken "vessels" below. The result of this chaotic and catastrophic dispersal of divine light was the imprisonment of holy sparks in the lower world, the realm of material reality.

Since these sparks of divine light seek to be liberated and returned to their source, the human task, according to Isaac Luria, is to bring about such liberation through proper devotional means. Known as *tiqqun,* the "mending" or "restitution" of the life of God, this effort is, at its core, a contemplative one. Every religious action requires contemplative concentration in order to "raise up the fallen sparks." The successful struggle on the part of the community will result in the final separation of holiness from materiality, and a return of all divine light to the state of primordial unity that preceded the creation of the world. Lurianic mysticism exercised great influence and had enduring appeal long after Safad itself ceased to be a prominent center of Jewish life. It gave mythic expression to the notion that collective religious action could transform the course of history to redeem both the people of Israel and God.

SEE ALSO Qabbalah.

BIBLIOGRAPHY

A general introduction to the teachings of Isaac Luria is found in Gershom Scholem's *Major Trends in Jewish Mysticism* (1941; reprint, New York, 1961), as well as in Scholem's *Kabbalah* (New York, 1974), especially pp. 128–144. An important study of Lurianic rituals is Scholem's essay "Tradition and New Creation in the Ritual of the Kabbalists," in his book *On the Kabbalah and Its Symbolism* (New York, 1965). Those able to read Hebrew will want to consult a lucid study of Lurianic ideas by Isaiah Tishby, *Torat ha-ra' ve-ha-qelippah be-qabbalat ha-Ariy* (Jerusalem, 1942). Special customs and rituals practiced by Isaac Luria are found in my study *Safed Spirituality: Rules of Mystical Piety; The Beginning of Wisdom* (New York, 1984), and for the techniques he taught, see my articles "Maggidic Revelation in the Teachings of Isaac Luria," in *Mystics, Philosophers, and Politicians: Essays in Jewish Intellectual History in Honor of Alexander Altmann,* edited by Jehuda Reinharz and David Swetschinski (Durham, N.C., 1982), and "The Contemplative Practice of Yiḥudim in Lurianic Kabbalah," in *History of Jewish Spirituality,* edited by Arthur Green (New York, 1986).

New Sources

Fine, Lawrence. *Physician of the Soul, Healer of the Cosmos: Isaac Luria and His Kabbalistic Fellowship.* Stanford Studies in Jewish History and Culture. Stanford, Calif., 2003.

Magid, Shaul. "From Theosophy to Midrash: Lurianic Exegesis and the Garden of Eden." *AJS Review* 22 (1997): 37–75.

Wineman, Aryeh. "The Dialectic of 'Tikkun' in the Legends of the Ari." *Prooftexts* 5 (1985): 33–44.

LAWRENCE FINE (1987)
Revised Bibliography

LURIA, SHELOMOH (c. 1510–1574), known by the acronym MaHaRSHaL (Morenu ha-Rav ["our teacher the rabbi"] Shelomoh Luria); Polish Talmudist and scholar. Luria was born in Poznan to a family that claimed descent from the great medieval Jewish exegete Rashi and that included many of the luminaries of the Ashkenazic rabbinical world. He was trained as a rigorous exponent of the Ashkenazic tradition in Talmudic exegesis, to which he added a distinctive commitment to relentless exactitude in the interpretation of sacred texts. His idiosyncratic method of study caused him to part company with many of the rabbinical authorities of his age and established his reputation as a brilliant, if demanding, Talmud scholar.

Shelomoh Luria appears to have held several rabbinical posts in Lithuania before settling first in the town of Brest-Litovsk, then in the important community of Ostrog, and finally in Lublin, where he died in 1574. In all of these centers Luria established academies that met opposition from the disciplines of his erstwhile teacher and colleague, Shalom Shakhna of Lublin, the primary exponent in Poland of the regnant method of Talmudic hermeneutics known as *pilpul* (dialectic reasoning). Luria fiercely condemned this approach as contrary to the true meaning of the text and argued instead for a "return to the Talmud," a careful explication of the sources, diction, and plain meaning of the Talmud and its later, especially Ashkenazic, interpreters. Particularly irksome to Luria were the corruptions that had recently crept into the Talmudic text through scribal errors and that had become accepted as a result of the new technology of printing; in his *Ḥokhmat Shelomoh* he set about to correct these errors and offered bold emendations and alternate readings that would be celebrated by critical scholars centuries after his death.

In line with this basic stance toward textual criticism, Luria also insisted on a firm command of Hebrew grammar and the Bible and opposed the study of Jewish philosophy. Perhaps most important, he not only rejected the codifications of Jewish law published in his own time, by Yosef Karo of Safad and by Luria's relative and friend Mosheh Isserles of Kraków, but he rejected Maimonides' code, the *Mishneh Torah,* as well. Objecting vehemently to both the form and the goal of these codes, Luria decided to write his own summary of rabbinic law in order to correct their errors. In his *Yam shel Shelomoh,* he cited all relevant authorities, examined the differing interpretations, and then selected the most cogent view, not necessarily the consensus. This ambitious task proved too massive even for Luria, and he was able to complete work on only a few tractates. Nonetheless, his contributions to jurisprudence and Talmudic scholarship marked him as one of the most important rabbis of his age and perhaps the leading eastern European Jewish scholar until the eighteenth century.

BIBLIOGRAPHY

There is no complete critical study of Luria or his works. The most useful analyses are two essays in Hebrew: Simha Assaf's "Mashehu le-toledot ha-Maharshal," in the *Sefer ha-yovel li-khvod Levi Ginzberg,* issued by the American Academy for Jewish Research (New York, 1945), pp. 45–63, and Haim Chernowitz's essay on Luria in *Toledot ha-posqim,* vol. 3 (New York, 1947), pp. 74–91. For an English source, parts of Moses A. Shulvass's *Jewish Culture in Eastern Europe: The Classic Period* (New York, 1975) may also be consulted.

New Sources

Rafeld, Me'ir. "Ha-Maharshal veha-'Yam shel Shelomoh." Ph.D. diss., Bar-Ilan University, Ramat Gan, Israel, 1991.

MICHAEL STANISLAWSKI (1987)
Revised Bibliography

LUSTRATIO. Lustrations, or purifications by sacrifice, played a primordial role in Roman religion, both public and private, inasmuch as they were celebrated every time there was a transition or the likelihood of a transition in the life of an individual or a city, and every time there was need to repel aggressions or at least threats from outside. Lustration rites were celebrated either in a complex liturgy that repeated the act of lustration at length or in a single ritual that effected the desired separation. Whatever the degree of ritual complexity, however, a lustration was always an act of definition. It was a definition, first, in that it distinguished and delimited in time and space two realities that are opposed, such as, for example, living and dead, civilized and savage, good and bad, peaceful and hostile, pure and defiled. A lustration was a definition, second, because this act of disjunction was usually accompanied by a reflection on the reality in question, an inspection, a clear and definite ordering, a verification. This twofold defining that a lustration accomplished may explain why the (still disputed) etymology of *lustrum/ lustrare* points in the direction of "inspection, gaze, light shed on" as well as that of "purification."

Lustrations therefore had a central place in the rites of birth and death, whereby the family firmly asserted the separation between what was not yet (or no longer) living and the world of the living, using rituals that enabled it to accompany the deceased or newly born person in his crucial passage without itself being adversely affected. At the community level certain festivals, and even the entire month of February, were given over to the lustration of families; in this way the city established a clear and definite break between its past and its future.

The most typical lustrations were those practiced in regard to fields, territory, city, or citizens. In these cases the lustration took a precise form, that of a procession, a circumambulation by the sacrificial victims around the object to be purified, the integrity of which was verified (i.e., emphasized), as were the threats—human, natural, or supernatural—that impended. The victims were sacrificed at the end of the procession. There were a variety of victims for a variety of divinities, as for instance a sow for Ceres. But in a lustration proper the victims were a boar, a ram, and a bull (or what was called *suovetaurilia*) and they were offered solely to Mars, who was invoked as defender of the city and territory or of an individual's fields (an interpretation denied by some scholars). The most spectacular lustrations, however, were those whose object was a group of citizens either under arms or in civilian dress but ready to form an army. Every five years (but under the empire, only sporadically) one of the censors, after inspecting and setting to rights the affairs of the Roman people, celebrated a solemn *lustrum* in the Campus Martius (Field of Mars) by walking the *suovetaurilia* around the citizens, who were organized in voting units (*centuriae*). The effect of this lustration was not only to ascertain and assert the perfection of the civic body but also to draw around it a strict boundary that Mars was to defend. The danger threatening the citizens was above all the danger of war; it is not surprising, therefore, that in a critical situation the generals led the sacrificial *suovetaurilia* around their legions or vessels.

SEE ALSO Purification.

BIBLIOGRAPHY

Volume 13 of the *Real-Encyclopädie der classischen Altertumswissenschaft*, edited by Georg Wissowa (Stuttgart, 1927), includes two articles of particular interest: "Lustrum," by Helmut Berve, and "Lustratio," by Fritz Boehme. Also recommended are W. Warde Fowler's *The Religious Experience of the Roman People from the Earliest Times to the Age of Augustus* (London, 1911), pp. 209–218; Carl Koch's *Gestirnverehrung im alten Italien: Sol Indiges und der Kreis der Di Indigetes* (Frankfurt, 1933); and Georges Dumézil's *Archaic Roman Religion* (Chicago, 1970).

New Sources

Gagé, Jean. "Les rites anciens de lustration du populus et les attributs triomphaux des censeurs." *Mélanges Ecole Française de Rome* 82 (1970): 43–71.

Munier, Frédérique. "La lustration du peuple d'Iguvium." In *Hommage à René Braun, vol. 1: De la préhistoire à Virgile: philologie, littératures et histoires anciennes*, edited by Jean Granarolo and Michèle Biraud, pp. 117–135. Paris, 1990.

Versnel, Henk S. "Sacrificium lustrale. The Death of Mettius Fufetius (Livy I, 28). Studies in Roman Lustration-Ritual I." *Mededelingen van het Nederlands Instituut te Rome* 37 (1975): 97–115.

JOHN SCHEID (1987)
Translated from French by Matthew J. O'Connell
Revised Bibliography

LUTHER, MARTIN (1483–1546), German theologian and reformer of the Christian church. Luther was born in Eisleben on November 10, the son of Hans Luder, who was engaged in copper mining. After moving to nearby Mansfeld, the family increasingly acquired modest prosperity. Because Hans Luder appears prominently in Luther's later recollections as a stern and oppressive presence, the question has arisen whether the son's development was significantly affected by intense conflict with his father. No satisfactory answer to this question has been given.

After initial schooling in Mansfeld, Martin Luther attended the cathedral school in Magdeburg from 1497 to 1498, where he came into contact with the Brethren of the Common Life, one of the most spiritual of late medieval religious movements. Between 1498 and 1501 he attended school in Eisenach, and, in 1501, he matriculated at the University of Erfurt to pursue the customary study of the seven liberal arts. Luther was declared ineligible for financial aid, an indirect testimonial to the economic successes of his father. The philosophical climate at the university was that of Ockhamism, which undoubtedly exerted its influence upon the young student. Upon receiving the master's degree in 1505, Luther began the study of law in the summer of that year, in accordance with the wishes of his father. Less than two months later, however, the experience of a terrifying thunderstorm near Stotterheim prompted his vow to Saint Anne to become a monk, resulting in the abandonment of his legal studies.

Undoubtedly, spiritual anxiety and uncertainty about his vocational choice combined to precipitate the determination to carry out the vow. On July 17, 1505, Luther entered the Monastery of the Eremites of Saint Augustine in Erfurt. His choice of this monastic order is explained not only by its strictness but also by its philosophical and theological orientation, to which Luther had been exposed during his earlier studies.

Two years later, on February 27, 1507, Luther was ordained to the priesthood. In his later recollections his first celebration of the Mass stood out as an awesome experience. Afterward, at the behest of his monastic superior, Johann von Staupitz, Luther began graduate studies in theology, first at Erfurt and then, in the fall of 1508, at the recently founded university at Wittenberg, because of his transfer to the Augustinian monastery there. In accordance with custom, he served as philosophical lecturer in the liberal arts curriculum. In 1509 he received his first theological degree, the *baccalaureus biblicus.*

In the fall of 1509 Luther was transferred back to Erfurt, where he continued his theological studies. Sometime thereafter (the exact date is uncertain) he was sent to Rome on monastic business. In his reflections of later years, he attributed great significance to that trip: the Rome that he had presumed to be the epitome of spiritual splendor had turned out to be terribly worldly. Soon after his return from Rome, Luther transferred a second time to Wittenberg, completing his doctorate in theology there in October 1512. He then assumed the *lectura in Biblia,* the professorship in Bible endowed by the Augustinian order.

The first academic courses that Luther taught were on *Psalms* (1513–1515), *Romans* (1515–1516), *Galatians* (1516–1517), *Hebrews* (1517–1518), and another on *Psalms* (1519). His lecture notes, which have been analyzed intensively, chronicle his theological development: his shift from the traditional exegetical method, his increasing concentration on questions of sin, grace, and righteousness, his preoccupation with Augustine of Hippo, and—last but by no means least—his alienation from scholastic theology. At the same time Luther acquired increasing responsibilities in his monastic order. In 1515 he became preacher at the parish church in Wittenberg and was appointed district vicar of his order. The latter position entailed the administrative oversight of the Augustinian monasteries in Saxony.

In his later years Luther spoke of having had a profound spiritual experience or insight (dubbed by scholars his "evangelical discovery"), and intensive scholarly preoccupation has sought to identify its exact date and nature. Two basic views regarding the time have emerged. One dates the experience, which Luther himself related to the proper understanding of the concept of the "righteousness of God" (*Rom.* 1:17), as having occurred about 1514, the other in about 1518. The matter remains inconclusive, partly because nowhere do Luther's writings of the time echo the dramatic notions that the reformer in later years associated with his experience. The import of the issue lies both in the precise understanding of what it was that alienated Luther from the Catholic church, and in understanding the theological frame of mind with which Luther entered the indulgences controversy of 1517. The dating of the experience before or after 1517 is thus important. Placing the experience in 1518 seems to be the most viable interpretation.

The Ninety-five Theses of October 31, 1517 (the traditional notion that Luther nailed them to the door of the Wittenberg castle church has recently been questioned) catapulted Luther into the limelight. These theses pertained to the ecclesiastical practice of indulgences that had not as yet been dogmatically defined by the church. Luther's exploration of the practice was therefore a probing inquiry.

Almost immediately after the appearance of the Ninety-five Theses, a controversy ensued. Undoubtedly it was fanned by the fact that Luther had focused not merely on a theological topic but had also cited a number of the popular grievances against Rome, thus touching upon a political issue. In addition to sending copies of the theses to several friends, Luther sent a copy to Archbishop Albert of Hohenzollern, whom he held responsible for a vulgar sale of indulgences in the vicinity of Wittenberg, together with a fervent plea to stop the sale. Luther was unaware that the sale was part and parcel of a large fiscal scheme by which Albert hoped to finance his recent elevation to the politically important post of archbishop of Mainz. Albert's response was to ask the University of Mainz to assess the theses and, soon thereafter, to request the Curia Romana to commence the *processus inhibitorius,* the proceedings by which Luther's orthodoxy would be ascertained. Thus the theses and Luther became an official matter for the church. The commencement of official proceedings against Luther added far-reaching notoriety to the affair, as did the related accusation of heresy by several theological opponents. The ensuing debate therefore became a public one, eventually allowing for the formation of a popular movement.

In April 1518 Luther presented a summary of his theological thought, which he called the "theology of the cross," at a meeting of the Augustinian order in Heidelberg. In presenting a caricature of scholastic theology, Luther appropriately emphasized its one-sidednesses. Soon afterward he was ordered to appear in Rome in conjunction with the proceedings against him, but the intervention of his territorial ruler, Elector Frederick, caused the interrogation to take place in Augsburg, Germany. With Cardinal Legate Cajetan representing the Curia, the meeting proved unsuccessful, since Luther refused to recant. Luther fled from Augsburg and, upon his return to Wittenberg, issued an appeal to a general council.

Overwhelmed by the unexpected notoriety of the affair, Luther agreed to refrain from further participation in the controversy. All the same, he was inadvertently drawn into a disputation held in Leipzig in July 1519. In the context of a wide-ranging, if tedious, discussion of the fundamental issues in the controversy, Luther's opponent, Johann Eck, professor of theology at Ingolstadt, was intent on branding him a heretic and succeeded in eliciting Luther's acknowledgment that the church's general councils had erred. Luther posited a difference between the authority of the church and that of scripture, a notion that late medieval thinkers had never seen as problematic.

After the election of Charles V as the new emperor, which had preoccupied the Curia for some time, official proceedings against Luther were resumed. In June 1520 the papal bull *Exsurge Domine* (Arise, O Lord) condemned forty-one sentences from Luther's writings as "heretical, offensive, erroneous, scandalous for pious ears, corrupting for simple minds and contradictory to Catholic teaching." Luther was given sixty days to recant. His response was to burn the bull in a public spectacle on 10 December 1520. On January 3, 1521, the bull *Decet Romanum Pontificem* (It Pleases the Roman Pontiff) excommunicated Luther. It was now incumbent upon the political authorities to execute the ecclesiastical condemnation, but Luther was given the opportunity to appear before the German diet at Worms in April 1521.

Several factors converged to bring about the unusual citation. Luther had begun to precipitate a popular movement, in part playing on prevailing anti-Roman and anticlerical sentiment. There was apprehension about popular restlessness. Moreover, Luther claimed persistently that he had not received a fair hearing. To invite Luther to appear at Worms, and, indeed, give him an opportunity to recant, seemed to be to everyone's advantage. When he appeared before the diet, Luther acknowledged that he had been too strident in tone, but he refused to recant anything of theological substance. After several weeks of deliberation, and despite some reluctance, a rump diet promulgated an edict that declared Luther (and all of his followers) political outlaws and called for the suppression of his teachings.

By that time, however, Luther had disappeared from the public scene. At the instigation of his ruler Elector Frederick, he had been taken on his return to Wittenberg to a secluded castle, the Wartburg, where he was to spend almost a full year in hiding. A period of self-doubt, it was also an exceedingly creative time, part of which he spent in translating the New Testament from Greek into German. He returned to Wittenberg in March 1522 to calm the restlessness that had surfaced there over the nature of the reform movement. In a series of sermons he enunciated a conservative notion of ecclesiastical reform, and his stance left its imprint on the subsequent course of the Reformation.

Luther resumed his professorial responsibilities and continued his prolific literary activities, clarifying theological themes and offering guidelines for undertaking ecclesiastical reform. His own theological formation was essentially complete by 1521; his theological work thereafter consisted in amplification and clarification.

The year 1525 proved to be a major theological and personal watershed for Luther: he became embroiled in two major controversies—with Erasmus and Thomas Müntzer—that resulted in a marked division in the reform movement. On June 13 of that same year he married Katharina von Bora, a former nun who had left her convent the previous year. Even though the marriage—coming as it did on the heels of the German Peasants' War—was a subject of notoriety among Luther's enemies, it set the tone for a Protestant definition of Christian marriage for which the term "school for character" was aptly coined.

The next several years were overshadowed by Luther's growing controversy with Huldrych Zwingli over Communion. The controversy reached its culmination in October 1529 with a colloquy held at Marburg at the instigation of Landgrave Philipp of Hesse, who viewed the split of the Reformation movement over this issue as a major political liability. Luther was a reluctant participant in the colloquy, for he saw the theological differences between Zwingli and himself to be so fundamental as to make conciliation impossible. The major issue debated at Marburg was the bodily presence of Christ in the Communion elements. It is unclear whether for Luther the politically more prudent course of action would have been theological conciliation (which would have presented a unified Reformation movement) or intransigence (which by its separation from Zwingli would have underscored the proximity of the Lutheran and the Catholic positions). No agreement was reached at Marburg; as a result, at the diet at Augsburg the following year, the Protestants appeared divided.

As a political outlaw, Luther was unable to be present at Augsburg. He stayed at Coburg (as far south as he was able to travel on Saxon territory), and his close associate Philipp Melanchthon functioned as spokesman for the Lutherans. Several of Luther's most insightful publications appeared during that summer—a tract on translating, an exposition of Psalm 118, and *Exhortation That Children Should Be Sent to School.*

The unsuccessful outcome of the discussions at Augsburg and the subsequent formation of the League of Smalcald (1531) were accompanied by Luther's reconsideration of his views on the right of resistance to the emperor, which he had previously rejected. The 1530s brought Luther's extensive involvement in the reorganization of the University of Wittenberg (1533–1536). His extensive participation in the academic disputations that were now resumed were evidence of the richness and fullness of his thought.

Luther's final years were overshadowed by his growing antagonism toward the papal church, and the consequences of his well-meant but misunderstood counsel to Landgrave Philipp of Hesse that bigamy was permissible under certain circumstances. In addition, the Lutheran movement was torn by several internal conflicts, and Luther was concerned about the increasing role of the political authorities in ecclesiastical affairs.

Luther's recognition that his norm of authority—scripture—did not preclude disagreement in interpretation and that the papal church was unwilling to accept the primacy of the word of God undoubtedly serve to explain—along with his increasing physical ailments—the vehemence of his last publications, especially those against the papacy and the Jews. He was plagued by insomnia and, from 1525 onward, by kidney stones, which in 1537 almost led to his demise. In February 1546 Luther traveled, together with two of his sons and Philipp Melanchthon, to Luther's birthplace, Eisleben, to mediate in a feud among the counts of Mansfeld. There, having succeeded in that assignment, he died on 16 February.

Not surprisingly, Martin Luther has received considerable scholarly and theological attention throughout the centuries. Assessments of Luther have always been staunchly partisan, with a clear demarcation between Protestant and Catholic evaluations. The former, while uniformly positive, have tended to follow the intellectual or theological currents of their particular time, such as the eighteenth-century Enlightenment or nineteenth-century German nationalism.

In the twentieth century, particularly in the latter part, the biographical and theological evaluation of Martin Luther focused on a number of specific aspects. There was a preoccupation with the "young" Luther, that is, Luther between 1512 and 1518, and particularly with Luther's "evangelical discovery," his formulation of a new understanding of the Christian faith. This new understanding has generated much speculation about Luther's relationship to the late Middle Ages, the medieval exegetical tradition, the significance of Augustine, Ockham, and mysticism. The "older" or "mature" Luther, generally defined as Luther after 1526, is only beginning to receive widespread attention; this part of his life has not attracted much scholarly interest because it lacks the excitement of Luther's earlier years. The general question is whether the "older" Luther should be seen in continuity or in discontinuity with the young Luther.

A key theme in Luther's theology is that of the sole authority of scripture, formulated as the notion of *sola scriptura;* this notion, because it implied the possibility of a divergence of tradition from scripture, raised a startling new question. Late medieval theology had formulated the issue of authority in terms of the possible divergency of pope and council. A related theme in Luther's theology was the relationship of law and gospel, which provided the key to the understanding of scripture. God reveals himself as both a demanding and a giving God, two qualities that Luther loosely assigned to the Old and New Testaments respectively; but in truth, so Luther asserted, grace is found in the Old Testament even as law is found in the New.

The notion of justification by faith is traditionally cited as the heart of Luther's thought. It is, in fact, his major legacy to the Protestant tradition. In contradistinction to the medieval notion of a cooperative effort between man and God, between works and grace, Luther only stressed grace and God. Such grace is appropriated by faith, which affirms the reality of the grace of forgiveness, despite the reality of sin. Luther's "theology of the cross" affirmed that God always works contrary to experience.

These themes must be considered in the context of Luther's general affirmation of traditional dogma. His sacramental teaching repudiated the medieval notion of transubstantiation and affirmed a "real presence" of Christ in the bread and wine of Communion. Besides the sacrament of Communion, only that of baptism was affirmed. At least in his early years, Luther advocated a congregationally oriented concept of the church, with the "priesthood of all believers," another key motif, as an important corollary. Luther's teaching of the "two kingdoms" sought to differentiate the Christian principles applicable in society.

SEE ALSO Reformation.

BIBLIOGRAPHY

The definitive Weimar edition of Luther's works, *D. Martin Luthers Werke: Kritische Gesammtausgabe,* edited by J. K. F. Knaake and others (Weimar, 1883–1974), in more than a hundred volumes, continues to be the basic tool for Luther research. An exhaustive sampling of Luther in English can be found in his *Works,* 55 vols., edited by Jaroslav Pelikan (Saint Louis, 1955–1976). The *Luther-Jahrbuch* (Munich, 1919–) publishes an annual bibliography, as does, less comprehensively, the Archiv für Reformationsgeschichte (Leipzig and Berlin, 1903–). A useful general introduction to facets and problems of Luther scholarship is found in Bernhard Lohse's *Martin Luther: Eine Einführung* (Munich, 1981). Of the numerous Luther biographies, the following deserve to be mentioned: Roland H. Bainton, *Here I Stand* (Nashville, 1955); Heinrich Bornkamm, *Martin Luther in der Mitte seines Lebens* (Göttingen, 1979); H. G. Haile, *Luther* (Garden City, N. Y., 1980); and Eric H. Erikson, *Young Man Luther* (New York, 1958), a controversial psychoanalytic study. Two useful collections of sources are *Martin Luther,* edited by E. G. Rupp and Benjamin Drewery (New York, 1970), and Walther von Löwenich's *Martin Luther: The Man and His Work* (Minneapolis, 1983).

Important studies on specific aspects of Luther's life and thought are Erwin Iserloh's *The Theses Were Not Posted* (Boston, 1968); Wilhelm Borth's *Die Luthersache (causa Lutheri)*

1517–1524 (Lübeck, 1970); and Mark U. Edwards, Jr.'s *Luther and the False Brethren* (Stanford, Calif., 1975) and *Luther's Last Battles* (Ithaca, N. Y., 1983). A creative statement of Luther's theology is Gerhard Ebeling's *Luther* (Philadelphia, 1970).

HANS J. HILLERBRAND (1987)

LUTHERANISM. Martin Luther's Roman Catholic opponents were the first to label the sixteenth-century reform movements "Lutheran." His supporters first called themselves "evangelical" (from the Greek *euaggelion,* "gospel") and then, after 1530, "the churches of the Augsburg Confession."

TEACHING AND WORSHIP. Lutheran teachings, which have remained determinative for Lutheranism until today, are preserved in the Book of Concord of 1580. By prefacing this collection of teachings with the three ecumenical creeds (Nicene, Apostles', and Athanasian), Lutherans demonstrate their basic agreement with the ancient trinitarian tradition. The collection includes Luther's Large and Small Catechisms of 1529, his Smalcald Articles of 1537, Philipp Melanchthon's Augsburg Confession of 1530 and its Apology of 1531, and the Formula of Concord, drafted in 1577 by a group of Lutheran church leaders to resolve intra-Lutheran controversies in Germany.

Luther's doctrine of "justification through grace by faith alone, apart from works of law," echoing Paul in his letter to the Romans (3:28), forms the core of Lutheranism. A person is right with God (i.e., "justified") by completely trusting the work of Christ (i.e., "by faith") and not by making any human effort to appease God (i.e., "apart from works of law"). Christ's atonement is communicated both verbally, in preaching and teaching, and visibly, in the celebration of the sacraments. Thus to Luther the doctrine of justification was not one among many doctrines, as medieval theology taught, but was the "chief article of faith" that establishes the norm for Christian faith and life. Consequently the word of God must be seen in its careful distinction between "law" and "gospel." The law, be it divine (especially the First Commandment of the Decalogue) or human (as manifested in the rule of temporal princes), creates necessary order in the face of evil and reveals the human inability to appease God. Through Christ, the gospel, which is communicated in words and sacraments, reveals God's unconditional love for all creatures. Trusting in Christ rather than in one's own efforts restores one's relationship with God. God may indeed reward good and punish evil, but believers no longer need worry about God's justice. Instead, they are free to enjoy God's mercy and thus help the "neighbor" in need. So viewed, all of life is a thanksgiving for what God did in Christ.

In worship, Lutherans have tried to be faithful to the ecumenical tradition of the Mass by regarding its center, the sacrament of Holy Communion, as the means of grace that strengthens and sustains Christians in a world of sin, death, and evil. Luther changed little in the liturgy of the Roman Mass, removing only what he called the "sacrifice of the Mass," namely, the prayers of thanksgiving that surround the act of consecrating bread and wine. He found these prayers too self-righteous, too full of words intended to appease God, rather than offering joyful thanks for what God did in Christ.

Following Luther's careful liturgical reforms in Wittenberg, Lutherans have insisted on the use of the vernacular in the liturgy, introduced congregational singing, and stressed preaching. Worship is thus the basic response to baptism, which discloses God's unconditional promise to be forever with those who trust God in Christ. Lutherans retained the practice of baptizing infants not only because it had been the custom from the beginning of Christianity but also because infant baptism demonstrates that God's grace is not conditioned by human response.

Lutherans recognize only two sacraments, baptism and the Lord's Supper, because Luther could find no clear evidence that Christ instituted any other sacraments. Baptism commissions all believers to a common ministry, but for the sake of enduring witness and good order in the church, there is a divinely instituted, special, ordained ministry. Lutherans have not always agreed on the precise differences between the ministry of all the baptized (the "common priesthood of all believers") and the ministry of the ordained, but they have nevertheless rejected any notion of a divinely instituted structure of hierarchical priesthood. An ordained Lutheran pastor is a baptized Christian who is called to the public ministry of word and sacraments after proper training and examination, and the rite of ordination is the solemn commissioning to be faithful to this call.

The core of Luther's reform movement was the proposal that the church return to the Christocentric stance that he had found in scripture and in the early church fathers. His fundamental insights were neither well understood nor satisfactorily evaluated either by Catholics or by many Lutherans. Nontheological factors seemed to help the spread of Lutheranism more than theological factors.

HISTORY. The doctrine of baptism proved to be the most revolutionary aspect of Lutheranism, since it allowed Luther to invite territorial princes to become "emergency bishops" of the new churches. Thus German princes interested in liberating themselves from the domination of Rome established Lutheranism in their own territories and encouraged it to spread, especially to the east. Princes, peasants, patricians, priests, and even bishops joined the Lutheran cause, mainly to break from Rome. Danish and Swedish kings declared Lutheranism the religion of their lands between 1527 and 1593. However, when, in 1525, peasants in Saxony rebelled against their landlords in the name of Luther's call to Christian freedom, Luther sided with the princes, who crushed the rebellion by force; he refused to see his cause identified with liberation from the yoke of feudalism.

The pope and the emperor were forced to soften their implacable opposition to Lutheranism because they needed the support of German princes to meet the threat of Turkish invasion from the south. At the request of Emperor Charles V, the Lutherans submitted a confession of their faith to the Diet of Augsburg in 1530. The signers of the Augsburg Confession included seven princes and two city magistrates, clearly demonstrating the strong political support Lutheranism had achieved. But subsequent negotiations between Lutheran and Catholic theologians failed to produce sufficient agreement to cease hostilities. The Council of Trent (1545–1563) was finally convened a year before Luther's death in 1546, but Lutherans were not invited to attend. In 1547, German Lutherans and Catholics faced each other in military battles; the war ended within a year with the defeat of the Lutheran Smalcald League. But Emperor Charles V was willing to compromise, and the resulting 1555 Peace of Augsburg tolerated "the religion of the Augsburg Confession," although it took almost a century and the Thirty Years' War (1618–1648) before the Peace of Westphalia accepted Lutheranism as a legitimate religion in the empire.

The Formula of Concord used medieval scholastic terminology and Aristotelian philosophical categories to provide a theological system to protect Lutheranism from both Catholic and Calvinist influences and to resolve the dispute between followers of Melanchthon, known as Philippists, and Gnesio-Lutherans (from the Greek *gnesios,* "authentic"). The result was a systematic, rational interpretation of the doctrines of sin, law, and grace, the cornerstones of a Lutheran theology grounded in the forensic notion that God declared humankind righteous by faith in Christ. The formula rejected both the Catholic notion of cooperation between human nature and divine grace through free will and Calvin's doctrine of Christ's spiritual (not real or bodily) presence in the Lord's Supper. The formula also insisted that all teachings must be subject to the authority of the prophetic and apostolic writings of scripture, thus opening the door to a biblicism that has at times produced a biblical fundamentalism.

Between 1580 and 1680, German Lutherans favored a uniform religion that fused pure doctrine with Christian laws. The resulting alliance between church and state created seventeenth-century Lutheran orthodoxy. Assisted by orthodox theologians, territorial princes dictated what people should believe and how they should behave, and obedience to political authority became the core of Christian ethics. But Lutheran orthodoxy gave rise to a new reform movement, nicknamed "pietist," which stressed a "religion of the heart" rather than the prevalent "religion of the head." Led by Philipp Jakob Spener, August Hermann Francke, and Nikolaus Zinzendorf, Lutheran Pietism emphasized individual conversion, lay ministry, and a morality distinct from worldly ethics. By the nineteenth century, the pietist impulse had created an "inner mission" movement in Germany that established a female diaconate, built hospitals and orphanages, instituted educational programs, cared for the mentally retarded, and advocated prison reform. The University of Halle trained missionaries for foreign missions, particularly for India and the United States. But social and ecumenical concerns were frequently overshadowed by a narrow-minded moralism. Thus both Lutheran orthodoxy and Lutheran Pietism tended to pervert the original purpose of Lutheranism: to be a reform movement within the church catholic. Both orthodox rationalism and pietist moralism had lost sight of the original Lutheran, ecumenical, holistic vision.

During the eighteenth-century Enlightenment, Lutheranism again succumbed to rationalist and secularist tendencies. Frederick II of Prussia (r. 1740–1786), for example, initiated an attitude of toleration that valued religion only as it served the general purposes of the state. Lutheran theologians like Johann Semler (1725–1791) considered the doctrine of justification nonessential and supported the general notion of Lutheranism as a moral teaching. In Germany and Scandinavia, however, some Lutheran theological faculties and church leaders reacted against this trend by nurturing a strong historical consciousness and intensive biblical studies, which led to frequent attempts to revive the spirit of Luther and the Lutheran confessions. These "Neo-Lutherans" called for a return to strong biblical and confessional norms to counteract the prevalent cultural Protestantism that had virtually eliminated Lutheranism's distinctive character. By 1817, three hundred years after Luther's posting of the Ninety-five Theses, Neo-Lutherans had produced a significant revival of old Lutheran norms and ideas. German Lutherans founded the Common Lutheran Conference in Prussia in 1868 to provide communication between the various territorial churches. Danish churchman Nikolai F. S. Grundtvig (1783–1872) promoted an ecumenical Lutheranism based on the apostolic tradition and on the creeds; he also revived liturgy and church music.

In the United States, Henry Melchior Mühlenberg (1711–1787), who had come from Halle to Philadelphia, organized the first American Lutheran synod in Pennsylvania in 1748. Synods were organized by regions and were headed by presidents; they met regularly in convention to decide matters of church polity and faith. Lutheran theological seminaries, colleges, and journals were soon founded in regions where Lutherans predominated. Samuel S. Schmucker (1799–1873), president of the oldest Lutheran seminary in the United States (founded in Gettysburg in 1826), envisaged an "American Lutheranism" that would be the leading force to unite all the major Protestant denominations. But he did not receive sufficient support to realize his vision. The country was too vast, and Lutherans were too estranged from one another, especially by ethnic background, to make Lutheran unity a realistic goal. The Lutheran Church-Missouri Synod, consisting of German Lutherans who were disenchanted with Lutheran attempts in Prussia to form a union with the Reformed church, was organized in 1847. Soon there were German, Danish, Norwegian, Swedish, and Finnish groups who cherished their own ethnic traditions more than unity with one another. During the Civil War, the United Lutheran Synod of the South was formed in response to political and cultural pressures. It was not until after World War I that Lutherans in the United States managed to form larger denominations through mergers.

The Nazi tyranny in Germany (1933–1945) strongly affected German Lutherans. A small minority of Lutheran pastors and congregations resisted Hitler, but the great majority of Lutherans either remained silent or actively cooperated with the Nazi regime. The resistance, which called itself the "Confessing church,"was opposed by those who called themselves the "German Christians," who were in basic agreement with the government's desire to link Lutheranism with Nazism. Danish and Norwegian Lutherans refused to cooperate with the German occupation forces, which did not react with persecution. All these groups looked to the Lutheran confessional documents for support of their positions.

After World War II, some 184 delegates representing about 80 million Lutherans from 49 churches in 22 countries organized the Lutheran World Federation in 1947. Headquartered in Geneva (which is also the headquarters of the World Council of Churches) the Lutheran World Federation unites Lutheran churches from around the world in common social-action projects and in regular world assemblies but otherwise has no authority over the churches. The trend toward Lutheran unity also continued in the United States. The Lutheran Council in the United States was established in 1967 to facilitate communication and common action among the larger Lutheran denominations and to represent them at the Lutheran World Federation.

Since the 1960s, there have been ongoing official dialogues between Lutherans and other Christian churches. In 1982 the Lutheran Church in America and the American Lutheran Church were able to agree with the Episcopal Church in the United States on an "interim sharing of the eucharist," hoping for total reconciliation between Lutherans and Anglicans in the future. In view of their beginnings, Lutherans have considered their relations with Roman Catholics particularly important. Official Lutheran-Catholic dialogues began in the 1960s and have taken place without interruption in the United States since 1965. There has always been a creative tension between Lutheranism as a movement and the Lutheran denominations. If Lutherans are guided by their confessional convictions, they will remain in this tension.

See Also Luther, Martin; Melanchthon, Philipp; Pietism; Reformation.

Bibliography

The most comprehensive treatment of Lutheranism, albeit from an American perspective, is offered in E. Clifford Nelson's *The Rise of World Lutheranism: An American Perspective* (Philadelphia, 1982). The same author also has written a readable history, *Lutheranism in North America, 1914–1970* (Minneapolis, 1972). In addition, there is a useful historical survey, stressing European and American Lutheranism, by Conrad Bergendoff, *The Church of the Lutheran Reformation* (Saint Louis, 1967). Normative Lutheran teachings, "the Lutheran confessions," are made available in translation in *The Book of Concord*, edited and translated by Theodore G. Tappert (Philadelphia, 1959). The historical roots and theological significance of the Lutheran confessions are described and analyzed by me and Robert W. Jenson in *Lutheranism: The Theological Movement and Its Confessional Writings* (Philadelphia, 1976). The distinctive features of Lutheranism, especially compared with other traditions in the United States, are sketched in Arthur C. Piepkorn's "Lutheran Churches," in volume 2 of *Profiles of Belief* (San Francisco, 1978). The theological center of Lutheranism has been explored, with an eye on ecumenical implications, in Wilhelm Dantine's *The Justification of the Ungodly*, translated by me and Ruth C. Gritsch (Saint Louis, 1968), and in Gerhard O. Forde's *Justification by Faith: A Matter of Death and Life* (Philadelphia, 1982). Detailed information on Lutheran worship is contained in Luther D. Reed's *The Lutheran Liturgy* (Philadelphia, 1947). Basic information on Lutheranism can be quickly obtained in *The Encyclopedia of the Lutheran Church*, 3 vols., edited by Julius Bodensieck (Minneapolis, 1965).

New Sources

Gassmann, Gunther, Duane H. Larson, and Mark W. Oldenburg. *Historical Dictionary of Lutheranism.* Lanham, Md., 2001.

Gritsch, Eric W. *A History of Lutheranism.* Minneapolis, 2002.

Mead, Frank Spencer, and Samuel S. Hill. Rev. by Craig D. Atwood. "Lutheran." In *Handbook of Denominations in the United States.* 11th ed. Nashville, 2001.

Truscott, Jeffrey A. *The Reform of Baptism and Confirmation in American Lutheranism.* Lanham, Md., 2003.

Eric W. Gritsch (1987)
Revised Bibliography

LU XIANGSHAN (1139–1193) was the literary name of Lu Jiuyuan, also known by the style name of Lu Zijing. A pivotally important thinker in the Southern Song period (1127–1279), he contributed to the forging of the intellectual movement of what came to be known in the West as neo-Confucianism, whose cultural mission was no less than the revivification and redefinition of the Confucian Way (*dao*). By reformulating and extending the teachings of Mengzi (391–308 BCE) on the mind-heart and human nature, Lu Xiangshan is supposed to have initiated the so-called "learning of the mind-heart" (*xinxue*) within the neo-Confucian tradition, as opposed to the "learning of principle" (*lixue*), first espoused by Zheng Yi (1033–1107) and later elaborated by Lu's good friend and intellectual nemesis, Zhu Xi (1130–1200). Passionate about the neo-Confucian enterprise, Lu argued that the fulfillment and implementation of the Way could not be achieved through the discursive and external pursuit of bookish knowledge. Rather, it hinged on the realization of the goodness of the mind-heart through virtuous actions and practical deeds.

Lu was born in the Jiangxi province into an elite family that had migrated from the north. The distinguished social pedigree of the Lus as local magnates notwithstanding, his family's material fortunes had been gradually dwindling. By the time Lu came into the world his family no longer owned land, but they were by no means poor, thanks to a prosperous business in medicines. Even though, from the generation of Lu's great-great grandfather to his father's, none of the Lus had held government office, the family continued to produce scholars of great repute, and its social and genealogical luster in the locality remained burnished. Lu Xiangshan himself secured the highest degree of *jinshi* (literally, "a presented scholar") in 1172. While Lu served studiously and successfully in a succession of official appointments on the local level, he was always engaged in teaching and lecturing. Late in his life, he led the White Elephant (Xiangshan) Academy in his home province, where, as an inspiring thinker and popular teacher, he attracted thousands of pupils and admirers. Although Lu did not write prolifically, he established an estimable scholarly reputation by dint of his profound views on learning and moral self-cultivation.

In his debate with Zhu Xi at Goose Lake temple in 1175, Lu famously declared that his program of learning was focused, direct, and "easy," in that it sought the illumination and revelation of one's intrinsic, original mind-heart (*ming benxin*) before the broad quest for extrinsic knowledge. By contrast, Lu found Zhu's project to be distracting, circuitous, and in the final analysis "fragmented," insofar as it considered the indiscriminate amassing of external know-how to be prior to the development of an enveloping, guiding inner vision. Lu also found fault with Zhu's dualistic metaphysical scheme of principle (*li*) and material force (*qi*), wherein the former was conceived as the supreme ontological entity of pure possibilities, and the latter the source of concrete things and their movements. Accordingly, Zhu's philosophical anthropology identified principle solely with human nature (*xing*), associating emotions (*qing*) with material force while recognizing the mind-heart (*xin*) as the vital link between nature and emotions, to the extent that it was the faculty endowed with the most subtle of material forces. Consciously in contention with this finicky architectonics, Lu's philosophy was propelled by the rage for an all-embracing unity and oneness, which he ascertained in his ontological conception of the mind-heart.

Whereas Zhu presupposed the inadequacy of the mind-heart in the absence of the guidance of principle qua nature, Lu asserted pristine humanity in terms of it. In fact, he posited the oneness of principle (endowed in humanity by heaven) and the mind-heart: "The mind-heart is one and principle is one." Lu construed the perfect truth of reality as a unity, inasmuch as "the mind-heart and principle can never be separated into two." For Lu, this unity was what Confucius had in mind when he made the oft-quoted statement that "there is one thread that runs through my teachings." Similarly, it was what Mengzi referred to when he stated that "the Way is one and only one." In other words, humanity was the same as the mind-heart and principle, which Lu further elucidated in terms of Mengzi's theory of innate goodness. This mind-heart/principle is the source of the sense of horror and commiseration when one sees a child about to tumble into a well; it is that which makes people ashamed of shameful things and makes them deplore the deplorable. It constitutes filial piety, respect for elders, the sense of right and wrong, and the virtues of rightness *(yi)* and reverence (*jing*). To put it another way, the mind-heart consists of the four moral sprouts (*siduan*) that define the goodness of nature: the sense of compassion, the sense of shame, the sense of humility, and the sense of right and wrong. Since all goodness and all things are already complete within us, Mengzi rightly admonished us that there is no greater joy than the examination of oneself in an effort to realize one's authentic self.

Lu also identifies the mind-heart with the Way (*dao*) that fills the universe. With reference to heaven, the Way is yin and yang, and with respect to earth, it may be described in terms of strength and weakness. Most significant, as regards humanity, the Way is the fundamental virtues of *ren* and *yi.* The former is the very human faculty or human-heartedness that defines humanity; the latter is the corresponding ability to act rightly and righteously. These two cardinal virtues, at once the embodiment and manifestation of the Way, are the original mind-heart.

To the extent that principle, or the Way, inheres in the mind-heart, which is our heaven-endowed moral nature, the quest for the Way must begin with the inward look toward the mind-heart, purposefully seeking to build and nurture what Mengzi calls the "greater part of our being." Lu was fond of saying that what he taught came spontaneously from deep within his being, such that "the six classics are annotations on myself," just as "I am annotations of the six classics." The thousands of words that he uttered were nothing other than expressions that issued from within him. Small wonder that he rejected Zhu Xi's program of learning, whose point of departure was "following the path of inquiry and learning" (*dao wenxue*), or seeking erudition through broad investigations of things. Such an epistemological premise was fundamentally flawed. Lu maintained that true understanding and knowledge of reality stemmed from and began with "honoring moral nature" (*zun dexing*), that is, the critical reflection on and examination of the self distinguished by the mind-heart. To learn, in its essentials, is to seek to return and preserve the mind-heart, which may be lost or obscured as a result of aggrandizement by undue and excessive desires. Therefore, no amount of empirical knowledge and experiential learning would enable human flourishing if, to begin with, people do not recognize that the mind-heart, endowed with innate moral nature and embodying the entire universe, is the locus of knowing and acting. To honor moral nature is to establish the moral, and indeed transcendent, goals and purposes of learning. Otherwise, study is a misguided, undirected, and ultimately irrelevant adventure of the mind that yields no meaningful moral-ethical consequences—namely to uplift oneself through empathy with and amelioration of others in the human community.

Because Lu appealed directly to the mind-heart, recommended deep introspection of the inner self through meditation and quiet-sitting, and espoused an "easy" method of cultivation that apparently spurned words and texts, since the time of Zhu Xi he has traditionally been considered to be a speculative thinker much preoccupied with the abstruse and recondite quest for spiritual enlightenment in the Chan Buddhist mode. As Zhu Xi's teaching came to be consolidated and accepted as orthodoxy, such characterization took hold. In point of fact, however, nothing could be further from the truth. Lu's effort to locate the ontological center of being and reality in the mind-heart bespeaks his earnest desire to concentrate on the moral-ethical agency of every human being. The unmitigated focus on the mind-heart points not to its self-referential capacity in an other-worldly sense, but rather to its ineluctable verification and validation through this-worldly practical learning, beginning with self-cultivation, which is in turn expanded into transformative deeds as they are brought to bear on community and society. As Lu takes pains to point out, principle is not some transcendent metaphysical entity out there; it is the ritual complex and order forged in history. At the same time that principle, embodied in the mind-heart, reveals our innate moral conscience and consciousness, it is manifested in the proper workings of social relations, rites, institutions, and laws. Principle is order-conferring and assent-eliciting insofar as it is understood not only cosmologically but also morally, socially, and historically. It is no accident that the towering Ming-dynasty thinker Wang Yangming (1472–1529), who expanded Lu's philosophical anthropology anchored on the mind-heart—and who thereby rekindled attention to and interest in this Song master's views—propounded the powerful injunction that knowing and acting are one.

In brief, the religio-philosophical mystique of Lu's holistic conception of the mind-heart as all-encompassing reality lies not in its putative vertical identification with some transcendent ideality, but in its horizontal association with the immanent (hence human and social) world of quotidian moral actions.

See Also Confucianism, overview article; Mengzi; Zhu Xi.

Bibliography

Birdwhistell, Anne D. "Dichotomies in Social Experience in the Thought of Lu Jiuyuan (1139–1193)." *Journal of Sung-Yuan Studies* 27 (1997): 1–26.

Birdwhistell, Anne D. "Social Reality and Lu Jiuyuan (1139–1193)." *Philosophy East and West* 47, no. 1 (1997): 47–65.

Cady, Lyman Van Law. "The Philosophy of Lu Hsiang-shan, a Neo-Confucian Monist Idealist." Ph.D. diss., Union Theological Seminary, New York, 1939.

Ching, Julia. "The Goose Lake Monastery Debate (1175)." *Journal of Chinese Philosophy* 1 (1974): 161–178.

Foster, Robert Wallace. "Differentiating Rightness from Profit: The Life and Thought of Lu Jiuyuan (1139–1193)." Ph.D. diss., Harvard University, 1997.

Fukuda, Shigeru. *Riku Shozan bunshu.* Tokyo, 1972.

Gao Zhuanxi. *Lixin zhi jian: Zhu Xi he Lu Jiuyuan de lixue.* Beijing, 1992.

Huang, Chin-shing. "Chu Hsi versus Lu Hsiang-shan: A Philosophical Interpretation." *Journal of Chinese Philosophy* 14, no. 2 (1987): 179–208.

Huang, Siu-chi. *Lu Hsiang-shan: A Twelfth-Century Chinese Idealist Philosopher.* New Haven, 1944.

Hymes, Robert P. "Lu Chiu-yuan, Academies, and the Problem of the Local Community." In *Neo-Confucian Education: The Formative Stage,* edited by Wm. Theodore de Bary and John W. Chaffee, pp. 432–456. Berkeley, 1989.

Kim, Oaksook Chun. "Chu Hsi and Lu Hsiang-shan: A Study of Philosophical Achievements and Controversy in Neo-Confucianism." Ph.D. diss., University of Iowa, 1980.

Li Jipiing. *Lu Xiangshan yanjiu.* Taipei, 1973.

Li Zhijian. *Lu Jiuyuan zhexue sixiang yanjiu.* Henan, People's Republic of China, 1985.

Lu Jiuyuan. *Lu Jiuyuan ji.* Beijing, 1980.

Mahony, Robert Joseph. "Lu Hsiang-shan and the Importance of Oral Communication in Confucian Education." Ph.D. diss., Columbia University, 1986.

Zhang Liwen. *Zouxiang xinxue zhi lu: Lu Xiangshan sixiang de zuji.* Beijing, 1992.

On-cho Ng (2005)

LU XIUJING (406–477), Daoist scholar and liturgical master active during the Liu Song dynasty (420–479) in China. Regarded as the seventh patriarch of the Celestial Master sect (*Tianshi Dao*), founded by Zhang Daoling in Sichuan province in the second century, Master Lu was a key figure in the development of the Daoist church during the Six Dynasties period (317–618). He has traditionally been credited with the earliest organization of the Daoist canon (*Daozang*) into its three major sections. Further, by editing and teaching the so-called Lingbao (Spiritual Treasure) scriptures, upon which he based his instructions for Lingbao rites, Master Lu laid down basic and enduring patterns for the subsequent development of Daoist liturgical life.

Born in Zhejiang province, Lu is said to have left his family and official career in order to collect and study Daoist scriptures. Although he withdrew to Mount Lu (Lushan) in Jiangxi province, he nonetheless enjoyed close connections with the courts of several Liu Song emperors, and as a result, both Mount Lu and the Chongxu monastery, which was built for him outside the capital (modern Nanjing), became renowned centers of Lingbao Daoism. Traditional accounts of his life include stories of omens surrounding his birth, his healing of Emperor Mingdi (r. 465–473), and dramatic victories over the learned Buddhists of his day in public debates. His most prominent disciple, Sun Youyue, was in turn a teacher of the great Daoist scholar Tao Hongjing, to whom much of Lu's scriptural collection was passed down.

Textual references to the earliest form of the Daoist canon date back to the year 437, when Master Lu signed himself "Disciple of the Three Caverns." These "caverns" (*dong*), evoking traditional beliefs that divine treasures are hidden in caves under the earth, were in fact the collected scriptural revelations of several Daoist groups: the Shangqing (Supreme Purity) scriptures; the Lingbao scriptures; and the Sanhuang (Three Sovereigns) scriptures. *Master Lu's Catalog of the Scriptures of the Three Caverns,* no longer extant but quoted elsewhere, was perhaps the first comprehensive listing of all these texts. Although the notion of three caverns probably did not originate with Master Lu, his early catalog not only served to define what was deemed authentic and Daoist at that time, but may well have established the notion of a single canon common to the various early movements of the emerging tradition.

Master Lu dedicated much of his career to the exposition of the Lingbao scriptures, which were claimed to have been revealed over a hundred years earlier. In fact, they were composed in the late 390s by Ge Chaofu, whose remarkable set of "revelations" not only drew upon Shangqing and Buddhist texts circulating then, but also upon the extensive library of his renowned great-uncle, Ge Hong. The popularity of these scriptures provoked so many forgeries and imitations that some fifty years after their initial release Master Lu undertook the difficult task of identifying and editing the original corpus. His catalog of the Lingbao scriptures, of which only the preface (*Lingbao jingmu xu*) remains extant in the Daoist canon, has recently been reconstructed from documents uncovered at Dunhuang.

Actively extolling the ultimate primacy of these particular scriptures and the effectiveness of Lingbao rites, Master Lu formulated a set of rituals for lay followers, as well as rites for the ordination of Daoist masters and the transmission of sacred scriptures. These liturgical writings helped develop an institutional structure within Daoism by combining Han dynasty (206 BCE–220 CE) court ceremonies with the practices of both the early Celestial Master sect and the old traditions and cults of southern China. Fundamental liturgical practices included the internalization of protective deities within the body of the initiated Daoist (the *daoshi*) and their projection as messengers in the course of the rite; the use of talismans (especially the five Lingbao written talismans) to orient and bind the various levels of heaven, earth, and underworld in each of the five directions (four cardinal points and the center); and the proclamation and burning (to effect their transmission heavenward) of official petitions for such ends as the release of ancestors from the sufferings of the underworld and the protection of the state. Basic to Master Lu's liturgies is a macrocosm-microcosm identity of the extended universe and the internal geography of the body, combined with a bureaucratic mediation of proper relations among spiritual realms. These features served to define a distinctive type of religious authority in the centuries of religious innovation after the fall of the Han dynasty, an authority that was not only formally invested, hierarchical, and stable, but also simultaneously holistic and deeply rooted in the practices of local traditions. The Lingbao liturgies codified by Master Lu were amplified and embellished until the middle of the Song dynasty (960–1279), when there were major changes and innovations in the ritual tradition as a whole. Even today, however, the rites of ordained Daoist masters in Taiwan still contain sections that faithfully preserve the instructions first penned by Master Lu.

SEE ALSO Daoism, article on Daoist Literature; Ge Hong; Tao Hongjing.

BIBLIOGRAPHY

The sources on Lu Xiujing's life and work are detailed in Chen Guofu's *Daozang yuanliu kao* (1949; rev. ed. Beijing, 1963), pp. 38–44. Special studies in Western languages include Ofuchi Ninji's "On *Ku Ling-Pao-Ching,*" *Acta Asiatica* 27 (1974): 33–56, and Max Kaltenmark's "*Ling-pao:* Note sur un terme du taoïsme religieux," *Mélanges publiées par l'Institut des Hautes Études Chinoises* 2 (1960): 559–588. For general background on this period of Daoist history, consult Rolf A. Stein's "Religious Taoism and Popular Religion from the Second to the Seventh Centuries," in *Facets of Taoism,* edited by Holmes Welch and Anna Seidel (New Haven, 1979), pp. 53–81; and Michel Strickmann's "The Mao Shan Revelations: Taoism and the Aristocracy," *T'oung pao* 63 (1977): 1–64.

New Sources

Nickerson, Peter. "Abridged Codes of Master Lu for the Daoist Community." In *Religions of China in Practice,* edited by Donald S. Lopez, Jr., pp. 347–359. Princeton, 1996.

Pregadio, Fabrizion. *The Encyclopedia of Taoism.* Richmond, Va., 2001.

Yamada, Toshiaki. "The Evolution of Taoist Ritual: K'ou Ch'ien-chih and Lu Xiujing." *Acta Asiatica* 68 (1995): 69–83.

CATHERINE M. BELL (1987)
Revised Bibliography

LYCANTHROPY SEE WOLVES

M

MABINOGION. The eleven native prose tales extant in Middle Welsh are known collectively as the *Mabinogion.* This convenient modern title, based on a scribal error in a single medieval manuscript, may convey a false impression of the homogeneity of these stories. Found in two related manuscripts of the fourteenth century, the White Book of Rhydderch and the Red Book of Hergest, they are literary compositions ranging in date from the late eleventh century to the mid-thirteenth century. They are derived, as complete tales or their episodes, from traditional oral narratives, and they bear witness, however imperfectly, to a large body of traditional material (Wel., *cyfarwyddyd),* other relics of which are extant in the collections of triads, the *Stanzas of the Graves,* and other allusions. The sources reflected are diverse—mythological, legendary, and international folkloric. The most clearly mythological are those tales known as the "Four Branches" of the *Mabinogion* (c. 1060–1120).

An attempt has been made to associate *mabinogi* with the name of the youth god Maponos (Wel., Mabon), son of Matrona (Wel., Modron), the mother goddess, and to suggest the meaning "Mabonalia," but the word occurs elsewhere in Middle Welsh meaning "childhood" or "beginnings," and there refers to the deeds of the precocious youthful hero which are portents of his future greatness. An extended meaning may be simply a tale of heroes or, perhaps, of ancestors.

The Four Branches are independent stories linked by cross-references and motivating episodes, but accretions and restructuring over a long period have so complicated the narrative that it is difficult to postulate what the original hero-tale may have been. W. J. Gruffydd's attempt to re-create a heroic biography of one major character, Pryderi, is too ambitious and is based on a misinterpretation of the Old Irish tale-types; Brinley Rees, following Georges Dumézil, offers a scheme of three functions as an original, unifying structure. Contemporary scholarship, however, regards the Four Branches of the Ma-

Clockwise from top left corner. Mayan vase with relief depicting the head of the sun, c. seventh to tenth century. Naturhistorisches Museum, Vienna, Austria. *[©Giraudon/Art Resource, N.Y.]*; Greek vase depicting Circe mixing a magical potion to transform the companions of Odysseus into animals. *[Photograph ©2004 Museum of Fine Arts, Boston]*; Late-nineteenth-century Alaskan Eskimo mask representing the spirit of the moon as a face encompassed by the air (board), the cosmos (hoops), and the stars (feathers). Sheldon Jackson Museum, Sitka, Alaska. *[©Werner Forman/Art Resource, N.Y.]*; Ummayad Mosque in Damascus, Syria. *[©Christine Osborne/Corbis]*; The Abbey of Mont-Saint-Michel, France. *[©Archivo Iconografico, S.A./Corbis]* .

binogi as the work of a single author and looks for an authorial thematic unity which has brought together a numer of disparate narratives.

The First Branch contains the birth-tale of Pryderi, son of Pwyll, lord of Dyfed (in southwestern Wales); Pwyll was known as "head of Annwn" because of his stay in the otherworld in the guise of its king, who had called upon him to help overcome an adversary. Upon his return Pwyll marries Rhiannon and they have a son, but the infant disappears from his crib. The child is subsequently discovered at the court of another nobleman, Teyrnon, some seventy miles distant, when a giant arm is amputated as it attempts to steal a foal on May Eve. There are many inconsistencies and gaps in the narrative, which seems to be a conflation of the motifs of the calumniated wife, the monster hand, and the congenital animals, but presumably it was intended to give an account of the birth of the hero in Annwn or to divine parents. Rhiannon is a Welsh counterpart of *Rigantona, queen-goddess, and is to be compared with Teyrnon, or *Tigernonos, king-god; her name and function are close to those of Matrona, whose son Maponos was taken from his mother's side when three nights old, according to an allusion in the eleventh-century story *Culhwch and Olwen.* She is probably identical with Epona, shown in Gaulish iconography as riding a horse, which recalls Rhiannon's associations with horses. Both Rhiannon and her son Pryderi are abducted in the Third Branch, and his loss is reflected in the wasting of his lordship of Dyfed.

The Third and Fourth Branches are complex narratives, both located in Gwynedd in northwestern Wales. The protagonists of the Fourth Branch are members of the divine family of Dôn (cf. Irish Tuatha Dé Danann)—Gwydion, the magician; Aranrhod, who gave birth to Lleu (cf. Irish Lugh; Gaulish Lugus) and Dylan, who was the son of the Wave and had the nature of a fish; Amaethon, the divine plowman; and Gofannon (cf. Irish Goibhniu), the divine smith. The story relates how Gwydion fashioned a wife from flowers for his nephew Lleu, cursed by his mother never to have a name, arms, or a wife.

The Second Branch describes the tragic result of the marriage of Branwen, daughter of Llŷr, to the Irish king Mathonwy and the devastation caused when her brother Brân, the giant king of Britain, and his brother Manawydan rescue her. *Llŷr* is possibly cognate with the Irish *ler* ("sea"), and there is probably some relationship between the Welsh characters and the Irish Manannán mac Lir and Bran of *The Voyage of Bran,* although the stories in Welsh and Irish do not correspond closely.

The other stories of the *Mabinogion* are briefer and simpler narratives. *Cyfranc Lludd a Llefelys,* first found as an interpolation in a Welsh translation by Geoffrey of Monmouth in his *Historia regum Britanniae* (c. 1200), is an extended triad. It may be a popular version of a mythological account of the winning of Britain by waves of invaders—otherworldly, Roman, and Saxon—or, according to another analysis, its three episodes, about fairy creatures, fighting dragons, and the food thief, reflect the Indo-European tripartite functions of sagacity, warfare, and provision. The *Dream of Maxen* is popular history, an account of the marriage of the Roman emperor Magnus Maximus (r. 383–388) with a British princess and the subsequent foundation of Brittany. *Culhwch and Olwen* (c. 1060) is an extended version of the folk tales *Six Go through the World* and *The Giant's Daughter;* the *Dream of Rhonabwy* (thirteenth century?) is a pastiche of traditions and themes put together as social satire and a parody of literary modes. The three romances, *Geraint, Owain,* and *Peredur,* are related to three romances by the twelfth-century French poet Chrétien de Troyes, although the nature of the interdependence is still problematic. The ultimate sources, however, are Celtic (Welsh or Breton), and they seem to contain examples of the sovereignty myth (better evidenced in Irish) wherein the hero, or king, marries the titular goddess of his land, thereby ensuring its fruitfulness. In the extant versions the significance of the myth has been lost, and little of its primitive value remained for either authors or audiences.

Bibliography

All these stories are translated into English in Gwyn Jones and Thomas Jones's *The Mabinogion* (London, 1993). Patrick K. Ford translates seven of them and discusses their possible mythological bases in *The Mabinogi and Other Medieval Welsh Tales* (Berkeley, 1977). Proinsias Mac Cana's *Celtic Mythology* (London, 1983) is an excellent introduction to the broader mythological themes, while Rachel Bromwich, *Trioedd Ynys Prydein: The Welsh Triads,* 2d ed. (Cardiff, 1978) discusses many of the characters of Welsh myth and legend. W. J. Gruffydd's *Math vab Mathonwy* (Cardiff, 1928) and *Rhiannon* (Cardiff, 1953) were pioneer studies of the structure of the Four Branches but need to be used with care; Brinley Rees, *Ceinciau'r Mabinogi* (1975; Llandysul, 1999) is an interesting Dumézilian study. Proinsias Mac Cana, *The Mabinogi* (Cardiff, 1992) and Sioned Davies, *The Four Branches of the Mabinogi* (Llandysul, 1993) cover a number of topics. Other useful studies of the narrative tradition are: Kenneth Jackson, *The International Popular Tale and Early Welsh Tradition* (Cardiff, 1961), W. J. Gruffydd, *Folklore and Myth in the Mabinogion* (Cardiff, 1958), J. K. Bollard, "The Role of Myth and Tradition in the Four Branches of the Mabinogi," *Cambridge Medieval Celtic Studies* 6 (1983): 67–86, Andrew Welsh, "The Traditional Narrative Motifs of the Four Branches of the Mabinogi," *Cambridge Medieval Celtic Studies* 15 (1988): 51–62, Juliette Wood, "The Calumniated Wife in Medieval Welsh Literature," *Cambridge Medieval Celtic Studies* 10 (1985): 25–38, P. K.Ford, "Prolegomena to a Reading of the *Mabinogi*: 'Pwyll' and 'Manawydan,'" *Studia Celtica* 16/17 (1981–1982): 110–25, Georges Dumézil, "La quatrième branche du Mabinogi et la thèologie des trois functions," *Rencontres des religions* (Paris, 1986): 25–38. For mythological themes in *Cyfranc Lludd a Llefelys* see the edition by Brynley F.Roberts (Dublin, 1975), Georges Dumézil, "Triades de calamités et triades de délits a valeur trifonctionelle chez divers peuples indo-européens," *Latomus* 14 (1955): 173–185.

BRYNLEY F. ROBERTS (1987 AND 2005)

MACUMBA SEE AFRO-BRAZILIAN RELIGIONS

MADHHAB. For lack of a better term, "legal school" is the most acceptable translation of *madhhab*, and it is preferable to both "sect" and "rite," terms which have been used in earlier works. A legal school implies a body of doctrine taught by a leader, or imam, and followed by the members of that school. The imam must be a leading *mujtahid*, one who is capable of exercising independent judgment. In his teaching, the imam must apply methods and principles which are peculiar to his own school independent of others. A *madhhab* must also have followers who assist their leader in the elaboration and dissimination of his teachings. A *madhhab* does not imply, however, a definite organization, a formal teaching, or an official status, nor is there a strict uniformity of doctrine within each *madhhab*. The membership of the present-day *madhhabs* is ascertainable on the basis of both individual confession and a loosely defined association of a country or a group to a particular *madhhab*. Legal school is a fitting description of *madhhab* simply because law is the main area in which the schools have widely disagreed. Their differences on the principles of the faith, at least among the Sunnī schools, are negligible. But disagreement on subsidiary matters (*furūʿ*) extends to almost every subject.

THE EARLIEST SCHOOLS. The first major split occurred between the Sunnī and the Shīʿī schools of law barely three decades after the death of the Prophet, about 660 CE. The secession of the Shīʿah from the main body of the Muslims, the Sunnīs, took place on political grounds, owing mainly to their differences on the nature and devolution of political authority. The Sunnīs accepted as legitimate the leadership of the four "Rightly Guided" caliphs, the Khulafāʾ Rashidun. But the Shīʿah claimed that ʿAlī, the fourth caliph and the cousin and son-in-law of the Prophet, had a superior claim to leadership over any of his three predecessors, hence their name, the Shīʿah ("party") of ʿAlī.

The bitter controversies which arose in the early period of Islam led to the formation of numerous groupings. The range of contested issues must have been extremely diverse: some five hundred schools are said to have disappeared at or about the beginning of the third Muslim century (ninth century CE). But even then the schools had not yet settled down to the number they are now. The real formation of Islamic law starts, at the hands of individual jurists, in the latter part of the first century AH (seventh century CE). This period is followed in the early second/eighth century by the emergence of two geographical centers of juristic activity in the Hejaz and Iraq. Each of these was further divided into two centers: Mecca and Medina in the Hejaz, and Basra and Kufa in Iraq. Of these four centers, usually referred to as the ancient schools of law, Medina and Kufa were the most important. With their further development in the latter half of the second century, geographical schools gave way to personal schools, named after an individual master whom the members of the school followed.

The ancient schools of law adopted two different approaches to jurisprudence. The jurists of Mecca and Medina, cities where the Prophet had lived and Islam had its origin and early development, laid emphasis on tradition as their standard for legal decisions. They thus acquired the name *ahl al-ḥadīth*, or "partisans of tradition." Being away from the Hejaz and culturally more advanced, the Iraqi schools, on the other hand, resorted more readily to personal opinion (*raʾy*), which is why they acquired the name *ahl al-raʾy*, or "partisans of opinion." This group had a tendency to imagine hypothetical cases in order to determine their legal solutions. They had a flair for scholasticism and technical subtlety. The *ahl al-ḥadīth*, on the other hand, were averse to abstract speculation; they were more pragmatic and concerned themselves with concrete cases. Abū Ḥanīfah was the leading figure of the Iraqi school, whereas Mālik, and after him al-Shāfiʿī, led the Hejazi school of legal thought.

THE ḤANAFĪYAH. The founder of the Ḥanafī school, Abū Ḥanīfah Nuʿmān ibn Thābit (d. 767), was born in Kufa, where he studied jurisprudence with Ibrāhīm al-Nakhaʿī and Ḥammād ibn Abī Sulaymān. He delivered lectures to a small circle of students who later compiled and elaborated his teaching. *Qiyās*, or analogical reasoning, which became one of the four sources of law, receives the greatest support from Abū Ḥanīfah. Because of this, and his extensive use of *raʾy*, Abū Ḥanīfah was criticized by the traditionists for emphasizing speculative opinion at the cost of the *ḥadīth*. Abū Ḥanīfah has left no work except a small volume on dogmatics, *Al-fiqh al-akbar* (The greater understanding). His teachings were documented and compiled mainly by two of his disciples, Abū Yūsuf and al-Shaybānī. The Ḥanafī school was favored by the ruling Abbasid dynasty. Abū Yūsuf, who became the chief justice of the caliph Hārūn al-Rashīd (r. 786–809), composed, at Hārūn's request, a treatise on fiscal and public law, the *Kitāb al-kharāj*.

Muḥammad ibn Ḥasan al-Shaybānī, a disciple of both Abū Ḥanīfah and Abū Yūsuf, compiled the *corpus juris* of the Ḥanafī school. Six of his juristic works, collectively called the *Ẓāhir al-rawāyah*, or works devoted to principal matters, became the basis of many future works on jurisprudence. All of the six works were later compiled in one volume entitled *Al-kāfī* (The concise), by al-Marwazī, better known as al-Ḥākim al-Shahid (d. 965). This was subsequently annotated by Shams al-Din al-Sarakhsi in thirty volumes, entitled *Al-mabsūṭt* (The comprehensive). Ḥanafī law is the most humanitarian of all the schools concerning the treatment of non-Muslims and war captives, and its penal law is considered to be more lenient.

The Ḥanafīyah has the largest following of all the schools, owing to its official adoption by the Ottoman Turks in the early sixteenth century. It is now predominant in Turkey, Syria, Jordan, Lebanon, Pakistan, Afghanistan, and among the Muslims of India, and its adherents constitute about one-third of the Muslims of the world.

THE MĀLIKĪYAH. The Mālikī school was founded by Mālik ibn Anas al-Aṣbaḥī (d. 795), who spent his entire life in Medina except for a brief pilgrimage to Mecca. He served as an official jurisconsult *(muftī)*, which may explain why he broke away from the casuistic practices of his predecessors and attempted to formulate the principles underlying the tradition, to which he devoted his famous work, *Al-muwaṭṭaʾ* (The leveled path). Mālik is distinguished by the fact that he added another source of law to those known to other schools, namely the practice of the Medinese (*ʿamal ahl Madīnah*). Since the Medinese followed each generation immediately preceding them, the process would have gone back to the generation that was in contact with the teachings and actions of the Prophet. In Mālik's opinion, the practice of the Medinese thus constitutes basic legal evidence. This pragmatic feature of Mālik's doctrine has been retained to the present in the legal practice (*ʿamal)* of the Maghreb, which takes more notice than other schools of the prevailing conditions and customs. (Islamic law in general does not recognize custom as a source of law although it may validly operate in a subsidiary capacity.) The major reference book of the Mālikī school is *Al-mudawwanah* (The enactment), compiled by Asad al-Furāt, and later edited and arranged by Saḥnūn, who published it under the name *Al-mudawwanah al-kubrā* (The greater enactment). The Mālikī school is currently predominant in Morocco, Algeria, Tunisia, Upper Egypt, the Sudan, Bahrain, and Kuwait.

THE SHĀFIʿĪYAH. The third major surviving school is called the Shāfiʿīyah, after its founder, Muḥammad ibn Idrīs al-Shāfiʿi (d. 819). A pupil of Mālik, he formulated the classical theory of jurisprudence in the form that it has largely retained ever since. This theory teaches that Islamic law is based on four basic principles, or roots, of jurisprudence (*uṣūl al-fiqh*): the word of God in the Qurʾān, the divinely inspired conduct or *sunnah* of the Prophet, consensus of opinion (*ijmāʿ*), and reasoning by analogy (*qiyās*). Al-Shāfiʿi studied the works of his predecessors and found that despite the existence of traditions from the Prophet, the early jurists occasionally preferred the opinion of the companions, or ignored traditions when they were contrary to local practice. Insisting on the overriding authority of tradition, al-Shāfiʿi said that authentic traditions must always be accepted. Whereas Abū Ḥanīfah and Mālik felt free to set aside a tradition when it conflicted with the Qurʾān, for al-Shāfiʿi a tradition could not be invalidated on this ground: he took it for granted that the Qurʾān and tradition did not contradict each other.

Al-Shāfiʿi also differed with both Abū Ḥanīfah and Mālik on the meaning of *ijmāʿ*. To al-Shāfiʿi's predecessors *ijmāʿ* meant the consensus of the scholars, but al-Shāfiʿi denied the existence of any such consensus. There could only be one valid consensus—that of the entire Muslim community. He thus restricted the scope of *ijmāʿ* to obligatory duties, such as the daily prayer, on which such a consensus could be said to exist. But the legal theory which prevailed after al-Shāfiʿi returned to the concept of the consensus of the scholars, when it considers infallible in the same way as the general consensus of the Muslims.

Al-Shāfiʿi essentially restricted the sources of law to the Qurʾān and the *sunnah*. Should there be no provision in these sources for a particular case, then the solution must be found through the application of analogy, which basically entails extending the logic of the Qurʾān and the *sunnah*. Any expression of opinion which is not related to these sources is arbitrary and excessive. Al-Shāfiʿi thus restricted the scope of *ijtihād* (independent reasoning) by subjecting it to the requirements of strict analogical reasoning; hence he considers *ijtihād* and *qiyās* synonymous.

Al-Shāfiʿi has left many works, of which the most important on jurisprudence are the *Risālah* (Letter) and the seven-volume *Kitāb al-umm* (The book of essentials). The Shāfiʿi school is now prevalent in Lower Egypt, southern Arabia, East Africa, Indonesia, and Malaysia and has many followers in Palestine, Jordan, and Syria.

THE ḤANĀBILAH. Even al-Shāfiʿi's degree of emphasis on tradition did not satisfy the uncompromising traditionists, who preferred not to use any human reasoning in law and chose, as much as possible, to base their doctrine on the Qurʾān and the *ḥadīth*. This was the avowed purpose of the two new schools which emerged in the third century AH (ninth century CE). The first and the only successful one of these was the Ḥanbalī school, founded by Aḥmad ibn Ḥanbal (d. 855), the orthodox opponent of the rationalists and the *ahl al-raʾy* (the other was the Ẓāhirī school of Dāwūd al-Ẓāhirī which is now extinct). Ibn Ḥanbal's reliance on tradition was so total that for some time he and his adherents were regarded not as real jurists (*fuqahāʾ*) but as mere traditionists. His main work, *Al-musnad* (The verified), is a collection of some twenty-eight thousand traditions. He uses *qiyās* very little and draws mainly on the sacred texts. Ibn Ḥanbal's teaching was later refined and developed by his disciples and commanded a widespread following, but in spite of a series of brilliant scholars and representatives over the centuries, the numbers suffered a continuous diminution after the fourteenth century CE. In the eighteenth century, the Wahhābīyah, the puritanical movement in the Arabian Peninsula, derived their doctrine and inspiration from the Ḥanābilah as it had been expressed by the celebrated jurist and theologian Ibn Taymīyah (d. 1328).

Ironically, the Ḥanābilah are in some respects more liberal than the other schools. Ḥanbalī law, for example, adopts the doctrine of *ibāḥah* (lit., "permissibility") on matters which are not expressly prohibited by law. It presumes that the validity of acts and transactions is overruled only by the existence of proof to the contrary. For example, only Ḥanbalī law would allow the stipulation of a clause in a marriage contract to prevent the husband from entering into a polygamous contract in the future. While the other schools regard this as interference with the *sharīʿah*, Ḥanbalī law maintains that the basic purpose of the law is fulfilled by monogamy; since polygamy is merely permitted by the law, it may be validly restricted in this manner. Other examples of this nature that may be cited include Ibn Qayyim al-Jawzīyah's validation of one witness of just character as legal proof, and his approval of the acts of a bona fide catalyst (*fuḍūlī*), both of which the other schools have rejected. The Ḥanbalī school is currently predominant in Saudi Arabia, Qatar, and Oman.

SHĪʿĪ SCHOOLS. In Sunnī law, the head of state, or caliph, is to be elected to office, and his main duty is to supervise the proper implementation of the *sharīʿah*, the divine law of Islam. Shīʿī law, on the other hand, maintains that leadership, the imamate, belongs to the descendants of ʿAlī through hereditary succession. Of the numerous Shīʿī schools, only three have survived to this day: Ithnā ʿAsharī (Twelver), Zaydī, and Ismāʿīlī. The differences among these groups stem from their divergence over the line of succession after the fourth imam. The Twelvers, who are the largest of the three groups, recognize twelve imams, hence their name, Ithnā ʿAsharīyah, or Twelvers, as opposed to the Ismāʿīlīyah, who are also called Sabʿīyah, or Seveners, because they differed with the other Shīʿī groups over the identity of the seventh imam. According to Twelver dogma, the twelfth imam, the imam of the age, who disappeared in 873 CE, will reappear to establish the rule of justice on earth.

For the Sunnīs, divine revelation, manifested in the Qurʾān and the *sunnah*, ceased with the death of the Prophet. For the Shīʿāh, however, divine revelation continued to be transmitted, after the death of the Prophet, to the line of their recognized imams. Accordingly, they maintain that in addition to the Qurʾān and the *sunnah*, the pronouncements of their imams, whom they believe infallible (*maʿṣūm*), constitute divine revelation and therefore binding law. The Shīʿāh, moreover, accept only those traditions whose chain of authority (*isnād*) goes back to one of their recognized imams; they also have their own *ḥadīth* collections. Since the imam is divinely inspired, the Shīʿāh basically do not recognize *ijmāʿ*. Twelver doctrine, however, permits *ijmāʿ* as interpretation of the command of the imams on a particular question by the jurist *(mujtahid)*. The Twelvers are divided into two branches, the Akhbārī and the Uṣūlī. The Akhbarīyah do not recognize *qiyās*, but the Uṣūlīyah do. Shīʿī law, which mainly originates in the teaching of the sixth imam, Jaʿfar al-Ṣādiq (d. 765) bears similarity to Shāfiʿī law but differs with it on many issues. Temporary marriage, or *mutʿah*, for example, is valid only in Shīʿī law. The Shīʿī law of inheritance is also very different from the law of any other school in this field. Twelver doctrine was officially adopted in Persia under the Safavids in 1501; it still commands the largest following in Iran, and it has also followers in Iraq, Lebanon, and Syria.

According to the Ismāʿīlī dogma, the esoteric meaning of the Qurʾān and its allegorical interpretation is known only to the imam, whose knowledge and guidance is indispensible to salvation. The Ismāʿīlīyah are divided into two groups, eastern and western. The former are centered in India, Pakistan, and Central Asia, and their leader is the present Aga Khan, forty-ninth imam in the line of succession. The Western Ismāʿīlīyah followed al-Mustaʿlī, the ninth Fatimid caliph. This line went to the twenty-first imam, al-Ṭayyib, but he became *mastūr* (occult). This group resides in southern Arabia and Syria.

The Zaydīyah follow Zayd ibn ʿAlī, the fifth imam in the order of the Shīʿī imams. They endorse the legitimacy of the caliphs who preceded ʿAlī on the belief that an acceptable leader has a legitimate title notwithstanding the existence of a superior claimant. Their legal doctrine is the nearest of the Shīʿī schools to the Sunnīs, and they mainly reside in the Yemen.

CONSENSUS AND DIVERGENCE AMONG THE SCHOOLS. To summarize, disagreement among jurists is basically a consequence of the freedom of *ijtihād* which they enjoyed, particularly in the first three centuries of Islam. They have differed mainly in four areas: interpretation of the Qurʾān, acceptance and interpretation of the *ḥadīth*, rationalist doctrines, and subsidiary matters. Concerning the Qurʾān, the jurists have disagreed over the abrogation (*naskh*) of some of the Qurʾanic verses by others where two verses provide divergent rulings on the same subject, or when the *ḥadīth* overrules a Qurʾanic verse. While al-Shāfiʿī's doctrine of *naskh* is based on the rule that the Qurʾān can only be abrogated by the Qurʾān and *sunnah* only by *sunnah*, the other three schools add that the Qurʾān and the *sunnah* may also abrogate one another.

The words of the Qurʾān are divided into general (*ʿāmm*) and specific (*khāṣṣ*). The jurists have disagreed regarding the meaning and implications of such words. For example, X is unable to pay his debt. His brother Y pays it while acting on his own initiative and out of good will. The question arises as to whether Y, who is called *fuḍūlī*, or catalyst, is entitled to claim his money back from X. Mālikī and Ḥanbalī law answer this question in the affirmative on the authority of surah 55:60 of the Qurʾān: "Is the reward of goodness (*iḥsān*) aught but goodness?" But for the Ḥanafīyah and Shāfiʿīyah the words of this verse are too general to be applied to the case in question; hence they deny the *fuḍūlī* the right to a repayment.

The scope of disagreement concerning the *sunnah* is even wider, for in this area differences extend not only to the interpretation of *ḥadīth* but also to its authenticity. Whereas the Ḥanafīyah, and to some extent the Shāfiʿīyah, apply strict rules to verify the authenticity of *ḥadīth*, the Mālikīyah and Ḥanābilah are relatively uncritical. Al-Shāfiʿi and Ibn

Ḥanbal, for example, accept a solitary (*aḥād*) tradition, one which is reported by a single narrator, but Abū Ḥanīfah and Mālik accept it only under certain conditions. The jurists have also applied different rules to cases of conflict and abrogation between traditions. Whereas the majority would not, for example, allow the abrogation of a *mutawātir* (a tradition reported by numerous narrators) by an *aḥād*, the Ḥanafīyah permit this in principle.

Disagreement over rationalist doctrines such as *ra'y*, consensus, analogy, and *ijtihād* has already been discussed. It may be added here that Ḥanafī law applies *istiḥsān*, or juristic preference, as a doctrine of equity where strict implementation of analogy leads to hardships and undesirable results. The Mālikī school, however, adopts *istiṣlāḥ* (regard for the public interest), which is essentially similar to *istiḥsān*, albeit with some difference of detail. Al-Shāfiʿī rejects both *istiḥsān* and *istiṣlāḥ*, which he considers as no more than frivolous and arbitrary interference with the *sharīʿah*. Alternately, the Shāfiʿīyah, the Ḥanābilah, and the Twelver Shīʿah adopt *istiṣḥāb*, or deduction by presumption of continuity. *Istiṣḥāb*, for example, assumes freedom from liability to be a natural state until the contrary is proved.

Differences of *ijtihād* concerning subsidiary matters need not be elaborated, as the abundance of legal doctrines and schools within the *sharīʿah* is indicative of such diversity. By the beginning of the fourth century AH there was a consensus established to the effect that all essential issues had been thoroughly discussed and finally settled. With this "closing of the door of *ijtihād*," as it was called, *ijtihad* gave way to *taqlīd*, or "imitation." From then on every Muslim was an imitator *(muqallid)* who had to belong to one of the recognized schools. By consensus also the four schools were accepted, and accepted one another, as equally orthodox. Notwithstanding the emergence of prominent scholars in later centuries (including Ibn Taymīyah and Ibn Qayyim al-Jawzīyah) who objected to *taqlīd*, no one actually provided an independent interpretation of the *sharīʿah*. *Taqlīd* remained a dominant practice for about a thousand years until the reform movements of the late nineteenth century (notably the Salafīyah, whose prominent figure is Muḥammad ʿAbduh) and the modernist school of thought in the present century which challenged *taqlīd* and called for a return to *ijtihād*.

A Muslim may join any orthodox school he or she wishes, or change from one school to another, without formalities. Furthermore, Islamic countries have made frequent use of divergent opinions of other schools, including Shīʿī legal doctrines, in modern legislation. In order to achieve desired results, modern reformers have utilized procedural expedients permitted in the *sharīʿah*, such as *takhayyur* and *talfīq*. *Takhayyur*, or "selection," enables the jurist to adopt from the various interpretations of the *sharīʿah* that which is deemed to be most suitable. Reformers in the area of personal status, for example, have frequently adopted a variant doctrine of a recognized school as the basis of reform. Sometimes the view of an early jurist outside the established schools has been so selected. Furthermore, legal rules have been occasionally constructed by combining part of the doctrine of one school or jurist with part of the doctrine of another school or jurist. This variation of *takhayyur* is known as *talfīq*, or "patching," a procedure which has been employed in the modern laws of the Middle East. (For interesting illustrations and details on these procedural devices see Coulson's *A History of Islamic Law*.)

SEE ALSO Abū Ḥanīfah; Abū Yūsuf; Ḥadīth; Ḥanābilah; Ibn Taymīyah; Ijmāʿ; Ijtihād; Islamic Law; Mālik ibn Anas; Qiyās; Shāfiʿi, al-; Sunnah; Uṣūl al-Fiqh.

BIBLIOGRAPHY

A useful biography of the well-known Sunnī and Shīʿī Jurists of early Islam, including the founders of the schools and their doctrines, can be found in Muhammad al-Khuḍarī's *Ta'rīkh a-ltashrīʿ al-islāmī*, 4th ed. (Cairo, 1934). Subhī Rajab Mahmassani's *Falsafat al-tarshrīʿ fī al-Islām: The Philosophy of Jurisprudence in Islam*, translated by Farhat J. Ziadeh (Leiden, 1961), contains more condensed information on both the Sunnī and Shīʿī *madhhabs*. This book also provides a useful bibliography of Arabic works on the subject. An accurate exposition of the roots of jurisprudence (*uṣūl al-figh*) in the Sunnī schools can be found in Muhammad Ma'ruf al-Dawalibi's *Al-madkhal ila 'ilm usul al-figh*, 5th ed. (Cairo, 1965). Noel J. Coulson's *A History of Islamic Law* (1964; reprint, Edinburgh, 1971) and Joseph Schacht's *An Introduction to Islamic Law* (Oxford, 1964) remain the best English works on the jurisprudence and history of the Sunnī *madhhabs*. There is also much useful information, and a bibliography, on the subject in Nicolas P. Aghnides's *Muhammadan Theories of Finance* (New York,1916). And finally, Ignázc Goldziher's *Introduction to Islamic Theology and Law*, translated by Andreas Hamori and Ruth Hamori (Princeton, 1981), is comprehensive on the Shīʿī *madhhabs* and their theological doctrines.

M. HASHIM KAMALI (1987)

MADHVA (1238–1317), also known as Anandatīrtha or Pūrnaprajñā; founder of the Dvaita Vedānta school of Indian philosophy. Born in Pajakakṣetra near Udipi in the Tulu country of the Indian state of Karnataka, Madhva attracted attention as a young renunciate by his prodigious abilities in reciting, interpreting, and criticizing scriptural and exegetical texts. Gathering pupils at his classes in Udipi, he made numerous trips throughout India accompanied by his disciples, including at least two visits to Badrinath in the Himalayas. It is believed that he debated a number of prominent scholars during his lifetime.

Madhva established his main temple, consecrated to the god Kṛṣṇa, at Udipi, and installed in it the idol of Bāla Kṛṣṇa secured from Dwarka. The temple has flourished to this day in the charge of a steady line of successors stemming from Madhva and his disciples. Tradition holds that in the year 1317, in the middle of delivering a lecture, Madhva vanished and retired permanently to Badrinath.

Madhva is credited with some thirty-seven works, including commentaries on the *Bhagavadgītā,* the *Brahma Sūtras,* and ten of the older Upaniṣads; ten independent treatises on Dvaita philosophy; short commentaries on the *Bhāgavata Purāṇa,* the *Mahābhārata,* and part of the *Ṛgveda;* and a number of other brief works of a varied nature. Many of these treatises were subsequently commented upon by Jayatīrtha, Vyāsatīrtha, and other famous Dvaitins; the resulting large body of literature forms the basis of Dvaita Vedānta.

Dvaita stands in strong contrast to Śaṅkara's Advaita system in its conception of *brahman* as a personal God, independent of all other things and different from them. Madhva's God, who is Viṣṇu, possesses transcendent attributes of creation, preservation, dissolution, control, enlightenment, obscuration, bondage, and release, and God himself is considered the cause of all causes productive of these results. Each individual self is by nature a reflection of God; however, no one is aware of this until, through study of the scriptures, he comes to understand his real nature, upon which he undertakes fervent devotion to the Lord, who responds by bestowing his grace upon the devotee according to the latter's capacity. The devotee then abides in a state of servitude to God forever, and this state constitutes his liberation.

Dvaita Vedānta is also known for its sophisticated analyses of matters pertaining to logic, epistemology, and metaphysics; many of these investigations were first raised in Madhva's writings.

The influence of Dvaita Vedānta has been felt throughout India, but most profoundly in the South. It has been claimed by some scholars that the direct influence of Madhva's thought played a part in the later development of Bengali Vaiṣṇavism. Certainly, later Dvaita writers were among the most formidable opponents of Advaita Vedānta, and these doctrinal differences led to the famous controversy between Vyāsatīrtha (1478–1539), the Dvaitin author of the *Nyāyāmṛta,* and Madhusūdana Sarasvatī (c. 1540–1600), author of the *Advaitasiddhi,* an extensive response to the *Nyāyāmṛta* and the most celebrated later work of Advaita polemics.

SEE ALSO Vedānta.

BIBLIOGRAPHY

A good overall introduction to the thought of Madhva is B. N. K. Sharma's *A History of the Dvaita School of Vedānta and Its Literature,* 2d rev. ed., 2 vols. (Bombay, 1981).

KARL H. POTTER (1987)

MĀDHYAMIKA.

The Mādhyamika, or Madhyamaka, school is one of the four great schools of Indian Buddhism, along with the Sarvāstivāda, Sautrāntika, and Yogācāra (Vijñānavāda) traditions. The name Mādhyamika ("one who follows the middle way") is derived from the word *madhyamaka,* found in the title *Madhyamakakārikā,* perhaps the most important work of Nāgārjuna, the founder of the school. The school is referred to as Dbu ma pa ("the school of the middle") in Tibet, San-lun-tsung ("the three-treatises school") in China, and Sanronshū ("the three-treatises school") in Japan. Historically, Indian Mādhyamika may be divided into three stages, early, middle, and late.

THE EARLY PERIOD. This period is marked by two great figures, Nāgārjuna and Āryadeva, and a lesser one, Rāhulabhadra. Nāgārjuna (c. 150–250 CE), born in South India, was the author of a number of works variously extant in Sanskrit, Tibetan, and/or Chinese (as subsequently indicated by the parenthetical abbreviations S, T, and C). He was associated with a king of the Śātavāhana dynasty, as is seen from his works, the *Ratnāvalī* (S partially, T) and the *Suhṛllekha* (T), both consisting of admonitions, moral as well as religious, given to the king. His main works comprise five philosophical treatises: the *Madhyamakakārikā* (S, T, C), the *Yuktiṣaṣṭikā* (T), and the *Śūnyatāsaptati* (T), all of which are written in verse and develop the philosophy of *śūnyatā* ("emptiness"); and the *Vigrahavyāvartanī* (S, T, C) and the *Vaidalyasūtra* (T), written in verse and in aphorisms, respectively, both of which are accompanied by autocommentaries in prose. The last two contain Nāgārjuna's criticism of the rules governing traditional Indian logic, especially those of the Naiyāyika. Another genuine work of Nāgārjuna's is, without doubt, the *Pratītyasamutpādahṛdaya* (S partially, T, C), as well as the autocommentary (*Pratītyasamutpādahṛdayavyākhyāna,* S partially, T, C). In this last work, consisting of seven verses and a commentary in prose, the course of transmigration of sentient beings owing to defilements, deeds, and suffering is explained in the light of the theory of twelve-membered dependent co-origination. At the same time, however, the text emphasizes that because everything is devoid of own being or essential nature there is actually no one who moves from this world to another. Many other works are traditionally ascribed to Nāgārjuna; some, for example, the *Mahāprajñāpāramitopadeśa* (Chin., *Ta chih-tu lun,* extant only in Chinese), have influenced the development of Buddhist exegetics, and some, for example, the *Daśabhūmikavibhāṣā* (C), that of Pure Land Buddhism in China and Japan. However, nothing definite can be said as to the authenticity of authorship of these works.

The philosophy of emptiness is found in such early Buddhist *sūtras* as the *Ti-i-i-kung ching* (T. D. 2.92c) and the *Aggi-Vacchagotta Suttanta* (*Majjhima Nikāya,* no. 72) and thus did not originate with Nāgārjuna, who declared that he revived the true teaching of the Buddha. However, Nāgārjuna also relied heavily on the Prajñāpāramitā Sūtras, the *Daśabhūmika Sūtra,* and the *Kāśyapaparivarta* in forming his philosophy. His philosophy of emptiness was a criticism of Indian realism, which was represented by Indian philosophical systems of the Sāṃkhya, the Vaiśeṣika, and the Naiyāyika, and by such Hīnayāna Buddhists as the Sarvāstivādas and other Abhidharma philosophers, who believed that human ideas, insofar as they are rational, have substances that correspond to them in the external world.

In speaking of emptiness Nāgārjuna meant to say not that nothing exists but that everything is empty of *svabhāva* ("own being"), that is, of an independent, eternal, and unchanging substance. All things are, like images in a dream or an illusion, neither substantially existent nor nonexistent absolutely. Nāgārjuna's negation of a self-dependent substance, which he holds to be nothing but a hypostatized concept or word, is derived from the traditional Buddhist idea of dependent origination (*pratītya-samutpāda*), the idea that whatever exists arises and exists dependent on other things. Nāgārjuna, however, introduces into that theory the concept of mutual dependency. Just as the terms *long* and *short* take on meaning only in relation to each other and are themselves devoid of independent qualities (longness or shortness), so too do all phenomena (all *dharmas*) lack own being (*svabhāva*). If a thing were to have an independent and unchanging own being, then it would follow that it is neither produced nor existent, because origination and existence presuppose change and transiency. All things, physical as well as mental, can originate and develop only when they are empty of own being. This idea of emptiness necessitates the truth of nonduality. *Saṃsāra* and *nirvāṇa* (defilements and liberation), like any other pair of contradictions, are nondual because both members of the pair are empty of own being.

Āryadeva (c. 170–270), a direct disciple of Nāgārjuna, was also active in South India. He wrote three works: the *Catuhsataka*, his main work (S fragment, T, C latter half only); the *Satasastra* (C), which has been studied throughout China and Japan; and the *Aksarasataka* (T, C), a small work consisting of a hundred words and his autocommentary. Āryadeva inherited Nāgārjuna's philosophy. Nothing is known about Rāhulabhadra except that he left two hymns, the *Prajñāpāramitāstotra* and the *Saddharmapuṇ-ḍarīkastotra*, and a few fragmentary verses quoted in the Chinese texts.

THE MIDDLE PERIOD. Tradition reports that eight Indian scholars wrote commentaries on the *Madhyamakakārikā:* Nāgārjuna himself (*Akutobhayā*, T); Buddhapālita (c. 470–540; *Buddhapālita-Mūlamadhyamakavṛtti*, T); Candrakīrti (c. 600–650; *Prasannapadā*, S, T); Devaśarman (fifth to six centuries; *Dkar po 'char ba*, T fragment); Guṇaśri (fifth to sixth centuries; title unknown); Guṇamati (fifth to sixth centuries; title unknown, T fragment); Sthiramati (c. 510–570; *Ta-sheng chung-kuan shih-lun*, C); and Bhavya (also known as Bhāvaviveka; c. 500–570; *Prajñāpradipa*, T, C).

The *Akutobhayā* is partially identical with Buddhapālita's commentary, and its authenticity is doubtful. Two fragments from Devaśarman's commentary are cited with appreciation by Bhāvaviveka. A fragment from Guṇamati's commentary is criticized by Bhāvaviveka. The works of Devaśarman and Guṇamati are not extant. Nothing is known about Guṇaśri or his work. The fact that Guṇamati and Sthiramati, both well-known Yogācārins, commented on the *Madhyamakakārikā* shows that Nāgārjuna was revered not only by Mādhyamikas but also by philosophers of other schools. In addition, there is Ch'ing-mu's commentary extant in Kumārajīva's Chinese translation. The *Shun-chung lun* (C) by Asaṅga (c. 320–400), another Yogācārin, is a general interpretation of Nāgārjuna's verse of salutation found at the very beginning of the *Madhyamakakārikā.*

The middle period is characterized by the split of the Mādhyamika into two subschools, the Prāsaṅgika, represented by Buddhapālita and Candrakīrti, and the Svātantrika, represented by Bhāvaviveka and Avalokitavrata. The names Prāsaṅgika and Svātantrika are not attested to in any Sanskrit texts and thus were probably coined by later Tibetan doxographers. However, the names so appropriately describe the tenets of the two subschools that they are widely used even by modern scholars.

In his arguments Nāgārjuna often used dilemmas and tetralemmas. In *Madhyamakakārikā* 1.1, for instance, he states that things produced from themselves, from others, from both themselves and others, or from no cause at all can be found nowhere. Buddhapālita, the founder of the Prāsaṅgika school, divided this tetralemma into four different *prasaṅga* arguments, or arguments *reductio ad absurdum.* He pointed out that (1) production of a thing from itself would be quite useless because, having own being, the thing would already exist and such production would thus involve the logical fault of overextension (*ati prasaṅga*), for a thing already existing by own being would, under this assumption, never cease being produced; (2) if things are produced from another, all things could be produced from all other things; (3) if things are produced from both themselves and another, the faults attached to the two preceding alternatives would combine in this third one; and (4) if things are produced from no cause, all things would be produced always and from all things.

Nāgārjuna himself used *prasaṅga* as often as dilemmas and tetralemmas, but Buddhapālita, analyzing even dilemmas and tetralemmas into plural *prasaṅgas*, considered the latter to be the main method of Mādhyamika argumentation. As a form of argument, *prasaṅga* had been known among logicians since the time of the *Nyāya Sūtra* (codified in the third century) under the name *tarka.* In the eighth century it was formalized by Buddhist logicians into a syllogistic form under the name *prasaṅga-anumāna* ("inference by *prasaṅga*"). If, for example, seeing smoke on a mountain, we want to prove the existence of fire to someone who objects by denying the existence of fire there, we can argue that if there were no fire on the mountain, there would be no smoke there either. At the same time we would be pointing out the fact that smoke is actually rising on the mountain. This form of argument is known as *pra-sanga*, the essence of which is to indicate that an absurd conclusion would follow, given the opponent's claim. The above example can be put into the following categorical syllogism: wherever there is smoke, there is fire (*p*); that mountain has smoke (*q*); therefore, that mountain has fire (*r*). This syllogism (*pq? r*) can be transformed into the following *prasaṅga-anumāna* (*p* ~*r*? *q*): wherever there is no fire, there is no smoke (the contraposition of *p*); (if) the mountain has no fire (~*r*), (it would follow that) the mountain has no smoke (~*q*), which is contrary to fact. Likewise, Buddhapālita's *prasaṅga* may be written: production of things from themselves is useless (*p*); (if) this thing is produced from itself (~*r*), then (it would follow that) its production is useless (~*q*). These examples of *prasaṅga-anumāna* are hypothetical syllogisms because the minor premise (~*r*) is hypothesized by the advocator and only claimed by the opponent and because the conclusion (~*q*), necessarily following from the two premises, is false.

Bhāvaviveka criticized Buddhapālita, saying that his argument was a mere *prasaṅga*, lacking both a true probans (i.e., minor premise) and an example (i.e., major premise). Furthermore, Buddhapālita may be understood to maintain a counterposition to the probans as well as to the example because of the nature of *prasaṅga*. This is to say, Buddhapālita's own opinion would be as follows: a thing is produced from another, et cetera (*r*), and its production is useful (*q*). Understood in that way, Buddhapālita's assertion would be contrary to Nāgārjuna, who denied not only production from the thing itself but also production from another, from both, and from no cause. Until some Buddhist logicians came, in the eighth century, to recognize *prasaṅga* as a form of formal inference, it was not regarded as authentic; in fact, although it had been admitted as supplementary to the categorical syllogism, it was classified as erroneous knowledge because its conclusion was false to the arguing party.

Bhāvaviveka was strongly influenced by his senior contemporary Dignāga, the reformer of Buddhist logic and epistemology. Accordingly, it was Bhāvaviveka's contention that the Mādhyamikas had to employ categorical syllogisms to prove the truth of their philosophy. In his commentary on the *Madhyamakakārikā* as well as in his other works, Bhāvaviveka formed innumerable categorical syllogisms, the so-called *svatantra-anumāna* ("independent inference"). This is why he came to be called a Svātantrika, in contradistinction to Buddhapālita, who was termed a Prāsaṅgika.

For instance, in commenting on Nāgārjuna's denial of production of things from themselves (*Madhyamakakārikā* 1.1), Bhāvaviveka uses the following syllogistic form, which may be rewritten according to Aristotelian logic thus:

> *Major Premise:* whatever exists is not produced from itself, for example, *caitanya* (an eternal, unchanging spirit in the Sāṃkhya philosophy). *Minor Premise:* the cognitive organs (eye, ear, nose, etc.) exist. *Conclusion:* therefore, from the standpoint of the highest truth (*paramarthatah*) they have not been produced from themselves.

In constituting this kind of syllogism, Bhāvaviveka included three unusual modifications: the word *paramārthataḥ* ("from the standpoint of the highest truth") is added; the negation in this syllogism should be understood as *prasajya-pratiṣedha* ("the negation of a proposition," opposite to *paryudāsa*, "the negation of a term"), in which the negative particle is related to the verb, not to the nominal, so that not from themselves may not mean from another; and no counterexample is available, that is, no member of the class contradictory to the probandum is available, which means that the contraposition of the major premise (i.e., what is produced from itself is nonexisting) is not supported by actual examples.

Bhāvaviveka's logic, however, had its own difficulties, for which it was criticized by Sthiramati and Candrakīrti as well as by the Naiyāyikas. If the restrictive *from the standpoint of the highest truth* governs not only the conclusion but also the whole syllogism, the minor premise would not be permissible because all things, including the cognitive organs, would be nonexistent from the standpoint of the highest truth according to the Mādhyamika. If, on the contrary, the restriction governed only the conclusion and not the two premises, then the cognitive organs in the minor premise would have to be regarded as existent when seen from the standpoint of truth on the conventional level (*saṃvṛti*, *vyavahāra*), while the same organs in the conclusion would be nonexistent when seen from the highest truth. Therefore, Bhāvaviveka is to be criticized for using the term *the cognitive organs* on two different levels of discourse. In both cases he commits a logical fallacy.

Candrakīrti says that the negation used by all Mādhyamikas should be regarded as *prasajya-pratiṣedha*. When there is a defect in the counterexample, that is, when the contraposition of the major premise is not attested to in actuality, how can there be certainty with regard to the validity of the original major premise? Candrakīrti, citing one of Nāgārjuna's verses, argued that the Mādhyamikas, having no assertion of their own, should not rely on the syllogistic method and that *prasaṅga* is the only and the best way of argumentation for them.

The commentary on the *Madhyamakakārikā* was Buddhapālita's sole work. Bhāvaviveka, in addition to the *Prajñāpradīpa*, wrote the *Madhyamakahṛdayakārikā* (S, T) with his autocommentary *Tarkajvālā* (T), in which he discussed the truth of the Mādhyamika philosophy in chapters 1, 2, and 3 and the doctrines of Hīnayāna Buddhism, Yogācāra, Sāṃkhya, Vaiśeṣika, Vedānta, and other schools in the following chapters. His *Ta-sheng chang-chen lun* (*Karatalaratna*?) is extant only in Chinese. The authenticity of two other works ascribed to Bhāvaviveka, the *Madhyamakaratnapradīpa* and the *Madhyamakārthasaṃgraha*, is doubtful. In addition to the *Prasannapadā*, Candrakīrti left a great work entitled *Madhyamakāvatāra* (T), consisting of verses and an autocommentary, in which he explicated the essentials of the Mādhyamika philosophy in accordance with the ten perfections (*pāramitā*) of the *bodhisattva*. He was a prolific writer: the *Pañcaskandhaprakaraṇa* and the commentaries on the *Śūnyatāsaptati*, the *Yuktiṣaṣṭika*, and the *Catuḥśataka*, all extant only in Tibetan, are known to be his works. Avalokitavrata (seventh century), a Svātantrika, wrote a bulky and informative commentary (T) on Bhāvaviveka's *Prajñāpradīpa.* Śāntideva, who tended to be a Prāsaṅgika, wrote the *Śikṣaṣāmuccaya* (S, T, C), a collection of teachings about learnings and practices of the *bodhisattva,* and the *Bodhicaryāvatāra* (S, T, C), which consisted of more than nine hundred verses and which also taught practices of the *bodhisattva* according to the six *pāramitās.* The *Sūtrasamuccaya,* a collection of passages from Māhāyana *sūtras,* is ascribed by Tibetans to Nāgārjuna, but it is closely related to the *Śikṣaṣāmuccaya* and suggests that Śāntideva may have added more *sūtra* passages to Nāgārjuna's original text.

THE LAST PERIOD. Philosophers of the middle period of Indian Mādhyamika can be characterized as follows: they wrote their own commentaries on the *Madhyamakakārikā;* they were divided into the Prāsaṅgika and the Svātantrika, according to whether they adopted either *prasaṅga* (*"reductio ad absurdum"*) or *svātantra-anu-mana* ("independent syllogism") as a means for establishing the truth of the Mādhyamika philosophy; and they regarded the Yogācāra school as their opponent and criticized its philosophy. In contrast, philosophers of the last period were influenced by Dharmakīrti, the greatest scholar of the Buddhist logico-epistemological school, as much as they were by Nāgārjuna; with a few exceptions, almost all of them belonged to the lineage of the Svātantrika school; and they appreciated the philosophy of the Yogācāra school and even introduced it as part of the Mādhyamika philosophy. Consequently, beginning with Śāntirakṣita, they came to be called the Yogācāra-Mādhyamika-Svātantrika by Tibetans. In contrast, the later Tibetan scholars called Bhāvaviveka a Sautrāntika-Mādhyamika-Svātantrika, as he adopted the Sautrāntika theory of the imperceptible but real external world from the standpoint of truth on the conventional level (*saṃvṛti*).

The greatest figure of this last period is Śāntirakṣita (c. 725–784), a disciple of Jñānagarbha (eighth century), of whom very little is known except that he was the author of the *Satyadvayavibhaṅga* (T), his autocommentary the *Satyadvayavibhaṅgavṛtti,* and the *Yogabhāvanāmārga* (T). A scholar at Nālandā Monastery, Śāntirakṣita was invited to Tibet by a Tibetan king. There he established the first Tibetan Buddhist monastery (at Bsam yas) in cooperation with Padmasambhava, and ordained the first six Tibetan monks. He wrote two works, the *Tattvasaṃgraha* (S, T) and the *Madhyamakālaṃkāra* (T), and a commentary on the *Satyadvayavibhaṅga,* the main work of his master. The *Tattvasaṃgraha,* written in 3,645 verses, introduces the philosophies of various Indian schools, non-Buddhist as well as Buddhist, and also provides a criticism of them. Accompanied by a large commentary by Kamalaśīla, his worthy disciple, this work is extant in Sanskrit and is extremely valuable for the information it imparts on the world of Indian philosophy at that time. In the *Madhyamakālaṃkāra,* to which there exist his autocommentary, the *Madhyamakālaṃkāravṛtti* (T), and Kamalaśīla's subcommentary, the *Madhyamakālaṃkārapañ-jika* (T), he criticizes the Buddhist philosophies of the Sarvāstivāda, Sautrāntika, and Yogācāra schools as well as non-Buddhist philosophies, and proclaims the Mādhyamika as the last and highest doctrine of all. The principle underlying his criticism against all other schools that regard specific entities as ultimate metaphysical realities is that they are empty of reality because they are devoid of both singular and plural own beings.

Like the Mīmāṃsā, Vaiśeṣika, Naiyāyika, and other schools, the Sarvāstivāda holds that knowledge, like a clean slate, is pure and is not endowed with the image of an object and that cognition takes place through the contact of mind, a cognitive organ, and an external object, all of which exist at the same moment. Epistemologically, this is a copyist theory of knowledge, called in India *nirākārajñānavāda* ("the theory of knowledge not endowed with the image of the object"). On the other hand, like the Sāṃkhya, Vedānta, and Yogācāra schools, the Sautrāntika contends that what is cognized is not an external object but an image thrown into knowledge by the external reality, which always remains something imperceptible. Knowledge is an effect of an external object that is its cause and that has already disappeared at the moment the knowledge arises. This is the representationalist's theory of knowledge and is called *sākārajñānavāda* ("the theory of knowledge endowed with the image of the object"). But the Sautrāntika, unlike the Yogācāra, does not deny the existence of the external reality. For it, an external reality, though never perceived, must be postulated as existing. According to the Yogācāra, it is unnecessary to postulate the existence of the external reality because what knowledge cognizes is an image that is given not by an external object but by the immediately preceding moment of the knowledge. The mind is a stream of moments containing impressions of experiences accumulated since the beginningless past. The world is nothing but the representations of mind; external objects are in reality nonexistent. Yogācāra holds, as does the Sautrāntika, that knowledge is endowed with an image (*sākārajñāna*). However, the Yogācāras are divided into two groups as regards the nature of that image. One maintains that the image is as real as the self-cognition (*svasaṃvedana*) of knowledge. The other contends that the image is unreal, although self-cognition is real. We often grasp an erroneous image, say of a silver coin that we realize a moment later is nothing but a shell. According to the latter opinion, this means that all images can be unreal, while the illumination (*prakāśa*) itself, which exists with both the silver coin and the shell, is real. This illumination or self-cognition is the only reality. This view is called *alīkākāravāda* ("the theory of the unreal image of cognition"). According to the former opinion, however, the illumination alone is never cognized separately from the image. The image of a silver coin is as real as the illumination because it is not contradicted by the image of a shell. This is because the latter exists not at the same moment as the former but a moment later. What is unreal is not the image but the conception that interprets the image as something other than what it is. This is called *satyākāravāda* ("the theory of the real image").

Śāntirakṣita preferred the Sautrāntika to the Sarvāstivāda and the Yogācāra to the Sautrāntika. As for the Satyākāravādins and Alīkākāravādins, Śāntirakṣita holds that both parties are unable to explain the reason why knowledge, which is unitary, has an image that always appears as a gross or a plural thing. So long as it appears with a dimension, even an image of cognition can be analyzed and broken down into parts or, ultimately, into "atoms of knowledge" (*jñāna-paramāṇu*) and therefore is plural. If the image is real, knowledge must be plural; if self-cognition alone is real, why is it not cognized separately? But both cases are not true because, after all, knowledge has neither a single own being nor a plural one and it is empty of own being. Thus the Yogācāra is superseded by the Mādhyamika, which points out that all things, external as well as internal, are empty.

Kamalaśīla (c. 740–797), a great student of Śāntirakṣita's, wrote the *Tattvasaṃgrahapañjikā* (S, T) and the *Madhyamakālaṃkāravṛttipañjikā* (T), commentaries on two main works of his teacher. Kamalaśīla entered Tibet after his master had passed away there and was victorious at the famous Bsam yas debate between himself and Mahāyāna Hwa-shaṅ, a Chinese Chan monk who had considerable influence on Tibetan Buddhism at that time. In order to introduce Tibetans to Buddhism, he wrote three books, all entitled *Bhāvanākrama* (The Steps of Buddhist Meditative Practice; 1 and 3 in S; 1, 2, and 3 in T; and 1 in C). He also wrote the *Madhyamakāloka* (T), his main work; the *Sarvadharmaniḥsvabhāvasiddhi* (T), a résumé of the *Madhyamakāloka;* and the *Tattvāloka* (T). Because of his victory in the debate at Bsam yas and his great effort thereafter, Mādhyamika Buddhism became firmly established in Tibet. His three *Bhāvanākramas* were considered by the Tibetans at that time to be the best introductions to the Yogācāra-Mādhyamika form of Indian Buddhism; the same can be said even for modern students of Buddhism. In them, the necessity for the gradual training toward enlightenment is stressed and the sudden enlightenment proclaimed by Chinese Ch'an is denounced.

Vimuktisena (eighth century), the author of the *Abhisamayālaṃkāravṛtti* (S partially, T), and Haribhadra (eighth century), the author of the *Abhisamayalamkaraloka* (S, T) and its résumé, the *Abhisamayālaṃkāraśāstravṛtti* (T), claimed a close relationship between the Yogācāra-Mādhyamika philosophy and the *Abhisamayālaṃkāra*, a synopsis of the *Pañcaviṃśatisāhasrikā-prajñāpāramitā Sūtra* ascribed to Maitreyanātha. They developed their philosophies in commenting on the *Abhisamayālaṃkāra.*

Jitāri, Bodhibhadra, Advayavajra (all eleventh to twelfth century), and others were Mādhyamikas whose interest extended to either Tantric Buddhism, logico-epistemology, or both. Jitāri, Bodhibhadra, and Advayavajra are known for having written the compendia of the four great Buddhist schools, the *Sugatamatavibhaṅga* (T), the *Jñānasārasamuccayanibandhana* (T), and the *Tattvaratnāvālī* (S, T), respectively. In these works, the specific doctrines of the four schools are introduced, and in the case of Bodhibhadra, non-Buddhist Indian philosophical schools are included. The schools are arranged in order from lowest to highest, according to their respective estimations. This style of compendium became the model after which later Tibetan Buddhists composed numerous *grubmtha'* (Skt., *siddhānta*) or compendia of doctrinal classification of Buddhist (and non-Buddhist) schools.

Kambala (Lwa-ba-pa or La-ba-pa; date uncertain) wrote the *Prajñāpāramitānavaśloka* and the *Ālokamālā*, and, according to Sahajavajra, belonged to the Alīkākāravāda-Yogācāra-Mādhyamika school. Ratnākaraśānti (eleventh century), an Alīkākāravādin, disputed with Jñānaśrīmitra (eleventh century), a Satyākāravādin. Ratnakarasanti claimed that the Yogācāra and the Mādhyamika were not different; consequently, he is counted sometimes as a Yogācāra-Mādhyamika and others as a Vijñaptimatra-Mādhyamika. He was a great logician as well, and introduced the theory of *antar-vyapti* (internal determination of universal concomitance) into Buddhist logic.

TIBET. Two or three decades after the debate at Bsam yas (794), Ye shes de, the first Tibetan Mādhyamika scholar, wrote the *Ltab''i khyadpar* (Differences in doctrines), in which he described the history of Indian Mādhyamika, its divisions into the Yogācāra- and Sautrāntika-Mādhyamikas, and other important Buddhist doctrines. During the ninth and the tenth centuries, Buddhism, as represented by Jñānagarbha, Śāntira-kṣita, and Kamalaśīla, flourished in Tibet. After the persecution of Buddhism by King Glang dar ma and the fall of the Tibetan dynasty, Atisa, a great scholar of Vikramaśīla Monastery, entered Tibet in 1041 to reestablish Buddhism there. He revered Candrakīrti and Śāntideva, rather than Bhāvaviveka and Śāntirakṣita, and founded the Bka'gdams pa school. He also erected the Gsang phu Temple, which became the center of Tibetan Buddhism under the guidance of Phywa pa Chos kyi Seng ge (1109–1169). Ñi ma grags (1055–?) translated all Candrakīrti's works. He was probably the first to use the names Prāsaṅgika and Svātantrika. Tsong kha pa (1375–1419), the greatest Mādhyamika in Tibet and the first abbot of Dga' ldan Monastery, founded the Dge lugs pa order, wrote many works, including the *Lam rin chen mo* (Great work on the gradual way), and synthesized Mādhyamika philosophy with the Tantras. The so-called *grubmtha'* literature, written by such scholars as Sa skya Paṇḍita (1182–1251), Dbus pa Blo gsal (fourteenth century), 'Jambyangs Bshad pa (1648–1722), and Dkon mchog 'Jigs med Dbang po (1728–1791), in which Buddhist and non-Buddhist schools are arranged as gradual steps culminating in Mādhyamika thought, is unique to Tibetan Buddhism.

CHINA AND JAPAN. It was Kumārajīva (350–409) who introduced Nāgārjuna's philosophy into China by translating the *Madhyamakakārikā*, the *Shih-erh-men lun* (Dvādaśamukha?), the *Po lun* (an interpretation of Āryadeva's *Catuḥśataka*), and the *Ta-chih-tu lun* (*Mahāprajñāpāra-*

mitopadeśa?). However, the authenticity of the second and fourth works, ascribed to Nāgārjuna, is doubtful. The third is not a direct translation of Āryadeva's work.

Chi-tsang (549–623) of the Sui dynasty, regarding the thoughts of Nāgārjuna and Āryadeva as the core of Buddhist doctrine, founded the San-lun tradition. *San-lun* ("three treatises") refers to the first three of the above-mentioned works. Chi-tsang wrote the *San-lun hsüan-i* (Deep Meaning of the Three Treatises) and also commented on the three treatises. He propagated the Middle Way and the eight kinds of negation that appear in the salutation verse of Nāgārjuna's *Madhyamakakārikā*. The tradition flourished during the early T'ang period but began to decline after Hsüan-tsang's transmission of the works of the Yogācāra school to China. Ekan, a Korean monk, introduced the San-lun doctrine to Japan, where, as the Sanronshū, it enjoyed a brief efflorescence as one of the six schools of the Nara period (seventh century). In China as well as in Japan, the school was short-lived and was overtaken by popular Buddhism as propagated by such traditions as Pure Land, Zen, and others.

SEE ALSO Āryadeva; Atīśa; Bhāvaviveka; Buddhapālita; Buddhism, Schools of, article on Tibetan and Mongolian Buddhism; Candrakīrti; Dharma, article on Buddhist Dharma and Dharmas; Dharmakīrti; Dignāga; Jizang; Kamalaśīla; Kumarajiva; Nāgārjuna; Pratītya-samutpāda; Śāntideva; Śāntarakṣita; Sarvāstivāda; Sautrāntika; Sthiramati; Śūnyam and Śūnyatā; Tsong kha pa; Yogācāra.

BIBLIOGRAPHY

Bhattacharya, Kamaleswar, trans. *The Dialectical Method of Nāgārjuna.* New Delhi, 1978. An English translation of Nāgārjuna's *Vigrahavyavartani* with the romanized text.

Iida, Shotarō. *Reason and Emptiness: A Study in Logic and Mysticism.* Tokyo, 1980. A study of Bhāvaviveka's philosophy with partial translations of related documents.

Matics, Marion L., trans. *Entering the Path of Enlightenment.* New York, 1970. An English translation of Śāntideva's *Bodhicaryāvatāra.*

Murti, T. R. V. *The Central Philosophy of Buddhism.* 2d ed. London, 1970. A readable account of the Mādhyamika philosophy based mainly on the *Prasannapadā of Candrakīrti.*

Ruegg, David S. *The Literature of the Madhyamaka School of Philosophy in India.* Wiesbaden, 1981. A valuable conspectus, containing the history, philosophers, doctrines, and documents of the school and a detailed bibliography of studies by modern scholars.

Sopa, Geshe Lhundup, and Jeffrey Hopkins. *Practice and Theory of Tibetan Buddhism.* New York, 1976. An English translation of Dkon mchog 'Jigs med Dbang po's compendium of the four great schools of Indian Buddhism.

New Sources

Berger, Douglas L. "The Social Meaning of the Middle Way: The Madhyamika Critique of Indian Ontologies of Identity and Difference." *Journal of Dharma* 26, no. 3 (2001): 282–310.

Burton, D. *Emptiness Appraised: A Critical Study of Nagarjuna's Philosophy.* Richmond, VA, 1999.

Candrakirti, and Mi pham rgya mtsho. *Introduction to the Middle Way: Candrakirti's Madhyamakavatara with Commentary by Ju Mipham.* Boston, 2002.

Garfield, J. L. *Empty Words: Buddhist Philosophy and Cross-Cultural Interpretation.* New York, 2002.

Napper, E. *Dependent-Arising and Emptiness: A Tibetan Buddhist Interpretation of Madhyamika Philosophy Emphasizing the Compatibility of Emptiness and Conventional Phenomena.* Boston, 2003.

Ruegg, D. S. *Studies in Indian and Tibetan Madhyamaka Thought.* Wien, 2000.

Thupten, J. *Self, Reality and Reason in Tibetan Philosophy: Tsongkhapa's Quest for the Middle Way.* New York, 2002.

Viévard, L. *Vacuité (Sunyata) et Compassion (Karuna) dans le Bouddhisme Madhyamaka.* Paris, 2002.

KAJIYAMA YŪICHI (1987)
Revised Bibliography

MADRASAH.

MADRASAH. The *madrasah* is an educational institution devoted to advanced studies in the Islamic religious sciences. Its origin has been much debated, but evidence that the term was in use in the eastern Iranian area as early as the late ninth century nullifies the hypothesis that it arose as the Sunnī competitor to the Azhar mosque school in Cairo, founded in 972 for the Ismāʿīlī Shīʿī sect. The same evidence likewise casts doubt on the idea that the Sunnīs copied the institution from the then-fledgling Karrāmīyah sect of Muslims, whose founder died in 869. It is also uncertain when the *madrasah* came to be associated with its characteristic architectural form, a rectangular courtyard with a broad arched area (*īwān*) centered on each side and one or two stories of small student cells occupying the remainder of the interior wall space. This form, considered in the light of certain texts, has given rise to the hypothesis that the *madrasah* may ultimately derive from a Buddhist monastic model.

Prior to the mid-eleventh century, *madrasahs* were confined to eastern Iran and played a number of educational roles. Mysticism (Sufism) and the traditions of Muḥammad (*ḥadīth*) were as likely to be studied as Islamic law, which later took pride of place in the *madrasah* curriculum. Consequently, the earliest sense of the word itself is "place of study," a noun of place from the verb meaning "to study." An alternative suggestion that it means "place for studying Islamic law" and that it comes from another form of the verb does not fit the earliest usages.

The early Seljuk period of the mid-eleventh century marks a turning point in the history of the institution. Construction and endowment of *madrasahs* by pious private citizens had earlier been the rule, although pre-Seljuk instances of patronage by rulers or officials are not unknown. From the early Seljuks on, however, the *madrasah* became increasingly linked to official patronage. The first Seljuk sultan, Ṭughril Beg, sponsored a *madrasah* in the northeastern Iranian city of Nishapur, but a far more significant development was the construction of a string of *madrasahs* by Niẓām al-Mulk, the famous vizier of Ṭughril Beg's two successors, Alp Arslān and Malikshāh. The earliest and most important Niẓāmīyah *madrasahs*, as they were called, were erected in Nishapur (1058) and Baghdad (1067). Legal science (*fiqh*) of a single interpretive school (*madhhab*) was the primary subject taught, and this subsequently became the dominant pattern, although eventually more than one school of law might be taught in the same *madrasah*.

The significance of the Niẓāmīyahs has been variously explained: they were training centers for Sunnī officials to help the Seljuks supplant Shīʿī functionaries; they provided financial support for staff and students at an unprecedented level; they initiated the process of using patronage to exert government control over the elite of previously independent religious scholars. Yet there is no substantial evidence that bureaucrats attended Niẓāmīyahs; too little is known about earlier institutions to confirm a change in manner or level of funding; and it is apparent that Niẓām al-Mulk and other founding patrons of the period acted more in a private capacity than in a governing capacity.

Possibly the Niẓāmīyah in Baghdad was most influential because it was the first *madrasah* west of Iran; in Baghdad, teaching had previously been practiced in mosques, shrines, shops, and so forth. The Niẓāmīyah *madrasah* became the prototype for the *madrasahs* that spread throughout the western Islamic world from the twelfth century on, and the word *madrasah* became synonymous with Islamic higher education.

In its fully evolved form, the *madrasah* was typically founded by someone who endowed property in perpetuity (*waqf*, "endowment") for the pious purpose of religious education. The founder, whether a private person or a member of the ruling elite, could maintain a degree of control over the endowment during his or her lifetime and oversee the curriculum and the hiring of faculty, but ultimately, jurisdiction over *madrasahs* and their income reverted to the judge (*qāḍī*) of the Islamic court or to religious authorities designated by the government. The curriculum did not depart from the religious sciences, including jurisprudence, traditions of the Prophet, Arabic grammar, recitation of the Qurʾān. Secular subjects were taught elsewhere until the nineteenth century, when educational reform efforts in various countries forced some expansion of the traditional curriculum. Certification of the completion of specific courses took the place of an overall diploma.

Madrasah attendance seems always to have been quite popular, perhaps in part because of the financial support offered to students. But the *madrasah* education was more a certification of acquisition of religious knowledge than a specific preprofessional training. To be sure, religious judges, jurisconsults, mosque heads, professors, and the like normally had some amount of *madrasah* training, and in the Ottoman Empire there evolved a regular *cursus honorum* for such religious officials in certain elite *madrasahs*, which were the most common feeders into the higher ranks. Many students, however, attended simply to improve their knowledge of religion and make manifest their family's piety with no intention of seeking religious employment. Thus the *madrasah* came to serve a general educational function in society as well as a specialized one.

While some of the most important *madrasahs*, such as al-Azhar in Cairo, the Qarawīyīn *madrasah* in Fés, and various Shīʿī institutions in Qom and elsewhere, have survived to the present day as centers of religious education, most have been supplanted or diminished in importance through the growth of secular, government-supported school systems. Those that have survived educationally often have done so under financial and administrative regimes different from those of the pre-modern period, frequently within a government ministry, and as a consequence have suffered a diminution of their intellectual independence. Today, the *madrasah* is no longer the exclusive institution for advanced study of Islam.

SEE ALSO Niẓām al-Mulk; Waqf.

BIBLIOGRAPHY

Discussion of issues surrounding the origin of the *madrasah* can be found in George Makdisi's "Muslim Institutions of Learning in Eleventh-Century Baghdad," *Bulletin of the School of Oriental and African Studies* 24 (1961): 1–56, and his *The Rise of Colleges* (Edinburgh, 1981); in my *The Patricians of Nisha-pur* (Cambridge, Mass., 1972), appendix 1; and in A. L. Tibawi's "Origin and Character of *al-Madrasah*," *Bulletin of the School of Oriental and African Studies* 25 (1962): 225–238. Representative of the largely uncritical accounts of Islamic educational history is Ahmad Shalaby's *History of Muslim Education* (Beirut, 1954). For studies of recent *madrasah* education in Iran and Morocco, see Michael M. J. Fischer's *Iran: From Religious Dispute to Revolution* (Cambridge, Mass., 1980), chaps. 2–4, and Dale F. Eickelman's "The Art of Memory: Islamic Knowledge and Its Social Reproduction," *Comparative Studies in Society and History* 20 (1978): 485–516.

RICHARD W. BULLIET (1987)

MA GCIG LAB SGRON (MACHIG LABDRON)

MA GCIG LAB SGRON (MACHIG LABDRON) (c. 1055–1149) is the best-known woman in Tibetan Buddhist history. Undoubtedly a historical figure, she is revered both as a role model for life as a female yogi, and for creating an extremely popular meditative ritual used throughout Tibetan religion, the Gcod (Chöd) rite.

Ma gcig flourished towards the beginning of Tibet's Buddhist renaissance, or "New" (*gsar ma*) transmission period, that occurred after the fall of the Yarlung dynasty. It was a time of decentralized political power during which many lamas, both lay and monastic, established small communities of Buddhist practice and learning throughout central, western, and southern Tibet. The social climate also apparently allowed the emergence of a number of outstanding female Buddhist leaders and practitioners, more than most other periods of Tibetan Buddhist history. Several of these women were dubbed *Ma gcig,* literally, "One Mother." Ma gcig Lab sgron seems to have gained particular eminence during her lifetime, and her story was preserved in a number of biographical sketches.

It is not possible to substantiate the details of the longer and most widely known versions of her life, but this basic outline seems probable: She was born in Lab phyi (Labchi) in the Himalayan regions of southern Tibet. She achieved early notoriety as a talented reader of scripture, a service that religious figures performed for lay persons in order to generate merit. At the home of one such lay sponsor Ma gcig met a traveling yogi from India, with whom she coupled and had several children. She was vilified for this union and for having abandoned her status as a nun, and moved with her family eventually to the mountain retreat Zangs ri Khang dmar (Zangri Khangmar), which remained her base for the rest of her life. She separated from her partner some years later, and also left her children alone for periods in order to study with Buddhist masters. Her most significant teacher was Pha Dam pa Sangs rgyas (Pha Dampa Sangye), a somewhat mysterious figure who probably was from India, and who transmitted a cycle of Buddhist meditative teachings in Tibet that spawned its own set of lineages, called the "Pacification" (Zhi byed) transmission.

Pha Dam pa is said to have taught Ma gcig the techniques of the Gcod ("Cutting") meditative rite, but there is little evidence for this. It is just as likely that it is a technique of Ma gcig's own invention, drawing creatively upon Buddhist ideas and other meditative practices from the region. It provocatively features a visualized sequence in which the meditator identifies with the female Tantric deity Vajrayoginī, who then cuts off the top half of the skull of the meditator's visualized body. Vajrayoginī proceeds to cut up the rest of the meditator's corpse, and then boils it in the bowl made from the severed skull. This gruesome stew is then served to invited guests: the demons, goblins, and ghouls of the neighborhood, as well as beings to whom the meditator owes a karmic debt. Meanwhile, the meditator imagines having achieved unity with the enlightened deity Vajrayoginī.

The visualized sequence of Gcod is performed widely in traditional Tibetan society, along with distinctive and haunting tunes, often to the beat of a two-sided drum. It is employed both as a means of personal realization for the practitioner, and as a service to the community. The rite is thought to serve to exorcise demons and burdensome karmic debts in the region where it is chanted. Ma gcig herself is said to have used the technique to reverse the epilepsy of one of her sons. After her death, her teachings were preserved and transmitted by several of her children, and soon were adopted as a popular practice for wandering yogis as well as monks and nuns from virtually all schools of Tibetan Buddhism.

In addition to being credited widely with creating the Gcod tradition, Ma gcig is the subject of a cult of veneration for her yogic prowess. She is also revered for symbolizing an independent woman with charisma and self-conviction. Along with Ye shes mtsho rgyal (Yeshe Tsogyal), Ma gcig is one of the most common female figures with whom religious Tibetan women are identified, or considered to be emanations. In the twentieth century the Central Tibetan nun Ani Lochen was renowned as an emanation of Ma gcig, and she became a respected *guru* for many people in the government and leadership echelon of Lhasa and environs.

Ma gcig's hagiography claims that she is the only Tibetan to have introduced a Buddhist tradition to Indians, a notion based on the story that several "fleet-footed" Indian yogis came to visit her in her mountain retreat to study Gcod. Whatever the veracity of this story, it indicates a recognition of her creative contribution to Tibetan Buddhism, a recognition uncommon for Tibetan historiography, which almost always attributes the creation of new techniques to an inspiration of the Buddha or other Indic source. It is impossible to know how much of the meditation is actually of Ma gcig's authorship as such. Still, the tradition continues to be attributed to her today, and it retains its popularity both inside Tibet and in the exiled community in South Asia.

See Also Ani Lochen; Ye shes Mtsho rgyal (Yeshe Tsogyal).

BIBLIOGRAPHY

Edou, Jerome. *Machig Labdrön and the Foundations of Chöd.* Ithaca, N.Y., 1996.

Evans-Wentz, W. Y., ed. *Tibetan Yoga and Secret Doctrines.* London, 1960. See pages 301–334.

Gyatso, Janet. "The Development of the gCod Tradition." In *Soundings in Tibetan Civilization,* edited by Barbara Aziz and Matthew Kapstein, pp. 74–98. Delhi, 1985.

Janet Gyatso (2005)

MAGEN DAVID.

The Magen David (Shield of David, Scutum Davidis), a hexagram or six-pointed star, has been at home in many cultures and civilizations, albeit without any readily identifiable meaning until the present century. In the Middle Ages, the Magen David appeared frequently in the decorations of Hebrew manuscripts from Europe and Islamic lands and even in the decorations of some synagogues, but it seems to have had then no distinct Jewish symbolic connotation. The Magen David, also called the Seal of Solomon (Sigillum Salomonis), was employed in the Middle Ages by Jews, Christians, and Muslims as a symbol with magic or amuletic power.

In the seventeenth century, the followers of the messianic pretender Shabbetai Tsevi adopted the Magen David. Amulets of the movement bore the hexagram with the Hebrew letters *MBD,* standing for *Mashiaḥ ben David,* "Messiah, son of David." Thus the hexagram came to be identified with the shield of the son of David, the hoped-for messiah.

In the late eighteenth century, the Magen David came into popular use in western Europe, perhaps as a meaningful new sign that could express or symbolize Judaism. As late as the nineteenth century, however, the Magen David was not yet accepted as a symbol by Orthodox Jews. Yitsḥaq Elḥanan Spektor, an influential Orthodox rabbi in Kovno (modern-day Kaunas), Lithuania, warned the local Reform congregations to remove the Magen David that graced their houses of worship.

The use of the Magen David was reinforced by two major events. First, in 1897, at Basel, Switzerland, the Magen David was officially adopted as the symbol of the newly formed Zionist Movement at the first Zionist Congress. Since 1948, the Magen David has appeared on the official flag of the state of Israel. Second, in the 1930s and 1940s the Nazis forced all Jews in lands under their control to wear a badge of shame: a yellow Magen David bearing the word *Jude* ("Jew"). Today the Magen David serves to identify most Jewish houses of worship, traditionalist as well as liberal, and it remains a positive symbol of Judaism.

SEE ALSO Amulets and Talismans; Geometry.

BIBLIOGRAPHY

The best single source on the Magen David is Gershom Scholem's article "Magen David" in the *Encyclopaedia Judaica* (Jerusalem, 1971), which includes an extensive bibliography.

New Sources

Oegema, Gerbern S. *The History of the Shield of David: The Birth of a Symbol.* Frankfurt am Main and New York, 1996.

JOSEPH GUTMANN (1987)
Revised Bibliography

MAGI. The Greek word *magos* (Latin *magus*), borrowed from Old Persian *magu-*, has two distinct meanings. First, it refers to a Zoroastrian priest and usually has a neutral or positive meaning. Second, it describes someone who engages in private types of ritual with the intent to influence the world or the course of history, for which most languages only have words with negative overtones (magician, wizard, and sorcerer). Although this second meaning has had a lasting impact on the common vocabulary of modern Western languages (in the word *magic* and its derivatives), the fact that the magi originally were a priestly class among the Persians was rarely forgotten in Greco-Roman antiquity.

THE MAGI IN ZOROASTRIANISM. The Old Persian word *magu-* is of uncertain etymology and meaning. Its Avestan counterpart is only found once in the Avesta in a difficult passage (*Yasna* 65.7), where it supposedly means "member of a tribe." It has been suggested that this is in fact the original meaning of the word and that it came to be used in western Iran in the meaning "member of the (priestly) tribe" and hence "priest," but this is uncertain. It can be concluded that the word was not a term used for "priest" by the eastern Iranian Zoroastrians, who were responsible for the composition of the Avesta.

The word *magu-*, "priest," is well attested in western Iran from the Achaemenid period (550–330 BCE) onward. It is found in the royal Old Persian inscriptions and in administrative documents (in Elamite) found in Persepolis. *Magu-* is also well attested in contemporary non-Iranian sources, chiefly in Greek. This wide range of sources notwithstanding, it is difficult to specify what these priests really were or did. In the Old Persian inscriptions, the word is only used in the context of Darius's accession to power, which revolved around his struggle against the usurper Gaumata, who is consistently described as a magus. The relevance of this is unclear. Herodotos follows Darius's version of the story, but both in the Iranian and in the Greek materials the fact that the usurper king was a magus is not given much more thought. One piece of evidence from Herodotos has often been adduced as a possible solution to this problem: he mentions magi as a name of one of the six tribes of the Medes (*Histories* 1.101). This passage has been invoked many times to suggest that the magi were "originally" a priestly clan among the Medes, and this suggestion has opened the floodgates for a large number of speculations, most of which attribute many of the aspects of Zoroastrianism that seemed difficult to understand to the pernicious influence of these Median magi. This simple trick allowed scholars to shape for themselves a pristine Zoroastrian theology, going back to the prophet Zarathushtra, which had been perverted by later generations and especially by the Median magi. However, Herodotos's testimony is much too weak to support this type of reconstruction.

Some of the characteristics Herodotos attributes to the magi moreover are typical of Zoroastrianism. He writes that most of the Persians bury their dead, but not the magi: they leave the body unburied, to be eaten by dogs and birds (*Histories* 1.140). In the same passage Herodotos records that the magi kill as many ants, snakes, and other flying and creeping animals as they can. These are both characteristic elements of evolved Zoroastrianism and strongly suggest that the information Herodotos had assembled on the magi concerned Zoroastrian priests, even though Herodotus never mentions Zoroaster and pays little attention to the religious beliefs of the Persians. In Herodotos's *Histories*, the magi perform a variety of functions, which are all compatible with functions performed by Zoroastrian priests known from other sources. The magi accompany the Persian armies, performing libations and sacrifices. Their presence is required for every sacrifice, because they have to sing a special hymn, they interpret signs, dreams, and portents, and they also have functions that seem to be entirely unconnected with the religion, functioning as court officials and in administrative and legal positions.

Many of these aspects return time and again in Greek literature on the magi. A few generations after Herodotos, two important extra functions came to be attached to the magi: their role in Persian education and their role as theologians who spread and interpreted the ideas of Zoroaster. The evidence from the large number of Greek sources available has been shown to be fully compatible with what can be reconstructed of priestly duties from Iranian sources.

For the Achaemenid period the most important evidence comes from the Elamite Persepolis tablets, chiefly administrative documents recording the transfer of amounts of wine, grain, and other foodstuffs, frequently for services rendered. The magi occur numerous times in these texts as specialists in ritual (for a large number of gods) and in other, not clearly religious, functions. This situation is similar to the evidence from the Greek sources and is in fact typical for the later history of the magi.

Most of the evidence for that later history comes from the Sassanian period (224–642 CE). In post-Sassanian Zoroastrian sources (the Pahlavi books), the word *mogh*, the Middle Persian descendant of Old Persian *magu-*, is hardly ever attested. Instead of this generic word, more specific titles are always given that reflect a hierarchy and a specialization of functions. Even though the high priestly title *mowbed* certainly contains the word (it is derived from an unattested **magupati-*, "leader of the magi"), the generic title became unpopular among the Zoroastrians of Iran in the early centuries after the Arab conquests. Since many reconstructions of Sassanian history are based on sources from those later periods, the existence of the word in Sassanian Iran has sometimes been obscured. It is, however, not only frequently found in non-Iranian Sassanian sources (Syriac, Armenian, Greek) but also well attested on the most reliable Iranian sources from the period itself, namely personal seals. In fact the word *mogh* (written *mgw*) is one of the most common words on Sassanian seals and bullae. The word also had a long and distinguished career in Islamic Persian poetry, which shows that it had not disappeared from the common speech of the Persians. The question therefore arises why the Zoroastrians who formulated their tradition in the ninth century, the authors of the Pahlavi books, wanted to get rid of it; so far no reasonable hypothesis has been suggested for this problem. The only suggestion that makes sense is that the Arabic word *majūs* (borrowed from Syriac) was used not just to refer to Persian priests but to Zoroastrians in general and that the term came to be felt to be misleading for those who wanted to distinguish themselves as members of the priestly class.

The duties of Zoroastrian priests in the Sassanian period were varied. Apart from ritual and theology, magi also occupied themselves with administrative work in general and legal affairs in particular. Sassanian society is often depicted as a static society, in which the social classes (priests, warriors, and others) could not and did not intermingle. While it is generally acknowledged nowadays that that image does not give an accurate picture of Sassanian society (it is based largely on descriptions of the "ideal" organization of a Zoroastrian society), it is true that the priesthood and the military apparatus had separate hierarchies with representatives spread all over the empire. The extant evidence is not sufficient to understand the whole system, but it seems that a priestly hierarchy (which was never stable in the Sassanian Empire but subject to continuing modifications) was in place already in the third century CE. Its backbone was and remained the network of fire-temples that covered the whole empire and was one of the most important economic factors of Sassanian Iran. Priests thus controlled vast sums of money (and also land, slaves, and goods) that had been donated to the temples as pious gifts or deposited temporarily. Associated with these fire-temples, in all likelihood, were priestly schools (*hērbedestān*), where future priests were educated and where lay Zoroastrians received religious instruction.

Apart from their evident religious functions in theology and ritual, priests were found at court, as advisers to the king, and as interpreters of signs and dreams. They are also, as already mentioned, well represented in functions now defined as purely secular: the administration of the empire and the judiciary. Evidence for priests in these functions comes from seals and legal texts but also in significant quantities from Christian literature, chiefly in Syriac and Armenian, where the magi are always represented as the chief imperial force attempting to stem the tide of conversion to Christianity by trying and executing Zoroastrian apostates.

With the Arab invasions of the seventh century and the slow process of Islamization of Iran, the priesthood underwent dramatic changes. The first to disappear almost immediately were the court priests and the priests in secular offices. The evidence for priestly functions from the ninth century still shows a great variety in functions, but eventually a simple system replaced the earlier hierarchy. Among the Parsi Zoroastrians there are basically three priestly titles: the *ervad* (Middle Persian *hērbed*, "priestly teacher") is a priest in minor orders, the *mobed* is a fully ordained priest, and the *dastur* (Middle Persian *dastwar*, "someone in authority") is a priest of the highest rank associated with the most prestigious type of fire-temple. In modern Zoroastrianism, priesthood is hereditary. The question whether it has always been strictly hereditary is difficult to answer, but it is likely that it was. There is no evidence to suggest that priesthood became hereditary only in a later period of the religion.

Their administrative business aside, it is evident that the core of priestly duties consisted of ritual, theology, and the transmission of Zoroastrian literature. The latter function is critical for the first two mentioned. Almost all Zoroastrian literature from the premodern period that survived is priestly literature. This consists of several distinct collections. The Avesta, in its own language, chiefly consists of ritual texts. Most nonritual texts in Avestan have been lost, but there is some information on their contents from summaries in Middle Persian. The second important part of Zoroastrian priestly literature consists of exegetical translations of the Avestan texts. These are collectively known as *Zand* (a word presumably meaning "knowledge"). Far from being only a translation of Avestan texts, the *Zand* texts are interspersed with explanatory notes and exegetical discussions. The third part of

Zoroastrian priestly literature consists of theological, historical, and other works that are based on the *Zand.* The fourth part, finally, are priestly compendia and answers to questions posed by members of the community. The latter two categories are clearly part of the priestly tradition from a period when writing had come to be accepted: they are written compositions. This is not the case with the first two collections. For a variety of reasons, there are signs that writing came to be used for the transmission of religious texts only late in the development of Zoroastrianism. The evidence is strongest for the Avesta itself, for a special alphabet was designed for it, covering all the nuances of priestly pronunciation of the holy texts in ritual, that cannot have originated before the fourth or even the fifth century CE. Even after the invention of this alphabet, it seems that the oral transmission of the holy texts and their commentaries continued as the normal procedure. Since priests had to use both hands in the rituals they performed, they could not hold a book and had no use for it in most rituals.

Before the fourth century CE the transmission of religious knowledge was an exclusively oral process. Since the Avesta was composed in an eastern Iranian language but has been preserved among western Iranian priests, it is likely that the texts of the Avesta were memorized word-by-word by the western Iranian priests from a very early period (i.e., the sixth century BCE) and that the corpus of the Avesta thus became fixed. To facilitate comprehension of the texts, they were provided with a translation in the local language, which was transmitted alongside the Avestan texts. This translation grew in size considerably over time with the addition of glosses and learned comments. The amount of texts thus orally transmitted was large, and there are clear signs of specialization to make this oral transmission possible. First, the texts were divided over numerous specialists who memorized part of the sacred literature. A further development, evident from later sources, divided the priesthood into two different classes: those whose chief responsibility was the performance of rituals and those whose responsibility lay in education and theology. Ritual priests memorized the Avestan texts with their accompanying rituals, and teacher-priests memorized the Avestan texts with their commentaries. The latter class of priests was therefore unsuited for the performance of many rituals, but it is this class that was responsible for the development of Zoroastrian theology.

The main evidence for this theology in Iran itself comes from the Sassanian and Islamic periods, but the evidence from Greek literature shows much earlier traces of recognizably Zoroastrian theologies attributed to (Zoroaster and) the magi. Since the majority of Avestan texts have been lost, a firm chronology of the development of Zoroastrian ideas is not possible. There are many different versions of the crucial Zoroastrian story of the creation of the world and the mixture of good and evil in it and also of ideas about how history will come to an end in the perfection of creation and the separation of evil from good. This seems to support the idea that a systematic view of Zoroastrian theology was developed in priestly circles on the basis of a large number of selected passages from Avesta and *Zand.* The early attestation of systematic views on this subject in Greek literature moreover shows that a priestly synthesis was reached comparatively early in the development of the tradition. As one would expect, it was constantly refined and adapted to new social, political, and cultural settings. In addition to a variety that arose in the course of history, one would expect different views to have been propounded in different regions of the Iranian world, in different priestly schools, and in different social settings. Evidently the requirements of the Sassanian court and large urban centers, where all subjects of learning and philosophy from Iran and the rest of the world were pursued, were different from those in rural parts of the empire.

This may explain, for instance, the matter of Zurvanism. Some priests held that the good and the evil spirits had been born from a primal deity, Zurvan, the god of time. This idea was based on the exegesis of difficult passages from the Avesta and it is attested chiefly in Armenian, Syriac, and Greek sources. It is almost entirely absent from Zoroastrian texts. Scholars have often seen a willful excision of this theology from Zoroastrian literature and interpreted this as a sign of a fierce sectarian struggle, for which there is, however, no evidence. If one assumes that Zurvanite ideas, which show a much stronger influence of Greek philosophy than most Zoroastrian texts, were characteristic of the type of theology developed in court circles, then their absence from most Zoroastrian texts, which derive from a single priestly family in southwestern Iran, is no longer surprising.

THE IMAGE OF THE MAGI IN THE ANCIENT WORLD. As noted above, important evidence for the activities of the magi is in Greek and Latin literature. The word *magos* was borrowed in an early stage of contact between Iranians and Greeks, presumably in the sixth century BCE. From the early sources onward the word has the double meaning of "Persian priest" and "magician." As Persian priests the magi appear chiefly as the followers of Zoroaster, heritors of an old tradition of wisdom. Their chief use in many discussions is to illustrate the philosophical position of positing two primal, eternal realities (good and evil), in other words, dualism.

In many more passages, however, magi appear as magicians. In an early development, Greeks started applying the term to non-Persians as well, and eventually Greek individuals began to apply it to themselves. The Persian magi were thought to have special powers in visiting the realm of the dead, in guiding souls to the otherworld, or evoking the spirits of the dead. They excelled in magic, using herbs, stones, and spells for their purposes, and they developed a reputation for astrological knowledge and interests. It should be noted that in this context the word is not always used in a negative sense. Even Christian literature shows a certain ambivalence in this respect. The despised figure of Simon Magus shows the negative use of the term, whereas the Magi who first recognized the newborn king of the Jews (*Mt.* 2:1–12) show the lasting impact of the positive reputation of these "Persian" wise men in the realms of astrology and divination. In general, however, the Western traditions on the magi are a Western invention fueled by stereotyped views of the East as a place from which one could expect both unfathomable wisdom and acute danger.

SEE ALSO Saoshyant.

BIBLIOGRAPHY

Benveniste, Émile. *Les mages dans l'ancien Iran.* Paris, 1938.

Bidez, Joseph, and Franz Cumont. *Les mages hellénisés: Zoroastre, Ostanès et Hystaspe d'après la tradition grecque.* Paris, 1938.

Boyce, Mary. *A History of Zoroastrianism,* vol. 2: *Under the Achaemenians.* Leiden, 1989.

Boyce, Mary, and Frantz Grenet. *A History of Zoroastrianism,* vol. 3: *Zoroastrianism under Macedonian and Roman Rule.* Leiden, 1991.

De Jong, Albert. *Traditions of the Magi: Zoroastrianism in Greek and Latin Literature.* Leiden, 1997.

Kingsley, Peter. "Meetings with Magi: Iranian Themes among the Greeks, from Xanthus of Lydia to Plato's Academy." *Journal of the Royal Asiatic Society* (1995): 173–209.

Kreyenbroek, Philip G. "The Zoroastrian Priesthood after the Fall of the Sassanian Empire." In *Transition Periods in Iranian History,* pp. 151–166. Paris, 1987.

Kreyenbroek, Philip G. "The Dādestān ī Dēnīg on Priests." *Indo-Iranian Journal* 30 (1987): 185–208.

Moulton, James Hope. *Early Zoroastrianism: The Origins, the Prophet, the Magi.* London, 1913.

ALBERT DE JONG (2005)

MAGIC

This entry consists of the following articles:

MAGIC: THEORIES OF MAGIC

Magic is a word with many definitions, an English word that is linked to others in most European languages but for which there may be no precise equivalent elsewhere. In most known societies, magic forms an integral part of the sphere of religious thought and behavior, that is, with the sacred, set apart from the everyday. In some societies, especially in the industrialized West, it is generally accepted as superstition and even as a form of sleight of hand used for entertainment. In addition it has almost always been considered to mark a distinction between Western and so-called primitive societies, or between Christian and non-Christian religions. Therefore it is not really feasible to consider "magic" apart from "religion," with which it often has been contrasted, as many of its defined elements refer to their opposition to what both local adherents and outside observers consider the more orthodox elements of religion.

Magic has usually been without any agreed detailed content of belief and behavior. But there is a general consensus as to what this content is. Most peoples in the world perform acts by which they intend to bring about certain events or conditions, whether in nature or among people, that they hold to be the consequences of these acts. If Western terms and assumptions are used, the cause and effect relationship between the act and the consequence is mystical, not scientifically validated. The acts typically comprise behavior such as manipulation of objects and recitation of verbal formulas or spells. Not everyone in a given society may actually perform magic, which may be done only by a specialist magician. As an example, in parts of Melanesia, it is reported that a man may plant a yam, fertilize it, weed it, and, when the tuber is ripe, harvest it: this is a straightforward technical activity. He may also perform rites or say spells that are thought to help the yam grow and ripen, and perhaps grow larger than those of his neighbors. To a Western farmer, these are magical acts and any link between them and their intended consequences is a mystical one, existing in the mind of the performer and not in any scientifically verifiable actuality. Conversely many Western farmers insist on planting crops during a full moon or other point in the calendar, and consider this to be essentially a technical or scientifically effective act; but the Melanesian would disagree and consider it superstitious, ineffectual, or merely stupid. Two kinds of performance may therefore be distinguished, but whereas external observers may make this distinction, the magical performers may not, regarding both performances as necessarily complementary and effective.

Studies of magic as a superstitious form or aspect of religion, and especially as a "traditional" or "premodern" form of belief and practice, are misleading. It has usually been taken for granted that magic declines in "modern" technologically and scientifically "advanced" societies, becoming a superstition that loses meaning and believed effectiveness. This may be the opinion of Western scholars concerned with religious truth and counter-beliefs, concepts held essentially by adherents of "world" religions with religious books and texts. For them, the religions of peoples without written texts are defined as lacking any ultimate truth; they are considered and defined to include all manner of beliefs in magic, witchcraft, sorcery, and divination (all forming the occult). They typically define "true" religions more narrowly, omitting the occult as outside the religious. Conventional studies of the Old Testament, for example, discuss witchcraft as a sign of early and pre-Christian modes of thought, while orthodox Muslims may deny beliefs in magic or witchcraft as linked to Satanic, unorthodox, and erroneous forms of knowledge that do not merit acceptance as orthodox. In brief, the inclusion of magic as part of a religion generally makes that religion, as viewed from Western eyes, "primitive," theologically untrue, and even as unworthy of serious study by those who consider themselves to be orthodox believers. It may become virtually impossible to consider magic as having any purpose or function that is morally acceptable, socially positive or productive, or efficacious in promoting the common good.

Much of the evidence offered for magic is inaccurate, sensational, and inadmissible, the kind of material to be found in many travelers' tales of mysterious powers by exotic practitioners they have not actually witnessed or in the accusations of conjuring the Devil by accused witches in late medieval Europe. There are, however, two other kinds of evidence. One is exemplified by the accounts of trained anthropological observers, who can speak the local languages and ask questions of the actual practitioners; the other is exemplified by the writings of scholars of past societies where there is reliable documentation from original sources. An example of the first kind is the work of Bronislaw Malinowski (1884–1942), who witnessed and described yam planting and other magical acts in Melanesia. Another example is in the writing of Edward Evans-Pritchard (1902–1973), who researched the use of magic in southwestern Sudan. Accounts of this kind have the immense advantage of being placed in the contexts in which the rites are carried out. Examples of the second kind are by G. E. R. Lloyd on the ancient Greeks and Keith V. Thomas on post-seventeenth-century England.

Scholars of many kinds have been writing about magic, its aims, its origins, its methods, and its believed efficacy for centuries, even before the days of the ancient Greeks. It seems sensible here not to attempt a historical survey about magic using as sources those who have accepted its validity for themselves; it is more productive to deal with the writers who have tried to understand the practice of magic among other societies whose systems of thought they have not shared at the outset but that they have come to understand during their research. Relatively little can be gained from the writings of those who could not remain objective observers. For example, the writings of the late medieval inquisitors or of King James I of England are important as data for analysis, but in themselves they throw no more light on theories of magic than would the verbal statements of a Melanesian yam magician.

Certain basic questions that have been asked by writers on magic include those tracing the relationship of magic to science and to religion, and researching its instrumental and technical efficacy, its social and psychological functions, its symbolism, and the nature of its thought. If the once popular concern with magic's evolutionist implications—that it marks an archaic stage of cultural evolution—are omitted, these questions essentially concern either the functions and efficacy of magic or the nature and processes of the system of thought that is claimed to lie behind it. It has generally been accepted by those studying magic that magical performances do not "work" in an immediately technical or instrumental sense. Melanesian yams are not affected by magical spells, other than in the indirect sense that a yam farmer might take greater care of magically protected yams and that neighbors might be wary of damaging them. Clearly many cases lie on the borderline; alchemy, which contained much that is generally accepted as magic, did at times stumble onto scientifically correct relations between phenomena and events.

Questions of systems of thought deal with these same problems, but at another level at which arise questions of symbolism, interpretation, and translation between cultures. Perhaps the most long-standing problem is that anthropology (and, to a lesser extent, psychology, history, and philosophy) involves the distinction between the notions of "primitive" and "civilized," a distinction with such pejorative implications that the terms are now rarely used, although there are scholars who use the word "primitive" in the sense of "primal." Theories of magic have essentially been concerned with the problem of the relationship between what are often referred to as "traditional" and "scientific" modes of thought. Other terms that have been used in this context include prelogical/logical, prescientific/scientific, irrational/rational, preliterate/literate, and "closed/open" beliefs in magic, the performance of magical rites being identified with the first term in each of the above pairs. Discussion of whether these are meaningful distinctions that actually exist between societies goes back to the work of Lucien Lévy-Bruhl, discussed below. Much later work has been devoted to refining, refuting, and assessing the worth of his findings, especially once it became clear that if there are indeed two contrasting modes of thought, they are normally found together in any particular society, so that references to a dichotomy between "primitive" and "civilized" are misleading.

At the risk of oversimplification, it may be said that in the history of theories of magic the battle has been between what have been called the "literalists" and the "symbolists." Briefly, the literalists suggest that performance of magical actions is instrumental, so that the thought behind them (depending on the views of the writer) is either similar or dissimilar to that behind scientific experiments. Therefore the world may be divided into those societies whose magicians try to achieve a cause-and-effect relationship in events, whether technical or psychological, and those where the magician's place is taken by the scientist. The symbolists argue that this distinction misses the point. What is important for them is that magicians and scientists may or may not be trying to achieve the same results but are using different conceptual systems. They speak different languages, the one symbolic and the other concrete, and translation or interpretation between them is meaningless until this fact is taken into account. The main questions, therefore, are those of the nature of the different modes of thought and how they may be translated into one another.

MAGIC IN SOCIAL AND CULTURAL EVOLUTION. The first important writers on magic whose views retain currency—or at least interest—are those nineteenth-century evolutionists generally known as the intellectualists because they based much of their work on their opinions of what prehistoric and archaic peoples might have thought about the world, as imagined from their academic armchairs.

The most influential of these writers were E. B. Tylor (1832–1917) and James G. Frazer (1854–1941). Both distinguish magic from religion as distinct modes of thought and ritual performance. Both claim to base their definitions and analyses on ethnographic material, although much of it was in fact erroneous and faulty. Their method, which they rather bizarrely referred to as "comparative," suffered because they failed to place the data in its social and cultural contexts; their approaches were essentially psychological in the sense that they depended upon their own assumptions about what might have been the behavior of other peoples rather than on categories formulated by those peoples themselves.

Tylor defined magical knowledge and performance as "pseudo-science": the magician and his public (Tylor's "savages") postulated a direct cause and effect link between the magical act and the intended result, whereas the link was not scientifically valid but based on the association of ideas only. Tylor considered magic to be "one of the most pernicious delusions that ever vexed mankind" but nevertheless regarded it as based on a rational process of analogy that has been called the symbolic principle of magic.

His predecessors had taken a belief in magic as a sign of the infantile and ignorant thinking of early mankind. To argue that "savages" were capable of rational thought, even in a scientifically unfounded context, was a significant advance. He was also interested in learning why "savages," capable of rationality, accepted magic even though it was clearly ineffective. His views, which have been accepted by most later anthropologists, were that magical and empirical behavior are often coterminous, in that natural processes often achieve what the magician claims to do; that failure can be attributed to hostile magical forces on the part of rival magicians or to the breaking of taboos; that there is great plasticity of definitions of success and failure; and that the weight of cultural tradition and authority validates the practice of magic. Finally Tylor maintained that "magic" and "religion" are complementary parts of a single cultural phenomenon and are thus not merely stages in the evolutionary development of mankind, although he believed that magical belief and practice decreased in the later stages of human history.

The other great evolutionist of the period, Frazer, held rather different views that have long persisted in popular thought on the subject. He built up an evolutionary schema with three main stages of thought, each paramount in turn. He placed magical thought as the most primitive, then religious thought, and finally scientific thought. He contrasted magic with religion and with science, although he discerned certain resemblances between magical and scientific thought. He placed magic at an earlier stage in human development for three reasons: (1) because in his view it was logically simpler; (2) because it persisted as superstition even in industrial societies and so forms an underlying and persistent substratum; and (3) because the Australian Aborigines (at that time taken as the extreme case of an archaic remnant people) believed in magic rather than in religion (in this, Frazer's ethnographic facts were simply incorrect). So in his schema, magic was the earliest form of thought and behavior involving the supernatural. As people came to realize that magical techniques were ineffective, they postulated the existence of omnipotent gods that controlled nature and needed to be supplicated and propitiated. Finally, men began to recognize the existence of empirical natural laws, first by alchemy and later by true science, and religion came to join magic as a superstition. The "evidence" for this development was virtually nonexistent outside Frazer's mind, but he fit a vast amount of data into "proving" his deductive hypothesis.

Frazer defined the magical according to his belief that magical performances are sympathetic rites based upon his Law of Similarity, by which like produces like, and the Law of Contact, by which things that have been in physical contact then act upon one another even at a distance. He defined magic based on similarity as Homeopathic Magic and that based on contact as Contagious Magic, and he added taboo as negative magic acting according to the same "laws." Since much of science seemed to him also to be based on the same premises, he linked it with magic by accepting Tylor's earlier view of the existence of a rational link between cause and effect in the magician's mind. It is easy today to point to the flaws in these intellectualist arguments, citing their authors' projection of their own modes of thought onto other cultures, but at the time, these theories were highly influential.

Tylor and Frazer were followed by many less original scholars who refined their predecessors' somewhat crude schemata of evolution. In England were R. R. Marett (1866–1943), Andrew Lang (1844–1912), A. E. Crawley (1869–1924), and others. Marett maintained that in the earliest stages of human evolution, religion could not be differentiated from magic, because at that prior pre-animistic stage of development, religion did not condemn magic as mere superstition. He coined the term magico-religious, a blanket term that has muddled the issue of the natures of magic and religion for almost a century. Marett held that magic arises from the recourse to make-believe acts that the magician considers symbolic and different from their realization, and as a means of resolving emotional tensions. Magic is a substitute activity that gives courage and confidence, a view later reflected in the work of Malinowski. Crawley, writing less specifically, held that "primitive" peoples' mentalities are totally religious or superstitious, so that magic cannot be differentiated from religion, because both are based on fear in the face of an omnipotent unknown. In the United States, Alexander A. Goldenweiser (1880–1940) made the point against Frazer that magic and science are in fact not similar, in that only the scientist sees order and the working of regularities in nature, whereas the magician is unaware of them; he suggested that in early societies, magic was closely linked with religion but that later they grew apart, religion becoming more centrally associated with the formal structure of society and magic assuming a place on the fringes of legality and organized religion.

These were not the only psychologically minded scholars to discuss the nature of magic. Another important figure was Wilhelm Wundt (1832–1920), who held that magical thinking, as the earliest phase in the development of religious thought, was based on emotional processes, the principal one being the fear of nature, which appears as hostile to human well-being and which is conceptualized as an evil force that can be controlled by magic. In the same line of development came Gerardus van der Leeuw (1890–1950), who maintained that the magician believes that he can control the external world by the use of words and spells, and Sigmund Freud (1856–1939), whose notion of the omnipotence of thought was basic to his argument. Primitive magical rites and words correspond to the obsessional actions and spell-like speech of neurotics, who believe that they can affect reality by their own thoughts and wishes. Freud accepted the gross evolutionist schema of Frazer as a parallel to the psychological development of the individual. It is tension in the face of the sense of impotence that gives rise to magical thought both in the child and in early man: magic is wish fulfillment. Unfortunately this analogy has no basis in the ethnographic data supplied by anthropologists and must be considered a "just-so story." It puts a pattern of coherence into Freud's psychological work but tells little of the nature of magic and magical thought.

The Sociology of Magic. In the years around 1900, the works of other kinds of thinkers became influential and have continued to be more so than that of the evolutionists and intellectualists. The principal theorists among these more sociologically minded scholars were Émile Durkheim (1858–1917), Marcel Mauss (1872–1950), and Lucien Lévy-Bruhl (1857–1939) in France and Max Weber (1864–1920) in Germany. All saw the social as more important than the individual or psychological.

The three French writers followed Auguste Comte in substituting sociological explanations of social processes for psychological ones. For them religion, including magic, is a social fact, brought into existence by collective action and then possessing an autonomy of its own; it is not merely an illusion (Durkheim realized that the religious and the magical both persist in "scientifically" based societies). The "religious" is defined as sacred, a realm set apart by the religion's adherents, whose beliefs and rites unite them into a single moral community or church whose members' ritual, linked to the sacred, fortifies their faith as members of a single community. The religious is a collective practice, there being no religion without a church in that sense. Magic, however, is an individual affair in the sense that the magician has a clientele and not a church. In magic, therefore, the function of ritual to fortify the faith of the group is lacking, and instead the magician attempts to bring about certain consequences by the use of magical or sacred objects and words. Durkheim's study of magic formed an unimportant part of his main study of Australian Aboriginal religion and seems to be included mainly for completeness of his treatment of what had conventionally been included under the "religious." However, in a sense the gap had already been filled by Marcel Mauss's essay eight years earlier, wherein he set out his general theory of magic. Both Mauss and Durkheim defined magic not by the structure of its rites but by the circumstances in which these rites occur. Much of Mauss's book is taken up with the relationship of magic to religion and science, the latter being similar to magic by analogy, the former being similar to magic in that both are based on beliefs in mana and the sacred.

Lévy-Bruhl did not present any theories of magic as such, but he was centrally concerned with the associated mode of thought, which he called prelogical or prescientific, that most later writers have associated with belief in magic. He argued that modern Western societies are scientifically oriented in their thought whereas "primitive" societies are mystically oriented toward using the supernatural to explain unexpected and anomalous events. Prescientific "collective representations" inhibit cognitive activities that would contradict them, so that events attributed to causes that are prescientific are not put to objective verification. "Prescientific" or "prelogical" thought (Lévy-Bruhl was later to withdraw the latter term) contravenes the rules of science and Western logic, but otherwise it is rational and builds up into a single coherent system. Examples are beliefs in the effects of witchcraft or of magical rainmaking. It is important that Lévy-Bruhl stressed the content of thought, which is determined by a society's culture, and not the process of thinking, which is not a social phenomenon but a psychological and physical one (a point on which he has often been misunderstood). A person's perceptions are determined by his or her culture's notions of the social and ritual value of those elements of experience that are perceived rather than merely being seen. That is to say, "primitives" do not perceive "mystically" because they are some way mentally inferior but perceive certain phenomena as significant because of the mystical properties given to them by their culture. Lévy-Bruhl called such thought "mystical" because "primitive" thought, unlike Western scientific thought, does not distinguish between the "natural" and the "supernatural" but considers them to be a single system of experience. There is therefore a "mystical participation" between the "primitive" and what Western science would call the natural, the social, and the supernatural, a participation that composes the "primitive's" total social personality.

In Germany the scholar Max Weber was working on somewhat different yet related problems. Particularly interested in the problem of rationality and its relationship to economic and political growth and development, he based his work mainly on comparisons between precapitalist religions in Europe, China, and India. His main argument was that magic had been the most widespread from of popular religion in pre- and proto-industrial societies, and in many parts of the world (especially in Asia, where capitalism might have been expected to develop early but did not), the recourse to magic prevented the rationalization of economic life. The power of magic might be broken by the appearance of prophets (of whom magicians were the precursors) who introduced new and rational schemes of reward and salvation. Much of the significance of Weber's work lies precisely in his views as to the relationship between the decline of magic and advances in technology. For him the former was a necessary forerunner of the latter, a view that has since met with considerable and sustained opposition from more literalist writers.

Magic in Its Social and Cultural Setting. The writers just mentioned were the last of the classic anthropologists and sociologists to have written about magic. Their successors based their findings and hypotheses on their own field research, where the importance of what people who believe in and use magic actually do and say about it and of the social contexts of their actions and statements become evident. The era of armchair scholars, however brilliant, was over. On the other hand, more recent work may be seen at one level to be based largely on proving, disproving, and refining the theories of the classic scholars. The later researchers and reports may usefully be divided into the literalists and the large and more diverse group of "symbolists," although it must be stressed that these labels are only rough and ready ways of identifying them.

The leading literalist was the Polish-born Bronislaw Malinowski, the first important anthropologist to present a coherent theory of magic based upon his own field research in the Trobriand Islands of Melanesia during the First World War. He insisted that among the Trobriand Islanders what is generally defined as magic is quite different from religion as religion refers to the fundamental issues of human existence while magic always regards specific, concrete, and detailed problems. For the Trobriand Islanders, magic was of several kinds and had several functions. First, its use lessened chance and risk and induced confidence in activities where risk was high and/or linked to techniques that may therefore easily be ineffective. His famous example was that of the use of magic when fishing in the open sea but not when fishing in the shallow lagoon. Besides acting as an extension to the technical, magic extended one's abilities into the realm of the miraculous, as with love magic, by which an ugly man attracts beautiful women, old men become rejuvenated, or a clumsy dancer becomes an agile one. And magic can also extend into the super-material or super-moral, as with the use of black or evil magic, or sorcery, that was thought to kill at a distance. Magic was to be expected and generally to be found whenever one came to an unbridgeable gap, a hiatus in his or her knowledge or powers of practical control.

However, Malinowski went further, in an important way. He stressed that the islanders' land was well watered and fertile and their sea rich in fish, so that the use of magic was not merely an extension of technical competence. The production of food provided, in addition to physical nourishment, a means of gift-giving and exchange whereby interpersonal bonds were recognized and prestige made and kept. Magic protected people from failure and enabled them to achieve success in which emotional and social involvement were high. Magic raised the psychological self-confidence of its believers, may have helped them achieve higher stages of technological and moral development, and may have enabled them better to organize their labor and to control the cooperative work on which the well-being of society's members depends. Magic "ritualizes man's optimism" (Malinowski, 1978, p. 70). Malinowski stressed also that among the Trobriand Islanders, the basis of magic lay in the immaculate saying and transmission of words and spells, which were validated by myth that created an inviolable tradition as to the magic's efficacy.

Malinowski projected his findings among the Trobriand Islanders onto all humankind, making their particular cultural beliefs, thoughts, motives, and actions into universals, and he has rightly been criticized for so doing. But at the same time, he did witness and participate in the magical practices of a "primitive" people. He was not adducing the functions of magic from his own thoughts as to what they might do and think but started from the ethnographic experience itself. It is true that, although he came to know the Trobrianders well, he may be suspected of projecting his own thoughts, emotions, and motives onto them when discussing the psychological functions of magic that he considered so central. Nonetheless, Malinowski revolutionized the study of magic.

Malinowski was essentially a successor to Frazer, who wrote the introduction to Malinowski's original book on the Trobriand Islanders in 1922. The first important immediate successor to the writers of the sociological school of Durkheim and Mauss was A. R. Radcliffe-Brown (1881–1955), who carried out research among the Andaman Islanders of the Bay of Bengal ten years before Malinowski's Trobriand work. Publishing *The Andaman Islanders* in 1922, Radcliffe-Brown created a book that was a landmark in the development of anthropological studies of religion and magic. In his work he did not rigidly differentiate between religion and magic. The Andamanese recognized certain objects and substances as possessing magical qualities in the sense that a magician may use them to cure sickness, control the weather, and the like. The magician acquired magical power and knowledge by coming into contact with spirits that possessed a mystical power, both dangerous and beneficial, for which Radcliffe-Brown used the Polynesian word *mana.*

He argued that the power of spirits and the substances and objects in which mana is manifest, or can be made manifest by a magician, was used to mark the importance of social position when it was being changed (e.g., at birth, death, in sickness). When undergoing these transitions, people became vulnerable to the dangers inherent in mana, and so they observed taboos and fears of pollution, which were removed by the use of this power in a magical performance. By this means the community was kept aware of the importance of cooperative ties between its members and, thus, of their sense of interdependence. The rites both gave confidence to the individual and (more importantly, in Radcliffe-Brown's view) demonstrated the importance of the activities magic delineates in this way—fishing for large animals, for example. These were important precisely because they represented communal activities and dangers and so emphasized the importance of members' dependence on one another. In brief, Radcliffe-Brown introduced to theories of magic the new dimension of ritual and social value and played down its relationship to technical knowledge and science.

The Later "Symbolists." Behind the work of both Malinowski and Radcliffe-Brown lay the problem raised by Lévy-Bruhl, that of the nature of the "prelogical" or magical mode of thought and worldview, for which the terms "mythopoeic" and "prescientific" have also been used. Since his work there has been continual discussion on the points that he raised. The most important figure in this context has been E. E. Evans-Pritchard, whose *Witchcraft, Oracles, and Magic among the Azande* (1937) has been the most influential of all writings on these topics. Evans-Pritchard carried out extensive field research among the Azande people of the southwestern Sudan, largely with the intention of testing Lévy-Bruhl's hypotheses. His book deals with Zande views on mystical causation in the contexts of accusations of witchcraft, of the use and working of oracles and divination to determine the identity of witches, and of the recourse to magic and the performances of magicians. He presented a detailed firsthand account of Zande magical beliefs and practices, setting them in their social contexts and stressing especially the modes of thought and the "collective representations" that lay behind them. Zande magic was based on the use of "medicines," mainly plants and vegetable substances, in which existed magical powers that were inert until activated by the verbal spells of the "owner," the magician, and which may be used for protection, production, and punishment of evildoers. Most magical performances were private, carried out by individuals, but there were also public magicians who performed magic that had consequences such as war, rain, and vengeance for death. Magic was in the hands of men, who were considered more responsible to use these powers than were women.

In an earlier paper, published in 1929, Evans-Pritchard contrasted Zande magic with that of the Trobriand Islanders as described by Malinowski. Among the former, there was no concept akin to that of mana that provided the power of magical objects for the Trobrianders, and the spell was of less importance and used essentially as a directive to the mystical power of the "medicines." Whereas among the Trobrianders, magic was "owned" by clans, as were the myths that validated it, among the Azande, it was spread out among the entire community, the distinction being due to differences in social organization and political authority. Evans-Pritchard emphasized the social context far more than did Malinowski and also stressed that magic could not be understood as an isolated phenomenon but only as part of a "ritual complex" (which one might call the occult), composed of magic, witchcraft, divination, and oracles. Indeed, without belief in witchcraft, Zande magic would have little meaning. Making an important point that went back to one made earlier by Radcliffe-Brown, Evans-Pritchard concluded that the main objective of the use of magic was not to change nature but rather to combat mystical powers and events caused by other people. In his research, the long-argued link between magic and science falls away, replaced with a network of social links, tensions, and conflicts of central importance.

Evans-Pritchard also discussed the reasons that magic persisted despite what would appear to be its frequent failure: believers in magic had a "closed" system of thought that inhibited "scientific" verification. His argument goes back to Lévy-Bruhl and has been taken up by later writers who have contrasted closed and open systems of thought, a dichotomy that has perpetuated the long-standing contrast between magic and science. Lévy-Bruhl had remarked that ignorance is culturally determined, and Evans-Pritchard stressed that what appeared to be failures in magical performances were attributed by the Azande not to their inefficacy in a technical sense but to failure of the magician to perform the magical rites correctly and to the counter-activities of hostile magicians or witches. The system answered its own problems in its own terms.

Later writers, in particular Robin Horton, have enlarged on the contrast between open systems of thought, where efforts are made objectively to prove or disprove hypothesized causal relations between scientific acts and natural consequences, and closed systems of thought, where this kind of verification is not attempted and success and failure are seen in the light of the already culturally accepted world-view. Other writers, especially those in collections of essays edited by Bryan Wilson in 1970 and by Horton and Ruth Finnegan in 1973, enlarged on the social and cultural factors, like literacy or division of labor, associated with this basic distinction between closed and open systems.

The discussion was taken further by suggesting that although the causal links in both magic and science are based on analogy, as had been said by Frazer and all later writers on magic (although using such terms as metaphor, metonymy, homeopathy, and the like), the analogies were of different kinds. Stanley J. Tambiah, for example, distinguishes "scientific" analogy from "persuasive," "rationalizing," or "evocative" analogy. He points out that the Azande themselves recognized the analogical or metaphorical basis of magical performances that have as their aim the transferal of a particular property or quality to a recipient person or object. Because of the similarity and/or difference between two objects, the magical rite transferred the desirable quality of the one to the other. The performance of the magical rites achieved and marked changes of quality or state through the "activation" of the analogy by the "performative" rite of magic.

The implication of these remarks is that the discussion of magic has widened in recent years from its relationships to religion and science to the mode of culturally determined thought behind it and to the social contexts of magical performances. The discussion has relied largely on the pioneering work of Lévy-Bruhl and Evans-Pritchard, but it has not all taken place among their anthropological followers. Important work has been done by philosophers such as Peter Winch and Martin Hollis, classicists such as G. E. R. Lloyd and E. R. Dodds, and others. A historian whose work merits mention here is Keith V. Thomas; his *Religion and the Decline of Magic* is concerned with the decline of magic in England from the seventeenth century onward. He stresses that, historically, magic cannot be separated from astrology and witchcraft, the relationship between them being both intellectual and practical.

Before the seventeenth century, religion and magic could not easily be distinguished, but with the rise in England of forms of Protestantism, there came a separation between the two, and the importance of magic declined. Thomas follows Weber in seeing this decline as permitting the "rationalization" of economic life, but he analyzes the historical situation with greater subtlety. He suggests that factors that led to the decline of magic included the growth of popular literacy and education, greater individual mobility, the development of forms of banking and insurance, and the rise of the new disciplines of economics, sociology, and statistics that were to remove much chance and uncertainty from everyday life. He also stresses the importance of optimism and aspirations in science and in medicine. Even though available technology had not yet greatly advanced, people considered that it could and would. For the history of English magic, at least, he considers the views of Weber as of more relevance than those of Malinowski. Even if the latter are correct for the Trobriand Islanders, they are not for what have become industrial societies. Malinowski's view, put neatly by Godfrey and Monica Wilson as "magic is dominant when control of the environment is weak," can be shown not to hold for "historical" and industrial societies (1968, p. 95).

A highly influential scholar in this context is Claude Lévi-Strauss, who has been concerned for many years with the nature of the magical worldview. He makes the point that by his performance, the magician is making "additions to the objective order of the universe," filling in links in a chain of causation between events that are distant from each other in space or in time (1966, p. 221). Magic may therefore be seen as a "naturalization of human actions—the treatment of certain human actions as if they were an integral part of physical determination," whereas in contrast religious rites bring about a "humanization of natural laws" (1966, p. 221). Religion and magic imply each other and are in that sense complementary and inseparable, neither having priority of any kind over the other.

Lévi-Strauss has suggested that the notion is similar to that of mana. Both are subjective notions, used by Westerners to mark off "outside" thought as different from "scientific" thought and by the Azande (for example) to distinguish surrounding peoples as more involved with magic and thus inferior to themselves (much as Westerners might call other cultures "superstitious" rather than "religious"). If magic is a subjective notion in that sense, it can have little or no meaning in cross-cultural analysis and understanding. The concept of magic is in itself empty of meaning and thus susceptible to the recognition of any meaning that one cares to give to it. Following this, Lévi-Strauss has implied that the category of magic must be abandoned.

Lévi-Strauss's observations notwithstanding, magic remains a category that has been and is used in accounts of systems of belief and ritual and so does merit continued discussion. Rather like the notion of totemism, which has also been "dissolved" by Lévi-Strauss, its shadow remains, and to understand most writings on comparative religion, its history as a concept must be analyzed in the wider contexts of differentiation between culturally determined modes of thought and forms of society rather than in the earlier terms of its relationship to religion and science.

Many more recent studies of magic, mainly by anthropologists and based on actual observation of its living believers and practitioners, have been concerned with the questions earlier discussed by Thomas in his work on the decline of magic and its link to modernization. In addition, writers have tended to follow Evans-Pritchard and to see magic as one element in the wider complex of the occult. The occult includes beliefs and practices of witchcraft, sorcery, divination, and sometimes of spirit possession. Unfortunately the word has acquired an implied quality of the uncanny and mysterious. This is an outsider's view and usually not that of local believers and practitioners. The "occult" is in practice part of the "everyday." It is considered normal, sensible, accepted. It may at times be seen as evil, as "black," but evil is everywhere, an accepted aspect of everyday life, even if unwelcome or feared. Like all religion, the occult is intimately linked to power and control of some people or forces over others. Practitioners, whether or good or evil, exert power and control; have to undergo training, acquisition of knowledge, and initiation; are professionals and experts; and can often pervert their skills. The normality of magic and the occult is an essential quality. It is not that everyone can practice professionally nor know much about it. But it is open to all to use it if they wish and can afford it. As with all forms of medicine, the "doctor" is trained and may monopolize the skill needed to make use of the occult, but his or her skills are part of total local knowledge.

In many places magic has indeed declined, but witchcraft, charismatic, and modern "deliverance" Christian cults have flourished and increased in importance. Many societies, throughout the world, undergo processes of modernization, globalization, and industrialization. They witness increases in the ambiguities and contradictions of morality; confusion of good and evil; breakdown of kinship, familial, and community ties and obligations; and greater differences between rich and poor, powerful and weak, and women and men. These factors are reflected in beliefs and practices of the occult that are considered to lie behind and to explain them, and are used to counter them. The occult becomes an important element in rivalry between modern political factions, ethnic groups, and inter-regional religious movements. The weak and poor may use the occult to give themselves some control over the powerful and wealthy; and the latter may use it to keep the former in their inferior place. Although magic may at times decline, its decline cannot be understood in isolation but only as part of the persistence of the entire occult complex, any element of which may rise or fall in importance with changes in the structure and organization of any particular society and community over time. Most earlier analyses of magic failed by merely distinguishing "magic," defined in the observer's own ethnocentric terms, as opposed to "religion."

To see magic as part of the occult (and so perhaps overcome the problem of translation of Eurocentric terms like "witchcraft" and "sorcery"), one may follow Lévi-Strauss in accepting its lack of value as explanatory phenomenon, and to single it out as being in "decline" may miss understanding it. Magic does not stand on its own but is part of the occult, which varies from one society to the next. It is the very normality of magic and the occult, as wide-ranging yet put into action or controlled by ordinary people, as a weapon in everyday relations and competition, that enables them to persist in ever-changing form.

SEE ALSO Miracles; Spells; Superstition; Witchcraft.

BIBLIOGRAPHY

Three important studies of theories of religion in general warrant mention here. E. E. Evans-Pritchard's *Theories of Primitive Religion* (Oxford, 1965) is an excellent summary of anthropological theories of religion and magic, with emphasis on the work of Tylor, Frazer, Durkheim, and Lévy-Bruhl. *Rationality,* edited by Bryan Wilson, (Oxford, 1970) and *Modes of Thought,* edited by Robin Horton and Ruth Finnegan, (London, 1973) are valuable collections of essays on the differences between magical and scientific world-views, and Claude Lévi-Strauss's *La pensée sauvage* (Paris, 1962), translated as *The Savage Mind* (London, 1966), is a brilliant discussion of the same problem. Other works on the basic problem of thought include J. Goody's *The Domestication of the Savage Mind* (Cambridge, U.K., 1977) and C. Hallpike's *The Foundation of Primitive Thought* (Oxford, 1979).

Of the numerous works on magic, five are classic. James G. Frazer's *The Golden Bough,* abbreviated edition, (London, 1922) is a summary of his twelve-volume third edition, a mass of ill-comprehended data that has had enormous influence far beyond its real importance. Henri Hubert and Marcel Mauss's "Esquisse d'une théorie générale de la magie," *Année sociologique* 7 (1904), translated as *A General Theory of Magic* (London, 1972)—the first sociologically oriented discussion of magic—is based on acute analysis of the data then available. Émile Durkheim's *Les formes élémentaires de la vie religieuse* (Paris, 1912), translated as *The Elementary Forms of the Religious Life* (1915; reprint, New York, 1965), is a highly influential study of Australian totemic religion. Lucien Lévy-Bruhl's *Les fonctions mentales dans les sociétés inferieures* (Paris, 1910), translated as *How Natives Think* (London, 1926), is a seminal work that, although outdated, has led to much fruitful work on the magical worldview. Max Weber's *The Sociology of Religion,* edited and translated by Talcott Parsons, (Boston, 1963) contains passages on the problems of rationality from several of Weber's original German works.

Later basic anthropological accounts of magic include Bronislaw Malinowski's *Coral Gardens and Their Magic,* two volumes, (London, 1935), a detailed ethnographic account of Trobriand magic, and *Magic, Science, and Religion* (New York, 1948), a collection of earlier papers on Trobriand religion and magic. A. R. Radcliffe-Brown's *The Andaman Islanders* (1922; 3d ed., Glencoe, Ill., 1948) is an ethnographic account that has had great influence. E. E. Evans-Pritchard's *Witchcraft, Oracles, and Magic among the Azande* (1937; 2d ed., Oxford, 1950), the most important anthropological account yet published on the working of magic, has influenced all later work on the subject. Also noteworthy is his brilliant comparative essay "The Morphology and Function of Magic: A Comparative Study of Trobriand and Zande Ritual and Spell," *American Anthropologist* 31, (1929): 619–641, reprinted in *Myth and Cosmos,* edited by John Middleton, (Garden City, N.Y., 1967). For a discussion of magic according to Malinowski, see Godfrey and Monica Wilson, *The Analysis of Social Change Based on Observations in Central Africa* (London, 1968).

Finally, there are two important historical works that deserve mention: Keith V. Thomas's *Religion and the Decline of Magic* (London, 1971), a historical account of the decline of magic in England since the seventeenth century, and G. E. R. Lloyd's *Magic, Reason, and Experience: Studies in the Origins and Development of Greek Science* (Cambridge, U.K., 1979), an innovative study of the relationships between magic and science.

JOHN MIDDLETON (1987 AND 2005)

MAGIC: MAGIC IN INDIGENOUS SOCIETIES

Magic, in the view of many anthropologists and other scholars of small-scale societies—those in which effective political control is restricted to a village or group of villages—is the manipulation of enigmatic forces for practical ends. Magical means are said to be extranatural or supernatural, and the objectives of magical intervention, natural. The magician prepares a variety of special objects or "bundles," "spells," "incantations," or "potions," which are thought to bring about, in some mysterious way, real changes in a person, object, or event.

In the simplest foraging societies everyone knows some magic, and a shaman is usually a part-time specialist in healing and divination who may be called on for public religious ritual. In agrarian and other, more complex societies magicians tend to work for private clients in curing illnesses, in ensuring a positive outcome of an intended act, or in modifying the behavior of a third party. Magic in these societies, where there is greater specialization, tends to be practiced in private and, at times, against the public interest.

Some anthropologists of the late nineteenth and early twentieth centuries believed that so-called primitive peoples confused magical causality and natural causality. Today most anthropologists hold that magicians can distinguish the one from the other. Magic is used to coax nature to do its job, not to replace it; that is, the magician tries to engender a desired natural process as opposed to some other natural process, and this he accomplishes principally through the use of metaphor—the "power of words"—or other magical formulas. The magician may also deceive the client into imagining that some noxious natural substance "removed" from the client's body is the source of his sickness or whatever supernatural harm has befallen him (when, in fact, the magician comes upon the substance through a trick and does not remove it from the client's body). Magic may be used to supplement natural causality so that no chances are taken. When natural causality is not known, use of magic may still be rational: that is, given that many actual or perceived dangers are beyond human control, one must at least try something.

Typically, magic is contrasted with science and religion. It differs from both in that its purposes are practical, not theoretical or cosmic. It shares with science the desire to obtain a utilitarian understanding of everyday events, and with religion the use of extranatural processes. Thus magic is neither primitive science nor the religion of primitive people, contrary to views prevalent among nineteenth-century theorists; rather it supplements each. In small-scale societies magic may be entwined with science and religion to such a degree that their disengagement is arbitrary. Observers of these societies tend to label communal rituals and beliefs "religion" and private uses of mysterious forces for personal gain "magic." In such societies, applied science is craft—the ability to make utilitarian tools and other objects—or the practical knowledge of planting, hunting, or curing. Here again magic is inexorably tied to science in a supplementary way, in that magical procedures give the craftsperson, gardener, or herbalist a measure of confidence in a risky endeavor: magic can protect a newly built canoe against sinking, keep insects out of gardens, and heal the sick. Magic is never an alternative to practical science or technology; rather it is an attempt to tip the odds in the favor of the practitioner in the likely event that scientific knowledge is limited.

In small-scale societies magic may represent the instrumental aspect of religious belief: the same myths—the stories that explain a people's origins or an ultimate cause—validate religion and magic. However, in religion the myths are believed to be universally applicable and are used to support the public good or the established order, whereas in magic the myths are fragmented and used for individual purposes. Thus the conflict between the social good and individual need sometimes finds expression as a conflict between religion and magic. As manifested in Europe, that conflict involved the church and the practice of witchcraft. Anthropologists have applied the term *witchcraft* to practices outside Europe, but the conflict with well-established religion that the use of this term suggests is not necessarily present in simple societies.

The terms *sorcery* and *divination* have also been applied to magical traditions outside Europe. Although there is substantial variation from society to society and among scholars who use these terms to describe indigenous beliefs, witchcraft usually refers to the involuntary practice of magic, and sorcery to the deliberate practice of magic. Witchcraft is thought to be involuntary, since at times the witch may be unaware of the condition. Furthermore, a witch may be possessed against his or her own will. Witchcraft receives greater attention in the literature than does sorcery, possibly because witchcraft appears to be more common and because anthropologists are interested in the social implications of accusations of witchcraft. Witchcraft activities may have good intentions ("white" magic), or they may have evil intentions ("black" magic), although here again field data suggest that such a distinction is not always clear. Divination is not identical to magic, as no manipulation of natural events is sought. Yet it is not entirely separate from magic. Divination is the attempt to reveal hidden information by "reading" the mystical symbolism found in otherwise ordinary objects or action. The oracle exposes the probable result of an intended action. The person who consults the oracle may then choose the action if that result is desired, or he may select some other course of action if it is not. Divination may not necessarily involve foretelling the future. An oracle may reveal the cause of some community problem: someone is a witch and so is the source of harm. Identifying the problem suggests its solution: exorcise the witch. Thus the diviner taps the same mystical forces that the magician employs. But, unlike the magician, the diviner does not attempt to change events; rather he seeks to know what has happened or what will happen.

An early interpretation of magic was set forth by James G. Frazer (1854–1941) in *The Golden Bough*, a massive study of supernatural practices around the world. In common with many social philosophers of the late nineteenth century, Frazer held that use of magic was typical of early societies. Human thought progressed from magic to religion and thence to science. Magic is like science in that both explain the causality of ordinary events by suggesting that cause A has effect B. However, magic is pseudoscience in that it confuses supernatural efficacy with natural results. Today most anthropologists disagree with Frazer on this point and follow the interpretation of Bronislaw Malinowski (1884–1942), who held that the magician is well aware of the distinction between the supernatural and natural realms.

Scholars look more kindly upon Frazer's classification of types of magic, if only for the sake of convenience. According to Frazer, magic follows the "law of sympathy": magical causes may have distinct effects through one or the other of two procedures. The first is homeopathic magic: the magician acts out a procedure on models of the intended victim, and what he does is mysteriously transmitted to the victim himself. "Like produces like" is the principle here. A pin stuck in a doll that represents the victim causes harm to the victim himself. The second type of sympathetic magic is contagious magic: items that have been in contact with the victim, such as his hair or nail clippings, may be magically manipulated to produce harm in the victim.

Malinowski best explicated what is today a commonly held view among scholars: that magic and science supplement each other and are not to be confused. In extensive fieldwork among inhabitants of the Trobriand Islands off northeast New Guinea (1914–1920), Malinowski found that these gardening and seafaring people were highly empirical in their approach to horticulture, canoe building, and sailing. Yet they consistently tempered their pragmatism with magic. In sailing, they ordinarily relied on their craft skills and seamanship, but they understood, too, that native craftsmanship and seamanship were at times insufficient aids in withstanding the unexpected foreboding condition, like a capricious storm on open water. For these possibilities the Trobrianders used magic: it seemed to make the unknown amenable to human action and therefore provided psychological reassurance for a potentially perilous voyage. For Malinowski, then, there is no evolution from magic to religion and ultimately to science; rather these three facets of human behavior must be understood together, as aspects of a cultural system.

In his classic study of a people of Zaire, *Witchcraft, Oracles, and Magic among the Azande* (1937), E. E. Evans-Pritchard (1902–1974) took up Malinowski's argument that magic has its own logic. If one accepts the Zande worldview, then belief in magic follows. "Witchcraft, oracles, and magic are like three sides to a triangle," wrote Evans-Pritchard. "Oracles and magic are two different ways of combatting witchcraft" (p. 387). Consultation of oracles in divination can locate the source of witchcraft, and use of magic can combat it. For example, the Zande hold that all human death is caused by witchcraft. True, if a man walks under a cliff, is struck by a rock, and subsequently dies, the Zande would not deny empirical causality: surely the rock caused the death. Yet they would also claim an attendant causality: what, it could be asked, caused that person to walk under the cliff in the first place? Why did the rock fall just as the person was under the cliff? Surely some witch was responsible. To discover the identity of the witch, the Zande would consult the oracles.

The pioneering work of Malinowski and Evans-Pritchard contributed much to the development of the modern anthropological view of magic: specifically, that it has social, cultural, and psychological functions; that it is a rational activity akin to but separate from science; and that its use is not restricted to the so-called primitive peoples but may also be found in complex societies. These scholars emphasized the practical use of magic, as a private act in a social matrix. But there is a related stream of anthropological thought that concerns magic as an individual's ritual or cognitive act.

In his *Elementary Forms of the Religious Life*, Émile Durkheim (1858–1917) saw magic and religion as embedded in each other. Both contain beliefs and rites, but whereas religious rites are concerned with the sacred, magical rites are directed toward the utilitarian. Religion works toward communal goals while magic deals with private ends. It is this that explains the abhorrence with which organized religions reject magical practices. Religion involves a church operating in public, while magic involves an individual operating in private.

Marcel Mauss (1872–1950), Durkheim's son-in-law and intellectual heir, saw magic as "private, secret, mysterious and tending at the margin towards the forbidden rite" (Lukes, in Sills, 1968, p. 80). Like Durkheim, Mauss emphasized the similarity between magic and religion. In Mauss's view, both involve mystical power. Magic is a "social fact," a fundamental unit of society. Every rite that is not communal involves magic. For peoples of Oceania, the supernatural or mystical force in magic is *mana*, a nonsentient supernatural power. Similar notions are found in many other parts of the world, and anthropologists have labeled them *mana* as well. *Mana* may be located in objects or people. It is the power transmitted through the laying on of hands when one is cured of illness. *Mana* resides in the "ghost shirt," a special garment worn by some nineteenth-century Plains Indians to protect against bullets. And *mana* is to be found in all lucky charms. The transfer of *mana*, or the aura given off by an object or person with *mana*, is at the heart of many magical practices: the transfer is said to ensure supernatural protection.

Central to any discussion of magic are a number of puzzling questions. How can people actually believe that a special garment will protect them against bullets? Why do people let themselves be duped by the hocus-pocus of the magician? Are people so credulous as to believe that placing a photograph of an intended victim in a coffin will actually harm that person?

Lucien Lévi-Bruhl (1857–1939) provided one answer to these questions. Like Frazer, Lévi-Bruhl developed an evolutionary scheme to account for cultural differences. He focused on human thought, however, not social institutions. For most of his career he held to what was essentially an elaboration of the racist notion that so-called primitive peoples are less fully evolved than "civilized" peoples, and that their thinking, which Lévi-Bruhl labeled "prelogical," is fundamentally childlike. Civilized peoples, in his view, think rationally, logically. Prelogical thinking involves a different order of perception: mystic properties are attached to inanimate objects or to living things. Magic is thus part of prelogical thinking, as are many other aspects of so-called primitive culture: language, enumeration, memory. Toward the end of his career, Lévi-Bruhl modified his position on the inherent difference of certain groups of human beings. Humans taken as a whole, he came to believe, have capacities for the various styles of thought: prelogical mentality is to be found everywhere, but it is emphasized more in primitive societies.

This brings us close to Claude Lévi-Strauss's view of the "savage mind." Magical action is, in his view, a subset of analogical thought, the mental activity emphasized in simple societies. Magic involves an assumption that metaphors work according to physical or natural laws. The case of the Zande peripatetic hit by a falling rock might be solved in this fashion: human intent of harm to that individual was paralleled by the natural event of the falling stone.

Lévi-Strauss formulated his own contrast between magic and religion: religion is "a humanization of natural laws," while magic is "a naturalization of human actions—the treatment of certain human actions as if they were an integral part of physical determinism" (1962, p. 221). Lévi-Strauss envisages no evolutionary sequence beginning with magic: magic, religion, and science all shade into one another, and each one has a place in human society.

S. J. Tambiah also sees analogy at work in science. Science, however, begins with known causal relationships between phenomena and then, through analogy, discovers the identical causal relations between unknown phenomena. Meaning imbued in the magical act is analogously transferred to the natural activity. This is not, Tambiah argues, faulty science but a normal activity of human thought: magic is a specialized use of analogy and the imputation of meaning from the magical procedure to a natural referent. Thus magic does what science cannot: it helps create a world of meaning. Seemingly bizarre magical behavior is to be understood as an exercise in the exploration of meaning in practical activity, not as a refutation of natural law.

Many anthropologists would argue that magic is part of the normal daily routines of people in modern, complex societies. Clearly magic is involved when a baseball player, in order to get a hit, crosses himself or picks up a bit of dirt before batting. *Mana* is the "charisma" of the persuasive individual; it is also the "prestige" of the person of high social station. Magical protection is afforded the automobile driver who places the statue of a saint on the dashboard. And magic is involved in the daily ritual of personal ablutions and grooming: "I must always wear this tie with that suit," "If my hair is not styled just so, I won't feel right." The doctor says, "Take two pills and call me if you don't feel better in twenty-four hours," and we take his advice, since, like most laypeople, we tend to see the science of the expert as a form of magic. And this is necessarily so, as we cannot all be experts in everything, yet we still need to reduce our anxiety and gain a sense of order and meaning in our lives.

BIBLIOGRAPHY

With the publication of *The Golden Bough: A Study in Magic and Religion*, 2 vols. (London, 1890), James Frazer put the study of magic forever on the agenda of anthropologists, folklorists, and all scholars of small-scale societies. Frazer's library study eventually grew to twelve volumes (3d ed., rev. & enl.; London, 1911–1915) plus an *Aftermath* (London, 1936). An abridged, single-volume version, entitled *The New Golden Bough*, edited by Theodor H. Gaster, was published in 1959 (New York).

In a theoretical essay entitled *Magic, Science, and Religion* (New York, 1948) Bronislaw Malinowski criticized Frazer's armchair scholarship, and it is with Malinowski's *Coral Gardens and Their Magic*, 2 vols. (Bloomington, Ind., 1935), that the modern anthropological field study of magic really begins. E. E. Evans-Pritchard's *Witchcraft, Oracles, and Magic among the Azande*, 2d ed. (1937; Oxford, 1950), is a classic field study of magic among a traditional African group. Religion in small-scale societies, especially among the indigenous peoples of Australia, is the subject of Émile Durkheim's *The Elementary Forms of the Religious Life* (1915; New York, 1965). Greater depth is given to the Durkheimian approach to magic in Henri Hubert and Marcel Mauss's "Esquisse d'une théorie générale de la magie," *L'année sociologique* 7 (1904). Subsequently translated as *A General Theory of Magic* (London, 1972), this important essay is quoted by Steven Lukes in his article on Mauss in the *International Encyclopedia of the Social Sciences*, edited by David L. Sills (New York, 1968), vol. 9, pp. 78–82. The racist position that the use of magic is an outcome of "primitive" thought is set forth by Lucien Lévy-Bruhl, especially in his *Primitive Mentality* (New York, 1923).

The nature of magical thought, as a species of normal human thought, is spelled out by Claude Lévi-Strauss in his classic essay *The Savage Mind* (Paris, 1962). Summations of anthropological ideas concerning magic and religion in simple societies can be found in Ruth Benedict's "Magic," in the *Encyclopaedia of the Social Sciences* (New York, 1933), vol. 10, pp. 39–44; Nur Yalman's "Magic," in the *International Encyclopedia of the Social Sciences* (New York, 1968), vol. 9, pp. 521–527; E. E. Evans-Pritchard's *Theories of Primitive Religion* (Oxford, 1965); and the various editions of *The Reader in Comparative Religion: An Anthropological Approach*, edited by William A. Lessa and Evon Z. Vogt. Stanley J. Tambiah's article entitled "The Form and Meaning of Magical Acts: A Point of View" appears in the fourth edition (New York, 1979) of the reader.

DONALD R. HILL (1987)

MAGIC: MAGIC IN GRECO-ROMAN ANTIQUITY

From the beginning, magic was an essential part of Greco-Roman culture and religion. Over the course of history, however, it changed in appearance, scope, and importance from being an element of simple rituals to becoming highly complex systems claiming the status of science and philosophy. To the extent that magical ideas were presupposed in early agrarian and sacrificial rites, purifications, and burial customs, magic even preceded the culture of the Greeks. Later, magical beliefs and practices steadily grew in significance and diversity. In the Hellenistic period that followed Alexander the Great (d. 323 BCE), magical material increased considerably. In Classical Greece of the sixth to fifth centuries BCE, Thessaly and Egypt had already been known as the prime sources of magical knowledge; but only Hellenistic syncretism produced the abundance of material now available. Within the Greco-Roman world magic formed to some extent a common tradition, yet at the same time each cultural region put its own stamp on it. The main traditions were those of Greek, Greco-Egyptian, Roman, Jewish, and Christian magic. While clearly distinguishable, these cultural contexts also overlapped to a considerable degree and produced a variety of syncretic forms.

SOURCES. The material to be considered falls into two categories. First, there is an abundance of primary sources: amulets, magical gems (often with pictorial and verbal inscriptions), curse tablets, spells on papyrus and on strips or sheets of metal, inscriptions, symbols, drawings, paintings, small figurines and larger sculptures, tools, and finally handbooks of magicians that collect the materials they used (especially the Greek Magical Papyri). Second, there is also a vast amount of secondary source material. Almost every ancient author presents literary and artistic descriptions of magical beliefs and practices. There are also many short references to such beliefs and practices as they existed at the time. Philosophers discussed the matter from early on. Scholarly investigations from the Hellenistic and Roman periods are extant (Plutarch's *On Superstition*; Pliny's *Natural History* 30). At that time the distinction between acceptable and unacceptable forms of magic became common, making it possible for even the educated to use magic in some positive way. Legal provisions had to be developed to deal with magic, especially with forms of it that were reputedly used to harm others.

Despite its reputation as illicit, fraudulent, and superstitious, magic was an essential part of daily life at all levels of society. The uses of magic seem to have been unlimited. In any case, they were also connected with legitimate forms of ritual, myth, symbol, and even language in general. Magic was presupposed in all forms of the miraculous, and in medicine, alchemy, astrology, and divination. Even so, magic retained its dubious reputation, and there were always those few who viewed it with total skepticism.

TERMINOLOGY. The phenomenon of magic is designated by several Greek terms, especially *mageia*, *pharmakeia*, and *goēteia*. The term *mageia* is derived from *magos* (pl., *magoi*), originally a Persian word (*magush*). Herodotus describes the Magoi (Magians) as a Median tribe. Later they were assumed to be priests and scholars of astrology, divination, and related subjects. Whereas Plato (*Alcibiades* 1.122) still speaks of *mageia* in a positive sense as referring to "the magian lore of Zarathushtra," Aristotle uses the term also in a negative sense as we do today (frag. 36; also Theophrastus, *History of Plants* 9.15.7). This negative meaning, which has little to do with the original meaning, becomes predominant in the Hellenistic period, when new words develop besides *magos* and *mageia*, as for instance *mageuein* and *magikos*. The positive meaning, however, is found in the writings of the magicians themselves, especially in the Greek Magical Papyri.

The negative meaning was taken over by the Romans; in Latin the terms are *magia*, *magicus*, and *magus*, as well as *maleficium* and *maleficus*. Modern English has inherited this negative meaning, with the exception of the Magi of *Matthew* 2:1.

DESCRIPTIONS OF MAGIC. What constitutes magic was already disputed in antiquity. Roman officials and intellectuals reflect the negative reputation that magic had acquired. Pliny (*Natural History* 30.1–2) points out its fraudulent and dangerous character and has a theory about its origins as a decadent mixture of elements from medicine, astronomy, and religion. Apuleius (*Apology* 26) sums up the view of it as being vulgar and making preposterous claims. By contrast, practitioners of magic provide favorable descriptions of the art (Apuleius, *Apology* 26; Greek Magical Papyri, passim), or they distinguish between lower and higher forms; *goēteia* became the lower, *mageia* the general, and *theourgia* the higher magic. This distinction allowed Neoplatonic philosophers, especially Iamblichus and Proclus, to accept theurgy as a form of philosophical magic.

GREEK AND ROMAN MAGIC. For reasons of methodology it is important to distinguish between primary (performative) and secondary (descriptive) material.

Primary sources. Primary sources for ancient magic consist of various kinds of artifacts, images, symbols, and written texts. Collections of such sources are today housed by public museums and libraries or with private collectors. The cataloging and publishing of these widely dispersed materials are still in progress.

Amulets. Greco-Roman antiquity has left us a large number of amulets of different kinds and purposes. The word *amuletum* occurs in Pliny and corresponds to the Greek *phulaktērion*. Amulets were magically potent objects that averted evil or increased a person's or a deity's divine power. They were worn around the neck or on the head, or arm, or were posted in various places in the house (on doors, at thresholds, etc.). Amulets come in many shapes and forms. Best known are the Egyptian scarab, the hand showing the *fica* (the obscene gesture called "the fig"), the phallus, the eye. Other forms are divine symbols and figurines, replicas of other parts of the human body, animals, and plants. Precious and semiprecious gems engraved with images of deities, inscriptions, and magical symbols were very popular. Often amulets were placed in capsules (*bullae*). While Egypt was the classical land of amulets, they were known in all parts of the ancient world. Among Jews the *tefillin* and the *mezuzah* should be mentioned, and among Christians the cross and the fish.

Curse tablets. Curse tablets, or *defixiones* (from Lat. *defixio*, "binding spell"; Gr., *katadesmos*), are known from Greece since the time of Homer. A large number of lead lamellae are extant from fifth-century Greece, but curse tablets exist also in the form of ostraca, seashells, and papyri, upon which the curse formulas were inscribed, often with the names of the cursed and the curser. The tablets were deposited in the ground near places where the spirits of the dead were believed to be or in such places as houses, baths, and sports arenas, so as to be communicated to avenging underworld deities (especially Hermes, Hekate, Persephone, and Typhon). Curse tablets were used for a variety of purposes, especially in erotic magic, court trials, political intrigues, and sports (gladiators, horse races). From the earlier and simpler curse developed the later, more elaborate, syncretistic forms of the Hellenistic and Roman eras; besides the magical formulas, inscriptions often included so-called *voces magicae*, characters, or drawings. A special form was the magical letter to the underworld deities.

Curse figurines. Curse figurines, of which several examples and descriptions have survived, were also widely used. To curse someone, one made a wax or clay figurine of the person and then stuck needles or nails into the figurine or mutilated it, while curse formulas were spoken over it. Like curse tablets, the figurines were deposited in the ground. This form of curse was apparently popular in erotic magic.

Drawings. Drawings have magical power in themselves, as extant magical papyri show. The subjects of the drawings can be deities, persons, or animals.

Tools. Magical tools are known to have existed and have in fact been found (nails, disks, etc.). The most important discovery was a set of tools found in Pergamum.

Symbols. A large number of magical signs and symbols appear on amulets, gems, and tablets. Although seemingly in use since Pythagoras (see Lucian, *Pro lapsu* 5), most of them are still unexplained today. The magicians called them *charactēres*. In Gnosticism they were also taken over by Christian magic (*Book of Jeu*, *Pistis Sophia*).

Incantations. Incantations belong to the magic of the word. They consist of magical formulas, prayers, and chants. The term comes from the Latin *incantamentum*, "incantation, spell" (Gr., *epoide*). Many examples of *incantamenta* are found in inscriptions, papyri, and literature, where they are quoted or described. They were widely used in medicine (healings, exorcisms), weather magic, cultic invocations of gods and demons, and erotic magic. Their significance for philosophy and rhetoric was recognized by the Sophists and Plato. They also appear as literary motifs in sagas, novels, myths, aretalogies, mystery cults, and collections of oracles.

Hymns. Hymns to the gods are closely related to incantations. In terms of poetry and religion, hymns are more and even highly developed forms. They were composed metrically and sung, with accompanying cithara and dance. Their basic form included the invocation of the gods, the gods' names and epithets (expressed in relative clauses, participles, adjectives, etc.), and the petition. Hymns existed from Archaic times on. Major extant collections include the Homeric Hymns (mainly from the eighth to the sixth centuries BCE), the Orphic Hymns (probably from the second century CE), and the hymn fragments inserted in the Greek Magical Papyri, some of which may be ancient.

Magical handbooks. Magicians collected the material they needed in handbooks, some of which are extant, as for example the great magical papyri of Berlin, Leiden, London, and Paris. Such handbooks include a wide variety of spells to be used by the magicians themselves or to be sold to customers. There are also rituals for acquiring assistant demons (*paredroi daimones*), initiation rituals, deification rituals, invocations for oracular séances with deities, and procedural matters (preparation of ingredients, instructions about when various procedures can be undertaken, etc.). Among the spells, those designed to attract a lover, harm an enemy, or restrain anger are most numerous. Other spells have to do with various illnesses, bedbugs, business problems, catching thieves, and horse races. To find out what the future holds, a host of mantic spells and longer rituals are provided. Outstanding among all these collections are the so-called Mithraic Liturgy, which exhibits yet unexplained relationships to the Mithraic cult, and the "Eighth Book of Moses," which contains three different versions of an initiation ritual. In addition to collecting magical material, the handbooks told magicians how to make and use amulets, curse tablets, figurines, and drawings, and how to use tools.

Secondary sources. Whereas primary sources present magical practices and beliefs directly, secondary sources presuppose, describe, or discuss them. The literature of Greek and Roman antiquity contains innumerable examples of such secondary sources, but careful distinctions must be made: while many authors have real knowledge of popular magic or even access to primary sources of magical literature, there is at the same time a purely literary tradition in which the same themes, motifs, and terms show up again and again. Therefore some authors simply imitate the descriptions of magical acts found in earlier authors or attempt to supersede them. While both kinds of authors may flourish simultaneously, some authors may have received their information from secondary sources exclusively.

Literary texts. Magic is a common literary motif in both Greek and Latin literature. Homer's *Iliad* and *Odyssey* contain many allusions to and descriptions of magical acts. Pliny (*Natural History* 30.1) states that the *Odyssey* in particular was recognized simply as a book of magic. In fact, Homeric verses were used later as magical formulas. Magic plays a role in Odysseus's encounter with the witch Circe (*Odyssey* 10.274ff.) and his descent into Hades and consultation with the seer Teiresias (*Odyssey* 11.14ff.). The Homeric Hymns have numerous references to magic, some of which (depending on whether the hymns actually were used in the cult) may be primary rather than merely secondary sources. The *Hymn to Demeter* 228–230 is especially important because of its reference in the Demophon episode to a ritual baptism of fire. From the beginning, literary interests were focused not only on erotic magic but also on death and the underworld with its deities, especially Hekate and Persephone (e.g., Hesiod's Hekate episode in *Theogony* 411–452). There is also, of course, a close relationship between the literary and the pictorial art. Greek drama took to the subject as well, expressing it either in episodes (e.g., the calling up of the ghost of Darius in Aeschylus's *Persae* 619–842) or in whole tragedies (e.g., Euripides' *Medea,* treating one of the great witches of antiquity). Ancient comedy used magic for its own purposes, as in the description of a *goēs* ("quack") in Aristophanes' *Plutus* (649–747) or Menander's *Deisidaimon* and *Theophoroumene.* Theocritus's second idyll, entitled *Pharmakeutria* (The Witch), became a literary prototype for many later poets.

The superstitious man as a literary and ethical type was described by Theophrastus (*Characters* 16). The hymnic tradition was continued by the third-century BCE poet Callimachus (*Hymn to Demeter* 3–6; *On the Bath of Pallas* 9) and his pupil Apollonius of Rhodes, whose *Argonautica* included several magical sections (3.7ff., invocation to Erato; 744–911, Medea's preparation of magical drugs; 1163–1224, Jason's nocturnal sacrifice to Hekate; 1225–1407, Jason's magical defeat of the giants). Especially popular were descriptions of scenes of necromancy. In the Roman period the second-century Greek satirist Lucian of Samosata provides an almost complete inventory of magical beliefs and practices, as did the Greek novels.

In Roman literature the tradition continues with an increasing interest in the dramatic and the bizarre. Vergil's eighth eclogue (64–110) describes a magical ritual performed by a deserted lover that shows exact knowledge of magical details, although it is based upon Theocritus's second idyll. In the *Aeneid,* dramatic magical scenes are connected with the death of Dido (4.504–676). Horace's fifth epode has a macabre scene of the abduction and murder of a child.

Philosophical and scientific investigations. According to ancient tradition, philosophers have been preoccupied with magic since pre-Socratic times. The names of Heraclitus, Pythagoras, Empedocles, and Democritus appear several times in connection with magic, and spells under the names of Pythagoras and Democritus are found in the Greek Magical Papyri. Although the historical value of these references is doubtful, philosophers seem to have investigated magical phenomena since Pythagoras, who also may have been the first to make a positive use of it.

Greek philosophy in general rejected magic. The Skeptics, Epicureans, and Cynics produced an entire literature combating magic. But the attitude gradually changed with the development of demonology, mantic, and astrology. The Hermetic writings and the Neoplatonic philosophers Iamblichus and Proclus (and probably even Plotinus) accepted forms of magic and integrated them into their systems.

Scientific compendia of magical beliefs and practices are extant from the Roman period. Pliny's *Natural History* contains a history and theory of what he calls the *magicae vanitates* (30.1–18) and a large collection of remedies (see also book 28). Although written as an apology, Apuleius's *Apologia* (*De magia*) is in fact a compendium of magic. Apuleius's other works are also valuable sources for the magical beliefs of his time (see especially the *Metamorphoses*).

Legal provisions. Ancient law had no provisions for prosecuting magicians for the practice of magic. However, there are numerous accounts of trials in which magic played a role. These were trials not only of magicians and witches but also of philosophers (e.g., Anaxagoras, Socrates, Apollonius of Tyana, and Apuleius of Madaura). According to ancient writers, these persons were accused of murder by poisoning (*pharmakōn*) or of failure to honor the gods properly (*asebeia*), accusations broad enough to add emotional furor to a wide range of charges. If magic as such was not a reason for prosecution, harming a person by means of magic was. Plato included legal provisions against such injury in his *Laws* (11.933. D). The Romans went further and included property damages caused by weather or agricultural magic in the *Tabulae XII.*

JEWISH MAGIC. Magic played a somewhat different role in Judaism as compared with neighboring religions. The Old Testament shows that Israelite religion was well aware of the importance of magic in the religions of Egypt and Babylon, but on the whole it viewed magic negatively. For the Old Testament, magic is either foreign or marginal. Magicians are called in by Pharaoh (*Ex.* 7–10) or Nebuchadrezzar (*Dn.* 2:2); they serve Jezebel (*2 Kgs.* 9:22) and Manasseh (*2 Chr.* 33:6). The prophets warn against magic (*Is.* 47:9–15, *Jer.* 27:9, *Ez.* 13:17–19, *Na.* 3:4, *Mal.* 3:5, *Mi.* 5:11–12). The religion of Israel is believed to be more powerful than all magic, which is excluded by law (*Ex.* 22:18; *Lv.* 19:26, 19:31, 20:6, 20:27; *Dt.* 18:9–22). Especially important is the necromancy in the story of the witch of Endor (*1 Sm.* 28).

This picture, however, is deceptive. Pre-Israelite religions, most of them saturated with magic, have left numerous traces in Israelite religion; furthermore, popular Israelite religion must not be confused with what the Old Testament conveys. In this popular religion, magic has a firm place that was often approved of even by "official" religion (e.g., Moses' and Elijah's magical wands in *Ex.* 4:20, 17:8–13; *2 Kgs.* 4:29, 4:31; Urim and Tummim, ephod and terafim in *1 Sm.* 2:18, 14:3, 14:18; *Jgs.* 17–18; *Dt.* 33:8). More important than amulets and rituals was the magic of the word, especially curses and blessings and above all the name of Yahveh (see especially *Jgs.* 13:6, 13:17–18; *Ex.* 3:14). The name of Yahveh became the most important magical element in Judaism and, beyond it, in Hellenistic syncretism. Therefore the God Iao plays an enormous role in the Greek Magical Papyri, and on the magical gems and amulets of the Hellenistic and Roman period.

These various developments persist on a far broader scale in rabbinic Judaism. The official rejection of magic in rabbinic literature must be seen against the background of popular religion and the whole mystical tradition

(Merkavah, Qabbalah), both of which were very open to magical beliefs and practices.

Christian Magic. For early Christianity, magic presented difficulties. On the one hand, Christians had inherited Judaism's negative attitude toward magic (see *Gal.* 5:20, and the typical attitudes expressed in *Acts* 8:9–24, 13:6–12, 19:13–19). On the other hand, the emphasis on miracles and sacraments implied approval of some forms of magic. Jesus' activities as a miracle worker were soon attacked as being the work of a magician possessed by Beelzebub (*Mk.* 3:22–27 and parallels). Beginning with the presynoptic sources of the Gospels, New Testament apologetics was increasingly preoccupied with defending Jesus against classification with the magicians. Since his exorcisms and miracle work could not be ignored, distinctions were introduced to separate miracles from magic. Similarly, miracles worked by Christian healers had to be separated from those of non-Christians. This was accomplished by treating the latter as acts done by magicians.

Problems arose also because of the close affinities between the epiphanies of the crucified and resurrected Christ and the magical concept of the return as demons of persons who had died of violence (*biaiothanatoi*) (see especially *Lk.* 24:36–43, *Jn.* 20:19–23). Moreover, magical presuppositions in the rituals of baptism and the Eucharist led to practices approved by some and disapproved by others (see especially Paul, who tried to correct misuse in *1 Cor.* 1:10–16, 8:1–11:1, 11:17–34, and in *Rom.* 6:3–10). Paul first distinguished between abuse (magical misconceptions) and proper use (sacraments) of these rituals. The fundamental theological problems stated or implied in these early texts continued to assert themselves throughout the history of Christianity and have led to ever new conceptualizations.

From the second century on, popular Christian religion showed greater interest in amulets, relics, symbols, and signs (see the apocryphal gospels and *Acts*). The gnostics also made positive use of magic (see especially the *Book of Jeu*, the *Pistis Sophia*, and the writings found at Nag Hammadi, Egypt). The official church, through its bishops, synods, and the writings of the church fathers, was forced to combat and suppress new Christian forms of magic and superstition. The extant wealth of amulets, spells, relics, holy places, symbols, and images indicates that complete suppression was impossible. Still, Christian theology was able to contain and restrain the lower forms of magic by accepting some forms of christianized magic while eliminating other, unwanted forms. Liturgy and sacramental theology developed special kinds of magic thought to be compatible with the doctrines of the church. By the end of antiquity, the church had become the home of many forms of magic that coexisted in an uneasy and tenuous symbiosis. Some magic was banned, some was tolerated, some was approved, but none achieved domination.

See Also Amulets and Talismans; Cursing; Incantation; Theurgy.

Bibliography

No complete collection of the vast remains of ancient magic exists, but there are useful editions and translations, indices, and surveys of literature. For new publications, see the annual bibliography in Marouzeau, *L'annee philologique*, section on "Magica."

Texts and Translations

Betz, Hans Dieter, ed. *The Greek Magical Papyri in Translation, Including the Demotic Spells.* 2 vols. Chicago, 1986.

Kropp, Angelicus M. *Ausgewählte koptische Zaubertexte.* 3 vols. Brussels, 1930–1932. Volume 1 has the edition of Coptic texts; volume 2 has their German translation; volume 3 is introductory.

Preisendanz, Karl. *Papyri Graecae Magicae: Die griechischen Zauberpapyri.* 2 vols. Edited by Albert Henrichs. 2d ed. Stuttgart, 1973–1974. Edition of Greek texts, with German translation, notes, and bibliography.

Studies

Abt, Adam. *Die Apologie des Apuleius von Madaura und die antike Zauberei.* Giessen, 1908.

Aune, David E. "Magic in Early Christianity." In *Aufstieg und Niedergang der römischen Welt*, vol. 2.23.2 (Berlin and New York, 1969), pp. 1507–1557. A comprehensive bibliographical report.

Bonner, Campbell. *Studies in Magical Amulets, Chiefly Graeco-Egyptian.* Ann Arbor, 1950.

Burkert, Walter. *Griechische Religion der archaischen und klassischen Epoche.* Stuttgart, 1977. Translated as *Greek Religion* (Cambridge, Mass., 1985). Important and up-to-date comments on various aspects of magic in the archaic and classical periods of Greek religion.

Grant, Robert M. *Miracle and Natural Law in Graeco-Roman and Early Christian Thought.* Amsterdam, 1952.

Herzig, Otto. *Lukian als Quelle für die antike Zauberei.* Würzburg, 1940.

Hopfner, Theodor. *Griechisch-ägyptischer Offenbarungszauber.* 2 vols. Leipzig, 1921–1924. Still the best survey of the entire range of material.

Hopfner, Theodor. "Mageia." In *Real-Encyclopädie der classischen Altertumswissenschaft*, vol. 14 (Stuttgart, 1928), pp. 301–393. Mostly a summary of the former work.

Luck, Georg. *Arcana Mundi. Magic and the Occult in the Greek and Roman Worlds.* Baltimore and London, 1985. A useful collection of sources in translation, with brief introductions and notes.

Nilsson, Martin P. *Geschichte der griechischen Religion.* 3d ed. 2 vols. Munich, 1967–1974. Has important sections on magic at the various stages of development in Greek religion.

Scholem, Gershom. "Der Name Gottes und die Sprachtheorie der Kabbala." *Eranos-Jahrbuch* 39 (1970): 243–297.

Thee, Francis C. R. *Julius Africanus and the Early Christian View of Magic.* Tübingen, 1984. The volume contains the *Kestoi* of Julius Africanus (c. 160–240 CE) in translation, together with commentary, extensive introduction, and a survey of the early Christian views on magic.

Thorndike, Lynn. *A History of Magic and Experimental Science*, vols. 1–2, *The First Thirteen Centuries of Our Era.* New York, 1923. Written from the perspective of the history of science; incomplete series of studies.

Trachtenberg, Joshua. *Jewish Magic and Superstition* (1939). Reprint, New York, 1982.

Trumpf, Jürgen. "Fluchtafel und Rachepuppe." *Mitteilungen des Deutschen Archäologischen Instituts*, Athenische Abteilung, 73 (1958): 94–102.

Widengren, Geo. *Religionsphänomenologie.* Berlin, 1969. References on various aspects of magic can be found in the index, s. v. v. *Magie, Magier.*

HANS DIETER BETZ (1987)

MAGIC: MAGIC IN MEDIEVAL AND RENAISSANCE EUROPE

Information about medieval and early modern notions of magic is derived mainly from two types of source: (1) theological writings that describe and condemn magic, generally referring to it explicitly by the term *magic*, and (2) other works telling in greater or lesser detail how to perform particular types of magical operation, which are usually not identified explicitly as magical. The word *magic* is mainly an abstract and analytical term used in the theological literature. Practitioners more often described the purposes their operations served (e.g., healing, cursing, arousing love), without troubling to place these operations in an abstract category such as *magic*. In the fifteenth century this distinction broke down, and individuals who prescribed and practiced magic began referring to themselves as magicians or workers of magic. Apart from the theological works dealing with magic and the descriptions of concrete magical procedures, the study of law codes and the records of prosecution also provide some insights.

Magical techniques mentioned in medieval and early modern sources are largely identical with those found in many other cultures: manipulation of images to afflict another person physically or emotionally, administration of potions for these same ends, recitation of charms for healing or curses for harm, placing curative or apotropaic substances on a client's body, placing harmful substances in a victim's bed or under the threshold, gazing into reflective surfaces to divine the future or learn about hidden affairs, and conjuring spirits and bidding them to provide aid.

THE THEOLOGICAL TRADITION. Many early Christian writers condemned magical practices, which they associated with the pagan traditions of Greco-Roman society. The North African writer Tertullian (c. 200 CE) represented magic as a kind of fraud taught by demons to impressionable women. Origen (c. 185–c. 254) discussed magic chiefly in his work against the pagan writer Celsus. He too represented magic as an art taught by demons, but he emphasized the real efficacy of words, whether sacred or magical. The early Christian attacks on magic were transmitted to the medieval West primarily by *The City of God* and other writings of Augustine of Hippo (354–430). Although Augustine wrote after the Roman emperor Constantine (d. 337) and his successors had given Christianity an official status as an established religion, he still felt a need to respond to pagan critics of Christianity, and one part of his argument was the link between paganism and magic. For Augustine, magic was taught by demons and worked through the power of demons. Magical plants and stones might seem to have inherent power, but it is demons who disclose this power. Augustine conceded that there are objects in nature (such as the magnet) that do have inexplicable properties, but what he referred to specifically as magic was for him a form of pagan idolatry.

From the seventh century into the twelfth, the theological tradition was passed down through writers, including Isidore of Seville (c. 560–636) and Hincmar of Rheims (c. 806–882), who continued to draw on early Christian literature. This tradition's concern was fourfold: (1) to trace the origins of magic, seen as largely the invention of Zoroaster; (2) to categorize various types of magic, particularly forms of divination such as pyromancy (divination by fire), aeromany (air), hydromancy (water), geomancy (earth), and necromancy (consultation of spirits); (3) to expose the effects of magic as largely illusory; and (4) to explain its real effects as caused by the aid of demons. Within this tradition, magicians were so named because of the greatness of their evil acts—the noun *magus* (magician) is derived from the adjective *magnus* (great). They cause storms by disrupting the elements, they transform natural objects, they cause disturbance to people's minds, and, by the power of incantations, they can kill their victims.

John of Salisbury's (1120–1180) *Polycraticus* stands within this tradition. John divided magic into three primary categories: illusions (*praestigia*), bewitchments (*maleficia*), and divination (*mathematica*). He took over from classical and early medieval sources various subdivisions of divination, depending on the means used for divining the future. Among the many practitioners he catalogued are *vultivoli*, who use figures of wax or clay to bewitch people; *imaginarii*, who use images to gain control over spirits; *specularii*, who gaze into reflecting surfaces such as mirrors or basins and foretell the future according to what they see. If these arts have any efficacy, it can only be through their reliance on demons. John himself was exposed to the operations of the *specularii* when he was a boy, and he was sent to learn Latin from a priest who engaged in these practices and used his pupils as mediums.

Hugh of Saint Victor (d. 1142) in his *Didascolicon* gave a classification of the types of magic similar to John of Salisbury's categories. He argued that magic is alien both to philosophy and religion, that it is immoral and illegal, and that it is false and thus deceptive. True law, religion, and erudition, he insisted, all repudiate it.

Thomas Aquinas (c. 1225–1274) spoke of magic as used for purposes such as disclosing the future and finding hidden treasure, opening closed doors, making people invisible, causing inanimate bodies to move about and speak, and summoning spirits. He believed that magicians make use of herbs and other natural objects, verbal formulas, and inscribed figures and characters. They use rituals such as sacrifices and prostrations. With astrological calculation, they observe the proper times for obtaining their effects. He also described the notory art (*ars notoria*), which claims to acquire knowledge through rituals of fasting and prayer, along with occult figures and formulas. However, the underlying cause of these effects is the working of demons. Still, Thomas recognized in his letter "On the Occult Works of Nature" that many wondrous effects are possible through manipulation of occult forces within the natural order. But many practices that might elsewhere have been categorized as magic he included under the category of superstition, which he defined as the inappropriate veneration of a proper object or the directing of veneration to an improper object.

The position of Albert the Great (1193–1280) is more difficult to summarize. In his strictly theological writings he repeats traditional condemnations of magic, but his scientific works tend to portray magic in a more benign light. He recognizes plants as having divine or magical effects, and he writes with apparent approbation about the efficacy of magical stones and inscriptions. The *Speculum astronomiae*, plausibly attributed to Albert, is concerned mainly with distinguishing between the valid prescriptions of astrological magic (i.e., operations making use of inscribed astrological symbols for exploiting the powers of heavenly bodies) and the reprobate operations of necromancy (which appeal to demonic powers). Also complex was the position of William of Auvergne (c. 1180–1249), who had studied and condemned works of demonic necromancy but explicitly recognized natural magic as a branch of science that might be rarified (many of its operations required substances that might be plentiful in India and other lands but were rare in Europe) but was not forbidden.

THE LITERATURE OF MAGICAL INSTRUCTIONS. Before the twelfth century, works telling how to make use of occult—or magical, to the theologians—powers fell mainly into three categories: (1) works of medicinal magic that might combine Galenic conceptions of healing with the use of occult substances and formulas; (2) instructions for divination; and (3) lists of the wondrous properties to be found in gems and other natural objects.

Medicine could be classed as magical if it made use of symbolic remedies or adjurations. The late Anglo-Saxon text *Lacnunga* recommended, for example, that a pregnant woman fearful of miscarrying should obtain milk from a cow that is of one color, pour it into running water, retrieve the water and drink it, return from the stream by a route different from the one she took in approaching it, enter into a different house from the one she left, and throughout the procedure remain silent and take care not to look around. The symbolic meanings in this operation are not obvious, but it is at least clear that by taking these measures the woman is ensuring that she will bear a child and have milk for it to drink, and that, with the variations in her route, she is breaking from a past experience of a presumably difficult pregnancy. Medical adjurations are usually more explicit in their meaning: An adjuration is a type of charm addressed to the disease itself, or to the disease agent (pictured as a demon, a worm, an elf, or some other maleficent being), which is commanded to depart. Adjurations and other medicinal charms were widely recommended and used, sometimes by physicians, throughout medieval Europe. The body parts of animals and birds (e.g., the various organs of the vulture) were also sometimes catalogued according to their medical utility.

Instructions for divination were various and ranged from simple lists (e.g., of favorable or unfavorable days for various undertakings) to more complicated procedures for telling the future. One particularly famous text, the *Sortes Sangallenses* (Saint Gall Oracles) is found in a manuscript from around the year 600. Individuals wanting to know about medical prognoses, fortunes in love, the outcome of judicial business, or other matters could consult these oracles, using dice to find the correct answers to their questions. Astrology could furnish more sophisticated counsel about one's fortunes and was also popularized in simpler forms of lunar astrology—in particular, by giving almanac-like indications of what one might expect for each day in the moon's phases.

Of the works on the wonders of nature, one of the more famous was the lapidary written by Marbode of Renne (1035–1123). Writing in literary Latin, Marbode recommended using a sapphire to gain the favor of God and of mortals, chalcedony to obtain victory in battle, selenite to reconcile quarreling lovers, and other gems for a wide range of purposes—although it is difficult to know whether readers actually used these gems with the expectation of obtaining concrete results or merely read the compilation for the excitement of knowing about marvelous magical effects.

The literature of magical instructions was greatly expanded in the twelfth and thirteenth centuries, when interaction between Christians and Muslims (especially in Spain) resulted in the transmission of a substantial mass of astrological and magical learning to western Europe that had long been preserved in Arabic. Adelard of Bath (1075–1160) was a particularly important Christian student of the Arabic occult sciences and did much to make them available to Europeans in the twelfth century. The most famous work of Arabic astrological magic, translated into Spanish and Latin in the thirteenth century at the behest of King Alfonso the Wise of Castile (1252–1284), was a compilation known in the West as *Picatrix.* This book told in detail how to conjure the spirits associated with the planets, how to inscribe on metal the images of the heavenly bodies to accomplish one's purposes (including bodily harm to individuals and groups), and how to use other magical procedures and objects. The book also gives instructions on how to use fumigations to attract spirits with the smoke of particular plants and other substances and on how to manufacture a magical mirror, which must be fumigated with a mixture of effluvia from the human body. More explicitly than most magical texts, *Picatrix* recognizes magic as a noble science and the magician as an exalted and honorable figure.

The astrological magic of *Picatrix* was at times referred to as necromancy, but in the later Middle Ages this term more often referred to conjuring of demons. The term originally meant summoning the spirits of the deceased, but in late medieval Europe the terms *necromantia* (necromancy) and *nigromantia* (roughly, black magic) were fundamentally interchangeable. Works describing how to conjure demons were, not surprisingly, often prey to inquisitorial fires, but some have survived. They center mainly on verbal formulas commanding the demons to present themselves and to carry out the will of the necromancer. The terms *coniuro* (I conjure), *exorcizo* (I exorcize), and *impero* (I command) meant the same thing: a conjuration or an exorcism was a command addressed to a demon, whether it was being ordered to come or to depart. The necromancer typically made reference to sacred names and sacred events as sources of magical power over the demons; thus, the conjuration "I conjure you by the passion and death of Christ" might be used to invoke a demon to appear and perform some service. Necromancers often stood within circles, which served mainly as further means of magical power but also could be seen as protecting the necromancer from the demons summoned. Practitioners of necromancy were expected to know Latin and basic liturgical formulas. They clearly were, for the most part, clerics. Writings on the conjuration of demons continued to circulate in the early modern period, when they became known as *grimoires.*

Although the magic of Western Christendom from the twelfth century onward was heavily indebted to Arabic sources, it drew also on Jewish tradition for inspiration. One particularly interesting example is the notory art ascribed in the later Middle Ages to King Solomon. This was a method of prayers and meditations meant to instill command of the liberal arts and other knowledge. There was a long Jewish tradition of gaining knowledge through magical contact with angels, and the *ars notoria* built on this tradition.

THE MAGICIANS OF RENAISSANCE EUROPE. For the most part, the literature of magical instruction either was anonymous or was pseudonymously ascribed (e.g., to Solomon, to Aristotle, or to Albert the Great). Beginning in the later fifteenth century, it was far more common for notable figures in society to practice and to write about what they themselves called magic. Their practices might be indebted to the Arabic tradition of the occult sciences, but two further sources that commanded attention from the 1480s onward were the writings from antiquity ascribed to the mythical Hermes Trismegistus titled *Hermetic Corpus* and the aspect of Jewish mysticism known as practical Qabbalah.

The Italian humanist Marsilio Ficino (1433–1499), in his *Three Books on Life* (completed 1489), provided one of the most important and influential syntheses of magical literature. Ficino was associated with Cosimo de' Medici (1519–1574), at whose urging he translated the *Hermetic Corpus* into Latin. He was also well acquainted with the third-century Neoplatonist philosopher Plotinus (205–270), from whom he took the notion of the universe as a great living being whose members worked in sympathetic harmony one with another; the fourth-century Neoplatonist Iamblichus, who had taught how to summon and make use of spirits by means of magical procedures; the *Picatrix*, which he used as a source for some of his prescriptions; and other works of Arabic astrological magic. His main interest was in using the beneficent influence of heavenly bodies (particularly the Sun and Jupiter) to enhance human life and health. This might be done by fashioning astrological images with the symbols of these celestial bodies, but in general Ficino was more favorably disposed to astrological "medicines" by which astral influences could be transmitted more effectively to humans: Saffron and honey, for example, were good repositories of solar virtue. Ficino also made use of Orphic hymns for their beneficent effect. Anticipating criticism for his use of magic, he pointed out that the magi in Matthew's gospel were honorable models for imitation, that Jesus had exercised healing arts, and that it was thus fitting for a priest and healer such as Ficino himself to use magical techniques to promote health and enhanced life. He insisted that he was advocating only natural magic, not demonic magic, although he did see astral powers as coming from heavenly bodies that were associated with attendant spirits, and he left himself open to the suspicion that these spirits were demonic.

Ficino's younger contemporary, Giovanni Pico della Mirandola (1463–1494), was also eclectic in his use of material but, unlike Ficino, he ascribed special importance to the magical efficacy of the practical Qabbalah—in particular, the power found in Hebrew words. In 1486 Pico proposed nine hundred theses for public debate at Rome—many of which had to do with natural magic and Qabbalah. In the theses and in his defense of them, he was concerned more with the theory of these arts than with concrete prescriptions for its practice. He provoked a systematic refutation of his arguments (published 1489) by the Spaniard Pedro Garcia, who refused to acknowledge that there was such an art as natural magic as distinct from the demonic sort.

In northern Europe, the most comprehensive Renaissance articulation of magic was that of Heinrich Cornelius Agrippa (1486–1535), whose encyclopedic *Three Books on Occult Philosophy* showed how natural substances, astral powers, mathematical figures, sacred names, and rituals could be used to magical effect. Agrippa wrote his work in 1510 as a young man, and he later condemned all occult learning as vain. Yet he finally published his compendium in 1533, perhaps because he had renewed confidence in its validity, but possibly (as some have suggested) in a cynical quest of publicity. The incorporation of demonic magic only hinted at in Ficino is more explicit in Agrippa, who explains how demons may be conjured and commanded, although he warns that the magician must do this with the aid of good spirits.

The image of the Renaissance magician gave rise to the legend of Doctor Faust, who conjured and made a pact with the demon Mephistopheles, resigning his soul to Satan in return for twenty-four years in which Mephistopheles would be at his service. Loosely based on the report of a historical person, this legend was popularized in a German *Faust Book* published in 1587, which inspired Christopher Marlowe to write his play, *The Tragical History of Doctor Faustus.* The assumption behind the legend is that Renaissance magicians were more like necromancers than they themselves claimed to be.

Giordano Bruno (1548–1600) is sometimes viewed as bringing Renaissance magic to its culmination, chiefly for his use of the Hermetic corpus and Qabbalah. His work *On Magic,* written late in his life, advocated the use of imagination as a way of gaining access to demonic power and discussed means for "binding" spirits. But this work was not published until 1891, and Bruno's notoriety in his own time was based mostly on his cosmological and philosophical theories. Still, *On Magic* is important in the history of Renaissance magic for its frank acknowledgment of the demonic element in magic. In Bruno, the complex relationship between natural and demonic magic that runs through Renaissance tradition from Ficino onward finds a striking resolution.

Bibliography

The most general and comprehensive study of the history of magic is Lynn Thorndike, *The History of Magic and Experimental Science* (New York, 1923–1958). For medieval magic in particular, see Edward Peters, *The Magician, the Witch, and the Law* (Philadelphia, 1978), Richard Kieckhefer, *Magic in the Middle Ages* (Cambridge, U.K., 1989), Valerie I. J. Flint, *The Rise of Magic in Early Medieval Europe* (Princeton, N.J., 1991), and Bengt Ankarloo and Stuart Clark, eds., *Witchcraft and Magic in Europe,* vol. 3, *The Middle Ages* (Philadelphia, 2002).

Numerous texts of magical instruction from medieval Europe have been edited, translated, and studied. For example, see Godfrid Storms, ed., *Anglo-Saxon Magic* (The Hague, 1948), Karen Louise Jolly, *Popular Religion in Late Saxon England: Elf Charms in Context* (Chapel Hill, N.C., 1996), Marbode of Renne, *De lapidibus,* edited by John M. Riddle and translated by C. W. King (Wiesbaden, 1977), Charles Burnett, *Magic and Divination in the Middle Ages: Texts and Techniques in the Islamic and Christian Worlds* (Aldershot, U.K., 1996), and David Pingree, ed., *Picatrix: The Latin Version of the Ghāyat Al-Ḥakīm* (London, 1986). For a discussion of necromancy and related forms of ritual magic, see Richard Kieckhefer, *Forbidden Rites: A Necromancer's Manual of the Fifteenth Century* (Stroud, U.K., 1997; reprint, University Park, Penn., 1998), and Claire Fanger, ed., *Conjuring Spirits: Texts and Traditions of Medieval Ritual Magic* (University Park, Pa., 1998).

For general studies of Renaissance magic, see Daniel P. Walker, *Spiritual and Demonic Magic: From Ficino to Campanella* (University Park, Pa., 2000), and Frances A. Yates, *Giordano Bruno and the Hermetic Tradition* (London, 1964). More specific texts and studies include Marsilio Ficino, *Three Books on Life,* with introduction and notes by Carol V. Kaske and John R. Clark (Binghamton, N.Y., 1989), Giovanni Pico della Mirandola, *Syncretism in the West: Pico's 900 Theses (1486): The Evolution of Traditional, Religious, and Philosophical Systems: Text, Translation, and Commentary,* translated by S. A. Farmer (Tempe, Ariz., 1998), Henry Cornelius Agrippa, *Three Books of Occult Philosophy,* translated by James Freake and edited by Donald Tyson (St. Paul, Minn., 1993), and Charles Garfield Nauert, *Agrippa and the Crisis of Renaissance Thought* (Urbana, Ill., 1965).

Richard Kieckhefer (2005)

MAGIC: MAGIC IN EASTERN EUROPE

Demonology, introduced by Christian religious thought in the fifteenth and sixteenth centuries, profoundly affected western European thought with respect to its conception of magic. The transformation of the witch into an expression of the demon who seeks to ensure his power on earth and prepare for his own advent obscured popular thinking, which possessed its own type of representations and its own system of values inherited from a rather deep-rooted paganism. In eastern Europe, where this intervention did not occur in the same way, the phenomenon of magic continued to evolve in its primary form, as a unified practice anchored in a popular culture of which it represented only one facet.

For so long isolated from the historical and sociological upheavals that affected western Europe, the peoples of eastern Europe still hold to a different worldview and use different means to account for the human condition. As Mircea Eliade states in his *De Zalmoxis à Gengis-Khan* (1970): "As in all other provinces of the Roman Empire, autochthonous religious realities outlived, more or less transformed, both the romanizing and the christianizing processes. There is enough proof of a pagan heritage" (p. 73). The common inherited substratum preserved by the Romanian and Balkan populations is considered by Eliade as "the principal unifying element in the entire Balkan peninsula" (ibid., p. 183). As early as the 1930s, Pierre Bogatyrev, in the introduction to his *Actes magiques, rites et croyances en Russie subcarpathique* (1929), noted a renaissance of paganism among ethnic groups practicing orthodox religions, even though he insists that this renaissance evidently took place "under the aegis of the Revolution and Soviet government." He adds: "Orthodox religion and witchcraft, the rival sisters, . . . form an unexpected ensemble. All of village Russia is divided into witchcraft parishes that do not yield to ecclesiastical parishes."

Given the importance of the pagan heritage (not to mention the circulation of motifs, sociocultural exchanges, and so on), it is not surprising that a rather large body of magical practices is shared by the majority of the traditional societies of southeastern Europe. In fact, there is no domain in which magic is not practiced; magic crosscuts all spheres in which human beings move. But recourse to magic becomes especially obligatory for the different phases of the life cycle; in this way it ensures its principal function, that of integrating individuals into their own collectivity and their own development. Throughout this region, for example, the Fates, those fabulous beings whom the Bulgars call "women or fairies of fate" and whom the Greeks name simply Morai ("fates"), participate in the "programming" of an entire life, from birth to death, including marriage. They are the ones to whom a woman addresses herself (even today, in a hospital setting) on the third day after childbirth:

> You, the Saints, You the Good Ones, You the Fates Predestine this child, This newborn. Come as sweet as honey, Come as smooth as water, And as good as bread, As gay as wine, As limpid as water, And give him intelligence and wisdom. To this child newborn, Give him health and good fortune in life. May he be protected by God.

In Romania, especially in the region known as Little Walachia, the Fates intervene in the principal magical rites dealing with marriage and love through the intermediary of their plant, the mandrake. When, for example, a mandrake is unearthed during rites designed to determine a young woman's mate, the Fates are addressed in the same terms as those used to ask about a child's destiny: "You, the Saints, / You the Good Ones, / You the Pure, / I give you honey, wine, bread, and salt. / Let me know the destiny of [so-and-so]." The Fates are also invoked through their plant in incantations that accompany magical rites aiming to reunite separated couples:

> You mandrake, You the Benefactress, Herb of the Saints, Know her lot. And if her husband had been destined to marry, If this union be his fate, Bring him back And reunite them, Keep them bound forever. . . . Give them a second chance. . . . If God had wanted them to separate, May they separate. But if not, Bring them together, you, Benefactress, Herb of the saints. Unite them a second time. Enliven her home. . . .

At times of death, the Fates through their plant are once again asked to intervene in a sort of ritual magic that is experienced and felt as a form of euthanasia. After the mandrake is unearthed "in order to summon death," an act performed in complete silence and sadness; it is boiled and the ill person is bathed with the decoction; at this time the Fates are invoked and asked to declare the lot they have selected for the sufferer: death or life. If it is death (as is usually the case), they are asked to palliate the victim's suffering: "May his fate be decided. / If it be death may it come quickly. / May he not suffer any longer." This type of magic ritual also appears in the Balkans, at least among the Bulgars, as Christo Vakarelski (1969) demonstrates.

Many other magical practices are shared by these traditional societies. Among them, the most important are the rites aiming to vitiate the contamination associated with childbirth and those aiming to avoid the contamination of death—all intended to ensure the separation of worlds that should not intersect. An extended comparative study, for example, could be undertaken on the magical precautions taken so that the dead remain dead and do not transform themselves into vampires, who are today still dreaded, feared, and fought. Represented as wild or monstrous carnivorous animals, these eternally unsatisfied beings are doomed to seek out earthly pleasures. They refuse to be relegated to the beyond and, instead, assume human form in order to finish on earth what they could not realize in life. In order to make sure the dead do not become vampires, certain preventive measures can be undertaken. One can, for example, deposit nine stones, nine marble chips, and nine millet grains under the person's head and utter the following incantation:

> Your mouth, I petrify. Your lips, I marbleize. Your teeth, to millet I transform. So that harm shall you never wreak.

Numerous magical practices (echoing religious rites) are also associated with the cyclical succession of the seasons and with the household. Incantations surrounding the home usually seek to expel malevolent forces and bring good luck:

> Just as the waters melt in March, Just as they are transported by the torrent And just as they clean and carry All the rust, All the trash, May my home and all those who live in it also be Cleansed Of all malfeasance, all bad luck, All illness, all ill will That may be in its walls.

These incantations and the rites they accompany are essential, for they situate man in a context of rituals that integrate him with nature and the order of the cosmos. In fact, it is in this domain that, from Romania to Bulgaria to Russia to Greece and Albania, the magical rites most resemble each other in both form and content.

Magical practices are also directed at administrative and legal authorities. For villagers the power of persuasion is the best weapon against these authorities with whom they are usually involved in a "battle of words." Silencing the authorities is seen as the ultimate form of persuasion, and many incantations thus request that they be silenced just like the dead:

> Just as the dead have now grown cold, May all members of the tribunal grow as cold. May no one be able to proclaim my guilt. May they stop speaking, May they lose their voice Just as the dead have lost theirs. The arms of the dead are crossed over their chest. May the case made against me grow as cold as they. May it go away.

In many regions of eastern Europe one could say that folk culture was not profoundly modified by the more or less important changes that occurred in modes of production. It is, however, not easy to speak of magic and witchcraft as it is currently practiced and experienced in these countries, because both official discourse and research data relegate these practices to an obscure past or consider them forms of charlatanism. A series of field trips conducted in Romania in recent years, however, confirms that folk beliefs remain very much alive and that recourse to magical practices in frequent, especially when it concerns the health of children, the prosperity of the home, the productivity of animals, and so on. In fact, one does not have recourse to magic merely on an occasional basis; it is the imaginary fabric into which all individuals are enveloped. There are few mothers, for example, who do not know one or another incantation to neutralize the effects of the evil eye (belief in the evil eye is found throughout the Mediterranean Basin and elsewhere). The following Romanian example is expressed in extremely violent terms:

> May he burst, the envious one. Evil eye he cast. May he explode. If a virgin spellbinds him, May her braids fall off. If his wife spellbinds him, May her milk dry up, May her breasts wither, May her child die of hunger. If a youth spellbinds him, May he burst completely.

Many practices and incantations form part of any individual's basic knowledge, but one seeks recourse to magic only if one has the gift, the power, the desire, and the daring to do so. The specialists commonly known as witches possess the gift and the daring to practice a distinct form of magic. A witch is frequently described as someone who uses supernatural forces to do evil (although most witches will say they do what they do for the good of humankind). Witches were and still are enormously feared because they are said to "give life or death." Consulting them always means incurring some form of danger, especially since they are thought to collaborate with the Devil (who appears in his diverse forms during the séance). Access to witches is also difficult and troublesome: they live often in faraway places (necessitating a tiresome journey, waiting one's turn among the others who have come for consultations, sleeping in a strange place); one can only see them on specific days and at specific times (at night, for example); one must be recommended to them by someone in whom the witch has confidence. Thus access to specialized magic could be said to presuppose a kind of punitive expiatory path.

People have recourse to witchcraft especially in cases of serious disequilibrium or when a significant disturbance has disrupted the natural order of things. Witches are especially sought out, for example, in cases in which a marriage is endangered by the intervention of a third party (usually the husband's mistress, a rival who wishes to substitute herself for his legitimate wife). Indeed, marital relations and extramarital ties are a source of great conflict and violence, and the greater part of specialized forms of magic is played out in this arena.

To control her husband, who should not waste his energies elsewhere, a woman has recourse to two forms of specialized magic, both of which aim to reunite the legitimate couple. In the first form the wife attempts to kill the intruder (the "rival," the "stranger") or to eliminate her from the protected sphere. In the process, the two women enter into a kind of magical battle using a number of possible weapons: a charmed knife that must symbolically reach the other; dolls made from scraps of the man's or the mistress's clothing: a yellow plant (*dosnica*), described as "terrifying," which causes the rival to wander to the ends of the earth; the mandrake, which can make people go mad; and an insect or a frog (seen as the mistress's substitute) captured under special conditions and made to suffer the worst treatments.

Specific procedures accompany the use of any of these means. For example, while piercing a symbol representing her rival with the charmed knife, the woman will utter the following incantation:

> You, charmed knife, Go into her body. Beat her, Crush her, So that her blood spouts forth. If she is alive, pierce her heart. If she is dead, seek her out in the Beyond.

While thinking of her rival a woman may prick an insect with a needle or a knife and utter:

> May the one who is breaking my home, The one who does not let me live with my man, The one who gives me no peace, May that one die and disappear.

In the second form—identified as the "magic of filth"—the wife will simply attempt to dissolve the soiled relationship in which her husband is involved in order to reestablish her original tie with him. She will use decoctions made from urine, semen, menstrual blood, fecal matter, sweat, or other secretions of intimate life (which serve as substitutes for the people concerned). These decoctions may be clandestinely fed to the husband. If he eats his own secretions (an act of autocannibalism), he is said to devour himself, thus reintegrating the forces and energies he seeks to dispense elsewhere. If he eats the substitutes of his wife, he is said to become impregnated by her, filled with her person.

Incantations accompany the administration of these decoctions; if, for example, the wife uses menstrual blood, she utters the following words (similar to those used in practices on certain Greek islands today):

> Just as the menses are cyclical, Have their hour and time, So, to each of my words May he likewise return. May he return to my body, May he return to my desire. . . . May my husband cling to me, May he explode, may he burst, May he not do without me.

The wife may also manipulate these secretions in other ways. She may, for example, take the earth on which her rival has trod and place it on her husband's feces, uttering an incantation all the while.

One could speak at length about these and other forms of magic still practiced in Romania and other east European countries. Indeed, despite all the sociocultural modifications and modernizing trends that have taken place in this part of the world, magic has adapted itself to its new environment. It is not a survival of a bygone era but an integral aspect of popular culture; it provides people with the power and know-how to understand their world and their position within it. Magic is still the arena through which different communities find a common language, a discourse through which they recognize themselves.

See Also Incantation.

Bibliography

Argenti, Philip P., and H. J. Rose. *The Folk-Lore of Chios.* Cambridge, 1949.

Bîrlea, Ovidiu. "Descîntecul." In his *Folclorul românesc,* vol. 2. Bucharest, 1983.

Bîrlea, Ovidiu, and Ion Muslea. *Tipologia folclorului: Din raspunsurile la chestionarele lui B. P. Hasdeu.* Bucharest, 1970.

Bogatyrev, Pierre. *Actes magiques, rites et croyances en Russie subcarpathique.* Paris, 1929.

Eliade, Mircea. *De Zalmoxis à Gengis-Khan.* Paris, 1970. Translated as *Zalmoxis, the Vanishing God: Comparative Studies in the Religions and Folklore of Dacia and Eastern Europe* (Chicago, 1972).

Eliade, Mircea. *Occultism, Witchcraft, and Cultural Fashions: Essays in Comparative Religions.* Chicago, 1976.

Gorovei, Arthur. *Descîntecele românilor.* Bucharest, 1931.

Kabbadias, Georgios B. *Pasteurs-Nomades méditéranéens: Les Saracatsans de Grèce.* Paris, 1965.

Krauss, Friedrich S. *Slavische Volksforschungen.* Leipzig, 1908.

Lorint, F. E., and Jean Bernabé. *La sorcellerie paysanne.* Brussels, 1977.

Megas, George A. *Greek Calendar Customs.* 2d ed. Athens, 1963.

Stahl, Paul-Henri. "L'organisation magique du territoire villageois roumain." *L'homme* 13 (1973): 150–162.

Vakarelski, Christo. *Bulgarische Volkskunde.* Berlin, 1969.

New Sources

Aleksieva, Ekaterina, and Dinna Ancheva. *Ancient Magic in Bulgarian Folklore: Perls of Syncretic Folk Art, Village of Bistritsa, Bulgaria.* Sofia, Bulgaria, 1991.

Brzozowska-Krajka, Anna. *Polish Traditional Folklore: The Magic of Time.* Translated by Wieslaw Krajka. East European Monographs, no. 498. Boulder; New York, 1998.

Petzoldt, Ruth, and Paul Neubauer, eds. *Demons, Mediators between this World and the Other: Essays on Demonic Beings from the Middle Ages to the Present.* Frankfurt am Main; New York, 1998.

Ryan, William Francis. *The Bathhouse at Midnight: An Historical Survey of Magic and Divination in Russia.* University Park, Pa., 1999.

Voiculescu, Vasile. *Tales of Fantasy and Magic.* Translated from the Romanian by Ana Cartianu. Bucharest, 1986.

Yovino-Young, Marjorie. *Pagan Ritual and Myth in Russian Magic Tales: A Study of Patterns.* Lewiston, N.Y., 1993.

Ionna Andreesco-Miereanu (1987)
Translated from French by Brunhild Biebuyck
Revised Bibliography

MAGIC: MAGIC IN ISLAM

Magic in Islam forms part of what are called *ʿulūm al-ghayb,* "the occult sciences," which include divination, astrology, oneiromancy, and all fields of learning relating to prophecy. Magic (Arab., *siḥr*) is an important branch, like divination and astrology, with which some forms of magic overlap.

Following the very rich literature of magic in Islam, I shall here treat the various categories of *siḥr* in three sections: black magic (*ʿilm al-siḥr*), theurgy (*ʿilm al-khawāṣṣ wa-al-ṭalāsim*), and white or natural magic (*ʿilm al-ḥiyal wa-al-shaʿwadhah*). The first section will deal with divinatory magic, exorcism of demons, spells and the summoning of spirits into bodily forms. The second section will examine the properties of divine names, numbers and certain spells, sympathetic magic or sorcery, amulets, talismans and potions, charms, and the properties of medicinal plants. The third section will consider the mutual connections between effective and efficient forces, the ability to vanish instantly from sight, and prestidigitation.

Black Magic. From the many Qurʾanic verses relating to magic (sixty-six, of which only three were revealed in Medina), one might conclude that the phenomenon of *siḥr* occurs in the revelation only in the form of a condemnation of pagan practices. In certain verses, however, magic appears as a fragment of a celestial knowledge that was given to humans by fallen angels such as Hārūt and Mārūt (*sūrah* 2:102). These angels revealed to humans secrets "that they ought not to have known" (*Apocalypse of Enoch* 64:10). Thus, "God decided, in his justice, that all the inhabitants of the world would die [by flood], for they knew all the secrets of the angels, and possessed the hateful power of the demons, the power of magic" (ibid., 64:6). Another group of verses, condemning this almost instinctive quest by humans to penetrate the will of God, connects magic with divination.

Divinatory magic. The boundaries between magic and divination remain blurred. In their classification of the sciences, the Muslim encyclopedists, such as al-Afkānī, Tāshköprüzade, and Ḥājjī Khalīfah, call divination a branch of magic. According to Edmond Doutté, the transition from magic to mantic takes place via a phenomenon of "objectivization of the desire" (Doutté, 1909, p. 352). Whether inductive or intuitive, divination partakes of magic in certain of its techniques. One of the sources of knowledge common to the magician and the seer is demonic inspiration. Furthermore, the Arab seer (*kāhin*), and especially the female seer, practiced magic and divination concurrently (see my book *La divination arabe,* Leiden, 1966, pp. 92ff.), so that in Islamic magical literature, the two run parallel without mingling. Both make use of supernatural means to predict natural elements; both share a practical and nontheoretical character. One searches in vain for a theoretical definition of magic in the Qurʾān or the *ḥadīth* (prophetic traditions).

Exorcism and spells. If divinatory magic has recourse to secrets revealed by fallen angels, the magic of incantations and spells is meant to compel the *jinn* and the demons to accomplish a desired end, by pronouncing the formula "ʾAzamtu ʿalaykum" ("I command you"). The Qurʾān and the *ḥadīth* say nothing of this, but theological consideration led to the following conclusion, formulated by Ḥājjī Khalīfah:

> This thing is possible and lawful, according to reason and the law; whoever denies it is not highly regarded, because he winds up failing to acknowledge the omnip-

otence of God: to subjugate the spirits, to humble them before him, and to make them subordinate to men, is one of the miracles of [God's] creation. (Ḥājjī Khalīfah, ed. Flügel, 1955–1958, vol. 4, pp. 205–207)

Two kinds of conjuring, however, may be distinguished. One variety consists in directing the mind toward an object other than God, and thus being unfaithful to him. When this unfaithfulness appears as one of the elements making up the magical act through one of the means used to realize it, it becomes forbidden magic. In this case, the magician acts in a manner that is wicked and harmful to others, and, indeed, a controversy arose among medieval jurists concerning the question of knowing "whether they must be killed because of the unbelief which is antecedent to the practice [of sorcery], or because of their corrupting activity and the resulting corruption of created beings" (Ibn Khaldūn, trans. Rosenthal, 1967, vol. 3, p. 159.).

On the other hand, the conjuring of spirits is permissible when it is performed "with perfect piety and the complete absence of all unlawfulness, in solitude and isolation from the world and in surrender to God" (Ḥājjī Khalīfah, op. cit., pp. 205–207). This interpretation is basically consistent with the demonological conception of Islam, which considers the *jinn* servants of God, somewhat in the manner of humans and angels.

The writers differ on how this power derived from God is applied. Fakhr al-Dīn al-Rāzī sums up the opinion of the theologians thus:

When the conditions are brought together and the incantations pronounced, God makes the latter like a mighty devastating fire, encircling the demons and the *jinn,* until the [four] corners of the world close in around them, and there is no place left for them to hide, nor any other choice than to come out and resign themselves to do as they are commanded. What is more, if the performer is skillful, being of good conduct and praiseworthy morals, God will dispatch powerful, rough, and strong angels to the demons to inspire them and lead them to obey and serve him. (quoted in Ḥājjī Khalīfah, loc. cit.)

Summarizing the views of the Muslim theologians, Ḥājjī Khalīfah adds: "The obedience of demons and *jinn* to humans is not something unimaginable, either from the standpoint of reason or from the standpoint of accepted practice." The best illustration of this conception of magical incantation is given by certain exalted mystics, the North African marabouts, or *ṭālibs*, who transform the old pagan magic and subordinate it to the omnipotence of the one God. How, in this case, can obtaining a miracle by divine favor be distinguished from the effects of magic?

For the philosophers, whose views are summed up by Ibn Khaldūn,

The difference between miracles and magic is this: a miracle is a divine power that arouses in the soul [the ability] to exercise influence. The [worker of miracles] is supported in his activity by the spirit of God. The sorcerer, on the other hand, does his work by himself and with the help of his own psychic power, and, under certain conditions, with the support of devils. The difference between the two concerns the idea, reality, and essence of the matter. (Ibn Khaldūn, op. cit.)

Ibn Khaldūn himself locates the distinction in external criteria, which he defines as follows;

Miracles are found [to be wrought] by good persons for good purposes and by souls that are entirely devoted to good deeds. Moreover, [they include] the 'advance challenge' [*taḥaddī*] of the claim to prophecy. Sorcery, on the other hand, is found [practiced] only by evil persons and as a rule is used for evil actions, such as causing discord between husband and wife, doing harm to enemies, and similar things. And it is found [practiced] by souls that are entirely devoted to evil deeds. (ibid.)

He adds that "this is also the view of the metaphysicians," and he concludes that "among the Sufis some who are favored by acts of divine grace are also able to exercise an influence upon worldly conditions. This, however, is not counted as a kind of sorcery. It is effected with divine support" (ibid.).

One should point out, finally, that wishing does not make a magician; indeed, to be a magician presupposes a disposition and a preparation not required of the worker of miracles. "This art," the Pseudo-Majrīṭī tells us, "can be practiced and applied only by one who has [the power of] it in his nature" (al-Majrīṭī, ed. Ritter, 1933, p. 187), and Ibn Khaldūn says that the philosophers "think that a sorcerer does not acquire his magical ability but has, by nature, the particular disposition needed for exercising that type of influence" (op cit., p. 167). This disposition is called *al-tiba' al-tamm,* "the perfect nature"; the person who possesses it attains "knowledge of the secrets of creation, of natural causes, and of the mode of being of things" (al-Majrīṭī, op. cit., p. 187; cf. Fahd, 1966, p. 192, n. 29). Pseudo-Majrīṭī's quotation from the so-called *Book of Hermes the Sage* defines this perfect nature in these terms:

The microcosm that is man, if he possesses the perfect nature, has a soul like the solar disc, unmoving in the heavens and illuminating every horizon with its rays. It is the same with the perfect nature whose ray is found in the soul; it flashes out, touches the translucent forces of wisdom, and draws them to the soul that is its point [of origin], just as the sun's radiance attracts the forces of the universe and lifts them up into the atmosphere. (al-Majrīṭī, op. cit., pp. 193–194)

The progressive assimilation of the magician to the forces that he conjures, evokes, or invokes contributes to the effectiveness of his work and the success of his endeavor. The spiritual beings (*rūḥanīyah*) then appear to him as if in person, speaking to him and teaching him all things.

Evocation of spirits. In conjuring and incantation, the magician relies on the service of *jinn* and demons to accomplish his ends; in evocation, he compels the spirits of the dead, the demons, and the planets to carry out his wishes.

Necromancy, which really belongs with divination, is steeped in black magic. Like the summoning of demons, it generally involves two phases: a material phase, consisting of the preparation of a mixture of various products belonging to a special pharmacopoeia and fumigations of every kind, plus an intellectual phase, consisting of the formulation of a prayer naming all the qualities and attributes of the spirit invoked and stating the wishes to be realized.

The evocation of the spirits of the planets is based on the knowledge of the qualities and properties of each of them: its color (red-gray for Saturn, white-gray for Jupiter, the yellow-green-red of red-gold for Mars, red-gold for Venus, a mixture of all colors for Mercury, and green-white for the Moon), its odor, and its flavor (for details, see al-Majrīṭī, op. cit., pp. 140, 150–156). To evoke the spirit of a planet, one must be dressed in its color and perfumed with its scent; further, by means of ingestion, one must assume its essence and flavor. Having done so, one must watch for the moment when the planet reaches the point corresponding to it in the zodiac, on a direct line that does not cross the line of another planet of a different nature. When this is so, the line from the planet to earth will be straight and uninterrupted.

Next, from metals attributed to the planet, one must fashion a cross, hollow from top to bottom and with a hole at the top, resting on two feet. This cross is to be mounted on the image of whatever it is one plans to ask of the spirit invoked: that of a lion, for example, or a serpent, in case one desires to go to war or to overcome an enemy, that of a bird if one wishes to escape danger, of a man seated on a throne if one aspires to fame, power, or respect, and so on. Likewise, to gain control of someone, one carves that person's likeness from a stone characteristic of the planet that presided over his birth, at the proper time and in the position described above. This image then serves as a base for the cross. The choice of a cross has to do with the fact that every body takes this shape; thus it serves to establish a connection between the higher spiritual entity and an image that resembles it. An incense burner made of the same metals as the cross is also used; it must have only one opening at the top of the cover, for the smoke to escape.

To summon a celestial spirit, a proper location must be selected, completely open to the sky. The ground should be strewn with plants of the same properties as the planet whose strength is to be attracted, on the principle that like attracts like; there must be nothing else on the ground or in the area. Incense of the same essence as the planet being evoked must be burned so that the fumes, escaping from the single opening in the burner, will pass through the hollow cross from bottom to top. All this must be done at a propitious time. If all these conditions are met, the upper world will be in harmony with the lower and thus the request will be received favorably. (See al-Majrīṭī, op. cit., pp. 182–186; for a French translation, see Fahd, 1966, pp. 170–171.)

THEURGY. Other techniques aimed at tapping the planetary and stellar virtues lie on the borders between magic and theurgy. The distinction between the two, according to Ibn Khaldūn, lies in the fact that

> the sorcerer does not need any aid, while those who work with talismans seek the aid of the spiritualities of the stars, the secrets of numbers, the particular qualities of existing things, and the positions of the sphere that exercise an influence upon the world of the elements, as the astrologers maintain. The philosophers, therefore, say that sorcery is a union of spirit with spirit, while the talisman is a union of spirit with body. (Ibn Khaldūn, op. cit., p. 166)

"As they understand it," Ibn Khaldūn continues, "that means that the high celestial natures are tied together with the low [terrestrial] natures, the high natures being the spiritualities of the stars. Those who work with [talismans], therefore, as a rule, seek the aid of astrology" (ibid., p. 167).

Such is the theory, but in practice it is rare to find mention in the texts of a magical act carried out without recourse to a material support. While the talismanic art assumes a perfect technique, grounded in astronomical, astrological, and other data, this is not required for the practice of magic, which is performed with the help of prayers, evocations, and attempts to unite spirits, demons, and stars by magical means.

The talisman. According to Ḥājjī Khalīfah, the art of talismanry is intended

> to combine the active celestial forces with the passive earthly forces at moments favorable to the desired action and influence, with the help of vapors [able] to strengthen and attract the spirit of the talisman, with the intent of producing unusual manifestations in the world of generation and decay. In comparison with magic, this science is more accessible, for both its principles and its causes are known. Its usefulness is obvious, but mastery comes only after a great deal of effort. (Ḥājjī Khalīfah, op. cit., pp. 165ff.)

In fact, skill in talismanry can be acquired only by one who understands its principles, which spring from the branches of knowledge making up natural philosophy, in particular mathematics, physics, and metaphysics.

A great many elements come into play in the creation of a talisman. In addition to ease and efficiency, sympathy and antipathy, time and place, there is relativity, a basic principle of the talismanic art, the relationship between the planet and the object of the talisman as well as the similarities and parallels among its various components. To be effective, these connections should be located on the straight line crossing the talisman's field of influence.

Time plays a fundamental role in talismanry. Indeed, the proper moment is a condition *sine qua non* for the success of the undertaking. In order to seize it, one must observe the planet until it arrives at its operative position, the most favorable point in its influence, its conjunction with the other planets and its position with respect to them, the exact instant when the talisman must be set in place, and so forth. Position plays an equally important part, in particular the observer's vantage point, the spot where the talisman is made and set up, and the place of origin of the materials used to fabricate it. Numbers, as the measure of time and moment, are, like speech, necessary for the expression of quantity.

Quality, meanwhile, is equivalent in talismanry to causality. The object on which the talisman acts must bear a perfect resemblance to the quality transferred to it, so that its sphere of activity can spread. This is the basis of the connection between the higher and lower natures. Quality here is none other than inherent nature, the source of causality. Its role is therefore essential, not only in the discovery of the limited properties and influences of the planets but also in the diffusion of these same properties and influences. This leads to an increase in the quality of the material of which the talisman is made, by causing equivalent qualities to act upon it (al-Majrīṭī, op. cit., pp. 99–100).

The properties. In the words of Paul Kraus, the properties of beings are

> the virtues proper to minerals, plants, and animals, their sympathies and antipathies, as well as the use of these virtues in the various arts and in medicine. The miraculous occupies an important place here, and affinities with magic are undeniable. Men, animals, and plants are no longer considered objects of reasoned inquiry, but are endowed with occult powers, able to heal any malady and to procure happiness and miraculous power of man. (Kraus, 1942–1943, vol. 2, p. 61)

Among the physical properties, those of stones hold pride of place in talismanic practice, and knowledge of them is one of the essential conditions for a talisman's success, likewise for the properties of animal bodies, where magic comes to the aid of medicine; the latter are considered healthful even for incurable diseases. Plants possess many properties used in the rich magical repertoire of fumigations. A large number of these are found in the geographical compilation known as *Nabatean Agriculture*, and Pseudo-Majrīṭī also collected many of them. Among the plants used in magical operations are laurel, marshmallow, mandrake, elm, pennyroyal, myrtle, olive, horseradish, darnel, rice, beans, chickpeas, watermelon, and chicory.

The magical powers of plants are commonly connected with the natures of the planets. These natures impart their virtues to whatever responds to them. The fact that a plant sprouts in one soil and not in another comes not from the particular nature of the soil but from the marriage of a fixed disposition with given conditions of air and water. "The prime cause of this lies on the line crossing the horizon of this piece of ground and marking the zone of influence of certain planets on certain countries; thus the existence of plants and specific features in a given country to the exlusion of others" (al-Majrīṭī, op. cit., pp. 385ff.).

This learned theurgy, which systematically and "rationally" exploits the virtues of animal, vegetable, and mineral kingdoms, is marked by its Hellenistic origins and by the rich syncretism from which it emanates. Popular magic in Islam has preserved this spirit, while opening it to new influences in the various Islamized countries, hence the existence of magical practices peculiar to each of the major Muslim regions.

There are innumerable survivals of ancient theurgy in Muslim tradition, where many instances are ascribed to the Prophet himself, and in the abundant magical literature that spread out throughout the Muslim world. A saying attributed to the Prophet reflects an important principle of ancient magic, namely the magical power of the spoken word: "There is," he is supposed to have said, "a kind of utterance that is none other than magic" (quoted in al-Majrīṭī, op. cit., p. 9). By virtue of this principle, onomatomancy became widespread in Muslim lands, and the ninety-nine "most beautiful names" of God, like the most ancient *sūrahs* of the Qurʾān, played a very great role in spells, amulets, and potions. Muslim magic was based in large part on the knowledge of the letters that made up the supreme name of God. At the base of these speculations, we find the theory asserting that the letters of the alphabet, being at the root of creation, represent the "materialization" of the divine word.

However, according to Ibn Khaldūn, there is

> a real difference between persons who practice talismanry and those who work with the secret virtues of names, regarding the manner in which the soul is made to act on living beings). . . . This soul has inherently the ability to encompass nature and control it, but its effect, among those who operate by means of talismans, is limited to drawing down from above the spirits of the spheres and tying them to certain figures or numerical supports. . . . It is otherwise with those who, to give their souls the ability to act, make use of the secret properties of names; they must be illuminated by the celestial light and sustained by divine help. (Ibn Khaldun, op. cit., pp. 175ff.)

These latter avoid giving the name of magic to practices consisting of the use of secret properties of letters, numbers, and names. Nonetheless, in practice, "they fall under the idea of sorcery" (ibid., p. 181), although they tend to locate their activities in the legitimate realm of natural magic.

WHITE OR NATURAL MAGIC. The branch of magic known in English as white magic, or natural magic, is denoted in Arabic by two terms: one, *simiyāʾ*, of Greek origin (*sēmeia*), and the other, *nīrinjāt*, Persian (*neyrang*). Both are applied generally to illusionism, prestidigitation, fakery, and legerdemain.

According to Ḥājjī Khalīfah (op. cit., pp. 646–647), natural magic involves imaginary phenomena, occurring in space and having no correspondence to anything palpable. Their production and causes remain a secret known only to the practitioners. Often it includes mixtures concocted by the magician out of natural essences, ointments, liquified materials, or even special words with suggestive powers. The range of such practices is very large: aerial illusions, atmospheric vapors, playing with fire, tricks with bottles, cups, and glasses, illusions with eggs, fruits produced out of season, wax figures, animal taming, discovery of hidden objects, preparation of magic ink, and so on.

In the *Ghāyat al-ḥakīm* of Pseudo-Majrīṭī, the term *nīrinjāt* is applied to charms that have an extraordinary power over human beings and natural phenomena alike, such as a magic ring that transfixes anyone who looks at it, amulets that ward off bad weather or neutralize weapons held by enemies, and so on (al-Majrīṭī, op. cit., pp. 242ff.). The making of these *nīrinjāt* requires extreme precision and careful handling of the poisonous materials used in their composition. These are potions that act by mans of absorption or fumigations of various powders and oils. The anticipated effects of these potions vary, and their application depends upon astrological conditions, as in all magical activity, and on the simultaneous utterance of a formulaic spell containing incomprehensible names.

In the same class of magical activity belongs the rainmaker, who commands the stars and who alternates between a demanding, coercive, and occasionally even insulting tone toward the heavens and flattery toward God. The imprecations he pronounces have a clearly magical character: often they include the use of the divine names with the aim of bending the will of heaven. The author of the *Theology of Aristotle*, followed by Ibn Sīnā (Avicenna), affirms that "prayer influences the sun and the stars, by imparting a certain motion to them, because the parts of the world form a single whole, like a 'single animal'" (quoted in A. Goichon, *Directives et remarques*, Paris, 1951, p. 250). For greater effectiveness, the rainmaker stood inside a circle (*mandil*) or a magic square.

In this same category is also included the evil eye. Ibn Sīnā explains it as "an admiring tendency of the soul that exercises, by this property, a weakening influence on the object of its admiration" (ibid., p. 523). For Ibn Khaldūn, the effect is

> natural and innate. It cannot be left alone. It does not depend on the free choice of its possessor. It is not acquired by him. [It is] an influence exercised by the soul of the person who has the evil eye. A thing or situation appears pleasing to the eye of a person, and he likes it very much. This [circumstance] creates in him envy and the desire to take it away from its owner. Therefore he prefers to destroy him. (Ibn Khaldūn, op. cit., pp. 170–171)

It may be concluded from the foregoing that Islam, the heir of ancient civilizations, has preserved for us, in its rich cultural and folkloric patrimony, remnants of Semitic and Hellenistic notions that were developed and intermingled in the wide expanse of the ancient and medieval Near East.

SEE ALSO Theurgy.

BIBLIOGRAPHY

Primary Sources

Buni, Ahmad ibn ʿAlī al-. *Shams al-maʿārif wa-laṭāʾif al-ʿawārif.* 4 vols. Cairo, 1905. A most important source for practical and theoretical understanding of Islamic magic. There are three versions of this work: short, medium and long. It exists in several lithographs and numerous manuscripts.

Ḥājjī Khalīfah. *Kashf al-ẓunūn.* 8 vols. Edited by O. Flügel. London, 1955-1958. A large encyclopedia with material arranged in alphabetical order. See especially the articles on *siḥr, simiyāʾ, ṭalāsim,* and the keywords given therein.

Ibn Khaldūn. *Al-muqaddimah.* Edited by M. Quatremère. Paris, 1858–. Translated by Franz Rosenthal as *The Muqaddimah: An Introduction to History,* 2d ed., 3 vols. (Princeton, 1967). The emphasis in this work is on the theoretical aspect of magic.

Majrīṭī, Maslamah ibn Aḥmad al-. *Ghāyat al-ḥakim.* Edited by H. Ritter. Leipzig, 1933. Translated by H. Ritter and M. Plessner as *"Picatrix": Das Ziel des Weisen Pseudo-Majrīṭī* (London, 1962). A study of magic and theurgy from the double perspective of theory (*ʿilmī*) and practice (*ʿmalī*). Completed in AH 395/1004 CE, it is the most important work in this field. On the question of its attribution to Maslamah al-Majrīṭī ("of Madrid"), see H. Ritter's article in *Vorträge der Bibliothek Warburg* 1 (1921–1922): 95–124.

Secondary Sources

Doutté, Edmond. *Magie et religion dans l'Afrique du Nord.* Algiers, 1909. An important study on magical practices in North Africa.

Fahd, Toufic. "Le monde du sorcier en Islam." In *Le monde du sorcier,* pp. 157–204. Paris, 1966. Includes an extensive bibliography. The present article owes much to this study.

Kovalenko, Anatoly. *Magie et Islam.* Geneva, 1981. A 721-page volume containing a detailed description of magical procedures, with an exhaustive bibliography. This is an invaluable reference work.

Kraus, Paul. *Jābir Ibn Ḥayyān.* 2 vols. Cairo, 1942–1943. A valuable tool for the study of the occult sciences in Islam and their relationship to Hellenism.

Mauchamps, Émile. *La sorcellerie au Maroc.* Paris, n.d. A posthumous work preceded by a study on the author and the work by Jules Bris. Mauchamps's investigation into magical practices in Morocco is an exemplary model; every Muslim region needs such an inquiry.

TOUFIC FAHD (1987)
Translated from French by David M. Weeks

MAGIC: MAGIC IN SOUTH ASIA

Since the beginning of modern Indology in the writings of travelers, missionaries, and administrators, Hinduism has been described as a religion saturated with magic and superstition. The work of the missionary-traveler Abbé Jean-Antoine Dubois (1765–1848) set the tone for this type of discourse, but the British utilitarians who administered India were more influential in differentiating the magical from religious and scientific rationality. Major dimensions of Hinduism were reduced to the animistic practices and beliefs of peasants, a "lower" form of religion that was designated pejoratively as magical. Sir Monier Monier-Williams, for instance, identified village gods with tutelary powers that warded off demons and evil spirits pervading the countryside. Peasants worshiped fetishes, symbols endowed with intrinsic powers, and were far more interested in the avoidance of harm than in spiritual goals.

The distinction between "high" Brahmanic religion and the lower folk superstitions thus marked a boundary, on one side of which lay two types of rationality—religious and scientific—and on the other side of which lay what E. B. Tylor and James G. Frazer codified as homeopathic magic. Even the great German sociologist, Max Weber, who emphasized the ideological foundations of socioeconomic practices in India, succumbed to this distinction. Subsequent Western scholarship, including the specialized textual studies of magic by Willem Caland, Victor Henry, and Maurice Bloomfield, were thoroughly taken in by the distinction between religion and science on the one hand, and magic on the other. The mid-twentieth-century scholars who followed in their footsteps (for example, Jan Gonda and Louis Dumont) continued to regard Indian magic as a domain that, if not limited to folk religion, is certainly a type of attitude that displays belief in supernatural causality, the faith in a ritual's power over nature and gods, and the intrinsic value of the fetish object (Gonda, 1980, pp. 249–250).

Recent developments in a number of disciplines bearing on South Asian cultures, among others, make the distinction between magic and religion hard to sustain, however. Medical anthropology and ethnomedicine (including ethnopsychiatry), performative and ritual theories based on the work of John Austin (and Stanley J. Tambiah), cognitive theories such as those of John Skorupski and Pascal Boyer, the use of postcolonial approaches, and the increasing focus on women's religious practices now allow researchers to understand so-called magic in a more inclusive manner. Numerous practices previously labeled magical can be seen as sharing a basic rationality with either religion or medicine, psychiatry, conflict resolution, or even technology. The rickshaw driver in Banaras who hangs a bottle of Ganges water in his vehicle could be symbolically articulating a wish for good fortune rather than trying to influence his fate. The pervasive practice of *vrata,* votive rituals in which practitioners, usually women, enact ritual performances in order to effect the well-being of others, cannot be seen either as exclusively magical or exclusively religious.

Still, the languages of South Asia contain dozens of terms that are either associated with magical practices, or in some way connote magic. This may be one of the main reasons that the conceptual distinction between magic and religion (or science) is still influential among many contemporary scholars.

Magical Terms and Practices. Due to the prevalence of magical practices throughout the subcontinent, from Nepal to Sri Lanka and from the tribal communities such as the Bhils, Warlis, or Gonds to the upper classes of Mumbai, the variety of terms is impressive. A very brief sample of various terms in Sanskrit, Hindi, Tamil, Newari, Sinhala, and other languages includes *yātū* or *jādū, māyā, karman, kṛtyā, śānti, abhicāra, tonā, ṭoṭakā, tantra-mantra, bhūt, mantravaadi, peey, peey-pisasu, tuna, mikhā, syākāḥ, kaiphaṭ, najar, abhicārin, ojhā, sokhā, gunia, baiga, bhagat, yakku, koḍivina, mantrayas, diṣṭiya,* and *yakṣa.*

These refer to a number of concepts, practices, and types of specialist, both in ancient times and today. The most common area of magical concern is the healing of humans (adults and children), animals, and even machinery such as vehicles. Since the time of the *Atharvaveda,* the dominant folk etiology has ascribed numerous health problems—when witchcraft or sorcery was not suspected—to the invasion of the person by ghosts or spirits (*bhūt-pret, piśāc, jinn* in Hindi/Urdu). Healing has often taken the form of exorcism, either at home or at specialized locations such as Bharatpur, or Baba Bahadur Sayyid in Banaras. These rituals are usually performed by specialists such as *ojhās* or *sokhās* or *gunia* in Nepal. The rites take the form of an expulsion, driving the invading agent out by mimicry and with the use of *mantras* and the help of the goddess, and imprisoning it in the body of an animal such as a fish or bird, which is then released into the wild. Patients are often given protective amulets (*kavac*) to prevent future problems.

The single most pervasive concern may be failure to conceive or safely deliver a child. Magical treatments range from exorcism to bathing in certain well-known pools, such as the Lorlark Kund in Banaras, the ritual offering of specially manipulated (and pricked) fruit such as coconuts, straddling Śiva-*liṅgams,* and chanting *mantras.* The specific problem and its remedy may be identified througha variety of divinatory rituals that includes the spinning of sticks, the throwing of dice, or the painting of fingernails with lampblack or collyrium *(kājjal).* Some diviners specialize in locating lost relatives and may work with the aid of reluctant spirits who whisper into their left ear, having been brought under control through so-called tantric rituals (Svoboda, 1986).

Despite the enormous technological and educational changes taking place throughout South Asia, few areas of human concern are untouched by magical technique. Even many of the trucks that speed along on highways display signs that threaten: "he who casts the evil eye (*najar*) will get a black face." The concept of evil eye—the damage done by an unfavorable glance—is extremely pervasive, and children are often armed (with facial paint) against it. Astrologers still do a booming business, from coordinating marriage matches to establishing auspicious travel dates. Art in villages, especially wall art, along with the ritual application of abstract diagrams (*kōḷam* in Tamil, *rangoli* in Maharashtra, etc.) on thresholds throughout the subcontinent, is associated with protection and auspiciousness. House construction, boat-building, and rickshaw and car purchase may be accompanied by special *pūjā* rituals for the pacification of evil influences and the peaceful enjoyment of ownership. Life-cycle rituals—especially those connected with young children (first solid feeding, cutting of hair, naming) and weddings—as well as the *vrata* rituals that religious practitioners (usually women) undertake are all associated with symbolic performances, *mantras,* and beliefs that may be interpreted as magical. The same even applies to yoga technique—Patañjali's *Yoga Sūtra* promises extraordinary powers to advanced practitioners—and tantric *sādhana,* and even the common *pūjā* that most Hindus perform frequently utilizes techniques and tools of magic.

Magical Tools and Technique. Magic in South Asia is not a failure of scientific rationality or transcendental metaphysics. It is the daily application of a subtle ideology that enchants the world of the senses by means of divine power. The tools and techniques vary from one region to the next, but a number of basic features prevail universally. The first and foremost is the *mantra,* which is used as a verbal formula for blessing, cursing, mind-altering, spells, and so forth. The *mantras* vary from Vedic and Atharvavedic versions (*Viṣeṇa hanmi te viṣam,* "with poison I kill your poison") to tantric ones: "*hrīṁ, śrīṁ, krīṁ, pa-ra-me-śva-ri, svā-hā*" and even ad-hoc formulas such as "Śānte śān, glory of Ali, hit my enemy with a thousand arrows." *Mantras* may be sung, chanted, whispered, and even blown into a bottle or onto the head of patients. Scholars have debated the meaning and function of *mantras,* but in magical practice they are regarded as the single most powerful tool in the magician's bag.

Mantras are often associated with or replaced by geometric designs—*yantras* and *maṇḍalas*—that depict in spatial terms the meaning of the *mantra,* or embody the power and attributes of a god or goddess. The diagrams utilize precise geometric symbols, but also rely on an elaborate color symbolism (for instance, white, red, black, and yellow all have symbolic meaning) or on numbers. These symbolic systems owe their significance to tantric alchemical ideas, *Atharvaveda* authority, Āyurveda medical cosmology, or local traditions (Goudriaan, 1978, pp. 175–190).

Regional variations also determine the types of herbs, plants, oils, and other remedies used, the kinds of animals regarded as beneficial or harmful, and the tombs, shrines, trees, ponds, or hills which constitute centers of healing, fertility, or exorcism. For example, in Banaras, muscle or joint pain might require the rubbing of fish oil, while in Rajasthan, lizard oil serves as the remedy. Pastoral tribes may favor the goat for curing asthma while settled villagers may rely on buffalo or perhaps the leaves of the nim tree. In every case the performance of magical rituals reveals a close familiarity with the natural environment, an acuity of sensory perception, and a sophisticated attention to the social and psychological needs of patients.

Intellectual Foundations of Indian Magic. One of the basic and most frequently discussed aspects of Hindu thought is the Vedic cosmological continuity between the transcendent and mundane realms, or between the sphere of gods (*adhidevata*) and the sphere of humans (*adhyātman*). The two realms resemble or correspond to each other through an infinitely rich system of homologies (*nidāna*). These correspondences are instantiated—with a one-to-one precision—within the Vedic sacrifice (*yajña*), which is the ritual that mediates between the two realms while forming yet a third. This foundational conception has been very fecund in sprouting several distinct traditions, which have included the ritualistic sciences of the *brāhmaṇa* texts, the mystical speculations of the Upaniṣads, the medical systems of Āyurveda, the physio-psychology of yoga, and the alchemy of Tantra to name but a few. At the most basic level, these traditions shared the insight that a connection between the human/individual realm and the divine/transcendent is possible, as long as it was produced through a specialized technique, knowledge, or healing substance. An early and vivid example of this connection can be seen in the *Bṛhadāraṇyaka Upaniṣad's* opening line: "The head of the sacrificial horse, clearly, is the dawn—its sight is the sun." Cosmology and ritual (sacrifice) mirror each other and form a seamless continuity, which the ritual specialist can exploit.

Throughout Indian history the sacrificial ritual has played a role not only in cosmology, but also in other contexts as well. Tantric traditions, as David Gordon White shows, are systems of (alchemical) mediations based on the science of the sacrifice. Fluids, semen, moon, and mercury on the one hand, and fire, blood, sun, and sulfur on the other are mediated by air, wind, and breath to unify the macrocosm with the microcosm. Similarly, as the oldest medical knowledge (Āyurveda) was becoming systematized and situated within the normative traditions of *dharma,* it was the sacrifice that provided the primary method of linking the work of the surgeon to religious cosmology: the Āyurvedic surgeon was merely replicating the work of the divine Aśvin twins who had learned from Prajāpati (and Brahmā) how to reattach the head of the sacrifice severed by Rudra (*Suśruta Saṃhitā* 1:17–20).

Although the three broad traditions (Upaniṣads, Tantra, Āyurveda) are distinct in most ways of reckoning, all assume some continuity between the divine and mundane realms. In fact, most traditions inspired by the Vedic ethos refuse to differentiate categorically between speculative (or "scientific") and pragmatic concerns. The Vedic sacrifice itself is as much about prosperity and health as it is about obtaining heaven, immortality, or the selfless nurturing of the gods.

A ready example of this combined orientation is the literature on domestic rituals. Systematically expounded in the Gṛhyasūtras, domestic rituals ensure the correct maintenance of the household, but are equally attentive to the threefold knowledge (of gods, *ātman*—the mystical self—and sacrifice) that defines the worthiest Brāhmaṇ. The same texts that describe how to part the hair of a pregnant woman with a porcupine quill in order to obtain a son, also explain what is superior knowledge and why it is so (*Śāṅkhāyana Gṛhyasūtra*). Another way of putting the matter is that the techniques most closely associated with *mukti* (liberation)—namely concentration, austerities, self-control, recitation—are also conducive to *bhukti* (enjoyment): long life, health, power, children, and wealth (*Chāndogya Upaniṣad* 5:19:2).

Within this worldview, no insurmountable boundary separates the "arts" of magic from mystical speculation. According to the *Ṛgvidhāna* (1:15:4), a mystical *mantra,* chanted in reverse, can be used to destroy one's foes: it has the power of *brahman,* which is the hidden potency of the Vedic ritual, and is the underlying principle of the *brāhmaṇa* texts and the Upaniṣads. Much of what is generally regarded as mystical (transcendent, speculative) is also magical (mundane, pragmatic) and vice versa.

Two intersecting and overlapping concepts that underscore this point are "Indra's net" (*Indrajāla*) and *māyā* (illusion). In the *Ṛgveda,* Indra (or Maghavan) is a magician-god who can change forms at will, "changing shape by the use of magic" (3.53.8; 7.99.4). Indra uses his magic to bring rains, using the lightning as his magician's wand. His net is a powerful tool with a profound effect on human perception: "Indra's net is vast, as big as this world, and with Indra's net—this magic—I enmesh, entrap, those people with darkness." Lee Siegel argues that these ideas indicate the intimate link between ancient Indian conceptions of magic and conjuring: both involve deception and illusion, resting as they do on the vulnerable nature of human perception.

As Jan Gonda has observed, "*māyā* is an incomprehensible wisdom and power enabling its possessor, or being able itself, to create, devise, contrive, effect, or do something." (Gonda, 1965, p. 216) The possessor may be divine or human, but in either case the power to create has a profound phenomenal upshot: it fashions a sense-based reality that is both wondrous and powerful in hiding what is ultimately real. It is the card up the magician's sleeve.

In short, Indra's net, the snare with which God rules over the sensory world and over humans, is his power, his *māyā.* This is how Śaṅkara, the ninth-century philosopher, interprets the passage in the *Bhagavadgītā* in which Kṛṣṇa says to Arjuna: "My *māyā* is hard to overcome" (7:14). The net is a fitting image to describe the power of God because it is sensory perception that binds humans in this world. At the same time that it binds, however, sensory perception also provides a connection to God's creative energy (Goudriaan, 1978, p. 216). What is perceived by humans in this world corresponds to elements of the divine order, creating a bond, a correspondence that is sense-based and lies at the root of the homological rationality that one sees in much of India's traditional thinking: the elaborate system of resemblances and correspondences that misled James Frazer and Victorian scholars into perceiving what they encountered as homeopathic and superstitious. The principle underlying this way of sorting out the world is not an expression of "magical" thinking, but rather a privileging of sensory experience as the index of God's creative energy, and a recognition of its potential to further one's interests.

By recognizing the connection between divine power (*māyā*) and sense perception, humans can transcend empirical reality (*mukti*) and *māyā,* but they can also use this recognition to live a good life (*bhukti*). This is possible only as long as the meshes of the phenomenal net, so to speak, are not broken. In fact, all practical magic commences with a problem, a tear in the net or web of perceived relations. The health problems of humans and animals, failure to conceive, or bad luck in business—all problems brought to the attention of the magician—may be understood implicitly as the rip in Indra's net.

LITERARY SOURCES OF MAGIC. Due to the difficulty of isolating a distinct magical domain within Indian culture and literature, it is hard to name uniquely magical texts. Only two texts within the ancient corpus can be regarded as almost completely magical works in the sense that they focus exclusively on rites and *mantras* conforming to the ideology outlined above. One of these is the *Atharvaveda,* the fourth and latest addition to the Vedic canon. It is primarily a collection of verbal formulas uttered by the *atharvaṇ* priest in a wide array of circumstances: The majority focus on health matters, but many deal with procreation, love, wealth, warfare, property disputes, travel, justice and, of course, the counteracting of sorcery.

The other primarily magical text is the *Kauśika Sūtra* (c. 700 BCE), which either reflects an ancient ritual tradition that paralleled the atharvanic formulas, or was artificially composed to illustrate the ritual contexts in which the *Atharvaveda* was meant to be used. Hundreds of rituals, most of them nearly indecipherable without the much later commentaries of Darila and Keśava Kāśmīrin, cover matters of concern similar to those of the *Atharvaveda.*

But, more broadly, the *Ṛgveda* (and *Ṛgvidhāna*) with its *mantras* and mythical allusions, and the *Yajurveda* and, later, the *brāhmaṇas* with their sacrificial rituals, are also rich sources of magical ideas and performances. In fact, Mīmāṃsā philosophy explains that what makes Vedic rituals powerful and efficacious is the *adṛṣta* type of action, the action that has no visible or empirical utility. For instance, the ritual's insistence on facing in a particular direction is more efficacious in producing results than cleansing the ritual utensils.

The Gṛhyasūtras prescribe the rituals and *mantras* that must be used in the household, governing the life stages (including pregnancy, birth, feeding, and naming) of twice-born members of society from the moment of conception until death. They describe in some detail, occasionally intersecting with the prescriptions of the *Kauśika Sūtra,* the verbal and ritual parameters that have to be observed in every stage of life. For instance, the *gurū* must initiate the student by sprinkling him with water three times—neither more nor less—as the student joins his hands in greeting (*Śāṅkhāyana Gṛhyasūtra* 2.2.10). During the wedding ceremony the groom seizes the bride by the thumb if he desires boys, by the other fingers if he wishes to bear girls (*Āśvalāyana Gṛhyasūtra* 1.7.3–4).

What makes these rituals "magical" is not that they are regarded as *yātū* or *abhicāra,* or that they seem to manifest magical thinking of the type defined by Frazer or even current theorists. The operative criterion is a recognition, based on sensory perception and performed symbolically, that life is constituted by interrelated phenomena (the number three, water, fingers, and children) that are both meaningful and controllable when properly understood. Numerous additional examples can be found in the *Suśruta Saṃhitā* and the *Caraka Saṃhitā,* the two major texts of Āyurveda medicine. Both texts are encyclopedic in range, covering every known medical topic, from medical philosophy (and cosmology) to diets, prognostics, surgery, pharmacology, and others. Both are based on a sophisticated humoral theory and both contain hundreds of healing procedures.

The legal texts, for example *Mānava Dharmaśāstra,* also describe rituals that could be characterized as magical by these ideological standards. The courtroom is a sacrificial hall and the criminal, especially the one who willingly confesses and submits to punishment, is a sacrificial player (the victim) who benefits by the punishment. Similarly, the *Kāmasūtra* is renowned for its use of carefully prescribed procedures designed to help in seduction, perpetuate or enhance love, improve sex, enrich the diet, and restore health. Even the pragmatic *Arthaśāstra* of Kauṭilya describes the use of special procedures for complementing the normal devices of statecraft—for instance, using *mantras* and potions to confuse and subdue one's enemies.

The *Mahābhārata* and *Rāmāyaṇa* both feature episodes involving magicians, although few rituals are explicitly prescribed. In contrast, some Purāṇa texts dating to the first millennium of the common era, most notably the *Agni Purāṇa,* contain large collections of spells, procedures, and formulas (including diets and herbal concoctions) for a variety of purposes: healing, undermining enemies, victory in battle, health, longevity, interpretation of dreams, astrological success, and so on. Other Purāṇas are not as detailed, but the *Devī Purāṇa* provides lengthy verbal formulas with detailed descriptions of their use.

A vast repository of magical practices and verbal formulas can be found in the literature that is broadly termed Tantra. Such texts as *Rasārṇava* (tenth–eleventh centuries CE), or the *Rasahṛdaya Tantra* of Govinda (tenth–eleventh century CE), contain spells and chants (*mantras*), geometric designs, alchemy, color symbolism, medical practices, and exorcism procedures.In popular street usage in India today, the word *tantra* has come to mean magic, due to the prestige of the tradition, along with its accessibility compared to the Vedic and Āyurvedic literature.

SEE ALSO Alchemy, article on Indian Alchemy; Mantra; Māyā.

BIBLIOGRAPHY

Bloomfield, Maurice. *Hymns of the Atharvaveda.* Sacred Books of the East, vol. 42. New York, 1969. Extensive translations of *Kauśika Sūtra* rituals alongside the *Atharvaveda* material, with useful commentaries.

Bloomfield, Maurice, ed. *The Kauśika Sūtra of the Atharvaveda.* Delhi, 1972. The full text, edited with the major commentaries, but not yet available in English.

Caland, Willem. *Altindisches Zauberritual: Probe eines (Übersetzung der wichtigsten Theile des Kauśika Sūtra).* Amsterdam, 1900. The most extensive translation of the *Kauśika Sūtra* rituals, with dated analysis of magic.

Desjarlais, R. R. *Body and Emotion: The Aesthetics of Illness and Healing in the Nepal Himalayas.* Philadelphia, 1992.

Freed, Ruth S., and Stanley A. Freed. *Ghosts: Life and Death in North India.* New York, 1993. A comprehensive survey and analysis of practices related to the belief in ghost possession and exorcism.

Gangadharan, N., trans. *The Agni Purāṇa, Parts I–II.* Delhi, 1985.

Gellner, David N. *The Anthropology of Buddhism and Hinduism: Weberian Themes.* New Delhi, 2001. A sociological analysis of Newari practices and beliefs in Nepal, including extensive discussions of magic, especially possession and healing.

Glucklich, Ariel. *The End of Magic.* New York, 1997. A theoretical and descriptive interpretation of magic, including a new theory of magic, based on material from Banaras.

Gonda, Jan. *Change and Continuity in Indian Religion.* Leiden, 1965.

Gonda, Jan. *Vedic Ritual: The Non-Solemn Rites.* Leiden, 1980. Contains a brief but detailed discussion of ancient Indian magic, based on the rituals of the Vedas, Gṛhyasūtras, and *Kauśika Sūtra.*

Goudriaan, Teun. *Māyā Divine and Human.* Delhi, 1978. A detailed textual study of the ideological foundations in *māyā* and Indra's net of Indian magic.

Henry, Victor. *La magie dans l'Inde antique.* Paris, 1904. A mostly descriptive study of magic in ancient India based on the *Atharvaveda* and *Kauśika Sūtra.*

Jayakar, Pupul. *The Earth Mother.* New Delhi, 1990. Somewhat informal but useful look at the mutual influences between Vedic and tantric traditions and tribal/folk cultures, especially in the domain of art and magic.

Kapferer, Bruce. *A Celebration of Demons: Exorcism and the Aesthetics of Healing in Sri Lanka.* 2d ed. Oxford, 1991.

Oldenberg, Hermann, trans. *The Grihya Sutras, Parts I–II.* Sacred Books of the East, vols. 29–30. Delhi, 1989.

Scott, David. *Formations of Ritual: Colonial and Anthropological Discourses on the Sinhala Yaktovil.* Minneapolis, 1994. A historical ethnography of Sinhala ideological and ritual discourses on malevolent spirits.

Siegel, Lee. *Net of Magic: Wonders and Deceptions in India.* Chicago, 1991. Studies the link between the arts of conjuration and ancient Indian cosmology.

Stutley, Margaret. *Ancient Indian Magic and Folklore: An Introduction.* Boulder, Colo., 1980. A clear and accessible survey that relies primarily on the work of Bloomfield.

Svoboda, Robert E. *Aghora: At the Left Hand of God.* New Delhi, 1986. A biographical and vivid account of the work of a contemporary Aghori tantric sorcerer.

White, David Gordon. *The Alchemical Body: Siddha Traditions in Medieval India.* Chicago, 1996. A close examination of the homological cosmology, based on fire and fluids, at the heart of alchemical magic within tantric literature.

ARIEL GLUCKLICH (2005)

MAGIC: MAGIC IN EAST ASIA

Magic and mantic arts are endemic in Chinese life and prominent in the religions of China, both in popular religion and in Buddhism and Daoism. The same is true of Korea and Japan, where indigenous beliefs have been overlaid by the cultural influence of China. The magical practices of China found ready acceptance in Korea and Japan. Although many of the practices traveled on their own, religion—chiefly Buddhism, which had already absorbed elements of Chinese popular beliefs and of Daoism—was an important vehicle for the transfer of Chinese magic. The result was an amalgam of magical lore in East Asia, with Chinese knowledge often providing a frame to which specifically Korean or Japanese practices and permutations were affixed.

CHINA. In general, one should distinguish between magic, which provides a means to accomplish specific ends (through spells, gestures, amulets, talismans, and the like), and various occult sciences (such as yarrow-stalk divination with the *Book of Changes,* astrology, hemerology, geomancy, and alchemy), even though this distinction was not strongly maintained in the traditional Chinese schema of magic and the occult. There was in fact a fluid boundary between magic (where there was no cause for rationalization) and occult sciences, which were elaborated in terms of a theory of symbolic correspondence based on the concepts of *yin-yang* dualism and of Five Actions (*wuxing:* water, fire, wood, metal, and earth). Not only was this theory the product of prior conceptions of the magical power of fire, water, and other primary forces in nature (e.g., wind), but even after its full elaboration the symbolic correspondences did not negate the validity of magical practices. Not infrequently, occult theory supplied a *modus operandi* for magic and religious worship. For example, an astrological instrument designed to calculate the position of the Big Dipper (Chinese archaeology has recently brought to light a second-century BCE specimen of the device) was used by the usurper Wang Mang to direct the power of the Dipper against his enemies in 23 CE. From the beginning, this astrological instrument served as one means for conjuring the god of the Dipper and polestar (talismanic replicas of the constellation cast in metal were also used). The same instrument was influential in Daoist star magic, and it was the model for an astrological *maṇḍala* in the esoteric Buddhism of the Tang period (618–907 CE). Similarly, the hemerological symbols of the calendrical cycle were not simply neutral signs marking the passage of time; they constituted a succession of spirits whose magical powers could be summoned through spells and talismans.

The Warring States (403–221 BCE), Qin (221–206 BCE), and Han (206 BCE–220 CE) periods were the formative age for Chinese magic. Earlier, magic was employed in dealings with the spirits and was important in the royal ancestral religion of the Shang and early Zhou (c. sixteenth–eighth centuries BCE). But the proliferation of magical arts, and an increasing differentiation between magic as employed in archaic religion and magic for its own sake, began during the Warring States and continued to develop in Qin-Han times. The history of Chinese magic in later centuries followed from the developments of this period. It was during the same period that the theory of symbolic correspondence was formulated, and developments in occult sciences paralleled significantly those in magic.

Before the Warring States the principal practitioners of magic were the *wu,* a class of female (and in lesser numbers, male) shamans who mediated between the human and spirit worlds. Their methods included trances in which spirits might descend into their bodies or in which the shaman might journey into the spirit world, invocations and maledictions, and the utilization of magical materials to either attract or repel the spirits. Their functions overlapped those of incantators (*chu*) and other ritual officiants; however, the latter did not engage in ecstatic trances. The Warring States and Qin-Han periods witnessed the decline in prestige of these shamans, who came to be increasingly associated with witchcraft; the rise of occult specialists (*fangshi,* literally "masters of recipes"), whose skills extended to magical operations; and the formation of a Daoist clergy, who adapted magic to fill the needs of the newly emergent religion (organized Daoist religious communities made their first appearance in the second century CE). The general populace also practiced forms of superstitious magic in the course of daily life.

Historical records of Han rulers who favored shamans and masters of recipes provide an important source of information about ancient Chinese magic. Liu Che (posthumously titled Wu Di; r. 140–87 BCE), for example, established cults for shamans and made his court a gathering place for masters of recipes who claimed to possess magical powers and the secrets of immortality. One master of recipes, Li Shaoweng, was a psychopomp who gained Liu Che's favor by conjuring the ghost of the ruler's recently deceased concubine; he was executed after he was exposed for fabricating portents. Near the end of Liu Che's reign the court was paralyzed by an outbreak of a type of shamanic witchcraft known as *gu.* The word *gu* referred to a demonic affliction that attacked its victim as the result of witchcraft. According to some accounts, *gu* was a poison produced by sealing certain creatures in a vessel until only one remained, which became the *gu.* The tradition that the *gu* is a magical potion cultivated by women and passed down through generations is still alive today. Those who ingested the *gu* were believed to die and become the demon-slaves of the *gu* and its keeper. In two of the witchcraft incidents at Liu Che's court the *gu* agent was discovered to be a wooden effigy buried in the ground, where it was intended to bring harm to the ruler. There were other cases of witchcraft during the Han period in which shamans were hired to work black magic.

Accusations of charlatanism against masters of recipes and fear of shamanic witchcraft were widespread during the Han period. A negative perception of magical practices crystallized around the government's concern for its own political and spiritual authority. All magic and occultism were potentially subversive. They incited social unrest and infringed upon the holiness of the monarch, whose position as the Son of Heaven made him the only legitimate authority to oversee dealings with the spirit world. Popular religious cults not under the direct control of the government were branded "abusive worship" (*yinsi*), and ordinary citizens could be executed if caught illicitly performing magic or uttering imprecations. Such practices were identified as the "way of the left" (*dso-dao*). The word *left* did not connote the sinister aspects Western cultures associate with the left. Rather, in cosmoritual symbolism the left was the ruler's position of honor, and those who practiced the way of the left were abusing powers belonging properly to the ruler.

The Daoist sects that arose in the second century CE inveighed against those who placed their faith in shamans, worshiped demons, and believed the occultists' shams. These practices were an offense to the true deities of the Dao. Daoist liturgy incorporated many elements of popular worship, however, and the clergy engaged in many of the magical practices that they condemned in others. Indeed, in the eyes of the Han government the Daoist sects were rebel organizations whose religion represented simply another outbreak of "abusive worship." For the Daoist sects the fundamental issue was heterodoxy—the use of magic not sanctioned by religious authority. But in the continual process of syncretization that occurred over the centuries as Daoism interacted with popular religion and with Buddhism, the standard of orthodoxy fluctuated.

The Buddhist attitude toward magic was similar. Illicit magical practices fell under the category of the "arts of Mara" (*moshu*), Mara being the tempter and chief of malevolent demons. *Moshu* parallels other Chinese terms such as "shamanic arts" (*wushu*) and "way of the left" in referring to the forms of magic prohibited by the orthodox church (and the government). However, as early as the fifth century CE there was a tradition of Buddhist spell-casting in China rivaling the Daoist practices. Buddhist magic was most prominent in the esoteric practices of Tantrism. The Tantric literature contained magical formulas to be used to gain prosperity or harm adversaries; Tantric *mantras*, *mudrās*, and *maṇḍalas* were utilized as instruments for working magic. Tantric magic incorporated elements of native Chinese magic and occultism, while at the same time enriching Daoist and popular practices.

Most existing knowledge of actual magical procedures in premodern times comes from Daoist and Buddhist writing, which naturally reflect the practices of Daoism and Buddhism. Recently, Chinese archaeologists have discovered manuscripts from the third and second centuries BCE that describe magic as it was practiced in the ancient popular religion and occult tradition. Two of the manuscripts are almanacs that are strikingly similar to Chinese almanacs in use today and attest to a continuity in magic and occult practice. The Chinese almanacs combine information on portents to watch for during the year with material on spells, talismans, and other magical devices.

Many of the common forms of magic described in premodern sources are still practiced. There are spells to summon deities and to drive off demons (versions of popular, Daoist, and Buddhist spells are preserved). Spitting and spouting water over which a spell has first been uttered is another common device (sometimes Daoist or Buddhist priests will spout ignited alcohol). Substances believed to have magical properties are often identified in traditional materia medica. Amber, for example, wards off nightmare demons and is used in making headrests. Amulets to be hung in the open or worn on the body exist in many forms. Peachwood amulets are perhaps the most ancient. Talismans (*fu*) made from strips of silk and inscribed with undecipherable writing have been discovered in a second century BCE tomb. A medical manuscript discovered in the same tomb includes a recipe for curing *gu* witchcraft by burning a talisman, scattering its ashes over sheep broth, and bathing the victim with the brew. Water over which the ashes of talismans have been scattered has been used in Daoism to cure sickness since the time of the earliest Daoist sects. Daoism talismans inscribed with symbols and magic writing have many uses. The deities are summoned with talismans, which may be used in conjunction with spells. And, in addition to using the ashes, Daoists may wear talismans as phylacteries or swallow them in order for them to take effect. Love magic is represented in a second century BCE manuscript that provides recipes for two philters with which a person can "obtain the object of desire." Another example in the same manuscript is a recipe that instructs a person engaged in a lawsuit to write the opponent's name on a slip and insert it in a shoe, magically trampling the opponent.

KOREA AND JAPAN. In Korea, cults formed around female shamans were a source of native Korean magic. This popular religion is known as Mu-sok ("shamanic customs"). Contacts between Korea and China began well before the Tang, but increased markedly during that period. Knowledge of Chinese magic and occultism was part of the general flow of Chinese culture into Korea. And the initial impact of Chinese religion—before, for example, there was a more sophisticated understanding of Buddhist theology—was an admiration for its great magical power as compared with native practices.

Chinese political institutions and ethics were also influential in the formation of the early Korean kingdoms. In general, the antagonism between government and practitioners of magic, and between Buddhism and popular religion, followed along lines similar to the situation in China.

In the native religion of Japan, which came to be known as Shintō ("way of the spirits") after Buddhism took hold, there were two categories of religious personnel. The *miko* (female shaman) was a medium into whose body a spirit might descend, sharing essential characteristics with shamans throughout East Asia. The *kannushi* (spirit controller) was more in the nature of a priest who oversaw the worship of the spirits. As with the shamans in China, the *miko* were increasingly associated with witchcraft, whereas the *kannushi* came to function as officiants in the state cult. Esoteric tantric Buddhism had a strong influence in Japan, leading to a syncretism of Shintō and Chinese-Buddhist magic. Buddhist ascetics called *hijiri* (sage) and *yamabushi* (mountain recluse) traced their origins to the eighth century CE and were renowned for their magical powers. As in Korea, in Japan other forms of Chinese magic and occultism were absorbed into the culture.

BIBLIOGRAPHY

Blacker, Carmen. *The Catalpa Bow.* London, 1975. A well-documented and groundbreaking study of shamanistic traditions in Japan, both from a historical and contemporary perspective.

Chang Chu-keun. "Mu-sok: The Shaman Culture of Korea." In *Folk Culture in Korea,* edited by Chun Shin-yong, pp. 59–88. Seoul, 1982. A more popular account of Korean shamanism.

Groot, J. J. M. de. *The Religious System of China* (1892–1910). 6 vols. Reprint, Taipei, 1967. A comprehensive description of religion in China, valuable for its copious translations of primary sources.

Haguenauer, Charles M. "Sorciers et sorcières de Corée." *Bulletin de la Maison Franco-Japonaise* (Tokyo) 2 (1929): 47–65. A scholarly examination of shamanism and magic in Korea.

Ngo Van Xuyet. *Divination, magie et politique dans la Chine ancienne.* Paris, 1976. An excellent study of magic and occultism in the formative Qin-Han period, including a translation of the chapter of biographies of occult specialists in the *Hou Han shu* (Documents of the Later Han).

Sieffert, René. "Le monde du sorcier au Japon." In *Le monde du sorcier,* "Sources orientales," vol. 7, pp. 355–389. Paris, 1966. An excellent survey of the practice of magic in Japan, with a detailed discussion of magic in Buddhism and Shintō.

DONALD HARPER (1987)

MAGNA MATER SEE CYBELE

MAGYAR RELIGION SEE HUNGARIAN RELIGION

MAHĀBHĀRATA. Hindu India's national epic takes its name from Bharata, an ancestor of the central family of heroes. It is the story of his descendants, the Bhāratas or Kurus. The *Mahābhārata* (Great story of the Bhāratas) is a massive encyclopedic text. In one famous verse it claims to contain everything. It is said to consist of 100,000 verses, although no known recension comes to quite that number. The text is also known as *Jaya* (Victory), a reference to its concern with the victory of *dharma* over *adharma* as assured by Kṛṣṇa, who as the incarnation of Viṣṇu guides the main action of the story. The text is further called the *Kārṣṇaveda* (Veda of Kṛṣṇa), a reference whose ambiguity may be intended since the text not only is concerned with this Kṛṣṇa but is alleged to have been written by Kṛṣṇa Dvaipāyana, the "island-born Kṛṣṇa," whose more familiar name is Vyāsa. Finally, it is called the "fifth Veda," indicating the importance that the epic's *brahman* poets attached to its prolongation of the Vedic heritage. The epic is a *smṛti* ("traditional") rather than *śruti* ("revealed") text, but its reputed author, Vyāsa, is the very person whom epic and classical mythology credits with the "division" of the Vedas into four.

The actual composition of the epic seems to have been carried out between about 500 BCE to 400 CE. The authors, however, probably drew on older bardic traditions with roots in Aryan lore of much greater antiquity. The central story is set in the area of the Ganges-Yamunā doab, and recalls tribal kingdoms that had settled in and around that area, after earlier residence in the Punjab, from about 1000 to 500 BCE. It is sometimes assumed that the Painted Gray Ware culture of this period provided the historical setting for a real war, of which the text of the *Mahābhārata* is but an embellished account. More likely, if the Painted Gray Ware peoples transmitted an early version of the story, it was as part of their mythology, for the epic has an Indo-European mythological structure.

Scholarly work since the 1940s, initiated by Stig Wikander and Georges Dumézil, has shown that the text is essentially mythological, though not denying that it integrates much "didactic" material, particularly in its postwar books. It prolongs the Vedic heritage by correlating the epic story and its leading characters with Vedic, and in some cases para-Vedic and Indo-European, mythological figures and narrative (particularly eschatological) themes. More recent work has focused on the epic's treatment of the war as a "sacrifice of battle," relating the narrative to Indian sacrificial traditions, particularly from the Brāhmaṇas. Most notably, Madeleine Biardeau has shown that the treatment of Vedic mythology and Brahmanic sacrifice in the epic forms part of a *bhakti* rereading of the Vedic revelation (*śruti*). From this perspective the epic is the first and grandest monument of *bhakti,* focused on Kṛṣṇa as the *avatāra* (incarnation) of Viṣṇu.

The main story begins when Viṣṇu and other gods descend or in some way assume human forms to relieve the burden of the goddess Earth, who is oppressed by demons. Following a succession crisis in the Lunar (i.e., Bhārata) dynasty, which rules India's "middle region," demons (*asuras*) infiltrate the royal lineages of the other kingdoms. In this situation two groups of cousins are born into the central lineage, each with its own succession claims: the five sons of King Pāṇḍu (the Pāṇḍavas) and the hundred sons (the Kauravas) of Pāṇḍu's older brother, Dhṛtarāṣṭra, who is prevented by blindness from ruling. The Pāṇḍavas are actually sons of gods, and their birth is part of the divine plan to rescue Earth. By means of a mantra their mothers (Kuntī, the senior wife of Pāṇḍu, and Mādrī, the junior wife) had invoked deities to sire them, thus circumventing a curse that would have caused Pāṇḍu's death had he had sexual relations with his wives. Thus, with Kuntī, the god Dharma sired Yudhiṣṭhira, Vāyu sired Bhīma, and Indra sired Arjuna; with Mādrī, the twin Aśvins sired the twins Nakula and Sahadeva.

Following the interpretation of Wikander and Dumézil, these groups of gods and heroes may be seen to represent a hierarchical axis within the Vedic (and Indo-European) pantheon that further evokes the order of the upper three Aryan classes (*varṇas*) and, more archaically, what Dumézil has called the three functions: (1) religious sovereignty and law (Dharma and Yudhiṣṭhira), (2) warfare (Vāyu and Bhīma, Indra and Arjuna), and (3) economic welfare and service (the Aśvins and the twins). While the Pāṇḍavas thus represent the nucleus of social and divine hierarchy and the principle of *dharma*, their hundred cousins—incarnations of *rākṣasas* (disruptive goblins), except for the eldest, Duryodhana, who is an incarnation of the *asura* Kali (Discord), the demon of the *kaliyuga*—represent undifferentiated chaos and *adharma*.

During their youth the two groups of cousins vie with each other and form alliances that continue into the war. Thus Karṇa, son of Kuntī and the sun god Sūrya (Kuntī had first tried out her mantra with Sūrya before marriage, and then abandoned the son), allies with Duryodhana. At the Pāṇḍavas' polyandric wedding with Draupadī (incarnation of Śrī, goddess of prosperity), they ally themselves with Draupadī's brother Dhṛṣṭadyumna, the incarnation of Agni (Fire), who will lead their army. It is also at the marriage of Draupadī that the Pāṇḍavas first meet their cousin Kṛṣṇa (who is Kuntī's brother's son) and consolidate their relation with him.

For a brief period the two parties divide the kingdom; the Kauravas retain the ancestral throne at Hāstinapura, while the Pāṇḍavas build a new palace at Indraprastha. But when Yudhiṣṭhira performs a Rājasūya sacrifice to lay claim to universal sovereignty, Duryodhana is inconsolable until his friends suggest he invite the Pāṇḍavas to a dice match and win their wealth at gambling. At the dice match Yudhiṣṭhira gambles away everything; the last stakes are his brothers, himself, and finally Draupadī. Duryodhana then orders his vilest brother, Duḥśāsana, to drag Draupadī into the assembly hall, and when she protests, Karṇa commands Duḥśāsana to disrobe her. But Duḥśāsana is unsuccessful, for new saris keep descending upon Draupadī—according to most versions, thanks to her prayer to Kṛṣṇa—to keep her covered. When Draupadī is thus miraculously saved, Dhṛtarāṣṭra grants her husbands their freedom and returns their weapons, which the Pāṇḍavas will use in the war to fulfill their vows to destroy Draupadī's offenders.

In a second gambling match the Pāṇḍavas lose again, and together with Draupadī they are exiled for thirteen years. The last year must be spent incognito if they are to get back their kingdom. They adopt disguises and escape detection, yet when the thirteen years are over Duryodhana refuses to return the Pāṇḍavas' half of the kingdom. But the brothers have spent their exile in pilgrimage and penance (Arjuna in particular has done *tapas* to get weapons from Śiva). Their last year in exile has the character of a *dīkśā* (consecration preparatory to a sacrifice), and they have thus prepared themselves for the sacrifice of battle.

As the war looms, Kṛṣṇa's role becomes increasingly central. Although he serves as the Pāṇḍavas' peace ambassador and is himself sworn to noncombatancy, he actually prepares both sides for war. Then, just before the first day's battle, as Arjuna's charioteer he "sings" the *Bhagavadgītā*, thus convincing Arjuna of his duty to fight. The eighteen-day war on the plain of Kurukṣetra (an ancient sacrificial terrain) then follows, in which all the divine and demonic forces converge in a vast holocaust that has been variously interpreted as a sacrifice or as the end of the universe (*pralaya*). By leading the Pāṇḍavas to victory, Kṛṣṇa as *avatāra* achieves his task of relieving Earth's burden and renovating the *dharma* at the juncture between the *dvāpara* and *kaliyugas*, the latter of which is our present age.

See Also Arjuna; Bhagavadgītā; Epics; Indo-European Religions, overview article; Kṛṣṇa; Kurukṣetra.

Bibliography

The most accessible full translation is that by P. C. Roy and K. M. Ganguli, *The Mahabharata of Krishna-Dwaipayana Vyasa*, 12 vols. (1884–1896), 2d ed. (Calcutta, 1970). A partial translation by J. A. B. van Buitenen, *The Mahābhārata*, 3 vols. (Chicago, 1973–1978), covers five of the epic's eighteen books and is now being continued by several translators. C. V. Narasimhan's *The Mahābhārata* (New York, 1965) is the best abridgment.

Early work on the *Mahābhārata* culminates and is best summarized in E. Washburn Hopkins's *The Great Epic of India* (1901; reprint, Calcutta, 1969) and *Epic Mythology* (1915; reprint, New York, 1969). Stig Wikander's "Pāṇḍava-sagan och Mahābhāratas mytiska forutsattningar," *Religion och Bibel* 6 (1947): 27–39, can also be read in French in Georges Dumézil's *Jupiter Mars Quirinus*, vol. 4, *Explication de textes indiens et latins* (Paris, 1948). Dumézil's own most comprehensive treatment of the *Mahābhārata* can be found in his *Mythe et épopée*, vol. 1, *L'idéologie des trois fonctions dans les épopées des peuples indo-européens* (Paris, 1968).

Other works that develop various views in connection with Indo-European and Indian myth and ritual include Madeleine Biardeau's "Études de mythologie hindoue, Chap. II, Bhakti et avatāra," *Bulletin de l'École Française d'Extrême Orient* 63 (1976): 111–263 and 65 (1978): 87–238; Alf Hiltebeitel's *The Ritual of Battle: Krishna in the "Mahābhārata"* (Ithaca, N.Y., 1976); Heino Gehrts's *Mahābhārata: Das Geschehen und seine Bedeutung* (Bonn, 1975); and Jacques Scheuer's *Śiva dans le Mahābhārata* (Paris, 1982). See also Vishnu S. Sukthankar's *On the Meaning of the Mahābhārata* (Bombay, 1957), which emphasizes the epic's reliance upon Upanisadic formulations, and B. B. Lal's "Excavation at Hastināpura and Other Explorations in the Upper Gangā and Sutlej Basins, 1950–52," *Ancient India* 10/11 (1954/55): 5–151, which discusses epic place names in relation to Painted Gray Ware.

New Sources

Hiltebeitel, Alf. *Rethinking the Mahabharata: A Reader's Guide to the Education of the Dharma King.* Chicago, 2001.

ALF HILTEBEITEL (1987)
Revised Bibliography

MAHĀMUDRĀ

MAHĀMUDRĀ is a multivalent term of great importance in later Indian Buddhism and Tibetan Buddhism. It also occurs occasionally in Hindu and East Asian Buddhist esotericism. Best translated from Sanskrit as "the great seal," *mahāmudrā* denotes a ritual hand-gesture, one of a sequence of "seals" in Tantric practice, the nature of reality as emptiness, a meditation procedure focusing on the nature of mind, an innate blissful gnosis cognizing emptiness nondually, or the supreme attainment of buddhahood at the culmination of the Tantric path. *Mahāmudrā* is best known as a central feature of the philosophical view, meditative practice, and conception of enlightenment in the Bka' brgyud (Kagyu) sect of Tibetan Buddhism, but it has a place in most Tibetan Buddhist traditions, as it did in late Indian Buddhist Tantric literature. It has inspired devout meditation, profound philosophy, and brilliant poetry throughout the Indo-Tibetan Buddhist world for over a millennium. Any attempt to write a "history" of *mahāmudrā* is complicated by the concept's complexity, as well as uncertainties about the Indian and Tibetan texts and authors crucial to understanding it. With these difficulties in mind, this survey will attempt to reflect general scholarly consensus on the evolution of the concept of *mahāmudrā* in India, its articulation in Tibet, practices characteristic of it in Bka' brgyud tradition, and controversies over its interpretation.

***MAHĀMUDRĀ* IN INDIA.** The history of *mahāmudrā* in India may tentatively be traced through the roughly chronological Tantric traditions that arose there and the works of the great adepts (*mahāsiddhas*) who expounded on Tantric themes in song and treatise.

***Mahāmudrā* in the Tantras.** In the ritually focused *kriyā* and *caryā* Tantras, as in much Indian yogic literature, the term *mudrā* refers to a hand-position that "seals" religious procedures. Perhaps the first text to mention *mahāmudrā* is the *Mañjuśrīmūlakalpa* (c. seventh century), where the term refers primarily to a "five-peaked" hand-position said to be the "heart-gesture of the *tathāgatas*," pure and stainless, the accomplishment of all worldly and ultimate aims, the highest of all *dharmas*. *Mahāmudrā* is mentioned with increasing frequency in the more soteriologically oriented yoga Tantras (first appearing in the late seventh century). In such texts as the *Tattvasaṁgraha* and the *Vajraśekhara-tantra*, *mahāmudrā* is linked with three other *mudrās*—the action (*karma*), pledge (*samaya*), and *dharma* seals—employed to confirm particular meditative attainments. *Mahāmudrā* here connotes a series of hand positions, *mantra* recitations, and visualizations that symbolize and help to effect one's complete identification with a deity's divine form or awakening mind (*bodhicitta*). The *mahāyoga* Tantras (first appearing around the eighth century) maintain the yoga Tantras' concern with complex, *maṇḍala*-based meditative practices (the "creation stage," *utpattikrama*), but also emphasize yoga within the human subtle body (the "completion stage," *utpannakrama*), and explicitly evoke erotic, violent, and other transgressive themes. In the *Guhyasamāja*, an important *mahāyoga* Tantra, *mahāmudrā* has multiple meanings, including a contemplation-recitation conducive to the adamantine body, speech, and mind of the *tathāgatas*; and the object—emptiness—through realization of which "all is accomplished." Elsewhere, the *Guhyasamāja* describes the awakening mind—synonymous with *māhamudrā*—as primordially unborn, empty, unarisen, nonexistent, devoid of self, naturally luminous, and immaculate like the sky.

In the elaborate, sexually charged, and profoundly gnostic *yoginī* Tantras (first appearing around the late eighth century), *mahāmudrā* emerges as a major Buddhist concept. Though still connected there to creation-stage *maṇḍala*-practice, it is more often related to completion-stage meditations involving the manipulation of mental and physical forces in the subtle body so as to produce a divine form and a luminous, blissful, nonconceptual gnosis. In the completion-stage discussions in such Tantric systems as the Hevajra, Cakrasaṁvara, and Kālacakra, *mahāmudrā* has three especially important meanings. First, it may refer to a practitioner's female consort in sexual yoga practices. Second, as before, it is one of a sequence of *mudrās* corresponding to various Buddhist concepts, experiences, and path-stages. Here, though, it usually is the culmination of the series, a direct realization of the nature of mind and reality that transcends and perfects other, more conventional seals, including those involving actual or visualized sexual yoga. Third, *mahāmudrā* by itself connotes the ultimate truth, realization, or achievement of *yoginī* Tantra practice: the great seal that marks all phenomena and experiences; a synonym for suchness, sameness, emptiness, space, and the goddess Nairātmyā (no-self); unchanging bliss beyond object and subject, shape, thought, or expression; and the ultimate gnostic attainment, *mahāmudrā-siddhi*.

The *Mahāsiddhas*. Despite *mahāmudrā*'s apparent origin in the Tantras, the "canons" of *mahāmudrā* texts identified later by Tibetan scholars consist primarily of collections of Tantric commentaries, treatises, and songs attributed to the elusive, charismatic, and unconventional *mahāsiddhas* who were prominent in north Indian Buddhism before and just after 1000 CE. Many of these *mahāsiddhas* practiced the *yoginī* Tantras, and thus placed *mahāmudrā* near the center of their conceptual world, alongside such related notions as the *yoginī* or *ḍākinī*, emptiness, great bliss, the innate (*sahaja*), and nonduality—and the gnosis comprehending all of these. They often expressed themselves in colorful and paradoxical language, and utilized a "rhetoric of immediacy" to emphasize a natural, nonconceptual approach to life and liberation.

Three of their collections were given special attention by Tibetan traditions. The "Seven Texts on Attainment," including Padmavajra's *Guhyasiddhi*, Indrabhūti's *Jñānasiddhi*, and Lakṣmīṅkarā's *Advayasiddhi*, are poetic commentaries on themes in the *mahāyoga* and *yoginī* Tantras. *Mahāmudrā* is mentioned occasionally, usually denoting "ultimates" such as the nature of mind, nonconceptual awareness, and a buddha's *dharma* body; *mahāmudrā* also is explicitly synonymous with such common terms as the innate and nonduality. The "Trilogy on the Essential" comprises the "King," "Queen," and "People" couplet-treasuries (*dohākoṣas*) credited by Tibetan tradition to Saraha. These texts seldom refer to *mahāmudrā*, but they do mention related concepts like the innate, nonduality, great bliss, the *yoginī*, and buddhahood; other songs ascribed to Saraha mention *mahāmudrā* often, describing it as, for instance, "the lamp of innate gnosis," the union of method and wisdom, emptiness, uninterrupted bliss, and mind itself. The "Twenty-Five [Texts] on the *Dharma* of Unthinking," attributed to Maitrīpa (1007–1085), contain few overt references to either *mahāmudrā* or unthinking (*amanasikāra*), but do discuss the attainment of a nonconceptual realization equivalent to *mahāmudrā*. Maitrīpa addresses *mahāmudrā* frequently in other texts ascribed to him, most notably the *Mahāmudrākanakamālā*, which provides a long list of "ultimate" synonyms for it, and concludes that "the path of *mahāmudrā* is unthinking."

Other *siddhas* also expounded on *mahāmudrā*, including Nāgārjuna, Śavaripa, Tilopa, Nāropa, Virūpa, and Vajrāpani. The *mahāsiddhas* not only sang *mahāmudrā*'s praises, but sometimes analyzed it in terms of other Tantric *mudrās*, as well as Mahāyanā "Perfection Vehicle" concepts like emptiness, mind-only, and *tathāgata-garbha*, or buddha-nature. They also divided *mahāmudrā* into sequences of basis, path, and result—or view, meditation, action, and result—and increasingly identified it as a distinct style of meditation in which, by various means, one settles nonconceptually into contemplation of the nature of mind as empty, luminous, blissful gnosis.

By the end of the Buddhist period in India, *mahāmudrā* evoked a variety of meanings, whether ritual, yogic, ontological, or soteriological, and it had become a crucial Buddhist term that could describe the nature of reality and of the mind, a ritual or meditative procedure for seeing that nature, and the enlightenment ensuing from that realization. Its usages sometimes were deeply Tantric, as when related to completion-stage notions like great bliss and luminosity, and sometimes more evocative of philosophical and meditative themes in Mahāyanā wisdom traditions, including Madhyamaka and Yogācāra. Though these Tantric and non-Tantric approaches would eventually be distinguished, in the syncretic milieu of late Indian Buddhism, they were virtually inseparable.

***MAHĀMUDRĀ* IN TIBET.** Some Tibetan Buddhists probably were familiar with *mahāmudrā* (Tib., *phyag rgya chen po*) as early as the ninth century, during the imperial period, when Indian Tantras using the term were first translated into Tibetan. *Mahāmudrā*'s real importance in Tibet, however, dates from the eleventh-century "renaissance" of Buddhism there. Traditions originating in this period all were shaped by the *mahāyoga* and, especially, *yoginī* Tantra systems that dominated late Indian Buddhism, so they usually accounted for *mahāmudrā* in their descriptions of the Buddhist path. *Mahāmudrā* was relatively peripheral among the Bka' gdams (Kadam), who de-emphasized the Tantras in favor of practices concerned with renunciation, compassion, and wisdom; the Sa skya (Sakya), who were heir to many *mahāsiddha* traditions, but tended to restrict the term to the final result of the Tantric path, *mahāmudrā-siddhi*; and the Rnying ma (Nyingma), whose central concern was the Great Perfection (*Rdzogs chen*), which is described much like *mahāmudrā*, but arose from different Tantric contexts. *Mahāmudrā* was more central to Zhi byed, Gcod, and Shangs pa Bka' brgyud, where it was closely connected to both Tantric practices and Mahāyāna wisdom perspectives. These traditions never developed strong institutional bases, and their practices eventually were absorbed by other sects.

Early Bka' brgyud. It was in the traditions of the Dvags po Bka' brgyud (Dakpo Kagyu) that *mahāmudrā* became central, and their long-term success helped assure *mahāmudrā*'s place in Tibetan religious discourse. The Tibetan progenitor of the Dvags po Bka' brgyud was Mar pa Chos kyi blo gros (Marpa, 1012–1097), a farmer and translator who traveled to India to acquire texts and teachings, and who studied there with the *mahāsiddha* Maitrīpa, under whose guidance he claimed to have attained *mahāmudrā*-realization. Tradition also claims he met the scholar-yogin Nāropa (c. 966–1040), who taught him the completion-stage practices called the "Six *Dharmas* of Nāropa" (inner heat, illusory body, dream, clear light, intermediate state, and consciousness-transfer), as well as *mahāmudrā* instructions received from his teacher, Tilopa (fl. tenth century). Mar pa and his greatest disciple, the ascetic yogin Mi la ras pa (Milarepa, 1028/40–1111/23), adapted Indian Tantric song styles to Tibetan forms, and *mahāmudrā* is often referred to in poems attributed to them. Their usages are multiple, but two are especially prominent: *mahāmudrā* as related to Tantric completion-stage practices like the Six Dharmas of Nāropa, and *mahāmudrā* as a wisdom-tradition technique for directly seeing the nature of mind as primordially empty, luminous, and blissful—though Mar pa and Mi la ras pa probably did not make such a distinction.

Mi la ras pa's disciple Sgam po pa Bsod nams rin chen, or Dvags po lha rje (Gampopa Sonam Rinchen, 1079–1153), however, apparently took *mahāmudrā* to connote realization of the ultimate either through completion-stage Tantric practice (the "path of means") or "Perfection Vehicle" wisdom and insight (the "path of liberation"). For the latter, initiation is not required; one must, rather, secure the blessings (*byin rlabs*) of one's *guru,* who gives a direct indication (*ngo sprod*) of mind's nature. Sgam po pa also described *mahāmudrā* as an "essential vehicle" beyond sūtra or Tantra, a realization that seals all phenomena and leads to enlightenment, either gradually through four yogas—one-pointedness, simplicity, single taste, and nonmeditation—or suddenly, in an insight given such names as the "thunder-strike" (*thog babs*) and the "white medicinal simple" (*dkar po gcig thub*). By combining Tantric and *mahāmudrā* teachings learned from Mi la ras pa with virtue-based practices drawn from the Bka' gdams, Sgam po pa laid the basis for later Bka' brgyud ideology and praxis, and his disciples and subdisciples—who included both scholarly monks and "crazy" (*smyon pa*) hermits—founded numerous subsects that became the backbone of institutional Bka' brgyud, most notably the Kar ma, 'Brug pa (Drukpa), and 'Bri gung (Drikung).

In subsequent centuries, 'Bri gung 'Jig rten gsum mgon (Drikung Jikten Sumgön, 1143–1217) promulgated the Fivefold (*lnga ldan*) *Mahāmudrā,* in which realization of the mind's true nature is the culmination of gradual practices drawn from Mahāyāna and the Tantras; and the more radical Single Intention (*dgongs gcig*), where all principles and procedures are subsumed under a single gnostic realization. Zhang tshal pa Brtson du grags (Zhangtselpa Tsöndudrak, 1123–1193) emphasized the sudden realization of *mahāmudrā* as the "white medicinal simple," but also explored it in terms of sūtra-based Buddhist philosophical schools and paths to liberation; slow, rapid, and instantaneous practices; the four yogas; and so on—as with 'Jig rten gsum mgon, *mahāmudrā* became a concept embracing all of Buddhism. The 'Brug pa master Gtsang pa Rgya ras pa (Tsangpa Gyarepa, 1161–1211) and others began to describe a "canon" of Indian *mahāmudrā* texts drawn from the songs and treatises of the *mahāsiddhas,* the Tantras, and such Mahāyāna texts as the Prajñāpāramitā sūtras, *Samādhirāja-sūtra,* and *Uttaratantra-śāstra.* They also identified a number of lineages of *mahāmudrā* instruction, the most important of which went back to Mar pa, thence in India either to Tilopa and Nāropa (the near lineage) or Saraha, Nāgārjuna, Śavaripa, and Maitrīpa (one version of a distant lineage).

Later developments. The third Karma pa, Rang byung rdo rje (Rangjung Dorje, 1284–1339), wrote a popular poetic epitome of *mahāmudrā,* analyzed it in terms of philosophical concepts like *tathāgata-garbha* and extrinsic emptiness (*gzhan stong*), and explored similarities between *mahāmudrā* and the Rnying ma Great Perfection. Gtsang smyon Heruka (Tsangnyön Heruka, 1452–1507) composed classic hagiographies of Mar pa and Mi la ras pa, and the definitive collection of Mi la's songs; *mahāmudrā* features prominently in all three. Dvags po Bkra shis rnam rgyal (Dakpo Tashi Namgyel, 1512–1587) wrote a still-influential compendium on *mahāmudrā* covering sūtra and Tantra sources, gradual and sudden paths, calm and insight meditation, and the four yogas. 'Brug chen Padma dkar po (Drukchen Pema Karpo, 1527–1592) composed *mahāmudrā* meditation manuals, a history of Bka' brgyud lineages, and treatises examining *mahāmudrā* in relation to Tantric theory and Madhyamaka philosophy. Synthetic trends emerged, too. Partly inspired by the Bka' brgyud, the first Panchen Lama, Blo bzang chos kyi rgyal mtshan (Lobsang Chökyi Gyaltsen, 1570–1662), revealed a Dge lugs (Geluk) *mahāmudrā* tradition—involving both sūtra and Tantra approaches—that was traced to Indian *mahāsiddhas,* but more directly credited to the sect's founder, Tsong kha pa Blo bzang grags pa (Tsongkapa Lobsang Drakpa, 1357–1419), who supposedly received it in a vision from the wisdom *bodhisattva,* Mañjuśrī. Rnying ma pas absorbed *mahāmudrā* into their Great Perfection system, while Karma chags med (Karma Chakme, 1613–1678) brought the Great Perfection within the compass of Bka' brgyud *mahāmudrā* schemes. The nonsectarian (*ris med*) master 'Jam mgon kong sprul Blo gros mtha' yas (Jamgön Kongtrul Lodrö Taye, 1813–1899) wrote extensively on *mahāmudrā,* published Indian and Tibetan *mahāmudrā* texts, and entered into comparative discussion of "ultimates" with members of other traditions.

In the modern era, *mahāmudrā* has continued to be central to Bka' brgyud (and to a lesser degree, Dge lugs) theory and practice. It often has been taught by modern lamas, and has great appeal for Western Buddhists, who often regard it as a simple and natural approach to spiritual life, free of the categories and complexities of more "culturally embedded" Buddhist practices.

Characteristic practices. Though the articulation of *mahāmudrā* was an ongoing process, and formulations of its practice were various, certain patterns eventually emerged. In a typical Bka' brgyud account, *mahāmudrā* generally is divisible into basis, path, and result, or, alternatively, view, meditation, action, and result. The basis is usually *tathāgata-garbha,* the mind's actual or potential enlightened nature. Rightly viewing the basis provides the motive for entering the path. Paths are multiple, and divisible into meditation and action. In an instantaneous path, one abides in the nature of mind and acts spontaneously and compassionately right from the beginning. In a Tantric path, one identifies with a deity such as Vajrayoginī and masters completion-stage practices like the Six Dharmas of Nāropa, attaining perfect gnosis and skill in acting, even if unconventionally, for the sake of others. In a gradual non-Tantric path (the one most commonly described), meditation commences with standard devotional practices directed to one's *guru* and various deities. One next attains mental tranquility through concentration on a single object—usually the nature of mind itself—thereby experiencing clarity, bliss, and nonduality. With the mind concentrated effortlessly on itself, one proceeds to insight meditation, in which an analytic search for any nonmental phenomenon anywhere, or any truly existent mind of any sort, yields literally nothing—or emptiness. One moves then through the four phases of *mahāmudrā* yoga: one-pointedness, where one is fixated on the nature of mind; simplicity, where all mental elaboration is stilled in the experience of emptiness; single taste, where all phenomena are seen to be sealed by emptiness; and nonmeditation, where the distinctions between meditation and action, between sentient being and Buddha—indeed, all dualities—are resolved in a perfectly integrated understanding. As meditative realization deepens, one's actions are increasingly natural, joyous, and beneficial to others. When one is utterly delusion-free and completely identified with the luminous, blissful, nondual gnosis that is one's inmost nature, one achieves the path's result: the *dharma*, enjoyment, and emanation bodies of a fully enlightened buddha—which are no different from the emptiness, luminosity, and appearances of the mind itself. This is *mahāmudrā-siddhi.*

Controversies. Discussions of *mahāmudrā* in Tibet raised several important philosophical and religious issues, which were debated vigorously. Sa skya Paṇḍita Kun dga' rgyal mtshan (Sakya Paṇḍita, 1182–1251) argued that some Bka' brgyud *mahāmudrā* teachings derived not from pure Indian lineages, but from discredited Chinese Chan influences; that there could be no such thing as a sūtra-based *mahāmudrā* because *mahāmudrā-siddhi* only can result from advanced Tantric practice; and that the Bka' brgyud rhetoric of immediacy was spiritually dangerous because it suggested that enlightenment was attainable through sudden insight alone, without recourse to gradual, virtue-based religious methods. Later Bka' brgyud (and Dge lugs) scholars rejected Sa skya Paṇḍita criticisms, asserting that *mahāmudrā*'s Indian roots were unassailable, its meaning articulated in both sūtras and Tantras, and its "sudden" rhetoric inclusive of virtue—and intended only for advanced practitioners.

Controversies also arose over whether *mahāmudrā* as a gnosis realizing emptiness is intrinsically empty of inherent existence just as worldly phenomena are (the *rang stong* view), or empty solely of worldly qualities extrinsic to it, itself being pure and permanent (the *gzhan stong* view); whether meditative experiences of clarity, bliss, and nonduality reflect genuine attainment, or are merely deceptions; and whether the multiple terms by which Tibetan Buddhists described the ultimate (*mahāmudrā*, Great Perfection, Madhyamaka, and so on) had identical or different referents. This latter discussion resonates still among contemporary Buddhists, who debate how *mahāmudrā* might relate to other Tibetan notions of ultimacy, to ideas and practices in other Buddhist traditions (especially Zen and *vipassana* meditation), and to reports of mystical experience the world around. Thus, though *mahāmudrā* is a concept specific to Indian and Tibetan Buddhist cultural settings, its implications transcend those contexts and suggest pan-Buddhist and universal human religious concerns.

See Also Buddhism, article on Buddhism in Tibet.

Bibliography

Broido, Michael M. "Padma dKar-po on the Two *Satyas.*" *Journal of the International Association of Buddhist Studies* 8, no. 2 (1985): 7–60. One of a number of scholarly and philosophically sophisticated articles by Broido on the philosophy of Padma dkar po.

Chang, Garma C. C., trans. and ed. *The Hundred Thousand Songs of Milarepa: The Life-Story and Teaching of the Greatest Poet-Saint Ever to Appear in the History of Buddhism.* 2 vols. New Hyde Park, N.Y., 1962; reprint, Boston, 1989. The greatest collection of the poems of Tibet's greatest poet, with ample references to *mahāmudrā.* For songs attributed to a range of Bka' brgyud masters, see Nālandā Translation Committee, *The Rain of Wisdom* (Boulder, Colo., 1980).

Dalai Lama, H. H., XIV, and Alexander Berzin. *The Gelug/Kagyü Tradition of Mahamudra.* Ithaca, N.Y., 1997. Detailed commentary on the first Panchen Lama's seminal Dge lugs *mahāmudrā* text. For an account of completion-stage Tantric *mahāmudrā* according to the Dge lugs, see Geshe Kelsang Gyatso, *Clear Light of Bliss: Mahamudra in Vajrayana Buddhism* (London, 1982; 2d ed., 1992).

The Eighth Situpa and the Third Karma pa. *Mahāmudrā Teachings of the Supreme Siddhas.* Translated by Lama Sherab Dorje. Ithaca, N.Y., 1995. Includes the third Karma pa's popular "Aspiration Prayer of *Mahāmudrā,*" with a learned and citation-rich commentary on it by the eighteenth-century scholar Si tu paṇ chen Chos kyi byung gnas.

Farrow, G. W., and I. Menon, eds. and trans. *The Concealed Essence of the Hevajra Tantra, with the Commentary Yogaratnamālā.* Delhi, 1992. Includes Sanskrit and English of the root-Tantra, and English translation of Kāṇha/Kṛṣṇācārya's commentary on it. See also David Snellgrove's two-volume edition and translation of the root-Tantra: *The Hevajra Tantra* (London, 1959).

'Gos lo tsā ba Gzhon nu dpal. *The Blue Annals.* Translated by George N. Roerich. Calcutta, 1949–1953; reprint, Delhi, 1979. This great chronicle, written by a Bka' brgyud pa, contains countless references to *mahāmudrā* traditions in Tibet from the eleventh to fifteenth century.

Guenther, Herbert V., trans. *Ecstatic Spontaneity: Saraha's Three Cycles of Doha.* Berkeley, 1993. Idiosyncratic and philosophically challenging translation of Saraha's "Trilogy on the Essential." Earlier works by Guenther include *The Life and Teaching of Nāropa* (London, 1963), which is a translation of a hagiography of Nāropa, with detailed discussion of the Tantric practices he received from Tilopa, including *mahāmudrā* and the Six *Dharmas*; and *The Tantric View of Life* (Boulder, Colo., 1972), which contains frequent references to *mahāmudrā*, and many quotations from little-studied texts by Indian Buddhist *mahāsiddhas.*

Gyaltsen, Khenpo Könchog, trans. and ed., and Katherine Rogers, co-trans. and ed. *The Garland of Mahamudra Practices: A Translation of Kunga Rinchen's Clarifying the Jewel Rosary of the Profound Fivefold Path.* Ithaca, N.Y., 1986. A sixteenth-century account of the 'Bri gung Bka' brgyud Fivefold *Mahāmudrā* practice.

Gyatso, Janet. "Healing with Fire: The Facilitations of Experience in Tibetan Buddhism." *Journal of the American Academy of Religion* 67, no. 1 (1999): 113–147. Discusses the concept of "experience" in relation to Tibetan Buddhist meditation traditions, including the Great Perfection and, especially, *mahāmudrā.*

Hookham, Susan K. *The Buddha Within: Tathagatagarbha Doctrine according to the Shentong Interpretation of the Ratnagotravibhaga.* Albany, N.Y., 1991. Discussion of Tibetan disputes over intrinsic and extrinsic emptiness, with special focus on the *Uttaratantra,* an Indian poetic treatise regarded by Bka' brgyud pas as central to Perfection-Vehicle *mahāmudrā.*

Jackson, David P. *Enlightenment by a Single Means: Tibetan Controversies on the "Self-Sufficient White Remedy."* Vienna, 1994. Analysis of the debate over *mahāmudrā* between Sa skya pas and Bka' brgyud pas; contains much useful information on and extracts from the writings of Sgam po pa and Zhang tshal pa.

Jackson, Roger R., trans. and ed. *Tantric Treasures: Three Collections of Mystical Verse from Buddhist India,* pp. 53–116. Oxford, 2004. Includes original texts and translations of Saraha's "People" *Dohākoṣa,* and *dohākoṣas* by Kāṇha and Tilopa. For Indian Buddhist songs in a related genre, see Per Kvaerne, *An Anthology of Buddhist Tantric Songs: A Study of the Caryāgīti* (Oslo, 1977).

Karma Chagmé. *A Spacious Path to Freedom: Practical Instructions on the Union of Mahamudra and Atiyoga.* Translated by B. Alan Wallace. Ithaca, N.Y., 1998. One of several translations of the most famous attempt at a *mahāmudrā*/Great Perfection synthesis; includes commentary by a modern Rnying ma lama, Gyatrul Rinpoche.

Kragh, Ulrich. "Culture and Subculture: A Study of the *Mahāmudrā* Teachings of Sgam po pa." M.A. research paper (*speciale*), University of Copenhagen, 1998. Surveys Sgam po pa's literary output and discusses his complex views on the nature of *mahāmudrā.*

Kvaerne, Per. "On the Concept of *Sahaja* in Indian Buddhist Tantric Literature." *Temenos* 11 (1975): 88–135. Pioneering study of a term often regarded as synonymous with *mahāmudrā,* especially in its Indian context. For a more recent study, see Ronald M. Davidson, "Reframing *Sahaja*: Genre, Representation, Ritual, and Lineage." *Journal of Indian Philosophy* 30 (2002): 45–83.

Martin Dan. "A Twelfth-Century Tibetan Classic of *Mahāmudrā*: *The Path of Ultimate Profundity: The Great Seal Instructions of Zhang.*" *Journal of the International Association of Buddhist Studies* 15 (1992): 243–319. Pioneering translation of Zhang tshal pa's great poem on *mahāmudrā.*

Mishra, Ramprasad. *Advayasiddhi: The Tantric View of Lakṣmīṅkarā.* New Delhi, 1993. Sanskrit text, English translation, and commentary on one of the "Seven [Texts] on Accomplishment."

Namgyal, Takpo Tashi. *Mahāmudrā: The Quintessence of Mind and Meditation.* Translated and annotated by Lobsang P. Lhalungpa. Boston, 1986. Excellent, if under-annotated, translation of Dvags po Bkra shis rnam rgyal's classic tome, the *Phyag chen zla ba'i 'od zer* (Moonbeams of *mahāmudrā*); a wealth of philosophical analysis, practical advice, and textual citations. For other *mahāmudrā* manuals, see Stephan Beyer, trans., *The Buddhist Experience: Sources and Interpretations,* pp. 154–161 (Encino, Calif., 1974), which is meditation advice from Padma dkar po; Tsele Natsok Rangdrol, *The Lamp of Mahamudra,* translated by Eric Pema Kunsang (Boston, 1989), an account by a modern lama; and Jamgon Kongtrul III, *Cloudless Sky: The Mahamudra Path of the Tibetan Buddhist Kagyü School,* edited and translated by Tina Drasczyk, Alex Drasczyk, and Richard Gravel (Boston, 1992), which includes a poem on *mahāmudrā* by the first Jam mgon kong sprul, and a practical commentary on it by a recent successor.

Robinson, James B., trans. *Buddha's Lions: The Lives of the Eighty-Four Siddhas.* Berkeley, 1975. Straightforward translation of Abhayadattaśrī's *Caturaśītisiddhapravṛtti,* the most influential Indian collection of *mahāsiddha* hagiographies; it also includes a list of all works attributed to the *mahāsiddhas* in the Peking Tibetan Tripiṭaka. For an alternative translation, see Keith Dowman, *Masters of Mahāmudrā* (Albany, N.Y., 1985).

Ruegg, David Seyfort. "A Kar ma bKa' brgyud Work on the Lineages and Traditions of the Indo-Tibetan dBu ma (Madhyamaka)." In *Orientalia Iosephi Tucci Memoriae Dicata,* edited by G. Gnoli and L. Lanciotti, pp. 1249–1280. Rome, 1988. This study of a sixteenth-century work includes interesting material on the relation among Tantra, Madhyamaka, and *mahāmudrā.*

Snellgrove, David L. *Indo-Tibetan Buddhism.* 2 vols. Boston, 1987. Classic account of Indian Buddhist Tantra and the early Tibetan renaissance; helpful for understanding *mahāmudrā* within its broader social and religious context. For a briefer, but still authoritative discussion of Indian Buddhist Tantra, see Paul Williams, with Anthony Tribe, *Buddhist Thought: A Complete Introduction to the Indian Tradition,* pp. 192–244 (London, 2000).

Tāranātha. *The Seven Instruction Lineages: bKa' babs bdun ldan.* Translated and edited by David Templeman. Dharamsala, India, 1983. See pages 2–14. Life stories of the lineage holders of various Indian practice-traditions, including that of *mahāmudrā,* by a sixteenth-century Tibetan philosopher and historian.

Tatz, Mark. "The Life of the *Siddha*-Philosopher Maitrīgupta." *Journal of the American Oriental Society* 107 (1987): 695–711. The best scholarly study of the life of the great eleventh-century Indian *mahāmudrā* master.

Thaye, Jampa. *A Garland of Gold: The Early Kagyu Masters of India and Tibet.* Bristol, UK, 1990. Includes brief biographies of Indian and Tibetan teachers crucial to Bka' brgyud *mahāmudrā* traditions, and translations of *dohās* by Tilopa, Nāropa, Śavaripa, Mar pa, and Mi la ras pa. For more extensive biographies, drawn from an early Bka' brgyud source, see Khenpo Könchog Gyaltsen, trans., *The Great Kagyu Masters:*

The Golden Lineage Treasury, edited by Victoria Huckenpahler (Ithaca, N.Y., 1990).

ROGER R. JACKSON (2005)

MAHARAL OF PRAGUE SEE LÖW, YEHUDAH BEN BETSAL'EL OF PRAGUE

MAHĀSĀṂGHIKA.

MAHĀSĀṂGHIKA. One of the earliest of the non-Mahāyāna Buddhist "sects" (the so-called Eighteen Schools of Hīnayāna Buddhism), the Mahāsāṃghika has been generally considered the precursor of Mahāyāna. However, although the Mahāsāṃghika and its subschools espoused many of the most radical views later attributed to the "Great Vehicle," other factors and early schools also contributed to the development of this movement.

EARLY DEVELOPMENT. Traditional accounts differ on the occasion and reason for the schism that gave rise to the Mahāsāṃghika. Some accounts claim that the Mahāsāṃghika separated from the Sthavira at the time of the Second Buddhist Council (Vaiśālī, c. 340 BCE), others, that it occurred during a third council (sometimes confused with *the* Third Council held at Pāṭaliputra under King Aśoka, 244 BCE). The reasons for the schism have also been much debated. It is agreed that the split was motivated by matters of monastic discipline, but scholars disagree on the precise issues at stake. Most Western scholars are inclined to accept that the Mahāsāṃghika represented the more lax position in matters of discipline. Less common is the position of those who would claim the opposite, pointing to the fact that the Mahāsāṃghika had a very conservative Vinaya and that its Prātimokṣa was as strict as that of other Hīnayāna schools. It seems therefore unlikely that laxness in monastic regulations was the motive for the split.

Moreover, recent scholarship tends to distinguish the dispute that provoked the Second Council, which ended in reconciliation in the order, from a dispute that probably occurred shortly thereafter (anywhere between sixteen and sixty years later). It was this latter dispute that produced the schism that divided the Hīnayāna schools into its two major camps, the Sthaviras and the Mahāsāṃghikas. Be that as it may, it seems obvious that the Mahāsāṃghika criticized the *arhat* ideal and exalted the image of the Buddha, turning the historical life of the founder into an event of secondary importance and the *arhat* ideal into an inferior goal. In this sense they were making an argument against tradition, and whatever the significance of their Vinaya may be, their doctrinal positions were clearly innovative.

LITERATURE. The Mahāsāṃghika tendency to innovate can be seen also in the content and structure of their Tripiṭaka. Although in its early stages it is believed to have been comprised of only three parts (Sūtra, Vinaya, and Abhidharma), the Sūtra Piṭaka was later expanded so that the *Kṣudraka Āgama* became a separate Piṭaka called Saṃyukta Piṭaka. According to some sources this section came to include "*vaipulya sūtras*," an expression that could refer to Mahāyāna texts. The last addition to the Mahāsāṃghika Tripiṭaka was a fifth section, the Dhāraṇī Piṭaka, a collection of spells and incantations. Some accounts, however, say that the fifth Piṭaka was a Bodhisattva Piṭaka, which presumably refers to a collection of Mahāyāna texts.

Unfortunately, little remains of this canon and it is now impossible to confirm or even clarify such general statements. The Prātimokṣa of the Mahāsāṃghika survives in its original Sanskrit, and part of the Vinaya survives in the Sanskrit work *Mahāvastu*, which claims in its colophon to be a work of the Lokottaravādin Mahāsāṃghika of Central India. Apart from these and a few fragments of the Vinaya and the Sūtra section of their canon found at Bāmiyān, the rest of the Indian texts of the school are lost. Even in translation only a few texts survive. There is a Chinese translation of their Vinaya by Faxian, and what seems to be part of their Sūtra Piṭaka (*Ekottarāgama*). The latter text appears to be a translation from a prakritic language. There is also a distinct Mahāsāṃghika influence on a Dharmaguptaka text, the *Śāriputrābhidharma Śāstra.*

The *Mahāvastu*—the Buddhist Hybrid Sanskrit text of which was preserved in Nepal as a Mahāyāna Sūtra—represents only that section of the Vinaya that establishes the "historical" basis for monastic institutions, that is, the life and early ministry of the Buddha. It is primarily a biography of the Buddha from his meeting with Dīpaṃkara to his first sermon and the conversion of the first disciples. It also contains a number of *avadānas*. But it contains no material on matters of monastic discipline and its main narrative is interpolated with numerous digressions, mostly stories of the *jātaka* or *avadāna* genre. Although the oldest portions of this work must go back to the early stages of the formation of canonical Buddhism, it contains numerous late interpolations that place the extant recension in the fifth century CE.

Although the *Mahāvastu* is regarded as a transitional work, for the most part it does not show doctrinal leanings radically distinct from those of most Vinayas. There are, however, a few clear signs of those elements of doctrine and language that have been traditionally considered characteristics of Mahāsāṃghika, some of which also define Mahāyāna. The text speaks of the Buddha's *lokottara* ("supramundane") status, of his presence in the world only by dint of an illusion created in order to conform to the aspirations and perceptions of living beings. The fact that the *Mahāvastu* is written in Hybrid Sanskrit would seem to confirm the tradition according to which the Mahāsāṃghika used some form of Prakrit in their religious literature.

DOCTRINAL DEVELOPMENTS. The most characteristic doctrine of the Mahāsāṃghika group are the famous "Five Points of Mahādeva" (sometimes attributed to a certain Bhadra), an attack on the *arhat* that has been the object of at least two interpretations: it can be regarded as an argument for more lax moral standards or it can be seen as an indirect way of arguing for the value of the *bodhisattva* ideal. These five points are (1) that an *arhat* can be seduced by another (*para-upahṛta*—meaning that he can have nocturnal emissions accompanied by an erotic dream); (2) that ignorance (*ajñāna*) is not totally absent in an *arhat* (his spiritual insight does not give him knowledge of profane matters); (3) that an *arhat* can have doubts (*kaṃkṣā*); (4) that an *arhat* can be surpassed by another (*para-vitīrṇa*—a term of obscure meaning); and (5) that an *arhat* can enter the higher stages of the path by uttering a phrase (*vacibheda*) such as "Oh, sorrow!" The exact meaning of these doctrines is far from obvious. Even the general intent is not transparent; one may ask if the Five Points imply that the *arhat* is more human than he was thought to be in other schools, or that he is weaker than others believe. Or is the implication that the *bodhisattva* path is superior?

Other doctrines attributed to the Mahāsāṃghika are equally tantalizing. For instance, it is said that they held that only *prajñā* liberates, a thesis that may reflect an early emphasis on *prajñā* such as would have led to the eventual centrality of the Perfection of Wisdom (Prajñāpāramitā) literature in Mahāyāna. The Mahāsāṃghika seem also to have claimed that all word of the Buddha are *nītārtha*; that is, they are in no need of interpretation. But this may mean not so much that the canon needs no exegesis as that the Buddha when he preaches has no hidden intent except for what living beings may find in his words, according to their capacities. At least this would be the only way this doctrine could accord with other statements attributed to the Mahāsāṃghikas, for they held that the Buddha preaches all *dharmas* with one word, that he preaches even when he does not speak, and that there is no conventional truth (*saṃvṛtti-satya*) in his Dharma.

BUDDHOLOGY. Also characteristic of the Mahāsāṃghika is the belief that there are many Buddhas in all of the ten directions and at all times in the past, the present, and the future. In this they differ from more conservative Buddhists who believe that a Buddha is a rare phenomenon. But the Mahāsāṃghika claim may be another side of the doctrine that has been called "Buddhist docetism," that is, the belief that Buddhas do not lead a human life, even when they seem to be appearing in history. Perhaps related to this doctrine is the notion that *bodhisattvas* make a vow (*praṇidhāna*) to remain in the cycle of transmigration for the sake of sentient beings. They prolong their stay voluntarily; in fact, *bodhisattvas* may choose a life in hell for the sake of living beings.

SECTARIAN OUTGROWTHS. Of the various sects that issued from the Mahāsāṃghika, the most important are the Lokottaravādins and the Prajñaptivādins. It has been suggested that these two branches represent two major doctrinal departures as well as two geographical centers of activity. Although both branches and their derivatives were active in more than one part of India, the Lokottaravādin group centered in the North (Mathura), the Prajñaptivādin groups in the southeast of India. It also seems that the northern groups preferred Sanskrit as their canonical language, whereas the groups in the South used Prakrit. Doctrinally, however, the distinction is difficult to maintain, since the traditional sources are often contradictory.

Lokottaravā. The Lokottaravādins seem to have emphasized the general docetic tendencies of the Mahāsāṃghika more than did the other subschools. Unfortunately, as the sources seem to conflate all doctrines of the Mahāsāṃghika splinter groups into their general description of the Mahāsāṃghika, it is difficult to distinguish one from the other or from the parent school. The tenet from which the Lokottaravā derives its name, the belief that the "career," or sequence of lives leading to and including the complete enlightenment of Buddhas, is only a series of apparitional events, is also attributed to the main school. According to this doctrine, Buddhas are supramundane; that is, they are not human beings but perfectly pure spiritual beings, free from the limitations of a physical body. This doctrine can be recognized in at least one key passage in the *Mahāvastu*, but it is far from being the dominant theme in that work. This does not necessarily prove that the belief was not as central to the school as claimed by the doxographers. It may be that much of the Mahāsāṃghika doctrinal speculation took place in the Abhidharma and the commentarial literature of the school—all of which is now lost. The monastic, meditational, and liturgical life of the communities probably did not reflect the doctrinal rifts that defined the schools.

Prajñaptivāda. In contrast to the general Mahāsāṃghika view, this subschool held that all statements of doctrine are merely of provisional or purely conventional meaning. Still, the Prajñaptivādins appear to have preserved some distinction between absolute and relative truths. In spite of the obscurity of this notion, one can see the connection between it and certain ideas of the Bahuśrutīyas. This may be due to a common origin from the Gokulika branch of the Mahāsāṃghika.

From the Prajñaptivāda arose other groups, the most important being the Aparaśailas and the Pūrvaśailas, whose main center of activity was in Dhānyakaṭaka (modern Andhra Pradesh). They seem to have counted in their literature some works of Mahāyāna tendency, perhaps even Prajñāpāramita texts in Prakrit.

If the Bahuśrutīya school is also an offshoot of the parent Mahāsāṃghika line then we would have to count among Mahāsāṃghika literature Harivarman's scholastic treatise, the Satyasiddhisastra (third century CE). This work clearly occupies an intermediate position between the Abhidharma of the Hīnayāna schools and the philosophical treatises of Mahāyāna.

INFLUENCE. Direct Mahāsāṃghika influence did not extend beyond the Indian subcontinent. But through its influence in the formation of Mahāyāna the school left its mark in the history of Buddhism in East Asia and Tibet. Its key doctrines—the centrality of *prajñā*, the *bodhisattva* vows, the apparitional life of the Buddha, the distinction between conventional and absolute truth—even today continue to affect Buddhist Mahāyāna perception of the world and of the Buddhist tradition.

See Also Arhat; Bodhisattva Path; Buddha; Buddhism, Schools of; Language, article on Buddhist Views of Language.

Bibliography

Aung, Shwe Zan, and C. A. F. Rhys Davids, trans. *Points of Controversy.* London, 1915. Classical Theravāda polemics against the doctrines of the Eighteen Schools.

Bareau, André. "Les sectes bouddhiques du Petit Véhicule et leurs Abhidharmapiṭaka." *Bulletin de l'École Française d'Extrême-Orient* 50 (1952): 1–11. Bareau is the leading scholar on the early history of the Hīnayāna schools. See also his "Trois traités sur les sectes bouddhiques attribués à Vasumitra, Bhavya et Vinītadeva," *Journal asiatique* 242 (1954): 229–266; 244 (1956): 167–200; *Les premiers conciles bouddhiques* (Paris, 1955); *Les sectes bouddhiques du petit véhicule* (Saigon, 1955); and "Les controverses rélatives à la nature de l'arhant dans le bouddhisme ancien," *Indo-Iranian Journal* 1 (1957): 241–250.

Bareau, André, and H. G. A. van Zeyst. "Andhakas." In the *Encyclopaedia of Buddhism,* vol. 1, edited by G. P. Malalasekera. Colombo, 1965. Analysis of a representative group of "southern" Mahāsāṃghikas.

Bechert, Heinz. "Zur Frühgeschichte des Mahāyāna-Buddhismus." *Zeitschrift der Deutschen Morgenländischen Gesellschaft* 113 (1963): 530–535. Summarizes contemporary understanding of the breadth and complexity of Hīnayāna sources for Mahāyāna.

Demiéville, Paul. "L'origine des sectes bouddhiques d'après Paramartha." In *Mélanges chinois et bouddhiques,* vol. 1, pp. 15–62. Brussels, 1931–1932. See also his "À propos du concile de Vaiśālī," *T'oung pao* 40 (1951): 239–296.

Dutt, Nalinaksha. *Early History of the Spread of Buddhism and the Buddhist Schools* (1925). Reprint, New Delhi, 1980. See also Dutt's *Aspects of Mahāyāna Buddhism and Its Relation to Hīnayāna* (London, 1930), and "The Second Buddhist Council," *Indian Historical Quarterly* 35 (March 1959): 45–56. Most of Dutt's earlier work on the sects, found hidden in various journals, was compiled in *Buddhist Sects in India* (Calcutta, 1970).

Jones, J. J., trans. *The Mahāvastu.* 3 vols. London, 1949–1956. This is the English translation of one of the few surviving Mahāsāṃghika texts.

Lamotte, Étienne. "Buddhist Controversy over the Five Propositions." *Indian Historical Quarterly* 32 (1966): 148–162. The material collected in this article is also found, slightly augmented, in Lamotte's great *Histoire du bouddhisme indien: Des origines à l'ère Saka* (Louvain, 1958), pp. 300–319, 542–543, 575–606, and 690–695. This erudite work is still the standard reference on the history of early Indian Buddhism.

La Vallée Poussin, Louis de. "Mahāvastu." In *Encyclopaedia of Religion and Ethics,* edited by James Hastings, vol. 8. Edinburgh, 1915. This article and the one by Rhys Davids listed below are dated, but they contain valuable information and historical hypotheses still defended by some scholars.

Masuda Jiryō. "Origins and Doctrines of Early Indian Buddhist Schools." *Asia Major* 2 (1925): 1–78.

Prebish, Charles S. "A Review of Scholarship on the Buddhist Councils." *Journal of Asian Studies* 33 (February 1974): 239–254. Prebish has dedicated serious reflection to the problem of the early schools, especially to the history and significance of their Vinaya. See also "The Prātimokṣa Puzzle: Facts versus Fantasy," *Journal of the American Oriental Society* 94 (April–June 1974): 168–176, and *Buddhist Monastic Discipline: The Sanskrit Prātimokṣa Sūtras of the Mahāsāṃghikas and Mulasarvastivadins* (University Park, Pa., 1975).

Prebish, Charles S., and Janice J. Nattier. "Mahāsāṃghika Origins: The Beginnings of Buddhist Sectarianism." *History of Religions* 16 (February 1977): 237–272. A well-argued challenge to the perception of Mahāsāṃghikas as "Liberals."

Rhys Davids, T. W. "Sects (Buddhist)." In *Encyclopaedia of Religion and Ethics,* edited by James Hastings, vol. 11. Edinburgh, 1920.

Wayman, Alex. "The Mahāsāṅghika and the Tathāgatagarbha." *Journal of the International Association of Buddhist Studies* 1 (1978): 35–50. Discusses possible connections between the Mahāsāṃghika subsects of Andhra and the development of Mahāyāna.

New Sources

Braarvig, Jens, et al., eds. *Buddhist Manuscripts in the Schøyen Collection* Vol. 1. Oslo, 2000. See pages 53–62 and pages 233–242.

Harrison, Paul. "Sanskrit Fragments of a Lokottaravādin Tradition." In *Indological and Buddhist Studies: Volume in Honour of Professor J. W. de Jong on His Sixtieth Birthday,* edited by L. Hercus and et al., pp. 211–234. Delhi, 1982.

Hirakawa, Akira. *Monastic Discipline for the Buddhist Nuns: An English Translation of the Chinese Text of the Mahāsāṃghika-Bhiksuni-Vinaya.* Patna, 1982.

Prebish, Charles S. "Saiksa-Dharmas Revisited: Further Considerations of Mahasamghika Origins." *History of Religions* 35 (1996): 258–270.

Yuyama, Akira, ed. *The Mahāvastu-avadāna: In Old Palm-Leaf and Paper Manuscripts.* Tokyo, 2001.

Luis O. Gómez (1987)
Revised Bibliography

MAHĀSIDDHAS. The Buddhist *mahāsiddha* ("fully perfected one"), or simply *siddha* ("perfected one"), is the central enlightened ideal of Tantric or Vajrayāna Buddhism, the last major developmental phase of Indian Buddhism and particularly prominent on the subcontinent between the eighth and twelfth centuries CE. Best known are the list of eighty four of the greatest Buddhist *siddhas* (as enumerated by the twelfth-century Indian author Abhayadatta) and the grouping of *siddhas* into seven lineages (by the Tibetan author Tāranātha). Like the Buddha for earliest Buddhism, the *arhat* for the pre-Mahāyāna tradition, and the *bodhisattva* for the Mahāyāna, the *siddha* stands as the preeminent model of an accomplished person for the Vajrayāna tradition. And like those earlier ideals for their traditions, the *siddha* embodies in his person the particular character and ideals of the Vajrayāna, with its emphasis on meditation, personal realization, the master-disciple relationship, and the nonmonastic ways of life of the householder and the wandering yogin.

SOURCES. Our knowledge of the Buddhist *siddhas* comes from a considerable amount of biographical material that survives chiefly in Tibetan texts, which are either translations of, or are based directly or indirectly on, Indian written and oral tradition. These biographies of the *siddhas*, which vary in length from a few lines to hundreds of pages, tell the "liberation story" (*rnam thar*) of their subjects, recounting their individual journeys from the ordinary human state to one of full awakening.

The biographies of the *siddhas* are especially characterized by strong mythological, symbolic, and magical overtones. As in the case of the Buddha Śākyamuni in his biographies, but to a much greater degree, the *siddhas* are depicted as beings whose lives are charged with the transcendent and supernatural. At the same time, the *siddhas* are shown as real men and women with specific connections to the everyday, historical world. Their stories depict them as coming from particular places, belonging to certain castes, and following this or that occupation. Their teachers, Tantric practices, and lineages are carefully noted. The greatest among them figure as great teachers, lineage founders, monastic officials, and prolific authors of extant Tantric texts. Many *siddhas* are known historically to have played important roles in the transmission of the Vajrayāna from India to Tibet, China, and Southeast Asia, and are part of the social and political history of those countries. This confluence of the mythological and transcendent on the one hand, and the historically tangible and specific on the other, is one of the particular marks of the *siddhas* and of the Vajrayāna in general.

STRUCTURE OF THE SIDDHA IDEAL. The *siddhas* are depicted in their biographies both as particular individuals and as members of a common type: their lives share a certain general structure or pattern, resumed here, that marks them as Buddhist *siddhas*.

Before enlightenment. The *siddha*'s life story generally begins with his birth, sometimes in the great Tantric areas of Kāmarūpa (northeast India), Uḍḍiyāna (northwest India), or Nāgārjunikoṇḍa (southeast India), sometimes in some other region. There typically follow details of caste status. In contrast to earlier Buddhism, where the higher castes are implicitly regarded as preferable, the *siddhas* come not only from the high castes (*brāhmaṇa* and *kṣatriya*) but as often from the low; some of the greatest *siddhas* were originally hunters, fishers, herdsmen, weavers, cobblers, blacksmiths, prostitutes, and even thieves. This diversity of social origins gives particularly vivid expression to the classical Buddhist insistence that caste and social distinctions are not spiritually rooted or inherent in reality, and that enlightenment can occur equally in any conditioned situation, whatever its conventionally stated social value.

The *siddhas* are typically depicted at the beginning of their careers as ordinary people who possess some often unspecified longing. They are men and women, monks and laypeople, privileged and destitute, but they all share a sense of unavoidable dissatisfaction and circularity in their lives. They reach a critical point in their religious career when they encounter a Tantric teacher who presents them with the possibility of a spiritual path—of meditation, of the shedding of habitual patterns, and of awakening. Their response is often a mixture of attraction and fear, but they share a feeling of connection with the teacher and with the message he articulates. Following this encounter, the future *siddhas* begin a demanding course of training under their *gurus*. The importance of the teacher-disciple relationship in each *siddha*'s biography reflects the Vajrayāna emphasis on the primacy of individual awakening and of the necessity of a realized, personal teacher to that process.

There follows in each *siddha*'s life a period of study with a teacher, whom the pupil sometimes attends for many years, and sometimes meets only periodically for new instructions. Formless meditation and liturgical Tantric practice (*sādhana*) are unremitting parts of the student's training, but so is activity "in the world"; many of these later-to-be-*siddhas* are instructed to carry out caste occupations and to marry. Some are instructed to perform tasks that are anathema to their former identities, such as the *brahmans* Bhadrapa and Lūyipa, who are told to make their living cleaning latrines and serving a prostitute, respectively. In general, hard tasks and humiliation of previous ego ideals marks the testing and training of the *siddhas* during their student days and their journey toward classic Buddhist realization of egolessness.

Siddhas as enlightened figures. After many years of arduous training, the *siddhas* emerge as fully enlightened people. In contrast to the Buddha, who was regarded as one of a kind thus far in our world age, to the *arhat*, whose enlightenment was seen as less than the Buddha's, and to the *bodhisattva*, who is enjoined to postpone his full awakening, the *siddhas* are depicted as having attained full awakening, thus fulfilling the Vajrayāna intention to make possible "enlightenment in this very lifetime."

As enlightened figures, the *siddhas* manifest a lively individuality as householders, yogins, or monks. Although the *siddhas* represent a basically nonmonastic ideal, they not infrequently turn up as followers of monastic discipline outwardly, but realized *siddhas* within.

The classical Vajrayāna understands itself as a development of the Mahāyāna; the *siddhas* are depicted as *bodhisattvas* whose primary motivation is to work for the benefit of others. Thus, the realized *siddhas* are all primarily teachers of others. Later Tibetan tradition explains the great diversity of origins, training, and teaching methodologies of the *siddhas* as a fulfillment of the Mahāyāna *bodhisattva* vow to help sentient beings in all stations and conditions by adopting their way of life.

This compassionate motivation is also given in explanation of the *siddhas*' undeniable unconventionality. As already noted, teachers sometimes send their students into situations conventionally forbidden to their caste. The *siddhas* themselves often break social and religious taboos as part of their teaching. The depiction of such unconventional activity is intended to reinforce the Tantric insistence that genuine spirituality cannot be identified with any particular external social form. Here, the *siddhas* give characteristic expression to the ancient dictum of the Buddha: awakening is a matter of seeing the conditioned structure of the world as such, not of slavishly identifying with a particular way of life or religious norm.

Magical elements. Magic also plays an important role in the lives of the realized *siddhas*. On one level, the *siddha* biographies articulate the traditional Buddhist (and pan-Indian) belief that spiritual awakening puts one in possession of miraculous powers. In this sense, the *siddha* carries on a motif present in the depiction of the Buddha, of some of the *arhats*, and of the *bodhisattvas* of higher attainment. But in the *siddhas*' lives, magic plays a more prominent role than it does in the earlier hagiographical traditions. This greater prominence is probably due to a combination of (1) the great emphasis in the Vajrayāna on practice and realization; (2) its alignment with nonmonastic, and thus yogic and lay, life; and (3) its bent toward breaking what it sees as the conservatism and stolid fixations of earlier Buddhism.

Some accounts of magic appear to be metaphorical, such as when *siddhas* turn others into stone, "petrifying" them with their unconventional teaching. Other feats, such as the production of jewels from a worthless substance, are perhaps psychological, indicating the way in which the *siddhas* can, through their insight, transform apparently worthless passions of the personality into the highest prize of enlightenment. Other examples of magic, such as Saraha's walking on water, may illustrate the *siddhas*' freedom from cause and effect. In all these examples the *siddhas*' use of magic points to the basic Vajrayāna (and classical Buddhist) teaching that the commonsense world is not as definite and fixed as it appears, but in fact contains unlimited freedom, power, and sacredness.

A final characteristic of the realized *siddha* is his passing away, which is understood not as a death in the ordinary sense but as a passing into a state that is invisible, but nevertheless real and potentially available. The *siddhas*, we are told, do not die, but rather go to a celestial realm from which they may appear at any time.

HISTORICITY AND THE SIDDHA BIOGRAPHIES. The historical concreteness of the *siddha* biographies, the existence of texts, songs, and lineages they created, their social and political impact, and the existence of the Vajrayāna itself leave little doubt that the *siddhas* were historical individuals. But to what extent are their stories simple historical accounts and to what extent do they represent a gathering of originally disparate elements around a particular figure?

Study of the Vajrayāna biographies themselves shows that it would be a mistake to take them simply as accounts of single individuals, at least in the ordinary sense. Many sometimes different, sometimes apparently contradictory accounts are given in the same and different texts about a single *siddha*. In addition, one finds the same motifs and even entire stories appearing in the lives of several different *siddhas*. In light of these factors, one perhaps best understands the *siddhas*' lives as sacred biographies, some elements of which undoubtedly emerged originally in the lives of those individuals, and others of which originated from elsewhere. These became the general property of the tradition, to be used and reused to clarify the nature of the *siddha* ideal itself through the medium of specific biographies.

Does this rather flexible approach to writing history reflect a lack of historical awareness on the part of Vajrayāna biographers? The temptation to answer this question in the affirmative must be resisted, at least until the particular Vajrayāna attitude toward history is clearly understood. The lives of the *siddhas* do not restrict themselves to what we in the West have typically understood as the legitimate domain of a person's "life," beginning with birth and ending with death. The "life" of a *siddha* may include "events" that precede birth and postdate death, and may also include dreams, visions, and supranormal experiences other respected persons may have had of those *siddhas* before, during, and after their human lives. This more inclusive attitude taken by the Vajrayāna toward a *siddha*'s life is due not so much to its lack of historical awareness, but rather to the particular understanding of history that it possesses. The *siddhas* are real people who are significant precisely because they embody cosmic, timeless, and universal dimensions of human reality. They may express themselves equally from their ordinary human as well as their transhuman aspects. For the tradition itself, contradictory stories about a *siddha* may simply indicate multiple manifestations of that person, while the repetition of the same stories in several lives may just mean a later *siddha* is teaching according to an earlier, typical pattern. Such elements are considered in the Vajrayāna not only a legitimate but a necessary part of proper historical writing about the *siddhas*.

Finally, it is necessary to mention the important impact of liturgy and of certain later Tibetan Tantric masters' lives on the understanding of the *siddhas*' biographies. What is understood as the universal and timeless essence of the *siddhas* makes it possible to invoke the living and tangible presence of the *siddhas* through liturgy. Moreover, many of the most famous *siddhas* are understood to be present, in later incarnations, in the persons of Tibetan *tulkus* (incarnate lamas). The living example of the *tulkus* and the invocation of the presence of the *siddhas* in ritual contribute significantly to the making present and interpreting of the *siddhas* whose lives and teachings can be read in the texts.

HISTORICAL ROLE OF THE SIDDHAS. The major historical legacy of the *siddhas* is the tradition they represented and the

Vajrayāna lineages they helped build, many of which are alive today. On a more restricted front, the *siddhas* were the authors of a great many Tantric works, hundreds of which survive in Tibetan translation. The most characteristic compositions of the *siddhas* are perhaps their *dohās* ("enlightenment songs"), which survive in independent collections, in biographies, and in the Tantras themselves. These songs are supposed usually to have been composed in liturgical situations to express the individuality and sacredness of that moment of awakened experience. The *siddhas* also composed other varieties of texts, including commentaries on the *tantras*, biographies of great masters, liturgical texts, and so on. A list of some six hundred works by Indian *siddhas* is given in the Tantric section of the Tibetan Bstan 'gyur (Tanjur); works of the *siddhas* are also included in other parts of the Tanjur and in Tibetan collections of Indian Buddhist texts.

The *siddhas* also played an important part in the history of Indian and Asian Buddhism. In India, the *siddhas* were the prime carriers of the Vajrayāna for a millennium, in its early formative period (pre-eighth century CE), during the time of its prominence (eighth to twelfth century CE), in the several centuries following the Islamic decimation of monastic Buddhism at the end of the twelfth century, through the sixteenth century, when contemporary Tibetan accounts give a first hand picture of a strong and vital Vajrayāna tradition in India. In the history of Tibetan Buddhism, it was the *siddhas* who carried the Vajrayāna to that land. All four of the major surviving schools, and many that did not survive, ultimately derive from Indian *siddhas*: the Bka' brgyud pa from Ti lo pa (988–1069) and Nā ro pa (1016–1100); the Rnying ma pa from Padmasambhava and Vimalamitra (both eighth century); the Sa skya pa from 'Brog mi (922–1022); and the Dge lugs pa from Atisa (982–1054), who, while not himself a *siddha*, inherited some of their traditions.

Siddhas such as Śubhākarasiṃha, Vajrabodhi, and Amoghavajra, all of whom journeyed to Tang China in the eighth century, were responsible for bringing the Vajrayāna to that land. Although their unconventional and wonder-working activity proved ultimately discordant with the Chinese outlook, and although the Vajrayāna they brought did not long survive in China, their activity provided the foundation for the transmission of the Vajrayāna to Japan by Kūkai (774–835), who founded the Shingon school there. The *siddha* ideal played an indirect role in the religious history of the Mongols as well, following Mongol appropriation of Tibetan Buddhism in the thirteenth century.

Finally, the *siddhas* carried the Vajrayāna to Southeast Asia, where there is evidence of their activity in Java, Sumatra and Kamboja from the early ninth century onward. The Vajrayāna continued there until the sixteenth century at least, when the Indian Vajrayānist Buddhaguptanātha visited that area and gave firsthand accounts of the Tantric tradition there.

SEE ALSO Amoghavajra; Arhat; Atīśa; Bodhisattva Path; Dge lugs pa; Mar pa; Mi la ras pa; Nā ro pa; Padmasambhava; Shingonshū; Śubhākarasiṃha; Tsong kha pa; Vajrabodhi; Zhenyan.

BIBLIOGRAPHY

Abhayadatta's *Caturśīti-siddha-pravṛtti* (History of the Eighty-four Siddhas), the most important extant Indian text on the *siddhas*, has been translated from the Tibetan by James B. Robinson as *Buddha's Lions* (Berkeley, 1979). The extended Tibetan biographies of two of the most important Indian *siddhas*, Padmasambhava and Nā ro pa, are given respectively in W. Y. Evans-Wentz's *The Tibetan Book of the Great Liberation* (Oxford, 1954) and *The Life and Teachings of Naropa*, translated by Herbert Guenther (Oxford, 1963). Per Kvaerne's *An Anthology of Buddhist Tantric Songs* (Oslo and New York, 1977) analyzes an important collection of the Indian *siddhas*' songs. Shashibhusan Dasgupta's *Obscure Religious Cults*, 3d ed. (Calcutta, 1969), attempts to see the Indian *siddhas* in their larger religious context; my "Accomplished Women in Tantric Buddhism of Medieval India and Tibet," in *Unspoken Worlds*, edited by Nancy A. Falk and Rita M. Gross (New York, 1980), pp. 227–242, discusses Indian women *siddhas*. Several works provide useful summaries of the role of the Indian *siddhas* and of the Vajrayāna outside of India. For Tibet, see David L. Snellgrove and Hugh Richardson's *A Cultural History of Tibet*, (New York, 1968; reprint, Boulder, 1980), pp. 95–110 and 118ff.; for China, see Kenneth Ch'en's *Buddhism in China* (1964; reprint, Princeton, 1972), pp. 325–337; for Japan, see Daigan and Alicia Matsunaga's *Foundation of Japanese Buddhism* (Los Angeles, 1974), vol. 1, pp. 171–200; and for Southeast Asia, see Nihar-Ranjan Ray's *Sanskrit Buddhism in Burma*, (Calcutta, 1936), pp. 12–14 and 62–99.

New Sources

Davidson, Ronald M. *Indian Esoteric Buddhism: A Social History of the Tantric Movement.* New York, 2002.

Katz, N. *Buddhist Images of Human Perfection: The Arahant of the Sutta Pitaka Compared with the Bodhisattva and the Mahasiddha.* Delhi, 1989.

Mar pa, et al. *The Life of the Mahasiddha Tilopa.* Dharamsala, 1995.

Ray, Reginald. "The Mahasiddha." In *Buddhism and Asian History*, edited by Joseph Mitsuo Kitagawa and Mark D. Cummings. See pages 389–394. New York, 1989.

Urban, Hugh B. *The Economics of Ecstasy: Tantra, Secrecy, and Power in Colonial Bengal.* New York, 2001.

White, David G. *The Alchemical Body: Siddha Traditions in Medieval India.* Chicago, 1996.

White, David G. *Kiss of the Yogini: "Tantric Sex" in its South Asian Contexts.* Chicago, 2003.

REGINALD RAY (1987)
Revised Bibliography

MAHATMA GANDHI SEE GANDHI, MOHANDAS

MAHĀVAIROCANA

MAHĀVAIROCANA (lit., "the great illuminator"), the Great Sun Buddha, is the transcendent and cosmocratic apotheosis of the historical Buddha, Śākyamuni. Under the earlier designation *Vairocana* ("the luminous one"), he represents Buddhism's most profound speculation on the emptiness and interpenetration of all elements in the universe *(dharmadhātu).* As Mahāvairocana he is concretely envisaged as the all-encompassing lord of the cosmos and is the object of worship for a form of Tantric Buddhism that spread from India to Sumatra, China, Japan, and Tibet.

In India, the name *Virocana* appears in the *Ṛgveda* in connection with celestial phenomena and the luminous residence of Varuṇa. Other Vedic contexts link Virocana variously with Sūrya, the solar deity; Candra, the lunar deity; and Agni, god of fire. In the *Chandogya Upaniṣad,* Virocana, king of the *asuras* (anti-gods), loses a competition for true knowledge of the Self to his counterpart Indra, king of the *devas* (gods). Pali Buddhist literature identifies the deity Verocana with the demon Bali, and in the *Saṃyutta Nikāya* he again opposes his nemesis Sakka (Indra), this time in seeking knowledge from the Buddha.

Vairocana is mentioned in other Buddhist texts such as the *Mahāvastu* and the *Lalitavistara,* but his role as a symbol of ultimate reality is developed only in Mahāyāna scriptures such as the *Daśabhūmikā Sūtra* and the *Gaṇḍavyūha Sūtra,* both found in the huge collection known as the *Avataṃsaka Sūtra.* According to the Chinese Huayan and the Japanese Kegon traditions, both of which are grounded in the *Avataṃsaka Sūtra,* Śākyamuni, the Buddha who preached the *Avataṃsaka,* had like all buddhas before him spent aeons as a *bodhisattva* striving toward enlightenment. On the night of his final enlightenment, he ascended to the palace of the Akaniṣṭha Heaven—the summit of the cosmos—where *abhiṣeka* ("initiation, consecretion") was conferred upon him by the buddhas of the Ten Quarters. He thus attained the "body of enjoyment" *(sambhogakaya)* and came to reign from the Akaniṣṭha Heaven as the celestial sovereign who preaches to highly advanced *bodhisattvas.* Simultaneously with this attainment, Śākyamuni realized his identity with the *dharmakāya* (reality as total, transcendent, and ineffable). The earthly body of Śākyamuni took up his preaching, but that body, as well as the "body of enjoyment," were now recognized as manifestations of the transcendent *dharmakāya.* Thus, Vairocana represents ultimate reality and at the same time permeates all levels of the manifest cosmos and the beings in it. The universe is his infinite body. All things are in him, and his presence shines in all things.

This notion of interpenetration—of the part in the whole and the whole in every part—is closely linked with images of light and illumination in the mythology of Vairocana/Mahāvairocana. The *Gaṇḍhavyūha Sūtra* describes reality as a universe of infinitely reflected light. As the solar deity, Vairocana is the center of the cosmos, its ruler and sovereign. He is above the cosmos, yet all its variations are reflections of him. A frequently used image is that of Indra's net. The net constitutes the universe, and at each knot there is a jewel that reflects all the other jewels in the net.

MAHĀVAIROCANA AND TANTRA. The name Vairocana points to an ultimate perspective to be realized through insight. Mahāvairocana, in contrast, is realized concretely in ritual practice. Mahāvairocana, the chief deity in much of the Buddhist Tantric tradition, rose to prominence sometime between the fifth and seventh century CE. While sharing Vairocana's symbolism, Mahāvairocana's distinctiveness in iconography, doctrine, and ritual is signaled by the Sanskrit prefix *mahā* ("great"). The principal scriptures that extol Mahāvairocana and describe his cult, the *Mahāvairocana Sūtra* and the *Tattvasaṃgraha,* are no longer fully extant in Sanskrit, but their Chinese translations are the basis of the Chinese Zhenyanand Japanese Shingon (mantra) schools of Buddhism. Tibetan translations of these scriptures are regarded as the root texts of two of the four classes of Tantra in that country, Carya Tantras and Yoga Tantras. Although Mahāvairocana was important in Tibetan Buddhism, his cult was overshadowed by deities of the Anuttarayoga Tantras. For the Tibetans the buddha Akṣobhya, the "primordial buddha" (Ādibuddha), and the dialectical symbolism of cosmic sexuality represented by *yab-yum,* or "father-mother," images found in the *Guhyasamaja Tantra* and *Hevajra Tantra,* were more compelling.

MAHĀVAIROCANA IN EAST ASIA. The *Mahāvairocana Sūtra* and the *Tattvasaṃgraha* were brought to China by two Indian *ācāryas* ("teachers") from the North Indian monastic university at Nālandā, which in the seventh century CE had become a center for Tantric studies. Śubhākarasiṃha (637–735) and Vajrabodhi (671–741) arrived to missionize the Tang court in 716 and 720 respectively. Through their efforts and those of their disciples, the major texts and commentaries concerning Mahāvairocana were translated. A small but stable cult was established under the cautious patronage of the pro-Daoist Emperor Xuanzong (r. 712–756). Mahāvairocana as he is revealed in what became known as Esoteric Buddhism (Chin., Mi-chiao; Jpn., Mikkyō) assumes the symbolism of Vairocana. Mahāvairocana is described as the lord of the vast palace of the *vajradharmadhātu* that has been created by his wondrous power of transformation *(adhiṣṭhāna).* This palace is identified both as the Akaniṣṭha Heaven and as the entire cosmos. Like Vairocana, Mahāvairocana has received initiations (*abhiṣekas*) from all the Buddhas, and the Akaniṣṭha Heaven is the scene of these initiations as well as of the revelation of the new Tantric scriptures. In the *Mahāvairocana Sūtra,* Mahāvairocana is portrayed as the light and sustenance of the manifest cosmos and as its supreme sovereign. He is at once the cosmocrat and the active participant in all manifestation; his presence is felt not only in the salvific action of *bodhisattvas* but also in weather, constellations, and all other phenomena. The *Tattvasaṃgraha* tends to emphasize the cosmos as it is reflected in Mahāvairocana. He is the Lord of Light, and the universe is an endless series of reflections of him.

Iconography and Worship. Mahāvairocana's distinctiveness is apparent in his texts, which are almost entirely devoted to ritual. While Vairocana represents absolute reality, to be realized through insight developed over long aeons, Mahāvairocana is realized through an active and immediate ritual participation in his very being. Practice is a ritual drama based upon iconographic conventions detailed in *maṇḍalas*, or cosmograms, drawn from the two major texts, and it consists of two intertwined acts. The disciple first attempts to realize his identity with the deity through imitating the iconographic conventions, or "marks," of the deity as revealed in the texts, and through oral instruction. His body and hand posture *(mudrā),* ritual incantation (mantra), and meditative vision *(samādhi)* seek to duplicate the very consciousness of the divinity he worships. Success in this *imitatio* is termed *siddhi* ("accomplishment"). The disciple undergoes a series of initiations *(abhiṣeka)* identifying him with deities at various levels of the *maṇḍala.* Should he be deemed fit, he may attain final realization of his identity with Mahāvairocana, reenacting the Buddha's quest and final ascent to the Akaniṣṭha Heaven to become an *ācārya.* Having realized his identity with the deity, he may now exercise that deity's powers for the good of others. This second act is also called *siddhi.*

Under the aegis of Vajrabodhi's disciple Amoghavajra (d. 774), under his Chinese successors, and under Kūkai (774–835), the Japanese founder of Shingon, the iconography of Esoteric Buddhism took a definitive form. Certain *maṇḍalas* were drawn from the *Mahāvairocana Sūtra* and the *Tattvasaṃgraha* to produce the Womb Maṇḍala (Garbhakośadhātu Maṇḍala) and the Diamond Maṇḍala (Vajradhātu Maṇḍala). Mahāvairocana of the Womb Maṇḍala is usually golden, seated in meditative posture on a lunar disk that rests on a red lotus blossom. He is regally adorned as the master of the cosmos and represents the final achievement of buddhahood. Other divinities depicted in the *maṇḍala* represent his compassionate activity *(karuṇā)* in all phenomena and the possibility of illumination. The Diamond Maṇḍala is composed of nine *maṇḍalas* selected from the *Tattvasaṃgraha.* They represent Mahāvairocana's consciousness or wisdom *(prajñā).* The central image of Mahāvairocana is usually white or blue, seated upon a lotus blossom resting on a lunar disk. He is adorned and crowned and his hands are clasped in the Gesture of All-Embracing Wisdom (Jñānamuṣṭi Mudra). Shingon tradition describes the *maṇḍala* as representative of the cosmos as Mahāvairocana sees it, the timeless universe of the interpenetrating light of wisdom. These two *maṇḍalas*, which like conditional reality and ultimate reality are said to be nondual, provide a framework for classifying all phenomena. Initiation and ritual practice were organized around the new scheme, and therefore an *ācārya* must be initiated into both *maṇḍalas*. Kūkai introduced several refinements, the most important of which is the identification of the first five material elements of the cosmos with the Womb Maṇḍala and the sixth element, mind, with the Diamond Maṇḍala. Thus, for Kūkai, the material cosmos was the body of the transcendent *dharmakāya,* not an ontologically secondary manifestation as might be surmised from Huayan doctrine.

The Religious Meaning of Mahāvairocana. The Great Sun Buddha Mahāvairocana represents one of the world's most profound religious conceptions. Like the physical sun, Mahāvairocana Buddha is the pivot of the manifest cosmos, the source of light and life. Yet this is far from pantheism, since Mahāvairocana transcends the universe just as he *is* the universe. Nor is this docetism. Indeed, no better term may be found than that coined by Masaharu Anesaki (1915), who speaks of Shingon's "cosmotheism." The full meaning of Mahāvairocana is apprehended in Tantric practice, for there Mahāvairocana functions as an icon, as both the embodiment of the divine and as a symbol pointing to divine transcendence. Thus, in the ritual drama of Tantra the practitioner realizes his own iconic nature. He is both the worshiper and the object of worship; he experiences the paradox of divinity that is the world and yet transcends the world. He is Mahāvairocana in this very body.

See Also Amoghavajra; Buddhas and Bodhisattvas, article on Celestial Buddhas and Bodhisattvas; Maṇḍalas, article on Buddhist Maṇḍalas; Shingonshū; Śubhākarasiṃha; Sun; Vajrabodhi.

Bibliography

The best introduction to the cult of Mahāvairocana in the context of Tibetan Tantric practice is David L. Snellgrove's *Buddhist Himalaya* (Oxford, 1957). On Vairocana and his symbolism in the Huayan and Kegon traditions see Francis D. Cook's *Huayan Buddhism: The Jewel Net of Indra* (University Park, Pa., 1977) and Thomas Cleary's *Entry into the Inconceivable: An Introduction to Hua-yen Buddhism* (Honolulu, 1983). The only study of the Zhenyan school in China is Chou I-liang's excellent annotated translation (with introductions) of the lives of Śubhākarasiṃha, Vajrabodhi, and Amoghavajra, "Tantrism in China," *Harvard Journal of Asiatic Studies* 8 (1945): 241–332. Studies of Esoteric Buddhism and thus of Mahāvairocana from the doctrinal perspective of Japanese Shingon are Minoru Kiyota's *Shingon Buddhism* (Los Angeles, 1978), which includes an explanation of the two *maṇḍalas*, and a hard-to-find but excellent work in French by the Shingon priest Tajima Ryūjun, *Étude sur le Mahāvairocana-sūtra* (Paris, 1936). Tajima's study includes a translation of the first chapter of this important text. Yoshito S. Hakeda has provided a fine introduction to Kūkai's life and thought and translations of some of his works in his *Kūkai: Major Works* (New York, 1972). The best study of the Shingon *maṇḍalas* is also by Tajima Ryūjun but again his *Les deux grands maṇḍalas et la doctrine de l'ésotérisme Shingon,* "Bulletin de la maison franco-japonaise," n.s. vol. 6 (Tokyo, 1959), is in French and hard to obtain. Somewhat easier to find is Beatrice Lane Suzuki's article on the Womb Maṇḍala, "The Shingon School of Mahāyāna Buddhism," part 2, "The Mandara," *Eastern Buddhist* 7 (May 1936): 1–38. Finally, a brief but excellent understanding of the two *maṇḍalas* may be found in Masaharu Anesaki's "Buddhist Cosmotheism and the Symbolism of Its Art" in his *Buddhist Art in Its Relation to Buddhist Ideals* (1915; reprint, New York, 1978).

New Sources

Abé, Ryūichi. *The Weaving of Mantra: Kūkai and the Construction of Esoteric Buddhist Discourse.* New York, 1999.

Hodge, Stephen. *The Mahā-Vairocana-Abhisambodhi Tantra: with Buddhaguhya's Commentary.* London, 2003.

Payne, Richard K., ed. *Re-visioning "Kamakura" Buddhism.* Honolulu, 1998.

Wayman, Alex, and R. Tajima. *The Enlightenment of Vairocana: Book I Study of the Vairocanabhisambodhitantra: Book II Study of the Mahavairocana-Sutra.* Delhi, 1992.

Yamamoto, Chikyo. *Mahāvairocana-sūtra: Translated into English from Ta-p'i lu che na ch'eng-fo shen-pien chia-ch'ih ching, the Chinese Version of Śubhākarasiṁha and I-hsing,* A.D. *725.* New Delhi, 1990.

CHARLES D. ORZECH (1987)
Revised Bibliography

MAHĀVĪRA. Among the numerous philosophers and religious teachers who preached in eastern India during the sixth century BCE was the Jina ("conqueror"), considered to be the founder and systematizer of Jainism. The name given to him by his parents was Vardhamāna ("prospering"), for soon after his conception, it is said, things began to flourish and prosper for him and for those around him. The gods called him Mahāvīra ("great hero"), because, they claimed, "he stands fast in the midst of dangers and fears" (*Jinacaritra* 108). He is regarded as the twenty-fourth *tīrthaṃkara* ("fordmaker") or prophet, and the reformer of Jainism. Mahāvīra's symbol is the lion; like other *tīrthaṃkaras*, he is sometimes represented with his two guardian deities.

HAGIOGRAPHY. The main episodes of Mahāvīra's life and religious career are often described in Jain literature and are prominent in the Śvetāmbara canon. The five principal "auspicious moments" of his life—his conception, birth, renunciation, enlightenment, and passing into *nirvāṇa*—are celebrated by his followers to this day.

According to the Jains, Mahāvīra was born seventy-five years and eight and a half months before the end of the fourth descending period of the current *avasarpiṇī* era (or 599 BCE); by the calculations of Western scholars, the event probably took place at least some fifty years later. He was born in Kuṇḍagrāma, apparently a village near Vaiśālī, to the north of modern-day Patna in northern Bihar—where a Mahāvīra memorial has been erected and where the Research Institute of Prakrit, Ahiṃsā, and Jainology was founded by the government of Bihar in 1956.

Like all *tīrthaṃkaras*, Vardhamāna was alleged to have come from a princely family; the Jains hold that he had a *kṣatriya* lineage and that his mother, Triśalā, was closely related to the Vaiśālī ruler. The Śvetāmbara scriptures and miniatures even show the transplantation of his embryo, following Indra's orders, from the womb of a *brahman* mother, Devānandā, into that of Triśalā. This episode, which is reminiscent of the Kṛṣṇa legend, is rejected by the Digambaras. As will be seen, the two churches disagree on certain points in the biography of the twenty-fourth *tīrthaṃkara.* Both agree, however, that his conception was foretold to his mother in a series of fourteen (or sixteen) auspicious dreams by a white elephant, a white bull, a lion, the goddess Śrī, the full moon, the rising sun, an ocean of milk, and so forth. These dreams are frequently described in the literature and represented in manuscripts and in temples.

While still in the womb Vardhamāna began to practice *ahiṃsā:* He was careful not to cause his mother any pain, and even vowed not to renounce the world before his parents' death. His birth was the occasion of universal rejoicing and liberality. As a boy he received a princely education and his family appears to have followed the doctrine of the twenty-third *tīrthaṃkara,* Pārśva, whose teachings Mahāvīra was to reconsider and complete, but not, apparently, to oppose. According to the Śvetāmbaras he married the princess Yaśodā, who gave birth to a daughter; their daughter's husband was later to start the first schism of Jainism. The Digambaras, however, consider that Vardhamāna had no such worldly ties. They emphasize that Mahāvīra was one of an unending succession of *tīrthaṃkaras*: His earlier births are linked with Ṛṣabha (through one of the latter's grandsons), while one of his disciples, King Śreṇika Bimbisāra, will be reborn as the first *tīrthaṃkara* of the next *utsarpiṇī* age.

By the time Vardhamāna was thirty years old his parents had died. Having gained the consent of his elder brother he distributed his property, plucked out his hair, and renounced the world; this is an event commonly depicted in Jain iconography, with Indra devotedly receiving the saint's hair in his hands. Thereafter, Mahāvīra led the hard, solitary life of a wandering ascetic (*śramaṇa*), begging for food and shelter, moving from place to place (except during the four months of the rainy season) in the eastern region of the Ganges Valley. According to the Digambaras, Mahāvīra immediately abandoned clothing as well as ornaments, whereas the Śvetāmbaras hold that this occurred only after thirteen months of renunciation. Such discussions again reflect a difference of opinion, in this case concerning the importance of nakedness in the holy life.

Both sects do agree that the prophet shunned all violence to living beings, took nothing that was not explicitly given to him, spoke no lies, strictly avoided unchaste behavior in thought, word, and deed, and had no possessions—in short, he followed what were to become the five major vows of the Jain monk. Moreover, he endured severe hardships (due to nature, animal, and humanity) and practiced systematic penances that involved many kinds of prolonged and complicated fasts, "exerting himself," according to the *Jinacaritra* (119), "for the suppression of the defilement of *karman.*" He gained disciples, with whom he conversed in a Prakrit language. In this way he spent twelve years, six months, and fifteen days on the mendicant's path. Finally, on a summer night, near a sal tree on the bank of the river Ṛjupālikā, he attained omniscience (*kevala-jñāna*), "which is infinite, supreme, unobstructed, unimpeded, and full. . . . He knew and saw all conditions of all living beings in the world—what they thought, spoke, or did at any moment" (*Jinacaritra* 120–121). He had in fact acquired full knowledge of the world (and the nonworld), and of the past, present, and future of its inhabitants, whether divine, infernal, animal, or human. Concerning the state of enlightenment there are again differences between the Śvetāmbaras, who consider that even a *kevalin* eats and complies with constraints of the body without any defilement, and the Digambaras, who believe that following enlightenment one is free from all human imperfections (such as hunger) and only sits in perfect omniscience while a divine sound emanates from his person and instructs his hearers, directly or otherwise.

After attaining omniscience Mahāvīra preached the truth to immense assemblies of listeners and successfully organized the fourfold Jain community of monks, nuns, male laity, and female laity. He was assisted in this task by eleven *gaṇadharas* (chiefs of religious communities): The first chief was Indrabhūti Gautama, who is responsible for having retained and handed down Mahāvīra's teachings. One of Mahāvīra's earlier disciples was Gośāla, who turned against him to become head of the Ājīvika sect.

Finally, at the age of seventy-two, sitting "single and alone . . . , reciting the fifty-five lectures that detail the results of *karman,*" Mahāvīra passed into *nirvāṇa.* According to tradition, this occurred in the town of Papa, near Patna, toward the end of the monsoon in the year 527 BCE. This year was to become the starting point of the era known as the Vīra Saṃvat; nevertheless, Western scholars tend to place Mahāvīra's death in 467 or 477–476 BCE, or even later. Be that as it may, at that time (which was a fast-day) the neighboring kings "instituted an illumination. . . . For they said: 'Since the spiritual light is gone, let us make a material illumination'" (*Jinacaritra* 128). As it happened, this homage coincided with the Hindu festival of Dīvālī, so that Hindus and Jains simultaneously conduct these two different celebrations.

MAHĀVĪRA'S TEACHINGS. Although the various discrepancies between the Digambara and Śvetāmbara accounts of Mahāvīra's career naturally imply doctrinal differences, the fundamental tenets upheld by the two churches are, nonetheless, basically similar, and can be regarded as deriving from Mahāvīra. Mahāvīra defined a pluralist substantialism that, typical of Jainism, is characterized by seven (or nine) *tattvas* (principles).

The first *tattva* is the soul or "life" *(jīva)*; it is immaterial, eternal, characterized by consciousness, and capable of cognition. The *tattvas* serve to explain the mechanism of transmigration, the innumerable reincarnations of the soul, and the soul's final liberation. In this context Mahāvīra explained *jīva* and its opposite, *ajīva;* the influx of karmic matter into the soul; bondage; stoppage of karmic influx; expulsion of previously accumulated karmic matter; and the final accomplishment of "perfection" *(siddhi)*, when karmic matter has been exhausted and the *jīva* has regained its pure spiritual nature.

This ultimate goal cannot be attained except by those who tread "the ford" that Mahāvīra built to the other shore of *saṃsāra.* They must train themselves to follow the ideal pattern of life, which has been set by the Jina, and they must master the "three jewels" of right (Jain) faith, right knowledge, and right conduct; "right conduct" necessitates performing the difficult and constant ascetic exercises that were undertaken by the Jina himself. As a consequence, from the beginning great importance has been attached to religious life and to the organization of the community, in which the female devotees seem to have been particularly active and numerous. According to the *Jinacaritra* (134–137), "the Venerable Ascetic Mahāvīra had an excellent community of 14,000 *śramaṇas* with Indrabhūti at their head; 36,000 nuns with Candanā at their head; 159,000 lay votaries with Śaṅkhaśataka at their head; 318,000 female lay votaries with Sulasā and Revatī at their head. . . ."

MAHĀVĪRA'S SIGNIFICANCE IN THE INDIAN TRADITION. It cannot be denied that in the traditional biography of Mahāvīra some episodes are stereotypes that systematically serve elsewhere to describe the career of other "great men" (*mahāpuruṣas*). Additionally, there are many discrepancies concerning the date and place of his birth, his *nirvāṇa,* and so forth. Nevertheless, there is no reason to doubt the historicity of this vigorous original thinker and extremely capable organizer. While naturally accepting many of the basic assumptions of his society and his era, he was one of the first to oppose the Brahmanic ritualistic orthodoxy and to suceed in building a coherent system aimed at explaining the laws of the universe and the place of humankind therein, thus clearly linking metaphysics with ethics and speculation with social organization.

It has been justly emphasized that Jainism (like early Buddhism) integrated many older beliefs and practices that had previously been nurtured only by isolated Brahmanic ascetics. With Mahāvīra, these ideas appear to have gained in influence. Jainism has thus been equated with some of the most typically Indian tendencies and ideals; indeed, Jainism did much to enrich Indian ideals of spirituality. Among its contributions are the belief in the powers of asceticism, in the spiritual benefit to be derived from fasting (even unto death), and in the absolute necessity of avoiding injury to life (*ahiṃsā*), whether in thought, word, or deed. This last ideal constitutes the first vow of the Jains, which is a dedication to tolerance, unabated benevolence, and vegetarianism.

The Jain movement probably owes much of its influence to the missionary zeal and gifts of Mahāvīra, and to his ability to organize a coherent society of religious and lay believers. The well-structured Jain community of monks and nuns was, together with the Buddhist *saṃgha,* one of the first to exist in India. In the course of time it proved to be remarkably dynamic, capable of continuing Mahāvīra's action, and even, as he himself is alleged to have done, of gaining the sympathy and support of many rulers. Following his path and the example he had set, Jain *nirgranthas* (religious mendicants) as well as laypersons have achieved the material as well as the spiritual glory of Jainism.

SEE ALSO Ahiṃsā; Ājīvikas; Gośāla; Jainism; Mokṣa; Tīrthaṃkaras.

BIBLIOGRAPHY

All standard books on Jainism discuss the life of Mahāvīra. The Digambara views are clearly presented in Padmanabh S. Jaini's *The Jaina Path of Purification* (Berkeley, Calif., 1979). Two valuable books are Bimala Churn Law's *Mahāvīra: His Life and Teachings* (London, 1937) and Hiralal Jain and A. N. Upadhye's *Mahāvīra: His Times and His Philosophy of Life* (New Delhi, 1974).

Two important Śvetāmbara canonical texts tell the story of Mahāvīra's life: One text is included in the first book of the canon (*Ācārāṅga Sūtra* 1.8); the other forms a major part of the *Jinacaritra* (Lives of the Jinas), edited in 1882 and 1879 respectively by Hermann Jacobi, and translated from Prakrit into English by Jacobi in volume 1 of *Jaina Sûtras,* "Sacred Books of the East," vol. 22 (1884; reprint, Delhi, 1964). The teachings of Mahāvīra are somewhat discursively presented in other canonical books, among them the *Sūtrakṛtāṅga* and *Uttarādhyayana,* also translated by Hermann Jacobi, in volume 2 of *Jaina Sūtras,* "Sacred Books of the East," vol. 45 (1895; reprint Delhi, 1964).

Comparisons between the Buddha and the Jina have been attempted by Ernst Leumann in *Buddha und Mahāvīra, die beiden indischen Religionsstifter* (Munich, 1921). Mahāvīra's career is the subject of a number of Jain quasi-epic poems from both the Digambara and Śvetāmbara traditions, and an important chapter in the *Triṣaṣṭiśalākāpuruṣacaritra,* translated by Helen M. Johnson as *Triṣaṣṭiśalākāpuruṣacaritra, or The Lives of Sixty-Three Illustrious Persons by Hemacandra,* "Gaekwad's Oriental Series," vols. 51, 77, 108, 125, 139, and 140 (Baroda, 1931–1962).

COLETTE CAILLAT (1987)

MAHĀYĀNA BUDDHISM SEE BUDDHISM, SCHOOLS OF, *ARTICLE ON* MAHĀYĀNA PHILOSOPHICAL SCHOOLS OF BUDDHISM

MAHDISM SEE MESSIANISM, *ARTICLE ON* MESSIANISM IN THE MUSLIM TRADITION

MAḤZOR SEE SIDDUR AND MAḤZOR

MAID OF LUDMIR

(c. 1805/1815–c. 1892). A semi-legendary figure, the Maid of Ludmir is reputed to have been one of the few women in Hasidism who functioned as a fully fledged spiritual master (*tsaddiq* or *rebbe*). Most of the information about her originates in oral traditions of "old women in Volhynia," first collected and published in 1909 by the historian Shmuel Abba Horodetzky. These were subsequently subjected to his own as well as others' elaborations and expansions, which appeared in a variety of popular-historical, belletristic, journalistic, and memoiristic works. Significantly, the hagiographical literature of nineteenth-century Hasidism does not refer to her at all, nor is any mystical or ethical teaching attributed to her in other genres of Hasidic writing. She is, however, mentioned briefly in an 1883 satirical work by an eastern European *maskil,* and, following the publication of Horodetzky's reports, in a handful of twentieth-century hagiographical anthologies.

As the oral tradition has it, the Maid, known as Hannah Rachel, was the only daughter of Monesh Verbermacher, an educated and well-to-do Jew in the Volhynian town of Ludmir (Vladimir). From an early age she distinguished herself not only by her beauty but also—unusually for a girl—by her ardor in prayer and remarkable aptitude for scholarship. Her betrothal to a beloved childhood playmate, which entailed the customary separation of bride and groom until the wedding, distressed the Maid and led to her withdrawal from society. This was exacerbated by the sudden death of her mother, following which she became a recluse, never leaving her room except to visit her mother's grave. On one of her visits to the cemetery she fell into unconsciousness followed by a prolonged and mysterious illness. When she recovered she claimed to have been given "a new and elevated soul." She broke off her engagement and declared that she would never marry, having "transcended the world of the flesh." From then on she adopted the full rigor of male ritual observance, and absorbed herself, like a male pietist, in intense study and prayer. She became known as the "Holy Maid" or the "Virgin" of Ludmir, and acquired a reputation for miracle working. Men and women, including rabbis and scholars, flocked to her study house in Ludmir, which functioned as her Hasidic court. She would grant blessings on request and deliver her weekly Hasidic teaching at the third Sabbath meal, as was customary among the male *tsaddiqim.* While her popular following grew, the male leadership of the movement disapproved, viewing her activities as a pathological manifestation of the powers of evil and impurity. Pressure was put on the Maid to abandon the practice of tsaddiqism and to resume her rightful female role in marriage. Following the personal intervention of Mordecai of Chernobyl—the most eminent *tsaddiq* of the region—she reluctantly agreed to marry, but the marriage was never consummated and soon ended in divorce. She married again, but divorced once more, apparently remaining a "maiden" to the end of her life. However, her marriages did have the desired effect of putting an abrupt end to her career as a *rebbe.* She eventually immigrated to the Holy Land—a remote corner of nineteenth-century Hasidism—where, as is almost certainly confirmed by archival documentation from the 1860s and 1870s, she spent the last years of her life as a childless widow affiliated to the Volhynian Hasidic community of Jerusalem.

The Maid of Ludmir was exceptional among the cluster of women reputed to have exercised charismatic authority within the Hasidic world of their day. Unlike most of them, she was not related by family ties—as mother, daughter, sister, or widow—to any of the illustrious male *tsaddiqim.* She could not, therefore, draw on the associative authority that some Jewish women could always derive from their connection to distinguished male relatives, and her charismatic powers were entirely her own. Nevertheless, while her career is often celebrated as a pioneering "feminist" success, the very terms in which the Maid tradition has been preserved present her case as an instructive failure. It serves precisely to reinforce, not to undermine, the traditional gender boundaries she attempted to cross.

The phenomenon of a spiritually empowered holy virgin, so common in the wider Christian environment of Hasidism, was alien to the Jewish tradition, which had always prized, albeit within limits, the practice of sexual abstinence by some men, while greeting with suspicion and ascribing no value to the adoption of celibacy by women. The anomaly of the celibate female *rebbe* was therefore perceived as an aberration of nature and a social deviation that the Hasidic leadership was quick to suppress. Only in the twentieth century, under the impact of modern feminism and the egalitarian elements of Zionist ideology, could the Maid of Ludmir tradition be presented as an inspirational model for national revival and proof of the alleged eradication of gender boundaries in Hasidism.

SEE ALSO Gender and Religion, article on Gender and Judaism; Hasidism; Tsaddiq.

BIBLIOGRAPHY

Deutsch, Nathaniel. "New Archival Sources on the Maiden of Ludmir." *Jewish Social Studies* 9, no. 1 (2002): 164–172.

Deutsch, Nathaniel. *The Maiden of Ludmir: A Jewish Holy Woman and Her World.* Berkeley, 2003.

Horodetzky, Shmuel Abba. "Ludmirskaya Dyeva (Di Ludmirer Moyd)." *Eveiskaya Starina* 1, no. 2 (1909): 219–222.

Horodetzky, Shmuel Abba. *Ha-ḥasidut ve-ha-ḥasidim.* 2d ed., vol. 4, pp. 67–71. Tel Aviv, 1943.

Rapoport-Albert, Ada. "On Women in Hasidism, S. A. Horodetzky, and the Maid of Ludmir Tradition." In *Jewish History: Essays in Honour of Chimen Abramsky,* edited by Ada Rapoport-Albert and Steven J. Zipperstein. London, 1988. With additional bibliographical references in note 2, and an expanded version in *Zaddik and Devotees: Historical and Sociological Aspects of Hasidism* (in Hebrew), edited by David Assaf (Jerusalem, 2001).

Winkler, Gershon. *They Called Her Rebbe: The Maiden of Ludomir.* New York, 1991.

ADA RAPOPORT-ALBERT (2005)

MAIMONIDES, ABRAHAM

MAIMONIDES, ABRAHAM ben Moses (1186–1237) was a theologian, jurist, mystical pietist, communal leader, and physician. He was born in Fustat, Egypt, the only son of the great Jewish philosopher Moses Maimonides (1135/8–1204). Exceptionally gifted at a precocious age, Abraham Maimonides studied rabbinics, philosophy, and medicine with his father. Upon the latter's demise, though still a mere youth of eighteen, Abraham was elected to the esteemed position of *nagid,* leader of Egyptian Jewry. He was the first to occupy this office in his family, where, largely on account of Maimonides' aura, it became hereditary for almost two centuries. Despite the temporal and spiritual turmoil of the period, he proved to be an able administrator, a charismatic teacher, and an influential scholar. As court physician to the Ayyūbid ruler al-Malik al-Kamil (r. 1218–1238), he enjoyed personal relations with the Muslim authorities and men of letters, including the historian Ibn Abi Usaybi.

LITERARY WORKS. Though hampered by his pastoral responsibilities, Maimonides' literary activity produced notable works in four main areas: polemics, *halakhic* jurisprudence, ethics, and exegesis. Of the first category, a fair part responded to the *halakhic* and philosophical detractors of his father's works. His masterful *Milhamot ha-shem* (Wars of the Lord), written after 1235, was singularly directed against the criticism of the rabbis of Provence and contributed towards the consolidation of his own prestige. As head of the Rabbinical Court in Cairo, he was consulted on legal matters from as far afield as Yemen and Provence and has left a sizeable collection of *responsa.* As a thinker and moralist, Abraham upheld his father's elitist philosophical system, of which he considered himself the interpreter and continuator. Nonetheless, his mature views diverged widely from those of Moses Maimonides. The latter had considered knowledge of God to be the ultimate human aim, but his son stressed ethical perfection. Indeed, his markedly ascetic mysticism earned him the epithet by which he is often referred to in later literature, Abraham *he-hasid* ("the Pious").

His *magnum opus,* the *Kifāyat al-ʿabidin* (Complete guide for devotees), written circa 1230, sets out his own religious theosophy. Written in a lively and attractive Arabic, this monumental compendium of jurisprudence and ethics is not extant in toto, but substantial manuscripts survive in Genizah collections. It circulated widely, reaching Provence, and was read at least into the seventeenth century. Its initial sections rehearse Maimonides' legal rulings, albeit with a distinctively spiritualized tone, whereas the fourth and final section, on the "special way," highlights the virtues of the *ṭarīq* (the path) advocated by Abraham. These turn out to be the stations (*maqāmat*), well known from classical Ṣūfī manuals: sincerity, mercy, generosity, gentleness, humility, faith, contentedness, abstinence, mortification, and solitude, whose mystical goal, *wusul* ("arrival"), was the encounter with God and the certitude of his light. Abraham Maimonides openly admires the Muslim Ṣūfīs, whose practices, he claims, ultimately derive from the prophets of Israel. Thus he finds biblical counterparts for Ṣūfī self-mortifications, such as combating sleep, solitary retreats in dark places, weeping, nightly vigils, and daily fasts. Notable is the obligation of the novice to take as his guide an experienced teacher who has traversed all the stages of the path in order to initiate him into the intricacies of mystical discipline before bestowing on him his mantle, as Elijah did on Elisha.

Departing from the juridical mode of his father's legal code, *Mishneh Torah,* Abraham stresses the spiritual significance of the traditional Jewish precepts (*mitsvot,* "divine commandments") and the "mysteries" they conceal, in much the same manner as al-Ghazālī did in his classical Islamic summa, *Iḥyāʾ ʿulūm ad-dīn* (Revival of the religious sciences).

Ṣūfī Influences. Abraham championed a pietistic circle whose adepts were dissatisfied with formal religion. Their number included his father-in-law, Hananel ben Samuel, and his own son Obadyah (1228–1265), author of the mystical *al-Maqāla al-hawdiyya* (Treatise of the pool). Partly inspired by Abraham ar-Rabia (d. 1223), also known as *hehasid,* whom he calls "our Master in the Way," Abraham Maimonides infused traditional Judaism with Ṣūfī ideals and practices.

Using to the utmost his prerogative as *nagid,* he endeavored to enforce on the larger community these far-reaching measures, which included such Islamic-influenced practices as ablution of the feet before prayer, standing in rows during prayer, kneeling and bowing, and raising the hands in supplication.

Abraham justified the adoption of Muslim customs and symbols with the idea that he had rediscovered lost mysteries of Jewish origin in traditions preserved by the Ṣūfīs but long forgotten by the Jews in the tribulations of their exile. Calling themselves "the disciples of the prophets," the Jewish pietists confidently awaited the imminent renewal of prophecy in Israel. The ancient Jewish traditions recovered from the Ṣūfīs were integral to the "prophetical tradition." Restoration of that discipline was a prerequisite to the return of prophecy itself, whose occurrence Moses Maimonides had predicted for an unspecifiable date.

Abraham also composed a biblical commentary. Although he intended to comment on the whole Bible, only the sections on *Genesis* and *Exodus* seem to have been completed. Here, as in the *Kifāya al-ʿabidin,* he projects his own mystical leanings into the patriarchal past, depicting ancient biblical figures as pietists, similar to the manner in which Ṣūfī literature perceives of Muḥammad and his companions as early Ṣūfīs. He often alludes to an esoteric interpretation of the "subtle mysteries" of the Pentateuch. Although he continually refers to his father's interpretations, these are not the latter's philosophical doctrines but rather point to his own pietistic concepts.

Perhaps due to his influence, later Judeo-Arabic exegetes, such as Tanhum Yerushalmi, and Syrian and Yemenite authors include certain Ṣūfī elements in their works. As for his ritual reforms, although intended to improve the spiritual decorum of the synagogue, they were not to go unchallenged. Despite his office and familial prestige, which considerably furthered the pietists' aims, Abraham confronted fierce opponents, who went as far as to denounce him to the Muslim authorities, accusing the Jewish pietists of introducing into the synagogue "false ideas," "unlawful changes," and "gentile customs."

This opposition, as well as the movement's own elitist character, seriously impeded its spread. With the general decline of oriental Jewry, Abraham Maimonides' construction of a Ṣūfī-influenced Jewish pietism gradually sank into oblivion, though some of its mystical elements were probably absorbed into the nascent Qabbalah.

See Also Jewish Thought and Philosophy, article on Premodern Philosophy; Maimonides, Moses; Sufism.

Bibliography

Cohen, Gerson. "The Soteriology of R. Abraham Maimuni." In *Studies in the Variety of Rabbinic Cultures,* pp. 209–242. Philadelphia, 1991.

Fenton, Paul. "Abraham Maimonides (1187–1237): Founding a Mystical Dynasty." In *Jewish Mystical Leaders and Leadership in the 13th Century,* edited by Moshe Idel and Mortimer Ostow, pp. 127–154. Northvale, N.J., 2000.

Rosenblatt, Samuel. *The High Ways to Perfection of Abraham Maimonides.* 2 vols. Baltimore and New York, 1927–1938.

Paul B. Fenton (2005)

MAIMONIDES, MOSES (c. 1135/8–1204), hellenized name of Mosheh ben Maimon; also known by the acronym RaMBaM (Rabbi Mosheh ben Maimon); distinguished Talmudist, philosopher, and physician, and one of the most illustrious figures of Jewish history. He had a profound and pervasive impact on Jewish life and thought, and his commanding influence has been widely recognized by non-Jews as well as Jews. His epoch-making works in the central areas of Jewish law (*halakhah*) and religious philosophy are considered to be unique by virtue of their unprecedented comprehensiveness, massive erudition, and remarkable originality and profundity. Their extraordinary conjunction of halakhic authority and philosophic prestige has been widely acknowledged. While the generations before the age of Maimonides produced philosophically trained Talmudists—scholars well versed in both Greek science and rabbinic lore—the extent to which Maimonides thoroughly and creatively amalgamated these disciplines and commitments is most striking. Many people of differing ideological inclinations throughout successive generations tend to find in or elicit from his great oeuvre a kind of *philosophia perennis.*

Early Life and Works. Maimonides was born in Córdoba, Spain, to a family of scholars. In 1148 Córdoba was conquered by the Almohads, a fanatical Islamic confederation.

To escape religious persecution, the family fled the city; they wandered through southern Spain and North Africa from 1148 to 1158 and settled in Fez for several years. In 1165 Maimonides resumed his wanderings, going from Morocco to the Land of Israel, which was then the scene of the Crusades, turbulent and inhospitable. He was unable to take root there, and after making his way southward from the Crusaders' port city of Acre through Jerusalem to Hebron, stopping for prayer in the holy sites, he settled in Fusṭāṭ (Old Cairo). He began to practice medicine and became the house physician of Saladin's vizier. In a candid letter to his favorite disciple, Maimonides comments revealingly about his medical practice:

> I inform you that I have acquired in medicine a very great reputation among the great, such as the chief *qāḍī*, the princes . . . and other grandees. . . . This obliges me continually to waste my day in Cairo visiting the [noble] sick. When I return to Fusṭāṭ, the most I am able to do . . . is to study medical books, which are so necessary for me. For you know how long and difficult this art is for a conscientious and exact man who does not want to state anything which he cannot support by argument and without knowing where it has been said and how it can be demonstrated.

Simultaneously, Maimonides emerged as the untitled leader of the Jewish community, combining the duties of rabbi, local judge, appellate judge, administrative chief responsible for appointing and supervising community officials, and overseer of philanthropic foundations. He refused all remuneration for these services, a practice that reflected his religious and philosophical principles. His only son, Avraham, who was to become the official head *(nagid)* of the Jewish community and the author of important exegetical and philosophical works, was born in 1187; his writings are a significant source of Maimonidean doctrine.

Maimonides' biography underscores a noteworthy paradox. A philosopher by temperament and ideology, a zealous devotee of the contemplative life who eloquently portrayed and yearned for the serenity of solitude, he nevertheless led a relentlessly active life that regularly brought him to the brink of exhaustion. He was a harassed physician, subject to the pressures and whims of court service, and a conscientious leader of his community, sensitive to the physical and spiritual needs of its members. Yet he combined this arduous routine with constant scholarship and literary productivity in a way that reflected his conviction that superior leaders should combine intellectual perfection with practical and moral virtue (*Guide of the Perplexed* 3.54).

His determination to preserve his economic independence is completely consonant with his belief that scholars or religious functionaries should not seek or receive communal support. Some of his most passionate and animated prose (e.g., *Mishneh Torah*, Study of the Torah 3.10, Sanhedrin 23.5; *Commentary on the Mishnah*, Avot 4.7) was elicited by his distaste for this practice and his unyielding opposition to the existence of an institutionalized and salaried rabbinate dependent upon the largesse of patrons or charitable collections. But history did not favor the Maimonidean view, and such a rabbinate did emerge.

The natural integration of traditional Torah study and philosophy, which was a pivot of his massive literary achievement and an axiom of his understanding of Judaism, is emphasized even in existential contexts. In a plaintive letter written in 1184, after the completion of his fourteen-volume code of law, the *Mishneh Torah*, and while he was working on the *Guide of the Perplexed*, he underscored his devotion to these two disciplines: "Were not the study of the Torah my delight, and did not the study of wisdom divert me from my grief, I should then have perished in mine affliction." This is related, of course, to his intellectual open-mindedness and his conviction that one should "accept the truth from whatever source it proceeds." Hence he affirms concerning a certain work "that the ideas presented . . . are not of my own invention . . . but I have gleaned them from the words of the wise occurring in the midrashim, in the Talmud, and in other of their works as well as from the words of the philosophers, ancient and recent." Torah and philosophy are consistently juxtaposed as sources of his teaching and as natural companions.

Finally, Maimonides' creativity reflects a strong pedagogic drive. His youthful works (*Millot ha-higgayon*, on logic, and *Ma'amar ha-'ibbur*, on the astronomical principles of the Jewish calendar) were composed in response to specific requests. Throughout his life he wrote hundreds of *responsa* (*teshuvot*)—decisions concerning the interpretation or application of the law—and letters of advice, comfort, or arbitration to all parts of the world, including Yemen, Baghdad, Aleppo, Damascus, Jerusalem, Alexandria, Marseilles, and Lunel. *Iggeret ha-shemad* (Epistle on Conversion) and *Iggeret Teiman* (Epistle to Yemen) are especially noteworthy. His code of law was intended for "small and great"; indeed, law for him was an educative force leading to ethical and intellectual perfection, and his code was intended to be not only a manual of commands but an instrument of education and instruction. His multifaceted erudition and constructive expository skills were widely appreciated, and he freely shared their fruits with inquirers and readers. Failure to share one's knowledge with others would be tantamount to "robbing one who deserves the truth of the truth, or begrudging an heir his inheritance" (*Guide*, intro. to part 3).

Maimonides' major works are the *Perush ha-Mishnah* (Commentary on the Mishnah), *Sefer ha-mitsvot* (Book of the Commandments), *Mishneh Torah* (Review of the Torah; also known as *Yad ha-ḥazaqah*), and *Moreh nevukhim* (*Guide of the Perplexed*). He also wrote some ten medical treatises that illustrate his vast erudition and the high ethical standards he brought to medicine. They are based to a large extent on Arabic medical literature. One of them deals with Galen and contains a rejoinder to Galen's criticisms of the Mosaic Torah.

***Commentary on the Mishnah* and *Book of the Commandments*.** The pioneering, comprehensive *Commentary on the Mishnah*, which engaged the attention of Maimonides for about ten years (1158–1168), was intended as both an introduction to and a review of the Talmud. Because it was composed in Arabic and translated into Hebrew in installments over the next two centuries, it did not have as great or immediate an impact as his other works. It combines minute textual study, even lexicographical annotation, with conceptual analysis. Maimonides often digresses to elaborate a theological principle or elucidate a philosophic or scientific issue, for, as he confesses, "expounding a single principle of religion is dearer to me than anything else that I might teach." The book includes noteworthy discussions of many problems: prophecy; the reconciliation of physics with the traditional understanding of the biblical account of creation (*maʿaseh bereʾshit*) and of metaphysics with traditional interpretations of Ezekiel's vision of the divine chariot (*maʿaseh merkavah*); the reconciliation of belief in free will with belief in predestination; reward and punishment; the history of religion; magic, medicine, and miracles; immortality and the world to come; and the proper methodological use of allegory.

In the *Commentary* Maimonides was already preoccupied with a problem that was to engage him intermittently for the rest of his life and that was also becoming a staple theme of Jewish religious thought: the metaphorical interpretation of the *aggadah*, the sections of the Talmud that deal with lore rather than law. Maimonides had planned to write a special commentary that would classify, explain, and rationalize the *aggadah*, but abandoned the idea; the *Guide of the Perplexed*, which was devoted in great part to matters of exegesis and allegory, was, by his own account, intended as a partial replacement for this work. The interest shown by Maimonides in *aggadic* interpretation gives that subject more prestige and also suggests that the *Guide* is part of the aggadic as well as the philosophic tradition.

Embedded in the *Commentary* are three separate monographs. The general introduction is a comprehensive inquiry into the theoretical, historical, and doctrinal foundations of the oral law—its origin in the act of revelation at Sinai and, in particular, the ongoing process of its transmission and interpretation. Maimonides emphasizes that the oral law is a completely rational enterprise, subject to its own canons of interpretation and brooking no suprarational interference. Even prophecy is of little relevance to the juridical process. Only the prophecy of Moses was legislative; all subsequent prophecy was merely exhortatory and could not produce new laws (see also *Guide* 2.39).

Chapter Ten (*pereq ḥeleq*) of the Talmudic tractate *Sanhedrin*, beginning "All Israelites have a share in the world to come," provides an occasion for Maimonides to include a lengthy excursus on Jewish belief. After criticizing crude, materialistic conceptions of the world to come and identifying the religious concept of the world to come with the philosophical notion of the immortality of the soul, Maimonides defines the term *Israelites* by formulating the famous thirteen principles, or articles of faith, that every Israelite is expected to endorse. The thirteen principles may be reduced to three basic groups: God—his existence, unity, incorporeality, and eternity, and the prohibition of idolatry; the law—prophecy, the uniqueness of Mosaic prophecy, the divine origin of the written and oral law, and the eternity and immutability of the law; beliefs relating to reward and punishment—God's omniscience, divine compensation for good and evil, the coming of the Messiah, and resurrection. All subsequent discussion of dogma by Jewish thinkers relates to this Maimonidean formulation.

Maimonides' introduction to *Pirqei avot* (Ethics of the Fathers), entitled "Eight Chapters," is a psychological-ethical treatise: its basis is an analysis of the soul and its powers, while its goal is a full presentation of Maimonides' theory of the golden mean. Maimonides defines virtues as psychological dispositions situated between extremes of excess and deficiency; a good deed is one that maintains the mean between these two bad extremes. This theory is the basis for a forceful repudiation by Maimonides of asceticism and all forms of extremism. Maimonides criticizes Jews who imitate "the followers of other religions" (probably Sufism) by adopting self-mortification and renunciation of "every joy." The last chapter contains an unequivocal affirmation of human freedom and, concomitantly, the rejection of all views (e.g., astrology and divine predestination) that would undermine free will. These introductions or excursuses, with their philosophical, psychological, and ethical disquisitions, enable the reader to take a rather accurate measure of the Maimonidean temper. Some scholars suggest that the *Guide* contradicts these earlier writings of Maimonides on many points (including, for example, free will).

In preparation for his great code of law, Maimonides wrote the *Book of the Commandments*, which provides a complete list of the 613 commandments thereby helping him to guard against forgetfulness and omissions and ensuring the comprehensiveness of the code. A major achievement of this work is the introduction, which defines fourteen guiding principles that determine which laws should be included in the enumeration of the 613. The ninth principle introduces an interesting classification of laws: (1) beliefs and opinions (e.g., to acknowledge the unity of God); (2) actions (e.g., to offer sacrifices); (3) virtues and traits of character (e.g., to love one's neighbor); (4) speech (e.g., to pray). This fourfold classification is significant for its all-inclusiveness and its repudiation—intentional or incidental—of narrow "legalism," in the pejorative sense that is often attached to the term as a description of Judaism.

***Mishneh Torah*.** Completed around the year 1178, the *Mishneh Torah* is a presentation of Jewish law without precedent or sequel in rabbinic literature. It is distinguished by five major characteristics: its codificatory form, its scope, its system of classification, its language and style, and its fusion of *halakhah* and philosophy.

1. *Codificatory form.* Maimonides presented the massive material in crisp, concise form, eliminating indeterminate debate and conflicting interpretations and formulating unilateral, undocumented decisions. He occasionally cites sources, mentions names of authorities, presents more than one view, includes exegetical and explanatory material, and describes personal views and practices.

2. *Scope.* One of the most revolutionary aspects of the code is its all-inclusive scope, which obliterates accidental distinctions between the practical and the theoretical. Maimonides opposed the pervasive tendency to study only those parts of the Talmud that were practical and relevant. He insisted that the abstruse, "antiquated" sections of the Talmud were not inferior to the popular, practical sections and should receive equal time and consideration. Laws concerning sacrifices or the messianic period were codified by him as precisely and comprehensively as laws concerning prayer and marital relations.

3. *Classification.* Maimonides abandoned the sequence of the Mishnah and created a new topical and pedagogical arrangement. Classification is, of course, a prerequisite for codification and necessitates interpretation, sustained conceptualization, a large measure of abstraction, and a synoptic view of the entire body of material. Legal classification concerns itself not only with the sum total of individual laws but with the concept of law per se. The ruling passion of Maimonides' life was order, system, conceptualization, and generalization, and this received its finest expression in *Mishneh Torah.*

4. *Language and style.* Maimonides chose the Hebrew of the Mishnah rather than the Hebrew of the Bible or the Aramaic of the Talmud and developed a rich, flexible style characterized by precision, brevity, and elegance. As a result, the *Mishneh Torah* contains substantial portions of the Talmud translated into fluent, felicitous Hebrew.

5. *Fusion of halakhah and philosophy.* Maimonides sought to bring about the unity of practice and concept, external observance and inner meaning, visible action and invisible experience, law and philosophy. This unification of the practical, theoretical, and theological components is underscored by Maimonides in a letter in which he describes the twofold objective of the *Mishneh Torah* as the provision of an authoritative compilation both of laws and of "true beliefs."

Book 1 of the *Mishneh Torah* (*Sefer ha-madda'*, Book of Knowledge) is a summary of the essential beliefs and guiding concepts that constitute the ideological and experiential substructure of Judaism. Maimonides explains that he could not compose a comprehensive work on the details of practical precepts while ignoring the fundamentals of essential beliefs, those commandments that are the "root" (*'iqqar*) of Mosaic religion and that should be known before anything else. The systematic treatment of metaphysics and ethics; the use of separate sections for laws of study (*talmud torah*) and laws of repentance (*teshuvah*); the devotion of a section to idolatry, including a history of religion and a review of superstitions and magical practices that must be uncompromisingly rejected—all these are combined in book 1, which serves as an introduction to, as well as an integral part of, the entire code.

Philosophic comments, rationalistic directives, ethical insights, and theological principles are also incorporated in other parts of the *Mishneh Torah.* Maimonides' systematization of the *halakhah* includes a good measure of ethical interpretation, spiritualization, and rationalization—the whole system of *ṭa'amei ha-mitsvot,* the reasons for the commandments. While not too many laws are actually rationalized, the mandate to engage in rationalization, to penetrate to the essence and the real motive powers of the commandments, is clearly issued in the *Mishneh Torah.* It is thus most significant that this code reveals Maimonides as jurist and philosopher simultaneously.

The *Mishneh Torah,* all the criticism of it notwithstanding, exercises a decisive, extensive, nearly constant influence on the study and practice of *halakhah.* This tightly structured work has become a prism through which passes practically all reflection on and analysis of Talmudic study. There is hardly a major literary development in the broad field of rabbinic literature—not only in the field of codification—that does not relate in some way to the *Mishneh Torah,* a work that remains *sui generis,* unprecedented and unrivaled.

Guide of the Perplexed. Maimonides' philosophic testament *par excellence,* his *Guide of the Perplexed,* was composed in Arabic sometime between 1185 and 1190 and was translated into Hebrew just prior to Maimonides' death by Shemu'el ibn Tibbon (c. 1150–c. 1230). It is divided into three parts and covers a wide spectrum of philosophic problems. Maimonides deals with the basic problems that engaged all medieval religious philosophers: faith and reason, or the relation of philosophy to scripture; the existence, unity, incorporeality, and freedom of God; God's relation to the world in terms of its origin and government; communication between God and man through revelation; and the issues of ethics, free will, and human destiny, including immortality and doctrines of eschatology. The *Guide* was used extensively by Jewish thinkers and also by Christian scholastics, most notably Thomas Aquinas.

Why and for whom was the *Guide* written? Specifically, Maimonides composed it for his student Yosef ben Yehudah Sham'un; generally, he addresses himself to the "perplexed," who is characterized as "a religious man for whom the validity of our law has become established in his soul and has become actual in his belief—such a man being perfect in his religion and character, and having studied the sciences of the philosophers and come to know what they signify." Maimonides is not concerned to teach "the vulgar or beginners in speculation nor those who have not engaged in any study other than the science of the law, I mean the legalistic study of the law. For the purpose of this treatise . . . is the science of law in its true sense." His reader is a religious intellectual, well versed in Jewish law and classical philosophy, who is perplexed because he wants to preserve the integrity of both and is unwilling to renounce either. Maimonides undertakes to achieve this objective by explaining metaphysics, revealing the mistakes of the philosophers, and interpreting the esoteric meaning of the Hebrew Bible and Talmud.

Maimonides emphasizes his insistence upon intellectual rigor and proper method in achieving these goals; hence his determination to expose the mistakes of certain "philosophers, particularly the followers of the *kalām*," who frequently "violate that which is perceived by the senses." He gives primacy to purity of method. The esoteric meaning of the Bible is elicited by proper use of the method of allegory—that is, the identification of the supraliteral sense of the religious texts. This is one way of affirming that the religious tradition contains the basic truths of philosophy. Moreover, there is essential harmony between faith and reason. In common with other medieval religious philosophers, Maimonides adds revelation to reason and sense perception as sources of knowledge. It is this epistemological assumption that alters classical epistemology and that accounts for Maimonides' axiom of the compatibility of religious tradition and philosophic reasoning. While there is no contradiction between them, Maimonides believed that demonstrated belief is superior to faith—he held what the historian of religion Harry A. Wolfson called a "single-faith theory of the rationalist type."

Maimonides' ideal was a blending of "the science of law, i.e., the legalistic study of the law" with "the science of the law in its true sense." The phrase "legalistic study of the law" is not a tautology. Maimonides here establishes in one bold stroke that law is two-dimensional: legal (in the restricted, positive sense) and metalegal or philosophical. Both, in Maimonides' view, are components of the oral law. According to his history of philosophy (*Guide* 1.71), which was shared by many Jewish, Christian, and Muslim writers down to the beginning of the modern era, the Jews in antiquity cultivated the sciences of physics and metaphysics, which they later neglected for a variety of historical and theological reasons; they did not borrow from Greek thought because philosophy was an integral part of their religious tradition. This dovetails perfectly with Maimonides' halakhic formulation (*Mishneh Torah*, Study of the Torah 1.11, 1.12), which grafts philosophy onto the substance of the oral law and makes its study mandatory. This is Maimonides' intellectual conviction and philosophic position: the essential relationship and constant intersection of philosophy and *halakhah*. For him, the issue is not the legitimacy of philosophy in religion, but the legitimacy of religion without philosophy. Just as Yehudah ha-Levi considered philosophy an unwelcome intrusion, Maimonides considered its absence undesirable and intolerable.

A third issue in Maimonides' treatment of philosophy—in addition to the epistemological issue (reason and revelation as twin sources of knowledge) and the historical issue (the existence of philosophy as a part of traditional Jewish lore)—is cultural: philosophy implies a measure of universality. Hence Maimonides assumes the identity of the lost classical philosophic tradition of Judaism with the study of philosophy that was in his own day being restored under foreign influence. He does not need to be uncomfortable when in his reconstruction of the history of philosophy he acknowledges the non-Jewish, primarily Muslim, stimulus for the medieval revival of Jewish philosophy. "We have already explained that all these views do not contradict anything said by our prophets and the sustainers of our law. . . . When in consequence of all this [exile and loss of wisdom] we grew up accustomed to the opinions of the ignorant, these philosophic views appeared to be, as it were, foreign to our law, just as they are foreign to the opinions of the ignorant. However, matters are not like this" (*Guide* 2.11). In a letter to his translator, Shemu'el ibn Tibbon, he mentions his main philosophic sources: Aristotle, whose books are "the roots and foundations of all works in the sciences"; al-Fārābī, whose "writings are faultlessly excellent—one ought to study and understand them"; and the important commentaries on Aristotle by Alexander of Aphrodisias, Themistius, and Ibn Rushd (Averroës).

Maimonidean philosophy is full of problems and dialectical pressures. In order to enlighten some readers without disconcerting others, Maimonides abandoned his fastidious organization, separated a unified presentation of views into unrelated sections, and even introduced premeditated, carefully wrought contradictions. Reading the *Guide* is thus a major challenge. To this day this dialectic continues to befuddle students of the *Guide*, who disagree concerning Maimonides' true intention and actual religious-philosophic stance.

There is, of course, a basic tension in the very attempt to combine Aristotelian philosophy with Judaism, and it is not certain that the two sides of Maimonides—the sovereign master of *halakhah* and the zealous disciple of Aristotle—could be completely at ease together. Given the supremacy of the contemplative life for Maimonides, what significance did the practical religious life have for him? Is there a genuine incompatibility between the meaningful observance of *mitsvot* and the serious study and appreciation of physics and metaphysics?

All difficulties notwithstanding—and he himself (*Guide* 1.33) mentions the view of those who contend that philosophic inquiry "undermines the foundations of law"—Maimonides remained unswervingly committed to his brand of rationalism. Indeed, he believed that there is a religious obligation to apply one's intellect to the study of God and the world. "One only loves God with the knowledge with which one knows him; according to the knowledge will be the love. If the former be little or much, so will the latter be little or much. A person ought therefore to devote himself to the understanding and comprehension of those sciences and studies which will inform him concerning his master, as far as it lies in human faculties to understand and comprehend."

Achievement and Legacy. Maimonides' lifework—the fastidious interpretation and thoughtful reformulation of Jewish belief and practice—seems to have been clear in his mind from an early age. There is a conscious unity and progressive continuity in his literary career. It is striking how early his ideas, ideals, and aspirations were formed, how logically they hang together, and how consistently and creatively they were applied. As his work moves from textual explication to independent exposition, and from one level of exposition to another, the reader, moving with it, feels that Maimonides had from the very beginning a master plan to achieve one overarching objective: to bring *halakhah* and philosophy, two apparently incongruous attitudes of mind, into fruitful harmony.

Maimonides consistently espoused a sensitized view of religion and morality, demanding an uncompromising observance of the law, openly disdaining the perfunctory view of the masses, searching for the ultimate religious significance of every human action, and urging a commitment to, and quest for, wisdom and perfection. He pursued a vision of a meaningful observance of *mitsvot* combined with a genuine appreciation of philosophy. Routine piety and unreflective behavior he denigrated; Talmudism divorced from spiritual animation he found wanting. He emphasized the nobility of philosophic religion, in which rationalism and piety are natural companions and through which human perfection is advanced. As a religious rationalist, he was convinced of the interrelatedness and complementarity of divine and human wisdom and strove doggedly for their integration.

Maimonides knew that this could not be done easily or indiscriminately, but he was convinced that the very attempt, full of tension and problems, was indispensable for the achievement of true religious perfection. It may be said that Maimonides allowed religious rationalism, which had led a sort of subliminal existence in earlier rabbinic writing, to claim and obtain legitimacy and dignity. Maimonides picked up the various strands of rationalism and, by criticizing, refining, and extending them, emerged as the symbol of the religious rationalist mentality and the harbinger of a new direction in religious thought. To a great extent, subsequent Jewish religious-intellectual history may be seen as a debate concerning the wisdom and effectiveness of the Maimonidean position.

Bibliography

Altmann, Alexander. "Maimonides' 'Four Perfections.'" Israel Oriental Studies 2 (1972): 15–24.

Bacher, Wilhelm, Marcus Brann, and David Jacob Simonsen, eds. *Moses ben Maimon.* 2 vols. Leipzig, 1908–1914; reprint, Hildesheim, 1971.

Baron, Salo W., ed. *Essays on Maimonides.* New York, 1941.

Berman, Lawrence. "Maimonides, the Disciple of Alfārābī." *Israel Oriental Studies* 4 (1974): 154–178.

Epstein, Isidore, ed. *Moses Maimonides.* London, 1935.

Halkin, Abraham, and David Hartman. *Crisis and Leadership: Epistles of Maimonides.* Philadelphia, 1985.

Hartman, David. *Maimonides: Torah and Philosophic Quest.* Philadelphia, 1976.

Lerner, Ralph. "Maimonides' Letter on Astrology." *History of Religions* 8 (November 1968): 143–158.

Maimonides, Moses. *The Book of Divine Commandments.* Translated and edited by Charles B. Chavel, London, 1940.

Maimonides, Moses. *The Code of Maimonides.* 15 vols. to date. Yale Judaica Series. New Haven, 1949–.

Maimonides, Moses. *Guide of the Perplexed.* Translated by Shlomo Pines with introductory essay by Leo Strauss. Chicago, 1963.

Twersky, Isadore, ed. *A Maimonides Reader.* New York, 1972.

Twersky, Isadore. *Introduction to the Code of Maimonides (Mishneh Torah).* New Haven, Conn., 1980.

Wolfson, Harry A. *Studies in the History of Philosophy and Religion,* vol. 2. Cambridge, Mass., 1977.

New Sources

Buijs, Joseph A., ed. *Maimonides: A Collection of Critical Essays.* Notre Dame, Ind., 1988.

Dobbs-Weinstein, Idit. *Maimonides and St. Thomas on the Limits of Reason.* Albany, 1995.

Fox, Marvin. *Interpreting Maimonides: Studies in Methodology, Metaphysics, and Moral Philosophy.* Chicago, 1990.

Kellner, Menachem Marc. *Maimonides on Judaism and the Jewish People.* Albany, 1991.

Kraemer, Joel L., ed. *Perspectives on Maimonides: Philosophical and Historical Studies.* New York, 1991.

Kreisel, Howard T. *Maimonides' Political Thought: Studies in Ethics, Law, and the Human Ideal.* Albany, 1999.

Leaman, Oliver. *Moses Maimonides.* New York, 1990.

Twersky, Isadore. *Studies in Maimonides.* Harvard Judaic Texts and Studies, 7. Cambridge, Mass., 1991.

Isadore Twersky (1987)
Revised Bibliography

MAITREYA.

Among the pantheon of Buddhist personages none offers such a complex array of incarnations as does Maitreya. His first and most important role is that of successor to Śākyamuni as a buddha who achieves the ultimate state of enlightenment after having been born as a human. The notion of Maitreya as the future Buddha is found within the traditions of all Buddhists, although there is no universal agreement about his life history or about the way in which he will realize the destiny set forth by his position as the next Buddha.

Textual Accounts. A survey of the literature provides us with some indication of the ways the Maitreya story has developed and increased in importance. The Pali canon, the source of much of our information on the early teaching, does not give Maitreya much significance, mentioning his name in only one of the early texts, the *Cakkavattisīhanāda Sutta.* In the noncanonic literature, two works are devoted primarily to Maitreya, the *Anagatavaṃsa* and the *Maitreyavyākaraṇa,* but the origin of these works and their precise dating are not known. An expanded version of the Maitreya story can be found in the *Divyāvadāna* of the Mūlasarvāstivādin school. Among this collection of tales is a story of a *bodhisattva* who wishes to perform an extreme act of ascetic practice and donate his head to a brahman teacher as a sign of his sincerity to pursue truth. But a deity, watching over the garden in which this scene occurs, attempts to save the *bodhisattva*'s life by keeping the brahman at a distance. The *bodhisattva* pleads with the deity to allow him to proceed because it was in this very garden that Maitreya had previously turned away from his desire to sacrifice his life for his teacher, thus failing to fulfill his highest aspirations, a flaw that should not be repeated.

The *Mahāvastu,* a text from the Mahāsāṃghika sect, provides a list of future Buddhas, placing Maitreya's name at the top. In this early account we find the name Ajita used to refer to Maitreya in his past lives. Later, Theravādins became quite interested in Ajita, and the story of his life was the focus of much attention by the fifth and sixth centuries. Ajita's identification as the son of King Ajātasattu of Magadha allowed the *saṃgha* to determine exactly where and how the *bodhisattva* will make his appearance when he achieves buddhahood. According to a section on Maitreya's life in the *Mahāvaṃsa,* a well-known history of Sri Lanka, Maitreya will reside in Tuṣita Heaven before descending to his earthly birth and maturation. The timing of this event is noted clearly. After Śākyamuni's *parinirvāṇa,* the world will enter a period of social and cosmological decline; five thousand years after the last buddha, the teaching will have fallen to a low ebb, and the human life-span will have been reduced to ten years. At this time the cycle will be reversed: life will improve until the length of an average life-span on earth will be eighty-thousand years. In this world of long life and an environment that will be conducive to the teaching of the Buddha, there will be a ruler, a *cakravartin,* who will provide for the welfare of the people and promote the teachings of the Buddha. When this paradise is ready, Maitreya will descend from Tuṣita Heaven, realize his full potential as a buddha, and teach the Dharma to advanced beings. Mahākāśyapa, one of the major disciples of Śākyamuni, will arise from the trance state he entered after the *parinirvāṇa* of his former teacher to once again serve a buddha and hear the teaching of the enlightened one.

This millenarian view of Maitreya is still held in the Buddhist areas of South and Southeast Asia, and in northern Myanmar (Burma) there is a belief that a contemporary teacher known as Bodaw was a universal king as well as the future Buddha Maitreya. The identification of Maitreya with leaders and founders is found consistently throughout Buddhist Asia.

Scholars have suggested that the idea of the future Buddha may be derived from the Iranian concept of the savior Saoshyant. In this light, Maitreya would represent the establishment of a world in which there is peace and abundance and where the Dharma will be taught and fully understood. Others, however, take the position that these ideas were already present in India at the time of Śākyamuni. The Buddhists, as well as the Ājīvikas and Jains, taught that there would be new *tīrthaṃkaras, jinas,* and Buddhas in the future. P. S. Jaini suggests that the source for the Maitreya development was within the Mahāsāṃghika school. Whereas the Theravāda paid little attention to Maitreya, giving only one canonic reference, the *Mahāvastu* of the Mahāsāṃghikas devotes a number of paragraphs to Maitreya, noting his name as Ajita, detailing events from his past lives, and telling of Śākyamuni's prediction of buddhahood for him. Thus, there is ample material to justify the study of Maitreya as a part of the Indian cultural and religious domain, without having to rely on a diffusionist theory of external influences to account for the notion of the future buddha.

The Mahāyāna tradition has given much attention to Maitreya, and we find in the literature many references to his life and activities. Since the Mahāyāna has emphasized the career and development of the *bodhisattva,* it is understandable that it would place Maitreya in this honored group. As with the earlier tradition, all Mahāyāna groups believe that Maitreya will follow in the footsteps of Śākyamuni. In the pantheon of *bodhisattvas,* Maitreya is not always given the highest place; he shares with such *bodhisattvas* as Mañjuśrī and Avalokiteśvara the esteem of the community of believers. In the Prajñāpāramitā texts, Maitreya is involved in dialogue with the Buddha and a group of disciples made up of *bodhisattvas* and *arhats.* The *arhats,* even the famous followers of Śākyamuni, are ranked far below the *bodhisattvas* in terms of their level of understanding. Thus the Prajñāpāramitā literature depicts Maitreya as ranking above an *arhat* such as Śāriputra. But Maitreya is not always portrayed so flatteringly in Mahāyāna literature. For example, in an account from the *Saddharmapuṇḍarīka Sūtra,* Mañjuśrī tells Maitreya that in the past, when he had taught the Dharma to Maitreya, Maitreya was a slothful student more interested in fame than understanding. Thus, in this meeting with his old teacher, Maitreya still needs answers to his questions. The question of whether Maitreya and Śākyamuni had ever met in any of their former lives also arises in Mahāyāna literature. The *Mahākarmavibhaṅga* states that the Buddha had indeed met Maitreya and praised him for his desire to live as a *bodhisattva.*

The Tantric tradition of later Mahāyāna seems to have had little interest in Maitreya. This tradition's dismissal of Maitreya may be seen in the *Guhyasamāja Tantra,* in which Maitreya is described as afraid and upset when he hears the Vajrayāna teaching. Because he is of limited learning, he is not able to comprehend this advanced instruction. The same questioning of Maitreya's level of comprehension is found in the *Vimalakīrtinirdeśa,* in which Maitreya is unable to give a proper response to the layman Vimalakīrti, who challenges the prediction of buddhahood by questioning whether the three times (past, present, and future) can be accepted as real. If they are not real, asks Vimalakīrti, in what sense can one say that a past prediction will result in future events? Unable to respond, Maitreya is reduced to silence. Thus the Mahāyāna texts present a varied view of this *bodhisattva,* showing him as destined for a great position in the future but still lacking the training necessary for a full understanding of the highest teaching within the tradition.

A much more glorified depiction of Maitreya occurs in the *Gaṇḍhavyuha Sūtra.* Here, Maitreya appears as a teacher of the young Sudhana, who travels about searching for answers from more than fifty teachers. Upon entering Maitreya's palace, Sudhana experiences, through the power of Maitreya, a trance in which he has visions of important places in the life of the future Buddha, including the place where Maitreya achieved the trance called *maitra* ("kind, amicable") that is the basis for his name. Sudhana then witnesses a long line of incarnations of Maitreya, including the life in which the *bodhisattva* was a king and another in which he was the king of the gods. Finally, Sudhana sees the Tuṣita Heaven, where Maitreya's rebirth will occur just prior to buddhahood. Maitreya tells Sudhana that they will meet again when the final birth has been accomplished. Even the texts that teach the superiority of the Pure Land of Amitābha and are usually considered affiliated with a school that was in competition with the Maitreya cult indicate that Sudhana is one of the privileged ones who have the ability to see the realm of Amitābha.

CULT. The practice that has grown up around the figure of Maitreya goes far beyond the aspects that have been noted in the canonical and popular literature.

China. When Buddhism arrived in China (c. first century CE), there was considerable interest in Maitreya, in part because of the Daoist belief in the ever-possible appearance of a sage capable of giving salvation to an elite band of devotees. As early as the Eastern Jin dynasty (317–420), Buddhist cultic life was directed toward Maitreya. Indeed, one of China's most famous monks, Daoan, took a vow to be reborn in Tuṣita Heaven in order to be near Maitreya and with him when he descends to earth. In the succeeding centuries, the Northern Wei (386–535) carved two great cave complexes, the first at Yungang and the other at Longmen. At Yungang, the earlier of the two sites, the Maitreya figures are prominent, and even today visitors can see him depicted in a number of poses. The caves at Longmen also contain many Maitreya figures, most dating to the first part of the sixth century. Tsukamoto Zenryū, who charted the number of images made in Longmen, has shown that although Śākyamuni and Maitreya were the chief models in the early days, by the seventh century attention was centered instead on Amitābha and Avalokiteśvara. (See his *Shina bukkyōshi kenkyū: Hokugi-hen,* Tokyo, 1942, pp. 355ff.)

Interest in the Pure Land teaching reached a high level during the seventh century and continued to have support throughout the Tang period (618–907); consequently, Maitreya's image was hardly ever depicted. But while Maitreya was no longer a popular subject for cave paintings or court-sponsored projects, he was not forgotten. At this time the Chinese people transformed him into a folk deity of great importance. Although majestic images of Maitreya carved in the caves disappeared from the repetoire of artists, a new form of Maitreya—as a fat, laughing, pot-bellied person—emerged in the Song dynasty. There is evidence that this vision of Maitreya was based on a popular historical figure, a tenth-century wandering sage. He is said to have been a native of Zhejiang and to have carried a hemp bag wherever he went. Children were especially attracted to him, and he is often depicted surrounded by them. Many stories arose about his miraculous abilities, including one that tells of the discovery of a third eye on his back. Because of the eye people called him a buddha, even though he begged them not to spread the word about his characteristics. Such stories led to the belief that this wanderer was none other than Maitreya himself, who had come down to earth and taken this unlikely form, attracting people through his wisdom and loving patience. Today, the figure of Maitreya in this guise is placed at the main entrance of Chinese monasteries, where he is revered by all laymen who wish for good fortune and prosperity.

Because he was conceived as a future Buddha who will come at a time when a great king rules, Maitreya was often used by those who wanted to secure political power or give themselves a legitimate basis for ruling. As early as the seventh century, Chinese rulers and would-be leaders were declaring themselves his incarnation or claiming they were destined to prepare the nation for the advent of the new Buddha. In 613, for example, Song Zixian, calling himself Maitreya, planned a revolt against the dynasty; later, during the Tang, Empress Wu made the same claim when she came to power. The Song dynasty (960–1279) saw the emergence of secret societies oriented to the notion that Maitreya was already in the world or that the world needed to be changed to accommodate him. The political use of Maitreya by those who challenged established authority may be one reason for the decline of royal patronage of artworks using this *bodhisattva* as a theme.

In Chinese cultic life Maitreya came to be associated with the three stages of cosmic time; he is the herald of the last age. In *baojuan* ("precious scroll") literature, which reflects the attitudes and beliefs of folk religion, we find the notion that he is a messenger who comes to earth during the last age as an ambassador of the Great Mother in order to save the sinful. A seventeenth-century *baojuan* text describes Maitreya as the controller of the heavens during the third age, which is symbolized by the color white. He sits on his throne, a nine-petaled lotus blossom, and waits for the time when he will rule for 108,000 years.

Maitreya was an important part of Chinese Buddhist development, in part because many millenarian movements could make full use of him without considering that he was anything but a Chinese deity; his foreign origin was forgotton. An example of the way in which motifs can spread from one culture to another is the case of Doan Minh Huyen, the charismatic Vietnamese leader who preached in regions devastated by the cholera epidemics of the nineteenth century. Doan advocated the founding of communities of believers who would teach followers and lead them to a state of spiritual perfection, thus ensuring that they would be protected from the upcoming holocaust. According to Doan, Maitreya would descend from Tuṣita Heaven to the mountains near Cambodia to preside over the Dragon Flower Assembly and bring about a new era.

The more orthodox Buddhists among the monastic and lay community were interested in Maitreya because they faced the uncertainity of living in a time when the "true teaching" was thought to be disappearing. In Maitreya, the Chinese found a deity that met their needs at many levels, and they did not hesitate to invest him with a variety of costumes, abilities, and cultic functions.

Korea. Another East Asian nation, Korea, has also paid much attention to Maitreya, in part because Buddhism was introduced on the peninsula at a time when the Maitreya cult was at the pinnacle of its importance in China. Since Maitreya practice was one of the first to be introduced, Korea held it in high esteem and continued to do so long after Chinese interest in the traditional aspects of Maitreya had died. The belief in Maitreya came to Korea from the Northern Wei and the kingdoms that followed it, and we can see him depicted in triad compositions from both the Paekche and Koguryŏ periods. Some scholars maintain that Maitreya practice in Korea was divided into two distinct approaches. Under Paekche rule, believers assumed that the nation had to prepare a proper environment for Maitreya before he would descend. During the Silla kingdom, on the other hand, it was thought that Maitreya would descend to the world and operate within it even if the times were troubled.

During the Three Kingdoms period (late fourth century–668), a semimilitary organization of young men, known as Hwarang, came to have a special relationship to Maitreya. Their association with Maitreya may be rooted in a sixth-century story about a monk who wished to have Maitreya reborn in the world so that he could pay homage to him. During a dream he discovered that Maitreya had already come into the world and had taken the form of a *hwarang* ("flower boy"). Identification of the *hwarang* with Maitreya was widespread, and it may be that the images of the *bodhisattva* that depict him as a pensive prince with one leg crossed over the knee of the other are visual representations of this association. During the Koryŏ period, there was much interest in the three periods of the teaching, and many believed that the final period, in which the true teaching would disappear to be replaced with a misunderstood one, had approached. Since the sūtras taught that this era would be reached fifteen hundred years after the *parinirvāṇa* of the Buddha, the Koreans assumed that the evil age was to start in the year 1052. There was much in subsequent centuries to justify the notion that an evil time had indeed come, and during these times of social disorder many understandably longed for the appearance of Maitreya in his role of protector. Even in the present, believers look to Maitreya for protection and assistance. Local people in Korea still approach statues of Maitreya to pray for good fortune, the birth of a son, the cure to an illness, and for protection in times of trouble.

The most distinctive images of Maitreya in Korea show a large platform secured to the top of his head, with either a tiered or a rounded form placed upon it. This headpiece may represent the stupa that Maitreya characteristically wears on the head.

The role of Maitreya in fertility cults is most easily seen in the practice now found in Korea's Cheju Island, in the northern East China Sea. At one site on the island an image of Maitreya has been placed next to a phallic stone; women come to the spot to touch the stone in the hope that this act will result in the birth of a son. When one takes an inventory of the objects toward which prayers for sons are directed, Maitreya is found alongside the Dragon King, the Mountain Spirit, and the Seven Stars. Of all the figures in the Buddhist pantheon, Maitreya was the one thought to be most able to answer particular prayers for children. This may explain the fat belly and surrounding children found in the Chinese form.

Maitreya also appears as a major element in the messianic groups that have arisen in Korea. One of these is a new religion founded in the late nineteenth century known as Chungsan-gyo, whose followers believe that a disease is present in the Kunsan area that, if not controlled, could spread throughout the world and bring destruction to the human race. Chungsan, the founder of this sect, taught that he alone had the magical spell necessary to control the disease. His followers believe that he was an incarnation of Maitreya and that he had descended to earth and for thirty years lived within an image of Maitreya. A more recent group, which has grown up around Yi Yu-song, teaches that Hananim, the primordial deity of Korean epics, the ruler of Heaven, will descend to Korea in the form of Maitreya Buddha.

Korean Buddhists continue to recognize Maitreya; twenty-seven major images of him in his majestic standing position have been constructed. Although the Chogye order of monks and nuns pays little attention to this *bodhisattva*, the laypeople of Korea, like those of China, refuse to let Maitreya fade from their religious practice.

Japan. The Japanese received the first information about Maitreya from Korea, a transmission that included images of the *bodhisattva*. Most of the monasteries said to have been founded by Shōtoku Taishi (574–622) contain statues of Maitreya in the pose of the pensive prince. It is probable that the Japanese viewed Maitreya as a *kami*, able to bring long life and prosperity, and thus rituals directed toward him were similar to those performed for indigenous spirits. During the later Heian period (794–1185), many felt that the time of the false teaching had been reached and found solace in the thought that Maitreya would soon descend to the earth and preach three sermons under the Dragon Flower Tree. Among those who hoped to see Maitreya was Kūkai (774–835), the founder of the Shingon sect, who proclaimed on his deathbed that he would be born into Tuṣita Heaven, where he would spend thousands of years in the presence of the future Buddha before descending with him to the world.

Later developments of the Maitreya cult can still be seen in Japan. In Kashima, for example, it is believed that the rice-laden Ship of Maitreya will one day come from a paradise out in the sea. During the Edo period (1600–1868) the Kashima area was the site of Maitreya dances in which the priestess of the shrine gave an oracle that foretold the coming year's fortune. In this capacity she reached out to the world of Maitreya, a paradise of abundance.

Some groups expect that Maitreya's future appearance will take place in Japan, on top of Kimpusan, where the Golden Land will be established and Maitreya will teach his three sermons. Followers in each of the major Buddhist areas in Asia have put forth the belief that Maitreya will be born within their own region and thus can be considered as one of their own rather than a foreigner.

Many of those who, by virtue of their membership in a Maitreya group, consider themselves an elite hope to remain on earth until Maitreya descends. In other cases, devotees believe that he has already appeared. For example, in 1773 a group known as Fujikō claimed that Maitreya had manifested himself on top of Mount Fuji. The leader, a priest named Kakugyō, announced the advent of the World of Maitreya. Later, Kakugyō sealed himself in a cell, drinking only water until his death, which his followers believe is but a stage of waiting for the new age with the future Buddha. The Fujikō articulated the hopes and aspirations of agrarian communities of the time. During the peasant rebellions of the Edo, large numbers of the group went on a pilgrimage called *eejanaika*, making the Ise Shrine the focus of their attention. Dancing themselves into ecstatic states, the pilgrims proclaimed that Maitreya would bring abundant harvests.

The twentieth century was a time of great interest in the "new religions" (*shinkō shūkyō*), which manifested the continuing thread of belief in the future Buddha and his appearance in the world. The Ōmotokyō, for example, have close ties with Maitreya. In 1928, Deguchi Onisaburo declared himself an incarnation of Maitreya. This proclamation was made during the year of the dragon, which the oracle had described as the year when great changes would take place. Another new group, the Reiyūkai, was founded by Kubo Kakutarō and his sister-in-law Kotani Kimi, who was renowned as a faith healer and called a living Buddha by her followers. After her death the sect established a mountain training center in which her teachings are the center of attention. The identification of Kotani with Maitreya can be seen in the name of the retreat, Mirokusan, or Maitreya's Mountain.

CONCLUDING REMARKS. Maitreya has been a significant figure in Buddhist thought wherever the religion has found support. For lay followers, the Maitreya cult was one method of creating good karma (Skt., *karman*) for themselves and of assuring that the future would be one of bliss. The element of hope for the future is a crucial part of the idea that Maitreya will or has appeared to lead humankind toward a better time. Since the story of Maitreya has yet to be completed, he can play a part in an infinite variety of scenarios, each established to meet the requirements of a specific time and place.

SEE ALSO Amitābha; Buddhas and Bodhisattvas, article on Celestial Buddhas and Bodhisattvas; Buddhism, article on Buddhism in Korea; Cakravartin; Dao'an; Korean Religion; Mañjuśrī; Millenarianism, article on Chinese Millenarian Movements; Ōmotokyō; Reiyūkai Kyōdan; Saoshyant.

BIBLIOGRAPHY

Primary Sources

"The *Anagata-vamsa.*" Edited by J. Minayeff. *Journal of the Pali Text Society* (1886): 33–53.

Aṣṭasāhasrikāprajñāpāramitāsūtra. Edited by Wogihara Unrai. Tokyo, 1932–1935.

Dīgha Nikāya. 3 vols. Edited by T. W. Rhys-Davids and J. Estlin Carpenter. Pali Text Society Series. London, 1890–1911. Translated by T. W. Rhys-Davids and C. A. F. Rhys-Davids as *Dialogues of the Buddha*, "Sacred Books of the Buddhists," vols. 2–4 (London, 1889–1921).

Divyāvadāna. Edited by E. B. Cowell and R. A. Neill. Cambridge, U.K., 1886.

Gaṇḍhavyuha Sūtra. Edited by D. T. Suzuki and Idzumi Hokei. Kyoto, 1934–1936.

Guhyasamāja Tantra. Edited by Benoytosh Bhattacharyya. Gaekwad's Oriental Series, no. 53. Baroda, 1931.

Le Mahāvastu. 3 vols. Edited by Émile Senart. Paris, 1882–1897. Translated by J. J. Jones as *The Mahāvastu*, "Sacred Books of the Buddhists," vols. 16, 18, 19 (London, 1949–1956).

Maitreyavyākaraṇa. Edited by Sylvain Lévi. Paris, 1932.

Saddharmapuṇḍarīkasūtra. Edited by Hendrik Kern and Bunyiu Nanjio. Bibliotheca Buddhica. Saint Petersburg, 1914. Translated by Hendrik Kern as *Saddharma-Puṇḍarīka; or, The Lotus of the Good Law*, "Sacred Books of the Buddhists," vol. 21 (1884; reprint, New York, 1963). Kumārajīva's fifth-century Chinese translation of the *Lotus* has been translated by Leon N. Hurvitz as *Scripture of the Lotus Blossom of the Fine Dharma* (New York, 1976).

Sukhāvativyūhasūtra. Edited by F. Max Müller and Bunyiu Nanjio. Anecdota Oxonensia Aryan Series. Oxford, 1883. Translated into English by F. Max Müller in *Buddhist Mahāyāna Texts*, edited by E. B. Cowell et al., "Sacred Books of the East," vol. 49 (1894; reprint, New York, 1969).

Vimalakīrtinirdeśa. Translated from Tibetan by Robert A. F. Thurman as *The Holy Teaching of Vimalakīrti: A Mahāyāna Scripture* (University Park, Penn., 1976).

Secondary Sources

Hayami Tasuku. *Miroku shinkō-mō hitotsu no jōdō shinkō.* Nihonjin no kōdō to shisō, vol. 12. Tokyo, 1971.

Miyata Noboru. *Miroku shinkō no kenkyū.* Tokyo, 1975.

Murakami Shigeyoshi. *Japanese Religion in Modern Century.* Translated by H. Byron Earhart. Tokyo, 1980.

Sponberg, Alan, and Helen Hardacre, eds. *Maitreya.* Princeton, 1986.

Tsuruoka Shizuo. "Nihon ni okeru Miroku geshō shinkō ni tsuite." *Shūkyō kenkyū* 144 (1955): 22–35.

New Sources

Elverskog, Johan. *Uygur Buddhist Literature.* Turnhout, 1997. See pp. 139–145 for an extensive bibliography on the Old Turkish text, the *Maitrismit nom bitig.*

Ji Xianlin, Werner Winter, and Georges-Jean Pinault. *Fragments of the Tocharian A Maitreyasamiti-Nāṭaka of the Xinjiang Museum, China.* Berlin, 1998.

Kassapathera. *Anagatavamsa Desana. The Sermon of the Chronicle-To-Be.* Edited with an introduction by John Holt and translated by Udaya Maddegama. New Delhi, 1993.

Kim, Inchang. *The Future Buddha Maitreya: An Iconological Study.* New Delhi, 1997.

Miyata Noboru. "Maitreya and Popular Religion in Early Twentieth Century Korea." In *Korea between Tradition and Modernity: Selected Papers from the Fourth Pacific and Asian Conference on Korean Studies,* edited by Yun-shik Chang et al., pp. 274–279. Vancouver, 2000.

Nattier, Jan. *Once upon a Future Time: Studies in a Buddhist Prophecy of Decline.* Berkeley, 1991.

Rhodes, Robert. "Recovering the Golden Age: Michinaga, Jokei and the Worship of Maitreya in Medieval Japan." *Japanese Religions* 23, nos. 1–2 (1998): 53–71.

Zieme, Peter. "Zum Maitreya-Kult in uigurischen Kolophonen." *Rocznik Orientalistyczny* 49 (1994): 219–230.

LEWIS R. LANCASTER (1987)
Revised Bibliography

MAJLISĪ, AL- (AH 1037–1110/11, 1627–1699/1700 CE), Muḥammad Bāqir ibn Muḥammad Taqī, preeminent Persian Shīʿī theologian in the late Safavid period. Born to a family of renowned scholars, he was made leader of the Friday prayers in Isfahan sometime after the death of his father in 1659. Shah Sulaymān appointed him as *shaykh al-Islām,* the highest religious official in the land, in 1687, and he reached the zenith of his power under Shah Sulṭān Ḥusayn, the last Safavid ruler (1694–1722). He died and was buried in Isfahan.

Al-Majlisī's career epitomizes the increasing predominance of the Shīʿī religious hierarchy. He used his influence in court circles to propagate his brand of Shiism, to persecute Ṣūfīs and non-Muslims, and to encourage the often forcible conversion of Sunnīs to Twelver Shiism. In order to reach beyond the learned circles in which Arabic was used as a means of expression he produced a large number of works in Persian, of which the best known are *Ḥayāt al-qulūb* (Life of the Hearts), a work of biographies of the prophets and imams, and *Ḥaqq al-yaqīn* (Certain Truth), his last completed work, which sets out the main tenets of Twelver Shiism.

In his Arabic works, al-Majlisī dealt with a variety of doctrinal issues; he also composed commentaries on some of the classical Shīʿī legal texts. Yet he is best known for his *Biḥār al-anwār* (Oceans of Light), a voluminous encyclopedia containing a vast number of Shīʿī traditions from various sources. As such, it spans virtually all major aspects of Twelver Shīʿī religious thought: the unity of God and the divine attributes; the concepts of knowledge, belief and unbelief, and free will and predestination; the lives of the prophets and imams and the pilgrimages to their graves; the position of the Qurʾān; and positive law.

Thanks to the *Biḥār,* much of the corpus of Shīʿī tradition was saved from oblivion and returned to center stage. In preparing the work, al-Majlisī relied heavily on the help of pupils and enlisted the financial backing of the Safavid court to obtain manuscripts of rare or inaccessible works. The first volume of the *Biḥār* appeared in 1666, and by the time of al-Majlisī's death seventeen of the twenty-six projected volumes had been finished. The rest were completed by his pupil ʿAbd Allāh Efendī. A lithograph edition of the entire work was first published between 1885 and 1897, and a new edition containing 110 volumes has been published in Tehran. Various volumes of the *Biḥār* have been translated into Persian, and the many excerpts, abridgments, and supplements in existence attest to the continuing influence of the work.

BIBLIOGRAPHY

The fullest account to date of al-Majlisī's life and works, with special emphasis on his *magnum opus,* is Karl-Heinz Pampus's *Die theologische Enzyklopädie Biḥār al-Anwār des Muḥammad Bāqir al-Maǧlisi, 1037–1110 AH = 1627–1699 AD.* (Bonn, 1970). There is a useful analysis of some aspects of al-Majlisī's theology on pages 93–95 of Said Amir Arjomand's "Religion, Political Action and Legitimate Domination in Shiʿite Iran: Fourteenth to Eighteenth Centuries A.D.," *European Journal of Sociology* 20 (1979): 59–109. Al-Majlisī's influence on Safavid policies is discussed in Laurence Lockhart's *The Fall of the Ṣafavī Dynasty and the Afghan Occupation of Persia* (Cambridge, 1958). Abdul-Hadi Hairi's "Madjlisī" in *The Encyclopaedia of Islam,* new ed. (Leiden, 1960–), contains a good bibliography. A highly competent rendition of selected passages from the *Biḥār* is included in *A Shīʿite Anthology,* edited and translated by William C. Chittick (Albany, N. Y., 1981).

ETAN KOHLBERG (1987)

MAKARIOS OF EGYPT (300–390), also known as the Presbyter and Makarios the Great; Christian ascetic and monastic leader. Known from childhood for his prudence and virtue, Makarios was characterized as a "child-old man," that is, a child in age and an old man in conduct. At the age of thirty he renounced the worldly life and went to the desert to become a monk. He repeatedly visited Antony of Egypt and was influenced both by his way of thinking and by his manner of life, which stressed flight from the world, austere asceticism, and constant struggle against Satan. In order to avoid the esteem and praise of others, Makarios went to Scete, in the remote part of the desert, south of Nitria. Because the inhospitality of the place made the ascetic life there difficult, only the most disciplined were able to endure it.

The reputation of Makarios as a saintly man, and his deeds, attracted many ascetics to Scete. In a short time, under his spiritual direction, the monastic center of Scete was enlarged and reorganized. The monks' work, their *ergocheiron* as it is called in monastic language, consisted of the preparation of baskets woven with straw cut from the marsh. They prayed at appointed hours of the day, and on Saturdays and Sundays they all gathered from the huts scattered around the church for the Divine Liturgy, which was usually celebrated by Makarios himself. Makarios had been ordained a priest at the age of forty, at which time he received the title of Mark the Presbyter. Once a day the monks ate a meal consisting of bread and vegetables, without oil, which was used only on Saturdays and Sundays. During the periods of the great fasts, their diet was more severe. Silence was regarded as one of the greater virtues.

During the more than sixty years that Makarios remained in the desert, he acquired the reputation of a great saint and wonder-worker. He was exiled for a short time to a small island in the Nile by the Arian bishop Lucius and died at the age of ninety. In the Orthodox church his feast day is January 10; in the Western church it is January 15.

The main works that come from the mouth, if not the hand, of Makarios are his *Forty-six Sayings,* included in *Gerontica* (narratives on the ascetical accomplishments of the Gerontes, or elders, of Scete). Gennadius of Marseilles mentions a letter of Makarios's that probably is the same as the first letter, *Ad filios Dei,* of the Latin collection. There is another short ascetical text of about two hundred lines, preserved in the Codex Jerusalemitus 113.

Some collections of homilies, discourses, and letters attributed to Makarios probably do not belong to him. Current research regards Asia Minor or Syria as their place of origin and the ascetic Symeon of Mesopotamia as their author. Preeminent among these is the collection of fifty homilies known as the *Spiritual Homilies.* However, the question of authorship of the *Spiritual Homilies* still remains open. Also attributed to Makarios are three other collections of various numbers of homilies; four letters (among which is the *Great Epistle*); seven treatises, or ascetical discourses; and two prayers, still used in the Greek Orthodox church.

In his writings Makarios presents the struggle of the faithful against evil, the world, and the passions. The believer can, with the help of divine grace, keep the senses of the soul clean so that they may be inundated by the divine light and become entirely light and spirit. Denial of the desires of the world, of material cares, and of earthly bonds is carried out so that one can receive the Holy Spirit and through the Spirit be enlightened and deified. Because of their mystical and ascetical character, Makarios's writings are highly esteemed, especially in the East. They exerted a great influence on the mystical theology of the Orthodox church, for example in the work of Gregory Palamas. Makarios's influence is also evident through the monastic figure and spiritual writer Evagrios of Pontus, his disciple.

BIBLIOGRAPHY

Davids, E. A. *Das Bild vom neuen Menschen.* Salzburg, 1968.

Desprez, V. *Pseudo-Macarie: Œuvres spirituelles,* vol. 1. *Sources chrétiennes,* vol. 275. Paris, 1980.

Dörries, Hermann. *Symeon von Mesopotamien: Die Überlieferung der messalianischen "Makarios" Schriften.* Leipzig, 1941.

Jaeger, Werner. *Two Rediscovered Works of Ancient Christian Literature: Gregory of Nyssa and Macarius.* Leiden, 1954. See pages 233–301. Includes the Great Epistle.

Makarios. *Patrologia Graeca,* edited by J.-P. Migne, vol. 34. Paris, 1860. Includes his letter *Ad filios Dei.*

Makarios. *Die 50 geistlichen Homilien des Makarios.* Edited by Hermann Dörries, Erich Klostermann, and Matthias Kroeger. Berlin, 1964.

THEODORE ZISSIS (1987)
Translated from Greek by Philip M. McGhee

MALALASEKERA, G. P. (1899–1973), Buddhist scholar, founder of the World Fellowship of Buddhists, and a dominant figure in the cultural life of Ceylon (now Sri Lanka). Born in Panadura, the son of a prosperous family, Gunapala Piyasena Malalasekera grew up in a scholarly atmosphere. As a schoolboy he was tutored in the Sinhala, Sanskrit, and Pali classics by his father, an Ayurvedic physician. During his formative years, Malalasekera was also deeply influenced by learned monks whom he came to know through his father, and he was inspired by men like Anagārika Dharmapāla (1864–1933), a leader in the Buddhist revivalist movement that had arisen in the age of British colonial repression of nationalistic aims and aspirations.

Preparing to follow in his father's footsteps, Malalasekera entered the Medical College in Colombo in 1917, but he had to abandon his medical studies the following year, upon his father's untimely death. Via external registration at the University of London, he then turned to the study of Western classics, graduating with first-class honors in 1919. In 1921 he joined the premier Buddhist school in Colombo, Ānanda College, as a teacher, and in ensuing years he became first its vice-principal and then its acting principal.

Upon the return of Ānanda's principal, Patrick de Silva Kularatne (1893–1976), Malalasekera was profoundly influenced by him in matters both educational and nationalistic. He went abroad for postgraduate studies at the University of London and obtained both the M.A. and the Ph.D. degrees in 1925. On his return home in 1926 he was appointed principal of Nālandā Vidyālaya, the new sister school of Ānanda, and within a year developed it to some stature. He was then appointed lecturer in Sinhala, Sanskrit, and Pali at University College, Colombo, and for most of the next three decades he pursued a brilliant academic career. He held the chair of Pali and Buddhist studies from the establishment of the University of Ceylon in 1942 until his resignation in 1959. As professor and dean for the greater part of this period, which saw the rapid expansion of the Faculty of Oriental Studies, he was a highly respected member of the academic community.

In 1957 Malalasekera was appointed ambassador to the Soviet Union, and he represented Ceylon at the ambassadorial level in Canada, the United Nations, and the United Kingdom until 1967, when he was called home to chair the National Council of Higher Education, a post in which he served with distinction for five years. Despite the demands of diplomatic assignments and administrative responsibilities, his scholarly activities were undiminished.

Malalasekera's major works include *The Pali Literature of Ceylon* (London, 1928); *Vaṃsatthappakāsinī* (London, 1935), a critical edition of the exegesis on the *Mahāvaṃsa* (Great Chronicle of Sri Lanka); the *Extended Mahāvaṃsa* (Colombo, 1937); *The Dictionary of Pali Proper Names* (London, 1937); and *An English-Sinhalese Dictionary* (Colombo, 1948). He wrote a large number of other scholarly books and articles, and he contributed extensively to popular journals both in Ceylon and abroad. His highest intellectual achievement, however, was the work he did on the *Encyclopaedia of Buddhism,* whose completion he, as editor in chief, did not live to see. This undertaking, sponsored by the government of Ceylon in commemoration of twenty-five hundred years of Buddhism, was commenced in 1956 and is still in progress. As a contribution to Buddhist learning, it will stand as a monument to Malalasekera's love of scholarship and great perseverance as a student of the divers aspects of Buddhist thought, culture, and civilization.

Throughout his life, Malalasekera participated in various spheres of interest in Ceylon, religious and social, cultural and intellectual. At government level his advice was sought in many fields and was acceptable to people of all shades of political opinion, for he discreetly steered clear of party politics. He stood for equity and social justice, always taking up the cause of the underprivileged. As a social worker, he traveled the country at his own expense and addressed gatherings large and small. He was frequently heard over Radio Ceylon. His was a receptive mind, and he was noted for his ability to expound with precision and clarity on topics from fine arts and humanities to social sciences and current affairs. As a religious leader, for twenty-five years Malalasekera was president of the All-Ceylon Buddhist Congress (ACBC), an important platform for shaping public opinion, and he was principally responsible for the founding, in May 1950, of the World Fellowship of Buddhists, modeled largely after the ACBC.

Until that time, the voice of the Buddhist population, which forms more than a fifth of the human race, had not been heard, nor its views adequately expressed, nor its aspirations respected in world assemblies. Communication among Buddhists of various lands had been limited, and Buddhists the world over had had no forum to air their grievances or to redress injustices. The differences between the Mahāyāna and Theravāda schools had led to disunity. It was Malalasekera's indefatigable efforts that brought them together. As a sequel to a resolution passed at the twenty-eighth session of the ACBC in 1947, a resolution was passed at a conference of world Buddhist leaders held in 1950 in the historic Temple of the Tooth, in Kandy, to establish the World Fellowship of Buddhists. Malalasekera was founder-president from 1950 to 1958. During his lifetime it grew into a dynamic organization, expressing Buddhist opinion and unifying Buddhists under the six-hued flag bearing the emblem of the *dharmacakra,* the Wheel of the Law, as a symbol of peace.

BIBLIOGRAPHY

Dharmabandhu, T. S. *Siṃhala vīrayō.* Colombo, 1949. In Sinhala.

Guruge, Ananda, ed. *Return to Righteousness: A Collection of Speeches, Essays and Letters of the Anagarika Dharmapala.* Colombo, 1965.

Hewage, L. G., et al., eds. *All Ceylon Buddhist Congress: Malalasēkara anusmaraṇa saṅgrahaya.* Colombo, 1973. In Sinhala.

Wijesekera, O. H. de A., ed. *Malalasekera Commemoration Volume.* Colombo, 1976.

Wijewardena, Don Charles. *The Revolt in the Temple.* Colombo, 1953.

New Sources

Freiberger, Oliver. "The Meeting of Traditions: Inter-Buddhist and Inter-Religious Relations in the West." *Journal of Global Buddhism* 2 (2001).

N. A. JAYAWICKRAMA (1987)
Revised Bibliography

MALBIM, acronym (MaLBIM) of Me'ir Loeb ben Yeḥi'el Mikha'el (1809–1879), European rabbi and exegete. Born in Volhynia, Russia, Malbim was chief rabbi of Romania from 1858 to 1864, having earlier served as rabbi to a number of communities in eastern Europe.

Malbim's life coincided with the struggle of European Jewry to achieve political rights. Some Jews, considering that the Judaism of the ghetto impeded their acceptance by their Christian neighbors, drifted away from Judaism. Others, who called themselves reformers, questioned the binding authority of the oral law, much of which seemed to them incompatible with the spirit of their age and therefore an impediment to emancipation. Malbim, a passionate and unyielding exponent of traditional Judaism, challenged the new Reform movement in his sermons and in his major work, a multivolume commentary on the entire Hebrew Bible. *Ha-Torah ve-ha-mitsvah,* his commentary on the Pentateuch, and *Miqra'ei qodesh,* his commentary on the Prophets and Hagiographa, were published between 1845 and 1876. In them, Malbim undertook to demonstrate that both the written law and the oral law form a unity, each component of which can be understood only through the other, and that, since the entire corpus of law and lore contained in the Talmud and Midrash had been revealed at Sinai together with the written law, no provision of either could be abrogated or amended. His stern refusal to compromise his convictions brought him into repeated conflict with the leaders of the communities he served, and his rabbinate was not a happy one.

Malbim introduces his commentary to *Leviticus* with a detailed analysis of 613 features of Hebrew lexicography, grammar, and biblical style that he insists had been forgotten by the medieval Jewish exegetes. He denies, for example, that true synonyms are to be found in the Hebrew Bible. Instead, an apparent synonym really introduces a new thought that demands its own exposition. Every word in scripture is the only word that could have been used in that particular context, and every verse conveys its own sublime meaning, though often that lofty message can be fathomed only by reference to Talmud, Midrash, and the literature of the Jewish mystics.

Because of his vigorous advocacy of traditional Judaism, Malbim remains a revered figure in Orthodox Jewish circles. Unfortunately, he is little known to the world of biblical scholarship because few of his writings have been published in English.

BIBLIOGRAPHY

Malbim's commentary on the Hebrew Bible has been republished in four volumes in the series "Otsar ha-perushim" (Jerusalem, 1956–1957). Volume 1, on *Genesis,* has been translated into English by Zvi Faier in two volumes (Jerusalem, 1978–1979). M. M. Yoshor has written a biography in Hebrew, *Ha-ga'on Malbim* (Jerusalem, 1976). Yehoshua Horowitz's brief article on Malbim in the *Encyclopaedia Judaica* (Jerusalem, 1971) is the best source of information on Malbim in English.

A. STANLEY DREYFUS (1987)

MALCOLM X (1925–1965) was an American Black Muslim leader, born Malcolm Little on May 19, 1925, in Omaha, Nebraska. His father, the Reverend Earl Little, a follower of Marcus Garvey and a Baptist minister, died when Malcolm was six years old, and his mother, the sole support of nine children, was later committed to an insane asylum. Malcolm attended school in East Lansing, Michigan, dropped out at the eighth grade, and then moved to live with an older sister in the Roxbury section of Boston. There he became involved in petty criminal activities. As an unemployed street hustler and the leader of an interracial gang of thieves in Roxbury, and later in Harlem, he was known as "Detroit Red" for the reddish tinge of his hair. During his prison years (1946–1952), he underwent the first of his two conversion experiences when he converted to the Nation of Islam led by Elijah Muhammad. Following the tradition of the Nation of Islam, he replaced his surname with an *X,* symbolizing what he had been and what he had become: "Ex-smoker. Ex-drinker. Ex-Christian. Ex-slave."

An articulate public speaker, charismatic personality, and indefatigable organizer, Malcolm X expressed the rage and anger of the black masses during the major phase of the civil rights movement from 1956 to 1965. He organized Muslim temples throughout the country and founded the newspaper *Muhammad Speaks* in the basement of his home. He articulated the Nation of Islam's beliefs in racial separation and rose rapidly through the ranks to become minister of Boston Temple No. 11 and was later rewarded with the post of minister of Temple No. 7 in Harlem, the largest and most prestigious temple of the Nation of Islam after the Chicago headquarters. Recognizing Malcolm's talents and abilities, Elijah Muhammad also named him "national representative" of the Nation of Islam, second in rank to Elijah Muhammad himself.

In 1963, after his public comments on President John F. Kennedy's assassination, Malcolm X was ordered by Elijah Muhammad to undergo a period of silence, an order that reflected the deep tensions and disputes among Black Muslim leaders. In March 1964, Malcolm left the Nation of Islam and founded his own Muslim Mosque, Inc. During his pilgrimage to Mecca that same year, he experienced a second conversion, embraced the orthodox universal brotherhood of Sunnī Islam, and adopted the Muslim name el-Hajj Malik el-Shabazz. He then renounced the separatist beliefs of the Nation of Islam. In 1965, he founded the Organization for Afro-American Unity as a political vehicle to internationalize the plight of black Americans, to make common cause with Third World nations, and to move from civil rights to human rights. On February 21, 1965, Malcolm X was assassinated while delivering a lecture at the Audubon Ballroom in Harlem. His martyrdom, ideas, and speeches contributed to the development of black nationalist ideology and the black power movement in the late 1960s in the United States.

SEE ALSO Elijah Muhammad.

BIBLIOGRAPHY

Breitman, George, ed. *Malcolm X Speaks.* New York, 1965. A collection of Malcolm X's speeches.

Goldman, Peter. *The Death and Life of Malcolm X.* New York, 1973. Focuses on the last year of Malcolm X's life and on the events, personalities, and controversies surrounding his assassination.

Lincoln, C. Eric. *The Black Muslims in America.* Boston, 1961. Remains the best historical overview of the development of the Nation of Islam under the leadership of Elijah Muhammad and Malcolm X.

Malcolm X, with the assistance of Alex Haley. *The Autobiography of Malcolm X.* New York, 1965. Still the best source of insights regarding Malcolm X's life and the development of his views, including his conversion experiences and the reasons for his dispute with other Black Muslim leaders.

Mamiya, Lawrence H. "From Black Muslim to Bilalian: The Evolution of a Movement." *Journal for the Scientific Study of Religion* 21 (June 1982): 138–152. Examines Malcolm X's influence on the leaders of the major schismatic groups in the Black Muslim movement—Warith D. Muhammad and Louis Farrakhan—and their divergent directions.

LAWRENCE H. MAMIYA (1987)

MĀLIK IBN ANAS (d. 795), was a renowned Muslim jurist and the eponymous founder of the Mālikī school. Mālik was born sometime between 708 and 715 in Medina, where he spent most of his life and where he died. Biographical tradition records that for a while he was a professional singer, but because he was ugly, his mother advised him to give up that career. Instead, he became, like an uncle and a grandfather before him, a religious scholar. Mālik studied with a number of well-known scholars of Medina and then, as his fame spread, acquired many pupils of his own.

In 762 he lent the weight of his reputation to an Alid revolt against the Abbasid caliph al-Manṣūr. When that failed, he was punished by the governor of Medina. But his prestige did not suffer, and he regained royal favor. The next three caliphs, al-Mahdi, al-Hadi, and Hārūn al-Rashīd, were personally interested in his work, and Hārūn, while on a pilgrimage in the last year of Mālik's life, even attended one of his lectures. The *Fihrist* of Ibn al-Nadim (composed 987) reports that Mālik addressed a treatise on the land tax to Hārūn, a counterpart to the famous *Kitāb al-kharaj* of the Iraqi jurist Abū Yūsuf (d. 798), but some scholars consider this apocryphal. After spending his entire life in Medina, Mālik died in 795 and was buried there in al-Baqiʿ Cemetery.

The two main sources for Mālik's legal scholarship are his *Kitāb al-muwatta'* (Book of the smoothed path) and the *Mudawwana* (The recorded book) of Sahnun (d. 854), a student of Mālik's student Ibn al-Qasim (d. 806). The textual histories of both works are complex, and Norman Calder has suggested that neither was an "authored text" but came into their present forms in about 890 and 864, respectively. Before this they existed only as open texts belonging to a semi-oral school tradition. Calder's datings have been pushed earlier by subsequent scholarship based on extant manuscripts, but the *Muwatta'* especially seems nevertheless to have been subject to organic growth and redaction. It existed in fifteen known recensions, of which eight have been preserved at least partially. The most influential of these is the "Vulgate" of Yahya ibn Yahya al-Laythi (d. 848); the recensions of al-Shaybani (d. 805) and Ibn Wahb (d. 812) depart from that recension considerably, others somewhat less. Jonathan Brockopp argues on the basis of fragments of *al-Mukhtasar al-kabir fi al-fiqh* by Abd Allah ibn Abd al-Hakam that this text and the *Muwatta'* probably preserve a core of authentic juridical dicta which may be attributed reliably to Mālik himself.

Mālik's intellectual activity belongs to the period of Islamic jurisprudence when the explicit legislative legacy provided by the Qurʾān and the Prophet Muḥammad was proving insufficiently complete for the needs of the rulers of the expanding empire, and they were turning for further guidance to religious specialists such as Mālik. It became the task of these early jurists to ensure the Islamic character of public administration as well as to suggest ways in which individual Muslims could lead more pious lives. Before Mālik's time, legal literature consisted of compendia of *ḥadīth* (traditions)—biographical reports of the actions and statements of the Prophet and his contemporaries that were considered authoritative guidelines for behavior—and compendia of the decisions of authoritative scholars on various theoretical and practical issues. Mālik's achievement was to combine these two sources of authority. Mālik set forth, drawing on the *ḥadīth,* the legal practices that had evolved in Medina. He at times based legal doctrines on the actual practice *(ʿamal)* of Medina, at times appealed to the consensus among the authoritis of Medina, and at times drew on sound opinion (*raʿy*) or consideration of what is best (*istihsan*). The subsequent Mālikī tradition emphasized the first two principles but downplayed that latter two. Unlike later jurists, Malik does not restrict *ḥadīth* or the concept of *sunnah* (revered practice) to the Prophet Muḥammad alone. Despite the inconsistencies of his own procedure, the use of *ḥadīth* to support existing legal opinion came to play a vital role in the subsequent systematization of Islamic legal thinking and in the codification of Islamic law.

The *Muwatta'* is arranged in chapters that deal with the ritual and legal concerns of the Muslim community, and it represents the accepted legal practice of Medina as it was taught by Mālik and his contemporaries. The enduring and widespread influence of the *Muwatta'* may in part be due to the middle-of-the-road quality of the Medinese doctrine it presents but should be attributed even more to the activities and geographical distribution of successive generations of Mālik's pupils, who gradually came to think of themselves as followers of a distinctive school. Soon after Mālik's death, Fustat in Egypt became a major center for the elaboration of Mālikī legal doctrine; Qayrawan in Tunisia and Córdoba in Spain quickly followed. An eastern branch of the Mālikī school boasted considerable influence in Baghdad in the late ninth century and the tenth century but dwindled thereafter.

The Mālikī school still predominates in North Africa and in the other Muslim communities of Africa.

BIBLIOGRAPHY

Abbott, Nabia. *Studies in Arabic Literary Papyri,* vol. 2: *Qur'ānic Commentary and Tradition.* Chicago, 1967. A valuable study of early Muslim scholarly activity.

Brockopp, Jonathan E. *Early Māikī Law: Ibn Abd al-Hakam and His Major Compendium of Jurisprudence.* Leiden, Netherlands, 2000. Translation and study of manuscript fragments of an early-ninth-century compendium of Mālikī law found in Qairawan.

Calder, Norman. *Studies in Early Muslim Jurisprudence.* Oxford, 1993. Revisionist work suggesting that many of the seminal works of Islamic law, including the *Muwatta',* are the product of organic growth and revision and cannot be dated as early as supposed.

Dutton, Yasin. *The Origins of Islamic Law: The Qur'an, the Muwatta' and Madinan 'Amal.* Surrey, U.K., 1999. Argues along traditional lines that the *Muwatta'* preserves authentic legal material going back to the nascent Muslim community.

Goldziher, Ignácz. *Muslim Studies,* vol. 2. Edited by S. M. Stern, translated by Stern and C. R. Barber. Chicago, 1973. The fundamental work on the development of *ḥadīth* in Islamic thought.

Muranyi, Miklos. *Materialien zur malikitischen Rechtsliteratur.* Wiesbaden, Germany, 1984.

Muranyi, Miklos. *Ein altes Fragment medinensischer Jurisprudenz aus Qairawan: Aus dem Kitab al-Hagg des 'Abd al-'Aziz b. 'Abd Allah b. Abi Salama al-Magisun (st. 164/780–81).* Stuttgart, Germany, 1985.

Muranyi, Miklos. *'Abd Allah b. Wahb (125/743–197/812): Leben und Werk: al-Muwatta', Kitab al-Muharaba.* Wiesbaden, Germany, 1992.

Muranyi, Miklos. *Beiträge zur Geschichte der Hadit- und Rechtsgelehrsamkeit der Malikiyya in Nordafrika bis zum 5. Jh. d.H.: Bio-bibliographische Notizen aus der Moscheebibliothek von Qairawan.* Wiesbaden, Germany, 1997.

Muranyi, Miklos. *Die Rechtsbücher des Qairawaners Sahnun B. Sa'id: Entstehungsgeschichte und Werküberlieferung.* Stuttgart, Germany, 1999. Muranyi's studies, based primarily on early manuscripts extant in Qairawan (Tunisia), give the fullest and most exact and authoritative account of the transmission of Malik's teachings and legal doctrines.

Schacht, Joseph. *An Introduction to Islamic Law.* Oxford, 1964. Anauthoritative general introduction with a valuable bibliography.

SUSAN A. SPECTORSKY (1987)
DEVIN J. STEWART (2005)

MALINOWSKI, BRONISLAW

MALINOWSKI, BRONISLAW (1884–1942), Polish-English social anthropologist. Born into an educated and aristocratic family, Bronislaw Kasper Malinowski received his Ph.D. in physics and mathematics from the Jagiellonian University of his native Cracow in 1908. Switching from the natural sciences to the human sciences, he entered the London School of Economics in 1910 and received a D.Sc. in 1916. He later traced his decision to study anthropology to his reading of James G. Frazer's *The Golden Bough.* The tribute was apt, for Malinowski became the leading British anthropologist of the generation following Frazer's, but also ironic, for no one did more to repudiate Frazer's method.

Malinowski's first contact with primitive society came during five months among the Mailu of Toulon Island off the southern coast of New Guinea in 1914–1915. In June 1915 he began the first of two extended periods of observation on the Trobriand Islands, to the east of New Guinea. Although colored by personal stress and ambivalence toward the natives, his twenty-one months in the Trobriands shaped his entire career. He became the apostle and exemplar of a new standard of anthropological fieldwork: ethnography must rely, he believed, on the participation of the ethnographer in the society under observation, rather than on the reports of travelers, missionaries, and hasty surveys. His fieldwork completed, Malinowski married Elsie Masson, daughter of a Melbourne chemistry professor. He began teaching at the London School of Economics after completing the manuscript of *Argonauts of the Western Pacific* (1922), the first of his many books on the Trobriands. In 1927 he became the first professor of anthropology at the University of London.

Malinowski's approach to anthropology was psychological, but not psychoanalytic. His most celebrated work among nonspecialists was probably *Sex and Repression in Savage Society* (1927), in which he denies Sigmund Freud's claim that the Oedipus complex is universal. In this book Malinowski argues that among the Trobriand Islanders matrilineal descent (reinforced by ignorance of physiological paternity) diverted a boy's hostility from his father to the distant authority figure of his maternal uncle. Trobriand men repressed sexual desire for their sisters, not their mothers. Malinowski rejects Freud's claim in *Totem and Taboo* (1913) that an original Oedipal "crime" had established human culture: Freud's Lamarckian group psychology is simply wrong, Malinowski argues, and any other means of perpetuating the memory of the act requires the preexistence of culture.

Malinowski's attack on Freud reflected no personal reluctance to generalize; he had none of the methodological caution of his American contemporary Franz Boas. Malinowski's generalizations were rarely the product of systematic cross-cultural comparison: having rejected the Victorians' reliance on written sources, he went to the other extreme and generalized from his own intensive but necessarily limited fieldwork. His theory—"functionalism"—stressed the role of human culture in satisfying a hierarchy of human needs, consisting of those that are basic (i.e., biological), derived (i.e., cultural or social), and integrative (i.e., normative). He attacked the evolutionists' concept of "survivals" and the diffusionists' concept of "culture complexes," with their implications that cultures are heterogeneous accumulations of sometimes useless objects and institutions. While his American contemporaries, notably Ruth Benedict, saw cultural unity in terms of a culture's dominant style or personality, he saw it in the fulfillment of individual and group needs. In part because of Malinowski's own work, evolutionism and diffusionism were both in retreat by the 1930s. As they receded from view, functionalism lost much of its original force, and after his death Malinowski the ethnographer was praised above Malinowski the theorist.

Malinowski never wrote an account of Trobriand culture as a whole; he studied individual institutions in their social settings. The attention he paid to Trobriand economics and sex was in line with the premises of functional theory. His book *Argonauts of the Western Pacific* describes the complex and highly ritualized interisland trade known as *kula; The Sexual Life of Savages* (1929) deals with sex and the family; and *Coral Gardens and Their Magic* (1935) discusses Trobriand agriculture. In all these works Malinowski deemphasizes the "primitive" nature of Trobriand life by stressing the rational organization of economic life and focusing on the nuclear family rather than on the segmentary kinship system.

Malinowski also applied functional analysis to less obviously useful activities. In *Myth in Primitive Psychology* (1926), he argues that myths are neither explanations of natural phenomena nor poetry; instead, they are validations of the social order. The mythic "charter" strengthens tradition by appealing to the design and experience of a supernatural past. Myths of origin, for example, explain the relative superiority and inferiority of different Trobriand clans. Malinowski's explanation of magic denies both Lucien Lévy-Bruhl's claim that primitive thought is "prelogical" and Frazer's theory of an evolutionary progression from magic to religion to science. In "Magic, Science and Religion," an essay in *Science, Religion and Reality*, edited by Joseph Needham (London, 1925), Malinowski argues that magic provides psychological encouragement and a rationale for group cooperation in those activities where primitives lack the knowledge or technical ability to ensure success. Magic is a supplement to, not a substitute for, practical activity.

Malinowski's analysis of religion was not only less original but also less successful than his treatments of myth and magic. He denied Émile Durkheim's claim that the object of worship is society itself, although conceding that religion is socially organized. Religion is man's consolation in the face of tragedy and uncertainty, not a means of social cohesion. It can be distinguished from magic by the absence of an external goal, in that worship is an end in itself. Malinowski never resolved the tension between his individualistic analysis of religious motivation and his sociological analysis of religious practice. The absence of worship on the Trobriand Islands may have denied him the stimulus necessary for a more sustained inquiry.

Elsie Malinowski died in 1935, after a long illness. At the end of 1938, Malinowski left London for an American sabbatical; rather than return to Europe during World War II, he was for three years a visiting professor at Yale University. In 1940 he married Valetta Swann, an artist. During the summers of 1940 and 1941 he went into the field again to study Mexican peasant markets in conjunction with a young Mexican ethnologist, Julio de la Fuente. In early 1942 he accepted Yale's offer of a permanent professorship effective that October. He never took up the appointment; his death of a heart attack on May 16, 1942, caught him in the midst of new beginnings. Doubly an émigré, he lost the chance to play in America the commanding role he had held in British social science between the wars.

Bibliography

A full list of Malinowski's works appears in the essential secondary work, *Man and Culture; An Evaluation of the Work of Bronislaw Malinowski*, edited by Raymond Firth (London, 1957). Malinowski's *A Diary in the Strict Sense of the Term* (New York, 1967) covers his Mailu research and his second stay in the Trobriands. Malinowski's and Julio de la Fuente's *Malinowski in Mexico: The Economics of a Mexican Market System*, edited by Susan Drucker-Brown (London, 1982), is the result of his last fieldwork. *The Ethnography of Malinowski: The Trobriand Islands, 1915–18*, edited by Michael W. Young (London, 1979) is a convenient reader, and its editorial notes cite recent work on both Malinowski and the Trobriands. The first comprehensive challenge to *Sex and Repression* is Melford E. Spiro's *Oedipus in the Trobriands* (Chicago, 1982).

New Sources

Ellen, R. F. *Malinowski between Two Worlds: The Polish Roots of an Anthropological Tradition*. Cambridge U.K.; New York, 1988.

Gonzalez, Roberto J. "Between Two Poles: Bronislaw Malinowski, Ludwik Fleck, and the Anthropology of Science." *Current Anthropology* 36, no. 5 (1995): 177–204.

Stocking, George W. *Malinowski, Rivers, Benedict, and Others: Essays on Culture and Personality*. Madison, Wis., 1986.

Strenski, Ivan. *Malinowski and the Work of Myth*. Princeton, N.J., 1992.

Young, Michael W. "Malinowski and the Function of Culture." In *Creating Culture: Profiles in the Study of Culture*, edited by Diane J. Austin-Broos, pp. 124–140. Sydney, 1987.

MICHAEL A. BAENEN (1987)
Revised Bibliography

MAMI WATA (Water as Mother) is a pidgin designation for a class of African water divinities and spirits or, occasionally, for the primordial divinities collectively. Mami Wata is a complex transcultural phenomenon composed of elements from widely disparate places and traditions that coalesced on the continent probably by the end of the nineteenth century. Shrines to Mami Wata are frequently found in coastal, riverine, or lacustrine areas of the continent. The roots of Mami Wata began with the traditional water divinities that were elaborated by the fifteenth century to include European influences, including the mermaid-man that Africans adopted as a new representation of the water divinities. Light skin and non-African features (markers of the spirit realm as well as of ethnicity), sunglasses, powder, and perfume also became familiar in representations of Mami Wata. Africans transplanted by slavery to Surinam in the seventeenth century discovered there a tradition about a riverine water divinity Watra Mamma, who in the eighteenth and nineteenth centuries was credited with helping slaves secure their liberation. The idea of water as mother was common to many cultures despite the difference in names ascribed to the divinity. These traditions were brought back to Africa in the nineteenth century, probably by Kru sailors, and Watra Mamma was identified in peoples' minds with local water divinities. The conflation of various traditions of water divinities in nineteenth-century West Africa created Mami Wata.

Devotees established shrines for Mami Wata decorated with objects reminiscent of the various traditions. Boats reminiscent of those the slaves on Surinam used to escape captivity became familiar objects at Mami Wata shrines. A nineteenth-century German chromolith of a female snake charmer with rich black hair inspired the additional representation of Mami Wata as a dark-skinned snake charmer dressed in exotic clothing. By the early twentieth century representations of Hindu divinities and cultic practices brought to the continent by traders from India also found a place in Mami Wata representations and praxis. African devotees acknowledge icons of divinity, such as mermaids and snake charmers, as symbolic revelations of the transcendent, and they are open to these new manifestations of the divine. At the same time they recognize that the spirits they represent are traditional. So despite the obvious layering of multiple cultural traditions in Mami Wata representations, she or he is generally not considered a new divinity or spirit by Africans.

Like other African water divinities known for their dispositional fluidity, Mami Wata can favor devotees with riches of all kinds, including spiritual wisdom, healing and divinatory powers, and beauty and wealth. Or she or he can create natural disasters and reverse traditional social expectations. Mami Wata is consulted for a variety of human concerns and is considered to be well suited to dealing with the problems of modernity introduced by colonialism and postcolonialism. Mami Wata's power is considered so great that she or he is petitioned by people from all classes, stations in life, and religious traditions who seek physical, spiritual, social, and economic assistance.

Although Mami Wata evolved from multiple cultural traditions, the divinity's praxis is culture specific. African communities situate Mami Wata in an existing community of divinities in which she or he has a particular place and genealogy. Mami Wata is normally worshipped traditionally, with invocations, sacrifices, and dances as other divinities are honored, but she or he is also honored with specific dance forms, rhythms, and rituals.

The gender system of a culture also affects the conceptualization of Mami Wata. Mami Wata can be represented as either female or male; indeed it would be unusual for an African divinity not to have a counterpart of the opposite gender. The male-gendered representation of Mami Wata is sometimes called Papa Wata. In some communities, the male Mami Wata is said to marry his female devotees and the female Mami Wata to marry her male devotees.

The exercise of priesthood by a Mami Wata priest (who is also a chief) in one patrilineal culture reflects the gendered role designated for males in his society. He has a spousal relationship to a female Mami Wata but one that does not include the experience of female receptivity through possession. He nourishes his community through animal and other sacrifices to Mami Wata and the divinities. In return he receives power from Mami Wata to protect and sustain his community through healing and to provide guidance through divination. In a matrilineal culture with a dual-gender system and a matrilocal or duolocal residence pattern, Mami Wata mermaid representations are gendered not by sexual characteristics but by the traditional symbols of a pot for the female and a fish for the male. A Mami Wata priestess in this community acts as a vessel to receive the divinity through possession, thus producing sustenance for the community. She constructs her election by Mami Wata as a commitment to a matrilineage in which the divinity is her mother and exercises control over her life, rather than as a marriage relationship. Her descriptions of Mami Wata's home under the sea resemble those of the homes of important women in her community. She does not maintain her own shrine for Mami Wata; instead, she goes to the shrines and festivals where she is invited, and in a state of possession, she provides healing remedies and inspired guidance for the community.

Mami Wata scholarship has explored the origins and representations of Mami Wata and its devotional service, and newer studies have focused on Mami Wata's role and function in particular cultures as a member of the community of divinities who protect and guide the community. At the level of praxis, the global interconnections characteristic of Mami Wata's origins continue, as Mami Wata devotional service is spread outside of Africa by both Africans and non-Africans. Mami Wata has a particular appeal for diasporic African people who seek to reclaim their roots and to identify with the power of their ancestral traditions, but non-Africans are also drawn to this powerful Water Mother. It is impossible to predict how Mami Wata traditions, representations, and praxis will change in response to this global reappropriation. But as long as Mami Wata continues to be efficacious, humans will find Mami Wata a source of solace and guidance.

See Also African Religions, overview article.

Bibliography

Caulder, Sharon. *Mark of Voodoo: Awakening to My African Spiritual Heritage.* St. Paul, Minn., 2002.

Drewal, Henry J. "Interpretation, Invention, and Representation in the Worship of Mami Wata." In *Performance in Contemporary African Arts,* edited by Ruth M. Stone, pp. 101–139. Bloomington, Ind., 1988.

Drewal, Henry J. "Mami Wata Shrines: Exotica and the Construction of Self." In *African Material Culture,* edited by Mary Jo Arnoldi, Christraud Geary, and Kris L. Hardin, pp. 308–333. Bloomington, Ind., 1996.

Gore, Charles, and Joseph Nevadomsky. "Practice and Agency in Mammy Wata Worship in Southern Nigeria." In *African Arts* 30, no. 2 (1997): 60–69, 95.

Isichei, Elizabeth. *Voices of the Poor in Africa.* Rochester, N.Y., 2002.

Opoku, Kofi Asare, and Kathleen O'Brien Wicker. "Abidjan Mami Water Festival 1994." *Religious Studies News* (November 1994): 18–19.

Rosenthal, Judy. *Posession, Ecstasy, and Law in Ewe Voodoo.* Charlottesville, Va., 1998.

Wicker, Kathleen O'Brien. "Mami Water in African Religion and Spirituality." In *African Spirituality: Forms, Meanings and Expressions,* edited by Jacob K. Olupona, pp. 198–222. New York, 2000.

KATHLEEN O'BRIEN WICKER (2005)

MAN SEE MASCULINE SACRALITY

MANA.

MANA. A generic Polynesian term for self-effecting or self-transcending efficacy ("power") that is at once personal and impersonal, sacred and secular, contained and containing. In scholarly usage the term exemplifies a vogue, commonplace in the "evolutionist" and "diffusionist" phases of anthropological speculation, for appropriating exotic terminologies and making universalist claims upon them. *Mana* belongs to a small set of anthropological "markers" for concepts that are very difficult to put into words. Some of the others include the Siouan *wakan,* Iroquois *orenda,* Aztec *nagual,* and Arabic *baraka.*

If it takes a certain amount of power even to comprehend what *power* itself might be, then terms of this sort provide an explicit ethnographic contextualization for a sense of power or empowerment that is wellnigh universal. *Mana* is not merely "power," in the sense of an efficient causality ("energy," "skill," "artisanship") necessary to effect the felicituous outcome of some human task or intention, but rather an exponential (power times power) or second-order derivative of the potency at issue. Electricity, one might say, *has mana,* but the invention of electricity *is mana.* So the Maori of New Zealand, who often use electricity or electrical current as an explanatory analogy for *mana* (for example, one may generate it, apply it, use it, or lose it) would have to face the charge that although electrical energy may be bought or sold (or at least rented) *mana* itself is nonnegotiable. One cannot buy it or sell it, or take currency for its use, and its only direct analogue in the realm of purchase and exchange would be those priceless "heirloom" valuables that are never circulated.

Hence, although one may specify *kinds* of *mana* according to the requirements of certain tasks, such as the *mana* of woodcarving, of curing, or of deep-sea navigation, *mana* itself is not specific or specifiable in that way. It is not overspecific but *underspecific,* like the role of the denominator in a fraction, determining a quotient. John Keats might well have had Shakespeare's *mana* in mind when he spoke of the Bard's talent as *negative capability,* "that is, when a man is capable of being in uncertainties, mysteries, doubts, without any irritable reaching after fact and reason."

The *mana* of an American president would have less to do with the job description, the vote count in the election, or the fact of being an elected representative of the people than with personal qualities over and above the demands of the office. So the determination and rhetorical skill of an Abraham Lincoln, the feckless bravado of a Theodore Roosevelt, or the social standing and charisma of a John F. Kennedy would be particular to the *mana* of those individuals. A woman president might add "gender" to that list, provided she were the first to be elected. The presidency, in no uncertain terms, *has mana,* but the personality of the president, as a unique reinvention of the office, *is mana.*

Remarkably, then, a truly omnipotent deity, unless it could transcend itself like the Norse Odin, might have all the power in the universe but no *mana.* Hence the need for the mediating figure, the prophet, savior, demiurge, the president who is *answerable* to God but not divine, to serve as a common denominator of divine immanence, dividing it into measurable components of efficacy. Conversely, possessors of heroic *mana,* like Hercules and Perseus, make the opposite trade-off, losing earthly potency when elevated to the status of constellations, mere "superstars" of the night sky.

Imagine, then, the *mana* of the black hole, which exhausts the empirical criteria for existence to become, as astronomers have put it, "the most potent source of energy in the known cosmos." "You do not *play* with *mana,*" the Maori might want to add, "except that it plays with you." This feature of the concept, its agency in subject-object transformation, may be the secret of ancient Maori sorcery training. A story tells of the veteran Maori sorcerer who calls his young apprentice to him and tells him he must use all the techniques and self-discipline he has learned to kill his own mother. Appalled at the very thought of this, the apprentice has a major crisis, and then marshalls his thoughts and his feelings and eventually accomplishes the deed. Morally demolished, but full of pride, he returns to his mentor to ask whether he has now truly become a sorcerer. "Almost," says the veteran, "but not quite. Now you must kill *me.*" As a *legacy, mana* is made of very stern stuff.

To what extent can *mana* be moral? To the extent that the morality in question has *mana.* Otherwise it becomes a superficial and empty category, like those "politically correct" agendas and protocols of the late twentieth century that were either coldly indifferent to, or cruelly patronizing of, the "minorities" they pretended to justify. *Mana* has no pathos, and no false empathy either.

Mana is the most practical and "natural," and the least idealistic or "supernatural," force in the world. It could only be called "magical" or "mystical" in cases when it does not work (for then it is not *mana* either), and someone is obliged to make apologies or excuses for it. Mana never apologizes; the Maori apprentice in the story becomes unimpeachable (not "innocent") by killing all the witnesses to his deadly acts. Conversely, the magical or supernatural must always leave little traces of its cunning lying around to assure the skeptical that some sort of cheating was going on. *Mana* does not leave clues.

As the prime organizer of human tasks, crafts, rowers, and vocations, *mana* not only guarantees the social hierarchy but actually substitutes for it, assurring the secrecy and sanctity of social status and position. There is a *mana* of leadership, closely akin to that of oratory; the king of traditional Tonga was considered to be the actual begetter of his subjects. Otherwise *mana* does not obey boundaries or limits without, as a liminal quality, transcending them, so that the need to differentiate in some final sense pairs the concept with another indispensable Polynesian original, that of *taboo. Mana* knows no limits; taboo knows nothing else; together they comprise the form and content of the comprehehnsible world.

The real epistemological challenge, for the outsider as well as the Polynesian subject, would be to authenticate each of them as an objective, independently existing entity. There must be a *mana* of knowing just exactly what *mana* is all about, a single, convergent, and perfectly understandable "yes" that controls all the difficult, dangerous, and divergent forms of "no," the quotient of an infinite divisor. Would that be the same thing as the one single and singular *taboo* that banishes all others? Or would it be totally different? We do not know.

Hence, if an unconditional taboo were placed upon the very existence of *mana,* that *mana* inherent in that taboo itself would increase beyond all measure, swallowing the world in a generic potency of its own particulars. The very intransigence of the concept, like that of the Chinese *tao,* renders it invincible (as it is said of death, that it is "not only *educational,* but perfectly *safe*"). If gravity, for instance, were to be reconceptualized as a general taboo placed on straight-line navigation, then the old Polynesian adage that "the sea closes upon itself" would make sport of our terrestrial geometries.

Like the "big bang" theory of modern cosmology, or the notion that the universe came into being through the disintegration of a gigantic proto-atom, *mana* simplifies the eternal problem of creation ex nihilo by supplementing it with a transformation instead. A quality that increases in direct proportion to the resistance offered it, and does so quite simply by identifying itself as the force behind that resistance, has no necessary relation to the beginnings and endings of things. Polynesians might argue about the relative strengths and weaknesses of their gods or mythic heroes—what parts they played in the creation and even why they may have played them—but there would be no question as to what they used to do it. *Mana* is inherent in the created things of this world (for example, all natural objects, elements, and processes) for the same reason it inhabits the artifacts of a skilled craftsman.

In one respect *mana* resembles the concept of the dreaming (formerly "dreamtime") among the Australian Aboriginal peoples. Understood as an alternative "phase" of everyday reality, the dreaming is only incidentally attributable to the past (for the purpose of certain stories or illustrative accounts) and is fully *present* to its own ritual enactments. In that way *mana* might be understood as the inceptive energy coefficient of the objects, persons, and actions to which it is attributed. It is nonlinear, and one could no more escape its effectiveness than one could avoid dreaming at night.

Philosophically, then, *mana* is not only explanatory but self-explanatory and plays a role in Polynesian thought not unlike that of gravity or energy in the physical sciences, evolution in the life sciences, and culture in the social sciences. It is at once the mirror of our artifice, and the artificer of our mirror. Science performs its observations and experiments to discover the truth of things; *mana,* immanent at one and the same time in both the test and the result, the cause and the effect, the question and the answer, is *the thing of the truth.* Everyone can know, down to minute particulars, exactly what science has done and wants to do; no one can really know, despite all the energy expended on its definition, what *mana* may truly be. All we can do is say its name and hope that something really good will come of it.

Mana is the power of the named over the nameless (*cf.* Laozi: "The *named* is the mother of the myriad creatures"), the existent over the nonexistent, the creative over the uncreated. It is the divine part of the human and the human part of the divine, the least visible part of the metaphor that controls the visible world. Might it not be the case that the early explorers and anthropologists who named the Polynesians as "savages" or "barbarians" had their categories reversed, that the people did not drift randomly to their remote islands, in fear of some uncertainty, but actively navigated the wave trains to find homes for themselves at the center of infinity? Or so the name of Kapingamarangi, a remote Polynesian outlier, would tell us. Literally translated, it means "The Place That Is Held Together by the Horizon."

If there were a Nobel Prize for the naming of things, the old Polynesians might at least expect an honorable mention. And a niche in navigation's hall of fame: all one has to do is keep to the latitude where the star Arcturus (*Hokulea,* "The Star of Joy") is on the zenith, and sooner or later one will run into Hawai'i. That is part of the *mana* of finding

Hawai'i, the actuarial value of which has increased exponentially since the days of Captain Cook.

Real *mana,* of course, does not profit a smile; it eschews negotiability and must pursue a fugitive existence in those islands. It is not begged, borrowed, or stolen. We have superstars whose voices or countenances run into the millions, but all that might be said of the *mana* of image, including its bizarre narcosis in the modern "global" culture, was said by William Shakespeare in one of his sonnets: "They are the lords and owners of their faces." Real *mana* is something much more civilized than we could possibly imagine. We have a difficult enough time with *aroha* (*arofa, aloha*), commonly translated as "love."

Like the distinctive face or personality, *mana* inheres solely in the one who possesses it (or, more properly, is possessed by it), so that "teaching" it or "passing it on" implies qualities of holism and autonomy that are largely incommensurate with those terms. One would not learn it or acquire it but *teach onesself to it.* Tattooing the skin, a practice favored especially by the Maori, would, if accomplished with the requisite *mana,* effectively embody the social power of "face." And the *mana* of the expert woodcarver would transfer the stamp of personality inherent in that transformation to the utensils, objects, houses, and canoes of the surrounding world. *Mana* is only the specific, Polynesian version of a conceptual motif found widespread in the Pacific region. "Now you see me as I am," a lavishly decorated dancer at Mount Hagen, in New Guinea, once told the anthropologist Marilyn Strathern, meaning that he had turned himself inside out, showing the beautiful intentions of his soul (*numan*) in the befeathered lineaments of his outer body, that he had *taught himself* to the dance.

Mana is not the self, but the *artistry* of the self. It has no other ego. Examples of this sort suggest that although the total effect of *mana* resembles that of abstraction in many ways, its power is actually opposite to what we know by that term. Scientific abstractions depend for their explanatory power upon known and testable qualities, which are then extended over the range of phenomenal experience. *Mana,* which is *noumenal* rather than phenomenal in Kant's terminology, does not so much explain as it transforms, and the result is always something that is very concrete and specific. To abstract is to derive, generalize, render a subject remote and incorporeal, control the mind with intellectual fictions. *Mana,* which controls by nonfictions, makes its sense, or makes *sense* of the world, in a totally different way: the cold eroticism of the long, dark Pacific. There might be a *mana* of logic, but never a logic of *mana.*

SEE ALSO Atua; Polynesian Religions, overview article; Power; Taboo.

BIBLIOGRAPHY

Best, Elsdon. *Maori Religion and Mythology.* Wellington, N.Z., 1976. A classic ethnographic sourcebook, including many evocations of basic cultural concepts by Maori people in their own words.

Caro, Niki. *Whale Rider.* New Zealand Film Commission, 2003. Film. The dramatic understatement of *mana* in this film of contemporary Maori life makes it the most powerful representation of the concept ever produced.

Handy, E. S. G. *Polynesian Religion.* Honolulu, 1927. A synthesis of one of the world's most dispersed religiosities.

Hiroa, Te Rangi (Sir Peter Buck). *The Coming of the Maori.* Whitcoulls, N.Z., 1949. Romantic account of Maori history and concept.

Schwimmer, Eric. *The World of the Maori.* Wellington, N.Z., 1966. A distinguished contemporary analysis of the working concepts in Maori life and thought.

ROY WAGNER (2005)

MANCO CAPAC AND MAMA OCLLO (probably thirteenth century), first Inca ruler, demigod ancestor of succeeding Inca rulers, and the founder, possibly legendary, of the Inca capital city of Cuzco, in the southern highlands of Peru. Early Spanish chroniclers reported various Inca creation myths. In one version, the Sun, taking pity on the miserable world, sent down his own son—presumably Manco Capac—and daughter to govern the people. According to another version, after the creation of the world the Sun summoned Manco Capac and, "speaking like an older brother," told him that the Inca would rule the world and that they must proudly regard the Sun as their father and worship him appropriately. In the most frequent variation, four brothers and four sisters emerged from a "window," or cave, in a rock at Pacaritambo ("inn of origin"), not far from Cuzco. After a period of wandering, one brother, Ayar Manco (later Manco Capac), having sent word that his father was the Sun, went to a hill above what is now Cuzco. The people of the valley looked up to see him dressed in gold ornaments that reflected dazzling sunlight. He founded Cuzco with a simple shrine on what would be the site of the great Temple of the Sun. He is said to have taught the people not only social and religious structure and ritual but also irrigation, planting, and harvesting.

When he was about to die, Manco Capac told his people that he must return to the sky, for his father had summoned him. His body was adored as a *huaca,* a sacred object. The Spaniards, seeking to destroy idolatry, removed the mummified bodies of other Inca rulers, but they could not find that of Manco Capac, which was kept in a village outside Cuzco. It was said to have turned into a stone (stone was particularly sacred to the Inca). This stone, elaborately dressed and adorned, was one of the most holy Inca objects, and ceremonies and sacrifices were held before it.

SEE ALSO Atahuallpa.

BIBLIOGRAPHY

Bernabé Cobo's mid-seventeenth-century *History of the Inca Empire* (Austin, 1979) is a rich source of lore about Manco Capac. Harold Osborne's *South American Mythology* (London, 1968) contains a number of Inca origin myths. J. H. Rowe's "Inca Culture at the Time of the Spanish Conquest," in the *Handbook of South American Indians*, edited by Julian H. Steward, vol. 2 (Washington, D.C., 1946), presents the legends in their general cultural context.

ELIZABETH P. BENSON (1987)

MANDA D'HIIA ("knowledge of life") is the primary savior, messenger, and instructor in Mandaeism, a still-surviving gnostic religion in Iraq and Iran. Dispatched from the world above, the Lightworld, to the lower realms, Manda d'Hiia brings saving knowledge, warnings, and consolation to human beings and to deficient Lightworld beings stranded between the earth and the Lightworld. His descents and ascents parallel the route of the soul, which, having come from the Lightworld, returns to its home at the body's death. The "life" of which Manda d'Hiia is "knowledge" is the upper, ultimate Lightworld principle, in some texts called the King of Light and other names. The names *Manda d'Hiia* and *Life* are pronounced over Mandaeans at baptism, and Manda d'Hiia's name occurs frequently in prayer formulas.

The savior appears most often in the two main collections of Mandaean mythological speculation, *Ginza*, separated into *Right Ginza* and *Left Ginza*, and the Mandaean *Book of John*. The *Right Ginza*, the larger part of *Ginza*, contains cosmologies and mythologies dealing mainly with the earthly world, while the smaller *Left Ginza* centers primarily on the ascent of the soul toward the Lightworld. In *Right Ginza 3*, Manda d'Hiia descends to the underworld, vanquishing the evil powers there. His devastating effect on the evil ones on earth is described in *Right Ginza* 5.2. This tractate makes use of the Old Testament's Psalm 114 in portraying the frenzied reaction of mountains and ocean to the savior's appearance. In *Right Ginza* 11, as in 15.17, Manda d'Hiia battles with Ruha, the personified female spirit, and with the planets, the wicked world-rulers who ensnare human beings.

According to *Left Ginza* 1.3, Manda d'Hiia released Hawwa, Adam's wife, from the world, and warned against mourning for the dead, a behavior repudiated by Mandaeism. *Right Ginza* 5.4 tells of the death of John the Baptist, the Mandaean prophet. Manda d'Hiia appears to John in the guise of a small boy who wishes to be baptized. When John takes the boy to the river, it floods, owing to the presence of the savior. John nearly drowns, but Manda d'Hiia makes the water recede. As birds and fishes praise Manda d'Hiia, John realizes that his baptism candidate is the very Lightbeing in whose name John performs his baptisms. This baptism turns out to be John's last: Manda d'Hiia has come to take him away from the world. The baptist's body is left on the riverbank, the savior covering it with sand, and the two ascend together to the Lightworld.

Occasionally, Manda d'Hiia is portrayed unflatteringly. The *Book of John* 2 informs us that the savior has caused strife in the Lightworld by revealing the secrets of salvation to Ruha, his adversary. In the eighth tractate of the same book, a messenger pleads for Yushamin, a rebellious, jailed Lightbeing. The King of Light is favorably inclined toward Yushamin, but Manda d'Hiia thinks that Yushamin deserves no forgiveness. To this the King of Light responds that Manda d'Hiia harbors a long-standing jealousy toward Yushamin: Manda d'Hiia hates Yushamin because the latter once refused him a wife.

In general, though, Manda d'Hiia is a positive figure. He was the guardian of Adam's epoch, the first of the four ages of the world. Today we live in the fourth age, an evil age, which will end when no Mandaeans are left on earth.

SEE ALSO Ginza; Mandaean Religion.

BIBLIOGRAPHY

The two main Mandaean sources that present Manda d'Hiia have been published in German under the editorship of Mark Lidzbarski as *Ginza: Der Schatz; oder, Das grosse Buch der Mandäer* (Göttingen, 1925) and *Das Johannesbuch der Mandäer* (1915; reprint, Berlin, 1966). Excerpts from myths found in these texts appear in *Gnosis: A Selection of Gnostic Texts*, vol. 2, *Coptic and Mandean Sources* (Oxford, 1974), edited by Werner Foerster. Kurt Rudolph's *Theogonie, Kosmogonie und Anthropogonie in den mandäischen Schriften* (Göttingen, 1965) devotes considerable space to myths in which Manda d'Hiia appears.

New Sources

Lupieri, Edmondo. *I Mandei. Gli ultimi gnostici.* Brescia, 1993. English translation as *The Mandaeans: The Last Gnostics.* Grand Rapids, Mich., 2002.

JORUNN JACOBSEN BUCKLEY (1987)
Revised Bibliography

MANDAEAN RELIGION. The religion of the Mandaeans (from *manda*, "knowledge") is a self-contained, unique system belonging in the general stratum of the Gnosticism of late antiquity. Thus Mandaeism shows affinities with Judaism and Christianity. For geographical reasons, it also exhibits certain early influences from the Iranian religious milieu. The Mandaeans live, as their ancestors did, along the rivers and waterways of southern Iraq and Khuzistan, Iran. Known by their neighbors as Subbi (baptizers), they form a Gnostic baptist community.

The Mandaeans can be traced to the second or third century of the common era. A hypothesis based on their language and literature indicates that they emigrated, during the first centuries of the common era, from the Jordan Valley area eastward to the environs of Haran, on the border between present-day Turkey and Syria, and finally to southern Babylonia. According to their text *Haran Gawaita* (Inner Haran), they fled persecution and traveled east under the protection of one of the three Parthian kings named Ardban who ruled from the early first century to 227 CE.

An East Aramaic dialect, the Mandaean language nevertheless contains West Syrian linguistic elements that point to the probability of a migration from west to east. Examples of these are *yardna* (running water; also designates the river Jordan), *sba* (baptize), *kushta* (truth, ritual handshake), *manda* (knowledge), and *nasuraiia* (observant ones). The last term (in English, Nasoraeans), also used by early Christians, refers primarily to the Mandaean priests. According to Rudolf Macuch, the date 271–272 CE may be argued as that appearing, in the hand of a Mandaean copyist, in the colophon of a hymnal (*qulasta*), published in *The Canonical Prayerbook of the Mandaeans* (1959). This colophon may well be the oldest extant Mandaean text. Macuch also dates Mandaean script on coins from what is now Luristan and Khuzistan as from the second and third centuries CE. Inscriptions on leather and lead strips, on clay tablets, and on magical bowls (labeled "magical" because they are used on a "folk religion" level) belong largely to the younger sources.

The Mandaean codex and scroll literature is found in the voluminous book *Ginza*, which is divided into *Right Ginza* and *Left Ginza*. It is a collection of mythological, revelatory, hortatory, and hymnic material. The *Right Ginza* contains generally cosmological, "this worldly" prose material, whereas the *Left Ginza*, much of it in verse, centers on the "otherworldly" fate of the soul. Symbolism of "right" and "left" is pervasive in Mandaeism, but in the case of the *Ginza* titles these terms are puzzling, for the right is usually connected to the beyond and the left to the earthly world. The Mandaean *Book of John* contains a variety of myths and legends. *The Canonical Prayerbook* includes hymns, liturgies, and instructions for priests. Central mythical and ritual material in this work and in the *Ginza* dates from the third and fourth centuries CE. Comments, exegeses, and instructions for rituals attested in *The Canonical Prayerbook* are in the texts *The Thousand and Twelve Questions*, *The Original Great World*, *The Original Small World*, and *The Coronation of the Great Shishlam*. The Mandaeans also have illustrated scrolls, such as *The Scroll of Abatur* and *The Scroll of the Rivers*, and a book on astrology, *The Book of the Zodiac*. Much of this literature was probably collected and edited after the seventh century CE, although most of the material is older.

Traditionally hostile to both Judaism and Christianity, the Mandaeans were confronted with the Islamic conquest in the seventh century CE. In response the Mandaean leaders declared the *Ginza* to be their holy scripture and proclaimed John the Baptist as the Mandaean prophet, since a holy book and a prophet were the Islamic requirements for recognition as a "People of the Book" (i.e., Jews, Christians, and Sabaeans), exempt from forcible conversion. The Mandaeans endured hardships under Islamic rule, but they were generally left in peace. Never aspiring to secular power or political expansion, the traditionally endogamous Mandaeans survived. The group was threatened by an outbreak of cholera in 1831 that eliminated the priestly class, but new priests were drawn from the ranks of literate laymen. Again as secularization set in during the twentieth century, scholars considered Mandaean culture to be in danger of extinction; however, a cultural, if not traditionally religious, revival seems to be taking hold. In Iraq two new baptismal pools and a new *mandi* (a clay and reed hut used by priests) were constructed in the 1970s. Mandaeans translated into Arabic Ethel S. Drower's *The Mandaeans of Iraq and Iran*, first published in 1937. In 1972 these translators compiled a Mandaean catechism for the benefit of the laity, who formerly were not allowed even to touch Mandaean books.

In bulk the Mandaean corpus exceeds anything transmitted from other Gnostic traditions, except perhaps that of Manichaeism. Relationships to other forms of Gnosticism are difficult to trace, but in 1949 Torgny Säve-Söderbergh demonstrated that the Manichaean *Psalms of Thomas*, dating from 250 to 275 CE, depend on a Mandaean original. In addition the long-held view that Mani had his roots in Mandaeism has been refuted by the discovery of the *Cologne Mani Codex*. However, the Syrian *Odes of Solomon* and a number of the Nag Hammadi tractates do show correspondences with Mandaean ideas.

In the sixteenth and seventeenth centuries Portuguese missionaries were among the first to bring Mandaean manuscripts out of the Orient. Thinking they had found the "Christians of Saint John," a misnomer for the Mandaeans, the missionaries were eager to trace the Mandaeans back to their putative origins. The possibilities of such a Christian connection contributed to the heyday of studies in Mandaeism in the first half of the twentieth century. Debates on Mandaeism's relationship to early Christianity have continued, although the question of a pre-Christian Mandaeism no longer holds the fascination it once did. Comparative issues are still central, but Mandaeism is also studied for its own sake. The relationship between the mythological and the cultic components remains a crucial issue, for in Mandaeism one faces a gnosis closely aligned with cultic practices. Kurt Rudolph in particular has sought to unravel the historical development of the Mandaean mythology and cult and to reconstruct the sequence of the variegated segments in the sources.

MYTHOLOGY. Mandaeism testifies to a basic framework of dualism in which diametrically opposed entities clash but also intertwine and to some extent recognize one another's claims. Good and evil, light and darkness, soul and matter vie for control from the very inception of the world. Mandaean mythological speculations center on the preexistent Lightworld (the upper, "heavenly" realm), on the creation of the earth and of human beings, and on the soul's journey back to its Lightworld origin. The primary Lightworld entity is "the Great Life" (also called by various other names), who resides with his consort "Treasure of Life" and numerous Lightbeings (*'utria*), the prototypes of earthly priests. The *'utria* gradually become involved in the creation, an entanglement causing their degradation and accrual of their sins. One of them, Ptahil, the pathetically unsuccessful creator of the earthly world and of human beings, fails to make Adam stand upright, for the creature is wholly material. A soul is brought—sometimes reluctantly—from the Lightworld, making Adam complete. The soul not only causes erect posture but functions as a revealer, instructing Adam and his wife Hawwa in *nasiruta,* the totality of Mandaean gnosis and cult.

Adam is taught to free his soul and spirit to return to the Lightworld, leaving the body behind. Of the three human constituents, *ruha* (spirit) is the middle, ambiguous component torn between body and soul. There is also a personified *ruha,* at times called Ruha d-Qudsha (holy spirit), who was originally fetched from the underworld prior to the creation of earth and human beings. By necessity Ptahil enters into fateful cooperation with this personified spirit, who has a stake in the human being. Ruha also enlists the planets and the zodiac spirits, her children, to help her. Together they demonize time and space. Arranging a noisy party to blot out the soul's revelatory voice in Adam, Ruha and her cohorts merely manage to frighten Adam, reawakening his quest for salvation beyond the earth (*Right Ginza,* 3).

In addition to the *'utria* Yushamin, Abatur, and Ptahil, there are others less stained by involvement in the lower realms. Manda d-Hiia (knowledge of life) and his son-brother Hibil are Lightworld envoys, revealers, and saviors busily shuttling between the Lightworld and the earth. Anosh-Utra, who imitates and competes with Jesus, and Shitil, the biblical Seth, are two less-central messengers. Shitil appears both as one of the *'utria* and as the first son of Adam. In the latter capacity Shitil dies vicariously for his father, who at the ripe age of one thousand years refuses to die. As a reward for his sacrifice, Shitil ascends and becomes the pure soul against which all human souls are weighed in the scales of Abatur on the threshold of the Lightworld.

Between Earth and the Lightworld the *matarata,* "purgatories" or "heavenly hells," provide tests and tribulations for ascending souls and spirits. The *matarata*—depicted in *The Scroll of Abatur*—present an inverted parallel to the underworlds mapped by Hibil before the creation of the earth. Demons, including some of the degraded *'utria,* serve as purgatory keepers, performing the thankless task of testing and punishing. Depending on the realm in which they appear, *'utria* and other divine beings may show themselves as good or evil. Abatur has been demoted from *rama* (elevated) to "lord of the scales." He must carry out his task until the end of time, though complaining bitterly (*Book of John,* 70–72).

Nonbelievers do not escape the *matarata.* Jesus, an apostate Mandaean, is doomed—unlike his mother Miriai, who converted from Judaism to Mandaeism, thus serving as the prototype of the west-to-east migrating Mandaean. In the *Book of John* 30 Jesus seeks baptism from John the Baptist, who at first hesitates, knowing Jesus' wicked intentions. John relents owing to a command from Abatur, but at the moment of baptism Ruha makes the sign of the cross over the Jordan, which immediately loses its luster, taking on many colors—a bad omen.

RITUALS. Among the Mandaeans, repeated baptism (*masbuta*) takes place on Sundays and special festival days. Two small rites of ablution, *rishama* and *tamasha,* are performed by the individual Mandaean and, unlike the *masbuta,* require no priest. At baptism the male candidates, clothed in white, and female candidates, who wear a black cloak over the white garment, line up on the riverbank. One at a time, each descends into the water and immerses himself or herself three times, whereupon the priest, in full ritual garb, submerges him or her thrice again. As the candidates crouch in the water, each receives a triple sign on the forehead with water and drinks three handfuls of water. Investiture with a tiny myrtle wreath—a symbol of spirit and of life—follows. Baptisms completed, the candidates sit on the riverbank. Now each is anointed on the forehead with sesame oil and partakes in a meal of bread (*pihta*) and water (*mambuha*). Finally, each baptized person exchanges a ritual handshake (*kushta*) with the priest. The entire ceremony is accompanied throughout by set prayers, formulas, and hymns uttered by the priest.

The laity undergo baptism as often as they wish. Moreover baptism is required on specific occasions: at marriage, after childbirth (for a woman), and as close to the moment of death as possible. Water not only cleanses sins and other impurities; it also represents the Lightworld as reflected in the earthly world. *Masbuta* anticipates and in some sense parallels the death mass, the *masiqta* (raising up), a complicated, lengthy, and essentially secret ritual celebrated for the dead and shielded from the view of the laity. Because baptismal river water symbolizes the Lightworld, the *masbuta* can be said to constitute a "horizontal" *masiqta*: immersion in water here on earth prepares for ascension at life's end.

The *masiqta* conveys spirit and soul from the dead body into the Lightworld. Three days after burial the "seals" put on the grave are broken, for spirit and soul are now ascending on their perilous journey through the *matarata* to the Lightworld. On this third day several priests celebrate the *masiqta.* In handling objects that symbolize the ascending spirit and soul, the priests' aim is threefold: to join spirit and soul; to create a new, Lightworld body for this joined entity; and to incorporate the new body into the community of deceased Mandaeans living in the Lightworld.

The majority of the symbolic objects in the *masiqta* are foodstuffs that feed the departed and act as creation material. Food links the living to the dead, maintaining the *laufa,* the connection between earth and the Lightworld. The priests personify the ascending spirit and soul, act as parents for the new body, and impersonate Lightbeings. As mediators priests are Lightbeings on earth, carrying out on earth rituals that have their models in the Lightworld. *Ganzibra* (treasurer) and *tarmida* (from *talmid,* "disciple") are the two surviving priestly ranks, each of which requires special initiation ceremonies; the supreme office of the *rishama* (head of the people) has been extinct since the mid-nineteenth century. Constituting the "Right," the Lightworld, the priests are complemented by the laity, who belong to the "Left," the material world. Neither can do without the other; the laity is required as witnesses for public rituals carried out by priests. This arrangement furnishes one among many examples of the carefully tempered dualism prevalent in the religion. The dualism and the relationship between myth and ritual remain among the most urgent issues confronting scholarship on Mandaeism, as do the editing and translating of unpublished Mandaean manuscripts.

History of Study. As far as is known, the first Westerner to come into contact with the Mandaeans was the monk Ricoldo da Montecroce in around 1290. The story of the encounter is set out in a kind of travel diary, an *Itinerarium* or *The Book of Travels in Eastern Parts*, written in his later years in the quiet of the convent of Santa Maria Novella in Florence. The Mandaeans are defined as a kind of "monstrous" spiritual reality in a merciless way, even if the description is thorough. The Mandaeans are not mentioned again until 1555, by Jesuit missionaries in Mesopotamia, this time confused with the Christians of Saint John the Apostle and Evangelist (Lupieri [2002] describes the contacts between the missionaries and the Mandaean community, in which their presumed "Christian" origin is finally recognized).

At the beginning of the seventeenth century European knowledge of Mandaeanism expanded as a result of the accounts of travelers, such as the Roman aristocrat Pietro Della Valle and missionaries like Basilio di San Francesco, a Portuguese Carmelite who applied himself to the conversion of the Mandaeans with great fervor, founding the Catholic mission at Basra among others. The work of Basilio was continued by another Carmelite, Ignatius a Jesu, who was responsible for a kind of handbook on the conversion of the Mandaeans with the long title *Narratio originum, rituum, et errorum Christianorum Sancti Ioannis* . . . (1652). Just like previous missionaries, Ignatius was convinced that the Mandaeans had originally or in the past been Christians and thus their conversion really amounted to a return to the faith from which they had lapsed.

The interpretation of Mandaeanism offered by Ignatius was initially favorably received in Rome, but at the beginning of the eighteenth century it was replaced by a radical critical reappraisal by two Maronite priests, Abraham Ecchellensis and Joseph Simeon Assemani. Ecchellensis in particular was the first European to note the Gnostic dualistic nature of Mandaeism.

From the end of the eighteenth century European and especially German academic scholarship played a decisive part. Among the many scholars of theology, history, and Oriental languages who were interested in Mandaeism, an important position was occupied by the Swedish scholar Matthias Norberg. Between 1815 and 1816 Norberg published the *Codex Nasaraeus*, complete with relevant lexical material, but namely an erroneous transcription of the entire *Ginza* in Syriac alphabet. Following the fantastic stories of the Maronite Germano Conti di Aleppo, Norberg identified the Nusairi in an Islamic brotherhood of Lebanon (the text and theory are, from a scientific point of view, unreliable). Although criticized by subsequent scholars, the work of Norberg marks a significant stage, allowing an even wider audience to have access to Mandaean texts. He paved the way for Orientalists such as Heinrich Petermann, the scholar responsible for beginning the scientific study of Mandaeism, above all the Mandaean edition of the *Ginza* (1867), still used as a reference work in studies of Mandaean religion.

Among the more serious writing on the subject, the works of two German Orientalists, Theodore Nöldeke and Mark Lidzbarski, are extremely important. In 1875 the former compiled an essential Mandaean grammar, and the latter published and translated the most important texts. Setting Mandaeism in the broader context of the comparative history of religion may be dated to Wilhelm Brandt, followed by Richard Reitzenstein, Rudolf Bultmann, Hans Jonas, and latterly Kurt Rudolph, Edwin Yamauchi, and Jorunn J. Buckley. With the exception of Yamauchi, their studies have proved that Mandaean literature provides significant evidence of a Gnostic religion that flourished in late antiquity but with roots that presumably go back to a more remote, pre-Christian period. The Mandaeans are thus the last living witnesses of this religion and are important in the religious history of late antiquity. Intense speculation has sought to ascribe their origins in the history of early Christianity by identifying them as descendants of an ancient group of followers of John the Baptist. This point of view, as seen earlier, was already shared by the seventeenth-century Portuguese missionaries in Iraq; hence the long-standing practice of calling the Mandaeans "the Christians of Saint John." Even if it is not possible to support this theory, one can definitely state that Mandaean literature has preserved in its oldest writings evidence of the milieu, in the Orient, in which early Christianity developed, evidence that can be used to interpret certain New Testament writings (especially Johannine texts). Studies such as those by Viggo Schou-Pedersen, Eric Segelberg, Geo Widengren, Rudolf Macuch, and Kurt Rudolph have confirmed this.

Since the nineteenth century there have been numerous different attempts to understand surviving Mandaean oral tradition by greater understanding of their texts, including those by the German Orientalist Heinrich Petermann and the French vice consul of Mosul Nicolas Siouffi; in 1880 the latter wrote one of the most extensive and detailed accounts of Mandaeism to date. However, the extraordinary undertaking of collecting these sources was the work of the English scholar Lady Ethel Stefana Drower, the wife of the British consul in Baghdad. She used her abilities and indefatigable energy to record in precise detail the daily expressions of religion and worship of the religious community, and she obtained a series of previously unknown texts, available only to Mandaean priests, and published them in part. Thanks to the work of Drower scholars are thus in a position to obtain a much more accurate impression of the Mandaeans than was previously possible, especially as regards their worship and certain "secret" teachings. Along with this the works of Macuch have cast a new and detailed light on the development of the Mandaic language. He has been responsible for research and study on the Neo-Mandaic dialect as it is still spoken by the Mandaeans of Iran (particularly in Khuzistan). For a long time the lack of a dictionary of the Mandaean language was keenly felt, but one was published in 1963, compiled by Drower and Macuch, who made use of the works and largely unpublished notes of Mark Lidzbarski.

Modern studies on Mandaean religion have been boosted by two important conferences at Harvard in 1999 and Oxford in 2002. One should also note the dissemination of Mandaean culture by Majid Fandi Al-Mubaraki, a Mandaean who has published a variety of literary texts, including lesser ones, through his small publishing company. Philologists who have worked on Neo-Mandaic literature include the Italians Fabrizio A. Pennacchietti and his pupil Roberta Borghero.

ORIGINS AND INFLUENCES. A chronology of Mandaic literature is difficult because of the lack of historical evidence. It is possible to date only several parts of the *Ginza* and certain magical texts (magic bowls) with greater accuracy to the third and fourth centuries CE (according to Macuch, the second and third centuries CE). Their existence may be inferred from the doctrinal content of the main texts. Theodore bar Koni, a seventh-century CE Syrian heresiologist who wrote *Ketaba d-ʾeskolyon* or *Scholion*, in which he describes the "Dostheans" or Mandaeans, quotes several passages from the *Ginza.*

There are two possible approaches that may be adopted when studying this subject: to examine contemporary non-Mandaic evidence (Gnostic or Manichaean, for example) or to carry out internal textual analysis, studying the themes and literary style, examining the particular doctrinal contents of the text to establish a history of the tradition. The first method has been adopted by the Swedish Egyptologist Torgny Säve-Söderbergh, for example, who has shown through a comparison of parallel texts that part of a Mandaean hymnology already existed in the third century CE.

The Mandaeans consider their religion a direct divine emanation, created directly from the World of Light. Nonetheless certain clues may provide an answer to the question of their origin. Several texts have preserved a mythical geographical tradition describing a persecution of the community (or 360 "followers," *tarmide)* in Jerusalem by the Jews under the guidance of Adonai, Ruha, and their seven sons (the Planets), after which Jerusalem was destroyed as a punishment. In a quasi-historical text, the *Haran Gawaita,* it is mentioned that the Nasurai stayed in the "Mountain of the Maddai" (Tura d-Madai) or "inner Harran," where they took refuge under a king called Ardban (Artabanus), fleeing from the ruling Jews. The precise identity of this Artabanus is uncertain: Macuch has identified him with the Parthian king Artabanus III or Artabanus IV or V. Generally it seems that this may be placed within the context of a tradition describing in a mythical or legendary manner the penetration (perhaps only partial) of the group into territory that was then Iranian (between Harran and Nisibi or Media) during the late Parthian period (first or second century CE). Further on the same text describes the establishment of a community at Baghdad or in Mesopotamia and the Mandaeans' subsequent fortunes under the Sassanids.

This tradition also includes the events in Jerusalem, which here take place on the Euphrates, and the Mandaean legend of John the Baptist (Iahia, Iuhana), who is here called "the Prophet of the Kushta" (Truth) and "the Messenger of the King of Light." John is also mentioned in other texts, and the Mandaeans regard him as one of their own, representing him as their "Prophet" to Muslims. He is described as opposing Christ. As mentioned above, it has previously been inferred that the Mandaeans were descendants of the followers of John the Baptist. However, this theory has not been fully proven. Thus it is not possible to demonstrate that the Mandaeans possess their own independent tradition dating back to that period. It is clear that they had embraced and given a Mandaean interpretation to legends from heretical Christian (that is, Gnostic) circles, preserving the opposition between Jesus and John the Baptist. Furthermore John the Baptist is not a particularly central figure in Mandaean tradition.

A relationship between Mandaic traditions and Aramaic (i.e. Syro-Palestinian) Christianity can be established via stylistic analysis, especially of Johannine writings. Mandaean literature does not give any reason to believe that this religious community had been Christian during some earlier period, considering the extremely vehement hostility shown toward Christianity as a whole (Christ is regarded in an entirely negative light). On the other hand, based upon a large number of traditional and lexical indications and notwithstanding the harsh anti-Jewish polemic (Moses is regarded as the prophet of the evil "spirit" Ruha and Adonai as a false, evil god), the Jewish origin of this group appears, according to Macuch, to be incontrovertible. Another passage in the *Haran Gawaita* states that until the coming of Christ the Mandaeans "loved Lord Adonai." This could be a heterodox Jewish sect that, like the Essenes, openly held different opinions from official Judaism, embracing powerful Iranian and Gnostic influences and thus gradually isolating themselves. This clearly distinct position—in regard to the Jewish wars of liberation—led to the persecution of the community and ultimately to their emigration from the region of the Jordan (and indeed Jordan, that is, Yardna, is what they call the waters of baptism) to the east, first to Harran and the mountainous region of Media (Tura d-Madai) and then to the southern part of Mesopotamia (Caracene, Maisan).

The exodus from the west must have occurred during the second century CE at the latest, because certain Mesopotamian and Iranian-Parthian elements imply a rather lengthy period in the east. The theory is corroborated by links with trans-Jordan baptist sects (including with the one at Qumran) and with so-called Syrian Gnosis (*The Odes of Solomon*, the Sethians, the Naassenes, *Acts of Thomas*), also from certain surprising ancient Syrian lexical components in their language and mythology. It has been thought that Mani, the founder of Manichaeism, had absorbed Mandaean elements in his later works. The Manichaean *Psalms of Thomas* make clear the links, sometimes friendly and sometimes hostile, existing between the two religions. On the other hand, in the ninth book of the *Right Ginza* there is a dispute with the followers of Mar Mani.

The long-lasting settlement in the lands at the confluence of the Tigris and the Euphrates (the Shatt al-ʿArab) also brought about new developments within the community, such as the introduction of the Frash-Ziwa (the shining Euphrates) in place of the Jordan, the later development of ritual worship and religious hierarchy, the evolution of other Iranian ideas, and clearly also the re-creation in the new homeland of the situation in Palestine during the early days of the sect. There is also an increasing contrast with Christianity and the Christian missionary church, especially the Byzantine part. Christ "the Roman" is one who oppresses the community, whom it must be on its guard against.

In contrast to what occurred during the Arsacid period, under whom the sect enjoyed a tranquil existence (as shown by king Artabanus in the legendary story in the *Haran Gawaita*), relations with the Sassanids were not good. The *Haran Gawaita* talks of a considerable reduction in the number of Mandaean temples during that period. It is known only that under Shāpūr I (242–273 CE) there took place a persecution of foreign religions, including that of the Nasoreans (Kirdir inscription). Mandaean documents repeatedly mention curses against Muḥammad and his religion (especially in colophons). Islam also instigated other persecutions, despite the tolerance accorded to the "Sabaeans." Thus the persecuted community withdrew to more and more inaccessible marsh regions of southern Iraq, where it continues to exist, alongside other Aramaic Christian groups, dreaming about and longing for their own particular past, convinced that wickedness will soon disappear from this world.

The fundamental importance of the Mandaean religion lies in the fact that in its original essentials it may be considered as an expression—organized in a baptismal community—of Syrian Mesopotamian Gnosis, a clearly defined entity, a peculiar Aramaic social and linguistic unit, something that has not been proven for any Gnostic school. Its rich traditions offer the opportunity of studying this religious model of late antiquity with its typically Oriental origins, which by this time had disappeared from every other point of view, and in this way gaining some idea of the religious nature and inner life of a Gnostic community.

This is the generally accepted reconstruction of scholars (Rudolph is among the most influential). Yet clear links with the *Gospel of John*, the *Odes of Solomon*, and several Gnostic texts leave open the possibility that Mandaean traditions date back to a pre-Christian age, a theory that at the beginning of the twentieth century enthralled leading scholars, such as Reitzenstein or Bultmann, who formulated a major philological historiographical construct based upon a theory of this kind.

The oldest evidence of Mandaic writing comes from second and third century CE Caracene coinage. According to Macuch, these reveal surprising similarities with the Elymean inscriptions at Tang-e Sarwak in Khuzistan. On the other hand, these indicate knowledge of the Nabatean alphabet. Macuch was completely convinced that the ancient Mandaeans should be regarded as an important link between the Nabatean and Elymean cultures, namely that they had brought the script with them from the west and had passed it on to the Elymeans. Clearly this assumes that the Mandaeans effectively either "invented" or transmitted this writing system. Furthermore Macuch maintained that the Mandaeans should be associated with Aramean penetration of Khuzistan and Caracene. If so the Mandaeans should no longer be regarded as isolated and self-contained but rather as an important means by which Aramean culture was diffused throughout the Orient as well as linked to the development of the Middle-Persian Pahlavi script. The Iranian theory of Widengren is based upon such speculation. According to the distinguished Swedish scholar, the Mandaean religion is the result of the development of three main religious environments that are at times clearly distinguishable. The first, the Judeo-Semitic and Western, constitutes the Palestinian milieu in which Mandaeism was born and developed. The essentially Jewish aspects of Mandaean Gnosis, including the figure of John the Baptist, in fact come from this layer, which is the oldest. The Mesopotamian component is next, made up of archaic Babylonian traditional elements, recognizable in the large number of Akkadian linguistic loan-words as well as in a large number of mythical and ritual themes, not least the sacred kingship. Finally, there is the Iranian part, which is imbued with religious ideas and concepts most probably taken from the doctrines of the Mazdean-Zurvanite Magi of Media Atropatene, in particular beliefs concerning human redemption expressed in the dogma of Savior Saved may be derived from these.

Such ideas, originating from an Iranian milieu, would define the characteristics of Mandaeism in terms of Gnosticism and dualism. Thus it is likely that Mani, the founder of the "Religion of Light," grew in a community of baptists linked to the Mandaeans, the Elchasaites. Given what has been said so far, one must therefore agree with Widengren that "without a detailed understanding of Mandaic language and literature, it is impossible to have a genuine and precise concept of ancient Gnosticism" (*Handbuch der Orientalistik, VIII*, 1961, p. 98). It is not necessary to suppose a Palestinian Judeo-Semitic milieu, because Jewish communities were present in Mesopotamia since at least the sixth century BCE.

See Also Ablutions; Baptism; Ginza; Gnosticism, article on Gnosticism from Its Origins to the Middle Ages; Manda d'Hiia; Manichaeism, overview article.

Bibliography

Two Mandaean collections were published in German under the editorship of Mark Lidzbarski, *Das Johannesbuch der Mandäer* (Giessen, 1915; reprint, Berlin, 1966) and *Ginzā: Der Schatz; Oder, Das grosse Buch der Mandäer* (Göttingen, Germany, 1925, 1978). Ethel S. Drower, trans., *The Canonical Prayerbook of the Mandaeans* (Leiden, 1959), contains a great number of Mandaean hymns and prayers. Representative excerpts from these three texts (as well as from other Mandaean sources) are in Werner Foerster, *Gnosis: A Selection of Gnostic Texts*, vol. 2, *Coptic and Mandean Sources*, edited by Robert M. Wilson (Oxford, 1974), which includes an introduction by Kurt Rudolph. The classical eyewitness account of Mandaean religious life is Ethel S. Drower, *The Mandaeans of Iraq and Iran* (Oxford, 1937; reprint, Leiden, Netherlands, 1962). Kurt Rudolph, *Die Mandäer*, vol. 1, *Prolegomena: Das Mandäerproblem*, vol. 2, *Der Kult* (Göttingen, Germany, 1960–1961), is a comprehensive treatment of Mandaeism. The bibliography in this work should be supplemented by that in Rudolf Macuch, *Handbook of Classical and Modern Mandaic* (Berlin, 1965). A list of works on Mandaeism after 1965 is in Macuch, ed., *Zur Sprache und Literatur der Mandäer*, Studia Mandaica I (Berlin, 1976).

The history of Mandaic historiography (especially their origins) is dealt with in Edmondo Lupieri, *The Mandaeans: The Last Gnostics* (Grand Rapids, Mich., 2002). New mythological studies, along with primary ethnographic evidence, are in the valuable work by Jorunn Jacobsen Buckley, *The Mandaeans: Ancient Texts and Modern People* (New York, 2002). Buckley also translated the Mandaic *Diwan malkuta 'laita: The Scroll of Exalted Kingship* (New Haven, Conn., 1993). Relations with the Sabeans have been investigated by Şinasi Gündüz, *The Knowledge of Life* (Oxford, 1994). The subject of magic and so-called magic bowls is dealt with in Shaul Shaked, "Bagdana, King of the Demons, and Other Iranian Terms in Babylonian Aramaic Magic," in *Papers in Honour of Professor Mary Boyce*, Acta Iranica 24–25, ser. 2, Hommages et Opera minora, 10–11 (Leiden, 1985), pp. 511–525; J. B. Segal and Erica C. D. Hunter, *Catalogue of the Aramaic and Mandaic Incantation Bowls in the British Museum* (London, 2000); and Marco Moriggi, *La lingua delle coppe magiche siriache* (Florence, 2004). For individual mythological, cosmological, and ritual topics, see the various studies collected in Geo Widengren, *Der Mandäismus* (Darmstadt, Germany, 1982); Edwin M. Yamauchi, *Gnostic Ethics and Mandaean Origins* (Cambridge, Mass., 1970); Eric Segelberg, *Gnostica Mandaica Liturgica* (Uppsala, Sweden, 1990); Waldemar Sundberg, *Kushta: A Monograph on a Principal Word in Mandaean Texts*, vol. 1, *The Descending Knowledge*, vol. 2, *The Ascending Soul* (Lund, Sweden, 1993–1994); Majella Franzmann, "Living Water: Mediating Element in Mandaean Myth and Ritual," *Numen* 36 (1990): 156–172; D. Kruisheer, "Theodore Bar Koni's *Ketaba d-'eskolyon* as a Source for the Study of Early Mandaeism," *Jaarbericht Ex Oriente Lux* 33 (1993): 151–169; Kurt Rudolph, "Die Mändaer heute: Ein Zwischenbilanz ihrer Erforschung und ihres Wandels in der Gegenwart," *Zeitschrif für Religionsgeschichte* 94 (1994): 161–184; Erica C. D. Hunter, "Aramaic-Speaking Communities of Sasanid Mesopotamia," *Aram* 7 (1995): 319–335; Ezio Albrile, "Il 'Bianco Monte' dei Magi: La montagna paradisiaca nel sincretismo iranico-mesopotamico," *Annali dell'Istituto Orientale di Napoli* 57 (1997): 145–161; and Ezio Albrile, "I Magi e la 'Madre celeste,'" *Antonianum* 75 (2000): 311–332. The proceedings of the conference on the Mandaeans held at Harvard University in June 1999 were published in *Aram* 11–12 (1999–2000): 197–331.

Jorunn Jacobsen Buckley (1987)
Ezio Albrile (2005)
Translated from Italian by Paul Ellis

MAṆḌALAS

This entry consists of the following articles:

MAṆḌALAS: HINDU MAṆḌALAS

The *maṇḍala*, a complex geometric design, is used in Hindu rituals in order to involve the whole cosmos in the ritual act. *Maṇḍalas* were first described in Tantric texts, but they already appear there in such detail and in such highly evolved forms that an earlier, unrecorded tradition of *maṇḍala* construction must be assumed.

The interest of the early Hindus in geometric designs with cosmological implications is attested by the careful construction of Vedic altars mentioned in the *Taitti-rīya Saṃhitā* (5.4.11) and in the *Baudhāyana Śulvaśāstra* and the *Āpasthamba Śulvaśāstra.* The best-known design is the falcon-shaped altar for the Agnicayana ritual. In this design, well-defined places are demarcated as seats for the gods during the ritual. Other geometrically shaped altars were in the forms of triangles, wheels, and so forth. They all developed out of a basic design, called *caturaśraśyenacit*, a fire altar "resembling a falcon [constructed] from squares." The shape of a particular *maṇḍala* depends on the special purpose of the sacrifice.

Another description of the geometrical designs for ritualistic purposes is found in the Vastuśātras, the handbooks on architecture. Instead of an outline in reduced scale, the Indian architect used a square (*vastumaṇḍala*) consisting of a grid of 64, 81, or more small squares as the starting point of a temple construction. Such a *vastumaṇḍala* was regarded as the body of the cosmic being (*vastupuruṣa*) in whose various parts the main deity, auxiliary deities, and temple guardians resided. The *vastumaṇḍala* is often closely connected with the actual design of the building and assures the builder of the presence of the gods.

Square forms, in contrast to the circular plans of Hindu and Jain cosmology, are also the basis for Hindu *maṇḍalas* used in Pāñcarātra (Vaiṣṇava Tantra) as well as Śaiva and Śākta Tantric rituals. The most elaborate designs to appear in the Pāñcarātra ritual are described in the *Lakṣmī Tantra* (c. tenth century CE), which contains a whole chapter on *maṇḍala* construction, and in the earlier *Jayākhya Saṃhitā.*

These texts prescribe at the beginning of the worship the construction of a square, which is divided into 256 small squares. The 16 small squares at the center and 8 squares of identical size at the margins are filled with one lotus each. The great square has gates and is surrounded by *śobhās* (ramparts; literally, "ornaments") and *koṇas* ("corners"). This *maṇḍala* is called Navapadma Maṇḍala ("*maṇḍala* of nine lotuses." The texts state that no matter whether the deity is worshiped in an image, in a pitcher, or under any other circumstances, the worshiper should always "recall to his mind the nine lotuses" of the *maṇḍala,* "which contains the whole world and is the exalted home of all gods, which encompasses all [other] loci and is the paramount abode" (*Lakṣmī Tantra* 37.22, 37.25). The Pañcarātrins also used a Cakrābja Maṇḍala ("*maṇḍala* having a lotus circle"), in which a large lotus fills the entire great square. A third form, the Navanābha Maṇḍala ("*maṇḍala* of the nine navels") has the great square divided into nine smaller squares, in each of which is a seat (*bimba*) for one of the nine manifestations of Lakṣmī (i.e., Vāsudeva, Saṃkarṣaṇa, Pradyumna, Aniruddha, Nārāyaṇa, Virāṭṭ, Viṣṇu, Narasiṃha, and Varāha).

In several North Indian Tantric Śaiva and Śākta texts, *maṇḍala* worship is mentioned along with the *dīkṣā* ("initiation") ceremony, (e.g., *Prapañcasāra Tantra* 5.36–70). The similarities in preparation and designs with those of the Pāñcarātrins is striking: in both traditions a pavilion must be erected over the prepared ground on which the *maṇḍala* is to be constructed. Of four *maṇḍalas,* mentioned in Tantric texts, the first, called Sarvatobhadra Maṇḍala ("*maṇḍala* that is auspicious on every side"), is identical with the Navapadma Maṇḍala; the second is only its smaller variant. The third, the Navanabha *Maṇḍala,* is identical in form with the *maṇḍala* of the same name of the Pāñcarātrins, but instead of the nine seats for deities it has five lotuses and four *svāstikas.* The fourth *maṇḍala* is identical with the third but has only five lotuses and no *svāstikas.* Therefore, it is called Pañcābja Maṇḍala ("*maṇḍala* of five lotuses"). During the initiation ceremony among the Pāñcarātrins and among Tantrics, the blindfolded adept is led to the *maṇḍala* and throws flowers upon it. The deity on whose seat the flowers fall will provide him with a name or will become his special object of worship.

In their daily and thus more private rituals, Tantrics of all denominations start the ritual with the drawing of geometrical designs in vermilion or red sandalwood paste on a purified surface. For the devotee, these diagrams are a source of cosmic power and the place on which the deity dwells during the ritual. Although such diagrams are also often called *maṇḍalas* and their function of providing a proper abode for the deity is the same as in the *dīkṣā* rituals, it has become customary to call the simpler designs for daily worship *yantras,* and to reserve the term *maṇḍala* for the larger ones in public ceremonies where the whole cosmos has to be present.

Hindu *maṇḍalas* have attracted the curiosity of modern symbolists and psychoanalysts such as Mircea Eliade and C. G. Jung. However, as their interpretations are not always based on the evidence of the available texts, the explanatory value of these studies is limited. A definitive history of the geometric designs used in Hindu rituals has yet to be written.

SEE ALSO Tantrism; Temple, article on Hindu Temples; Yantra.

BIBLIOGRAPHY

Bürk, Albert. "Das Āpastamba-Śulva Sūtra." *Zeitschrift der Deutschen Morgenländischen Gesellschaft* 56 (1902): 327–391.

Gupta, Sanjukta, trans. and ed. *Lakṣmī Tantra: A Pāñcarātra Text.* Leiden, 1972.

Gupta, Sanjukta, and Teun Goudriaan. "Hindu Tantric and Śākta Literature." In *History of Indian Literature,* edited by Jan Gonda, vol. 2, fasc. 2. Wiesbaden, 1981.

Gupta, Sanjukta, Dirk Jan Hoens, and Teun Goudriaan. *Hindu Tantrism.* Leiden, 1979.

Kramrisch, Stella. *The Hindu Temple.* 2 vols. Calcutta, 1946.

Meister, Michael W. "Maṇḍala and Practice in Nagara Architecture in North India." *Journal of the American Oriental Society* 99 (1979): 204–219.

Pott, P. H. *Yoga and Tantra: Their Interrelation and Their Significance for Indian Archeology* (1946). Translated from Dutch by Rodney Needham. The Hague, 1966.

New Sources

Bühnemann, Gudrun. *Mandalas and Yantras in the Hindu Traditions.* Leiden and Boston, 2003.

PETER GAEFFKE (1987)
Revised Bibliography

MAṆḌALAS: BUDDHIST MAṆḌALAS

In general terms, the Sanskrit word *maṇḍala* (Tib., *dkyil 'khor*) refers to something that is round or circular. *Maṇḍala* also designates a region, terrestrial division, domain, assembly, or group. In Tantric traditions, the term *maṇḍala* often refers to a space with a specific structure that is enclosed and delimited by a circumferential line into which a deity or deities are invited by means of *mantras.* This space is often a circle, but may also appear as a square, a triangle, or another shape.

The center of a *maṇḍala* contains an image or symbol of the main deity, the *maṇḍaleśa* or *maṇḍala* lord, for which the *maṇḍala* is named. The *maṇḍaleśa* is identified with the whole *maṇḍala,* and the surrounding deities are the *maṇḍaleśa's* aspects. The number of residents of a *maṇḍala* (e.g., buddhas, *bodhisattvas,* deities, consorts, offering goddesses, and gatekeepers) differs according to specific schools, giving rise to many varieties of *maṇḍalas,* which are difficult to classify. A simple *maṇḍala* has only one *maṇḍaleśa* with four surrounding deities situated in the four cardinal directions. This simple structure can be expanded by adding four more divine beings in the intermediate directions. Thus, the divinities surrounding the *maṇḍaleśa* usually number eight or multiples of eight. Greater complexity of the basic structure is achieved by increasing the number of divinities surrounding the center, by varying their spatial relationship to the center, and by grouping them around the center in circles of increasing distance.

Maṇḍalas can be classified structurally as unicyclic, with only one inner circle; bi-cyclic, with a second circle; tricyclic; and quadricyclic. The circles within some tricyclic *maṇḍalas* are called the body *maṇḍala*, the speech *maṇḍala*, and the mind *maṇḍala*, according to the way in which the deities are represented. Generally, the deities can be represented in one of three ways. They may appear as images with iconographic characteristics, in symbolic form, or as seed syllables (*bīja*), which are *mantras* of deities and are thus considered identical to them. The symbols are often identical with the attributes held by the images. In the body *maṇḍala*, the deities are represented as anthropomorphic images with iconographic attributes; in the speech *maṇḍala*, they are represented by their seed syllables; and in the mind *maṇḍala*, they are represented by their symbols.

Composite *maṇḍalas* consist of several individual *maṇḍalas*, each with a central deity. While the simplest *maṇḍala* houses one to five deities, more complex *maṇḍalas* may accommodate several hundred or more than one thousand deities. The *maṇḍala* structure can function as an important device for representing the pantheon of deities in a system or school, as well as the hierarchy of deities within the system. The hierarchical status of the *maṇḍala* inhabitants declines as one moves away from the center, and those in the outermost ring generally function only as guardians. The element of distance from the *maṇḍala's* center assumed importance when it came to including Brahmanic and Hindu deities, who were regularly assigned to the periphery of the *maṇḍala*.

There is no single uniform *maṇḍala* pattern. *Maṇḍalas* display various shapes and consist of different constituent parts, depending on the traditions of different schools, the ritual application, the deity worshiped, and the practitioner's qualifications and goals. It must be emphasized, however, that the *maṇḍala* is not merely a physical structure with a specific design. It is the place in which the practitioner beholds the deities who have been invoked into the *maṇḍala* and so have become an integral part of the structure.

One basic structural element of *maṇḍalas* (and *yantras*) is the lotus design. The lotus is a South Asian symbol of creation, purity, transcendence, and the sphere of the absolute, but it is especially known as a symbol of the female reproductive organ. In *maṇḍalas* of lotus design, the central deity is positioned in the pericarp, with the emanations or subordinate deities in the petals. A lotus design may feature one or more concentric rings of petals. Four-petaled and eight-petaled lotus designs are the most common. The petals of an eight-petaled lotus ideally point in the cardinal and intermediate directions and are thus well suited for positioning deities in their respective directions. Eight-petaled lotus designs are commonly found in the center of Buddhist (and also Hindu and Jain) *maṇḍalas*, such as in some versions of the *maṇḍala* of the Eight Great Bodhisattvas. The free-standing lotus *maṇḍalas*, which were manufactured in India from brass and later in Tibet from other metals, also feature an eight-petaled lotus with a statue of a *tathāgata* in the center and small statues of surrounding deities on the lotus petals. A pattern of nine lotuses arranged in groups of three placed one above the other appears in several important *maṇḍalas*, including versions of the Buddhist *vajradhātumaṇḍala*; this pattern also appears in Hindu Tantric *maṇḍalas*, such as versions of the *Pāñcarātra navapadmamaṇḍala* and the *Śaiva navanābhamaṇḍala*.

Maṇḍalas of the goddess Vajravārāhī (Vajrayoginī) include a hexagram consisting of two superimposed equilateral triangles, one pointing upwards and the other downwards. The triangles, which are also found in Hindu *maṇḍalas* and *yantras*, symbolize the union of the female and male principles. The hexagram is a widespread symbol and has been used for decorative purposes or as a magical sign in many cultures. It is also known as Magen David, the Shield of David, or as the Seal of Solomon.

Maṇḍalas have been used in different ways in various traditions. Indian Buddhist Tantric texts attest to their use in rituals, most importantly in Tantric consecration or empowerment (*abhiṣeka*) rites, which form part of a ritual initiation by a Tantric teacher. The number of empowerments received by the disciple differs according to the type of initiation. In the garland empowerment, a blindfolded initiate casts a flower on the *maṇḍala* in front of him. The initiate's buddha family is then determined from the place in the *maṇḍala* where the flower has fallen. A similar ritual is also known in Hindu Tantric traditions. *Maṇḍalas* for such temporary use in a specific ritual are prepared from various materials, including colored powders. After they have fulfilled their purposes, the *maṇḍalas* are ritually obliterated. The actual size of *maṇḍalas* differs according to the practitioner's means and goals. At times they are large enough for the practitioner to enter and move along pathways in them. *Maṇḍalas* are also visualized as part of Tantric *sādhanas* (described below).

MAṆḌALAS IN INDIAN BUDDHIST TEXTS. Descriptions of *maṇḍalas* for visualization appear in Indian *sādhana* texts in such collections as the *Sādhanamālā*. Some of these texts may date back to the ninth century CE or earlier. The term *sādhana* refers both to the methods employed by Tantric practitioners for the worship of a particular deity and the texts written to guide practitioners, often called yogins, in worship. As part of a *sādhana*, the practitioner may mentally create a *maṇḍala* of a deity in the following manner. After completing certain preliminary rites, the practitioner visualizes in succession: (1) an outer enclosure of ritual thunderbolt scepters (*vajra*); (2) a pavilion made of thunderbolt scepters; (3) a floor of adamantine stones; and (4) an outer boundary. Next the practitioner visualizes a white downward-pointing triangle inside the pavilion; this is the symbol of the female generative principle, called the "origin of existents" (*dharmodayā*), which is said to consist of space. Such an inverted triangle is also common in Hindu *maṇḍalas* and *yantras*, where it is a symbol of the female pubic triangle, sex organ, and womb. In the center of the triangle the practitioner visualizes a lotus with multicolored petals, and in its pericarp a five-pronged crossed thunderbolt scepter (*viśvavajra*) having the form of space. The spheres of the four great elements (wind, fire, water, earth), arising through the transformation of specific seed syllables, are configured atop one another in the center of the crossed thunderbolt scepter. Generated from the transformation of the four elements, the practitioner then visualizes a square palace, made from various jewels, with four gates, eight columns (two at each gate), four verandas, and four arches. The palace is decorated with garlands, half-garlands, mirrors, fly-whisks, various banners, bells, and other ornaments. In its innermost part the practitioner visualizes an eight-petaled lotus within whose pericarp the deity is enthroned.

Other patterns for *maṇḍala* visualization do not feature the origin of existents but call for the palace to be situated in the pavilion made of thunderbolt scepters and to rest on the five-pronged thunderbolt scepter, which is inside the pericarp of a huge lotus with multicolored petals. The lotus in turn rests on Mount Sumeru, which is surrounded by the oceans, continents, and subcontinents.

Structural elements of *maṇḍalas* appear more clearly in complex three-dimensional *maṇḍalas* made of such materials as wood, metal, or even precious stones. Three-dimensional *maṇḍalas* are already mentioned in the *Dharmamaṇḍalasūtra* by Buddhaguhya, a text composed in the eighth century and extant only in its Tibetan translation. This work deals with various aspects of the *maṇḍala* and its symbolism. The *Niṣpannayogāvalī* and *Vajrāvalī*, two complementary works by Abhayākaragupta that were written around 1100, are important documents for the study of late Indian Tantric *maṇḍalas*. Both texts describe in great detail twenty-six *maṇḍalas* from various Tantric traditions, including a version of the *kālacakramaṇḍala*. The *Niṣpannayogāvalī* focuses on the three-dimensional forms of these *maṇḍalas* for visualization (*bhāvyamaṇḍala*) and describes in detail the iconography of deities. The *Vajrāvalī* explains the construction and ritual use of two-dimensional *maṇḍalas*, which are to be drawn or painted (*lekhyamaṇḍala*) on the ground. In visualized *maṇḍalas*, the deities are mentally seen with their distinct iconographic characteristics, whereas in drawn *maṇḍalas* they are usually only represented by corresponding symbols (*cihna*, *samaya*). The elaborate ritual descriptions in the *Vajrāvalī* begin with the selection and purification of the site and the drawing of the lines of the *maṇḍala*, and include important details of the consecration rituals.

MAṆḌALAS IN THE TIBETAN AND NEVĀR BUDDHIST TRADITIONS. Permanent *maṇḍalas* painted on cloth are known as *paṭa* (Skt.), *thaṅka* (Tib.), and *paubhāḥ* or *paubāhāḥ* (Nevārī). Such *maṇḍalas* on cloth are commonly found in the Tibetan and Nevār Buddhist traditions as objects of general worship, and must have been popular in India as well since simpler versions, which assign anthropomorphic images of deities in the directions and have been called proto-*maṇḍalas*, are described in the *Mañjuśrīmūlakalpa* (eighth to eleventh century). Important painted *maṇḍala* collections of the later Tibetan tradition include the Ṅor collection, a set of 132 *maṇḍalas* produced at Ṅor Monastery, the headquarters of the Tibetan Sa skya (Sakya) pa Ṅor sect. The collection forms part of a voluminous work, the *Rgyud sde kun btus* (Compendium of Tantras), which is based on earlier *maṇḍala* texts and encompasses all Tibetan Tantric traditions, with an emphasis on the Sa skya sect. The text was compiled and the *maṇḍala* paintings were produced in Eastern Tibet during the latter half of the nineteenth century.

Maṇḍalas are also painted on the walls and ceilings of temples in the Tibetan and Nevār Buddhist traditions, a practice that continues today. The painting of *maṇḍalas* became part of the Bon tradition of Tibet, which is still active as an organized religion and has absorbed considerable Buddhist influence. In addition to the painting of *maṇḍalas*, a tradition of manufacturing and installing stone *maṇḍalas* of Dharmadhātuvāgīśvara, a form of Mañjuśrī, for the purposes of worship started around the seventeenth century among Nevār Buddhists. Many such stone *maṇḍalas* can be found in the Kathmandu Valley.

A two-dimensional painted or drawn *maṇḍala* represents a three-dimensional *maṇḍala* structure from a bird's-eye view. The outer parts of Tibetan painted *maṇḍalas* are often made up of several concentric rings. The outermost rim consists of a circle of fire, with the flames represented by a line of scrollwork. This flame barrier is usually depicted in five colors: blue, red, green, white, and yellow. Contiguous to the circle of fire is a dark, impenetrable wall of thunderbolt scepters. Some texts identify it with the ring mountain of Buddhist cosmology, the world's most exterior boundary. Such a circle of thunderbolt scepters can appear in different positions on a *maṇḍala*. Its general function is that of a separator between the outer rings of the *maṇḍala*.

In some cases, especially in *maṇḍalas* of wrathful deities, a circle containing eight cremation grounds (*śmaśāna*) follows. They are represented as places of religious practice, with four in the cardinal and four in the intermediate directions. The cremation grounds are modeled on a detailed iconographic plan. Each site has been assigned a specific mountain, relic shrine (stupa), river, tree, and ascetic who practices there. An ocean appears between each of the cremation grounds. In some *maṇḍalas* the circle of cremation grounds is found in the outermost part of the *maṇḍala*, outside the circle of fire. The cremation grounds encircle a ring of multicolored lotus petals. These are the petals of the huge lotus, which is conceived of as supporting the entire *maṇḍala* structure. Inside these enclosures is a park-like courtyard, often filled with water or cloud motifs, or displaying symbols of victory and auspiciousness.

A square palace appears in the center of the *maṇḍala.* Each of the four sides of the palace is interrupted by a T-shaped gate guarded by a gatekeeper. The palace rests on a foundation consisting of a crossed thunderbolt scepter, whose prongs project beyond the T-shaped gates. The palace has an inner courtyard of four basic colors that represent the four directions, usually white (east), yellow (south), red (west), and green (north). The center of the palace, usually marked off by another circle, contains the throne of the deity, which takes such shapes as that of a lotus flower or a wheel. These structural parts of the *maṇḍala* may be adorned elaborately in various ways.

A comparison between the structural elements of some extant painted *maṇḍalas* in the Tibetan tradition and those of the visualized *maṇḍalas* described in Indian *sādhana* texts shows many similarities. The fire circle of the painted *maṇḍala* corresponds to the outer boundary, which is visualized as surrounding the whole *maṇḍala* structure on all sides like a fire. According to some *sādhana* texts this circle is visualized in five colors, as in the Tibetan *maṇḍala* paintings. The circle of ritual thunderbolt scepters corresponds to the outer enclosure of thunderbolt scepters, which is identified with the ring mountain in cosmology. The huge crossed thunderbolt scepter of painted *maṇḍalas,* upon which the *maṇḍala* palace stands, corresponds to the crossed thunderbolt scepter (*viśvavajra*) visualized as resting on the lotus inside the origin of existents. The multicolored lotus petals in the painted *maṇḍalas* are the petals of this lotus.

Offering *maṇḍalas*. While the basic structure of the *maṇḍala* suggests that it was originally intended to portray the central deity as a king on a throne surrounded by his court inside a palace, various theological and philosophical concepts and schemes became associated with the *maṇḍala* structure when the *maṇḍala* symbolism evolved to more intricate and complex levels in the course of time. Such elements as the four gates of the *maṇḍala* were identified with categories of the Buddhist path. Iconographic characteristics of the *maṇḍala* deities were interpreted as expressing Buddhist truths. This development naturally led to various interpretations of the *maṇḍala* structure. The interpretations are extremely varied so that even a single text may provide more than one interpretation of the structural elements of a *maṇḍala.*

In *The Theory and Practice of the Maṇḍala,* Giuseppe Tucci called the *maṇḍala* "a map of the cosmos" and a "psychocosmogram" (Tucci, 1961, p. 23). These terms have been taken over by many later authors, who speak about the *maṇḍala* as a "cosmogram." This can be misleading, since we do not find representations of the continents in deity *maṇḍalas,* although cosmological notions often became associated with them. The "world" depicted in a deity *maṇḍala* is mostly a divine, transcendent world, distinguishable from the universe offered up in another kind of *maṇḍala,* the offering *maṇḍala.*

The offering *maṇḍala* or Mount Meru *maṇḍala,* which is widely known in the Tibetan tradition, is the symbolic offering of the spheres of the universe to a deity or preceptor. This *maṇḍala* represents the component parts of the universe according to ancient Indian cosmology: Mount Meru, the four continents, the eight subcontinents, the sun and moon, and the symbols of wealth and auspiciousness. The offering is made in containers of various shapes and materials. The most commonly used container consists of a round plate topped by hollow concentric metal rings of decreasing diameter and held in position by the grain offering that is placed inside. A decoration, which may include the wheel of the law, is placed on the top of the *maṇḍala.* Handfuls of grain, signifying the components of the universe, are generally heaped into the concentric rings. In this way the donor makes an offering of the universe in miniature. A similar scheme is also represented by free-standing brass, silver, beaded, or wooden structures, which are often placed on altars. Similar to the Tibetan offering *maṇḍala* is the *gurumaṇḍala,* which figures prominently in rituals of Nevār Buddhists. It is an ancient ritual offering of Mount Meru and the continents to the *gurū,* identified with the transcendental Buddha Vajrasattva.

MAṆḌALAS IN JAPANESE SHINGON BUDDHISM. *Maṇḍalas* also play an important role in the Shingon and Tendai esoteric schools of Japanese Buddhism. Kūkai (774–835 CE), who received a Buddhist Tantric transmission of Indian origin from his teacher Hui-ko (746–805) in China, is credited with bringing to Japan copies of a pair of *maṇḍalas.* The paired *maṇḍalas* assumed a prominent role in the ritual of the Shingon school that Kūkai subsequently founded, which aims at integrating the individual with the Buddha. The two *maṇḍalas* are said to represent the two aspects of the *dharma,* the knower and the known, which are viewed as two aspects of the same reality. One is the so-called Womb or Matrix *Maṇḍala* (Skt., *garbhamaṇḍala* or [*mahākaruṇā*]-*garbhodbhavamaṇḍala*; Jpn., *taizō mandara* or *daihi taizō shō mandara*), meaning "*maṇḍala* generated from the womb of Great Compassion." The other *maṇḍala* is the Thunderbolt Realm *Maṇḍala* (Jpn., *kongōkai mandara*), which is one of several known versions of a *vajradhātumaṇḍala.* The Womb *Maṇḍala* features in its center the familiar pattern of an eight-petaled lotus with Mahāvairocana occupying the throne. The Thunderbolt Realm *Maṇḍala* can best be categorized as a composite *maṇḍala,* an aggregate of originally nine individual *maṇḍalas* arranged horizontally and vertically in rows of three. When viewed collectively, these individual *maṇḍalas* are referred to as the "assemblies." Structurally, the Thunderbolt Realm *Maṇḍala* can be compared to the above-mentioned nine-lotus *maṇḍalas.* In addition to these two fundamental *maṇḍalas,* other *maṇḍalas* are also known in these esoteric Japanese traditions.

SPECULATIONS ON THE ORIGINS OF THE *MAṆḌALA*. The origins of the Buddhist Tantric *maṇḍala* are not yet clearly understood. Several scholars have suggested that all Tantric *maṇḍalas* are rooted in Vedic traditions. The layout of Vedic altars is taken as indicative of an early interest in geometric designs endowed with cosmological symbolism. The method of determining the lines of the compass for the construction of sacrificial altars, the consecration of bricks on the surface of a *cayana* altar by means of *mantras* and the locating of deities on the bricks are essential features of Vedic rituals, and aspects of these rituals recur in the practice of constructing *maṇḍalas* and invoking deities into their parts. The sacred space of *maṇḍalas* and *yantras* can be seen as a continuation of the Vedic sacrificial site, and the square enclosure of many Tantric *maṇḍalas* can be seen as an analogue of the sacred fire altar. But the similarities between the two traditions are limited, since the patterns displayed by Tantric *maṇḍalas* are distinctly different, as are the details of the rites and the *mantras* and deities invoked. Influences from other traditions must also have played an important role in the development of the *maṇḍala.*

Ronald M. Davidson pointed out similarities between Buddhist *maṇḍala* structures and structural elements of political systems. He suggested a derivation of the form and functions of Buddhist *maṇḍalas* from the political situation in early medieval India, with the *maṇḍala* replicating the feudal system of vassals (*sāmanta*) and the relationship between overlords and peripheral states. This derivation, however, can only account for selected *maṇḍala* patterns. Earlier, Stanley J. Tambiah had interpreted *maṇḍalas* as patterns for social organization.

Some scholars have considered the Wheel of Existence (*bhavacakra*) as an antecedent of the Buddhist Tantric *maṇḍala.* The Wheel of Existence, whose earliest representation is a fifth-century painting found on the wall of cave 17 in Ajaṇṭā, is a graphic and pictorial didactic device for explaining Buddhist teachings, namely the endless cycle of birth and death. It differs considerably from a *maṇḍala* in its nature and function, since it is not concerned with deities and their emanations in the way *maṇḍalas* are. The *kasiṇa* disks used as concentration devices in early Buddhism and recommended, for example, in Buddhaghosa's *Visuddhimagga,* have also been invoked as antecedents of *maṇḍalas.* However, these are plain disks and, unlike *maṇḍalas,* do not represent sacred space. Others have pointed to the symbolism and architectural form of stupas as contributing factors to the development of the Tantric *maṇḍala.* In contrast, Siegbert Hummel assumed that *maṇḍalas* originated outside India, probably in Tibet or China. Tucci believed that the symbolism of the *maṇḍala* was derived from the ziggurats of ancient Mesopotamia. These were towers built of mud brick with a square foundation and five (later seven) terraces, outside staircases, and a shrine at the summit.

Maṇḍala-like patterns are also found on Chinese mirrors, which led Schuyler Cammann to postulate the derivation of the Tibetan *maṇḍala* paintings from the Han dynasty's "TLV" mirrors. Cammann studied TLV patterns—three sets of angles, resembling the letters *T, L,* and *V*—on the backsides of Chinese mirrors used between 100 BCE and 100 CE. TLV patterns seem to represent the universe, but the symbolism of the mirror designs is still a matter of debate. The Chinese mirrors depict the square earth—that is, the Middle Kingdom, or China—at the center of the world with four T-shaped gates. In Tibetan *maṇḍalas* the T-shaped gates are also visible, but they are crowned with elaborate structures. Squares with T-shaped gates (called *earth squares*) are common elements of Hindu *yantras* as well. In the Chinese mirrors, the outer circle is thought to represent the sky, as indicated by a continuous string of clouds or "drifting cloud" design. In the Tibetan *maṇḍala,* however, the scrollwork on the outer ring represents fire.

SEE ALSO Buddhist Meditation, article on Tibetan Buddhist Meditation; Labyrinth; Mahāvairocana; Tantrism, overview article; Temple.

BIBLIOGRAPHY

Giuseppe Tucci's *The Theory and Practice of the Maṇḍala, with Special Reference to the Modern Psychology of the Subconscious,* translated by A. H. Brodrick (London, 1961), remains a readable general source on *maṇḍalas.* This is a translation of Tucci's original Italian work, *Teoria e pratica del maṇḍala, con particolare riguardo alla moderna psicologia de profondo* (Rome, 1949). However, Tucci's book, which was influenced by Jung's theory of archetypes, has become somewhat dated and suffers from generalizations and at times a confusing mix of Hindu and Buddhist materials. Also dated, but still a mine of information culled from Indo-Tibetan sources, is Reginald A. Ray's "Maṇḍala Symbolism in Tantric Buddhism," an unpublished doctoral dissertation submitted to the Divinity School of the University of Chicago in 1973. Detailed descriptions of thirty-seven major *maṇḍalas* in Indian Tantric Buddhist texts can be found in Marie-Thérèse de Mallmann, *Introduction à l'iconographie du tântrisme bouddhique* (Paris, 1986), pp. 39–82. Buddhaguhya's *Dharmamaṇḍalasūtra* was translated by Erberto Lo Bue as "The *Dharmamaṇḍala-Sūtra,*" in *Orientalia Iosephi Tucci Memoriae Dicata,* edited by G. Gnoli and L. Lanciotti (Rome, 1987), vol. 2, pp. 787–818. See also Siegbert Hummel, *Der Ursprung des tibetischen Maṇḍalas,* Ethnos 23 (1958): 158-171; and S. J. Tambiah, *World Conqueror and World Renouncer* (London, 1976).

For an interpretation of the Buddhist *maṇḍala* as replicating the Indian medieval feudal system, see Ronald M. Davidson, *Indian Esoteric Buddhism: A Social History of the Tantric Movement* (New York, 2002), pp. 131–144. A comprehensive treatment of the Tibetan *maṇḍala* can be found in Martin Brauen, *The Mandala: Sacred Circle in Tibetan Buddhism,* translated by Martin Willson (Boston, 1998). The book is a translation of the original German work, *Das Mandala: Der heilige Kreis im tantrischen Buddhismus* (Cologne, Germany, 1992).

Photographs of Tibetan *maṇḍalas* from different periods and traditions are reproduced in many exhibition catalogues, including Denise P. Leidy and Robert A. F. Thurman, *Mandala: The Architecture of Enlightenment* (New York, 1997). For the Tibetan Ṅor *maṇḍalas,* see *The Ngor Mandalas of Tibet,* vol. 1: *Plates,* edited by bSod nams rgya mtsho and Musashi Tachikawa (Tokyo, 1989), and vol. 2: *Listings of the Mandala Deities,* by bSod nams rgya mtsho, revised by Tachikawa, S. Onoda, K. Noguchi, and K. Tanaka (Tokyo, 1991).

For a comprehensive treatment of the two main *maṇḍalas* of the Japanese Shingon and Tendai schools, see Adrian Snodgrass, *The Matrix and Diamond World Mandalas in Shingon Buddhism* (New Delhi, 1988), and Michael Saso, *Homa Rites and Maṇḍala Meditation in Tendai Buddhism* (New Delhi, 1991). Nepalese stone *maṇḍalas* are described in Adalbert Gail, "Stone Maṇḍalas in Nepal," *East and West* 50 (2000): 309–358. For the Tibetan offering or Mount Meru *maṇḍalas,* see Stephan Beyer, *The Cult of Tārā: Magic and Ritual in Tibet* (Berkeley, 1973), pp. 167–170, and Alex Wayman, *The Buddhist Tantras: Light on Indo-Tibetan Esotericism* (London, 1995), pp. 101–106. For the *gurumaṇḍala* of the Nevār Buddhists, see David N. Gellner, "Ritualized Devotion, Altruism, and Meditation: The Offering of the Guru Maṇḍala in Newar Buddhism," *Indo-Iranian Journal* 34 (1991): 161–197.

For research on *maṇḍala* and landscape the reader may consult the essays in A. W. Macdonald, ed., *Maṇḍala and Landscape* (New Delhi, 1997). Buddhist *yantras* in Southeast Asia have been described in François Bizot, "Notes sur les *yantra* bouddhiques d'indochine," in *Tantric and Taoist Studies in Honour of R. A. Stein,* edited by Michel Strickmann (Brussels, 1981), vol. 1, pp. 155–191; see also François Bizot and Oskar von Hinüber, *La guirlande de joyaux* (Paris, 1994). For a discussion of the designs of Chinese mirrors and a comparison with Tibetan *maṇḍala* designs, see the following two articles by Schuyler Cammann: "The 'TLV' Pattern on Cosmic Mirrors of the Han Dynasty," in *Journal of the American Oriental Society* 68 (1948): 159–167; and "Suggested Origin of the Tibetan Mandala Paintings," in *The Art Quarterly* 13 (1950): 106–119.

GUDRUN BÜHNEMANN (2005)

MANI, the founder of Manichaeism—an important Gnostic and universal religion with pronounced syncretic tendencies and a marked missionary driving force—was born in the year 527 of the Seleucid calendar, which was calculated in Babylon as starting on April 3, 311 BCE. According to the evidence of al-Birunial-Bīrūnī, this equates to the year 216–217 CE, during the reign of the last Arsacid Parthian ruler, Ardawan (r. 213–224 CE). A comparison with Chinese and Coptic sources allows an even more accurate dating of his birth, in the spring of April 14, 216.

The Greek name *Manichaios* (Latin, *Manichaeus*) is a transcription of a name of Semitic origin, *Mani Hayya* (Mani the Living). The epithet *Hayya* (Living) indicated a particular quality of divine beings or benign individuals providing healing and life-giving power. The term thus represents an important feature of the spiritual life work of Mani: namely, his desire to establish himself as a doctor and healer of both body and soul, performing various miraculous cures that are mentioned in the stories and hagiographic accounts of his life. The honorific title "Lord Mani" (*Mar Mani*), was also known to the Chinese via the transcription *Mo-mo-ni* and to the Tibetans as *Mar Ma-ne.* The form *Manes* (the madman) was used in etymological wordplay (*mania,* "madness") by opponents in order to attack what they considered the absurd nature of his teaching. In the same way, the original Aramaic word *mana* (vessel), was turned around so that instead of being the "vessel of life" (*mana hayya*), insulting epithets were coined, such as the "vessel of Evil" (Ephraim) or "vessel of the Anti-Christ" (*Acta Archelai*).

INTRODUCTION. Third-century CE Mesopotamia was a flourishing province of Parthian, and later the Sassanid, empire. It had a high level of civilization and urban and commercial development (in contrast to the Iranian upland, with its agricultural economy and its predominantly warrior, feudal society). This aristocratic environment, based upon particular, overtly national values, was encouraged by Sassanid Zoroastrianism and the priestly cast of the magi, whose ascendancy was growing thanks to the groundwork of the high priest Kirdīr.

It was this aristocratic environment of Mesopotamia that came into conflict with the universalism of Mani and his ascetic teachings (preaching abstinence from agricultural labor and marriage), a situation that risked jeopardizing the religious, social, and economic basis of the empire. This increased importance of trade was not well-regarded in Zoroastrian ethical thought, in contrast to Manichaeism, in which we find an imaginary merchant ship (in the figurative language of its parables) and metaphors such as the Treasure and the Pearl, or the Merchant traveling in search of valuable merchandise, representing the itinerant nature of the seeker of knowledge, a feature common to both Manichaeism and Buddhism.

The extensive movement of peoples and goods in Mesopotamia encouraged religious, philosophical, and cultural interchange. The close proximity of beliefs from the Hellenism of late antiquity, Chaldean astrology, esoteric and Gnostic communities, and elements of Semitic paganism all produced a particularly syncretic environment. Furthermore, the vigor and growing spread of Christian proselytism now existed alongside Judaism, which had become entrenched over several centuries, and both Zoroastrianism and Buddhism had a presence in those areas adjacent to the great caravan routes that had encouraged the spread of Buddhism from India to Central Asia.

All of these belief systems influenced the spiritual development of Mani to varying degrees. Such an auspicious situation, in terms of geography and culture—cosmopolitan, eclectic, and with flourishing trade—opened a wide range of possibilities in terms of religious and philosophical opportunities. The distinctive features that caused the emergence of Mani, in the context of a varied and dynamic social outlook, were suffused with a concern for metaphysical and religious inquiry. His father, Patek, was no stranger to these views, for he belonged to the Elkasite baptismal community (the *Mughtasilah*—"those who are washed, who are purified"—mentioned bythe Arabic chronicler al-Nadīm [d. 995]).

BEGINNINGS. Mani was born in a place in northern Babylon, at Gaukhai in the Bēth Derāyē region, of Iranian parents. His father, Patek, was from Hamadan and his mother, Maryam, was from the noble Parthian Kamsaragan family. Mani's origins were a source of pride to him; he was aware that he came from an important part of the world in terms of its cultural, social, and religious relevance—a clear indication of its spiritual vitality. Mani *al-babiliyu* ("the Babylonian") as he was called in Arabic sources, would refer to the land of his birth on numerous occasions, with gratitude that he came from a cosmopolitan, eclectic land, a privileged starting point for his universalistic and missionary impulse. This drove him to spread his message in far-off lands: "A thankful pupil am I (Mani), I have come from the land of Babylon, I have come from the land of Babylon and I am posted at the door of Truth . . . I have come forth from the land of Babylon so that I might shout a call into the world" (M4a, Parthian).

The ancient prestige of Babylon—"gateway of the gods" (*bāb-ilāni*), as its name means—would thus be enhanced according to new needs of faith and salvation as a "gateway of Truth," as a means of getting to heaven, in line with the symbolism found in the language of various Gnostic and Manichaean passages, which regard religious teaching as a "gateway of salvation" (*dar ī uzēnišn*; M 5714, Middle Persian). The gates were opened by a savior who would proclaim a "call," launched by Mani to begin the missionary preaching drive, starting with the apostle himself, who was the first of the "heralds" of the message of salvation to be spread throughout the world.

Descriptions of Mani also survive in the polemical and heresiological works of Christian writers and confirm that his physical appearance was twofold—both Iranian and Mesopotamian, as when, in the *Acta Archelai* (XIV.3), Mani is described arriving dressed in "a multi-colored cloak of a somewhat ethereal appearance, while in his hand he held a very strong staff made of ebony-wood. He carried a Babylonian book under his left arm and he had covered his legs with trousers of different colors, one of them scarlet and the other colored leek-green, and his appearance was like that of an old Persian magician or warlord." Persian in appearance, like a wise man or magician as well as a warrior—for his clothes resembled that of a priest of the god Mithras (again, according to the *Acta Archelai* [XL.7])—this description of Mani is a clear and figurative representation of the dual nature of his ethnic and cultural roots—Iranian and Mesopotamian—and also illustrates another extremely important detail of the missionary activity and artistic and cultural output of Manichaeism—namely, the book.

Another epithet, "apostle," also appears in a Syriac inscription ("Mani, Apostle of Jesus Christ," a formula used by Mani to refer to himself that occurs in the *Epistula Fundamenti* passed on by Augustine) inscribed on rock crystal, on which there also appears what seems to be a picture of Mani in the center of a triptych of figures. He is wearing a hat and a band, his hair is flowing, and he has a long beard with a parting in the middle. Another representation, on a copper plate from the Oldenburg expedition in Turkestan, instead shows an image with oriental features. Here, Mani has long hair over his shoulders and a Middle Persian inscription, "the face of the Apostle of Light." Another probable depiction, more Chinese in style, is on a wall painting of Kočo (VIII-IX sec.), showing him as a church dignitary surrounded by his elect, with a beard and mustache, a richly-decorated hat, and a halo consisting of a lunar crescent surrounding a reddish-white solar disk.

THE PHYSICAL BODY AND FIRST TEACHINGS. According to the Arabic sources—the *Fihrist* of al-Nadīm—Mani was lame, but this reference to a physical disability can be interpreted in one of two ways. It may be seen as a term of condemnation and contempt by a religious opponent (normal practice in heresiological Muslim literature) intended to emphasize the physical (and hence psychological and spiritual) deformity of the heretical adversary, variously described as lame, cross-eyed, or a leper. On the other hand, it may be seen as a physical symbol of otherness, and of a lopsided walk (compared to the normal, erect posture) that is typical of exceptional individuals such as fortune-tellers, healers, shamans, and therapists. These types of individuals—like Oedipus, Melampus, Jason, or indeed Jacob—have been studied by Carlo Ginzburg (1992, pp. 206–224), who finds they are geographically and culturally closer to Mani, who after his night battle with the angel beside the river Yabboq limps because of a dislocated hip.

Walking lopsidedly is thus the sign of a physical abnormality, of an otherness that characterizes ecstatic experiences and journeys that anticipate going into the world of the dead, into a supernatural dimension involving those who are apparently dead. This could correspond to a side of Mani's character—namely, his ability as a wise man and healer, as well as his ability to wield miraculous powers (Middle Persian, *warz*). It was this aspect of Mani that influenced those who met him to convert. One such convert was the king of Turan, who was convinced of the merit of Mani's teaching because of his ability to levitate. In another episode, Mani miraculously showed to the skeptical king of Messenia the Paradise of Light with all of the gods in the immortal Air of Life, causing the king to faint. Mani then brought him back to consciousness by laying a hand on his head.

The miraculous, restorative power of Mani is thus shown mainly in cures. For this reason he is described—and describes himself—as a doctor, a therapist who treats both body and soul, wounded and imprisoned in the world of Matter. Thus, his healing was a means of conversion, a tangible sign of his message of salvation effected by restorative words (*salubria verba* in the *Epistula Fundamenti*), fully justifying the epithet "living" (*hayya*) that follows his name.

Yet these healing powers also resulted in his condemnation. In his last appearance before the Sassanid king, Wahrām I (prompted by the Zorastrian priests), the king accused him of being unskilled in war and hunting, and also of being an inattentive and ineffective doctor. Mani's defense—reminding the king of the benefits he had given to his family, the exorcisms that had given release to his servants and those who had been cured of fevers and deadly illnesses—was of no avail. The possession of miraculous healing powers was part of a whole raft of spiritual abilities gained during mystic and ecstatic experiences in visions and revelations by angelic beings and, in particular, by the angel known as "the Twin" (Greek, *syzygos*; Middle Persian, *narjamīg*; Arabic, *al-Tawm*).

The first revelation, which Mani experienced at the age of twelve, led him to renounce the rituals of the Elkasite baptist community in pursuit of more interior knowledge. It was the spiritual double of Mani, his protective angelic twin, who revealed to him the hidden mysteries of *gnōsis*. This was the main feature of his message, a *gnōsis* involving both knowledge and understanding of the human condition—and the pursuit of a regime of physical and mental asceticism—in order to achieve the appropriate separation within the individual life of the "mixture" of the two "principles" (or "natures," "substances," "roots") of Light/Wisdom, as opposed to Darkness/Ignorance. The mythical development of "two principles" was regarded as taking place in three "periods" of time (*initium*, *medium*, and *finis*, according to Augustine). These represent a first phase, in which Good and Evil were separate; a second phase, corresponding to mankind's present existence, in which the two principles were mingled after the onset of Matter' and a third future stage at the final apocatastasis, when Evil would be defeated and the two principles would separate once more. This outline forms the basis of the cosmological, soteriological, and eschatological myth of Mani's dualist system, a radical and absolute dualism that considered not just myth and metaphysics but also anthropology and ethics, so that microcosm and macrocosm reflected one other. Thus, the drama of the creation of the world and the redemption of Light imprisoned by Matter was the same as the inner experience of the Manichaean believer, with his existence enlightened by *gnōsis* and the *Nous* that would redeem his soul.

THE INITIAL TEACHINGS. Mani's first teachings were subject to many Jewish and Gnostic influences, as well as to teachers such as Marcion (d. 160?) and Bardaisan (154–222 CE). Mani probably inherited from Marcion a number of his views opposing the Old Testament, even if in the system of Mani various heterodox Jewish positions, like those of Qumran (Reeves, 1991), should be stressed. They are particularly recognizable in the structure of the Elkasite baptismal community into which Mani was introduced by his father and where he had his first religious experiences. It is far from insignificant that during this period apocryphal, apocalyptic literature (by Adam, Seth, Enoch, Shem, and Enosh) that was Gnostic in character was circulating; these works, along with the Christian Gospels, the Pauline Epistles, and the Acts (of John, Peter, Paul, Andrew, and Thomas) influenced Mani's initial spiritual training. Paul and Thomas were particular favorites of Mani, the former as an example of the ideal apostle who went all over the world and spread the message of salvation, regardless of adversity and persecution, and the latter because he had set out to preach the gospel in India and was thus the predecessor of Mani, whose own first mission was also to India.

From the philosophy of Bardaisan, who lived during the second and third centuries and was an exponent of Syriac Gnosticism derived from Greek and Iranian ideas, Mani was probably influenced by the idea of the two principles of Light and Darkness and their intermingling, and, therefore, by a number of mythical personifications that were remarkably similar (such as the Father of Greatness and the Mother of Light, which recall the Father of Life and Mother of Life in Bardaisan). He must also have inherited from Christians and Bardesanites the use of music as a way of elevating and purifying the soul. His knowledge of Zoroastrian religious teaching should also be mentioned, especially as regards the two principles, the three periods of time, and the importance of the complete nature of the separation. The Buddhist element—remarked upon by al-Bīrūnī, who mentions an Indian influence on the doctrine of transmigration—must also have influenced Mani's monastic organization and some of his injunctions, such as the nonviolence prescribed for the elect.

The aspect of Mani's teaching that is most different from the various forms of ascetic Gnosticism and proselytizing was his own prophetic and apostolic mission—via preaching—with a missionary zeal that spread his message of universal salvation both east and west. Once again it was his angel twin who ordained his missionary calling when he was in his twenty-fourth year (240 CE), driving Mani to divorce himself from the Elkasite community in order to undertake a missionary enterprise that would last for a further thirty-five years, during which time he would gain converts and encourage missions and those who followed him. He began by sailing to India, to the kingdom of Tūrān and—following the positive reception of Šābuhr—throughout the provinces of the empire: Persia, Media, Parthia, Adiabene, Babylon, Messenia, and Sushan. He also sent missions beyond the empire, and in the West, in Syria and Egypt, under the leadership of Addā, he succeeded in gaining important converts in the city of Palmyra, converting Nafšā, the sister of the queen Zenobia (and perhaps even Zenobia herself).

While in the East, under the leadership of Ammō, there were missions in Margiana and in Bactria, beyond the Oxus, and perhaps even in Armenia. In his missionary drive following the "call" proclaiming the words of salvation to mankind, Mani took the apostle Paul as his example and attempted to make himself the final link in a whole chain of redeeming figures. Beginning from the biblical line of Adam, Seth, Enosh, Enoch, Shem, and Noah—and with the addition of

Zoroaster, Buddha (even Laozi, according to the Chinese *Compendium*), and Jesus—this line of apostolic succession was ended with Mani himself, fulfilling the prophecy that depicted him, as he was called in Islamic sources, as the "Seal of the Prophets" (*khātim al-nabiyyīn*). The purpose of his coming was to perfect and fulfill the religions that had gone before him. Their teachings had been incomplete and imperfect before Mani's supreme revelation and his words of life, which he passed on in "living books."

THE SPREAD OF MANI'S TEACHINGS. The dissemination of Mani's message led to his being known in Central Asia in a large number of different ways and by many different expressions, such as the returning "Messiah-God," from a Christian perspective, or as "Mani the Buddha of Light" (*Mo-ni-guang-fo*), or as the "All-knowing king of the law" in Chinese texts, according to Buddhist phraseology that identified him with the future Buddha, Maitreya, and thus called him Buddha (*burxan*) or God (*tängri*). The eclectic and syncretic aspect of his teaching was not always well-received, and in some cases, as recorded in an eighth- or ninth-century Tibetan text, he was addressed as "the deceitful Persian Mar Ma-ne," and accused of dressing up his message in Buddhist guise, borrowing various beliefs in order to construct his own completely different versions.

Yet this chameleon-like ability, which encouraged the widespread expansion of his teaching, was the distinctive characteristic of Mani and his successors, enabling them to blend "wisdom and action" (M 5794, *wihīh ud kirdagān*), "wisdom and ability" (Mani Codex of Cologne 5.4: *sophia kai eumēchania*), and finding, as the Chinese texts remark, the "skillful means" (*fang bian*) that allowed them to adapt themselves to every geographical, cultural, and social situation in order to boost conversions and establish communities and institutions. With this practical wisdom, Manichaean *gnōsis* displayed the dual Buddhist ideas of *prajñā* (awareness) and *upāya* (means), showing a practical and industrious attitude that would enable it to flourish in a variety of places and obtain widespread recognition.

From this point of view, Mani was not an ascetic who was cut off from the world, and even if he preached detachment from Matter, involving fasting and abstinence, his approach toward daily life was anything but pessimistic and rejectionist. On the contrary, his clever strategy of promotion and general consensus was optimistic and proactive, cleverly avoiding any "radical" fundamentalist and anti-universal attitude, though with unfortunate political consequences resulting in his conflict with royal authority.

From the start of his missionary career, Mani sought the support of government and the Sassanid royal family, and he was staunchly supported by Šābuhr, even becoming part of the royal entourage (*komitaton*) and traveling with him to the provinces of the empire and on a campaign against the Romans. Perhaps it was also because of his Parthian noble ancestry, and for this reason—not just as a Gnostic metaphor—he was called "son of the king" (Puech, 1949, p. 36). Because of his attendance at court, Mani's religious imagery depicted royal and feudal institutions of the palace of Ctesiphon. Beginning with the figure of the Father of Greatness and his heavenly entourage of Eons, Kingdoms, and Divinities—which made up the "retinue" (*padwāz*) of the King of Paradise—other characters were added, including the "friends," those who stood in the presence of the King (*parwānag*), and the "guardian of the gate" (*darbān*).

Mani's ascension into heaven after his death on February 27, 277 CE, when he was sixty (following his suffering in prison), is the subject of a story (M5569) that mixes royal and warrior images, a story that became the paradigm for the fate of the devoted followers of his teachings. Much like a king who dons armor and is given divine garb, a diadem of light, and a marvelous garland, the Apostle Mani ascends to heaven in an apotheosis of light and glory to reach the Father.

THE PREACHINGS AND AUTHORED WORKS. Mani's preaching was thus strategically aimed at the royal circle, as is shown by the stories of famous conversions—such as the brother of the King of Kings, Mihršāh—and hence his first work was a book dedicated to his protector, the King of Kings, Šābuhr, titled *Šābuhragān* (*Nībēg;* "Book dedicated to Šābuhr"), written in Middle Persian and containing cosmology, prophecy, and apocalyptics.

Mani also wrote eight books in Eastern Aramaic: the *Living Gospel*, a kind of New Testament, which put forward a new version of the four Gospels and the Epistles of Paul, explaining the purpose of his mission; the *Treasure of Life*, a work of theology and apologetics; the *Mysteries* (al-Nadīm gives us the titles of eighteen chapters); the *Pragmateia*, a collection of Manichaean mythology; the *Image*, a collection of pictures representing teachings; the *Giants*, inspired by the Book of Giants and dealing with apocalyptics; the *Letters*, important organizational and missionary documents; and, finally, the *Psalms* and *Prayers*.

In Mani's versatile linguistic competence (he spoke Aramaic and Middle Persian), there are signs of the universal nature of his message, disseminated in many scripts and languages (Greek, Latin, Coptic, Iranian, Turkish, and Chinese). His writings were inventive, and he created a simplified Eastern Syriac alphabet (for the Iranic languages) that eliminated the complicated use of scribal heterograms, thus facilitating a better understanding and use of the languages (Parthian, Middle Persian, Sogdian) that spread his teachings. Thus, one of the prayers dedicated to Mani praises him as "interpreter of religion" (M 38 Parthian). His new gospel message continued to be translated into new languages and scripts.

The fundamental importance of the book as a secure means of transmitting truthfully his spiritual teaching and avoiding any possibility of misrepresentation reveals another important aspect of Mani's character. In addition to being a preacher, he was also an artist who gained a reputation as a tremendous communicator. He did this not simply via stories that had cumulative symbolic effect, but rather by accompanying these stories with pictures illustrating his baroque and impressionist mythology. The use of these pictures demonstrated that his missionary work did not involve only religion and writing, but that Mani was a painter as well.

CONCLUSION. The art of Manichaean manuscripts became famous in posterity, consisting of refined, finely-decorated miniatures with ornamental floral arrangements and bright colors. This work verified Mani's reputation as a calligrapher and as a painter (in Islamic sources) able to draw a large perfect circle. He was also regarded as the inventor of a kind of lute.

Mani, the Apostle of Light, was thus a custodian of divine revelation, a conscious syncretist, a miracle worker, a wise and able man, a rhetorician, a lyric and epic storyteller, and a dramatist. His original intellectual and artistic character indicates that he was a poet and visionary rather than a theologian and philosopher. Mani was detested and cursed as the founder of a heretical religion by the major religions of his day, Zoroastrianism and Christianity, and subsequently by Islam. Yet he was lauded as the Savior in hymns by the faithful, as well as in festivals such as Bēma—the day commemorating his death and his spiritual presence among believers.

SEE ALSO Bardaisan; Gnosticism, article on Gnosticism from Its Origins to the Middle Ages; Manichaeism, overview article and articles on Manichaeism and Christianity, Manichaeism in Central Asia and China, Manichaeism in Iran, and Manichaeism in the Roman Empire; Marcion.

BIBLIOGRAPHY

Ginzburg, Carlo. *Storia notturna. Per una decifrazione del sabba.* Torino, 1989. English translation *Ecstasies: Deciphering the Witch's Sabbath.* New York, 1992.

Gnoli, Gherardo. "Introduzione generale." In *Il Manicheismo, volume I: Mani e il Manicheismo*, edited by Gherardo Gnoli, with the assistance of Andrea Piras, pp. XI-LXVII. Milan, Italy, 2003. Translation and comment of Manichaean texts: Greek (Luigi Cirillo) Coptic (Serena Demaria, Sergio Pernigotti), Iranian (Enrico Morano, ElioProvasi), Turkish (Peter Zieme), Chinese (Antonello Palumbo), Arabic (Alberto Ventura).

Gulácsi, Zsuzsanna. *Manichaean Art in Berlin Collections.* Turnhout, Belgium, 2001.

Klimkeit Hans-Joachim. *Gnosis on the Silk Road.* San Francisco, 1993. Translation of Iranian and Turkish texts.

Klimkeit Hans-Joachim. "Jesus, Mani and Buddha as Physicians in the Texts of the Silk Road." In *La Persia e l'Asia Centrale. Da Alessandro al X secolo*, pp. 589-595. Rome, 1996.

Hegemonius, *Acta Archelai (The Acts of Archaelaus)*, translated by Mark Vermes, introduction and commentary by Samuel N.C. Lieu, with the assistance of Kevin Katz. Turnhout, Belgium, 2001.

Lieu, Samuel N.C. "A New Figurative Representation of Mani?" In *Studia Manichaica*, edited by Ronald E. Emmerick et al., pp. 380-386. Berlin, 2000.

Panaino, Antonio. "Strategies of Manichaean Religious Propaganda." In *Turfan Revisited—The First Century of Research: The Arts and Cultures of the Silk Road*, edited by D. Durkin-Meisterernst et al., pp. 249-255. Berlin, 2004

Puech, Henri-Charles. *Le manichéisme: son fondateur, sa doctrine.* Paris, 1949.

Reeves, John C. "The 'Elchasaite' Sanhedrin of the Cologne Mani Codex in Light of Second Temple Jewish Sectarian Sources." *Journal of Jewish Studies* 43 (1991): 68-91.

Richter, Siegfried G. *The Manichaean Coptic Papyri in the Chester Beatty Library. Psalm Book, Die Erakleides-Psalmen.* Turnhout, Belgium, 1998.

Skjærvø, Prods Oktor."Bardesanes." In *Encyclopædia Iranica* III, edited by Ehsan Yarshater, cols. 780b-785b. London and New York, 1989.

Stein, Rolf Aurel. "Une mention du manichéisme dans le choix du bouddhisme comme religion d'état par le roi tibétain Khri-sroṅ. lde-bcan." In *Indianisme et bouddhisme. Mélanges offerts à Mgr Étienne Lamotte*, pp. 329-337. Louvain-la-Neuve, 1980.

Tardieu, Michel. *Le manichéisme.* Paris, 1981.

Tardieu, Michel. "La conception de Dieu dans le manichéisme." In *Knowledge of God in the Graeco-Roman World*, edited by T. Baarda et al., pp. 262-270. Leiden, 1988.

Van Tongerloo, Alois. "Manichaeus Medicus." In *Studia Manichaica*, edited by Ronald E. Emmerick et al., pp. 613-621. Berlin, 2000.

Widengren, Geo. *Mesopotamian Elements in Manichaeism.* Uppsala, Sweden, 1946.

Widengren, Geo. *Mani and Manichaeism.* New York, 1965.

Wurst, Gregor. *The Manichaean Coptic Papyri in the Chester Beatty Library. Psalm Book, Die Bema-Psalmen.* Turnhout, Belgium, 1996.

ANDREA PIRAS (2005)

MANICHAEISM

This entry consists of the following articles:

MANICHAEISM: AN OVERVIEW

The doctrine professed by Mani and the path to salvation that he revealed constitute a form of gnosis. It originated during the first half of the third century in Mesopotamia, a region of the Parthian empire in which a number of different religious and philosophical schools were actively present, notably Christianity, Judaism, and Zoroastrianism. The sects and communities of the region reflected the influence of one or the other of these cults to varying degrees and were often characterized by an evident Gnostic orientation. Hellenism was well rooted and widespread in Mesopotamia (as in neighboring Syria), especially in the urban centers of Seleucid origin. Open to commercial and cultural exchanges, Mesopotamia was the region within the vast Parthian empire that was most likely to absorb syncretic and eclectic cultural and spiritual trends. Manichaeism, however, was not only a gnosis in the narrow sense; it was primarily a universal Gnostic religion—the only great universal religion to arise from the Near Eastern Gnostic tradition. No other Gnostic school was as successful as Manichaeism, and no other aimed, as it did, to establish itself as a truly universal religion, founded and nurtured by an enterprising missionary spirit.

As with all Gnostic movements, Manichaeism holds that knowledge leads to salvation and that this is achieved through the victory of the good light over evil darkness. As with all Gnosticism, Manichaeism is permeated by a deep and radical pessimism about the world, which is seen as dominated by evil powers, and by a strong desire to break the chains holding the divine and luminous principle inside the prison of matter and of the body. Knowledge leads to salvation through an anamnesis, in which the initiate recognizes that his soul is a particle of light, consubstantial with the transcendental God.

MANICHAEAN LITERATURE AND SOURCES. Very little remains of the rich and varied Manichaean literature. We know the canon of its scriptures mainly through the titles of individual works, of which seven were attributed to Mani himself, and through fragments preserved in quotations by authors who were hostile to Manichaeism. Sometimes we do have most of the text, as, for example, in the *Living Gospel,* which was translated from Syriac to Greek. So too was the *Treasure of Life,* some passages of which were quoted by Augustine and by al-Bīrūnī; the *Mysteries,* of which we know the subtitles quoted by Ibn al-Nadīm and a few passages preserved by al-Bīrūnī; the *Treatise,* the *Book of Giants,* and the *Epistles,* of which Ibn al-Nadīm gives a list; and the *Psalms* and *Prayers.* All of these works were attributed to the founder of the faith, and rare and scattered fragments of them have been preserved in Manichaean texts from Central Asia (Turfan) and Egypt (Fayum). Two more works were attributed to Mani but are outside of the canon: the *Image* and the *Shābuhragān,* the book dedicated to the Sassanid king Shāpūr I. The purpose of the *Image* was to illustrate the main themes of the doctrine in a way that would be clear even to those not able to read. The *Shābuhragān,* the only work written in Middle Persian—Mani usually wrote in Syriac or Eastern Aramaic—discussed cosmology, anthropogony, and eschatology and is known to us through fragments preserved in the Turfan manuscripts and through an essential quotation by al-Bīrūnī concerning the Seal of the Prophecy.

Manichaean patrology is relatively better known to us than Mani's writings, mainly through the texts discovered at Turfan around the beginning of this century and those found at Fayum in 1930. Among the hagiographic works, we should mention the Manichaean Codex of Cologne, a Greek translation of a Syriac original, dating from the fifth century, and the Coptic *Homilies;* among the doctrinal ones, the Coptic *Kephalaia* and the *Chinese Treatise* of Dunhuang; among the hymns, the Coptic *Psaltery* and the Iranian hymn books, in Middle Persian and in Parthian, found in Turfan, as well as those in Chinese from Dunhuang; among the practical and liturgical writings, the *Compendium of Doctrines and Rules of the Buddha of Light, Mani,* a treatise dating from 731, found in Dunhuang, that was translated from Parthian into Chinese for use in the administration of the cult. To the last category also belonged the *Khwāstwānēft,* a handbook of formulas for the confession of sins, which has come down to us in a Uighur text from Central Asia.

Thus the discoveries of the twentieth century have brought to light, albeit only partially and in a fragmented fashion, a literature that in many cases, especially in the psalms and hymns, is distinguished by its considerable literary value and by its strong and delicate poetic sensibility. These writings substantially modified the picture of Manichaeism that had been reconstructed through indirect sources before the end of the nineteenth century.

These sources, however, are still valuable, and they contribute now in a more balanced way to a reconstruction of Manichaean doctrine and history. They are numerous, and all by hostile authors, Neoplatonic, Christian, Zoroastrian, Muslim. There are Greek sources, from Alexander of Nicopolis to the *Acta Archelai;* Latin sources, from the Pseudo-Marius Victorinus to Augustine; Syrian sources, from Aphraates and Ephraem of Syria in the fourth century to Theodoros bar Kōnaī in the eighth; Middle Persian and Pahlavi sources, from passages in the *Dēnkard* (The acts of religion) to a chapter of the *Shkand-gumānīg Wizār* (The definitive solution to doubts), a Zoroastrian apologetic work (ninth and tenth centuries); Arabic and Persian Muslim sources, from al-Yaʿqūbī (ninth century), al-Ṭabarī, al-Masʿūdī, and Ibn al-Nadīm (tenth century) to al-Bīrūnī, Ṭaʿālibī (eleventh century), al-Sharastānī (twelfth century), Abū'l-Fidā, and Mirkhwānd (fourteenth and fifteenth centuries).

Until Manichaean literature was rediscovered, the works of Augustine, al-Bīrūnī, Ibn al-Nadīm, and the *Acta Archelai* were the cornerstones of Manichaean studies. Although the situation has undoubtedly changed considerably thanks to the more recent discoveries, the accounts of some anti-Manichaean authors remain extremely important, especially when viewed alongside those passages in Manichaean literature that discuss similar or identical subjects. It is now easier to distinguish between that which was written in polemic and apologetic ardor and that which resulted from accurate and intelligent information concerning Manichaean doctrines. Some of the sources are particularly relevant since they provide likely and precious data: for example, *de Moribus Manichaeorum, de duabus animabus, de Genesi contra Manichaeos,* the writings against Adimantus, Faustus, Felix, Fortunatus, Secundinus by Augustine, the Manichaean cosmogony of Theodoros bar Kōnaī, and a few quotations and excerpts by al-Bīrūnī and Ibn al-Nadīm.

The Fundamental Doctrines. Manichaean doctrine places great importance on the concept of dualism, which is deeply rooted in Iranian religious thought.

Dualism. Like Zoroastrian cosmology, which we know through relatively late texts (ninth century CE), Manichaean dualism is based on the doctrine of the two roots, or principles, of light and darkness and the three stages of cosmic history: the golden age before the two principles mixed together; the middle, or mixed, period; the present age, in which the powers of light and darkness battle for ultimate control of the cosmos; and the last age, when the separation of that which had become mixed, and between followers of good and evil, occurs. According to the Zoroastrian doctrine, this is the time of *frashgird* (MPers., "rehabilitation"; Av., *frashōkereti*) in which the two poles of good and evil will once again be distinguished. The holy books that he himself has revealed are those of the two principles and three stages. The two principles are light and darkness; the three stages are the past, the present, and the future; this information comes to us from a fragment of a Chinese text. This is the doctrine to which Augustine makes reference—*initium, medium, et finis*—in his anti-Manichaean treatises *Against Felix* and *Against Faustus.* It is more fully expressed in another Chinese text:

> First of all, we must distinguish between the two principles. He who wishes to join this religion must know that the two principles of light and darkness have absolutely distinct natures; if he cannot distinguish this, how can he practice the doctrine? Also, it is necessary to understand the three stages, that is, the prior stage, the middle stage, the posterior stage. In the prior stage, heaven and earth do not yet exist: there are only light and darkness, and they are separate from each other. The nature of light is wisdom, the nature of darkness is ignorance. In all motion and in all repose, these two are opposed to each other. At the middle stage, darkness has invaded light. The latter lunges forward to drive it back and thus itself enters the darkness and attempts at all costs to drive it out. Through the great calamity we acquire disgust, which, in turn, drives us to separate our selves from our bodies; in the burning abode the vow is made to attempt an escape. (Chavannes and Pelliot, 1913)

The "great calamity" is a metaphor for the body, and the "burning abode" stands for the world, seen as a burning house from which one is saved by escaping. The text continues: "At the later stage, instruction and conversion are accomplished, truth and falsehood have returned each to its roots: light has returned to the great light, and darkness has returned to the mass of darkness. The two principles are reconstituted" (Chavannes and Pelliot, 1913).

The two roots are not generated and have nothing in common: they are irreducible opposites in every way. Light is good, equated with God; darkness is evil, equated with matter. Because good and evil are coeval, the problem of the origin of evil (a central dilemma of Christian doctrine) is resolved, in the most radical and extreme way. Its existence cannot be denied; it is everywhere, it is eternal and can only be defeated by knowledge (gnosis), which leads to salvation through the separation of light and darkness.

The way in which the two principles are represented is reminiscent of the two spirits, or *mainyus*, in the original Zoroastrian concept. Spenta Mainyu and Angra Mainyu are opposites in all things (*Yasna* 30.3–6), and their choice between good and evil, between *asha* ("truth") and *druj* ("falsehood"), is also prototypical of the choice that must be made by humankind. The ethical value of Manichaean dualism is no less strong, although its answer to the problem of evil is, of course, more typically Gnostic. The Manichaeans refused to consider Ōhrmazd and Ahriman, the Pahlavi equivalents of the two *mainyus*, as two brothers who are opposed one to the other. The Uighur text *Khwāstwānēft* states: "If we once asserted that Khormuzta [Ōhrmazd] and Shīmnu [Ahriman] are brothers, one the cadet, one the firstborn . . . I repent of it . . . and I beg to be forgiven for that sin" (1c.3–4). Thus they were not so much addressing the dualism of the *Gāthās,* as opposing the later dualism of Zurvanism, which had demoted Ahura Mazdā to the role of a symmetrical opposite of Angra Mainyu and placed Zurwān, who personified infinite time, above the dualistic formula. In fact, it is interesting to observe how the Manichaeans restored Ōhrmazd to a central role in the drama of salvation and in the very Gnostic approach to the *prōtos anthrōpos,* while considering *Zurwān* as one of the names—the other Iranian name was *Srōshaw*—for the Father of Greatness, "sovereign god of the heaven of light," "god of truth," that is, one of the two terms of the dualistic formula. Terms for the opposite pole are *Devil, Satan, Ahriman, Shīmnu, Hulē, Matter, Evil,* the *Great Archon,* and the *Prince of Darkness.*

Rather than metaphysical speculation, we find at the root of Manichaean dualism a merciless analysis of the human condition, a pessimism largely common to all forms of gnosis and to Buddhism. By the mere fact of being incarnate, humans suffer; they are prey to evil, forgetful of their luminous nature as long as they remain asleep and dimmed by ignorance in the prison of matter. While the two principles remain mixed, all is waste, torture, death, darkness: "Liberate me from this deep nothingness, from this dark abyss of waste, which is naught but torture, wounds unto death, and where there is no rescuer, no friend. There can be no salvation here, ever! All is darkness . . . all is prisons, and there is no exit" (Parthian fragment T2d.178).

This pessimistic attitude toward the world and toward life, which perpetuates itself in the snares of matter, accompanied Manichaeism throughout its history, increasingly strengthened by the bitter and often violent confrontations between its followers and the other established religions of the eastern and western empires. It was probably also at the root of an antinomic tendency of these "subversives," who could see nothing good in a world full of horror, evil, and injustice. This was probably also an important reason for the fierce persecutions they suffered—as is evident from the testimony of Zoroastrian sources (*Dēnkard,* Madan edition, pp. 216–218)—as well as for their refusal to conform to traditional customs and practices. It also helped to bring about that *damnatio memoriae* to which Mani and Manichaeism were universally subjected.

Knowledge as the path to salvation. An essential and specific characteristic of Manichaeism is its Gnosticism, that is, its mixture of religion and science in a sort of theosophy. Manichaeism was attempting to give a universal explanation of the world, and it did not believe that mere faith and dogma were effective instruments in the search for redemption. On the contrary, Manichaean soteriology was based on knowledge. So it is understandable that Augustine should confess that he had most been attracted by precisely this aspect of Manichaeism during the years of his adherence to it (377–382), that is, to the promise that humankind could be freed of the authority of faith and tradition and led back to God simply by the strength of reason.

Manichaeans did not accept tradition, be it that of the New Testament or that of the Zoroastrian scriptures (*Kephalaia* 7), without first making a distinction between what they recognized as true and authentic in them and what, in their view, was simply the result of deceitful manipulations and interpolations by ignorant or insincere disciples. Only Mani's authority was worthy of trust, as it was based on reason and drawn from revelation. It was also set down in writing by him with extreme care and with the precise intent of not letting his teachings be misrepresented. Manichaeans, therefore, prided themselves on not asserting any truth without a logical and rational demonstration thereof, and without first opening the doors of knowledge.

Such knowledge was, ultimately, an anamnesis, an awakening; that is, gnosis was an *epignosis,* a recognition, a memory of self, knowledge of one's true ego and, at the same time, knowledge of God, the former being consubstantial with the latter, a particle of light fallen into matter's obfuscating mix. Thus God is a "savior saved," or one to be saved: a transcendental, luminous principle, spirit, or intelligence *(nous).* It is the superior portion of humankind's ego, exiled in the body, and is the subject of the act of knowledge, thanks to which we will know where we are, where we come from, and where we are going. Humans have forgotten their nature, a blend of light and darkness, spirit and matter. The enlightening power of knowledge makes them understand their own nature, that of the universe, and their destiny. It is, therefore, a universal science, blending theology, cosmology, anthropology, and eschatology. It includes everything: physical nature as well as history. Reason can penetrate anything: "Man must not believe until he has seen the object with his own eyes" (*Kephalaia* 142).

The cosmogonic and anthropogonic myths. It may appear paradoxical to find that the doctrine of Manichaeism, founded in reason, whose ability and dignity it praised, was expressed in a language of myth, one that was crowded with figures and images and painted in strong, often dark colors. In fact, its mythology, which was invented by Mani himself, is intellectualistic and reflexive, almost metaphorical in character: Manichaean myths serve the purpose of illustrating the truth about the drama of existence, both macrocosmic and microcosmic. They achieve their objective with the aid of powerful images, most of which are derived from the mythological heritage of previous traditions—a fact that lent them greater weight and authority—and by the use of divine figures, both angelic and demoniacal, familiar, at least in part, to the popular imagination. Because Mani's teachings were directed to all the world's peoples, the actors in the great play could, to be more easily understood, adopt different names in different countries, drawing from local pantheons. Thus, Manichaean mythology is like a great album of pictures arranged in a sequence aimed at awakening in the adept reminiscences and intuitions that will lead him to knowledge. Small wonder, then, that Mani, who was famous for his paintings, should also use a book of illustrations, the *Image* (Gr., *Eikon;* MPers., and Pth., *Ārdahang*), to convey his doctrine, or that his disciples later continued to do the same in their missionary activities.

Such a mythology must, of necessity, have keys to its interpretation. The first of these is the omnipresent dominant theme: that of the soul which has fallen into matter and is freed by its *nous.* Next, in order to understand what are often described as the aberrations of Manichaean myths—those repugnant acts of cannibalism and sexual practices with which they are studded, as well as the self-destructiveness and autophagia of matter—one must keep in mind two basic concepts: the Indo-Iranian idea of the equivalence of spirit, light, and seed (Eliade, 1971, pp. 1–30) and that of the distillation of light through the "gastric machine" of the elect, an act that corresponds to the great purification of the luminous elements (Syr., *zīwānē*), which was carried out by the demiurge and his children at the beginning of time (Tardieu, 1981). The premise of the first concept is that light resides in the seed and through procreation is decanted from one body into another, undergoing the painful cycles of births and deaths (Skt., *saṃsāra*). This follows the related doctrine of metempsychosis (Syr., *tashpīkā;* Lat., *revolutio;* Gr., *metangismos*), an idea that originally came from India and that Mani adopted as pivotal to his system. The premise of the second is that just as the universe is the place in which all luminous bodies are healed, so the stomach is like a great alchemist's alembic, in which the elect, thanks to the high degree of purification he has attained, is able to separate the light present in food from all impurities, through a double cycle of filtering and return. This cycle is a microcosm, whose corresponding macrocosm is the distillation of the *zīwānē* into the moon and the sun (Tardieu, 1981).

The Manichaean origin myth is based on the doctrine of two principles (light and darkness) and three stages of creation. During the first stage of existence, the two principles, personified as the Father of Greatness and the Prince of Darkness, are separate, residing, respectively, in the north and in the south, kept apart by a border between their two kingdoms. The Prince of Darkness—that is, agitated and disorderly matter—wishes to penetrate the kingdom of the Father of Greatness. Thus begins the second stage, in which the Father of Greatness, not wishing to compromise his five "dwellings" (Intelligence, Science, Thought, Reflection, and Conscience), decides to battle the Prince of Darkness and engenders an avatar, the Mother of the Living, who, in turn, produces Primordial Man. But the Prince of Darkness defeats Primordial Man and devours his five children. The avidity and greed of the Prince of Darkness, however, bring about his downfall; the five children of Primordial Man are like a poison within his stomach.

The Father of Greatness responds by creating a second being: the Living Spirit (who corresponds to the Persian god Mithra). The Living Spirit, who is also the father of five children, and Primordial Man confront the demons of the powers of darkness, and so the demiurgic action begins: from the bodies of the demons arise the skies, the mountains, the soil, and, finally, from a first bit of liberated light, the sun, moon, and stars. The Father of Greatness then creates a third being, called the Messenger, who incarnates *nous;* he is also called the Great Wahman, the Good Thought (Av., Vohu Manah). The Messenger calls forth twelve Virgins of Light, and they show themselves nude to the demons, both male and female, so that they will all ejaculate at the sight of such beauty and thus free the elements of light that they had ingested and imprisoned. The seed spilled on the dry earth gives life to five trees: thus is accomplished the creation of the world.

The creation of the human race then occurs as follows. The she-demons, thus impregnated, thanks to the Messenger's ruse, give birth to monsters, who swallow plants in order to absorb the light contained within them. Then Matter (darkness), in the guise of Az, the personification of concupiscence, in order to imprison the elements of light in a more secure fashion, causes the demons Ashaqlun and Namrael, male and female, to devour all the monsters, and then to mate. They then generate the first human couple, Adam and Eve. At this point, the work of salvation begins: Adam, kept wild and ignorant by the snares of darkness, is awakened from this state by the savior, the son of God, sent by the powers above. The savior is identified with Primordial Man, Ōhrmazd, or, later, with the transcendental Jesus, or the god of *nous.* The savior awakens Adam from his slumber, opens his eyes, shows him his soul, which is suffering in the material world, and reveals to him the infernal origins of his body and the heavenly origins of his spirit. Thus Adam acquires knowledge of himself, and his soul, thanks to gnosis, is resuscitated.

The third stage is the Great War between the forces of good and evil, characterized on the one hand by the desperate attempt of the Prince of Darkness to spread evil throughout the world by means of procreation—that is, by the creation of more and more corporeal prisons to entrap the elements of light—and on the other hand by the efforts of the Father of Greatness to spread good. Through the practice of the laws of the religion and, in particular, by interrupting the cycle of reincarnation, light is liberated; that is, the soul is freed by knowledge. When the church of justice triumphs, the souls will be judged, and those of the elect will rise to Heaven. The world will then be purified and destroyed by a fire lasting 1,468 years. All, or most, of the light particles, will be saved; Matter, in all its manifestations, and with its victims (the damned), will be forever imprisoned in a globe inside a gigantic pit covered with a stone. The separation of the two principles will thus be accomplished for all eternity.

ORIGINS. We now know something more about the origins of the Manichaean religion, by comparing the Manichaean Codex of Cologne to other available sources, mainly the Arabic ones. Mani was raised in the environment of a Judeo-Christian Gnostic and baptist sect, which had been founded by a figure, almost more mythical than historical, by the name of Elchasai (Gr., Alkhasaios; Arab., al-Khasayh). Elchasaism was a particularly widespread movement during the third and fourth centuries in Syria, Palestine, Mesopotamia, Transjordan, and northern Arabia. It survived for many centuries and is mentioned by the Arabic encyclopedist Ibn al-Nadīm as still existing during the fourth century AH in what is today southeastern Iraq.

It would, however, be a mistake to view the origins of Manichaeism only, or even mainly, in the light of such information, for one might erroneously conclude that the principal inspiration for the Manichaean doctrine was Judeo-Christian Gnosticism. The origins of Manichaeism are still open to question (as are, in fact, those of Gnosticism). The most likely interpretation would recognize the dominating imprint of Iranian dualism since without a doubt the dualistic doctrine is central and pivotal to Mani's thought and to the teachings and practices of his church. We must, however, consider the presence of three different forms of religious doctrine: the Iranian, which is basically Zoroastrian; the Christian or Judeo-Christian; and the Mahāyāna Buddhist. Of these, the Iranian form held the key to the Manichaean system and provided the essence of the new universalistic religious concept that developed from the main themes and aspirations of Gnosticism. If we were to separate the Manichaean system from its Christian and Buddhist elements, it would not suffer irreparably.

Manichaeism was long thought of as a Christian heresy, but this interpretation was already being abandoned during the nineteenth century and has now been entirely rejected. We must also reject the approach that perceives the Judeo-Christian components, more or less affected by Hellenism, as dominant (Burkitt, 1925; Schaeder, 1927). There is a widespread tendency today to give equal emphasis to what we have called the three forms of Manichaeism and to consider it a great and independent universal religion, although such an approach is sometimes still weighted in favor of the relationship between Manicheaism and Christianity (Tardieu, 1981). Nevertheless, if we discount certain obvious differences, we can assert that Manichaeism has its roots in the Iranian religious tradition and that its relationship to Mazdaism, or Zoroastrianism, is more or less like that of Christianity to Judaism (Bausani, 1959, p. 103).

HISTORY. We can trace the beginnings of the religion to the second revelation received by the prophet at the age of twenty-four, that is, on the first of Nisan of 551 of the Seleucid era, which corresponds to April 12, 240 CE (his first occurred at the age of twelve while he was living in the baptist community). It was then that there appeared to him an angel, his "twin" (Gr., *suzugos;* Arab., *al-Tawm*), described as the "beautiful and sublime mirror" of his being, and it was then that Mani began his prophetic and apostolic ministry, breaking off from Elchasaism and its strict legalistic ritualism. He presented himself as the Seal of the Prophets and preached a new doctrine aimed at all peoples—Buddhists, Zoroastrians, and Christians.

A number of factors lead us to believe that, at the beginning of his ministry, Mani saw the universalistic religion he was founding as one that could be adapted to the new political reality of the Persian empire of the Sassanids, founded by Ardashīr I. To the emperor Shāpūr he dedicated a work, written in Middle Persian, that opened with a declaration of the universalistic idea of the Seal of the Prophecy. Any ambitions that great Sassanid ruler might have harbored for a universal empire would have found congenial a religious doctrine that presented itself as the sum and perfection of all the great prior religious traditions.

A missionary spirit moved Manichaeism from its very inception. Mani traveled first in the direction of the "country of the Indians" (perhaps in the footsteps of the apostle Thomas), with the hope of converting the small Christian communities scattered along the coast of Fars and Baluchistan (Tardieu, 1981) and perhaps, also, in order to penetrate lands in which Buddhism was already widespread. Manichaean tradition remembers this first apostolic mission by its conversion of Tūrān-shāh, that is, the Buddhist ruler of Tūrān, a kingdom in the Iranian world. That mission was a relatively brief one owing to the turn of events in the Sassanid empire. The death of Ardashīr and the accession to the throne of Shāpūr, the "king of kings of Ērānshahr," recalled Mani to Persia. Manichaeism began at that time to spread to Iran, where it acquired a prominent position, thanks also to the conversion of high court officials and even members of the royal family, and encouraged, to a certain degree, by the king's support. In fact, the image of Shāpūr in Manichaean tradition is a positive one: Manichaeism almost became the official religion of the Persian empire. Mani himself, after obtaining a successful audience with Shāpūr, joined the ruler's court and obtained his permission to preach the new creed throughout the empire, under the protection of local authorities. During this fortunate period for Manichaean propaganda in Iran, in the 250s, Mani wrote the *Shābuhragān,* a work he dedicated to his royal protector and which has reached us only in a fragmented form.

Once the work of its founder had established it as a real church, Manichaeism soon spread beyond the borders of Persia, both in the Roman Empire and in the east, southeast, and south. Mani wrote: "My hope [that is, the Manichaean church] has reached the east of the world and all inhabited regions of the earth, both to the north and to the south. . . . None of the [previous] apostles has ever done anything like this" (*Kephalaia* 1).

The political good fortune of Manichaeism in the Persian empire lasted only a few years. The official state religion, Zoroastrianism, grew increasingly hostile as the Magian clergy, guided by influential figures such as the high priest Kerdēr, organized it into a real national church, with its own strict orthodoxy and a strong nationalistic spirit. The reasons for the conflict between the Zoroastrianism of the Magi and Manichaeism during the third century are numerous: a hereditary clerical caste within a hierarchical social structure based on caste tended to be conservative and traditionalist; the eastern empire's cultural and spiritual horizons were narrow, typical of an agrarian and aristocratic society such as that of the Iranian plateau and very different from the ethnically and culturally diverse and composite one in the westernmost regions of the empire, where there had arisen a flourishing and cosmopolitan urban civilization. The alliance between the throne and the Magi, which remained strong despite some internal contrasts for the entire duration of the Sassanid empire, did not allow Manichaeism to take over and, by subjecting it to periodical and fierce persecutions, finally weakened its drive and confined it to a minority position.

On the one hand, Manichaeism accurately reflected the most widespread anxieties and aspirations of that period's religious preoccupations, through its soteriology, the idea of knowledge as freedom, and the value it placed on personal experience of the divine; on the other hand, the restored Zoroastrianism of the Magi reflected a tendency, widespread during the third century in both the Persian and Roman empires, toward the formation of a national culture. From this standpoint, we can view Manichaeism more as heir to Parthian eclecticism and syncretism—"one of the last manifestations of Arsacid thought" (Bivar, 1983, p. 97)—than as an interpreter of the vast cultural and political changes witnessed in Iran upon the ascent to power of the Sassanid dynasty.

The first anti-Manichaean persecution in the Iranian state began, after the death of Shāpūr and of his successor, Hormīzd I, with the killing of Mani himself, ordered by Bahrām I, probably around the beginning of the year 277. Many other episodes followed, affecting Manichaean communities in all regions of the empire, from Khorasan to Mesopotamian Seleucia (Ctesiphon), the seat of the Manichaean papacy. Manichaeism, however, was not completely eradicated from the Iranian world; in fact, it survived for centuries. Under the caliphate of the Umayyads it remained alive in those territories that had been Sassanid, despite internal schisms and disciplinary controversy.

During the third and fourth centuries Manichaeism moved west, into the Roman Empire. It spread through Egypt, North Africa, Palestine, Syria, Asia Minor, Dalmatia, and Rome and as far north as southern Gaul and Spain. Its adherents were the subjects of persecution by both central and peripheral imperial authorities, meeting everywhere with the strong hostility of the political and religious establishment. The Manichaeans were seen by Rome as a dangerous subversive element and were often thought to be agents of the rival Persian power. Despite persecutions and imperial edicts, such as that of Diocletian in 297, the faith for the most part persisted, except in some western areas of the Roman Empire. Manichaeism was perceived as a threat well into the Christian era. Repressive measures were repeatedly taken by Roman imperial and church authorities (notably Pope Leo the Great, in 445); nevertheless, in 527 the emperors Justin and Justinian still felt the need to promulgate a law inflicting capital punishment on the followers of Mani's teachings.

Like Zoroastrianism and Christianity, Islam had at first been tolerant of Manichaeism but in the end acted with equal violence against it. The advent of the Abbasid caliphate marked a renewal of bloody repressive measures, which succeeded in pushing the Manichaeans east, in the direction of Transoxiana, during the tenth century. It was in Khorasan, Chorasmia, and Sogdiana that the Manichaean faith expanded and gained strength, and there it became an outpost for the dissemination of Mani's gospel to China and Central Asia. In the last decades of the sixth century, the religion suffered a schism with the so-called Dēnāwars ("observers of *dēn,*" i.e., of the true religion), a rigorist and puritan sect. Samarkand became the new see of the Manicaean papacy.

Toward the end of the seventh century, Manichaeism reached the Far East. As the great caravan route from Kashgar to Kucha to Karashahr was reopened following the Chinese conquest of eastern Turkestan, Manichaeism made its appearance in China, mainly through Sogdian missionaries. In 732, an imperial edict allowed Manichaeans the freedom to practice their cult there. The religion also spread to Central Asia and Mongolia, to the vast empire of the Uighurs, who adopted Manichaeism as their official religion in 763. But political and military events following the fall, in 840, of the Uighur empire caused Manichaeism's supremacy in Central Asia to be short lived, although it probably survived there until the thirteenth century. In China, where the Manichaeans were persecuted during the ninth century and banned by edict in 843, just after the collapse of the Uighurs, Manichaeism nonetheless survived until the sixteenth century, protected by secret societies, alongside Daoism and Buddhism.

THE MANICHAEAN CHURCH. At the core of the ecclesiastical structure was a marked distinction among classes of clergy, which were subdivided into four. The first included teachers or apostles, never more than 12; the second, bishops, never more than 72; the third, stewards, never more than 360; and the fourth were the elects (that is, the elects in general). The laity made up a fifth class. Only men could belong to the first three classes, that is, the true clergy, and above these stood the leader of the faithful, the Manichaean pope. The clergy lived in monasteries in the cities and supported itself through the gifts and foundations of the laity, according to a system clearly derived from Buddhist, rather than Christian, monasticism (Baur, 1831; Widengren, 1965).

Different moral codes governed the clergy and the lay population. The former was required to observe the five commandments: truth, nonviolence, sexual abstinence, abstinence from meat and from food and drink that were considered impure, poverty. The laity was required (1) to observe the ten laws of good behavior, which, among other things, prescribed a strictly monogamous marriage and abstinence from all forms of violence, both against men and against animals; (2) to pray four times a day (at dawn, midday, sunset, and night), after observing particular rituals of purification; (3) to contribute the tenth, or the seventh, part of their worldly goods to support the clergy; (4) to fast weekly (on Sundays) and yearly for the thirty days preceding the celebration of the festival of the Bēma; and (5) to confess their sins weekly (on Mondays), as well as during a great yearly collective confession at the end of the fasting period.

The liturgy was simple: it recalled episodes of the life of Mani, his martyrdom, and that of the first apostles. The principal festivity was the Bēma (Gr.; MPers., *gāh;* "pulpit, throne, tribunal"), which, on the vernal equinox, celebrated Mani's passion through gospel worship; the collective confession of sins; the recitation of three hymns to Mani; the reading of the apostle's spiritual testament, the *Letter of the Seal;* chants glorifying the triumphant church; and a sacred banquet offered to the elect by the listeners. In Manichaean holy places the *bēma,* a throne on five steps, was left empty in memory of the one who, having left the world, nonetheless remained as an invisible guide and judge of his church. The empty throne was probably originally a Buddhist symbol.

HERITAGE AND SURVIVING ELEMENTS. The survival of Manichaeism as a source of inspiration for a number of medieval heresies in the West poses complex questions. Manichaean dualism has been adduced as an explanation for the origin of those heretical movements that were based on dualism, on moral asceticism, and on a more or less pronounced antinomism. Accusations of Manichaeism—the most widely despised of Christian heresies—were pronounced by adversaries against heretics to show their relation to the doctrines of Mani, although such a connection has been generally hard to prove beyond doubt.

Priscillianism, which arose in Spain at the end of the fourth century, was probably not related to Manichaeism, although Paulicianism, in seventh-century Armenia, probably was, as was Bogomilism. The latter arose in Bulgaria during the tenth century and spread along the Balkan Peninsula to the coastline of Asia Minor, along with the Cathari in southern France and northern Italy during the twelfth and thirteenth centuries; together they were considered links in the same chain, which might be called "medieval Manichaeism" or "Neo-Manichaeism." A connection among these movements is probable, and in fact such a link is certain between the Bogomils and the Cathari. However, it is not possible to prove their derivation from Manichaeism. Their popular character, the social environment in which they developed, and the typically Gnostic nature of Manichaeism all suggest a generalized influence rather than a direct derivation, that is, a background inspiration from the great dualistic religion of late antiquity. It now appears certain that in some instances Manichaeism itself did survive in the West in clandestine groups and secret forms, especially in Roman Africa, despite the proscriptions and persecutions of the sixth century.

The problem is analogous in the East, except in China, where we know that Manichaeism did survive, camouflaged in Daoist or Buddhist guise, until the sixteenth century. A Manichaean origin has been ascribed to Mazdakism, a religious and social movement of Sassanid Iran between the fifth and sixth centuries (Christensen, 1925), and some degree of Manichaean influence upon it is undeniable, although a more accurate perception would probably see the movement as a heretical form of Zoroastrianism. There has been an occasional attempt to consider Manichaean any Muslim *zindīq* (Arab., "heretic, free thinker"). The word derives from the Middle Persian *zandīg,* used by Zoroastrians to describe those who used the *Zand,* the Middle Persian translation of and commentary on the Avesta, in a heterodox manner. Although it is true that *zindīq* is often used to mean "Manichaean," its sense is actually broader; *zandaqah* cannot, therefore, be strictly identified with Manichaeism.

In any case, Manichaeism survived in the Islamic world, even through the persecutions of the Abbasid caliphate, and exercised some degree of influence on Gnostic currents in this world. Finally, there is a great likelihood of a direct connection between Manichaeism and some Tibetan cosmological concepts (Tucci, 1970).

See Also Frashōkereti; Mani; Mazdakism.

Bibliography

A work that by now belongs to the prehistory of Manichaean studies is Isaac de Beausobre's *Histoire critique de Manichée et du manichéisme,* 2 vols. (Amsterdam, 1734–1739), which presented Manichaeism as a reformed Christianity. A hundred years later, Manichaean studies reached a turning point with F. C. Baur's *Das manichäische Religionssystem nach den Quellen neu untersucht und entwickelt* (Tübingen, 1831), which gave particular consideration to the Indo-Iranian, Zoroastrian, and Buddhist backgrounds.

In the years following, a number of general studies were published that still remain important—G. Flügel's *Mani, seine Lehre und seine Schriften* (Leipzig, 1862); K. Kessler's *Mani: Forschungen über die manichäische Religion* (Berlin, 1889); F. C. Burkitt's *The Religion of the Manichees* (Cambridge, 1925); and H. H. Schaeder's *Urform und Fortbildungen des manichäischen Systems* (Leipzig, 1927)—even though more recent studies and discoveries have, by now, gone beyond them. Also useful are A. V. W. Jackson's *Researches on Manichaeism, with Special Reference to the Turfan Fragments* (New York, 1932) and H.-J. Polotsky's *Abriss des manichäischen Systems* (Stuttgart, 1934).

A quarter of a century apart, two important status reports concerning the question of Manichaean studies were published: H. S. Nyberg's "Forschungen über den Manichäismus," *Zeitschrift für die neutestamentliche Wissenschaft und die Kunde der älteren Kirche* 34 (1935): 70–91, and Julien Ries's "Introduction aux études manichéennes," *Ephemerides Theologicae Lovanienses* 33 (1957): 453–482 and 35 (1959): 362–409.

General works that remain valuable, although they give a partially different picture of Manichaeism, are Henri-Charles Puech's *Le manichéisme: Son fondateur, sa doctrine* (Paris, 1949) and Geo Widengren's *Mani and Manichaeism* (London, 1965). We are also indebted to Puech for a very useful collection of essays, *Sur le manichéisme et autres essais* (Paris, 1979), and to Widengren for another, with an important introduction, *Der Manichäismus* (Darmstadt, 1977), pp. ix–xxxii, as well as for a more recent essay, "Manichaeism and Its Iranian Background," in *The Cambridge History of Iran,* vol. 3, edited by Ehsan Yarshater (Cambridge, 1983), pp. 965–990.

The volume *Der Manichäismus* contains some of the most important contributions to Manichaean studies, reprinted entirely or partially (all in German), by H. S. Nyberg, F. C. Burkitt, H. H. Schaeder, Richard Reitzenstein, H.-J. Polotsky, Henri-Charles Puech, V. Stegemann, Alexander Böhlig, Mark Lidzbarski, Franz Rosenthal, W. Bang-Kaup, A. Baumstark, Charles R. C. Allberry, Prosper Alfaric, W. Seston, J. A. L. Vergote, W. B. Henning, Georges Vajda, Carsten Colpe, and A. V. W. Jackson. Two noteworthy syntheses of Manichaeism in French are François Decret's *Mani et la tradition manichéenne* (Paris, 1974) and M. Tardieu's *Le manichéisme* (Paris, 1981); the latter is particularly full of original suggestions.

Two works from the 1960s are dedicated more to Mani himself than to Manichaeism, one concerning mainly the social and cultural background from which Manichaeism emerged and the other mainly dedicated to the religious personality of the founder: Otakar Klíma's *Manis Zeit und Leben* (Prague, 1962) and L. J. R. Ort's *Mani: A Religio-Historical Description of His Personality* (Leiden, 1967).

Although the once-classic work on Manichaean literature, Prosper Alfaric's *Les écritures manichéennes,* 2 vols. (Paris, 1918–1919), is now quite dated, there is a wealth of more recent works to which we can turn. A whole inventory of Iranian documents from Central Asia can be found in Mary Boyce's *A Catalogue of the Iranian Manuscripts in Manichaean Script in the German Turfan Collection* (Berlin, 1960). Excellent editions of Iranian and Turkic texts are due to F. W. K. Müller, A. von Le Coq, Ernst Waldschmidt and Wolfgang Lentz,

W. Bang, and Annemarie von Gabain, F. C. Andreas, and W. B. Henning, published in the *Abhandlungen* and in the *Sitzungsberichte* of the Prussian Academy of Sciences between 1904 and 1936. W. B. Henning's pupil, Mary Boyce, has also published, in addition to the above-mentioned catalog, two other important contributions to Manichaean studies, *The Manichaean Hymn Cycles in Parthian* (Oxford, 1954) and *A Reader in Manichaean Middle-Persian and Parthian,* "Acta Iranica," no. 9 (Tehran and Liège, 1975). Editions of Iranian texts, as well as a number of extremely careful philological studies, can be found in W. B. Henning's *Selected Papers,* 2 vols., "Acta Iranica," nos. 14–15 (Tehran and Liège, 1977), where are reprinted also Henning's fundamental *Mitteliranische Manichaica aus Chinesisch-Turkestan,* written in collaboration with F. C. Andreas between 1932 and 1934.

W. Sundermann and P. Zieme, two scholars from the Academy of Sciences in Berlin, are currently responsible for continuing research in the Iranian and Turkish texts from Turfan, which are preserved in Berlin. We owe to them, among other things, Sundermann's *Mittelpersische und parthische kosmogonische und Parabeltexte der Manichäer* (Berlin, 1973), *Mitteliranische manichäische Texte kirchengeschichtlichen Inhalts* (Berlin, 1981), *Ein manichäisch-soghdisches Parabelbuch* (Berlin, 1985), *Der Sermon vom Licht-Nous* (Berlin, 1992), *Der Sermon von der Seele* (Turnhout, Belgium, 1997), and Zieme's *Manichäisch-türkische Texte* (Berlin, 1975), *Altun Yaruq Sudur. Eine Lehrschrift des östlichen Manichäismus* (Turnhout, Belgium, 1996). On the state of research into Iranian texts, see also Sundermann's "Lo studio dei testi iranici di Turfan," in *Iranian Studies,* edited by me (Rome, 1983), pp. 119–134. Recent research on Sogdian Manichaean texts has been done by N. Sims-Williams (London) and E. Morano (Turin), following the lead of Ilya Gershevitch (Cambridge). Again in the context of Central Asian texts, the handbook for the confession of sins has been carefully edited, after the work of W. Bang and W. B. Henning, and with an ample commentary, by Jes P. Asmussen in *X*^{v}*āstānīft: Studies in Manichaeism* (Copenhagen, 1965); the *Shābuhragān* is the subject of an extremely useful work by D. N. MacKenzie, "Mani's *Šābuhragān,*" *Bulletin of the School of Oriental and African Studies* 42 (1979): 500–534 and 43 (1980): 288–310.

Concerning the Chinese texts, the following are useful works. On the *Treatise,* see Édouard Chavannes and Paul Pelliot's "Un traité manichéen retrouvé en Chine," *Journal asiatique* (1911): 499–617 and (1913): 99–392. On the *Compendium,* see Chavannes and Pelliot's "Compendium de la religion du Buddha de Lumière, Mani," *Journal asiatique* (1913): 105–116 (Pelliot fragment), and Gustav Haloun and W. B. Henning's "The Compendium of the Doctrines and Styles of the Teaching of Mani, the Buddha of Light," *Asia Major,* n.s. 3 (1952): 184–212 (Stein fragment). On the London Chinese hymn book, see, in addition to the work of Ernst Waldschmidt and Wolfgang Lentz, Tsui Chi's "Mo-ni-chiao hsia-pu tsan," *Bulletin of the School of Oriental and African Studies* 11 (1943): 174–219.

On the Coptic texts of Fayum, a survey of the state of research can be found in Alexander Böhlig's "Die Arbeit an den koptischen Manichaica," in *Mysterion und Wahrheit* (Leiden, 1968), pp. 177–187. Among editions of the texts are *Manichäische Homilien,* by H.-J. Polotsky (Stuttgart, 1934), *Kephalaia,* by C. Schmidt, H.-J. Polotsky, and Alexander Böhlig (Stuttgart, 1935–1940; Berlin, 1966), and Charles R. C. Allberry's *A Manichaean Psalm-Book,* vol. 2 (Stuttgart, 1938). On the Manichaean Codex of Cologne, see Albert Henrichs and Ludwig Koenen's "Ein griechischer Mani-Codex," *Zeitschrift für Papyrologie und Epigraphik* 5 (1970): 97–216, 19 (1975): 1–85, and 32 (1979): 87–200, and Ludwig Koenen and Cornelia Römer, *Der Kölner Mani-Kodex. Über das Werden seines Leibes* (Opladen, 1988).

Of indirect sources, I shall mention here only the following few. On Augustine, see R. Jolivet and M. Jourion's *Six traités anti-manichéens,* in *Oeuvres de Saint Augustin,* vol. 17 (Paris, 1961); on Theodoros bar Konai, see Franz Cumont's *Recherches sur le manichéisme,* vol. 1 (Brussels, 1908); on Zoroastrian sources, see J.-P. de Menasce's *Une apologétique mazdéenne du neuvième siècle 'Škand-gumānīk vicār'* (Fribourg, 1945); and on Islamic sources, see Carsten Colpe's "Der Manichäismus in der arabischen Überlieferung" (Ph.D. diss., University of Göttingen, 1954).

Three valuable anthologies of Manichaean texts are A. Adams's *Texte zum Manichäismus,* 2d ed. (Berlin, 1962), Jes P. Asmussen's *Manichaean Literature* (Delmar, N.Y., 1975), Alexander Böhlig and Jes P. Asmussen's *Die gnosis,* vol. 3 (Zurich, 1980), Hans-Joachim Klimkeit. *Gnosis on the Silk Road.* San Francisco 1998, and *Il Manicheismo,* edited by Gherardo Gnoli, vol. 1. Milan, 2003.

Concerning the spread of Manichaeism in Asia, in North Africa, and in the Roman Empire, there are numerous works. The old text by E. de Stoop, *Essai sur la diffusion du manichéisme dans l'Empire romain* (Ghent, 1909), heads the list, followed by Paul Pelliot's "Les traditions manichéennes au Fou-kien," *T'oung pao* 22 (1923): 193–208; M. Guidi's *La lotta tra l'Islam e il manicheismo* (Rome, 1927); Uberto Pestalozza's "Il manicheismo presso i Turchi occidentali ed orientali," *Rendiconti del Reale Istituto Lombardo di Scienze e Lettere,* 2d series, 67 (1934): 417–497; Georges Vajda's "Les Zindiqs en pays d'Islam au debout de la période abbaside," *Rivista degli Studi Orientali* 17 (1937): 173–229; Giuseppe Messina's *Cristianesimo, buddhismo, manicheismo nell'Asia antica* (Rome, 1947); H. H. Schaeder's "Der Manichäismus und sein Weg nach Osten," in *Glaube und Geschichte: Festschrift für Friedrich Gogarten* (Giessen, 1948), pp. 236–254; O. Maenchen-Helfen's "Manichaeans in Siberia," in *Semitic and Oriental Studies Presented to William Popper* (Berkeley, 1951), pp. 161–165; Francesco Gabrieli's "La *zandaqa* au premier siècle abbasside," in *L'élaboration de l'Islam* (Paris, 1961), pp. 23–28; Peter Brown's "The Diffusion of Manichaeism in the Roman Empire," *Journal of Roman Studies* 59 (1969): 92–103; François Decret's *Aspects du manichéisme dans l'Afrique romaine* (Paris, 1970); and S. N. C. Lieu's *The Religion of Light: An Introduction to the History of Manichaeism in China* (Hong Kong, 1979) and *Manichaeism in the Later Roman Empire and Medieval China* (Manchester, 1985).

Among studies devoted to special topics, note should be taken of Charles R. C. Allberry's "Das manichäische Bema-Fest," *Zeitschrift für die neutestamentliche Wissenschaft und die Kunde der älteren Kirche* 37 (1938): 2–10; Geo Widengren's *The Great Vohu Manah and the Apostle of God* (Uppsala, 1945) and *Mesopotamian Elements in Manichaeism* (Uppsala, 1946); Henri-Charles Puech's "Musique et hymnologie manichéennes," in *Encyclopédie des musiques sacrées,* vol. 1 (Paris, 1968), pp. 353–386; and Mircea Eliade's "Spirit, Light, and Seed," *History of Religions* 11 (1971): 1–30. Of my own works, I may mention "Un particolare aspetto del simbolismo della luce nel Mazdeismo e nel Manicheismo," *Annali dell'Istituto Universitario Orientale di Napoli* n.s. 12 (1962): 95–128, and "Universalismo e nazionalismo nell'Iran del III secolo," in *Incontro di religioni in Asia tra il III e il X secolo,* edited by L. Lanciotti (Florence, 1984), pp. 31–54.

In the most exhaustive treatment of Manichaeism to have appeared in an encyclopedic work, Henri-Charles Puech's "Le manichéisme," in *Histoire des religions,* vol. 2, edited by Puech (Paris, 1972), pp. 523–645, we also find a full exposition of the problem concerning the heritage and survival of Manichaeism, with a bibliography to which one should add Raoul Manselli's *L'eresia del male* (Naples, 1963).

Despite the length of the present bibliography, there are some works cited in the text of my article that have not yet been mentioned here. On the relationship between Manichaeism and Zoroastrianism, see Alessandro Bausani's *Persia religiosa* (Milan, 1959); on the Parthian heritage in Manichaeism, see A. D. H. Bivar's "The Political History of Iran under the Arsacids," in *The Cambridge History of Iran,* vol. 3, edited by Ehsan Yarshater (Cambridge, 1983), pp. 21–97; and on the influence of Manichaeism in Tibet, see Giuseppe Tucci's *Die Religionen Tibets* (Stuttgart, 1970), translated as *The Religions of Tibet* (Berkeley, 1980).

After 1987, among individual and collective works, proceedings of international conferences, etc., see: Julien Ries, *Les études manichéennes. Des controverses de la Réforme aux découvertes du XX? siècle* (Louvain-la-Neuve, 1988); *Manichaica Selecta. Studies Presented to Professor Julien Ries,* edited by Aloïs van Tongerloo and Søren Giversen (Louvain, 1991); Alexander Böhlig and Christoph Markschies, *Gnosis und Manichäismus* (Berlin, 1994); *The Manichaen NOYΣ,* edited by Aloïs van Tongerloo and J. van Oort (Louvain, 1995); *Turfan, Khotan und Dunhuang,* edited by Ronald E. Emmerick, W. Sundermann, Ingrid Warnke and Peter Zieme (Berlin, 1996); *Emerging from Darkness,* edited by Paul Mirecki and Jason BeDuhn (Leiden, 1997); Samuel N. C. Lieu, *Manichaeism in Central Asia and China* (Leiden, 1998); Jason BeDuhn, *The Manichaean Body in Discipline and Ritual* (Baltimore, 2000); Xavier Tremblay, *Pour une histoire de la Sérinde. Le manichéisme parmi les peuples et religions d'Asie Centrale d'après les sources primaires* (Vienna, 2001); *Augustine and Manichaeism in the Latin West,* edited by Johannes van Oort, Otto Wermelinger, Gregor Wurst (Leiden, 2001), *The Light and the Darkness,* edited by Paul Mirecki and Jason BeDuhn (Leiden, 2001).

GHERARDO GNOLI (1987)
Translated from Italian by Ughetta Fitzgerald Lubin

MANICHAEISM: MANICHAEISM IN IRAN

Manichaeism, a basically Gnostic religion founded by Mani, was widespread in antiquity. In Iran, this religion very strongly made use of Zoroastrian motifs to look like a genuine Iranian religion. This fact led both to intensive interaction between Manichaeism and other Iranian religions, also stimulating some aspects of those religions, and to severe persecution of Manichaeans alike.

THE LIFE OF MANI. Mani (216–277) was born into an Iranian family, but at the age of four his father took him to live with the religious community of the Elkasaites. Mani's father, Pattik, may have been of Arsacid stock, so it is assumed that Mani was well acquainted with Iranian and Zoroastrian tradition.

At the age of twenty-four, Mani began preaching. In 241, after Shāpūr I (r. 241–272) had become king of the Sasanian empire, Mani began to spread his teaching at the Sassanian court. He was introduced by Pērōz, a high-ranking member of the nobility, possibly the king's brother. The central themes in his message were the "two principles of light and darkness" and the "three times." Both ideas have their roots in Zoroastrian cosmology: first, the original time when the realms of light and darkness existed side by side with equal strength but separated by a boundary; second, the time of mixture after the combat between light and darkness; and third, the time of the renewed separation of the two principles.

Mani strongly depended on and made use of Zoroastrian religious thoughts combined with his own Gnostic teachings to provide an Iranian framework for his cosmogonical and eschatological myth. He not only adopted the terminology and the dualistic mythology of the Zoroastrians, but also made dualism even more exclusive: The material world was considered the devil's (or Ahreman's) realm; only the spiritual world was good.

Shāpūr, who was driven to acquire and introduce new knowledge into his kingdom, listened to Mani because Mani presented his religion as a kind of "reform" of Zarathushtra's (Zoroaster's) ancient teachings. Further, according to Mani's teachings, all former religions had been included in this new religion. This idea fit Shāpūr's dream of establishing a large empire incorporating different peoples and their different creeds. Therefore, Shāpūr viewed Manichaeism as a suitable syncretistic yet still Iranian religion to serve as a common bond for all people in the emerging empire: for Christians in the West, due to the Gnostic tradition picked up in Manichaeism; for Zoroastrians, due to Mani's attempt to present himself as a "new Zoroaster;" and for Buddhists in eastern Iran, as a result of the Manichaean missionary Mār Ammō's journeys during the middle of the third century. Thus Manichaeism flourished for thirty years within the Sassanian Empire. Mani himself stayed in the Persis and western Iran, where he developed a good deal of his missionary work and his church organization.

This situation changed after Shāpūr's death. Although King Hormīzd (r. 272–273) favored Mani, the religio-political career of the Zoroastrian priest Kerdīr (mid-third to early fourth century) started during this time. Following Hormīzd's short reign, his elder brother Wahrām I (r. 274–

277) became king. Kerdīr managed to influence the new king, strengthening Zoroastrianism and thus weakening Manichaeism. Mani was summoned to the court at Bēt Lāpāt (Gundēshābuhr) by Wahrām I and interrogated about his religion. Although Mani could heal Wahrām's servants from demons and fever, Wahrām sentenced him to prison in order to settle Zoroastrian accusations against Mani, possibly raised by Kerdīr. Mani died in prison on February 26, 277.

The years following Mani's death resulted in persecutions of the members of Mani's church, reaching their climax with the martyrdom of Sisinnos, then leader of the religion, in 286 during the reign of Wahrām II (r. 277–293). These years focused on Kerdīr's career and his promotion of Zoroastrianism as the only religion in the Sassanian Empire. This led to the persecution of other religions, as stated in Kerdīr's inscription from Naqsh-i Rostam:

> And the creed of Ahreman and the dēws was driven out of the land and deprived of credence. And Jews and Buddhists and Brahmans and Aramaic and Greek-speaking Christians and Baptisers and Manichaeans were assailed in the land. And images were overthrown, and the dens of demons were (thus) destroyed, and the places and abodes of the Yazads were established. (Boyce, 1984, p. 112).

THE SPREAD OF MANICHAEISM. Persecutions of the Manichaeans resulted in an exodus of Manichaeans from central Iran to Mesopotamia and the eastern provinces of the Roman Empire. Other refugees found shelter with the Arab king Amaro of Hira (end of third to beginning of fourth centuries), who in the last decade of the third century convinced the Sassanian king Narseh (r. 293–302) to put an end to the persecutions of Manichaeans in Iran. Narseh had another reason to end the repression of the Manichaeans: when the Roman emperor Diocletian (r. 284–305) issued an edict against the Manichaeans in 297, Narseh saw a chance to get Manichaean support for his military agitations against the Romans.

For some years the Manichaeans managed to live calmly, but during the reign of Narseh's successor Hormīzd II (r. 302–309), the Zoroastrian priests again voted for the extirpation of the Manichaean creed. Once again the kingdom of Hira helped many Manichaeans to flee from Iran to the west; others sought refuge in eastern Iran, spreading Manichaeism along the Silk Road as far as central Asia in the following centuries. In eastern Iran (present-day Turkmenistan), Manichaeism had been known since the middle of the third century, due to the missionary efforts of Mār Ammō, and in the early fourth century, refugees could find shelter there. As a result, Iranian Manichaeism came into intensive contact with Buddhism that spread westward from the Kushāna Empire, thus leading to the further adaptation of Buddhist traditions by Manichaean missionaries, who partly adapted Buddhist terminology like *nirvāṇa* (Parthian: *prnybr'n*) or "salvation" (Parthian: *mwxš*) for Manichaean theological ideas.

In the sixth century, Manichaeism reached its climax in eastern Iran, with Samarkand as the religious and administrative center, independent from the Manichaean west. Shād-Ohrmezd (d. 600) was the most prominent East Iranian leader of the community of the Dēnāwars, the "Pure Ones"; he was very engaged in preserving and spreading Iranian Manichaean literature. Besides Parthian missionaries, Sogdians began to play an important part in transmitting Iranian religious ideas farther to the east. However, Manichaeism was accepted among Sogdians only from the end of the sixth century—after Zoroastrianism, Christianity, and Buddhism had spread among them.

ZOROASTRIAN PERSECUTION OF THE MANICHAEANS. Even though Mani spent most of his life establishing his religion in the core area of Iran, from the early fourth century on, Manichaeism had its centers elsewhere and there are relatively few extant original Manichaean sources in Iran. From the *Dēnkard*, a theological compendium of the Zoroastrians in Middle Persian language, it is written that during the reign of Shāpūr II (r. 309–379), the Zoroastrian priest Ādurbād ī Māraspandān (mid-fourth century) was the main adversary of Manichaeism, and the third book of the *Dēnkard* brings to light Ādurbād's refutation of Mani's doctrine, opening with the line: "Ten injunctions which the crippled demon Mani clamoured against those of the restorer of righteousness, Ādurbād ī Māraspandān." These refutations showed some differences between Manichaeism and Zoroastrianism, mainly that the Zoroastrian world view was believed to be much more in agreement with the cosmos and not as anticosmic as Manichaeism. It is probable that this theological refutation of Mani's religion by an important Zoroastrian priest of the time gave an ideological justification for the persecution of Manichaeans during the mid-fourth century.

Although the persecution of Manichaeans during the reign of Shāpūr II seemed to be less fierce than the persecution of Christians by the same king, there is one interesting Syriac text referring to the martyrdom of the Christian Aitāllāh: The Sassanian authorities tried to persuade Aitāllāh to abstain from his faith by referring to the example of an imprisoned Manichaean who, after being tortured, had anathemized Mani and his faith. To prove his abrogation from his former religion, this Manichaean even killed an ant to show that he no longer followed the Manichaean prohibition of killing any animal. Manichaeans believed that some part of the divine light was included in every being, thus killing even an ant would harm the divine element in it. This episode not only highlighted the persecution of Manichaeans in the Sassanian Empire, it also indicated the attempts to reconvert them to Zoroastrianism. By killing the ant, the (former) Manichaean not only showed his willingness to break with his former religious behavior, but also acted according to Zoroastrian behavior: Killing ants and other creatures of this kind, which are Ahreman's creations bringing evil to the world, is a religious act to partake as a Zoroastrian in the cosmic battle against Ahreman's creations.

During the fourth century Zoroastrians tried to convince Manichaeans to convert to Zoroastrianism, even through pressure. But the Zoroastrian clergy also reacted against the still-practicing Manichaeans in another way. Several scholars have argued that the appreciation Manichaeans gave to their canonical "holy books" led to the creation of a written *Avesta* by the Zoroastrian clergy during the fourth century (see cf. Hutter, 2000, p. 314). This book was produced to compete with the Manichaean books. In theological disputes, Zoroastrians no longer had to rely solely on the oral tradition; they now had a book showing that it was not Zoroastrianism that had failed, but Mani who had falsified the teaching of Zoroaster.

With such a book, Zoroastrian priests and judges could act against Manichaeism. In the early fifth century, during the reign of Yazdegerd I (r. 339–420), the persecutions of Manichaeans had been renewed. In the legal textbook *Mādigān ī hazār dādestān* (Book of thousand judgments), it is written that the property of heretics should be confiscated; heretics (*zandīq*) in this passage referred to Manichaeans. Also Mazdak's movement during the reign of Kawād (r. 488–497 and 499–531) was not always distinguished from Manichaeism. Mazdak (about 460–524) was a charismatic figure whose doctrine combined Gnostic thoughts with Zoroastrian, Manichaean, and Greek elements. His doctrine focuses on a good god, but man is bound to earth in a pessimistic way. When man comes in contact with the divine he is able to remove all his earthly bonds. Mazdak also tried to abolish social distinctions and and reach equality among all people.

Still, during the reign of Khosrow I (Anūshirvaān, r. 531–579), there lived some Manichaeans in the area of present-day Iran. Thus despite persecution, Manichaeans formed a part of the religious pluralism within the Sassanian Empire. After the decisive victory of the Arabs over the Persians in 637, the initial tolerance of the Arabs gave rise to Manichaeism in western Iran for a short period, with some Manichaeans returning from Khorasan and eastern Iran. But this was only a brief revival before the end of Manichaeism in Iran proper at the end of the seventh or at the beginning of the eighth centuries.

MANICHAEAN THOUGHT IN IRANIAN RELIGIOUS HISTORY. From the discoveries of Manichaean literature in the Turfan oasis in Chinese Turkestan during the early twentieth century, it has been determined that the Middle Persian language remained—even in central Asia—the ritual language for Manichaeans, at least at a symbolic level. There are passages in this language inserted in Parthian and Sogdian liturgical texts showing that the origin of Manichaeism in the core area of the early Sassanian Empire was long influential.

Manichaean thought also lived on in Iran proper, influencing later periods. When Ādurbād ī Māraspandān opposed Manichaeism in the fourth century, he supported the positive Zoroastrian stance to the material world against the pessimistic and negative tendencies of the Manichaeans. On the other hand, the "heretical" Zurwānite interpretation of Zoroastrianism, showing the material world in a negative light and as Ahreman's work, was comparable to the Manichaean worldview. Such ascetic aspects in parts of the Zoroastrian religion that try to avoid contact with the material world are possibly the result of Manichaean influence on Zoroastrianism.

Another important aspect is the Manichaean symbolism of the divine light: the Column of Light/Glory (*bāmistūn*) and the Maiden of Light (*kanīgrōšn*) are also adapted within Zoroastrianism, as well as partly in Sufism and even in the recent Bahā'ī religion. Mani's concept of the heavenly twin (*yamag*) may also have had some impact on Ṣūfī mystics. The idea that the succession of prophets, sent by God to different peoples at different times, was adopted by Mani to prove his claim to be God's last prophet for humankind. This same idea was taken up in Islamic thought (and transferred to Muḥammad), as well as in the middle of the nineteenth century—through Islamic intermediation—when it was taken as the cornerstone of Bahā'ī theology. The founder of Bahā'ī, Bahā'u'llāh, saw himself as the latest in a line of subsequent messengers, continuing God's revelation.

Manichaeism as a living religion flourished in the central parts of Iran only for a relatively short period, but nevertheless Iranian influence remained integral for Manichaeism, and Manichaeism had a lasting effect on Iran. Mani's ideas form one important branch in the religious history of Iran, leaving an impact on Zoroastrianism, Iranian Islam, and the Bahā'ī faith.

BIBLIOGRAPHY

Bausani, Alessandro. *Religion in Iran: From Zoroaster to Baha'ullah* (1959). Translated by J. M. Marchesi. New York, 2000.

Buck, Christopher. "Unique Eschatological Interface. Bahá'u'lláh and Cross-Cultural Messianism." In *Studies in Bábí and Bahá'í History.* Vol. 3, edited by Peter Smith, pp. 157–179. Los Angeles, 1986. Article focuses on continuing revelation according to Bahā'ī theology, also covering Mani's concept of prophetic succession within Iranian religions.

Corbin, Henry. *The Man of Light in Iranian Sufism.* Translated by Nancy Pearson. Boulder, Colo., 1978.

Gignoux, Philippe. *Les quatre inscriptions du mage Kirdīr.* Paris, 1991.

Gignoux, Philippe, ed. *Recurrent Patterns in Iranian Religions from Mazdaism to Sufism.* Paris, 1992. Important collection of essays, covering also Manichaean topics.

Hutter, Manfred. "Manichaeism in the Early Sasanian Empire." In *Numen* 40 (1993): 2–15.

Hutter, Manfred. "Manichaeism in Iran in the Fourth Century." In *Studia Manichaica. IV. Internationaler Kongress zum Manichaeismus,* edited by Ronald E. Emmerick, Werner Sundermann, and Peter Zieme, pp. 308–317. Berlin, 2000.

Hutter, Manfred. "Die frühe manichäische Mission unter Buddhisten im Ostiran." In *Zeitschrift für Religionswissenschaft* 10 (2002): 19–32. This is a series of three articles covering most of the history and religious history of Manichaeism in connection to the religious pluralism in the Sassanian Empire.

Lieu, Samuel N. C. *Manichaeism in the Later Roman Empire and Medieval China.* 2d ed. Tübingen, Germany, 1992. An overview on the historical development, especially pp. 106–115.

Olsson, Tord. "The Refutation of Manichaean Doctrines in Denkard 3.200." In *Manichaeica Selecta. Studies Presented to Professor Julien Ries on the Occasion of His Seventieth Birthday,* edited by Alois van Tongerloo and Soren Giverson, pp. 273–293. Louvain, Belgium, 1991.

Sundermann, Werner. "Studien zur kirchengeschichtlichen Literatur der iranischen Manichäer I–III." In *Altorientalische Forschungen* 13 (1986): 40–92; 239–317; *Altorientalische Forschungen* 14 (1987): 41–107. Very detailed study of the Iranian literature and historical sources for Manichaeism.

Tremblay, Xavier. *Pour une Histoire de la Sérinde. Le Manichéisme parmi les peoples et religions de l'Asie Centrale d'après les sources primaires.* Vienna, 2001. Focusing mainly on eastern Iran and the Sogdians, also with a valuable appendix containing many details on all relevant written sources for Manichaean history in eastern Iran.

MANFRED HUTTER (2005)

MANICHAEISM: MANICHAEISM IN THE ROMAN EMPIRE

The early diffusion of Manichaeism in the late Roman Empire was achieved directly through the missionary vision of Mani and the evangelistic endeavors of his earliest disciples. Patronized by the Sassanid monarch Shāpūr I, Mani disseminated his teaching both within the Sassanid Empire and in the frontier regions of the Roman Empire, which had recently come under Persian domination. According to Manichaean texts, a mission led by Adda was active along the Syrian frontier at the time of the ascendancy of Odaenathus at Palmyra (c. 262–266). The mission appears to have spent some time in Palmyra and later reached Egypt, especially Alexandria; a number of communities were established, which might have later influenced the development of early Christian monasticism. It is possible that a separate mission to Egypt, probably via Eilat and the Red Sea ports, was also dispatched, and Luxor (Lycopolis) eventually became its center. The sect had reached Syria, North Africa, Asia Minor, the Balkans, and Italy, including Rome, by end of the third century CE.

The study of the history of the sect in the Roman Empire was greatly advanced by the recovery of genuine Manichaean writings in the form of ancient manuscripts and not merely citations transmitted in polemical writings by their enemies. The first manuscripts to come to light, between 1915 and 1919, were a small number of papyrus fragments in Syriac, written in the distinctive Manichaean Estrangela script, recovered from Oxyrhynchus in Egypt. A more substantial but highly fragmentary text in Latin was recovered from Theveste (Roman Tabessa) in North Africa in 1918. This text, probably a letter, was written in Latin by a Manichaean elect using Christian scriptures (both the Gospels and the Pauline epistles) to justify the apparently privileged position of the elect and the theological reasons for their needing the service of the hearers to attend to their daily needs. The elect members of the sect were the priests who were not permitted to engage in harvesting or thrashing or milling of the wheat or barley nor in the act of baking for fear of damaging the Light-particles which according to Manichaean teaching are found in plant-life. Their livelihood therefore depended on the service of the hearers who were members of the second rank. A substantial find of Manichaean texts were made at Medinet Madi (Roman Narmouthis) in Egypt, between 1929 and 1930, consisting of seven codices in the Lycopolitan (specifically dialect L4) or the Sub-Achmimic B dialect of the Coptic language, which was not native to the area where the texts were found. It is highly possible that the texts were originally translated from Syriac near Luxor (Roman Lycopolis) and brought to Medinet Madi in the late fourth century CE by Manichaean missionaries who hid them for fear of confiscation by the Christian Roman authorities. The cache was split up by the workmen who discovered it; some were purchased by the Irish-American collector Chester Beatty, and the rest by the Berlin Academy. The division is as follows:

In Berlin, at the Bode Museum for Egyptology:

1. The *Letters* of Mani.
2. The *Kephalaia of the Teacher* (i.e., Mani).
3. The *Synaxeis* Codex, which appears to contain a commentary on the *Living Gospel* (a canonical work of Mani's) and a text that remains unidentified.
4. A historical work that includes a life of Mani and the early history of the sect (the so-called *Acta* Codex).

In Dublin, the Chester Beatty Collection, originally in London:

5. The *Homilies.*
6. The *Psalm-Book.*
7. The *Kephalaia of the Wisdom of My Lord Mani.*

Unfortunately, substantial sections of the codices containing the *Letters* of Mani and the historical work were lost in the aftermath of World War II before the leaves were conserved and photographed. Nevertheless, the texts, which are still in the process of being edited and translated, throw an enormous amount of light on the earliest phase of the history of the sect in its original Mesopotamian homeland. To these texts from Medinet Madi must be added a miniature parchment codex containing an autobiographical account of the early life of Mani in Greek, which might have originally been recovered from Lycopolis in Egypt and is now housed and exhibited in the Papyrussammlung of Cologne University (the so-called *Cologne Mani Codex*). A Coptic version of this Greek text might have formed the first part of the now almost completely lost historical text in Coptic recovered from Medinet Madi. This text describes Mani's upbringing in a community of "baptists," who claimed Elchasaios, a Jewish

Christian known from Christian polemical writings, as one of the founders of their sect. The successful deciphering of this text in 1970 caused a sensation and completely altered the direction of research on Manichaean origins; scholars now had to look more closely at the esoteric fringes of Second Temple Judaism and at Gnostic Christianity for the ancestry of some of Mani's ideas, both on cosmogony and on ethics.

The existence of a Manichaean community at Kellis in the Dakleh Oasis in Egypt during the late Roman period (fourth century CE) came as a complete surprise to scholars. Manichaean texts in Coptic, Greek, and Syriac were recovered as part of the ongoing excavations at Ismant el-Kharab by an international team led by scholars from Australia. The texts recovered so far consist of papyrus codices, as well as inscribed wooden boards. These contain psalms and prayers and a substantial number of fragments of the canonical *Letters of Mani.* There are also bilingual Syriac and Coptic word lists, and the same Estrangela script that was used on the fragments from Oxyrhynchus was also used for these texts. This script is standard for the copying of Manichaean texts in Central Asia in Middle Iranian as well as Turkic languages. Because the texts from Kellis were recovered from a clearly recorded archaeological context, they show that the religion was widespread in the oasis and that the followers regarded themselves as true Christians. The discovery of a substantial section of Paul's epistle to the Romans shows that the sect was well versed in Christian literature, and it is clear from the unique private letters of the believers that the reading of both Manichaean and what is now called apocryphal Christian literature (e.g., *Acts of John*) was prescribed. The community disappeared when the oasis site was abandoned at the end of the fourth century CE.

The spread of Manichaeism in the Roman Empire was assisted above all by the conversion of the Empire to Christianity. This opened many missionary possibilities for a religion that claimed to be a superior form of Christianity and that was proclaimed by a prophet who styled himself the "Apostle of Jesus Christ" and the promised Paraclete. It is clear that Mani saw himself as a latter-day Saint Paul who could claim apostleship through special visionary appearances by his divine alter ego (his *syzygos*). It is also clear that Mani was familiar with both Christian literature and the hyper-Pauline and anti-Judaic writings of Marcion.

In the Roman Empire, when the religion was first disseminated under the last pagan regime prior to Constantine, its polytheism was thinly disguised. But as the religion circulated under Christian emperors it became a form of Christian dualism (between spirit and body, as well as between good and evil) with strong emphasis on asceticism, especially for the elect members of the sect. The Manichaean community at Kellis, for instance, clearly regarded itself as a sect of Gnostic Christianity, and the surviving correspondence of its members abounded in Christian (and Gnostic) terminology and shows familiarity with Christian (including apocryphal) writings. Persecution against the sect, instigated probably by the pagan emperor Diocletian or his colleague Galerius in 302, was probably instrumental in the establishment of a major Manichaean community at Kellis. The earliest Manichaean missionaries were undoubtedly Syriac speakers, but the sect's literature was soon translated into Greek, Latin, and Coptic. As in Central Asia, the copying of Manichaean texts was held in high esteem by the sect and was normally carried out by hearers. Manichaean books were handsomely bound, and extant examples display a uniformly high standard of calligraphy.

One of the best-known Roman converts to the sect was Augustine of Thagaste in North Africa, who became a hearer while he was a university student and teacher at Carthage (c. 373–382). After his famous conversion to a more orthodox Christianity (via Neoplatonism) in Milan in 386, he would devote a great deal of his intellectual energy into refuting the basic tenets of the sect, especially its dualism, its use of Christian scriptures, and its pseudo-asceticism, through his vast literary output. A particular source of concern for Christian polemicists like Augustine was the sect's claim to be a superior form of Christianity through its interpretation of Christian rather than Manichaean scriptures. The sect's rejection of the Old Testament—save for stories concerning certain figures like Seth and Enoch (who were also revered in Gnostic teaching)—as relevant for salvation would have been popular among pagans who wished to be converted to Christianity but who abhorred Judaism. The sect claimed to revere the crucified Christ; the long-term imprisonment of light by matter in the physical universe was, according to Manichaean teaching, personified by the "suffering Jesus" (*Jesus patibilis*). This allowed the sect to give a mystical interpretation to the crucifixion, and their use of the historical Jesus as a messianic figure who heralded the mission and "martyrdom" of Mani also enforced the appeal of the sect to a recently Christianized populace.

Christian leaders therefore had to demonstrate that Manichaean Christology had no scriptural basis and was founded on themes in apocryphal Christian literature, such as the *Acts of John* and the *Acts of Thomas.* They were also concerned that Manichaean belief in a dualistic creation myth could lead to the denial of the role of human volition in sin and the attribution of evil to a secondary deity that would challenge the omnipotence of the Christian God (the Father). Augustine, the most effective of the Christian polemicists on this score took the battle to the Manichaeans by accusing them of rendering the Judeo-Christian God less than omnipotent by removing him entirely from the horror of human existence. The God that Augustine presents to his Manichaean opponents is imbued with qualities that are more Neoplatonic than Christian. He is almighty, all-seeing, all-knowing, wise, loving, and above all creative, because all these qualities are not for his own gratification but emanate from him into the whole of creation. The world was created out of nothing (*ex nihilo*), and by "nothing" Augustine means absolute nonbeing, thereby rejecting the pagan view that the world was created out of "not anything."

Into this modified Neoplatonic picture of creation as emanation, Augustine injects the important Christian doctrine that God saw that everything he created was good (*Gn.* 1:10). The identification of creation with goodness is fundamental to him. Matter, in that it was created, is not in itself evil, as the Manichaeans would argue, but formless. Upon this basic substance God imposed "measure, form, and order" (*modus, species, et ordo*) in different ways to bring about the variety of his creation. Evil is not to be found in creation but in the way a certain object is deficient in its measure, form, and order. Evil is a negative force because it is a privation of good (*privatio boni*). Therefore, one cannot say that evil exists in the same way that good exists, because it is a corruption of good and hence parasitic in its existence. In short, evil exists only as a less desirable aspect of some actual unity that is intrinsically good, although it may have fallen far below the state that God intended. An earlier contemporary writer against the sect, Titus of Bostra, would argue that all suffering, including natural disasters, is the result of sin and not the work of a malignant deity. Human beings, according to Titus, are born neither good nor bad but fair. People acquire goodness through education and training. From birth they are imbued with the knowledge of good and evil. Consequently, they are able to reflect on the consequences of sinful actions and come to right decisions. What Titus advocates, therefore, is an all-out assault on evil by Christians in their daily living, rather than remaining on the defensive like the father of light in the Manichaean myth, waiting for the prince of darkness, his opponent, to take the initiative.

The much-vaunted ascetical commandments of the Manichaeans were seen by their Christian opponents as being based on the sect's belief in the evil nature of matter and not on genuine efforts to combat human desires. Manichaean leaders were frequently accused (e.g., by Augustine) of gluttony and overindulgence in expensive (vegetarian) food and (fruit) drinks. The sect was also labeled as libertines who used innumerable methods of contraception to enable the elect to practice sexual intercourse without leading to human birth and generation, which would prolong the "crucifixion" of light-particles in matter.

The religion, as already mentioned, was banned by the pagan emperor Diocletian in 302 for being a Persian sect that could endanger the moral values of patriotic Romans. The ban was later renewed by Christian emperors, who accused the sect of being a secretive cult, and Manichaeanism was heavily persecuted from Theodosius I onward as the most dangerous of Christian heresies. The standard punishment was the denial of rights of Roman citizenship, a punishment that prohibited members from making wills, which rendered any form of gift to the sect difficult. By the early Byzantine period, the death penalty was commonly inflicted on the leaders of the sect. The church was highly active in promoting polemical writings against the sect, especially a fictional life of Mani known as the *Acta Archelai*, in which Mani was portrayed as a failed miracle-worker who plagiarized his teachings from Christian sources. This and other polemical writings constituted the main source on the history of the sect until the beginning of the twentieth century. Moreover, they were used regularly by the Byzantine and Catholic churches in the Middle Ages against "Neo-Manichaean" sects, such as Paulicianism, Bogomilism, and Catharism. The actual religion itself was probably extinguished by persecution under Justinian, since no genuine Manichaean texts appear to be cited by, nor known by name to, the sect's medieval and Byzantine opponents.

See Also Mani.

Bibliography

Primary Sources

The series *Corpus fontium Manichaeorum,* published by Brepols and edited by Alois van Tongerloo, Samuel N. C. Lieu, and J. van Oort, aims eventually to publish all Manichaean texts. Already published are two sections of the *Psalm-Book* (Turnhout, Belgium, 1996) in the *Series Coptica* and a volume in the *Series Latina* on the anti-Manichaean writings of Pope Leo the Great (Turnhout Belgium, 2002). The publication of the Coptic Manichaean codices found at Medinet Madi in 1929 is underway. The volumes include: Hans Jakob Polotsky, *Manichäische Homilien,* Manichäische Handschriften der Sammlung A, Chester Beatty (Stuttgart, Germany, 1934); C. R. C. Allberry, *A Manichaean Psalm-Book: Part II,* Manichaean Manuscripts in the Chester Beatty Collection (Stuttgart, Germany, 1938); Hans Jakob Polotsky and Alexander Böhlig, *Kephalaia,* Manichäische Handschriften der staatlichen Museen Berlin, Seite 1–243 (Stuttgart, Germany, 1940); Alexander Böhlig, *Kephalaia,* Manichäische Handschriften der staatlichen Museen Berlin, Zweite Hälfte, Lieferung 11–12, Seite 244–291 (Stuttgart, Germany, 1966); and Wolf Peter Funk, Lieferung 13–14, Seite 292–366 (Stuttgart, Germany, 1999), and Lieferung 15–16, Seite 367–440, (Stuttgart, Germany, 2001).

The standard edition of the *Cologne Mani Codex* is Ludwig Koenen and Cornelia Römer, *Der Kölner Mani-Kodex* (Opladen, Germany, 1988). The texts from Kellis are published in *Kellis Literary Texts:* Vol. 1, edited by Iain Gardner (Oxford, 1996). See also the *Coptic Documentary Texts from Kellis*: Vol. 1, edited by Iain Gardner, Anthony Alcock, and Wolf Peter Funk (Oxford, 1999), which includes a collection of private correspondence from the Manichaean community in Kellis. A convenient edition and translation of the *Tebessa Codex* is Jason BeDuhn and Geoffrey Harrison, "The *Tebessa Codex*: A Manichaean Treatise on Biblical Exegesis and Church Order," in Paul Mirecki and Jason BeDuhn, eds., *Emerging from Darkness: Studies in the Recovery of Manichaean Sources* (Leiden, 1997), pp. 33–88. The *Acta Archelai* (attributed to Hegemonius) has been translated by Mark Vermes and annotated by Samuel N. C. Lieu, *Acta Archelai* (Turnhout, Belgium, 2001). A dictionary covering genuine Manichaean documents in Syriac, Coptic, Greek, and Latin was published as part of the Corpus Fontium Manichaeorum Project: Sarah Clackson, Erica Hunter, Samuel N. C. Lieu, and Mark Vermes, eds., *Dictionary of Manichaean Texts*, vol. 1, *Texts from the Roman Empire (Texts in Syriac, Greek, Coptic, and Latin)* (Turnhout, Belgium, 1998). A substantial collection of Manichaean texts from the Roman Empire in English translation can now be found in I. Gardner and S.N.C. Lieu. eds., *Manichaean Texts from the Roman Empire* (Cambridge, U.K., 2004). A detailed bibliography is also available: Gunner Mikkelsen, *Bibliographia Manichaica: A Comprehensive Bibliography of Manichaeism through 1996* (Turnhout, Belgium, 1997).

Studies

Samuel N. C. Lieu, *Manichaeism in the Later Roman Empire and Medieval China*, 2d ed. (Tübingen, Germany, 1992), gives a detailed overall survey of the history of the religion across Eurasia; the sections on Egypt have been updated by Iain Gardner and Lieu, "From Narmouthis (Medinet Madi) to Kellis (Ismant el-Kharab), Manichaean Documents from Roman Egypt," *Journal of Roman Studies* 86 (1996): 146–169, and by the same two authors, *Manichaean Texts from the Roman Empire* (New York, 2004). A thought-provoking study on the relationship between *gnōsis* and *ascesis* in Manichaeism is Jason BeDuhn, *The Manichaean Body in Discipline and Ritual* (Baltimore, 2001). Studies in more specialized aspects of the religion in the Roman Empire include: François Decret, *Aspects du manichéisme dans l'Afrique romaine* (Paris, 1970); François Decret, *L'Afrique manichéenne, Étude historique et doctrinale*, 2 vols. (Paris, 1978.); and Samuel N. C. Lieu, *Manichaeism in Mesopotamia and the Roman East* (Leiden, 1999). A classic study of the influence of Manichaeism on Augustine's theology, especially on his concept of the "two cities," is J. van Oort, *Jerusalem and Babylon: A Study into Augustine's City of God and the Sources of His Doctrine of the Two Cities* (Leiden, 1991). The *Manichaean Studies Newsletter*, an important annual newsletter (with bibliographical details of the year's publications) has been published by the International Association of Manichaean Studies and Brepols (Turnhout, Belgium) since 1988.

SAMUEL N. C. LIEU (2005)

MANICHAEISM: MANICHAEISM AND CHRISTIANITY

The teaching of Mani (216–277 CE) was essentially Gnostic, its constituent elements deriving from Judaism, Judeo-Christianity, and Iranian religion, especially Zoroastrianism in its Zurwānist form. It incorporated features from Marcion of Pontus (d. c. 160 CE) and from pluralistic Syriac Christianity represented by Bardesanes (Bardaisan) of Edessa (154–222 CE). According to the *Cologne Mani Codex* and several other primary texts discovered in Egypt, it is basically correct to see early Manichaeism as a kind of Christian heresy. Mani considered himself an apostle of Jesus Christ and, moreover, the Paraclete promised by Jesus. Within the Roman Empire the Manichaeans claimed to be the true Christian believers (*veri Christiani*), while they saw the members of the Catholic Christian Church as "semi-Christians." According to his *Capitula*, handed over by Augustine of Hippo (c. 400 CE), Faustus, the itinerant Manichaean bishop originating from Milevis (Algeria), declared his acceptance of the preaching of Jesus and his belief in a kind of Trinity. For many years the future Catholic bishop Augustine did the same (cf., e.g., *Confessions* III.6.10).

Mani himself believed he was promulgating a new universal religion that would supersede all others. The "prophet from the land of Babylon" was born on April 14, 216 CE, near the southern Mesopotamian town of Seleucia-Ctesiphon on the Tigris River. His father's name was Pattīg or Pattēg; in all probability the (Jewish) name of his mother was Marjam (Mirjam). After receiving several revelations from his heavenly Twin, Mani started his missionary journeys inside and outside the Persian Empire in 240 CE, at first accompanied only by his father and two other members of the Judeo-Christian (Elchasaite) sect of his youth.

Following the example of the apostles of Jesus, missionaries were sent out, and Mani himself journeyed in 241 CE by boat to India and up the Indus Valley to Turan, where he won over the king. Soon after the accession of Shāpūr I (242–273 CE) as the sole king of kings of the Persian Empire, Mani seems to have delivered to him his only Middle Persian writing, the *Shābuhragān*. His admittance into Shāpūr's entourage accorded him unique opportunities to propagate his new prophecy. After Shāpūr's death, Mani also found a willing ear with Hormīzd (Ōhrmazd, 272–273). At the beginning of the second year of the reign of Bahrām I (274–276/7), this benevolent attitude changed. Kardēr, the head of the Zoroastrian magi, began to persuade the great king to take action against the new prophet. Mani was summoned before Bahrām, duly accused, put in chains, and tortured. After twenty-six days in prison, Mani died. In several Manichaean sources his death is described as a crucifixion. Mani's religion soon spread from Mesopotamia to the Atlantic in the west and finally as far as the Pacific in the east.

Although Mani failed to make his revelation the official religion of Iran, he succeeded in what he really intended: the establishment of a new world religion or church. The firm interior organization of this church seems to date from Mani's times and, in essence, may even be a creation of the prophet himself. The church was headed by Mani and later by his deputy *archēgos*. Immediately following this *archēgos* or *princeps* there were, in the order of three subordinate ranks, the 12 apostles or teachers, the 72 bishops, and the 360 presbyters. The fourth rank was constituted by the elect, both men and women, and finally, the fifth rank consisted of the wide circle of auditors. In order to firmly establish the doctrine of his church, Mani composed a sevenfold canon of authoritative writings:

1. *The Living Gospel* (or Great Gospel);
2. *The Treasure of Life;*
3. The *Pragmateia* (or Treatise, Essay);
4. *The Book of Mysteries* (Secrets);
5. *The Book of the Giants;*

6. The *Letters*;
7. The *Psalms* and *Prayers*.

All of these writings only survive in fragmentary form, but in many cases its Jewish and in particular (Judeo-)Christian parallels are evident. The discovery of the *Cologne Mani Codex* shortly before 1970 produced a highly significant extract from the first and most important of Mani's writing, that is, his *Living Gospel*.

Like his followers in the West, Mani regarded himself as a true disciple of Jesus: he assumed the title "apostle of Jesus Christ." However, this title seems not to be fashioned after the example and role of the apostles of Jesus in the New Testament Gospels. Mani preeminently followed in the footsteps of the apostle Paul. In the case of Mani the concept of apostle should be taken in an even wider sense. In the *Cologne Mani Codex*, as in several other Manichaean writings, Paul functions as a link in a long chain of "apostles of truth." These apostles include such Jewish forefathers as Adam, Sethel, Enos, Sem, and Henoch, but also religious figures like the Buddha and Zoroaster had been called to become the apostle for their own time. The idea of the cyclical incarnation of the true apostle (or prophet or savior or evangelist: in many Manichaean texts these terms are interchangeable) was well known in Judeo-Christian circles. Moreover it is likely that, for the Manichaeans, Mani was also the seal of the prophets. Later on Muḥammad seems to have adopted this concept of being both the apostle (*rasūl*) of God and the seal of the prophets.

When Manichaeism moved east, much of its essential structure remained the same. In southern China, Mani was presented as a reincarnation of Laozi, the founder of Daoism; to many others, he was the Buddha of Light. Yet eastern and western Manichaeism were to a certain extent identical, though the eastern texts represent a much later and far more syncretistic form of Manichaeism. In all its varieties, however, the figure of Jesus had a certain place.

In order to understand both Mani's claim of being an apostle of Jesus Christ and the universal place of Jesus himself within the Manichaean system, some key elements of the Manichaean myth will be highlighted. According to this myth, a series of emanations took place in the heavenly world. From the Father of Greatness came forth the Messenger of Light, and from him emanated Jesus the Splendor, who in turn brought forth the Light-Mind, or Light-Nous. This Nous called forth the Apostle of Light, and during the course of world history this (heavenly) apostle became incarnate in great religious leaders, such as the Buddha, Zoroaster, Jesus the Messiah, and Mani. When Mani assumed the title of apostle of Jesus Christ, he actually considered himself an apostle of Jesus the Splendor and not of the historical Jesus. The figure of Jesus the Messiah was, in fact, well known in Manichaeism, but in comparison to the other apostles, he did not have any unique significance (as in mainstream Christendom). He also was an apostle of the Light-Nous, and thus of Jesus the Splendor.

Mani and his followers taught a cosmogony of a definitely dualistic kind: evil is an eternal cosmic force, not the result of a fall. Two realms or kingdoms—that of light and that of darkness, good and evil, God and matter—oppose each other implacably. This dualism, however, is not the Hellenistic dualism of spirit and matter but one of two substances: the divine light is a visible, spatial, and quantifiable element, as is the evil substance of darkness, the active principle of lust, the "thought of death."

The Myth. In the kingdom of light the Father of Greatness rules, and this kingdom is an extension of himself. It has four divine attributes (purity, light, power, wisdom), and the Father resides in his five intellectual powers or "limbs" (reason, mind, intelligence, thought, and understanding, which are otherwise substantially detailed as the five elements of living air, light, wind, water, and fire). Surrounding the Father are the twelve aeons, equally distributed toward the four directions of heaven and refracted into myriads of "aeons of the aeons."

Opposed to the kingdom of light is the realm of darkness, a kingdom that is essentially the domain of evil matter. It is disorderly and dominated by the Prince of Darkness, who is the product of (and even identified with) evil matter. This kingdom also consists of five areas or worlds (dark reason, dark mind), which are also referred to as the five elements of smoke, fire, wind, water, and darkness. In this area countless demons are actively present; they fight and devour each other. Because there was an accidental shift of these disorganized movements, the Prince of Darkness once glimpsed the radiance of light, desired to possess its life, and therefore attacked the kingdom of light. In the ensuing struggle, the Father of Light called forth the Mother of Life, who in turn evoked the First Man. This was the first series of "evocations." After that, the First Man, the "firstborn" Son of God, was called forth and, being equipped with the five light powers as his "sons" or "arms," went into battle. But Primal Man was defeated, and his fivefold armor or Living Soul was devoured by the powers of evil. This being the case, the divine Soul (also termed the Living Self that is suspended on the Cross of Light and, particularly in the West, personified as the suffering Jesus, *Jesus patibilis*) was mixed with the dark elements of matter and thus became in need of redemption.

The First Man, being vanquished, lay unconscious in the depths. In order to redeem him, the Father of Light called forth a second series of evocations: a new divine Trinity. First, the Father sent forth the Beloved of the Lights; from him came the Great Builder; he in turn produced the Living Spirit. This Living Spirit (also termed the Father of Life) sent his Call from the lowest boundary of the world of light to the First Man lying in the depths. First Man aroused from his unconscious state and responded by an Answer. Then the Living Spirit, together with its five sons and the Mother of Life, descended to the First Man and led him up to the world of light. To rescue the light still captured through the compound of the divine Soul with evil matter, the Living Spirit constructed, with the help of its sons, ten heavens and eight earths.

It is especially noteworthy that, according to the Manichaean cosmogonic myth, this act of creation is performed by a light god, not by an evil demiurge. Thus, in Manichaeism, unlike most other Gnostic systems, the structure of the universe is divinely devised. In order to create the cosmos, however, use had to be made of material of a mixed substance (light and darkness). The sun and the moon are considered to be vessels of pure light, being made from the particles of light completely unaffected by darkness. The planets and stars, however, are evil rulers because they are created from material contaminated with darkness.

With the world so constructed—as a well-ordered prison for the forces of darkness and also as a place where the divine Soul has been captured—the process of salvation could begin. To this end a third evocation of deities occurred. The Father of Greatness called forth the Third Messenger or Ambassador, who was charged to extract and purify the light still retained by the powers of darkness and contained in their bodies. By taking advantage of the innate lust of the male and female archons chained in the heavens, this Tertius Legatus and his female doublet, the Virgin of Light (also represented as the Twelve Maidens, each corresponding to a sign of the zodiac), made them relinquish the light they had devoured. It was concentrated in particular in their semen and in their wombs. The sins of the male archons fell upon the earth when they saw the beautiful Maiden(s). Out of that part of their semen that had dropped into water a monster arose, but this fearful beast was subjugated by the Adamas of Light. From the semen that had fallen on the dry ground, five trees sprang up, and from them all other forms of plant life originated.

When the female archons, pregnant by their own evil nature, saw the naked form of the Third Messenger, they were also agitated, and their fetuses fell down upon the earth. These abortions not only survived their premature births but also devoured the fruits of the trees that had grown out of the semen of the male archons. Driven by sexual lust, they united with each other and gave birth to the innumerable species of animals now known. The light that was not saved was thus transferred to the earth, where it is still scattered and bound in plants and, to a lesser degree, in the bodies of animals.

The next episodes of the Manichaean myth may be summarized, still with a certain emphasis on Christian parallels, as succinctly as possible. In order to continue the liberation of the light, the Third Messenger called forth the Column of Glory (who is also referred to as the New or Perfect Man; cf. *Eph.* 4:12–13) and set in motion the work of "the ships of light" (i.e., the sun and moon) in order to transport the light to the New Paradise that had been built by the Great Builder. This process frightened the powers of darkness, and in a desperate attempt to preserve some of the captive particles of light, they created the first human couple, Adam and Eve. Hence man was fabricated by the demons, but after the image of the Third Messenger (and so ultimately after the image of God), which the demons had seen on high. Man was thus rooted in two worlds, but at first he was unconscious of his high descent. However, Jesus the Luminous descended to bring him the saving knowledge; this revelation by Jesus to Adam is the archetype of all future human redemption. Gradually this liberation will be achieved. In order to bring about the redemption of the light, Jesus evoked the Light-Mind, or Light-Nous (Intelligence). This Nous in turn summoned forth the Apostle of Light, who became incarnate in the world's great religious leaders.

The final stage of history will be introduced by the Great War between the forces of good and evil. When the church of the righteous ones triumphs, all the souls will be judged, and those of the chosen will rise to heaven. After that the world will be destroyed and purified by a fire lasting 1,468 years. All or most of the light particles will be saved; evil matter, in all its manifestations and with its victims (the damned), will be forever imprisoned in a globe (*bôlos, globus*). Then the separation of light and darkness will be accomplished for all eternity.

This is an eclectic account of the myth. However complex its ramifications became in the course of many centuries, its essentials remained the same. It is Mani's doctrine that there are two principles and three "moments": the time before the commingling and the struggle, when the two kingdoms of light and darkness were opposed; the time of the commingling, the present world's existence; and future time, in which the two kingdoms will again be (and now definitively) separated. In essence this doctrine is typically Gnostic: the Nous (the heavenly revelation) rescues the Psyche (the divine spark of light in man) from Hyle (evil matter).

SPREAD OF MANICHAEISM. In the fourth century Manichaeism made great strides in Egypt and North Africa. In 373 Augustine joined the sect in Carthage, and he remained an ardent follower of Manichaeism for more than ten years. Later on, during his career as a Catholic presbyter and bishop, he opposed his former coreligionists in a great number of writings. Nevertheless it is still debated whether the most influential father of the Western church was also positively influenced by Manichaeism. Many of Mani's adherents became refugees with the onslaught of the vandals in the course of the fifth century CE. Hence in Rome, Pope Leo the Great (r. 440–461) actively sought out Manichaean refugees in order to suppress them. In 527 CE there were lawsuits against them in Constantinople. However, Manichaeism survived in North Africa until at least the eighth century CE.

In the East, on the other hand, especially in Chinese Turkestan, there is evidence that Manichaeans were still active in the thirteenth century. A Manichaean temple built in the fourteenth century is still standing on Hua-piao Hill not far from the modern city of Quanzhou on the South China Coast.

Statements by Catholic Christian writers in the Middle Ages suggest that Manichaeism persisted in the West. The Paulicians, the Bogomils, and the Cathari, as well as those who followed Priscillian were all charged with being Manichaeans. In fact, all these authorities were using *Manichaean* as a synonym for *dualist*, and any teaching that manifested a tendency toward dualism was accordingly called Manichaean. The teaching of Priscillian (c. 370 CE) is by no means easy to define, but it is doubtful that the epithet Manichaean is applicable. The Paulicians, first noted in Armenia in the seventh century CE, seem to have been straightforward Gnostics; they had a direct influence on the Bogomils, who emerged in Bulgaria in the tenth century. In the eleventh century the Cathari began to achieve notoriety in Italy, Germany, and France—being commonly called Albigensians in France—but it has yet to be proved that there was an evident historical connection between any of these and the ancient Manichaeans.

See Also Cathari.

Bibliography

Koenen, Ludwig, and Cornelia Römer. *Der Kölner Mani-Kodex.* Opladen, Germany, 1988.

Leo I, Pope. *Sermons and Letters against the Manichaeans.* Edited by Hendrik Gerhard and Johannes van Oort. Turnhout, Belgium, 2000.

Lieu, Samuel N. C. *Manichaeism in the Later Roman Empire and Medieval China.* Tübingen, Germany, 1992.

Oort, Johannes van. *Mani, Manichaeism, and Augustine.* Tbilisi, Republic of Georgia, 2001.

Oort, Johannes van, Otto Wermelinger, and Gregor Wurst, eds. *Augustine and Manichaeism in the Latin West.* Leiden and Boston, 2001.

Polotsky, Hans Jacob. *Abriss des manichäischen Systems.* Stuttgart, 1935. Reprinted in Polotsky, *Collected Papers*, pp. 699–714. Jerusalem, 1971.

Rudolph, Kurt. *Gnosis: The Nature and History of an Ancient Religion.* Edinburgh, 1983.

Johannes van Oort (2005)

MANICHAEISM: MANICHAEISM IN CENTRAL ASIA AND CHINA

The diffusion of Manichaeism in Central Asia is documented only in Manichaean historical sources found in Chotcho near Turfan by German explorers at the beginning of the twentieth century. These were recovered in fragmentary condition, but they clearly once belonged to handsome codices produced in the Uighur kingdom in the tenth and eleventh centuries CE, when Manichaeism was the dominant state religion. From these historical texts we learn that the religion was under the leadership of Mar Ammo, one of the best known of Mani's disciples, who was chosen for the evangelization of Eastern Iran because of his knowledge of the Parthian language. He was accompanied by translators, which explains why Manichaean texts in Parthian often show traces of direct translation from Mani's original Syriac. Mar Ammo was also honored in later Manichaean tradition as the first missionary to cross the River Oxus into Khorasan.

Once established in the territories of the former Kushan Empire, Manichaeism came into competition and synthesis with Buddhism, and Manichaean texts in Parthian in particular acquired a large number of Buddhist terms and concepts, such as *vairocana*, *parinirvāṇa* and *saṃsāra.* In addition, Mani came to be worshiped as the Buddha of Light, but the Feast of the Bema, which commemorates Mani's death, remained a unique and important ceremony for the sect. At some point, Middle Persian-speaking Manichaeans also migrated into Central Asia, and the city of Merv probably became a merging point for both the Parthian-speaking and Middle Persian-speaking branches of the sect. As Manichaean missionaries moved eastward along the Silk Road, many of their converts would have been Sogdians or Sogdian-speakers, and their religious texts were translated into Sogdian, and also into Bactrian and Tocharian. Along the Silk Road, Manichaean missionaries probably performed a variety of roles, including those of musicians, scribes, and information gatherers (especially on prices of goods and exchange rates). Manichaeism was unique among religions in Central Asia in that it maintained three principal languages (Middle Persian, Parthian, and Sogdian) for its scripture. There are some examples of texts (such as Mani's *Evangelium*, of which only a few leaves have survived) that are diglottal (Middle Persian and Sogdian).

At the end of the seventh century CE, an important schism broke out between the followers of Mihr (the Mihrijja) and those of Miqlas (the Miqlasijja) in Mesopotamia over how strictly certain rules governing daily living should be followed. This dispute was continued by Manichaean communities in Central Asia, which generally followed the stricter Miqlasijja branch. The Sogdian Manichaeans also paid considerable attention to the hierarchical distinction between the elect and the hearers. The Sogdian Manichaeans also paid considerable attention to the hierarchical distinction between the elect who were committed to a life of ascetical living and the hearers who were members of the second rank and who were more involved with commercial activities along the Silk Road. The elect members who were mainly priests had to rely on the hearers for their sustenance and in return they absolved the hearers from their sins. The religion became synonymous with the *dynd'r* or *dyn'br* (Sogdian for "elect"), and when the Chinese Buddhist pilgrim Xuanzang traversed Bactria and Tocharistan circa 630 CE, he noted that the religion of the Tinaba was a heresy among the Persians. Recent archaeological discoveries suggest that Manichaeism was already established in the Turfan area prior to the conversion of the Uighur Khaghan in 762 CE.

The Early History of Manichaeism in China. Little was known of the precise history of Manichaeism in China until the discovery of genuine Manichaean texts in Chinese from the Cave of a Thousand Buddhas in Dunhuang in the first decade of the twentieth century. These came as a surprise to Sinologists who believed that traditional China was highly impervious to foreign religious influences other than those of Buddhism and Islam. No account of the gradual diffusion of the religion from Eastern Iran to China via the Silk Road had come down to us from a Manichaean source. Chinese sources mention the sending of Mozak (a Manichaean priest of a high grade) by Tes, the King of Cazanistan and Tocharistan, to the Tang court in 719 CE. Mozak was reportedly well-received by the court because of his skills in astrology. Moreover, the Manichaeans in China preserved the tradition that the spread of the religion in the Middle Kingdom was brought about by the earlier arrival of Mozak during the reign of Emperor Gaozong of the Tang dynasty. Mozak's pupil, Mihr-Ōhrmazd (Mi-we-mo-ssu), who held the rank of *aftadan* (*fu-to-tan,* or *episcopus*), later also came to China and presented himself to the royal court, where he was granted an audience by the Empress Wu. According to later Buddhist sources in Chinese, Mihr-Ōhrmazd presented to the court a Manichaean work entitled the *Sūtra of the Two principles,* which was to become the most popular Manichaean scripture in China.

The religion was clearly popular among the Sogdian (i.e., East Iranian) merchants and there were attempts to win Chinese converts. In 731 CE a Manichaean priest was asked to provide a summary of the main tenets of the religion. It is interesting to note that the version of the summary (the *Compendium of the Teachings of Mani the Buddha of Light*) that was found among the Dunhuang documents already shows clear attempts to depict Manichaeism as a form of Buddhism; Mani was seen as an *avatar* (reincarnation or remanifestation) of Laozi, the traditional founder of Daoism in China. Many Chinese believed that Laozi had not died but had gone to the west, where he reappeared as the Buddha. This legend was used by the Manichaeans as a passport to the multireligious scene of Tang China. The legend was also welcomed by syncretistic Daoists who were keen to absorb the new religion into the mainstream of Chinese religions through this putative connection with the founder of Daoism. The response of the Tang government to the *Compendium,* however, was the prompt passage of a law in 731 that restricted the dissemination of the religion among foreigners in China and banned its spread among the indigenous Chinese. By then a substantial number of Manichaean texts had already been translated into Chinese from Parthian and Sogdian; one of the longest Manichaean texts in Chinese, a version of the *Sermon of the Light-Nous* (a popular Manichaean text in Central Asia) contains a character that was forbidden after the reign of Empress Wu.

In addition, the third of the three Chinese texts from Dunhuang, the *Hymnscroll,* contains hymns that are both transliterated and translated from Parthian, indicating an early period of contact with Manichaean communities in Central Asia. Some canonical Manichaean texts (non-extant) were listed among the Nestorian Christian texts translated by the famous Nestorian missionary Jing-jing, which may explain why the sacred writings of the Nestorians and Manichaeans in Chinese shared some common theological vocabulary. Beyond that, there was very little in common between the two sects, except that the Chinese authorities considered both to be of Persian origin until the Nestorians petitioned successfully in 745 to have the epithet "Persian" replaced by "Roman" in the title of their religion.

MANICHAEISM AS THE OFFICIAL RELIGION OF THE UIGHUR KINGDOM. A major landmark in the history of Manichaeism in China was the conversion of Moyu (Bogu) Khan of the Uighur Turks to the religion in 762. Since 755, Tang China had been fatally weakened by the so-called An Lushan rebellion; the Uighurs became the only effective fighting force in the service of the Tang government, and their troops garrisoned the sensitive frontier between China and Tibet. The conversion that was proclaimed on a trilingual (Old Turkish in runic script, Sogdian, and Chinese) inscription found at Karabalghasun at the end of the nineteenth century proudly announces the adoption of strict prohibitions, such as vegetarianism and the abstention from alcohol. Under the patronage of the Uighurs, Manichaean temples were permitted to be established in both the capitals of China (Chang'an and Luoyang), as well as four other major cities in North and Central China. The sudden collapse of the Uighur Empire in 840 led to the closure of most of the temples, and after the proscription against Buddhism and other foreign religions in 843, Manichaean priests were publicly humiliated and executed. The remnants of the Uighur Turks were resettled in the region round Chotcho.

Manichaeism continued to flourish and followers were rewarded with productive agricultural lands, which, despite the religion's rules against intoxication, were used for the cultivation of wine grapes. The brief period of foreign patronage probably only lasted a century, but it was the period in which most of the Manichaean texts that were recovered by the German Turfan expeditions were produced by highly professional scribes and artists.

MANICHAEISM AS A SECRET RELIGION IN CHINA. The religion reemerged during the Five Dynasties period (907–960) as a popular secret religion in Central and, in particular, South China. The earlier use of the myth of the Buddha Mani as an *avatar* of Laozi enabled the Manichaeans to pass themselves off as Buddhists or as Daoists. The religion was particularly popular south of the Yangtze, especially in and around the cosmopolitan port city of Quanzhou (Zaitun in Western medieval sources). The followers of the religion were sufficiently well connected for some of their scriptures to be accepted into the Daoist canon in 1019 (since then removed).

In 1120 a major rebellion took place under the leadership of Fang La, the owner of a lacquer grove, in protest against a special impost on luxury goods. It was widely believed by the authorities that many of the rebels were members of secret religious sects (castigated by authorities as "vegetarian demon worshipers") and that their meeting places were loci of political protest. This led to widespread crackdowns on unauthorized religious assemblies and the confiscation of noncanonical scriptures. A list of the latter was given in a memorial of 1120, which shows that much of the typical Manichaean terminology found in texts translated from Central Asian languages during the Tang period was still in use by members of the sect in South China. An exchange of letters between a Daoist abbot of a former Manichaean temple and a Confucian scholar, composed in 1204, shows that the strict commandments of the sect (on vegetarianism and sexual abstinence, as well as a requirement to pray seven times a day) still had admirers in Central China, though there were few devotees.

Manichaeism in South China under the Mongols. The Mongol conquest of South China in 1280 brought a century of freedom of persecution for the Manichaeans in that region. It is highly probable that the secretive "Christians" whom Marco Polo and his uncle Maffeo encountered in Fuzhou were in fact Manichaeans. Nestorianism also returned to China; many of the Mongol administrators and military commanders were Turkic-speaking Nestorians. Bishop Mar Solomon (d. 1313) is given the title "Bishop of the Manichaeans and Nestorians of the various circuits of Jiangnan" on a bilingual Turko-Syriac (i.e., Turkish written in Nestorian Syriac script with Syriac loanwords) and Chinese inscription discovered during the Sino-Japanese War (1937–1945) at Quanzhou. It was under the Mongols that the Manichaeans took over a Buddhist temple on Huabiao Hill in Jinjiang near Quanzhou and refurbished it as a Manichaean temple with a statue of Mani as the Buddha of Light. This statue, which was recovered from a former Manichaean temple in North China, shows many similar features, especially in the design of its garments, with the famous portrait of a Manichaean leader as depicted on a wall painting from Chotcho that was destroyed in World War II.

The Nestorian community in South China, judging from the abundant remains of their funerary monuments in syncretistic Buddhist and Christian art forms and inscriptions in half a dozen languages (including Chinese and Turko-Syriac), was clearly reintroduced from Central Asia by Mongols to serve as administrators. Their presence in Quanzhou and their high social status probably enabled the Manichaeans to claim protection as a privileged foreign religion. However, as soon as the Mongols were expelled in 1368, Manichaeism found itself once more under persecution with the accession of a more inward-looking Ming dynasty. Nevertheless, as late as the fifteenth century, the followers of the sect would still count Jesus and the "primal man" among the religion's chief deities. The religion probably finally died out in the first decades of the twentieth century in South China. The temple on Huabiao Hill, which local worshipers call a *cao'an* (thatched nunnery), is still used daily as a Buddhist temple in which Mani is worshiped as a local Buddhist deity with special powers.

See Also Chinese Religion, overview article; Mani.

Bibliography

Primary Sources

Of the three genuine Chinese Manichaean texts recovered in Dunhuang, the longest is a version of the *Sermon of the Light-Nous*, which is well represented in Parthian, Sogdian, and Old Turkish. The best edition, translation, and study remains Edouard Chavannes and Paul Pelliot, *Un traité manichéen retrouvé en Chine I* (Paris, 1912; reprinted from *Journal Asiatique* [1911]: 499–617). The second longest, the *Hymnscroll*, was translated by Tsui Chi as "*Mo-ni chiao hsia-pu tsan*, the Lower (Second?) Section of the Manichaean Hymns," *Bulletin of the School of Oriental and African Studies* 11 (1943): 174–219. The third, known commonly as the *Compendium*, was partially translated by Gustav Haloun and W. B. Henning as "The Compendium of the Doctrines and Styles of the Teaching of Mani, the Buddha of Light," *Asia Major* n.s. 3 (1952): 184–212. This text was more completely translated by Nahal Tajadod, *Mani, le Bouddha de Lumière: Catéchisme manichéen chinois* (Paris, 1990). All three texts were translated into German by Helwig Schmidt-Glintzer, *Chinesische Manichaica: Mit textkritischen Anmerkungen und einem Glossar* (Wiesbaden, 1987).

A small number of Manichaean fragments in Chinese were also found in Turfan. On these see Th. Thilo, "Einige Bemerkungen zu zwei chinesisch-manichäischen Textfragmenten der Berliner Turfan-Sammlung," in Horst Klengel and Werner Sundermann, eds., *Ägypten, Vorderasien, Turfan: Probleme der Edition und Bearbeitung altorientalischer Handschriften* (Berlin, 1991), pp. 161–170.

Secondary Sources

The second and third parts of the monograph by Edouard Chavannes and Paul Pelliot, *Un traité manichéen retrouvé en Chine II* (Paris, 1913; reprinted from *Journal Asiatique* [1913]: 99–199 and 261–394), remain a mine of high quality information. Samuel N. C. Lieu, *Manichaeism in the Later Roman Empire and Medieval China* (Tübingen, Germany, 1992), pp. 219–304, gives a general study. A useful study on Manichaeism among Sogdian merchants is Étienne de la Vaissière, *Histoire des marchands sogdiens* (Paris, 2002). Peter Bryder, *The Chinese Transformation of Manichaeism: A Study of Chinese Manichaean Terminology* (Löberöd, Sweden, 1985), is a seminal work, and the same author's ". . .Where the Faint Traces of Manichaeism Disappear," *Altorientalische Forschungen* 15, no. 1 (1988): 201–208, traces the history of the sect in South China. More specialized aspects of the history of the sect in China are dealt with by Samuel N. C. Lieu in *Manichaeism in Central Asia and China* (Leiden, Netherlands, 1998). For bibliographic information, see Gunner B. Mikkelsen, *Bibliographica Manichaica: A Comprehensive Bibliography of Manichaeism through 1996* (Turnhout, 1997), especially pp. 281–301.

Samuel N. C. Lieu (2005)

MĀṆIKKAVĀCAKAR (ninth century CE), Tamil poet-saint devoted to the god Śiva. Māṇikkavācakar ("he whose speech is like rubies") is generally acknowledged to have been the greatest poet of Tamil Śaivism. For at least the past thousand years he has also enjoyed the status of a saint in South Indian temples consecrated to Śiva, where one frequently sees his image and hears his hymns sung by professional reciters (*ōtuvārs*) as part of the regular temple ritual.

Māṇikkavācakar probably flourished about the middle of the ninth century. He was born in the *brahman* settlement at Tiruvātavūr, a village near Madurai. According to the *Tiruvātavūrar Purāṇam*, a fifteenth-century hagiography, he was a precocious child and at an early age entered the service of the Pandya king at Madurai; there he soon became prime minister. His high position notwithstanding, Māṇikkavācakar harbored religious longings that remained unfulfilled until, while on a trip to Perunturai (modern-day Avadayarkoyil in Pudukkottai District), he unexpectedly met and was initiated by a guru who was none other than Śiva himself. This abrupt change led to a series of bizarre and amusing incidents revolving around the interactions of Māṇikkavācakar kar, the Pandya king, and Śiva in various guises—all counted among Śiva's "sacred sports" as narrated in the *Tiruviḷaiyāṭal Purāṇam*, the sacred history of the great Mīnākṣī-Sundareśvara temple in Madurai.

After gaining release from the king's service, Māṇikkavācakar is reputed to have visited several shrines of Śiva in the Tamil country, composing hymns as he went. He eventually settled in Chidambaram, site of the Naṭarāja temple. Here he composed more poems, defeated Buddhists from Lanka in a debate, and finally, according to the hagiography, disappeared into the inner sanctum of the temple, having merged with the god.

Two works are ascribed to Māṇikkavācakar. His premier poem is the *Tiruvācakam* (Sacred speech), a collection of fifty-one hymns addressed to Śiva. The *Tiruvācakam* displays a rich variety of poetic forms skillfully utilized. Some of the poems are based on women's folk songs that accompany certain domestic activities or village games. In these instances, form and theology coincide, for in the *Tiruvācakam* Māṇikkavācakar typically casts himself as a female who is in love with Śiva. The hymns of the *Tiruvācakam* have long been venerated by Tamil speakers not just for their musicality but also for their paradigmatic expression of devotion. These hymns frequently give voice to the intense emotions of longing for, separation from, and union with the deity. They celebrate a god who overwhelms his devotee, resulting in an experience of melting and surrender. Viewed historically, the *Tiruvācakam* forms a bridge between early Tamil devotional poetry with its inheritance of forms and images drawn from the Caṅkam period, and the later systematic treatises of the Tamil Śaiva Siddhānta school of philosophy.

Māṇikkavācakar's other work, the *Tirukkōvaiyār*, is a poem of four hundred quatrains modeled on Caṅkam *akam* ("inner," i.e., love) poetry. Ostensibly an erotic poem, the *Tirukkōvaiyār* has traditionally been interpreted as an allegory on the relationship between Śiva and the soul. Along with the far more popular *Tiruvācakam*, it comprises the eighth section of the twelve-part Tirumurai, the canonical poetry of Tamil Śaivism.

In addition to the deep reverence many Tamils have for the *Tiruvācakam*, the cult of the saint is still prominent at several locations in modern Tamil Nadu. Especially noteworthy is the Śrī Ātmanātacuvāmi temple in Avadayarkoyil, marking the site of Māṇikkavācakar's initiation. Here the saint is ritually identified with the god, for only the saint's image, decorated to look like various forms of Śiva, is carried in procession at festivals. Also, both major annual festivals of this temple conclude with a dramatic ritual reenactment of Māṇikkavācakar's initiation by Śiva.

See Also Śaivism, articles on Nāyaṉārs, Śaiva Siddhānta; Tamil Religions.

Bibliography

Besides numerous Tamil editions of the *Tiruvācakam*, there have been several translations of the text into English and German. The first English translation was that of G. U. Pope, *The Tiruvaçagam or "Sacred Utterances" of the Tamil Poet, Saint and Sage Manikkavaçakar* (1900; reprint, Madras, 1970). While Pope's translation is in a late Victorian style of English poetry that is now outdated, his work contains the Tamil text and a lengthy introductory "appendix" that is still useful. A translation into more modern English by a Tamil devotee of Śiva is *Pathway to God through Tamil Literature*, vol. 1, *Through the Thiruvaachakam*, translated and edited by G. Vanmikanathan (New Delhi, 1971). The translator's 100-page introduction interprets the *Tiruvācakam* as a "handbook of mystical theology." A recent study that discusses Māṇikkavācakar and the religio-historical context of his major work is my own *Hymns to the Dancing Śiva: A Study of Māṇikkavācakar's Tiruvācakam* (Columbia, Mo., 1982).

New Sources

Sivapriya. *True History and Time of Manikkavasaghar from His Work*. Delhi, 1996.

Glenn E. Yocum (1987)
Revised Bibliography

MANISM (from Lat. *manes*, "departed spirit, ghost") was a theory of the origin of religion briefly advocated in the late nineteenth century by the popular British philosopher Herbert Spencer (1820–1903) and by one of his disciples, the Canadian-born Grant Allen (1848–1899). It bears no relation to, and should not be confused with, theories based on the concept of *mana*.

That the spirits of the dead occupy an important place in the history of religion is verifiable simply by observation. All primal and many later cultures have regarded the dead—and particularly the newly dead—as continuing to be active and concerned members of their respective families. Having passed beyond the limitations of earthly life, they are in possession of power greater than that of mortals. This power may be turned to the advantage of the living if the memory of the dead is respected and offerings continue to be made at the graveside or elsewhere. The unburied or uncremated dead, who have not been sent into the afterlife with the proper rituals, or those neglected by their families, are, on the other hand, liable to be dangerous. Always, however, they are believed to occupy a relatively lowly position in the supernatural hierarchy. They have power, but their power is limited as a rule to the circles within which they moved while still alive. Naturally, those who possessed greater power and influence during their lifetimes (chieftains and kings, for instance) were held to wield greater, though still limited, power after death.

The first attempt to link belief in the power of departed spirits with the world of religion was made in the early third century BCE, by the Greek writer Euhemerus (c. 340–260 BCE), in his *Hiera anagraphē* (Sacred history). Euhemerus claimed that all the gods had been prominent men and women of their own day, revered when alive and worshiped after death. In fact, of course, examples abound in societies past and present of human beings accorded divine honors after death, and similar theories have often been put forward to account for the otherwise obscure origins of several deities. Snorri Sturluson in his *Prose Edda*, for example, traced the ancestry of Þórr (Thor) and Óðinn (Odin) back to the heroes of the Trojan War. This type of explanation is generally called "euhemerism," after its first advocate.

But euhemerism seeks not to account for the origins of religion as such but only for the worship of particular deities. The theory is certainly sound, if kept within appropriate limits, since the deification process is well attested historically. Manism, on the other hand, sought to explain—or to explain away—the whole of religion on this one principle.

Herbert Spencer's essay "Manners and Fashion" was first published in the *Westminster Review* in April 1854, thus antedating E. B. Tylor's *Primitive Culture* (London, 1871) by seventeen years. In it, Spencer claimed to have established a close relation between "Law, Religion, and Manners," in the sense that those who presided over these three areas of human activity ("Deity, Chief, and Master of the Ceremonies") were identical. Reflecting further on the role of chiefs and medicine men in primitive belief, Spencer came to the conclusion that "the aboriginal god is the dead chief: the chief not dead in our sense, but gone away, carrying with him food and weapons to some rumoured region of plenty, some promised land, whither he had long intended to lead his followers, and whence he will presently return to fetch them. This hypothesis, once entertained, is seen to harmonize with all primitive ideas and practices" (Spencer, *Essays*, vol. 3, London, 1891, p. 7). Thus humankind's earliest deity had been a deified "big man," a deceased chief, whose power had been sufficiently great to have become a tradition and whose power was believed still to be operative from the other side of the gulf between life and death.

In 1862 Spencer published the first volume of his massive composite work of "sociology," appropriately called *First Principles* (these principles were, however, greatly revised in subsequent editions). There he stated:

> As all ancient records and traditions prove, the earliest rulers are regarded as divine personages. The maxims and commands they uttered during their lives are held sacred after their deaths, and are enforced by their divinely-descended successors; who in their turn are promoted to the pantheon of the race, there to be worshipped and propitiated along with their predecessors; the most ancient of whom is the supreme god, and the rest subordinate gods. (Spencer, *First Principles*, London, 1862, pp. 158–159)

This was, in essence, Spencer's theory of what subsequently came to be called "manism," also known as the "ghost theory" of the origin of religion.

Following the publication in 1876 of the first volume of Spencer's *Principles of Sociology*, in which the theory was again stated, E. B. Tylor made perhaps his only entry into the field of public controversy. He reviewed Spencer's book in the journal *Mind* (2, no. 6, April 1877, pp. 141–156); Spencer replied in the same journal (pp. 415–419), with a further rejoinder by Tylor (pp. 419–423), by Spencer again (pp. 423–429), and a final short contribution by Tylor (p. 429). Tylor's contention was that "Mr. Spencer seems to stretch the principle of deities being actual ancestors deified somewhat far," that his contentions often could not be tested, and that when they could, his cases "hardly look encouraging." His theory, Tylor concluded, was "in conflict not merely with the speculations of mythologists, but with the canons of sober historical criticism." Spencer, who did not like to be criticized and seldom ventured into public controversy, nevertheless penned a reply, suggesting that Tylor actually was in agreement with him "in regarding the ghost-theory as primary and other forms of superstitions as derived . . . [although] it appears that he does not hold this view in the unqualified form given to it by me." Tylor answered, virtually accusing Spencer of plagiarism on some points, but stating that although Spencer had the right to hold his "ghost theory" (which closely resembled the theory put forth by Euhemerus), "I look on this theory as only partly true, and venture to consider Mr. Spencer's attempt to carry it through unreservedly as one of the least satisfactory parts of his system."

The trouble was that it was so hard to envisage any process by which ghosts could become the other inhabitants of the spiritual world. Andrew Lang sketched the broad outlines of this hypothetical process: "The conception of ghosts of the dead is more or less consciously extended, so that spirits who never were incarnate as men become credible beings. They may inform inanimate objects, trees, rivers, fire, clouds, earth, sky, the great natural departments, and thence polytheism results" (*Cock Lane and Common Sense*, London, 1894, p. 339). This Lang did not accept. He was moving steadily in the direction of his theory of the existence of "high gods" and was disposed to question not only Spencer's "ghost theory" but also Tylor's theory of animism (which resembled Spencer's theory on certain points) as being inadequate explanations of the origin of the concept of deity. Lang appears actually to have believed in ghosts—which neither Spencer nor Tylor did—and was a keen psychical researcher (or at least a theorist about the researches of others). He was unable to discern any connection between ghosts and the higher gods, though "a few genuine wraiths, or ghosts . . . would be enough to start the animistic hypothesis, or to confirm it notably, if it was already started" (ibid., p. 346).

Although Herbert Spencer was enormously widely read in the late nineteenth and early twentieth centuries, his popularity was due to the completeness of his system of "synthetic philosophy" rather than to his theory of manism, which won very few adherents. But in 1897 Grant Allen produced his book *The Evolution of the Idea of God* (abr. ed., London, 1903; reprint, London, 1931), which accepted the manism theory with very few modifications. Allen maintained that "in its simplest surviving savage type, religion consists wholely and solely in certain acts of deference paid by the living to the persons of the dead" (1931 ed., p. 18). But religion is not mythology; indeed, Allen, following Spencer, insisted that mythology, cosmogony, ontology, and ethics were all "extraneous developments," which sprang from different roots and had "nothing necessarily in common with religion proper" (ibid., p. 25). Religion, then, had developed from corpse worship to ghost worship and then to shade worship. All else had developed later and need not be considered as an essential part of religion.

Writing to Allen in 1892, James G. Frazer had stated his agreement with the manism thesis: "so far as I believe ancestor-worship, or the fear of ghosts, to have been on the whole the most important factor in the evolution of religious belief" (quoted in Edward Clodd, *Grant Allen: A Memoir*, London, 1900, p. 145). Others at the time certainly concurred, wholly or in part, though they preferred the more comprehensive term *animism* to describe the same set of phenomena and recognized that the theory of manism could accommodate other spirit phenomena only with the greatest difficulty.

Manism in the form proposed by Spencer and Allen was too narrow to account for the genesis of more than a certain selection of religious phenomena. It therefore appealed to very few scholars. Exceptions included, however, Julius Lippert (1839–1909) of Berlin, who applied it to the biblical material in *Der Seelenkult in seinen Beziehungen zur althebräischen Religion* (Berlin, 1881) and other works produced during the 1880s. It might also be argued that the manism theory exercised a certain indirect influence on the Myth and Ritual school. In his book *Kingship* (London, 1927), Arthur M. Hocart (1883–1939) stated categorically that "the earliest known religion is a belief in the divinity of kings . . . in the earliest records known, man appears to us worshiping gods and their earthly representatives, namely kings" (p. 7). But this connection was at best oblique.

Summing up, we may say that what binds together Euhemerus and Herbert Spencer (for manism might well also be called neo-euhemerism) marks a genuinely important aspect of the history of religion. It cannot, however, be seriously put forward as the origin of religion per se without very serious distortion. This was true even in the high period of evolutionary theory; today, Spencer's manism remains no more than a historical curiosity.

SEE ALSO Ancestors; Preanimism; Spencer, Herbert.

BIBLIOGRAPHY

The fullest expression of Herbert Spencer's theory is in his *Principles of Sociology*, vol. 1 (London, 1876), pp. 304–440. For a good short account of Spencer's system of thought, see J. W. Burrow's *Evolution and Society: A Study in Victorian Social Theory* (Cambridge, 1970), pp. 179–227. On Grant Allen, see Edward Clodd's *Grant Allen: A Memoir* (London, 1900), pp. 142–147, and Allen's own *The Evolution of the Idea of God*, new ed. (London, 1931). See also Henri Pinard de la Boullaye's *L'étude comparée des religions*, 3d ed., vol. 1, *Son histoire dans le monde occidental* (Paris, 1919), pp. 381–382. Reference may also be made to the series of articles "Ancestor-Worship and Cult of the Dead," by William Crooke and others, in the *Encyclopaedia of Religion and Ethics*, edited by James Hastings, vol. 1 (Edinburgh, 1908), pp. 425–467; in discussing Spencer's theory, Crooke comments, "Needless to say, these views have not met with general acceptance" (p. 427).

ERIC J. SHARPE (1987)

MANITOU is the Algonquian name for a powerful and dangerous entity, especially one who appears in a nonhuman form and who controls a vital human resource, such as a food, medicine, pathway, or premonition. Although the numbers and types of manitous are believed to be indefinite and manifold, some common examples include animals, lakes, rapids, cliffs, winds, thunders, inspirations, visions, and dreams. Best translated as "spirit," *manitou* also refers to an individual's seat of personhood and agency. While the term originates specifically from the Algoquian-speaking tribes of the Great Lakes and Saint Lawrence River valley, the concept is ubiquitous among all indigenous peoples of the Great Lakes and Eastern Woodlands. Known by other names, including *oki, pilotois,* and *powwow* in the various languages of this vast region, *manitou* is the more prominent term among indigenous peoples and scholars alike.

The concept of manitou reflects an anthropomorphic outlook shared by the indigenous peoples of the Great Lakes and Eastern Woodlands, according to which all living things possess the same fundamental human characteristics. Rather than drawing sharp ontological distinctions between different classes of beings, such as humans, gods, plants, and animals, indigenous peoples of the region endow every living thing with the same type of tangible life force, or spirit, with the conjoined sense of personhood and power. According to this perspective, all beings possess similar (human) needs, emotions, motivations, and behaviors.

Conversely, the physical appearance of any particular living thing is understood as a nonessential, sometimes impermanent, feature of the person. This idea is evident in the indigenous oral traditions of the Great Lakes and Eastern Woodlands, where metamorphosis is a recurring theme. Some narratives, for instance, describe the circumstances in which certain ancestors transmogrified into the cliffs, lakes, hills, and other prominent physical features of the environment. Other stories relate occasions in which animals have transmogrified into human forms.

It is traditionally believed that while a person dreams the spirit wanders from the body and that at death it departs for the land of the dead or moves into a newborn's body. Thus it is the spirit that ultimately defines the person. Consequently, it is difficult and misleading in this context to speak of different classifications of manitous based on appearances, since these qualitative differences belie a common essential character that indigenous peoples confer to all living things.

But precisely what things, according to this perspective, are living? Given the variability that they associate with life-forms, it is perhaps not surprising that the indigenous peoples of the Great Lakes and Northeast Woodlands detect and classify sprits according to quantitative rather than qualitative measures. While all living things are persons, according to this perspective, a living presence itself is indicated by agency—that is, by a movement, force, or power of any kind. Hence, all powers are persons.

While there are an indefinite number of living entities, it is the powerful, the especially spirited who command the attention of others. Likewise, while there are an indefinite number of nonhuman forces that might occupy any given locality in the form of such things as plants, animals, winds, and rocks, it is the powerful among spirits—the particularly awesome, beautiful, or striking objects of experience—that indigenous peoples typically refer to as manitous. This may include wolves, bears, eagles, thunders, rapids, dreams, inspirations, and other impressive nonhuman entities. Like powerful human beings, these entities are honored and respected because their impressiveness is an ominous indicator of their ability to dispense fortune or misfortune. Prayer, song, tobacco, or other gifts of gratitude are humbly offered to them in hope of arousing their favor and calming their temper.

Likewise, many of these indigenous communities received their first European visitors, along with their guns, brass kettles, and other strange and impressive wares, as manitous. Thus, rather than honoring a manitou according to a rigid taxonomy of living things, indigenous peoples honor any given manitou in direct correlation to the spiritual capacity that they perceive in it, him, or her.

As they view all spirits within the same ontological frame of reference, indigenous peoples apply ordinary social protocols of exchange and reciprocity to guide and interpret their interactions with manitous. According to the ethics of reciprocal gift exchange, in lieu of an even trade, material goods are exchanged for political capital—that is, in exchange for honor and respect. Consequently, these societies are led traditionally by the accomplished hunters, fishermen, healers, and orators of their communities, that is, those who amass honor in return for the food, medicine, wisdom, and other precious commodities that they provide.

Likewise, indigenous peoples pay homage to the nonhuman forces to which they attribute their fortunes and misfortunes. Thus, in fishing, hunting, healing, traveling, and all other important enterprises that are subject to fortuitous circumstances, indigenous peoples seek the aid or forbearance of associated spirits by presenting prayer, song, tobacco, or other ceremonial offerings. By placing tobacco in a lake at the outset of a fishing expedition, for instance, the fisherman intends to compel the lake manitou to reciprocate by releasing its bounty.

In many of these traditions, an individual seeks his or her own personal spirit helper by performing a vision quest, often at the time of adolescence. Upon envisioning an eagle, bear, thunder, or some other manitou while fasting in isolation, the quester finds a charm that represents the manitou, such as a feather, claw, bone, shell, or stone, which he or she thenceforth carries in a medicine bundle.

The anthropomorphic outlook embraced by the indigenous peoples of the Great Lakes and Eastern Woodlands, which underscores the mutability of life forms, reflects a religious orientation that is ultimately grounded in a method, rather than an orthodoxy, for deciphering spirits. Although the characteristics of specific manitous are certainly conveyed by the many narrative traditions of the region, it is important to recognize that a people's oral tradition is in constant flux due to their ongoing encounters with the actual objects of experience that they consider manitous. In other words, while stories describe the anthropomorphic characteristics of a particular plant, animal, or landscape feature, these characteristics are shaped by the practical economic relationships that indigenous peoples have with them. As a people's relationships to various manitous shift over time, so do the corresponding myths and stories.

See Also North American Indians, articles on Indians of the Northeast Woodlands, Indians of the Plains.

Bibliography

Boatman, John. *My Elders Taught Me: Aspects of Western Great Lakes American Indian Philosophy.* Lanham, Md., 1992.

Hallowell, A. Irving. *Ojibwa Ontology and World View.* Chicago, 1960.

Hilger, M. Inez. *Chippewa Child Life and Its Cultural Background.* St. Paul, Minn., 1951.

Johnston, Basil. *Ojibwa Ceremonies.* Lincoln, Nebr., 1982.

Johnston, Basil. *The Manitous: The Spiritual World of the Ojibwa.* New York, 1995.

Spindler, George, and Louise Spindler. *Dreamers with Power: The Menominee.* Prospect Heights, Ill., 1984.

Vecsey, Christopher. *Traditional Ojibwa Religion and Its Historical Changes.* Philadelphia, 1983.

JAMES B. JEFFRIES (2005)

MAÑJUŚRĪ, an important figure in the Mahāyāna Buddhist pantheon, is a *bodhisattva*, one of a number of celestial heroes whose compassion has led them to postpone the bliss of final enlightenment until all other beings are freed of suffering. Especially associated with wisdom, Mañjuśrī is a key figure in numerous Mahāyāna scriptures, and he has been the focus of significant cultic activity throughout Mahāyāna Buddhist countries. His name means "gentle glory." Many of his alternate names and epithets refer to his relation to speech (Vāgīśvara, "lord of speech") and to his youth (Kumārabhūta, "in the form of a youth" or "having become the crown prince"). Because he is destined soon to become a Buddha, Mañjuśrī is often called "prince of the teachings"; for his role as master of the wisdom teachings (*prajñāpāramitā*) he is frequently described as "progenitor of the Buddhas."

Mañjuśrī's role in Mahāyāna scriptures is often that of interlocutor; as a senior *bodhisattva* at teaching assemblies, he frequently questions Śākyamuni Buddha and requests teachings of him. Although he is not highlighted in the early Mahāyāna texts on the perfection of insight, Mañjuśrī came to be known for his profound wisdom, and is associated with this textual tradition as its patron lord. The most common artistic representations and literary descriptions of Mañjuśrī (including scriptures, ritual texts, and meditation manuals) depict him as a golden-complexioned sixteen-year-old prince wearing a five-peaked crown. In his right hand he wields the sword of discriminating insight, which cuts through all ignorance and illusion, penetrating to the truth. In his left hand he grasps a book, the *Prajñāpāramitā Sūtra* (Scripture on the perfection of insight), whose teachings he has mastered and upholds. He sits upon a lion, which represents the roar of sovereign truth.

Mañjuśrī has been the focus of significant cultic activity. Perhaps the most extraordinary site for this has been a mountain complex in northern China named Wutai Shan, Five Terrace Mountain, where—until the mid-twentieth century—pilgrims from all over Asia have traveled in quests for visions of the *bodhisattva*. Beginning as a local mountain cult, the numinous precincts of this region eventually were identified as the special earthly domain of Mañjuśrī, and by the mid-eighth century it had become a thriving international Buddhist center, with seventy-two notable monasteries and temples, as well as numerous retreat huts.

Mañjuśrī traditionally is believed to be a celestial *bodhisattva* of the tenth stage *(bhūmi)*, the highest level prior to attaining buddhahood. He dwells continually in a meditative trance known as "heroic valor" *(sūraṃgamasamādhi)*, and is thus able to manifest himself at will throughout the universe, including Mount Wutai, in order to aid all beings. Wutai Shan was identified as Mañjuśrī's principal seat of manifestation through two means: time and again notable persons had visions of the *bodhisattva* there; and these visions received scriptural legitimation in the form of prophecies in a series of texts. The most significant of these texts is the *Avataṃsaka Sūtra* (Flower garland scripture), in which Śākyamuni declared that in a future age Mañjuśrī would dwell on a five-peaked mountain in northern China. According to pilgrims' accounts of these visions, the *bodhisattva* manifests himself on the mountain in several forms, most typically as a sphere of glowing light, as a five-colored cloud, as a lion-riding youth, or as an old man. Further mountain sites in the Himalayas and central Asia, including Mount Gośṛṅga in Khotan, were identified as sacred to the *bodhisattva*, but, unlike Mount Wutai, they never gained international recognition and acceptance. As a further element in the mountain theme, Mañjuśrī popularly plays a role in the founding tales of Nepal: with his sword, he cut an opening in the mountains to drain a great lake, thus creating the Kathmandu Valley.

Mañjuśrī has been especially venerated in the Chan and Zen traditions of East Asia for his uncompromising quest for insight. He is also linked closely to the teachings of the Tantric schools, both as lord of profound knowledge and as a potent protector and guide of those on this path. While Mañjuśrī's special role within the Buddhist pantheon is to protect and uphold the wisdom teachings and to inspire students of these teachings, a wide range of scriptures, ritual texts, and popular traditions makes clear the multifaceted nature of his cult, which was extended far beyond Buddhist scholastic circles.

SEE ALSO Mountains.

BIBLIOGRAPHY

The standard cross-cultural monograph on Mañjuśrī, containing much information organized in a systematic way, is Étienne Lamotte's "Mañjuśrī" (in French), *T'oung pao* 48 (1960): 1–96. Intensive analysis of a group of East Asian paintings of Mañjuśrī, emphasizing religious dimensions and including a chapter on the Wu-t'ai Shan cult in T'ang China, may be found in my *Studies on the Mysteries of Mañjuśrī*, Society for the Study of Chinese Religions Monograph No. 2 (Boulder, 1983). The translation of an important Tantric text in praise of Mañjuśrī, the *Mañjuśrī-nāma-saṅgīti Sūtra*, has been made by Alex Wayman, *Chanting the Names of Mañjuśrī* (Boston, 1985).

New Sources

Lopez, Donald S. *Religions of India in Practice.* Princeton, 1995.

Lopez, Donald S. *Religions of China in Practice.* Princeton, 1996.

Wallis, G. *Mediating the Power of Buddhas: Ritual in the Manjusrimulakalpa.* Albany, N.Y., 2002.

RAOUL BIRNBAUM (1987)
Revised Bibliography

MANNHARDT, WILHELM (1831–1880), pioneer of scientific folklore in Germany. He was born on March 26, 1831, in Schleswig, the son of a Mennonite pastor; five years later the family moved to Danzig. Mannhardt was always in very poor health, having been afflicted with curvature of the spine at about the age of seven. Unsuited to active life, he read assiduously and showed an early interest in both Germanic mythology and folklore. The shape of his early thinking was established by 1848, when he read Jakob Grimm's *Deutsche Mythologie* (Göttingen, 1835). While still at school he began his inquiries into the oral traditions of northern Germany, and was on one occasion suspected by one of his informants of being one of the dwarfs about which he was asking—he was at the time only one and a half meters tall.

Mannhardt studied German language and literature at the universities of Tübingen and Berlin, receiving his doctorate at Tübingen in 1854 and his habilitation at Berlin three years later. In 1855 he assumed the editorship of the *Zeitschrift für deutsche Mythologie und Sittenkunde*, a journal which survived only four years. In autumn 1855 he came into contact with the brothers Grimm, whose work he admired greatly, and in 1858 he published his first book, *Germanische Mythen*, extending his inquiries to cover not only European but also Indian material. He was perhaps the first scholar to compare the Germanic Þórr (Thor) with the Vedic Indra as two deities associated with thunder. In the early 1860s Mannhardt was forced by ill health to return to Danzig; there he obtained a librarian's post, which he held until 1873.

It was in Danzig that Mannhardt began the research work for which he was to become famous. He planned a comprehensive work to be called *Monumenta mythica Germaniae*, to be based not only on written sources but on first-hand information from the rural community (which was, however, even then beginning to change under the impact of scientific farming). The great work was never completed, but in its preparation Mannhardt circulated a questionnaire, and in so doing created a technique. The original questionnaire contained twenty-five questions (later expanded to thirty-five) concerning popular beliefs and practices connected with the harvest *(Erntesitten)*. His methodology was in general that of the emerging sciences of geology and archaeology, and was aimed at uncovering lower "layers" of belief, which might finally contribute to a "mythology of Demeter." Mannhardt also traveled widely in search of material in northern Europe, and interviewed prisoners of war in and near Danzig. After writing two preliminary studies, *Roggenwolf und Roggenhund* (1865) and *Die Korndämonen* (1867), he published in 1875 and 1876 the work for which he is chiefly known today, the two volumes of *Wald- und Feldkulte*. But his health was unequal to the sustained effort which his program required, and on Christmas Day 1880, at the age of forty-nine, he died, leaving behind a vast collection of material that has been little used.

Perhaps intimidated by the thoroughness of Mannhardt's methods, scholars for many years tended to accept his results virtually unaltered. His work provided most of the European material for James G. Frazer's *The Golden Bough*, and in general was used more by scholars of comparative religion than by folklorists. And certainly his studies marked an epoch in comparative study. In recent years scholars have begun to examine Mannhardt's material afresh. The emphasis is in process of shifting from beliefs in "spirits of the corn" to the function of harvest rituals in preindustrial, agrarian societies, but the irreplaceable material that Mannhardt collected remains a lasting memorial to his pioneering effort.

BIBLIOGRAPHY

Schmidt, Arno. *Wilhelm Mannhardts Lebenswerk.* Danzig, 1932.

Sydow, C. W. von. *Selected Papers on Folklore.* Copenhagen, 1948. See the papers on pages 89–105 and 146–165.

Weber-Kellermann, Ingeborg. *Erntebrauch in der ländlichen Arbeitswelt des 19. Jahrhunderts auf Grund der Mannhardtbefragung in Deutschland von 1865.* Marburg, 1965. Includes a biographical sketch on pages 9–24.

New Sources

Tybjerg, Tove. "Wilhelm Mannhardt: A Pioneer in the Study of Rituals." In *The Problem of Ritual,* edited by Tore Alhbäck, pp. 27–37. Stockholm, 1993.

ERIC J. SHARPE (1987)
Revised Bibliography

MANSI RELIGION SEE KHANTY AND MANSI RELIGION

MANTRA is, most concisely, a sacred utterance, incantation, or invocation repeated aloud or in meditation in order to bring about a prescribed effect, such as the calming of the mind or a vision of a deity. The *mantra* may be with or without conventional meaning, but it contains esoteric or mystical potentialities.

The word *mantra* is derived from the Sanskrit verbal root *man,* "to think," and the suffix *-tra,* indicating instrumentality. Thus the word indicates, literally, a means or instrument of thought. More practically, a *mantra* is an efficacious sound or utterance. Its translation can be difficult, and is often inexact. In the earliest Indian text, the *Ṛgveda,* it often had the sense of "invocation," while in later literature it is closer to "incantation," "word(s) of power," "(magic) formula," "sacred hymn," "name of God," or sometimes simply "thought." Because by the twenty-first century the word has entered common English, it is best to leave it untranslated and allow context to determine its meaning.

Mantras were originally, and commonly, used in religions that originated in South Asia, particularly in Hinduism and its Vedic predecessors, as well as in Buddhism. Jainism and Sikhism, two other major South Asian religions, also employ *mantras* prolifically, but unlike Buddhism and Hinduism, Jainism and Sikhism did not contribute much to theorizing *mantra.*

Mantras can range from an entire verse with a conventional meaning to single syllables in which the meaning is esoteric, multileveled, and all but secret except to the initiated. A common element of *mantras* is that they are in Sanskrit (though arguments have been made that single-syllable *mantras* participate in a linguistic encoding beyond any conventional syntactically oriented language). As the word literally indicates, *mantras* are useful sounds or collocations of sounds. They are useful, powerful, or efficacious for several reasons: first, because the sounds themselves are said to bear their meaning; second, because they are used in ritual, in which the action lies within the sphere of liminality, which renders both words and actions unconventional and therefore (in a manner of thinking) more direct and effective; and third, because they are said to be transformative to the speaker in ways that ordinary language is not. Among the ritual settings in which they are used, *mantras* function as vehicles to meditation; as verbal accompaniments to offerings to a deity, which are thought to bring about the results of particular desires; and as linguistic or sonic embodiments of deities or other structures.

According to the orthodox Hindu theology of the Pūrvamīmāṃsā, the Vedas are uncreated, they are not the products of human endeavor (*apauruṣeya*). This elevates the words of the Vedas to the status of *mantra,* as their meaning is no longer simply conventional, representative, or marked by syntactic context. They are thus eternal, the products of the extraordinary vision of Vedic seers (*ṛṣi, kavi*), their phonetic embodiment equivalent with their meaning and materiality. Thus the Vedic hymns (*sūkta,* "well-spoken") are regarded as collections of *mantras,* expressing the true nature and structure of the cosmos. This ideology is the main reason why, in the later Vedic traditions, it became unimportant for those who studied the Vedas to know the meaning of the verses; it was sufficient to memorize the texts—precisely, with fastidious attention to pronunciation and accent. A byproduct of this was the rise of the discipline of linguistics in India after about the sixth century BCE, particularly in a series of texts called *prātiśākhyas* dedicated to analysis of the pronunciation of the words in each textual branch (*śākhā*) of the Veda.

Several centuries earlier than these treatises on phonetics, however, in the late second millennium BCE, the texts on ritual use of the *Sāmaveda* showed an array of meaningless sounds, or, more accurately, sounds whose meaning was nothing but their sound. These undecipherable sounds, such as *bham* and *bhā,* were called *stobhas*, and they were recited within and surrounding more conventional Samavedic verse *mantras.* Slightly later, in the middle Vedic period, the centuries around the turn of the first millennium BCE, the theologians of the *brāhmaṇa* texts considered that the whispered utterance (*upāṃśu*), particularly of Vedic verses in ritual contexts, was superior to the audible one, and that the best of all was the silent (*tuṣṇīm*) or mental (*mānasa*) utterance. One such text, the *Śatapatha Brāhmaṇa* (5.4.4.13), states that undefined or unmanifest (*anirukta*) speech represents the innumerable, the unlimited. This notion of the inseparability of speech and thought was to have a great impact on future ideologies of *mantra.*

Mantra achieved its highest development in Hindu and Buddhist Tantras, beginning in about the sixth century CE, though many non-Tantric Hindu theologians realized its importance as well. Tantric teaching on *mantra* revolved around the concept of *vāc,* both the deity and concept of speech, as well as the female energy principle. It is regarded as the force that animates the male principle, Śiva. The dynamics of *vāc* embody the threefold process of creation, manifestation, and resorption, a topic that receives considerable attention in the Tantras. The doctrine of speech, then, is essentially the "science of *mantra*" (*mantravidyā, mantraśāstra*).

The following *mantras* deserve mention:

- The syllable *oṃ* is regarded as the supreme *mantra,* containing within its sounds *a-u-m* the entire articulatory apparatus, and thus the sum total of all sounds and *mantras.* This *mantra* is said to have flashed forth in the heart of Brahmā, the creator, while he was in deep meditation, and to have unfolded in the form of Gāyatrī, the mother of the Vedas.
- The Gāyatrī Mantra is widely hailed as the most characteristic Vedic *mantra*—(Oṃ bhūr bhuvaḥ svaḥ) Tatsavitur vareṇyaṃ bhargo devasya dhīmahi; Dhiyo yo naḥ pracodayā't: "(Om. Earth! Mid-region! Celestium!) Let us meditate on that excellent radiance of the god Savitṛ; may he impel our visions" (*Ṛgveda* 3.62.10). This is to be recited a certain number of times (usually 108) two or three times per day by all *brahmans* initiated into the rites of the "twice-born." It served as a model for a substantial number of other *gāyatrīs* dedicated to different deities. (*Gāyatrī* is the name of the metrical pattern consisting of three times eight syllables, with the major division after the first two strophes.)
- Agne vratapate vrataṃ cariṣyāmi (*Vājasaneyī-Saṃhitā* of the *Śukla* [White] *Yajurveda* 1.5): "O Agni Lord of Vows, I will observe my vow." This *mantra* has been prescribed for nearly three millennia for a person or married couple about to undertake a vow of abstinence or penance. Agni is both the sacred fire and the deity of that fire who transmits oblations to the other deities. Thus, this *mantra* is recited while invoking the deity Agni in the form of fire as witness to the vow.
- Oṃ namaḥ śivāya: "Om, obeisance to Śiva." This is the famous "five-syllable *mantra*" (the *oṃ* is an addition) to the great Hindu deity Śiva. Large numbers of religious mendicants and lay people alike mutter this *mantra*

hundreds or even thousands of times daily. As with most *mantras* that mention the name of a deity directly or obliquely, it is believed that the number of times it is repeated is important in "attaining perfection" (*siddhi*) in the *mantra*. This means that after extensive "practice" of a *mantra*, the aspirant gains the ability to invoke the deity at will or even identify him or herself with that deity. This could mean either merging with the deity or becoming the deity.

- The well-known Hare Krishna *mantra*—Hare kṛṣṇa hare kṛṣṇa kṛṣṇa kṛṣṇa hare hare; hare rāma hare rāma rāma rāma hare hare: "O Hare, O Kṛṣṇa, etc.; O Hara, O Rāma, etc." This example of a *mantra* that contains only divine names was memorialized by Bengali mystic Śrī Caitanya (1486–1533).
- Oṃ namo bhagavate vāsudevāya: "Om, obeisance to the illustrious Vāsudeva (*Kṛṣṇa*)." This *mantra* is one of the most commonly recited by Vaiṣṇavas, followers of the different sects dedicated to the worship of Viṣṇu or Kṛṣṇa.
- Oṃ aiṃ hrīm klīṃ chāmuṇḍāyai vicche: "Om Aiṃ Hrīm Klīṃ, to the goddess Chāmuṇḍā, Vicche." This string of monosyllabic or "seed" (*bīja*) *mantras*, with one of the names of the goddess appended, followed by the peculiar bisyllabic seed *mantra vicche*, is one of the most commonly used *mantras* in offerings to various forms of the goddess. *Bīja mantras* are regarded as the phonic representations of different deities, though many of them, such as *hrīm* and *klīṃ*, are used for several different deities.
- Oṃ maṇi padme hūṃ: "Om (O heart of Avalokiteśvara), in the lotus made of jewels." This is the most popular *mantra* in Tibetan Buddhism. Its recitation is said to lead to rebirth in worlds contained within the hair pores of Avalokiteśvara's body.
- Sauḥ. This *bīja mantra* has received a great deal of attention and analysis in esoteric Śaiva Tantras, where its phonic components are broken down and assigned extreme cosmic importance. *Sauḥ* is considered the "heart *bīja*," holding within it the entire cosmos. The great Śaiva philosopher Abhinavagupta (c. 975–1025), in his massive *Tantrāloka* (4.186–189), breaks this *mantra* into three parts, *s-au-ḥ*: *s* equals being (*sat*); *au* is the three energies of precognitive impulse, cognition, and action; and *ḥ* (*visarga*) is emission, that which is projected outward by the supreme consciousness.

These are by no means the only *mantras* that deserve discussion; dozens of others are accorded equal or greater status by different sectarian traditions in South Asia and beyond (e.g., the *Heart Sūtra* is treated as a *mantra* by millions of Buddhists across East Asia, who recite it constantly because of its supposed esoteric effects). Thus, *mantras* are, and always have been, an integral and integrative part of Indian and pan-Asian religions, as religion across Asia has been intimately influenced by the use and ideology of *mantra* in South Asia.

SEE ALSO Buddhism, Schools of, article on Tantric Ritual Schools of Buddhism; Buddhist Books and Texts, article on Canon and Canonization; Hindu Tantric Literature; Oṃ; Tantrism.

BIBLIOGRAPHY

Alper, Harvey, ed. *Mantra.* Albany, N.Y., 1989. This important book contains ten chapters and an excellent conclusion by leading scholars on the subject of *mantra* in different branches of Indic religion and philosophy.

Gonda, Jan. "The Indian Mantra." *Oriens* 16 (1963): 244–297. Reprinted in Gonda's *Selected Studies*, vol. 4, *History of Ancient Indian Religion*, pp. 248–301. Leiden, 1975. This article presents the clearest and most detailed picture of *mantra* in Vedic, and discusses the development of *mantra* in medieval India.

Padoux, André. *Mantras et diagrammes rituels dans l'Hindouisme.* Paris, 1986. This collection of articles by leading scholars explicates the relationship between *mantras* and cosmograms (*maṇḍalas* and *yantras*) in Indian religion, architecture, and medicine.

Padoux, André. *Vāc: The Concept of the Word in Selected Hindu Tantras.* Translated by Jacques Gontier. Albany, N.Y., 1990. This is the definitive book on the theology and construction of *mantras* in Hindu Tantra, especially as it is found in the Śaiva texts of Kashmir.

Studholme, Alexander. *The Origins of Om Manipadme Hum: A Study of the Karaṇḍavyūha Sūtra.* Albany, N.Y., 2002. This is a deep study of the religious context of this Buddhist *mantra* and the little-known sūtra text in which it is first celebrated.

FREDERICK M. SMITH (2005)

MANU

MANU. There is no general agreement on the origin and etymology of the Sanskrit name *Manu.* It obviously is related to the verbal root *man-*, "think," and to various words meaning "human being, man," including *manuṣa, manuṣya*, and so on.

As early as the *Ṛgveda* (c. 1200 BCE), expressions such as "Father Manu [or Manuṣ]" seem to indicate that Manu was already conceived at that time as the progenitor of the human race. As such, he has often been compared with Mannus, the "origo gentis" in Tacitus's *Germania* (2.3). Manu most definitely is characterized as the father of mankind in a well-known story from the *Śatapatha Brāhmaṇa* (1.8.1), dating to around 900 BCE. Following the advice of a fish, Manu builds a ship and, with the fish's help, survives the great flood alone among men. After the water recedes, he worships and performs penance. As a result, a woman, Iḍā (also Iḷā or Ilā), is produced, by whom "he begets this offspring of Manu."

Manu was not only the first man but also the first king. All royal lineages, in some way or other, descend from him. His principal son, Ikṣvāku, reigned at Ayodhyā. One of Ikṣvāku's sons, Vikukṣi, carried on the Aikṣvāku dynasty, also known as the solar race, at Ayodhyā, whereas his other son, Nimi, established the dynasty of Videha. Manu's second son, Nābhānediṣṭha, founded the kingdom of Vaiśāli; his third son, Śaryāti, the kingdom of Ānanta; and his fourth son, Nābhāga, the dynasty of the Rathītaras. Manu's "daughter," Iḍā, also had a son, Purūravas, who became the founder of the Aila, or lunar race, at Pratiṣṭhāna. Purūravas's romance with the *apsara* Urvaśī became one of the most popular stories in Sanskrit literature.

Certain texts refer to Manu as being the first to have kindled the sacrificial fire. According to the *Śatapatha Brāhmaṇa* (1.5.1.7), "Manu, indeed, worshiped with sacrifices in the beginning; imitating that, this offspring of his performs sacrifices." More particularly, Manu's name is connected with the origin of the Śrāddha, the ritual for the dead (*Āpastamba Dharmasūtra* 2.7.16.1).

In addition, Manu is considered to have been the originator of social and moral order. Many texts quote maxims relating to various aspects of *dharma*, and attribute them to Manu. In this connection he also became the *ṛṣi* who revealed the most authoritative of the Dharmaśāstras.

In later literature Manu—or rather a succession of Manus—can be seen to play a role in the Hindu cyclical view of time. Each *kalpa*, or "day," of Brahmā, corresponding to one thousand *caturyuga*s or *mahāyuga*s, is divided into fourteen *manvantara*s, "periods of Manu." In the most sophisticated system a *manvantara* consists of seventy-one *caturyuga*s, or 306,720,000 human years. The *manvantara*s are separated by fifteen transitional periods (Skt., *saṃdhi*s) of four-tenths of a *caturyuga*. Each *manvantara* is presided over by a different Manu. In the present *Śvatavārāhakalpa*, six *manvantara*s have by now elapsed (presided over by Svāyambhuva, Svārociṣa, Auttami, Tāmasa, Raivata, and Cākṣuṣa, respectively). The present, seventh Manu is Manu Vaivasvata, who will be succeeded by Sāvarṇi, Dakṣasāvarṇi, Brahmasāvarṇi, Dharmasāvarṇi, Rudrasāvarṇi, Raucya or Devasāvarṇi, and Bhautya or Indrasāvarṇi.

See Also Śāstra Literature.

Bibliography

Many Sanskrit passages dealing with Manu have been collected and translated in John Muir's *Original Sanskrit Texts*, vol. 1 (1872; reprint, Amsterdam, 1967). See also Georg Bühler's introduction to *The Laws of Manu* (1886), "Sacred Books of the East," vol. 25 (reprint, Delhi, 1964).

New Sources

The Laws of Manu. Introduction and notes translated by Wendy Doniger with Brian K. Smith. London; New York, 1991.

Ludo Rocher (1987)
Revised Bibliography

MAORI RELIGION [FIRST EDITION].

New Zealand is the southernmost island group in Polynesia and was one of the last places in the world to be settled. Its native inhabitants, a Polynesian people who call themselves Maori, reached New Zealand not much more than six hundred years before the Dutch explorer Abel Tasman became the first European to lay eyes on the country, in 1642. No other European arrived until James Cook's visit in 1769, which inaugurated regular and steadily increasing outside contact. At that time, the Maori numbered about one hundred thousand, the great majority of them residing on North Island.

Gods and Their Influence. In common with other Polynesians, the Maori conceived of reality as divided into two realms: the world of physical existence (*te ao marama,* "the world of light") and the world of supernatural beings (comprising both *rangi,* "the heavens," and *po,* "the underworld"). Communication between the two realms was frequent. Birth, for example, was regarded as the passage of a human spirit from the spiritual realm into this one, and death marked the return of the spirit to its point of origin.

Gods or spirits, termed *atua*s, were frequent visitors to the physical world, where they were extremely active. Indeed, any event for which no physical cause was immediately apparent was attributed to the gods. This included winds, thunder and lightning, the growth of plants, physical or mental illness, menstruation, involuntary twitches in the muscles, the fear that gripped a normally brave warrior before battle, the skill of an artist, even—after the arrival of Europeans—the operation of windmills. As the naturalist Ernest Dieffenbach summarized the Maori view, "*atua*s are the secret powers of the universe" (Dieffenbach, 1843, vol. 2, p. 118).

Another critical concept in traditional Maori religion is *tapu* (a term widespread in the Pacific, often rendered in English as "taboo"). Numerous definitions of the Maori *tapu* have been advanced, some identifying it as a set of rules regarding proper and forbidden conduct, others as a condition diverse enough to cover both the "sacred" and the "polluted." Perhaps the most useful view is that of the nineteenth-century magistrate and physician Edward Shortland, who defined *tapu* simply as the state of being under the influence of some *atua.* Because the influencing *atua* might be of any nature, from a protecting and strengthening god to an unwelcome, disease-dealing demon, the condition of a *tapu* person or thing could be anything from sacred to uncommonly powerful or brave; from dangerous to sick, deranged, or dead.

In the last analysis, Maori religion was concerned with the exercise of human control over the movements and activities of *atua*s in the physical world. It attempted to direct the influence of the gods into areas where their influence was deemed beneficial and to expel it where it was not, or where it was no longer desired.

Establishing *tapu*. Directing the influence of the gods was primarily pursued by means of ritual. One common way of instilling *tapu* (that is, inviting the gods to extend their influence over someone or something) was through ritual incantations called *karakia.* Many of these are long and difficult to translate, but one brief and simple example is a *karakia* recorded by the nineteenth-century missionary Richard Taylor, which might be chanted for a war party setting out on a campaign:

> E te rangi, ho mai he riri! E te atua, ho mai he riri!
> O heaven, give us fury! O god, give us fury!

Maori gods did not look into the hearts of their devotees; impeccable delivery was sufficient for a *karakia* to work its power. One man, in fact, was within the bounds of orthodoxy when he had the incantation necessary for planting sweet potatoes and other crops recited by a talking bird.

Another means of attracting *atuas* and disposing them to lend their influence to human affairs was to give them gifts. Many Maori rituals included the preparation of several ovens; the food cooked in one of them was reserved for the gods. When an important new canoe was launched, the heart of a human sacrifice might be offered to the gods for protection of the craft.

The influence of *atuas* was considered to be highly contagious, readily spreading from things that were *tapu* to things that were not. One common pathway was physical contact. Death was highly *tapu,* and anything that came in contact with a corpse—the tree on which it was exposed during decomposition, the people who scraped the bones a year after death, the place where the bones were finally deposited—became *tapu* as well. The supreme conductor of *tapu* was cooked food, which drew the *atua* influence from whatever it contacted and transferred this influence to anything it subsequently touched. One young woman, for example, died within forty-eight hours of being informed that a sweet potato she was eating had grown on a spot where an important chief was buried. The *tapu* of death, particularly stemming from someone of such high rank, was more than she could sustain.

Another avenue for the passage of *tapu* was resemblance. In the early 1840s, the artist George French Angas encountered stiff resistance in the Lake Taupo region whenever he wished to sketch *tapu* persons or things. The loss or contamination of *tapu* was thought to be detrimental, and the Maori reasoned that godly influence would pass from someone or something to its representation, and thus to anything with which the representation might come in contact. The Maori also feared that desecration would occur if sketches of *tapu* persons or objects were stored in the same portfolio—or were executed with the same pencil—as sketches of lowly or defiling objects.

The principles of *tapu* contagion were used ritually to introduce godly influence into places or situations where it was desired. One means of doing this was to put rudely carved stone images in sweet potato fields during the growing season. These *taumata atuas* were resting-places that attracted the gods, whose influence would then permeate the field and stimulate the growth of the crop. Similar reasoning underpinned the notion that certain rocks or trees, which virile gods were thought to frequent, had the power to impregnate barren women who embraced them. Another rite designed to enlist the aid of a deceased ancestor in easing a difficult childbirth called for music to be played on a flute made from one of his bones.

Dispelling *tapu.* *Tapu* was by no means an invariably desirable state. Disease, as already noted, was thought to be the work of certain gods or demons noted for their maliciousness. *Atua kahu,* for example, were a special class of supernatural beings that originated in human stillbirths. Nasty by nature, to be *tapu* from their influence was to succumb to illness, anxiety, or confusion. Well-known mischief workers in the Rotorua area were Te Makawe, an *atua* who caused people to be scalded by geysers or hot pools, and the *atua* Tatariki, who rejoiced in swelling people's toes and ankles.

Even the *tapu* so necessary for the achievement of desired ends had its drawbacks. A fine house or canoe was *tapu* while under construction, because *atuas* animated the creative work of the craftsmen. That same *tapu,* however, precluded ordinary use of the house, or canoe, once completed. Likewise, the craftsmen themselves were *tapu* during construction, as were priests performing rituals or warriors on campaign. Being in a state of *tapu,* while essential for the successful accomplishment of their goals, placed a number of restrictions on one's activities. Given the propensity of *tapu* to spread, such persons exercised great caution regarding contact with other persons or things; one of the more irksome constraints was that they might not use their hands while eating.

The disadvantages associated with undesirable *tapu*—as also with desirable *tapu,* once its benefits had been realized—meant that quite often it was important for persons and things to be released from this state, to be rendered *noa,* free from the influence of *atuas.* The Maori had a number of means for terminating the *tapu* state. One was simply to leave the area. Many *atuas* were limited in their activities to a certain locale; thus one cure for disease was to take a long trip and thereby escape the afflicting *atua*'s sphere of influence. The most common procedure, however, was to perform a ritual of the type known as *whakanoa* ("to make *noa*"). Most of these rituals involved the use of one of the following agents: water, the latrine, a female, or cooked food.

Whakanoa rituals, designed to dispel *tapu,* were as important in Maori religion as those used to instill it. The study of *whakanoa* rituals is fascinating, largely because of the initial implausibility in Western eyes of some of the agents used (such as the latrine), and the challenge of working out the rationale peculiar to each one. Scholarly consensus has yet to be reached in this area; the following are some contemporary theories under consideration.

The property of cooked food as supreme conductor of *atua* influence has already been mentioned; this apparently has to do with growth. In Maori eyes, growth was an unmistakable sign of *atua* activity. Hence a sweet potato field during the growing season was extremely *tapu,* and the head—as the site of the most vigorous growth of hair—was the most *tapu* part of the body. By exposure to fire or intense heat, cooking destroys the capacity of food for growth. Thus a proverb that may be applied to someone who has not yet accomplished much, but from whom great things are expected, runs *iti noa ana, he pito mata* ("only a little morsel, but it has not been cooked"). It still has, that is, the capacity for growth. If, upon removing food from an earthen oven, a morsel was found that had not been cooked, it was suspected that an *atua* was lurking in it. Cooking, then, was thought to rout *atua* influence, leaving the food a veritable vacuum for *tapu.* Therefore, a cooked sweet potato or piece of fern root might be passed ritually over the hands of someone who had engaged in a *tapu* activity, such as tattooing or cutting the hair of a chief. The *atua* influence would be drawn into the food, leaving the hands *noa,* and the now-*tapu* food might then be thrown into a stream, deposited at the latrine, or eaten, often by a woman.

Water was thought to remove *atua* influence by washing it away. Those who had handled a corpse or who had been involved in the *tapu* activity of teaching or learning sacred lore might return to the *noa* state by immersing themselves in water, preferably the flowing water of a stream.

Women frequently played important roles in *whakanoa* rituals. A war party might be released from *tapu* by a rite in which a woman would eat the ear of the first enemy they had killed. A newly constructed house could be rendered *noa* by a ceremony in which a woman stepped over the threshold. Women had to be careful of their movements because they might inadvertently dispel beneficial *tapu.* The arrival of a woman at the site could spoil the construction of a house or canoe, drive cockles from a beach or birds from the forest, blight sweet potatoes in a garden, even stop the black mud that was used to dye flax from "growing." These female powers were intensified during menstruation.

Opinions vary as to the basis of the female's capacity to dispel *tapu.* Some scholars hold that women were repulsive to the gods; thus at the approach of a female the gods would withdraw, leaving a *noa* state behind them. Given this interpretation, however, it is difficult to explain the fact that women were able to instill *tapu* ritually as well as to dispel it. Students might be rendered *tapu* prior to training in sacred lore, for example, by eating a piece of food that had been passed under the thigh of a woman.

Another view is that women could make *tapu* things *noa* because they were thought to attract *atuas*, not repel them. According to this theory, the female—specifically her genitalia—represented a passageway between the two realms of existence. When brought in proximity with a woman, an *atua* would be drawn into and through her, and thereby repatriated to the spiritual realm. This would leave the person or thing that had been *tapu,* by merit of that *atua*'s influence, in a *noa* state.

The Maori viewed birth as the transit of a human spirit from the world of the gods to the physical world. That transit, of course, occurred via female genitalia. The female was also significant at death, when the spirit would leave this world and return to the realm of the *atuas*. This point is expressed mythologically in the story of the death of the culture hero Maui. He resolved to give humankind eternal life by killing Hine-nui-te-po, the personification of death. Maui intended to kill the huge woman by entering her vagina as she slept, passing through her body and emerging at the mouth. But she awoke as Maui was entering her, clenched her thighs, and crushed him to death. And it is the common fate of all of us, claimed a Maori who recounted this story, to be drawn at death into the genitals of Hine-nui-te-po. As with human spirits, other *atuas* might enter and leave the physical world by means of the female. This theory might account for the capacity of women to instill and to dispel *tapu.*

The remaining *whakanoa* agent to be discussed is the latrine. Built on the edge of a cliff or brow of a hill, the Maori latrine was made with a low horizontal beam supported by two upright, often carved, posts. The user placed his feet on the beam while squatting, preserving his balance by grasping hand grips planted in the ground in front of the beam. A person could be ritually released from a *tapu* state by biting the latrine's horizontal beam. This might be done instead of, or in addition to, immersion in water by students following a teaching session. Maori mythology provides a further example: the pedigree of humankind begins with the union of the god Tane with Hine-hau-one, a female being who was formed from the earth to be Tane's mate. The formation, vivification, and impregnation of Hine-hau-one were *tapu* procedures, at the conclusion of which she became *noa* by biting a latrine beam.

The latrine beam marked a sharp line of separation: before it was the village, humming with life; behind it was a silent, shunned area where excrement fell and where people ventured only for murderous purposes, such as to learn witchcraft. In Maori culture the latrine beam became a metaphor for the notion of separation in general and, most specifically, for the separation between life and death. Since the dead belong to *po,* part of the realm of the *atuas*, the latrine beam can further be understood to represent the threshold between the two realms of existence. From this perspective, *whakanoa* rituals utilizing the latrine are susceptible to the same sort of interpretation suggested above for those involving women. *Tapu* persons or things were taken to a portal between the two worlds, where the godly influence was ritually repatriated to the spiritual realm.

Also in common with the female, the latrine sometimes constituted a point of entry into, or departure from, the physical world for *atuas* and their influence. For instance, at the beginning of the construction of an important house or canoe, a chip from the carving work would be placed at the latrine. This can be interpreted as contributing to the *tapu* quality of the project by imbuing the chip (and therefore, by extension, the undertaking as a whole) with the influence of the gods. The clearest example, however, is the consecration of the Takitumu canoe. According to traditional history, Takitumu was one of the canoes that brought the Maori ancestors from their original homeland of Hawaiki to New Zealand. Before setting sail, Takitumu was rendered *tapu* so as to be under the gods' protection during the long voyage. This was accomplished by literally hauling the canoe up to a latrine. There, certain images that had been stored in a burial cave were placed on board, and the gods themselves—particularly Kahukura, a rainbow god—were ritually invited to embark.

MODERN MAORI RELIGION. Christianity was introduced to New Zealand in 1814, when Samuel Marsden, chaplain of the penal colony at New South Wales in Australia, preached a sermon at the Bay of Islands on Christmas Day. Conversion proceeded rapidly after 1825, and by midcentury nearly the entire North Island was covered by Anglican, Roman Catholic, and Wesleyan missions. Today, the Maori belong to a variety of Christian denominations, the largest of which are the Anglican, Roman Catholic, Methodist, and Mormon churches. Also important are two Christian sects unique to New Zealand: Ringatu ("upraised hand") was founded in the 1860s by the Maori warrior and preacher Te Kooti; Ratana, a larger sect, was established in the 1920s by the reformed alcoholic and visionary Tahupotiki Wiremu Ratana. The Ratana church, which stresses faith healing, has been a major force in Maori politics.

BIBLIOGRAPHY

Among the many fascinating accounts of Maori life written by early visitors to New Zealand, two are George French Angas's *Savage Life and Scenes in Australia and New Zealand,* 2d ed., 2 vols. (London, 1847), and Ernest Dieffenbach's *Travels in New Zealand,* 2 vols. (London, 1843). Two other nineteenth-century works with considerable information on religion are the missionary Richard Taylor's *Te Ika a Maui, or, New Zealand and Its Inhabitants* (London, 1855) and the magistrate Edward Shortland's *Traditions and Superstitions of the New Zealanders,* 2d ed. (London, 1856). An important collection of exclusively Maori myths (despite its title) is George Grey's *Polynesian Mythology* (1855), edited by W. W. Bird (New York, 1970). The anthropologist Elsdon Best has written many works on Maori religion (as on all aspects of Maori culture), among them *Some Aspects of Maori Myth and Religion* (1922; reprint, Wellington, 1954), *Spiritual and Mental Concepts of the Maori* (1922; reprint, Wellington, 1954), *Maori Religion and Mythology* (Wellington, 1924), and *Tuhoe: The Children of the Mist* (Wellington, 1925). Important monographs by the historian of religion J. Prytz Johansen are *The Maori and His Religion in Its Non-Ritualistic Aspects* (Copenhagen, 1954) and *Studies in Maori Rites and Myths* (Copenhagen, 1958). Two recent anthropological studies are Jean Smith's *Tapu Removal in Maori Religion* (Wellington, 1974) and *Counterpoint in Maori Culture* (London, 1983) by F. Allan Hanson and Louise Hanson.

F. ALLAN HANSON (1987)

MAORI RELIGION [FURTHER CONSIDERATIONS].

By the twelfth century the Maori people who migrated from eastern Polynesian had fully adapted their habitations to the cooler climate of land and sea in the austral islands of Aotearoa. New Zealand scholars initially believed the migrants arrived in one great fleet of canoes around 1350 CE, but subsequent research established that multiple canoe migrations began several centuries earlier and that occasional back-and-forth voyages between Aotearoa and the ancestral island of Hawaiki had taken place.

The Maori remained undisturbed by contact with foreigners until the late eighteenth century, when Europeans named New Zealand and began to harvest seals, whales, and timber from the South and the North Islands. Missionaries from Australia arrived in December 1814, and on Christmas Day Samuel Marsden celebrated the first Christian service in the islands, erecting a flagstaff and raising "'the flag of old England, the flag that has braved a thousand years'" (Rosenfeld, 1999, p. 29). He was unaware that Maori tribes claimed unoccupied land by setting up a pole and kindling fires. The ritual pole symbolizes the cosmic tree of Tane-mahuta, who separated his father, the Sky, from his mother, the Earth, by standing on his head and pushing them apart to form the human realm.

Sacred space is a fundamental feature of Maori religion. A tribe's land is marked by *wahi tapu,* "sacred places" named for what happened there and commemorated in *whakapapa,* "oral genealogies." Novelist Witi Ihimaera's protagonist in *The Matriarch* (1986) calls walking the land with his grandmother "my custom," a way of recalling the significant detail of what he had been told as a child (p. 102).

Before contact, conversion, and colonization, oral genealogies were redacted by schools of poets and recited during public gatherings on the *marae,* an open space near the house of a chief. This ritual has persisted throughout two hundred years of dynamic interaction between Maori and European settlers. Without the recitation of *whakapapa,* the indigenous people would have lost their identity. Whether the story of the descent group is told by a grandparent standing on the land or an appointed orator standing on the *marae,* the future is made possible in Maori terms by presenting the past as the domain of the ancestors and as the days that lie in front. In Maori story, Hawaiki is both the place of origin and the destination of the dead. The time before creation is conceived of as an undifferentiated womb out of which all things are born or as a serpent swallowing its tail.

The details of genealogy recited on the *marae* vary with each kin group's ancestors and experiences, and there are also different existing versions of primal myths. After the full translation of the Old Testament into Maori was published in 1858, a group of *tohunga*, "religious experts," redacted a more uniform version of cosmogonic myth that revealed a preexistent, supreme god, Io, whose essence fertilized the womb of potential being and set in motion the creation of the world. The reconciled cosmogony reflects the nineteenth-century preoccupation with *urmonotheismus*, but it also proves that indigenous religion authentically develops in response to experience. The controversy over Io continues to enliven discourse about Maori religion.

When they were baptized as Anglicans or Methodists, Maori converts were required to renounce their customs as things of the devil. As the number of conversions accelerated in the 1830s, some chiefs and charismatic leaders asserted their control over tribal space. Between 1844 and 1845, Hone Heke cut down the British flagstaff three times in a dispute with the governor over customs duties. Poles and borders became symbols of resistance in subsequent resistance movements. In 1856 chiefs representing the tribes of the North Island and the South Island gathered around a flagstaff to ritually convey their *mana* over their combined territories to the first Maori king and placed a *tapu* boundary around the center of the North Island.

The primal power of *mana* and the prohibitions of *tapu* maintain order in the social world. *Mana* is divine power made manifest in the human realm; it dwells in chosen members of society and natural species, as well as places and things. *Mana* has been defined as "prestige," "authority," "charisma," "dignity," and, especially, the "power to act." *Mana* can rise and fall, like the water level in a lake, and the loss of *mana* leaves the holder weak and impotent. *Tapu* is a condition of being. People, places, activities, and things are made *tapu* and set apart from the ordinary. *Tapu* is contagious and can kill; it designates what is out of bounds, prohibited, and restricted, and some define it as sacred. Tapu contagion is removed by *whakanoa* rites. Whatever has *mana* is *tapu* and vice versa (Metge, 1989, pp. 62–66).

Mana o te whenua, "power over the land," was a stipulated authority that was increasingly invoked by Maori leaders as their ancestral space was sold off, confiscated, or removed from their control by special legislation during the nineteenth and twentieth centuries. In 1835 the British resident and the northern chiefs signed "A Declaration of the Independence of New Zealand" that recognized the chiefs' *mana i te wenua* (the spelling changed over time), or "authority within the territory" of the New Zealand tribes (Moon and Fenton, 2002, p. 56). In 1840 thirty-five chiefs signed New Zealand's founding document, the Treaty of Waitangi, which substituted a foreign word for *mana* and precipitated a debate over sovereignty that is still being waged.

By the 1850s, the Maori and settler populations had reached near parity. Muskets, diseases, alcoholism, infertility, and land selling had reduced the Maori, hastening the abandonment of traditional villages. People unintentionally trespassed on neglected *tapu* sites and incurred an illness that was removed by male or female healers, who sometimes combined traditional rites with Bible-derived practices to remove the spiritual contagion.

Disputes between colonial officials and Maori chiefs precipitated a series of Land Wars between 1860 and 1872 that resulted in punitive confiscations of territory from tribes that resisted assimilation. Charismatic leaders rose up and initiated millenarian movements with their own flags, poles, rituals, offices, liturgies, holidays, prophets, and messiahs that grafted biblical branches onto the ancient tree of *tapu* and *mana*. The pentecostal "Good and Peaceful" ritual of the *niu* pole called down the sacred winds that endued all believers with god-given power to speak in tongues and resist harm in battle. As the *niu* cult swept over the North Island, Christian pastors withdrew from their missions and sought protection in largely European settlements until the wars ceased.

The charismatic prophet Te Kooti attacked his Maori and European rivals, who occupied his ancestral land after he was sent to prison on the false charge of spying for the Good and Peaceful movement in 1866. Two years later, he escaped with three hundred prisoners and founded the Ringatu sect, which became a licit church after his death.

During the Land Wars, the British crown colony grew into a self-governing nation. Regional militias fought pitched battles with disciples of unconventional *tohunga* imbued with *mana* from the Holy Ghost, Gabriel, and Michael, as well as the gods of their respective tribes. In the Old Testament these Maori *poropiti*, "prophets," found a disenfranchised people like themselves, who were led by Jehovah out of slavery and to their promised land. At the end of the century, one prophet took the name Kenana, or "Canaan," and marched his dispossessed disciples to the foot of his tribe's sacred mountain. They built a settlement with a *tapu* precinct, including a house called New Jerusalem for the prophet and his wives—all high-born women with lands he consolidated under his *mana*. When Rua Kenana first heard the call to be a savior for his people, he responded, "If your wish is for me to save only people, I won't help, but if it is to save the land, then I shall carry out this task" (Webster, 1979, p. 158).

Diverse religious movements revived Maori customs, including *mana* and *tapu*, while their members claimed Jewish descent from Noah's son, Shem, and worshiped Jehovah. Mormon missionaries began to attract Maori converts in the 1880s. In 1918 the prophet Wiremu Ratana preached repentance and conducted healings. Over the next forty years, the nondenominational Ratana church gathered in so many adherents that it was able to align itself with the Labour Party and elect Ratana followers to all four Maori seats in Parliament. Yet special land legislation continued to reduce the territory of the tribes, until only 1.2 million hectares remained in their possession at the end of the twentieth century.

By 1929 a symbolic substitute for the land was emerging. Over the course of a century, the communal plaza and the chief's dwelling had developed into a single ritual complex combining the *marae* and the *whare whakairo*, "meeting house," where funerals, weddings, and important meetings took place. The beams, pillars, art, and sculpture of the meeting house express the motifs of *whakapapa* and symbolize the body of the ancestor. The *marae* is the gathering place in front of the house, where parties meet to discuss issues of importance. Visitors must be called onto the *marae* by a woman with a welcoming song, which removes any pollution they bring with them. The elaborate protocol of the *hui*, "meeting," reinforced the system of *tapu* and *mana*, connecting the living with the ancestors and binding the present to the past.

After World War II, 70 percent of the Maori population gradually migrated to towns and cities. Political leaders, such as Sir Apirana Ngata and Te Puea Herangi, led the struggle for visibility and authority in a new milieu, where Maori neighborhoods formed islands in a largely European sea. Maori then comprised about 10 percent of New Zealand's total population. Urban leaders founded new clubs and associations that mobilized support for protests and focused public attention on longstanding claims to tribal fishing grounds, habitations, and reserves guaranteed to the tribes under the Treaty of Waitangi but subsequently removed from their possession. In 1975 the legislature set up the extraordinary Waitangi Tribunal to hear Maori claims under the treaty provisions and to recommend to Parliament their terms of settlement. Parliament and the courts have listened to the tribunal's powerful judgments and have restored fishing rights, paid compensation, and returned lands to Maori descent groups, enforcing the Treaty of Waitangi, redressing grievances, and demonstrating that even after two hundred years of tumultuous change, the divine gift of *mana* remains an efficacious ordering principle of the Maori social world.

See Also Mana.

Bibliography

Binney, Judith. *The Legacy of Guilt: A Life of Thomas Kendall.* Oxford, 1968. The book's Appendix I contains the first description by a lay missionary of the northernmost tribes' primal myths.

Binney, Judith. "The Ringatu Traditions of Predictive History." *Journal of the Polynesian Society* 23, no. 2 (October 1988): 167–174. Includes primary data on the symbolic world of a nineteenth-century new religious movement.

Binney, Judith. *Redemption Songs: A Life of Te Kooti Arikirangi Te Turuki.* Auckland, New Zealand, 1995. A detailed and comprehensive presentation of the life and times of the extraordinary guerrilla leader and prophet who founded the Ringatu church.

Cowan, James. *The New Zealand Wars.* Vol. 1: *1845–64.* Wellington, New Zealand, 1922; reprinted with amendments, 1983. The first volume of a two-volume history of conflicts between Maori and Europeans over the land. Includes an account of the ritual that granted *mana* over the center of the North Island to the Maori king.

Elsmore, Bronwyn. *Mana from Heaven: A Century of Maori Prophets in New Zealand.* Tauranga, New Zealand, 1989. Discusses more than forty renewal and resistance movements and churches that arose in the historical context of Christianization during the nineteenth and twentieth centuries.

Ihimaera, Witi. *The Matriarch.* Wellington, New Zealand, 1986. A novel about inherited *mana* and its use for good and evil by a contemporary Maori writer who tells the story of Te Kooti in language that transcends historiography.

Marsden, Maori. "God, Man and Universe: A Maori View." In *Te Ao Hurihuri: Aspects of Maoritanga,* edited by Michael King, pp. 118–137. Auckland, New Zealand, 1992. A Maori elder and Anglican cleric presents the reconciled version of the Maori creation story of the supreme god, Io, and explicates other major aspects of the holy in Maori religion of the late nineteenth and early twentieth centuries.

Metge, Joan. *In and Out of Touch: Whakamaa in Cross Cultural Context.* Wellington, New Zealand, 1989. A concise and insightful explication of *mana* and the loss of *mana* gathered from contemporary Maori sources by a twentieth-century anthropologist.

Moon, Paul, and Sabine Fenton. "Bound into a Fateful Union: Henry Williams' Translation of the Treaty of Waitangi into Maori in February 1840." *Journal of the Polynesian Society* 111, no 1 (March 2002): 51–63. Argues that the missionary translator of the Treaty of Waitangi intentionally avoided using the word *mana* to translate the concept of sovereignty over tribal resources and substituted the neologism *kawanatanga,* "governance," instead.

Rosenfeld, Jean E. *The Island Broken in Two Halves: Land and Renewal Movements among the Maori of New Zealand.* University Park, Pa., 1999. Examines four different, but related, new religious movements that attempted to renew and maintain the Maori world by holding fast to the land under the threat of cultural assimilation during a century of conflict.

Salmond, Anne. *Hui, a Study of Maori Ceremonial Gatherings.* Wellington, New Zealand, 1975. A clear presentation of the complex protocol of the ritual meeting.

Salmond, Anne. "'Te Ao Tawhito': A Semantic Approach to the Traditional Maori Cosmos." *Journal of the Polynesian Society* 87, no. 1 (March 1978): 5–28. An explanation of the male and female complements and their attributes, which characterize the physical, spiritual, and social dimensions of the Maori world.

Smith, Jonathan Z. *Imagining Religion: From Babylon to Jonestown.* Chicago, 1982. In this collection of Smith's essays, see "The Unknown God: Myth in History" (pp. 66–89), in which Smith complements Marsden's inside view of Io with a scholarly review of the data in the historical record.

Sorrensen, M. P. K. "Land Purchase Methods and Their Effect on Maori Population, 1865–1901." *Journal of the Polynesian Society* 65, no. 3 (1956): 183–199. Important study that relates the loss of Maori land to the decline of the Maori population in the late nineteenth century.

Walker, Ranginui. *Ka Whawhai Tanu Matou (Struggle without End).* New York, 1990. A comprehensive history of the Maori people from the canoe migrations to the Waitangi Tribunal by a Maori scholar and orator.

Walker, Ranginui. "Marae: A Place to Stand." In *Te Ao Hurihuri: Aspects of Maoritanga,* edited by Michael King, pp. 15–27.

Auckland, New Zealand, 1992. Describes the development of the ritual complex of the *marae* and the meeting house during the era after European contact.

Webster, Peter. *Rua and the Maori Millennium.* Wellington, New Zealand, 1979. Webster's extraordinary study of the confrontation between a Maori messiah and a government determined to destroy his *mana* contributes to our general knowledge about the phenomena of revitalization movements around the world.

JEAN E. ROSENFELD (2005)

MAPONOS, a Celtic deity associated with youth, but of otherwise uncertain attributes, was identified by the conquering Romans with Apollo. The name is attested by several Romano-British and Gallo-Roman inscriptions in insular Britain and Gaul. It has also been found in an inscription in Gaulish at Chamalières (Puy-de-Dôme). In insular Britain, an inscription found in Ribchester, County Durham, reads "Deo sancto Apollini Mapono(o)," and another found in Hexham, County Northumberland, reads "Apollini Mapono" (*Corpus inscriptionum Latinarum,* Berlin, 1863, vol. 7, nos. 218, 1345). These indicate with exactitude the *interpretatio Romana:* Maponos is Apollo in his aspect of youth, an interpretation that takes into account the meaning "young man" associated with the stem *map-* ("son") and the theonymic suffix *-ono-s.*

Although no accounts of Gaulish theology survive, the name is enough to prove that the two aspects of the Celtic Apollo that are attested in Ireland—god of youth and leech god—also existed in Gaul and in insular Britain. The Irish equivalent is Mac ind Óg ("young son"), whose other name is Oenghus ("only choice"), son of Daghdha and of Boann, wife of Elcmhaire. Mapono's conception is recounted in the first version of the cycle of Édaín: Daghdha has sent Elcmhaire away and has magically suspended the course of the sun—and consequently the march of time—for nine months. The child is thus born on the evening of the day he was conceived. For this reason he is both the symbol of youth and the god of time, in opposition and complementarity to his father, the god of eternity.

Under the name of Mac ind Óg he is the hero of the adventure known as *The Taking of the Sid,* and, under the name of Oenghus, he is one of the principal personages of the cycle of Édaín. To him befalls the adventure of *The Dream of Oenghus,* a tale of a quest for sovereignty disguised as an amorous anecdote. And it is he who, at the end of the cycle, will vainly fight with Patrick over Eithne (Édaín), a personification of Ireland.

The Welsh form *Mabon mab Modron* ("Mabon son of Modron": *Modron* from **matrona,* "mother") is attested on several occasions, for example in the story *Culhwch and Olwen.* But this account gives only very brief indications as to his character: It is said only that he is kept prisoner from birth and that King Arthur ends up releasing him during the quest for marvelous objects needed for the marriage of Culhwch and Olwen.

BIBLIOGRAPHY

Guyonvarc'h, Christian-J., and Françoise Le Roux. *Textes mythologiques irlandais,* vol. 1. Rennes, 1980.

Le Roux, Françoise. "Notes d'histoire des religions, V. 9: Introduction à une étude de l' 'Apollon celtique.'" *Ogam* 12 (1960): 59–72.

Mac Cana, Proinsias. *Celtic Mythology.* Rev. ed. Feltham, U.K., 1983.

FRANÇOISE LE ROUX (1987)
CHRISTIAN-J. GUYONVARC'H (1987)
Translated from French by Erica Meltzer

MAPPŌ. The Japanese term *mappō* (Chin., *mofa*) denotes the third and eschatologically decisive period in the history of the Buddha's Dharma as revealed in certain texts that were to have a significant impact on the evolution of East Asian Buddhism, particularly the Pure Land tradition. The three-stage periodization of which it is a part includes the period of the True Dharma (*shōbō*), when the Buddha's teachings were correctly practiced and people thereby attained enlightenment; the period of the Counterfeit Dharma (*zōbō*), when the teachings existed but very few upheld the practices and none attained enlightenment; and the period of Final Dharma (*mappō,* often translated as the "Latter Days of the Law"), when only the teachings remained, the practices were no longer pursued, and enlightenment was a mere word. In the view of those who espoused this eschatology, such a declining view of history, which was ascribed to the growing spiritual deficiencies of the *saṃgha,* spelled doom for the traditional schools of Buddhism. As many Buddhists came to believe that the traditional teachings had lost their relevance to the times and to the religious needs of the people, the Pure Land path emerged on the stage of history, claiming to have been especially prepared by the Buddha for the age of *mappō.*

The concept of the three stages of Dharma culminating in *mofa* appeared in the form we know it today in China during the second half of the sixth century, where it is first mentioned in the *Lishi yuanwen* (Vows) of the Tiantai master Huisi (515–577), composed in the year 558. A few years later, a Mahāyāna *sūtra,* the *Daji yuezang jing,* was translated into Chinese, introducing a variety of similar eschatological views concerning the period of Final Dharma. The Japanese scholar Yamada Ryūjō has shown that this *sūtra* was the product of four major strands of scriptures woven together, each containing various forebodings on the destiny of the Buddhist *saṃgha.* One of the earliest mentions of the three stages of Dharma is found in another text of the period, the *Dasheng tongxing;* however, the precise source of Huisi's formulation remains unclear.

The notion of three stages of Dharma evolved gradually through the centuries in the historical experience of Buddhism, incorporating the multiple and variegated factors that contributed to the progressive decline of the church. These factors, some of which had existed since the time of Śākyamuni Buddha himself, became exacerbated with the passage of time: the violation of monastic precepts, debates surrounding the ordination of women, sectarian rivalries, a tendency to adhere to the letter, rather than the spirit, of the teachings, corruption in the monastic centers, the emergence of anti-Buddhist despots in India and central Asia, social and political unrest throughout Buddhist Asia, and finally, the devastation of Buddhist communities in Gandhāra by the Ephthalites in the sixth century, an event that convinced many of the impending destruction of the *saṃgha.*

Prior to the mid-sixth century, various texts had made reference to the eras of True and Counterfeit Dharma, but none to the period of Final Dharma. However, the appearance of the *Daji yuezang jing,* coinciding with the wholesale devastation of institutional Buddhism during the Northern Zhou persecution of 574–577, confirmed the arrival of the age of Final Dharma foretold in that and other texts. In response to this historical crisis two powerful movements emerged, both proclaiming their teachings as eminently suited for the times: the Three Stages (Sanjie) school of Xinxing (540–595) and the Pure Land path of Daochou (562–645).

Ultimately, four basic chronologies emerged, each reckoned on the basis of the Buddha's decease, universally accepted in China as having occurred in 949 BCE:

1. True Dharma, 500 years; Counterfeit Dharma, 1,000 years
2. True Dharma, 1,000 years; Counterfeit Dharma, 500 years
3. True Dharma, 500 years; Counterfeit Dharma, 500 years
4. True Dharma, 1,000 years; Counterfeit Dharma, 1,000 years

Calculated on the basis of the first of these chronologies, the prevailing belief was that the period of Final Dharma, which was to last for ten thousand years, had begun in 552 CE. Although this belief was inherited by Japanese Buddhists, the year 1052 was also widely embraced in medieval Japan as the beginning of the age of Final Dharma, based on the fourth of the above-mentioned chronologies.

Belief in the three stages was combined with another popular view concerning the destiny of the *saṃgha,* one that divided Buddhist history into five five-hundred-year periods. This notion too had a complex history, but in its final form characterized the gradual eclipse of the Dharma as follows; an age in which enlightenment was the dominant feature of the religious life, an age in which meditative practices were firmly established, an age in which the study of scripture was firmly established, an age in which the building of stupas and temples was firmly established, and an age in which fighting and bickering and the decline and disappearance of the Dharma were the dominant features of the religious life. The period of Final Dharma was identified with the last of these ages. Another prevalent view, intimately connected with that of *mappō,* characterized our time as one of Five Defilements, in which the age itself, all religious views, all desires, all sentient beings, and all human life are defiled.

Mofa is mentioned by almost all of the eminent Buddhist writers of the Sui and Tang dynasties, but it was Xinxing and Daochou who refused to regard it as merely descriptive of external historical events and actually incorporated it into the very foundation of their teachings. That is, both thinkers affirmed the reality of the end time in their own religious awakening and realized the extent to which the fundamental ignorance (*avidyā*) of all beings precluded the mastery of traditional practices leading to supreme enlightenment. Such an admission of contemporary deficiencies, both inner and outer, justified in their view a new path to salvation.

In the case of Xinxing, this new path called for the universal recognition of the buddha nature in all beings and the consequent practice of selfless acts of compassion toward everyone, regardless of status, as an antidote to the blind ignorance and profound egocentricity of the age. For Daochou it meant entrusting the ego-self to the saving vows of the Buddha Amitābha (Chin., Womituofo; Jpn., Amida) as the only viable means of deliverance from the ocean of *saṃsāra.* Xinxing's Three Stages school experienced a turbulent history and eventually disappeared during the Huichang persecution of Buddhism in 845, but the Pure Land lineage of Daochou gained wide acceptance and became a major force in East Asian Buddhism.

In China, the implications of the concept of *mofa* were mitigated by the continuing vigor of mainstream Mahāyāna Buddhism, which insisted on the observance of precepts, adherence to meditative practices, and cultivation of wisdom as essential for supreme enlightenment. Daochou and the subsequent Pure Land masters, while proclaiming a new path suited for the age of *mofa,* were not entirely free from the weight of this great tradition and continued to advocate a variety of more traditional Buddhist practices. By contrast, in Japan a foreboding sense of doom permeated the whole of medieval society, involving all of the Buddhist schools. Recognition of the advent of *mappō* was thus a decisive factor in the formation of the major schools of Japanese Buddhism in the thirteenth century—Jōdo, Jōdo Shin, Nichiren, and Zen—and even affected the earlier schools founded during the Nara (710–784) and Heian (794–1185) periods.

The first nonscriptural citation of the term in Japan appears in the *Nihon ryōiki* (Miraculous stories from the Japanese Buddhist tradition), compiled in the ninth century. A lament in this text states, "We are already in the age of Degenerate Dharma. How can we live without doing good? My heart aches for all beings. How can we be saved from calamity in the age of Degenerate Dharma?" The nature of *mappō* is also the topic of the *Mappō tōmyōki* (The lamp to illuminate the age of final Dharma), attributed to Saichō (767–823), the founder of the Japanese Tendai school. According to Saichō, each of the three stages of history is characterized by practices relevant to that particular age. The practices suited to the period of True Dharma include observance of the precepts and the practice of meditative disciplines. Those practices endemic to the period of Counterfeit Dharma are the violation of the precepts and the accumulation of property by monks. In the period of Final Dharma all monks must be honored, even though they violate or disregard the precepts, since the very nature of the times precludes the very existence and validity of the precepts.

Such a view of the end time, widely held by both clerics and laity, meant not only the bankruptcy of the Buddhist *saṃgha* but appeared also to herald the end of the world itself through the operation of inexorable historical forces. In the twelfth and thirteenth centuries a variety of events seemed to confirm the reality of *mappō:* the impotence of imperial rule, the decline of the aristocracy, social upheaval, local uprisings, internecine warfare, natural calamities and pestilence, and conflagrations that destroyed the capital.

This sense of impending collapse generated a variety of responses among the Buddhist clergy. These were of two basic types. One vigorously rejected this pessimistic view of history and reaffirmed the power of traditional paths to enlightenment. The other accepted the fact of *mappō* as the manifestation of the basic human condition—weak, imperfect, vulnerable, and subject to temptations—and saw the working of Dharma in the very midst of such karmic limitations, whether through the Nembutsu, containing the saving vows of Amida Buddha, or in the Daimoku, manifesting the miraculous salvific powers of the *Lotus Sūtra.*

It was Hōnen (1133–1212), one of the pioneering figures of the Kamakura period (1185–1333), who incorporated the implications of the doctrine of *mappō* into a virtual revolution in Japanese Buddhism. For him, the end time of history did not signal the decline and destruction of the Buddhist *saṃgha* but rather the opening up of the true *saṃgha* to both men and women, upper and lower classes, clergy and laity alike. For Hōnen, *mappō* did not mean the rampant violation of precepts but the disintegration of the sacrosanct authority of precepts that discriminated against certain groups of people. Since the age of *mappō* meant the nonexistence of precepts, the path of enlightenment was now open to people considered evil in the eyes of traditional Buddhism: those who made a living by taking life (hunters, fishermen, peasants, and warriors) and those who were outcasts from society (traders and merchants, prostitutes, monks and nuns who had violated the precepts, and others). Such people he proclaimed to be the primary concern of Amida Buddha's Primal Vow (*hon-gan*), the ultimate manifestation of true compassion. On the basis of this conviction Hōnen proclaimed the founding of an independent Jōdo (Pure Land) school in 1175.

Thus, while *mappō* spelled doom and despair for the established sects, it was an age of boundless hope and optimism for the disenfranchised. More fundamentally, in this view history became witness to the truth and relevance of the Pure Land path to enlightenment, as had been prophesied by Śākyamuni in the Pure Land sūtras. The end time of history was here and now, but it was in the here and now that Amida's compassionate vow had become fully operative.

Shinran (1173–1263) pushed this acute sense of historical crises even more radically into an existential realization of the human condition. He saw the particular evils of the age of *mappō* as revealing the very ground of self-existence. For Shinran, evil, though particularized in the individual, forms the essence of humanity in *saṃsāra.* But this realization of profound karmic evil is not final, for deeper and wider still is the working of Amida's compassionate vow, operating through samsaric existence to deliver the self, as well as all suffering beings, into the Pure Land.

For Shinran, then, *mappō* was no longer a particular period of history but the fundamental reality of life itself, embracing all ages, past, present, and future. The Primal Vow of Amida is working not only in the end time but has always been responding to the deepest yearnings of humanity, whether in the period of True Dharma, Counterfeit Dharma, or Final Dharma, whenever and wherever man is steeped in brutish egoism. It took the radical breakdown of history, however, for this truth to surface within human consciousness. As Shinran wrote in the *Shōzōmatsu wasan* (Hymns on the last age):

> Throughout the three periods of True, Counterfeit, and Final Dharma Amida's Primal Vow has been spread. In this world at the end of the Counterfeit Dharmaand and in the Final Dharma age All good acts have entered the Palace of the Dragon.

SEE ALSO Amitābha; Daochuo; Hōnen; Jingtu; Jōdo Shinshū; Jōdoshu; Saichō; Shinran; Xinxing.

BIBLIOGRAPHY

The groundwork for the study of the origin of *mappō* is found in Yamada Ryūjō's *Daijō bukkyō seiritusuron josetsu* (Kyoto, 1959), pp. 567–592. A discussion of Xinxing's Three Stages sect can be found in Kenneth Ch'en's *Buddhism in China: A Historical Survey* (Princeton, 1964), pp. 297–300. Readers of Japanese will want to consult Yabuki Keiki's monumental study of the sect, *Sangaikyō no kenkyū* (Tokyo, 1927). There is no adequate study of the *mappō* concept in Western languages, but Shinran's view may be seen in the English translation of his *Shōzōmatsu wasan* (Hymns on the last age), Ryūkoku Translation Series, vol. 7 (Kyoto, 1981). An attempt to relate the three stages of history to the dialetical evolution of Shinran's faith and thought is found in *The Heart of Buddhism* by Takeuchi Yoshinori (New York, 1983), pp. 48–60.

New Sources

Chappell, David W. "Early Forebodings of the Death of Buddhism." *Numen* 27, no. 1 (1980): 122–154.

Deeg, Max. "Das Ende des Dharma und die Ankunft des Maitreya. Endzeit- und Neue-Zeit-Vorstellungen im Buddhismus mit einem Exkurs zur K āś yapa-Legende." *Zeitschrift für Religionswissenschaft* 7 (1999): 145–169.

Hubbard, Jamie. "Mo Fa, the Three Levels Movement, and the Theory of Three Periods." *Journal of the International Association of Buddhist Studies* 19, no. 1 (1996): 1–17.

Hubbard, Jamie. *Absolute Delusion, Perfect Buddahood: The Rise and Fall of a Chinese Heresy.* Honolulu, 2000.

Marra, Michele. "The Development of Mappo Thought in Japan." *Japanese Journal of Religious Studies* 15 (1988): 25–54.

Nattier, Jan. *Once upon a Future Time: Studies in a Buddhist Prophecy of Decline.* Berkeley, 1991.

Stone, Jackie. "Seeking Enlightenment in the Last Age: Mappo Thought in Kamakura Buddhism." *Eastern Buddhist* 18, no. 1 (1985): 28–56.

TAITETSU UNNO (1987)
Revised Bibliography

MAPUCHE RELIGION. The Mapuche currently live in Chile and Argentina. In Chile, they have settled between the Bio-Bio River to the north and the Channel of Chacao to the south, a territory that encompasses the provinces of Arauco, Bio-Bio, Malleco, Cautin, Valdivia, Osorno, and Llanquihue (approximately between 37° and 41° south latitude). In Argentina, they are found at similar latitudes in the northern Patagonian province of Neuquén and, to a lesser extent, in the Río Negro and Chubut provinces; to the north there are scattered and isolated groups in the Pampas region. The most optimistic calculations estimate that there are 500,000 Mapuche in Chile and fifty thousand in Argentina.

The Mapuche belong to the Araucana-chon linguistic family. Most of the Mapuche live in small settlements in a pattern of scattered encampments. The basic economic activity among the Chilean Mapuche is agriculture; the Argentinians rely on sheep and goat herding, as dictated by varying ecological settings. Patrilineal descent, patrilocal residence, and matrilateral marriage are the most noteworthy traits of contemporary Mapuche society. Patrilineage or, in many cases, a subdivision thereof, as well as the residential family, increasingly constitute the minimal units of the settlement in economic, social, and religious terms.

The structural changes undergone by the Mapuche in the past hundred years—a product of their adaptation to a new natural and social environment—have transformed Mapuche economy and, to a lesser degree, Mapuche society. Nonetheless, despite insistent missionary activity by Roman Catholics and Protestants (particularly fundamentalists), the foundation of their system of religious beliefs and practices remains practically intact in many regions.

To describe their mythico-religious beliefs even briefly, to characterize the numerous major deities, both regional and local, and to elucidate the symbolic content and meanings of each of the many rites of this people are tasks far beyond the scope of this work. I have therefore chosen to summarize them, making use of two cognitive structures common to them all, which will allow me to piece together the complex Mapuche belief system of religious practices and images and to outline their internal logic.

The first structure—apparently the most widespread—is dualism, which orders and defines two polar elements according to their relationships of opposition and complementarity. The second is the tetradic division generated as a result of a first bipartition that brings two opposed couples face to face and a second bipartition of degree that defines in each couple a climax and its attenuation.

The vast Mapuche pantheon is divided into two great antithetical and complementary spheres. The first is made up of beneficent deities, organized into a tetradic family based on a combination of sex and age (old man and old woman, young boy and young girl). These deities are the agents of good, health, and prosperity, and their tetradic nature symbolizes perfection. Cosmologically and vertically, they are found in the celestial sphere, or *wenú mapú,* which is the summit of the positive aspect of the four vertical components of the universe. Horizontally, some of them are ranked, with varying degrees of positivity, with the four regions of the world (the east, south, north, and west cardinal points). Temporally, they are associated with clarity. Given that the tetradic division is also the ordering principle of the day, they have their most exact manifestations in *epewún* ("dawn"), a superlative concretion of *anti-* ("clarity"), whose sign is positive, and in *ki-ri-ni-f* ("dusk"), the attenuation of *pún* ("darkness"), whose sign is negative. Finally, they are associated with positive colors—blue (the most important) and white-yellow (denoting attenuation).

The second sphere of this theophanic dualism is made up of the malefic beings, of *wekufi-,* who appear isolated, in odd numbers, and of indeterminate age and sex. They are agents of evil, illness, and chaos, and they symbolize imperfection. Their place in the cosmos is ambiguous; some groups place them in the *anká wenú,* or middle heaven, but generally they are considered to belong to the *pu mapú,* or netherworld—the climax of the negative aspect in the vertical conception of the universe. The temporal acts of the *wekufi-* are most evident during *rangi-n púñ* ("midnight"), the most negative moment, and, to a lesser extent, during *rangíñ ánti* ("midday"), the attenuation of the positive pole. *Wekufi-* that are associated with red and black, the malefic hues, play an even greater role in determining the qualities attributed to them.

The implied symbolic network arises from various levels of discourse, such as the *ngetrán* (accounts of mythical or historical events characterized by truthfulness) and the decoding of dreams and signs—present events that anticipate the qualities of future occurrences. The social correlative of this theophanic dualism is incarnated in the figures of the *máchi* ("shaman") and *kalkú* ("witch"), who manipulate the forces of good and evil, respectively. The paraphernalia of the *máchi* include, among other things, the *kultrún* (a kettledrum), which serves as a symbolic microcosm; the *wáda* (a rattle); and the *kaskawílla* (a girdle with small bells). The *máchi* are assisted by benevolent deities and are responsible for staving off illnesses caused by the *kalkú,* who are assisted by the *wekufi-* beings.

Shamanic rites include Machiluwún, an initiatory rite carried out after the *máchi* has undergone a period of revelation through illness or dreams and after he has received instruction from an initiated shaman, and the Ngejkurrewén, a postinitiatory rite of power renewal. The Pewutún is a diagnostic ritual. There are two therapeutic rites: the Datwún, for serious illnesses, and the Ulutún, for minor ailments. All these rites and their associated artifacts and actions—including the *réwe,* a wood carving representing the cosmic stages; branches from sacred trees; ritual displacements of objects from the right (positive) to the left (negative), facing east and counting in twos, fours, or multiples thereof; songs and dances beseeching the benevolent gods to act; blue and white flags; and the moments (dawn and dusk) when the rites are performed—are symbolic expressions denoting supplication to the forces of good and the restoration of health.

In contrast, the witch directly or indirectly causes *kalkutún* ("harm") by throwing objects with malefic powers around the victim's house or by working magic on the victim's nails, hair, clothing, sweat, or footprints. The witch may poison the victim, or may enlist the help of a *wekufi*—such as a *witranálwe,* the soul of a dead man that has been captured by the *kalkú.* The nocturnal appearance of the *witranálwe* in the form of a great, resplendent, cadaverous horseman causes illness and death.

Community members take part in numerous rituals outside of the specialized orbit of shamanism and witchcraft. The funerary rites, or Awn, are still practiced in the Chilean settlements. Their object is twofold: to ensure that the soul of the dead can cross into the world where the ancestors live (a site that some scholars say is very close to, or is associated with, the domain of the benevolent deities) and to prevent the spirit of the dead person from being captured by a witch and transformed into his aide during his nocturnal ambushes.

The term *ngillatún* alludes to the act of prayer and connotes diverse practices on individual, family, and group levels. Strictly speaking, on the group level it designates a "ritual complex" that varies in several respects according to the traditions of the community performing it. These variations include the number and affiliation of the participants, the extent of group cohesion, the ritual's duration, its association with agrarian or pastoral economic cycles, and its occasional or periodic nature, that is, whether it is carried out to counteract natural phenomena or to observe crucial dates of the annual cycle. Despite this great diversity, what finally defines the *ngillatún* is its strongly propitiatory nature, its characters—varying with the time it is performed—as restorer of the cosmic order, and its enrichment of coherence and meaning within communal life through the ritual congregation.

Within this cultural domain, the symbolic network also impregnates with meaning each of the ritual episodes—for example, the forms of spoken and sung prayer, ritual sprinkling, ritual painting, women's songs, men's dances and mixed dances, sacrifices, libations, and horseback rides. It is this network that determines the temporal bounds of the episodes, the meaning of the displacements, and the colors used, as well as the number of times (twice, four times, or a multiple thereof) that each action must be repeated.

This summary, centered around the ideological principles that serve to organize and define a large part of the symbolic beliefs, rites, and images of the Mapuche, should not lead the reader to suppose that this is a closed system lacking flexibility. The history of the Mapuche people indicates exactly the opposite. They have adapted to new conditions while preserving their traditional knowledge and beliefs, even if these have sometimes been modified or given new meanings.

BIBLIOGRAPHY

Among the classic studies of the subject, the most noteworthy for the Chilean region include Ricardo E. Latcham's *La organización social y las creencias religiosas de los antiguos araucanos* (Santiago, 1924) and Tomas Guevara's *Folklore araucano* (Santiago, 1911) and *Historia de Chile: Chile prehispánico,* 2 vols. in 1 (Santiago, 1925–1927). The North American anthropologist Louis C. Faron, who spent several years living in Chilean settlements, offers an excellent analysis of Mapuche society and its connections with religious practices in *Mapuche Social Structure: Institutional Reintegration in a Patrilineal Society of Central Chile* (Urbana, Ill., 1961); one of his many articles on this ethnic group, "Symbolic Values and the Integration of Society among the Mapuche of Chile," *American Anthropologist* 64 (1962): 1151–1163, deals with the dualism of the Mapuche worldview and offers valuable contributions. Other articles that should be cited, both because of the wealth of their data and the new outlooks they bring to the subject, are Maria E. Grebe's "Mitos, creencias y concepto de enfermedad en la cultura mapuche," *Acta psiquiatrica y psicologica de America Latina* (Buenos Aires) 17 (1971): 180–193, and "Cosmovision mapuche," *Cuadernos de la realidad nacional* (Santiago) 14 (1972): 46–73.

One of the most extensive monographs on the religion of the Argentinian Mapuche is Rodolfo M. Casamiquela's *Estudio del nillatún y la religión araucana* (Bahía Blanca, 1964). The compilations and observations of Bertha Koessler-Ilg in *Tradiciones araucanas* (La Plata, 1962) are a good addition. Other books worthy of mention are Else Marta Waag's *Tres entidades 'weku-fü' en la cultura mapuche* (Buenos Aires, 1982), which is outstanding for its wealth of information, and the anthology of essays *Congreso del Area Araucana Argentina* (Buenos Aires, 1963). The theoretical and methodological bases as well as the development and exemplification within different cultural domains of the two cognitive structures summarized in this article can be found in two essays by C. Briones de Lanata and me: "Che Kimí-n: Un aborde a la cosmologica Mapuche," *Runa: Archivo para las ciencias del hombre* (Buenos Aires) 15 (1985) and "Estructuras cognitivas e interacción social: El caso de la brujeria entre los Mapuche argentinos," in *Actas del 45° Congreso Internacional de Americanistas* (Bogotá, 1985).

New Sources

Calvo, Mayo. *Secretos y Tradiciones Mapuches,* Santiago, 1992.

Foerster, Rolf. *Introducción a la Religiosidad Mapuche.* Santiago, 1993.

Kuramochi, Yosuke, ed. *Cultura Mapuche.* Quito, Ecuador, 1997.

Kuramochi, Yosuke, and Juan Luis Nass, eds. *Mitología Mapuche.* Quito, Ecuador, 1991.

Sierra, Malú. *Mapuche, Gente de la Tierra.* Santiago, 2002.

MIGUEL ANGEL OLIVERA (1987)
Translated from Spanish by Erica Meltzer
Revised Bibliography

MĀRA. Although Māra appears in the Atharvaveda as a personification of death associated with the god Yama, it is in Buddhism that he comes to the fore. There he takes on the role of a mythological antagonist or metaphorical opponent of the Buddha, his teachings, and his community. Māra, one of whose epithets is "the Evil One" (Skt., Pāpīyāṃs; Pali, Pāpimant), has sometimes been compared to Satan; in fact, he is a god, the chief deity of the Realm of Desire (Kāmadhātu), a position he earned by virtue of a meritorious deed in a past life. As such, he rules over most sentient beings who are caught up in *saṃsāra* (including humans and the lower deities). He resides in the Sixth Heaven of Buddhist cosmology, the dwelling place of the Paranirmita-vaśavartin gods, and so is sometimes called Vaśavartin (Pali, Vasavattī; "controlling"), or, in East Asia, King of the Sixth Heaven. As Lord of the Kāmadhātu, Māra is best understood as a divine king who wants to keep sentient beings under his command, that is, in his realm of life and death, of desire and ignorance. Hence he actively opposes anyone who seeks to escape from his dominion by attaining enlightenment.

This opposition takes on many forms in Buddhist myth and legend. Most prominently, it is featured in a number of encounters Māra is said to have with the Buddha. He tries, for instance, to block the Buddha from going forth on his Great Departure from his father's palace, an episode often featured in Southeast Asian art and sometimes reenacted in ordination rituals. Later, under the bodhi tree at Bodh Gayā, Māra plagues the Buddha in a variety of ways. Desperate to keep the Blessed One from becoming enlightened, he musters a huge army of monsters, all armed with dreadful weapons, in an attempt to scare him away. Their attack, however, comes to naught. The weapons they fling at the Buddha turn to flowers and perfumes, and the Buddha remains unperturbed in meditation. Māra then challenges the Buddha's right to sit on the seat of enlightenment. He calls on his hordes to bear witness to his own merits, and they all shout that the bodhi seat—the highest point in this world—belongs to Māra. In response, the Buddha reaches down and touches the surface of the earth with the tip of his right hand, calling on it to bear witness to his merits. This earth-touching *(bhūmisparśa)* gesture, which became famous iconographically in countless Buddha images, elicits a response from the earth goddess, who affirms in no uncertain terms the Buddha's supremacy. In one version of the story, she appears physically and wrings out the water from her hair, causing a flood (symbolic of the Buddha's merits) that sweeps away the forces of Māra. In some biographical traditions, at this point or a bit later, Māra makes yet another attempt to counter the Buddha's enlightenment by sending his three daughters to seduce him. Needless to say, he is unmoved by their wiles. Having been unsuccessful in preventing the Buddha's enlightenment, Māra then tries to encourage him to pass promptly into *parinirvāṇa* (complete extinction) so as no longer to be a threat to his (Māra's) dominion.

Māra, however, did not limit his attentions to the Buddha alone. The *Samyutta Nikāya,* for instance, contains two collections of stories in which Māra variously tries to tempt, frighten, or trick not only the Buddha but ordinary monks and nuns. Sometimes he seeks to disrupt their practice or meditation; other times he tries to convince them of the truth of heretical doctrines. In doing so, he may take on various forms, even the guise of the Buddha himself. Thus, for example, he appears to the monk Śūra in the form of the Blessed One and deceitfully announces that he had lied when previously he had told him that all five *skandhas* (personality aggregates) are impermanent, marked by suffering, and without self, when in fact some of them are actually permanent, stable, and eternal. Śūra, luckily, is not duped by this. In other contexts, Hīnayānists are sometimes said to view the new Mahāyāna teachings not as the "Word of the Buddha" but as the "Word of Māra."

More broadly, any form of contradiction or opposition—from crude to subtle—to the practice and doctrine of Buddhism, however it is defined, may be thought to be an act of Māra. In Southeast Asia, if bad weather, drunkenness, or petty thievery mar the celebration of a Buddhist festival, it is said to be because of Māra. In East Asia, monks who are remiss in their observance of the precepts are sometimes said to be followers of "the way of Māra" (Jpn., *Madō*). In Tibet, Māra came to be associated with indigenous demonic divinities *(bdud)* whose subservience to Buddhism needed periodically to be reasserted. In China, due in part to linguistic confusion, Māra was identified with the god Īśvara, that is, Maheśvara (Śiva), or with the ambivalently-esteemed protector of the northeastern quarter, Īśāna. In Japan, in medieval times, a persistent creation myth told of the attempt by King Māra (Ma-ō)'s to block the creation of the Japanese islands themselves because he knew that Buddhism would thrive there. He only gave his imprimatur to the cosmogonic project when Amaterasu, the sun goddess, agreed to keep Buddhism at bay in her land, an agreement that she did not honor but which is why a taboo was established on Buddhist images, monks, and sūtras at the grand shrine of Ise. Māra's written contract with Amaterasu, moreover, came to be identified as the divine seal *(shinshi),* one of the three regalia of the Japanese imperial line.

Less mythically perhaps, throughout the Buddhist world, Māra came to be seen as a metaphor for various passions and impediments on the path. Thus practitioners are enjoined to recognize multiple Māras associated with the personality aggregates *(skandha-māra)* or the defilements *(kleśa-māraś).* Māra's daughters are said to symbolize pleasure, restlessness, and desire; and various troops in Māra's army are identified with lust, sloth, doubt, hypocrisy, ignorance, and so on.

Yet Māra is not always ultimately maligned and condemned. In contexts in which the doctrine of the potential enlightenment of all beings is asserted, the story is told of Māra's conversion to Buddhism by the arhat Upagupta, who first tames the "Evil One" by binding corpses around his neck, but then releases him when he agrees to stop harassing Buddhist monks, or when, in one version of the tale, he actually makes a vow for future buddhahood.

SEE ALSO Buddha.

BIBLIOGRAPHY

For a general overview of Māra, including references to his appearance in Vedic literature and his association with death, see Louis de La Vallée Poussin, "Māra," in *Encyclopaedia of Religion and Ethics,* edited by James Hastings (Edinburgh, 1915), vol. 8, pp. 406–407. See also Alex Wayman, "Studies in Yama and Māra," *Indo-Iranian Journal* 3 (1959): 112–125. For a classic presentation of the textual history of the Māra legend, see Ernst Windisch, *Māra und Buddha* (Leipzig, 1895). For a study based on Pali sources, see Trevor O. Ling, *Buddhism and the Mythology of Evil* (London, 1962). For a comparative perspective, see James W. Boyd, *Satan and Māra: Christian and Buddhist Symbols of Evil* (Leiden, 1975). For accounts of Māra's interactions with various nuns and monks (including the Buddha), see C. A. F. Rhys Davids, *The Book of Kindred Sayings (Samyutta-Nikāya)* (London, 1917), vol. 1, pp. 128–170. On the story of Māra and Śūra, see Edmund Hardy, "Mara in the Guise of Buddha," *Journal of the Royal Asiatic Society* (1901): 951–955. On the role of Māra in China and in the Japanese creation myth, see Nobumi Iyanaga, "Le Roi Māra du sixième ciel et le mythe médiéval de la création du Japon," *Cahiers d'Extrême-Asie"* 9 (1996–1997): 323–396. On the conversion of Māra by Upagupta, see John S. Strong, *The Legend and Cult of Upagupta* (Princeton, 1992), pp. 93–117. Finally, for a perspective on Māra that highlights the art historical record, see Patricia Karetzky, "Māra, Buddhist Deity of Death and Desire," *East and West* 32 (1982): 75–92.

JOHN S. STRONG (2005)

MĀRA (AND GREAT MOTHERS).

A mythological female deity with features and functions of the Great Mother is frequently mentioned in the folk songs, legends, folk beliefs, and magic incantations of Latvian folklore. Opinion differs regarding the origin of the name *Māra.* In the first half of the twentieth century a group of Latvian folklorists and religious scholars that included Pēteris Šmits, Ludvigs Bērziņš, and Ludvigs Adamovičs tried to see a greater impact of Christian concepts in Latvian folklore, primarily based on phonetic similarities in the names Māra and Marija. They attempted to prove that Māra is nothing more than a phonetically transformed Holy Mary (Latvian, Svētā Marija). But one only needs to look at the text of a few folk songs, or *dainas,* that mention Māra to see that she is not Mary, the Christian Mother of God, but an independent mythological being. In Latvian folklore, Māra can be seen as a protectress of cows. She may be found sitting in a willow or under an aspen tree, and she is mentioned as guiding a boat of orphans across dangerous waters, but in some folklore texts she is also described as a harmful being, one who, for instance, takes away or disturbs sleep.

Other scholars have not expressed as categorical an opinion regarding the origin of Māra's image. The Latvian-born Swedish theologian Haralds Biezais believes that Māra incorporates features of an ancient fertility goddess whose name Latvians have long forgotten, so they now call her Holy Mary (Biezais, 1955, pp. 323–337). In 1940 Mārtiņš Bruņenieks had advanced a hypothesis that partially corresponds to Biezais's theory. According to Bruņenieks, Māra's name was borrowed from Mary, the Christian Mother of God, replacing the Latvian goddess of fate Laima, while retaining Laima's functions as a deity of fate. However, this presents an obvious contradiction because both the names Māra and Laima can be found in Latvian folklore, even though their functions, such as the protection of women in labor, are partially duplicated.

An opposing point of view was proposed in the first half of the twentieth century by the brothers Ernests and Arvīds Brastiņš. They believed that both in function and name Māra is a genuine Latvian goddess—a giver and taker of life and protectress of fertility, birth, and productivity.

During the Soviet occupation of Latvia (between 1940 and 1990), the topic of Māra was off limits to Latvian scholars. It was only during the second half of the 1980s that various scholars returned, with qualifications, to the hypothesis advanced by the brothers Brastiņš. Among them were Vjačeslav Ivanov and Vladimir Toporov, Moscow linguists and scholars of Baltic languages and mythology; Konstantīns Karulis, a linguist from Riga; Māra Zālīte, an author and folklore scholar; and, during the 1990s, the folklorist Janīna Kursīte. Their theory that Māra was not Holy Mary borrowed from Christianity but an independent female deity was based on both Latvian folklore and comparative source material from other Indo-European peoples. In this case, the name Māra hypothetically had been derived from the Indo-

European root form *$m\bar{a}$-, which was used to denote the concept of mother and archetypal maternal beginnings. Expanded by *r*, the *$m\bar{a}$-root expresses the active creative force, the goddess of creation, and the goddess of destruction.

With the passage of time the female goddess or female chthonic spirit who carried this name (and had the ambivalent role of both giver and taker of life) took on different forms within the traditions of the various Indo-European peoples. For some, including Latvians, the name denoted a primarily constructive goddess who promotes fertility and productivity. For others, such as the Slavic peoples, it referred to a harmful spirit who comes at night to disturb human sleep and nocturnal peace, on occasion appearing as a forerunner of death or actual death itself. For Czechs and Poles she is Marena or Marana, a goddess associated with rituals devoted to the change of winter and spring seasons and the calling for rain. In Russian mythology she is Mara or Kikimora, a spirit who is either tiny or exactly the opposite—a tall, bent, and ugly woman with matted hair who lives under the floor and at night weaves the thread of human lives and brings harm in various ways. A related comparison in English is the word *nightmare*, where *mare*, the second part of the compound word, incorporates the abovementioned Indo-European root.

For Latvians, Māra appears in traditional folk beliefs, legends, and folk songs either as a woman in white clothing, a mooing cow heavy with milk, or a toad or snake. Usually Māra is called either Mīļā Māra (Dear Māra) or Svētā Māra (Holy Māra). In the first case this is a word formula, which people use to directly or indirectly approach Māra with a plea for her to be kind and protective to humans, which does not mean that the goddess is always kind and protective. The second word formula (Svētā Māra) has furnished an additional argument for scholars who have linked the origin of Māra's name to the Christian Holy Mary. Both the linguist Jānis Endzelīns and Pēteris Šmits proposed the theory in the first half of the twentieth century that Latvians had derived the word *svēts* (holy, sacred, blessed, or saint, before a word), along with the Christian religion, from their neighboring Russians. In fact, the word *svēts* is a Christian ecclesiastic term that originates in the ancient Russian language. It does not mean, however, that this word could not have existed before in the Latvian language as a way to refer to the concept of sanctity (*svētums*) in the pre-Christian context, because the word is based on the Indo-European root **kuei* (shining, bright, or white). If this ancient word *svēts* had arrived in the Latvian language by derivation, then there would not be as many toponyms and, in particular, ancient hydronyms throughout the Latvian and Lithuanian territory derived from this root form (e.g., Svētupe, Svēte, and Sventeļi). Moreover this root form appears in the synonym *svētelis* (literally, "white" or "shining"), used for the bird stork. More precisely Svētā Māra in its oldest, pre-Christian sense was seemingly used to describe the deity's essence and appearance, as in Baltā spīdošā Māra (White shining Māra).

Among Māra's specific functions, of significance is her protectorship of cows (as well as milk and butter). Māra is the giver of milk as a sacral drink to those going through puberty initiation rites. Thus, an etiological myth that has survived to the present day explains why the willow tree has slippery shiny leaves:

> *Aiz ko auga vītoliņš Glumajām lapiņām? —Mīļā Māra sviestu sita, Vītolā rokas slauka.* Why doth the willow tree grow With slippery leaves Dear *Māra* churning butter, Wipes her hands on the willow.

The gift of cows to an orphan girl about to be wed is dependant upon Māra's benevolence, since the orphan girl has neither father nor mother to provide her with the necessary dowry (property, goods, and farm animals, which were mandatory when getting married):

> *Mīļā Māra govis skaita Vītolā sēdēdama; Visas bija raibaļiņas, Dūmaliņas vien nebija; Nakti veda sērdienīti, Tai iedeva dūmaliņu.* Dear Māra counts her cows Sitting in a willow; All of them spotted cows, None of them smoke dark; At night the orphan girl was wed, She was given the smoke-dark one.

The being, deity or human, who is able to count cows or other such things in great numbers, is considered the owner of those things. The spotted cows mentioned in the folk song, in accordance with Baltic mythological concepts, are the most fertile and productive of cows, more so than the smoke-dark cow. In giving it as a gift to the orphan girl, Māra demonstrates her benevolence but she also indirectly indicates the social status of the orphan as one without the usual rights. For instance, the orphan girl is wed at night and not during the day, as is customary. In this and other folk songs it can be seen that Māra's tree is the willow, which shows Māra's link with ancient healing rituals—as well as fertility, which in Latvian folk songs is often symbolized by the shiny leaves of the willow. Māra is expert in, and in charge of, healing herbs. *Māras paparde*, the legendary fern blossom linked in Latvian folklore to the summer solstice, is described through the use of a possessive adjective as belonging to Māra. Māra is the creator of the spotted flowers of the bean plant, a death and rebirth ritual plant, symbolizing fertility:

> *Pupiņai raibi ziedi, Kas tos raibus darināja? —Mīļā Māra darināja, Debesīs sēdēdama.* The bean has spotted flowers, Who has made them spotted?—Dear Māra made them so, While she sat in heaven.

The structure of this folk song, which can be found in other folk songs mentioning Māra's name, is that of a sacral dialogue similar to the ancient Indian sacral dialogues *brahmodia*, which were created as oral components of a cosmogonic ritual.

Māra is invoked in magic incantations aimed at stopping bleeding (*asinsvārdos;* literally, "blood words"). In these verses Māra appears with a gold broom in her hand and is asked to sweep away the raven's blood or the fast-flowing river, the latter being a euphemism for the taboo words of human blood. An important role for Māra is the healing of breaks and bruises. In several mythological folk songs, Māra pieces together a broken jug (renewing the cosmos or microcosmos). As she renews the cosmos she mends a broken limb or heals bruises:

> *Dieviņš krūzu (kannu) sadauzīja, Svēta Māra salasīja, Sastīpoja sudraba stīpiņām, Lai nesāp, lai netūkst, Lai netek kā akmeņam. Dieviņš* [dim. of *Dievs*] broke a jug, Holy Māra picked up the pieces, Circled the jug with silver hoops, So it would not hurt, would not swell, Would not leak as if [made] of stone. (Straubergs, 1939, no. 395)

Māra is appealed to with special invocations in instances of birth complications during a woman's labor. Sometimes in folk beliefs and in magic incantations Māra is personified as a woman's uterus. In such instances Māra (= *dzemde* in Latvian = uterus) is invoked to come and replace the uterus of a woman experiencing birth complications, and if Māra will not take the place of the woman's uterus she is threatened with black cats or dogs who will bark and tear her to pieces:

> *Mīļā Māriņa, svētā Māriņa, Stāvi savā vietiņā, guli savā vietiņā! Necilājies, negrozies! Ja tu cilāsies, ja tu grozīsies, Nāks trejdeviņiem striķiem, trejdeviņiem pinekļiem, tevi tīstīs, tevi saistīs.* Dear Māriņa [dim. of Māra], blessed Māriņa, Stay in your place, sleep in your place! Don't shift, don't move! If you shift, if you move, They'll come with thrice nine ropes, [They'll come] with thrice nine hobbles, To tie you up, to bind you. (Straubergs, 1938, no. 394)

Māra is also called upon in instances of snakebites, and as a precautionary measure against meeting up with snakes in the woods. Snakes as killers or as healers are under Māra's supervision and, therefore, it is she and no other deity who is entreated by anyone wishing to evade snakebites. Māra is mentioned in many folk songs as a deity who does harm and is feared by humans, and against whose appearance from the sea or other waters people try to protect themselves. Humans wind a silver hoop around their houses so that Māra will not appear as a destroyer of flowers in cases where flowers are associated with life. In other folk-song texts Māra is shown as standing under an aspen tree, shaking and making it tremble. The aspen tree is most often associated with dying and the underworld in Baltic religious beliefs. Depicting Māra as standing under an aspen tree obviously underlines her ambivalent nature and her link to the kingdom of the dead and her role as overseer of the underworld.

People, especially women, made offerings and sacrifices to Māra to encourage her to appear more frequently in her benevolent rather than her destructive and harmful form. The most common sacrifice was a hen or a sheep. Sheep's wool and colored strands of wool were placed as offerings to Māra on the branches or in the hollows of trees, which most often were linden trees.

Māra's opposite, a masculine deity, is Dievs, the god of light, who is in charge of the higher world, the heavens, whereas Māra is in charge of the netherworld and earth. In several Latvian mythological folk songs, Dievs is shown as the ultimate judge over humans, the deity who brings on a monstrous flood as punishment for some unnamed violation, while Māra is the one who averts Dievs's anger:

> *Grib Dieviņš šo zemīti Ar ūdeni slīcināt; Mīļā Māra Dievu lūdza, Ap galviņu glāsīdama.* Dieviņš [dim. of Dievs] wants to drown This small land in flood waters; Dear Māra appeals to Dievs, Tenderly caressing his head.

Māra is associated with water. She helps fishermen threatened with danger and guides sailors' boats safely ashore, as well as a boat of orphans across the sea. She is the one who controls thunderstorms, tempests, and other natural disasters. The concept of Māras *avots* (Māra's spring) is connected to fertility. This is a special spring in which, during the summer solstice or other major ritual festivities, women wash themselves to gain fertility, health, and energy. In the best-known sanctuaries in Latvia, such as *zilie kalni* (blue hills), Māra's spring is often mentioned as a sacred object. The concept of Māras *baznīca* (Māra's church) also figures in folk beliefs and legends, often as a place (forest, cave, pile of stones, etc.) where Māra endows humans (primarily women) with their share or what they deserve of wealth or good fortune, or even poverty or ill fortune if the goddess has not received sufficient offerings.

Māra appears in mythological folk songs as the protectress of the world of the dead, most often together with the sons of Dievs. On the far side of a bridge fashioned of bones, across a river of blood, "shaking and trembling," she welcomes the souls of soldiers fallen in battle. This is a word formula that suggests an ecstatic emotional experience or epiphany and a transitional crisis situation.

Thursday night, the fifth night, specifically the time between Thursday and Friday, is frequently mentioned in references to Māra. Certain tasks primarily done by women, such as knitting and weaving, were forbidden on Thursday evening. This was considered to be the night of Māra's birth and this taboo was observed up until the nineteenth century (and even as late as the twentieth century in several far corners of the Latvian countryside). On this night one could not whistle or make any kind of noise because people believed that on the fifth night all magicians and witches had been born, and noise could accidentally call them forth. Certain parallels can be drawn with similar beliefs about the fifth night in other European countries. Thus, for example, *Friday* in English is derived from the German and Scandinavian chthonic goddess Freyja.

Māra's image among Catholics in the Baltics is quite different. This pertains, first of all, to Lithuania, and secondly to eastern Latvia, where the Catholic region of Latgale is located. Here the pre-Christian Māra's image has fused with the Catholic image of Holy Mary (Svēta Marija in Latvian). Prayers to Marija/Māra, the Mother of God, have become an important component of the Catholic faith practiced by the people. Thus, in Latgale on August 15 each year, on *Svātōs Marijas debesbraukšonas dīna* (Feast of the Assumption of Holy Mary into heaven), there are mass pilgrimages to Aglona Cathedral, where an altar painting of the Virgin Mary that is considered to be a special source of miracles is located. Māra's/Marija's sacred spring, whose healing power is renowned from ancient times, is located near the cathedral. However, the majority of Latvians have retained in their traditional folk consciousness their own Great "Mother of all Mothers" image—that of Māra from pre-Christian times. In Latvian folk beliefs a special Māra's day is celebrated several times per year in honor of Māra.

See Also Goddess Worship.

BIBLIOGRAPHY

Biezais, Haralds. *Die Hauptgöttinnen der alten Letten.* Uppsala, Sweden, 1955.

Brastiņš, Arvīds. *Māte Māra.* Cleveland, 1967.

Bruņenieks, Mārtiņš. *Senlatviešu Laima.* Riga, Latvia, 1940.

Gimbutas, Marija. *The Language of the Goddess.* San Francisco, 1989. See page 134.

Gimbutas, Marija. *The Living Goddesses.* Berkeley, 1999. See pages 159 and 202–203.

Karulis, Konstantīns. "Vai latviešu Māra ir Svētā Marija?" *Literatūra un Māksla* 8, no. 7 (1988): 4.

Kursīte, Janīna. "Māra." In *Latviešu folklora mītu spogulī,* pp. 258–300. Riga, Latvia, 1996.

Riekstiņš, Hugo. "Māras dienas parašas." *Labietis* 4 (1939): 274–280.

Rode, Ojārs. "Māra Afganistānā." *Dievturu Vēstnesis* 4 (1990): 17–20.

Ryžakova, Svetlana. "'Svjataja Mara' v latyšskoj narodnoj kul'ture." *Živaja Starina* (Moscow) 2 (1996): 42–46.

Straubergs, Kārlis. *Latviešu buramie vārdi.* 2 vols. Rīga, 1939–1941.

Vīķis-Freibergs, Vaira. "The Major Gods and Goddesses of Ancient Latvian Mythology." In *Linguistics and Poetics of Latvian Folk Songs,* pp. 91–113. Kingston, Ontario, and Montreal, 1989.

Zālīte, Māra. "Pilna Māras istabiņa jeb tautasdziesmu Māras meklējumos." *Varavīksne,* pp. 118–156. Riga, Latvia, 1985.

Janīna Kursīte (2005)

Translated by Margita Gailītis and Vija Kostoff

MARANKE, JOHN (1912–1963), African religious prophet and founder of the Apostolic Church of John Maranke. John (or Johane) Maranke was born Muchabaya Ngomberume in 1912. His birthplace is believed to be near Bondwe Mountain in the Maranke Tribal Trust Land of Southern Rhodesia. His father, Mombe-rume, was part of the royal Sithole lineage, and his mother was the daughter of the Shona chief Maranke.

Church records indicate that Maranke was baptized a Methodist under the name of Roston at the local mission. Some of his instructors thought that he would eventually enter the Methodist ministry. In July of 1932, however, John, as he is referred to by his followers, received a spiritual calling to start the Apostolic church. An account of the visionary experiences leading to his calling is presented in the *Humbowo Hutswa we Vapostori* (The New Revelation of the Apostles), a book composed in the Shona language by Maranke and viewed by the movement as a major ecclesiastical text.

When John was five years old, he began to hear strange voices and see visions. After a year of Methodist primary school, he claimed that he had been visited by the Holy Spirit. He prayed continually and stood on top of anthills preaching to the trees. During this time, John was plagued by a mysterious childhood illness that could not be diagnosed. Following this illness, he lived for a short period of time in the mountains and was thought by his relatives and friends to be dead.

On the evening of July 17, 1932, near Mount Nyengwe in Umtali District, John allegedly witnessed a bright light and heard a heavenly voice that said: "You are John the Baptist, an Apostle. Now go and do my work. Go to every country and preach and convert people." John regarded this vision as a divine calling from the Holy Spirit to found the Apostolic church.

Between 1932 and 1934, John's church grew rapidly. After the initial spiritual revelation, John, his brothers Conorio and Anrod, and his uncle Peter Mupako went to spread the news to the neighboring settlements. Ruka (Luke) Mataruka, John's brother-in-law, became the first convert and evidenced signs of his spiritual calling immediately. John himself was baptized by Ruka. As the news of John's revelation spread beyond his extended family, people from all parts of the district flocked to him to receive spiritual healing.

On Saturday, July 20, 1932, the first Apostolic Sabbath was held near the Murozi, or "Jordan," River, in which the new converts were baptized. It is estimated that approximately 150 new members were baptized on that day. Ruka was made the first evangelist of the church. Two of John's cousins, Simon (Mushati) and Gwati, were designated respectively as the first prophet and first secretary of the church; his brother Conorio became the first healer. Momberume, John's father, was also baptized then and was made the elder judge (*mutongi*) of the church, charged with resolving disputes.

On August 24, 1934, the Passover (*Paseka* or *Pendi*) of the Apostolic church was held. This celebration was a combined reenactment of the Last Supper and a Eucharist. It was also intended to commemorate the moment at which John Maranke received his initial calling from the Holy Spirit and, hence, was also known as the Pendi, or Pentecost. After John's death, the date of the celebration was changed to July 17, in honor of the date of John's first calling. During the Passover, Apostles from all regions gather to confess sins of the preceding year and to celebrate spiritual renewal. As the church has grown, the importance of this celebration has increased.

Eventually, a leadership hierarchy consisting of four spiritual gifts (*bipedi*) and three ranks (*mianza*) was established for each Apostolic congregation. The spiritual gifts are designated as works of healing, evangelism, prophecy, and baptism. Members are ordained within each spiritual gift. The ranks within each gift are derived from the sacred word *Lieb-Umah* that John Maranke received in a prophetic revelation. The Apostles assert that this word means "he who speaks with God." John specified that each Apostolic congregation should contain three Lieb-Umahs, or priests, for each of the four gifts. Together, all of the men holding degrees of the Lieb-Umah rank within a single congregation constitute the Committee of Twelve Elders charged with its governance.

John and his relatives controlled the church from its center in Bocha, Zimbabwe (then Southern Rhodesia), until his death (allegedly by poisoning) in 1963. In the late 1940s, however, Ruka Mataruka gained a considerable following of his own and broke away from the parent church. John challenged Ruka's bid for power and was ultimately able to regain many of the dissident followers. After John's death, a schism again divided the Zimbabwean branch of the church when Simon Mushati formed another rival group. Simon argued that he had always been second to John in the leadership structure of the church and challenged the right of John's eldest son, Abel, to succeed his father. Invoking Shona customary law, John's brother Anrod performed a christianized version of the traditional inheritance ceremony and passed on the leadership to John's eldest sons, Abel and Makebo. By this time, the church was so large that it was necessary to travel to outlying districts and to other countries to perform the Passover. Abel, as John's legitimate successor, was given the power to perform the Passover and to lead the church. He divided these responsibilities with his younger brother Makebo, who traveled north to Nyasaland (now Malawi) and east to Mozambique on his behalf. By the 1960s, there were an estimated fifty thousand Maranke Apostles in Zimbabwe alone.

THE APOSTOLIC MOVEMENT ON AN INTERNATIONAL SCALE. The Apostolic church entered Zambia (then Northern Rhodesia) and Malawi (then Nyasaland) by 1948. Initially, the Shona evangelist Kasimil visited these areas and baptized many new converts who subsequently spread the word among their relatives and in neighboring villages. The early congregations also contained many Shona members who had migrated north in search of work.

In 1952, Nawezi Petro, a Zairian of Lunda origin, encountered the Shona Apostles on a visit to Southern Rhodesia. He claimed that they healed his wife of tuberculosis after a series of European doctors had failed to do so. Nawezi and his wife immediately converted and returned home to introduce the church to Katanga Province (now Shaba). Meanwhile, the church spread northward to the Kasai Province of Zaire and to the capital, Kinshasa (then Léopoldville). Kasanda Vincent and Mujanaie Marcel, the first spokesmen for the group in the Kasai area, quickly acquired a large following. Over the years, several schisms developed in the Zairian branch of the Apostolic church. The major rift took place when Nawezi's brother-in-law Musumbu Pierre broke away from the Katanga congregation and acquired a large local following in the Kasai region. This struggle between Musumbu and Nawezi was finally resolved in 1974 when the church center acknowledged Musumbu's status as the first leader of the Zairian branch and the official representative of the Zairian congregations.

A similar pattern of growth took place in Angola and Mozambique, where the Apostolic church went through the characteristic pattern of rapid growth and subsequent schism. By the early 1980s, there were an estimated three hundred thousand members of the Maranke Apostolic church in six central and southern African nations: Zimbabwe, Zaire, Angola, Mozambique, Malawi, and Zambia. The largest membership is concentrated in eastern Zimbabwe and southwestern Zaire.

THE IMPACT OF THE APOSTOLIC CHURCH IN CENTRAL AND SOUTHERN AFRICA. Apostolic theology is highly moralistic, emphasizing the keeping of commandments, observation of food and other taboos, and the regular confession of sins. The Apostles accept the Old and New Testaments of the Bible equally as the foundation for their belief. Saturday is kept as the sabbath day. Biblical teachings are supplemented by John's prophetic book *New Witness of the Apostles,* which is considered to provide spiritual and moral directives for a better life. Emphasis is placed on Holy Spirit inspiration and faith healing.

Apostolic doctrine involves a clear reaction to the mission churches. Voluntary polygamy is condoned, and church members are encouraged to avoid Western medical treatment. At the same time, Apostles eschew many aspects of traditional religion, including the veneration of the ancestors and the use of herbal medicines and charms. The role of women as ceremonial leaders is emphasized in the church, and they hold the positions of prophetesses and healers. Although marriage is not considered a sacrament among the Apostles, the customary dowry is de-emphasized and the importance of the family unit is stressed.

Ceremonies are conducted in multiple languages, and church liturgy varies somewhat from one congregation to another, although the basic format of worship remains consistent. While the influence of John Maranke as a prophet and founder is acknowledged by all congregations, there has been no attempt to elevate him to divine or messianic status. He is considered to be a messenger of God and a reformer whose interpretation of Christianity has made it relevant to large segments of the African population. The movement contains an innovative combination of African customs and Christianity. The charismatic appeal of the church and an ability to absorb cultural variations have accounted for its spread and popularity across several African nations.

BIBLIOGRAPHY

Aquina, Mary, O.P. "The People of the Spirit: An Independent Church in Rhodesia." *Africa* 37 (1967): 203–219. Contains a brief account of the Apostolic movement in the Karanga area of Southern Rhodesia during the 1950s with an explanation of its doctrine and rituals. Emphasis is placed on the role of confession for church members.

Daneel, M. L. *Old and New in Southern Shona Independent Churches,* vol.1, *Background and Rise of the Major Movements.* The Hague, 1971. A detailed historical account of the background and rise of several Shona traditional cults and independent churches, including a discussion of the early years of the Apostolic Church of John Maranke in eastern Zimbabwe.

Jules-Rosette, Bennetta. *African Apostles: Ritual and Conversion in the Church of John Maranke.* Ithaca, N. Y., 1975. A study of the Apostolic Church of John Maranke in Zaire, Zambia, and Zimbabwe, containing a detailed account of the Zairian branch and discussion of ritual and the conversion process in the church based on firsthand ethnographic materials.

Jules-Rosette, Bennetta, ed. *The New Religions of Africa.* Norwood, N. J., 1979. An edited collection of eleven essays on new African religious movements containing an article on the role of women as leaders in the Maranke Apostolic church and an introductory comparison of the Maranke Apostles with related movements in the same region.

Maranke, John. *The New Witness of the Apostles.* Translated by J. S. Kusotera. Bocha, Rhodesia, 1953. A mimeographed pamphlet, giving an autobiographical account of the spiritual visions of John Maranke and the history of the founding of the church from his perspective; outlines the commandments and moral directives governing church membership.

Murphree, Marshall W. *Christianity and the Shona.* New York, 1969. A study of Christianity among the Shona of the Budja area of Mtoko District in Zimbabwe, containing an account of the relationships among the Methodists, the Roman Catholics, and the Maranke Apostles in the area. A description of Apostolic doctrine and ritual is included.

BENNETTA JULES-ROSETTE (1987)

MARATHI RELIGIONS.

The Marathi language, which has demarcated the area in western India called Maharashtra for almost a thousand years, is an Indo-European language of North India that includes elements from the Dravidian languages of South India as well. Other elements of Maharashtrian culture—food, marriage customs, the patterns of caste groupings, and many aspects of religion—also reflect the fact that the Marathi-speaking area is a bridge between North and South. To the mix of Indo-European and Dravidian is added a mix of Vaiṣṇava and Śaiva traditions, and the whole is contained by a remarkable sense of the area's unity and integrity.

The major persistent natural and cultural subregions of Maharashtra are the coastal strip between the Arabian Sea and the Sahyādri Mountains (Western Ghāṭs), called the Koṅkan; the fertile northeastern region of Vidarbha, in central India; and, between these, the Deś, the Marathi-speaking part of the Deccan plateau, including the upper reaches of the Godāvarī and Kṛṣṇa river systems. The upper Godāvarī valley is also called Marāṭhvāḍā.

THE DEVELOPMENT OF MARATHI AND MAHARASHTRIAN RELIGION. The earliest examples of the Marathi language are found in inscriptions from the eleventh century. By the late thirteenth century, when the Yadava kingdom governed most of the area known as Maharashtra and Marathi literature began to appear, the language was already well developed. Three sorts of writings came into being at about the same time, setting in motion very different religious movements.

In Vidarbha, a court-supported philosopher, Mukuṇḍarājā, wrote the *Vivekasindhu,* a philosophical treatise in the Advaita Vedānta tradition of Śaṅkara. Mukuṇḍarājā created no cult or school, but his influence is reflected in later work, particularly that of the seventeenth-century Rāmdās, a religio-political saint contemporaneous with the birth of the Marāṭhā nation under Śivaji.

The thirteenth century also saw the beginnings of two religious movements that continue in the early twenty-first century. The Vārkarī sect, which is the area's most popular devotional religious movement and which has an important literature, understands itself to have begun with Jñāneśvar. Jñāneśvar was the author of an approximately nine-thousand-verse commentary on the *Bhagavadgītā* called the *Jñāneśvarī,* a work strongly influenced by the Advaita of Śaṅkara. A number of devotional poems (*abhaṅgas*) addressed to the deity Viṭhobā of Paṇḍharpūr are also ascribed to Jñāneśvar; it is on the basis of these that he is considered the first of a line of poet-saints who composed songs in honor of Viṭhobā, whom Vārkarīs take to be a form of Kṛṣṇa. These poet-saints, numbering around forty, include Nāmdev, a contemporary of Jñāneśvar to whom Hindi as well as Marathi poems are ascribed; Cokhāmeḷā, an untouchable; Eknāth, a sixteenth-century brahman from Paiṭhaṇ on the Godāvarī River; and Tukārām, the most popular Maharashtrian poet-saint, a seventeenth-century *śūdra* grocer who lived in Dehu, near Pune (Poona). Members of the Vārkarī sect, virtually all of whom are Maharashtrians, still sing the songs of these poet-saints and carry images of their footwear in an annual pilgrimage to Paṇḍharpūr.

The Mahānubhāv sect is not so widely popular today as the Vārkarī sect, but it has an important place in the religious history of Maharashtra. Founded by the thirteenth-century Cakradhar, the Mahānubhāv sect produced a large body of prose hagiographies and poetry. The sect spread primarily in the valley of the Godāvarī River and in Vidarbha. Like the Vārkarīs, Mahānubhāvs are devotees of Kṛṣṇa; but they exceed the Vārkarīs in their rejection of Brahmanic caste and pollution rules, and in their espousal of an ascetic way of life.

Another sect important in medieval Maharashtra was that of the Nāths, whose influence can be discerned in the early history and literature of the Vārkarīs and Mahānubhāvs. The Nāths were a sect of ascetics and yogins who specialized in various kinds of occult knowledge and who were devoted to the god Śiva. Aside from legends concerning the Navanāth, or Nine Nāths, the strongest Nāth influence today is probably in the figure of Dattātreya, to be discussed below.

MAHARASHTRIAN DEITIES. Although the two *bhakti* (devotional) sects of the Vārkarīs and the Mahānubhāvs are more pronouncedly Vaiṣṇava (or, rather, Kṛṣṇaite) than Śaiva, there is evidence of a Śaiva background against which they spread. And in the village and pastoral cults of Maharashtra, goddesses and Śaiva gods are far more prominent than Visnu or Kṛṣṇa.

Pilgrimage deities. The most important pilgrimage deity of Maharashtra is Viṭhobā of Paṇḍharpūr, whose primary mythological indentification is with Kṛṣṇa, but who also has strong connections with Śiva and who may have originated in a pastoral hero cult. Besides Viṭhobā, most other major Maharashtrian pilgrimage deities are goddesses and Śaiva gods. Of the many Śiva temples in Maharashtra, the two most important to Indian pilgrimage traditions may be Bhīmaśaṅkar in Pune District and Tryambakeśvar in Nasik District. Both temples are basic to the Maharashtrian landscape, since they are at the sources of the important Bhīma and Godāvarī rivers, respectively. Along with several other Maharashtrian Śiva temples, these two claim to be among the most important Śiva temples in all of India, the twelve *jyotirliṅgas*. Tryambakeśvar, together with the nearby city of Nāsik, is one of the four sites of the twelve-year cycle of Kumbha Melās.

Several other important pilgrimage deities, more or less closely identified with Śiva, appear to be deities of pastoralists, tribals, and warriors, eventually adopted by settled agriculturalists as well. Perhaps the most prominent of these is Khaṅḍobā, whose temples at Jejurī, near Pune, and at Māḷegāv (Nanded District) attract large numbers of pilgrims from a wide range of castes. Other extremely popular pilgrimage deities of this sort are Śambhu Mahādev at Singṇāpūr (Satara District) and Jyotibā at Vāḍī Ratnāgiri (Kolhapur District).

Four goddess temples that ring the Marathi-speaking area are also among the principal Maharashtrian pilgrimage places: the temple of Mahalaksmī at Kolhāpūr, that of Bhavānī at Tuḷjāpūr (Usmanabad District), that of Reṇukā at Māhūr (Nanded District), and that of Saptaśṛṅgī, at Vaṇī near Nāsik. These temples are linked to the religious geography of all of India as three and a half of the 108 *śakti pīṭhas*, places where, according to a Purānic story, body parts of Śiva's wife Satī were scattered throughout India; Saptaśṛṅgī is said to be the one-half *pīṭha* and thus is somewhat less important than the other three. Although they are all identified as *śakti pīṭhas*, each goddess has her own history and individuality as well. Bhavānī, for example, was worshiped by the seventeenth-century Marāṭhā king Śivājī in the form of his sword.

Distinct from temple priests, who in Śaiva and goddess temples are not necessarily brahmans but often belong to the *gurav* caste, there are special types of mendicant devotee-performers attached to several of the major pilgrimage deities of Maharashtra. *Vāghyās* and *muraḷīs*, for instance, are such devotees, dedicated to Khaṅḍobā: *muraḷīs* are women dancers and *vāghyās* are male devotees whose devotional performances sometimes involve acting like dogs, since a dog accompanies Khaṅḍobā. The most popular of such folk-religious figures are *gondhaḷīs*, who are devotees of goddesses, particularly of Reṇukā of Māhūr and Tuljā Bhavāni. Their performance, the *gondhaḷ*, combines music and storytelling, usually at a wedding or other family occasion, but the *gondhaḷī* also serves as bard, singing the heroic *pavāḍās* that celebrate Maharashtrian bravery from the time of Śivājī on.

Other deities. The figure of Dattātreya illustrates a Maharashtrian reworking of religious influences from both North and South, as well as the synthesizing of Śaiva and Vaiṣṇava motifs. A *ṛsi* ("seer") in Sanskrit epic and Purāṇic literature, Datta first appears in Marathi literature as one of the five Mahānubhāv incarnations of the supreme God, Parameśvara. By the sixteenth century, however, Datta is clearly in the mainstream Hindu tradition, and has begun to be represented as the Brahmā-Viṣṇu-Śiva triad, in one body with three heads. Shortly before that time, incarnations of the god began to appear on Maharashtrian soil, and many believe that Datta has appeared in modern times, as Sāī Bābā, as the Svāmī of Akkalkoṭ, or as some other *avatāra.* Datta's chief and very popular pilgrimage center is at Gāṅgāpūr, located to the south of Maharashtra in northern Karnataka state. As in the northern tradition, Datta is seen as the patron deity of ascetics. Another element in Maharashtrian Datta worship is that while he is seen as a brahman, he has also become *guru* for people in all walks of life, even, it is said, for prostitutes, and his three-headed image or an image of one of his *avataras* is found at all levels of society.

The elephant-headed god Gaṇeśa or Gaṇapati is also particularly important in Maharashtra. There is a formal pilgrimage route of eight centers, all fairly near Pune, where *svayambhū* ("self-formed") elephant-headed stones bestow blessings as images of Gaṇeśa, but much more frequently worshiped are the representations of Gaṇeśa fixed over the doors of homes, brilliant with red coloring; among the stone sculptures on temple walls; and appearing here and there in the open countryside or in small shrines on city streets. Gaṇeśa was the family deity of the Peṣvās, the Citpāvan brahmans who ruled from Pune after the time of Śivājī, and the numerically small in numbers but nevertheless influential Citpāvans are still among Gaṇapati's principal worshipers. The annual Gaṇeśa festival has become a widely popular public event since 1893, when the nationalist leader Bal

Gangadhar Tilak organized it as a way to celebrate patriotism through religious means.

The god Rām is found in temples throughout Maharashtra, but seems not to carry the cultural importance found in great public events like the Rāmlīlā in the Hindi-speaking area. Rām's devotee, the monkey god Māruti (Hanumān), is tightly woven into Maharashtrian rural life; a Māruti temple is found in almost every Maharashtrian village or on its outskirts. Other deities prominent as village protectors are goddesses with names ending in *āī* ("mother"), *bāī* ("lady") or *devī* ("goddess"), such as Marīāī, the goddess of pestilence.

RITUALS. The ritual life of Maharashtrian Hindus includes festivals regulated by the calendar, celebrations of events in the human life cycle, and rituals performed in response to individual or collective crises.

Calendrical rites. Rituals occurring annually include pilgrimage festivals (*jatrās*) to particular places at particular times, and festivals celebrated locally or domestically in an annual cycle. Maharashtrian Hindus follow the luni-solar calendar, ending months with the no-moon day (the *amānta* system), as in South India, rather than with the full-moon day (the *pūrṇimānta* system), as in North India. The greatest concentration of pilgrimage festivals occurs during the month of Caitra (March–April), the first month of the Hindu calendar, but such festivals take place throughout the year. The pilgrimage deities mentioned above account for only a fraction of the thousands of *jatrās* occurring every year in Maharashtra.

Of local and domestic festivals, some of the most popular in Maharashtra are the following.

- Divāḷī: a complex of several festival days occurring at the end of the month of Āśvin and the beginning of the month of Kārtik (generally in October), celebrated domestically, most prominently by decorating homes with lighted lamps.
- Navarātra: a festival in honor of goddesses celebrated for the first nine days of the month of Āśvin (September–October); Navarātra culminates on the tenth day with Dasarā or Vijayadaśamī, a festival of triumph that is traditionally considered an auspicious day for inaugurating military campaigns or other enterprises.
- The Gaṇeśa festival: a ten-day festival ending on the fourteenth day of the month of Bhādrapad (August–September), in which temporary images of the elephant-headed deity Gaṇeśa are worshiped in home shrines (and, following Tilak's innovations, in elaborate neighborhood shrines in cities and towns as well); in some homes, women set up temporary shrines in honor of the goddess Gaurī (Pārvatī) for three days during the Gaṇeśa festival.
- Vaṭasāvitrī: a *vrata* (a fast and ritual) performed by married women on the full moon day of the month of Jyeṣṭha (May–June) for their husbands' welfare.
- Nāg Pañcamī: one of the many days of fasting and worship during the month of Śrāvaṇ (July–August), this festival is held on the fifth day of the month and is characterized by the worship of snakes and by women's songs and games.
- Polā: a festival usually celebrated on the no-moon day at the end of the month of Śrāvaṇ, a day on which the bullocks used in agricultural work are decorated, worshiped, and led in procession around the village.

In addition to such annual festivals, there are certain days of each fortnight and of each week that are especially dedicated to particular gods and that are observed by special worship of those gods and/or by fasting in their honor. For example, Monday is for Śiva, Tuesday and Friday for goddesses, Thursday for Dattātreya, Saturday for Śani (Saturn), Sunday for Khaṅḍobā, the fourth day of each fortnight for Gaṇeśa, the eleventh day of the fortnight for Viṭhobā, the thirteenth day for Śiva, and so on.

Life-cycle rites. Besides marriage and funeral rituals, those of the classical Hindu life-cycle rites (*saṃskāras*) most commonly celebrated in Maharashtra today are the ceremony of naming a child (this is performed on or near the twelfth (*bārāvā*) day after the child's birth and is hence called *bārseṃ*), and the ceremony, primarily among brahmans, of initiating young boys and investing them with the sacred thread (*muñja*). In addition, there are several rituals celebrating the early married life and pregnancy of young women. These rituals are generally performed by women and are not included in the classical list of *saṃskāras*. Such, for example, are Maṅgaḷā Gaurī, the worship of the goddess Gaurī and playing of women's games on a Tuesday of the month of Śrāvaṇ, for the first five years of a woman's married life, and Ḍohāḷejevaṇ, a celebration in honor of a pregnant woman, named for the cravings of pregnancy (*ḍohālā*).

Crisis rites. Rituals of crisis in Maharashtra most commonly take the form of a *navas:* one promises a deity that one will perform a particular fast or pilgrimage in his or her honor, or make some particular offering, if one gets a certain desired object—most typically, the birth of a son. If that object is attained, one must keep one's promise (*navas pheḍaṇeṃ*). With the notable exception of Viṭhobā of Paṇḍharpūr, many of the chief pilgrimage deities of Maharashtra are said to answer such prayers (*navasālā pāvaneṃ*); and many Maharashtrian pilgrimages, whether at special festival times or otherwise, are made in fulfillment of a *navas.*

In addition, there are village deities, such as Marīāī (the cholera goddess) and Śītalā (the smallpox goddess), who are especially propitiated for curing individuals of disease and for averting or bringing to an end such disasters as epidemics and droughts which affect an entire village. Marīāī is served by a *potrāj*—always, until the contemporary conversion to Buddhism, an untouchable *mahār*—who carries a whip and a burning rope, wears a skirt made of women's blouse pieces, and acts as priest for the goddess.

A popular but elaborate ritual called the Satyanārāyaṇ Pūjā is most common in modern, urban environments. It is performed in fulfillment of a *navas,* for thanksgiving, for safety on a journey, or for prosperity or success of some sort.

Changes in Hinduism in Modern Maharashtra. Modern changes in Maharashtrian religion are many and varied, ranging from the training of women as ritual priests to a large-scale conversion from Hinduism to Buddhism (see below). Two streams of change in the nineteenth century affected the intellectual history of Hinduism, but seem not to have influenced common practice. Gopal Hari Deshmukh (1823–1892), writing as Lokahitavāḍī ("he who is concerned for the people's welfare"), set in motion a reform and liberalization of Hindu practice that was later organized as the Prārthanā Samāj, the "prayer society." This was the Maharashtrian counterpart of the Bengali Brāhmo Samāj, but was not as separated from mainstream Hindu life as the latter. The "non-brahman movement" begun by Jotibā Phule (1828–1890) was also liberalizing and rationalizing, but carried the additional message that brahman dominance was socially, politically, and, indeed, religiously destructive to the welfare of the lower classes. Phule's Satyashodhak Samāj (Truth Seeking Society) brought his religious ideas and ideals to every corner of the Des and Vidarbha. The chief carryover of Phule's movement in the first half of the twentieth century, however, was political rather than religious. Phule is revered today in the Ambedkar movement.

The institutional changes in Hinduism in the modern period incude the Gaṅapati festival as reorganized by Tilak; the formation of the Rāṣṭrīya Svayaṃsevak Saṅgh, a paramilitary service organization with a religious base for young men with a branch for women, and the training of women as sannyasis and as priests. While the Rāṣṭrīya Svayaṃsevak Saṅgh (RSS) has spread over much of India, it originated in the city of Nagpur in Vidarbha, and is still of great importance all over Maharashtra, particularly among brahmans. Begun by Dr. K. B. Hedgewar (1889–1940), the RSS was both a Hindu revival organization that combined Sanskrit prayer with military drill and a nationalistic service organization. Its leadership is celibate and promises lifelong dedication to the organization, but the majority of its members become associated with the youth groups of the RSS and maintain their formal affiliation only as long as they are students. The RSS is linked to the conservative Bhāratīya Janatā Pakṣa (BJP) political party, but retains its separate existence as a non-political body. It traces its intellectual heritage to the Hindu revivalistic thought of Bal Gangadhar Tilak and Vīr Savarkar, both also ardent nationalists.

Women have been of consequence in Maharashtrian religion from the days of Cakradhar and Jñāneśvar, and Muktābāī, Janābāī, Soyrābāī, and Bahiṇābāī are important figures in the Vārkarī movement. A pattern of prominent women devotees of even more prominent male saints was repeated in the twentieth century as Godāvarī Mātā succeeded Upāsanī Bābā at the important ashram at Sakori in Ahmadnagar District. Here the Kanyā Kumārī Sthān, a young women's religious training institute, was established, enabling women to become full-fledged ascetics. The most recent development is a program in Pune that trains women as Vedic ritual priests.

Maharashtra is home also of many gurus and their ashrams, the best known being Meher Bābā's center at Ahmadnagar, Muktānanda's at Ganeshpuri near Mumbai, and Rajneesh's in Pune. All of these have Western as well as Indian adherents. There are also many gurus whose followers are all Indian, such as Gajānan Mahāraj of Shegaon and Swāmī Samarth of Akkalkot.

Religious Minorities. Of the non-Hindu religions in Maharashtra, Buddhism, Islam, and Christianity account for roughly 7, 8, and 1.5 percent of the population, respectively. Jains are few in number but important as merchants as are the Muslim merchant groups of Bohras, Khojas, and Memons. There is little writing on either contemporary Islam or Christianity in the Maharashtrian context, but there is much information on the most recent change in religion, the conversion to Buddhism.

The initial Buddhist conversion took place in the city of Nagpur in 1956 and has spread all over Maharashtra (and to many urban areas of India); the conversion movement is still gaining adherents. After a series of frustrated attempts on the part of untouchables to enter temples, B. R. Ambedkar (1891–1956), an untouchable *mahar* educator, reformer, and statesman, declared in 1935 that he "would not die a Hindu." The conversion was postponed for twenty years while political activities took precedence, but just before his death, Dr. Ambedkar publicly became a Buddhist and called for conversion to that once-important Indian religion. More than six million adherents, the majority of them in Maharashtra, now list themselves as Buddhist, and a Buddhist literature in Marathi, a growing order of Buddhist monks, and a program of building Buddhist *viharas* (temples) now mark the Maharashtrian scene. Many of the converts draw inspiration from the world-famous ancient Buddhist cave-temples in Maharashtra, especially the complexes at Ajanta and Ellora.

The writing on contemporary Islam in the state is almost non-existent, but there seems to have been a considerable mixture of Hinduism and Islam in the past. Shaykh Muḥammad was an honored saint-poet within the *bhakti* tradition in the fifteenth century; the god Dāttatreya often appeared as a *faqīr,* or Muslim holy man, to his disciples; Sāī Baba of Shirdi was a Muslim but now is chiefly worshiped by Hindus, who flock to his center and pray to him for material well-being. The sea shrine of Hājī Ālī in Mumbai, accessible at low tide, is visited by Indians of all religions. Muḥarram is the name of the first month of the Muslim year, and the first ten days of that month are an important festival also known by that name. In the past Hindus participated in great numbers in the Muharram festival, and visited the shrines of Ṣūfī saints. There is less participation in Muharram today, but the festival continues to be important to Shīʿā Muslims. It is a solemn occasion associated with the memory of Ḥusayn, son of the Prophet's daughter by ʿAlī, and commemorates the death of Ḥusayn in the battle of Karbala in 680 CE. The festival involves a temporary structure called an *imāmbāra* for gatherings; the standard of a hand placed on a pole, emblematic of the five members of the family of the Prophet; a procession carrying a replica of Ḥusayn's tomb, called a *tābūt,* which culminates in its immersion in the river (at least in Pune); and a feast, which is also observed by Sunnis. Muslims observe the ninth month of the Muslim year, Rāmadān, with fasting.

Christian conversion in the area, outside of the Portuguese presence in Goa, began in the nineteenth century, with the American Marathi Mission being the most important of the foreign groups. Justin Abbott and others of this mission did much to translate the Vārkarī poets into English, and one famous convert of the mission, Narayan Vaman Tilak, wrote Christian *bhakti* hymns in Marathi. Another influential convert, not connected to any Maharashtrian institution, was Pandita Ramabai, who wrote on social and women's issues, established a home for girls, and introduced Braille to India. The educational institutions, particularly the colleges, established by both Protestants and Catholics, are very important. Festivals are also important, especially the feast of Mary's Nativity at the famous shrine of Our Lady of the Mount in Bandra in Mumbai. While the feast is held in other parts of the West Coast on September 8, coincident with the harvest, the Bandra festival goes on for a week with several hundred thousand people venerating the ancient statue in the shrine and attending the Bandra fair. There is also a feast for St. Gonsalo Garcia, the first Indian born saint, and an older feast for St. Francis Xavier, whose tomb is in Goa, on December 3.

The small but culturally and economically important group of Parsis, eighth-century Zoroastrian immigrants from Persia, is primarily based in Mumbai and other large cities of Maharashtra.There is also a small group of Marathi-speaking Jews, the Bene Israeli, most of whom have migrated to Israel.

SEE ALSO Ambedkar, B. R.; Brāhmo Samāj; Hindu Religious Year; Indian Religions, article on Rural Traditions; Parsis; Pilgrimage, article on Hindu Pilgrimage; Poetry, article on Indian Religious Poetry; Rites of Passage, article on Hindu Rites; Tilak, Bal Gangadhar.

BIBLIOGRAPHY

The most thorough and prolific writer on the religious traditions of Maharashtra, including folk traditions, is R. C. Dhere, who writes in Marathi. His *Viṭṭhal, Ek Mahāsamanvay* (Poona, 1984) is the most comprehensive work on the Viṭhobā cult to date. The standard work on this subject in English is G. A. Deleury's *The Cult of Viṭhobā* (Poona, 1960). A recent account is *Palkhi: A Pilgrimage to Paṇḍharpūr* by D. B. Mokashi, translated by Philip C. Engblom (Albany, N. Y., 1987), which adds to the reality of the Vārkarī pilgrimage. Dilip Chitre's translations of the bhakta Tukārām, *Tuka Says,* first published as a Penguin Classic, is now available in a more comprehensive edition published by the Sontheimer Cultural Association in Pune. Shankar Gopal Tulpule's *Classical Marathi Literature from the Beginning to AD 1818* in *A History of Indian Literature,* vol. 9, fasc. 4, edited by Jan Gonda (Wiesbaden, 1979), gives a thorough survey of Vārkarī and Mahānubhāv literature, as well as of other premodern religious literature in Marathi; this work includes generous bibliographical footnotes. An earlier work, R. D. Ranade's *Indian Mysticism: The Poet-Saints of Maharashtra* (1933; reprint, Albany, N. Y., 1983) provides extensive summaries of the thought of Ramdas and most of the Vārkarī poet saints.

Madhukar Shripad Mate's *Temples and Legends of Maharashtra* (Bombay, 1962) describes several of the most important pilgrimage temples of Maharashtra; and thousands of pilgrimage festivals are listed in *Fairs and Festivals in Maharashtra,* vol. 10 of *Census of India, 1961,* part 7B (Bombay, 1969). Günther-Dietz Sontheimer's *Pastoral Dieties in Western India,* translated from the German by Anne Feldhaus (New York, 1989), is a richly detailed study of the religious traditions of Maharashtrian pastoralists, including myths of Birobā, Mhaskobā, and Khaṅḍobā. John M. Stanley analyzes the meaning of a Khaṅḍobā festival in "Special Time, Special Power," *Journal of Asian Studies* 37 (1977): 37–48. Anne Feldhaus's *Water and Womanhood: Religious Meanings of Rivers in Maharashtra* (New York, 1995) is based on extensive fieldwork in the state. Two older works containing a wealth of information on Maharashtrian folklore are R. E. Enthoven's *The Folklore of Bombay* (London, 1924) and John Abbott's *The Keys of Power: A Study of Indian Ritual and Belief* (1932; reprint, Secaucus, N. J., 1974).

For developments in the modern period, see Matthew Lederle's *Philosophical Trends in Modern Maharastra* (Bombay, 1976), which provides a good survey of the major religious-philosophical thinkers. Eleanor Zelliot's *From Untouchable to Dalit: Essays on the Ambedkar Movement* (3d edition, New Delhi, 2001) provides material on the Buddhist conversion. *The Experience of Hinduism: Essays on Religion in Maharashtra,* edited by Eleanor Zelliot and Maxine Berntsen (Albany, N. Y., 1988) contains essays on contemporary religion, including V. M. Sirsikar on "My Years in the R.S.S.," and the last *kīrtan* of the reformer-saint Gadge Maharaj.

ELEANOR ZELLIOT (1987 AND 2005)
ANNE FELDHAUS (1987 AND 2005)

MARCION (d. 160?), founder of an independent Christian church in the second century and influential exponent of the idea that God's sole attribute is goodness. Marcion was born toward the end of the first century in Sinope, a city in Pontus, on the southern coast of the Black Sea. A shipowner by profession and a man of wealth, he was a member of the Christian church in his home city (where, according to some sources, his father was bishop), but he left there after being ejected by the church. He lived for a time in western Asia Minor but again left because his ideas found little acceptance. In Rome he became a member of that city's more cosmopolitan congregation, presenting it with the large gift of 200,000 sesterces, and came under the influence of Cerdo, a Christian teacher from Asia. As his ideas became more clearly defined, he ran into conflict with the leaders of the church in Rome, and in 144 he founded his own church (his money was returned), which spread rapidly throughout the Roman Empire and came to rival the Catholic Church. By the end of the century, there were Marcionite congregations in cities throughout the Roman world, and writers in Greek (Justin Martyr), Latin (Tertullian), and Syriac (Bardesanes, or Bardaisan) were refuting his views.

Both because of his success in establishing an organization parallel to the "great" church, with its own bishops, elders, catechumens, liturgy, and canon of holy scripture, and his radical conception of God as love, Marcion is a significant figure in early Christian history. He taught that Christianity has no relation to the Judaism from which it sprang, he rejected the Hebrew scriptures in their entirety, and he abbreviated the New Testament to conform to his teaching. He believed that the God of Jesus Christ has nothing to do with, and is superior to, the God of the Hebrew scriptures who created the world, and he believed that Jesus came to reveal an utterly new and strange God, who is of pure goodness and mercy and without wrath or judgment. Marcion claimed to have learned this message from the apostle Paul, who, he believed, was alone among the early Christian leaders in understanding the revelation in Christ. While most Christians saw continuity between the covenant with Israel and the new covenant initiated under Jesus, Marcion saw only contradiction and opposition, and by a selective reading of the scriptures he sought to restore and repristinate the original and authentic faith that had been obscured by Christian teachers. He did not, however, make any claims for himself, either as a prophet or as a holy man. He saw himself as a teacher and a man of learning who pointed beyond himself to the teachings of Jesus and Paul.

Like other Christian thinkers from this period whose views were not accepted by the growing consensus, Marcion has gone down in history as a "heretic," but this epithet should not obscure his importance. At a time when questions such as the relation of Christianity to Judaism, the place of the Hebrew scriptures (Christian Old Testament) in Christian life and thinking, the proper method for interpreting scripture (especially passages that describe God as capricious, despotic, or vindictive), and indeed the very terms in which the Christian faith would be expressed, were matters of intense dispute, Marcion provided clear and unequivocal answers. He also emphasized a central element in Christianity, the boundless grace of God, a point that was lost on his critics. Marcion repudiated all attempts to see Christ as the fulfillment of ancient prophecy. Christ is wholly unique and must be set apart from everything, that is, from Judaism, the created world, and the God who made the world.

His critics classified him among the Gnostics, but he does not fit easily into this classification. On certain points—his contrast between the creator God and the high God who is the father of Jesus, his depreciation of the world, his dualism, his docetic Christology (his view that Christ did not have a real human body), and his rejection of the Old Testament—there were affinities with Gnosticism, perhaps through the influence of Cerdo and others he met at Rome. But Marcion had little sympathy for the speculative systems of the Gnostic teachers: he did not think that salvation comes through *gnōsis* ("knowledge"), and he had a different anthropology (there is no "spark of light" in human beings; they are wholly the work of the creator God) and a different view of redemption.

Marcion was the first Christian to put together a collection of books (a canon) as a standard for Christian life and teaching. His canon of the New Testament, in contrast to the generally accepted Christian collection of twenty-seven books, comprised an edited version of the gospel of Luke (omitting such parts as the infancy narratives, genealogy, baptism, and temptation) and ten epistles of Paul (not including *1 Timothy*, *2 Timothy*, and *Titus*) with the references to God as judge and passages dealing with punishment or the fulfillment of Jewish prophecy edited out. His effort to provide an original and authentic witness to the gospel was a powerful impetus toward the adoption of an approved list of books by the Catholic Church. Marcion also figures in the history of textual criticism of the New Testament, although recent scholarship has tended to see his work less as that of an independent witness and more as a testimony to one branch of the textual tradition.

Marcion wrote one book, *Antitheses*, which is known only through fragments and allusions in the writings of his critics. It consisted of a series of contradictory statements setting forth opposition between the creator God of the Old Testament and the good and benevolent God of Jesus, between the Jewish law and the Christian gospel. Though designed as a polemical and theological work, it assumed a creedlike status as a confession of faith within the Marcionite congregations and served as a key for interpreting the scriptures.

Besides taking an active part in the formation of the biblical canon, Marcion indirectly forced Christian thinkers of the second and third centuries to clarify their ideas on the relation between the Old Testament and the New Testament and led them to affirm that the Hebrew scriptures were not to be discarded by the church. In modern times, largely through the historical and theological interpretation of the nineteenth-century German church historian Adolf von Harnack, there has been renewed interest in Marcion as an original Christian thinker with an alternative vision of the Christian faith; his admirers have included figures as diverse as the Marxist Ernst Bloch and the historian Arnold Toynbee.

BIBLIOGRAPHY

Aland, Barbara. "Marcion: Versuch einer neuen Interpretation," *Zeitschrift für Theologie und Kirche* 70 (1973): 420–447.

Blackman, Edwin C. *Marcion and His Influence.* London, 1948.

Harnack, Adolf von. *Marcion: Das Evangelium vom fremden Gott; Eine Monographie zur Geschichte der Grundlegung der katholischen Kirche.* Leipzig, 1921. A fundamental study, with a collection of the most important texts.

Hoffman, R. Joseph. *Marcion and the Restitution of Christianity.* Chico, Calif., 1984.

ROBERT L. WILKEN (1987)

MARCIONISM. The movement known as Marcionism was founded in the second century by Marcion, an early Christian teacher from Sinope in Asia Minor. Of the many early Christian sects the Marcionites were among the most successful, creating a parallel organization to the Catholic Church. The Marcionite church existed in recognizable form for over three hundred years, until the middle of the fifth century. The oldest inscription from any Christian church building is from a Marcionite church in a small village south of Damascus. The inscription, in Greek, identifies the building as the "gathering place [*synagoge*] of the Marcionites of the village of Lebabon of the Lord and Savior Jesus Christ under the leadership of Paul the presbyter" and is dated 318–319. This inscription is evidence not only of the continuation of the Marcionite movement into the fourth century, but of the benefit it received from the toleration extended to the Catholic Church. The use of the word *Marcionite,* a term of opprobrium to other Christians, shows the veneration in which the founder was held.

Marcion broke with the Catholic Church in Rome in 144. By the end of the second century, Marcionite churches could be found in cities throughout the Roman Empire. The central elements of Marcionism are rejection of the Old Testament (the Hebrew scriptures) and the creator God portrayed there; belief in a strange God who has nothing to do with the world and who is revealed in Jesus Christ; acceptance of Marcion's Bible, a pared-down version of the New Testament comprising an edited text of the gospel of Luke and ten epistles of Paul; and acceptance of Marcion's own work, *Antitheses,* used as a key to the interpretation of the scriptures. The Marcionites followed a strict ascetic life that forbade marriage and encouraged the avoidance of wine and meat (but allowed fish). Perforce the movement spread through the winning of new converts, not by birth, and yet was extraordinarily successful.

Marcionism developed its own brand of orthodoxy, but under Apelles, a disciple who eventually broke with his master, there was an effort to modify Marcion's dualism and to trace all things back to a single principle. Apelles also taught that Christ had a real body though he did not undergo a human birth. Over the centuries, however, the main ideas of the group remained remarkably durable.

Evidence of the survival of Marcionism can be found from the third, fourth, and fifth centuries in all parts of the Roman world: Asia Minor, Crete, western and eastern Syria, Palestine, Alexandria, Carthage, and Rome. To untutored Christians its churches could hardly be distinguished from the Catholic Church, so similar were they in organization and ritual. To bishops and theologians, however, Marcionism was a deadly foe, and a series of key thinkers opposed it vigorously. It is mentioned by such diverse writers as Irenaeus, Tertullian, Origen, Cyril of Jerusalem, Basil of Caesarea, Epiphanius of Cyprus, Adamantius, Bardesanes (Bardaisan), Theodore of Mopsuestia, and Theodoret of Cyrrhus. A fourth-century creed from Laodicea, a city on the Syrian coast, confesses "one God, ruler, God of the law and the gospel," suggesting that the framers thought it necessary to separate Catholic Christianity from Marcionism. As late as the fifth century some villages in Syria were predominantly Marcionite. After that time little is known about the movement.

BIBLIOGRAPHY

Blackman, Edwin C. *Marcion and His Influence.* London, 1948.

Harnack, Adolf von. *Marcion: Das Evangelium vom fremden Gott; Eine Monographie zur Geschichte der Grundlegung der katholischen Kirche.* Leipzig, 1921.

ROBERT L. WILKEN (1987)

MARDUK (also known as Bel, "lord") was a god of the city of Babylon who rose from being an obscure god of the Sumerian pantheon to become head of the Babylonian pantheon by the first millennium BCE. The name was probably pronounced *Marutuk,* which possibly had the short form *Marduk.* Etymologically it is probably derived from *amar-Utu* ("bull calf of the sun god Utu"). This name may not be genealogically accurate, since Marduk was normally considered to be the son of Enki, the god of underground fresh waters. It may reflect an earlier genealogy, or may have had a political origin, in which case it would indicate that the city of Babylon was in the cultural orbit of the more important city of Sippar (whose god was Utu, the sun god) in the Early Dynastic times (early third millennium BCE). Marduk was probably already the god of Babylon in this early period, but he first became a great god with the rise of Babylon as capital of the Old Babylonian kingdom under Hammurabi in the eighteenth century BCE. The kings of the Old Babylonian dynasty owed special allegiance to Marduk as god of Babylon, and he became in effect the royal god.

Marduk continued to rise in popularity after the decline of the Old Babylonian period. When his (captured) cult statue was returned to Babylon during the reign of Nebuchadrezzar I in the twelfth century BCE, Marduk was officially recognized as head of the Babylonian pantheon. His rise was effected in theological terms through his identification with Asarluhi, the god of the minor southern city of Kuaru, who was closely associated with Enki and was considered his first-born son. The process of identifying Marduk and Asarluhi began before the establishment of the Old Babylonian kingdom, for it is attested in a letter-prayer of King Siniddinam of Larsa in which Asarluhi is called "god of Babylon." Marduk became known as the firstborn of Enki, and he took Asarluhi's place as Enki's assistant/partner in the magical literature. The identification of Marduk with Asarluhi was eventually so thorough that Asarluhi ceased to be remembered as an originally distinct god, and the name "Asarluhi" was simply used as the name for Marduk, both in Akkadian literature and in the Sumerian portion of bilingual Sumerian-Akkadian literature (where Marduk appears in the parallel Akkadian line).

The ultimate rise of Marduk to become king of the Babylonian pantheon is described in *Enuma elish,* the most important mythological work in which Marduk appears. This lengthy myth was written in the second half of the second millennium, probably circa 1200 BCE. It declares its main purpose to be the exaltation of the god Marduk. *Enuma elish* was a state myth, and it was read aloud to the assembled populace as part of the Akitu festival, the spring New Year celebration, in the first millennium BCE.

Marduk's political fortunes are also mythologized in an esoteric text called the *Tribulations of Marduk* or the *Ordeal of Marduk.* Although it was originally understood to be a tale of a dying and resurrected god, there is no basis for this interpretation and no evidence at all that Marduk was a vegetation-type dying god. The text is cast in the form of an esoteric cultic commentary, possibly of events of the New Year ritual. Unlike other extant esoteric commentaries, this one was written for wide distribution. It relates cultic elements of the ritual to the misfortunes of Marduk, who has been captured, sentenced, and imprisoned by other gods; at the time of the text someone is interceding on behalf of Marduk, and there is a hint in the text that Marduk is or is about to be freed. The text is manifestly political, with the enmity between Ashur and Marduk alluding to that between Assyria and Babylonia. There may also be an allusion to the return of the statue of Marduk in 669 BCE from the "Assyrian captivity" it had remained in since Sennacherib's destruction of the temple of Marduk twenty years earlier. The celebration of the statue's return as a vindication of Marduk may be analogous to the composition of *Enuma elish* on the occasion of an earlier return of the god's statue.

Marduk is prominent in the magical literature, particularly in the Marduk-Ea (originally, Asarluhi-Enki) type of incantation. In these texts, a problem situation (such as illness) is described. Asarluhi (Marduk) relates the problem to Enki (Ea), who responds with a formulaic "My son, what do I know that you do not know, to your knowledge what can I add?" Enki then spells out a ritual to be followed to alleviate the problem. Here Asarluhi-Marduk is seen as almost the overseer of humanity. This involvement with humanity is also underscored in *Shurpu,* a ritual text used to relieve the distress of someone suffering for a sin of which he has no knowledge; in it Marduk is addressed as the god who is able to preserve and restore his worshipers. Marduk was considered a powerful and fierce god who punished sinners but who at the same time could be merciful and pardon his followers. In this judgmental role he is the subject of several literary prayers and of *Ludlul bel ne-meqi* ("I will praise the wise lord"), sometimes called "the Babylonian *Job,*" a wisdom work about a righteous sufferer whose fortunes declined abysmally but who was ultimately restored by Marduk.

SEE ALSO Akitu; Dying and Rising Gods; Enuma Elish; Mesopotamian Religions, overview article.

BIBLIOGRAPHY

Frymer-Kensky, Tikva. "The Tribulations of Marduk: The So-Called 'Marduk Ordeal Text.'" *Journal of the American Oriental Society* 103 (January–March 1983): 131–141.

Lambert, W. G. "Three Literary Prayers of the Babylonians." *Archiv für Orientforschung* 19 (1959–1960): 47–66.

Lambert, W. G. *Babylonian Wisdom Literature.* Oxford, 1960. See pages 21–62.

Lambert, W. G. "The Reign of Nebuchadnezzar I." In *The Seed of Wisdom: Essays in Honor of Theophile James Meek,* edited by W. S. McCullough, pp. 3–13. Toronto, 1964.

Lambert, W. G. "Studies in Marduk." *Bulletin of the School of Oriental and African Studies* 47 (1984): 1–9.

Soden, Wolfram von. "Gibt es ein Zeugnis defür, dass die Babylonier an die Wiederauferstehung Marduks geglaubt haben?" *Zeitschrift für Assyriologie* 51 (May 1955): 130–166.

Sommerfeld, Walter. *Der Aufstieg Marduks: Die Stellung Marduks in der babylonischen Religion des zweiten Jahrtausends v. Chr.* "Alter Orient und Altes Testament," vol. 213. Neukirchen-Vluyn, 1982.

New Sources

Black, Jeremy A. *Gods, Demons and Symbols of Ancient Mesopotamia.* Austin, 1992.

Bottéro, Jean. *Mesopotamia: Writing, Reasoning, and the Gods.* Chicago, 1995.

Bottéro, Jean. *Religion in Ancient Mesopotamia.* Chicago, 2001.

Greenspahn, Frederick E. *Essential Papers on Israel and the Ancient Near East.* New York, 1991.

Janzen, J. Gerald. "On the Moral Nature of God's Power: Yahweh and the Sea in Job and Deutero-Isaiah." *Catholic Bible Quarterly* 56 (July 1994): 458–479.

TIKVA FRYMER-KENSKY (1987)
Revised Bibliography

MARDU RELIGION.

The name *Mardu* refers collectively to Aborigines belonging to a number of language-named groups in Western Australia, principally the Kartujarra, Manyjilyjarra, and Warnman. Their traditional homelands lie in the vicinity of Lake Disappointment, a huge salt lake in the Gibson Desert, between 22° to 25° south latitude and 122° to 126° east longitude. It is impossible to estimate accurately the population of these groups prior to contact with Europeans, but today they number about 1,600. Many of them live in incorporated communities, run by elected Aboriginal councillors, at Jigalong, Parnngurr and Punmu, and in towns such as Newman, Nullagine, Marble Bar and Port Hedland. The Mardu speak mutually intelligible dialects of the Western Desert language, which covers one-sixth of the continent.

Since the mid-1960s, when the last groups of previously uncontacted desert people moved into settlements, there have been no fully nomadic hunter-gatherers living beyond the range of white Australian cultural influences. In the Western Desert region, their migration into settlements was gradual, beginning around the late 1800s. Some of the small, scattered bands that had exploited large overlapping tracts in their arid homelands began making contact with Europeans living at outposts on the pastoral frontier. Since then, their sedentarisation and increasing involvement with whites has wrought many changes: today they wear clothes, live in houses, watch television, shop in supermarkets, and so on, and continue to battle with the pernicious consequences of colonization, including high rates of unemployment, "life-style" diseases such as diabetes, kidney failure, and problems arising from alcohol misuse. Yet the Mardu retain strong continuities with their past in major beliefs and behaviors pertaining to kinship, religion, and values. Much of their rich religious life has been maintained into the present, because religion was absolutely fundamental to their culture. It is tenaciously maintained, albeit in a progressively more attenuated form, and still underpins Mardu worldview. Some Mardu have become Christians, but usually as a complement to, rather than a replacement for, the traditional religion.

It is important to stress that, despite the use of the present tense, this account refers to a past era, prior to and following initial contacts with the invading Europeans. It is, however, constructed on the basis of direct observation and interviews occurring during field research since 1963. Over this period, this author has observed many changes, and although the religious life has become less vigorous, it remains highly significant in the lives of most Mardu.

THE SPIRITUAL IMPERATIVE. Traditional Australian Aboriginal cultures are notable for the striking contrast they exhibit between comparatively simple material technologies and social and religious forms that reveal great richness and complexity. Clear proof of the adaptational skills of the Aborigines can be seen in their success in colonizing all of a continent that is almost three-quarters arid. Yet to appreciate fully their cultural accomplishments it is vital to understand how completely religion pervades their lives. The Aborigines base their existence firmly in the belief that spiritual beings are the sources and controllers of all power. As they understand it, spiritual power flows freely into the human realm as long as they act out their lives in accordance with the grand design originally laid out by their spiritual forefathers in the world-creating era. Aborigines learn obedience to the dictates of a heritage that, while transmitted by their ancestors, is nonetheless believed to have its origins in spiritual, not human, actions. Since all knowledge and power are said to derive from the spiritual realm, the Aborigines in effect deny the human innovatory component in their culture. They understand history in cosmic rather than chronological terms, and they grant primacy to spiritual conceptions of cause, being, and purpose. This certainly does not mean that people are denied their individuality, but simply that creativity is not admissible as part of the measure of a person's social worth. In the Aboriginal view, human worth is based on conformity to the founding design and on its perpetuation, which ensures that power will continue to flow from the spiritual realm and thus maintain the fertility of all life forms.

At the heart of Aboriginal religion is the Dreaming, a complex concept that embodies a creative era long past but also implicates the present and the future. During the Dreaming powerful ancestral beings, singly or in groups, are believed to have transformed the face of Australia in the course of their wanderings and creative activities. They hunted and gathered in much the same way as their human descendants, but much of their behavior was on a grander scale and sometimes more excessive than that permitted the first people they left behind as pioneers of human society. Aborigines point to a host of topographical features as undeniable proof of the Dreaming's reality. The eternal verities of the Dreaming are also encoded in mythology, rituals, songs, and objects, and all relate back to the land, the bedrock of metaphysical conceptions that formulate an indivisible unity of spirit and substance.

When their earthly wanderings ended, the creative beings "died," and they metamorphosed into landforms or celestial bodies, where their spiritual essence remains, withdrawn from, but watchful of, human affairs. The creative beings release enabling power into the human realm in response not to prayer or sacrifice, which have no place in Aboriginal religion, but to ritual performance. Individuals who are able to transcend their human consciousness for brief periods (during dreams, dances, visions, or heightened emotional states) may also bring about a release of power. The withdrawn creative ancestors use spirit beings as intermediaries for direct intervention in human affairs, most often while people are sleeping, and such encounters result in the transference of new knowledge and power from the spiritual realm. To maintain the unity they perceive in their cosmic order, the Mardu must, as their spiritual imperative demands of them, perform rituals regularly and in the proper manner, and they must also obey the dictates of the life design that is the legacy of the Dreaming.

THE TOTEMIC CONNECTION. The Mardu see themselves as quite distinct from the natural world because of their culture and their ritual control over all fertility, yet they acknowledge their intimate relationship with it. Totemic beliefs express and affirm this link, by positing a unity between individuals or groups and elements of the natural world. To the Mardu, the animals, birds, plants, or minerals that are identified as totems are signs or exemplifiers of the link between humans and nature, so their religious significance lies not in the particular identity of the totem, but in the linkage it represents. There are totemic connections linking Mardu *groups* to natural species, but these are much less significant than the ways in which totemism connects *individuals* to their spiritual origins. These ascribed affiliations are experienced as enduring and unbreakable bonds uniting every individual to the great powers of the Dreaming. The two most important forms of individual totemism, which are closely related in Mardu thought, can most aptly be termed "ancestral" and "conception." Wherever creative beings traveled during the Dreaming, they left behind inexhaustible supplies of life essence or power from which tiny spirit-children emanate. Thus a person's ancestral totem derives from whichever creative being or group of beings "left him or her behind." The totem is identified by linking the area or site where an individual was conceived with knowledge regarding the particular creative beings known to have traveled through or lived there during the Dreaming. Before entering its human mother, the spirit-child disguises itself in some plant, animal, or mineral form, which, when recognized by the parents, becomes the child's conception totem. People may share the same object or species as a totem, but never exactly the same set of circumstances or events that mark their "coming into being." So, in combination, these two forms of totemic affiliation not only enable everyone to establish his or her descent from the marvels of the Dreaming epoch but also provide each individual with a unique facet of social identity. The medium of the totem itself is less important culturally than the message of a personalized link between the individual and the associated spirit-child and Dreaming event.

LIFE CYCLE AND MALE INITIATION. The Mardu do not possess reincarnation beliefs, but they view life as cyclical in that it begins and ends with a spirit or soul that is indestructible. The life crises of birth, menarche, and marriage are not ritualized. A young woman's change of status to wife and mother is unheralded, and involves an essential continuity in activities, for she is already an accomplished food provider. Males, by comparison, undergo a protracted and richly detailed initiation into social adulthood and are not permitted to marry until they have passed through a long series of named initiatory stages. They learn to endure physical operations, to obey their elders, to observe strict taboos, to hunt meat for the older men in payment for ritual knowledge, and to assist in the supervision and care of younger novices.

At about age sixteen, after they have undergone minor rites involving tooth evulsion and the piercing of the nasal septum, youths are circumcised amid a great deal of ceremonial that is modeled symbolically on death and rebirth. The large ceremonies that conclude several months of preparation focus the energy and attention of the community on the several novices who are circumcised together. Within a year full manhood will be attained via subincision, an operation in which the ventral surface of the penis is slit open. Of the initiatory stages that follow, the most important is the Mirdayidi, a ceremonial feast held at the site of a group's secret cache of sacred objects, which are then revealed to the novice for the first time. After his introduction to the spiritual roots of his own being, a young man must subsequently go through the same ritual in neighboring territories and thus gain formal admission to the natural resources and ritual activities in those areas. The final initiatory stages entail the cutting and carving of sacred objects symbolizing the novice's links to his home territory, its creative beings, and the Dreaming. This stage completed, a man is entitled to claim his betrothed in marriage. Throughout the rest of his life he continues to acquire more knowledge through participation in rituals, and by middle age he is referred to as a *nindibuga* ("knowledgeable one"). With old age comes increased wisdom, respect, and a less physically active role in ritual life.

WOMEN'S ROLE IN THE RELIGIOUS LIFE. Men control the secret and sacred core of the religion and the major rituals whose performance is considered by all Mardu to be essential to the future of their society. Women do not dispute men's dominance of the religious life. They, too, are actively involved in many aspects of it, and have their own secret-sacred rituals and associated objects, but they devote much less time to religious activities than men do and must arrange their activities to fit in with the plans of the men, not vice versa. Women collect the bulk of the food supply and maintain the life of the camp while men are engaged in religious activity, but they are also active participants in many rituals that are held in the camping area. In a passive sense, too, women and children provide a vital baseline or antithesis for men's division of life into dangerous-exclusive and mundane-inclusive dimensions. The conviction of mature men that only they have the knowledge to control powerful and dangerous spiritual forces invests their religious life with much of its tension and excitement.

MYTHOLOGY AND SONG SEQUENCE. Mardu learn much about their spiritual heritage and about the Dreaming from a rich mythology, which relates how things came to be as they are and outlines the memorable events of the Dreaming era. Long narrative myths chronicle the travels of the creative beings, following the paths they took and dwelling on the naming of places, but details of their secret-sacred doings are known only to initiated men. Together with song sequences and, in many cases, rituals, these narratives broaden people's horizons by providing vivid mental and "historical" maps of areas that may as yet be unseen, so that when people do visit such places for the first time they already "know" them in a religious sense. There are times and situations that are conducive to the telling of myths, even when this is an informal affair: for example, when children have the spiritual significance of landforms explained to them, or when initiates view secret-sacred objects for the first time and have extra details added to the version of the myth they already know.

All major rituals have an associated sequence of songs, which follows the movement of the creative beings concerned and highlights in cryptic fashion the more notable events of the Dreaming. Rote learning of the hundreds of songs in a given sequence is made easier by the brevity of each song, which consists only of a few words, and by repetition (each is sung several times). There is great variation in pitch, tempo, and loudness, and the singing often generates great excitement among performers and audience alike. In some public rituals women and children join in the singing and sometimes dance. The song sequence and myth associated with a given ritual are often very similar in theme, but the song sequence is not a mnemonic for the myth such that it would be possible to reconstruct the myth from the songs.

RITUAL. Mardu group rituals are culturally more important than individual rites, but both have the same aim: to induce the flow of power from the spiritual realm for human benefit. The manipulative aspects of ritual as communication are most evident in individual rites, most of which are publicly performed and socially approved. However, some individuals and groups are believed to practice sorcery, which is invoked at times as an explanation for serious illness or sudden death. Most individual ritual acts are spontaneous, as when magic is used to make a strong wind abate or to beckon a rain-bearing cloud. Although any adult with the requisite knowledge can perform such acts, they are most often the task of diviner-curers (*mabarn*), who are said to possess stronger psychic and magical powers than others. These part-time specialists use their diagnostic and curative skills for the benefit of sick individuals and the community at large.

One vitally important ritual that involves relatively few actors is the "increase" rite. This generally simple and brief rite is performed annually at particular sites, scattered throughout the Western Desert, that are the spirit homes of many different plants and animals. The purpose of the increase rite is to summon the spirits concerned to emerge, scatter, and be plentiful. There is at least one such site within the home area of every local group, so the Mardu and their neighbors are mutually dependent in ensuring through ritual the continued supply of food resources.

The major focus of group rituals is the *japal* ("big meeting"), a large assembly of bands from a wide area, who meet perhaps once or twice a year at a prearranged site when food and water resources permit. These gatherings mark the high points of the Mardu social calendar, when much activity is crammed into a short space of time in an atmosphere of excitement and intensified sociality. Besides their vitally important religious functions, Big Meetings provide an occasion for settling major disputes, arranging marriages, gift exchanges, and disseminating a large amount of information and gossip. Initiatory rituals usually form the major focus of religious activity, but many other ceremonies are held as well, and the exchange of religious lore is a major item of business. Initially there is an important division between hosts and visitors, but this soon dissolves in favor of kinship considerations in the conduct of the affairs at hand. The timing and coordination of large numbers of people and a complex division of labor demand planning and direction. An informal gathering of mature men directs the meeting, and the host group is most active in master-of-ceremonies roles. There is much discussion and consultation between the sexes and among the groups present. Ritual leadership is situational and changes as the rituals performed change. Ritual activities usually alternate between the camp area and secret bush grounds that are tabooed to women and children. Singing and dancing sometimes continue day and night.

Both men and women attain senior ritual status by repeated participation in the religious life over a period of many years and by diligent performance of their allotted tasks. The men with the highest status are generally elderly; they prepare food for ceremonial feasts, advise and direct rituals, dance the major secret-sacred dances, and caretake the caches of sacred objects. Next in the hierarchy are the active middle-aged men, who manage the ritual activity, transmit directives from those above them, and perform many important dances. Below them are the legmen, who play major roles as hunters and as supervisors of novices. At the lowest level are the partly initiated young male novices, who must obey all instructions, look on in silence, and learn.

Group rituals may be organized, too, when enough bands are assembled to provide the needed personnel. The death of anyone older than an infant is an occasion for ritual, which is performed by members of bands that are in the vicinity at the time, and the reburial of the bones, which occurs a year or two later, is the more significant ritual event.

The Mardu have two major ritual categories: *manganyjanu*, said to have been passed down from the Dreaming; and *bardunjarijanu* ("from the dream spirit"), which have been revealed to humans during their dreams. The Dreaming rituals predominate, but it is highly likely that they were originally of the second type, wherein spirit-being intermediaries of the creative beings encounter humans during dreams and reveal ritual information. Men share these revelations with others, who then have similar dream experiences and add details concerning the necessary body decorations, song lyrics and tunes, and dances. When a new ritual comes into being, the old one is passed on to other groups and, with the passage of time and over great distances, becomes identified as a Dreaming ritual. The great appeal of the dream-spirit ritual is that it requires no special ground and can be staged with a minimum of preparation by small groups. Women and children join in the singing and a little of the dancing, and are excluded from only a small part of the proceedings. Although its secret-sacred element is not large, dream-spirit ritual is taken just as seriously by the men as are the important Dreaming rituals.

The Mardu identify some of their rituals in terms of a specific, primary purpose, such as rainmaking or increase of species, but all their rituals fulfill very important functions in the culture. As acts of communication and commemoration, rituals maintain the relevance of the Dreaming in the present. They are educational because novices are invariably involved, and they are beneficial because participants acquire strength and protection against malevolent powers through contact with the spiritual realm. To be effective, rituals require the harmonious unity of participants and the complete absence of conflict. In the Western Desert, group rituals override many other kinds of allegiances and thus serve to dilute rather than reinforce any tendencies toward local parochialism. The widely shared major rituals, in particular, force people's attention outward to regional concerns and wider bonds of interdependence, in which survival in this extremely harsh land is ultimately grounded.

Sites and Portable Objects. Particular landforms and a variety of portable objects provide tangible reminders of the reality and power of the Dreaming. The sites created in the epoch of the Dreaming elicit powerful emotions of belonging that anchor a people to their home territory. Portable objects derive sacredness and power from their believed origins in, or close association with, the Dreaming. The most sacred are stones said to be the metamorphosed parts of the bodies of ancestral beings and wooden boards that men carve in representation of similar power-laden objects that were carried by the creative beings. In addition to these highly valued group-owned objects are those that are individually owned. Each man has a bundle of secret and nonsecret paraphernalia; these are often items of gift exchange and are frequently displayed and discussed when groups of men meet informally.

Conclusion. The genius in Mardu religion resides in its successful accommodation of two strongly contradictory elements: the everyday reality of an inherently dynamic culture and a dominant ideology that stresses continuity and changelessness. This ideology is founded in the concept of the Dreaming, which ordained a life design that is held to be fixed and immutable, so as to assure (prior to the European invasion, that is) the continuity of present and future with the founding past. Throughout the desert there is a continual diffusion and circulation of religious lore, and Aborigines are regularly engaged in the creation, acquisition, performance, and transmission of their religion. How, then, can the Mardu accommodate the undeniable facts of change in an ideological framework that entertains no notion of progress or evolution?

A close examination of the structure of their rituals provides an important clue. Each "new" ritual is in fact a unique recombination of already existing constituent elements rather than a structure fabricated from hitherto unknown components. The assimilation of incoming rituals is made easy because they contain so much that is already familiar. In their long history of isolation from the rest of the world, Aborigines were spared the trauma of confronting radically different or alien cultural forms. Thus the kinds of change and innovation they have encountered are those which "fit the forms of permanence," as W. E. H. Stanner so aptly put it in his seminal work *On Aboriginal Religion* (1968, p. 168).

Not all the knowledge derivable from the Dreaming is embodied in the life-design legacy that the Mardu faithfully perpetuate. Further knowledge and power are available to the living through the mediating activities of spirit beings, which link the spiritual and human realms. How, then, can newly acquired knowledge undergo transformation from peripheral, individually experienced phenomena into communally shared and supposedly timeless structures of the religious life? One example of this process was provided above, in the brief description of the creation of dream-spirit rituals from what initially are highly individual experiences. But once in existence, both ritual structures and song sequences become highly circumscribed in performance, and the necessity for faithful reproduction precludes them from becoming common avenues for the incorporation of new religious knowledge that is individually acquired. Mythology, on the other hand, has an inherent flexibility that makes it an ideal vehicle for incorporative purposes. In the easy and informal atmosphere of myth telling, people are free to indulge in elaboration and character development while leaving intact the main story line and theme. But myths also lend themselves readily to expansion to accommodate new information flowing from dream revelations and the discovery of hitherto unlocated sacred objects. Once new knowledge is embedded within existing myths, the Aborigines may examine the associated song sequence, if one exists, and reinterpret the meaning of the cryptic references therein, so as to accord with the truths of the expanded myth. In this way, and in the absence of the written word, changing political, social, and religious realities are validated and absorbed effortlessly into the ahistorical, cosmological flow of time. Thus is the "is-now" transformed into the "ever-was" of the Dreaming.

See Also Australian Indigenous Religions, overview article; Dreaming, The.

Bibliography

Two monographs that deal with the past and present of Mardu religion are my own *The Jigalong Mob: Aboriginal Victors of the Desert Crusade* (Menlo Park, Calif., 1974) and *The Mardu Aborigines: Living the Dream in Australia's Desert* (revised and enlarged 2d ed., Fort Worth, 1991). Aspects of Western Desert religion are discussed in Ronald M. Berndt's *Australian Aboriginal Religion,* 4 vols. (Leiden, 1974), in Ronald M. Berndt and Catherine H. Berndt's *The World of the First Australians,* 2d ed. (Canberra, 1988), and in an early monograph by the same authors, *A Preliminary Account of Field Work in the Ooldea Region, Western South Australia* (Sydney, 1945). A book by noted ethno-archaeologist Richard A. Gould, *Yiwara: Foragers of the Australian Desert* (New York, 1969), contains details concerning desert ritual and belief.

Robert Tonkinson (1987 and 2005)

MARETT, R. R. (1866–1943), British philosopher and anthropologist, who introduced the theory of preanimism and the term *animatism* into the scholarly debate. Robert Ranulph Marett was born on the Channel Island of Jersey on June 13, 1866. He was educated at Balliol College, Oxford, specializing in the classics, philosophy, and ethics, and in 1891 he was elected fellow of Exeter College, Oxford, where he remained for the whole of his academic career. His anthropological interests were fired by reading his fellow-Oxonian Andrew Lang's book *Custom and Myth* (1884) and after 1893 by association with E. B. Tylor (1832–1917), whose friend and disciple he became. In 1893 he submitted a prize essay titled "The Ethics of Savage Races," which was examined by Tylor. Despite the difference in their ages, a close friendship began, and as Tylor's powers began to wane, Marett became his assistant. Marett later wrote a bibliographical memoir, *Tylor* (1936).

On Tylor's retirement, Marett was appointed in 1910 reader in social anthropology at Oxford, a post which he held until 1936, when he was succeeded by A. R. Radcliffe-Brown. For some years he was also rector (i.e., president) of Exeter College. He traveled widely in Europe, visited Australia once, in 1914, and in 1930 delivered the Lowell Lectures in Boston. He was Gifford Lecturer at the University of Saint Andrews twice, in 1931–1932 and 1932–1933, and the two published volumes of these lectures, *Faith, Hope and Charity in Primitive Religion* (1932) and *Sacraments of Simple Folk* (1933), Marett believed to embody his best work. He also had an interest in prehistoric archaeology, and he conducted and supervised excavations at the Mousterian site of La Cotte de Saint Brelade on his native island of Jersey. He died on February 18, 1943.

As an anthropological theorist, Marett's reputation was made virtually overnight, by the publication in 1900 of his paper "Preanimistic Religion" (*Folklore*, June 1900), in which he called into question Tylor's theory of "animism" and introduced the terms *preanimism* and *animatism* (which are not synonyms). During the next few years he wrote extensively on this theme, suggesting that *tabu* is best understood as "negative magic" and emphasizing the importance of the Melanesian—actually common Pacific—word *mana* as its positive counterpart. *Mana* he explained most fully in a paper, "The Conception of *Mana*," delivered at the Oxford Science of Religion Congress in 1908, and in an article, "Mana," in Hastings's *Encyclopaedia of Religion and Ethics*, vol. 8 (1915).

Where Marett differed most strikingly from other late Victorian anthropologists in Britain was in his degree of fellow-feeling with and indebtedness to the French sociologists of the *Année sociologique* school. This made him, in effect, the first of the British social anthropologists and gave his later work especially a dimension largely absent from the writings of his predecessors.

Marett's style was always admirably lucid, often being further illuminated by wit and a certain irony. Today he tends to be evaluated chiefly for work done between 1899 and 1910, to the neglect of his more mature writings. He will, however, always have an important place in the history of both anthropology and comparative religion, and he was also highly significant as an advocate of academic anthropology and as a trainer of anthropologists.

See Also Animism and Animatism; Preanimism; Tylor, E. B.

Bibliography

Works by Marett

In addition to works cited in the text, Marett's *Anthropology* (London, 1911) should be consulted, as should *The Threshold of Religion*, 3d ed. (London, 1915), a collection of his important early papers. Included in this collection are "Preanimistic Religion" (1900) and "The Conception of *Mana*" (1908). *A Jerseyman at Oxford* (Oxford, 1941) is Marett's highly informative and entertaining autobiography.

Works about Marett

There is no biography or full critical study, but see *Custom Is King: Essays Presented to R. R. Marett on His Seventieth Birthday*, edited by Leonard Halford Dudley Buxton (London, 1936). This work contains a personal appreciation by the editor and a full bibliography. See also the entry on Marett by John N. Mavrogordato in the *Dictionary of National Biography, 1941–1950* (Oxford, 1959), and the discussion in my book *Comparative Religion: A History* (London, 1975), pp. 65–71.

New Sources

Marett, R. R. *The Early Sociology of Religion: Vol. 7 The Threshold of Religion by R.R. Marrett.* Edited by Bryan Turner. London, 1997.

Eric J. Sharpe (1987)
Revised Bibliography

MARI AND MORDVIN RELIGION.

The Mari and Mordvin languages together form the so-called Volga group within the Finno-Ugric linguistic family. In international literature, the Mari people are better known as the Cheremis (from the Old Russian name *Chermisy*). The Mari republic lies in western Russia in a heavily forested region north of the Volga river. The Mari may be divided into three groups based on their differing environments: the Mountain Mari, the smallest group; the Meadow Mari, the largest group; and the so-called Eastern Mari, which is the youngest group, having developed only in the seventeenth century.

The Mordvins (from the Old Russian name *Mordva*) consist of two related groups, speaking the Erzä and Mokša dialects of the Mordvin language. They differ from each other to such an extent that the speakers of Erzä and Mokša do not understand one another. Two separate literary languages have been formed accordingly. The Mordvin republic, Mordvinia, lies to the east of the Mari homeland in the Russian federation. In addition, there are some separated settlements in the Tatar and Bashkir republics. The population of the Erzä is approximately twice that of the Mokša. The Erzä could also be called Western Mordvins, living on the banks of the Sura River, and the Mokša of the Mokša River could be called Eastern Mordvins.

The Mari and Mordvin languages, with the Balto-Finnic and Saami (Lapp) languages, are believed to stem from a common Volga Finnic protolanguage, spoken from 1500 to 500 BCE. Around the beginning of the common era, Mari and Mordvin started to develop into separate languages. Although they possess a common linguistic background, the Mari and Mordvin cultures have, in the course of centuries, undergone diverse developments under the influence of Tatar and, later, Russian domination. For this reason, the Mari and Mordvins are culturally quite different from each other, particularly in their religious views and activities. There are very few common features in Mari and Mordvin religion, and many differences become manifest in the comparison of their specific cultural groups as well.

SOURCES. The first mention of the Mordvins is in the chronicle of the historian Jordanes (551 CE). He relates that in the fourth century, Ermanarik, the king of the East Goths, subjugated a people called Mordens. Nestor, on the other hand, tells in his eleventh-century chronicle of three peoples living at the Oka River where it meets the Volga: the Cheremis, the Mordvins, and the Muromans, a distinct third group. Giovanni da Pian del Carpini, the papal emissary, wrote in his report of 1245 that the Tatars occupied the domain of the Mordui people, living between Russians and Bulgars. Marco Polo, on the other hand, mentions Mordui as one of the groups under Mongolian power.

The influence of the foreign cultures, beginning with the Tatar hegemony of the medieval period, is evident in Mari and Mordvin religion. The conversion to Christianity began in the middle of the sixteenth century, when the Russians finally overthrew the Tatar khanate of Kazan. The often quite violent mission was strengthened in the seventeenth century, with the result that many features of pre-Christian Mari and Mordvin religion gradually disappeared. Many fieldworkers of the nineteenth and twentieth centuries have, however, been able to report religious beliefs and practices that clearly belong to the autochthonous elements of the Mari and Mordvin cultures.

Our earliest information on Mordvin religion comes from an earlier Italian explorer, G. Barbaro, who visited the district now called Eastern Russia in 1446. He gives an account of the horse sacrifices of the Mokša. In regard to the Mari, some valuable information can be found in the report published by an envoy from Holstein, Adam Olearius (1663), on Mari offering rituals. The sources of the eighteenth century include the accounts by N. Witzen, P. J. Strahlenberg, G. F. Müller, I. Lepeshchin, J. P. Georgi, N. Rytshkov, and P. S. Pallas. A valuable study on Mordvin religion is the Russian manuscript written by a surveyor named Mil'kovich in 1783. In addition to Russian scholars, several Finnish ethnographers, including Albert Hämäläinen, Heikki Paasonen, and Uno Holmberg Harva, have done fieldwork among the Mari and Mordvins in the late nineteenth and early twentieth centuries. Their collections have been published by the Finno-Ugric Society in Helsinki. Uno Holmberg Harva edited the monographs on the religion of the Mari (1914) and Mordvin (1942). Holmberg's study of Finno-Ugric mythology published in volume 4 (1927) of *The Mythology of All Races* is still a classic in its field, a comparative survey of Finno-Ugric worldviews. More recent publications include N. F. Mokshin's work on Mordvin religion (1968) and Thomas A. Sebeok and Frances J. Ingemann's work on Mari religion (1956).

Mari and Mordvin ethnic religions are described here mainly on the basis of the folklore sources of the nineteenth and twentieth centuries. As a result of the Russian socialist revolution, Mari and Mordvin cultures have undergone rapid changes that have had great influence on their religious views (secularization and acculturation).

LIFE AND DEATH. Both the Mari and the Mordvins employ a complex system of soul concepts. The Mordvins describe physical death with such expressions as *"ojm'eze l'iśś"* ("his spirit left") or *"ojm'enze noldaś"* ("he overthrew his spirit"). Various terms for soul denote the life-keeping elements, breathing, or simply "up"; in Mokša languages, *ojm'e* or *vajm'ä*, in Erzä, *arńe*, in Mari, *šüloš*. The life of this kind of soul is related to the length of the life of the individual whose body it inhabits, beginning with the first symptoms of physical life and ending with body's last breath. The soul then leaves the body like warm air or smoke. This kind of soul is linear, living only once with its personal character. The cyclical soul concept, in which the soul lives on after the physical death, in manifest in such words as *tšopatša* (Erzä), *šopatša* (Mokša), and *ört* (Mari). These souls are described as living with the body both in its lifetime in this world and after death in the place where the corpse has been buried. The *ört* may leave the body during a trance or dream or when a person is senseless. After death, the *ört* may appear as a ghost who disturbs relatives or wanders through the home. It is the *ört* that is moved to the land of the dead. The *tšopatša* is conceived of as a kind of personal guardian spirit that is embodied in the shadow or a picture of its carrier. It also lives after the physical death of its corporeal carrier and often takes the form of a soul bird.

Family cult rites associated with death are organized by the dead person's relatives. Life after death was regarded as a direct continuation of earthly life. The departed were believed to live in much the same way as they had upon earth, in log cabins within fenced groves that were called *šugarla* (Mari), *kalmazur* (Erzä), or *kalma-kuža* (Mokša). The articles used by them in life were carefully carried to the cemetery and placed beside their bodies in the grave. In death as in life family and kin remain together, so that the graveyard is simply the counterpart of the village. In this view, there is no realm of the dead in the universal sense. It was thus natural to construct the cabin of the dead in such a way that a window faced home; there also was a hole to allow the *ört* or *tšopatša* to revisit the living members of the family.

Each family worships its own dead. Festivals in honor of a departed individual were celebrated during the first year after death: immediately after burial, six weeks (or the fortieth day) after death, and one year after death. After this last ritual, the deceased was no longer honored as an individual but rather as a member of the collective group of the family dead in ceremonies celebrated annually in accordance with the economic and religious calendar.

Twice a year the Mordvins hold a festival called Pokštšat Babat or At'at Babat ("grandfathers and grandmothers") for all departed ancestors. The ancestors are then requested to participate in a banquet shared between the living and dead members of the family. Formerly, animal sacrifices, often horses, were offered to the departed. Heikki Paasonen points out that this practice may derive from an earlier practice of human sacrifice. He also believes that the worship of some gods *(pas)* is related to the ancestor cult. The Erzä annually worship Staka, a god resembling a Turkic ruler or prince; in addition, the Erzä and Mokša worship a god called Keremet, who is given the title *soltan* ("sultan"), which seems to be a manifestation of a former local hero cult.

UNIVERSE AND NATURE. According to a Mordvin myth recorded by the Russian clergyman Fedor Saverskii in 1853, there were a pair of creators in the beginning of time. God was sitting on a rock in the midst of the huge proto-ocean contemplating the creation of the universe. A devil *(šaitan)* appeared and promised to help him in the act of creation. God asked him to dive into the depth of the ocean and to bring sand from the bottom. After having succeeded in his third attempt, the devil brought the material but hid some of it in his mouth, planning to create his own world. God threw the sand he had been given on the surface of the proto-ocean and it started to grow both there as well as in the devil's mouth, forcing him to empty it. Because of this dualistic conflict, there is evil as well as good in the universe.

The creator god is called Niške-pas or Niške in Mordvin languages, literally meaning "the great procreator." According to Erzä and Mokša folklore, he created heaven and earth, the rising sun, the wandering moon, black forests, and green grass. He also created the world sea and placed in it three mythical fish who support the universe on their backs. According to Mordvin incantations, the fish are white beings, probably whales; their movements cause earthquakes. According to this same myth, the Erzä were created as the first human beings to cut the forest and harvest the grass. The Erzä man is put to plow and sow; his position is superior to that of his wife, whose duty it is to cook.

In international literature, there are scholarly accounts of complex hierarchical systems of deities of the universe in Mari and Mordvin religions. However, they follow the well-known theoretical patterns of the supreme being, lord of the earth, and the Olympic idea of a system of twelve gods to such an extent that it is more probable that the theory has arranged the cultural material than vice versa. In spite of this, we may refer to the interesting account by Strahlenberg, who states that the highest deity of the Mordvins (meaning the Erzä) is Jumishipas, the sky god. The first part of the name is the same as the Mari *Jumo* and Finnish *Jumala,* meaning "God"; the latter part is equivalent to *Škipas,* the name of the sun god. There probably was some kind of sun worship in both Mari and Mordvin cultures.

Nature and culture were divided among the various supernatural beings, each of whom had control over a certain building or an area in nature. It was believed that these guardian spirits existed in order to aid the people in their struggles with neighboring tribes, competitive outgroups, and unknown supernatural powers. They also controlled the affairs and actions that took place in the area in their charge, warned for danger, and punished for wrong, immoral, or improper behavior. In Mari and Mordvin folklore, there are plenty of narratives about personal encounters with the supernatural in the natural and cultural realms. In family and clan festivals held during certain seasons of the economic year, sacrifices, for example, food offerings, were offered to them as a part of family or regional cult practice.

The Erzä and Mokša had a guardian spirit called Mastorava, an earth mother who was thought to grant good harvests and good health upon the tillers of the fields. Each tilled field was thought to have its own particular spirits. The guardian spirits of forests, water, and fire were often conceived of as female supernatural beings, as evidenced by their feminine names. Among the Mordvins, there were such spirits as Vir-ava ("forest mother"), Vedmastor-ava ("water mother"), and Tol-ava ("fire mother"). The first person buried in a graveyard was considered to be the guardian spirit of that particular cemetery. The important economy of the beehives was also guarded by a guardian spirit, P'erna-azor-ava, the hostess or keeper of the bees. She was given the first taste of the annual harvest of honey.

The guardian spirits of the cultural realm watched over their own buildings and controlled behavior there. The dwelling place as a whole, that is, the courtyard, the house, and its adjoining buildings, were later called *jurt (yurt),* a word borrowed from the Tatar language. The spirit of this area was called Jurt-ava ("mother of the dwelling place"). This concept, particularly among the Erzä, replaced such former Finno-Ugrian concepts as Kudon'-tšin ("house god") or the Mokša Kud-ava ("house mother"). The word *kud* is similar to the Finnish *koti* or Saami *kota,* meaning "home."

Christianity, accepted by the Mari and Mordvins in its Russian Orthodox form, replaced the guardian spirits of the former autochthonous religion with the names of the saints and patrons of the Orthodox church. The functions of the spirits were easily mixed with the attributes and patronages of the Christian saints. The cult was transferred from the *keremet* (sacred groves) and so on to the cemeteries and neighborhood of the church. Some syncretic religious movements also appeared as a result of the encounter between the old and new religions, as, for example, the Kugu Sorta ("big candle") movement among the Mari at the end of the nineteenth century, combining monastic asceticism with pre-

Christian blood sacrifices in the old sacred groves and the worship of pre-Christian deities.

SEE ALSO Finnish Religions; Finno-Ugric Religions, overview article.

BIBLIOGRAPHY

Beke, Ödön, comp. *Tscheremissische Texte zur Religion und Volkskunde.* Oslo, 1931.

Hämäläinen, A. *Tseremissien uhritapoja.* Helsinki, 1908.

Harva (Holmberg), Uno. *Die religiosen Vorstellungen der Mordwinen.* Helsinki, 1952.

Holmberg, Uno. *Die Religion der Tscheremissen.* Helsinki, 1926.

Holmberg, Uno. *The Mythology of All Races,* vol. 4, *Finno-Ugric, Siberian.* Boston, 1927; reprint, New York, 1964.

Mokshin, N. F. "Proiskhozhdenie i sushchnost' mordovskikh dokhristianskikh religioznykh prazdnikov (ozks'ov)." In *Uche-nye zapiski Mordovskogo gosudarstvennogo universiteta (seri-ia istorischeskikh nauk).* Saransk, 1965.

Mokshin, N. F. *Religioznye verovaniia Mordvy.* Saransk, 1968.

Paasonen, Heikki. "Mordvins." In *Encyclopaedia of Religion and Ethics,* edited by James Hastings, vol. 8. Edinburgh, 1915.

Paasonen, Heikki, and Paavo Ravila. *Mordwinische Volksdichtung.* 4 vols. Helsinki, 1938–1947.

Shakhmatov, A. A. *Mordovskii etnograficheskii sbornik.* Saint Petersburg, 1910.

JUHA PENTIKÄINEN (1987)

MARIE DE L'INCARNATION, originally called Marie Guyart, was born in Tours, France, on October 28, 1599. The fourth of eight children of Florent Guyart and Jeanne Michelet, she was a contemporary of René Descartes, who was born in Tours three years earlier. As a young girl she wanted to become a nun, but her mother considered her too lighthearted for this, guiding her instead toward a marriage with Claude Martin, which took place in 1617. Martin died in October 1619, leaving Marie with a six-month-old child, named Claude after his father, and a business that was so unsound she dissolved it. During the twelve years that followed, while taking care of her son, she ran the transport business of her brother-in-law, Paul Buisson, with whom she and Claude were living. Despite family pressures, she decided not to remarry. Her free time was dedicated to a solitary life of prayer and meditation and she began having regular mystic experiences, which she recorded. When her son was twelve, she made the difficult decision to entrust him to her sister"s care and on January 25, 1631, entered the Ursuline convent at Tours. Eight years later, following various spiritual, social, and political developments, she went to New France with Marie-Madeleine de Chauvigny de la Peltrie, a wealthy lay benefactor, thus becoming the first missionary nun to work abroad. In 1639 she founded the first Ursuline monastery in Quebec. She threw herself body and soul into prayer, the temporal and spiritual administration of the monastery, and the education of young immigrant and native girls in the colony. A woman of exceptional spirituality, she also was eminently practical, and gave advice to both religious and political authorities. Marie died at the monastery on April 30, 1672.

Marie de l'Incarnation left an enormous volume of writing, more than 13,000 letters according to some estimates, of which several hundred, the most important, have been preserved and published. There are two reasons for there being such a large number. On the one hand, letter writing was the only way of keeping in touch with her family and of passing on her wishes. On the other hand, her son had become a Benedictine monk at the convent at Saint-Maur shortly after his mother had left for New France, and a sustained, very intimate exchange of letters between them took place. In addition to these letters, Marie produced two autobiographical *Relations:* the first at the convent in Tours in 1633 at the request of the Jesuit Georges de la Haye, and the second in Quebec in 1654 for her son. Finally, in note form there are fragments of talks or discussions with young novices.

Marie never wrote with a view to being published. It was her son who, realizing the quality and profound nature of her writings, collected, selected, and edited them for publication. It is uncertain to what extent he touched up his mother's work so that it would meet his own stylistic and theological standards. In any event, the style and content of her writing are captivating. Her innermost soul is bared, without any attempt at argument or persuasion. In sharing her experience of God and of those whom she encounters, she narrates rather than debates. Her writing is not so much a matter of understanding but rather of listening. For her, the important thing is "that words have resonance." They have resonance in expressing her intimate experience of the infinite nature of God in relation to her own existential nothingness. Furthermore, throughout her letters words echo her own cultural transformation as she meets and learns about the Huron tribes, their languages, customs, and spirituality. In 1640 Marie wrote, "Canada was portrayed as a horrible place, we were told that it was a district of Hell, that there was no more wretched country in the entire world. Our experience is precisely the opposite, here we have found a heavenly place, which for my part I am unworthy to inhabit. There are savage young girls who have not a trace of barbarism" (*Correspondance,* Lettre XLVII). This attitude contrasted sharply with that of many of Marie's contemporaries, who regarded the Iroquois as agents of the devil who were beyond salvation. Studies on the challenges Marie de l'Incarnation faced in meeting "the enemies of God and the faith" shed light on the emerging tension between the mental images of the European Christian culture to which she belonged and her divine experience.

The Ursuline order of which she was a member and the Benedictine order to which her son Claude belonged knew of her literary output from 1677. However it took more than two and a half centuries and the prescient vision of the literary critic and religious historian Henri Bremond (1865–1933) for scholars such as François Jamet and Guy-Marie Oury to undertake critical editions of the writings of Marie de l'Incarnation. In addition to provoking new thinking in the field of spiritual theology, her works have been picked up by academics in other disciplines, mostly women, who have subjected them to secular analysis. This has contributed to their recognition as powerful writings that express and provide evidence of the experience of a seventeenth-century woman well aware of the sociopolitical realities of her age, realities apprehended in the context of a lively and inspired intimacy with God. Since the 1990s an increasing number of scholars, novelists, theologians, psychologists, historians, and sociologists have discovered in Marie de l'Incarnation's writings a fruitful source for their theses, essays, and novels. For them, she has much to say concerning the relationship between a woman and her body, a mother and her son, a "bride of Christ" and her divine husband, a nun and her ecclesiastical institution, and a missionary and Native Americans. Two international conferences, held in 1999 in Tours and Quebec on the occasion of the four-hundredth anniversary of her birth, have resulted in two collections, presenting a range of excellent analyses of current scholarship concerning the life and work of a woman who lived, in every condition of life, in close intimacy with God.

Bibliography

New editions of the writings of Marie de l'Incarnation have been published in the twentieth century and are therefore for the most part readily available in large libraries. There are also many studies concerning her. As of 2004, a search in the catalogue of Univérsité Laval (Quebec) using her name as the subject returned around two hundred works.

Brodeur, Raymond, ed. *Femme, mystique, et missionnaire: Marie Guyart de l'Incarnation."* Sainte-Foy, Quebec, 2001.

Bruneau, Marie-Florine. *Women Mystics Confront the Modern World: Marie de l'Incarnation (1599–1672) and Madame Guyon (1648–1717)."* Albany, N.Y., 1998.

Davis, Natalie Zemon. *Women on the Margins: Three Seventeenth-Century Lives.* Cambridge, Mass., 1995.

Deroy-Pineau, Françoise, ed. *Marie Guyard de l'Incarnation: Un destin transocéanique (Tours 1599–Québec 1672)."* Paris, 2000.

Maître, Jacques. *Anorexies religieuses, anorexie mentale: Essai de psychanalyse sociohistorique: De Marie de l'Incarnation à Simone Weil."* Paris, 2000.

Mali, Anya. *Mystic in the New World: Marie de l'Incarnation (1599–1672)."* Leiden, and New York, 1996.

Marie de l'Incarnation. *Correspondance.* Edited by Guy Oury. Solesmes, 1971.

Rosario Adriazola, Maria-Paul del. *La Connaissance spirituelle chez Marie de l'Incarnation, la Thérèse du Nouveau Monde."* Paris, 1989.

Raymond Brodeur (2005)
Translated from French by Paul Ellis

MARITAIN, JACQUES (1882–1973), French Neo-Thomist philosopher. Born in Paris, he was baptized in the French Reformed church and received religious instruction from the liberal Protestant theologian Jean Réville. During his youth, Maritain considered himself an unbeliever. He studied at the Sorbonne (1901–1906) but found the dominant positivism and rationalism—epitomized in the influence of the philosopher Auguste Comte and the historian and writer Ernest Renan—spiritually barren. At the Sorbonne, Maritain joined a circle of friends that included the writer Charles Péguy and a young Russian Jew, Raïssa Oumansoff. He also attended the lectures of the philosopher Henri Bergson at the Collège de France. Bergson's vitalistic philosophy liberated Maritain from positivism and made possible for him the rehabilitation of metaphysical thinking.

In 1904 Maritain married Raïssa Oumansoff, and soon they came under the influence of the fiery, uncompromising Catholic writer Léon Bloy. Primarily through Bloy's tutorship and personal example, they were baptized in the Roman Catholic church in 1906. Maritain spent the next two years in Heidelberg studying with the distinguished biologist and neovitalist Hans Dreisch. On returning to France he began reading the *Summa theologiae* of Thomas Aquinas. Thomas's philosophical realism became for Maritain a second and more decisive intellectual deliverance. For the rest of his long life, he revered Thomas as his master and saw as his own vocation the application of the perennial wisdom of Thomism to contemporary philosophy, art, politics, and education. "Woe unto me," he wrote, "should I not thomistize!"

Maritain served as professor of philosophy at the Institut Catholique de Paris (1914–1933), the Institute of Medieval Studies in Toronto (1933–1945), and Princeton University (1948–1952), as well as at other North American universities. At the invitation of Charles de Gaulle, he served as French ambassador to the Vatican from 1945 to 1948. During his years in North America, Maritain's influence on Catholic thought, as well as on arts and letters, was enormous.

Raïssa Maritain died in 1960, and the following year Maritain returned to France and retired to Toulouse to live with the Little Brothers of Jesus, a Dominican monastic order. In 1969 he entered the order. In 1966 Maritain published *The Peasant of the Garonne,* a sharp warning to the post-Vatican II reformers in the Roman church. Because Maritain had championed some liberal influences in the church, especially in the field of politics, the book surprised many and provoked widespread discussion. However, the work reflects a long-standing tension in Maritain between adherence to tradition and openness to new ideas, as well as his disdain of any modern ways that deviate from Thomas.

Maritain's literary output was prodigious, including about forty books published over a span of some sixty years. He ranged over almost every aspect of philosophy, and all his works—from *La philosophie bergsonienne* (1914) to his penultimate book, *On the Church of Christ* (1970)—are informed by the thought of Thomas Aquinas. Maritain traces what he perceives to be a cultural breakdown in the West to a disease of the mind. That disease has its beginnings in the early modern repudiation of Thomistic philosophy, first in William of Ockham's nominalism and rejection of Aristotelian metaphysics; then in Luther's severing of faith from reason; in Descartes's rationalism, in which reason is divorced from sensory experience and existing things; and, finally, in Rousseau's sentimental appeal to the inner feelings of the heart. Maritain sees metaphysical thinking brought to a close with Kant, and the future turned over to scientism and positivism on the one hand and subjectivism and relativism on the other.

Maritain's genius lay not only in his skill in demonstrating the inadequacies of a good deal of modern philosophy but also in exhibiting how the authentic truths of modern thought are consistent with, and conceptually more adequate when understood in terms of, Thomistic realism. Existentialism is a case in point. Its emphasis on action, and on what Maritain calls its "imprecatory posture," isolates the idea of existence from a genuine knowledge of being, since it involves philosophizing in a posture of dramatic singularity. Maritain argues that one can never know pure subjective existence. Objective philosophic knowledge necessarily involves a distinction between essence and existence, for the essence of a thing is what makes it intelligible as a being, what defines its nature. Essence and existence are correlative and inseparable. Maritain therefore insists that an "authentic" existentialism must go beyond the cry and agony of the subject to a genuine analysis of being.

Such an analysis will lead reflection beyond finite existence to that being whose essence is to exist, who exists necessarily (God). In works such as *Approaches to God* (1954), Maritain attempts to show that the Thomistic cosmological proofs of the existence of God are the development of a primordial, prephilosophical intuition of being. Furthermore, he seeks to demonstrate that Kant's widely approved critique of the Thomistic cosmological proofs—which holds that they imply the ontological argument—is in error. Maritain reconceives the five Thomistic proofs by appropriating ideas from modern physics and the philosophy of science. However, the philosophical critics of natural theology remain largely unconvinced.

Among modern religious philosophers, Maritain stands preeminent in his reflections on aesthetics, for example, in works such as *Art and Scholasticism* (1920; Eng. ed., 1962) and *Creative Intuition in Art and Poetry* (1953). Maritain's discussion of poetic intuition and knowledge and of the relationship between art and morality are profound and have influenced numerous writers and critics.

In *Scholasticism and Politics* (1940), *True Humanism* (1936; Eng. ed., 1938), and *Man and the State* (1951), Maritain argues eloquently for the dignity of the person, for human rights and liberty, and for what is essentially an American model of church-state relations. Maritain's writings on the person and on society and politics have had wide influence and are reflected in the documents of Vatican II.

Maritain represents, perhaps better than any other thinker, the intellectual confidence, indeed the aggressiveness, of Roman Catholicism in the 1940s and 1950s. Like the Protestant theologian Reinhold Niebuhr, Maritain was a brilliant critic of secular culture and a superb apologist for the Christian life. He was also, like Niebuhr, a "relative" pessimist who nevertheless held out hope for the recovery of an integral, Christian humanism—a humanism permeated by works of genuine sanctity.

Many Catholic intellectuals consider Maritain's Thomism as no longer an adequate guide and call instead for a philosophical pluralism in the church. The form of Thomism that does continue to have a wide following, the "transcendental" Thomism associated with Joseph Maréchal (1878–1944) and, more recently, with Karl Rahner, was repudiated by Maritain. While his work is presently in eclipse and his future influence is uncertain, Maritain will be remembered as one of the intellectual giants in the period between the two world wars.

Bibliography

Maritain's greatest work on metaphysics and the theory of knowledge is *Distinguish to Unite, or the Degrees of Knowledge*, translated under the supervision of Gerald B. Phelen (New York, 1959). In *Approaches to God*, translated by Peter O'Reilly (New York, 1954), Maritain restates the five ways of Thomas Aquinas to demonstrate the existence of God and proposes a "sixth way." *True Humanism*, translated by Margot Adamson (New York, 1938), is Maritain's most important work in social philosophy, and *Man and the State* (Chicago, 1951) is his most comprehensive examination of political philosophy. *Creative Intuition in Art and Poetry* (New York, 1953) is Maritain's masterpiece in the philosophy of art. *Challenges and Renewals*, edited by Joseph W. Evans and Leo R. Ward (Notre Dame, Ind., 1966), is a useful selection of writings by Maritain covering all aspects of his philosophy.

No definitive critical study of Maritain has been written. Joseph W. Evans's *Jacques Maritain: The Man and His Achievement* (New York, 1963) includes a variety of essays on aspects of Maritain's work. Julie Kernan's *Our Friend, Jacques Maritain: A Personal Memoir* (Garden City, N. Y., 1975) is a rather full biographical account. The definitive bibliography of works by and about Maritain up to 1961 is Donald Gallagher and Idella Gallagher's *The Achievement of Jacques and Raïssa Maritain: A Bibliography, 1906–1961* (New York, 1962).

James C. Livingston (1987)

MARK OF EPHESUS (1392–1444), a leader of the Greek Orthodox resistance against the unionist movement with the Western church. A native of Constantinople, Mark studied under prominent teachers and then opened a private higher school. He was elected metropolitan of Ephesus and participated in the Council of Ferrara-Florence as a representative of the patriarchate of Antioch at the expressed wish of the emperor John VIII Palaeologus. However, he became the strongest adversary of union with the Roman church. Mark abstained from the sessions of the council and was the only Eastern bishop to refuse to sign the decisions of the council in 1439. When Pope Eugenius IV—for whom unanimity and the support of Mark were determinant factors for union—learned of his refusal, he said, "Therefore, we have accomplished nothing."

After his return to Constantinople, Mark was offered the patriarchal see by the emperor and bishops in the hope that his zeal against union would decrease under the burden of the great responsibilities of office. Mark refused the offer. Attempting to go to Mount Athos, probably with the aim of mobilizing the monks against union, he was seized on the island of Lemnos by the imperial police and was not allowed to leave the island for two years. After his liberation, he directed the struggle in Constantinople. Shortly before his death he persuaded Gennadios Scholarios, the future patriarch of Constantinople, to succeed him in his function as head of the antiunionists.

Mark's theology is basically hesychastic with occasional use of Aristotelian categories to support his arguments. His work *Syllogistic Chapters on the Divine Essence and Energy* reveals his spiritual and intellectual origins. His polemics against the Roman church are included in various writings, of which the most important is *Syllogistic Chapters against the Latins.* By an encyclical letter, *To Christians All Over the Earth,* he directed the attention of Orthodox believers to the danger from those who were wavering and finding themselves in agreement with both Easterners and Westerners; he called these people "Greco-Latins."

Mark believed that differences with the Westerners over such matters as the procession of the Holy Spirit, purgatory, and the use of unleavened bread for the Eucharist were dogmatic differences; therefore, he considered the Latins heretics. A summary of his position may be found in his statement regarding a patriarch who favored union: "The further I stay from this man and others like him the nearer I come to God and to the faithful and holy fathers."

BIBLIOGRAPHY

A lengthy sketch of Mark's person and work may be found in Louis Petit's article "Marc Eugénicos," in *Dictionnaire de théologie catholique,* vol. 9 (Paris, 1927), and a shorter sketch in Hans Georg Beck's *Kirche und theologische Literatur im byzantinischen Reich* (Munich, 1959), pp. 755–758. The most complete study is Katerina Mamoni's *Marcos Eugenicos* (Athens, 1954). Mark's ecclesiastical policy from the Roman Catholic point of view is treated by Joseph Gill in *Personalities of the Council of Florence* (Oxford, 1964). Constantine N. Tsirpanlis provides the Greek Orthodox point of view in *Mark Eugenicus and the Council of Florence: A Historical Reevaluation of His Personality* (New York, 1979).

Panagiotis C. Christou (1987)

MARK THE EVANGELIST, traditionally the author of the second canonical gospel, who wrote in Rome during the emperor Nero's persecution of Christians (early to mid–60s). Mark was not one of the twelve disciples of Jesus. Whether the evangelist is mentioned in the New Testament depends on the accuracy of the commonly accepted identification of him with the John Mark of Jerusalem mentioned in *Acts* and Paul's letters.

John Mark first appears in *Acts* 12:12: Peter is said to go "to the house of Mary, the mother of John, whose other name was Mark." (John would have been Mark's Semitic, Jewish name; Marcus is a common Latin, Roman name.) He is referred to in a similar way again in *Acts* 12:25 and 15:37, but in 15:39 he is called simply Mark. Elsewhere he is called only Mark (*Col.* 4:10, *2 Tm.* 4:11, *Phlm.* 24, *1 Pt.* 5:13). In *Colossians,* we read that Mark was the cousin of Barnabas, with whom he continued missionary labors after the break with Paul (*Acts* 15:38–39). Significantly, he is there grouped with the Jewish members of Paul's company (*Col.* 4:11), which fits the identification with John Mark. Since *2 Timothy* was almost certainly not written by Paul and the Pauline authorship of *Colossians* is questionable, *Philemon* 24 is the only unimpeachable Pauline reference to Mark as one of Paul's fellow workers. Yet all these references are significant because they show the traditional association of Mark with Paul. The same is true for *1 Peter* 5:13, which suggests Mark's association also with Peter in Rome (i. e., "Babylon").

The earliest statements about Mark the evangelist by Christian writers, beginning with those of Bishop Papias of Hierapolis in the first half of the second century, do not identify him explicitly with John Mark, but almost unanimously associate him with Peter as Peter's interpreter (cf. Eusebius's *Church History* 3.39.15). Frequently it is said that Mark and Peter worked together in Rome, and this, of course, accords with ancient church tradition about Peter's final place of abode, as well as with *1 Peter* 5:13. A somewhat later tradition recounts that Mark was the first to preach and to found churches in Egypt (*Church History* 2.16.1), and that he became the first bishop of Alexandria. A recently discovered letter of Clement of Alexandria, which, if genuine, dates from the end of the second century, relates how Mark came to Alexandria with the early canonical gospel and there augmented it for the sake of a special spiritual elite.

That the *Gospel of Mark* is actually the work of someone of that name is probable; that he was associated with Peter in Rome is possible, although that association would not entirely explain the character and content of the gospel; that he was actually John Mark cannot be said with certainty, nor can it be denied categorically. If Mark the evangelist was John Mark of Jerusalem it is at least striking that in his gospel Jesus' ministry is centered in Galilee (in contrast to the *Gospel of John,* which centers the ministry in Jerusalem) and that the disciples are encouraged to look to Galilee for the fulfillment of their hopes and plans whether by their own mission or by Jesus' return (*Mk.* 14:28, 16:7). Moreover, the gospel seems to assume a gentile-Christian rather than a Jewish-Christian readership (cf. *Mk.* 7:3–4).

Legend has it that Mark was martyred in Alexandria during Nero's reign and that his remains eventually were moved to Venice. The evangelist's symbol, the lion, became the emblem of that city, in which the cathedral is named for Mark. The symbolism, as old as the second century, is probably drawn from *Revelation* 4:7 and ultimately from *Ezekiel* 1:10. Mark's feast is celebrated on April 25.

BIBLIOGRAPHY

Aside from the New Testament the most important primary source is Eusebius's *Church History,* which brings together earlier testimony of Christian writers on the origin and authorship of the Gospels. The most convenient edition is the two-volume "Loeb Classical Library" text and translation of Kirsopp Lake, J. E. L. Oulton, and Hugh J. Lawlor (Cambridge, Mass., 1926).

Vincent Taylor's *The Gospel According to St. Mark* (London, 1952), pp. 1–8, cites fully and discusses the patristic evidence on Mark, taking the position that the evangelist was, in fact, John Mark. Werner G. Kümmel's *Introduction to the New Testament,* rev. ed. (Nashville, 1975), pp. 95–98, states a more skeptical critical consensus. Old and new evidence of Mark's relation to Alexandria is given and discussed in Morton Smith's *Clement of Alexandria and a Secret Gospel of Mark* (Cambridge, Mass., 1973), pp. 19–44, 446. Yet the certainty of this consensus is at least questioned by Raymond E. Brown, *Introduction to the New Testament* (New York, 1997), pp. 158–161, and by Joel Marcus, *Mark 1–8* (New York, 2000), pp. 17–24. On the identity of Mark, and tradition about him, see C. Clifton Black, *Mark: Images of an Apostolic Interpreter* (Columbia, S. C., 1994).

D. MOODY SMITH (1987 AND 2005)

MAROON RELIGIONS SEE AFRO-SURINAMESE RELIGIONS; CARIBBEAN RELIGIONS, *ARTICLE ON* AFRO-CARIBBEAN RELIGIONS

MAR PA (Marpa, 1002/1012–1097) is acknowledged as the "forefather" who introduced the Lineage of the Oral Precepts (Bka' brgyud), later one of the four major schools of the Buddha's doctrine (the Kagyü), in Tibet. After the collapse of the Tibetan empire with the death of King Glang dar ma (Langdarma, r. 836–841), who had done away with the centers of monastic learning in the Land of Snows, the Buddhist tradition soon degenerated, creating a situation akin to one documented in a remote Himalayan valley in the early twenty-first century (Sihle, 2001). Some ritual techniques were preserved, but uninterrupted master–disciple transmission of the initiations and meditational instructions gave way to a legitimacy based solely on clan descendance and mere ownership of the books. Especially lacking was a cohesive overview of Buddhist learning, and the ability therein to distinguish the essence.

The responsibility for a potential revival rested on the shoulders of Tibetan aspirants willing to make the difficult journey to the firya lands, acquaint themselves with the spoken and written idiom of the country, study at the great monastic universities, or train under individual masters in India and Nepal. Among these, Mar pa Chos kyi blo gros ("*Dharma* Intellect" from the Mar clan) stands out as the *lo tsā ba* (yogin-translator) par excellence. One of the earliest *Golden Garland* redactions (by the thirteenth-century Rgyal thang pa Bde chen rdo rje [Dechen Dorje from Gyalthang]) that relates Mar pa's life in the context of a Bka brgyud lineage history introduces the subject by way of his previous birth as an Indian *brahman,* thus accounting for his future relative ease in picking up Sanskrit and the Indian vernaculars.

Mar pa Lo tsā ba was born in Lho brag (Lhotrak, "Southcliff"), the youngest of four siblings. An older sister, a Rdzogs chen (Dzogchen, "Great Perfection") practitioner, achieved the rainbow body. An older brother is explicitly mentioned as "being remarkable for his patience," the very trait that the young Mar pa entirely lacked, for he is described as a wild youth who quarreled with everyone. His relatives were more than willing to sponsor his removal to a monastery in distant Mu gu lung (Mugu Valley), headed by the long-term India resident 'Brog mi Lo tsāba (Drokmi Lotsāwa, c. 992/3–1043/1072). But when the latter exacted fees far beyond Mar pa's means for every meditational instruction imparted, young Mar pa decided to travel to the south.

Further funding by his relatives was meager compared to that of (the future) Gnyos Lo tsā ba (Nyö Lotsāwa) from Kha rag, whom Mar pa encountered en route, and who traveled in grand style, with a large entourage. Mar pa became his servant, setting up camp, cooking meals, fetching water, sweeping, and so forth. In the Nepal Valley they came across a huge religious gathering, presided over by two of the disciples of Nāropa (1016–1100), the Newar "Bald Head" (Bal po Spyi ther pa) and Guru Pentapa (probably Paindapa, "the alms gatherer"), and attended largely by the local "twice-born" (*brahmans*). The former granted Mar pa the Hevajra initiation; under Pentapa he continued his Sanskrit studies. Most important of all, they dispatched a messenger to India with an introduction letter to Mahā shrī Nāropa.

At the monastic university of Nālandā, Gnyos tried to dissuade Mar pa from studying under Nāropa, since the latter had switched from being a respected Doorkeeper Scholar to a possessionless Kusulu jungle-dweller. Mar pa remained adamant, and in the course of three journeys to India studied, under Nāropa and a number of other masters, all the main cycles of the Tantras, especially of the Mother and Father class in Highest Yoga. The range of his learning became extremely wide. No wonder, then, that even during his lifetime, Mar pa was regarded as a living buddha, and he is depicted as such on the well-preserved fresco portrait at the Nine-Storied Prince's Castle built by Mi la ras pa (Milarepa,

1028/40-1111/23) in Lho brag, wherein Mar pa is shown seated on a Buddha's lion throne and attended by standing *bodhisattvas* in old Indian attire.

Back in the Lho brag area, he established his own teaching center at Gro bo lung (Trowo Valley). There he became responsible for the transmission of: (1) the six yogas of Nāropa, directly obtained from that master, and (2) the "great sealing gesture" or *mahāmudrā*, specifically taught to him by Maitripa Mahāsiddha (c. 1007–1085). Elements thereof eventually spread to the other main schools. The cycles centered on the Mother Tantras gained major ascendancy in the Bka' brgyud line.

In one long episode (missing from Gtsang smyon Heruka's [Tsang Nyön Heruka, "the mad saint from Tsang"] fifteenth-century biography of Mar pa) Rgyal thang pa insists on the emanational (*nirmāṇakāya*) nature of Mar pa, his wife Bdag med ma (Dagmema), and their seven sons, all of them *bodhisattvas*. As proof he points out that the sons all died in ascending order, from the youngest up to Dar ma sdo sde Dar ma mdo sde (Tarma Dode), who dissolved into Bdag med ma who dissolved into Mar pa, whose consciousness dissolved into a rainbow. He likens this to the dissolving of the *maṇḍala* deities at the end of the Hevajra meditation scenario. (This is counter to Gtsang smyon Heruka's narrative of Dar ma mdo sde's transmigration into the body of a *brahman* boy in India, and his own rebirth as Ti phu pa.) In a view entirely in tune with the more important role accorded to Bdag med ma by Rgyal thang pa, upon Mar pa's return to Gro bo lung, Lord Nāro appeared to him in a dream and delivered a verse injunction to take Bdag med ma as his wife. This markedly differs from the somewhat misogynous tone of Gtsang smyon Heruka's redaction, which contains several snide remarks aimed at her (e.g., "A woman leading a meeting [is like] a goat leading the way, [like] a prairie dog serving as a sentry," 1986, p. 166).

The translation of Gtsang smyon Heruka's *Life of Marpa* has each chapter prefixed by a calligraphed *nges don* (definitive meaning), which applies to the instructions embedded in the spiritual songs. Much historical research is reflected in the notes, although Gtsang smyon Heruka's own intention was, rather, the creation of a flawless, near-filmic scenario, similar to a jewel box in which to enshrine the songs of instruction—the ones translated and commented upon in a masterly fashion in Trungpa Rinpoche's introduction. Studied in conjunction with a step-by-step *mahāmudrā* instruction like Si tu Pa chen's spirited commentary to the root verses by the third Karma pa, the uniqueness of Mar pa Lo tsā ba's heritage retains a sense of timeless wonder.

SEE ALSO Buddhism, article on Buddhism in Tibet; Buddhism, Schools of, article on Tibetan and Mongolian Buddhism; Mahāsiddhas; Mi la ras pa; Nā ro pa.

BIBLIOGRAPHY

Rgyal thang pa Bde chen rdo rje's thirteenth-century *Dkar brgyud gser 'phreng* (Golden garland of the white [cotton robes] transmission) is so far unavailable in English translation, except for the root verses of the Tilopa chapter, which can be found in Fabrizio Torricelli's "A Thirteenth Century Tibetan Hymn to the Siddha Tilopa," *The Tibet Journal* 23, no. 3 (1998): 18–24. The only complete translation of a Mar pa biography is Chögyam Trungpa and the Nālandā Translation Committee, *The Life of Marpa the Translator, Seeing Accomplishes All*, by Gtsang smyon Heruka (Boston and London, 1982; reprints, 1986 and 1995). A superb introduction to Mar pa's *mahāmudrā* heritage is Lama Sherap Dorje, trans., *Mahāmudrā Teachings of the Supreme Siddhas: The Eighth Situ-pa Tenpa'i Nyinchay on the Third Gyalwa Karmapa Rangjung Dorje's "Aspiration Prayer of Mahāmudrā of Definitive Meaning"* (Ithaca, N.Y., 1995). Its adaptation in the Dge lugs (Geluk) system is flawlessly presented in Alexander Berzin, trans., *The Gelug/Kagyü Tradition of Mahamudra: H.H. the Dalai Lama's Commentary to the First Panchen Lama, Lobsang Chökyi Gyaltsen's "A Root Text for the Precious Gelug/Kagyü Tradition of Mahamudra"* (Ithaca, N.Y., 1997). Although not intended as such, Nicholas Sihle's unpublished Ph.D. dissertation, "Les tantristes tibétains (*ngakpa*): Religieux dans le monde, religieux du rituel terrible: Étude de Ch'ongkor, communauté villageoise de tantristes du Baragaon (nord du Népal)," Université de Paris (2001), probably presents the most authentic image of the state of much post-Glang dar ma Buddhism in Tibet. Hubert Decleer's preliminary study, "*The Melodious Drumsound All-Pervading*, Sacred Biography of Rwa Lotsāwa, about early Lotsāwa *rnam thar* and *chos 'byung*," *Proceedings of the International Association for Tibetan Studies*, Narita, 1989 (1992): 13–28, offers a few introductory remarks about the historical problems involved.

HUBERT DECLEER (2005)

MARRANOS, a term of opprobrium designating Jews (and, occasionally, Muslims) converted to Christianity (and their descendants), was used in the Iberian world in late medieval and early modern times. The Castilian word *marrano* (deriving from an Arabic word for "prohibited," or "illicit") means "swine," or "pork" and either expressed the same abhorrence toward converts as the converts had previously felt toward the ritually unclean animal or insinuated suspicions regarding the converts' continued loyalties to Judaism. Usage of the term appears to have been limited to common parlance and satirical literature. In modern times, Jewish historians revived the term to underscore the uniqueness of the "Marrano" phenomenon in Iberian and Jewish history.

More commonly, and more neutrally, the converts and their descendants are designated *conversos* (converts), *cristianos nuevos* (Span.), *cristãos novos* (Port.), or "New Christians." Referring specifically to *conversos* suspected or found guilty of practicing or adhering to some form of Judaism, Inquisitorial documents employ the term *judaizante,* meaning "judaizer" (or, in modern variations, the terms *secret* or *crypto-Jew*). In premodern and modern Hebrew sources, the *conversos* are designated as *anusim* (forced [converts]). To avoid the confusions of earlier historiography, present historians use *converso* and New Christian synonymously to refer strictly to the social group of converts and descendants, and reserve *judaizer* and *Marrano* as synonyms for those *conversos* whose retention of some form of Judaism may be demonstrated or suspected.

The "*Converso* Problem." The large and problematical *converso* population and the concomitant Marrano phenomenon were the outcome of unprecedented, large-scale conversions of Spanish and Portuguese Jews between 1391 and 1497. In 1391 and 1392, social resentment of prospering urban Jewish minorities and religious militancy nurtured by a pugnacious Spanish tradition of spiritual warfare provoked a nationwide chain of pogroms, in the course of which large numbers of Jews fell victim to forced, legally irreversible baptism. The unrelenting persistence of anti-Jewish pressures resulted, in subsequent decades, in a second wave of more or less voluntary conversions, creating an initial population of tens of thousands of *conversos* of questionable religious sincerity.

Envy of the *conversos'* social and economic gains, made possible by their liberation from anti-Jewish restrictions, and lingering suspicions of their secret and private loyalty to Judaism, rekindled popular anger and violence against them (which also might have developed into antiroyalist sentiment) and gave birth to a social and religious "*converso* problem" that was politically threatening in that it potentially harbored antiroyalist sentiment. In 1478 a Castilian Inquisition, whose appointments were controlled by the crown, was established to deal with the problem's religious dimension; that is, to prosecute and punish insincere judaizing individuals and thus protect the purity of Catholic orthodoxy and, at the same time, lay to rest the popular suspicions and the indiscriminate, anti-*converso* scapegoating that were viewed as a political danger. Addressing the social dimension, "purity of blood" (Span., *limpieza de sangre;* Port., *limpeza de sangue*) statutes—the earliest was adopted (but nullified) in 1449 in Toledo—sought, whenever the circumstances proved opportune, to exclude the New Christians as a group from upper-echelon ecclesiastical, civil, and military positions by virtue of their Jewish or Muslim descent. The statutes became a more widely adopted mode of anti-*converso* social discrimination after 1555–1556, when, in the midst of a vociferous debate, the archbishop of Toledo, Juan Martínez Silíceo (1486–1557), obtained papal and royal ratification of a *limpieza* statute excluding New Christians from positions in the cathedral chapter of Toledo.

The remaining Jews of Spain, meanwhile, were implicated in fostering the persistence of Jewish loyalties among the *conversos* and in subverting the new state-church-city alliance. They were expelled by the Catholic rulers, Isabella of Castile (r. 1474–1504) and Ferdinand of Aragon (r. 1479–1516), from Andalusia, the scene of the first Inquisitorial discoveries of widespread judaizing, in 1483 and from the rest of Castile and Aragon in 1492. Seeking to avoid exile, many Spanish Jews hastily converted or returned converted after a temporary exile and joined the ranks of a not insignificant *converso* minority of approximately 2–3 percent of the total Spanish population. An estimated 150,000 Jews fled—between 80,000 and 120,000 to neighboring Portugal, where they raised the Jewish population to about 10 percent of the total population, and the rest to North Africa, Italy, and the Ottoman Empire. During 1496 and 1497, Manuel I, king of Portugal (1495–1521), forcibly converted the vast majority of Portuguese Jews, including the new arrivals from Spain, in a move meant to both rid his kingdom of the Jews, in compliance with a condition set forth by the Catholic king whose daughter he was to marry, and retain their services, which were deemed important for the country's (and its colonies') economic development.

In Portugal, too, the "unsatisfactory" (i.e., forced) conversions, as well as the social and economic advances of the *conversos,* created a proportionally more substantial "*converso* problem," notwithstanding royal promises not to investigate the *conversos'* religious life made in the expectation of their eventual total assimilation. Despite vigorous New Christian efforts to stave off its institution, a Portuguese Inquisition on the Spanish model was established in 1536. And, in ensuing years, Portuguese institutions adopted "purity of blood" statutes to turn the tide of upwardly mobile New Christians tainted by suspicions of judaizing (willfully retaining Jewish loyalties and practices) that were seemingly confirmed by Inquisitorial proceedings. As the Spanish and Portuguese colonies attracted larger populations, Inquisitorial tribunals were established in Goa (1560), Lima (1570), Mexico (1571), and in Cartagena, Colombia (1610). Only Brazil was treated differently and remained under the jurisdiction of the Lisbon tribunal, which sent periodic "visitors" (that is, small and occasional commissions of inquiry) to the colony.

Historical Sources. The records of the Inquisition, preserved in great abundance, are our primary and often exclusive source of information about the extent and nature of the Marrano phenomenon—that is, the secret and heretical (by definition of the church) retention of Jewish doctrines, rites, and customs by groups and individuals within the larger *converso* populations. The reliability of these documents is the subject of continual debate. Some historians deny them all validity because they originated from an entirely self-contained and secret organization whose stated aims of religious orthodoxy they dismiss. Most historians accept them as a faithful record of the Inquisitorial proceedings: some without further questioning, others with more or less serious reservations about Inquisitorial (as opposed to accusatorial) procedure. For the Inquisition operated without external checks and balances and, as accuser, judge, and jury, controlled every aspect of the trial, in complete secrecy. Its decisions to prosecute (whom and when), imprison (and for how long), torture (and how often), and sentence (and how harshly) were, wittingly or unwittingly, exposed to—and generally unprotected from—internal infusions of malice, prejudice, bias, error, or misunderstanding. Only a complete statistical and comparative profile of all the Inquisition's tribunals, as is now being assembled, might reveal where and when any such infusion must be suspected and taken into consideration. Inquisitorial procedure may also have influenced the accusations, testimonies, and confessions of witnesses and defendants. Inasmuch as witnesses as well as defendants communicated with the inquisitors, they often had to bridge a social and cultural gap and speak in a voice not quite their own—and they might, therefore, have intentionally or unintentionally misconstrued the realities under discussion. Only a complete reexamination of accusation, testimony, and confession might reveal the manner in which "translation" and misconstruction may have affected the reliability of any given Inquisitorial record.

The Nature of the Marrano Phenomenon. Inquisitorial documents (such as manuals, edicts of faith, testimonies, and confessions) and statistics about the numbers of judaizers are helpful in charting the extent of the phenomenon, but do not afford a rounded picture of its nature. The Inquisition's definition of heresy, moreover, inspired a preoccupation with the external manifestations but rarely with the spiritual content of judaizing and thus deprives us of a significant dimension of the phenomenon. Within these limitations, little more than a catalogue of judaizing practices—constituting a maximum of observance rarely, if ever, attained by any individual Marrano—can be offered. The following summary focuses on the "full-fledged" Marranism of the later sixteenth and seventeenth centuries. When Jews were still present and memories yet alive, the earliest transitional generations of Marranos no doubt practiced a wider range of observances and traditions.

Loyalty to Judaism. Echoing Inquisitorial parlance, the Marranos defined themselves as those who believed salvation could be achieved only through the Law of Moses (by which they meant Judaism). This thoroughly un-Jewish formula clearly reveals the two elements in Marrano religion: a rejection of salvation through Jesus and a loyalty to the Law of Moses. As either one constituted in itself sufficient proof of heresy, the Inquisition never queried deeper to establish which of the two elements weighed heavier.

The Marranos' loyalty to Judaism, encumbered by the need for secrecy, expressed itself in an ever more restricted variety of Jewish observances and traditions, a restriction that was due to the loss of knowledge about Jewish law and, especially, Jewish doctrines, and the virtual absence of sources of Jewish education. Fairly rapid to disappear were circumcision, ritual slaughtering, the covering of the head during prayer, the use of phylacteries, and such festivals as Ro'sh ha-Shanah, Shavu'ot, and Ḥanukkah. Passover and Sukkot survived here and there but were celebrated in attenuated forms.

The Sabbath, fasts, prayers, and certain domestic traditions formed the main staples of Marrano Judaism. These observances and customs not only lend themselves well to concealment but have also been central to the home-based daily rhythm of traditional Judaism. The cleaning of the house, the changing of linen and clothes, the taking of baths, the preparation of food—including the so-called *adafina* (a stew prepared before the onset of the Sabbath)—and the kindling of lights are mentioned in connection with the Marrano observance of the Sabbath. On the Sabbath itself, Marranos abstained from work as often as the opportunity presented itself and whenever the spirit moved them, that is to say, with a definite measure of irregularity. Some Marranos contented themselves with an abstention from work "in intention" only.

Fasting occupied a particularly prominent place in Marrano religious life. Not only was it easy to conceal, it also mirrored and opposed, to some extent, Christian practice. Yom Kippur (Day of Atonement) and the Fast of Esther were the holiest days of the Marrano calendar. As the Marranos had lost count of the Jewish lunar calendar, the dates of these fasts were computed on the basis of a mixed lunar-solar calendar: Yom Kippur was observed on the tenth day after the New Moon in September (or, sometimes, on the tenth of September) and the Fast of Esther on the full moon of February. On Yom Kippur, Marranos customarily extended mutual forgiveness to each other, but only rarely does one encounter a Marrano who went barefoot on that day, as did Jews. Either on the eve of Yom Kippur or on that of the Sabbath, Marrano fathers often blessed their children, even when the children had as yet no knowledge of the Jewish origin of this custom. The Fast of Esther, on the eve of Purim, has minor importance in traditional Judaism. As Purim itself fell into oblivion, Marranos retained and expanded the fast, especially in Portugal, undoubtedly because of the similarity between their situation and that of Queen Esther, who had also been forced to hide her ancestral religion in order to survive in an alien environment.

On the Sabbath and Yom Kippur and other festive or special occasions, Marranos recited—rather than chanted, as in traditional fashion—Jewish prayers. As the original Hebrew prayers were lost and memory of their content dimmed, Marranos resorted to readings of the Psalms of David and vernacular creations of their own to replace the Qiddush, grace after meals, and other prayers. These vernacular prayers—some transcribed verbatim in the Inquisitorial documents—stress the unity, omnipotence, and mercy of Adonai ("my Lord," one of the few Hebrew words to survive among the Marranos), the God of the heavens, creator and ruler of the universe, in conscious opposition to Christian trinitarianism. Several prayers beseech God to deliver the Marranos from their tribulations. A great many of these locally or familially transmitted prayers were still current among the Marranos of twentieth-century Portugal.

Among the domestic traditions recorded, some may be termed culinary or dietary, while others are associated with rites of passage. Whereas ritual slaughtering other than that of an occasional fowl fell into desuetude, the kosher preparation of meat—the draining of blood, the removal of nerves, and the salting of meat—did not. This is, perhaps, the reason that Marranos, not having a chance to prepare meat properly, preferred meals of fish and vegetables when breaking a fast. As much as possible and as desired, again irregularly, Marranos avoided eating meats and seafoods traditionally declared nonkosher—pork, rabbit, octopus, and eel, in particular. And when baking bread, some Marrano women had a habit of throwing three small balls of dough into the fire, in imitation of a *ḥallāh*-baking custom. In rites-of-passage traditions, there was a great deal of local variety. Jewish names were generally lost, except in a few particularly "noble" Jewish families that retained a memory of their ancestral family name. Otherwise, Marranos adopted Christian first names and surnames. In many places, a festive ceremony called Hadas ("fate"?) took place on the eighth night after a child's birth. The origin and the meaning of this custom are uncertain. Death and burial rites associated with traditional Judaism were quite common. The washing and dressing in shrouds of the corpse and the meals taken during the period of mourning, as well as sundry superstitious acts, are mentioned with relative frequency.

REJECTION OF CHRISTIANITY. The Marranos' rejection of Christianity consisted not only of a denial of salvation through the law of Jesus, of their opposition to the Trinity, and of their appropriation of the Paternoster for Marrano purposes. In early years, it sometimes included a ceremony intended to undo baptism. Later, Marranos more commonly were lax in their attendance at the Mass—which, however, was also not infrequently neglected by Christians. Some Marranos used to recite a deprecatory formula denying the efficacy of the sacraments or the veneration of images before entering a church. Others remained silent or mumbled through Christological parts of the liturgy or bent rather than kneeled at the requisite times. Evidence of Marranos' spewing out the Host after Communion is sparse, and accusations of Marranos' desecrating the Host may reflect the preconception of malevolent witnesses more than actual practice.

MESSIANIC INCLINATIONS. One final aspect of Marrano religion remains largely in the dark: messianism. Many Marrano prayers reflect a commitment to traditional Jewish messianism, but the degree to which this commitment explains New Christian participation in specific, often Christian messianic movements remains a matter for speculation. In the early years following the expulsion of the Jews, several reports from various parts of Spain speak of visionary experiences by *conversos* with more or less explicitly messianic overtones, especially around 1500 when three prophetic figures (including a charismatic twelve-year-old named Inés of Herrera) gained a large following almost overnight. Later, the Jewish adventurer David Reubeni's visit to Portugal and reception by the king from 1525 to 1527 stirred *converso* emotions, perhaps so deeply as to have provoked messianic expectations. And toward the end of the sixteenth century, messianic beliefs surrounding the deceased King Sebastian of Portugal, who had fallen in battle in 1578, again attracted *converso* attention and may even have been inspired by *conversos.* The participation of Spanish and Portuguese *conversos* in messianically inclined popular movements appears undisputed. On the basis of our meager sources, however, it is difficult to gauge whether they responded so eagerly as Marranos who rejected Jesus and retained Jewish messianic hopes, as New Christians prompted by a radical desire to alter the contemporary situation of Inquisitorial repression and socioreligious discrimination, or whether they were swept up by a general enthusiasm that also drew Old Christians *(cristianos viejos,* or *cristãos velhos)* into these movements.

THE TRANSMISSION OF MARRANISM. Originally, the transmission of Marranism was confined to the *converso* population. After the first generation, as more and more New Christians intermarried with Old Christians, their "partially" New Christian descendants often proved as susceptible to judaizing as did the "pure" New Christians. For reasons that smack of racialist prejudice, the Portuguese Inquisition made a point of carefully noting the exact degree of *converso*-parentage of its suspects. Only rarely does one encounter a "pure" Old Christian among the Inquisition's judaizer victims.

Most commonly, Marranism was transmitted through the family. In Inquisitorial documents, parents, grandparents, and close relatives figure most prominently as the teachers of the Marrano heresy. In fact, the Inquisition generally dismissed as incomplete any confessions that failed to reveal this familial link. Neither in "pure" nor in "partial" New Christian families was judaizing always continual: sometimes the Marrano tradition skipped a generation and was revived only among the grandchildren. Within the family, women played an important role in fostering the continuity of Marrano traditions. Less exposed to the assimilatory pressures of public life than men were, wives, mothers, grandmothers, and aunts perpetuated the essentially domestic rites and customs of Marranism. They thus maintained a Marrano home within which the male members of the family, exposed to public denigration and suspicion of *conversos,* found solace, approval, and peace of mind. During certain periods and in certain locales, there were more women accused by the prosecution than men; in addition, the wording of the accusations frequently differed, as the women were assumed to have taken a more active role than the men in judaizing. In the Marrano communities of twentieth-century Portugal, spiritual leadership rested, more often than not, on the shoulders of highly venerated older women. In general, children were not informed of the judaizing meaning of family ceremonies until they were between the ages of ten and fifteen, to protect the family against slips of the juvenile tongue or inopportune revelations before ever-vigilant Inquisitorial authorities.

Another channel of transmission ran through professional associations. In the earliest days, some Marranos refused to do business with other Marranos until the latter had sworn a Jewish oath. Later, such formal arrangements disappeared, yet informally shared and avowed Marranism appears to have infused subsequent commercial associations with highly prized trust and stability. In turn, and up to a point, this trust, based on a common loyalty and kept secret, contributed significantly to the socially created momentum of Marranism. Universities, too, with their colleges and student organizations, their relatively large concentrations of New Christians, and their pervasive preoccupation with purity of blood, proved important centers of judaizing. Especially in medicine, a profession traditionally associated with Jews and generally mistrusted by the religious establishment, Marranos reinforced each other's ancestral loyalties and, where opportune, drew into their orbit wavering *conversos,* who felt the attraction of New Christian solidarity or were reacting against Old Christian antagonism.

The religious education of the Marranos was extremely limited. For the most part, judaizers had to rely on family traditions of Jewish practices and prayers. Those who wished to deepen their intellectual understanding of Judaism culled information from the Vulgate translation of the Hebrew Bible—including the Apocrypha and Pseudepigrapha, which are not part of the rabbinic canon—and the abundant vernacular literature on biblical themes. Marranos also turned anti-Jewish texts to their advantage, for polemic literature and Inquisitorial edicts of faith never tired of denouncing innumerable Jewish practices and ideas, and thus publicized forbidden traditions. Genuinely Jewish literature was occasionally smuggled in from the vernacular Spanish and Portuguese presses established by former *conversos* in Italy and Holland.

THE INQUISITION. In Spain the initial Inquisitorial hunt for judaizers was begun by district, in stages between 1480 and 1495, depending on the tribunal. Its duration varied widely from jurisdiction to jurisdiction: until about 1510 in most of Old Castile, into the 1520s in Valencia, and into the 1590s in Cuenca. In most of Spain, judging from Inquisitorial documentation, judaizing would appear to have been eradicated within one or two generations after the expulsion and the final wave of conversion, except where it appeared sporadically in isolated regions and in Majorca, where there were dramatic proceedings against several hundred "Xuetas" (probably, "little Jews") from 1675 to 1691. In Portugal, prosecution of judaizers started in 1536 and lasted without major interruptions until the 1760s—that is, across almost ten generations.

The activity of the Portuguese Inquisition is particularly uneven when viewed over time. Dramatic increases in Inquisitorial vigilance occurred between the years 1618 and 1640, between 1660 and 1674, and during the 1720s and 1730s. During the same period, Portuguese judaizers also made their appearance outside of Portugal. Under the union of the Spanish and Portuguese crowns (1580–1640), large numbers of Portuguese New Christians sought economic opportunities or respite from the Portuguese Inquisition, or both, in Spain and its American colonies. The Portuguese rebellion of 1640 rendered these somewhat suspect and increasingly more prosperous immigrants political enemies and provoked retaliation in Spain and its territories in America that lasted into the 1660s. Some Portuguese New Christians nonetheless remained in Spain, and their descendants became the final object of anti-judaizing activity in Spanish Inquisitorial history, from as early as 1630 and up until between 1720 and 1731. Ultimately, the Portuguese Marrano phenomenon survived Inquisitorial repression, and distinct vestiges of judaizing were discovered in Beira Alta and Trás-os-Montes provinces in the twentieth century and have persisted until today.

Some evidence suggests that women were as numerous as men among the judaizer victims of the Inquisitions. During certain periods, such as the first century of the Portuguese Inquisition, women may even have outnumbered men. Two groups stand out as constant and ubiquitous targets of Inquisitorial vigilance: professionals (especially physicians) and merchants of various ilk and size. Almost as numerous are the artisans and public servants, but their incidence varied more, presumably in accordance with local conditions. An occasional cleric is encountered, more apparently before the widespread introduction of *limpieza* statutes. In the earliest days of the Spanish Inquisition, the Jeronymite order, among others, was discovered to harbor a relatively large number of judaizers who had found in the monastery the perfect shelter for their secret activities.

A number of historical circumstances may account for the greater persistence and larger extension of the Marrano phenomenon in Portugal than in Spain. The coexistence of *conversos* and Jews in Spain from 1391 until 1492 forged a clear and permanent distinction between sincere and judaizing *conversos* and undermined *converso* solidarity. In Portugal, where the entire Jewish community was converted at once, ancestral loyalties remained latent, and so acted as a catalyst of group solidarity. Conversion there was even harder for the Spanish exiles, who by their act of emigration had already expressed a strong attachment to Judaism. The forty years that elapsed between the conversion and the institution of the Portuguese Inquisition, moreover, gave judaizers an opportunity to adjust themselves to the exigencies of secrecy. Finally, as former Spanish exiles, the vast majority of Portuguese New Christians (only a very small minority of whom were the descendants of the 20,000 native Portuguese Jews) constituted a distinct ethnic group whose primordial ties reinforced ancestral religious commitments.

Some of the geographic, chronological, and professional variations in Inquisitorial repression are undoubtedly a reflection of differences in the persistence and preponderance of judaizers. The 1618 Oporto arrests (and others of the same sort), the periodic increases in Portuguese Inquisitorial vigilance, and the anti-Portuguese campaign of the Spanish and American Inquisitions smack of arbitrariness and extra-religious inspiration. In these instances, victimization occurred in an atmosphere of commercial rivalry, xenophobia, political discontent, or economic decline. It is difficult, however, to pinpoint exactly how political or economic tension engendered a widening or deepening of Inquisitorial repression. Historians who accept the reality of the Marrano phenomenon and the reliability of Inquisitorial recording seek—but have not yet found, by reason of the sheer magnitude of such a project—reverberations of extrareligious considerations in the trial records themselves: in increases in spontaneous accusations and extorted denunciations, in a greater readiness (on flimsier evidence) to prosecute, or in a slackening of procedural rigor.

The Marrano phenomenon also extended beyond the Iberian world. Most New Christians who emigrated to non-Iberian Europe or to America returned to Judaism; some immediately, others after several generations, depending on the climate of toleration in the land of settlement. These ex-*conversos* founded Jewish communities during the sixteenth century in North Africa, Italy, Ottoman Greece and Turkey, and, during the seventeenth century, in southwestern France, Amsterdam, Hamburg, London, the Caribbean, and North America. The reasons behind their emigration are the subject of an interminable scholarly debate. Some *conversos* migrated in search of economic opportunities, others to re-embrace their ancestral Judaism. Most, however, appear to have fled the threat or experience of Inquisitorial persecution. At first, immediately following the institution of the Portuguese Inquisition, this threat gave rise to a general fear, prompting many *conversos,* including those not directly threatened, to flee the country. Later, the Inquisitorial threat became particularized and was feared primarily by families that had relatives or close associates who had been incarcerated and might be forced, by Inquisitorial pressure or torture, to denounce their judaizing associates.

Interpretations of the Marrano Phenomenon. Theories about the Marranos are almost as numerous as the scholars who have studied the subject. Difficulty arises from the nearly total lack of sources in the Marrano voice and the need, therefore, to rely almost entirely on the documentation of the Inquisition, a not disinterested adversary, for information. Some have seen the Inquisition as an instrument of the seignorial class designed to combat, through incarceration and expropriation, the economic, social, and political advances of a rising and largely *converso* middle class. Others have viewed the Inquisitorial persecution of the *conversos* as a continuation of the age-old anti-Jewish struggle of the church inspired by ecclesiastical paranoia. Both views considered the reality of Marranism an Inquisitorial myth and dismissed Inquisitorial documentation as a malicious or misguided fabrication. The *conversos,* they opined, had completely assimilated into Christian society, give or take an occasional atavistic Jewish custom.

At the other extreme, some historians have been convinced that many *conversos* consciously attempted to remain Jews to the degree that their enforced clandestinity permitted. The Inquisitorial efforts to stamp out all remaining traces of Judaism were therefore a response to a reality that an intolerant church defined as heretical, and Inquisitorial documentation reveals more or less substantial snippets of a vibrant and tenacious crypto-Judaism. The subsequent resettlement of many Marranos in Jewish communities in more tolerant parts of Europe and America confirms, according to these historians, their unwavering loyalty to Judaism.

Most historians today probably reject both interpretations. No matter what motivation one imputes to the inquisitors, the once secret and immensely detailed archives of the Inquisition are there now for everyone to see, examine, and compare, and the stories they tell are clearly beyond the powers of even the most devious imagination. On the other hand, a simple loyalty to Judaism is inadequate to account for the regional and chronological differences in the manifestations of Marranism, to explain why some and not other Jewish traditions were retained, or to justify the protracted and voluntary lingering of most Marranos in Portugal, Spain, and the colonies.

Historians now generally acknowledge the variety of *converso* religious commitments spanning a spectrum from the sincere Christian via the indifferent or wavering *converso* to the sincere judaizer. They accept that the social experiences of the New Christians, such as "purity of blood" discrimination and pressures to assimilate, influenced the *conversos'* religious commitment so that every New Christian was a potential Marrano who by any one of a number of social accidents or personal idiosyncrasies could become an active judaizer. For them, Marranism was "a potential Judaism, which entry into a Jewish community transformed most often into a real Judaism" (Révah, 1959–1960, p. 55).

Another avenue of approach recognizes Marranism as a popular tradition—that is, as the continuation of a popular Jewish tradition that, even when Judaism was a licit religion in Spain and Portugal, had always differed from the Judaism of the rabbinically educated elite. The domestic centrality of popular religion lodges it primordially in a network of familial and ethnic ties at the same time that its private nature renders it less susceptible to public dynamics. The fortunes of popular religion and of Marranism, therefore, fluctuate with the individual's relation to their family, extended group of families, or ethnic community. This relation, in turn, is shaped by the family or ethnic community's place in society at large. Under the conditions of social discrimination prevailing in Portugal and Spain, the New Christian family or ethnic community experienced differing and intermittent forms of social rejection. At this point, Marranism became the focus of a counterculture, a rejection of the religious principles under which the New Christians were refused their equal place as Christians in Iberian society. The variety of *converso* commitments to Marranism, therefore, spans a spectrum from a more or less witting retention of popular Jewish traditions to a more or less willful embrace of New Christian counterculture.

Aftermath and Impact. The impact of the *converso* problem and the Marrano phenomenon on Iberian and Jewish history cannot be denied, however difficult it may be to gauge its profundity precisely. Scholarly estimations, therefore, vary widely, but the following observations have found a certain general acceptance.

Originally founded to inquire into the religious orthodoxy of the *conversos,* the Spanish and Portuguese Inquisitions usurped the supervision of many other religious affairs, set the strictest limits on religious dissension and innovation, and, in the end, encouraged Iberian Catholicism's drift toward conformism and ritualism. On the other side, the *conversos'* forced induction into Christianity, their rejection by Iberian society, and their involuntary marginality could not but have complicated New Christian attitudes toward Christianity in particular and toward religion in general. Some *conversos* vented their misgivings at contemporary Iberian Catholicism or sought satisfaction in more profound religious experiences than were available through the official church. New Christians were particularly numerous among the anticlerical, antiritualistic Erasmian humanists and pietists (e.g., Luis de León, 1527–1591, a poet and writer), some of whom (e.g., the Sevillian cleric Constantino Ponce de la Fuente) were confusedly accused of Lutheranism. Other New Christians were attracted to the urbane, reformist, heterodox mysticism of the *alumbrados,* who claimed direct, unmediated divine illumination (e.g., the brothers Ortiz), or to the enlightened and militant spirituality of the Jesuits (e.g., Laínez and Polanco, generals of the Jesuit order; possibly Juan de Mariana, a historian; and Baltasar Gracián y Morales, a writer). A few exceptional individuals (e.g., the cleric and reformer John of Ávila, Teresa of Ávila, and, possibly, the priest Miguel de Molinos) formulated their personal, mystical "innovations" in such orthodox terms that they passed even the rigorous examinations of the Inquisition. Other New Christians evaded the complication and retreated into religious indifference or a more or less radical rejection of any and all religions, with or without a public facade of piety and devotion. All in all, the criticism and spiritual quest, as well as the contrasting indifference of many sincerely Christian *converses,* left an indelible mark on the Christianity of sixteenth-century Spain and Portugal.

Various significant religious developments in seventeenth-century Jewish history, too, have been explained as reverberations of the Marrano phenomenon. Not surprisingly, among several first-generation Marrano refugees who reconverted to Judaism, one encounters an apologetic need to defend Jews and Judaism, as well as a polemic urge to counter the claims of Christianity, that is more common and more strong than that found among traditional Jews. Several of the apologetic works (e.g., those by Menasseh ben Israel, Isaac Cardoso, and Isaac Orobio de Castro) were published in the vernacular, became classics, and have influenced modern perceptions of Jews and Judaism. For reasons of law and self-censorship, the polemic treatises (e.g., by Eliau Montalto, Saul Levi Morteira, Orobio de Castro, and Abraham Gomes Silveyra) circulated in manuscript, in Spanish and Portuguese, among Jews only and have been brought to public attention only recently.

Scholars have also pointed to an unmistakable note of disillusionment with revealed and institutional religion among another group of ex-Marranos. They argue—differing in the weight they give this argument—that some Marranos carried their forceful rejection of Christianity over into a critique of parts or all of the Jewish tradition. Having lost faith in both the Christian and the Jewish traditions, these ex-Marranos joined the growing European community of skeptics; thus, each in a personal way projected a distinctly modern alternative to traditional revealed religion. Uriel da Costa (1585–1640) embraced Epicureanism; Barukh Spinoza pursued and reworked Cartesian philosophy to the point of *amor Dei (sive Naturae) intellectualis* (an intellectual love of God [or Nature]); and Isaac La Peyrère, according to one theory, envisioned a meta-Judeo-Christian messianism inspired by the manner in which the Marranos had combined and transcended both the Jewish and the Christian traditions.

Finally, ex-Marrano Jews played a leading role in the most important new Jewish movement of the seventeenth century, that of the pseudomessiah Shabbetai Tsevi. They were among the first and most ardent followers as soon as news of Shabbetai's messianic mission reached the European Jewish communities, and some (e.g., Abraham Cardoso) became prominent advocates of the heretical Shabbatean movement, which retained faith in Shabbetai's messiahship even after his apostasy. In the early days of the movement, ex-Marranos saw in Shabbetai Tsevi a confirmation of the Jewish messianic expectations many of them, as Marranos, had nurtured for several generations in the face of insistent Christian denunciations. Shabbetai's claims that he had apostatized for a messianic purpose reminded a few ex-Marranos of their former double life, and their acceptance of these claims helped put their guilt-laden memories in a new and positive light. Distinct echoes of the Marrano experience, therefore, resound in the two most novel Jewish movements of the seventeenth century: skepticism and mystical messianism.

NON-IBERIAN PARALLELS TO MARRANISM. Jewish loyalties among converted Jews survived elsewhere and at other times in Jewish history. A certain degree of Marranism attended every instance of a forced conversion of Jews. In most cases, the forcibly converted Jews either fled and returned to Judaism, were eventually assimilated completely into the native population, or were permitted by a subsequent decree to return to Judaism. In a few cases, however, the forcibly converted Jews remained a group apart. Thus, in Italy in the early 1290s, the Jews of Apulia were forcibly converted. Throughout the fourteenth and much of the fifteenth centuries, sources continue to speak of the *neofiti* (neophytes) or *mercanti* (merchants), the descendants of these converted Jews, as a group that had not completely abandoned its ancestral Jewish practices.

The other documented cases of Marranism occurred in Persia, whose *conversos* are referred to as Jedidim. In the middle of the seventeenth century, first the Jews of Isfahan and later those of the rest of Persia were forcibly converted. The converts and their descendants were known as *Jadid al-Islam* (New Muslim). In 1839 the Jews of Mashhad were forcibly converted and also called *Jadid al-Islam.* In both cases the Jedidim successfully resisted pressures to intermarry with the rest of the Muslim population. The ultimate fate of the earlier Jedidim is not known. The Mashhad Jedidim, however, maintained themselves as a community through endogamy, religious leadership, and communal observances and instruction. Some settled elsewhere either as Jedidim or as Jews (as in Jerusalem in the 1890s) and so gave rise to an economically important *Jadid* diaspora; others remained in Persia, where they still formed a distinct Judeo-Muslim group as late as the 1940s.

In sum, Marrano-like survivals of Jewish loyalties among converted Jews appeared where the converted Jews chose to stay in their native land, where the religious and social intolerance that had given rise to the forced conversion persisted unabatedly for many subsequent generations, and where the Jewish, neophyte, or Jadid community constituted a more or less distinct and cohesive socioeconomic group. The extent to which variations in the intensity of Jewish commitments prior to conversion played a role in emergent Marranism cannot be precisely assessed.

Marranos in the Western Hemisphere. In the sixteenth century, Spanish *conversos* began to arrive in the Western Hemisphere along with the conquistadors. Some were seeking economic opportunities, and all were relieved to be far from the Spanish Inquisition's reach. Among them were judaizers, many of whom were tried by the Inquisitions established in Mexico and Peru during the sixteenth and seventeenth centuries. Some moved north to territories that would later become part of the United States, while others remained in Mexico, Brazil, Peru, and elsewhere.

Many of these crypto-Jews passed on traditions to their children, but as time passed, this transmission became more and more problematic. The majority experienced life as Catholics (some as Protestants), yet some retained a sense of identity as Jews or continued hidden religious observances, such as candle lighting or baking special types of bread. Near the end of the twentieth century (in 1990, to be precise), a great deal of media attention began to be paid to those who are or claim to be their descendants. There is considerable controversy about the nature of their identity, their genuineness, and their motives, and about how to receive them. Quite a few crypto-Judaic societies have been established, especially in the Southwest United States (New Mexico, Texas, Arizona, and Colorado) while in Latin America many individuals have sought out rabbis or chosen to convert; some have even gone to Israel to study, convert, and live as Jews.

See Also Domestic Observances, article on Jewish Practices; Heresy, article on Christian Concepts; Inquisition, The, article on The Inquisition in the Old World; Judaism; Messianism, article on Jewish Messianism; Polemics, article on Jewish-Christian Polemics; Rites of Passage, article on Jewish Rites; Shabbetai Tsevi; Spinoza, Barukh.

Bibliography

General Studies

The first book-length study of the Marranos was Cecil Roth's *A History of the Marranos* (Philadelphia, 1932), which is now outdated and not always reliable. Roth summarized the then limited state of knowledge almost entirely on the basis of far from satisfactory secondary literature. Shorter, updated, better informed, and fully annotated is Israel S. Révah's "Les Marranos," *Revue des études juives* 108 (1959–1960): 2–77. A compilation of Marrano customs appears in David M. Gitlitz's *Secrecy and Deceit: The Religion of the Crypto-Jews* (Philadelphia, 1996). A comparative history of the *conversos* appears in Renée Levine Melammed's *A Question of Identity: Iberian Conversos in Historical Perspective* (New York, 2004).

Marranism in Spain and Portugal

For Spain we possess two substantial overviews: Julio Caro Baroja's *Los Judíos en la España moderna y contemporánea,* 3 vols. (Madrid, 1962), an uneven, but, when used with discrimination, extremely informative history by a well-known anthropologist; and Antonio Domínguez Ortiz's *Los Judeoconversos en España y América* (Madrid, 1971), a sober and judicious account by one of Spain's most eminent historians. The early history of the Marranos of Ciudad Real is covered on the basis of all available Inquisitorial documentation in Haim Beinart's *Conversos on Trial* (Jerusalem, 1981); a more exhaustive and surefooted treatment, especially of the Jewish element in Marranism, than the previous overviews. On the basis of contemporary Hebrew sources, Benzion Netanyahu's *The Marranos of Spain from the Late Fourteenth to the Early Sixteenth Century* (New York, 1966) argues against the theory of a persistent and vibrant judaizing among the forced converts. The unique role of women is analyzed in Renée Levine Melammed's *Heretics or Daughters of Israel: The Crypto-Jewish Women of Castile* (New York, 1999).

For Portugal, the classic account of João Lúcio d'Azevedo, *História dos cristãos novos portugueses* (Lisbon, 1921), focuses more on the political history of the New Christian problem than on the evolution of the Marrano phenomenon. Although primarily a history of the fierce political struggle surrounding the establishment of the Portuguese Inquisition, Alexandre Herculano's *History of the Origin and Establishment of the Inquisition in Portugal,* translated by John C. Branner (Stanford, Calif., 1926), contains much invaluable information on the early-sixteenth-century history of the Portuguese Marranos. António José Saraiva's *Inquisição e cristãos-novos* (Oporto, Portugal, 1969) interprets the Inquisition's prosecution of the Portuguese New Christians in terms of a class struggle. The best study of the Marranos in the Spanish and Portuguese colonies is Anita Novinsky's *Cristãos novos na Bahia* (São Paulo, 1972), which stresses the anti-Catholic, defensive nature of the Marrano phenomenon.

Marranos in a Non-Iberian Context

Surveying the Marranos in a non-Iberian context, Brian Pullan's *The Jews of Europe and the Inquisition of Venice, 1550–1670* (Oxford, 1983) offers a new and promising perspective on Marranism in general.

Biographic Sources

Marranism has been studied successfully in a number of excellent biographies. Yosef Hayim Yerushalmi's *From Spanish Court to Italian Ghetto: Isaac Cardoso; A Study in Seventeenth-Century Marranism and Jewish Apologetics* (New York, 1971) delivers far more than the title indicates and probes deeply into the intellectual world of a Marrano who returned to Judaism. In Hebrew, Yosef Kaplan's *From Christianity to Judaism: The Life and Work of Isaac Orobio de Castro* (Jerusalem, 1982) meticulously reconstructs the life of another ex-Marrano. Martin A. Cohen's *The Martyr: The Story of a Secret Jew and the Mexican Inquisition in the Sixteenth Century* (Philadelphia, 1973) beautifully tells the story of the famous adventurer, Luis Carvajal the Younger.

Works of Related Interest

Edward Glaser's "Invitation to Intolerance: A Study of the Portuguese Sermons Preached at Autos-da-fé," *Hebrew Union College Annual* 27 (1956): 327–385, offers keen insights into the anti-*converso* mentality of the inquisitors. Albert A. Sicroff's *Les controverses des statuts de "pureté de sang" en Espagne du quinzième au dix-septième siècle* (Paris, 1960) gives a detailed outline of the intellectual debate surrounding the "purity of blood" statutes.

DANIEL M. SWETSCHINSKI (1987)
RENÉE LEVINE MELAMMED (2005)

MARRIAGE. Every culture of the world recognizes some form of the institution of marriage. In most cultures and religions neither man nor woman is considered complete, after reaching maturity, without a spouse. Many religions consider marriage as a sacred act that originates from a god or as the union of souls or spirits with the sacred realm.

Jewish beliefs trace the origin of marriage to Adam and Eve and view their union as a part of the fabric of creation. The nuptial blessings emphasize marriage in the scheme of creation and speak of the state of marriage as paradise regained. As a blessing from God, Jewish marriage should not only perpetuate humankind but should also enhance and complete the partners' personal growth.

Christian marriage is also identified with the sacred union of Adam and Eve and is regarded as a vocation. The ceremony joins the bride and groom into one spirit in union with Christ and God. In Christianity, marriage is also a metaphor for the marriage of the church to Christ. In this sense the bride and groom become the "bride" of Christ and are heirs together of the grace of life through the spirit of Christ.

For the Hindu, marriage is also a sacred institution whereby man and woman become one in spirit. Hindu marriage is also a social duty, and in the Vedic period it was a moral and religious obligation as well. Marriage and the siring of male children was the only possible way in which a man could repay his debt to his ancestors.

Marriage among the Zinacantecos, a Maya Indian group in central Mexico, is a mixture of native Indian religion and sixteenth-century Catholicism, as it is in most Latin American cultures. In these societies the celebration of a Christian marriage was urged on the native Indians by the Spanish conquerors as the only means to attain heaven at death. Marriage here takes place on two levels. It is not simply the relationship between two individuals and their families, but it is also a bond between the souls of the bride and groom.

Among the Hopi Indians of the American Southwest, a woman initiates a marriage and brings a husband to her father's house. The marriage is necessary for the girl's life after death. The wedding clothes that are provided by her husband's male relatives will become her shroud upon her death and will transport her spirit into the afterworld. And so, without entering into marriage, one cannot truly die.

PURPOSE OF MARRIAGE. The purpose of marriage and the beliefs that surround this institution must be viewed differently for every culture. Marriage in industrialized societies is very different from that in societies where kinship relations and the alliances created through those relations will be the most important part of an individual's life. Here, the marriage arrangements may not take individual choice into account. There are three major categories of belief about the purposes of marriage: Marriage may be viewed as existing primarily for the continuation of the family and society through procreation; it may be considered most importantly as an alliance, that is, the means to bring about the integration of society by setting up kinship ties and kinship terminology; and finally, the union of bride and groom may be perceived as a complex system of exchanges between groups and/or individuals. These categories will be validated through the religious beliefs of the society.

Continuation of society. The institution of marriage perpetuates society by socially recognizing the union of man and woman and incorporating their offspring into the fabric of social life. There are variants of marriage forms that exist in many cultures to allow for the continuation of the family and of society in the event that one of the marriage partners dies. The two best known forms are the levirate and the sororate. In the levirate, when the husband of a marriage dies, an approved male relative of his may live with the widow and the children. This replacement husband will conceive more children for the deceased as if he were the deceased. In the sororate, the place of a deceased wife is taken by her sister.

The Nuer and Zulu societies of Africa practice another variant of the more traditional marriage in order that the family of the deceased may continue. There are two types of this "ghost marriage." If a man is engaged and dies before the marriage, his fiancée should marry one of his kinsmen and conceive children for the dead man, in much the same way as in the levirate. A man may also "waken" a dead relative who was never married by marrying a wife to his name and conceiving children for him. Also among these two groups, women may "become" men to carry on the male line. A rich, important woman, or the eldest daughter in a family with no sons, can marry another woman and become the father of her wife's children who are conceived by some male relative of the female husband. The importance of all these forms of marriage is that they allow for the perpetuation of the family line, and indirectly the entire society, through the existing structure of social relations.

While these forms of marriage perpetuate society through those who have died, many societies ensure their continuation into the future by marrying off those individuals not yet born. Among the Tiwi of Australia, a young girl is contracted for her future marriage before her birth, at her mother's wedding ceremony. When the girl enters puberty her wedding ceremony is held. This ceremony is attended by the girl, her father, and her husband, as well as her future sons-in-law. For in the same way that she has been married since her mother's wedding, here at her wedding she also marries her daughters to their future husbands.

Alliance. The importance placed upon marriage in many societies is in its role in integrating society. Marriage is the starting point for the kinship ties that run across and between different and independent kinship or descent groups. A marriage will be used to create an alliance between two lines of descent with very little focus upon the relationship between the bride and groom. In many cases these will be arranged marriages, often making use of go-betweens to reach an agreement between the two families. Love is not a requirement here, but the affection that exists after many years of successful marriage is a product of the marriage. Among Georgian Jews, when dowry is unavailable, a love marriage may be effected by elopement, the legitimacy of which is later recognized if the match appears to be successful.

System of exchange. In the final category of marriage beliefs, marriage represents the gift or exchange of women between two descent groups. The position of giving or receiving wives sets up a constantly changing mechanism by which status is expressed and validated between the two kinship groups. The ideal exchange is for both descent groups to exchange sisters, thereby maintaining the status of each group as equal. Marrying a woman in compensation for the death of a man is also an exchange recognized as equivalent in many cultures for the settlement of quarrels.

When women are not exchanged equally, then the balance between the two groups remains unequal and must be achieved through other means. This balancing may take the form of payments made on behalf of the husband to the man or the family who has given up the wife. These payments are viewed as equivalent to the reproductive powers of the woman who is being given to another group as well as a return on the labor and usefulness the bride's family will lose upon her marriage. These payments are known as "bride-price" or "bride-wealth."

Postmarital residence or marriage service may be used in a similar way as bride-price or may even be combined with bride-wealth payments. To repay the bride's family for the loss of a daughter, the groom will serve his in-laws for an agreed-upon time. In the Hebrew scriptures, for example, this type of service is described in *Genesis* 29, which tells of Jacob's serving his father-in-law for seven years for each of his wives, Leah and Rachel.

Dowry is not the opposite of bride-price; rather, it is an endowment of property upon the bride from her own family and is generally viewed as her share of the family inheritance. In some instances, however, dowry may closely resemble the practice of paying bride-price, as in marriages between castes in India and Sri Lanka. Most Hindu marriages are traditionally made between members of the same caste, and no dowry will be given. However, when a girl marries into a higher caste she will be accompanied by a substantial dowry in symbolic payment for her movement to a higher status. This practice is known as hypergamy.

Exchange relationships at marriage may be expressed primarily through the flow of gifts between families, and frequently these expenses will be about equal on both sides. The power of the gift is not only in the object as gift but in the relationships that lie behind the gifts. It is the exchange itself that is essential to the completion and success of the marriage. This exchange of gifts is often an important part of the religious ceremony of marriage.

FORMS OF MARRIAGE. There are two basic forms of marriage: monogamy, the union of one man with one woman, and polygamy, the union of a man or a woman with multiple marriage partners. Polygamy can also be divided into two types: polyandry, in which a woman has more than one husband, and, conversely, polygyny, in which a man has more than one wife. Polygyny is the most common form of multiple marriage, and the plurality of wives is mainly the privilege of older men and their wealth. Polygyny augments the power of a man by increasing his alliances and following. But it may cause conflict among co-wives, as among the Ndembu of Zambia. Conflict between wives is very common in Islamic lands. The Tiv of Nigeria manage the problem differently: the first wife becomes the "husband" of the "little wives," and grows very attached to them.

The classic case of polyandry is in Tibet, where a group of brothers may jointly marry a wife. The wedding takes place when the eldest brother has reached the appropriate age, and on formal occasions it is he who will perform the role of father, although all brothers are viewed as the father to the children of the marriage. One effect of polyandry is to keep down the population, an important goal where arable land is a scarce resource. There is, however, an alternative to polyandrous marriage open to younger brothers: they may become monks and commit themselves to a life of celibacy. Such a "marriage" to religion or to God is an avenue available to both sexes in most societies.

Societies regulate not only how many spouses one can have but from what general categories these individuals should be selected. Exogamy, marriage outside a defined kinship group, is primarily concerned with incest prohibitions. Brother-sister and parent-child unions are forbidden in nearly every culture; cousin marriage is forbidden in the third degree of the collateral line among Roman Catholics, while it is recommended among many peoples of Africa. Endogamy is marriage within a defined group as required by custom or law. This group may be defined by culturally recognized kinship ties or by a religious tradition. Pious Roman Catholics and Jews obey the rule of endogamy and take a spouse from within their own religion. Good Hindus will keep marriage within their own caste, except when practicing hypergamy.

MARRIAGE AS A RITE OF PASSAGE. A rite of passage is a vehicle for moving an individual or a group of individuals from one way of being to another through a series of culturally recognized stages. A marriage ceremony moves the bride and groom from being unmarried to being husband and wife. Just as the definition of what marriage is will vary cross-culturally, so will the manner in which the union of marriage is created and recognized. The rite of passage may extend over a long period of time and include great finery and complex symbolism, or there may be no traditional ceremony at all, simply an action conducted in public view.

MARRIAGE RITUAL. The ceremonials of marriage may be entirely of a religious nature, include both religious and secular elements, or be entirely within the secular and legal realm. Two elements are used to mark a marriage, whether there is a ceremony or not: the sharing of food between the bride and groom (or some passage of food or other substance between them) and the necessity of a public statement or the requirement of witnesses to the marriage event, which may even include proof of virginity and consummation, as among Arabs.

Among the Mundurucú of South America, a marriage is marked only when the man brings the day's kill to his bride instead of to one of his close female relatives. The Ndembu of Africa, like the Tiwi of Australia, combine the puberty rites for a young girl with her marriage ceremony. Here the emphasis is upon fertility. The rites take place where the groom has planted his arrow by the "milk tree," a tree that represents the matrilineage. Among Trobriand Islanders, a man and a woman may have been sleeping together for a long while, but their marriage is not acknowledged until they eat yams together in public. The Burmese wedding ceremony does not create marriage but is, rather, the public statement that a couple intend to live together as husband and wife. The symbol of marriage here is the sharing of food from the same bowl by the bride and groom after the ceremony.

The Jewish marriage ceremony must have witnesses for the signing of the marriage contract and for the symbolic consummation, the *yiḥud,* or time of privacy. It is during this time of privacy that the couple break their fast and eat together for the first time. When they emerge from their seclusion, they are husband and wife and will then share a meal with their guests.

The wedding ceremony in Burma is not attended by Buddhist monks. This ceremony is a secular affair contained within religious rites. The Buddhist monks are fed a special meal in the bride's home the morning before the wedding. This feast acquires merit for the couple to be married and for the parents of the bride. A religious ceremony is held the evening after the wedding at the village shrine and offerings are made by the bride, her mother, and the mother of the groom to the guardian spirits of the village and to the spirits of the ancestors. During the secular wedding ceremony the couple are instructed to worship their parents and the Buddha. Their hands are held together and immersed in a bowl of water so that "their union should be as indivisible as water."

Christian marriage may be regarded as a sacrament, one of the outward signs of inward grace, and may include the Eucharist within the ceremony, the sacred sharing of the mystical body of Christ that unites all participants with God. In most Christian churches this is an optional rite, but a wedding will usually be followed by a sharing of food and drink with guests. This part of the ceremony is not sacred. One can also be a Christian and include few if any religious elements in the marriage ceremony—which may be performed entirely within the secular domain by various officers of law. Or a couple may become married simply by living together for a set period of years, thus forming a marriage in "common law." These options to the traditional marriage ceremony are available in other religions as well.

The necessity for consummation to occur in order for a marriage to be legally binding is not universal but is culturally and religiously specific. Although the Virgin Mary bore Christ without intercourse with her husband, any Christian marriage can be annulled or canceled if the couple do not consummate the marriage. In Hinduism, however, the most important rite for validation of a marriage is the ceremony called Saptapadi, the "taking of seven steps" by the couple before the sacred nuptial fire. Legally the marriage is complete with the seventh step, for according to the Hindu Marriage Act of 1955 consummation is not necessary to make marriage complete and binding.

The marriage ceremony of Java is a syncretism of Hinduism, Islam, and folk religion from the villages. The evening before the ceremony, a feast called the Slametan is held. Then the bride must sit by herself for five hours until midnight. At midnight an angel enters her and will remain in her until five days after the wedding. The actual wedding begins the next day when the groom makes a trip to the office of the government religious official to register and legalize the marriage. For Javanese Muslims, this is the important part of the marriage ceremony, for it is here that the marriage is made official in the eyes of God and the government. However, according to the folk religion the couple is not married until they exchange their *kembang majang* ("blossoming flowers"), which stand for their virginity. And then they must eat from one another's dish but they must not finish their food. Consummation of the marriage is believed to have occurred when this food begins to smell in five days, or when the angel has left the bride.

CREATION MYTHS AND THE INSTITUTION OF MARRIAGE. Many origin myths that explain the creation of the world and of humankind also explain marriage. In Samoa the marriage of the creator god Tangaloa with a woman he has created begins the world and, through their union, all of mankind. The Makasar of Indonesia believe that the son of the sky deity was sent to earth on a rainbow to prepare the world for humans. This god married six female deities and their offspring became the peoples of the world. The union of the Japanese gods Izanagi and Izanami consolidates and fertilizes the moving earth. Through their union, they produced the islands of Japan. The marriage of Osiris, one of the greatest of ancient Egyptian deities, with his sister Isis accounts for the continuation of the pharaohs and their practice of marrying their sisters. And, for Jews, Christians, and Muslims alike, the marriage of Adam and Eve, two beings created by God, generates all of humankind.

SEE ALSO Hieros Gamos; Mystical Union; Rites of Passage; Sacrament, article on Christian Sacraments.

BIBLIOGRAPHY

One of the first scholars to concern himself with marriage practices was Lewis Henry Morgan in *Ancient Society* (New York, 1877). Following this evolutionary approach, Edward A. Westermarck compiled his classic *The History of Human Marriage* (1891), 3 vols., 5th ed. (1921; reprint, New York, 1971). This three-volume set treats everything believed to be related to marriage in that time, including marriage rites, customs, and kinship organizations. One of the classic studies of the constitution of social groups and their unity was written by W. Robertson Smith following the precedents set by Morgan and Westermarck. Smith's *Kinship and Marriage in Early Arabia,* edited by Stanley A. Cook (1903; Oosterhuit, 1966), goes beyond these first works and is particularly concerned with the laws of marriage and how this institution functioned within the tribal organization in Arabia at the time of Muhammad. The theories of primitive promiscuity and group marriage as the earliest forms of marriage in human history that are put forth by all of these books have never been substantiated, but these works provide valuable insights into human society.

For a contemporary view of love and marriage in the Jewish religion and its place in society, see Maurice Lamm's *The Jewish Way in Love and Marriage* (San Francisco, 1980). This book also includes a thorough description of a contemporary Jewish wedding ceremony. The best review of marriage and kinship beliefs for cultures of Africa is *African Systems of Kinship and Marriage,* edited by A. R. Radcliffe-Brown and Daryll Forde (Oxford, 1962). This book considers marriage in relation to other aspects of culture including economic, political, and religious beliefs. Melford E. Spiro's *Kinship and Marriage in Burma: A Cultural and Psychodynamic Analysis* (Berkeley, 1977) is an excellent presentation of kinship beliefs in Burma and includes a full account of Burmese Buddhist views on marriage. Clifford Geertz's seminal work *The Religion of Java* (Glencoe, Ill., 1960) describes the syncretism of Hindu, Islamic, and folk beliefs that comprise Javanese religion. This book focuses on the five major occupations of the population and their religious beliefs that shape the moral organization of the culture of Java. The mixture of Catholic and Maya Indian beliefs is explored in Evon Z. Vogt's *Zinacantan: A Maya Community in the Highlands of Chiapas* (Cambridge, Mass., 1969). An extensive study of the Tzotzil-speaking Indians of Guatemala, it includes a full account of their religious beliefs and marriage practices, especially the relationships created between families and *compadres,* or ritual godparents. For an excellent view of marriage as a life process, begun before the birth of the bride and occurring in gradual stages as she matures, see Jane C. Goodale's *Tiwi Wives: A Study of the Women of Melville Island, North Australia* (Seattle, 1971).

EDITH TURNER (1987)
PAMELA R. FRESE (1987)

MARS. The Latin name *Mars,* found throughout Italy, lacks any Indo-European etymology. It appears in both a simple form and in doubled form. The Latin *Mars* coexists with an ancient form, *Mavors* (kept in use by poets), as well as a contracted form, *Maurs* (see *Corpus inscriptiorum Latinarum,* Berlin, 1863, vol. 1, no. 49). As for the doubled form, *Marmar,* it very likely stems from **Mar-mart-s;* it is found in the *Carmen Arvale* along with *Marmor,* which seems an odd form. *Mamers,* which the ancients identified as an Oscan term (Paulus-Festus, ed. Lindsay, 1913, p. 150 L.), derived from **Mamars* by apophony of the second vowel. A god Maris is known among the Etruscan gods, but the identification with Mars is doubtful, since Laran is the Etruscan god of war. The Umbrian ritual of the seven Iguvine Tables (from ancient Iguvium, modern Gubbio) attests to the worship of Mars in that region: Table VIb1 mentions the sacrifice of three oxen to Mars Grabovius. With Jupiter and Vofionus, Mars receives the epithet "Grabovius" (the link with Latin *Gradivus,* epithet of Mars, is uncertain) and is the second god of the so-called "Grabovian trinity." Mars is the god to whom is dedicated the *ver sacrum,* an Italic ritual, originally Sabin (Strabo 5.4.12), in which the god is offered all that is born and produced during the spring. This evidence indicates that the Mamertini (whose name is linked with Mamars), when a plague spread in the Samnium, entered Bruttium in 288 BCE and then settled in Messana (Festus, p. 150 L). Such a ritual attests to the Italic dimension of Mars. The dative *Mamartei,* read in an inscription at Satricum dating from the sixth century BCE, implies the existence of a nominative, **Mamars.* The *Lapis Satricanus,* found in the foundation of a temple of Mater Matuta, mentions, in an archaic genitive form, the name of Valerius Publicola (consul in Rome at the beginning of the Republic), and a dedication or offering by his *sodales* to Mars (*popliosio valesiosio suodales mamartei*).

Mars is the Roman god of power, particularly of war. He held the second position in the archaic triad of Jupiter, Mars, and Quirinus, which, according to Georges Dumézil, pre-existed the Capitoline triad. He received the second share of the *spolia opima* in the threefold distribution of the highest military spoils established by the law of Numa (Festus, p. 204 L.). He had not only a particular priest, the *flamen Martialis,* but also a specific kind of offering: the *suovetaurilia,* a set of three victims (boar, ram, and bull) sacrificed as part of the Capitoline triad, a purification ritual called the *lustratio populi* celebrated by the Roman censors at the closing of the *lustrum* in the Campus Martius.The old brotherhood of the Salii, created by Numa (Livy, 1.20. 4), was specially concerned with the war rituals and the god of war. The Salii, divided into two twelve-member groups called the Salii Palatini and the Salii Collini, were under the protection of Jupiter, Mars, and Quirinus (Servius, *Ad Aeneidem* 8.663). It is probable that the opening service for the military season in spring was handled by the Salii Palatini, with Mars as their patron, and the closing service by the Salii Collini, with Quirinus as their patron.

Two sets of feasts, in March and October, correspond to the opening and closing of the military season. The first, in the spring, began on March 1, when the Salii Palatini went out of their *Curia* on the Palatine and the Salii Collini left the *Sacrarium* on the Quirinal to reach the Regia and offer a sacrifice to Mars. This cycle comprised the following feasts: the horse races on March 14 for the Equirria on the Field of Mars; on the same day, an old man would be expelled from the city in the Mamuralia, a reenactment of the legend of Mamurius Veturius (Mamurius Veturius, whose name recalled the god, was the smith who fabricated the shields, *ancilia,* of the Salii. One of the shields was said to have dropped from the sky—see Ovid, *Fasti* 3.369 ff.); a sacrifice called Agonium Martiale was celebrated on March 17; the lustration of arms took place at the Quinquatrus on March 19 and that of battle trumpets at the Tubilustrium on March 23. Before beginning operations, a Roman general entered the Sacrarium Martis in the Regia and exclaimed, "Mars uigila!" ("Mars, wake up!") If the lances of the god vibrated, it was a good omen and the war could begin.

The second cycle, in autumn, included the rite of purification at the Tigillum Sororium on October 1 (purification rites in memory of Horatius, who killed the Curatii and his own sister); the sacrifice of a war horse during the rites of the Equus October (October Horse), on October 15; and the lustration of arms, Armilustrium, on October 19. In spring, as in autumn, the priestly brotherhood of the Salii danced at the feasts (a dance called *tripudium*) while brandishing lances and shields. In ordinary times these arms were kept in the *sacrarium* of Mars within the Regia.

The god's military character was well established, but scholars of the predeistic shool, such as Herbert Jenkins Rose or Gustav Hermansen, who thought that Roman religion was based on *numen* (something like the Melanesian *mana*) and not on anthropomorphism, developed the theory of an agrarian Mars. This opinion seems to be based on a confusion between the god's intrinsic nature and the range of applications for his intervention. His power could be employed not only in warfare but also in agriculture. At an Eitrem Conference held in Oslo in 1955 Herbert Jenkins Rose insisted that the Equus October was sacrified *ob frugum euentum* (for the gathering of crops, but Georges Dumézil demonstrated that with this ritual the Romans intended to thank the god of war for preserving the harvest from enemies and allowing them to gather in their crops. If the lance of Mars is important in the ritual (Arnobius, *adv. nationes* 6.11, said that according to Varro the ancient Romans had *pro Marte hastam*) and can give a good omen with its vibrations, we cannot come to the conclusion that the Romans first worshiped the *hasta* and only later conceived a god with the human features of a warrior.

The name of the god does not appear in the fragments of the *Carmina Saliorum,* but Gellius (13. 23. 2) mentions it in an old prayer associated with *Nerio* and the *Moles,* two aspects of his power. In the *Carmen Arvale,* the Arval brothers prayed to "fierce Mars" *(fere Mars)* to protect Roman territory by "leaping to the border" *(limen sali).* Likewise, Cato the Elder's peasant, celebrating a private sacrifice of a pig, a sheep, and a bull, called *suovetaurile* for a *lustratio agri,* invoked Mars "to halt, rebuff, and cast away visible and invisible maladies" (*De agricultura* 141).

The god's most ancient place of worship was situated on the Field of Mars at the *ara Martis,* the altar near which D. Junius Brutus Callaicus erected a temple in 138 BCE. The most important sanctuary, outside the Porta Collina, near the Via Appia, had been dedicated on June 1, 338 BCE, and was the starting point for the annual cavalry parade (Dionysius of Halicarnassus, 6.13.4).

At the beginning of the Second Punic War, in 217 BCE, Mars was associated in a *lectisternium* with Venus, after the pattern of Ares and Aphrodite, in order to exalt the connection between Romulus, son of Mars, and Venus, ancestor of the Aeneades. Later, Augustus created the cult of Mars the avenger (Mars Ultor)—avenger of the Roman disaster suffered by M. Licinius Crassus at Carrhae in 53 BCE, and also avenger of the assassination of Julius Caesar (the victory at Philippi in 42 BCE). In 20 BCE, a round temple was erected upon the Capitoline in honor of Mars Ultor and, in 2 BCE, the great temple, situated in its own forum, was built (Dio Cassius, 54.8.3 and 60.5.3). Thus Mars enjoyed new prestige.

SEE ALSO Flamen; Lustratio; Roman Religion, article on The Early Period.

BIBLIOGRAPHY

Dumézil, Georges. *Archaic Roman Religion.* 2 vols. Translated by Philip Krapp. Chicago, 1970. Discusses the theory of the agrarian Mars.

Dumézil, Georges. *Fêtes romaines d'été et d'automne.* Paris, 1975. Pages 139–156 and 177–219 treat the Equus October.

Hermansen, Gustav. *Studien über den italischen und den römischen Mars.* Copenhagen, 1940. Supports the theory of the agrarian Mars.

Heurgon, Jacques. *Trois études sur le "ver sacrum."* Brussels, 1957. See pages 20–35.

Poultney, James Wilson. *The Bronze Tables of Iguvium.* Baltimore, 1959.

Ramat, Anna Giscalone. "Studi intorno ai nomi del dio Marte." *Archivio glottologico italiano* 47 (1962): 112–142.

Rose, Herbert Jenkins. *Ancient Roman Religion.* London, 1948.

Rose, Herbert Jenkins. "Some Problems of Classical Religion." The Eitrem lectures delivered at the University of Oslo, March 1955. Oslo, 1958, pp. 1–17.

Schilling, Robert. *La religion romaine de Vénus.* 2nd ed. Paris, 1982. Pages 107 and following treat the association between Mars and Venus in the *lectisternium* of 217 BCE.

Scholz, U. W. *Studien zum altitalischen und altrömischen Marskult und Marsmythos.* Heidelberg, 1970.

Stibbe, C. M., et al. *Lapis Satricanus: Archaeological, Epigraphical, Linguistic, and Historical Aspects of the New Inscription from Satricum.* The Hague, 1980.

Versnel, H. S. "Die neue Inschrift von Satricum in historischer Sicht." *Gymnasium* 89 no. 3 (1982): 193–235.

Versnel, H. S. "Transition and Reversal in Myth and Ritual" and "Apollo and Mars One Hundred Years after Roscher." In *Inconsistencies in Greek and Roman Religion.* Leiden and New York, 1990–1993.

Wagenvoort, Henobrik. *Roman Dynamism.* Oxford, 1947.

Wissowa, Georg. *Religion und Kultus der Römer.* 2d ed. Munich, 1912. See pages 141 and following.

ROBERT SCHILLING (1987)
CHARLES GUITTARD (2005)
Translated from French by Paul C. Duggan

MARSILIUS OF PADUA (c. 1275–1342), originally Marsilio dei Mainardini; Italian political theorist. Marsilius probably studied medicine at the University of Padua. In 1313 he was rector of the University of Paris, where he met such leading Averroists as Peter of Abano and John of Jandun. He is famous chiefly for his antipapalist treatise *Defensor pacis* (Defender of Peace; 1324), a landmark in the history of political philosophy. When his authorship of this work became known in 1326, he was forced to flee to the court of Louis of Bavaria in Nuremberg; Pope John XXII thereupon branded him a heretic. Marsilius subsequently assisted Louis in various imperial ventures in Italy.

The primary purpose of the *Defensor pacis* was to refute the papalist claims to "plenitude of power" as advanced by Pope Innocent IV, Egidius of Rome, and others in the thirteenth and fourteenth centuries. The papal position had held that secular rulers must be subject to the papacy even in "temporal" affairs, so that they must be established, judged, and, if necessary, deposed by the pope. Marsilius, in contrast, undertook to demonstrate that the papacy and the priesthood in general must be subject not only in temporal but even in "spiritual" affairs to the whole people, with the powers of the priesthood reduced to the administration of the sacraments and the teaching of divine law.

Marsilius's doctrine overthrew the attempt to base human society on religious values under priestly control; instead, the way was opened for a purely secular society under the control of a popularly elected government. Hence, it is understandable that Marsilius has been hailed as a prophet of the modern world. His treatise exerted a marked influence on the conciliar movement and during the period of the Reformation.

Equally as important as these revolutionary conclusions are the three premises from which Marsilius derived them. These premises are found in his general theory of the state. The first is the Aristotelian teleological view of the state as subserving the good life. The various parts of the state, including government, are defined by the contribution they make to the rational "fulfillment" of man's natural desire for the highest ends of a "sufficient life," which include the common benefit and justice.

The second theme, in contrast, is a negative and minimal utilitarianism. It emphasizes the inevitability of conflicts among persons and the consequent need for the formal instrumentalities of coercive law and government in order to regulate these conflicts and avert the destruction of human society. In developing this theme, Marsilius presents a positivistic concept of law, which stands in contrast to his nonpositivistic conception of justice (a distinction often overlooked in discussions of his ideas). Marsilius, unlike most medieval political philosophers, holds that justice is not a necessary condition of law. What is necessary is that the legal rules have coercive force. These rules and the government that enforces them must be unitary in the sense that, if a society is to survive, it cannot have two or more rival coercive bodies of law and government.

The third theme of Marsilius's political theory is that the people are the only legitimate source of all political authority. It is the people, the whole body of citizens or its "weightier part," who must make the laws either by themselves or through elected representatives, and it is also the people who must elect, "correct," and, if necessary, depose the government.

Although all three themes of Marsilius's general political theory were found in earlier medieval political philosophers, no other philosopher had given the second and third themes as central a position as did Marsilius. The full consequence of these emphases emerges in the applications he makes of his general political theory to the problems of ecclesiastical politics.

In keeping with his first theme, Marsilius views the Christian priesthood as one of the parts of the state dedicated to achieving the "sufficient life" for all believers. Unlike the other parts of the state, however, the priesthood subserves the "sufficient life" to be attained primarily "in the future world" rather than the present one. Marsilius manifests skepticism about the rational demonstrability of such a future life; nevertheless, he officially accepts the Christian doctrine that the future life is superior to the present life. He also holds, however, that secular and religious values are in basic opposition.

Here he seems to be applying in the realm of the practical the Averroist doctrine of the contrariety of reason and faith in theoretical philosophy.

At this point, however, Marsilius's second and third themes have their effect. Since the essence of political authority is the coerciveness required for the minimal end of preserving society, it follows that the higher end subserved by the priesthood does not entitle it to superior political authority. The question of the order of political superiority and inferiority is thus separated from the question of the order of moral and religious values. According to Marsilius's second theme, the secular government, as bearer of coercive authority, must be politically superior to the priesthood. If the priests refuse to obey the government and its laws, then they must be compelled to do so, because such disobedience threatens that unity of coercive authority without which society cannot survive.

In addition to this political argument against diverse centers of coercive power in any society, Marsilius also stresses, from within the religious tradition itself, that religious belief, in order to be meritorious, must be purely voluntary. Hence, in order to fulfill its mission, divine law and the priesthood that teaches and administers it cannot be coercive in this world.

Marsilius's third theme, republicanism, also plays an important role in the political subordination of the priesthood and papacy. The only rules and persons entitled to the status of being coercive laws and government officials are those ultimately chosen by the people; hence, there can be no crediting the claims of divine law and the priesthood to a separate derivation of coercive political authority from God. Because the whole people is superior in virtue to any of its parts and because freedom requires popular consent or election, the priesthood itself must be elected by the people of each community rather than being appointed by an oligarchically chosen pope. Also, the pope himself must be elected by the whole of Christendom. Similarly, the whole people must elect general councils to provide authoritative interpretations of the meaning of divine law. In these ways Marsilius's general political theory leads to a republican structure for the church as opposed to its traditional monarchical structure.

BIBLIOGRAPHY

There are two critical editions of *Defensor pacis,* one edited by C. W. Previté-Orton (Cambridge, 1928), the other edited by Richard Scholz in *Fontes juris Germanici antiqui* of the *Monumenta Germaniae Historica* (Hanover, 1932). I have translated it in volume 2 of my *Marsilius of Padua, the Defender of Peace* (New York, 1956). This translation has been reprinted in several later editions.

For studies of Marsilius's doctrines, see my *Marsilius of Padua and Medieval Political Philosophy* (1951; reprint, New York, 1979); Georges de Lagarde's *La naissance de l'esprit laïque au déclin du moyen age,* vol. 3, *Le defensor pacis* (Louvain, 1970); and Jeannine Quillet's *La philosophie politique de Marsile de Padoue* (Paris, 1970). Two volumes of essays from the Convegno Internazionale su Marsilio da Padova, held at the University of Padua in 1980, are in the historical journal *Medioevo: Rivista di storia della filosofia medievale* 5–6 (1979–1980).

ALAN GEWIRTH (1987)

MARTIAL ARTS

This entry consists of the following articles:

MARTIAL ARTS: AN OVERVIEW

The role of the warrior has been a position of importance to many cultures historically, with the efficacy of combat strategies and warrior skills often determining the course of history and the continued existence of groups of people. In the cultures of South Asia, Southeast Asia, and the Far East, religious beliefs and teachings often interpenetrated the martial traditions. Just as the physical forms of these arts have varied from one country to the next, so too have their religious and meditative components. For some martial traditions, these spiritual elements constitute the highest levels of practice. This article will introduce the varied religious and meditative dimensions of martial traditions as found in India, China, Japan, and Indonesia—an orientation often overlooked by practitioners of such disciplines, who prefer to concentrate upon the physical dimensions of practice. Regrettably, most of what is known about many martial arts is limited to information transmitted by oral tradition. Hence, even theories about the origins of the martial arts remain speculative and nebulous. However, most historians agree that some of the earliest traceable roots lead either to India or China.

INDIA. The origins of the martial traditions of India are difficult to trace and verify, but vestiges of fighting techniques used in ancient India do remain. Early references to combative situations can be found in such classic epics as the *Ṛgveda,* the *Rāmāyaṇa,* and the *Mahābhārata.* Contemporary writings generally emphasize wrestling forms *(kuṣṭhi, varja-muṣṭi, binoṭ, masti)* and weaponry (e.g., *bāṇa, pharī-gatkā, lāṭhī, paṭā, cilampam).* Wrestling flourished in India before the beginnings of the Aryan invasions (c. 1500 BCE).

Aside from wrestling and weaponry, there exists surprisingly little information concerning any organized martial disciplines. Some systems are mentioned sporadically in the literature, including *aṭitaṭa, cilampam, kuttu varicai* (Tamil), and *mukkebazi,* though no reference to religious practices is to be found. However, recent Western investigations of the Indian martial system known as *kaḷarippayaṯṯu* have begun to uncover the association between religious and physical aspects of practice in Indian culture today.

Kaḷarippayaṯṯu (*kaḷari,* "fencing school"; *payaṯṯu,* "fencing exercise"; *kaḷarippayaṯṯu,* "place where martial exercises are taught") is a system of martial training found in Kerala which, in its present form, dates back to at least the twelfth century CE. It was developed primarily to prepare Kerala's martial caste (Nairs) for combat, although higher-caste Yatra *brahmans,* lower-caste Tiyyas, and many Muslims and Christians were also proficient in the form. This system rests upon preliminary physical culture training (physical exercise and body massage) that is later followed by practice in unarmed combat as well as a variety of weapons.

In *kaḷarippayattu,* in-depth knowledge of the *marma*—vulnerable points of the human body—is required in order to know where to attack one's opponent, how to protect one's own body, and how to treat injuries to these vital spots during training or battle. Further, the use of breathing exercises, repetition of *mantras*, visual concentration, and performance of special rituals (paying respects to deities and teachers) all aid in achieving proper mind-body coordination and may lead to the development of power *(śakti).* The lower abdominal region referred to as the *nabhi* or *nabhi mūla(m),* as well as the three lower *cakras* of *kuṇḍalinīyoga,* may also be stressed in *kaḷarippayattu.* The *nahbi mūla(m)* corresponds to the second yogic *cakra, svādhiṣṭhāna,* and is recognized as the source of *prāṇa-vāyu* ("energy").

Attempting to articulate the spiritual dimensions of an Indian martial system is difficult in a culture that possesses such an indigenous spiritual tradition as yoga. It is evident that some of the techniques and practices employed in *kaḷarippayattu* overlap with yoga. However, within most schools, the process of spiritual emancipation *(mokṣa)* is overtly reserved for the discipline of yoga. These *kaḷarippayattu* masters familiar with yoga acknowledge that both disciplines develop the ability to focus at will on one point (i.e., the ability to "concentrate") but beyond this similarity the practices diverge, with yoga continuing as a self-conscious path of meditation. Among the Ṣūfī *kaḷarippayattu* practitioners of the Cannanore area of northern Kerala, however, great emphasis is placed upon spiritual training and development. Advanced training in meditation involves progressing through a series of rituals known as *dhikrs* (Arab., lit., "remembrance, recollection" of God), which are performed silently or aloud. Such practices can lead to experiences of ecstasy, realization of the internal white light, and union with God. As the connection between Indian martial traditions and religious practices is evident historically, it is safe to assume that additional investigations will provide more information on the practices and aims associated with the overlap of these martial traditions with meditative techniques and philosophies.

CHINA. Though lacking in strong documentation, historical reviews generally credit Bodhidharma (c. 448–527 CE) with playing a central role in the development of a systematized martial discipline in China. Bodhidharma is an obscure figure. However, he is generally acknowledged to be the first patriarch of the Chan (Jpn., Zen) school in China. Although no Indian records of his life are known to exist, Chinese sources indicate that he was trained in Buddhist meditation in Kāñcīpuram, a province south of Madras. Upon the death of his master Prajñātara, he reportedly left India for China, in part due to the decline of Buddhism in those areas outside of India proper. After visiting with the emperor at Nanking, Bodhidharma proceeded north to the Shao-lin Temple in Henan province. In his teaching there he reportedly became disturbed by the inability of monks to stay awake during meditation. To eliminate this tendency as well as to improve their health, Bodhidharma allegedly introduced a systematized set of exercises to strengthen the body and mind—exercises that purportedly marked the beginning of the *shaolin* style of temple boxing. These exercise forms were transmitted orally and transcribed by later monks in the *Yijin jing* and *Xishui jing.*

In addition to his contributions in the area of physical training, Bodhidharma was also said to have been centrally involved in transmitting the *Laṅkāvatāra Sūtra* to his disciple Huike, insisting that it represented the key to buddhahood. The teaching of the *Laṅkāvatāra Sūtra* focuses upon enlightenment, with specific reference to such doctrines as "mind-only" *(vijñāptimātra)* and "all-conserving consciousness" *(ālaya-vijñāna).* It essentially records the Buddha's own inner experience *(pratyātmagata)* concerning the religious teachings of Mahāyāna Buddhism. A central theme of the *Laṅkāvatāra Sūtra* is the importance of transmission of doctrine from mind to mind without reliance upon written texts. In keeping with the Chan tradition, it appeals directly to the enlightened mind as its source of authority, rather than depending upon words to convey its message.

Many of these teachings were later incorporated into Chinese philosophy, interspersed with the already prevailing Daoist precepts of the *dao, yin-yang,* and the principle of dualism and change, the importance given to deep breathing *(lianqi)* and its relationship to the goal of longevity or immortality, and the doctrines of "nonaction" *(wuwei)* and "natural spontaneity" *(ziran).* The interpretation of Buddhist and Daoist precepts transformed martial and nonmartial teachings into a new form, the early search for *dao* being later replaced by the goal of *qianxing* ("illumination"), because of the Chan Buddhist influences noted above.

Contemporary Chinese martial arts are said to be derived from the original *shaolin* techniques introduced by Bodhidharma. These forms of *gongfu* are generally divided into two groups—"internal" *(neijia zhuanfa),* or "soft" *(rou),* and "external" *(waijia zhuanfa),* or "hard" *(gang).* In addition to stressing the importance of the Daoist and Buddhist philosophical-experiential principles described above, the "internal" system also concentrates on the will *(yi),* vital energy *(qi),* and internal strength. Further, Daoist deep breathing techniques of *qigong* are practiced to cultivate *qi* in the *dantian* ("cinnabar fields"), where it is collected and stored. Styles falling within the "internal" category include *taiji, bagua,* and *xingyi,* while *shaolin* boxing is classified as "external." Principles of Daoist philosophy and cosmogony are reflected in the three primary internal styles. Ironically, while the internal styles clearly draw upon the principles of Daoist and Chan teachings in the employment of specific self-defense techniques, strategies, and forms, few of the internal schools today emphasize the transformative religious goals stressed by the classical meditative systems and by some of the earlier practitioners of these martial disciplines.

JAPAN. From roughly the eighth century to the end of the sixteenth century CE, Japan was beset by numerous domestic wars. This sociopolitical climate provided the classical professional warriors *(bushi)* with not only a prominent role in molding the natural character of Japan, but also an opportunity to further develop and refine the combative techniques of the *bujutsu* (martial arts). During these centuries martial traditions *(ryū)* were founded with the specific purpose of formalizing and perpetuating practical combat systems. It was during the Kamakura period (1185–1333 CE) that Zen Buddhism was introduced to Japan from China, largely through the work of the Japanese Buddhist priests Eisai (1141–1215) and Dōgen (1200–1253), who had studied Chan in China. Through the efforts of their followers Tokiyori (1227–1263) and Tokimune (1251–1284), Chan, as Zen, was introduced into Japanese life, having a distinct impact upon the life of the samurai. The successful cooperation of the martial and spiritual disciplines led to the creation of Bushidō, the warrior code, which idealized such virtues as loyalty and courage and espoused the goal of achieving that state of mind in which the warrior's thoughts would transcend life and death *(seishi o chōetsu).*

In 1603, the Tokugawa military government *(bakufu)* was founded by Tokugawa Ieyasu, an event that marked the end of war as a pervasive aspect of the Japanese culture and the beginning of the Edo period (1603–1867 CE). In this era of peace, maintained by strict tyrannical rules, governmental influences stressed the redirection of the people's attention to the ideals of the past. This marked a notable shift in social awareness for *bushi* and commoner alike, leading to the development of the classical *budō* forms. Influenced by the Confucian interpretation of the Dao, the Japanese culture took the principle of *dao—dō* in Japanese—and modified it in such a way as to be compatible with Japanese feudal society and applicable to man in his social relationships. The shift from *bujutsu* (*bu,* "military [martial] affairs"; *jutsu,* "art") to *budō* (*dō,* "way") signified a change in emphasis from combat training to cultivation of man's awareness of his spiritual nature. The primary goal of classical *budō* was enlightenment as outlined in Zen teachings—a shift again from simply external perfection of (martial) techniques to self-mastery via "spiritual forging" *(seishin tanren).* The distinction between *bujutsu* ("martial arts") and *budō* ("martial ways") still holds true today.

The formation of specific *budō* systems began during the early seventeenth century. *Kenjutsu* ("sword art") was transformed into *kendo* ("sword way"); and the essence of *iaido* ("sword drawing technique") as a spiritual discipline appeared at this time in contrast to *iaijutsu.* Weaponless *budō* systems, such as *jikishinryu,* also appeared. The classical *budō* forms continued to evolve until the latter part of the nineteenth century when, with the rise of ultranationalism among the Japanese people, both the aims of classical *budō* and classical *bujutsu* disciplines were redirected to support this effort.

Modern *bujutsu* and modern *budō* are generally viewed as beginning in 1868, after the overthrow of the Tokugawa government. However, there are significant differences between these modern martial traditions and their classical counterparts. Collectively speaking, the modern disciplines are generally characterized as methods of self-defense or as tactics for sparring or grappling with an opponent. Modern *bujutsu* consists of hand-to-hand combat systems that are used as methods of self-defense and spiritual training. Modern *budō* consists of various systems of physical exercise or sport seen as methods of self-defense or as spiritual training aimed at bringing man into harmony with a peace-seeking international society. Examples of modern *budō* include modern *kendō,* modern *jūdō, karatedō, aikidō, (nippon) shōrinji kenpō,* and *kyūdō.*

In many cases, a comparison of the modern *budō* to their classical counterparts (which are still practiced today in Japan) reveals major differences in purpose. While the proclaimed concern for discipline, morals, and the importance of "spirit" carries over from the classical traditions, the concept of *dō* is largely distorted in the modern disciplines. Modern exponents have been accused of reinterpreting the *dō* to fit their own subjective interpretation of their personal role and needs in the world, rather than focusing upon classical martial-meditative goals. However, to dismiss all of the modern *budō* systems as poor imitations of once-thriving, authentic spiritual disciplines may be premature. For example, select schools of modern *kendō* and *kyūdō* do stress goals associated with the classical *(budō)* disciplines. It may be that the individual practitioners within a particular discipline remain the best measure of the degree to which the classical *budō* aims are stressed, realized, and exemplified.

INDONESIA. Throughout its history, Indonesia has been subject to the cultural and combative influences of other countries, including India, China, and Indochina. Furthermore, Java, its cultural and political core, has always been a center of magical and mystical beliefs and practices, which have become even more widespread since independence from the Dutch in 1949. With ongoing migrations of peoples of the many Indonesian islands and the combative and mystical elements continuing to evolve over time, highly sophisticated martial arts have developed, which are currently referred to as *pukulan.*

While several major combative forms are presently found in Indonesia, the martial art known as *pencak-silat* is the dominant self-defense discipline and the one with the strongest spiritual roots. It reportedly first developed on the Riouw archipelago in the eleventh century CE. By the 1300s it had become a highly sophisticated technical art that was open solely to members of nobility and the ruling classes. Indian, Chinese, Arabic and, later, Japanese influences permeated in varying degrees a number of the styles. These developments as well as travel between the different islands further modified its combative form (which was no longer limited exclusively to select social classes) leading to rapid diversification. There are now hundreds of different styles.

Though varying definitions exist, *pencak* usually connotes skillful body movements in variation, while *silat* refers to the fighting application of *pencak. Pencak-silat* is known to have been influenced by Hindu religious elements and to have evolved further through contact with a rich Islamic spiritual tradition. The emphasis placed on the spiritual aspects of the art will vary from one style to another, but most systems start with physical training aimed at learning and applying various techniques for avoiding physical harm at the hands of an assailant. Upon successful acquisition of these motor skills, the practitioner may develop his inner power, which can be expressed in varying forms. For example, the practitioner of the Joduk style of Bali is able to engage in mystic, trancelike states—an ability that distinguishes the individual as a *guru* ("teacher"). Further internal development in the various styles of *pencak-silat* leads to the title of *maha guru* ("master teacher") while those who have attained the summit of technique are given the title of *pendekar* ("fighter"; also connotes "spiritualist" and leader or champion who has obtained an understanding of true—inner—knowledge).

The final stage of training in *pencak-silat* is referred to as *kebatinan.* Importance is placed on inner emotional experience and personal revelation as derived from the practice of the mystical discipline, although the practices and methods employed as one advances on the mystical path vary noticeably from one sect to another. The path of *kebatinan* stresses intuitive feeling *(rasa)* and surrender *(sujud);* man rids himself of impulses and bodily desires by emptying himself so as to be filled with the divine presence of God—the revelation of the divine residing within the heart *(batin).* The path of *kebatinan* is no easy understanding. Overcoming one's attachment to the outward aspects of existence *(lahir)* may involve ascetic practices *(tapa):* fasting, prayer, meditation (particularly visual concentrative techniques), sexual abstinence, remaining awake throughout the night, or retreating to the mountains and into caves. It should be pointed out, however, as noted earlier with other martial systems, that the degree to which the mystical practices are pursued and realized will vary from one practitioner to another. For example, some *pendekar* avoid all involvement with mysticism and *kebatinan,* while others practice also the noncorporeal, mystical aspects of their discipline.

CONCLUSIONS. While the spiritual dimensions of several martial systems of India, China, Japan, and Indonesia have been briefly outlined, the meditative-religious dimensions of martial arts and martial traditions of other countries still need to be critically and comprehensively assessed. Today, the spiritual dimensions of practice are often overlooked, although increased interest in the concept of the "spiritual warrior" has begun to appear. Inclusion of this important component will serve to broaden our understanding of the interrelationship between the physical and spiritual sides of human existence.

SEE ALSO Attention; Bodhidharma; Bushidō; Spiritual Discipline; War and Warriors.

BIBLIOGRAPHY

A scholarly overview of Asian martial systems can be found in Donn F. Draeger and Robert W. Smith's *Comprehensive Asian Fighting Arts* (New York, 1980), originally published as *Asian Fighting Arts* (Tokyo and Palo Alto, Calif., 1969); discussions of religious dimensions are limited, as are references supporting textual material. A less critical discussion of Indian martial arts is in the *Encyclopedia of Indian Physical Culture,* edited by Dattatraya C. Mujumdar (Baroda, India, 1950). Excellent discussions of *kaḷarippayaṯṯu* appear in Phillip B. Zarrilli's *When the Body Becomes All Eyes* (Delhi and New York, 1998). Perhaps the best historical review of the Chinese martial arts can be found in *A Source Book in the Chinese Martial Arts,* 2 vols., edited by James I. Wong (Stockton, Calif., 1978). Donn F. Draeger's three volumes on the martial arts and martial ways of Japan—*Classical Bujutsu* (New York, 1973), *Classical Budo* (New York, 1973), and *Modern Bujutsu and Budo* (New York, 1974)—are among the best writings on the topic. For the Indonesian martial arts, Draeger's *Weapons and Fighting Arts of the Indonesian Archipelago* (Rutland, Vt., 1972) remains the definitive source. Finally, an in-depth discussion of the religious dimensions of martial traditions appears in my forthcoming *Meditative-Religious Traditions of Fighting Arts and Martial Ways.*

New Sources

Grave, J. *Initiation Rituelle et Arts Martiaux: Trois écoles de Kanuragan Javanais.* Paris, 2001.

Green, T. A. *Martial Arts of the World: An Encyclopedia.* Santa Barbara, Calif., 2001.

Jones, D. E. *Combat, Ritual, and Performance: Anthropology of the Martial Arts.* Westport, Conn., 2002.

McCarthy, P., et al. *Ancient Okinawan Martial Arts: koryu uchinadi.* Boston, 1999.

McFarlane, Stewart. "Mushin, Morals, and Martial Arts—a Discussion of Keenan's Yogacara Critique." *Japanese Journal of Religious Studies* 17 (1990): 397–420.

McFarlane, Stewart. "Fighting Bodhisattvas and Inner Warriors: Buddhism and the Martial Traditions of China and Japan." *Buddhist Forum* (1994): 185–210.

Mol, S. *Classical Weaponry of Japan: Special Weapons and Tactics of the Martial Arts.* New York, 2003.

MICHAEL MALISZEWSKI (1987)
Revised Bibliography

MARTIAL ARTS: CHINESE MARTIAL ARTS

The Chinese term *wushu* (martial arts) is usually applied to fighting techniques practiced by individuals in a nonmilitary setting, as distinct from the training methods (*bingfa*) of soldiers in a regular army. Individual techniques within the martial arts tradition are usually called in Chinese *quan* or, less commonly, *zhang*. There are dozens of *quan* styles; some of the most famous are Shaolin Quan (Shaolin Hand-Combat), Taiji Quan (Great-Ultimate Hand-Combat), Xingyi Quan (Form-and-Intention Hand-Combat), and Bagua Zhang (Eight-Trigrams Hand-Combat).

The terms *quan* (literally, "fist") and *zhang* (literally, "palm") evince the significance of unarmed hand-combat in the Chinese martial arts. Even though each and every *quan* system has developed its own techniques of armed combat (usually with swords, spears, and staffs, but sometimes with such quintessential weaponry as metal-tipped fans), the foundation of all is empty-handed combat. Another characteristic of the Chinese martial arts is the stringing together of fixed positions into determined practice sequences, which define a given *quan* style. The invention of new body or weapon postures, or the combination of existing ones into new sequences, amounts to the creation of a new style, or substyle, of fighting.

The Chinese martial arts, of course, are first and foremost effective fighting techniques. However, their appeal to people of diverse interests, ages, and social backgrounds indicates that they have other dimensions as well. Young and old alike attest that the martial arts contribute to physical health and mental well-being. Whereas for some they are a competitive sport (some *quan* styles are included in international competitions such as the Asian Games), others consider them a performing art. (In traditional China, martial artists often made a living by giving public performances on holidays and at temple fairs, and some of their outstanding descendants—Bruce Lee [Li Xiaolong, 1940–1973] and Li Lianjie [Jet Li, b. 1963] for example—have made careers in the movies.) Finally, the martial arts are embedded in a rich matrix of Chinese religious and philosophical ideas. It is this unique combination of military, therapeutic, athletic, theatrical, and religious goals that is one of the martial arts' most striking features.

HISTORY. The history of the Chinese martial arts became the subject of critical inquiry during China's Republican period (1911–1948). Its pioneering scholars were Tang Hao (1897–1959) and Xu Zhen (1898–1967), who were followed, beginning in the 1970s, by such scholars as Lin Boyuan, Matsuda Ryūchi, Ma Mingda, Cheng Dali, and Douglas Wile. Despite their outstanding achievements, however, the history of Chinese martial arts is not yet fully charted. The following brief outline is therefore tentative only.

Ancient foundations. Contemporary Chinese martial arts share at least some similarities with ancient Chinese gymnastics. An elaborate gymnastics system called *daoyin* (literally, "guiding and pulling") is described in texts and paintings from the first centuries BCE. Individual *daoyin* exercises were often named—like training sequences in the modern martial arts—after specific animals that they purported to imitate, including, for example, the monkey, swallow, bear, tiger, deer, dragon, and toad. Another similarity between *daoyin* gymnastics and the later martial arts is the emphasis on breathing techniques and the internal circulation of vital energy, *qi*. Thus, in both systems external limb movement is joined by internal meditative practice.

Ancient Chinese literature highlights the therapeutic efficacy of *daoyin* gymnastics, classifying it as a branch of the medical science of "nourishing life" (*yangsheng*). Archaeology has shed light on this medical significance: In 1973 an annotated illustration of *daoyin* exercises was unearthed in Hunan, and in 1983 a *daoyin* manual was discovered in Hubei. Dating from the second century BCE, both the illustration (known as *Daoyin tu*) and manual (titled *Yinshu*) assign specific *daoyin* exercises for the treatment of specific illnesses. Four centuries later, the famous physician Hua Tuo (d. 208) created "Five Animals Exercises," which were each intended for the cure of a particular disease.

The medical significance of *daoyin* gymnastics was joined by religious import. In the course of the first centuries CE, *daoyin* exercises were incorporated into the emerging Daoist religion. Gymnastics was integrated with dietary, alchemical, and meditative techniques in search of the Daoist goal of immortality. Thus, *daoyin* gymnastics share with the martial arts not only certain principles of practice, but also medical and religious goals. The major difference concerns the latter's expressed martial purpose. Unlike the martial arts, ancient gymnastics was not combat related. The available sources do not assign *daoyin* any military significance.

As distinct from *daoyin* gymnastics, there also existed in ancient China a system of empty-handed combat called *shoubo*, which some scholars regard as the predecessor of *quan*-style fighting. Even though the available sources on *shoubo* are limited, Ma Mingda claims to perceive in it the four principles of kick (*ti*), grasp, (*na*), throw (*die*), and hit (*da*), which characterize the later period martial arts.

The emergence of *quan* systems. Even though *daoyin* gymnastics, and possibly *shoubo* combat, contributed to the evolution of martial arts, the emergence of distinctive *quan* styles occurred much later. The earliest evidence of individual unarmed techniques characterized by quintessential sequences of positions dates from the Ming period (1368–1644). Sixteenth-century military experts such as Qi Jiguang (1528–1588), Zheng Ruoceng (fl. 1505–1580), Tang Shunzhi (1507–1560), and He Liangchen (fl. 1565) allude to over ten *quan* styles, including, for example, Wenjia Quan (Wen-Family Hand-Combat), Song Taizu Chang Quan (Emperor Song Taizu's Long Hand-Combat), Hou Quan (Monkey Hand-Combat), E Quan (Decoy Hand-Combat), and Tongzi Bai Guanyin Shen Quan (Acolyte Worships Guanyin Miraculous Hand-Combat). The Ming period also witnessed the publication of the earliest extant manual of *quan* fighting: Qi Jiguang's *Quan jing jieyao* (Essentials of the classic of hand-combat, c. 1562), in which the famous general selected what he considered to be the best positions of earlier styles.

Ming-period *quan* techniques served as the foundation for the Qing-period (1644–1911) evolution of fighting styles with which we are familiar today: Taiji Quan, Xingyi Quan (originally called Liuhe Quan), Bagua Zhang, and Shaolin Quan all date from the Qing. The origins of at least some of these styles can be traced back to the dynasty's early days. Taiji Quan and Xingyi Quan, for example, are usually ascribed to the seventeenth-century martial artists Chen Wangting (from Henan) and Ji Jike (from Shanxi) respectively. As for the Shaolin Monastery's Buddhist monks, they too turned their attention to *quan* techniques in the course of the Ming-Qing transition. Shaolin clerics had been practicing fighting ever since the Tang period (618–907), when they lent military support to Emperor Li Shimin (600–649). However, all through the Ming period their quintessential weapon was the staff (*gun*). Only in the course of the seventeenth century did unarmed *quan* fighting eclipse staff training in the monastery's regimen.

Daoyin vocabulary already figured in some Ming-period martial arts; however, only in the course of the Qing period was the ancient gymnastics tradition fully integrated into unarmed fighting, creating a synthesis of martial, therapeutic, and religious goals. Most Qing-period *quan* styles combine external limb movement with internal meditative practice. *Qi* circulation techniques figure prominently in Qing-period martial arts manuals, such as *Taiji quan jing* (Taiji classic; c. nineteenth century) and the writings of Chang Naizhou (fl. eighteenth century). A similar emphasis upon "internal strength" and spiritual perfection is also apparent in the *Yijin jing* (Sinews-transformation classic), which is significant as the earliest source of the legend of Bodhidharma (fl. 500 CE). Even though it was authored in the seventeenth century, the manual presents itself as if it had been compiled a millennium earlier by the Indian saint (in his native Sanskrit). Thus, the *Yijin jing* initiated the widespread legend according to which Bodhidharma invented the Shaolin martial arts.

The integration of martial arts and *daoyin* gymnastics occurred, at least in part, in the context of armed sectarian activities. Leaders of popular messianic uprising, such as Wang Lun (fl. 1770s) taught their disciples *quan* and *qi* circulation alike. Often they began their careers as itinerant martial artists, making a living by public demonstrations of martial skills, as well as by healing. The intimate connection between martial arts, religion, and rebellion is apparent in shared nomenclature. Fighting techniques and sectarian groups sometimes shared the same titles: Eight Trigrams (Bagua), for example, was the name of a group that revolted in 1813.

During the late Qing and Republican periods the martial arts were incorporated into the rhetoric of national rejuvenation. The disintegration of the Qing regime and the incursion of Western (and Japanese) colonial powers threatened the existence of a Chinese political entity, and created fears lest China's cultural identity be lost as well. As in the case of other national movements, it was argued that the recreation of a Chinese political body necessitated a rejuvenation of its citizens' physical bodies. Being native, the martial arts were deemed appropriate for the task. Now renamed "national arts" (*guoshu*), fighting techniques such as Taiji Quan spread from isolated agricultural areas into China's biggest cities.

By the second half of the twentieth century, the Chinese martial arts had been internationalized. Chinese masters who traveled abroad and foreign students who studied in Taiwan, Hong Kong, and mainland China brought the martial arts to millions of Western practitioners. Native lineages of Taiji Quan, Shaolin Quan, and other fighting styles emerged in numerous countries, where local martial arts manuals and magazines are published in a variety of languages.

RELIGION. Arguably, the religious significance of the martial arts has been an important factor in their popularity outside their homeland. Chinese *quan* styles combine the goal of physical strength with the search of spiritual perfection. This synthesis is apparent not only in martial arts manuals, but also in the tradition's artistic representations. Martial arts novels such as Jin Yong's (Louis Cha) *Tianlong babu* (Extraordinary beings, date) and award-winning movies such as Ang Lee's *Crouching Tiger, Hidden Dragon* (*Wohu canglong*, 2000) present the perfect warrior as spiritually enlightened. His or her religious attainments are articulated—in novels, films, and martial arts manuals alike—by a rich language that draws on diverse textual traditions. Even though they are often combined, it is possible to discern at least three religious vocabularies within the martial tradition: Daoism, Chinese cosmology, and Buddhism.

Daoism. Ancient *daoyin* gymnastics evolved partially in the context of Daoist religious practice. By the time this calisthenics tradition was incorporated into the late Ming and Qing martial arts, it was imbued with a rich Daoist vocabulary, which depicted the religious goal of immortality, as well as the various means—dietary, medical, alchemical, and meditative—of attaining it. For example, in some Daoist visualization practices the adept concocts in his brain, which serves as a crucible, an elixir. By drinking it, the practitioner creates an imperishable internal body, which, shedding the external one, emerges to immortality. This mystical language is reflected in Qing-period martial arts manuals, as in the following passage by Chang Naizhou:

> Training the body unifies our external form; training the *qi* solidifies our internal aspect. When we are as strong and firm as iron, we naturally develop an indestructible golden elixir body. In this way, we transcend the common, enter sagehood, and attain the highest level. If it is said that an enemy does not fear us, this is of little significance. (Wile, 1996)

Chinese cosmology. The unity of microcosm and macrocosm, which characterizes much of traditional Chinese philosophy, implies that the martial artist can reenact cosmic processes within his or her body, thereby attaining unity with the universe's underlying principles, or, as the Western scholar would term them, the divine.

The Chinese worldview does not recognize an external creator god. Instead the world is usually regarded as having evolved through a process of differentiation from a primordial unity called *taiji* ("great ultimate"). In this process of evolution several stages, or forces, are discernible, including *yin* and *yang*, the five elements (*wuxing*: water, fire, wood, metal, and earth), and the eight trigrams (*bagua*), which form the core of the ancient *Yi jing* (Classic of changes). In such fighting styles as Taiji Quan and Bagua Zhang—which are consciously named after the cosmology—the practitioner reenacts the process of universal differentiation. The practice sequence opens in the quiescence of the primordial *taiji*, and proceeds through the interplay of *yin* and *yang*, the five elements, and the eight trigrams to a profusion, which equals the myriad phenomena. The training sequence does not end however in this state of multiplicity. Rather, the practitioner goes back in time to the origins of the universe, receding from the myriad things to the eight trigrams and five elements, contracting further to the two cosmic principles *yin* and *yang*, and culminating in the tranquility of *taiji*. Thus, the martial artist achieves, in his or her body, a mystical experience of unity with the undifferentiated whole that preceded cosmic fragmentation.

Buddhism. As early as the Tang period, Chinese Buddhist martial practice was related to Buddhist martial mythology. Despite the religion's prohibition of violence, it featured a significant number of military gods, who could be relied upon as an excuse for warfare. Thus, Shaolin's tutelary deity was the fearsome Vajrapāṇi (Chin., Jingangshen), also known as Nārāyaṇa (Chin., Naluoyanshen), who was believed to bestow physical strength on fighting monks. As indicated by his name, Vajrapāṇi's original weapon was the mythic *vajra* (literally, "diamond"). However, in the course of the Ming period, when they developed techniques of staff fighting, Shaolin monks altered Vajrapāṇi's image, arming him with a staff. The relation between martial deities and martial monks was thus reciprocal: Fighting gods such as Vajrapāṇi sanctioned monastic violence, at the same time that fighting monks changed the deities' weaponry to suit their own military training.

Twentieth-century martial arts manuals associate the Shaolin fighting style not only with Buddhist mythology but also with the Buddhist search for enlightenment. Shaolin's abbot Yongxin (b. 1965) describes Shaolin Quan as "martial Chan" (*wuchan*), arguing that it is no different from meditation, the reading of scriptures, or any other form of self-cultivation practiced in the Chan (Jap., Zen) school. Some practitioners argue further that it is possible to perceive a Chan logic within Shaolin Quan's sequences of positions, which create patterns only to destroy them, thereby liberating the practitioner from preconceived notions.

It remains to be examined, however, when Chan vocabulary was first integrated into Chinese fighting styles such as Shaolin Quan. Preliminary investigations suggest that it is lacking from Shaolin-related literature all through the sixteenth century. But we know that Japanese Chan masters such as Takuan Sōhō (1573–1645) associated the martial arts with Buddhist self-cultivation. It is possible, therefore, that Chan rhetoric was introduced to the Chinese martial arts through Japanese influence. The notion that Chan could contribute to martial courage, for example, has been shown by Tang Hao to have been borrowed from Nitobe Inazō's *Bushidô: The Soul of Japan* (1899) into the *Shaolin quanshu mijue* (Shaolin hand-combat method secret formulas), first published in 1911.

SEE ALSO Bodhidharma; Buddhism, overview article; Chan; Daoism, overview article; Taiji; Yinyang Wuxing.

BIBLIOGRAPHY

Cheng Dali. *Zhongguo wushu: Lishi yu wenhua.* Chengdu, People's Republic of China, 1995.

Despeux, Catherine. "Gymnastics: The Ancient Tradition." In *Taoist Meditation and Longevity Techniques,* edited by Livia Kohn, pp. 225–261. Ann Arbor, Mich., 1989.

Lin Boyuan. *Zhongguo tiyu shi,* vol. 1: *Shangce, gudai.* Beijing, 1987.

Ma Mingda. *Shuo jian cong gao.* Lanzhou, People's Republic of China, 2000. An excellent collection of articles on various aspects of the Chinese martial arts by a leading expert.

Matsuda Ryūchi. *Zusetsu Chugoku bujutsu shi.* Translated into Chinese as *Zhongguo wushu shilue.* Taipei, Taiwan, 1986. An excellent general history of the Chinese martial arts.

Shahar, Meir. "Ming-Period Evidence of Shaolin Martial Practice." *Harvard Journal of Asiatic Studies* 61, no. 2 (2001): 359–413.

Tang Hao. *Shaolin quanshu mijue kaozheng.* Shanghai, 1941.

Tang Hao. *Shaolin Wudang kao* (1930). Reprint, Hong Kong, 1968.

Wile, Douglas. *Lost T'ai-chi Classics from the Late Ch'ing Dynasty.* Albany, N.Y., 1996.

Wile, Douglas. *T'ai Chi's Ancestors: The Making of an Internal Martial Art.* New York, 1999.

Xu Zhen (Zhedong). *Guoji lunlue* (1929). Reprint in series no. 1, vol. 50, *Minguo congshu.* Shanghai, 1989.

Zhongguo wushu baike quanshu. Beijing, 1998. A comprehensive encyclopedia that summarizes twentieth-century research on the Chinese martial arts.

MEIR SHAHAR (2005)

MARTINEAU, JAMES

MARTINEAU, JAMES (1805–1900), English Unitarian. Born in Norwich, England, and educated at Manchester College, Martineau served as a minister, principally in Liverpool (1831–1857), and as a professor, and later principal, of Manchester College (1840–1885).

An early devotee of the materialistic philosophical determinism that Joseph Priestley (1733–1804) had absorbed from David Hartley (1705–1757) and transmitted to the English Unitarians, Martineau turned away from that position in the mid-1830s, in part under the influence of William Ellery Channing (1780–1842). He gave up external proof for intuition, metaphysics for ethics, and determinism for conscience and free will, and gradually abandoned his early belief in the historical validity of the scriptural miracles. Study in Germany in 1848–1849 reinforced the biblical skepticism that had led him to give up his belief in the evidential value of miracles. In his struggle to break the Priestleyan hold on his denomination, the passing of time and changing sensibilities gave Martineau a victory of sorts by the 1860s, but he had made many enemies in the older school, and he watched younger colleagues turn away from the theism to which he remained loyal to preach antisupernaturalism, humanism, and a variety of enthusiasms. In his later works, the impact of Darwinism and other scientific developments led him to a vast expansion of the argument from design, while the centrality he assigned to divine will bears some resemblance to his former determinism.

For most of his career, Martineau was highly controversial. A brilliant critic, he could be deliberately provocative, sometimes unscrupulous, and often wounding. He was denied the chair in philosophy at University College, London, after agitation by leading anticlerical intellectuals, among them his sister Harriet Martineau (1802–1876), whose book celebrating her conversion to free thought he had gratuitously and savagely reviewed in 1851. From the 1830s on, he rejected the Unitarian name, seeing it as sectarian and preferring the older Presbyterian or newer Free Christian labels, but few of his co-religionists followed him in this, and his plan in 1888 for sweeping denominational reform was a failure. But his prolonged and more irenic old age brought him almost universal admiration, and his stature in Unitarian history ranks with that of Priestley.

Martineau's subtle, complex, and self-consciously lyrical preaching was highly influential, as were his collections of hymns and liturgical services. His principal works are *The Rationale of Religious Enquiry* (1836), *A Study of Spinoza* (1882), *Types of Ethical Theory* (1885), *A Study of Religion* (1888), and *The Seat of Authority in Religion* (1890).

Bibliography

The principal collection of Martineau's papers is in Manchester College, Oxford, but there are other major collections in many places. His most important sermons, reviews, and occasional papers are collected in *Essays, Reviews, and Addresses*, 4 vols. (London, 1890–1891). The two biographies are by students and close associates. The best is J. Estlin Carpenter's *James Martineau, Theologian and Teacher: A Study of His Life and Thought* (London, 1905), but James Drummond and C. B. Upton's *The Life and Letters of James Martineau*, 2 vols. (London, 1902), contains much valuable material. As yet there is no satisfactory extended study of English Unitarianism, but there is an excellent brief sketch: H. L. Short's "Presbyterians under a New Name," in *The English Presbyterians: From Elizabethan Puritanism to Modern Unitarianism*, by C. Gordon Bolam and others (Boston, 1968).

R. K. Webb (1987)

MARTYRDOM.

[*This entry deals with religious witness that involves loss of life. For discussion of ritual death in a cross-cultural context, see* Suicide. *For death suffered because of religious identity, see* Persecution.]

The badge of martyrdom is awarded by the leadership of a community to men and women who offer their lives voluntarily in solidarity with their group in conflict with another, ideologically contrasting, group. The martyr and his or her slayer are delegates, champions, or defenders of their societies. A few martyrs are suicides, but most are slain by judicial, military, police, religious, or other functionaries. These functionaries execute the martyr as a terrorist, a criminal, or a heretic who threatens fundamental social values or the physical safety of members of the society. The societies of the slayer and the slain struggle to control the meaning of the slaying: is it to be understood by the world as martyrdom or as judicial retribution?

Martyrs may be "witnesses," the literal meaning of the Greek term, of politically disestablished groups claiming self-determination or heroes of the expansionist wars of established groups. Contemporary images race before our eyes—a self-immolating Buddhist monk in Vietnam, an Irish Republican Army soldier dying of starvation in a British jail, a Japanese kamikaze diving his bomb-plane into an American warship. Martyrdom is an attempt to break through the ideological and social boundaries between the conflicting groups with hierocratic, religiously based power. A minority's religious power invokes a higher, purifying vengeance (Jacoby, 1983) upon a dominant adversary, who in turn vengefully slays the martyr.

The confrontation may unite the martyr's people, strengthening their opposition as they, under charismatic leadership, inch toward their own organizational power. The exemplary act of a martyr strengthens people's courage to bear their daily tribulations and directs their anger to the cruel, murderous adversary, the source of these tribulations. The martyrdom may also strengthen the adversary's will to repress the martyr's society. Martyrdom politicizes the relationship between the groups.

Martyrdom seems not to have appeared until rather late in history, perhaps the fourth century BCE. The identification of ideology as an independent cultural reality has been a prerequisite for martyrdom. The ideologies at issue serve as symbols of mobilization, principles around which the societies rally, reinforcing, even radicalizing, more mundane economic or political conflicts.

The religions of Egypt and Mesopotamia and Greek philosophy treat ideologies as distinct cultural realities already hosting the seeds of the ideas of active good and evil and heroism. Zoroastrian dualism proposed an independent evil force, and Judaism of the Maccabean age adapted this view of a struggle with evil for monotheism. Hellenism brought a personalistic element to the ideologies in the image of the ascetic philosopher. Oriental Christianity synthesized the dualistic idea with that of the individual hero and so previewed Islamic ideas of martyrdom, including the pledge of eternal life to martyrs, forgiveness of sins, exemption from the Last Judgment, and the intercessory ability of the souls of martyrs.

Martyrdom imbues economic and political conflict with sacred meaning, subjecting it to what Max Weber called "the ethic of absolute ends," the pursuit of goals with little attention to the cost. In fact, action guided by an "ethic of responsibility," the value of the goal weighed against the cost of the means, discourages martyrdom.

Martyrdom is a free voluntary act. It is also an altruistic act. The martyr may avoid death by conceding to the adversary, but nevertheless accepts, affirms or even seeks death. A soldier, even a gladiator, strives to defeat the adversary without being hurt or killed. If death occurs, it is an accident of the situation. Only when that situation is sacralized, as in the case of the Muslim *jihād*, is the slain soldier a martyr.

This article develops some elements of a social theory of martyrdom. The basic queries are: under what conditions does a society generate martyrs; what are the types of martyrs; and what special social circumstances give rise to each type?

HOW MARTYRDOM FITS INTO SOCIAL LIFE. Martyrdom infuses a mundane event with divine grace. The symbolism parallels that of a sacrificial animal attaining a sacred quality. The animal victim disappears, either eaten by the worshipers, delivering its sanctity to their fellowship, or, as a burnt offering, rising as a sweet savor to the Lord. The martyr, a human sacrifice, attains an indelible sanctity. The sanctity may take the form of a redemptory promise, softening the pain or enabling the martyr to persist despite pain. Early Christians imprisoned and awaiting martyrdom were believed to have the power to forgive sins. Those released might retain this power, perhaps becoming presbyters of the church.

The martyr dies convinced of his or her legitimate authority, an authority challenging that of the executioners. A religious martyr may believe himself or herself to be an incarnation of the Holy Ghost, as did Montanus (Frend, 1972); the Spirit of God, al-Ḥaqq, as did al-Ḥallāj (Massignon, 1982); or a receiver of the Torah, as did ʿAqivaʾ ben Yosef.

The martyr, deceased, is a sacred symbol of an authority around which the society rallies. The authority created is charismatic, untethered by tradition. Such charismatic authority discards an older order in a breakthrough to a new social and cultural order, often conceived as a spiritual order.

Martyrdom is exemplary. A martyr is often a model for lesser forms of martyrdom. In Islam the idea of a martyr's death "in the way of Allāh" is applied metaphorically to the giving of *ṣadaqah*, or alms.

While suicide, being self-inflicted, is rarely accepted as martyrdom, asceticism, also self-inflicted, is a minor martyrdom. The adversary of the ascetic is bodily desire. The conquest of desire is a propaedeutic for the conquest of the social adversary.

The martyr demonstrates the human possibility of the act. That a person of flesh and blood succeeds in dying, sometimes painfully, facilitates the recruitment of future martyrs. Such a death is also a message deterring future deviance. That a member of a despised minority can show such commitment challenges the courage of members of the dominant group. The adversary may attempt to obscure the event. To be exemplary, martyrdom must be public and publicized. A private act, meaningful only to the martyr and the executioner, fails in this exemplary function. The martyr's group may be denied the benefits of its champion as witness. Undoubtedly, unrecorded martyrs died in dungeons with their ashes cast into the sea. However, martyrologies reveal no martyrs who sought social concealment.

In Jewish tradition, death for *qiddush ha-shem*, sanctifying of the name—or better, the reputation—of God, is intended to impress the Gentiles. This norm derives from a reading of the phrase in *Ezekiel*, "in the sight of the nations." Publicity for the Islamic *shahīd* ("martyr") is implicit in the idea of the *jihād* as a collective, rather than a personal obligation. Ibn Rushd (Averroës) wrote in his twelfth-century work on the *jihād*, *Bidāyat al-mujtahid*, that for *shahīds* to cancel the obligation for others, these others must know and recognize the volunteer's martyrdom. (Averroës, in Peters, 1977).

Martyrdom is political. Martyrdom is a political act affecting the allocation of power between two societies, or between a subgroup and the larger society. The Maccabean Revolt, which offered early and paradigmatic martyrs, was the action of a small community seeking a measure of local cultural independence. The Christian communities of Asia Minor, in the first and second centuries, offered martyrs to the Roman authorities in their struggle to limit the power of Rome to coerce particular expressions of loyalty. Certain religious martyrs may refuse to inflict physical violence on an adversary, but, as a political act, martyrdom is never a passive submission. The nonviolent martyr strikes the enemy psychologically.

The martyr's cry for vengeance mobilizes action against the adversary. The martyrdom of Mary Stuart followed a religious struggle over the crown of England. Elizabeth Tudor feared a bitter religious war were Mary to come to the throne. Mattingly (1959) writes of Catholic kings beyond the seas more eager to avenge the Queen of Scots dead than to keep her alive. Her shed blood cried out for vengeance on her enemies more unmistakably than her living voice could ever have done.

Where hierocratic power appears, political power may not be far behind. Sometimes one is transformed into the other. In this sense, the pope commands battalions. The Irish

Republican Army tapped the church's hierocratic power to support its struggle for Irish independence from Great Britain.

Martyrdom aims to reduce political authority to ineffectiveness by challenging the sacred basis of the legitimacy of the adversary's authority. The potential martyr is a rival claimant to authority and this political claim may be religiously legitimated.

The political struggle may be internal: an established society and a schismatic minority may share a faith and a political system. The Maccabees, Arnold of Brescia, Jan Hus, and Savonarola, for example, accused the leaders of their established groups of treason. The minority attack was treated as heretical, endangering the faith.

The eleventh-century Persian-born Ṣūfī ʿAyn al-Quḍāt al-Hamadhānī challenged Islamic authorities. The authorities' claim to power rested on Qurʾanic revelation and the *sunnah*, the traditions deriving from it. He claimed that divine grace poured down on him with all manner of esoteric knowledge and precious revelations, and he was thus an independent source of law.

Jan Hus (1373–1415) was directly political. Hus challenged the legitimacy of the papacy, the see of Peter, by preaching that Peter is not the head of the church, that ultimate appeal must be made directly to Christ. Condemned at the Council of Constance in 1414 and imprisoned, he wrote a characteristic martyr's message to a friend in Prague: "In prison and in chains expecting tomorrow to receive sentence of death, full of hope in God that I shall not swerve from the truth nor abjure errors imputed to me by false witnesses." He was urged to recant after being tied to the stake but replied, as is the custom of martyrs, "God is my witness that I have never taught nor preached that which false witnesses have testified against me. . . . I now joyfully die."

The fire was kindled and Hus repeated the Kyrie Eleison until stifled by the smoke. His ashes were scattered in the river, a final device to control the meaning of the event, discouraging a sepulchral shrine. After his death, Hussites fought in Prague and established the ecclesiastical organization of Tábor, recognizing only two sacraments, baptism and communion, and rejecting most of the ceremonial of the Roman Catholic church.

The minority may organize as a secret society, a sect practicing an uncommon cult. The twelfth-century Tanchelm in the Low Countries and Edus de l'Étoile in Brittany both declared themselves sons of God. Their sectarian followers were repressed, and they were imprisoned and martyred (Cohn, 1961). Ecstatics and ascetics, critical of the established church, gather around such claimants and perpetuate the movements.

MARTYR TYPES: POLITICAL INDEPENDENCE AND ACTION ORIENTATION. The relative political power of the conflicting communities determines the task of martyrdom and the characteristics of the martyrs selected to carry out that task. Crescive, self-determining, and decaying societies all generate a peculiar form of martyrdom.

Christian communities within the Roman Empire were a politically crescive minority. The martyrs of this minority suffered passively, inviting violence but inflicting only moral or psychological pressure on the adversary. An expansive Islam in its early centuries exemplifies the self-determining society. Its martyrs were active and belligerent. The post-Enlightenment Jewish community of western Europe was a politically decaying society. Jews who died at the hand of their adversaries were not, by and large, martyrs but mere victims of pogroms and, lately, of the Holocaust.

The attitude of the society toward worldly action is a second influence on the type of martyrdom. Orientation to action may be primarily "otherworldly" or primarily "innerworldly," to borrow Max Weber's terms. These two orientations are related dialectically. The active political innerworldly understanding of life is a minor motif for crescive and decaying societies, but a major motif for a self-determining society. Segments of the society animated by innerworldly orientations tend not to be at peace with otherworldly segments. Heterodoxy is the case in which internal schismatics, themselves in a crescive stage, offer a religious otherworldly counterpoint to the political orientation of a ruling self-determining society.

The discussion will be organized in terms of the degrees of political independence of the societies. References to inner- or otherworldly attitudes are subsumed within the social type.

Martyrdom in crescive societies. A crescive society is one that is politically powerless but beginning to stir, perhaps renascent. The resistance of Jews to Hellenization under the Seleucid ruler Antiochus Epiphanes in the second century BCE is an early model. The elderly Eleazar, according to the apocryphal *2 Maccabees*, is the martyr type, choosing to give his life rather than eat pork in an already desecrated Temple in Jerusalem. That image is reconstituted in the second-century Judean rebellion against Hadrianic Rome in which the scholar and political leader ʿAqivaʾ ben Yosef joined with Bar Kokhba, the leader of the revolt. Tradition has it that ʿAqivaʾ was burned, wrapped in a Torah scroll, in a Roman arena.

The exemplar of Christian martyrdom is the trial and the crucifixion on Golgotha as that event is related in the Gospels. Later martyrs strive to imitate Christ. The sacrificed Lamb of God survives, not in this world, but in the world beyond. Anomalously the divinely designated executioners were pagans. Ordinarily, only a priest could perform a valid sacrifice. This point was not lost on the eleventh-century Jews of Mainz, who, facing impending slaughter by Crusaders, slew their children and then themselves. They sanctified the sacrifice by their "priestly" hands, symbolically reviving the temple rite in Mainz. (Gentile slaughterers would have polluted the offering.) The adversary is made impotent by delivering to him dead bodies, the ultimate in noncooperation, and the spiritual strength and authority of the martyr's society is affirmed.

Martyrdom in crescive societies creates authority, escalates the struggle, unifies the minority, and legitimates the new culture by demonstrating its priority over nature. Furthermore, martyrs propel a politically crescive society toward self-determination, toward social and cultural freedom. The establishment of new authority is a step in this process, the martyr's group, for instance, becoming infused with the Holy Spirit (Klawitzer, 1980). The death of the martyr makes the ideological choice a matter of life and death. This escalates the struggle, perhaps expediting the resolution in favor of the minority. As the society moves toward increased responsibility, the culture itself changes. Ironically, the values for which the early martyrs surrendered their lives may not be significant to members of a succeeding and successful self-determining society.

Radicalizing and escalating the conflict unifies the two parties internally. The grievous injustice of the slaying of the defenseless martyr and the gruesome inhuman circumstances under which the slaying occurs leave few individuals on the sidelines. Martyrdom further unifies and strengthens the group in its struggle. If social solidarity is a prerequisite for martyrdom, how does the precrescive, perhaps fractured, group find its initial martyrs? Part of the answer to this question is that the martyrs constitute a small group within the minority. Intense primary relations in this group enable it to stand against the powerful larger group.

The unity of the minority community may be thwarted by a defection of some of its members to the majority. During the Christian conquest of Spain, from the thirteenth to the fifteenth century, for example, a number of Muslims and Jews manifestly accepted Christianity, while surreptitiously continuing to practice their previous faiths. Both Muslim and Jewish societies were decaying. The Inquisition struck at these New Christians and, at the same time, urged the state to expel those who had remained Jews and Muslims. Some unification was achieved by the Jewish émigrés in their Diaspora.

A crystallizing around a self-assertive core of a divided minority is necessary before serious manifest resistance is thinkable. The tragedy of unification amidst disunity is dramatized in the apocalypse in the *Gospel of Mark* (13:9–13), where it is written that brother shall betray brother, and father his child, and the children shall rise up against their parents and have them put to death.

With martyrdom, the culture of the minority, its ideology and law, is sanctified, a covenant established, stamped with blood. It is written in *Mekhilta'*, a Jewish interpretative work, that every commandment that the Israelites have not died for is not really established, and every commandment that they have died for will be established among them (Herr, 1967).

Martyrdom, by placing ideology ahead of physical survival, affirms the priority of culture over nature and the group's life, law, and civilization over biological self-interest. A crescive society that values individual life above group survival and above its cultural survival is not ready to become self-determining.

The self-determining society: heroic martyrs. The self-determining society has achieved political control of its life. Examples are fourth-century Christians in Asia Minor following the victory of Constantine, Islam of the Umayyad caliphate in eighth-century Damascus, and the Yishuv, the Jewish community of Palestine during the 1920s led by the Va'ad Le'umi, the National Council. Martyrs in such a society are active, aiding the society in its expansion, openly propagandizing, sending missionaries to the unconverted, and warring against adversaries. In Islam the *jihād* is a religious obligation and the martyr, the *shahīd*, one who dies in this sacred battle. The European Christian society that sent an armed pilgrimage to Jerusalem under Pope Gregory VII, in the words of Cohn (1961), raced toward a mass sacrifice, a mass apotheosis in Jerusalem. Defending against external enemies is the major problem; the achievement of internal unity is a minor social problem. Nevertheless, the self-determining society suffers its internal schisms. Islamic historians say little about Muslim martyrs executed by Arab pagans, the early opposition group, beyond the early oppression in Yathrib. The record is clear on Islamic martyrs of internecine conflict, Muslim martyrs killed by Muslims during the crescive and during the self-determining periods are remembered by their sects. The historic example is Muḥammad's grandson, Ḥusayn, the son of ʿAlī, slain by the soldiers of Yazid, the son of the caliph Muʿāwiyah, to prevent Ḥusayn's accession to the caliphate. This martyrdom is commemorated yearly with flagellation, imitative suffering, in Shīʿī circles. The ideological conflict was between Shīʿī insistence on blood succession from the Prophet and an elective basis of caliphal legitimacy.

The politically decaying society: victims and anti-martyrs. The politically decaying society is losing its ability to be self-determining. Roman provincial societies were decaying as they were co-opted by a victorious Christianity. Zoroastrian society became a weak minority in Persia, with a diaspora in India, shortly after the Islamic conquest. The world's smaller societies, such as those of the North American Indian civilization and of the Polynesian islands, were submerged by modern imperial powers.

The cause and the characteristic of this decay is loss of political autonomy. The society's symbols fail to command the loyalty of its members. Western European Jewish society, by the late eighteenth century, fits this mold. Local Jewish community control, supported by charters, was weakened as new concepts of statehood and citizenship took hold in Europe. Christian or secular frames of reference and values began to control the interpretations of Jewish tradition itself. The Jewish Haskalah, or Enlightenment, was built on the back of such intellectual symbols. Major civilizational contributions of Jews were made, not to Jewish society, as such, but to the environing societies. Heine, Mahler, Freud, and Einstein contributed to their German and Austrian cultures.

Martyrdom is latent in a decaying society. The adversary claims mere victims who affirm no ideology by their deaths. Jewish leaders tend to remember the victims of the Holocaust as martyrs for the sanctification of God's name. Breslauer (1981), in a dissent, writes that they were on the whole not sacred witnesses but passive victims, not proud martyrs for a cause but political pawns.

Leaders of a decaying society may dismiss resistance and martyrdom in favor of negotiation with the adversary. Rubenstein (1975) charges the Hungarian Jewish community leaders during World War II with near complicity in their own destruction. Though they knew about Auschwitz, one meeting with Eichmann convinced them that they had nothing to fear if they cooperated with the Schutzstaffel (SS) in enforced ghettoization, confiscation of real and personal property, and deportation for "labor service" in Poland.

Jewish resistance, independent and in cooperation with local partisans, produced genuine martyrs but was rarely supported by the officials of the Judenrat, the Jewish councils of the ghetto. The Warsaw ghetto uprising, authorized by ghetto leaders, was a final suicidal thrust, Samson at the temple of Dagon. Self-immolation requires a residue of moral strength, a will to protect the group's honor. Slaves may commit suicide, like concentration camp inmates throwing their bodies against the electrified wire, in order to relieve their suffering.

The negotiating victims may become collaborators or even converts. They may even become anti-martyrs. An anti-martyr may be a convert to the dominant ideology, remaining a leader of the minority and seeking to manage the conflict by collaborating with the dominant group. This effort may cost them their own lives. Anti-martyrs may strive to suppress martyrs whom they consider wrong-headed. They are not opportunistic turncoats, moved by personal avarice, but quislings, deeply committed to an enemy ideology, believing it best for their group. If they lose, they die unrelenting. The anti-martyr may meet his death at the hands of his new associates after they lose faith in him. Some new Christians, accused by the Spanish Inquisition of reverting to Judaism, went to the stake holding a cross. Leaders who suppress martyrdom out of a survivalist instinct without accepting the adversary are not anti-martyrs in the sense used here.

A martyr is delegated by the community and apotheosized by it. Anti-martyrs act individually or as members of a small separatist cadre. The minority condemns them as traitors and their apotheosis as evil.

How a Group Produces Martyrs. Martyr candidates may not always be found when needed. How does a community recruit and prepare individuals to sacrifice themselves? Ignatius of Antioch, seeking martyrdom, pleaded with his co-religionists in Rome not to try to rescue him but to allow him to die. At the same time, some bishops of the church denied their faith and fled to avoid court proceedings (Riddle, 1931). Not all sectors of the minority society are equally productive of martyrs. The level of devotion of most members of the community is insufficient to sustain martyrs. Zealots form cells within the wider community of devotees. These cells become a foundry for martyrs, supporting them throughout their ordeal.

The martyrs of politically crescive minorities, being leaders, tend to be recruited from its nobility. By and large these martyrs are males, not because females resist martyrdom, but because martyrs are drawn from the religio-political leadership. Female martyrs die affirming family principles. Barbara, one of a group of Catholic virgin martyrs, said to have been a follower of Origen in the third century, was immured in a tower, and ultimately beheaded by her father when he learned of her conversion to Christianity. Cecilia reportedly died as a martyr during the reign of Marcus Aurelius, along with her husband and friends whom she had converted.

What are the psychological characteristics, the motives of those who seek suffering and are willing to die? Although some writers tend to cite self-enhancing motives, such as a promise of redemption, or, as in Augustine's view, a way of avoiding a sin, one can safely say that altruism is the central motive. The basic commitment to moral action transcends the martyr's immediate interest in his personal fate. Sustaining such commitment requires ego integrity and the ability to overcome instinctive drives to escape.

Doubtless, some individuals throw themselves into martyrdom out of a mental derangement. But psychotics must be rare among martyrs, since they cannot usually establish and maintain the human bonds required in martyr cells. Many a stable mind, however, must become deranged during the tortures that can precede execution.

A martyr is prepared through life in a cell, that is, by social support. There he or she finds succor. The act is clothed ideologically and the potential martyr rehearsed. A martyr's ideology centers on the meaning of life in relation to death. It does not aim simply to attenuate the pain of martyrdom through a fantasy of a future life but provides a meaning for dying continuous with the meaning of the martyr's life. The martyr goes forward despite the pain.

Martyrologies, narrative or cultic, praise martyrs and expose evil. They prepare martyrs by example and encourage popular minor martyrdoms. A Christian cult of the martyr, in place by the end of the second century, exhibited relics—a bone, a lock of hair or some drops of blood—upon the anniversary of a martyrdom (Riddle, 1931). The more contemporary training of the kamikaze included worship at a special shrine for those who had died in training or in combat. There the trainees sought spiritual "intoxication" (Warner and Warner, 1982).

Exemplary martyrs need not be from one's own group. Invidiousness and pride can be as important as anger in strengthening the resolve to endure physical pain and degradation. The early Christians, not yet distinctively non-Jewish, identified with Maccabean martyrs. Gandhi, while struggling against the Boers in the Transvaal, praised the stalwart Boer women who survived an abominable incarceration by the English during the Boer War.

Ideology for preparing the martyr argues for the sanctity of the mission and the satanic quality of the adversary. It evokes earlier exemplary martyrs, including some from other groups. The lifelong preparation for the confrontation is materialized in a rehearsal for martyrdom. The rehearsal begins with the study of martyrologies, a vicarious experience, and follows with exercise of the minor martyrdoms—giving charity, fasting, and receiving the sacraments.

The early Christians offered organized rehearsals for the ordeal. The Roman process, being judicial, was predictable. Its stages included arrest, examination, threatening and persuasion, acquittal for recantation, and, as a test of loyalty, the performance by the recanter of pagan rites. Persons likely to be examined were trained in prepared responses for each stage.

How Society Controls Its Own Martyrs. A practical danger to a politically crescive minority is that some members will initiate open political action, perhaps open rebellion, before the community is ready to support such an act and, therefore, to succeed. Martyrdom, a harbinger of an uprising, is also a temporary alternative to it. A community must control its martyrs as it does its military zealots.

The community sets rules governing the occasions for martyrdom. Which principles are worth dying for? Who should die? When should one not die? The loss of such control among the Judean provincials during the latter part of the first century BCE was fatal for Jewish autonomy and nearly fatal for Jewry as a whole.

The thoroughness of the Jewish defeat in the Judean rebellion of 70 CE, which led to the destruction of the Temple, was symbolized in the redesignation of the Temple mount as Aeolia Capitolina. The subsequent Bar Kokhba Revolt (c. 132–135) was severely suppressed. The community, not prepared for these acts of desperation, had not widely supported Bar Kokhba. These catastrophes shifted the center of Jewish life to the Diaspora. The evidence is that the edicts of Hadrian, such as the edict forbidding circumcision, which were cited as giving the Jews no choice but to rebel, actually followed the rebellion as martial law.

Control is also a matter of ruling when martyrdom is not expected. A Muslim is forbidden to wish for death or for an encounter with the enemy. The *ṭalab al-shahādah*, the seeking of martyrdom, even on the battlefield, is too close to suicide for Islamic jurists. Mahmud Shaltiut, a recent Shaykh al-Azhar, allows the community but three reasons for declaring *jihād:* to repel aggression, to protect the mission of Islam, and to defend religious freedom, that is, the freedom of Muslims to practice their faith in non-Muslim lands (Shaltiut, in Peters, 1977).

The Talmudic laws of martyrdom were formulated at the Council of Lydda in the second century. These laws governed a minority in a province of pagan Rome. By the Middle Ages, Jews were a minority in powerful Islamic states from Arabia to Spain and in equally powerful European Christian states. From time to time the pressure on the Jews to convert increased to the point where martyrdom became an issue. Group, not simply individual, survival was also a sacred obligation. Moses Maimonides (Mosheh ben Maimon), writing his *Epistle on Apostasy* in 1162–1163, warned that the death of the martyr condemns all of his potential descendants to nonbeing (Maimonides, 1979). For this and other reasons, Maimonides sought to restrict the occasions for obligatory martyrdom.

The rabbis of the Talmud had restricted martyrdom to avoiding public worship of strange gods, incest or adultery, and murder. Under pressure it is permissible, writes Maimonides, to utter the Shahādah, the Muslim declaration of the unity of God and the prophetic mission of Muḥammad. The coerced Jew could think whatever he wished. If a Jew is coerced to violate publicly commands of the Torah other than the three specificed above, Maimonides advises submission, a position not repeated in his *Epistle to Yemen,* nor in his *Mishneh Torah,* his major work. It is not unlike Muslim dissimulation—acting when under pressure as if one has abandoned Islam. The person is culpable, however, if the violations are of his own free will. Maimonides recommends migration to more friendly shores, rather than awaiting the Messiah in the land of oppression.

Rules control the candidacy for martyrdom. Candidates who might not stand up to the adversary, who cannot assure that their action is voluntary, are to be discouraged. The rules given by Ibn Rushd (Averroës) for recruiting for a *jihād* recall the biblical rules limiting military service according to age, marital status, and attitude to danger. The *shahīd* should not recoil from fighting if the number of enemies is but twice the number of his own troops, an estimate based on a Qurʾanic verse (surah 8:66), but should flee before a greater disproportion (Shaltiut, 1977).

The Suppression of Martyrdom by the Dominant Group. A dominant group may strive to prevent martyrdom when it cannot exploit the public meaning of the event. Potential martyrs may be co-opted or suppressed.

The adversary group may, for instance, assimilate a sympathetic sector of the minority. The new "converts," given positions in the dominant society, may become a showcase for attenuating minority resistance. (This approach misfires when it polarizes the minority, inciting the resisters to attack the assimilationists, as in the case of the Maccabean assault on the Hellenizing Jews.) Since martyrdom depends on charismatic authority, any move toward rationalizing the social order gives the minority a sense of justice and order and undermines martyrdom.

Repressive measures may parallel co-optive measures in a kind of carrot-and-stick process. The martyr-producing cells may be attacked, for instance, by an infiltrating agent provocateur. Resistance cells may be made illegal and their members executed as part of a "witchhunt." Government-sponsored terror against the primary community may deprive the resisting cells of support.

Other ways of raising the penalty for martyrdom include inflicting more painful deaths or executing more martyrs, thus overtaxing the minority's supply of martyrs. Such increased viciousness may be an act of desperation. Its very horror may further radicalize the minority in its thrust against the dominant society.

Persecutions involve centrally sponsored repressions of the minority, not unique or local actions against potential martyrs. Christian tradition speaks of ten persecutions, including those under the emperors Decius, Valerian, and Diocletian. Under Valerian, for instance, an edict was issued in 257 CE compelling acts of submission in conformity with the Roman religion. Christians refusing them were condemned to the mines, beaten with whips and rods, branded on their foreheads, and shaven on one side so that if they escaped they could be recognized as runaway slaves or criminals. This extreme persecution occurred but two generations before Constantine's victory.

If martyrs must be taken, the impact of the martyrdom on the adversary's society may be limited by isolating the killing from view. Assigning the killing to specialists is one way to accomplish this. As there is preparation of martyrs, so there is preparation of their specialized slayers. The SS in Nazi Germany conceived of itself as a sacred order, an elite trusted to guard the messianic Führer. The concentration camps were a training ground toughening them for the task. Prisoners were thought of as belonging to inferior races, shiftless and asocial; subjected to starvation and unsanitary conditions, they came to resemble the walking dead. Any SS officer who showed compassion could be eliminated from the group. Those who made common cause with the prisoners were stripped of their rank, given twenty-five lashes, and consigned to the company of the "subhuman" (Kogon, 1973).

Precisely the opposite approach is to encourage wide public participation in the repression of the minority community as a whole. The goal is to eliminate or demoralize it to the extent that it cannot function as a hinterland for martyrs. Elements putatively out of the control of the authorities may carry out the establishment's justice, and so mask its intent. Operating with two faces, the dominant community may pretend to provide legal and police protection, diverting the minority from a planned defense. The same objective situation may occur, without duplicity, when more than one authority exists in society. In medieval Germany and in Poland, for instance, Jews resided under charter from the local bishop or nobility. This guarantee of safety was ineffective when Jews were attacked by soldiers and mobs during the Crusades and in the early Polish pogroms. The lynching of blacks in the post–Civil War American South has the same character of mob action, sometimes disapproved of, sometimes condoned by the authorities.

A society may deprive martyrs of an exemplary function by declaring them criminals. Justice is done by removing them from the society. By the second century the Romans had developed a literature justifying the suppression of the Christians and defining their martyrdom as insane. The works of Marcus Cornelius Fronto and Lucian, for instance, attacked Christians as public enemies, atheists, a fanatical species enamored of death, who ran to the cruelest tortures as to a feast. To discredit the ideology, these works ridiculed Christians who claimed that Jesus was born of a virgin into a poor family in a small town in Judaea, when, in reality, his mother had been cast off by her husband for committing adultery with a soldier named Panthera.

The meaning of the event is controlled in subsequent time by myths about the meanings of the event. The martyr views the battle as a prelude to the subjugation of his executioner and then as taking vengeance on the executioner and his society. The dominant society, seeing the event as punishment or vengeance, hopes that it will have no sequel, that the cycle is complete, the criminal punished, justice achieved.

Destruction of records is aimed to control later historical reconstruction. Allard (1971) reports that during the Diocletian persecutions (285–323 CE), churches were burned along with their manuscripts, which included passions of the ancient martyrs. Books were burned at public book burnings. The persecutors, having failed to stop the apostasies, attempted to abolish their memories.

Perhaps the greatest weapon of the state, particularly the modern state, is its ability to make martyrdom appear obsolete and meaningless. Bureaucratizing the killing accomplishes this end. Rubenstein (1975) says that the Holocaust could only have been carried out by an advanced political community with a highly trained, tightly disciplined police and civil service bureaucracy. The moral barrier to the riddance of a surplus population was overcome by taking the project out of the hands of bullies and hoodlums and delegating it to the bureaucrats.

SEE ALSO Holocaust, The; Jihād.

BIBLIOGRAPHY

Allard, Paul. *La persecution de Dioclétian et le triomphe de l'église.* 3d rev. ed. 2 vols. Rome, 1971.

Ben Sasson, H. H. "Kiddush Hashem: Historical Aspects." In *Encyclopaedia Judaica.* Jerusalem, 1971.

Bickerman, Elias J. *The God of the Maccabees.* Leiden, 1979.

Breslauer, S. Daniel. "Martyrdom and Charisma: Leo Baeck and a New Jewish Theology." *Encounter* 42 (Spring 1981): 133–142.

Cohn, Norman R. C. *The Pursuit of the Millennium.* 3d ed. New York, 1970.

Coogan, Tim Pat. *On the Blanket: The H Block Story.* Dublin, 1980.

Frend, W. H. C. *Martyrdom and Persecution in the Early Church.* Oxford, 1965.

Gandhi, M. K. *Satyagraha in South Africa.* Translated by Yalji Govindji Desair. Madras, 1928.

Hazrat, Ahmad. *Ahmadiyyat or the True Islam.* New Delhi, 1980.

Historical Society of Israel. *Milḥemet qodesh u-marṭirologyah.* Jerusalem, 1967.

Jacobs, I. "Eleazar ben Yair's Sanction for Marytrdom." *Journal for the Study of Judaism in the Persian, Hellenistic, and Roman Period* 13 (December 1982): 183–186.

Jacoby, Susan. *Wild Justice: The Evolution of Revenge.* New York, 1983.

Klawitzer, Frederick C. "The Role of Martyrdom and Persecution in Developing the Priestly Authority of Women in Early Christianity: A Case Study of Montanism." *Church History* 49 (September 1980): 251–261.

Kogon, Eugen. *The Theory and Practice of Hell.* New York, 1973.

Lamm, Norman. "Kiddush Ha-shem and Hillul Ha-shem." In *Encyclopaedia Judaica.* Jerusalem, 1971.

Maimonides, Moses. *Epistle to Yemen.* New York, 1952.

Maimonides, Moses. *Iggeret ha-shemad.* In *Iggrot ha-Rambam,* pp. 13–68. Jerusalem, 1979.

Massignon, Louis. *The Passion of al-Hallaj: Mystic and Martyr of Islam.* Princeton, 1982.

Mattingly, Garrett. *The Armada.* Boston, 1959.

Peters, Rudolph, trans. *Jihād in Medieval and Modern Islam.* Leiden, 1977.

Poliakov, Leon. *La causalité diabolique: Essai sur l'origine des persécutions.* Paris, 1980.

Rahner, Karl. *On the Theology of Death.* New York, 1961.

Riddle, Donald W. *The Martyrs: A Study in Social Control.* Chicago, 1931.

Rosenberg, Bruce A. *Custer and the Epic of Defeat.* University Park, Pa., 1974.

Rubenstein, Richard L. *The Cunning of History: The Holocaust and the American Future.* New York, 1975.

Sachedina, Abdulaziz Abdulhussein. *Islamic Messianism: The Idea of Mahdi in Twelver Shi'ism.* Albany, N.Y., 1981.

Szaluta, Jacques. "Apotheosis to Ignominy: The Martyrdom of Marshall Petain." *Journal of Psychohistory* 7 (Spring 1980): 415–453.

Vööbus, Arthur. *History of Asceticism in the Syrian Orient.* Corpus Scriptorum Christianorum Orientalium, vol. 189. Louvain, 1958.

Warner, Dennis, and Peggy Warner. *The Sacred Warriors: Japan's Suicide Legions.* New York, 1982.

Wensinck, A. J. "The Oriental Doctrine of the Martyrs." In *Semietische Studien uit de Nalatenschap.* Leiden, 1941.

Zerubavel, Yael. "The Last Stand: On the Transformation of Symbols in Modern Israeli Culture." Ph.D. diss., University of Pennsylvania, 1980.

New Sources

Boyarin, Daniel. *Dying for God: Martyrdom and the Making of Christianity and Judaism.* Stanford, Calif., 1999.

Clar, Gillian. "Bodies and Blood: Late Antique Debate on Martyrdom, Virginity, and Resurrection." In *Changing Bodies, Changing Meanings: Studies on the Human Body in Antiquity,* edited by Dominic Montserrat, pp. 99–115. New York, 1998.

Cunningham, Lawrence. "Saints and Martyrs: Some Contemporary Considerations." *Theological Studies* 60 (1999): 529–537.

Davis, Joyce M. *Martyrs: Innocence, Vengeance and Despair in the Middle East.* New York, 2003.

Fenech, Louis. "Martyrdom and the Execution of Guru Arjan in Early Sikh Stories." *Journal of the American Orientalist Society* 121 (January–March 2001): 20–32.

Gregory, Brad S. *Salvation at Stake: Christian Martyrdom in Early Modern Europe.* Cambridge, Mass., 1999.

Leyerle, Blake. "Blood Is Seed." *Journal of Religion* 81 (January 2001): 26–44.

Salisbury, Joyce. *Perpetua's Passion: The Death and Memory of a Young Roman Woman.* New York, 1997.

SAMUEL Z. KLAUSNER (1987)
Revised Bibliography

MARX, KARL (1818–1883), German social and economic theorist. Marx was born in Trier on May 5, 1818. Both his grandfather and his uncle had been rabbis in the city and so had several of his paternal grandmother's ancestors. His mother also descended from a long line of rabbis in Holland. His father, Heinrich, had in 1817 converted to Protestantism in order to retain his position as a lawyer at the High Court of Appeals in Trier when the Rhineland, formerly French, became, through annexation, subject to the discriminatory laws of Prussia. Marx was baptized in 1824. During his high school years he enjoyed the literary tutelage of his father's friend, Baron Ludwig von Westphalen, whose daughter Jenny he would later marry.

In 1835 Marx registered in the faculty of law at the University of Bonn. A year later he transferred to the University of Berlin, but there he soon became ill through overwork. The following months of convalescence in the country completely changed his intellectual outlook. At first a romantic, vaguely religious idealist, he now converted to Hegel's philosophy. He joined a discussion group of "Young Hegelians," consisting of instructors and advanced students in a variety of disciplines, mostly of radical political and religious leanings. For them Hegel's dialectical method, separated from its conservative content, provided a powerful weapon for the critique of established religion and politics. The leading voices in the *Doktorklub,* as the group was called, were those of the theologians David Friedrich Strauss and Bruno Bauer. In his *Life of Jesus* Strauss had interpreted the gospel narratives as mythologizing the aspirations of the early Christian community. After some initial criticism, Bauer went even further: those narratives contained no truth at all, while the faith based on them had become the main obstacle on the road to political and cultural progress.

The young Marx extended these critical conclusions to all religion. His doctoral dissertation, *On the Difference between the Philosophies of Nature in Democritus and Epicurus*, which he submitted in 1841 to the Jena faculty of philosophy, was prefaced by a motto taken from Aeschylus's *Prometheus:* "In one word, I hate all the gods."

In 1843 Marx married Jenny von Westphalen. After his wedding and a prolonged vacation near Trier, he returned to Bonn, where he started writing for the radical Cologne paper *Die Rheinische Zeitung*. His first contribution consisted of a series of critical articles on the proceedings of the Rhineland parliament dealing with freedom of the press and the debates concerning the punishment of wood thefts. Other reports, on religious disputes, were censored and never appeared. In October 1842 Marx, having been appointed editor-in-chief, moved to Cologne. Six months later the paper folded under the pressure of Prussian censorship. In October 1843 Marx left the Rhineland for Paris, where he expected to find more freedom as well as make direct contact with French revolutionary workers' movements.

During his final year in Germany Marx's political position had developed from radically democratic to communist. At the same time he had increasingly come under the influence of that other critical interpreter of Hegel's philosophy, Ludwig Feuerbach. In *The Essence of Christianity* (1841) Feuerbach had applied Hegel's concept of alienation to all divine reality: in religion man projects his own nature into a supernatural realm and thus "alienates" from himself what rightly belongs to him. Marx instantly embraced the theory of religion as alienation, but he found Feuerbach's interpretation of the origin of the religious attitude inadequate. Religion, Marx asserted, mythically justifies a fundamental social frustration. Far from constituting the essence of human alienation, the need for religion implies a tacit protest against the existing, dehumanizing conditions of society. In that sense Marx called it "the opium of the people" in his essay "Introduction to a Critique of Hegel's Philosophy of Right" (1844), published in the Paris-based *Deutsch-Franzözische Jahrbücher*. "The abolition of religion as the illusory happiness of men is a demand for real happiness. The call to abandon their illusions about this condition is the *call to abandon a condition which requires illusions*." Full emancipation demands that the social structures that create the need for religion be changed.

The secondary character of religious beliefs with respect to social-economic conditions appears in another essay Marx published in the same issue of the *Jahrbücher*, "On the Jewish Question." Bauer had proposed the thesis that the Jewish problem could be solved instantly if Jews would cease to claim religious privileges from the state. By so doing, they maintained the religious state and prevented their own as well as other people's emancipation. Bauer held that emancipation of man required a secular state that recognizes neither Christians nor Jews. Marx agreed that the existence of religion always indicates an incomplete emancipation, but he denied that religion is the cause of the problem or, for that matter, that political rights are the solution. Bauer had simply identified religion with alienation and political equality with emancipation. But political emancipation is by no means human emancipation. "To be *politically* emancipated from religion is not to be finally and completely emancipated from religion, because political emancipation is not the final and absolute form of human emancipation." Even if the state should suppress religion, its own existence would remain a profane expression of an alienation that in time would irresistibly produce its religious form. So instead of being a remedy for religious alienation, the secular state is the purest symptom of its presence. Even more than religion, the state keeps alive the inhuman conditions that separate the individual from his fellow human beings and thereby prevent humankind from realizing its full potential. If religion means deception, the state is more religious than the church.

Henceforth Marx devoted his critical efforts entirely to the critique of the state. But under the influence of an essay by Friedrich Engels on political economy, published in the same issue of the *Jahrbücher* that had featured Marx's own two essays, he saw that political attitudes are rooted in economic conditions. This "genial" insight inspired the so-called *Economic Philosophical Manuscripts* of 1844, which would remain unpublished until 1927. Here, for the first time, Marx aims his attacks exclusively at the capitalist economy itself, a system that alienates the worker from the very activity through which he should achieve his humanization as well as from the kind of social cooperation required by genuine humanization.

In 1845 the French government (under Prussian pressure) forbade Marx all political activity and threatened him with imprisonment. Once again Marx emigrated, this time to Brussels, where he would remain until March 1848. This second stage of his mature life was to be a very productive one, even though little of his literary activity ever reached print.

Foremost among his unpublished writings from this period is *The German Ideology* (1845–1846). In it Marx developed the crucial concept of ideology and, with it, the basic principles of a powerful theory of history. Not what human beings think or imagine, not conscious decisions or theoretical schemes, but social-economic relations are the primary determining factors of history. Ideas, shaped by language, emerge from social-economic structures. The division between mental and physical labor, severing thinking from its vital, social roots, has given birth to an independent realm of abstract speculation. In fact, the theories accepted in a particular society express the interests and aspirations of the ruling class. As soon as one class acquires control over the process of material production, it falls heir to the "means of mental production" and begins to impose such ideas as best serve its dominion. Detached from its social-economic basis, theory turns into ideology. The term *ideology* refers to any theory that ignores the social conditioning of ideas and presents itself with a semblance of intellectual autonomy.

Engels later qualified Marx's position by suggesting that conscious processes, developed through the impact of social relations, in turn influence these relations. Unfortunately, Marx's later metaphorical reformulation of the relation (in the preface to his *Critique of Political Economy*) as one between base and superstructure confirmed the "derived" character of ideas rather than eliminating it. Clearly, religion considered as a "superstructure" can hardly do more than "reflect" its social origins.

In Brussels, Marx and Engels, who had met in Paris in 1844 and by now had become constant, though often distant, collaborators, intensified their revolutionary activity. For the newly founded Communist League they wrote their famous *Manifesto* (1848), an entirely new vision of history. Since his early Paris days, the social-economic category of class had, for Marx, come to dominate all others. In the *Manifesto*'s scenario, the class of the bourgeoisie, created by the capitalist system, would function as the revolutionary lever toward the communist society of the future. An unprecedented social and cultural mover in its own development, the bourgeoisie is now destined to terminate the class structure of society itself. It does so by creating an underclass, the proletariat, that will increase in numbers and in misery until its members, for the sake of sheer survival, will be forced to rise throughout the entire industrialized world. "What the bourgeoisie, therefore, produces above all else, is its own gravediggers."

In the same year, 1848, revolutions started all over the European continent. But when the Belgian authorities learned of an imminent republican putsch, they expelled Marx from the country for illegal political agitation. The exile barely interrupted Marx's revolutionary activity. Returning to Paris on March 5 with the papers of the Communist League, which a few days earlier had had its headquarters transferred from London to Brussels, Marx was, on March 10, elected as its president. In his French headquarters his attention remained fixed on Germany, where he still expected a "total" revolution to take place. Through his speeches to the German Working Men's Club (based in Paris) and his articles in the new communist paper of Cologne, the *Neue Rheinische Zeitung*, Marx continuously bombarded the German community with his revolutionary messages.

The June revolution in Paris confirmed at least part of Marx's theories, for in it social issues clearly prevailed over political ones. Meanwhile, Marx again had moved to Cologne to direct the *Neue Reinische*, which, not surprisingly, was gradually censored into extinction. Its editor was expelled from Prussian territory for having instigated open rebellion. During that same summer of 1848 Marx definitively settled down in London.

Here, amidst extreme poverty, domestic tragedy (several of his children died, possibly due to their living conditions), occasional family turmoil (his young servant bore him a child), and constant polemics, Marx completed the third stage of his career. Apart from revolutionary activity (mainly through the reorganized Communist League), he devoted himself entirely to his lifetime theoretical project: a definitive social critique of the capitalist economy. Only two parts of his voluminous theoretical writing during this period reached completion before his death: the *Contribution to the Critique of Political Economy* (1859) and the first volume of what by then had already become a reduced project, *Capital* (1867).

In all his later writings Marx criticizes capitalist theories in categories often borrowed from the classical economists, especially Adam Smith and David Ricardo. Even his central concept of surplus value, the value generated by labor beyond the cost of wages and tools, appears in Ricardo. But the perspective differs substantially. For Marx shows how capitalist theory merely expresses the practice of a society at a particular historical stage of its development. Indeed, capitalism is now approaching the point where its internal "contradictions" (in fact, mostly social conflicts) must openly erupt and destroy the system itself. Throughout his development Marx never wavered in his confidence that bourgeois society would break down in a social revolution that would result in a socialist state and, in due time, generate a stateless communist society.

Yet during this same period Marx also produced an enormous output of noneconomic writings, most important among them, two historical studies on the French revolution of 1848 and the subsequent events leading to the Second Empire of Napoleon III: *The Class Struggles in France* (1850) and *The Eighteenth Brumaire of Louis Napoleon* (1852). In addition, he wrote hundreds of newspaper articles for the *New York Daily Tribune* and for the *Neue Oder-Zeitung*, his main source of support (beside the gifts of the ever-generous Engels) during that period.

From 1870 on Marx's health steadily declined. He increasingly suffered from respiratory problems, which, after 1880, forced him for prolonged periods to seek refuge from the damp, polluted London air in Margate, the Isle of Wight, Karlsbad (where he took the baths), Nice, and even North Africa. Yet despite his poor health his literary activity continued unabatedly, and his travels provided him with opportunities for establishing new revolutionary contacts as far away as Algiers. Still, it became gradually obvious that he would never complete his lifework, and during his final years he felt increasingly reluctant even to attempt bringing some order to his papers. Thus when he died on March 14, 1883, he left an enormous estate of unpublished manuscripts. Out of the more than a thousand pages of notes Marx had accumulated for the sequel of *Capital*, Engels published *Capital II* (1885) and *Capital III* (1894). In addition, in 1927 Karl Kautsky published the historical notes, *Theories of Surplus Value*, under the title *Capital IV*. In 1953 Marx's earlier preparatory notes for *Capital* appeared under the title *Grundrisse der Kritik der politischen Ökonomie* (in English, simply *Grundrisse*).

BIBLIOGRAPHY

Dupré, Louis. *The Philosophical Foundations of Marxism*. New York, 1966.

Kolakowski, Leszek. *Main Currents of Marxism: Its Rise, Growth, and Dissolution*, vol. 1, *The Founders*. Oxford, 1978.

Marx, Karl, and Friedrich Engels. *On Religion*. New York, 1964.

Marx, Karl, and Friedrich Engels. *Collected Works*. 50 vols. Translated by Richard Dixon et al. New York, 1975–.

McLellan, David. *Karl Marx: His Life and Thought*. London, 1973.

Rubel, Maximilien, and Margaret Manale. *Marx without Myth: A Chronological Study of His Life and Work*. Oxford, 1975.

New Sources

Hartley, George. *The Abyss of Representation: Marxism and the Postmodern Sublime*. Durham, N.C., 2003.

McLellan, David. "Then and Now: Marx and Marxism." *Political Studies*, 47 (December 1999): 955–967.

Negri, Antonio. *Marx beyond Marx*. New York, 1989.

Read, Jason. *The Micro-politics of Capital: Marx and the Prehistory of the Present*. Albany, 2003.

Wheen, Francis. *Karl Marx*. New York, 2000.

LOUIS DUPRÉ (1987)
Revised Bibliography

ISBN 0-02-865741-1
90000
9 780028 657417